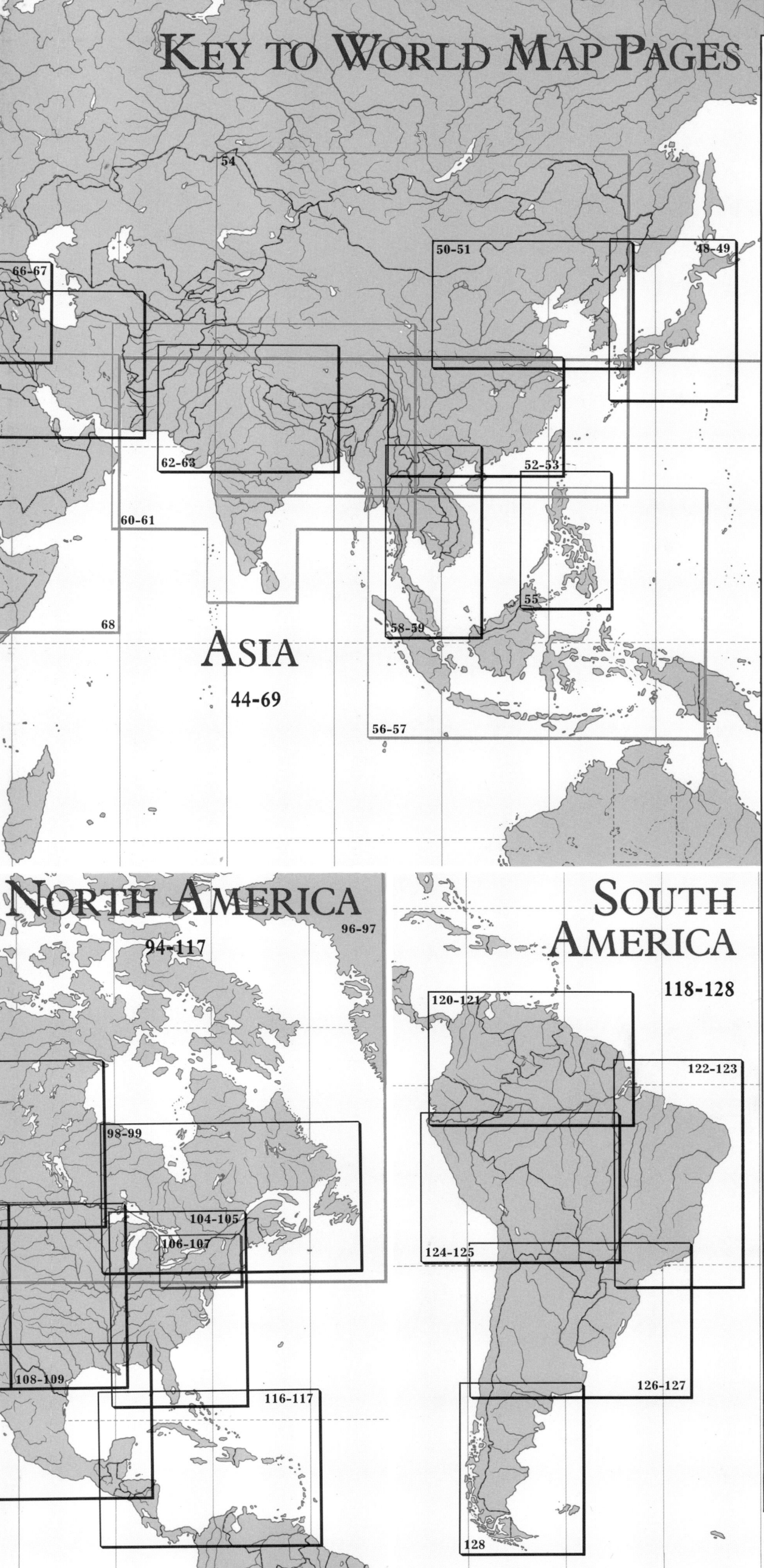

KEY TO WORLD MAP PAGES

COUNT

D0811262

Afghanistan		Latvia	
Albania	38-39	Lebanon	69
Algeria	74-75	Lesotho	85
Angola	80-81	Liberia	78
Argentina	126, 128	Libya	73
Armenia	67	Lithuania	40
Australia	88-91	Luxembourg	17
Austria	19, 20-21		
Azerbaijan	67	Madagascar	85
		Malawi	83
Bahamas	116-117	Malaysia	55-56
Bangladesh	61	Mali	78-79
Barbados	117	Malta	37
Belgium	17	Mauritania	78
Belize	116	Mauritius	71
Belorussia	40	Mexico	114-115
Benin	79	Moldavia	42
Bhutan	61	Mongolia	54
Bolivia	124-125	Morocco	74
Botswana	84-85	Mozambique	83
Brazil	120-127		
Brunei	55	Namibia	84
Bulgaria	38-39	Nepal	63
Burkina Faso	78-79	Netherlands	16-17
Burma	61	New Zealand	87
Burundi	82	Nicaragua	116
		Niger	79
Cambodia	58-59	Nigeria	79
Cameroon	82	Northern Ireland	15
Canada	96-101	Norway	8-9
Central African			
Republic	82	Oman	68
Chad	73		
Chile	126, 128	Pakistan	62
China	50-54	Panama	116
Colombia	120	Papua New Guinea	86
Congo	82	Paraguay	126-127
Costa Rica	116	Peru	124
Croatia	21	Philippines	55
Cuba	116-117	Poland	20
Cyprus	37	Portugal	30-31
Czechoslovakia	20-21	Puerto Rico	117
Denmark	11	Qatar	65
Djibouti	68		
Dominican Republic	117	Romania	38
		Russia	40-45
Ecuador	120	Rwanda	82
Egypt	76		
El Salvador	116	Saudi Arabia	68
England	12-13	Scotland	14
Equatorial Guinea	82	Senegal	78
Estonia	40	Sierra Leone	78
Ethiopia	68, 77	Singapore	59
		Slovenia	33
Fiji	87	Somali Republic	68
Finland	8-9	South Africa	84-85
France	24-27	Spain	28-31
French Guiana	121	Sri Lanka	60
		Sudan	77
Gabon	80	Surinam	121
Gambia	78	Swaziland	85
Georgia	43	Sweden	8-9
Germany	18-19	Switzerland	22-23
Ghana	78-79	Syria	67
Greece	39		
Greenland	4	Taiwan	53
Guatemala	116	Tajikistan	44
Guinea	78	Tanzania	82-83
Guinea-Bissau	78	Thailand	58-59
Guyana	121	Togo	79
		Trinidad and	
Haiti	117	Tobago	117
Honduras	116	Tunisia	75
Hong Kong	53	Turkey	66-67
Hungary	21	Turkmenistan	44
Iceland	8	Uganda	82
India	60-63	Ukraine	42
Indonesia	56-57	United Arab Emirates	65
Iran	64-65	United Kingdom	12-15
Iraq	64-65	USA	102-113
Irish Republic	15	Uruguay	126-127
Israel	69	Uzbekistan	44
Italy	32-35		
Ivory Coast	78	Venezuela	120-121
		Vietnam	58-59
Jamaica	116		
Japan	48-49	Wales	12-13
Jordan	69		
Kazakhstan	44	Yemen	68
Kenya	82	Yugoslavia	38-39
Kirghizia	44		
Korea, North	51	Zaïre	80-81
Korea, South	51	Zambia	83
Kuwait	64-65	Zimbabwe	83

ASIA

44-69

NORTH AMERICA

94-117

96-97

SOUTH AMERICA

118-128

54

50-51

48-49

66-67

62-63

60-61

68

52-53

55

58-59

56-57

98-99

104-105

106-107

108-109

116-117

120-121

122-123

124-125

126-127

128

PHILIP'S

GREAT WORLD ATLAS

PHILIP'S

GREAT WORLD ATLAS

Published by George Philip Limited
59 Grosvenor Street, London W1X 9DA

ISBN 0-540-05687-1

Printed in Hong Kong

PHILIP'S WORLD MAPS

The reference maps which form the main body of this atlas have been prepared in accordance with the highest standards of international cartography to provide an accurate and detailed representation of the earth. The scales and projections used have been carefully chosen to give balanced coverage of the world, while emphasizing the most densely populated and economically significant regions. A hallmark of Philip's mapping is the use of hill shading and relief colouring to create a graphic impression of landforms: this makes the maps exceptionally easy to read. However, knowledge of the key features employed in the construction and presentation of the maps will enable the reader to derive the fullest benefit from the atlas.

Map sequence

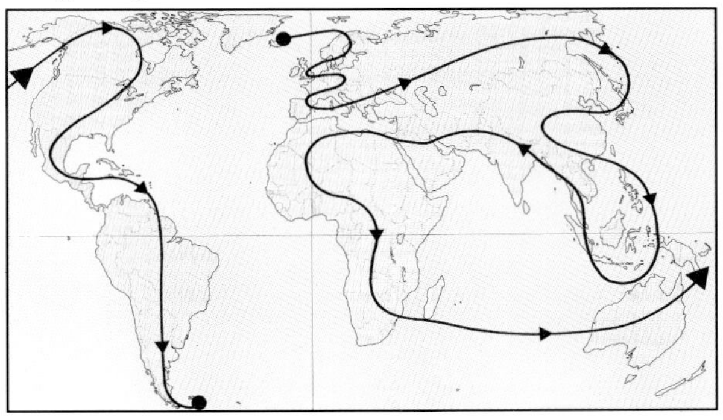

The atlas covers the earth continent by continent: first Europe; then its land neighbour Asia (mapped north before south, in a clockwise sequence), then Africa, Australia and Oceania, North America and South America. This is the classic arrangement adopted by most cartographers since the 16th century. For each continent, there are maps at a variety of scales. First, physical relief and political maps of the whole continent. Then a series of larger-scale maps of the regions within the continent, each followed, where required, by still larger-scale maps of the most important or densely populated areas. The governing principle is that by turning the pages of the atlas, the reader moves steadily from north to south through each continent, with each map overlapping its neighbours. A key map showing this sequence, and the area covered by each map, can be found on the endpapers of the atlas.

Map presentation

With very few exceptions (eg for the Arctic and Antarctic), the maps are drawn with north at the top, regardless of whether they are presented upright or sideways on the page. In the borders will be found the map title; a locator diagram showing the area covered and the page numbers for maps of adjacent areas; the scale; the projection used; the degrees of latitude and longitude; and the letters and figures used in the index for locating place names and geographical features. Physical relief maps also have a height reference panel identifying the colours used for each layer of contouring.

Map symbols

Each map contains a vast amount of detail which can only be conveyed clearly and accurately by the use of symbols. Points and circles of varying sizes locate and identify the relative importance of towns and cities; different styles of type are employed for administrative, geographical and regional place names. A variety of pictorial symbols denote landscape features such as glaciers, marshes and reefs, and man-made structures including roads, railways, airports, canals and dams. International borders are shown by red lines. Where neighbouring countries are in dispute, for example in the Middle East, the maps show the *de facto* boundary between nations, regardless of the legal or historical situation. The symbols are explained on the first page of the World Maps section of the atlas.

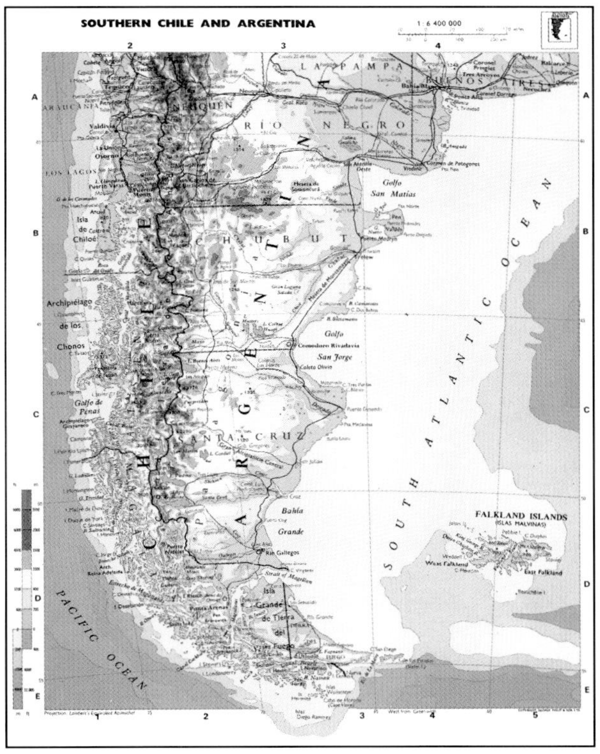

Map scales

1: 16 000 000
1 inch = 252 statute miles

The scale of each map is given in the numerical form known as the 'representative fraction'. The first figure is always one, signifying one unit of distance on the map; the second figure, usually in millions, is the number by which the map unit must be multiplied to give the equivalent distance on the earth's surface. Calculations can easily be made in centimetres and kilometres, by dividing the earth units figure by 100 000 (ie deleting the last five 0s). Thus 1:1 000 000 means 1 cm = 10 km. The calculation for inches and miles is more laborious, but 1 000 000 divided by 63 360 (the number of inches in a mile) shows that 1:1 000 000 means approximately 1 inch = 16 miles. The table below provides distance equivalents for scales down to 1:50 000 000.

LARGE SCALE		
1: 1 000 000	1 cm = 10 km	1 inch = 16 miles
1: 2 500 000	1 cm = 25 km	1 inch = 39.5 miles
1: 5 000 000	1 cm = 50 km	1 inch = 79 miles
1: 6 000 000	1 cm = 60 km	1 inch = 95 miles
1: 8 000 000	1 cm = 80 km	1 inch = 126 miles
1: 10 000 000	1 cm = 100 km	1 inch = 158 miles
1: 15 000 000	1 cm = 150 km	1 inch = 237 miles
1: 20 000 000	1 cm = 200 km	1 inch = 316 miles
1: 50 000 000	1 cm = 500 km	1 inch = 790 miles
SMALL SCALE		

Measuring distances

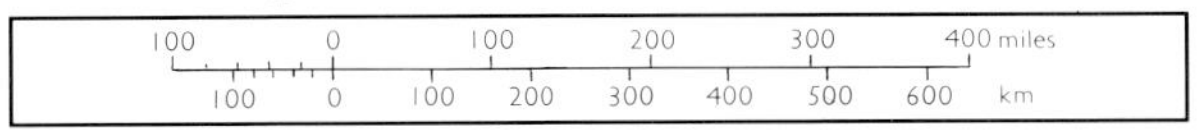

Although each map is accompanied by a scale bar, distances cannot always be measured with confidence because of the distortions involved in portraying the curved surface of the earth on a flat page. As a general rule, the larger the map scale (ie the lower the number of earth units in the representative fraction), the more accurate and reliable will be the distance measured. On small-scale maps such as those of the world and of entire continents, measurement may only be accurate along the 'standard parallels', or central axes, and should not be attempted without considering the map projection.

Map projections

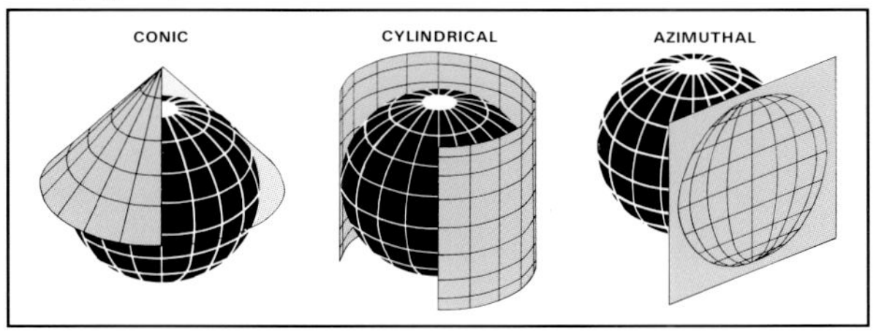

Unlike a globe, no flat map can give a true scale representation of the world in terms of area, shape and position of every region. Each of the numerous systems that have been devised for projecting the curved surface of the earth on to a flat page involves the sacrifice of accuracy in one or more of these elements. The variations in shape and position of landmasses such as Alaska, Greenland and Australia, for example, can be quite dramatic when different projections are compared.

For this atlas, the guiding principle has been to select projections that involve the least distortion of size and distance. The projection used for each map is noted in the border. Most fall into one of three categories - conic, cylindrical or azimuthal - whose basic concepts are shown above. Each involves plotting the forms of the earth's surface on a grid of latitude and longitude lines, which may be shown as parallels, curves or radiating spokes.

Latitude and longitude

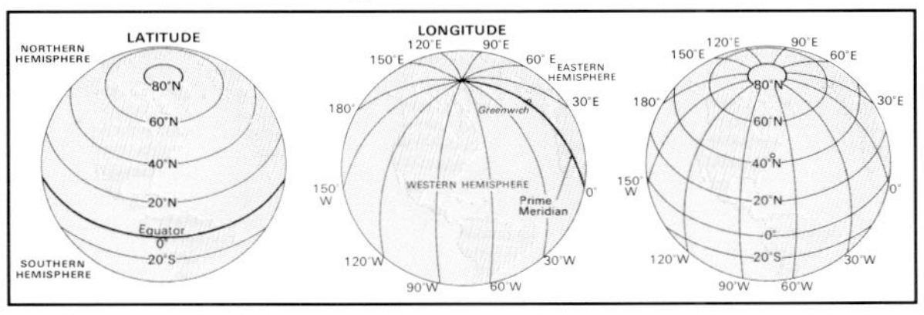

Accurate positioning of individual points on the earth's surface is made possible by reference to the geometrical system of latitude and longitude. Latitude *parallels* are drawn west-east around the earth and numbered by degrees north and south of the Equator, which is designated 0° of latitude. Longitude *meridians* are drawn north-south and numbered by degrees east and west of the *prime meridian,* 0° of longitude, which passes through Greenwich in England. By referring to these co-ordinates and their sub-divisions of minutes (1/60th of a degree) and seconds (1/60th of a minute), any place on earth can be located to within a few hundred yards. Latitude and longitude are indicated by blue lines on the maps; they are straight or curved according to the projection employed. Reference to these lines is the easiest way of determining the relative positions of places on different maps, and for plotting compass directions.

Name forms

For ease of reference, both English and local name forms appear in the atlas. Oceans, seas and countries are shown in English throughout the atlas; country names may be abbreviated to their commonly accepted form (eg Germany, not Federal Republic of Germany). Conventional English forms are also used for place names on the smaller-scale maps of the continents. However, local name forms are used on all large-scale and regional maps, with the English form given in brackets only for important cities - the large-scale map of European Russia thus shows Moskva (Moscow). For countries which do not use a Roman script, place names have been transcribed according to the systems adopted by the British and US Geographic Names Authorities. For China, the Pin Yin system has been used, with some more widely known forms appearing in brackets, as with Beijing (Peking). Both English and local names appear in the index, the English form being cross-referenced to the local form.

CONTENTS

WORLD STATISTICS

Countries x
Cities xi
Distances xii
Climate xiii
Physical
Dimensions xiv-xv

INTRODUCTION TO WORLD GEOGRAPHY

The Universe 2-3
The Solar System 4-5

THE EARTH
Time and Motion 6-7
Geology 8-9
Oceans 10-11
Atmosphere 12-13
Climate 14-15
Water 16-17
Landscape 18-19
Environment 20-21

PEOPLE
Demography 22-23
Cities 24-25
The Human Family 26-27
Conflict and
Cooperation 28-29

PRODUCTION
Agriculture 30-31
Energy 32-33
Minerals 34-35
Manufacturing 36-37
Trade 38-39

QUALITY OF LIFE
Wealth 40-41
Standards 42-43
Health 44-45
Environment 46-47

WORLD MAPS

1-128

THE WORLD

Map Symbols

1

The World: Political
1:64 000 000

2-3

Arctic Ocean 1:28 000 000
Greenland

4

Antarctica 1:28 000 000

5

EUROPE

Europe: Physical
1:16 000 000

6

Europe: Political
1:16 000 000

7

Scandinavia and the
Baltic Lands 1:4 000 000
Norway, Sweden, *Finland*,
Iceland

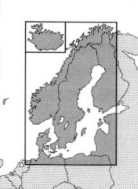

8-9

Denmark and Southern
Sweden 1:2 000 000
Denmark, *Norway*, *Sweden*

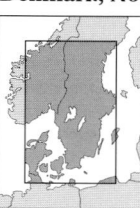

10-11

England and Wales
1:1 600 000
Isle of Man, Channel Islands

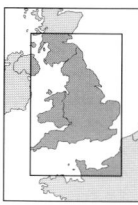

12-13

Scotland 1:1 600 000

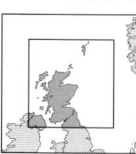

14

Ireland 1:1 600 000
Irish Republic, Northern Ireland

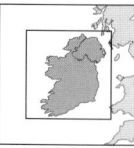

15

NOTE
The titles to the World Maps
list the main countries, states
and provinces covered by
each map. A name given in
italics indicates that only part
of the country is shown on
the map.

Netherlands, Belgium and Luxembourg 1:1 000 000

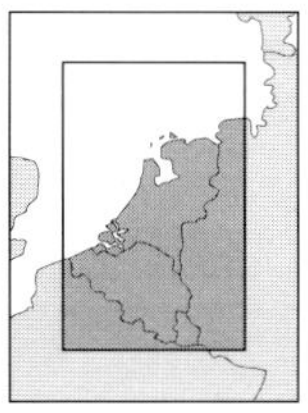

16-17

Germany 1:2 000 000

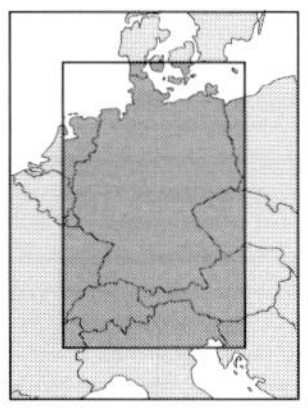

18-19

Middle Europe 1:2 800 000
Austria, Czechoslovakia, Hungary, Poland

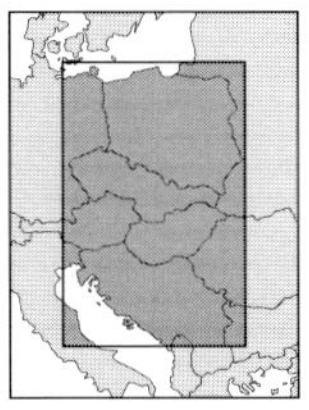

20-21

Switzerland 1:800 000
Liechtenstein

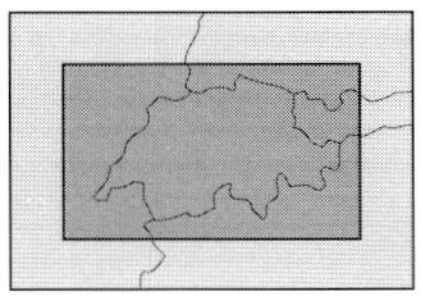

22-23

Northern France 1:2 000 000

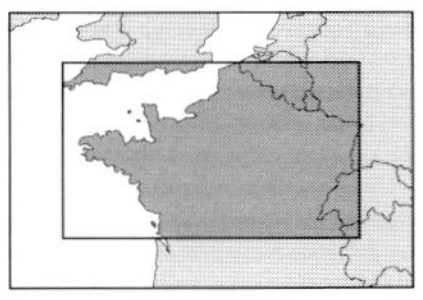

24-25

Southern France 1:2 000 000
Corsica, Monaco

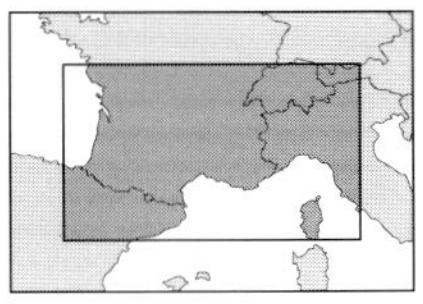

26-27

Eastern Spain 1:2 000 000
Andorra

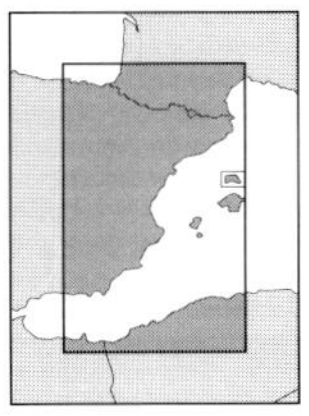

28-29

Western Spain and Portugal 1:2 000 000

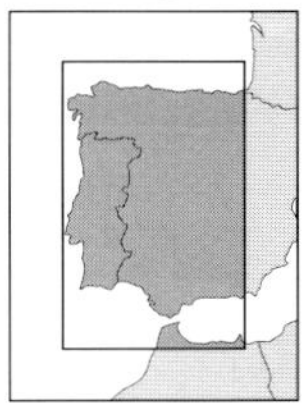

30-31

Northern Italy, Slovenia and Croatia
1:2 000 000
San Marino, Slovenia, *Croatia*

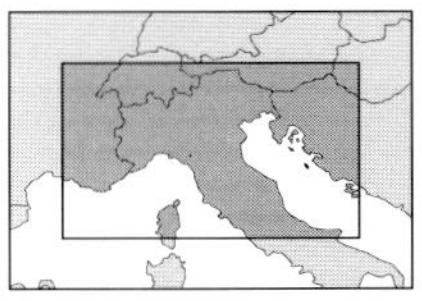

32-33

Southern Italy 1:2 000 000
Sardinia, Sicily

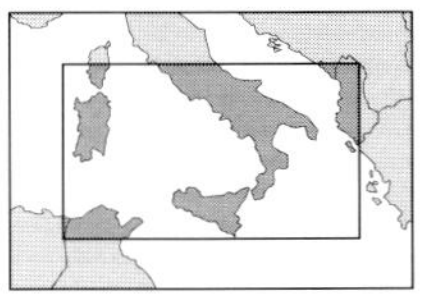

34-35

Balearics, Canaries and Madeira 1:800 000 / 1:1 040 000
Mallorca, Menorca, Ibiza, Tenerife

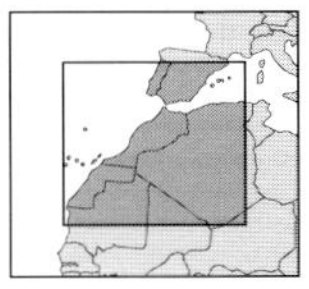

36

Malta, Crete, Corfu, Rhodes and Cyprus
1:800 000 / 1:1 600 000

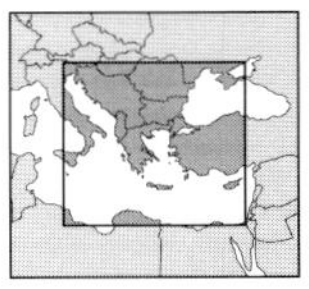

37

The Balkans 1:2 800 000
Yugoslavia, Romania, Bulgaria, Greece, Albania

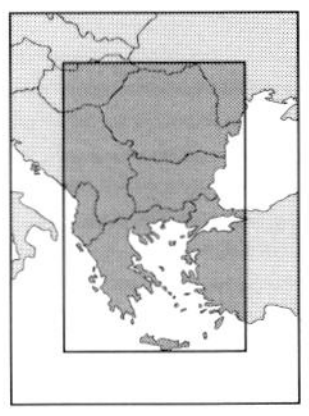

38-39

Western Russia, Belorussia and the Baltic States 1:4 000 000
Russian Fed., Estonia, Latvia, Lithuania, Belorussia, *Ukraine*

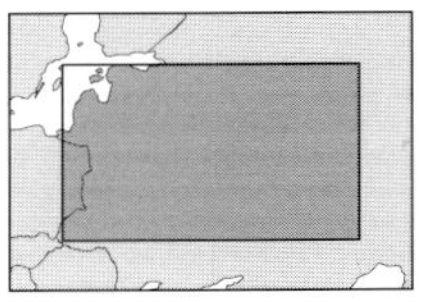

40-41

Ukraine, Moldavia and the Caucasus 1:4 000 000
Russian Fed., Ukraine, Georgia, *Armenia, Azerbaijan,* Moldavia

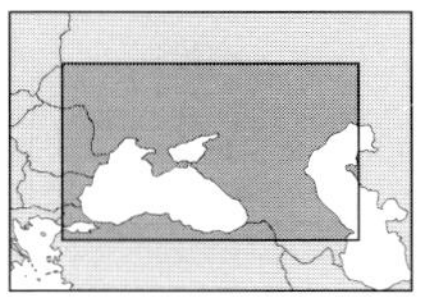

42-43

ASIA

Russia and Central Asia
1:16 000 000
Russian Fed., Kazakhstan, Turkmenistan, Uzbekistan

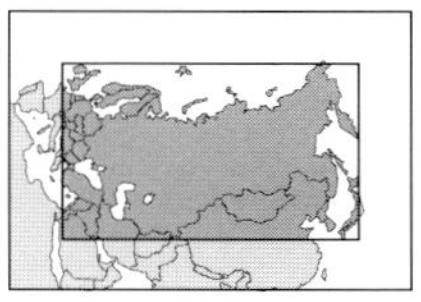

44-45

Asia: Physical
1:40 000 000

46

Asia: Political
1:40 000 000

47

Japan 1:4 000 000
Ryukyu Islands

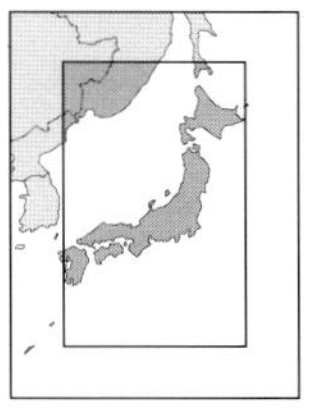

48-49

Northern China and Korea
1:4 800 000
North Korea, South Korea

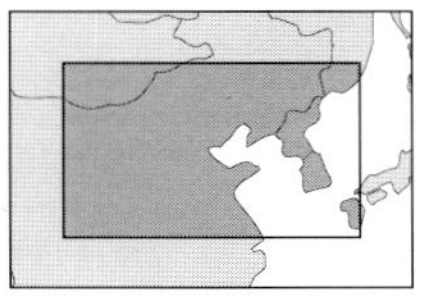

50-51

Southern China 1:4 800 000
Hong Kong, Taiwan, Macau

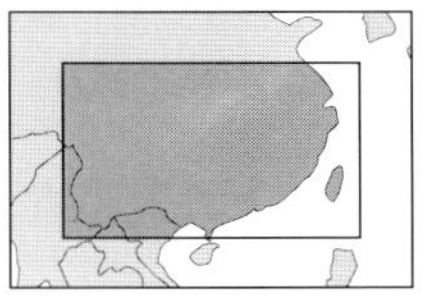

52-53

China 1:16 000 000
Mongolia

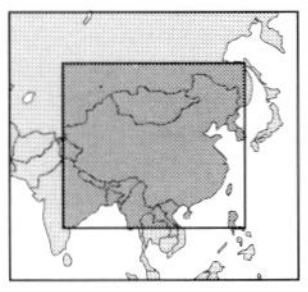

54

Philippines 1:6 000 000

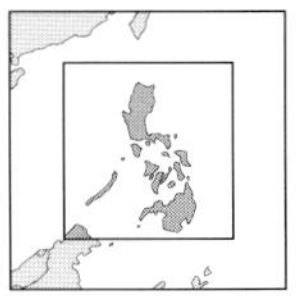

55

Indonesia 1:10 000 000
Malaysia, Singapore, Brunei

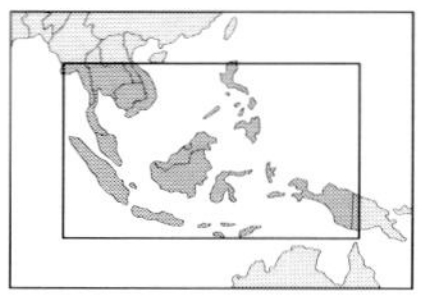

56-57

Mainland South-East Asia
1:4 800 000
Thailand, Vietnam, Cambodia, Laos

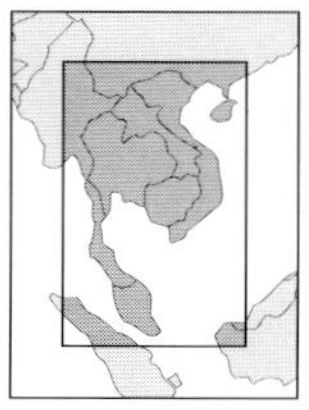

58-59

South Asia 1:8 000 000
India, Pakistan, Bangladesh, Burma, Sri Lanka, Afghanistan

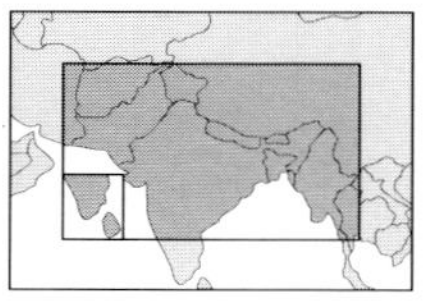

60-61

The Indo-Gangetic Plain
1:4 800 000
India, Pakistan, Nepal, Kashmir

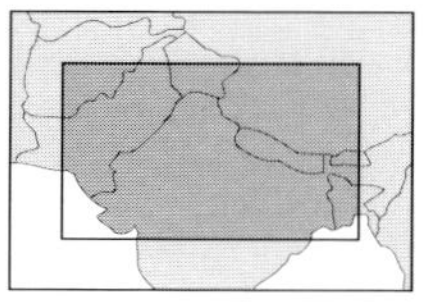

62-63

The Middle East 1:5 600 000
Iran, Iraq, *Saudi Arabia*, United Arab Emirates, Kuwait, Qatar

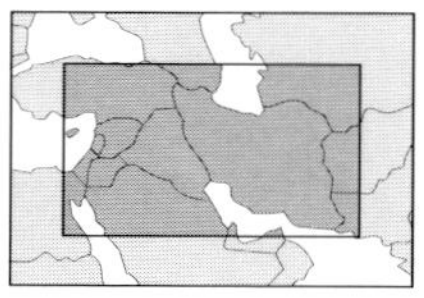

64-65

Turkey 1:4 000 000
Syria

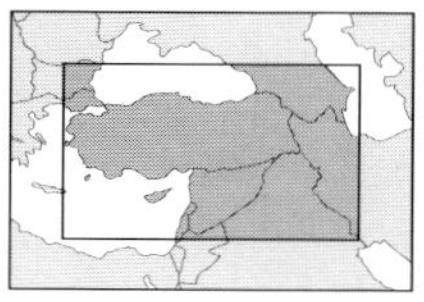

66-67

Arabia and the Horn of Africa 1:12 000 000
Saudi Arabia, Oman, Yemen, *Somalia*, Ethiopia, Djibouti

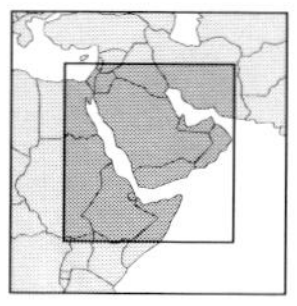

68

The Near East 1:2 000 000
Israel, Lebanon, *Jordan*

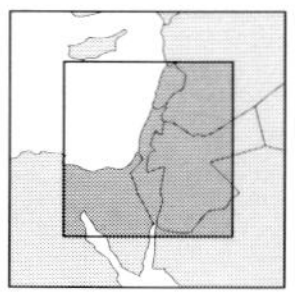

69

AFRICA

Africa: Physical
1:32 000 000
70

Africa: Political
1:32 000 000
71

Northern Africa 1:12 000 000
Libya, Chad, Niger

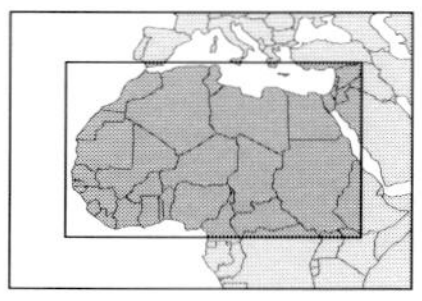

72-73

North-West Africa
1:6 400 000
Algeria, Morocco, Tunisia, *Mauritania, Niger, Mali*

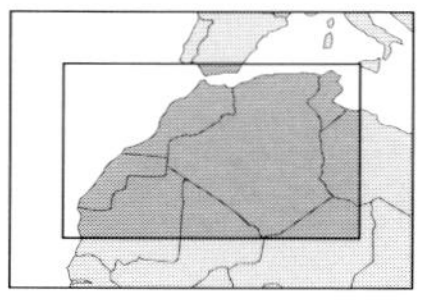

74-75

The Nile Valley 1:6 400 000
Egypt, Sudan, *Ethiopia*
The Nile Delta 1:3 200 000

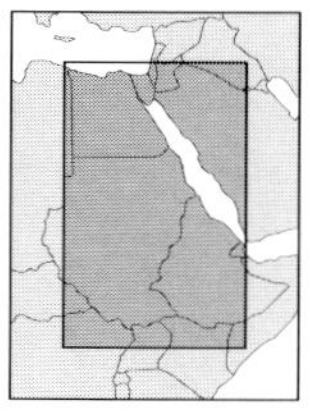

76-77

West Africa 1:6 400 000
Nigeria, Ivory Coast, Ghana, Senegal, Guinea, Burkina Faso

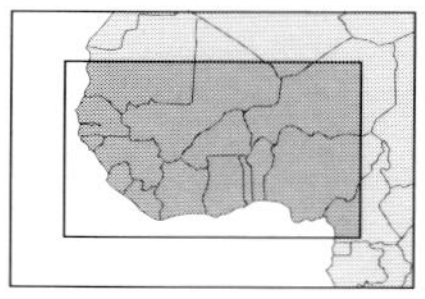

78-79

Central and Southern Africa 1:12 000 000
Zaïre, Angola, Cameroon, Congo, Gabon, Central African Republic

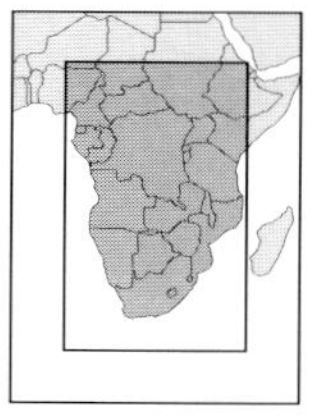

80-81

East Africa 1:6 400 000
Kenya, Tanzania, Zambia, Uganda, Malawi

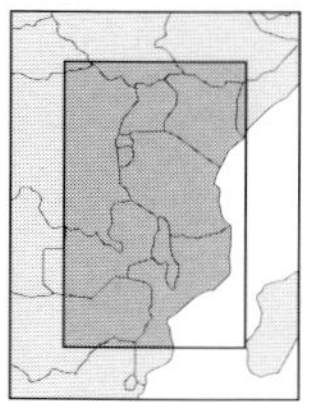

82-83

Southern Africa 1:6 400 000
South Africa, Zimbabwe, Madagascar, *Mozambique*, Botswana, Namibia

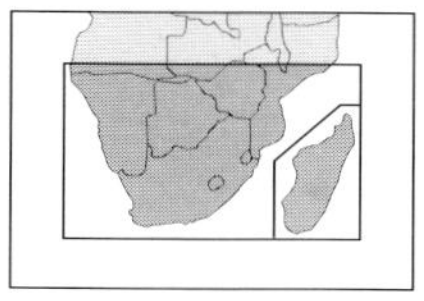

84-85

VIII

AUSTRALIA AND OCEANIA

Australia and Oceania: Physical and Political
1:32 000 000
86

New Zealand 1:4 800 000
Fiji, Tonga, Samoa

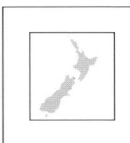
87

Western Australia
1:6 400 000
Northern Territory

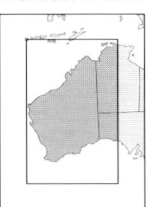
88-89

Eastern Australia 1:6 400 000
New South Wales, Queensland, Victoria, *South Australia*, Tasmania

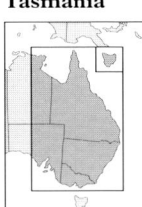
90-91

Pacific Ocean 1:43 200 000
Kiribati, Vanuatu, New Caledonia, Tuvalu, Micronesia, French Polynesia
92-93

NORTH AMERICA

North America: Physical
1:28 000 000
94

North America: Political
1:28 000 000
95

Canada 1:12 000 000
North West Territories, Yukon Alaska 1:24 000 000

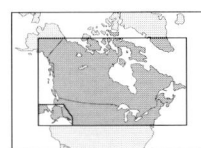
96-97

Eastern Canada 1:5 600 000
Quebec, *Ontario*, Newfoundland

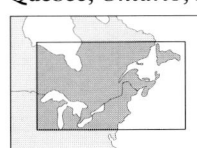
98-99

Western Canada 1:5 600 000
British Columbia, Alberta, Saskatchewan, Manitoba

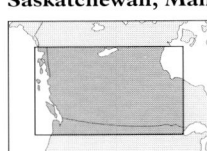
100-101

United States 1:9 600 000
Hawaii 1:8 000 000

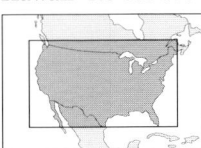
102-103

Eastern United States
1:4 800 000

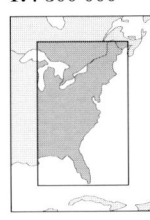
104-105

North-Eastern United States 1:2 000 000
New York, New England, *Pennsylvania*

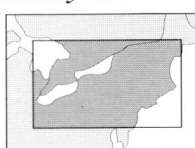
106-107

Middle United States
1:4 800 000

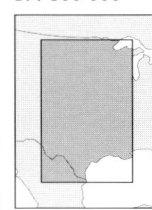
108-109

Western United States
1:4 800 000

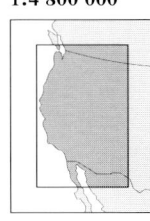
110-111

Central and Southern California and Washington 1:2 000 000

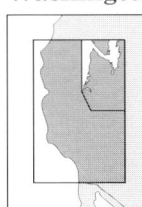
112-113

Mexico 1:6 400 000

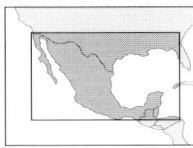
114-115

Central America and the West Indies 1:6 400 000
Guatemala, Nicaragua, Cuba, Jamaica, Panama, Haiti

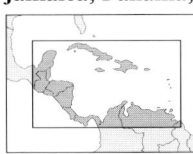
116-117

SOUTH AMERICA

South America: Physical
1:24 000 000
118

South America: Political
1:24 000 000
119

South America - North-West 1:6 400 000
Colombia, Venezuela, *Brazil*, Ecuador, Guyana

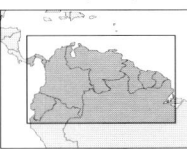
120-121

Eastern Brazil 1:6 400 000

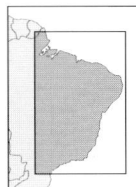
122-123

South America - West
1:6 400 000
Peru, Brazil, Bolivia

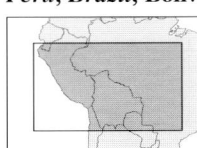
124-125

Central South America
1:6 400 000
Argentina, Chile, Brazil, Paraguay, Uruguay

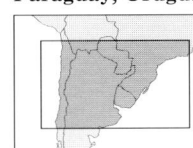
126-127

Southern Chile and Argentina 1:6 400 000

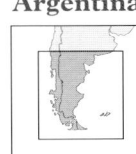
128

INDEX TO WORLD MAPS

129-224

WORLD STATISTICS: COUNTRIES

This alphabetical list includes all the countries and territories of the world. If a territory is not completely independent, then the country it is associated with is named. The area figures give the total area of land, inland water and ice. Units for areas and populations are thousands. The annual income is the Gross National Product per capita in US dollars. The figures are the latest available, usually 1989-91.

Country/Territory	Area km² Thousands	Area miles² Thousands	Population Thousands	Capital	Annual Income US $
Adélie Land (Fr)	432	167	0.03	-	
Afghanistan	652	25	16,433	Kabul	450
Albania	28.8	11.1	3,250	Tiranë	1,000
Algeria	2,382	920	24,960	Algiers	2,060
American Samoa (US)	0.20	0.08	39	Pago Pago	6,000
Amsterdam Is. (Fr)	0.05	0.02	0.03	-	
Andorra (Fr/Spain)	0.45	0.17	52	Andorre-la-Vella	
Angola	1,247	481	10,020	Luanda	620
Anguilla (UK)	0.40	0.09	8	The Valley	
Antigua & Barbuda	0.44	0.17	77	St. John's	4,600
Argentina	2,767	1,068	32,322	Buenos Aires	2,370
Armenia	29.8	11.5	3,300	Yerevan	
Aruba (Neths)	0.19	0.07	60	Oranjestad	6,000
Ascension Is. (UK)	0.09	0.03	1.5	Georgetown	
Australia	7,687	2,968	17,086	Canberra	17,080
Austral. Antarc. Terr.	6,120	2,363	0	-	
Austria	83.9	32.4	7,712	Vienna	19,240
Azerbaijan	86.6	33.4	7,000	Baku	
Azores (Port)	2.2	0.87	260	Ponta Delgada	
Bahamas	13.9	5.4	253	Nassau	11,510
Bahrain	0.68	0.26	503	Manama	6,500
Bangladesh	144	56	115,594	Dacca	200
Barbados	0.43	0.17	255	Bridgetown	6,540
Belau (US)	0.46	0.18	15	Koror	
Belgium	30.5	11.8	9,845	Brussels	15,440
Belize	23.0	8.9	188	Belmopan	1,970
Belorussia	207.6	80.1	10,200	Minsk	
Benin	113	43	4,736	Porto-Novo	360
Bermuda (UK)	0.05	0.02	61	Hamilton	25,000
Bhutan (India)	47.0	18.1	1,517	Thimphu	190
Bolivia	1,099	424	7,400	La Paz/Sucre	620
Botswana	582	225	1,291	Gaborone	2,040
Bouvet Is. (Nor)	0.05	0.02	0.02	-	
Brazil	8,512	3,286	153,322	Brasilia	2,680
Brit. Antarctic Terr. (UK)	1,709	660	0.3	Stanley	
Brit. Ind. Oc. Terr. (UK)	0.08	0.03	3	-	
Brunei	5.8	2.2	266	Bandar Seri Begawan	6,000
Bulgaria	111	43	9,011	Sofia	2,210
Burkina Faso	274	106	9,001	Ouagadougou	330
Burma (Myanmar)	677	261	41,675	Rangoon	500
Burundi	27.8	10.7	5,438	Bujumbura	210
Cambodia	181	70	8,246	Phnom Penh	300
Cameroon	475	184	11,834	Yaoundé	940
Canada	9,976	3,852	26,522	Ottawa	20,450
Canary Is. (Spain)	7.3	2.8	1,700	Las Palmas/S.Cruz	
Cape Verde Is.	4.0	1.6	370	Praia	890
Cayman Is. (UK)	0.26	0.10	27	Georgetown	
Cent. African Rep.	623	241	3,039	Bangui	390
Chad	1,284	496	5,679	Ndjamena	190
Chatham Is. (NZ)	0.96	0.37	0.05	Waitangi	
Chile	757	292	13,386	Santiago	1,940
China	9,597	3,682	1,139,060	Beijing	370
Christmas Is. (Aus)	0.14	0.05	2.3	The Settlement	
Cocos (Keeling) Is. (Aus)	0.01	0.005	0.70	-	
Colombia	1,139	440	32,987	Bogotá	1,240
Comoros	2.2	0.86	551	Moroni	480
Congo	342	132	2,271	Brazzaville	1,010
Cook Is. (NZ)	0.24	0.11	18	Avarua	900
Costa Rica	51.1	19.7	2,994	San José	1,910
Croatia	56.5	21.8	4,680	Zagreb	
Crozet Is. (Fr)	0.51	0.19	35	-	
Cuba	111	43	10,609	Havana	3,000
Cyprus	9.3	3.6	702	Nicosia	8,040
Czechoslovakia	128	49	15,678	Prague	3,140
Denmark	43.1	16.6	5,140	Copenhagen	22,090
Djibouti	23.2	9.0	409	Djibouti	1,000
Dominica	0.75	0.29	83	Roseau	1,940
Dominican Rep.	48.7	18.8	7,170	Santo Domingo	820
Ecuador	284	109	10,782	Quito	960
Egypt	1,001	387	53,153	Cairo	600
El Salvador	21.0	8.1	5,252	San Salvador	1,100
Equatorial Guinea	28.1	10.8	348	Malabo	330
Estonia	44.7	17.4	1,600	Tallinn	
Ethiopia	1,222	472	50,974	Addis Ababa	120
Falkland Is. (UK)	12.2	4.7	2	Stanley	
Faroe Is. (Den)	1.4	0.54	47	Tórshavn	22,090
Fiji	18.3	7.1	765	Suva	1,770
Finland	338	131	4,986	Helsinki	26,070
France	552	213	56,440	Paris	19,480
French Guiana (Fr)	90.0	34.7	99	Cayenne	2,500
French Polynesia (Fr)	4.0	1.5	206	Papeete	6,000
Gabon	268	103	1,172	Libreville	3,220
Gambia, The	11.3	4.4	861	Banjul	260
Georgia	69.7	26.9	5,500	Tbilisi	
Germany	357	138	79,479	Berlin/Bonn	17,000
Ghana	239	92	15,028	Accra	390
Gibraltar (UK)	0.007	0.003	31	-	4,000
Greece	132	51	10,269	Athens	6,000
Greenland (Den)	2,176	840	60	Godthåb	6,000
Grenada	0.34	0.13	85	St. George's	2,120
Guadeloupe (Fr)	1.7	0.66	344	Basse-Terre	7,000
Guam (US)	0.55	0.21	119	Agana	6,000
Guatemala	109	42	9,197	Guatemala City	900
Guinea	246	95	5,756	Conakry	480
Guinea-Bissau	36.1	13.9	965	Bissau	180
Guyana	215	83	796	Georgetown	370
Haiti	27.8	10.7	6,486	Port-au-Prince	370
Honduras	112	43	5,105	Tegucigalpa	590
Hong Kong (UK)	1.1	0.40	5,801	-	11,540
Hungary	93.0	35.9	10,344	Budapest	2,780
Iceland	103	40	255	Reykjavik	21,150
India	3,288	1,269	843,931	Delhi	350
Indonesia	1,905	735	179,300	Jakarta	560
Iran	1,648	636	58,031	Tehran	2,450
Iraq	438	169	18,920	Baghdad	2,000
Ireland	70.3	27.1	3,523	Dublin	9,550
Israel	27.0	10.4	4,659	Jerusalem	10,970
Italy	301	116	57,663	Rome	16,850
Ivory Coast	322	125	11,998	Abidjan	730
Jamaica	11.0	4.2	2,420	Kingston	1,510
Jan Mayen Is. (Nor)	0.38	0.15	0.06	-	
Japan	378	146	123,537	Tokyo	25,430
Johnston Is. (US)	0.002	0.0009	0.30	-	
Jordan	89.2	34.4	4,009	Amman	1,240
Kazakhstan	2,717	1,049	16,500	Alma Ata	
Kenya	580	224	24,032	Nairobi	370
Kerguelen Is. (Fr)	7.2	2.8	0	-	
Kermadec Is. (NZ)	0.03	0.01	0	-	
Kirghizia	199	76.5	4,300	Bishkek	
Kiribati	0.72	0.28	66	Tarawa	760
Korea, North	121	47	21,773	Pyongyang	900
Korea, South	99.0	38.2	43,302	Seoul	5,400
Kuwait	17.8	6.9	2,143	Kuwait City	16,380
Laos	237	91	4,139	Vientiane	200
Latvia	63.1	24.6	2,700	Riga	
Lebanon	10.4	4.0	2,701	Beirut	2,000
Lesotho	30.4	11.7	1,774	Maseru	470
Liberia	111	43	2,607	Monrovia	500
Libya	1,760	679	4,545	Tripoli	5,800
Liechtenstein	0.16	0.06	29	Vaduz	33,000
Lithuania	65.2	25.4	3,751	Vilnius	
Luxembourg	2.6	1.0	384	Luxembourg	28,770
Macau (Port)	0.02	0.006	479	-	2,000
Madagascar	587	227	11,197	Antananarivo	230
Madeira (Port)	0.81	0.31	280	Funchal	
Malawi	118	46	8,556	Lilongwe	200
Malaysia	330	127	17,861	Kuala Lumpur	2,340
Maldives	0.30	0.12	215	Malé	440
Mali	1,240	479	8,156	Bamako	270
Malta	0.32	0.12	354	Valletta	6,630
Mariana Is. (US)	0.48	0.18	22	Saipan	
Marshall Is. (US)	0.18	0.07	42	Majuro	
Martinique (Fr)	1.1	0.42	341	Fort-de-France	4,000
Mauritania	1,025	396	2,050	Nouakchott	500
Mauritius	1.9	0.72	1,075	Port Louis	2,250
Mayotte (Fr)	0.37	0.14	84	Mamoundzou	
Mexico	1,958	756	86,154	Mexico City	2,490
Micronesia, Fed. Stat (US)	0.70	0.27	103	Kolonia	
Midway Is. (US)	0.005	0.002	0.45	-	
Moldavia	33.7	13.0	4,300	Kishinev	
Monaco	0.002	0.0001	29	-	20,000
Mongolia	1,567	605	2,190	Ulan Bator	400
Montserrat (UK)	0.10	0.04	13	Plymouth	
Morocco	447	172	25,061	Rabat	950
Mozambique	802	309	15,656	Maputo	80
Namibia	824	318	1,781	Windhoek	1,000
Nauru	0.02	0.008	10	Domaneab	
Nepal	141	54	18,916	Katmandu	170
Netherlands	41.9	16.2	15,019	Amsterdam	17,330
Neths. Antilles (Neths)	0.99	0.38	189	Willemstad	6,000
New Caledonia (Fr)	19.0	7.3	168	Nouméa	4,000
New Zealand	269	104	3,429	Wellington	12,680
Nicaragua	130	50	3,871	Managua	800
Niger	1,267	489	7,732	Niamey	310
Nigeria	924	357	108,542	Lagos (Abuja)	270
Niue (NZ)	0.26	0.10	3	Alofi	
Norfolk Is. (Aus)	0.03	0.01	2	Kingston	
Norway	324	125	4,242	Oslo	23,120
Oman	212	82	1,502	Muscat	5,220
Pakistan	796	307	112,050	Islamabad	380
Panama	77.1	29.8	2,418	Panama City	1,830
Papua New Guinea	463	179	3,699	Port Moresby	860
Paraguay	407	157	4,277	Asunción	1,110
Peru	1,285	496	22,332	Lima	1,160
Peter 1st Is. (Nor)	0.18	0.07	0	-	
Philippines	300	116	61,480	Manila	730
Pitcairn Is. (UK)	0.03	0.01	0.06	Adamstown	
Poland	313	121	38,180	Warsaw	1,700
Portugal	92.4	35.7	10,525	Lisbon	4,890
Puerto Rico (US)	8.9	3.4	3,599	San Juan	6,470
Qatar	11.0	4.2	368	Doha	15,860
Queen Maud Land (Nor)	2,800	1,081	0	-	
Réunion (Fr)	2.5	0.97	599	St.-Denis	4,000
Romania	238	92	23,200	Bucharest	1,640
Ross Dependency (NZ)	435	168	0	-	
Russia	17,075	6,591	147,400	Moscow	
Rwanda	26.3	10.2	7,181	Kigali	310
St. Christopher/Nevis	0.36	0.14	44	Basseterre	3,300
St. Helena (UK)	0.31	0.12	7	Jamestown	
St. Lucia	0.62	0.24	151	Castries	1,900
St. Paul Is. (Fr)	0.007	0.003	0	-	
St. Pierre & Miquelon (Fr)	0.24	0.09	6	St. Pierre	
St. Vincent/Grenadines	0.39	0.15	116	Kingstown	1,610
San Marino	0.06	0.02	24	San Marino	
São Tomé & Príncipe	0.96	0.37	121	São Tomé	380
Saudi Arabia	2,150	830	14,870	Riyadh	6,230
Senegal	197	76	7,327	Dakar	710
Seychelles	0.28	0.11	67	Victoria	4,670
Sierra Leone	71.7	27.7	4,151	Freetown	240
Singapore	0.62	0.24	3,003	Singapore	12,310
Slovenia	20.3	7.8	1,940	Ljubljana	
Solomon Is.	28.9	11.2	321	Honiara	580
Somalia	638	246	7,497	Mogadishu	150
South Africa	1,221	471	35,282	Pretoria	2,520
South Georgia (UK)	3.8	1.4	0.05	-	
South Sandwich Is. (UK)	0.38	0.15	0	-	
Spain	505	195	38,959	Madrid	10,920
Sri Lanka	65.6	25.3	16,993	Colombo	470
Sudan	2,506	967	25,204	Khartoum	450
Surinam	163	63	422	Paramaribo	3,050
Svalbard (Nor)	62.0	23.9	4	Longyearbyen	
Swaziland	17.4	6.7	768	Mbabane	820
Sweden	450	174	8,618	Stockholm	23,680
Switzerland	41.3	15.9	6,712	Bern	32,790
Syria	185	71	12,116	Damascus	990
Taiwan	36.0	13.9	20,300	Taipei	6,600
Tajikistan	143	55.2	5,100	Dushanbe	
Tanzania	945	365	25,635	Dar es Salaam	120
Thailand	513	198	57,196	Bangkok	1,420
Togo	56.8	21.9	3,531	Lome	410
Tokelau (NZ)	0.01	0.005	2	Nukunonu	
Tonga	0.75	0.29	95	Nuku'alofa	1,010
Trinidad & Tobago	5.1	2.0	1,227	Port of Spain	3,470
Tristan da Cunha (UK)	0.11	0.04	0.33	Edinburgh	
Tunisia	164	63	8,180	Tunis	1,420
Turkey	779	301	57,326	Ankara	1,630
Turkmenistan	488	186	3,500	Ashkhabad	
Turks & Caicos Is. (UK)	0.43	0.17	10	Grand Turk	
Tuvalu	0.03	0.01	10	Funafuti	600
Uganda	236	91	18,795	Kampala	220
Ukraine	604	232	51,700	Kiev	
United Arab Emirates	83.6	32.3	1,589	Abu Dhabi	19,860
United Kingdom	244	94	57,405	London	16,070
United States	9,373	3,619	249,928	Washington	21,700
Uruguay	177	68	3,094	Montevideo	2,560
Uzbekistan	447	173	19,900	Tashkent	
Vanuatu	12.2	4.7	147	Port Vila	1,060
Vatican City	0.0004	0.0002	1.0	-	
Venezuela	912	352	19,735	Caracas	2,560
Vietnam	332	127	66,200	Hanoi	300
Virgin Is. (UK)	0.15	0.06	13	Road Town	
Virgin Is. (US)	0.34	0.13	117	Charlotte Amalie	12,000
Wake Is.	0.008	0.003	0.30	-	
Wallis & Futuna Is. (Fr)	0.20	0.08	18	Mata-Utu	
Western Sahara (Mor)	266	103	179	El Aiun	
Western Samoa	2.8	1.1	164	Apia	730
Yemen	528	204	11,282	San'a	640
Yugoslavia	179	69.4	17,144	Belgrade	3,060
Zaire	2,345	906	35,562	Kinshasa	230
Zambia	753	291	8,073	Lusaka	420
Zimbabwe	391	151	9,369	Harare	640

WORLD STATISTICS: CITIES

This list shows the principal cities with more than 500,000 inhabitants (for China only cities with more than 1 million are included). The figures are taken from the most recent census or estimate available, and as far as possible are the population of the metropolitan area, eg greater New York, Mexico or London. All the figures are in thousands. The top 20 world cities are indicated with their rank in brackets following the name.

Afghanistan
Kabul — 1,127
Algeria
Algiers — 1,722
Oran — 664
Angola
Luanda — 1,200
Argentina
Buenos Aires [8] — 10,728
Cordoba — 1,055
Rosario — 1,016
Mendoza — 668
La Plata — 611
San Miguel Tucuman — 571
Armenia
Yerevan — 1,199
Australia
Sydney — 3,531
Melbourne — 2,965
Brisbane — 1,215
Perth — 1,083
Adelaide — 1,013
Austria
Vienna — 1,483
Azerbaijan
Baku — 1,757
Bangladesh
Dacca — 4,770
Chittagong — 1,840
Khulna — 860
Rajshahi — 430
Belgium
Brussels — 970
Antwerp — 500
Belorussia
Minsk — 1,589
Gomel — 500
Bolivia
La Paz — 993
Brazil
São Paulo [3] — 16,832
Rio de Janeiro [7] — 11,141
Belo Horizonte — 3,446
Recife — 2,945
Pôrto Alegre — 2,924
Salvador — 2,362
Fortaleza — 2,169
Çuritiba — 1,926
Brasilia — 1,557
Nova Iguaçu — 1,325
Belem — 1,296
Santos — 1,200
Goiâna — 928
Campinas — 845
Manaus — 834
São Gonçalo — 731
Guarulhos — 718
Duque de Caxias — 666
Santo Andre — 637
Osasco — 594
São Bernado do Campo — 566
São Luis — 564
Natal — 512
Bulgaria
Sofia — 1,129
Burma
Rangoon — 2,459
Mandalay — 533
Cambodia
Phnom Penh — 500
Cameroon
Douala — 1,030
Yaoundé — 654
Central African Rep.
Bangui — 597
Chad
Ndjamena — 512
Canada
Toronto — 3,427
Montréal — 2,921
Vancouver — 1,381
Ottawa-Hull — 819
Edmonton — 785
Calgary — 671
Winnipeg — 623
Québec — 603
Hamilton — 557

Chile
Santiago — 4,858
China
Shanghai [5] — 12,320
Beijing [10] — 9,750
Tianjin — 5,459
Shenyang — 4,285
Wuhan — 3,493
Canton — 3,359
Chongqing — 2,832
Harbin — 2,668
Chengdu — 2,642
Xi'an — 2,387
Zibo — 2,329
Nanjing — 2,290
Nanchang — 2,289
Lupanshui — 2,247
Taiyuan — 1,929
Changchun — 1,908
Dalian — 1,682
Zhaozhuang — 1,612
Zhengzhou — 1,610
Kunming — 1,516
Jinan — 1,464
Tangshan — 1,410
Guiyang — 1,403
Lanzhou — 1,391
Linyi — 1,385
Pingxiang — 1,305
Qiqihar — 1,301
Anshan — 1,298
Qingdao — 1,273
Xintao — 1,272
Hangzhou — 1,271
Fushun — 1,270
Yangcheng — 1,265
Yulin — 1,255
Dongguang — 1,230
Chao'an — 1,227
Xiaogan — 1,219
Fuzhou — 1,205
Suining — 1,195
Changsha — 1,193
Shijiazhuang — 1,187
Jilin — 1,169
Xintai — 1,167
Puyang — 1,125
Baotou — 1,119
Bozhou — 1,112
Zhongshan — 1,073
Luoyang — 1,063
Laiwu — 1,054
Leshan — 1,039
Urumchi — 1,038
Ningbo — 1,033
Datong — 1,020
Huainan — 1,019
Heze — 1,017
Handan — 1,014
Linhai — 1,012
Macheng — 1,010
Changshu — 1,004
Colombia
Bogotá — 4,185
Medellin — 1,506
Cali — 1,397
Barranquilla — 920
Cartagena — 560
Congo
Brazzaville — 596
Croatia
Zagreb — 1,175
Cuba
Havana — 2,059
Czechoslovakia
Prague — 1,194
Denmark
Copenhagen — 1,339
Dominican Rep.
Santo Domingo — 1,313
Ecuador
Guayaquil — 1,301
Quito — 1,110
Egypt
Cairo [18] — 6,325
Alexandria — 2,893
El Giza — 1,858
Shubra el Kheima — 711
El Salvador
San Salvador — 973

Ethiopia
Addis Ababa — 1,686
Finland
Helsinki — 987
France
Paris [13] — 8,510
Lyons — 1,170
Marseilles — 1,080
Lille — 935
Bordeaux — 628
Toulouse — 523
Georgia
Tbilisi — 1,194
Germany
Berlin — 3,301
Hamburg — 1,594
Munich — 1,189
Cologne — 928
Essen — 623
Frankfurt — 619
Dortmund — 584
Düsseldorf — 563
Stuttgart — 552
Leipzig — 545
Bremen — 533
Duisburg — 525
Dresden — 518
Hanover — 500
Ghana
Accra — 965
Greece
Athens — 3,027
Thessalonika — 872
Guatemala
Guatemala — 2,000
Guinea
Conakry — 705
Haiti
Port-au-Prince — 1,144
Honduras
Tegucigalpa — 605
Hong Kong
Kowloon — 2,302
Hong Kong — 1,176
Tsuen Wan — 690
Hungary
Budapest — 2,115
India
Calcutta [11] — 9,194
Bombay [14] — 8,243
Delhi — 5,729
Madras — 4,289
Bangalore — 2,922
Ahmadabad — 2,548
Hyderabad — 2,546
Poona — 1,686
Kanpur — 1,639
Nagpur — 1,302
Jaipur — 1,015
Lucknow — 1,008
Coimbatore — 920
Patna — 919
Surat — 914
Madurai — 908
Indore — 829
Varanasi — 797
Jabalpur — 757
Agra — 747
Vadodara — 744
Cochin — 686
Dhanbad — 678
Bhopal — 671
Jamshedpur — 670
Allahabad — 650
Ulhasnagar — 649
Tiruchchirappalli — 610
Ludhiana — 606
Srinagar — 606
Vishakhapatnam — 604
Amritsar — 595
Gwalior — 556
Calicut — 546
Vijayawada — 543
Meerut — 537
Dharwad — 527
Trivandrum — 520
Salem — 519
Solapur — 515
Jodhpur — 506
Ranchi — 503

Indonesia
Jakarta [17] — 7,348
Surabaya — 2,224
Medan — 1,806
Bandung — 1,567
Semarang — 1,026
Palembang — 787
Ujung Pandang — 709
Malang — 512
Iran
Tehran [19] — 6,043
Mashhad — 1,464
Esfahan — 987
Tabriz — 971
Shiraz — 848
Ahvaz — 580
Bakhtaran — 561
Qom — 543
Iraq
Baghdad — 4,649
Basra — 617
Mosul — 571
Ireland
Dublin — 921
Italy
Rome — 2,817
Milan — 1,464
Naples — 1,203
Turin — 1,012
Palermo — 731
Genoa — 712
Ivory Coast
Abidjan — 1,850
Bouaké — 640
Jamaica
Kingston — 525
Japan
Tokyo [6] — 11,829
Yokohama — 2,993
Osaka — 2,636
Nagoya — 2,116
Sapporo — 1,543
Kyoto — 1,479
Kobe — 1,411
Fukuoka — 1,160
Kawasaki — 1,089
Kitakyushu — 1,056
Hiroshima — 1,044
Sakai — 818
Chiba — 789
Sendai — 700
Okayama — 572
Kumamoto — 556
Kagoshima — 531
Higashiosaka — 523
Hamamatsu — 514
Amagasaki — 509
Funabashi — 507
Jordan
Amman — 1,160
Irbid — 680
Kazakhstan
Alma Ata — 1,108
Karaganda — 614
Astrakhan — 509
Kenya
Nairobi — 1,429
Mombasa — 500
Kirghizia
Bishkek — 616
Korea, North
Pyongyang — 2,639
Hamhung — 775
Chongjin — 754
Chinnampo — 691
Sinuiju — 500
Korea, South
Seoul [9] — 10,513
Pusan — 3,754
Taegu — 2,206
Inchon — 1,604
Kwangju — 1,165
Taejon — 866
Ulsan — 551

Benghazi — 650
Lithuania
Vilnius — 582
Madagascar
Antananarivo — 703
Malaysia
Kuala Lumpur — 1,103
Mali
Bamako — 646
Mauritania
Nouakchott — 500
Mexico
Mexico City [1] — 18,748
Guadalajara — 2,587
Monterrey — 2,335
Puebla — 1,218
León — 947
Torreón — 730
San Luis Potosi — 602
Ciudad Juárez — 596
Mérida — 580
Culiacán Rosales — 560
Mexicali — 511
Moldavia
Kishinev — 565
Mongolia
Ulan Bator — 500
Morocco
Casablanca — 2,158
Rabat-Salé — 893
Fès — 548
Mozambique
Maputo — 1,070
Netherlands
Rotterdam — 1,040
Amsterdam — 1,038
The Hague — 684
Utrecht — 526
New Zealand
Auckland — 851
Nicaragua
Managua — 682
Nigeria
Lagos — 1,097
Ibadan — 1,060
Ogbomosho — 527
Norway
Oslo — 643
Pakistan
Karachi — 5,208
Lahore — 2,953
Faisalabad — 1,104
Rawalpindi — 795
Hyderabad — 752
Multan — 722
Gujranwala — 659
Peshawar — 556
Panama
Panama City — 625
Paraguay
Asunción — 708
Peru
Lima-Callao — 4,605
Arequipa — 592
Philippines
Manila — 1,728
Quezon City — 1,326
Cebu — 552
Caloocan — 524
Poland
Warsaw — 1,671
Lodz — 852
Krakow — 744
Wroclaw — 640
Poznan — 586
Portugal
Lisbon — 1,612
Oporto — 1,315
Puerto Rico
San Juan — 1,816
Romania
Bucharest — 2,014
Russia
Moscow [12] — 8,967
St Petersburg — 5,020
Nizhniy Novgorod — 1,438
Novosibirsk — 1,436
Yekaterinburg — 1,367
Samara — 1,257
Chelyabinsk — 1,179

Omsk — 1,148
Kazan — 1,094
Perm — 1,091
Ufa — 1,083
Rostov — 1,020
Volgograd — 999
Krasnoyarsk — 912
Saratov — 905
Voronezh — 887
Vladivostok — 648
Izhevsk — 635
Yaroslavl — 633
Togliatti — 630
Irkutsk — 626
Simbirsk — 625
Krasnodar — 620
Barnaul — 602
Khaborovsk — 601
Novokuznetsk — 600
Orenburg — 547
Penza — 543
Tula — 540
Kemerovo — 520
Ryazan — 515
Tomsk — 502
Naberezhniye-Chelni — 501
Saudi Arabia
Riyadh — 2,000
Jedda — 1,400
Mecca — 618
Medina — 500
Senegal
Dakar — 1,382
Singapore
Singapore — 2,600
Somali Rep.
Mogadishu — 1,000
South Africa
Cape Town — 1,912
Johannesburg — 1,762
East Rand — 1,038
Durban — 982
Pretoria — 823
Port Elizabeth — 652
West Rand — 647
Vereeniging — 540
Spain
Madrid — 3,123
Barcelona — 1,694
Valencia — 739
Seville — 668
Zaragoza — 596
Malaga — 595
Sri Lanka
Colombo — 1,412
Sudan
Omdurman — 600
Khartoum — 510
Sweden
Stockholm — 1,471
Gothenburg — 720
Malmö — 500
Switzerland
Zurich — 839
Syria
Damascus — 1,361
Aleppo — 1,308
Taiwan
Taipei — 2,680
Kaohsiung — 1,343
Taichung — 715
Tainan — 657
Panchiao — 506
Tajikistan
Dushanbe — 595
Tanzania
Dar es Salaam — 1,100
Thailand
Bangkok — 5,609
Tunisia
Tunis — 774
Turkey
Istanbul — 5,495
Ankara — 2,252
Izmir — 1,490
Adana — 776
Bursa — 614
Uganda
Kampala — 500

Ukraine
Kiev — 2,587
Kharkhov — 1,611
Dnepropetrovsk — 1,179
Odessa — 1,115
Donetsk — 1,110
Zaporozhye — 884
Lvov — 790
Krivoy Rog — 713
Mariupol — 529
Lugansk — 509
Nikolayev — 503
United Kingdom
London [17] — 6,378
Manchester — 1,669
Birmingham — 1,400
Liverpool — 1,060
Glasgow — 730
Newcastle — 617
Uruguay
Montevideo — 1,248
United States
New York [2] — 18,120
Los Angeles [4] — 13,770
Chicago [15] — 8,181
San Francisco [20] — 6,042
Philadelphia — 5,963
Detroit — 4,620
Dallas — 3,766
Boston — 3,736
Washington — 3,734
Houston — 3,642
Miami — 3,001
Cleveland — 2,769
Atlanta — 2,737
Saint Louis — 2,467
Seattle — 2,421
Minneapolis-SP. — 2,388
San Diego — 2,370
Baltimore — 2,343
Pittsburgh — 2,284
Phoenix — 2,030
Tampa — 1,995
Denver — 1,858
Cincinnati — 1,729
Kansas City — 1,575
Milwaukee — 1,572
Portland — 1,414
Sacramento — 1,385
Norfolk — 1,380
Columbus — 1,344
San Antonio — 1,323
New Orleans — 1,307
Indianapolis — 1,237
Buffalo — 1,176
Providence — 1,118
Charlotte — 1,112
Hartford — 1,108
Salt Lake City — 1,065
San Jose — 712
Memphis — 653
Jacksonville — 610
Uzbekistan
Tashkent — 2,073
Venezuela
Caracas — 3,247
Maracaibo — 1,295
Valencia — 1,135
Maracay — 857
Barquisimeto — 718
Vietnam
Ho Chi Minh — 3,900
Hanoi — 3,100
Haiphong — 1,279
Da-Nang — 500
Yemen
San'a — 500
Yugoslavia
Belgrade — 1,470
Skopje — 505
Zaïre
Kinshasa — 2,654
Lubumbashi — 543
Zambia
Lusaka — 900
Zimbabwe
Harare — 681
Bulawayo — 500

WORLD STATISTICS: DISTANCES

The table shows air distances in miles and kilometres between thirty major cities. Known as 'Great Circle' distances, these measure the shortest routes between the cities, which aircraft use where possible. The maps show the world centred on six individual cities, and illustrate, for example, why direct flights from Japan to northern America and Europe are across the Arctic regions, and Singapore is on the direct line route from Europe to Australia. The maps have been constructed on an Azimuthal Equidistant projection, on which all distances measured through the centre point are true to scale. The circular lines are drawn at 5,000, 10,000 and 15,000 km from the central city.

Distances in the upper-right triangle are in **miles**; distances in the lower-left triangle are in **kilometres (Kms)**.

	Berlin	Bombay	Buenos Aires	Cairo	Calcutta	Caracas	Chicago	Copenhagen	Darwin	Hong Kong	Honolulu	Johannesburg	Lagos	Lisbon	London	Los Angeles	Mexico City	Moscow	Nairobi	New York	Paris	Peking	Reykjavik	Rio de Janeiro	Rome	Singapore	Sydney	Tokyo	Toronto	Wellington
Berlin	—	3907	7400	1795	4370	5241	4402	222	8044	5440	7310	5511	3230	1436	557	5785	6047	1000	3958	3967	545	4860	1482	6230	734	6179	10002	5545	4037	11272
Bombay	6288	—	9275	2706	1034	9024	8048	3990	4510	2683	8024	4334	4730	4982	4467	8700	9728	3126	2816	7793	4356	2956	5179	8332	3837	2432	6313	4189	7760	7686
Buenos Aires	11909	14925	—	7341	10268	3167	5599	7498	9130	11481	7558	5025	4919	5964	6917	6122	4591	8374	6463	5298	6867	11972	7106	1214	6929	9867	7332	11410	5650	6202
Cairo	2890	4355	11814	—	3541	6340	6127	1992	7216	5064	8838	3894	2432	2358	2180	7580	7687	1803	2197	5605	1994	4688	3272	6149	1325	5137	8959	5947	5737	10268
Calcutta	7033	1664	16524	5699	—	9609	7978	4395	3758	1653	7048	5256	5727	5639	4946	8152	9494	3438	3839	7921	4883	2031	5398	9366	4486	1800	5678	3195	7805	7055
Caracas	8435	14522	5096	10203	15464	—	2502	5215	11221	10166	6009	6847	4810	4044	4664	3612	2228	6175	7173	2131	4738	8947	4297	2825	5196	11407	9534	8801	2406	8154
Chicago	7084	12953	9011	3206	12839	4027	—	4250	9361	7783	4247	8689	5973	3991	3949	1742	1694	4971	8005	711	4132	6588	2956	5311	4809	9369	9243	6299	435	8358
Copenhagen	357	6422	12067	9860	7072	8392	6840	—	8017	5388	7088	5732	3436	1540	592	5594	5912	970	4167	3845	638	4475	1306	6345	951	6195	9968	5403	3892	11160
Darwin	12946	7257	14693	11612	6047	18059	15065	12903	—	2654	5369	6611	8837	9391	8605	7888	9091	7053	6472	9971	8582	3735	8632	9948	8243	2081	1957	3375	9630	3309
Hong Kong	8754	4317	18478	8150	2659	16360	12526	8671	4271	—	5543	6669	7360	6853	5980	7232	8775	4439	5453	8047	5984	1220	6015	11001	5769	1615	4582	1786	7810	5857
Honolulu	11764	12914	12164	14223	11343	9670	6836	11407	8640	8921	—	11934	10133	7821	7228	2558	3781	7036	10739	4958	7437	5070	6081	8290	8026	6721	5075	3854	4638	4669
Johannesburg	8870	6974	8088	6267	8459	11019	13984	9225	10639	10732	19206	—	2799	5089	5637	10362	9063	5692	1818	7979	5426	7276	6797	4420	4811	5381	6860	8418	8310	7308
Lagos	5198	7612	7916	3915	9216	7741	9612	5530	14222	11845	16308	4505	—	2360	3118	7713	6879	3886	2366	5268	2929	7119	4175	3750	2510	6925	9643	8376	5560	9973
Lisbon	2311	8018	9600	3794	9075	6501	6424	2478	15114	11028	12587	8191	3799	—	987	5668	5391	2427	4015	3369	903	6007	1832	4805	1157	7385	11295	6928	3565	12163
London	928	7190	11131	3508	7961	7507	6356	952	13848	9623	11632	9071	5017	1588	—	5442	5552	1552	4237	3463	212	5057	1172	5778	889	6743	10558	5942	3545	11691
Los Angeles	9311	14000	9852	12200	13120	5812	2804	9003	12695	11639	4117	16676	12414	9122	8758	—	1549	6070	9659	2446	5645	6251	4310	6310	6332	8776	7502	5475	2170	6719
Mexico City	9732	15656	7389	12372	15280	3586	2726	9514	14631	14122	6085	14585	11071	8676	8936	2493	—	6664	9207	2090	5717	7742	4635	4780	6365	10321	8058	7024	2018	6897
Moscow	1610	5031	13477	2902	5534	9938	8000	1561	11350	7144	11323	9161	6254	3906	2498	9769	10724	—	3942	4666	1545	3600	2053	7184	1477	5237	9008	4651	4637	10283
Nairobi	6370	4532	10402	3536	6179	11544	12883	6706	10415	8776	17282	2927	3807	6461	6819	15544	14818	6344	—	7358	4029	5727	5395	5548	3350	4635	7552	6996	7570	8490
New York	6385	12541	8526	9020	12747	3430	1145	6188	12647	12950	7980	12841	8477	5422	5572	3936	3364	7510	11842	—	3626	6828	2613	4832	4280	9531	9935	6741	356	8951
Paris	876	7010	11051	3210	7858	7625	6650	1026	13812	9630	11968	8732	4714	1454	342	9085	9200	2486	6485	5836	—	5057	1384	5708	687	6671	10539	6038	3738	11798
Peking	7822	4757	19268	7544	3269	14399	10603	7202	6011	1963	8160	11710	11457	9668	8138	10060	12460	5794	9216	10988	8217	—	4897	10773	5049	2783	5561	1304	6557	6700
Reykjavik	2385	8335	11437	5266	8687	6915	4757	2103	13892	9681	9787	10938	6718	2948	1887	6936	7460	3304	8683	4206	2228	7882	—	6135	2048	7155	10325	5469	2600	10725
Rio de Janeiro	10025	13409	1953	9896	15073	4546	8547	10211	16011	17704	13342	7113	6035	7734	9299	10155	7693	11562	8928	7777	9187	17338	9874	—	5725	9763	8389	11551	5180	7367
Rome	1180	6175	11151	2133	7219	8363	7739	1531	13265	9284	12916	7743	4039	1861	1431	10188	10243	2376	5391	6888	1105	8126	3297	9214	—	6229	10143	6127	4399	11523
Singapore	9944	3914	15879	8267	2897	18359	15078	9969	3349	2599	10816	8660	11145	11886	10852	14123	16610	8428	7460	15339	10737	4478	11514	15712	10025	—	3915	3306	9350	5298
Sydney	16096	10160	11800	14418	9138	15343	14875	16042	3150	7374	8168	11040	15519	18178	16992	12073	12969	14497	12153	15989	16962	8949	16617	13501	16324	6300	—	4861	9800	1383
Tokyo	8924	6742	18362	9571	5141	14164	10137	8696	5431	2874	6202	13547	13480	11149	9562	8811	11304	7485	11260	10849	9718	2099	8802	18589	9861	5321	7823	—	6410	5762
Toronto	6497	12488	9093	9233	12561	3873	700	6265	15498	12569	7465	13374	8948	5737	5704	3492	3247	7462	12183	574	6015	10552	4184	8336	7080	15047	15772	10316	—	8820
Wellington	18140	12370	9981	16524	11354	13122	13451	17961	5325	9427	7513	11761	16050	19575	18814	10814	11100	16549	13664	14405	18987	10782	17260	11855	18545	8526	2226	9273	14194	—

MEXICO CITY
19 26N 99 4W

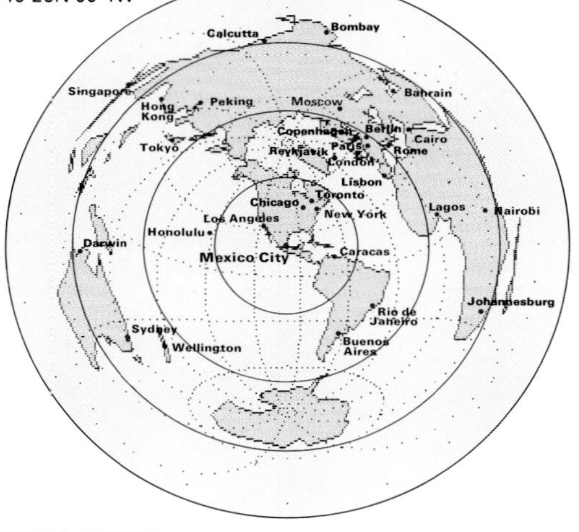

LONDON
51 28N 0 27W

TOKYO
35 33N 139 46E

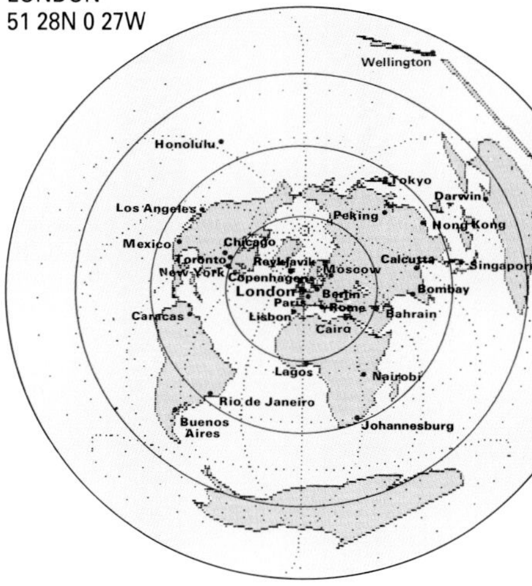

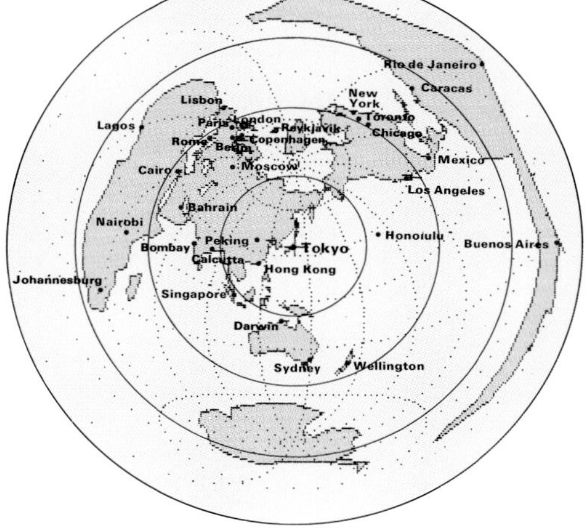

RIO DE JANEIRO
22 50S 43 15W

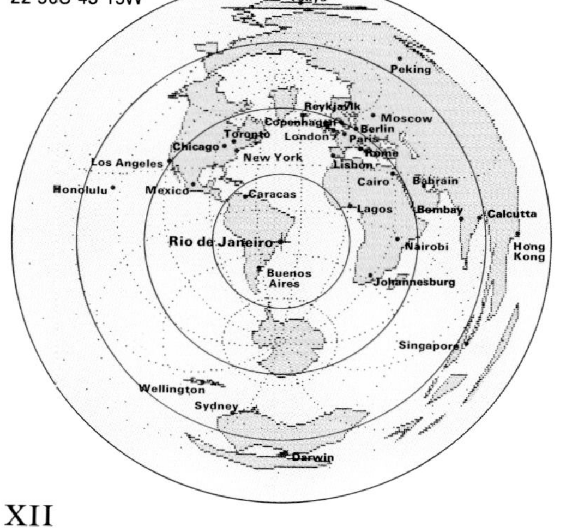

SINGAPORE
1 21N 103 54E

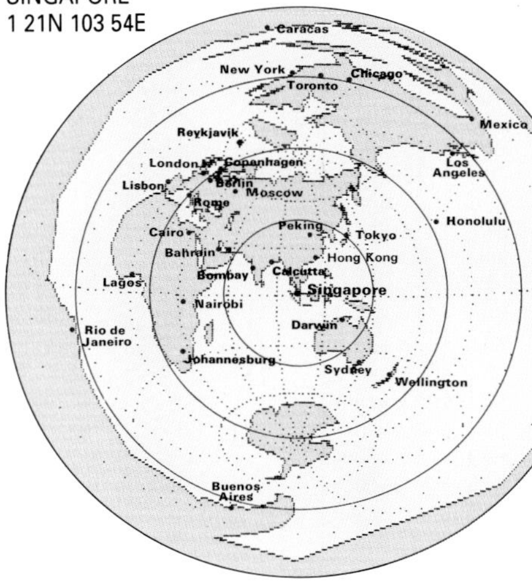

SYDNEY
33 56S 151 10E

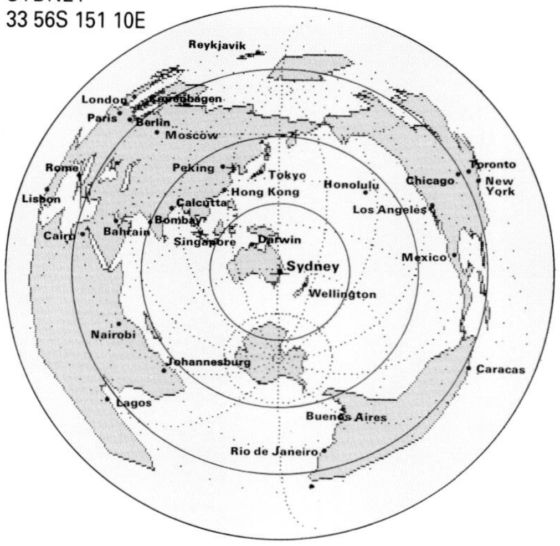

WORLD STATISTICS: CLIMATE

Rainfall and temperature figures are provided for more than 70 cities around the world. As climate is affected by altitude, the height of each city is shown in metres beneath its name. For each month, the figures in red show average temperature in degrees Celsius or centigrade, and in blue the total rainfall or snow in millimetres; the average annual temperature and total annual rainfall are at the end of the rows.

EUROPE

	Jan.	Feb.	Mar.	Apr.	May	June	July	Aug.	Sept.	Oct.	Nov.	Dec.	Year
Athens, Greece	62	37	37	23	23	14	6	7	15	51	56	71	402
107 m	10	10	12	16	20	25	28	28	24	20	15	11	18
Berlin, Germany	46	40	33	42	49	65	73	69	48	49	46	43	603
55 m	-1	0	4	9	14	17	19	18	15	9	5	1	9
Istanbul, Turkey	109	92	72	46	38	34	34	30	58	81	103	119	816
114 m	5	6	7	11	16	20	23	23	20	16	12	8	14
Lisbon, Portugal	111	76	109	54	44	16	3	4	33	62	93	103	708
77 m	11	12	14	16	17	20	22	23	21	18	14	12	17
London, UK	54	40	37	37	46	45	57	59	49	57	64	48	593
5 m	4	5	7	9	12	16	18	17	15	11	8	5	11
Málaga, Spain	61	51	62	46	26	5	1	3	29	64	64	62	474
33 m	12	13	16	17	19	29	25	26	23	20	16	13	18
Moscow, Russia	39	38	36	37	53	58	88	71	58	45	47	54	624
156 m	-13	-10	-4	6	13	16	18	17	12	6	-1	-7	4
Odessa, Ukraine	57	62	30	21	34	34	42	37	37	13	35	71	473
64 m	-3	-1	2	9	15	20	22	22	18	12	9	1	10
Paris, France	56	46	35	42	57	54	59	64	55	50	51	50	619
75 m	3	4	8	11	15	18	20	19	17	12	7	4	12
Rome, Italy	71	62	57	51	46	37	15	21	63	99	129	93	744
17 m	8	9	11	14	18	22	25	25	22	17	13	10	16
Shannon, Irish Republic	94	67	56	53	61	57	77	79	86	86	96	117	929
2 m	5	5	7	9	12	14	16	16	14	11	8	6	10
Stockholm, Sweden	43	30	25	31	34	45	61	76	60	48	53	48	554
44 m	-3	-3	-1	5	10	15	18	17	12	7	3	0	7

ASIA

	Jan.	Feb.	Mar.	Apr.	May	June	July	Aug.	Sept.	Oct.	Nov.	Dec.	Year
Bahrain	8	18	13	8	<3	0	0	0	0	0	18	18	81
5 m	17	18	21	25	29	32	33	34	31	28	24	19	26
Bangkok, Thailand	8	20	36	58	198	160	160	175	305	206	66	5	1,397
2 m	26	28	29	30	29	29	28	28	28	28	26	25	28
Beirut, Lebanon	191	158	94	53	18	3	<3	<3	5	51	132	185	892
34 m	14	14	16	18	22	24	27	28	26	24	19	16	21
Bombay, India	3	3	3	<3	18	485	617	340	264	64	13	3	1,809
11 m	24	24	26	28	30	29	27	27	27	28	27	26	27
Calcutta, India	10	31	36	43	140	297	325	328	252	114	20	5	1,600
6 m	20	22	27	30	30	30	29	29	29	28	23	19	26
Colombo, Sri Lanka	89	69	147	231	371	224	135	109	160	348	315	147	2,365
7 m	26	26	27	28	28	27	27	27	27	27	26	26	27
Harbin, China	6	5	10	23	43	94	112	104	46	33	8	5	488
160 m	-18	-15	-5	6	13	19	22	21	14	4	-6	-16	3
Ho Chi Minh, Vietnam	15	3	13	43	221	330	315	269	335	269	114	56	1,984
9 m	26	27	29	30	29	28	28	28	27	27	27	26	28
Hong Kong	33	46	74	137	292	394	381	361	257	114	43	31	2,162
33 m	16	15	18	22	26	28	28	28	27	25	21	18	23
Jakarta, Indonesia	300	300	211	147	114	97	64	43	66	112	142	203	1,798
8 m	26	26	27	27	27	27	27	27	27	27	26	26	27
Kabul, Afghanistan	31	36	94	102	20	5	3	3	<3	15	20	10	338
1,815 m	-3	-1	6	13	18	22	25	24	20	14	7	3	12
Karachi, Pakistan	13	10	8	3	3	18	81	41	13	<3	3	5	196
4 m	19	20	24	28	30	31	30	29	28	28	24	20	26
Kazalinsk, Kazakhstan	10	10	13	12	15	5	5	8	8	10	13	15	125
63 m	-12	-11	-3	6	18	23	25	23	16	8	-1	-7	7
New Delhi, India	23	18	13	8	13	74	180	172	117	10	3	10	640
218 m	14	17	23	28	33	34	31	30	29	26	20	15	25
Omsk, Russia	15	8	8	13	31	51	51	51	28	25	18	20	318
85 m	-22	-19	-12	-1	10	16	18	16	10	1	-11	-18	-1
Shanghai, China	48	58	84	94	94	180	147	142	130	71	51	36	1,135
7 m	4	5	9	14	20	24	28	28	23	19	12	7	16
Singapore	252	173	193	188	173	173	170	196	178	208	254	257	2,413
10 m	26	27	28	28	28	28	28	27	27	27	27	27	27
Tehran, Iran	46	38	46	36	13	3	3	3	3	8	20	31	246
1,220 m	2	5	9	16	21	26	30	29	25	18	12	6	17
Tokyo, Japan	48	74	107	135	147	165	142	152	234	208	97	56	1,565
6 m	3	4	7	13	17	21	25	26	23	17	11	6	14
Ulan Bator, Mongolia	<3	<3	3	5	10	28	76	51	23	5	5	3	208
1,325 m	-26	-21	-13	-1	6	14	16	14	8	-1	-13	-22	-3
Verkhoyansk, Russia	5	5	3	5	8	23	28	25	13	8	5	5	134
100 m	-50	-45	-32	-15	0	12	14	9	2	-15	-38	-48	-17

AFRICA

	Jan.	Feb.	Mar.	Apr.	May	June	July	Aug.	Sept.	Oct.	Nov.	Dec.	Year
Addis Ababa, Ethiopia	<3	3	25	135	213	201	206	239	102	28	<3	0	1,151
2,450 m	19	20	20	20	19	18	18	18	19	21	22	21	20
Antananarivo, Madagas.	300	279	178	53	18	8	8	10	18	61	135	287	1,356
1,372 m	21	21	21	19	18	15	14	15	17	19	21	21	19
Cairo, Egypt	5	5	5	3	3	<3	0	0	<3	<3	3	5	28
116 m	13	15	18	20	25	28	28	28	26	24	20	16	22
Cape Town, South Africa	15	8	18	48	79	84	89	66	43	31	18	10	508
17 m	21	21	20	17	14	13	12	13	14	16	18	19	17
Johannesburg, S. Africa	114	109	89	38	25	8	8	8	23	56	107	125	709
1,665 m	20	20	18	16	13	10	11	13	16	18	19	20	16

	Jan.	Feb.	Mar.	Apr.	May	June	July	Aug.	Sept.	Oct.	Nov.	Dec.	Year
Khartoum, Sudan	<3	<3	<3	<3	3	8	53	71	18	5	<3	0	158
390 m	24	25	28	31	33	34	32	31	32	32	28	25	29
Kinshasa, Zaïre	135	145	196	196	158	8	3	3	31	119	221	142	1,354
325 m	26	26	27	27	26	24	23	24	25	26	26	26	25
Lagos, Nigeria	28	46	102	150	269	460	279	64	140	206	69	25	1,836
3 m	27	28	29	28	28	26	26	25	26	26	28	28	27
Lusaka, Zambia	231	191	142	18	3	<3	<3	<3	0	10	91	150	836
1,277 m	21	22	21	21	19	16	16	18	22	24	23	22	21
Monrovia, Liberia	31	56	97	216	516	973	996	373	744	772	236	130	5,138
23 m	26	26	27	27	26	25	24	25	25	25	26	26	26
Nairobi, Kenya	38	64	125	211	158	46	15	23	31	53	109	86	958
1,820 m	19	19	19	19	18	16	16	16	18	19	18	18	18
Timbuktu, Mali	<3	<3	3	<3	5	23	79	81	38	3	<3	<3	231
301 m	22	24	28	32	34	35	32	30	32	31	28	23	29
Tunis, Tunisia	64	51	41	36	18	8	3	8	33	51	48	61	419
66 m	10	11	13	16	19	23	26	27	25	20	16	11	18
Walvis Bay, South Africa	<3	5	8	3	3	<3	<3	3	<3	<3	<3	<3	23
7 m	19	19	19	18	17	16	15	14	14	15	17	18	18

AUSTRALIA, NEW ZEALAND AND ANTARCTICA

	Jan.	Feb.	Mar.	Apr.	May	June	July	Aug.	Sept.	Oct.	Nov.	Dec.	Year
Alice Springs, Australia	43	33	28	10	15	13	9	8	8	18	31	38	252
579 m	29	28	25	20	15	12	12	14	18	23	26	28	21
Christchurch, N. Zealand	56	43	48	48	66	66	69	48	46	43	48	56	638
10 m	16	16	14	12	9	6	6	7	9	12	14	16	11
Darwin, Australia	386	312	254	97	15	3	<3	3	13	51	119	239	1,491
30 m	29	29	29	29	28	26	25	26	28	29	30	29	28
Mawson, Antarctica	11	30	20	10	44	180	14	40	3	20	0	0	362
14 m	0	-5	-10	-14	-15	-16	-18	-18	-19	-13	-5	-1	-11
Perth, Australia	8	10	20	43	130	180	170	149	86	56	20	13	881
60 m	23	23	22	19	16	14	13	13	15	16	19	22	18
Sydney, Australia	89	102	127	135	127	117	117	76	73	71	73	73	1,181
42 m	22	22	21	18	15	13	12	13	15	18	19	21	17

NORTH AMERICA

	Jan.	Feb.	Mar.	Apr.	May	June	July	Aug.	Sept.	Oct.	Nov.	Dec.	Year
Anchorage, Alaska, USA	20	18	15	10	13	18	41	66	66	56	25	23	371
40 m	-11	-8	-5	2	7	12	14	13	9	2	-5	-11	2
Chicago, Ill., USA	51	51	66	71	86	99	84	81	79	66	61	51	836
251 m	-4	-3	2	9	14	20	23	22	19	12	5	-1	10
Churchill, Man., Canada	15	13	18	23	32	44	46	58	51	43	39	21	402
13 m	-28	-26	-20	-10	-2	6	12	11	5	-2	-12	-22	-7
Edmonton, Alta., Canada	25	19	19	22	43	77	89	78	39	17	16	25	466
676 m	-15	-10	-4	5	11	15	17	16	11	6	-4	-10	3
Honolulu, Hawaii, USA	104	66	79	48	25	18	23	28	36	48	64	104	643
12 m	23	18	19	20	22	24	25	26	26	24	22	19	22
Houston, Tex., USA	89	76	84	91	119	117	99	99	104	94	89	109	1,171
12 m	12	13	17	21	24	27	28	29	26	22	16	12	21
Kingston, Jamaica	23	15	23	31	102	89	38	91	99	180	74	36	800
34 m	25	25	25	26	26	28	28	28	27	27	26	26	26
Los Angeles, Calif., USA	79	76	71	25	10	3	<3	<3	5	15	31	66	381
95 m	13	14	14	16	17	19	21	22	21	18	16	14	17
Mexico City, Mexico	13	5	10	20	53	119	170	152	130	51	18	8	747
2,309 m	12	13	16	18	19	19	17	18	18	16	14	13	16
Miami, Fla., USA	71	53	64	81	173	178	155	160	203	234	71	51	1,516
8 m	20	20	22	23	25	27	28	28	27	25	22	21	24
Montréal, Que., Canada	72	65	74	74	66	82	90	92	88	76	81	87	946
57 m	-10	-9	-3	-6	13	18	21	20	15	9	2	-7	6
New York, N.Y., USA	94	97	91	81	81	84	107	109	86	89	76	91	1,092
96 m	-1	-1	3	10	16	20	23	23	21	15	7	2	11
St Louis, Mo., USA	58	64	89	97	114	114	89	86	81	74	71	64	1,001
173 m	0	1	7	13	19	24	26	26	22	15	8	2	14
San José, Costa Rica	15	5	20	46	229	241	211	241	305	300	145	41	1,798
1,146 m	19	19	21	21	22	21	21	21	21	20	20	19	20
Vancouver, B.C., Canada	154	115	101	60	52	45	32	41	67	114	150	182	1,113
14 m	3	5	6	9	12	15	17	17	14	10	6	4	10
Washington, D.C., USA	86	76	91	84	94	99	112	109	94	74	66	79	1,064
22 m	1	2	7	13	18	23	25	24	20	14	8	3	13

SOUTH AMERICA

	Jan.	Feb.	Mar.	Apr.	May	June	July	Aug.	Sept.	Oct.	Nov.	Dec.	Year
Antofagasta, Chile	0	0	0	<3	3	3	5	3	3	3	<3	0	13
94 m	21	21	20	18	16	15	14	14	15	16	18	19	17
Buenos Aires, Argentina	79	71	109	89	76	61	56	61	79	86	84	99	950
27 m	23	23	21	17	13	9	10	11	13	15	19	22	16
Lima, Peru	3	<3	<3	<3	<3	5	8	8	8	3	3	<3	41
120 m	23	24	24	22	19	17	16	16	17	18	19	21	20
Manaus, Brazil	249	231	262	221	170	84	58	38	46	107	142	203	1,811
44 m	28	28	28	27	28	28	28	28	29	29	29	28	28
Paraná, Brazil	287	236	239	102	13	<3	3	21	25	127	231	310	1,582
260 m	23	23	23	22	21	20	20	21	23	24	24	24	23
Rio de Janeiro, Brazil	125	122	130	107	79	53	41	43	66	79	104	137	1,082
61 m	26	26	25	24	22	21	21	21	21	22	23	25	23

WORLD STATISTICS: PHYSICAL DIMENSIONS

Each topic list is divided into continents and within a continent the items are listed in size order. The order of the continents is as in the atlas, Europe through to South America. Certain lists down to this mark ▷ are complete; below they are selective. The world top ten are shown in square brackets; in the case of mountains this has not been done because the world top thirty are all in Asia. The figures are rounded as appropriate.

WORLD, CONTINENTS, OCEANS

	km²	miles²	%
The World	509,450,000	196,672,000	
Land	149,450,000	57,688,000	29.3
Water	360,000,000	138,984,000	70.7
Asia	44,500,000	17,177,000	29.8
Africa	30,302,000	11,697,000	20.3
North America	24,241,000	9,357,000	16.2
South America	17,793,000	6,868,000	11.9
Antarctica	14,100,000	5,443,000	9.4
Europe	9,957,000	3,843,000	6.7
Australia & Oceania	8,557,000	3,303,000	5.7
Pacific Ocean	179,679,000	69,356,000	49.9
Atlantic Ocean	92,373,000	35,657,000	25.7
Indian Ocean	73,917,000	28,532,000	20.5
Arctic Ocean	14,090,000	5,439,000	3.9

SEAS

Pacific	km²	miles²
South China Sea	2,318,000	895,000
Bering Sea	2,268,000	875,000
Sea of Okhotsk	1,528,000	590,000
East China & Yellow	1,249,000	482,000
Sea of Japan	1,008,000	389,000
Gulf of California	162,000	62,500
Bass Strait	75,000	29,000

Atlantic	km²	miles²
Caribbean Sea	2,766,000	1,068,000
Mediterranaen Sea	2,516,000	971,000
Gulf of Mexico	1,543,000	596,000
Hudson Bay	1,232,000	476,000
North Sea	575,000	223,000
Black Sea	452,000	174,000
Baltic Sea	397,000	153,000
Gulf of St. Lawrence	238,000	92,000

Indian	km²	miles²
Red Sea	438,000	169,000
The Gulf	239,000	92,000

MOUNTAINS

Europe		m	ft
Mont Blanc	France/Italy	4,807	15,771
Monte Rosa	Italy/Switzerland	4,634	15,203
Dom	Switzerland	4,545	14,911
Weisshorn	Switzerland	4,505	14,780
Matterhorn/Cervino	Italy/Switzerland	4,478	14,691
Mt. Maudit	France/Italy	4,465	14,649
Finsteraarhorn	Switzerland	4,275	14,025
Aletschhorn	Switzerland	4,182	13,720
Jungfrau	Switzerland	4,158	13,642
Barre des Ecrins	France	4,103	13,461
Gran Paradiso	Italy	4,061	13,323
Piz Bernina	Italy/Switzerland	4,052	13,294
Ortles	Italy	3,899	12,792
Monte Viso	Italy	3,841	12,602
Grossglockner	Austria	3,797	12,457
Wildspitze	Austria	3,774	12,382
Weisskügel	Austria/Italy	3,736	12,257
Dammastock	Switzerland	3,640	11,942
Tödi	Switzerland	3,623	11,886
Presanella	Italy	3,556	11,667
Monte Adamello	Italy	3,554	11,660
Mulhacén	Spain	3,478	11,411
Pico de Aneto	Spain	3,404	11,168
Marmolada	Italy	3,342	10,964
Etna	Italy	3,340	10,958
▷ Musala	Bulgaria	2,925	9,596
Olympus	Greece	2,917	9,570
Gerlach	Czechoslovakia	2,655	8,711
Galdhöpiggen	Norway	2,469	8,100
Pietrosul	Romania	2,305	7,562
Hvannadalshnúkur	Iceland	2,119	6,952
Narodnaya	Russia	1,894	6,214
Ben Nevis	UK	1,343	4,406

Asia		m	ft
Everest	China/Nepal	8,848	29,029
Godwin Austen (K2)	China/Kashmir	8,611	28,251
Kanchenjunga	India/Nepal	8,598	28,208
Lhotse	China/Nepal	8,516	27,939
Makalu	China/Nepal	8,481	27,824
Cho Oyu	China/Nepal	8,201	26,906
Dhaulagiri	Nepal	8,172	26,811
Manaslu	Nepal	8,156	26,758
Nanga Parbat	Kashmir	8,126	26,660
Annapurna	Nepal	8,078	26,502
Gasherbrum	China/Kashmir	8,068	26,469
Broad Peak	India	8,051	26,414
Gosainthan	China	8,012	26,286
Disteghil Sar	Kashmir	7,885	25,869
Nuptse	Nepal	7,879	25,849
Masherbrum	Kashmir	7,826	25,676
Nanda Devi	India	7,817	25,646
Rakaposhi	Kashmir	7,788	25,551
Kamet	India	7,756	25,446
Namcha Barwa	China	7,756	25,446
Gurla Mandhata	China	7,728	25,354
Muztag	China	7,723	25,338
Kongur Shan	China	7,719	25,324
Tirich Mir	Pakistan	7,690	25,229
▷ Saser	Kashmir	7,672	25,170
Pik Kommunizma	Tajikistan	7,495	24,590
Aling Gangri	China	7,315	23,999
Elbrus	Russia	5,633	18,481
Demavand	Iran	5,604	18,386
Ararat	Turkey	5,165	16,945
Gunong Kinabalu	Malaysia (Borneo)	4,101	13,455
Yu Shan	Taiwan	3,997	13,113
Fuji-san	Japan	3,776	12,388
Rinjani	Indonesia	3,726	12,224
Mt. Rajang	Philippines	3,364	11,037
Pidurutalagala	Sri Lanka	2,524	8,281

Africa		m	ft
Kilimanjaro	Tanzania	5,895	19,340
Mt. Kenya	Kenya	5,199	17,057
Ruwenzori	Uganda/Zaire	5,109	16,762
Ras Dashan	Ethiopia	4,620	15,157
Meru	Tanzania	4,565	14,977
Karisimbi	Rwanda/Zaïre	4,507	14,787
Mt. Elgon	Kenya/Uganda	4,321	14,176
Batu	Ethiopia	4,307	14,130
Gughe	Ethiopia	4,200	13,779
Toubkal	Morocco	4,165	13,665
Irhil Mgoun	Morocco	4,071	13,356
Mt. Cameroon	Cameroon	4,070	13,353
Teide	Spain (Tenerife)	3,718	12,198
Thabana Ntlenyana	Lesotho	3,482	11,424
Emi Kussi	Chad	3,415	11,204
▷ Mt. aux Sources	Lesotho/S. Africa	3,282	10,768
Mt. Piton	Réunion	3,069	10,069

Oceania		m	ft
Puncak Jaya	Indonesia	5,029	16,499
Puncak Mandala	Indonesia	4,760	15,617
Puncak Trikora	Indonesia	4,750	15,584
Mt. Wilhelm	Papua New Guinea	4,508	14,790
▷ Mauna Kea	USA (Hawaii)	4,208	13,806
Mauna Loa	USA (Hawaii)	4,169	13,678
Mt. Cook	New Zealand	3,753	12,313
Mt. Balbi	Solomon Is.	2,743	8,999
Orohena	Tahiti	2,241	7,352
Kosciusko	Australia	2,230	7,316

North America		m	ft
Mt. McKinley	USA (Alaska)	6,194	20,321
Mt. Logan	Canada	6,050	19,849
Citlaltepetl	Mexico	5,700	18,701
Mt. St.Elias	USA/Canada	5,489	18,008
Popocatepetl	Mexico	5,452	17,887
Mt. Foraker	USA (Alaska)	5,304	17,401
Ixtaccihuatl	Mexico	5,286	17,342
Lucania	USA (Alaska)	5,226	17,145
Mt. Steele	Canada	5,011	16,440
Mt. Bona	USA (Alaska)	5,005	16,420
Mt. Blackburn	USA (Alaska)	4,996	16,391
Mt. Sanford	USA (Alaska)	4,949	16,237
Mt. Wood	Canada	4,848	15,905
Nev. de Toluca	Mexico	4,670	15,321
Mt. Fairweather	USA (Alaska)	4,663	15,298
Mt. Whitney	USA	4,418	14,495
Mt. Elbert	USA	4,399	14,432
Mt. Harvard	USA	4,395	14,419
Mt. Rainier	USA	4,392	14,409
Blanca Peak	USA	4,364	14,317
Long's Peak	USA	4,345	14,255
Nev. de Colima	Mexico	4,339	14,235
Mt. Shasta	USA	4,317	14,163
Tajumulco	Guatemala	4,217	13,835
Gannett Peak	USA	4,202	13,786
▷ Mt. Waddington	Canada	3,994	13,104
Mt. Robson	Canada	3,954	12,972
Ch. Grande	Costa Rica	3,837	12,589
Loma Tinta	Haiti	3,175	10,417

South America		m	ft
Aconcagua	Argentina	6,960	22,834
Illimani	Bolivia	6,882	22,578
Bonete	Argentina	6,872	22,546
Ojos del Salado	Argentina/Chile	6,863	22,516
Tupungato	Argentina/Chile	6,800	22,309
Pissis	Argentina	6,779	22,241
Mercedario	Argentina/Chile	6,770	22,211
Huascaran	Peru	6,768	22,204
Llullaillaco	Argentina/Chile	6,723	22,057
Nudo de Cachi	Argentina	6,720	22,047
Yerupaja	Peru	6,632	21,758
N. de Tres Cruces	Argentina/Chile	6,620	21,719
Incahuasi	Argentina/Chile	6,601	21,657
Ancohuma	Bolivia	6,550	21,489
Sajama	Bolivia	6,520	21,391
Coropuna	Peru	6,425	21,079
Ausangate	Peru	6,384	20,945
Cerro del Toro	Argentina	6,380	20,932
Ampato	Peru	6,310	20,702
Chimborasso	Ecuador	6,267	20,561
▷ Cotopaxi	Ecuador	5,897	19,347
Cayambe	Ecuador	5,796	19,016
S. Nev.de S. Marta	Colombia	5,775	18,947
Pico Bolivar	Venezuela	5,007	16,427

Antarctica		m	ft
Vinson Massif		4,897	16,066
Mt. Kirkpatrick		4,528	14,855
Mt. Markham		4,349	14,268

OCEAN DEPTHS

Atlantic Ocean	m	ft	
Puerto Rico (Milwaukee) Deep	9,200	30,183	[7]
Cayman Trench	7,680	25,197	[10]
Gulf of Mexico	5,203	17,070	
Mediterranean	5,121	16,801	
Black Sea	2,211	7,254	
North Sea	310	1,017	
Baltic Sea	294	965	
Hudson Bay	111	364	

Indian Ocean	m	ft
Java Trench	7,450	24,442
Red Sea	2,266	7,434
Persian Gulf	73	239

Pacific Ocean	m	ft	
Mariana Trench	11,022	36,161	[1]
Tonga Trench	10,822	35,505	[2]
Japan Trench	10,554	34,626	[3]
Kuril Trench	10,542	34,586	[4]
Mindanao Trench	10,497	34,439	[5]
Kermadec Trench	10,047	32,962	[6]
Peru-Chile Trench	8,050	26,410	[8]
Aleutian Trench	7,822	25,662	[9]
Middle American Trench	6,662	21,857	

Arctic Ocean	m	ft
Molloy Deep	5,608	18,399

LAND LOWS

		m	ft
Caspian Sea	Europe	-28	-92
Dead Sea	Asia	-400	-1,312
Lake Assal	Africa	-156	-512
Lake Eyre North	Oceana	-16	-52
Death Valley	N. America	-86	-282
Valdés Peninsula	S. America	-40	-131

RIVERS

Europe

		km	miles	
Volga	Caspian Sea	3,700	2,300	
Danube	Black Sea	2,850	1,770	
Ural	Caspian Sea	2,535	1,574	
Dnieper	Volga	2,285	1,420	
Kama	Volga	2,030	1,260	
Don	Volga	1,990	1,240	
Petchora	Arctic	1,790	1,110	
Oka	Volga	1,480	920	
Belaya	Kama	1,420	880	
Dniester	Black Sea	1,400	870	
Vyatka	Kama	1,370	850	
Rhine	North Sea	1,320	820	
N. Dvina	Arctic	1,290	800	
Desna	Dnieper	1,190	740	
Elbe	North Sea	1,145	710	
Vistula	Baltic Sea	1,090	675	
Loire	Atlantic	1,020	635	
Thames	North Sea	335	210	

Asia

		km	miles	
Yangtse	Pacific	6,380	3,960	[3]
Yenisei-Angara	Arctic	5,550	3,445	[5]
Ob-Irtysh	Arctic	5,410	3,360	[6]
Hwang Ho	Pacific	4,840	3,005	[7]
Amur	Pacific	4,510	2,800	[9]
Mekong	Pacific	4,500	2,795	[10]
Lena	Arctic	4,400	2,730	
Irtysh	Ob	4,250	2,640	
Yenisei	Arctic	4,090	2,540	
Ob	Arctic	3,680	2,285	
Indus	Indian	3,100	1,925	
Brahmaputra	Indian	2,900	1,800	
Syr Darya	Aral Sea	2,860	1,775	
Salween	Indian	2,800	1,740	
Euphrates	Indian	2,700	1,675	
Vilyuy	Lena	2,650	1,645	
Kolyma	Arctic	2,600	1,615	
Amu Darya	Aral Sea	2,540	1,575	
Ural	Caspian Sea	2,535	1,575	
Ganges	Indian	2,510	1,560	
Si Kiang	Pacific	2,100	1,305	
Irrawaddy	Indian	2,010	1,250	
Tarim-Yarkand	Lop Nor	2,000	1,240	
Tigris	Indian	1,900	1,180	
Angara	Yenisei	1,830	1,135	
Godavari	Indian	1,470	915	
Sutlej	Indian	1,450	900	
Yamuna	Indian	1,400	870	

Africa

		km	miles	
Nile	Mediterranean	6,670	4,140	[1]
Zaïre/Congo	Atlantic	4,670	2,900	[8]
Niger	Atlantic	4,180	2,595	
Zambezi	Indian	2,740	1,700	
Oubangi/Uele	Zaïre	2,250	1,400	
Kasai	Zaïre	1,950	1,210	
Shaballe	Indian	1,930	1,200	
Orange	Atlantic	1,860	1,155	
Cubango	Okavango Swamps	1,800	1,120	
Limpopo	Indian	1,600	995	
Senegal	Atlantic	1,600	995	
Volta	Atlantic	1,500	930	
Benue	Niger	1,350	840	

Australia

		km	miles	
Murray-Darling	Indian	3,720	2,310	
Darling	Murray	3,070	1,905	
Murray	Indian	2,575	1,600	
Murrumbidgee	Murray	1,690	1,050	

North America

		km	miles	
Mississippi-Missouri	Gulf of Mexico	6,020	3,740	[4]
Mackenzie	Arctic	4,240	2,630	
Mississippi	Gulf of Mexico	3,780	2,350	
Missouri	Mississippi	3,725	2,310	
Yukon	Pacific	3,185	1,980	
Rio Grande	Gulf of Mexico	3,030	1,880	
Arkansas	Mississippi	2,340	1,450	
Colorado	Pacific	2,330	1,445	
Red	Mississippi	2,040	1,270	
Columbia	Pacific	1,950	1,210	
Saskatchewan	L Winnipeg	1,940	1,205	
Snake	Columbia	1,670	1,040	
Churchill	Hudson Bay	1,600	990	
Ohio	Mississippi	1,580	980	
Brazos	Gulf of Mexico	1,400	870	
St Lawrence	Atlantic	1,170	730	

South America

		km	miles	
Amazon	Atlantic	6,430	3,990	[2]
Paraná-Plate	Atlantic	4,000	2,480	
Purus	Amazon	3,350	2,080	
Madeira	Amazon	3,200	1,990	
São Francisco	Atlantic	2,900	1,800	
Paraná	Plate	2,800	1,740	
Tocantins	Atlantic	2,640	1,640	
Paraguay	Paraná	2,550	1,580	
Orinoco	Atlantic	2,500	1,550	
Pilcomayo	Paraná	2,500	1,550	
Araguaia	Tocantins	2,250	1,400	
Juruá	Amazon	2,000	1,240	
Xingu	Amazon	1,980	1,230	
Ucayali	Amazon	1,900	1,180	
Maranón	Amazon	1,600	990	
Uruguay	Plate	1,600	990	
Magdalena	Caribbean	1,540	960	

LAKES

Europe

		km²	miles²	
Lake Ladoga	Russia	18,400	7,100	
Lake Onega	Russia	9,700	3,700	
Saimaa system	Finland	8,000	3,100	
Vänern	Sweden	5,500	2,100	
Rybinsk Res.	Russia	4,700	1,800	

Asia

		km²	miles²	
Caspian Sea	Asia	371,000	143,000	[1]
Aral Sea	Kazakh/Uzbek	36,000	13,900	[6]
Lake Baikal	Russia	31,500	12,200	[9]
Tonlé Sap	Cambodia	20,000	7,700	
Lake Balkhash	Kazakhstan	18,500	7,100	
Dongting Hu	China	12,000	4,600	
Issyk Kul	Kirghizia	6,200	2,400	
Lake Urmia	Iran	5,900	2,300	
Koko Nur	China	5,700	2,200	
Poyang Hu	China	5,000	1,900	
Lake Khanka	China/Russia	4,400	1,700	
Lake Van	Turkey	3,500	1,400	
Ubsa Nur	China	3,400	1,300	

Africa

		km²	miles²	
Lake Victoria	E. Africa	68,000	26,000	[3]
Lake Tanganyika	C. Africa	33,000	13,000	[7]
Lake Malawi/Nyasa	E. Africa	29,000	11,000	[10]
Lake Chad	C. Africa	25,000	9,700	
Lake Turkana	Ethiopia/Kenya	8,500	3,300	
Lake Volta	Ghana	8,500	3,300	
Lake Bangweulu	Zambia	8,000	3,100	
Lake Rukwa	Tanzania	7,000	2,700	
Lake Mai-Ndombe	Zaïre	6,500	2,500	
Lake Kariba	Zambia/Zimbabwe	5,300	2,000	
Lake Mobutu	Uganda/Zaïre	5,300	2,000	
Lake Nasser	Egypt/Sudan	5,200	2,000	
Lake Mweru	Zambia/Zaïre	4,900	1,900	
Lake Cabora Bassa	S. Africa	4,500	1,700	
Lake Kyoga	Uganda	4,400	1,700	
Lake Tana	Ethiopia	3,630	1,400	
Lake Kivu	Rwanda/Zaïre	2,650	1,000	
Lake Edward	Uganda/Zaïre	2,200	850	

Australia

		km²	miles²	
Lake Eyre	Australia	9,000	3,500	
Lake Torrens	Australia	5,800	2,200	
Lake Gairdner	Australia	4,800	1,900	

North America

		km²	miles²	
Lake Superior	Canada/USA	82,200	31,700	[2]
Lake Huron	Canada/USA	59,600	23,000	[4]
Lake Michigan	USA	58,000	22,400	[5]
Great Bear Lake	Canada	31,500	12,200	[8]
Great Slave Lake	Canada	28,700	11,100	
Lake Erie	Canada/USA	25,700	9,900	
Lake Winnipeg	Canada	24,400	9,400	
Lake Ontario	Canada/USA	19,500	7,500	
Lake Nicaragua	Nicaragua	8,200	3,200	
Lake Athabasca	Canada	8,000	3,100	
Smallwood Res.	Canada	6,530	2,520	
Reindeer Lake	Canada	6,400	2,500	
Lake Winnipegosis	Canada	5,400	2,100	
Nettilling Lake	Canada	5,500	2,100	
Lake Nipigon	Canada	4,850	1,900	
Lake Manitoba	Canada	4,700	1,800	

South America

		km²	miles²	
Lake Titicaca	Bolivia/Peru	8,200	3,200	
Lake Poopo	Peru	2,800	1,100	

ISLANDS

Europe

		km²	miles²	
Great Britain	UK	229,880	88,700	[8]
Iceland	Atlantic Ocean	103,000	39,800	
Ireland	Ireland/UK	84,400	32,600	
Novaya Zemlya (N)	Russia	48,200	18,600	
W. Spitzbergen	Norway	39,000	15,100	
Novaya Zemlya (S)	Russia	33,200	12,800	
Sicily	Italy	25,500	9,800	
Sardinia	Italy	24,000	9,300	
NE.Spitzbergen	Norway	15,000	5,600	
Corsica	France	8,700	3,400	
Crete	Greece	8,350	3,200	
Zealand	Denmark	6,850	2,600	

Asia

		km²	miles²	
Borneo	S E. Asia	737,000	284,000	[3]
Sumatra	Indonesia	425,000	164,000	[6]
Honshu	Japan	230,000	88,800	[7]
Celebes	Indonesia	189,000	73,000	
Java	Indonesia	126,700	48,900	
Luzon	Philippines	104,700	40,400	
Mindanao	Philippines	95,000	36,700	
Hokkaido	Japan	78,400	30,300	
Sakhalin	Russia	76,400	29,500	
Sri Lanka	Indian Ocean	65,600	25,300	
Taiwan	Pacific Ocean	36,000	13,900	
Kyushu	Japan	35,700	13,800	
Hainan	China	34,000	13,100	
Timor	Indonesia	33,600	13,000	
Shikoku	Japan	18,800	7,300	
Halmahera	Indonesia	18,000	6,900	
Ceram	Indonesia	17,150	6,600	
Sumbawa	Indonesia	15,450	6,000	
Flores	Indonesia	15,200	5,900	
Samar	Philippines	13,100	5,100	
Negros	Philippines	12,700	4,900	
Bangka	Indonesia	12,000	4,600	
Palawan	Philippines	12,000	4,600	
Panay	Philippines	11,500	4,400	
Sumba	Indonesia	11,100	4,300	
Mindoro	Philippines	9,750	3,800	
Buru	Indonesia	9,500	3,700	
Bali	Indonesia	5,600	2,200	
Cyprus	Mediterranean	3,570	1,400	
Wrangel I.	Russia	2,800	1,000	

Africa

		km²	miles²	
Madagascar	Indian Ocean	587,000	226,600	[4]
Socotra	Indian Ocean	3,600	1,400	
Réunion	Indian Ocean	2,500	965	
Tenerife	Atlantic Ocean	2,350	900	
Mauritius	Indian Ocean	1,865	720	

Oceania

		km²	miles²	
New Guinea	Indon./Pap. NG	780,000	301,080	[2]
New Zealand (S)	New Zealand	150,500	58,100	
New Zealand (N)	New Zealand	114,400	44,200	
Tasmania	Australia	67,800	26,200	
New Britain	Papua NG	37,800	14,600	
New Caledonia	Pacific Ocean	16,100	6,200	
Viti Levu	Fiji	10,500	4,100	
Hawaii	Pacific Ocean	10,450	4,000	
Bougainville	Papua NG	9,600	3,700	
Guadalcanal	Solomon Is	6,500	2,500	
Vanua Levu	Fiji	5,550	2,100	
New Ireland	Papua NG	3,200	1,200	

North America

		km²	miles²	
Greenland	Greenland	2,175,600	839,800	[1]
Baffin I.	Canada	508,000	196,100	[5]
Victoria I.	Canada	212,200	81,900	[9]
Ellesmere I.	Canada	212,000	81,800	[10]
Cuba	Cuba	114,500	44,200	
Newfoundland	Canada	96,000	37,100	
Hispaniola	Atlantic Ocean	76,200	29,400	
Banks I.	Canada	67,000	25,900	
Devon I.	Canada	54,500	21,000	
Melville I.	Canada	42,400	16,400	
Vancouver I.	Canada	32,150	12,400	
Somerset I.	Canada	24,300	9,400	
Jamaica	Caribbean	11,400	4,400	
Puerto Rico	Atlantic Ocean	8,900	3,400	
Cape Breton I.	Canada	4,000	1,500	

South America

		km²	miles²	
Tierra del Fuego	Argentina/Chile	47,000	18,100	
Falkland I. (E.)	Atlantic Ocean	6,800	2,600	
South Georgia	Atlantic Ocean	4,200	1,600	
Galapagos (Isabela)	Pacific Ocean	2,250	870	

INTRODUCTION TO WORLD GEOGRAPHY

THE UNIVERSE

4: ORBITS OF THE
    PLANETS
    PLANETARY DATA

About 15 billion years ago, time and space began with the most colossal explosion in cosmic history: the 'Big Bang' that initiated the universe. According to current theory, in the first millionth of a second of its existence it expanded from a dimensionless point of infinite mass and density into a fireball about 30 billion kilometres across; and it has been expanding ever since.

It took almost a million years for the primal fireball to cool enough for atoms to form. They were mostly hydrogen, still the most abundant material in the universe. But the new matter was not evenly distributed around the young universe, and a few billion years later atoms in relatively dense regions began to cling together under the influence of gravity, forming distinct masses of gas separated by vast expanses of empty space. These first proto-galaxies, to begin with, were dark places: the universe had cooled. But gravitational attraction continued its work, condensing matter into coherent lumps inside the galactic gas clouds. About three billion years later, some of these masses had contracted so much that internal pressure produced the high temperatures necessary to bring about nuclear fusion: the first stars were born.

There were several generations of stars, each feeding on the wreckage of its extinct predecessors as well as the original galactic gas swirls. With each new generation, progressively larger atoms were forged in stellar furnaces and the galaxy's range of elements, once restricted to hydrogen, grew larger. About ten billion years after the Big Bang, a star formed on the outskirts of our galaxy with enough matter left over to create a retinue of planets. Some 4.7 billion years after that, a few planetary atoms had evolved into structures of complex molecules that lived, breathed and eventually pointed telescopes at the sky.

They found that their Sun is just one of more than 100 billion stars in the home galaxy alone. Our galaxy, in turn, forms part of a local group of 25 or so similar structures, some much larger than our own; there are at least 100 million other galaxies in the universe as a whole. The most distant ever observed, a highly energetic galactic core known only as Quasar PKS 2000-330, lies about 15 billion light-years away.

LIFE OF A STAR

For most of its existence, a star produces energy by the nuclear fusion of hydrogen into helium at its core. The duration of this hydrogen-burning period – known as the main sequence – depends on the star's mass; the greater the mass, the higher the core temperatures and the sooner the star's supply of hydrogen is exhausted. Dim, dwarf stars consume their hydrogen slowly, eking it out over a thousand billion years or more. The Sun, like other stars of its mass, should spend about 10 billion years on the main sequence; since it was formed less than five billion years ago, it still has half its life left.

Once all a star's core hydrogen has been fused into helium, nuclear activity moves outward into layers of unconsumed hydrogen. For a time, energy production sharply increases: the star grows hotter and expands enormously, turning into a so-called red giant. Its energy output will increase a thousandfold, and it will swell to a hundred times its present diameter.

After a few hundred million years, helium in the core will become sufficiently compressed to initiate a new cycle of nuclear fusion: from helium to carbon. The star will contract somewhat, before beginning its last expansion, in the Sun's case engulfing the Earth and perhaps Mars. In this bloated condition, the Sun's outer layers will break off into space, leaving a tiny inner core, mainly of carbon, that shrinks progressively under the force of its own gravity: dwarf stars can attain a density more than 10,000 times that of normal matter, with crushing surface gravities to match. Gradually, the nuclear fires will die down, and the Sun will reach its terminal stage: a black dwarf, emitting insignificant amounts of energy.

However, stars more massive than the Sun may undergo another transformation. The additional mass allows gravitational collapse to continue indefinitely: eventually, all the star's remaining matter shrinks to a point, and its density approaches infinity – a state that will not permit even sub-atomic structures to survive.

The star has become a black hole: an anomalous 'singularity' in the fabric of space and time. Although vast coruscations of radiation will be emitted by any matter falling into its grasp, the singularity itself has an escape velocity that exceeds the speed of light, and nothing can ever be released from it. Within the boundaries of the black hole, the laws of physics are suspended, but no physicist can ever observe the extraordinary events that may occur.

THE END OF THE UNIVERSE

The likely fate of the universe is disputed. One theory (top) dictates that the expansion begun at the time of the Big Bang will continue 'indefinitely', with ageing galaxies moving farther and farther apart in an immense, dark graveyard. Alternately, (bottom) gravity may overcome the expansion. Galaxies will fall back together until everything is again concentrated at a single point, followed by a new Big Bang and a new expansion, in an endlessly repeated cycle. The first theory is supported by the amount of visible matter in the universe; the second assumes there is enough dark material to bring about the gravitational collapse.

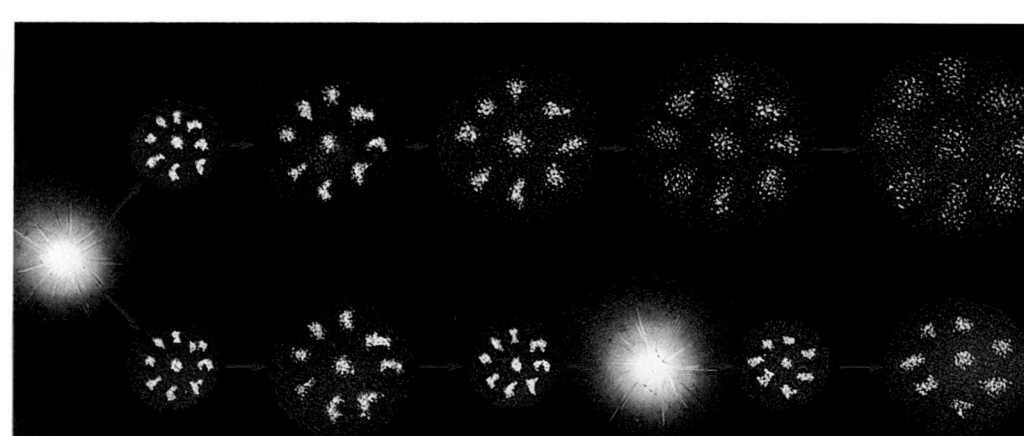

GALACTIC STRUCTURES

The universe's 100 million galaxies show clear structural patterns, originally classified by the American astronomer Edwin Hubble in 1925. Spiral galaxies like our own (top row) have a central, almost spherical bulge and a surrounding disc composed of spiral arms. Barred spirals (bottom row) have a central bar of stars across the nucleus, with spiral arms trailing from the ends of the bar. Elliptical galaxies (far left) have a uniform appearance, ranging from a flattened disc to a near sphere. So-called SO galaxies (left row, right) have a central bulge, but no spiral arms. A few have no discernible structure at all. Galaxies also vary enormously in size, from dwarfs only 2,000 light-years across to great assemblies of stars 80 or more times larger.

THE HOME GALAXY

The Sun and its planets are located in one of the spiral arms, a little less than 30,000 light-years from the galactic centre and orbiting around it in a period of more than 200 million years. The centre is invisible from the Earth, masked by vast, light-absorbing clouds of interstellar dust. The galaxy is probably around 12 billion years old and, like other spiral galaxies, has three distinct regions. The central bulge is about 30,000 light-years in diameter. The disc in which the Sun is located is not much more than 1,000 light-years thick but 100,000 light-years from end to end. Around the galaxy is the halo, a spherical zone 150,000 light-years across studded with globular star-clusters and sprinkled with individual suns.

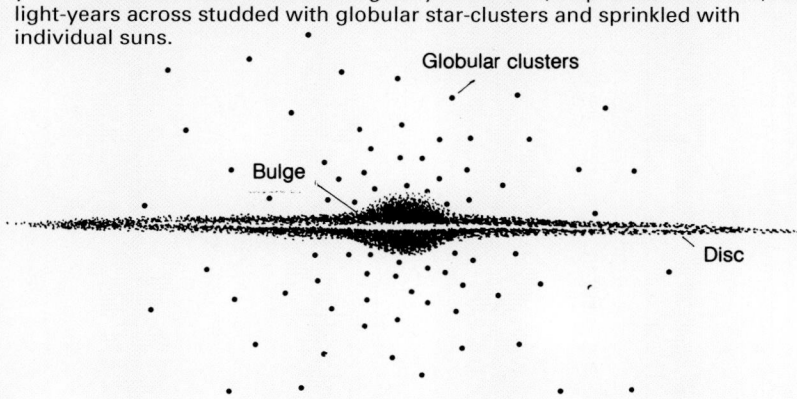

Globular clusters

Bulge

Disc

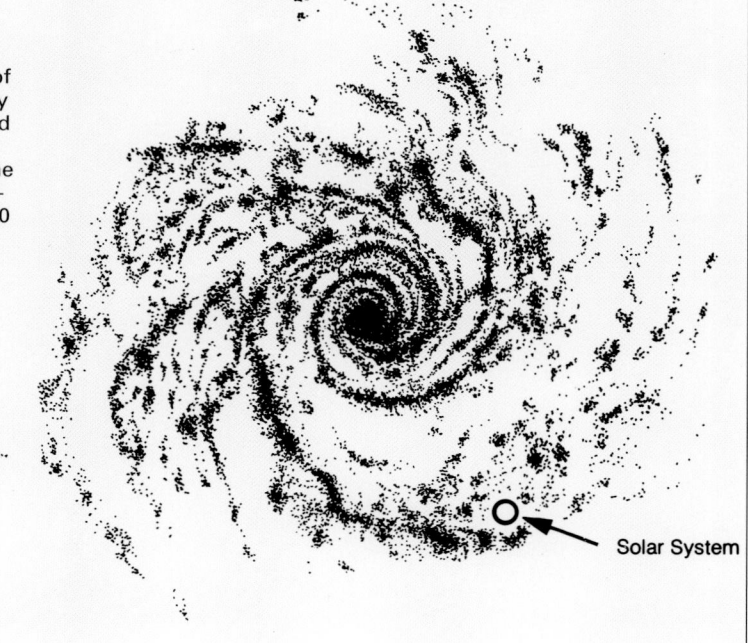

Solar System

Star charts are drawn as projections of a vast, hollow sphere with the observer in the middle. Each circle below represents one hemisphere, centred on the north and south celestial poles respectively – projections of the Earth's poles in the heavens. At the present era, the north pole is marked by the star Polaris; the south pole has no such convenient reference point. The rectangular map shows the stars immediately above and below the celestial equator.

Astronomical coordinates are normally given in terms of 'Right Ascension' for longitude and 'Declination' for latitude or altitude. Since the stars appear to rotate around the Earth once every 24 hours, Right Ascension is measured eastward – anti-clockwise – in hours and minutes. One hour is equivalent to 15 angular degrees; zero on the scale is the point at which the Sun crosses the celestial equator at the spring equinox, known to astronomers as the First Point in Aries. Unlike the Sun, stars always rise and set at the same point on the horizon. Declination measures (in degrees) a star's angular distance above or below the celestial equator.

NORTHERN HEAVENS

SOUTHERN HEAVENS

THE CONSTELLATIONS

The constellations and their English names

Andromeda	Andromeda	Circinus	Compasses	Lacerta	Lizard	Piscis Austrinus	Southern Fish
Antila	Air Pump	Columba	Dove	Leo	Lion	Puppis	Ship's Stern
Apus	Bird of Paradise	Coma Berenices	Berenice's Hair	Leo Minor	Little Lion	Pyxis	Mariner's Compass
Aquarius	Water-carrier	Corona Australis	Southern Crown	Lepus	Hare	Reticulum	Net
Aquila	Eagle	Corona Borealis	Northern Crown	Libra	Scales	Sagitta	Arrow
Ara	Altar	Corvus	Crow	Lupus	Wolf	Sagittarius	Archer
Aries	Ram	Crater	Cup	Lynx	Lynx	Scorpius	Scorpion
Auriga	Charioteer	Crux	Southern Cross	Lyra	Harp	Sculptor	Sculptor
Boötes	Herdsman	Cygnus	Swan	Mensa	Table	Scutum	Shield
Caelum	Chisel	Delphinus	Dolphin	Microscopium	Microscope	Serpens	Serpent
Camelopardalis	Giraffe	Dorado	Swordfish	Monoceros	Unicorn	Sextans	Sextant
Cancer	Crab	Draco	Dragon	Musca	Fly	Taurus	Bull
Canes Venatici	Hunting Dogs	Equuleus	Little House	Norma	Level	Telescopium	Telescope
Canis Major	Great Dog	Eridanus	Eridanus	Octans	Octant	Triangulum	Triangle
Canis Minor	Little Dog	Fornax	Furnace	Ophiuchus	Serpent Bearer	Triangulum Australe	Southern Triangle
Capricornus	Goat	Gemini	Twins	Orion	Orion	Tucana	Toucan
Carina	Keel	Grus	Crane	Pavo	Peacock	Ursa Major	Great Bear
Cassiopeia	Cassiopeia	Hercules	Hercules	Pegasus	Winged Horse	Ursa Minor	Little Bear
Centaurus	Centaur	Horologium	Clock	Perseus	Perseus	Vela	Sails
Cepheus	Cepheus	Hydra	Water Snake	Phoenix	Phoenix	Virgo	Virgin
Cetus	Whale	Hydrus	Sea Serpent	Pictor	Easel	Volans	Flying Fish
Chamaeleon	Chameleon	Indus	Indian	Pisces	Fishes	Vulpecula	Fox

THE NEAREST STARS

The 20 nearest stars, excluding the Sun, with their distance from Earth in light-years*

Proxima Centauri	4.3
Alpha Centauri A	4.3
Alpha Centauri B	4.3
Barnard's Star	6.0
Wolf 359	8.1
Lal 21185	8.2
Sirius A	8.7
Sirius B	8.7
UV Ceti A	9.0
UV Citi B	9.0
Ross 154	9.3
Ross 248	10.3
Epsilon Eridani	10.8
L 789-6	11.1
Ross 128	11.1
61 Cygni A	11.2
61 Cygni B	11.2
Procyon A	11.3
Procyon B	11.3
Epsilon Indi	11.4

Many of the nearest stars, like Alpha Centauri A and B, are doubles, orbiting about the common centre of gravity and to all intents and purposes equidistant from Earth. Many of them are dim objects, with no name other than the designation given by the astronomers who investigated them. However, they include Sirius, the brightest star in the sky, and Procyon, the seventh brightest. Both are far larger than the Sun: of the nearest stars only Epsilon Eridani is similar in size and luminosity.

* A light-year equals approx. 9,500,000,000,000 kilometres

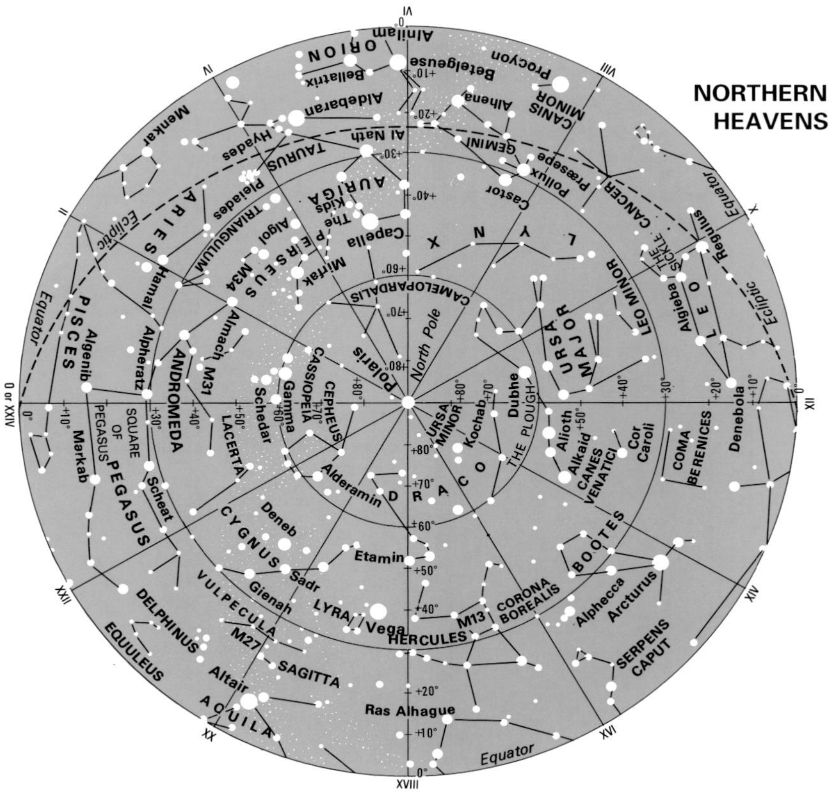

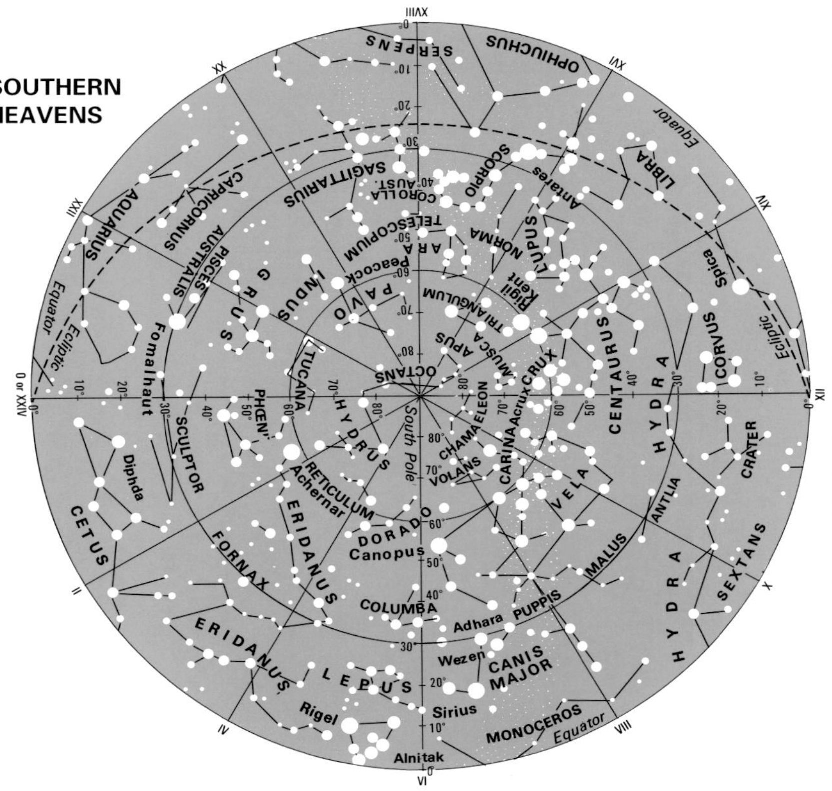

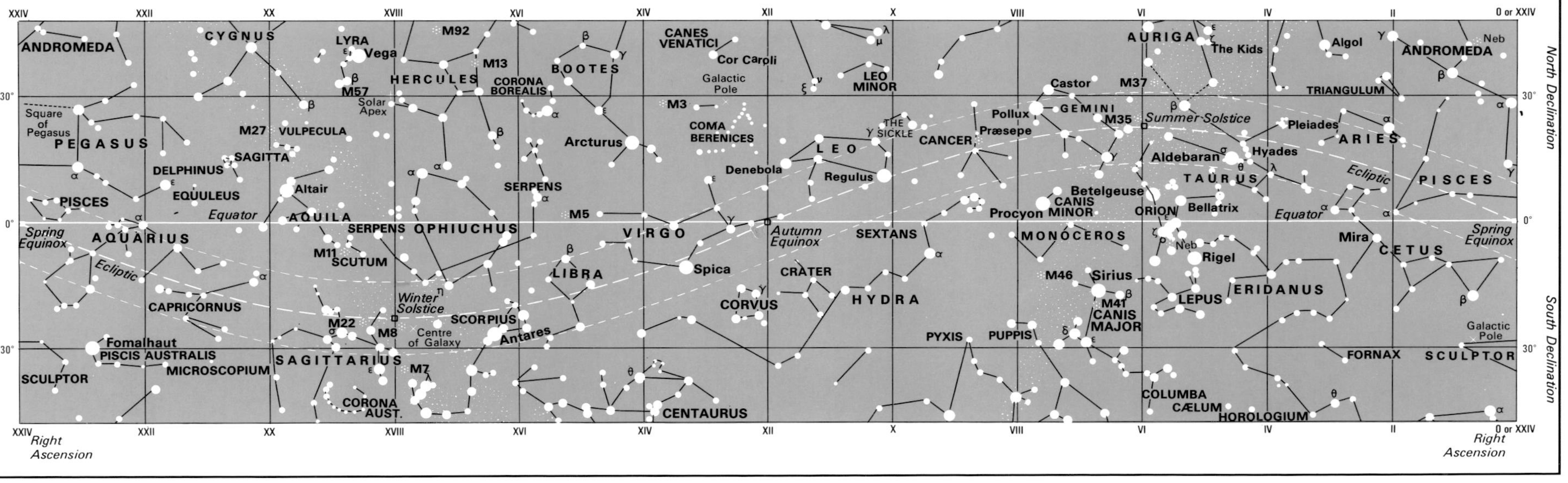

THE SOLAR SYSTEM

2: THE HOME GALAXY

6: THE SEASONS
   DAY & NIGHT

7: THE MOON

Lying 27,000 light years from the centre of one of billions of galaxies that comprise the observable universe, our solar system contains nine planets and their moons, innumerable asteroids and comets and a miscellany of dust and gas, all tethered by the immense gravitational field of the Sun, the middling-sized star whose thermonuclear furnaces provide them all with heat and light. The solar system was probably formed about 4.6 billion years ago, when a spinning cloud of gas, mostly hydrogen but seeded with other, heavier elements, condensed enough to ignite a nuclear reaction and create a star. The Sun still accounts for almost 99.9% of the system's total mass; one planet, Jupiter, contains most of the remainder.

By composition as well as distance, the planetary array divides quite neatly in two: an inner system of four small, solid planets, including the Earth, and an outer system, from Jupiter to Neptune, of four huge gas giants. Between the two groups lies a scattering of asteroids, perhaps as many as 40,000; possibly the remains of a planet destroyed by some unexplained catastrophe, they are more likely to be debris left over from the solar system's formation, prevented by the gravity of massive Jupiter from coalescing into a larger body. The ninth planet, Pluto, seems to be a world of the inner system type: small, rocky and something of an anomaly.

By the 1990s, the solar system also included some newer anomalies: several thousand spacecraft. Most were in orbit around the Earth, but some had probed far and wide around the system. The information beamed back by these robotic investigators has transformed our knowledge of our celestial environment.

Much of the early history of science is the story of people trying to make sense of the errant points of light that were all they knew of the planets. Now, men have themselves stood on the Earth's Moon; probes have landed on Mars and Venus and orbiting radars have mapped far distant landscapes with astonishing accuracy. In the 1980s, the US Voyagers skimmed all four major planets of the outer system, bringing new revelations with each close approach. Only Pluto, inscrutably distant in an orbit that takes it 50 times the Earth's distance from the Sun, remains unvisited by our messengers.

ORBITS OF THE PLANETS

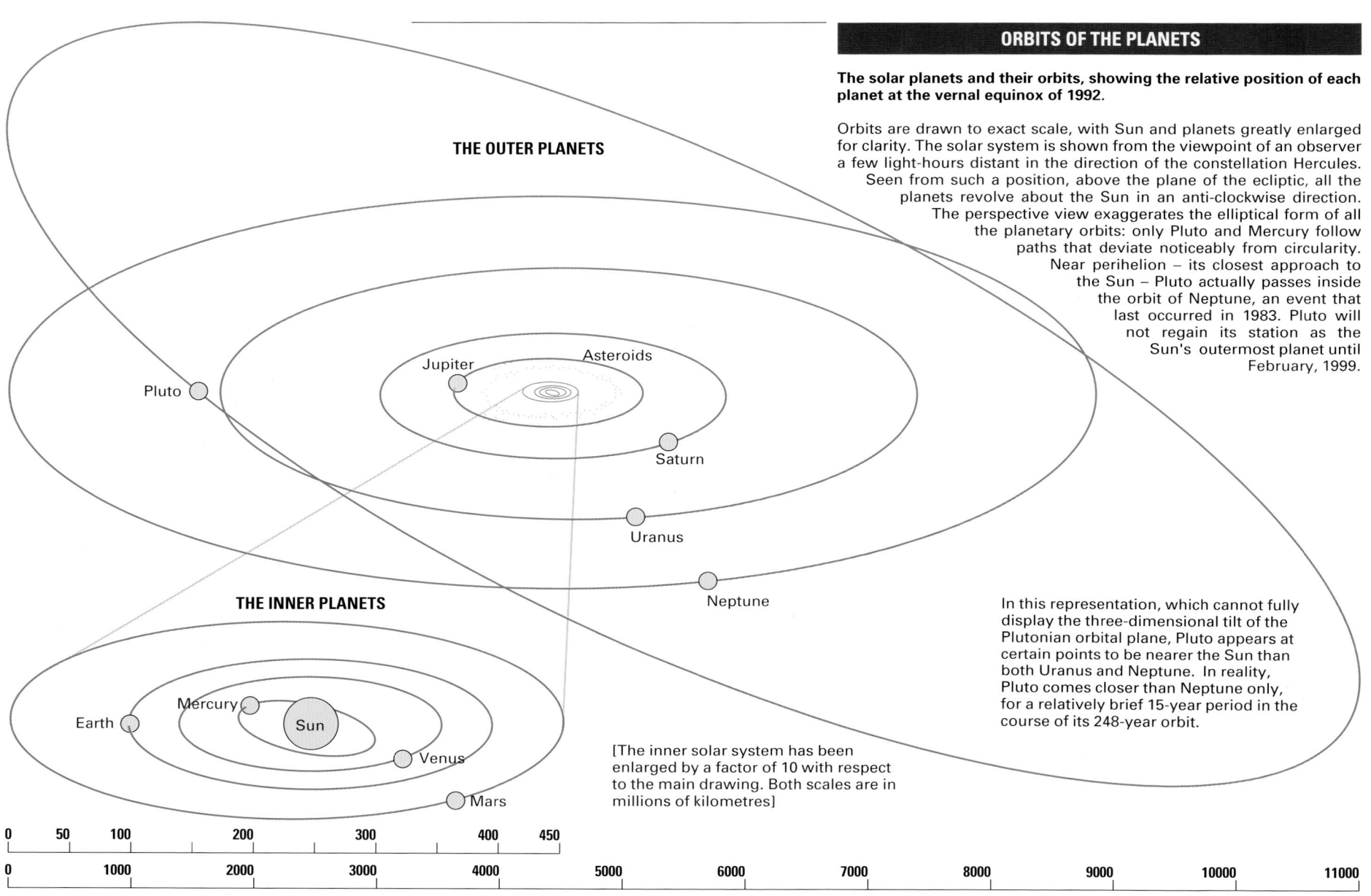

The solar planets and their orbits, showing the relative position of each planet at the vernal equinox of 1992.

Orbits are drawn to exact scale, with Sun and planets greatly enlarged for clarity. The solar system is shown from the viewpoint of an observer a few light-hours distant in the direction of the constellation Hercules. Seen from such a position, above the plane of the ecliptic, all the planets revolve about the Sun in an anti-clockwise direction. The perspective view exaggerates the elliptical form of all the planetary orbits: only Pluto and Mercury follow paths that deviate noticeably from circularity. Near perihelion – its closest approach to the Sun – Pluto actually passes inside the orbit of Neptune, an event that last occurred in 1983. Pluto will not regain its station as the Sun's outermost planet until February, 1999.

THE OUTER PLANETS

Pluto Jupiter Asteroids Saturn Uranus Neptune

THE INNER PLANETS

Earth Mercury Sun Venus Mars

In this representation, which cannot fully display the three-dimensional tilt of the Plutonian orbital plane, Pluto appears at certain points to be nearer the Sun than both Uranus and Neptune. In reality, Pluto comes closer than Neptune only, for a relatively brief 15-year period in the course of its 248-year orbit.

[The inner solar system has been enlarged by a factor of 10 with respect to the main drawing. Both scales are in millions of kilometres]

0 50 100 200 300 400 450

0 1000 2000 3000 4000 5000 6000 7000 8000 9000 10000 11000

PLANETARY DATA

	Mean distance from Sun (million km)	Mass (Earth = 1)	Period of orbit (Earth years)	Period of rotation (Earth days)	Equatorial diameter (km)	Average density (water = 1)	Surface gravity (Earth = 1)	Escape velocity (km/sec)	Number of known satellites
Sun	-	332,946	-	25.38	1,392,000	1.41	27.9	617.5	-
Mercury	58.3	0.06	0.241	58.67	4,878	5.5	0.38	4.27	0
Venus	107.7	0.8	0.615	243	12,104	5.25	0.90	10.36	0
Earth	149.6	1.0	1.00	0.99	12,756	5.52	1.00	11.18	1
Mars	227.3	0.1	1.88	1.02	6,794	3.94	0.38	5.03	2
Jupiter	777.9	317.8	11.86	0.41	142,800	1.33	2.64	60.22	16
Saturn	1,427.1	95.2	29.63	0.42	120,000	0.706	1.16	36.25	17
Uranus	2,872.3	14.5	83.97	0.45	52,000	1.70	1.11	22.4	15
Neptune	4,502.7	17.2	164.8	0.67	48,400	1.77	1.21	23.9	8
Pluto	5,894.2	0.002	248.63	6.38	3,000	5.50	0.47	5.1	1

Planetary days are given in sidereal time -- that is, with respect to the stars rather than the Sun. Most of the information in the table was confirmed by spacecraft and often obtained from photographs and other data transmitted back to the Earth. In the case of Pluto, however, only earthbound observations have been made, and no spacecraft can hope to encounter it until well into the next century. Given the planet's small size and great distance, figures for its diameter and rotation period cannot be definitive.

Since Pluto does not appear to be massive enough to account for the perturbations in the orbits of Uranus and Neptune that led to its 1930 discovery, it is quite possible that a tenth and even more distant planet may exist. Once Pluto's own 248-year orbit has been observed for long enough, further discrepancies may give a clue as to any tenth planet's whereabouts. Even so, distance alone would make it very difficult to locate, especially since telescopes powerful enough to find it are normally engaged in galactic study.

THE PLANETS

Mercury is the closest planet to the Sun and hence the fastest-moving. It has no significant atmosphere and a cratered, wrinkled surface very similar to that of Earth's moon.

Venus has much the same physical dimensions as Earth. However, its carbon dioxide atmosphere is 90 times as dense, accounting for a runaway greenhouse effect that makes the Venusian surface, at 475°C, the hottest of all the planets. Radar mapping shows relatively level land with volcanic regions whose sulphurous discharges explain the sulphuric acid rains reported by soft-landing space probes before they succumbed to Venus's fierce climate.

Earth seen from space is easily the most beautiful of the inner planets; it is also, and more objectively, the largest, as well the only home of known life. Living things are the main reason why the Earth is able to retain a substantial proportion of corrosive and highly reactive oxygen in its atmosphere, a state of affairs that contradicts the laws of chemical equilibrium; the oxygen in turn supports the life that constantly regenerates it.

Mars was once considered the likeliest of the other planets to share Earth's cargo of life: seasonal expansion of dark patches strongly suggested vegetation and the planet's apparent icecaps indicated the vital presence of water. But close inspection by spacecraft brought disappointment: chemical reactions account for the seeming vegetation, the icecaps are mainly frozen carbon dioxide and whatever oxygen the planet once possessed is now locked up in the iron-bearing rock that covers its cratered surface and gives it its characteristic red hue.

Jupiter masses almost three times as much as all the other planets together; had it scooped up a little more matter during its formation, it might have evolved into a small companion star for the Sun. The planet is mostly gas, under intense pressure in the lower atmosphere above a core of fiercely compressed hydrogen and helium. The upper layers form strikingly-colored rotating belts, the outward sign of the intense storms created by Jupiter's rapid diurnal rotation. Close approaches by spacecraft have shown an orbiting ring system, and discovered several previously unknown moons: Jupiter has at least 16.

Saturn is structurally similar to Jupiter, rotating fast enough to produce an obvious bulge at its equator. Ever since the invention of the telescope, however, Saturn's rings have been the feature that has attracted most observers. Voyager probes in 1980 and 1981 sent back detailed pictures that showed them to be composed of thousands of separate ringlets, each in turn made up of tiny icy particles, interacting in a complex dance that may serve as a model for the study of galactic and even larger structures.

Uranus was unknown to the ancients: although it is faintly visible to the naked eye, it was not discovered until 1781. Its composition is broadly similar to Jupiter and Saturn, though its distance from the Sun ensures an even colder surface temperature. Observations in 1977 suggested the presence of a faint ring system, amply confirmed when Voyager 2 swung past the planet in 1986.

Neptune is always more than four billion kilometres from Earth, and despite its diameter of almost 50,000 km it can only be seen by telescope. Its 1846 discovery was the result of mathematical predictions by astronomers seeking to explain irregularities in the orbit of Uranus, but until Voyager 2 closed with the planet in 1989 little was known of it. Like Uranus, it has a ring system; Voyager's photographs revealed a total of eight moons.

Pluto is the most mysterious of the solar planets, if only because even the most powerful telescopes can scarcely resolve it from a point of light to a disc. It was discovered as recently as 1930, like Neptune as the result of perturbations in the orbits of the two then outermost planets. Its small size as well as its eccentric and highly tilted orbit have led to suggestions that it is a former satellite of Neptune, somehow liberated from its primary. In 1978 Pluto was found to have a moon of its own, Charon, apparently half the size of Pluto itself.

Mean distance from Sun in million kilometres	
Mercury	58.3
Venus	107.7
Earth	149.6
Mars	227.9
Jupiter	777.9
Saturn	1,427.1
Uranus	2,872.3
Neptune	4,502.7
Pluto	5,894.2

THE EARTH: TIME & MOTION

4: ORBITS OF THE PLANETS
11: OCEAN CURRENTS
12: CIRCULATION OF THE AIR

The basic unit of time measurement is the day, one rotation of the Earth on its axis. The subdivision of the day into hours, minutes and seconds is arbitrary and simply for our convenience. Our present calendar is based on the solar year of 365.24 days, the time taken by the Earth to orbit the Sun. As the Earth rotates from west to east, the Sun appears to rise in the east and set in the west. When the Sun is setting in Shanghai, on the opposite side of the world New York is just emerging into sunlight. Noon, when the sun is directly overhead, is coincident at all places on the same meridian, with shadows pointing directly toward the poles.

Calendars based on the movements of the Sun and Moon have been used since ancient times. The Julian Calendar, with its leap year, introduced by Julius Caesar, fixed the average length of the year at 365.25 days, which was about 11 minutes too long (the Earth completes its orbit in 365 days, 5 hours, 48 minutes and 46 seconds of mean solar time). The cumulative error was rectified by the Gregorian Calendar, introduced by Pope Gregory XIII in 1582, when he decreed that the day following October 4 was October 15, and that century years do not count as leap years unless divisible by 400. England did not adopt the reformed calendar until 1752, when it found itself 11 days behind the continent.

Britain imposed the Gregorian Calendar on all its possessions, including the American colonies. All dates preceding September 2 were marked O.S., for Old Style.

EARTH DATA

Maximum distance from the Sun (Aphelion): 152,007,016 km.
Minimum distance from Sun (Perihelion): 147,000,830 km.
Obliquity of the ecliptic: 23° 27' 08".
Length of year - solar tropical (equinox to equinox): 365.24 days
Length of year - sidereal (fixed star to fixed star): 365.26 days
Length of day - mean solar day: 24h, 03m, 56s.
Length of day - mean sidereal day: 23h, 56m, 04s.

Superficial area: 510,000,000 sq. km.
Land surface: 149,000,000 sq. km. (29.2%)
Water surface: 361,000,000 sq. km. (70.8%)
Equatorial circumference: 40,077 km.
Meridional circumference: 40,009 km.
Equatorial diameter: 12,756.8 km.
Polar diameter: 12,713.8 km.
Equatorial radius: 6,378.4 km.
Polar radius: 6,356.9 km.
Volume of the Earth: 1,083,230 x 10^6 cu. km.
Mass of the Earth: 5.9 x 10^21 tonnes

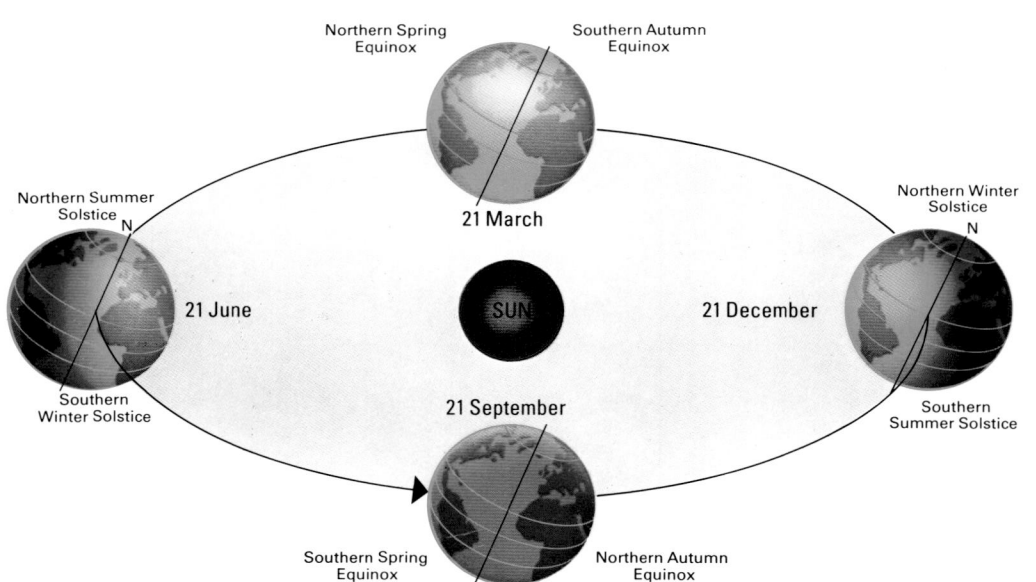

THE SEASONS

The Earth revolves around the Sun once a year in an 'anti-clockwise' direction, tilted at a constant angle, 66½°. In June, the northern hemisphere is tilted towards the Sun: as a result it receives more hours of sunshine in a day and therefore has its warmest season, summer. By December, the Earth has rotated halfway round the Sun so that the southern hemisphere that is tilted towards the Sun and has its summer; the hemisphere that is tilted away from the Sun has winter. On 21 June the Sun is directly overhead at the Tropic of Cancer (23½° N), and this is midsummer in the northern hemisphere. Midsummer in the southern hemisphere occurs on 21 December, when the Sun is overhead at the Tropic of Capricorn (23½° S).

DAY & NIGHT

The Sun appears to rise in the east, reach its highest point at noon, and then set in the west, to be followed by night. In reality it is not the Sun that is moving but the Earth revolving from west to east.

At the summer solstice in the northern hemisphere (21 June), the Arctic has total daylight and the Antarctic total darkness. The opposite occurs at the winter solstice (21 December). At the equator, the length of day and night are almost equal all year.

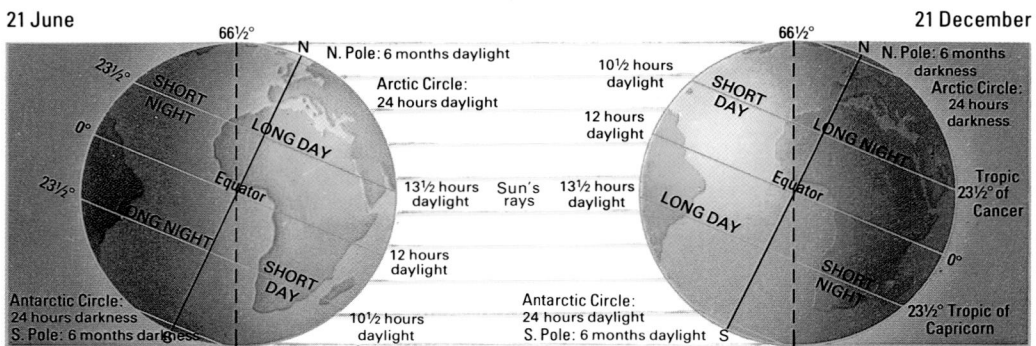

THE SUN'S PATH

The diagrams on the left illustrate the apparent path of the Sun at (A) the equator, (B) in mid-latitude (45°), (C) at the Arctic Circle (66½°) and (D) at the North Pole, where there are six months of continuous daylight and six months of continuous night.

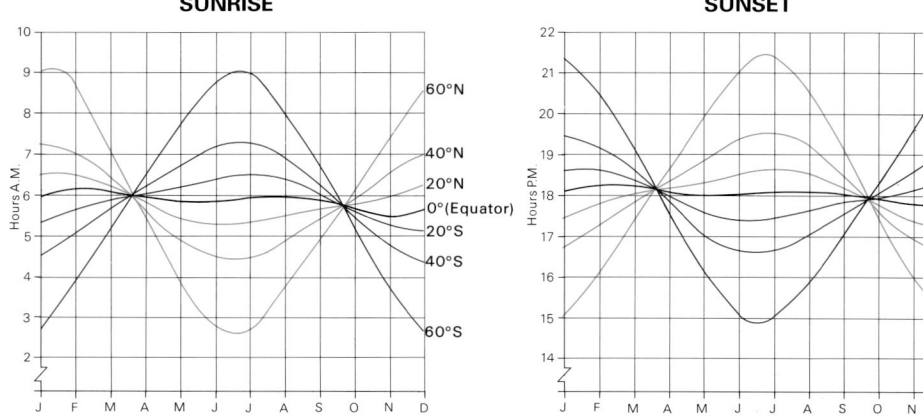

MEASUREMENTS OF TIME

Astronomers distinguish between solar time and sidereal time. Solar time derives from the period taken by the Earth to rotate on its axis: one rotation defines a solar day. But the speed of the Earth along its orbit around the Sun is not constant. The length of day - or 'apparent solar day' - as defined by the apparent successive transits of the Sun - is irregular because the Earth must complete more than one rotation before the Sun returns to the same meridian. The constant sidereal day is defined as the interval between two successive apparent transits of a star, or the first point of Aries, across the same meridian. If the Sun is at the equinox and overhead at a meridian one day, then the next day it will be to the east by approximately 1°. Thus the Sun will not cross the meridian until four minutes after the sidereal noon.

From the diagrams on the right it is possible to discover the time of sunrise or sunset on a given date and for latitudes between 60°N and 60°S.

THE MOON

PHASES OF THE MOON

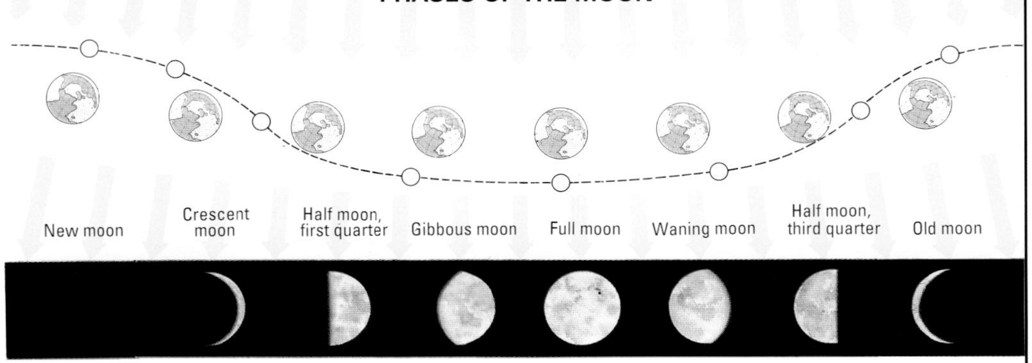

New moon	Crescent moon	Half moon, first quarter	Gibbous moon	Full moon	Waning moon	Half moon, third quarter	Old moon

The Moon rotates more slowly than the Earth, making one complete turn on its axis in just over 27 days. Since this corresponds to its period of revolution around the Earth, the Moon always presents the same hemisphere or face to us, and we never see 'the dark side'. The interval between one full Moon and the next (and between new Moons) is about 29½ days - a lunar month. The apparent changes in the shape of the Moon are caused by its changing position in relation to the Earth; like the planets, it produces no light of its own and shines only by reflecting the rays of the Sun.

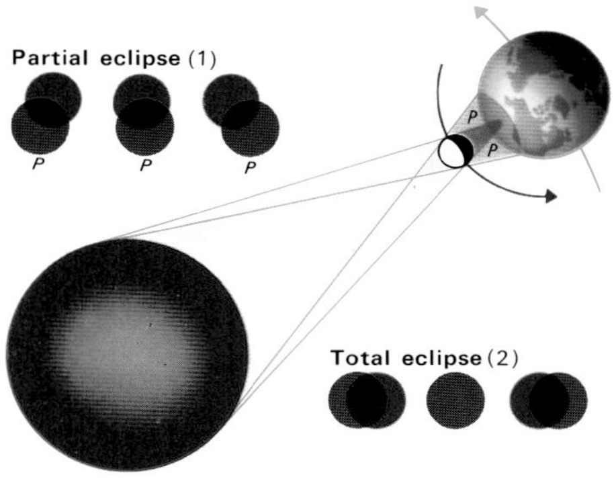

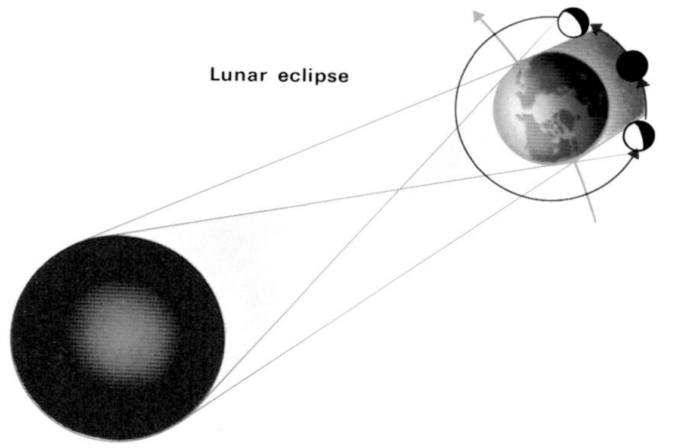

Partial eclipse (1)

Lunar eclipse

Total eclipse (2)

ECLIPSES

When the Moon passes between the Sun and the Earth it causes a partial eclipse of the Sun (1) if the Earth passes through the Moon's outer shadow (P), or a total eclipse (2) if the inner cone shadow crosses the Earth's surface. In a lunar eclipse, the Earth's shadow crosses the Moon and, again, provides either a partial or total eclipse. Eclipses of the Sun and the Moon do not occur every month because of the 5° difference between the plane of the Moon's orbit and the plane in which the Earth moves. In the 1990s only 14 lunar eclipses are possible, for example, seven partial and seven total; each is visible only from certain, and variable, parts of the world. The same period witnesses 13 solar eclipses - six partial (or annular) and seven total.

TIDES

The daily rise and fall of the ocean's tides are the result of the gravitational pull of the Moon and that of the Sun, though the effect of the latter is only 46.6% as strong as that of the Moon. This effect is greatest on the hemisphere facing the Moon and causes a tidal 'bulge'. When lunar and solar forces pull together, with Sun, Earth and Moon in line (near new and full Moons), higher 'spring tides' (and lower low tides) occur; when lunar and solar forces are least coincidental with the Sun and Moon at an angle (near the Moon's first and third quarters), 'neap tides' occur, which have a small tidal range.

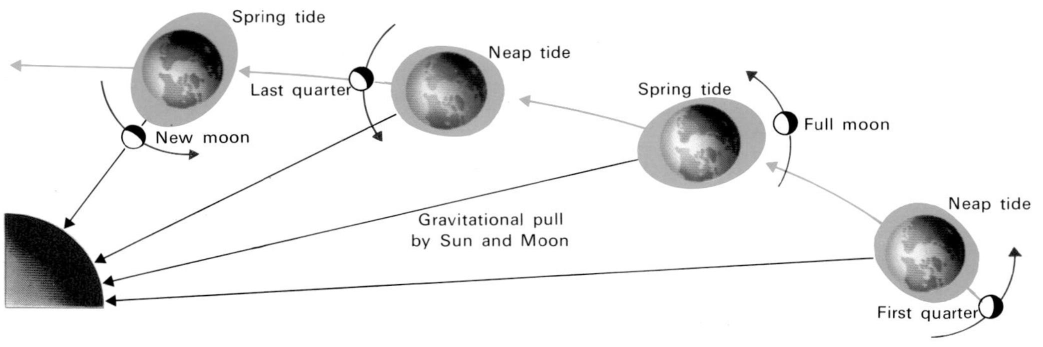

Spring tide
Neap tide
Last quarter
Spring tide
New moon
Full moon
Gravitational pull by Sun and Moon
Neap tide
First quarter

MOON DATA

Distance from Earth: The Moon orbits at a mean distance of 384,199.1 km, at an average speed of 3,683 km/h in relation to the Earth.

Size & mass: The average diameter of the Moon is 3,475.1 km. It is 400 times smaller than the Sun but is about 400 times closer to the Earth, so we see them as the same size. The Moon has a mass of 7.348×10^{19} tonnes, with a density 3.344 times that of water.

Visibility: Only 59% of the Moon's surface is directly visible from Earth. Reflected light takes 1.25 seconds to reach Earth - compared to 8 minutes 27.3 seconds for light from the Sun.

Temperature: With the Sun overhead the temperature on the lunar equator can reach 117.2°C [243°F]. At night it can sink to -162.7°C [-261°F].

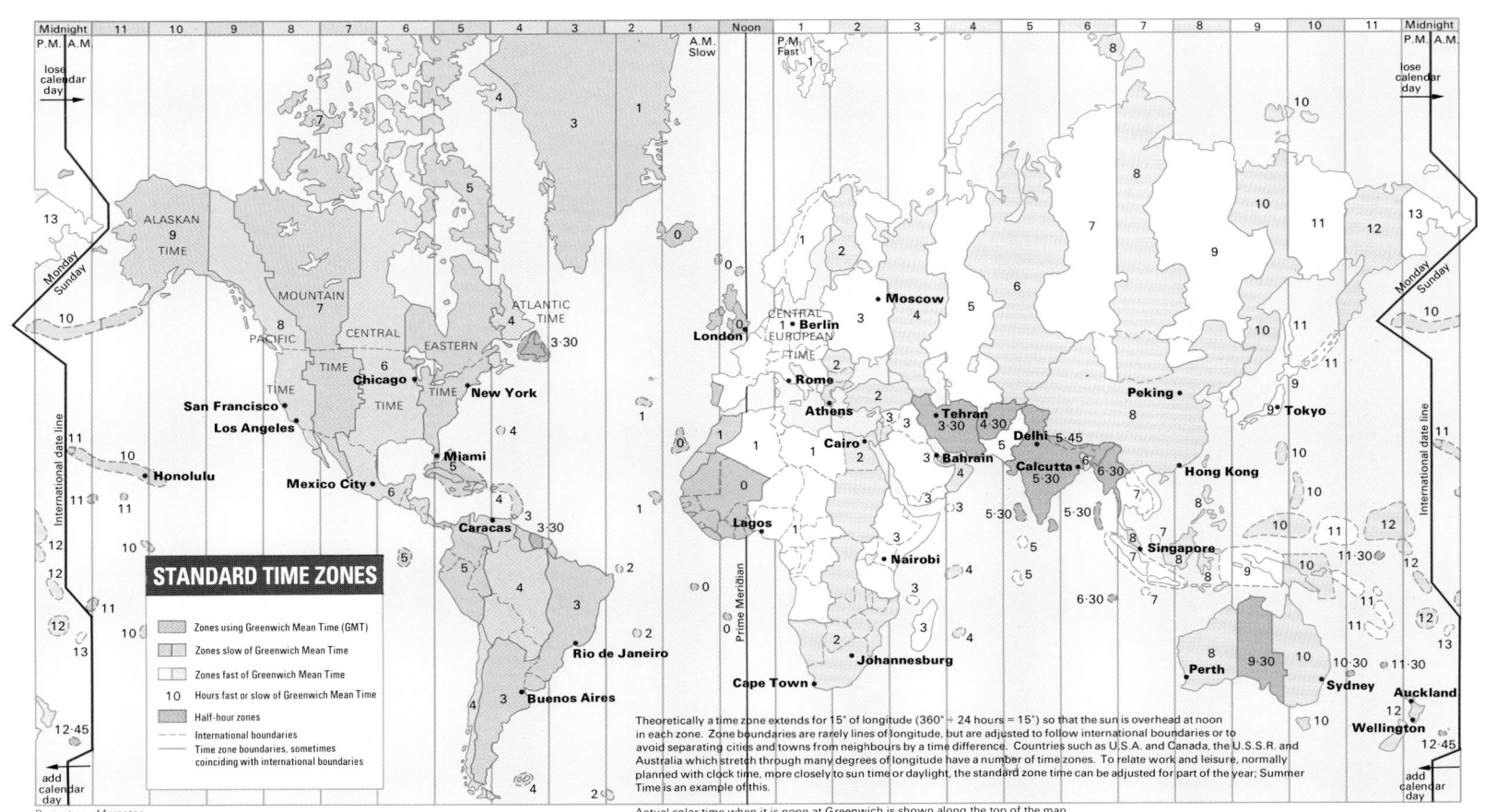

STANDARD TIME ZONES

- Zones using Greenwich Mean Time (GMT)
- Zones slow of Greenwich Mean Time
- Zones fast of Greenwich Mean Time
- 10 Hours fast or slow of Greenwich Mean Time
- Half-hour zones
- International boundaries
- Zone boundaries, sometimes coinciding with international boundaries

Theoretically a time zone extends for 15° of longitude (360° ÷ 24 hours = 15°) so that the sun is overhead at noon in each zone. Zone boundaries are rarely lines of longitude, but are adjusted to follow international boundaries or to avoid separating cities and towns from neighbours by a time difference. Countries such as U.S.A. and Canada, the U.S.S.R. and Australia which stretch through many degrees of longitude have a number of time zones. To relate work and leisure, normally planned with clock time, more closely to sun time or daylight, the standard zone time can be adjusted for part of the year; Summer Time is an example of this.

Projection: Mercator

Actual solar time when it is noon at Greenwich is shown along the top of the map

TIME ZONES

The Earth rotates through 360° in 24 hours, and therefore it moves 15° every hour. The world is divided into 24 standard time zones, each centred on lines of longitude at 15° intervals, so that every country falls within one or more agreed zones. The Greenwich meridian, based on the location of the Royal Observatory in London, lies at the centre of the first zone. All places to the west of Greenwich are one hour behind for every 15° of longitude; places to the east are ahead by one hour for every 15°.

When it is 12 noon at the Greenwich meridian, 180° east it is midnight of the same day – while 180° west the day is only just beginning. To overcome this the International Date Line was established, approximately following the 180° meridian. Thus if you travelled eastwards from Japan (140° East) to Samoa (170° West) you would pass from Sunday night into Sunday morning.

THE EARTH: GEOLOGY

18:	THE SPREADING EARTH TYPES OF ROCK MOUNTAIN BUILDING
19:	MOULDING THE LAND
21:	THE CARBON CYCLE
34:	MINERALS

The complementary, almost jigsaw-puzzle fit of the Atlantic coasts led to Alfred Wegener's proposition of continental drift in Germany (1915). His theory suggested that an ancient super-continent, which he called Pangaea, incorporating all the Earth's land masses, gradually split up to form the continents we know today. By 180 million years ago Pangaea had divided into two major groups and the southern part, Gondwanaland, had itself begun to break up with India and Antarctica-Australia becoming isolated. By 135 million years ago the widening of the splits in the North Atlantic and Indian Oceans persisted, a South Atlantic gap had appeared and India continued to move 'north' towards Asia. By 65 million years ago South America had completely split from Africa.
To form today's pattern India 'collided' with Asia (crumpling up sediments to form the Himalayas); South America rotated and moved west to connect with North America; Australia separated from Antarctica and moved north; and the familiar gap developed between Greenland and Europe.

The origin of the Earth is still open to conjecture, although the most widely accepted theory is that it was formed from a solar cloud consisting mainly of hydrogen 4,600 million years ago. The cloud condensed, forming the planets. The lighter elements floated to the surface of the Earth, where they cooled to form a crust; the inner material remained hot and molten. The first rocks were formed over 3,500 million years ago, but the Earth's surface has since been constantly altered.

The crust consists of a brittle, low-density material varying from 5 to 50 kilometres deep beneath the continents, consisting predominately of silica and aluminium: hence its name, sial . Below the sial is a basaltic layer known as sima , comprising mainly silica and magnesium. The crust accounts for only 1.5 per cent of the Earth s volume.

Immediately below the crust the mantle begins, with a distinct change in density and chemical properties. The rock is rich in iron and magnesium silicates, and temperatures reach 1,600°C. The rigid upper mantle extends down to a depth of about 1,000 kilometres, below which is a more viscous lower mantle about 1,900 kilometres thick.

The outer core, measuring about 2,100 kilometres thick, consists of molten iron and nickel at 2,100°C to 5,000°C, possibly separated from the less dense mantle by an oxidized shell. About 5,000 kilometres below the surface is a liquid transition zone, below which is the solid inner core, a sphere of about 2,700 kilometres diameter where rock is three times as dense as in the crust. The temperature at the centre of the Earth is probably about 5,000°C.

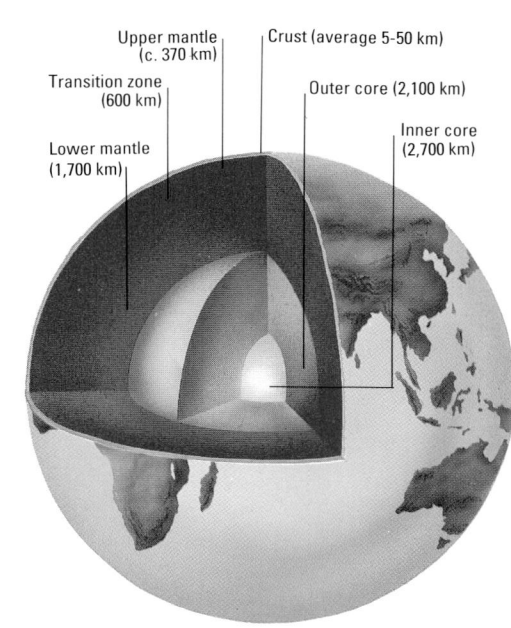

Upper mantle (c. 370 km)
Crust (average 5-50 km)
Transition zone (600 km)
Outer core (2,100 km)
Lower mantle (1,700 km)
Inner core (2,700 km)

CONTINENTAL DRIFT

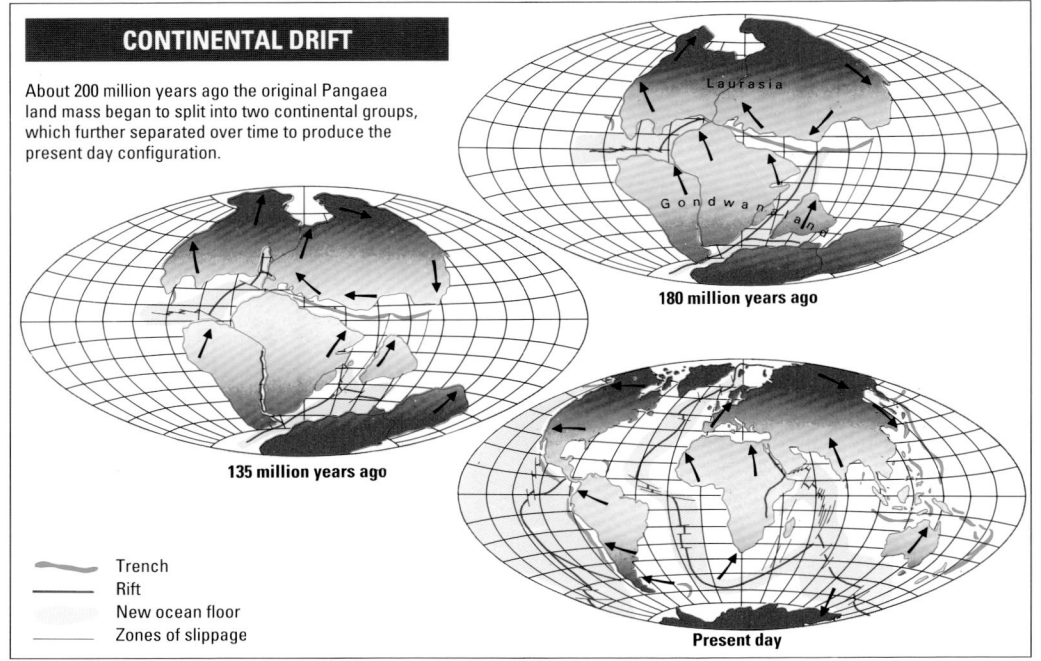

About 200 million years ago the original Pangaea land mass began to split into two continental groups, which further separated over time to produce the present day configuration.

Laurasia

180 million years ago

Gondwanaland

135 million years ago

Present day

Trench
Rift
New ocean floor
Zones of slippage

PLATE TECTONICS

The original debate about the drift theory of Wegener and others formed a long prelude to a more radical idea: plate tectonics. The discovery that the continents are carried along on the top of slowly-moving crustal plates (which float on heavier liquid material – the lower mantle – much as icebergs do on water) provided the mechanism for the drift theories to work. The plates converge and diverge along margins marked by seismic and volcanic activity. Plates diverge from mid-ocean ridges where molten lava pushes up and forces the plates apart at a rate of up to 40 mm a year; converging plates form either a trench (where the oceanic plates sink below the lighter continental rock) or mountain ranges (where two continents collide).

The debate about plate tectonics is not over, however. In addition to abiding questions such as what force actually moves the plates (massive convection currents in the Earth's interior is the most popular explanation), and why many volcanoes and earthquakes occur in mid-plate (such as Hawaii and central China), evidence began to emerge in the early 1990s that, with more sophisticated equipment and models, the whole theory might be in doubt.

EARTHQUAKES

Earthquake magnitude is usually rated according to either the Richter or the Modified Mercalli scale, both devised by seismologists in the 1930s. The Richter scale measures absolute earthquake power with mathematical precision: each step upwards represents a ten-fold increase in shockwave amplitude. Theoretically, there is no upper limit, but the largest earthquakes measured have been rated at between 8.8 and 8.9. The 12–point Mercalli scale, based on observed effects, is often more meaningful, ranging from I (earthquakes noticed only by seismographs) to XII (total destruction); intermediate points include V (people awakened at night; unstable objects overturned), VII (collapse of ordinary buildings; chimneys and monuments fall); and IX (conspicuous cracks in ground; serious damage to reservoirs).

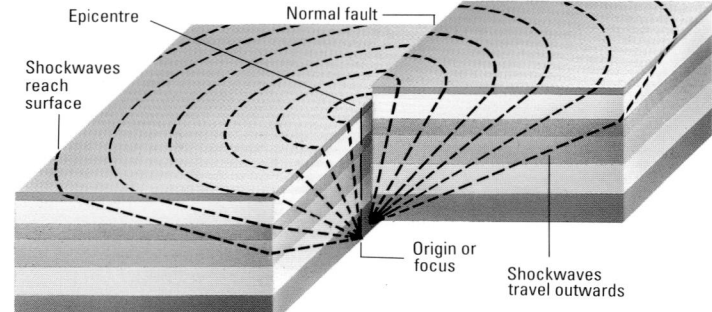

Epicentre
Normal fault
Shockwaves reach surface
Origin or focus
Shockwaves travel outwards

NOTABLE EARTHQUAKES SINCE 1900

Year	Location	Mag.	Deaths
1906	San Francisco, USA	8.3	503
1906	Valparaiso, Chile	8.6	22,000
1908	Messina, Italy	7.5	83,000
1915	Avezzano, Italy	7.5	30,000
1920	Gansu, China	8.6	180,000
1923	Yokohama, Japan	8.3	143,000
1927	Nan Shan, China	8.3	200,000
1932	Gansu, China	7.6	70,000
1934	Bihar, India/Nepal	8.4	10,700
1935	Quetta, India*	7.5	60,000
1939	Chillan, Chile	8.3	28,000
1939	Erzincan, Turkey	7.9	30,000
1960	Agadir, Morocco	5.8	12,000
1962	Khorasan, Iran	7.1	12,230
1963	Skopje, Yugoslavia	6.0	1,000
1964	Anchorage, Alaska	8.4	131
1968	N. E. Iran	7.4	12,000
1970	N. Peru	7.7	66,794
1972	Managua, Nicaragua	6.2	5,000
1974	N. Pakistan	6.3	5,200
1976	Guatemala	7.5	22,778
1976	Tangshan, China	8.2	650,000
1978	Tabas, Iran	7.7	25,000
1980	El Asnam, Algeria	7.3	20,000
1980	S. Italy	7.2	4,800
1985	Mexico City, Mexico	8.1	4,200
1988	N.W. Armenia, USSR	6.8	55,000
1990	N. Iran	7.7	36,000

The highest magnitude recorded on the Richter scale is 8.9, in Japan on 2 March 1933 (2,990 deaths). The most devastating quake ever was at Shaanxi (Shensi), central China, on 24 January 1566, when an estimated 830,000 people were killed.

* now Pakistan

DISTRIBUTION

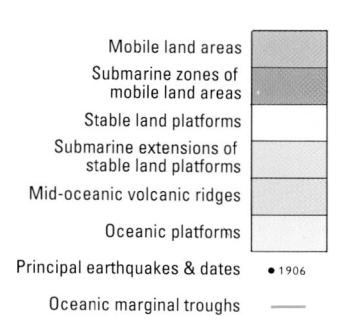

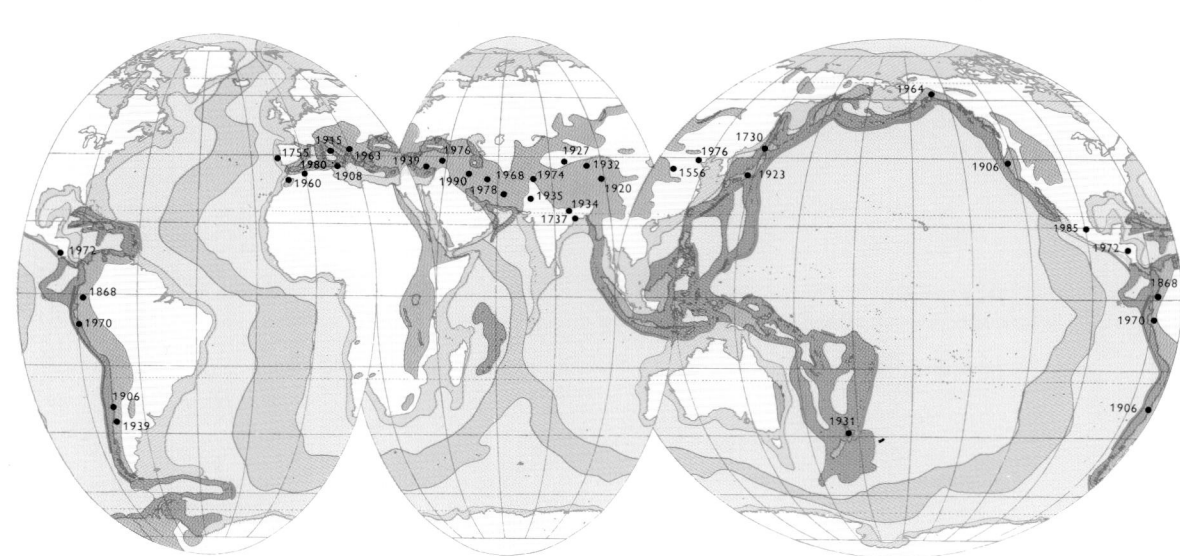

Mobile land areas
Submarine zones of mobile land areas
Stable land platforms
Submarine extensions of stable land platforms
Mid-oceanic volcanic ridges
Oceanic platforms
Principal earthquakes & dates ● 1906
Oceanic marginal troughs —

Earthquakes are a series of rapid vibrations originating from the the slipping or faulting of parts of the Earth's crust when stresses within build to breaking point, and usually occur at depths between 8 and 30 kilometres.

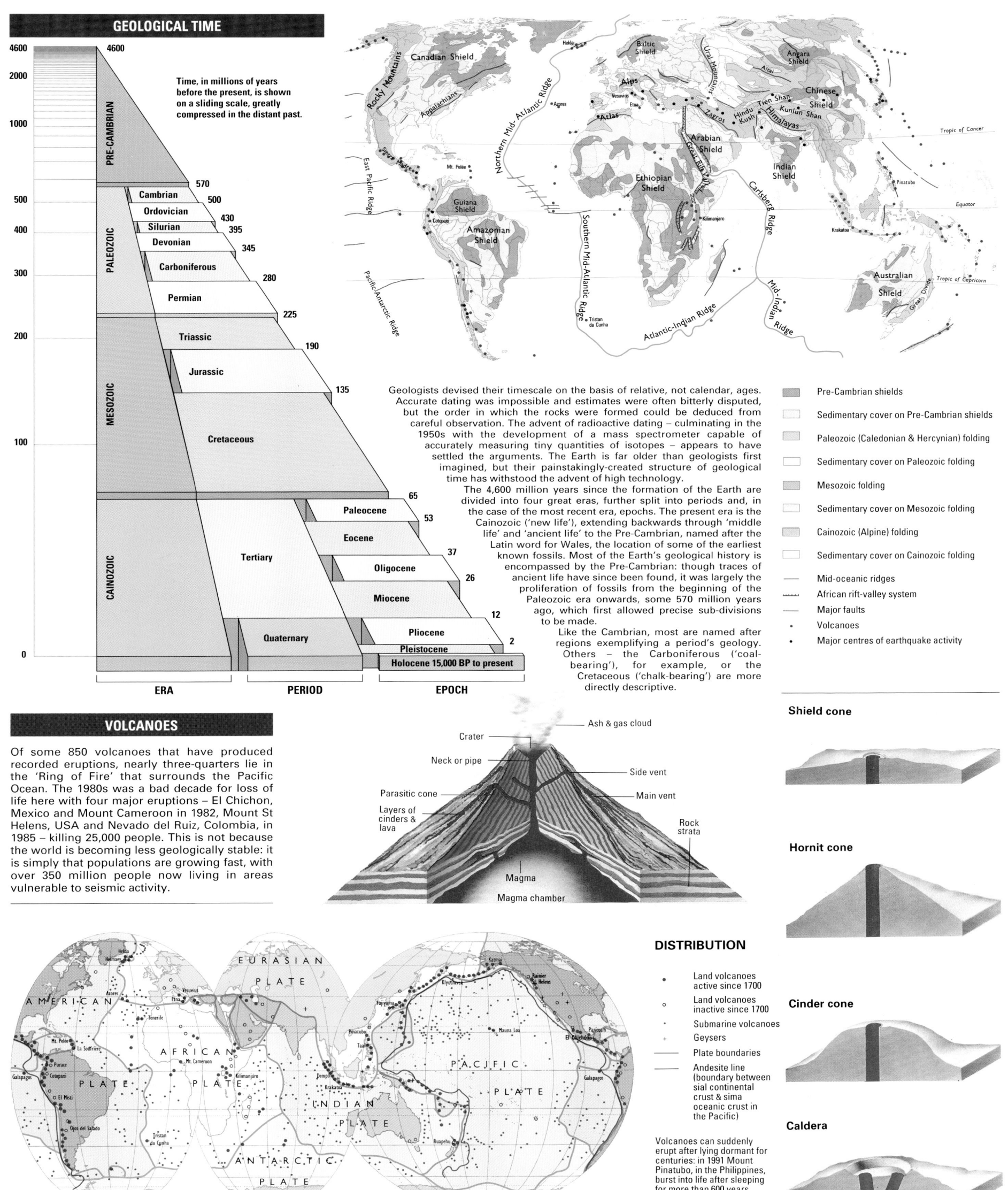

GEOLOGICAL TIME

Time, in millions of years before the present, is shown on a sliding scale, greatly compressed in the distant past.

ERA	PERIOD	EPOCH
PRE-CAMBRIAN		
PALEOZOIC	Cambrian 570	
	Ordovician 500	
	Silurian 430	
	Devonian 395	
	Carboniferous 345	
	Permian 280	
MESOZOIC	Triassic 225	
	Jurassic 190	
	Cretaceous 135	
CAINOZOIC	Tertiary	Paleocene 65
		Eocene 53
		Oligocene 37
		Miocene 26
	Quaternary	Pliocene 12
		Pleistocene 2
		Holocene 15,000 BP to present

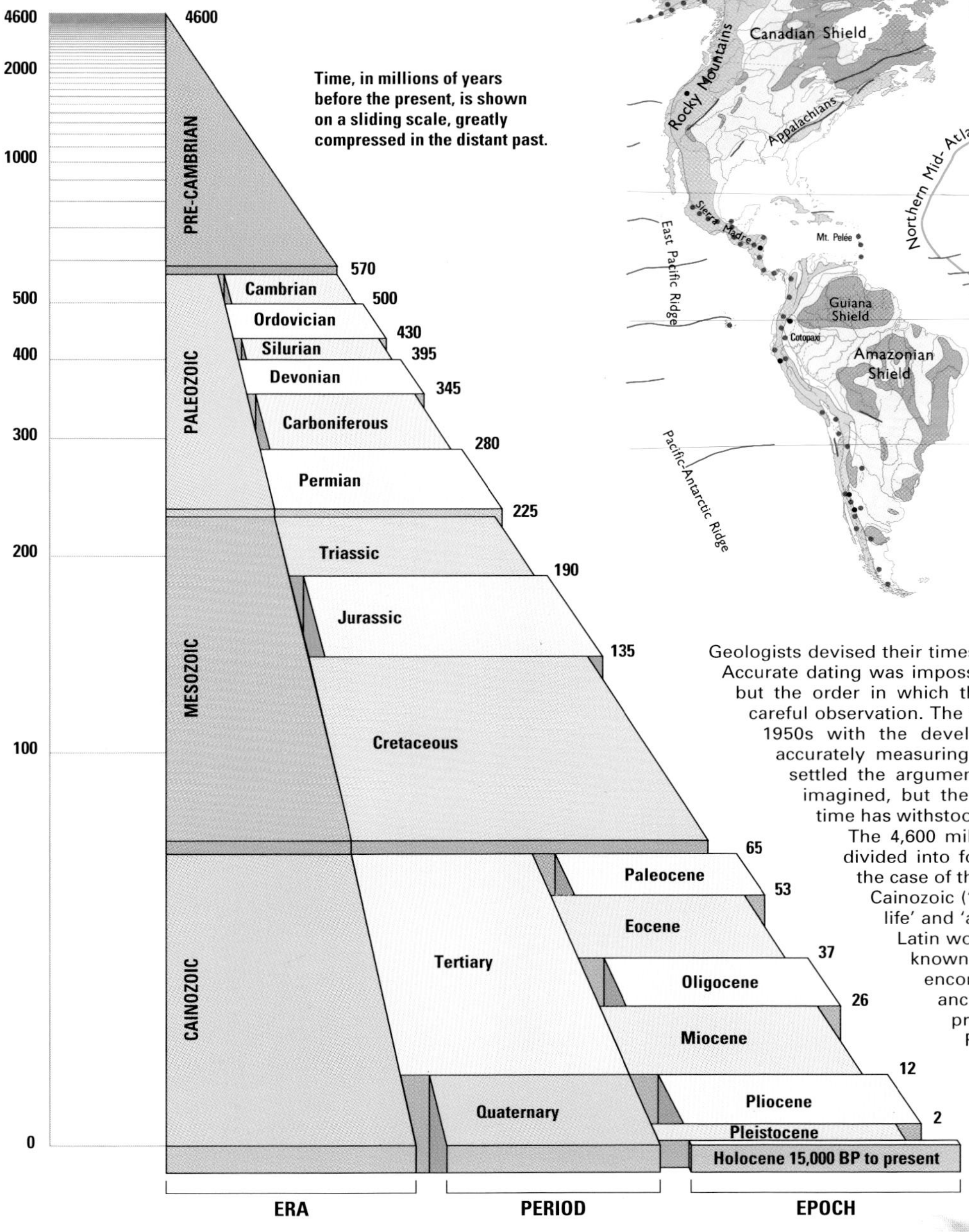

4600 2000 1000 500 400 300 200 100 0

Geologists devised their timescale on the basis of relative, not calendar, ages. Accurate dating was impossible and estimates were often bitterly disputed, but the order in which the rocks were formed could be deduced from careful observation. The advent of radioactive dating – culminating in the 1950s with the development of a mass spectrometer capable of accurately measuring tiny quantities of isotopes – appears to have settled the arguments. The Earth is far older than geologists first imagined, but their painstakingly-created structure of geological time has withstood the advent of high technology.

The 4,600 million years since the formation of the Earth are divided into four great eras, further split into periods and, in the case of the most recent era, epochs. The present era is the Cainozoic ('new life'), extending backwards through 'middle life' and 'ancient life' to the Pre-Cambrian, named after the Latin word for Wales, the location of some of the earliest known fossils. Most of the Earth's geological history is encompassed by the Pre-Cambrian: though traces of ancient life have since been found, it was largely the proliferation of fossils from the beginning of the Paleozoic era onwards, some 570 million years ago, which first allowed precise sub-divisions to be made.

Like the Cambrian, most are named after regions exemplifying a period's geology. Others – the Carboniferous ('coal-bearing'), for example, or the Cretaceous ('chalk-bearing') are more directly descriptive.

- Pre-Cambrian shields
- Sedimentary cover on Pre-Cambrian shields
- Paleozoic (Caledonian & Hercynian) folding
- Sedimentary cover on Paleozoic folding
- Mesozoic folding
- Sedimentary cover on Mesozoic folding
- Cainozoic (Alpine) folding
- Sedimentary cover on Cainozoic folding
- — Mid-oceanic ridges
- ⸴⸴⸴ African rift-valley system
- — Major faults
- • Volcanoes
- • Major centres of earthquake activity

VOLCANOES

Of some 850 volcanoes that have produced recorded eruptions, nearly three-quarters lie in the 'Ring of Fire' that surrounds the Pacific Ocean. The 1980s was a bad decade for loss of life here with four major eruptions – El Chichon, Mexico and Mount Cameroon in 1982, Mount St Helens, USA and Nevado del Ruiz, Colombia, in 1985 – killing 25,000 people. This is not because the world is becoming less geologically stable: it is simply that populations are growing fast, with over 350 million people now living in areas vulnerable to seismic activity.

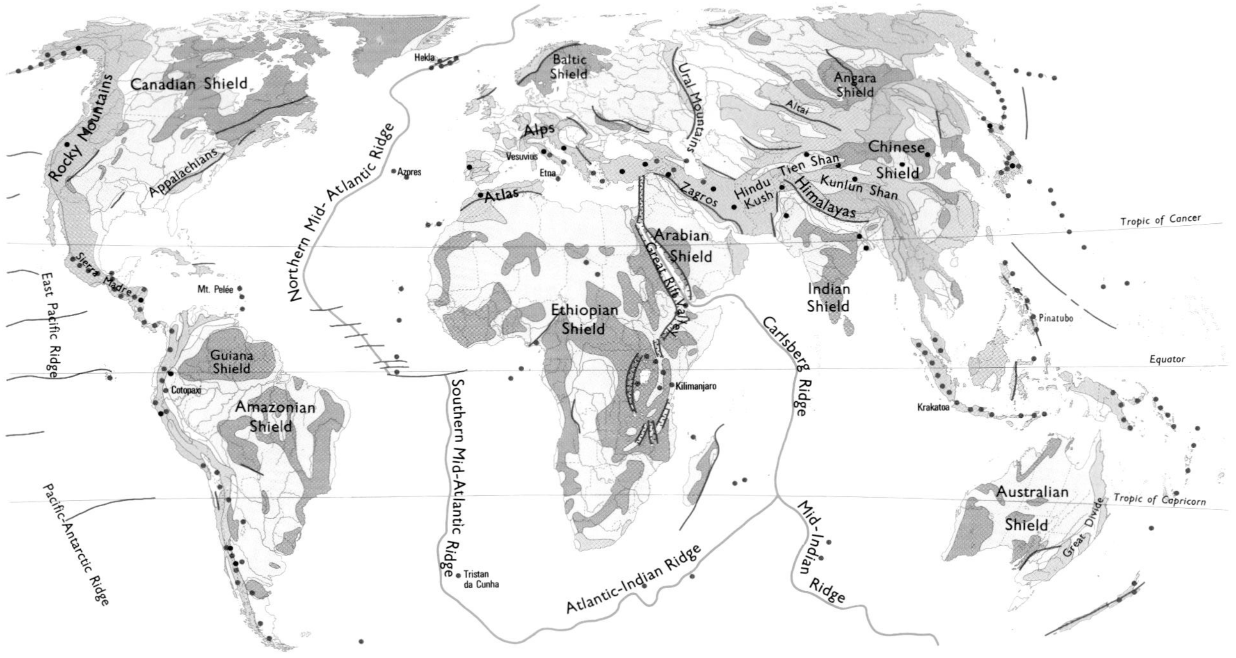

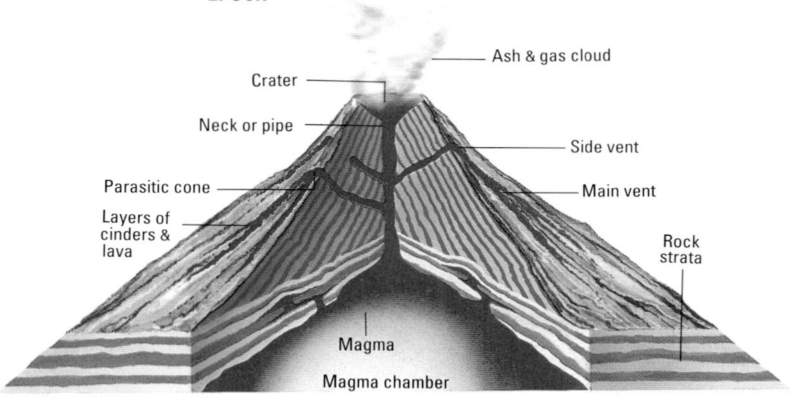

Crater — Ash & gas cloud
Neck or pipe
Parasitic cone — Side vent
Layers of cinders & lava — Main vent
Rock strata
Magma
Magma chamber

Shield cone
Hornit cone
Cinder cone
Caldera

DISTRIBUTION

- • Land volcanoes active since 1700
- ○ Land volcanoes inactive since 1700
- · Submarine volcanoes
- + Geysers
- — Plate boundaries
- Andesite line (boundary between sial continental crust & sima oceanic crust in the Pacific)

Volcanoes can suddenly erupt after lying dormant for centuries: in 1991 Mount Pinatubo, in the Philippines, burst into life after sleeping for more than 600 years.

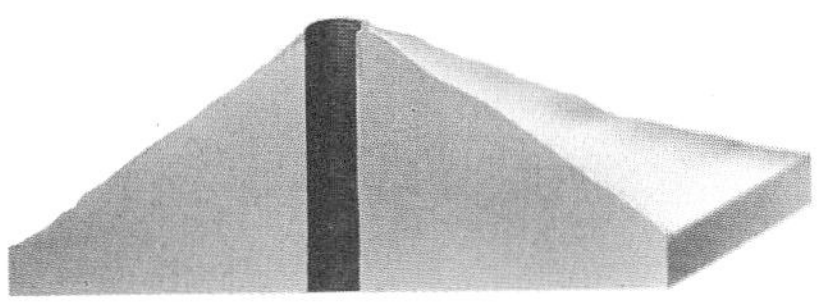

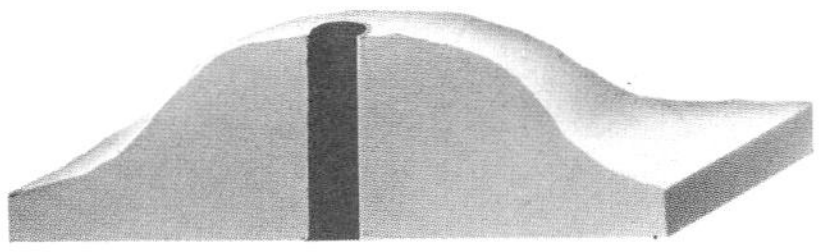

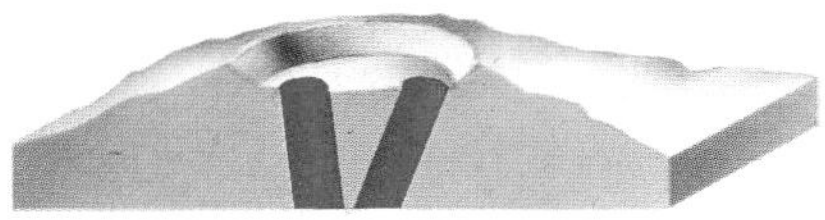

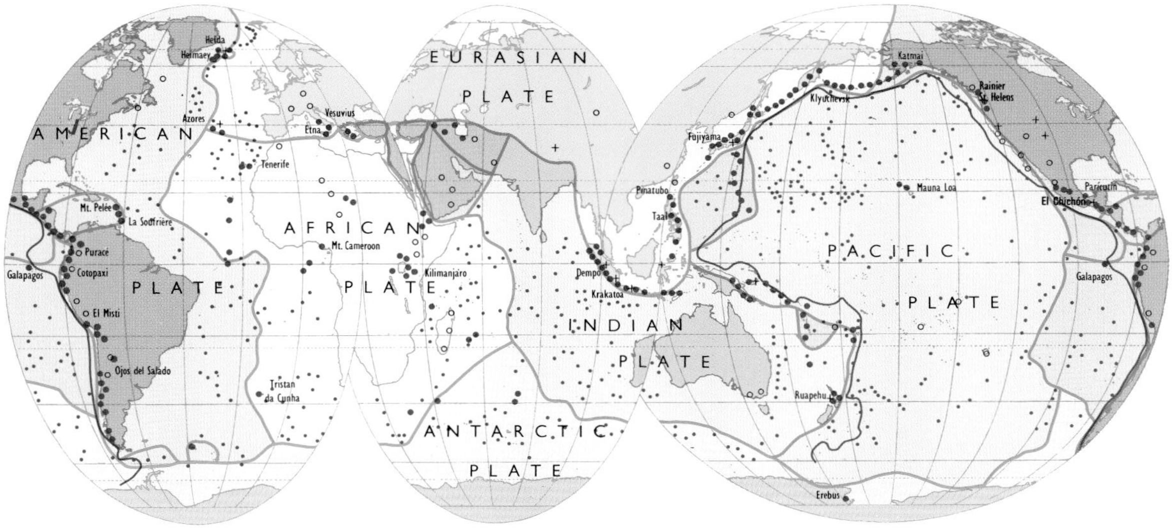

EURASIAN PLATE
AMERICAN PLATE
AFRICAN PLATE
INDIAN PLATE
PACIFIC PLATE
ANTARCTIC PLATE

THE EARTH: OCEANS

7:	TIDES
16:	HYDROLOGICAL CYCLE WATER DISTRIBUTION
17:	WATERSHEDS
18:	THE SPREADING EARTH
39:	SHIPPING
47:	WATER POLLUTION

The Earth is a misnamed planet: almost 71% of its total surface area – 360,059,000 square kilometres – is covered by its oceans and seas. This great cloak of liquid water gives the planet its characteristic blue appearance from space, and is one of two obvious differences between the Earth and its near-neighbours in space, Mars and Venus. The other difference is the presence of life, and the two are closely linked.

In a strict geographical sense, the Earth has only three oceans: the Atlantic, the Pacific and the Indian. Sub-divided vertically instead of horizontally, however, there are many more. The most active is the sunlit upper layer, home of most sea-life and the vital interface between air and water. In this surface zone, huge energies are exchanged between the oceans and the atmosphere above; it is also a kind of membrane through which the ocean breathes, absorbing enormous quantities of carbon dioxide and partially exchanging them for oxygen, largely through the phytoplankton, tiny plants that photosynthesize solar energy and provide the food base for all other marine life.

As depth increases, light and colour fade away, the longer wavelengths dying first. At 50 metres, the ocean is a world of green and blue and violet; at 100 metres, only blue remains; by 200 metres, there is only a dim twilight. The temperature falls away with the light until some time before 1,000 metres – the precise depth varies – there occurs a temperature change almost as abrupt as the transition between air and water far above.

Below this thermocline, at a near-stable 3°C, the waters are forever unmoved by the winds of the upper world and are stirred only by the slow action of deep ocean currents. The pressure is crushing, touching 1,000 atmospheres in the deepest trenches: a force of one tonne bearing down on every square centimetre.

Yet even here the oceans support life, and not only the handful of strange, deep-sea creatures that find a living in the near-empty abyss. The deep ocean serves as a gigantic storehouse both for heat and for assorted atmospheric chemicals, regulating and balancing the proportions of various trace compounds and elements and ensuring a large measure of stability for both the climate and the ecology that depend on it.

— Sea level

— 200 metres

— 500 metres

— 1,000 metres

— 1,500 metres

— 2,000 metres

— 6,000 metres

— 11,000 metres

From the tidal zone at the coastline, the continental shelf, geologically still part of the continental landmass, drops gently to about 200 metres. At the end of the shelf, the seabed falls away in the steeper angle of the continental slope, exaggerated in this drawing, in which the horizontal scale has been greatly compressed. The subsequent descent to the deep ocean floor, known as the continental rise, is more gentle, with gradients between 1 in 100 and 1 in 700 until the abyssal plains, at between 2,500 and 6,000 metres below the surface. Most marine life is confined to the first 200 metres, where sunlight can still penetrate.

ATOLL BUILDING

A coral atoll begins existence as a bare volcanic peak, thrusting above the ocean surface. A colony of coral - marine organisms called polyps, with skeletons of rigid calcium carbonate - forms itself in the shallow water around the peak. Its seafloor eruption over, the volcano slowly sinks, leaving the coral forming a ring around its remnant. In time, all obvious trace of the volcano vanishes, and the barrier reef of an atoll is all that remains.

For the most part, the sea bottom is flat, seldom descending below 6,000 metres. A few ocean trenches, however, slice almost twice as far into the Earth's crust, especially in the Pacific, where six trenches reach more than 10,000 metres, including the 11,022-metre Mariana Trench. The deepest Atlantic trench is the Puerto Rico trough (Milwaukee Deep), at 9,200 metres. Deep ocean water circulates very slowly, often remaining in place for thousands of years at a time.

Life is very scarce in the deep ocean, but a few organisms have been found even in the abyssal darkness of the great trenches, feeding on the trickle of organic debris that reaches the seafloor from far above.

PROFILE OF AN OCEAN

The deep ocean floor is no more uniform than the surface of the continents, although it was not until the development of effective sonar equipment that it was possible to examine submarine contours in detail. The Atlantic (right) and the Pacific show similar patterns. Off-shore comes the continental shelf, sliding downwards to the continental slope and the steeper continental rise, after which the seabed rolls onward into the abyssal plains. In the wide Pacific, these are interrupted by gently-rising abyssal hills; in both oceans, the plains extend all the way to the mid-oceanic ridges, where the upwelling of new crustal material is constantly forcing the oceans wider. Volcanic activity is responsible for the formation of seamounts and tablemounts or guyots, their flat-topped equivalents. In this cross-section, only the Azores are high enough to break the surface and become islands.

Massachusetts (Nantucket sound)

Kelvin seamounts

Corne seamour

2,000 metres

4,000 metres

Abyssal plain

OCEAN CURRENTS

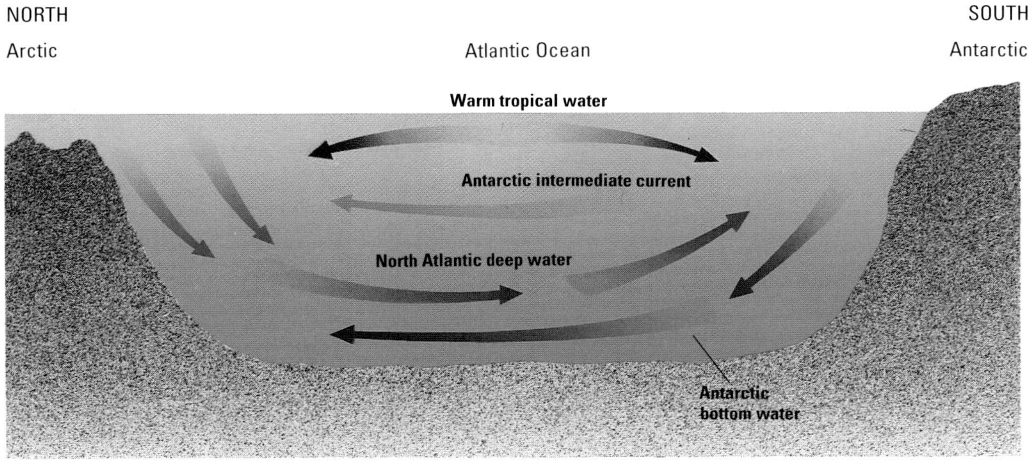

NORTH
SOUTH
Arctic
Atlantic Ocean
Antarctic
Warm tropical water
Antarctic intermediate current
North Atlantic deep water
Antarctic bottom water

Moving immense quantities of energy as well as billions of tonnes of water every hour, the ocean currents are a vital part of the great heat engine that drives the Earth's climate. They themselves are produced by a twofold mechanism. At the surface, winds push huge masses of water before them; in the deep ocean, below an abrupt temperature gradient that separates the churning surface waters from the still depths, density variations cause slow vertical movements.

The pattern of circulation of the great surface currents is determined by the displacement known as the Coriolis effect. As the Earth turns beneath a moving object - whether it is a tennis ball or a vast mass of water - it appears to be deflected to one side. The deflection is most obvious near the equator, where the Earth's surface is spinning eastward at 1700 km/h; currents moving poleward are curved clockwise in the northern hemisphere and anti-clockwise in the southern.

The result is a system of spinning circles known as gyres. The Coriolis effect piles up water on the left of each gyre, creating a narrow, fast-moving stream that is matched by a slower, broader returning current on the right. North and south of the equator, the fastest currents are located in the west and in the east respectively. In each case, warm water moves from the equator and cold water returns to it. Cold currents often bring an upwelling of nutrients with them, supporting the world's most economically important fisheries. Depending on the prevailing winds, some currents on or near the equator may reverse their direction in the course of the year - a seasonal variation on which Asian monsoon rains depend, and whose occasional failure can bring disaster to millions of people.

CURRENTS & TEMPERATURES

(Northern Hemisphere: winter)

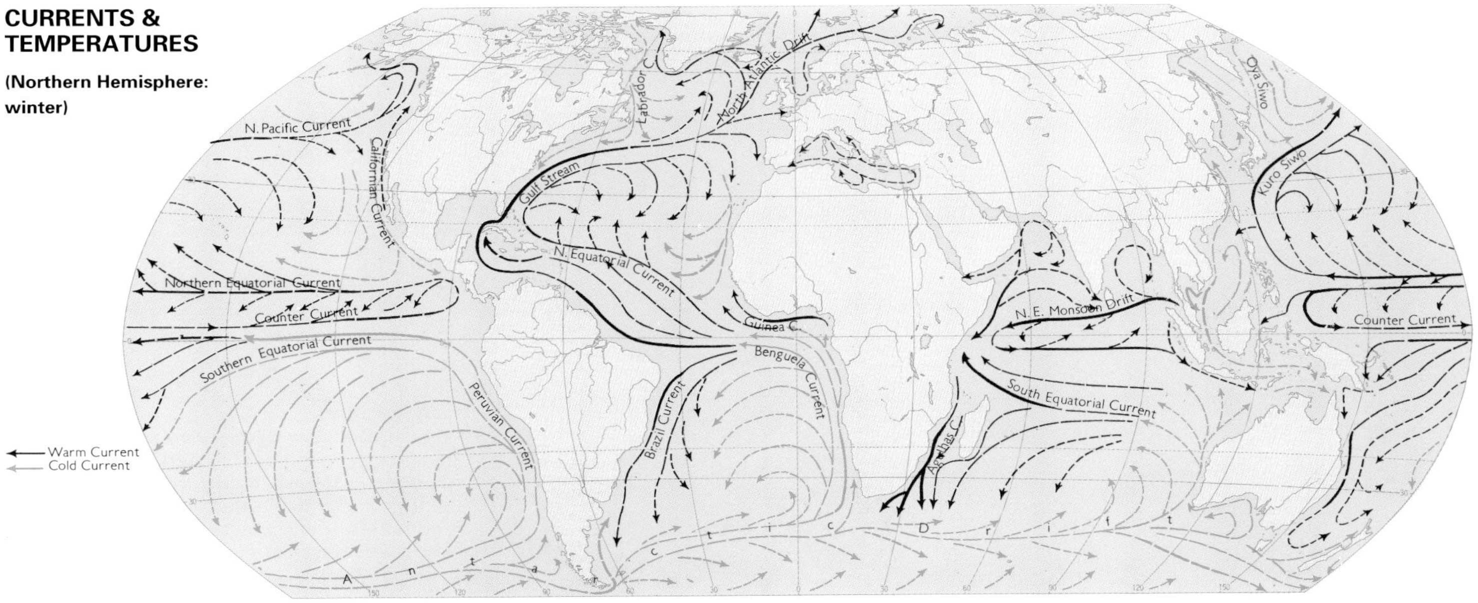

Warm Current
Cold Current
N. Pacific Current
Californian Current
Labrador
North Atlantic Drift
Gulf Stream
N. Equatorial Current
Northern Equatorial Current
Counter Current
Southern Equatorial Current
Peruvian Current
Guinea C.
Benguela Current
Brazil Current
Oya Siwo
Kuro Siwo
N. E. Monsoon Drift
Counter Current
South Equatorial Current
Agulhas C.
A n t a r c t i c D r i f t

CURRENTS & TEMPERATURES

(Northern Hemisphere: summer)

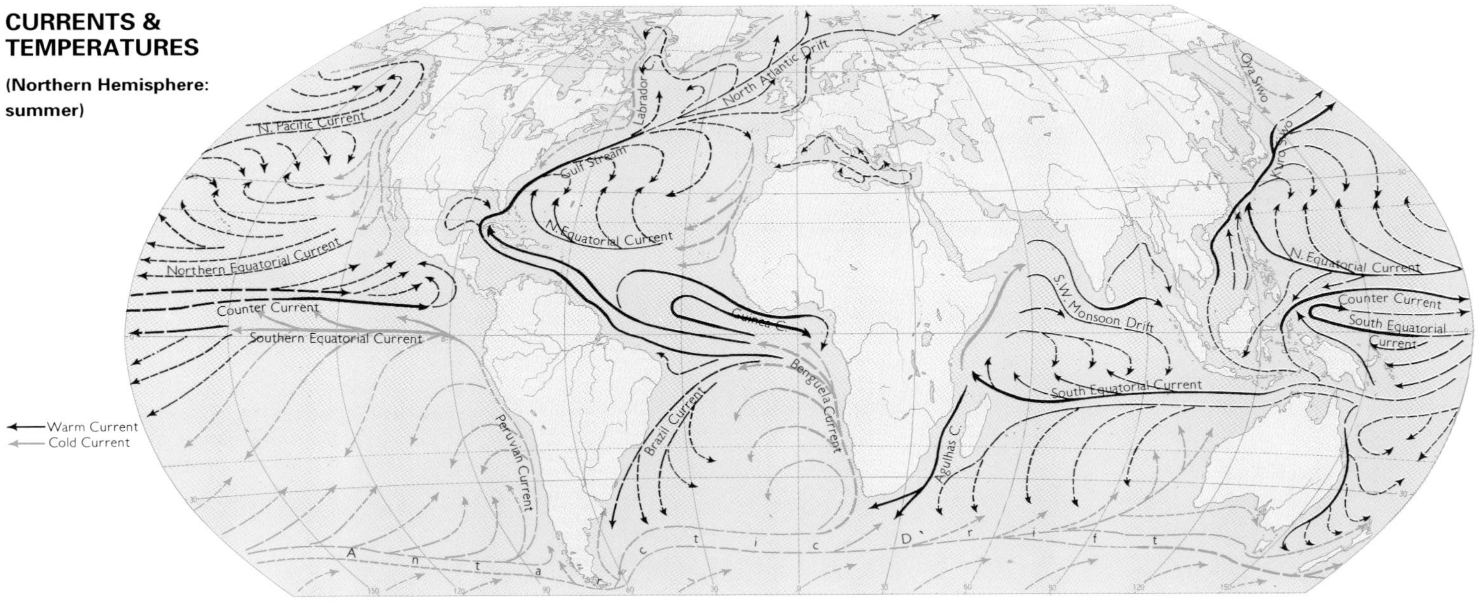

Warm Current
Cold Current
N. Pacific Current
Labrador
North Atlantic Drift
Gulf Stream
N. Equatorial Current
Northern Equatorial Current
Counter Current
Southern Equatorial Current
Peruvian Current
Guinea C.
Benguela Current
Brazil Current
Oya Siwo
N. Equatorial Current
Counter Current
South Equatorial Current
S.W. Monsoon Drift
South Equatorial Current
Agulhas C.
A n t a r c t i c D r i f t

SEAWATER

The chemical composition of the sea, in grams per tonne of seawater, excluding the elements of water itself

Chlorine	19400
Sodium	10800
Magnesium	1290
Sulphur	904
Calcium	411
Potassium	392
Bromine	67
Strontium	8.1
Boron	4.5
Fluorine	1.3
Lithium	0.17
Rubidium	0.12
Phosphorus	0.09
Iodine	0.06
Barium	0.02
Arsenic	0.003
Cesium	0.0003

Seawater also contains virtually every other element, although the quantities involved are too small for reliable measurement. In natural conditions, its composition is broadly consistent across the world's seas and oceans; but especially in coastal areas, variations, sometimes substantial, may be caused by the presence of industrial waste and sewage sludge.

Mid-Atlantic ridge
Atlantic seamount
Azores
Josephine seamounts
Gettysburg seamounts
Gibraltar

COPYRIGHT GEORGE PHILIP LTD.

11:	OCEAN CURRENTS
15:	BEAUFORT WIND SCALE
21:	SOLAR ENERGY GREENHOUSE EFFECT
46:	GREENHOUSE POWER
47:	ACID RAIN

Extending from the surface far into space, the atmosphere is a meteor shield, a radiation deflector, a thermal blanket and a source of chemical energy for the Earth's diverse inhabitants. Five-sixths of its mass is found in the first 15 kilometres, the troposphere, no thicker in relative terms than the skin of an onion. Clouds, cyclonic winds, precipitation and virtually all the phenomena we call weather occur in this narrow layer. Above, a thin layer of ozone blocks ultra-violet radiation. Beyond 100 kilometres, atmospheric density is lower than most laboratory vacuums, yet these tenuous outer reaches, composed largely of hydrogen and helium, trap cosmic debris and incoming high-energy particles alike.

CIRCULATION OF THE AIR

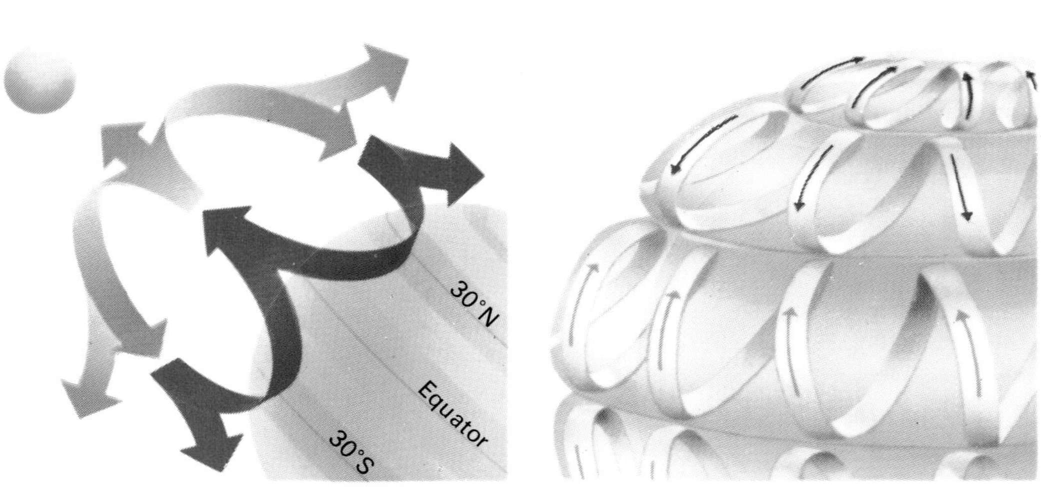

30°N
Equator
30°S

STRUCTURE OF ATMOSPHERE

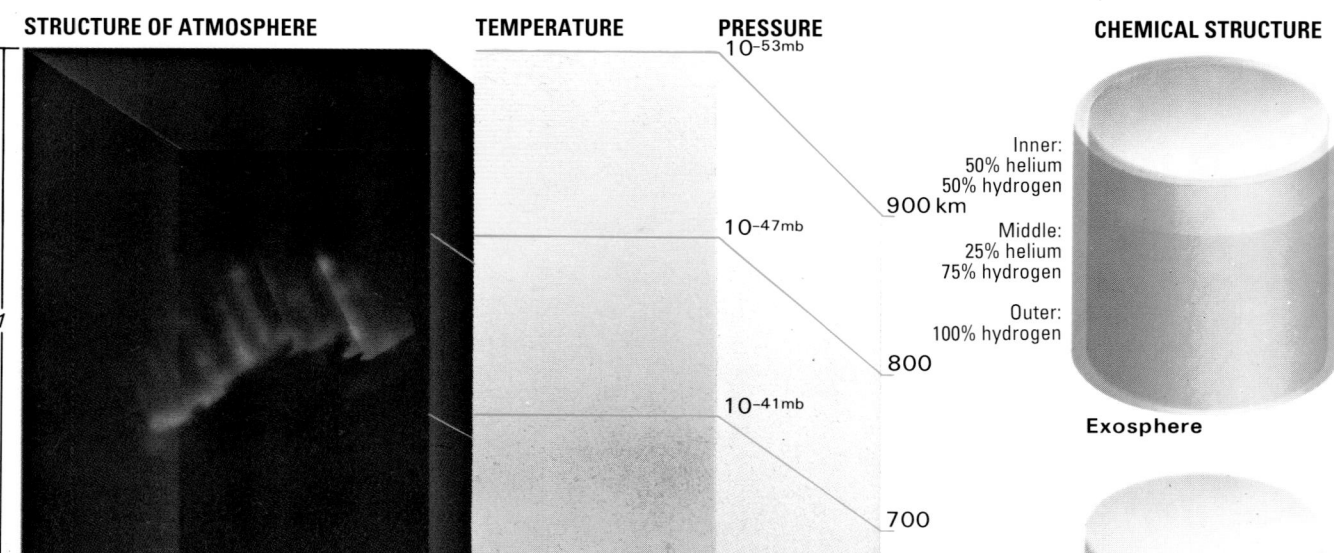

F2
F1
E
D
Mesosphere
Ozone layer
Tropopause

TEMPERATURE

ca. 2 200 °C
ca. 1 500 °C
ca. 750 °C
−58 °C
−91 °C
−93 °C
−33 °C
−8 °C
−12 °C
−38 °C
−53 °C
15 °C

PRESSURE

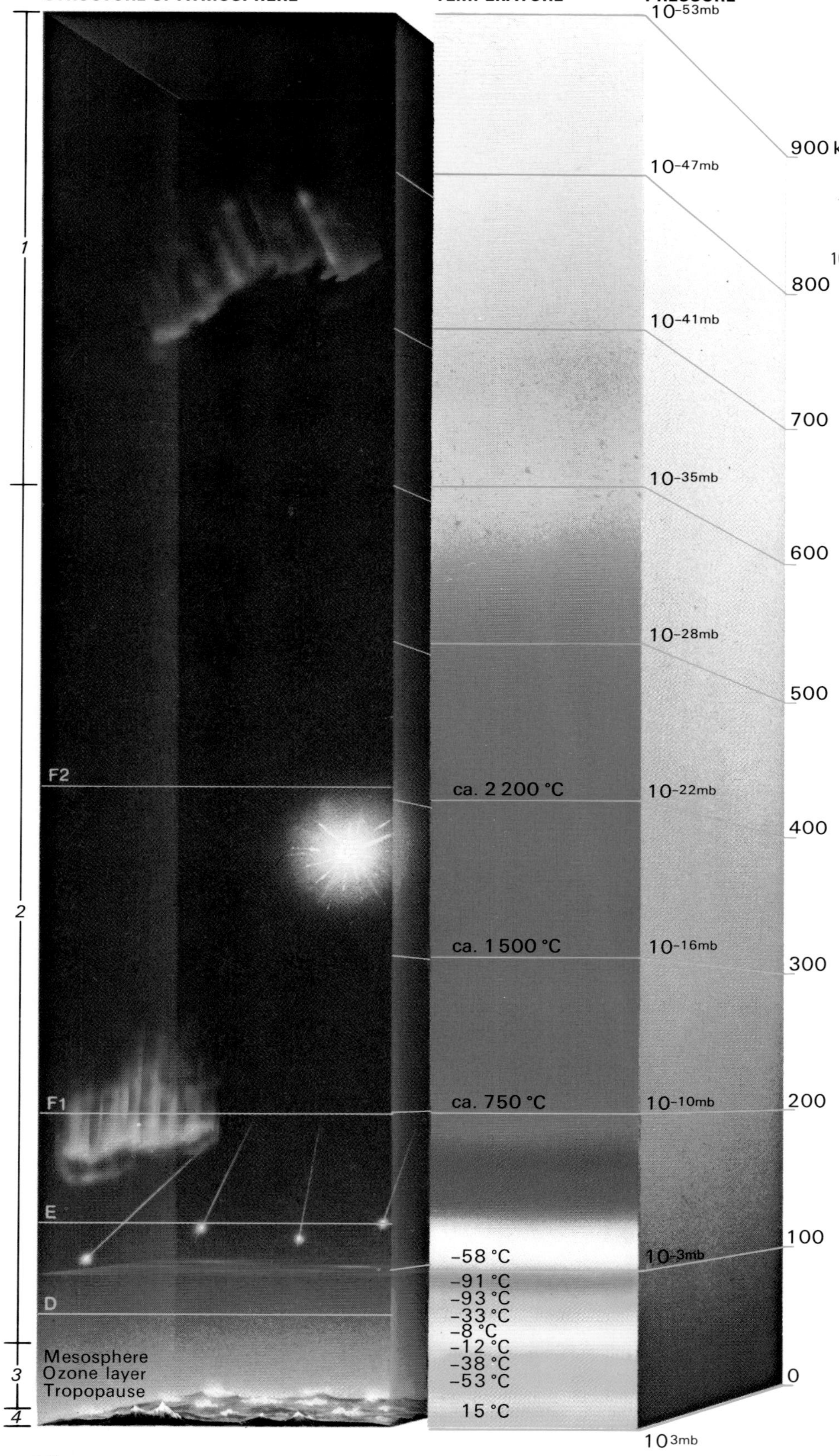

10^{-53} mb
10^{-47} mb
10^{-41} mb
10^{-35} mb
10^{-28} mb
10^{-22} mb
10^{-16} mb
10^{-10} mb
10^{-3} mb
10^{3} mb

900 km
800
700
600
500
400
300
200
100
0

CHEMICAL STRUCTURE

Inner: 50% helium 50% hydrogen
Middle: 25% helium 75% hydrogen
Outer: 100% hydrogen

Exosphere

15% helium
15% oxygen & atomic oxygen
70% nitrogen

Ionosphere

1% ozone
1% argon
18% oxygen
80% nitrogen

Stratosphere

1% argon
21% oxygen
78% nitrogen

Troposphere

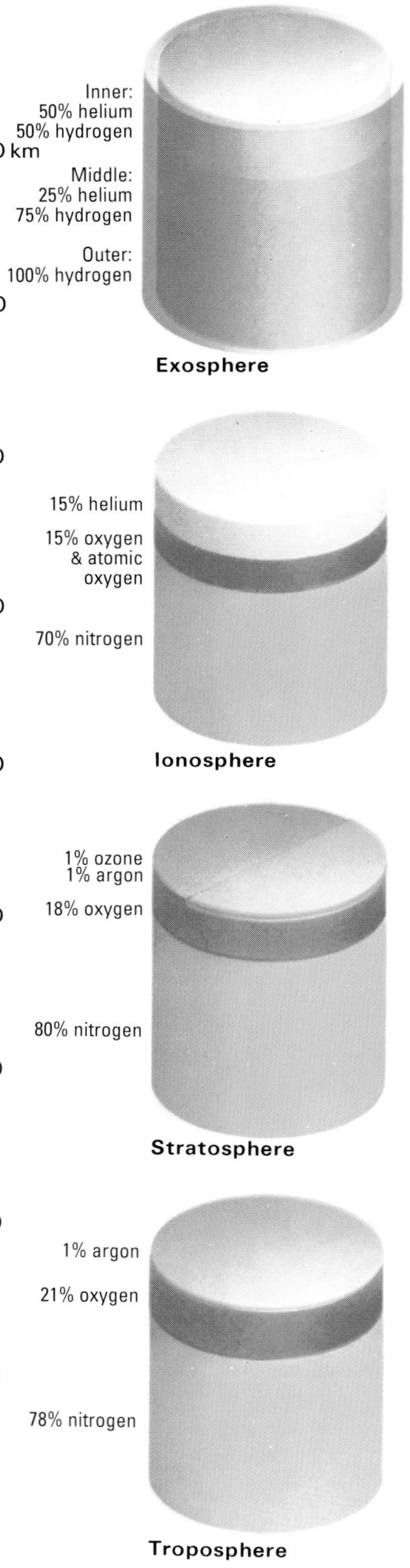

Exosphere

The atmosphere's upper layer has no clear outer boundary, merging imperceptibly with interplanetary space. Its lower boundary, at an altitude of approximately 600 kilometres, is almost equally vague. The exosphere is mainly composed of hydrogen and helium in changing proportions, with a small quantity of atomic oxygen up to 600 kilometres. Helium vanishes with increasing altitude, and above 2,400 kilometres the exosphere is almost entirely hydrogen.

Ionosphere

Gas molecules in the ionosphere, mainly helium, oxygen and nitrogen, are electrically charged - ionized - by the Sun's radiation. Within the ionosphere's range of 50 to 600 kilometres in altitude, they group themselves into four layers, known conventionally as D, E, F1 and F2, all of which can reflect radio waves of differing frequencies. The high energy of ionospheric gas gives it a notional temperature of more than 2,000°C, although its density is negligible. The auroras - *aurora borealis* and its southern counterpart, *aurora australis* - occur in the ionosphere when charged particles from the Sun interact with the Earth's magnetic fields, at their strongest near the poles.

Stratosphere

Separated at its upper and lower limits by the distinct thresholds of the stratopause and the tropopause, the stratosphere is a remarkably stable layer between 50 kilometres and about 15 kilometres. Its temperature rises from −55°C at its lower extent to approximately 0°C near the stratopause, where a thin layer of ozone absorbs ultra-violet radiation. "Mother-of-pearl" or nacreous cloud occurs at about 25 kilometres' altitude. Stratospheric air contains enough ozone to make it poisonous, although it is in any case far too rarified to breathe.

Troposphere

The narrowest of all the atmospheric layers, the troposphere extends up to 15 kilometres at the equator but only 8 kilometres at the poles. Since this thin region contains about 85% of the atmosphere's total mass and almost all of its water vapour, it is also the realm of the Earth's weather. Temperatures fall steadily with increasing height by about 1°C for every 100 metres above sea level.

Heated by the relatively high surface temperatures near the Earth's equator, air expands and rises to create a belt of low pressure. Moving northward towards the poles, it gradually cools, sinking once more and producing high pressure belts at about latitudes 30° North and South. Water vapour carried with the air falls as rain, releasing vast quantities of energy as well as liquid water when it condenses.

The high and low pressure belts are both areas of comparative calm, but between them, blowing from high to low pressure areas, are the prevailing winds. The atmospheric circulatory system is enormously complicated by the Coriolis effect brought about by the spinning Earth: winds are deflected to the right in the northern hemisphere and to the left in the southern, giving rise to the typically cyclonic pattern of swirling clouds carried by the moving masses of air.

Although clouds appear in an almost infinite variety of shapes and sizes, there are recognizable features that form the basis of a classification first put forward by Luke Howard, a London chemist, in 1803 and later modified by the World Meteorological Organization. The system derives from the altitude of clouds and whether they form hairlike filaments ('cirrus'), heaps or piles ('cumulus') or layers ('stratus'). Each characteristic carries some kind of message – not always a clear one – to forecasters about the weather to come.

CLASSIFICATION OF CLOUDS

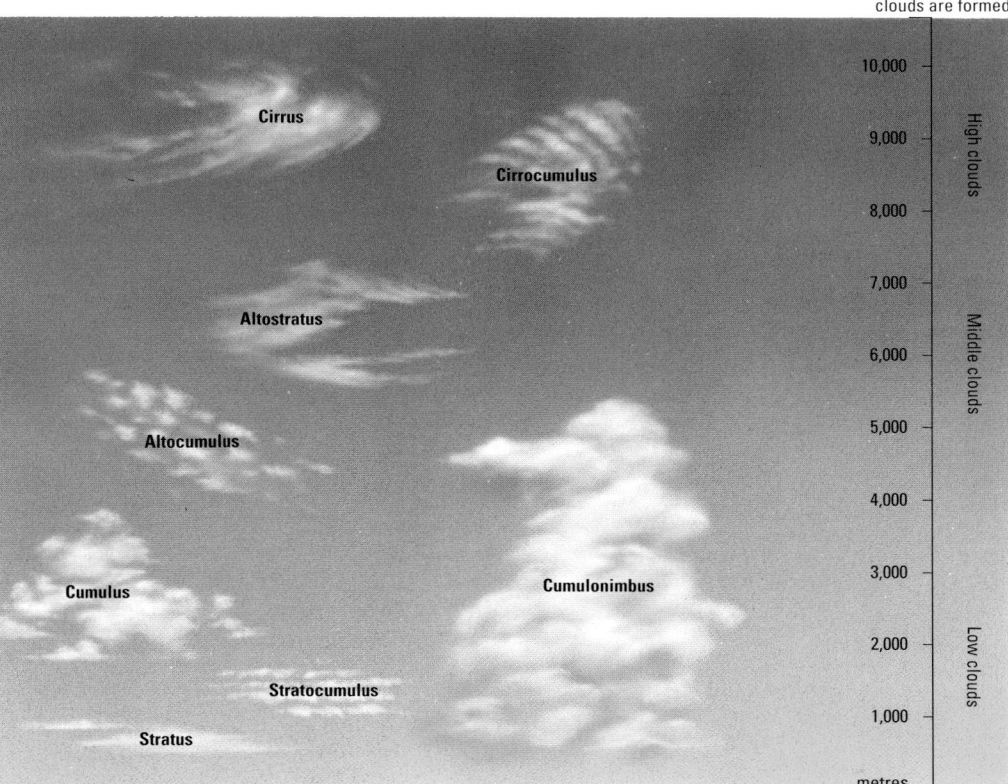

Altitude at which clouds are formed

	metres
High clouds	10,000
	9,000
	8,000
Middle clouds	7,000
	6,000
	5,000
	4,000
Low clouds	3,000
	2,000
	1,000

Cirrus
Cirrocumulus
Altostratus
Altocumulus
Cumulus
Cumulonimbus
Stratocumulus
Stratus

Clouds form when damp, usually rising, air is cooled. Thus they form when a wind rises to cross hills or mountains; when a mass of air rises over, or is pushed up by, another mass of denser air; or when local heating of the ground causes convection currents. The types of clouds are classified according to altitude as high, middle, or low. The high ones, composed of ice crystals, are cirrus, cirrostratus and cirrocumulus. The middle clouds are altostratus, a grey or bluish striated, fibrous, or uniform sheet producing light drizzle, and altocumulus, a thicker and fluffier version of cirrocumulus. The low clouds include nimbostratus, a dark grey layer that brings almost continuous rain or snow; cumulus, a detached 'heap' – brilliant white in sunlight but dark and flat at the base; and stratus, which forms dull, overcast skies at low altitudes. Cumulonimbus, associated with storms and rains, heavy and dense with flat base and a high, fluffy outline, can be tall enough to occupy middle as well as low altitudes.

PRESSURE & WINDS

January

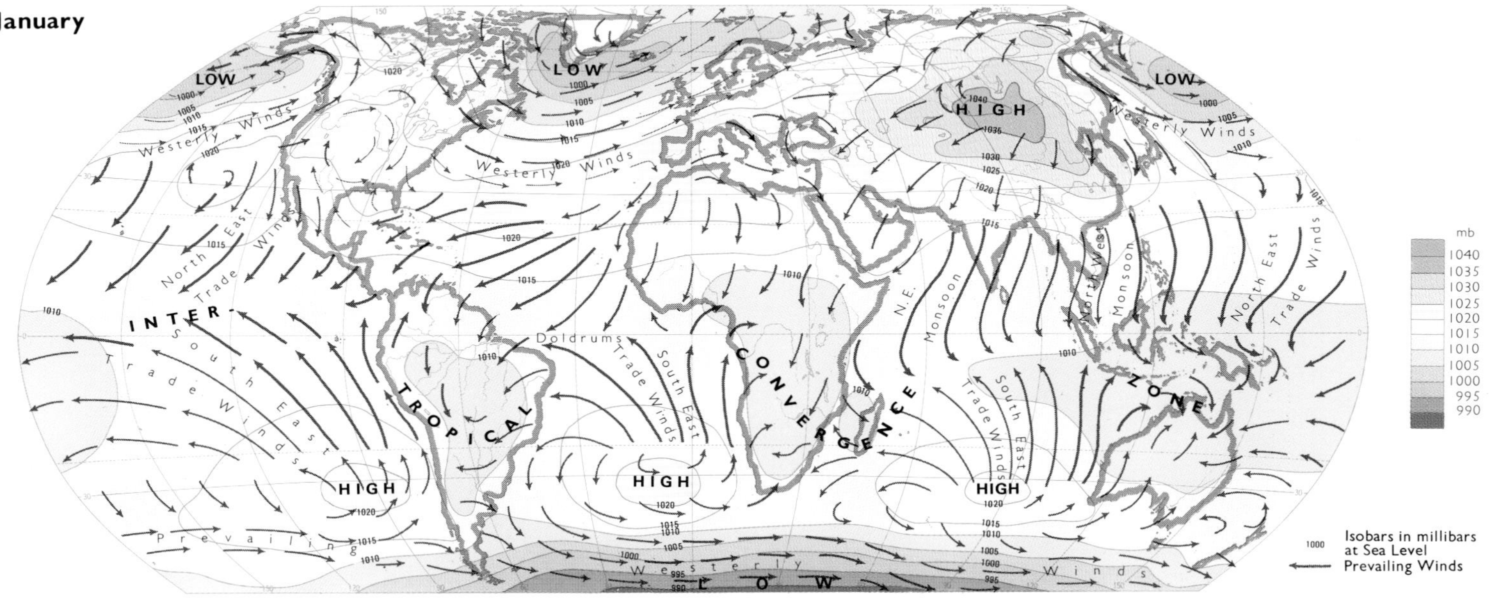

July

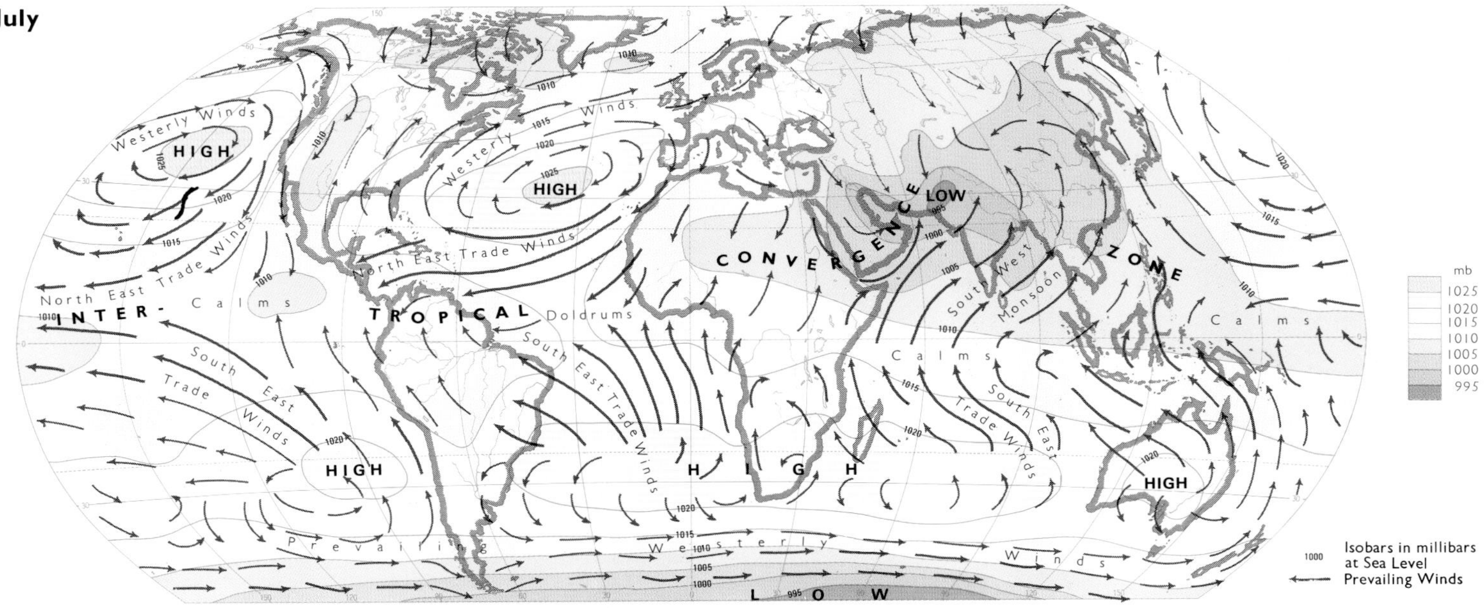

Isobars in millibars at Sea Level
Prevailing Winds

mb
1040
1035
1030
1025
1020
1015
1010
1005
1000
995
990

mb
1025
1020
1015
1010
1005
1000
995

CLIMATE RECORDS

Pressure & Winds

Highest barometric pressure: Agata, Siberia, USSR, 1,083.8 mb [32 in] at altitude 262 m [862 ft], 31 Dec. 1968.

Lowest barometric pressure: Typhoon Tip, 480 km [300 mls] west of Guam, Pacific Ocean, 870 mb [25.69 in], 12 Oct. 1979.

Highest recorded windspeed: Mt Washington, New Hampshire, USA 371 kph [231 mph], 12 Apr. 1934. This is three times as strong as hurricane force on the Beaufort Scale.

Windiest place: Commonwealth Bay, George V Coast, Antarctica, where gales frequently reach over 320 kph [200 mph].

Worst recorded storm: Bangladesh (then East Pakistan) cyclone*, 13 Nov. 1970 – over 300,000 dead or missing. The 1991 cyclone, Bangladesh's and the world's second worst in terms of loss of life, killed an estimated 138,000.

Worst recorded tornado: Missouri/Illinois/Indiana, USA, 18 Mar. 1925 – 792 deaths. The tornado was only 275 m (300 yds) wide.

* Tropical cyclones are known as hurricanes in Central and North America and as typhoons in the Far East

THE EARTH: CLIMATE

11:	OCEAN CURRENTS
12:	CIRCULATION OF THE AIR
13:	CLASSIFICATION OF CLOUDS PRESSURE & WINDS
16:	HYDROLOGICAL CYCLE
17:	NATURAL VEGETATION
21:	GREENHOUSE EFFECT
30:	LAND USE
46:	GLOBAL WARMING

Climate is weather in the long term: the seasonal pattern of hot and cold, wet and dry, averaged over time. At the simplest level, it is caused by the uneven heating of the Earth. Surplus heat at the equator passes towards the poles, levelling out the energy differential. Its passage is marked by a ceaseless churning of the atmosphere and the oceans, further agitated by the the Earth's diurnal spin and the motion it imparts to moving air and water. The heat's means of transport – by winds and ocean currents, by the continual evaporation and recondensation of water molecules – is the weather itself.

There are four basic types of climate, each open to considerable sub-division: tropical, desert, temperate and polar. But although latitude is obviously a critical factor, it is not the only determinant. The differential heating of land and sea, the funnelling and interruption of winds and ocean currents by landmasses and mountain ranges, and the transpiration of vegetation: all combine to add complexity. New York, Naples and the Gobi Desert share almost the same latitude, for example, but their climates are very different. And although the sheer intricacy of the weather system often defies day-to-day prediction in these or any other places – despite the satellites and number-crunching supercomputers with which present-day meteorologists are equipped – their climatic patterns retain a year-on-year stability.

They are not indefinitely stable, however. The planet regularly passes through long, cool periods of around 100,000 years: these are the ice ages, probably caused by recurring long-term oscillations in the Earth's orbital path and fluctuations in the Sun's energy output. In the present era, the Earth is nearest to the Sun in the middle of the northern hemisphere's winter; 11,000 years ago, at the end of the last ice age, the northern winter fell with the Sun at its most distant.

Left to its own devices, the climate even now should be drifting towards another glacial period. But global warming caused by increasing carbon dioxide levels in the atmosphere, largely the result of 20th-century fuel-burning and deforestation, may well precipitate change far faster than the great, slow cycles of the solar system.

CLIMATE REGIONS

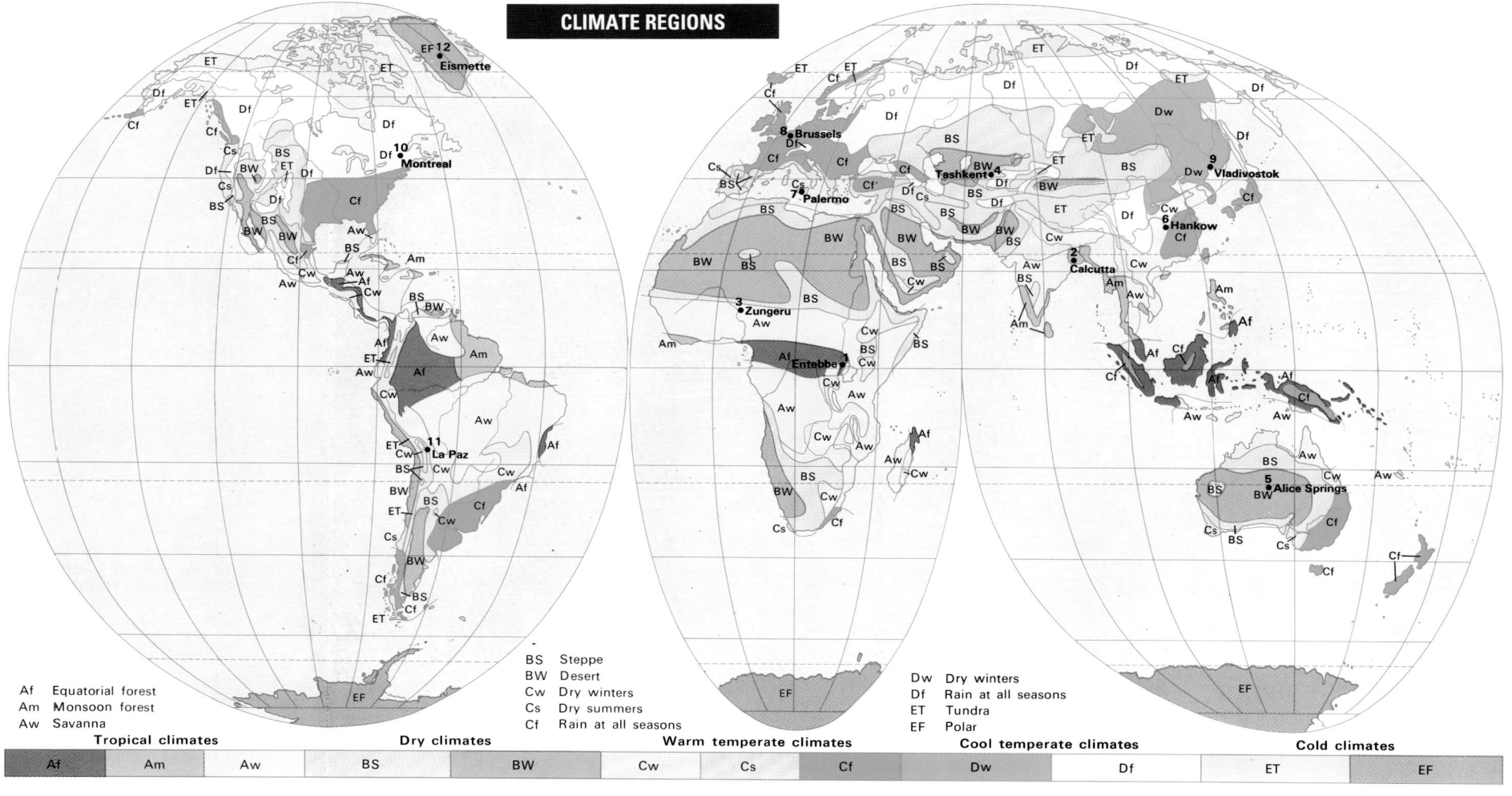

Af	Equatorial forest	
Am	Monsoon forest	
Aw	Savanna	
BS	Steppe	
BW	Desert	
Cw	Dry winters	
Cs	Dry summers	
Cf	Rain at all seasons	
Dw	Dry winters	
Df	Rain at all seasons	
ET	Tundra	
EF	Polar	

Tropical climates			Dry climates		Warm temperate climates			Cool temperate climates			Cold climates
Af	Am	Aw	BS	BW	Cw	Cs	Cf	Dw	Df	ET	EF

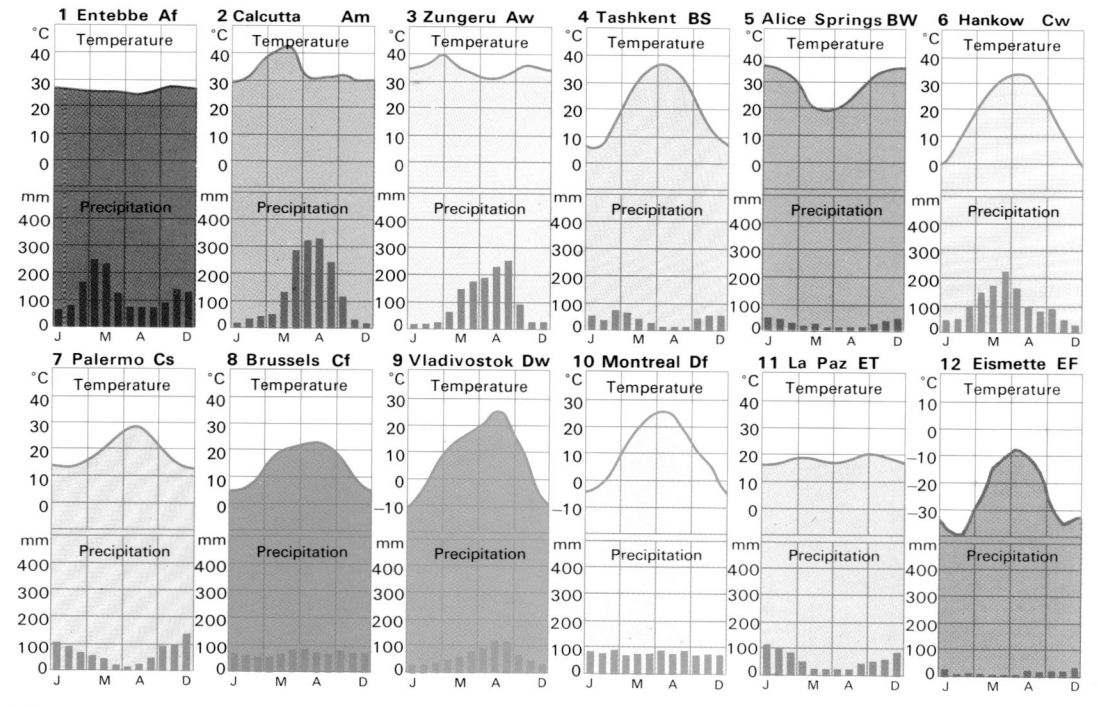

1 Entebbe Af — 2 Calcutta Am — 3 Zungeru Aw — 4 Tashkent BS — 5 Alice Springs BW — 6 Hankow Cw — 7 Palermo Cs — 8 Brussels Cf — 9 Vladivostok Dw — 10 Montreal Df — 11 La Paz ET — 12 Eismette EF

CLIMATE & WEATHER TERMS

Absolute humidity: amount of water vapour contained in a given volume of air.
Cloud cover: amount of cloud in the sky; measured in oktas (from 1 - 8), with 0 clear, & 8 total cover.
Condensation: the conversion of water vapour, or moisture in the air into liquid.
Cyclone: violent storm resultinig from counter clockwise rotation of winds in the northern hemisphere & clockwise in the southern: called hurricane in N. America, typhoon in the Far East.
Depression: approximately circular area of low pressure.
Dew: water droplets condensed out of the air after the ground has cooled at night.
Dew point: temperature at which air becomes saturated (reaches a relative humidity of 100%) at a constant pressure.
Drizzle: precipitation where drops are less than 0.5 mm (0.02 in) in diameter.
Evaporation: conversion of water from liquid into vapour, or moisture in the air.
Frost: dew that has frozen when the air temperature falls below freezing point.
Hail: frozen rain; small balls of ice, often falling during thunder storms.
Hoar frost: formed on objects when the dew point is below freezing point.
Humidity: amount of moisture in the air.
Isobar: cartographic line connecting places of equal atmospheric pressure.
Isotherm: cartographic line connecting places of equal temperature.
Lightning: massive electrical discharge released in thunderstorm from cloud to cloud or cloud to ground, the result of the tip becoming positively charged & the bottom negatively charged.
Precipitation: measurable rain, snow, sleet or hail.
Prevailing wind: most common direction of wind at a given location.
Rain: precipitation of liquid particles with diameter larger than 0.5 mm (0.02 in).
Relative humidity: amount of water vapour contained in a given volume of air at a given temperature.
Sleet: translucent or transparent ice-pellets (partially melted snow).
Snow: formed when water vapour condenses below freezing point.
Thunder: sound produced by the rapid expansion of air heated by lightning.
Tidal wave: giant ocean wave generated by earthquakes (tsunami) or cyclonic winds.
Tornado: severe funnel-shaped storm that twists as hot air spins vertically (waterspout at sea).
Whirlwind: rapidly rotating column of air, only a few metres across made visible by dust.

WINDCHILL FACTOR

In sub-zero weather, even moderate winds significantly reduce effective temperatures. The chart below shows the windchill effect across a range of speeds. Figures in the pink zone are not dangerous to well-clad people; in the blue zone, the risk of serious frostbite is acute.

Wind speed (km/h)

	16	32	48	64	80
0°C	-8	-14	-17	-19	-20
-5°C	-14	-21	-25	-27	-28
-10°C	-20	-28	-33	-35	-36
-15°C	-26	-36	-40	-43	-44
-20°C	-32	-42	-48	-51	-52
-25°C	-38	-49	-56	-59	-60
-30°C	-44	-57	-63	-66	-68
-35°C	-51	-64	-72	-74	-76
-40°C	-57	-71	-78	-82	-84
-45°C	-63	-78	-86	-90	-92
-50°C	-69	-85	-94	-98	-100

BEAUFORT WIND SCALE

Named for the 19th-century British naval officer who devised it, the Beaufort Scale assesses wind speed according to its effects. It was originally designed as an aid for sailors, but has since been adapted for use on land.

Scale	Wind speed kph	mph	Effect
0	0-1	0-1	**Calm** Smoke rises vertically
1	1-5	1-3	**Light air** Wind direction shown only by smoke drift
2	6-11	4-7	**Light breeze** Wind felt on face; leaves rustle; vanes moved by wind
3	12-19	8-12	**Gentle breeze** Leaves and small twigs in constant motion; wind extend small flag
4	20-28	13-18	**Moderate** Raises dust and loose paper; small branches move
5	29-38	19-24	**Fresh** Small trees in leaf sway; crested wavelets on inland waters
6	39-49	25-31	**Strong** Large branches move; difficult to use umbrellas; overhead wires whistle
7	50-61	32-38	**Near gale** Whole trees in motion; difficult to walk against wind
8	62-74	39-46	**Gale** Twigs break from trees; walking very difficult
9	75-88	47-54	**Strong gale** Slight structural damage
10	89-102	55-63	**Storm** Trees uprooted; serious structural damage
11	103-117	64-72	**Violent Storm** Widespread damage
12	118+	73+	**Hurricane**

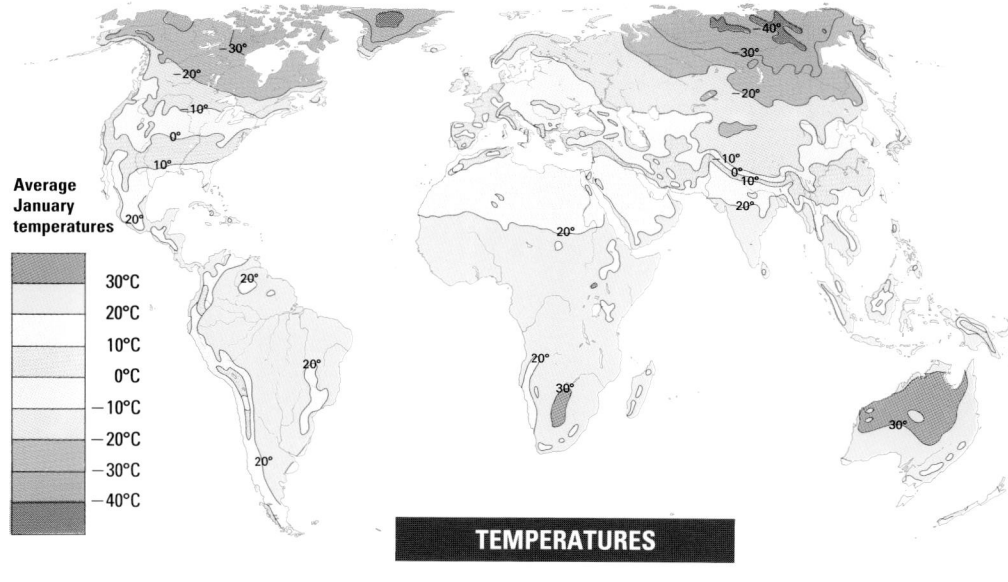

Average January temperatures

30°C / 20°C / 10°C / 0°C / −10°C / −20°C / −30°C / −40°C

TEMPERATURES

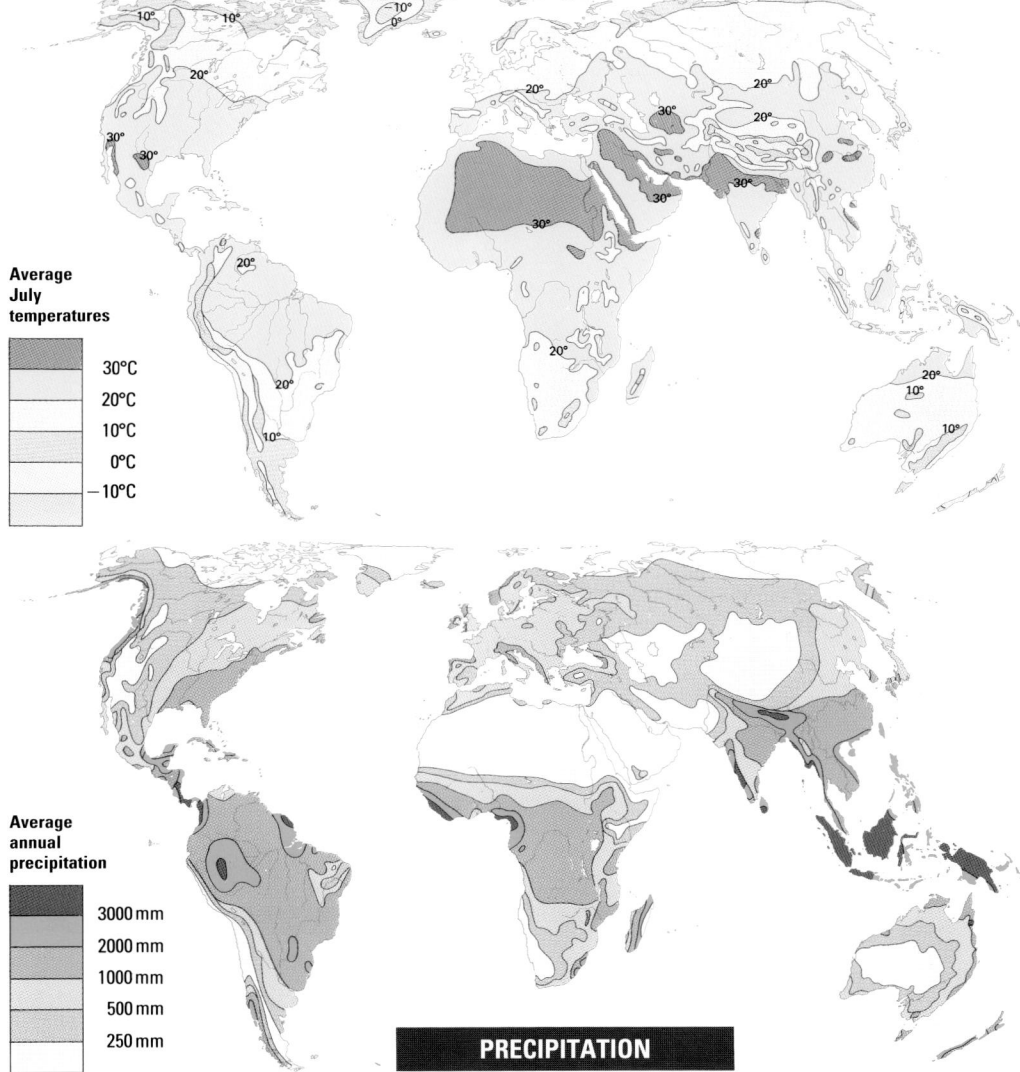

Average July temperatures

30°C / 20°C / 10°C / 0°C / −10°C

Average annual precipitation

3000 mm / 2000 mm / 1000 mm / 500 mm / 250 mm

PRECIPITATION

CLIMATE RECORDS

Temperature

Highest recorded temperature: Al Aziziyah, Libya, 58°C [136.4°F], 13 Sep. 1922.

Highest mean annual temperature: Dallol, Ethiopia, 34.4°C [94°F], 1960-66.

Longest heatwave: Marble Bar, W. Australia, 162 days over 38°C [100°F], 23 Oct. 1923 - 7 Apr. 1924.

Lowest recorded temperature (outside poles): Verkhoyansk, Siberia, USSR -68°C [-90°F], 6 Feb. 1933. Verkhoyansk also registered the greatest annual range of temperature: - 70°C to 37°C [-94°F to 98°F].

Lowest mean annual temperature: Polus Nedostupnosti, Pole of Cold, Antarctica, -57.8°C [-72°F].

Precipitation

Driest place: Arica, N. Chile, 0.8mm [0.3 in] per year (60-year average).

Longest drought: Calama, N. Chile: no recorded rainfall in 400 years to 1971.

Wettest place (average): Tututendo, Colombia: mean annual rainfall 11,770 mm [463.4 in].

Wettest place (12 months): Cherrapunji, Meghalaya, N.E. India, 26,470 mm [1,040 in], Aug. 1860 to Aug. 1861. Cherrapunji also holds the record for rainfall in one month: 930 mm [37 in] July 1861.

Wettest place (24 hours): Cilaos, Réunion, Indian Ocean, 1,870 mm [73.6 in], 15-16 Mar. 1952.

Heaviest hailstones: Gopalganj, Bangladesh, up to 1.02 kg [2.25 lb], 14 Apr. 1986 (killed 92 people).

Heaviest snowfall (continuous): Bessans, Savoie, France, 1730 mm [68 in] in 19 hours, 5-6 Apr. 1969.

Heaviest snowfall (season/year): Paradise Ranger Station, Mt Rainier, Washington, USA, 31,102 mm [1,224.5 in], 19 Feb. 1971 to 18 Feb. 1972.

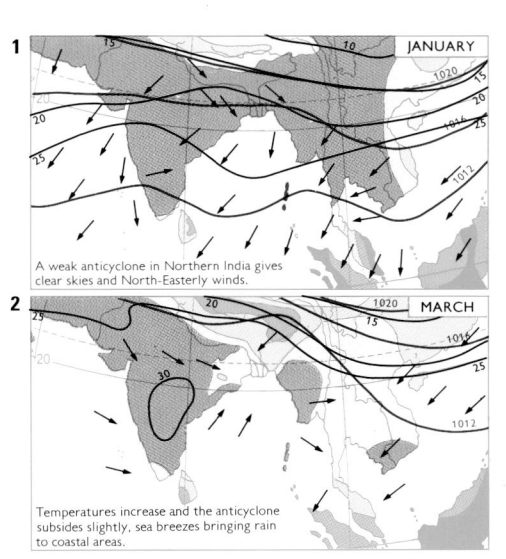

JANUARY
A weak anticyclone in Northern India gives clear skies and North-Easterly winds.

MARCH
Temperatures increase and the anticyclone subsides slightly, sea breezes bringing rain to coastal areas.

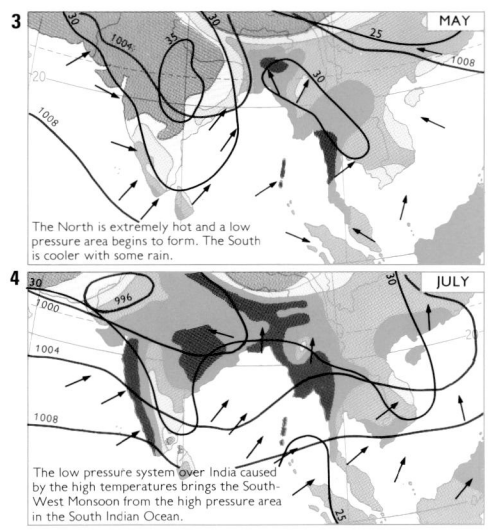

MAY
The North is extremely hot and a low pressure area begins to form. The South is cooler with some rain.

JULY
The low pressure system over India caused by the high temperatures brings the South-West Monsoon from the high pressure area in the South Indian Ocean.

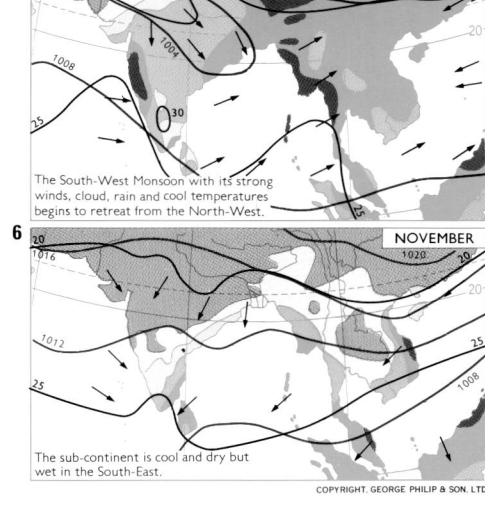

SEPTEMBER
The South-West Monsoon with its strong winds, cloud, rain and cool temperatures begins to retreat from the North-West.

NOVEMBER
The sub-continent is cool and dry but wet in the South-East.

COPYRIGHT. GEORGE PHILIP & SON. LTD.

THE MONSOON

While it is crucial to the agriculture of South Asia, the monsoon that follows the dry months is unpredictable - in duration as well as intensity. A season of very heavy rainfall, causing disastrous floods, can be succeeded by years of low precipitation, leading to serious drought.

Monthly rainfall

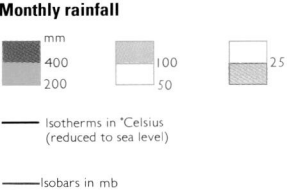

mm
400 / 200 / 100 / 50 / 25

— Isotherms in °Celsius (reduced to sea level)

— Isobars in mb

→ Prevailing winds

THE EARTH: WATER

14: TYPES OF PRECIPITATION

15: RAINFALL
THE MONSOON
CLIMATE RECORDS

19: SHAPING FORCES:
RIVERS & GLACIERS

Fresh water is essential to all terrestrial life, from the humblest bacterium to the most advanced technological society. Yet freshwater resources form a minute fraction of the Earth's 1.41 billion cubic kilometres of water: most human needs must be met from the 2,000 cubic kilometres circulating in rivers at any one time. Agriculture accounts for huge quantities: without large-scale irrigation, most of the world's people would starve. And since fresh water is just as essential for most industrial processes – smelting a tonne of nickel, for example, requires about 4,000 tonnes of water – the combination of growing population and advancing industry has put water supplies under strain.

Fortunately water is seldom used up: the planet's hydrological cycle circulates it with benign efficiency, at least on a global scale. More locally, though, human activity can cause severe shortages: water for industry and agriculture is being withdrawn from many river basins and underground aquifers faster than natural recirculation can replace it.

THE HYDROLOGICAL CYCLE

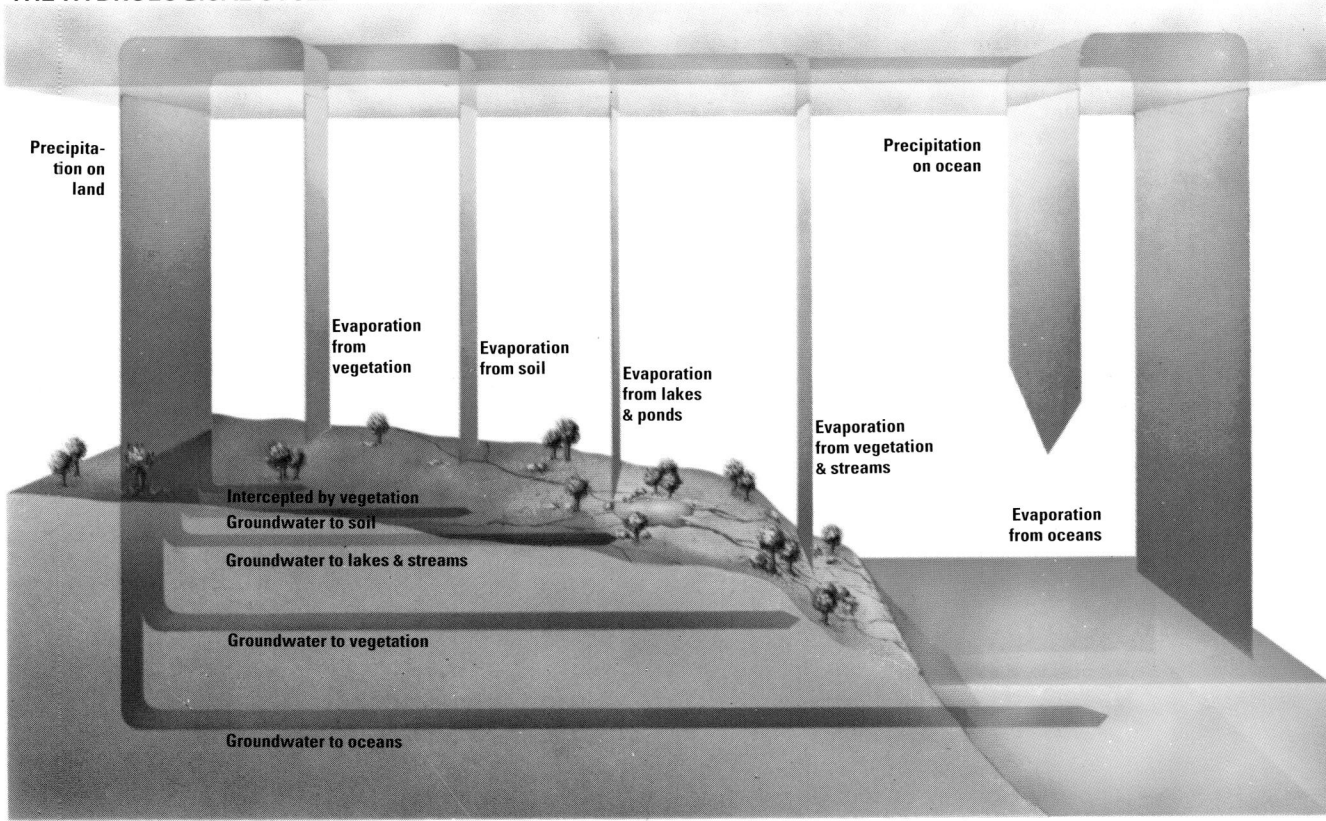

Precipitation on land

Precipitation on ocean

Evaporation from vegetation

Evaporation from soil

Evaporation from lakes & ponds

Evaporation from vegetation & streams

Evaporation from oceans

Intercepted by vegetation
Groundwater to soil

Groundwater to lakes & streams

Groundwater to vegetation

Groundwater to oceans

WATER DISTRIBUTION

The distribution of planetary water, by percentage. Oceans and icecaps together account for more than 99% of the total; the breakdown of the remainder is estimated.

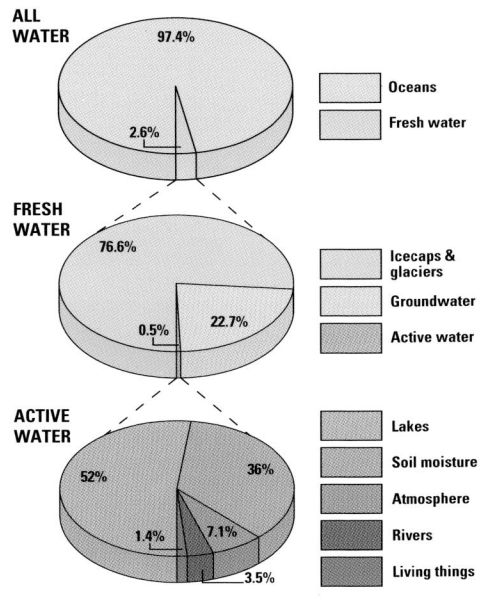

ALL WATER
- 97.4% — Oceans
- 2.6% — Fresh water

FRESH WATER
- 76.6% — Icecaps & glaciers
- 0.5% — Groundwater
- 22.7% — Active water

ACTIVE WATER
- 52% — Lakes
- 36% — Soil moisture
- 7.1% — Atmosphere
- 1.4% — Rivers
- 3.5% — Living things

Almost all the world's water is 3,000 million years old, and all of it cycles endlessly through the hydrosphere, though at different rates. Water vapour circulates over days, even hours, deep ocean water circulates over millenia and ice-cap water remains solid for millions of years.

Water vapour is constantly drawn into the air from the Earth's rivers, lakes, seas and plant transpiration. In the atmosphere, it circulates around the planet, transporting energy as well as water itself. When the vapour cools it falls as rain or snow, and returns to the surface to evaporate once more. The whole cycle is driven by the Sun.

WATER RUNOFF

Annual freshwater runoff by continent in cubic kilometres

- Asia
- North America
- South America
- Australasia
- Europe
- Africa

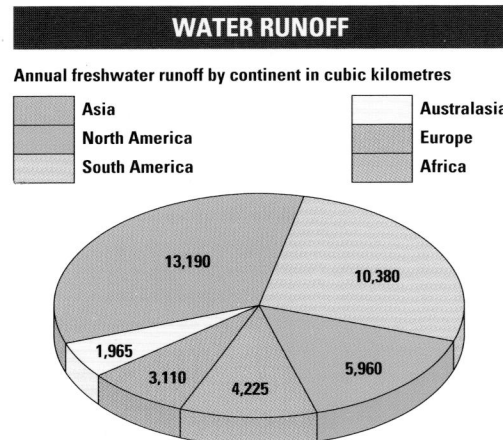

- 13,190
- 10,380
- 5,960
- 4,225
- 3,110
- 1,965

WATER UTILIZATION

The percentage breakdown of water usage by sector, selected countries (1980s)

Legend: Domestic | Industrial | Agriculture

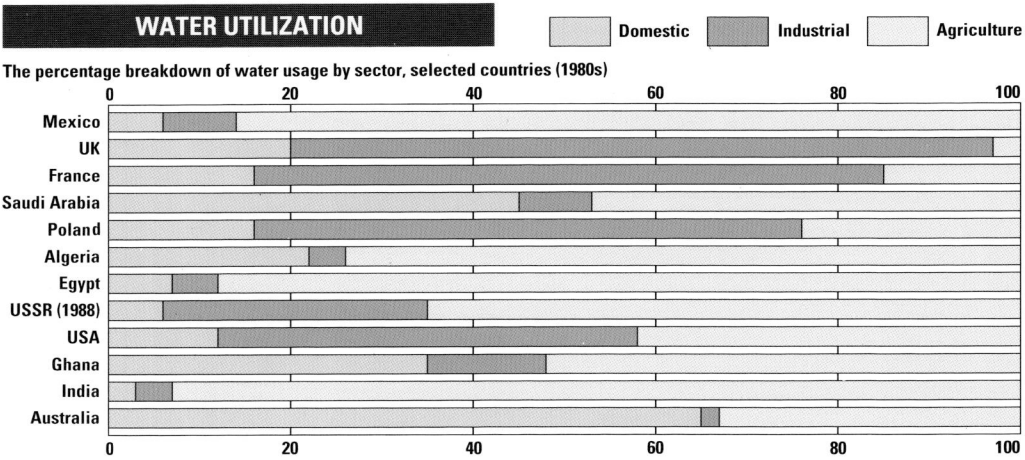

- Mexico
- UK
- France
- Saudi Arabia
- Poland
- Algeria
- Egypt
- USSR (1988)
- USA
- Ghana
- India
- Australia

WATER SUPPLY

Percentage of total population with access to safe drinking water (latest available year, 1980s)

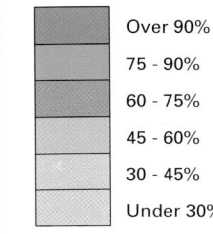

- Over 90%
- 75 - 90%
- 60 - 75%
- 45 - 60%
- 30 - 45%
- Under 30%

Least well provided countries (rural areas only):

Paraguay 8%	Guinea 15%
Mozambique 12%	Mauritania 17%
Uganda 12%	Malawi 17%
Angola 15%	Morocco 17%

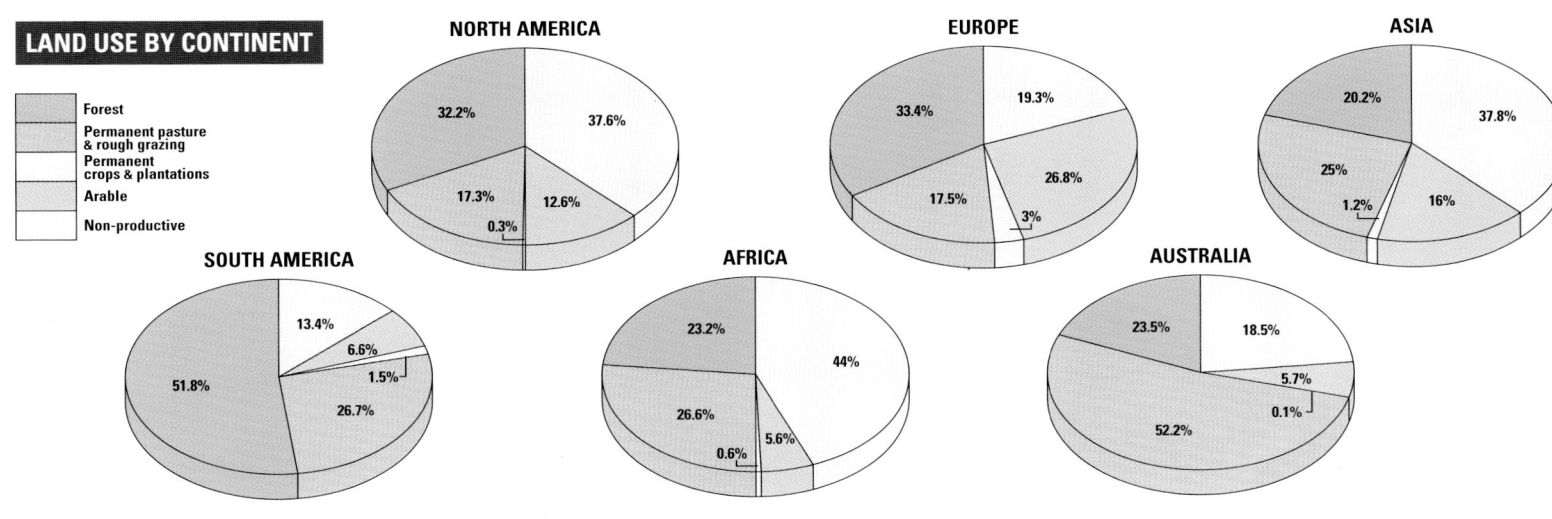

WHERE THE RIVERS RUN

- Pacific Ocean
- Indian Ocean
- Arctic Ocean
- Atlantic Ocean
- Caribbean Sea
- Mediterranean Sea
- Inland basins

ARCTIC OCEAN

Yukon • Mackenzie • Yenisey • Lena • Ob • Angara • Amur • Irtysh

Peace • Nelson • Rhine • Volga • Syr Darya • Hwang Ho

Columbia • Missouri • St. Lawrence • Danube • Tigris • Amu Darya • Yangtze-Kiang • Si-Kiang

Colorado • Rio Grande • Mississippi • Mediterranean Sea • Nile • Euphrates • Brahmaputra • Ganges • Irrawaddy • Salween

ATLANTIC OCEAN

PACIFIC OCEAN

Caribbean Sea

Indus • Arabian Sea • Bay of Bengal • Mekong

Orinoco • Amazon • Negro • Volta • White Nile • Niger

Japurá • Tocantins • Zaïre

Ucayali • Madeira • São Francisco

INDIAN OCEAN

Paraguay • Zambezi

Orange

Paraná

Darling

Murray

WATERSHEDS

The world's major rivers; those named are the longest, led by the Nile and the Amazon

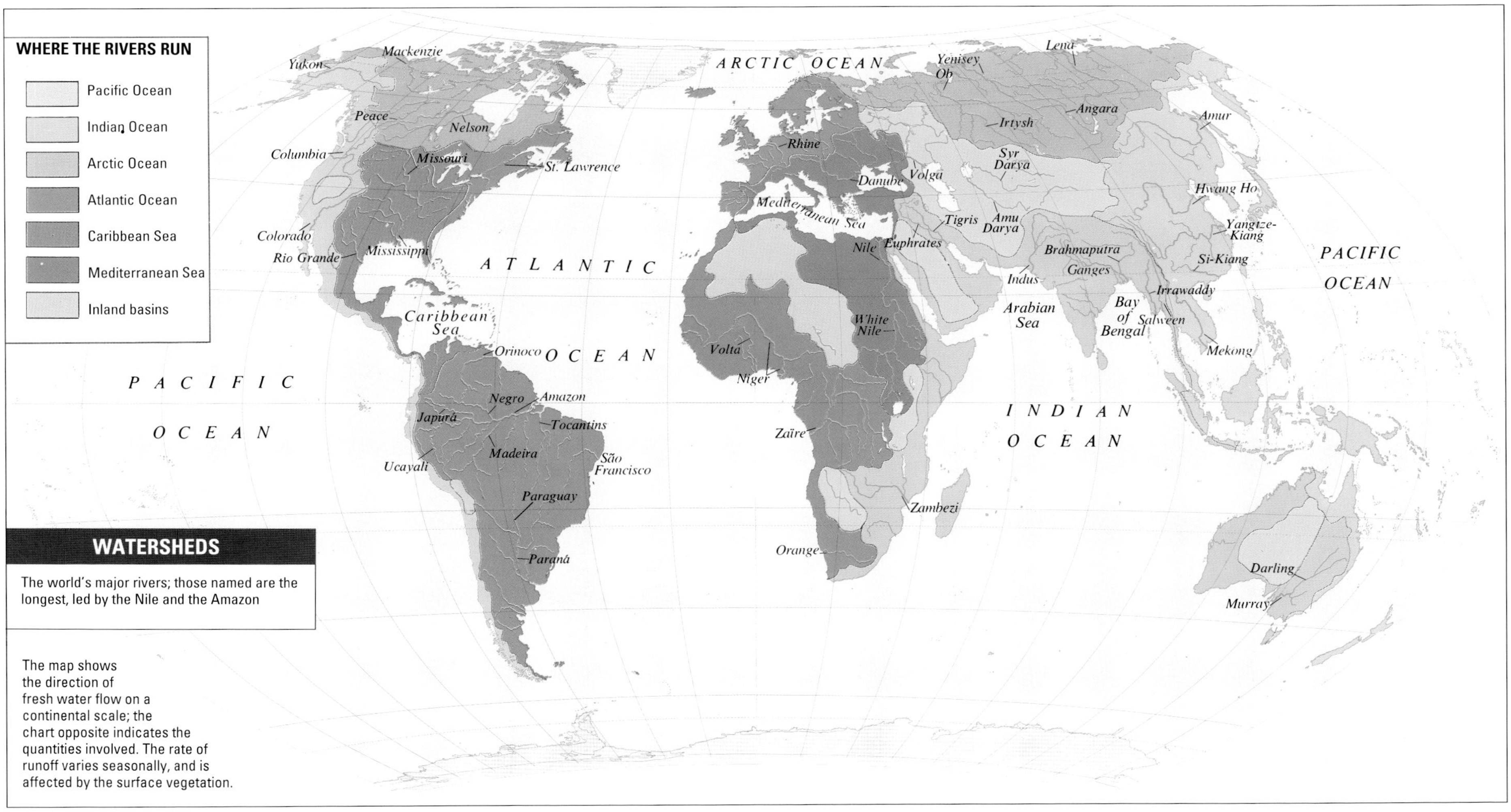

The map shows the direction of fresh water flow on a continental scale; the chart opposite indicates the quantities involved. The rate of runoff varies seasonally, and is affected by the surface vegetation.

LAND USE BY CONTINENT

- Forest
- Permanent pasture & rough grazing
- Permanent crops & plantations
- Arable
- Non-productive

NORTH AMERICA
32.2% | 37.6% | 17.3% | 0.3% | 12.6%

EUROPE
33.4% | 19.3% | 17.5% | 26.8% | 3%

ASIA
20.2% | 37.8% | 25% | 1.2% | 16%

SOUTH AMERICA
13.4% | 6.6% | 1.5% | 51.8% | 26.7%

AFRICA
23.2% | 44% | 26.6% | 0.6% | 5.6%

AUSTRALIA
23.5% | 18.5% | 5.7% | 52.2% | 0.1%

The proportion of productive land has reached its upper limit in Europe, and in Asia more than 80% of potential cropland is already under cultivation. Elsewhere, any increase is often matched by corresponding losses due to desertification and erosion; projections for 2025 show a decline in cropland per capita for all continents, most notably in Africa.

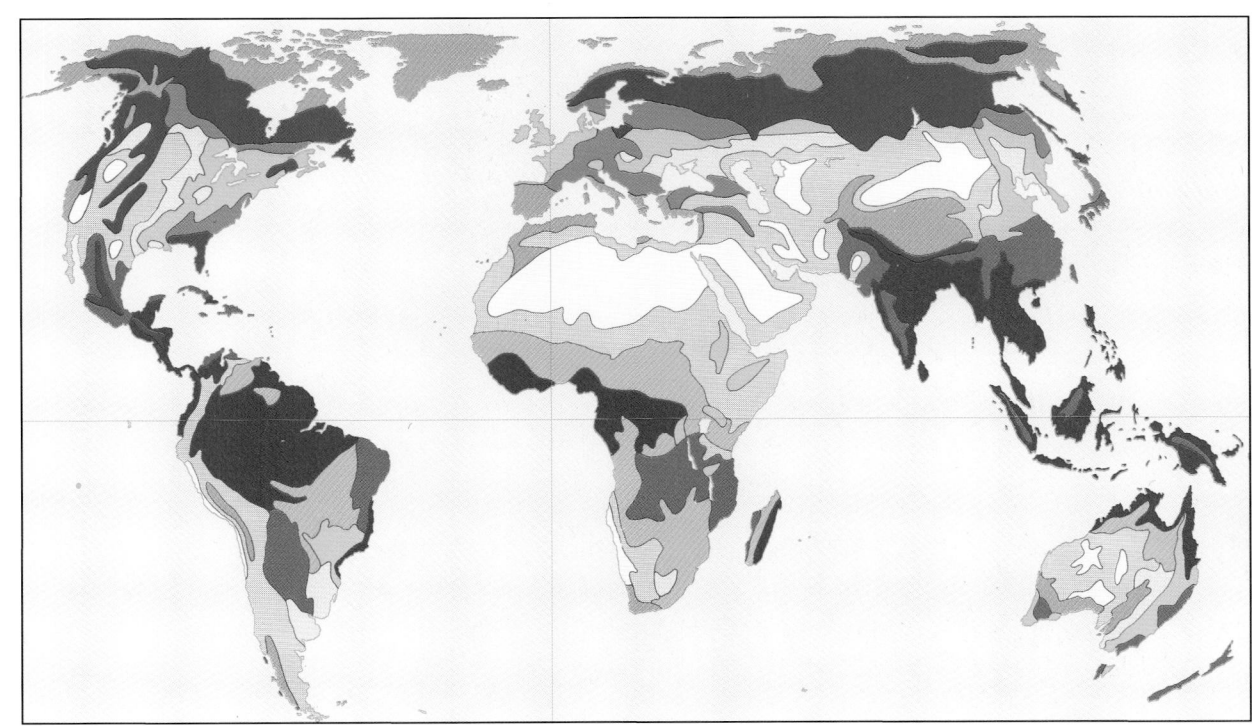

NATURAL VEGETATION

Regional variation in vegetation

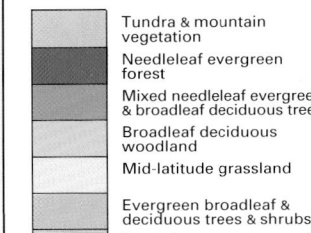

- Tundra & mountain vegetation
- Needleleaf evergreen forest
- Mixed needleleaf evergreen & broadleaf deciduous trees
- Broadleaf deciduous woodland
- Mid-latitude grassland
- Evergreen broadleaf & deciduous trees & shrubs
- Semi-desert scrub
- Desert
- Tropical grassland (savanna)
- Tropical broadleaf rainforest & monsoon forest
- Sub-tropical broadleaf & needleleaf forest

The map illustrates the natural climax vegetation of a region, as dictated by its climate and topography. In most cases, human agricultural activity has drastically altered the vegetation pattern. Western Europe, for example, lost most of its broadleaf forest many centuries ago, and irrigation has turned some natural semi-desert into productive land.

THE EARTH: LANDSCAPE

8:	THE EARTH'S STRUCTURE
	PLATE TECTONICS
9:	GEOLOGICAL TIME
	VOLCANOES
10:	OCEANS
16:	HYDROLOGICAL CYCLE
34:	STRUCTURAL REGIONS

Above and below the surface of the oceans, the features of the Earth's crust are constantly changing. The phenomenal forces generated by convection currents in the molten core of our planet carry the vast segments or 'plates' of the crust across the globe in an endless cycle of creation and destruction. New crust emerges along the central depths of the oceans, where molten magma flows from the margins of neighbouring plates to form the massive mid-ocean ridges. The sea floor spreads, and where ocean plates meet continental plates, they dip back into the earth's core to melt once again into magma.

Less dense, the continental plates 'float' among the oceans, drifting into and apart from each other at a rate which is almost imperceptibly slow. A continent may travel little more than 25 millimetres per year – in an average lifetime, Europe will move no more than a man's height – yet in the vast span of geological time, this process throws up giant mountain ranges and opens massive rifts in the land's surface.

The world's greatest mountain ranges have been formed in this way – the Himalayas by the collision of the Indo-Australian and Eurasian plates, the Andes by the meeting of the Nazca and South American plates. The Himalayas are a classic example of 'fold mountains', formed by the crumpling of the Earth's surface where two land masses have been driven together. The coastal range of the Andes, by contrast, was formed by the upsurge of molten volcanic rock created by the friction of the continent 'overriding' the ocean plate.

Destruction of the landscape, however, begins as soon as it is formed. Wind, water, ice and sea, the main agents of erosion, mount a constant assault that even the hardest rocks cannot withstand. Mountain peaks may dwindle by as little as a few millimetres each year, but if they are not uplifted by further movements of the crust they will eventually be reduced to rubble. Water is the most powerful destroyer – it has been estimated that 100 billion tonnes of rock is washed into the oceans every year.

When water freezes, its volume increases by about nine per cent, and no rock is strong enough to resist this pressure. Where water has penetrated tiny fissures or seeped into softer rock, a severe freeze followed by a thaw may result in rockfalls or earth-slides, creating major destruction in a few minutes. Over much longer periods, acidity in rainwater breaks down the chemical composition of porous rocks like limestone, eating away the rock to form deep caves and tunnels. Chemical decomposition also occurs in riverbeds and glacier valleys, hastening the process of mechanical erosion.

Rivers and glaciers, like the sea itself, generate much of their effect through abrasion – pounding the landscape with the debris they carry with them. But as well as destroying they also create new landscapes, many of them spectacular : vast deltas, as at the mouth of the Mississippi or the Nile; cliffs, rock arches and stacks, as on the south coast of Australia; and the fjords cut by long-melted glaciers in British Columbia, Norway and New Zealand.

The vast ridges that divide the Earth's crust beneath each of the world's major oceans mark the boundaries between tectonic plates which are moving very gradually in opposite directions. As the plates shift apart, molten magma rises from the Earth's core to seal the rift and the sea floor slowly spreads towards the continental landmasses. The rate of sea floor spreading has been calculated by magnetic analysis of the rock – at about 40 mm [1.5 in] a year in the North Atlantic. Near the ocean shore, underwater volcanoes mark the line where the continental rise begins. As the plates meet, much of the denser ocean crust dips beneath the continental plate and is melted back into the magma.

THE SPREADING EARTH

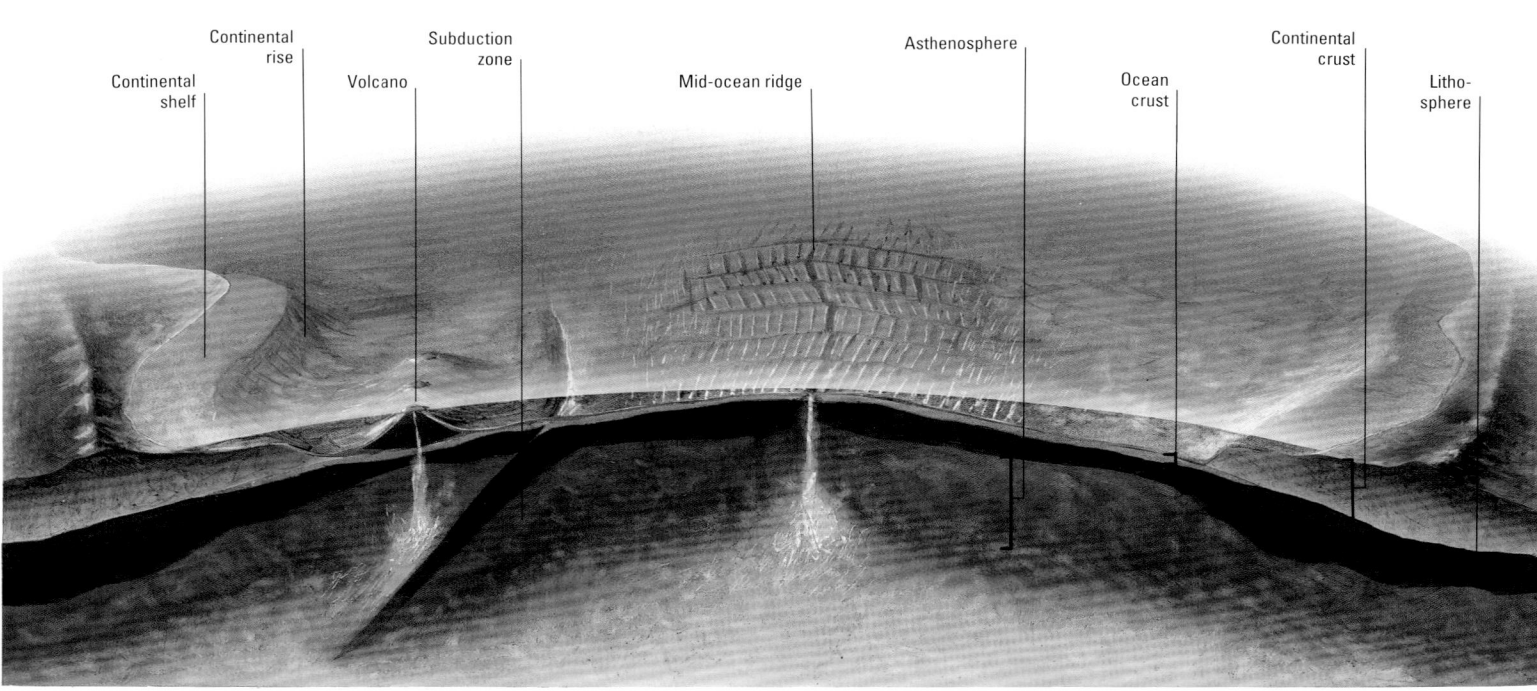

Continental shelf — Continental rise — Volcano — Subduction zone — Mid-ocean ridge — Asthenosphere — Ocean crust — Continental crust — Lithosphere

TYPES OF ROCK

Rocks are divided into three types, according to the way in which they are formed:

Igneous rocks, including granite and basalt, are formed by the cooling of magma from within the Earth's crust.

Metamorphic rocks, such as slate, marble and quartzite, are formed below the Earth's surface by the compression or baking of existing rocks.

Sedimentary rocks, like sandstone and limestone, are formed on the surface of the Earth from the remains of living organisms and eroded fragments of older rocks.

MOUNTAIN BUILDING

Mountains are formed when pressures on the Earth's crust caused by continental drift become so intense that the surface buckles or cracks. This happens most dramatically where two tectonic plates collide : the Rockies, Andes, Alps, Urals and Himalayas resulted from such impacts. These are all known as fold mountains, because they were formed by the compression of the rocks, forcing the surface to bend and fold like a crumpled rug.

The other main building process is when the crust fractures to create faults, allowing rock to be forced upwards in large blocks; or when the pressure of magma within the crust forces the surface to bulge into a dome, or erupts to form a volcano. Large mountain ranges may reveal a combination of those features; the Alps, for example, have been compressed so violently that the folds are fragmented by numerous faults and intrusions of molten rock.

Over millions of years, even the greatest mountain ranges can be reduced by erosion to a landscape known as a peneplain.

Types of fold: Geographers give different names to the degrees of fold that result from continuing pressure on the rock strata. A simple fold may be symmetric, with even slopes on either side, but as the pressure builds up, one slope becomes steeper and the fold becomes asymmetric. Later, the ridge or 'anticline' at the top of the fold may slide over the lower ground or 'syncline' to form a recumbent fold. Eventually, the rock strata may break under the pressure to form an overthrust and finally a nappe fold.

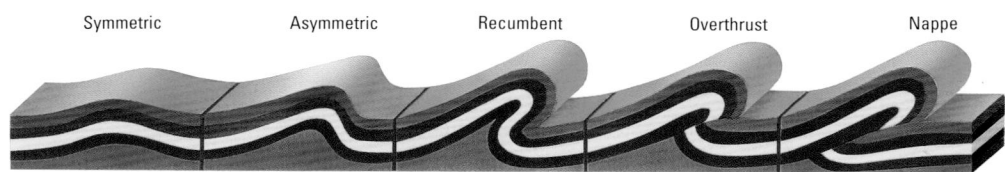

Symmetric — Asymmetric — Recumbent — Overthrust — Nappe

Types of fault: Faults are classified by the direction in which the blocks of rock have moved. A normal fault results when a vertical movement causes the surface to break apart; compression causes a reverse fault. Sideways movement causes shearing, known as a strike-slip fault. When the rock breaks in two places, the central block may be pushed up in a horst fault, or sink in a graben fault.

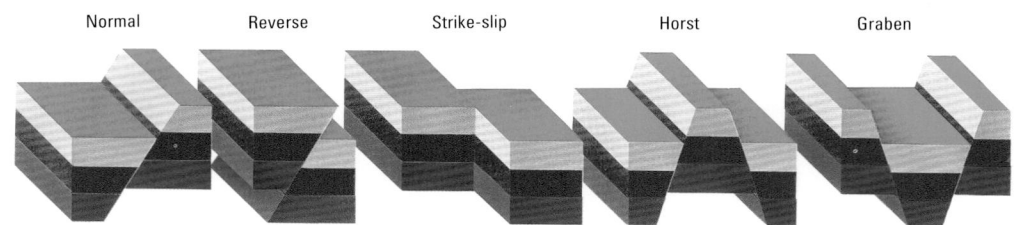

Normal — Reverse — Strike-slip — Horst — Graben

MOULDING THE LAND

While hidden forces of extraordinary power are moving the continents from below the Earth's crust, the more familiar elements of wind and water, heat and cold combine to sculpt the surface of the landscape. Erosion by weathering is seen in desert regions, where rocks degrade imperceptibly into sand through the effects of changing temperatures and strong winds.

The power of water is fiercer still. Coastlines change faster than most landscape features, both by erosion and by the build-up of sand and pebbles carried by the sea. In severe storms, giant waves pound the shoreline with rocks and boulders, and frequently destroy concrete coastal defences; but even in quieter conditions, the sea steadily erodes cliffs and headlands and creates new land in the form of sand-dunes, spits and salt-marshes.

Rivers, too, are incessantly at work shaping the landscape on their way to join the sea. In highland regions, where the flow is rapid, they cut deep gorges and V-shaped valleys. As they reach more gentle slopes, rivers release some of the debris they have carried downstream, broadening out and raising levees along their banks by depositing mud and sand. In the lowland plains, they may drift into meanders, depositing more sediment and even building deltas when they finally approach the sea.

Ice has created some of the world's dramatic landscapes. As glaciers move slowly downhill, they scrape away rock from the mountains and valley sides, creating spectacular landscape features.

SHAPING FORCES: THE SEA

In areas of hard rock, waves cut steep cliffs and form underwater platforms; debris is deposited as a terrace. Bays are formed when sections of soft rock are carved away between headlands of harder rock; these are then battered until the headlands are reduced to rock arches and stacks.

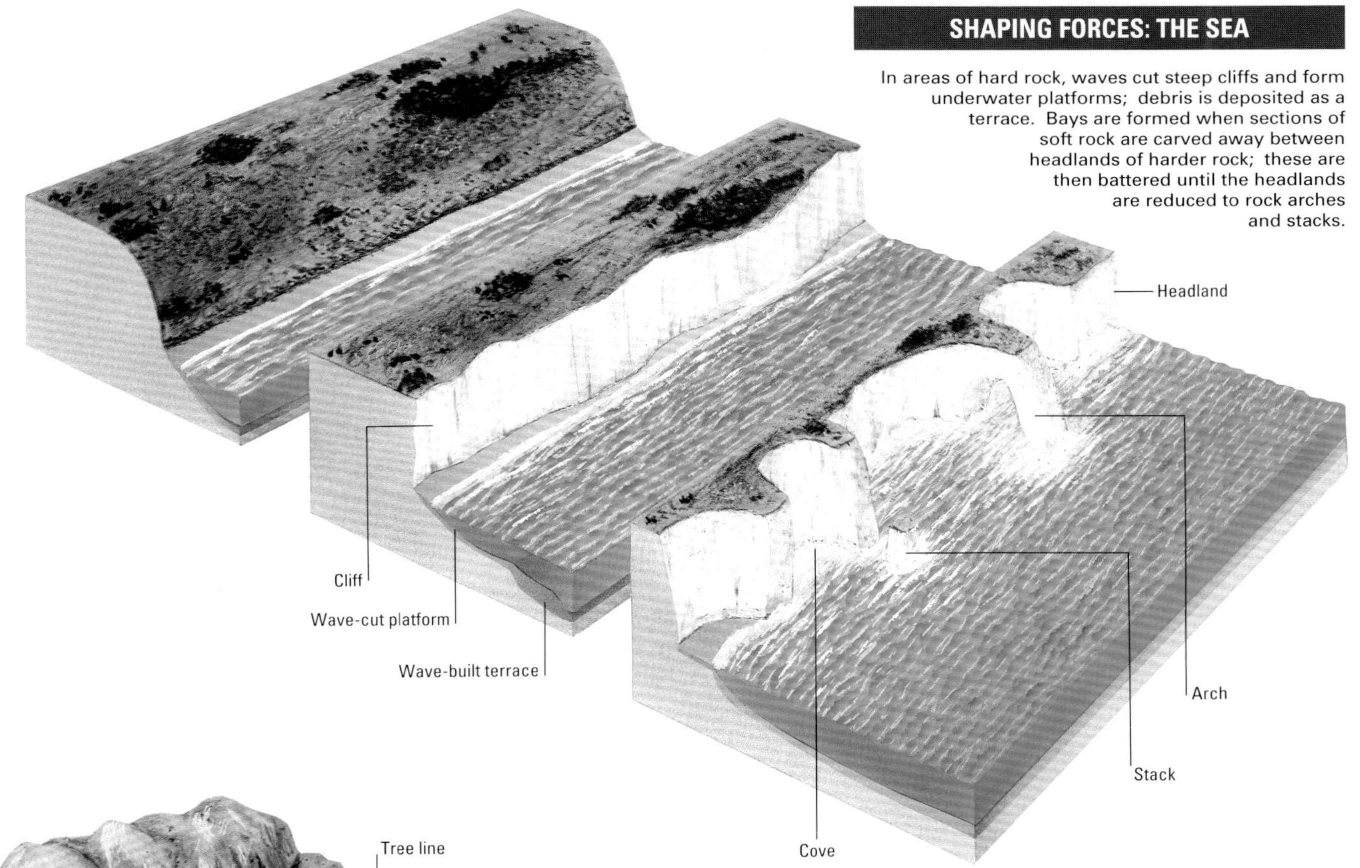

Headland

Cliff

Wave-cut platform

Wave-built terrace

Arch

Stack

Cove

SHAPING FORCES: RIVERS

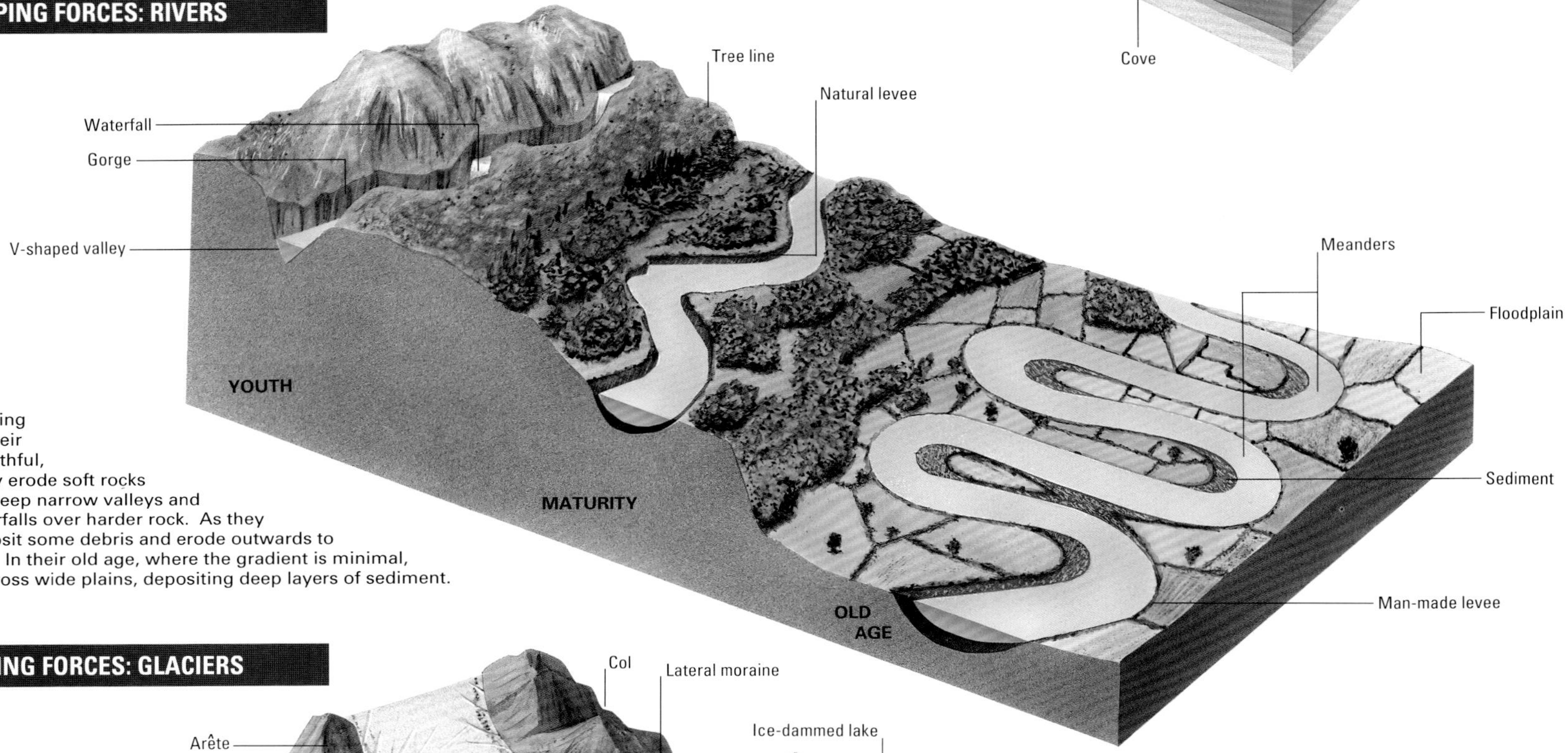

Tree line

Natural levee

Waterfall

Gorge

V-shaped valley

Meanders

Floodplain

YOUTH

Rivers shape the landscape according to the speed of their flow. In their youthful, upland stage they erode soft rocks quickly, cutting steep narrow valleys and tumbling in waterfalls over harder rock. As they mature they deposit some debris and erode outwards to widen the valley. In their old age, where the gradient is minimal, they meander across wide plains, depositing deep layers of sediment.

MATURITY

Sediment

OLD AGE

Man-made levee

SHAPING FORCES: GLACIERS

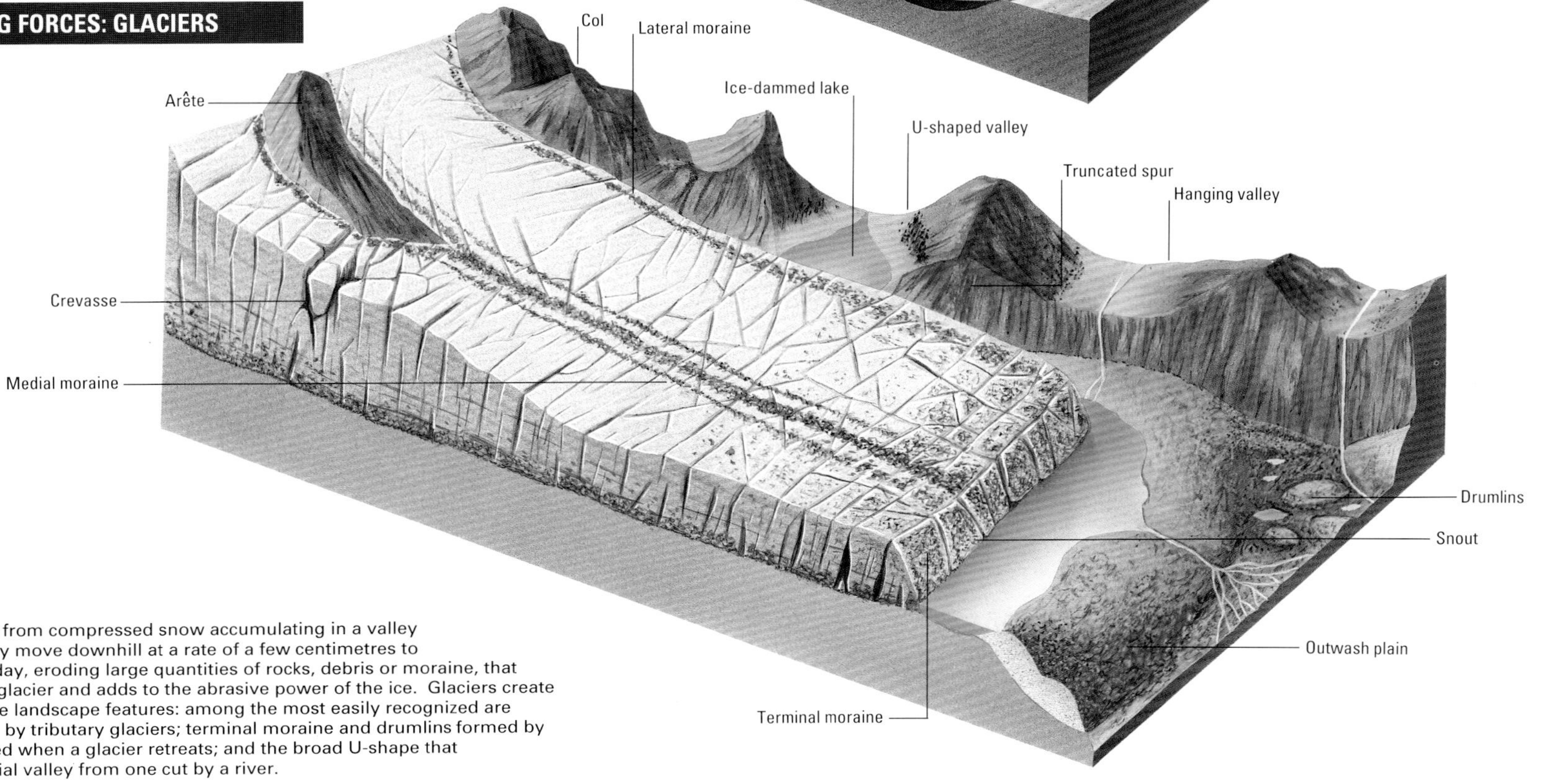

Col

Lateral moraine

Ice-dammed lake

U-shaped valley

Arête

Truncated spur

Hanging valley

Crevasse

Medial moraine

Drumlins

Snout

Outwash plain

Terminal moraine

Glaciers are formed from compressed snow accumulating in a valley head or cirque. They move downhill at a rate of a few centimetres to several metres per day, eroding large quantities of rocks, debris or moraine, that is caught up by the glacier and adds to the abrasive power of the ice. Glaciers create numerous distinctive landscape features: among the most easily recognized are hanging valleys, cut by tributary glaciers; terminal moraine and drumlins formed by rock debris deposited when a glacier retreats; and the broad U-shape that distinguishes a glacial valley from one cut by a river.

19

THE EARTH: ENVIRONMENT

10: OCEANS

12: ATMOSPHERE

17: NATURAL VEGETATION

46: CARBON DIOXIDE
GREENHOUSE POWER
GLOBAL WARMING

47: ACID RAIN
DESERTIFICATION
DEFORESTATION
WATER POLLUTION

Unique among the planets, the Earth has been the home of living creatures for most of its existence. Precisely how these improbable assemblies of self-replicating chemicals ever began remains a matter of conjecture, but the planet and its passengers have matured together for a very long time. Over three billion years, life has not only adapted to its environment: it has also slowly changed that environment to suit itself.

The planet and its biosphere – the entirety of its living things – function like a single organism. The British scientist James Lovelock, who first stated this 'Gaia hypothesis' in the 1970s, went further: the planet, he declared, actually was a living organism, equipped on a colossal scale with the same sort of stability-seeking

mechanisms used by lesser lifeforms like bacteria and humans to keep themselves running at optimum efficiency.

Lovelock's theory was inspired by a study of the Earth's atmosphere, whose constituents he noted are very far from the state of chemical equilibrium observed elsewhere in the solar system. The atmosphere has contained a substantial amount of free oxygen for the last two billion years; yet without constant renewal, the oxygen molecules would soon be locked permanently in oxides. The nitrogen, too, would find chemical stability, probably in nitrates (accounting for some of the oxygen). Without living plants and algae to remove it, carbon dioxide would steadily increase from its present-day 0.03%; in a few million

years, it would form a thick blanket similar to the atmosphere of lifeless Venus, where surface temperatures reach 475°C.

It is not enough, however, for the biosphere simply to produce oxygen. While falling concentrations would be first uncomfortable and ultimately fatal for most contemporary life, at levels above the current 21% even moist vegetation is highly inflammable, and a massive conflagration becomes almost inevitable – a violent form of negative feedback to set the atmosphere on the path back to sterile equilibrium.

Fortunately, the biosphere has evolved over eons into a subtle and complex control system, sensing changes and reacting to them quickly but gently, tending always to maintain the balance it has achieved.

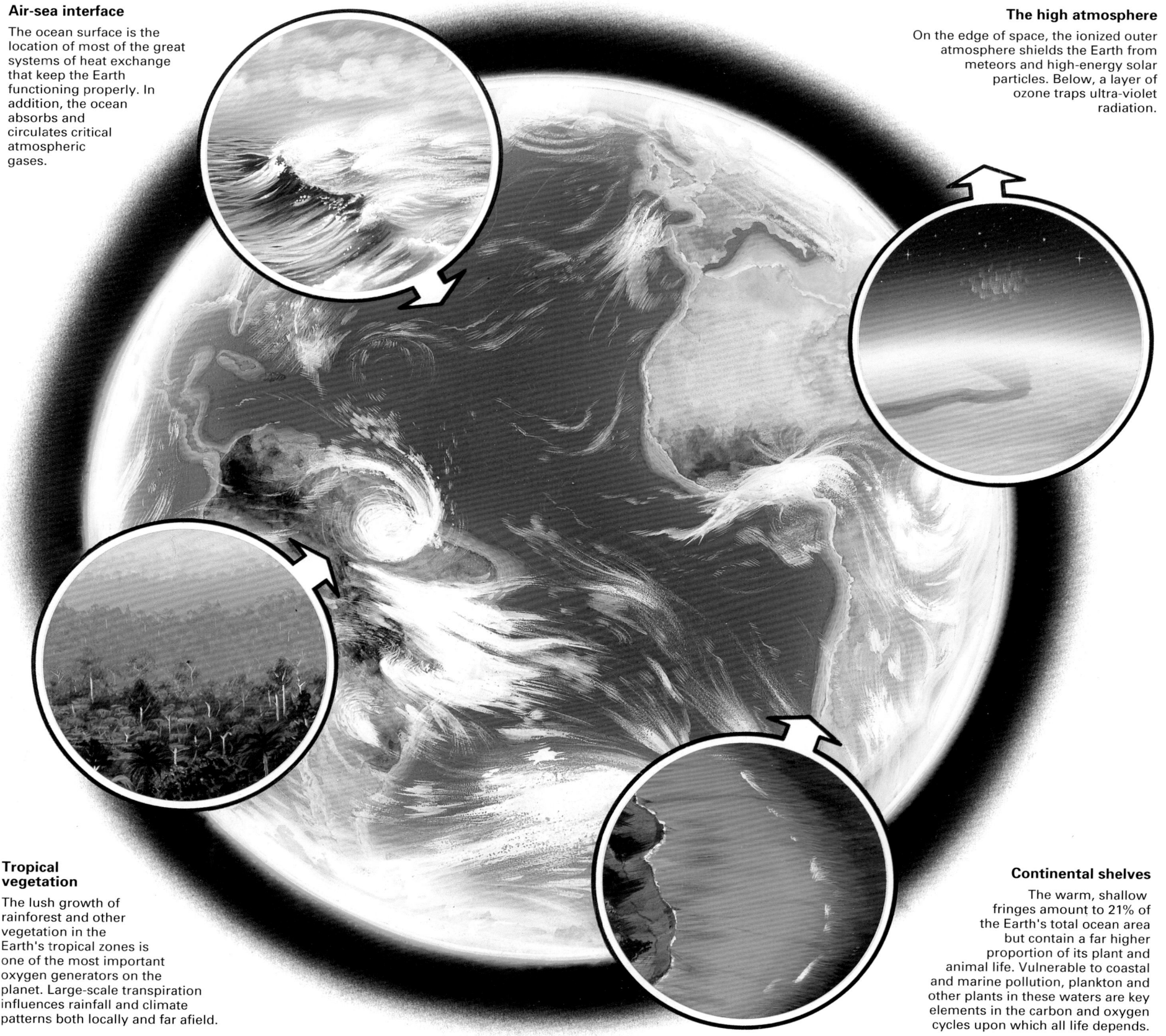

Air-sea interface

The ocean surface is the location of most of the great systems of heat exchange that keep the Earth functioning properly. In addition, the ocean absorbs and circulates critical atmospheric gases.

The high atmosphere

On the edge of space, the ionized outer atmosphere shields the Earth from meteors and high-energy solar particles. Below, a layer of ozone traps ultra-violet radiation.

Tropical vegetation

The lush growth of rainforest and other vegetation in the Earth's tropical zones is one of the most important oxygen generators on the planet. Large-scale transpiration influences rainfall and climate patterns both locally and far afield.

Continental shelves

The warm, shallow fringes amount to 21% of the Earth's total ocean area but contain a far higher proportion of its plant and animal life. Vulnerable to coastal and marine pollution, plankton and other plants in these waters are key elements in the carbon and oxygen cycles upon which all life depends.

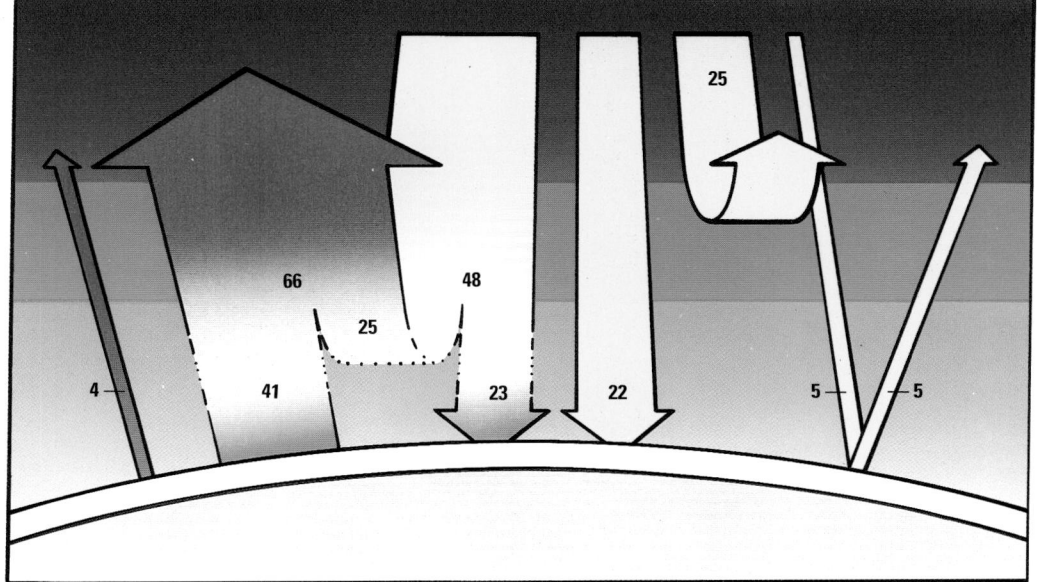

THE EARTH'S ENERGY BALANCE

Apart from a modest quantity of internal heat from its molten core, the Earth receives all its energy from the Sun. If the planet is to remain at a constant temperature, it must re-radiate exactly as much as it receives. Even a minute surplus would lead to a warmer Earth, a deficit to a cooler one; because the planetary energy budget is constantly audited by the laws of physics, which do not permit juggling, it must balance with absolute precision. The temperature at which thermal equilibrium is reached depends on a multitude of interconnected factors. Two of the most important are the relative brightness of the Earth – its index of reflectivity, called the albedo – and the heat-trapping capacity of the atmosphere – the celebrated 'greenhouse effect'.

Because the Sun is very hot, most of its energy arrives in the form of relatively short-wave radiation: the shorter the waves, the more energy they carry. Some of the incoming energy is reflected straight back into space, exactly as it arrived; some is absorbed by the atmosphere on its way towards the surface; some is absorbed by the earth itself. Absorbed energy heats the Earth and its atmosphere alike. But since its temperature is very much lower than that of the Sun, outgoing energy is emitted at much longer infra-red wavelengths. Some of the outgoing radiation escapes directly into outer space; some of it is reabsorbed by the atmosphere. Atmospheric energy eventually finds its way back into space, too, after a complex series of interactions. These include the air movements we call the weather and, almost incidentally, the maintenance of life on Earth.

This diagram does not attempt to illustrate the actual mechanisms of heat exchange, but gives a reasonable account (in percentages) of what happens to 100 energy 'units'. Short-wave radiation is shown in yellow, long-wave in red.

THE CARBON CYCLE

Most of the constituents of the atmosphere are kept in constant balance by complex cycles in which life plays an essential and indeed a dominant part. The control of carbon dioxide, which left to its own devices would be the dominant atmospheric gas, is possibly the most important, although since all the Earth's biological and geophysical cycles interact and interlock, it is hard to separate them even in theory and quite impossible in practice.

The Earth has a huge supply of carbon, only a small quantity of which is in the form of carbon dioxide. Of that, around 98% is dissolved in the sea; the fraction circulating in the air amounts to only 340 parts per million of the atmosphere, where its capacity as a greenhouse gas is the key regulator of the planetary temperature. In turn, life regulates the regulator, keeping carbon dioxide concentrations below danger level.

If all life were to vanish tomorrow from the Earth, the atmosphere would begin the process of change immediately, although it might take several million years to achieve a new, inorganic stability. First, the oxygen content would begin to fall away; with no more assistance than a little solar radiation, a few electrical storms and its own high chemical potential, oxygen would steadily combine with atmospheric nitrogen and volcanic outgassing. In doing so, it would yield sufficient acid to react with carbonaceous rocks such as limestone, releasing carbon dioxide. Once carbon dioxide levels exceeded about 1%, its greenhouse power would increase disproportionately. Rising temperatures – well above the boiling point of water would speed chemical reactions; in time, the Earth's atmosphere would consist of little more than carbon dioxide and superheated water vapour.

Living things, however, circulate carbon. They do so first by simply existing: after all, the carbon atom is the basic building block of living matter. During life, plants absorb atmospheric carbon dioxide, incorporating the carbon itself into their structure – leaves and trunks in the case of land plants, shells

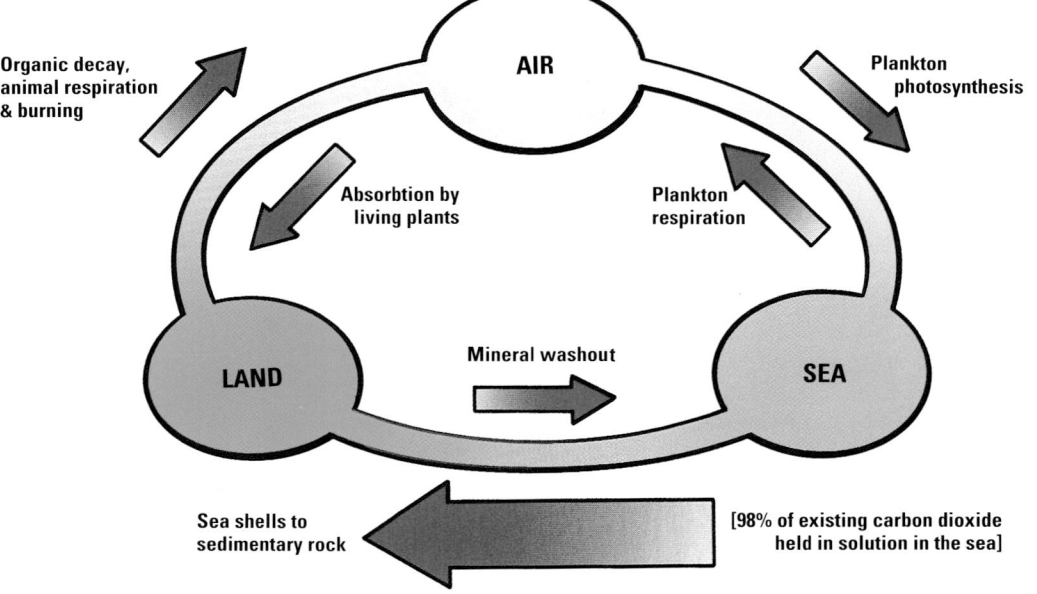

in the case of plankton and the tiny creatures that feed on it. The oxygen thereby freed is added to the atmosphere, at least for a time. Most plant carbon is returned to circulation when the plants die and decay, combining once more with the oxygen released during life. However, a small proportion – about one part in 1000 – is removed almost permanently, buried beneath mud on land, at sea sinking as dead matter to the ocean floor. In time, it is slowly compressed into sedimentary rocks such as limestone and chalk.

But in the evolution of the Earth, nothing is quite permanent. On an even longer timescale, the planet's crustal movements force new rock upward in mid-ocean ridges. Limestone deposits are

moved, and sea levels change; ancient limestone is exposed to weathering, and a little of its carbon is released to be fixed in turn by the current generation of plants.

The carbon cycle has continued quietly for an immensely long time, and without gross disturbance there is no reason why it would not continue almost indefinitely in the future. However, human beings have found a way to release fixed carbon at a rate far faster than existing global systems can recirculate it. Oil and coal deposits represent the work of millions of years of carbon accumulation; but it has taken only a few human generations of high-energy scavenging to endanger the entire complex regulatory cycle.

THE GREENHOUSE EFFECT

Constituting barely 0.03% of the atmosphere, carbon dioxide has a hugely disproportionate effect on the Earth's climate and even its habitability. Like the glass panes in a greenhouse, it is transparent to most incoming short-wave radiation, which passes freely to heat the planet beneath. But when the warmed earth re-transmits that energy, in the form of longer-wave infra-red radiation, the carbon dioxide functions as an opaque shield, so that the planetary surface (like the interior of a greenhouse) stays relatively hot.

Recent increases in CO_2 levels are causing alarm: global warming associated with a runaway greenhouse effect could bring disaster. But a serious reduction would be just as damaging, with surface temperatures falling dramatically; during the last ice age, for example, the carbon dioxide concentration was around 180 parts per million, and a total absence of the gas would likely leave the planet a ball of ice, or at best frozen tundra.

The diagram shows incoming sunlight as yellow; high-energy ultra-violet (blue) is trapped by the ozone layer while outgoing heat from the warmed Earth (red) is partially retained by carbon dioxide.

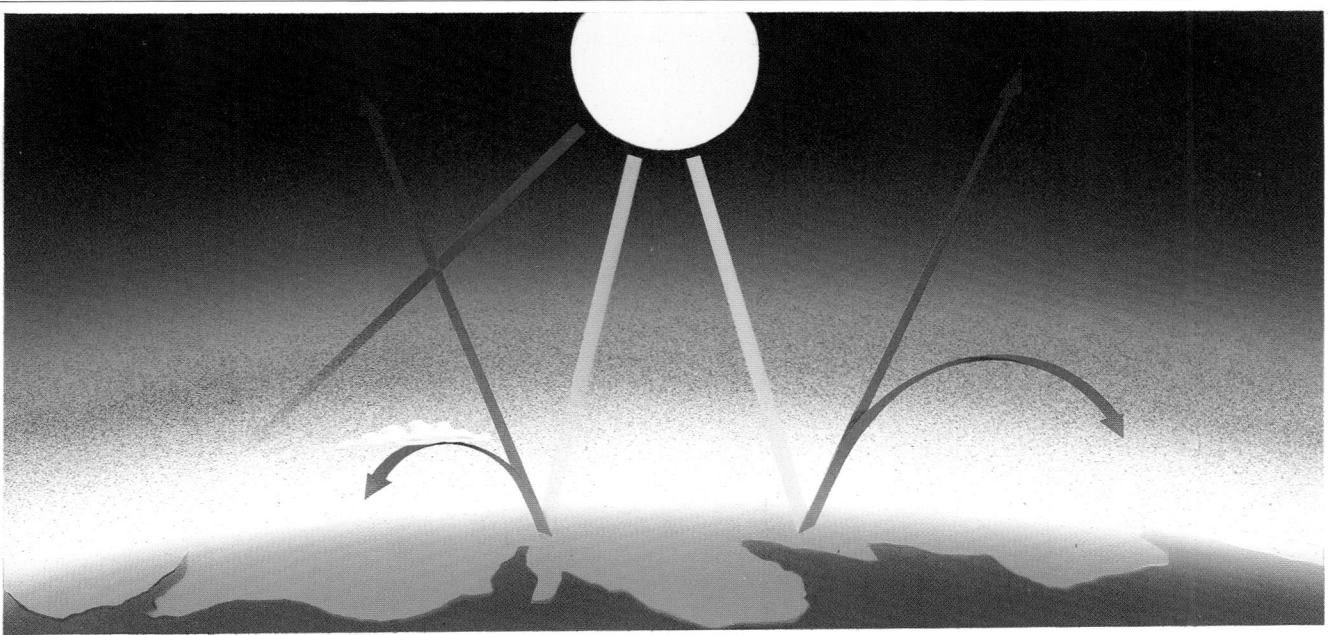

PEOPLE: DEMOGRAPHY

24: URBANIZATION OF
THE EARTH
URBAN POPULATION

25: LARGEST CITIES

31: FOOD & POPULATION

40: WEALTH & POPULATION

46: HUMAN EXPANSION

As the 20th century draws to its close, the Earth's population increases by nearly 10,000 every hour – enough to fill a new major city every week. The growth is almost entirely confined to the developing world, which accounted for 67% of total population in 1950 and is set to reach 84% by 2025. In developed countries, populations are almost static, and in some places, such as Germany, are actually falling. In fact, there is a clear correlation between wealth and low fertility: as incomes rise, reproduction rates drop.

The decline is already apparent. With the exception of Africa, the actual rates of increase are falling nearly everywhere. The structure of populations, however, ensures that human numbers will continue to rise even as fertility diminishes. Developed nations, like the UK, have an even spread across ages, and usually a growing proportion of elderly people: the over-75s often outnumber the under-5s, and women of child-bearing age form only a modest part of the total. Developing nations fall into a pattern somewhere between that of Kenya and Brazil: the great majority of their people are in the younger age groups, about to enter their most fertile years. In time, even Kenya's population profile should resemble the developed model, but the transition will come about only after a few more generations' growth.

It remains to be seen whether the planet will tolerate the population growth that seems inevitable before stability is reached. More people consume more resources, increasing the strain on an already troubled environment. However, more people should mean a greater supply of human ingenuity – the only commodity likely to resolve the crisis .

LARGEST NATIONS

The world's most populous nations, in millions (1989)

1.	China	1120
2.	India	812
3.	USA	250
4.	Indonesia	179
5.	Brazil	147
6.	Russia	147
7.	Japan	123
8.	Nigeria	109
9.	Pakistan	109
10.	Bangladesh	107
11.	Mexico	84
12.	Germany	79
13.	Vietnam	66
14.	Philippines	60
15.	Italy	58
16.	UK	57
17.	Turkey	57
18.	France	56
19.	Thailand	55
20.	Iran	55
21.	Egypt	53
22.	Ukraine	52
23.	Ethiopia	51
24.	S. Korea	43
25.	Burma	41

CROWDED NATIONS

Population per square kilometre (1989), exc. nations of less than one million

1.	Hong Kong	5826.2
2.	Singapore	4401.6
3.	Bangladesh	795.4
4.	Mauritius	577.3
5.	Taiwan	554.2
6.	Netherlands	439.0
7.	S. Korea	432.3
8.	Puerto Rico	412.9
9.	Belgium	328.5
10.	Japan	327.0
11.	Lebanon	283.2
12.	Rwanda	280.1
13.	India	273.1
14.	Sri Lanka	259.6
15.	El Salvador	251.3
16.	Trinidad & Tobago	246.2
17.	UK	236.8
18.	Germany	224.9
19.	Israel	224.6
20.	Jamaica	219.3

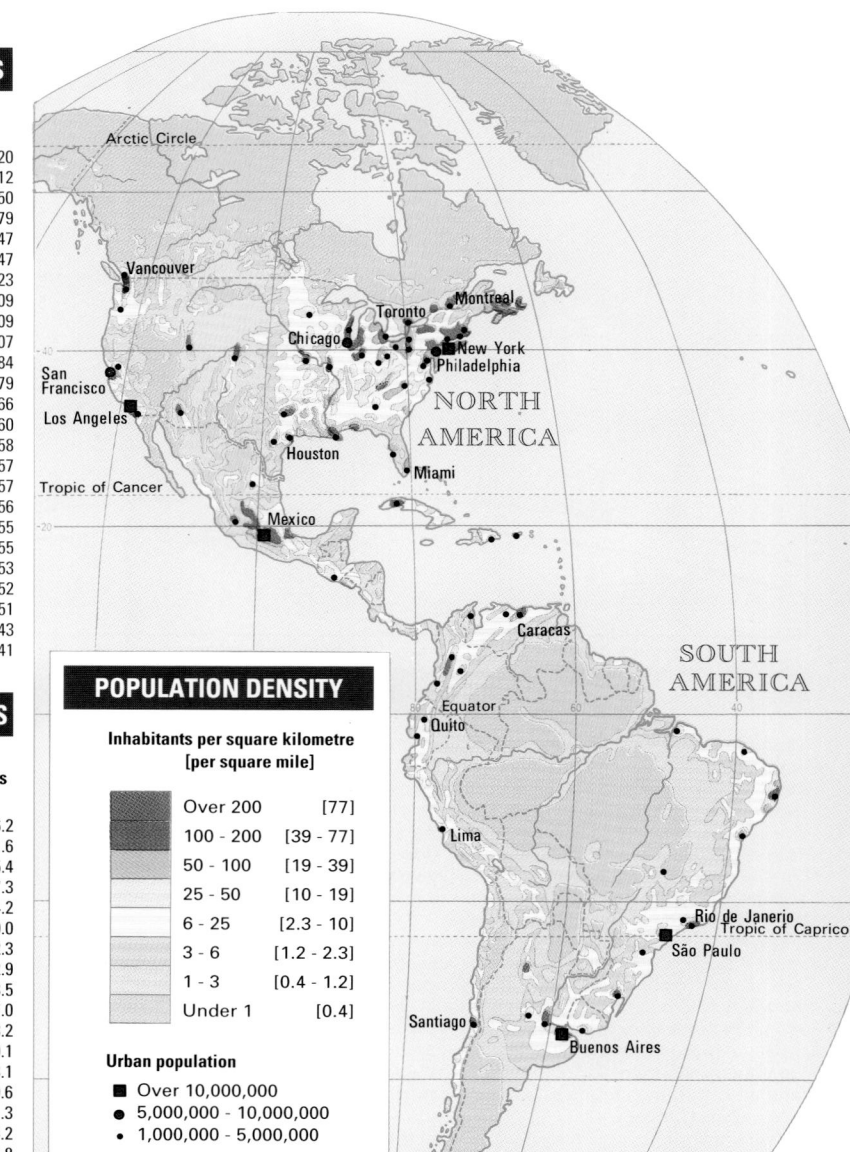

POPULATION DENSITY

Inhabitants per square kilometre [per square mile]

	Over 200	[77]
	100 - 200	[39 - 77]
	50 - 100	[19 - 39]
	25 - 50	[10 - 19]
	6 - 25	[2.3 - 10]
	3 - 6	[1.2 - 2.3]
	1 - 3	[0.4 - 1.2]
	Under 1	[0.4]

Urban population

■ Over 10,000,000
● 5,000,000 - 10,000,000
• 1,000,000 - 5,000,000

Places marked are conurbations, not city limits; San Francisco itself, for example, has an official population of less than a million.

Projection : Mollweide's Interrupted Homolographic

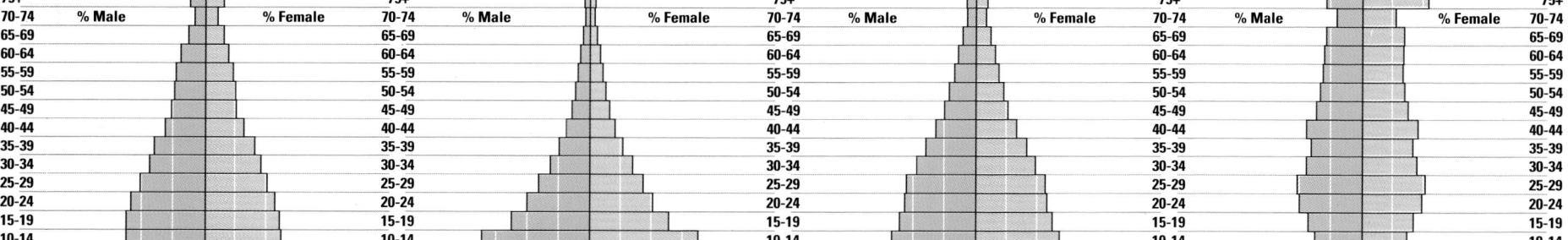

Population pyramids: WORLD, Kenya, Brazil, UK (% Male / % Female by age group 0-4 to 75+)

RATES OF GROWTH

Apparently small rates of population growth lead to dramatic increases over two or three generations. The table below translates annual percentage growth into the number of years required to double a population.

% change	Doubling time
0.5	139.0
1.0	69.7
1.5	46.6
2.0	35.0
2.5	28.1
3.0	23.4
3.5	20.1
4.0	17.7

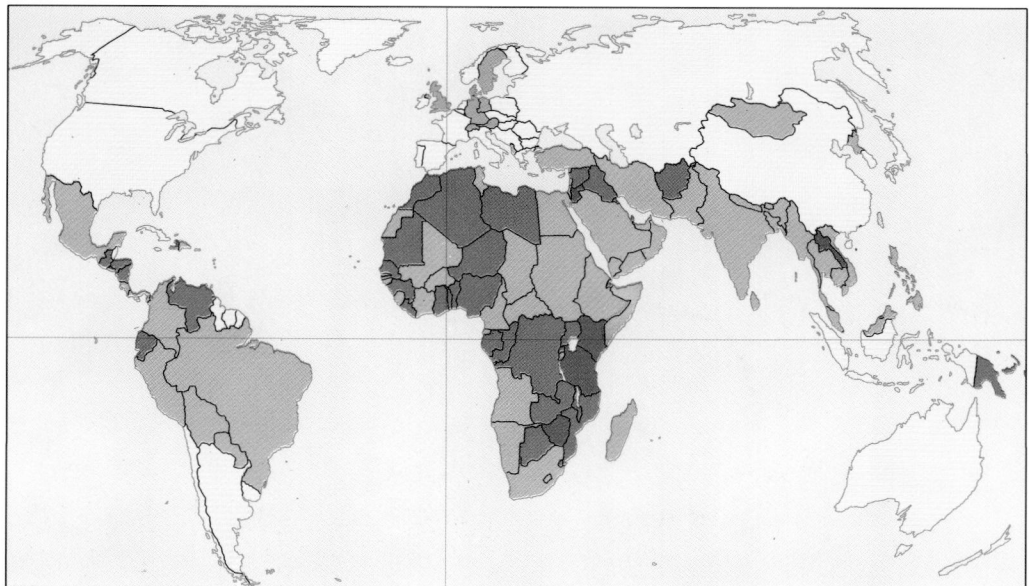

POPULATION CHANGE

Estimated percentage change in total population, 1988-2000

	Over 60%	
	40 - 60%	
	20 - 40%	
	0 - 20%	[USA 0.8%] [UK 0.3%]
	Loss or no change	

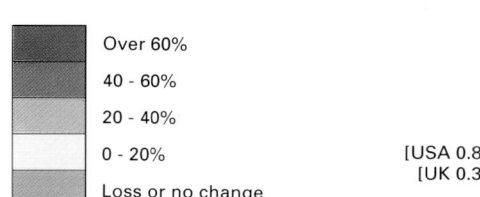

Highest expected gain*		Lowest expected gain	
Haiti	+84%	Andorra	-15%
Kenya	+82%	Switzerland	-10%
El Salvador	+77%	Oman	-5%
Jordan	+75%	Sweden	-4%
Tanzania	+74%	Germany	-2%

* India (191 million), China (187), Nigeria (49), Pakistan (48), Indonesia (38), Bangladesh (36) & Brazil (34) are expected to gain most in total population over the same period

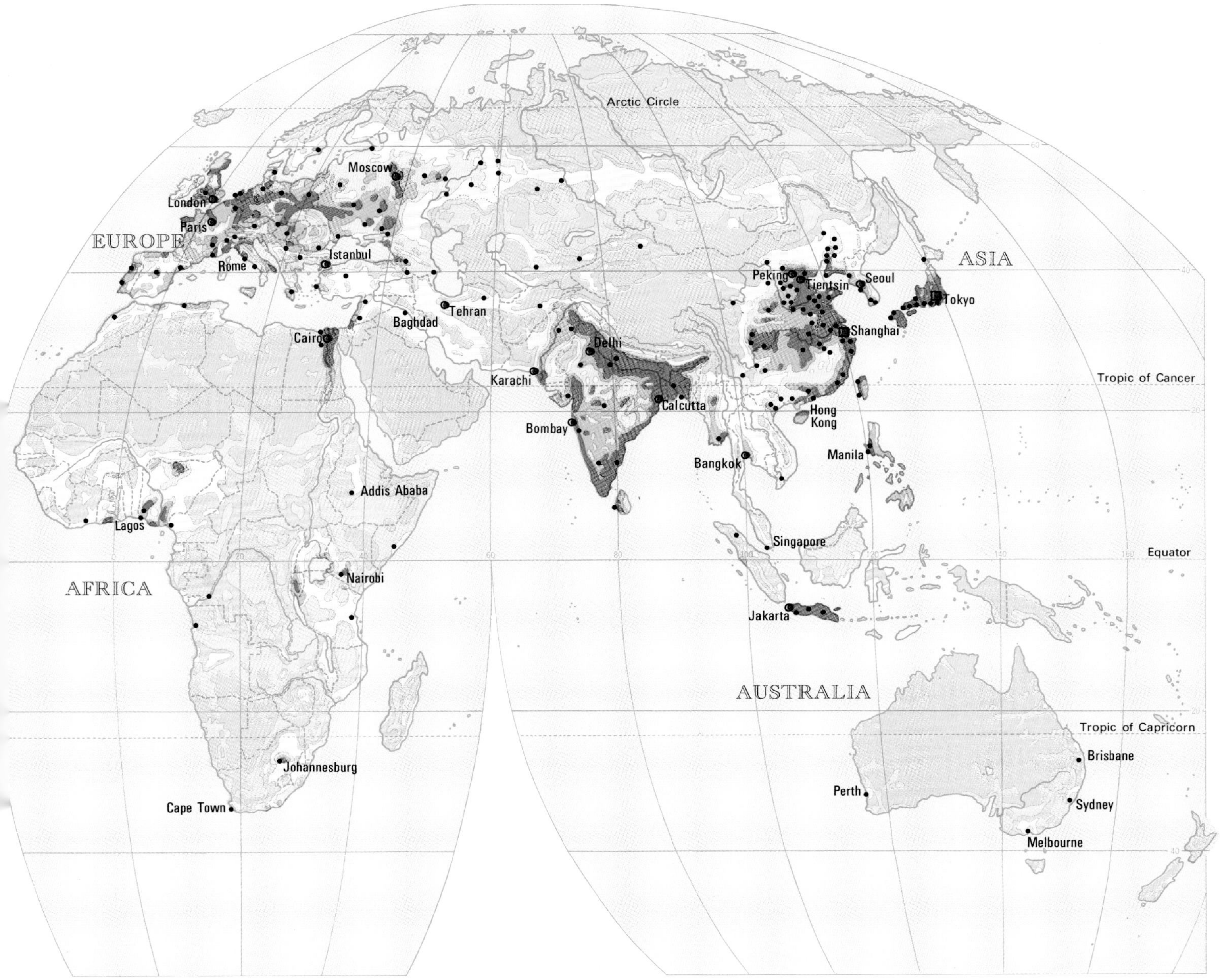

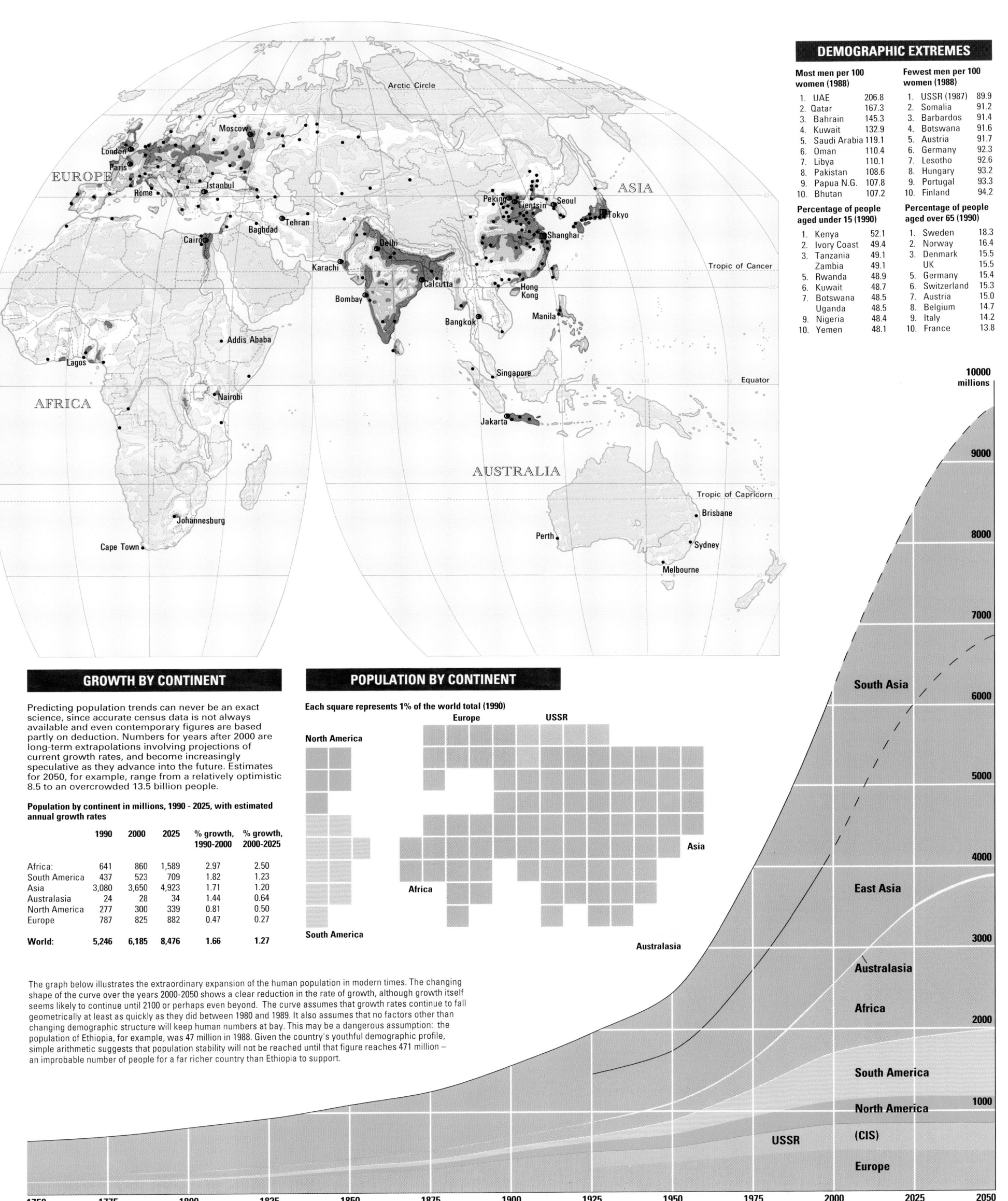

Most men per 100 women (1988)		Fewest men per 100 women (1988)	
1. UAE	206.8	1. USSR (1987)	89.9
2. Qatar	167.3	2. Somalia	91.2
3. Bahrain	145.3	3. Barbardos	91.4
4. Kuwait	132.9	4. Botswana	91.6
5. Saudi Arabia	119.1	5. Austria	91.7
6. Oman	110.4	6. Germany	92.3
7. Libya	110.1	7. Lesotho	92.6
8. Pakistan	108.6	8. Hungary	93.2
9. Papua N.G.	107.8	9. Portugal	93.3
10. Bhutan	107.2	10. Finland	94.2

Percentage of people aged under 15 (1990)		Percentage of people aged over 65 (1990)	
1. Kenya	52.1	1. Sweden	18.3
2. Ivory Coast	49.4	2. Norway	16.4
3. Tanzania	49.1	3. Denmark	15.5
Zambia	49.1	UK	15.5
5. Rwanda	48.9	5. Germany	15.4
6. Kuwait	48.7	6. Switzerland	15.3
7. Botswana	48.5	7. Austria	15.0
Uganda	48.5	8. Belgium	14.7
9. Nigeria	48.4	9. Italy	14.2
10. Yemen	48.1	10. France	13.8

GROWTH BY CONTINENT

Predicting population trends can never be an exact science, since accurate census data is not always available and even contemporary figures are based partly on deduction. Numbers for years after 2000 are long-term extrapolations involving projections of current growth rates, and become increasingly speculative as they advance into the future. Estimates for 2050, for example, range from a relatively optimistic 8.5 to an overcrowded 13.5 billion people.

Population by continent in millions, 1990 - 2025, with estimated annual growth rates

	1990	2000	2025	% growth, 1990-2000	% growth, 2000-2025
Africa:	641	860	1,589	2.97	2.50
South America	437	523	709	1.82	1.23
Asia	3,080	3,650	4,923	1.71	1.20
Australasia	24	28	34	1.44	0.64
North America	277	300	339	0.81	0.50
Europe	787	825	882	0.47	0.27
World:	5,246	6,185	8,476	1.66	1.27

The graph below illustrates the extraordinary expansion of the human population in modern times. The changing shape of the curve over the years 2000-2050 shows a clear reduction in the rate of growth, although growth itself seems likely to continue until 2100 or perhaps even beyond. The curve assumes that growth rates continue to fall geometrically at least as quickly as they did between 1980 and 1989. It also assumes that no factors other than changing demographic structure will keep human numbers at bay. This may be a dangerous assumption: the population of Ethiopia, for example, was 47 million in 1988. Given the country's youthful demographic profile, simple arithmetic suggests that population stability will not be reached until that figure reaches 471 million – an improbable number of people for a far richer country than Ethiopia to support.

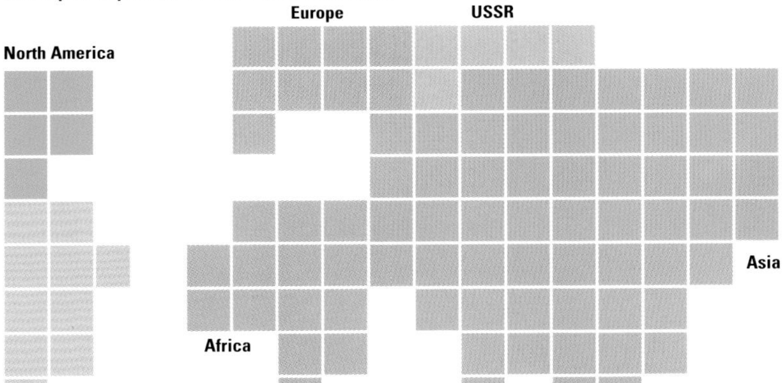

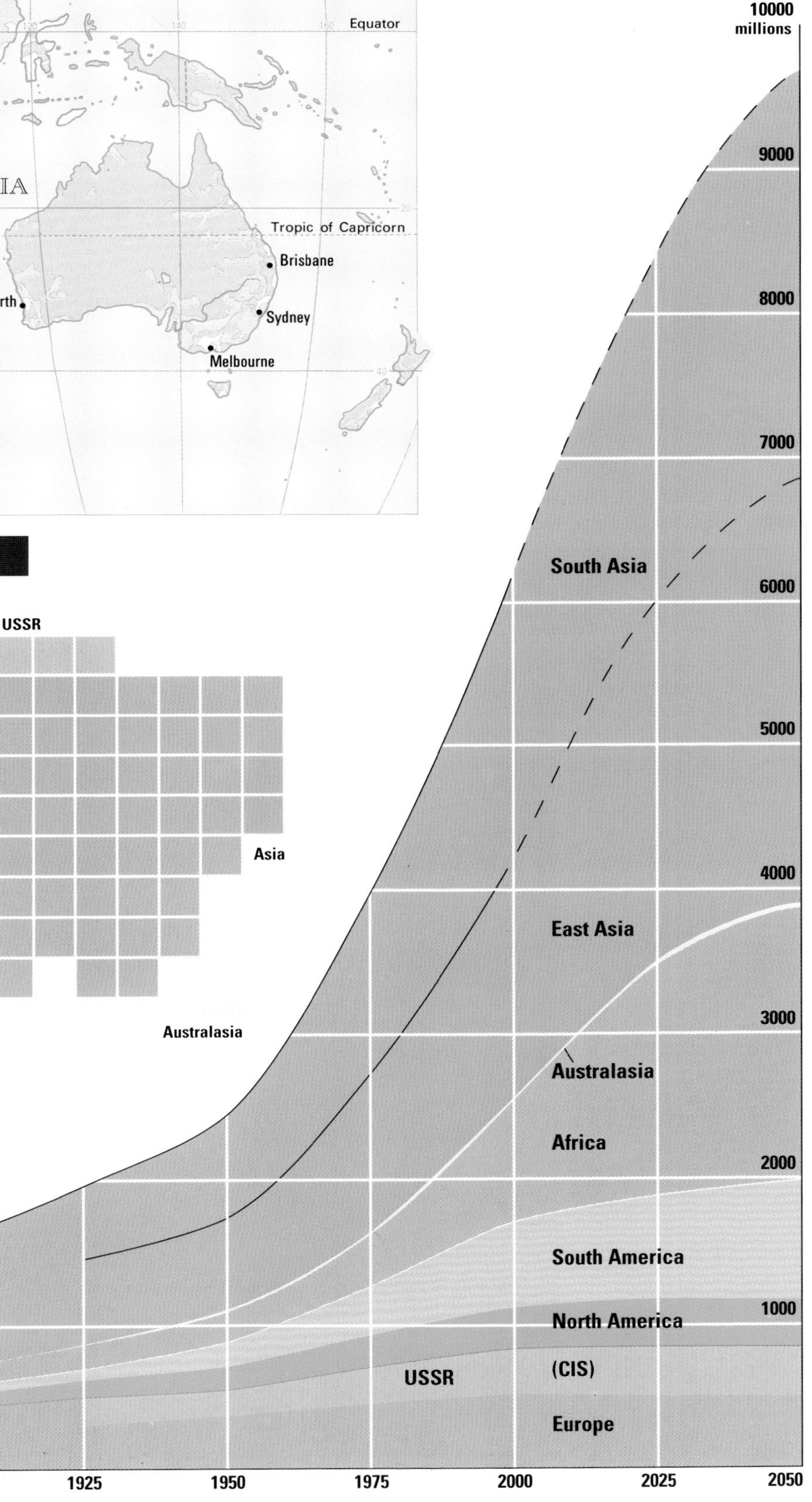

POPULATION BY CONTINENT

Each square represents 1% of the world total (1990)

PEOPLE: CITIES

16: WATER SUPPLY

22: POPULATION DENSITY

39: THE GREAT PORTS

In 1750, barely three humans in every hundred lived in a city; by 2000, more than half of a vastly greater world population will find a home in some kind of urban area. In 1850, only London and Paris had more than a million inhabitants; by 2000, at least 24 cities will each contain over ten million people. The increase is concentrated in the Third World, if only because levels of urbanization in most developed countries - more than 90% in the UK and Belgium, and almost 75% in the USA, despite that country's great open spaces - have already reached practical limits.

Such large-scale concentration is relatively new to the human race. Although city life has always attracted country-dwellers in search of trade, employment or simply human contact, until modern times they paid a high price. Crowding and poor sanitation ensured high death rates, and until about 1850, most cities needed a steady flow of incomers simply to maintain their populations: there were 600,000 more deaths than births in 18th-century London, for example, and some other large cities showed an even worse imbalance.

With improved public health, cities could grow from their own human resources, and large-scale urban living became a commonplace in the developed world. Since about 1950, the pattern has been global. Like their counterparts in 19th-century Europe and the USA, the great new cities are driven into rapid growth by a kind of push-pull mechanism. The push is generated by agricultural overcrowding: only so many people can live from a single plot of land, and population pressure drives many into towns; The pull comes from the possibilities of economic improvement, an irresistible lure to the world's rural hopefuls.

Such improvement is not always obvious: the typical Third World city, with millions of people living (often illegally) in shanty towns and many thousands existing homelessly on the ill-made streets, does not present a great image of prosperity. Yet modern shanty towns are healthier than industrializing Pittsburgh or Manchester in the last century, and these

human ant-hills teem with industry as well as squalor: throughout the world, above-average rates of urbanization have gone hand-in-hand with above-average economic growth. Surveys consistently demonstrate that Third World city-dwellers are generally better off than their rural counterparts, whose poverty is less concentrated but often more desperate. This only serves to increase the attraction of the city for the rural poor.

However, the sheer speed of the urbanization process threatens to overwhelm the limited abilities of city authorities to provide even rudimentary services and administration. The 24 million people expected to live in Mexico City by 2000, for example, would swamp a more efficient local government than Mexico can provide. Improvements are often swallowed up by the relentless rise in urban population: although safe drinking water should reach 75% of Third World city-dwellers by the end of the century - a considerable achievement - population growth will add 100 million to the list of those without it.

THE URBANIZATION OF THE EARTH
City-building, 1850-2000; each white spot represents a city of at least one million inhabitants.

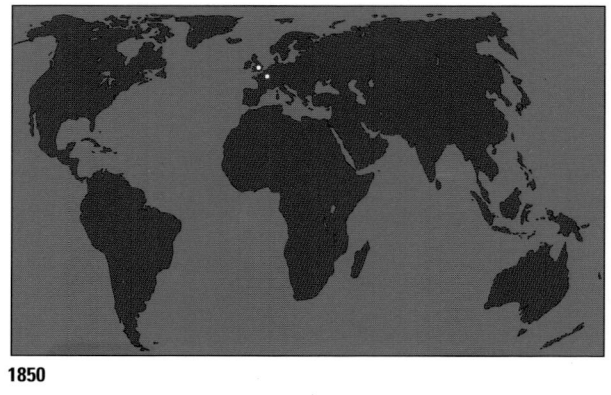

1850

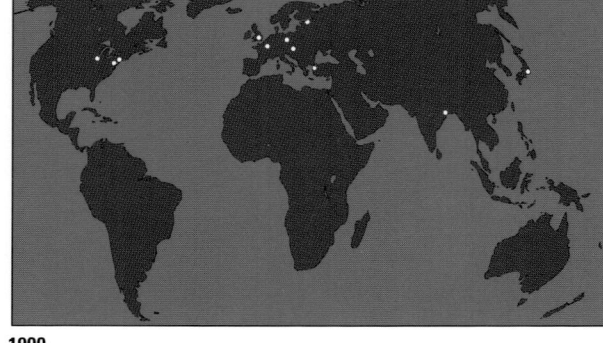

1900

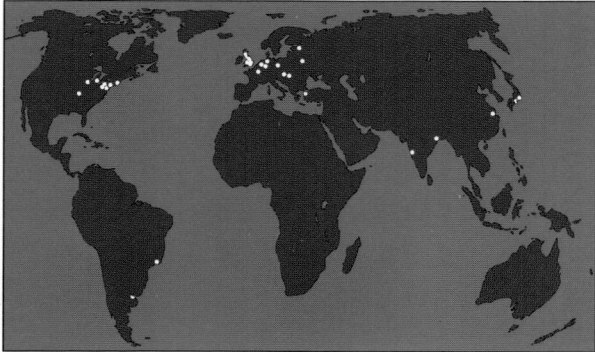

1925

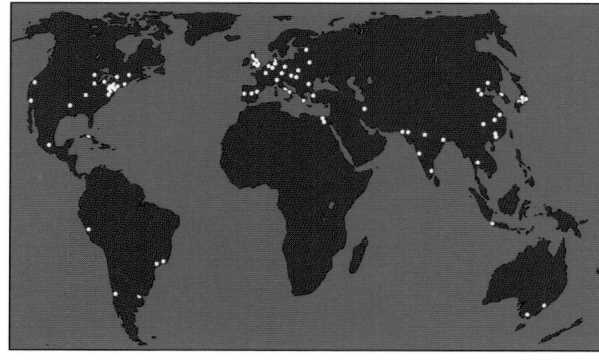

1950

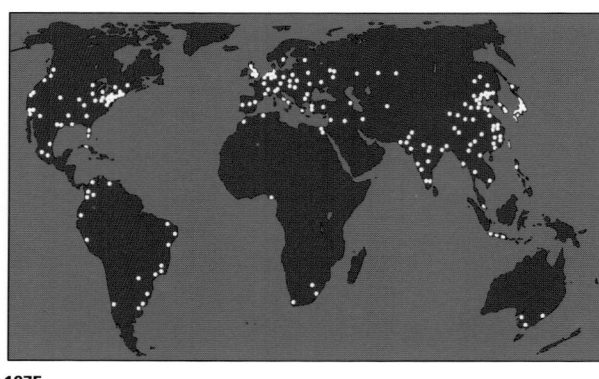

1975

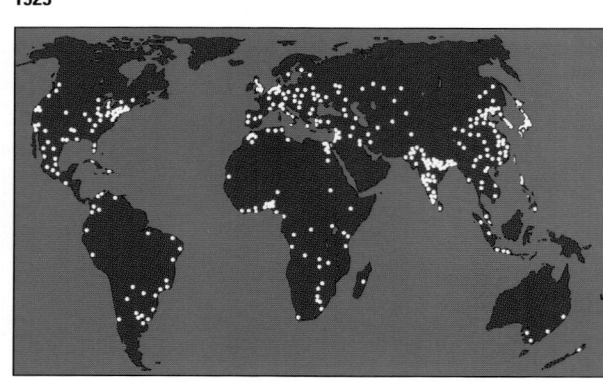

2000

URBAN POPULATION

Percentage of total population living in towns & cities (1990)

[UK 92.5%]

[USA 74.0 %]

Over 75%

50 - 75%

25 - 50%

10 - 25%

Under 10%

Highest urban population*		Lowest urban population	
Macau	98.7%	Bhutan	5.3%
Belgium	96.9%	Burundi	7.3%
Kuwait	95.6%	Rwanda	7.7%
Hong Kong	93.2%	Burkina Faso	9.0%
UK	92.5%	Nepal	9.6%
Israel	91.6%	Uganda	10.4%
Iceland	90.5%	Oman	10.0%

* Several countries, including Bermuda, Monaco, Singapore & Vatican City, are designated as '100% urban'

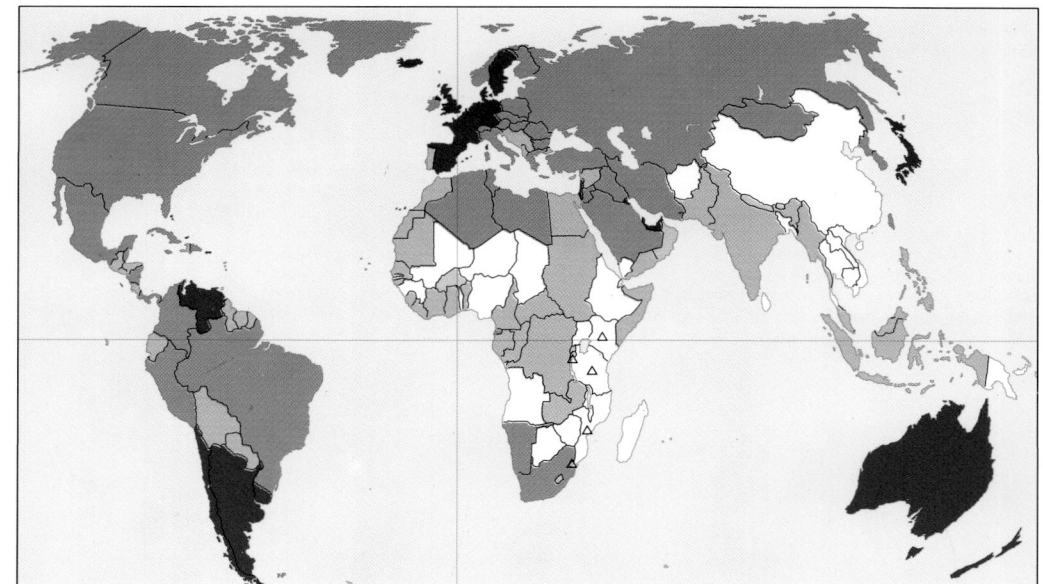

EXPANDING CITIES

The growth of the world's largest cities, 1950-2000. Intermediate rings indicate relative size in 1970 & 1985.

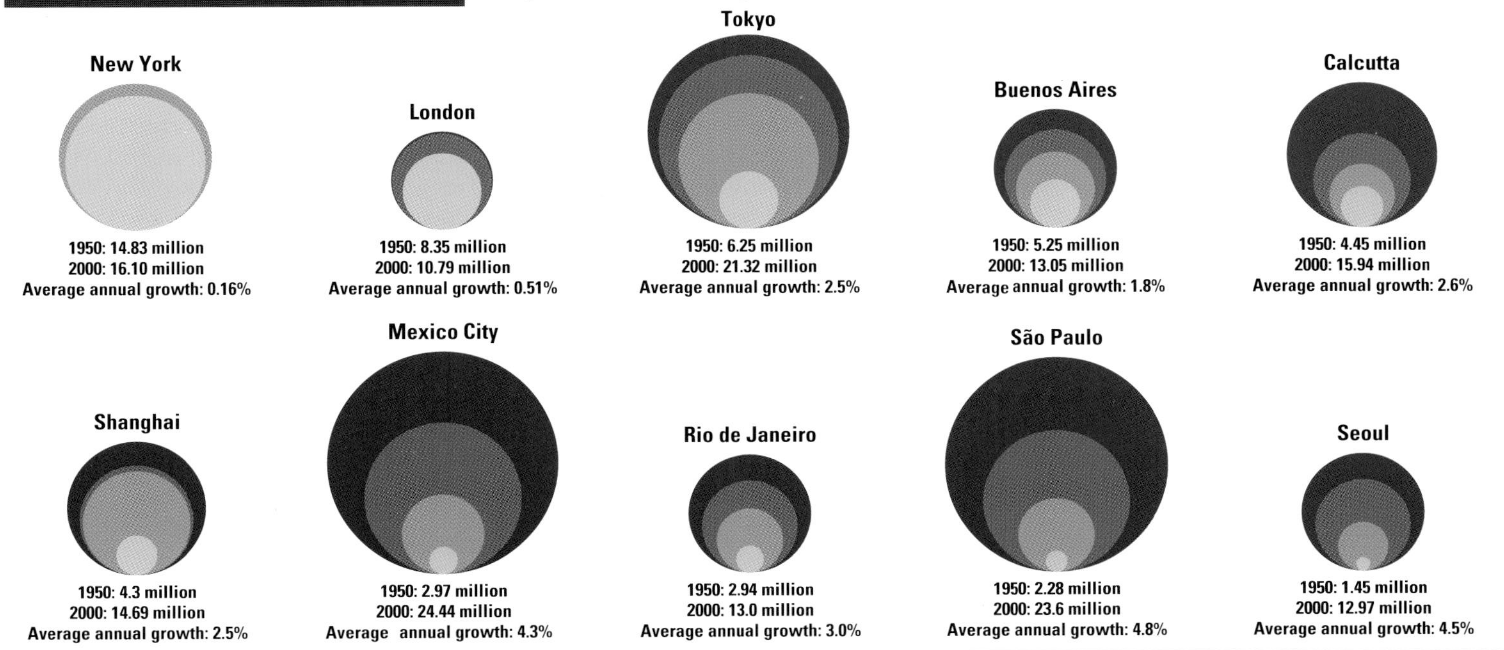

New York
1950: 14.83 million
2000: 16.10 million
Average annual growth: 0.16%

London
1950: 8.35 million
2000: 10.79 million
Average annual growth: 0.51%

Tokyo
1950: 6.25 million
2000: 21.32 million
Average annual growth: 2.5%

Buenos Aires
1950: 5.25 million
2000: 13.05 million
Average annual growth: 1.8%

Calcutta
1950: 4.45 million
2000: 15.94 million
Average annual growth: 2.6%

Shanghai
1950: 4.3 million
2000: 14.69 million
Average annual growth: 2.5%

Mexico City
1950: 2.97 million
2000: 24.44 million
Average annual growth: 4.3%

Rio de Janeiro
1950: 2.94 million
2000: 13.0 million
Average annual growth: 3.0%

São Paulo
1950: 2.28 million
2000: 23.6 million
Average annual growth: 4.8%

Seoul
1950: 1.45 million
2000: 12.97 million
Average annual growth: 4.5%

Each set of circles illustrates a city's size in 1950, 1970, 1985 and 2000. In most cases, expansion has been steady and, often, explosive. New York and London, however, went through patches of negative growth during the period. In New York, the world's largest city in 1950, population reached a peak around 1970. London shrank slightly between 1970 and 1985 before resuming a very modest rate of increase. In both cases, the divergence from world trends can be explained in part by counting methods: each is at the centre of a great agglomeration, and definitions of where 'city limits' lie may vary over time. But their relative decline also matches a pattern often seen in mature cities in the developed world, where urbanization, already at a very high level, has reached a plateau.

CITIES IN DANGER

As the 1980s advanced, most industrial countries, alarmed by acid rain and urban smog, took significant steps to limit air pollution. These controls, however, are expensive to install and difficult to enforce, and clean air remains a luxury most developed as well as developing cities must live without.

Those taking part in the United Nations' Global Environment Monitoring System (right) frequently show dangerous levels of pollutants ranging from soot to sulphur dioxide and photochemical smog; air in the majority of cities without such sampling equipment is likely to be at least as bad.

URBAN AIR POLLUTION

The world's most polluted cities: number of days each year when sulphur dioxide levels exceeded the WHO threshold of 150 micrograms per cubic metre (average over 4 to 15 years, 1970s - 1980s)

Sulphur dioxide is the main pollutant associated with industrial cities. According to the World Health Organization, more than seven days in a year above 150 µg per cubic metre bring a serious risk of respiratory disease: at least 600 million people live in urban areas where SO_2 concentrations regularly reach damaging levels.

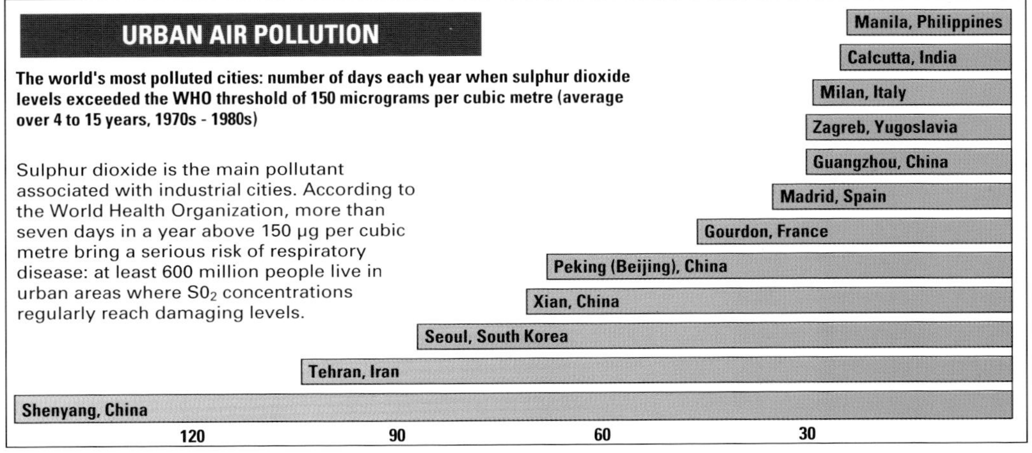

Manila, Philippines
Calcutta, India
Milan, Italy
Zagreb, Yugoslavia
Guangzhou, China
Madrid, Spain
Gourdon, France
Peking (Beijing), China
Xian, China
Seoul, South Korea
Tehran, Iran
Shenyang, China

120   90   60   30

LARGEST CITIES

The world's most populous cities, in millions of inhabitants, based on estimates for the year 2000*

	City	
1.	Mexico City	24.4
2.	São Paulo	23.6
3.	Tokyo-Yokohama	21.3
4.	New York	16.1
5.	Calcutta	15.9
6.	Bombay	15.4
7.	Shanghai	14.7
8.	Tehran	13.7
9.	Jakarta	13.2
10.	Buenos Aires	13.1
11.	Rio de Janeiro	13.0
12.	Seoul	13.0
13.	Delhi	12.8
14.	Lagos	12.4
15.	Cairo-Giza	11.8
16.	Karachi	11.6
17.	Manila-Quezon	11.5
18.	Peking (Beijing)	11.5
19.	Dhaka	11.3
20.	Osaka-Kobe	11.2
21.	Los Angeles	10.9
22.	London	10.8
23.	Bangkok	10.3
24.	Moscow	10.1
25.	Tientsin (Tianjin)	10.0
26.	Lima-Callao	8.8
27.	Paris	8.8
28.	Milan	8.7
29.	Madras	7.8
30.	Baghdad	7.7
31.	Chicago	7.0
32.	Bogotá	6.9
33.	Hong Kong	6.1
34.	St Petersburg	5.8
35.	Pusan	5.8
36.	Santiago	5.6
37.	Shenyang	5.5
38.	Madrid	5.4
39.	Naples	4.5
40.	Philadelphia	4.3

[City populations are based on urban agglomerations rather than legal city limits. In some cases, such as Tokyo-Yokohama and Cairo-Giza, where two adjacent cities have merged into one concentration, they have been regarded as a single unit]

* For list of largest cities in 1990, see page XI

INFORMAL CITIZENS

Proportion of population living in squatter settlements, selected cities in the developing world (1980s)

Urbanization in most Third World countries has been coming about far faster than local governments can provide services and accommodation for the new city-dwellers. Many – in some cities, most – find their homes in improvized squatter settlements, often unconnected to power, water and sanitation networks. Yet despite their ramshackle housing and marginal legality, these communities are often the most dynamic part of a city economy. They are also growing in size; and given the squatters' reluctance to be counted by tax-demanding authorities, the percentages shown here are likely to be underestimates.

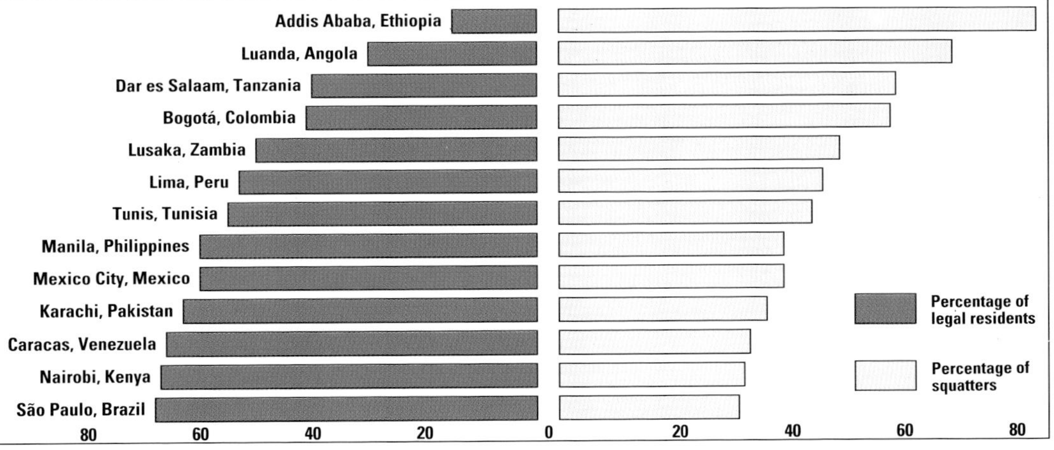

Addis Ababa, Ethiopia
Luanda, Angola
Dar es Salaam, Tanzania
Bogotá, Colombia
Lusaka, Zambia
Lima, Peru
Tunis, Tunisia
Manila, Philippines
Mexico City, Mexico
Karachi, Pakistan
Caracas, Venezuela
Nairobi, Kenya
São Paulo, Brazil

80 60 40 20 0 20 40 60 80

Percentage of legal residents

Percentage of squatters

URBAN ADVANTAGES

Despite overcrowding and poor housing, living standards in the developing world's cities are almost invariably better than in the surrounding countryside. Resources - financial, material and administrative - are concentrated in the towns, which are usually also the centres of political activity and pressure. Governments - frequently unstable, and rarely established on a solid democratic base - are usually more responsive to urban discontent than rural misery. In many countries, especially in Africa, food prices are often kept artificially low, appeasing underemployed urban masses at the expense of agricultural development. The imbalance encourages further cityward migration, helping to account for the astonishing rate of post-1950 urbanization and putting great strain on the ability of many nations to provide even modest improvements for their people.

RELATIVE MORTALITY

Infant deaths per 1,000 live births in rural & urban areas of selected developing countries (1986-1988)

Urban
Rural

Bangladesh, Kenya, Peru, Senegal, Indonesia, Colombia

150 120 90 60 30

RELATIVE LITERACY

Adult literacy rates (%) in urban & rural areas of selected developing countries (1986-1988)

Urban
Rural

Chile, Philippines, Bolivia, Cameroon, India, Tunisia

100 80 60 40 20

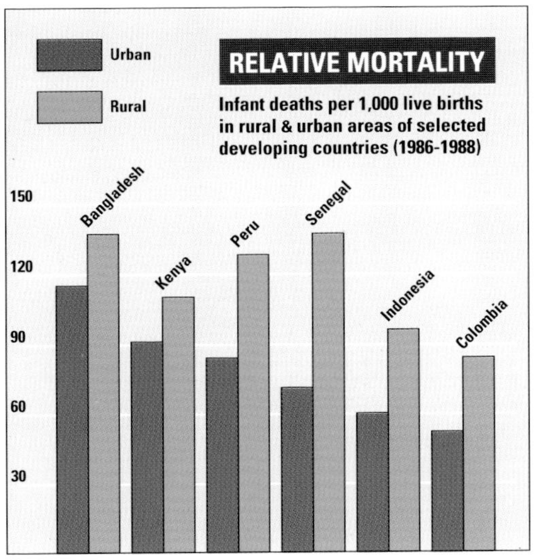

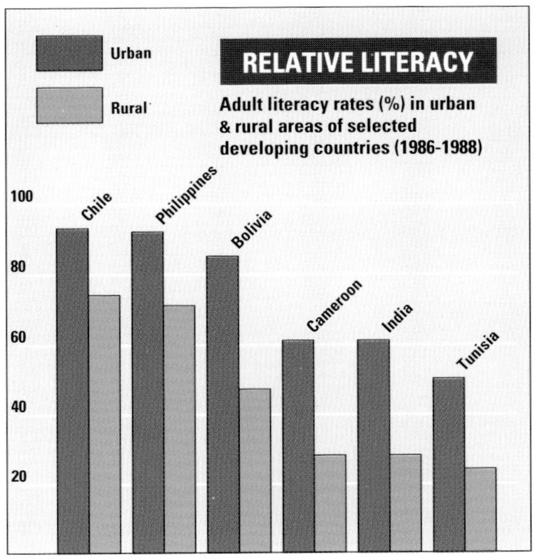

PEOPLE: THE HUMAN FAMILY

22: POPULATION DENSITY

28: THE WORLD'S REFUGEES
    WAR SINCE 1945

29: UNITED NATIONS
    INTERNATIONAL ORGANIZATIONS

46: THE HISTORY OF HUMAN EXPANSION

Strictly speaking, all human beings belong to a single race: *Homo sapiens* has no sub-species. But although all humans are inter-fertile, anthropologists and geneticists distinguish three main racial types, whose differences reflect not so much evolutionary origin as long periods of separation.

Racial affinities are not always obvious. The Caucasoid group stems from Europe, North Africa and India, but still includes Australian aboriginals within its broad type; Mongoloid peoples comprise American Indians and Eskimos as well as most Chinese, central Asians and Malays; Negroids are mostly of African origin, but also include the Papuan peoples of New Guinea.

Migration in modern times has mingled racial groups to an unprecedented extent, and most nations now have some degree of racially mixed population.

Language is almost the definition of a particular human culture; the world has well over 5,000, most of them with only a few hundred thousand speakers. In one important sense, all languages are equal: although different vocabularies and linguistic structures greatly influence patterns of thought, all true human languages can carry virtually unlimited information. But even if there is no theoretical difference in the communicative power of English and one of the 500 or more tribal languages of Papua New Guinea, for example, an English speaker has access to very much more of the global culture than a Papuan who knows no other tongue.

Like language, religion encourages the internal cohesion of a single human group at the expense of creating gulfs of incomprehension between different groups. All religions satisfy a deep-seated human need, assigning men and women to a comprehensible place in what most of them still consider a divinely ordered world. But religion is also a means by which a culture can assert its individuality: the startling rise of Islam in the late 20th century is partly a response by large sections of the developing world to the secular, Western-inspired world order from which many non-Western peoples feel excluded. Like uncounted millions of human beings before them, they find in their religion not only a personal faith but a powerful group identity.

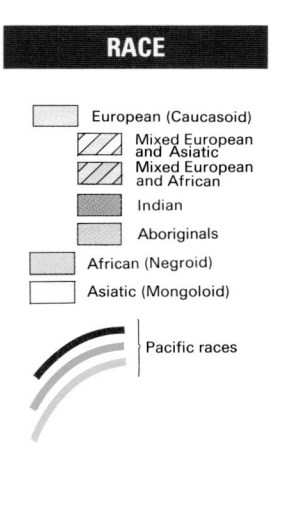

RACE

- European (Caucasoid)
- Mixed European and Asiatic
- Mixed European and African
- Indian
- Aboriginals
- African (Negroid)
- Asiatic (Mongoloid)
- Pacific races

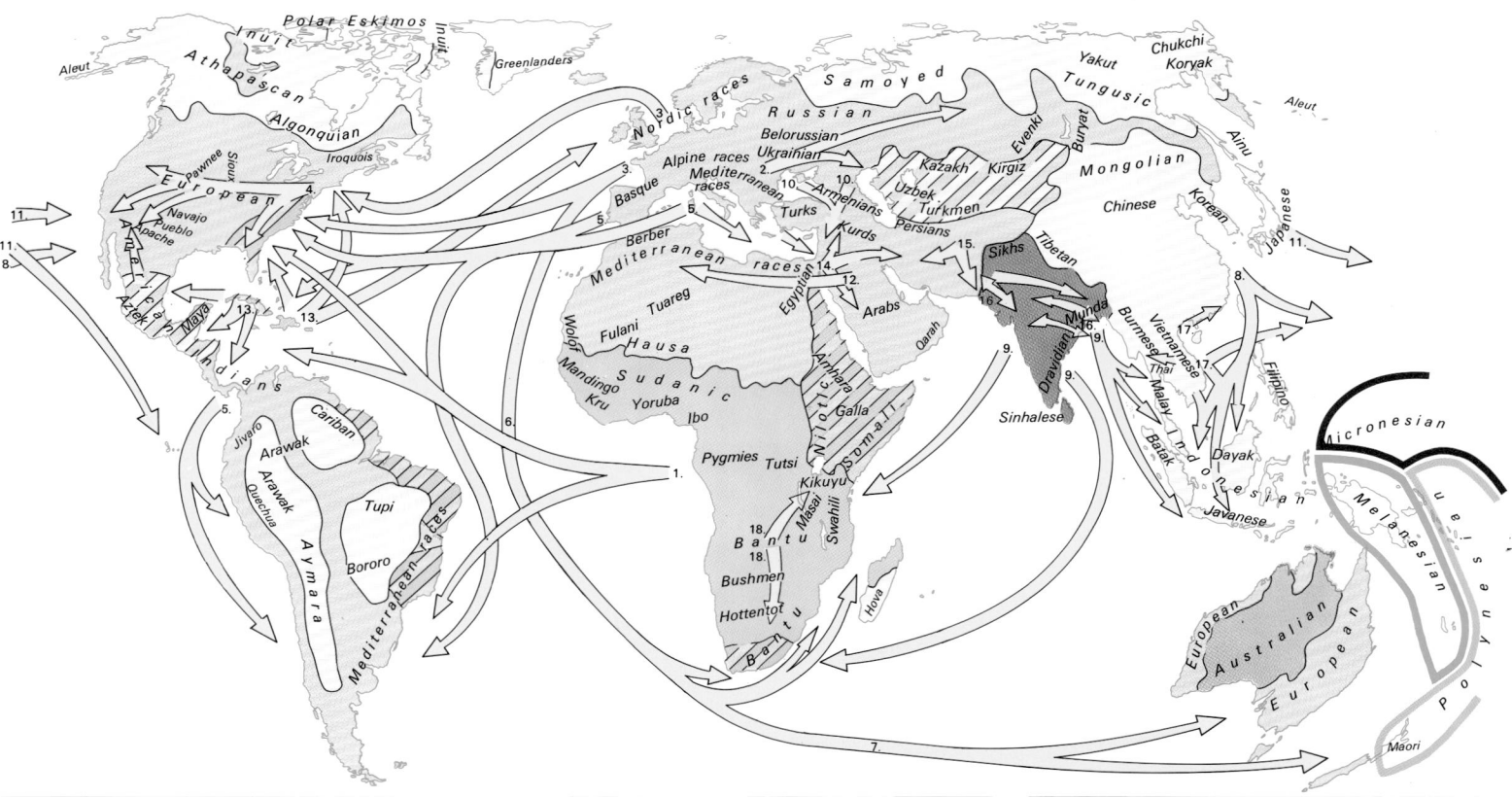

MOVEMENTS OF POPULATION

1. Africa to America (slaves), c. 1500-1860
2. Western Russia to Siberia, c. 1850-1950
3. W., E. & N. Europe to N. America, c. 1850-1900
4. From East Coast N. America, c. 1860-1960
5. Southern Europe to America, c. 1880-1920
6. Europe to S., E. & Central Africa, c. 1880-1950
7. Europe to Australia & N. Zealand, c. 1840-1950
8. China to S-E Asia & N. America, c. 1900-1950
9. India to Africa & South-East Asia, c. 1860-1910

Major migrations of peoples since 600 AD

10. European & N. American Jews to Israel, 1948-
11. Japan to N. & S. America, c. 1870-1910
12. Arabs to North Africa, 7th-9th centuries
13. C. America to N. America & Europe, c. 1950-1970
14. Migration in the Middle East, c. 1950-
15. Refugees from Afghanistan, 1979-
16. Migration in India, 1946-
17. Migration in & from South-East Asia, c. 1960-
18. Spread of the Bantu peoples, c. 1700-1900

BUILDING THE USA

U.S. Immigration 1820-1990

'Give me your tired, your poor/Your huddled masses yearning to breathe free....'

So starts Emma Lazarus's poem *The New Colossus*, inscribed on the Statue of Liberty. For decades the USA was the magnet that attracted millions of immigrants, notably from Central and Eastern Europe, the flow peaking in the early years of this century.

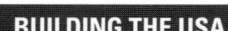
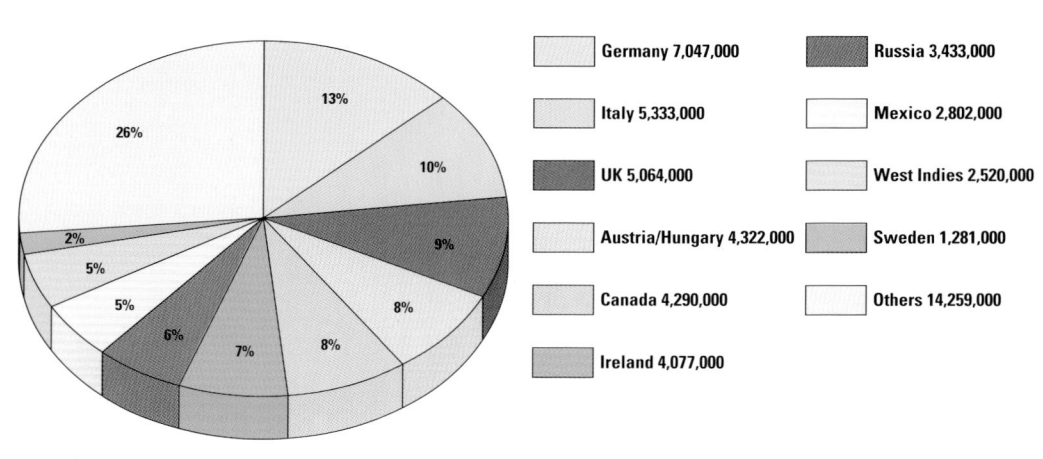

- Germany 7,047,000
- Italy 5,333,000
- UK 5,064,000
- Austria/Hungary 4,322,000
- Canada 4,290,000
- Ireland 4,077,000
- Russia 3,433,000
- Mexico 2,802,000
- West Indies 2,520,000
- Sweden 1,281,000
- Others 14,259,000

MIGRATION

The movement of migrants in thousands (1985-1990)

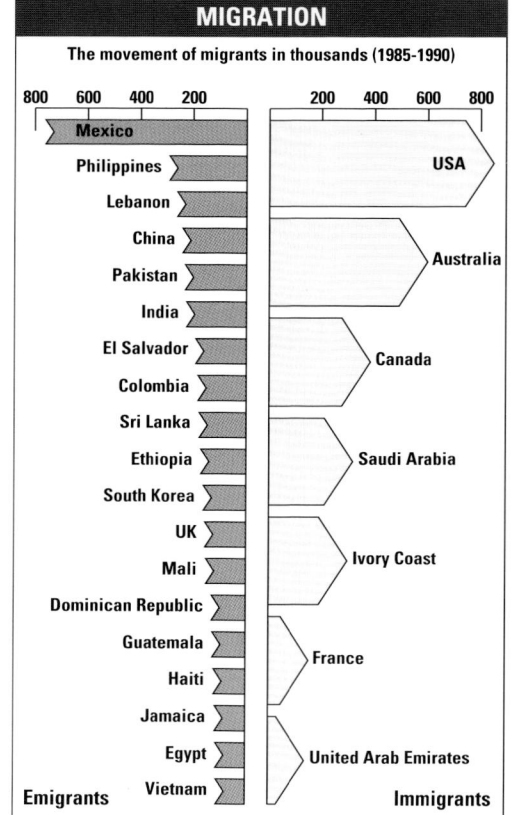

Emigrants — Immigrants

(Emigrants) Mexico, Philippines, Lebanon, China, Pakistan, India, El Salvador, Colombia, Sri Lanka, Ethiopia, South Korea, UK, Mali, Dominican Republic, Guatemala, Haiti, Jamaica, Egypt, Vietnam

(Immigrants) USA, Australia, Canada, Saudi Arabia, Ivory Coast, France, United Arab Emirates

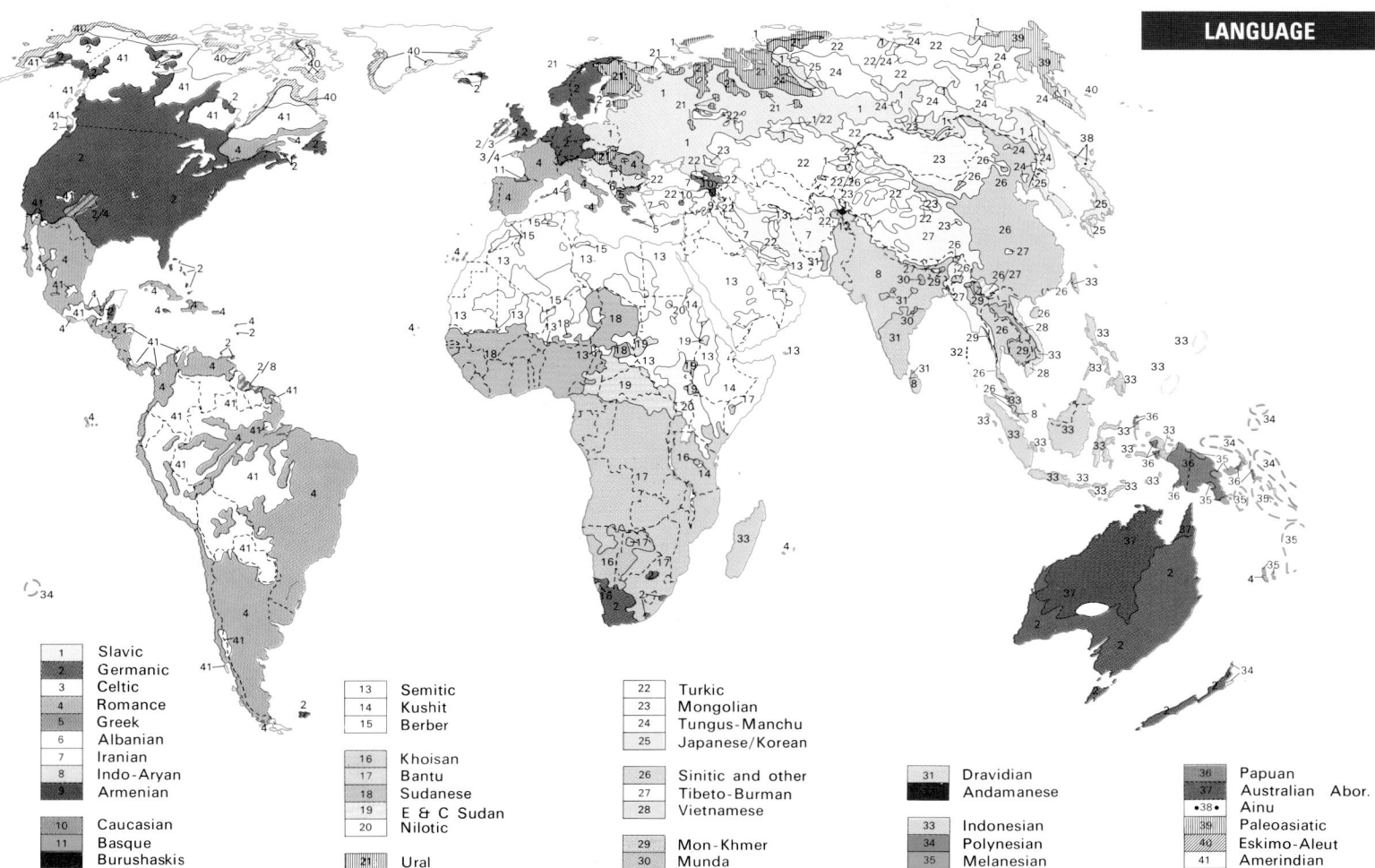

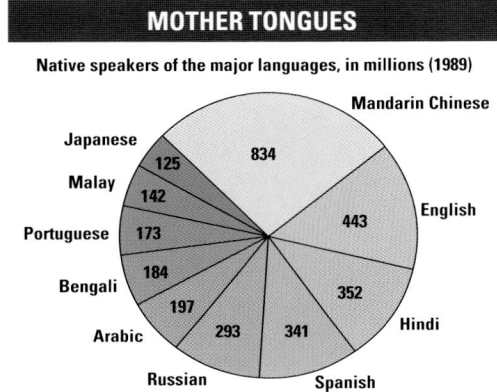

OFFICIAL LANGUAGES

Language	Total population	World %
English	1400m	27.0%
Chinese	1070m	19.1%
Hindi	700m	13.5%
Spanish	280m	5.4%
Russian	270m	5.2%
French	220m	4.2%
Arabic	170m	3.3%
Portuguese	160m	3.0%
Malay	160m	3.0%
Bengali	150m	2.9%
Japanese	120m	2.3%

Key (languages):

1 Slavic
2 Germanic
3 Celtic
4 Romance
5 Greek
6 Albanian
7 Iranian
8 Indo-Aryan
9 Armenian

10 Caucasian
11 Basque
12 Burushaskis

13 Semitic
14 Kushit
15 Berber

16 Khoisan
17 Bantu
18 Sudanese
19 E & C Sudan
20 Nilotic

21 Ural

22 Turkic
23 Mongolian
24 Tungus-Manchu
25 Japanese/Korean

26 Sinitic and other
27 Tibeto-Burman
28 Vietnamese

29 Mon-Khmer
30 Munda

31 Dravidian
Andamanese

33 Indonesian
34 Polynesian
35 Melanesian

36 Papuan
37 Australian Abor.
38 Ainu
35 Paleoasiatic
40 Eskimo-Aleut
41 Amerindian

Languages form a kind of tree of development, splitting from a few ancient proto-tongues into branches that have grown apart and further divided with the passage of time. English and Hindi, for example, both belong to the great Indo-European family, although the relationship is only apparent after much analysis and comparison with non-Indo-European languages such as Chinese or Arabic; Hindi is part of the Indo-Aryan subgroup; English is a member of Indo-European's Germanic branch; French, another Indo-European tongue, traces its descent through the Latin, or Romance, branch. A few languages – Basque is one example – have no apparent links with any other, living or dead. Most modern languages, of course, have acquired enormous quantities of vocabulary from each other.

MOTHER TONGUES

Native speakers of the major languages, in millions (1989)

Mandarin Chinese 834
English 443
Hindi 352
Spanish 341
Russian 293
Arabic 197
Bengali 184
Portuguese 173
Malay 142
Japanese 125

Religions are not as easily mapped as the physical contours of landscape. Divisions are often blurred and frequently overlapping: most nations include people of many different faiths – or no faith at all. Some religions, like Islam and Christianity, have proselytes worldwide; others, like Hinduism and Confucianism, are restricted to a particular area, though modern migrations have taken some Indians and Chinese very far from their cultural origins. It is also difficult to show the degree to which religion exercises control over daily life: Christian Western Europe, for example, is nowadays far less dominated by its religion than are the Islamic nations of the Middle East. Similarly, figures for the major faiths' adherents make no distinction between nominal believers enrolled at birth and those for whom religion is a vital part of existence.

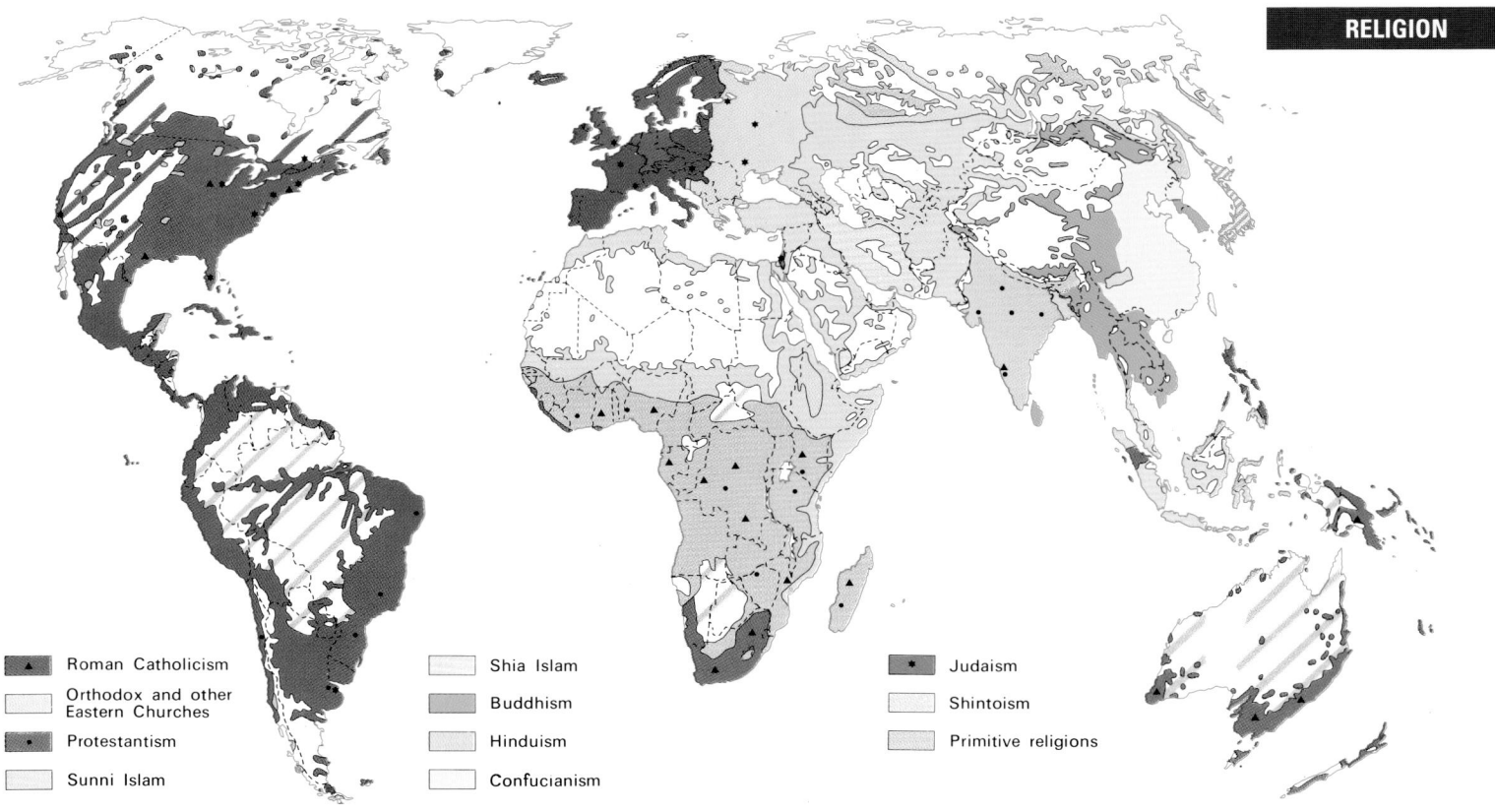

RELIGIOUS ADHERENTS

Christian	1667m
Roman Catholic	952m
Protestant	337m
Orthodox	162m
Anglican	70m
Other Christian	148m
Muslim	881m
Sunni	841m
Shia	40m
Hindu	663m
Buddhist	312m
Chinese folk	172m
Tribal	92m
Jewish	18m
Sikhs	17m

Key (religion):

- Roman Catholicism
- Orthodox and other Eastern Churches
- Protestantism
- Sunni Islam
- Shia Islam
- Buddhism
- Hinduism
- Confucianism
- Judaism
- Shintoism
- Primitive religions

27

PEOPLE: CONFLICT & COOPERATION

26: RACE
    MIGRATION

27: RELIGION

46: HUMAN EXPANSION

Humans are social animals, rarely functioning well except in groups. Evolution has made them so: hunter-gatherers in cooperative bands were far more effective than animals that prowled alone. Agriculture, the building of cities and industrialization are all developments that depended on human cooperative ability – and in turn increased the need for it.

Unfortunately, human groups do not always cooperate so well with other human groups, and friction between them sometimes leads to cooperatively organized violence. War is itself a very human activity, with no real equivalent in any other species. Always murderous, it is sometimes purposeful and may even be very effective. The colonization of the Americas and Australia, for example, was in effect the waging of aggressive war by well-armed Europeans against indigenous peoples incapable of offering a serious defence.

More often, war achieves little but death and ruin. However, the great 20th-century wars appear to have cured the notoriously aggressive Europeans of their previous bad habits, although at the cost of between 50 and 100 million dead. The relative peace in the postwar developed world is at least partly due to the nuclear weapons with which rival powers have armed themselves – weapons so powerful that their use would leave a scarcely habitable planet with no meaningful distinction between victor and vanquished.

Yet warfare remains endemic: the second half of the 20th century was one of the bloodiest periods in history, and death by organized violence remains unhappily common. The map below attempts to show the serious conflicts that have scarred the Earth since 1945. Most are civil wars in poor countries, rather than international conflicts between rich ones; some of them are still unresolved, while others, like apparently extinct volcanoes, may erupt again at intervals, adding to the world's miserable population of refugees.

THE WORLD'S REFUGEES

Refugees and their national origin; the host nations and the relative size of their refugee populations (1991)

Refugees in millions

Refugees as a proportion of host country's population

The pie-chart shows the origins of the world's refugees, the bar-chart their destinations. According to the United Nations High Commissioner for Refugees in 1990, there were almost 15 million of them, a number that continued to increase and was almost certain to be amplified during the decade. Some have fled from climatic change, some from economic disaster and others from political persecution; the great majority are the victims of war.
All but a few who make it overseas seek asylum in neighbouring countries, which are often the least equipped to deal with them and where they are rarely welcome. Lacking any rights or power, they frequently become an embarrassment and a burden to their reluctant hosts.
Usually, the best any refugee can hope for is rudimentary food and shelter in temporary camps that all to often become semi-permanent, with little prospect of assimilation by host populations: many Palestinians, for example, have been forced to live in camps since 1948.

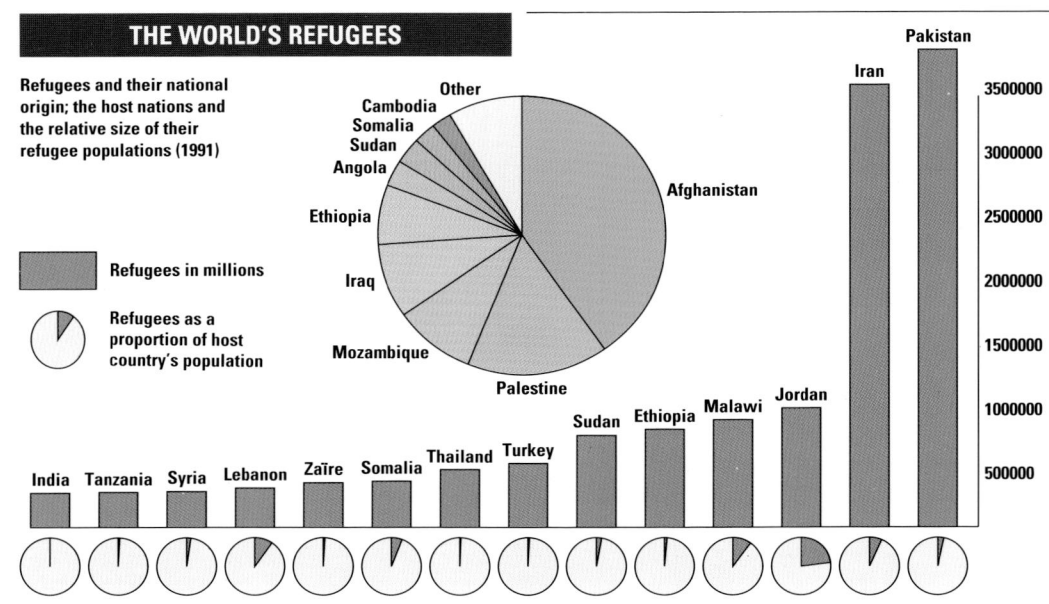

WAR SINCE 1945

Past	Current	
☆	★	Major international war
☆	★	Minor international war
◎	◉	Major civil war
◎	◉	Minor civil war
○	●	Long-running terrorist campaigns

UNITED NATIONS

The United Nations Organization was born as World War II drew to its conclusion. Six years of strife had strengthened the world's desire for peace, but an effective international organization was needed to help achieve it. That body would replace the League of Nations which, since its inception in 1920, had signally failed to curb the aggression of at least some of its member nations. At the United Nations Conference on International Organization held in San Francisco, the United Nations Charter was drawn up. Ratified by the Security Council and signed by 51 nations, it came into effect on 24 October 1945.

The Charter set out the aims of the organization: to maintain peace and security, and develop friendly relations between nations; to achieve international cooperation in solving economic, social, cultural and humanitarian problems; to promote respect for human rights and fundamental freedoms; and to harmonize the activities of nations in order to achieve these common goals.

By 1992, the UN had expanded to more than 160 member countries; it is the largest international political organization, employing 23,000 people worldwide; its headquarters in New York accounts for 7,000 staff and it also has major offices in Rome, Geneva and Vienna.

The United Nations has six principal organs:

The General Assembly
The forum at which member nations discuss moral and political issues affecting world development, peace and security meets annually in September, under a newly-elected President whose tenure lasts one year. Any member can bring business to the agenda, and each member nation has one vote. Decisions are made by simple majority, save for matters of very great importance, when a two-thirds majority is required. While the General Assembly has no powers of enforcement, its recommendations to member nations are regarded as persuasive and it is empowered to instruct UN organs or agencies to implement its decisions.

The Security Council
A legislative and executive body, the Security Council is the primary instrument for establishing and maintaining international peace by attempting to settle disputes between nations. It has the power to dispatch UN forces to stop aggression, and member nations undertake to make armed forces, assistance and facilities available as required. The Security Council has ten temporary members elected by the General Assembly for two-year terms, and five permanent members - China, France, Russia, UK and USA. On questions of substance, the vote of each of the permanent members is required within the necessary nine-vote majority.

The Economic and Social Council
By far the largest United Nations executive, the Council operates as a conduit between the General Assembly and the many United Nations agencies it instructs to implement Assembly decisions, and whose work it coordinates. The Council also sets up commissions to examine economic conditions, collects data and issues studies and reports, and may make recommendations to the Assembly. The Council's overall aim is to help the peoples of the world with education, health and human rights. It has 54 member countries, elected by the General Assembly to three-year terms.

The Secretariat
This is the staff of the United Nations, and its task is to administer the policies and programmes of the UN and its organs, and assist and advise the Head of the Secretariat, the Secretary-General – a full-time, non-political, appointment made by the General Assembly.

The Trusteeship Council
The Council administers trust territories with the aim of promoting their advancement. Only one remains - the Trust Territory of the Pacific Is. (Palau), administered by the USA.

The International Court of Justice (the World Court)
The World Court is the judicial organ of the United Nations. It deals only with United Nations disputes and all members are subject to its jurisdiction, which includes both cases submitted to it by member nations and matters especially provided for in the Charter or in treaties. The Court's decisions are only binding in respect of a particular dispute; failure to heed a judgement may involve recourse to the Security Council. There are 15 judges, elected for nine-year terms by the General Assembly and the Security Council. The Court sits in The Hague.

United Nations agencies and programmes, and inter-governmental agencies coordinated by the UN, contribute to harmonious world development. Social and humanitarian operations include:

United Nations Development Programme (UNDP): plans and funds projects to help developing countries make better use of resources. Voluntary pledges of $1.3 billion were made for 1990, to fund almost 7,000 projects in 152 countries.

United Nations International Childrens' Fund (UNICEF): created at the General Assembly's first session in 1945 to help children in the aftermath of World War II, it now provides basic healthcare and aid worldwide. Voluntarily funded, three-quarters of its income is derived from government donations.

United Nations Fund for Population Activities (UNFPA): promotes awareness of population issues and family planning, providing appropriate assistance.

Food & Agriculture Organization (FAO): aims to raise living standards and nutrition levels in rural areas by improving food production and distribution.

United Nations Educational, Scientific & Cultural Organization (UNESCO): promotes international cooperation through broader and better education.

World Health Organization (WHO): promotes and provides for better health care, public and environmental health and medical research.

Membership: There are 13 independent states who are not members of the UN – Andorra, Kiribati, Liechtenstein, N. Korea, S. Korea, Monaco, Nauru, San Marino, Switzerland, Taiwan, Tonga, Tuvalu and Vatican City. By 1992, the successor states of the former USSR had either joined or were planning to join. There were 51 members in 1945. Official languages are Chinese, English, French, Russian, Spanish and (a recent addition) Arabic.

Funding: The UN budget for 1988-1989 was US $ 1,788,746,000. Contributions are assessed by members' ability to pay, with the maximum 25% of the total, the minimum 0.01%. Contributions for 1988-1989 were: USA 25%, Japan 11.38%, USSR 9.99%, W. Germany 8.08%, France 6.25%, UK 4.86%, Italy 3.99%, Canada 3.09%, Spain 1.95%, Netherlands 1.65% (others 23.75%).

Peacekeeping: The UN has been involved in 18 peacekeeping operations worldwide since 1945, five of which (Afghanistan/Pakistan, Iran/Iraq, Angola, Namibia and Honduras) were initiated in 1988-1989. In June 1991 UN personnel totalling over 11,000 were working in eight separate areas.

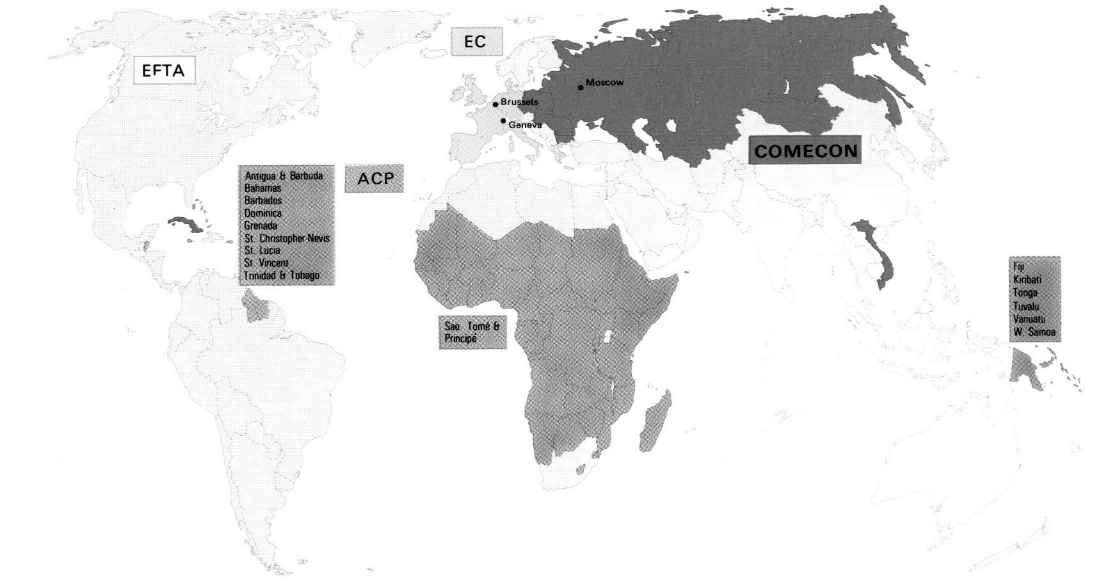

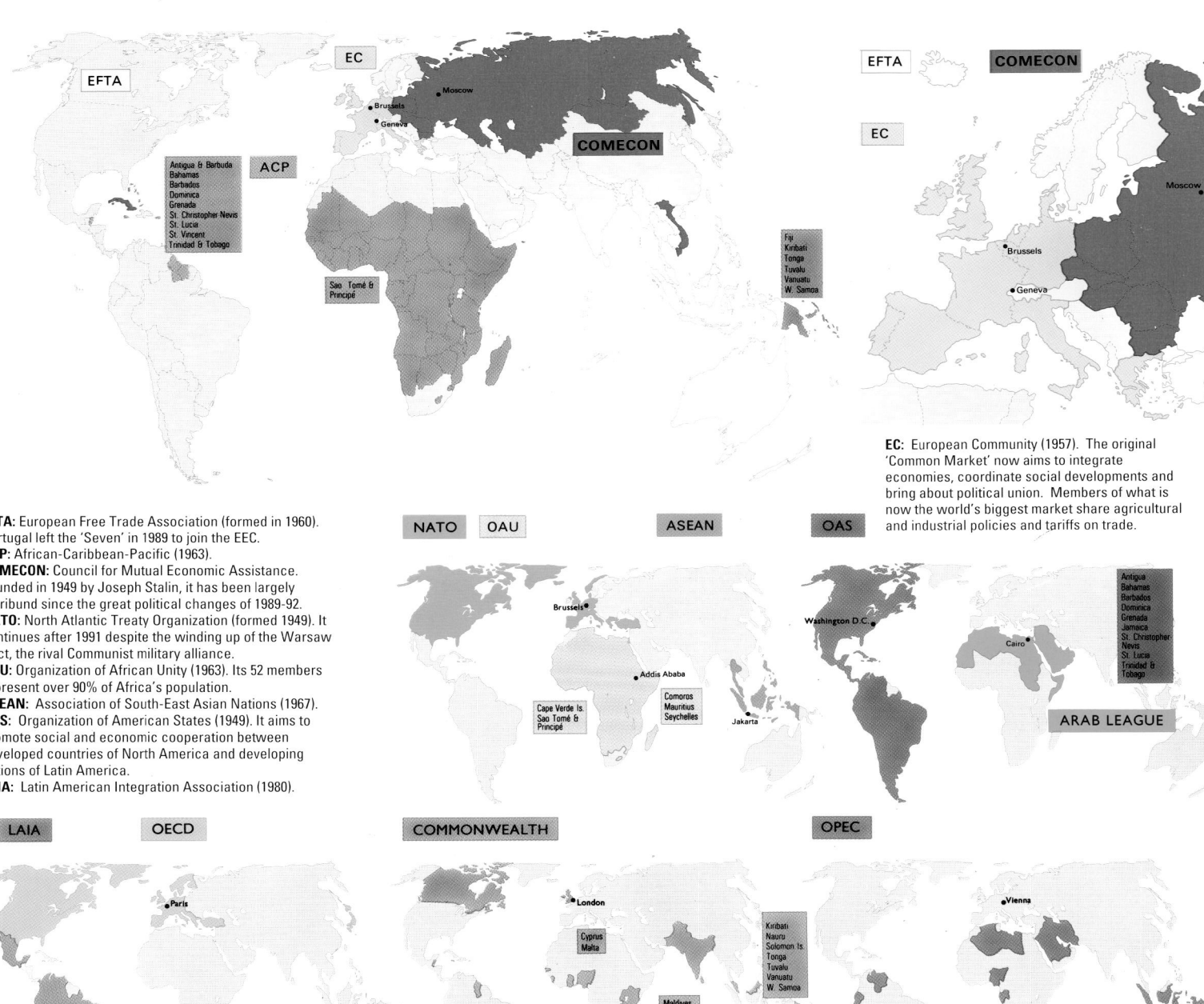

EFTA: European Free Trade Association (formed in 1960). Portugal left the 'Seven' in 1989 to join the EEC.

ACP: African-Caribbean-Pacific (1963).

COMECON: Council for Mutual Economic Assistance. Founded in 1949 by Joseph Stalin, it has been largely moribund since the great political changes of 1989-92.

NATO: North Atlantic Treaty Organization (formed 1949). It continues after 1991 despite the winding up of the Warsaw Pact, the rival Communist military alliance.

OAU: Organization of African Unity (1963). Its 52 members represent over 90% of Africa's population.

ASEAN: Association of South-East Asian Nations (1967).

OAS: Organization of American States (1949). It aims to promote social and economic cooperation between developed countries of North America and developing nations of Latin America.

LAIA: Latin American Integration Association (1980).

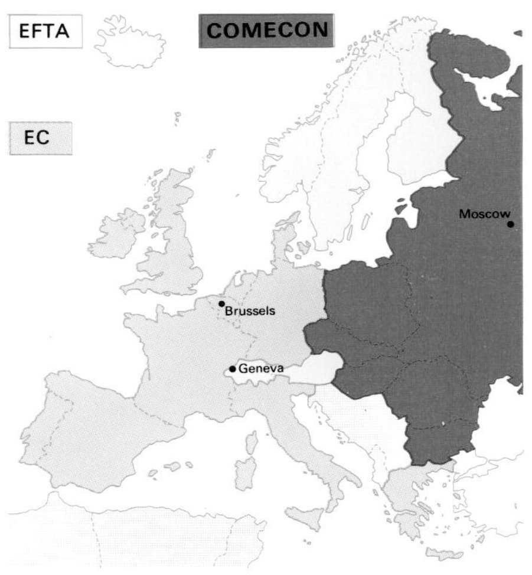

EC: European Community (1957). The original 'Common Market' now aims to integrate economies, coordinate social developments and bring about political union. Members of what is now the world's biggest market share agricultural and industrial policies and tariffs on trade.

United Nations agencies are involved in many aspects of international trade, safety and security:

General Agreement on Tariffs and Trade (GATT): sponsors international trade negotiations and advocates a common code of conduct.

International Maritime Organization (IMO): promotes unity amongst merchant shipping, especially in regard to safety, marine pollution and standardization.

International Labour Organization (ILO): seeks to improve labour conditions and promote productive employment to raise living standards.

World Meteorological Organization (WMO): promotes cooperation in weather observation, reporting and forecasting.

World Intellectual Property Organization (WIPO): seeks to protect intellectual property such as artistic copyright, scientific patents and trademarks.

Disarmament Commission: considers and makes recommendations to the General Assembly on disarmament issues.

International Atomic Energy Agency (IAEA): fosters development of peaceful uses for nuclear energy, establishes safety standards and monitors the destruction of nuclear material designed for military use.

The World Bank comprises three United Nations agencies:

International Monetary Fund (IMF): cultivates international monetary cooperation and expansion of trade.

International Bank for Reconstruction & Development (IBRD): provides funds and technical assistance to developing countries.

International Finance Corporation (IFC): Encourages the growth of productive private enterprise in less developed countries.

OECD: Organization for Economic Cooperation and Development (1961). The 24 major Western free-market economies plus Yugoslavia as an associate member. 'G7' is its 'inner group' of USA, Canada, Japan, UK, Germany, Italy and France.

COMMONWEALTH: The Commonwealth of Nations evolved from the British Empire; it comprises 18 nations recognizing the British monarch as head of state and 32 nations with their own heads of state.

OPEC: Organization of Petroleum Exporting Countries (1960). It controls three-quarters of the world's oil supply.

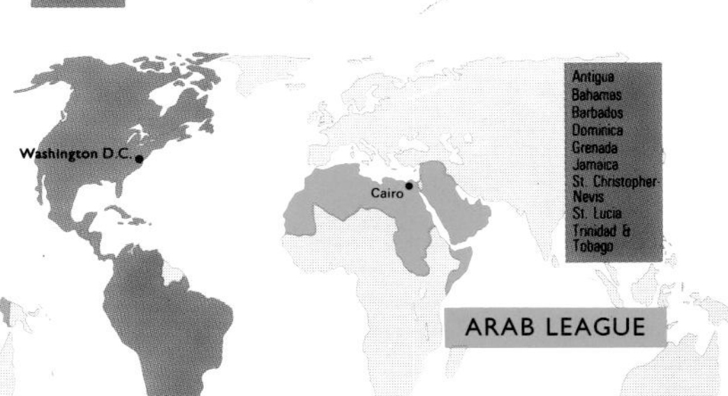

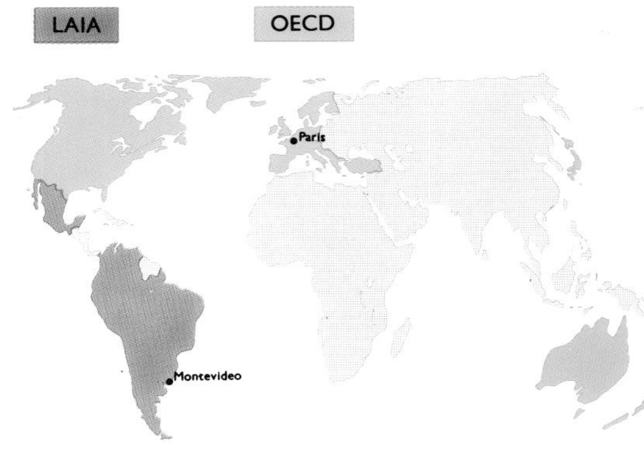

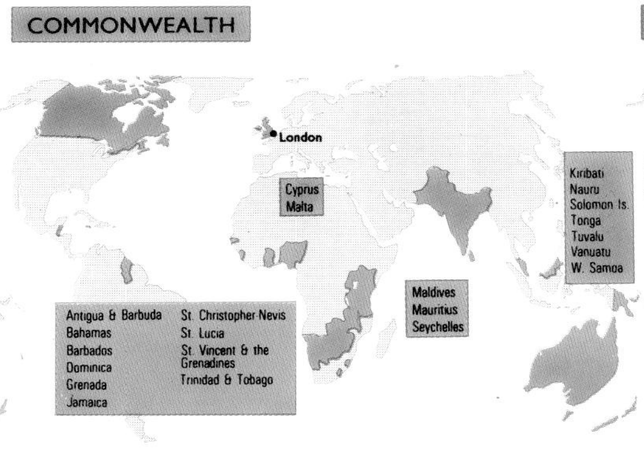

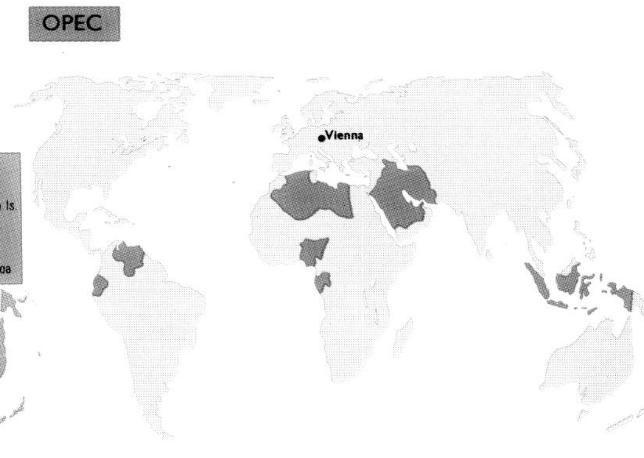

PRODUCTION: AGRICULTURE

14:	CLIMATE REGIONS
15:	TEMPERATURE & PRECIPITATION
16:	WATER UTILIZATION
17:	NATURAL VEGETATION LAND USE BY CONTINENT
36:	DIVISION OF EMPLOYMENT
46:	HUMAN EXPANSION

The invention of agriculture transformed human existence more than any other development, though it may not have seemed much of an improvement to its first practitioners. Primitive farming required brutally hard work, and it tied men and women to a patch of land, highly vulnerable to local weather patterns and to predators, especially human predators – drawbacks still apparent in much of the world today. It is difficult to imagine early humans being interested in such an existence while there were still animals around to hunt and wild seeds and berries to gather. Probably the spur was population pressure, with consequent overhunting and scarcity.

Despite its difficulties, the new life-style had a few overwhelming advantages. It supported far larger populations, eventually including substantial cities, with all the varied cultural and economic activities they allowed. Later still, it furnished the surpluses that allowed industrialization, another enormous step in human development.

Machines relieved many farmers of their burden of endless toil, and made it possible for relatively small numbers to provide food for more than five billion people.

Now as in the past, the whole business of farming involves the creation of a severely simplified ecology, under the tutelage and for the benefit of the farmer. Natural plant life is divided into crops, to be protected and nurtured, and weeds, the rest, to be destroyed. From the earliest days, crops were selectively bred to increase their food yield, usually at the expense of their ability to survive, which became the farmer's responsibility; 20th-century plant geneticists have carried the technique to highly productive extremes. Due mainly to new varieties of rice and wheat, world grain production has increased by 70% since 1965, more than doubling in the developing countries, although such high yields demand equally high consumption of fertilizers and pesticides to maintain them. Mechanized farmers in North America and Europe

continue to turn out huge surpluses, although not without environmental costs.

Where production is inadequate, the reasons are as likely to be political as agricultural. Africa, the only continent where food production per capita is actually falling, suffers acutely from economic mis-management, as well as from the perennial problems of war and banditry. Dismal harvests in the USSR, despite its excellent farmland, helped bring about the collapse of the Soviet system.

There are other limits to progress. Increasing population puts relentless pressure on farmers not only to maintain high yields but also to increase them. Most of the world's potential cropland is already under the plough. The over-working of marginal land is one of the prime causes of desertification; new farmlands burned out of former rainforests are seldom fertile for long. Human numbers may yet outrun the land's ability to feed them, as they did almost 10,000 years ago.

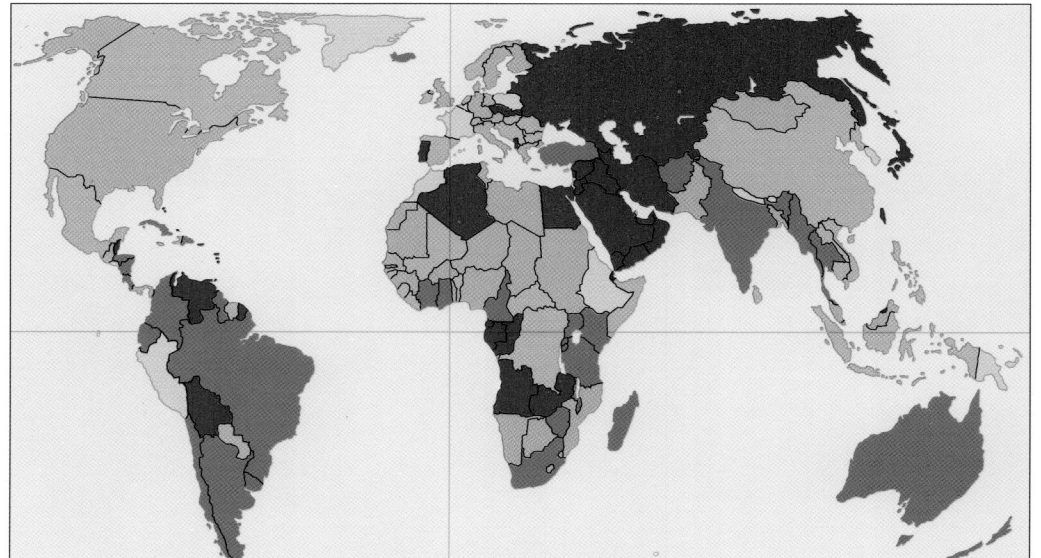

SELF-SUFFICIENCY IN FOOD

Balance of trade in food products as a percentage of total trade in food products (1988)

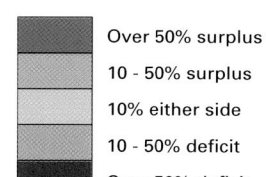

- Over 50% surplus
- 10 - 50% surplus
- 10% either side
- 10 - 50% deficit
- Over 50% deficit

Most self-sufficient		Least self-sufficient	
Uganda	93%	Algeria	-97%
Argentina	92%	Saudi Arabia	-95%
Burma	86%	Czechoslovakia	-92%
Chile	82%	Venezuela	-92%
Iceland	82%	Gabon	-88%
Uruguay	82%	Oman	-88%
Kenya	80%	Syria	-88%
New Zealand	80%	Egypt	-86%
Costa Rica	79%	Japan	-85%

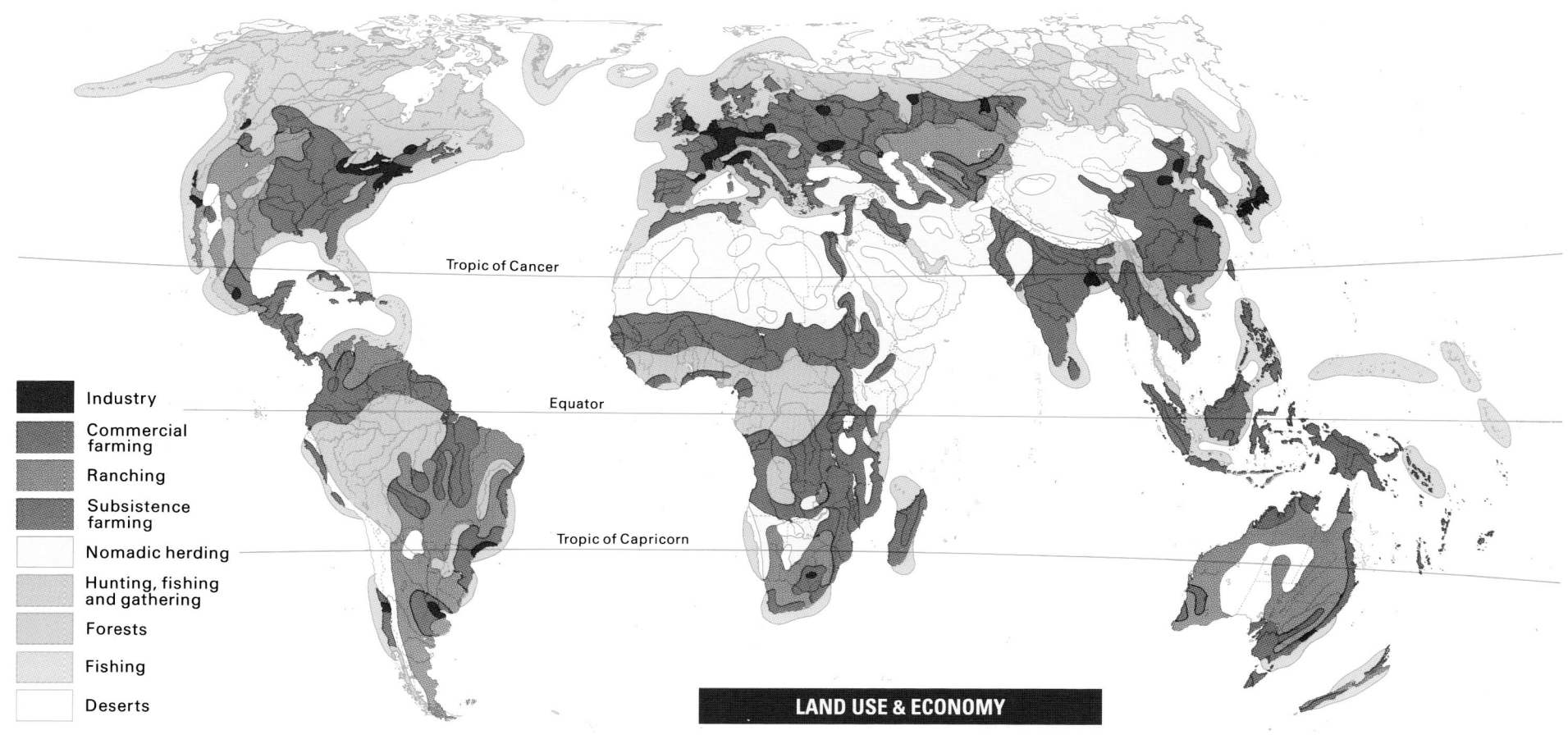

- Industry
- Commercial farming
- Ranching
- Subsistence farming
- Nomadic herding
- Hunting, fishing and gathering
- Forests
- Fishing
- Deserts

Tropic of Cancer

Equator

Tropic of Capricorn

LAND USE & ECONOMY

STAPLE CROPS

Separate figures for Russia, Ukraine and the other successors of the defunct USSR are not yet available

Wheat: Grown in a range of climates, with most varieties - including the highest-quality bread wheats - requiring temperate conditions. Mainly used in baking, it is also used for pasta and breakfast cereals.

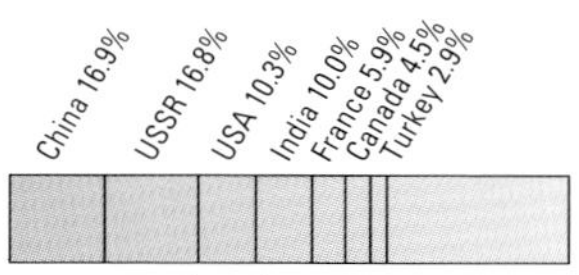
China 16.9%
USSR 16.8%
USA 10.3%
India 10.0%
France 5.9%
Canada 4.5%
Turkey 2.9%

World total (1989): 538,056,000 tonnes

Maize: Originating in the New World and still an important human food in Africa and Latin America, in the developed world it is processed into breakfast cereals, oil, starches and adhesives. It is also used for animal feed.

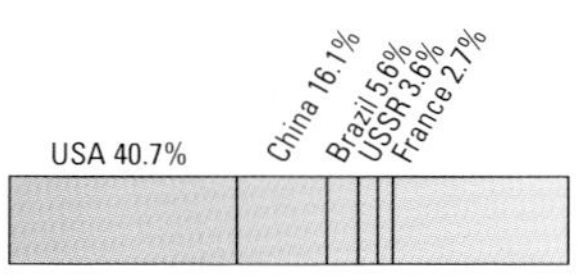
USA 40.7%
China 16.1%
Brazil 5.6%
USSR 3.6%
France 2.7%

World total (1989): 470,318,000 tonnes

Oats: Most widely used to feed livestock, but eaten by humans as oatmeal or porridge. Oats have a beneficial effect on the cardio-vascular system, and human consumption is likely to increase.

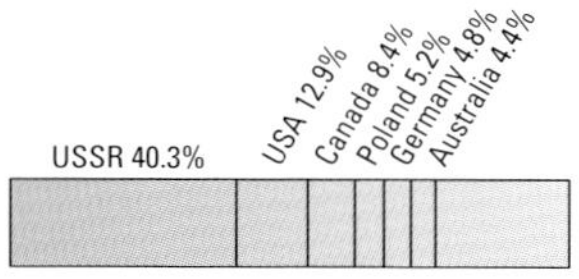
USSR 40.3%
USA 12.9%
Canada 8.4%
Poland 5.2%
Germany 4.8%
Australia 4.4%

World total (1989): 42,197,000 tonnes

Millet: The name covers a number of small grained cereals, members of the grass family with a short growing season. Used to produce flour and meal, animal feed and fermented to make beer, especially in Africa.

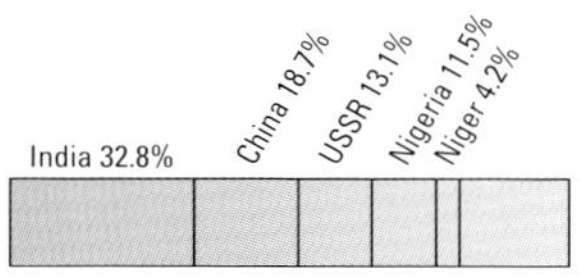
India 32.8%
China 18.7%
USSR 13.1%
Nigeria 11.5%
Niger 4.2%

World total (1989): 30,512,000 tonnes

Cassava: A tropical shrub that needs high rainfall (over 1000 mm annually) and a 10 - 30 month growing season to produce its large, edible tubers. Used as flour by humans, as cattle feed and in industrial starches.

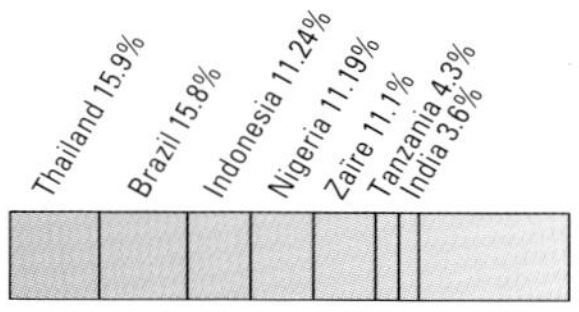
Thailand 15.9%
Brazil 15.8%
Indonesia 11.24%
Nigeria 11.19%
Zaire 11.1%
Tanzania 4.3%
India 3.6%

World total (1989): 147,500,000 tonnes

Rice: Thrives on the high humidity and temperatures of the Far East, where it is the traditional staple food of half the human race. Usually grown standing in water, rice responds well to continuous cultivation, with three or four crops annually.

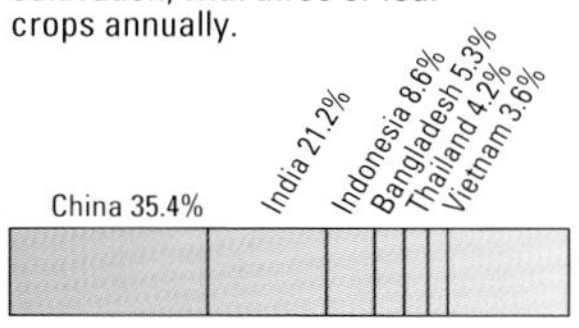
China 35.4%
India 21.2%
Indonesia 8.6%
Bangladesh 5.3%
Thailand 4.2%
Vietnam 3.6%

World total (1989): 506,291,000 tonnes

Barley: Primarily used as animal feed, but widely eaten by humans in Africa and Asia. Elsewhere, malted barley furnishes beer and spirits. Able to withstand the dry heat of sub-arid tropics, its growing season is only 80 days.

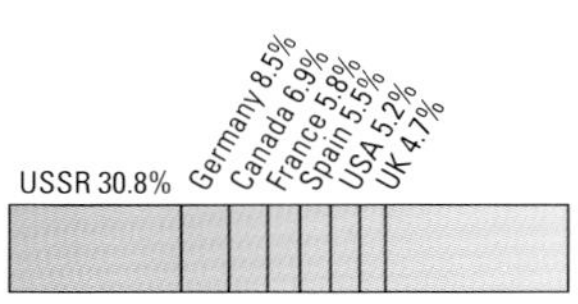
USSR 30.8%
Germany 8.5%
Canada 6.9%
France 5.8%
Spain 5.5%
USA 5.2%
UK 4.7%

World total (1989): 168,964,000 tonnes

Rye: Hardy and tolerant of poor and sandy soils, it is an important foodstuff and animal feed in Central and Eastern Europe. Rye produces a dark, heavy bread as well as alcoholic drinks.

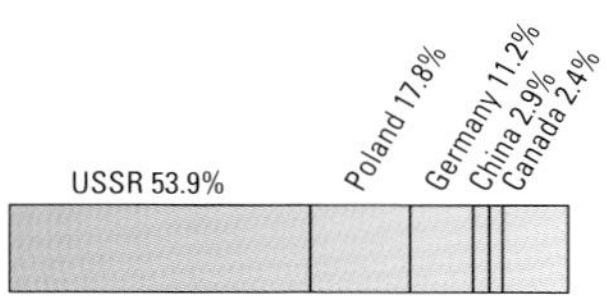
USSR 53.9%
Poland 17.8%
Germany 11.2%
China 2.9%
Canada 2.4%

World total (1989): 34,893,000 tonnes

Potatoes: The most important of the edible tubers, potatoes grow in well-watered, temperate areas. Weight for weight less nutritious than grain, they are a human staple as well as an important animal feed.

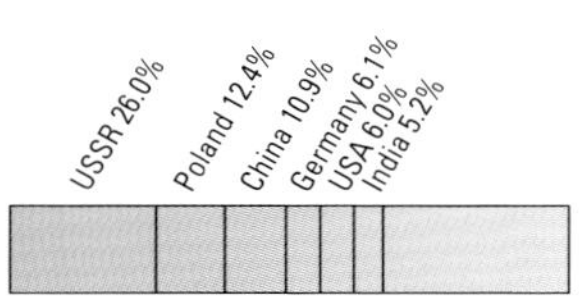
USSR 26.0%
Poland 12.4%
China 10.9%
Germany 6.1%
USA 6.0%
India 5.2%

World total (1989): 276,740,000 tonnes

Soya: Beans from soya bushes are very high - 30-40% - in protein. Most are processed into oil and proprietary protein foods. Consumption since 1950 has tripled, mainly due to the health-conscious developed world.

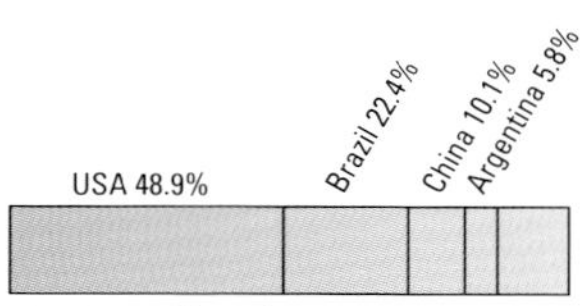
USA 48.9%
Brazil 22.4%
China 10.1%
Argentina 5.8%

World total (1989): 107,350,000 tonnes

Cereals are grasses with starchy, edible seeds; every important civilization has depended on them as a source of food. The major cereal grains contain about 10% protein and 75% carbohydrate; grain is easy to store, handle and transport, and contributes more than any other group of foods to the energy and protein content of human diet. If all the cereals were consumed directly by man, there would be no shortage of food in the world, but a considerable proportion of the total output is used as animal feed.

Starchy tuber crops or root crops, represented here by potatoes and cassava, are second in importance only to cereals as staple foods; easily cultivated, they provide high yields for little effort and store well – potatoes for up to six months, cassava for up to a year in the ground. Protein content is low (2% or less), starch content high, with some minerals and vitamins present, but populations that rely heavily on these crops may suffer from malnutrition.

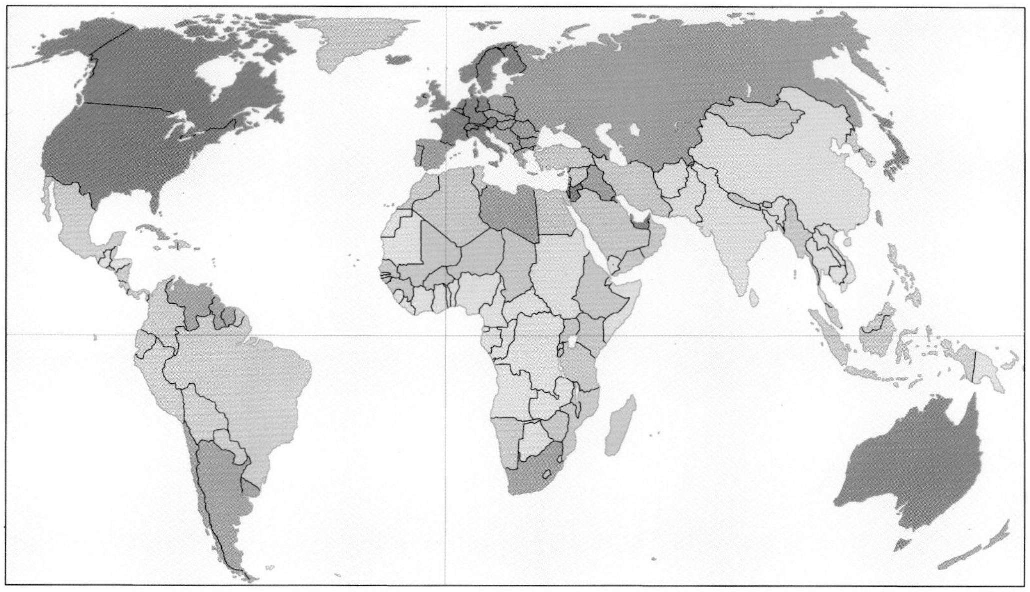

IMPORTANCE OF AGRICULTURE

Percentage of the total population dependent on agriculture (1989)

- Over 75%
- 50 - 75%
- 25 - 50%
- 10 - 25%
- Under 10%

Most dependent		**Least dependent**	
Nepal	91.5%	Singapore	1.0%
Burundi	91.4%	Hong Kong	1.3%
Bhutan	90.9%	Bahrain	1.8%
Niger	87.7%	Belgium[1]	1.9%
Burkina Faso	84.6%	UK	2.0%
Mozambique	81.9%	USA	2.4%
Mali	81.4%	UAE	2.7%
Tanzania	81.4%	Puerto Rico	3.0%

[1] includes Luxembourg

FOOD & POPULATION

Comparison of food production and population by continent (1989). The left column indicates percentage shares of total world food production; the right shows population in proportion.

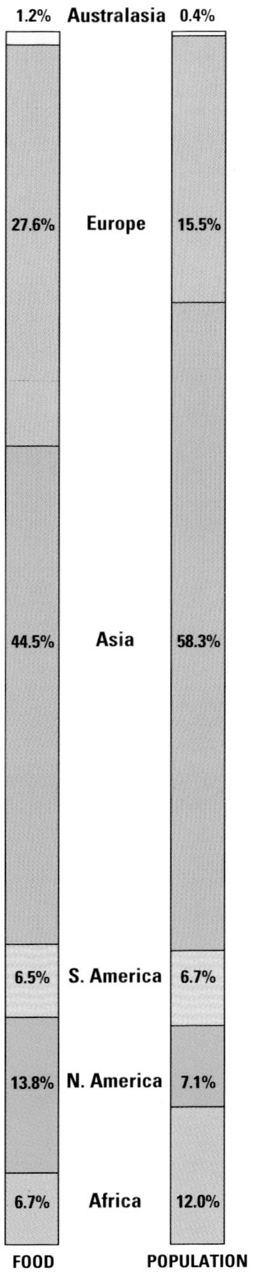
1.2% Australasia 0.4%
27.6% Europe 15.5%
44.5% Asia 58.3%
6.5% S. America 6.7%
13.8% N. America 7.1%
6.7% Africa 12.0%
FOOD
POPULATION

ANIMAL PRODUCTS

Separate figures for Russia, Ukraine and the other successors of the defunct USSR are not yet available

Traditionally, food animals subsisted on land unsuitable for cultivation, supporting agricultural production with their fertilizing dung. But free-ranging animals grow slowly and yield less meat than those more intensively reared; the demands of urban markets in the developed world have encouraged the growth of factory-like production methods. A large proportion of staple crops, especially cereals, are fed to animals, an inefficient way to produce protein but one likely to continue as long as people value meat and dairy products in their diet.

Cheese: Least perishable of all dairy products, cheese is milk fermented with selected bacterial strains to produce a foodstuff with a potentially immense range of flavours and textures. The vast majority of cheeses are made from cow's milk, although sheep and goat cheeses are highly prized.

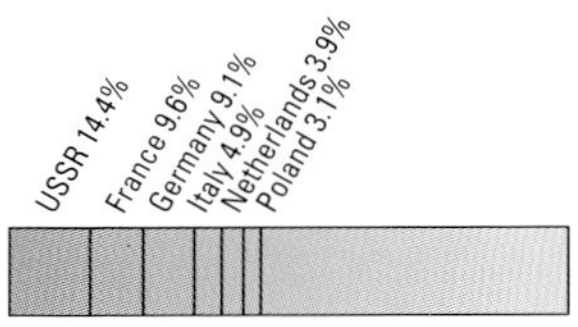
USSR 14.4%
France 9.6%
Germany 9.1%
Italy 4.9%
Netherlands 3.9%
Poland 3.1%

World total (1989): 14,475,276 tonnes

Lamb & Mutton: Sheep are the least demanding of domestic animals. Although unsuited to intensive rearing, they can thrive on marginal pastureland incapable of supporting beef cattle on a commercial scale. Sheep are raised as much for their valuable wool as for the meat that they provide, with Australia the world leader.

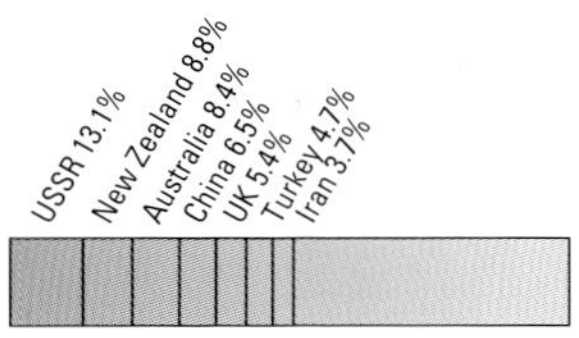
USSR 13.1%
New Zealand 8.8%
Australia 8.4%
China 6.5%
UK 5.4%
Turkey 4.7%
Iran 3.7%

World total (1989): 6,473,000 tonnes

Beef & Veal: Most beef and veal is reared for home markets, and the top five producers are also the biggest consumers. The USA produces nearly a quarter of the world's beef and eats even more. Australia, with its small domestic market, is by far the largest exporter.

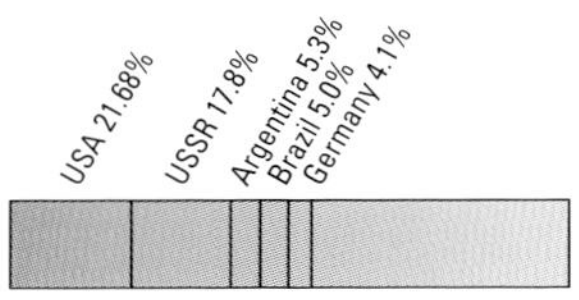
USA 21.68%
USSR 17.8%
Argentina 5.3%
Brazil 5.0%
Germany 4.1%

World total (1989): 49,436,000 tonnes

SUGARS

Sugar cane: Confined to tropical regions, cane sugar accounts for the bulk of international trade in the commodity. Most is produced as a foodstuff, but some countries, notably Brazil and South Africa, distill sugar cane and use the resulting ethyl alcohol to make motor fuels.

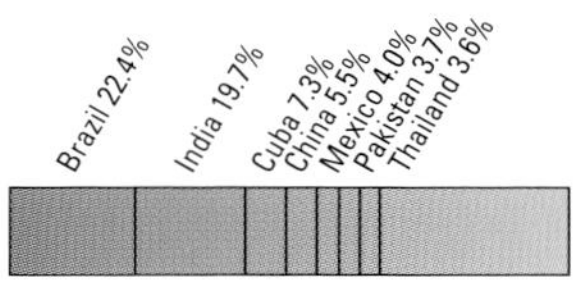
Brazil 22.4%
India 19.7%
Cuba 7.3%
China 5.5%
Mexico 4.0%
Pakistan 3.7%
Thailand 3.6%

World total (1989): 1,007,184,000 tonnes

Milk: Many human groups, including most Asians, find raw milk indigestible after infancy, and it is often only the starting point for other dairy products such as butter, cheese and yoghurt. Most world production comes from cows, but sheep's milk and goats' milk are also important.

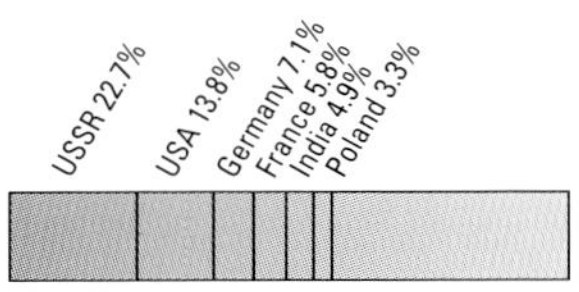
USSR 22.7%
USA 13.8%
Germany 7.1%
France 5.8%
India 4.9%
Poland 3.3%

World total (1989): 474,020,000 tonnes

Butter: A traditional source of vitamin A as well as calories, butter has lost much popularity in the developed world for health reasons, although it remains a valuable food. Most butter from India, the world's second-largest producer, is clarified into ghee, which has religious as well as nutritional importance.

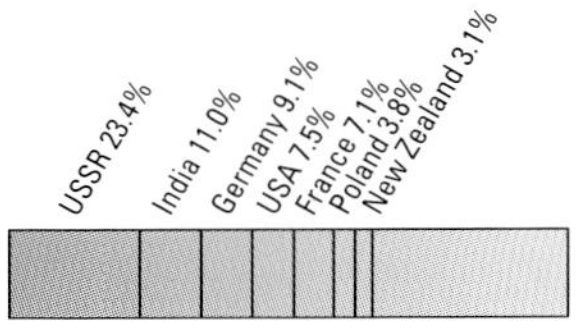
USSR 23.4%
India 11.0%
Germany 9.1%
USA 7.5%
France 7.1%
Poland 3.8%
New Zealand 3.1%

World total (1989): 7,611,826 tonnes

Pork: Although pork is forbidden to many millions, notably Muslims, on religious grounds, more is produced than any other meat in the world, mainly because it is the cheapest. It accounts for about 90% of China's meat output, although per capita meat consumption is relatively low.

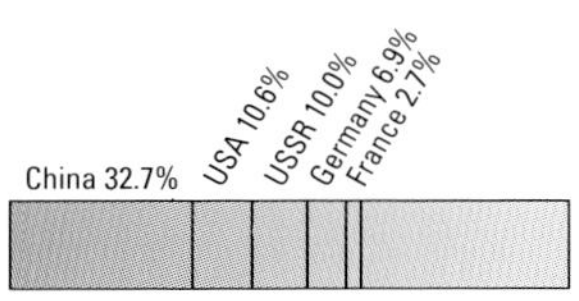
China 32.7%
USA 10.6%
USSR 10.0%
Germany 6.9%
France 2.7%

World total (1989): 67,460,000 tonnes

Fish: Commercial fishing requires large shoals of fish, often of only one species, within easy reach of markets. Although the great majority are caught wild in the sea, fish-farming of both marine and freshwater species is assuming increasing importance, especially as natural stocks become depleted.

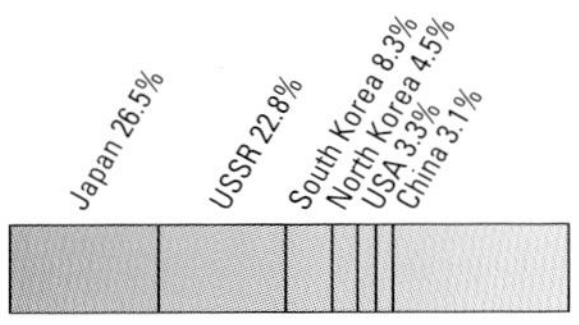
Japan 26.5%
USSR 22.8%
South Korea 8.3%
North Korea 4.5%
USA 3.3%
China 3.1%

World total (1989): 14,143,923 tonnes

Sugar beet: A temperate crop closely related to the humble beetroot, sugar beet's yield after processing is indistinguishable from cane sugar. Sugar beet is steadily replacing sugar cane imports in Europe, to the detriment of the developing countries that rely on it as a major cash crop.

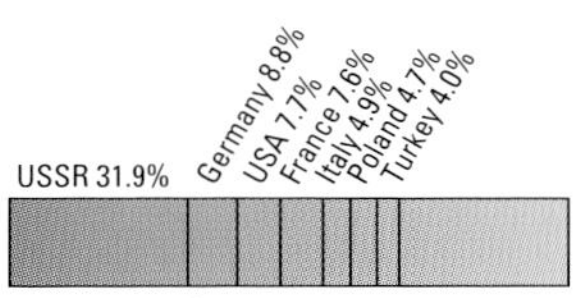
USSR 31.9%
Germany 8.8%
USA 7.7%
France 7.6%
Italy 4.9%
Poland 4.7%
Turkey 4.0%

World total (1989): 305,882,000 tonnes

PRODUCTION: ENERGY

39:	WORLD SHIPPING
46:	CARBON DIOXIDE GREENHOUSE POWER CO₂ PRODUCERS GLOBAL WARMING
47:	MARINE POLLUTION

We live in a high-energy civilization. While vast discrepancies exist between rich and poor – a North American consumes 13 times as much energy as a Chinese, for example – even developing nations have more power at their disposal than was imaginable a century ago. Abundant energy supplies keep us warm or cool, fuel our industries and our transport systems, even feed us: high-intensity agriculture, with its fertilizers, pesticides and machinery, is heavily energy-dependent.

Unfortunately, most of the world's energy comes from fossil fuels: coal, oil and gas deposits laid down over many millions of years. These are the Earth's capital, not its income, and we are consuming that capital at an alarming rate (see box, opposite). New discoveries have persistently extended the known reserves: in 1989, the reserves-to-production ratio for oil assured over 45 years' supply, an improvement of almost a decade on the 1970 situation. But despite the effort and ingenuity of prospectors, stocks are clearly limited. They are also very unequally distributed, with the Middle East accounting for most oil reserves, and the CIS, especially Russia,

possessing an even higher proportion of the world's natural gas. Coal reserves are more evenly shared, and also more plentiful: coal will outlast oil and gas by a very wide margin.

It is possible to reduce energy demand by improving efficiency: most industrial nations have dramatically increased output since the 1970s without a matching rise in energy consumption. But as fossil stocks continue to diminish, renewable energy sources – solar, wave and wind power, as well as more conventional hydro-electricity – must take on steadily greater importance.

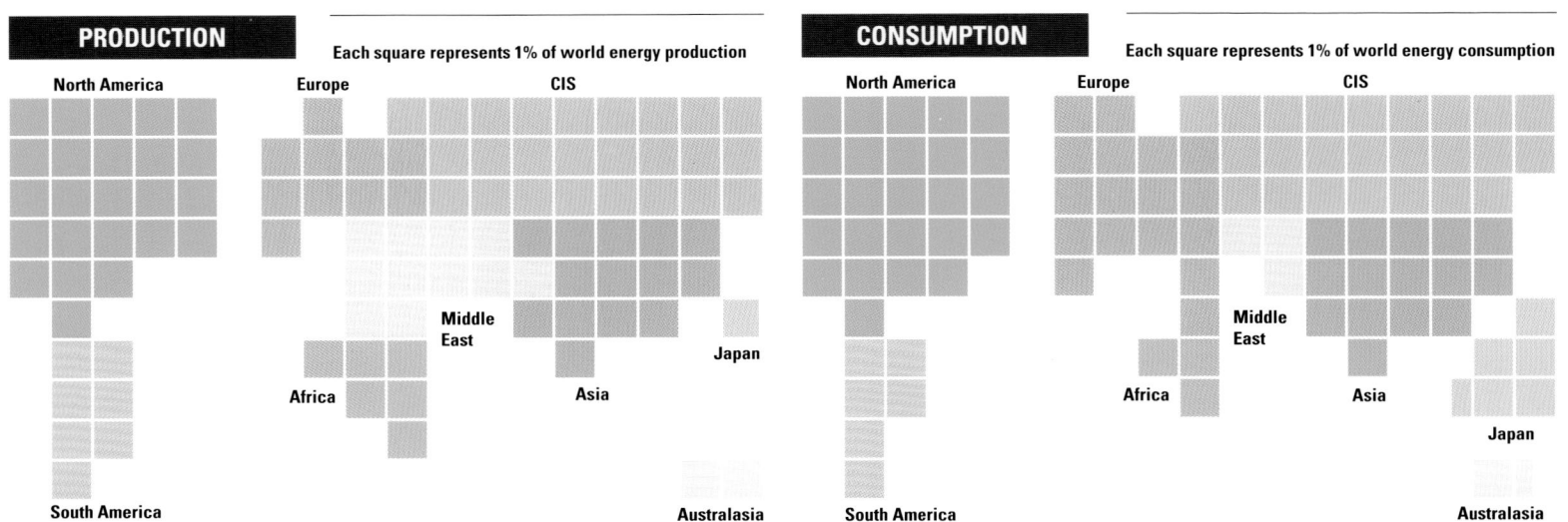

PRODUCTION — Each square represents 1% of world energy production

North America · Europe · CIS · Africa · Middle East · Asia · Japan · South America

CONSUMPTION — Each square represents 1% of world energy consumption

North America · Europe · CIS · Africa · Middle East · Asia · Japan · South America · Australasia

CONVERSIONS

For historical reasons, oil is still traded in barrels. The weight and volume equivalents shown below are all based on average density 'Arabian light' crude oil, and should be considered approximate.

The energy equivalents given for a tonne of oil are also somewhat imprecise: oil and coal of different qualities will have varying energy contents, a fact usually reflected in their price on world markets.

1 barrel:
0.136 tonnes
159 litres
35 Imperial gallons
42 US gallons

1 tonne:
7.33 barrels
1185 litres
256 Imperial gallons
261 US gallons

1 tonne oil:
1.5 tonnes hard coal
3.0 tonnes lignite
12,000 kWh

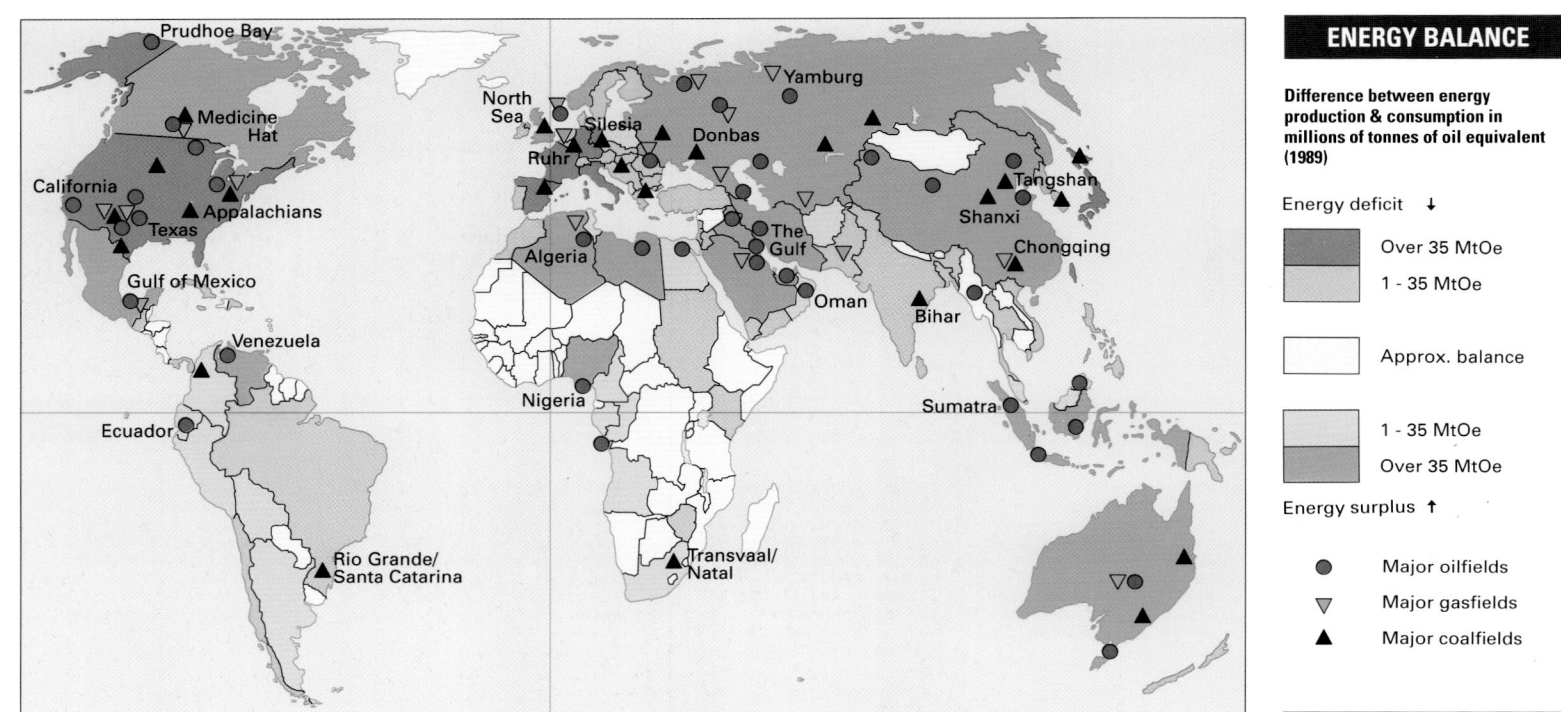

Prudhoe Bay · Medicine Hat · California · Appalachians · Texas · Gulf of Mexico · Venezuela · Ecuador · Rio Grande/Santa Catarina · North Sea · Ruhr · Silesia · Donbas · Algeria · The Gulf · Oman · Nigeria · Transvaal/Natal · Yamburg · Tangshan · Shanxi · Chongqing · Bihar · Sumatra

ENERGY BALANCE

Difference between energy production & consumption in millions of tonnes of oil equivalent (1989)

Energy deficit ↓
- Over 35 MtOe
- 1 – 35 MtOe

Approx. balance

Energy surplus ↑
- 1 – 35 MtOe
- Over 35 MtOe

- ● Major oilfields
- ▽ Major gasfields
- ▲ Major coalfields

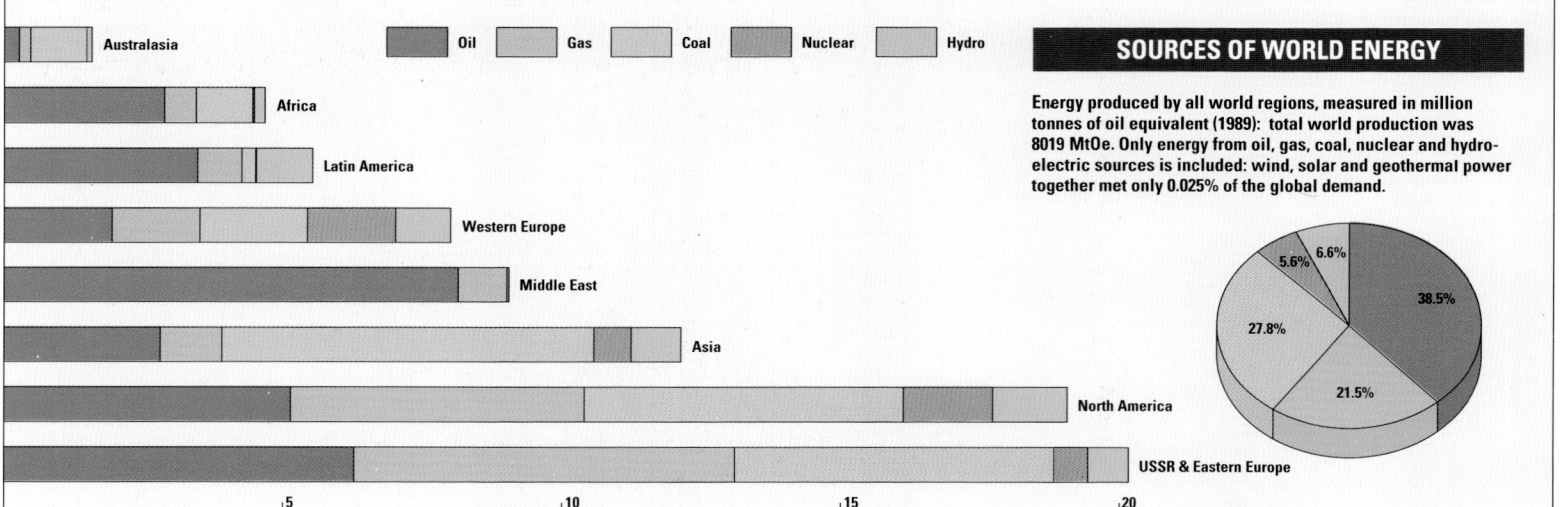

Oil · Gas · Coal · Nuclear · Hydro

Australasia · Africa · Latin America · Western Europe · Middle East · Asia · North America · USSR & Eastern Europe

5 · 10 · 15 · 20

SOURCES OF WORLD ENERGY

Energy produced by all world regions, measured in million tonnes of oil equivalent (1989): total world production was 8019 MtOe. Only energy from oil, gas, coal, nuclear and hydro-electric sources is included: wind, solar and geothermal power together met only 0.025% of the global demand.

38.5% · 21.5% · 27.8% · 5.6% · 6.6%

FOSSIL FUEL RESERVES

Known world reserves in years as a multiple of annual production, 1970, 1980 and 1989

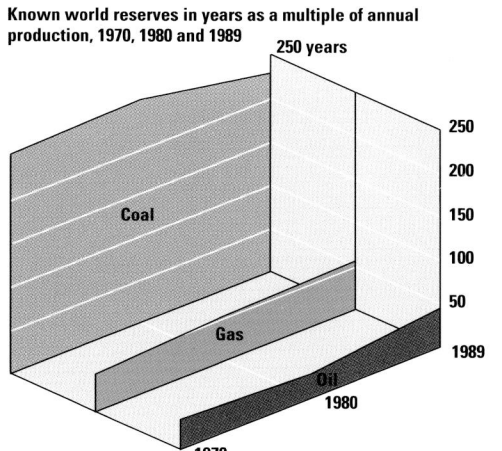

ENERGY AND OUTPUT

Tonnes of oil equivalent consumed to produce US $1000 of GDP, four industrial nations (1973-89)

Intensity of energy use is a rough indicator of efficiency: the 1973-4 oil crisis caused a dramatic improvement in each of the countries illustrated, although the USA remains relatively profligate. Reliable figures for Russia and the other republics of the former USSR are hard to obtain, but estimates suggest that for equivalent production they use up to four times as much energy as the USA.

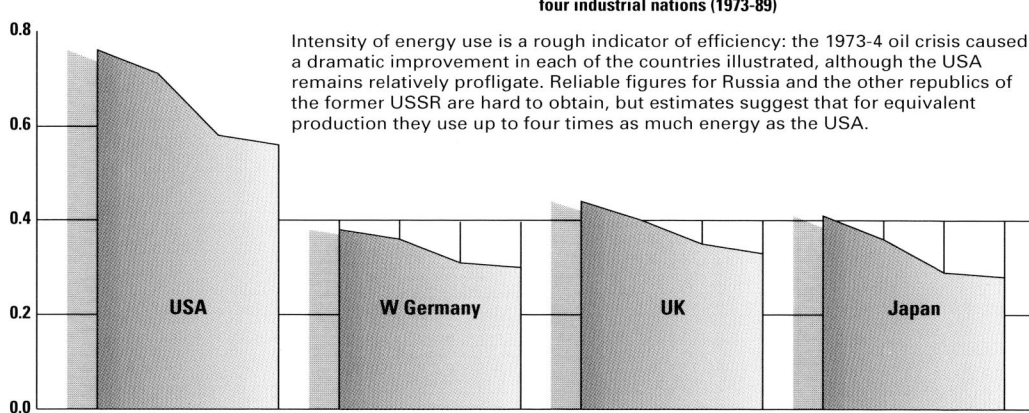

COAL RESERVES

World coal reserves by region & country, thousand million tonnes (1988)

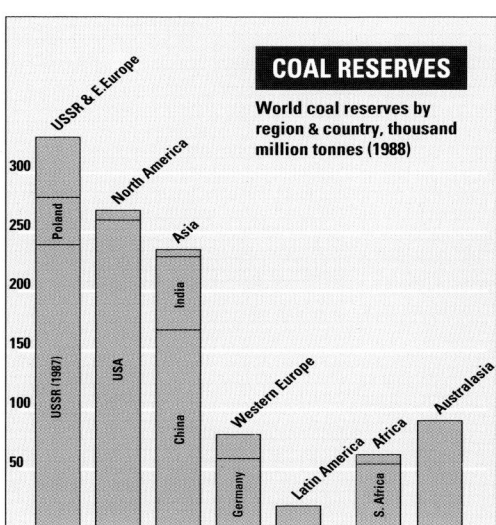

GAS RESERVES

World natural gas reserves by region & country, thousand million tonnes (1988)

Ca: Canada
In: Indonesia
Ma: Malaysia
AD: Abu Dhabi
SA: Saudi Arabia
Qa: Qatar
Iq: Iraq
No: Norway
Ne: Netherlands
Ve: Venezuela
Mx: Mexico
Al: Algeria
Ni: Nigeria

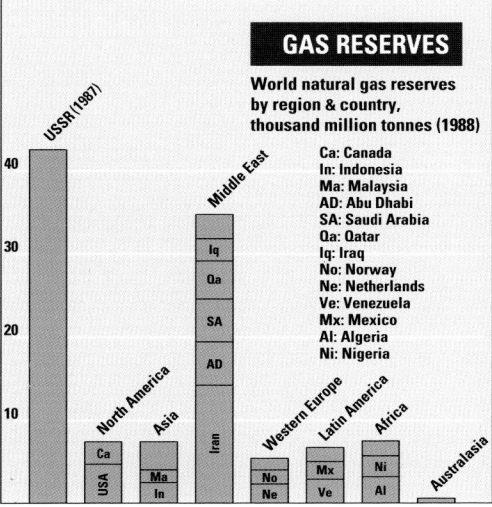

OIL RESERVES

World oil reserves by region & country, thousand million tonnes (1988)

AD: Abu Dhabi
Ve: Venezuela
Mx: Mexico

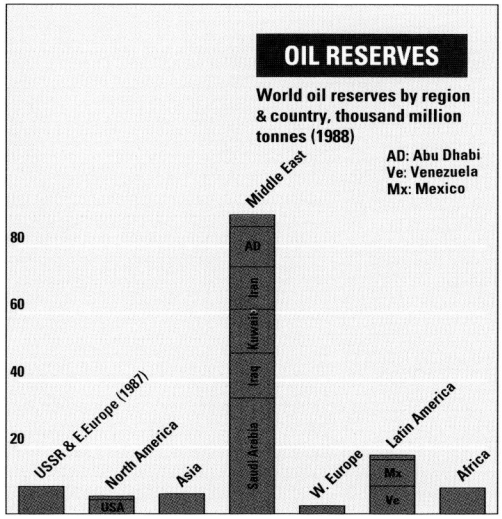

OIL MOVEMENTS

Major world movements of oil in millions of tonnes (1989)

Middle East to Western Europe	195.5
Middle East to Japan	150.0
Middle East to Asia (exc. Japan and China)	127.5
Latin America to USA	126.1
Middle East to USA	94.1
USSR to Western Europe	78.1
North Africa to Western Europe	93.5
West Africa to Western Europe	39.6
West Africa to USA	59.8
Canada to USA	45.0
South-East Asia to Japan	42.2
Latin America to Western Europe	28.7
Western Europe to USA	28.7
Middle East to Latin America	20.5

Total world movements: 1577 million tonnes

Only inter-regional movements in excess of 20 million tonnes are shown. Other Middle Eastern oil shipments throughout the world totalled 47.4 million tonnes; miscellaneous oil exports of the then USSR amounted to 88.8 million tonnes.

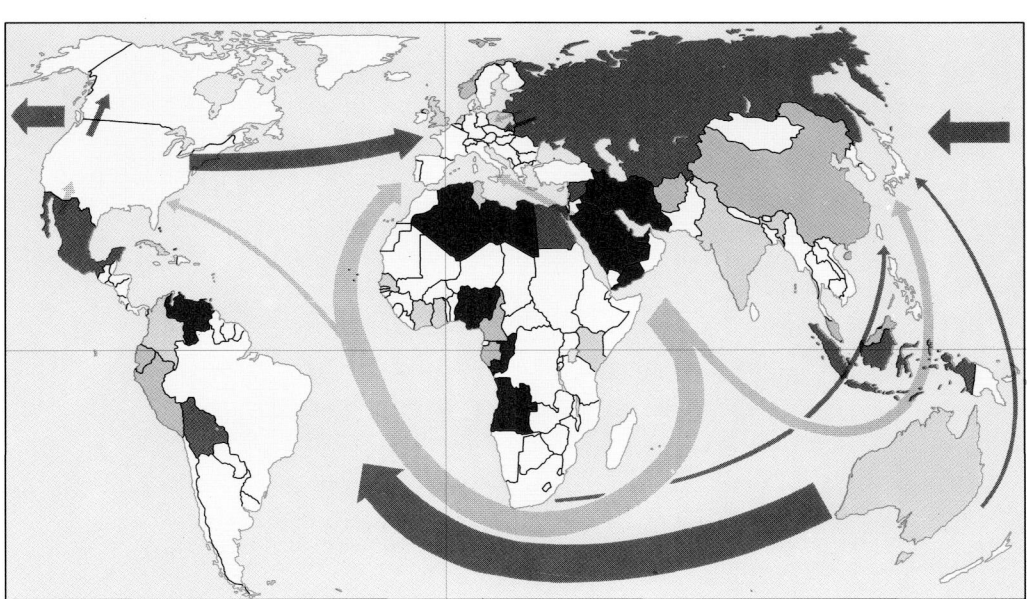

FUEL EXPORTS

Fuels as a percentage of total value of all exports (1986)

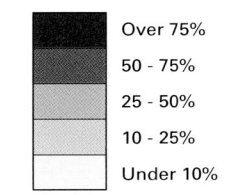

	Over 75%
	50 - 75%
	25 - 50%
	10 - 25%
	Under 10%

Direction of trade

Coal

Oil

Arrows show the major trade direction of selected fuels, & are proportional to export value

NUCLEAR POWER

Percentage of electricity generated by nuclear power stations, leading nations (1988)

1. France	70%	11. Germany (W)	34%
2. Belgium	66%	12. Japan	28%
3. Hungary	49%	13. Czechoslovakia	27%
4. South Korea	47%	14. UK	18%
5. Sweden	46%	15. USA	17%
6. Taiwan	41%	16. Canada	16%
7. Switzerland	37%	17. Argentina	12%
8. Finland	36%	18. USSR (1989)	11%
9. Spain	36%	19. Yugoslavia	6%
10. Bulgaria	36%	20. Netherlands	5%

The decade 1980-1990 was a bad time for the nuclear power industry. Major projects regularly ran vastly over-budget, and fears of long-term environmental damage were heavily reinforced by the 1986 Soviet disaster at Chernobyl. Although the number of reactors in service continued to increase throughout the period, orders for new plant shrank dramatically, and most countries cut back on their nuclear programmes.

HYDRO-ELECTRICITY

Percentage of electricity generated by hydro-electrical power stations, leading nations (1988)

1. Paraguay	99.9%	11. Laos	95.5%
2. Zambia	99.6%	12. Nepal	95.2%
3. Norway	99.5%	13. Iceland	94.0%
4. Congo	99.1%	14. Uruguay	93.0%
5. Costa Rica	98.3%	15. Brazil	91.7%
6. Uganda	98.3%	16. Albania	87.2%
7. Rwanda	97.7%	17. Fiji	81.4%
8. Malawi	97.6%	18. Ecuador	80.7%
9. Zaïre	97.4%	19. C. African Rep.	80.4%
10. Cameroon	97.2%	20. Sri Lanka	80.4%

Countries heavily reliant on hydro-electricity are usually small and non-industrial: a high proportion of hydro-electric power more often reflects a modest energy budget than vast hydro-electric resources. The USA, for instance, produces only 8% of power requirements from hydro-electricity; yet that 8% amounts to more than three times the hydro-power generated by all of Africa.

ALTERNATIVE ENERGY SOURCES

Solar: Each year the sun bestows upon the Earth almost a million times as much energy as is locked up in all the planet's oil reserves, but only an insignificant fraction is trapped and used commercially. In some experimental installations, mirrors focus the sun's rays on to boilers, whose steam generates electricity by spinning turbines. Solar cells turn the sunlight into electricity directly, and although efficiencies are still low, advancing technology offers some prospect of using the sun as the main world electricity source by 2100.

Wind: Caused by uneven heating of the Earth, winds are themselves a form of solar energy. Windmills have been used for centuries to turn wind power into mechanical work; recent models, often arranged in banks on gust-swept high ground, usually generate electricity.

Tidal: The energy from tides is potentially enormous, although only a few installations have been built to exploit it. In theory at least, waves and currents could also provide almost unimaginable power, and the thermal differences in the ocean depths are another huge well of potential energy. But work on extracting it is still in the experimental stage.

Geothermal: The Earth's temperature rises by 1°C for every 30 metres' descent, with much steeper temperature gradients in geologically active areas. El Salvador, for example, produces 39% of its electricity from geothermal power stations. More than 130 are operating worldwide.

Biomass: The oldest of human fuels ranges from animal dung, still burned in cooking fires in much of North Africa and elsewhere, to sugar cane plantations feeding high-technology distilleries to produce ethanol for motor vehicle engines. In Brazil and South Africa, plant ethanol provides up to 25% of motor fuel. Throughout the developing world most biomass energy comes from firewood: although accurate figures are impossible to obtain, it may yield as much as 10% of the world's total energy consumption.

PRODUCTION: MINERALS

19: GEOLOGY

37: PATTERNS OF PRODUCTION

39: WORLD SHIPPING

Even during the Stone Age, when humans often settled near the outcrops of flint on which their technology depended, mineral resources have attracted human exploiters. Their descendants have learned how to make use of almost every known element. These elements can be found, in one form or another, somewhere in the Earth's bountiful crust. Iron remains the most important, but modern industrial civilization has a voracious appetite for virtually all of them.

Mineral deposits once dictated the site of new industries; today, most industrial countries are heavily dependent on imports for many of their key materials. Most mining, and much refining of raw ores, is done in developing countries, where labour is cheap.

The main map below shows the richest sources of the most important minerals at present; some reserves – lead and mercury, for example – are running very low. The map takes no account of undersea deposits, most of which are considered inaccessible. Growing shortages, though, may encourage submarine mining: plans have already been made to recover the nodules of manganese found widely scattered on ocean floors.

MINERAL EXPORTS

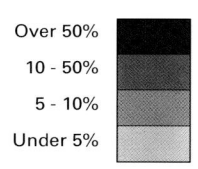

Minerals & metals as a percentage of total exports (1986)

Over 50%

10 - 50%

5 - 10%

Under 5%

Direction of trade

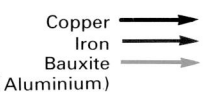

Copper

Iron

Bauxite (Aluminium)

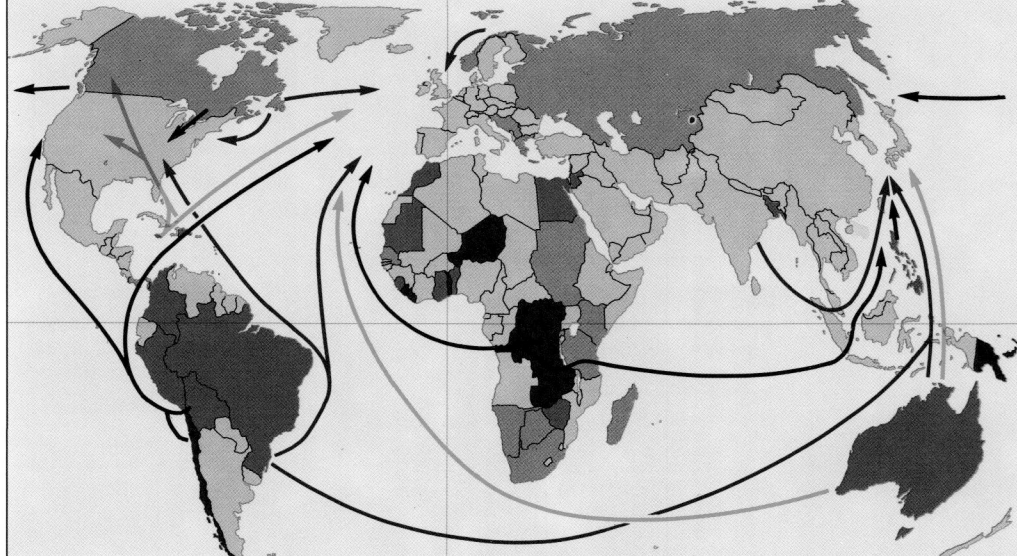

URANIUM

In its pure state, uranium is an immensely heavy, white metal; but although spent uranium is employed as projectiles in anti-missile cannon, where its mass ensures a lethal punch, its main use is as a fuel in nuclear reactors, and in nuclear weaponry. Uranium is very scarce: the main source is the rare ore pitchblende, which itself contains only 0.2% uranium oxide. Only a minute fraction of that is the radioactive U^{235} isotope, though so-called breeder reactors can transmute the more common U^{238} into highly radioactive plutonium.

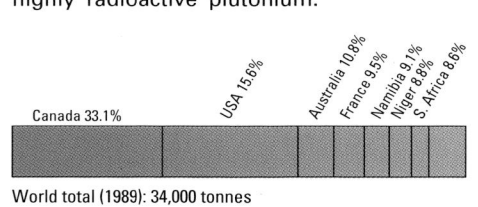

Canada 33.1% | USA 15.6% | Australia 10.8% | France 9.5% | Namibia 9.1% | Niger 8.9% | S. Africa 8.6%

World total (1989): 34,000 tonnes

METALS

Separate figures for Russia, Ukraine and the other successors of the defunct USSR are not as yet available

Aluminium: Produced mainly from its oxide, bauxite, which yields 25% of its weight in aluminium. The cost of refining and production is often too high for producer-countries to bear, so bauxite is largely exported. Lightweight and corrosion resistant, aluminium alloys are widely used in aircraft, vehicles, cans and packaging.

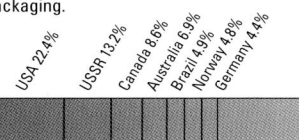

USA 22.4% | USSR 13.2% | Canada 8.6% | Australia 6.9% | Brazil 4.9% | Norway 4.8% | Germany 4.3%

World total (1989): 18,000,000 tonnes*

Copper: Derived from low-yielding sulphide ores, copper is an important export for several developing countries. An excellent conductor of heat and electricity, it forms part of most electrical items, and is used in the manufacture of brass and bronze. Major importers include Japan and Germany.

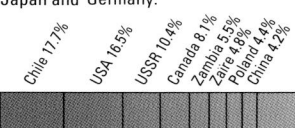

Chile 17.7% | USA 16.5% | USSR 10.4% | Canada 8.1% | Zambia 5.5% | Zaire 4.8% | Poland 4.4% | China 4.2%

World total (1989): 9,100,000 tonnes*

Lead: A soft metal, obtained mainly from galena (lead sulphide), which occurs in veins associated with iron, zinc and silver sulphides. Its use in vehicle batteries accounts for the USA's prime consumer status; lead is also made into sheeting and piping. Its use as an additive to paints and petrol is decreasing.

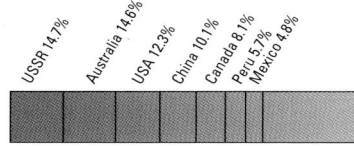

USSR 14.7% | Australia 14.6% | USA 12.3% | China 10.1% | Canada 8.1% | Peru 5.7% | Mexico 4.8%

World total (1989): 3,400,000 tonnes*

Mercury: The only metal that is liquid at normal temperatures, most is derived from its sulphide, cinnabar, found only in small quantities in volcanic areas. Apart from its value in thermometers and other instruments, most mercury production is used in anti-fungal and anti-fouling preparations, and to make detonators.

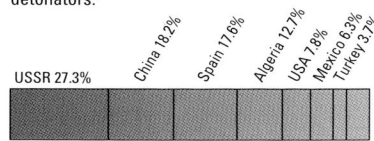

USSR 27.3% | China 18.2% | Spain 17.6% | Algeria 12.7% | USA 7.8% | Mexico 6.3% | Turkey 3.7%

World total (1989): 5,500,000 kilograms*

DIAMOND

Most diamond is found in kimberlite, or "blue ground", a basic peridotite rock; erosion may wash the diamond from its kimerlite matrix and deposit it with sand or gravel on river beds. Only a small proportion of the world's diamond, the most flawless, is cut into gemstones - "diamonds"; most is used in industry, where the material's remarkable hardness and abrasion resistance finds a use in cutting tools, drills and dies, as well as in styluses. Australia, not among the top 12 producers at the beginning of the 1980s, had by 1986 become world leader and by 1989 was the source of 37.5% of world production. The other main producers were Zaire (18.9%), Botswana (16.3%), then USSR (11.8%) and South Africa (9.7%). Between them, these five nations accounted for over 94% of the world total of 96,600,000 carats - at 0.2 grams per carat, almost one tonne.

Tin: Soft, pliable and non-toxic, used to coat 'tin' (tin-plated steel) cans, in the manufacture of foils and in alloys. The principal tin-bearing mineral is cassiterite (SnO_2), found in ore formed from molten rock. Producers and refiners were hit by a price collapse in 1991.

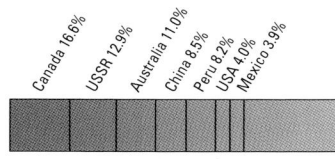

Brazil 22.5% | China 14.8% | Malaysia 14.4% | Indonesia 14.2% | Bolivia 7.1% | Thailand 6.6% | USSR 6.3%

World total (1989): 223,000 tonnes*

Zinc: Often found in association with lead ores, zinc is highly resistant to corrosion, and about 40% of the refined metal is used to plate sheet steel, particularly vehicle bodies – a process known as galvanizing. Zinc is also used in dry batteries, paints and dyes.

Canada 16.6% | USSR 12.9% | Australia 11.0% | China 8.5% | Peru 8.2% | USA 4.0% | Mexico 3.9%

World total (1989): 7,300,000 tonnes*

Gold: Regarded for centuries as the most valuable metal in the world and used to make coins, gold is still recognized as the monetary standard. A soft metal, it is alloyed to make jewellery; the electronics industry values its corrosion resistance and conductivity.

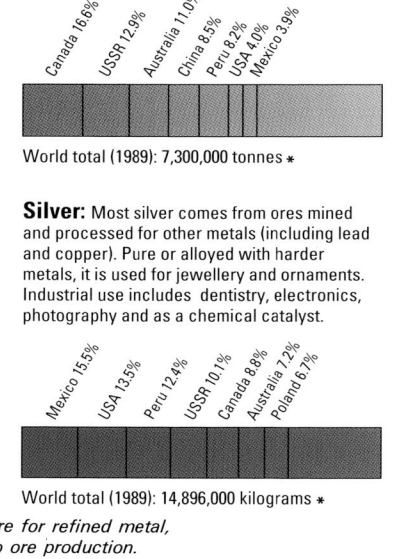

S. Africa 29.9% | USSR 14.1% | USA 13.1% | Australia 10.0% | Canada 7.9% | China 4.2% | Brazil 2.4%

World total (1989): 2,026,000 kilograms*

Silver: Most silver comes from ores mined and processed for other metals (including lead and copper). Pure or alloyed with harder metals, it is used for jewellery and ornaments. Industrial use includes dentistry, electronics, photography and as a chemical catalyst.

Mexico 15.5% | USA 13.5% | Peru 12.4% | USSR 10.1% | Canada 8.8% | Australia 7.2% | Poland 6.7%

World total (1989): 14,896,000 kilograms*

Figures for aluminium are for refined metal, all other figures refer to ore production.

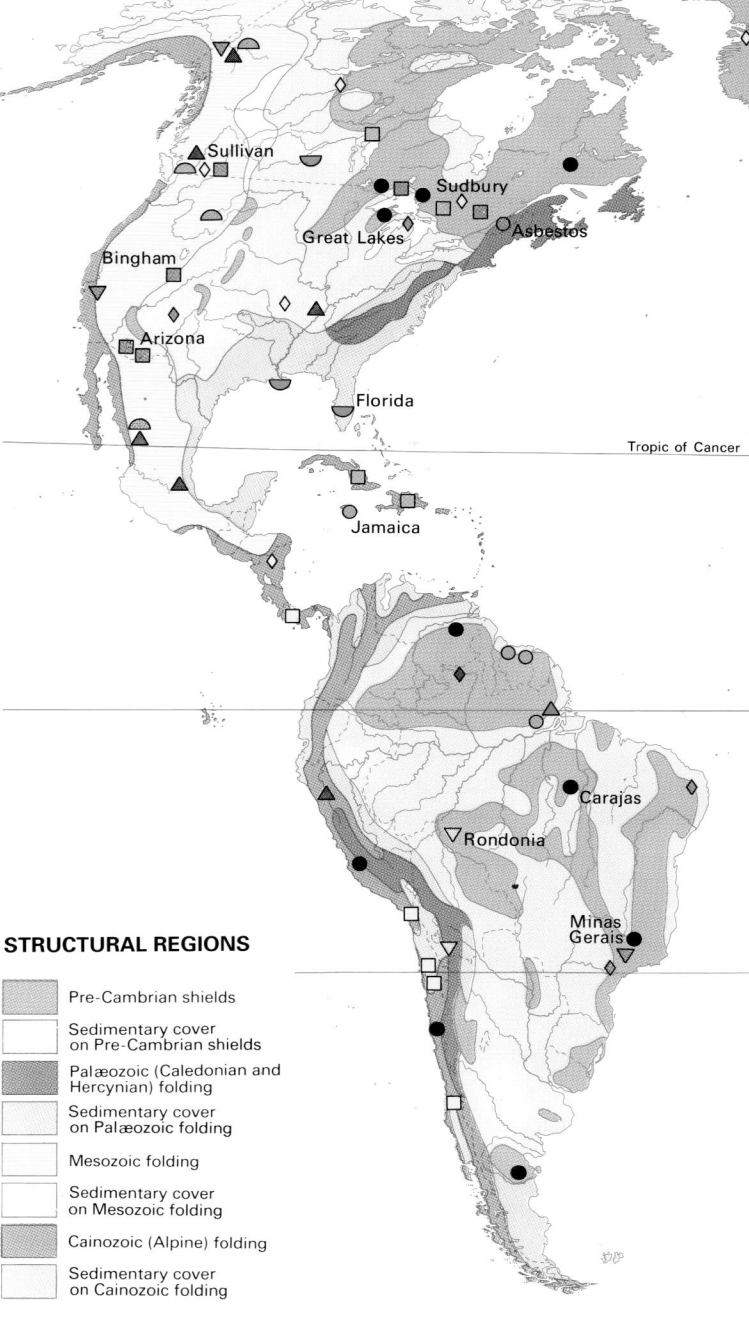

STRUCTURAL REGIONS

Pre-Cambrian shields

Sedimentary cover on Pre-Cambrian shields

Palæozoic (Caledonian and Hercynian) folding

Sedimentary cover on Palæozoic folding

Mesozoic folding

Sedimentary cover on Mesozoic folding

Cainozoic (Alpine) folding

Sedimentary cover on Cainozoic folding

Tropic of Cancer

Sullivan

Sudbury

Great Lakes

Asbestos

Bingham

Arizona

Florida

Jamaica

Carajas

Rondonia

Minas Gerais

IRON & FERRO-ALLOYS

Ever since the art of high-temperature smelting was discovered, some time in the second millennium BC, iron has been by far the most important metal known to man. The earliest iron ploughs transformed primitive agriculture and led to the first human population explosion, while iron weapons - or the lack of them - ensured the rise or fall of entire cultures.

Widely distributed around the world, iron ores usually contain 25-60% iron; blast furnaces process the raw product into pig-iron, which is then alloyed with carbon and other minerals to produce steels of various qualities. From the time of the Industrial Revolution steel has been almost literally the backbone of modern civilization, the prime structural material on which all else is built.

Iron-smelting usually developed close to sources of ore and, later, to the coalfields that fueled the furnaces. Today, most ore comes from a few richly-endowed locations where large-scale mining is possible. Iron and steel plants are generally built at coastal sites so that giant ore carriers, which account for a sizeable proportion of the world's merchant fleet, can easily discharge their cargoes.

World production of pig iron and ferro-alloys (1988). All countries with an annual output of more than one million tonnes are shown

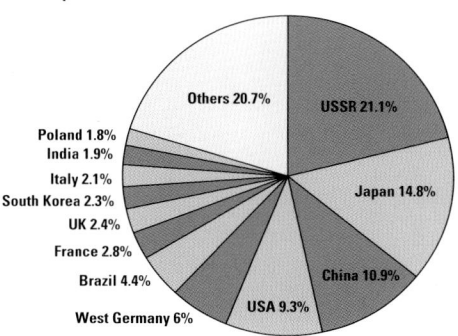

Others 20.7%
USSR 21.1%
Japan 14.8%
China 10.9%
USA 9.3%
West Germany 6%
Brazil 4.4%
France 2.8%
UK 2.4%
South Korea 2.3%
Italy 2.1%
India 1.9%
Poland 1.8%

Total world production: 545 million tonnes

Development of world production of pig iron and ferro-alloys (1945-1988) in million tonnes

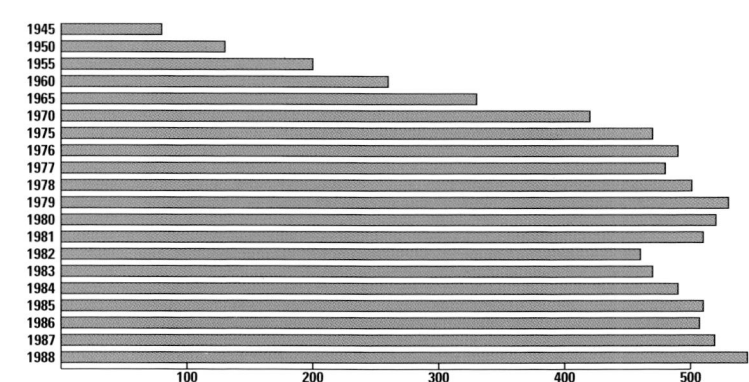

Chromium: Most of the world's chromium production is alloyed with iron and other metals to produce steels with various different properties. Combined with iron, nickel, cobalt and tungsten, chromium produces an exceptionally hard steel, resistant to heat; chrome steels are used for many household items where utility must be matched with appearance - cutlery, for example. Chromium is also used in production of refractory bricks, and its salts for tanning and dyeing leather and cloth.

Manganese: In its pure state, manganese is a hard, brittle metal. Alloyed with chrome, iron and nickel, it produces abrasion-resistant steels; manganese-aluminium alloys are light but tough. Found in batteries and inks, manganese is also used in glass production. Manganese ores are frequently found in the same location as sedimentary iron ores. Pyrolusite (MnO_2) and psilomelane are the main economically-exploitable sources.

Nickel: Combined with chrome and iron, nickel produces stainless and high-strength steels; similar alloys go to make magnets and electrical heating elements. Nickel combined with copper is widely used to make coins; cupro-nickel alloy is very resistant to corrosion. Its ores yield only modest quantities of nickel - 0.5 to 3.0% - but also contain copper, iron and small amounts of precious metals. Japan, the USA, the UK, Germany and France are the principal importers.

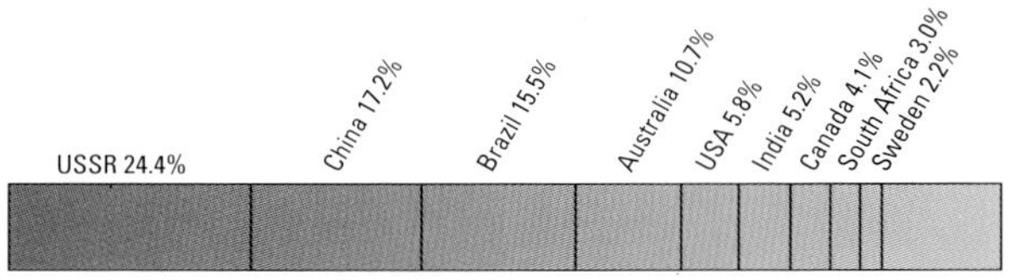

USSR 24.4% | China 17.2% | Brazil 15.5% | Australia 10.7% | USA 5.8% | India 5.2% | Canada 4.1% | South Africa 3.0% | Sweden 2.2%

World total production of iron ore (1989): 989,000,000 tonnes

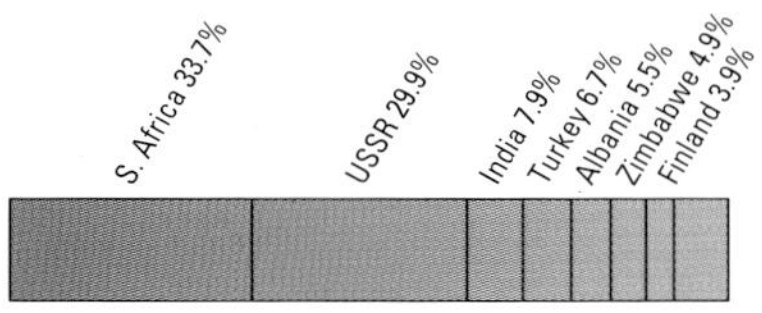

S. Africa 33.7% | USSR 29.9% | India 7.9% | Turkey 6.7% | Albania 5.5% | Zimbabwe 4.9% | Finland 3.9%

World total (1989): 12,700,000 tonnes

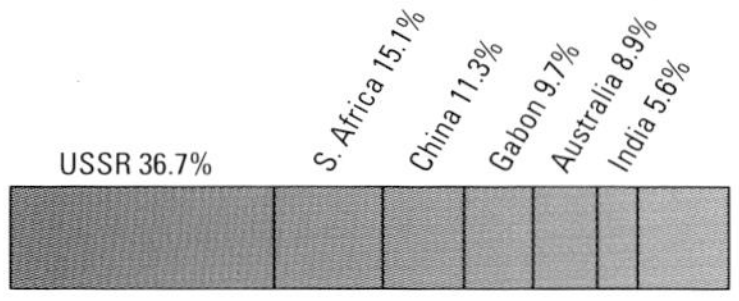

USSR 36.7% | S. Africa 15.1% | China 11.3% | Gabon 9.7% | Australia 8.9% | India 5.6%

World total (1989): 24,000,000 tonnes

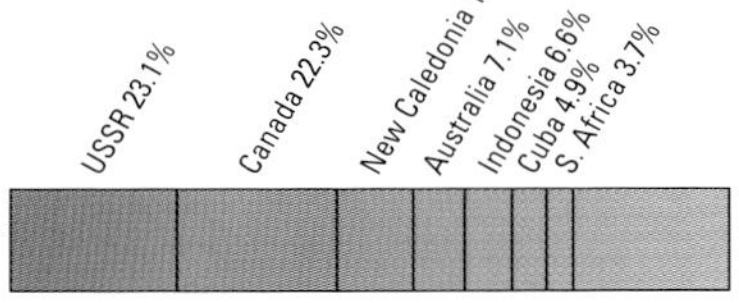

USSR 23.1% | Canada 22.3% | New Caledonia 10.6% | Australia 7.1% | Indonesia 6.0% | Cuba 4.9% | S. Africa 3.7%

World total (1989): 910,000 tonnes

DISTRIBUTION

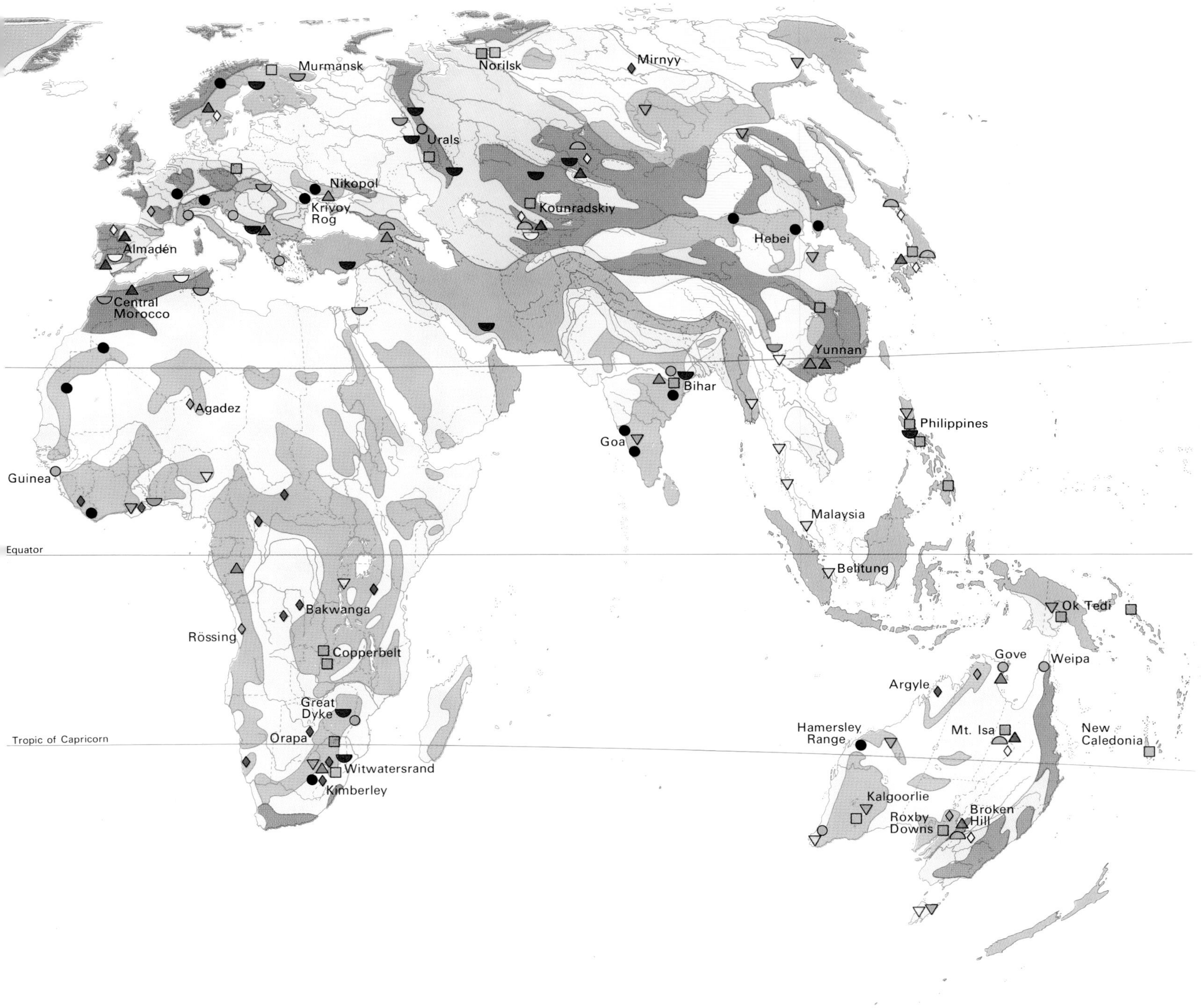

Base metals
- ▢ Copper
- ▲ Lead
- ▽ Mercury
- ▽ Tin
- ◇ Zinc

Iron and ferro-alloys
- ● Iron
- ◗ Chrome
- ▢ Nickel
- ▲ Manganese

Light metals
- ◉ Bauxite

Rare metals
- ◇ Uranium

Precious metals
- ▽ Gold
- ⌂ Silver

Precious stones
- ◆ Diamonds

Mineral fertilizers
- ⌁ Phosphates

Industrial minerals
- ◉ Asbestos

Map labels: Murmansk, Norilsk, Mirnyy, Urals, Nikopol, Krivoy Rog, Kounradskiy, Hebei, Almadén, Central Morocco, Agadez, Yunnan, Bihar, Goa, Philippines, Malaysia, Belitung, Guinea, Equator, Bakwanga, Rössing, Copperbelt, Great Dyke, Orapa, Tropic of Capricorn, Witwatersrand, Kimberley, Ok Tedi, Gove, Weipa, Argyle, Hamersley Range, Mt. Isa, New Caledonia, Kalgoorlie, Roxby Downs, Broken Hill

PRODUCTION: MANUFACTURING

16: WATER UTILIZATION

30: LAND USE & ECONOMY

34: MINERAL PRODUCTION

35: IRON & FERRO-ALLOYS

38: TRADING NATIONS
    MAJOR EXPORTS
    TRADED PRODUCTS

In its broadest sense, manufacturing is the application of energy, labour and skill to raw materials in order to transform them into finished goods with a higher value than the various elements used in production.

Since the early days of the Industrial Revolution, manufacturing has implied the use of an organized workforce harnessed to some form of machine. The tendency has consistently been for increasingly expensive human labour to be replaced by increasingly complex machinery, which has evolved over time from water-powered looms to fully-integrated robotic plants.

Obviously, not all industries – or manufacturing countries - have reached the same level. Textiles, for example, the foundation of the early industrial revolution in the West, can be mass-produced with fairly modest technology; today, they are usually produced in developing countries, mostly in Asia, where low labour costs compensate for the large workforce the relatively simple machinery requires. Nevertheless, the trend towards high-technology production, however uneven, seems inexorable. Gains in efficiency make up for the staggering cost of the equipment itself, and the outcome is that fewer and fewer people are employed to produce more and more goods.

One paradoxical result of the increase in industrial efficiency is a relative decline in the importance of the industrial sector of a nation's economy. The economy has already passed through one transition, generations past, when workers were drawn from the land into factories. The second transition releases labour into what is called the service sector of the economy: a diffuse but vital concept that includes not only such obvious services as transport and administration, but also finance, insurance and activities as diverse as fashion design or the writing of computer software.

The process is far advanced in the mature economies of the West, with Japan not far behind. Almost two-thirds of US wealth, for example, is now generated in the service sector, and less than half of Japanese Gross National Product comes from industry. The shrinkage, though, is only relative: between them, these two industrial giants produce almost twice as much manufactured goods as the rest of the world put together. And it is on the solid base of production that their general prosperity is founded.

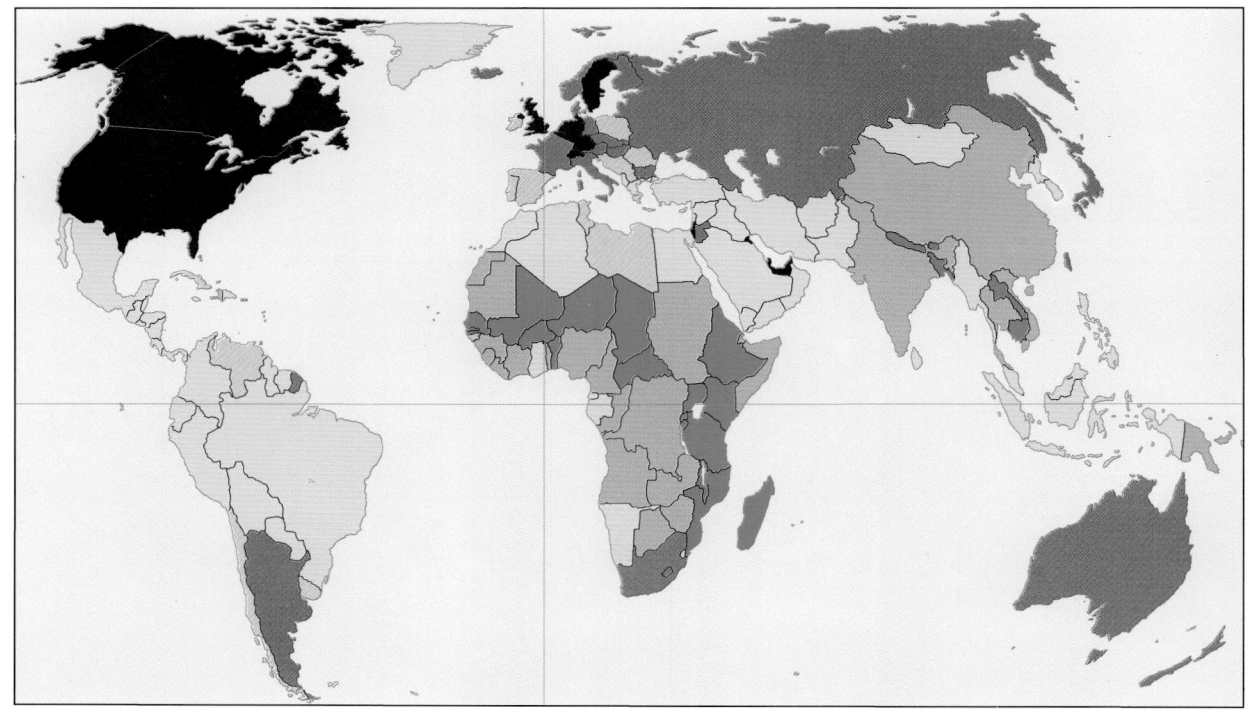

EMPLOYMENT

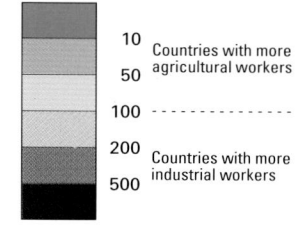

The number of workers employed in manufacturing for every 100 workers engaged in agriculture

10
50 — Countries with more agricultural workers
100 - - - - - - - - - -
200
500 — Countries with more industrial workers

Selected countries (latest available figure, 1986-1989)

Singapore	6,166
Hong Kong	2,632
UK	912
Belgium	751
Germany (W)	749
USA	641
Sweden	615
France	331
Japan	320
Czechoslovakia	286

DIVISION OF EMPLOYMENT

Distribution of workers between agriculture, industry and services, selected countries (late 1980s)

The six countries selected illustrate the usual stages of economic development, from dependence on agriculture through industrial growth to the expansion of the services sector.

- Agriculture
- Industry
- Services

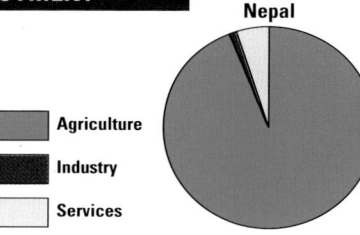 Nepal
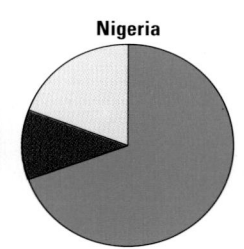 Nigeria
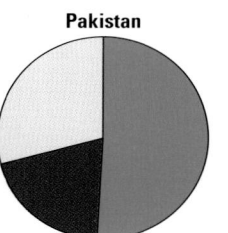 Pakistan
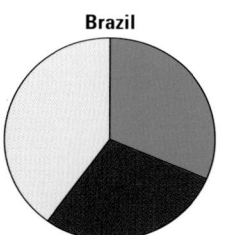 Brazil
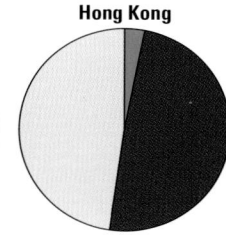 Hong Kong
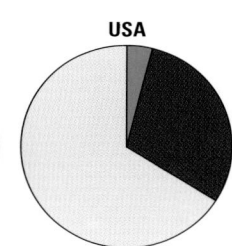 USA

THE WORKFORCE

Percentages of men and women between 15 and 64 in employment, selected countries (late 1980s)

The figures include employees and self-employed, who in developing countries are often subsistence farmers. People in full-time education are excluded. Because of the population age structure in developing countries, the employed population has to support a far larger number of non-workers than its industrial equivalent. For example, more than 52% of Kenya's people are under 15, an age group that makes up less than a tenth of the UK population.

Men   Women

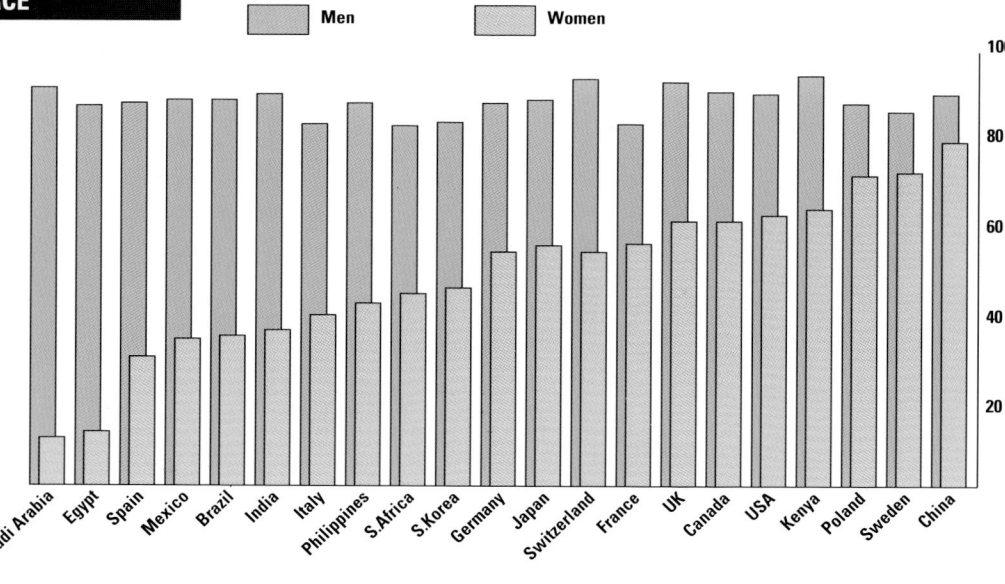

Saudi Arabia, Egypt, Spain, Mexico, Brazil, India, Italy, Philippines, S.Africa, S.Korea, Germany, Japan, Switzerland, France, UK, Canada, USA, Kenya, Poland, Sweden, China

WEALTH CREATION

The Gross National Product (GNP) of the world's largest economies, US $ billion (1989)

1.	USA	5,237,707	21.	Denmark	105,263
2.	Japan	2,920,310	22.	Norway	92,097
3.	Germany	1,272,959	23.	Saudi Arabia	89,986
4.	France	1,000,866	24.	Indonesia	87,936
5.	Italy	871,955	25.	South Africa	86,029
6.	UK	834,166	26.	Turkey	74,731
7.	Canada	500,337	27.	Argentina	68,780
8.	China	393,006	28.	Poland	66,974
9.	Brazil	375,146	29.	Thailand	64,437
10.	Spain	358,352	30.	Hong Kong	59,202
11.	India	287,383	31.	Yugoslavia	59,080
12.	Australia	242,131	32.	Greece	53,626
13.	Netherlands	237,451	33.	Algeria	53,116
14.	Switzerland	197,984	34.	Venezuela	47,164
15.	South Korea	186,467	35.	Israel	44,131
16.	Sweden	184,230	36.	Portugal	44,058
17.	Mexico	170,053	37.	Philippines	42,754
18.	Belgium	162,026	38.	Pakistan	40,134
19.	Austria	131,899	39.	New Zealand	39,437
20.	Finland	109,705	40.	Colombia	38,607

There are no accurate figures available for either the USSR or its successor nations.

PATTERNS OF PRODUCTION

Breakdown of industrial output by value, selected countries (1987)

	Food & agriculture	Textiles & clothing	Machinery & transport	Chemicals	Other
Algeria	26%	20%	11%	1%	41%
Argentina	24%	10%	16%	12%	37%
Australia	18%	7%	21%	8%	45%
Austria	17%	8%	25%	6%	43%
Belgium	19%	8%	23%	13%	36%
Brazil	15%	12%	24%	9%	40%
Burkina Faso	62%	18%	2%	1%	17%
Canada	15%	7%	25%	9%	44%
Denmark	22%	6%	23%	10%	39%
Egypt	20%	27%	13%	10%	31%
Finland	13%	6%	24%	7%	50%
France	18%	7%	33%	9%	33%
Germany	12%	5%	38%	10%	36%
Greece	20%	22%	14%	7%	38%
Hong Kong	6%	40%	20%	2%	33%
Hungary	6%	11%	37%	11%	35%
India	11%	16%	26%	15%	32%
Indonesia	23%	11%	10%	10%	47%
Iran	13%	22%	22%	7%	36%
Israel	13%	10%	28%	8%	42%
Ireland	28%	7%	20%	15%	28%
Italy	7%	13%	32%	10%	38%
Japan	10%	6%	38%	10%	37%
Kenya	35%	12%	14%	9%	29%
Malaysia	21%	5%	23%	14%	37%
Mexico	24%	12%	14%	12%	39%
Netherlands	19%	4%	28%	11%	38%
New Zealand	26%	10%	16%	6%	43%
Norway	21%	3%	26%	7%	44%
Pakistan	34%	21%	8%	12%	25%
Philippines	40%	7%	7%	10%	35%
Poland	15%	16%	30%	6%	33%
Portugal	17%	22%	16%	8%	38%
Singapore	6%	5%	46%	8%	36%
South Africa	14%	8%	17%	11%	49%
South Korea	15%	17%	24%	9%	35%
Spain	17%	9%	22%	9%	43%
Sweden	10%	2%	35%	8%	44%
Thailand	30%	17%	14%	6%	33%
Turkey	20%	14%	15%	8%	43%
UK	14%	6%	32%	11%	36%
USA	12%	5%	35%	10%	38%
Venezuela	23%	8%	9%	11%	49%
Yugoslavia	13%	17%	25%	6%	39%

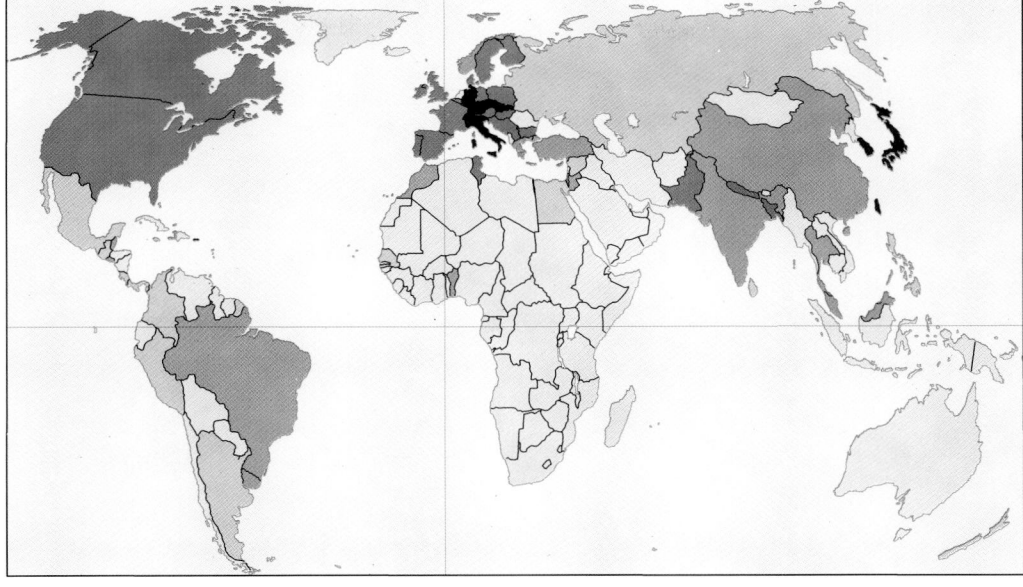

INDUSTRY & TRADE

Manufactured goods as a percentage of total exports (1989)

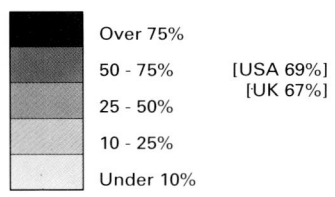

- Over 75%
- 50 – 75% [USA 69%] [UK 67%]
- 25 – 50%
- 10 – 25%
- Under 10%

The Far East & South-East Asia (Japan 99.5%, Macau 98.5%, Taiwan 96.8%, Hong Kong 96.1%, S. Korea 95.9%) is most dominant, but many countries in Europe (eg Austria 98.4%) are also heavily dependent on manufactured goods.

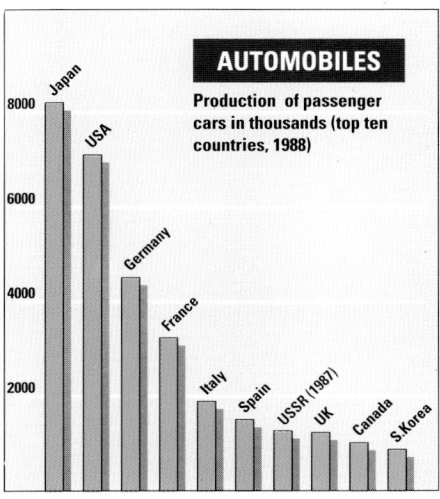

AUTOMOBILES

Production of passenger cars in thousands (top ten countries, 1988)

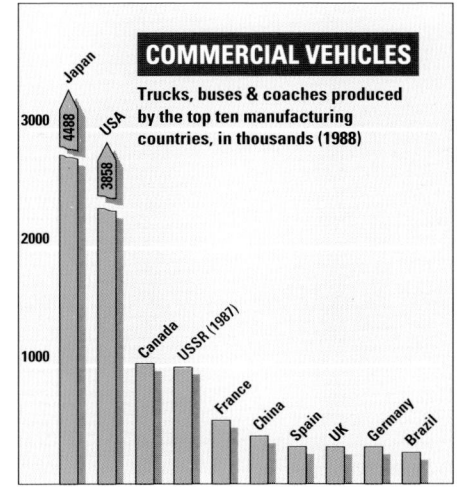

COMMERCIAL VEHICLES

Trucks, buses & coaches produced by the top ten manufacturing countries, in thousands (1988)

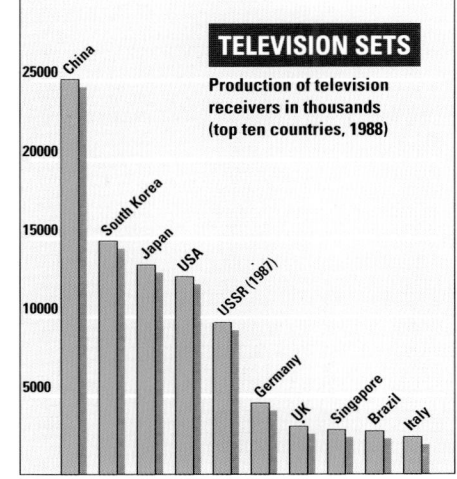

TELEVISION SETS

Production of television receivers in thousands (top ten countries, 1988)

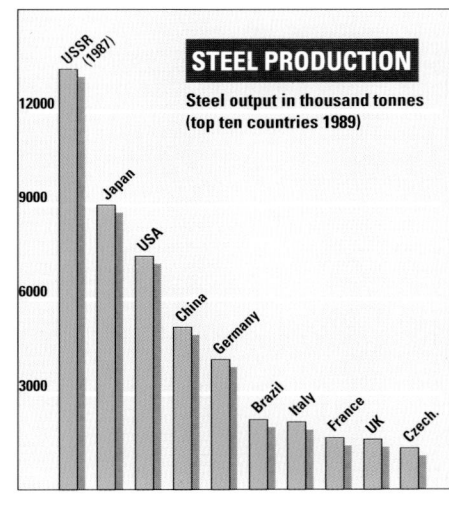

STEEL PRODUCTION

Steel output in thousand tonnes (top ten countries 1989)

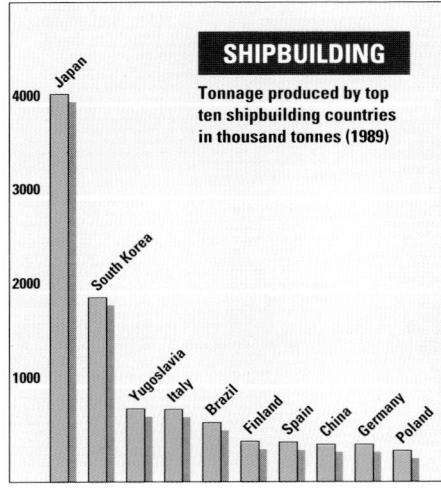

SHIPBUILDING

Tonnage produced by top ten shipbuilding countries in thousand tonnes (1989)

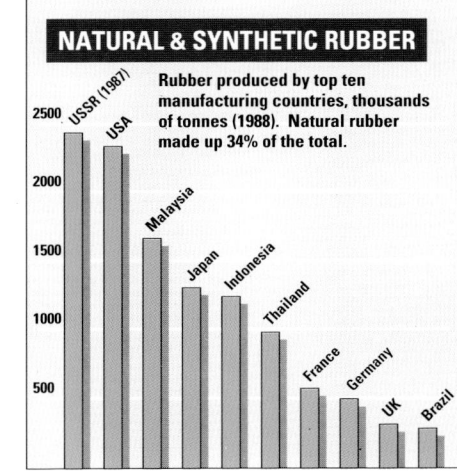

NATURAL & SYNTHETIC RUBBER

Rubber produced by top ten manufacturing countries, thousands of tonnes (1988). Natural rubber made up 34% of the total.

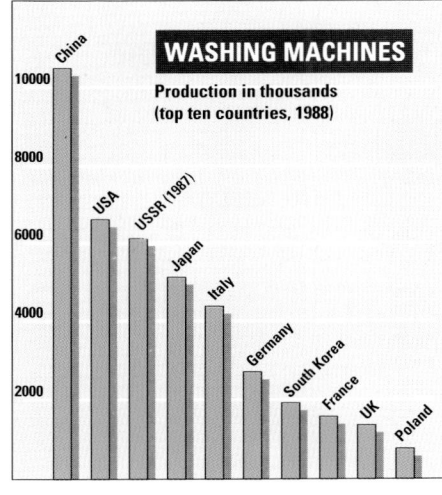

WASHING MACHINES

Production in thousands (top ten countries, 1988)

INDUSTRIAL POWER

Industrial output (mining, manufacturing, construction, energy & water production), top 40 nations, US $ billion (1988)

1.	USA	1,249.54	21. Austria	50.63
2.	Japan	1,155.41	22. Belgium	46.88
3.	Germany	479.69	23. Poland	39.52
4.	USSR	326.54	24. Finland	35.50
5.	France	304.95	25. South Africa	35.46
6.	UK	295.00	26. Saudi Arabia	33.36
7.	Italy	286.00	27. Denmark	30.79
8.	China	174.05	28. Iraq	30.27
9.	Canada	171.06	29. Czechoslovakia	30.18
10.	Spain	126.60	30. Yugoslavia	29.32
11.	Brazil	116.13	31. Indonesia	29.03
12.	Netherlands	76.48	32. Norway	28.74
13.	Sweden	75.17	33. Argentina	26.27
14.	South Korea	74.00	34. Turkey	26.07
15.	India	72.69	35. Israel	24.15
16.	Australia	72.63	36. Algeria	22.88
17.	E. Germany	64.66	37. Venezuela	22.70
18.	Switzerland	63.37	38. Romania	22.19
19.	Mexico	61.57	39. Iran	19.90
20.	Taiwan	54.81	40. Thailand	18.62

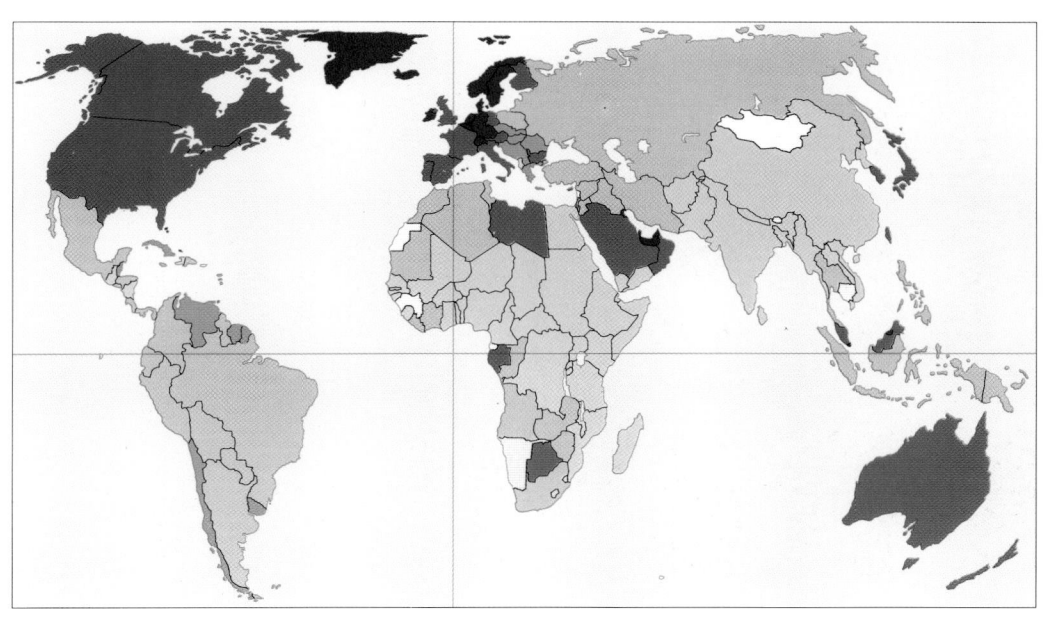

EXPORTS PER CAPITA

Value of exports in US $, divided by total population (1988)

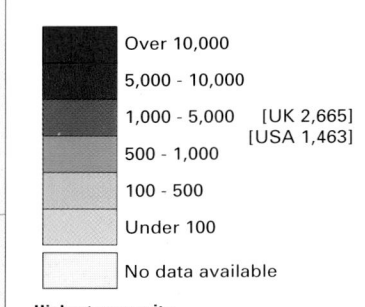

- Over 10,000
- 5,000 – 10,000
- 1,000 – 5,000 [UK 2,665] [USA 1,463]
- 500 – 1,000
- 100 – 500
- Under 100
- No data available

Highest per capita

Singapore	16,671
Hong Kong	12,676
UAE	10,217
Belgium	10,200
Bahamas	8,580
Qatar	8,431

PRODUCTION: TRADE

29: INTERNATIONAL ORGANISATIONS

30: SELF-SUFFICIENCY IN FOOD

33: FUEL EXPORTS MOVEMENTS OF OIL

34: MINERAL EXPORTS

37: INDUSTRY & TRADE EXPORTS PER CAPITA

43: TOURISM

Thriving international trade is the outward sign of a healthy world economy – the obvious indicator that some countries have goods to sell and others the wherewithal to buy them. Despite local fluctuations, trade throughout the 1980s grew consistently faster than output, increasing in value by almost 50% in the decade 1979-89. It remains dominated by the wealthy, industrialized countries of the Organization for Economic Development: between them, the 24 OECD members account for almost 75% of world imports and exports in most years. OECD dominance is just as marked in the trade in 'invisibles' - a column in the balance sheet that includes, among other headings, the export of services, interest payments on overseas investments, tourism and even remittances from migrant workers abroad. In the UK, 'invisibles' account for more than half all trading income.

However, the size of these great trading economies means that imports and exports usually comprise a fraction of their total wealth: in the case of the famously export-conscious Japanese, trade in goods and services amounts to less than 18% of GDP. In poorer countries, trade - often in a single commodity - may amount to 50% GDP or more. And there are oddities: import-export figures for the entrepôt economy of Singapore, for example, the transit point for much Asian trade, are almost double that small nation's total earnings.

WORLD TRADE

Percentage of total world exports by value (1989)

- Over 10%
- 5 - 10%
- 1 - 5%
- 0.5 - 1%
- 0.25 - 0.5%
- Under 0.25%

[USA 15.7%] [UK 6.3%]

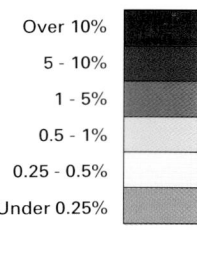

THE GREAT TRADING NATIONS

The imports and exports of the top ten trading nations as a percentage of world trade (1989). Each country's trade in manufactured goods is shown in orange.

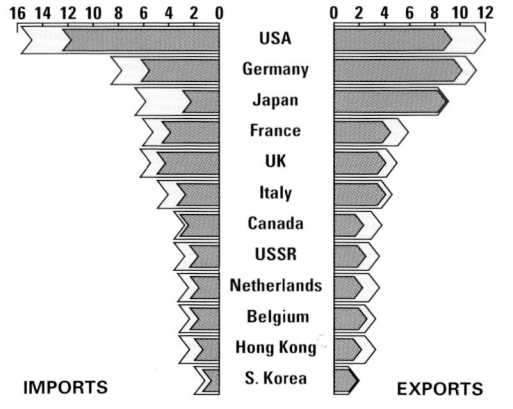

IMPORTS — USA, Germany, Japan, France, UK, Italy, Canada, USSR, Netherlands, Belgium, Hong Kong, S. Korea — EXPORTS

MAJOR EXPORTS

Leading manufactured items and their exporters, by percentage of world total in US dollars (late 1980s)

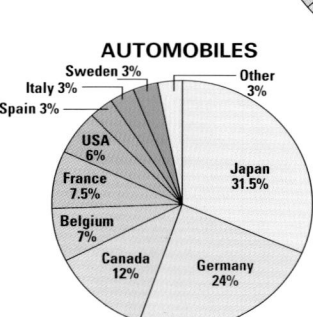

AIRCRAFT
- Italy 3%
- Canada 5%
- Other 11%
- France 8%
- Germany 9%
- UK 13%
- USA 51%

TELECOMMUNICATIONS GEAR
- Italy 3%
- Canada 4%
- Hong Kong 4%
- Sweden 4%
- UK 5%
- France 5%
- Germany 9%
- Other 19%
- Japan 33%
- USA 14%

DATA PROCESSING EQUIPMENT
- Singapore 4%
- Italy 4%
- Canada 4%
- Ireland 5%
- France 6%
- UK 6%
- Other 14%
- USA 24%
- Japan 22%
- Germany 11%

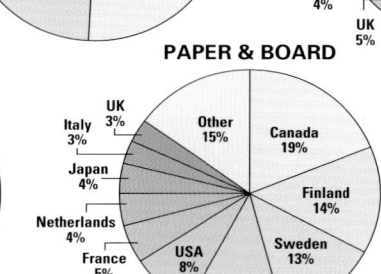

AUTOMOBILES
- Sweden 3%
- Italy 3%
- Spain 3%
- Other 3%
- USA 6%
- France 7.5%
- Belgium 7%
- Canada 12%
- Japan 31.5%
- Germany 24%

PAPER & BOARD
- UK 3%
- Italy 3%
- Japan 4%
- Netherlands 4%
- France 5%
- Other 15%
- Canada 19%
- Finland 14%
- Sweden 13%
- Germany 12%
- USA 8%

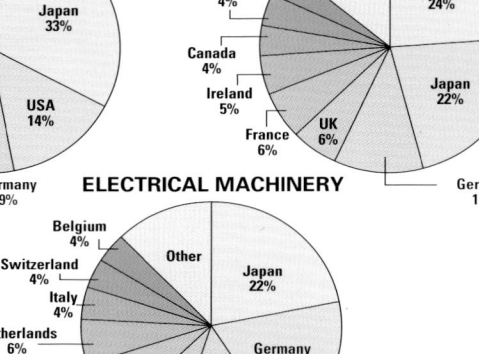

ELECTRICAL MACHINERY
- Belgium 4%
- Switzerland 4%
- Italy 4%
- Netherlands 6%
- France 7%
- UK 8%
- Other
- Japan 22%
- Germany 19%
- USA 14%

TRADED PRODUCTS

Top ten manufactures traded, by value in billions of US $ (late 1980s)

Automobiles, Engines & vehicle parts, Data processing equipment, Telecommunications, Transistors etc, Aircraft, Paper & board, Trucks, Meas. & control instruments, Electrical machinery

DEPENDENCE ON TRADE

Value of exports as a percentage of Gross Domestic Product (1988)

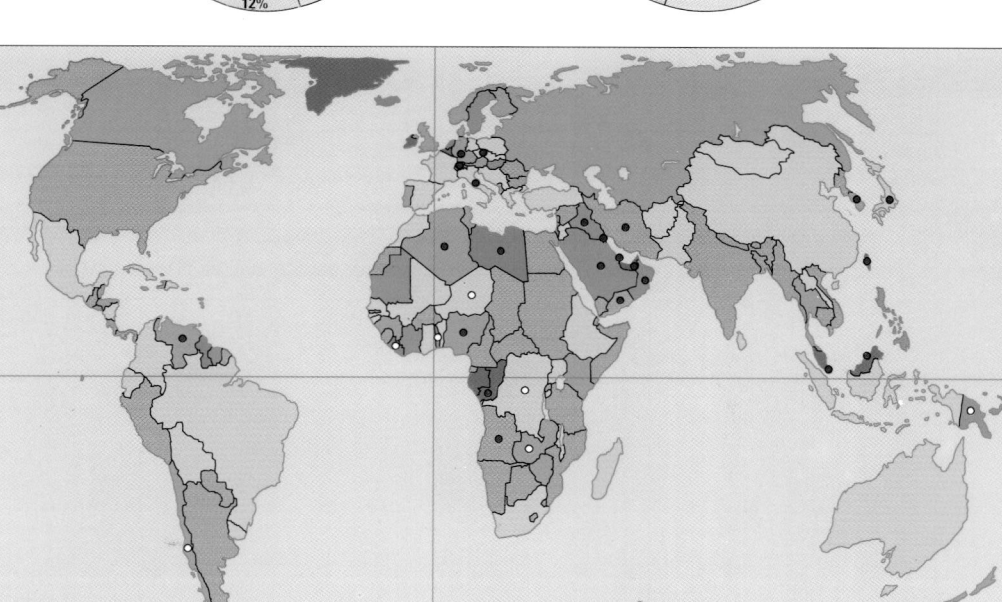

- Over 50%
- 40 - 50%
- 30 - 40%
- 20 - 30%   [UK 21%]
- 10 - 20%   [USA 6.5%]
- Under 10%

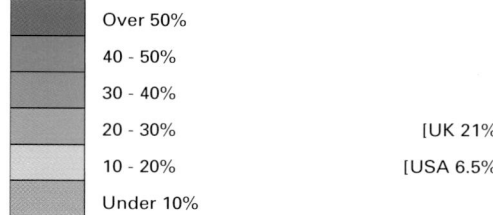

- Most dependent on industrial exports (over 75% of total exports)
- Most dependent on fuel exports (over 75% of total exports)
- Most dependent on mineral & metal exports (over 75% of total exports)

COPYRIGHT GEORGE PHILIP LTD.

WORLD SHIPPING

While ocean passenger traffic is now relatively modest, sea transport still carries most of world trade. Oil and bulk carriers make up the majority of the world fleet, although the general cargo category was the fastest growing in 1989, a year in which total tonnage increased by 1.5%.

Almost 30% of world shipping sails under a 'flag of convenience', whereby owners take advantage of low taxes by registering their vessels in a foreign country the ships will never see, notably Panama and Liberia.

MERCHANT FLEETS

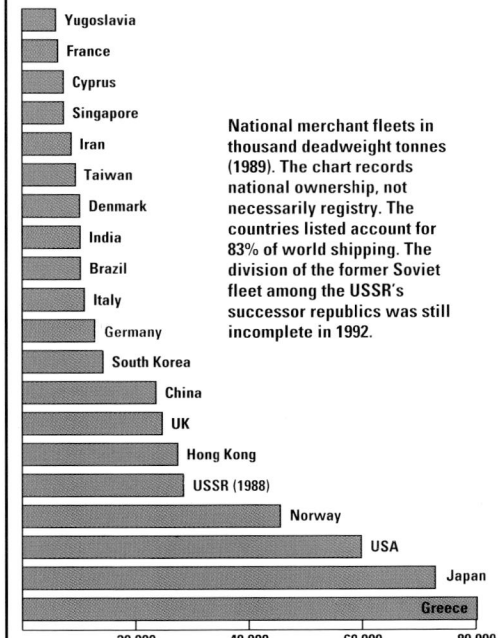

Yugoslavia
France
Cyprus
Singapore
Iran
Taiwan
Denmark
India
Brazil
Italy
Germany
South Korea
China
UK
Hong Kong
USSR (1988)
Norway
USA
Japan
Greece

20,000   40,000   60,000   80,000

National merchant fleets in thousand deadweight tonnes (1989). The chart records national ownership, not necessarily registry. The countries listed account for 83% of world shipping. The division of the former Soviet fleet among the USSR's successor republics was still incomplete in 1992.

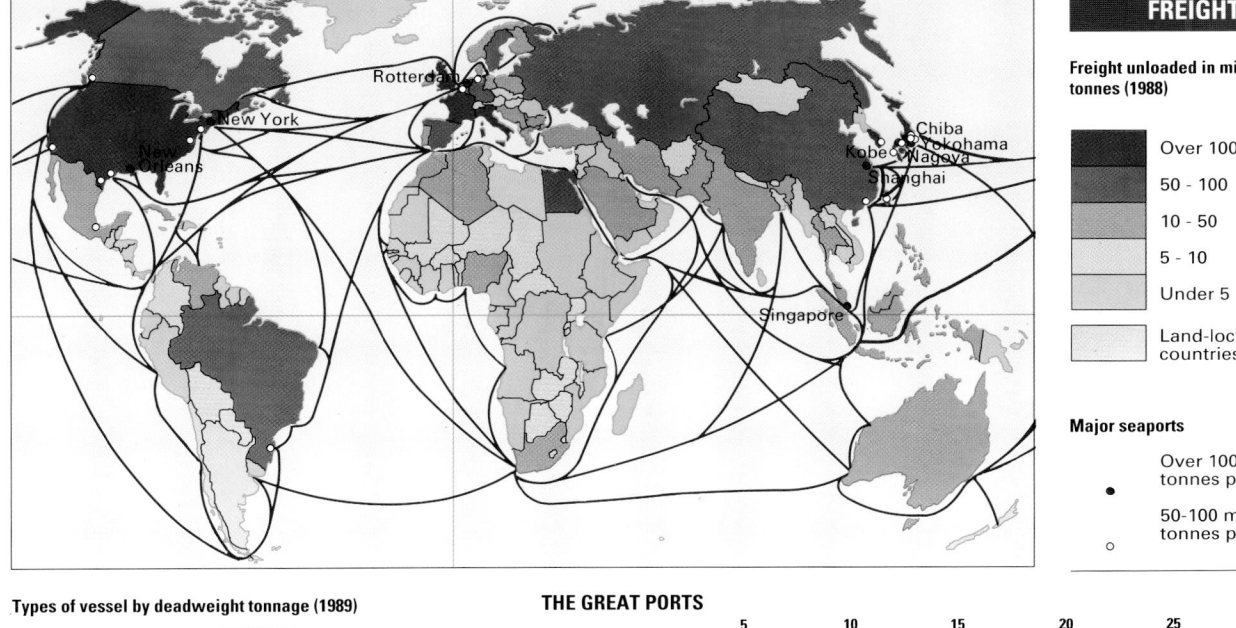

Rotterdam
New York
New Orleans
Chiba
Kobe Yokohama
Nagoya
Shanghai
Singapore

FREIGHT

Freight unloaded in millions of tonnes (1988)

- Over 100
- 50 - 100
- 10 - 50
- 5 - 10
- Under 5
- Land-locked countries

Major seaports

- Over 100 million tonnes per year
- ○ 50-100 million tonnes per year

Types of vessel by deadweight tonnage (1989)

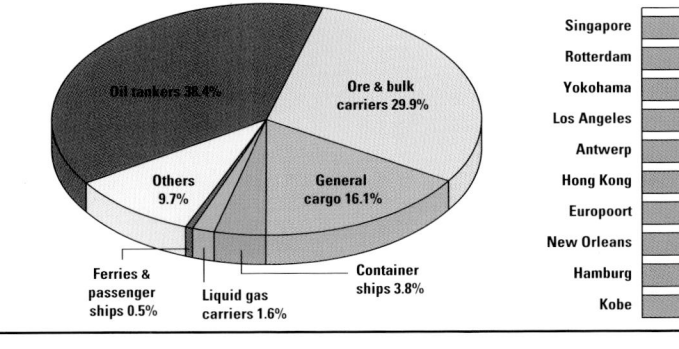

Oil tankers 38.4%
Ore & bulk carriers 29.9%
Others 9.7%
General cargo 16.1%
Ferries & passenger ships 0.5%
Liquid gas carriers 1.6%
Container ships 3.8%

THE GREAT PORTS

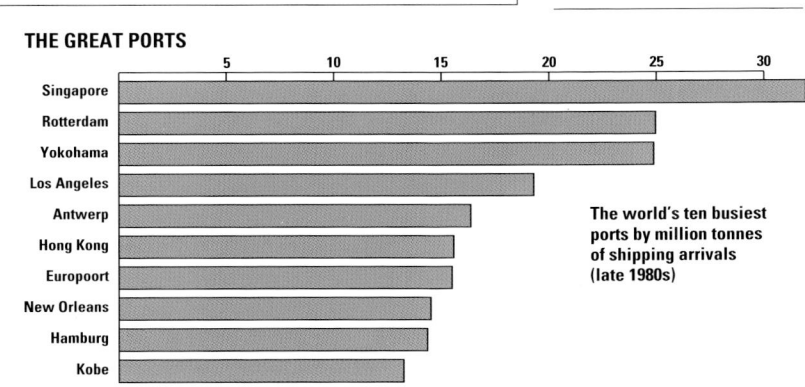

5   10   15   20   25   30

Singapore
Rotterdam
Yokohama
Los Angeles
Antwerp
Hong Kong
Europoort
New Orleans
Hamburg
Kobe

The world's ten busiest ports by million tonnes of shipping arrivals (late 1980s)

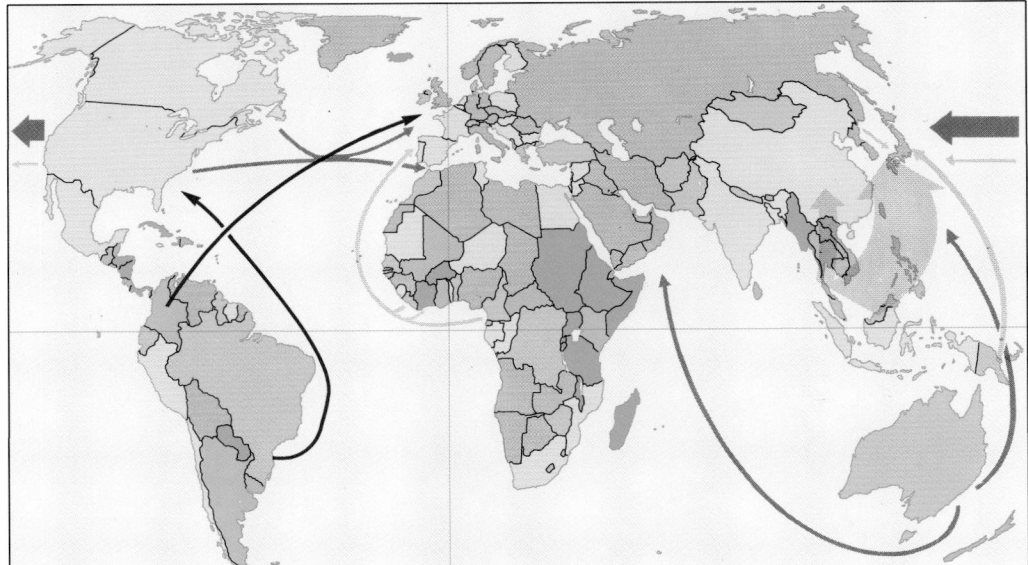

TRADE IN PRIMARY PRODUCTS

Exports in primary products (excluding fuels, minerals & metals) as a percentage of total exports (1988)

- Over 75%
- 50 - 75%
- 25 - 50%
- 10 - 25%   [USA 17.6%]
- Under 10%   [UK 9%]

Direction of trade

- ➡ Major movements of wheat
- → Major movements of coffee
- ➡ Major movements of hardwoods

Arrows show the major trade direction of selected primary products, & are proportional to export value

BALANCE OF TRADE

Value of exports in proportion to the value of imports (1988)

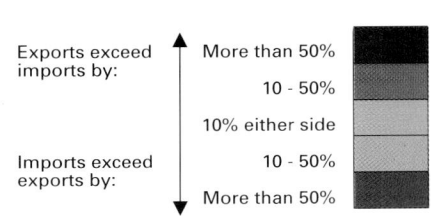

Exports exceed imports by:
- More than 50%
- 10 - 50%

10% either side

Imports exceed exports by:
- 10 - 50%
- More than 50%

The total world trade balance should amount to zero, since exports must equal imports on a global scale. In practice, at least $100 billions in exports go unrecorded, leaving the world with an apparent deficit and many countries in a better position than public accounting reveals. However, a favourable trade balance is not necessarily a sign of prosperity: many poorer countries must maintain a high surplus in order to service debts, and do so by restricting imports below their real requirements.

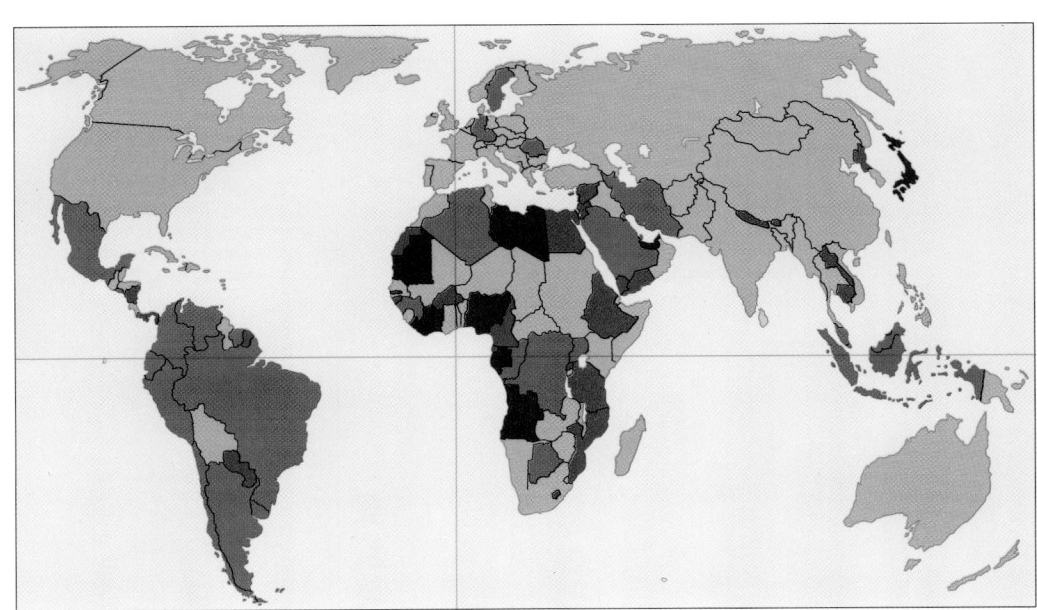

QUALITY OF LIFE: WEALTH

36: WEALTH CREATION

37: INDUSTRIAL POWER
    EXPORT PER CAPITA

38: WORLD TRADE
    MAJOR EXPORTS

39: BALANCE OF TRADE

43: DISTRIBUTION OF
    SPENDING
    DISTRIBUTION OF
    INCOME

Throughout the 1980s, most of the world became at least slightly richer. There were exceptions: in Africa, the poorest of the continents, many incomes actually fell, and the upheavals in Eastern Europe in 1989 left whole populations awash with political freedom but worse off financially in economies still teetering towards capitalism.

Most of the improvements, however, came to those who were already, in world terms, extremely affluent: the gap between rich and poor grew steadily wider. And in those developing countries that showed significant statistical progress, advances were often confined to a few favoured areas while conditions in other, usually rural, districts went from bad to worse.

The pattern of world poverty varies from region to region. In most of Asia, the process of recognized development is generally under way, with production increases outpacing population growth. By 2000, less than 10% of the Chinese population should be officially rated 'poor': without the means to buy either adequate food or the basic necessities required to take a full part in everyday life. Even India's lower growth rate should be enough to reduce the burden of poverty for at least some of its people. In Latin America, average per capita production is high enough for most countries to be considered 'middle income' in world rankings. But although adequate resources exist, Latin American wealth is distributed with startling inequality. According to a 1990 World Bank report, a tax of only 2% on the richest fifth would raise enough money to pull every one of the continent's 437 million people above the poverty line.

In Africa, solutions will be harder to find. The bane of high population growth has often been aggravated by incompetent administration, a succession of natural disasters and war. Population is the crux of the problem: numbers are growing anything up to twice as fast as the economies that try to support them. Aid from the developed world is only a partial solution; although Africa receives more than any other continent, much has been wasted on over-ambitious projects or lost in webs of inexperienced or corrupt bureaucracy. Yet without aid, Africa seems doomed to permanent crisis.

The rich countries can afford to increase their spending. The 24 members of the Organization for Economic Cooperation and Development comprise only 16% of the world's population, yet between them the nations accounted for almost 80% of total world production in 1988, a share that is likely to increase as 2000 approaches.

CURRENCIES

Currency units of the world's most powerful economies

1. USA: US Dollar($,US$)
   = 100 cents
2. Japan: Yen (Y,¥)
   = 100 sen
3. Germany: Deutsche Mark (DM)
   = 100 Pfennige
4. France: French Franc (Fr)
   = 100 centimes
5. Italy: Italian Lira (L, £, Lit)
6. UK: Pound Sterling (£)
   = 100 pence
7. Canada: Canadian Dollar
   (C$, Can$) = 100 cents
8. China: Renminbi Yuan
   (RMBY, $, Y) = 10 jiao = 100 fen
9. Brazil: Cruzado (Cr$)
   = 100 centavos
10. Spain: Peseta (Pta, Pa)
    = 100 céntimos
11. India: Indian Rupee (Re, Rs)
    = 100 paisa
12. Australia: Australian Dollar ($A)
    = 100 cents
13. Netherlands: Guilder, Florin
    (Gld, f) = 100 centimes
14. Switzerland: Swiss Franc
    (SFr, SwF) = 100 centimes
15. South Korea: Won (W)
    = 100 Chon
16. Sweden: Swedish Krona (SKr)
    = 100 ore
17. Mexico: Mexican Pesos (Mex$)
    = 100 centavos
18. Belgium: Belgian Franc (BFr)
    = 100 centimes
19. Austria: Schilling (S, Sch)
    = 100 groschen
20. Finland: Markka (FMk)
    = 100 penni
21. Denmark: Danish Krone (DKr)
    = 100 ore
22. Norway: Norwegian Krone
    (NKr) = 100 ore
23. Saudi Arabia: Riyal (SAR, SRI$)
    = 100 halalah
24. Indonesia: Rupiah (Rp)
    = 100 sen
25. South Africa: Rand (R)
    = 100 cents

CONTINENTAL SHARES

Shares of population and of wealth (GNP) by continent

Generalized continental figures show the startling difference between rich and poor but mask the successes or failures of individual countries. Japan, for example, with less than 4% of Asia's population, produces almost 70% of the continent's output.

POPULATION

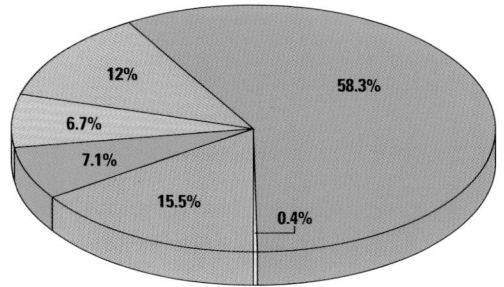

12%
6.7%
7.1%
15.5%
58.3%
0.4%

GNP

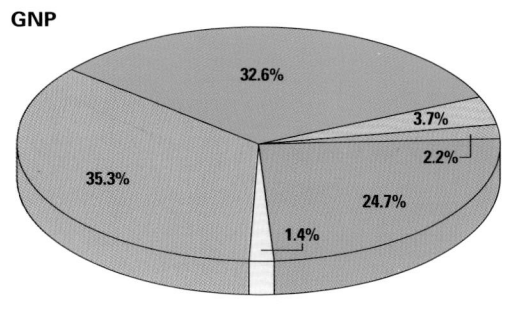

32.6%
3.7%
2.2%
24.7%
1.4%
35.3%

 Europe
 Australia
 Asia
 Africa
 South America
 North America

LEVELS OF INCOME

Gross National Product per capita: the value of total production divided by population (1986)

- Over 400%
- 200 - 400%
- 100 - 200%

[World average wealth per person US $2,940]

- 50 - 100%
- 25 - 50%
- Under 25%

[Gross National Product (GNP) is the value of a nation's total production plus or minus the net balance of foreign financial transactions – including investments, banking and insurance]

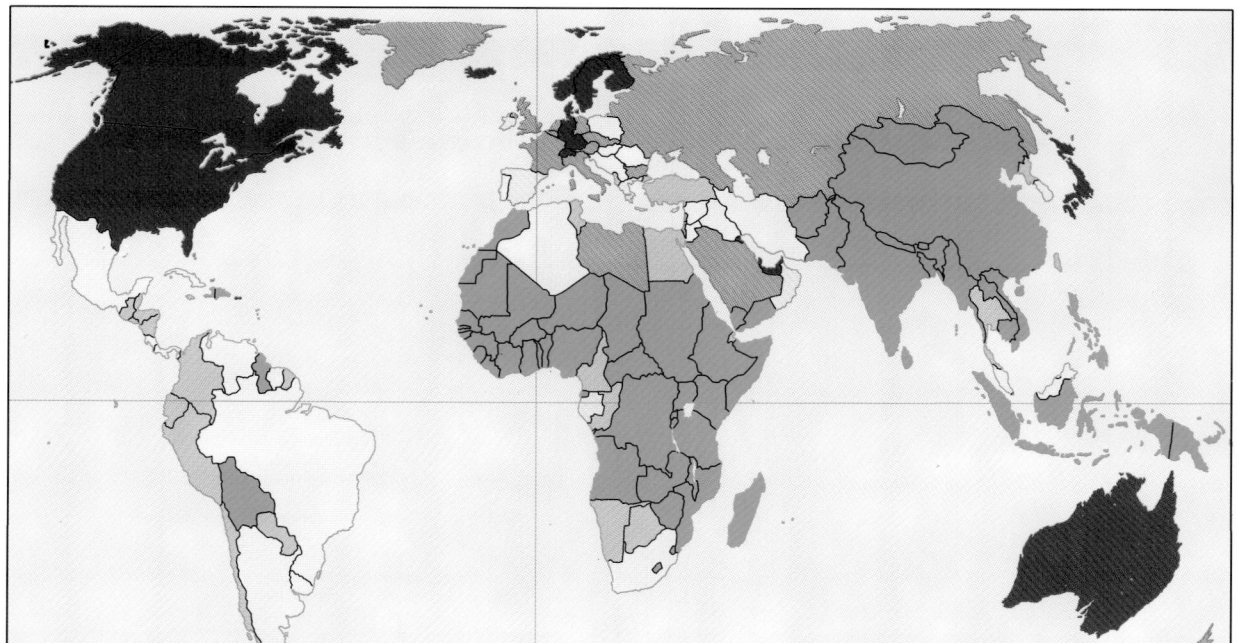

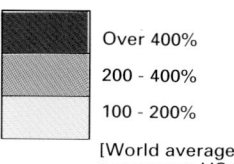

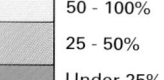

INDICATORS

The gap between the world's rich and poor is now so great that it is difficult to illustrate it on a single graph. Car ownership in the USA, for example, is almost 2,000 times as common as it is in Bangladesh. Within each income group, however, comparisons have some meaning: the affluent Japanese on their overcrowded island have far fewer cars than the Americans; the Chinese, perhaps because of propaganda value, have more television sets than the Indians, whose per capita income is similar, while Nigerians prefer to spend their money on vehicles.

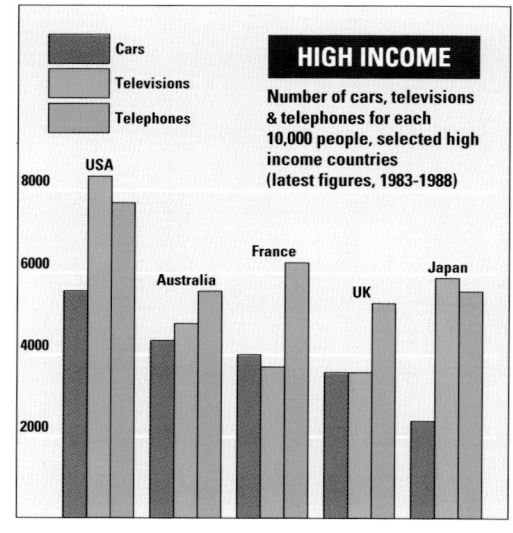

HIGH INCOME

Number of cars, televisions & telephones for each 10,000 people, selected high income countries (latest figures, 1983-1988)

Cars / Televisions / Telephones

USA France Australia UK Japan

8000 / 6000 / 4000 / 2000

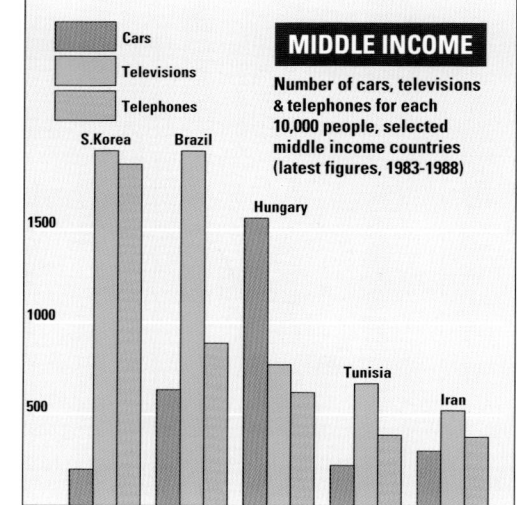

MIDDLE INCOME

Number of cars, televisions & telephones for each 10,000 people, selected middle income countries (latest figures, 1983-1988)

Cars / Televisions / Telephones

S.Korea Brazil Hungary Tunisia Iran

1500 / 1000 / 500

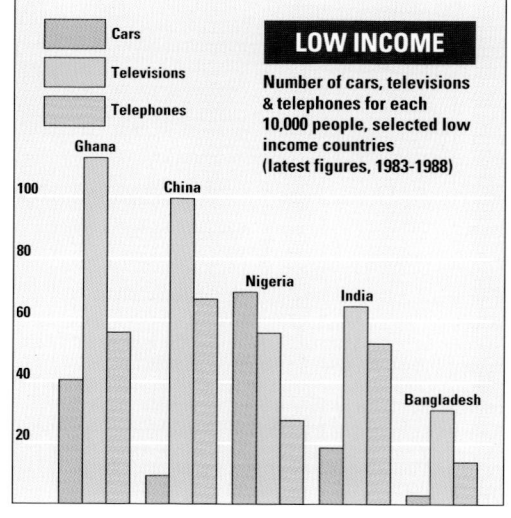

LOW INCOME

Number of cars, televisions & telephones for each 10,000 people, selected low income countries (latest figures, 1983-1988)

Cars / Televisions / Telephones

Ghana China Nigeria India Bangladesh

100 / 80 / 60 / 40 / 20

40

International debtors and the development aid they receive (1989)

■ Debt, $ per capita

□ Aid, $ per capita

Although aid grants make a vital contribution to many of the world's poorer countries, they are usually dwarfed by the burden of debt that developing economies are expected to repay. In the case of Mozambique, aid amounted to more than 70% of GNP. In 1990, the World Bank rated Mozambique as the world's poorest country; yet debt interest payments came to almost 75 times its entire export earnings.

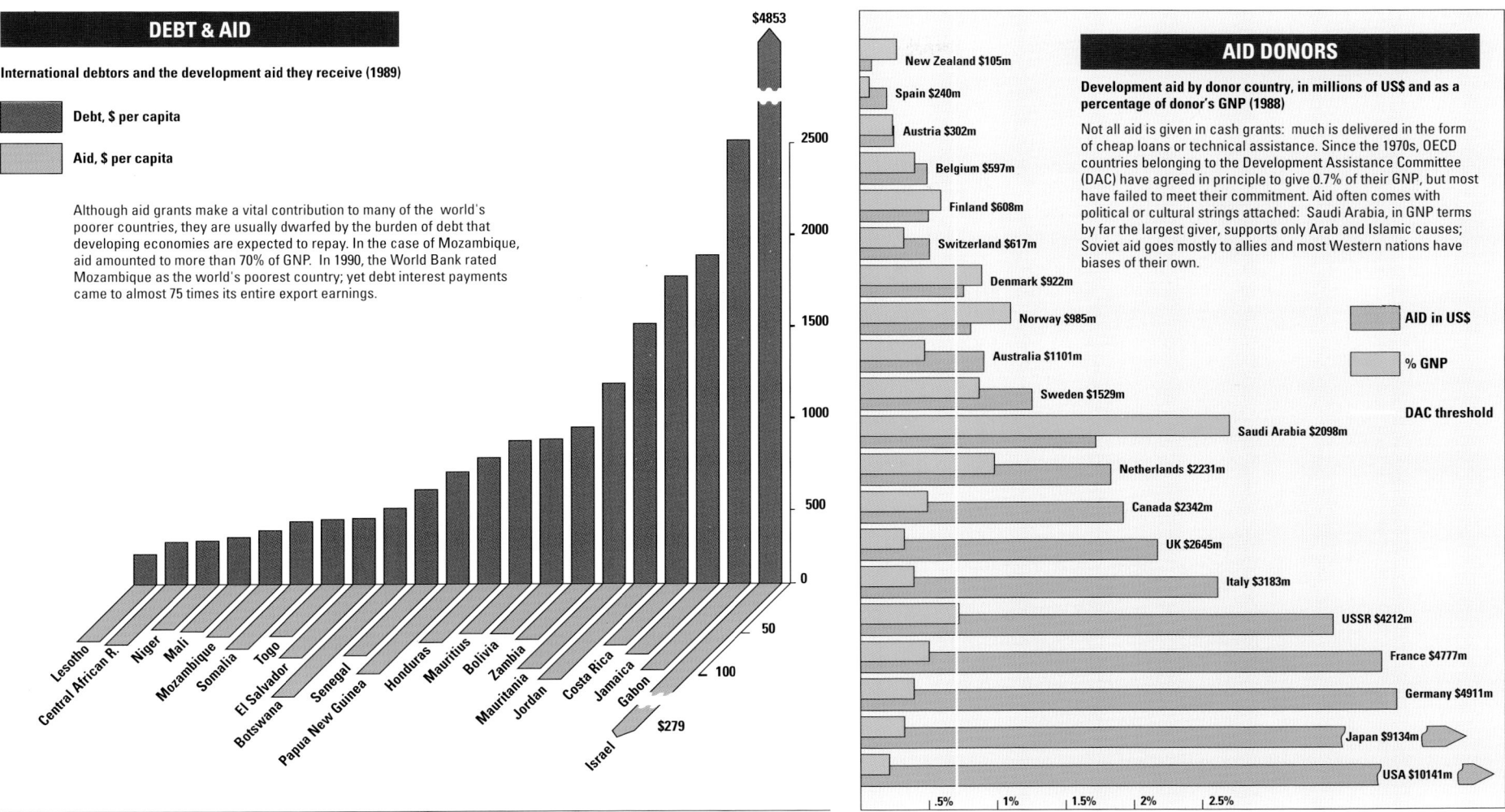

AID DONORS

Development aid by donor country, in millions of US$ and as a percentage of donor's GNP (1988)

Not all aid is given in cash grants: much is delivered in the form of cheap loans or technical assistance. Since the 1970s, OECD countries belonging to the Development Assistance Committee (DAC) have agreed in principle to give 0.7% of their GNP, but most have failed to meet their commitment. Aid often comes with political or cultural strings attached: Saudi Arabia, in GNP terms by far the largest giver, supports only Arab and Islamic causes; Soviet aid goes mostly to allies and most Western nations have biases of their own.

□ AID in US$

□ % GNP

DAC threshold

New Zealand $105m
Spain $240m
Austria $302m
Belgium $597m
Finland $608m
Switzerland $617m
Denmark $922m
Norway $985m
Australia $1101m
Sweden $1529m
Saudi Arabia $2098m
Netherlands $2231m
Canada $2342m
UK $2645m
Italy $3183m
USSR $4212m
France $4777m
Germany $4911m
Japan $9134m
USA $10141m

Inflation (right) is an excellent index of a country's financial stability, and usually its prosperity or at least its prospects. Inflation rates above 20% are generally matched by slow or even negative growth; above 50%, an economy is left reeling. Most advanced countries during the 1980s had to wrestle with inflation that occasionally touched or even exceeded 10%; in Japan, the growth leader, price increases averaged only 1.8% between 1980 and 1988.

Government spending (below right) is more difficult to interpret. Obviously, very low levels indicate a weak state, and high levels a strong one; but in poor countries, the 10-20% absorbed by the government may well amount to most of the liquid cash available, whereas in rich countries most of the 35-50% typically in government hands is returned in services.

GNP per capita figures (below) should also be compared with caution. They do not reveal the vast differences in living costs between different countries: the equivalent of US $100 is worth considerably more in poorer nations than it is in the USA itself.

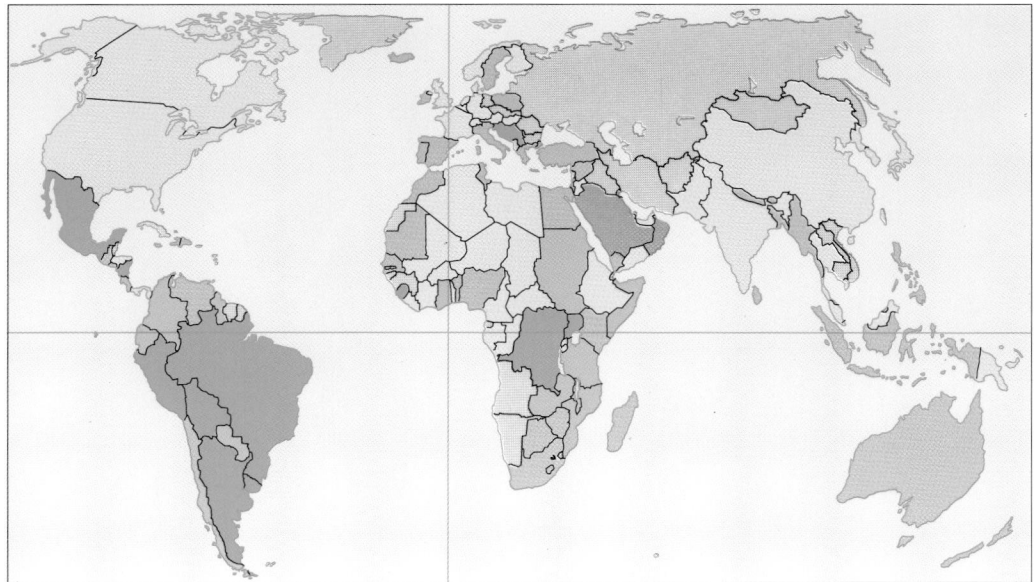

INFLATION

Average annual rate of inflation (1980-1988)

Over 50%

20 - 50%

7.5 - 20%

0 - 7.5%

Negative inflation

No data available

Highest inflation
Bolivia 483%
Argentina 291%
Brazil 189%

Lowest inflation
Oman ....-6.5%
Saudi Arabia ....-4.2%
Kuwait ....-3.9%

[UK 5.7%] [USA 4.0%]

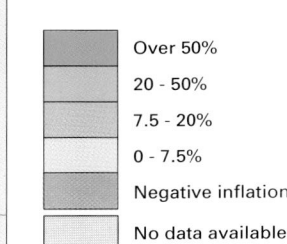

THE WEALTH GAP

The world's richest & poorest countries, by Gross National Product per capita in US $ (1989)

1.	Liechtenstein	33,000	1. Mozambique	80
2.	Switzerland	30,270	2. Ethiopia	120
3.	Bermuda	25,000	3. Tanzania	120
4.	Luxembourg	24,860	4. Laos	170
5.	Japan	23,730	5. Nepal	170
6.	Finland	22,060	6. Somalia	170
7.	Norway	21,850	7. Bangladesh	180
8.	Sweden	21,710	8. Malawi	180
9.	Iceland	21,240	9. Bhutan	190
10.	USA	21,100	10. Chad	190
11.	Denmark	20,510	11. Sierra Leone	200
12.	Canada	19,020	12. Burundi	220
13.	UAE	18,430	13. Gambia	230
14.	France	17,830	14. Madagascar	230
15.	Austria	17,360	15. Nigeria	250
16.	Germany	16,500	16. Uganda	250
17.	Belgium	16,390	17. Mali	260
18.	Kuwait	16,380	18. Zaïre	260
19.	Netherlands	16,010	19. Niger	290
20.	Italy	15,150	20. Burkina Faso	310

GNP per capita is calculated by dividing a country's Gross National Product by its population. The UK ranks 21st, with US $14,570.

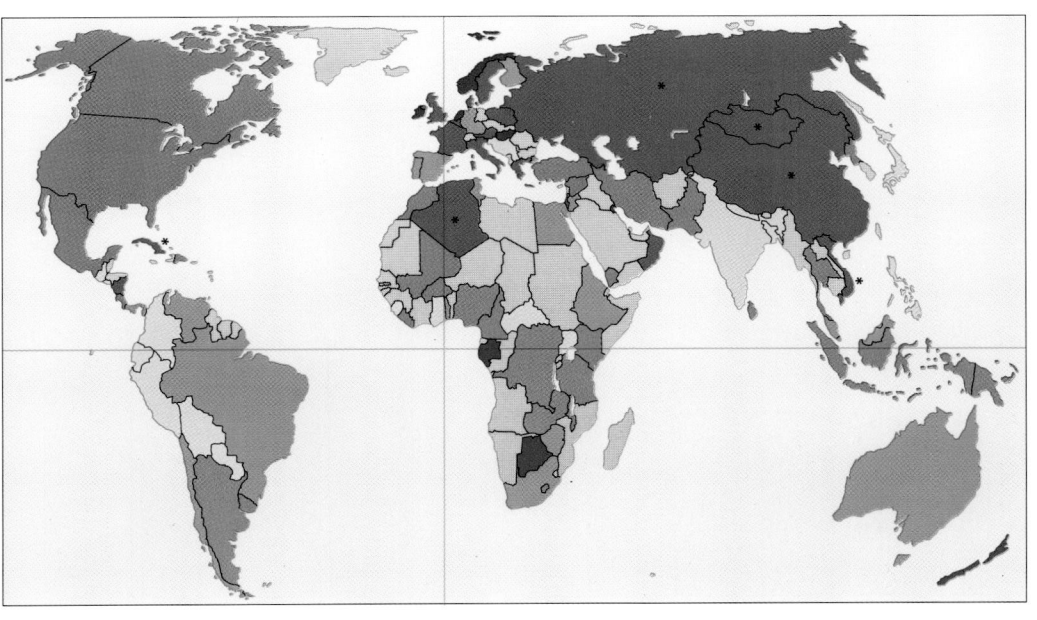

STATE REVENUE

Central government revenue as a percentage of GNP (1988) [* estimate]

Over 45%

35 - 45%

25 - 35%

15 - 25%

0 - 15%

No data available

Highest proportion
Botswana 74%
Hungary 58%
Kuwait 52%
Netherlands 51%
Gabon 47%

[UK 36.4%] [USA 19.7%]

QUALITY OF LIFE: STANDARDS

16: WATER SUPPLY

22: POPULATION DENSITY

25: URBAN POLLUTION
     INFORMAL CITIZENS
     URBAN ADVANTAGES

28: WORLD'S REFUGEES
     WAR SINCE 1945

36: EMPLOYMENT
     THE WORK FORCE

40: THE WEALTH GAP

41: DEBT & AID

45: LIFE EXPECTANCY
     INFANT MORTALITY
     CRIME & PUNISHMENT

At first sight, most international contrasts are swamped by differences in wealth. The rich not only have more money, they have more of everything, including years of life. Those with only a little money are obliged to spend most of it on food and clothing, the basic maintenance costs of existence; air travel and tourism are unlikely to feature on the lists of their expenditure. However, poverty and wealth are both relative: slum-dwellers living on social security payments in an affluent industrial country have far more resources at their disposal than an average African peasant, but feel their own poverty none the less acutely. A middle-class Indian lawyer cannot command a fraction of the earnings of a counterpart in New York, London or Rome; nevertheless, he rightly sees himself as prosperous.

In 1990 the United Nations Development Programme published its first Human Development Index, an attempt to construct a comparative scale by which at least a simplified form of well-being might be measured. The index, running from 1 to 100, combined figures for life expectancy and literacy with a wealth scale that matched incomes against the official poverty lines of a group of industrialized nations. National scores ranged from a startling 98.7 for Sweden to a miserable 11.6 for Niger, reflecting the all too familiar gap between rich and poor.

Comparisons between nations with similar incomes are more interesting, showing the effect of government policies. For example, Sri Lanka was awarded 78.9 against 43.9 for its only slightly poorer neighbour, India; Zimbabwe, at 57.6, had more than double the score of Senegal, despite no apparent disparities in average income. Some development indicators may be interpreted in two ways. There is a very clear correlation, for example, between the wealth of a nation and the level of education that its people enjoy. Education helps create wealth, of course; but are rich countries wealthy because they are educated, or well-educated because they are rich? Women's fertility rates appear to fall almost in direct proportion to the amount of secondary education they receive; but high levels of female education are associated with rich countries, where fertility is already low.

Not everything, though, is married to wealth. The countries cited on these pages have been chosen, representatively, to give a range covering different cultures as well as different economic power, revealing disparities among rich and among poor as well as between the two obvious groups. Income distribution, for example, shows that in Brazil (following the general pattern of Latin America) most national wealth is concentrated in a few hands; Bangladesh is much poorer, but what little wealth there is is more evenly spread.

Among the developed countries the USA, with its poorest 20% sharing less than 5% of the national cake, has a noticeably less even distribution than Japan, where despite massive industrialization traditional values act as a brake against poverty. Hungary, still enmeshed in Communism when these statistics were compiled, shows the most even distribution of all, which certainly matches with Socialist theory. However, the inequalities in Communist societies, a contributing factor in the demise of most of them in the late 1980s, are not easily measured in money terms: Communist élites are less often rewarded with cash than with power and privilege, commodities not easily expressed statistically.

There are other limits to statistical analysis. Even without taking account of such imponderables as personal satisfaction, it will always be more difficult to measure a reasonable standard of living than a nation's income or its productivity. Lack of money certainly brings misery, but its presence does not guarantee contentment.

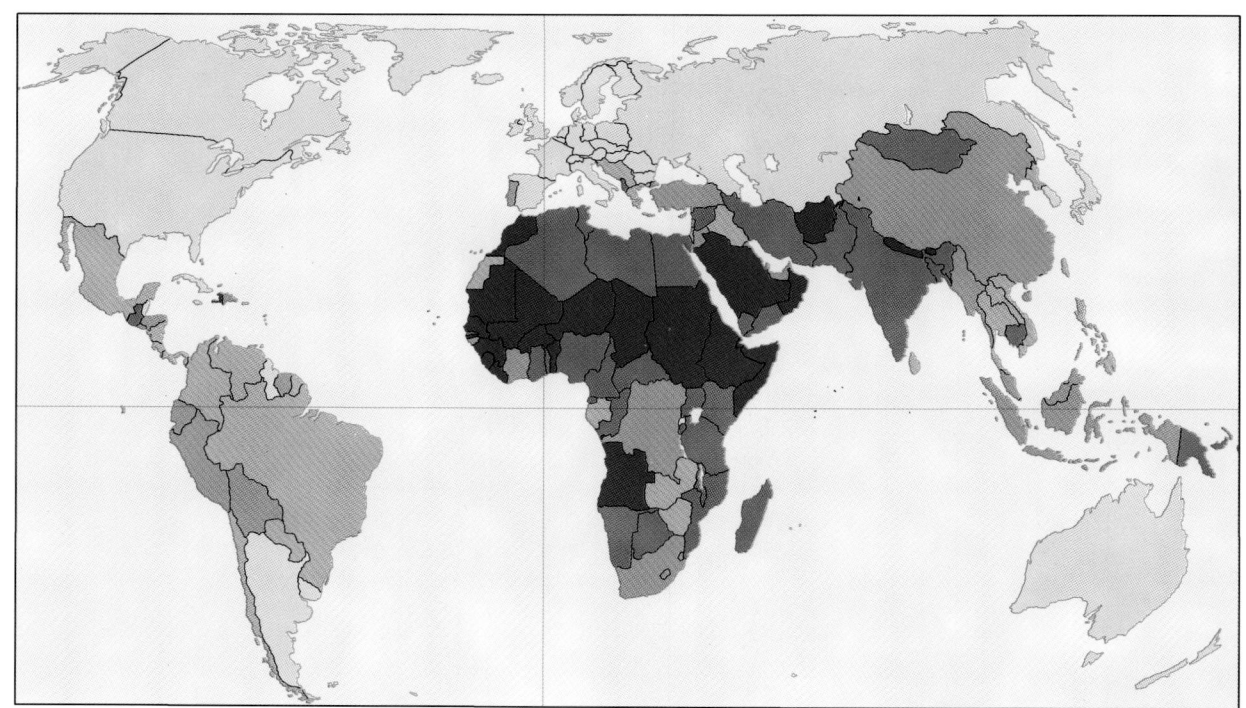

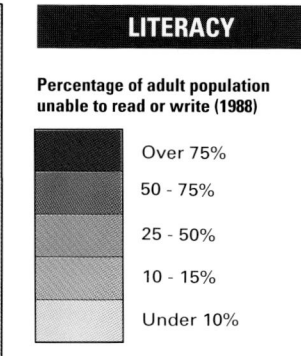

LITERACY

Percentage of adult population unable to read or write (1988)

Over 75%

50 - 75%

25 - 50%

10 - 15%

Under 10%

Highest rates of illiteracy

Somalia	88%
Burkina Faso	87%
Niger	86%
Mali	83%
Mauritania	83%
Chad	78%
Benin	76%
Nepal	76%
Guinea	75%

[UK 4.86%]   [USA 4%]

EDUCATION

The developing countries made great efforts in the 1970s and 1980s to bring at least a basic education to their people. Primary school enrolments rose above 60% in all but the poorest nations. Figures often include teenagers or young adults, however, and there are still an estimated 300 million children worldwide who receive no schooling at all. Secondary and higher education are expanding far more slowly, and the gap between rich and poor is probably even larger than it appears from the charts here, while the bare statistics provide no real reflection of educational quality.

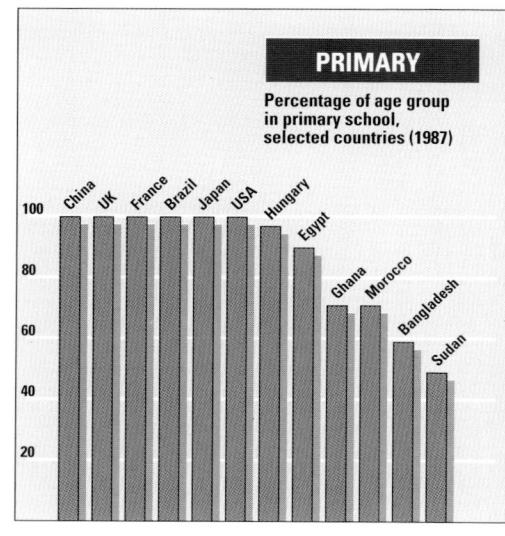

PRIMARY

Percentage of age group in primary school, selected countries (1987)

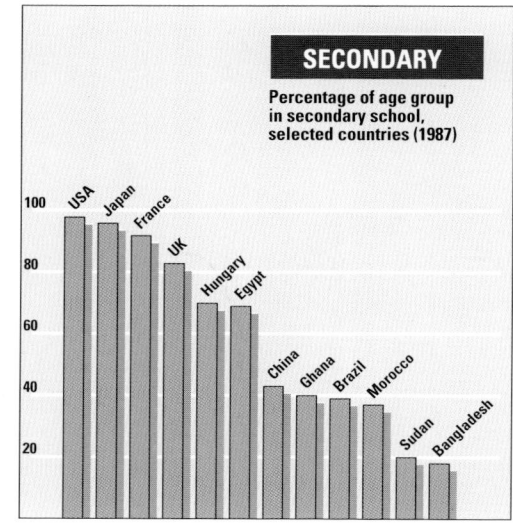

SECONDARY

Percentage of age group in secondary school, selected countries (1987)

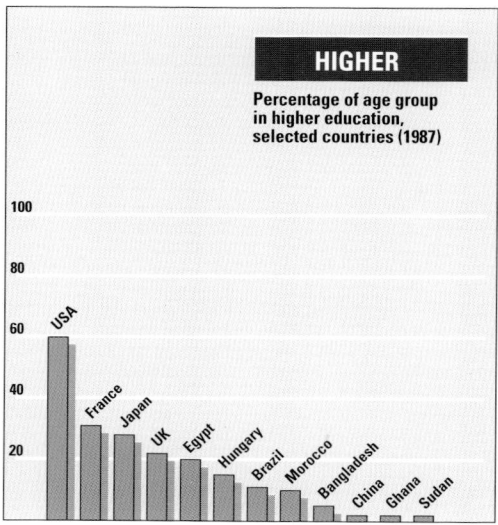

HIGHER

Percentage of age group in higher education, selected countries (1987)

DISTRIBUTION OF SPENDING

Percentage share of household spending, (1989)

- Food
- Medicine & Education
- Clothing
- Transport
- Energy & Housing
- Other

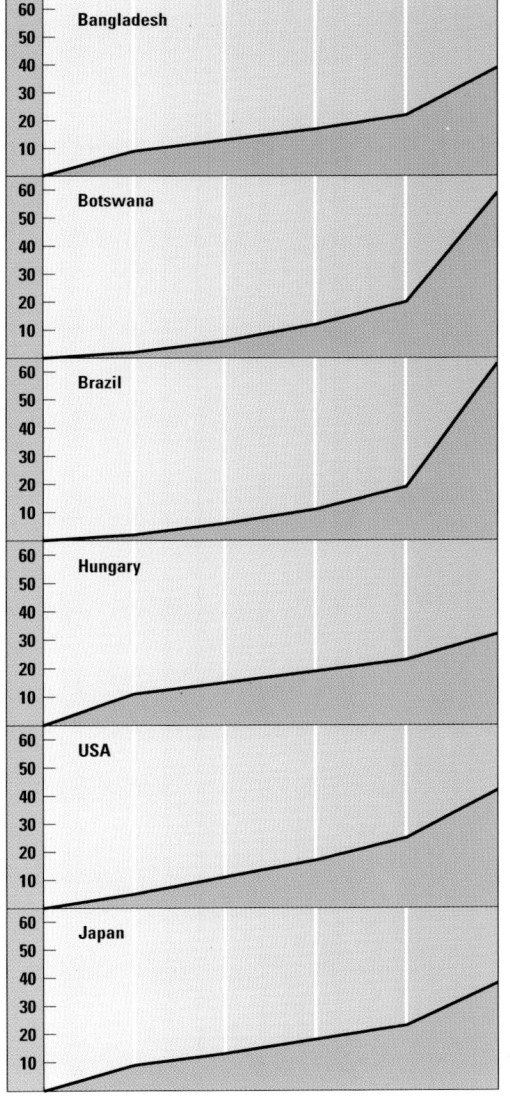

UK USA Japan Hungary Brazil Egypt Nigeria B'desh

DISTRIBUTION OF INCOME

Percentage share of household income from poorest fifth to richest fifth, selected countries (1989)

Bangladesh
Botswana
Brazil
Hungary
USA
Japan

FERTILITY & EDUCATION

- Fertility rate: average number of children borne per woman
- Percentage of female age group in secondary education

Fertility rates compared with female education, selected countries (1988)

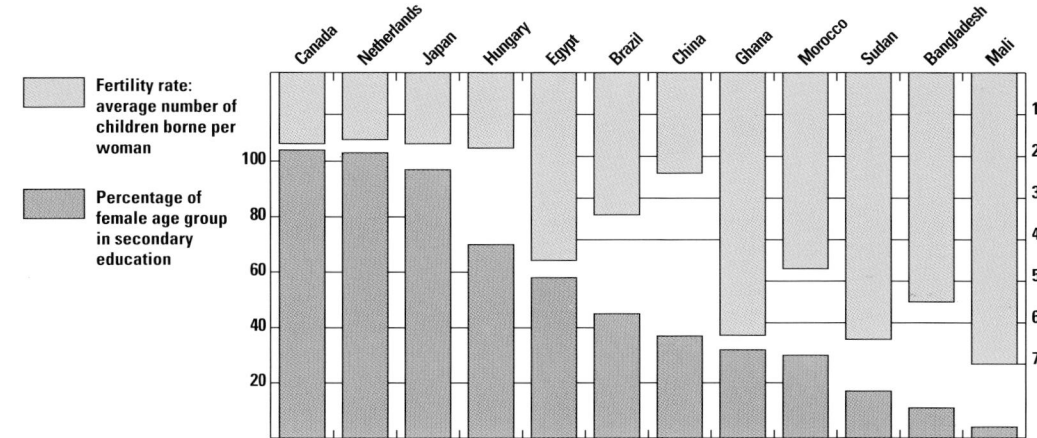

Canada Netherlands Japan Hungary Egypt Brazil China Ghana Morocco Sudan Bangladesh Mali

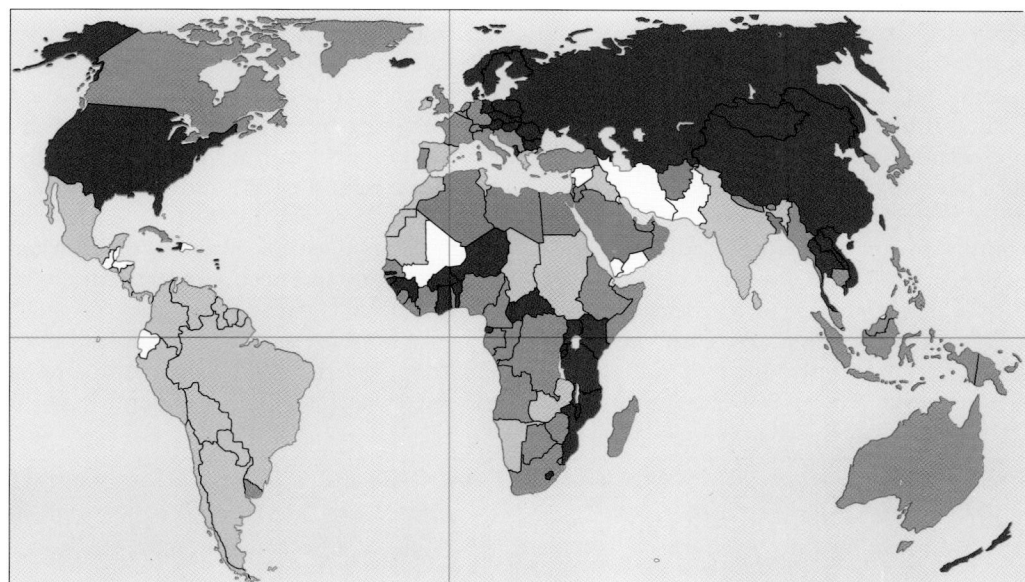

TOURIST SPENDING

Nations spending the most on overseas tourism, US $ (1987)

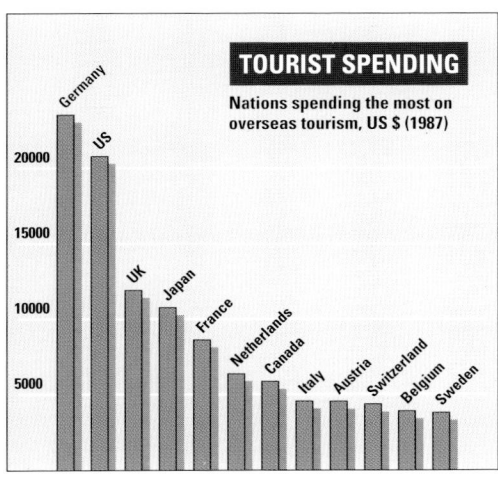

Germany US UK Japan France Netherlands Canada Italy Austria Switzerland Belgium Sweden

TOURIST EARNING

Nations receiving the most from overseas tourism, US $ (1987)

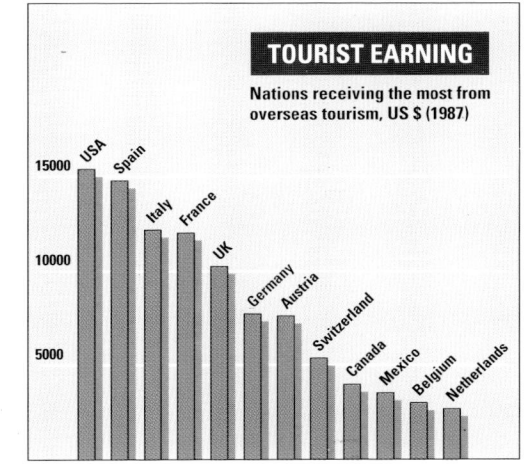

USA Spain Italy France UK Germany Austria Switzerland Canada Mexico Belgium Netherlands

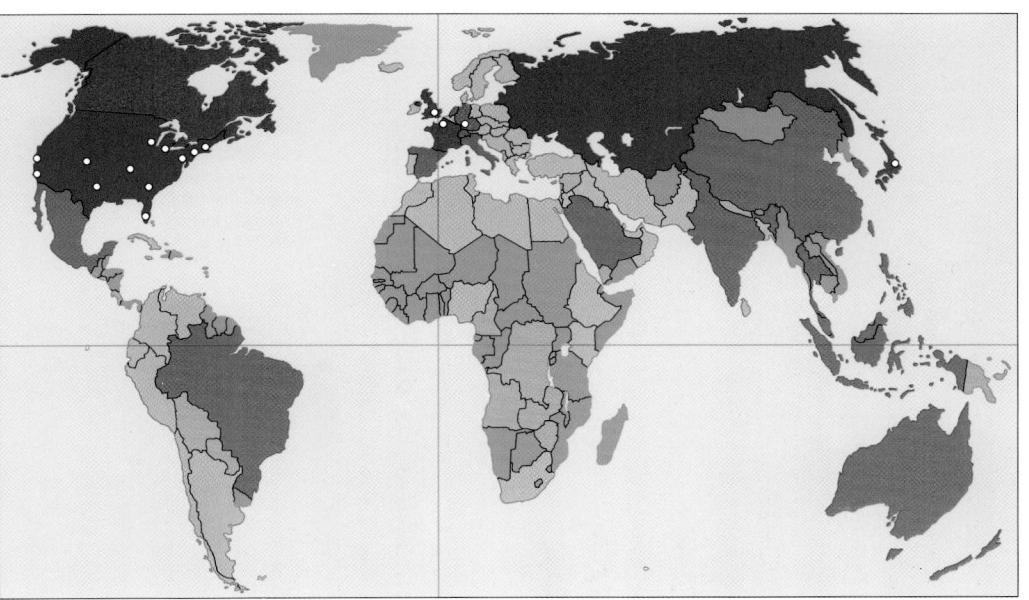

Since the age group for secondary schooling is usually defined as 12 to 17 years, percentages for countries with a significant number of 11- or 18-year-olds in secondary school may actually exceed 100. A high proportion of employed women may indicate either an advanced, industrial economy where female opportunities are high, or a poor country where many women's lives are dominated by agricultural toil. The lowest rates are found in Islamic nations, whose religious precepts often exclude women even from field-work.

WOMEN AT WORK

Women in paid employment as a percentage of the total workforce (1989)

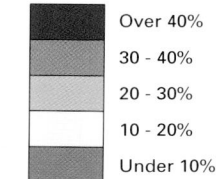

- Over 40%
- 30 - 40%
- 20 - 30%
- 10 - 20%
- Under 10%

Highest proportion
Burundi.............................. 53%
Ghana 51%
Mozambique 48%

Lowest proportion
UAE 6%
Saudi Arabia 7%
Bangladesh 7%

[UK 42%] [USA 44%]

Small economies in attractive areas are often completely dominated by tourism: in some West Indian islands, tourist spending provides over 90% of total income. In cash terms the USA is the world leader: its 1987 earnings exceeded 15 billion dollars, though that sum amounted to only 0.4% of its GDP.

AIR TRAVEL

Millions of passenger km [number carried, international & domestic, multiplied by distance flown by each from airport of origin] (1988)

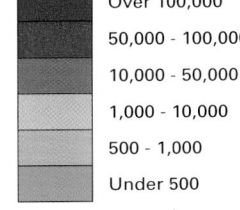

- Over 100,000
- 50,000 - 100,000
- 10,000 - 50,000
- 1,000 - 10,000
- 500 - 1,000
- Under 500

○ Major airports (over 20 million passengers a year)

The world's busiest airport in terms of total passengers is Chicago's O'Hare; the busiest international airport is Heathrow, the largest of London's airports.

QUALITY OF LIFE: HEALTH

16: WATER SUPPLY

25: URBAN POLLUTION
INFORMAL CITIZENS
URBAN ADVANTAGES

31: FOOD & POPULATION

43: DISTRIBUTION OF
SPENDING

According to statistics gathered in the late 1980s and early 1990s, a third of the world's population has no access to safe drinking water: malaria is on the increase; cholera, thought vanquished, is reappearing in South America; an epidemic of the terrifying AIDS virus is gathering force in Africa; and few developing countries can stretch their health care budgets beyond US $2 per person per year.

Yet human beings, by every statistical index, have never been healthier. In the richest nations, where food is plentiful, the demands of daily work are rarely onerous and medical care is both readily available and highly advanced, the average life expectancy is often more than 75 years – approaching the perceived limits for human longevity. In middle-income nations such as Brazil and the Philippines, life expectancy usually extends at least to the mid-60s; in China, it has already reached 70. Even in poverty-stricken Ethiopia and Chad, lifespans are close to 50. Despite economic crisis, drought, famine and even war, every country in the world reported an increase between 1965 and 1990.

It was not always so, even in countries then considered rich. By comparison, in 1880 the life expectancy of an average Berliner was under 30 years and infant mortality in the United Kingdom, then the wealthiest nation, stood at 144 per thousand births – a grim toll exceeded today only by three of the poorest African countries (Mali, Sierra Leone and Guinea). Even by 1910, European death rates were almost twice as high as the world average less than 80 years later; infant mortality in Norway, Europe's healthiest country, was then higher than in present-day Indonesia. In far less than a century, human prospects have improved beyond recognition.

In global terms, the transformation is less the result of high technology medicine – still too expensive for all but a minority, even in rich countries – than of improvements in agriculture and hence nutrition, matched by the widespread diffusion of the basic concepts of disease and public health. One obvious consequence, as death rates everywhere continue to fall, is sustained population growth. Another is the rising expectation of continued improvement felt by both rich and poor nations alike.

In some ways, the task is easier for developing countries, striving with limited resources to attain health levels to which the industrialized world has only recently become accustomed. As the tables below illustrate, infectious disease is rare among the richer nations, while ailments such as cancer, which tend to kill in advanced years, do not seriously impinge on populations with shorter lifespans.

Yet infectious disease is relatively cheap to eliminate, or at least reduce, and it is likely to be easier to raise life expectancy from 60 to 70 than from 75 to 85. The ills of the developed world and its ageing population are more expensive to treat – though most poor countries would be happy to suffer from the problems of the affluent. Western nations regularly spend more money on campaigns to educate their citizens out of over-eating and other bad habits than many developing countries can devote to an entire health budget – an irony that marks the dimensions of the rich-poor divide.

Indeed, wealth itself may be the most reliable indicator of longevity. Harmful habits are usually the province of the rich; yet curiously, though the dangerous effects of tobacco have been proved beyond doubt, the affluent Japanese combine very high cigarette consumption with the longest life expectancy of all the major nations. Similarly, heavy alcohol consumption seems to have no effect on longevity: the French, world leaders in 1988 and in most previous surveys, outlive the more moderate British by a year, and the abstemious Indians by almost two decades.

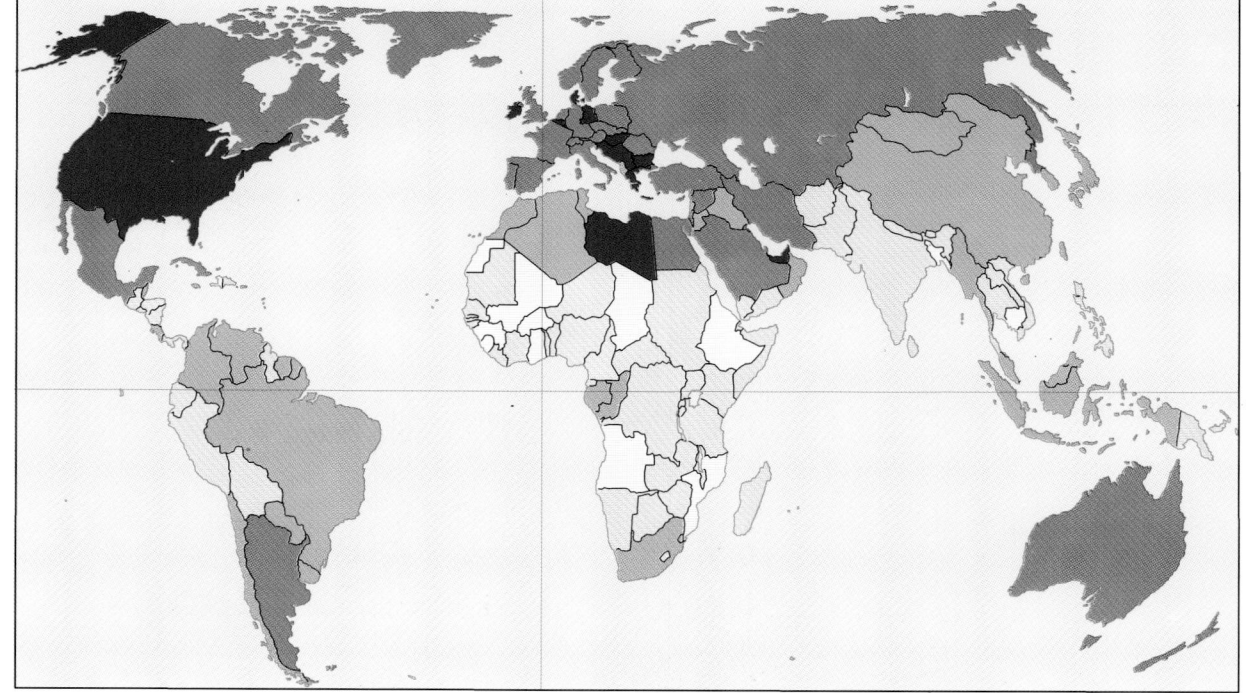

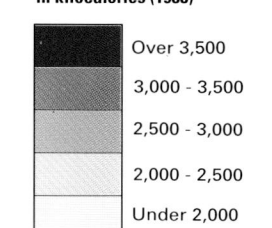

FOOD CONSUMPTION

Average daily food intake per person in kilocalories (1988)

- Over 3,500
- 3,000 - 3,500
- 2,500 - 3,000
- 2,000 - 2,500
- Under 2,000

Highest intake

Germany (E)	3,814
UAE	3,733
Greece	3,688
USA	3,645
Bulgaria	3,642

Lowest intake

Mozambique	1,595
Chad	1,717
Ethiopia	1,749
Guinea	1,776
Ghana	1,949

[USA 3,645] [UK 3,256]

CAUSES OF DEATH

The rich not only live longer, on average, than the poor; they also die from different causes. Infectious and parasitic diseases, all but eliminated in the developed world, remain a scourge in poorer countries. On the other hand, more than two-thirds of the populations of OECD nations eventually succumb to cancer or circulatory disease; the proportion in Latin America is only about 45%. In addition to the three major diseases shown here, respiratory infection and injury also claim more lives in developing nations, which lack the drugs and medical skills required to treat them.

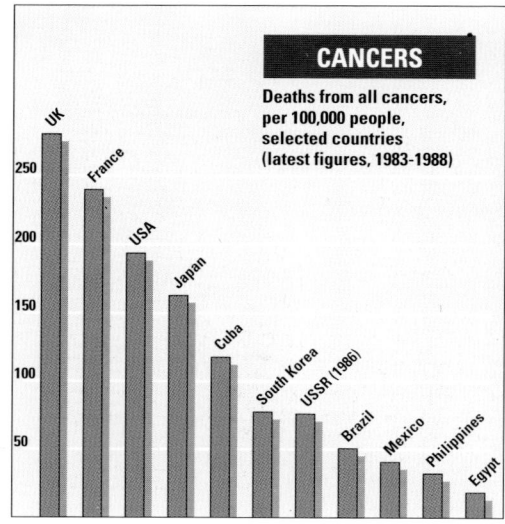

CANCERS

Deaths from all cancers, per 100,000 people, selected countries (latest figures, 1983-1988)

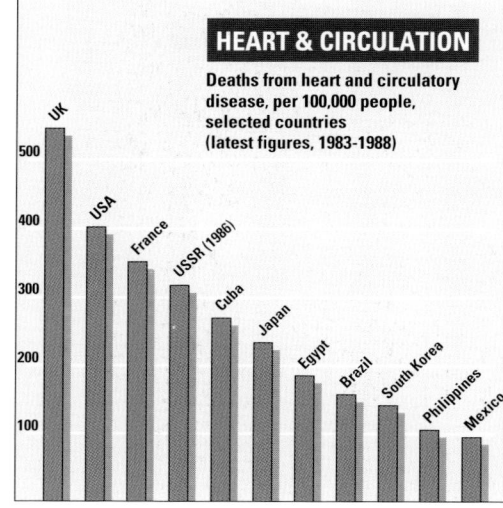

HEART & CIRCULATION

Deaths from heart and circulatory disease, per 100,000 people, selected countries (latest figures, 1983-1988)

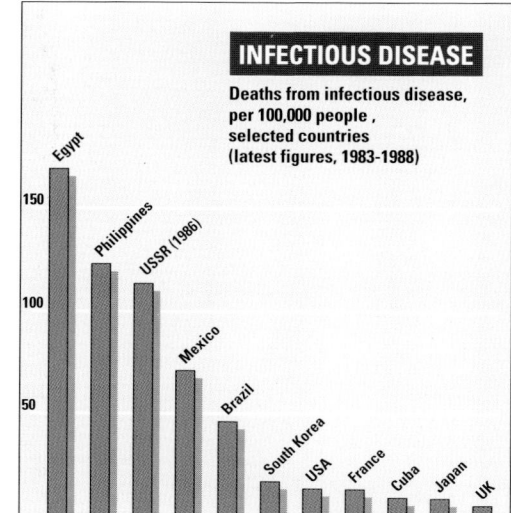

INFECTIOUS DISEASE

Deaths from infectious disease, per 100,000 people, selected countries (latest figures, 1983-1988)

LIFE EXPECTANCY

Years of life expectancy at birth, selected countries (1988-1989)

The chart shows combined data for both sexes. On average, women live longer than men worldwide, even in developing countries with high maternal mortality rates. Overall, life expectancy is steadily rising, though the difference between rich and poor nations remains dramatic.

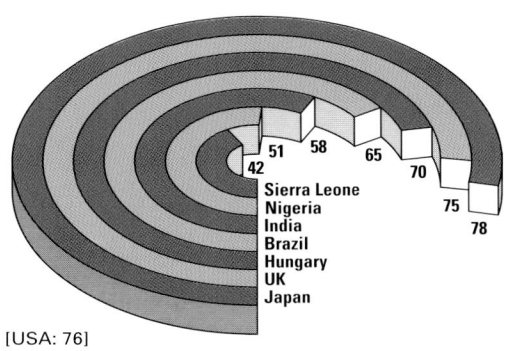

42 51 58 65 70 75 78

Sierra Leone
Nigeria
India
Brazil
Hungary
UK
Japan

[USA: 76]

INFANT MORTALITY

Number of babies who die before the age of one year, per thousand live births (1988)

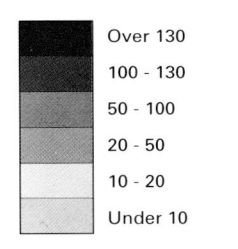

- Over 130
- 100 - 130
- 50 - 100
- 20 - 50
- 10 - 20
- Under 10

Highest infant mortality

Afghanistan 172
Ethiopia 154

Lowest infant mortality

Iceland 3
Japan 5

[USA 10] [UK 9]

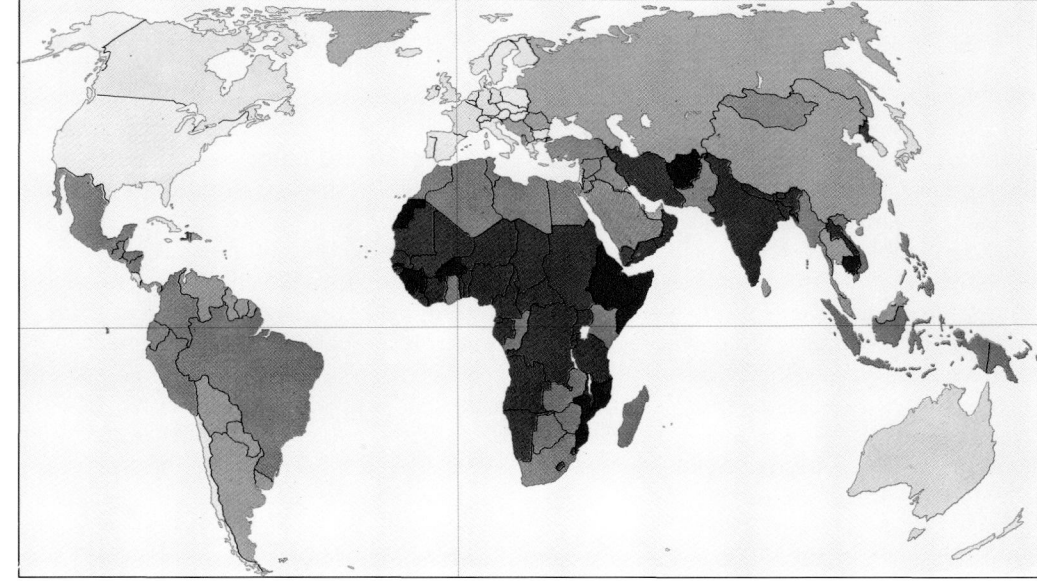

HOSPITAL CAPACITY

Hospital beds available for each 1,000 people (1983-1988)

Highest capacity		Lowest capacity	
Finland	14.9	Bangladesh	0.2
Sweden	13.2	Nepal	0.2
France	12.9	Ethiopia	0.3
USSR (1986)	12.8	Mauritania	0.4
Netherlands	12.0	Mali	0.5
North Korea	11.7	Burkina Faso	0.6
Switzerland	11.3	Pakistan	0.6
Austria	10.4	Niger	0.7
Czechoslovakia	10.1	Haiti	0.8
Hungary	9.1	Chad	0.8

[UK 8] [USA 5.9]

The availability of a bed can mean anything from a private room in a well-equipped Californian teaching hospital to a place in the overcrowded annexe of a rural African clinic. In the Third World especially, quality of treatment can vary enormously from place to place within the same country.

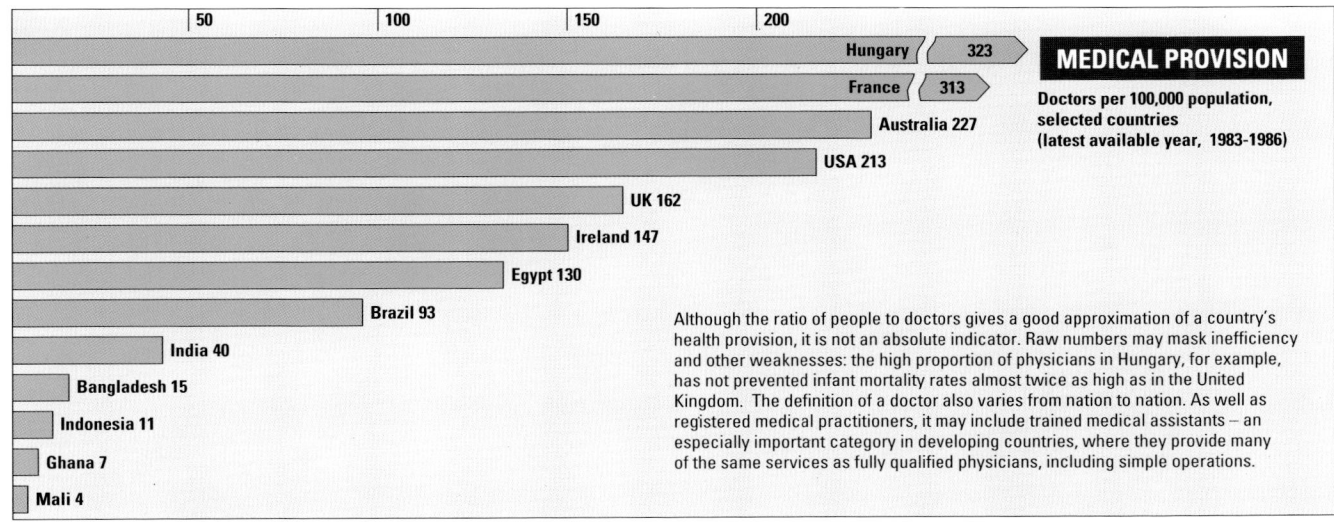

50 100 150 200

Hungary 323
France 313
Australia 227
USA 213
UK 162
Ireland 147
Egypt 130
Brazil 93
India 40
Bangladesh 15
Indonesia 11
Ghana 7
Mali 4

MEDICAL PROVISION

Doctors per 100,000 population, selected countries (latest available year, 1983-1986)

Although the ratio of people to doctors gives a good approximation of a country's health provision, it is not an absolute indicator. Raw numbers may mask inefficiency and other weaknesses: the high proportion of physicians in Hungary, for example, has not prevented infant mortality rates almost twice as high as in the United Kingdom. The definition of a doctor also varies from nation to nation. As well as registered medical practitioners, it may include trained medical assistants – an especially important category in developing countries, where they provide many of the same services as fully qualified physicians, including simple operations.

THE AIDS CRISIS

The Acquired Immune Deficiency Syndrome was first identified in 1981, when American doctors found otherwise healthy young men succumbing to rare infections. By 1984, the cause had been traced to the Human Immunodeficiency Virus (HIV), which can remain dormant for many years and perhaps indefinitely: only half of those known to carry the virus in 1981 had developed AIDS ten years later.

By 1991 the World Health Organization knew of more than 250,000 AIDS cases worldwide and suspected the true number to be at least four times as high. In Western countries in the early 1990s, most AIDS deaths were among male homosexuals or needle-sharing drug-users. However, the disease is spreading fastest among heterosexual men and women, which is its usual vector in the Third World, where most of its victims live. Africa is the most severely hit: a 1992 UN report estimated that 2 million African children will die of AIDS before the year 2000 – and some 10 million will be orphaned.

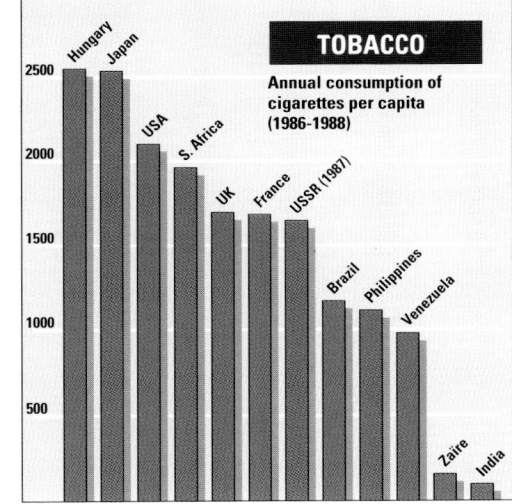

TOBACCO

Annual consumption of cigarettes per capita (1986-1988)

2500 Hungary Japan
2000 USA S. Africa
UK France USSR (1987)
1500
Brazil Philippines Venezuela
1000
500
Zaire India

CRIME & PUNISHMENT

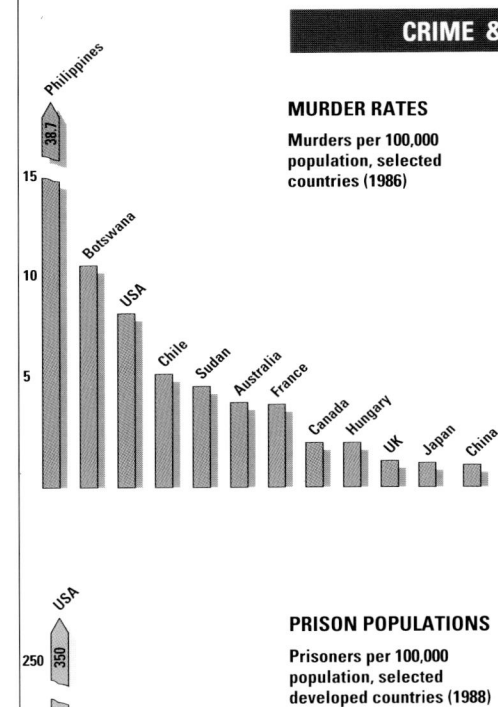

Philippines 38.7

MURDER RATES

Murders per 100,000 population, selected countries (1986)

15 Botswana
USA
10 Chile Sudan Australia France
5 Canada Hungary UK Japan China

Crime rates are difficult to compare internationally. Standards of reporting and detection vary greatly, as do the definitions of many types of crime. Murder is probably the best detected as well as the most heinous, but different legal systems make different distinctions between murder and manslaughter or other forms of culpable homicide. By any reckoning, however, the USA's high murder rate stands out against otherwise similar Western countries, although it is dwarfed by the killings recorded in the very different culture of the Philippines.

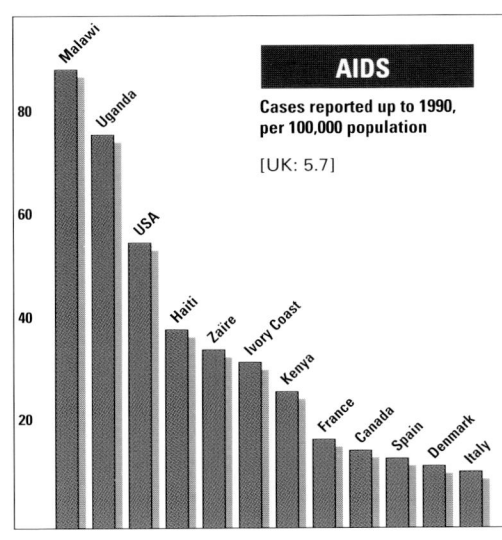

AIDS

Cases reported up to 1990, per 100,000 population

[UK: 5.7]

80 Malawi Uganda
USA
60
Haiti Zaire Ivory Coast
40 Kenya
France Canada Spain Denmark Italy
20

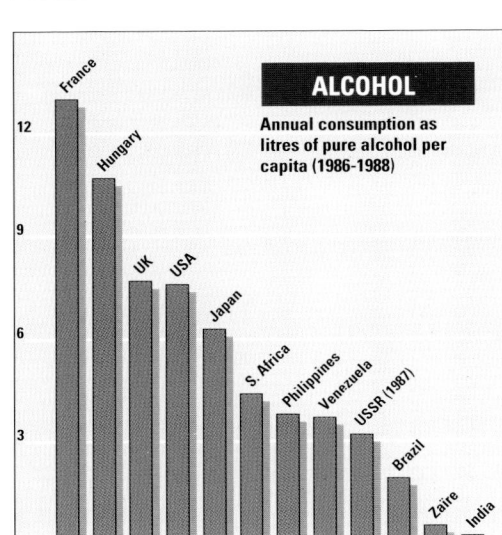

ALCOHOL

Annual consumption as litres of pure alcohol per capita (1986-1988)

12 France Hungary
UK USA Japan
9
S. Africa Philippines Venezuela USSR (1987)
6
Brazil
3
Zaire India

PRISON POPULATIONS

Prisoners per 100,000 population, selected developed countries (1988)

USA 350
250
200
150 Canada UK Turkey Germany (W) Portugal France Spain Australia Denmark Sweden Netherlands
100
50

Differences in prison population reflect penal policies as much as the relative honesty or otherwise of different nations, and by no means all governments publish accurate figures. In more than 50 countries, people are still regularly imprisoned without trial, in 60 torture is a normal part of interrogation, and some 130 retain the death penalty, often administered for political crimes and in secret. Over 2,000 executions were recorded in 1990 by the civil rights organization Amnesty International

QUALITY OF LIFE: ENVIRONMENT

10: OCEANS

12: ATMOSPHERE

14: CLIMATE

21: GREENHOUSE EFFECT

25: URBAN POLLUTION

Humans, have always had a dramatic effect on their environment, at least since the invention of agriculture almost 10,000 years ago. Generally, the Earth has accepted human interference without obvious ill effects: the complex systems that regulate the global environment have absorbed substantial damage while maintaining a stable and comfortable home for the planet's trillions of lifeforms. But advancing human technology and the rapidly expanding populations it supports are now threatening to overwhelm the Earth's ability to cope.

Industrial wastes, acid rainfall, expanding deserts and large-scale deforestation all combine to create environmental change at a rate far faster than the Earth can accommodate. Equipped with chain-saws and flame-throwers, humans can now destroy more forest in a day than their ancestors could in a century, upsetting the balance between plant and animal, carbon dioxide and oxygen, on which all life ultimately depends. The fossil fuels that power industrial civilization have pumped enough carbon dioxide and other green~house gases into the atmosphere to make climatic change a near-certainty. Chlorofluorocarbons (CFCs) and other man-made chemicals are rapidly eroding the ozone layer, the planet's screen against ultra-violet radiation.

As a result, the Earth's average temperature has risen by approximately 0.5°C since the beginning of this century. Further rises seem inevitable, with 1990 marked as the hottest year worldwide since records began. A warmer Earth probably means a wetter Earth, with melting icecaps raising sea levels and causing severe flooding in some of the world's most densely populated regions. Other climatic models suggest an alternative doom: rising temperatures could increase cloud cover, reflecting more solar energy back into space and causing a new ice age.

Either way, the consequences for humans could be disastrous – perhaps the Earth's own way of restoring ecological balance over the next few thousand years. Fortunately, there is a far faster mechanism available. Human ingenuity has provoked the present crisis; but human ingenuity, inspired if need be by fear, can respond to it. Production of CFCs is already almost at a standstill, and the first faltering steps towards stabilization and ultimately reduction of carbon dioxide have been taken, with Denmark pioneering the way by taxing emissions in 1991.

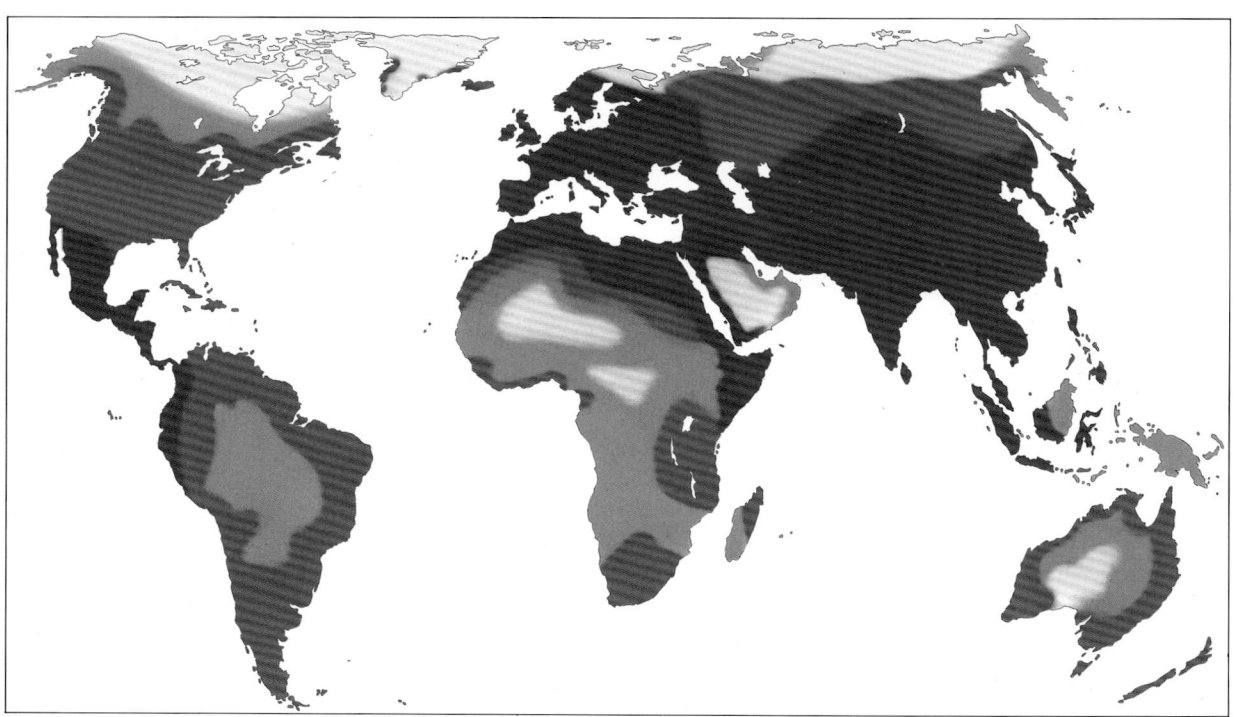

THE HISTORY OF HUMAN EXPANSION

The growth of ecological control: areas where human activity dominates the environment, from primitive times to the year 2000

- By 1500 AD
- By 1900 AD
- By 2000 AD
- Areas not dominated by human activity

THE RISE IN CARBON DIOXIDE

Emissions of carbon dioxide in millions of tonnes, 1950-1991

Atmospheric concentration of carbon dioxide, parts per million, 1750-2000. Pre-1950 data were obtained from air samples trapped in Antarctic ice.

Since the beginning of the Industrial Revolution, human activity has pumped steadily more carbon dioxide into the atmosphere. Most was quietly absorbed by the oceans, whose immense 'sink' capacity meant that 170 years were needed for levels to increase from the pre-industrial 280 parts per million to 300 (inset graph). But the vast increase in fuel-burning since 1950 (main graph) has overwhelmed even the oceanic sink. Atmospheric concentrations are now rising almost as steeply as carbon dioxide emissions themselves.

GREENHOUSE POWER

Relative contributions to the greenhouse effect by the major heat-absorbing gases in the atmosphere

The chart combines greenhouse potency and volume. Carbon dioxide has a greenhouse potential of only 1 but its concentration of 350 parts per million, makes it predominate. CFC 12 , with 25,000 times the absorption capacity of CO_2, is present only as 0.00044 ppm.

- Carbon dioxide
- Ozone
- Methane
- Nitrous oxide
- CFC 12
- CFC 11

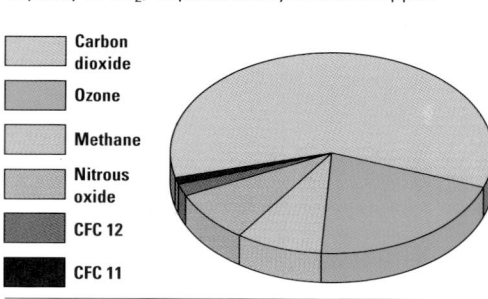

CARBON DIOXIDE

Carbon dioxide released in millions of tonnes (1980s)

Although most of the net increase in atmospheric carbon dioxide comes from fossil fuel combustion, deforestation and changing land use also contribute

- Fuel burning
- Deforestation

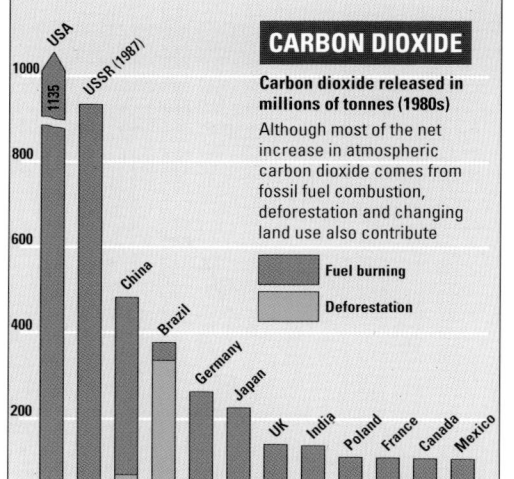

GLOBAL WARMING

The rise in average temperatures caused by carbon dioxide and other greenhouse gases (1960-2020)

- assumes present trends continue
- assumes drastic emissions cuts in the 1990s

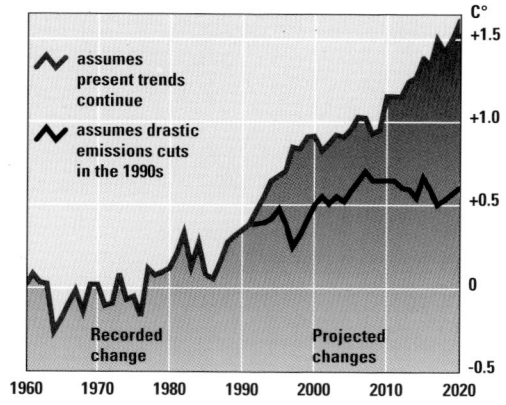

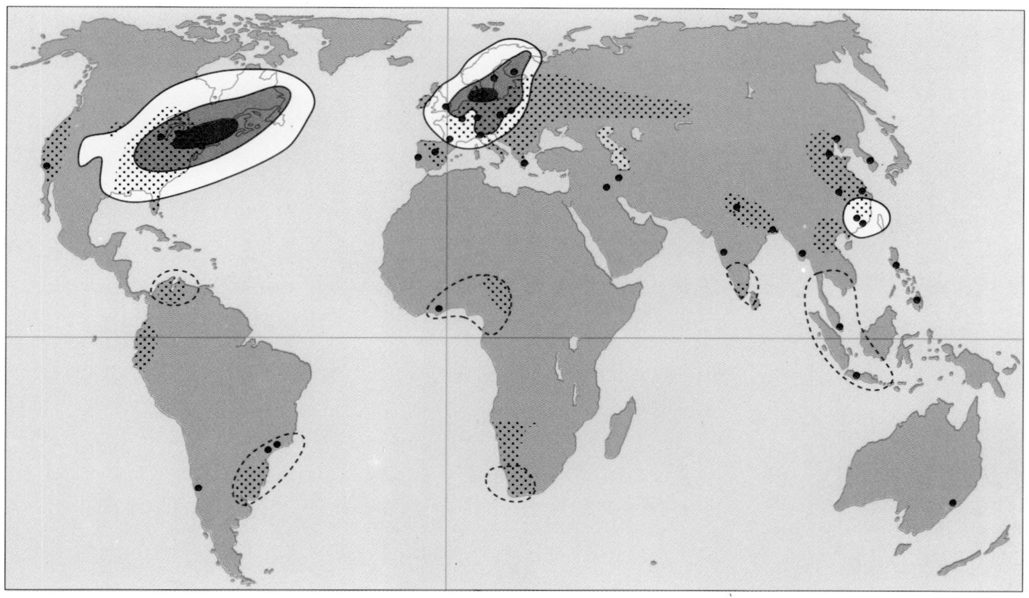

ACID RAIN

Acid rainfall & sources of acidic emissions (1980s)

Acid rain is caused when sulphur & nitrogen oxides in the air combine with water vapour to form sulphuric, nitric & other acids.

Regions where sulphur and nitrogen oxides are released in high concentrations, mainly from fossil fuel combustion.

• Major cities with high levels of air pollution (including nitrogen & sulphur emissions)

Areas of heavy acid deposition

pH numbers indicate acidity, decreasing from a neutral 7. Normal rain, slightly acid from dissolved carbon dioxide, never exceeds a pH of 5.6.

pH less than 4.0 (most acidic)
pH 4.0 to 4.5
pH 4.5 to 5.0

Areas where acid rain is a potential danger

THE ANTARCTIC

The vast Antarctic ice-sheet, containing some 70% of the Earth's fresh water, plays a crucial role in the circulation of atmosphere and oceans and hence in determining the planetary climate. The frozen southern continent is also the last remaining wilderness – the largest area to remain free from human colonization.

Ever since Amundsen and Scott raced for the South Pole in 1911, various countries have pressed territorial claims over sections of Antarctica, spurred in recent years by its known and suspected mineral wealth: enough iron ore to supply the world at present levels for 200 years, large oil reserves and, probably, the biggest coal deposits on Earth.

However, the 1961 Antarctic Treaty set aside the area for peaceful uses only, guaranteeing freedom of scientific investigation, banning waste disposal and nuclear testing, and suspending the issue of territorial rights. By 1990, the original 12 signatories had grown to 25, with a further 15 nations granted observer status in subsequent deliberations. However, the Treaty itself was threatened by wrangles between different countries, government agencies and international pressure groups.

Finally, in July, 1991, the belated agreement of the UK and the US assured unanimity on a new accord to ban all mineral exploration for a further 50 years. The ban can only be rescinded if all present signatories, plus a majority of any future adherents, agree. While the treaty has always lacked a formal mechanism for enforcement, it is firmly underwritten by public concern generated by the efforts of environmental pressure groups such as Greenpeace, foremost in the campaign to have Antarctica declared a 'World Park'.

It seems likely that the virtually uninhabited continent will remain untouched by tourism, nuclear-free and dedicated to peaceful scientific research.

DESERTIFICATION

Existing deserts
Areas with a high risk of desertification
Areas with a moderate risk of desertification
Former areas of rainforest
Existing rainforest

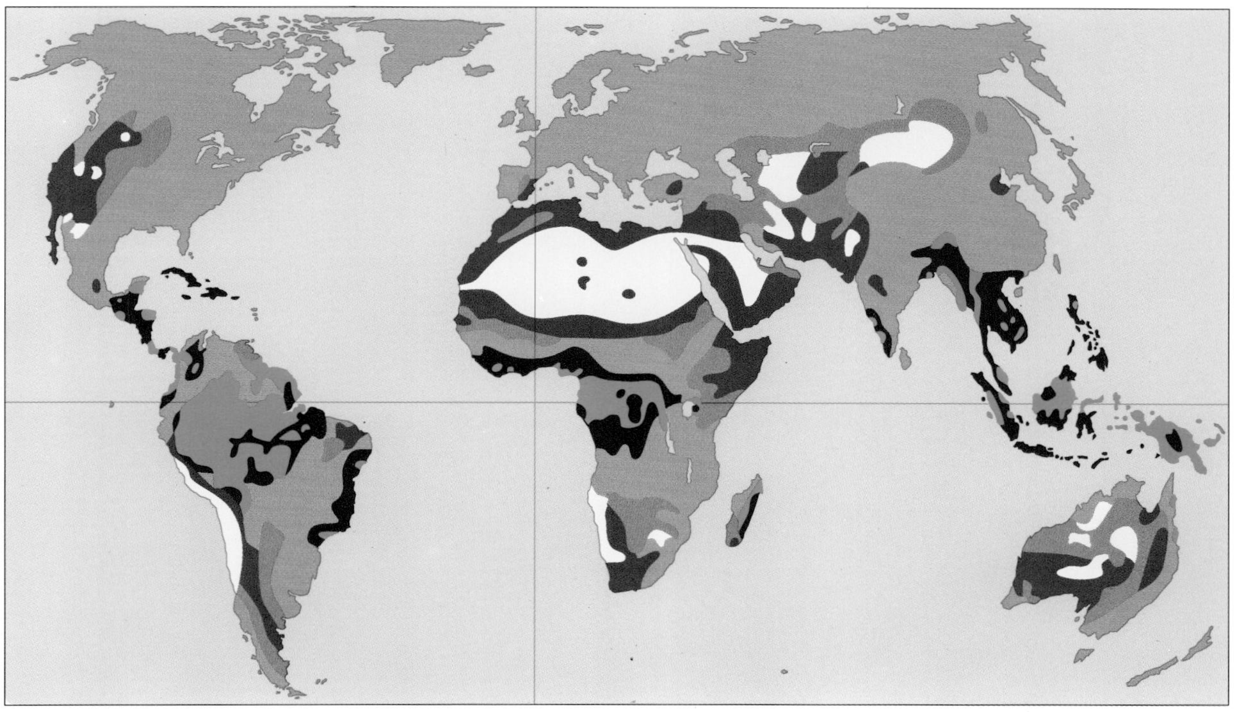

DEFORESTATION

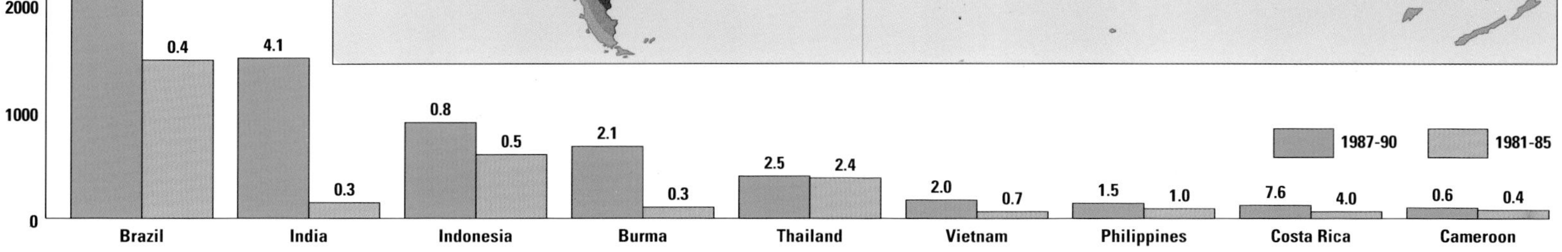

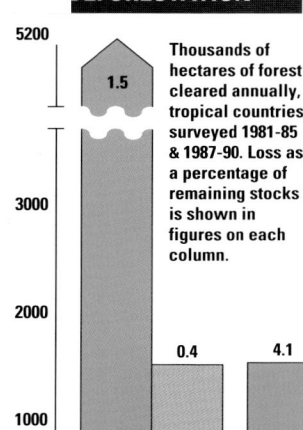

5200

1.5

Thousands of hectares of forest cleared annually, tropical countries surveyed 1981-85 & 1987-90. Loss as a percentage of remaining stocks is shown in figures on each column.

3000

2000

1000

0

	1987-90	1981-85
Brazil	0.4	
India	4.1	0.3
Indonesia	0.8	0.5
Burma	2.1	0.3
Thailand	2.5	2.4
Vietnam	2.0	0.7
Philippines	1.5	1.0
Costa Rica	7.6	4.0
Cameroon	0.6	0.4

WATER POLLUTION

Severely polluted sea areas & lakes
Less polluted sea areas & lakes
Areas of frequent oil pollution by shipping
Major oil tanker spills ▶
Major oil rig blow outs ▲
Offshore dumpsites for industrial & municipal waste ▼
Severely polluted rivers & estuaries

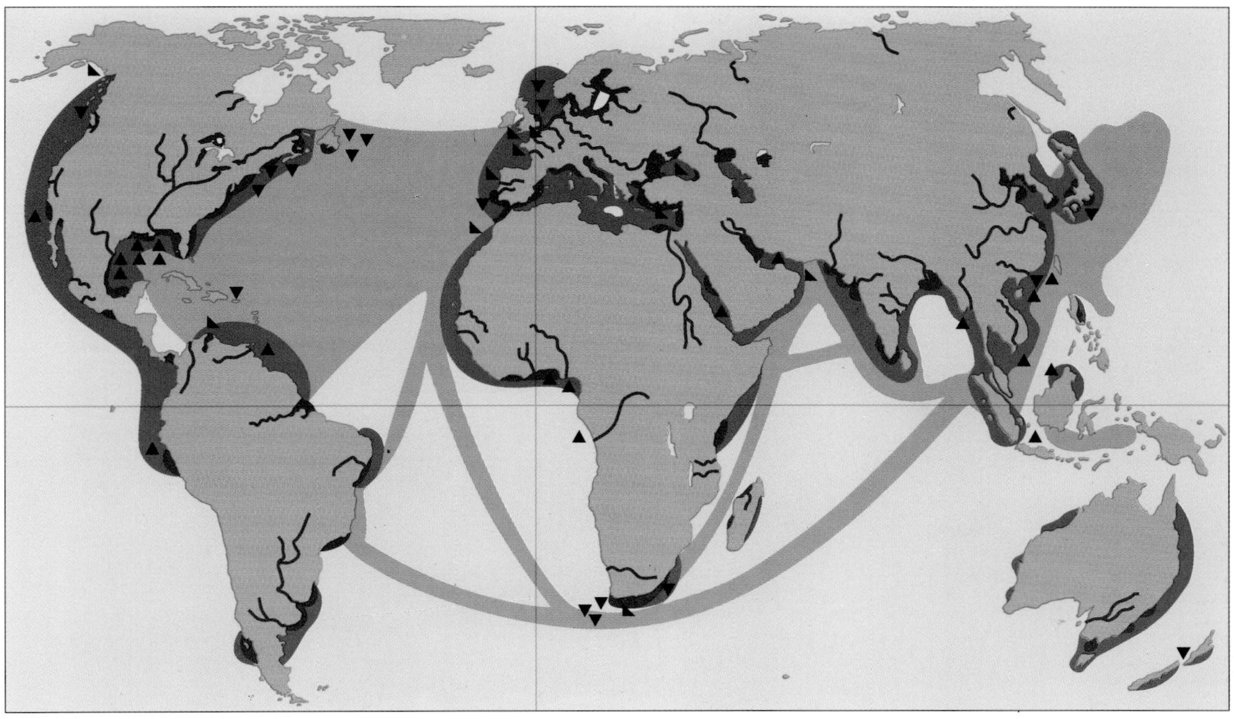

Poisoned rivers, domestic sewage and oil spillage have combined in recent years to reduce the world's oceans to a sorry state of contamination, notably near the crowded coasts of industrialized nations. Shipping routes, too, are constantly affected by tanker discharges. Oil spills of all kinds, however, declined significantly during the 1980s, from a peak of 750,000 tonnes in 1979 to under 50,000 tonnes in 1990. The most notorious tanker spill of that period – when the *Exxon Valdez* (94,999 grt) ran aground in Prince William Sound, Alaska, in March 1989 – released only 267,000 barrels, a relatively small amount compared to the results of blow-outs and war damage. 2,500,000 barrels were spilled during the Gulf War of 1991; the worst tanker accident in history occurred in July 1979, when the *Atlantic Empress* and the *Aegean Captain* collided off Trinidad, polluting the Caribbean with 1,890,000 barrels of crude oil.

WORLD MAPS

MAP SYMBOLS

SETTLEMENTS

◻ PARIS   ◼ Berne   ◉ Livorno   ◉ Brugge   ◎ Algeciras   ◉ Fréjus   ○ Oberammergau   ○ Thira

Settlement symbols and type styles vary according to the scale of each map and indicate the importance of towns on the map rather than specific population figures

∴   Ruins or Archæological Sites   ⌣   Wells in Desert

ADMINISTRATION

——— International Boundaries

— — — International Boundaries (Undefined or Disputed)

········· Internal Boundaries

National Parks

Country Names

NICARAGUA

Administrative Area Names

KENT

CALABRIA

International boundaries show the *de facto* situation where there are rival claims to territory

COMMUNICATIONS

——— Principal Roads

⌣ Other Roads

-·-·- Trails and Seasonal Roads

⨝ Passes

✧ Airfields

⌣ Principal Railways

··-·- Railways Under Construction

⌣ Other Railways

⌐--⌐ Railway Tunnels

··········· Principal Canals

PHYSICAL FEATURES

⌣ Perennial Streams

········· Intermittent Streams

◯ Perennial Lakes

⬭ Intermittent Lakes

⬭ Swamps and Marshes

▭ Permanent Ice and Glaciers

▴ 8848   Elevations in metres

• 8050   Sea Depths in metres

1134   Height of Lake Surface Above Sea Level in metres

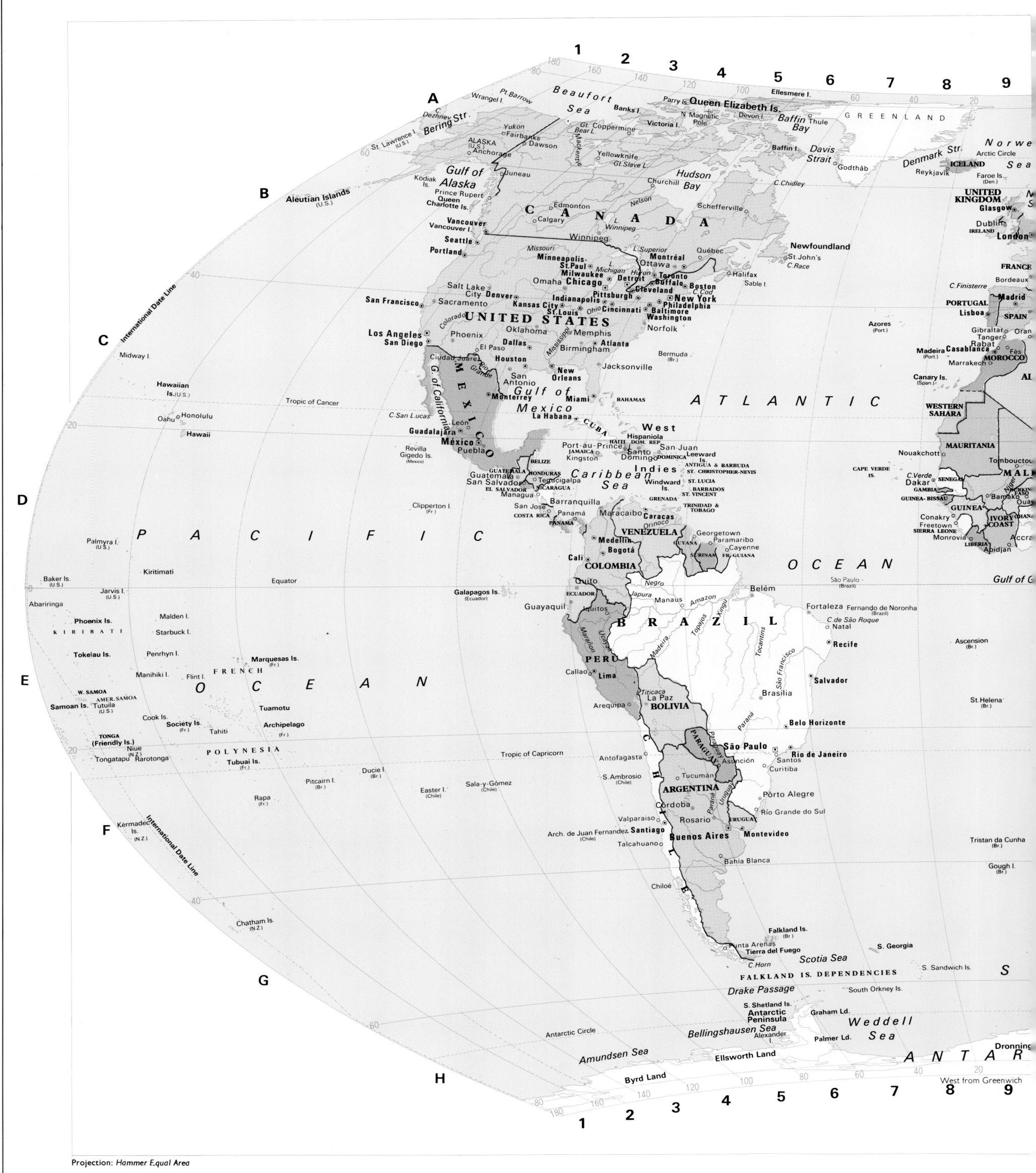

A

Wrangel I.
Pt. Barrow
Beaufort Sea
Banks I.
Parry Is.
N Magnetic Pole
Victoria I.
Devon I.
Queen Elizabeth Is.
Ellesmere I.
Baffin Bay
Thule
GREENLAND

Dezhnev Str.
Bering Str.
St. Lawrence I. (U.S.)
Yukon
Fairbanks
Dawson
ALASKA (U.S.)
Anchorage
Gt. Coppermine
Bear L.
Mackenzie
Yellowknife
Gt. Slave L.
Hudson Bay
Baffin I.
Davis Strait
Godthåb
Denmark Str.
Arctic Circle
Faroe Is. (Den.)
Norwe
Sea
ICELAND
Reykjavik

B
Aleutian Islands (U.S.)
Gulf of Alaska
Kodiak Is.
Prince Rupert
Queen Charlotte Is.
Vancouver
Vancouver I.
CANADA
Edmonton
Calgary
Winnipeg
Nelson
Churchill
C Chidley
Schefferville
Newfoundland
St. John's
C. Race
Halifax
Sable I.
UNITED KINGDOM
Glasgow
Dublin
IRELAND
London
FRANCE
Bordeaux
C. Finisterre

Seattle
Portland
Missouri
L. Superior
Minneapolis-St. Paul
Milwaukee
Michigan
Ottawa
Montréal
Québec
St. Paul
Huron
Detroit
Toronto
Buffalo
Boston
C. Cod
New York

C
San Francisco
Sacramento
Salt Lake City
Denver
Colorado
UNITED STATES
Omaha
Kansas City
St. Louis
Ohio
Indianapolis
Pittsburgh
Cleveland
Cincinnati
Philadelphia
Baltimore
Washington
Norfolk
International Date Line
Midway I.

Los Angeles
San Diego
Phoenix
El Paso
Oklahoma
Dallas
Memphis
Birmingham
Atlanta
Jacksonville
Bermuda (Br.)
Azores (Port.)
PORTUGAL
Lisboa
SPAIN
Madrid
Gibraltar
Tanger
Rabat
Madeira (Port.)
Casablanca
Fès
MOROCCO
Marrakech

Hawaiian Is. (U.S.)
Tropic of Cancer
Ciudad Juárez
Rio Grande
San Antonio
Houston
New Orleans
Miami
Gulf of Mexico
BAHAMAS
ATLANTIC
Canary Is. (Span.)
WESTERN SAHARA
Al

Oahu
Honolulu
Hawaii
C. San Lucas
MÉXICO
G. of California
León
Monterrey
La Habana
CUBA
West
Hispaniola
HAITI
DOM. REP.
San Juan
Leeward Is.
Nouakchott
MAURITANIA
Tombouctou

Revilla Gigedo Is. (Mexico)
Guadalajara
México
Puebla
Port-au-Prince
Santo Domingo
Kingston
JAMAICA
DOMINICA
ANTIGUA & BARBUDA
ST. CHRISTOPHER-NEVIS
CAPE VERDE IS.
C. Verde
Dakar
SENEGAL
MALI
Bamako

D
GUATEMALA
BELIZE
HONDURAS
San Salvador
Tegucigalpa
EL SALVADOR
NICARAGUA
Managua
Indies
Caribbean Sea
ST. LUCIA
Windward Is.
BARBADOS
ST. VINCENT
GRENADA
TRINIDAD & TOBAGO
GUINEA-BISSAU
GAMBIA
Conakry
Freetown
SIERRA LEONE
GUINEA
Ouas
IVORY COAST
Accra

San Jose
COSTA RICA
Panamá
Barranquilla
PANAMA
Maracaibo
Caracas
Georgetown
Paramaribo
Cayenne
Monrovia
LIBERIA
Abidjan

PACIFIC
Palmyra I. (U.S.)
Kiritimati
VENEZUELA
Medellín
Bogotá
GUYANA
SURINAM
FR. GUIANA
OCEAN

Baker Is. (U.S.)
Jarvis I. (U.S.)
Equator
COLOMBIA
Cali
Quito
Negro
São Paulo (Brazil)
Gulf of G

Abariringa
Phoenix Is.
Malden I.
Galapagos Is. (Ecuador)
ECUADOR
Guayaquil
Iquitos
Japura
Manaus
Amazon
Belém
Fortaleza
Fernando de Noronha (Brazil)
C. de São Roque
Natal
Ascension (Br.)

KIRIBATI
Starbuck I.
BRAZIL
Madeira
Tapajós
Xingu
Tocantins
Recife

Tokelau Is.
Penrhyn I.
Marquesas Is. (Fr.)
PERÚ
Marañón
Ucayali
São Francisco
Salvador

E
W. SAMOA
AMER. SAMOA
Samoan Is. Tutuila (U.S.)
Manihiki I.
Flint I.
FRENCH
Tuamotu
Callao
Lima
Titicaca
La Paz
BOLIVIA
Arequipa
Brasília
St. Helena (Br.)

OCEAN
Cook Is.
Society Is. (Fr.)
Tahiti
Archipelago (Fr.)
Belo Horizonte

TONGA (Friendly Is.)
Niue (N.Z.)
Tongatapu
Rarotonga
POLYNESIA
Tubuai Is. (Fr.)
Tropic of Capricorn
Antofagasta
Paraná
Paraguay
São Paulo
PARAGUAY
Asunción
Santos
Rio de Janeiro
Curitiba

Pitcairn I. (Br.)
Ducie I. (Br.)
Easter I. (Chile)
Sala-y-Gómez (Chile)
S. Ambrosio (Chile)
Tucumán
Pôrto Alegre
Río Grande do Sul

Rapa (Fr.)
Córdoba
ARGENTINA
Paraná
Uruguay
URUGUAY

F
Kermadec Is. (N.Z.)
International Date Line
Valparaíso
Arch. de Juan Fernandez (Chile)
Santiago
Rosario
Buenos Aires
Montevideo
Tristan da Cunha (Br.)

Talcahuano
Bahía Blanca
Gough I. (Br.)

Chiloé
Falkland Is. (Br.)
S. Georgia

G
Chatham Is. (N.Z.)
Punta Arenas
Tierra del Fuego
C. Horn
Scotia Sea
S. Sandwich Is.
S
FALKLAND IS. DEPENDENCIES

Drake Passage
South Orkney Is.

S. Shetland Is.
Antarctic Peninsula
Graham Ld.
Weddell Sea

Antarctic Circle
Bellingshausen Sea
Alexander
Palmer Ld.
Dronning

Amundsen Sea
Ellsworth Land
ANTAR

H
Byrd Land
West from Greenwich

Projection: Hammer Equal Area

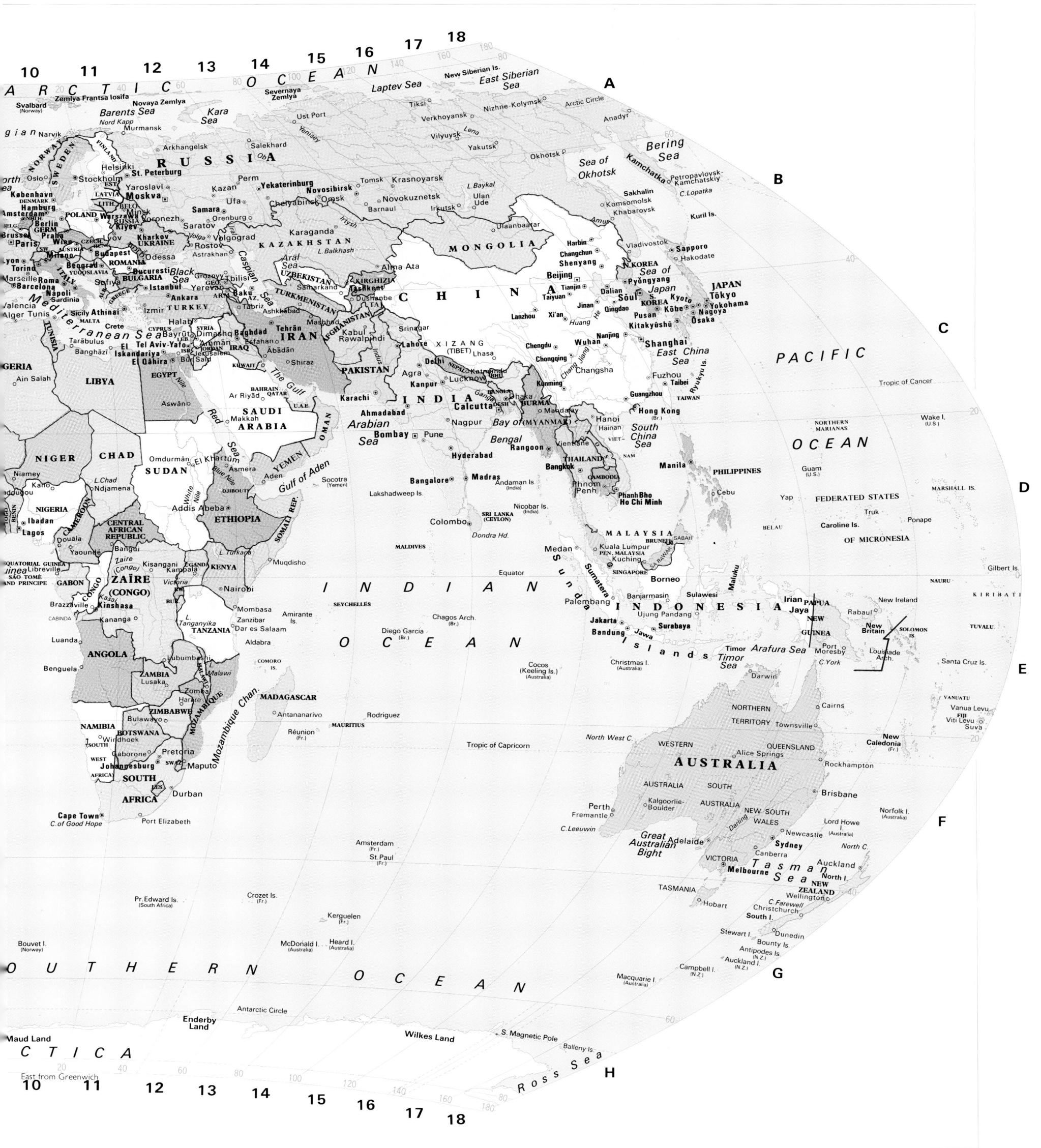

18
17
16
15
14
13
12
11
10

A R C T I C   O C E A N

A

Svalbard (Norway)   Zemlya Frantsa Iosifa   Novaya Zemlya   Severnaya Zemlya
Nord Kapp   Murmansk   Kara Sea   Ust Port   Tiksi   Verkhoyansk   Nizhne-Kolymsk   Arctic Circle
Barents Sea   Salekhard   Yenisey   Lena   Vilyuysk   Yakutsk   Okhotsk   Anadyr   Bering Sea
Narvik   Arkhangelsk   Ob   Bering Sea

NORWAY   Oslo   SWEDEN   FINLAND   Helsinki   **RUSSIA**   Kamchatka   Petropavlovsk-Kamchatskiy   **B**
Stockholm   St. Peterburg   Yekaterinburg   Tomsk   Krasnoyarsk   L. Baykal   Sea of Okhotsk
Kobenhavn   ESTLATVIA   Moskva   Perm   Novosibirsk   Ulan Ude   Sakhalin   C. Lopatka
DENMARK   LITH. BELO.   Kazan   Yaroslavl   Chelyabinsk   Omsk   Novokuznetsk   Irkutsk   Khabarovsk   Kuril Is.
Hamburg   Amsterdam   POLAND   Warszawa   Samara   Orenburg   Barnaul   Ulaanbaatar   Amur   Vladivostok   Sapporo
Berlin   GERM.   Minsk   RUSSIA   Saratov   Harbin   Hakodate
Brussel   Praha   CZECH.   Kiyev   Voronezh   KAZAKHSTAN   Changchun   N.KOREA   Sea of   JAPAN
Paris   AUSTRIA   UKRAINE   Kharkov   Rostov   Karaganda   Alma Ata   Shenyang   Pyongyang   Japan
Lyon   Torino   Budapest   ROMANIA   Volgograd   Astrakhan   L. Balkhash   Beijing   Dalian   KOREA   Kyoto   Tokyo
Milano   YUGOSLAVIA   Beograd   Bucuresti   Black Sea   Aral Sea   Tianjin   Taiyuan   Jinan   Qingdao   Soul   Pusan   Kobe   Yokohama
Marseille   Roma   ITALY   Sofiya   BULGARIA   Grozny   GEO.   Tbilisi   UZBEKISTAN   KIRGHIZIA   Lanzhou   Xi'an   Huang   **C H I N A**   Nagoya   Osaka
Barcelona   Napoli   GREECE   Istanbul   Ankara   Yerevan   ARM.   Baku   Tashkent   Samarkand   Kitakyushu
Valencia   Sardinia   Sicily   Athinai   TURKEY   Izmir   AZ.   Caspian Sea   TURKMENISTAN   Dushanbe   Chengdu   Chongqing   Chang Jiang   Wuhan   Shanghai   **C**
Alger   Tunis   Crete   CYPRUS   Halab   SYRIA   Tabriz   Ashkhabad   AFGHANISTAN   TAJ.   XIZANG (TIBET)   Lhasa   Changsha   East China Sea
Mediterranean Sea   MALTA   Bayrut   Dimashq   Tehran   **I R A N**   Mashhad   Kabul   Srinagar   Kunming   Fuzhou   Ryukyu Is.
TUNISIA   Tel Aviv-Yafo   LEB.   Baghdad   Esfahan   Rawalpindi   Lahore   NEPAL   Kathmandu   Guangzhou   Taibei
El Iskandariya   ISR.   JORDAN   IRAQ   Abadan   Delhi   Kanpur   BHU.   Chongqing   Hong Kong (Br.)   TAIWAN
El Qahira   Amman   KUWAIT   Shiraz   PAKISTAN   Agra   Lucknow   BANGL.   Nanjing   Tropic of Cancer
Tropic of Cancer
ALGERIA   Ar Riyad   BAHRAIN   The Gulf   Karachi   **I N D I A**   Dhaka   BURMA   Hanoi   South China Sea   PACIFIC
Ain Salah   QATAR   U.A.E.   Ahmadabad   Calcutta   (MYANMAR)   Mandalay   Hainan   NORTHERN MARIANAS   Wake I. (U.S.)
LIBYA   EGYPT   Makkah   SAUDI   OMAN   Bombay   Nagpur   Bay of   Rangoon   VIET.   OCEAN
Aswan   Nile   ARABIA   Arabian   Pune   Bengal   THAILAND   NAM   Guam (U.S.)
Red Sea   Hyderabad   Bangkok   CAMBODIA   Manila   PHILIPPINES
NIGER   CHAD   Omdurman   El Khartum   YEMEN   Sea   Bangalore   Madras   Andaman Is.   Phnom   Cebu   MARSHALL IS.   **D**
Niamey   Kano   SUDAN   Blue Nile   Asmera   Aden   Socotra (Yemen)   (India)   Penh   Ho Chi Minh   Yap   FEDERATED STATES
Ndjamena   DJIBOUTI   Gulf of Aden   Lakshadweep Is.   Nicobar Is.   Phanh Bho   Truk   Ponape
NIGERIA   CAMEROON   CENTRAL   Addis Abeba   SOMALI REP.   (India)   MALAYSIA   BRUNEI   SABAH   BELAU   Caroline Is.   OF MICRONESIA
Ibadan   AFRICAN   ETHIOPIA   Colombo   SRI LANKA (CEYLON)   Kuala Lumpur   Kuching   SARAWAK
Lagos   REPUBLIC   Bangui   Dondra Hd.   PEN. MALAYSIA   Borneo
EQUATORIAL GUINEA   Yaounde   Zaire (Congo)   UGANDA   KENYA   MALDIVES   Medan   SINGAPORE
Libreville   Kisangani   Kampala   Equator   Sumatera   Banjarmasin   Sulawesi   NAURU
SAO TOME AND PRINCIPE   GABON   ZAIRE   Victoria   Nairobi   Palembang   **I N D O N E S I A**   Irian   PAPUA   KIRIBATI
Brazzaville   (CONGO)   BUR.   Mombasa   Amirante Is.   SEYCHELLES   Chagos Arch. (Br.)   Ujung Pandang   Jaya   New Ireland   Gilbert Is.
CABINDA   Kinshasa   L. Tanganyika   Zanzibar   Jakarta   Jawa   Surabaya   NEW   Rabaul
Kananga   TANZANIA   Dar es Salaam   Diego Garcia (Br.)   Bandung   GUINEA   New Britain   SOLOMON IS.
Luanda   Aldabra   Timor   Arafura Sea   Port   Louisiade   TUVALU
ANGOLA   Benguela   Lubumbashi   COMORO IS.   Christmas I. (Australia)   Sunda Islands   Timor Sea   Moresby   C. York   Arch.   Santa Cruz Is.   **E**
ZAMBIA   Lusaka   Malawi   MADAGASCAR   Cocos (Keeling Is.) (Australia)   Darwin   VANUATU
NAMIBIA   ZIMBABWE   Zomba   Antananarivo   Rodriguez   NORTHERN   Cairns   Vanua Levu   FIJI
Bulawayo   Harare   MAURITIUS   TERRITORY   Townsville   New   Viti Levu   Suva
Windhoek   BOTSWANA   MOZAMBIQUE   Mozambique Chan.   Reunion (Fr.)   Caledonia (Fr.)
Gaborone   Pretoria   SWAZ.   Tropic of Capricorn   North West C.   WESTERN   QUEENSLAND
Johannesburg   LES.   Amsterdam (Fr.)   Alice Springs   Rockhampton
SOUTH   Maputo   St. Paul (Fr.)   **A U S T R A L I A**   Brisbane
AFRICA   Durban   AUSTRALIA   SOUTH   New   Norfolk I. (Australia)   **F**
Cape Town   Port Elizabeth   Perth   Kalgoorlie-   AUSTRALIA   NEW SOUTH   Lord Howe (Australia)
C. of Good Hope   Fremantle   Boulder   WALES   Newcastle   North C.
Pr. Edward Is. (South Africa)   Crozet Is. (Fr.)   C. Leeuwin   Great   Adelaide   Darling   Sydney   Auckland   North I.
Australian   VICTORIA   Canberra   NEW
Kerguelen (Fr.)   Bight   Melbourne   Tasman Sea   ZEALAND
Bouvet I. (Norway)   McDonald I.   Heard I. (Australia)   TASMANIA   Wellington
(Australia)   C. Farewell   Christchurch   South I.
S O U T H E R N   O C E A N   Hobart   Stewart I.   Dunedin   **G**
Bounty Is. (N.Z.)
Macquarie I. (Australia)   Campbell I. (N.Z.)   Antipodes Is. (N.Z.)
Auckland Is. (N.Z.)
Antarctic Circle
Maud Land   Enderby Land   Wilkes Land   S. Magnetic Pole   Balleny Is.   **H**
CTICA   Ross Sea

East from Greenwich
10   11   12   13   14   15   16   17   18

1 : 28 000 000

200 100   0   200   400   600 miles
400   200   0   200   400   600   800   1200 km

18   17   16   15

JAPAN

PACIFIC OCEAN

Aleutian Islands
Near Is.
Dutch Harbor
Unimak I.
Pribilof Is.
Komandorskiye Ostrova
Vlk. Klyuchevskaya 4850
▼7822

Bering Sea

Mys Lopatka
Kurilskiye Ostrova
La Perouse St.
Hokkaidō

Kodiak I.
Alaska Pen.
Bristol Bay
Nunivak
St. Matthew (U.S.A.)
Mys Navarin
St. Lawrence I. (U.S.A.)
Anadyrskiy Zaliv
Mys Olyutorski
Ostrov Karaginskiy
Poluostrov Kamchatka
Petropavlovsk-Kamchatskiy
Penzhinskaya G.
Gizhiginskaya Guba

Sea of Okhotsk

Sakhalin
Tatarskiy Proliv
Sovetskaya Gavan
Amur
Nikolayevsk
Ulbanskiy Zaliv
Udskaya Guba
Khabarovsk

G. of Alaska
Cook Inlet
Pr. William Sd.
Seward
Anchorage
Cordova
Mt. St. Elias 5489
Mt. Logan 6050
Mt. McKinley 6194
Fairbanks
Sitka
Juneau
Skagway
Whitehorse
Lewes

ALASKA

Yukon
Kuskokwim
St. Michael
Nome
Norton Sd.
Mys Chukotskiy
C. Pr. of Wales
Kotzebue Sd.
Koyukuk
Noatak
Pt. Hope
C. Lisburne
Pt. Barrow
Prudhoe Bay
Harrison B.
C. Halkett
C. Belcher
Proliv Longa
Ostrova Vrangelya

Chukchi Sea

Anadyr
Penzhina
Okhotsko Kolymskoye
Chukotskiy Khrebet
Nizhne Kolymsk
Kolyma
Sredne Kolymsk
Alazeya
Chaunskaya G.
Russkoye Ustie
Indigirka
Zashiversk
Verkhoyansk
Yana
Kazache
Verkhoyanskiy Khrebet
Aldan
Yakutsk
Lena
Olekma
Stanovoy Khrebet

Rocky Mountains
Pr. Rupert
Skeena
Dawson Creek

Liard
Peace
Fort Vermilion
Athabasca
Fort Simpson
Fort Norman
Fort Good Hope
Mackenzie
C. Bathurst
Herschel
Fort McPherson
Mackenzie Bay
Port Brabant

Great Bear Lake

Beaufort Sea

3767

Novosibirskiye Ostrova
Lyakhovskiye Ostrova
O. Kotelnyy
Lena
Bulun
Tiksi
Olenek
Anabar

Laptev Sea

Zhigansk
Vilyuy

SIBERIA

NORTH AMERICA

Yellowknife
Gt. Slave Lake
Coppermine
Athabasca L.
Dubawnt L.
Churchill

Victoria Island
Banks I.
C. Kellett
C. Pr. Alfred
Wollaston Pen.
Melville I.
M'Clure Str.
Pr. Albert Pen.
Pr. Patrick
Parry Is.
Borden I.
3700
Ellef Ringnes I.
Melville Sd.
King William I.
Boothia Pen.
Somerset I.
Axel Heiberg I.
Sverdrup Is.
Nansen Sd.
Eureka
2104

ARCTIC OCEAN

Canada Basin

Mendeleyev Ridge
3327

Alpha Cordillera 4007
Makarov Basin
Lomonosov Ridge
NORTH POLE
Fram Basin 4418
3741
Nansen Cordillera 4100
Nansen Basin 4484
3849
3545

O. Bennetta

O. Petra
Nordvik
Kotuy
Poluostrov Taymyr
Severnaya Zemlya
O. Oktyabrskoy Revolyutsii
O. Uedineniya
O. Ushakova
O. Vise
Ostrov Graham Bell
Z. Vilcheka
Zemlya Frantsa Iosifa
Alexandra Ld.

Oz. Taymyr
Pyasina
Norilsk
Dudinka
Igarka
Yenisey
Turukhansk
Taz
Urengoy
Plato Putorana
Kheta
Golchikha
Podkamennaya Tunguska
Nizhnyaya Tunguska

Hudson Bay
Southampton I.
Coats I.
Mansel
Rivers Welcome Sd.
Chesterfield

Melville Pen.
Foxe Channel
Fury & Hecla Str.
G. of Boothia
Pr. Regent Inlet
Barrow Str.
Lancaster Sd.
Bylot I.
Devon I.
Jones Sd.
Ellesmere I.
C. Columbia
Alert
Lincoln Sea
Robeson Ch.
Smith Sd.
Kane Basin
Thule
Dundas
Humboldt Gletscher
Markham I.
K. Morris Jesup
Peary Ld.
Rasmussen Land
Knud

Magnetic Pole 1990
Bathurst I.

McKinley Sea

Nordkapp
A
B

Ostrov Belyy
Poluostrov Yamal
Kara Sea
Baydaratskaya Guba
Novaya Zemlya
Novy Port
Nadym
Salekhard
Surgut
Ob

C. Wolstenholme
Nettilling
2399
K. York
Baffin Bay
Frobisher B.
Hudson Str.
Cumberland Sd.
Resolution I.
C. Chidley
Ungava B.
Feuilles R.
Labrador
C. Dyer
Disko B.
Disko
Godhavn
Umanak
Upernavik

Baffin Island

Davis Str.

Kong Frederik IX.s. Land

GREENLAND (Denmark)

Kong Christian IX.s Land
Kong Christian X.s Land
K. Franz Joseph Fd.
Kong Oscar Fj.
Scoresbysund
Mont Forel 3360
Gunnbjørn Field 3700
K. Brewster

Greenland Sea

2571
Vestspitsbergen
Longyearbyen
Svalbard (Norway)
Edgeøya
Nordaustlandet
Nordkapp

Barents Sea

Bjørnøya

Ostrov Kolguyev
Mys Kanin Nos
Pechora
Vorkuta
Khabarovo
Berezovo
Narodnaya 1894
Uralskie Gory
Tobolsk

Godthåb
Frederikshåb
Julianehåb
Sydprøven
C. Charles
Hamilton Inlet

Kong Frederik VI.s Kyst
Angmagssalik
Horn
Breiðafjörður
Reykjavík
Hekla 1491
Øræfajökull

ICELAND

Denmark Strait
Iceland Plateau
Jan Mayen
3800
Faroe Is.

Norwegian Sea

Arctic Circle

Tromsø
Lofoten
Hammerfest
Vadsø
Varangerfjord
Murmansk
Kolskiy Poluostrov
Beloye More
Arkhangelsk
Mezen
Onega
Sev. Dvina
Vychegda
Ufa
Perm
Yekaterinburg

NORWAY
SWEDEN
Trondheim
Oslo
Bergen
Stockholm

FINLAND
Gulf of Bothnia
Helsinki
Tornio
Ladozhskoye Ozero
Onezhskoye Ozero
Tallinn
St. Peterburg
Chudskoye Ozero

RUSSIA
Moskvá
Saratov
Volga
Volgograd
Samara
Rostov

Shetland Is.
Orkney Is.
Hebrides
Rockall
4755

Mid-Atlantic Ridge

ATLANTIC OCEAN

BRITISH ISLES
SCOTLAND
Glasgow
Edinburgh
Belfast
IRELAND
Dublin
Liverpool
ENGLAND
WALES
C. Clear
Cork

North Sea

DENMARK
København
Skagerrak
Kattegat
Baltic Sea
Gdańsk
Szczecin
Hamburg
Elbe
Berlin
Leipzig
Köln
Amsterdam
NETH.
GERMANY
London
Praha
Wrocław
Łódź
POLAND
Wisła
Warszawa
Kiev
Odessa
Black Sea
Riga
Vilnius
Kaliningrad
Nemen

Riga
Gulf of Finland

Maximum extent of sea ice

Summer extent of sea ice

Ice caps and permanent ice shelf

ft   m
12 000 4000
6000 2000
4500 1500
3000 1000
1200 400
600 200
0 0
500 1500
2000 6000
3000 9000
4000 12 000
5000 15 000
m ft

Projection: Zenithal Equidistant

West from Greenwich   East from Greenwich

6   7   8   9

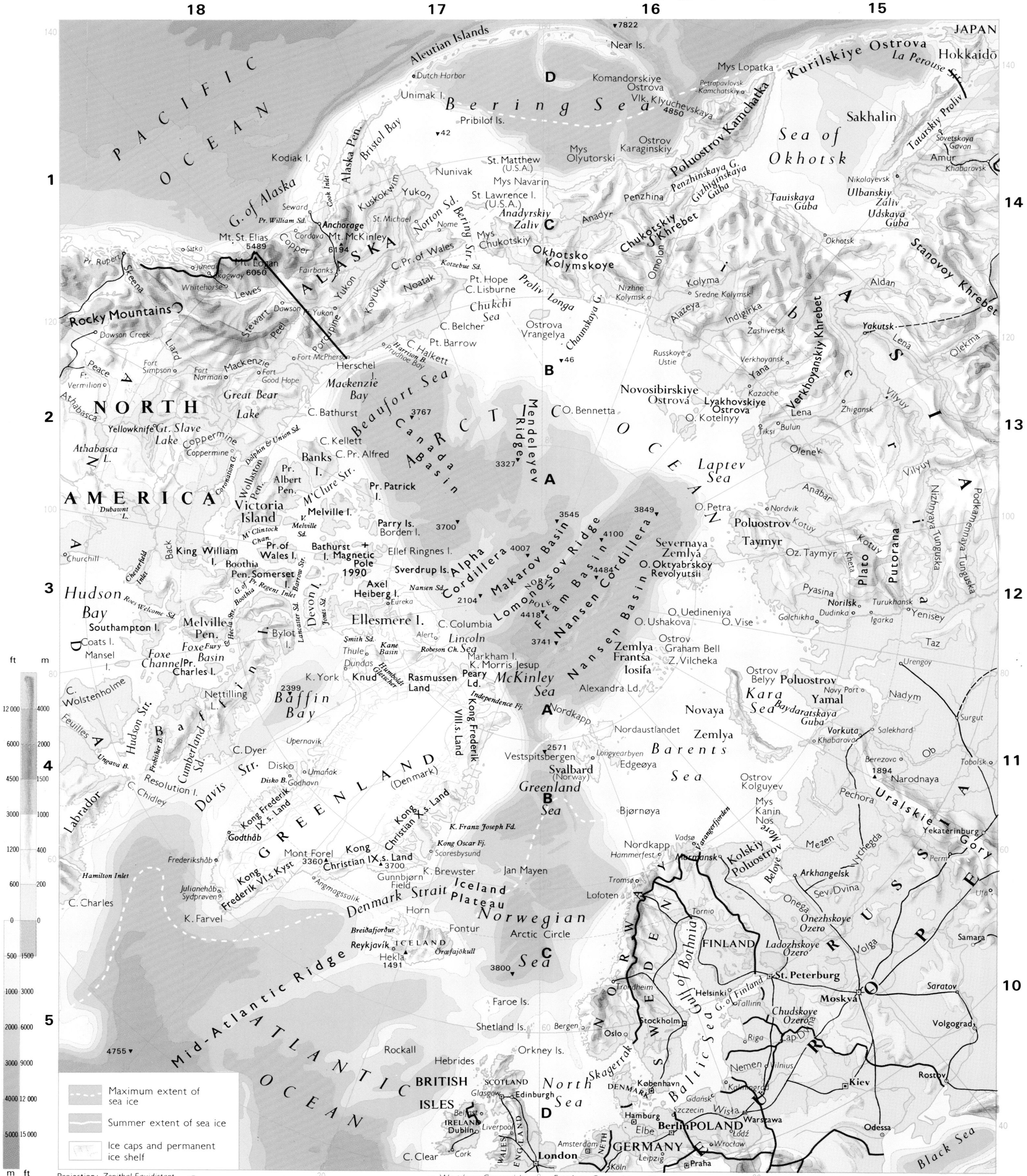

1 : 28 000 000

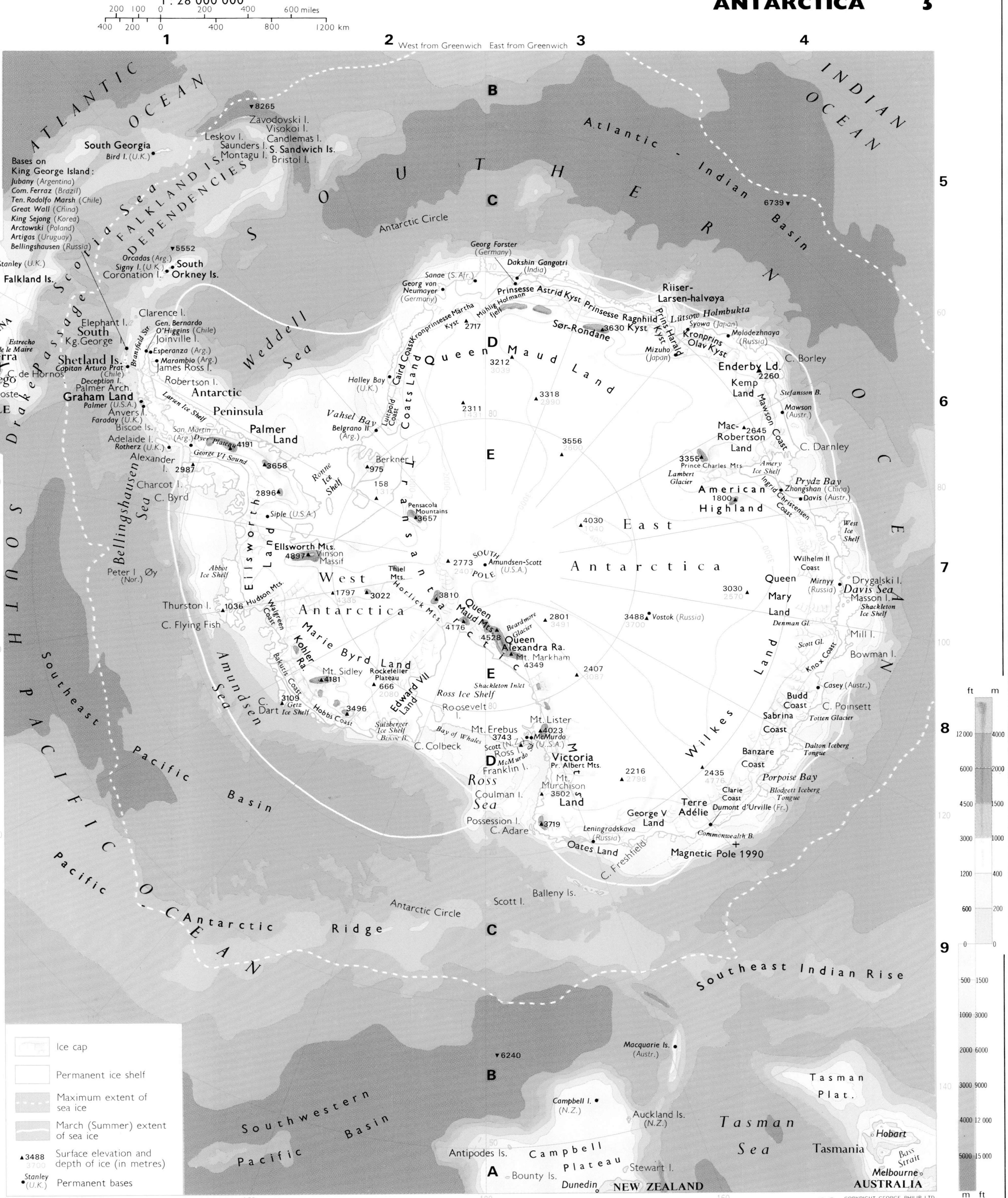

200 100 0 200 400 600 miles
400 200 0 400 800 1200 km

West from Greenwich   East from Greenwich

ATLANTIC   OCEAN

SOUTHERN

Atlantic - Indian Basin

INDIAN OCEAN

Antarctic Circle

▼8265

South Georgia
Bird I. (U.K.)

Bases on King George Island:
Jubany (Argentina)
Com. Ferraz (Brazil)
Ten. Rodolfo Marsh (Chile)
Great Wall (China)
King Sejong (Korea)
Arctowski (Poland)
Artigas (Uruguay)
Bellingshausen (Russia)

Leskov I.
Visokoi I.
Candlemas I.
Saunders I. S. Sandwich Is.
Montagu I.
Bristol I.

Zavodovski I.

Stanley (U.K.)
Falkland Is.

FALKLAND IS. DEPENDENCIES
Scotia Sea
Drake Passage

▼5552

Orcadas (Arg.)
Signy I. (U.K.) South
Coronation I. Orkney Is.

Georg Forster (Germany)
Dakshin Gangotri (India)
Sanae (S. Afr.)
Georg von Neumayer (Germany)

Prinsesse Astrid Kyst Prinsesse Ragnhild Kyst
Riiser-Larsen-halvøya

6739▼

Clarence I.
Elephant I.
South Kg. George
Gen. Bernardo O'Higgins (Chile)
Joinville I.
Esperanza (Arg.)
Marambio (Arg.)
James Ross I.
Capitan Arturo Prat (Chile)
Deception I.
Shetland Is.
Palmer Arch.
Robertson I.

Prinsesse Martha Kyst
Muhlig Holmann fjella
2717
Sør-Rondane
3630

Kronprins Olav Kyst
Lützow Holmbukta
Syowa (Japan)
Mizuho (Japan)
Molodezhnaya (Russia)

Queen Maud Land

C. Borley

ARGENTINA
Tierra del Fuego
C. de Hornos
I. Hoste
CHILE
Estrecho de le Maire

Graham Land
Palmer (U.S.A.)
Anvers I.
Faraday (U.K.)
Biscoe Is.
Adelaide I.
Rotherz (U.K.)
Alexander I.

Weddell Sea

Antarctic Peninsula

Palmer Land

Vahsel Bay
Belgrano II (Arg.)

Halley Bay (U.K.)

3212
3318
2311
3556

Enderby Ld.
2260
Kemp Land
Mawson (Austr.)
Stefansson B.

3039

4191
3658
2987
2896
158
975
3657

George VI Sound

Larsen Ice Shelf

San Martin (Arg.) Dyer Plateau

Berkner I.
Ronne Ice Shelf

Transantarctic Mts.

Coats Land
Caird Coast
Ronne Ice Shelf

Pensacola Mountains

Mac-Robertson Land
2645
3355
Prince Charles Mts.
Lambert Glacier
Amery Ice Shelf

1800

Siple (U.S.A.)

Charcot I.
C. Byrd

Ellsworth Land

Ellsworth Mts.
4897 Vinson Massif

Bellingshausen Sea

Abbot Ice Shelf

SOUTH POLE
2773
Amundsen-Scott (U.S.A.)

East Antarctica

Prydz Bay
Zhongshan (China)
Davis (Austr.)
American Highland

Ingrid Christensen Coast

West Ice Shelf

OCEAN

Peter I Øy (Nor.)

Thurston I.
C. Flying Fish

1036
1797
3022
3810
4176

Thiel Mts.

Horlick Mts.

West Antarctica

Queen Maud Mts.

Hudson Mts.
Walgreen Coast

Wilhelm II Coast
3030
Vostok (Russia)
3488

Queen Mary Land

Mirnyy (Russia)
Drygalski I.
Davis Sea
Masson I.
Shackleton Ice Shelf

Marie Byrd Land
Kohler Ra.
Mt. Sidley 4181
3743
3109
C. Dart
3496
Getz Ice Shelf
Hobbs Coast
Bakutis Coast

Rockefeller Plateau
666
Edward VII Land
Roosevelt I.

Beardmore Glacier
2801
4528
Queen Alexandra Ra.
Mt. Markham 4349

Shackleton Inlet

Ross Ice Shelf

2407

Denman Gl.
Scott Gl.
Knox Coast
Mill I.
Bowman I.

Budd Coast
Casey (Austr.)
Sabrina Coast
C. Poinsett
Totten Glacier
Dalton Iceberg Tongue

Amundsen Sea

Sulzberger Ice Shelf
Bay of Whales
Biscoe B.

Mt. Erebus 3743
McMurdo
Scott (N.Z.)
McMurdo (U.S.A.)
Ross I.

Mt. Lister 4023

Victoria Land
Pr. Albert Mts.

Wilkes Land

Banzare Coast
Porpoise Bay
Blodgett Iceberg Tongue

C. Colbeck

Ross Sea

Franklin I.
Mt. Murchison 3502
Coulman I.
Possession I.
C. Adare 3719

2216
2435

Clarie Coast
Dumont d'Urville (Fr.)
Terre Adélie

Southeast Pacific Basin

Pacific Basin

Pacific Ocean

Antarctic Ridge

Leningradskaya (Russia)
Oates Land
C. Freshfield

George V Land

Commonwealth B.
+ Magnetic Pole 1990

Southeast Indian Rise

Antarctic Circle
Scott I.
Balleny Is.

▼6240

Southwestern Basin

Macquarie Is. (Austr.)

Tasman Plat.

Campbell I. (N.Z.)
Auckland Is. (N.Z.)

Tasman Sea

Pacific Basin

Antipodes Is.
Campbell Plateau
Bounty Is.
Stewart I.
Dunedin NEW ZEALAND

Tasmania
Hobart
Bass Strait
Melbourne
AUSTRALIA

Legend:

Ice cap
Permanent ice shelf
Maximum extent of sea ice
March (Summer) extent of sea ice
▲3488 Surface elevation and depth of ice (in metres)
3700
Stanley (U.K.) Permanent bases

Projection: *Zenithal Equidistant*

ft   m
12 000 4000
        2000
6000   1500
4500
3000   1000
        400
1200
600

500   1500
1000 3000
2000 6000
3000 9000
4000 12 000
5000 15 000
m   ft

COPYRIGHT GEORGE PHILIP LTD.

The Antarctic Treaty was signed in Washington in 1959 so that scientific and technical research could continue unhampered by international politics.

All territorial claims covering land areas south of latitude 60°S have been suspended. Those claims were:

Norwegian claim   45°E – 20°W
Australian claims   { 45°E – 136°E
                       142°E – 160°E
French claim   136°E – 142°E
New Zealand claim   160°E – 150°W
Chilean claim   90°W – 53°W
British claim   80°W – 20°W
Argentine claim   74°W – 53°W

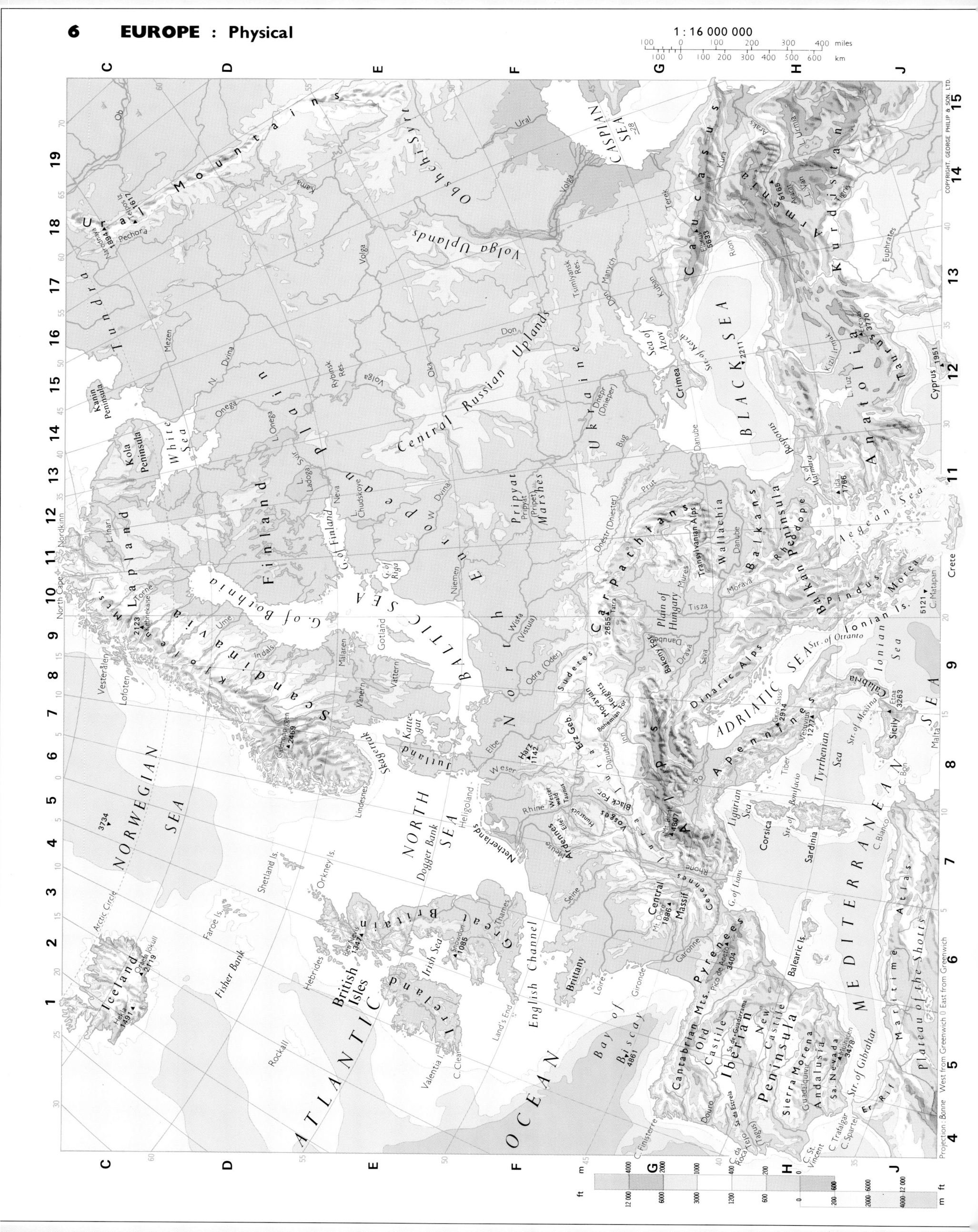

1 : 16 000 000

Projection: Bonne West from Greenwich 0 East from Greenwich

1: 16 000 000
miles
km
ATLANTIC OCEAN
NORTH SEA
NORWEGIAN SEA
BALTIC SEA
BLACK SEA
CASPIAN SEA
MEDITERRANEAN SEA
ADRIATIC SEA
Tyrrhenian Sea
Ionian Sea
BAY OF BISCAY
English Channel
White Sea
ICELAND
Reykjavik
Faroe Is. (Dan.)
UNITED KINGDOM
IRELAND
Dublin
LONDON
NORWAY
Oslo
SWEDEN
Stockholm
FINLAND
Helsinki
DENMARK
COPENHAGEN
ESTONIA
Tallinn
LATVIA
Riga
LITHUANIA
Vilnius
BELORUSSIA
Minsk
POLAND
WARSAW
GERMANY
BERLIN
NETHERLANDS
Amsterdam
BELGIUM
Brussels
LUX.
FRANCE
PARIS
SWITZERLAND
Bern
AUSTRIA
VIENNA
CZECHOSLOVAKIA
PRAGUE
HUNGARY
BUDAPEST
ROMANIA
BUCHAREST
BULGARIA
Sofia
YUGOSLAVIA
Belgrade
SLOVENIA
Ljubljana
CROATIA
Zagreb
ALBANIA
Tirana
GREECE
ATHENS
ITALY
Rome
SPAIN
MADRID
PORTUGAL
Lisbon
UKRAINE
Kiev
MOLDAVIA
Kishinev
RUSSIA
MOSCOW
KAZAKHSTAN
GEORGIA
Tbilisi
ARMENIA
Yerevan
AZERBAIJAN
Baku
TURKEY
Ankara
CYPRUS
Nicosia
SYRIA
IRAQ
Baghdad
IRAN
MOROCCO
Rabat
ALGERIA
Algiers
TUNISIA
Tunis
MALTA
Valletta
LONDON Capital Cities
Projection: Bonne
West from Greenwich 0 East from Greenwich
COPYRIGHT GEORGE PHILIP & SON LTD

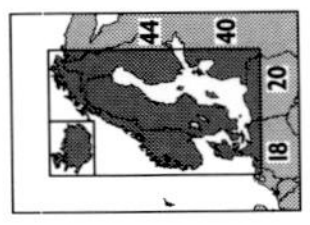

NORWEGIAN SEA
GULF OF BOTHNIA
FINNMARK
TROMS
NORDLAND
NORRBOTTEN
VÄSTERBOTTEN
JÄMTLAND
LAPPI
OULU
VAASA
KESKI-SUOMEN
KUOPIO
NORD-TRØNDELAG
SØR-TRØNDELAG
MØRE OG ROMSDAL
Lofoten
Vesterålen
Vestfjorden
Hammerfest
Vadsø
Tromsø
Narvik
Kiruna
Gällivare
Luleå
Boden
Piteå
Skellefteå
Umeå
Lycksele
Östersund
Härnösand
Sundsvall
Kramfors
Örnsköldsvik
Bodø
Mosjøen
Namsos
Steinkjer
Levanger
Trondheim
Kristiansund
Molde
Ålesund
Rovaniemi
Kemi
Tornio
Haparanda
Oulu
Kajaani
Kokkola
Jakobstad
Vaasa
Kristinestad
Jyväskylä
Kuopio
Inari
Arctic Circle
Kvarken
ICELAND
on the same scale as general map
Reykjavík
Akureyri
Húsavík
Ísafjörður
Keflavík
Hafnarfjörður
Akranes
Vatnajökull
Hofsjökull
Langjökull
Mýrdalsjökull
Faxaflói
Húnaflói
Skagafjörður
Eyjafjörður
Seyðisfjörður
Vestmannaeyjar
Hekla
West from Greenwich

1 : 4 000 000
50 0 50 100 miles
50 0 50 100 150 km
NORWAY
SWEDEN
FINLAND
ESTONIA
LATVIA
LITHUANIA
RUSSIA
BELORUSSIA
POLAND
GERMANY
DENMARK
NETH.
BALTIC SEA
GULF OF FINLAND
Skagerrak
Kattegat
The Sound
Rīgas Jūras Līcis (Gulf of Riga)
Zatoka Gdańska
Ålands hav
Svealand
Götaland
STOCKHOLM
OSLO
HELSINKI (Helsingfors)
KØBENHAVN (Copenhagen)
Tallinn
Riga
Vilnius
Göteborg
Malmö
Bergen
Stavanger
Gdańsk
Kaliningrad
Szczecin (Stettin)
Hamburg
Gotland
Öland
Bornholm
Saaremaa (Ösel)
Hiiumaa (Dagö)
Åland (Ahvenanmaa)
Projection: Conical with two standard parallels
East from Greenwich
COPYRIGHT, GEORGE PHILIP & SON, LTD.
9 10 11 12 13 14 15 16 17 18
F G H J K
ft m
6000 2000
4500 1500
3000 1000
1200 400
600 200
0 0
200 600
m ft

Gulf of Bothnia
Trondheim
Östersund
Sundsvall
Härnösand
Hudiksvall
Söderhamn
Gävle
Uppsala
Stockholm
Södertälje
Västerås
Eskilstuna
Örebro
Karlstad
Falun
Borlänge
Mora
Oslo
Drammen
Lillehammer
Hamar
Fredrikstad
Sarpsborg
Halden
Skien
Porsgrunn
Kristiansund
Röros
JÄMTLANDS LÄN
VÄSTERNORRLANDS LÄN
GÄVLEBORGS LÄN
KOPPARBERGS LÄN
VÄRMLANDS LÄN
ÖREBRO LÄN
VÄSTMANLANDS LÄN
UPPSALA LÄN
STOCKHOLMS LÄN
SÖDERMANLANDS LÄN
SØR TRØNDELAG FYLKE
MØRE OG ROMSDAL FYLKE
OPPLAND FYLKE
HEDMARK FYLKE
BUSKERUD FYLKE
TELEMARK FYLKE
VESTFOLD FYLKE
ØSTFOLD FYLKE
AKERSHUS FYLKE
Jotunheimen
Dovrefjell
Rondane
Mälaren
Hjälmaren
Siljan
Transtrands-fjällen

1: 2 000 000
Skagerrak
Norskerenna
Kattegat
BALTIC SEA
GERMANY
POLAND
Göteborg
Malmö
København (Copenhagen)
Ålborg
Århus
Odense
Esbjerg
Helsingborg
Helsingør
Lund
Kalmar
Karlskrona
Växjö
Jönköping
Linköping
Norrköping
Nyköping
Västervik
Visby
Gotland
Öland
Bornholm
Rønne
Flensburg
Kiel
Schleswig
Rendsburg
Rugen
Słupsk
Lębork
JYLLAND
SJÆLLAND
FYN
LOLLAND
FALSTER
HALLANDS LÄN
KRONOBERGS LÄN
JÖNKÖPINGS LÄN
KALMAR LÄN
BLEKINGE LÄN
KRISTIANSTADS LÄN
MALMÖHUS LÄN
SKARABORGS LÄN
ÖSTERGÖTLANDS LÄN
GÖTEBORGS OCH BOHUS LÄN
AUST-AGDER FYLKE
Jammerbugt
Ålborg Bugt
Store Bælt
Lille Bælt
Femer Bælt
Kieler Bucht
Hanöbukten
Bornholmsgattet
Kalmarsund
Projection: Conical with two standard parallels
East from Greenwich
COPYRIGHT. GEORGE PHILIP & SON. LTD.

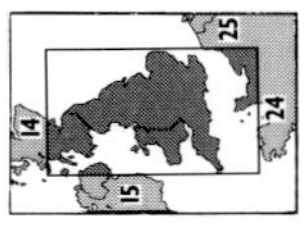

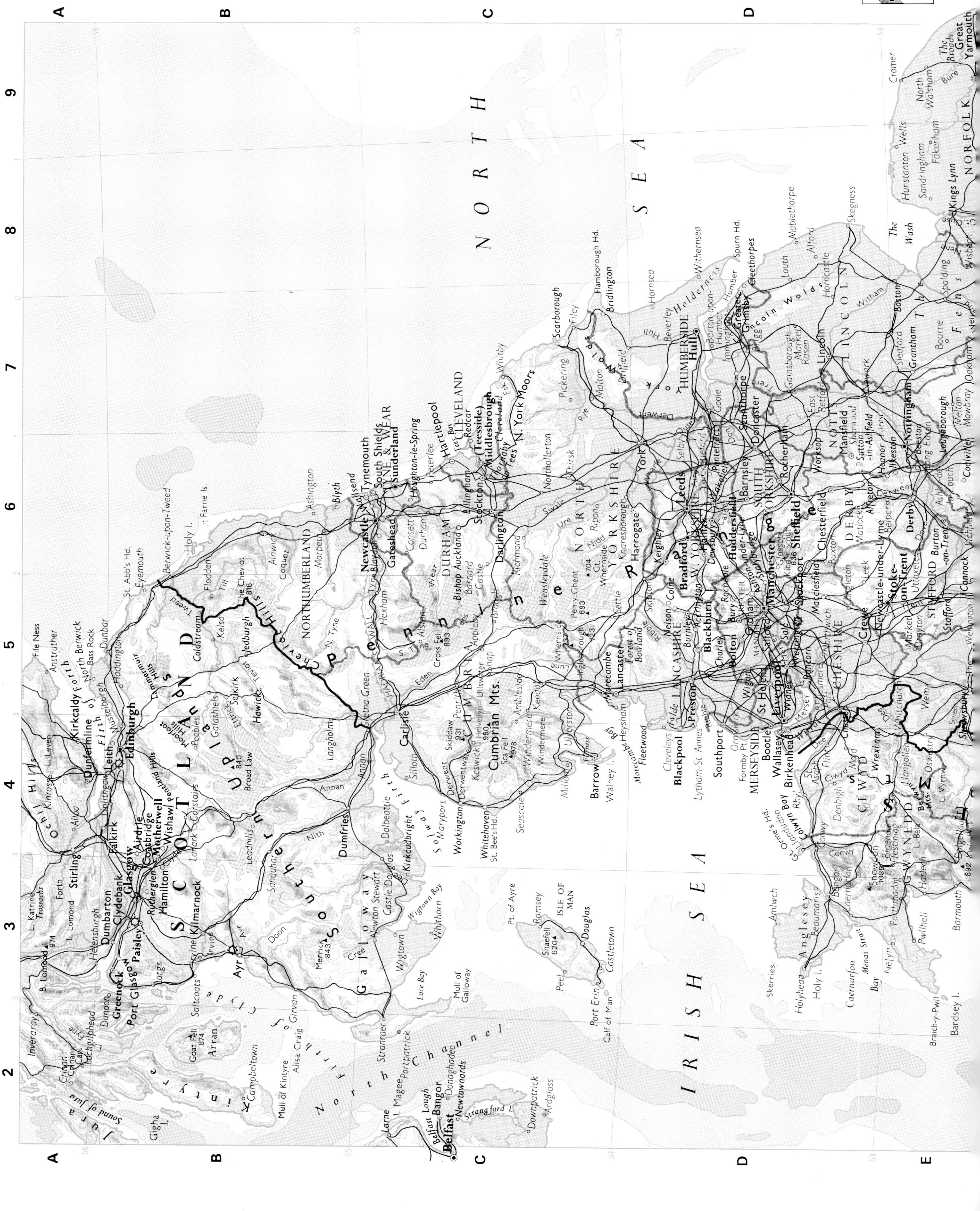

A   B   C   D

NORTH   SEA

SCOTLAND

Southern   Uplands

L. Katrine
Trossachs
L. Lomond
B. Lomond 974
Inveraray
Crinan
Cairn
Lochgilphead
Dunoon
Helensburgh
Dumbarton
Greenock
Port Glasgow Paisley
Glasgow
Clydebank
Rutherglen
Hamilton
Kilmarnock
Irvine
Saltcoats
Largs
Ayr
Campbeltown
Mull of Kintyre
Ailsa Craig
Gigha I.
Jura
Sound of Jura
Kintyre
Firth of Clyde
Arran
Goat Fell 874

Ochil Hills
Stirling
Alloa
Kinross
L. Leven
Dunfermline
Kirkcaldy
Forth
Firth of Forth
Leith
Edinburgh
Whitburn
Bathgate
Falkirk
Airdrie
Coatbridge
Motherwell
Wishaw
Pentland Hills
Lanark Carstairs
Peebles
Galashiels
Selkirk
Moorfoot Hills
Lammermuir Hills
Broad Law 840
Leadhills
Sanquhar

North Berwick
Bass Rock
Dunbar
Haddington
Musselburgh
St. Abb's Hd.
Eyemouth
Coldstream
Berwick-upon-Tweed
Tweed
Flodden
Kelso
Jedburgh
Hawick
Teviot
The Cheviot 816
Cheviot Hills

NORTHUMBERLAND
Alnwick
Coquet
Morpeth
Ashington
Blyth
Holy I.
Farne Is.
Till

Dumfries
Nith
Annan
Gretna Green
Solway Firth
Kirkcudbright
Castle Douglas
Dalbeattie
Newton Stewart
Wigtown
Wigtown Bay
Whithorn
Merrick 843
Cree
Doon
Galloway
Stranraer
Portpatrick
Luce Bay
Mull of Galloway

IRISH SEA

North Channel
Larne
Magee
Donaghadee
Bangor
Newtownards
Belfast
Belfast Lough
Strangford L.
Downpatrick
Ardglass

ISLE OF MAN
Pt. of Ayre
Ramsey
Snaefell 620
Douglas
Peel
Port Erin
Calf of Man
Castletown

PENNINES
Carlisle
CUMBRIA
Cumbrian Mts.
Skiddaw 931
Penrith
Keswick
Helvellyn 950
Derwent
Derwentwater
Ullswater
Sca Fell 978
Ambleside
Windermere
Windermere
Kendal
Workington
Maryport
Whitehaven
St. Bee's Hd.
Seascale
Millom
Barrow
Walney I.
Ulverston
Morecambe Bay
Morecambe
Heysham
Fleetwood
Cleveleys
Blackpool
Lytham-St. Annes
Southport
Formby Pt.

Gosforth
Eden
S. Tyne
N. Tyne
Hadrian's Wall
Hexham
Haltwhistle
Cross Fell 893
Appleby
Bishop Auckland
Barnard Castle
Richmond
Swaledale
Wensleydale
Ure
Ingleborough
Settle
Pen-y-Ghent 693
Whernside
Ribble
Forest of Bowland
Clitheroe
Nelson
Colne
Burnley
Accrington
Blackburn
Preston
LANCASHIRE
Chorley
Bolton
Bury
Rochdale

Newcastle upon Tyne
Gateshead
Tynemouth
South Shields
TYNE & WEAR
Sunderland
Houghton-le-Spring
Peterlee
Consett
DURHAM
Durham
Wear
Stockton
Middlesbrough
CLEVELAND
(Teesside)
Hartlepool
Redcar
Tees
Billingham
Darlington
Northallerton
Thirsk
Whitby
Robin Hood's Bay
N. York Moors
Pickering
Scarborough
Filey
Flamborough Hd.
Bridlington
Hornsea
Driffield
Malton
Rye
Derwent
NORTH YORKSHIRE
York
Harrogate
Knaresborough
Ripon
Nidd
Skipton
Keighley
Bradford
Leeds
WEST YORKSHIRE
Halifax
Huddersfield
Wakefield
Barnsley
Dewsbury
SOUTH YORKSHIRE
Doncaster
Rotherham
Sheffield

HUMBERSIDE
Hull
Beverley
Holderness
Withernsea
Spurn Hd.
Humber
Great Grimsby
Cleethorpes
Barton-upon-Humber
Immingham
Goole
Selby
Gainsborough
Market Rasen
Lincoln Wolds
Lincoln
LINCOLN
Louth
Mablethorpe
Alford
Horncastle
Skegness
Witham
Retford
Worksop
Mansfield
Sutton-in-Ashfield
Newark
Sleaford
Grantham
Bourne
The Fens
Spalding
Boston

St. Helens
Liverpool
Bootle
Wallasey
Birkenhead
MERSEYSIDE
Warrington
Widnes
Runcorn
Manchester
Salford
Sale
Stockport
Altrincham
Macclesfield
CHESHIRE
Chester
Crewe
Nantwich
Northwich
Newcastle-under-Lyme
Stoke-on-Trent
Leek
STAFFORD
Stafford
Uttoxeter
Cannock
Burton-on-Trent
DERBY
Derby
Chesterfield
Matlock
Buxton
Ashbourne
Belper
Alfreton
Ilkeston
Nottingham
Loughborough
Melton Mowbray
Oakham

Dee
CLWYD
Wrexham
Denbigh
Ruthin
Flint
Rhyl
Prestatyn
Colwyn Bay
Llandudno
Conwy
Bangor
Beaumaris
Anglesey
Holyhead
Holy I.
Amlwch
Menai Strait
Caernarfon
GWYNEDD
Snowdon 1085
Harlech
Bala
Blaenau Ffestiniog
Ffestiniog
Llangollen
Oswestry
Shrewsbury
Severn
Welshpool
Newtown
POWYS
Pwllheli
Nefyn
Braich-y-Pwll
Bardsey I.
Cardigan Bay
Barmouth
Dolgellau

NORFOLK
Cromer
Great Yarmouth
The Broads
Bure
North Walsham
Sandringham
Fakenham
Hunstanton
The Wash
Kings Lynn
Wisbech
Nene

1 : 1 600 000
50 miles
80 km
ENGLISH CHANNEL
Bristol Channel
Channel Islands
FRANCE
SCILLY ISLES
On same Scale
Isles of Scilly
St. Mary's
Land's End
Penzance
St. Ives
Lundy
Guernsey
Alderney
Sark
St. Peter Port
Jersey
St. Helier
ISLE OF WIGHT
CORNWALL
DEVON
DORSET
SOMERSET
AVON
WILTS
HANTS
BERKS
WEST SUSSEX
EAST SUSSEX
SURREY
KENT
ESSEX
SUFFOLK
CAMBRIDGE
NORTHAMPTON
BEDFORD
HERTFORD
BUCKS
OXFORD
GLOUCESTER
HEREFORD & WORCESTER
WARWICK
WEST MIDLANDS
SHROPSHIRE
POWYS
DYFED
GWENT
MID GLAMORGAN
WEST GLAMORGAN
SOUTH GLAMORGAN
LONDON
Birmingham
Bristol
Cardiff
Swansea
Plymouth
Exeter
Southampton
Portsmouth
Bournemouth
Brighton
Dover
Ipswich
Cambridge
Oxford
Reading
Le Havre
Cherbourg
Rouen
Dieppe
Caen
Projection: Conical with two standard parallels.
West from Greenwich
East from Greenwich
COPYRIGHT, GEORGE PHILIP & SON, LTD.

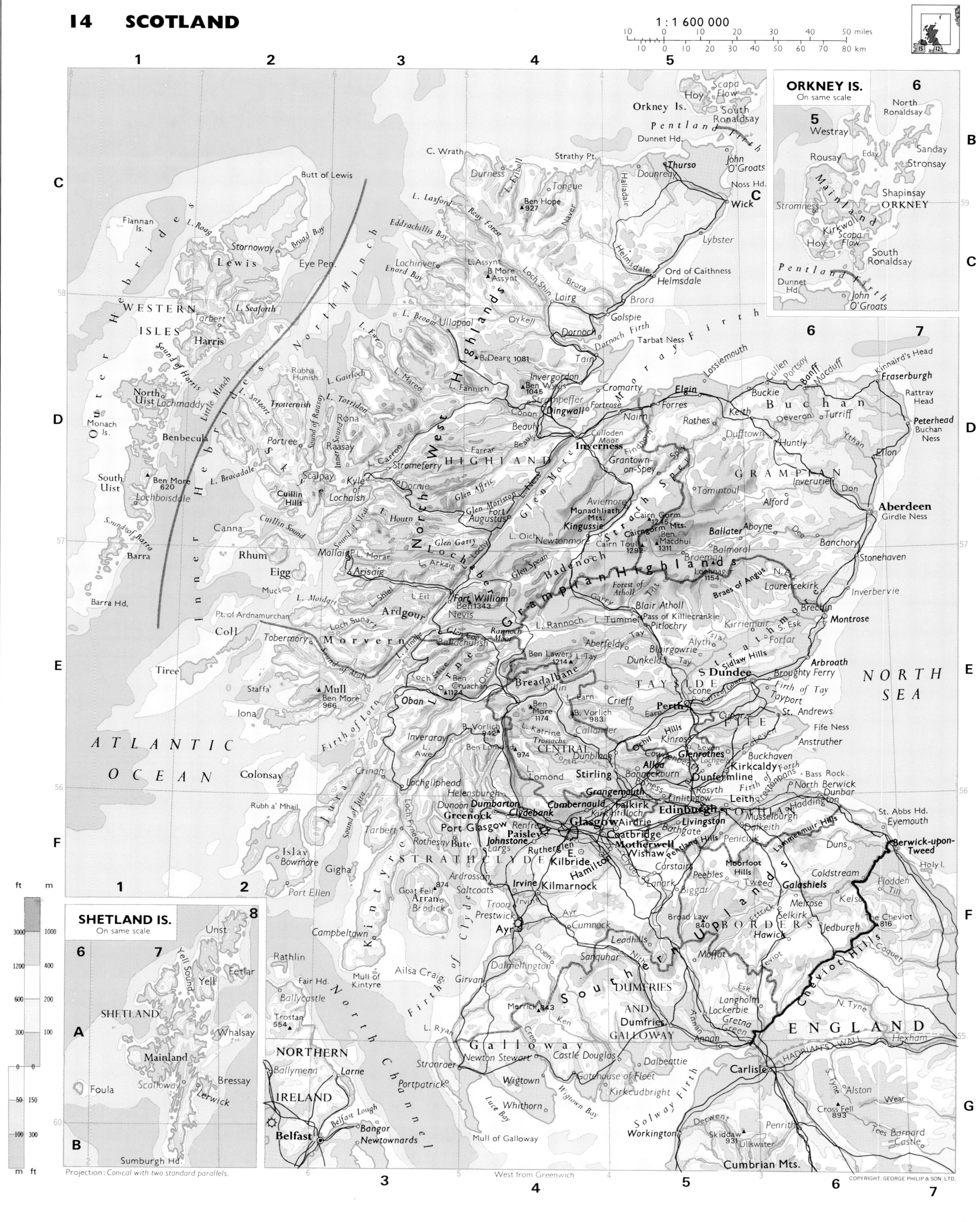

1 : 1 600 000

ORKNEY IS.
On same scale

SHETLAND IS.
On same scale

Projection: Conical with two standard parallels.

West from Greenwich

COPYRIGHT. GEORGE PHILIP & SON. LTD.

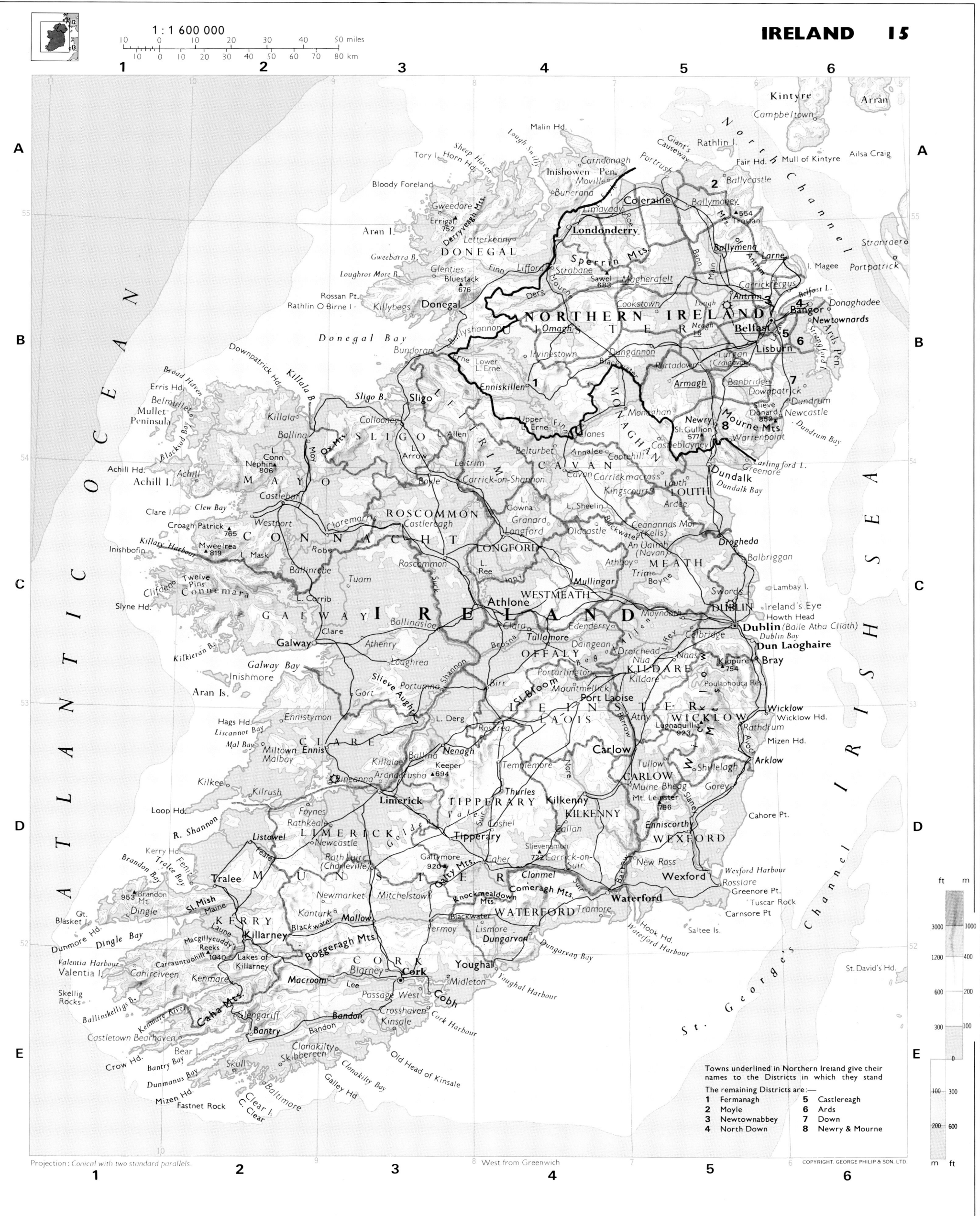

1 : 1 600 000

Projection: Conical with two standard parallels.

West from Greenwich

COPYRIGHT. GEORGE PHILIP & SON LTD.

Towns underlined in Northern Ireland give their
names to the Districts in which they stand
The remaining Districts are:—

1	Fermanagh	5	Castlereagh
2	Moyle	6	Ards
3	Newtownabbey	7	Down
4	North Down	8	Newry & Mourne

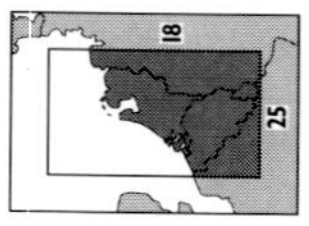

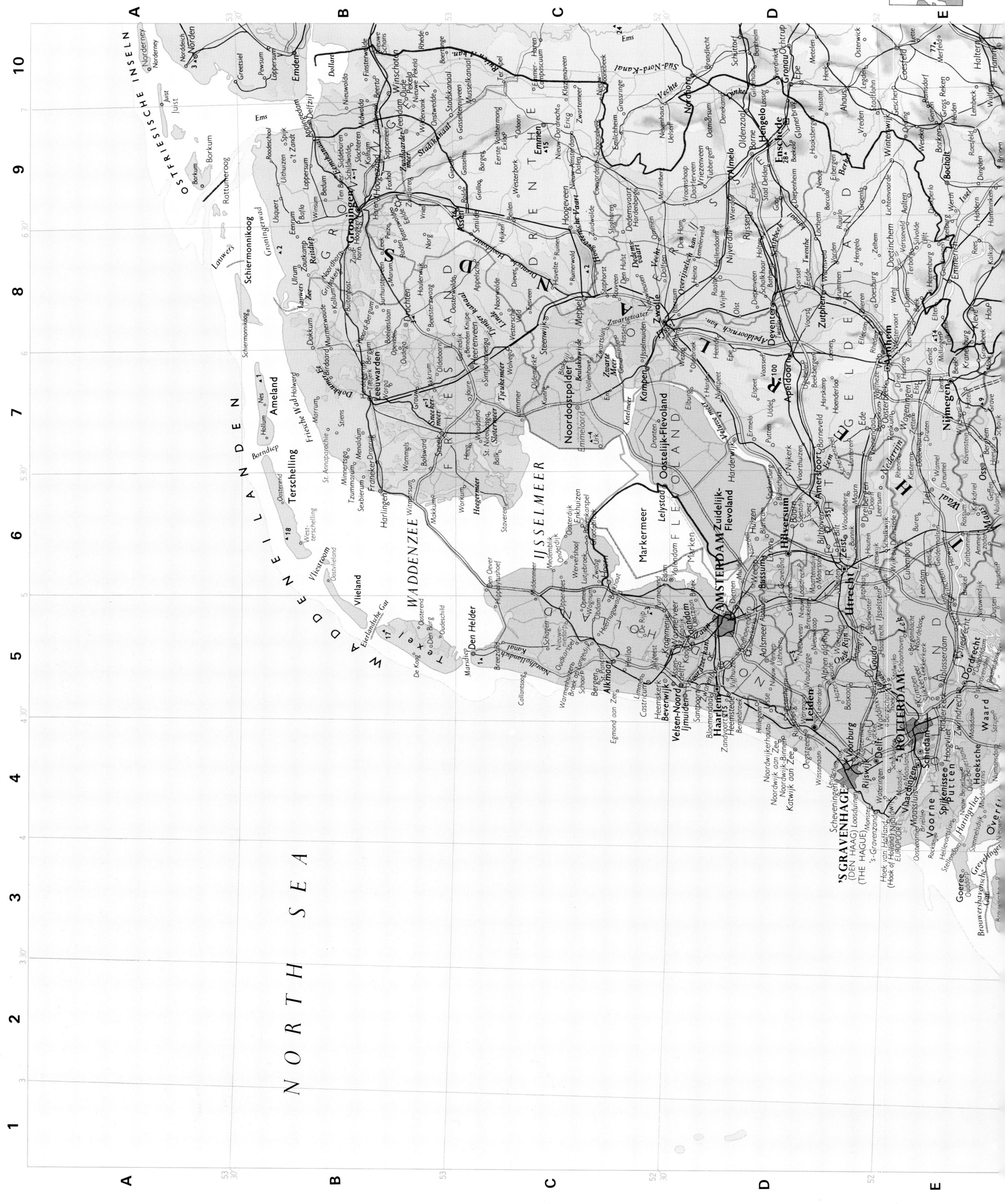
NORTH SEA
WADDENZEE
IJSSELMEER
WADDENEILANDEN
OSTFRIESISCHE INSELN
Markermeer
Noordoostpolder
AMSTERDAM
ROTTERDAM
'S GRAVENHAGE
(DEN HAAG)
(THE HAGUE)
Utrecht
Groningen
Leeuwarden
Zwolle
Arnhem
Nijmegen
Apeldoorn
Enschede
Hengelo
Emmen
Haarlem
Leiden
Dordrecht
Den Helder
Alkmaar
Lelystad
Amersfoort
Hilversum
Deventer
Zutphen
Kampen
Meppel
Assen
Harlingen
Texel
Vlieland
Terschelling
Ameland
Schiermonnikoog
Borkum
Juist
Norderney
Emden
Norden
Dollart
Bocholt
Emmerich
Kleve
Ems
Vecht
Waal
Lek
Nederrijn
Schiedam
Vlaardingen
Delft
Rijswijk
Voorburg
Gouda
Alphen a/d Rijn
Zaanstad
Purmerend
Hoorn
Enkhuizen
Sneek
Heerenveen
Drachten
Steenwijk
Hoogeveen
Coevorden
Almelo
Oldenzaal
Winterswijk
Doetinchem
Ede
Wageningen
Tiel
Oss
FRIESLAND
DRENTHE
OVERIJSSEL
GELDERLAND
FLEVOLAND
Oostelijk-Flevoland
Zuidelijk-Flevoland
Spijkenisse
Voorne
Putten
Goeree
A B C D E
1 2 3 4 5 6 7 8 9 10

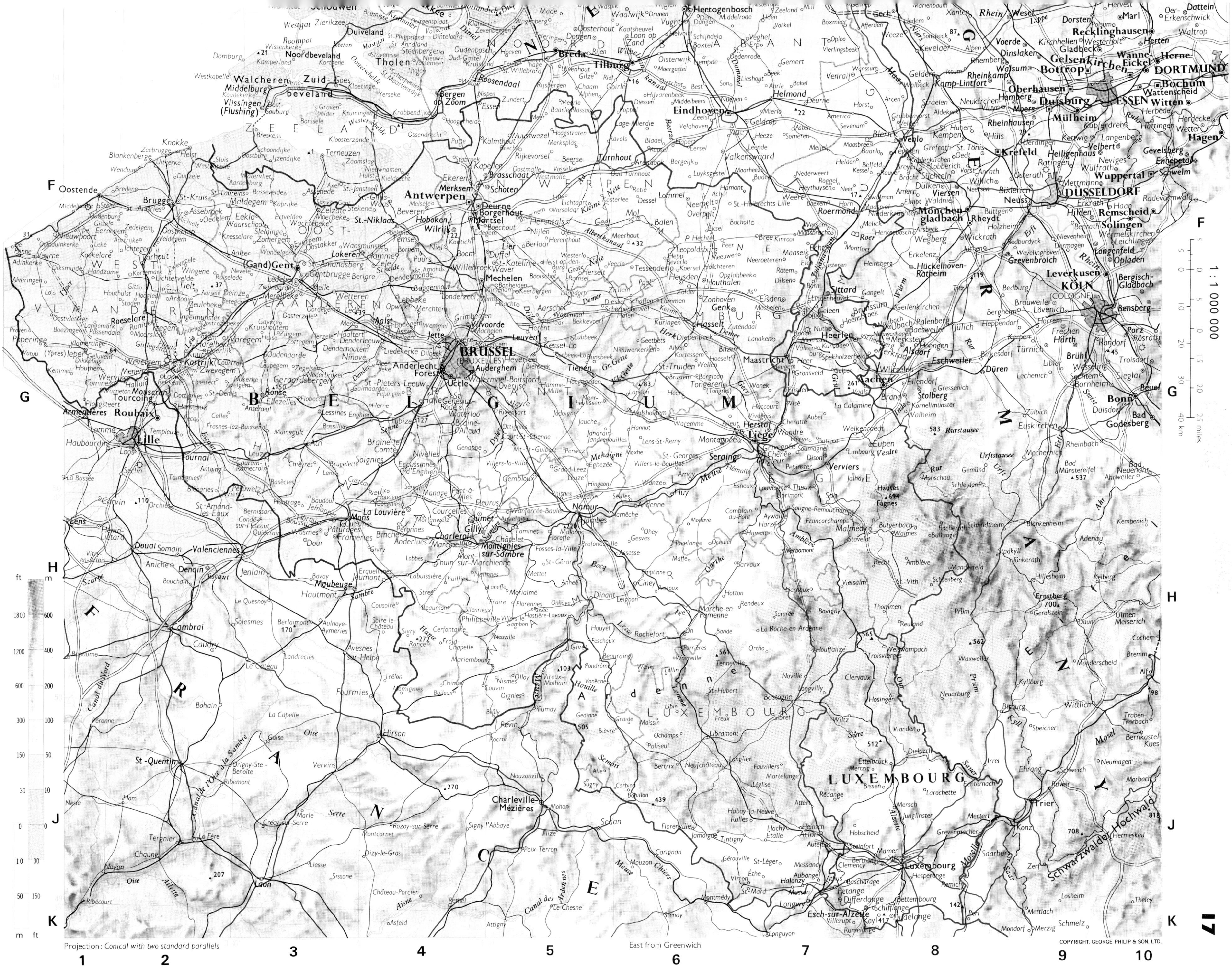
1 : 1 000 000
5 0 5 10 15 20 25 miles
5 0 10 20 30 40 km
BELGIUM
LUXEMBOURG
GERMANY
FRANCE
NOORD BRABANT
ZEELAND
ANTWERPEN
LIMBURG
LUXEMBOURG
OOST-VLAANDEREN
WEST-VLAANDEREN
HAINAUT
Ardennes
BRUSSEL
(BRUXELLES)
Antwerpen
(Gand) Gent
Brugge
Oostende
Lille
Roubaix
Tourcoing
Mons
Charleroi
Namur
Liège
Maastricht
Aachen
Köln
(COLOGNE)
Düsseldorf
Essen
Dortmund
Bonn
Eindhoven
Tilburg
Breda
's-Hertogenbosch
Luxembourg
Trier
Valenciennes
Cambrai
St-Quentin
Laon
Charleville-Mézières
Sedan
Schwarzwalder Hochwald
Projection: Conical with two standard parallels
East from Greenwich
COPYRIGHT, GEORGE PHILIP & SON, LTD.
ft m
1800 600
1200 400
600 200
300 100
150 50
30 10
0 0
10 30
50 150
m ft

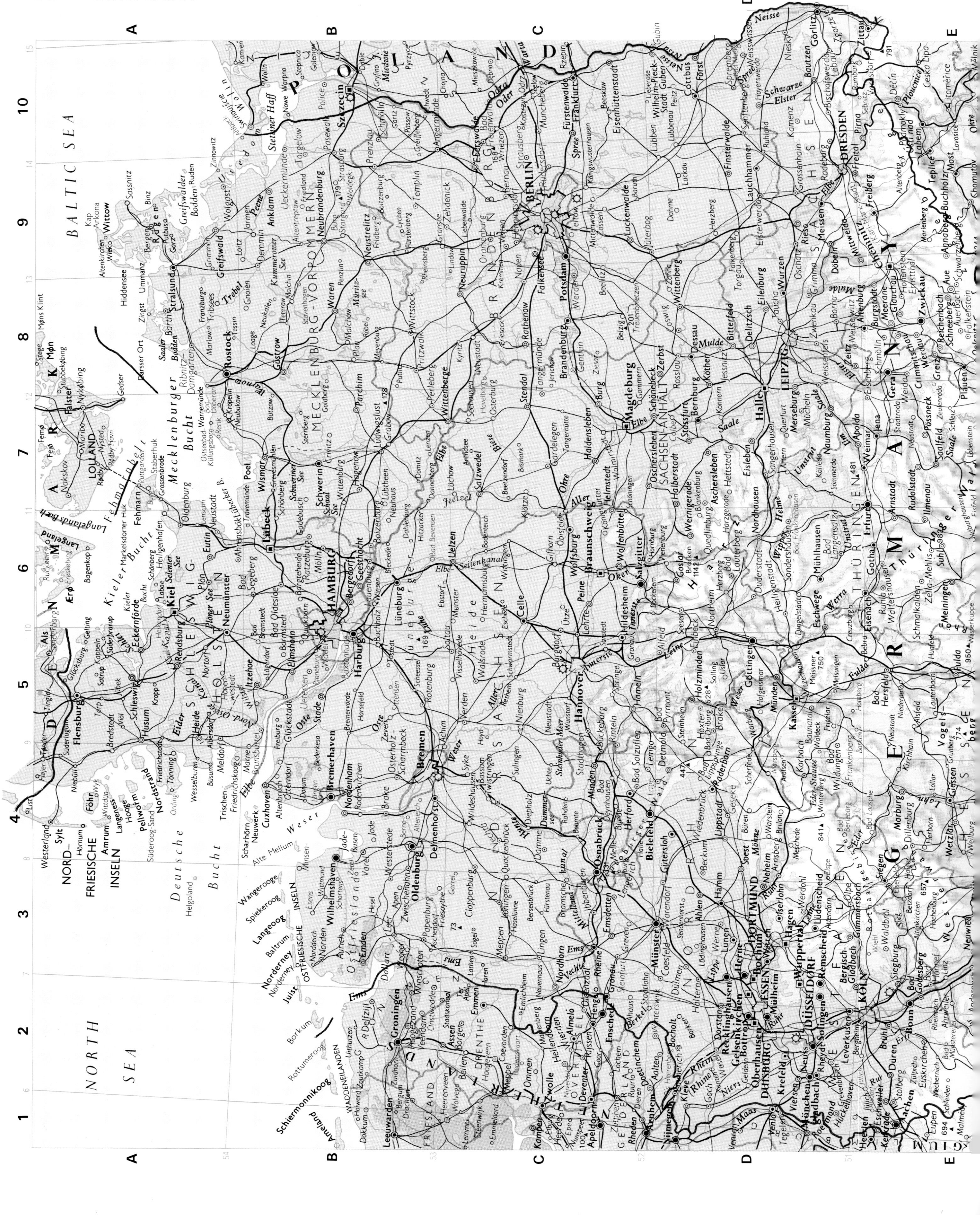
BALTIC SEA
NORTH SEA
DENMARK
POLAND
GERMANY
NORD-FRIESISCHE INSELN
OSTFRIESISCHE INSELN
WADDENEILANDEN
Deutsche Bucht
Mecklenburger Bucht
Kieler Bucht
Fehmarnbelt
Stettiner Haff
SCHLESWIG-HOLSTEIN
MECKLENBURG-VORPOMMERN
BRANDENBURG
NIEDERSACHSEN
SACHSEN-ANHALT
SACHSEN
THÜRINGEN
NORDRHEIN-WESTFALEN
HESSEN
Lüneburger Heide
Harz
Rügen
Fehmarn
Lolland
Falster
Møn
Als
Ærø
Langeland
Sylt
Föhr
Amrum
Pellworm
Helgoland
Borkum
Juist
Norderney
Baltrum
Langeoog
Spiekeroog
Wangerooge
Hiddensee
Usedom
Wolin
HAMBURG
BERLIN
Bremen
Bremerhaven
Hannover
Kiel
Lübeck
Rostock
Stralsund
Greifswald
Wismar
Schwerin
Flensburg
Neumünster
Szczecin
Potsdam
Magdeburg
Braunschweig
Halle
LEIPZIG
DRESDEN
Chemnitz
Zwickau
Gera
Jena
Weimar
Erfurt
Göttingen
Kassel
Osnabrück
Münster
Bielefeld
Oldenburg
Emden
Wilhelmshaven
Cuxhaven
Groningen
DORTMUND
ESSEN
DUISBURG
DÜSSELDORF
KÖLN
Bonn
Aachen
Wuppertal
Bochum
Gelsenkirchen
Wolfsburg
Salzgitter
Hildesheim
Celle
Lüneburg
Uelzen
Frankfurt
Cottbus
Görlitz
Dessau
Wittenberg
Elbe
Weser
Ems
Oder
Rhein
Saale
Spree
Havel
Aller
Leine

1 : 2 000 000

10   0   10   20   30   40   50 miles
10   0   10 20 30 40 50 60 70 80 km

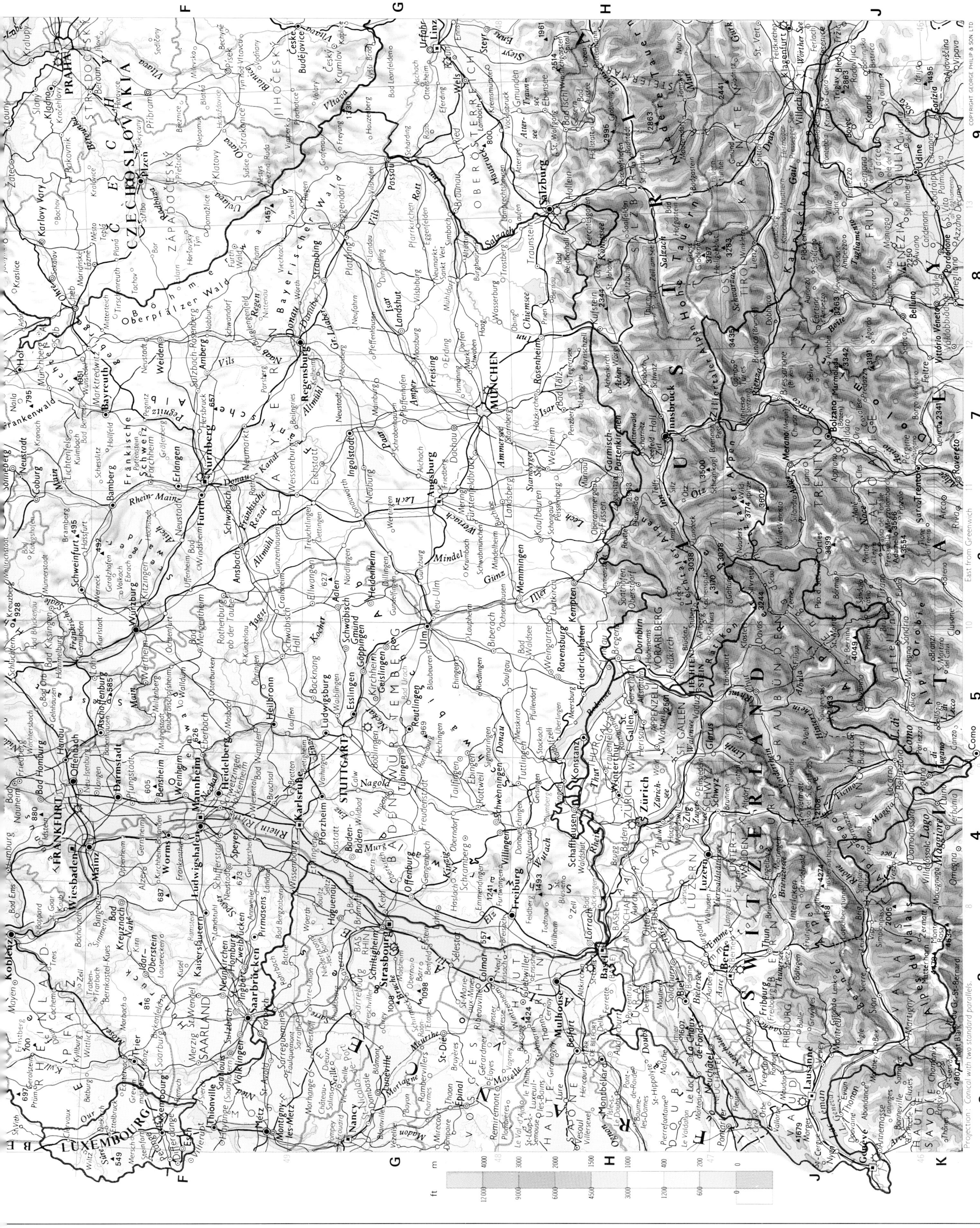

F   G   H   J   K

PRAHA

ČESKOSLOVENSKO

ČECHY

STŘEDOČESKÝ

ZÁPADOČESKÝ

JIHOČESKÝ

Karlovy Vary

Plzeň

Linz

OBERÖSTERREICH

Salzburg

STEIERMARK

Klagenfurt

KÄRNTEN

B A Y E R N

Bayreuth

Nürnberg

Fürth

Erlangen

Bamberg

Regensburg

Donau

Amberg

Weiden

MÜNCHEN

Augsburg

Ingolstadt

Freising

Rosenheim

Innsbruck

T I R O L

SÜD TIROL

BOZEN · Bolzano

TRENTINO

Trento

Rovereto

VENEZIA GIULIA

Udine

FRIULI

Belluno

Vittorio Veneto

Feltre

STUTTGART

Ulm

Neu-Ulm

Heidelberg

Mannheim

Ludwigshafen

Worms

Speyer

Karlsruhe

Pforzheim

Reutlingen

Tübingen

BADEN WÜRTTEMBERG

Esslingen

Heilbronn

Göppingen

Memmingen

Kempten

Kaufbeuren

Friedrichshafen

Ravensburg

Konstanz

VORARLBERG

Bregenz

Feldkirch

LIECHTENSTEIN

Vaduz

St. Gallen

APPENZELL

Winterthur

Zürich

Zürich-see

GRAUBÜNDEN

Davos

Chur

S W I T Z E R L A N D

Luzern

Zug

Schwyz

Basel

Solothurn

Biel

Bern

Fribourg

Thun

Interlaken

VALAIS · WALLIS

BERN

Lausanne

VAUD

NEUCHÂTEL

La Chaux-de-Fonds

Neuchâtel

Yverdon

Colmar

Mulhouse

Belfort

Montbéliard

Strasbourg

HAUT RHIN

BAS RHIN

VOSGES

Épinal

HAUTE SAÔNE

DOUBS

SAVOIE

HAUTE SAVOIE

Annemasse

FRANKFURT

Wiesbaden

Mainz

Offenbach

Darmstadt

Aschaffenburg

Würzburg

Schweinfurt

Coburg

HESSEN

RHEINLAND PFALZ

Koblenz

Bad Kreuznach

Idar-Oberstein

SAARLAND

Saarbrücken

Neunkirchen

Homburg

Pirmasens

Zweibrücken

Kaiserslautern

LUXEMBOURG

Thionville

Metz

Nancy

Lombardia

Como

Lecco

Sondrio

APS. OROBIE

ALPI

ITALIA

Projection: Conical with two standard parallels.

East from Greenwich

m 4000 3000 2000 1500 1000 400 200 0
ft 12000 9000 6000 4500 3000 1200 600 0

BALTIC SEA

LITHUANIA

(RUSSIA)

BELORUSSIA

UKRAINE

POLAND

GERMANY

CZECHOSLOVAKIA

DENMARK

Kaliningrad (Königsberg)

Gdańsk (Danzig)

Szczecin (Stettin)

BERLIN

WARSZAWA (Warsaw)

PRAHA (PRAGUE)

WROCŁAW (Breslau)

KRAKÓW

ŁÓDŹ

Poznań

DRESDEN

LEIPZIG

Chemnitz (Karl-Marx-Stadt)

Brno

Lvov

Brest

Grodno

Lublin

Košice

Rostock

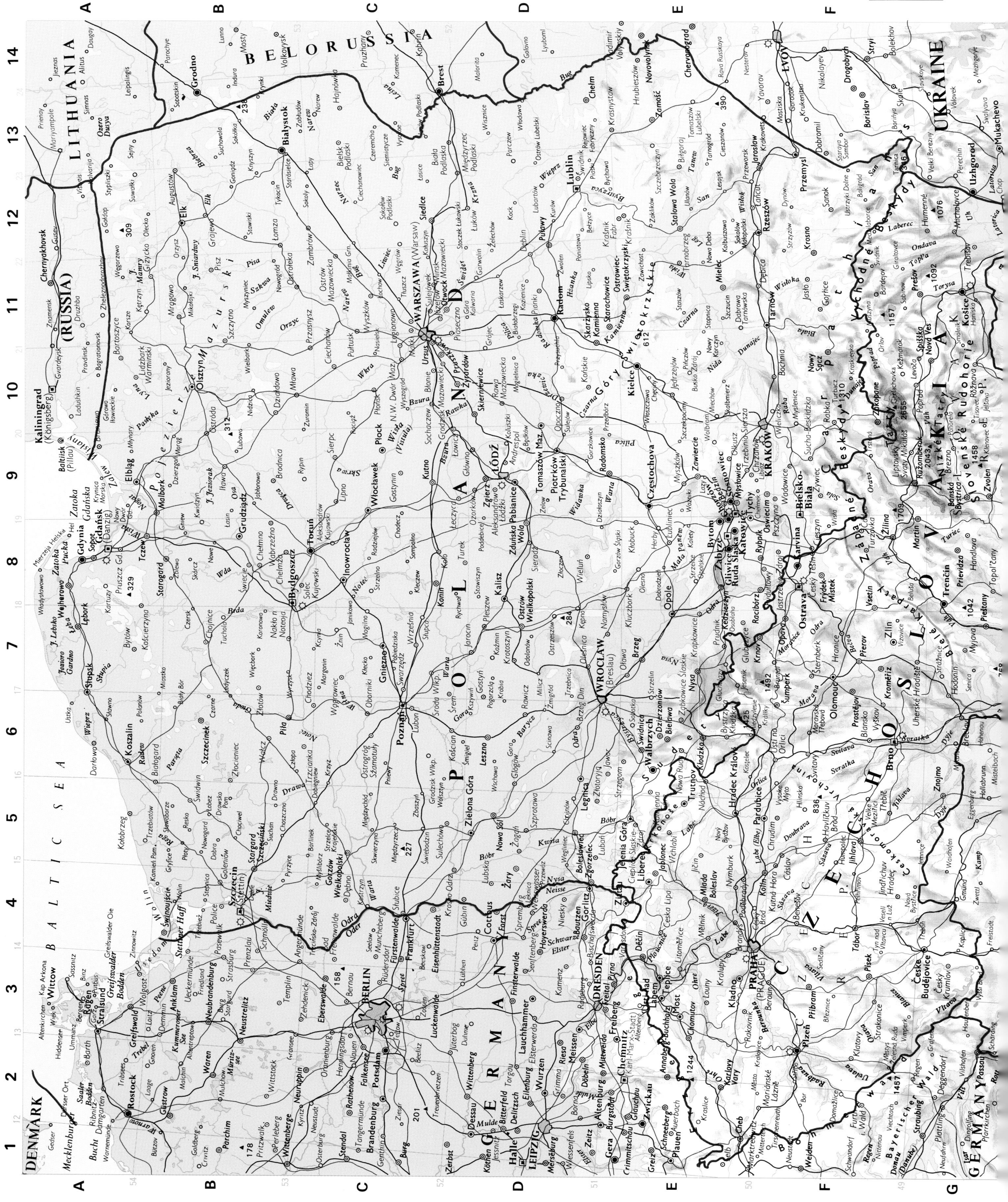

1 : 2 800 000

100 miles

150 km

Projection: Conical with two standard parallels

East from Greenwich

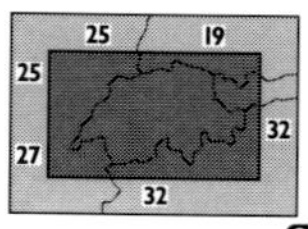

FRANCE

HAUTE-SAÔNE

SUNDGAU

HAUT RHIN

MULHOUSE
BELFORT
BASEL (BASLE)
Lörrach
Rheinfelden
Waldshut
Säckingen
Brugg
Windisch
Aarau
Olten
LANDSCHAFT AARGAU

JURA
Delémont
Porrentruy
Moutier
SOLOTHURN
Solothurn
Grenchen
Biel (Bienne)
Langenthal
Burgdorf
LUZERN

BESANÇON
DOUBS
Besançon
Montbéliard
Audincourt
Pontarlier

La Chaux-de-Fonds
Le Locle
St-Imier
Chasseral 1607
NEUCHÂTEL
Neuchâtel
St-Blaise
Ins
Kerzers
Murten
BERN (BERNE)
Köniz
Ostermundigen
Worb
Münsingen
Langnau i. E.
EMMENTAL
Entlebuch

Lac de Neuchâtel
Yverdon
Grandson
Ste-Croix
Chasseron 1607
Payerne
Estavayer-le-Lac
FRIBOURG (Freibourg)
Schwarzenburg
Marly
Romont
Bulle
Gruyère
FRIBOURG
BERN
Thun
Steffisburg
Thunersee
Spiez
Brienzersee
Interlaken
Meiringen

JURA
Morez
Le Sentier
Mt Tendre 1679
Le Brassus
Vallorbe
Orbe
Echallens
Moudon
Lausanne
Morges
Lutry
Vevey
Montreux
Villeneuve
Aigle
Leysin
Château-d'Oex
Gstaad
Lenk
Oberland
Bernese Alps
Adelboden
Kandersteg
Frutigen
Wildstrubel 3243
Wildhorn 3248

St-Claude
Nyon
Thonon-les-Bains
Évian-les-Bains
Léman (L. Geneva)
GENÈVE (GENEVA)
Vernier
Annemasse
HAUTE-SAVOIE
Chablais
Faucigny
Monthey
Bex
St-Maurice
Martigny
VALAIS
Sion
Sierre
Visp
Brig
Simplon
Leuk
Zermatt
Matterhorn 4478 (Mte Cervino)
Weisshorn 4505
Dom 4545
Saas Fee
Weissmies 4023
Monte Leone 3553
Dufourspitze
Monte Rosa

Oyonnax
Bellegarde-s.-V.
Annecy
Lac d'Annecy
Rumilly
St-Gervais-les-B.
Megève
Sallanches
Chamonix-Mont-Blanc
Mt Blanc 4807
Col du Gd St-Bernard 2469
Aosta
VALLE D'AOSTA
Courmayeur
La Thuile
Petit St-Bernard 2188
Albertville
Aix-les-Bains
Belley
Lac du Bourget
SAVOIE

PIEMONTE

Projection: Conical with two standard parallels

ft m
9000 3000
6000 2000
4500 1500
3000 1000
1200 500
600 200

ENGLAND

English Channel

CHANNEL ISLANDS

Baie de la Seine

NORMANDIE

BRETAGNE

Mer d'Iroise

F R A N C E

DÉPARTEMENTS IN THE PARIS AREA

1 Ville de Paris   3 Val-de-Marne
2 Seine-St.-Denis   4 Hauts-de-Seine

Projection: Conical with two standard parallels

West from Greenwich   East from Greenwich

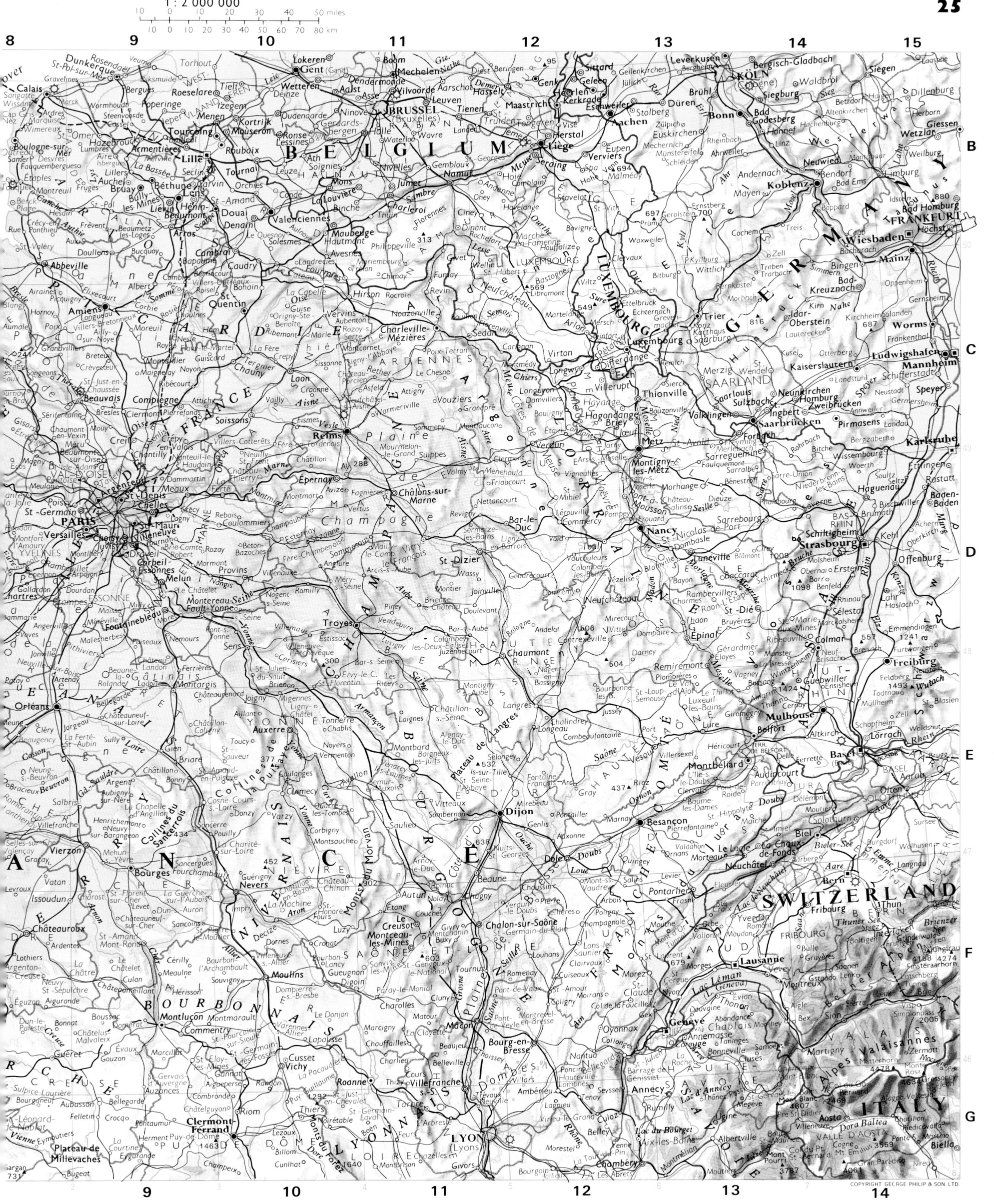

1 : 2 000 000

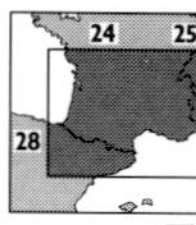

ATLANTIC OCEAN

Golfe de Gascogne

DEUX-SÈVRES · VENDÉE · AUNIS · SAINTONGE · ANGOUMOIS · CHARENTE · GIRONDE · LANDES · GASCOGNE · ARMAGNAC · BÉARN · NAVARRE · PYRÉNÉES-ATLANTIQUES · HAUTES-PYRÉNÉES · FOIX · ARIÈGE · ROUSSILLON · PYRÉNÉES-ORIENTALES · AUDE · HÉRAULT · TARN · AVEYRON · LOT · DORDOGNE · PÉRIGORD · LIMOUSIN · HAUTE-VIENNE · CREUSE · MARCHE · CORRÈZE · CANTAL · AUVERGNE · PUY-DE-DÔME · BOURBONNAIS · NIVERNAIS

La Rochelle · Niort · Poitiers · Châteauroux · Bourges · Nevers · Moulins · Montluçon · Vichy · Clermont-Ferrand · Thiers · Limoges · Angoulême · Saintes · Rochefort · Cognac · Périgueux · Brive-la-Gaillarde · Tulle · Aurillac · Bordeaux · Bergerac · Agen · Cahors · Rodez · Millau · Montauban · Toulouse · Albi · Castres · Béziers · Montpellier · Sète · Narbonne · Carcassonne · Perpignan · Foix · Tarbes · Lourdes · Pau · Bayonne · Biarritz · St-Jean-de-Luz · Dax · Mont-de-Marsan · Arcachon

San Sebastián · Pamplona · NAVARRA · Tudela · Calahorra · Zaragoza (Saragossa) · Huesca · Jaca · Sierra de la Peña · Sierra de Guara · ARAGÓN · Barbastro · Lérida · Gerona · Figueras · Manresa · BARCELONA · ANDORRA · ROUSSILLON

Pic d'Aneto 3404 · Vignemale 3298 · Pic du Midi 2886 · Aigoual 1567 · Plomb du Cantal 1858 · Puy de Sancy 1886

Projection: Conical with two standard parallels — West from Greenwich — East from Greenwich

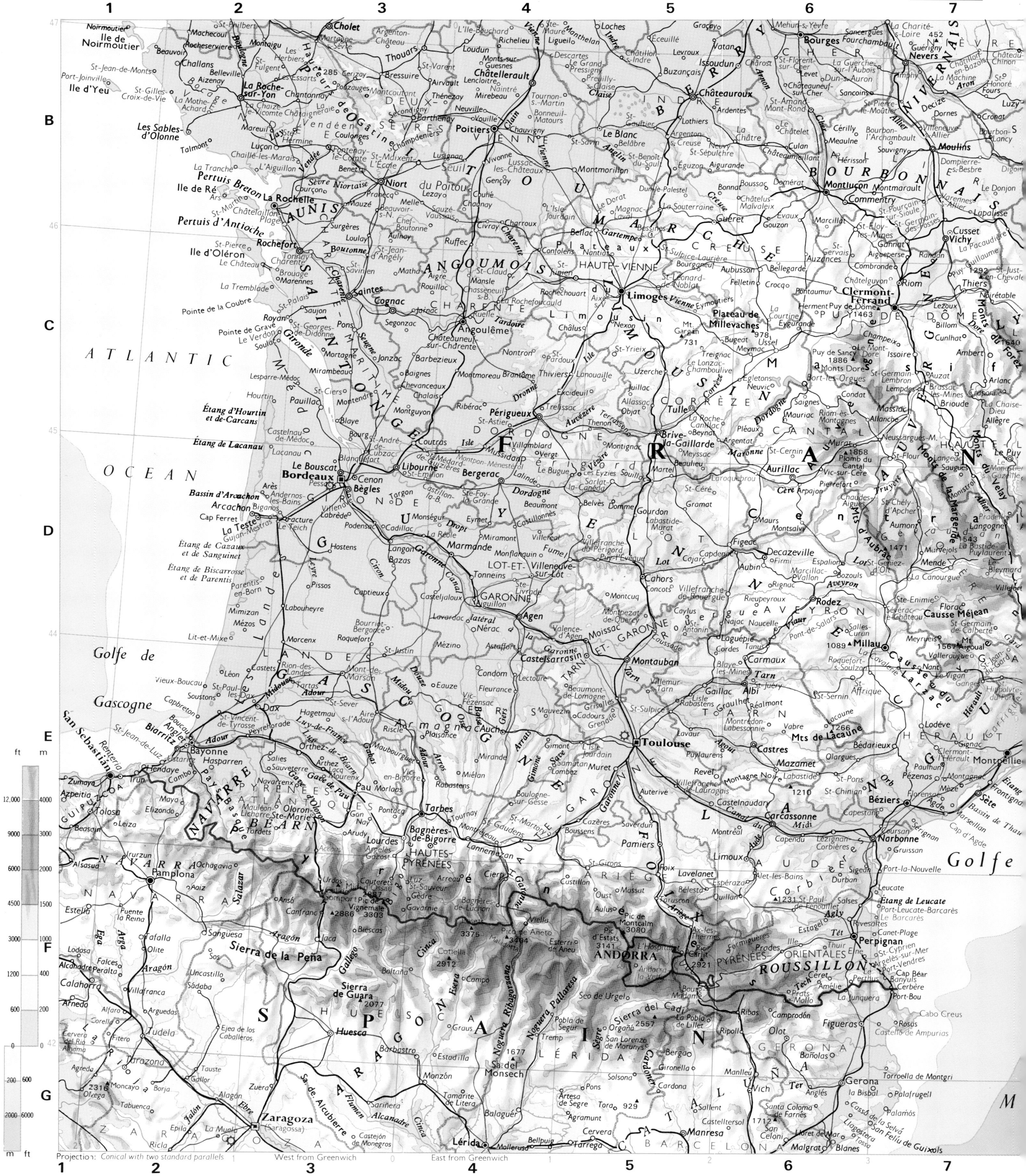

1 : 2 000 000

10   0   10   20   30   40   50 miles
10   0   10   20   30   40   50   60   70   80 km

8   9   10   11   12   13   14

B

C

D

E

F

G

Golfo di Génova

LIGURIAN SEA

du Lion

MEDITERRANEAN SEA

CORSICA

SWITZERLAND

ITALY

FRANCE

MARSEILLE

Toulon

Nîmes

LYON

St-Étienne

Grenoble

Valence

Avignon

Aix-en-Provence

Arles

Genève

Lausanne

Bern

FRIBOURG

Luzern

Schwyz

Davos

St. Moritz

Milano
(Milan)

Bergamo

Brescia

Torino

Novara

Pavia

Asti

Alessandria

Parma

Carrara

Massa

Cúneo

Savona

GÉNOVA
(Genoa)

La Spézia

Livorno

San Remo

MONACO
Monte-Carlo

Nice

Cannes

Bastia

Ajaccio

HAUTE CORSE

CORSE DU SUD

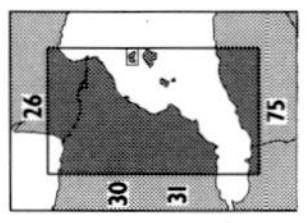

BAY OF BISCAY
Golfe de Gascogne
FRANCE
SPAIN
ANDORRA
PYRÉNÉES
ROUSSILLON
BARCELONA
Zaragoza (Saragossa)
Pamplona
Bilbao
San Sebastián
Toulouse
Perpignan
Tarragona
Lérida
Huesca
Logroño
Burgos
MADRID
Teruel
Castellón de la Plana
Menorca (Minorca)
Mallorca (Majorca)
Palma
ISLAS BALEARES
Sa. de Alcubierre
Los Monegros
Sierra de la Peña
Mts. del Maestrazgo
Montes Universales
Serranía de Cuenca
Sierra de la Demanda
Sa. del Moncayo
Golfo de San Jorge
Costa Brava
Costa Dorada
NAVARRE
BÉARN
GASCOGNE
ARAGÓN
CATALUÑA
LA RIOJA
PAÍS VASCO
CANTABRIA
LANGUEDOC
B
C
D
E
F
1
2
3
4
5
6
7
8

1 : 2 000 000

10 0 10 20 30 40 50 miles
10 0 10 20 30 40 50 60 70 80 km

F G H J K

8 7 6 5 4 3 2 1

Spain / Mediterranean

509
Isla Conejera
Cabrera
Cabo de Salines
Santanyí
Campos
Bahía de Palma
Cabo Blanco
Lluchmayor

Isla Grosa
San Juan Bautista
Punta Grosa
Isla de Tagomago
Ibiza (Iviza)
San Miguel
San Antonio
Sta. Eulalia
Ibiza
Isla Cunillera
San José
475
I. Espalmador
Formentera
192
Isla del Vedra
San Francisco
Punta de Cala Codolar
Cabo Berbería

B A L E A R E S

M E D I T E R R A N E A N   S E A

2850

VALENCIA
Valencia
Albufera de Valencia
Sueca
Cullera
Alcira
Játiva
Tabernes de Valldigna
Gandía
Grao de Gandía
Oliva
Denia
Cabo de San Antonio
Jávea
Cabo de la Nao
Benidorm
Villajoyosa
Alcoy
Sa. de Aitana
1558
Alicante
Santa Pola
Isla de Tabarca
Elche
Crevillente
Orihuela
Murcia
Cartagena
Mar Menor
Cabo de Palos

ALGERIA
ALGER (Algiers)
Boufarik
El Affroun
Blida
Koléa
Bou Ismail
Medéa
Berrouaghia
Ksar el Boukhari
Miliana
Khemis Miliana
Chérchel
Gouraya
Ténès
Ech-Cheliff
1985
Tiaret
Mostaganem
Azzew
Mohammadia
Sig
ORAN
Mascara
Arzew
Sidi-Bel-Abbès
Aïn Témouchent
Beni Saf
Ghazaouet
Nedroma
Berkane
Melilla (Sp.)
Nador
C. Tres Forcas
Alborán (Sp.)

M O R O C C O

Almería
Golfo de Almería
Guadix
Granada
Sierra Nevada
Mulhacén 3478
Sierra de Gádor
Motril

Albacete
Sierra de Segura
Sierra de Alcaraz

East from Greenwich
West from Greenwich

Projection: Conical with two standard parallels

COPYRIGHT GEORGE PHILIP & SON, LTD.

m ft
3000 9000
2000 6000
1500 4500
1000 3000
600 1800
400 1200
200 600
0 0
200 600
2000 6000

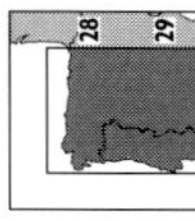

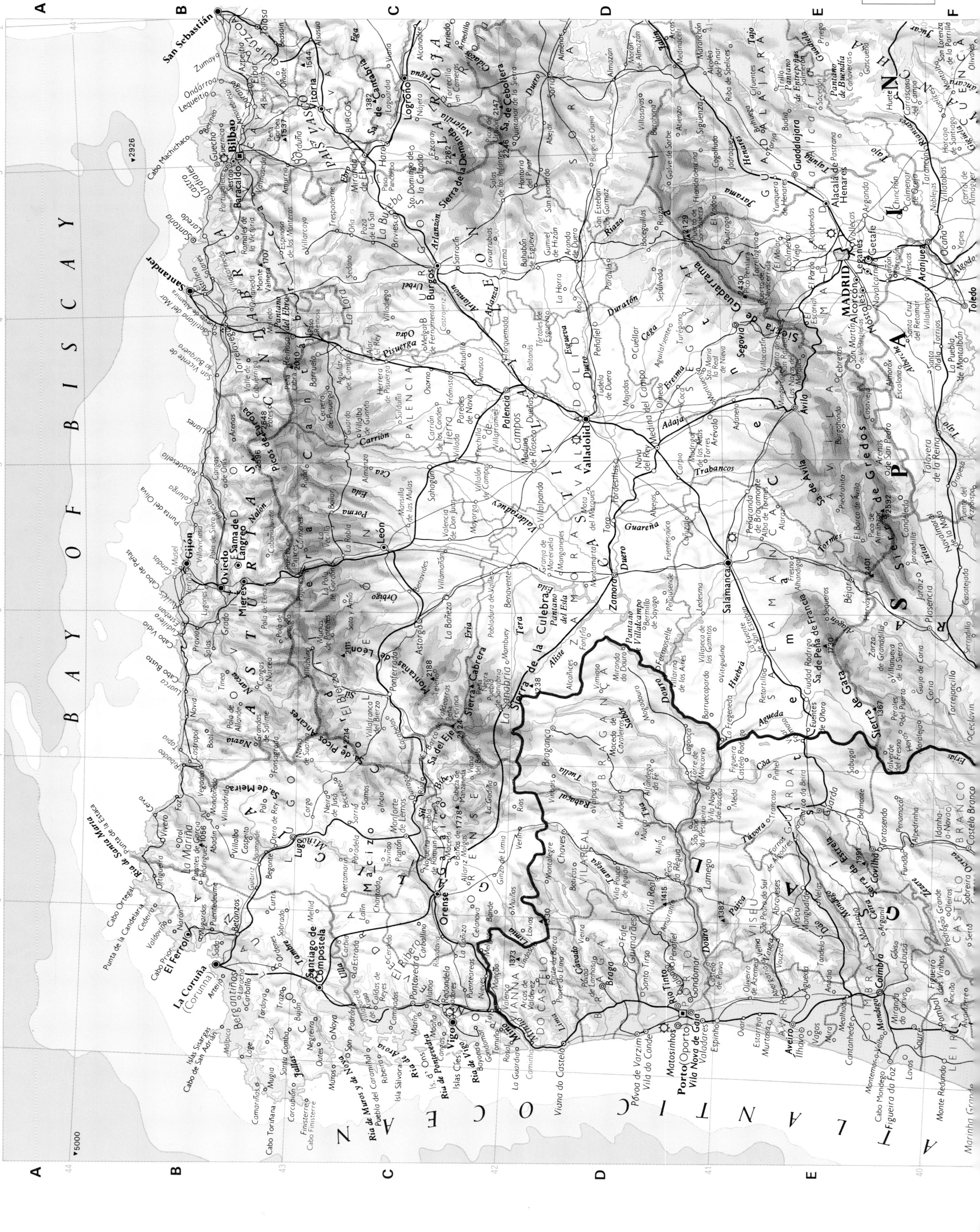

BAY OF BISCAY

ATLANTIC OCEAN

PAÍS VASCO

CANTABRIA

ASTURIAS

GALICIA

LUGO

LEÓN

PALENCIA

BURGOS

LA RIOJA

GUADALAJARA

CUENCA

MADRID

San Sebastián

Bilbao

Baracaldo

Santander

Gijón

Oviedo

Vitoria

Logroño

Burgos

Palencia

Valladolid

Segovia

Ávila

Salamanca

Zamora

León

Orense

Vigo

Pontevedra

Santiago de Compostela

La Coruña (Coruña)

El Ferrol

Lugo

Porto (Oporto)

Vila Nova de Gaia

Matosinhos

Coimbra

Viseu

Lamego

Vila Real

Braga

Guarda

Aranjuez

Toledo

Alcalá de Henares

Guadalajara

Sierra de Guadarrama

Sierra de Gredos

Picos de Europa

Sierra de la Demanda

Sierra de la Culebra

Serra da Estrela

Duero

Douro

Tajo

Ebro

1 : 2 000 000

10   0   10   20   30   40   50 miles
10   0   10   20   30   40   50   60   70   80 km

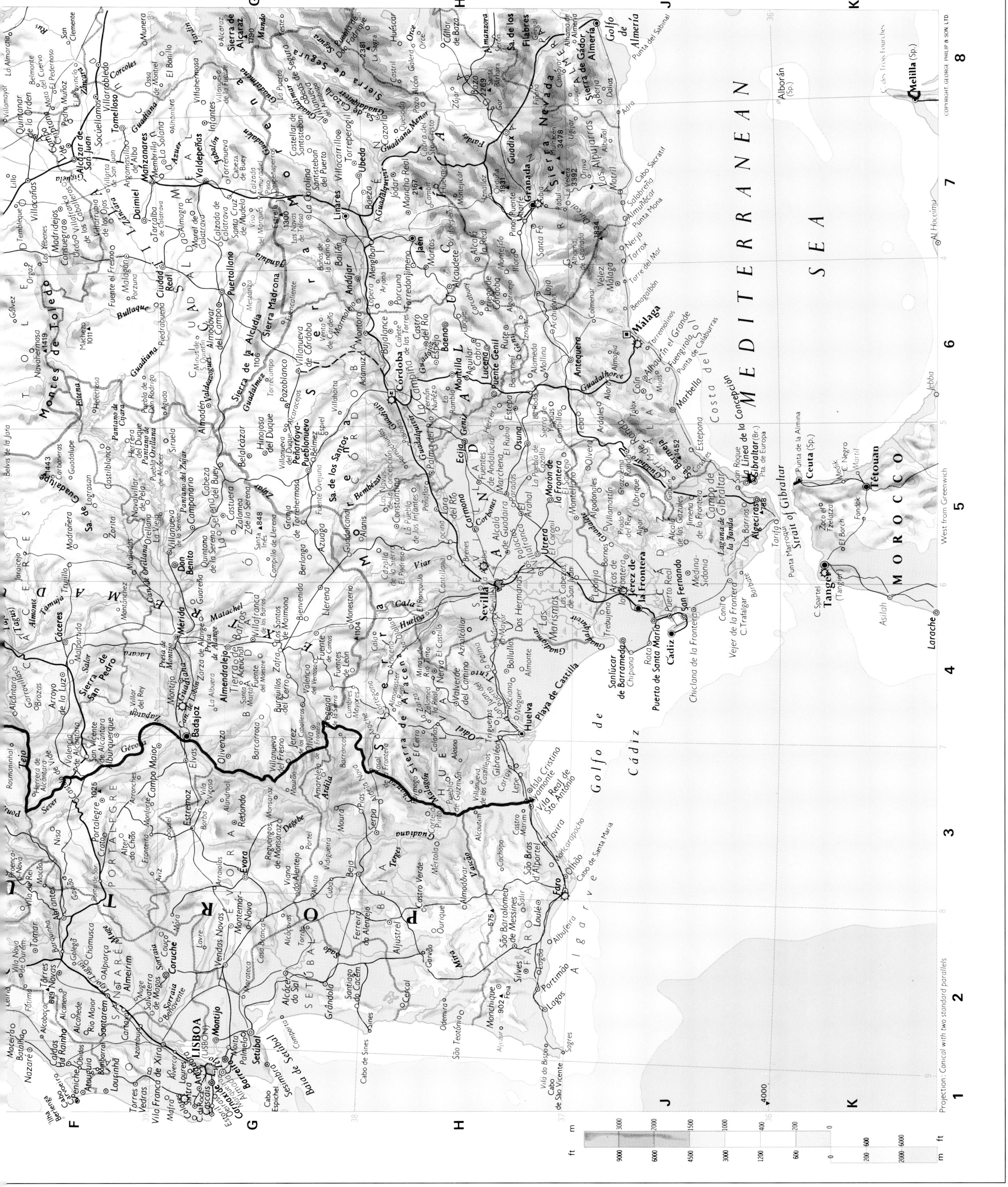

MEDITERRANEAN SEA

MOROCCO

Golfo de Cádiz

Projection: Conical with two standard parallels

West from Greenwich

COPYRIGHT GEORGE PHILIP & SON LTD

Montes de Toledo

Sierra Nevada

Sierra de Segura

LISBOA (LISBON)

Sevilla

Córdoba

Málaga

Granada

Cádiz

Badajoz

Mérida

Cáceres

Ciudad Real

Valdepeñas

Jaén

Gibraltar (Br.)

Ceuta (Sp.)

Tánger (Tanger)

Tétouan

Melilla (Sp.)

Algeciras

Huelva

Faro

Évora

Strait of Gibraltar

Golfo de Almería

Alborán (Sp.)

m   ft
9000
6000
4500
3000
1200
600
0

SWITZERLAND

VORARLBERG

LIECHTENSTEIN

FRANCHE-COMTÉ

VAUD

VALAIS

GRAUBÜNDEN

TICINO

LUZERN

BERN

FRIBOURG

Genève (GENEVA)

Lausanne

Bern

Luzern

Zürich-see

Lago Maggiore

L. di Como

Lago d'Iseo

Lago di Garda

MILANO (Milan)

TORINO (Turin)

Bérgamo

Bréscia

Novara

Vercelli

Vigévano

Pavia

Piacenza

Cremona

Mántova

Parma

Réggio

Módena

PIEMONTE

LOMBARDIA

EMILIA-ROMAGNA

Alessandria

Asti

Cúneo

Mondovì

GÉNOVA (Genoa)

Savona

La Spezia

Carrara

Massa

ALPES MARITIMES

ALPES-DE-HAUTE-PROVENCE

HAUTE-SAVOIE

SAVOIE

DAUPHINÉ

PROVENCE

BOUCHES-DU-RHÔNE

VAUCLUSE

DRÔME

Lyon (Lyons)

Grenoble

Chambéry

Annecy

Valence

Montélimar

Avignon

Arles

Salon

Aix-en-Provence

MARSEILLE (Marseilles)

Toulon

La Seyne

Hyères

ILES D'HYÈRES

Côte d'Azur

Cannes

Nice

Antibes

MONACO

Monte-Carlo

Menton

Ventimiglia

San Remo

Imperia (Maurizio-Oneglia)

Albenga

GOLFO DI GÉNOVA

LIGURIAN SEA

Rapallo

Chiávari

Sestri

Lucca

Pisa

Livorno (Leghorn)

Pistóia

Viareggio

Pietrasanta

TOSCANA

Volterra

Piombino

Elba

Arcipelago Toscano

Bastia

Calvi

L'Ile Rousse

Ajaccio

CORSE (CORSICA)

HAUTE CORSE

CORSE-DU-SUD

G. de St-Florent

G. de Porto

G. de Sagone

G. d'Ajaccio

Montecristo

Pianosa

Giglio

Capraia

Gorgona

1 : 2 000 000

10 0 10 20 30 40 50 miles
10 0 10 20 30 40 50 60 70 80 km

8   9   10   11   12   13   14

A

B

C

D

E

F

G

HUNGARY

SLOVENIA

CROATIA

YUGOSLAVIA

BOSNIA

HERZEGOVINA

Innsbruck

Graz

Klagenfurt

Villach

Maribor

Ljubljana

Zagreb

Trieste

Venézia (Venice)

Golfo di Venézia

Pádova (Padua)

Vicenza

Verona

Ferrara

Bologna

Ravenna

Rímini

SAN MARINO

Ancona

Perúgia

Firenze (Florence)

Arezzo

ADRIATIC SEA

ADRIA

Split

Zadar

Šibenik

Dugi Otok

Hvar

Korčula

Lastovo

Mljet

Pula

Rijeka (Fiume)

Karlovac

Banja Luka

Pescara

Chieti

L'Aquila

Teramo

ROMA (ROME)

Vatican City

Civitavécchia

Terni

Spoleto

UMBRIA

MARCHE

LAZIO

ABRUZZI

MOLISE

VENETO

FRIULI

VENEZIA GIULIA

DALMACIJA

Dinara Planina

Vieste

Monte Sant'Ángelo

COPYRIGHT GEORGE PHILIP & SON LTD.

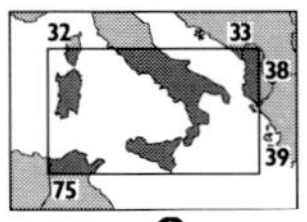

CORSE
CORSICA
CORSE-DU-SUD

Iles Sanguinaires
G. d'Ajaccio
C. di Muro
G. de Valinco
Sartène
Propriano
Pétreto
Tarcco
Zonza
Levie
Favone
Solenzara
Incudine
2136

Bonifacio
I. de Cavallo
Bouches de Bonifacio
Santa Teresa Gallura
La Maddalena
Maddalena
Caprera
Pto. Cervo
Arzachena
Costa Smeralda
Iles Cerbicales
Pórto-Vecchio

Asinara
Punta dello Scorno
Golfo dell' Asinara
Coghinas
Áqqius
Calangiánus
Golfo Aranci
G. di Ólbia
Tavolara

Porto Tórres
Sorso
Sennori
C. dell'Argentiera
Sássari
Osilo
Óschiri
Ttémpio Pausania
M. Limbara
1362
L. al Coghinas
Posada
Ólbia

Ferúlia
Íttiri
Alghero
Villanova Monteleone
Ozieri
Pattada
Búdduso
Bitti
Siniscola
C. Comino

Bosa
Bonorva
1259
Macomer
Temo
Nuoro
Oliena
Dorgali
Golfo di Orosei

SARDEGNA
Ghilarza
L. del Tirso
Fonni
Monti del Gennargentu
1834
SARDEGNA
Baunei
C. di Monte Santu

C. Mannu
Sórgono
Sórgono

Golfo di Oristano
Cábras
Oristano
M. Arci
812
Láconi
Nurri
Arbatax
Láusei

Arborea
Terralba
Jerzu
SARDINIA

C. Pécora
Flumínimaggiore
1236
M. Línas
Güspini
Montévecchio
Arbus
Gonnosfanádiga
Villacidro
Santuri
Serramanna
Mándas
Seníorbi
S. Vito
Villaputzu
Muravera

Iglésias
Fiumendosa
Assémini
Dolíanova
Sínnai
1069
S. Sperate
C. Ferrato

Portoscuso
Gonnesa
Cíxerri
Sílíqua
Sestu
Selárgíus
Quartu Sant'Elena
Serpentara

Carloforte
Carbonia
1116
Santadi
Cagliari
Golfo di Cágliari
C. Carbonara

San Pietro
Sant'Antíoco
Sant' Antíoco
Porto Botte
Pula
Teulada
Serpentara

G. di Palmas
C. Spartivento

T Y R R H E N I A N   S E A

3719

3589

Ustica

ROMA
(Rome)
Vatican City
Tívoli
Subiaco
Carsoli
Conca del Fúcino
2283

Fregene
Lido di Óstia
(Lido di Roma)
Fiumicino
Fosso
Frascati
Albano Laziale
Velletri
Palestrina
Valmontone
Anagni
Alatri
Véroli
Sora
Isola del Liri
Monte S. Giovanni

Láncio
Cisterna di Latina
Cori
Ferentino
Frosinone
Ceprano
Pontecorvo
Cassino

Ánzio
Nettuno
Sezze
Priverno
Sonnino
Ceccano

Monte Circeo
541
Sabáudia
Terracina
Fondi
1533
Fórmia
Sessa Aurunca

Palmarola
Zannone
Gaeta
Minturno
Gariqliano
Mondragone

Ísole Ponziane
Ponza
283
Golfo di Gaeta
Volturno
Casal di
Giugliano

Ventotene
Poz.
Prócida
788
Íschia
(Naples)

PALERMO
Bagheria
Golfo di Castellammare
Castellammare del Golfo
Terrasini
Favarotta
C. Gallo
Monreale
Mísilmeri
Términi Imerese

C. San Vito
Érice
1110
Trápani
S. Giuseppe Iato
Partinico
Campofelice

Levanzo
Ísole Égadi
Alcamo
Páceco
Camporeale
Corleone
1613
Lercara
Alía

Maréttimo
Favignana
Stagnone
Calatafimi
Salemi
Gibellina
Prizzi
Belsito

Marsala
Partanna
Bisacquino
Sambuca di Sicilia
Fiddia

Castelvetrano
Castelvetrano
Mazara del Vallo
Menfi
Burgio
Sciacca
Mussomeli
Caltanis

Campobello di Mazara
Belice
Ribera
Platani
Racalmuto
San Cataldo

Sicilian Channel
Cattólica Eráclea
Siciliana Aragona
Canicat

Porto Empédocle
Agrigento
Náro
Favara
Licata

Palma di Montechiaro
Campobello di Licata
Ravanu

Pantelleria
Pantelleria
836
(It.)
1319

Iles de la Galite
Galite

Bizerte (Binzert)
C. Blanc
Cani
Plane

Menzel-Bourguiba
Zembra
C. Serrat
Mateur
Golfe de Tunis
C. Bon

El Kala
Tabarka
Téboursouk
TUNIS
Halq el Oued
Kelibia

ALGERIA
Bou Salem
Béja
Tébourba
Menzel-Temime

TUNISIA
Medjerda
Soliman
Nabeul

Téboursouk
Zaghouan
Hammamet

M E D I T E

Projection: Conical with two standard parallels

East from Greenwich

ft m
9000 3000
6000 2000
4500 1500
3000 1000
1200 400
600 200
0 0
200 600
2000 6000
4000 12.000
m ft

1 : 2 000 000

ADRIATIC SEA

IONIAN SEA

MEDITERRANEAN SEA

Strait of Otranto

ALBANIA

Tirana (Tirone)
Durrësi (Durazzo)
Vlora (Valona)

Kérkira (Corfu)

G. di Manfredónia
Monte Sant'Angelo
Testa del Gargano
Fóggia
Manfredónia
Barletta
Trani
Biscéglie
Molfetta
Bari
Bitonto
Monopoli
Cerignola
Canosa
Andria
Corato
Terlizzi

Benevento
Caserta
Avellino
Salerno
NÁPOLI
Sorrento
Capri
G. di Salerno

BASILICATA
Potenza
Matera
Táranto
Golfo di Táranto
Bríndisi
Lecce
Nardò
Galátina
Gallípoli
Otranto
C. Santa Maria di Leuca

CALABRIA
Cosenza
Rossano
Crotone
Catanzaro
Golfo di Sant'Eufémia
Golfo di Squillace
Vibo Valéntia
Palmi
Réggio di Calábria
Messina
Str. di Messina

Isole Eólie o Lípari (Æolian Is.)
Strómboli
Salina
Lípari
Vulcano

SICILIA
Milazzo
Barcellona
Monti Nébrodi
Etna 3340
Catánia
Golfo di Catánia
Siracusa
Augusta
Ragusa
Módica
Noto
C. Passero
Gela
Vittória

COPYRIGHT. GEORGE PHILIP & SON LTD

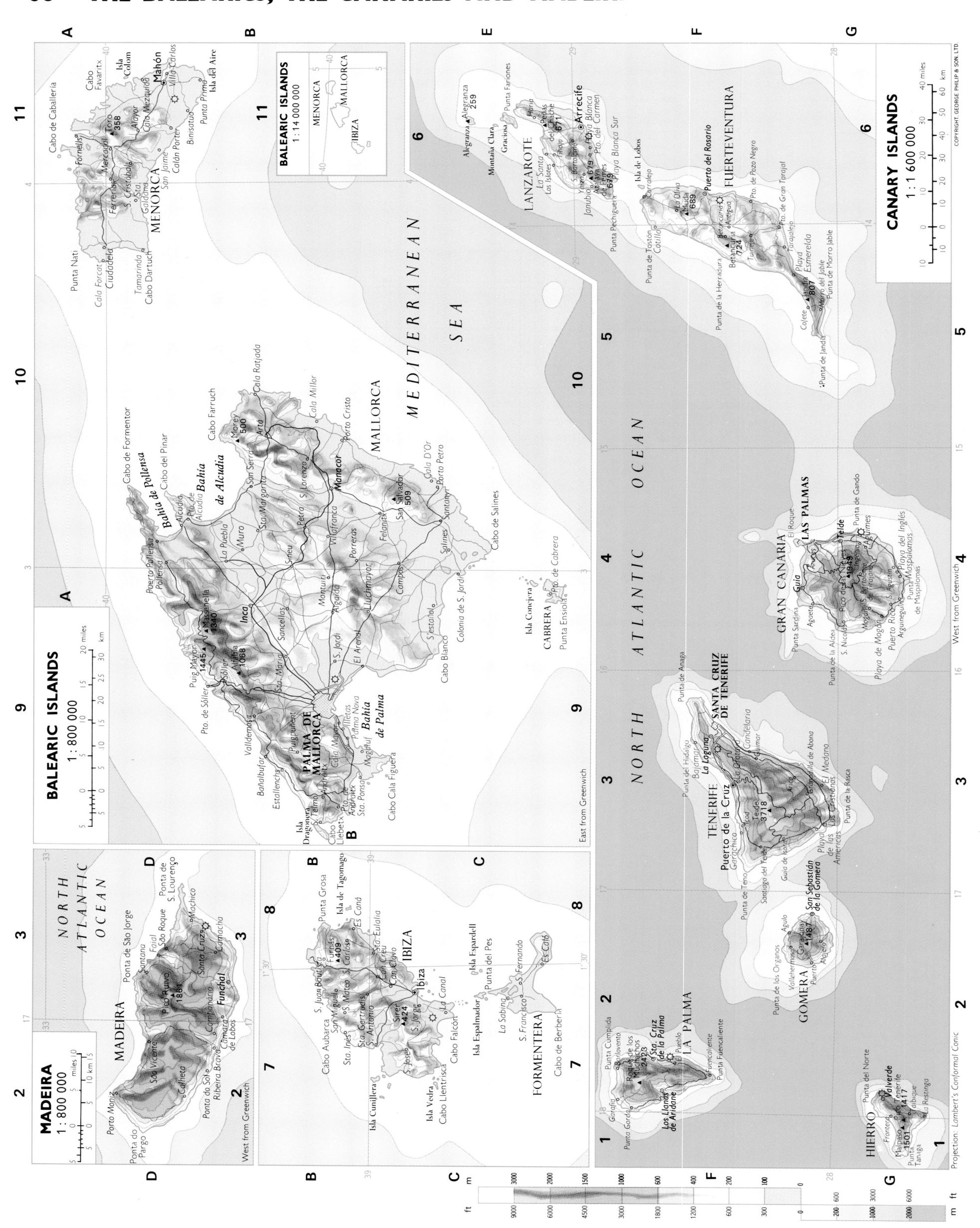

BALEARIC ISLANDS
1:14 000 000

MENORCA

MALLORCA

IBIZA

BALEARIC ISLANDS
1:800 000

MENORCA

Cabo de Caballeria
Cabo Caballeria
Fornells
Cala Forcat
Ciudadela
Tamarinda
Cabo Dartuch
Punta Nati
Punta Prima
Isla del Aire
Villa Carlos
Mahón
Isla Colom
Alayor
Cala Mezquida
Toro 358
Mercadal
Ferrerias
Sta.
Galdana
Cristobal
San Jaime
Calan Porter
Binisatló

MALLORCA
Cabo de Formentor
Puerto Pollensa
Pollensa
Bahía de Pollensa
Cabo del Pinar
Pto. de
Alcudia
Alcudia
Bahía
de Alcudia
La Puebla
Muro
Sta. Margarita
Ca'n Picafort
Son Serra
Cala Ratjada
Artá
Morey 500
Cala Millor
Capdepera
Cabo Farruch
Son San Lorenzo
Manacor
Porto Cristo
Porto Petro
Cala D'Or
MALLORCA
Sóller
Puig Mayor 1445
Massanella 1340
Alfabia 1068
Inca
Sineu
Sta. Maria
Montuiri
Petra
Vilafranca
Felanitx
San Salvador 509
Santanyí
Cabo de Salines
Cabo Blanco
Porreras
Lluchmayor
Campos
Salines
S. Jordi
S'Estañol
El Arenal
Bahía de Palma
PALMA DE MALLORCA
Valldemosa
Estellenchs
Bañalbufar
Pto. de Sóller
Puigpuñent
Calviá
Magalluf
Palma Nova
Illetas
Andraitx
Pto. de Andraitx
Sta. Ponsa
Cabo Cala Figuera
Isla Dragonera
Cabo Llebetx

MEDITERRANEAN SEA

Isla Conejera
CABRERA
Punta Ensiola
Pto. de Cabrera
Colonia de S. Jordi

NORTH ATLANTIC OCEAN

CANARY ISLANDS
1:1 600 000

LANZAROTE
Alegranza 259
Graciosa
Montaña Clara
Punta Fariones
Haría
Peñas del Chache 671
Arrecife
Costa Teguise
Sta. Bárbara 679
Tahiche
Yaiza
Janubio
Los Islotes
La Santa
Playa Blanca
Pto. del Carmen
Punta Pechiguera
Punta de Papagayo

FUERTEVENTURA
Isla de Lobos
Corralejo
Punta de Tostón
Cotillo
La Oliva
Muda 689
Betancuria
Puerto del Rosario
Antigua
Tuineje
Gran Tarajal
Pto. de Pozo Negro
Pajara
Betancuria 724
Pta. de la Entallada
Playa Esmeralda
Jandia 807
Cofete
Punta de Jandia
Morro del Jable
Punta de la Herradura

GRAN CANARIA
LAS PALMAS
El Roque
Telde
Pico de las Nieves 1949
Guia
Punta Sardina
Agaete
S. Nicolás
Mogán
Puerto Rico
Maspalomas
Playa del Inglés
Punta de Maspalomas
San Bartolomé
San Agustín
Arguineguín
Punta de la Aldea
Pta. de Gando

TENERIFE
SANTA CRUZ DE TENERIFE
La Laguna
Candelaria
Güimar
Punta de Anaga
Punta del Hidalgo
Bajamar
Tacoronte
La Orotava
Pto. de la Cruz
Puerto de la Cruz
Icod
Teide 3718
Vilaflor
Guía de Isora
Adeje
El Médano
Los Cristianos
Playa de las Américas
Punta de la Rasca
Buenavista
Garachico
Punta de Teno
Santiago del Teide

GOMERA
San Sebastián de la Gomera
Hermigua
Agulo
Vallehermoso
Chipude 1487
Playa de Santiago
Punta de los Organos

LA PALMA
Santa Cruz de la Palma
Roque de los Muchachos 2423
Pueblo
Fuencaliente
Punta Fuencaliente
Barlovento
Punta Cumplida
Los Llanos de Aridane
El Paso
Punta Gorda
Grafía

HIERRO
Valverde
Pico de Tenerife 1501
Frontera
Taibique
La Restinga
Punta del Norte
Punta Tanga

MADEIRA
1:800 000

NORTH ATLANTIC OCEAN

MADEIRA
Porto Moniz
Ponta de São Jorge
São Roque
Faial
Santana
Machico
Santa Cruz
São Vicente
Camacha
Pico Ruivo 1861
Funchal
Câmara de Lobos
Santa
Campanário
Ribeira Brava
Ponta do Sol
Calheta
Ponta do Pargo

IBIZA
Punta Grosa
Isla de Tagomago
Es Caná
Sta. Eulalia
S. Juan Bautista
Portinatx
S. Carlos 409
S. Miguel
S. Mateo
Sta. Inés
S. Antonio
Sta. Gertrudis
Ibiza
S. José 424
S. Jorge
Cabo Aubarca
Isla Conillera
Isla Vedra
Cabo Llentrisca
La Sabina
La Canal

FORMENTERA
Isla Espardell
Punta del Pes
Isla Espalmador
S. Francisco
S. Fernando
Es Caló
Cabo de Berbería

West from Greenwich

East from Greenwich

COPYRIGHT GEORGE PHILIP & SON, LTD.

Projection: Lambert's Conformal Conic

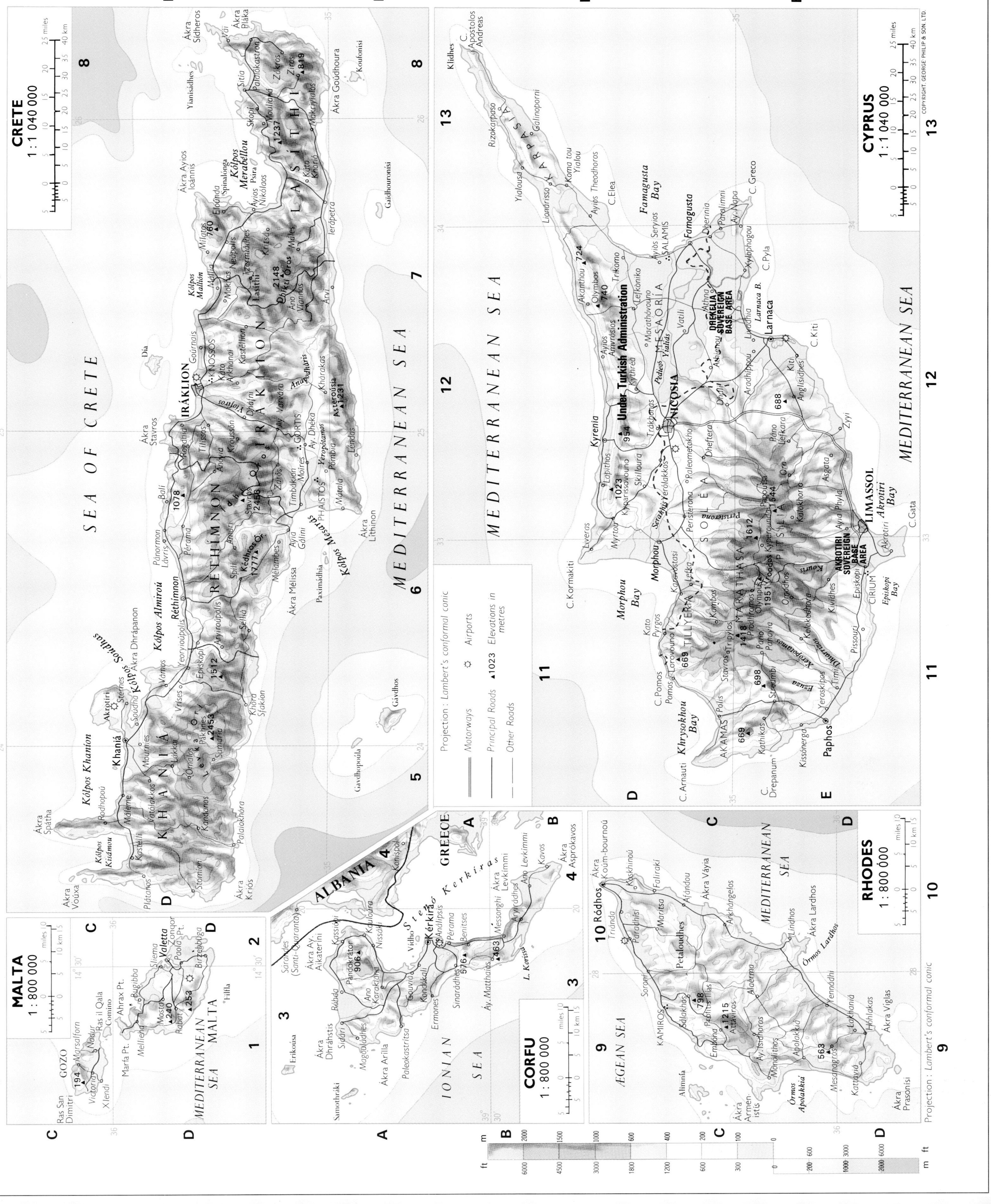
CRETE
1 : 1 040 000
SEA OF CRETE
MEDITERRANEAN SEA
Khaniá
Réthimnon
Iráklion
KNOSSOS
GORTIS
PHAISTOS
Kólpos Khanion
Kólpos Almiroú
Kólpos Merabéllou
Kólpos Mesarás
Ierápetra
Sitía
Gávdhos
Dia
KHANIÁ
RÉTHIMNON
IRÁKLION
LASÍTHI
CYPRUS
1 : 1 040 000
MEDITERRANEAN SEA
NICOSIA
Under Turkish Administration
Famagusta
Famagusta Bay
Larnaca
Larnaca B.
LIMASSOL
Akrotiri Bay
Paphos
Kyrenia
Morphou
Morphou Bay
Khrysokhou Bay
Episkopi Bay
KARPASIA
MESAORIA
TROODOS
AKROTIRI SOVEREIGN BASE AREA
DHEKELIA SOVEREIGN BASE AREA
SALAMIS
C. Apostolos Andreas
C. Greco
C. Gata
C. Kiti
C. Arnauti
C. Kormakiti
MALTA
1 : 800 000
GOZO
Comino
Valletta
Sliema
Mosta
Rabat
Birzebbuga
MEDITERRANEAN SEA
Filfla
CORFU
1 : 800 000
Kérkira
ALBANIA
GREECE
IONIAN SEA
Stenó Kerkiras
L. Korissía
RHODES
1 : 800 000
Ródhos
Líndhos
AEGEAN SEA
MEDITERRANEAN SEA
Kólpos Lárdhos
Projection: Lambert's conformal conic
Motorways
Principal Roads
Other Roads
Airports
Elevations in metres
COPYRIGHT GEORGE PHILIP & SON LTD.

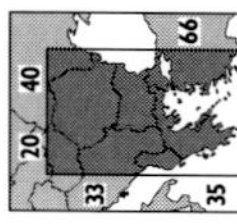
20
40
66
33
35

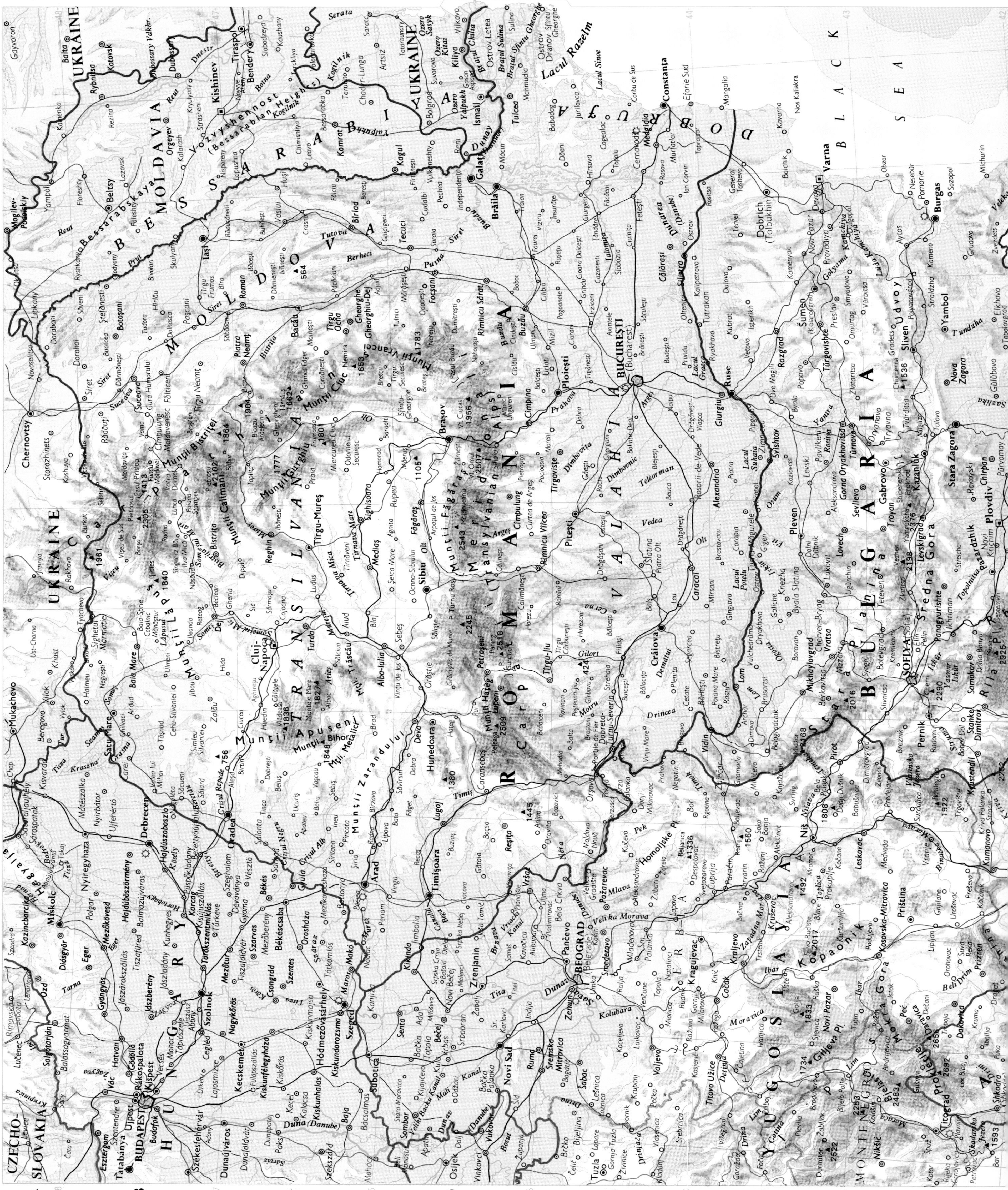
A
B
C
D
E
F
G
1
2
3
4
5
6
7
8
9
10
11
12
ROMANIA
BULGARIA
YUGOSLAVIA
HUNGARY
UKRAINE
MOLDAVIA
BESSARABIA
TRANSILVANIA
VALAHIA
DOBRUJA
MONTENEGRO
CZECHO-SLOVAKIA
BLACK SEA
BUCUREŞTI (Bucharest)
SOFIYA (Sofia)
BEOGRAD (Belgrade)
BUDAPEST
Kishinev
Cluj-Napoca
Timişoara
Constanţa
Varna
Burgas
Plovdiv
Craiova
Braşov
Iaşi
Galaţi
Brăila
Ploieşti
Debrecen
Szeged
Novi Sad
Ruse
Pleven

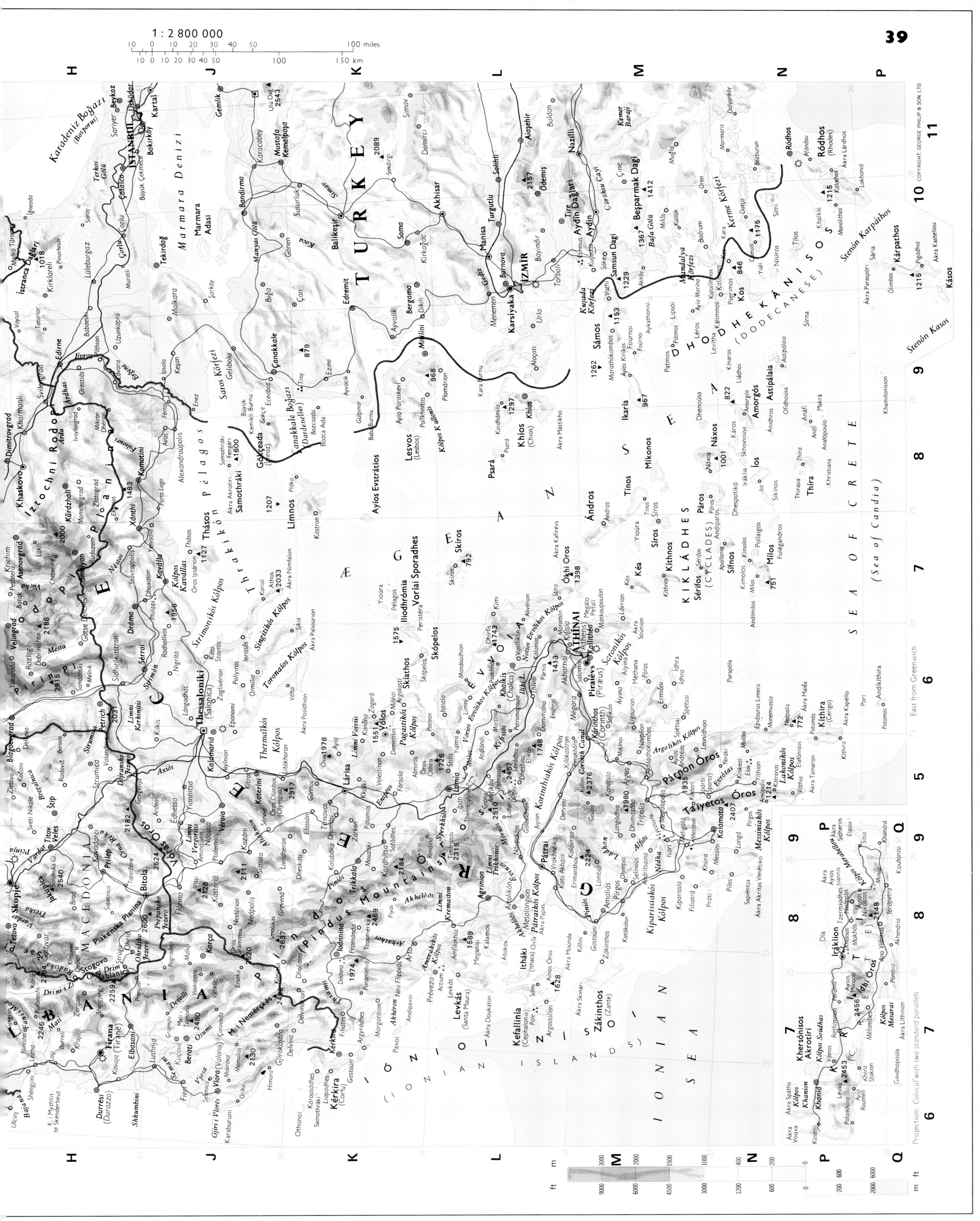
1 : 2 800 000
100 miles
150 km
TURKEY
MACEDONIA
IONIAN SEA
SEA OF CRETE
(Sea of Candia)
KIKLÁDHES
(CYCLADES)
DHODHEKÁNISOS
(DODECANESE)
Marmara Denizi
Thrakikón Pélagos
Iztochni Rodopi
Pindus Mountains
Karadeniz Boğazı (Bosporus)
İSTANBUL
İZMİR
ATHÍNAI (Athens)
Thessaloníki (Salonica)
Piraiévs (Piraeus)
Tirana (Tiranë)
Durrësi (Durazzo)
Skopje
Edirne
Lárisa
Vólos
Pátrai
Kórinthos (Corinth)
Kalamata
Iráklion
Khaniá
Ródhos (Rhodes)
Kérkira (Corfu)
Zákinthos (Zante)
Kefallinía (Cephalonia)
Levkás (Santa Maura)
Itháki (Ithaca)
Lesvos (Lesbos)
Khíos (Chios)
Sámos
Ikaría
Náxos
Páros
Thíra
Mílos
Kárpathos
Kásos
Kíthira (Cerigo)
Límnos
Samothráki
Thásos
Gökçeada (İmroz)
Çanakkale Boğazı (Dardenelles)
Saros Körfezi
Thermaïkós Kólpos
Korinthiakós Kólpos
Vorías Sporadhes
Skíros
Ándros
Tínos
Síros
Mikonos
Áyios Evstrátios
Bursa
Balıkesir
Manisa
Aydın
Çorlu
Tekirdağ
Stenón Kárpathos
Stenón Kasos
Projection: Conical with two standard parallels
East from Greenwich
COPYRIGHT GEORGE PHILIP & SON, LTD.
ft
m
9000
6000
4500
3000
1200
600
200
0
3000
2000
1500
1000
400
200
0

1 2 3 4 5 6 7 8 9

Orno 20 22 24 G. of FINLAND Bol'shoy 28 Kronshtadt 30 Novaya Syasstroy 34
Gotska Tyuters Lomonosov Ladoga
Sandon Paldiski SANKT PETERBURG Volkhov
Tallinn Kunda Ust Luga Pushkin (Leningrad) Pasha
Kärdla Kohtla Ivangorod Gatchina Kolpino Tikhvin Pikalevo
Hiiumaa Rapla Tapa Järve Kingisepp Tosno Kirishi Boksitogorsk
(Khiuma) Rakvere Narva Volosovo Lyuban Nebolchi
Haapsalu Paide Tamsalu Narvskoye Chudovo Khvoynaya Chagoda
Saaremaa Virtsu Vdkhr. Slantsy Luga Malaya Lyubytino
(Sarema) ESTONIA Vishera Lesnoye
Kuressaare Gdov Tolmachevo Komarovo
(Kingisepp) Pärnu Viljandi Plyussa Luga Torkovichi Novgorod Pestovo
Ruhnu Moisakula Chudskoye Polna Plyussa Shimsk Parakhino Borovichi
Gotland Ainaži Ozero Seredka Struga Krasnyye Oz. Ilmen Paddubye Okulovka
Rizhskiy Tartu Shelon Krettsy Lesnoye
Zaliv Väru Pskov Porkhov Staraya Valday Bologoye
Ventspils (Gulf of Riga) Valga Pechory Dno Russa Klimovichi
Munamagi Kachanovo Soltsy Demyansk Vyshniy
318 Valka Ostrov Volochek
Valmiera Novorzhev 343 Torzhok
Kuldiga Cesis Gulbene Pytalovo 328 Opochka R U Kuvshinovo
Aizpute Sigulda Aluksne Lovat Toropets Ostashkov Likhoslavl
Tukums Gauja Kholm Oz. Seliger Staritsa
Liepaja Riga Madona Oz. Lubana Andreapol Selizharovo Rzhev
Priekule Jelgava Jaunjelgava 311 Rezekne Novosokolniki Zapadnaya Dvina Zubtsov
Skuodas Možeikiai Bauska Plavinas Ludza Nelidovo Volga
Mažeikiai Jekabpils Sebezh Velikiye Olenino Starisa
Klaipeda Telšiai Birzai Daugava Idritsa Luki Zap. Dvina Zharkovskiy Rzhev
Kretinga Joniskis Nevel Belyy Tupik Sychevka
Neringa Plunge Kuršenai Rokiskis Daugavpils Disna Novopolotsk Demidov Dukhovshchina Moska
Silute 228 Radviliskis Panevezys Verkhnedvinsk Polotsk Gorodok Vyazma
Taurage Šiauliai Seduva (Drissa) Disna Surazh (Gagarin) 320
Zelenogradsk Kedainiai Ukmerge Zarasai Glubokoye Vitebsk Yartsevo Borodino
Polessk LITHUANIA Vidzy Vyazma
Kaliningrad Neman Jonava Postavy Krulevshchina Beshenkovichi Safonovo
(RUSSIA) Sakiai Lyntupy Senno Lepel Lyozno Smolensk
(Bagrationovsk) Gusev Kaunas Vilya Naujoji Vilnia Kobylnik Dolginovo Rudnya Dorogobuzh Ugra
Chernyakhovsk Lentvaris Vilnius Smorgan Osintorf Krasnyy Yukhnov
Lyna Kietzyn Alitus Ostrovets Vileyka (Krasnyye) Yelnya Mosalsk
309 Varena Vilya Tolochin Orsha Pochinok Spas-Demensk Meshchovsk
Druskininkai Smorgan Molodechno Kopys Desna
Suwalki Osmyany Slavnoye Shklov Rostavl Kirov Sukhinichi
Augustów Yaratishky Borisov Mstislavl Lyudinovo Kozelsk
Grodno Lida Volozhin Zhodino Mogilev Gorki Kletnya Zhizdra
Bialystok 238 Lyubcha Rakov 346 Dzerzhinsk Minsk Cherven Bykhov Krichev Dyatkovo Fokino
Nowy Dwor Knyszyn Novogrudok Gродzyanka Petukhovka Cherikov Zhukovka Bezhitsa
Ostrołęka Ostrów Mosty Stolbtsy BELORUSSIA Kostyukovichi Bryansk
Mazowiecka Łapy Dyatlovo Nesvizh Osipavichi Surazh Mglin Karachev
Pułtusk Zabludow Slonim Baranovichi Bobruysk Drut Rogachev Klintsy Unecha Pochep
Ciechanów Bielsk Volkovysk Lyakhovichi Kletsk Slutsk Zhlobin Klimovichi Navlya 277
Wegrów Podlaski Byten Soligorsk Glussk Svetlogorsk Iput Starodub Trubchevsk Kromy
Wołomin Bialowieza Gantsevichi Oktyabrskiy Rechitsa Surazh Novozybkov Dmitrovsk-
WARSZAWA Siedlce Hajnówka Pruzhany Telekhany Gomel Dobrush Orlovskiy
(Warsaw) Siemiatycze Biala Zhabinka Bereza Pripyat (Pripet) 316 Novobelitsa Zheleznogorsk
Otwock Podlaska Brest Drogichin Yaselda Luninets Kalinkovichi Semenovka Sevsk Dmitriev-
Łuków Ivanovo Pinsk Polesye Mozyr Gorodnya Novgorod-Severskiy Lgovskiy
Miedzyrzec Kobrin Pripyat Petrikov Vasilevichi Novgorod-Severskiy
Radom Podlaski Bialystok Stolin David Gorodok (Pripet Yelsk Khoyniki Loyev Rylsk Lgov
Zyrardów Lublin Włodawa Vysotsk Marshes) Chernobyl Shchors Desna Shostka Ka
Kozienice Lubartów Ubort Dubrovitsa Olevsk Ovruch Uzh Chernigov Berezna Glukhov Krolevets
Puławy Kovel Sarny Voronezh Konotop Seym Korenevo
Ostrowiec Opole Lubelskie Lyuboml Kamen Kashirskiy Staryy Belokorovichi Korosten Borzna Bakhmach Buryn Sudzha
Świętokrzyski Kraśnik Chelm Chartoriysk Goryn Oster Nezhin Belopolye Okhtyrka
Zawichost Zawada Novovolynsk Rozhishche Kiyevskoye Nosovka Romny Sumy Rokitno
Opatów Zaklików Zamość Vladimir Styr Sluch Gorodnitsa Vdkhr. Ichnya Lokhvitsa
Tarnobrzeg Stalowa Wola 390 Volynskiy Kivertsy Kostopol Malin Priluki Lebedin
Nisko Gorokhov Lutsk Karets Radomyshl Irpen Brovary Piryatin Trostyanets
Mielec Leżajsk Chervonograd Rovno Zdolbunov Korostyshev KIYEV Jagotin Grebenka Bogodukhov
Rzeszów Łańcut Rava Dubno Ostrog Novograd- Zhitomir (Kiev) Sula Gadyach Grayvoron
Przemysl Przeworsk Russkaya Berestechko Izyaslav Volynskiy Fastov Pereyaslav Lubny Romodan Krasnokutsk
Kramenka Slavuta Polonnoye Khmelnitskiy Akhtyrka
Krosno Sanok Bugskaya Brody Shepetovka Vasilkov Dnepr Mirgorod Poltava
Jasło Lesko Gorodok Zolochev Kremenets Berdichev Belaya Tserkov Khorol Zolotonosha Kremenchugskoye
Lvov Starokonstantinov Skvira Cherkassy Vdkhr.
Drogobych Rogatin Zbarazh 471 Vinnitsa Smela Karlovka
Uzhgorod Stryi Ternopol Khmelnitskiy Tetiyev Zolotonosha Krasnograd
Dnestr Berezhany Skalat Grimaylov Khmelnik 384 Svetlovodsk Poltava
CZECHOSLOVAKIA Bolekhov Kalush Monastyriska Trembovlya Kopychintsy Gorodok Vinnitsa Tyashlyk Vorskla
1346 Ivano-Frankovsk Tlumach Chortkov Komenets- Zhashkov Chigirin Kabelyaki
Mukachevo (Stanislav) Kolomyya Gorodenka Zaleshchiki Skala Podolskaya Podolskiy Zhmerinka Zvenigorodka Shpola Kremenchug Krasnograd
1881 Perechin

Projection: Conical with two standard parallels East from Greenwich

ft m
3000 1000
1200 400
600 200
0 0
200 600
m ft

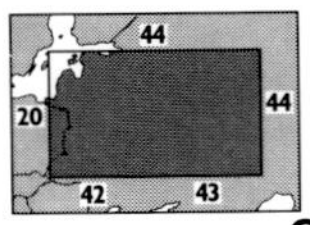

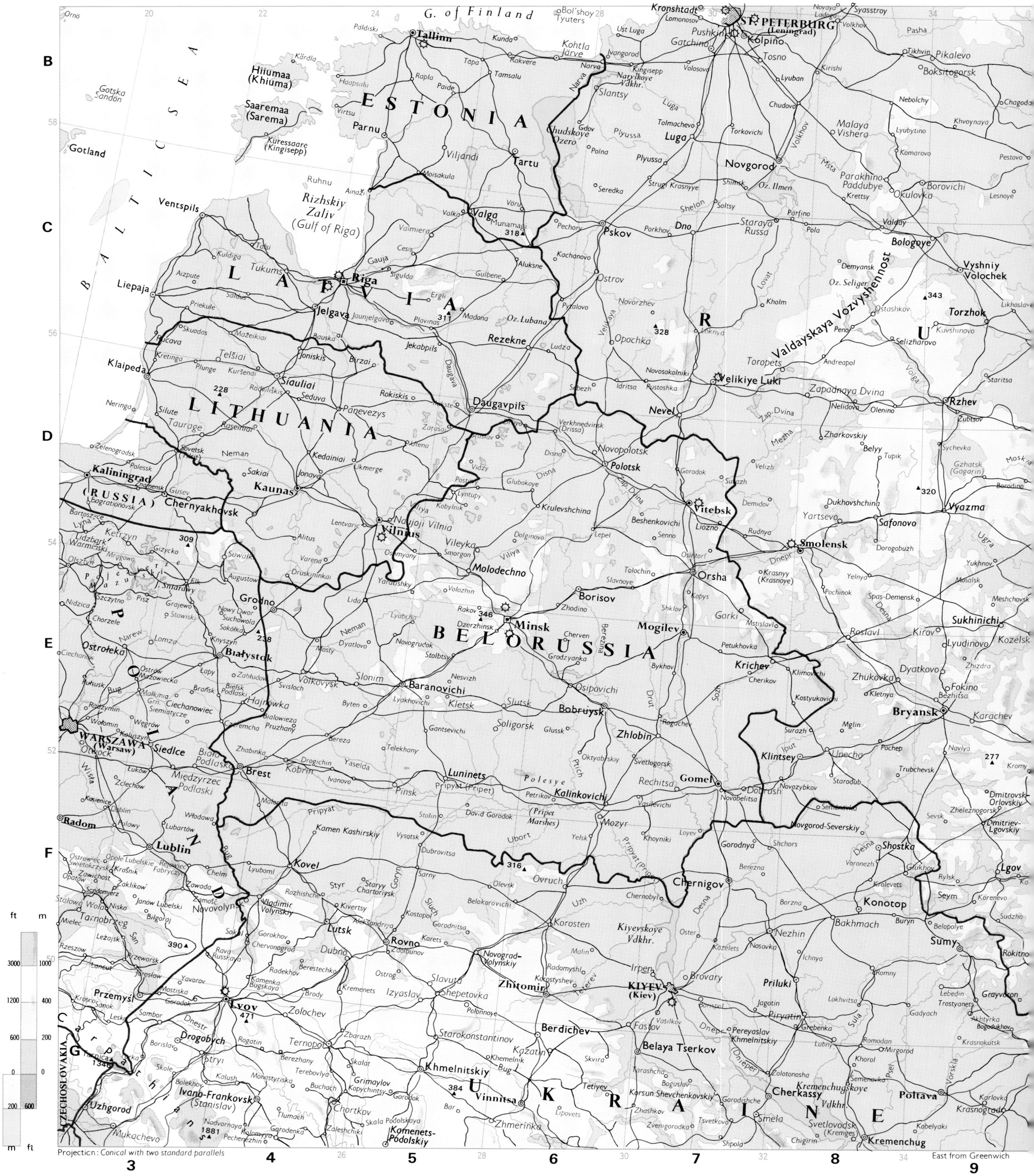

1 : 4 000 000

50   0   50   100 miles
50   0   50   100   150 km

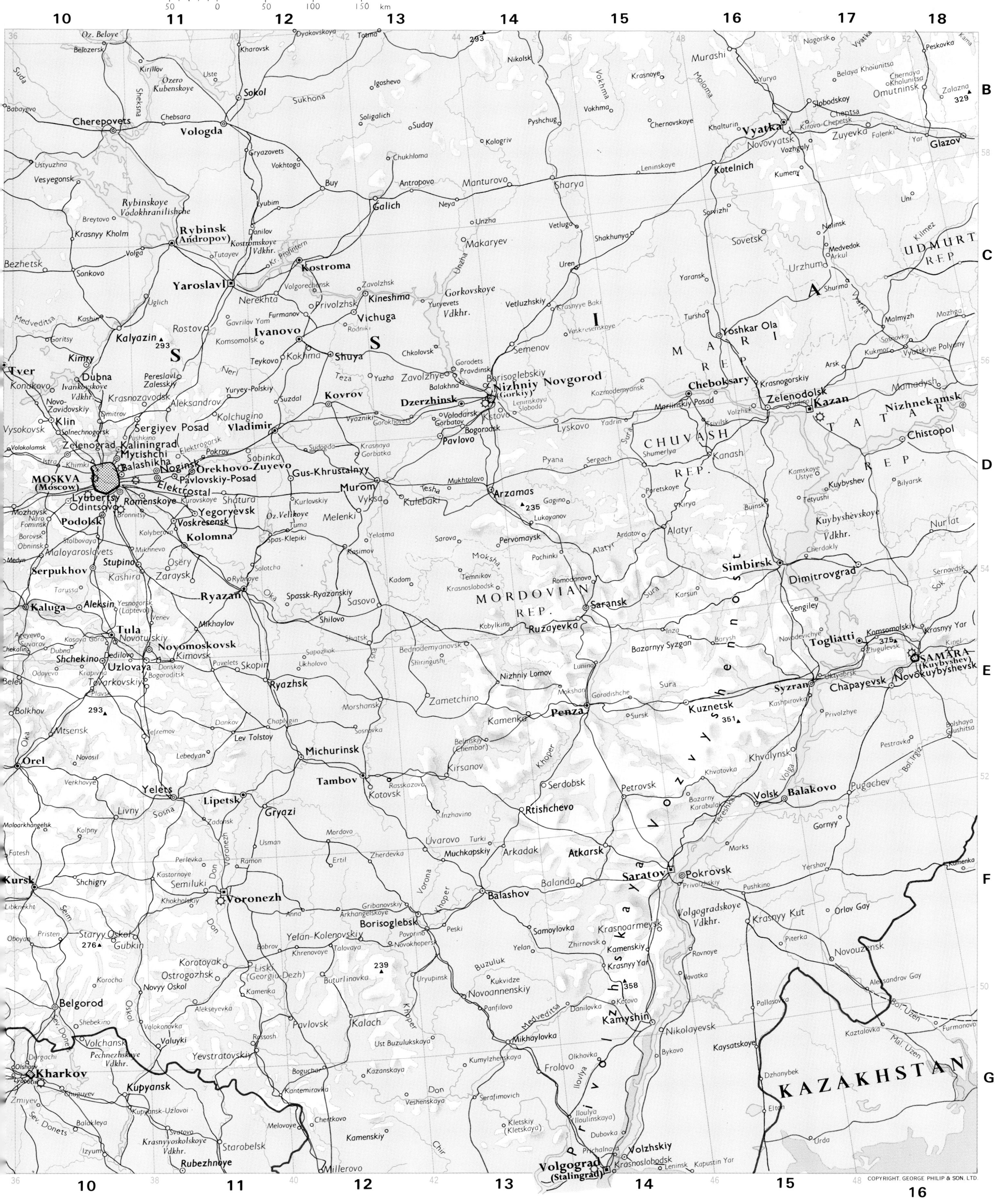

10 11 12 13 14 15 16 17 18

B
Oz. Beloye
Belozersk
Kirillov
Dyakovskaya
Kharovsk
Totma
293
Nikolsk
Krasnoye
Murashi
Nagorsk
Vyatka
Peskovka
Kama
Suda
Babayevo
Uste
Ozero Kubenskoye
Sheksna
Sukhona
Igoshevo
Vokhma
Molona
Yurya
Slobodskoy
Chernaya
Okholunitsa
Omutninsk
Zalazna
329
Cherepovets
Vologda
Sokol
Soligalich
Suday
Pyschug
Chernovskoye
Khalturin
Vyatka
Kirovo-Chepetsk
Zuyevka
Falenki
Glazov
58
Ustyuzhna
Chebsara
Gryazovets
Chukhloma
Kologriv
Manturovo
Sharya
Leninskoye
Kotelnich
Kumeny
Novovyatsk
Vozhgaly
Yar
UDMURT REP.
Vesyegonsk
Breytovo
Lyubim
Buy
Antropovo
Neya
Vetluga
Shakhunya
Svechinskiy
Sovetsk
Sorvizhi
Nolinsk
Uni
Krasnyy Kholm
Rybinskoye Vodokhranilishche
Rybinsk (Andropov)
Danilov
Galich
Unzha
Uren
Yaransk
Urzhum
Medvedok
Arkul
Malmyzh
Mozhga
C
Bezhetsk
Volga
Tutayev
Kostromskoye
Makaryev
Yaranskoye
Shurma
Kilmez
Sonkovo
Uglich
Nerekhta
Volgorechensk
Kineshma
Gorkovskoye Vdkhr.
Yuryevets
Vetluzhskiy
Krasnyye Baki
Shumya
Vyatskiye Polyany
Kukmor
Arsk
Sovizhi
56
Medveditsa
Kashin
Rostov
Gavrilov Yam
Privolzhsk
Vichuga
Rodniki
Semenov
MARI REP.
Yoshkar Ola
Krasnogorskiy
Mamadysh
Kalyazin
293
Ivanovo
Kohma
Shuya
Chkalovsk
Gorodets
Pravdinsk
Kozmodemyansk
Cheboksary
Zelenodolsk
Kazan
Nizhnekamsk
S S
Kimry
Tver
Dubna
Pereslavl Zalesskiy
Teykovo
Yuzha
Zavolzhye
Borisoglebskiy
Nizhniy Novgorod (Gorkiy)
Leninskaya Sloboda
Marinskiy Posad
Volzhsk
TATAR REP.
Chistopol
Konakovo
Ivankovskoye Vdkhr.
Krasnozavodsk
Aleksandrov
Yuryev-Polskiy
Suzdal
Kovrov
Vyazniki
Gorokhovets
Volodarsk
Gorbatov
Kstovo
Lyskovo
Yadrin
CHUVASH REP.
Kanash
Kamskoye Ustye
Kuybyshev
Bilyarsk
D
Vysokovsk
Klin
Solnechnogorsk
Dmitrov
Novo-Zavidovskiy
Zelenograd
Kaliningrad
Mytishchi
Sergiyev Posad
Pushkino
Elektrogorsk
Pokrov
Vladimir
Sudogda
Krasnaya Gorbatka
Pavlovo
Bogorodsk
Pyana
Sergach
Shumerlya
Tetyushi
Buinsk
Kuybyshevskoye Vdkhr.
Nurlat
Volokolamsk
Istra
Khimki
Balashikha
Noginsk
Orekhovo-Zuyevo
Gus-Khrustalnyy
Murom
Vyksa
Kulebaki
Arzamas
235
Gagino
Kirya
Cherdakly
MOSKVA (Moscow)
Lyubertsy
Odintsovo
Ramenskoye
Pavlovskiy-Posad
Elektrostal
Pavlovskiy Posad
Kurlovskiy
Melenki
Yelatma
Sarova
Pervomaysk
Pochinki
Lukoyanov
Ardatov
Alatyr
Simbirsk
Dimitrovgrad
Sernovodsk
Mozhaysk
Nara
Fominsk
Bronnitsy
Yegoryevsk
Voskresensk
Oz. Velikoye
Tuma
Kasimov
Moksha
Temnikov
Romodanovo
Karsun
Inza
Sengiley
Sok
Podolsk
Stolbovaya
Kolomna
Spas-Klepiki
Salotcha
Kadom
Krasnoslobodsk
Saransk
Sura
Barysh
Togliatti
375
Zhigulevsk
Komsomolskiy
Krasnyy Yar
Kinel
Borovsk
Obninsk
Maloyaroslavets
Mikhnevo
Kolybelnoye
Rybnoye
Oka
Spassk-Ryazanskiy
MORDOVIAN REP.
Bazarnyy Syzgan
Novodevichye
SAMARA (Kuybyshev)
Medyn
Serpukhov
Stupino
Zaraysk
Ryazan
Sasovo
Ruzayevka
Bednodemyanovsk
Syzran
Novokuybyshevsk
E
Kaluga
Aleksin
Yesnogorsk (Laptevo)
Venev
Mikhaylov
Kashira
Shilovo
Shatsk
Sapozhok
Nizhniy Lomov
Lunino
Gorodishche
Kashpirovka
Privolzhye
Tarussa
Novotulskiy
Dedilovo
Donskoy
Pavelets
Skopin
Likholovo
Shiringushi
Sura
Kuznetsk
Bolshaya Glushitsa
Ageyevo
Kosaya Gora
Tula
Novomoskovsk
Bogoroditsk
Ryazhsk
Zametchino
Mokshan
Penza
Pestravka
Dubna
Shchekino
Kimovsk
Dankov
Chaplygin
Morshansk
Sosnovka
Kamenka
Sursk
351
Belev
Tovarkovskiy
Uzlovaya
Plavsk
Yefremov
Lev Tolstoy
Belinskiy (Chembar)
Serdobsk
Khvatovka
Khvalynsk
Volsk
Mtsensk
293
Novosil
Lebedyan
Michurinsk
Kirsanov
Inzhavino
Bazarny Karabulak
Volga
Balakovo
Bolkhov
Oka
Krapivna
Odoyev
Verkhovye
Yelets
Gryazi
Tambov
Kotovsk
Rasskazovo
Rtishchevo
Petrovsk
Bazarny Karabulak
Marks
Orel
Livny
Sosna
Lipetsk
Mordovo
Usman
Uvarovo
Turki
Arkadak
Atkarsk
Saratov
Pokrovsk
Yershov
Kamenka
F
Kursk
Shchigry
Semiluki
Zadonsk
Voronezh
Anna
Ertil
Zherdevka
Muchkapskiy
Balashov
Serdobsk
Balanda
Privolzhskiy
Pushkino
52
Moloarkhangelsk
Kolpny
Kastornoye
Perlevka
Ramon
Voronezh
Gribanovskiy
Borisoglebsk
Peski
Samoylovka
Krasnoarmeysk
Volgogradskoye Vdkhr.
Krasnyy Kut
Orlov Gay
Fatesh
Seim
Pristen
Staryy Oskol
276
Gubkin
Korotoyak
Ostrogozhsk
Lisky (Georgiu-Dezh)
Buturlinovka
239
Yelan-Kolenovskiy
Talovaya
Povorino
Novokhopersk
Yelan
Zhirnovsk
Kamenskiy
Krasnyy Yar
Novatka
Pallasovka
Novouzensk
Belgorod
Oskol
Korocha
Novyy Oskol
Kamenka
Bobrov
Khrenovoye
Uryupinsk
Buzuluk
Kukvidze
Novoannenskiy
358
Kotovo
Kamyshin
Nikolayevsk
Kaztalovka
G
Kharkov
Shebekino
Volokonovka
Pavlovsk
Kalach
Khoper
Ust Buzulukskaya
Panfilovo
Medveditsa
Danilovka
Mikhaylovka
Bykovo
Dzhanybek
Kupyansk
Alekseyevka
Kamenka
Boguchar
Kazanskaya
Kumylzhenskaya
Frolovo
Olkhovka
Kaysatskoye
KAZAKHSTAN
Zmiyev
Sev. Donets
Valuyki
Rossosh
Kantemirovka
Veshenskaya
Serafimovich
Ilovlya
Prichalnaya
Volzhskiy
Eltan
Urda
Chuguyev
Pechenezhskoye Vdkhr.
Olshany
Kupyansk-Uzlovyy
Svatovo
Millerovo
Chernkovo
Chir
Don
Kletskiy (Kletskaya)
Dubovka
Volgograd (Stalingrad)
Krasnoslobodsk
Leninsk
Kapustin Yar
Mal Uzen
Bol Uzen
Dergachi
Izyum
Starobelsk
Kamenskiy
Melovoye
Kletskiy
Ilovlya (Ilovlinskaya)
Pichuga
Balakleya
Krasnyyaskolskoye Vdkhr.
Rubezhnoye

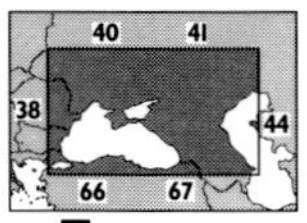

1 2 3 4 5 6 7

A

Sokal Chervonograd Gorokhov Dubno Rovno Aleksandriya Korets Gorodnitsa Korosten Oster Kozelets Nosovka Nezhin Bakhmach Belopolye Sudzha Obyan Pristen Staryy Oskol 276

Kamenka-Bugskaya Radekhov Berestechko Ostrog Slavuta Shepetovka Novograd-Volynskiy Radomyshl Malin Irpen Brovary KIYEV (Kiev) Priluki Romny Lokhvitsa Akhtyrka Graivoron Rokitnoye Karocha Novyy Oskol

L'vov Zolochev Brody Kremenets Izyaslav Zhitomir Radomyshl Vasilkov Borispol Piryatin Pereyaslav-Khmelnitskiy Sula Gadyach Bogodukhov Belgorod Volokonovka Valuik

B

▲471 Rogatin Ternopol Zbarazh Starokonstantinov Berdichev Fastov Dnepr Jagotin Pereyaslav Lubny Khorol Mirgorod Romodan Krasnokutsk Olshany Kharkov Pechnezhskoye Vdkhr. Volchansk

Ivano-Frankovsk (Stanislav) Berezhany Grimaylov 384 Khmelnitskiy Kazatin Skvira Belaya Tserkov Tarashcha Zolotonosha Semenovka Yorskla Poltava Karlovka Krasnograd Izyum Zmiyev Chuguyev Kupyansk-Uzlovoy Svatovo Kupyansk

Chortkov Skala Podolskaya Kopychintsy Gorodok Bar UKRAINE Vinnitsa Zhmerinka Bug Boguslav Korsun Shevchenkovskiy Gorodishche Cherkassy Kremenchugskoye Vdkhr. Kobelyaki Orel Lozovaya Krasnyy Liman Barvenkovo Krasnyyoskolskoye Vdkhr. Kremennaya

C

Nadvornaya Gorodenka Kolomyya Snyatyn Khotin Kemenets-Podolskiy Dnestr Mogilev-Podolskiy Tulchin Gaysin Uman Novomirgorod Malaya Viska Znamenka Kamenka Aleksandrovka Svetlovodsk (Kremges) Tsarichanka Dneprodzerzhinskoye Vdkhr. Slavyansk Kramatorsk Artemovsk Lisichansk

Pechenezhin Zaleshchiki Novoselitsa Kupkani MOLDAVIA Pervomaysk Bolshaya Vradyevka Balta Olshanka Novoukrainka Zheltyye Vody Pyatikhatki Dneprodzerzhinsk Novomoskovsk Aleksandriya Verchovtsevo Dnepropetrovsk Pavlograd Konstantinovka

Chernovtsy Storozhinets Radauti Beltsy Soroki Rybnitsa Kotovsk Ananyev Bobrinets Pomoshnaya 269 Dolinskaya Sofevka Sinelnikovo Krasnoarmeysk Gorlovka Yenakiyevo Makeyevka

2102 ▲ Pietrosul Tirgu-Neamt 429 Dubossary Vdkhr. Kornesthy Ungeny Orgeyev Tsebrikovo Arbuzinka Bug Ingulets Krivoy Rog Ingulets Volchya Volnovakha Donetsk (Stalino) Mospino Detailovo

Gheorgheni Praid Odorheiul Secuiesc Topita Piatra-Neamt Roman Bistrita Iasi Kishinev Bendery Tiraspol Razdelnaya Berezovka Voznesensk Novy Bug Apostolovo Nikopol Marganets Ordzhonikidze Kamenka-Dneprovskaya Orekhov Pologi Gulyaypole Kuybyshevo Novoazovsk

C ROMANIA Miercurea Ciuc Bacau Vaslui Husi Komrat Tsebrikovo Nikolayev Snigirevka Ingulets Velikaya Lepetikha Kakhovskoye Vdkhr. Malaya Belozerka Mikhailovka Bolshoy Tokmak Molochansk Molochnaya 324 ▲ Mariupol (Zhdanov) Taganrogskiy Yeysk

D

Sfintu Gheorghe Olt Adjud Focsani Tecuci Barlad Siret (Sereth) Vulkaneshty Bolgrad Chatyr-Lunga Artsiz Belgorod-Dnestrovskiy Zhovtnevoye (Oktyabrskoye) Ochakov Berislav Novaya Kakhovka Akimovka Melitopol Primorskoye (Nogaysk) Priazovskoye Berdyansk

Vf. Omul ▲2507 Ramnicu Sarat Galati Kagul Bessarabka Tatarbunary Odessa Ilyichevsk Ovidiopol Kherson Golaya Pristen Skadovsk Genichesk AZOVSKOYE MORE (Sea of Azov) ▼14 Primorsko-Akhtarsk

Buzau Braila Ismail Kiliya Vilkovo Sulina M. Tarkhankut Chernomorskoye Razdolnoye Karkinitskiy Zaliv Krasnoperekopsk Arbatskaya Strelka Biryuchiy

Tirgoviste Ploiesti Buzau Faurei Tulcea Dobroge Dzhankoi Krasnogvardyesk Krymskiy P.-ov. (Crimea) Salgir Nizhnegorskiy Lenino Kerch Taman Temryuk Slavyansk-na-Kubani Kubar Krymsk Abinsk

D

Valahia Arges Urziceni Tandarei Yevpatoriya Saki Lenskoye Vladislavovka Feodosiya Anapa Novorossiysk 921 ▲

Silic BUCURESTI (Bucharest) Calarasi Cernavoda Mamaia Simferopol Belogorsk Krym Sudak Gelendzhik Kabardinka

Giurgiu Ruse (Ruscuk) Oltenita Silistra Constanta Sevastopol Bakhchisaray Gora Roman-Kosh 1545 Alushta Yalta Alupka

Razgrad Dobrich Balchik M. Sarych

BULGARIA Popovo Balchik Nos Kaliakra

E

Turgoviste Preslav Kolarovgrad (Shumen) Varna

Sliven Chatal Balkan Aitos Karnobat Burgas

BLACK SEA

2135 ▼ 2211 ▼ 2137 ▼

F

Elkhovo Yambol

Svilengrad Kirklareli 1018 Istranca Daglari Demirkoy Ignada Burnu Ince-Burnu Sinop Gerze Bafra Burnu

Edirne Babaeski Vize Inebolu Ayancik KUZEY

Dhidhimotikhon Uzunkoprü Luleburgaz Karadeniz Bogazi (Bosporus) Zonguldak Filyos Bartin Kure Kastamonu Taskopru Durağan Bafra Samsun Terme

Corlu Catalca Sile Eregli Caycuma Devrek Arac Vezirkopru Merzifon Havza Carsamba Unye Fatsa Ordu Giresun

Tekirdag 1261 Istanbul Uskudar Gebze Izmit Kandira Karabuk 2565 ▼ Tosya Kargi Osmancik Iskilip Ladik 2062 ▲ Gümüshacikoy

G

Gelibolu (Gallipoli) MARMARA DENIZI (Sea of Marmara) Marmara Yalova Iznik Golü Golcuk Sapanca Adapazari Bolu Gerede Gumushacikoy Corum Mecitozu Amasya Niksar Dereli

Imrali Bandirma Mudanya Mudurnu Goynuk Ortakoy Kursunlu Kizil Irmak Ilgaz Cankiri Amasya Turhal Zile 3095 ▲ Sebinkarahisar

Balikesir Edremit Bursa 2543 ▲ Sakarya Beypazari Ayas Kizilcahamam 2378 ▲ Kalecik Ankara Elmadağ Deveci Daği Tokat Koyulhisar

Projection: Conical with two standard parallels

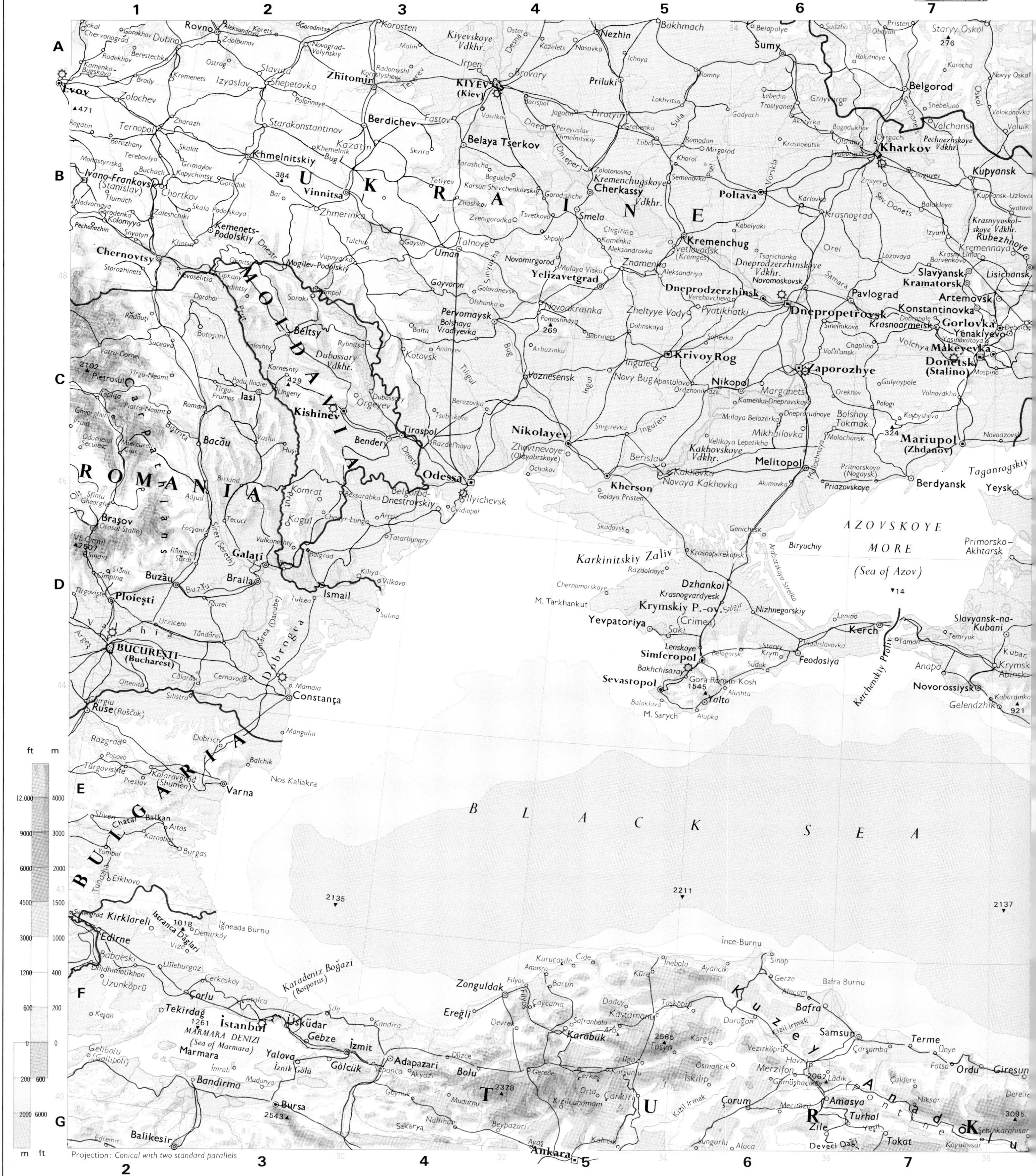

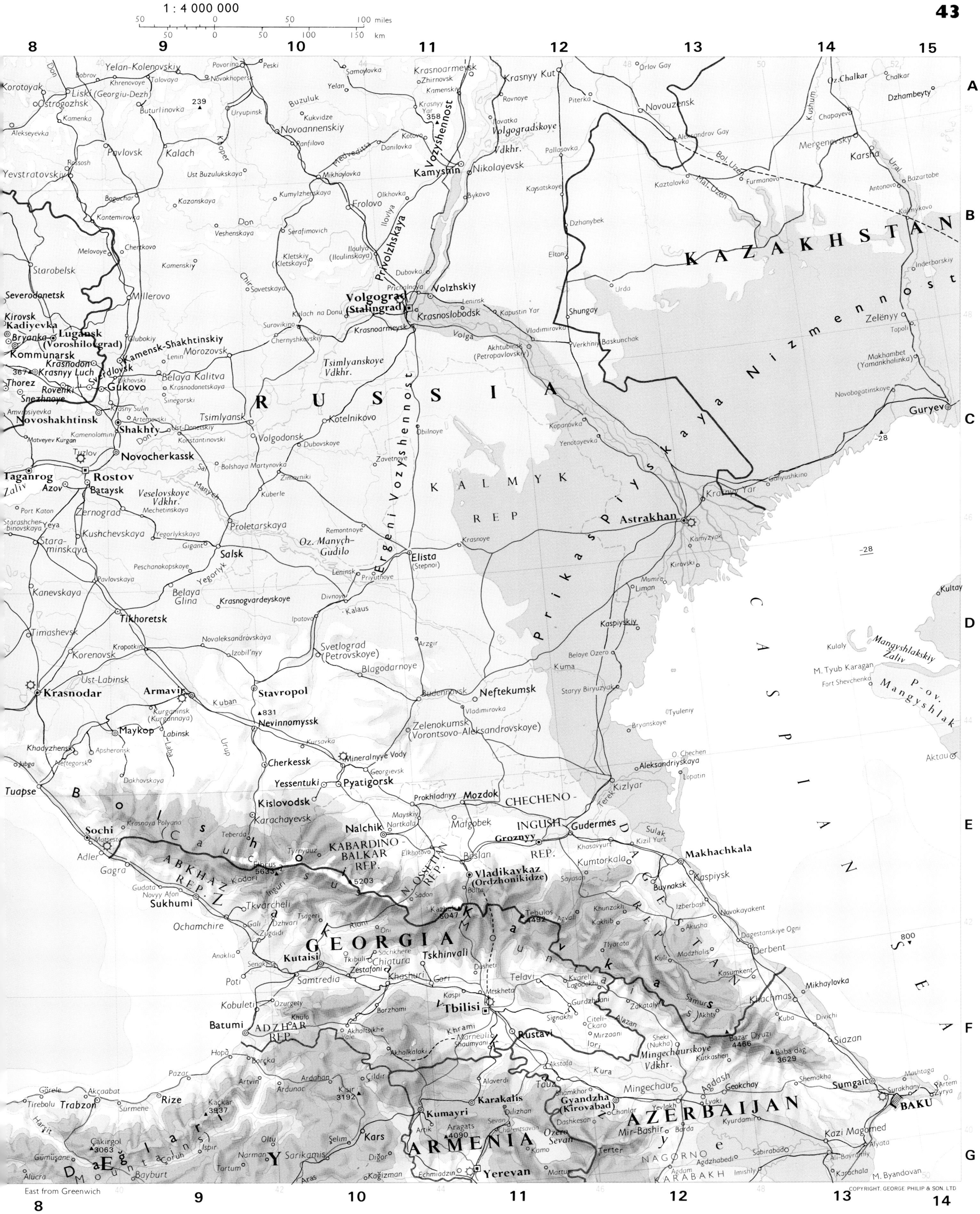

1 : 4 000 000

50   0   50   100 miles

50   0   50   100   150   km

8   9   10   11   12   13   14   15

A

Korotoyak   Yelan-Kolenovskiy   Povorino   Peski   Orlov Gay   Oz.Chalkar   Chalkar
Ostrogozhsk   Liski (Georgiu-Dezh)   Novokhopersk   Samoylovka   Krasnoarmeysk   Krasnyy Kut   Novouzensk   Dzhambeyty
Alekseyevka   Dobrov   Khrenovoye   Talovaya   Yelan   Zhirnovsk   Piterka   Rovatka   Aleksandrov Gay   Kushum   Chapayeva   Karsha
Kamenka   Buturlinovka   239   Uryupinsk   Buzuluk   Kukvidze   Krasnyy Yar   358   Ravnoye   Mergenevskiy   Bazartobe
Yevstratovskiy   Pavlovsk   Kalach   Koper   Novoannenskiy   Mikhaylovka   Kamyshin   Nikolayevsk   Volgogradskoye   Vdkhr.   Antonovo

B

KAZAKHSTAN
Starobelsk   Boguchar   Panfilovo   Vozyshennost   Volzhskiy   Dzhanybek   Urda   Inderborskiy
Bogorov   Millerovo   Don   Veshenskaya   Serafimovich   Iloulya (Iloulinskaya)   Dubovka   Elton   Bol.Uzen   Kalmykovo
Kirovsk   Kletskiy (Kletskaya)   Privolzhskaya   Krasnoslobodsk   Vladimirovka   Verkhniy Baskunchak   Makhambet (Yamankhalinka)
Kadiyevka   Lugansk (Voroshilovgrad)   Glubokiy   Surovikino   Kalach na Donu   Volgograd (Stalingrad)   Krasnoarmeysk   Akhtubinsk (Petropavlovskiy)   Topoli
Bryanka   Krasnodon   Krasny Sulin   Belaya Kalitva   Morozovsk   Chernyshkovskiy   Volga   Shungay
Kommunarsk   Krasnyy Luch   Gukovo   Tsimlyanskoye   Vdkhr.   Novobogatinskoye

C

Thorez   Sverdlovsk   Tikhovskiy   RUSSIA   Guryev
Rovenki   Snezhnoye   Shakhty   Tsimlyansk   Ust-Donetskiy   Kotelnikovo   Obilnoye   Kopanovka   −28
Novoshakhtinsk   Kamenolomni   Novocherkassk   Volgodonsk   Dubovskoye   Zavetnoye   Yenotayevka   Krasnyy Yar   Ganyushkino
Matveyev Kurgan   Tuzlov   Don   Konstantinovskiy   Bolshaya Martynovka   Zimovniki   KALMYK   Kamyzyak
Taganrog   Rostov   Bataysk   Sal   Manych   Küberle   REP   Astrakhan

D

Azov   Zaliv   Veselovskoye   Vdkhr.   Mechetinskaya   Proletarskaya   Remontnoye   Krasnoye   Mumra   CASPIAN
Port Katon   Zernograd   Yegorlykskaya   Gigant   Oz. Manych-Gudilo   Priyutnoye   Liman   Kultay
Starashcher-binovskaya   Yeya   Kushchevskaya   Salsk   Yegorlyk   Leninsk   Elista (Stepnoi)   Beloye Ozero   Kulaly   Mangyshlakskiy Zaliv
Kanevskaya   Belaya Glina   Peschanokopskoye   Krasnogvardeyskoye   Divnoye   Kalaus   Kuma   M. Tyub Karagan   P-ov Mangyshlak
Timashevsk   Tikhoretsk   Novaleksandrovskaya   Svetlograd (Petrovskoye)   Blagodarnoye   Staryy Biryuzyak   Fort Shevchenko
Korenovsk   Ust-Labinsk   Kropotkin   Izobil'nyy   Budennovsk   Neftekumsk   Tyuleniy   −28   Aktau

D/E

Krasnodar   Armavir   Kurganinsk (Kurgannaya)   Stavropol   Nevinnomyssk   Kursavka   Zelenokumsk (Vorontsovo-Aleksandrovskoye)   O. Chechen   Aktau
Maykop   Labinsk   Kuban   831   Vladimirovka   Aleksandriyskaya   800
Khadyzhensk   Apsheronsk   L-Laba   Urup   Cherkessk   Mineralnyye Vody   Georgiyevsk   Kislyar   Lopatin
Yubga   Neftegorsk   Dakhovskaya   Yessentuki   Pyatigorsk   Prokhladnyy   Mozdok   CHECHENO-   Kizlyar
Tuapse   B   Krasnaya Polyana   Kislovodsk   Karachayevsk   Mayskiy   INGUSH   Gudermes   Sulak
    o   Teberda   Nalchik   Nartkala   Malgobek   Groznyy   REP.   Khasavyurt   Kizil Yurt   Makhachkala

E

Sochi   l   Caucasus   KABARDINO-   Elkhotovo   Beslan   Kumtorkala   Kaspiysk
Adler   Matsesta   s   BALKAR   5203   N. OSSETIN   Sayasan   Buynaksk
Gagra   ABKHAZ   h   Tyrnyauz   REP.   REP.   Vladikaykaz (Ordzhonikidze)   Khunzakh   Novokayakent
    REP. Z   o   Elbrus 5633   K   Kazbek 5047   Tebulos 4492   Agvali   Izberbash   Derbent
Gudauta   Novyy Afon   u   Kodori   a   Balta   Tlyarata   Akusha   Dagestanskiye Ogni
Sukhumi   Tkvarcheli   Inguri   u   Dasheti   u   Kuli   Madzhalis
Ochamchire   Gali   Dzhari   Tsageri   z   Telavi   v   Kasumkent
    Rioni   Oni   b   Kvareli   k   Samur   Akhty

F

GEORGIA   Tskhinvali   e   Lagodekhi   a   Bazar Dyuzi 4466   Khachmas
Kutaisi   Sachkhere   Gori   Telavi   Zakataly   Kutkashen   Mikhaylovka
Poti   Samtredia   Zestafoni   Khashuri   Kaspi   Mtskheta   Sheki (Nukha)   Baba dag 3629   Kuba
Kobuleti   Ozurgety   Khulo   Borzhomi   Tbilisi   Alazan   Mingechaurskoye   Vdkhr.   Divichi
Batumi   ADZHAR   Akhaltsikhe   Khrami   Rustavi   Gurdzhaani   Iori   Agdash   Siazan
    REP.   Akhalkalaki   Marneuli Shaumyan   Signakhi   Mirzaani   Kura   Geokchay   Sumgait

G

Hopa   Borçka   Ardahan   Çildir   Citeli Tskaro   Alazan   Kutkashen   Shemakha   Maştaga
Pazar   Artvin   Ardanuç   Kisir 3192   Akhalkalaki   Akstafa   Tauz   Mingechaur   Lyaki   BAKU
Gürele   Akçaabat   Kaçkar 3937   Oltu   Şelim   Alaverdi   Mir-Bashir   Barda   Surakhany   Zyra
Tirebolu   Trabzon   Rize   Sürmene   İspir   Kars   Karakalis   Sevan   Dilizhan   Chanlar   Kazi Magomed   Kazi Magomed
Harşit   3063 Çakirgol   D   Narman   Sarikamis   Kumayri   Aragats 4090   Ozero Sevan   Gyandzha (Kirovabad)   Agdam   Sabirabad   Ali-Bayramly
Gümüşane   E   Mountains   Tortum   Echmiadzin   Artik   Kamo   Terter   Aras   NAGORNO   Imishly   Bilyasar   M. Byandovan
    N   G   E   Y   Bayburt   Yerevan   KARABAKH   Agdzhabedi   Yalyata   Gorchala

COPYRIGHT. GEORGE PHILIP & SON, LTD.

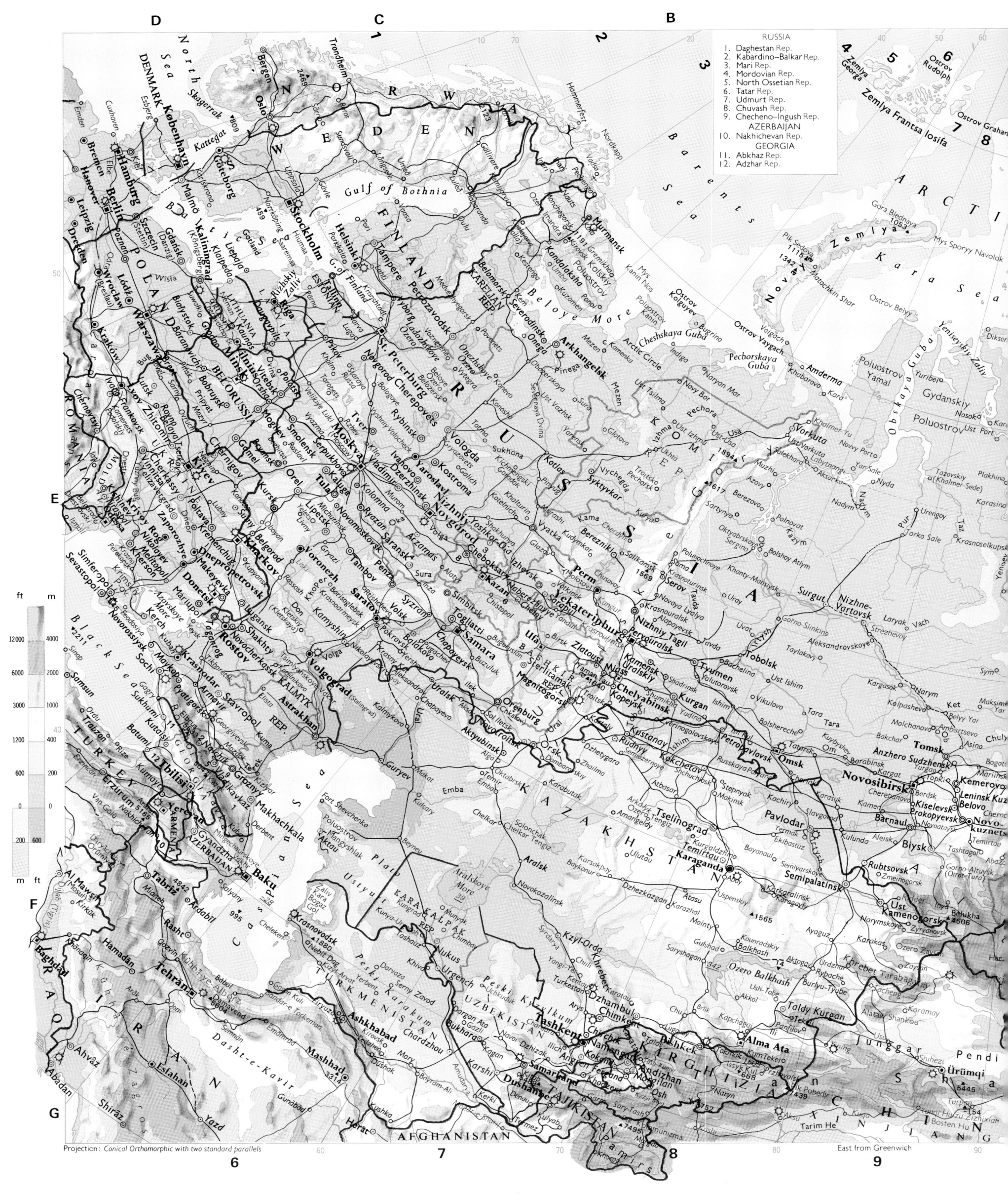

RUSSIA
1. Daghestan Rep.
2. Kabardino–Balkar Rep.
3. Mari Rep.
4. Mordovian Rep.
5. North Ossetian Rep.
6. Tatar Rep.
7. Udmurt Rep.
8. Chuvash Rep.
9. Checheno–Ingush Rep.
AZERBAIJAN
10. Nakhichevan Rep.
GEORGIA
11. Abkhaz Rep.
12. Adzhar Rep.

Projection: Conical Orthomorphic with two standard parallels

East from Greenwich

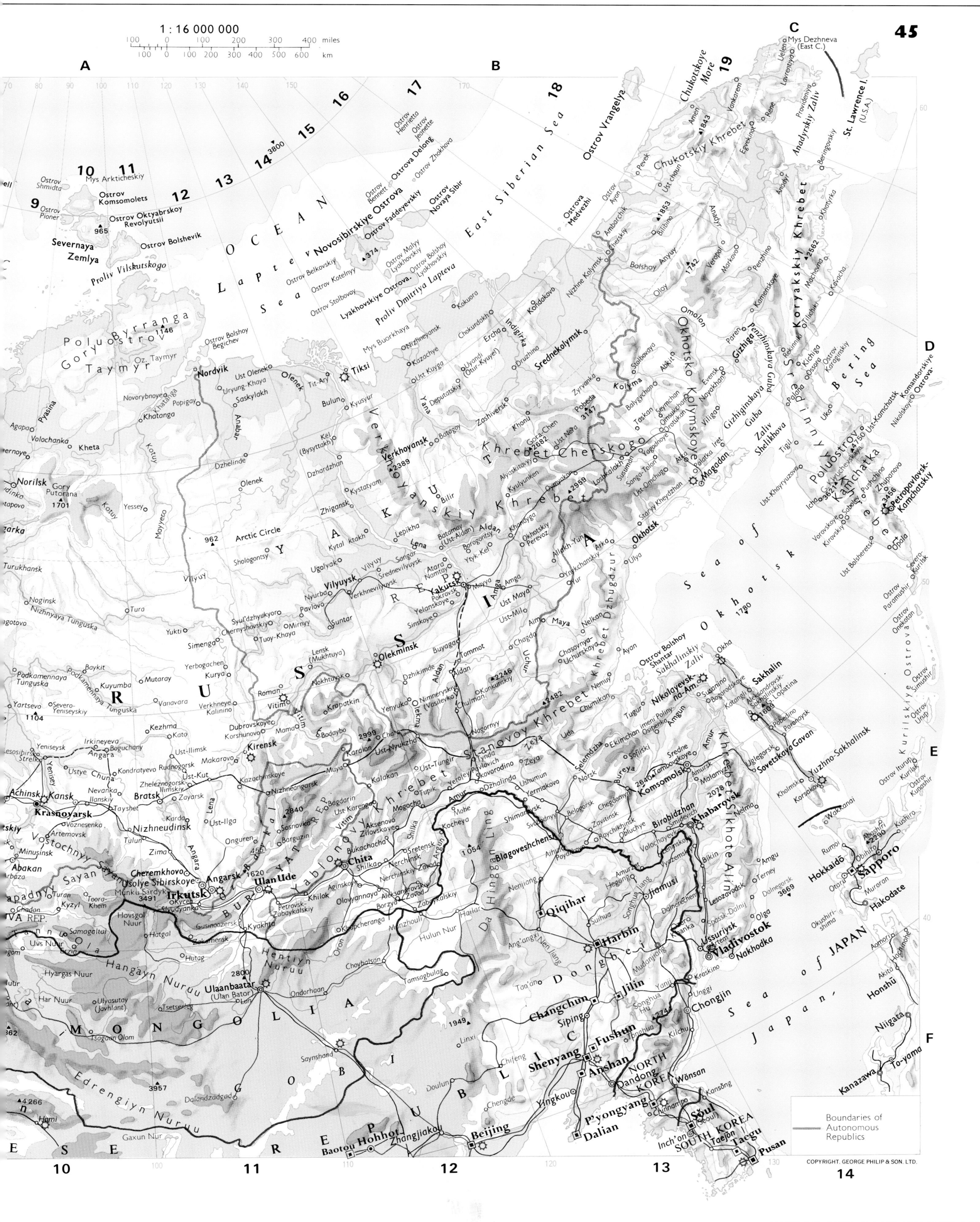

1 : 16 000 000

100   0   100   200   300   400 miles
100 0 100 200 300 400 500 600 km

A   B   C

OCEAN

Laptev Sea   East Siberian Sea   Chukotskoye More   Bering Sea

Severnaya Zemlya

Poluostrov Taymyr
Gory Byrranga

Norilsk

Mys Dezhneva (East C.)

St. Lawrence I. (U.S.A.)

Koryakskiy Khrebet

Sredinnyy Khrebet

Poluostrov Kamchatka

Petropavlovsk-Kamchatskiy

Khrebet Cherskogo

Verkhoyansk

Yakutsk

Verkhoyanskiy Khrebet

R U S S I A N   R E P.

Sea of Okhotsk

Magadan

Okhotsk

Sakhalin

Nikolayevsk-na-Am.

Sovetskaya Gavan

Yuzhno-Sakhalinsk

Kurilskiye Ostrova

Hokkaidō

Sapporo

Hakodate

Khabarovsk

Komsomolsk

Birobidzhan

Blagoveshchensk

Stanovoy Khrebet

Yablonovyy Khrebet

Bratsk

Krasnoyarsk

Kansk

Achinsk

Nizhneudinsk

Abakan

Kirensk

Cheremkhovo
Usolye Sibirskoye
Angarsk
Irkutsk
Ulan Ude

Chita

TUVA REP.

Hovsgol Nuur

Hangayn Nuruu

Ulaanbaatar (Ulan Bator)

M O N G O L I A

Hentiyn Nuruu

G O B I

Qiqihar

Harbin

Changchun

Jilin

Fushun

Shenyang
Anshan

Da Hinggan Ling

Dong bei

Sikhote Alin

Vladivostok
Ussuriysk
Nakhodka

Sea of Japan

JAPAN

Honshū

Niigata

Kanazawa

To-yama

NORTH KOREA

P'yongyang

Wŏnsan

Dandong

Dalian

Yingkou

Beijing

Zhangjiakou

Baotou   Hohhot

R E P U B L I C

Sŏul
SOUTH KOREA
Inch'on
Taejŏn
Taegu
Pusan

COPYRIGHT. GEORGE PHILIP & SON. LTD.

Boundaries of Autonomous Republics

10   11   12   13   14

1 : 40 000 000

250   0   250   500   750   1000 miles
250   0   500   1000   1500 km

Projection: Bonne

COPYRIGHT GEORGE PHILIP & SON, LTD.

East from Greenwich

1 : 40 000 000

COPYRIGHT GEORGE PHILIP & SON, LTD

Projection: Bonne

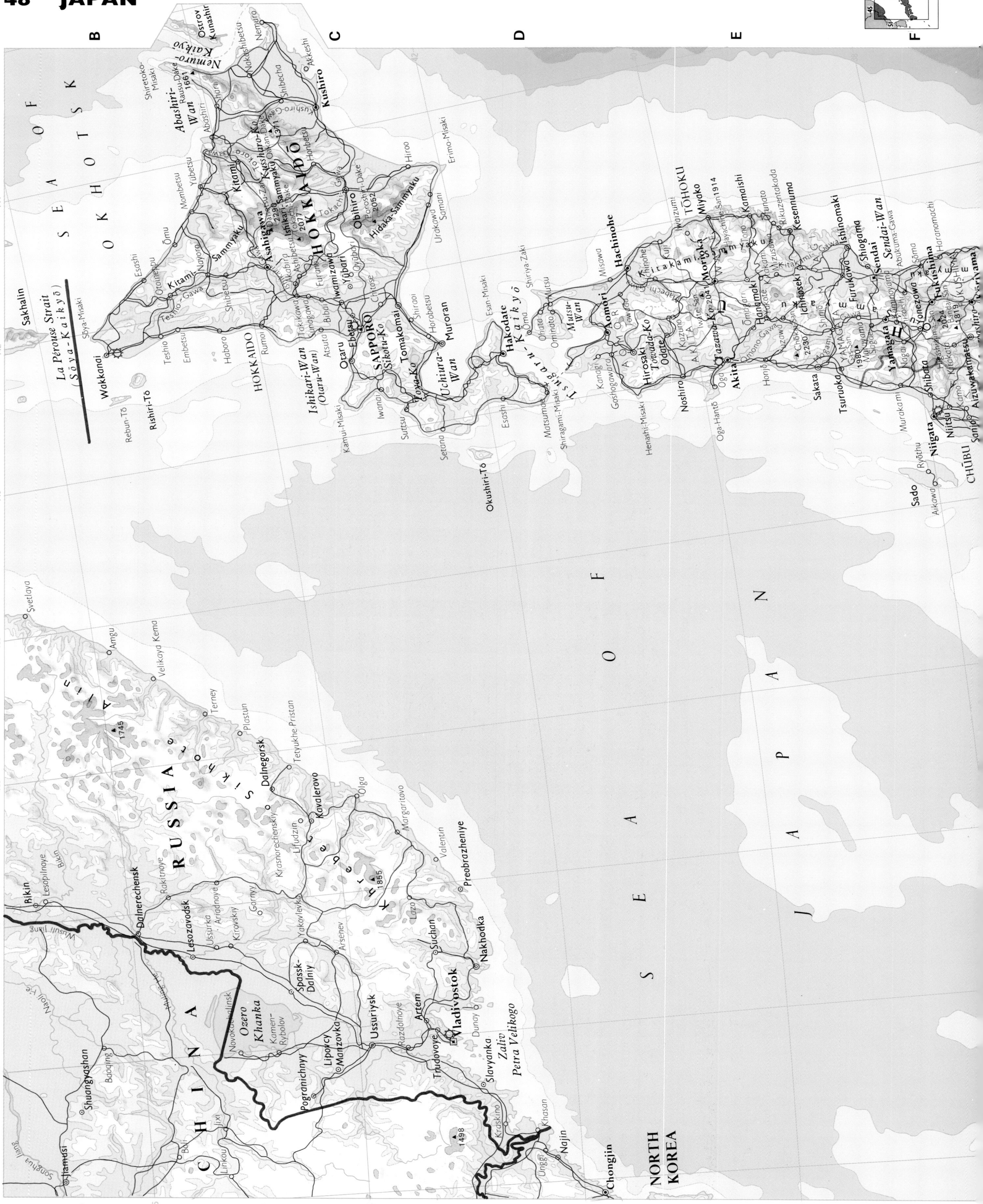
SEA OF OKHOTSK
SEA OF JAPAN
RUSSIA
CHINA
NORTH KOREA
HOKKAIDO
TŌHOKU
CHŪBU
Sakhalin
La Pérouse Strait (Sōya-Kaikyō)
Tsugaru-Kaikyō
Nemuro-Kaikyō
Ostrov Kunashir
Wakkanai
Rishiri-Tō
Rebun-Tō
Abashiri-Wan
Abashiri
Kitami
Asahikawa
Sapporo
Otaru
Ishikari-Wan (Otaru-Wan)
Tomakomai
Muroran
Uchiura-Wan
Hakodate
Obihiro
Kushiro
Nemuro
Hidaka-Sammyaku
Erimo-Misaki
Okushiri-Tō
Mutsu-Wan
Aomori
Hachinohe
Hirosaki
Towada-Ko
Noshiro
Akita
Morioka
Miyako
Kamaishi
Kesennuma
Ichinoseki
Ishinomaki
Sendai
Sendai-Wan
Sakata
Tsuruoka
Yamagata
Fukushima
Niigata
Sado
Vladivostok
Nakhodka
Ussuriysk
Artem
Dalnegorsk
Dalnerechensk
Lesozavodsk
Spassk-Dalniy
Ozero Khanka
Zaliv Petra Velikogo
Preobrazheniye
Kavalerovo
Terney
Chongjin
Najin
Khasan
Jiamusi
Shuangyashan
Jixi
Sikhote Alin
Svetlaya
Amgu

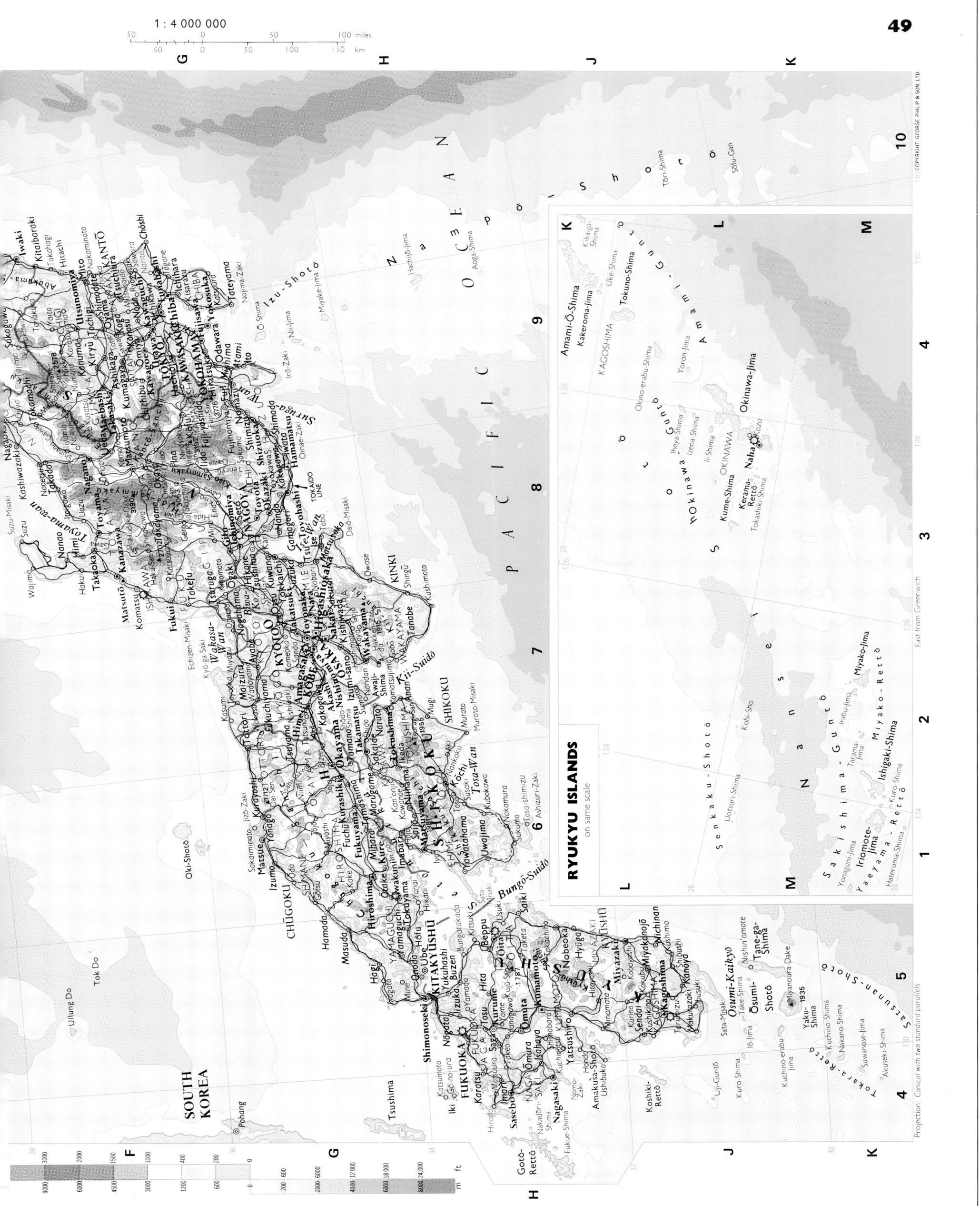

1 : 4 000 000
50
0
50
100 miles
50
0
50
100
150 km
G
H
J
K
F
RYUKYU ISLANDS
on same scale
SOUTH KOREA
PACIFIC OCEAN
Nampō-Shotō
Tsushima
Ullung Do
Tok Do
Pohang
Oki-Shotō
CHŪGOKU
SHIKOKU
KINKI
KANTŌ
KYŪSHŪ
KYOTO
KOBE
ŌSAKA
NAGOYA
TŌKYŌ
YOKOHAMA
KAWASAKI
Chiba
Hiroshima
Okayama
FUKUOKA
KITAKYŪSHŪ
Shimonoseki
Kumamoto
Nagasaki
Kagoshima
Miyazaki
Ōita
Beppu
Matsuyama
Kōchi
Takamatsu
Tokushima
Wakayama
Nara
Kanazawa
Toyama
Fukui
Gifu
Shizuoka
Hamamatsu
Toyohashi
Maebashi
Utsunomiya
Mito
Iwaki
Chōshi
Tottori
Matsue
Izumo
Hamada
Masuda
Hagi
Sasebo
Saga
Kurume
Sendai
Miyakonojō
Nobeoka
Uwajima
Tosa-Wan
Kii-Suidō
Bungo-Suidō
Ise-Wan
Suruga-Wan
Wakasa-Wan
Toyama-wan
Izu-Shotō
Ōsumi-Kaikyō
Ōsumi-Shotō
Satsunan-Shotō
Tokara-Rettō
Tane-ga-Shima
Yaku-Shima
Koshiki-Rettō
Gotō-Rettō
Amakusa-Shotō
Amami-Ō-Shima
Tokuno-Shima
Okinawa-Jima
Naha
Okinawa-Guntō
Amami-Guntō
Miyako-Jima
Ishigaki-Shima
Iriomote-Jima
Sakishima-Guntō
Senkaku-Shotō
Nansei-Shotō
Yaeyama-Rettō
Miyako-Rettō
TOKAIDO LINE
Projection: Conical with two standard parallels
East from Greenwich
m
ft
COPYRIGHT GEORGE PHILIP & SON, LTD

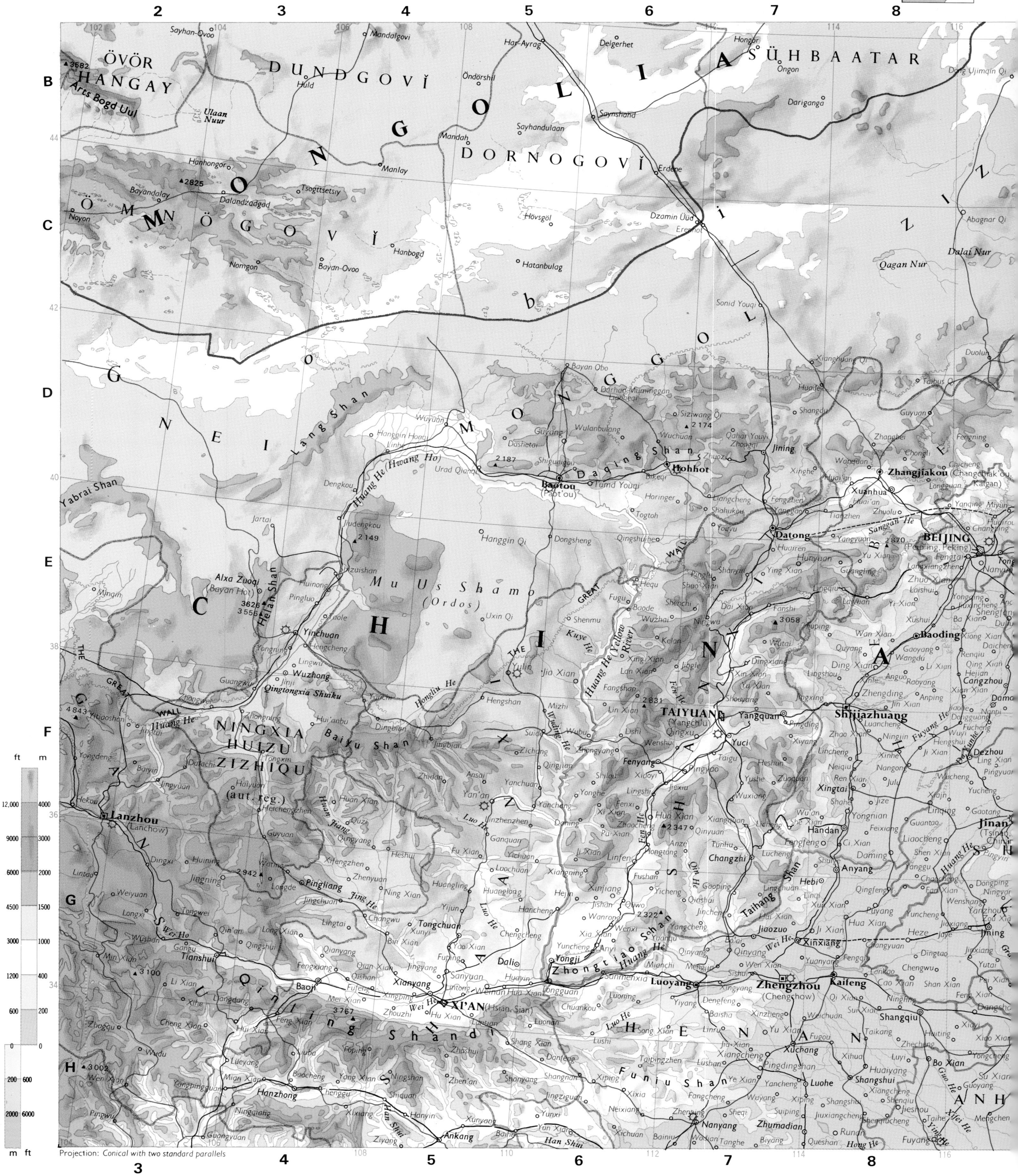

45
54 49
52 53

2 3 4 5 6 7 8

MONGOLIA

ÖVÖR HANGAY
▲3682
Arts Bogd Uul
Sayhan-Ovoo
102 104
Mandalgovi
Delgerhet
106
Har-Ayrag
Hongor
108
SÜHBAATAR
Ongon
Daing Ujimqin Qi

B

DUNDGOVĬ
Huld
Öndörshil
Saynshand
Dariganga

Ulaan Nuur
44
Hanhongor
Manlay
Sayhandulaan
DORNOGOVĬ
Erdene

▲2825
Mandah

ÖMNÖGOVĬ
Bayandalay
Dalandzadgad
Tsogttsetsiy
Dzamin Üüd
Ereen
Abagnar Qi

C
Noyon
Hovsgöl
Hanbogd
Hatanbulag
Qagan Nur
Dalai Nur

Nomgon
Bayan-Ovoo
Sonid Youqi

42
b
NEI
MONGGOL

Xianghuang Qi
Duolun

D
Bayan Obo
Darhan Muminggan Lianheqi
▲2174 Siziwang Qi
Shangdu
Guyuan
Tabus Qi
Fengning

Lang Shan
Weiyuan
Guyang
Wulanbulang
Wuchuan
Qahar Youyi Zhongqi
Xinghe
Zhangbei
Chongli
Chicheng

Hangjin Houqi
Linhe
▲2187 Shiguaigou
Daqing Shan
Hohhot
Jining
Wanquan
Zhangjiakou (Changchak'ou, Kalgan)

Yabrai Shan
Dengkou
Huang He (Hwang Ho)
Urad Qianqi
Baotou (Pao't'ou)
Tumd Youqi
Bikeqi
Horinger
Liangcheng
Fengzhen
Xuanhua
Huai'an
Yanqing Miyun

40
Jartai
Judengkou
▲2149
Hanggin Qi
Dongsheng
Qingshuihe
Togtoh
Youyu
Datong
Yangyuan
Sanggan He
Changping
BEIJING (Peiping, Peking)

E
Alxa Zuoqi (Bayan Hot)
Dzuishan
Hequ
Fugu
Huairen
Shanyin
Ying Xian
Guangling
Lanxiangzhen
Tong
Nanyuan

Mingin
Helan Shan
▲3628 ▲3556
Pingluo
Taole
MU US SHAMO (ORDOS)
Uxin Qi
Shenmu
Baode
Wuzhai
Dai Xian
Fanshi
Wutai
▲3058
Fuping
Wan Xian
Baoding
Xiong Xian
Daicheng

38
Yinchuan
Yongning
Hengcheng
Yulin
Jia Xian
Huang He Yellow River
Kuye He
Kelan
Xin Xian
Ningwu
Shouyang
Yi Xian
Gaoyang
Li Xian
Renqiu
Cangzhou

THE GREAT WALL
Lingwu
Wuzhong
Qingtongxia Shuiku
Hongliu He
Hengshan
Fangshan
Fen He
Jingle
Ya Xian
Lingshou
Ding Xian
Quyang
Renqiu
Hejian

4843 Yitiaoshan
THE GREAT WALL
Zhongning
Hui'anbu
Baiyu Shan
Jingbian
Mizhi
Lin Xian
▲2831
Wuding He
Wubu
Lishi
Wenshui
Taiyuan (Yangch'u)
Yangquan
Pingding
Shijiazhuang
Huolu

F
Lanzhou (Lanchow)
Huang He
Baiyu Shan
Dingbian
Ansai
Yanchuan
Yonghe
Lingshi
Jiexiu
Yuci
Xiyang
Zhao Xian
Ningjin
Fuyang
Hengshui
Xinhe
Dezhou
Lingcheng
Pingyuan

36
Hekou
Tongxin
Zhidan
Yan'an
Yanchang
Fenxi
Pingyao
Yushe
Zuoquan
Wuxiang
Julu
Xingtai
Yucheng

Dingxi
Huining
▲2942
Pingliang
Jing He
Ning Xian
Fu Xian
Yichuan
Luochuan
Xiangning
Fushan
Gaoping
Lingchuan
Handan
Ci Xian
Daming
Linqing
Guantao
Jinan (Tsinan)

G
NINGXIA HUIZU ZIZHIQU (aut. reg.)
Wei Ho
Qin'an
Changwu
Huangling
Heyang
Jishan
Yicheng
Qiwo
▲2322
Qinyuan
Changzhi
Anyang
Hebi
Qingfeng
Puyang
Yuncheng
Yanzhou

34
Tianshui
▲3100
Li Xian
Baoji
Xianyang
XI'AN (Hsian, Sian)
Tongguan
Luoyang
Mianchi
Jiaozuo
Wen Xian
Xinxiang
Yuanyang
Zhengzhou (Chengchow)
Kaifeng
Heze

QINLING SHANDI
▲3767
Wei Ho
Zhouzhi
Chuankou
Lushi
Song Xian
Yiyang
Dengfeng
Xinzheng
Weichuan
Xuchang
Luohe

H
▲3002
Hanzhong
Ningqiang
Han Shui
Ankang
Shiquan
Zhen'an
Shangnan
Xixia
Neixiang
FUNIU SHAN
Nanyang
Fangcheng
Pingdingshan
Shangshui
ANH

3 104 4 108 5 110 6 112 7 114 8 116

ft m
12,000 4000
9000 3000
6000 2000
4500 1500
3000 1000
1200 400
600 200
0 0
200 600
2000 6000
m ft

1 : 4 800 000

50   0   50   100   150 miles

50   0   50   100   150   200   km

9   10   11   12   13   14   15   16

H I   Q I U

Horqin Youyi Qianqi

Zhenlai   Nen   Bin Xian   Jixi

HARBIN

(Haerhpin)   Acheng   Yanshou   Turiy Rog

Batcheng   Maoxing   Zhaoyuan   Shuangcheng   Ozero
Khanka

Hulin He   Tuquan   Tao'an   Da'an   Songhua   Shangzhi   U   S   S   R

Jiang   Yimianpo   Hengdaohezi   Maqiaohe

Tongyu   Qian Gorlos   Fuyu   Changchunling   Sanchahe   Lahu He   Wuchang   Mudanjiang   Xiachengzi   Pogranichnyy

Jarud Qi   Beizhengzhen   Nong'an   Dehui   Yushu   Shulan   Shanhetun   Hailin   Muling   Suiyang   Sufenhe

Beitaolaizhao   Songhua   Gangyao   Wulajie   Jilin   Jiaohe   Huangsongdian   Ning'an   Dongjingcheng

Changling   Jiutai   Jiang   (Kirin,   Emu   Jingpo   Luozigou   Golenki

Jinxi   Fulongquan   Chilin)   Xinzhan   Hu   Dongning   Pokrovka   Ussuriysk

Changchun   Fanjiatun   690   Zhang guang cai Ling   (Voroshilov)

Huaidezhen   Panshi   Huadian   Chunyang   Wangqing   Razdolnoye

Shuangliao   Huaide   Shuangyang   Yitong   Jiaohe   Erdao   Jiang   Helong   Antu   Shixian   Mingyuezhou   Vladivostok

Lishu   Huanan   Fusong   Yanji   Tumen   Hunchun   Slavyanka

Siping   Liaoyuan   Dongfeng   Huinan   Chan   1677   Muson   Nojin

Bamiancheng   Zhangwu   Dongfeng   Liuhe   bai   Kyongsong   Posyet

Jargalang   Xifeng   Linjiang   Shan   Puryong   Chongjin

Xiliao He   Kangping   Kaiyuan   Hailong   Changbai   2541   Nanam   Chhuronjang

Jinxi   WALL   Faku   Liao He   Shanchengzhen   Chungang up   Paektu-san   Kyongsong

Willow   Tieling   Qingyuan   Xinbin   Hyesan   Irhyangdong   Ondaejin   Musudan

Fushun   Qingyuan   Xinbin   Tonghua   Kapsan   Simpungdong   Kilju

Xinmin   Xinlitun   SHENYANG   1845   Manpojin   Pungson   Kosongni   Kimchaek

(Mukden)   Liaoyang   Huajiang   Kasan-dong   (Songjin)

Benxi   Qingchengzi   Koin   2522   Pujon-chosuji   Changhungni   Tanchon

Jinzhou   Liaoyang   Huan   2522   Kwangdaeri

Anshan   Jiang   Yalu   Chosan   Changjin-   Pukchong

Niuzhuang   Panshan   Lianshanguan   Kuandian   Koin dong   chosuji   Sinhung   Sinpo

Yingkou   Haicheng   Fengcheng   Supung   Pyoktong   NORTH   Oro   Shori

Yingkou   Gai Xian   Xiuyan   Sk.   Sinuiju   KOREA   Hamhung   Hungnam

Liaodong   Xiongyuecheng   Wanfu   1131   Dandong   Anping   Taegwan   Tangchon ni

Wan   Fu Xian   Gushan   Donggou   Yongampo   Sonchon   Hamhung   Tongjoson

Jin Xian   Xinjin   Pikou   Zhuanghe   Yalu Jiang   Anju   Yongbyon   Man

Lüshun   Pengnae   Sukchon   Unsan   Yonghung   Kowan

Dalian   Cho-do   Chinnampo   Anbyon   Wonsan   Kojo

Korea   Sariwon   Koksan   Hoeyang   1638   Kosong

Bay   Suan   Chiha-ri   Pyonggang   Changdo-ri   Kangson   Yangyang

Changyon   Haeju   Kumchon   Sinmak   Nam-chon   Hwachon-   Chumunjin

P'YONGYANG   Chunghwa   1578

Paengnyong-do   Ongjin   Kaesong   Panmunjom   Uijongbu   Kangnung

Cease Fire Line   Kumhwa   Hongchon

Chunchon   Samchok   Ullung-do

Inch'on   Kanghwa   SEOUL   Hoengsong   Yongwol   Ulchin

(Soul)   Ichon   Wonju   Yongwol

Yongdungpo   Suwon   Chongju   Chungju   Chechon   Ulchin

Osan   Pyongtaek   Chungju

SOUTH   Yechon   Andong   Yongdok

Chonan   Chochiwon   KOREA   Yongju   Chongha

Anmyon-do   Taechon-ni   Nonsan   Taejon   Sangju   Uisong   Pohang

Onyang   Kumi   Waegwan   Kimchon   Yongchon

Kunsan   Iri   Chonju   Koryong   TAEGU   Chongdo   Kyongju

Puan   Songju   Kyongju   Ulsan

Chongup   Namwon   Chinju   1915   Masan   Miryang   Tongnae

Kwangju   Hadong   Chinhae   PUSAN

Sago-ri   Tamyang   Samchonpo   Chungmu

Mokpo   Sunchon   Posong   Polgyo-ri   Yosu   Chindo   Sasuna

Changhung   Haenam   Izuhara   Karatsu

Korea   Tsushima   Iki

Strait   JAPAN   Imari

Cheju   Cheju-do   Nakadori-jima   Sasebo   Kashima

Hallim   1950   Onpyong-ni   Omura   Isahaya

Mosulpo   Sogwi-po   Kuchinotsu   Nagasaki

Fukue-jima

SEA   OF   JAPAN

H E I L O N G J I A N G

H E I L O N G

Maoxing

Shuangcheng

D o n g b e i   (M a n c h u r i a)

L I A O N I N G

1949

2029   Linxi

Bairin Youqi

Hexigten Qi   2020   Ongniud Qi

Xar Moron He   Wutonghaolai   Xiawa

Laoha   He   Hure Qi

Chifeng   Heishui   Beipiao

Weichang   1885   Chaoyang   Yi Xian   Goubangzi   Niuzhuang

Chengde   Jianchang   Ningcheng   Jinzhou   Beizhen

Luanping   Shangbanchengzi   Jinxi   Jianchangying

Langhua   Lingyuan   Xingcheng   Liaodong

Pingquan   Suizhong   Wan

Miyun   Zunhua   Qinhuangdao   Changli

Sk.   Fengrun   Luan Xian   Leting

Xinglong   Lulong   Funing

Jixian   Tangshan

Hangu   (Tientsin,   Tanggu

TIANJIN   T'ienching)   Dagu   Oikou

Yangcunzhuang   Bo Hai

Wuqing   (Gulf of Chihli)

Langfang   Huang He   Longkou   Penglai   Yantai   Weihai

Zhanhua   Huang Xian   Daxinzhuang   Fushan   Muping

Huimin   Kenli   Beizhen   Laizhou   Zhaoyuan   Qixia   923   Wendeng

Deping   Wudi   Wan   Ye Xian   Rushan

Shanghe   Guangrao   Shouguang   Shandong   Bandao   Nanhuang   Shidao

Qingcheng   Huantai   Changyi   Pingdu   Laixi   Haiyang

Zhoucun   Zibo   Yidu   Fangzi   Weifang   Gaomi   Jimo

Jiyang   Linzi   Anqiu   Changyang

Tai Shan   Boshan   Linqu   Zhucheng   QINGDAO

524   Laiwu   1108   Ju Xian   Lancun   (Ch'ingtao)

S H A N D O N G   Yishui   Wulian   Jiaozhou Wan

Xintai   Mengyin   Titie

Sishui   Feng   Tangtou   Rizhao   HUANG HAI

Fei Xian   Pingyi   Shijiusuo   (Yellow Sea)

Teng Xian   Linyi   Andongwei

Teng Xian   Zaozhuang   Ganyu   Haizhou Wan

Weishan   Hanzhuang   Tancheng   Lianyungang

J I A N G S U   Lianyungang

Xuzhou   Pixian   (Hsinhailien)

Suchow   Shuangg   Guannan   Xiangshui   Binhai

Suining   Suqian   Shuyang   Yancheng

Lingbi   Qingjiang   Huai'an   Funing

Guzhen   Si Xian   Da Yunhe   Lanshui

Hongze   Huai'an   Baoying   Liuzhuang

Hudiyuan   Hu   Gaoyou   Xinghua

Bengbu   Fengyang   Hu   Dongtai

East from Greenwich

9   10   11   12   13   14   15

COPYRIGHT. GEORGE PHILIP & SON. LTD.

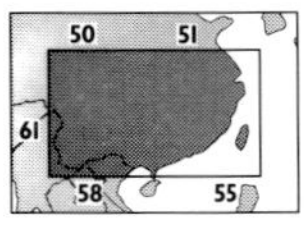

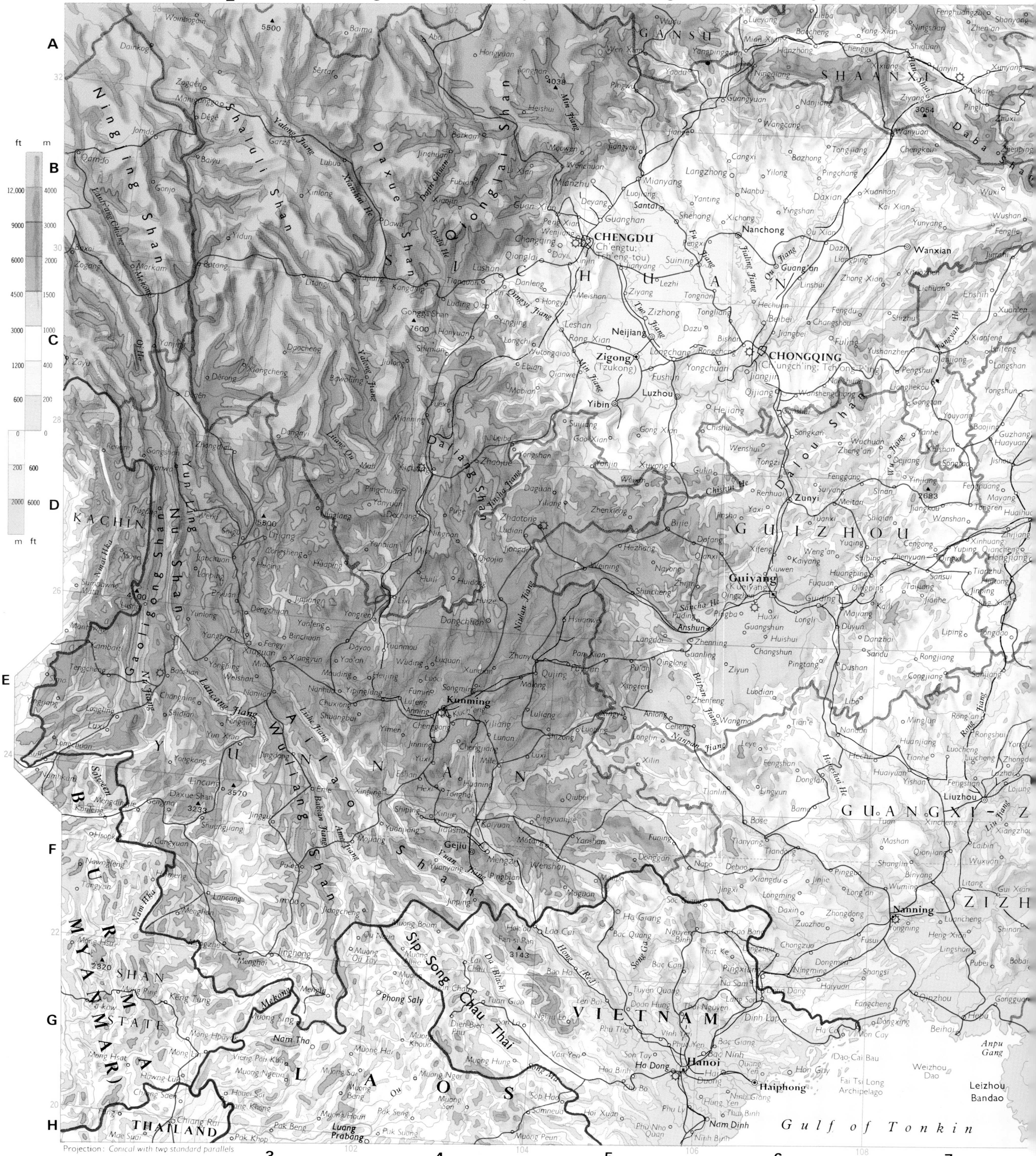

1 2 3 4 5 6 7
A B C D E F G H
ft m
12,000 4000
9000 3000
6000 2000
4500 1500
3000 1000
1200 400
600 200
0 0
200 600
2000 6000
m ft
GANSU
SHAANXI
SICHUAN
GUIZHOU
YUNNAN
GUANGXI-ZHUANG ZIZHIQU
VIETNAM
LAOS
THAILAND
BURMA (MYANMAR)
SHAN STATE
KACHIN
CHENGDU
(Ch'engtu; Tch'eng-tou)
CHONGQING
(Ch'ung-ch'ing; Tch'ong-k'ing)
Guiyang
(Kueiyang)
Kunming
(Kun-ming)
Nanning
Hanoi
Haiphong
Nam Dinh
Ha Dong
Luang Prabang
Nanchong
Wanxian
Zigong
(Tzukong)
Neijiang
Yibin
Luzhou
Zunyi
Anshun
Liuzhou
Gejiu
Bose
Ningjing Shan
Shaluli Shan
Daxue Shan
Qionglai Shan
Min Shan
Daba Shan
Dalou Shan
Daliang Shan
Yun Ling
Nu Shan
Gaoligong Shan
Wuliang Shan
Ailao Shan
Sip Song Chau Thai
Jinsha Jiang
Yalong Jiang
Min Jiang
Dadu He
Lancang Jiang
Nu Jiang
Mekong
Salween
Hong (Red)
Da (Black)
Chishui He
Wu Jiang
Nanpan Jiang
Beipan Jiang
Hongshui He
Jialing Jiang
Han Shui
Yuan Jiang
Gonggga Shan
7600
5500
4038
3054
2683
3570
3233
3143
2320
4700
Gulf of Tonkin
Leizhou Bandao
Weizhou Dao
Fai Tsi Long Archipelago
Projection: Conical with two standard parallels

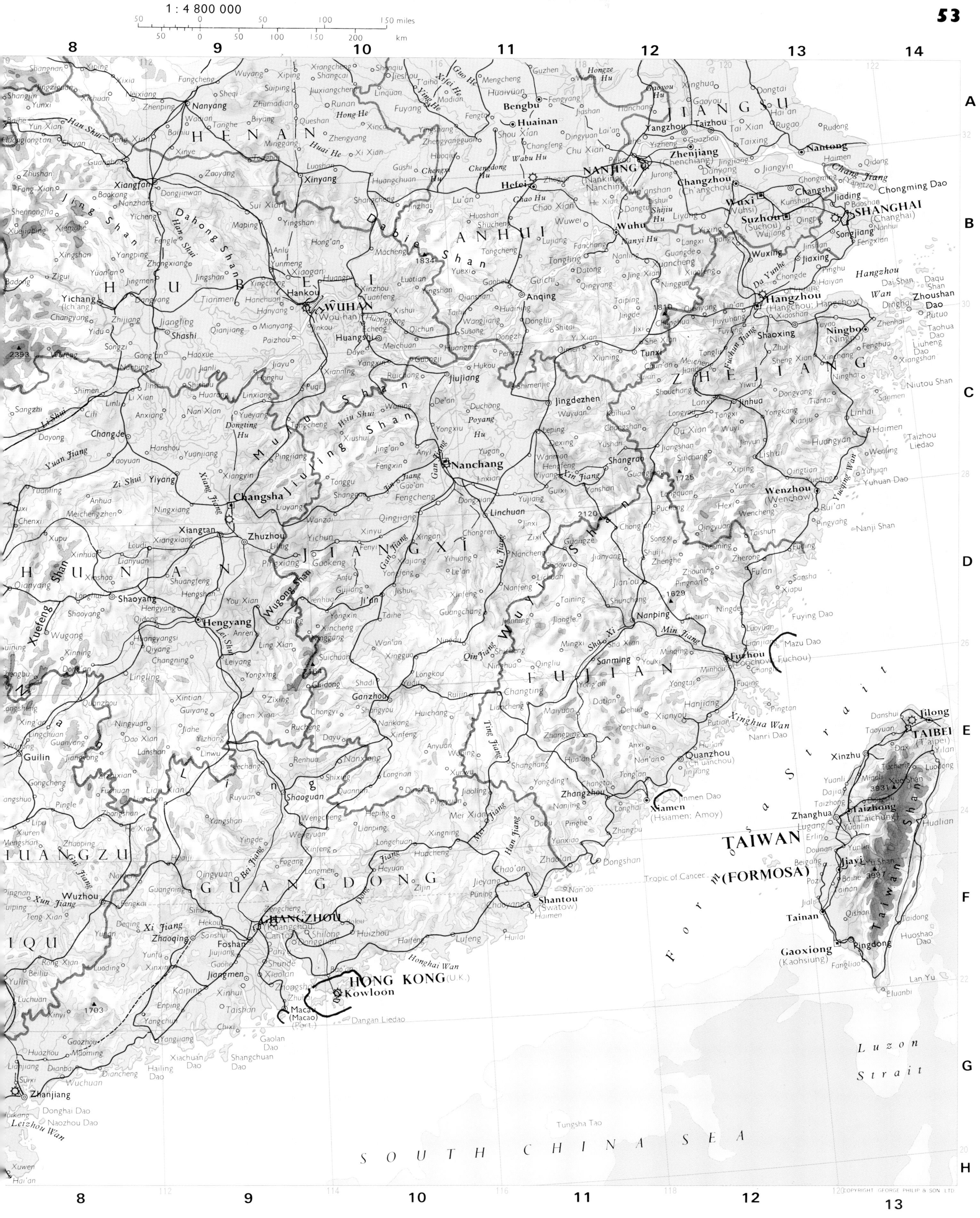
1 : 4 800 000
miles
km
HENAN
HUBEI
ANHUI
JIANGSU
ZHEJIANG
JIANGXI
HUNAN
FUJIAN
GUANGDONG
TAIWAN
(FORMOSA)
WUHAN
(Wu-han)
Hankou
NANJING
(Nanking: Nanching)
SHANGHAI
(Changhai)
Hangzhou
(Hangchou: Hangchow)
Nanchang
Changsha
Fuzhou
(Foochow: Fuchou)
Xiamen
(Hsiamen: Amoy)
GUANGZHOU
(Kuangchou: Canton)
HONG KONG
(U.K.)
Kowloon
Macau
(Macao)
(Port.)
TAIBEI
(T'aipei)
Jilong
Gaoxiong
(Kaohsiung)
Tainan
Taizhong
(T'aichung)
Shantou
(Swatow)
Wenzhou
(Wenchow)
Ningbo
(Ningpo)
Suzhou
(Suchou)
Wuxi
(Wuhsi)
Changzhou
(Ch'angchou)
Zhenjiang
(Chenchiang)
Hefei
Bengbu
Huainan
Anqing
Jiujiang
Jingdezhen
Wuhu
Nanyang
Xiangfan
Yichang
(Ich'ang)
Shashi
Huangshi
Hengyang
Zhuzhou
Xiangtan
Shaoyang
Ganzhou
Shaoguan
Zhangzhou
Quanzhou
(Ch'uanchou)
Sanming
Nanping
Foshan
Jiangmen
Zhanjiang
Wuzhou
Guilin
Dabie Shan
Jiuling Shan
Mufu Shan
Wuyi Shan
Wugong Shan
Poyang Hu
Dongting Hu
Chang Jiang
(Yangtze)
Gan Jiang
Xiang Jiang
Min Jiang
Xi Jiang
Bei Jiang
Dong Jiang
Han Shui
Taiwan Shan
Formosa Strait
Luzon Strait
SOUTH CHINA SEA
Tropic of Cancer
Chongming Dao
Zhoushan Dao
Hangzhou Wan
Honghai Wan
Leizhou Wan
Xinghua Wan
Mazu Dao
Jinmen Dao
Donghai Dao
Naozhou Dao
Dangan Liedao
Tungsha Tao
Lan Yu
COPYRIGHT GEORGE PHILIP & SON LTD

1 : 16 000 000

100 0 100 200 300 400 miles
100 0 100 200 300 400 500 600 km

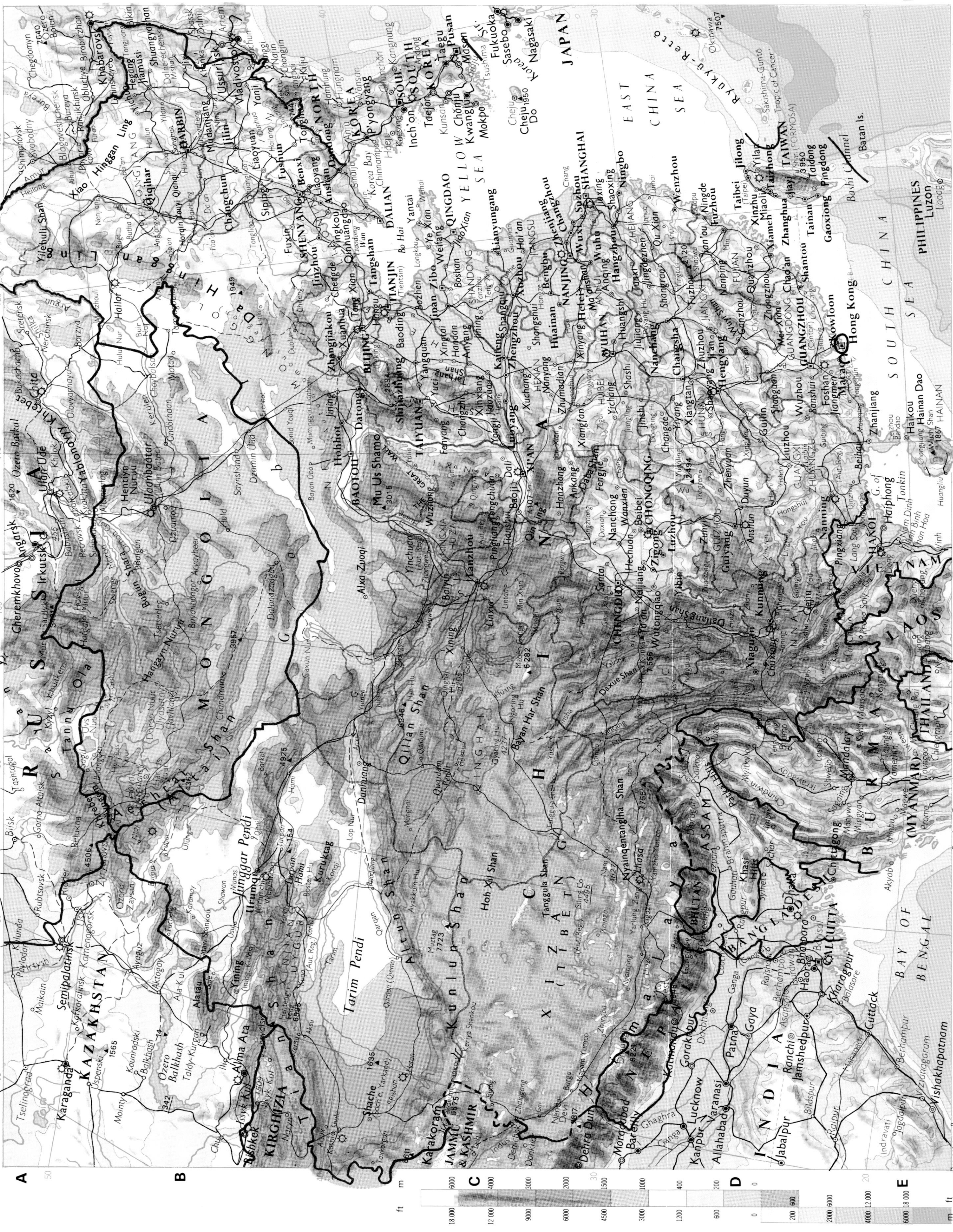

COPYRIGHT GEORGE PHILIP & SON LTD

R U S S I A

M O N G O L I A

KAZAKHSTAN

KIRGHIZIA

C H I N A

XINJIANG

XIZANG (TIBET)

QINGHAI

GANSU

SICHUAN

YUNNAN

GUIZHOU

GUANGXI

GUANGDONG

HUNAN

JIANGXI

FUJIAN

ZHEJIANG

JIANGSU

ANHUI

HUBEI

HENAN

SHANXI

SHAANXI

NINGXIA

HEBEI

SHANDONG

LIAONING

JILIN

HEILONGJIANG

NEIMONGGOL

NORTH KOREA

SOUTH KOREA

JAPAN

TAIWAN (FORMOSA)

PHILIPPINES

VIETNAM

LAOS

THAILAND

BURMA (MYANMAR)

BANGLADESH

INDIA

NEPAL

BHUTAN

ASSAM

JAMMU & KASHMIR

BEIJING

TIANJIN

SHANGHAI

CHONGQING

CHENGDU

WUHAN

NANJING

GUANGZHOU

Hong Kong

Macao

Kowloon

SHENYANG

HARBIN

DALIAN

QINGDAO

TAIYUAN

BAOTOU

ZIGONG

KUNMING

Lhasa

Ulaanbaatar

Irkutsk

Ulan-Ude

Khabarovsk

Vladivostok

SEOUL

Pyongyang

Pusan

Fukuoka

Nagasaki

Taibei

Gaoxiong

HANOI

Haiphong

DHAKA

CALCUTTA

Patna

Varanasi

Lucknow

Allahabad

Alma Ata

Semipalatinsk

Karaganda

YELLOW SEA

EAST CHINA SEA

SOUTH CHINA SEA

BAY OF BENGAL

Korea Strait

Ryukyu-Retto

Tarim Pendi

Junggar Pendi

Tien Shan

Altai

Tien Shan

Tarim Pendi

Kunlun Shan

Altun Shan

Qilian Shan

Himalaya

Gobi

Mu Us Shamo

Great Wall

Huang He

Chang Jiang

Xi Jiang

Tropic of Cancer

East from Greenwich

Projection: Bonne

m ft
6000 18 000
4000 12 000
3000 9000
2000 6000
1500 4500
1000 3000
600 1200
400
200 600
0 0
200
600 2000
4000 12 000
6000 18 000

ft m

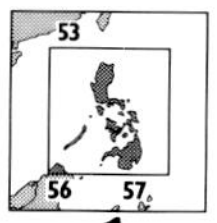

1 : 6 000 000

50   0   50   100   150   200 miles
50   0   50   100   150   200   250   300 km

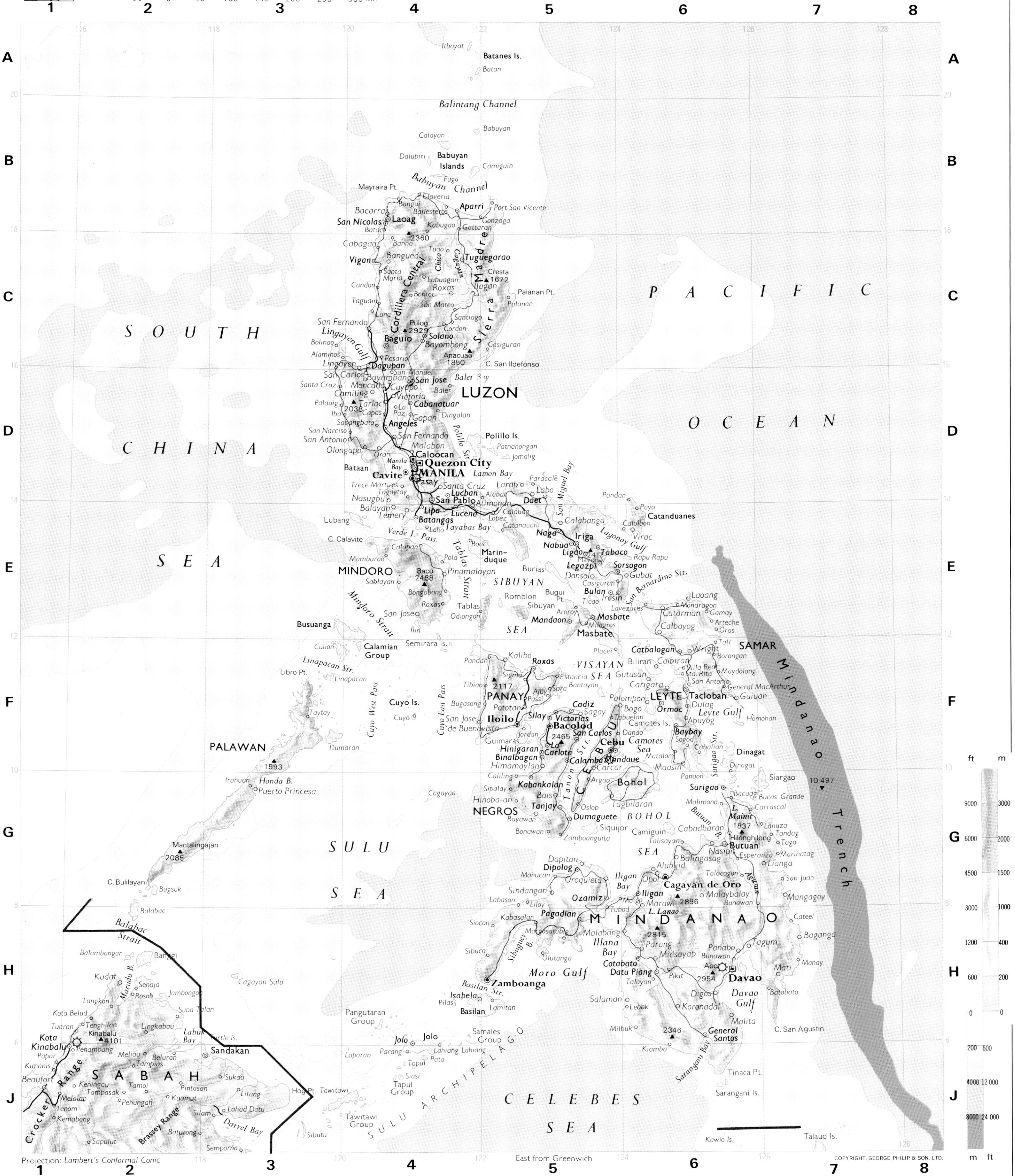

Projection: Lambert's Conformal Conic

East from Greenwich

COPYRIGHT. GEORGE PHILIP & SON. LTD.

PACIFIC

OCEAN

SOUTH

CHINA

SEA

LUZON

Batanes Is.
Batan
Itbayat

Balintang Channel

Calayan

Babuyan
Islands
Camiguin
Dalupiri
Fuga
Babuyan

Mayraira Pt.
Babuyan Channel
Bacarra
Claveria
Aparri
Port San Vicente
San Nicolas
Bangui
Bollesteros
Gonzaga
Laoag
Batac
Kabugao
Gattaran
▲2360
Banna
Tuao
Tuguegarao
Vigan
Bangued
Chico
Cresta
1672
Santa
Cordillera Central
Lubuagan
Ilagan
Maria
Roxas
Bontoc
San Mateo
Sierra Madre
Candon
Tagudin
Santiago
Palanan Pt.
Luna
Cordon
Palanan
San Fernando
Pulog
Solano
Baguio
▲2929
Bayombong
Casiguran
Lingayen Gulf
Rosario
Bolinao
Anacuao
1850
Alaminos
Dagupan
San Manuel
C. San Ildefonso
Lingayen
San Carlos
Bayambang
San Jose
Baler Bay
Santa Cruz
Moncada
Cuyo
Baler
Camiling
Victoria
▲2038
Tarlac
La
Dingalan
Palauig
Capas
Paz
Iba
Sapangbato
Gapan
San Narciso
Angeles
San Fernando
San Antonio
Malabon
Polillo Is.
Olongapo
Orani
Caloocan
Patnanongan
Bataan
Manila
Quezon City
Jomalig
Bay
Cavite ◉**MANILA**
Trece Martires
Pasay
Lamon Bay
Larap
Labo
Paracale
Pandan
Nasugbu
Santa Cruz
Lucban
Alabat
Daet
Tagaytay
San Pablo
Atimonan
San Miguel Bay
Balayan
Lipa
Lucena
Calauag
Lopez
Calabanga
Catanauan
Naga
Iriga
Batangas
Boac
Tayabas Bay
Nabua
Verde I.
Marin-
Lagonoy Gulf
Virac
Pass.
Lobo
duque
Catanduanes
C. Calavite
Ligao
Tabaco
Mamburao
Calapan
Legazpi
Sorsogon
Donsol
Gubat
MINDORO
Baco
Burias
Bulan
▲2488
Sablayan
Ticao
Irosin
San Jose
Pinamalayan
SIBUYAN
Casiguran
Bongabong
Romblon
Laoang
Roxas
Tablas
Sibuyan
Lun Bernardino Str.
Mondragon
Odiongan
SEA
Aroroy
Catarman
Gamay
Busuanga
Mandaon
Masbate
Lavezares
Arteche
Culion
Calamian
Group
Masbate
Milagros
Calbayog
Oras
Linapacan Str.
Placer
Catbalogan
Taft
Libro Pt.
Linapacan
SAMAR
Wright
Borongan
Semirara Is.
Kalibo
Biliran
Caibiran
Pandan
Roxas
VISAYAN
General MacArthur
Cuyo Is.
Tibiao
Sigma
Estancia
SEA
Gutusan
Guiuan
Taytay
▲2117
Ajuy
Sara
Carigara
Sta. Rita
Maydolong
Cuyo
PANAY
Passi
Bantayan
Palompon
San Antonio
Cuyo East Pass
Bugasong
Pototan
LEYTE
Tacloban
Dumaran
San Jose
Cadiz
Bogo
Ormoc
Dulag
de Buenavista
Iloilo
Sagay
Camotes
Homonhon
Cagayan
Silay
Victorias
Tubigon
Leyte Gulf
Bacolod
San Carlos
Cebu
Camotes
Baybay
PALAWAN
Guimaras
Jordan
▲2465
Dando
Sea
Sogod
Abuyog
Irahuan
Honda B.
Hinigaran
La
Calamba
Cabalian
Puerto Princesa
Binalbagan
Carlota
Mandaue
Maasin
Dinagat
▲1593
Himamaylan
Carcar
Panaon
Siargao
Caliling
Kabankalan
Argao
10 497
Sipalay
Baio
Bohol
Malimono
Bucas Grande
Cagayan
Hinoba-an
Surigao
Carrascal
Tanjay
Oslob
Butuan
NEGROS
Dumaguete
Siquijor
Tagbilaran
Bacuog
Cabadbaran
Lanuza
Mantalingajan
Bayawan
Tandag
▲2085
Bonawan
Zamboanguita
BOHOL
Camiguin
Hilonghilong
Tago
C. Bulilayan
SEA
Maimit
Bugsuk
Dapitan
1837
Esperanza
Marihatag
SULU
Balabac
Dipolog
Nasipit
Lianga
Balambangan
Balabac Str.
Manucan
Butuan
Bangui
Sindangan
Iligan
Opol
San Juan
Bay
Talacogon
Kudat
Cagayan Sulu
Oroquieta
Cagayan de Oro
Mangagoy
SEA
Liloy
Talacogon
Maruda B.
Loboc
Ozamiz
Iligan
Malaybalay
Marawi
▲2896
Kota Belud
Labason
Cateel
Tenghilan
Kabasalan
Pagadian
MINDANAO
Langkon
Kabugao
Siocon
L. Lanao
Baganga
▲4101
Labuk
Kinabatangan B.
Kasatuba
Malabang
▲2815
Penampang
Sandakan
Parang
Panabo
Kota
Meliau
Sibuco
Illana
Midsayap
Tagum
Kinabalu
Beluran
Bay
Parang
Panabo
Papar
Tampias
Kimanis
Pintasan
Labuk
Olutanga
Cotabato
Davao
Beaufort
Tuaran
Sukau
Pangutaran
Bunawan
▲2954
Group
Datu Piang
Apo
Pikit
SABAH
Litang
Samales
Zamboanga
Talayan
Digos
Davao
Keningau
Tamoi
Group
Basilan Str.
Kuamut
Crocker Range
Isabela
Salaman
Lebak
Koronadal
Gulf
Melalap
Pintasan
Jolo
Malita
Brassey Range
Basilan
Lamitan
Kiamba
Tenom
Silam
Jolo
▲2346
C. San Agustin
Kemabong
Darvel Bay
Lahad Datu
Parang
General
Milbuk
Sapulut
Baturong
Tapul
Group
Santos
Kawio Is.
Talaud Is.
Sibutu
Tawitawi
Tapul
Saranga Bay
Tinaca Pt.
1.5
Semporna
Group
Sarangani Is.
SULU ARCHIPELAGO
Tawitawi
Lahiang Lahiang
Laparan
CELEBES
Pata
Parang
Siasi
SEA
Pangutaran

ft   m
9000   3000
6000   2000
4500   1500
3000   1000
1200   400
600   200
0   0
200   600
4000   12 000
8000   24 000
m   ft

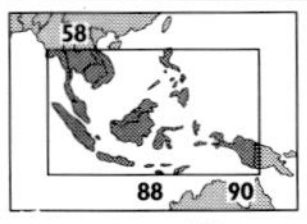

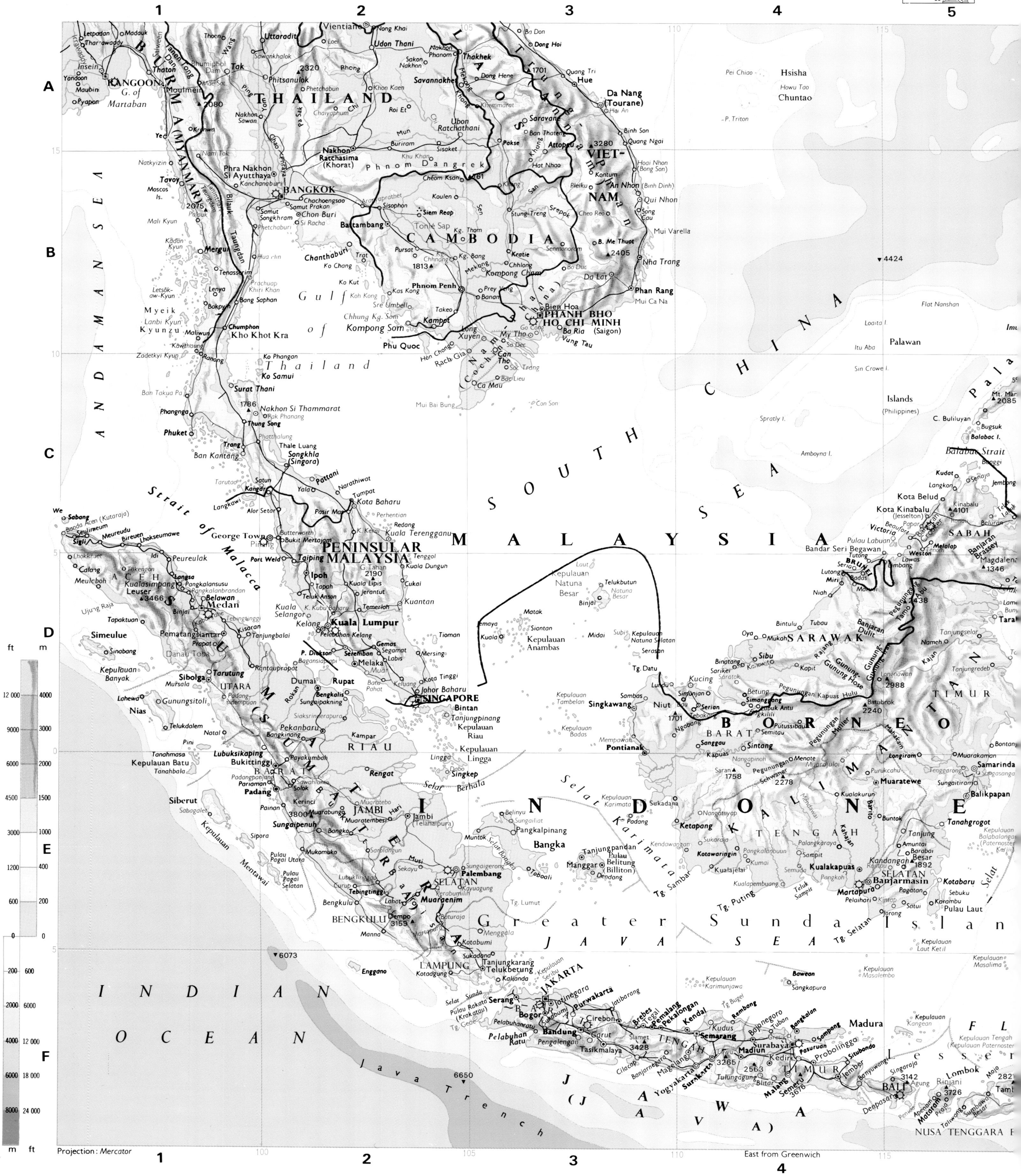

THAILAND
BURMA / MYANMAR
LAOS
VIET-NAM
CAMBODIA
PENINSULAR MALAYSIA
MALAYSIA
SINGAPORE
INDONESIA
BORNEO / KALIMANTAN
SARAWAK
SABAH
BRUNEI
SUMATERA
JAWA (JAVA)

ANDAMAN SEA
SOUTH CHINA SEA
Gulf of Thailand
Strait of Malacca
INDIAN OCEAN
Java Trench
JAVA SEA
Greater Sunda Islands

RANGOON
BANGKOK
PHANH BHO HO CHI MINH (Saigon)
PHNOM PENH
Hue
Da Nang (Tourane)
KUALA LUMPUR
Medan
Padang
Palembang
JAKARTA
Bandung
Semarang
Surabaya
Pontianak
Banjarmasin
Balikpapan
Samarinda
Kota Kinabalu (Jesselton)
Bandar Seri Begawan
Kuching

Phnom Dangrek
Tonle Sap
Mekong
Danau Toba
Kepulauan Natuna Besar
Kepulauan Anambas
Kepulauan Riau
Kepulauan Lingga
Bangka
Pulau Belitung (Billiton)
Madura
BALI
Lombok

4424
3280
4101
3726
6073
6650
3466
3800
3155
3428
3265
2563
3676
3142
2821

Projection: Mercator
East from Greenwich

m ft
12 000 4000
9000 3000
6000 2000
4500 1500
1200 400
600 200
0 0
200 600
2000 6000
4000 12 000
6000 18 000
8000 24 000

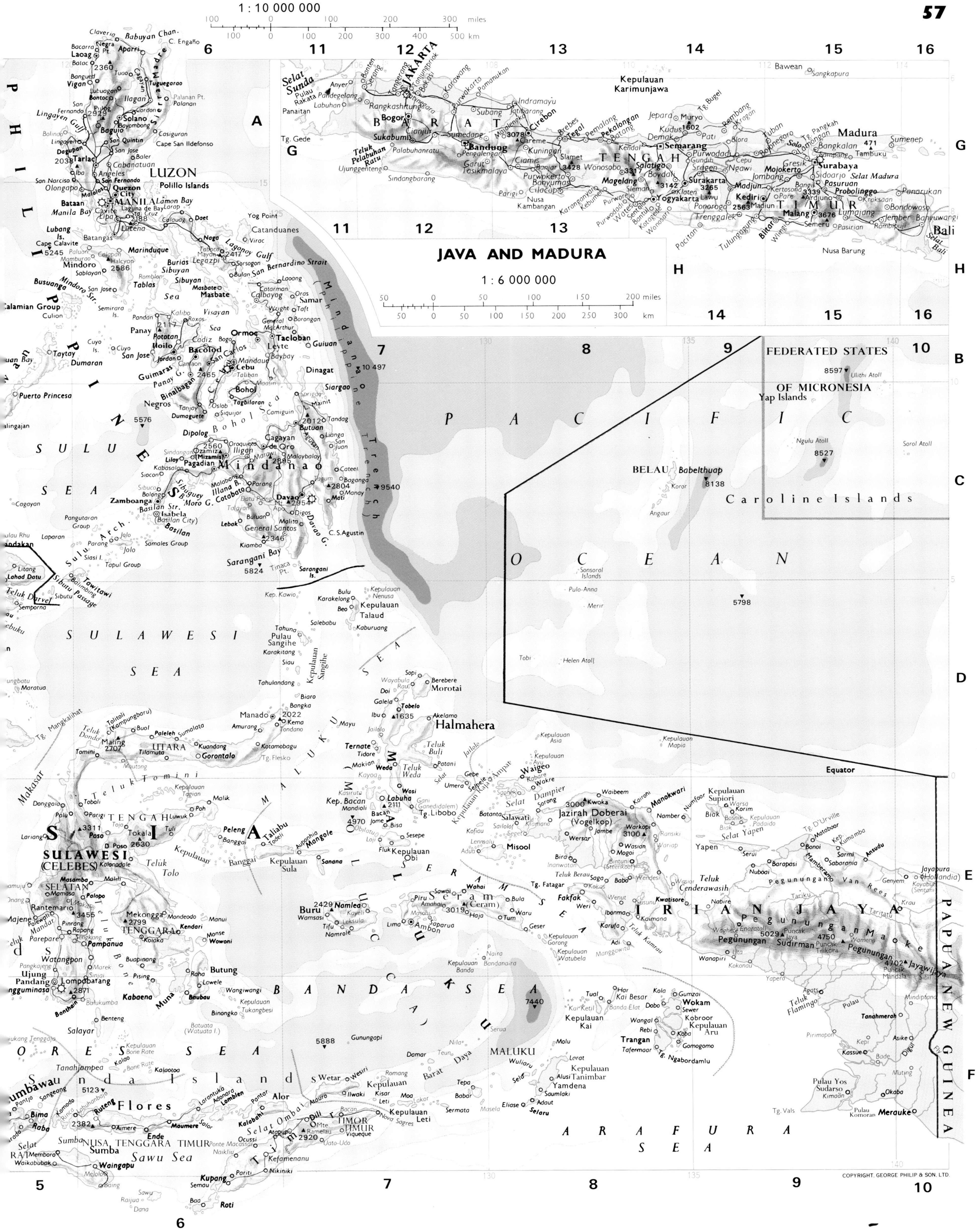
1 : 10 000 000
miles
km
JAVA AND MADURA
1 : 6 000 000
miles
km
LUZON
Polillo Islands
Babuyan Chan.
C. Engaño
Laoag
Vigan
Tuguegarao
Ilagan
Baguio
Solano
Lingayen Gulf
Dagupan
Tarlac
Cabanatuan
Cape San Ildefonso
San Fernando
Olongapo
Bataan
Manila Bay
MANILA
Quezon City
Lamon Bay
Lucena
Batangas
Lubang Is.
Cape Calavite
Mindoro
Marinduque
Catanduanes
Lagonoy Gulf
Legazpi
San Bernardino Strait
Burias
Sibuyan
Sibuyan Sea
Masbate
Tablas
Busuanga
Calamian Group
Samar
Catbalogan
Leyte
Tacloban
Guiuan
Ormoc
Panay
Iloilo
Bacolod
Cebu
Bohol
Negros
Dumaguete
Puerto Princesa
Dinagat
Siargao
Bohol Sea
Cagayan de Oro
Iligan
Butuan
Dipolog
Pagadian
Mindanao
Cotabato
Zamboanga
Basilan
Isabela
Davao
Davao G.
General Santos
Sarangani Bay
Sarangani Is.
C. S. Agustin
Mati
SULU SEA
Sulu Arch.
Jolo
Tawitawi
Sibutu Passage
Lahad Datu
Teluk Darvel
SULAWESI SEA
PHILIPPINES
Mindanao Trench
(Philippine Trench)
10 497
9540
Kepulauan Talaud
Kepulauan Nenusa
Pulau Sangihe
Kepulauan Sangihe
Tahuna
Siau
Manado
Gorontalo
UTARA
Teluk Tomini
Tomini
Tolitoli
SULAWESI (CELEBES)
TENGAH
Poso
Palu
Donggala
Makasar
Kepulauan Togian
Luwuk
Peleng
Banggai
Kepulauan Banggai
Teluk Tolo
SELATAN
Masamba
Palopo
Rantemario
Majene
Parepare
Watampone
Ujung Pandang
Lompobatang
Bulukumba
Salayar
TENGGARA
Kendari
Kolaka
Mekongga
Muna
Butung
Baubau
Kabaena
Wowoni
Teluk Bone
Kepulauan Tukangbesi
Kepulauan Sula
Sanana
Mangole
Taliabu
MALUKU SEA
Morotai
Halmahera
Ternate
Tidore
Teluk Buli
Teluk Weda
Weda
Labuha
Kep. Bacan
Obi
Kepulauan Obi
Waigeo
Salawati
Selat Dampier
Misool
Sorong
Jazirah Doberai (Vogelkop)
Manokwari
Kepulauan Supiori
Biak
Selat Yapen
Yapen
Teluk Cenderawasih
Nabire
Fakfak
Kaimana
IRIAN JAYA
Pegunungan Van Rees
Jayapura (Hollandia)
Pegunungan Sudirman
Puncak Jaya
5029
Puncak Trikora
4750
Pegunungan Jayawijaya
Puncak Mandala
4702
Pegunungan Maoke
Wamena
Teluk Flamingo
Tanahmerah
Merauke
Pulau Yos Sudarso
Kimaan
Pulau Komoran
Tg. Vals
PAPUA NEW GUINEA
Seram
Ambon
Buru
Namlea
Masohi
Bula
Kepulauan Gorong
Kepulauan Watubela
Kepulauan Banda
BANDA SEA
7440
Kepulauan Kai
Tual
Kepulauan Aru
Dobo
Wokam
Kobroor
Trangan
MALUKU
Kepulauan Tanimbar
Yamdena
Saumlaki
Selaru
Babar
Kepulauan Leti
Wetar
Alor
Kalabahi
Flores
Ende
Maumere
Ruteng
Sumbawa
Bima
Raba
FLORES SEA
Sunda Islands
TIMOR
Dili
Atambua
Kupang
Roti
Sawu Sea
NUSA TENGGARA TIMUR
Sumba
Waingapu
Selat Ombai
Timor
ARAFURA SEA
PACIFIC OCEAN
Equator
BELAU
Babelthuap
Koror
Angaur
8138
FEDERATED STATES OF MICRONESIA
Yap Islands
Ulithi Atoll
Ngulu Atoll
Sorol Atoll
Caroline Islands
Sonsorol Islands
Pulo Anna
Merir
Tobi
Helen Atoll
5798
8597
8527
Selat Sunda
Pulau Rakata
Anyer
Panaitan
Tg. Gede
Teluk Pelabuhan Ratu
Sukabumi
Bogor
JAKARTA
BARAT
Bandung
Garut
Tasikmalaya
Cirebon
Indramayu
Tegal
Pekalongan
Semarang
Kudus
Pati
TENGAH
Magelang
Yogyakarta
Surakarta
Madiun
Kediri
Blitar
Malang
TIMUR
Surabaya
Madura
Probolinggo
Jember
Bondowoso
Banyuwangi
Bali
Kepulauan Karimunjawa
Bawean
Selat Madura
Nusa Barung
Nusa Kambangan
Cilacap
Slamet
3428
3078
3142
3265
3339
3676
2563
1602

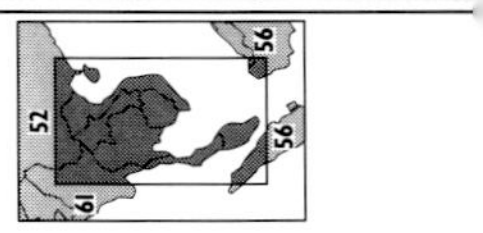

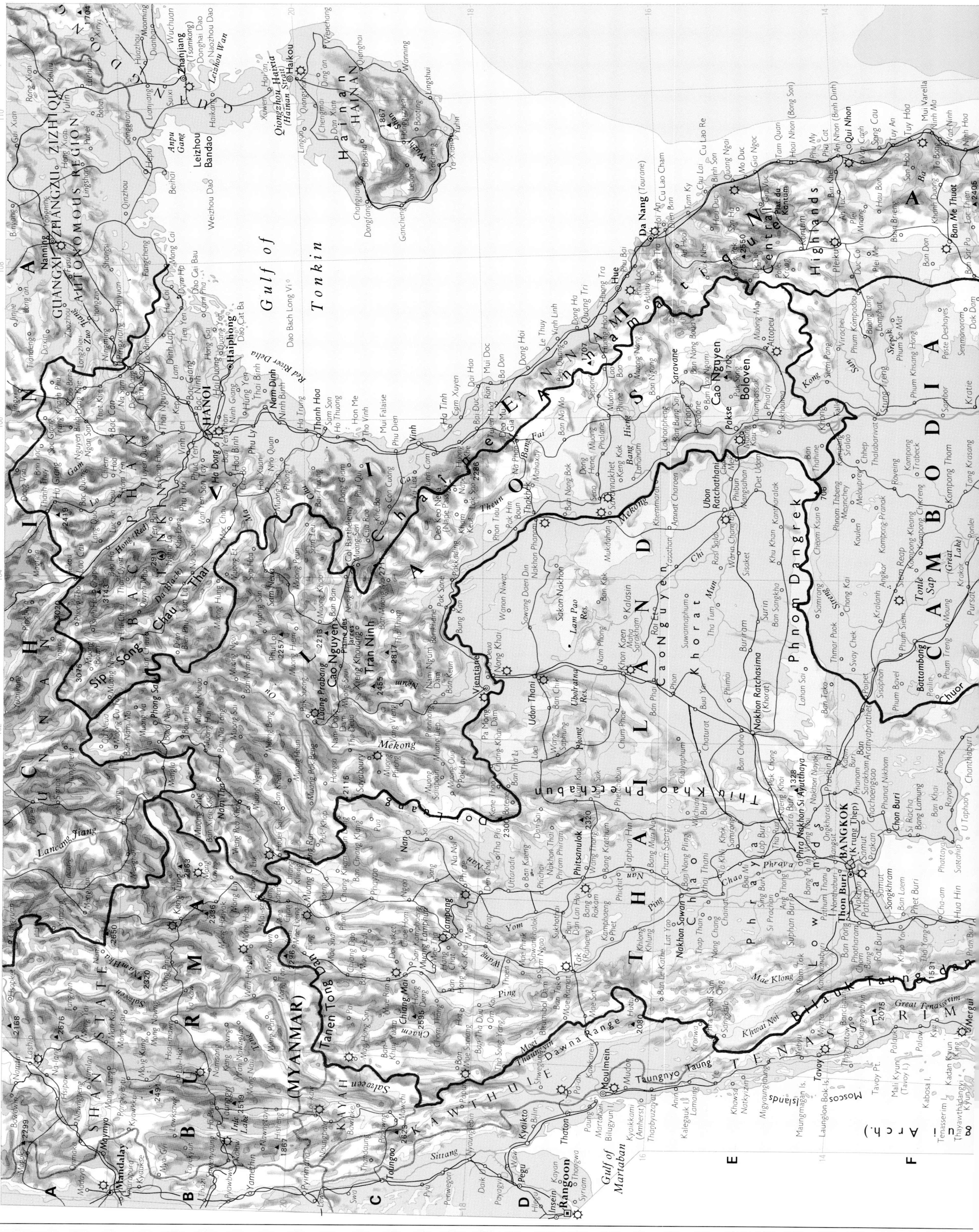

GUANGXI ZHUANGZU ZIZHIQU AUTONOMOUS REGION
YUNNAN
Gulf of Tonkin
Hainan
HAINAN
Haikou
Zhanjiang (Tsamkong)
Leizhou Bandao
Red River Delta
HANOI
Haiphong
Nam Dinh
Thanh Hoa
Vinh
Hue
Da Nang (Tourane)
Qui Nhon
Ban Me Thuot
Central Highlands
Cao Nguyen Boloven
Cao Nguyen Tran Ninh
Pakse
Saravane
Attopeu
Luang Prabang
Vientiane
Udon Thani
Khon Kaen
Nakhon Ratchasima (Khorat)
Ubon Ratchathani
Phnom Dangrek
Tonle Sap (Great Lake)
Battambang
Kratie
Mekong
THAILAND
CAMBODIA
BANGKOK (Krung Thep)
Thon Buri
Phra Nakhon Si Ayutthaya
Chon Buri
Phitsanulok
Lampang
Chiang Mai
Nan
Tak (Rahaeng)
BURMA (MYANMAR)
SHAN STATE
KAYAH
Tanen Tong Dan
Dawna Range
Mandalay
Maymyo
Toungoo
Thaton
Pegu
Rangoon
Moulmein
Gulf of Martaban
Tavoy
Mergui
Taunggyi
Inle Lake
Salween
Sittang
Sip Song Chau Thai
Lancang Jiang

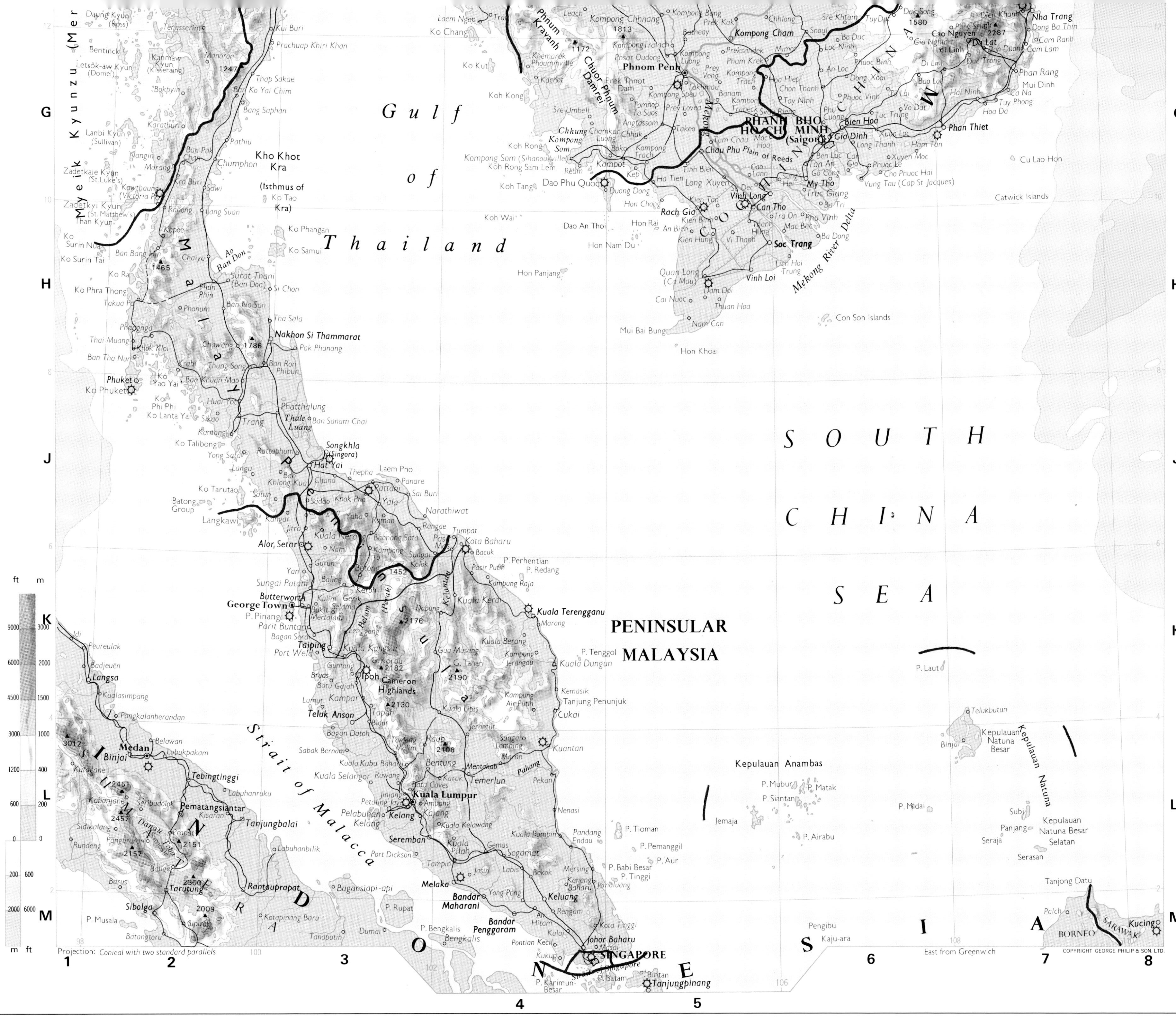
1 : 4 800 000
SOUTH CHINA SEA
Gulf of Thailand
PENINSULAR MALAYSIA
Strait of Malacca
Kho Khot Kra (Isthmus of Kra)
Mekong River Delta
Phnom Penh
THANH PHO HO CHI MINH (Saigon)
Kuala Lumpur
SINGAPORE
George Town
Medan
Nha Trang
Phan Thiet
Kota Baharu
Kuala Terengganu
Kuantan
Ipoh
Melaka
Johor Baharu
Hat Yai
Nakhon Si Thammarat
Phuket
Kepulauan Anambas
Kepulauan Natuna
Con Son Islands
Catwick Islands
Kuching
SARAWAK
BORNEO
Projection: Conical with two standard parallels
East from Greenwich
COPYRIGHT GEORGE PHILIP & SON LTD.

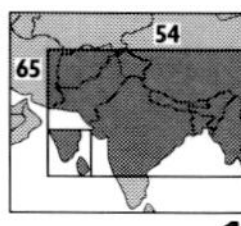

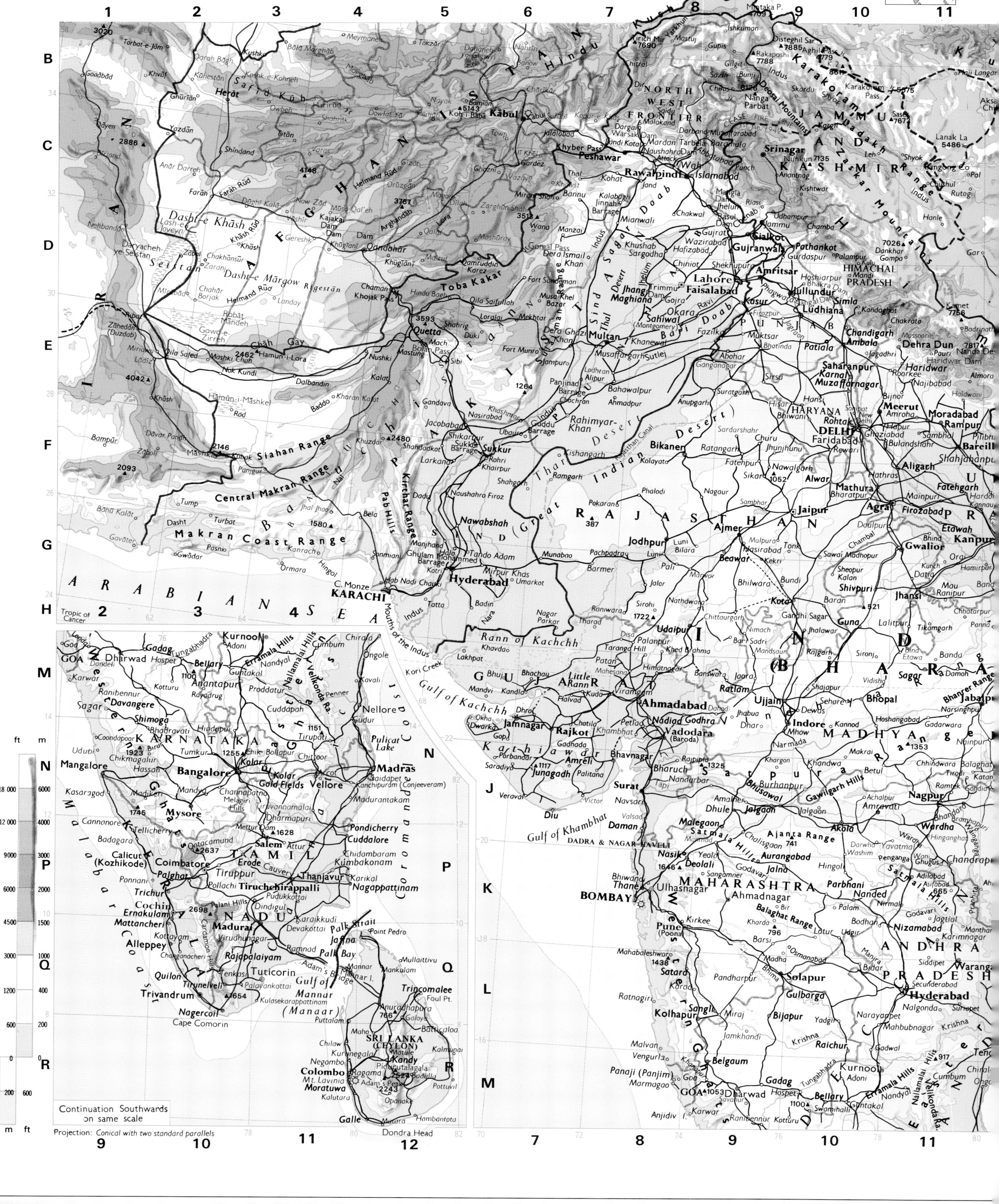

Continuation Southwards
on same scale

Projection: Conical with two standard parallels

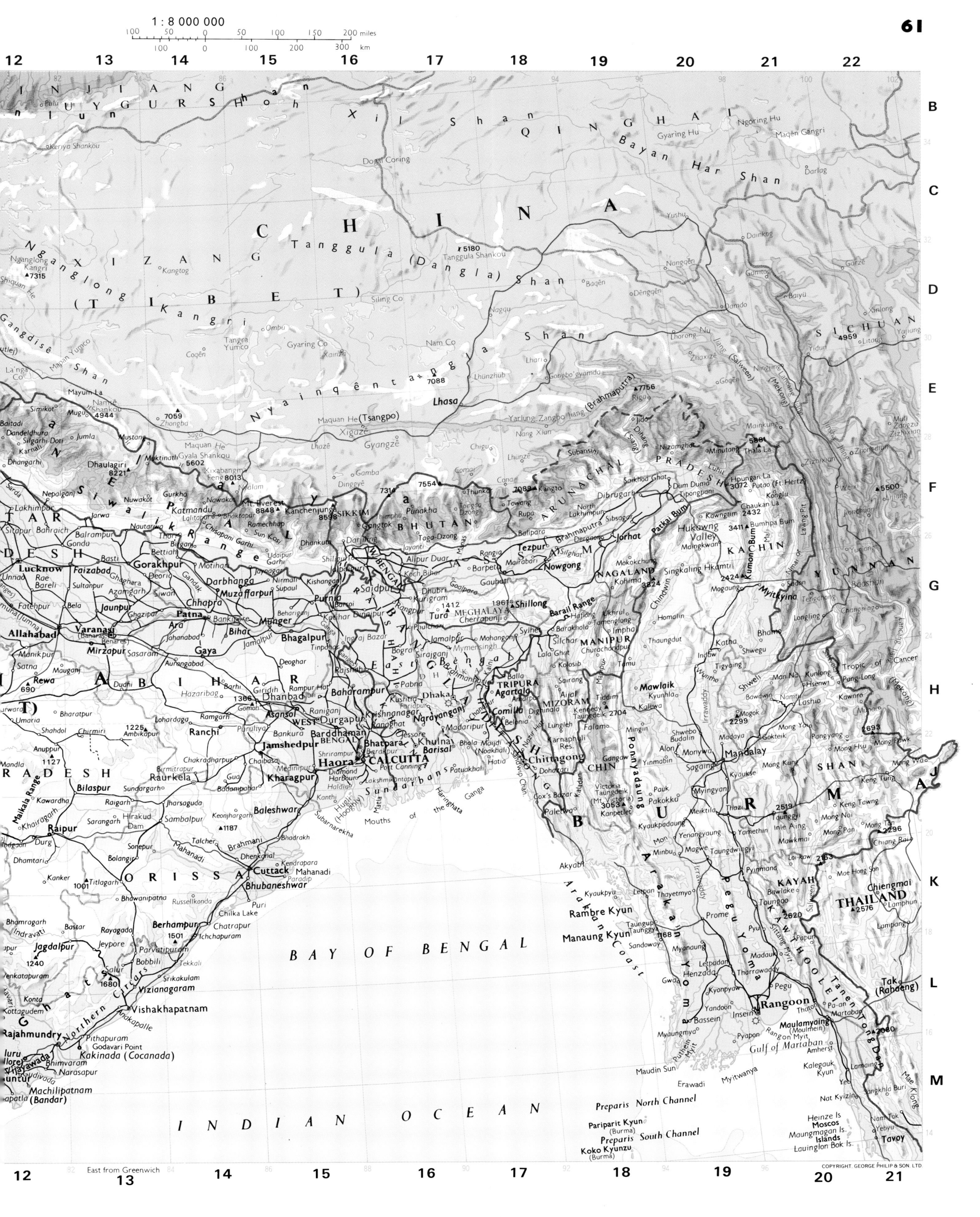

1 : 8 000 000

100 50 0 50 100 150 200 miles
100 0 100 200 300 km

East from Greenwich

COPYRIGHT. GEORGE PHILIP & SON. LTD.

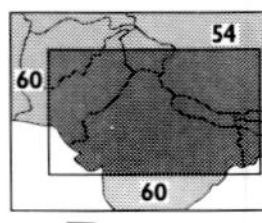

AFGHANISTAN

DASHT-I-NAWAR

N.W. FRONTIER PROVINCE

PAKISTAN

BALUCHISTAN

PUNJAB

SIND

THAL DESERT

KASHMIR

JAMMU AND KASHMIR

HIMACHAL PRADESH

PUNJAB

HARYANA

RAJASTHAN

THAR DESERT (Great Indian Desert)

MADHYA PRADESH

GUJARAT

Rann of Kachchh

Little Rann

Gulf of Kachchh

ARABIAN SEA

Mouths of the Indus

Tropic of Cancer

Kabul · Peshawar · Islamabad · Rawalpindi · Srinagar · Jammu · Amritsar · Lahore · Multan · Quetta · Karachi · Hyderabad · Jodhpur · Jaipur · Ajmer · Udaipur · Ahmadabad · Vadodara · Rajkot · Bhavnagar · Delhi · New Delhi · Meerut · Agra · Gwalior · Indore · Bhopal · Ujjain · Chandigarh · Ludhiana

Gir Hills

Pab Hills

Kirthar Range

Sulaiman Range

Pir Panjal Range

Zaskar

Salt Range

Projection: Conical with two standard parallels

ft m
18,000 6000
12,000 4000
9000 3000
6000 2000
4500 1500
3000 1000
1200 400
600 200
0 0
200 600
2000 6000
m ft

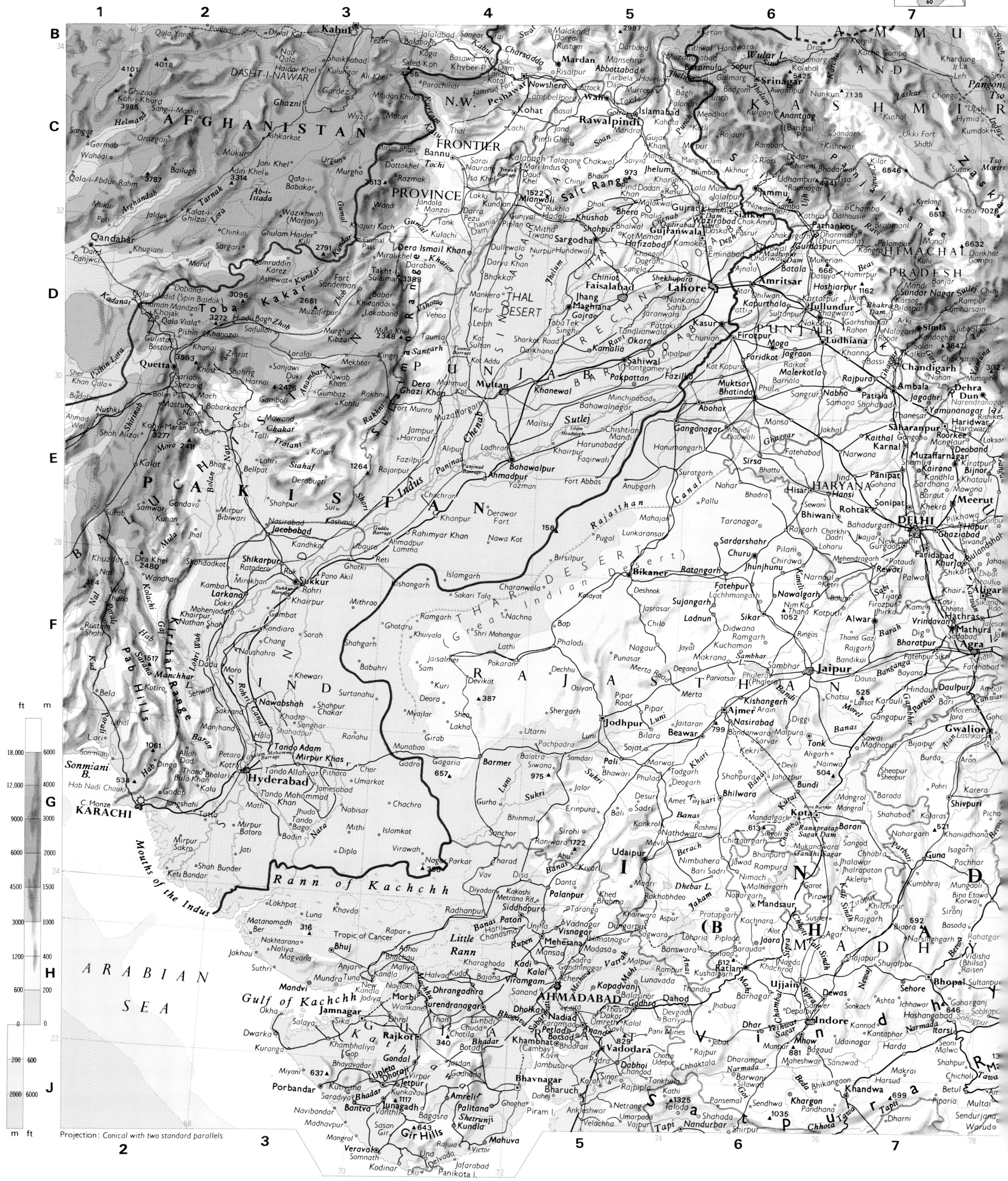

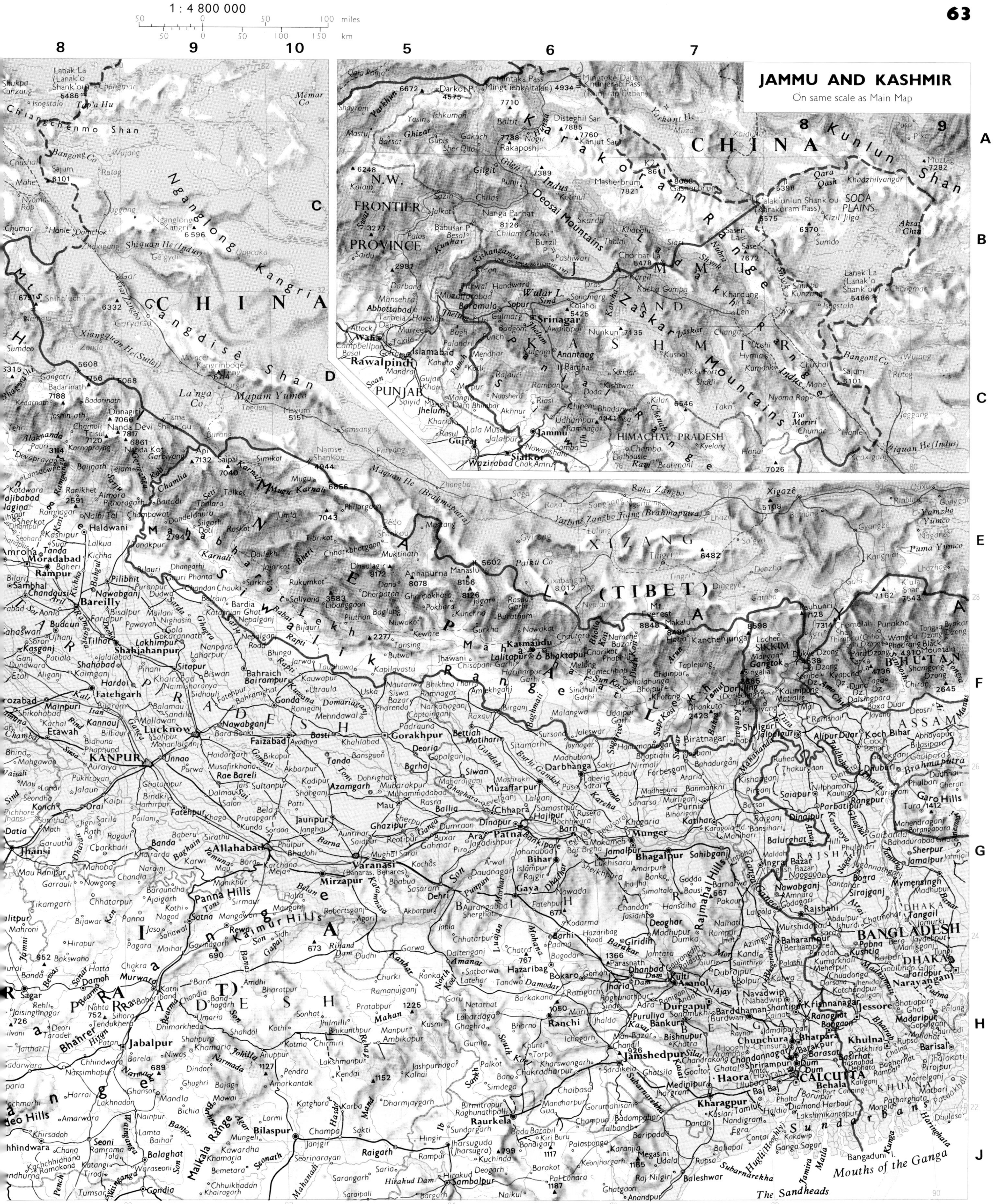

1 : 4 800 000

50   0   50   100 miles
50   0   50   100   150 km

JAMMU AND KASHMIR
On same scale as Main Map

CHINA

Kunlun Shan

Karakoram Range

N.W. FRONTIER PROVINCE

Gilgit

Nanga Parbat

Skardu

SODA PLAINS

Zaskar Mountains

Wular L.
Srinagar
Gulmarg
Baramula
Sopur
Anantnag

Leh

Muzaffarabad
Abbottabad
Mansehra

Rawalpindi
Islamabad

PUNJAB

Jammu
Sialkot
Wazirabad
Gujrat

HIMACHAL PRADESH

Tso Moriri

CHINA

Nganglong Kangri

Gangdise Shan

Mapam Yumco

Shiquan He (Indus)

Nanda Devi

TIBET

XIZANG (TIBET)

Mt. Everest 8848

Makalu

Kanchenjunga

SIKKIM
Gangtok

BHUTAN

Kathmandu
Lalitpur
Bhaktapur

Mahabharat Range

Pokhara

NEPAL

Darjeeling

ASSAM

Brahmaputra

Koch Bihar

Moradabad
Rampur
Bareilly
Budaun

Lucknow
Kanpur

Faizabad
Gorakhpur

Allahabad
Varanasi (Banaras, Benares)
Mirzapur

UTTAR PRADESH

Patna
Gaya

BIHAR

Bhagalpur
Munger

Darbhanga
Muzaffarpur

Purnia

Rajshahi

BANGLADESH
DHAKA

Mymensingh

Jabalpur

MADHYA PRADESH

Bilaspur

Raipur

Ranchi
Jamshedpur
Dhanbad
Asansol
Durgapur

Raurkela

Jessore
Khulna

Kharagpur
Haora
CALCUTTA

WEST BENGAL

ORISSA

Sundarbans

Mouths of the Ganga

The Sandheads

East from Greenwich

COPYRIGHT. GEORGE PHILIP & SON, LTD.

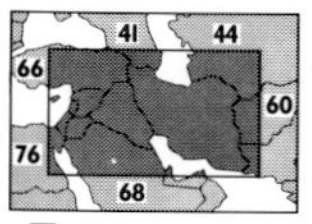

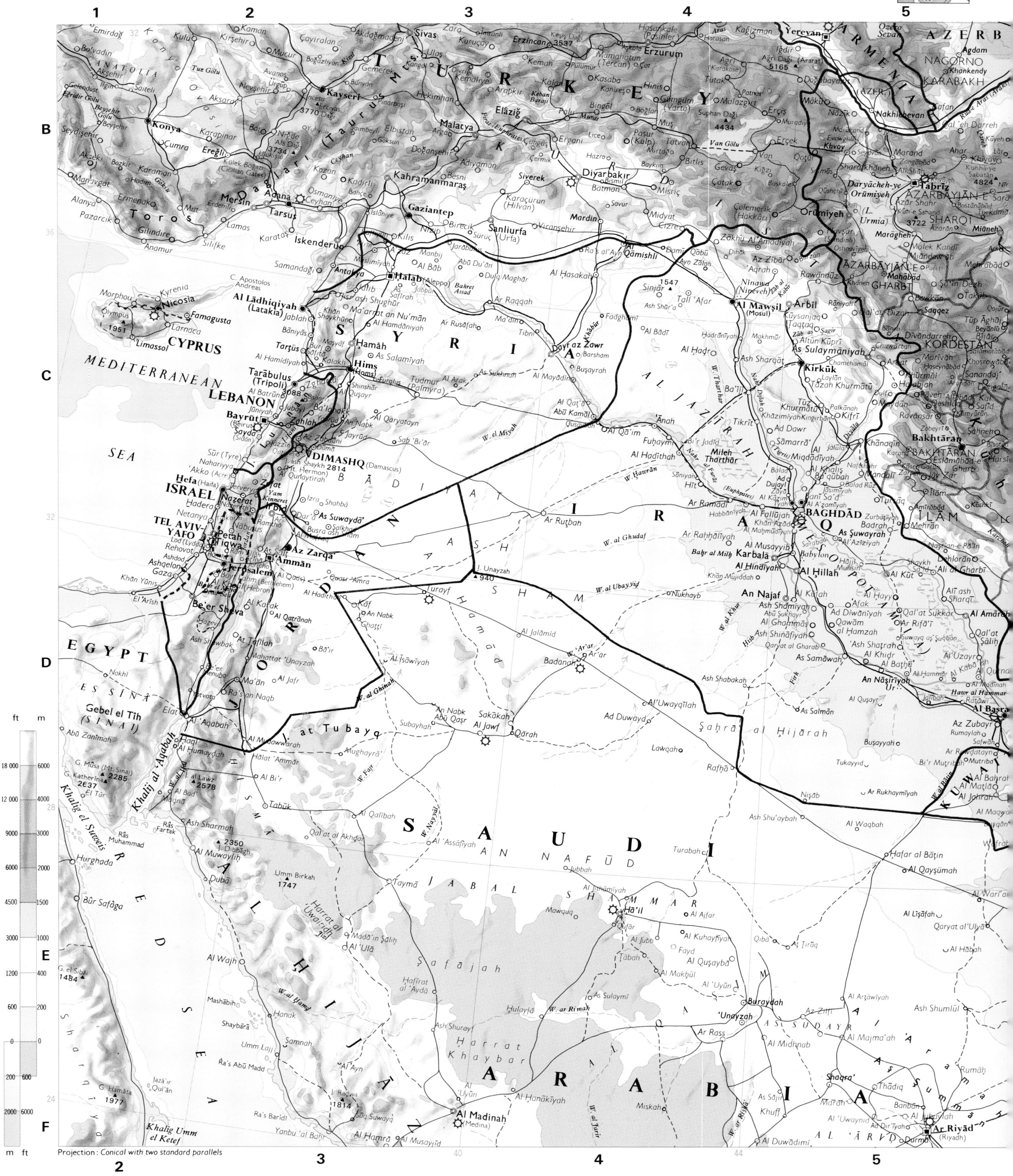

TURKEY
SYRIA
IRAQ
JORDAN
LEBANON
ISRAEL
CYPRUS
EGYPT
SAUDI ARABIA
ARMENIA
MEDITERRANEAN SEA
RED SEA
ANATOLIA
Toros
AL JAZĪRAH
MESOPOTAMIA
BĀDIYAT ASH SHĀM
AN NAFŪD
JABAL SHAMMAR
AL ḤIJĀZ
ES SÎNÂ
Gebel el Tih (SINAI)
Ṣaḥrā' al Ḥijārah
Harrat Khaybar
NAGORNO KARABAKH
AZARBAYJAN-E SHARQI
AZARBAYJAN-E GHARBI
KORDESTAN
BAKHTARAN
ILAM
KUWAIT
Sivas
Erzurum
Yerevan
Kayseri
Konya
Malatya
Elâzığ
Diyarbakır
Adana
Mersin
Tarsus
Gaziantep
Kahramanmaraş
Sanliurfa (Urfa)
Mardin
İskenderun
Nicosia
Famagusta
Limassol
Larnaca
Ḥalab (Aleppo)
Al Lādhiqīyah (Latakia)
Ḥamāh
Ḥimṣ (Homs)
Tudmur (Palmyra)
Dayr az Zawr
Ar Raqqah
Al Ḥasakah
Al Qāmishlī
Ṭarābulus (Tripoli)
Bayrūt (Beirut)
Ṣaydā (Sidon)
Ṣūr (Tyre)
DIMASHQ (Damascus)
Hefa (Haifa)
TEL AVIV-YAFO
Jerusalem
Be'er Sheva
Gaza
'Ammān
Az Zarqā'
Irbid
Al 'Aqabah
Elat
Al Mawṣil (Mosul)
Arbīl
Kirkūk
As Sulaymānīyah
BAGHDĀD
Karbalā'
An Najaf
Al Ḥillah
Al Kūt
An Nāṣirīyah
Al Baṣrah
Tabrīz
Orūmīyeh
Bakhtarān
Ar Ruṭbah
Ḥā'il
Buraydah
'Unayzah
Al Madīnah (Medina)
Ar Riyāḍ (Riyadh)
Tabūk
Al Jawf
Rafḥā
Hafar al Bāṭin
Al Wajh
Hurghada
Khalīj al 'Aqabah
Khalig el Suweis
Projection: Conical with two standard parallels
ft m
18 000 6000
12 000 4000
9000 3000
6000 2000
4500 1500
3000 1000
1200 400
600 200
0 0
200 600
2000 6000
m ft

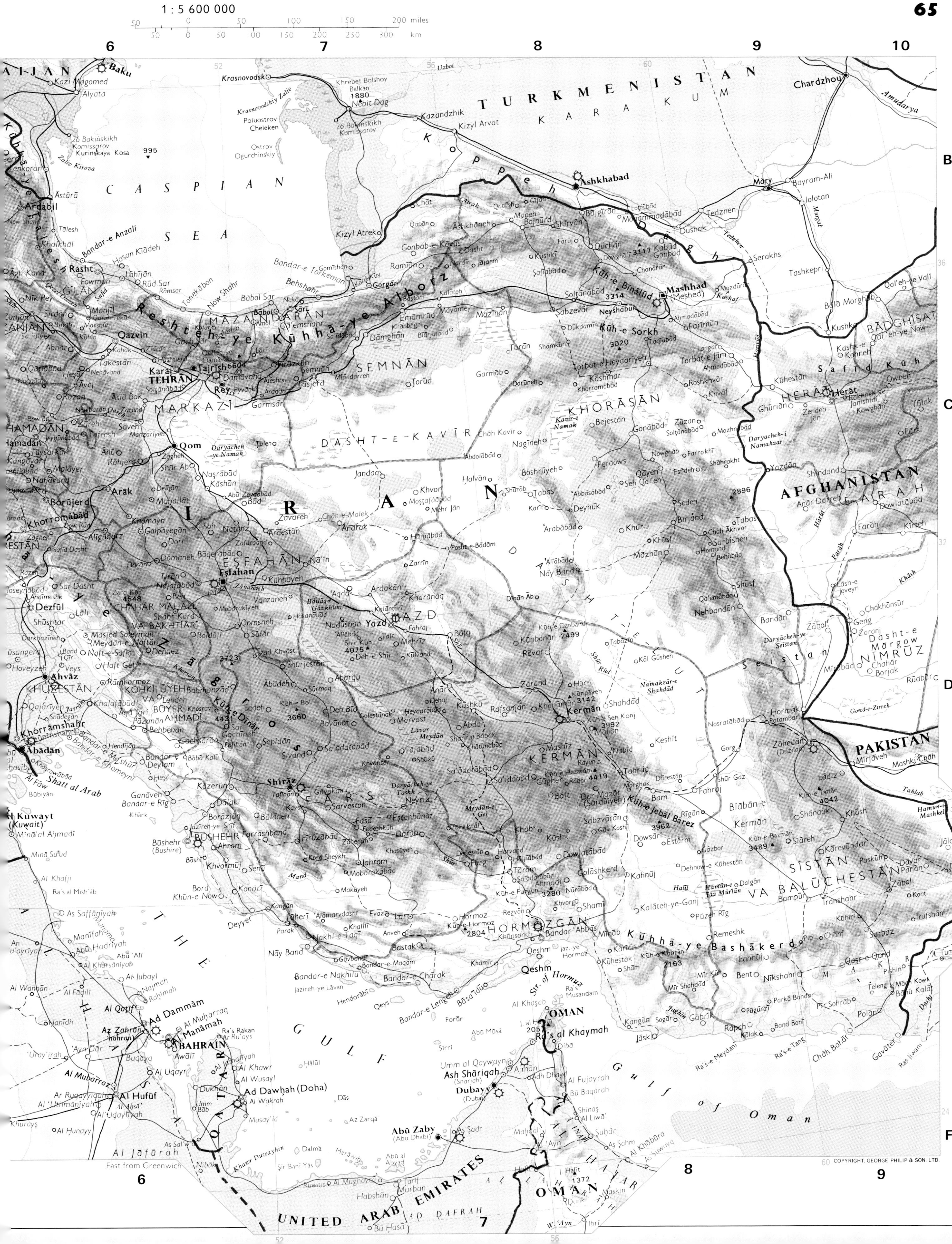

1 : 5 600 000

50 0 50 100 150 200 miles
50 0 50 100 150 200 250 300 km

6   7   8   9   10

TURKMENISTAN

KARA KUM

CASPIAN SEA

IRAN

AFGHANISTAN

PAKISTAN

KHORĀSĀN

DASHT-E-KAVĪR

HERĀT

TEHRĀN

Mashhad (Meshed)

Ashkhabad

Chardzhou

Baku

Ardabīl

Rasht

Qazvīn

HAMADĀN

Qom

Arāk

Borūjerd

Khorramābād

Dezfūl

Ahvāz

KHŪZESTĀN

Khorramshahr

Ābādān

Esfahan

ESFAHĀN

YAZD

Yazd

KERMĀN

Kermān

Shīrāz

FĀRS

BŪSHEHR (Bushire)

HORMOZGĀN

Bandar 'Abbās

Qeshm

Str. of Hormuz

SĪSTĀN VA BALŪCHESTĀN

Zāhedān (Duzdab)

THE GULF

GULF of Oman

OMAN

UNITED ARAB EMIRATES

Dubayy (Dubai)

Abū Zaby (Abu Dhabi)

Ash Shāriqah (Sharjah)

BAHRAIN

Al Manāmah

QATAR

Ad Dawḥah (Doha)

Al Kuwayt (Kuwait)

Ad Dammām

Az Zahrān

Al Hufūf

East from Greenwich

COPYRIGHT. GEORGE PHILIP & SON. LTD

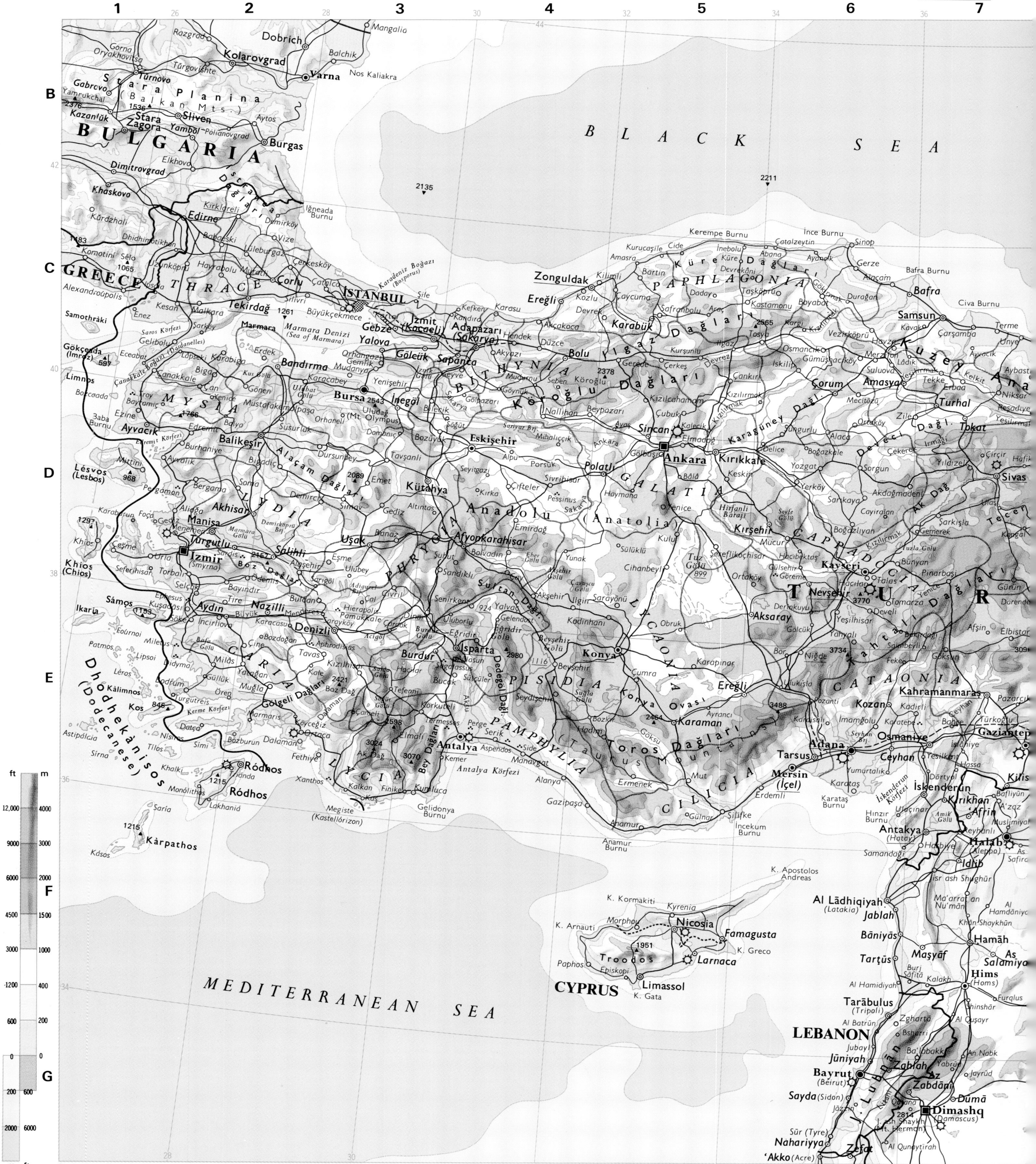

BULGARIA

GREECE

THRACE

BLACK SEA

MEDITERRANEAN SEA

CYPRUS

LEBANON

Map labels (selected):

Mangalia, Dobrich, Varna, Burgas, Nos Kaliakra, Balchik, Kolarovgrad, Razgrad, Gorna Oryakhovitsa, Turnovo, Gabrovo, Sliven, Stara Zagora, Kazanlŭk, Yambol, Khaskovo, Dimitrovgrad, Kŭrdzhali, Edirne, Kırklareli, İğneada Burnu, Demirköy, Vize, Komotini, Alexandroúpolis, Samothráki, Gökçeada (İmroz), Eceabat, Çanakkale, Gelibolu, Tekirdağ, Corlu, Çatalca, İSTANBUL, Karadeniz Boğazı (Bosporus), İzmit (Kocaeli), Gebze, Yalova, Adapazarı (Sakarya), Düzce, Bolu, Zonguldak, Ereğli, Karabük, Safranbolu, Kastamonu, Sinop, İnebolu, Samsun, Çarşamba, Terme, Ünye, Ordu, Bafra, Amasya, Çorum, Tokat, Turhal, Bursa, Uludağ, İnegöl, Eskişehir, Kütahya, Ankara, Kırıkkale, Sivas, Yozgat, Kırşehir, Nevşehir, Kayseri, Aksaray, Konya, Karaman, Ereğli, Niğde, Adana, Tarsus, Mersin (İçel), Osmaniye, Gaziantep, Kahramanmaraş, İskenderun, Kırıkhan, Antakya (Hatay), Kilis, Manisa, İzmir (Smyrna), Turgutlu, Salihli, Uşak, Afyonkarahisar, Akhisar, Aydın, Nazilli, Denizli, Isparta, Burdur, Antalya, Fethiye, Muğla, Bodrum, Marmaris, Kös, Ródhos, Kárpathos, Sámos, Ikaría, Léros, Pátmos, Khíos (Chios), Lésvos (Lesbos), Anadolu (Anatolia), Halab (Aleppo), İdlib, Al Lādhiqiyah (Latakia), Jablah, Bāniyās, Hamāh, Hims (Homs), Tartūs, Tarābulus (Tripoli), Bayrut (Beirut), Sayda (Sidon), Sūr (Tyre), Dimashq (Damascus), Nicosia, Famagusta, Kyrenia, Larnaca, Limassol, Paphos, Troódos

Projection: Conical with two standard parallels

Provinces in Turkey are named after the chief towns which are underlined.

Division between Greeks and Turks in Cyprus; Turks to the North.

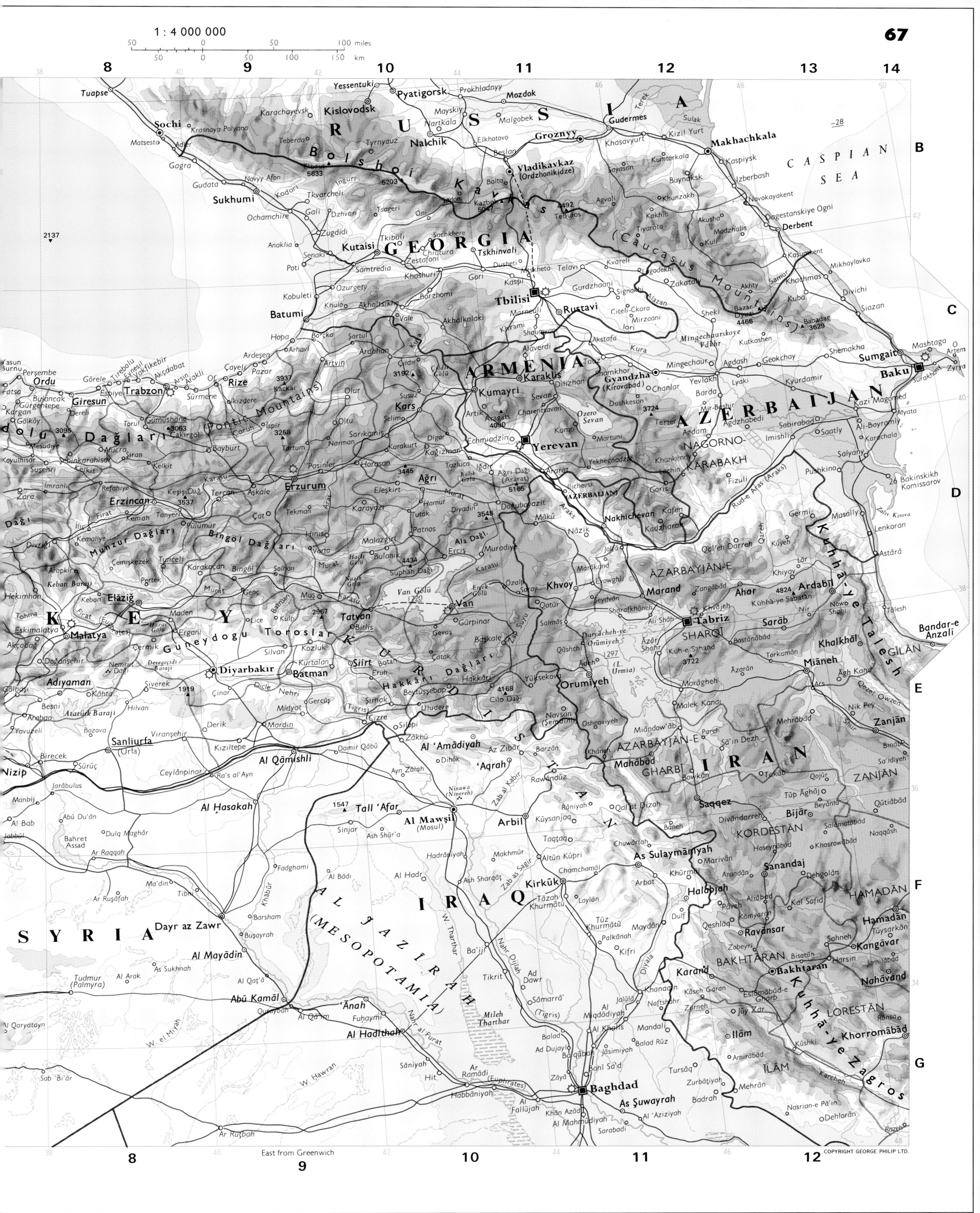

1 : 4 000 000

50   0   50   100 miles

50   40   0   50   100   150 km

East from Greenwich

COPYRIGHT GEORGE PHILIP LTD.

RUSSIA

Tuapse
Sochi
Matsesta
Adler
Gagra
Gudata
Sukhumi
Ochamchire
Gali
Anaklia
Zugdidi

Krasnaya Polyana
Teberda
Karachayevsk
Kislovodsk
Yessentuki
Pyatigorsk
Prokhladnyy
Mozdok
Mayskiy
Nalchik
Nartkala
Elkhotovo
Beslan
Malgobek
Groznyy
Gudermes
Khasavyurt
Kizil Yurt
Sulak
Makhachkala
Kaspiysk

Tyrnyauz
Nartkala

Bolshoi Kavkaz
5633
5203
Kazbek
5047
Tebulos
4492

Vladikavkaz
(Ordzhonikidze)
Balta
Salugardon

Kumtorkala
Buynaksk
Izberbash
Dagestanskiye Ogni
Derbent

CASPIAN
SEA
−28

GEORGIA
Kutaisi
Tkibuli
Chiatura
Sachkhere
Oni
Kodori
Tkvarcheli
Dzhvari
Tsageri
Senaki
Poti
Samtredia
Khashuri
Zestafoni
Kobuleti
Ozurgety
Khulo
Akhaltsikhe
Borzhomi
Vale
Akhalkalaki
Batumi
Hopa
Tskhinvali
Dusheti
Mtskheta
Telavi
Gori
Kaspi
Tbilisi
Rustavi
Marneuli
Gurdzhaani
Signakhi
Lagodekhi
Citeli-Ckaro
Mirzaani
Kvareli
Telavi

Akhtala
Agvali
Khunzakh
Tiyarota
Kakhib
Kuli
Akusha
Madzhalis
Kasumkent
Mikhaylovka

Caucasus Mountains
Bazar-Dyuzi
4466
Babadag
3629
Zakataly
Sheki
Kutkashen
Kuba
Divichi
Siazan
Khashmas
Samur
Akhty

ARMENIA
Kumayri
Karaklis
Dilizhan
Alaverdi
Akstafa
Artik
Aragats
4090
Charentsavan
Sevan
Ozero
Sevan
Martuni
Yekhegnadzor
Echmiadzin
Yerevan
Vedi
Ararat

Gyandzha
(Kirovabad)
Dashkesan
3724
Chanlar
Mingechaur
Mingechaurskoye Vdkhr.
Yevlakh
Barda
Agdash
Geokchay
Terter
Agdam
NAGORNO-
KARABAKH
Khankendi
Fizuli
Goris
Kafan
Kadzharan
Qareh
Germi

AZERBAIJAN
Mir-Bashir
Kyurdamir
Lyaki
Kazi Magomed
Ali-Bayramly
Salyany
Pushkino
26 Bakinskikh
Komissarov
Zaliv Kirova
Lenkoran
Astara

Shemakha
Sumgait
Mashtaga
Artem
Baku
Surakhani
Zyrya
Ali-Bayramly
Saatly
Karachala

TURKEY / TÜRKİYE region
Persembe
Yason
Burnu
Ordu
Fatsa
Görele
Tirebolu
Giresun
Gürgentepe
Kargan
Gölköy
Dereli
Espiye
Akçaabat
Trabzon
Sürmene
Rize
Çayeli
Pazar
Ardeşen
Arhavi
Artvin
Olur
393
Çakirgöl
Gümüşhane
3063
3095
Anadolu Dağları
Mesudiye
Refahiye
Koyulhisar
Susehri
İmranlı
Zara
Kelkit
Torul
Bayburt
3258
İspir
Çoruh
Tortum
İkizdere
Şavşat
Çıldır
Çıldır Gölü
3192
Susuz
Selimo
Kars
Karakurt
Kağızman
Tuzluca
Iğdır

Erzincan
3537
Kemah
Tanyeri
Tercan
Aşkale
Pasinler
Erzurum
Horasan
3445
Ağrı
Eleşkirt
Karaydzi
Tutak
Hamur
Patnos
3546
Ağrı Dağı
(Ararat)
5165
Diyadın
Doğubayazıt
Karasu
Balık
Gölü

Dağı
Divriği
Arapkir
Keban Baraji
Keban
Çemişkezek
Tunceli
Karakoçan
Bingöl
Muş
Varto
Hınıs
4434
Süphan Dağı
Malazgirt
Ercis
Muradiye
Van Gölü
1720
Van
Ala Dağl.
Özalp
Saray
Zab Suyu
Karasu

Hekimhan
Kangal
Darende
Elazığ
Maden
Lice
Kulp
2967
Genç
Bingöl Dağları
Muhur Dağları
Munzur Dağları
Malatya
Eskimalatya
Akçadağ
Ergani
Çermik
Silvan
Kozluk
Siirt
Eruh
Şırnak
Çatak
Gevaş
Gürpınar
Başkale

Muş
Bitlis
Tatvan

KEY (map labels)
Toroslar
Güneydoğu
Diyarbakır
Batman
Hakkâri
Hakkâri Dağları
4168
Cilo Dağı
Yüksekova
Beytüşşebap
Uludere

Adıyaman
Kâhta
Besni
Gölbaşı
Doğanşehir
Nemrut
Dağı
Devegeçidi
Baraji
Çınar
Ergani
Siverek
1919
Hilvan
Bozova
Atatürk Baraji
Yavuzeli
Araban
Birecik
Nizip
Manbij
Jarābulus
Süruç
Şanlıurfa
(Urfa)
Viranşehir
Ceylanpınar
Ra's al 'Ayn
Derik
Kızıltepe
Mardin
Midyat
Gercüş
Kurtalan
Silopi
Cizre
Zakhū
Al Qāmishli
Al Ḥasakah
Ayn Zālah
Dihōk
Al 'Amādiyah
'Aqrah
Barzān
Rawāndūz

Ninawa (Nineveh)
Zab al Kabir
Al Mawṣil
(Mosul)
Arbil
Altūn Küprü
Makhmūr
Küysanjaq
Taqtaq
Chamchamal
As Sulaymāniyah
Halabjah
Marivān
Arbat

SYRIA
Dayr az Zawr
Al Mayādin
Tudmur
(Palmyra)
Al Arak
As Sukhnah
Abū Kamāl
Quṣaybah
Al Qā'im
'Ānah
Fuḥaymī
Al Ḥadīthah
Sab 'Bi'ar
Al Qaryatayn
Bahret
Assad
Dulq Maghār
Ar Ruṣāfah
Ar Raqqah
Tibni
Khābūr
Ma'din
Barsham
Buṣayrah
Fadghami
Al Bādī
Al Hadr
Hadrāniyah
Ash Sharqāt
Ash Shūr'a
Sinjar
Tall 'Afar
1547

IRAQ
AL JAZIRAH
(MESOPOTAMIA)
W. Tharthar
Mileh
Tharthar
Buḥayrat
Ath Tharthar
Ba'jī
Tikrit
Ad
Dawr
Sāmarrā'
Balad
Ad Dujayl
Al Khāliṣ
Khānaqīn
Mandali
Jaṣāniyah
Balad Rūz
Al Miqdādiyah
Jalūlā'
Diyālā
Naft Khāneh
Karand
Qaṣr-e
Shīrīn
Mehrān
Kirkūk
Tāzah
Khurmātū
Tūz
Khurmātū
Laylān
Kifri
Dukān
Qal'at Dizah
Rāniyah
Qal'at
Sāqir
Chuwārtah
Bāneh
Saqqez
Bijār
Takāb

Ar
Ramādī
(Euphrates)
W. Ḥawran
Ar Ruṭbah
Zāya
Al
Fallūjah
Khān Āzād
Al Mahmūdīyah
Al 'Azīzīyah
Baghdad
As Suwayrah
Banī Sa'd
Zubāṭiyah
Badrah
Naṣrān-e Pā'īn
Dehlorān

IRAN
Khvoy
Marand
Ahar
Tabriz
SHARQĪ
ĀZARBĀYJĀN-E
Sarāb
Mārākand
Jolfa
NĀZIK
Nakhichevan
Qal'eh Darreh
Kūyeh
Rud-e Aras (Araks)
Ardabil
4824
Kūhhā-ye Sabālān
Masally
Nīr
Novo
Ashtar
GĪLĀN
Khalkhāl
Kūhhā-ye Talesh
Mīāneh
Zanjan
Nīk Pey
Qezel Owzan
Āgh Kand
Bandar-e
Anzalī
Tālesh
Āstārā

Qūshchī
Orūmīyeh
Duryācheh-ye
Orūmīyeh
(L. Urmia)
1297
'Adeh
Ali Shāh
Kūh-e Sahand
3722
Āzarān
Marāgheh
Bostānābād
Khvājeh
Zenagād
Zangabād

Miāndow'āb
Pareh
Bōwkān
Saqqez
Divāndarreh
Hoseynābād
Khosrowābād
KORDESTĀN
Sanandaj
Dehgolān
Salāmātābād
Qūtiābād
Naqqāsh
Qūjūr
Sa'idīyeh
ZANJAN
Bīnāb

Mahābād
GHARBĪ
ĀZARBĀYJĀN-E
Naqadeh
(Soldūz)
Oshgavīyeh
Navsān
(Şemdīn)
Sardasht
Mīrābād

HAMADAN region
HAMADAN
Hamadan
Tüysarkān
Kangāvar
Sahneh
Kamyarān
Kal Safid
Arandān
Aliābād
Ravānsar
Pāveh
BAKHTARAN
Bakhtaran
Harsin
Bīsotūn
Jamīlābād
Nahāvand
Zobeyri
Qeshlāq
Kūshki
Karkheh
ĪLĀM
LORESTĀN
Khorromābād
Kūhhā-ye Zagros
Ranāo
Amīrābād
Zorneh
Esfandābād-e Gharb
Jūy Zar
Zarneh
 Qaleh

2137
2967

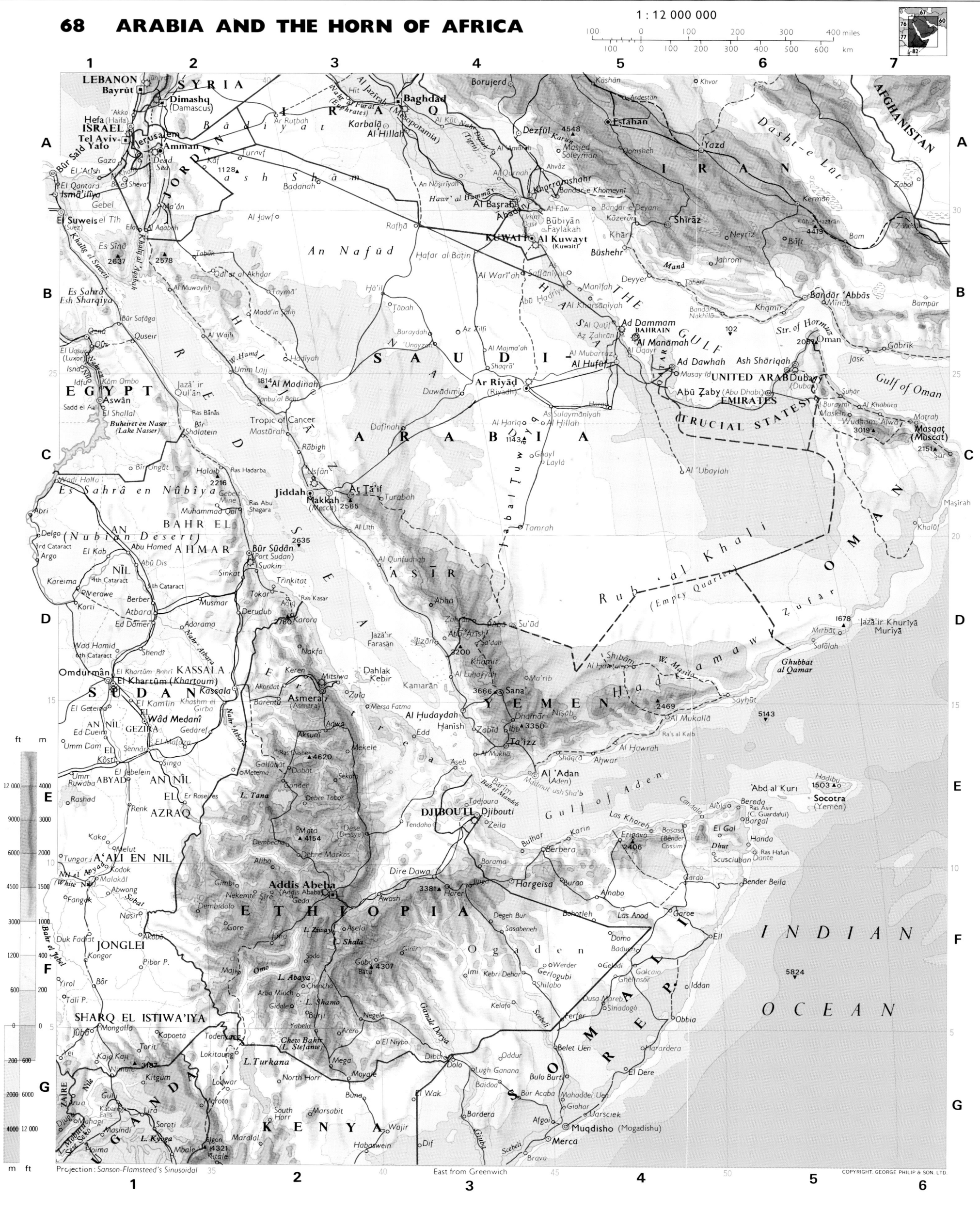

1 : 12 000 000

100   0   100   200   300   400 miles
100   0   100   200   300   400   500   600 km

1   2   3   4   5   6   7

A   LEBANON   SYRIA   AFGHANISTAN
Bayrūt   Hit   Al Jazīrah   Baghdad   Borujerd   Kāshān   Khvor   Ardestān
Dimashq   Nahr al Furāt   Dezfūl   4548   Eşfahān
(Damascus)   (Euphrates)   Karbalā'   Qomsheh   Yazd
Hefa (Haifa)   Al Hillah   Ahvāz   Dasht-e Lūt
ISRAEL   Jerusalem   Al Qurnah   Khorramshahr   Shīrāz   Kermān   Zābol
Tel Aviv-Yafo   Amman   Al Başrah   Abādān   Bandar-e Khomeynī   Bam   4419
Būr Sa'īd Yafo   Gaza   Al 'Amārah   Al Fāw   Kāzerūn   Neyrīz   Zāhedān
El 'Arīsh   Beer Sheva   Badanah   An Nāşirīyah   Hawr al Hammār   Būbiyān   Bandar-e Deyam
El Qantara   Dead Sea   1128   Faylakah   Khār
Ismā'īlīya   Ma'ān   Rafhā   KUWAIT   Al Kuwayt   Būshehr   Bandar 'Abbās
Gebel   Al Jawf   (Kuwait)   Mīnāb

B   Es Sahrā   2637   2578   An Nafūd   Hafar al Bāţin   Az Zilfī   Bandar Nakhīlū   Bampūr
Esh Sharqīya   Qâl'at al Akhdar   Hā'il   Al Warī'ah   Deyyer   Khamīr   Oman
Khalīg el Suweis   Tabūk   Taymā'   Manīfah   THE   102
Būr Safāga   Madā'in Şālih   Burayḍah   S'Al Qaţīf   Ad Dammam   GULF
Quseir   Al Wajh   Hā'il   'Unayzah   Az Zahrān   BAHRAIN   Ash Shāriqah   Jāsk

C   El Uqsur   Hurghada   Umm Lajj   1814 Al Madīnah   Al Majma'ah   Al Manāmah   UNITED ARAB   Dubayy
(Luxor)   Jazā'ir   Yanbu' al Baḥr   Duwādimī   Ar Riyāḍ   Ad Dawhah   (Dubai)
Isna   Qul'ān   Rābigh   (Riyadh)   QATAR   Abū Zaby (Abu Dhabi)   Şuhār
Aswān   Ras Bānās   Mastūrah   As Sulaymānīyah   Musay'īd   EMIRATES   Buraymī   Al Khābūra
El Shallal   Bīr   Tropic of Cancer   Al Hilllah   Al Hufūf   TRUCIAL STATES   Maskin   3019   Maşqaţ
Buheiret en Naser   Shalatein   Al Hariq   1143   Harād   Wudhām   'Alwa   (Muscat)
(Lake Nasser)   Halaib   2216   Nsfan   Jiddah   Ghayl   Layla   2151   Şūr

D   Wadi Halfa   Es Sahrâ en Nûbiya   Makkah (Mecca)   2565   Al 'Ubaylah   Masīrah
Abri   BAHR EL   Ras Hadarba   At Tā'if   Al Lith   Rub' al Khali   Khalūf
Delgo   (Nubian Desert)   Turabah   (Empty Quarter)   Zufār   1678   Jazā'ir Khurīyā Murīyā
3rd Cataract   El Kab   AHMAR   2635   Tamrah   Mirbāt   Salālah
Argo   Būr Sūdân   Al Qunfudhah   Ghubbat al Qamar
Kareima   Abū Dis   (Port Sudan)   Abhā   Shibām   W. Masīla   Mirbāt
Merowe   4th Cataract   Suakin   'ASĪR   Al Huwaysh   3200   Sayhūt   5143
Korti   Berber   Sinkat   Zuhrah   Abū 'Arīsh   Sa'dah   Ma'rib   Ḥaḍramawt
Atbara   Musmar   Trinkitat   3666   Al Mukallā
Ed Dāmer   Adarama   Tokar   Jazā'ir Farasān   Jīzān   Khamir   2469   Ra's al Kalb

E   Omdurmân   El Khartūm Bahrī   KASSALA   Derudub   2786 Karora   Nakfa   Kamarān   Sana'   Nişāb   'Abd al Kuri   Hadibu   Socotra
El Khartūm (Khartoum)   Keren   Mitsiwa   Dahlak Kebir   YEMEN   Al Mukallā   1503   (Yemen)
SUDAN   Kassala   Akordat   Zula   Al Hudaydah   Dhamār   3350   Ghubbat al Qamar
AN NÎL   Khashm el Girba   Asmera   Hanish   Zabīd   Ra's Asir (C. Guardafui)
El Kamlin   (Asmara)   Barentu   Ta'izz   Al Hawrah   Bereda   Bargal
Wâd Medanî   Adwa   Edd   Aseb   Al Mukhā   Al 'Adan (Aden)   Ahwar   Candala   El Gal   Handa
GEZIRA   Gedaref   Aksum   Mersa Fatma   Mādinat ush Sha'b   Ahwar   Alūla   Bosaso   Dhut

F   ABYAD   AN NÎL   Ras Dashen 4620   Mekele   Bāb el Mandeb   Las Khoreh   Karin   Ras Hafun Dante
EL AZRAQ   Er Roseires   Gallabat   Dobāt   DJIBOUTI   Djibouti   Scusciuban
Rashad   Metema   Sekota   Tadjoura   Zeila   Erigavo   2406
Renk   A'ALI EN NÎL   Mota   Gonder   Dese (Dessye)   Tendaho   Bulhar   Berbera   Bender Beila
Kaka   Debre Tabor   4154   Borama   Burao
Umm Ruwaba   Tungarú   Dembecha   Dire Dawa   Hargeisa   Anabo   Gardo
Melut   Debre Markos   3381   Harer   Degeh Bur   Las Anod   Garoe
El Jebelein   Alibo   Awash   Sasabeneh   Domo   Eil
NH-el Abyad   Kodok   Gimbi   Addis Abeba   Bohotleh   Badoweyn
(White Nile)   Malakal   Nekemte   (Addis Ababa)   Asela   Ogaden   Badueyn

G   JONGLEI   Abwong   Gore   L. Ziwai   Ginir   Imi   Kebri Dehar   Geladi   Dusa Mareb   5824   INDIAN
Fangok   Jima   L. Abaya   Goba   4307   Shilabo   Galcaio   Gheinsor   Iddan   OCEAN
Duk Fadiat   Nasir   Sodo   Chencha   Werder   Gerlogubi   Obbia
Kongor   Akobo   ETHIOPIA   Shala   Kelafo   Sinadogo
Pibor P.   Arba Minch   L. Shamo   SOMALI   REP.   Scebeli   Ferfer
Yirol   Gidole   Burji   Negele   Ganale Dorya   Domo   Eil
Bôr   Majri   Chew Bahir   Arero   El Niybo   Dību   Oddur   Bardera   Hararardera   El Dere
SHARQ EL ISTIWA'IYA   Omo   (L. Stefanie)   Mega   Moyale   Dolo   Lugh Ganana   Bulo Burti
Jûba   Yabelo   Dibb   Belet Uen
ZAIRE   Mongalla   Kapoeta   L. Turkana   North Horr   Wajir   Bur Acaba   Mahaddei Uen
UGANDA   Torit   Todenyang   Muqdisho (Mogadishu)
Arua   Lokitaung   South Horr   Marsabit   Dif   Merca
Gulu   3187   Lodwar   Baidoa   Afgoi   Uarsciek
Kabaret Falls   Kitgum   Marâlal   Baardheere   Gíohar   Brava
L. Albert   Soroti   Elgon   4321   Habaswein   KENYA
Masindi   L. Kyoga   Mbale   Scebeli

ft   m
12 000   4000
9000   3000
6000   2000
4500   1500
3000   1000
1500   500
600   200
0   0
200   600
2000   6000
4000   12 000
m   ft

Projection: Sanson-Flamsteed's Sinusoidal

35   East from Greenwich   40   45   50

1   2   3   4   5   6

COPYRIGHT. GEORGE PHILIP & SON, LTD.

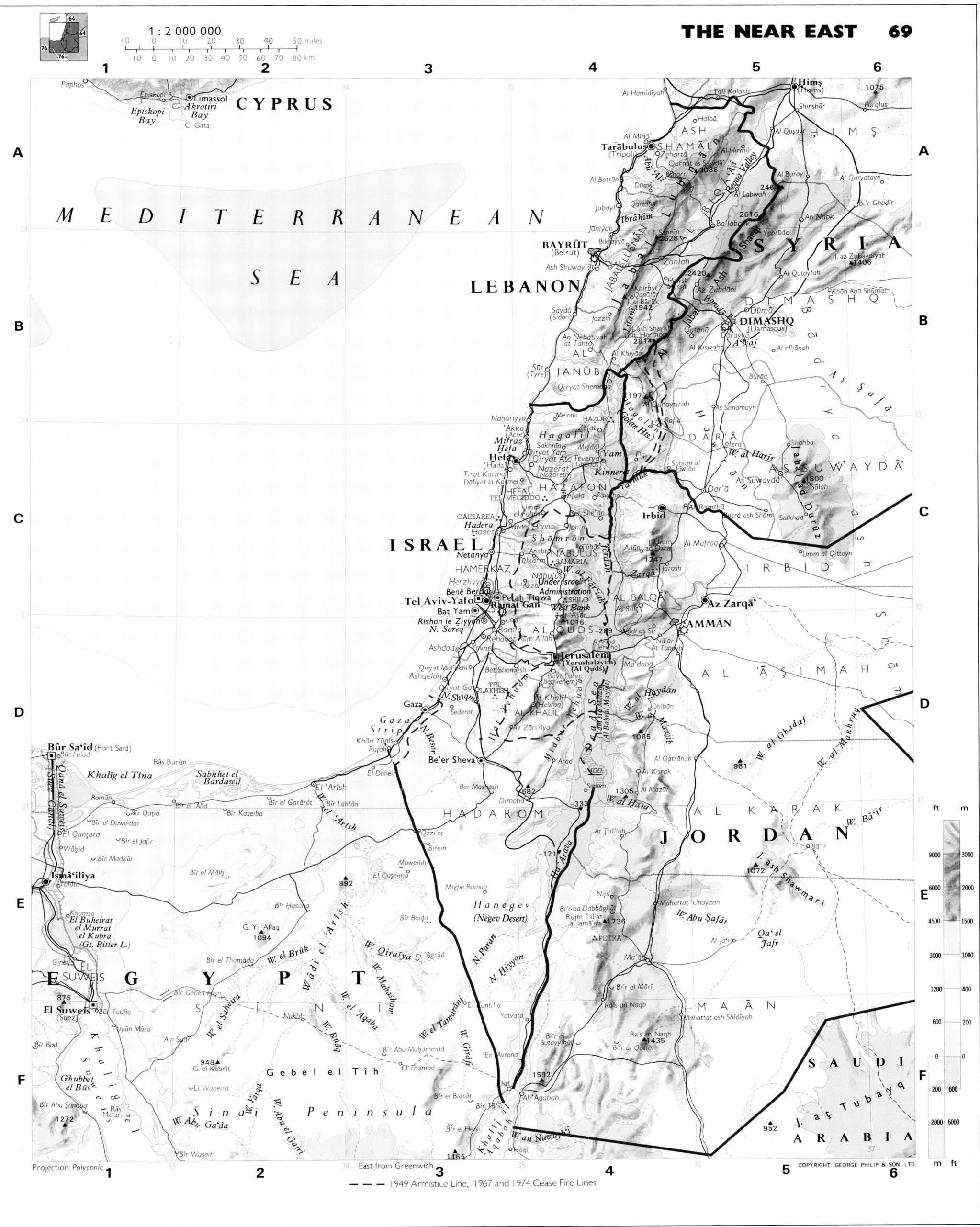

1 : 2 000 000

10   0   10   20   30   40   50 miles
10 0 10 20 30 40 50 60 70 80 km

CYPRUS

Paphos
Episkopi
Limassol
Akrotiri
Episkopi Bay
Bay
C. Gata

M E D I T E R R A N E A N

S E A

A

B

C

D

E

F

Al Hamidiyah
Al Mina'
Tarābulus
(Tripoli)
Al Batrūn
Jubayl
Jūniyah
Ibrāhīm
BAYRŪT
(Beirut)
Ash Shuwayfāt
Alayh
Saydā
(Sidon)
Jazzīn
An Nabatīyah
at Tahta

Tall Kalakh
Ḥalba
Zgharta
Qartaba
Dūmā
Bikfayyā
Zaḥlah
Khirbat
al Barūk
Ash Shaykh
Ḥāṣbayyā
Al Khiyām

Ḥimṣ
(Homs)
Shinshār
Al Quṣayr
Al Hirmil
3088
2616
'An 'Nabk
2628
Sannīn
2420
Ash
2814
Qaṭanā

Furqlus
Bi'r Ghadīr
Al Qaryatayn
Al Burayj
246
Al Labwah
Yabrūd
J. az Zubaydīyah
1406
Al Quṭayfah
Dūmā
DIMASHQ
(Damascus)
A'waj
Khān Abū Shāmāt
Al Hijānah

HIMS

SYRIA

DIMASHQ

AL
JANŪB
Sūr
(Tyre)
Qiryat Shemona

Me'ona
HAZOR
Zefat
Naharīyya
'Akko
(Acre)
Mifraz
Hefa
Ḥefa
(Haifa)
Tirat Karmel
Daliyat el Karmel
HEFA'
TEL MEGIDDO
CAESAREA
Ḥadera
Ḥadera
Netanya
HAMERKAZ
Herzliyya
Benē Beraq
Tel Aviv-Yafo
Bat Yam
Rishon le Ziyyon
N. Soreq
Ashdod
Qiryat Mal'akhi
Ashqelon
Qiryat Gat
Gaza
Gaza Strip
Khān Yūnis
Rafah

Ḥagalil
Sakhnīn
Qiryat Yam
Qiryat Ata Teverya
(Tiberias)
Nazerat
Nazareth
HAZAFON
'Afula
Umm
el Fahm
Bet She'an
Janin
Shōmrōn
Anabta
Tulkarm
NABULUS
SAMARIA
Nāblus
'Azzūn
Under Israeli
Administration
SHILO
West Bank
1016
Ramla
Lod
Rām Allāh
Rehovot
Yavne
Bet Shemesh
Bayt Lahm
(Bethlehem)
TEL
LAKHISH
N. Shiqma
Sederot
AL KHALIL
Az Zāhirīya

1974
Golan Hts.
Yam
Kinneret
Fiq
Yarmūk
Irbid
Ailūn
1247
Zarqā'
Jarash
Az Zarqā'
AMMĀN
Wādī as Sīr
'Arrā
Wādī Mūsā
Ma'daba
AL BALQĀ'
As Salṭ
AL QUDS
Jerusalem
(Yerushalayim)
(Al Quds)
299
Arīḥā
(Jericho)
Al Ḥaydān
Dhibān
1065
W. al Mūjib
Al Karak
981
W. al Khanzīr

197
Al Qunayṭirah
Ṣafd
As Sanamayn
Ḥarrah
DAR'Ā
'Ira
Shaqrā' al
'awīnīn
Dar'ā
Al Ḥarīr
Shahba
Aṣ Ṣuwaydā
1800
Ṣalah
Salkhad

AS SUWAYDĀ'
J A B A L   A D   D U R Ū Z

IRBID

Umm al Qittayn
Umm ad Darak
Al Mafraq

ISRAEL

LEBANON

Bir Sa'id
(Port Said)
Būr Fu'ad
Khalīg el Tīna
Qand el Suweis
Suez Canal
Ismâ'ilîya
Ismailia
El Qantara
Wāhid
Bir Madkūr
Khamsa
El Buheirat
el Murrat
el Kubra
(Gt. Bitter L.)
El Suweis
El Suweis
(Suez)
875
Bir Taufiq
Bir Bad'
Ghubbet
el Būs
Bir Abu Sandūq
1272
Rās
Matarma
Uyūn Mūsa
'Ain Sudr
Khalîg

Rās Burūn
Sabkhet el
Bardawil
Romāni
Bir el Abd
Bir el Garārāt
Bir el Duweidar
El Qantara
Bir Qaṭia
Bir el Jafir
Wâdi el 'Arîsh
Bir Gebel Ḥisn
Wâdî el Brûk
G. Yi 'Allaq
1094
Bir el Thamâda
S I N A I
Wâdi el Girâfi
Nakhl
W. el 'Aqaba
948
G. el Kabrît
El Wabeira
Gebel el Tîh
El Thamad

El 'Arîsh
Bir Lahfan
Bir Kaseiba
Abu Aweigila
Qeziot
Bireln
El Quseima
Muweilih
Bir Hasana
Bir Beiḍa
Mizpe Ramon
Hanegev
(Negev Desert)
Bir el Mālhi
892
Wâdi Qiratya
El 'Agrûd
W. Mahaḑkam
N. Paran
N. Hiẓyon
Wâdi el Tamarûni
Yotvata
'En Avrona
W. Giraif
El Tuntilla
Bir Abu Muḥammad
Bir el Biârât
Bir el Ḥeisi
Gir
1165

Be'er Sheva
Bor Mashash
Dimona
O'Arad
HADAROM
682
Qeziot
333
121
Ha 'Arava
1305

Mizpe Ramon
Nijil
Mahattat 'Unayzah
Ruim Tal'at
al Jamā'ah
1736
W. Abu Ṣafāt
Qa' el
Jafr
'En
PETRA
Bi'r al Mārī
Rā's an Naqb
Mahattat ash Shidīyah
1435
Bi'r al Qattār
952
J. aṭ Tubayq

W. el Ḥasa
At Tafīlah
Al Mazār
Al Qaṭrānah
W. al Ghafaf
W. al Makhrūq
1072
J. ash Shawmari
Al Qatrānah
'En
AL 'ĀSIMAH

AL KARAK

JORDAN

M A' Ā N
Ma'ān

EGYPT

Al 'Aqabah
Al 'Aqabah
Bîr Ṭaba
Khalîg Aqaba
Ḥaql
W. an Nuwaybi'

SAUDI

ARABIA

Projection: Polyconic

East from Greenwich

COPYRIGHT GEORGE PHILIP & SON, LTD.

1   2   3   4   5   6

- - - - 1949 Armistice Line, 1967 and 1974 Cease Fire Lines

ft   m
9000   3000
6000   2000
4500   1500
3000   1000
1200   400
600   200
0   0
200   600
2000   6000
m   ft

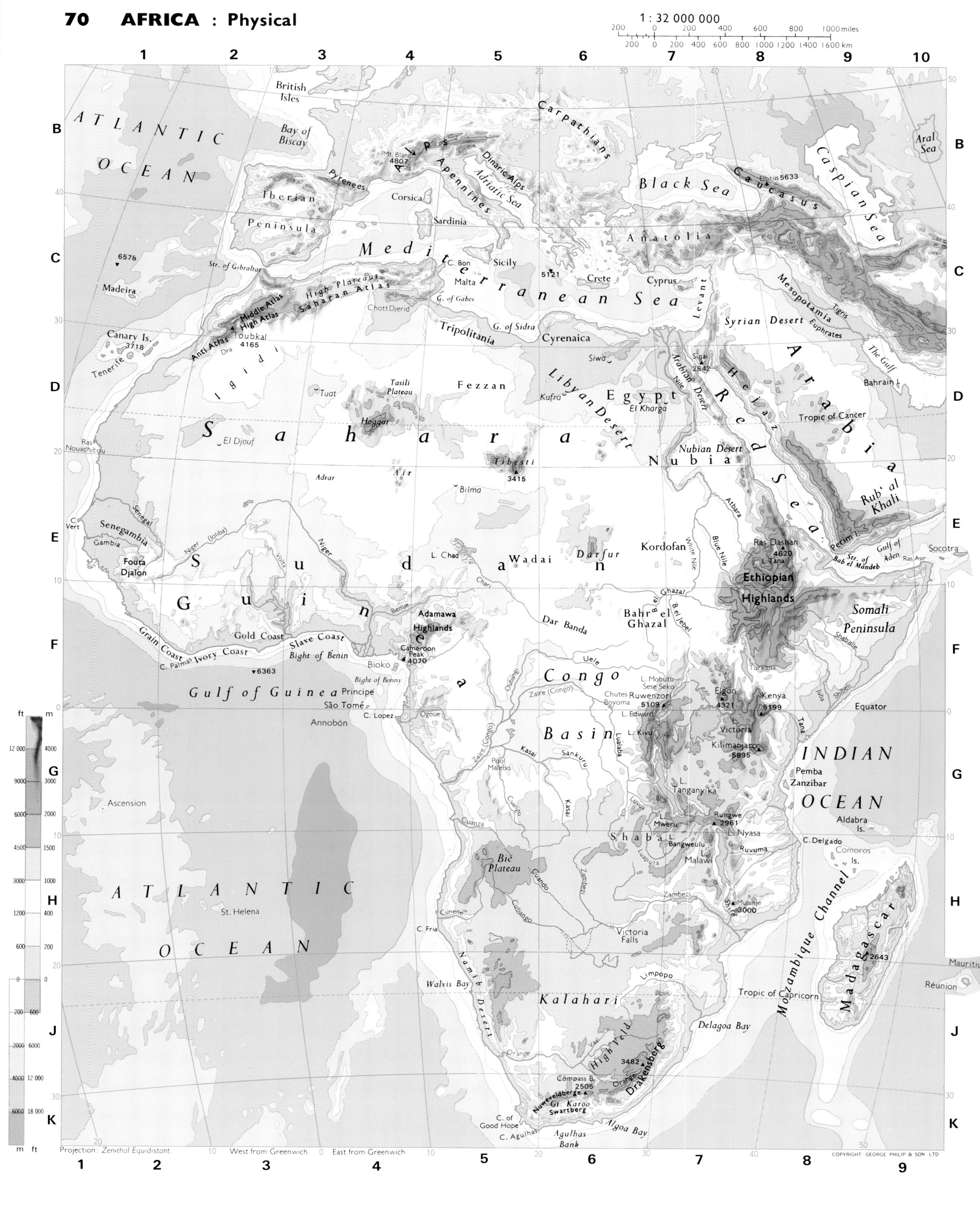

1 : 32 000 000

Projection: Zenithal Equidistant.   West from Greenwich   East from Greenwich   COPYRIGHT GEORGE PHILIP & SON LTD

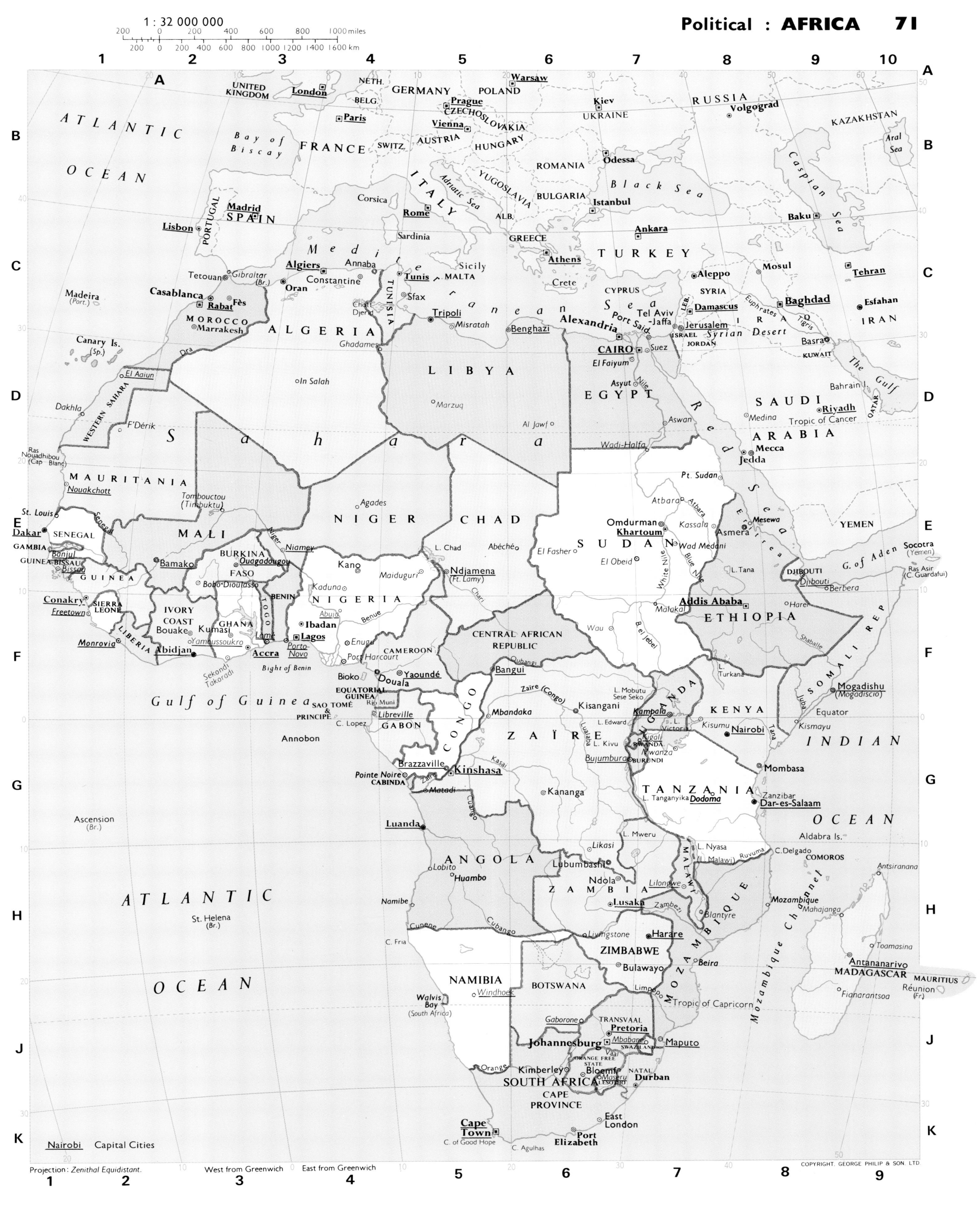

1 : 32 000 000

200   0   200   400   600   800   1000 miles
200   0   200 400 600 1000 1200 1400 1600 km

1   2   3   4   5   6   7   8   9   10

ATLANTIC

OCEAN

Bay of Biscay

UNITED KINGDOM
London
NETH.
BELG.
GERMANY
POLAND
Warsaw
Paris
Prague
CZECHOSLOVAKIA
Vienna
AUSTRIA
HUNGARY
SWITZ.
FRANCE
Kiev
UKRAINE
RUSSIA
Volgograd
KAZAKHSTAN
Aral Sea

Madrid
Lisbon
SPAIN
PORTUGAL
Corsica
ITALY
Rome
Sardinia
Adriatic Sea
YUGOSLAVIA
ROMANIA
BULGARIA
Black Sea
Odessa
Istanbul
Ankara
Baku
Caspian Sea

Casablanca
Rabat Fès
MOROCCO
Marrakesh
Tetouan
Gibraltar (Br.)
Oran
Algiers
Annaba
Constantine
TUNISIA
Tunis
Sfax
MALTA
Sicily
Crete
GREECE
Athens
CYPRUS
Aleppo
SYRIA
Damascus
Tel Aviv-Jaffa
LEB.
Jerusalem
ISRAEL
JORDAN
Baghdad
IRAQ
Basra
Euphrates
Tigris
Esfahan
Tehran
Mosul
IRAN

Madeira (Port.)
Canary Is. (Sp.)
ATLANTIC OCEAN

Mediterranean Sea

Algiers
ALGERIA
Chott Djerid
Tripoli
Misratah
Ghadames
Benghazi
LIBYA
Alexandria
Port Said
CAIRO
Suez
El Faiyum
EGYPT
Asyut
Aswan
Al Jawf
Marzuq
In Salah
Dra
WESTERN SAHARA
El Aaiun
Dakhla
F'Dérik
Ras Nouadhibou (Cap Blanc)
S   a   h   a   r   a
Nile
Tropic of Cancer
SAUDI
ARABIA
Medina
Mecca
Jedda
Riyadh
QATAR
Bahrain I.
The Gulf
KUWAIT
Wadi Halfa

Nouakchott
MAURITANIA
Tombouctou (Timbuktu)
Agades
NIGER
CHAD
Abéché
SUDAN
El Fasher
El Obeid
Omdurman
Khartoum
Wad Medani
Kassala
Atbara
Atbara
Pt. Sudan
YEMEN
G. of Aden
Socotra (Yemen)
Ras Asir (C. Guardafui)
Berbera
DJIBOUTI
Djibouti
Asmera
Mesewa
ERITREA
L. Tana
Addis Ababa
ETHIOPIA
Harer
Shabelle
SOMALI REP.

St. Louis
Dakar
SENEGAL
GAMBIA
Banjul
GUINEA-BISSAU
Bissau
Conakry
Freetown
SIERRA LEONE
GUINEA
LIBERIA
Monrovia
Senegal
MALI
Bamako
BURKINA FASO
Ouagadougou
Bobo-Dioulasso
Niamey
Niger
Kano
Kaduna
Maiduguri
L. Chad
Ndjamena (Ft. Lamy)
Chari
NIGERIA
Abuja
Ibadan
Lagos
Porto-Novo
BENIN
TOGO
GHANA
Accra
Lomé
IVORY COAST
Bouake
Kumasi
Yamoussoukro
Abidjan
Sekondi-Takoradi
Bight of Benin
Enugu
Port Harcourt
CENTRAL AFRICAN REPUBLIC
Wau
Malakal
White Nile
Blue Nile
L. Turkana
Benue
Bangui
CAMEROON
Yaoundé
Douala
Bioko
EQUATORIAL GUINEA
SAO TOMÉ & PRINCIPE
Rio Muni
C. Lopez
Libreville
GABON
Annobon
Gulf of Guinea

Bangui
Oubangui
Zaire (Congo)
CONGO
Brazzaville
Pointe Noire
CABINDA
Matadi
Kinshasa
Kisangani
Mbandaka
ZAIRE
L. Mobutu Sese Seko
L. Edward
L. Kivu
Bujumbura
BURUNDI
RWANDA
Kigali
Mwanza
UGANDA
Kampala
L. Victoria
Kisumu
Nairobi
KENYA
Equator
Kismayu
Mogadishu (Mogadiscio)
Juba
Tana
INDIAN
OCEAN
Mombasa
Zanzibar
TANZANIA
Dodoma
Dar-es-Salaam
L. Tanganyika
Kananga
Kasai
Lualaba
Ascension (Br.)

Luanda
ANGOLA
Lobito
Huambo
Namibe
Kwango
Zaire
Kananga
Likasi
Lubumbashi
L. Mweru
ZAMBIA
Ndola
Lusaka
Zambezi
Lilongwe
MALAWI
L. Nyasa (L. Malawi)
Ruvuma
C. Delgado
COMOROS
Antsiranana
MOZAMBIQUE
Mozambique
Mahajanga
Toamasina
MADAGASCAR
Antananarivo
MAURITIUS
Réunion (Fr.)
Fianarantsoa
Mozambique Channel
Blantyre

ATLANTIC
OCEAN
St. Helena (Br.)
Walvis Bay (South Africa)
NAMIBIA
Windhoek
C. Fria
Cunene
Cubango
Livingstone
Harare
Bulawayo
ZIMBABWE
BOTSWANA
Gaborone
Limpopo
Beira
Tropic of Capricorn

Orange
Kimberley
Bloemfontein
ORANGE FREE STATE
Maseru
LESOTHO
TRANSVAAL
Pretoria
Johannesburg
Mbabane
SWAZILAND
Maputo
NATAL
Durban
SOUTH AFRICA
CAPE PROVINCE
Cape Town
C. of Good Hope
C. Agulhas
East London
Port Elizabeth

Nairobi   Capital Cities

Projection : Zenithal Equidistant.

West from Greenwich   East from Greenwich

COPYRIGHT. GEORGE PHILIP & SON. LTD.

1   2   3   4   5   6   7   8   9

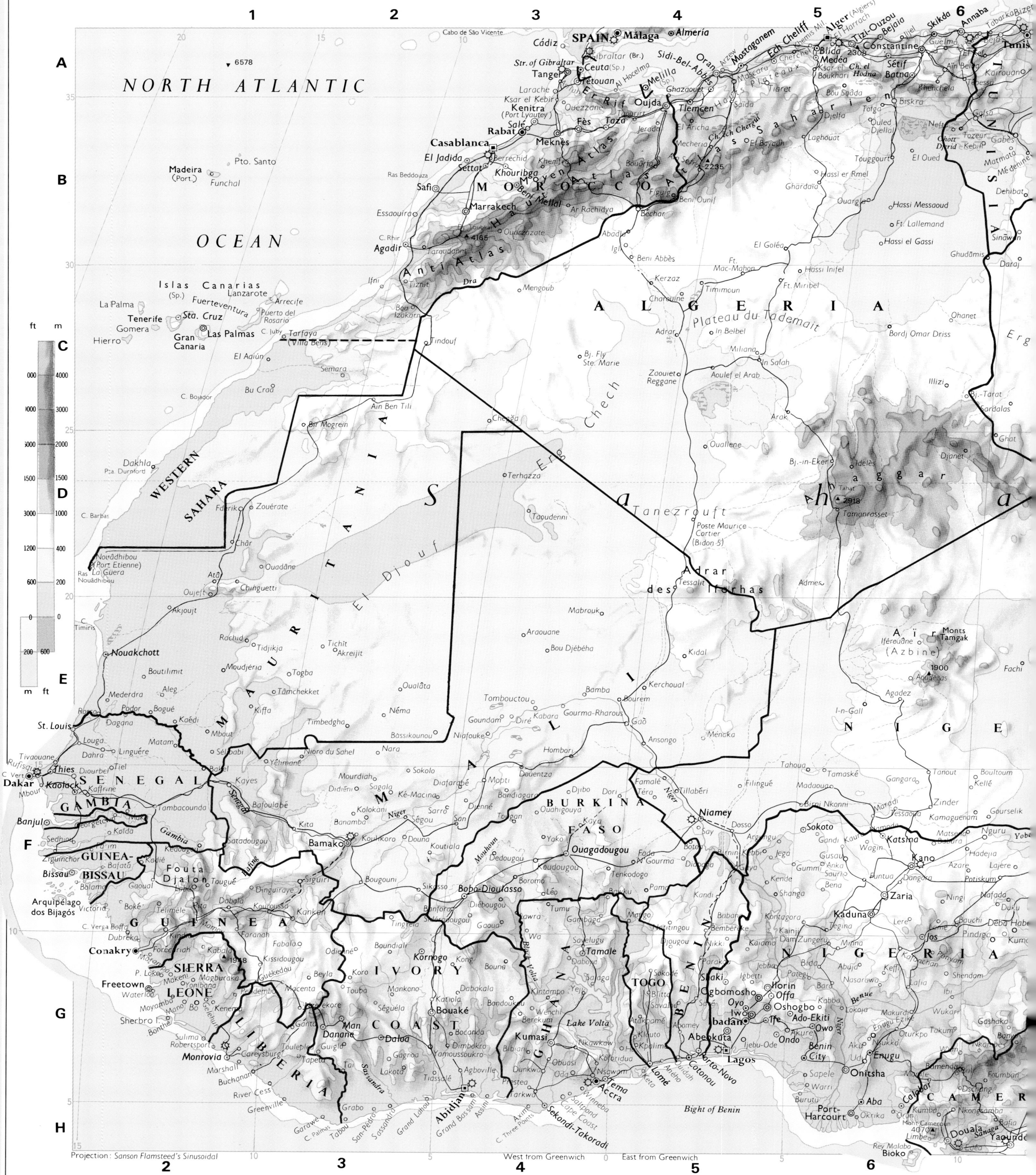

NORTH ATLANTIC

OCEAN

SPAIN

MOROCCO

ALGERIA

WESTERN SAHARA

MAURITANIA

MALI

NIGER

SENEGAL

GAMBIA

GUINEA-BISSAU

GUINEA

SIERRA LEONE

LIBERIA

IVORY COAST

GHANA

BURKINA FASO

TOGO

BENIN

NIGERIA

TUNISIA

CAMEROON

Madeira (Port.)

Islas Canarias (Sp.)

Casablanca
Rabat
Marrakech
Agadir
Tanger
Tetouan
Fès
Meknès
Oujda
Tlemcen
Oran
Alger (Algiers)
Constantine
Tunis

Nouakchott
Nouâdhibou (Port Etienne)
Dakar
St. Louis
Banjul
Bissau
Conakry
Freetown
Monrovia
Abidjan
Accra
Lomé
Porto-Novo
Lagos
Cotonou
Ibadan
Kano
Kaduna
Abuja
Niamey
Ouagadougou
Bamako
Tombouctou
Gao
Tamanrasset
Agadez

Bight of Benin

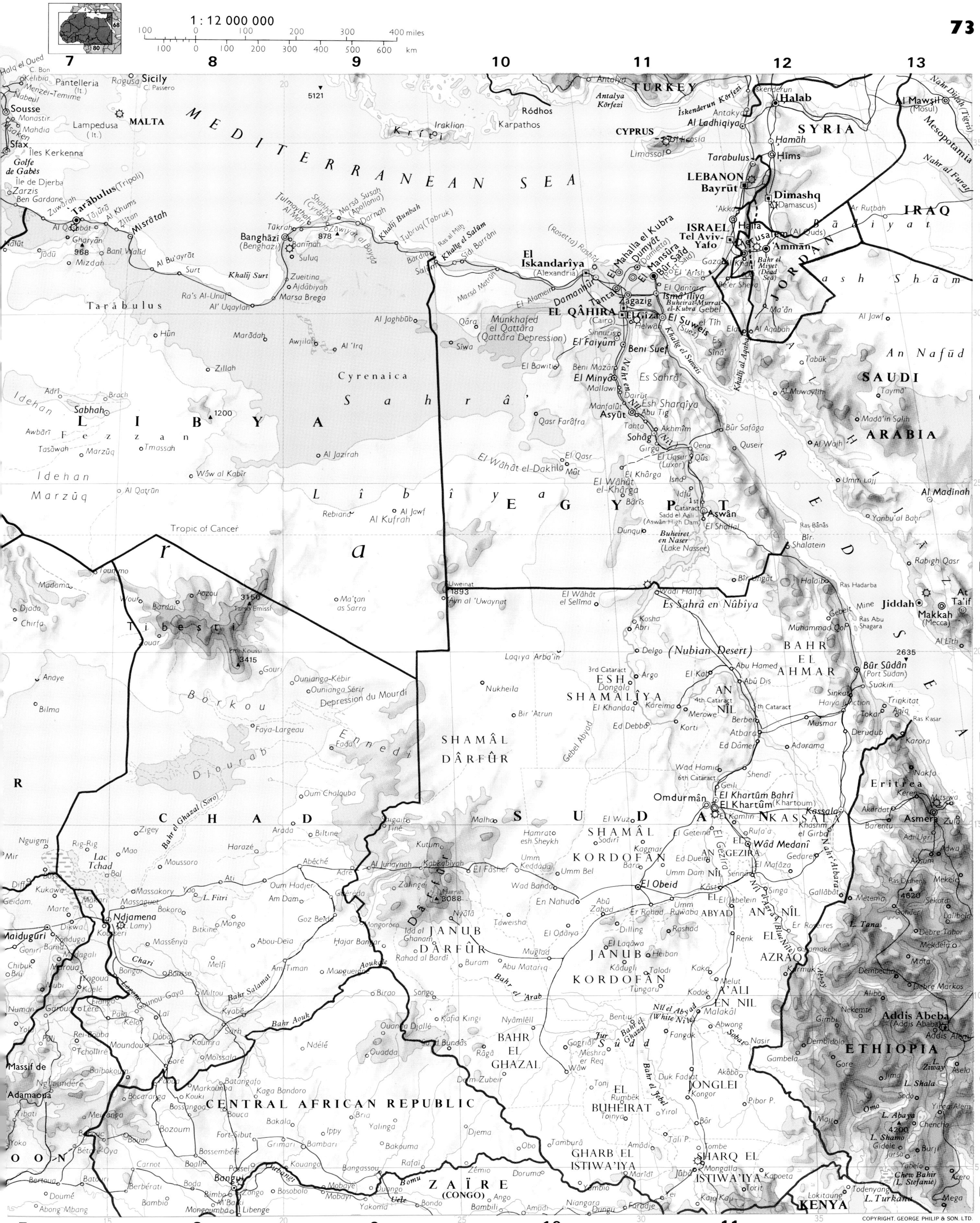

1 : 12 000 000

MEDITERRANEAN SEA

TURKEY

CYPRUS

SYRIA

IRAQ

LEBANON
Bayrût

ISRAEL
Tel Aviv-Yafo
Jerusalem

JORDAN
Amman

SAUDI ARABIA

LIBYA

Tarâbulus (Tripoli)

Banghāzī (Benghazi)

EGYPT

EL QÂHIRA (Cairo)
El Gîza
El Iskandarîya (Alexandria)
El Suweis
El Faiyûm
Beni Suef
El Minyâ
Asyût
Sohâg
El Ugsur (Luxor)
Aswân
Buheiret en Naser (Lake Nasser)

Tropic of Cancer

Makkah (Mecca)
Jiddah
At Ta'if

Bûr Sûdân (Port Sudan)

CHAD

Ndjamena
Lac Tchad

SUDAN

El Khartûm (Khartoum)
El Khartûm Bahrî
Omdurmân
Kassala
El Obeid
Wâd Medanî

SHAMÂL DÂRFÛR
JANUB DÂRFÛR
SHAMÂL KORDOFÂN
JANUB KORDOFÂN
ESH SHAMALÎYA
AN NÎL
AN NÎL EL AZRAQ
A'ALI EN NÎL
EL GEZIRA
ABYAD
BAHR EL GHAZAL
BUHEIRAT
JONGLEI
GHARB EL ISTIWA'IYA
SHARQ EL ISTIWA'IYA
BAHR EL AHMAR

Jûba

ETHIOPIA
Addis Abeba (Addis Ababa)
L. Tana

Eritrea
Asmera

CENTRAL AFRICAN REPUBLIC
Bangui

ZAÏRE (CONGO)

KENYA
L. Turkana

MALTA
Sicily

An Nafûd

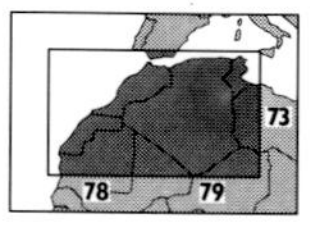

A

B

C

D

E

1 2 3

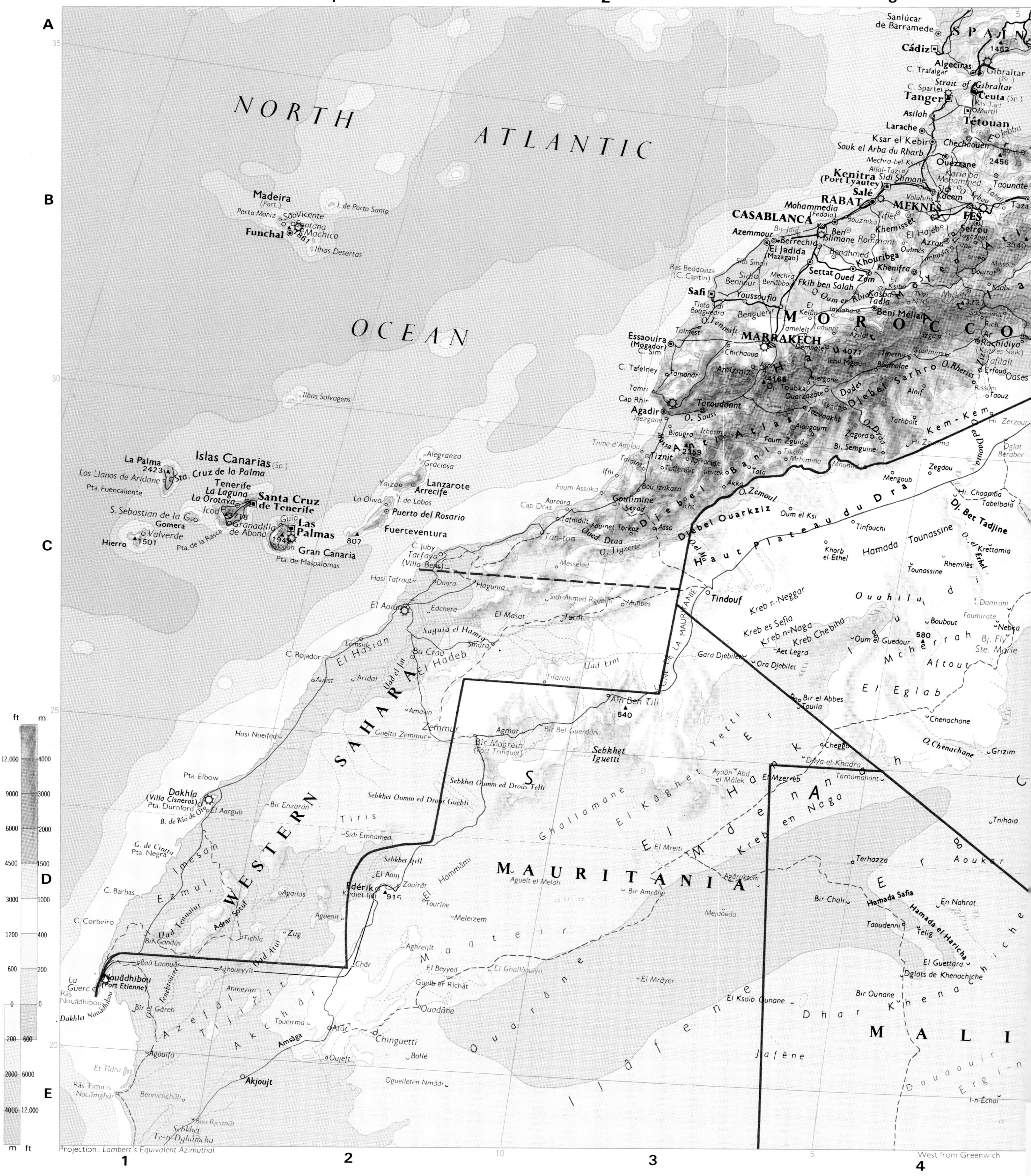

NORTH

ATLANTIC

OCEAN

Madeira (Port.)
Porto Moniz I. de Porto Santo
Santana São Vicente
Funchal Machico
861 Ilhas Desertas

Ilhas Salvagens

Islas Canarias (Sp.)
La Palma 2423
Los Llanos de Aridane Sta. Cruz de la Palma
Tenerife Lanzarote
La Laguna 3718 Arrecife
La Orotava **Santa Cruz de Tenerife**
Pta. Fuencaliente Icod Graciosa
S. Sebastián de la Go. Guia Yaizao Alegranza
Gomera Granadilla de Abona La Oliva I. de Lobos
Valverde 1949 **Las Palmas** **Puerto del Rosario**
Hierro 1501 Pta. de la Rasca 807
Gran Canaria **Fuerteventura**
Pta. de Maspalomas

C. Juby
Tarfaya
(Villa Bens)
Hasi Tafraut
Daora Hagunia
El Aaiún Edchera Sidi Ahmed Rgueibt Manbes
Lemsid Tucat El Masat
C. Bojador Smara Uad Erni
Aarist El Hāsian Bu Craa
Aridal El Hadeb Tifarati
Hadej el Jir

WESTERN SAHARA

Amasin
Zemmur
Guelta Zemmur Agmar Aouinet Torkoz
Bir Mogrein Bir Bel Guerdāne
(Fort Trinquet)
Pta. Elbow Sebkhet Iguetti
Dakhla Sebkhet Oumm ed Drous Telli
(Villa Cisneros) Bir Enzaran Sebkhet Oumm ed Drous Guebli
Pta. Durnford Oro El Aargub
B. de Río de Oro
Tiris
G. de Cintra
Pta. Negra Sebkhet Ijill
El Aouj
Bir el Gareb Fdérik Zouirat
915 Tourine
C. Barbas Aguelt el Melah
Aguelal Agailas

MAURITANIA

C. Corbeiro Meleizem
La Guéra Bir Gandūs Bir Amrane
Nouâdhibou Adrar Aouil Zug Aguénit
(Port Etienne) Char Mejâoūda
Dakhlet Nouâdhibou Ahmeyim
Rás Nouâdhibou El Beyyed
Bir el Gāreb El Ghallouiya
Agouifa Guelb er Richāt
Amsaga Ouadāne
Et Tidra Toueirma
Rás Timiris **Akjoujt** Chinguetti
Nouâmghâr Oujeft
Bennichâb Bôli
Sebkhet Ogueileten Nmâdi
Te-n-Dghâmcha

SPAIN
Sanlúcar de Barrameda
Cádiz Algeciras 1452
C. Trafalgar Gibraltar
C. Spartel Strait of Gibraltar **Ceuta** (Sp.)
Ras Tarf Martil
Tanger **Tétouan**
Asilah Chechaouen Jebha
Larache 2456
Ksar el Kebir Ouezzane
Souk el Arba du Rharb Taounate
Mechra-bel-Ksiri Taza
Kénitra Sidi Slimane
(Port Lyautey) Allal-Tazi **FÈS**
Volubilis Sefrou 3340
Salé **RABAT** **MEKNÈS**
Mohammedia El Hajeb
(Fedala) Azrou
CASABLANCA Khemisset Ifrane
Azemmour Bir Jdid Benahmed Boulmane
El Jadida Settat Oued Zem Midelt
(Mazagan) Khouribga Khenifra Rich
Ras Beddouza Fkih ben Salah Rachidiya
(C. Cantin) Beni Mellal (Ksar es Souk)
Safi Youssoufia Tadla Tafilalt
Tleta Sidi Oum er Rbia Erfoud Oases
Bou Guedra Azilal Rissani
Benguerir **MARRAKECH** Djebel Sarhro
Essaouira Chichaoua 4071 O. Rheriss
(Mogador) C. Sim Ouarzazate Alnif
Tamanar Amizmiz Dadès
Tamri Asni 3165 Zagora Foum Zguid
Cap Rhir Taroudannt 4165 Anergane Bi. Semguine
Agadir Toubkal Mengoub Zegdou
Inezgane Igherm Tata
O. Souss Tinerhir Hi. Chagma
Tine d'Anglou 2359 Foum Zguid Tabelbala
Tiznit Talaint Di. Bet Tadjine
Ifni Tuffermit Kem-Kem Zerzour
Foum Assaka Mrhimina Daoura
Goulimine Akka O. Draa
Seyad Bou Izakarn Oued el Ksi Khorb el Ethel
Cap Draa Assa Hamada Tounassine
Aoreora O. Zemoul Tinfouchi
Tan-tan Haut Plateau du Dra Tounassine
Oued Draa Rhemilès
O. Tigzerte Tindouf Krettamia
Messeled Kreb r. Neggar
Kreb es Sefia Ouahila Damrani
Kreb n-Naga Foumirate
Kreb Chebiha Oum el Guedour 580 Nebka
Aet Legra Bi. Fly
Gara Djebilet Ora Djebilet Mcherrah Ste. Marie
Aftout
Ain Ben Tili Bir el Abbes El Eglab
540 Touila Chenachane
Bir Abbes
Djarf el Khadra Grizim
Chegga Chenachane
Ayoûn Abd Tarhamanant
el Mâlek El Mzerreb
Ghallamane El Kâghet Yetti Terhazza
El Hank Medenane Aoukar
Kreb en Naga
El Mreiti Tniहaia
Agôraktem Bir Chali Hamada Safia
Matġeir En Nahrat
El Beyyed Hamada el Haricha
Taoudenni Telig
Guelb er Richât El Guettara
El Mrâyer El Guettara
Ouarâne Dglats de Khenachiche
El Ksaib Ounane
Bir Ounane **MALI**
Dhar Tichit
Aguelt el Melah Jafène
Ouadāne
Jafène
Ergin
Douaouir
I-n-Échal

ft m
12,000 4000
9000 3000
6000 2000
4500 1500
3000 1000
1200 400
600 200
0 0
200 600
2000 6000
4000 12,000
m ft

1 2 3 4

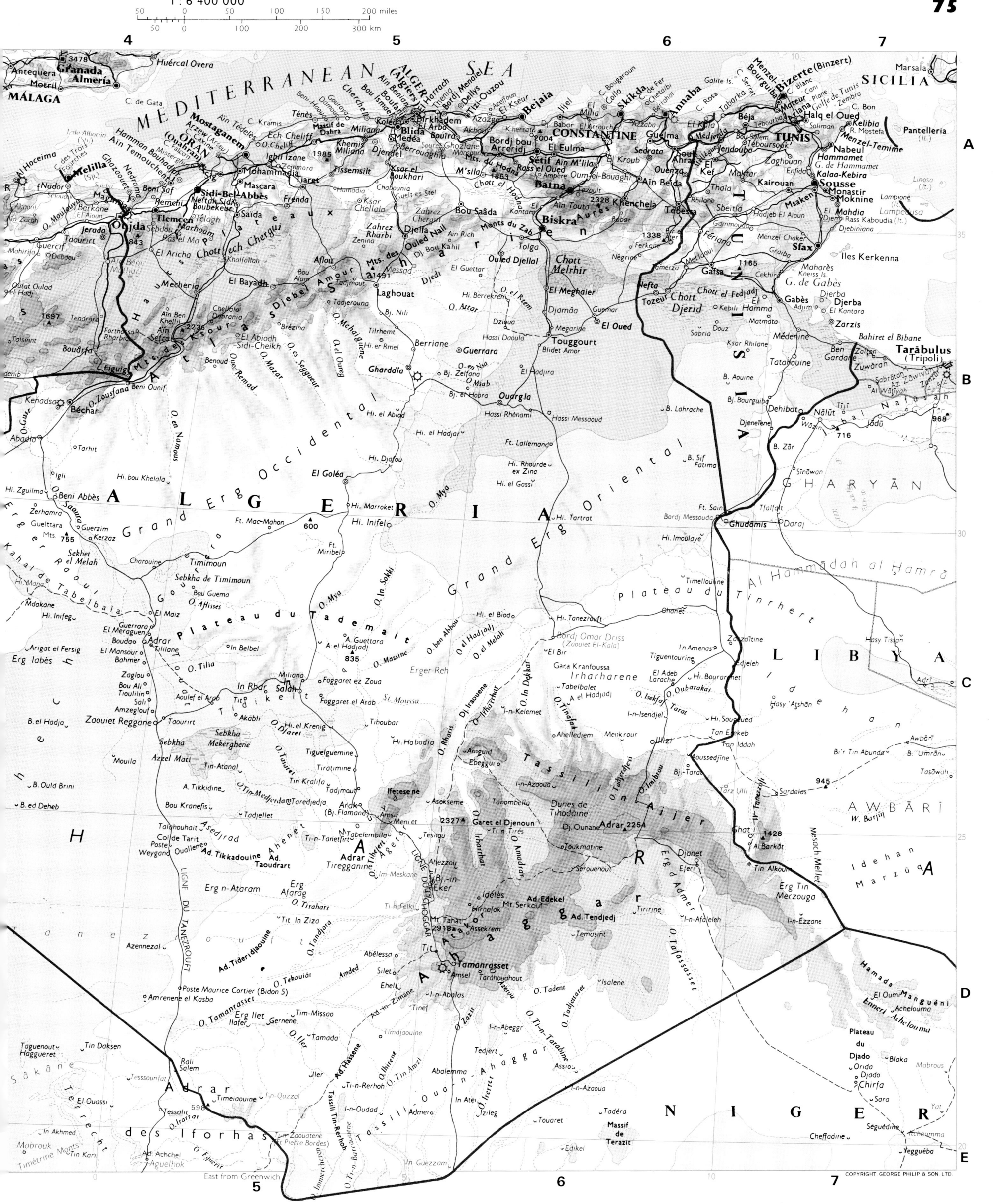

1 : 6 400 000

MEDITERRANEAN SEA

MÁLAGA

ALGERIA

TUNISIA

LIBYA

NIGER

SICILIA

COPYRIGHT. GEORGE PHILIP & SON. LTD

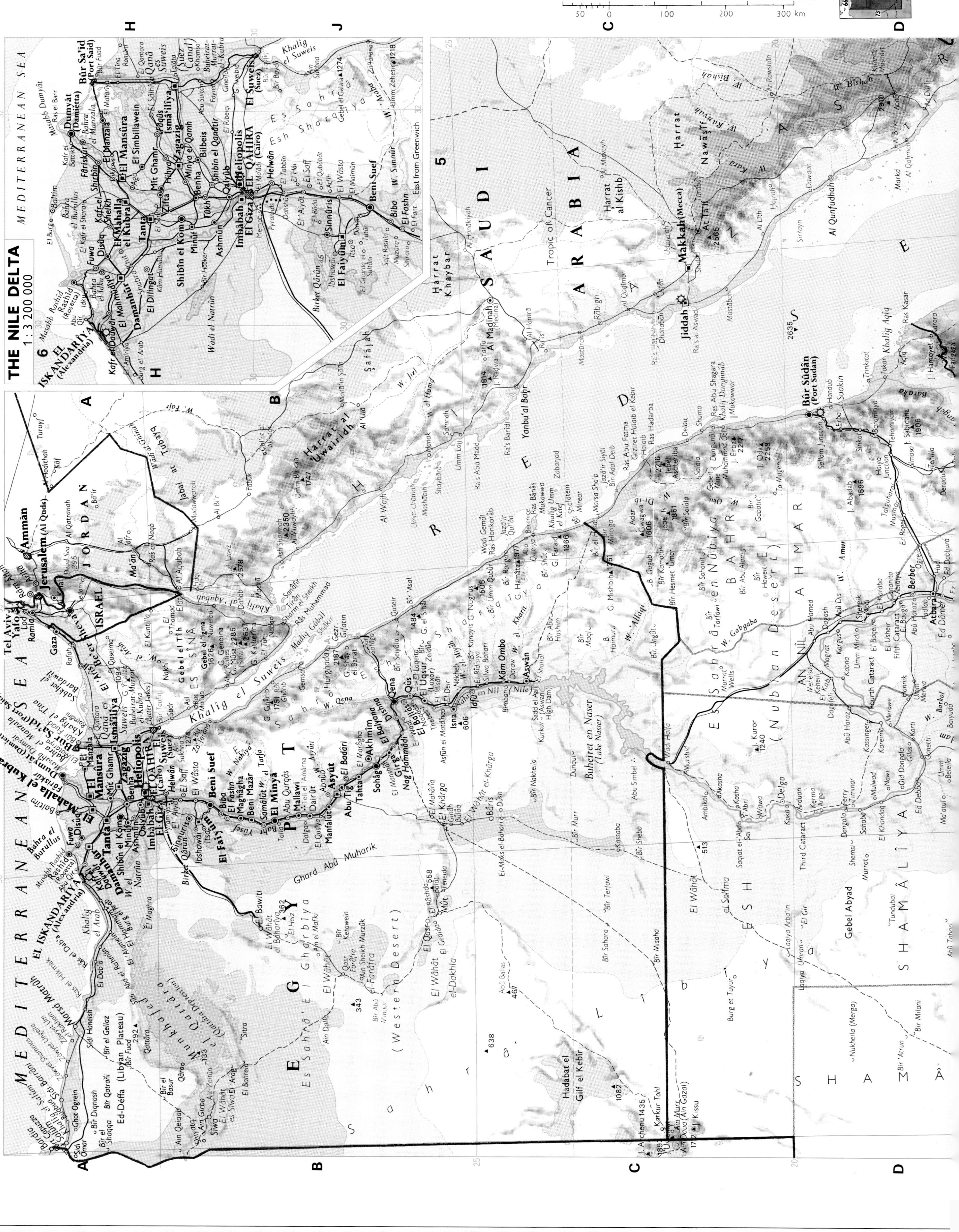

1 : 6 400 000

50 0 50 100 150 200 miles

50 0 100 200 300 km

THE NILE DELTA
1 : 3 200 000

MEDITERRANEAN SEA

MEDITERRANEAN SEA

SAUDI ARABIA

Makkah (Mecca)

Al Madīnah (Medina)

Jiddah

Bûr Sûdân (Port Sudan)

Tropic of Cancer

East from Greenwich

EGYPT

JORDAN

ISRAEL

Amman

Jerusalem (Al Quds)

Tel Aviv-Yafo

Gaza

EL QÂHIRA (Cairo)

EL ISKANDARÎYA (Alexandria)

Bûr Sa'îd (Port Said)

Dumyât (Damietta)

El Mansûra

Tanta

Zagazig

El Faiyûm

Beni Suef

El Minyâ

Asyût

Sohâg

Qena

El Uqsur (Luxor)

Aswân

Kôm Ombo

Buheiret en Naser (Lake Nasser)

Sadd el Aali (Aswan High Dam)

Abu Simbel

AN NÎL

BAHR EL AHMAR

ESH SHAMÂLÎYA

Es Sahrâ' en Nûbîya (Nubian Desert)

Es Sahrâ' el Gharbîya (Western Desert)

Es Sahrâ' esh Sharqîya

Red Sea

Khalîg el 'Aqaba

Khalîg el Suweis (Gulf of Suez)

Suez Canal

El Suweis (Suez)

Ismâ'îlîya

Sinâ

Gebel el Tîh

Gebel Mûsa 2285

Gebel Katharîna 2637

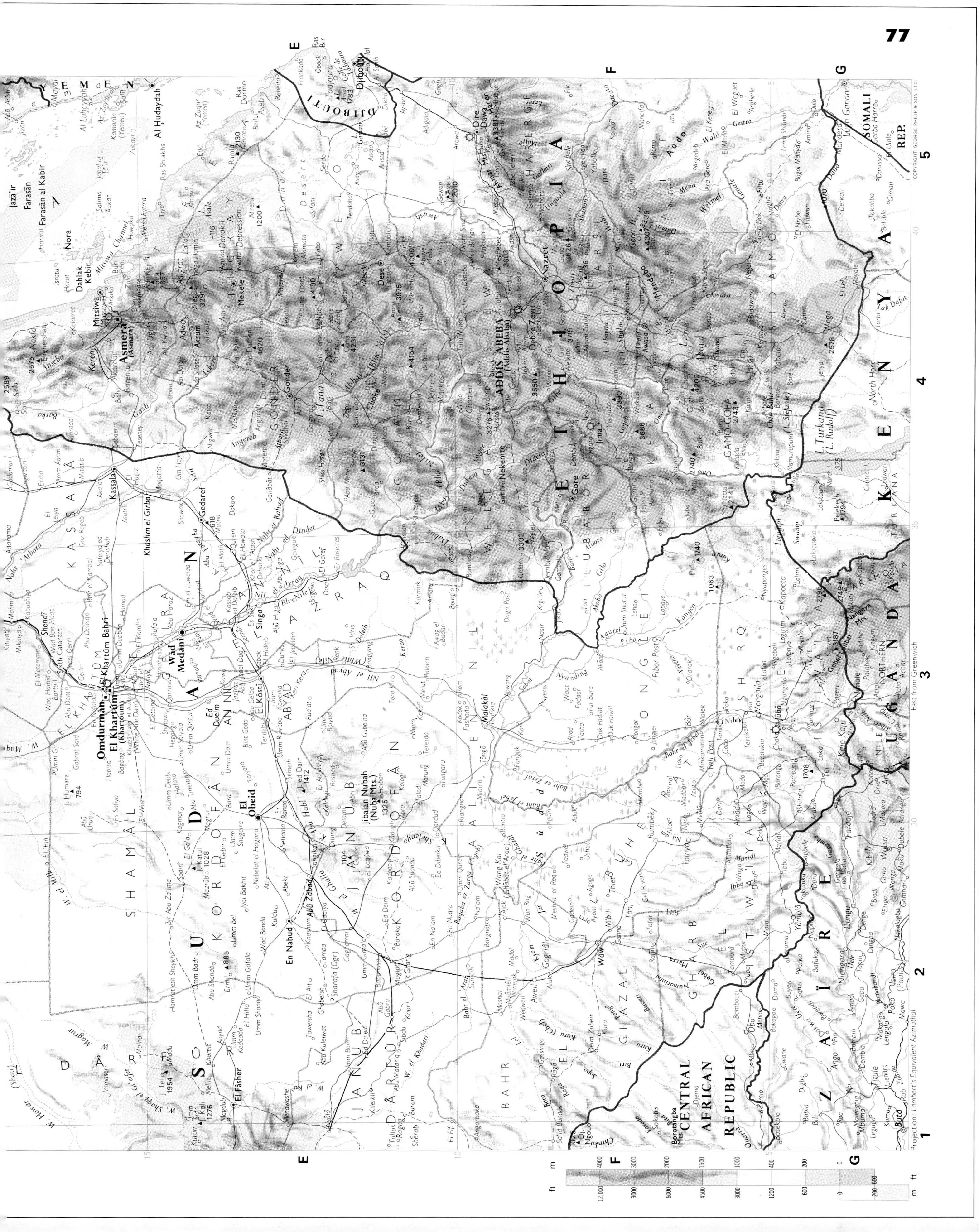

ETHIOPIA

SUDAN

KENYA

UGANDA

ZAÏRE

CENTRAL AFRICAN REPUBLIC

SOMALI REP.

DJIBOUTI

YEMEN

DÂRFÛR

KASSALĀ

KURDUFĀN

GAMO GOFA

SIDAMO

HARERGE

WELO

TIGRA

GONDER

GOJAM

SHEWA

ARSI

BALE

WELEGA

ILUBABOR

KEFA

EL GHAZAL

EL BUHEYRAT

SHARQIYA

Addis Abeba (Addis Ababa)

Asmera (Asmara)

El Khartûm (Khartoum)

Omdurmân

Khartûm Bahri

Wâd Medani

El Obeid

En Nahud

El Fasher

Kassalā

Gedaref

Mekele

Aksum

Gonder

Dese

Nazret

Debre Zeyit

Dire Dawa

Harer

Jima

Gore

Nekemte

Keren

Mitsiwa

Djibouti

Al Hudaydah

Ed Dueim

El Kosti

Malakal

Juba

L. Tana

L. Turkana (L. Rudolf)

Blue Nile (Bahr el Azraq)

White Nile (Bahr el Abyad)

Jibalan Nubah (Nuba Mts.)

Danakil Desert

Danakil Depression

Projection: Lambert's Equivalent Azimuthal

East from Greenwich

COPYRIGHT GEORGE PHILIP & SON LTD

m ft

12,000 9000 6000 4500 3000 1200 600 200 0

4000 3000 2000 1500 1000 400 200 0 m ft 200 600

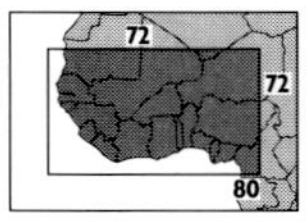

M A U R I T A N I A

Nouakchott

SENEGAL

DAKAR
Rufisque
Thiès
Diourbel
Mbour
Kaolack

Sénégal
St. Louis
Louga

GAMBIA
Banjul
Brikama

GUINEA-
Arquipélago dos Bijagós
BISSAU

Bissau

GUINEA

Conakry

Fouta Djalon

Kankan
Kindia

Boké

SIERRA
LEONE
Freetown
Makeni
Bo

NORTHERN
EASTERN
SOUTHERN
WESTERN

LIBERIA

Monrovia
Buchanan
Paynesville

Grain Coast

MALI

Bamako
Kayes
Koulikoro
Ségou
Sikasso
Bobo-Dioulasso
Mopti
Bandiagara

BURKINA FASO

Koudougou
Ouagadougou

IVORY COAST

Bouaké
Korhogo
Ferkéssédougou
Daloa
Gagnoa
Yamoussoukro
Abidjan
Grand Bassam

Man
Danané

G U L F

West from Greenwich

Projection: Lambert's Equivalent Azimuthal

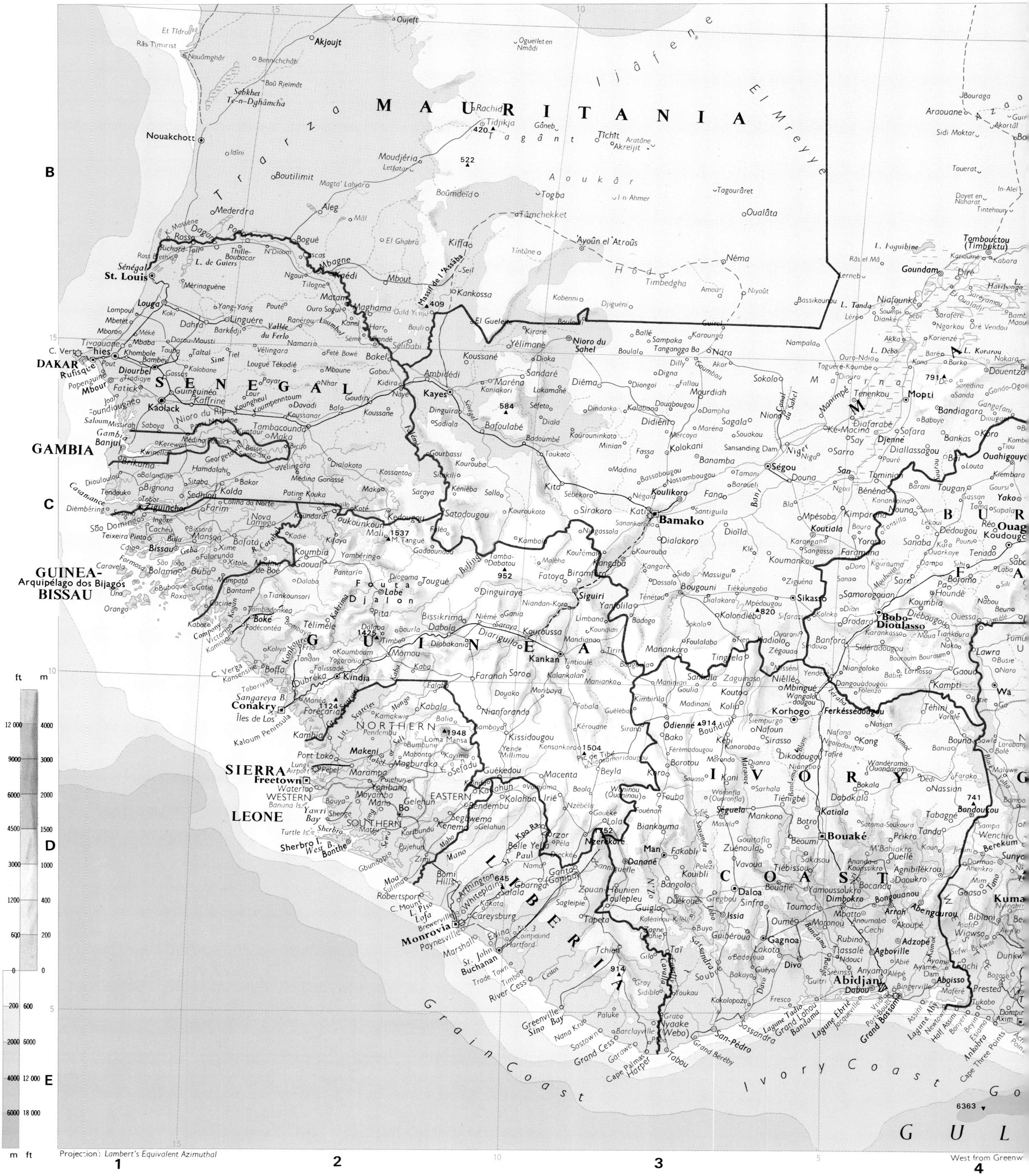

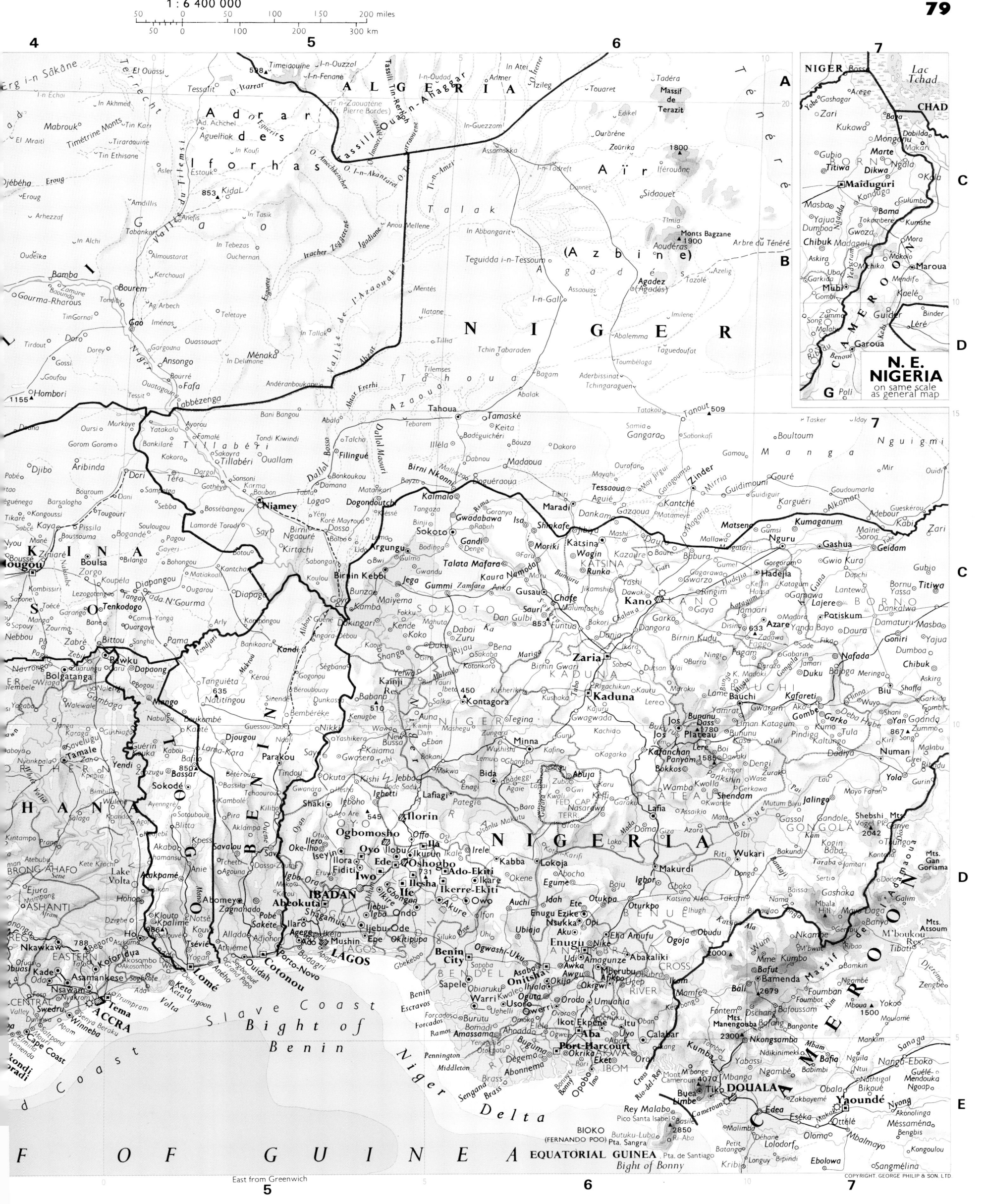

N. E. NIGERIA
on same scale
as general map

COPYRIGHT. GEORGE PHILIP & SON. LTD

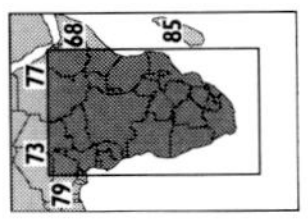

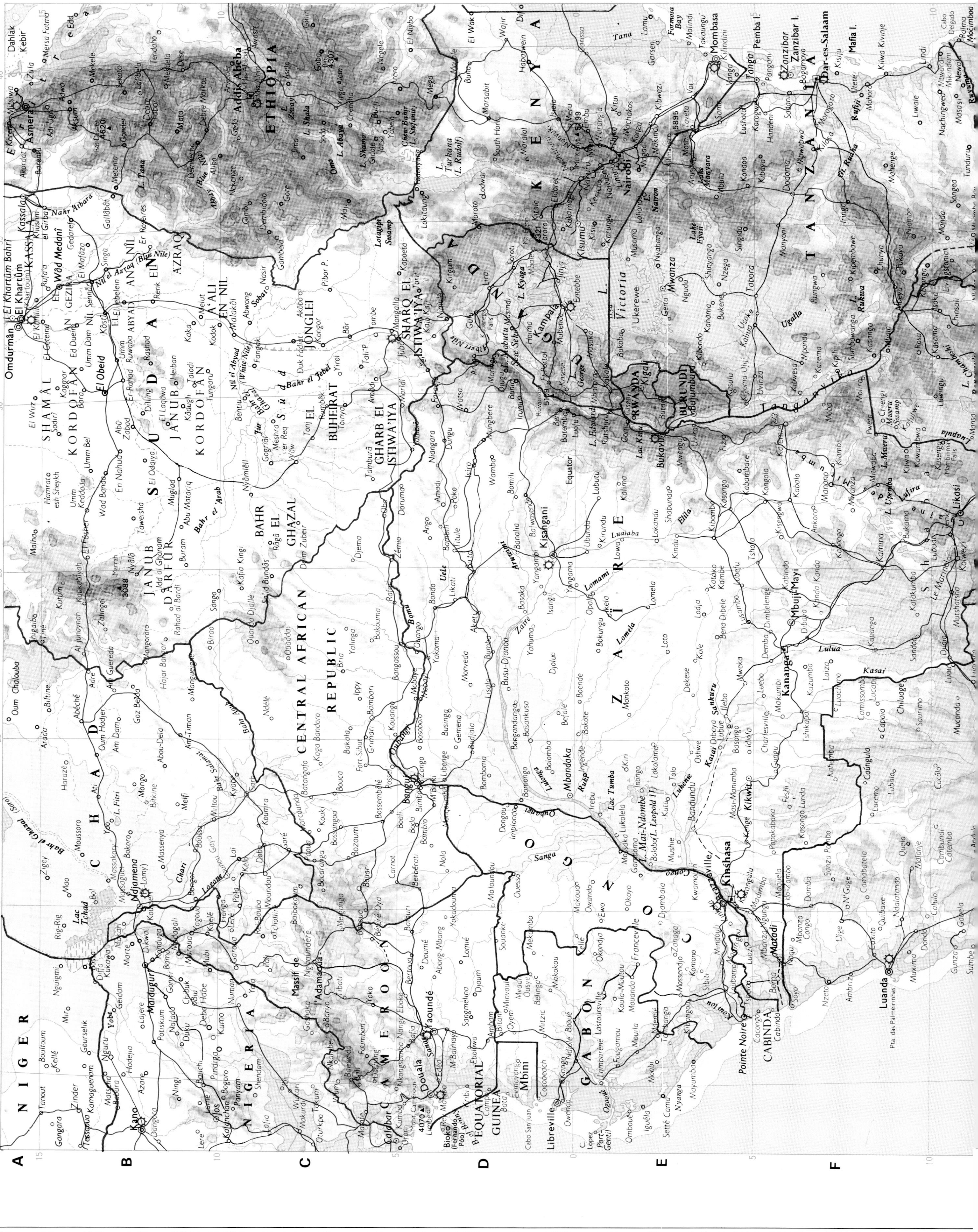

Countries and major features (map labels):

NIGER · NIGERIA · CHAD · CAMEROON · CENTRAL AFRICAN REPUBLIC · SUDAN · ETHIOPIA · KENYA · UGANDA · RWANDA · BURUNDI · TANZANIA · ZAIRE · CONGO · GABON · EQUATORIAL GUINEA · CABINDA · ANGOLA

Regions: SHAMÂL KORDOFAN · JANUB KORDOFAN · JANUB DARFUR · BAHR EL GHAZAL · GHARB EL ISTIWA'IYA · SHARQ EL ISTIWA'IYA · BUHEIRAT · ADAMAOUA

Major cities and places: Asmara · El Khartûm (Khartoum) · Omdurmân · El Khartûm Bahri · Wâd Medani · El Obeid · Addis Abeba · Nairobi · Mombasa · Zanzibar I. · Dar-es-Salaam · Kampala · Kigali · Bujumbura · Bukavu · Kisangani · Ndjamena · Bangui · Douala · Yaoundé · Libreville · Brazzaville · Kinshasa · Luanda · Pointe Noire · Mbandaka · Kikwit · Kananga · Mbuji-Mayi · Lac Tchad

Lakes and rivers: L. Tana · Blue Nile · Nil el Azraq · An Nîl · White Nile · Nil el Abyad · L. Turkana (L. Rudolf) · L. Victoria · L. Kyoga · L. Kivu · L. Tanganyika · L. Rukwa · L. Leopold II (L. Mai-Ndombe) · Zaïre · Lualaba · Kasai · Sankuru · Lomami · Ubangi · Chari · Bahr el Ghazal

Grid references A8 through F1

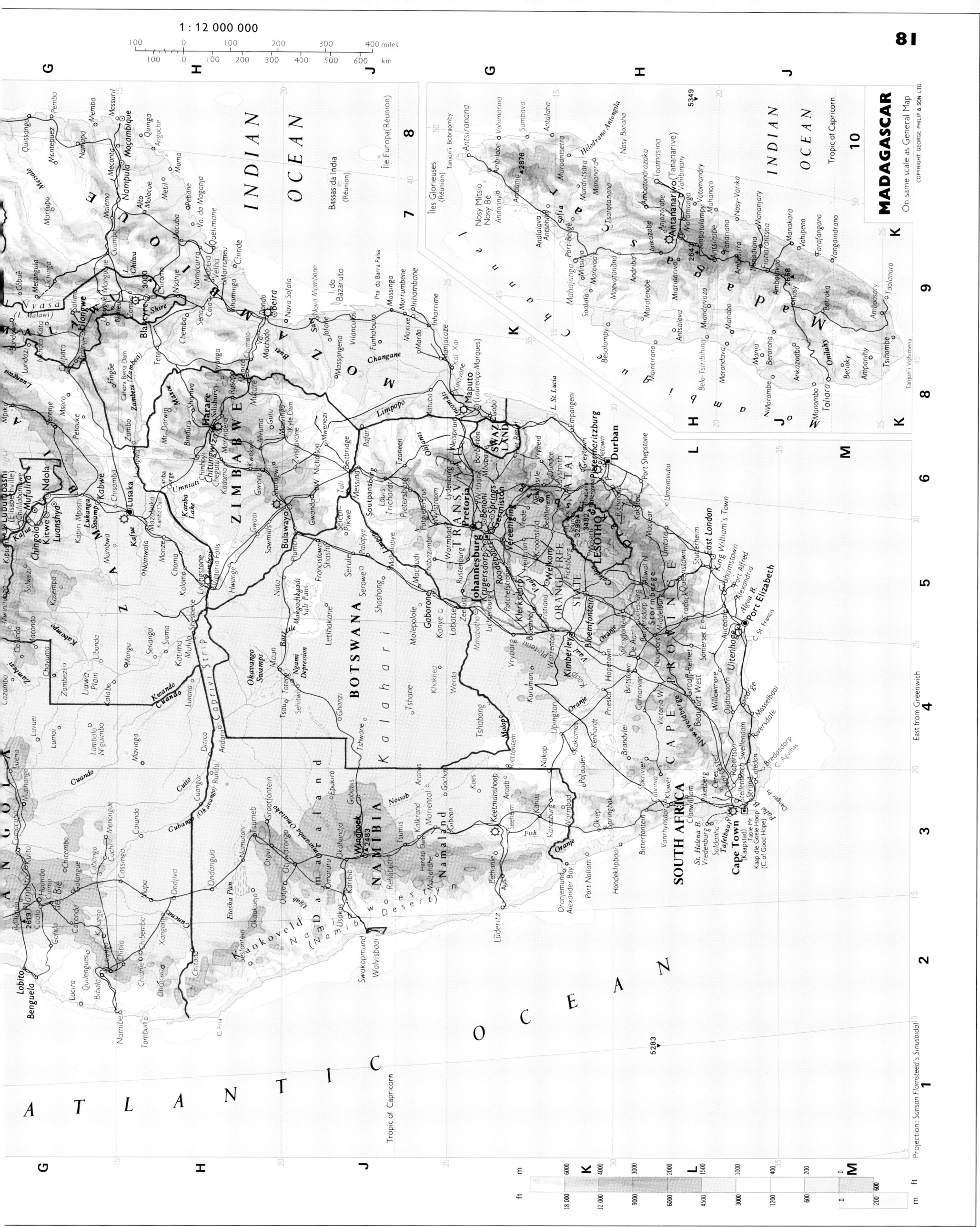

1 : 12 000 000

100   0   100   200   300   400 miles
100   0   100   200   300   400   500   600 km

MADAGASCAR
On same scale as General Map

INDIAN OCEAN

I N D I A N

O C E A N

A T L A N T I C   O C E A N

Tropic of Capricorn

East from Greenwich

Projection: Sanson Flamsteed's Sinusoidal

ANGOLA

NAMIBIA

BOTSWANA

Kalahari

ZIMBABWE

SOUTH AFRICA

CAPE PROVINCE

Cape Town

Durban

MADAGASCAR

Antananarivo (Tananarive)

ft   m
18 000   6000
12 000   4000
        3000
9000   2000
6000   1500
        1000
4500
3000   400
1200   200
600   0
0   m   ft
200   600

K   L   M

ft

m

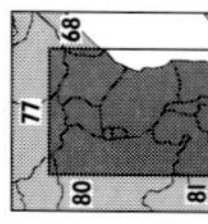

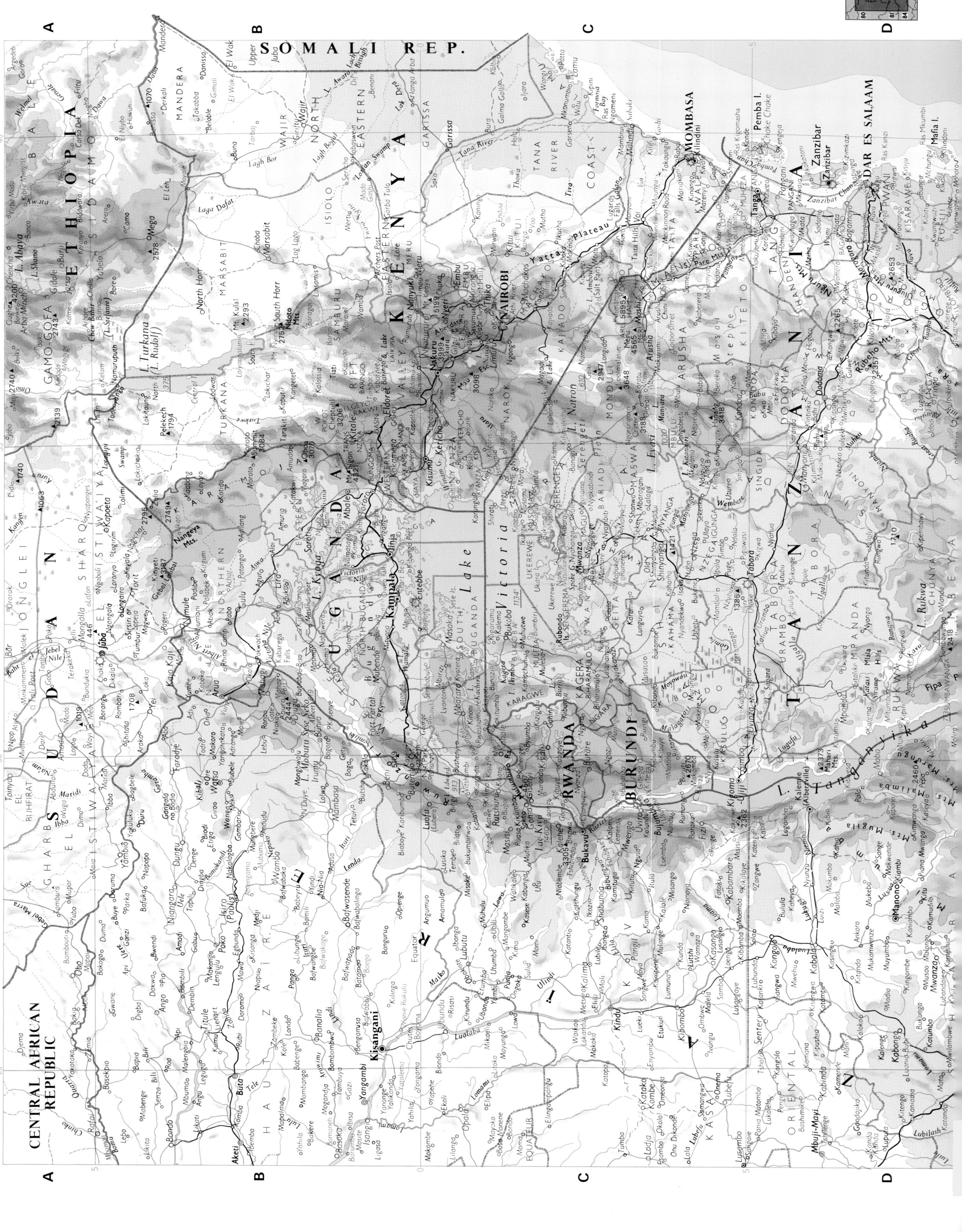

SOMALI REP.

ETHIOPIA

KENYA

UGANDA

TANZANIA

SUDAN

CENTRAL AFRICAN REPUBLIC

ZAIRE

RWANDA

BURUNDI

NAIROBI

MOMBASA

DAR ES SALAAM

Zanzibar

Pemba I.

Mafia I.

Kisangani

Kampala

Entebbe

Jinja

Juba

Lake Victoria

L. Turkana (L. Rudolf)

L. Kyoga

L. Albert

L. Tanganyika

L. Kivu

L. Mobutu Sese Seko

Arusha

Moshi

Tabora

Dodoma

Tanga

Kigoma

Bukavu

EQUATOR

RIFT VALLEY

Nakuru

Meru

Embu

Thika

Kitale

Eldoret

Kisumu

Kericho

Marsabit

Wajir

Garissa

Tana River

COAST

SERENGETI

Zanzibar

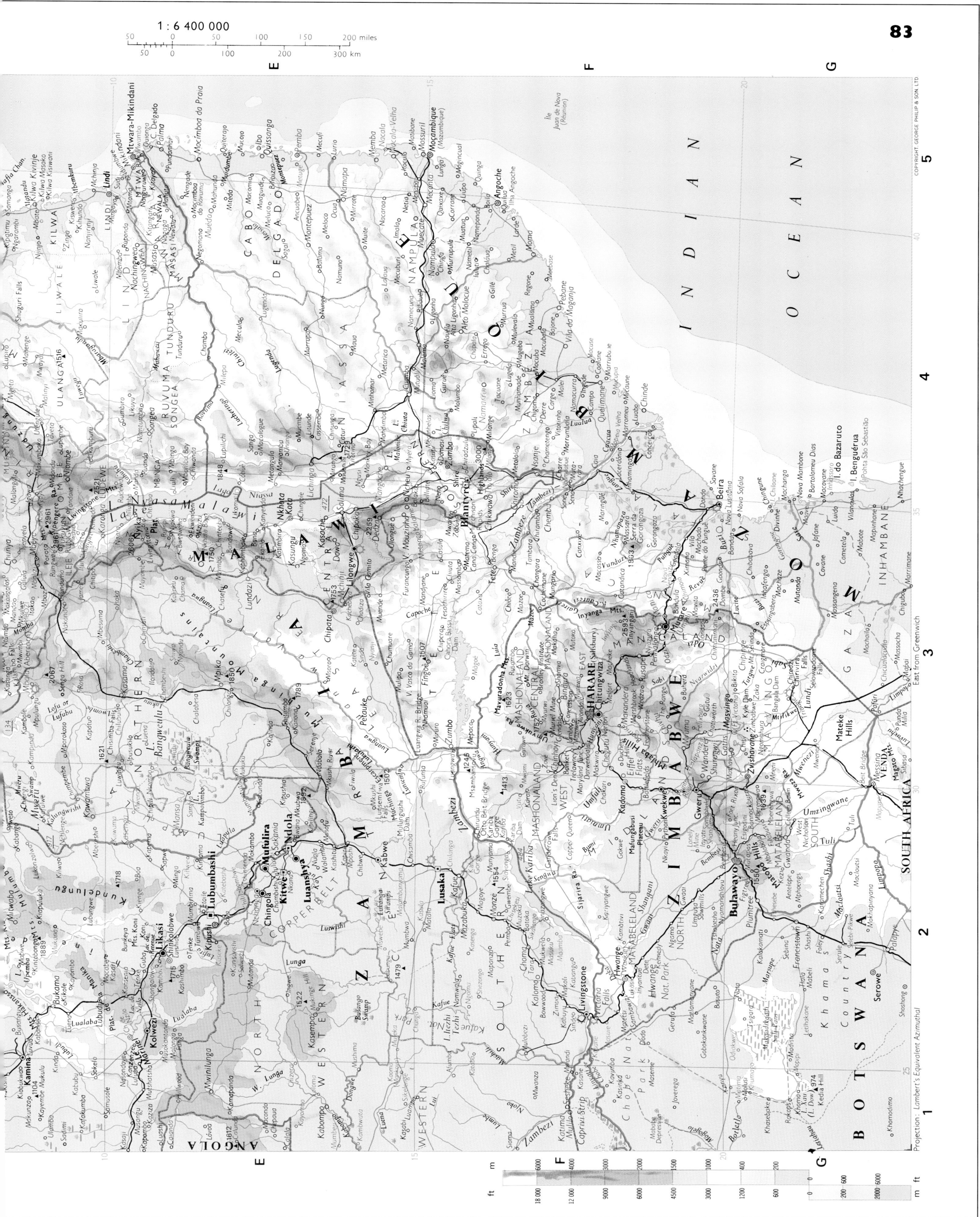

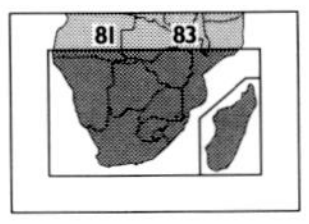

ANGOLA

NAMIBIA

BOTSWANA

SOUTH AFRICA

CAPE PROVINCE

ORANGE FREE STATE

BOPHUTHATSWANA

CISKEI

ZAMBIA

WESTERN

CUANDO CUBANGO

Caprivi Strip

ATLANTIC OCEAN

Tropic of Capricorn

Kalahari

Namaqualand

Damaraland

Namaland

Kaokoveld (Northern Namib)

Namib Desert

Great Karoo

Little Karoo

Okavango Swamps

Khamas Country

Kaukauveld

Sandveld

Projection: Lambert's Equivalent Azimuthal

Livingstone
Victoria Falls
Hwange
Hwange Nat. Park
Chobe Nat. Park

Windhoek
Swakopmund
Walvisbaai (Walvis Bay) (Cape Province)
Keetmanshoop
Lüderitz
Tsumeb
Grootfontein
Otavi
Otjiwarongo
Okahandja
Rehoboth
Mariental
Gobabis

Upington
Kimberley
Bloemfontein
Welkom
Virginia
Kroonstad
Klerksdorp
Krugersdorp
Carletonville
Potchefstroom
Vanderbijl
Vryburg
Mafikeng
Zeerust
Rustenburg
Gaborone
Lobatse
Kanye
Molepolole
Mochudi
Serowe
Palapye
Mahalapye
Maun

Cape Town (Kaapstad)
Stellenbosch
Paarl
Worcester
Table Mt. 1086
Kaap die Goeie Hoop (Cape of Good Hope)
Simonstown
Strand
Somerset West
Swellendam
Mosselbaai
George
Oudtshoorn
Beaufort West
Graaff-Reinet
Cradock
Queenstown
Port Elizabeth
Uitenhage
Port Alfred
Grahamstown
Fort Beaufort
East London
Middelburg
De Aar
Carnarvon
Victoria West
Richmond
Noupoort

Namibe
Ponta Albina
Pta. da Marca
Baynes Mts. 2195
Hartmannberge
Steilrandberge
Joubertberge
Brandberg 2606
Erongo 2350

Tsumeb 2148
Karasberg
Groot Karasberg 2204
Hunsberge 1655

Tsodilo Hill 1300
Ghanzi
L. Dow 1974
Kedia Hill

Oranjemund
Alexander Bay
Port Nolloth
Springbok
Saldanha
Vredenburg

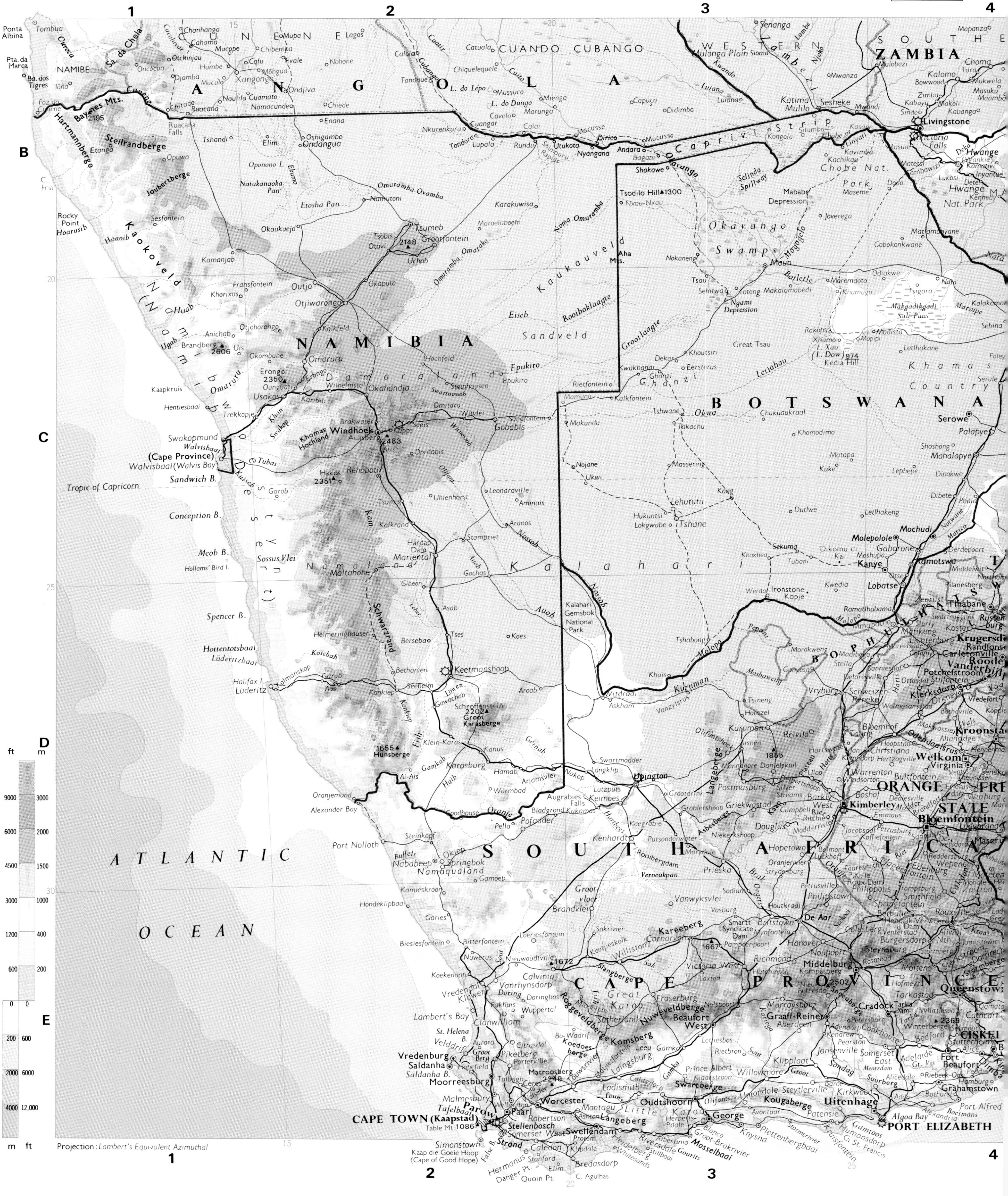

MADAGASCAR

On same scale as General Map

COPYRIGHT. GEORGE PHILIP & SON. LTD.

1 : 32 000 000

Top map (Physical)

Sula Is. · Celebes · Ceram · Buru · Ambon · Banda Sea · 7440 · Tanimbar Is. · Aru Is. · G. of Sarera · Puntjak Djaja 5029 · Maoke Mts. · Sepik · Admiralty Is. · Bismarck Archipelago · New Ireland · New Guinea · New Britain · 9103 · Bougainville · Solomon Is. · Malaita · Guadalcanal · S. Cristobal · Sta. Cruz Is. · Ellice Is. · Rotuma

PACIFIC

Espiritu Santo I. · Mallikolo I. · New Hebrides · 7570 · Loyalty Is. · Vanua Levu · Fiji Is. · Viti Levu · Samoa Is. · Savaii · Upolu

Flores Sea · Sumbawa · Flores · Timor · Sumba · Timor Sea · INDIAN OCEAN · N.W. Cape · Ashburton · Gascoyne · Shark Bay · Geographe B. · C. Naturaliste · C. Leeuwin · Darling Ra. · Mt. Bruce 1227 · Musgrave Ra. · Macdonnell Ra.

Arafura Sea · Thursday I. · Torres Str. · C. York · C. Arnhem · Gulf of Carpentaria · Melville I. · Arnhem L. · King Sound · Fitzroy · L. Woods · Tanami Desert · Barkly Tableland · Flinders · Victoria · L. Mackay · L. Disappointment · L. Amadeus

C. York Pen. · Great Barrier Reef · Great Dividing Ra. · Coral Sea · Chesterfield Is. · G. of Papua · Owen Stanley Ra. · Fly · D'Entrecasteaux Arch. · Louisiade Arch. · New Caledonia

AUSTRALIA · L. Eyre · Cooper Cr. · Warrego · L. Frome · L. Torrens · Darling · Lachlan · Darling Downs · New England Ra. · C. Byron · Hervey B. · Sandy C. · Gt. Sandy I. · Botany B. · Norfolk I. · Lord Howe I. · Tropic of Capricorn · Tongatabu I. · Tonga Is. (Friendly) · 10 822

OCEAN · Kermadec Is. · 10 047

L. Barlee · Nullarbor Plain · Eyre Pen. · Gardner · Flinders Ras. · Spencer Gulf · Kangaroo I. · Encounter B. · Murray · Australian Alps · Mt. Kosciusko 2230 · C. Howe · Three Kings I. · North C.

Great Australian Bight · P. Phillip · King I. · Bass Strait · Flinders I. · South C. · TASMANIA · Tasman Sea · SOUTH I. · Southern Alps · Mt. Cook 3764 · NEW ZEALAND · NORTH I. · Mt. Egmont · L. Taupo · R. Ruapehu · Hawke B. · B. of Plenty · Cook Strait · East C. · Stewart I. · Canterbury Bight · Chatham I.

Bottom map (Political)

INDONESIA · Ujung Pandang · Celebes · Buru · Ceram · Sula Is. · Banda Sea · Aru Is. · Tanimbar Is. · IRIAN JAYA · New Guinea · Papua · Fly · Torres Str. · Port Moresby · Madang · Lae · New Britain · Rabaul · New Ireland · PAPUA NEW GUINEA · Choiseul · Ysabel · Bougainville · SOLOMON IS. · Honiara · Guadalcanal · Malaita · S. Cristobal · Sta. Cruz Is. · KIRIBATI · Funafuti · TUVALU · Tokelau Is. (N.Z.)

Flores Sea · Sumbawa · Flores · Timor · Kupang · Sumba · Timor Sea · Arafura Sea · Darwin · Katherine · Gulf of Carpentaria · Coral Sea Islands Territory · Espiritu Santo · Rotuma · Vila · VANUATU · WESTERN SAMOA · Savaii · Upolu · Apia · AMER. SAMOA

Wyndham · Broome · NORTHERN TERRITORY · Cooktown · Cairns · Townsville · QUEENSLAND · Charters Towers · Mt. Isa · Chesterfield Is. (Fr.) · New Caledonia (Fr.) · Loyalty Is. (Fr.) · Nouméa · Vila · Vanua Levu · FIJI · Viti Levu · Suva · TONGA (Friendly)

Dampier · Onslow · WESTERN AUSTRALIA · Alice Springs · Longreach · Rockhampton · Toowoomba · Charleville · Quilpie · Cunnamulla · Warwick · Brisbane · PACIFIC · Tropic of Capricorn · Norfolk I. (Aust.) · Nuku'alofa

Geraldton · Wiluna · Laverton · Oodnadatta · L. Eyre · SOUTH AUSTRALIA · Darling · Bourke · NEW SOUTH WALES · Broken Hill · Hay · Newcastle · Sydney · Goulburn · Lord Howe I. (Aust.) · Kermadec Is. (N.Z.)

Kalgoorlie–Boulder · P. Pirie · Mildura · Murray · Canberra · OCEAN

Perth · Fremantle · Esperance · Great Australian Bight · Adelaide · Bendigo · Ballarat · VICTORIA · Geelong · Melbourne · King I. · Bass Strait · Launceston · Tasman Sea · NORTH I. · Auckland · Hamilton · New Plymouth · Wellington · Napier · International Date Line

Albany · TASMANIA · Hobart · SOUTH I. · Greymouth · Nelson · NEW ZEALAND · Chatham I.

Invercargill · Dunedin · Christchurch

Vila Capital Cities

Projection: Bonne · East from Greenwich · West from Greenwich · COPYRIGHT GEORGE PHILIP & SON LTD.

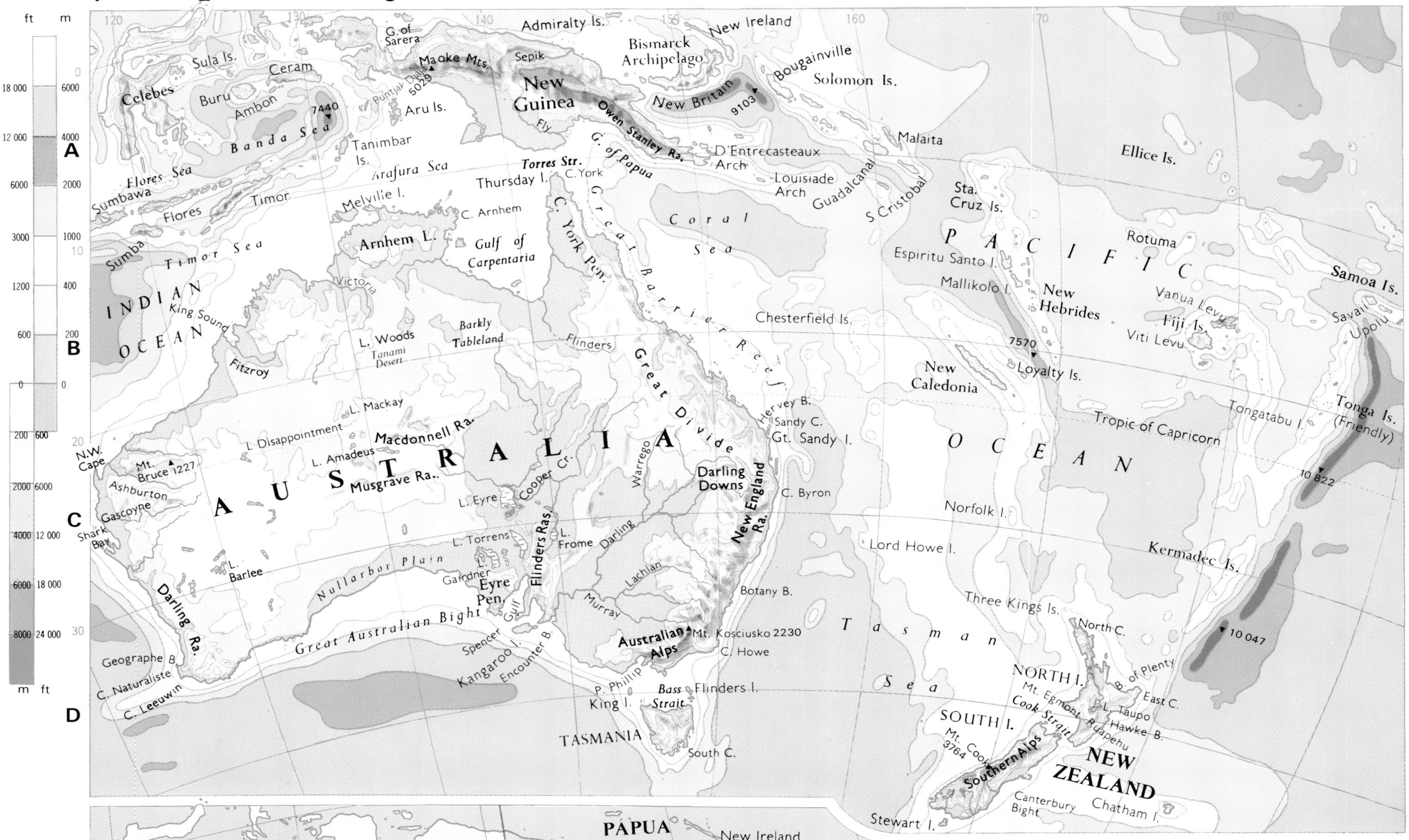

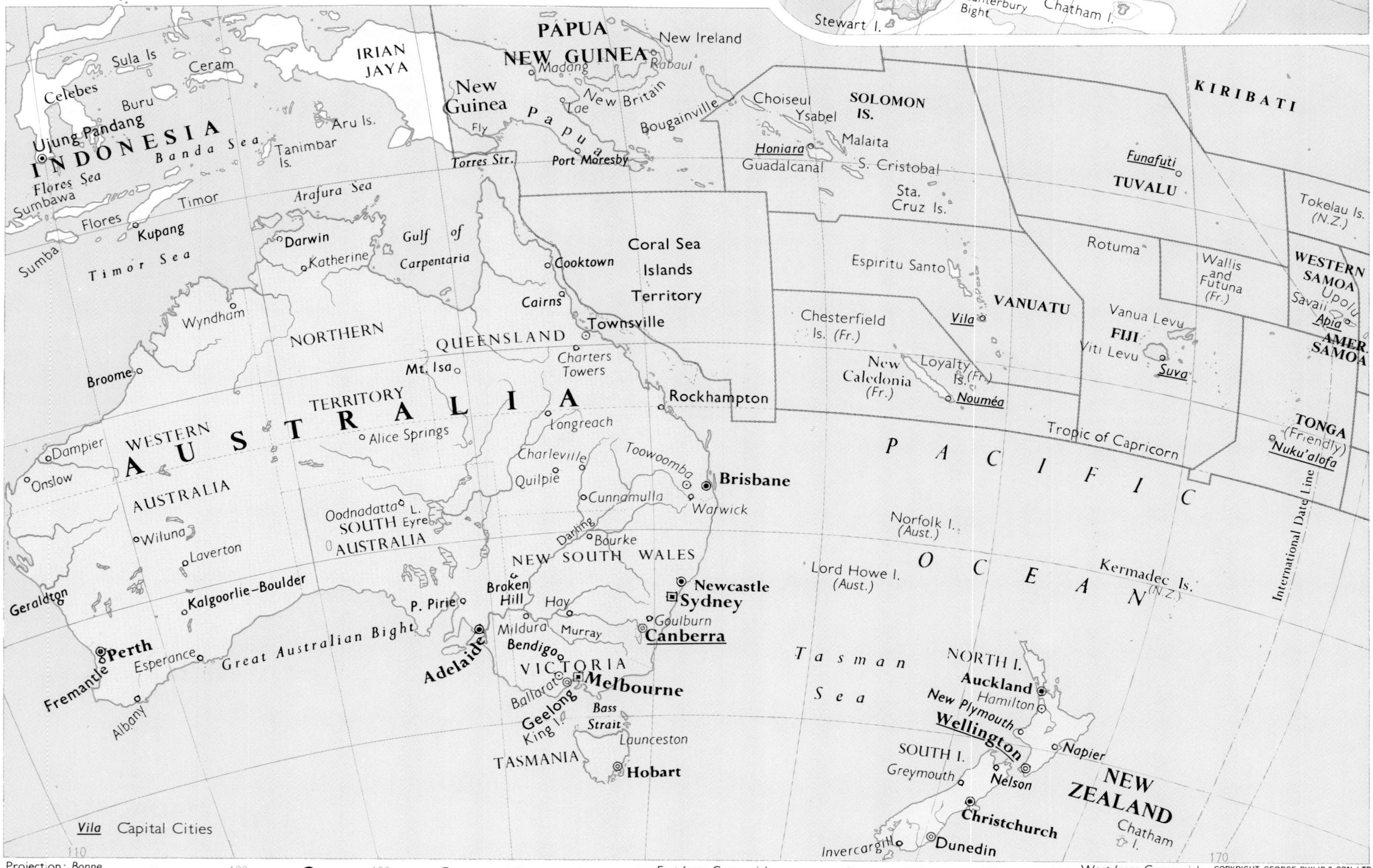

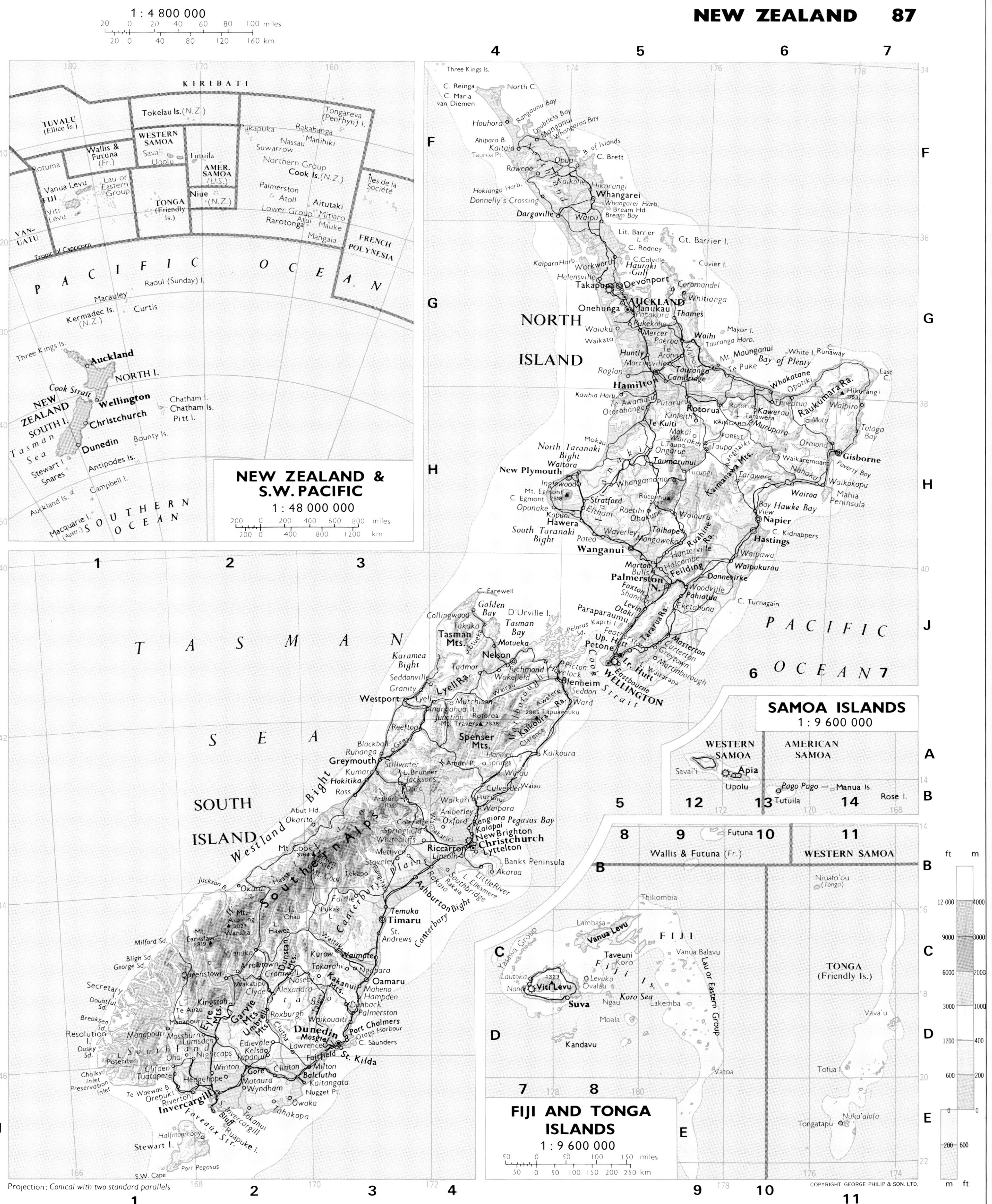

1 : 4 800 000

20 0 20 40 60 80 100 miles
20 0 40 80 120 160 km

KIRIBATI

TUVALU
(Ellice Is.)

Tokelau Is.(N.Z.)

WESTERN
SAMOA

Wallis &
Futuna
(Fr.)

Rotuma

Savaii Upolu
Tutuila
AMER.
SAMOA
(U.S.)

Vanua Levu

FIJI
Viti Levu

Lau or
Eastern
Group

TONGA
(Friendly
Is.)

Niue
(N.Z.)

Tongareva
(Penrhyn) I.

Pukapuka
Rakahanga
Nassau Manihiki
Suwarrow

Northern Group
Cook Is.(N.Z.)

Palmerston
Atoll

Aitutaki
Lower Group Mitiaro
Atui Mauke
Rarotonga

Mangaia

Îles de la
Société

FRENCH
POLYNESIA

VAN-
UATU

Tropic of Capricorn

P A C I F I C   O C E A N

Macauley
Raoul (Sunday) I.

Kermadec Is.
(N.Z.)
Curtis

Three Kings I.
Auckland
NORTH I.

NEW
ZEALAND
SOUTH I.

Cook Strait
Wellington

Christchurch

Chatham I.
Chatham Is.
Pitt I.

Dunedin

Tasman
Sea

Stewart I.
Snares
Antipodes Is.

Bounty Is.

Auckland Is.
Campbell I.

Macquarie I.
(Austr.)

S O U T H E R N   O C E A N

**NEW ZEALAND &
S.W. PACIFIC**
1 : 48 000 000

200 0 200 400 600 800 miles
200 0 400 800 1200 km

NORTH
ISLAND

Three Kings Is.
C. Reinga North C.
C. Maria
van Diemen
Houhora
Rangaunu Bay
Doubtless Bay
Mongonui Whangaroa Bay
Ahipara B.
Kaitaia B. of Islands
Tauroa Pt. C. Brett
Rawene Opua
Hokianga Harb. Kaikohe Hikurangi
Donnelly's Crossing Whangarei
Dargaville Whangarei Harb.
Waipu Bream Hd.
Bream Bay
Lit. Barr. I.
Gt. Barrier I.
C. Rodney
Kaipara Harb. C.Colville
Warkworth Cuvier I.
Helensville Hauraki Coromandel
Takapuna Gulf Whitianga
Devonport
AUCKLAND
Onehunga Manukau Thames
Papakura
Pukekohe Mayor I.
Waiuku Mercer Waihi
Waikato Paeroa Tauranga Harb.
Huntly Te Bay of Plenty
Raglan Aroha Tauranga White I. C. Runaway
Morrinsville Te Puke Whakatane East
Kawhia Harb. Hamilton Cambridge Opotiki C.
Te Awamutu Kawerau Raukumara Ra.
Putaruru Rotorua Tarawera Whangaparaoa Hikurangi
Otorohanga Kinleith Murupara Waipiro
North Taranaki Te Kuiti KAINGAROA Tolaga
Bight Mokau FOREST Bay
Waitara Mangakino L.Taupo Motu
New Plymouth Taumarunui Waikaremoana Gisborne
Inglewood Whangamomona Turangi Nuhaka Poverty Bay
Mt.Egmont Ruapehu Kaimanawa Mts. Waikokopu
C. Egmont Stratford Waiouru Wairoa Mahia
Opunake Eltham Raetihi Tarawera Peninsula
Kapuni Ohakune Bay Hawke Bay
Hawera Taihape Napier
South Taranaki Waverley Mangaweka Hastings
Bight Patea Hunterville Waipawa
Wanganui Marton Feilding Waipukurau
Bulls Holcombe Woodville C. Kidnappers
Palmerston N. Dannevirke
Foxton Shannon Pahiatua C. Turnagain
Levin Otaki Woodville
Paraparaumu Eketahuna
Up. Hutt Masterton
Lr. Hutt Carterton
Petone WELLINGTON Greytown Martinborough
Eastbourne Featherston
Strait

PACIFIC

OCEAN

C. Farewell
Golden Bay
Collingwood D'Urville I.
Takaka Tasman
Tasman Bay
Mts. Motueka
Nelson
Karamea Tadmor Richmond
Bight Picton
Seddonville Havelock
Granity Lyell Ra. Pelorus Sd.
Westport Murchison Wairau Blenheim
Lyell Inangahua Seddon
Junction Ward
Reefton Mt. Travers
Blackball Grey Clarence
Runanga Spenser
Greymouth Mts. Hanmer Kaikoura
Stillwater Springs
Kumara L. Brunner Arthur's P. Waiau
Hokitika Jacksons Culverden Waiau
Ross Arthur's Pegasus Bay
Pass Waikari
Amberley Waipara
Abut Hd. Oxford Rangiora Kaiapoi
Okarito Coalgate New Brighton
Springfield Christchurch
WESTLAND Whitecliffs Lyttelton
Riccarton Lincoln
Mt. Cook Staveley Banks Peninsula
Methven Akaroa
Jackson B. Okuru L. Coleridge
Mt. Cook L. Ellesmere
Haast Fairlie Rakaia Southbridge
Southern Alps Pukaki L. Little River
Hawea Tekapo
Temuka
Timaru
Wanaka St. Canterbury
Milford Sd. Mt. Aspiring Andrews Bight
Mt. Earnslaw Cromwell Waitaki
Wanaka
Arrowtown Kurow
Queenstown Clyde Naseby Oamaru
Te Anau Alexandra Maheno
Wakatipu Roxburgh Hampden
Manapouri Dunback
Te Anau Palmerston
Kingston Ettrick
Lumsden Clutha Waikouaiti
Mossburn Edievale Port Chalmers
Secretary I. Ohai Kelso Lawrence Otago Harbour
Doubtful Winton Tapanui Dunedin
Sd. Clinton Mosgiel
Breaksea Sd. Nightcaps Milton St. Kilda
Resolution I. Clinton Fairfield C. Saunders
Dusky Sd. Riverton Gore Balclutha
Chalky Inlet Invercargill Mataura Kaitangata
Preservation Te Waewae B. Edendale Wyndham Nugget Pt.
Inlet Orepuki Kapuka
Tuatapere Owaka
Invercargill Tokanui
Bluff Ruapuke I.
Foveaux Str.
Stewart I.
Halfmoon Bay
Port Pegasus
S.W. Cape

TASMAN SEA

SOUTH
ISLAND

Westland Bight

SAMOA ISLANDS
1 : 9 600 000

WESTERN
SAMOA
AMERICAN
SAMOA

Savai'i Apia
Upolu Pago Pago Manua Is.
Tutuila Rose I.

**FIJI AND TONGA
ISLANDS**
1 : 9 600 000

50 0 50 100 150 miles
50 0 50 100 150 200 250 km

Wallis & Futuna (Fr.)
Futuna
WESTERN SAMOA

Niuafo'ou
(Tonga)

Thikombia
Lambasa
Vanua Levu
Taveuni FIJI
Yasawa Group Koro Vanua Balavu
Lautoka Levuka
Nana Viti Levu Ovalau Fiji Is. Lau or Eastern Group
Suva Ngau Lakemba
Koro Sea
Moala
TONGA
(Friendly Is.)
Kandavu
Vatoa
Vava'u
Tofua I.
Tongatapu Nuku'alofa

Projection: Conical with two standard parallels

COPYRIGHT. GEORGE PHILIP & SON. LTD.

ft m
12 000 4000
9000 3000
6000 2000
3000 1000
1200 400
600 200
0 0
200 600
m ft

NORTHERN TERRITORY

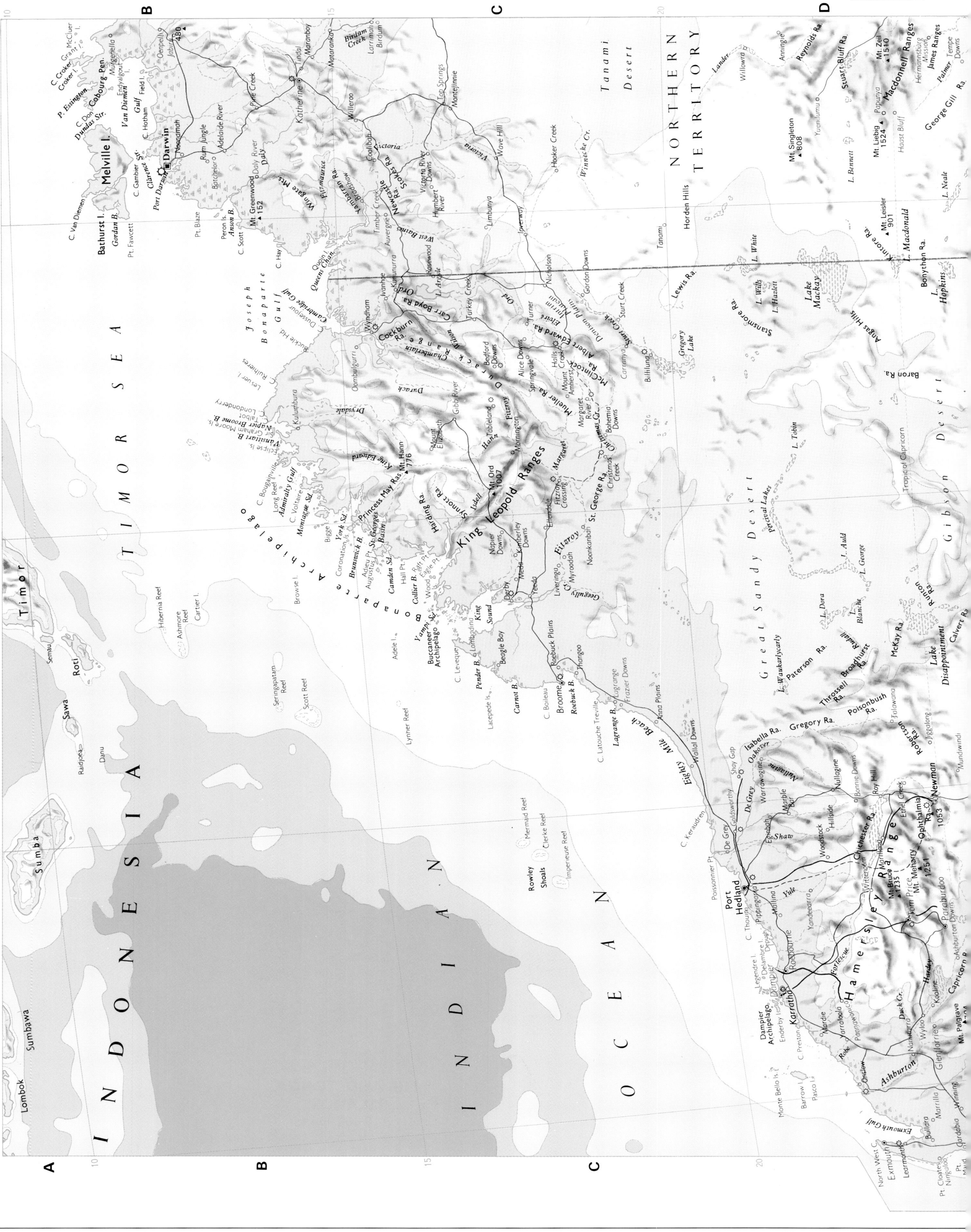

INDONESIA

TIMOR SEA

INDIAN OCEAN

Timor

Sumba

Sumbawa

Lombok

Roti

Sawu

Melville I.

Bathurst I.

Darwin

Joseph Bonaparte Gulf

Cambridge Gulf

Bonaparte Archipelago

King Leopold Ranges

Durack Ra.

Carr Boyd Ra.

Chamberlain Ra.

Black Ra.

McCrinloch Ra.

Mueller Ra.

Stansmore Ra.

Baron Ra.

Great Sandy Desert

Gibson Desert

Tanami Desert

Macdonnell Ranges

James Ranges

Reynolds Ra.

Mt. Zeil 1510

Mt. Liebig 1524

Mt. Leisler 901

Mt. Singleton 808

Lake Mackay

L. White

L. Auld

L. Disappointment

Lake Dora

L. Blanche

Throssell Ra.

Broadhurst Ra.

McKay Ra.

Paterson Ra.

Calvert Ra.

Hamersley Range

Chichester Ra.

Ophthalmia Ra. 1053

Mt. Meharry 1251

Mt. Bruce 1235

Isabella Ra.

Gregory Ra.

Port Hedland

Broome

Roebuck Plains

Eighty Mile Beach

Ninety Mile Beach

Dampier Archipelago

Karratha

Ashburton

Exmouth Gulf

Monte Bello Is.

Barrow I.

Fitzroy

King Sound

Yampi Sd.

Buccaneer Archipelago

C. Leveque

Derby

Admiralty Gulf

Princess May Ra.

Mt. Hann 776

Mt. Ord 1007

Wyndham

Kununurra

Argyle

Halls Creek

Tropic of Capricorn

Scott Reef

Ashmore Reef

Hibernia Reef

Cartier I.

Rowley Shoals

Mermaid Reef

Clerke Reef

Imperieuse Reef

Lynher Reef

Long Reef

Adele I.

Lacepede Is.

Pine Creek

Katherine

Victoria River

Daly River

Wave Hill

Hooker Creek

Egg Springs

Horden Hills

Angas Hills

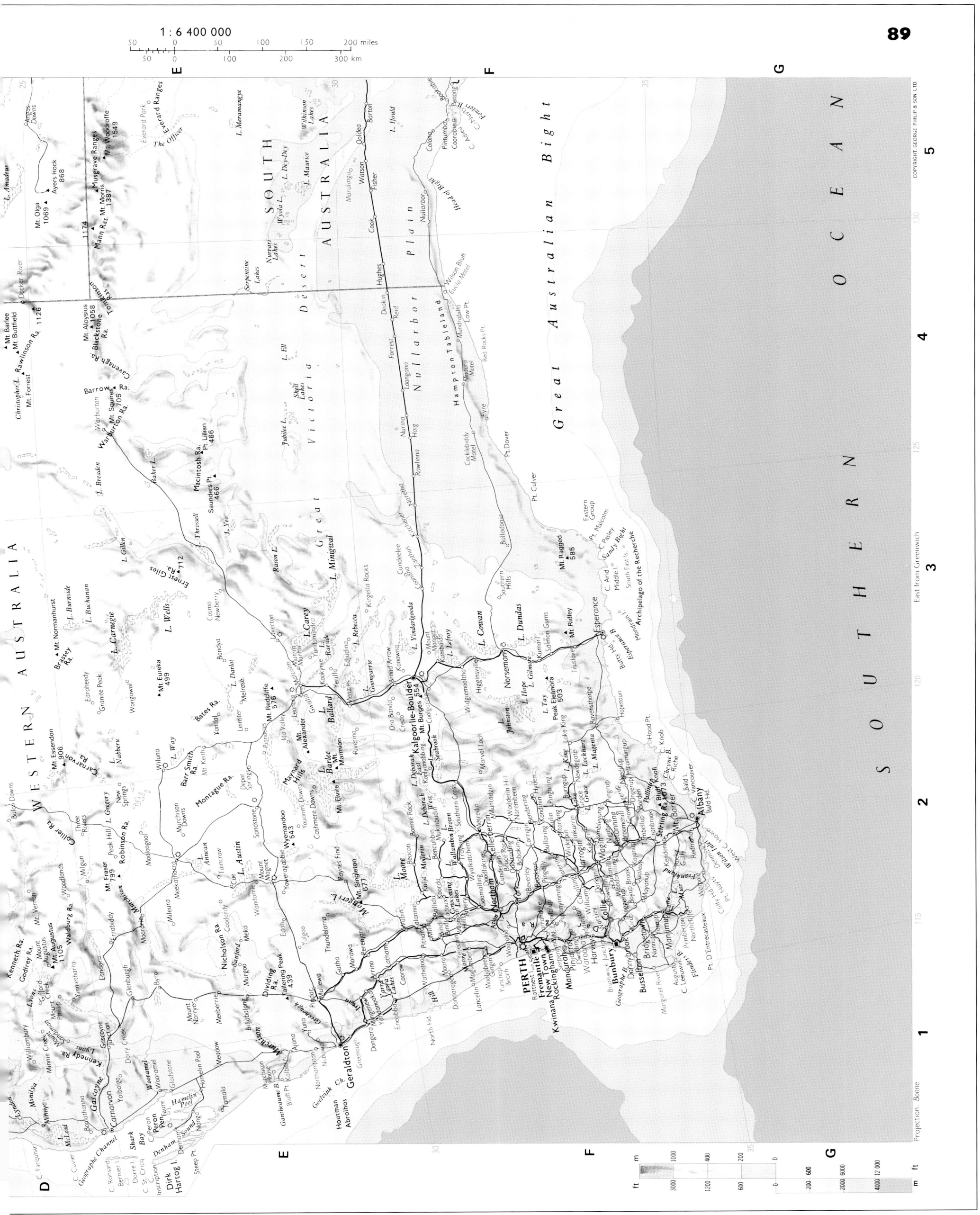

1 : 6 400 000

50   0   50   100   150   200 miles

50   0   100   200   300 km

Projection, Bonne

COPYRIGHT GEORGE PHILIP & SON LTD

East from Greenwich

WESTERN AUSTRALIA

SOUTH

AUSTRALIA

Great Victoria Desert

Nullarbor Plain

Hampton Tableland

Great Australian Bight

SOUTHERN OCEAN

PERTH

Fremantle

Albany

Esperance

Kalgoorlie-Boulder

Geraldton

Carnarvon

ft   m
12 000   4000
6000   2000
2000   600
600   200
0   0
-200   -200
600   ...
1200   ...
3000   1000

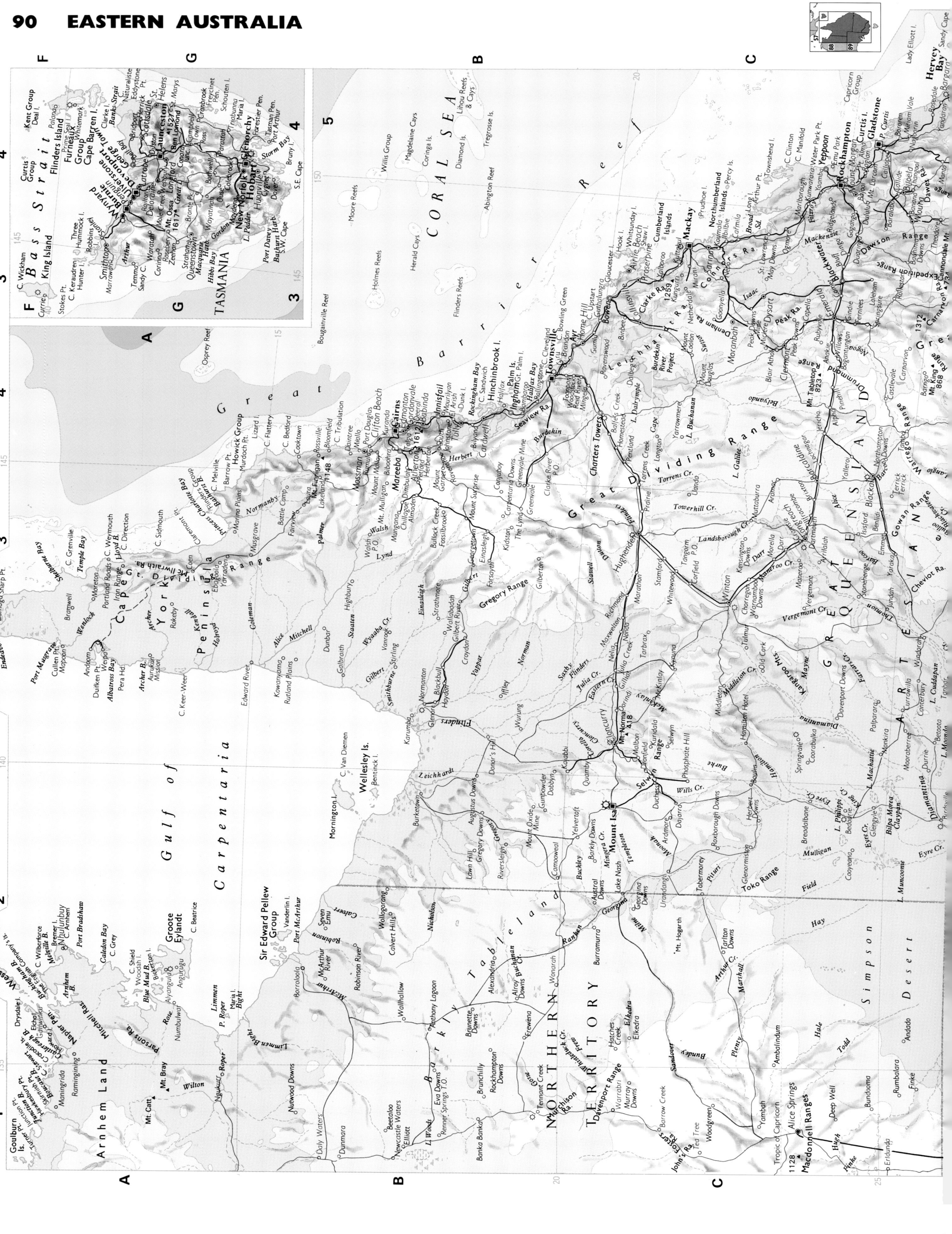

CORAL SEA
Great Barrier Reef
Gulf of Carpentaria
Cape York Peninsula
Great Dividing Range
QUEENSLAND
NORTHERN TERRITORY
Barkly Tableland
Simpson Desert
Arnhem Land
GREAT ARTESIAN BASIN
TASMANIA
Bass Strait
Flinders Island
King Island
Hobart
Launceston
Cairns
Townsville
Mackay
Rockhampton
Gladstone
Mount Isa
Alice Springs
Charters Towers
Winton
Longreach
Cloncurry
Wellesley Is.
Groote Eylandt
Sir Edward Pellew Group
Nhulunbuy
Macdonnell Ranges
Tropic of Capricorn

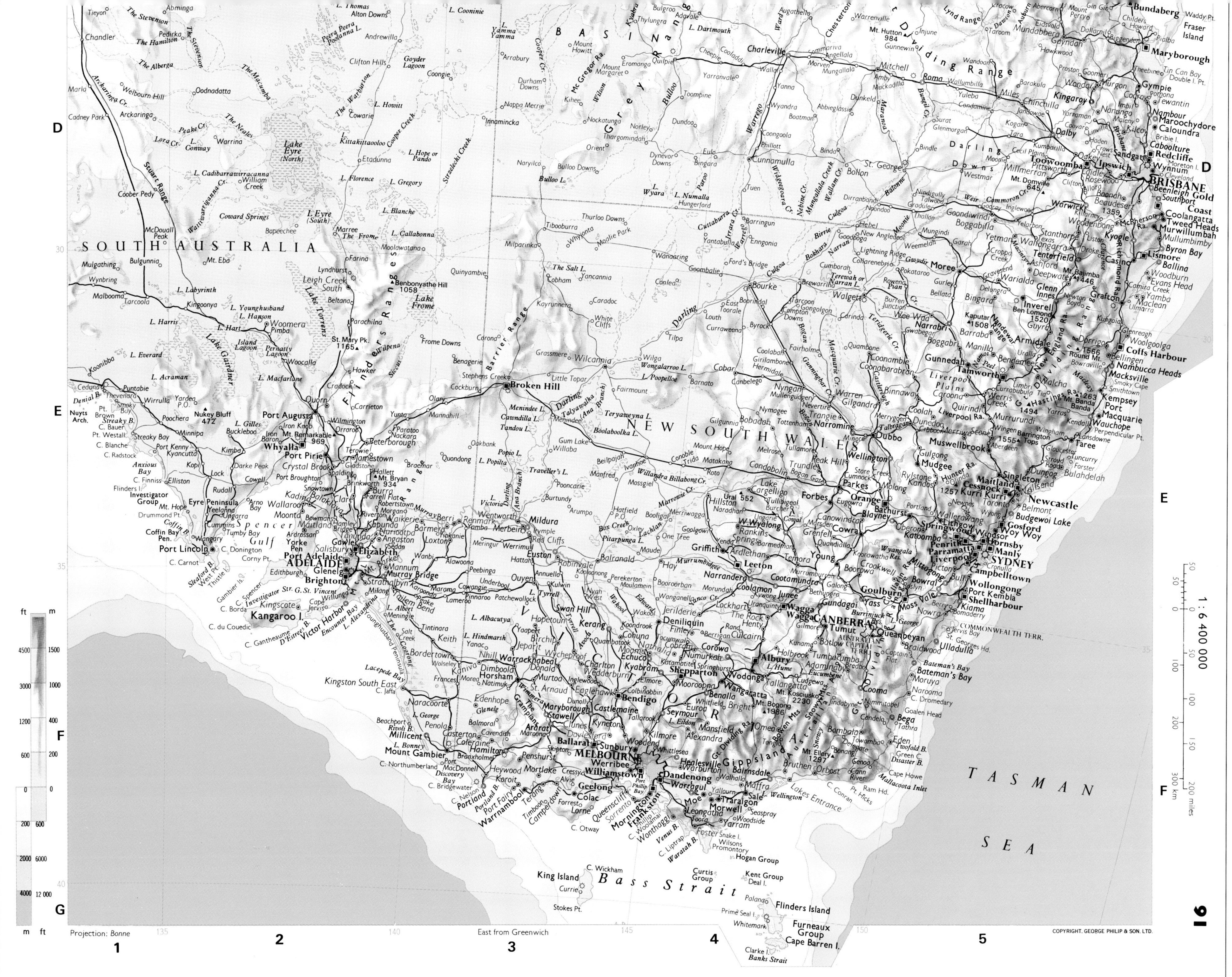
1 : 6 400 000
50 0 50 100 150 200 miles
50 0 100 200 300 km
SOUTH AUSTRALIA
NEW SOUTH WALES
VICTORIA
TASMAN SEA
Bass Strait
ADELAIDE
MELBOURNE
SYDNEY
CANBERRA
BRISBANE
AUSTRALIAN CAPITAL TERR.
COMMONWEALTH TERR.
Great Dividing Range
Grey Range
Flinders Ranges
Barrier Range
Lake Eyre (North)
Lake Torrens
Lake Gairdner
Lake Frome
Spencer Gulf
Gulf St. Vincent
Kangaroo I.
King Island
Flinders Island
Furneaux Group
Cape Barren I.
Broken Hill
Port Augusta
Whyalla
Port Pirie
Port Lincoln
Mildura
Wagga Wagga
Albury
Bendigo
Ballarat
Geelong
Newcastle
Wollongong
Toowoomba
Maryborough
Bundaberg
Gold Coast
Coffs Harbour
Dubbo
Bourke
Charleville
Projection: Bonne
East from Greenwich
COPYRIGHT, GEORGE PHILIP & SON, LTD.
ft m
4500 1500
3000 1000
1200 400
600 200
0 0
200 600
2000 6000
4000 12 000
m ft

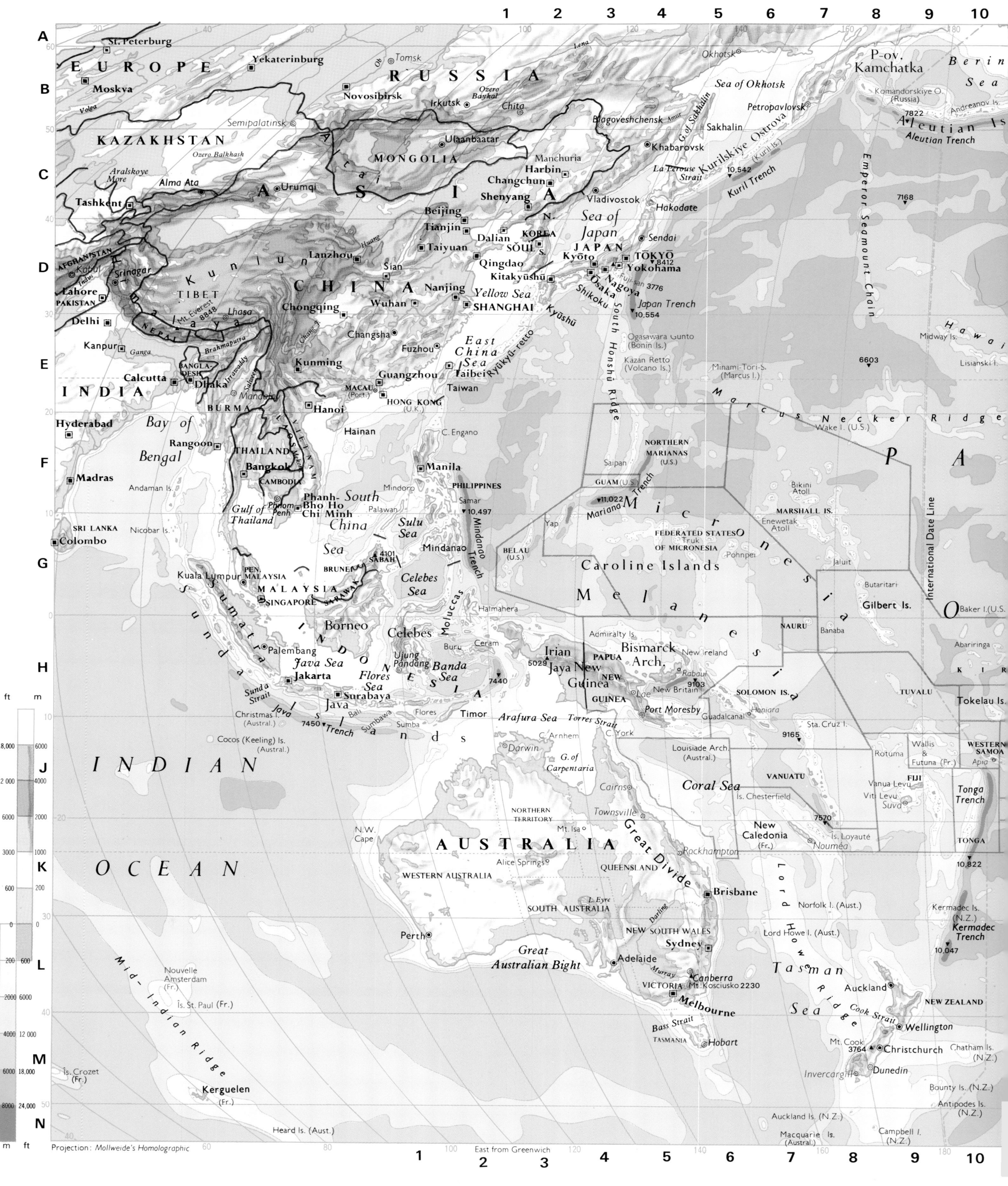

1 2 3 4 5 6 7 8 9 10

A St. Peterburg

E U R O P E Yekaterinburg Tomsk Lena Okhotsk P-ov. Kamchatka Berin Sea
Moskva RUSSIA Sea of Okhotsk
B Novosibirsk Ozero Baykal Chita Blagoveshchensk Amur Komandorskiye O. (Russia) Andreanov Is.
Volga Irkutsk Sakhalin Petropavlovsk 7822 Aleutian Is.
KAZAKHSTAN Semipalatinsk Khabarovsk La Perouse Strait 10.542 Aleutian Trench
Ozero Balkhash MONGOLIA Ulaanbaatar Kurilskiye Ostrova (Kuril Is.) Kuril Trench
C Aralskoye More Alma Ata Urumqi A S I A Harbin Manchuria Vladivostok Hakodate 7168
Tashkent Changchun N. Sea of Japan Emperor Seamount Chain
Shenyang KOREA Sendai
Beijing Dalian SŎUL JAPAN
AFGHANISTAN Kabul Tianjin S. Kyōto TŌKYŌ Hawai
D Srinagar Lanzhou Taiyuan Qingdao Ōsaka Nagoya Yokohama 8412
Lahore K u n l u n Sian Kitakyūshū Shikoku Fuji-san 3776 Midway Is.
PAKISTAN CHINA Nanjing Yellow Sea Kyūshū South Honshū Ridge Japan Trench 10.554
Delhi TIBET Lhasa Chongqing Wuhan SHANGHAI 6603 Lisianski I.
Mt.Everest 8848 Changsha East China Sea Ogasawara Gunto (Bonin Is.)
Kanpur Ganga Brahmaputra NEPAL Himalaya Fuzhou Taibei Ryūkyū-retto Kazan Retto (Volcano Is.) Minami-Tori-S. (Marcus I.)
E Kunming Guangzhou Taiwan Necker Ridge
Calcutta BANGLA-DESH Dhaka MACAU (Port.) HONG KONG (U.K.) Marcus Wake I. (U.S.) P A
INDIA BURMA Mandalay Irrawaddy Salween Hainan C. Engano NORTHERN MARIANAS (U.S.)
Hyderabad Rangoon Bay of Bengal Saipan Bikini Atoll
F THAILAND VIETNAM Manila GUAM (U.S.) Micronesia MARSHALL IS.
Madras Bangkok PHILIPPINES 11,022 Mariana Trench FEDERATED STATES OF MICRONESIA Enewetak Atoll
Andaman Is. CAMBODIA Mindoro Samar 10,497 Yap Truk Pohnpei Jaluit
SRI LANKA Phanh-Bho Ho Chi Minh South China Sea Palawan Sulu Sea BELAU (U.S.) Butaritari
G Phnom Penh Gulf of Thailand 4101 SABAH Mindanao Mindanao Trench Caroline Islands Gilbert Is.
Nicobar Is. Kuala Lumpur PEN. MALAYSIA BRUNEI Celebes Sea Halmahera Melanesia NAURU Banaba Baker I.(U.S.)
Colombo MALAYSIA SARAWAK Moluccas Ceram Admiralty Is. New Ireland Abariringa
SINGAPORE Borneo Celebes Buru Irian Jaya New Guinea Bismarck Arch. New Britain K I R
H Sumatra Palembang Ujung Pandang Banda Sea 5029 PAPUA NEW GUINEA Rabaul 9103 TUVALU
Sunda INDONESIA Java Sea Flores Sea 7440 Lae Port Moresby SOLOMON IS. Honiara Tokelau Is.
Jakarta Surabaya Bali Sumbawa Sumba Timor Guadalcanal Sta. Cruz I. WESTERN SAMOA
Sunda Strait Java Flores Arafura Sea Torres Strait 9165 Rotuma Wallis & Futuna (Fr.) Apia
I N D I A N Sunda Islands 7450 Java Trench C. Arnhem C. York VANUATU Vanua Levu FIJI
J Christmas I. (Austral.) Darwin G. of Carpentaria Louisiade Arch. (Austral.) Coral Sea Viti Levu Suva Tonga Trench
Cocos (Keeling) Is. (Austral.) NORTHERN TERRITORY Mt. Isa Cairns Is. Chesterfield New Caledonia (Fr.) 7570 Is. Loyauté TONGA
O C E A N Townsville Great Divide Rockhampton Nouméa 10,822
K WESTERN AUSTRALIA AUSTRALIA Alice Springs QUEENSLAND Lord Howe I. (Aust.) Norfolk I. (Aust.) Kermadec Is. (N.Z.)
Nouvelle Amsterdam (Fr.) L. Eyre Brisbane Kermadec Trench 10.047
Îs. St. Paul (Fr.) SOUTH AUSTRALIA Darling NEW SOUTH WALES Lord Howe I. (Aust.)
L Perth Great Australian Bight Sydney Tasman Sea Auckland NEW ZEALAND
Mid-Indian Ridge Adelaide Murray Canberra Mt. Kosciusko 2230 Cook Strait Wellington
VICTORIA Melbourne Lord Howe Ridge Mt. Cook 3764 Christchurch Chatham Is. (N.Z.)
M Is. Crozet (Fr.) Bass Strait TASMANIA Hobart Invercargill Dunedin Bounty Is. (N.Z.)
Kerguelen (Fr.) Antipodes Is. (N.Z.)
N Heard Is. (Aust.) Macquarie Is. (Austral.) Campbell I. (N.Z.)
Auckland Is. (N.Z.)

Projection: Mollweide's Homolographic East from Greenwich

ft m
18,000 6000
12 000 4000
6000 2000
3000 1000
600 200
0 0
200 600
2000 6000
4000 12 000
6000 18,000
8000 24,000
m ft

1 2 3 4 5 6 7 8 9 10

1 : 43 200 000

11 **12** **13** **14** **15** **16** **17** **18** **19** **20**

ALASKA
(U.S.)

Bristol Bay

Gulf of Alaska
Prince of Wales I.
Prince Rupert
Kitimat
Queen Charlotte Is.
Juneau
6050

GREENLAND
C. Farewell
U.K.

Hudson Bay

C A N A D A

Labrador

N O R T H   A M E R I C A

N O R T H

Edmonton

L. Winnipeg

Newfoundland

Vancouver
Vancouver I.
Victoria
Seattle
Calgary
Regina
Winnipeg
St. Lawrence
Montréal
Quebec
Pr. Edward I.
Saint John

Portland
Boise
Snake
Missouri
L. Superior
L. Michigan
Ottawa
Toronto
L. Ontario
L. Erie
Buffalo
Boston
C. Sable

C. Mendocino
Minneapolis
CHICAGO
Pittsburgh
Detroit
Cincinnati
NEW YORK
Philadelphia
Baltimore
Washington

Salt Lake City
Denver
Kansas City
St. Louis
Memphis

ATLANTIC

San Francisco
4418
Mountains
UNITED STATES
Oklahoma
Dallas
Mississippi
Atlanta
C. Hatteras

6741

Los Angeles
San Diego
Ciudad Juárez
6225
San Antonio
Houston
New Orleans
Jacksonville
Bermuda (U.K.)

OCEAN

Sierra Madre
M E X I C O
Monterrey
Gulf of Mexico
Miami

Tropic of Cancer
Hawaiian Is.
(U.S.)
Honolulu
Oahu
Hawaii

Gulf of California
Is. Revilla Gigedo
(Mexico)
Guadalajara
México
Puebla 5700
Acapulco

La Habana
Florida Strait
BAHAMAS
CUBA
Yucatán Channel
Mérida
West Indies
Hispaniola
HAITI
DOM. REP.
9200
7680
JAMAICA
Kingston
PUERTO RICO (U.S.)
Leeward Is.

Johnston I. (U.S.)

P A C I F I C

Laysan I.

an Ridge

Christmas Island Ridge
Palmyra Is. (U.S.)
Teraina
Tabuaeran
Kiritimati

Jarvis I.
(U.S.)

GUATEMALA
Guatemala
4662
BELIZE
HONDURAS
EL SALVADOR
San Salvador
NICARAGUA
Managua
CENTRAL AMERICA
San José
COSTA RICA
PANAMA
Panama
Colón
Canal

I. Clipperton (Fr.)

Barranquilla
Maracaibo
Caracas
BARBADOS
Windward Is.
TRINIDAD & TOBAGO
Caribbean Sea

I. del Coco
(Costa Rica)

VENEZUELA
Orinoco

O C E A N

Canterbury I.
Phoenix Is.
K I R I B A T I
Malden I.
Starbuck I.

Medellín
Bogotá
Cali
COLOMBIA

Equator

Galápagos
(Ecuador)
Guayaquil
Quito
ECUADOR
Manaus
Amazonas
Iquitos
C. Pariñas
BRAZIL

N.Z.
Tongareva
Penrhyn Is.
Manihiki
Suwarrow Is.
ukapuka
Vostok I.
Flint I.

Îs. Marquises

Trujillo
SOUTH

tuila
SAMOA
U.S.
Cook Islands
(N.Z.)

Îs. de la Société
Caroline I.
Îs. Tuamotu

6369
PERU
Lima
Cuzco
A M E R I C A

Niue
(N.Z.)
Manuae
Austral
Rarotonga
Tahiti
FRENCH POLYNESIA
Tuamotu Ridge

Arequipa
L. Titicaca
Illampu & Ancohuma
6550
6866
Peru
La Paz
BOLIVIA

Seamount Chain
Îs. Tubuai
(Îs. Australes)
Rapa

Iquique
Chile
8050
Antofagasta
Trench

Tropic of Capricorn
Pitcairn I. (U.K.)
Ducie I. (U.K.)

PARAGUAY
Asunción

East Pacific Ridge

I. de Pascua
(Easter I.)
(Chile)
Sala-y-Gomez
San Félix (Chile)
San Ambrosio (Chile)
Tucumán

PTO. Alegre

Arch. de Juan Fernández
(Chile)
6960
Córdoba
Rosario
URUGUAY
Montevideo

Pacific-Antarctic Ridge

Valparaíso
Santiago
Concepción
Buenos Aires
ARGENTINA
Río de la Plata

Chile Rise

Patagonia

SOUTH

ATLANTIC

6212

OCEAN

Punta Arenas
Str. of Magellan
Tierra del Fuego
C. Horn
Falkland Is. (U.K.)
South Georgia

1 : 28 000 000

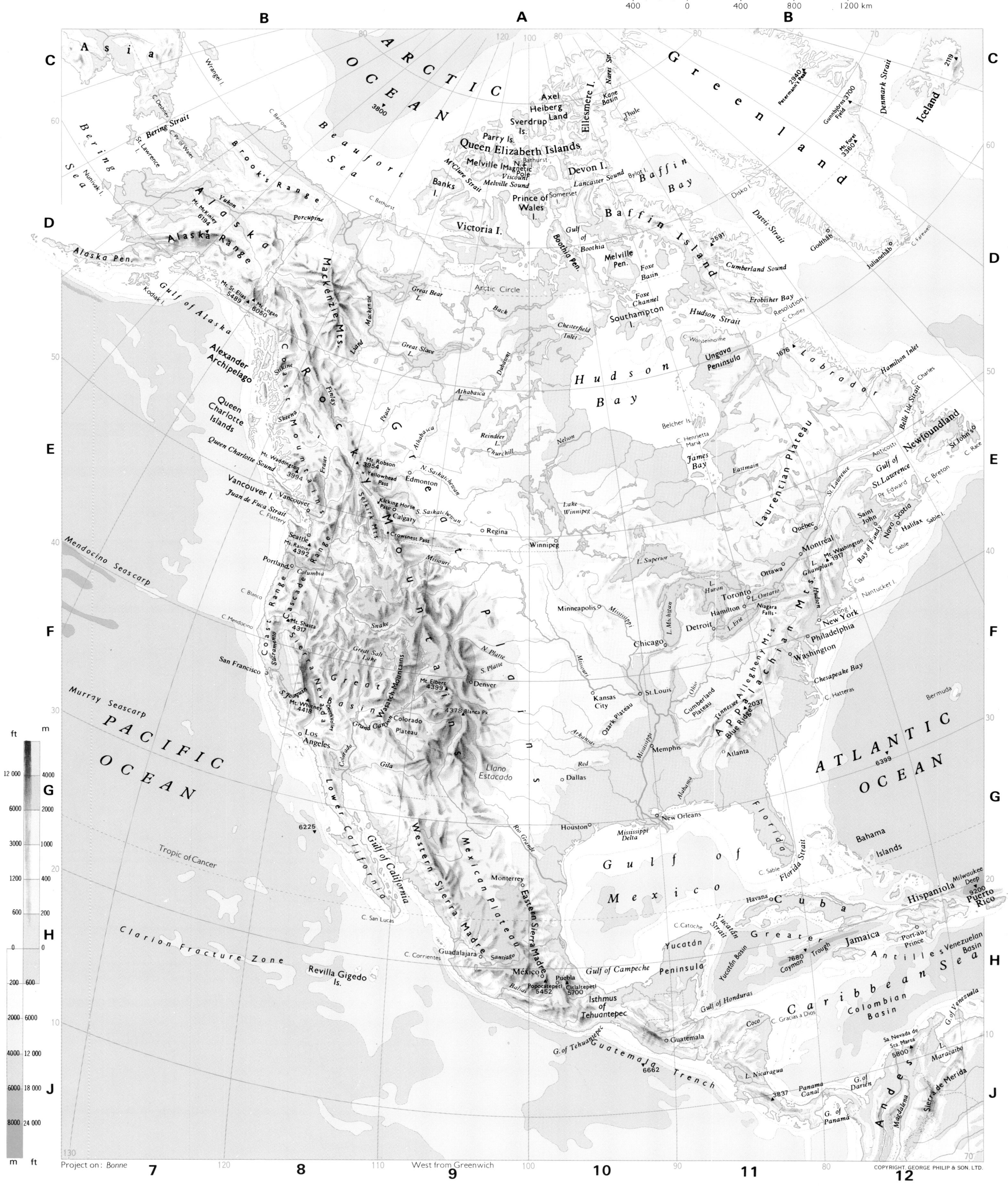
Asia
ARCTIC OCEAN
Greenland
Iceland
Denmark Strait
Bering Sea
Bering Strait
Beaufort Sea
Queen Elizabeth Islands
Axel Heiberg Land
Ellesmere I.
Devon I.
Banks I.
Victoria I.
Prince of Wales I.
Baffin Bay
Baffin Island
Davis Strait
Brook's Range
Alaska Range
Alaska
Alaska Pen.
Gulf of Alaska
Mt. McKinley 6194
Mt. St. Elias 5489
Mt. Logan 6050
Mackenzie Mts.
Great Bear L.
Great Slave L.
Arctic Circle
Hudson Bay
Hudson Strait
Southampton I.
Ungava Peninsula
Labrador
Newfoundland
Gulf of St. Lawrence
James Bay
Laurentian Plateau
Alexander Archipelago
Queen Charlotte Islands
Coast Mountains
Rocky Mountains
Great Plains
Vancouver I.
Mt. Robson 3954
Edmonton
Calgary
Regina
Winnipeg
Lake Winnipeg
Mendocino Seascarp
Murray Seascarp
PACIFIC OCEAN
Seattle
Mt. Rainier 4392
Portland
Cascade Range
Coast Range
Mt. Shasta 4317
San Francisco
Sierra Nevada
Mt. Whitney 4418
Great Basin
Great Salt Lake
Wasatch Mountains
Colorado Plateau
Grand Canyon
Los Angeles
Mt. Elbert 4399
Denver
Llano Estacado
L. Superior
L. Michigan
L. Huron
L. Erie
L. Ontario
Minneapolis
Chicago
Detroit
Toronto
Montréal
Québec
Ottawa
New York
Philadelphia
Washington
Chesapeake Bay
Appalachian Mts.
Blue Ridge 2037
St. Louis
Kansas City
Memphis
Atlanta
Dallas
Houston
New Orleans
Mississippi
Florida
ATLANTIC OCEAN
Bermuda
Gulf of Mexico
Tropic of Cancer
Lower California
Gulf of California
Western Sierra Madre
Mexican Plateau
Eastern Sierra Madre
Monterrey
Guadalajara
México
Popocatepetl 5452
Citlaltepetl 5700
Gulf of Campeche
Isthmus of Tehuantepec
Yucatán Peninsula
Guatemala
Cuba
Havana
Hispaniola
Puerto Rico
Jamaica
Bahama Islands
Caribbean Sea
Colombian Basin
Greater Antilles
Clarion Fracture Zone
Revilla Gigedo Is.
Guatemala Trench 6662
Panama Canal
G. of Panamá
Andes
Sierra de Merida
Project on: Bonne
West from Greenwich

1 : 28 000 000

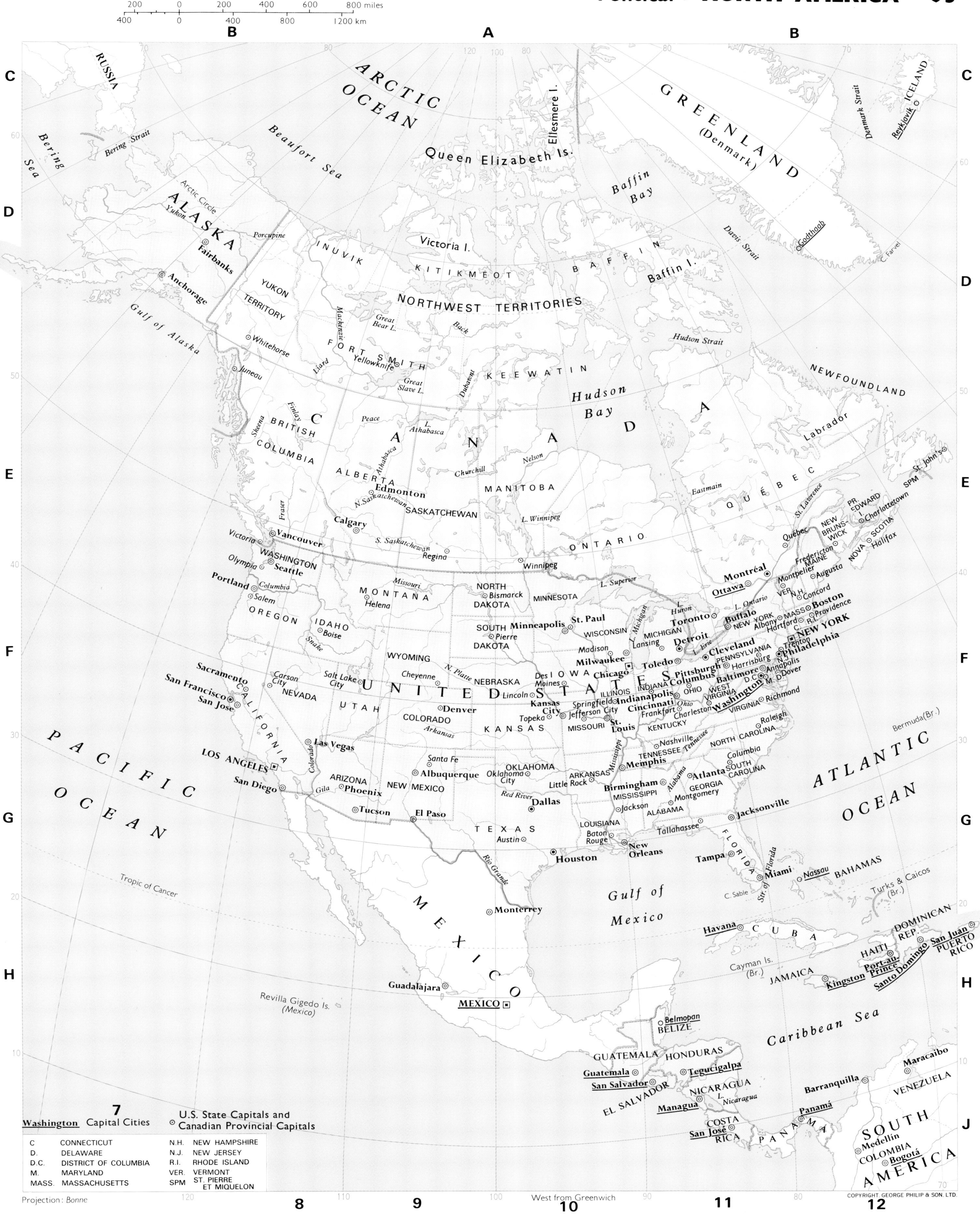

200   0   200   400   600   800 miles
400   0   400   800   1200 km

B   A   B

C RUSSIA   ARCTIC OCEAN   GREENLAND   ICELAND C
(Denmark)   Reykjavik

Bering Strait   Queen Elizabeth Is.   Ellesmere I.
Denmark Strait

Bering Sea   Beaufort Sea   Baffin Bay

Arctic Circle   Victoria I.   Baffin   Godthåb
D ALASKA   KITIKMEOT   BAFFIN   C. Farewel D
Yukon   Fairbanks   NORTHWEST TERRITORIES   Baffin I.
Anchorage   INUVIK
YUKON TERRITORY   Great Bear L.   Back
Whitehorse   FORT SMITH   Hudson Strait
Gulf of Alaska   Mackenzie   KEEWATIN
Juneau   Yellowknife   NEWFOUNDLAND
Liard   Great Slave L.   Dubawnt   Hudson Bay

E Finlay   C A N A D A   Labrador E
Skeena   Peace   L. Athabasca
BRITISH COLUMBIA   Nelson   Eastmain   QUÉBEC   SPM St. John's
ALBERTA   N. Saskatchewan   Churchill   MANITOBA   Québec   NEW BRUNS-   NOVA SCOTIA   Charlottetown
Edmonton   Athabasca   ONTARIO   WICK   Halifax
Victoria   Calgary   SASKATCHEWAN   L. Winnipeg   St. Lawrence   PR. EDWARD   Fredericton   MAINE
Vancouver   S. Saskatchewan   Montréal   Augusta
WASHINGTON   Seattle   Regina   Winnipeg   L. Superior   Ottawa   Montpelier   N.H.   Concord
Olympia   MONTANA   L. Huron   Toronto   Buffalo   VER.
Portland   Columbia   Missouri   NORTH DAKOTA   MINNESOTA   Lansing   MICHIGAN   L. Ontario   NEW YORK   Albany   MASS.   Boston
Salem   Bismarck   St. Paul   Minneapolis   WISCONSIN   Detroit   Cleveland   Hartford   R.I.   Providence
OREGON   IDAHO   Helena   SOUTH DAKOTA   Madison   Milwaukee   L. Erie   PENNSYLVANIA   Harrisburg   C.   NEW YORK

F Boise   Pierre   Chicago   Toledo   Pittsburgh   Trenton   Philadelphia F
Snake   WYOMING   N. Platte   NEBRASKA   IOWA   Des Moines   INDIANA   Columbus   OHIO   WEST   Baltimore   N.J.   Dover
Sacramento   Carson City   Cheyenne   Lincoln   Springfield   Indianapolis   Cincinnati   VIRGINIA   Annapolis   M. D.C.
San Francisco   NEVADA   Salt Lake City   Denver   Kansas City   Jefferson City   Frankfort   Ohio   VIRGINIA   Washington   Richmond
San Jose   CALIFORNIA   UTAH   COLORADO   Topeka   St. Louis   KENTUCKY   Charleston
Las Vegas   Colorado   Arkansas   KANSAS   MISSOURI   Nashville   NORTH CAROLINA   Raleigh
Santa Fe   Mississippi   TENNESSEE   Tennessee   Columbia
G LOS ANGELES   ARIZONA   Albuquerque   OKLAHOMA   Memphis   Alabama   SOUTH CAROLINA G
San Diego   Phoenix   NEW MEXICO   Oklahoma City   ARKANSAS   Birmingham   Atlanta   ATLANTIC OCEAN
Gila   Red River   Little Rock   MISSISSIPPI   GEORGIA   Jacksonville   Bermuda (Br.)
PACIFIC OCEAN   Tucson   El Paso   TEXAS   Dallas   Jackson   ALABAMA   Montgomery
LOUISIANA   Tallahassee   FLORIDA
Austin   Baton Rouge   Tampa   C. Sable
Tropic of Cancer   Rio Grande   Houston   New Orleans   Miami   Nassau   BAHAMAS   Turks & Caicos (Br.)
MEXICO   Gulf of Mexico   Str. of Florida

Monterrey   Havana   CUBA   DOMINICAN REP.
Revilla Gigedo Is.   Cayman Is. (Br.)   HAITI   San Juan   PUERTO RICO
(Mexico)   Port-au-   Santo Domingo
H Guadalajara   JAMAICA   Kingston   Prince H
MEXICO   Caribbean Sea
Belmopan   Maracaibo
BELIZE   SOUTH
GUATEMALA   HONDURAS   Barranquilla   VENEZUELA
Guatemala   Tegucigalpa   Medellín
San Salvador   NICARAGUA   Panamá   COLOMBIA
EL SALVADOR   Managua   L. Nicaragua   Bogotá
J COSTA RICA   PANAMA   AMERICA J
San José

7   Capital Cities   U.S. State Capitals and
Washington   Canadian Provincial Capitals

C   CONNECTICUT   N.H.   NEW HAMPSHIRE
D.   DELAWARE   N.J.   NEW JERSEY
D.C.   DISTRICT OF COLUMBIA   R.I.   RHODE ISLAND
M.   MARYLAND   VER.   VERMONT
MASS.   MASSACHUSETTS   SPM   ST. PIERRE ET MIQUELON

Projection: Bonne

120   110   100   West from Greenwich   90   80   70
8   9   10   11   12

COPYRIGHT GEORGE PHILIP & SON. LTD.

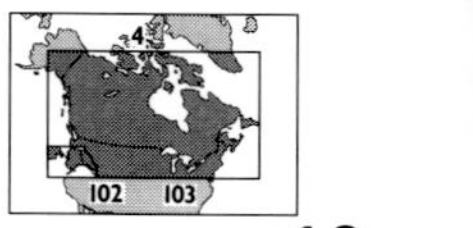

PACIFIC OCEAN

ALASKA

YUKON TERRITORY

NORTHWEST TERRITORIES

BRITISH COLUMBIA

ALBERTA

SASKATCHEWAN

MANITOBA

INUVIK

KITIKMEOT

KEEWATIN

Anchorage
Mt Gerdine
Talkeetna
Big Delta
Fairbanks
Tanana
Eagle
Dawson
Yukon
Old Crow
Aklavik
Ft McPherson
Inuvik
Arctic Red R.
Tuktoyaktuk
Banks Island
Prince Albert Pen.
Melville Island
Viscount Melville Sound
Prince of Wales Island
Somerset Island

Mt Sanford
Wrangell Mts.
Mt St. Elias
Mt Lucania
Mt Logan
Cordova
Valdez
Seward
Whitehorse
Skagway
Juneau
Sitka
Carcross
Teslin
Atlin

Amundsen Gulf
Victoria Island
M'Clintock Channel
Boothia Peninsula
Franklin Str.
King William I.
Gjoa Haven
Spence Bay

Coronation Gulf
Coppermine
Cambridge Bay
Kent Pen.
Queen Maud Gulf
Bathurst Inlet
Chantrey Inlet
Adelaide Pen.

Mackenzie Mountains
Fort Norman
Norman Wells
Ft. Good Hope
Fort Franklin
Gt. Bear Lake
Great Bear
Keith Arm
Smith Arm
Dease Arm
Echo Bay
Port Radium
Burnside

Rocky Mountains
Cassiar Mountains
Coast Mountains
Stikine
Telegraph Creek
Dease Lake
Skeena
Hazelton
Smithers
Babine
Prince Rupert
Queen Charlotte Is.
Pr. of Wales I.
Ketchikan
Wrangell
Petersburg

Fort Nelson
Ft. Nelson
Fort Liard
Liard
Trout
Fort Providence
Yellowknife
L. de Gras
Clinton Colden L.
Aylmer
Pelly
L. Macdougall
Arctic

Fort Simpson
Wrigley
Rae
Fort Resolution
Great Slave
Snowdrift
Fort Reliance
Dubawnt L.
Baker L.
Chesterfield Inlet
Rankin Inlet
Whale Cove
Eskimo Pt.
Thlewiaza

Fort Vermilion
Hay River
Ft. Smith
Caribou Mts.
Meander River
Peace
Slave
L. Claire
Fort Chipewyan
Lake Athabasca
Uranium City
Fond-du-Lac
Wholdaia L.
Kasba L.
Nueltin L.
Yathkyed L.

Edmonton
Calgary
Red Deer
Leduc
Wetaskiwin
Camrose
Stettler
Drumheller
Lethbridge
Medicine Hat
Grande Prairie
Peace River
Fort McMurray
Fort Mackay
Lesser Slave
McLennan
Lac la Biche
Vegreville
Vermilion
Lloydminster
Wainwright

Saskatoon
Regina
Moose Jaw
Prince Albert
North Battleford
Battleford
Swift Current
Yorkton
Melville
Nipawin
Tisdale
Melfort
Humboldt
Rosthern
Biggar
Kerrobert
Kindersley
Rosetown
Weyburn
Estevan
Assiniboia
Shaunavon

Reindeer Lake
Lac la Ronge
Flin Flon
Churchill
Cree Lake
Wollaston L.
Brochet
Cedar Lake
The Pas
Lynn Lake
Southern Indian L.
Sherridon
Norway House
Gods L.

Winnipeg
L. Manitoba
L. Winnipegosis
Dauphin
Brandon
Portage la Prairie
St. Boniface
Selkirk
Neepawa
Minnedosa
Virden
Souris
Morden
Kenora
Emerson
L. of the Woods
Rainy L.
Lac Seul
Lake Winnipeg

Port Nelson
York Factory
Nelson
Hayes
Gods L.
Island L.
Sandy L.
Cape Churchill

Vancouver
Victoria
Nanaimo
Vancouver I.
New Westminster
Kamloops
Kelowna
Penticton
Revelstoke
Nelson
Trail
Prince George
Williams Lake
Quesnel
Bella Coola
Waddington
Squamish
Comox
Port Alberni
Campbell River
Cumberland
Mt. Robson
Yellowhead P.
Kicking Horse P.
Cranbrook
Fernie

WASHINGTON
Seattle
Tacoma
Spokane
Olympia
Bellingham
Everett
Yakima
Wenatchee
Port Angeles
Juan de Fuca Str.
C. Flattery

MONTANA
NORTH DAKOTA
SOUTH DAKOTA
MINNESOTA
WYOMING
NEBRASKA
IOWA
WISCONSIN

Great Falls
Helena
Lewistown
Glasgow
Miles City
Glendive
Billings
Missouri
Milk
Fort Peck
Yellowstone

Minot
Williston
Devils Lake
Grand Forks
Jamestown
Valley City
Bismarck
Mandan
Dickinson
Fargo
Wahpeton
Crookston
Thief River Falls
Red Lake
Grafton

Pierre
Aberdeen
Watertown
Huron
Rapid City
Black Hills
Mobridge
Mitchell
Sioux Falls
Yankton
Chadron
Alliance

Minneapolis
St. Paul
Duluth
St. Cloud
Brainerd
Moorhead
Mankato
Rochester
Winona
Willmar
Bemidji
Virginia
Hibbing
Eveleth
Ely
Superior
Ashland

Omaha
Des Moines
Council Bluffs
Sioux City
North Platte
Grand Island
Norfolk
Lincoln
Waterloo
Cedar Rapids
Dubuque
Davenport
Mason City
Fort Dodge
Ames
Austin
La Crosse
Madison

UNITED STATES
CANADA

ALASKA
1 : 24 000 000

ft m
9000 3000
6000 2000
4500 1500
3000 1000
1200 400
600 200
0 0
600 200
6000 2000
m ft

100 0 100 200 300 miles
100 0 200 400 km

RUSSIA
Korakskij Khr.
Anadyr
Ossora
Karaginskij
Providenija
Ugolnyi
Cukotskoje More (Chukchi Sea)

BERING SEA
St. Lawrence I. (US)
St. Matthew I.
Nunivak
Pribilof Is.
Kuskokwim Bay
Bristol Bay
Bethel

Barrow
Wainwright
Pt. Barrow
Prudhoe Bay
Harrison Bay
Colville
Brooks Range
Baird Mts.
Kotzebue
Shungnak
Noatak
Seward Pen.
Nome
Council
Arctic Circle

Fairbanks
College
Mt. McKinley
Nenana
Healy
Circle
Fort Yukon
Eagle

Anchorage
Kenai
Soldotna
Seward
Homer
Valdez
Cordova
Wrangell Mts.
Mt St. Elias
Whitehorse
Skagway
Juneau
Sitka
Petersburg
Wrangell
Ketchikan
Prince Rupert

GULF OF ALASKA
Kodiak
Kodiak I.
Afognak I.
Alaska Peninsula
Shumagin Is.
Trinity Is.
Unimak I.
Dutch Harbor
Unalaska I.
Aleutian Is.
Andreanof Is.
Near Is.
Amchitka I.
Attu

Chichagof I.
Baranof I.
Alexander Archipelago
Queen Charlotte Is.
Graham I.
Moresby I.

PACIFIC OCEAN

West from Greenwich

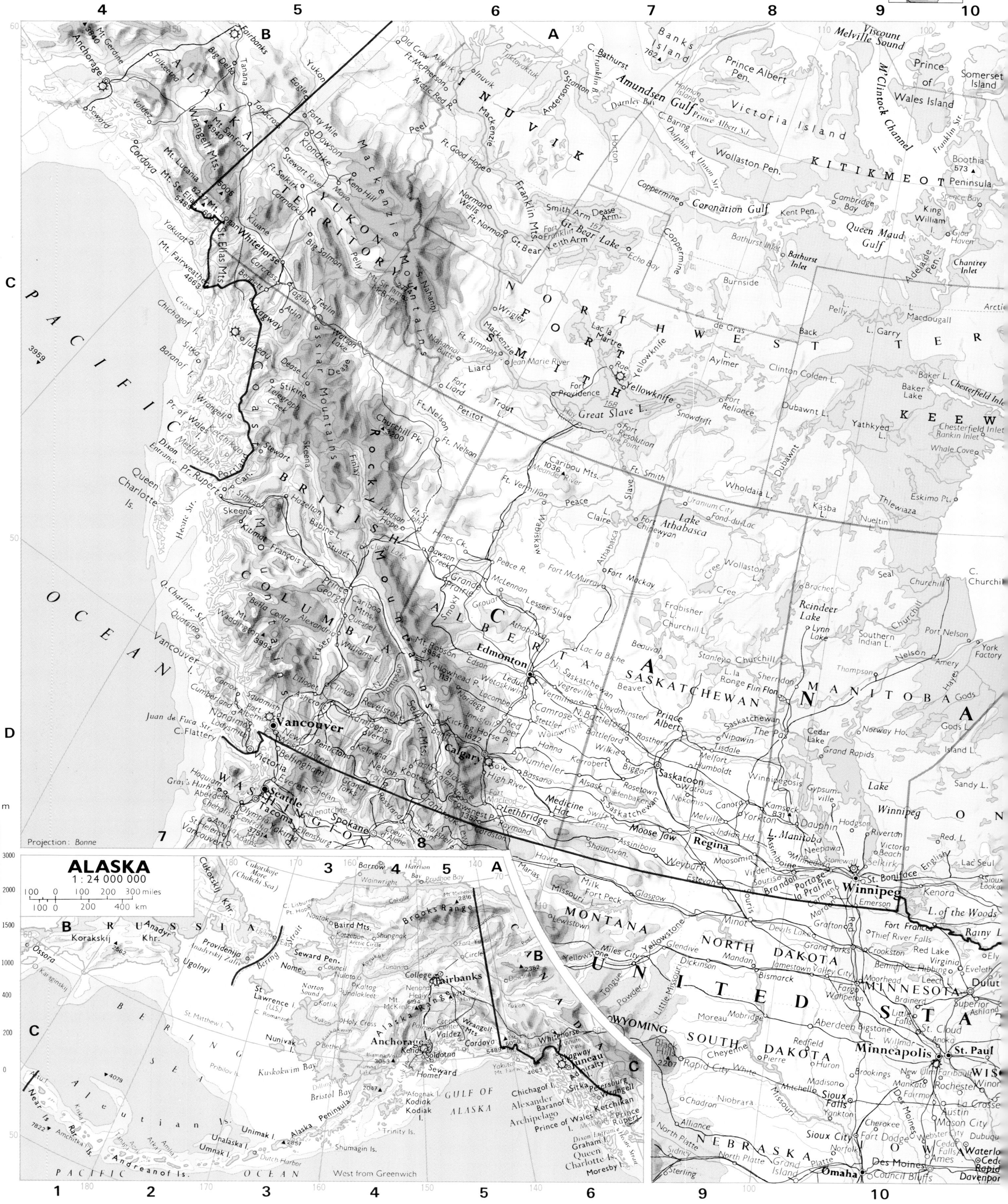

1 : 12 000 000

200   100   0   100   200   300   400 miles

100   0   100   200   300   400   500   600 km

11   12   13   14   15   16

Devon Island
Lancaster Sound
Baffin Bay
Svartenhuk
Halvø
Angmagssalik

G R E E N L A N D

Arctic Bay
Bylot I.
Pond Inlet
Disko
Christianshåb
Kong Frederik VI.s Kyst
Brodeur
Peninsula
Milne
Inlet
Pond Inlet
Disko
B.
Holsteinsborg
Sondre Stromfjord

B

Fury & Hecla Str.
Igloolik
Island
C. Hewett
Clyde
Sukkertoppen

Gulf
of
Boothia
Melville
Pen.
Hall
Lake
Prince
Charles
2591
Cumberland
Peninsula
Pangnirtung
Godthåb
Frederikshåb

Pelly B.
Committee B.
Basin
Foxe
Foxe
Peninsula
C. Dorchester
Amadjuak
2599
C. Dyer
Cape
Dyer
Hoare B.
Ivigtut
Rae Isthmus
Circle
Repulse
Bay
C. Mercy
Cumberland Sd.
Julianehåb
Kap Farvel

Wager B.
Wager
Bay
Ross Welcome Sd.
Southampton
I.
Coral Harbour
Coats
I.
Cape Dorset
Amadjuak
Lake
Amadjuak
Iqaluit
Frobisher Bay
3809

ATIN
Southampton
I.
Bell
Pen.
Lake
Harbour
Resolution I.

ATLANTIC

Digges Is.
Invujivik
Saglouk
(Suglak)
Koartac
(Notre Dame
de Koartac)
Akpatok
I.

Mansel
I.
Maricourt
(Wakeham)
Arnaud (Bell.)
(Payne Bay)
Ungava Bay
1676
Port Nouveau-Québec
George R.
Hebron
Nutak

Hudson
Payne
Portland
Promontory
Peninsula
Inoucdjouac
(Port Harrison)
Koksoak
Feuilles
Kuujjuaq
George
Whale
Nain
Hopedale
Ottawa
Isl.
257
L. Minto
Mélèzes
Kaniapiskau

Bay
Sleeper Is.
King
George Is.
King George Is.
Baker's
Dozen
Is.
La L'Eau Claire
Lac Bienville
L.
Kaniapiskau
L. Harrison
Indian Harbour
Rigolet
N E W F.

Belcher
Is.
Grand Baleine
Poste-de-
la-Baleine
(Great Whale River)
Kanaaupscow
Scheffervile
Petitsikapau
COAST OF LABRADOR
North West R.
Churchill
Falls
Goose
Bay
L. Melville
Cartwright
Battle Harb.
Belle Isle

Ft. Severn
C. Henrietta
Maria
Pte.
Louis-XIV
A
Ft. George
La Grande
Ashuanipi
Churchill
St. Augustin
Saguenay
Str. of Belle Isle
Twillingate
Lewisporte
Gander
Bonavista
Trinity B.

D
Winisk
James Bay
Nouveau Comptoir
(Paint Hills)
1128
Gognon
Moisie
Romaine
Natashquan
Grand
Falls
Carbonear
St. John's

Big
Trout L.
Attawapiskat
Akimiski
I.
Eastmain
QUEBEC
Moisie
Mingan
I. d'Anticosti
Corner Brook
Port aux Basques
Placentia
Trepassey
C. Race

Ft. Albany
Charlton
I.
Fort Rupert
(Rupert
House)
Rupert
Mistassini
L. Albanel
Péribonca
Sept-Îles
Port-Cartier
NEWFOUNDLAND

TARIO
Albany
Albany
Moosonee
Nottaway
Chibougamau
Manicouagan
R. St. Lawrence
Gaspé
Pen. de Gaspé
C. de Gaspé
St. Lawrence
Cabot Str.
C. North
Ray
Glace Bay

L. St. Joseph
Harricana
Matagami
Dolbeau
St-Jean
Baie-Comeau
Betsiamites
Rimouski
Matane
Campbellton
Dalhousie
Îs. de la Madeleine
Cape Breton I.
Sydney
Port Hawkesbury

Armstrong
Nakina
Kenogami
Missinaibi
Rès. de Gouin
Roberval
Chicoutimi
Jonquière
Saguenay
1190
Rivière-
du-Loup
St. Léonard
Bathurst
Chatham
PR. EDWARD I.
Charlottetown
Summerside

L.
Nipigon
Hearst
L. Abitibi
Taschereau
Senneterre
Val-d'Or
Dolbeau
Chicoutimi
NEW
BRUNSWICK
Moncton
Northumberland Str.
Amherst
New Glasgow
Mulgrave

Thunder Bay
Cochrane
Timmins
Notre-Dame-
du-Nord
Rouyn
La Tuque
Shawinigan
Québec
Lévis
Thetford Mines
St. Léonard
Woodstock
Fredericton
Newcastle
Springhill
Kentville
Truro
Windsor
Dartmouth
Sable I.
(Nova Scotia)

Michipicoten
Heron Bay
Oba
Franz
Kirkland Lake
Haileybury
Cobalt
Témiscamingue
Rès. de
Cabonga
L. d'Or
Trois-Rivières
St. Hyacinthe
Sorel
Drummondville
Sherbrooke
MAINE
Saint
John
B. of Fundy
Bridgewater
Liverpool
Shelburne
C. Sable
Yarmouth
NOVA SCOTIA
Halifax

Sault Ste. Marie
Sudbury
Copper Cliff
North Bay
Ottawa
Hull
Pembroke
Arnprior
Cornwall
1917
VT.
N.H.
Augusta
Lewiston
Portland

Lake Superior
Copper Harbor
Keweenaw
Marquette
Sault Ste. Marie
Parry
Sound
Georgian
Bay
Owen Sound
Orillia
Belleville
Kingston
Watertown
Burlington
L. Champlain
NEW
HAMPSHIRE
Concord
Manchester
Lowell

Ironwood
Iron Mt.
Manistique
Cheboygan
Lake
Huron
Collingwood
Oshawa
TORONTO
Cobourg
Rochester
Syracuse
Utica
Worcester
MASS.
Boston
C. Cod

Wausau
Green
Bay
Antigo
Menominee
Traverse
City
Cadillac
Saginaw
Guelph
Kitchener
London
Stratford
Brantford
Hamilton
Niagara
Falls
Buffalo
NEW
YORK
Albany
Springfield
CONN.
Providence

Milwaukee
Racine
Sheboygan
Manitowoc
Ludington
Muskegon
Grand
Rapids
Lansing
Flint
Sarnia
Windsor
Detroit
Toledo
Erie
Elmira
Binghamton
Scranton
Wilkes-Barre
New Haven
Bridgeport
R.I.
DEL.

CHICAGO
Gary
Evanston
South Bend
INDIANA
OHIO
Cleveland
Akron
Youngstown
PENNSYLVANIA
Williamsport
Jamestown
Reading
Allentown
Trenton
NEW JERSEY
Newark
Jersey City
NEW YORK

Madison
Rockford
Kenosha
ILLINOIS
WISCONSIN

West from Greenwich

COPYRIGHT GEORGE PHILIP & SON, LTD.

11   12   13   14

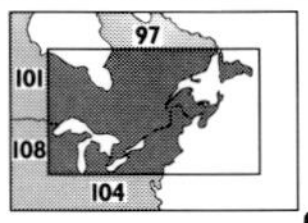

MANITOBA

N.W. TERRITORIES

HUDSON BAY

JAMES BAY

Belcher Islands

North Belcher Is.
Baker's Dozen Is.
Kugong I.
Tukarak I.
Flaherty I.
Innetalling I.
Merry I.

L. Minto
Mélèzes
Nastapoka
Lacs des Loups-Marin
L. Guillaume-Delisle
L. à l'Eau Claire
Petite Baleine
Lac D'Iberville
Grand Baleine
Lac Bienville

Akimiski I.
North Twin I.
South Twin I.
Weston I.
Charlton
Tradely I.
Eastmain
Fort Rupert
Rupert House
Nemiscau
Broadback
Nottaway

ONTARIO

QUEBEC

Polar Bear Provincial Park
Winisk
Attawapiskat
Ekwan
Albany
Fort Albany
Moose Factory
Moosonee
Moose River

LAKE SUPERIOR

Thunder Bay
Duluth
Superior
Ashland
Isle Royale

WISCONSIN
MICHIGAN

Marquette
Sault Ste. Marie
Sudbury
North Bay
Timmins
Kirkland Lake
Kapuskasing
Cochrane
Rouyn
Val-d'Or

LAKE MICHIGAN
LAKE HURON
Georgian Bay
Parry Sound
Manitoulin

GREEN BAY
Milwaukee
Madison
Rockford
CHICAGO
Green Bay
Appleton
Oshkosh

ILLINOIS
INDIANA
OHIO
PENNSYLVANIA

DETROIT
Windsor
Grand Rapids
Flint
Lansing
Kalamazoo
Toledo
CLEVELAND
Lorain
Sandusky

LAKE ERIE
LAKE ONTARIO

TORONTO
HAMILTON
St. Catharines
Niagara Falls
BUFFALO
London
Kitchener
Guelph
Brantford
Barrie
Peterborough
Kingston
OTTAWA
Cornwall
Brockville
Belleville
Oshawa

Rochester
Syracuse
Utica
Albany
Binghamton
Elmira

Adirondack Mountains
Plattsburg
Watertown
Tupper Lake
Saranac Lake

MONTRÉAL
Trois-Rivières
Shawinigan
Grand-Mère
Joliette
Hull
Pembroke

PARC PROV. DU MONT-TREMBLANT
ALGONQUIN PROV. PARK
PARC NAT. DE LA GATINEAU
PARC PROV. DE LA VÉRENDRYE

L. Nipigon
L. Seul
Lac Mistassini
L. St-Jean

Lambert's Equivalent Azimuthal

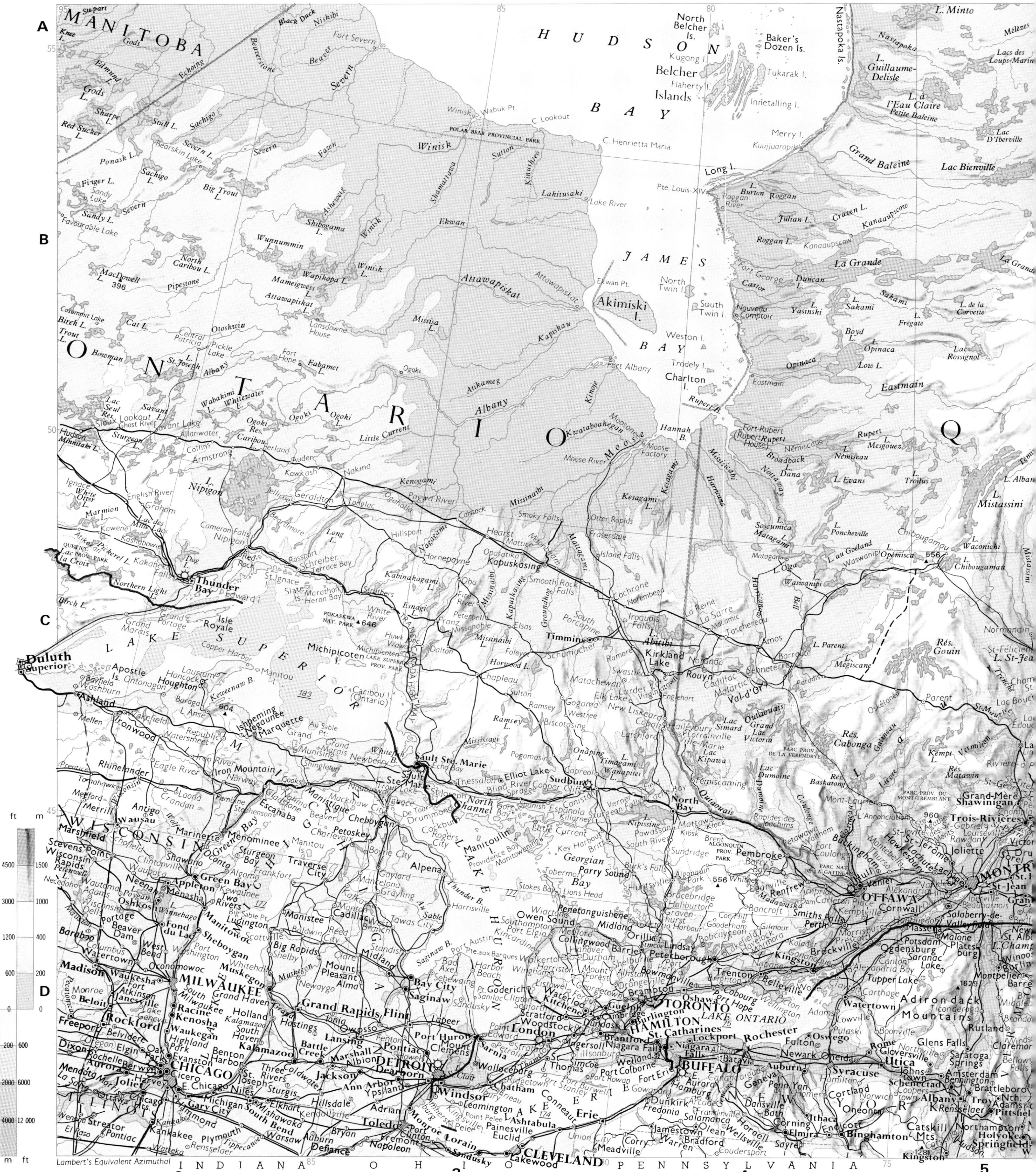

1 : 5 600 000

50 0 50 100 150 200 miles
50 0 50 100 150 200 250 300 km

6 **7** **8** **9**

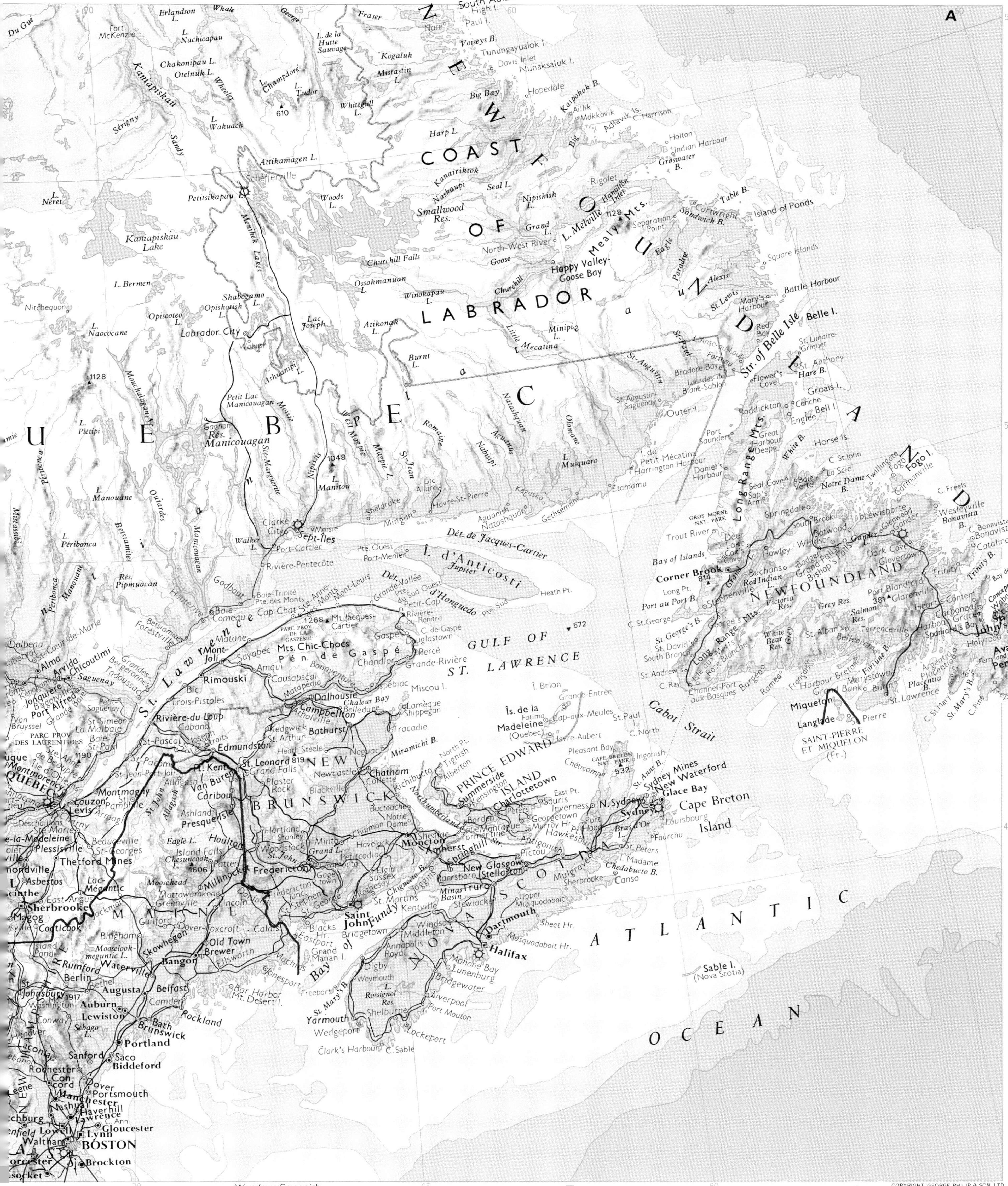

A 55

NEW
COAST

Z

Du Gué
Erlandson L. Whale L. Fraser L. George South Aulatsivik I.
Fort McKenzie High I.
L. Nachicapau L. de la Hutte Sauvage Nain
Chakonipau L. Paul I.
Otelnuk L. Mistastin L. Voisey's B. Tunungayualok I.
Kogaluk Davis Inlet
Nunaksaluk I.
L. Champdoré
L. Tudor Big Bay Hopedale
610 Whitegull L. Kaipokok B.
Harp L. Aillik Makkovik
Kanairiktok C. Harrison
Indian Harbour
Grôswater B.
Attikamagen L.

OF
Petitsikapau L. Seal L. Nipishish Holton
Kanairiktok Rigolet Hamilton Inlet
Naskaupi Cartwright
L. Néret Smallwood Res. North-West River Goose Sandwich B.
Woods L. Churchill Falls L. Melville 1128 Separation Pt. Island of Ponds
Kaniapiskau Lake L. Bermen Square Islands

B

Shabogamo Churchill Happy Valley- Table B.
Opiskotish L. Ossokmanuan Goose Bay
Nitchequon Opiscoteo Winokapau L. Paradise
Churchill Eagle
LABRADOR
N

Gagnon 1128 Mishikamau Ashuanipi L. Burnt Minipi St. Lewis
L. Plétipi Res. Manicouagan L. Joseph Atikonak L. L. du Little Mary's
L. Naococane Labrador City a Petit-Mécatina Harbour
Manicouagan Wabush St. Paul Red B.
Petit Lac St-Augustin Anse-au-Loup Belle I.
L. Péribanca Manicouagan Bradore Bay Flower's Strait of Belle Isle
L. Manouane Lourdes-de- Cove Hare B.
West Magpie Blanc-Sablon Groais I.
Bétsiamites Magpie L. St-Augustin- St. Anthony
Nipissis 1048 Romaine Saguenay Conche
Rés. St-Jean Natashquan Englee Bell I.
Pipmuacan L. Manitou Aguanus Olomane Roddickton
Nabisipi White B. Horse Is.
Manic L. Allard Musquaro Kegaska C. St. John
L. Péribonca Lac Havre-St-Pierre Etamamu Port au Choix La Scie
Sheldrake Mingan Gethsemani Port Saunders Notre Dame B.
Clarke Sept-Îles Aguanish Natashquan Baie Twillingate Fogo I.
City Walker L. Port-Cartier Verte
Godbout Rivière-Pentecôte NEWFOUNDLAND
Dét. de Jacques-Cartier South Brook Carmanville
Pte. Ouest Springdale Lewisporte
Baie-Trinité Port-Menier GROS MORNE Botwood Westeyville
Pte. des Monts Î. d'Anticosti NAT. PARK Trout River Deer Bonavista
Baie- Grande-Vallée Jupiter Lake Grand Bonavista B.
Comeau Cap-Chat Ste-Anne Pte. Sud Heath Pt. Bay of Islands Falls Gander Catalina
1268 Mt. Jacques- Pte. Ouest d'Honguedo Corner Brook 814 Buchans Glenwood Trinity B.
PARC PROV. DE Cartier 572 Red Indian Bishop's Falls Bay de Verde
LA GASPÉSIE Douglastown Long Pt. L. Windsor Trinity Conception B.
Dolbeau Matane Gaspé Port au Port B. St. George's Victoria Badger Blandford Carbonear
Alma Arvida Mts. Chic-Chocs Pén. de Gaspé C. de Gaspé Long Range Mts. Res. 381 Glarenville Harbour Grace
Chicoutimi Sayabec Pén. Percé St-George C. St. John C. Freels
Jonquière Amqui Bonaventure Chandler Grand- GULF OF St. David's White Grey Res. Spaniard's Bay
Saguenay Causapscal Grande-Rivière St. Andrew's Bear Salmon Mt.
Port Rimouski Paspébiac Rivière Res. Long St. Alban's Terrenceville St. John's
Alfred Bic Matapédia Miscou I. ST. LAWRENCE Long Range Mts. Bellevile Holyrood
St. Siméon Trois-Pistoles Dalhousie Chaleur Bay Î. Brion C. Ray Rose Blanche Fortune Avalon
La Malbaie Campbellton Lamèque Channel-Port Harbour Breton Marystown PENINSULA
Baie- Rivière-du-Loup Atholville Shippegan Î. Brion aux Basques Burgeo Fortune B. C. Race
PARC PROV. St-Paul Edmundston Bathurst Tracadie Grande-Entrée Rameau Placentia B. Bull's
DES LAURENTIDES St-Pascal Kedgwick St. Arthur Îs. de la Miquelon Placentia Bride
1190 Heath Steele Miramichi B. Madeleine St. Pierre Langlade St. Lawrence C. St. Mary's
Cabano Cap-aux-Meules St. Lawrence C. Passey
Montmorency St-Jean-Port-Joli St. Léonard 819 NEW Newcastle North Pt. (Quebec) Havre-Aubert SAINT-PIERRE
QUÉBEC St-Pacôme Grand Falls Chatham Tignish ET MIQUELON
Montmagny St. Jean Van Buren BRUNSWICK Blackville Richibucto Alberton Havre-Aubert C. North (Fr.)
Lauzon St-Pamphile Caribou Plaster Rock PRINCE EDWARD St. Paul Cape Breton
Lévis Van Buren Minto Havelock Summerside ISLAND Pleasant Bay
Deschaillons St-Jean- Ashland Doaktown Chipman Northumberland Borden Ingonish Ingonish
Ste-Marie Port-Joli Presque Isle Stanley Dorchester Kensington Charlottetown Chéticamp CAPE BRETON
Plessisville Armagh Hartland Fredericton Souris East Pt. 532 NAT. PARK
St-Georges Eagle L. Houlton Woodstock Chipman Peters Georgetown Inverness New Waterford
Thetford Mines Island Falls Grand L. Moncton Shediac Murray Hr. N. Sydney Glace Bay
Beauceville Chesuncook L. Patten Minto Sackville Cape Tormentine Pt. Hood Sydney Mines Sydney Cape Breton
Asbestos Lincoln Dorchester Amherst Springhill St. Anns B. Louisbourg Island
Lac-Mégantic Millinocket Fredericton Gagetown Joggins Brâs d'Or
L. St-Hyacinthe Moosehead Junction St. Stephen Parrsboro New Glasgow Mulgrave
Sherbrooke Greenville Oromocto NOVA Chignecto B. Stellarton St. Peters Canso
MAINE Mattawamkeag St. George Sussex Truro Sherbrooke
East Angus Lincoln Minas Basin Antigonish Chedabucto B.
Magog Bingham Calais Eastport SCOTIA Stewiacke Upper Musquodoboit
Coaticook Mooselookmeguntic L. Dover-Foxcroft St. Martins Kentville Windsor
Skowhegan Old Town 1606 Saint Fredericton Bay of Fundy Musquodoboit
Johnsbury Rumford Waterville Brewer John Hr. St. Mary's
1917 Augusta Ellsworth St. Stephen Digby Dartmouth Musquodoboit Hr. Sheet Hr.
Berlin Bethel Bangor Bar Harbor Annapolis Bridgetown Middleton Halifax ATLANTIC
Auburn Belfast Mt. Desert I. Grand Manan I. Royal Mahone Bay
Lewiston Camden Blocks Weymouth Lunenburg Sable I.
Sanford Saco Rockland Yarmouth St. Mary's B. Bridgewater (Nova Scotia)
Rochester Biddeford Wedgeport Rossignol Liverpool
Dover Portsmouth Lockeport
Concord Portland Clark's Harbour Shelburne Port Mouton
Manchester Brunswick Sebago Shelburne C. Sable OCEAN
Nashua Bath
Haverhill Laconia Sebago L.
Lawrence
Lowell Gloucester C. Ann
BOSTON Lynn
Waltham Brockton

D 45

C

West from Greenwich 70 65 60

6 **7** **8**

COPYRIGHT GEORGE PHILIP & SON LTD.

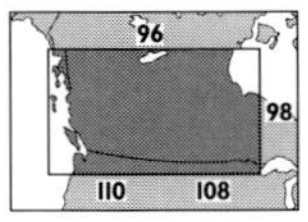

YUKON TERRITORY

NORTHWEST TERRITORIES

BRITISH COLUMBIA

ALBERTA

ALASKA

PACIFIC OCEAN

GREAT SLAVE LAKE

WOOD BUFFALO NATIONAL PARK

ROCKY MOUNTAINS

Skeena Mountains

Cassiar Mountains

Cariboo Mountains

Selkirk Mountains

Birch Mountains

Caribou Mts.

VANCOUVER ISLAND

QUEEN CHARLOTTE ISLANDS

ALEXANDER ARCH.

WASHINGTON

IDAHO

Whitehorse

Yellowknife

Fort Simpson

Fort Nelson

Hay River

Fort Smith

Fort McMurray

Prince Rupert

Kitimat

Prince George

Dawson Creek

Grande Prairie

EDMONTON

Red Deer

Calgary

Lethbridge

Jasper

Banff

Kamloops

Kelowna

Penticton

Cranbrook

Nelson

VANCOUVER

New Westminster

North Vancouver

Victoria

Nanaimo

Port Alberni

Powell River

SEATTLE

Everett

Bremerton

Bellingham

Juneau

Sitka

Ketchikan

Wrangell

Petersburg

Projection: Lambert's Equivalent Azimuthal

West from Greenwich

ft m
12 000 4000
9000 3000
6000 2000
3000 1000
1200 400
600 200
0 0
200 600
2000 6000
m ft

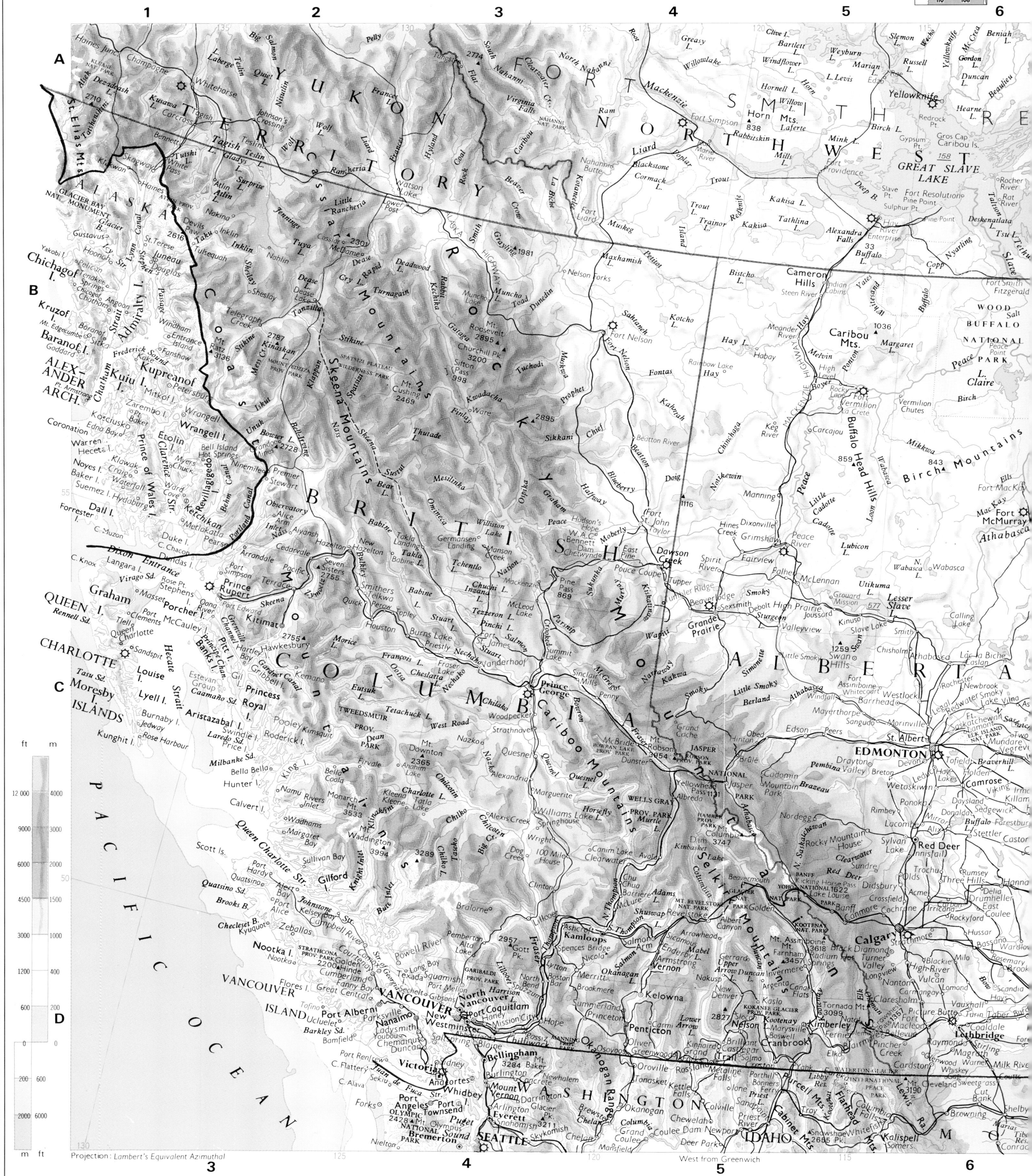

1 : 5 600 000

50   0   50   100   150   200 miles
50 0 50 100 150 200 250 300 km

7   8   9   10   11

A

REGION   KEEWATIN   REGION

TERRITORIES

HUDSON

BAY

257

B

Lake Athabasca

524   396   Wollaston

350   Reindeer L.

Southern Indian L. 254

Churchill

C. Churchill

Churchill

C. Tatnam

55

478   Cree L.

Key Lake

Reindeer L.

MANITOBA

ONTARIO

SASKATCHEWAN

680

Flin Flon

Island L.

C

LAKE WINNIPEG   217

Prince Albert

Lake Winnipegosis   252

Saskatoon

1831

Yorkton

Dauphin

Manitoba   248

50

876

Regina

WINNIPEG

Kenora

Lake of the Woods

Moose Jaw

Brandon

Swift Current

Medicine Hat   1466

Cypress Hills

Weyburn

Estevan

762

International Falls

D

MONTANA

NORTH   DAKOTA

MINNESOTA

Virginia

Minot

Grand Forks

Bemidji

Hibbing

Grand Rapids

Duluth

Cloquet

Williston

Fort Peck Res.

7   8   9   10

COPYRIGHT GEORGE PHILIP & SON LTD

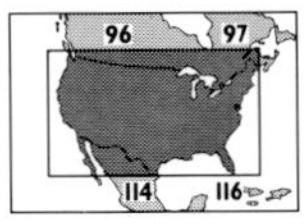

PACIFIC OCEAN

BRITISH COLUMBIA

ALBERTA · SASKATCHEWAN · MANITOBA

WASHINGTON · OREGON · IDAHO · MONTANA · NORTH DAKOTA · SOUTH DAKOTA · NEBRASKA · WYOMING

NEVADA · UTAH · COLORADO · KANSAS

CALIFORNIA · ARIZONA · NEW MEXICO · OKLAHOMA · TEXAS

BAJA CALIFORNIA NORTE · BAJA CALIFORNIA SUR · SONORA · CHIHUAHUA · COAHUILA · DURANGO

MEXICO

Vancouver · Victoria · Seattle · Tacoma · Spokane · Portland · Salem · Eugene · Boise · Great Falls · Helena · Billings · Bismarck

Sacramento · San Francisco · Oakland · Berkeley · Stockton · Modesto · San Jose · Fresno · Bakersfield · Reno · Salt Lake City · Ogden · Denver · Colorado Springs · Pueblo

Los Angeles · Long Beach · Anaheim · Santa Ana · Riverside · San Bernardino · Pasadena · Glendale · San Diego · Tijuana · Mexicali · Phoenix · Mesa · Tucson · Albuquerque · Amarillo · Lubbock · Fort Worth

El Paso · Ciudad Juárez · Hermosillo · Chihuahua · Nuevo Laredo · Laredo · Monterrey · Matamoros · Corpus Christi · San Antonio · Austin · Midland · Odessa · San Angelo

Great Salt Lake · Lake Mead · Lake Powell · Grand Canyon Nat. Park · Yellowstone National Park · Lake Tahoe · Colorado · Rio Grande

Golfo de California

HAWAII 1 : 8 000 000

Kauai · Niihau · Kaula · Oahu · Honolulu · Pearl City · Molokai · Lanai · Maui · Kahoolawe · Hawaii

Hawaiian Islands

Mauna Kea · Mauna Loa 4170 · Kilauea Crater 1247 · Hilo · Kailua · Hana

Projection: Albers Equal Area

West from Greenwich

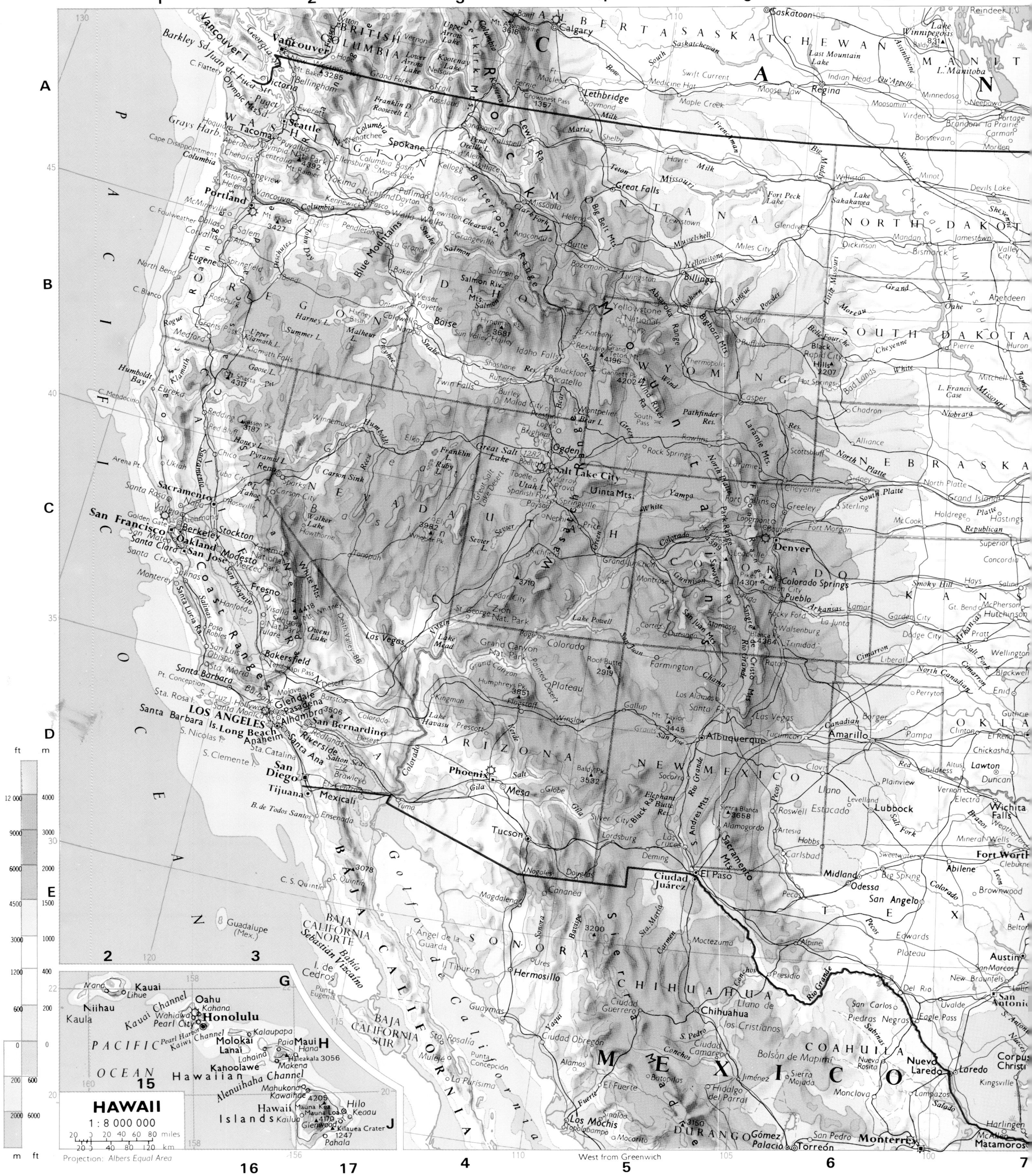

1 : 9 600 000

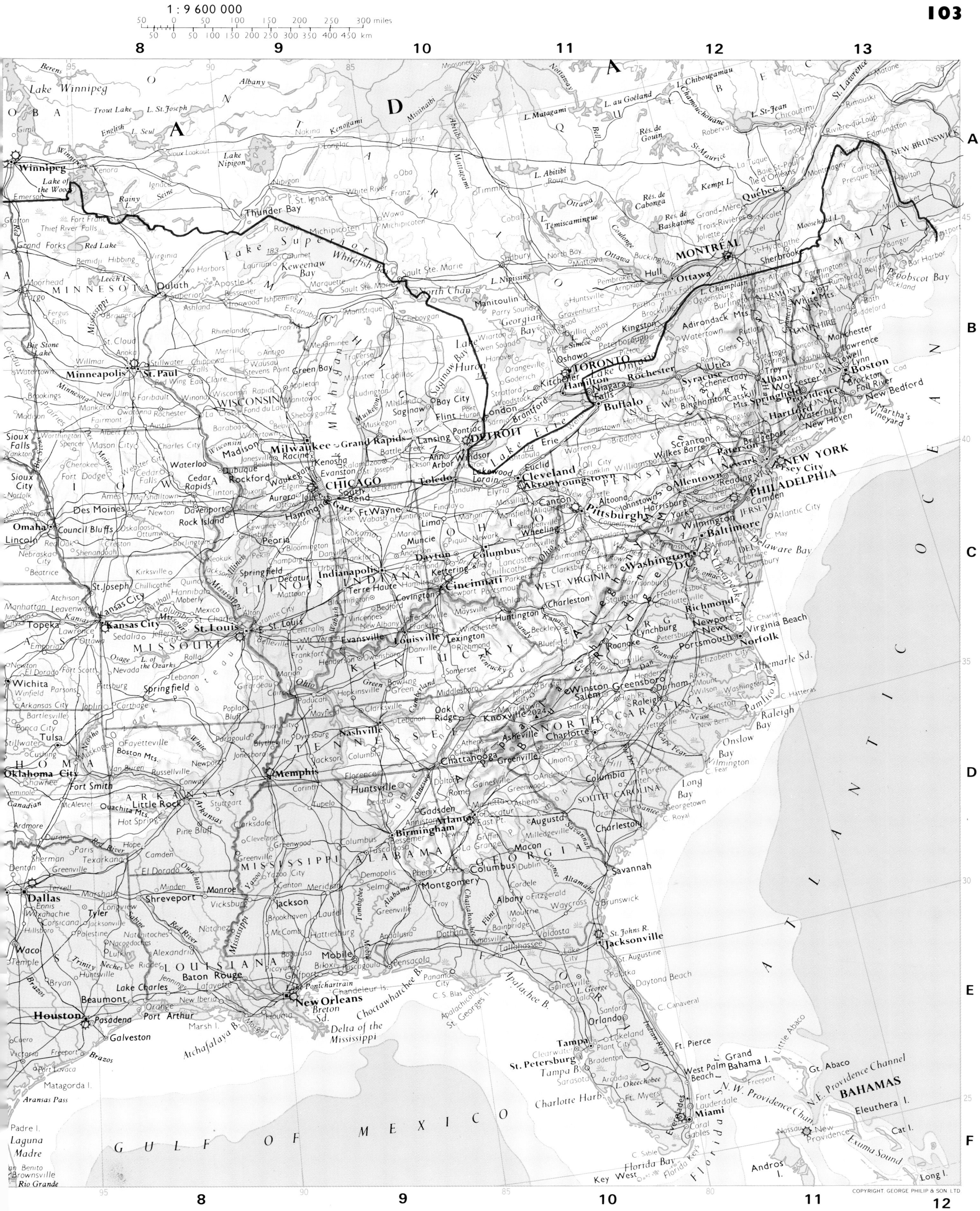

8
9
10
11
12
13
A
B
C
D
E
F
CANADA
ONTARIO
QUEBEC
NEW BRUNSWICK
Lake Winnipeg
Winnipeg
Lake of the Woods
Thunder Bay
Lake Superior
Lake Nipigon
Lake Huron
Lake Michigan
Lake Ontario
Lake Erie
Sault Ste. Marie
Sudbury
Ottawa
MONTREAL
Québec
TORONTO
Hamilton
Buffalo
Rochester
Syracuse
Albany
Boston
Providence
Hartford
NEW YORK
PHILADELPHIA
Baltimore
Washington D.C.
Richmond
Norfolk
Pittsburgh
Cleveland
DETROIT
Toledo
Columbus
Cincinnati
Indianapolis
CHICAGO
Milwaukee
Minneapolis
St. Paul
Duluth
Des Moines
Omaha
Kansas City
St. Louis
Louisville
Nashville
Memphis
Chattanooga
Knoxville
Atlanta
Birmingham
Charlotte
Columbia
Charleston
Savannah
Jacksonville
Tampa
St. Petersburg
Orlando
Miami
Key West
New Orleans
Baton Rouge
Houston
Dallas
Oklahoma City
Tulsa
Wichita
Little Rock
Shreveport
Jackson
Mobile
MINNESOTA
WISCONSIN
MICHIGAN
IOWA
ILLINOIS
INDIANA
OHIO
PENNSYLVANIA
NEW YORK
MAINE
VERMONT
NEW HAMPSHIRE
MASS.
CONN.
R.I.
NEW JERSEY
MARYLAND
DEL.
WEST VIRGINIA
VIRGINIA
KENTUCKY
TENNESSEE
NORTH CAROLINA
SOUTH CAROLINA
GEORGIA
FLORIDA
ALABAMA
MISSISSIPPI
LOUISIANA
ARKANSAS
MISSOURI
KANSAS
OKLAHOMA
TEXAS
ATLANTIC OCEAN
GULF OF MEXICO
BAHAMAS
Grand Bahama I.
Andros I.
Eleuthera I.
Nassau
Delta of the Mississippi
Appalachian Mts.
Blue Ridge
Chesapeake Bay
Delaware Bay
Long Bay
Onslow Bay
C. Hatteras
C. Canaveral
Florida Keys
Florida Bay
8
9
10
11
12

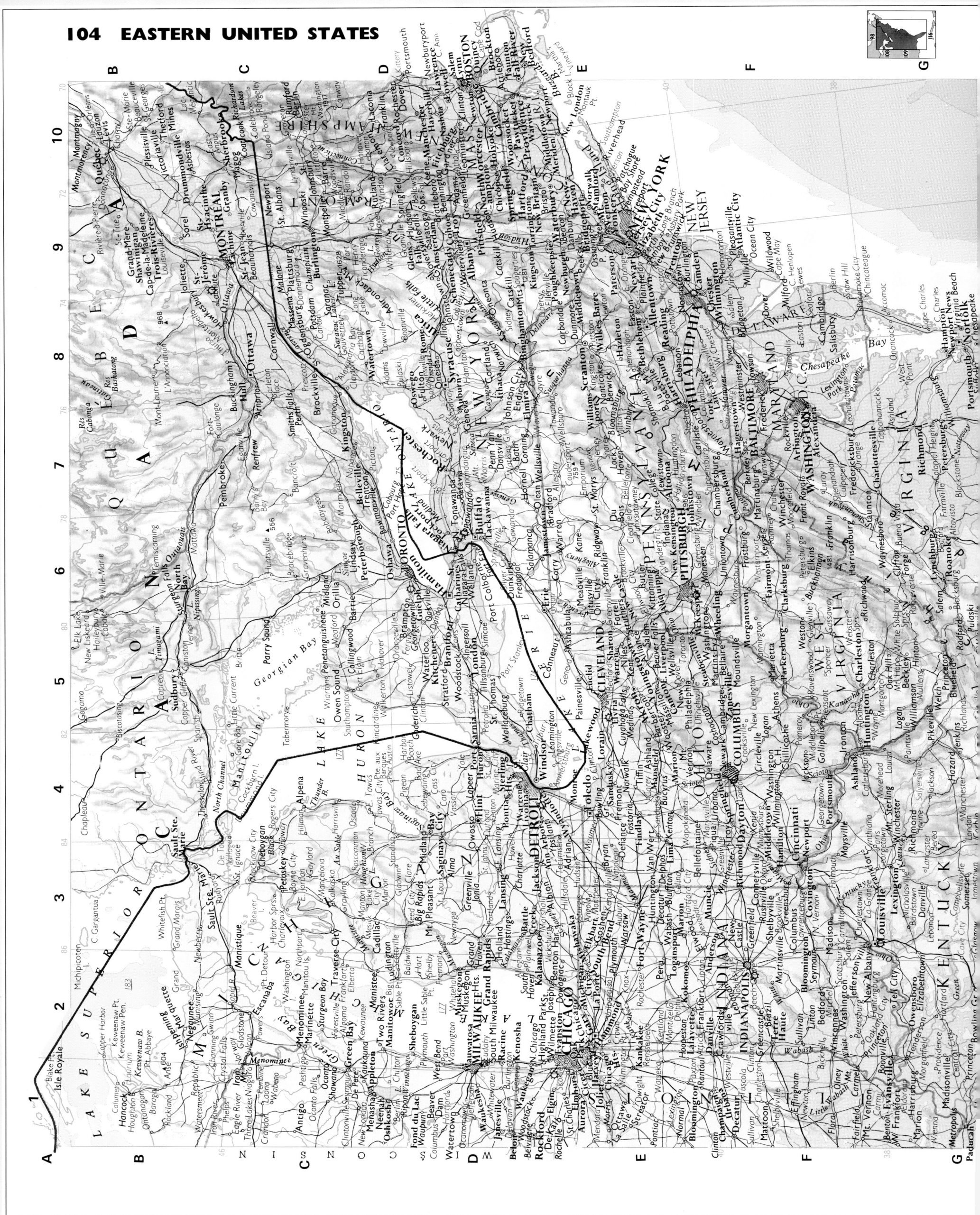

LAKE SUPERIOR
LAKE MICHIGAN
LAKE HURON
LAKE ERIE
LAKE ONTARIO
Georgian Bay
Green Bay
Chesapeake Bay
ONTARIO
QUÉBEC
CANADA
MICHIGAN
WISCONSIN
ILLINOIS
INDIANA
OHIO
KENTUCKY
WEST VIRGINIA
VIRGINIA
MARYLAND
DELAWARE
PENNSYLVANIA
NEW JERSEY
NEW YORK
VERMONT
NEW HAMPSHIRE
MASS.
CONN.
R.I.
CHICAGO
MILWAUKEE
DETROIT
CLEVELAND
PITTSBURGH
COLUMBUS
INDIANAPOLIS
PHILADELPHIA
BALTIMORE
WASHINGTON D.C.
NEW YORK
BOSTON
MONTRÉAL
Ottawa
TORONTO
Hamilton
Buffalo
Rochester
Syracuse
Albany
London
Windsor
Toledo
Lansing
Grand Rapids
Cincinnati
Dayton
Louisville
Erie
Scranton
Harrisburg
Richmond
Norfolk
Québec
Sudbury
Sault Ste. Marie

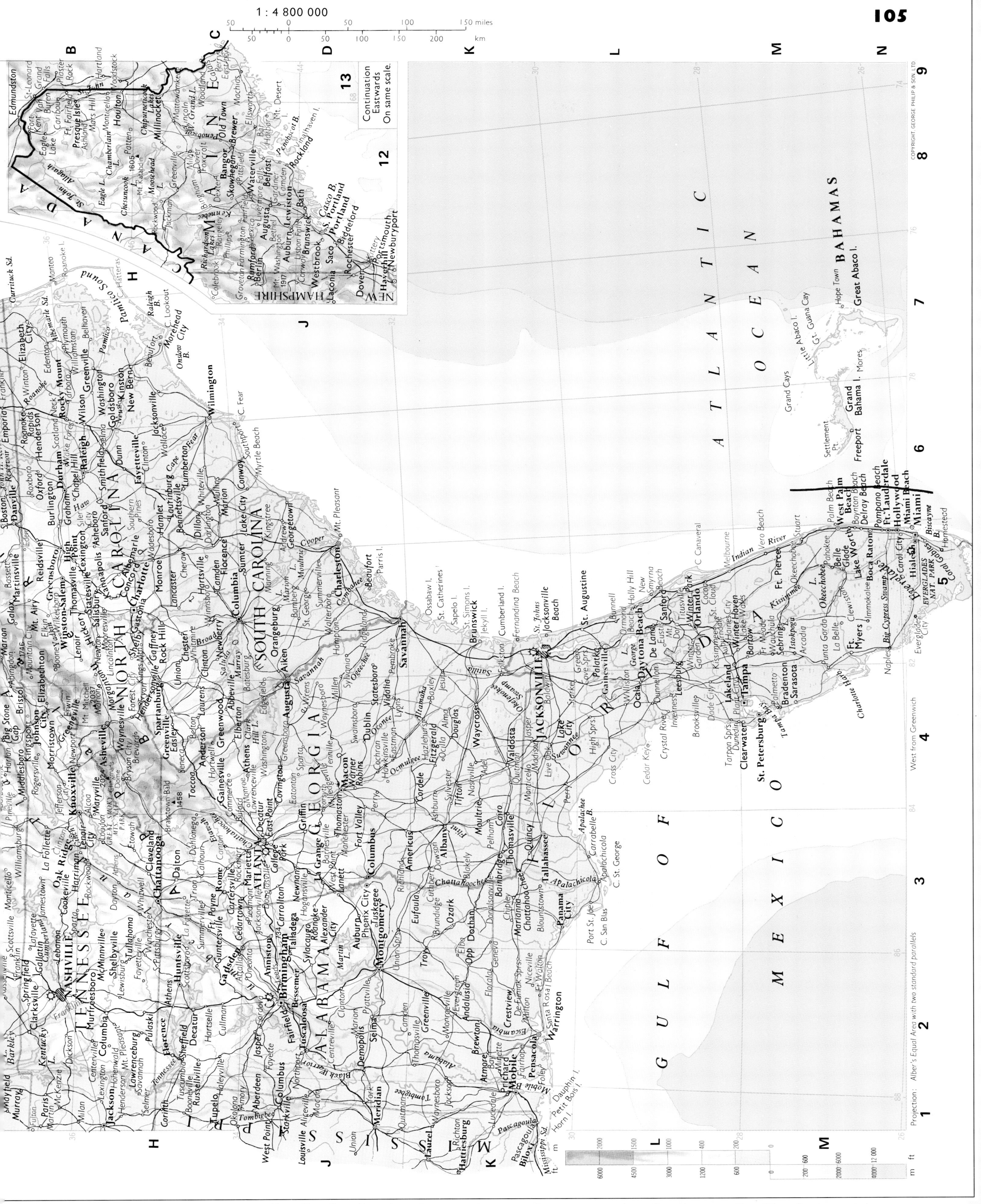

1 : 4 800 000
50 0 50 100 150 miles
50 0 50 100 150 200 km
13
12
Continuation Eastwards On same scale.
NORTH CAROLINA
SOUTH CAROLINA
GEORGIA
ALABAMA
TENNESSEE
FLORIDA
MAINE
NEW HAMPSHIRE
CANADA
BAHAMAS
ATLANTIC OCEAN
GULF OF MEXICO
Great Abaco I.
Grand Bahama I.
Freeport
Nashville
Knoxville
Chattanooga
Atlanta
Birmingham
Montgomery
Mobile
Pensacola
Tallahassee
Jacksonville
Savannah
Charleston
Columbia
Charlotte
Raleigh
Wilmington
Orlando
Tampa
St. Petersburg
Miami
Augusta
Macon
Columbus
Greenville
Asheville
Portland
Bangor
Augusta
Projection: Alber's Equal Area with two standard parallels
West from Greenwich
COPYRIGHT GEORGE PHILIP & SON, LTD
m ft
6000 4500 3000 1200 600 200 0
2000 1500 1000 400 200
200 600 2000 4000
600 6000 12 000

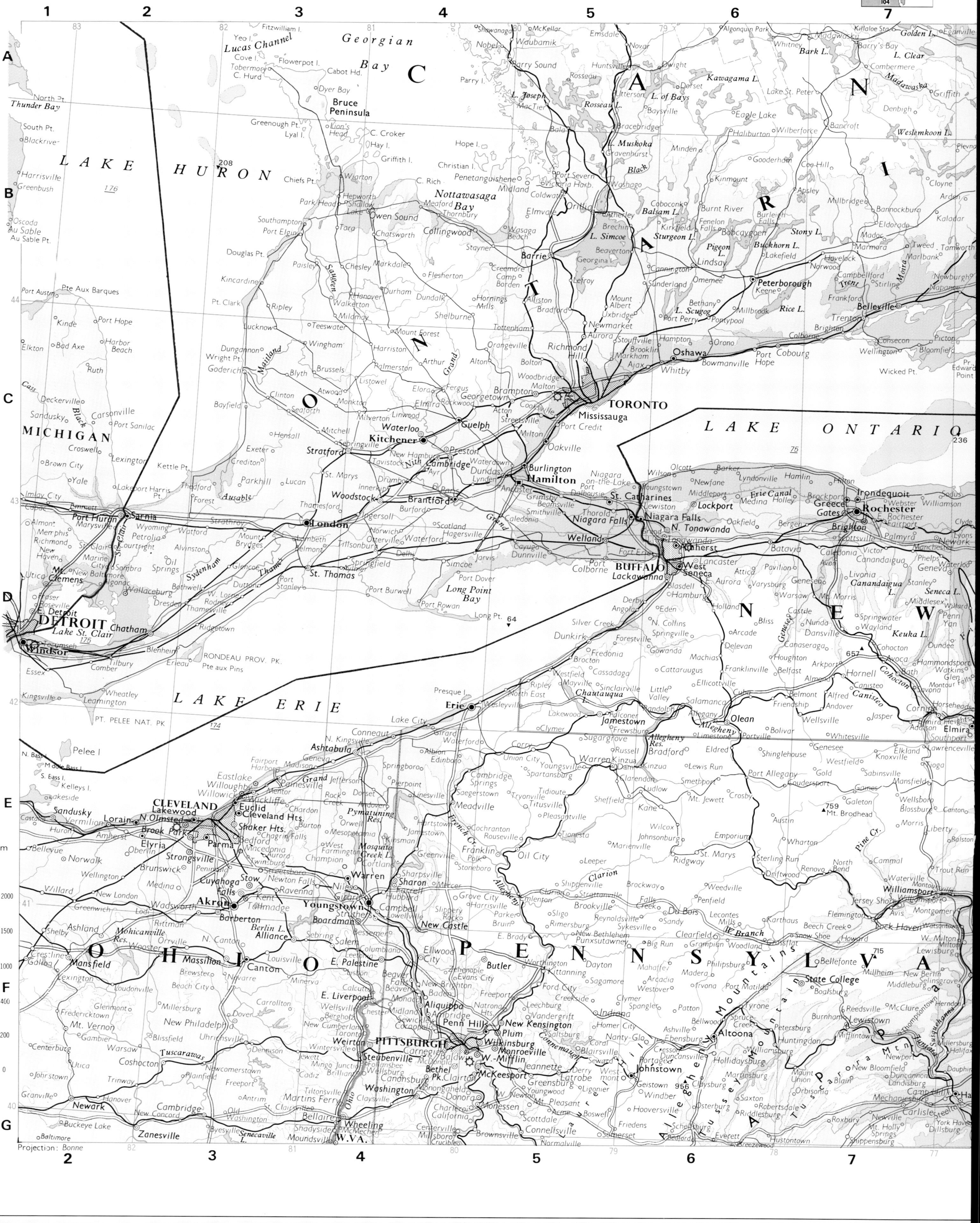

1   2   3   4   5   6   7

A B C D E F G

Georgian Bay

LAKE HURON

Bruce Peninsula

Nottawasaga Bay

MICHIGAN

ONTARIO

Owen Sound · Collingwood · Barrie · L. Simcoe · Orillia · Lindsay · Peterborough

Waterloo · Kitchener · Guelph · Brampton · **TORONTO** · Mississauga

Stratford · Cambridge · Hamilton · Burlington · Oakville

London · Brantford · St. Catharines · Niagara Falls · Welland

LAKE ONTARIO

Buffalo · Lackawanna · Tonawanda · N. Tonawanda · Amherst

Rochester · Greece · Gates · Brighton · Irondequoit

LAKE ERIE

Sarnia · Port Huron · **DETROIT** · Windsor · Lake St. Clair

Long Point Bay · Long Pt. · Dunkirk

Erie · Jamestown · Chautauqua · Olean · Hornell · Elmira

Cleveland · Lakewood · Euclid · Cleveland Hts. · Shaker Hts. · Parma

Sandusky · Lorain · Elyria · Akron · Youngstown · Warren

NEW YORK

OHIO **PENNSYLVANIA**

Mansfield · Canton · Massillon · New Castle · Butler

PITTSBURGH · Wilkinsburg · McKeesport · Monroeville · Penn Hills

Washington · Wheeling · **W.VA.**

Steubenville · Weirton · Johnstown · Altoona · State College

Zanesville · Newark

ft m

6000 2000
4500 1500
3000 1000
1200 400
600   200
0   0
200   600

m ft

1 : 2 000 000

State/region names: ONTARIO · QUEBEC · NEW YORK · VERMONT · NEW HAMPSHIRE · MAINE · MASSACHUSETTS · CONNECTICUT · RHODE ISLAND · NEW JERSEY · PENNSYLVANIA

MONTREAL · Ottawa · Hull · PHILADELPHIA · NEW YORK · Long Island · ATLANTIC OCEAN

West from Greenwich

COPYRIGHT GEORGE PHILIP & SON, LTD.

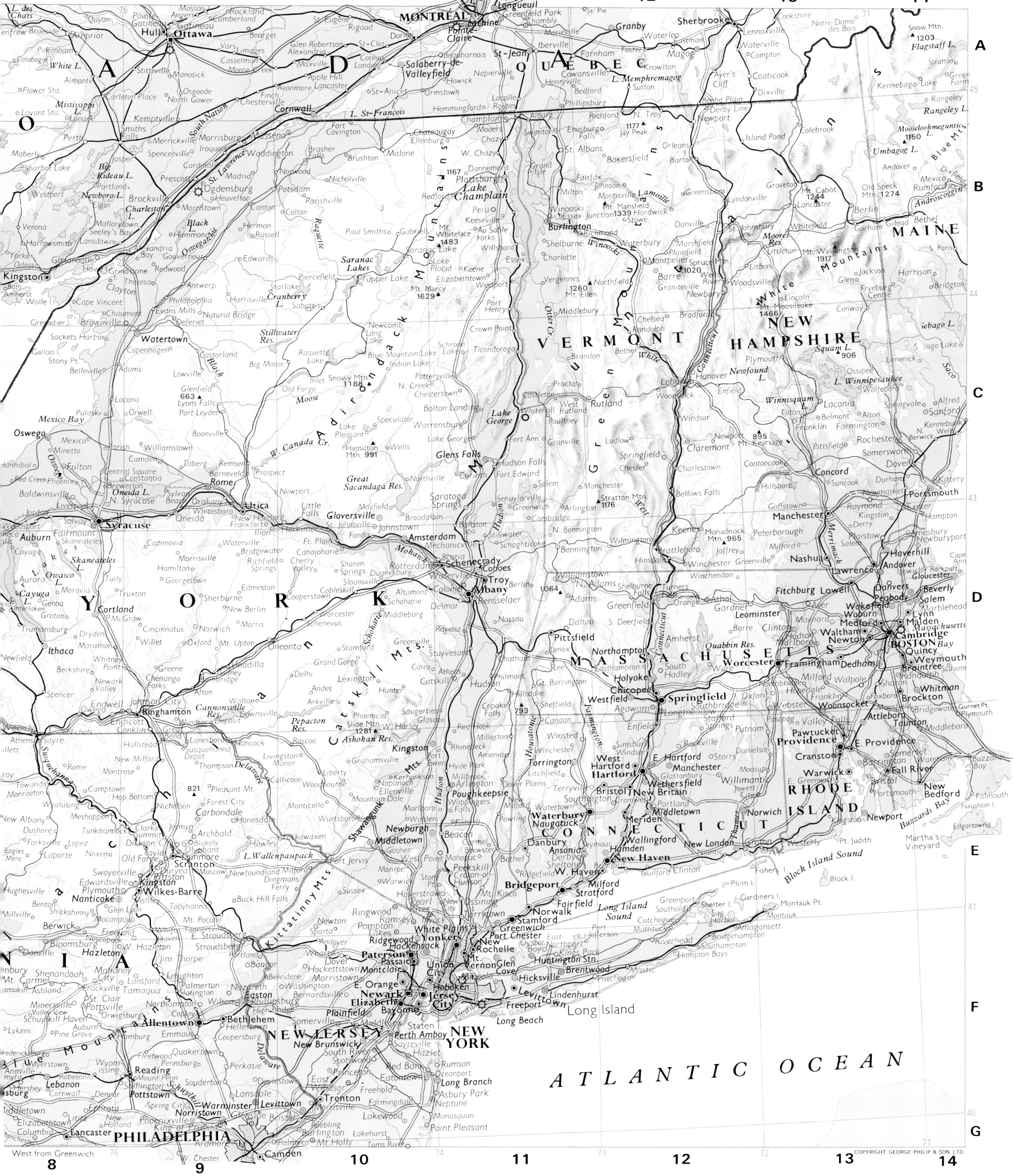

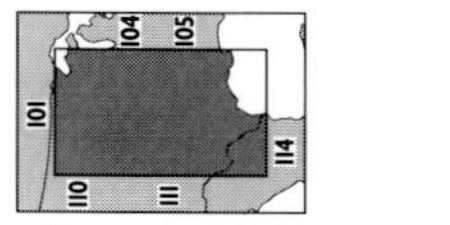

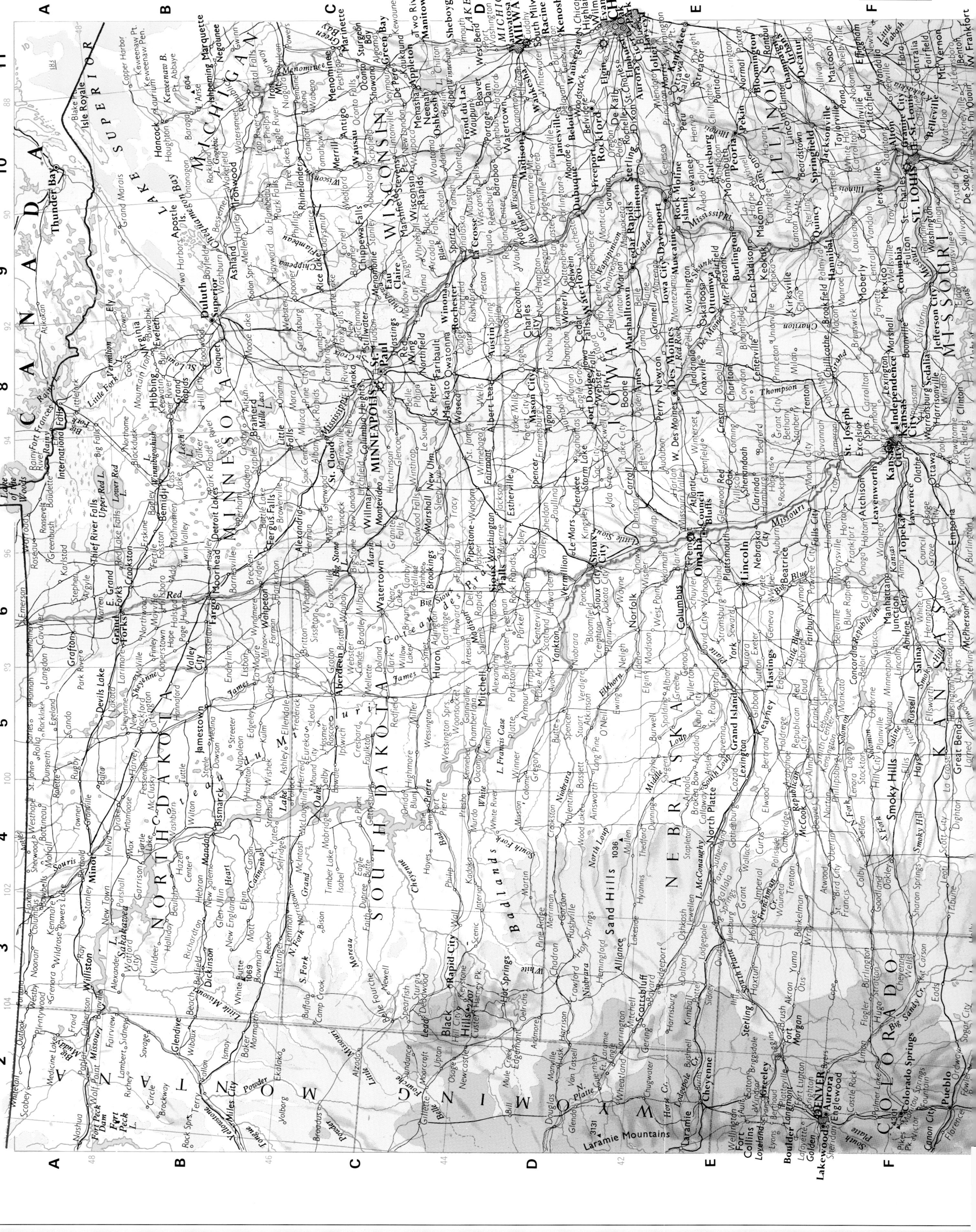

CANADA
NORTH DAKOTA
SOUTH DAKOTA
NEBRASKA
KANSAS
MINNESOTA
IOWA
WISCONSIN
MICHIGAN
ILLINOIS
MISSOURI
MONTANA
WYOMING
COLORADO
LAKE SUPERIOR
LAKE MICHIGAN
CHICAGO
MILWAUKEE
MINNEAPOLIS
St. Paul
ST. LOUIS
Kansas City
Omaha
DENVER
Des Moines
Duluth
Bismarck
Lincoln
Cheyenne
Sioux City
Rapid City
Black Hills
Badlands
Sand Hills
Smoky Hills
Laramie Mountains
Lake of the Woods
Thunder Bay
Isle Royale
Missouri
Mississippi
Platte
Red
Yellowstone

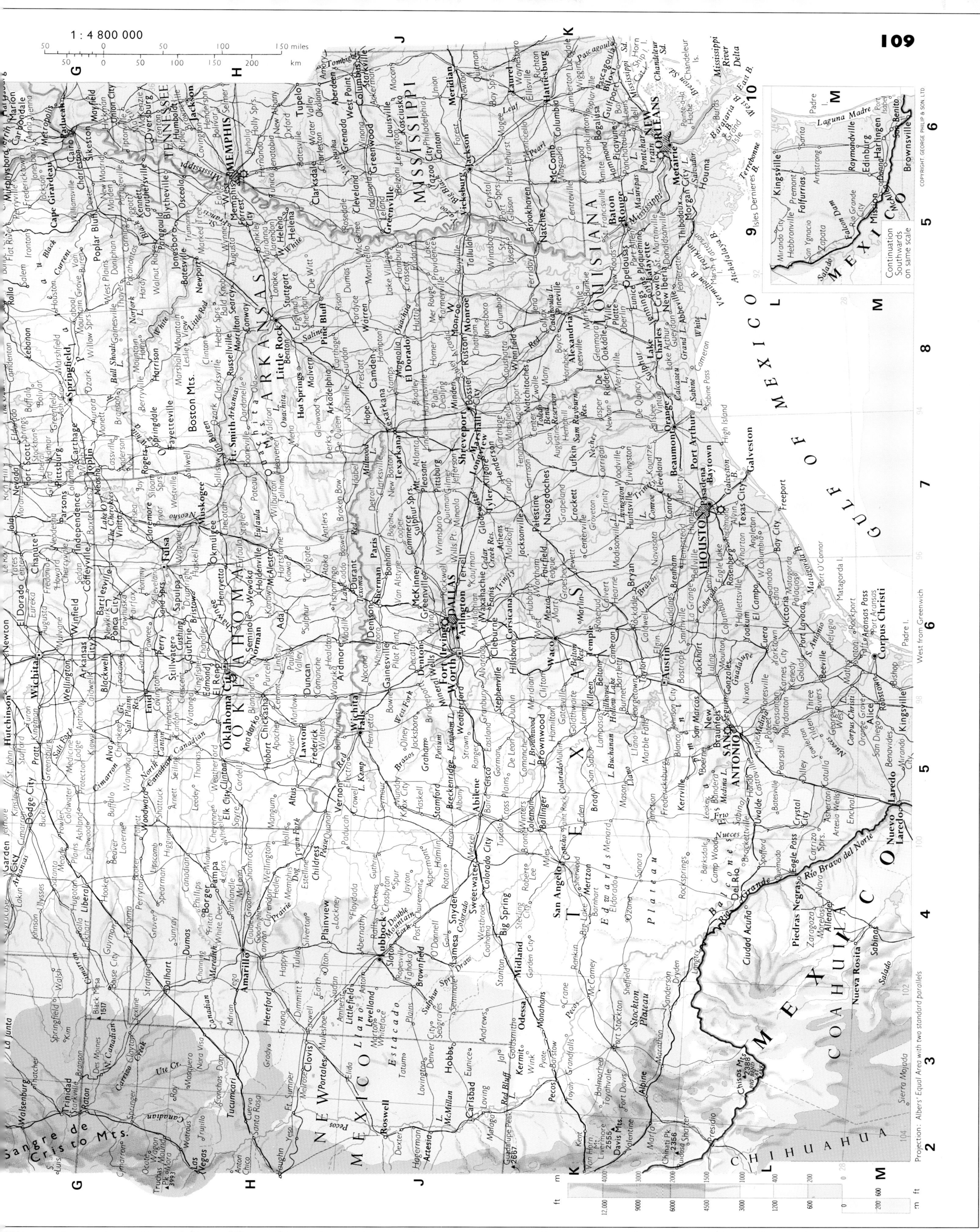

1 : 4 800 000

50   0   50   100   150 miles
50 0 50 100 150 200 km

G   **H**   **J**   **K**

TENNESSEE

MEMPHIS

MISSISSIPPI

Meridian

New ORLEANS

Metairie

Baton Rouge

LOUISIANA

ARKANSAS

Little Rock

Hot Springs

Texarkana

Shreveport

OKLAHOMA

Oklahoma City

Norman

Tulsa

DALLAS

Fort Worth

Arlington

Irving

Waco

Austin

Houston

Pasadena

Baytown

Beaumont

Port Arthur

Galveston

Corpus Christi

T E X A S

San Antonio

Laredo

Nuevo Laredo

Wichita

Hutchinson

Dodge City

Amarillo

Lubbock

Odessa

Midland

San Angelo

Big Spring

N E W   M E X I C O

Roswell

Carlsbad

Sangre de Cristo Mts.

M E X I C O

C O A H U I L A

C H I H U A H U A

Ciudad Acuña

Piedras Negras

GULF OF MEXICO

Laguna Madre

Brownsville

McAllen

Padre I.

COPYRIGHT GEORGE PHILIP & SON, LTD

M

10

Pascagoula

Mississippi River Delta

Chandeleur Is.

9 Isles Dernières B.

Continuation Southwards on same scale

6

5

8

7

6

5

4

3

2

West from Greenwich

Projection: Albers' Equal Area with two standard parallels

G   **H**   **J**   **K**   **L**   **M**

ft   m
12,000   3000
9000
6000   1500
4500
3000   1200
600
0   200 600

1 : 4 800 000

50 0 50 100 miles

50 0 50 100 150 km

100
108
109
114

WASHINGTON
OREGON
IDAHO
MONTANA
WYOMING
NEVADA
BRITISH COLUMBIA
ALBERTA
SASKATCHEWAN
CANADA
Vancouver
Seattle
Tacoma
Olympia
Portland
Salem
Eugene
Spokane
Boise
Pocatello
Idaho Falls
Missoula
Helena
Butte
Great Falls
Billings
Casper
Ogden
Salt Lake City
Great Salt Lake
Reno
Sacramento
Bighorn Mountains
Medicine Bow Mts.
Uinta Mountains
Clearwater Mountains
Salmon River Mountains
Blue Mountains
Cabinet Mountains
Lemhi Range
Great Sandy Desert
Olympic Mts.
Juan de Fuca Strait

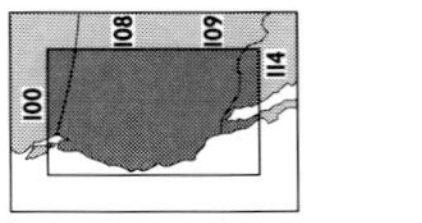

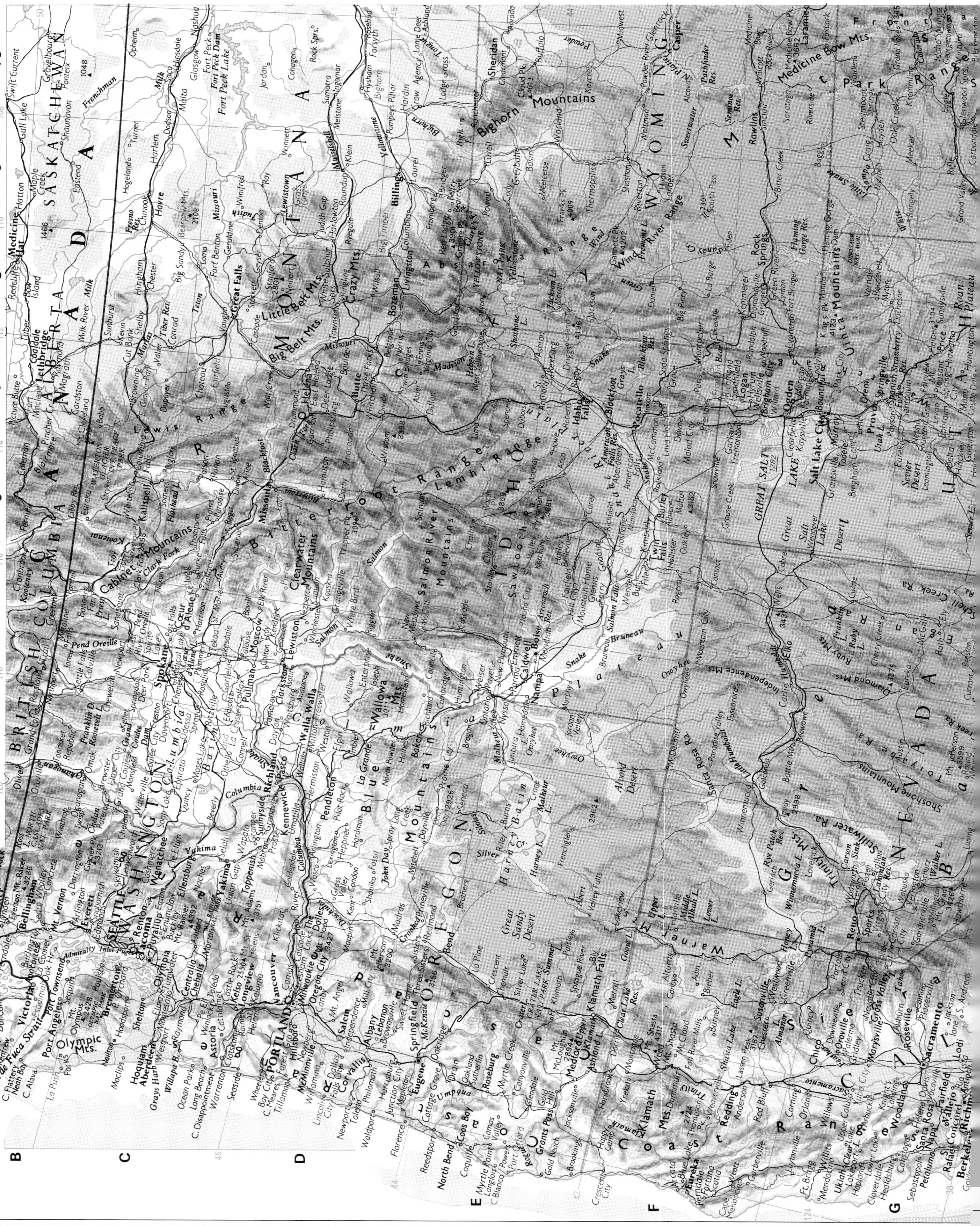

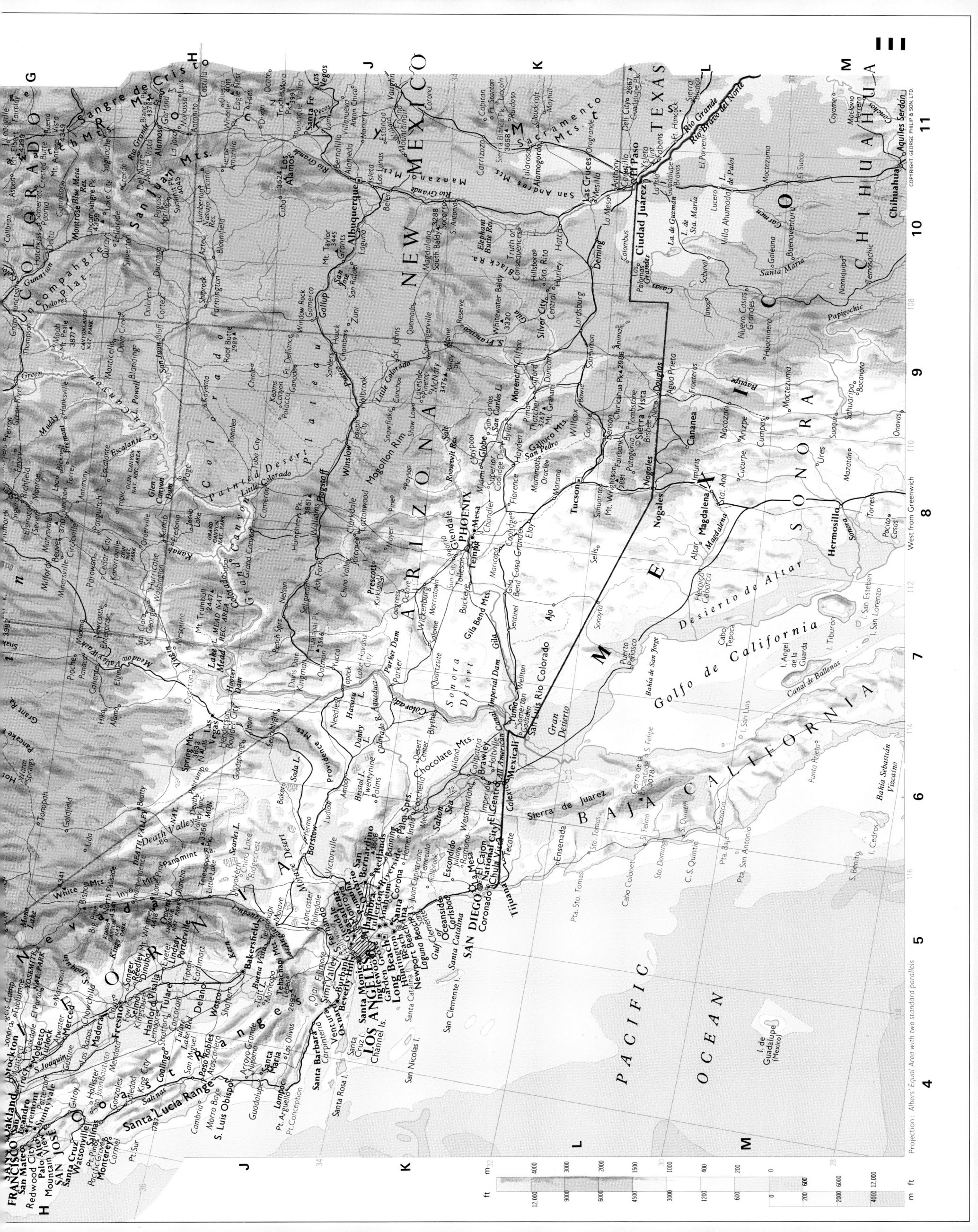

COLORADO
NEW MEXICO
ARIZONA
TEXAS
CALIFORNIA
MEXICO
SONORA
CHIHUAHUA
BAJA CALIFORNIA
PACIFIC OCEAN
Golfo de California
Desierto de Altar
Gran Desierto
Sonora Desert
Mojave Desert
Death Valley
Colorado Plateau
Painted Desert
Grand Canyon
Santa Lucia Range
Sierra de Juarez
San Juan Mts.
Sacramento Mts.
Uncompahgre Plat.
FRANCISCO
Oakland
SAN JOSE
LOS ANGELES
SAN DIEGO
PHOENIX
Tucson
Albuquerque
Santa Fe
El Paso
Ciudad Juárez
Las Vegas
Fresno
Bakersfield
Hermosillo
Nogales
Mexicali
Tijuana
Yuma
Flagstaff
Chihuahua
Las Cruces
Santa Barbara
Long Beach
Lake Mead
Hoover Dam
Parker Dam
Salton Sea
Rio Grande
Colorado
Gila
Channel Is.
I. de Guadalupe (Mexico)
Projection: Albers' Equal Area with two standard parallels
West from Greenwich
COPYRIGHT, GEORGE PHILIP & SON, LTD.

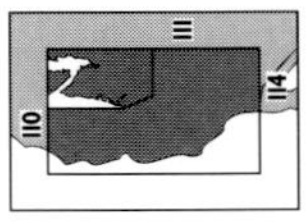

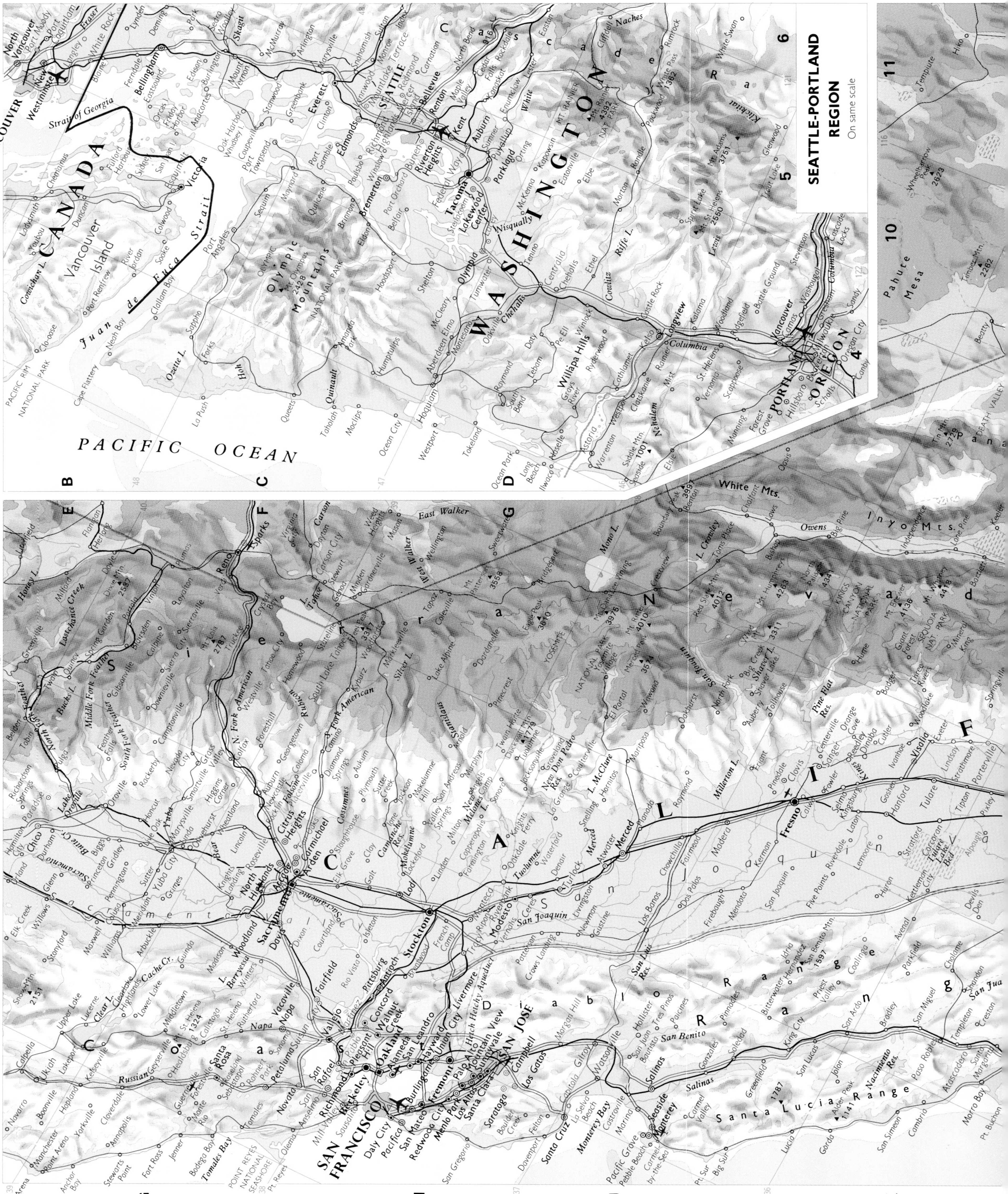

SEATTLE-PORTLAND REGION
On same scale

CANADA

Vancouver Island

Strait of Georgia

Juan de Fuca Strait

Olympic Mountains

NATIONAL PARK

PACIFIC OCEAN

WASHINGTON

SEATTLE

Tacoma

Olympia

PORTLAND

OREGON

Columbia

Willapa Hills

Pahute Mesa

DEATH VALLEY

White Mts.

Inyo Mts.

Owens

Sierra Nevada

YOSEMITE NAT. PARK

KINGS CANYON NAT. PARK

SEQUOIA NAT. PARK

SACRAMENTO

Sacramento Valley

Stockton

San Joaquin

Fresno

Merced

Modesto

Visalia

SAN FRANCISCO

Oakland

Berkeley

SAN JOSE

Santa Cruz

Monterey Bay

Salinas

Santa Lucia Range

Coast Ranges

Reno

Sparks

Carson City

Lake Tahoe

Mono L.

Napa

Santa Rosa

Vallejo

Concord

Livermore

Fremont

Palo Alto

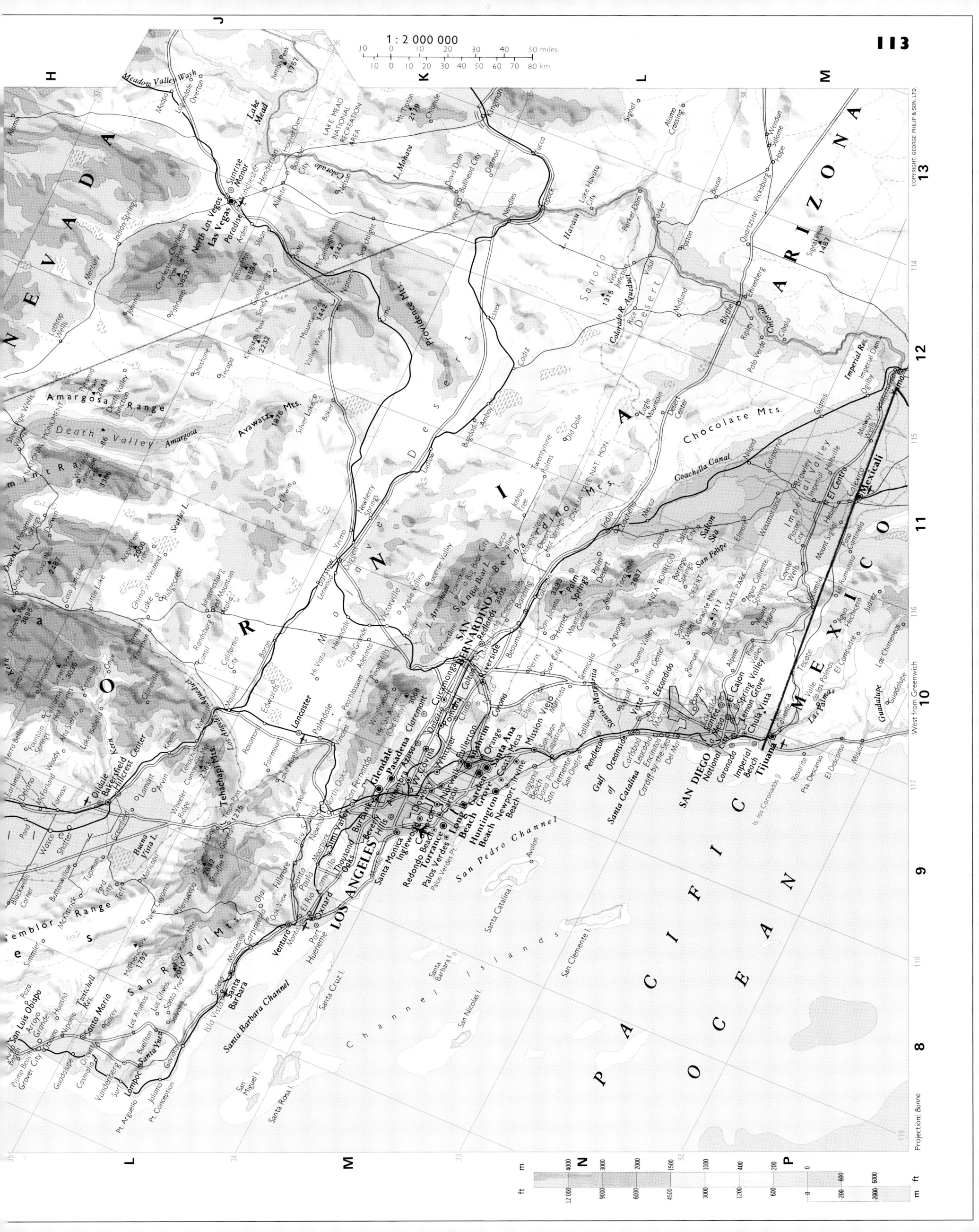
1 : 2 000 000
NEVADA
CALIFORNIA
ARIZONA
MEXICO
PACIFIC OCEAN
LOS ANGELES
SAN DIEGO
SAN BERNARDINO
Las Vegas
North Las Vegas
Lake Mead
LAKE MEAD NATIONAL RECREATION AREA
Mojave Desert
Death Valley
Amargosa Range
Avawatz Mts.
Providence Mts.
Chocolate Mts.
Sonora Desert
Salton Sea
Coachella Canal
Colorado R. Aqueduct
Imperial Valley
Mexicali
Tijuana
Santa Barbara Channel
San Pedro Channel
Gulf of Santa Catalina
Channel Islands
Santa Catalina I.
San Clemente I.
Santa Cruz I.
Santa Rosa I.
San Miguel I.
San Nicolas I.
Santa Barbara
Ventura
Oxnard
Bakersfield
Lancaster
Palmdale
Glendale
Pasadena
Long Beach
Santa Ana
Riverside
Palm Springs
Escondido
Oceanside
El Centro
Yuma
Blythe
Needles
Kingman
Barstow
San Luis Obispo
Santa Maria
Lompoc
Tehachapi Mts.
Colorado
Projection: Bonne
West from Greenwich
COPYRIGHT GEORGE PHILIP & SON LTD.

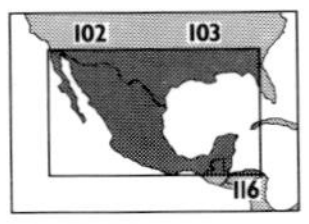

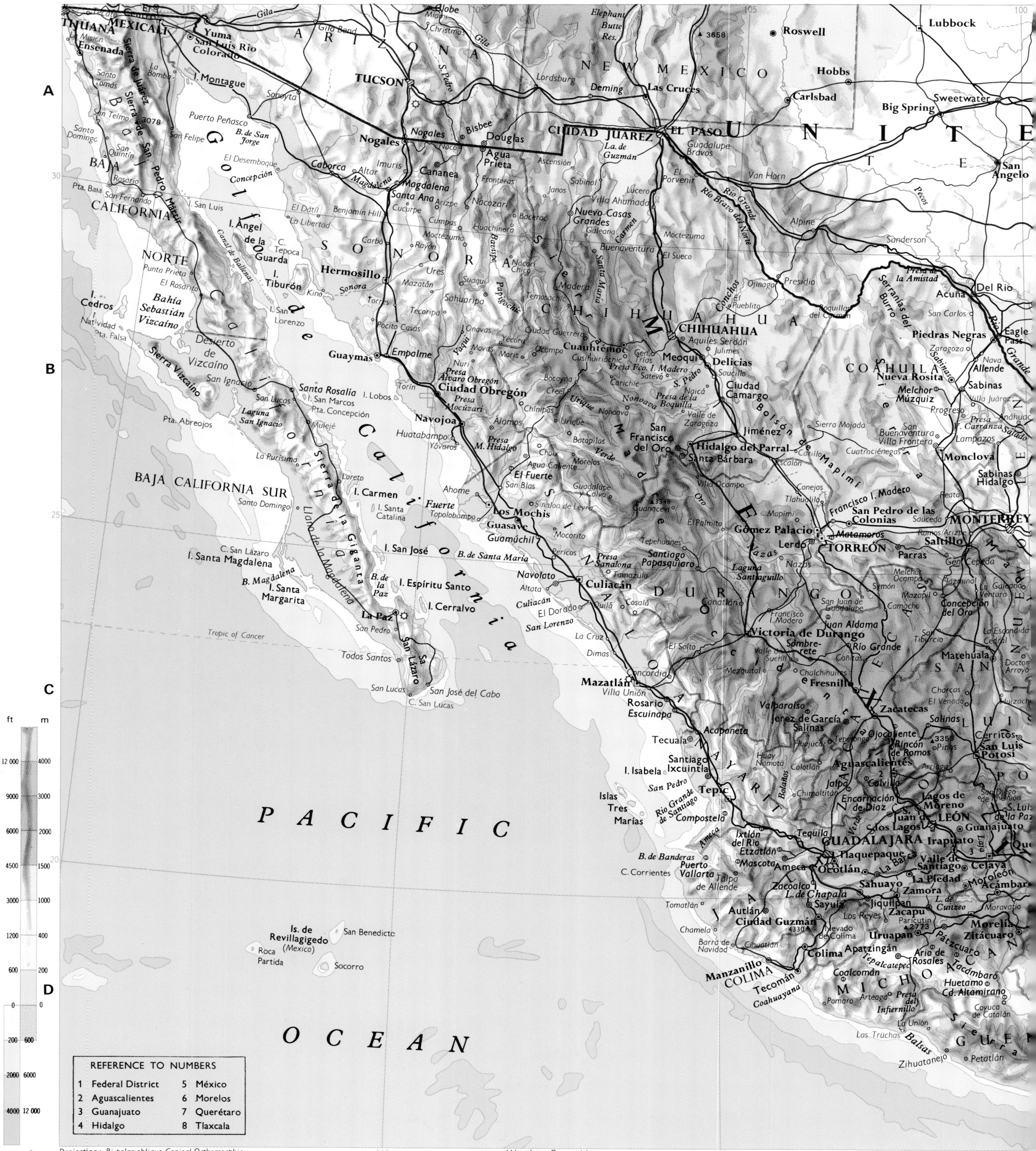

Grid references
1 2 3 4

A B C D

Place names

United States / borders
Tijuana, Mexicali, Yuma, San Luis Rio Colorado, Ensenada, El Centro
ARIZONA, NEW MEXICO
TUCSON, Globe, Miami, Christmas, Gila Bend, S. Pedro, Gila
Elephant Butte Res., 3658, Roswell, Lubbock
Lordsburg, Deming, Las Cruces, Hobbs, Carlsbad
CIUDAD JUAREZ, EL PASO, UNITED
Nogales, Bisbee, Douglas, Agua Prieta
Van Horn, Alpine, Sanderson, Big Spring, Sweetwater
San Angelo, Del Rio, Acuña, Eagle Pass, Piedras Negras

Baja California
BAJA CALIFORNIA NORTE, Sierra de Juárez, 3078
Santo Tomás, San Telmo, San Quintín, Santo Domingo, El Rosario
Pta. Baja, San Fernando, Rosario, Punta Prieta, El Rosarito
I. Cedros, I. Natividad, Pta. Falsa
Bahía Sebastián Vizcaíno, Desierto de Vizcaíno, Sierra Vizcaíno
BAJA CALIFORNIA SUR
Santa Rosalía, San Ignacio, Laguna San Ignacio, Mulegé, Loreto
Sierra de la Giganta, Llano de la Magdalena
La Purísima, Santo Domingo, San José del Cabo
C. San Lázaro, I. Santa Magdalena, I. Santa Margarita
B. Magdalena, B. de la Paz, I. Espíritu Santo, I. Cerralvo
La Paz, San Pedro, Todos Santos, San Lucas, C. San Lucas
Puerto Peñasco, B. de San Jorge, San Felipe, I. Ángel de la Guarda
C. Tepoca, I. Tiburón, El Desemboque, La Libertad

Gulf of California
Golfo de California / Gulf of California
I. San Luis, I. Lobos, I. San Marcos, I. San José, I. Carmen
I. Santa Catalina, I. San Lorenzo

Sonora
SONORA, Caborca, Altar, Magdalena, Santa Ana, Imuris, Cananea
Cucurpe, Arizpe, Nacozari, Fronteras
Hermosillo, Ures, Mazatán, Sonora, Kino, Torres, Pócito Casas
Guaymas, Empalme, Ciudad Obregón, Navojoa, Huatabampo
Presa Álvaro Obregón, Presa Mocúzari, Yávaros
Benjamin Hill, El Dátil, Sahuaripa, Técoripa, Onavas, Yécora
Moctezuma, Huachinera, Nácori Chico

Chihuahua
CHIHUAHUA, Cuauhtémoc, Meoqui, Delicias, Saucillo
Ciudad Camargo, Jiménez, Hidalgo del Parral, Santa Bárbara
San Francisco del Oro, Villa Ahumada, Nuevo Casas Grandes
Ciudad Guerrero, Madera, Temosachic, Creel, Batopilas, Urique
Gómez Palacio, Lerdo, TORREÓN
La de Guzmán, Ascensión, El Porvenir, Ojinaga, Presidio
Aquiles Serdán, Julimes, Satevó, Boquilla

Sinaloa
SINALOA, Los Mochis, Guasave, Guamúchil, Culiacán, Navolato
El Fuerte, Ahome, Topolobampo, San Blas
Mazatlán, Villa Unión, Rosario, Escuinapa, Concordia
El Dorado, San Lorenzo, Dimas, El Salto

Durango
DURANGO, Victoria de Durango, Santiago Papasquiaro
Canatlán, Río Grande, Sombrerete, Nazas, El Palmito

Coahuila / Nuevo León
COAHUILA, Nueva Rosita, Melchor Múzquiz, Sabinas
Monclova, Sabinas Hidalgo, MONTERREY, Saltillo, Parras
San Pedro de las Colonias, Francisco I. Madero, Matehuala
Ramos Arizpe

Zacatecas / San Luis Potosí
ZACATECAS, Fresnillo, Valparaíso, Jerez de García, Salinas
SAN LUIS POTOSÍ, San Luis Potosí, Cerritos, Charcas, Venado
Concepción del Oro

Jalisco / Aguascalientes / Guanajuato
GUADALAJARA, Tlaquepaque, Aguascalientes, Calvillo
Encarnación de Díaz, Lagos de Moreno, LEÓN, Guanajuato
San Juan de los Lagos, Tequila, Irapuato, Celaya
Ixtlán del Río, Etzatlán, Ameca, Mascota, Autlán, Zacoalco
Ocotlán, La Barca, La Piedad, Sahuayo, Zamora

Nayarit
NAYARIT, Tepic, Compostela, Tecuala, Acaponeta
Santiago Ixcuintla, San Pedro, Islas Tres Marías
Rincón de Romos, Jalpa, Colotlán

Colima / Michoacán
COLIMA, Manzanillo, Tecomán, Colima, Coalcomán
MICHOACÁN, Ciudad Guzmán, Uruapan, Apatzingán, Zitácuaro
Morelia, Pátzcuaro, Zacapu, Jiquilpan, Sayula
Ario de Rosales, Tacámbaro, Huetamo, Cd. Altamirano
Zihuatanejo, Petatlán, Las Truchas

Water / other
PACIFIC OCEAN
Río Grande, Rio Brano del Norte, Río Conchos, Pecos
Tropic of Cancer
Is. de Revillagigedo (México), San Benedicto, Roca Partida, Socorro
B. de Banderas, Puerto Vallarta, C. Corrientes, Talpa de Allende
B. de Santa María, B. de la Paz
Laguna Santiaguillo, Presa Sanalona, Presa de la Amistad
Presa de la Boquilla, Presa Fco. I. Madero
Río Grande de Santiago, L. de Chapala, L. de Cuitzeo

ft	m
12 000	4000
9000	3000
6000	2000
4500	1500
3000	1000
1200	400
600	200
0	0
200	600
2000	6000
4000	12 000

m ft

REFERENCE TO NUMBERS

1	Federal District	5	México
2	Aguascalientes	6	Morelos
3	Guanajuato	7	Querétaro
4	Hidalgo	8	Tlaxcala

102 103
116

1 : 6 400 000

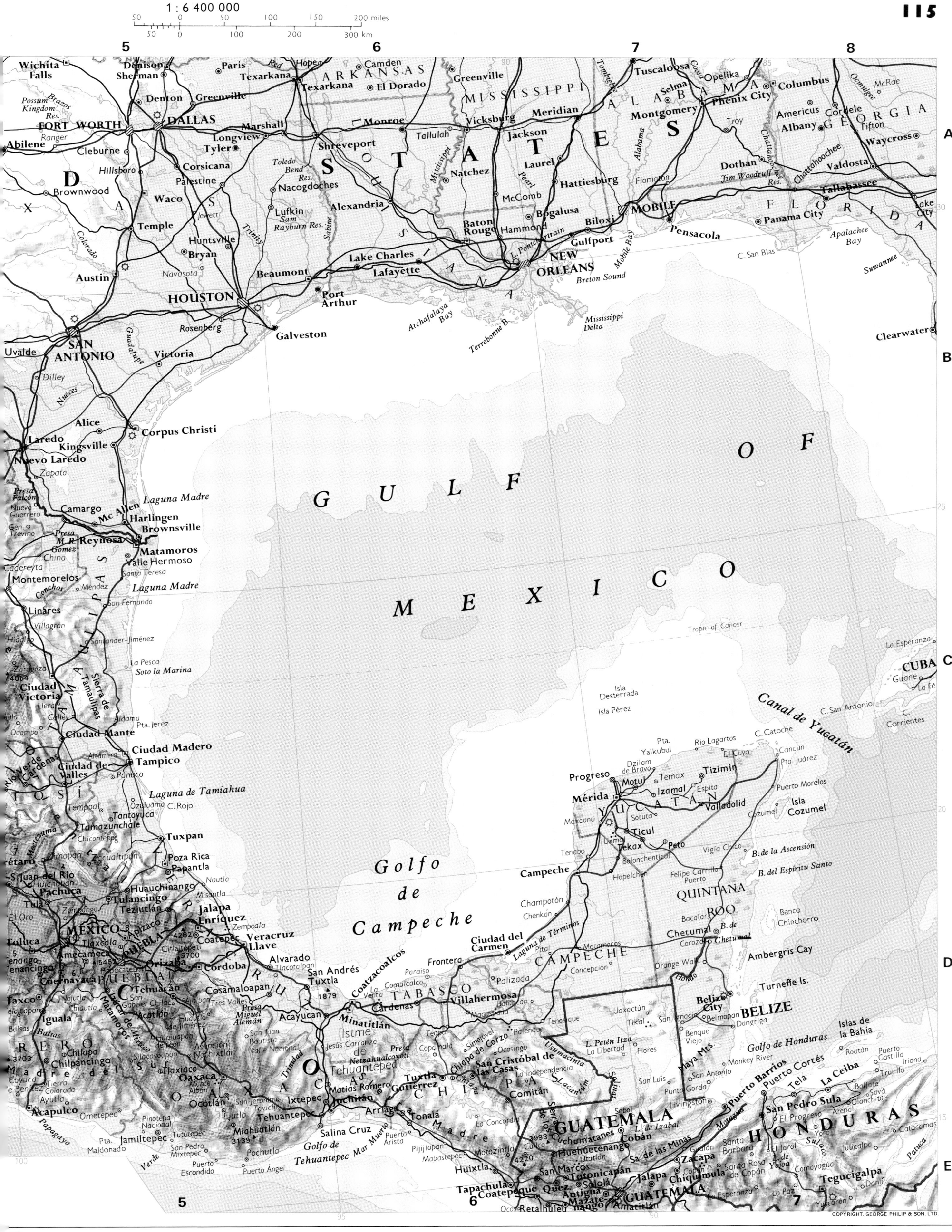

50   0   50   100   150   200 miles
50   0   100   200   300 km

5   **6**   **7**   **8**

Wichita
Falls
Denison
Sherman   Paris   Red   Hope   Camden   Greenville   Tuscaloosa   Opelika
Texarkana   Texarkana   El Dorado   MISSISSIPPI   Columbus   McRae
Denton   Greenville   ARKANSAS   Greenville   Montgomery   Phenix City   Americus   Cordele   A
FORT WORTH   DALLAS   Longview   Marshall   Monroe   Vicksburg   Meridian   ALABAMA   Montgomery   Albany   GEORGIA   Tifton   Waycross
Abilene   Ranger   Cleburne   Tyler   Shreveport   Jackson   Troy   Valdosta
Hillsboro   Corsicana   Palestine   Toledo   Natchez   Laurel   Dothan   Jim Woodruff   Chattahoochee   Tallahassee
Brownwood   Waco   Nacogdoches   Alexandria   McComb   Hattiesburg   Flomaton   Res.   FLORIDA   Lake City
Temple   Lufkin   Sam   Baton   Bogalusa   MOBILE   Pensacola   Panama City   Apalachee   Bay
Huntsville   Rayburn Res.   Rouge   Hammond   Biloxi   Bay
Bryan   Trinity   Lake Charles   New   Gulfport   Mobile Bay   C. San Blas   Suwannee   B
Austin   Beaumont   Lafayette   ORLEANS   Breton Sound
HOUSTON   Port   Atchafalaya   Mississippi
Rosenberg   Arthur   Bay   Terrebonne B.   Delta   Clearwater
SAN   Victoria   Galveston
ANTONIO
Uvalde   Dilley   Nueces

Alice   Corpus Christi

GULF   OF

Laredo   Kingsville
Nuevo Laredo   Zapata
Presa   Camargo   McAllen   Harlingen   **MEXICO**
Falcón   Reynosa   Brownsville   C
Nuevo   Matamoros
Guerrero   Valle Hermoso   Laguna Madre
Montemorelos   Santa Teresa
Linares   San Fernando   Laguna Madre   Tropic of Cancer   La Esperanza   CUBA
Villagrán   Guane   La Fé
Ciudad   Soto la Marina   Isla   Canal de Yucatán   C. San Antonio
Victoria   La Pesca   Desterrada   Corrientes
Isla Pérez   Pta.   Río Lagartos   C. Catoche
Ciudad Mante   Yalkubul   El Cuyo   Cancún
Progreso   Dzilam   Temax   Tizimín   Pto. Juárez
Ciudad Madero   de Bravo   Motul   Izamal   Espita   Puerto Morelos
Tampico   Mérida   Valladolid   Isla
Ciudad   Sotuta   YUCATÁN   Cozumel   D
Valles   Laguna de Tamiahua   Maxcanú   Ticul   Cozumel
Tantoyuca   Uxmal   Tekax   Peto
Tuxpan   Tenabo   Bolonchentical   Vigía Chico   B. de la Ascensión
Poza Rica   Campeche   Hopelchén   QUINTANA
Papantla   Champotón   Felipe Carrillo   ROO   B. del Espíritu Santo
Huauchinango   Chenkán   Puerto   Banco
Tulancingo   Golfo   Bacalar   Chinchorro
Jalapa   de   Chetumal   B. de
MÉXICO   Enríquez   Campeche   Ciudad del   Laguna de Términos   Chetumal
Veracruz   Carmen   Matamoros   Corozal   Ambergris Cay
Cuernavaca   Llave   Frontera   Orange Walk   Turneffe Is.
Taxco   Córdoba   Alvarado   Paraíso   CAMPECHE   Belize   D
Iguala   Orizaba   San Andrés   Coatzacoalcos   Palizada   City   BELIZE
Tuxtla   Concepción   Uaxactún   Belmopan   Dangriga
Acayucan   Villahermosa   TABASCO   Benque   Golfo de
Chilpancingo   Minatitlán   Cárdenas   Tikal   Viejo   Islas de
Acapulco   TEHUANTEPEC   Palenque   L. Petén Itzá   Maya Mts.   la Bahía
Oaxaca   San Cristóbal de   Flores   Monkey River   Roatán   Puerto
Ixtepec   las Casas   San Luis   Castilla
Tehuantepec   Tuxtla   La Independencia   Punta   San Antonio   La Ceiba
Gutiérrez   CHIAPAS   Comitán   Gorda   Puerto Barrios   Trujillo
Salina Cruz   Tonalá   Arriaga   GUATEMALA   Puerto Cortés   E
Golfo de   Cobán   Zacapa   San Pedro Sula   HONDURAS
Miahuatlán   Tehuantepec   Huehuetenango   L. de Izabal   Chiquimula
Tapachula   GUATEMALA   Jalapa   Tegucigalpa
Coatepeque   GUATEMALA   Juticalpa

COPYRIGHT GEORGE PHILIP & SON LTD.

Projection: Bi-polar oblique Conical Orthomorphic

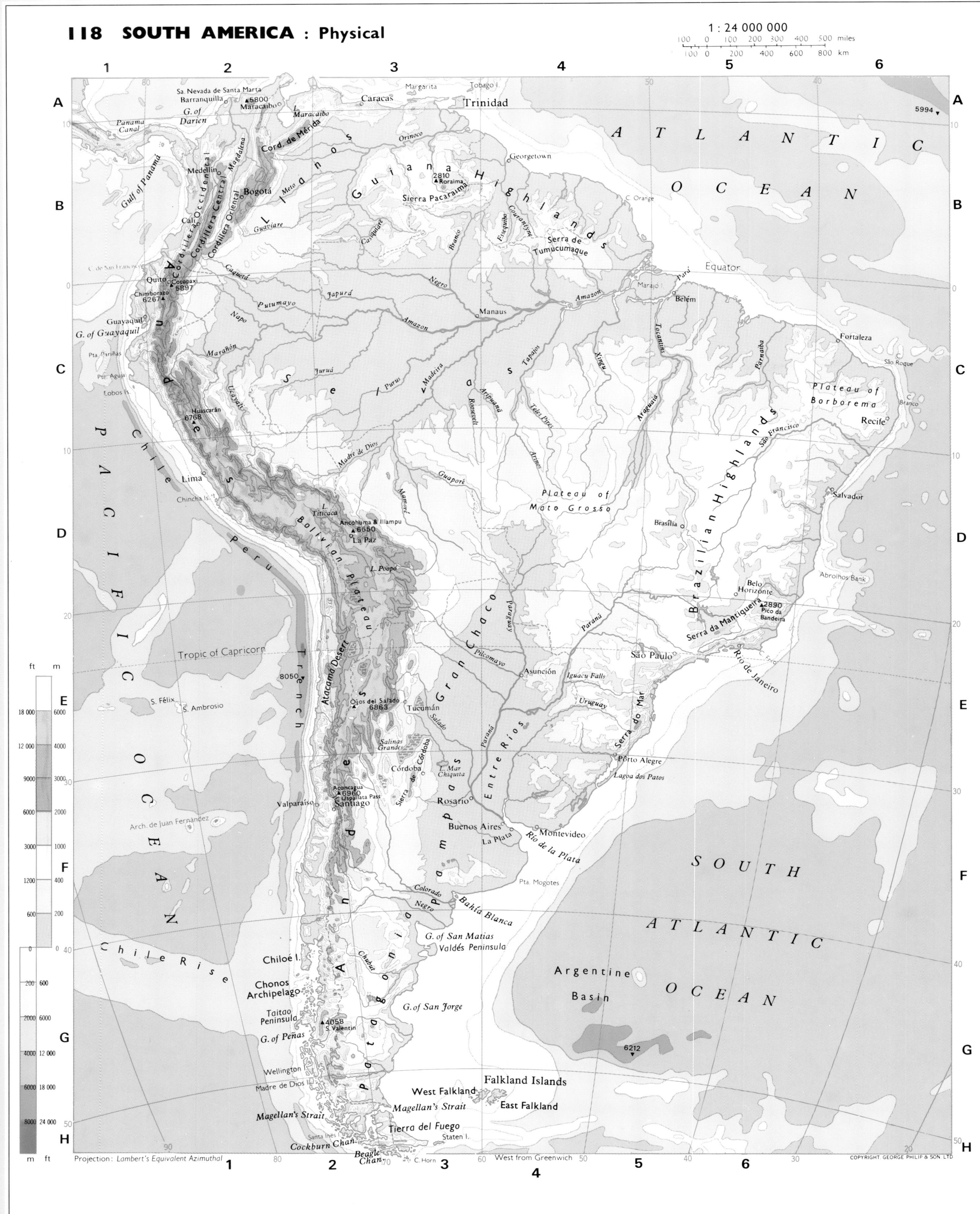

118 SOUTH AMERICA : Physical

1 : 24 000 000

100   0   100 200 300 400 500 miles
100   0   200   400   600   800 km

1 : 24 000 000

100 0 100 200 300 400 500 miles
100 0 200 400 600 800 km

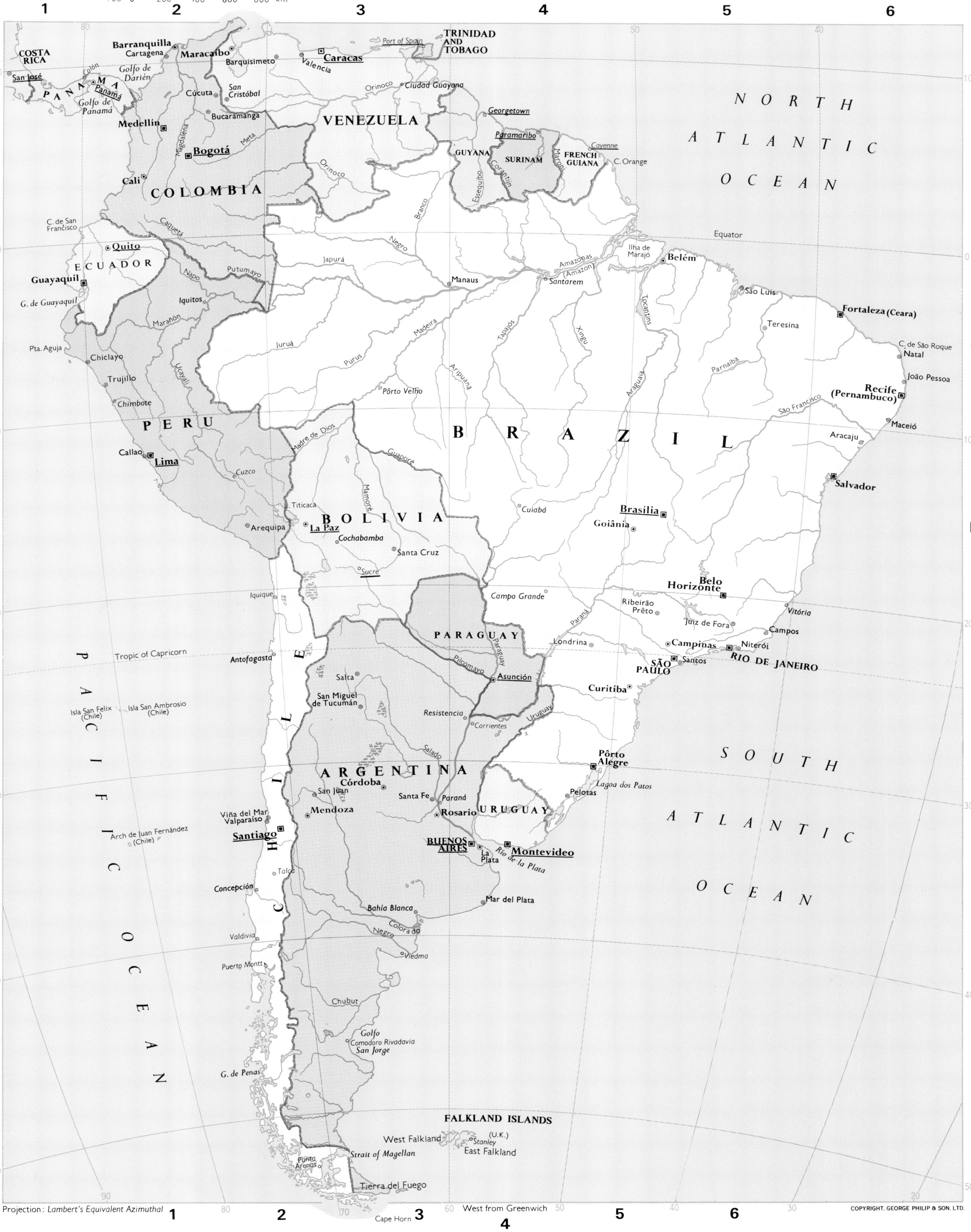

1   2   3   4   5   6

A

COSTA RICA
Barranquilla
Cartagena
Maracaibo
Barquisimeto
Valencia
Caracas
TRINIDAD AND TOBAGO
Port of Spain
San José
Colón
PANAMA
Panamá
Golfo de Darién
Golfo de Panamá
Cúcuta
San Cristóbal
Orinoco
Ciudad Guayana
Medellín
Bucaramanga
Magdalena
VENEZUELA
Georgetown
Bogotá
Meta
GUYANA
Paramaribo
SURINAM
Cayenne
FRENCH GUIANA
C. Orange

B

Cali
COLOMBIA
Orinoco
Essequibo
Courantijn
Maroni

NORTH
ATLANTIC
OCEAN

C. de San Francisco
Caquetá
Negro
Branco
Equator

C

Quito
ECUADOR
Putumayo
Japurá
Amazonas
Ilha de Marajó
Belém
Guayaquil
Napo
Santarem
Amazon
São Luís
G. de Guayaquil
Iquitos
Manaus
Fortaleza (Ceará)
Marañón
Teresina
C. de São Roque
Pta. Aguja
Chiclayo
Juruá
Purus
Madeira
Tapajós
Xingu
Araguaia
Parnaiba
Natal
João Pessoa
Trujillo
Pôrto Velho
Recife (Pernambuco)
Chimbote
PERU
Ucayali
Aripuanã
São Francisco
Maceió
Aracaju

D

BRAZIL
Callao
Lima
Madre de Dios
Guaporé
Cuzco
Mamoré
Cuiabá
Salvador
Titicaca
BOLIVIA
Brasília
Arequipa
La Paz
Cochabamba
Santa Cruz
Sucre
Goiânia
Iquique
Campo Grande
Belo Horizonte
Ribeirão Prêto
Vitória

E

Tropic of Capricorn
Antofagasta
Paraná
PARAGUAY
Paraguay
Juiz de Fora
Campos
Campinas
Niterói
RIO DE JANEIRO
São Paulo
Santos
Londrina
Salta
Asunción
Pilcomayo
San Miguel de Tucumán
Curitiba
Isla San Felix (Chile)
Isla San Ambrosio (Chile)
Resistencia
Corrientes
Uruguay
Pôrto Alegre

SOUTH
ATLANTIC
OCEAN

F

PACIFIC OCEAN
CHILE
Salado
ARGENTINA
Córdoba
San Juan
Santa Fe
Paraná
URUGUAY
Pelotas
Lagoa dos Patos
Viña del Mar
Valparaíso
Mendoza
Rosario
Arch. de Juan Fernández (Chile)
Santiago
BUENOS AIRES
Montevideo
La Plata
Río de la Plata
Talca
Concepción
Mar del Plata
Bahía Blanca
Valdivia
Colorado
Negro

G

Puerto Montt
Viedma
Chubut
Golfo Comodoro Rivadavia
San Jorge
G. de Penas

H

FALKLAND ISLANDS
West Falkland
(U.K.)
Stanley
East Falkland
Strait of Magellan
Punta Arenas
Cape Horn
Tierra del Fuego

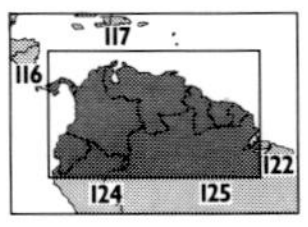

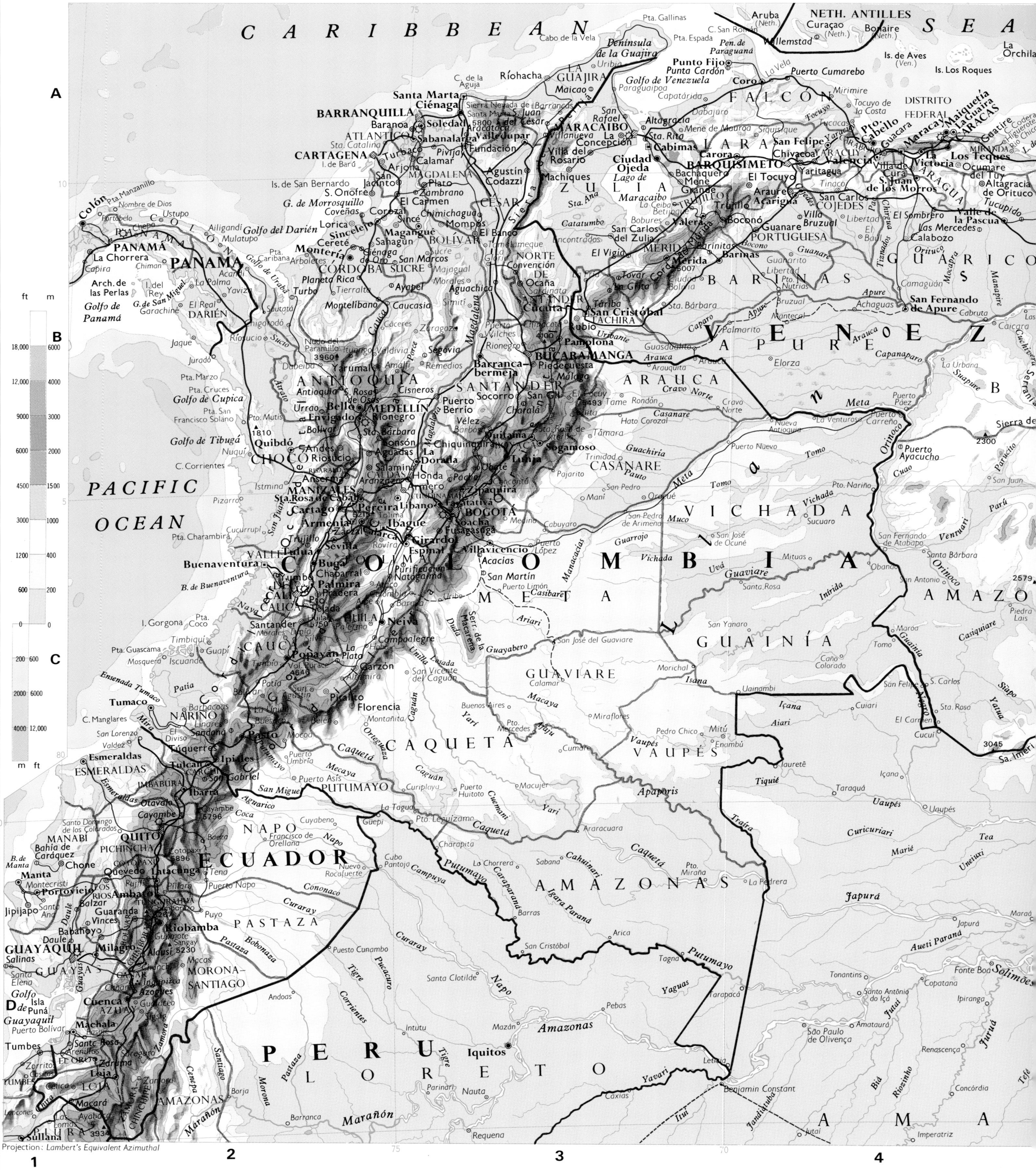

CARIBBEAN SEA

PACIFIC OCEAN

NETH. ANTILLES

COLOMBIA

VENEZUELA

ECUADOR

PERU

PANAMÁ

Projection: Lambert's Equivalent Azimuthal

ft m — 18,000 6000 — 12,000 4000 — 9000 3000 — 6000 2000 — 4500 1500 — 3000 1000 — 1200 400 — 600 200 — 0 — 200 600 — 2000 6000 — 4000 12,000 m ft

CARTAGENA · BARRANQUILLA · Santa Marta · Maracaibo · MARACAY · CARACAS · BARQUISIMETO · VALENCIA · MEDELLÍN · BOGOTÁ · CALI · Buenaventura · BUCARAMANGA · Cúcuta · San Cristóbal · Mérida · Barinas · San Fernando de Apure

QUITO · GUAYAQUIL · Cuenca · Machala · Manta · Portoviejo · Ambato · Riobamba

Iquitos · LORETO · AMAZONAS · CAQUETÁ · PUTUMAYO · VAUPÉS · GUAINÍA · VICHADA · META · CASANARE · ARAUCA · GUAVIARE · NARIÑO · CAUCA · CHOCÓ · ANTIOQUIA · SANTANDER · BOLÍVAR · CÓRDOBA · SUCRE · MAGDALENA · CESAR · ZULIA · FALCÓN · LARA · TRUJILLO · PORTUGUESA · GUÁRICO · APURE · DISTRITO FEDERAL · ARAGUA · MIRANDA

Golfo de Panamá · Golfo del Darién · Golfo de Venezuela · Lago de Maracaibo · Río Magdalena · Orinoco · Amazonas · Putumayo · Caquetá · Napo · Marañón

ATLANTIC OCEAN

1 : 6 400 000

50   0   50   100   150   200 miles
50   0   100   200   300 km

COPYRIGHT GEORGE PHILIP & SON LTD

Tropic of Capricorn

West from Greenwich

Projection: Lambert's Equivalent Azimuthal

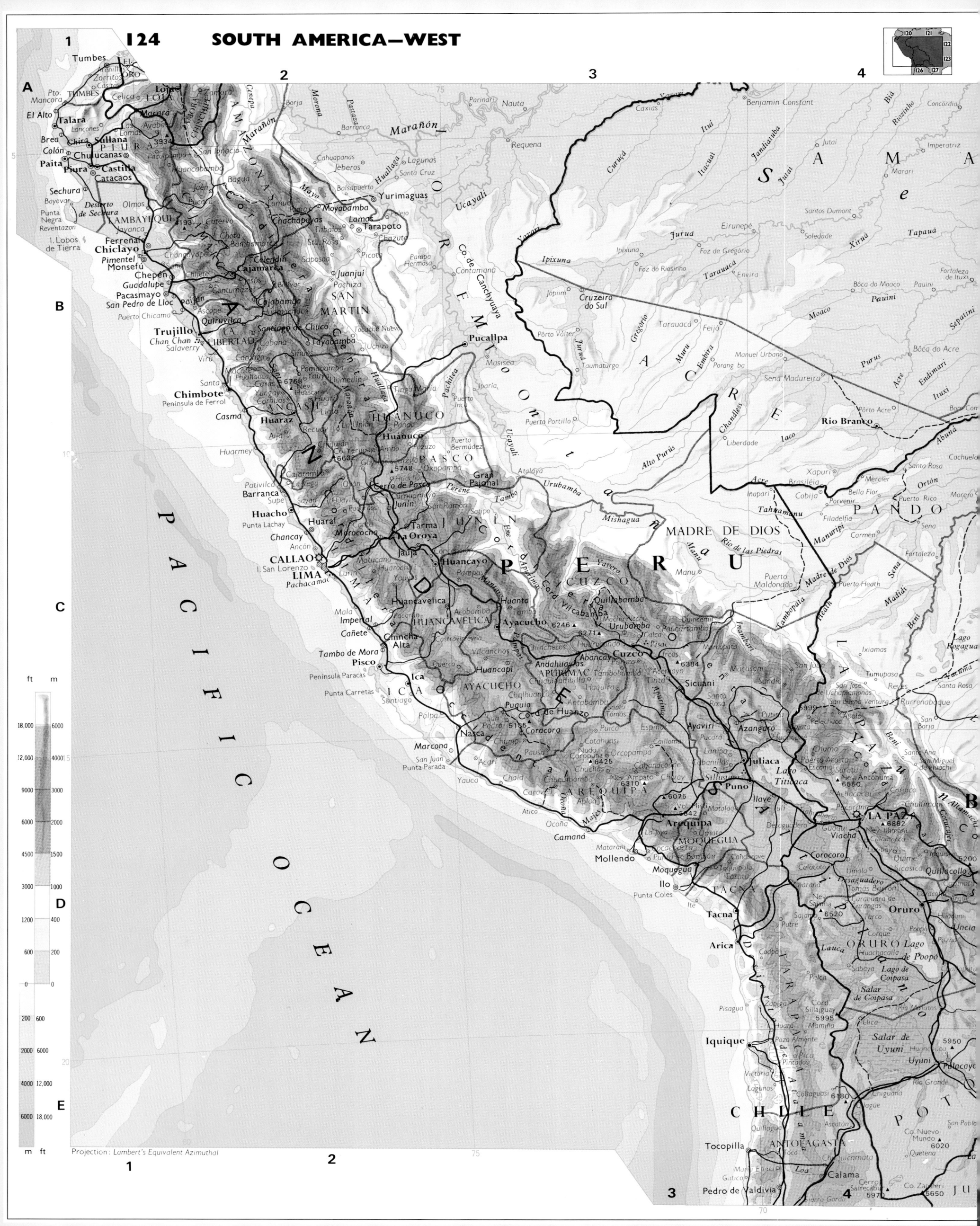

A

B

C

D

E

1

2

3

4

5

10

15

20

ft   m

18,000   6000

12,000   4000

9000   3000

6000   2000

4500   1500

3000   1000

1200   400

600   200

0   0

200   600

2000   6000

4000   12,000

6000   18,000

m   ft

Projection: Lambert's Equivalent Azimuthal

PACIFIC OCEAN

PERU

CHILE

Tumbes

Talara

Paita

Piura

Chiclayo

Trujillo

Chimbote

Huaraz

Callao

LIMA

Pisco

Ica

Nasca

Arequipa

Mollendo

Tacna

Arica

Iquique

Antofagasta

Pucallpa

Rio Branco

Cuzco

Puno

Lago Titicaca

LA PAZ

Oruro

Lago de Poopó

Salar de Uyuni

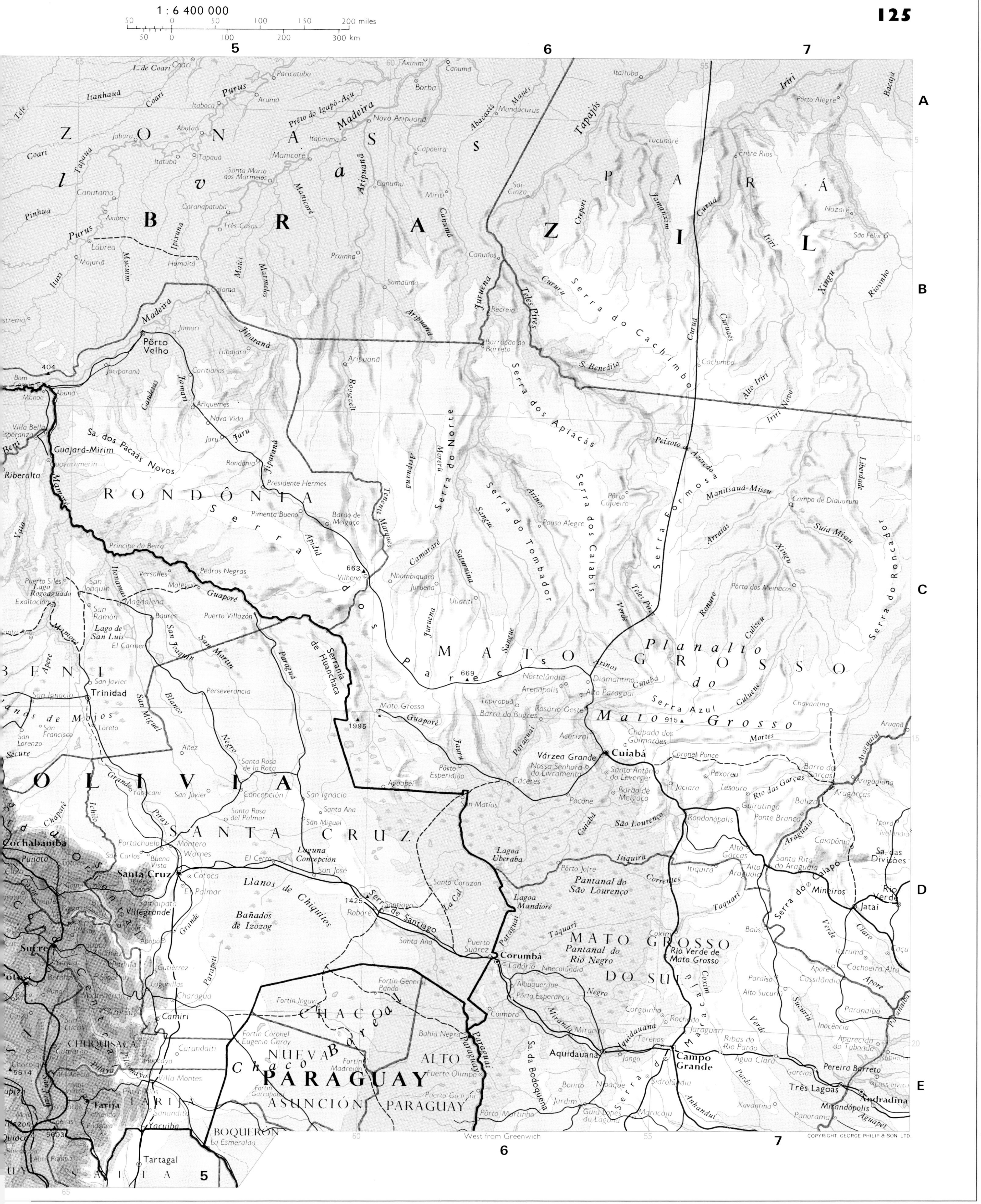

1 : 6 400 000

50   0   50   100   150   200 miles
50   0   100   200   300 km

5   **6**   **7**

A M A Z O N A S

B R A Z I L

Z O N A S

P A R Á

Coari Itanhauã L. de Coari Coari Paricatuba Arumã Borba Canumã Itaituba Pôrto Alegre Bacaiá

Purus Itaboca Novo Aripuanã Abacaxis Maués Mundacurus Tucunaré Entre Rios Iriri

Itapinima Manicoré Capoeira Miriti Sai Cinza Crepori Jamanxim São Félix Nazaré

Canutama Caranapatuba Três Casas Prainha Samaúma Canudos Serra do Cachimbo Curuá Xingu Riosinho

Pinhuã Purus Lábrea Ipixuna Humaitá Prêto do Igapó-Açu Madeira Aripuanã Juruena Recreio Teles Pires S. Benedito Serra dos Aplacás Cachimba

Itusi Majuriã Mucim Madeira Jamari Jiparaná Barracão do Barreto Curuá Alto Iriri Liberdade

Pôrto Velho Calama Tabajara Aripuanã Serra do Norte Peixoto de Azevedo Manitsauá-Missu

Abunã Jaciparaná Caritianas Serra dos Caiabis Campo de Diauarum

Manaá Villa Bella Guajará-Mirim Nova Vida Jaru Tiparaná Pôrto Cajueiro Suiá Missu Serra do Roncador

Riberalta Sa. dos Pacaás Novos Presidente Hermes Arinos Pouso Alegre Arraias Xingu Pôrto dos Meinacos

R O N D Ô N I A Pimenta Bueno Barão de Melgaço Serra do Tombador Serra Formosa Renuro Culiseu

Príncipe da Beira Apidiá Nhambiquara Juruena Utiariti Planalto GROSSO Serra do Roncador

Puerto Siles Lago Rogoaguado Versalles Pedras Negras Vilhena 663 Camararé M A T O GROSSO Culuene Chavantina

San Joaquín Mateguá Guaporé Serrania de Huanchaca 669 Arinos Nortelândia Diamantino Cuiabá Serra Azul 915

San Ramón El Carmen Perseverancia Mato Grosso Arenápolis Alto Paraguai M a t o G r o s s o Mortes

B E N I Lago de San Luis San Javier 1995 Guaporé Tapirapuã Rosário Oeste Chapada dos Guimarães Aruanã

Llanos de Mojos Trinidad San Martín Barra da Bugres Várzea Grande Cuiabá Coronel Ponce Barra do Garças

San Ignacio Loreto Jauru Acorizal Santo Antônio do Leverger Poxoreu Araguaiana Aragarças

B O L I V I A Concepción San Ignacio Pôrto Esperidião Cáceres Pocone Barão de Melgaço Jaciara Tesouro Rio das Garças

Cochabamba Santa Rosa del Palmar Santa Ana San Matías Cuiabá Rondonópolis Guiratinga Ponte Branca Serra do Mineiros

S A N T A C R U Z San Miguel Lagoa Uberaba São Lourenço Alto Garças Araguaia Caçapônua

Santa Cruz Montero Warnes El Cerro Laguna Concepción San José Pôrto Jofre Itiquira Itiquira Santa Rita do Araguaia Jataí

Villegrande Llanos de Chiquitos Santo Corazón Pantanal do São Lourenço Correntes Alto Araguaia Baús Serra do Verde

Sucre 1425 Robore Santa Ana Lagoa Mandioré M A T O G R O S S O Taquari Rio Verde de Mato Grosso Paraíso Aporé Cachoeira Alta

Potosí Bañados de Izozog Serra de Santiago Puerto Suárez Corumbá Pantanal do Rio Negro Coxim Sa. das Divisões

Gutierrez Lagunillas Charagua Ladário Albuquerque Negro Corguinho Alto Sucuriú Cassilândia Paranaíba

C H A C O Fortín General Pando Pôrto Esperança Coimbra Miranda Rochedo Inocência

Camiri Fortín Ingavi Bahia Negra Paraguai Sa. da Bodoquena Aquidauana Terenos Campo Grande Pereira Barreto

Fortín Coronel Eugenio Garay Carandaiti N U E V A C H A C O Fuerte Olimpo Aquidauana Jango Sidrolândia Ribas do Rio Pardo Aparecida do Taboado Três Lagoas

CHUQUISACA Boqueron P A R A G U A Y Bonito Nioaque Xavantina Anhandui Andradina

5614 Villa Montes ASUNCIÓN PARAGUAY Pôrto Martinho Jardim Anhandui Mirandópolis Aguapeí

Tarija Yacuíba Pilcomayo Fortín Madrejón ALTO Guia Lopes da Laguna Panorama

T A R I J A BOQUERON La Esmeralda West from Greenwich Maracaju

5603 Tartagal S A N T A

6   **7**

COPYRIGHT GEORGE PHILIP & SON LTD

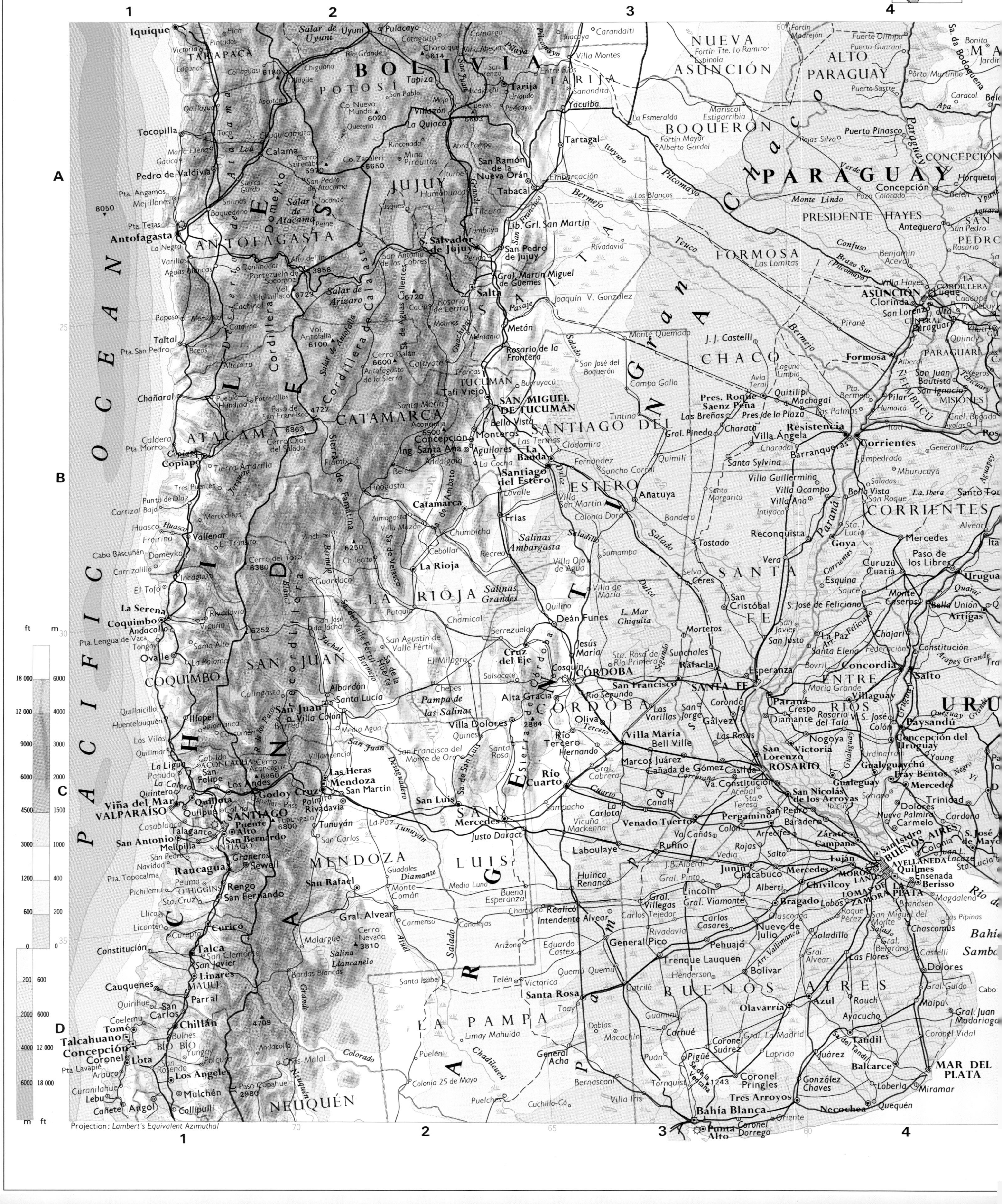

PACIFIC OCEAN

BOLIVIA
PARAGUAY

Countries / Regions:
TARAPACÁ · POTOSÍ · TARIJA · NUEVA ASUNCIÓN · ALTO PARAGUAY · BOQUERÓN · JUJUY · SALTA · FORMOSA · PRESIDENTE HAYES · CONCEPCIÓN · CHACO · PEDRO · ANTOFAGASTA · CATAMARCA · TUCUMÁN · SANTIAGO DEL ESTERO · SANTA FE · CORRIENTES · MISIONES · PARAGUARI · ATACAMA · LA RIOJA · CHILE · SAN JUAN · COQUIMBO · CÓRDOBA · ENTRE RÍOS · URUGUAY · MENDOZA · SAN LUIS · ARGENTINA · LA PAMPA · BUENOS AIRES · NEUQUÉN

Selected place names:
Iquique · Pica · Salar de Uyuni · Pulacayo · Cotagaita · Camargo · Carandaiti · Fortín Tte. 1o Ramiro · Fuerte Olimpo · Puerto Guaraní · Puerto Sastre · Pôrto Murtinho · Victoria · Pintados · Chorolque 5614 · Villa Abecia · Pilaya · Villa Montes · Espinola · Fortín Mayor Alberto Gardel · Rojas Silva · Puerto Pinasco · Lagunas · Collaguasi 6180 · Chiguana · Río Grande · Tupiza · San Juan · Mariscal Estigarribia · Mojo · La Esmeralda · Horqueta · Concepción · Tocopilla · Ollague · Villazón 6020 · La Quiaca 5603 · Yacuiba · La Lomitas · Pozo Colorado · Belén · Apa · Quetena · Rinconada · Mina Pirquitas · San Ramón de la Nueva Orán · Tartagal · Los Blancos · Monte Lindo · Presidente Hayes · Antequera · San Pedro · María Elena · Toco · Calama · Cerro Sairecábur 5970 · Co. Zapaleri 5650 · Abra Pampa · Tabacal · Embarcación · Bermejo · Teuco · Confuso · Benjamín Aceval · Clorinda · Pedro de Valdivia · Chuquicamata · Humahuaca · Tilcara · Rivadavia · Pirané · Asunción · Lorenzo · Luque · Pta. Angamos · Mejillones · Cerro del Indio · Portezuelo de Socompa 3858 · San Pedro de Atacama · Susques · S. Salvador de Jujuy · San Pedro de Jujuy · Perico · Formosa · Villa Hayes · Alberdi · San Juan Bautista · Quitilipi · Pilar · Humaitá · Neembucú · 8050 · Antofagasta · La Negra · Salar de Atacama · Peine · Tumbaya · Gral. Martín Miguel de Güemes · Joaquín V. González · Pta. Tetas · Varillas · Aguas Blancas · Alto del Inca · Tacones · San Antonio de los Cobres · Salta · Pasaje · Monte Quemado · J. J. Castelli · Laguna Limpia · Pres. Roque Saenz Peña · Machagai · Las Palmas · Cnel. Bogado · Ayolas · Paposo · Alemania · Catalina · Vol. Antofalla 6100 · Salar de Arizaro · Llullaillaco 6723 · Cachinal · Cachi · Rosario de Lerma 6720 · Molinos · Metán · Alemanía · Campo Gallo · Las Breñas · Pres. de la Plaza · Resistencia · Villa Ángela · Corrientes · Empedrado · General Paz · Taltal · Breas · Cafayate · Guachipas · Rosario de la Frontera · San José del Boquerón · Charata · Santa Sylvina · Villa Guillermina · Villa Ocampo · Villa Ana · Bella Vista · Sto. Tomé · Pta. San Pedro · Altamira · Cerro Galán 6600 · Santa María · Trancas · Tucumán · Quimilí · La Ibera · Chañaral · Pueblo Hundido · Paso de San Francisco 4722 · Aconquija 5500 · Tafí Viejo · Buruyacú · SAN MIGUEL DE TUCUMÁN · Tintina · Tostado · Reconquista · Mburucuyá · Bella Vista · La Serena · Goya · Caldera · Copiapó · Cerro Ojos del Salado 6863 · Concepción · Monteros · Bella Vista · La Banda · Clodomira · Fernández · Suncho Corral · Santa Margarita · Villa San Roque · Pta. Morro · Tierra Amarilla · Flambalá · Ing. Santa Ana · Aguilares · La Cocha · Santiago del Estero · Añatuya · Santa Clara · Curuzú Cuatiá · Carrizal Bajo · Tres Puentes · Andalgalá · Ambato · Lavalle · Villa San Martín · Bandera · Selva · Esquina · Sauce · Punta de Díaz · Cerro del Toro 6380 · Belén · Chumbicha · Salinas Ambargasta · Saladillo · Intiyaco · Ceres · San Javier · Santa Lucía · Mercedes · Huasco · Freirina · El Tránsito · Tinogasta · Frías · Colonia Dora · Vera · Corrientes · Monte Caseros · Bella Unión · Artigas · Cabo Bascuñán · Vallenar · Vinchina 6250 · Chilecito · Recreo · Sumampa · Villa Ojo de Agua · L. Mar Chiquita · Sta. 1 · Sgo. José de Feliciano · Uruguaiana · Quaraí · Carrizalillo · Domeyko · Sa. de Famatina · Cebollar · La Rioja · Quilino · Dean Funes · San Cristóbal · Morteros · La Paz · Chajarí · Federación · Constitución · El Tofo · Incaguasi · 6252 · San José de Jáchal · Patquía · Chamical · Serrezuela · Jesús María · Sunchales · Rafaela · Esperanza · Santa Elena · Concordia · Salto · La Serena · Coquimbo · Andacollo · Rivadavia · Vicuña · Guandacol · Salsacate · Cruz del Eje · Cosquín · CÓRDOBA · San Francisco · Santa Fe · Paraná · María Grande · Villaguay · Pta. Lengua de Vaca · Tongoy · Samo Alto · 6252 · Jáchal · El Milagro · Río Primero · Sta. Rosa del Río Segundo · Alta Gracia · Río Segundo · Las Varillas · Coronda · Crespo · Diamante · Ovalle · La Paloma · Calingasta · Albardón · Santa Lucía · Pampa de las Salinas · Villa Dolores · Oliva · Rosario del Tala · Gualeguay · Paysandú · Quillaicillo · Huentelauquén · San Juan · Villa Colón · San Francisco del Monte de Oro · Quines · 2884 · Río Tercero · Villa María · Bell Ville · Las Rosas · Nogoyá · Victoria · Concepción del Uruguay · Young · Las Vilos · Quilimari · Media Agua · Villavicencio · Santa Rosa · Río Cuarto · Gral. Cabrera · Marcos Juárez · Cañada de Gómez · Castro · Rosario · San Lorenzo · Gualeguaychú · Fray Bentos · Mercedes · La Ligua · Papudo · Cerro Aconcagua 6960 · Las Heras · Mendoza · San Martín · Gral. Deheza · San Jorge · Gálvez · Va. Constitución · Negro · Uruguay · Salamanca · San Felipe · Los Andes · Godoy Cruz · San Luis · Sampacho · La Carlota · Venado Tuerto · Pergamino · San Nicolás de los Arroyos · Soriano · Dolores · Nueva Palmira · Cardona · Viña del Mar · Quillota · Quilpué · Colina · Puente del Inca 6800 · Tupungato · Rivadavia · Mercedes · Pehuajó · Vicuña Mackenna · Va. Cañás · Rufino · Rojas · Arrecifes · Colón · Zárate · Campana · Luján · Buenos Aires · Trinidad · VALPARAÍSO · SANTIAGO · Talagante · San Bernardo · Tunuyán · La Paz · Tunuyán · Justo Daract · Laboulaye · Vedia · Junín · Chacabuco · Mercedes · Morón · Avellaneda · Quilmes · San Antonio · Melipilla · San Pedro · Navidad · Graneros · Sewell · San Carlos · San Mercedes · J.B. Alberdi · Gral. Pinto · Alberti · Bragado · Lobos · Zamora · La Plata · Ensenada · Berisso · Pta. Topocalma · Rancagua · O'Higgins · Rengo · San Fernando · Mendoza · Guadales · Diamante · Monte Comán · Huinca Renancó · Lincoln · Gral. Villegas · Gral. Viamonte · Chivilcoy · Lomas de Zamora · Magdalena · Pichilemu · Peumo · San Rafael · Media Luna · Buena Esperanza · Carlos Tejedor · Carlos Casares · Nueve de Julio · Saladillo · Gral. Belgrano · Chascomús · Bahía Sambo · Licantén · Gral. Alvear · Carmensa · Canalejas · Chara · Realicó · Intendente Alvear · Rivadavia · Pehuajó · General Pico · Trenque Lauquen · Henderson · Gral. Alvear · Las Flores · Castelli · Dolores · Constitución · Talca · San Clemente · San Javier · Linares · Maule · Malargüe · Cerro Nevado 3810 · Salina Llancanelo · Gral. Alvear · Arizona · Eduardo Castex · General Pico · Catriló · Bolívar · Olavarría · Azul · Rauch · Maipú · Gral. Guido · Cabo · Cauquenes · Quirihue · San Carlos · Parral · Santa Isabel · Telén · Victorica · Quemú Quemú · Guaminí · Carhué · Daireaux · Tandil · Gonzáles Chaves · Loberia · Miramar · Quequén · Coelemu · Tomé · Talcahuano · Concepción · Coronel · Lota · Bío Bío · Bulnes · Chillán · Yungay · Polcura · 4709 · Andacollo · Chos-Malal · Colorado · Limay Mahuida · Doblas · Macachín · Puán · Pigüé · Coronel Suárez · Laprida · Juárez · Balcarce · MAR DEL PLATA · Los Ángeles · Mulchén · Paso Copahue 2980 · Neuquén · Colonia 25 de Mayo · Puelches · General Acha · Cuchillo-Có · Villa Iris · Tornquist 1243 · Coronel Pringles · Tres Arroyos · Necochea · Lebu · Cañete · Angol · Collipulli · NEUQUÉN · Puelén · Chadileuvú · Bernasconi · Bahía Blanca · Coronel Dorrego · Oriente · Punta Alta

Scale (left margin):
ft · m
18 000 · 6000
12 000 · 4000
9000 · 3000
6000 · 2000
4500 · 1500
3000 · 1000
1200 · 400
600 · 200
0 · 0
200 · 600
2000 · 6000
4000 · 12 000
6000 · 18 000
m · ft

Projection: Lambert's Equivalent Azimuthal

1 : 6 400 000

50   0   50   100   150   200 miles

50   0   100   200   300 km

5   6   7

MATO GROSSO
DO SUL

PARANÁ

BRAZIL

SÃO PAULO

SÃO PAULO

RIO DE JANEIRO

BELO HORIZONTE

SANTA CATARINA

RIO GRANDE

DO SUL

URUGUAY

MONTEVIDEO

A T L A N T I C

O C E A N

Tropic of Capricorn

Tres Lagoas
Andradina
Araçatuba
Mirassol
S. José do Rio Prêto
Olímpia
Passos
Oliveira
Congonhas
Lima
Itabirito
Vitória
Itaguari
Vila Velha
Guarapari

Mirandópolis
Xavantina
Catanduva
Ribeirão Prêto
Batatais
S. Seb. do Paraíso
Campo Belo
São João del Rei
Ponte Nova
Pico da Bandeira 2890
Castêlo

Panorama
Birigui
Tietê
Taquaritinga
Mococa
Guaxupé
Três Pontas
Lavras
Barbacena
Leopoldina
Cachoeiro de Itapemirim

Adamantina
Tupã
Lins
Novo Horizonte
Casa Branca
Varginha
Ubá
Muriaé
Itaperuna

Presidente Prudente
Martinópolis
Marília
Araraquara
São Carlos
São João da Boa Vista
Poços de Caldas
Pouso Alegre
Três Corações
Juiz de Fora
Além Paraíba
Guarus
CAMPOS

Paranavaí
Assis
Rio Claro
Limeira
Mogi-Mirim
Itajubá 2787
Volta Redonda
Barra do Piraí
Nova Friburgo
Macaé
RIO DE JANEIRO
Cabo de São Tomé

Londrina
Rolândia
Cambará
Piracicaba
CAMPINAS
Americana
Guaratinguetá
Bananal
Barra Mansa
Nova Iguaçu
São Gonçalo
Cabo Frio

Umuarama
Maringá
Arapongas
Botucatu
Jundiaí
S. J. dos Campos
Taubaté
Petrópolis
DUQUE DE CAXIAS
NITERÓI
La. de Araruama

Apucarana
Avaré
Tatuí
Itu
Mogi das Cruzes
Angra dos Reis

Itapetininga
SÃO PAULO
SANTO ANDRÉ

Itararé
São Bernardo del Campo
São Vicente
SANTOS
Ilha de São Sebastião

PARANÁ
Ponta Grossa
CURITIBA
Antonina
Paranaguá
Ilha Comprida
Ilha do Cardoso

União da Vitória
Rio Negro
Mafra
São Francisco do Sul
Joinvile

Caçador
Blumenau
Itajaí

Joaçaba
SANTA CATARINA
Brusque
Rio do Sul

Lajes
Ilha de Santa Catarina
Florianópolis

Erechim
Vacaria
Tubarão
Laguna
Cabo Santa Marta Grande

Caràzinho
Passo Fundo
Criciúma
Araranguá

Cruz Alta
Guaporé
Bento Gonçalves
Caxias do Sul

Santa Maria
Santa Cruz do Sul
Nôvo Hamburgo
Taquara
Montenegro

Cachoeira do Sul
Canoas
São Leopoldo
Osorio
Viamão
PORTO ALEGRE

Santana do Livramento
São Gabriel
Dom Pedrito

Bagé

Pelotas
Lagoa dos Patos

Melo
Jaguarão
Rio Grande

Treinta y Tres
Santa Vitória do Palmar

Rocha
San Carlos
Maldonado

Plata

5304

COPYRIGHT. GEORGE PHILIP & SON. LTD

1 : 6 400 000

Projection: Lambert's Equivalent Azimuthal

West from Greenwich

COPYRIGHT GEORGE PHILIP & SON LTD

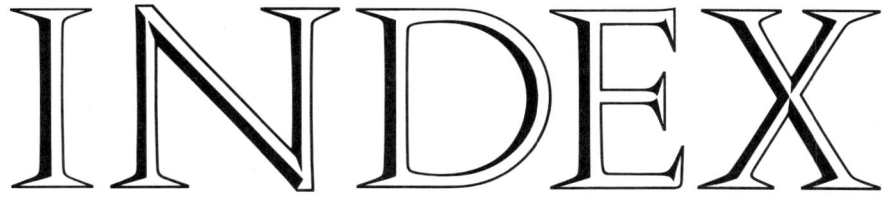

INDEX

The index contains the names of all the principal places and features shown on the World Maps. Each name is followed by an additional entry in italics giving the country or region within which it is located. The alphabetical order of names composed of two or more words is governed primarily by the first word and then by the second. This is an example of the rule:

Mīr Kūh, *Iran* **65 E8**
Mīr Shahdād, *Iran* **65 E8**
Miraj, *India* **60 L9**
Miram Shah, *Pakistan* **62 C4**
Miramar, *Mozam.* **126 D4**

Physical features composed of a proper name (Erie) and a description (Lake) are positioned alphabetically by the proper name. The description is positioned after the proper name and is usually abbreviated:

Erie, L., *N. Amer.* **106 D4**

Where a description forms part of a settlement or administrative name however, it is always written in full and put in its true alphabetic position:

Mount Morris, *U.S.A.* **106 D7**

Names beginning with M' and Mc are indexed as if they were spelt Mac. Names beginning St. are alphabetised under Saint, but Sankt, Sint, Sant', Santa and San are all spelt in full and are alphabetised accordingly. If the same place name occurs two or more times in the index and all are in the same country, each is followed by the name of the administrative subdivision in which it is located. The names are placed in the alphabetical order of the subdivisions. For example:

Jackson, *Ky., U.S.A.* **104 G4**
Jackson, *Mich., U.S.A.* **104 D3**
Jackson, *Minn., U.S.A.* **108 D7**

The number in bold type which follows each name in the index refers to the number of the map page where that feature or place will be found. This is usually the largest scale at which the place or feature appears. The letter and figure which are in bold type immediately after the page number give the grid square on the map page, within which the feature is situated. The letter represents the latitude and the figure the longitude.

In some cases the feature itself may fall within the specified square, while the name is outside. This is usually the case only with features which are larger than a grid square. Rivers are indexed to their mouths or confluences, and carry the symbol ➤ after their names. A solid square ■ follows the name of a country while, an open square □ refers to a first order administrative area.

ABBREVIATIONS USED IN THE INDEX

A.C.T. — Australian Capital Territory
Afghan. — Afghanistan
Ala. — Alabama
Alta. — Alberta
Amer. — America(n)
Arch. — Archipelago
Ariz. — Arizona
Ark. — Arkansas
Atl. Oc. — Atlantic Ocean
B. — Baie, Bahía, Bay, Bucht, Bugt
B.C. — British Columbia
Bangla. — Bangladesh
Barr. — Barrage
Bos.-H. — Bosnia-Herzegovina
C. — Cabo, Cap, Cape, Coast
C.A.R. — Central African Republic
C. Prov. — Cape Province
Calif. — California
Cent. — Central
Chan. — Channel
Colo. — Colorado
Conn. — Connecticut
Cord. — Cordillera
Cr. — Creek
Czech. — Czechoslovakia
D.C. — District of Columbia
Del. — Delaware
Dep. — Dependency
Des. — Desert
Dist. — District
Dj. — Djebel
Domin. — Dominica
Dom. Rep. — Dominican Republic
E. — East
El Salv. — El Salvador

Eq. Guin. — Equatorial Guinea
Fla. — Florida
Falk. Is. — Falkland Is.
G. — Golfe, Golfo, Gulf, Guba, Gebel
Ga. — Georgia
Gt. — Great, Greater
Guinea-Biss. — Guinea-Bissau
H.K. — Hong Kong
H.P. — Himachal Pradesh
Hants. — Hampshire
Harb. — Harbor, Harbour
Hd. — Head
Hts. — Heights
I.(s). — Île, Ilha, Insel, Isla, Island, Isle
Ill. — Illinois
Ind. — Indiana
Ind. Oc. — Indian Ocean
Ivory C. — Ivory Coast
J. — Jabal, Jebel, Jazira
Junc. — Junction
K. — Kap, Kapp
Kans. — Kansas
Kep. — Kepulauan
Ky. — Kentucky
L. — Lac, Lacul, Lago, Lagoa, Lake, Limni, Loch, Lough
La. — Louisiana
Liech. — Liechtenstein
Lux. — Luxembourg
Mad. P. — Madhya Pradesh
Madag. — Madagascar
Man. — Manitoba
Mass. — Massachusetts
Md. — Maryland

Me. — Maine
Medit. S. — Mediterranean Sea
Mich. — Michigan
Minn. — Minnesota
Miss. — Mississippi
Mo. — Missouri
Mont. — Montana
Moza. — Mozambique
Mt.(e). — Mont, Monte, Monti, Montaña, Mountain
N. — Nord, Norte, North, Northern, Nouveau
N.B. — New Brunswick
N.C. — North Carolina
N. Cal. — New Caledonia
N. Dak. — North Dakota
N.H. — New Hampshire
N.I. — North Island
N.J. — New Jersey
N. Mex. — New Mexico
N.S. — Nova Scotia
N.S.W. — New South Wales
N.W.T. — North West Territory
N.Y. — New York
N.Z. — New Zealand
Nebr. — Nebraska
Neths. — Netherlands
Nev. — Nevada
Nfld. — Newfoundland
Nic. — Nicaragua
O. — Oued, Ouadi
Occ. — Occidentale
O.F.S. — Orange Free State
Okla. — Oklahoma
Ont. — Ontario
Or. — Orientale

Oreg. — Oregon
Os. — Ostrov
Oz. — Ozero
P. — Pass, Passo, Pasul, Pulau
P.E.I. — Prince Edward Island
Pa. — Pennsylvania
Pac. Oc. — Pacific Ocean
Papua N.G. — Papua New Guinea
Pass. — Passage
Pen. — Peninsula, Péninsule
Phil. — Philippines
Pk. — Park, Peak
Plat. — Plateau
P-ov. — Poluostrov
Prov. — Province, Provincial
Pt. — Point
Pta. — Ponta, Punta
Pte. — Pointe
Qué. — Québec
Queens. — Queensland
R. — Rio, River
R.I. — Rhode Island
Ra.(s). — Range(s)
Raj. — Rajasthan
Reg. — Region
Rep. — Republic
Res. — Reserve, Reservoir
S. — San, South, Sea
Si. Arabia — Saudi Arabia
S.C. — South Carolina
S. Dak. — South Dakota
S.I. — South Island
S. Leone — Sierra Leone
Sa. — Serra, Sierra
Sask. — Saskatchewan
Scot. — Scotland

Sd. — Sound
Sev. — Severnaya
Sib. — Siberia
Sprs. — Springs
St. — Saint, Sankt, Sint
Sta. — Santa, Station
Ste. — Sainte
Sto. — Santo
Str. — Strait, Stretto
Switz. — Switzerland
Tas. — Tasmania
Tenn. — Tennessee
Tex. — Texas
Tg. — Tanjung
Trin. & Tob. — Trinidad & Tobago
U.A.E. — United Arab Emirates
U.K. — United Kingdom
U.S.A. — United States of America
Ut. P. — Uttar Pradesh
Va. — Virginia
Vdkhr. — Vodokhranilishche
Vf. — Vîrful
Vic. — Victoria
Vol. — Volcano
Vt. — Vermont
W. — Wadi, West
W. Va. — West Virginia
Wash. — Washington
Wis. — Wisconsin
Wlkp. — Wielkopolski
Wyo. — Wyoming
Yorks. — Yorkshire
Yug. — Yugoslavia

Aachen

A

Aachen, *Germany* 18 E2
Aadorf, *Switz.* 23 B7
Aalborg = Ålborg, *Denmark* 11 G3
Aalen, *Germany* 19 G6
A'âli en Nîl □, *Sudan* 77 F3
Aalsmeer, *Neths.* 16 D5
Aalst, *Belgium* 17 G4
Aalst, *Neths.* 17 F6
Aalten, *Neths.* 16 E9
Aalter, *Belgium* 17 F2
Aarau, *Switz.* 22 B6
Aarberg, *Switz.* 22 B4
Aardenburg, *Belgium* 17 F2
Aare →, *Switz.* 22 A6
Aargau □, *Switz.* 22 B6
Aarhus = Århus, *Denmark* 11 H4
Aarle, *Neths.* 17 E7
Aarschot, *Belgium* 17 G5
Aarsele, *Belgium* 17 G2
Aartrijke, *Belgium* 17 F2
Aarwangen, *Switz.* 22 B5
Aba, *China* 52 A3
Aba, *Nigeria* 79 D6
Aba, *Zaïre* 82 B3
Âbâ, Jazîrat, *Sudan* 77 E3
Abacaxis →, *Brazil* 121 D6
Ābādān, *Iran* 65 D6
Abade, *Ethiopia* 77 F4
Ābādeh, *Iran* 65 D7
Abadin, *Spain* 30 B3
Abadla, *Algeria* 75 B4
Abaeté, *Brazil* 123 E2
Abaeté →, *Brazil* 123 E2
Abaetetuba, *Brazil* 122 B2
Abagnar Qi, *China* 50 C9
Abai, *Paraguay* 127 B4
Abak, *Nigeria* 79 E6
Abakaliki, *Nigeria* 79 D6
Abakan, *Russia* 45 D10
Abalemma, *Niger* 79 B6
Abana, *Turkey* 66 C6
Abancay, *Peru* 124 C3
Abanilla, *Spain* 29 G3
Abano Terme, *Italy* 33 C8
Abapó, *Bolivia* 125 D5
Abarán, *Spain* 29 G3
Abariringa, *Kiribati* 92 H10
Abarqū, *Iran* 65 D7
Abashiri, *Japan* 48 B12
Abashiri-Wan, *Japan* 48 B12
Abaújszántó, *Hungary* 21 G11
Abay, *Kazakhstan* 44 E8
Abaya, L., *Ethiopia* 77 F4
Abaza, *Russia* 44 D10
Abbadia San Salvatore, *Italy* 33 F8
'Abbāsābād, *Iran* 65 C8
Abbay = Nîl el Azraq →, *Sudan* 77 D3
Abbaye, Pt., *U.S.A.* 104 B1
Abbé, L., *Ethiopia* 77 E5
Abbeville, *France* 25 B8
Abbeville, *La., U.S.A.* 109 K8
Abbeville, *S.C., U.S.A.* 105 H4
Abbiategrasso, *Italy* 32 C5
Abbieglassie, *Australia* 91 D4
Abbot Ice Shelf, *Antarctica* 5 D16
Abbotsford, *Canada* 100 D4
Abbotsford, *U.S.A.* 108 C9
Abbottabad, *Pakistan* 62 B5
Abcoude, *Neths.* 16 D5
Abd al Kūrī, *Ind. Oc.* 68 E5
Ābdar, *Iran* 65 D7
'Abdolābād, *Iran* 65 C8
Abéché, *Chad* 73 F9
Abejar, *Spain* 28 D2
Abekr, *Sudan* 77 E2
Abêlessa, *Algeria* 75 D5
Abengourou, *Ivory C.* 78 D4
Åbenrå, *Denmark* 11 J3
Abensberg, *Germany* 19 G7
Abeokuta, *Nigeria* 79 D5
Aber, *Uganda* 82 B3
Aberaeron, *U.K.* 13 E3
Aberayron = Aberaeron, *U.K.* 13 E3
Abercorn = Mbala, *Zambia* 83 D3
Abercorn, *Australia* 91 D5
Aberdare, *U.K.* 13 F4
Aberdare Ra., *Kenya* 82 C4
Aberdeen, *Australia* 91 E5
Aberdeen, *Canada* 101 C7
Aberdeen, *S. Africa* 84 E3
Aberdeen, *U.K.* 14 D6
Aberdeen, *Ala., U.S.A.* 105 J1
Aberdeen, *Idaho, U.S.A.* 110 E7
Aberdeen, *S. Dak., U.S.A.* 108 C5
Aberdeen, *Wash., U.S.A.* 112 D3
Aberdovey = Aberdyfi, *U.K.* 13 E3
Aberdyfi, *U.K.* 13 E3
Aberfeldy, *U.K.* 14 E5
Abergaria-a-Velha, *Portugal* 30 E2
Abergavenny, *U.K.* 13 F4
Abernathy, *U.S.A.* 109 J4
Abert, L., *U.S.A.* 110 E3
Aberystwyth, *U.K.* 13 E3
Abha, *Si. Arabia* 76 D5
Abhar, *Iran* 65 B6
Abhayapuri, *India* 63 F14
Abidiya, *Sudan* 76 D3
Abidjan, *Ivory C.* 78 D4
Abilene, *Kans., U.S.A.* 108 F6
Abilene, *Tex., U.S.A.* 109 J5
Abingdon, *U.K.* 13 F6
Abingdon, *Ill., U.S.A.* 108 E9
Abingdon, *Va., U.S.A.* 105 G5
Abington Reef, *Australia* 90 B4
Abitau →, *Canada* 101 B7
Abitau L., *Canada* 101 A7
Abitibi L., *Canada* 98 C4
Abiy Adi, *Ethiopia* 77 E4
Abkhaz Republic □, *Georgia* 43 E9
Abkit, *Russia* 45 C16
Abminga, *Australia* 91 D1
Abnûb, *Egypt* 76 B3
Abocho, *Nigeria* 79 D6
Abohar, *India* 62 D6
Aboisso, *Ivory C.* 78 D4
Aboméy, *Benin* 79 D5
Abondance, *France* 27 B10
Abong-Mbang, *Cameroon* 80 D2
Abonnema, *Nigeria* 79 E6
Abony, *Hungary* 21 H10
Aboso, *Ghana* 78 D4
Abou-Deïa, *Chad* 73 F8
Aboyne, *U.K.* 14 D6
Abra Pampa, *Argentina* 126 A2
Abrantes, *Portugal* 31 F2
Abraveses, *Portugal* 30 E3
Abreojos, Pta., *Mexico* 114 B2
Abreschviller, *France* 25 D14
Abri, *Esh Shamâliya, Sudan* 76 C3
Abri, *Janub Kordofân, Sudan* 77 E3
Abrolhos, Banka, *Brazil* 123 E4
Abruzzi □, *Italy* 33 F10
Absaroka Ra., *U.S.A.* 110 D9
Abū al Khaşīb, *Iraq* 65 D6
Abū 'Alī, *Si. Arabia* 65 E6
Abū 'Alī →, *Lebanon* 69 A4
Abu 'Arīsh, *Si. Arabia* 68 D3
Abû Ballas, *Egypt* 76 C2
Abu Deleiq, *Sudan* 77 D3
Abu Dhabi = Abū Z̧āby, *U.A.E.* 65 E7
Abû Dis, *Sudan* 76 D3
Abû Dom, *Sudan* 77 D3
Abū Du'ān, *Syria* 64 B3
Abu el Gairi, W. →, *Egypt* 69 F2
Abû Gabra, *Sudan* 77 E2
Abu Ga'da, W. →, *Egypt* 69 F1
Abû Gubeiha, *Sudan* 77 E3
Abu Habl, Khawr →, *Sudan* 77 E3
Abū Ḩadrīyah, *Si. Arabia* 65 E6
Abu Hamed, *Sudan* 76 D3
Abu Haraz, *An Nîl el Azraq, Sudan* 77 E3
Abû Haraz, *Esh Shamâliya, Sudan* 76 D3
Abû Higar, *Sudan* 77 E3
Abū Kamāl, *Syria* 64 C4
Abū Madd, Ra's, *Si. Arabia* 64 E3
Abu Matariq, *Sudan* 77 E2
Abu Qir, *Egypt* 76 H7
Abu Qireiya, *Egypt* 76 C4
Abu Qurqâs, *Egypt* 76 J7
Abu Şafāt, W. →, *Jordan* 69 E5
Abû Simbel, *Egypt* 76 C3
Abū Şukhayr, *Iraq* 64 D5
Abu Tig, *Egypt* 76 B3
Abu Tiga, *Sudan* 77 E3
Abû Zabad, *Sudan* 77 E2
Abū Z̧āby, *U.A.E.* 65 E7
Abū Zeydābād, *Iran* 65 C6
Abufari, *Brazil* 125 B5
Abuja, *Nigeria* 79 D6
Abukuma-Gawa →, *Japan* 48 E10
Abukuma-Sammyaku, *Japan* 48 F10
Abunã, *Brazil* 125 B4
Abunã →, *Brazil* 125 B4
Aburo, *Zaïre* 82 B3
Abut Hd., *N.Z.* 87 K3
Abwong, *Sudan* 77 F3
Åby, *Sweden* 11 F10
Aby, Lagune, *Ivory C.* 78 D4
Acacías, *Colombia* 120 C3
Acajutla, *El Salv.* 116 D2
Açailândia, *Brazil* 122 C2
Acámbaro, *Mexico* 114 C4
Acaponeta, *Mexico* 114 C3
Acapulco, *Mexico* 115 D5
Acarai, Serra, *Brazil* 121 C6
Acaraú, *Brazil* 122 B3
Acari, *Brazil* 122 C4
Acarí, *Peru* 124 D3
Acarigua, *Venezuela* 120 B4
Acatlán, *Mexico* 115 D5
Acayucan, *Mexico* 115 D6
Accéglio, *Italy* 32 D3
Accomac, *U.S.A.* 104 G8
Accous, *France* 26 E3
Accra, *Ghana* 79 D4
Accrington, *U.K.* 12 D5
Acebal, *Argentina* 126 C3
Aceh □, *Indonesia* 56 D1
Acerenza, *Italy* 35 B8
Acerra, *Italy* 35 B7
Aceuchal, *Spain* 31 G4
Achacachi, *Bolivia* 124 D4
Achaguas, *Venezuela* 120 B4
Achalpur, *India* 60 J10
Achao, *Chile* 128 B2
Achel, *Belgium* 17 F6
Acheng, *China* 51 B14
Achenkirch, *Austria* 19 H7
Achensee, *Austria* 19 H7
Acher, *India* 62 H5
Achern, *Germany* 19 G4
Achill, *Ireland* 15 C2
Achill Hd., *Ireland* 15 C1
Achill I., *Ireland* 15 C1
Achill Sd., *Ireland* 15 C2
Achim, *Germany* 18 B5
Achinsk, *Russia* 45 D10
Achol, *Sudan* 77 F3
Acıgöl, *Turkey* 66 E3
Acireale, *Italy* 35 E8
Ackerman, *U.S.A.* 109 J10
Acklins I., *Bahamas* 117 B5
Acme, *Canada* 100 C6
Acobamba, *Peru* 124 C3
Acomayo, *Peru* 124 C3
Aconcagua □, *Chile* 126 C1
Aconcagua, Cerro, *Argentina* 126 C2
Aconquija, Mt., *Argentina* 126 B2
Acopiara, *Brazil* 122 C4
Açores, Is. dos = Azores, *Atl. Oc.* 2 C8
Acorizal, *Brazil* 125 D6
Acquapendente, *Italy* 33 F8
Acquasanta, *Italy* 33 F10
Acquaviva delle Fonti, *Italy* 35 B9
Acqui, *Italy* 32 D5
Acraman, L., *Australia* 91 E2
Acre = 'Akko, *Israel* 69 C4
Acre □, *Brazil* 124 B3
Acre →, *Brazil* 124 B4
Acri, *Italy* 35 C9
Acs, *Hungary* 21 H8
Acton, *Canada* 106 C4
Açu, *Brazil* 122 C4
Ad Dammām, *Si. Arabia* 65 E6
Ad Dawhah, *Qatar* 65 E6
Ad Dawr, *Iraq* 64 C4
Ad Dir'īyah, *Si. Arabia* 64 E5
Ad Dīwānīyah, *Iraq* 64 D5
Ad Dujayl, *Iraq* 64 C5
Ad Durūz, J., *Jordan* 69 C5
Ada, *Ghana* 79 D5
Ada, *Serbia, Yug.* 21 K10
Ada, *Minn., U.S.A.* 108 B6
Ada, *Okla., U.S.A.* 109 H6
Adaja →, *Spain* 30 D6
Ådalslinden, *Sweden* 10 A10
Adam, Mt., *Falk. Is.* 128 D4
Adamantina, *Brazil* 123 F1
Adamaoua, Massif de l', *Cameroon* 79 D7
Adamawa Highlands = Adamaoua, Massif de l', *Cameroon* 79 D7
Adamello, Mt., *Italy* 32 B7
Adami Tulu, *Ethiopia* 77 F4
Adaminaby, *Australia* 91 F4
Adams, *Mass., U.S.A.* 107 D11
Adams, *N.Y., U.S.A.* 107 C8
Adams, *Wis., U.S.A.* 108 D10
Adams, Mt., *U.S.A.* 112 D5
Adam's Bridge, *Sri Lanka* 60 Q11
Adams L., *Canada* 100 C5
Adam's Peak, *Sri Lanka* 60 R12
Adamuz, *Spain* 31 G6
Adana, *Turkey* 66 E6
Adana □, *Turkey* 66 E6
Adanero, *Spain* 30 E6
Adapazarı, *Turkey* 66 C4
Adarama, *Sudan* 77 D3
Adare, C., *Antarctica* 5 D11
Adaut, *Indonesia* 57 F8
Adavale, *Australia* 91 D3
Adda →, *Italy* 32 C6
Addis Ababa = Addis Abeba, *Ethiopia* 77 F4
Addis Abeba, *Ethiopia* 77 F4
Addis Alem, *Ethiopia* 77 F4
Addison, *U.S.A.* 106 D7
Addo, *S. Africa* 84 E4
Adebour, *Niger* 79 C7
Ādeh, *Iran* 64 B5
Adel, *U.S.A.* 105 K4
Adelaide, *Australia* 91 E2
Adelaide, *Bahamas* 116 A4
Adelaide, *S. Africa* 84 E4
Adelaide I., *Antarctica* 5 C17
Adelaide Pen., *Canada* 96 B10
Adelaide River, *Australia* 88 B5
Adelanto, *U.S.A.* 113 L9
Adelboden, *Switz.* 22 D5
Adele I., *Australia* 88 C3
Adélie, Terre, *Antarctica* 5 C10
Ademuz, *Spain* 28 E3
Aden = Al 'Adan, *Yemen* 68 E4
Aden, G. of, *Asia* 68 E4
Adendorp, *S. Africa* 84 E3
Adh Dhayd, *U.A.E.* 65 E7
Adhoi, *India* 62 H4
Adi, *Indonesia* 57 E8
Adi Daro, *Ethiopia* 77 E4
Adi Keyih, *Ethiopia* 77 E4
Adi Kwala, *Ethiopia* 77 E4
Adi Ugri, *Ethiopia* 77 E4
Adieu, C., *Australia* 89 F5
Adieu Pt., *Australia* 88 C3
Adigala, *Ethiopia* 77 E5
Adige →, *Italy* 33 C9
Adigrat, *Ethiopia* 77 E4
Adilabad, *India* 60 K11
Adin, *U.S.A.* 110 F3
Adin Khel, *Afghan.* 60 C6
Adinkerke, *Belgium* 17 F1
Adirondack Mts., *U.S.A.* 107 C10
Adıyaman, *Turkey* 67 E8
Adiyaman □, *Turkey* 67 E8
Adjim, *Tunisia* 75 B7
Adjohon, *Benin* 79 D5
Adjud, *Romania* 38 C10
Adjumani, *Uganda* 82 B3
Adlavik Is., *Canada* 99 B8
Adler, *Russia* 43 E8
Adliswil, *Switz.* 23 B7
Admer, *Algeria* 75 D6
Admer, Erg d', *Algeria* 75 D6
Admiralty G., *Australia* 88 B4
Admiralty I., *U.S.A.* 96 C6
Admiralty Inlet, *U.S.A.* 110 C2
Admiralty Is., *Papua N. G.* 92 H6
Ado, *Nigeria* 79 D5
Ado Ekiti, *Nigeria* 79 D6
Adok, *Sudan* 77 F3
Adola, *Ethiopia* 77 E5
Adonara, *Indonesia* 57 F6
Adoni, *India* 60 M10
Adony, *Hungary* 21 H8
Adour →, *France* 26 E2
Adra, *India* 63 H12
Adra, *Spain* 29 J1
Adrano, *Italy* 35 E7
Adrar, *Algeria* 75 C4
Adré, *Chad* 73 F9
Adrī, *Libya* 75 C7
Ádria, *Italy* 33 C9
Adrian, *Mich., U.S.A.* 104 E3
Adrian, *Tex., U.S.A.* 109 H3
Adriatic Sea, *Europe* 6 G8
Adua, *Indonesia* 57 E7
Adula, *Switz.* 23 D8
Adwa, *Ethiopia* 77 E4
Adzhar Republic □, *Georgia* 43 F10
Adzopé, *Ivory C.* 78 D4
Ægean Sea, *Europe* 39 L8
Æolian Is. = Eólie, Is., *Italy* 35 D7
Aerhtai Shan, *Mongolia* 54 B4
Ærø, *Denmark* 11 K4
Ærøskøbing, *Denmark* 11 K4
Aesch, *Switz.* 22 B5
'Afak, *Iraq* 64 C5
Afándou, *Greece* 37 C10
Afarag, Erg, *Algeria* 75 D5
Afars & Issas, Terr. of = Djibouti ■, *Africa* 68 E3
Affreville = Khemis Miliana, *Algeria* 75 A5
Afghanistan ■, *Asia* 60 C4
Afgoi, *Somali Rep.* 68 G3
Afikpo, *Nigeria* 79 D6
Aflou, *Algeria* 75 B5
Afogados da Ingàzeira, *Brazil* 122 C4
Afognak I., *U.S.A.* 96 C4
Afragola, *Italy* 35 B7
Afrera, *Ethiopia* 77 E5
Africa 70 E6
'Afrīn, *Syria* 64 B3
Afşin, *Turkey* 66 D7
Afton, *U.S.A.* 107 D9
Aftout, *Algeria* 74 C4
Afuá, *Brazil* 121 D7
Afula, *Israel* 69 C4
Afyonkarahisar, *Turkey* 66 D4
Afyonkarahisar □, *Turkey* 66 D4
Aga, *Egypt* 76 H7
Agadès = Agadez, *Niger* 79 B6
Agadez, *Niger* 79 B6
Agadir, *Morocco* 74 B3
Agaete, *Canary Is.* 36 F4
Agailás, *Mauritania* 74 D2
Agapa, *Russia* 45 B9
Agar, *India* 62 H7
Agaro, *Ethiopia* 77 F4
Agartala, *India* 61 H17
Agassiz, *Canada* 100 D4
Agats, *Indonesia* 57 F9
Agbélouvé, *Togo* 79 D5
Agboville, *Ivory C.* 78 D4
Agdam, *Azerbaijan* 43 G12
Agdash, *Azerbaijan* 43 F12
Agde, *France* 26 E7
Agde, C. d', *France* 26 E7
Agdz, *Morocco* 74 B3
Agdzhabedi, *Azerbaijan* 43 F12
Agen, *France* 26 D4
Agersø, *Denmark* 11 J5
Ageyevo, *Russia* 41 D10
Agger, *Denmark* 11 H2
Àggius, *Italy* 34 B2
Āgh Kand, *Iran* 65 B6
Aghoueyyît, *Mauritania* 74 D1
Aginskoye, *Russia* 45 D12
Agira, *Italy* 35 E7
Ağlasun, *Turkey* 66 E4
Agly →, *France* 26 F7
Agnibilékrou, *Ivory C.* 78 D4
Agnita, *Romania* 38 D7
Agnone, *Italy* 35 A7
Agofie, *Ghana* 79 D5
Agogna →, *Italy* 32 C5
Agogo, *Sudan* 77 F2
Agon, *France* 24 C5
Agön, *Sweden* 10 C11
Ágordo, *Italy* 33 B9
Agout →, *France* 26 E5
Agra, *India* 62 F7
Agramunt, *Spain* 28 D6
Agreda, *Spain* 28 D3
Ağri, *Turkey* 67 D10
Ağri □, *Turkey* 67 D10
Agri →, *Italy* 35 B9
Ağrı Dağı, *Turkey* 67 D11
Ağrı Karakose, *Turkey* 67 D10
Agrigento, *Italy* 34 E6
Agrinion, *Greece* 39 L4
Agrópoli, *Italy* 35 B7
Água Branca, *Brazil* 122 C3
Agua Caliente, *Baja Calif. N., Mexico* 113 N10
Agua Caliente, *Sinaloa, Mexico* 114 B3
Agua Caliente Springs, *U.S.A.* 113 N10
Água Clara, *Brazil* 125 E7
Agua Hechicero, *Mexico* 113 N10
Agua Preta →, *Brazil* 121 D5
Agua Prieta, *Mexico* 114 A3
Aguachica, *Colombia* 120 B3
Aguada Cecilio, *Argentina* 128 B3
Aguadas, *Colombia* 120 B2
Aguadilla, *Puerto Rico* 117 C6
Aguadulce, *Panama* 116 E3
Aguanga, *U.S.A.* 113 M10
Aguanish, *Canada* 99 B7
Aguanus →, *Canada* 99 B7
Aguapeí, *Brazil* 125 D6
Aguapeí →, *Brazil* 123 F1
Aguapey →, *Argentina* 126 B4
Aguaray Guazú →, *Paraguay* 126 A4
Aguarico →, *Ecuador* 120 D2
Aguas →, *Spain* 28 D4
Aguas Blancas, *Chile* 126 A2
Aguas Calientes, Sierra de, *Argentina* 126 B2
Águas Formosas, *Brazil* 123 E3
Aguascalientes, *Mexico* 114 C4
Aguascalientes □, *Mexico* 114 C4
Agudo, *Spain* 31 G6
Águeda, *Portugal* 30 E2
Agueda →, *Spain* 30 D4
Aguié, *Niger* 79 C6
Aguilafuente, *Spain* 30 D6
Aguilar, *Spain* 31 H6
Aguilar de Campóo, *Spain* 30 C6
Aguilares, *Argentina* 126 B2
Aguilas, *Spain* 29 H3
Agüimes, *Canary Is.* 36 G4
Aguja, C. de la, *Colombia* 120 A3
Agulaa, *Ethiopia* 77 E4
Agulhas, C., *S. Africa* 84 E3
Agulo, *Canary Is.* 36 F2
Agung, *Indonesia* 56 F5
Agur, *Uganda* 82 B3
Agusan →, *Phil.* 55 G6
Agustín Codazzi, *Colombia* 120 A3
Agvali, *Russia* 43 E12
Aha Mts., *Botswana* 84 B3
Ahaggar, *Algeria* 75 D6
Ahamansu, *Ghana* 79 D5
Ahar, *Iran* 64 B5
Ahaus, *Germany* 18 C3
Ahelledjem, *Algeria* 75 C6
Ahipara B., *N.Z.* 87 F4
Ahiri, *India* 60 K12
Ahlen, *Germany* 18 D3
Ahmad Wal, *Pakistan* 62 E1
Ahmadabad, *India* 62 H5
Aḩmadābād, *Khorāsān, Iran* 65 C9
Aḩmadābād, *Khorāsān, Iran* 65 C8
Aḩmadī, *Iran* 65 E8
Ahmadnagar, *India* 60 K9
Ahmadpur, *Pakistan* 62 E4
Ahmar, *Ethiopia* 77 F5
Ahmedabad = Ahmadabad, *India* 62 H5
Ahmednagar = Ahmadnagar, *India* 60 K9
Ahoada, *Nigeria* 79 D6
Ahome, *Mexico* 114 B3
Ahr →, *Germany* 18 E3
Ahram, *Iran* 65 D6
Ahrax Pt., *Malta* 37 D1
Ahrensbök, *Germany* 18 A6
Ahrweiler, *Germany* 18 E3
Āhū, *Iran* 65 C6
Ahuachapán, *El Salv.* 116 D2
Ahvāz, *Iran* 65 D6
Ahvenanmaa = Åland, *Finland* 9 F16
Aḩwar, *Yemen* 68 E4
Ahzar, *Mali* 79 B5
Aiari →, *Brazil* 120 C4
Aichach, *Germany* 19 G7
Aichi □, *Japan* 49 G8
Aidone, *Italy* 35 E7
Aiello Cálabro, *Italy* 35 C9
Aigle, *Switz.* 22 D3
Aignay-le-Duc, *France* 25 E11
Aigoual, Mt., *France* 26 D7
Aigre, *France* 26 C4

Aigua, Uruguay 127 C5
Aigueperse, France 26 B7
Aigues →, France 27 D8
Aigues-Mortes, France 27 E8
Aigues-Mortes, G. d', France 27 E8
Aiguilles, France 27 D10
Aiguillon, France 26 D4
Aigurande, France 26 B5
Aihui, China 54 A7
Aija, Peru 124 B2
Aikawa, Japan 48 E9
Aiken, U.S.A. 105 J5
Ailao Shan, China 52 F3
Aillant-sur-Tholon, France 25 E10
Aillik, Canada 99 A8
Ailly-sur-Noye, France 25 C9
Ailsa Craig, U.K. 14 F3
'Ailūn, Jordan 69 C4
Aim, Russia 45 D14
Aimere, Indonesia 57 F6
Aimogasta, Argentina 126 B2
Aimorés, Brazil 123 E3
Ain □, France 27 B9
Ain →, France 27 C9
Aïn Beïda, Algeria 75 A6
Aïn Ben Khellil, Algeria 75 B4
Aïn Ben Tili, Mauritania 74 C3
Aïn Beni Mathar, Morocco 75 B4
Aïn Benian, Algeria 75 A5
Ain Dalla, Egypt 76 B2
Ain el Mafki, Egypt 76 B2
Ain Girba, Egypt 76 B2
Aïn M'lila, Algeria 75 A6
Ain Qeiqab, Egypt 76 B1
Aïn-Sefra, Algeria 75 B4
Ain Sheikh Murzûk, Egypt 76 B2
'Ain Sudr, Egypt 69 F2
Ain Sukhna, Egypt 76 J8
Aïn Tédelès, Algeria 75 A5
Aïn-Témouchent, Algeria 75 A4
Aïn Touta, Algeria 75 A6
Aïn Zeitûn, Egypt 76 B2
Aïn Zorah, Morocco 75 B4
Ainabo, Somali Rep. 68 F4
Ainaži, Latvia 40 C4
Aínos Óros, Greece 39 L3
Ainsworth, U.S.A. 108 D5
Aipe, Colombia 120 C2
Aiquile, Bolivia 125 D4
Aïr, Niger 79 B6
Air Hitam, Malaysia 59 M4
Airaines, France 25 C8
Airão, Brazil 121 D5
Airdrie, U.K. 14 F5
Aire →, France 25 C11
Aire →, U.K. 12 D7
Aire, I. del, Spain 36 B11
Aire-sur-la-Lys, France 25 B9
Aire-sur-l'Adour, France 26 E3
Airlie Beach, Australia 90 C4
Airolo, Switz. 23 C7
Airvault, France 24 F6
Aisch →, Germany 19 F7
Aisen □, Chile 128 C2
Aisne □, France 25 C10
Aisne →, France 25 C9
Aitana, Sierra de, Spain 29 G4
Aitkin, U.S.A. 108 B8
Aitolikón, Greece 39 L4
Aiuaba, Brazil 122 C3
Aiud, Romania 38 C6
Aix-en-Provence, France 27 E9
Aix-la-Chapelle = Aachen, Germany 18 E2
Aix-les-Bains, France 27 C9
Aixe-sur-Vienne, France 26 C5
Aiyansh, Canada 100 B3
Aíyina, Greece 39 M6
Aiyínion, Greece 39 J5
Aiyion, Greece 39 L5
Aizawl, India 61 H18
Aizenay, France 24 F5
Aizpute, Latvia 40 C2
Aizuwakamatsu, Japan 48 F9
Ajaccio, France 27 G12
Ajaccio, G. d', France 27 G12
Ajaju →, Colombia 120 C3
Ajalpan, Mexico 115 D5
Ajanta Ra., India 60 J9
Ajax, Canada 106 C5
Ajdâbiyah, Libya 73 B9
Ajdovščina, Slovenia 33 C10
Ajibar, Ethiopia 77 E4
Ajka, Hungary 21 H7
'Ajmān, U.A.E. 65 E7
Ajmer, India 62 F6
Ajo, U.S.A. 111 K7
Ajoie, Switz. 22 B4
Ajok, Sudan 77 F2
Ajuy, Phil. 55 F5
Ak Dağ, Antalya, Turkey 66 E3
Ak Dağ, Sivas, Turkey 66 D7
Akaba, Togo 79 D5
Akabira, Japan 48 C11
Akabli, Algeria 75 C5
Akaki Beseka, Ethiopia 77 F4
Akala, Sudan 77 D4
Akamas □, Cyprus 37 D11
Akanthou, Cyprus 37 D12
Akaroa, N.Z. 87 K4
Akasha, Sudan 76 C3
Akashi, Japan 49 G7
Akbou, Algeria 75 A5
Akçaabat, Turkey 67 C8
Akçakoca, Turkey 66 C4
Akchâr, Mauritania 74 D2
Akdağmadeni, Turkey 66 D6
Akelamo, Indonesia 57 D7
Akershus fylke □, Norway 10 E5
Aketi, Zaïre 80 D4
Akhalkalaki, Georgia 43 F10
Akhaltsikhe, Georgia 43 F10
Akharnaí, Greece 39 L6
Akhelóös →, Greece 39 L4
Akhendria, Greece 39 Q8
Akhéron →, Greece 39 K3
Akhladhókambos, Greece 39 M5
Akhmîm, Egypt 76 B3
Akhnur, India 63 C6
Akhtubinsk, Russia 43 B12
Akhty, Russia 43 F12
Akhtyrka, Ukraine 40 F9
Aki, Japan 49 H6
Akimiski I., Canada 98 B3
Akimovka, Ukraine 42 C6
Akita, Japan 48 E10
Akita □, Japan 48 E10
Akjoujt, Mauritania 78 B2
Akka, Morocco 74 C3
Akkeshi, Japan 48 C12
'Akko, Israel 69 C4
Akkol, Kazakhstan 44 E8
Akkrum, Neths. 16 B7
Aklampa, Benin 79 D5
Aklavik, Canada 96 B6
Akmolinsk = Tselinograd, Kazakhstan 44 D8
Akmonte, Spain 31 H4
Aknoul, Morocco 75 B4
Akō, Japan 49 G7
Ako, Nigeria 79 C7
Akobo →, Ethiopia 77 F3
Akola, India 60 J10
Akonolinga, Cameroon 79 E7
Akordat, Ethiopia 77 D4
Akosombo Dam, Ghana 79 D5
Akot, Sudan 77 F3
Akpatok I., Canada 97 B13
Akranes, Iceland 8 D3
Akreïjit, Mauritania 78 B3
Akrítas Venétiko, Ákra, Greece 39 N4
Akron, Colo., U.S.A. 108 E3
Akron, Ohio, U.S.A. 106 E3
Akrotiri, Cyprus 37 E11
Akrotíri, Ákra, Greece 39 J8
Akrotiri Bay, Cyprus 37 E12
Aksai Chih, India 63 B8
Aksaray, Turkey 66 D6
Aksarka, Russia 44 C7
Aksay, Kazakhstan 44 D6
Akşehir, Turkey 66 D4
Akşehir Gölü, Turkey 66 D4
Aksenovo Zilovskoye, Russia 45 D12
Akstafa, Azerbaijan 43 F11
Aksu, China 54 B3
Aksu →, Turkey 66 E4
Aksum, Ethiopia 77 E4
Aktogay, Kazakhstan 44 E8
Aktyubinsk, Kazakhstan 44 D6
Aku, Nigeria 79 D6
Akure, Nigeria 79 D6
Akureyri, Iceland 8 D4
Akuseki-Shima, Japan 49 K4
Akusha, Russia 43 E12
Akwa-Ibom □, Nigeria 79 E6
Akyab = Sittwe, Burma 61 J18
Akyazı, Turkey 66 C4
Al 'Adan, Yemen 68 E4
Al Aḩsā, Si. Arabia 65 E6
Al Ajfar, Si. Arabia 64 E4
Al Amādīyah, Iraq 64 B4
Al Amārah, Iraq 64 D5
Al 'Aqabah, Jordan 69 F4
Al Arak, Syria 64 C3
Al 'Aramah, Si. Arabia 64 E5
Al Arṭāwīyah, Si. Arabia 64 E5
Al 'Āṣimah □, Jordan 69 D5
Al' Assāfīyah, Si. Arabia 64 D3
Al 'Ayn, Oman 65 E7
Al 'Ayn, Si. Arabia 64 E3
Al A'ẓamīyah, Iraq 64 C5
Al 'Azīzīyah, Iraq 64 C5
Al 'Azīzīyah, Libya 75 B7
Al Bāb, Syria 64 B3
Al Bad', Si. Arabia 64 D2
Al Bādī, Iraq 64 C4
Al Baḩrah, Kuwait 64 D5
Al Balqā' □, Jordan 69 C4
Al Barkāt, Libya 75 D7
Al Bārūk, J., Lebanon 69 B4
Al Başrah, Iraq 64 D5
Al Baṭḩā, Iraq 64 D5
Al Batrūn, Lebanon 69 A4
Al Bi'r, Si. Arabia 64 D3
Al Bu'ayrāt, Libya 73 B8
Al Burayj, Syria 69 A5
Al Fallūjah, Iraq 64 C4
Al Fāw, Iraq 65 D6
Al Fujayrah, U.A.E. 65 E8
Al Ghadaf, W. →, Jordan 69 D5
Al Ghammās, Iraq 64 D5
Al Hābah, Si. Arabia 64 E5
Al Ḥadīthah, Iraq 64 C4
Al Ḥadīthah, Si. Arabia 64 D3
Al Hājānah, Syria 69 B5
Al Ḥāmad, Si. Arabia 64 D3
Al Hamdāniyah, Syria 64 C3
Al Ḥamidīyah, Syria 69 A4
Al Hammādah al Ḥamrā', Libya 75 C7
Al Ḥammār, Iraq 64 D5
Al Ḥarīr, W. →, Syria 69 C4
Al Ḥasā, W. →, Jordan 69 D4
Al Ḥasakah, Syria 64 B4
Al Ḥawrah, Yemen 68 E4
Al Ḥaydān, W. →, Jordan 69 D4
Al Ḥayy, Iraq 64 C5
Al Ḥijāz, Si. Arabia 68 B2
Al Ḥillah, Iraq 64 C5
Al Ḥillah, Si. Arabia 68 C4
Al Hirmil, Lebanon 69 A5
Al Hoceïma, Morocco 74 A4
Al Ḥudaydah, Yemen 68 E3
Al Hufūf, Si. Arabia 65 E6
Al Ḥumaydah, Si. Arabia 64 D2
Al Ḥunayy, Si. Arabia 65 E6
Al Irq, Libya 73 C9
Al Īsāwīyah, Si. Arabia 64 D3
Al Ittihad = Madīnat ash Sha'b, Yemen 68 E3
Al Jafr, Jordan 69 E5
Al Jaghbūb, Libya 73 C9
Al Jahrah, Kuwait 64 D5
Al Jalāmīd, Si. Arabia 64 D3
Al Jamalīyah, Qatar 65 E6
Al Janūb □, Lebanon 69 B4
Al Jawf, Libya 73 D9
Al Jawf, Si. Arabia 64 D3
Al Jazirah, Iraq 64 C5
Al Jazirah, Libya 73 C9
Al Jithāmīyah, Si. Arabia 64 E4
Al Jubayl, Si. Arabia 65 E6
Al Jubaylah, Si. Arabia 64 E5
Al Jubb, Si. Arabia 64 E4
Al Junaynah, Sudan 73 F9
Al Kabā'ish, Iraq 64 D5
Al Karak, Jordan 69 D4
Al Karak □, Jordan 69 E5
Al Kāzim Tyah, Iraq 64 C5
Al Khalīl, Jordan 69 D4
Al Khalīl □, Jordan 69 D4
Al Khawr, Qatar 65 E6
Al Khiḑr, Iraq 64 D5
Al Khiyām, Lebanon 69 B4
Al Kiswah, Syria 69 B5
Al Kufrah, Libya 73 D9
Al Kuhayfīyah, Si. Arabia 64 E4
Al Kūt, Iraq 64 C5
Al Kuwayt, Kuwait 64 D5
Al Labwah, Lebanon 69 A5
Al Lādhiqīyah, Syria 64 C2
Al Līth, Si. Arabia 76 C5
Al Liwā', Oman 65 E8
Al Luḩayyah, Yemen 68 D3
Al Madīnah, Iraq 64 D5
Al Madīnah, Si. Arabia 64 E3
Al-Mafraq, Jordan 69 C5
Al Maḩmūdīyah, Iraq 64 C5
Al Majma'ah, Si. Arabia 64 E5
Al Makhruq, W. →, Jordan 69 D6
Al Makḩūl, Si. Arabia 64 E4
Al Manāmah, Bahrain 65 E6
Al Maqwa', Kuwait 64 D5
Al Marj, Libya 73 B9
Al Maṭlā, Kuwait 64 D5
Al Mawjib, W. →, Jordan 69 D4
Al Mawşil, Iraq 64 B4
Al Mayādin, Syria 64 C4
Al Mazār, Jordan 69 D4
Al Midhnab, Si. Arabia 64 E5
Al Minā', Lebanon 69 A4
Al Miqdādīyah, Iraq 64 C5
Al Mubarraz, Si. Arabia 65 E6
Al Mughayrā', U.A.E. 65 E7
Al Muḩarraq, Bahrain 65 E6
Al Mukallā, Yemen 68 E4
Al Mukhā, Yemen 68 E3
Al Musayjīd, Si. Arabia 64 E3
Al Musayyib, Iraq 64 C5
Al Muwayliḩ, Si. Arabia 64 E2
Al Owuho = Otukpa, Nigeria 79 D6
Al Qā'im, Iraq 64 C4
Al Qalībah, Si. Arabia 64 D3
Al Qaryatayn, Syria 69 A6
Al Qaşabát, Libya 73 B7
Al Qaṭ'ā, Syria 64 C4
Al Qaṭīf, Si. Arabia 65 E6
Al Qatrānah, Jordan 69 D5
Al Qaṭrūn, Libya 73 D8
Al Qayşūmah, Si. Arabia 64 D5
Al Quds = Jerusalem, Israel 69 D4
Al Quds □, Jordan 69 D4
Al Qunaytirah, Syria 69 C4
Al Qunfudhah, Si. Arabia 76 D5
Al Qurnah, Iraq 64 D5
Al Quşayr, Iraq 64 D5
Al Quşayr, Syria 69 A5
Al Qutayfah, Syria 69 B5
Al' Uḑaylīyah, Si. Arabia 65 E6
Al 'Ulā, Si. Arabia 64 E3
Al Uqaylah ash Sharqīgah, Libya 73 B8
Al Uqayr, Si. Arabia 65 E6
Al 'Uwaynid, Si. Arabia 64 E5
Al' 'Uwayqīlah, Si. Arabia 64 D4
Al 'Uyūn, Si. Arabia 64 E4
Al 'Uyūn, Si. Arabia 64 E3
Al Wajh, Si. Arabia 64 E3
Al Wakrah, Qatar 65 E6
Al Wannān, Si. Arabia 65 E6
Al Waqbah, Si. Arabia 64 D5
Al Wari'āh, Si. Arabia 64 E5
Al Wātīyah, Libya 75 B7
Al Wusayl, Qatar 65 E6
Ala, Italy 32 C8
Ala Dağları, Turkey 67 D10
Alabama □, U.S.A. 105 J2
Alabama →, U.S.A. 105 K2
Alaca, Turkey 66 C6
Alaçam, Turkey 66 C6
Alaçam Dağları, Turkey 66 D3
Alaejos, Spain 30 D5
Alaérma, Greece 37 C9
Alagna Valsésia, Italy 32 C4
Alagoa Grande, Brazil 122 C4
Alagoas □, Brazil 122 C4
Alagoinhas, Brazil 123 D4
Alagón, Spain 28 D3
Alagón →, Spain 31 F4
Alajero, Canary Is. 36 F2
Alajuela, Costa Rica 116 D3
Alakamisy, Madag. 85 C8
Alalapura, Surinam 121 C6
Alalaú →, Brazil 121 D5
Alameda, Spain 31 H6
Alameda, Calif., U.S.A. 112 H4
Alameda, N. Mex., U.S.A. 111 J10
Alaminos, Phil. 55 C3
Alamo, U.S.A. 113 J11
Alamo Crossing, U.S.A. 113 L13
Alamogordo, U.S.A. 111 K11
Alamos, Mexico 114 B3
Alamosa, U.S.A. 111 H11
Åland, Finland 9 F16
Alandroal, Portugal 31 G3
Ålands hav, Sweden 9 G15
Alandur, India 60 N12
Alange, Presa de, Spain 31 G4
Alanis, Spain 31 G5
Alanya, Turkey 66 E4
Alaotra, Farihin', Madag. 85 B8
Alapayevsk, Russia 44 D7
Alar del Rey, Spain 30 C6
Alaraz, Spain 30 E5
Alaşehir, Turkey 66 D3
Alaska □, U.S.A. 96 B5
Alaska, G. of, Pac. Oc. 96 C5
Alaska Highway, Canada 100 B3
Alaska Pen., U.S.A. 96 C4
Alaska Range, U.S.A. 96 B4
Alássio, Italy 32 D5
Alataw Shankou, China 54 B3
Alatri, Italy 34 A6
Alatyr, Russia 41 D15
Alatyr →, Russia 41 D15
Alausi, Ecuador 120 D2
Álava □, Spain 28 C2
Alava, C., U.S.A. 110 B1
Alaverdi, Armenia 43 F11
Alawoona, Australia 91 E3
'Alayh, Lebanon 69 B4
Alayor, Spain 36 B11
Alazan →, Azerbaijan 43 F12
Alba, Italy 32 D5
Alba de Tormes, Spain 30 E5
Alba Iulia, Romania 38 C6
Albac, Romania 38 C6
Albacete, Spain 29 G3
Albacete □, Spain 29 G3
Albacutya, L., Australia 91 F3
Ålbæk, Denmark 11 G4
Ålbæk Bugt, Denmark 11 G4
Albaida, Spain 29 G4
Albalate de las Nogueras, Spain 28 E2
Albalate del Arzobispo, Spain 28 D4
Albania ■, Europe 39 J3
Albano Laziale, Italy 34 A5
Albany, Australia 89 G2
Albany, Ga., U.S.A. 105 K3
Albany, Minn., U.S.A. 108 C7
Albany, N.Y., U.S.A. 107 D11
Albany, Oreg., U.S.A. 110 D2
Albany, Tex., U.S.A. 109 J5
Albany →, Canada 98 B3
Albardón, Argentina 126 C2
Albarracín, Spain 28 E3
Albarracín, Sierra de, Spain 28 E3
Albatross B., Australia 90 A3
Albegna →, Italy 33 F8
Albemarle, U.S.A. 105 H5
Albemarle Sd., U.S.A. 105 H7
Albenga, Italy 32 D5
Alberche →, Spain 30 F6
Alberdi, Paraguay 126 B4
Alberes, Mts., Spain 28 C7
Alberique, Spain 29 F4
Albersdorf, Germany 18 A5
Albert, France 25 B9
Albert, L. = Mobutu Sese Seko, L., Africa 82 B3
Albert, L., Australia 91 F2
Albert Canyon, Canada 100 C5
Albert Edward Ra., Australia 88 C4
Albert Lea, U.S.A. 108 D8
Albert Nile →, Uganda 82 B3
Albert Town, Bahamas 117 B5
Alberta □, Canada 100 C6
Alberti, Argentina 126 D3
Albertinia, S. Africa 84 E3
Albertkanaal →, Belgium 17 F4
Alberton, Canada 99 C7
Albertville = Kalemie, Zaïre 82 D2
Albertville, France 27 C10
Albi, France 26 E6
Albia, U.S.A. 108 E8
Albina, Surinam 121 B7
Albina, Ponta, Angola 84 B1
Albino, Italy 32 C6
Albion, Idaho, U.S.A. 110 E7
Albion, Mich., U.S.A. 104 D3
Albion, Nebr., U.S.A. 108 E5
Albion, Pa., U.S.A. 106 E4
Alblasserdam, Neths. 16 E5
Albocácer, Spain 28 E5
Alborán, Medit. S. 31 K7
Alborea, Spain 29 F3
Ålborg, Denmark 11 G3
Ålborg Bugt, Denmark 11 H4
Alborz, Reshteh-ye Kūhhā-ye, Iran 65 C7
Albox, Spain 29 H2
Albreda, Canada 100 C5
Albufeira, Portugal 31 H2
Albula →, Switz. 23 C8
Albuñol, Spain 29 J1
Albuquerque, Brazil 125 D6
Albuquerque, U.S.A. 111 J10
Albuquerque, Cayos de, Caribbean 116 D3
Alburg, U.S.A. 107 B11
Alburno, Mte., Italy 35 B8
Alburquerque, Spain 31 F4
Albury, Australia 91 F4
Alby, Sweden 10 B9
Alcácer do Sal, Portugal 31 G2
Alcaçovas, Portugal 31 G2
Alcalá de Chisvert, Spain 28 E5
Alcalá de Guadaira, Spain 31 H5
Alcalá de Henares, Spain 28 E1
Alcalá de los Gazules, Spain 31 J5
Alcalá la Real, Spain 31 H7
Alcamo, Italy 34 E5
Alcanadre, Spain 28 C2
Alcanadre →, Spain 28 D4
Alcanar, Spain 28 E5
Alcanede, Portugal 31 F2
Alcanena, Portugal 31 F2
Alcañices, Spain 30 D4
Alcaníz, Spain 28 D4
Alcântara, Brazil 122 B3
Alcántara, Spain 31 F4
Alcantara L., Canada 101 A7
Alcantarilla, Spain 29 H3
Alcaracejos, Spain 31 G6
Alcaraz, Spain 29 G2
Alcaraz, Sierra de, Spain 29 G2
Alcaudete, Spain 31 H6
Alcázar de San Juan, Spain 29 F1
Alcira, Spain 29 F4
Alcoa, U.S.A. 105 H4
Alcobaça, Portugal 31 F2
Alcobendas, Spain 28 E1
Alcolea del Pinar, Spain 28 D2
Alcora, Spain 28 E4
Alcorcón, Spain 30 E7
Alcoutim, Portugal 31 H3
Alcova, U.S.A. 110 E10
Alcoy, Spain 29 G4
Alcubierre, Sierra de, Spain 28 D4
Alcublas, Spain 28 F4
Alcudia, Spain 36 B10
Alcudia, B. de, Spain 36 B10
Alcudia, Sierra de la, Spain 31 G6
Aldabra Is., Seychelles 3 E12
Aldama, Mexico 115 C5
Aldan, Russia 45 D13
Aldan →, Russia 45 C13
Aldea, Pta. de la, Canary Is. 36 G4
Aldeburgh, U.K. 13 E9
Aldeia Nova, Portugal 31 H3
Alder, U.S.A. 110 D7
Alder Pk., U.S.A. 112 K5
Alderney, Chan. Is. 13 H5
Aldershot, U.K. 13 F7
Aledo, U.S.A. 108 E9
Alefa, Ethiopia 77 E4
Aleg, Mauritania 78 B2
Alegranza, Canary Is. 36 E6
Alegranza, I., Canary Is. 36 E6
Alegre, Brazil 123 F3
Alegrete, Brazil 127 B4
Aleisk, Russia 44 D9
Aleksandriya, Ukraine 40 F5
Aleksandriya, Ukraine 42 B5
Aleksandriyskaya, Russia 43 E12
Aleksandrov, Russia 41 C11
Aleksandrovac, Serbia, Yug. 21 L11
Aleksandrovka, Ukraine 42 B5
Aleksandrovo, Bulgaria 38 F7
Aleksandrovsk-Sakhalinskiy, Russia 45 D15
Aleksandrovskiy Zavod, Russia 45 D12
Aleksandrovskoye, Russia 44 C8
Aleksandrów Kujawski, Poland 20 C8
Aleksandrów Łódźki, Poland 20 D9
Alekseyevka, Russia 41 F11
Aleksin, Russia 41 D10
Aleksinac, Serbia, Yug. 21 M11
Além Paraíba, Brazil 123 F3

Alemania

Alemania, *Argentina* 126 B2
Alemania, *Chile* 126 B2
Ålen, *Norway* 10 B5
Alençon, *France* 24 D7
Alenuihaha Chan., *U.S.A.* 102 H17
Aleppo = Ḩalab, *Syria* 64 B3
Aléria, *France* 27 F13
Alert Bay, *Canada* 100 C3
Alès, *France* 27 D8
Aleşd, *Romania* 38 B5
Alessándria, *Italy* 32 D5
Ålestrup, *Denmark* 11 H3
Ålesund, *Norway* 8 E9
Alet-les-Bains, *France* 26 F6
Aletschhorn, *Switz.* 22 D6
Aleutian Is., *Pac. Oc.* 96 C2
Aleutian Trench, *Pac. Oc.* 92 B10
Alexander, *U.S.A.* 108 B3
Alexander, Mt., *Australia* 89 E3
Alexander Arch., *U.S.A.* 100 B2
Alexander B., *S. Africa* 84 D2
Alexander Bay, *S. Africa* 84 D2
Alexander City, *U.S.A.* 105 J3
Alexander I., *Antarctica* 5 C17
Alexandra, *Australia* 91 F4
Alexandra, *N.Z.* 87 L2
Alexandra Falls, *Canada* 100 A5
Alexandretta = İskenderun, *Turkey* 66 E7
Alexandria = El Iskandarîya, *Egypt* 76 H6
Alexandria, *Australia* 90 B2
Alexandria, *B.C., Canada* 100 C4
Alexandria, *Ont., Canada* 98 C5
Alexandria, *Romania* 38 F8
Alexandria, *S. Africa* 84 E4
Alexandria, *Ind., U.S.A.* 104 E3
Alexandria, *La., U.S.A.* 109 K8
Alexandria, *Minn., U.S.A.* 108 C7
Alexandria, *S. Dak., U.S.A.* 108 D6
Alexandria, *Va., U.S.A.* 104 F7
Alexandria Bay, *U.S.A.* 107 B9
Alexandrina, L., *Australia* 91 F2
Alexandroúpolis, *Greece* 39 J8
Alexis →, *Canada* 99 B8
Alexis Creek, *Canada* 100 C4
Alfabia, *Spain* 36 B9
Alfambra, *Spain* 28 E3
Alfândega da Fé, *Portugal* 30 D4
Alfaro, *Spain* 28 C3
Alfeld, *Germany* 18 D5
Alfenas, *Brazil* 127 A6
Alfiós →, *Greece* 39 M4
Alfonsine, *Italy* 33 D9
Alford, *U.K.* 14 D6
Alfred, *Maine, U.S.A.* 107 C14
Alfred, *N.Y., U.S.A.* 106 D7
Alfreton, *U.K.* 12 D6
Alga, *Kazakhstan* 44 E6
Algaida, *Spain* 36 B9
Algar, *Spain* 31 J5
Algarinejo, *Spain* 31 H6
Algarve, *Portugal* 31 J2
Algeciras, *Spain* 31 J5
Algemesí, *Spain* 29 F4
Alger, *Algeria* 75 A5
Algeria ■, *Africa* 75 C5
Alghero, *Italy* 34 B1
Algiers = Alger, *Algeria* 75 A5
Algoa B., *S. Africa* 84 E4
Algodonales, *Spain* 31 J5
Algodor →, *Spain* 30 F7
Algoma, *U.S.A.* 104 C2
Algona, *U.S.A.* 108 D7
Algonac, *U.S.A.* 106 D2
Alhama de Almería, *Spain* 29 J2
Alhama de Aragón, *Spain* 28 D3
Alhama de Granada, *Spain* 31 J7
Alhama de Murcia, *Spain* 29 H3
Alhambra, *Spain* 29 G1
Alhambra, *U.S.A.* 113 L8
Alhaurín el Grande, *Spain* 31 J6
Alhucemas = Al Hoceïma, *Morocco* 74 A4
'Alī al Gharbī, *Iraq* 64 C5
Alī ash Sharqī, *Iraq* 64 C5
Ali Bayramly, *Azerbaijan* 43 G13
'Alī Khēl, *Afghan.* 62 C3
Ali Sahîh, *Djibouti* 77 E5
Alī Shāh, *Iran* 64 B5
Ália, *Italy* 34 E6
'Alīābād, *Khorāsān, Iran* 65 C8
Alīābād, *Kordestān, Iran* 64 C5
'Alīābād, *Yazd, Iran* 65 D7
Aliaga, *Spain* 28 E4
Aliağa, *Turkey* 66 D2
Aliákmon →, *Greece* 39 J5
Alibo, *Ethiopia* 77 F4
Alibunar, *Serbia, Yug.* 21 K10
Alicante, *Spain* 29 G4
Alicante □, *Spain* 29 G4
Alice, *S. Africa* 84 E4
Alice, *U.S.A.* 109 M5
Alice →, *Queens., Australia* 90 C3
Alice →, *Queens., Australia* 90 B3
Alice, Punta dell', *Italy* 35 C10
Alice Arm, *Canada* 100 B3
Alice Downs, *Australia* 88 C4
Alice Springs, *Australia* 90 C1
Alicedale, *S. Africa* 84 E4
Aliceville, *U.S.A.* 105 J1
Alick Cr. →, *Australia* 90 C3
Alicudi, I., *Italy* 35 D7
Alida, *Canada* 101 D8
Aligarh, *Raj., India* 62 G7
Aligarh, *Ut. P., India* 62 F8
Alīgūdarz, *Iran* 65 C6
Alijó, *Portugal* 30 D3
Alimena, *Italy* 35 E7
Alimnía, *Greece* 37 C9
Alingsås, *Sweden* 11 G6
Alipur, *Pakistan* 62 E4
Alipur Duar, *India* 61 F16
Aliquippa, *U.S.A.* 106 F4
Aliste →, *Spain* 30 D5
Alitus, *Lithuania* 40 D4
Alivérion, *Greece* 39 L7
Aliwal North, *S. Africa* 84 E4
Alix, *Canada* 100 C6
Aljezur, *Portugal* 31 H2
Aljustrel, *Portugal* 31 H2
Alkamari, *Niger* 79 C7
Alken, *Belgium* 17 G6
Alkmaar, *Neths.* 16 C5
All American Canal, *U.S.A.* 111 K6
Allada, *Benin* 79 D5
Allah Dad, *Pakistan* 62 G2
Allahabad, *India* 63 G9
Allakh-Yun, *Russia* 45 C14
Allal Tazi, *Morocco* 74 B3
Allan, *Canada* 101 C7
Allanche, *France* 26 C6
Allanmyo, *Burma* 61 K19
Allanridge, *S. Africa* 84 D4
Allanwater, *Canada* 98 B1
Allaqi, Wadi →, *Egypt* 76 C3
Allariz, *Spain* 30 C3
Allassac, *France* 26 C5
Alle, *Belgium* 17 J5
Allegan, *U.S.A.* 104 D3
Allegany, *U.S.A.* 106 D6
Allegheny →, *U.S.A.* 106 F5
Allegheny Plateau, *U.S.A.* 104 G6
Allegheny Res., *U.S.A.* 106 E6
Allègre, *France* 26 C7
Allen, *Argentina* 128 A3
Allen, Bog of, *Ireland* 15 C4
Allen, L., *Ireland* 15 B3
Allende, *Mexico* 114 B4
Allentown, *U.S.A.* 107 F9
Alleppey, *India* 60 Q10
Aller →, *Germany* 18 C5
Alleur, *Belgium* 17 G7
Allevard, *France* 27 C10
Alliance, *Surinam* 121 B7
Alliance, *Nebr., U.S.A.* 108 D3
Alliance, *Ohio, U.S.A.* 106 F3
Allier □, *France* 26 B6
Allier →, *France* 25 F10
Allingåbro, *Denmark* 11 H4
Alliston, *Canada* 98 D4
Alloa, *U.K.* 14 E5
Allora, *Australia* 91 D5
Allos, *France* 27 D10
Alluitsup Paa = Sydprøven, *Greenland* 4 C5
Alma, *Canada* 99 C5
Alma, *Ga., U.S.A.* 105 K4
Alma, *Kans., U.S.A.* 108 F6
Alma, *Mich., U.S.A.* 104 D3
Alma, *Nebr., U.S.A.* 108 E5
Alma, *Wis., U.S.A.* 108 C9
Alma Ata, *Kazakhstan* 44 E8
Almada, *Portugal* 31 G1
Almaden, *Australia* 90 B3
Almadén, *Spain* 31 G6
Almagro, *Spain* 31 G7
Almanor, L., *U.S.A.* 110 F3
Almansa, *Spain* 29 G3
Almanza, *Spain* 30 C5
Almanzor, Pico de, *Spain* 30 E5
Almanzora →, *Spain* 29 H3
Almas, *Brazil* 123 D2
Almazán, *Spain* 28 D2
Almazora, *Spain* 28 F4
Almeirim, *Brazil* 121 D7
Almeirim, *Portugal* 31 F2
Almelo, *Neths.* 16 D9
Almenar, *Spain* 28 D2
Almenara, *Brazil* 123 E3
Almenara, *Spain* 28 F4
Almenara, Sierra de, *Spain* 29 H3
Almendralejo, *Spain* 31 G4
Almería, *Spain* 29 J2
Almería □, *Spain* 29 H2
Almería, G. de, *Spain* 29 J2
Almirante, *Panama* 116 E3
Almirante Montt, G., *Chile* 128 D2
Almirós, *Greece* 39 K5
Almiroú, Kólpos, *Greece* 37 D6
Almodôvar, *Portugal* 31 H2
Almodóvar del Campo, *Spain* 31 G6
Almogia, *Spain* 31 J6
Almonaster la Real, *Spain* 31 H4
Almont, *U.S.A.* 106 D1
Almonte, *Canada* 107 A8
Almonte →, *Spain* 31 F4
Almora, *India* 63 E8
Almoradi, *Spain* 29 G4
Almorox, *Spain* 30 E6
Almoustarat, *Mali* 79 B5
Almuñécar, *Spain* 31 J7
Alnif, *Morocco* 74 B3
Alnwick, *U.K.* 12 B6
Aloi, *Uganda* 82 B3
Alon, *Burma* 61 H19
Alor, *Indonesia* 57 F6
Alor Setar, *Malaysia* 59 J3
Alora, *Spain* 31 J6
Alosno, *Spain* 31 H3
Alougoum, *Morocco* 74 B3
Aloysius, Mt., *Australia* 89 E4
Alpaugh, *U.S.A.* 112 K7
Alpedrinha, *Portugal* 30 E3
Alpena, *U.S.A.* 104 C4
Alpercatas →, *Brazil* 122 C3
Alpes-de-Haute-Provence □, *France* 27 D10
Alpes-Maritimes □, *France* 27 E11
Alpha, *Australia* 90 C4
Alphen, *Neths.* 17 F5
Alphen aan den Rijn, *Neths.* 16 D5
Alpiarça, *Portugal* 31 F2
Alpine, *Ariz., U.S.A.* 111 K9
Alpine, *Calif., U.S.A.* 113 N10
Alpine, *Tex., U.S.A.* 109 K3
Alpnach, *Switz.* 23 C6
Alps, *Europe* 6 F7
Alpu, *Turkey* 66 D4
Alrø, *Denmark* 11 J4
Alroy Downs, *Australia* 90 B2
Alsace, *France* 25 D14
Alsask, *Canada* 101 C7
Alsásua, *Spain* 28 C2
Alsen, *Sweden* 10 A7
Alsfeld, *Germany* 18 E5
Alsten, *Norway* 8 D12
Alta, *Norway* 8 B17
Alta, Sierra, *Spain* 28 E3
Alta Gracia, *Argentina* 126 C3
Alta Lake, *Canada* 100 C4
Alta Sierra, *U.S.A.* 113 K8
Altaelva →, *Norway* 8 B17
Altafjorden, *Norway* 8 A17
Altagracia, *Venezuela* 120 A3
Altagracia de Orituco, *Venezuela* 120 B4
Altai = Aerhtai Shan, *Mongolia* 54 B4
Altamachi →, *Bolivia* 124 D4
Altamaha →, *U.S.A.* 105 K5
Altamira, *Brazil* 121 D7
Altamira, *Chile* 126 B2
Altamira, *Colombia* 120 C2
Altamira, *Mexico* 115 C5
Altamira, Cuevas de, *Spain* 30 B6
Altamont, *U.S.A.* 107 D10
Altamura, *Italy* 35 B9
Altanbulag, *Mongolia* 54 A5
Altar, *Mexico* 114 A2
Altata, *Mexico* 114 C3
Altavista, *U.S.A.* 104 G6
Altay, *China* 54 B3
Altdorf, *Switz.* 23 C7
Alte Mellum, *Germany* 18 B4
Altea, *Spain* 29 G4
Altenberg, *Germany* 18 E9
Altenbruch, *Germany* 18 B4
Altenburg, *Germany* 18 E8
Altenkirchen, *Mecklenburg-Vorpommern, Germany* 18 A9
Altenkirchen, *Rhld-Pfz., Germany* 18 E3
Altenteptow, *Germany* 18 B9
Alter do Chão, *Portugal* 31 F3
Altıntas, *Turkey* 66 D4
Altiplano, *Bolivia* 124 D4
Altkirch, *France* 25 E14
Altmühl →, *Germany* 19 G7
Alto Adige = Trentino-Alto Adige □, *Italy* 32 B8
Alto Araguaia, *Brazil* 125 D7
Alto Cuchumatanes = Cuchumatanes, Sierra de los, *Guatemala* 116 C1
Alto del Inca, *Chile* 126 A2
Alto Garças, *Brazil* 125 D7
Alto Iriri →, *Brazil* 125 B7
Alto Ligonha, *Mozam.* 83 F4
Alto Molocue, *Mozam.* 83 F4
Alto Paraguai, *Brazil* 125 C6
Alto Paraguay □, *Paraguay* 126 A4
Alto Paraná □, *Paraguay* 127 B5
Alto Parnaíba, *Brazil* 122 C2
Alto Purús →, *Peru* 124 B3
Alto Río Senguerr, *Argentina* 128 C2
Alto Santo, *Brazil* 122 C4
Alto Sucuriú, *Brazil* 125 D7
Alto Turi, *Brazil* 122 B2
Alton, *Canada* 106 C4
Alton, *U.S.A.* 108 F9
Alton Downs, *Australia* 91 D2
Altoona, *U.S.A.* 106 F6
Altopáscio, *Italy* 32 E7
Altos, *Brazil* 122 C3
Altötting, *Germany* 19 G8
Altstätten, *Switz.* 23 B9
Altūn Kūprī, *Iraq* 64 C5
Altun Shan, *China* 54 C3
Alturas, *U.S.A.* 110 F3
Altus, *U.S.A.* 109 H5
Alubijid, *Phil.* 55 G6
Alucra, *Turkey* 43 F8
Aluksne, *Latvia* 40 C5
Alùla, *Somali Rep.* 68 E5
Alunite, *U.S.A.* 113 K12
Alupka, *Ukraine* 42 D6
Alushta, *Ukraine* 42 D6
Alusi, *Indonesia* 57 F8
Alustante, *Spain* 28 E3
Al'Uzayr, *Iraq* 64 D5
Alva, *U.S.A.* 109 G5
Alvaiázere, *Portugal* 30 F2
Älvängen, *Sweden* 11 G6
Alvarado, *Mexico* 115 D5
Alvarado, *U.S.A.* 109 J6
Alvarães, *Brazil* 121 D5
Alvaro Obregón, Presa, *Mexico* 114 B3
Alvdal, *Norway* 10 B4
Alvear, *Argentina* 126 B4
Alverca, *Portugal* 31 G1
Alveringen, *Belgium* 17 F1
Alvesta, *Sweden* 9 H13
Alvie, *Australia* 91 F3
Alvin, *U.S.A.* 109 L7
Alvinston, *Canada* 106 D3
Alvito, *Portugal* 31 G3
Älvkarleby, *Sweden* 9 F14
Älvros, *Sweden* 10 B8
Älvsborgs län □, *Sweden* 11 F6
Älvsbyn, *Sweden* 8 D16
Älvsered, *Sweden* 11 G6
Alwar, *India* 62 F7
Alxa Zuoqi, *China* 50 E3
Alyaskitovyy, *Russia* 45 C15
Alyata, *Azerbaijan* 43 G13
Alyth, *U.K.* 14 E5
Alzada, *U.S.A.* 108 C2
Alzano Lombardo, *Italy* 32 C6
Alzette →, *Lux.* 17 J8
Alzey, *Germany* 19 F4
Am Dam, *Chad* 73 F9
Am-Timan, *Chad* 73 F9
Amacuro □, *Venezuela* 121 B5
Amadeus, L., *Australia* 89 D5
Amâdi, *Sudan* 77 F3
Amadi, *Zaïre* 82 B2
Amadjuak, *Canada* 97 B12
Amadjuak L., *Canada* 97 B12
Amadora, *Portugal* 31 G1
Amagasaki, *Japan* 49 G7
Amager, *Denmark* 11 J6
Amakusa-Shotō, *Japan* 49 H5
Amalfi, *Colombia* 120 B2
Amalfi, *Italy* 35 B7
Amaliás, *Greece* 39 M4
Amalner, *India* 60 J9
Amambaí, *Brazil* 127 A4
Amambaí →, *Brazil* 127 A5
Amambay □, *Paraguay* 127 A4
Amambay, Cordillera de, *S. Amer.* 127 A4
Amami-Guntō, *Japan* 49 L4
Amami-Ō-Shima, *Japan* 49 L4
Amana →, *Venezuela* 121 B5
Amaná, L., *Brazil* 121 D5
Amanda Park, *U.S.A.* 112 C3
Amándola, *Italy* 33 F10
Amangeldy, *Kazakhstan* 44 D7
Amantea, *Italy* 35 C9
Amapá, *Brazil* 121 C7
Amapá □, *Brazil* 121 C7
Amapari, *Brazil* 121 C7
Amara, *Sudan* 77 E3
Amarante, *Brazil* 122 C3
Amarante, *Portugal* 30 D2
Amarante do Maranhão, *Brazil* 122 C2
Amaranth, *Canada* 101 C9
Amareleja, *Portugal* 31 G3
Amargosa, *Brazil* 123 D4
Amargosa →, *U.S.A.* 113 J10
Amargosa Ra., *U.S.A.* 113 J10
Amári, *Greece* 37 D6
Amarillo, *U.S.A.* 109 H4
Amaro, Mt., *Italy* 33 F11
Amaro Leite, *Brazil* 123 D2
Amarpur, *India* 63 G12
Amasra, *Turkey* 66 C5
Amassama, *Nigeria* 79 D6
Amasya, *Turkey* 66 C6
Amasya □, *Turkey* 66 C6
Amataurá, *Brazil* 120 D4
Amatikulu, *S. Africa* 85 D5
Amatitlán, *Guatemala* 116 D1
Amatrice, *Italy* 33 F10
Amay, *Belgium* 17 G6
Amazon = Amazonas →, *S. Amer.* 121 D7
Amazonas □, *Brazil* 125 B5
Amazonas □, *Peru* 124 B2
Amazonas □, *Venezuela* 120 C4
Amazonas →, *S. Amer.* 121 D7
Ambahakily, *Madag.* 85 C7
Ambala, *India* 62 D7
Ambalavao, *Madag.* 85 C8
Ambalindum, *Australia* 90 C2
Ambam, *Cameroon* 80 D2
Ambanja, *Madag.* 85 A8
Ambarchik, *Russia* 45 C17
Ambarijeby, *Madag.* 85 A8
Ambaro, Helodranon', *Madag.* 85 A8
Ambartsevo, *Russia* 44 D9
Ambato, *Ecuador* 120 D2
Ambato, Sierra de, *Argentina* 126 B2
Ambato Boeny, *Madag.* 85 B8
Ambatofinandrahana, *Madag.* 85 C8
Ambatolampy, *Madag.* 85 B8
Ambatondrazaka, *Madag.* 85 B8
Ambatosoratra, *Madag.* 85 B8
Ambenja, *Madag.* 85 B8
Amberg, *Germany* 19 F7
Ambergris Cay, *Belize* 115 D7
Ambérieu-en-Bugey, *France* 27 C9
Amberley, *N.Z.* 87 K4
Ambert, *France* 26 C7
Ambidédi, *Mali* 78 C2
Ambikapur, *India* 63 H10
Ambikol, *Sudan* 76 C3
Ambilobé, *Madag.* 85 A8
Ambinanindrano, *Madag.* 85 C8
Ambjörnarp, *Sweden* 11 G7
Ambleside, *U.K.* 12 C5
Amblève, *Belgium* 17 H8
Amblève →, *Belgium* 17 H7
Ambo, *Ethiopia* 77 E4
Ambo, *Peru* 124 C2
Ambodifototra, *Madag.* 85 B8
Ambodilazana, *Madag.* 85 B8
Ambohimahasoa, *Madag.* 85 C8
Ambohimanga, *Madag.* 85 C8
Ambohitra, *Madag.* 85 A8
Ambon, *Indonesia* 57 E7
Amboseli L., *Kenya* 82 C4
Ambositra, *Madag.* 85 C8
Ambovombé, *Madag.* 85 D8
Amboy, *U.S.A.* 113 L11
Amboyna I., *S. China Sea* 56 C4
Ambridge, *U.S.A.* 106 F4
Ambriz, *Angola* 80 F2
Amby, *Australia* 91 D4
Amchitka I., *U.S.A.* 96 C1
Amderma, *Russia* 44 C7
Ameca, *Mexico* 114 C4
Ameca →, *Mexico* 114 C3
Amecameca, *Mexico* 115 D5
Ameland, *Neths.* 16 B7
Amélia, *Italy* 33 F9
Amélie-les-Bains-Palalda, *France* 26 F6
Amen, *Russia* 45 C18
Amendolaro, *Italy* 35 C9
America, *Neths.* 17 F7
American Falls, *U.S.A.* 110 E7
American Falls Res., *U.S.A.* 110 E7
American Highland, *Antarctica* 5 D6
American Samoa ■, *Pac. Oc.* 87 B13
Americana, *Brazil* 127 A6
Americus, *U.S.A.* 105 J3
Amersfoort, *Neths.* 16 D6
Amersfoort, *S. Africa* 85 D4
Amery, *Australia* 89 F2
Amery, *Canada* 101 B10
Amery Ice Shelf, *Antarctica* 5 C6
Ames, *U.S.A.* 108 E8
Amesbury, *U.S.A.* 107 D14
Amfíklia, *Greece* 39 L5
Amfilokhía, *Greece* 39 L4
Amga, *Russia* 45 C14
Amga →, *Russia* 45 C14
Amgu, *Russia* 45 E14
Amgun →, *Russia* 45 D14
Amherst, *Burma* 61 L20
Amherst, *Canada* 99 C7
Amherst, *Mass., U.S.A.* 107 D12
Amherst, *N.Y., U.S.A.* 106 D6
Amherst, *Ohio, U.S.A.* 106 E2
Amherst, *Tex., U.S.A.* 109 H3
Amherst I., *Canada* 107 B8
Amherstburg, *Canada* 98 D3
Amiata, Mte., *Italy* 33 F8
Amiens, *France* 25 C9
Amindaion, *Greece* 39 J4
Amīrābād, *Iran* 64 C5
Amirante Is., *Seychelles* 3 E12
Amisk L., *Canada* 101 C8
Amistad, Presa de la, *Mexico* 114 B4
Amite, *U.S.A.* 109 K9
Amizmiz, *Morocco* 74 B3
Åmli, *Norway* 11 F2
Amlwch, *U.K.* 12 D3
Amm Adam, *Sudan* 77 D4
'Ammān, *Jordan* 69 D4
Ammanford, *U.K.* 13 F3
Ammassalik = Angmagssalik, *Greenland* 4 C6
Ammerån, *Sweden* 10 A10
Ammerån →, *Sweden* 10 A10
Ammersee, *Germany* 19 G7
Ammerzoden, *Neths.* 16 E6
Amnat Charoen, *Thailand* 58 E5
Amo Jiang →, *China* 52 F3
Āmol, *Iran* 65 B7
Amorebieta, *Spain* 28 B2
Amorgós, *Greece* 39 N8
Amory, *U.S.A.* 105 J1
Amos, *Canada* 98 C4
Åmot, *Buskerud, Norway* 10 E3
Åmot, *Telemark, Norway* 10 E2
Åmotsdal, *Norway* 10 E2
Amour, Djebel, *Algeria* 75 B5
Amoy = Xiamen, *China* 53 E12
Ampang, *Malaysia* 59 L3
Ampanihy, *Madag.* 85 C7
Ampasindava, Helodranon', *Madag.* 85 A8
Ampasindava, Saikanosy, *Madag.* 85 A8

Ampato, Nevado, *Peru* 124 D3
Ampenan, *Indonesia* 56 F5
Amper, *Nigeria* 79 D6
Amper →, *Germany* 19 G7
Ampère, *Algeria* 75 A6
Ampezzo, *Italy* 33 B9
Amposta, *Spain* 28 E5
Ampotaka, *Madag.* 85 D7
Ampoza, *Madag.* 85 C7
Amqui, *Canada* 99 C6
Amravati, *India* 60 J10
Amreli, *India* 62 J4
Amrenene el Kasba, *Algeria* 75 D5
Amriswil, *Switz.* 23 A8
Amritsar, *India* 62 D6
Amroha, *India* 63 E8
Amrum, *Germany* 18 A4
Amsel, *Algeria* 75 D6
Amsterdam, *Neths.* 16 D5
Amsterdam, *U.S.A.* 107 D10
Amsterdam, I., *Ind. Oc.* 3 F13
Amstetten, *Austria* 21 G4
Amudarya →, *Uzbekistan* 44 E6
Amundsen Gulf, *Canada* 96 A7
Amundsen Sea, *Antarctica* 5 D15
Amuntai, *Indonesia* 56 E5
Amur →, *Russia* 45 D15
Amurang, *Indonesia* 57 D6
Amuri Pass, *N.Z.* 87 K4
Amurrio, *Spain* 28 B1
Amursk, *Russia* 45 D14
Amurzet, *Russia* 45 E14
Amusco, *Spain* 30 C6
Amvrakikós Kólpos, *Greece* 39 L4
Amvrosiyevka, *Ukraine* 43 C8
Amzeglouf, *Algeria* 75 C5
An Bien, *Vietnam* 59 H5
An Hoa, *Vietnam* 58 E7
An Khe, *Vietnam* 58 F7
An Nabatīyah at Tahta, *Lebanon* 69 B4
An Nabk, *Si. Arabia* 64 D3
An Nabk, *Syria* 69 A5
An Nabk Abū Qaşr, *Si. Arabia* 64 D3
An Nafūd, *Si. Arabia* 64 D4
An Najaf, *Iraq* 64 C5
An Nāşirīyah, *Iraq* 64 D5
An Nhon, *Vietnam* 58 F7
An Nîl □, *Sudan* 76 D3
An Nîl el Abyad □, *Sudan* 77 E3
An Nîl el Azraq □, *Sudan* 77 E3
An Nu'ayrīyah, *Si. Arabia* 65 E6
An Nuwayb'ī, W. →, *Si. Arabia* 69 F3
An Thoi, Dao, *Vietnam* 59 H4
An Uaimh, *Ireland* 15 C5
Anabar →, *Russia* 45 B12
'Anabtā, *Jordan* 69 C4
Anaco, *Venezuela* 121 B5
Anaconda, *U.S.A.* 110 C7
Anacortes, *U.S.A.* 112 B4
Anacuao, Mt., *Phil.* 55 C4
Anadarko, *U.S.A.* 109 H5
Anadia, *Brazil* 122 C4
Anadia, *Portugal* 30 E2
Anadolu, *Turkey* 66 D4
Anadyr, *Russia* 45 C18
Anadyr →, *Russia* 45 C18
Anadyrskiy Zaliv, *Russia* 45 C19
Anáfi, *Greece* 39 N8
Anafópoulo, *Greece* 39 N8
Anaga, Pta. de, *Canary Is.* 36 F3
Anagni, *Italy* 34 A6
'Ānah, *Iraq* 64 C4
Anaheim, *U.S.A.* 113 M9
Anahim Lake, *Canada* 100 C3
Anáhuac, *Mexico* 114 B4
Anajás, *Brazil* 122 B2
Anajatuba, *Brazil* 122 B3
Anakapalle, *India* 61 L13
Anakie, *Australia* 90 C4
Anaklia, *Georgia* 43 E9
Analalava, *Madag.* 85 A8
Análipsis, *Greece* 37 A3
Anamã, *Brazil* 121 D5
Anambar →, *Pakistan* 62 D3
Anambas, Kepulauan, *Indonesia* 56 D3
Anambas Is. = Anambas, Kepulauan, *Indonesia* 56 D3
Anamoose, *U.S.A.* 108 B4
Anamosa, *U.S.A.* 108 D9
Anamur, *Turkey* 66 E5
Anamur Burnu, *Turkey* 66 E5
Anan, *Japan* 49 H7
Anand, *India* 62 H5
Anantnag, *India* 63 C6
Ananyev, *Ukraine* 42 C3
Anapa, *Russia* 42 D7
Anapodháris →, *Greece* 37 E7
Anápolis, *Brazil* 123 E2
Anapu →, *Brazil* 121 D7
Anār, *Iran* 65 D7
Anārak, *Iran* 65 C7
Anatolia = Anadolu, *Turkey* 66 D4
Anatone, *U.S.A.* 110 C5
Anatsogno, *Madag.* 85 C7
Añatuya, *Argentina* 126 B3
Anauá →, *Brazil* 121 C5
Anaunethad L., *Canada* 101 A8
Anavilhanas, Arquipélago das, *Brazil* 121 D5
Anaye, *Niger* 73 E7
Anbyŏn, *N. Korea* 51 E14
Ancash □, *Peru* 124 B2
Ancenis, *France* 24 E5
Ancho, Canal, *Chile* 128 D2
Anchor Bay, *U.S.A.* 112 G3
Anchorage, *U.S.A.* 96 B5
Anci, *China* 50 E9
Ancohuma, Nevada, *Bolivia* 124 D4
Ancón, *Peru* 124 C2
Ancona, *Italy* 33 E10
Ancud, *Chile* 128 B2
Ancud, G. de, *Chile* 128 B2
Andacollo, *Argentina* 126 D1
Andacollo, *Chile* 126 C1
Andado, *Australia* 90 D2
Andahuaylas, *Peru* 124 C3
Andalgalá, *Argentina* 126 B2
Åndalsnes, *Norway* 10 B1
Andalucía □, *Spain* 31 H6
Andalusia, *U.S.A.* 105 K2
Andalusia □ = Andalucía □, *Spain* 31 H6
Andaman Is., *Ind. Oc.* 46 H13
Andaman Sea, *Ind. Oc.* 56 B1
Andara, *Namibia* 84 B3
Andaraí, *Brazil* 123 D3
Andeer, *Switz.* 23 C8
Andelfingen, *Switz.* 23 A7
Andelot, *France* 25 D12
Andenne, *Belgium* 17 H6
Andéranboukane, *Mali* 79 B5
Anderlecht, *Belgium* 17 G4
Anderlues, *Belgium* 17 H4
Andermatt, *Switz.* 23 C7
Andernach, *Germany* 18 E3
Andernos-les-Bains, *France* 26 D2
Anderslöv, *Sweden* 11 J7
Anderson, *Calif., U.S.A.* 110 F2
Anderson, *Ind., U.S.A.* 104 E3
Anderson, *Mo., U.S.A.* 109 G7
Anderson, *S.C., U.S.A.* 105 H4
Anderson →, *Canada* 96 B7
Anderson, Mt., *S. Africa* 85 D5
Andes, *S. Amer.* 124 C2
Andes, Cord. de los, *S. Amer.* 124 C3
Andfjorden, *Norway* 8 B14
Andhra Pradesh □, *India* 60 L11
Andikíthira, *Greece* 39 P6
Andīmeshk, *Iran* 65 C6
Andímilos, *Greece* 39 N7
Andípaxoi, *Greece* 39 K3
Andizhan, *Uzbekistan* 44 E8
Andoany, *Madag.* 85 A8
Andoas, *Peru* 120 D2
Andong, *S. Korea* 51 F15
Andongwei, *China* 51 G10
Andorra ■, *Europe* 28 C6
Andorra La Vella, *Andorra* 28 C6
Andover, *U.K.* 13 F6
Andover, *Mass., U.S.A.* 107 D13
Andover, *N.Y., U.S.A.* 106 D7
Andover, *Ohio, U.S.A.* 106 E4
Andradina, *Brazil* 123 F1
Andrahary, Mt., *Madag.* 85 A8
Andraitx, *Spain* 36 B9
Andramasina, *Madag.* 85 B8
Andranopasy, *Madag.* 85 C7
Andreanof Is., *U.S.A.* 96 C2
Andreapol, *Russia* 40 C8
Andrespol, *Poland* 20 D9
Andrewilla, *Australia* 91 D2
Andrews, *S.C., U.S.A.* 105 J6
Andrews, *Tex., U.S.A.* 109 J3
Ándria, *Italy* 35 A9
Andriba, *Madag.* 85 B8
Andrijevica, *Montenegro, Yug.* 21 N9
Andrítsaina, *Greece* 39 M4
Androka, *Madag.* 85 C7
Andropov = Rybinsk, *Russia* 41 B11
Ándros, *Greece* 39 M7
Andros I., *Bahamas* 116 B4
Andros Town, *Bahamas* 116 B4
Andújar, *Spain* 31 G6
Andulo, *Angola* 80 G3
Anegada, B., *Argentina* 128 B4
Anegada I., *Virgin Is.* 117 C7
Anegada Passage, *W. Indies* 117 C7
Anécho, *Togo* 79 D5
Añelo, *Argentina* 128 A3
Anergane, *Morocco* 74 B3
Aneto, Pico de, *Spain* 28 C5
Añez, *Bolivia* 125 D5
Anfu, *China* 53 D10
Ang Thong, *Thailand* 58 E3
Angamos, Punta, *Chile* 126 A1
Ang'angxi, *China* 54 B7
Angara →, *Russia* 45 D10
Angarab, *Ethiopia* 77 E4
Angarsk, *Russia* 45 D11
Angas Downs, *Australia* 89 E5
Angas Hills, *Australia* 88 D4
Angaston, *Australia* 91 E2
Ånge, *Sweden* 10 B9
Ángel de la Guarda, I., *Mexico* 114 B2
Angel Falls, *Venezuela* 121 B5
Angeles, *Phil.* 55 D4
Ängelholm, *Sweden* 11 H6
Angellala, *Australia* 91 D4
Angels Camp, *U.S.A.* 111 G3
Anger →, *Ethiopia* 77 F4
Angereb →, *Ethiopia* 77 E4
Ångermanälven →, *Sweden* 10 B12
Angermünde, *Germany* 18 B10
Angers, *Canada* 107 A9
Angers, *France* 24 E6
Angerville, *France* 25 D8
Ängesån →, *Sweden* 8 C17
Anghiari, *Italy* 33 E9
Angical, *Brazil* 123 D3
Angikuni L., *Canada* 101 A9
Angkor, *Cambodia* 58 F4
Anglés, *Spain* 28 D7
Anglesey, *U.K.* 12 D3
Anglet, *France* 26 E2
Angleton, *U.S.A.* 109 L7
Angleur, *Belgium* 17 G7
Anglin →, *France* 26 B4
Anglisidhes, *Cyprus* 37 E12
Anglure, *France* 25 D10
Angmagssalik, *Greenland* 4 C6
Ango, *Zaïre* 82 B2
Angoche, *Mozam.* 83 F4
Angoche, I., *Mozam.* 83 F4
Angol, *Chile* 126 D1
Angola, *Ind., U.S.A.* 104 E3
Angola, *N.Y., U.S.A.* 106 D5
Angola ■, *Africa* 81 G3
Angoon, *U.S.A.* 100 B2
Angoulême, *France* 26 C4
Angoumois, *France* 26 C4
Angra dos Reis, *Brazil* 127 A7
Angren, *Uzbekistan* 44 E8
Angtassom, *Cambodia* 59 G5
Angu, *Zaïre* 82 B1
Anguang, *China* 51 B12
Anguilla, *W. Indies* 117 C7
Anguo, *China* 50 E8
Angurugu, *Australia* 90 A2
Angus, Braes of, *U.K.* 14 E5
Anhanduí →, *Brazil* 127 A5
Anhée, *Belgium* 17 H5
Anholt, *Denmark* 11 H5
Anhua, *China* 53 C8
Anhui □, *China* 53 B11
Anhwei □ = Anhui □, *China* 53 B11
Anichab, *Namibia* 84 C1
Anicuns, *Brazil* 123 E2
Ánidhros, *Greece* 39 N8
Anie, *Togo* 79 D5
Animas, *U.S.A.* 111 L9
Ånimskog, *Sweden* 11 F6
Anina, *Romania* 38 D4
Anivorano, *Madag.* 85 B8
Anjar, *India* 62 H4
Anjidiv I., *India* 60 M9
Anjou, *France* 24 E6
Anjozorobe, *Madag.* 85 B8
Anju, *N. Korea* 51 E13
Anka, *Nigeria* 79 C6
Ankaboa, Tanjona, *Madag.* 85 C7
Ankang, *China* 50 H5
Ankara, *Turkey* 66 D5
Ankara □, *Turkey* 66 D5
Ankaramena, *Madag.* 85 C8
Ankazoabo, *Madag.* 85 C7
Ankazobe, *Madag.* 85 B8
Ankisabe, *Madag.* 85 B8
Anklam, *Germany* 18 B9
Ankober, *Ethiopia* 77 F4
Ankoro, *Zaïre* 82 D2
Anlong, *China* 52 E5
Anlu, *China* 53 B9
Anmyŏn-do, *S. Korea* 51 F14
Ånn, *Sweden* 10 A6
Ann, C., *U.S.A.* 107 D14
Ann Arbor, *U.S.A.* 104 D4
Anna, *Russia* 41 F12
Anna, *U.S.A.* 109 G10
Anna Plains, *Australia* 88 C3
Anna Regina, *Guyana* 121 B6
Annaba, *Algeria* 75 A6
Annaberg-Buchholz, *Germany* 18 E8
Annalee →, *Ireland* 15 B4
Annam = Trung-Phan, *Vietnam* 58 E7
Annamitique, Chaîne, *Asia* 58 D6
Annan, *U.K.* 14 G5
Annan →, *U.K.* 14 G5
Annapolis, *U.S.A.* 104 F7
Annapolis Royal, *Canada* 99 D6
Annapurna, *Nepal* 63 E10
Annean, L., *Australia* 89 E2
Anneberg, *Sweden* 11 G6
Annecy, *France* 27 C10
Annecy, L. d', *France* 27 C10
Annemasse, *France* 27 B10
Anning, *China* 52 E4
Anningie, *Australia* 88 D5
Anniston, *U.S.A.* 105 J3
Annobón, *Atl. Oc.* 71 G4
Annonay, *France* 27 C8
Annot, *France* 27 E10
Annotto Bay, *Jamaica* 116 C4
Annuello, *Australia* 91 E3
Annville, *U.S.A.* 107 F8
Annweiler, *Germany* 19 F3
Áno Viánnos, *Greece* 37 D7
Anoka, *U.S.A.* 108 C8
Anorotsangana, *Madag.* 85 A8
Anóyia, *Greece* 37 D6
Anping, *Hebei, China* 50 E8
Anping, *Liaoning, China* 51 D12
Anpu Gang, *China* 52 G7
Anqing, *China* 53 B11
Anqiu, *China* 51 F10
Anren, *China* 53 D9
Ans, *Belgium* 17 G7
Ansai, *China* 50 F5
Ansbach, *Germany* 19 F6
Anseba →, *Ethiopia* 77 D4
Anserma, *Colombia* 120 B2
Anseroeul, *Belgium* 17 G3
Anshan, *China* 54 B7
Anshan, *Liaoning, China* 51 D12
Anshun, *China* 52 D5
Ansião, *Portugal* 30 F2
Ansirabe, *Madag.* 85 B8
Ansley, *U.S.A.* 108 E5
Ansó, *Spain* 28 C4
Anson, *U.S.A.* 109 J5
Anson B., *Australia* 88 B5
Ansongo, *Mali* 79 B5
Ansonia, *U.S.A.* 107 E11
Anstruther, *U.K.* 14 E6
Ansudu, *Indonesia* 57 E9
Antabamba, *Peru* 124 C3
Antakya, *Turkey* 66 E7
Antalaha, *Madag.* 85 A9
Antalya, *Turkey* 66 E4
Antalya □, *Turkey* 66 E4
Antalya Körfezi, *Turkey* 66 E4
Antananarivo, *Madag.* 85 B8
Antananarivo □, *Madag.* 85 B8
Antanimbaribe, *Madag.* 85 C7
Antarctic Pen., *Antarctica* 5 C18
Antarctica 5 E3
Antelope, *Zimbabwe* 83 G2
Antenor Navarro, *Brazil* 122 C4
Antequera, *Paraguay* 126 A4
Antequera, *Spain* 31 H6
Antero, Mt., *U.S.A.* 111 G10
Anthony, *Kans., U.S.A.* 109 G5
Anthony, *N. Mex., U.S.A.* 111 K10
Anthony Lagoon, *Australia* 90 B2
Anti Atlas, *Morocco* 74 C2
Anti-Lebanon = Ash Sharqi, Al Jabal, *Lebanon* 69 B5
Antibes, *France* 27 E11
Antibes, C. d', *France* 27 E11
Anticosti, I. d', *Canada* 99 C7
Antifer, C. d', *France* 24 C7
Antigo, *U.S.A.* 108 C10
Antigonish, *Canada* 99 C7
Antigua, *Canary Is.* 36 F5
Antigua, *Guatemala* 116 D1
Antigua, *W. Indies* 117 C7
Antigua & Barbuda ■, *W. Indies* 117 C7
Antilla, *Cuba* 116 B4
Antimony, *U.S.A.* 111 G8
Antioch, *U.S.A.* 112 G5
Antioche, Pertuis d', *France* 26 B2
Antioquia, *Colombia* 120 B2
Antioquia □, *Colombia* 120 B2
Antipodes Is., *Pac. Oc.* 92 M9
Antler, *U.S.A.* 108 A4
Antler →, *Canada* 101 D8
Antlers, *U.S.A.* 109 H7
Antofagasta, *Chile* 126 A1
Antofagasta □, *Chile* 126 A2
Antofagasta de la Sierra, *Argentina* 126 B2
Antofalla, *Argentina* 126 B2
Antofalla, Salar de, *Argentina* 126 B2
Antoing, *Belgium* 17 G2
Anton, *U.S.A.* 109 J3
Anton Chico, *U.S.A.* 111 J11
Antongila, Helodrano, *Madag.* 85 B8
Antonibé, *Madag.* 85 B8
Antonibé, Presqu'île d', *Madag.* 85 A8
Antonina, *Brazil* 127 B6
Antonito, *U.S.A.* 111 H10
Antonovo, *Kazakhstan* 43 B14
Antrain, *France* 24 D5
Antrim, *U.K.* 15 B5
Antrim □, *U.K.* 15 B5
Antrim, Mts. of, *U.K.* 15 B5
Antrim Plateau, *Australia* 88 C4
Antrodoco, *Italy* 33 F10
Antropovo, *Russia* 41 B13
Antsalova, *Madag.* 85 B7
Antsiranana, *Madag.* 85 A8
Antsohihy, *Madag.* 85 A8
Antsohimbondrona Seranana, *Madag.* 85 A8
Antu, *China* 51 C15
Antwerp = Antwerpen, *Belgium* 17 F4
Antwerp, *U.S.A.* 107 B9
Antwerpen, *Belgium* 17 F4
Antwerpen □, *Belgium* 17 F5
Anupgarh, *India* 62 E5
Anuradhapura, *Sri Lanka* 60 Q12
Anveh, *Iran* 65 E7
Anvers = Antwerpen, *Belgium* 17 F4
Anvers I., *Antarctica* 5 C17
Anxi, *Fujian, China* 53 E12
Anxi, *Gansu, China* 54 B4
Anxiang, *China* 53 C9
Anxious B., *Australia* 91 E1
Anyama, *Ivory C.* 78 D4
Anyang, *China* 50 F8
Anyi, *Jiangxi, China* 53 C10
Anyi, *Shanxi, China* 50 G6
Anyuan, *China* 53 E10
Anza, *U.S.A.* 113 M10
Anze, *China* 50 F7
Anzhero-Sudzhensk, *Russia* 44 D9
Ánzio, *Italy* 34 A5
Anzoátegui □, *Venezuela* 121 B5
Aoga-Shima, *Japan* 49 H9
Aoiz, *Spain* 28 C3
Aomori, *Japan* 48 D10
Aomori □, *Japan* 48 D10
Aonla, *India* 63 E8
Aosta, *Italy* 32 C4
Aoudéras, *Niger* 79 B6
Aouinet Torkoz, *Morocco* 74 C3
Aoukar, *Mali* 74 D4
Aouker, *Mauritania* 78 B3
Aoulef el Arab, *Algeria* 75 C5
Apa →, *S. Amer.* 126 A4
Apache, *U.S.A.* 109 H5
Apalachee B., *U.S.A.* 105 L3
Apalachicola, *U.S.A.* 105 L3
Apalachicola →, *U.S.A.* 105 L3
Apapa, *Nigeria* 79 D5
Apaporis →, *Colombia* 120 D4
Aparecida do Taboado, *Brazil* 123 F1
Aparri, *Phil.* 55 B4
Aparurén, *Venezuela* 121 B5
Apateu, *Romania* 38 C4
Apatin, *Serbia, Yug.* 21 K8
Apatzingán, *Mexico* 114 D4
Apeldoorn, *Neths.* 16 D7
Apeldoornsch Kanal →, *Neths.* 16 D8
Apen, *Germany* 18 B3
Apennines = Appennini, *Italy* 32 D7
Apere →, *Bolivia* 125 C4
Apia, *W. Samoa* 87 A13
Apiacás, Serra dos, *Brazil* 125 B6
Apiaú →, *Brazil* 121 C5
Apiaú, Serra do, *Brazil* 121 C5
Apidiá →, *Brazil* 125 C5
Apinajé, *Brazil* 123 D2
Apizaco, *Mexico* 115 D5
Aplao, *Peru* 124 D3
Apo, Mt., *Phil.* 57 C7
Apodi, *Brazil* 122 C4
Apolakkiá, *Greece* 37 C9
Apolakkiá, Órmos, *Greece* 37 C9
Apolda, *Germany* 18 D7
Apollonia = Marsá Susah, *Libya* 73 B9
Apollonia, *Greece* 39 N7
Apolo, *Bolivia* 124 C4
Apónguao →, *Venezuela* 121 C5
Aporé, *Brazil* 125 D7
Aporé →, *Brazil* 123 E1
Aporema, *Brazil* 122 A1
Apostle Is., *U.S.A.* 108 B9
Apóstoles, *Argentina* 127 B4
Apostolos Andreas, C., *Cyprus* 37 D13
Apostolovo, *Ukraine* 42 C5
Apoteri, *Guyana* 121 C6
Appalachian Mts., *U.S.A.* 104 G6
Appelscha, *Neths.* 16 C8
Appennini, *Italy* 32 D7
Appennino Ligure, *Italy* 32 D5
Appenzell, *Switz.* 23 B8
Appenzell-Ausser Rhoden □, *Switz.* 23 B8
Appenzell-Inner Rhoden □, *Switz.* 23 B8
Appiano, *Italy* 33 B8
Appingedam, *Neths.* 16 B9
Apple Hill, *Canada* 107 A10
Apple Valley, *U.S.A.* 113 L9
Appleby, *U.K.* 12 C5
Appleton, *U.S.A.* 104 C1
Approuague, *Fr. Guiana* 121 C7
Approuague →, *Fr. Guiana* 121 C7
Apricena, *Italy* 35 A8
Aprigliano, *Italy* 35 C9
Aprília, *Italy* 34 A5
Apsheronsk, *Russia* 43 D8
Apt, *France* 27 E9
Apuane, Alpi, *Italy* 32 D7
Apuaú, *Brazil* 121 D5
Apucarana, *Brazil* 127 A5
Apulia = Púglia □, *Italy* 35 B9
Apure □, *Venezuela* 120 B4
Apure →, *Venezuela* 120 B4
Apurímac □, *Peru* 124 C3
Apurimac →, *Peru* 124 C3
Apuseni, Munţii, *Romania* 38 C5
Aqabah = Al 'Aqabah, *Jordan* 69 F4
'Aqabah, Khalīj al, *Red Sea* 64 D2
'Aqdā, *Iran* 65 C7
Aqîq, *Sudan* 76 D4
Aqîq, Khalîg, *Sudan* 76 D4
Aqrah, *Iraq* 64 B4
Aquidauana, *Brazil* 125 E6
Aquidauana →, *Brazil* 125 D6
Aquiles Serdán, *Mexico* 114 B3
Aquin, *Haiti* 117 C5
Ar Rachidiya, *Morocco* 74 B4
Ar Rafīd, *Syria* 69 C4

Ar Raḥḥālīyah, *Iraq* 64 C4
Ar Ramādī, *Iraq* 64 C4
Ar Ramthā, *Jordan* 69 C5
Ar Raqqah, *Syria* 64 C3
Ar Rass, *Si. Arabia* 64 E4
Ar Rifā'i, *Iraq* 64 D5
Ar Riyāḍ, *Si. Arabia* 64 E5
Ar Ru'ays, *Qatar* 65 E6
Ar Rukhaymīyah, *Iraq* ... 64 D5
Ar Ruqayyidah, *Si. Arabia* 65 E6
Ar Ruṣāfah, *Syria* 64 C3
Ar Ruṭbah, *Iraq* 64 C4
Ara, *India* 63 G11
'Arab, Bahr el →, *Sudan* 77 F2
Arab, Khalîg el, *Egypt* .. 76 H6
'Arabābād, *Iran* 65 C8
Araban, *Turkey* 67 E7
Arabatskaya Strelka,
 Ukraine 42 D6
Arabba, *Italy* 33 B8
Arabelo, *Venezuela* 121 C5
Arabia, *Asia* 68 C4
Arabian Desert = Es
 Sahrâ' Esh Sharqîya,
 Egypt 76 B3
Arabian Gulf = Gulf, The,
 Asia 65 E6
Arabian Sea, *Ind. Oc.* ... 46 H10
Araç, *Turkey* 66 C5
Aracaju, *Brazil* 122 C4
Aracataca, *Colombia* 120 A3
Aracati, *Brazil* 122 B4
Araçatuba, *Brazil* 127 A5
Aracena, *Spain* 31 H4
Aracena, Sierra de, *Spain* 31 H4
Araçuaí, *Brazil* 123 E3
Araçuaí →, *Brazil* 123 E3
'Arad, *Israel* 69 D4
Arad, *Romania* 38 C4
Arada, *Chad* 73 F9
Aradhippou, *Cyprus* 37 E12
Arafura Sea, *E. Indies* .. 57 F8
Aragarças, *Brazil* 125 D7
Aragats, *Armenia* 43 F11
Aragón □, *Spain* 28 D4
Aragón →, *Spain* 28 C3
Aragona, *Italy* 34 E6
Aragua □, *Venezuela* 120 B4
Aragua de Barcelona,
 Venezuela 121 B5
Araguacema, *Brazil* 122 C2
Araguaçu, *Brazil* 123 D2
Araguaia →, *Brazil* 122 C2
Araguaiana, *Brazil* 125 D7
Araguaína, *Brazil* 122 C2
Araguari, *Brazil* 123 E2
Araguari →, *Brazil* 121 C8
Araguatins, *Brazil* 122 C2
Araioses, *Brazil* 122 B3
Arak, *Algeria* 75 C5
Arāk, *Iran* 65 C6
Arakan Coast, *Burma* ... 61 K19
Arakan Yoma, *Burma* ... 61 K19
Arakli, *Turkey* 67 C9
Araks = Aras, Rūd-e →,
 Iran 64 B5
Aral Sea = Aralskoye
 More, *Asia* 44 E7
Aralsk, *Kazakhstan* 44 E7
Aralskoye More, *Asia* ... 44 E7
Aramac, *Australia* 90 C4
Arambag, *India* 63 H12
Aran I., *Ireland* 15 B3
Aran Is., *Ireland* 15 C2
Aranda de Duero, *Spain* . 28 D1
Arandān, *Iran* 64 C5
Aranjuez, *Spain* 30 E7
Aranos, *Namibia* 84 C2
Aransas Pass, *U.S.A.* 109 M6
Aranzazu, *Colombia* 120 B2
Araouane, *Mali* 78 B4
Arapahoe, *U.S.A.* 108 E5
Arapari, *Brazil* 122 C2
Arapey Grande →,
 Uruguay 126 C4
Arapiraca, *Brazil* 122 C4
Arapkir, *Turkey* 67 D8
Arapongas, *Brazil* 127 A5
Ar'ar, *Si. Arabia* 64 D4
Araracuara, *Colombia* ... 120 D3
Araranguá, *Brazil* 127 B6
Araraquara, *Brazil* 123 F2
Ararás, Serra das, *Brazil* . 127 B5
Ararat, *Australia* 91 F3
Ararat, Mt. = Ağrı Dağı,
 Turkey 67 D11
Arari, *Brazil* 122 B3
Araria, *India* 63 F12
Araripe, Chapada do,
 Brazil 122 C3
Araripina, *Brazil* 122 C3
Araruama, L. de, *Brazil* . 123 F3
Araruna, *Brazil* 122 C4
Aras, Rūd-e →, *Iran* ... 64 B5
Araticu, *Brazil* 122 B2
Arauca, *Colombia* 120 B3
Arauca □, *Colombia* 120 B3
Arauca →, *Venezuela* 120 B4
Arauco, *Chile* 126 D1
Arauco □, *Chile* 126 D1
Araújos, *Brazil* 123 E2
Arauquita, *Colombia* 120 B3
Araure, *Venezuela* 120 B4
Arawa, *Ethiopia* 77 F5
Araxá, *Brazil* 123 E2

Araya, Pen. de, *Venezuela* 121 A5
Arba Minch, *Ethiopia* ... 77 F4
Arbat, *Iraq* 64 C5
Arbatax, *Italy* 34 C2
Arbaza, *Russia* 45 D10
Arbedo, *Switz.* 23 D8
Arbīl, *Iraq* 64 B5
Arbois, *France* 25 F12
Arboletes, *Colombia* 120 B2
Arbon, *Switz.* 23 A8
Arbore, *Ethiopia* 77 F4
Arborea, *Italy* 34 C1
Arborfield, *Canada* 101 C8
Arborg, *Canada* 101 C9
Arbrå, *Sweden* 10 C10
Arbroath, *U.K.* 14 E6
Arbuckle, *U.S.A.* 112 F4
Arbus, *Italy* 34 C1
Arbuzinka, *Ukraine* 42 C4
Arc, *France* 25 C12
Arc →, *France* 27 C10
Arcachon, *France* 26 D2
Arcachon, Bassin d',
 France 26 D2
Arcade, *U.S.A.* 106 D6
Arcadia, *Fla., U.S.A.* 105 M5
Arcadia, *La., U.S.A.* 109 J8
Arcadia, *Nebr., U.S.A.* .. 108 E5
Arcadia, *Pa., U.S.A.* 106 F6
Arcadia, *Wis., U.S.A.* ... 108 C9
Arcata, *U.S.A.* 110 F1
Arcévia, *Italy* 33 E9
Archangel = Arkhangelsk,
 Russia 44 C5
Archar, *Bulgaria* 38 F5
Archbald, *U.S.A.* 107 E9
Archena, *Spain* 29 G3
Archer →, *Australia* 90 A3
Archer B., *Australia* 90 A3
Archers Post, *Kenya* 82 B4
Archidona, *Spain* 31 H6
Arci, Monte, *Italy* 34 C1
Arcidosso, *Italy* 33 F8
Arcila = Asilah, *Morocco* 74 A3
Arcis-sur-Aube, *France* .. 25 D11
Arckaringa, *Australia* ... 91 D1
Arckaringa Cr. →,
 Australia 91 D2
Arco, *Italy* 32 C7
Arco, *U.S.A.* 110 E7
Arcola, *Canada* 101 D8
Arcos, *Spain* 28 D2
Arcos de los Frontera,
 Spain 31 J5
Arcos de Valdevez,
 Portugal 30 D2
Arcot, *India* 60 N11
Arcoverde, *Brazil* 122 C4
Arctic Bay, *Canada* 97 A11
Arctic Ocean, *Arctic* 4 B18
Arctic Red River, *Canada* 96 B6
Arda →, *Bulgaria* 39 H9
Arda →, *Italy* 32 D6
Ardabīl, *Iran* 65 B6
Ardahan, *Turkey* 67 C10
Ardakān = Sepīdān, *Iran* 65 D7
Ardales, *Spain* 31 J6
Årdalstangen, *Norway* ... 10 C1
Ardatov, *Russia* 41 D15
Ardea, *Greece* 39 J5
Ardèche □, *France* 27 D8
Ardèche →, *France* 27 D8
Ardee, *Ireland* 15 C5
Arden, *Canada* 106 B8
Arden, *Denmark* 11 H3
Arden, *Calif., U.S.A.* 112 G5
Arden, *Nev., U.S.A.* 113 J11
Ardenne, *Belgium* 25 C12
Ardennes □, *France* 25 C11
Ardentes, *France* 25 F8
Ardeşen, *Turkey* 67 C9
Ardestān, *Iran* 65 C7
Ardgour, *U.K.* 14 E3
Árdhas →, *Greece* 39 H9
Ardila →, *Portugal* 31 G3
Ardlethan, *Australia* 91 E4
Ardmore, *Australia* 90 C2
Ardmore, *Okla., U.S.A.* .. 109 H6
Ardmore, *Pa., U.S.A.* ... 107 G9
Ardmore, *S. Dak., U.S.A.* 108 D3
Ardnacrusha, *Ireland* ... 15 D3
Ardnamurchan, Pt. of,
 U.K. 14 E2
Ardooie, *Belgium* 17 G2
Ardore Marina, *Italy* 35 D9
Ardres, *France* 25 B8
Ardrossan, *Australia* 91 E2
Ardrossan, *U.K.* 14 F4
Ards □, *U.K.* 15 B6
Ards Pen., *U.K.* 15 B6
Ardud, *Romania* 38 B5
Ardunac, *Turkey* 43 F10
Åre, *Sweden* 10 A7
Arecibo, *Puerto Rico* 117 C6
Areia Branca, *Brazil* 122 B4
Arena, Pt., *U.S.A.* 112 G3
Arenales, Cerro, *Chile* ... 128 C2
Arenápolis, *Brazil* 125 C6
Arenas, *Spain* 30 B6
Arenas de San Pedro,
 Spain 30 E5
Arendal, *Norway* 11 F2
Arendonk, *Belgium* 17 F6
Arendsee, *Germany* 18 C7
Arenillas, *Ecuador* 120 D1

Arenys de Mar, *Spain* ... 28 D7
Arenzano, *Italy* 32 D5
Areópolis, *Greece* 39 N5
Arequipa, *Peru* 124 D3
Arequipa □, *Peru* 124 D3
Arere, *Brazil* 121 D7
Arero, *Ethiopia* 77 G4
Arès, *France* 26 D2
Arévalo, *Spain* 30 D6
Arezzo, *Italy* 33 E8
Arga →, *Spain* 28 C3
Argalastí, *Greece* 39 K6
Argamakmur, *Indonesia* . 56 E2
Argamasilla de Alba, *Spain* 29 F1
Arganda, *Spain* 28 E1
Arganil, *Portugal* 30 E2
Argelès-Gazost, *France* .. 26 F3
Argelès-sur-Mer, *France* . 26 F7
Argens →, *France* 27 E10
Argent-sur-Sauldre, *France* 25 E9
Argenta, *Italy* 33 D8
Argentan, *France* 24 D6
Argentário, Mte., *Italy* .. 33 F8
Argentat, *France* 26 C5
Argentera, *Italy* 32 D3
Argentera, Monte del, *Italy* 32 D4
Argenteuil, *France* 25 D9
Argentia, *Canada* 99 C9
Argentiera, C. dell', *Italy* . 34 B1
Argentière, Aiguilles d',
 Switz. 22 E4
Argentina ■, *S. Amer.* .. 128 B3
Argentina Is., *Antarctica* . 5 C17
Argentino, L., *Argentina* . 128 D2
Argenton-Château, *France* 24 F6
Argenton-sur-Creuse,
 France 26 B5
Argeş →, *Romania* 38 E9
Argeş □, *Romania* 38 E8
Arghandab →, *Afghan.* . 62 D1
Argo, *Sudan* 76 D3
Argolikós Kólpos, *Greece* . 39 M5
Argonne, *France* 25 C12
Árgos, *Greece* 39 M5
Argostólion, *Greece* 39 L3
Arguedas, *Spain* 28 C3
Arguello, Pt., *U.S.A.* 113 L6
Arguineguín, *Canary Is.* . 36 G4
Argun →, *Russia* 45 D13
Argungu, *Nigeria* 79 C5
Argus Pk., *U.S.A.* 113 K9
Argyle, *U.S.A.* 108 A6
Argyle, L., *Australia* 88 C4
Arhavi, *Turkey* 67 C9
Århus, *Denmark* 11 H4
Århus Amtskommune □,
 Denmark 11 H4
Ariadnoye, *Russia* 48 B7
Ariamsvlei, *Namibia* 84 D2
Ariana, *Tunisia* 75 A7
Ariano Irpino, *Italy* 35 A8
Ariano nel Polèsine, *Italy* . 33 D9
Ariari →, *Colombia* 120 C3
Aribinda, *Burkina Faso* .. 79 C4
Arica, *Chile* 124 D3
Arica, *Colombia* 120 D3
Arico, *Canary Is.* 36 F3
Arid, C., *Australia* 89 F3
Arida, *Japan* 49 G7
Aridha, *Syria* 64 C3
Arīḥā, *Syria* 64 C3
Arīlla, Ákra, *Greece* 37 A3
Arima, *Trin. & Tob.* 117 D7
Arinos →, *Brazil* 125 C6
Ario de Rosales, *Mexico* . 114 D4
Aripuanã, *Brazil* 125 B5
Aripuanã →, *Brazil* 125 B5
Ariquemes, *Brazil* 125 B5
Arisaig, *U.K.* 14 E3
Arîsh, W. el →, *Egypt* .. 76 H8
Arismendi, *Venezuela* ... 120 B4
Arissa, *Ethiopia* 77 E5
Aristazabal I., *Canada* ... 100 C3
Arivaca, *U.S.A.* 111 L8
Arivonimamo, *Madag.* ... 85 B8
Ariza, *Spain* 28 D2
Arizaro, Salar de,
 Argentina 126 A2
Arizona, *Argentina* 126 D2
Arizona □, *U.S.A.* 111 J8
Arizpe, *Mexico* 114 A2
Arjeplog, *Sweden* 8 C15
Arjona, *Colombia* 120 A2
Arjona, *Spain* 31 H6
Arjuno, *Indonesia* 57 G15
Arka, *Russia* 45 C15
Arkadak, *Russia* 41 F13
Arkadelphia, *U.S.A.* 109 H8
Arkaig, L., *U.K.* 14 E3
Arkalyk, *Kazakhstan* 44 D7
Arkansas □, *U.S.A.* 109 H8
Arkansas →, *U.S.A.* 109 J9
Arkansas City, *U.S.A.* ... 109 G6
Árkathos →, *Greece* 39 K4
Arkhángelos, *Greece* 37 C10
Arkhangelsk, *Russia* 44 C5
Arkhangelskoye, *Russia* . 41 F12
Arkiko, *Ethiopia* 77 D4
Arklow, *Ireland* 15 D5
Arkona, Kap, *Germany* .. 18 A9
Arkösund, *Sweden* 11 F10
Arkticheskiy, Mys, *Russia* 45 A10
Arkul, *Russia* 41 C17
Arlanc, *France* 26 C7

Arlanza →, *Spain* 30 C6
Arlanzón →, *Spain* 30 C6
Arlberg Pass, *Austria* ... 19 H6
Arlee, *U.S.A.* 110 C6
Arles, *France* 27 E8
Arlesheim, *Switz.* 22 B5
Arlington, *S. Africa* 85 D4
Arlington, *Oreg., U.S.A.* . 110 D3
Arlington, *S. Dak., U.S.A.* 108 C6
Arlington, *Va., U.S.A.* ... 104 F7
Arlington, *Wash., U.S.A.* 112 B4
Arlon, *Belgium* 17 J2
Arlöv, *Sweden* 11 J7
Arly, *Burkina Faso* 79 C5
Armagh, *U.K.* 15 B5
Armagh □, *U.K.* 15 B5
Armagnac, *France* 26 E4
Armançon →, *France* ... 25 E10
Armavir, *Russia* 43 D9
Armenia, *Colombia* 120 C2
Armenia ■, *Asia* 43 F11
Armenistís, Ákra, *Greece* . 37 C9
Armentières, *France* 25 B9
Armidale, *Australia* 91 E5
Armour, *U.S.A.* 108 D5
Armstrong, *B.C., Canada* 100 C5
Armstrong, *Ont., Canada* 98 B2
Armstrong, *U.S.A.* 109 M6
Armstrong →, *Australia* 88 C5
Arnarfjörður, *Iceland* 8 D2
Arnaud →, *Canada* 97 B12
Arnauti, C., *Cyprus* 37 D11
Arnay-le-Duc, *France* 25 E11
Arnedillo, *Spain* 28 C2
Arnedo, *Spain* 28 C2
Arnemuiden, *Neths.* 17 F3
Árnes, *Iceland* 8 C3
Årnes, *Norway* 10 D5
Arnett, *U.S.A.* 109 G5
Arnhem, *Neths.* 16 E7
Arnhem, C., *Australia* ... 90 A2
Arnhem B., *Australia* 90 A2
Arnhem Land, *Australia* . 90 A1
Arno →, *Italy* 32 E7
Arno Bay, *Australia* 91 E2
Arnold, *Calif., U.S.A.* ... 112 G6
Arnold, *Nebr., U.S.A.* ... 108 E4
Arnoldstein, *Austria* 21 J3
Arnon →, *France* 25 E9
Arnot, *Canada* 101 B9
Arnøy, *Norway* 8 A16
Arnprior, *Canada* 98 C4
Arnsberg, *Germany* 18 D4
Arnstadt, *Germany* 18 E6
Aro →, *Venezuela* 121 B5
Aroab, *Namibia* 84 D2
Aroche, *Spain* 31 H4
Aroeiras, *Brazil* 122 C4
Arolla, *Switz.* 22 D4
Arolsen, *Germany* 18 D5
Aron →, *France* 26 B7
Arona, *Italy* 32 C5
Aroroy, *Phil.* 55 E5
Arosa, *Switz.* 23 C9
Arosa, Ria de, *Spain* 30 C2
Arpajon, *France* 25 D9
Arpajon-sur-Cère, *France* . 26 D6
Arpino, *Italy* 34 A6
Arque, *Bolivia* 124 D4
Arrabury, *Australia* 91 D3
Arraias, *Brazil* 123 D2
Arraias →, *Mato Grosso,
 Brazil* 125 C7
Arraias →, *Pará, Brazil* . 122 C2
Arraiolos, *Portugal* 31 G3
Arran, *U.K.* 14 F3
Arrandale, *Canada* 100 C3
Arras, *France* 25 B9
Arrats →, *France* 26 D4
Arreau, *France* 26 F4
Arrecife, *Canary Is.* 36 F6
Arrecifes, *Argentina* 126 C3
Arrée, Mts. d', *France* ... 24 D3
Arriaga, *Chiapas, Mexico* . 115 D6
Arriaga, San Luis Potosí,
 Mexico 114 C4
Arrilalah P.O., *Australia* . 90 C3
Arrino, *Australia* 89 E2
Arrojado →, *Brazil* 123 D3
Arromanches-les-Bains,
 France 24 C6
Arronches, *Portugal* 31 F3
Arros →, *France* 26 E3
Arrou, *France* 24 D8
Arrow, L., *Ireland* 15 B3
Arrow Rock Res., *U.S.A.* 110 E6
Arrowhead, *Canada* 100 C5
Arrowhead, L., *U.S.A.* ... 113 L9
Arrowtown, *N.Z.* 87 L2
Arroyo de la Luz, *Spain* . 31 F4
Arroyo Grande, *U.S.A.* .. 113 K6
Års, *Denmark* 11 H3
Ars, *Iran* 64 B5
Ars-en-Ré, *France* 26 B2
Ars-sur-Moselle, *France* .. 25 C13
Arsenault L., *Canada* 101 B7
Arsenev, *Russia* 48 B6
Arsi □, *Ethiopia* 77 F4
Arsiero, *Italy* 33 C8
Arsin, *Turkey* 67 C8
Arsk, *Russia* 41 C16
Árta, *Greece* 39 K4
Artá, *Spain* 36 B10
Arteaga, *Mexico* 114 D4
Arteche, *Phil.* 55 E6

Arteijo, *Spain* 30 B2
Artem, *Russia* 48 C6
Artem, Ostrov, *Azerbaijan* 43 F14
Artemovsk, *Russia* 45 D10
Artemovsk, *Ukraine* 42 B8
Artemovski, *Russia* 43 C9
Artenay, *France* 25 D8
Artern, *Germany* 18 D7
Artesa de Segre, *Spain* ... 28 D6
Artesia = Mosomane,
 Botswana 84 C4
Artesia, *U.S.A.* 109 J2
Artesia Wells, *U.S.A.* 109 L5
Artesian, *U.S.A.* 108 C6
Arth, *Switz.* 23 B7
Arthez-de-Béarn, *France* . 26 E3
Arthington, *Liberia* 78 D2
Arthur →, *Australia* 90 G3
Arthur Cr. →, *Australia* . 90 C2
Arthur Pt., *Australia* 90 C5
Arthur's Pass, *N.Z.* 87 K3
Arthur's Town, *Bahamas* 117 B4
Artigas, *Uruguay* 126 C4
Artik, *Armenia* 43 F10
Artillery L., *Canada* 101 A7
Artois, *France* 25 B9
Artsiz, *Ukraine* 42 C3
Artvin, *Turkey* 43 F9
Artvin □, *Turkey* 67 C9
Aru, Kepulauan, *Indonesia* 57 F8
Aru Is. = Aru, Kepulauan,
 Indonesia 57 F8
Aru Meru □, *Tanzania* .. 82 C4
Arua, *Uganda* 82 B3
Aruanã, *Brazil* 123 D1
Aruba, *Neth. Ant.* 117 D6
Arucas, *Canary Is.* 36 F4
Arudy, *France* 26 E3
Arumã, *Brazil* 121 D5
Arumpo, *Australia* 91 E3
Arun →, *Nepal* 63 F12
Arunachal Pradesh □,
 India 61 E19
Arusha, *Tanzania* 82 C4
Arusha □, *Tanzania* 82 C4
Arusha Chini, *Tanzania* .. 82 C4
Aruwimi →, *Zaïre* 82 B1
Arvada, *U.S.A.* 110 D10
Arvayheer, *Mongolia* 54 B5
Arve →, *France* 27 B10
Árvi, *Greece* 37 E7
Arvida, *Canada* 99 C5
Arvidsjaur, *Sweden* 8 D15
Arvika, *Sweden* 9 G12
Arvin, *U.S.A.* 113 K8
Arxan, *China* 54 B6
Aryiráodhes, *Greece* 37 B3
Aryiroúpolis, *Greece* 37 D6
Arys, *Kazakhstan* 44 E7
Arzachena, *Italy* 34 A2
Arzamas, *Russia* 41 D13
Arzew, *Algeria* 75 A4
Arzgir, *Russia* 43 D11
Arzignano, *Italy* 33 C8
As, *Belgium* 17 F7
Aş Şadr, *U.A.E.* 65 E7
Aş Şafā, *Syria* 69 B6
'As Saffānīyah, *Si. Arabia* 65 D6
Aş Şafīrah, *Syria* 64 B3
Aş Şahm, *Oman* 65 E8
.As Sājir, *Si. Arabia* 64 E5
As Salamīyah, *Syria* 64 C3
As Salt, *Jordan* 69 C4
As Sal'w'a, *Qatar* 65 E6
As Samāwah, *Iraq* 64 D5
As Sanamayn, *Syria* 69 B5
As Sukhnah, *Syria* 64 C3
As Sulaymānīyah, *Iraq* .. 64 C5
As Sulaymī, *Si. Arabia* .. 64 E4
As Summān, *Si. Arabia* .. 64 E5
As Suwaydā', *Syria* 69 C5
As Suwaydā' □, *Syria* ... 69 C5
As Suwayrah, *Iraq* 64 C5
Asab, *Namibia* 84 D2
Asaba, *Nigeria* 79 D6
Asafo, *Ghana* 78 D4
Asahi-Gawa →, *Japan* ... 49 G6
Asahigawa, *Japan* 48 C11
Asale, L., *Ethiopia* 77 E5
Asamankese, *Ghana* 79 D4
Asansol, *India* 63 H12
Åsarna, *Sweden* 10 B8
Asbe Teferi, *Ethiopia* 77 F5
Asbesberge, *S. Africa* 84 D3
Asbestos, *Canada* 99 C5
Asbury Park, *U.S.A.* 107 F10
Ascensión, *Mexico* 114 A3
Ascensión, B. de la,
 Mexico 115 D7
Ascension I., *Atl. Oc.* 2 E9
Aschaffenburg, *Germany* . 19 F5
Aschendorf, *Germany* ... 18 B3
Aschersleben, *Germany* .. 18 D7
Asciano, *Italy* 33 E8
Áscoli Piceno, *Italy* 33 F10
Áscoli Satriano, *Italy* 35 A8
Ascona, *Switz.* 23 D7
Ascope, *Peru* 124 B2
Ascotán, *Chile* 126 A2
Aseb, *Ethiopia* 68 E3
Asedjrad, *Algeria* 75 D5
Asela, *Ethiopia* 77 F4
Asenovgrad, *Bulgaria* 39 G7
Asfeld, *France* 25 C11
Asfûn el Matâ'na, *Egypt* . 76 B3

Azovskoye More

Åsgårdstrand, *Norway* 10 E4
Asgata, *Cyprus* 37 E12
Ash Fork, *U.S.A.* 111 J7
Ash Grove, *U.S.A.* 109 G8
Ash Shamāl □, *Lebanon* 69 A5
Ash Shāmīyah, *Iraq* 64 D5
Ash Shāriqah, *U.A.E.* 65 E7
Ash Sharmah, *Si. Arabia* 64 D2
Ash Sharqāt, *Iraq* 64 C4
Ash Sharqi, Al Jabal, *Lebanon* 69 B5
Ash Shaṭrah, *Iraq* 64 D5
Ash Shawbak, *Jordan* 64 D2
Ash Shawmari, J., *Jordan* 69 E5
Ash Shaykh, J., *Lebanon* 69 B4
Ash Shināfīyah, *Iraq* 64 D5
Ash Shu'aybah, *Si. Arabia* 64 E5
Ash Shumlūl, *Si. Arabia* 64 E5
Ash Shūr'a, *Iraq* 64 C4
Ash Shurayf, *Si. Arabia* 64 E3
Ash Shuwayfāt, *Lebanon* 69 B4
Ashanti □, *Ghana* 79 D4
Ashau, *Vietnam* 58 D6
Ashburn, *U.S.A.* 105 K4
Ashburton, *N.Z.* 87 K3
Ashburton →, *Australia* 88 D1
Ashburton Downs, *Australia* 88 D2
Ashby de la Zouch, *U.K.* 12 E6
Ashcroft, *Canada* 100 C4
Ashdod, *Israel* 69 D3
Asheboro, *U.S.A.* 105 H6
Asherton, *U.S.A.* 109 L5
Asheville, *U.S.A.* 105 H4
Asheweig →, *Canada* 98 B2
Ashford, *Australia* 91 D5
Ashford, *U.K.* 13 F8
Ashford, *U.S.A.* 110 C2
Ashibetsu, *Japan* 48 C11
Ashikaga, *Japan* 49 F9
Ashizuri-Zaki, *Japan* 49 H6
Ashkarkot, *Afghan.* 62 C2
Ashkhabad, *Turkmenistan* 44 F6
Ashland, *Kans., U.S.A.* 109 G5
Ashland, *Ky., U.S.A.* 104 F4
Ashland, *Maine, U.S.A.* 99 C6
Ashland, *Mont., U.S.A.* 110 D10
Ashland, *Nebr., U.S.A.* 108 E6
Ashland, *Ohio, U.S.A.* 106 F2
Ashland, *Oreg., U.S.A.* 110 E2
Ashland, *Pa., U.S.A.* 107 F8
Ashland, *Va., U.S.A.* 104 G7
Ashland, *Wis., U.S.A.* 108 B9
Ashley, *N. Dak., U.S.A.* 108 B5
Ashley, *Pa., U.S.A.* 107 E9
Ashmont, *Canada* 100 C6
Ashmore Reef, *Australia* 88 B3
Ashmûn, *Egypt* 76 H7
Ashq'elon, *Israel* 69 D3
Ashtabula, *U.S.A.* 106 E4
Ashton, *S. Africa* 84 E3
Ashton, *U.S.A.* 110 D8
Ashton under Lyne, *U.K.* 12 D5
Ashuanipi, L., *Canada* 99 B6
Asia 46 E11
Asia, Kepulauan, *Indonesia* 57 D8
Āsīā Bak, *Iran* 65 C6
Asiago, *Italy* 33 C8
Asidonhoppo, *Surinam* 121 C6
Asifabad, *India* 60 K11
Asike, *Indonesia* 57 F10
Asilah, *Morocco* 74 A3
Asinara, *Italy* 34 A1
Asinara, G. dell', *Italy* 34 B1
Asino, *Russia* 44 D9
'Asīr □, *Si. Arabia* 68 D3
Asir, Ras, *Somali Rep.* 68 E5
Aşkale, *Turkey* 67 D9
Asker, *Norway* 10 E4
Askersund, *Sweden* 11 F8
Askham, *S. Africa* 84 D3
Askim, *Norway* 10 E5
Askja, *Iceland* 8 D5
Asl, *Egypt* 76 J8
Asmara = Asmera, *Ethiopia* 77 D4
Asmera, *Ethiopia* 77 D4
Asnæs, *Denmark* 11 J5
Asni, *Morocco* 74 B3
Ásola, *Italy* 32 C7
Asoteriba, Jebel, *Sudan* 76 C4
Asotin, *U.S.A.* 110 C5
Aspe, *Spain* 29 G4
Aspen, *U.S.A.* 111 G10
Aspendos, *Turkey* 66 E4
Aspermont, *U.S.A.* 109 J4
Aspiring, Mt., *N.Z.* 87 L2
Aspres-sur-Buëch, *France* 27 D9
Asprókavos, Ákra, *Greece* 37 B4
Aspromonte, *Italy* 35 D8
Aspur, *India* 62 H6
Asquith, *Canada* 101 C7
Assa, *Morocco* 74 C3
Assâba, *Mauritania* 78 B2
Assam □, *India* 61 F18
Assamakka, *Niger* 79 B6
Asse, *Belgium* 17 H4
Assebroek, *Belgium* 17 F2
Assekrem, *Algeria* 75 D6
Assémini, *Italy* 34 C2
Assen, *Neths.* 16 C9
Assendelft, *Neths.* 16 D5
Assenede, *Belgium* 17 F3
Assens, *Århus, Denmark* 11 H4
Assens, *Fyn, Denmark* 11 J3
Assesse, *Belgium* 17 H6
Assini, *Ivory C.* 78 D4
Assiniboia, *Canada* 101 D7
Assiniboine →, *Canada* 101 D9
Assis, *Brazil* 127 A5
Assisi, *Italy* 33 E9
Assynt, L., *U.K.* 14 C3
Astaffort, *France* 26 D4
Astara, *Azerbaijan* 67 D13
Asten, *Neths.* 17 F7
Asteroúsia, *Greece* 37 E7
Asti, *Italy* 32 D5
Astipálaia, *Greece* 39 N9
Astorga, *Spain* 30 C4
Astoria, *U.S.A.* 112 D3
Åstorp, *Sweden* 11 H6
Astrakhan, *Russia* 43 C13
Astudillo, *Spain* 30 C6
Asturias, *Spain* 30 B5
Asunción, *Paraguay* 126 B4
Asunción Nochixtlán, *Mexico* 115 D5
Asutri, *Sudan* 77 D4
Aswa →, *Uganda* 82 B3
Aswad, Ras al, *Si. Arabia* 76 C4
Aswân, *Egypt* 76 C3
Aswân High Dam = Sadd el Aali, *Egypt* 76 C3
Asyût, *Egypt* 76 B3
Asyûti, Wadi →, *Egypt* 76 B3
Aszód, *Hungary* 21 H9
At Ṭafīlah, *Jordan* 69 E4
At Tā'if, *Si. Arabia* 68 C3
Aṭ Ṭirāq, *Si. Arabia* 64 E5
Atacama □, *Chile* 126 B2
Atacama, Desierto de, *Chile* 126 A2
Atacama, Salar de, *Chile* 126 A2
Ataco, *Colombia* 120 C2
Atakor, *Algeria* 75 D6
Atakpamé, *Togo* 79 D5
Atalándi, *Greece* 39 L5
Atalaya, *Peru* 124 C3
Atalaya de Femes, *Canary Is.* 36 F6
Ataléia, *Brazil* 123 E3
Atami, *Japan* 49 G9
Atapupu, *Indonesia* 57 F6
Atâr, *Mauritania* 74 D2
Atara, *Russia* 45 C13
Ataram, Erg n-, *Algeria* 75 D5
Atarfe, *Spain* 31 H7
Atascadero, *U.S.A.* 111 J3
Atascadero, *Calif., U.S.A.* 112 K6
Atasu, *Kazakhstan* 44 E8
Atauro, *Indonesia* 57 F7
Atbara, *Sudan* 76 D3
'Atbara →, *Sudan* 76 D3
Atbasar, *Kazakhstan* 44 D7
Atchafalaya B., *U.S.A.* 109 L9
Atchison, *U.S.A.* 108 F7
Atebubu, *Ghana* 79 D4
Ateca, *Spain* 28 D3
Aterno →, *Italy* 33 F10
Atesine, Alpi, *Italy* 32 B8
Atessa, *Italy* 33 F11
Ath, *Belgium* 17 G3
Athabasca, *Canada* 100 C6
Athabasca →, *Canada* 101 B6
Athabasca, L., *Canada* 101 B7
Athboy, *Ireland* 15 C5
Athenry, *Ireland* 15 C3
Athens = Athínai, *Greece* 39 M6
Athens, *Ala., U.S.A.* 105 H2
Athens, *Ga., U.S.A.* 105 J4
Athens, *N.Y., U.S.A.* 107 D11
Athens, *Ohio, U.S.A.* 104 F4
Athens, *Pa., U.S.A.* 107 E8
Athens, *Tenn., U.S.A.* 105 H3
Athens, *Tex., U.S.A.* 109 J7
Atherley, *Canada* 106 B5
Atherton, *Australia* 90 B4
Athiéme, *Benin* 79 D5
Athienou, *Cyprus* 37 D12
Athínai, *Greece* 39 M6
Athlone, *Ireland* 15 C4
Athna, *Cyprus* 37 D12
Atholl, Forest of, *U.K.* 14 E5
Atholville, *Canada* 99 C6
Áthos, *Greece* 39 J7
Athus, *Belgium* 17 J7
Athy, *Ireland* 15 D5
Ati, *Chad* 73 F8
Ati, *Sudan* 77 E2
Atiak, *Uganda* 82 B3
Atico, *Peru* 124 D3
Atienza, *Spain* 28 D2
Atikokan, *Canada* 98 C1
Atikonak L., *Canada* 99 B7
Atimonan, *Phil.* 55 E4
Atka, *Russia* 45 C16
Atkarsk, *Russia* 41 F14
Atkinson, *U.S.A.* 108 D5
Atlanta, *Ga., U.S.A.* 105 J3
Atlanta, *Tex., U.S.A.* 109 J7
Atlantic, *U.S.A.* 108 E7
Atlantic City, *U.S.A.* 104 F8
Atlantic Ocean 2 E9
Atlántico □, *Colombia* 120 A2
Atlas Mts. = Haut Atlas, *Morocco* 74 B3
Atlin, *Canada* 100 B2
Atlin, L., *Canada* 100 B2
Atmore, *U.S.A.* 105 K2
Atoka, *U.S.A.* 109 H6
Átokos, *Greece* 39 L3
Atolia, *U.S.A.* 113 K9
Atouguia, *Portugal* 31 F1
Atoyac →, *Mexico* 115 D5
Atrak →, *Iran* 65 B8
Ätran, *Sweden* 11 G6
Atrato →, *Colombia* 120 B2
Atrauli, *India* 62 E8
Atri, *Italy* 33 F10
Atsbi, *Ethiopia* 77 E4
Atsoum, Mts., *Cameroon* 79 D7
Atsuta, *Japan* 48 C10
Attalla, *U.S.A.* 105 H2
Attáviros, *Greece* 37 C9
Attawapiskat, *Canada* 98 B3
Attawapiskat →, *Canada* 98 B3
Attawapiskat, L., *Canada* 98 B2
Attendorn, *Germany* 18 D3
Attert, *Belgium* 17 J7
Attica, *U.S.A.* 104 E2
Attichy, *France* 25 C10
Attigny, *France* 25 C11
Attikamagen L., *Canada* 99 A6
Attleboro, *U.S.A.* 107 E13
Attock, *Pakistan* 62 C5
Attopeu, *Laos* 58 E6
Attur, *India* 60 P11
Atuel →, *Argentina* 126 D2
Atvacik, *Turkey* 66 D2
Åtvidaberg, *Sweden* 11 F10
Atwater, *U.S.A.* 111 H3
Atwood, *Canada* 106 C3
Atwood, *U.S.A.* 108 F4
Au Sable →, *U.S.A.* 104 C4
Au Sable Pt., *U.S.A.* 98 C2
Aubagne, *France* 27 E9
Aubange, *Belgium* 17 J7
Aubarca, C., *Spain* 36 B7
Aube □, *France* 25 D11
Aube →, *France* 25 D10
Aubel, *Belgium* 17 G7
Aubenas, *France* 27 D8
Aubenton, *France* 25 C11
Auberry, *U.S.A.* 112 H7
Aubigny-sur-Nère, *France* 25 E9
Aubin, *France* 26 D6
Aubrac, Mts. d', *France* 26 D7
Auburn, *Ala., U.S.A.* 105 J3
Auburn, *Calif., U.S.A.* 112 G5
Auburn, *Ind., U.S.A.* 104 E3
Auburn, *N.Y., U.S.A.* 107 D8
Auburn, *Nebr., U.S.A.* 108 E7
Auburn, *Wash., U.S.A.* 112 C4
Auburn Ra., *Australia* 91 D5
Auburndale, *U.S.A.* 105 L5
Aubusson, *France* 26 C6
Auch, *France* 26 E4
Auchel, *France* 25 B9
Auchi, *Nigeria* 79 D6
Auckland, *N.Z.* 87 G5
Auckland Is., *Pac. Oc.* 92 N8
Aude □, *France* 26 E6
Aude →, *France* 26 E7
Auden, *Canada* 98 B2
Auderghem, *Belgium* 17 G4
Auderville, *France* 24 C5
Audierne, *France* 24 D2
Audincourt, *France* 25 E13
Audo, *Ethiopia* 77 F5
Audubon, *U.S.A.* 108 E7
Aue, *Germany* 18 E8
Auerbach, *Germany* 18 E8
Aueti Paraná →, *Brazil* 120 D4
Aufist, *W. Sahara* 74 C2
Augathella, *Australia* 91 D4
Augrabies Falls, *S. Africa* 84 D3
Augsburg, *Germany* 19 G6
Augusta, *Italy* 35 E8
Augusta, *Ark., U.S.A.* 109 H9
Augusta, *Ga., U.S.A.* 105 J5
Augusta, *Kans., U.S.A.* 109 G6
Augusta, *Maine, U.S.A.* 99 D6
Augusta, *Mont., U.S.A.* 110 C7
Augusta, *Wis., U.S.A.* 108 C9
Augustenborg, *Denmark* 11 K3
Augustów, *Poland* 20 B12
Augustus, Mt., *Australia* 88 D2
Augustus Downs, *Australia* 90 B2
Augustus I., *Australia* 88 C3
Aukan, *Ethiopia* 77 D5
Aukum, *U.S.A.* 112 G6
Auld, L., *Australia* 88 D3
Aulla, *Italy* 32 D6
Aulnay, *France* 26 B3
Aulne →, *France* 24 D2
Aulnoye-Aymeries, *France* 25 B10
Ault, *France* 24 B8
Ault, *U.S.A.* 108 E2
Aulus-les-Bains, *France* 26 F5
Aumale, *France* 25 C8
Aumont-Aubrac, *France* 26 D7
Auna, *Nigeria* 79 C5
Aunis, *France* 26 B3
Auponhia, *Indonesia* 57 E7
Aups, *France* 27 E10
Aur, P., *Malaysia* 59 L5
Auraiya, *India* 63 F8
Aurangabad, *Bihar, India* 63 G11
Aurangabad, *Maharashtra, India* 60 K9
Auray, *France* 24 E4
Aurès, *Algeria* 75 A6
Aurich, *Germany* 18 B3
Aurilândia, *Brazil* 123 E1
Aurillac, *France* 26 D6
Auronza, *Italy* 33 B9
Aurora, *Canada* 106 C5
Aurora, *S. Africa* 84 E2
Aurora, *Colo., U.S.A.* 108 F2
Aurora, *Ill., U.S.A.* 104 E1
Aurora, *Mo., U.S.A.* 109 G8
Aurora, *Nebr., U.S.A.* 108 E6
Aurora, *Ohio, U.S.A.* 106 E3
Aursmoen, *Norway* 10 E5
Aurukun Mission, *Australia* 90 A3
Aus, *Namibia* 84 D2
Auschwitz = Oświecim, *Poland* 20 E9
Aust-Agder fylke □, *Norway* 9 G9
Austin, *Minn., U.S.A.* 108 D8
Austin, *Nev., U.S.A.* 110 G5
Austin, *Pa., U.S.A.* 106 E6
Austin, *Tex., U.S.A.* 109 K6
Austin, L., *Australia* 89 E2
Austral Downs, *Australia* 90 C2
Austral Is. = Tubuai Is., *Pac. Oc.* 93 K12
Austral Seamount Chain, *Pac. Oc.* 93 K13
Australia ■, *Oceania* 92 K5
Australian Alps, *Australia* 91 F4
Australian Capital Territory □, *Australia* 91 F4
Austria ■, *Europe* 21 H4
Austvågøy, *Norway* 8 B13
Autazes, *Brazil* 121 D6
Autelbas, *Belgium* 17 J7
Auterive, *France* 26 E5
Authie →, *France* 25 B8
Authon-du-Perche, *France* 24 D7
Autlán, *Mexico* 114 D4
Autun, *France* 25 F11
Auvelais, *Belgium* 17 H5
Auvergne, *Australia* 88 C5
Auvergne, *France* 26 C7
Auvergne, Mts. d', *France* 26 C6
Auvézère →, *France* 26 C4
Auxerre, *France* 25 E10
Auxi-le-Château, *France* 25 B9
Auxonne, *France* 25 E12
Auzances, *France* 26 B6
Auzat-sur-Allier, *France* 26 C7
Avallon, *France* 25 E10
Avalon, *U.S.A.* 113 M8
Avalon Pen., *Canada* 99 C9
Avaré, *Brazil* 127 A6
Ávas, *Greece* 39 J8
Avawatz Mts., *U.S.A.* 113 K10
Aveiro, *Brazil* 121 D6
Aveiro, *Portugal* 30 E2
Aveiro □, *Portugal* 30 E2
Āvej, *Iran* 65 C6
Avelgem, *Belgium* 17 G2
Avellaneda, *Argentina* 126 C4
Avellino, *Italy* 35 B7
Avenal, *U.S.A.* 112 K6
Avenches, *Switz.* 22 C4
Averøya, *Norway* 10 A1
Aversa, *Italy* 35 B7
Avery, *U.S.A.* 110 C6
Aves, I. de, *W. Indies* 117 C7
Aves, Is. de, *Venezuela* 117 D6
Avesnes-sur-Helpe, *France* 25 B10
Avesta, *Sweden* 9 F14
Aveyron □, *France* 26 D6
Aveyron →, *France* 26 D5
Avezzano, *Italy* 33 F10
Aviá Terai, *Argentina* 126 B3
Aviano, *Italy* 33 B9
Avigliana, *Italy* 32 C4
Avigliano, *Italy* 35 B8
Avignon, *France* 27 E8
Ávila, *Spain* 30 E6
Ávila □, *Spain* 30 E6
Ávila, Sierra de, *Spain* 30 E5
Avila Beach, *U.S.A.* 113 K6
Avilés, *Spain* 30 B5
Avisio →, *Italy* 33 B8
Aviz, *Portugal* 31 F3
Avize, *France* 25 D11
Avoca, *Ireland* 15 D5
Avoca, *U.S.A.* 106 D7
Avoca →, *Australia* 91 F3
Avola, *Canada* 100 C5
Avola, *Italy* 35 F8
Avon, *N.Y., U.S.A.* 106 D7
Avon, *S. Dak., U.S.A.* 108 D5
Avon □, *U.K.* 13 F5
Avon →, *Australia* 89 F2
Avon →, *Avon, U.K.* 13 F5
Avon →, *Hants., U.K.* 13 G6
Avon →, *Warks., U.K.* 13 F5
Avondale, *Zimbabwe* 83 F3
Avonlea, *Canada* 101 D7
Avonmore, *Canada* 107 A10
Avonmouth, *U.K.* 13 F5
Avranches, *France* 24 D5
Avre →, *France* 24 D8
Awag el Baqar, *Sudan* 77 E3
A'waj →, *Syria* 69 B5
Awaji-Shima, *Japan* 49 G7
'Awālī, *Bahrain* 65 E6
Awantipur, *India* 63 C6
Awasa, L., *Ethiopia* 77 F4
Awash, *Ethiopia* 68 F3
Awash →, *Ethiopia* 77 E5
Awaso, *Ghana* 78 D4
Awatere →, *N.Z.* 87 J5
Awbārī, *Libya* 75 C7
Awbārī □, *Libya* 75 C7
Awe, L., *U.K.* 14 E3
Aweil, *Sudan* 77 F2
Awgu, *Nigeria* 79 D6
Awjilah, *Libya* 73 C9
Ax-les-Thermes, *France* 26 F5
Axarfjörður, *Iceland* 8 C5
Axel, *Neths.* 17 F3
Axel Heiberg I., *Canada* 4 B3
Axim, *Ghana* 78 E4
Axinim, *Brazil* 121 D6
Axintele, *Romania* 38 E9
Axioma, *Brazil* 125 B5
Axiós →, *Greece* 39 J5
Axminster, *U.K.* 13 G4
Axvall, *Sweden* 11 F7
Aÿ, *France* 25 C11
Ayabaca, *Peru* 124 A2
Ayabe, *Japan* 49 G7
Ayacucho, *Argentina* 126 D4
Ayacucho, *Peru* 124 C3
Ayaguz, *Kazakhstan* 44 E9
Ayamonte, *Spain* 31 H3
Ayan, *Russia* 45 D14
Ayancık, *Turkey* 42 F6
Ayapel, *Colombia* 120 B2
Ayas, *Turkey* 42 F5
Ayaviri, *Peru* 124 C3
Aybastı, *Turkey* 66 C7
Aydın, *Turkey* 66 E2
Aydin □, *Turkey* 66 E2
Aye, *Belgium* 17 H6
Ayenngré, *Togo* 79 D5
Ayer's Cliff, *Canada* 107 A12
Ayers Rock, *Australia* 89 E5
Ayiá, *Greece* 39 K5
Ayía Aikateríni, Ákra, *Greece* 37 A3
Ayia Dhéka, *Greece* 37 D6
Ayia Gálini, *Greece* 37 D6
Ayía Marína, *Greece* 39 M9
Ayia Napa, *Cyprus* 37 E13
Ayía Paraskeví, *Greece* 39 K9
Áyia Phyla, *Cyprus* 37 E12
Ayía Rouméli, *Greece* 39 P6
Ayia Varvára, *Greece* 37 D7
Áyios Amvrósios, *Cyprus* 37 D12
Áyios Andréas, *Greece* 39 M5
Ayíos Evstrátios, *Greece* 39 K7
Áyios Ioánnis, Ákra, *Greece* 37 D7
Áyios Isidhoros, *Greece* 37 C9
Áyios Kiríkos, *Greece* 39 M9
Áyios Matthaíos, *Greece* 37 B3
Áyios Mírono, *Greece* 39 P8
Áyios Nikólaos, *Greece* 37 D7
Áyios Seryios, *Cyprus* 37 D12
Ayios Theodhoros, *Cyprus* 37 D13
Aykathonisi, *Greece* 39 M9
Aylesbury, *U.K.* 13 F7
Aylmer, *Canada* 106 D4
Aylmer, L., *Canada* 96 B8
Ayna, *Spain* 29 G2
Ayolas, *Paraguay* 126 B4
Ayom, *Sudan* 77 F2
Ayon, Ostrov, *Russia* 45 C17
Ayora, *Spain* 29 F3
Ayr, *Australia* 90 B4
Ayr, *U.K.* 14 F4
Ayr →, *U.K.* 14 F4
Ayrancı, *Turkey* 66 E5
Ayre, Pt. of, *U.K.* 12 C3
Aysha, *Ethiopia* 77 E5
Aytos, *Bulgaria* 38 G10
Ayu, Kepulauan, *Indonesia* 57 D8
Ayutla, *Guatemala* 116 D1
Ayutla, *Mexico* 115 D5
Ayvacık, *Turkey* 66 C7
Ayvalık, *Turkey* 66 D2
Aywaille, *Belgium* 17 H7
Az Zabdānī, *Syria* 69 B5
Aẓ Ẓāhirīyah, *Jordan* 69 D3
Aẓ Ẓahrān, *Si. Arabia* 65 E6
Az Zarqā, *Jordan* 69 C5
Az Zāwiyah, *Libya* 75 B7
Az Zībār, *Iraq* 64 B5
Az-Zilfī, *Si. Arabia* 64 E5
Az Zubayr, *Iraq* 64 D5
Azambuja, *Portugal* 31 F2
Azamgarh, *India* 63 F10
Azangaro, *Peru* 124 C3
Azaouak, Vallée de l', *Mali* 79 B5
Āzār Shahr, *Iran* 64 B5
Āzarbāyjān-e Gharbī □, *Iran* 64 B5
Āzarbāyjān-e Sharqī □, *Iran* 64 B5
Azare, *Nigeria* 79 C7
Azay-le-Rideau, *France* 24 E7
A'zāz, *Syria* 64 B3
Azazga, *Algeria* 75 A5
Azbine = Aïr, *Niger* 79 B6
Azefal, *Mauritania* 74 D2
Azeffoun, *Algeria* 75 A5
Azemmour, *Morocco* 74 B3
Azerbaijan ■, *Asia* 43 F12
Azezo, *Ethiopia* 77 E4
Azimganj, *India* 63 G13
Aznalcóllar, *Spain* 31 H4
Azogues, *Ecuador* 120 D2
Azores, *Atl. Oc.* 2 C8
Azov, *Russia* 43 C8
Azov Sea = Azovskoye More, *Europe* 42 C7
Azovskoye More, *Europe* 42 C7

Azovy, *Russia* 44 C7
Azpeitia, *Spain* 28 B2
Azrou, *Morocco* 74 B3
Aztec, *U.S.A.* 111 H10
Azúa, *Dom. Rep.* 117 C5
Azuaga, *Spain* 31 G5
Azuara, *Spain* 28 D4
Azuay □, *Ecuador* 120 D2
Azuer →, *Spain* 31 F7
Azuero, Pen. de, *Panama* 116 E3
Azul, *Argentina* 126 D4
Azul, Serra, *Brazil* 125 C7
Azurduy, *Bolivia* 125 D5
Azusa, *U.S.A.* 113 L9
Azzaba, *Algeria* 75 A6
Azzano Décimo, *Italy* 33 C9
'Azzūn, *Jordan* 69 C4

B

Ba Don, *Vietnam* 58 D6
Ba Dong, *Vietnam* 59 H6
Ba Ngoi = Cam Lam, *Vietnam* 59 G7
Ba Ria, *Vietnam* 59 G6
Ba Tri, *Vietnam* 59 G6
Ba Xian, *China* 50 E9
Baa, *Indonesia* 57 F6
Baamonde, *Spain* 30 B3
Baar, *Switz.* 23 B7
Baarle Nassau, *Belgium* 17 F5
Baarlo, *Neths.* 17 F8
Baarn, *Neths.* 16 D6
Bab el Mandeb, *Red Sea* 68 E3
Baba Burnu, *Turkey* 66 D2
Baba dag, *Azerbaijan* 43 F13
Bābā Kalū, *Iran* 65 D6
Babaçulândia, *Brazil* 122 C2
Babadag, *Romania* 38 E11
Babaeski, *Turkey* 66 C2
Babahoyo, *Ecuador* 120 D2
Babakin, *Australia* 89 F2
Babana, *Nigeria* 79 C5
Babar, *Algeria* 75 A6
Babar, *Indonesia* 57 F7
Babar, *Pakistan* 62 D3
Babarkach, *Pakistan* 62 E2
Babayevo, *Russia* 41 B9
Babb, *U.S.A.* 110 B7
Babenhausen, *Germany* 19 F4
Babi Besar, P., *Malaysia* 59 L4
Babian Jiang →, *China* 52 F3
Babile, *Ethiopia* 77 F5
Babinda, *Australia* 90 B4
Babine, *Canada* 100 B3
Babine →, *Canada* 100 B3
Babine L., *Canada* 100 C3
Babo, *Indonesia* 57 E8
Bābol, *Iran* 65 B7
Bābol Sar, *Iran* 65 B7
Baboua, *C.A.R.* 80 C2
Babura, *Nigeria* 79 C6
Babusar Pass, *Pakistan* 63 B5
Babušnica, *Serbia, Yug.* 21 M12
Babuyan Chan., *Phil.* 55 B4
Babuyan Is., *Phil.* 55 B4
Babylon, *Iraq* 64 C5
Bac Can, *Vietnam* 58 A5
Bac Giang, *Vietnam* 58 B6
Bac Ninh, *Vietnam* 58 B6
Bac Phan, *Vietnam* 58 B5
Bac Quang, *Vietnam* 58 A5
Bacabal, *Brazil* 122 B3
Bacajá →, *Brazil* 121 D7
Bacalar, *Mexico* 115 D7
Bacan, *Indonesia* 57 F7
Bacan, Kepulauan, *Indonesia* 57 E7
Bacan, Pulau, *Indonesia* 57 E7
Bacarra, *Phil.* 55 B4
Bacău, *Romania* 38 C9
Baccarat, *France* 25 D13
Bacerac, *Mexico* 114 A3
Băceşti, *Romania* 38 C10
Bach Long Vi, Dao, *Vietnam* 58 B6
Bachaquero, *Venezuela* 120 B3
Bacharach, *Germany* 19 E3
Bachelina, *Russia* 44 D7
Bachuma, *Ethiopia* 77 F4
Bačina, *Serbia, Yug.* 21 M11
Back →, *Canada* 96 B9
Bačka Palanka, *Serbia, Yug.* 21 K9
Bačka Topola, *Serbia, Yug.* 21 K9
Bäckefors, *Sweden* 11 F6
Backnang, *Germany* 19 G5
Backstairs Passage, *Australia* 91 F2
Baco, Mt., *Phil.* 55 E4
Bacolod, *Phil.* 55 F5
Bacqueville-en-Caux, *France* 24 C8
Bácsalmás, *Hungary* 21 J9
Bacuag, *Phil.* 55 G6
Bacuk, *Malaysia* 59 J4
Bād, *Iran* 65 C7
Bad →, *U.S.A.* 108 C4
Bad Axe, *U.S.A.* 106 C2
Bad Bergzabern, *Germany* 19 F4
Bad Berleburg, *Germany* 18 D4
Bad Bevensen, *Germany* 18 B6
Bad Bramstedt, *Germany* 18 B5
Bad Brückenau, *Germany* 19 E5
Bad Doberan, *Germany* 18 A7
Bad Driburg, *Germany* 18 D5
Bad Ems, *Germany* 19 E3
Bad Frankenhausen, *Germany* 18 D7
Bad Freienwalde, *Germany* 18 C10
Bad Godesberg, *Germany* 18 E3
Bad Hersfeld, *Germany* 18 E5
Bad Hofgastein, *Austria* 21 H3
Bad Homburg, *Germany* 19 E4
Bad Honnef, *Germany* 18 E3
Bad Ischl, *Austria* 21 H3
Bad Kissingen, *Germany* 19 E6
Bad Königshofen, *Germany* 19 E6
Bad Kreuznach, *Germany* 19 F3
Bad Laasphe, *Germany* 18 E4
Bad Lands, *U.S.A.* 108 D3
Bad Langensalza, *Germany* 18 D6
Bad Lauterberg, *Germany* 18 D6
Bad Lippspringe, *Germany* 18 D4
Bad Mergentheim, *Germany* 19 F5
Bad Münstereifel, *Germany* 18 E2
Bad Muskau, *Germany* 18 D10
Bad Nauheim, *Germany* 19 E4
Bad Oeynhausen, *Germany* 18 C4
Bad Oldesloe, *Germany* 18 B6
Bad Orb, *Germany* 19 E5
Bad Pyrmont, *Germany* 18 D5
Bad Ragaz, *Switz.* 23 B9
Bad Reichenhall, *Germany* 19 H8
Bad Säckingen, *Germany* 19 H3
Bad Salzuflen, *Germany* 18 C4
Bad Segeberg, *Germany* 18 B6
Bad Tölz, *Germany* 19 H7
Bad Urach, *Germany* 19 G5
Bad Waldsee, *Germany* 19 H5
Bad Wildungen, *Germany* 18 D5
Bad Wimpfen, *Germany* 19 F5
Bad Windsheim, *Germany* 19 F6
Badagara, *India* 60 P9
Badagri, *Nigeria* 79 D5
Badajós, L., *Brazil* 121 D5
Badajoz, *Spain* 31 G4
Badajoz □, *Spain* 31 G4
Badalona, *Spain* 28 D7
Badalzai, *Afghan.* 62 E1
Badampahar, *India* 61 H15
Badanah, *Si. Arabia* 64 D4
Badarinath, *India* 63 D8
Badas, *Brunei* 56 D4
Badas, Kepulauan, *Indonesia* 56 D3
Baddo →, *Pakistan* 60 F4
Bade, *Indonesia* 57 F9
Baden, *Austria* 21 G6
Baden, *Switz.* 23 B6
Baden-Baden, *Germany* 19 G4
Baden-Württemberg □, *Germany* 19 G5
Badenoch, *U.K.* 14 E4
Badger, *Canada* 99 C8
Badger, *U.S.A.* 112 J7
Bādghīsāt □, *Afghan.* 60 B3
Badgom, *India* 63 B6
Badhoevedorp, *Neths.* 16 D5
Badia Polèsine, *Italy* 33 C8
Badin, *Pakistan* 62 G3
Badogo, *Mali* 78 C3
Badong, *China* 53 B8
Baduen, *Somali Rep.* 68 F4
Badulla, *Sri Lanka* 60 R12
Baena, *Spain* 31 H6
Baexem, *Neths.* 17 F7
Baeza, *Ecuador* 120 D2
Baeza, *Spain* 29 H1
Bafa Gölü, *Turkey* 66 E2
Bafang, *Cameroon* 79 D7
Bafatá, *Guinea-Biss.* 78 C2
Baffin B., *Canada* 4 B4
Baffin I., *Canada* 97 B12
Bafia, *Cameroon* 79 E7
Bafilo, *Togo* 79 D5
Bafing →, *Mali* 78 C2
Bafliyūn, *Syria* 64 B3
Baflo, *Neths.* 16 B9
Bafoulabé, *Mali* 78 C2
Bafoussam, *Cameroon* 79 D7
Bāfq, *Iran* 65 D7
Bafra, *Turkey* 42 F6
Bafra Burnu, *Turkey* 42 F6
Bāft, *Iran* 65 D8
Bafut, *Cameroon* 79 D7
Bafwasende, *Zaïre* 82 B2
Bagamoyo, *Tanzania* 82 D4
Bagamoyo □, *Tanzania* 82 D4
Bagan Datoh, *Malaysia* 59 L3
Bagan Serai, *Malaysia* 59 K3
Baganga, *Phil.* 55 H7
Bagani, *Namibia* 84 B3
Bagansiapiapi, *Indonesia* 56 D2
Bagasra, *India* 62 J4
Bagawi, *Sudan* 77 E3
Bagdad, *U.S.A.* 113 L11
Bagdarin, *Russia* 45 D12
Bagé, *Brazil* 127 C5
Bagenalstown = Muine Bheag, *Ireland* 15 D5
Baggs, *U.S.A.* 110 F10
Bagh, *Pakistan* 63 C5
Baghdād, *Iraq* 64 C5
Bagheria, *Italy* 34 D6
Baghlān, *Afghan.* 60 A6
Bagley, *U.S.A.* 108 B7
Bagnacavallo, *Italy* 33 D8
Bagnara Cálabra, *Italy* 35 D8
Bagnères-de-Bigorre, *France* 26 E4
Bagnères-de-Luchon, *France* 26 F4
Bagni di Lucca, *Italy* 32 D7
Bagno di Romagna, *Italy* 33 E8
Bagnoles-de-l'Orne, *France* 24 D6
Bagnoli di Sopra, *Italy* 33 C8
Bagnolo Mella, *Italy* 32 C7
Bagnols-sur-Cèze, *France* 27 D8
Bagnorégio, *Italy* 33 F9
Bagolino, *Italy* 32 C7
Bagotville, *Canada* 99 C5
Bagua, *Peru* 124 B2
Baguio, *Phil.* 55 C4
Bahabón de Esgueva, *Spain* 28 D1
Bahadurgarh, *India* 62 E7
Bahama, Canal Viejo de, *W. Indies* 116 B4
Bahamas ■, *N. Amer.* 117 B5
Baharampur, *India* 63 G13
Baharîya, El Wâhât al, *Egypt* 76 J6
Bahau, *Malaysia* 59 L4
Bahawalnagar, *Pakistan* 62 D5
Bahawalpur, *Pakistan* 62 E4
Bahçe, *Turkey* 66 E7
Baheri, *India* 63 E8
Bahi, *Tanzania* 82 D4
Bahi Swamp, *Tanzania* 82 D4
Bahía = Salvador, *Brazil* 123 D4
Bahía □, *Brazil* 123 D3
Bahía, Is. de la, *Honduras* 116 C2
Bahía Blanca, *Argentina* 126 D3
Bahía de Caráquez, *Ecuador* 120 D1
Bahía Honda, *Cuba* 116 B3
Bahía Laura, *Argentina* 128 C3
Bahía Negra, *Paraguay* 125 E6
Bahir Dar, *Ethiopia* 77 E4
Bahmanzād, *Iran* 65 D6
Bahmer, *Algeria* 75 C4
Bahönye, *Hungary* 21 J7
Bahr Aouk →, *C.A.R.* 80 C3
Bahr el Ahmar □, *Sudan* 76 C3
Bahr el Ghazâl □, *Sudan* 77 F2
Bahr Salamat →, *Chad* 73 G8
Bahr Yûsef →, *Egypt* 76 J7
Bahra el Burullus, *Egypt* 76 H7
Bahraich, *India* 63 F9
Bahrain ■, *Asia* 65 E6
Bahret Assad, *Syria* 64 C3
Bahror, *India* 62 F7
Bāhū Kalāt, *Iran* 65 E9
Bai, *Mali* 78 C4
Bai Bung, Mui, *Vietnam* 59 H5
Bai Duc, *Vietnam* 58 C5
Bai Thuong, *Vietnam* 58 C5
Baia Mare, *Romania* 38 B6
Baia-Sprie, *Romania* 38 B6
Baião, *Brazil* 122 B2
Baïbokoum, *Chad* 73 G8
Baicheng, *China* 51 B12
Baidoa, *Somali Rep.* 68 G3
Baie Comeau, *Canada* 99 C6
Baie-St-Paul, *Canada* 99 C5
Baie Trinité, *Canada* 99 C6
Baie Verte, *Canada* 99 C8
Baignes-Ste.-Radegonde, *France* 26 C3
Baigneux-les-Juifs, *France* 25 E11
Baihe, *China* 50 H6
Baihe, *Taiwan* 53 F13
Ba'ījī, *Iraq* 64 C4
Baikal, L. = Baykal, Oz., *Russia* 45 D11
Baile Atha Cliath = Dublin, *Ireland* 15 C5
Bailei, *Ethiopia* 77 F5
Bailén, *Spain* 31 G7
Băileşti, *Romania* 38 E6
Baileux, *Belgium* 17 H4
Bailique, Ilha, *Brazil* 122 A2
Bailleul, *France* 25 B9
Bailundo, *Angola* 81 G3
Baima, *China* 52 A3
Bain-de-Bretagne, *France* 24 E5
Bainbridge, *Ga., U.S.A.* 105 K3
Bainbridge, *N.Y., U.S.A.* 107 D9
Baing, *Indonesia* 57 F6
Bainiu, *China* 50 H7
Bainville, *U.S.A.* 108 A2
Bā'ir, *Jordan* 69 E5
Baird, *U.S.A.* 109 J5
Baird Mts., *U.S.A.* 96 B3
Bairin Youqi, *China* 51 C10
Bairin Zuoqi, *China* 51 C10
Bairnsdale, *Australia* 91 F4
Bais, *Phil.* 55 G5
Baisha, *China* 50 G7
Baïsole →, *France* 26 E4
Baissa, *Nigeria* 79 D7
Baitadi, *Nepal* 63 E9
Baixa Grande, *Brazil* 123 D3
Baiyin, *China* 50 F3
Baiyü, *China* 52 B2
Baiyu Shan, *China* 50 F4
Baiyuda, *Sudan* 76 D3
Baj Baj, *India* 63 H13
Baja, *Hungary* 21 J8
Baja, Pta., *Mexico* 114 B1
Baja California, *Mexico* 114 A1
Bajamar, *Canary Is.* 36 F3
Bajana, *India* 62 H4
Bājgīrān, *Iran* 65 B8
Bajimba, Mt., *Australia* 91 D5
Bajo Nuevo, *Caribbean* 116 C4
Bajoga, *Nigeria* 79 C7
Bajool, *Australia* 90 C5
Bakala, *C.A.R.* 73 G9
Bakar, *Croatia* 33 C11
Bakchar, *Russia* 44 D9
Bakel, *Neths.* 17 E7
Bakel, *Senegal* 78 C2
Baker, *Calif., U.S.A.* 113 K10
Baker, *Mont., U.S.A.* 108 B2
Baker, *Oreg., U.S.A.* 110 D5
Baker, Canal, *Chile* 128 C2
Baker, L., *Canada* 96 B10
Baker I., *Pac. Oc.* 92 G10
Baker L., *Australia* 89 E4
Baker Lake, *Canada* 96 B10
Baker Mt., *U.S.A.* 110 B3
Bakers Creek, *Australia* 90 C4
Baker's Dozen Is., *Canada* 98 A4
Bakersfield, *Calif., U.S.A.* 113 K7
Bakersfield, *Vt., U.S.A.* 107 B12
Bakhchisaray, *Ukraine* 42 D5
Bakhmach, *Ukraine* 40 F8
Bākhtarān, *Iran* 64 C5
Bakhtārān □, *Iran* 64 C5
Bakırdağı, *Turkey* 66 D6
Bakırköy, *Turkey* 39 H11
Bakkafjörður, *Iceland* 8 C6
Bakkagerði, *Iceland* 8 D7
Bakony →, *Hungary* 21 H7
Bakony Forest = Bakony Hegyseg, *Hungary* 21 H7
Bakony Hegyseg, *Hungary* 21 H7
Bakori, *Nigeria* 79 C6
Bakouma, *C.A.R.* 73 G9
Baku, *Azerbaijan* 43 F13
Bakutis Coast, *Antarctica* 5 D15
Bala, *Canada* 106 A5
Bâlâ, *Turkey* 66 D5
Bala, L., *U.K.* 12 E4
Balabac I., *Phil.* 55 H2
Balabac Str., *E. Indies* 56 C5
Balabagh, *Afghan.* 62 B4
Balabakk, *Lebanon* 69 A5
Balabalangan, Kepulauan, *Indonesia* 56 E5
Bălăciţa, *Romania* 38 E6
Balad, *Iraq* 64 C5
Balad Rūz, *Iraq* 64 C5
Bālādeh, *Fārs, Iran* 65 D6
Balādeh, *Māzandaran, Iran* 65 B6
Balaghat, *India* 60 J12
Balaghat Ra., *India* 60 K10
Balaguer, *Spain* 28 D5
Balakhna, *Russia* 41 C13
Balaklava, *Australia* 91 E2
Balaklava, *Ukraine* 42 D5
Balakleya, *Ukraine* 42 B7
Balakovo, *Russia* 41 E15
Balancán, *Mexico* 115 D6
Balanda, *Russia* 41 F14
Balashikha, *Russia* 41 D10
Balashov, *Russia* 41 F13
Balasinor, *India* 62 H5
Balasore = Baleshwar, *India* 61 J15
Balassagyarmat, *Hungary* 21 G9
Balât, *Egypt* 76 B2
Balaton, *Hungary* 21 J7
Balayan, *Phil.* 55 E4
Balazote, *Spain* 29 G2
Balboa, *Panama* 116 E4
Balbriggan, *Ireland* 15 C5
Balcarce, *Argentina* 126 D4
Balcarres, *Canada* 101 C8
Balchik, *Bulgaria* 38 F11
Balclutha, *N.Z.* 87 M2
Bald Hd., *Australia* 89 G2
Bald I., *Australia* 89 F2
Bald Knob, *U.S.A.* 109 H9
Baldock L., *Canada* 101 B9
Baldwin, *Fla., U.S.A.* 105 K4
Baldwin, *Mich., U.S.A.* 104 D3
Baldwinsville, *U.S.A.* 107 C8
Baldy Peak, *U.S.A.* 111 K9
Bale, *Croatia* 33 C10
Bale □, *Ethiopia* 77 F5
Baleares □, *Spain* 28 F7
Baleares, Is., *Spain* 36 B10
Balearic Is. = Baleares, Is., *Spain* 36 B10
Baleia, Pta. da, *Brazil* 123 E4
Balen, *Belgium* 17 F6
Baler, *Phil.* 55 D4
Baler Bay, *Phil.* 55 D4
Balerna, *Switz.* 23 E8
Baleshwar, *India* 61 J15
Balfate, *Honduras* 116 C2
Balfe's Creek, *Australia* 90 C4
Balfour, *S. Africa* 85 D4
Bali, *Cameroon* 79 D6
Balí, *Greece* 37 D6
Bali, *Indonesia* 56 F5
Bali □, *Indonesia* 56 F5
Bali, Selat, *Indonesia* 57 H16
Baligród, *Poland* 20 F12
Balık Gölü, *Turkey* 67 D10
Balikeşir, *Turkey* 66 D2
Balikeşir □, *Turkey* 66 D2
Balikpapan, *Indonesia* 56 E5
Balimbing, *Phil.* 57 C5
Baling, *Malaysia* 59 K3
Balintang Channel, *Phil.* 55 B4
Balipara, *India* 61 F18
Baliza, *Brazil* 125 D7
Balk, *Neths.* 16 C7
Balkan Mts. = Stara Planina, *Bulgaria* 38 F6
Balkhash, *Kazakhstan* 44 E8
Balkhash, Ozero, *Kazakhstan* 44 E8
Balla, *Bangla.* 61 G17
Ballachulish, *U.K.* 14 E3
Balladonia, *Australia* 89 F3
Ballarat, *Australia* 91 F3
Ballard, L., *Australia* 89 E3
Ballater, *U.K.* 14 D5
Ballenas, Canal de, *Mexico* 114 B2
Balleny Is., *Antarctica* 5 C11
Ballesteros, *Phil.* 55 B4
Ballia, *India* 63 G11
Ballidu, *Australia* 89 F2
Ballina, *Australia* 91 D5
Ballina, *Mayo, Ireland* 15 B2
Ballina, *Tipp., Ireland* 15 D3
Ballinasloe, *Ireland* 15 C3
Ballinger, *U.S.A.* 109 K5
Ballinrobe, *Ireland* 15 C2
Ballinskelligs B., *Ireland* 15 E1
Ballon, *France* 24 D7
Ballycastle, *U.K.* 15 A5
Ballymena, *U.K.* 15 B5
Ballymena □, *U.K.* 15 B5
Ballymoney, *U.K.* 15 A5
Ballymoney □, *U.K.* 15 A5
Ballyshannon, *Ireland* 15 B3
Balmaceda, *Chile* 128 C2
Balmazújváros, *Hungary* 21 H11
Balmhorn, *Switz.* 22 D5
Balmoral, *Australia* 91 F3
Balmoral, *U.K.* 14 D5
Balmorhea, *U.S.A.* 109 K3
Balonne →, *Australia* 91 D4
Balrampur, *India* 63 F10
Balranald, *Australia* 91 E3
Balş, *Romania* 38 E7
Balsapuerto, *Peru* 124 B2
Balsas, *Mexico* 115 D5
Balsas →, *Goiás, Brazil* 122 C2
Balsas →, *Maranhão, Brazil* 122 C3
Balsas →, *Mexico* 114 D4
Bålsta, *Sweden* 10 E11
Balsthal, *Switz.* 22 B5
Balston Spa, *U.S.A.* 107 D11
Balta, *Romania* 38 E5
Balta, *Russia* 43 E11
Balta, *Ukraine* 42 B3
Balta, *U.S.A.* 108 A4
Baltanás, *Spain* 30 D6
Baltic Sea, *Europe* 9 H15
Baltîm, *Egypt* 76 H7
Baltimore, *Ireland* 15 E2
Baltimore, *U.S.A.* 104 F7
Baltit, *Pakistan* 63 A6
Baltrum, *Germany* 18 B3
Baluchistan □, *Pakistan* 60 F4
Balurghat, *India* 63 G13
Balya, *Turkey* 66 D2
Balygychan, *Russia* 45 C16
Balzar, *Ecuador* 120 D2
Bam, *Iran* 65 D8
Bama, *China* 52 E6
Bama, *Nigeria* 79 C7
Bamako, *Mali* 78 C3
Bamba, *Mali* 79 B4
Bambamarca, *Peru* 124 B2
Bambari, *C.A.R.* 73 G9
Bambaroo, *Australia* 90 B4
Bamberg, *Germany* 19 F6
Bamberg, *U.S.A.* 105 J5
Bambesi, *Ethiopia* 77 F3
Bambey, *Senegal* 78 C1
Bambili, *Zaïre* 82 B2
Bambuí, *Brazil* 123 F2
Bamenda, *Cameroon* 79 D7
Bamfield, *Canada* 100 D3
Bāmīān □, *Afghan.* 60 B5
Bamiancheng, *China* 51 C13
Bamkin, *Cameroon* 79 D7
Bampūr, *Iran* 65 E9
Ban Aranyaprathet, *Thailand* 58 F4
Ban Ban, *Laos* 58 C4
Ban Bang Hin, *Thailand* 59 H2
Ban Chiang Klang, *Thailand* 58 C3
Ban Chik, *Laos* 58 D4
Ban Choho, *Thailand* 58 E4
Ban Dan Lan Hoi, *Thailand* 58 D2
Ban Don = Surat Thani, *Thailand* 59 H2
Ban Don, *Vietnam* 58 F6
Ban Don, Ao, *Thailand* 59 H2
Ban Dong, *Thailand* 58 C3
Ban Hong, *Thailand* 58 C2
Ban Kaeng, *Thailand* 58 D3
Ban Keun, *Laos* 58 C4
Ban Khai, *Thailand* 58 F3
Ban Kheun, *Laos* 58 B3
Ban Khlong Kua, *Thailand* 59 J3
Ban Khuan Mao, *Thailand* 59 J2
Ban Khun Yuam, *Thailand* 58 C1
Ban Ko Yai Chim, *Thailand* 59 G2

Ban Kok, *Thailand* 58 D4
Ban Laem, *Thailand* 58 F2
Ban Lao Ngam, *Laos* 58 E6
Ban Le Kathe, *Thailand* .. 58 E2
Ban Mae Chedi, *Thailand* .. 58 C2
Ban Mae Laeng, *Thailand* .. 58 B2
Ban Mae Sariang, *Thailand* . 58 C1
Ban Mê Thuôt = Buon Me
   Thuot, *Vietnam* 58 F7
Ban Mi, *Thailand* 58 E3
Ban Muong Mo, *Laos* 58 C4
Ban Na Mo, *Laos* 58 D5
Ban Na San, *Thailand* 59 H2
Ban Na Tong, *Laos* 58 B3
Ban Nam Bac, *Laos* 58 B4
Ban Nam Ma, *Laos* 58 A3
Ban Ngang, *Laos* 58 E6
Ban Nong Bok, *Laos* 58 D5
Ban Nong Boua, *Laos* 58 E6
Ban Nong Pling, *Thailand* . 58 E3
Ban Pak Chan, *Thailand* .. 59 G2
Ban Phai, *Thailand* 58 D4
Ban Pong, *Thailand* 58 F2
Ban Ron Phibun, *Thailand* . 59 H2
Ban Sanam Chai, *Thailand* . 59 J3
Ban Sangkha, *Thailand* ... 58 E4
Ban Tak, *Thailand* 58 D2
Ban Tako, *Thailand* 58 E4
Ban Tha Dua, *Thailand* ... 58 D2
Ban Tha Li, *Thailand* 58 D3
Ban Tha Nun, *Thailand* ... 59 H2
Ban Thahine, *Laos* 58 E5
Ban Xien Kok, *Laos* 58 B3
Ban Yen Nhan, *Vietnam* .. 58 B6
Baña, Punta de la, *Spain* .. 28 E5
Banaba, *Kiribati* 92 H8
Bañalbufar, *Spain* 36 B9
Banalia, *Zaïre* 82 B2
Banam, *Cambodia* 59 G5
Banamba, *Mali* 78 C3
Banana, *Australia* 90 C5
Bananal, I. do, *Brazil* 123 D1
Banaras = Varanasi, *India* . 63 G10
Banas →, *Gujarat, India* . 62 H4
Banas →, *Mad. P., India* . 63 G9
Bânâs, Ras, *Egypt* 76 C4
Banaz, *Turkey* 66 D3
Banbān, *Si. Arabia* 64 E5
Banbridge, *U.K.* 15 B5
Banbridge □, *U.K.* 15 B5
Banbury, *U.K.* 13 E6
Banchory, *U.K.* 14 D6
Bancroft, *Canada* 98 C4
Band Boní, *Iran* 65 E8
Band Qīr, *Iran* 65 D6
Banda, *India* 63 G9
Banda, Kepulauan,
   Indonesia 57 E7
Banda Aceh, *Indonesia* ... 56 C1
Banda Elat, *Indonesia* 57 F8
Banda Is. = Banda,
   Kepulauan, *Indonesia* .. 57 E7
Banda Sea, *Indonesia* 57 F7
Bandai-San, *Japan* 48 F10
Bandama →, *Ivory C.* ... 78 D3
Bandān, *Iran* 65 D9
Bandanaira, *Indonesia* ... 57 E7
Bandanwara, *India* 62 F6
Bandar = Machilipatnam,
   India 61 L12
Bandār 'Abbās, *Iran* 65 E8
Bandar-e Anzalī, *Iran* 65 B6
Bandar-e Chārak, *Iran* ... 65 E7
Bandar-e Deylam, *Iran* ... 65 D6
Bandar-e Khomeyni, *Iran* . 65 D6
Bandar-e Lengeh, *Iran* ... 65 E7
Bandar-e Maqām, *Iran* ... 65 E7
Bandar-e Ma'shur, *Iran* .. 65 D6
Bandar-e Nakhīlū, *Iran* .. 65 E7
Bandar-e Rīg, *Iran* 65 D6
Bandar-e Torkeman, *Iran* . 65 B7
Bandar Maharani = Muar,
   Malaysia 59 L4
Bandar Penggaram = Batu
   Pahat, *Malaysia* 59 M4
Bandar Seri Begawan,
   Brunei 56 C4
Bandawe, *Malawi* 83 E3
Bande, *Belgium* 17 H6
Bande, *Spain* 30 C2
Bandeira, Pico da, *Brazil* . 123 F3
Bandeirante, *Brazil* 123 D1
Bandera, *Argentina* 126 B3
Bandera, *U.S.A.* 109 L5
Banderas, B. de, *Mexico* . 114 C3
Bandiagara, *Mali* 78 C4
Bandırma, *Turkey* 66 C3
Bandon, *Ireland* 15 E3
Bandon →, *Ireland* 15 E3
Bandula, *Mozam.* 83 F3
Bandundu, *Zaïre* 80 E3
Bandung, *Indonesia* 57 G12
Bandya, *Australia* 89 E3
Bāneh, *Iran* 64 C5
Bañeres, *Spain* 29 G4
Banes, *Cuba* 117 B4
Banff, *Canada* 100 C5
Banff, *U.K.* 14 D6
Banff Nat. Park, *Canada* . 100 C5
Banfora, *Burkina Faso* ... 78 C4
Bang Fai →, *Laos* 58 D5
Bang Hieng →, *Laos* 58 D5
Bang Krathum, *Thailand* .. 58 D3

Bang Lamung, *Thailand* .. 58 F3
Bang Mun Nak, *Thailand* . 58 D3
Bang Pa In, *Thailand* 58 E3
Bang Rakam, *Thailand* ... 58 D3
Bang Saphan, *Thailand* ... 59 G2
Bangala Dam, *Zimbabwe* . 83 G3
Bangalore, *India* 60 N10
Bangante, *Cameroon* 79 D7
Bangaon, *India* 63 H13
Bangassou, *C.A.R.* 80 D4
Banggai, Kepulauan,
   Indonesia 57 E6
Banggi, P., *Malaysia* 56 C5
Banghāzī, *Libya* 73 B9
Bangil, *Indonesia* 57 G15
Bangjang, *Sudan* 77 E3
Bangka, P., Sulawesi,
   Indonesia 57 D7
Bangka, P., Sumatera,
   Indonesia 56 E3
Bangka, Selat, *Indonesia* . 56 E3
Bangkalan, *Indonesia* 57 G15
Bangkinang, *Indonesia* ... 56 D2
Bangko, *Indonesia* 56 E2
Bangkok, *Thailand* 58 F3
Bangladesh ■, *Asia* 61 H17
Bangolo, *Ivory C.* 78 D3
Bangong Co, *India* 63 B8
Bangor, *Down, U.K.* 15 B6
Bangor, *Gwynedd, U.K.* .. 12 D3
Bangor, *Maine, U.S.A.* .. 99 D6
Bangor, *Pa., U.S.A.* 107 F9
Bangued, *Phil.* 55 C4
Bangui, *C.A.R.* 80 D3
Bangui, *Phil.* 55 B4
Banguru, *Zaïre* 82 B2
Bangweulu, L., *Zambia* .. 83 E3
Bangweulu Swamp, *Zambia* 83 E3
Bani, *Dom. Rep.* 117 C5
Bani →, *Mali* 78 C4
Bani, Djebel, *Morocco* ... 74 C3
Bani Bangou, *Niger* 79 B5
Banī Sa'd, *Iraq* 64 C5
Banī Walīd, *Libya* 73 B7
Bania, *Ivory C.* 78 D4
Banihal Pass, *India* 63 C6
Banīnah, *Libya* 73 B9
Bānīyās, *Syria* 64 C3
Banja Luka, *Bos.-H., Yug.* 21 L7
Banjar, *Indonesia* 57 G13
Banjarmasin, *Indonesia* .. 56 E4
Banjarnegara, *Indonesia* . 57 G13
Banjul, *Gambia* 78 C1
Banka Banka, *Australia* .. 90 B1
Banket, *Zimbabwe* 83 F3
Bankilaré, *Niger* 79 C5
Bankipore, *India* 63 G11
Banks I., *B.C., Canada* .. 100 C3
Banks I., *N.W.T., Canada* . 96 A7
Banks Pen., *N.Z.* 87 K4
Banks Str., *Australia* 90 G4
Bankura, *India* 63 H12
Bann →, *Down, U.K.* ... 15 B5
Bann →, *L'derry., U.K.* . 15 A5
Banna, *Phil.* 55 C4
Bannalec, *France* 24 E3
Bannang Sata, *Thailand* .. 59 J3
Banning, *U.S.A.* 113 M10
Banningville = Bandundu,
   Zaïre 80 E3
Bannockburn, *Canada* ... 106 B7
Bannockburn, *U.K.* 14 E5
Bannockburn, *Zimbabwe* . 83 G2
Bannu, *Pakistan* 60 C7
Bañolas, *Spain* 28 C7
Banon, *France* 27 D9
Baños de la Encina, *Spain* . 31 G7
Baños de Molgas, *Spain* .. 30 C3
Banská Bystrica, *Czech.* .. 20 G9
Banská Štiavnica, *Czech.* . 21 G8
Banswara, *India* 62 H6
Bantayan, *Phil.* 55 F5
Banten, *Indonesia* 57 G12
Bantry, *Ireland* 15 E2
Bantry B., *Ireland* 15 E2
Bantul, *Indonesia* 57 G14
Bantva, *India* 62 J4
Banu, *Afghan.* 60 B6
Banyak, Kepulauan,
   Indonesia 56 D1
Banyo, *Cameroon* 79 D7
Banyuls-sur-Mer, *France* . 26 F7
Banyumas, *Indonesia* 57 G13
Banyuwangi, *Indonesia* .. 57 H16
Banzare Coast, *Antarctica* 5 C9
Banzyville = Mobayi, *Zaïre* 80 D4
Bao Ha, *Vietnam* 58 A5
Bao Lac, *Vietnam* 58 A5
Bao Loc, *Vietnam* 59 G6
Bao'an, *China* 53 F10
Baocheng, *China* 50 H4
Baode, *China* 50 E6
Baodi, *China* 51 E9
Baoding, *China* 50 E8
Baoji, *China* 50 G4
Baojing, *China* 52 C7
Baokang, *China* 53 B8
Baoshan, *Shanghai, China* 53 B13
Baoshan, *Yunnan, China* . 52 E2
Baotou, *China* 50 D6
Baoying, *China* 51 H10
Bap, *India* 62 F5
Bapatla, *India* 61 M12
Bapaume, *France* 25 B9
Bāqerābād, *Iran* 65 C6

Ba'qūbah, *Iraq* 64 C5
Baquedano, *Chile* 126 A2
Bar, *Montenegro, Yug.* .. 21 N9
Bar, *Ukraine* 42 B2
Bar Bigha, *India* 63 G11
Bar Harbor, *U.S.A.* 99 D6
Bar-le-Duc, *France* 25 D12
Bar-sur-Aube, *France* 25 D11
Bar-sur-Seine, *France* 25 D11
Barabai, *Indonesia* 56 E5
Barabinsk, *Russia* 44 D8
Baraboo, *U.S.A.* 108 D10
Baracaldo, *Spain* 28 B2
Baracoa, *Cuba* 117 B5
Baradero, *Argentina* 126 C4
Baraga, *U.S.A.* 108 B10
Barahona, *Dom. Rep.* ... 117 C5
Barahona, *Spain* 28 D2
Barail Range, *India* 61 G18
Baraka →, *Sudan* 76 D4
Barakhola, *India* 61 G18
Barakot, *India* 63 J11
Barakpur, *India* 63 H13
Barakula, *Australia* 91 D5
Baralaba, *Australia* 90 C4
Baralzon L., *Canada* 101 B9
Barameiya, *Sudan* 76 D4
Baramula, *India* 63 B6
Baran, *India* 62 G7
Baranoa, *Colombia* 120 A3
Baranof I., *U.S.A.* 100 B1
Baranovichi, *Belorussia* .. 40 E5
Barão de Cocais, *Brazil* .. 123 E3
Barão de Grajaú, *Brazil* .. 122 C3
Barão de Melgaço,
   Mato Grosso, Brazil ... 125 D6
Barão de Melgaço,
   Rondônia, Brazil 125 C5
Baraolt, *Romania* 38 C8
Barapasi, *Indonesia* 57 E9
Barasat, *India* 63 H13
Barat Daya, Kepulauan,
   Indonesia 57 F7
Barataria B., *U.S.A.* 109 L10
Baraut, *India* 62 E7
Baraya, *Colombia* 120 C2
Barbacena, *Brazil* 123 F3
Barbacoas, *Colombia* 120 C2
Barbacoas, *Venezuela* ... 120 B4
Barbados ■, *W. Indies* .. 117 D8
Barbalha, *Brazil* 122 C4
Barban, *Croatia* 33 C11
Barbastro, *Spain* 28 C5
Barbate, *Spain* 31 J5
Barberino di Mugello, *Italy* 33 D8
Barberton, *S. Africa* 85 D5
Barberton, *U.S.A.* 106 E3
Barbezieux, *France* 26 C3
Barbosa, *Colombia* 120 B3
Barbourville, *U.S.A.* 105 G4
Barbuda, *W. Indies* 117 C7
Barcaldine, *Australia* 90 C4
Barcarrota, *Spain* 31 G4
Barcellona Pozzo di Gotto,
   Italy 35 D8
Barcelona, *Spain* 28 D7
Barcelona, *Venezuela* 121 A5
Barcelona □, *Spain* 28 D7
Barcelonette, *France* 27 D10
Barcelos, *Brazil* 121 D5
Barcoo →, *Australia* 90 D3
Barcs, *Hungary* 21 K7
Barda, *Azerbaijan* 43 F12
Barda del Medio, *Argentina* 128 A3
Bardai, *Chad* 73 D8
Bardas Blancas, *Argentina* 126 D2
Barddhaman, *India* 63 H12
Bardejov, *Czech.* 20 F11
Bardera, *Somali Rep.* 68 G3
Bardi, *Italy* 32 D6
Bardia, *Libya* 73 B9
Bardolino, *Italy* 32 C7
Bardsey I., *U.K.* 12 E3
Bardstown, *U.S.A.* 104 G3
Bareilly, *India* 63 E8
Barentin, *France* 24 C7
Barenton, *France* 24 D6
Barents Sea, *Arctic* 4 B9
Barentu, *Ethiopia* 77 D4
Barfleur, *France* 24 C5
Barfleur, Pte. de, *France* . 24 C5
Barga, *China* 54 C3
Barga, *Italy* 32 D7
Bargal, *Somali Rep.* 68 E5
Bargara, *Australia* 90 C5
Barge, *Italy* 32 D4
Bargnop, *Sudan* 77 F2
Bargteheide, *Germany* ... 18 B6
Barguzin, *Russia* 45 D11
Barh, *India* 63 G11
Barhaj, *India* 63 F10
Barhi, *India* 63 G11
Bari, *India* 62 F7
Bari, *Italy* 35 A9
Bari Doab, *Pakistan* 62 D5
Bariadi □, *Tanzania* 82 C3
Barīm, *Yemen* 68 E3
Barima →, *Guyana* 121 B5
Barinas, *Venezuela* 120 B3
Barinas □, *Venezuela* 120 B4
Baring, C., *Canada* 96 B8
Baringo, *Kenya* 82 B4
Baringo □, *Kenya* 82 B4
Baringo, L., *Kenya* 82 B4
Barinitas, *Venezuela* 120 B3

Bariri, *Brazil* 123 F2
Bârîs, *Egypt* 76 C3
Barisal, *Bangla.* 61 H17
Barisan, Bukit, *Indonesia* . 56 E2
Barito →, *Indonesia* 56 E4
Barjac, *France* 27 D8
Barjols, *France* 27 E10
Barjūj, Wadi →, *Libya* .. 75 C7
Bark L., *Canada* 106 A7
Barka = Baraka →, *Sudan* 76 D4
Barkam, *China* 52 B4
Barker, *U.S.A.* 106 C6
Barkley Sound, *Canada* .. 100 D3
Barkly Downs, *Australia* . 90 C2
Barkly East, *S. Africa* 84 E4
Barkly Tableland, *Australia* 90 B2
Barkly West, *S. Africa* ... 84 D3
Barksdale, *U.S.A.* 109 L4
Barlee, L., *Australia* 89 E2
Barlee, Mt., *Australia* 89 D4
Barletta, *Italy* 35 A9
Barlinek, *Poland* 20 C5
Barlovento, *Canary Is.* .. 36 F2
Barlow L., *Canada* 101 A8
Barmedman, *Australia* ... 91 E4
Barmer, *India* 62 G4
Barmera, *Australia* 91 E3
Barmouth, *U.K.* 12 E3
Barmstedt, *Germany* 18 B5
Barnagar, *India* 62 H6
Barnard Castle, *U.K.* 12 C6
Barnato, *Australia* 91 E3
Barnaul, *Russia* 44 D9
Barnesville, *U.S.A.* 105 J3
Barnet, *U.K.* 13 F7
Barneveld, *Neths.* 16 D7
Barneveld, *U.S.A.* 107 C9
Barneville-Cartevert,
   France 24 C5
Barngo, *Australia* 90 D4
Barnhart, *U.S.A.* 109 K4
Barnsley, *U.K.* 12 D6
Barnstaple, *U.K.* 13 F3
Barnsville, *U.S.A.* 108 B6
Baro, *Nigeria* 79 D6
Baro →, *Ethiopia* 77 F3
Baroda = Vadodara, *India* 62 H5
Baroda, *India* 62 G7
Baroe, *S. Africa* 84 E3
Baron Ra., *Australia* 88 D4
Barpeta, *India* 61 F17
Barques, Pte. aux, *U.S.A.* 104 C4
Barquinha, *Portugal* 31 F2
Barquísimeto, *Venezuela* . 120 A4
Barr, *France* 25 D14
Barra, *Brazil* 122 D3
Barra, *U.K.* 14 E1
Barra, Sd. of, *U.K.* 14 D1
Barra da Estiva, *Brazil* ... 123 D3
Barra de Navidad, *Mexico* 114 D4
Barra do Corda, *Brazil* ... 122 C2
Barra do Mendes, *Brazil* . 123 D3
Barra do Piraí, *Brazil* 123 F3
Barra Falsa, Pta. da,
   Mozam. 85 C6
Barra Hd., *U.K.* 14 E1
Barra Mansa, *Brazil* 123 F3
Barraba, *Australia* 91 E5
Barração do Barreto, *Brazil* 125 B6
Barrackpur = Barakpur,
   India 63 H13
Barrafranca, *Italy* 35 E7
Barranca, *Lima, Peru* 124 C2
Barranca, *Loreto, Peru* ... 120 D2
Barrancabermeja, *Colombia* 120 B3
Barrancas, *Colombia* 120 A3
Barrancas, *Venezuela* 121 B5
Barrancos, *Portugal* 31 G4
Barranqueras, *Argentina* . 126 B4
Barranquilla, *Colombia* ... 120 A3
Barras, *Brazil* 122 B3
Barras, *Colombia* 120 D3
Barraute, *Canada* 98 C4
Barre, *Mass., U.S.A.* 107 D12
Barre, *Vt., U.S.A.* 107 B12
Barre de Bugres, *Brazil* .. 125 C6
Barreal, *Argentina* 126 C2
Barreiras, *Brazil* 123 D3
Barreirinha, *Brazil* 121 D6
Barreirinhas, *Brazil* 122 B3
Barreiro, *Portugal* 31 G1
Barreiros, *Brazil* 122 C4
Barrême, *France* 27 E10
Barren, Nosy, *Madag.* ... 85 B7
Barretos, *Brazil* 123 F2
Barrhead, *Canada* 100 C6
Barrie, *Canada* 98 D4
Barrier Ra., *Australia* 91 E3
Barrière, *Canada* 100 C4
Barrington, *U.S.A.* 107 E13
Barrington L., *Canada* ... 101 B8
Barrington Tops, *Australia* 91 E5
Barringun, *Australia* 91 D4
Barro do Garças, *Brazil* .. 125 D7
Barrow, *U.S.A.* 96 A4
Barrow →, *Ireland* 15 D4
Barrow, C., *U.S.A.* 94 B4
Barrow Creek, *Australia* .. 90 C1
Barrow I., *Australia* 88 D2
Barrow-in-Furness, *U.K.* . 12 C4
Barrow Pt., *Australia* 90 A3
Barrow Ra., *Australia* 89 E4
Barrow Str., *Canada* 4 B3
Barruecopardo, *Spain* 30 D4

Barruelo, *Spain* 30 C6
Barry, *U.K.* 13 F4
Barry's Bay, *Canada* 98 C4
Barsalogho, *Burkina Faso* . 79 C4
Barsat, *Pakistan* 63 A5
Barsham, *Syria* 64 C4
Barsi, *India* 60 K9
Barsø, *Denmark* 11 J3
Barsoi, *India* 61 G15
Barstow, *Calif., U.S.A.* .. 113 L9
Barstow, *Tex., U.S.A.* ... 109 K3
Barth, *Germany* 18 A8
Barthélemy, Col, *Vietnam* 58 C5
Bartin, *Turkey* 66 C5
Bartlesville, *U.S.A.* 109 G7
Bartlett, *Calif., U.S.A.* ... 112 J8
Bartlett, *Tex., U.S.A.* 109 K6
Bartlett, L., *Canada* 100 A5
Bartolomeu Dias, *Mozam.* 85 G4
Barton, *Australia* 89 F5
Barton upon Humber, *U.K.* 12 D7
Bartoszyce, *Poland* 20 A10
Bartow, *U.S.A.* 105 M5
Barú, I. de, *Colombia* 120 A2
Barú, Volcan, *Panama* ... 116 E3
Barumba, *Zaïre* 82 B1
Baruth, *Germany* 18 C9
Barvaux, *Belgium* 17 H6
Barvenkovo, *Ukraine* 42 B7
Barwani, *India* 62 H6
Barysh, *Russia* 41 E15
Barzān, *Iraq* 64 B5
Bas-Rhin □, *France* 25 D14
Bašaid, *Serbia, Yug.* 21 K10
Bāsa'idū, *Iran* 65 E7
Basal, *Pakistan* 62 C5
Basankusa, *Zaïre* 80 D3
Basawa, *Afghan.* 62 B4
Bascharage, *Lux.* 17 J7
Bascuñán, C., *Chile* 126 B1
Basècles, *Belgium* 17 G3
Basel, *Switz.* 22 A5
Basel-Stadt □, *Switz.* 22 A5
Baselland □, *Switz.* 22 B5
Basento →, *Italy* 35 B9
Bashi Channel, *Phil.* 54 D7
Bāshīn, *Iran* 65 D6
Bashkir Republic □, *Russia* 44 D6
Basilan, *Phil.* 55 H5
Basilan Str., *Phil.* 55 H5
Basildon, *U.K.* 13 F8
Basilicata □, *Italy* 35 B9
Basim = Washim, *India* .. 60 J10
Basin, *U.S.A.* 110 D9
Basingstoke, *U.K.* 13 F6
Baška, *Croatia* 33 D11
Başkale, *Turkey* 67 D10
Baskatong, Rés., *Canada* . 98 C4
Basle = Basel, *Switz.* 22 A5
Basoda, *India* 62 H7
Basodino, *Switz.* 23 D6
Basoka, *Zaïre* 82 B1
Basongo, *Zaïre* 80 E4
Basque, Pays, *France* 26 E2
Basque Provinces = País
   Vasco □, *Spain* 28 C2
Basra = Al Baṣrah, *Iraq* .. 64 D5
Bass Rock, *U.K.* 14 E6
Bass Str., *Australia* 90 F4
Bassano, *Canada* 100 C6
Bassano del Grappa, *Italy* . 33 C8
Bassar, *Togo* 79 D5
Bassas da India, *Ind. Oc.* . 81 J7
Basse Santa-Su, *Gambia* . 78 C2
Basse-Terre, *Guadeloupe* . 117 C7
Bassecourt, *Switz.* 22 B4
Bassein, *Burma* 61 L19
Basseterre,
   St. Christopher-Nevis . 117 C7
Bassett, *Nebr., U.S.A.* ... 108 D5
Bassett, *Va., U.S.A.* 105 G6
Bassevelde, *Belgium* 17 F3
Bassi, *India* 62 D7
Bassigny, *France* 25 E12
Bassikounou, *Mauritania* . 78 B3
Bassilly, *Belgium* 17 G3
Bassum, *Germany* 18 C4
Båstad, *Sweden* 11 H6
Bastak, *Iran* 65 E7
Baştām, *Iran* 65 B7
Bastar, *India* 61 K12
Bastelica, *France* 27 F13
Basti, *India* 63 F10
Bastia, *France* 27 F13
Bastia Umbra, *Italy* 33 E9
Bastogne, *Belgium* 17 H7
Bastrop, *U.S.A.* 109 K6
Bat Yam, *Israel* 69 C3
Bata, *Eq. Guin.* 80 D1
Bata, *Romania* 38 C5
Bataan, *Phil.* 55 D4
Batabanó, *Cuba* 116 B3
Batabanó, G. de, *Cuba* .. 116 B3
Batac, *Phil.* 55 B4
Batagoy, *Russia* 45 C14
Batak, *Bulgaria* 39 H7
Batalha, *Portugal* 31 F2
Batama, *Zaïre* 82 B2
Batamay, *Russia* 45 C13
Batan I., *Phil.* 55 A4
Batanes Is., *Phil.* 55 A4
Batang, *China* 52 B2
Batang, *Indonesia* 57 G13
Batangafo, *C.A.R.* 73 G8

Batangas, *Phil.* 55 E4
Batanta, *Indonesia* 57 E8
Batatais, *Brazil* 127 A6
Batavia, *U.S.A.* 106 D6
Bataysk, *Russia* 43 C8
Batchelor, *Australia* 88 B5
Bateman's B., *Australia* 91 F5
Batemans Bay, *Australia* 91 F5
Bates Ra., *Australia* 89 E3
Batesburg, *U.S.A.* 105 J5
Batesville, *Ark., U.S.A.* 109 H9
Batesville, *Miss., U.S.A.* 109 H10
Batesville, *Tex., U.S.A.* 109 L5
Bath, *U.K.* 13 F5
Bath, *Maine, U.S.A.* 99 D6
Bath, *N.Y., U.S.A.* 106 D7
Batheay, *Cambodia* 59 G5
Bathgate, *U.K.* 14 F5
Bathmen, *Neths.* 16 D8
Bathurst = Banjul, *Gambia* 78 C1
Bathurst, *Australia* 91 E4
Bathurst, *Canada* 99 C6
Bathurst, *S. Africa* 84 E4
Bathurst, C., *Canada* 96 A7
Bathurst B., *Australia* 90 A3
Bathurst Harb., *Australia* 90 G4
Bathurst I., *Australia* 88 B5
Bathurst I., *Canada* 4 B2
Bathurst Inlet, *Canada* 96 B9
Batie, *Burkina Faso* 78 D4
Batlow, *Australia* 91 F4
Batman, *Turkey* 67 E9
Batna, *Algeria* 75 A6
Batobato, *Phil.* 55 H7
Batoka, *Zambia* 83 F2
Baton Rouge, *U.S.A.* 109 K9
Batong, Ko, *Thailand* 59 J2
Batopilas, *Mexico* 114 B3
Batouri, *Cameroon* 80 D2
Battambang, *Cambodia* 58 F4
Batticaloa, *Sri Lanka* 60 R12
Battice, *Belgium* 17 G7
Battipáglia, *Italy* 35 B7
Battle, *U.K.* 13 G8
Battle →, *Canada* 101 C7
Battle Camp, *Australia* 90 B3
Battle Creek, *U.S.A.* 104 D3
Battle Ground, *U.S.A.* 112 E4
Battle Harbour, *Canada* 99 B8
Battle Lake, *U.S.A.* 108 B7
Battle Mountain, *U.S.A.* 110 F5
Battlefields, *Zimbabwe* 83 F2
Battleford, *Canada* 101 C7
Battonya, *Hungary* 21 J11
Batu, *Ethiopia* 68 F2
Batu, Kepulauan, *Indonesia* 56 E1
Batu Caves, *Malaysia* 59 L3
Batu Gajah, *Malaysia* 59 K3
Batu Is. = Batu, Kepulauan, *Indonesia* 56 E1
Batu Pahat, *Malaysia* 59 M4
Batuata, *Indonesia* 57 F6
Batumi, *Georgia* 43 F9
Baturaja, *Indonesia* 56 E2
Baturité, *Brazil* 122 B4
Bau, *Malaysia* 56 D4
Baubau, *Indonesia* 57 F6
Bauchi, *Nigeria* 79 C6
Bauchi □, *Nigeria* 79 C6
Baud, *France* 24 E3
Baudette, *U.S.A.* 108 A7
Baudour, *Belgium* 17 H3
Bauer, C., *Australia* 91 E1
Baugé, *France* 24 E6
Bauhinia Downs, *Australia* 90 C4
Bauma, *Switz.* 23 B7
Baume-les-Dames, *France* 25 E13
Baunatal, *Germany* 18 D5
Baunei, *Italy* 34 B2
Baures, *Bolivia* 125 C5
Bauru, *Brazil* 127 A6
Baús, *Brazil* 125 D7
Bauska, *Latvia* 40 C4
Bautzen, *Germany* 18 D10
Bavānāt, *Iran* 65 D7
Bavaria = Bayern □, *Germany* 19 F7
Båven, *Sweden* 10 F10
Bavi Sadri, *India* 62 G6
Bavispe →, *Mexico* 114 B3
Bawdwin, *Burma* 61 H20
Bawean, *Indonesia* 56 F4
Bawku, *Ghana* 79 C4
Bawlake, *Burma* 61 K20
Bawolung, *China* 52 C3
Baxley, *U.S.A.* 105 K4
Baxoi, *China* 52 B1
Baxter Springs, *U.S.A.* 109 G7
Bay, L. de, *Phil.* 57 B6
Bay Bulls, *Canada* 99 C9
Bay City, *Mich., U.S.A.* 104 D4
Bay City, *Oreg., U.S.A.* 110 D2
Bay City, *Tex., U.S.A.* 109 L7
Bay de Verde, *Canada* 99 C9
Bay Minette, *U.S.A.* 105 K2
Bay St. Louis, *U.S.A.* 109 K10
Bay Springs, *U.S.A.* 109 K10
Bay View, *N.Z.* 87 H6
Baya, *Zaïre* 83 E2
Bayamo, *Cuba* 116 B4
Bayamón, *Puerto Rico* 117 C6
Bayan Har Shan, *China* 54 C4
Bayan Hot = Alxa Zuoqi, *China* 50 E3
Bayan Obo, *China* 50 D5
Bayan-Ovoo, *Mongolia* 50 C4
Bayana, *India* 62 F7
Bayanaul, *Kazakhstan* 44 D8
Bayandalay, *Mongolia* 50 C2
Bayanhongor, *Mongolia* 54 B5
Bayard, *U.S.A.* 108 E3
Bayawan, *Phil.* 55 G5
Baybay, *Phil.* 55 F6
Bayburt, *Turkey* 67 C9
Bayerischer Wald, *Germany* 19 F8
Bayern □, *Germany* 19 F7
Bayeux, *France* 24 C6
Bayfield, *Canada* 106 C3
Bayfield, *U.S.A.* 108 B9
Bayindır, *Turkey* 66 D2
Baykal, Oz., *Russia* 45 D11
Baykit, *Russia* 45 C10
Baykonur, *Kazakhstan* 44 E7
Baynes Mts., *Namibia* 84 B1
Bayombong, *Phil.* 55 C4
Bayon, *France* 25 D13
Bayona, *Spain* 30 C2
Bayonne, *France* 26 E2
Bayonne, *U.S.A.* 107 F10
Bayovar, *Peru* 124 B1
Bayram-Ali, *Turkmenistan* 44 F7
Bayramiç, *Turkey* 66 D2
Bayreuth, *Germany* 19 F7
Bayrischzell, *Germany* 19 H8
Bayrūt, *Lebanon* 69 B4
Bayt Lahm, *Jordan* 69 D4
Baytown, *U.S.A.* 109 L7
Bayzo, *Niger* 79 C5
Baza, *Spain* 29 H2
Bazar Dyuzi, *Russia* 43 F12
Bazarny Karabulak, *Russia* 41 E15
Bazarnyy Syzgan, *Russia* 41 E15
Bazartobe, *Kazakhstan* 43 B14
Bazaruto, I. do, *Mozam.* 85 C6
Bazas, *France* 26 D3
Bazhong, *China* 52 B6
Bazmān, Kūh-e, *Iran* 65 D9
Beach, *U.S.A.* 108 B3
Beach City, *U.S.A.* 106 F3
Beachport, *Australia* 91 F2
Beachy Hd., *U.K.* 13 G8
Beacon, *Australia* 89 F2
Beacon, *U.S.A.* 107 E11
Beaconia, *Canada* 101 C9
Beagle, Canal, *S. Amer.* 128 E3
Beagle Bay, *Australia* 88 C3
Bealanana, *Madag.* 85 A8
Beamsville, *Canada* 106 C5
Bear →, *U.S.A.* 112 G5
Béar, C., *France* 26 F7
Bear I., *Ireland* 15 E2
Bear L., *B.C., Canada* 100 B3
Bear L., *Man., Canada* 101 B9
Bear L., *U.S.A.* 110 E8
Bearcreek, *U.S.A.* 110 D9
Beardmore, *Canada* 98 C2
Beardmore Glacier, *Antarctica* 5 E11
Beardstown, *U.S.A.* 108 F9
Béarn, *France* 26 E3
Bearpaw Mts., *U.S.A.* 110 B9
Bearskin Lake, *Canada* 98 B1
Beas de Segura, *Spain* 29 G2
Beasain, *Spain* 28 B2
Beata, C., *Dom. Rep.* 117 C5
Beata, I., *Dom. Rep.* 117 C5
Beatrice, *U.S.A.* 108 E6
Beatrice, *Zimbabwe* 83 F3
Beatrice, C., *Australia* 90 A2
Beatton →, *Canada* 100 B4
Beatton River, *Canada* 100 B4
Beatty, *U.S.A.* 111 H5
Beaucaire, *France* 27 E8
Beauce, Plaine de la, *France* 25 D8
Beauceville, *Canada* 99 C5
Beauchêne, I., *Falk. Is.* 128 D5
Beaudesert, *Australia* 91 D5
Beaufort, *Malaysia* 56 C5
Beaufort, *N.C., U.S.A.* 105 H7
Beaufort, *S.C., U.S.A.* 105 J5
Beaufort Sea, *Arctic* 4 B1
Beaufort West, *S. Africa* 84 E3
Beaugency, *France* 25 E8
Beauharnois, *Canada* 98 C5
Beaujeu, *France* 27 B8
Beaulieu →, *Canada* 100 A6
Beaulieu-sur-Dordogne, *France* 26 D5
Beaulieu-sur-Mer, *France* 27 E11
Beauly, *U.K.* 14 D4
Beauly →, *U.K.* 14 D4
Beaumaris, *U.K.* 12 D3
Beaumetz-lès-Loges, *France* 25 B9
Beaumont, *Belgium* 17 H4
Beaumont, *France* 26 D4
Beaumont, *Calif., U.S.A.* 113 M10
Beaumont, *Tex., U.S.A.* 109 K7
Beaumont-de-Lomagne, *France* 26 E4
Beaumont-le-Roger, *France* 24 C7
Beaumont-sur-Oise, *France* 25 C9
Beaumont-sur-Sarthe, *France* 24 D7
Beaune, *France* 25 E11
Beaune-la-Rolande, *France* 25 D9
Beaupréau, *France* 24 E6
Beauraing, *Belgium* 17 H5
Beauséjour, *Canada* 101 C9
Beauvais, *France* 25 C9
Beauval, *Canada* 101 B7
Beauvoir-sur-Mer, *France* 24 F4
Beauvoir-sur-Niort, *France* 26 B3
Beaver, *Alaska, U.S.A.* 96 B5
Beaver, *Okla., U.S.A.* 109 G4
Beaver, *Pa., U.S.A.* 106 F4
Beaver, *Utah, U.S.A.* 111 G7
Beaver →, *B.C., Canada* 100 B4
Beaver →, *Ont., Canada* 98 A2
Beaver →, *Sask., Canada* 101 B7
Beaver City, *U.S.A.* 108 E5
Beaver Dam, *U.S.A.* 108 D10
Beaver Falls, *U.S.A.* 106 F4
Beaver Hill L., *Canada* 101 C10
Beaver I., *U.S.A.* 104 C3
Beaverhill L., *Alta., Canada* 100 C6
Beaverhill L., *N.W.T., Canada* 101 A8
Beaverlodge, *Canada* 100 B5
Beavermouth, *Canada* 100 C5
Beaverstone →, *Canada* 98 B2
Beaverton, *Canada* 106 B5
Beaverton, *U.S.A.* 112 E4
Beawar, *India* 62 F6
Bebedouro, *Brazil* 127 A6
Beboa, *Madag.* 85 B7
Bebra, *Germany* 18 E5
Beccles, *U.K.* 13 E9
Bečej, *Serbia, Yug.* 21 K10
Becerreá, *Spain* 30 C3
Béchar, *Algeria* 75 B4
Beckley, *U.S.A.* 104 G5
Beckum, *Germany* 18 D4
Bečva →, *Czech.* 20 F7
Bédar, *Spain* 29 H3
Bédarieux, *France* 26 E7
Bédarrides, *France* 27 D8
Beddouza, Ras, *Morocco* 74 B3
Bedele, *Ethiopia* 77 F4
Bederkesa, *Germany* 18 B4
Bedeso, *Ethiopia* 77 F5
Bedford, *Canada* 98 C5
Bedford, *S. Africa* 84 E4
Bedford, *U.K.* 13 E7
Bedford, *Ind., U.S.A.* 104 F2
Bedford, *Iowa, U.S.A.* 108 E7
Bedford, *Ohio, U.S.A.* 106 E3
Bedford, *Pa., U.S.A.* 106 F6
Bedford, *Va., U.S.A.* 104 G6
Bedford, C., *Australia* 90 B4
Bedford Downs, *Australia* 88 C4
Bedfordshire □, *U.K.* 13 E7
Będków, *Poland* 20 D9
Bednja →, *Croatia* 33 B13
Bednodemyanovsk, *Russia* 41 E13
Bedónia, *Italy* 32 D6
Bedourie, *Australia* 90 C2
Bedretto, *Switz.* 23 C7
Bedum, *Neths.* 16 B9
Będzin, *Poland* 20 E9
Beech Grove, *U.S.A.* 104 F2
Beechy, *Canada* 101 C7
Beek, *Gelderland, Neths.* 16 E8
Beek, *Limburg, Neths.* 17 G7
Beek, *Noord-Brabant, Neths.* 17 E7
Beekbergen, *Neths.* 16 D7
Beelitz, *Germany* 18 C8
Beenleigh, *Australia* 91 D5
Be'er Menuha, *Israel* 64 D2
Be'er Sheva', *Israel* 69 D3
Beersheba = Be'er Sheva', *Israel* 69 D3
Beerta, *Neths.* 16 B10
Beerze →, *Neths.* 16 E6
Beesd, *Neths.* 16 E6
Beeskow, *Germany* 18 C10
Beeston, *U.K.* 12 E6
Beetaloo, *Australia* 90 B1
Beetsterzwaag, *Neths.* 16 B8
Beetzendorf, *Germany* 18 C7
Beeville, *U.S.A.* 109 L6
Befale, *Zaïre* 80 D4
Befandriana, *Madag.* 85 C7
Befotaka, *Madag.* 85 C8
Bega, *Australia* 91 F4
Bega, Canalul, *Romania* 38 D3
Bégard, *France* 24 D3
Bègles, *France* 26 D3
Begna →, *Norway* 10 D4
Begonte, *Spain* 30 B3
Begusarai, *India* 63 G12
Behābād, *Iran* 65 C8
Behara, *Madag.* 85 C8
Behbehān, *Iran* 65 D6
Behshahr, *Iran* 65 B7
Bei Jiang →, *China* 53 F9
Bei'an, *China* 54 B7
Beibei, *China* 54 D5
Beigang, *Taiwan* 53 F13
Beihai, *China* 52 G7
Beijing, *China* 50 E9
Beijing □, *China* 50 E9
Beilen, *Neths.* 16 C8
Beiliu, *China* 53 F8
Beilngries, *Germany* 19 F7
Beilpajah, *Australia* 91 E3
Beilul, *Ethiopia* 77 E5
Beipiao, *China* 51 D11
Beira, *Mozam.* 83 F3
Beirut = Bayrūt, *Lebanon* 69 B4
Beitaolaizhao, *China* 51 B13
Beitbridge, *Zimbabwe* 83 G3
Beiuş, *Romania* 38 C5
Beizhen, *Liaoning, China* 51 D11
Beizhen, *Shandong, China* 51 F10
Beizhengzhen, *China* 51 B12
Beja, *Portugal* 31 G3
Béja, *Tunisia* 75 A6
Beja □, *Portugal* 31 H3
Bejaia, *Algeria* 75 A6
Béjar, *Spain* 30 E5
Bejestān, *Iran* 65 C8
Bekasi, *Indonesia* 57 G12
Békés, *Hungary* 21 J11
Békéscsaba, *Hungary* 21 J11
Bekily, *Madag.* 85 C8
Bekkevoort, *Belgium* 17 G5
Bekoji, *Ethiopia* 77 F4
Bekok, *Malaysia* 59 L4
Bekwai, *Ghana* 79 D4
Bela, *India* 63 G9
Bela, *Pakistan* 62 F2
Bela Crkva, *Serbia, Yug.* 21 L11
Bela Palanka, *Serbia, Yug.* 21 M12
Bela Vista, *Brazil* 126 A4
Bela Vista, *Mozam.* 85 D5
Bélâbre, *France* 26 B5
Belalcázar, *Spain* 31 G5
Belarus = Belorussia ■, *Europe* 40 E5
Belau I., *Pac. Oc.* 92 G5
Belavenona, *Madag.* 85 C8
Belawan, *Indonesia* 56 D1
Belaya, *Ethiopia* 77 E4
Belaya Glina, *Russia* 43 C9
Belaya Kalitva, *Russia* 43 B9
Belaya Kholunitsa, *Russia* 41 B17
Belaya Tserkov, *Ukraine* 40 G7
Belcher Is., *Canada* 97 C12
Belchite, *Spain* 28 D4
Belden, *U.S.A.* 112 E5
Belém, *Brazil* 122 B2
Belém de São Francisco, *Brazil* 122 C4
Belén, *Argentina* 126 B2
Belén, *Colombia* 120 C2
Belén, *Paraguay* 126 A4
Belen, *U.S.A.* 111 J10
Bélesta, *France* 26 F5
Belet Uen, *Somali Rep.* 68 G4
Belev, *Russia* 41 E10
Belfair, *U.S.A.* 112 C4
Belfast, *S. Africa* 85 D5
Belfast, *U.K.* 15 B6
Belfast, *Maine, U.S.A.* 99 D6
Belfast, *N.Y., U.S.A.* 106 D6
Belfast □, *U.K.* 15 B6
Belfast L., *U.K.* 15 B6
Belfeld, *Neths.* 17 F8
Belfield, *U.S.A.* 108 B3
Belfort, *France* 25 E13
Belfort, Territoire de □, *France* 25 E13
Belfry, *U.S.A.* 110 D9
Belgaum, *India* 60 M9
Belgioioso, *Italy* 32 C6
Belgium ■, *Europe* 17 G5
Belgorod, *Russia* 41 F10
Belgorod-Dnestrovskiy, *Ukraine* 42 C4
Belgrade = Beograd, *Serbia, Yug.* 21 L10
Belgrade, *U.S.A.* 110 D8
Belhaven, *U.S.A.* 105 H7
Beli Drim →, *Europe* 21 N10
Beli Manastir, *Croatia* 21 K8
Belice →, *Italy* 34 E5
Belin-Béliet, *France* 26 D3
Belinga, *Gabon* 80 D2
Belinskiy, *Russia* 41 E13
Belinyu, *Indonesia* 56 E3
Belitung, *Indonesia* 56 E3
Beliu, *Romania* 38 C5
Belize ■, *Cent. Amer.* 115 D7
Belize City, *Belize* 115 D7
Beljanica, *Serbia, Yug.* 21 L11
Belkovskiy, Ostrov, *Russia* 45 B14
Bell →, *Canada* 98 C4
Bell Bay, *Australia* 90 G4
Bell I., *Canada* 99 B8
Bell-Irving →, *Canada* 100 B3
Bell Peninsula, *Canada* 97 B11
Bell Ville, *Argentina* 126 C3
Bella Bella, *Canada* 100 C3
Bella Coola, *Canada* 100 C3
Bella Flor, *Bolivia* 124 C4
Bella Unión, *Uruguay* 126 C4
Bella Vista, *Corrientes, Argentina* 126 B4
Bella Vista, *Tucuman, Argentina* 126 B2
Bellac, *France* 26 B5
Bellágio, *Italy* 32 C6
Bellaire, *U.S.A.* 106 F4
Bellary, *India* 60 M10
Bellata, *Australia* 91 D4
Belle Fourche, *U.S.A.* 108 C3
Belle Fourche →, *U.S.A.* 108 C3
Belle Glade, *U.S.A.* 105 M5
Belle-Ile, *France* 24 E3
Belle Isle, *Canada* 99 B8
Belle Isle, Str. of, *Canada* 99 B8
Belle-Isle-en-Terre, *France* 24 D3
Belle Plaine, *Iowa, U.S.A.* 108 E8
Belle Plaine, *Minn., U.S.A.* 108 C8
Belle Yella, *Liberia* 78 D3
Belledonne, Chaîne de, *France* 27 C10
Belledune, *Canada* 99 C6
Bellefontaine, *U.S.A.* 104 E4
Bellefonte, *U.S.A.* 106 F7
Bellegarde, *France* 25 E9
Bellegarde-en-Marche, *France* 26 C6
Bellegarde-sur-Valserine, *France* 27 B9
Bellême, *France* 24 D7
Belleoram, *Canada* 99 C8
Belleville, *Canada* 98 D4
Belleville, *France* 27 B8
Belleville, *Ill., U.S.A.* 108 F10
Belleville, *Kans., U.S.A.* 108 F6
Belleville, *N.Y., U.S.A.* 107 C8
Belleville-sur-Vie, *France* 24 F5
Bellevue, *Canada* 100 D6
Bellevue, *Idaho, U.S.A.* 110 E6
Bellevue, *Ohio, U.S.A.* 106 E2
Bellevue, *Wash., U.S.A.* 112 C4
Belley, *France* 27 C9
Bellin, *Canada* 97 B13
Bellingen, *Australia* 91 E5
Bellingham, *U.S.A.* 112 B4
Bellingshausen Sea, *Antarctica* 5 C17
Bellinzona, *Switz.* 23 D8
Bello, *Colombia* 120 B2
Bellows Falls, *U.S.A.* 107 C12
Bellpat, *Pakistan* 62 E3
Bellpuig, *Spain* 28 D6
Belluno, *Italy* 33 B9
Bellville, *U.S.A.* 109 L6
Bellwood, *U.S.A.* 106 F6
Bélmez, *Spain* 31 G5
Belmont, *Australia* 91 E5
Belmont, *Canada* 106 D3
Belmont, *S. Africa* 84 D3
Belmont, *U.S.A.* 106 D6
Belmonte, *Brazil* 123 E4
Belmonte, *Portugal* 30 E3
Belmonte, *Spain* 28 F2
Belmopan, *Belize* 115 D7
Belmullet, *Ireland* 15 B2
Belo Horizonte, *Brazil* 123 E3
Belo Jardim, *Brazil* 122 C4
Belo-sur-Mer, *Madag.* 85 C7
Belo-Tsiribihina, *Madag.* 85 B7
Belogorsk, *Russia* 45 D13
Belogorsk, *Ukraine* 42 D6
Belogradchik, *Bulgaria* 38 F5
Beloha, *Madag.* 85 D8
Beloit, *Kans., U.S.A.* 108 F5
Beloit, *Wis., U.S.A.* 108 D10
Belokorovichi, *Ukraine* 40 F6
Belomorsk, *Russia* 44 C4
Belonia, *India* 61 H17
Belopolye, *Ukraine* 40 F9
Belorussia ■, *Europe* 40 E5
Belovo, *Russia* 44 D9
Beloye More, *Russia* 44 C4
Beloye Ozero, *Russia* 43 D12
Belozersk, *Russia* 41 A10
Belpasso, *Italy* 35 E7
Belsele, *Belgium* 17 F4
Belsito, *Italy* 34 E6
Beltana, *Australia* 91 E2
Belterra, *Brazil* 121 D7
Beltinci, *Slovenia* 33 B13
Belton, *S.C., U.S.A.* 105 H4
Belton, *Tex., U.S.A.* 109 K6
Belton Res., *U.S.A.* 109 K6
Beltsy, *Moldavia* 42 C3
Belturbet, *Ireland* 15 B4
Belukha, *Russia* 44 E9
Beluran, *Malaysia* 56 C5
Belvedere Maríttimo, *Italy* 35 C8
Belvès, *France* 26 D5
Belvidere, *Ill., U.S.A.* 108 D10
Belvidere, *N.J., U.S.A.* 107 F9
Belvis de la Jara, *Spain* 31 F6
Belyando →, *Australia* 90 C4
Belyy, *Russia* 40 D8
Belyy, Ostrov, *Russia* 44 B8
Belyy Yar, *Russia* 44 D9
Belzig, *Germany* 18 C8
Belzoni, *U.S.A.* 109 J9
Bemaraha, Lembalemban' i, *Madag.* 85 B7
Bemarivo, *Madag.* 85 C7
Bemarivo →, *Madag.* 85 B8
Bemavo, *Madag.* 85 C8
Bembéréke, *Benin* 79 C5
Bembesi, *Zimbabwe* 83 F2
Bembesi →, *Zimbabwe* 83 F2
Bembézar →, *Spain* 31 H5
Bemidji, *U.S.A.* 108 B7
Bemmel, *Neths.* 16 E7
Ben, *Iran* 65 C6
Ben Cruachan, *U.K.* 14 E3
Ben Dearg, *U.K.* 14 D4
Ben Gardane, *Tunisia* 75 B7
Ben Hope, *U.K.* 14 C4
Ben Lawers, *U.K.* 14 E4
Ben Lomond, *N.S.W., Australia* 91 E5
Ben Lomond, *Tas., Australia* 90 G4
Ben Lomond, *U.K.* 14 E4
Ben Luc, *Vietnam* 59 G6
Ben Macdhui, *U.K.* 14 D5
Ben Mhor, *U.K.* 14 D1
Ben More, *Central, U.K.* 14 E4

Ben More, *Strath., U.K.* 14 E2
Ben More Assynt, *U.K.* 14 C4
Ben Nevis, *U.K.* 14 E4
Ben Quang, *Vietnam* 58 D6
Ben Slimane, *Morocco* 74 B3
Ben Tre, *Vietnam* 59 G6
Ben Vorlich, *U.K.* 14 E4
Ben Wyvis, *U.K.* 14 D4
Bena, *Nigeria* 79 C6
Bena Dibele, *Zaïre* 80 E4
Benagalbón, *Spain* 31 J6
Benagerie, *Australia* 91 E3
Benahmed, *Morocco* 74 B3
Benalla, *Australia* 91 F4
Benambra, Mt., *Australia* 91 F4
Benamejí, *Spain* 31 H6
Benares = Varanasi, *India* 63 G10
Bénat, C., *France* 27 E10
Benavente, *Portugal* 31 G2
Benavente, *Spain* 30 C5
Benavides, *Spain* 30 C5
Benavides, *U.S.A.* 109 M5
Benbecula, *U.K.* 14 D1
Benbonyathe, *Australia* 91 E2
Bencubbin, *Australia* 89 F2
Bend, *U.S.A.* 110 D3
Bendel □, *Nigeria* 79 D6
Bender Beila, *Somali Rep.* 68 F5
Bendering, *Australia* 89 F2
Bendery, *Moldavia* 42 C3
Bendigo, *Australia* 91 F3
Bendorf, *Germany* 18 E3
Benē Beraq, *Israel* 69 C3
Beneden Knijpe, *Neths.* 16 C7
Beneditinos, *Brazil* 122 C3
Benedito Leite, *Brazil* 122 C3
Bénéna, *Mali* 78 C4
Benenitra, *Madag.* 85 C8
Benešov, *Czech.* 20 F4
Bénestroff, *France* 25 D13
Benet, *France* 26 B3
Benevento, *Italy* 35 A7
Benfeld, *France* 25 D14
Benga, *Mozam.* 83 F3
Bengal, Bay of, *Ind. Oc.* 61 K16
Bengbu, *China* 51 H9
Benghazi = Banghāzī, *Libya* 73 B9
Bengkalis, *Indonesia* 56 D2
Bengkulu, *Indonesia* 56 E2
Bengkulu □, *Indonesia* 56 E2
Bengough, *Canada* 101 D7
Benguela, *Angola* 81 G2
Benguerir, *Morocco* 74 B3
Benguérua, I., *Mozam.* 85 C6
Benha, *Egypt* 76 H7
Beni, *Zaïre* 82 B2
Beni □, *Bolivia* 125 C4
Beni →, *Bolivia* 125 C4
Beni Abbès, *Algeria* 75 B4
Beni-Haoua, *Algeria* 75 A5
Beni Mazâr, *Egypt* 76 J7
Beni Mellal, *Morocco* 74 B3
Beni Ounif, *Algeria* 75 B4
Beni Saf, *Algeria* 75 A4
Beni Suef, *Egypt* 76 J7
Beniah L., *Canada* 100 A6
Benicarló, *Spain* 28 E5
Benicia, *U.S.A.* 112 G4
Benidorm, *Spain* 29 G4
Benidorm, Islote de, *Spain* 29 G4
Benin ■, *Africa* 79 D5
Benin, Bight of, *W. Afr.* 79 D5
Benin City, *Nigeria* 79 D6
Benisa, *Spain* 29 G5
Benitses, *Greece* 37 A3
Benjamin Aceval, *Paraguay* 126 A4
Benjamin Constant, *Brazil* 120 D3
Benjamin Hill, *Mexico* 114 A2
Benkelman, *U.S.A.* 108 E4
Benkovac, *Croatia* 33 D12
Benlidi, *Australia* 90 C3
Bennebroek, *Neths.* 16 D5
Bennekom, *Neths.* 16 D7
Bennett, *Canada* 100 B2
Bennett, L., *Australia* 88 D5
Bennett, Ostrov, *Russia* 45 B15
Bennettsville, *U.S.A.* 105 H6
Bennington, *U.S.A.* 107 D11
Bénodet, *France* 24 E2
Benoni, *S. Africa* 85 D4
Benoud, *Algeria* 75 B5
Benque Viejo, *Belize* 115 D7
Bensheim, *Germany* 19 F4
Benson, *U.S.A.* 111 L8
Bent, *Iran* 65 E8
Benteng, *Indonesia* 57 F6
Bentinck I., *Australia* 90 B2
Bentiu, *Sudan* 77 F2
Bento Gonçalves, *Brazil* 127 B5
Benton, *Ark., U.S.A.* 109 H8
Benton, *Calif., U.S.A.* 112 H8
Benton, *Ill., U.S.A.* 108 F10
Benton Harbor, *U.S.A.* 104 D2
Bentu Liben, *Ethiopia* 77 F4
Bentung, *Malaysia* 59 L3
Benue □, *Nigeria* 79 D6
Benue →, *Nigeria* 79 D6
Benxi, *China* 51 D12
Benzdorp, *Surinam* 121 C7
Beo, *Indonesia* 57 D7
Beograd, *Serbia, Yug.* 21 L10
Beowawe, *U.S.A.* 110 F5
Bepan Jiang →, *China* 52 E6
Beppu, *Japan* 49 H5
Berati, *Albania* 39 J2
Berau, Teluk, *Indonesia* 57 E8
Berber, *Sudan* 76 D3
Berbera, *Somali Rep.* 68 E4
Berbérati, *C.A.R.* 80 D3
Berberia, C. del, *Spain* 36 C7
Berbice □, *Guyana* 121 C6
Berbice →, *Guyana* 121 B6
Berceto, *Italy* 32 D7
Berchtesgaden, *Germany* 19 H8
Berdichev, *Ukraine* 42 B3
Berdsk, *Russia* 44 D9
Berdyansk, *Ukraine* 42 C7
Berea, *U.S.A.* 104 G3
Berebere, *Indonesia* 57 D7
Bereda, *Somali Rep.* 68 E5
Berekum, *Ghana* 78 D4
Berenice, *Egypt* 76 C4
Berens →, *Canada* 101 C9
Berens I., *Canada* 101 C9
Berens River, *Canada* 101 C9
Berestechko, *Ukraine* 40 F4
Bereşti, *Romania* 38 C10
Beretău →, *Romania* 38 B4
Berettyo →, *Hungary* 21 J11
Berettyóújfalu, *Hungary* 21 H11
Berevo, *Mahajanga, Madag.* 85 B7
Berevo, *Toliara, Madag.* 85 B7
Bereza, *Belorussia* 40 E4
Berezhany, *Ukraine* 40 G4
Berezina →, *Belorussia* 40 E7
Berezna, *Ukraine* 40 F7
Berezniki, *Russia* 44 D6
Berezovka, *Ukraine* 42 C4
Berezovo, *Russia* 44 C7
Berga, *Spain* 28 C6
Bergama, *Turkey* 66 D2
Bergambacht, *Neths.* 16 E5
Bérgamo, *Italy* 32 C6
Bergantiños, *Spain* 30 B2
Bergara, *Spain* 28 B2
Bergedorf, *Germany* 18 B6
Bergeijk, *Neths.* 17 F6
Bergen, *Germany* 18 A9
Bergen, *Neths.* 16 C5
Bergen, *Norway* 9 F8
Bergen, *U.S.A.* 106 C7
Bergen-op-Zoom, *Neths.* 17 F4
Bergerac, *France* 26 D4
Bergheim, *Germany* 18 E2
Berghem, *Neths.* 16 E7
Bergisch-Gladbach, *Germany* 18 E3
Bergschenhoek, *Neths.* 16 E5
Bergsjö, *Sweden* 10 C11
Bergues, *France* 25 B9
Bergum, *Neths.* 16 B7
Bergville, *S. Africa* 85 D4
Berhala, Selat, *Indonesia* 56 E2
Berhampore = Baharampur, *India* 63 G13
Berhampur, *India* 61 K14
Berheci →, *Romania* 38 C10
Bering Sea, *Pac. Oc.* 96 C1
Bering Str., *U.S.A.* 96 B3
Beringen, *Belgium* 17 F6
Beringen, *Switz.* 23 A7
Beringovskiy, *Russia* 45 C18
Berislav, *Ukraine* 42 C5
Berisso, *Argentina* 126 C4
Berja, *Spain* 29 J2
Berkane, *Morocco* 75 B4
Berkel →, *Neths.* 16 D8
Berkeley, *U.K.* 13 F5
Berkeley, *U.S.A.* 112 H4
Berkeley Springs, *U.S.A.* 104 F6
Berkhout, *Neths.* 16 C5
Berkner I., *Antarctica* 5 D18
Berkovitsa, *Bulgaria* 38 F6
Berkshire □, *U.K.* 13 F6
Berlaar, *Belgium* 17 F5
Berland →, *Canada* 100 C5
Berlanga, *Spain* 31 G5
Berlare, *Belgium* 17 F4
Berlenga, I., *Portugal* 31 F1
Berlin, *Germany* 18 C9
Berlin, *Md., U.S.A.* 104 F8
Berlin, *N.H., U.S.A.* 107 B13
Berlin, *Wis., U.S.A.* 104 D1
Bermeja, Sierra, *Spain* 31 J5
Bermejo →, *Formosa, Argentina* 126 B4
Bermejo →, *San Juan, Argentina* 126 C2
Bermeo, *Spain* 28 B2
Bermillo de Sayago, *Spain* 30 D4
Bermuda ■, *Atl. Oc.* 2 C6
Bern, *Switz.* 22 C4
Bern □, *Switz.* 22 C5
Bernado, *U.S.A.* 111 J10
Bernalda, *Italy* 35 B9
Bernalillo, *U.S.A.* 111 J10
Bernardo de Irigoyen, *Argentina* 127 B5
Bernardo O'Higgins □, *Chile* 126 C1
Bernasconi, *Argentina* 126 D3
Bernau, *Bayern, Germany* 19 H8
Bernau, *Brandenburg, Germany* 18 C9
Bernay, *France* 24 C7
Bernburg, *Germany* 18 D7
Berne = Bern, *Switz.* 22 C4
Berne = Bern □, *Switz.* 22 C5
Berner Alpen, *Switz.* 22 D5
Bernese Oberland = Oberland, *Switz.* 22 C5
Bernier I., *Australia* 89 D1
Bernina, Piz, *Switz.* 23 D9
Bernina, Pizzo, *Switz.* 23 D9
Bernissart, *Belgium* 17 H3
Bernkastel-Kues, *Germany* 19 F3
Beroroha, *Madag.* 85 C8
Béroubouay, *Benin* 79 C5
Beroun, *Czech.* 20 F4
Berounka →, *Czech.* 20 F4
Berovo, *Macedonia, Yug.* 39 H5
Berrahal, *Algeria* 75 A6
Berre, Étang de, *France* 27 E9
Berrechid, *Morocco* 74 B3
Berri, *Australia* 91 E3
Berriane, *Algeria* 75 B5
Berrouaghia, *Algeria* 75 A5
Berry, *Australia* 91 E5
Berry, *France* 25 F8
Berry Is., *Bahamas* 116 A4
Berryessa, L., *U.S.A.* 112 G4
Berryville, *U.S.A.* 109 G8
Bersenbrück, *Germany* 18 C3
Berthold, *U.S.A.* 108 A4
Berthoud, *U.S.A.* 108 E2
Bertincourt, *France* 25 B9
Bertoua, *Cameroon* 80 D2
Bertrand, *U.S.A.* 108 E5
Bertrange, *Lux.* 17 J8
Bertrix, *Belgium* 17 J6
Berufjörður, *Iceland* 8 D6
Beruri, *Brazil* 121 D5
Berwick, *U.S.A.* 107 E8
Berwick-upon-Tweed, *U.K.* 12 B5
Berwyn Mts., *U.K.* 12 E4
Berzasca, *Romania* 38 E4
Besal, *Pakistan* 63 B5
Besalampy, *Madag.* 85 B7
Besançon, *France* 25 E13
Besar, *Indonesia* 56 E5
Beshenkovichi, *Belorussia* 40 D6
Beslan, *Russia* 43 E11
Besnard L., *Canada* 101 B7
Besni, *Turkey* 67 E7
Besor, N. →, *Egypt* 69 D3
Bessarabiya, *Moldavia* 38 B11
Bessarabka, *Moldavia* 42 C3
Bessèges, *France* 27 D8
Bessemer, *Ala., U.S.A.* 105 J2
Bessemer, *Mich., U.S.A.* 108 B9
Bessin, *France* 24 C5
Bessines-sur-Gartempe, *France* 26 B5
Best, *Neths.* 17 E6
Bet She'an, *Israel* 69 C4
Bet Shemesh, *Israel* 69 D3
Bet Tadjine, Djebel, *Algeria* 74 C4
Betafo, *Madag.* 85 B8
Betancuria, *Canary Is.* 36 F5
Betanzos, *Bolivia* 125 D4
Betanzos, *Spain* 30 B2
Bétaré Oya, *Cameroon* 80 C2
Bétera, *Spain* 28 F4
Bethal, *S. Africa* 85 D4
Bethanien, *Namibia* 84 D2
Bethany, *S. Africa* 84 D4
Bethany, *U.S.A.* 108 E7
Bethel, *Alaska, U.S.A.* 96 B3
Bethel, *Vt., U.S.A.* 107 C12
Bethel Park, *U.S.A.* 106 F4
Bethlehem = Bayt Lahm, *Jordan* 69 D4
Bethlehem, *S. Africa* 85 D4
Bethlehem, *U.S.A.* 107 F9
Bethulie, *S. Africa* 84 E4
Béthune, *France* 25 B9
Béthune →, *France* 24 C8
Bethungra, *Australia* 91 E4
Betijoque, *Venezuela* 120 B3
Betim, *Brazil* 123 E3
Betioky, *Madag.* 85 C7
Beton-Bazoches, *France* 25 D10
Betong, *Thailand* 59 K3
Betoota, *Australia* 90 D3
Betroka, *Madag.* 85 C8
Betsiamites, *Canada* 99 C6
Betsiamites →, *Canada* 99 C6
Betsiboka →, *Madag.* 85 B8
Betsjoeanaland, *S. Africa* 84 D3
Bettembourg, *Lux.* 17 J8
Bettiah, *India* 63 F11
Bèttola, *Italy* 32 D6
Betul, *India* 60 J10
Betung, *Malaysia* 56 D4
Betzdorf, *Germany* 18 E3
Beuca, *Romania* 38 E7
Beuil, *France* 27 D10
Beulah, *U.S.A.* 108 B4
Beuvron →, *France* 24 E8
Beveren, *Belgium* 17 F4
Beverley, *Australia* 89 F2
Beverley, *U.K.* 12 D7
Beverlo, *Belgium* 17 F6
Beverly, *Mass., U.S.A.* 107 D14
Beverly, *Wash., U.S.A.* 110 C4
Beverly Hills, *U.S.A.* 113 L8
Beverwijk, *Neths.* 16 D5
Bex, *Switz.* 22 D4
Bey Dağları, *Turkey* 66 E4
Beyānlū, *Iran* 64 C5
Beyin, *Ghana* 78 D4
Beyla, *Guinea* 78 D3
Beynat, *France* 26 C5
Beyneu, *Kazakhstan* 44 E6
Beypazarı, *Turkey* 66 C4
Beyşehir Gölü, *Turkey* 66 E4
Beytüşşebap, *Turkey* 67 E10
Bezhetsk, *Russia* 41 C10
Bezhitsa, *Russia* 40 E9
Béziers, *France* 26 E7
Bezwada = Vijayawada, *India* 61 L12
Bhachau, *India* 60 H7
Bhadarwah, *India* 63 C6
Bhadrakh, *India* 61 J15
Bhadravati, *India* 60 N9
Bhagalpur, *India* 63 G12
Bhakkar, *Pakistan* 62 D4
Bhakra Dam, *India* 62 D7
Bhamo, *Burma* 61 G20
Bhandara, *India* 60 J11
Bhanrer Ra., *India* 62 H8
Bharat = India ■, *Asia* 60 K11
Bharatpur, *India* 62 F7
Bhatinda, *India* 62 D6
Bhatpara, *India* 63 H13
Bhaun, *Pakistan* 62 C5
Bhaunagar = Bhavnagar, *India* 62 J5
Bhavnagar, *India* 62 J5
Bhawanipatna, *India* 61 K12
Bhera, *Pakistan* 62 C5
Bhilsa = Vidisha, *India* 62 H7
Bhilwara, *India* 62 G6
Bhima →, *India* 60 L10
Bhimavaram, *India* 61 L12
Bhimbar, *Pakistan* 63 C6
Bhind, *India* 63 F8
Bhiwandi, *India* 60 K8
Bhiwani, *India* 62 E7
Bhola, *Bangla.* 61 H17
Bhopal, *India* 62 H7
Bhubaneshwar, *India* 61 J14
Bhuj, *India* 62 H3
Bhumiphol Dam = Phumiphon, Khuan, *Thailand* 58 D2
Bhusaval, *India* 60 J9
Bhutan ■, *Asia* 61 F17
Biá →, *Brazil* 120 D4
Biafra, B. of = Bonny, Bight of, *Africa* 79 E6
Biak, *Indonesia* 57 E9
Biała →, *Poland* 20 E10
Biała Podlaska, *Poland* 20 C13
Białogard, *Poland* 20 A5
Białystok, *Poland* 20 B13
Biancavilla, *Italy* 35 E7
Bīārjmand, *Iran* 65 B7
Biaro, *Indonesia* 57 D7
Biarritz, *France* 26 E2
Biasca, *Switz.* 23 D7
Biba, *Egypt* 76 J7
Bibai, *Japan* 48 C10
Bibala, *Angola* 81 G2
Bibane, Bahiret el, *Tunisia* 75 B7
Bibbiena, *Italy* 33 E8
Bibby I., *Canada* 101 A10
Biberach, *Germany* 19 G5
Biberist, *Switz.* 22 B5
Bibey →, *Spain* 30 C3
Bibiani, *Ghana* 78 D4
Biboohra, *Australia* 90 B4
Bibungwa, *Zaïre* 82 C2
Bic, *Canada* 99 C6
Bicaz, *Romania* 38 C9
Biccari, *Italy* 35 A8
Bichena, *Ethiopia* 77 E4
Bickerton I., *Australia* 90 A2
Bicknell, *Ind., U.S.A.* 104 F2
Bicknell, *Utah, U.S.A.* 111 G8
Bida, *Nigeria* 79 D6
Bidar, *India* 60 L10
Biddeford, *U.S.A.* 99 D5
Biddwara, *Ethiopia* 77 F4
Bideford, *U.K.* 13 F3
Bidon 5 = Poste Maurice Cortier, *Algeria* 75 D5
Bidor, *Malaysia* 59 K3
Bié, Planalto de, *Angola* 81 G3
Bieber, *U.S.A.* 110 F3
Biel, *Switz.* 22 B4
Bielawa, *Poland* 20 E6
Bielé Karpaty, *Czech.* 20 F7
Bielefeld, *Germany* 18 C4
Bielersee, *Switz.* 22 B4
Biella, *Italy* 32 C5
Bielsk Podlaski, *Poland* 20 C13
Bielsko-Biała, *Poland* 20 F9
Bien Hoa, *Vietnam* 59 G6
Bienfait, *Canada* 101 D8
Bienne = Biel, *Switz.* 22 B4
Bienvenida, *Spain* 31 G4
Bienvenue, *Fr. Guiana* 121 C7
Bienville, L., *Canada* 98 A5
Biescas, *Spain* 28 C4
Biese →, *Germany* 18 C7
Biesiesfontein, *S. Africa* 84 E2
Bietigheim, *Germany* 19 G5
Bievre, *Belgium* 17 J6
Biferno →, *Italy* 35 A8
Big →, *Canada* 99 B8
Big B., *Canada* 99 A7
Big Bear City, *U.S.A.* 113 L10
Big Bear L., *U.S.A.* 113 L10
Big Beaver, *Canada* 101 D7
Big Belt Mts., *U.S.A.* 110 C8
Big Bend, *Swaziland* 85 D5
Big Bend Nat. Park, *U.S.A.* 109 L3
Big Black →, *U.S.A.* 109 J9
Big Blue →, *U.S.A.* 108 F6
Big Cr. →, *Canada* 100 C4
Big Creek, *U.S.A.* 112 H7
Big Cypress Swamp, *U.S.A.* 105 M5
Big Falls, *U.S.A.* 108 A8
Big Fork →, *U.S.A.* 108 A8
Big Horn Mts. = Bighorn Mts., *U.S.A.* 110 D10
Big Lake, *U.S.A.* 109 K4
Big Moose, *U.S.A.* 107 C10
Big Muddy →, *U.S.A.* 108 A2
Big Pine, *U.S.A.* 111 H4
Big Piney, *U.S.A.* 110 E8
Big Quill L., *Canada* 101 C8
Big Rapids, *U.S.A.* 104 D3
Big River, *Canada* 101 C7
Big Run, *U.S.A.* 106 F6
Big Sable Pt., *U.S.A.* 104 C2
Big Sand L., *Canada* 101 B9
Big Sandy, *U.S.A.* 110 B8
Big Sandy Cr. →, *U.S.A.* 108 F3
Big Sioux →, *U.S.A.* 108 D6
Big Spring, *U.S.A.* 109 J4
Big Springs, *U.S.A.* 108 E3
Big Stone City, *U.S.A.* 108 C6
Big Stone Gap, *U.S.A.* 105 G4
Big Stone L., *U.S.A.* 108 C6
Big Sur, *U.S.A.* 112 J5
Big Timber, *U.S.A.* 110 D9
Big Trout L., *Canada* 98 B1
Biğa, *Turkey* 66 C2
Bigadiç, *Turkey* 66 D3
Biganos, *France* 26 D3
Bigfork, *U.S.A.* 110 B6
Biggar, *Canada* 101 C7
Biggar, *U.K.* 14 F5
Bigge I., *Australia* 88 B4
Biggenden, *Australia* 91 D5
Biggs, *U.S.A.* 112 F5
Bighorn, *U.S.A.* 110 C10
Bighorn →, *U.S.A.* 110 C10
Bighorn Mts., *U.S.A.* 110 D10
Bignona, *Senegal* 78 C1
Bigorre, *France* 26 E4
Bigstone L., *Canada* 101 C9
Bigwa, *Tanzania* 82 D4
Bihać, *Bos.-H., Yug.* 33 D12
Bihar, *India* 63 G11
Bihar □, *India* 63 G11
Biharamulo, *Tanzania* 82 C3
Biharamulo □, *Tanzania* 82 C3
Bihor, Munţii, *Romania* 38 C5
Bijagós, Arquipélago dos, *Guinea-Biss.* 78 C1
Bijaipur, *India* 62 F7
Bijapur, *Karnataka, India* 60 L9
Bijapur, *Mad. P., India* 61 K12
Bījār, *Iran* 64 C5
Bijeljina, *Bos.-H., Yug.* 21 L9
Bijelo Polje, *Montenegro, Yug.* 21 M9
Bijie, *China* 52 D5
Bijnor, *India* 62 E8
Bikaner, *India* 62 E5
Bikapur, *India* 63 F10
Bikeqi, *China* 50 D6
Bikfayyā, *Lebanon* 69 B4
Bikin, *Russia* 45 E14
Bikin →, *Russia* 48 A7
Bikini Atoll, *Pac. Oc.* 92 F8
Bikoué, *Cameroon* 79 E7
Bilara, *India* 62 F5
Bilaspur, *Mad. P., India* 63 H10
Bilaspur, *Punjab, India* 62 D7
Bilauk Taungdan, *Thailand* 58 F2
Bilbao, *Spain* 28 B2
Bilbeis, *Egypt* 76 H7
Bilbor, *Romania* 38 B8
Bíldudalur, *Iceland* 8 D2
Bileća, *Bos.-H., Yug.* 21 N8
Bilecik, *Turkey* 66 C4
Bilecik □, *Turkey* 66 C4
Bilgoraj, *Poland* 20 E12
Bilibino, *Russia* 45 C17
Bilibiza, *Mozam.* 83 E5
Bilir, *Russia* 45 C14
Biliran I., *Phil.* 55 F6
Bill, *U.S.A.* 108 D2
Billabalong, *Australia* 89 E2
Billiluna, *Australia* 88 C4
Billingham, *U.K.* 12 C6
Billings, *U.S.A.* 110 D9
Billiton Is. = Belitung, *Indonesia* 56 E3
Billom, *France* 26 C7
Bilma, *Niger* 73 E7
Bilo Gora, *Croatia* 21 K7
Biloela, *Australia* 90 C5
Biloku, *Guyana* 121 C6
Biloxi, *U.S.A.* 109 K10
Bilpa Morea Claypan, *Australia* 90 D2
Bilthoven, *Neths.* 16 D6
Biltine, *Chad* 73 F9
Bilyana, *Australia* 90 B4
Bilyarsk, *Russia* 41 D17
Bilzen, *Belgium* 17 G7
Bima, *Indonesia* 57 F5
Bimban, *Egypt* 76 C3
Bimbila, *Ghana* 79 D5

Bimbo, *C.A.R.* 80 D3
Bimini Is., *Bahamas* 116 A4
Bin Xian, *Heilongjiang, China* 51 B14
Bin Xian, *Shaanxi, China* 50 G5
Bina-Etawah, *India* 62 G8
Bināb, *Iran* 65 B6
Binalbagan, *Phil.* 55 F5
Binalong, *Australia* 91 E4
Bīnālūd, Kūh-e, *Iran* 65 B8
Binatang, *Malaysia* 56 D4
Binbee, *Australia* 90 C4
Binche, *Belgium* 17 H4
Binchuan, *China* 52 E3
Binda, *Australia* 91 D4
Bindle, *Australia* 91 D4
Bindura, *Zimbabwe* 83 F3
Bingara, *N.S.W., Australia* 91 D5
Bingara, *Queens., Australia* 91 D3
Bingen, *Germany* 19 F3
Bingerville, *Ivory C.* 78 D4
Bingham, *U.S.A.* 99 C6
Bingham Canyon, *U.S.A.* 110 F7
Binghamton, *U.S.A.* 107 D9
Bingöl, *Turkey* 67 D9
Bingöl □, *Turkey* 67 D9
Bingöl Dağları, *Turkey* 67 D9
Binh Dinh = An Nhon, *Vietnam* 58 F7
Binh Khe, *Vietnam* 58 F7
Binh Son, *Vietnam* 58 E7
Binhai, *China* 51 G10
Binisatua, *Spain* 36 B11
Binjai, *Indonesia* 56 D1
Binnaway, *Australia* 91 E4
Binongko, *Indonesia* 57 F6
Binscarth, *Canada* 101 C8
Bintan, *Indonesia* 56 D2
Bintulu, *Malaysia* 56 D4
Bintuni, *Indonesia* 57 E8
Binyang, *China* 52 F7
Binz, *Germany* 18 A9
Binzert = Bizerte, *Tunisia* 75 A6
Bío Bío □, *Chile* 126 D1
Biograd, *Croatia* 33 E12
Bioko, *Eq. Guin.* 79 E6
Biougra, *Morocco* 74 B3
Bir, *India* 60 K9
Bir, Ras, *Djibouti* 77 E5
Bîr Abu Hashim, *Egypt* 76 C3
Bîr Abu M'nqar, *Egypt* 76 B2
Bîr Abu Muḩammad, *Egypt* 69 F3
Bi'r ad Dabbāghāt, *Jordan* 69 E4
Bîr Adal Deib, *Sudan* 76 C4
Bi'r al Butayyihāt, *Jordan* 69 F4
Bi'r al Mārī, *Jordan* 69 E4
Bi'r al Qattār, *Jordan* 69 F4
Bir Aouine, *Tunisia* 75 B6
Bîr 'Asal, *Egypt* 76 B3
Bîr Autrun, *Sudan* 76 D2
Bîr Beiḑa, *Egypt* 69 E3
Bîr Diqnash, *Egypt* 76 A2
Bir el Abbes, *Algeria* 74 C3
Bîr el 'Abd, *Egypt* 69 D2
Bir el Ater, *Algeria* 75 B6
Bîr el Basur, *Egypt* 76 B2
Bîr el Biarât, *Egypt* 69 F3
Bîr el Duweidar, *Egypt* 69 E1
Bîr el Garârât, *Egypt* 69 D2
Bîr el Gellaz, *Egypt* 76 A2
Bîr el Heisi, *Egypt* 69 F3
Bîr el Jafir, *Egypt* 69 E1
Bîr el Mâlḩi, *Egypt* 69 E2
Bîr el Shaqqa, *Egypt* 76 A2
Bîr el Thamâda, *Egypt* 69 E2
Bîr Fuad, *Egypt* 76 A2
Bîr Gebeil Ḩişn, *Egypt* 69 E2
Bi'r Ghadīr, *Syria* 69 A6
Bîr Haimur, *Egypt* 76 C3
Bîr Ḩasana, *Egypt* 69 E2
Bi'r Jadīd, *Iraq* 64 C4
Bir Jdid, *Morocco* 74 B3
Bîr Kanayis, *Egypt* 76 C3
Bîr Kaseiba, *Egypt* 69 E2
Bîr Kerawein, *Egypt* 76 B2
Bîr Lahfân, *Egypt* 69 D2
Bir Lahrache, *Algeria* 75 B6
Bîr Madkûr, *Egypt* 69 E1
Bîr Maql, *Egypt* 76 C3
Bîr Misaha, *Egypt* 76 C2
Bir Mogrein, *Mauritania* 74 C2
Bîr Murr, *Egypt* 76 C3
Bi'r Muţribah, *Kuwait* 64 D5
Bîr Nakheila, *Egypt* 76 C3
Bîr Qaţia, *Egypt* 69 E1
Bîr Qatrani, *Egypt* 76 A2
Bîr Ranga, *Egypt* 76 C4
Bîr Sahara, *Egypt* 76 C2
Bîr Seiyâla, *Egypt* 76 B3
Bir Semguine, *Morocco* 74 B3
Bîr Shalatein, *Egypt* 76 C4
Bîr Shebb, *Egypt* 76 C2
Bîr Shût, *Egypt* 76 C4
Bîr Terfawi, *Egypt* 76 C2
Bîr Umm Qubûr, *Egypt* 76 C3
Bîr Ungât, *Egypt* 76 C3
Bîr Za'farâna, *Egypt* 76 J8
Bîr Zeidûn, *Egypt* 76 B3
Bira, *Indonesia* 57 E8
Bîra, *Romania* 38 B10
Biramféro, *Guinea* 78 C3
Birao, *C.A.R.* 73 F9
Birawa, *Zaïre* 82 C2
Bîrca, *Romania* 38 F6
Birch Hills, *Canada* 101 C7
Birch I., *Canada* 101 C9
Birch L., *N.W.T., Canada* 100 A5
Birch L., *Ont., Canada* 98 B1
Birch L., *U.S.A.* 98 C1
Birch Mts., *Canada* 100 B6
Birch River, *Canada* 101 C8
Birchip, *Australia* 91 F3
Bird, *Canada* 101 B10
Bird City, *U.S.A.* 108 F4
Bird I. = Aves, I. de, *W. Indies* 117 C7
Bird I., *S. Africa* 84 E2
Birdaard, *Neths.* 16 B7
Birdlip, *U.K.* 13 F5
Birdsville, *Australia* 90 D2
Birdum, *Australia* 88 C5
Birein, *Israel* 69 E3
Bireuen, *Indonesia* 56 C1
Birifo, *Gambia* 78 C2
Birigui, *Brazil* 127 A5
Birkenfeld, *Germany* 19 F3
Birkenhead, *U.K.* 12 D4
Birket Qârûn, *Egypt* 76 J7
Birkhadem, *Algeria* 75 A5
Bîrlad, *Romania* 38 C10
Birmingham, *U.K.* 13 E6
Birmingham, *U.S.A.* 105 J2
Birmitrapur, *India* 61 H14
Birni Ngaouré, *Niger* 79 C5
Birni Nkonni, *Niger* 79 C6
Birnin Gwari, *Nigeria* 79 C6
Birnin Kebbi, *Nigeria* 79 C5
Birnin Kudu, *Nigeria* 79 C6
Birobidzhan, *Russia* 45 E14
Birr, *Ireland* 15 C4
Birrie →, *Australia* 91 D4
Birs →, *Switz.* 22 B5
Birsilpur, *India* 62 E5
Birsk, *Russia* 44 D6
Birtin, *Romania* 38 C5
Birtle, *Canada* 101 C8
Birur, *India* 60 N9
Biryuchiy, *Ukraine* 42 C6
Birzai, *Lithuania* 40 C4
Bîrzava, *Romania* 38 C4
Birzebugga, *Malta* 37 D2
Bisa, *Indonesia* 57 E7
Bisáccia, *Italy* 35 A8
Bisacquino, *Italy* 34 E6
Bisalpur, *India* 63 E8
Bisbee, *U.S.A.* 111 L9
Biscarrosse et de Parentis, Étang de, *France* 26 D2
Biscay, B. of, *Atl. Oc.* 6 F5
Biscayne B., *U.S.A.* 105 N5
Biscéglie, *Italy* 35 A9
Bischofshofen, *Austria* 21 H3
Bischofswerda, *Germany* 18 D10
Bischofszell, *Switz.* 23 B8
Bischwiller, *France* 25 D14
Biscoe Bay, *Antarctica* 5 D13
Biscoe Is., *Antarctica* 5 C17
Biscostasing, *Canada* 98 C3
Biscucuy, *Venezuela* 120 B4
Biševo, *Croatia* 33 F13
Bisha, *Ethiopia* 77 D4
Bishah, W. →, *Si. Arabia* 76 C5
Bishan, *China* 52 C6
Bishkek, *Kirghizia* 44 E8
Bishnupur, *India* 63 H12
Bisho, *S. Africa* 85 E4
Bishop, *Calif., U.S.A.* 111 H4
Bishop, *Tex., U.S.A.* 109 M6
Bishop Auckland, *U.K.* 12 C6
Bishop's Falls, *Canada* 99 C8
Bishop's Stortford, *U.K.* 13 F8
Bisignano, *Italy* 35 C9
Bisina, L., *Uganda* 82 B3
Biskra, *Algeria* 75 B6
Bislig, *Phil.* 57 C7
Bismarck, *U.S.A.* 108 B4
Bismarck Arch., *Papua N. G.* 92 H6
Bismark, *Germany* 18 C7
Biso, *Uganda* 82 B3
Bison, *U.S.A.* 108 C3
Bīsotūn, *Iran* 64 C5
Bispfors, *Sweden* 8 E14
Bispgården, *Sweden* 10 A10
Bissagos = Bijagós, Arquipélago dos, *Guinea-Biss.* 78 C1
Bissau, *Guinea-Biss.* 78 C1
Bissett, *Canada* 101 C9
Bissikrima, *Guinea* 78 C2
Bistcho L., *Canada* 100 B5
Bistreţu, *Romania* 38 F6
Bistrica = Ilirska-Bistrica, *Slovenia* 33 C11
Bistriţa, *Romania* 38 B7
Bistriţa →, *Romania* 38 C9
Bistriţei, Munţii, *Romania* 38 B8
Biswan, *India* 63 F9
Bitam, *Gabon* 80 D2
Bitburg, *Germany* 19 F2
Bitche, *France* 25 C14
Bithynia, *Turkey* 66 C4
Bitkine, *Chad* 73 F8
Bitlis, *Turkey* 67 D10
Bitlis □, *Turkey* 67 D10
Bitola, *Macedonia, Yug.* 39 H4
Bitolj = Bitola, *Macedonia, Yug.* 39 H4
Bitonto, *Italy* 35 A9
Bitter Creek, *U.S.A.* 110 F9
Bitter L. = Buheirat-Murrat-el-Kubra, *Egypt* 76 H8
Bitterfeld, *Germany* 18 D8
Bitterfontein, *S. Africa* 84 E2
Bitterroot →, *U.S.A.* 110 C6
Bitterroot Range, *U.S.A.* 110 D6
Bitterwater, *U.S.A.* 112 J6
Bitti, *Italy* 34 B2
Bittou, *Burkina Faso* 79 C4
Biu, *Nigeria* 79 C7
Bivolari, *Romania* 38 B10
Biwa-Ko, *Japan* 49 G8
Biwabik, *U.S.A.* 108 B8
Bixad, *Romania* 38 B6
Biyang, *China* 50 H7
Biysk, *Russia* 44 D9
Bizana, *S. Africa* 85 E4
Bizen, *Japan* 49 G7
Bizerte, *Tunisia* 75 A6
Bjargtangar, *Iceland* 8 D1
Bjelasica, *Montenegro, Yug.* 21 N9
Bjelovar, *Croatia* 21 K6
Bjerringbro, *Denmark* 11 H3
Bjørnøya, *Arctic* 4 B8
Bjuv, *Sweden* 11 H6
Blace, *Serbia, Yug.* 21 M11
Black = Da →, *Vietnam* 58 B5
Black →, *Canada* 106 B5
Black →, *Ark., U.S.A.* 109 H9
Black →, *N.Y., U.S.A.* 107 C8
Black →, *Wis., U.S.A.* 108 D9
Black Diamond, *Canada* 100 C6
Black Forest = Schwarzwald, *Germany* 19 H4
Black Hills, *U.S.A.* 108 C3
Black I., *Canada* 101 C9
Black L., *Canada* 101 B7
Black L., *U.S.A.* 104 C3
Black Mesa, *U.S.A.* 109 G3
Black Mt. = Mynydd Du, *U.K.* 13 F4
Black Mts., *U.K.* 13 F4
Black Range, *U.S.A.* 111 K10
Black River, *Jamaica* 116 C4
Black River Falls, *U.S.A.* 108 C9
Black Sea, *Europe* 42 E6
Black Volta →, *Africa* 78 D4
Black Warrior →, *U.S.A.* 105 J2
Blackall, *Australia* 90 C4
Blackball, *N.Z.* 87 K3
Blackbull, *Australia* 90 B3
Blackburn, *U.K.* 12 D5
Blackduck, *U.S.A.* 108 B7
Blackfoot, *U.S.A.* 110 E7
Blackfoot →, *U.S.A.* 110 C7
Blackfoot Res., *U.S.A.* 110 E8
Blackie, *Canada* 100 C6
Blackpool, *U.K.* 12 D4
Blackriver, *U.S.A.* 106 B1
Blacks Harbour, *Canada* 99 C6
Blacksburg, *U.S.A.* 104 G5
Blacksod B., *Ireland* 15 B2
Blackstone, *U.S.A.* 104 G6
Blackstone →, *Canada* 100 A4
Blackstone Ra., *Australia* 89 E4
Blackville, *Canada* 99 C6
Blackwater, *Australia* 90 C4
Blackwater →, *Ireland* 15 E4
Blackwater →, *U.K.* 15 B5
Blackwater Cr. →, *Australia* 91 D3
Blackwell, *U.S.A.* 109 G6
Blackwells Corner, *U.S.A.* 113 K7
Bladel, *Neths.* 17 F6
Blaenau Ffestiniog, *U.K.* 12 E4
Blagodarnoye, *Russia* 43 D10
Blagoevgrad, *Bulgaria* 39 G6
Blagoveshchensk, *Russia* 45 D13
Blain, *France* 24 E5
Blaine, *U.S.A.* 112 B4
Blaine Lake, *Canada* 101 C7
Blainville-sur-l'Eau, *France* 25 D13
Blair, *U.S.A.* 108 E6
Blair Athol, *Australia* 90 C4
Blair Atholl, *U.K.* 14 E5
Blairgowrie, *U.K.* 14 E5
Blairmore, *Canada* 100 D6
Blairsden, *U.S.A.* 112 F6
Blairsville, *U.S.A.* 106 F5
Blaj, *Romania* 38 C6
Blake Pt., *U.S.A.* 108 A10
Blakely, *U.S.A.* 105 K3
Blâmont, *France* 25 D13
Blanc, C., *Tunisia* 75 A6
Blanc, Mont, *Alps* 27 C10
Blanca, B., *Argentina* 128 A4
Blanca Peak, *U.S.A.* 111 H11
Blanchard, *U.S.A.* 109 H6
Blanche, C., *Australia* 91 E1
Blanche, L., *S. Austral., Australia* 91 D2
Blanche, L., *W. Austral., Australia* 88 D3
Blanco, *S. Africa* 84 E3
Blanco, *U.S.A.* 109 K5
Blanco →, *Argentina* 126 C2
Blanco, C., *Costa Rica* 116 E2
Blanco, C., *Spain* 36 B9
Blanco, C., *U.S.A.* 110 E1
Blanda →, *Iceland* 8 D4
Blandford Forum, *U.K.* 13 G5
Blanding, *U.S.A.* 111 H9
Blanes, *Spain* 28 D7
Blangy-sur-Bresle, *France* 25 C8
Blanice →, *Czech.* 20 F4
Blankenberge, *Belgium* 17 F2
Blankenburg, *Germany* 18 D6
Blanquefort, *France* 26 D3
Blanquillo, *Uruguay* 127 C4
Blansko, *Czech.* 20 F6
Blantyre, *Malawi* 83 F4
Blaricum, *Neths.* 16 D6
Blarney, *Ireland* 15 E3
Blato, *Croatia* 33 F13
Blatten, *Switz.* 22 D5
Blaubeuren, *Germany* 19 G5
Blåvands Huk, *Denmark* 9 J10
Blaydon, *U.K.* 12 C6
Blaye, *France* 26 C3
Blaye-les-Mines, *France* 26 D6
Blayney, *Australia* 91 E4
Blaze, Pt., *Australia* 88 B5
Bleckede, *Germany* 18 B6
Bled, *Slovenia* 33 B11
Blednaya, Gora, *Russia* 44 B7
Bléharis, *Belgium* 17 G2
Blejeşti, *Romania* 38 E8
Blekinge län □, *Sweden* 9 H13
Blenheim, *Canada* 106 D2
Blenheim, *N.Z.* 87 J4
Bléone →, *France* 27 D10
Blerick, *Neths.* 17 F8
Bletchley, *U.K.* 13 F7
Blida, *Algeria* 75 A5
Blidet Amor, *Algeria* 75 B6
Blidö, *Sweden* 10 E12
Bligh Sound, *N.Z.* 87 L1
Blind River, *Canada* 98 C3
Blinnenhorn, *Switz.* 23 D6
Blitar, *Indonesia* 57 H15
Blitta, *Togo* 79 D5
Block I., *U.S.A.* 107 E13
Block Island Sd., *U.S.A.* 107 E13
Blodgett Iceberg Tongue, *Antarctica* 5 C9
Bloemendaal, *Neths.* 16 D5
Bloemfontein, *S. Africa* 84 D4
Bloemhof, *S. Africa* 84 D4
Blois, *France* 24 E8
Blokziji, *Neths.* 16 C7
Blönduós, *Iceland* 8 D3
Bloodvein →, *Canada* 101 C9
Bloody Foreland, *Ireland* 15 A3
Bloomer, *U.S.A.* 108 C9
Bloomfield, *Australia* 90 B4
Bloomfield, *Canada* 106 C7
Bloomfield, *Iowa, U.S.A.* 108 E8
Bloomfield, *N. Mex., U.S.A.* 111 H10
Bloomfield, *Nebr., U.S.A.* 108 D6
Bloomington, *Ill., U.S.A.* 108 E10
Bloomington, *Ind., U.S.A.* 104 F2
Bloomsburg, *U.S.A.* 107 F8
Blora, *Indonesia* 57 G14
Blossburg, *U.S.A.* 106 E7
Blouberg, *S. Africa* 85 C4
Blountstown, *U.S.A.* 105 K3
Bludenz, *Austria* 19 H5
Blue Island, *U.S.A.* 104 E2
Blue Lake, *U.S.A.* 110 F2
Blue Mesa Res., *U.S.A.* 111 G10
Blue Mts., *Oreg., U.S.A.* 110 D4
Blue Mts., *Pa., U.S.A.* 107 F8
Blue Mud B., *Australia* 90 A2
Blue Nile = An Nîl el Azraq □, *Sudan* 77 E3
Blue Nile = Nîl el Azraq →, *Sudan* 77 D3
Blue Rapids, *U.S.A.* 108 F6
Blue Ridge Mts., *U.S.A.* 105 G5
Blue Stack Mts., *Ireland* 15 B3
Blueberry →, *Canada* 100 B4
Bluefield, *U.S.A.* 104 G5
Bluefields, *Nic.* 116 D3
Bluff, *Australia* 90 C4
Bluff, *N.Z.* 87 M2
Bluff, *U.S.A.* 111 H9
Bluff Knoll, *Australia* 89 F2
Bluff Pt., *Australia* 89 E1
Bluffton, *U.S.A.* 104 E3
Blumenau, *Brazil* 127 B6
Blümisalphorn, *Switz.* 22 D5
Blunt, *U.S.A.* 108 C4
Bly, *U.S.A.* 110 E3
Blyth, *Canada* 106 C3
Blyth, *U.K.* 12 B6
Blyth Bridge, *U.K.* 12 E5
Blythe, *U.S.A.* 113 M12
Bø, *Norway* 10 E3
Bo, *S. Leone* 78 D2
Bo Duc, *Vietnam* 59 G6
Bo Hai, *China* 51 E10
Bo Xian, *China* 50 H8
Boa Esperança, *Brazil* 121 C5
Boa Nova, *Brazil* 123 D3
Boa Viagem, *Brazil* 122 C4
Boa Vista, *Brazil* 121 C5
Boac, *Phil.* 55 E4
Boaco, *Nic.* 116 D2
Bo'ai, *China* 50 G7
Boal, *Spain* 30 B4
Boardman, *U.S.A.* 106 E4
Boatman, *Australia* 91 D4
Bobadah, *Australia* 91 E4
Bobai, *China* 52 F7
Bobbili, *India* 61 K13
Bóbbio, *Italy* 32 D6
Bobcaygeon, *Canada* 98 D4
Böblingen, *Germany* 19 G5
Bobo-Dioulasso, *Burkina Faso* 78 C4
Boboc, *Romania* 38 D9
Bobonaza →, *Ecuador* 120 D2
Bobov Dol, *Bulgaria* 38 G5
Bóbr →, *Poland* 20 C5
Bobraomby, Tanjon' i, *Madag.* 85 A8
Bobrinets, *Ukraine* 42 B5
Bobrov, *Russia* 41 F12
Bobruysk, *Belorussia* 40 E6
Bobures, *Venezuela* 120 B3
Boca de Drago, *Venezuela* 121 A5
Bôca do Acre, *Brazil* 124 B4
Bôca do Jari, *Brazil* 121 D7
Bôca do Moaco, *Brazil* 124 B4
Boca Grande, *Venezuela* 121 B5
Boca Raton, *U.S.A.* 105 M5
Bocaiúva, *Brazil* 123 E3
Bocanda, *Ivory C.* 78 D4
Bocaranga, *C.A.R.* 73 G8
Bocas del Toro, *Panama* 116 E3
Boceguillas, *Spain* 28 D1
Bochnia, *Poland* 20 F10
Bocholt, *Belgium* 17 F7
Bocholt, *Germany* 18 D2
Bochum, *Germany* 18 D3
Bockenem, *Germany* 18 C6
Bocognano, *France* 27 F13
Boconó, *Venezuela* 120 B3
Boconó →, *Venezuela* 120 B4
Bocoyna, *Mexico* 114 B3
Bocq →, *Belgium* 17 H5
Boda, *C.A.R.* 80 D3
Bodaybo, *Russia* 45 D12
Boddington, *Australia* 89 F2
Bodega Bay, *U.S.A.* 112 G3
Bodegraven, *Neths.* 16 D5
Boden, *Sweden* 8 D16
Bodensee, *Europe* 23 A8
Bodenteich, *Germany* 18 C6
Bodhan, *India* 60 K10
Bodinga, *Nigeria* 79 C6
Bodio, *Switz.* 23 D7
Bodmin, *U.K.* 13 G3
Bodmin Moor, *U.K.* 13 G3
Bodoquena, Serra da, *Brazil* 125 E6
Bodrog →, *Hungary* 21 G11
Bodrum, *Turkey* 66 E2
Boechout, *Belgium* 17 F5
Boegoebergdam, *S. Africa* 84 D3
Boekelo, *Neths.* 16 D9
Boelenslaan, *Neths.* 16 B8
Boën, *France* 27 C8
Boende, *Zaïre* 80 E4
Boerne, *U.S.A.* 109 L5
Boertange, *Neths.* 16 B10
Boezinge, *Belgium* 17 G1
Boffa, *Guinea* 78 C2
Bogalusa, *U.S.A.* 109 K10
Bogan Gate, *Australia* 91 E4
Bogantungan, *Australia* 90 C4
Bogata, *U.S.A.* 109 J7
Bogatić, *Serbia, Yug.* 21 L9
Boğazlıyan, *Turkey* 66 D6
Bogense, *Denmark* 11 J4
Boggabilla, *Australia* 91 D5
Boggabri, *Australia* 91 E5
Boggeragh Mts., *Ireland* 15 D3
Bognor Regis, *U.K.* 13 G7
Bogø, *Denmark* 11 K6
Bogo, *Phil.* 55 F6
Bogodukhov, *Ukraine* 42 A6
Bogong, Mt., *Australia* 91 F4
Bogor, *Indonesia* 57 G12
Bogoroditsk, *Russia* 41 E11
Bogorodsk, *Russia* 41 C13
Bogorodskoye, *Russia* 45 D15
Bogoso, *Ghana* 78 D4
Bogotá, *Colombia* 120 C3
Bogotol, *Russia* 44 D9
Bogra, *Bangla.* 61 G16
Boguchany, *Russia* 45 D10
Boguchar, *Russia* 43 B9
Bogué, *Mauritania* 78 B2
Boguslav, *Ukraine* 42 B4
Bohain-en-Vermandois, *France* 25 C10
Bohemia Downs, *Australia* 88 C4
Bohemian Forest = Böhmerwald, *Germany* 19 F8
Bohena Cr. →, *Australia* 91 E4
Bohinjska Bistrica, *Slovenia* 33 B11
Böhmerwald, *Germany* 19 F8
Bohmte, *Germany* 18 C4
Bohol, *Phil.* 55 G6
Bohol Sea, *Phil.* 57 C6
Bohotleh, *Somali Rep.* 68 F4
Boi, *Nigeria* 79 D6
Boi, Pta. de, *Brazil* 127 A6
Boiaçu, *Brazil* 121 D5
Boiano, *Italy* 35 A7
Boileau, C., *Australia* 88 C3
Boipeba, I. de, *Brazil* 123 D4
Bois →, *Brazil* 123 E1
Boischot, *Belgium* 17 F5
Boise, *U.S.A.* 110 E5
Boise City, *U.S.A.* 109 G3
Boissevain, *Canada* 101 D8
Boîte →, *Italy* 33 B9
Boitzenburg, *Germany* 18 B9
Boizenburg, *Germany* 18 B6
Bojador C., *W. Sahara* 74 C2
Bojnūrd, *Iran* 65 B8

Bojonegoro, *Indonesia* 57 G14
Boju, *Nigeria* 79 D6
Boka Kotorska, *Montenegro, Yug.* 21 N8
Bokala, *Ivory C.* 78 D4
Boké, *Guinea* 78 C2
Bokhara →, *Australia* 91 D4
Bokkos, *Nigeria* 79 D6
Boknafjorden, *Norway* 9 G8
Bokoro, *Chad* 73 F8
Bokote, *Zaïre* 80 E4
Boksitogorsk, *Russia* 40 B8
Bokungu, *Zaïre* 80 E4
Bol, *Chad* 73 F7
Bol, *Croatia* 33 E13
Bolama, *Guinea-Biss.* 78 C1
Bolan Pass, *Pakistan* 60 E5
Bolaños →, *Mexico* 114 C4
Bolbec, *France* 24 C7
Boldājī, *Iran* 65 D6
Boldeşti, *Romania* 38 D9
Bole, *China* 54 B3
Bole, *Ethiopia* 77 F4
Bolekhov, *Ukraine* 40 G3
Bolesławiec, *Poland* 20 D5
Bolgatanga, *Ghana* 79 C4
Bolgrad, *Ukraine* 42 D3
Boli, *Sudan* 77 F2
Bolinao, *Phil.* 55 C3
Bolinao C., *Phil.* 57 A5
Bolívar, *Argentina* 126 D3
Bolívar, *Antioquía, Colombia* 120 B2
Bolívar, *Cauca, Colombia* 120 C2
Bolívar, *Peru* 124 B2
Bolivar, *Mo., U.S.A.* 109 G8
Bolivar, *Tenn., U.S.A.* 109 H10
Bolívar □, *Colombia* 120 B3
Bolívar □, *Ecuador* 120 D2
Bolívar □, *Venezuela* 121 B5
Bolivia ■, *S. Amer.* 125 D5
Bolivian Plateau, *S. Amer.* 118 D3
Bolkhov, *Russia* 41 E10
Bollène, *France* 27 D8
Bollnäs, *Sweden* 10 C10
Bollon, *Australia* 91 D4
Bollstabruk, *Sweden* 10 A11
Bollullos, *Spain* 31 H4
Bolobo, *Zaïre* 80 E3
Bologna, *Italy* 33 D8
Bologne, *France* 25 D12
Bologoye, *Russia* 40 C9
Bolomba, *Zaïre* 80 D3
Bolonchenticul, *Mexico* 115 D7
Bolong, *Phil.* 57 C6
Boloven, Cao Nguyen, *Laos* 58 E6
Bolpur, *India* 63 H12
Bolsena, *Italy* 33 F8
Bolsena, L. di, *Italy* 33 F8
Bolshaya Glushitsa, *Russia* 41 E17
Bolshaya Martynovka, *Russia* 43 C9
Bolshaya Vradiyevka, *Ukraine* 42 C4
Bolshereche, *Russia* 44 D8
Bolshevik, Ostrov, *Russia* 45 B11
Bolshoi Kavkas, *Asia* 43 E11
Bolshoy Anyuy →, *Russia* 45 C17
Bolshoy Atlym, *Russia* 44 C7
Bolshoy Begichev, Ostrov, *Russia* 45 B12
Bolshoy Lyakhovskiy, Ostrov, *Russia* 45 B15
Bolshoy Tokmak, *Ukraine* 42 C6
Bol'shoy Tyuters, *Estonia* 40 B5
Bolsward, *Neths.* 16 B7
Boltaña, *Spain* 28 C5
Boltigen, *Switz.* 22 C4
Bolton, *Canada* 106 C5
Bolton, *U.K.* 12 D5
Bolu, *Turkey* 66 C4
Bolu □, *Turkey* 66 C4
Boluo, *China* 53 F10
Bolvadin, *Turkey* 66 D4
Bolzano, *Italy* 33 B8
Bom Comércio, *Brazil* 125 B4
Bom Conselho, *Brazil* 122 C4
Bom Despacho, *Brazil* 123 E2
Bom Jesus, *Brazil* 122 C3
Bom Jesus da Gurguéia, Serra, *Brazil* 122 C3
Bom Jesus da Lapa, *Brazil* 123 D3
Boma, *Zaïre* 80 F2
Bomaderry, *Australia* 91 E5
Bombala, *Australia* 91 F4
Bombarral, *Portugal* 31 F1
Bombay, *India* 60 K8
Bomboma, *Zaïre* 80 D3
Bombombwa, *Zaïre* 82 B2
Bomi Hills, *Liberia* 78 D2
Bomili, *Zaïre* 82 B2
Bommel, *Neths.* 16 E4
Bomokandi →, *Zaïre* 82 B2
Bomongo, *Zaïre* 80 D3
Bomu →, *C.A.R.* 80 D4
Bon, C., *Tunisia* 75 A7
Bon Sar Pa, *Vietnam* 58 F6
Bonaduz, *Switz.* 23 C8
Bonaire, *Neth. Ant.* 117 D6
Bonang, *Australia* 91 F4
Bonanza, *Nic.* 116 D3
Bonaparte Arch., *Australia* 88 B3
Boñar, *Spain* 30 C5
Bonaventure, *Canada* 99 C6
Bonavista, *Canada* 99 C9
Bonavista, C., *Canada* 99 C9
Bonawan, *Phil.* 55 G5
Bondeno, *Italy* 33 D8
Bondo, *Zaïre* 82 B1
Bondoukou, *Ivory C.* 78 D4
Bondowoso, *Indonesia* 57 G15
Bone, Teluk, *Indonesia* 57 E6
Bone Rate, *Indonesia* 57 F6
Bone Rate, Kepulauan, *Indonesia* 57 F6
Bonefro, *Italy* 35 A7
Bo'ness, *U.K.* 14 E5
Bong Son = Hoai Nhon, *Vietnam* 58 E7
Bongabong, *Phil.* 55 E4
Bongandanga, *Zaïre* 80 D4
Bongor, *Chad* 73 F8
Bongouanou, *Ivory C.* 78 D4
Bonham, *U.S.A.* 109 J6
Bonheiden, *Belgium* 17 F5
Bonifacio, *France* 27 G13
Bonifacio, Bouches de, *Medit. S.* 34 A2
Bonin Is. = Ogasawara Gunto, *Pac. Oc.* 92 E6
Bonke, *Ethiopia* 77 F4
Bonn, *Germany* 18 E3
Bonnat, *France* 26 B5
Bonne Terre, *U.S.A.* 109 G9
Bonners Ferry, *U.S.A.* 110 B5
Bonnétable, *France* 24 D7
Bonneuil-Matours, *France* 24 F7
Bonneval, *France* 24 D8
Bonneville, *France* 27 B10
Bonney, L., *Australia* 91 F3
Bonnie Downs, *Australia* 90 C3
Bonnie Rock, *Australia* 89 F2
Bonny, *Nigeria* 79 E6
Bonny →, *Nigeria* 79 E6
Bonny, Bight of, *Africa* 79 E6
Bonny-sur-Loire, *France* 25 E9
Bonnyville, *Canada* 101 C6
Bonoi, *Indonesia* 57 E9
Bonorva, *Italy* 34 B1
Bonsall, *U.S.A.* 113 M9
Bontang, *Indonesia* 56 D5
Bonthain, *Indonesia* 57 F5
Bonthe, *S. Leone* 78 D2
Bontoc, *Phil.* 55 C4
Bonyeri, *Ghana* 78 D4
Bonython Ra., *Australia* 88 D4
Bookabie, *Australia* 89 F5
Booker, *U.S.A.* 109 G4
Boolaboolka L., *Australia* 91 E3
Booligal, *Australia* 91 E3
Boom, *Belgium* 17 F4
Boonah, *Australia* 91 D5
Boone, *Iowa, U.S.A.* 108 D8
Boone, *N.C., U.S.A.* 105 G5
Booneville, *Ark., U.S.A.* 109 H8
Booneville, *Miss., U.S.A.* 105 H1
Boonville, *Calif., U.S.A.* 112 F3
Boonville, *Ind., U.S.A.* 104 F2
Boonville, *Mo., U.S.A.* 108 F8
Boonville, *N.Y., U.S.A.* 107 C9
Boorindal, *Australia* 91 E4
Boorowa, *Australia* 91 E4
Boothia, Gulf of, *Canada* 97 A11
Boothia Pen., *Canada* 96 A10
Bootle, *Cumb., U.K.* 12 C4
Bootle, *Mersey., U.K.* 12 D4
Booué, *Gabon* 80 E2
Bophuthatswana □, *S. Africa* 84 D4
Boppard, *Germany* 19 E3
Boquerón □, *Paraguay* 125 E5
Boquete, *Panama* 116 E3
Boquilla, Presa de la, *Mexico* 114 B3
Boquillas del Carmen, *Mexico* 114 B4
Bor, *Czech.* 20 F2
Bor, *Serbia, Yug.* 21 L12
Bôr, *Sudan* 77 F3
Bor, *Turkey* 66 E6
Bor Mashash, *Israel* 69 D3
Boradā →, *Syria* 69 B5
Borah Pk., *U.S.A.* 110 D7
Borama, *Somali Rep.* 68 F3
Borang, *Sudan* 77 G3
Borås, *Sweden* 11 G6
Borāzjān, *Iran* 65 D6
Borba, *Brazil* 121 D6
Borba, *Portugal* 31 G3
Borborema, Planalto da, *Brazil* 122 C4
Borçka, *Turkey* 43 F9
Bord Khūn-e Now, *Iran* 65 D6
Borda, C., *Australia* 91 F2
Bordeaux, *France* 26 D3
Borden, *Australia* 89 F2
Borden, *Canada* 99 C7
Borden I., *Canada* 4 B2
Borders □, *U.K.* 14 F6
Bordertown, *Australia* 91 F3
Borðeyri, *Iceland* 8 D3
Bordighera, *Italy* 32 E4
Bordj bou Arreridj, *Algeria* 75 A5
Bordj Bourguiba, *Tunisia* 75 B7
Bordj el Hobra, *Algeria* 75 B5
Bordj Fly Ste. Marie, *Algeria* 74 C4
Bordj-in-Eker, *Algeria* 75 D6
Bordj Menaiel, *Algeria* 75 A5
Bordj Messouda, *Algeria* 75 B6
Bordj Nili, *Algeria* 75 B5
Bordj Omar Driss, *Algeria* 75 C6
Bordj-Tarat, *Algeria* 75 C6
Bordj Zelfana, *Algeria* 75 B5
Borensberg, *Sweden* 11 F9
Borgå, *Finland* 9 F18
Borgarnes, *Iceland* 8 D3
Børgefjellet, *Norway* 8 D12
Borger, *Neths.* 16 C9
Borger, *U.S.A.* 109 H4
Borgerhout, *Belgium* 17 F4
Borghamn, *Sweden* 11 F8
Borgholm, *Sweden* 9 H14
Bórgia, *Italy* 35 D9
Borgloon, *Belgium* 17 G6
Borgo San Dalmazzo, *Italy* 32 D4
Borgo San Lorenzo, *Italy* 33 E8
Borgo Valsugano, *Italy* 33 B8
Borgomanero, *Italy* 32 C5
Borgonovo Val Tidone, *Italy* 32 C6
Borgorose, *Italy* 33 F10
Borgosésia, *Italy* 32 C5
Borgvattnet, *Sweden* 10 A9
Borikhane, *Laos* 58 C4
Borislav, *Ukraine* 40 G3
Borisoglebsk, *Russia* 41 F13
Borisoglebskiy, *Russia* 41 C13
Borisov, *Belorussia* 40 D6
Borispol, *Ukraine* 40 F7
Borja, *Peru* 120 D2
Borja, *Spain* 28 D3
Borjas Blancas, *Spain* 28 D5
Borken, *Germany* 18 D2
Borkou, *Chad* 73 E8
Borkum, *Germany* 18 B2
Borlänge, *Sweden* 9 F13
Borley, C., *Antarctica* 5 C5
Bormida →, *Italy* 32 D5
Bórmio, *Italy* 32 B7
Born, *Neths.* 17 F7
Borna, *Germany* 18 D8
Borndiep, *Neths.* 16 B7
Borne, *Neths.* 16 D9
Bornem, *Belgium* 17 F4
Borneo, *E. Indies* 56 D5
Bornholm, *Denmark* 9 J13
Borno □, *Nigeria* 79 C7
Bornos, *Spain* 31 J5
Bornu Yassa, *Nigeria* 79 C7
Borobudur, *Indonesia* 57 G14
Borodino, *Russia* 40 D9
Borogontsy, *Russia* 45 C14
Boromo, *Burkina Faso* 78 C4
Boron, *U.S.A.* 113 L9
Borongan, *Phil.* 55 F6
Bororen, *Australia* 90 C5
Borotangba Mts., *C.A.R.* 77 F1
Borovan, *Bulgaria* 38 F6
Borovichi, *Russia* 40 B8
Borovsk, *Russia* 41 D10
Borrego Springs, *U.S.A.* 113 M10
Borriol, *Spain* 28 E4
Borroloola, *Australia* 90 B2
Borşa, *Romania* 38 B7
Borssele, *Neths.* 17 F3
Bort-les-Orgues, *France* 26 C6
Borth, *U.K.* 13 E3
Borujerd, *Iran* 65 C6
Borzhomi, *Georgia* 43 F10
Borzna, *Ukraine* 40 F8
Borzya, *Russia* 45 D12
Bosa, *Italy* 34 B1
Bosanska Dubica, *Bos.-H., Yug.* 33 C13
Bosanska Gradiška, *Bos.-H., Yug.* 21 K7
Bosanska Kostajnica, *Bos.-H., Yug.* 33 C13
Bosanska Krupa, *Bos.-H., Yug.* 33 D13
Bosanski Novi, *Bos.-H., Yug.* 33 C13
Bosanski Šamac, *Bos.-H., Yug.* 21 K8
Bosansko Grahovo, *Bos.-H., Yug.* 33 D13
Bosansko Petrovac, *Bos.-H., Yug.* 33 D13
Bosaso, *Somali Rep.* 68 E4
Boscastle, *U.K.* 13 G3
Boscotrecase, *Italy* 35 B7
Bose, *China* 52 F6
Boshan, *China* 51 F9
Boshoek, *S. Africa* 84 D4
Boshof, *S. Africa* 84 D4
Boshrūyeh, *Iran* 65 C8
Bosilegrad, *Serbia, Yug.* 21 N12
Boskoop, *Neths.* 16 D5
Bosna →, *Bos.-H., Yug.* 21 K8
Bosna i Hercegovina = Bosnia-Herzegovina □, *Bos.-H., Yug.* 21 L7
Bosnia-Herzegovina □, *Bos.-H., Yug.* 21 L7
Bosnik, *Indonesia* 57 E9
Bosobolo, *Zaïre* 80 D3
Bosporus = Karadeniz Boğazı, *Turkey* 66 C3
Bossangoa, *C.A.R.* 73 G8
Bossekop, *Norway* 8 B17
Bossembélé, *C.A.R.* 73 G8
Bossier City, *U.S.A.* 109 J8
Bosso, *Niger* 79 C7
Bostānābād, *Iran* 64 B5
Bosten Hu, *China* 54 B3
Boston, *U.K.* 12 E7
Boston, *U.S.A.* 107 D13
Boston Bar, *Canada* 100 D4
Bosut →, *Croatia* 21 K8
Boswell, *Canada* 100 D5
Boswell, *Okla., U.S.A.* 109 H7
Boswell, *Pa., U.S.A.* 106 F5
Botad, *India* 62 H4
Botan →, *Turkey* 67 E9
Botany B., *Australia* 91 E5
Botene, *Laos* 58 D3
Botevgrad, *Bulgaria* 38 G6
Bothaville, *S. Africa* 84 D4
Bothnia, G. of, *Europe* 8 E16
Bothwell, *Australia* 90 G4
Bothwell, *Canada* 106 D3
Boticas, *Portugal* 30 D3
Botletle →, *Botswana* 84 C3
Botoşani, *Romania* 38 B9
Botro, *Ivory C.* 78 D3
Botswana ■, *Africa* 84 C3
Bottineau, *U.S.A.* 108 A4
Bottrop, *Germany* 17 E9
Botucatu, *Brazil* 127 A6
Botwood, *Canada* 99 C8
Bou Alam, *Algeria* 75 B5
Bou Ali, *Algeria* 75 C4
Bou Djébéha, *Mali* 78 B4
Bou Guema, *Algeria* 75 C5
Bou Ismael, *Algeria* 75 A5
Bou Izakarn, *Morocco* 74 C3
Boû Lanouâr, *Mauritania* 74 D1
Bou Saâda, *Algeria* 75 A5
Bou Salem, *Tunisia* 75 A6
Bouaké, *Ivory C.* 78 D3
Bouar, *C.A.R.* 80 C3
Bouârfa, *Morocco* 75 B4
Bouca, *C.A.R.* 73 G8
Boucau, *France* 26 E2
Boucaut B., *Australia* 90 A1
Bouches-du-Rhône □, *France* 27 E9
Bouda, *Algeria* 75 C4
Boudenib, *Morocco* 74 B4
Boudry, *Switz.* 22 C3
Boufarik, *Algeria* 75 A5
Bougainville, C., *Australia* 88 B4
Bougainville Reef, *Australia* 90 B4
Bougaroun, C., *Algeria* 75 A6
Bougie = Bejaia, *Algeria* 75 A6
Bougouni, *Mali* 78 C3
Bouillon, *Belgium* 17 J6
Bouïra, *Algeria* 75 A5
Boulder, *Colo., U.S.A.* 108 E2
Boulder, *Mont., U.S.A.* 110 C7
Boulder City, *U.S.A.* 113 K12
Boulder Creek, *U.S.A.* 112 H4
Boulder Dam = Hoover Dam, *U.S.A.* 113 K12
Bouli, *Mauritania* 78 B2
Boulia, *Australia* 90 C2
Bouligny, *France* 25 C12
Boulogne →, *France* 24 E5
Boulogne-sur-Gesse, *France* 26 E4
Boulogne-sur-Mer, *France* 25 B8
Bouloire, *France* 24 E7
Boulsa, *Burkina Faso* 79 C4
Boultoum, *Niger* 79 C7
Boumalne, *Morocco* 74 B3
Boun Neua, *Laos* 58 B3
Boun Tai, *Laos* 58 B3
Bouna, *Ivory C.* 78 D4
Boundary Pk., *U.S.A.* 112 H8
Boundiali, *Ivory C.* 78 D3
Bountiful, *U.S.A.* 110 F8
Bounty Is., *Pac. Oc.* 92 M9
Bourbon-Lancy, *France* 26 B7
Bourbon-l'Archambault, *France* 26 B7
Bourbonnais, *France* 26 B7
Bourbonne-les-Bains, *France* 25 E12
Bourem, *Mali* 79 B4
Bourg, *France* 26 C3
Bourg-Argental, *France* 27 C8
Bourg-de-Péage, *France* 27 C9
Bourg-en-Bresse, *France* 27 B9
Bourg-St.-Andéol, *France* 27 D8
Bourg-St.-Maurice, *France* 27 C10
Bourg-St.-Pierre, *Switz.* 22 E4
Bourganeuf, *France* 26 C5
Bourges, *France* 25 E9
Bourget, *Canada* 107 A9
Bourget, L. du, *France* 27 C9
Bourgneuf, B. de, *France* 24 E4
Bourgneuf-en-Retz, *France* 24 E5
Bourgogne, *France* 25 F11
Bourgoin-Jallieu, *France* 27 C9
Bourgueil, *France* 24 E7
Bourke, *Australia* 91 E4
Bournemouth, *U.K.* 13 G6
Bourriot-Bergonce, *France* 26 D3
Bouse, *U.S.A.* 113 M13
Boussac, *France* 26 B6
Boussens, *France* 26 E4
Bousso, *Chad* 73 F8
Boussu, *Belgium* 17 H3
Boutilimit, *Mauritania* 78 B2
Bouvet I. = Bouvetøya, *Antarctica* 3 G10
Bouvetøya, *Antarctica* 3 G10
Bouznika, *Morocco* 74 B3
Bouzonville, *France* 25 C13
Bova Marina, *Italy* 35 E8
Bovalino Marina, *Italy* 35 D9
Bovec, *Slovenia* 33 B10
Bovenkarspel, *Neths.* 16 C6
Bovigny, *Belgium* 17 H7
Bovill, *U.S.A.* 110 C5
Bovino, *Italy* 35 A8
Bow Island, *Canada* 100 D6
Bowbells, *U.S.A.* 108 A3
Bowdle, *U.S.A.* 108 C5
Bowelling, *Australia* 89 F2
Bowen, *Australia* 90 C4
Bowen Mts., *Australia* 91 F4
Bowie, *Ariz., U.S.A.* 111 K9
Bowie, *Tex., U.S.A.* 109 J6
Bowkān, *Iran* 64 B5
Bowland, Forest of, *U.K.* 12 D5
Bowling Green, *Ky., U.S.A.* 104 G2
Bowling Green, *Ohio, U.S.A.* 104 E4
Bowling Green, C., *Australia* 90 B4
Bowman, *U.S.A.* 108 B3
Bowman I., *Antarctica* 5 C8
Bowmans, *Australia* 91 E2
Bowmanville, *Canada* 98 D4
Bowmore, *U.K.* 14 F2
Bowral, *Australia* 91 E5
Bowraville, *Australia* 91 E5
Bowron →, *Canada* 100 C4
Bowser L., *Canada* 100 B3
Bowsman, *Canada* 101 C8
Bowwood, *Zambia* 83 F2
Boxholm, *Sweden* 11 F9
Boxmeer, *Neths.* 17 E7
Boxtel, *Neths.* 17 E6
Boyabat, *Turkey* 42 F6
Boyaca = Casanare □, *Colombia* 120 B3
Boyce, *U.S.A.* 109 K8
Boyer →, *Canada* 100 B5
Boyle, *Ireland* 15 C3
Boyne →, *Ireland* 15 C5
Boyne City, *U.S.A.* 104 C3
Boynton Beach, *U.S.A.* 105 M5
Boyoma, Chutes, *Zaïre* 82 B2
Boyup Brook, *Australia* 89 F2
Boz Dağ, *Turkey* 66 E3
Boz Dağları, *Turkey* 66 D3
Bozburun, *Turkey* 66 E3
Bozdoğan, *Turkey* 66 E3
Bozeman, *U.S.A.* 110 D8
Bozen = Bolzano, *Italy* 33 B8
Bozkır, *Turkey* 66 E5
Bozouls, *France* 26 D6
Bozoum, *C.A.R.* 73 G8
Bozova, *Turkey* 67 E8
Bozovici, *Romania* 38 E5
Bozüyük, *Turkey* 66 D4
Bra, *Italy* 32 D4
Brabant □, *Belgium* 17 G5
Brabant L., *Canada* 101 B8
Brabrand, *Denmark* 11 H4
Brač, *Croatia* 33 E13
Bracadale, L., *U.K.* 14 D2
Bracciano, *Italy* 33 F9
Bracciano, L. di, *Italy* 33 F9
Bracebridge, *Canada* 98 C4
Brach, *Libya* 73 C7
Bracieux, *France* 25 E8
Bräcke, *Sweden* 10 B9
Brackettville, *U.S.A.* 109 L4
Brački Kanal, *Croatia* 33 E13
Brad, *Romania* 38 C5
Brádano →, *Italy* 35 B9
Bradenton, *U.S.A.* 105 M4
Bradford, *Canada* 106 B5
Bradford, *U.K.* 12 D6
Bradford, *Pa., U.S.A.* 106 E6
Bradford, *Vt., U.S.A.* 107 C12
Brădiceni, *Romania* 38 D6
Bradley, *Ark., U.S.A.* 109 J8
Bradley, *Calif., U.S.A.* 112 K6
Bradley, *S. Dak., U.S.A.* 108 C6
Bradley Institute, *Zimbabwe* 83 F3
Bradore Bay, *Canada* 99 B8
Bradshaw, *Australia* 88 C5
Brady, *U.S.A.* 109 K5
Brædstrup, *Denmark* 11 J3
Braemar, *Australia* 91 E2
Braeside, *Canada* 107 A8
Braga, *Portugal* 30 D2
Braga □, *Portugal* 30 D2
Bragado, *Argentina* 126 D3
Bragança, *Brazil* 122 B2
Bragança, *Portugal* 30 D4
Bragança □, *Portugal* 30 D4
Bragança Paulista, *Brazil* 127 A6
Brahmanbaria, *Bangla.* 61 H17
Brahmani →, *India* 61 J15
Brahmaputra →, *India* 63 G13
Braich-y-pwll, *U.K.* 12 E3
Braidwood, *Australia* 91 F4
Brăila, *Romania* 38 D10
Braine-l'Alleud, *Belgium* 17 G4
Braine-le-Comte, *Belgium* 17 G4
Brainerd, *U.S.A.* 108 B7
Braintree, *U.K.* 13 F8
Braintree, *U.S.A.* 107 D14
Brak →, *S. Africa* 84 D3

Brake, *Niedersachsen, Germany* 18 B4
Brake, *Nordrhein-Westfalen, Germany* 18 D5
Brakel, *Neths.* 16 E6
Brakwater, *Namibia* 84 C2
Brålanda, *Sweden* 11 F6
Bralorne, *Canada* 100 C4
Bramberg, *Germany* 19 E6
Bramminge, *Denmark* 11 J2
Brämön, *Sweden* 10 B11
Brampton, *Canada* 98 D4
Bramsche, *Germany* 18 C3
Bramwell, *Australia* 90 A3
Branco →, *Brazil* 121 D5
Branco, C., *Brazil* 122 C5
Brande, *Denmark* 11 J3
Brandenburg, *Germany* 18 C8
Brandenburg □, *Germany* 18 C9
Brandfort, *S. Africa* 84 D4
Brandon, *Canada* 101 D9
Brandon, *U.S.A.* 107 C11
Brandon B., *Ireland* 15 D1
Brandon Mt., *Ireland* 15 D1
Brandsen, *Argentina* 126 D4
Brandval, *Norway* 10 D6
Brandvlei, *S. Africa* 84 E3
Brandýs, *Czech.* 20 E4
Branford, *U.S.A.* 107 E12
Braniewo, *Poland* 20 A9
Bransfield Str., *Antarctica* 5 C18
Branson, *Colo., U.S.A.* 109 G3
Branson, *Mo., U.S.A.* 109 G8
Brantford, *Canada* 98 D3
Brantôme, *France* 26 C4
Branxholme, *Australia* 91 F3
Branzi, *Italy* 32 B6
Bras d'Or, L., *Canada* 99 C7
Brasiléia, *Brazil* 124 C4
Brasília, *Brazil* 123 E2
Brasília Legal, *Brazil* 121 D6
Braslav, *Belorussia* 40 D5
Braslovce, *Slovenia* 33 B12
Braşov, *Romania* 38 D8
Brass, *Nigeria* 79 E6
Brass →, *Nigeria* 79 E6
Brassac-les-Mines, *France* 26 C7
Brasschaat, *Belgium* 17 F4
Brassey, Banjaran, *Malaysia* 56 D5
Brassey Ra., *Australia* 89 E3
Brasstown Bald, *U.S.A.* 105 H4
Bratislava, *Czech.* 21 G7
Bratsk, *Russia* 45 D11
Brattleboro, *U.S.A.* 107 D12
Braunau, *Austria* 21 G3
Braunschweig, *Germany* 18 C6
Braunton, *U.K.* 13 F3
Brava, *Somali Rep.* 68 G3
Bråviken, *Sweden* 10 F10
Bravo del Norte →, *Mexico* 114 B5
Brawley, *U.S.A.* 113 N11
Bray, *Ireland* 15 C5
Bray, Mt., *Australia* 90 A1
Bray, Pays de, *France* 25 C8
Bray-sur-Seine, *France* 25 D10
Brazeau →, *Canada* 100 C5
Brazil, *U.S.A.* 104 F2
Brazil ■, *S. Amer.* 123 D2
Brazo Sur →, *S. Amer.* 126 B4
Brazos →, *U.S.A.* 109 L7
Brazzaville, *Congo* 80 E3
Brčko, *Bos.-H., Yug.* 21 L8
Brea, *Peru* 124 A1
Breadalbane, *Australia* 90 C2
Breadalbane, *U.K.* 14 E4
Breaden, L., *Australia* 89 E4
Breaksea Sd., *N.Z.* 87 L1
Bream B., *N.Z.* 87 F5
Bream Hd., *N.Z.* 87 F5
Breas, *Chile* 126 B1
Brebes, *Indonesia* 57 G13
Brechin, *Canada* 106 B5
Brechin, *U.K.* 14 E6
Brecht, *Belgium* 17 F5
Breckenridge, *Colo., U.S.A.* 110 G10
Breckenridge, *Minn., U.S.A.* 108 B6
Breckenridge, *Tex., U.S.A.* 109 J5
Breckland, *U.K.* 13 E8
Brecknock, Pen., *Chile* 128 D2
Břeclav, *Czech.* 20 G6
Brecon, *U.K.* 13 F4
Brecon Beacons, *U.K.* 13 F4
Breda, *Neths.* 17 E5
Bredasdorp, *S. Africa* 84 E3
Bredbo, *Australia* 91 F4
Bredene, *Belgium* 17 F1
Bredstedt, *Germany* 18 A4
Bree, *Belgium* 17 F7
Breezand, *Neths.* 16 C5
Bregalnica →, *Macedonia, Yug.* 39 H5
Bregenz, *Austria* 19 H5
Bréhal, *France* 24 D5
Bréhat, I. de, *France* 24 D4
Breiðafjörður, *Iceland* 8 D2
Breil-sur-Roya, *France* 27 E11
Breisach, *Germany* 19 G3
Brejinho de Nazaré, *Brazil* 122 D2
Brejo, *Brazil* 122 B3
Bremen, *Germany* 18 B4
Bremen □, *Germany* 18 B4
Bremer I., *Australia* 90 A2
Bremerhaven, *Germany* 18 B4
Bremerton, *U.S.A.* 112 C4
Bremervörde, *Germany* 18 B5
Bremsnes, *Norway* 10 A1
Brenes, *Spain* 31 H5
Brenham, *U.S.A.* 109 K6
Brenner Pass, *Austria* 19 H7
Breno, *Italy* 32 C7
Brent, *Canada* 98 C4
Brent, *U.K.* 13 F7
Brenta →, *Italy* 33 C9
Brentwood, *U.K.* 13 F8
Brentwood, *U.S.A.* 107 F11
Bréscia, *Italy* 32 C7
Breskens, *Neths.* 17 F3
Breslau = Wrocław, *Poland* 20 D7
Bresle →, *France* 24 B8
Bresles, *France* 25 C9
Bressanone, *Italy* 33 B8
Bressay, *U.K.* 14 A7
Bresse, *France* 25 F12
Bressuire, *France* 24 F6
Brest, *Belorussia* 40 E3
Brest, *France* 24 D2
Brest-Litovsk = Brest, *Belorussia* 40 E3
Bretagne, *France* 24 D4
Bretçu, *Romania* 38 C9
Breteuil, *Eure, France* 24 D7
Breteuil, *Oise, France* 25 C9
Breton, *Canada* 100 C6
Breton, Pertuis, *France* 26 B2
Breton Sd., *U.S.A.* 109 L10
Brett, C., *N.Z.* 87 F5
Bretten, *Germany* 19 F4
Breukelen, *Neths.* 16 D6
Brevard, *U.S.A.* 105 H4
Breves, *Brazil* 122 B1
Brevik, *Norway* 10 E3
Brewarrina, *Australia* 91 D4
Brewer, *U.S.A.* 99 D6
Brewer, Mt., *U.S.A.* 112 J8
Brewster, *N.Y., U.S.A.* 107 E11
Brewster, *Wash., U.S.A.* 110 B4
Brewster, Kap, *Greenland* 4 B6
Brewton, *U.S.A.* 105 K2
Breyten, *S. Africa* 85 D4
Breytovo, *Russia* 41 B10
Brezhnev = Naberezhnyye Chelny, *Russia* 44 D6
Brežice, *Slovenia* 33 C12
Brézina, *Algeria* 75 B5
Březnice, *Czech.* 20 F3
Breznik, *Bulgaria* 38 G5
Brezno, *Czech.* 20 G9
Bria, *C.A.R.* 73 G9
Briançon, *France* 27 D10
Briare, *France* 25 E9
Bribie I., *Australia* 91 D5
Bricquebec, *France* 24 C5
Bridgehampton, *U.S.A.* 107 F12
Bridgend, *U.K.* 13 F4
Bridgeport, *Calif., U.S.A.* 111 G4
Bridgeport, *Conn., U.S.A.* 107 E11
Bridgeport, *Nebr., U.S.A.* 108 E3
Bridgeport, *Tex., U.S.A.* 109 J6
Bridger, *U.S.A.* 110 D9
Bridgeton, *U.S.A.* 104 F8
Bridgetown, *Australia* 89 F2
Bridgetown, *Barbados* 117 D8
Bridgetown, *Canada* 99 D6
Bridgewater, *Canada* 99 D7
Bridgewater, *Mass., U.S.A.* 107 E14
Bridgewater, *S. Dak., U.S.A.* 108 D6
Bridgewater, C., *Australia* 91 F3
Bridgnorth, *U.K.* 13 E5
Bridgton, *U.S.A.* 107 B14
Bridgwater, *U.K.* 13 F4
Bridlington, *U.K.* 12 C7
Bridport, *Australia* 90 G4
Bridport, *U.K.* 13 G5
Brie, Plaine de la, *France* 25 D10
Brie-Comte-Robert, *France* 25 D9
Briec, *France* 24 D2
Brielle, *Neths.* 16 E4
Brienne-le-Château, *France* 25 D11
Brienon-sur-Armançon, *France* 25 E10
Brienz, *Switz.* 22 C6
Brienzersee, *Switz.* 22 C5
Brig, *Switz.* 22 D5
Brigg, *U.K.* 12 D7
Briggsdale, *U.S.A.* 108 E2
Brigham City, *U.S.A.* 110 F7
Bright, *Australia* 91 F4
Brighton, *Australia* 91 F2
Brighton, *Canada* 98 D4
Brighton, *U.K.* 13 G7
Brighton, *U.S.A.* 108 F2
Brignogan-Plage, *France* 24 D2
Brignoles, *France* 27 E10
Brihuega, *Spain* 28 E2
Brikama, *Gambia* 78 C1
Brilliant, *Canada* 100 D5
Brilliant, *U.S.A.* 106 F4
Brilon, *Germany* 18 D4
Bríndisi, *Italy* 35 B10
Brinje, *Croatia* 33 D12
Brinkley, *U.S.A.* 109 H9
Brinkworth, *Australia* 91 E2
Brinnon, *U.S.A.* 112 C4
Brion, I., *Canada* 99 C7
Brionne, *France* 24 C7
Brionski, *Croatia* 33 D10
Brioude, *France* 26 C7
Briouze, *France* 24 D6
Brisbane, *Australia* 91 D5
Brisbane →, *Australia* 91 D5
Brisighella, *Italy* 33 D8
Bristol, *U.K.* 13 F5
Bristol, *Conn., U.S.A.* 107 E12
Bristol, *Pa., U.S.A.* 107 F10
Bristol, *R.I., U.S.A.* 107 E13
Bristol, *S. Dak., U.S.A.* 108 C6
Bristol, *Tenn., U.S.A.* 105 G4
Bristol B., *U.S.A.* 96 C4
Bristol Channel, *U.K.* 13 F3
Bristol I., *Antarctica* 5 B1
Bristol L., *U.S.A.* 111 J5
Bristow, *U.S.A.* 109 H6
British Columbia □, *Canada* 100 C3
British Guiana = Guyana ■, *S. Amer.* 121 B6
British Honduras = Belize ■, *Cent. Amer.* 115 D7
British Isles, *Europe* 6 E5
Brits, *S. Africa* 85 D4
Britstown, *S. Africa* 84 E3
Britt, *Canada* 98 C3
Brittany = Bretagne, *France* 24 D4
Britton, *U.S.A.* 108 C6
Brive-la-Gaillarde, *France* 26 C5
Briviesca, *Spain* 28 C1
Brixton, *Australia* 90 C3
Brlik, *Kazakhstan* 44 E8
Brno, *Czech.* 20 F6
Bro, *Sweden* 10 E11
Broad →, *U.S.A.* 105 J5
Broad Arrow, *Australia* 89 F3
Broad B., *U.K.* 14 C2
Broad Haven, *Ireland* 15 B2
Broad Law, *U.K.* 14 F5
Broad Sd., *Australia* 90 C4
Broadhurst Ra., *Australia* 88 D3
Broads, The, *U.K.* 12 E9
Broadus, *U.S.A.* 108 C2
Broadview, *Canada* 101 C8
Broager, *Denmark* 11 K3
Broaryd, *Sweden* 11 G7
Brochet, *Canada* 101 B8
Brochet, L., *Canada* 101 B8
Brock, *Canada* 101 C7
Brocken, *Germany* 18 D6
Brockport, *U.S.A.* 106 C7
Brockton, *U.S.A.* 107 D13
Brockville, *Canada* 98 D4
Brockway, *Mont., U.S.A.* 108 B2
Brockway, *Pa., U.S.A.* 106 E6
Brocton, *U.S.A.* 106 D5
Brod, *Macedonia, Yug.* 39 H4
Brodarevo, *Serbia, Yug.* 21 M9
Brodeur Pen., *Canada* 97 A11
Brodick, *U.K.* 14 F3
Brodnica, *Poland* 20 B9
Brody, *Ukraine* 40 F4
Broechem, *Belgium* 17 F5
Broek, *Neths.* 16 D6
Broek op Langedijk, *Neths.* 16 C5
Brogan, *U.S.A.* 110 D5
Broglie, *France* 24 C7
Broken Bow, *Nebr., U.S.A.* 108 E5
Broken Bow, *Okla., U.S.A.* 109 H7
Broken Hill = Kabwe, *Zambia* 83 E2
Broken Hill, *Australia* 91 E3
Brokind, *Sweden* 11 F9
Brokopondo, *Surinam* 121 B7
Brokopondo □, *Surinam* 121 C6
Bromfield, *U.K.* 13 E5
Bromley, *U.K.* 13 F8
Brønderslev, *Denmark* 11 G3
Brong-Ahafo □, *Ghana* 78 D4
Bronkhorstspruit, *S. Africa* 85 D4
Bronnitsy, *Russia* 41 D11
Bronte, *Italy* 35 E7
Bronte, *U.S.A.* 109 K4
Bronte Park, *Australia* 90 G4
Brook Park, *U.S.A.* 106 E4
Brookfield, *U.S.A.* 108 F8
Brookhaven, *U.S.A.* 109 K9
Brookings, *Oreg., U.S.A.* 110 E1
Brookings, *S. Dak., U.S.A.* 108 C6
Brooklin, *Canada* 106 C6
Brookmere, *Canada* 100 D4
Brooks, *Canada* 100 C6
Brooks B., *Canada* 100 C3
Brooks L., *Canada* 101 A7
Brooks Ra., *U.S.A.* 96 B5
Brooksville, *U.S.A.* 105 L4
Brookville, *U.S.A.* 104 F3
Brooloo, *Australia* 91 D5
Broom, L., *U.K.* 14 D3
Broome, *Australia* 88 C3
Broomehill, *Australia* 89 F2
Broons, *France* 24 D4
Brora, *U.K.* 14 C5
Brora →, *U.K.* 14 C5
Brosna →, *Ireland* 15 C4
Broşteni, *Romania* 38 B8
Brotas de Macaúbas, *Brazil* 123 D3
Brothers, *U.S.A.* 110 E3
Brøttum, *Norway* 10 C4
Brou, *France* 24 D8
Brough, *U.K.* 13 C5
Broughton Island, *Canada* 97 B13
Broughty Ferry, *U.K.* 14 E6
Brouwershaven, *Neths.* 16 E3
Brouwershavensche Gat, *Neths.* 16 E3
Brovary, *Ukraine* 40 F7
Brovst, *Denmark* 11 G3
Browerville, *U.S.A.* 108 B7
Brown, Pt., *Australia* 91 E1
Brown Willy, *U.K.* 13 G3
Brownfield, *U.S.A.* 109 J3
Browning, *U.S.A.* 110 B7
Brownlee, *Canada* 101 C7
Brownsville, *Oreg., U.S.A.* 110 D2
Brownsville, *Tenn., U.S.A.* 109 H10
Brownsville, *Tex., U.S.A.* 109 N6
Brownsweg, *Surinam* 121 B6
Brownwood, *U.S.A.* 109 K5
Brownwood, L., *U.S.A.* 109 K5
Browse I., *Australia* 88 B3
Broye →, *Switz.* 22 C3
Brozas, *Spain* 31 F4
Bruas, *Malaysia* 59 K3
Bruay-en-Artois, *France* 25 B9
Bruce, Mt., *Australia* 88 D2
Bruce Pen., *Canada* 106 A3
Bruce Rock, *Australia* 89 F2
Bruche →, *France* 25 D14
Bruchsal, *Germany* 19 F4
Bruck an der Leitha, *Austria* 21 G6
Bruck an der Mur, *Austria* 21 H5
Brue →, *U.K.* 13 F5
Brugelette, *Belgium* 17 G3
Bruges = Brugge, *Belgium* 17 F2
Brugg, *Switz.* 22 B6
Brugge, *Belgium* 17 F2
Brühl, *Germany* 18 E2
Bruinisse, *Neths.* 17 E4
Brûlé, *Canada* 100 C5
Brûlon, *France* 24 E6
Brûly, *Belgium* 17 J5
Brumado, *Brazil* 123 D3
Brumado →, *Brazil* 123 D3
Brumath, *France* 25 D14
Brummen, *Neths.* 16 D8
Brumunddal, *Norway* 10 D4
Brunchilly, *Australia* 90 B1
Brundidge, *U.S.A.* 105 K3
Bruneau, *U.S.A.* 110 E6
Bruneau →, *U.S.A.* 110 E6
Brunei = Bandar Seri Begawan, *Brunei* 56 C4
Brunei ■, *Asia* 56 D4
Brunette Downs, *Australia* 90 B2
Brunflo, *Sweden* 10 A8
Brunico, *Italy* 33 B8
Brünig, P., *Switz.* 22 C6
Brunkeberg, *Norway* 10 E2
Brunna, *Sweden* 10 E11
Brunnen, *Switz.* 23 C7
Brunner, L., *N.Z.* 87 K3
Bruno, *Canada* 101 C7
Brunsbüttel, *Germany* 18 B5
Brunssum, *Neths.* 17 G7
Brunswick = Braunschweig, *Germany* 18 C6
Brunswick, *Ga., U.S.A.* 105 K5
Brunswick, *Maine, U.S.A.* 99 D6
Brunswick, *Md., U.S.A.* 104 F7
Brunswick, *Mo., U.S.A.* 108 F8
Brunswick, *Ohio, U.S.A.* 106 E3
Brunswick, Pen. de, *Chile* 128 D2
Brunswick B., *Australia* 88 C3
Brunswick Junction, *Australia* 89 F2
Bruntál, *Czech.* 20 F7
Bruny I., *Australia* 90 G4
Brus Laguna, *Honduras* 116 C3
Brusartsi, *Bulgaria* 38 F6
Brush, *U.S.A.* 108 E3
Brushton, *U.S.A.* 107 B10
Brusio, *Switz.* 23 D10
Brusque, *Brazil* 127 B6
Brussel, *Belgium* 17 G4
Brussels = Brussel, *Belgium* 17 G4
Brussels, *Canada* 106 C3
Brustem, *Belgium* 17 G6
Bruthen, *Australia* 91 F4
Bruxelles = Brussel, *Belgium* 17 G4
Bruyères, *France* 25 D13
Bryan, *Ohio, U.S.A.* 104 E3
Bryan, *Tex., U.S.A.* 109 K6
Bryan, Mt., *Australia* 91 E2
Bryanka, *Ukraine* 43 B8
Bryansk, *Russia* 40 E9
Bryanskoye, *Russia* 43 D12
Bryant, *U.S.A.* 108 C6
Bryne, *Norway* 9 G8
Bryson City, *U.S.A.* 105 H4
Brza Palanka, *Serbia, Yug.* 21 L12
Brzava →, *Serbia, Yug.* 21 K10
Brzeg, *Poland* 20 E7
Brzeg Din, *Poland* 20 D6
Bsharri, *Lebanon* 69 A5
Bū Baqarah, *U.A.E.* 65 E8
Bu Craa, *W. Sahara* 74 C2
Bū Ḩasā, *U.A.E.* 65 F7
Bua Yai, *Thailand* 58 E4
Buapinang, *Indonesia* 57 E6
Buayan, *Phil.* 57 C7
Buba, *Guinea-Biss.* 78 C2
Bubanza, *Burundi* 82 C2
Būbiyān, *Kuwait* 65 D6
Bucak, *Turkey* 66 E4
Bucaramanga, *Colombia* 120 B3
Bucas Grande I., *Phil.* 55 G6
Buccaneer Arch., *Australia* 88 C3
Bucchiánico, *Italy* 33 F11
Bucecea, *Romania* 38 B9
Buchach, *Ukraine* 40 G4
Buchan, *U.K.* 14 D6
Buchan Ness, *U.K.* 14 D7
Buchanan, *Canada* 101 C8
Buchanan, *Liberia* 78 D2
Buchanan, L., *Queens., Australia* 90 C4
Buchanan, L., *W. Austral., Australia* 89 E3
Buchanan, L., *U.S.A.* 109 K5
Buchanan Cr. →, *Australia* 90 B2
Buchans, *Canada* 99 C8
Bucharest = Bucureşti, *Romania* 38 E9
Buchholz, *Germany* 18 B5
Buchloe, *Germany* 19 G6
Buchon, Pt., *U.S.A.* 112 K6
Buchs, *Switz.* 23 B8
Bückeburg, *Germany* 18 C5
Buckeye, *U.S.A.* 111 K7
Buckhannon, *U.S.A.* 104 F5
Buckhaven, *U.K.* 14 E5
Buckie, *U.K.* 14 D6
Buckingham, *Canada* 98 C4
Buckingham, *U.K.* 13 F7
Buckingham B., *Australia* 90 A2
Buckinghamshire □, *U.K.* 13 F7
Buckle Hd., *Australia* 88 B4
Buckleboo, *Australia* 91 E2
Buckley, *U.S.A.* 110 C2
Buckley →, *Australia* 90 C2
Bucklin, *U.S.A.* 109 G5
Bucks L., *U.S.A.* 112 F5
Bucquoy, *France* 25 B9
Buctouche, *Canada* 99 C7
Bucureşti, *Romania* 38 E9
Bucyrus, *U.S.A.* 104 E4
Budafok, *Hungary* 21 H9
Budalin, *Burma* 61 H19
Budapest, *Hungary* 21 H9
Budaun, *India* 63 E8
Budd Coast, *Antarctica* 5 C8
Buddusò, *Italy* 34 B2
Bude, *U.K.* 13 G3
Budel, *Neths.* 17 F7
Budennovsk, *Russia* 43 D11
Budeşti, *Romania* 38 E9
Budge Budge = Baj Baj, *India* 63 H13
Budgewoi, *Australia* 91 E5
Búðareyri, *Iceland* 8 D6
Búðir, *Iceland* 8 D2
Budia, *Spain* 28 E2
Budjala, *Zaïre* 80 D3
Búdrio, *Italy* 33 D8
Buea, *Cameroon* 79 E6
Buellton, *U.S.A.* 113 L6
Buena Vista, *Bolivia* 125 D5
Buena Vista, *Colo., U.S.A.* 111 G10
Buena Vista, *Va., U.S.A.* 104 G6
Buena Vista L., *U.S.A.* 113 K7
Buenaventura, *Colombia* 120 C2
Buenaventura, *Mexico* 114 B3
Buenaventura, B. de, *Colombia* 120 C2
Buendía, Pantano de, *Spain* 28 E2
Buenópolis, *Brazil* 123 E3
Buenos Aires, *Argentina* 126 C4
Buenos Aires, *Colombia* 120 C3
Buenos Aires, *Costa Rica* 116 E3
Buenos Aires □, *Argentina* 126 D4
Buenos Aires, L., *Chile* 128 C2
Buesaco, *Colombia* 120 C2
Buffalo, *Mo., U.S.A.* 109 G8
Buffalo, *N.Y., U.S.A.* 106 D6
Buffalo, *Okla., U.S.A.* 109 G5
Buffalo, *S. Dak., U.S.A.* 108 C3
Buffalo, *Wyo., U.S.A.* 110 D10
Buffalo →, *Canada* 100 A5
Buffalo Head Hills, *Canada* 100 B5
Buffalo L., *Canada* 100 C6
Buffalo Narrows, *Canada* 101 B7
Buffels →, *S. Africa* 84 D2
Buford, *U.S.A.* 105 H4
Bug →, *Poland* 20 C11
Bug →, *Ukraine* 40 C4
Buga, *Colombia* 120 C2
Buganda, *Uganda* 82 C3
Buganga, *Uganda* 82 C3
Bugasong, *Phil.* 55 F5
Bugeat, *France* 26 C5
Bugel, Tanjung, *Indonesia* 56 F4
Buggenhout, *Belgium* 17 F4
Bugibba, *Malta* 37 D1
Bugsuk, *Phil.* 55 G2
Buguma, *Nigeria* 79 E6
Bugun Shara, *Mongolia* 54 B5
Buguruslan, *Russia* 44 D6
Buhăeşti, *Romania* 38 C10
Buheirat-Murrat-el-Kubra, *Egypt* 76 H8
Buhl, *Idaho, U.S.A.* 110 E6
Buhl, *Minn., U.S.A.* 108 B8
Buick, *U.S.A.* 109 G9
Builth Wells, *U.K.* 13 E4
Buinsk, *Russia* 41 D16
Buíque, *Brazil* 122 C4

Calamian Group

Buir Nur, *Mongolia* 54 B6
Buis-les-Baronnies, *France* 27 D9
Buitenpost, *Neths.* 16 B8
Buitrago, *Spain* 30 E7
Bujalance, *Spain* 31 H6
Buján, *Spain* 30 C2
Bujaraloz, *Spain* 28 D4
Buje, *Croatia* 33 C10
Bujumbura, *Burundi* 82 C2
Bukachacha, *Russia* 45 D12
Bukama, *Zaïre* 83 D2
Bukavu, *Zaïre* 82 C2
Bukene, *Tanzania* 82 C3
Bukhara, *Uzbekistan* 44 F7
Bukima, *Tanzania* 82 C3
Bukit Mertajam, *Malaysia* 59 K3
Bukittinggi, *Indonesia* 56 E2
Bukoba, *Tanzania* 82 C3
Bukoba □, *Tanzania* 82 C3
Bukuru, *Nigeria* 79 D6
Bukuya, *Uganda* 82 B3
Bula, *Guinea-Biss.* 78 C1
Bula, *Indonesia* 57 E8
Bülach, *Switz.* 23 A7
Bulahdelah, *Australia* 91 E5
Bulan, *Phil.* 55 E5
Bulancak, *Turkey* 67 C8
Bulandshahr, *India* 62 E7
Bulanık, *Turkey* 67 D10
Bûlâq, *Egypt* 76 B3
Bulawayo, *Zimbabwe* 83 G2
Buldan, *Turkey* 66 D3
Bulgan, *Mongolia* 54 B5
Bulgaria ■, *Europe* 38 G8
Bulgroo, *Australia* 91 D3
Bulgunnia, *Australia* 91 E1
Bulhar, *Somali Rep.* 68 E3
Buli, Teluk, *Indonesia* 57 D7
Buliluyan, C., *Phil.* 55 G2
Bulki, *Ethiopia* 77 F4
Bulkley →, *Canada* 100 B3
Bull Shoals L., *U.S.A.* 109 G8
Bullange, *Belgium* 17 H8
Bullaque →, *Spain* 31 G6
Bullara, *Australia* 88 D1
Bullaring, *Australia* 89 F2
Bullas, *Spain* 29 G3
Bulle, *Switz.* 22 C4
Bulli, *Australia* 91 E5
Bullock Creek, *Australia* 90 B3
Bulloo →, *Australia* 91 D3
Bulloo Downs, *Queens., Australia* 91 D3
Bulloo Downs, *W. Austral., Australia* 88 D2
Bulloo L., *Australia* 91 D3
Bulls, *N.Z.* 87 J5
Bully-les-Mines, *France* 25 B9
Bulnes, *Chile* 126 D1
Bulo Burti, *Somali Rep.* 68 G4
Bulsar = Valsad, *India* 60 J8
Bultfontein, *S. Africa* 84 D4
Bulu Karakelong, *Indonesia* 57 D7
Bulukumba, *Indonesia* 57 F6
Bulun, *Russia* 45 B13
Bumba, *Zaïre* 80 D4
Bumbiri I., *Tanzania* 82 C3
Bumhpa Bum, *Burma* 61 F20
Bumi →, *Zimbabwe* 83 F2
Buna, *Kenya* 82 B4
Bunawan, *Agusan del S., Phil.* 55 G6
Bunawan, *Davao del S., Phil.* 55 H6
Bunazi, *Tanzania* 82 C3
Bunbah, Khalīj, *Libya* 73 B9
Bunbury, *Australia* 89 F2
Buncrana, *Ireland* 15 A4
Bundaberg, *Australia* 91 C5
Bünde, *Germany* 18 C4
Bundey →, *Australia* 90 C2
Bundi, *India* 62 G6
Bundooma, *Australia* 90 C1
Bundoran, *Ireland* 15 B3
Bundukia, *Sudan* 77 F3
Bung Kan, *Thailand* 58 C4
Bungatakada, *Japan* 49 H5
Bungil Cr. →, *Australia* 90 D4
Bungo-Suidō, *Japan* 49 H6
Bungoma, *Kenya* 82 B3
Bungu, *Tanzania* 82 D4
Bunia, *Zaïre* 82 B3
Bunji, *Pakistan* 63 B6
Bunkie, *U.S.A.* 109 K8
Bunnell, *U.S.A.* 105 L5
Bunnik, *Neths.* 16 D6
Buñol, *Spain* 29 F4
Bunsbeek, *Belgium* 17 G5
Bunschoten, *Neths.* 16 D6
Buntok, *Indonesia* 56 E4
Bununu, *Nigeria* 79 D6
Bununu Dass, *Nigeria* 79 C6
Bünyan, *Turkey* 66 D6
Bunyu, *Indonesia* 56 D5
Bunza, *Nigeria* 79 C5
Buol, *Indonesia* 57 D6
Buon Brieng, *Vietnam* 58 F7
Buon Me Thuot, *Vietnam* 58 F7
Buong Long, *Cambodia* 58 F6
Buorkhaya, Mys, *Russia* 45 B14
Buqayq, *Si. Arabia* 65 E6
Buqbua, *Egypt* 76 A2
Bur Acaba, *Somali Rep.* 68 G3
Bûr Fuad, *Egypt* 76 H8
Bûr Safâga, *Egypt* 76 B3
Bûr Sa'îd, *Egypt* 76 H8
Bûr Sûdân, *Sudan* 76 D4
Bûr Taufiq, *Egypt* 76 J8
Bura, *Kenya* 82 C4
Burao, *Somali Rep.* 68 F4
Burāq, *Syria* 69 B5
Buras, *U.S.A.* 109 L10
Buraydah, *Si. Arabia* 64 E5
Burbank, *U.S.A.* 113 L8
Burcher, *Australia* 91 E4
Burdekin →, *Australia* 90 B4
Burdett, *Canada* 100 D6
Burdur, *Turkey* 66 E4
Burdur □, *Turkey* 66 E4
Burdur Gölü, *Turkey* 66 E4
Burdwan = Barddhaman, *India* 63 H12
Bure, *Ethiopia* 77 E4
Bure →, *U.K.* 12 E9
Büren, *Germany* 18 D4
Buren, *Neths.* 16 E6
Bureya →, *Russia* 45 E13
Burford, *Canada* 106 C4
Burg, *Sachsen-Anhalt, Germany* 18 C7
Burg, *Schleswig-Holstein, Germany* 18 A7
Burg el Arab, *Egypt* 76 H6
Burg et Tuyur, *Sudan* 76 C2
Burg Stargard, *Germany* 18 B9
Burgas, *Bulgaria* 38 G10
Burgdorf, *Germany* 18 C5
Burgdorf, *Switz.* 22 B5
Burgeo, *Canada* 99 C8
Burgersdorp, *S. Africa* 84 E4
Burges, Mt., *Australia* 89 F3
Burghausen, *Germany* 19 G8
Búrgio, *Italy* 34 E6
Bürglen, *Switz.* 23 C7
Burglengenfeld, *Germany* 19 F8
Burgo de Osma, *Spain* 28 D1
Burgohondo, *Spain* 30 E6
Burgos, *Spain* 28 C1
Burgos □, *Spain* 28 C1
Burgstädt, *Germany* 18 E8
Burgsvik, *Sweden* 9 H15
Burguillos del Cerro, *Spain* 31 G4
Burgundy = Bourgogne, *France* 25 F11
Burhou, *U.K.* 24 C4
Buri Pen., *Ethiopia* 77 D4
Burias, *Phil.* 55 E5
Burica, Pta., *Costa Rica* 116 E3
Burigi, L., *Tanzania* 82 C3
Burin, *Canada* 99 C8
Buriram, *Thailand* 58 E4
Buriti Alegre, *Brazil* 123 E2
Buriti Bravo, *Brazil* 122 C3
Buriti dos Lopes, *Brazil* 122 B3
Burj Sāfitā, *Syria* 64 C3
Burji, *Ethiopia* 77 F4
Burkburnett, *U.S.A.* 109 H5
Burke, *U.S.A.* 110 C6
Burke →, *Australia* 90 C2
Burketown, *Australia* 90 B2
Burkina Faso ■, *Africa* 78 C4
Burk's Falls, *Canada* 98 C4
Burley, *U.S.A.* 110 E7
Burlingame, *U.S.A.* 112 H4
Burlington, *Canada* 106 C5
Burlington, *Colo., U.S.A.* 108 F3
Burlington, *Iowa, U.S.A.* 108 E9
Burlington, *Kans., U.S.A.* 108 F7
Burlington, *N.C., U.S.A.* 105 G6
Burlington, *N.J., U.S.A.* 107 F10
Burlington, *Vt., U.S.A.* 107 B11
Burlington, *Wash., U.S.A.* 112 B4
Burlington, *Wis., U.S.A.* 104 D1
Burlyu-Tyube, *Kazakhstan* 44 E8
Burma ■, *Asia* 61 J20
Burnaby I., *Canada* 100 C2
Burnet, *U.S.A.* 109 K5
Burney, *U.S.A.* 110 F3
Burngup, *Australia* 89 F2
Burnham, *U.S.A.* 106 F7
Burnie, *Australia* 90 G4
Burnley, *U.K.* 12 D5
Burns, *Oreg., U.S.A.* 110 E4
Burns, *Wyo., U.S.A.* 108 E2
Burns Lake, *Canada* 100 C3
Burnside →, *Canada* 96 B9
Burnside, L., *Australia* 89 E3
Burnt River, *Canada* 106 B6
Burntwood →, *Canada* 101 B9
Burntwood L., *Canada* 101 B8
Burqān, *Kuwait* 64 D5
Burqin, *China* 54 B3
Burra, *Australia* 91 E2
Burramurra, *Australia* 90 C2
Burreli, *Albania* 39 H3
Burren Junction, *Australia* 91 E4
Burrendong Dam, *Australia* 91 E4
Burriana, *Spain* 28 F4
Burrinjuck Res., *Australia* 91 F4
Burro, Serranías del, *Mexico* 114 B4
Burruyacú, *Argentina* 126 B3
Burry Port, *U.K.* 13 F3
Bursa, *Turkey* 66 C3
Bursa □, *Turkey* 66 C3
Burseryd, *Sweden* 11 G7
Burstall, *Canada* 101 C7
Burton L., *Canada* 98 B4
Burton upon Trent, *U.K.* 12 E6
Burtundy, *Australia* 91 E3
Buru, *Indonesia* 57 E7
Burullus, Bahra el, *Egypt* 76 H7
Burûn, Râs, *Egypt* 69 D2
Burundi ■, *Africa* 82 C3
Bururi, *Burundi* 82 C2
Burutu, *Nigeria* 79 D6
Burwell, *U.S.A.* 108 E5
Bury, *U.K.* 12 D5
Bury St. Edmunds, *U.K.* 13 E8
Buryat Republic □, *Russia* 45 D11
Buryn, *Ukraine* 40 F8
Busalla, *Italy* 32 D5
Busango Swamp, *Zambia* 83 E2
Buşayrah, *Syria* 64 C4
Buşayyah, *Iraq* 64 D5
Busca, *Italy* 32 D4
Būshehr, *Iran* 65 D6
Būshehr □, *Iran* 65 D6
Bushell, *Canada* 101 B7
Bushenyi, *Uganda* 82 C3
Bushire = Būshehr, *Iran* 65 D6
Bushnell, *Ill., U.S.A.* 108 E9
Bushnell, *Nebr., U.S.A.* 108 E3
Busia □, *Kenya* 82 B3
Busie, *Ghana* 78 C4
Businga, *Zaïre* 80 D4
Buskerud fylke □, *Norway* 10 D3
Busko Zdrój, *Poland* 20 E10
Busoga □, *Uganda* 82 B3
Busovača, *Bos.-H., Yug.* 21 L7
Busra ash Shām, *Syria* 69 C5
Bussang, *France* 25 E13
Busselton, *Australia* 89 F2
Busseto, *Italy* 32 D7
Bussigny, *Switz.* 22 C3
Bussum, *Neths.* 16 D6
Bustamante, B., *Argentina* 128 C3
Busto, C., *Spain* 30 B4
Busto Arsizio, *Italy* 32 C5
Busu-Djanoa, *Zaïre* 80 D4
Busuanga, *Phil.* 55 E3
Büsum, *Germany* 18 A4
Buta, *Zaïre* 82 B1
Butare, *Rwanda* 82 C2
Butaritari, *Kiribati* 92 G9
Bute, *U.K.* 14 F3
Bute Inlet, *Canada* 100 C4
Butemba, *Uganda* 82 B3
Butembo, *Zaïre* 82 B2
Butera, *Italy* 35 E7
Bütgenbach, *Belgium* 17 H8
Butha Qi, *China* 54 B7
Butiaba, *Uganda* 82 B3
Butler, *Mo., U.S.A.* 108 F7
Butler, *Pa., U.S.A.* 106 F5
Bütschwil, *Switz.* 23 B8
Butte, *Mont., U.S.A.* 110 C7
Butte, *Nebr., U.S.A.* 108 D5
Butte Creek →, *U.S.A.* 112 F5
Butterworth = Gcuwa, *S. Africa* 85 E4
Butterworth, *Malaysia* 59 K3
Buttfield, Mt., *Australia* 89 D4
Button B., *Canada* 101 B10
Buttonwillow, *U.S.A.* 113 K7
Butty Hd., *Australia* 89 F3
Butuan, *Phil.* 55 G6
Butuku-Luba, *Eq. Guin.* 79 E6
Butung, *Indonesia* 57 E6
Buturlinovka, *Russia* 41 F12
Butzbach, *Germany* 18 E4
Bützow, *Germany* 18 B7
Buxar, *India* 63 G10
Buxton, *Guyana* 121 B6
Buxton, *S. Africa* 84 D3
Buxton, *U.K.* 12 D6
Buxy, *France* 25 F11
Buy, *Russia* 41 B12
Buyaga, *Russia* 45 D13
Buynaksk, *Russia* 43 E12
Büyük Menderes →, *Turkey* 66 E2
Büyükçekmece, *Turkey* 39 H11
Buzançais, *France* 24 F8
Buzău, *Romania* 38 D9
Buzău →, *Romania* 38 D10
Buzău, Pasul, *Romania* 38 D9
Buzen, *Japan* 49 H5
Buzet, *Croatia* 33 C10
Buzi →, *Mozam.* 83 F3
Buziaş, *Romania* 38 D4
Buzuluk, *Russia* 44 D6
Buzuluk →, *Russia* 41 F13
Buzzards Bay, *U.S.A.* 107 E14
Bwana Mkubwe, *Zaïre* 83 E2
Byala, *Bulgaria* 38 F8
Byala Slatina, *Bulgaria* 38 F6
Byandovan, Mys, *Azerbaijan* 43 G13
Bychawa, *Poland* 20 D12
Bydgoszcz, *Poland* 20 B8
Byelorussia = Belorussia ■, *Europe* 40 E5
Byers, *U.S.A.* 108 F2
Byesville, *U.S.A.* 106 G3
Byhalia, *U.S.A.* 109 H10
Bykhov, *Belorussia* 40 E7
Bykovo, *Russia* 43 B11
Bylas, *U.S.A.* 111 K8
Bylderup, *Denmark* 11 K3
Bylot I., *Canada* 97 A12
Byrd, C., *Antarctica* 5 C17
Byro, *Australia* 89 E2
Byrock, *Australia* 91 E4
Byron Bay, *Australia* 91 D5
Byrranga, Gory, *Russia* 45 B11
Byrum, *Denmark* 11 G5
Byske, *Sweden* 8 D16
Byske älv →, *Sweden* 8 D16
Bystrzyca Kłodzka, *Poland* 20 E6
Byten, *Belorussia* 40 E4
Bytom, *Poland* 20 E8
Bytów, *Poland* 20 A7
Byumba, *Rwanda* 82 C3

C

C.I.S. = Commonwealth of Independent States ■, *Eurasia* 45 D11
Ca →, *Vietnam* 58 C5
Ca Mau = Quan Long, *Vietnam* 59 H5
Ca Mau, Mui = Bai Bung, Mui, *Vietnam* 59 H5
Ca Na, *Vietnam* 59 G7
Caacupé, *Paraguay* 126 B4
Caála, *Angola* 81 G3
Caamano Sd., *Canada* 100 C3
Caapiranga, *Brazil* 121 D5
Caazapá, *Paraguay* 126 B4
Caazapá □, *Paraguay* 127 B4
Cabadbaran, *Phil.* 55 G6
Cabalian, *Phil.* 55 F6
Caballeria, C. de, *Spain* 36 A11
Cabana, *Peru* 124 B2
Cabanaconde, *Peru* 124 D3
Cabañaquinta, *Spain* 30 B5
Cabanatuan, *Phil.* 55 D4
Cabanes, *Spain* 28 E5
Cabanillas, *Peru* 124 D3
Cabano, *Canada* 99 C6
Čabar, *Croatia* 33 C11
Cabazon, *U.S.A.* 113 M10
Cabedelo, *Brazil* 122 C5
Cabeza del Buey, *Spain* 31 G5
Cabildo, *Chile* 126 C1
Cabimas, *Venezuela* 120 A3
Cabinda, *Angola* 80 F2
Cabinda □, *Angola* 80 F2
Cabinet Mts., *U.S.A.* 110 C6
Cabo Blanco, *Argentina* 128 C3
Cabo Frio, *Brazil* 123 F3
Cabo Pantoja, *Peru* 120 D2
Cabo Raso, *Argentina* 128 B3
Cabonga, Réservoir, *Canada* 98 C4
Cabool, *U.S.A.* 109 G8
Caboolture, *Australia* 91 D5
Cabora Bassa Dam = Cahora Bassa Dam, *Mozam.* 83 F3
Caborca, *Mexico* 114 A2
Cabot, Mt., *U.S.A.* 107 B13
Cabot Str., *Canada* 99 C8
Cabra, *Spain* 31 H6
Cabra del Santo Cristo, *Spain* 29 H1
Cábras, *Italy* 34 C1
Cabrera, I., *Spain* 36 B9
Cabrera, Sierra, *Spain* 30 C4
Cabri, *Canada* 101 C7
Cabriel →, *Spain* 29 F3
Cabruta, *Venezuela* 120 B4
Cabugao, *Phil.* 55 C4
Cabuyaro, *Colombia* 120 C3
Caçabelos, *Spain* 30 C4
Čačak, *Serbia, Yug.* 21 M10
Cacao, *Fr. Guiana* 121 C7
Cáceres, *Brazil* 125 D6
Cáceres, *Colombia* 120 B2
Cáceres, *Spain* 31 F4
Cáceres □, *Spain* 31 F4
Cache Bay, *Canada* 98 C4
Cache Cr. →, *U.S.A.* 112 G5
Cachepo, *Portugal* 31 H3
Cachéu, *Guinea-Biss.* 78 C1
Cachi, *Argentina* 126 B2
Cachimbo, *Brazil* 125 B7
Cachimbo, Serra do, *Brazil* 125 B6
Cachoeira, *Brazil* 123 D4
Cachoeira Alta, *Brazil* 123 E1
Cachoeira de Itapemirim, *Brazil* 123 F3
Cachoeira do Sul, *Brazil* 127 C5
Cachoeiro do Arari, *Brazil* 122 B2
Cachopo, *Portugal* 31 H3
Cachuela Esperanza, *Bolivia* 125 C4
Cacólo, *Angola* 80 G3
Caconda, *Angola* 81 G3
Cacongo, *Angola* 80 F2
Caçu, *Brazil* 123 E1
Caculé, *Brazil* 123 D3
Cadarache, *France* 27 E9
Čadca, *Czech.* 20 F8
Caddo, *U.S.A.* 109 H6
Cadell Cr. →, *Australia* 90 C3
Cadenazzo, *Switz.* 23 D7
Cader Idris, *U.K.* 12 E4
Cadí, Sierra del, *Spain* 28 C6
Cadibarrawirracanna, L., *Australia* 91 D2
Cadillac, *Canada* 98 C4
Cadillac, *France* 26 D3
Cadillac, *U.S.A.* 104 C3
Cadiz, *Phil.* 55 F5
Cádiz, *Spain* 31 J4
Cadiz, *U.S.A.* 106 F4
Cádiz □, *Spain* 31 J5
Cádiz, G. de, *Spain* 31 J4
Cadney Park, *Australia* 91 D1
Cadomin, *Canada* 100 C5
Cadotte →, *Canada* 100 B5
Cadours, *France* 26 E5
Cadoux, *Australia* 89 F2
Caen, *France* 24 C6
Caernarfon, *U.K.* 12 D3
Caernarfon B., *U.K.* 12 D3
Caernarvon = Caernarfon, *U.K.* 12 D3
Caerphilly, *U.K.* 13 F4
Caesarea, *Israel* 69 C3
Caeté, *Brazil* 123 E3
Caetité, *Brazil* 123 D3
Cafayate, *Argentina* 126 B2
Cafifi, *Colombia* 120 B3
Cafu, *Angola* 84 B2
Cagayan →, *Phil.* 55 B4
Cagayan de Oro, *Phil.* 55 G6
Cagayan Is., *Phil.* 55 G4
Cagayan Sulu I., *Phil.* 55 H3
Cagli, *Italy* 33 E9
Cágliari, *Italy* 34 C2
Cágliari, G. di, *Italy* 34 C2
Cagnano Varano, *Italy* 35 A8
Cagnes-sur-Mer, *France* 27 E11
Caguán →, *Colombia* 120 D3
Caguas, *Puerto Rico* 117 C6
Caha Mts., *Ireland* 15 E2
Cahama, *Angola* 84 B1
Caher, *Ireland* 15 D4
Cahersiveen, *Ireland* 15 E1
Cahora Bassa Dam, *Mozam.* 83 F3
Cahore Pt., *Ireland* 15 D5
Cahors, *France* 26 D5
Cahuapanas, *Peru* 124 B2
Cahuinari →, *Colombia* 120 D3
Cai Bau, Dao, *Vietnam* 58 B6
Cai Nuoc, *Vietnam* 59 H5
Caia, *Mozam.* 83 F4
Caiabis, Serra dos, *Brazil* 125 C6
Caianda, *Angola* 83 E1
Caiapó, Serra do, *Brazil* 125 D7
Caiapônia, *Brazil* 125 D7
Caibarién, *Cuba* 116 B4
Caibiran, *Phil.* 55 F6
Caicara, *Bolívar, Venezuela* 120 B4
Caicara, *Monagas, Venezuela* 121 B5
Caicó, *Brazil* 122 C4
Caicos Is., *W. Indies* 117 B5
Caicos Passage, *W. Indies* 117 B5
Cailloma, *Peru* 124 D3
Caine →, *Bolivia* 125 D4
Caird Coast, *Antarctica* 5 D1
Cairn Gorm, *U.K.* 14 D5
Cairn Toul, *U.K.* 14 D5
Cairngorm Mts., *U.K.* 14 D5
Cairns, *Australia* 90 B4
Cairo = El Qâhira, *Egypt* 76 H7
Cairo, *Ga., U.S.A.* 105 K3
Cairo, *Ill., U.S.A.* 109 G10
Cairo Montenotte, *Italy* 32 D5
Caithness, Ord of, *U.K.* 14 C5
Caiundo, *Angola* 81 H3
Caiza, *Bolivia* 125 E4
Cajabamba, *Peru* 124 B2
Cajamarca, *Peru* 124 B2
Cajamarca □, *Peru* 124 B2
Cajapió, *Brazil* 122 B3
Cajarc, *France* 26 D5
Cajatambo, *Peru* 124 C2
Cajàzeiras, *Brazil* 122 C4
Čajetina, *Serbia, Yug.* 21 M9
Çakirgol, *Turkey* 43 F8
Čakovec, *Croatia* 33 B13
Çal, *Turkey* 66 D3
Cala, *Spain* 31 H4
Cala →, *Spain* 31 H4
Cala Cadolar, Punta de, *Spain* 29 G6
Cala d'Or, *Spain* 36 B10
Cala Figuera, C., *Spain* 36 B9
Cala Forcat, *Spain* 36 A10
Cala Mayor, *Spain* 36 B9
Cala Mezquida, *Spain* 36 B11
Cala Millor, *Spain* 36 B10
Cala Ratjada, *Spain* 36 B10
Calabanga, *Phil.* 55 E5
Calabar, *Nigeria* 79 E6
Calabozo, *Venezuela* 120 B4
Calábria □, *Italy* 35 C9
Calaburras, Pta. de, *Spain* 31 J6
Calaceite, *Spain* 28 D5
Calacoto, *Bolivia* 124 D4
Calafate, *Argentina* 128 D2
Calahorra, *Spain* 28 C3
Calais, *France* 25 B8
Calais, *U.S.A.* 99 C6
Calais, Pas de, *France* 25 B8
Calalaste, Cord. de, *Argentina* 126 B2
Calama, *Brazil* 125 B5
Calama, *Chile* 126 A2
Calamar, *Bolívar, Colombia* 120 A3
Calamar, *Vaupés, Colombia* 120 C3
Calamarca, *Bolivia* 124 D4
Calamba, *Phil.* 55 F5
Calamian Group, *Phil.* 55 F3

Calamocha, *Spain* 28 E3
Calán Porter, *Spain* 36 B11
Calañas, *Spain* 31 H4
Calanda, *Spain* 28 E4
Calang, *Indonesia* 56 D1
Calangiánus, *Italy* 34 B2
Calapan, *Phil.* 55 E4
Călăraşi, *Romania* 38 E10
Calasparra, *Spain* 29 G3
Calatafimi, *Italy* 34 E5
Calatayud, *Spain* 28 D3
Calato = Kálathos, *Greece* 39 N11
Calauag, *Phil.* 55 E5
Calavà, C., *Italy* 35 D7
Calavite, C., *Phil.* 55 E4
Calayan, *Phil.* 55 B4
Calbayog, *Phil.* 55 E6
Calbe, *Germany* 18 D7
Calca, *Peru* 124 C3
Calcasieu L., *U.S.A.* 109 L8
Calci, *Italy* 32 E7
Calcutta, *India* 63 H13
Caldaro, *Italy* 33 B8
Caldas □, *Colombia* 120 B2
Caldas da Rainha, *Portugal* 31 F1
Caldas de Reyes, *Spain* 30 C2
Caldas Novas, *Brazil* 123 E2
Calder →, *U.K.* 12 D6
Caldera, *Chile* 126 B1
Caldwell, *Idaho, U.S.A.* 110 E5
Caldwell, *Kans., U.S.A.* 109 G6
Caldwell, *Tex., U.S.A.* 109 K6
Caledon, *S. Africa* 84 E2
Caledon →, *S. Africa* 84 E4
Caledon B., *Australia* 90 A2
Caledonia, *Canada* 106 C5
Caledonia, *U.S.A.* 106 D7
Calella, *Spain* 28 D7
Calemba, *Angola* 84 B2
Calenzana, *France* 27 F12
Caleta Olivia, *Argentina* 128 C3
Calexico, *U.S.A.* 113 N11
Calf of Man, *U.K.* 12 C3
Calgary, *Canada* 100 C6
Calheta, *Madeira* 36 D2
Calhoun, *U.S.A.* 105 H3
Cali, *Colombia* 120 C2
Calicut, *India* 60 P9
Caliente, *U.S.A.* 111 H6
California, *Mo., U.S.A.* 108 F8
California, *Pa., U.S.A.* 106 F5
California □, *U.S.A.* 111 H4
California, Baja, *Mexico* 114 A1
California, Baja, T.N. □, *Mexico* 114 B2
California, Baja, T.S. □, *Mexico* 114 B2
California, G. de, *Mexico* 114 B2
California City, *U.S.A.* 113 K9
California Hot Springs, *U.S.A.* 113 K8
Călimăneşti, *Romania* 38 D7
Călimani, Munţii, *Romania* 38 B8
Călineşti, *Romania* 38 D7
Calingasta, *Argentina* 126 C2
Calipatria, *U.S.A.* 113 M11
Calistoga, *U.S.A.* 112 G4
Calitri, *Italy* 35 B8
Calitzdorp, *S. Africa* 84 E3
Callabonna, L., *Australia* 91 D3
Callac, *France* 24 D3
Callan, *Ireland* 15 D4
Callander, *U.K.* 14 E4
Callantsoog, *Neths.* 16 C5
Callao, *Peru* 124 C2
Callaway, *U.S.A.* 108 E5
Calles, *Mexico* 115 C5
Callide, *Australia* 90 C5
Calling Lake, *Canada* 100 B6
Calliope, *Australia* 90 C5
Callosa de Ensarriá, *Spain* 29 G4
Callosa de Segura, *Spain* 29 G4
Calola, *Angola* 84 B2
Calolbon, *Phil.* 55 E6
Caloocan, *Phil.* 55 D4
Calore →, *Italy* 35 A7
Caloundra, *Australia* 91 D5
Calpe, *Spain* 29 G5
Calpella, *U.S.A.* 112 F3
Calpine, *U.S.A.* 112 F6
Calstock, *Canada* 98 C3
Caltabellotta, *Italy* 34 E6
Caltagirone, *Italy* 35 E7
Caltanissetta, *Italy* 35 E7
Calulo, *Angola* 80 G2
Calumet, *U.S.A.* 104 B1
Calunda, *Angola* 81 G4
Caluso, *Italy* 32 C4
Calvados □, *France* 24 C6
Calvert, *U.S.A.* 109 K6
Calvert →, *Australia* 90 B2
Calvert Hills, *Australia* 90 B2
Calvert I., *Canada* 100 C3
Calvert Ra., *Australia* 88 D3
Calvi, *France* 27 F12
Calvillo, *Mexico* 114 C4
Calvinia, *S. Africa* 84 E2
Calw, *Germany* 19 G4
Calwa, *U.S.A.* 112 J7
Calzada Almuradiel, *Spain* 29 G1
Calzada de Calatrava, *Spain* 31 G7
Cam →, *U.K.* 13 E8
Cam Lam, *Vietnam* 59 G7
Cam Pha, *Vietnam* 58 B6
Cam Ranh, *Vietnam* 59 G7
Cam Xuyen, *Vietnam* 58 C6
Camabatela, *Angola* 80 F3
Camacã, *Brazil* 123 E4
Camaçari, *Brazil* 123 D4
Camacha, *Madeira* 36 D3
Camacho, *Mexico* 114 C4
Camacupa, *Angola* 81 G3
Camaguán, *Venezuela* 120 B4
Camagüey, *Cuba* 116 B4
Camaiore, *Italy* 32 E7
Camamu, *Brazil* 123 D4
Camaná, *Peru* 124 D3
Camanche Res., *U.S.A.* 112 G6
Camaquã →, *Brazil* 127 C5
Câmara de Lobos, *Madeira* 36 D3
Camararé →, *Brazil* 125 C6
Camarat, C., *France* 27 E10
Camaret, *France* 24 D2
Camargo, *Bolivia* 125 E4
Camargue, *France* 27 E8
Camarillo, *U.S.A.* 113 L7
Camariñas, *Spain* 30 B1
Camarón, C., *Honduras* 116 C2
Camarones, *Argentina* 128 B3
Camarones, B., *Argentina* 128 B3
Camas, *U.S.A.* 112 E4
Camas Valley, *U.S.A.* 110 E2
Cambados, *Spain* 30 C2
Cambará, *Brazil* 127 A5
Cambay = Khambhat, *India* 62 H5
Cambil, *Spain* 29 H1
Cambo-les-Bains, *France* 26 E2
Cambodia ■, *Asia* 58 F5
Camborne, *U.K.* 13 G2
Cambrai, *France* 25 B10
Cambria, *U.S.A.* 111 J3
Cambrian Mts., *U.K.* 13 E4
Cambridge, *Canada* 98 D3
Cambridge, *Jamaica* 116 C4
Cambridge, *N.Z.* 87 G5
Cambridge, *U.K.* 13 E8
Cambridge, *Idaho, U.S.A.* 110 D5
Cambridge, *Mass., U.S.A.* 107 D13
Cambridge, *Md., U.S.A.* 104 F7
Cambridge, *Minn., U.S.A.* 108 C8
Cambridge, *N.Y., U.S.A.* 107 C11
Cambridge, *Nebr., U.S.A.* 108 E4
Cambridge, *Ohio, U.S.A.* 106 F3
Cambridge Bay, *Canada* 96 B9
Cambridge G., *Australia* 88 B4
Cambridge Springs, *U.S.A.* 106 E4
Cambridgeshire □, *U.K.* 13 E8
Cambrils, *Spain* 28 D6
Cambuci, *Brazil* 123 F3
Cambundi-Catembo, *Angola* 80 G3
Camden, *Ala., U.S.A.* 105 K2
Camden, *Ark., U.S.A.* 109 J8
Camden, *Maine, U.S.A.* 99 D6
Camden, *N.J., U.S.A.* 107 G9
Camden, *S.C., U.S.A.* 105 H5
Camden Sd., *Australia* 88 C3
Camdenton, *U.S.A.* 109 F8
Çameli, *Turkey* 66 E3
Camembert, *France* 24 D7
Cámeri, *Italy* 32 C5
Camerino, *Italy* 33 E10
Cameron, *Ariz., U.S.A.* 111 J8
Cameron, *La., U.S.A.* 109 L8
Cameron, *Mo., U.S.A.* 108 F7
Cameron, *Tex., U.S.A.* 109 K6
Cameron Falls, *Canada* 98 C2
Cameron Highlands, *Malaysia* 59 K3
Cameron Hills, *Canada* 100 B5
Cameroon ■, *Africa* 73 G7
Camerota, *Italy* 35 B8
Cameroun →, *Cameroon* 79 E6
Cameroun, Mt., *Cameroon* 79 E6
Cametá, *Brazil* 122 B2
Camiguin □, *Phil.* 55 G6
Camiguin I., *Phil.* 55 B4
Camiling, *Phil.* 55 D4
Caminha, *Portugal* 30 D2
Camino, *U.S.A.* 112 G6
Camira Creek, *Australia* 91 D5
Camiranga, *Brazil* 122 B2
Camiri, *Bolivia* 125 E5
Camissombo, *Angola* 80 F4
Cammal, *U.S.A.* 106 E7
Camocim, *Brazil* 122 B3
Camogli, *Italy* 32 D6
Camooweal, *Australia* 90 B2
Camopi, *Fr. Guiana* 121 C7
Camopi →, *Fr. Guiana* 121 C7
Camotes Is., *Phil.* 55 F6
Camotes Sea, *Phil.* 55 F6
Camp Crook, *U.S.A.* 108 C3
Camp Nelson, *U.S.A.* 113 J8
Camp Wood, *U.S.A.* 109 L4
Campagna, *Italy* 35 B8
Campana, *Argentina* 126 C4
Campana, I., *Chile* 128 C1
Campanário, *Madeira* 36 D2
Campanario, *Spain* 31 G5
Campania □, *Italy* 35 B7
Campbell, *S. Africa* 84 D3
Campbell, *Calif., U.S.A.* 112 H5
Campbell, *Ohio, U.S.A.* 106 E4
Campbell I., *Pac. Oc.* 92 N8
Campbell L., *Canada* 101 A7
Campbell River, *Canada* 100 C3
Campbell Town, *Australia* 90 G4
Campbellford, *Canada* 106 B7
Campbellpur, *Pakistan* 62 C5
Campbellsville, *U.S.A.* 104 G3
Campbellton, *Canada* 99 C6
Campbelltown, *Australia* 91 E5
Campbeltown, *U.K.* 14 F3
Campeche, *Mexico* 115 D6
Campeche □, *Mexico* 115 D6
Campeche, B. de, *Mexico* 115 D6
Camperdown, *Australia* 91 F3
Camperville, *Canada* 101 C8
Campi Salentina, *Italy* 35 B11
Campidano, *Italy* 34 C1
Campíglia Maríttima, *Italy* 32 E7
Campillo de Altobuey, *Spain* 28 F3
Campillo de Llerena, *Spain* 31 G5
Campillos, *Spain* 31 H6
Campina Grande, *Brazil* 122 C4
Campina Verde, *Brazil* 123 E2
Campinas, *Brazil* 127 A6
Campine, *Belgium* 17 F6
Campli, *Italy* 33 F10
Campo, *Cameroon* 80 D1
Campo, *Spain* 28 C5
Campo Belo, *Brazil* 123 F2
Campo de Criptana, *Spain* 29 F1
Campo de Diauarum, *Brazil* 125 C7
Campo de Gibraltar, *Spain* 31 J5
Campo Flórido, *Brazil* 123 E2
Campo Formoso, *Brazil* 122 D3
Campo Grande, *Brazil* 125 E7
Campo Maíor, *Brazil* 122 B3
Campo Maior, *Portugal* 31 G3
Campo Mourão, *Brazil* 127 A5
Campo Tencia, *Switz.* 23 D7
Campo Túres, *Italy* 33 B8
Campoalegre, *Colombia* 120 C2
Campobasso, *Italy* 35 A7
Campobello di Licata, *Italy* 34 E6
Campobello di Mazara, *Italy* 34 E5
Campofelice, *Italy* 34 E6
Camporeale, *Italy* 34 E6
Campos, *Brazil* 123 F3
Campos Altos, *Brazil* 123 E2
Campos Belos, *Brazil* 123 D2
Campos del Puerto, *Spain* 36 B10
Campos Novos, *Brazil* 127 B5
Campos Sales, *Brazil* 122 C3
Camprodón, *Spain* 28 C7
Camptonville, *U.S.A.* 112 F5
Campuya →, *Peru* 120 D3
Camrose, *Canada* 100 C6
Camsell Portage, *Canada* 101 B7
Çan, *Turkey* 66 C2
Can Clavo, *Spain* 36 C7
Can Creu, *Spain* 36 C7
Can Gio, *Vietnam* 59 G6
Can Tho, *Vietnam* 59 G5
Canaan, *U.S.A.* 107 D11
Canada ■, *N. Amer.* 96 C10
Cañada de Gómez, *Argentina* 126 C3
Canadian, *U.S.A.* 109 H4
Canadian →, *U.S.A.* 109 H7
Çanakkale, *Turkey* 39 J9
Çanakkale □, *Turkey* 66 C2
Çanakkale Boğazı, *Turkey* 66 C2
Canal Flats, *Canada* 100 C5
Canalejas, *Argentina* 126 D2
Canals, *Argentina* 126 C3
Canals, *Spain* 29 G4
Canandaigua, *U.S.A.* 106 D7
Cananea, *Mexico* 114 A2
Cañar, *Ecuador* 120 D2
Cañar □, *Ecuador* 120 D2
Canarias, Is., *Atl. Oc.* 36 F4
Canarreos, Arch. de los, *Cuba* 116 B3
Canary Is. = Canarias, Is., *Atl. Oc.* 36 F4
Canastra, Serra da, *Brazil* 123 F2
Canatlán, *Mexico* 114 C4
Canaveral, C., *U.S.A.* 105 L5
Cañaveras, *Spain* 28 E2
Canavieiras, *Brazil* 123 E4
Canbelego, *Australia* 91 E4
Canberra, *Australia* 91 F4
Canby, *Calif., U.S.A.* 110 F3
Canby, *Minn., U.S.A.* 108 C6
Canby, *Oreg., U.S.A.* 112 E4
Cancale, *France* 24 D5
Canche →, *France* 25 B8
Canchyuaya, Cordillera de, *Peru* 124 B3
Cancún, *Mexico* 115 C7
Candala, *Somali Rep.* 68 E4
Candarave, *Peru* 124 D3
Candas, *Spain* 30 B5
Candé, *France* 24 E5
Candeias →, *Brazil* 125 B5
Candela, *Italy* 35 A8
Candelaria, *Argentina* 127 B4
Candelaria, *Canary Is.* 36 F3
Candelaria, Pta. de la, *Spain* 30 B2
Candeleda, *Spain* 30 E5
Candelo, *Australia* 91 F4
Candia = Iráklion, *Greece* 37 D7
Candia, Sea of = Crete, Sea of, *Greece* 39 N8
Cândido de Abreu, *Brazil* 123 F1
Cândido Mendes, *Brazil* 122 B2
Candle L., *Canada* 101 C7
Candlemas I., *Antarctica* 5 B1
Cando, *U.S.A.* 108 A5
Candon, *Phil.* 55 C4
Canea = Khaniá, *Greece* 37 D6
Canela, *Brazil* 122 D2
Canelli, *Italy* 32 D5
Canelones, *Uruguay* 127 C4
Canet-Plage, *France* 26 F7
Cañete, *Chile* 126 D1
Cañete, *Peru* 124 C2
Cañete, *Spain* 28 E3
Cañete de las Torres, *Spain* 31 H6
Canfranc, *Spain* 28 C4
Cangas, *Spain* 30 C2
Cangas de Narcea, *Spain* 30 B4
Cangas de Onís, *Spain* 30 B5
Canguaretama, *Brazil* 122 C4
Canguçu, *Brazil* 127 C5
Cangxi, *China* 52 B5
Cangyuan, *China* 52 F2
Cangzhou, *China* 50 E9
Cani, I., *Tunisia* 75 A7
Canicattì, *Italy* 34 E6
Canicattini, *Italy* 35 E8
Canim Lake, *Canada* 100 C4
Canindé, *Brazil* 122 B4
Canindé →, *Brazil* 122 C3
Canindeyu □, *Paraguay* 127 A4
Canipaan, *Phil.* 56 C5
Canisteo, *U.S.A.* 106 D7
Canisteo →, *U.S.A.* 106 D7
Cañitas, *Mexico* 114 C4
Cañizal, *Spain* 30 D5
Canjáyar, *Spain* 29 H2
Çankırı, *Turkey* 66 C5
Çankırı □, *Turkey* 66 C5
Cankuzo, *Burundi* 82 C3
Canmore, *Canada* 100 C5
Cann River, *Australia* 91 F4
Canna, *U.K.* 14 D2
Cannanore, *India* 60 P9
Cannes, *France* 27 E11
Canning Town = Port Canning, *India* 63 H13
Cannington, *Canada* 106 B5
Cannock, *U.K.* 12 E5
Cannon Ball →, *U.S.A.* 108 B4
Cannondale Mt., *Australia* 90 D4
Caño Colorado, *Colombia* 120 C4
Canoas, *Brazil* 127 B5
Canoe L., *Canada* 101 B7
Canon City, *U.S.A.* 108 F2
Canora, *Canada* 101 C8
Canosa di Púglia, *Italy* 35 A9
Canowindra, *Australia* 91 E4
Canso, *Canada* 99 C7
Canta, *Peru* 124 C2
Cantabria □, *Spain* 30 B6
Cantabria, Sierra de, *Spain* 28 C2
Cantabrian Mts. = Cantábrica, Cordillera, *Spain* 30 C5
Cantábrica, Cordillera, *Spain* 30 C5
Cantal □, *France* 26 C6
Cantal, Plomb du, *France* 26 C6
Cantanhede, *Portugal* 30 E2
Cantaura, *Venezuela* 121 B5
Cantavieja, *Spain* 28 E4
Canterbury, *Australia* 90 D3
Canterbury, *U.K.* 13 F9
Canterbury □, *N.Z.* 87 K3
Canterbury Bight, *N.Z.* 87 L3
Canterbury Plains, *N.Z.* 87 K3
Cantil, *U.S.A.* 113 K9
Cantillana, *Spain* 31 H5
Canto do Buriti, *Brazil* 122 C3
Canton = Guangzhou, *China* 53 F9
Canton, *Ga., U.S.A.* 105 H3
Canton, *Ill., U.S.A.* 108 E9
Canton, *Miss., U.S.A.* 109 J9
Canton, *Mo., U.S.A.* 108 E9
Canton, *N.Y., U.S.A.* 107 B9
Canton, *Ohio, U.S.A.* 106 F3
Canton, *Okla., U.S.A.* 109 G5
Canton, *S. Dak., U.S.A.* 108 D6
Canton L., *U.S.A.* 109 G5
Cantù, *Italy* 32 C6
Canudos, *Brazil* 125 B6
Canumã, *Amazonas, Brazil* 121 D6
Canumã, *Amazonas, Brazil* 125 B5
Canumã →, *Brazil* 125 A6
Canutama, *Brazil* 125 B5
Canutillo, *U.S.A.* 111 L10
Canyon, *Tex., U.S.A.* 109 H4
Canyon, *Wyo., U.S.A.* 110 D8
Canyonlands Nat. Park, *U.S.A.* 111 G9
Canyonville, *U.S.A.* 110 E2
Canzo, *Italy* 32 C6
Cao Bang, *Vietnam* 58 A6
Cao He →, *China* 51 D13
Cao Lanh, *Vietnam* 59 G5
Cao Xian, *China* 50 G8
Cáorle, *Italy* 33 C9
Cap-aux-Meules, *Canada* 99 C7
Cap-Chat, *Canada* 99 C6
Cap-de-la-Madeleine, *Canada* 98 C5
Cap-Haïtien, *Haiti* 117 C5
Cap St.-Jacques = Vung Tau, *Vietnam* 59 G6
Capa, *Vietnam* 58 A4
Capa Stilo, *Italy* 35 D9
Capáccio, *Italy* 35 B8
Capaia, *Angola* 80 F4
Capanaparo →, *Venezuela* 120 B4
Capanema, *Brazil* 122 B2
Caparo →, *Barinas, Venezuela* 120 B3
Caparo →, *Bolívar, Venezuela* 121 B5
Capatárida, *Venezuela* 120 A3
Capbreton, *France* 26 E2
Capdenac, *France* 26 D6
Cape →, *Australia* 90 C4
Cape Barren I., *Australia* 90 G4
Cape Breton Highlands Nat. Park, *Canada* 99 C7
Cape Breton I., *Canada* 99 C7
Cape Charles, *U.S.A.* 104 G8
Cape Coast, *Ghana* 79 D4
Cape Dorset, *Canada* 97 B12
Cape Dyer, *Canada* 97 B13
Cape Fear →, *U.S.A.* 105 H6
Cape Girardeau, *U.S.A.* 109 G10
Cape Jervis, *Australia* 91 F2
Cape May, *U.S.A.* 104 F8
Cape May Pt., *U.S.A.* 103 C12
Cape Palmas, *Liberia* 78 E3
Cape Province □, *S. Africa* 84 E3
Cape Tormentine, *Canada* 99 C7
Cape Town, *S. Africa* 84 E2
Cape Verde Is. ■, *Atl. Oc.* 2 D8
Cape Vincent, *U.S.A.* 107 B8
Cape York Peninsula, *Australia* 90 A3
Capela, *Brazil* 122 D4
Capela de Campo, *Brazil* 122 B3
Capelinha, *Brazil* 123 E3
Capella, *Australia* 90 C4
Capendu, *France* 26 E6
Capestang, *France* 26 E7
Capim, *Brazil* 122 B2
Capim →, *Brazil* 122 B2
Capinópolis, *Brazil* 123 E2
Capinota, *Bolivia* 124 D4
Capitan, *U.S.A.* 111 K11
Capitán Aracena, I., *Chile* 128 D2
Capitán Pastene, *Chile* 128 A2
Capitola, *U.S.A.* 112 J5
Capivara, Serra da, *Brazil* 123 D3
Capizzi, *Italy* 35 E7
Čapljina, *Bos.-H., Yug.* 21 M7
Capoche →, *Mozam.* 83 F3
Capoeira, *Brazil* 125 B6
Cappadocia, *Turkey* 66 D6
Capraia, *Italy* 32 E6
Caprarola, *Italy* 33 F9
Capreol, *Canada* 98 C3
Caprera, *Italy* 34 A2
Capri, *Italy* 35 B7
Capricorn Group, *Australia* 90 C5
Capricorn Ra., *Australia* 88 D2
Caprino Veronese, *Italy* 32 C7
Caprivi Strip, *Namibia* 84 B3
Captainganj, *India* 63 F10
Captain's Flat, *Australia* 91 F4
Captieux, *France* 26 D3
Cápua, *Italy* 35 A7
Caquetá □, *Colombia* 120 C3
Caquetá →, *Colombia* 120 D4
Carabobo, *Venezuela* 120 A4
Carabobo □, *Venezuela* 120 A4
Caracal, *Romania* 38 E7
Caracaraí, *Brazil* 121 C5
Caracas, *Venezuela* 120 A4
Caracol, *Brazil* 122 C3
Caracollo, *Bolivia* 124 D4
Caradoc, *Australia* 91 E3
Caráglio, *Italy* 32 D4
Carahue, *Chile* 128 A2
Caraí, *Brazil* 123 E3
Carajás, Serra dos, *Brazil* 122 C1
Caranapatuba, *Brazil* 125 B5
Carandaiti, *Bolivia* 125 E5
Carangola, *Brazil* 123 F3
Carani, *Australia* 89 F2
Caransebeş, *Romania* 38 D5
Carantec, *France* 24 D3
Caraparaná →, *Colombia* 120 D3
Carapelle →, *Italy* 35 A8
Caras, *Peru* 124 B2
Caratasca, L., *Honduras* 116 C3
Caratinga, *Brazil* 123 E3
Caraúbas, *Brazil* 122 C4
Caravaca, *Spain* 29 G3
Caravággio, *Italy* 32 C6
Caravelas, *Brazil* 123 E4
Caraveli, *Peru* 124 D3
Caràzinho, *Brazil* 127 B5
Carballino, *Spain* 30 C2
Carballo, *Spain* 30 B2
Carberry, *Canada* 101 D9
Carbia, *Spain* 30 C2
Carbó, *Mexico* 114 B2
Carbon, *Canada* 100 C6
Carbonara, C., *Italy* 34 C2
Carbondale, *Colo., U.S.A.* 110 G10
Carbondale, *Ill., U.S.A.* 109 G10
Carbondale, *Pa., U.S.A.* 107 E9
Carbonear, *Canada* 99 C9
Carboneras, *Spain* 29 J3
Carboneras de Guadazaón, *Spain* 28 F3
Carbonia, *Italy* 34 C1
Carcabuey, *Spain* 31 H6
Carcagente, *Spain* 29 F4

Carcajou, *Canada* 100 B5
Carcar, *Phil.* 55 F5
Carcasse, C., *Haiti* 117 C5
Carcassonne, *France* 26 E6
Carche, *Spain* 29 G3
Carchi □, *Ecuador* 120 C2
Carcross, *Canada* 96 B6
Cardabia, *Australia* 88 D1
Çardak, *Turkey* 66 E3
Cardamon Hills, *India* 60 Q10
Cárdenas, *Cuba* 116 B3
Cárdenas, *San Luis Potosí, Mexico* 115 C5
Cárdenas, *Tabasco, Mexico* 115 D6
Cardenete, *Spain* 28 F3
Cardiel, L., *Argentina* 128 C2
Cardiff, *U.K.* 13 F4
Cardiff-by-the-Sea, *U.S.A.* 113 M9
Cardigan, *U.K.* 13 E3
Cardigan B., *U.K.* 13 E3
Cardinal, *Canada* 107 B9
Cardón, Punta, *Venezuela* 120 A3
Cardona, *Spain* 28 D6
Cardona, *Uruguay* 126 C4
Cardoner →, *Spain* 28 D6
Cardross, *Canada* 101 D7
Cardston, *Canada* 100 D6
Cardwell, *Australia* 90 B4
Careen L., *Canada* 101 B7
Carei, *Romania* 38 B5
Careiro, *Brazil* 121 D6
Careme, *Indonesia* 57 G13
Carentan, *France* 24 C5
Carey, *Idaho, U.S.A.* 110 E7
Carey, *Ohio, U.S.A.* 104 E4
Carey, L., *Australia* 89 E3
Carey L., *Canada* 101 A8
Careysburg, *Liberia* 78 D2
Cargèse, *France* 27 F12
Carhaix-Plouguer, *France* 24 D3
Carhuamayo, *Peru* 124 C2
Carhuas, *Peru* 124 B2
Carhué, *Argentina* 126 D3
Caria, *Turkey* 66 E3
Cariacica, *Brazil* 123 F3
Caribbean Sea, *W. Indies* 117 C5
Cariboo Mts., *Canada* 100 C4
Caribou, *U.S.A.* 99 C6
Caribou →, *Man., Canada* 101 B10
Caribou →, *N.W.T., Canada* 100 A3
Caribou I., *Canada* 98 C2
Caribou Is., *Canada* 100 A6
Caribou L., *Man., Canada* 101 B9
Caribou L., *Ont., Canada* 98 B2
Caribou Mts., *Canada* 100 B5
Carichic, *Mexico* 114 B3
Carigara, *Phil.* 55 F6
Carignan, *France* 25 C12
Carignano, *Italy* 32 D4
Carillo, *Mexico* 114 B4
Carinda, *Australia* 91 E4
Cariñena, *Spain* 28 D3
Carinhanha, *Brazil* 123 D3
Carinhanha →, *Brazil* 123 D3
Carini, *Italy* 34 D6
Carinola, *Italy* 34 A6
Caripito, *Venezuela* 121 A5
Caritianas, *Brazil* 125 B5
Carlbrod = Dimitrovgrad, *Serbia, Yug.* 21 M12
Carlentini, *Italy* 35 E8
Carleton Place, *Canada* 98 C4
Carletonville, *S. Africa* 84 D4
Carlin, *U.S.A.* 110 F5
Carlingford, L., *Ireland* 15 B5
Carlinville, *U.S.A.* 108 F10
Carlisle, *U.K.* 12 C5
Carlisle, *U.S.A.* 106 F7
Carlit, Pic, *France* 26 F5
Carloforte, *Italy* 34 C1
Carlos Casares, *Argentina* 126 D3
Carlos Chagas, *Brazil* 123 E3
Carlos Tejedor, *Argentina* 126 D3
Carlow, *Ireland* 15 D5
Carlow □, *Ireland* 15 D5
Carlsbad, *Calif., U.S.A.* 113 M9
Carlsbad, *N. Mex., U.S.A.* 109 J2
Carlyle, *Canada* 101 D8
Carlyle, *U.S.A.* 108 F10
Carmacks, *Canada* 96 B6
Carmagnola, *Italy* 32 D4
Carman, *Canada* 101 D9
Carmangay, *Canada* 100 C6
Carmanville, *Canada* 99 C9
Carmarthen, *U.K.* 13 F3
Carmarthen B., *U.K.* 13 F3
Carmaux, *France* 26 D6
Carmel, *U.S.A.* 107 E11
Carmel-by-the-Sea, *U.S.A.* 111 H3
Carmel Valley, *U.S.A.* 112 J5
Carmelo, *Uruguay* 126 C4
Carmen, *Bolivia* 124 C4
Carmen, *Colombia* 120 B2
Carmen, *Paraguay* 127 B4
Carmen →, *Mexico* 114 A3
Carmen, I., *Mexico* 114 B2
Carmen de Patagones, *Argentina* 128 B4
Cármenes, *Spain* 30 C5
Carmensa, *Argentina* 126 D2
Carmi, *U.S.A.* 104 F1
Carmichael, *U.S.A.* 112 G5
Carmila, *Australia* 90 C4
Carmona, *Spain* 31 H5
Carnarvon, *Queens., Australia* 90 C4
Carnarvon, *W. Austral., Australia* 89 D1
Carnarvon, *S. Africa* 84 E3
Carnarvon Ra., *Queens., Australia* 90 D4
Carnarvon Ra., *W. Austral., Australia* 89 E3
Carnation, *U.S.A.* 112 C5
Carnaxide, *Portugal* 31 G1
Carndonagh, *Ireland* 15 A4
Carnduff, *Canada* 101 D8
Carnegie, *U.S.A.* 106 F4
Carnegie, L., *Australia* 89 E3
Carnic Alps = Karnische Alpen, *Europe* 21 J3
Carniche Alpi = Karnische Alpen, *Europe* 21 J3
Carnot, *C.A.R.* 80 D3
Carnot, C., *Australia* 91 E2
Carnot B., *Australia* 88 C3
Carnsore Pt., *Ireland* 15 D5
Caro, *U.S.A.* 104 D4
Carol City, *U.S.A.* 105 N5
Carolina, *Brazil* 122 C2
Carolina, *Puerto Rico* 117 C6
Carolina, *S. Africa* 85 D5
Caroline I., *Kiribati* 93 H12
Caroline Is., *Pac. Oc.* 92 G6
Caron, *Canada* 101 C7
Caroni →, *Venezuela* 121 B5
Caroona, *Australia* 91 E5
Carora, *Venezuela* 120 A3
Carovigno, *Italy* 35 B10
Carpathians, *Europe* 20 F11
Carpaţii Meridionali, *Romania* 38 D8
Carpenédolo, *Italy* 32 C7
Carpentaria, G. of, *Australia* 90 A2
Carpentaria Downs, *Australia* 90 B3
Carpentras, *France* 27 D9
Carpi, *Italy* 32 D7
Carpina, *Brazil* 122 C4
Carpino, *Italy* 35 A8
Carpinteria, *U.S.A.* 113 L7
Carpio, *Spain* 30 D5
Carpolac = Morea, *Australia* 91 F3
Carr Boyd Ra., *Australia* 88 C4
Carrabelle, *U.S.A.* 105 L3
Carranya, *Australia* 88 C4
Carrara, *Italy* 32 D7
Carrascal, *Phil.* 55 G6
Carrascosa del Campo, *Spain* 28 E2
Carrauntoohill, *Ireland* 15 E2
Carretas, Punta, *Peru* 124 C2
Carrick-on-Shannon, *Ireland* 15 C3
Carrick-on-Suir, *Ireland* 15 D4
Carrickfergus, *U.K.* 15 B6
Carrickfergus □, *U.K.* 15 B6
Carrickmacross, *Ireland* 15 C5
Carrieton, *Australia* 91 E2
Carrington, *U.S.A.* 108 B5
Carrión →, *Spain* 30 D6
Carrión de los Condes, *Spain* 30 C6
Carrizal Bajo, *Chile* 126 B1
Carrizalillo, *Chile* 126 B1
Carrizo Cr. →, *U.S.A.* 109 G3
Carrizo Springs, *U.S.A.* 109 L5
Carrizozo, *U.S.A.* 111 K11
Carroll, *U.S.A.* 108 D7
Carrollton, *Ga., U.S.A.* 105 J3
Carrollton, *Ill., U.S.A.* 108 F9
Carrollton, *Ky., U.S.A.* 104 F3
Carrollton, *Mo., U.S.A.* 108 F8
Carrollton, *Ohio, U.S.A.* 106 F3
Carron →, *U.K.* 14 D3
Carron, L., *U.K.* 14 D3
Carrot →, *Canada* 101 C8
Carrot River, *Canada* 101 C8
Carrouges, *France* 24 D6
Carruthers, *Canada* 101 C7
Çarşamba, *Turkey* 66 C7
Carse of Gowrie, *U.K.* 14 E5
Carsoli, *Italy* 33 F10
Carson, *Calif., U.S.A.* 113 M8
Carson, *N. Dak., U.S.A.* 108 B4
Carson →, *U.S.A.* 112 F8
Carson City, *U.S.A.* 112 F7
Carson Sink, *U.S.A.* 110 G4
Carstairs, *U.K.* 14 F5
Cartagena, *Colombia* 120 A2
Cartagena, *Spain* 29 H4
Cartago, *Colombia* 120 C2
Cartago, *Costa Rica* 116 E3
Cartaxo, *Portugal* 31 F2
Cartaya, *Spain* 31 H3
Carteret, *France* 24 C5
Cartersville, *U.S.A.* 105 H3
Carterton, *N.Z.* 87 J5
Carthage, *Ark., U.S.A.* 109 H8
Carthage, *Ill., U.S.A.* 108 E9
Carthage, *Mo., U.S.A.* 109 G7
Carthage, *S. Dak., U.S.A.* 108 C6
Carthage, *Tex., U.S.A.* 109 J7
Cartier I., *Australia* 88 B3
Cartwright, *Canada* 99 B8
Caruaru, *Brazil* 122 C4
Carúpano, *Venezuela* 121 A5
Carutapera, *Brazil* 122 B2
Caruthersville, *U.S.A.* 109 G10
Carvalho, *Brazil* 121 D7
Carvin, *France* 25 B9
Carvoeiro, *Brazil* 121 D5
Carvoeiro, C., *Portugal* 31 F1
Casa Branca, *Brazil* 123 F2
Casa Branca, *Portugal* 31 G2
Casa Grande, *U.S.A.* 111 K8
Casablanca, *Chile* 126 C1
Casablanca, *Morocco* 74 B3
Casacalenda, *Italy* 35 A7
Casal di Principe, *Italy* 35 B7
Casalbordino, *Italy* 33 F11
Casale Monferrato, *Italy* 32 C5
Casalmaggiore, *Italy* 32 D7
Casalpusterlengo, *Italy* 32 C6
Casamance →, *Senegal* 78 C1
Casamássima, *Italy* 35 B9
Casanare □, *Colombia* 120 B3
Casanare □, *Colombia* 120 B3
Casanare →, *Colombia* 120 B4
Casarano, *Italy* 35 B11
Casares, *Spain* 31 J5
Casas Grandes, *Mexico* 114 A3
Casas Ibañez, *Spain* 29 F3
Casasimarro, *Spain* 29 F2
Casatejada, *Spain* 30 F5
Casavieja, *Spain* 30 E6
Cascade, *Idaho, U.S.A.* 110 D5
Cascade, *Mont., U.S.A.* 110 C8
Cascade Locks, *U.S.A.* 112 E5
Cascade Ra., *U.S.A.* 112 D5
Cascais, *Portugal* 31 G1
Cascavel, *Brazil* 127 A5
Cáscina, *Italy* 32 E7
Caselle Torinese, *Italy* 32 C4
Caserta, *Italy* 35 A7
Cashel, *Ireland* 15 D4
Cashmere, *U.S.A.* 110 C3
Cashmere Downs, *Australia* 89 E2
Casibare →, *Colombia* 120 C3
Casiguran, *Phil.* 55 C5
Casilda, *Argentina* 126 C3
Casino, *Australia* 91 D5
Casiquiare →, *Venezuela* 120 C4
Casitas, *Peru* 124 A1
Çaslan, *Canada* 100 C6
Čáslav, *Czech.* 20 F5
Casma, *Peru* 124 B2
Casmalia, *U.S.A.* 113 L6
Casola Valsenio, *Italy* 33 D8
Cásoli, *Italy* 33 F11
Caspe, *Spain* 28 D4
Casper, *U.S.A.* 110 E10
Caspian Sea, *Asia* 44 E6
Casquets, *Chan. Is.* 24 C4
Cass City, *U.S.A.* 104 D4
Cass Lake, *U.S.A.* 108 B7
Cassá de la Selva, *Spain* 28 D7
Cassano Iónio, *Italy* 35 C9
Cassel, *France* 25 B9
Casselman, *Canada* 107 A9
Casselton, *U.S.A.* 108 B6
Cassiar, *Canada* 100 B3
Cassiar Mts., *Canada* 100 B2
Cassilândia, *Brazil* 125 D7
Cassinga, *Angola* 81 H3
Cassino, *Italy* 34 A6
Cassis, *France* 27 E9
Cassville, *U.S.A.* 109 G8
Cástagneto Carducci, *Italy* 32 E7
Castaic, *U.S.A.* 113 L8
Castanhal, *Brazil* 122 B2
Casteau, *Belgium* 17 G4
Castéggio, *Italy* 32 C6
Castejón de Monegros, *Spain* 28 D4
Castel di Sangro, *Italy* 33 G11
Castel San Giovanni, *Italy* 32 C6
Castel San Pietro, *Italy* 33 D8
Castelbuono, *Italy* 35 E7
Casteldelfino, *Italy* 32 D4
Castelfiorentino, *Italy* 32 E7
Castelfranco Emília, *Italy* 32 D8
Castelfranco Véneto, *Italy* 33 C8
Casteljaloux, *France* 26 D4
Castellabate, *Italy* 35 B7
Castellammare, G. di, *Italy* 34 D5
Castellammare del Golfo, *Italy* 34 D5
Castellammare di Stábia, *Italy* 35 B7
Castellamonte, *Italy* 32 C4
Castellana Grotte, *Italy* 35 B10
Castellane, *France* 27 E10
Castellaneta, *Italy* 35 B9
Castellar de Santisteban, *Spain* 29 G1
Castelleone, *Italy* 32 C6
Castelli, *Argentina* 126 D4
Castelló de Ampurias, *Spain* 28 C8
Castellón □, *Spain* 28 E4
Castellón de la Plana, *Spain* 28 F4
Castellote, *Spain* 28 E4
Castelltersol, *Spain* 28 D7
Castelmáuro, *Italy* 35 A7
Castelnau-de-Médoc, *France* 26 C3
Castelnaudary, *France* 26 E5
Castelnovo ne' Monti, *Italy* 32 D7
Castelnuovo di Val di Cécina, *Italy* 32 E7
Castelo, *Brazil* 123 F3
Castelo Branco, *Portugal* 30 F3
Castelo Branco □, *Portugal* 30 F3
Castelo de Paiva, *Portugal* 30 D2
Castelo de Vide, *Portugal* 31 F3
Castelo do Piauí, *Brazil* 122 C3
Castelsarrasin, *France* 26 D5
Casteltérmini, *Italy* 34 E6
Castelvetrano, *Italy* 34 E5
Casterton, *Australia* 91 F3
Castets, *France* 26 E2
Castiglione del Lago, *Italy* 33 E9
Castiglione della Pescáia, *Italy* 32 F7
Castiglione della Stiviere, *Italy* 32 C7
Castiglione Fiorentino, *Italy* 33 E8
Castilblanco, *Spain* 31 F5
Castilla, *Peru* 124 B1
Castilla, Playa de, *Spain* 31 H4
Castilla La Mancha □, *Spain* 31 F7
Castilla La Nueva = Castilla La Mancha □, *Spain* 31 F7
Castilla La Vieja = Castilla y Leon □, *Spain* 30 D6
Castilla y Leon □, *Spain* 30 D6
Castillon, Barr. de, *France* 27 E10
Castillon-en-Couserans, *France* 26 F5
Castillon-la-Bataille, *France* 26 D3
Castillonès, *France* 26 D4
Castillos, *Uruguay* 127 C5
Castle Dale, *U.S.A.* 110 G8
Castle Douglas, *U.K.* 14 G5
Castle Rock, *Colo., U.S.A.* 108 F2
Castle Rock, *Wash., U.S.A.* 112 D4
Castlebar, *Ireland* 15 C2
Castleblaney, *Ireland* 15 B5
Castlegar, *Canada* 100 D5
Castlemaine, *Australia* 91 F3
Castlereagh, *Ireland* 15 C3
Castlereagh □, *U.K.* 15 B6
Castlereagh →, *Australia* 91 E4
Castlereagh B., *Australia* 90 A2
Castletown, *I. of Man* 12 C3
Castletown Bearhaven, *Ireland* 15 E2
Castlevale, *Australia* 90 C4
Castor, *Canada* 100 C6
Castres, *France* 26 E6
Castricum, *Neths.* 16 C5
Castries, *St. Lucia* 117 D7
Castril, *Spain* 29 H2
Castro, *Brazil* 127 A5
Castro, *Chile* 128 B2
Castro Alves, *Brazil* 123 D4
Castro del Río, *Spain* 31 H6
Castro Marim, *Portugal* 31 H3
Castro Urdiales, *Spain* 28 B1
Castro Verde, *Portugal* 31 H2
Castrojeriz, *Spain* 30 C6
Castropol, *Spain* 30 B3
Castroreale, *Italy* 35 D8
Castrovíllari, *Italy* 35 C9
Castroville, *Calif., U.S.A.* 112 J5
Castroville, *Tex., U.S.A.* 109 L5
Castrovirreyna, *Peru* 124 C2
Castuera, *Spain* 31 G5
Casummit Lake, *Canada* 98 B1
Çat, *Turkey* 67 D9
Cat Ba, Dao, *Vietnam* 58 B6
Cat I., *Bahamas* 117 B4
Cat I., *U.S.A.* 109 K10
Cat L., *Canada* 98 B1
Catacamas, *Honduras* 116 D2
Catacáos, *Peru* 124 B1
Cataguases, *Brazil* 123 F3
Catahoula L., *U.S.A.* 109 K8
Çatak, *Turkey* 67 D10
Catalão, *Brazil* 123 E2
Çatalca, *Turkey* 66 C3
Catalina, *Canada* 99 C9
Catalonia = Cataluña □, *Spain* 28 D6
Cataluña □, *Spain* 28 D6
Çatalzeytin, *Turkey* 66 C6
Catamarca, *Argentina* 126 B2
Catamarca □, *Argentina* 126 B2
Catanauan, *Phil.* 55 E5
Catanduanes, *Phil.* 55 E6
Catanduva, *Brazil* 127 A6
Catánia, *Italy* 35 E8
Catánia, G. di, *Italy* 35 E8
Catanzaro, *Italy* 35 D9
Cataonia, *Turkey* 66 E6
Catarman, *Phil.* 55 E6
Catbalogan, *Phil.* 55 F6
Cateel, *Phil.* 55 H7
Catende, *Brazil* 122 C4
Cathcart, *S. Africa* 84 E4
Cathlamet, *U.S.A.* 112 D3
Catio, *Guinea-Biss.* 78 C1
Catismiña, *Venezuela* 121 C5
Catita, *Brazil* 122 C3
Catlettsburg, *U.S.A.* 104 F4
Catoche, C., *Mexico* 115 C7
Catolé do Rocha, *Brazil* 122 C4
Catral, *Spain* 29 G4
Catria, Mt., *Italy* 33 E9
Catrimani, *Brazil* 121 C5
Catrimani →, *Brazil* 121 C5
Catskill, *U.S.A.* 107 D11
Catskill Mts., *U.S.A.* 107 D10
Catt, Mt., *Australia* 90 A1
Cattaraugus, *U.S.A.* 106 D6
Cattólica, *Italy* 33 E9
Cattólica Eraclea, *Italy* 34 E6
Catu, *Brazil* 123 D4
Catuala, *Angola* 84 B2
Catur, *Mozam.* 83 E4
Catwick Is., *Vietnam* 59 G7
Cauca □, *Colombia* 120 C2
Cauca →, *Colombia* 120 B3
Caucaia, *Brazil* 122 B4
Caucasia, *Colombia* 120 B2
Caucasus = Bolshoi Kavkas, *Asia* 43 E11
Caudebec-en-Caux, *France* 24 C7
Caudete, *Spain* 29 G3
Caudry, *France* 25 B10
Caulnes, *France* 24 D4
Caulónia, *Italy* 35 D9
Caúngula, *Angola* 80 F3
Cauquenes, *Chile* 126 D1
Caura →, *Venezuela* 121 B5
Caurés →, *Brazil* 121 D5
Cauresi →, *Mozam.* 83 F3
Causapscal, *Canada* 99 C6
Caussade, *France* 26 D5
Causse-Méjean, *France* 26 D7
Cauterets, *France* 26 F3
Cautín □, *Chile* 128 A2
Cauvery →, *India* 60 P11
Caux, Pays de, *France* 24 C7
Cava dei Tirreni, *Italy* 35 B7
Cávado →, *Portugal* 30 D2
Cavaillon, *France* 27 E9
Cavalaire-sur-Mer, *France* 27 E10
Cavalcante, *Brazil* 123 D2
Cavalese, *Italy* 33 B8
Cavalier, *U.S.A.* 108 A6
Cavalla = Cavally →, *Africa* 78 E3
Cavallo, I. de, *France* 27 G13
Cavally →, *Africa* 78 E3
Cavan, *Ireland* 15 C4
Cavan □, *Ireland* 15 C4
Cavárzere, *Italy* 33 C9
Cave City, *U.S.A.* 104 G3
Cavenagh Ra., *Australia* 89 E4
Cavendish, *Australia* 91 F3
Caviana, I., *Brazil* 121 C7
Cavite, *Phil.* 55 D4
Cavour, *Italy* 32 D4
Cavtat, *Croatia* 21 N8
Cavuşcu Gölü, *Turkey* 66 D4
Cawndilla L., *Australia* 91 E3
Cawnpore = Kanpur, *India* 63 F9
Caxias, *Brazil* 122 B3
Caxias do Sul, *Brazil* 127 B5
Caxine, C., *Algeria* 75 A4
Caxito, *Angola* 80 F2
Çay, *Turkey* 66 D4
Cay Sal Bank, *Bahamas* 116 B3
Cayambe, *Ecuador* 120 C2
Cayambe, *Ecuador* 120 C2
Çaycuma, *Turkey* 66 C5
Çayeli, *Turkey* 67 C9
Cayenne, *Fr. Guiana* 121 B7
Cayenne □, *Fr. Guiana* 121 C7
Cayeux-sur-Mer, *France* 25 B8
Cayiralan, *Turkey* 66 D6
Caylus, *France* 26 D5
Cayman Brac, *Cayman Is.* 116 C4
Cayman Is., *W. Indies* 116 C3
Cayo Romano, *Cuba* 117 B4
Cayuga, *Canada* 106 D5
Cayuga, *U.S.A.* 107 D8
Cayuga L., *U.S.A.* 107 D8
Cazalla de la Sierra, *Spain* 31 H5
Căzăneşti, *Romania* 38 E10
Cazaux et de Sanguinet, Étang de, *France* 26 D2
Cazères, *France* 26 E5
Cazin, *Bos.-H., Yug.* 33 D12
Čazma, *Croatia* 33 C13
Čazma →, *Croatia* 33 C13
Cazombo, *Angola* 81 G4
Cazorla, *Spain* 29 H1
Cazorla, *Venezuela* 120 B4
Cazorla, Sierra de, *Spain* 29 G2
Cea →, *Spain* 30 C5
Ceanannus Mor, *Ireland* 15 C5
Ceará = Fortaleza, *Brazil* 122 B4
Ceará □, *Brazil* 122 C4
Ceará Mirim, *Brazil* 122 C4
Cebaco, I. de, *Panama* 116 E3
Cebollar, *Argentina* 126 B2
Cebollera, Sierra de, *Spain* 28 D2
Cebreros, *Spain* 30 E6
Cebu, *Phil.* 55 F5
Ceccano, *Italy* 34 A6
Cechi, *Ivory C.* 78 D4
Čechy, *Czech.* 19 F9
Cecil Plains, *Australia* 91 D5
Cécina, *Italy* 32 E7
Cécina →, *Italy* 32 E7
Ceclavin, *Spain* 30 F4
Cedar →, *U.S.A.* 108 E9
Cedar City, *U.S.A.* 111 H7
Cedar Creek Res., *U.S.A.* 109 J6
Cedar Falls, *Iowa, U.S.A.* 108 D8
Cedar Falls, *Wash., U.S.A.* 112 C5
Cedar Key, *U.S.A.* 105 L4
Cedar L., *Canada* 101 C8
Cedar Rapids, *U.S.A.* 108 E9
Cedartown, *U.S.A.* 105 H3
Cedarvale, *Canada* 100 B3

Cedarville

Cedarville, *S. Africa* 85 E4
Cedarville, *U.S.A.* 110 F3
Cedeira, *Spain* 30 B2
Cedral, *Mexico* 114 C4
Cedrino →, *Italy* 34 B2
Cedro, *Brazil* 122 C4
Cedros, I. de, *Mexico* 114 B1
Ceduna, *Australia* 91 E1
Cefalù, *Italy* 35 D7
Cega →, *Spain* 30 D6
Cegléd, *Hungary* 21 H9
Céglie Messápico, *Italy* 35 B10
Cehegín, *Spain* 29 G3
Ceheng, *China* 52 E5
Cehu-Silvaniei, *Romania* 38 B6
Ceira →, *Portugal* 30 E2
Cekhira, *Tunisia* 75 B7
Celano, *Italy* 33 F10
Celanova, *Spain* 30 C3
Celaya, *Mexico* 114 C4
Celbridge, *Ireland* 15 C5
Celebes = Sulawesi □, *Indonesia* 57 E6
Celebes Sea, *Indonesia* 57 D6
Celendín, *Peru* 124 B2
Čelić, *Bos.-H., Yug.* 21 L8
Celica, *Ecuador* 120 D2
Celina, *U.S.A.* 104 E3
Celje, *Slovenia* 33 B12
Celle, *Germany* 18 C6
Celles, *Belgium* 17 G2
Celorico da Beira, *Portugal* 30 E3
Cement, *U.S.A.* 109 H5
Çemişgezek, *Turkey* 67 D8
Cenepa →, *Peru* 120 D2
Cengong, *China* 52 D7
Ceno →, *Italy* 32 D7
Centallo, *Italy* 32 D4
Centenário do Sul, *Brazil* 123 F1
Center, *N. Dak., U.S.A.* 108 B4
Center, *Tex., U.S.A.* 109 K7
Centerfield, *U.S.A.* 111 G8
Centerville, *Calif., U.S.A.* 112 J7
Centerville, *Iowa, U.S.A.* 108 E8
Centerville, *Pa., U.S.A.* 106 F5
Centerville, *S. Dak., U.S.A.* 108 D6
Centerville, *Tenn., U.S.A.* 105 H2
Centerville, *Tex., U.S.A.* 109 K7
Cento, *Italy* 33 D8
Central, *Brazil* 122 D3
Central, *U.S.A.* 111 K9
Central □, *Kenya* 82 C4
Central □, *Malawi* 83 E3
Central □, *U.K.* 14 E4
Central □, *Zambia* 83 E2
Central, Cordillera, *Bolivia* 125 D5
Central, Cordillera, *Colombia* 120 C2
Central, Cordillera, *Costa Rica* 116 D3
Central, Cordillera, *Dom. Rep.* 117 C5
Central, Cordillera, *Peru* 124 B2
Central, Cordillera, *Phil.* 55 C4
Central, Sistema, *Spain* 30 E5
Central African Republic ■, *Africa* 73 G9
Central City, *Ky., U.S.A.* 104 G2
Central City, *Nebr., U.S.A.* 108 E5
Central I., *Kenya* 82 B4
Central Makran Range, *Pakistan* 60 F4
Central Patricia, *Canada* 98 B1
Central Russian Uplands, *Europe* 6 E13
Central Siberian Plateau, *Russia* 46 C14
Centralia, *Ill., U.S.A.* 108 F10
Centralia, *Mo., U.S.A.* 108 F8
Centralia, *Wash., U.S.A.* 112 D4
Centreville, *Ala., U.S.A.* 105 J2
Centreville, *Miss., U.S.A.* 109 K9
Centúripe, *Italy* 35 E7
Cephalonia = Kefallinía, *Greece* 39 L3
Ceprano, *Italy* 34 A6
Cepu, *Indonesia* 57 G14
Ceram = Seram, *Indonesia* 57 E7
Ceram Sea = Seram Sea, *Indonesia* 57 E7
Cerbère, *France* 26 F7
Cerbicales, Is., *France* 27 G13
Cercal, *Portugal* 31 H2
Cercemaggiore, *Italy* 35 A7
Cerdaña, *Spain* 28 C6
Cerdedo, *Spain* 30 C2
Cère →, *France* 26 D5
Cerea, *Italy* 33 C8
Ceres, *Argentina* 126 B3
Ceres, *Brazil* 123 E2
Ceres, *Italy* 32 C4
Ceres, *S. Africa* 84 E2
Ceres, *U.S.A.* 112 H6
Céret, *France* 26 F6
Cereté, *Colombia* 120 B2
Cerfontaine, *Belgium* 17 H4
Cerignola, *Italy* 35 A8
Cerigo = Kíthira, *Greece* 39 N7
Cérilly, *France* 26 B6
Cerisiers, *France* 25 D10
Cerizay, *France* 24 F6
Çerkeş, *Turkey* 66 C5
Çerkezköy, *Turkey* 66 C2
Cerknica, *Slovenia* 33 C11
Çermik, *Turkey* 67 D8
Cerna →, *Romania* 38 E7
Cernavodă, *Romania* 38 E11
Cernay, *France* 25 E14
Cernik, *Croatia* 21 K7
Cerralvo, I., *Mexico* 114 C3
Cerreto Sannita, *Italy* 35 A7
Cerritos, *Mexico* 114 C4
Cerro Sombrero, *Chile* 128 D3
Certaldo, *Italy* 32 E8
Cervaro →, *Italy* 35 A8
Cervera, *Spain* 28 D6
Cervera de Pisuerga, *Spain* 30 C6
Cervera del Río Alhama, *Spain* 28 C3
Cérvia, *Italy* 33 D9
Cervignano del Friuli, *Italy* 33 C10
Cervinara, *Italy* 35 A7
Cervione, *France* 27 F13
Cervo, *Spain* 30 B3
César □, *Colombia* 120 B3
Cesaro, *Italy* 35 E7
Cesena, *Italy* 33 D9
Cesenático, *Italy* 33 D9
Cēsis, *Latvia* 40 C4
Česká Lípa, *Czech.* 20 E4
České Budějovice, *Czech.* 20 G4
Ceskomoravská Vrchovina, *Czech.* 20 F5
Český Brod, *Czech.* 20 E4
Český Krumlov, *Czech.* 20 G4
Český Těšin, *Czech.* 20 F8
Çeşme, *Turkey* 66 D2
Cessnock, *Australia* 91 E5
Cestos →, *Liberia* 78 D3
Cétin Grad, *Croatia* 33 C12
Cetina →, *Croatia* 33 E13
Cetraro, *Italy* 35 C8
Ceuta, *Morocco* 74 A3
Ceva, *Italy* 32 D5
Cévennes, *France* 26 D7
Ceyhan, *Turkey* 66 E6
Ceyhan →, *Turkey* 66 E6
Ceylânpınar, *Turkey* 67 E9
Ceylon = Sri Lanka ■, *Asia* 60 R12
Cèze →, *France* 27 D8
Cha-am, *Thailand* 58 F2
Chaam, *Neths.* 17 E5
Chabeuil, *France* 27 D9
Chablais, *France* 27 B10
Chablis, *France* 25 E10
Chabounia, *Algeria* 75 A5
Chacabuco, *Argentina* 126 C3
Chachapoyas, *Peru* 124 B2
Chachasp, *Peru* 124 D3
Chachoengsao, *Thailand* 58 F3
Chachran, *Pakistan* 60 E7
Chachro, *Pakistan* 62 G4
Chaco □, *Argentina* 126 B3
Chaco □, *Paraguay* 126 B3
Chad ■, *Africa* 73 E8
Chad, L. = Tchad, L., *Chad* 73 F7
Chadan, *Russia* 45 D10
Chadileuvú →, *Argentina* 126 D2
Chadiza, *Zambia* 83 E3
Chadron, *U.S.A.* 108 D3
Chadyr-Lunga, *Moldavia* 42 C3
Chae Hom, *Thailand* 58 C2
Chaem →, *Thailand* 58 C2
Chaeryŏng, *N. Korea* 51 E13
Chagai Hills, *Afghan.* 60 E3
Chagda, *Russia* 45 D14
Chagny, *France* 25 F11
Chagoda, *Russia* 40 B9
Chagos Arch., *Ind. Oc.* 46 K11
Chāh Ākhvor, *Iran* 65 C8
Chāh Bahār, *Iran* 65 E9
Chāh-e-Malek, *Iran* 65 D8
Chāh Kavīr, *Iran* 65 D7
Chahar Burjak, *Afghan.* 60 D3
Chaibasa, *India* 61 H14
Chaillé-les-Marais, *France* 26 B2
Chainat, *Thailand* 58 E3
Chaitén, *Chile* 128 B2
Chaiya, *Thailand* 59 H2
Chaj Doab, *Pakistan* 62 C5
Chajari, *Argentina* 126 C4
Chake Chake, *Tanzania* 82 D4
Chakhānsūr, *Afghan.* 60 D3
Chakonipau, L., *Canada* 99 A6
Chakradharpur, *India* 63 H11
Chakwal, *Pakistan* 62 C5
Chala, *Peru* 124 D3
Chalais, *France* 26 C4
Chalchihuites, *Mexico* 114 C4
Chalcis = Khalkís, *Greece* 39 L6
Chaleur B., *Canada* 99 C6
Chalfant, *U.S.A.* 112 H8
Chalhuanca, *Peru* 124 C3
Chalindrey, *France* 25 E12
Chaling, *China* 53 D9
Chalisgaon, *India* 60 J9
Chalkar, *Kazakhstan* 43 A14
Chalkar, Ozero, *Kazakhstan* 43 A14
Chalky Inlet, *N.Z.* 87 M1
Challans, *France* 24 F5
Challapata, *Bolivia* 124 D4
Challis, *U.S.A.* 110 D6
Chalna, *India* 63 H13
Chalon-sur-Saône, *France* 25 F11
Chalonnes-sur-Loire, *France* 24 E6
Châlons-sur-Marne, *France* 25 D11
Châlus, *France* 26 C4
Chalyaphum, *Thailand* 58 E4
Cham, *Germany* 19 F8
Cham, *Switz.* 23 B6
Cham, Cu Lao, *Vietnam* 58 E7
Chama, *U.S.A.* 111 H10
Chaman, *Pakistan* 60 D5
Chamba, *India* 62 C7
Chamba, *Tanzania* 83 E4
Chambal →, *India* 63 F8
Chamberlain, *U.S.A.* 108 D5
Chamberlain →, *Australia* 88 C4
Chambers, *U.S.A.* 111 J9
Chambersburg, *U.S.A.* 104 F7
Chambéry, *France* 27 C9
Chambly, *Canada* 107 A11
Chambord, *Canada* 99 C5
Chamchamal, *Iraq* 64 C5
Chamela, *Mexico* 114 D3
Chamical, *Argentina* 126 C2
Chamkar Luong, *Cambodia* 59 G4
Chamonix-Mont-Blanc, *France* 27 C10
Champa, *India* 63 H10
Champagne, *Canada* 100 A1
Champagne, *France* 25 D11
Champagne, Plaine de, *France* 25 D11
Champagnole, *France* 25 F12
Champaign, *U.S.A.* 104 E1
Champassak, *Laos* 58 E5
Champaubert, *France* 25 D10
Champdeniers, *France* 26 B3
Champeix, *France* 26 C7
Champlain, *Canada* 104 B9
Champlain, *U.S.A.* 107 B11
Champlain, L., *U.S.A.* 107 B11
Champotón, *Mexico* 115 D6
Chamusca, *Portugal* 31 F2
Chan Chan, *Peru* 124 B2
Chana, *Thailand* 59 J3
Chañaral, *Chile* 126 B1
Chanārān, *Iran* 65 B8
Chanasma, *India* 62 H5
Chancay, *Peru* 124 C2
Chancy, *Switz.* 22 D1
Chandannagar, *India* 63 H13
Chandausi, *India* 63 E8
Chandeleur Is., *U.S.A.* 109 L10
Chandeleur Sd., *U.S.A.* 109 L10
Chandigarh, *India* 62 D7
Chandler, *Australia* 91 D1
Chandler, *Canada* 99 C7
Chandler, *Ariz., U.S.A.* 111 K8
Chandler, *Okla., U.S.A.* 109 H6
Chandless →, *Brazil* 124 B4
Chandmani, *Mongolia* 54 B4
Chandpur, *Bangla.* 61 H17
Chandpur, *India* 62 E8
Chandrapur, *India* 60 K11
Chānf, *Iran* 65 E9
Chang, *Pakistan* 62 F3
Chang, Ko, *Thailand* 59 F4
Chang Jiang →, *China* 53 B13
Changa, *India* 63 C7
Changanacheri, *India* 60 Q10
Changane →, *Mozam.* 85 C5
Changbai, *China* 51 D15
Changbai Shan, *China* 51 C15
Changchiak'ou = Zhangjiakou, *China* 50 D8
Ch'angchou = Changzhou, *China* 53 B12
Changchun, *China* 51 C13
Changchunling, *China* 51 B13
Changde, *China* 53 C8
Changdo-ri, *N. Korea* 51 E14
Changfeng, *China* 53 A11
Changhai = Shanghai, *China* 53 B13
Changhua, *China* 53 B12
Changhŭng, *S. Korea* 51 G14
Changhŭngni, *N. Korea* 51 D15
Changjiang, *China* 54 E5
Changjin, *N. Korea* 51 D14
Changjin-chŏsuji, *N. Korea* 51 D14
Changle, *China* 53 E12
Changli, *China* 51 E10
Changling, *China* 51 B12
Changlun, *Malaysia* 59 J3
Changning, *Hunan, China* 53 D9
Changning, *Yunnan, China* 52 E2
Changping, *China* 50 D9
Changsha, *China* 53 C9
Changshan, *China* 53 C12
Changshou, *China* 52 C6
Changshu, *China* 53 B13
Changshun, *China* 52 D6
Changtai, *China* 53 E11
Changting, *China* 53 E11
Changwu, *China* 50 G4
Changxing, *China* 53 B12
Changyang, *China* 53 B8
Changyi, *China* 51 F10
Changyŏn, *N. Korea* 51 E13
Changyuan, *China* 50 G8
Changzhi, *China* 50 F7
Changzhou, *China* 53 B12
Chanhanga, *Angola* 84 B1
Chanlar, *Azerbaijan* 43 F12
Channapatna, *India* 60 N10
Channel Is., *U.K.* 13 H5
Channel Is., *U.S.A.* 113 M7
Channel-Port aux Basques, *Canada* 99 C8
Channing, *Mich., U.S.A.* 104 B1
Channing, *Tex., U.S.A.* 109 H3
Chantada, *Spain* 30 C3
Chanthaburi, *Thailand* 58 F4
Chantilly, *France* 25 C9
Chantonnay, *France* 24 F5
Chantrey Inlet, *Canada* 96 B10
Chanute, *U.S.A.* 109 G7
Chanza →, *Spain* 31 H3
Chao Hu, *China* 53 B11
Chao Phraya →, *Thailand* 58 F3
Chao Phraya Lowlands, *Thailand* 58 E3
Chao Xian, *China* 53 B11
Chao'an, *China* 53 F11
Chaocheng, *China* 50 F8
Chaoyang, *Guangdong, China* 53 F11
Chaoyang, *Liaoning, China* 51 D11
Chapada dos Guimarães, *Brazil* 125 D6
Chapala, *Mozam.* 83 F4
Chapala, L. de, *Mexico* 114 C4
Chaparé →, *Bolivia* 125 D5
Chaparral, *Colombia* 120 C2
Chapayevo, *Kazakhstan* 43 A14
Chapayevsk, *Russia* 41 E16
Chapecó, *Brazil* 127 B5
Chapel Hill, *U.S.A.* 105 H6
Chapleau, *Canada* 98 C3
Chaplin, *Canada* 101 C7
Chaplino, *Ukraine* 42 B7
Chaplygin, *Russia* 41 E12
Châr, *Mauritania* 74 D2
Chara, *Russia* 45 D12
Charadai, *Argentina* 126 B4
Charagua, *Bolivia* 125 D5
Charalá, *Colombia* 120 B3
Charambirá, Punta, *Colombia* 120 C2
Charaña, *Bolivia* 124 D4
Charapita, *Colombia* 120 D3
Charata, *Argentina* 126 B3
Charcas, *Mexico* 114 C4
Charcoal L., *Canada* 101 B8
Chard, *U.K.* 13 G5
Chardara, *Kazakhstan* 44 E7
Chardon, *U.S.A.* 106 E3
Chardzhou, *Turkmenistan* 44 F7
Charente □, *France* 26 C4
Charente →, *France* 26 C2
Charente-Maritime □, *France* 26 C3
Charentsavan, *Armenia* 43 F11
Chari →, *Chad* 73 F7
Chārīkār, *Afghan.* 60 B6
Chariton →, *U.S.A.* 108 F8
Charity, *Guyana* 121 B6
Charkhari, *India* 63 G8
Charkhi Dadri, *India* 62 E7
Charleroi, *Belgium* 17 H4
Charleroi, *U.S.A.* 106 F5
Charles, C., *U.S.A.* 104 G8
Charles City, *U.S.A.* 108 D8
Charles L., *Canada* 101 B6
Charles Town, *U.S.A.* 104 F7
Charleston, *Ill., U.S.A.* 104 F1
Charleston, *Miss., U.S.A.* 109 H9
Charleston, *Mo., U.S.A.* 109 G10
Charleston, *S.C., U.S.A.* 105 J6
Charleston, *W. Va., U.S.A.* 104 F5
Charleston Pk., *U.S.A.* 113 J11
Charlestown, *S. Africa* 85 D4
Charlestown, *U.S.A.* 104 F3
Charlesville, *Zaïre* 80 F4
Charleville = Rath Luirc, *Ireland* 15 D3
Charleville, *Australia* 91 D4
Charleville-Mézières, *France* 25 C11
Charlevoix, *U.S.A.* 104 C3
Charlieu, *France* 27 B8
Charlotte, *Mich., U.S.A.* 104 D3
Charlotte, *N.C., U.S.A.* 105 H5
Charlotte Amalie, *Virgin Is.* 117 C7
Charlotte Harbor, *U.S.A.* 105 M4
Charlottesville, *U.S.A.* 104 F6
Charlottetown, *Canada* 99 C7
Charlton, *Australia* 91 F3
Charlton, *U.S.A.* 108 E8
Charlton I., *Canada* 98 B4
Charmes, *France* 25 D13
Charny, *Canada* 99 C5
Charolles, *France* 27 B8
Chârost, *France* 25 F9
Charouine, *Algeria* 75 C4
Charre, *Mozam.* 83 F4
Charroux, *France* 26 B4
Charsadda, *Pakistan* 62 B4
Charters Towers, *Australia* 90 C4
Chartres, *France* 24 D8
Chascomús, *Argentina* 126 D4
Chasefu, *Zambia* 83 E3
Chasovnya-Uchurskaya, *Russia* 45 D14
Chasseneuil-sur-Bonnieure, *France* 26 C4
Chāt, *Iran* 65 B7
Chatal Balkan = Udvoy Balkan, *Bulgaria* 38 G9
Château-Arnoux, *France* 27 D10
Château-Chinon, *France* 25 E10
Château d'Oex, *Switz.* 22 D4
Château-du-Loir, *France* 24 E7
Château-Gontier, *France* 24 E6
Château-la-Vallière, *France* 24 E7
Château-Landon, *France* 25 D9
Château-Porcien, *France* 25 C11
Château-Renault, *France* 24 E7
Château-Salins, *France* 25 D13
Château-Thierry, *France* 25 C10
Châteaubourg, *France* 24 D5
Châteaubriant, *France* 24 E5
Châteaudun, *France* 24 D8
Châteaugiron, *France* 24 D5
Châteaulin, *France* 24 D2
Châteaumeillant, *France* 26 B6
Châteauneuf-du-Faou, *France* 24 D3
Châteauneuf-en-Thymerais, *France* 24 D8
Châteauneuf-sur-Charente, *France* 26 C3
Châteauneuf-sur-Cher, *France* 25 F9
Châteauneuf-sur-Loire, *France* 25 E9
Châteaurenard, *Bouches-du-Rhône, France* 27 E8
Châteaurenard, *Loiret, France* 25 E9
Châteauroux, *France* 25 F8
Châtel-St.-Denis, *Switz.* 22 C3
Châtelaillon-Plage, *France* 26 B2
Châtelaudren, *France* 24 D4
Chatelet, *Belgium* 17 H5
Châtelguyon, *France* 26 C7
Châtellerault, *France* 24 F7
Châtelus-Malvaleix, *France* 26 B6
Chatfield, *U.S.A.* 108 D9
Chatham, *N.B., Canada* 99 C6
Chatham, *Ont., Canada* 98 D3
Chatham, *U.K.* 13 F8
Chatham, *La., U.S.A.* 109 J8
Chatham, *N.Y., U.S.A.* 107 D11
Chatham, I., *Chile* 128 D2
Chatham Is., *Pac. Oc.* 92 M10
Chatham Str., *U.S.A.* 100 B2
Chatillon, *Italy* 32 C4
Châtillon-Coligny, *France* 25 E9
Châtillon-en-Bazois, *France* 25 E10
Châtillon-en-Diois, *France* 27 D9
Châtillon-sur-Indre, *France* 24 F8
Châtillon-sur-Loire, *France* 25 E9
Châtillon-sur-Marne, *France* 25 C10
Châtillon-sur-Seine, *France* 25 E11
Chatmohar, *Bangla.* 63 G13
Chatra, *India* 63 G11
Chatrapur, *India* 61 K14
Chats, L. des, *Canada* 107 A8
Chatsworth, *Canada* 106 B4
Chatsworth, *Zimbabwe* 83 F3
Chattahoochee →, *U.S.A.* 105 K3
Chattanooga, *U.S.A.* 105 H3
Chaturat, *Thailand* 58 E3
Chau Doc, *Vietnam* 59 G5
Chaudanne, Barr. de, *France* 27 E10
Chaudes-Aigues, *France* 26 D7
Chauffailles, *France* 27 B8
Chauk, *Burma* 61 J19
Chaukan La, *Burma* 61 F20
Chaulnes, *France* 25 C9
Chaumont, *France* 25 D12
Chaumont, *U.S.A.* 107 B8
Chaumont-en-Vexin, *France* 25 C8
Chaumont-sur-Loire, *France* 24 E8
Chaunay, *France* 26 B4
Chauny, *France* 25 C10
Chausey, Is., *France* 24 D5
Chaussin, *France* 25 F12
Chautauqua L., *U.S.A.* 106 D5
Chauvigny, *France* 24 F7
Chauvin, *Canada* 101 C6
Chavantina, *Brazil* 125 C7
Chaves, *Brazil* 122 B2
Chaves, *Portugal* 30 D3
Chavuma, *Zambia* 81 G4
Chawang, *Thailand* 59 H2
Chazelles-sur-Lyon, *France* 27 C8
Chazuta, *Peru* 124 B2
Chazy, *U.S.A.* 107 B11
Cheb, *Czech.* 20 E2
Cheboksary, *Russia* 41 C15
Cheboygan, *U.S.A.* 104 C3
Chebsara, *Russia* 41 B11
Chech, Erg, *Africa* 74 D4
Chechaouen, *Morocco* 74 A3
Chechen, Os., *Russia* 43 E12
Checheno-Ingush Republic □, *Russia* 43 E11
Chechon, *S. Korea* 51 F15
Chęciny, *Poland* 20 E10
Checleset B., *Canada* 100 C3
Checotah, *U.S.A.* 109 H7
Chedabucto B., *Canada* 99 C7
Cheduba I., *Burma* 61 K18
Cheepie, *Australia* 91 D4
Chef-Boutonne, *France* 26 B3
Chegdomyn, *Russia* 45 D14
Chegga, *Mauritania* 74 C3
Chegutu, *Zimbabwe* 83 F3
Chehalis, *U.S.A.* 112 D4

Cheiron, Mt., *France* 27 E10
Cheju Do, *S. Korea* 51 H14
Chekalin, *Russia* 41 D10
Chekiang = Zhejiang □, *China* 53 C13
Chel = Kuru, Bahr el →, *Sudan* 77 F2
Chela, Sa. da, *Angola* 84 B1
Chelan, *U.S.A.* 110 C4
Chelan, L., *U.S.A.* 110 C3
Cheleken, *Turkmenistan* 44 F6
Chelforó, *Argentina* 128 A3
Chéliff, O. →, *Algeria* 75 A5
Chelkar, *Kazakhstan* 44 E6
Chelkar Tengiz, Solonchak, *Kazakhstan* 44 E7
Chellala Dahrania, *Algeria* 75 B5
Chelles, *France* 25 D9
Chełm, *Poland* 20 D13
Chełmek, *Poland* 20 E9
Chełmno, *Poland* 20 B8
Chelmsford, *U.K.* 13 F8
Chelmsford Dam, *S. Africa* 85 D4
Chelmźa, *Poland* 20 B8
Chelsea, *Okla., U.S.A.* 109 G7
Chelsea, *Vt., U.S.A.* 107 C12
Cheltenham, *U.K.* 13 F5
Chelva, *Spain* 28 F4
Chelyabinsk, *Russia* 44 D7
Chelyuskin, C., *Russia* 46 B14
Chemainus, *Canada* 100 D4
Chembar = Belinskiy, *Russia* 41 E13
Chemillé, *France* 24 E6
Chemnitz, *Germany* 18 E8
Chemult, *U.S.A.* 110 E3
Chen, Gora, *Russia* 45 C15
Chen Xian, *China* 53 E9
Chenab →, *Pakistan* 62 D4
Chenachane, O. →, *Algeria* 74 C4
Chenango Forks, *U.S.A.* 107 D9
Chencha, *Ethiopia* 77 F4
Chenchiang = Zhenjiang, *China* 53 A12
Chênée, *Belgium* 17 G7
Cheney, *U.S.A.* 110 C5
Cheng Xian, *China* 50 H3
Chengbu, *China* 53 D8
Chengcheng, *China* 50 G5
Chengchou = Zhengzhou, *China* 50 G7
Chengde, *China* 51 D9
Chengdong Hu, *China* 53 A11
Chengdu, *China* 52 B5
Chenggong, *China* 52 E4
Chenggu, *China* 50 H4
Chengjiang, *China* 52 E4
Chengkou, *China* 52 B7
Ch'engtu = Chengdu, *China* 52 B5
Chengwu, *China* 50 G8
Chengxi Hu, *China* 53 A11
Chengyang, *China* 51 F11
Chenjiagang, *China* 51 G10
Chenkán, *Mexico* 115 D6
Chenxi, *China* 53 C8
Cheo Reo, *Vietnam* 58 F7
Cheom Ksan, *Cambodia* 58 E5
Chepelare, *Bulgaria* 39 H7
Chepén, *Peru* 124 B2
Chepes, *Argentina* 126 C2
Chepo, *Panama* 116 E4
Cheptsa →, *Russia* 41 B17
Cheptulil, Mt., *Kenya* 82 B4
Chequamegon B., *U.S.A.* 108 B9
Cher □, *France* 25 E9
Cher →, *France* 24 E7
Cherasco, *Italy* 32 D4
Cheratte, *Belgium* 17 G7
Cheraw, *U.S.A.* 105 H6
Cherbourg, *France* 24 C5
Cherchell, *Algeria* 75 A5
Cherdakly, *Russia* 41 D16
Cherdyn, *Russia* 44 C6
Cheremkhovo, *Russia* 45 D11
Cherepanovo, *Russia* 44 D9
Cherepovets, *Russia* 41 B10
Chergui, Chott ech, *Algeria* 75 B5
Cherikov, *Belorussia* 40 E7
Cherkassy, *Ukraine* 42 B5
Cherkessk, *Russia* 43 D10
Cherlak, *Russia* 44 D8
Chernaya Kholunitsa, *Russia* 41 B17
Cherni, *Bulgaria* 38 G6
Chernigov, *Ukraine* 40 F7
Chernobyl, *Ukraine* 40 F7
Chernogorsk, *Russia* 45 D10
Chernomorskoye, *Ukraine* 42 D5
Chernovskoye, *Russia* 41 B15
Chernovtsy, *Ukraine* 42 B1
Chernoye, *Russia* 45 B9
Chernyakhovsk, *Russia* 40 D2
Chernyshkovskiy, *Russia* 43 B10
Chernyshovskiy, *Russia* 45 C12
Cherokee, *Iowa, U.S.A.* 108 D7
Cherokee, *Okla., U.S.A.* 109 G5
Cherokees, L. O'The, *U.S.A.* 109 G7
Cherquenco, *Chile* 128 A2
Cherrapunji, *India* 61 G17
Cherry Creek, *U.S.A.* 110 G6
Cherry Valley, *U.S.A.* 113 M10
Cherryvale, *U.S.A.* 109 G7
Cherskiy, *Russia* 45 C17
Cherskogo Khrebet, *Russia* 45 C15
Chertkovo, *Russia* 43 B9
Cherven, *Belorussia* 40 E6
Cherven-Bryag, *Bulgaria* 38 F7
Chervonograd, *Ukraine* 40 F4
Cherwell →, *U.K.* 13 F6
Chesapeake, *U.S.A.* 104 G7
Chesapeake B., *U.S.A.* 104 F7
Cheshire □, *U.K.* 12 D5
Cheshskaya Guba, *Russia* 44 C5
Cheslatta L., *Canada* 100 C3
Chesley, *Canada* 106 B3
Cheste, *Spain* 29 F4
Chester, *U.K.* 12 D5
Chester, *Calif., U.S.A.* 110 F3
Chester, *Ill., U.S.A.* 109 G10
Chester, *Mont., U.S.A.* 110 B8
Chester, *Pa., U.S.A.* 104 F8
Chester, *S.C., U.S.A.* 105 H5
Chesterfield, *U.K.* 12 D6
Chesterfield, Is., *N. Cal.* 92 J7
Chesterfield Inlet, *Canada* 96 B10
Chesterton Ra., *Australia* 91 D4
Chesterville, *Canada* 107 A9
Chesuncook L., *U.S.A.* 99 C6
Chetaibi, *Algeria* 75 A6
Chéticamp, *Canada* 99 C7
Chetumal, B. de, *Mexico* 115 D7
Chetwynd, *Canada* 100 B4
Chevanceaux, *France* 26 C3
Cheviot, The, *U.K.* 12 B5
Cheviot Hills, *U.K.* 12 B5
Cheviot Ra., *Australia* 90 D3
Chew Bahir, *Ethiopia* 77 G4
Chewelah, *U.S.A.* 110 B5
Cheyenne, *Okla., U.S.A.* 109 H5
Cheyenne, *Wyo., U.S.A.* 108 E2
Cheyenne →, *U.S.A.* 108 C4
Cheyenne Wells, *U.S.A.* 108 F3
Cheyne B., *Australia* 89 F2
Chhabra, *India* 62 G7
Chhapra, *India* 63 G11
Chhata, *India* 62 F7
Chhatarpur, *India* 63 G8
Chhep, *Cambodia* 58 F5
Chhindwara, *India* 63 H8
Chhlong, *Cambodia* 59 F5
Chhuk, *Cambodia* 59 G5
Chi →, *Thailand* 58 E5
Chiamis, *Indonesia* 57 G13
Chiamussu = Jiamusi, *China* 54 B8
Chiang Dao, *Thailand* 58 C2
Chiang Kham, *Thailand* 58 C3
Chiang Khan, *Thailand* 58 D3
Chiang Khong, *Thailand* 58 B3
Chiang Mai, *Thailand* 58 C2
Chiang Saen, *Thailand* 58 B3
Chiange, *Angola* 81 H2
Chiapa →, *Mexico* 115 D6
Chiapa de Corzo, *Mexico* 115 D6
Chiapas □, *Mexico* 115 D6
Chiaramonte Gulfi, *Italy* 35 E7
Chiaravalle, *Italy* 33 E10
Chiaravalle Centrale, *Italy* 35 D9
Chiari, *Italy* 32 C6
Chiasso, *Switz.* 23 E8
Chiatura, *Georgia* 43 E10
Chiautla, *Mexico* 115 D5
Chiávari, *Italy* 32 D6
Chiavenna, *Italy* 32 B6
Chiba, *Japan* 49 G10
Chibabava, *Mozam.* 85 C5
Chibatu, *Indonesia* 57 G12
Chibemba, *Cunene, Angola* 81 H2
Chibemba, *Huila, Angola* 84 B2
Chibia, *Angola* 81 H2
Chibougamau, *Canada* 98 C5
Chibougamau L., *Canada* 98 C5
Chibuk, *Nigeria* 79 C7
Chic-Chocs, Mts., *Canada* 99 C6
Chicacole = Srikakulam, *India* 61 K13
Chicago, *U.S.A.* 104 E2
Chicago Heights, *U.S.A.* 104 E2
Chichagof I., *U.S.A.* 100 B1
Chichaoua, *Morocco* 74 B3
Chicheng, *China* 50 D8
Chichester, *U.K.* 13 G7
Chichibu, *Japan* 49 F9
Ch'ich'ihaerh = Qiqihar, *China* 54 B7
Chickasha, *U.S.A.* 109 H5
Chiclana de la Frontera, *Spain* 31 J4
Chiclayo, *Peru* 124 B2
Chico, *U.S.A.* 112 F5
Chico →, *Chubut, Argentina* 128 B3
Chico →, *Santa Cruz, Argentina* 128 C3
Chicomo, *Mozam.* 85 C5
Chicontepec, *Mexico* 115 C5
Chicopee, *U.S.A.* 107 D12
Chicoutimi, *Canada* 99 C5
Chicualacuala, *Mozam.* 85 C5
Chidambaram, *India* 60 P11
Chidenguele, *Mozam.* 85 C5
Chidley, C., *Canada* 97 B13
Chiede, *Angola* 84 B2
Chiefs Pt., *Canada* 106 B3
Chiem Hoa, *Vietnam* 58 A5
Chiemsee, *Germany* 19 H8
Chiengi, *Zambia* 83 D2
Chiengmai = Chiang Mai, *Thailand* 58 C2
Chienti →, *Italy* 33 E10
Chieri, *Italy* 32 D4
Chiers →, *France* 25 C11
Chiese →, *Italy* 32 C7
Chieti, *Italy* 33 F11
Chièvres, *Belgium* 17 G3
Chifeng, *China* 51 C10
Chigirin, *Ukraine* 42 B5
Chignecto B., *Canada* 99 C7
Chigorodó, *Colombia* 120 B2
Chiguana, *Bolivia* 126 A2
Chiha-ri, *N. Korea* 51 E14
Chihli, G. of = Bo Hai, *China* 51 E10
Chihuahua, *Mexico* 114 B3
Chihuahua □, *Mexico* 114 B3
Chiili, *Kazakhstan* 44 E7
Chik Bollapur, *India* 60 N10
Chikmagalur, *India* 60 N9
Chikwawa, *Malawi* 83 F3
Chilac, *Mexico* 115 D5
Chilako →, *Canada* 100 C4
Chilam Chavki, *Pakistan* 63 B6
Chilanga, *Zambia* 83 F2
Chilapa, *Mexico* 115 D5
Chilas, *Pakistan* 63 B6
Chilaw, *Sri Lanka* 60 R11
Chilcotin →, *Canada* 100 C4
Childers, *Australia* 91 D5
Childress, *U.S.A.* 109 H4
Chile ■, *S. Amer.* 128 B2
Chile Chico, *Chile* 128 C2
Chile Rise, *Pac. Oc.* 93 L18
Chilecito, *Argentina* 126 B2
Chilete, *Peru* 124 B2
Chilia, Braţul →, *Romania* 38 D12
Chililabombwe, *Zambia* 83 E2
Chilin = Jilin, *China* 51 C14
Chilka L., *India* 61 K14
Chilko →, *Canada* 100 C4
Chilko, L., *Canada* 100 C4
Chillagoe, *Australia* 90 B3
Chillán, *Chile* 126 D1
Chillicothe, *Ill., U.S.A.* 108 E10
Chillicothe, *Mo., U.S.A.* 108 F8
Chillicothe, *Ohio, U.S.A.* 104 F4
Chilliwack, *Canada* 100 D4
Chilo, *India* 62 F5
Chiloane, I., *Mozam.* 85 C5
Chiloé □, *Chile* 128 B2
Chiloé, I. de, *Chile* 128 B2
Chilpancingo, *Mexico* 115 D5
Chiltern Hills, *U.K.* 13 F7
Chilton, *U.S.A.* 104 C1
Chiluage, *Angola* 80 F4
Chilubi, *Zambia* 83 E2
Chilubula, *Zambia* 83 E3
Chilumba, *Malawi* 83 E3
Chilwa, L., *Malawi* 83 F4
Chimaltitán, *Mexico* 114 C4
Chimán, *Panama* 116 E4
Chimay, *Belgium* 17 H4
Chimbay, *Uzbekistan* 44 E6
Chimborazo, *Ecuador* 120 D2
Chimborazo □, *Ecuador* 120 D2
Chimbote, *Peru* 124 B2
Chimkent, *Kazakhstan* 44 E7
Chimoio, *Mozam.* 83 F3
Chimpembe, *Zambia* 83 D2
Chin □, *Burma* 61 J18
Chin Ling Shan = Qinling Shandi, *China* 50 H5
China, *Mexico* 115 B5
China ■, *Asia* 54 D6
China Lake, *U.S.A.* 113 K9
Chinacota, *Colombia* 120 B3
Chinan = Jinan, *China* 50 F9
Chinandega, *Nic.* 116 D2
Chinati Pk., *U.S.A.* 109 K2
Chincha Alta, *Peru* 124 C2
Chinchilla, *Australia* 91 D5
Chinchilla de Monte Aragón, *Spain* 29 G3
Chinchón, *Spain* 28 E1
Chinchorro, Banco, *Mexico* 115 D7
Chinchou = Jinzhou, *China* 51 D11
Chincoteague, *U.S.A.* 104 G8
Chinde, *Mozam.* 83 F4
Chindo, *S. Korea* 51 G14
Chindwin →, *Burma* 61 J19
Chineni, *India* 63 C6
Chinga, *Mozam.* 83 F4
Chingola, *Zambia* 83 E2
Chingole, *Malawi* 83 E3
Ch'ingtao = Qingdao, *China* 51 F11
Chinguetti, *Mauritania* 74 D2
Chingune, *Mozam.* 85 C5
Chinhae, *S. Korea* 51 G15
Chinhanguanine, *Mozam.* 85 D5
Chinhoyi, *Zimbabwe* 83 F3
Chiniot, *Pakistan* 62 D5
Chínipas, *Mexico* 114 B3
Chinju, *S. Korea* 51 G15
Chinle, *U.S.A.* 111 H9
Chinnampo, *N. Korea* 51 E13
Chino, *Japan* 49 G9
Chino, *U.S.A.* 113 L9
Chino Valley, *U.S.A.* 111 J7
Chinon, *France* 24 E7
Chinook, *Canada* 101 C6
Chinook, *U.S.A.* 110 B9
Chinsali, *Zambia* 83 E3
Chióggia, *Italy* 33 C9
Chíos = Khíos, *Greece* 39 L9
Chipata, *Zambia* 83 E3
Chipewyan L., *Canada* 101 B9
Chipinge, *Zimbabwe* 83 G3
Chipiona, *Spain* 31 J4
Chipley, *U.S.A.* 105 K3
Chipman, *Canada* 99 C6
Chipoka, *Malawi* 83 E3
Chippenham, *U.K.* 13 F5
Chippewa →, *U.S.A.* 108 C8
Chippewa Falls, *U.S.A.* 108 C9
Chiquián, *Peru* 124 C2
Chiquimula, *Guatemala* 116 D2
Chiquinquira, *Colombia* 120 B3
Chiquitos, Llanos de, *Bolivia* 125 D5
Chir →, *Russia* 43 B10
Chirala, *India* 60 M12
Chiramba, *Mozam.* 83 F3
Chirawa, *India* 62 E6
Chirchik, *Uzbekistan* 44 E7
Chirgua →, *Venezuela* 120 B4
Chiricahua Pk., *U.S.A.* 111 L9
Chiriquí, G. de, *Panama* 116 E3
Chiriquí, L. de, *Panama* 116 E3
Chirivira Falls, *Zimbabwe* 83 G3
Chirmiri, *India* 61 H13
Chiromo, *Malawi* 81 H7
Chirpan, *Bulgaria* 38 G8
Chirripó Grande, Cerro, *Costa Rica* 116 E3
Chisamba, *Zambia* 83 E2
Chisapani Garhi, *Nepal* 61 F14
Chisholm, *Canada* 100 C6
Chishtian Mandi, *Pakistan* 62 E5
Chishui, *China* 52 C5
Chishui He →, *China* 52 C5
Chisimba Falls, *Zambia* 83 E3
Chisone →, *Italy* 32 D4
Chisos Mts., *U.S.A.* 109 L3
Chistopol, *Russia* 41 D17
Chita, *Colombia* 120 B3
Chita, *Russia* 45 D12
Chitado, *Angola* 81 H2
Chitembo, *Angola* 81 G3
Chitipa, *Malawi* 83 D3
Chitose, *Japan* 48 C10
Chitral, *Pakistan* 60 B7
Chitré, *Panama* 116 E3
Chittagong, *Bangla.* 61 H17
Chittagong □, *Bangla.* 61 G17
Chittaurgarh, *India* 62 G6
Chittoor, *India* 60 N11
Chitungwiza, *Zimbabwe* 83 F3
Chiusa, *Italy* 33 B8
Chiusi, *Italy* 33 E8
Chiva, *Spain* 29 F4
Chivacoa, *Venezuela* 120 A4
Chivasso, *Italy* 32 C4
Chivay, *Peru* 124 D3
Chivhu, *Zimbabwe* 83 F3
Chivilcoy, *Argentina* 126 C4
Chiwanda, *Tanzania* 83 E3
Chixi, *China* 53 G9
Chizera, *Zambia* 83 E1
Chkalov = Orenburg, *Russia* 44 D6
Chkolovsk, *Russia* 41 C13
Chloride, *U.S.A.* 113 K12
Cho Bo, *Vietnam* 58 B5
Cho-do, *N. Korea* 51 E13
Cho Phuoc Hai, *Vietnam* 59 G6
Choba, *Kenya* 82 B4
Chobe National Park, *Botswana* 84 B3
Chochiwŏn, *S. Korea* 51 F14
Chociwel, *Poland* 20 B5
Chocó □, *Colombia* 120 B2
Choconta, *Colombia* 120 B3
Choctawhatchee B., *U.S.A.* 103 D9
Chodecz, *Poland* 20 C9
Chodziez, *Poland* 20 C6
Choele Choel, *Argentina* 128 A3
Choisy-le-Roi, *France* 25 D9
Choix, *Mexico* 114 B3
Chojnice, *Poland* 20 B7
Chojnów, *Poland* 20 D5
Chōkai-San, *Japan* 48 E10
Choke, *Ethiopia* 77 E4
Chokurdakh, *Russia* 45 B15
Cholame, *U.S.A.* 112 K6
Cholet, *France* 24 E6
Choluteca, *Honduras* 116 D2
Choluteca →, *Honduras* 116 D2
Chom Bung, *Thailand* 58 F2
Chom Thong, *Thailand* 58 C2
Choma, *Zambia* 83 F2
Chomen Swamp, *Ethiopia* 77 F4
Chomun, *India* 62 F6
Chomutov, *Czech.* 20 E3
Chon Buri, *Thailand* 58 F3
Chon Thanh, *Vietnam* 59 G6
Chonan, *S. Korea* 51 F14
Chone, *Ecuador* 120 D2
Chong Kai, *Cambodia* 58 F4
Chong Mek, *Thailand* 58 E5
Chong'an, *China* 53 D12
Chongde, *China* 53 B13
Chŏngdo, *S. Korea* 51 G15
Chŏngha, *S. Korea* 51 F15
Chŏngjin, *N. Korea* 51 D15
Chŏngju, *N. Korea* 51 E13
Chŏngju, *S. Korea* 51 F14
Chongli, *China* 50 D8
Chongming, *China* 53 B13
Chongming Dao, *China* 53 B13
Chongoyape, *Peru* 124 B2
Chongqing, *Sichuan, China* 52 C6
Chongqing, *Sichuan, China* 52 B4
Chongren, *China* 53 D11
Chŏngŭp, *S. Korea* 51 G14
Chongzuo, *China* 52 F6
Chŏnju, *S. Korea* 51 G14
Chonos, Arch. de los, *Chile* 128 C2
Chopim →, *Brazil* 127 B5
Chorbat La, *India* 63 B7
Chorley, *U.K.* 12 D5
Chorolque, Cerro, *Bolivia* 126 A2
Chorregon, *Australia* 90 C3
Chortkov, *Ukraine* 40 G4
Chŏrwŏn, *S. Korea* 51 E14
Chorzów, *Poland* 20 E8
Chos-Malal, *Argentina* 126 D1
Chosan, *N. Korea* 51 D13
Choszczno, *Poland* 20 B5
Chota, *Peru* 124 B2
Choteau, *U.S.A.* 110 C7
Chotila, *India* 62 H4
Chowchilla, *U.S.A.* 111 H3
Choybalsan, *Mongolia* 54 B6
Christchurch, *N.Z.* 87 K4
Christchurch, *U.K.* 13 G6
Christian I., *Canada* 106 B4
Christiana, *S. Africa* 84 D4
Christiansfeld, *Denmark* 11 J3
Christiansted, *Virgin Is.* 117 C7
Christie B., *Canada* 101 A6
Christina →, *Canada* 101 B6
Christmas Cr. →, *Australia* 88 C4
Christmas Creek, *Australia* 88 C4
Christmas I. = Kiritimati, *Kiribati* 93 G12
Christmas I., *Ind. Oc.* 92 J2
Christopher L., *Australia* 89 D4
Chrudim, *Czech.* 20 F5
Chrzanów, *Poland* 20 E9
Chtimba, *Malawi* 83 E3
Chu, *Kazakhstan* 44 E8
Chu →, *Vietnam* 58 C5
Chu Chua, *Canada* 100 C4
Chu Lai, *Vietnam* 58 E7
Chu Xian, *China* 53 A12
Ch'uanchou = Quanzhou, *China* 53 E12
Chuankou, *China* 50 G6
Chūbu □, *Japan* 49 F8
Chubut □, *Argentina* 128 B3
Chubut →, *Argentina* 128 B3
Chuchi L., *Canada* 100 B4
Chudovo, *Russia* 40 B7
Chudskoye, Oz., *Estonia* 40 B5
Chūgoku □, *Japan* 49 G6
Chūgoku-Sanchi, *Japan* 49 G6
Chuguyev, *Ukraine* 42 B7
Chugwater, *U.S.A.* 108 E2
Chukhloma, *Russia* 41 B13
Chukotskiy Khrebet, *Russia* 45 C18
Chukotskoye More, *Russia* 45 C19
Chula Vista, *U.S.A.* 113 N9
Chulman, *Russia* 45 D13
Chulucanas, *Peru* 124 B1
Chulumani, *Bolivia* 124 D4
Chulym →, *Russia* 44 D9
Chum Phae, *Thailand* 58 D4
Chum Saeng, *Thailand* 58 E3
Chuma, *Bolivia* 124 D4
Chumar, *India* 63 C8
Chumbicha, *Argentina* 126 B2
Chumerna, *Bulgaria* 38 G8
Chumikan, *Russia* 45 D14
Chumphon, *Thailand* 59 G2
Chumpi, *Peru* 124 D3
Chumuare, *Mozam.* 83 E3
Chumunjin, *S. Korea* 51 F15
Chuna →, *Russia* 45 D10
Chun'an, *China* 53 C12
Chunchŏn, *S. Korea* 51 F14
Chunchura, *India* 63 H13
Chunga, *Zambia* 83 F2
Chunggang-ŭp, *N. Korea* 51 D14
Chunghwa, *N. Korea* 51 E13
Chungju, *S. Korea* 51 F14
Chungking = Chongqing, *China* 52 C6
Chungmu, *S. Korea* 51 G15
Chungt'iaoshan = Zhongtiao Shan, *China* 50 G6
Chunian, *Pakistan* 62 D6
Chunya, *Tanzania* 83 D3
Chunya □, *Tanzania* 82 D3
Chunyang, *China* 51 C15
Chuquibamba, *Peru* 124 D3
Chuquibambilla, *Peru* 124 C3
Chuquicamata, *Chile* 126 A2
Chuquisaca □, *Bolivia* 125 E5
Chur, *Switz.* 23 C9
Churachandpur, *India* 61 G18
Churchill, *Canada* 101 B10
Churchill →, *Man., Canada* 101 B10
Churchill →, *Nfld., Canada* 99 B7
Churchill, C., *Canada* 101 B10
Churchill Falls, *Canada* 99 B7
Churchill L., *Canada* 101 B7
Churchill Pk., *Canada* 100 B3
Churfisten, *Switz.* 23 B8
Churu, *India* 62 E6
Churwalden, *Switz.* 23 C9

Chushal

Chushal, *India* 63 C8
Chusovoy, *Russia* 44 D6
Chuuronjang, *N. Korea* 51 D15
Chuvash Republic □, *Russia* 41 D15
Chuwārtah, *Iraq* 64 C5
Chuxiong, *China* 52 E3
Ci Xian, *China* 50 F8
Ciacova, *Romania* 38 D4
Cianjur, *Indonesia* 57 G12
Cibadok, *Indonesia* 57 G12
Cibatu, *Indonesia* 57 G12
Cibola, *U.S.A.* 113 M12
Cicero, *U.S.A.* 104 E2
Cícero Dantas, *Brazil* 122 D4
Cidacos →, *Spain* 28 C3
Cide, *Turkey* 42 F5
Ciechanów, *Poland* 20 C10
Ciego de Avila, *Cuba* 116 B4
Ciénaga, *Colombia* 120 A3
Ciénaga de Oro, *Colombia* 120 B2
Cienfuegos, *Cuba* 116 B3
Cieplice Słąskie Zdrój, *Poland* 20 E5
Cierp, *France* 26 F4
Cíes, Is., *Spain* 30 C2
Cieszyn, *Poland* 20 F8
Cieza, *Spain* 29 G3
Çifteler, *Turkey* 66 D4
Cifuentes, *Spain* 28 E2
Cihanbeyli, *Turkey* 66 D5
Cihuatlán, *Mexico* 114 D4
Cijara, Pantano de, *Spain* 31 F6
Cijulang, *Indonesia* 57 G13
Cikajang, *Indonesia* 57 G12
Cikampek, *Indonesia* 57 G12
Cilacap, *Indonesia* 57 G13
Çıldır, *Turkey* 43 F10
Çıldır Gölü, *Turkey* 67 C10
Cili, *China* 53 C8
Cilicia, *Turkey* 66 E5
Cilo Dağı, *Turkey* 67 E10
Cima, *U.S.A.* 113 K11
Cimahi, *Indonesia* 57 G12
Cimarron, *Kans., U.S.A.* 109 G4
Cimarron, *N. Mex., U.S.A.* 109 G2
Cimarron →, *U.S.A.* 109 G6
Cimone, Mte., *Italy* 32 D7
Cîmpina, *Romania* 38 D8
Cîmpulung, *Argeş, Romania* 38 D8
Cîmpulung, *Suceava, Romania* 38 B8
Çinar, *Turkey* 67 E9
Cinca →, *Spain* 28 D5
Cincinnati, *U.S.A.* 104 F3
Cîndeşti, *Romania* 38 D9
Çine, *Turkey* 66 E3
Ciney, *Belgium* 17 H6
Cíngoli, *Italy* 33 E10
Cinigiano, *Italy* 33 F8
Cinto, Mte., *France* 27 F12
Ciorani, *Romania* 38 E9
Čiovo, *Croatia* 33 E13
Cipó, *Brazil* 122 D4
Circeo, Monte, *Italy* 34 A6
Çirçir, *Turkey* 66 C7
Circle, *Alaska, U.S.A.* 96 B5
Circle, *Mont., U.S.A.* 108 B2
Circleville, *Ohio, U.S.A.* 104 F4
Circleville, *Utah, U.S.A.* 111 G7
Cirebon, *Indonesia* 57 G13
Cirencester, *U.K.* 13 F6
Cirey-sur-Vezouze, *France* 25 D13
Ciriè, *Italy* 32 C4
Cirium, *Cyprus* 37 E11
Cirò, *Italy* 35 C10
Ciron →, *France* 26 D3
Cisco, *U.S.A.* 109 J5
Ciskei □, *S. Africa* 85 E4
Cislău, *Romania* 38 D9
Cisneros, *Colombia* 120 B2
Cisterna di Latina, *Italy* 34 A5
Cisternino, *Italy* 35 B10
Citaré →, *Brazil* 121 C7
Citeli-Ckaro, *Georgia* 43 F12
Citlaltépetl, *Mexico* 115 D5
Citrus Heights, *U.S.A.* 112 G5
Citrusdal, *S. Africa* 84 E2
Città della Pieve, *Italy* 33 F9
Città di Castello, *Italy* 33 E9
Città Sant' Angelo, *Italy* 33 F11
Cittadella, *Italy* 33 C8
Cittaducale, *Italy* 33 F9
Cittanova, *Italy* 35 D9
Ciucaş, *Romania* 38 D8
Ciudad Altamirano, *Mexico* 114 D4
Ciudad Bolívar, *Venezuela* 121 B5
Ciudad Camargo, *Mexico* 114 B3
Ciudad Chetumal, *Mexico* 115 D7
Ciudad de Valles, *Mexico* 115 C5
Ciudad del Carmen, *Mexico* 115 D6
Ciudad Delicias = Delicias, *Mexico* 114 B3
Ciudad Guayana, *Venezuela* 121 B5
Ciudad Guerrero, *Mexico* 114 B3
Ciudad Guzmán, *Mexico* 114 D4
Ciudad Juárez, *Mexico* 114 A3
Ciudad Madero, *Mexico* 115 C5
Ciudad Mante, *Mexico* 115 C5
Ciudad Obregón, *Mexico* 114 B3
Ciudad Ojeda, *Venezuela* 120 A3
Ciudad Real, *Spain* 31 G7
Ciudad Real □, *Spain* 31 G7
Ciudad Rodrigo, *Spain* 30 E4
Ciudad Trujillo = Santo Domingo, *Dom. Rep.* 117 C6
Ciudad Victoria, *Mexico* 115 C5
Ciudadela, *Spain* 36 B10
Ciulniţa, *Romania* 38 E10
Civa Burnu, *Turkey* 66 C7
Cividale del Friuli, *Italy* 33 B10
Cívita Castellana, *Italy* 33 F9
Civitanova Marche, *Italy* 33 E10
Civitavécchia, *Italy* 33 F8
Civitella del Tronto, *Italy* 33 F10
Civray, *France* 26 B4
Çivril, *Turkey* 66 D3
Cixerri →, *Italy* 34 C1
Cizre, *Turkey* 67 E10
Clacton-on-Sea, *U.K.* 13 F9
Clain →, *France* 24 F7
Claire, L., *Canada* 100 B6
Clairemont, *U.S.A.* 109 J4
Clairton, *U.S.A.* 106 F5
Clairvaux-les-Lacs, *France* 27 B9
Clallam Bay, *U.S.A.* 112 B2
Clamecy, *France* 25 E10
Clanton, *U.S.A.* 105 J2
Clanwilliam, *S. Africa* 84 E2
Clara, *Ireland* 15 C4
Clara →, *Australia* 90 B3
Claraville, *U.S.A.* 113 K8
Clare, *Australia* 91 E2
Clare, *U.S.A.* 104 D3
Clare □, *Ireland* 15 D3
Clare →, *Ireland* 15 C2
Clare I., *Ireland* 15 C2
Claremont, *Calif., U.S.A.* 113 L9
Claremont, *N.H., U.S.A.* 107 C12
Claremont Pt., *Australia* 90 A3
Claremore, *U.S.A.* 109 G7
Claremorris, *Ireland* 15 C3
Clarence →, *Australia* 91 D5
Clarence →, *N.Z.* 87 K4
Clarence, I., *Chile* 128 D2
Clarence I., *Antarctica* 5 C18
Clarence Str., *Australia* 88 B5
Clarence Str., *U.S.A.* 100 B2
Clarence Town, *Bahamas* 117 B5
Clarendon, *Ark., U.S.A.* 109 H9
Clarendon, *Tex., U.S.A.* 109 H4
Clarenville, *Canada* 99 C9
Claresholm, *Canada* 100 C6
Clarie Coast, *Antarctica* 5 C9
Clarinda, *U.S.A.* 108 E7
Clarion, *Iowa, U.S.A.* 108 D8
Clarion, *Pa., U.S.A.* 106 E5
Clarion →, *U.S.A.* 106 E5
Clark, *U.S.A.* 108 C6
Clark, Pt., *Canada* 106 B3
Clark Fork, *U.S.A.* 110 B5
Clark Fork →, *U.S.A.* 110 B5
Clark Hill Res., *U.S.A.* 105 J4
Clarkdale, *U.S.A.* 111 J7
Clarke City, *Canada* 99 B6
Clarke I., *Australia* 90 G4
Clarke L., *Canada* 101 C7
Clarke Ra., *Australia* 90 C4
Clark's Fork →, *U.S.A.* 110 D9
Clark's Harbour, *Canada* 99 D6
Clarks Summit, *U.S.A.* 107 E9
Clarksburg, *U.S.A.* 104 F5
Clarksdale, *U.S.A.* 109 H9
Clarkston, *U.S.A.* 110 C5
Clarksville, *Ark., U.S.A.* 109 H8
Clarksville, *Tenn., U.S.A.* 105 G2
Clarksville, *Tex., U.S.A.* 109 J7
Claro →, *Brazil* 123 E1
Clatskanie, *U.S.A.* 112 D3
Claude, *U.S.A.* 109 H4
Claveria, *Phil.* 55 B4
Clay, *U.S.A.* 112 G5
Clay Center, *U.S.A.* 108 F6
Claypool, *U.S.A.* 111 K8
Claysville, *U.S.A.* 106 F4
Clayton, *Idaho, U.S.A.* 110 D6
Clayton, *N. Mex., U.S.A.* 109 G3
Cle Elum, *U.S.A.* 110 C3
Clear, C., *Ireland* 15 E2
Clear I., *Ireland* 15 E2
Clear L., *U.S.A.* 112 F4
Clear Lake, *S. Dak., U.S.A.* 108 C6
Clear Lake, *Wash., U.S.A.* 110 B2
Clear Lake Res., *U.S.A.* 110 F3
Clearfield, *Pa., U.S.A.* 104 E6
Clearfield, *Utah, U.S.A.* 110 F7
Clearlake Highlands, *U.S.A.* 112 G4
Clearmont, *U.S.A.* 110 D10
Clearwater, *Canada* 100 C4
Clearwater, *U.S.A.* 105 M4
Clearwater →, *Alta., Canada* 100 C6
Clearwater →, *Alta., Canada* 101 B6
Clearwater Cr. →, *Canada* 100 A3
Clearwater Mts., *U.S.A.* 110 C6
Clearwater Prov. Park, *Canada* 101 C8
Cleburne, *U.S.A.* 109 J6
Cleethorpes, *U.K.* 12 D7
Cleeve Hill, *U.K.* 13 F6
Clelles, *France* 27 D9
Clemency, *Lux.* 17 J7
Clerke Reef, *Australia* 88 C2
Clermont, *Australia* 90 C4
Clermont, *France* 25 C9
Clermont-en-Argonne, *France* 25 C12
Clermont-Ferrand, *France* 26 C7
Clermont-l'Hérault, *France* 26 E7
Clerval, *France* 25 E13
Clervaux, *Lux.* 17 H8
Cléry-St.-André, *France* 25 E8
Cles, *Italy* 32 B8
Cleveland, *Australia* 91 D5
Cleveland, *Miss., U.S.A.* 109 J9
Cleveland, *Ohio, U.S.A.* 106 E3
Cleveland, *Okla., U.S.A.* 109 G6
Cleveland, *Tenn., U.S.A.* 105 H3
Cleveland, *Tex., U.S.A.* 109 K7
Cleveland □, *U.K.* 12 C9
Cleveland, C., *Australia* 90 B4
Cleveland Heights, *U.S.A.* 106 E3
Clevelândia, *Brazil* 127 B5
Clevelândia do Norte, *Brazil* 121 C7
Clew B., *Ireland* 15 C2
Clewiston, *U.S.A.* 105 M5
Clifden, *Ireland* 15 C1
Clifden, *N.Z.* 87 M1
Cliffdell, *U.S.A.* 112 D5
Clifton, *Australia* 91 D5
Clifton, *Ariz., U.S.A.* 111 K9
Clifton, *Tex., U.S.A.* 109 K6
Clifton Beach, *Australia* 90 B4
Clifton Forge, *U.S.A.* 104 G6
Clifton Hills, *Australia* 91 D2
Climax, *Canada* 101 D7
Clinch →, *U.S.A.* 105 H3
Clingmans Dome, *U.S.A.* 105 H4
Clint, *U.S.A.* 111 L10
Clinton, *B.C., Canada* 100 C4
Clinton, *Ont., Canada* 98 D3
Clinton, *N.Z.* 87 M2
Clinton, *Ark., U.S.A.* 109 H8
Clinton, *Ill., U.S.A.* 108 E10
Clinton, *Ind., U.S.A.* 104 F2
Clinton, *Iowa, U.S.A.* 108 E9
Clinton, *Mass., U.S.A.* 107 D13
Clinton, *Mo., U.S.A.* 108 F8
Clinton, *N.C., U.S.A.* 105 H6
Clinton, *Okla., U.S.A.* 109 H5
Clinton, *S.C., U.S.A.* 105 H5
Clinton, *Tenn., U.S.A.* 105 G3
Clinton, *Wash., U.S.A.* 112 C4
Clinton C., *Australia* 90 C5
Clinton Colden L., *Canada* 96 B9
Clintonville, *U.S.A.* 108 C10
Clipperton, I., *Pac. Oc.* 93 F17
Clisson, *France* 24 E5
Clive L., *Canada* 100 A5
Cliza, *Bolivia* 125 D4
Cloates, Pt., *Australia* 88 D1
Clocolan, *S. Africa* 85 D4
Clodomira, *Argentina* 126 B3
Clonakilty, *Ireland* 15 E3
Clonakilty B., *Ireland* 15 E3
Cloncurry, *Australia* 90 C3
Cloncurry →, *Australia* 90 B3
Clones, *Ireland* 15 B4
Clonmel, *Ireland* 15 D4
Cloppenburg, *Germany* 18 C4
Cloquet, *U.S.A.* 108 B8
Clorinda, *Argentina* 126 B4
Cloud Peak, *U.S.A.* 110 D10
Cloudcroft, *U.S.A.* 111 K11
Cloverdale, *U.S.A.* 112 G4
Clovis, *Calif., U.S.A.* 111 H4
Clovis, *N. Mex., U.S.A.* 109 H3
Cloyes-sur-le-Loir, *France* 24 E8
Cluj-Napoca, *Romania* 38 C6
Clunes, *Australia* 91 F3
Cluny, *France* 27 B8
Cluses, *France* 27 B10
Clusone, *Italy* 32 C6
Clutha →, *N.Z.* 87 M2
Clwyd □, *U.K.* 12 D4
Clwyd →, *U.K.* 12 D4
Clyde, *N.Z.* 87 L2
Clyde, *U.S.A.* 106 C8
Clyde →, *U.K.* 14 F4
Clyde, Firth of, *U.K.* 14 F4
Clyde River, *Canada* 97 A13
Clydebank, *U.K.* 14 F4
Clymer, *U.S.A.* 106 D5
Cõa →, *Portugal* 30 D3
Coachella, *U.S.A.* 113 M10
Coachella Canal, *U.S.A.* 113 N12
Coahoma, *U.S.A.* 109 J4
Coahuayana →, *Mexico* 114 D4
Coahuayutla, *Mexico* 114 D4
Coahuila □, *Mexico* 114 B4
Coal →, *Canada* 100 B3
Coalane, *Mozam.* 83 F4
Coalcomán, *Mexico* 114 D4
Coaldale, *Canada* 100 D6
Coalgate, *U.S.A.* 109 H6
Coalinga, *U.S.A.* 111 H3
Coalville, *U.K.* 12 E6
Coalville, *U.S.A.* 110 F8
Coaraci, *Brazil* 123 D4
Coari, *Brazil* 121 D5
Coari →, *Brazil* 121 D5
Coari, L. de, *Brazil* 121 D5
Coast □, *Kenya* 82 C4
Coast Mts., *Canada* 100 C3
Coast Ranges, *U.S.A.* 112 E4
Coatbridge, *U.K.* 14 F4
Coatepec, *Mexico* 115 D5
Coatepeque, *Guatemala* 116 D1
Coatesville, *U.S.A.* 104 F8
Coaticook, *Canada* 99 C5
Coats I., *Canada* 97 B11
Coats Land, *Antarctica* 5 D1
Coatzacoalcos, *Mexico* 115 D6
Cobalt, *Canada* 98 C4
Cobán, *Guatemala* 116 C1
Cobar, *Australia* 91 E4
Cóbh, *Ireland* 15 E3
Cobham, *Australia* 91 E3
Cobija, *Bolivia* 124 C4
Cobleskill, *U.S.A.* 107 D10
Coboconk, *Canada* 106 B6
Cobourg, *Canada* 98 D4
Cobourg Pen., *Australia* 88 B5
Cobram, *Australia* 91 F4
Cobre, *U.S.A.* 110 F6
Cóbué, *Mozam.* 83 E3
Coburg, *Germany* 19 E6
Coca, *Spain* 30 D6
Coca →, *Ecuador* 120 D2
Cocachacra, *Peru* 124 D3
Cocal, *Brazil* 122 B3
Cocanada = Kakinada, *India* 61 L13
Cocentaina, *Spain* 29 G4
Cochabamba, *Bolivia* 125 D4
Coche, I., *Venezuela* 121 A5
Cochem, *Germany* 19 E3
Cochemane, *Mozam.* 83 F3
Cochin, *India* 60 Q10
Cochin China = Nam-Phan, *Vietnam* 59 G6
Cochise, *U.S.A.* 111 K9
Cochran, *U.S.A.* 105 J4
Cochrane, *Alta., Canada* 100 C6
Cochrane, *Ont., Canada* 98 C3
Cochrane →, *Canada* 101 B8
Cochrane, L., *Chile* 128 C2
Cockburn, *Australia* 91 E3
Cockburn, Canal, *Chile* 128 D2
Cockburn I., *Canada* 98 C3
Cockburn Ra., *Australia* 88 C4
Cocklebiddy Motel, *Australia* 89 F4
Coco →, *Cent. Amer.* 116 D3
Coco, Pta., *Colombia* 120 C2
Cocoa, *U.S.A.* 105 L5
Cocobeach, *Gabon* 80 D1
Côcos, *Brazil* 123 D3
Côcos →, *Brazil* 123 D3
Cocos, I. del, *Pac. Oc.* 93 G19
Cocos Is., *Ind. Oc.* 92 J1
Cod, C., *U.S.A.* 103 B13
Codajás, *Brazil* 121 D5
Codera, C., *Venezuela* 120 A4
Coderre, *Canada* 101 C7
Codigoro, *Italy* 33 D9
Codó, *Brazil* 122 B3
Codogno, *Italy* 32 C6
Codpa, *Chile* 124 D4
Codróipo, *Italy* 33 C10
Cody, *U.S.A.* 110 D9
Coe Hill, *Canada* 98 D4
Coelemu, *Chile* 126 D1
Coelho Neto, *Brazil* 122 B3
Coen, *Australia* 90 A3
Coeroeni →, *Surinam* 121 C6
Coesfeld, *Germany* 18 D3
Cœur d'Alene, *U.S.A.* 110 C5
Cœur d'Alene L., *U.S.A.* 110 C5
Coevorden, *Neths.* 16 C9
Cofete, *Canary Is.* 36 F5
Coffeyville, *U.S.A.* 109 G7
Coffin B., *Australia* 91 E2
Coffin Bay Peninsula, *Australia* 91 E2
Coffs Harbour, *Australia* 91 E5
Cofrentes, *Spain* 29 F3
Cogealac, *Romania* 38 E11
Coghinas →, *Italy* 34 B1
Coghinas, L. di, *Italy* 34 B2
Cognac, *France* 26 C3
Cogne, *Italy* 32 C4
Cogolludo, *Spain* 28 E1
Cohagen, *U.S.A.* 110 C10
Cohoes, *U.S.A.* 107 D11
Cohuna, *Australia* 91 F3
Coiba, I., *Panama* 116 E3
Coig →, *Argentina* 128 D3
Coihaique, *Chile* 128 C2
Coimbatore, *India* 60 P10
Coimbra, *Brazil* 125 D6
Coimbra, *Portugal* 30 E2
Coimbra □, *Portugal* 30 E2
Coín, *Spain* 31 J6
Coipasa, L. de, *Bolivia* 124 D4
Coipasa, Salar de, *Bolivia* 124 D4
Cojata, *Peru* 124 D4
Cojedes □, *Venezuela* 120 B4
Cojedes →, *Venezuela* 120 B4
Cojimies, *Ecuador* 124 A2
Cojocna, *Romania* 38 C6
Cojutepequé, *El Salv.* 116 D2
Cokeville, *U.S.A.* 110 E8
Colac, *Australia* 91 F3
Colares, *Portugal* 31 G1
Colatina, *Brazil* 123 E3
Colbeck, C., *Antarctica* 5 D13
Colbinabbin, *Australia* 91 F3
Colborne, *Canada* 106 B7
Colby, *U.S.A.* 108 F4
Colchagua □, *Chile* 126 C1
Colchester, *U.K.* 13 F8
Coldstream, *U.K.* 14 F6
Coldwater, *Canada* 106 B5
Coldwater, *U.S.A.* 109 G5
Colebrook, *Australia* 90 G4
Colebrook, *U.S.A.* 107 B13
Coleman, *Canada* 100 D6
Coleman, *U.S.A.* 109 K5
Coleman →, *Australia* 90 B3
Colenso, *S. Africa* 85 D4
Coleraine, *Australia* 91 F3
Coleraine, *U.K.* 15 A5
Coleraine □, *U.K.* 15 A5
Coleridge, L., *N.Z.* 87 K3
Colesberg, *S. Africa* 84 E4
Coleville, *U.S.A.* 112 G7
Colfax, *Calif., U.S.A.* 112 F6
Colfax, *La., U.S.A.* 109 K8
Colfax, *Wash., U.S.A.* 110 C5
Colhué Huapi, L., *Argentina* 128 C3
Cólico, *Italy* 32 B6
Coligny, *France* 27 B9
Coligny, *S. Africa* 85 D4
Colima, *Mexico* 114 D4
Colima □, *Mexico* 114 D4
Colima, Nevado de, *Mexico* 114 D4
Colina, *Chile* 126 C1
Colina do Norte, *Guinea-Biss.* 78 C2
Colinas, *Goiás, Brazil* 123 D2
Colinas, *Maranhão, Brazil* 122 C3
Coll, *U.K.* 14 E2
Collaguasi, *Chile* 126 A2
Collarada, Peña, *Spain* 28 C4
Collarenebri, *Australia* 91 D4
Collbran, *U.S.A.* 111 G10
Colle di Val d'Elsa, *Italy* 33 E8
Colle Salvetti, *Italy* 32 E7
Colle Sannita, *Italy* 35 A7
Collécchio, *Italy* 32 D7
Colleen Bawn, *Zimbabwe* 83 G2
College Park, *U.S.A.* 105 J3
Collette, *Canada* 99 C6
Collie, *Australia* 89 F2
Collier B., *Australia* 88 C3
Collier Ra., *Australia* 88 D2
Colline Metallifere, *Italy* 32 E7
Collingwood, *Canada* 98 D3
Collingwood, *N.Z.* 87 J4
Collins, *Canada* 98 B2
Collinsville, *Australia* 90 C4
Collipulli, *Chile* 126 D1
Collo, *Algeria* 75 A6
Collonges, *France* 27 B9
Collooney, *Ireland* 15 B3
Colmar, *France* 25 D14
Colmars, *France* 27 D10
Colmenar, *Spain* 31 J6
Colmenar de Oreja, *Spain* 28 E1
Colmenar Viejo, *Spain* 30 E7
Colne, *U.K.* 12 D5
Colo →, *Australia* 91 E5
Cologna Véneta, *Italy* 33 C8
Cologne = Köln, *Germany* 18 E2
Colom, I., *Spain* 36 B11
Coloma, *U.S.A.* 112 G6
Colomb-Béchar = Béchar, *Algeria* 75 B4
Colombey-les-Belles, *France* 25 D12
Colombey-les-Deux-Églises, *France* 25 D11
Colômbia, *Brazil* 123 F2
Colombia ■, *S. Amer.* 120 C3
Colombier, *Switz.* 22 C3
Colombo, *Sri Lanka* 60 R11
Colome, *U.S.A.* 108 D5
Colón, *Argentina* 126 C4
Colón, *Cuba* 116 B3
Colón, *Panama* 116 E4
Colón, *Peru* 124 A1
Colona, *Australia* 89 F5
Colonella, *Italy* 33 F10
Colonia, *Uruguay* 126 C4
Colonia de San Jordi, *Spain* 36 B9
Colonia Dora, *Argentina* 126 B3
Colonial Heights, *U.S.A.* 104 G7
Colonne, C. delle, *Italy* 35 C10
Colonsay, *Canada* 101 C7
Colonsay, *U.K.* 14 E2
Colorado □, *U.S.A.* 102 C5
Colorado →, *Argentina* 128 A4
Colorado →, *N. Amer.* 111 L6
Colorado →, *U.S.A.* 109 L7
Colorado City, *U.S.A.* 109 J4
Colorado Desert, *U.S.A.* 102 D3
Colorado Plateau, *U.S.A.* 111 H8
Colorado River Aqueduct, *U.S.A.* 113 L12
Colorado Springs, *U.S.A.* 108 F2
Colorno, *Italy* 32 D7
Colotlán, *Mexico* 114 C4
Colquechaca, *Bolivia* 125 D4
Colton, *Calif., U.S.A.* 113 L9
Colton, *N.Y., U.S.A.* 107 B10
Colton, *Wash., U.S.A.* 110 C5
Columbia, *La., U.S.A.* 109 J8
Columbia, *Miss., U.S.A.* 109 K10
Columbia, *Mo., U.S.A.* 108 F8
Columbia, *Pa., U.S.A.* 107 F8
Columbia, *S.C., U.S.A.* 105 H5
Columbia, *Tenn., U.S.A.* 105 H2
Columbia →, *N. Amer.* 110 C1
Columbia, C., *Canada* 4 A4
Columbia, District of □, *U.S.A.* 104 F7
Columbia, Mt., *Canada* 100 C5

Columbia Basin, *U.S.A.* .. 110 C4
Columbia Falls, *U.S.A.* ... 110 B6
Columbia Heights, *U.S.A.* 108 C8
Columbiana, *U.S.A.* 106 F4
Columbretes, Is., *Spain* ... 28 F5
Columbus, *Ga., U.S.A.* .. 105 J3
Columbus, *Ind., U.S.A.* .. 104 F3
Columbus, *Kans., U.S.A.* . 109 G7
Columbus, *Miss., U.S.A.* . 105 J1
Columbus, *Mont., U.S.A.* 110 D9
Columbus, *N. Dak., U.S.A.* 108 A3
Columbus, *N. Mex., U.S.A.* 111 L10
Columbus, *Nebr., U.S.A.* . 108 E6
Columbus, *Ohio, U.S.A.* . 104 F4
Columbus, *Tex., U.S.A.* .. 109 L6
Columbus, *Wis., U.S.A.* .. 108 D10
Colunga, *Spain* 30 B5
Colusa, *U.S.A.* 112 F4
Colville, *U.S.A.* 110 B5
Colville →, *U.S.A.* 96 A4
Colville, C., *N.Z.* 87 G5
Colwyn Bay, *U.K.* 12 D4
Coma, *Ethiopia* 77 F4
Comácchio, *Italy* 33 D9
Comalcalco, *Mexico* 115 D6
Comallo, *Argentina* 128 B2
Comanche, *Okla., U.S.A.* 109 H6
Comanche, *Tex., U.S.A.* . 109 K5
Comandante Luis Piedrabuena, *Argentina* . 128 C3
Comăneşti, *Romania* 38 C9
Comarapa, *Bolivia* 125 D5
Comayagua, *Honduras* ... 116 D2
Combahee →, *U.S.A.* ... 105 J5
Combeaufontaine, *France* . 25 E12
Comber, *Canada* 106 D2
Comblain-au-Pont, *Belgium* 17 H7
Combles, *France* 25 B9
Combourg, *France* 24 D5
Combronde, *France* 26 C7
Comeragh Mts., *Ireland* .. 15 D4
Comet, *Australia* 90 C4
Comilla, *Bangla.* 61 H17
Comines, *Belgium* 17 G1
Comino, *Malta* 37 C1
Comino, C., *Italy* 34 B2
Cómiso, *Italy* 35 F7
Comitán, *Mexico* 115 D6
Commentry, *France* 26 B6
Commerce, *Ga., U.S.A.* .. 105 H4
Commerce, *Tex., U.S.A.* . 109 J7
Commercy, *France* 25 D12
Commewijne □, *Surinam* . 121 B7
Committee B., *Canada* ... 97 B11
Commonwealth B., *Antarctica* 5 C10
Commonwealth of Independent States ■, *Eurasia* 45 D11
Commoron Cr. →, *Australia* 91 D5
Communism Pk. = Kommunizma, Pik, *Tajikistan* 44 F8
Como, *Italy* 32 C6
Como, L. di, *Italy* 32 B6
Comodoro Rivadavia, *Argentina* 128 C3
Comorin, C., *India* 60 Q10
Comoro Is. ■, *Ind. Oc.* .. 71 H8
Comox, *Canada* 100 D4
Compiègne, *France* 25 C9
Comporta, *Portugal* 31 G2
Compostela, *Mexico* 114 C4
Comprida, I., *Brazil* 127 A6
Compton, *U.S.A.* 113 M8
Compton Downs, *Australia* 91 E4
Con Cuong, *Vietnam* 58 C5
Con Son, Is., *Vietnam* 59 H6
Cona Niyeu, *Argentina* ... 128 B3
Conakry, *Guinea* 78 D2
Conara Junction, *Australia* 90 G4
Concarneau, *France* 24 E3
Conceição, *Brazil* 122 C4
Conceição, *Mozam.* 83 F4
Conceição da Barra, *Brazil* 123 E4
Conceição do Araguaia, *Brazil* 122 C2
Conceição do Canindé, *Brazil* 122 C3
Concepción, *Argentina* ... 126 B2
Concepción, *Bolivia* 125 D5
Concepción, *Chile* 126 D1
Concepción, *Mexico* 115 D6
Concepción, *Paraguay* 126 A4
Concepción, *Peru* 124 C2
Concepción □, *Chile* 126 D1
Concepción →, *Mexico* .. 114 A2
Concepción, Est. de, *Chile* 128 D2
Concepción, L., *Bolivia* .. 125 D5
Concepción, Punta, *Mexico* 114 B2
Concepción del Oro, *Mexico* 114 C4
Concepción del Uruguay, *Argentina* 126 C4
Conception, Pt., *U.S.A.* .. 113 L6
Conception B., *Namibia* .. 84 C1
Conception I., *Bahamas* .. 117 B4
Concession, *Zimbabwe* ... 83 F3
Conchas Dam, *U.S.A.* 109 H2
Conche, *Canada* 99 B8
Concho, *U.S.A.* 111 J9
Concho →, *U.S.A.* 109 K5
Conchos →, *Chihuahua, Mexico* 114 B4
Conchos →, *Tamaulipas, Mexico* 115 B5
Concord, *Calif., U.S.A.* .. 112 H4
Concord, *N.C., U.S.A.* ... 105 H5
Concord, *N.H., U.S.A.* ... 107 C13
Concordia, *Argentina* 126 C4
Concórdia, *Brazil* 120 D4
Concordia, *Mexico* 114 C3
Concordia, *U.S.A.* 108 F6
Concots, *France* 26 D5
Concrete, *U.S.A.* 110 B3
Condamine, *Australia* 91 D5
Condat, *France* 26 C6
Conde, *Brazil* 123 D4
Conde, *U.S.A.* 108 C5
Condé-sur-l'Escaut, *France* 25 B10
Condé-sur-Noireau, *France* 24 D6
Condeúba, *Brazil* 123 D3
Condobolin, *Australia* 91 E4
Condom, *France* 26 E4
Condon, *U.S.A.* 110 D3
Condove, *Italy* 32 C4
Conegliano, *Italy* 33 C9
Conejera, I., *Spain* 36 B9
Conejos, *Mexico* 114 B4
Conflans-en-Jarnisy, *France* 25 C12
Confolens, *France* 26 B4
Confuso →, *Paraguay* ... 126 B4
Congjiang, *China* 52 E7
Congleton, *U.K.* 12 D5
Congo = Zaïre →, *Africa* 80 F2
Congo, *Brazil* 122 C4
Congo (Kinshasa) = Zaïre ■, *Africa* 80 E4
Congo ■, *Africa* 80 E3
Congo Basin, *Africa* 70 G6
Congonhas, *Brazil* 123 F3
Congress, *U.S.A.* 111 J7
Conil, *Spain* 31 J4
Coniston, *Canada* 98 C3
Conjeeveram = Kanchipuram, *India* 60 N11
Conjuboy, *Australia* 90 B3
Conklin, *Canada* 101 B6
Conlea, *Australia* 91 E3
Conn, L., *Ireland* 15 B2
Connacht, *Ireland* 15 C3
Conneaut, *U.S.A.* 106 E4
Connecticut □, *U.S.A.* ... 107 E12
Connecticut →, *U.S.A.* .. 107 E12
Connell, *U.S.A.* 110 C4
Connellsville, *U.S.A.* 106 F5
Connemara, *Ireland* 15 C2
Connemaugh →, *U.S.A.* . 106 F5
Connerré, *France* 24 D7
Connersville, *U.S.A.* 104 F3
Connors Ra., *Australia* ... 90 C4
Conoble, *Australia* 91 E3
Cononaco →, *Ecuador* ... 120 D2
Cononbridge, *U.K.* 14 D4
Conquest, *Canada* 101 C7
Conrad, *U.S.A.* 110 B8
Conran, C., *Australia* 91 F4
Conroe, *U.S.A.* 109 K7
Conselheiro Lafaiete, *Brazil* 123 F3
Conselheiro Pena, *Brazil* . 123 E3
Consort, *Canada* 101 C6
Constance = Konstanz, *Germany* 19 H5
Constance, L. = Bodensee, *Europe* 23 A8
Constanţa, *Romania* 38 E11
Constantina, *Spain* 31 H5
Constantine, *Algeria* 75 A6
Constitución, *Chile* 126 D1
Constitución, *Uruguay* ... 126 C4
Consuegra, *Spain* 31 F7
Consul, *Canada* 101 D7
Contact, *U.S.A.* 110 F6
Contai, *India* 63 J12
Contamana, *Peru* 124 B3
Contarina, *Italy* 33 C9
Contas →, *Brazil* 123 D4
Contes, *France* 27 E11
Conthey, *Switz.* 22 D4
Contoocook, *U.S.A.* 107 C13
Contra Costa, *Mozam.* ... 85 D5
Contres, *France* 24 E8
Contrexéville, *France* 25 D12
Contumaza, *Peru* 124 B2
Convención, *Colombia* ... 120 B3
Conversano, *Italy* 35 B10
Conway = Conwy, *U.K.* .. 12 D4
Conway = Conwy →, *U.K.* 12 D4
Conway, *Ark., U.S.A.* ... 109 H8
Conway, *N.H., U.S.A.* ... 107 C13
Conway, *S.C., U.S.A.* ... 105 J6
Conway, L., *Australia* ... 91 D2
Conwy, *U.K.* 12 D4
Conwy →, *U.K.* 12 D4
Coober Pedy, *Australia* ... 91 D1
Cooch Behar = Koch Bihar, *India* 61 F16
Coodardy, *Australia* 89 E2
Cook, *Australia* 89 F5
Cook, *U.S.A.* 108 B8
Cook, B., *Chile* 128 E2
Cook, Mt., *N.Z.* 87 K3
Cook Inlet, *U.S.A.* 96 C4
Cook Is., *Pac. Oc.* 93 J11
Cook Strait, *N.Z.* 87 J5
Cookeville, *U.S.A.* 105 G3
Cookhouse, *S. Africa* 84 E4
Cookshire, *Canada* 107 A13
Cookstown, *U.K.* 15 B5
Cookstown □, *U.K.* 15 B5
Cooksville, *Canada* 106 C5
Cooktown, *Australia* 90 B4
Coolabah, *Australia* 91 E4
Cooladdi, *Australia* 91 D4
Coolah, *Australia* 91 E4
Coolamon, *Australia* 91 E4
Coolangatta, *Australia* ... 91 D5
Coolgardie, *Australia* 89 F3
Coolibah, *Australia* 88 C5
Coolidge, *U.S.A.* 111 K8
Coolidge Dam, *U.S.A.* ... 111 K8
Cooma, *Australia* 91 F4
Coonabarabran, *Australia* . 91 E4
Coonamble, *Australia* 91 E4
Coonana, *Australia* 89 F3
Coondapoor, *India* 60 N9
Coongie, *Australia* 91 D3
Coongoola, *Australia* 91 D4
Cooninie, L., *Australia* ... 91 D2
Cooper, *U.S.A.* 109 J7
Cooper →, *U.S.A.* 105 J6
Cooper Cr. →, *Australia* . 91 D2
Cooperstown, *N. Dak., U.S.A.* 108 B5
Cooperstown, *N.Y., U.S.A.* 107 D10
Coorabie, *Australia* 89 F5
Coorabulka, *Australia* 90 C3
Coorow, *Australia* 89 E2
Cooroy, *Australia* 91 D5
Coos Bay, *U.S.A.* 110 E1
Cootamundra, *Australia* .. 91 E4
Cootehill, *Ireland* 15 B4
Cooyar, *Australia* 91 D5
Cooyeana, *Australia* 90 C2
Copahue Paso, *Argentina* . 126 D1
Copainalá, *Mexico* 115 D6
Copán, *Honduras* 116 D2
Copatana, *Brazil* 120 D4
Cope, *U.S.A.* 108 F3
Cope, C., *Spain* 29 H3
Copenhagen = København, *Denmark* 11 J6
Copertino, *Italy* 35 B11
Copiapó, *Chile* 126 B1
Copiapó →, *Chile* 126 B1
Copley, *Australia* 91 E2
Copp L., *Canada* 100 A6
Copparo, *Italy* 33 D8
Coppename →, *Surinam* . 121 B6
Copper Center, *U.S.A.* ... 96 B5
Copper Cliff, *Canada* 98 C3
Copper Harbor, *U.S.A.* .. 104 B2
Copper Queen, *Zimbabwe* 83 F2
Copperbelt □, *Zambia* ... 83 E2
Coppermine, *Canada* 96 B8
Coppermine →, *Canada* . 96 B8
Copperopolis, *U.S.A.* 112 H6
Coquet →, *U.K.* 12 B6
Coquilhatville = Mbandaka, *Zaïre* 80 D3
Coquille, *U.S.A.* 110 E1
Coquimbo, *Chile* 126 B1
Coquimbo □, *Chile* 126 C1
Corabia, *Romania* 38 F7
Coração de Jesus, *Brazil* .. 123 E3
Coracora, *Peru* 124 D3
Coradi, Is., *Italy* 35 B10
Coral Gables, *U.S.A.* 105 N5
Coral Harbour, *Canada* .. 97 B11
Coral Sea, *Pac. Oc.* 92 J7
Corantijn →, *Surinam* ... 121 B6
Coraopolis, *U.S.A.* 106 F4
Corato, *Italy* 35 A9
Corbeil-Essonnes, *France* . 25 D9
Corbie, *France* 25 C9
Corbières, *France* 26 F6
Corbigny, *France* 25 E10
Corbin, *U.S.A.* 104 G3
Corbion, *Belgium* 17 J6
Corbones →, *Spain* 31 H5
Corby, *U.K.* 13 E7
Corby Glen, *U.K.* 13 E7
Corcoles →, *Spain* 29 F1
Corcoran, *U.S.A.* 111 H4
Corcubión, *Spain* 30 C1
Cordele, *U.S.A.* 105 K4
Cordell, *U.S.A.* 109 H5
Cordenons, *Italy* 33 C9
Cordes, *France* 26 D5
Cordisburgo, *Brazil* 123 E3
Córdoba, *Argentina* 126 C3
Córdoba, *Mexico* 115 D5
Córdoba, *Spain* 31 H6
Córdoba □, *Argentina* ... 126 C3
Córdoba □, *Colombia* ... 120 B2
Córdoba □, *Spain* 31 G6
Córdoba, Sierra de, *Argentina* 126 C3
Cordon, *Phil.* 55 C4
Cordova, *Ala., U.S.A.* ... 105 J2
Cordova, *Alaska, U.S.A.* . 96 B5
Corella, *Spain* 28 C3
Corella →, *Australia* 90 B3
Coremas, *Brazil* 122 C4
Corentyne →, *Guyana* ... 121 B6
Corfield, *Australia* 90 C3
Corfu = Kérkira, *Greece* . 37 A3
Corfu, Str of, *Greece* 37 A4
Corgo, *Spain* 30 C3
Corguinho, *Brazil* 125 D7
Cori, *Italy* 34 A5
Coria, *Spain* 30 F4
Corigliano Cálabro, *Italy* . 35 C9
Coringa Is., *Australia* 90 B4
Corinna, *Australia* 90 G4
Corinth = Kórinthos, *Greece* 39 M5
Corinth, *Miss., U.S.A.* ... 105 H1
Corinth, *N.Y., U.S.A.* 107 C11
Corinth, G. of = Korinthiakós Kólpos, *Greece* 39 L5
Corinth Canal, *Greece* 39 M6
Corinto, *Brazil* 123 E3
Corinto, *Nic.* 116 D2
Cork, *Ireland* 15 E3
Cork □, *Ireland* 15 E3
Cork Harbour, *Ireland* ... 15 E3
Corlay, *France* 24 D3
Corleone, *Italy* 34 E6
Corleto Perticara, *Italy* ... 35 B9
Çorlu, *Turkey* 39 H10
Cormack L., *Canada* 100 A4
Cormóns, *Italy* 33 C10
Cormorant, *Canada* 101 C8
Cormorant L., *Canada* ... 101 C8
Corn Is. = Maiz, Is. del, *Nic.* 116 D3
Cornélio Procópio, *Brazil* . 127 A5
Cornell, *U.S.A.* 108 C9
Corner Brook, *Canada* ... 99 C8
Corníglio, *Italy* 32 D7
Corning, *Ark., U.S.A.* ... 109 G9
Corning, *Calif., U.S.A.* ... 110 G2
Corning, *Iowa, U.S.A.* ... 108 E7
Corning, *N.Y., U.S.A.* ... 106 D7
Corno, Monte, *Italy* 33 F10
Cornwall, *Canada* 98 C5
Cornwall □, *U.K.* 13 G3
Corny Pt., *Australia* 91 E2
Coro, *Venezuela* 120 A4
Coroaci, *Brazil* 123 E3
Coroatá, *Brazil* 122 B3
Corocoro, *Bolivia* 124 D4
Corocoro, I., *Venezuela* .. 121 B5
Coroico, *Bolivia* 124 D4
Coromandel, *Brazil* 123 E2
Coromandel, *N.Z.* 87 G5
Coromandel Coast, *India* . 60 N12
Corona, *Australia* 91 E3
Corona, *Calif., U.S.A.* ... 113 M9
Corona, *N. Mex., U.S.A.* . 111 J11
Coronado, *U.S.A.* 113 N9
Coronado, B. de, *Costa Rica* 116 E3
Coronados, G. de los, *Chile* 128 B2
Coronados, Is. los, *U.S.A.* 113 N9
Coronation, *Canada* 100 C6
Coronation Gulf, *Canada* . 96 B8
Coronation I., *Antarctica* . 5 C18
Coronation I., *U.S.A.* 100 B2
Coronation Is., *Australia* . 88 B3
Coronda, *Argentina* 126 C3
Coronel, *Chile* 126 D1
Coronel Bogado, *Paraguay* 126 B4
Coronel Dorrego, *Argentina* 126 D3
Coronel Fabriciano, *Brazil* 123 E3
Coronel Murta, *Brazil* 123 E3
Coronel Oviedo, *Paraguay* 126 B4
Coronel Ponce, *Brazil* 125 D6
Coronel Pringles, *Argentina* 126 D3
Coronel Suárez, *Argentina* 126 D3
Coronel Vidal, *Argentina* . 126 D4
Corongo, *Peru* 124 B2
Coronie □, *Surinam* 121 B6
Coropuna, Nevado, *Peru* . 124 D3
Çorovoda, *Albania* 39 J3
Corowa, *Australia* 91 F4
Corozal, *Belize* 115 D7
Corozal, *Colombia* 120 B2
Corps, *France* 27 D9
Corpus, *Argentina* 127 B4
Corpus Christi, *U.S.A.* ... 109 M6
Corpus Christi, L., *U.S.A.* 109 L6
Corque, *Bolivia* 124 D4
Corral, *Chile* 128 A2
Corral de Almaguer, *Spain* 28 F1
Corralejo, *Canary Is.* 36 F6
Corrégio, *Italy* 32 D7
Corrente, *Brazil* 122 D2
Corrente →, *Brazil* 123 D3
Correntes →, *Brazil* 125 D6
Correntes, C. das, *Mozam.* 85 C6
Correntina, *Brazil* 123 D3
Corrèze □, *France* 26 C5
Corrèze →, *France* 26 C5
Corrib, L., *Ireland* 15 C2
Corrientes, *Argentina* 126 B4
Corrientes □, *Argentina* .. 126 B4
Corrientes →, *Argentina* . 126 C4
Corrientes →, *Peru* 120 D3
Corrientes, C., *Colombia* . 120 B2
Corrientes, C., *Cuba* 116 B3
Corrientes, C., *Mexico* ... 114 C3
Corrigan, *U.S.A.* 109 K7
Corrigin, *Australia* 89 F2
Corry, *U.S.A.* 106 E5
Corse, *France* 27 F13
Corse, C., *France* 27 E13
Corse-du-Sud □, *France* .. 27 G13
Corsica = Corse, *France* .. 27 F13
Corsicana, *U.S.A.* 109 J6
Corte, *France* 27 F13
Corte do Pinto, *Portugal* . 31 H3
Cortegana, *Spain* 31 H4
Cortez, *U.S.A.* 111 H9
Cortina d'Ampezzo, *Italy* . 33 B9
Cortland, *U.S.A.* 107 D8
Cortona, *Italy* 33 E8
Coruche, *Portugal* 31 G2
Çoruh →, *Turkey* 67 C9
Çorum, *Turkey* 66 C6
Çorum □, *Turkey* 66 C6
Corumbá, *Brazil* 125 D6
Corumbá →, *Brazil* 123 E2
Corumbá de Goiás, *Brazil* 123 E2
Corumbaíba, *Brazil* 123 E2
Corunna = La Coruña, *Spain* 30 B2
Corvallis, *U.S.A.* 110 D2
Corvette, L. de la, *Canada* 98 B5
Corydon, *U.S.A.* 108 E8
Cosalá, *Mexico* 114 C3
Cosamaloapan, *Mexico* ... 115 D5
Cosenza, *Italy* 35 C9
Coshocton, *U.S.A.* 106 F3
Cosmo Newberry, *Australia* 89 E3
Cosne-sur-Loire, *France* .. 25 E9
Coso Junction, *U.S.A.* ... 113 J9
Coso Pk., *U.S.A.* 113 J9
Cospeito, *Spain* 30 B3
Cosquín, *Argentina* 126 C3
Cossato, *Italy* 32 C5
Cossé-le-Vivien, *France* ... 24 E6
Cosson →, *France* 24 E8
Costa Blanca, *Spain* 29 G4
Costa Brava, *Spain* 28 D8
Costa del Sol, *Spain* 31 J6
Costa Dorada, *Spain* 28 E6
Costa Mesa, *U.S.A.* 113 M9
Costa Rica ■, *Cent. Amer.* 116 D3
Costa Smeralda, *Italy* 34 A2
Costigliole d'Asti, *Italy* ... 32 D5
Costilla, *U.S.A.* 111 H11
Cosumnes →, *U.S.A.* 112 G5
Coswig, *Germany* 18 D8
Cotabato, *Phil.* 55 H6
Cotacajes →, *Bolivia* 124 D4
Cotagaita, *Bolivia* 126 A2
Cotahuasi, *Peru* 124 D3
Côte d'Azur, *France* 27 E11
Côte-d'Ivoire ■ = Ivory Coast ■, *Africa* 78 D3
Côte d'Or, *France* 25 E11
Côte-d'Or □, *France* 25 E11
Coteau des Prairies, *U.S.A.* 108 C6
Coteau du Missouri, *U.S.A.* 108 B4
Coteau Landing, *Canada* . 107 A10
Cotegipe, *Brazil* 123 D3
Cotentin, *France* 24 C5
Côtes-d'Armor □, *France* . 24 D4
Côtes de Meuse, *France* .. 25 C12
Côtes-du-Nord = Côtes-d'Armor □, *France* 24 D4
Cotiella, *Spain* 28 C5
Cotillo, *Canary Is.* 36 F5
Cotina →, *Bos.-H., Yug.* 21 M8
Cotoca, *Bolivia* 125 D5
Cotonou, *Benin* 79 D5
Cotopaxi, *Ecuador* 120 D2
Cotopaxi □, *Ecuador* 120 D2
Cotronei, *Italy* 35 C9
Cotswold Hills, *U.K.* 13 F5
Cottage Grove, *U.S.A.* ... 110 E2
Cottbus, *Germany* 18 D10
Cottonwood, *U.S.A.* 111 J7
Cotulla, *U.S.A.* 109 L5
Coubre, Pte. de la, *France* 26 C2
Couches, *France* 25 F11
Couço, *Portugal* 31 G2
Coudersport, *U.S.A.* 106 E6
Couedic, C. du, *Australia* . 91 F2
Couëron, *France* 24 E5
Couesnon →, *France* 24 D5
Couhé, *France* 26 B4
Coulanges-sur-Yonne, *France* 25 E10
Coulee City, *U.S.A.* 110 C4
Coulman I., *Antarctica* ... 5 D11
Coulommiers, *France* 25 D10
Coulonge →, *Canada* 98 C4
Coulonges-sur-l'Autize, *France* 26 B3
Coulterville, *U.S.A.* 112 H6
Council, *Alaska, U.S.A.* .. 96 B3
Council, *Idaho, U.S.A.* ... 110 D5
Council Bluffs, *U.S.A.* ... 108 E7
Council Grove, *U.S.A.* ... 108 F6
Coupeville, *U.S.A.* 112 B4
Courantyne →, *S. Amer.* . 121 B6
Courcelles, *Belgium* 17 H4
Courçon, *France* 26 B3
Couronne, C., *France* 27 E9
Cours-la-Ville, *France* 27 B8
Coursan, *France* 26 E7
Courseulles-sur-Mer, *France* 24 C6
Court-St.-Etienne, *Belgium* 17 G5
Courtenay, *Canada* 100 D3
Courtland, *U.S.A.* 112 G5
Courtrai = Kortrijk, *Belgium* 17 G2
Courtright, *Canada* 106 D2
Courville-sur-Eure, *France* 24 D8
Coushatta, *U.S.A.* 109 J8
Coutances, *France* 24 C5
Couterne, *France* 24 D6
Coutras, *France* 26 C3
Coutts, *Canada* 100 D6

Couvet, *Switz.* 22 C3
Couvin, *Belgium* 17 H4
Covarrubias, *Spain* 28 C1
Coveñas, *Colombia* 120 B2
Coventry, *U.K.* 13 E6
Coventry L., *Canada* 101 A7
Covilhã, *Portugal* 30 E3
Covington, *Ga., U.S.A.* 105 J4
Covington, *Ky., U.S.A.* 104 F3
Covington, *Okla., U.S.A.* 109 G6
Covington, *Tenn., U.S.A.* 109 H10
Cowal, L., *Australia* 91 E4
Cowan, *Canada* 101 C8
Cowan, L., *Australia* 89 F3
Cowan L., *Canada* 101 C7
Cowangie, *Australia* 91 F3
Cowansville, *Canada* 107 A12
Cowarie, *Australia* 91 D2
Cowcowing Lakes, *Australia* 89 F2
Cowdenbeath, *U.K.* 14 E5
Cowell, *Australia* 91 E2
Cowes, *U.K.* 13 G6
Cowlitz →, *U.S.A.* 112 D4
Cowra, *Australia* 91 E4
Coxilha Grande, *Brazil* 127 B5
Coxim, *Brazil* 125 D7
Coxim →, *Brazil* 125 D7
Cox's Bazar, *Bangla.* 61 J17
Cox's Cove, *Canada* 99 C8
Coyame, *Mexico* 114 B3
Coyote Wells, *U.S.A.* 113 N11
Coyuca de Benítez, *Mexico* 115 D4
Coyuca de Catalan, *Mexico* 114 D4
Cozad, *U.S.A.* 108 E5
Cozumel, *Mexico* 115 C7
Cozumel, I. de, *Mexico* 115 C7
Craboon, *Australia* 91 E4
Cracow = Kraków, *Poland* 20 E9
Cracow, *Australia* 91 D5
Cradock, *S. Africa* 84 E4
Craig, *Alaska, U.S.A.* 100 B2
Craig, *Colo., U.S.A.* 110 F10
Craigavon = Lurgan, *U.K.* 15 B5
Craigmore, *Zimbabwe* 83 G3
Crailsheim, *Germany* 19 F6
Craiova, *Romania* 38 E6
Cramsie, *Australia* 90 C3
Cranberry Portage, *Canada* 101 C8
Cranbrook, *Tas., Australia* 90 G4
Cranbrook, *W. Austral., Australia* 89 F2
Cranbrook, *Canada* 100 D5
Crandon, *U.S.A.* 108 C10
Crane, *Oreg., U.S.A.* 110 E4
Crane, *Tex., U.S.A.* 109 K3
Cranston, *U.S.A.* 107 E13
Craon, *France* 24 E6
Craonne, *France* 25 C10
Craponne-sur-Arzon, *France* 26 C7
Crasna, *Romania* 38 C10
Crater, L., *U.S.A.* 110 E2
Crateús, *Brazil* 122 C3
Crati →, *Italy* 35 C9
Crato, *Brazil* 122 C4
Crato, *Portugal* 31 F3
Cravo Norte, *Colombia* 120 B3
Cravo Norte →, *Colombia* 120 B3
Crawford, *U.S.A.* 108 D3
Crawfordsville, *U.S.A.* 104 E2
Crawley, *U.K.* 13 F7
Crazy Mts., *U.S.A.* 110 C8
Crean L., *Canada* 101 C7
Crécy-en-Brie, *France* 25 D9
Crécy-en-Ponthieu, *France* 25 B8
Crediton, *Canada* 106 C3
Credo, *Australia* 89 F3
Cree →, *Canada* 101 B7
Cree →, *U.K.* 14 G4
Cree L., *Canada* 101 B7
Creede, *U.S.A.* 111 H10
Creel, *Mexico* 114 B3
Creighton, *U.S.A.* 108 D6
Creil, *France* 25 C9
Crema, *Italy* 32 C6
Cremona, *Italy* 32 C7
Crepori →, *Brazil* 125 B6
Crépy, *France* 25 C10
Crépy-en-Valois, *France* 25 C9
Cres, *Croatia* 33 D11
Cresbard, *U.S.A.* 108 C5
Crescent, *Okla., U.S.A.* 109 H6
Crescent, *Oreg., U.S.A.* 110 E3
Crescent City, *U.S.A.* 110 F1
Crescentino, *Italy* 32 C5
Crespino, *Italy* 33 D8
Crespo, *Argentina* 126 C3
Cressy, *Australia* 91 F3
Crest, *France* 27 D9
Cresta, Mt., *Phil.* 55 C5
Crested Butte, *U.S.A.* 111 G10
Crestline, *Calif., U.S.A.* 113 L9
Crestline, *Ohio, U.S.A.* 106 F2
Creston, *Canada* 100 D5
Creston, *Calif., U.S.A.* 112 K6
Creston, *Iowa, U.S.A.* 108 E7
Creston, *Wash., U.S.A.* 110 C4
Crestview, *Calif., U.S.A.* 112 H8
Crestview, *Fla., U.S.A.* 105 K2
Crete = Kríti, *Greece* 37 D7
Crete, *U.S.A.* 108 E6
Crete, Sea of, *Greece* 39 N8
Creus, C., *Spain* 28 C8
Creuse □, *France* 26 B6
Creuse →, *France* 26 B4
Creuzburg, *Germany* 18 D6
Crevalcore, *Italy* 33 D8
Crèvecœur-le-Grand, *France* 25 C9
Crevillente, *Spain* 29 G4
Crewe, *U.K.* 12 D5
Criciúma, *Brazil* 127 B6
Crieff, *U.K.* 14 E5
Crikvenica, *Croatia* 33 C11
Crimea = Krymskiy Poluostrov, *Ukraine* 42 D5
Crimmitschau, *Germany* 18 E8
Cristalândia, *Brazil* 122 D2
Cristino Castro, *Brazil* 122 C3
Crişul Alb →, *Romania* 38 C4
Crişul Negru →, *Romania* 38 C4
Crişul Repede →, *Romania* 38 C3
Crivitz, *Germany* 18 B7
Crixás, *Brazil* 123 D2
Crna Gora = Montenegro □, *Montenegro, Yug.* 21 N9
Crni Drim →, *Macedonia, Yug.* 39 H3
Črnomelj, *Slovenia* 33 C12
Croaghpatrick, *Ireland* 15 C2
Croatia ■, *Europe* 33 C13
Crocker, Banjaran, *Malaysia* 56 C5
Crockett, *U.S.A.* 109 K7
Crocodile = Krokodil →, *Mozam.* 85 D5
Crocodile Is., *Australia* 90 A1
Crocq, *France* 26 C6
Croisette, C., *France* 27 E9
Croisic, Pte. du, *France* 24 E4
Croix, L. La, *Canada* 98 C1
Croker, C., *Australia* 88 B5
Croker I., *Australia* 88 B5
Cromarty, *Canada* 101 B10
Cromarty, *U.K.* 14 D4
Cromer, *U.K.* 12 E9
Cromwell, *N.Z.* 87 L2
Cronat, *France* 25 F10
Cronulla, *Australia* 91 E5
Crooked →, *Canada* 100 C4
Crooked →, *U.S.A.* 110 D3
Crooked I., *Bahamas* 117 B5
Crooked Island Passage, *Bahamas* 117 B5
Crookston, *Minn., U.S.A.* 108 B6
Crookston, *Nebr., U.S.A.* 108 D4
Crooksville, *U.S.A.* 104 F4
Crookwell, *Australia* 91 E4
Crosby, *Minn., U.S.A.* 108 B8
Crosby, *N. Dak., U.S.A.* 101 D8
Crosby, *Pa., U.S.A.* 106 E6
Crosbyton, *U.S.A.* 109 J4
Cross →, *Nigeria* 79 E6
Cross City, *U.S.A.* 105 L4
Cross Fell, *U.K.* 12 C5
Cross L., *Canada* 101 C9
Cross Plains, *U.S.A.* 109 J5
Cross River □, *Nigeria* 79 D6
Cross Sound, *U.S.A.* 96 C6
Crossett, *U.S.A.* 109 J9
Crossfield, *Canada* 100 C6
Crosshaven, *Ireland* 15 E3
Croton-on-Hudson, *U.S.A.* 107 E11
Crotone, *Italy* 35 C10
Crow →, *Canada* 100 B4
Crow Agency, *U.S.A.* 110 D10
Crow Hd., *Ireland* 15 E1
Crowell, *U.S.A.* 109 J5
Crowley, *U.S.A.* 109 K8
Crowley, L., *U.S.A.* 112 H8
Crown Point, *U.S.A.* 104 E2
Crows Landing, *U.S.A.* 112 H5
Crows Nest, *Australia* 91 D5
Crowsnest Pass, *Canada* 100 D6
Croydon, *Australia* 90 B3
Croydon, *U.K.* 13 F7
Crozet Is., *Ind. Oc.* 3 G12
Crozon, *France* 24 D2
Cruz, C., *Cuba* 116 C4
Cruz Alta, *Brazil* 127 B5
Cruz das Almas, *Brazil* 123 D4
Cruz de Malta, *Brazil* 122 C3
Cruz del Eje, *Argentina* 126 C3
Cruzeiro, *Brazil* 123 F2
Cruzeiro do Oeste, *Brazil* 127 A5
Cruzeiro do Sul, *Brazil* 124 B3
Cry L., *Canada* 100 B3
Crystal Bay, *U.S.A.* 112 F7
Crystal Brook, *Australia* 91 E2
Crystal City, *Mo., U.S.A.* 108 F9
Crystal City, *Tex., U.S.A.* 109 L5
Crystal Falls, *U.S.A.* 104 B1
Crystal River, *U.S.A.* 105 L4
Crystal Springs, *U.S.A.* 109 K9
Csongrád, *Hungary* 21 J10
Csorna, *Hungary* 21 H7
Csurgo, *Hungary* 21 J7
Cu Lao Hon, *Vietnam* 59 G7
Cua Rao, *Vietnam* 58 C5
Cuácua →, *Mozam.* 83 F4
Cuamato, *Angola* 84 B2
Cuamba, *Mozam.* 83 E4
Cuando →, *Angola* 81 H4
Cuando Cubango □, *Angola* 84 B3
Cuangar, *Angola* 84 B2
Cuanza →, *Angola* 70 G5
Cuarto →, *Argentina* 126 C3
Cuatrociénegas, *Mexico* 114 B4
Cuauhtémoc, *Mexico* 114 B3
Cuba, *Portugal* 31 G3
Cuba, *N. Mex., U.S.A.* 111 J10
Cuba, *N.Y., U.S.A.* 106 D6
Cuba ■, *W. Indies* 116 B4
Cuballing, *Australia* 89 F2
Cubango →, *Africa* 84 B3
Çubuk, *Turkey* 66 C5
Cucamonga, *U.S.A.* 113 L9
Cuchi, *Angola* 81 G3
Cuchillo-Có, *Argentina* 128 A4
Cuchivero →, *Venezuela* 120 B4
Cuchumatanes, Sierra de los, *Guatemala* 116 C1
Cucuí, *Brazil* 120 C4
Cucurpe, *Mexico* 114 A2
Cucurrupí, *Colombia* 120 C2
Cúcuta, *Colombia* 120 B3
Cudahy, *U.S.A.* 104 D2
Cudalbi, *Romania* 38 D10
Cuddalore, *India* 60 P11
Cuddapah, *India* 60 M11
Cuddapan, L., *Australia* 90 D3
Cudgewa, *Australia* 91 F4
Cudillero, *Spain* 30 B4
Cue, *Australia* 89 E2
Cuéllar, *Spain* 30 D6
Cuenca, *Ecuador* 120 D2
Cuenca, *Spain* 28 E2
Cuenca □, *Spain* 28 F2
Cuenca, Serranía de, *Spain* 28 F3
Cuerdo del Pozo, Pantano de la, *Spain* 28 D2
Cuernavaca, *Mexico* 115 D5
Cuero, *U.S.A.* 109 L6
Cuers, *France* 27 E10
Cuervo, *U.S.A.* 109 H2
Cuesmes, *Belgium* 17 H3
Cuevas, Cerro, *Bolivia* 125 E4
Cuevas del Almanzora, *Spain* 29 H3
Cuevo, *Bolivia* 125 E5
Cuiabá, *Brazil* 125 D6
Cuiabá →, *Brazil* 125 D6
Cuilco, *Guatemala* 116 C1
Cuillin Hills, *U.K.* 14 D2
Cuillin Sd., *U.K.* 14 D2
Cuima, *Angola* 81 G3
Cuiseaux, *France* 27 B9
Cuité, *Brazil* 122 C4
Cuito →, *Angola* 84 B3
Cuitzeo, L. de, *Mexico* 114 D4
Cuiuni →, *Brazil* 121 D5
Cukai, *Malaysia* 59 K4
Culan, *France* 26 B6
Culbertson, *U.S.A.* 108 A2
Culcairn, *Australia* 91 F4
Culebra, Sierra de la, *Spain* 30 D4
Culemborg, *Neths.* 16 E6
Culgoa →, *Australia* 91 D4
Culiacán, *Mexico* 114 C3
Culiacán →, *Mexico* 114 C3
Culion, *Phil.* 55 F4
Culiseu →, *Brazil* 125 C7
Cúllar de Baza, *Spain* 29 H2
Cullarin Ra., *Australia* 91 E4
Cullen, *U.K.* 14 D6
Cullen Pt., *Australia* 90 A3
Cullera, *Spain* 29 F4
Cullman, *U.S.A.* 105 H2
Culloden Moor, *U.K.* 14 D4
Culoz, *France* 27 C9
Culpeper, *U.S.A.* 104 F7
Culuene →, *Brazil* 125 C7
Culver, Pt., *Australia* 89 F3
Culverden, *N.Z.* 87 K4
Cumaná, *Venezuela* 121 A5
Cumare, *Colombia* 120 C3
Cumari, *Brazil* 123 E2
Cumberland, *Canada* 100 D3
Cumberland, *Md., U.S.A.* 104 F6
Cumberland, *Wis., U.S.A.* 108 C8
Cumberland →, *U.S.A.* 105 G2
Cumberland I., *U.S.A.* 105 K5
Cumberland Is., *Australia* 90 C4
Cumberland L., *Canada* 101 C8
Cumberland Pen., *Canada* 97 B13
Cumberland Plateau, *U.S.A.* 105 H3
Cumberland Sd., *Canada* 97 B13
Cumborah, *Australia* 91 D4
Cumbres Mayores, *Spain* 31 G4
Cumbria □, *U.K.* 12 C5
Cumbrian Mts., *U.K.* 12 C4
Cumbum, *India* 60 M11
Cuminá →, *Brazil* 121 D6
Cuminapanema →, *Brazil* 121 D7
Cummings Mt., *U.S.A.* 113 K8
Cummins, *Australia* 91 E2
Cumnock, *Australia* 91 E4
Cumnock, *U.K.* 14 F4
Cumpas, *Mexico* 114 A3
Cumplida, Pta., *Canary Is.* 36 F2
Çumra, *Turkey* 66 E5
Cuncumén, *Chile* 126 C1
Cundeelee, *Australia* 89 F3
Cunderdin, *Australia* 89 F2
Cundinamarca □, *Colombia* 120 C3
Cunene →, *Angola* 84 B1
Cúneo, *Italy* 32 D4
Cunillera, I., *Spain* 36 C7
Cunlhat, *France* 26 C7
Cunnamulla, *Australia* 91 D4
Cuorgnè, *Italy* 32 C4
Cupar, *Canada* 101 C8
Cupar, *U.K.* 14 E5
Cupica, G. de, *Colombia* 120 B2
Ćuprija, *Serbia, Yug.* 21 M11
Curaçá, *Brazil* 122 C4
Curaçao, *Neth. Ant.* 117 D6
Curacautín, *Chile* 128 A2
Curahuara de Carangas, *Bolivia* 124 D4
Curanilahue, *Chile* 126 D1
Curaray →, *Peru* 120 D3
Curatabaca, *Venezuela* 121 B5
Cure →, *France* 25 E10
Curepto, *Chile* 126 D1
Curiapo, *Venezuela* 121 B5
Curicó, *Chile* 126 C1
Curicó □, *Chile* 126 C1
Curicuriari →, *Brazil* 120 D4
Curimatá, *Brazil* 122 D3
Curiplaya, *Colombia* 120 C3
Curitiba, *Brazil* 127 B6
Currabubula, *Australia* 91 E5
Currais Novos, *Brazil* 122 C4
Curralinho, *Brazil* 122 B2
Currant, *U.S.A.* 110 G6
Curraweena, *Australia* 91 E4
Currawilla, *Australia* 90 D3
Current →, *U.S.A.* 109 G9
Currie, *Australia* 90 F3
Currie, *U.S.A.* 110 F6
Currie, Mt., *S. Africa* 85 E4
Currituck Sd., *U.S.A.* 105 G8
Curtea de Argeş, *Romania* 38 D7
Curtis, *Spain* 30 B2
Curtis, *U.S.A.* 108 E4
Curtis Group, *Australia* 90 F4
Curtis I., *Australia* 90 C5
Curuá →, *Pará, Brazil* 121 D7
Curuá →, *Pará, Brazil* 125 B7
Curuá, I., *Brazil* 122 A1
Curuaés →, *Brazil* 125 B7
Curuápanema →, *Brazil* 121 D6
Curuçá, *Brazil* 122 B2
Curuguaty, *Paraguay* 127 A4
Curup, *Indonesia* 56 E2
Curupira, Serra, *S. Amer.* 121 C5
Cururu →, *Brazil* 125 B6
Cururupu, *Brazil* 122 B3
Curuzú Cuatiá, *Argentina* 126 B4
Curvelo, *Brazil* 123 E3
Cushing, *U.S.A.* 109 H6
Cushing, Mt., *Canada* 100 B3
Cusihuiriáchic, *Mexico* 114 B3
Cusna, Monte, *Italy* 32 D7
Cusset, *France* 26 B7
Custer, *U.S.A.* 108 D3
Cut Bank, *U.S.A.* 110 B7
Cutervo, *Peru* 124 B2
Cuthbert, *U.S.A.* 105 K3
Cutler, *U.S.A.* 112 J7
Cutral-Có, *Argentina* 128 A3
Cutro, *Italy* 35 C9
Cuttaburra →, *Australia* 91 D3
Cuttack, *India* 61 J14
Cuvier, C., *Australia* 89 D1
Cuvier I., *N.Z.* 87 G5
Cuxhaven, *Germany* 18 B4
Cuyabeno, *Ecuador* 120 D2
Cuyahoga Falls, *U.S.A.* 106 E3
Cuyapo, *Phil.* 55 D4
Cuyo, *Phil.* 55 F4
Cuyo East Pass, *Phil.* 55 F4
Cuyo West Pass, *Phil.* 55 F4
Cuyuni →, *Guyana* 121 B6
Cuzco, *Bolivia* 124 E4
Cuzco, *Peru* 124 C3
Cuzco □, *Peru* 124 C3
Cwmbran, *U.K.* 13 F4
Cyangugu, *Rwanda* 82 C2
Cyclades = Kikládhes, *Greece* 39 M7
Cygnet, *Australia* 90 G4
Cynthiana, *U.S.A.* 104 F3
Cypress Hills, *Canada* 101 D7
Cyprus ■, *Medit. S.* 37 E12
Cyrenaica, *Libya* 70 C6
Cyrene = Shaḥḥāt, *Libya* 73 B9
Czar, *Canada* 101 C6
Czarne, *Poland* 20 B6
Czechoslovakia ■, *Europe* 20 F7
Czersk, *Poland* 20 B7
Częstochowa, *Poland* 20 E9

D

Da →, *Vietnam* 58 B5
Da Hinggan Ling, *China* 54 B7
Da Lat, *Vietnam* 59 G7
Da Nang, *Vietnam* 58 D7
Da Qaidam, *China* 54 C4
Da Yunhe →, *China* 51 G11
Da'an, *China* 51 B13
Daarlerveen, *Neths.* 16 D9
Dab'a, Râs el, *Egypt* 76 H6
Daba Shan, *China* 52 B7
Dabai, *Nigeria* 79 C6
Dabajuro, *Venezuela* 120 A3
Dabakala, *Ivory C.* 78 D4
Dabeiba, *Colombia* 120 B2
Dabhoi, *India* 62 H5
Dąbie, *Poland* 20 B4
Dabie Shan, *China* 53 B10
Dabo, *Indonesia* 56 E2
Dabola, *Guinea* 78 C2
Dabou, *Ivory C.* 78 D4
Daboya, *Ghana* 79 D4
Dabrowa Tarnówska, *Poland* 20 E10
Dabu, *China* 53 E11
Dabung, *Malaysia* 59 K4
Dabus →, *Ethiopia* 77 E4
Dacato →, *Ethiopia* 77 F5
Dacca = Dhaka, *Bangla.* 63 H14
Dacca = Dhaka □, *Bangla.* 63 G14
Dachau, *Germany* 19 G7
Dadanawa, *Guyana* 121 C6
Daday, *Turkey* 42 F5
Dade City, *U.S.A.* 105 L4
Dades, Oued →, *Morocco* 74 B3
Dadiya, *Nigeria* 79 D7
Dadra and Nagar Haveli □, *India* 60 J8
Dadri = Charkhi Dadri, *India* 62 E7
Dadu, *Pakistan* 62 F2
Dadu He →, *China* 52 C4
Dăeni, *Romania* 38 E11
Daet, *Phil.* 55 D5
Dafang, *China* 52 D5
Dagana, *Senegal* 78 B1
Dagash, *Sudan* 76 D3
Dagestanskiye Ogni, *Russia* 43 E13
Daggett, *U.S.A.* 113 L10
Daghestan Republic □, *Russia* 43 E12
Daghfeli, *Sudan* 76 D3
Dagö = Hiiumaa, *Estonia* 40 B3
Dagu, *China* 51 E9
Daguan, *China* 52 D4
Dagupan, *Phil.* 55 C4
Dahab, *Egypt* 76 B3
Dahlak Kebir, *Ethiopia* 68 D3
Dahlenburg, *Germany* 18 B6
Dahlonega, *U.S.A.* 105 H4
Dahme, *Germany* 18 D9
Dahod, *India* 62 H6
Dahomey = Benin ■, *Africa* 79 D5
Dahong Shan, *China* 53 B9
Dahra, *Senegal* 78 B1
Dahra, Massif de, *Algeria* 75 A5
Dai Hao, *Vietnam* 58 C6
Dai-Sen, *Japan* 49 G6
Dai Shan, *China* 53 B14
Dai Xian, *China* 50 E7
Daicheng, *China* 50 E9
Daimiel, *Spain* 29 F1
Daingean, *Ireland* 15 C4
Dainkog, *China* 52 A1
Daintree, *Australia* 90 B4
Daiō-Misaki, *Japan* 49 G8
Dairût, *Egypt* 76 B3
Daisetsu-Zan, *Japan* 48 C11
Dajarra, *Australia* 90 C2
Dajia, *Taiwan* 53 E13
Dajin Chuan →, *China* 52 B3
Dak Dam, *Cambodia* 58 F6
Dak Nhe, *Vietnam* 58 E6
Dak Pek, *Vietnam* 58 E6
Dak Song, *Vietnam* 59 F6
Dak Sui, *Vietnam* 58 E6
Dakar, *Senegal* 78 C1
Dakhla, *Mauritania* 74 D1
Dakhla, El Wâhât el-, *Egypt* 76 B2
Dakhovskaya, *Russia* 43 D9
Dakingari, *Nigeria* 79 C5
Dakor, *India* 62 H5
Dakoro, *Niger* 79 C6
Dakota City, *U.S.A.* 108 D6
Đakovica, *Serbia, Yug.* 21 N10
Đakovo, *Croatia* 21 K8
Dalaba, *Guinea* 78 C2
Dalachi, *China* 50 F3
Dalai Nur, *China* 50 C9
Dālakī, *Iran* 65 D6
Dalälven, *Sweden* 9 F14
Dalaman, *Turkey* 66 E3
Dalaman →, *Turkey* 66 E3
Dalandzadgad, *Mongolia* 50 C3
Dalarö, *Sweden* 9 G15
Dālbandīn, *Pakistan* 60 E4
Dalbeattie, *U.K.* 14 G5
Dalbosjön, *Sweden* 11 F6
Dalby, *Australia* 91 D5
Dalby, *Sweden* 11 J7
Dalen, *Neths.* 16 C9
Dalen, *Norway* 10 E2
Dalfsen, *Neths.* 16 C8
Dalga, *Egypt* 76 B3
Dalgān, *Iran* 65 E8
Dalhart, *U.S.A.* 109 G3
Dalhousie, *Canada* 99 C6
Dalhousie, *India* 62 C6
Dali, *Shaanxi, China* 50 G5
Dali, *Yunnan, China* 52 E3
Dalian, *China* 51 E11
Daliang Shan, *China* 52 D4
Dalias, *Spain* 29 J2
Daling He →, *China* 51 D11
Dāliyat el Karmel, *Israel* 69 C4

Dergachi

Dalkeith, *U.K.* 14 F5
Dall I., *U.S.A.* 100 C2
Dallarnil, *Australia* 91 D5
Dallas, *Oreg., U.S.A.* 110 D2
Dallas, *Tex., U.S.A.* 109 J6
Dallol, *Ethiopia* 77 E5
Dalmacija = Dalmatia □, *Croatia* 21 M7
Dalmatia □, *Croatia* 21 M7
Dalmellington, *U.K.* 14 F4
Dalnegorsk, *Russia* 45 E14
Dalnerechensk, *Russia* 45 E14
Daloa, *Ivory C.* 78 D3
Dalou Shan, *China* 52 C6
Dalsjöfors, *Sweden* 11 G7
Dalskog, *Sweden* 11 F6
Daltenganj, *India* 63 G11
Dalton, *Canada* 98 C3
Dalton, *Ga., U.S.A.* 105 H3
Dalton, *Mass., U.S.A.* 107 D11
Dalton, *Nebr., U.S.A.* 108 E3
Dalton Iceberg Tongue, *Antarctica* 5 C9
Dalupiri I., *Phil.* 55 B4
Dalvík, *Iceland* 8 D4
Daly →, *Australia* 88 B5
Daly City, *U.S.A.* 112 H4
Daly L., *Canada* 101 B7
Daly Waters, *Australia* 90 B1
Dam Doi, *Vietnam* 59 H5
Dam Ha, *Vietnam* 58 B6
Daman, *India* 60 J8
Dāmaneh, *Iran* 65 C6
Damanhûr, *Egypt* 76 H7
Damanzhuang, *China* 50 E9
Damar, *Indonesia* 57 F7
Damaraland, *Namibia* 84 C2
Damascus = Dimashq, *Syria* 69 B5
Damaturu, *Nigeria* 79 C7
Damāvand, *Iran* 65 C7
Damāvand, Qolleh-ye, *Iran* 65 C7
Damba, *Angola* 80 F3
Dame Marie, *Haiti* 117 C5
Dāmghān, *Iran* 65 B7
Dămienesti, *Romania* 38 C10
Damietta = Dumyât, *Egypt* 76 H7
Daming, *China* 50 F8
Damīr Qābū, *Syria* 64 B4
Dammarie, *France* 24 D8
Dammartin-en-Goële, *France* 25 C9
Dammastock, *Switz.* 23 C6
Damme, *Germany* 18 C4
Damodar →, *India* 63 H12
Damoh, *India* 63 H8
Damous, *Algeria* 75 A5
Dampier, *Australia* 88 D2
Dampier, Selat, *Indonesia* 57 E8
Dampier Arch., *Australia* 88 D2
Damrei, Chuor Phnum, *Cambodia* 59 G4
Damville, *France* 24 D8
Damvillers, *France* 25 C12
Dan-Gulbi, *Nigeria* 79 C6
Dana, *Indonesia* 57 F6
Dana, L., *Canada* 98 B4
Dana, Mt., *U.S.A.* 112 H7
Danakil Depression, *Ethiopia* 77 E5
Danao, *Phil.* 55 F6
Danbury, *U.S.A.* 107 E11
Danby L., *U.S.A.* 111 J6
Dand, *Afghan.* 62 D1
Dandaragan, *Australia* 89 F2
Dandeldhura, *Nepal* 63 E9
Dandeli, *India* 60 M9
Dandenong, *Australia* 91 F4
Dandong, *China* 51 D13
Danfeng, *China* 50 H6
Danforth, *U.S.A.* 99 C6
Dangan Liedao, *China* 53 F10
Danger Is. = Pukapuka, *Cook Is.* 93 J11
Danger Pt., *S. Africa* 84 E2
Dangla, *Ethiopia* 77 E4
Dangora, *Nigeria* 79 C6
Dangrek, Phnom, *Thailand* 58 E5
Dangriga, *Belize* 115 D7
Dangshan, *China* 50 G9
Dangtu, *China* 53 B12
Dangyang, *China* 53 B8
Daniel, *U.S.A.* 110 E8
Daniel's Harbour, *Canada* 99 B8
Danielskuil, *S. Africa* 84 D3
Danielson, *U.S.A.* 107 E13
Danilov, *Russia* 41 B12
Danilovka, *Russia* 41 F14
Daning, *China* 50 F6
Danissa, *Kenya* 82 B5
Danja, *Nigeria* 79 C6
Dankalwa, *Nigeria* 79 C7
Dankama, *Nigeria* 79 C6
Dankhar Gompa, *India* 60 C11
Dankov, *Russia* 41 E11
Danleng, *China* 52 B4
Danlí, *Honduras* 116 D2
Dannemora, *Sweden* 9 F14
Dannemora, *U.S.A.* 107 B11
Dannenberg, *Germany* 18 B7
Dannevirke, *N.Z.* 87 J6
Dannhauser, *S. Africa* 85 D5
Danshui, *Taiwan* 53 E13
Dansville, *U.S.A.* 106 D7
Dantan, *India* 63 J12
Dante, *Somali Rep.* 68 E5
Danvers, *U.S.A.* 107 D14
Danville, *Ill., U.S.A.* 104 E2
Danville, *Ky., U.S.A.* 104 G3
Danville, *Va., U.S.A.* 105 G6
Danyang, *China* 53 B12
Danzhai, *China* 52 D6
Danzig = Gdańsk, *Poland* 20 A8
Dao, *Phil.* 57 B6
Dão →, *Portugal* 30 E2
Dao Xian, *China* 53 E8
Daocheng, *China* 52 C3
Daora, *W. Sahara* 74 C2
Daoud = Aïn Beïda, *Algeria* 75 A6
Daoulas, *France* 24 D2
Dapitan, *Phil.* 55 G5
Dapong, *Togo* 79 C5
Daqing Shan, *China* 50 D6
Daqu Shan, *China* 53 B14
Dar es Salaam, *Tanzania* 82 D4
Dar Mazār, *Iran* 65 D8
Dar'ā, *Syria* 69 C5
Dar'ā □, *Syria* 69 C5
Dārāb, *Iran* 65 D7
Daraj, *Libya* 75 B7
Dārān, *Iran* 65 C6
Daravica, *Serbia, Yug.* 21 N10
Daraw, *Egypt* 76 C3
Dārayyā, *Syria* 69 B5
Darazo, *Nigeria* 79 C7
Darband, *Pakistan* 62 B5
Darband, Kūh-e, *Iran* 65 D8
Darbhanga, *India* 63 F11
Darby, *U.S.A.* 110 C6
Dardanelle, *Ark., U.S.A.* 109 H8
Dardanelle, *Calif., U.S.A.* 112 G7
Dardanelles = Çanakkale Boğazı, *Turkey* 66 C2
Darende, *Turkey* 66 D7
Dārestān, *Iran* 65 D8
Darfo, *Italy* 32 C7
Dârfûr, *Sudan* 73 F9
Dargai, *Pakistan* 62 B4
Dargan Ata, *Uzbekistan* 44 E7
Dargaville, *N.Z.* 87 F4
Darhan Muminggan Lianheqi, *China* 50 D6
Dari, *Sudan* 77 F3
Darién, G. del, *Colombia* 120 B2
Darién, Serranía del, *Colombia* 120 B2
Dariganga, *Mongolia* 50 B7
Darjeeling = Darjiling, *India* 63 F13
Darjiling, *India* 63 F13
Dark Cove, *Canada* 99 C9
Darkan, *Australia* 89 F2
Darkhazīneh, *Iran* 65 D6
Darkot Pass, *Pakistan* 63 A5
Darling →, *Australia* 91 E3
Darling Downs, *Australia* 91 D5
Darling Ra., *Australia* 89 F2
Darlington, *U.K.* 12 C6
Darlington, *S.C., U.S.A.* 105 H6
Darlington, *Wis., U.S.A.* 108 D9
Darlot, L., *Australia* 89 E3
Darłowo, *Poland* 20 A6
Darmstadt, *Germany* 19 F4
Darnah, *Libya* 73 B9
Darnall, *S. Africa* 85 D5
Darnétal, *France* 24 C8
Darney, *France* 25 D13
Darnley, C., *Antarctica* 5 C6
Darnley B., *Canada* 96 B7
Daroca, *Spain* 28 D3
Darr, *Australia* 90 C3
Darr →, *Australia* 90 C3
Darrington, *U.S.A.* 110 B3
Darsser Ort, *Germany* 18 A8
Dart →, *U.K.* 13 G4
Dart, C., *Antarctica* 5 D14
Dartmoor, *U.K.* 13 G4
Dartmouth, *Australia* 90 C3
Dartmouth, *Canada* 99 D7
Dartmouth, *U.K.* 13 G4
Dartmouth, L., *Australia* 91 D4
Dartuch, C., *Spain* 36 B10
Darvaza, *Turkmenistan* 44 E6
Darvel, Teluk, *Malaysia* 57 D5
Darwha, *India* 60 J10
Darwin, *Australia* 88 B5
Darwin, *U.S.A.* 113 J9
Darwin, Mt., *Chile* 128 D3
Darwin River, *Australia* 88 B5
Dās, *U.A.E.* 65 E7
Dashetai, *China* 50 D5
Dashkesan, *Azerbaijan* 43 F12
Dasht, *Iran* 65 B8
Dasht →, *Pakistan* 60 G2
Dasht-e Mārgow, *Afghan.* 60 D3
Dasht-i-Nawar, *Afghan.* 62 C3
Daska, *Pakistan* 62 C6
Dassa-Zoume, *Benin* 79 D5
Dasseneiland, *S. Africa* 84 E2
Datça, *Turkey* 66 E2
Datia, *India* 63 G8
Datian, *China* 53 E11
Datong, *Anhui, China* 53 B11
Datong, *Shanxi, China* 50 D7
Datu, Tanjung, *Indonesia* 56 D3
Datu Piang, *Phil.* 55 H6
Daugava →, *Latvia* 40 C4
Daugavpils, *Latvia* 40 D5
Daule, *Ecuador* 120 D2
Daule →, *Ecuador* 120 D2
Daulpur, *India* 62 F7
Daun, *Germany* 19 E2
Dauphin, *Canada* 101 C8
Dauphin I., *U.S.A.* 105 K1
Dauphin L., *Canada* 101 C9
Dauphiné, *France* 27 C9
Daura, *Borno, Nigeria* 79 C7
Daura, *Kaduna, Nigeria* 79 C6
Dausa, *India* 62 F7
Davangere, *India* 60 M9
Davao, *Phil.* 55 H6
Davao, G. of, *Phil.* 55 H6
Dāvar Panāh, *Iran* 65 E9
Davenport, *Calif., U.S.A.* 112 H4
Davenport, *Iowa, U.S.A.* 108 E9
Davenport, *Wash., U.S.A.* 110 C4
Davenport Downs, *Australia* 90 C3
Davenport Ra., *Australia* 90 C1
David, *Panama* 116 E3
David City, *U.S.A.* 108 E6
David Gorodok, *Belorussia* 40 E5
Davidson, *Canada* 101 C7
Davis, *U.S.A.* 112 G5
Davis Dam, *U.S.A.* 113 K12
Davis Inlet, *Canada* 99 A7
Davis Mts., *U.S.A.* 109 K2
Davis Sea, *Antarctica* 5 C7
Davis Str., *N. Amer.* 97 B14
Davos, *Switz.* 23 C9
Davy L., *Canada* 101 B7
Dawa →, *Ethiopia* 77 G5
Dawaki, *Bauchi, Nigeria* 79 D6
Dawaki, *Kano, Nigeria* 79 C6
Dawes Ra., *Australia* 90 C5
Dawson, *Canada* 96 B6
Dawson, *Ga., U.S.A.* 105 K3
Dawson, *N. Dak., U.S.A.* 108 B5
Dawson, I., *Chile* 128 D2
Dawson Creek, *Canada* 100 B4
Dawson Inlet, *Canada* 101 A10
Dawson Ra., *Australia* 90 C4
Dawu, *China* 52 B3
Dax, *France* 26 E2
Daxi, *Taiwan* 53 E13
Daxian, *China* 52 B6
Daxin, *China* 52 F6
Daxindian, *China* 51 F11
Daxinggou, *China* 51 C15
Daxue Shan, *Sichuan, China* 52 B3
Daxue Shan, *Yunnan, China* 52 F2
Dayao, *China* 52 E3
Daye, *China* 53 B10
Dayi, *China* 52 B4
Daylesford, *Australia* 91 F3
Dayong, *China* 53 C8
Dayr az Zawr, *Syria* 64 C4
Daysland, *Canada* 100 C6
Dayton, *Nev., U.S.A.* 112 F7
Dayton, *Ohio, U.S.A.* 104 F3
Dayton, *Pa., U.S.A.* 106 F5
Dayton, *Tenn., U.S.A.* 105 H3
Dayton, *Wash., U.S.A.* 110 C4
Daytona Beach, *U.S.A.* 105 L5
Dayu, *China* 53 E10
Dayville, *U.S.A.* 110 D4
Dazhu, *China* 52 B6
Dazu, *China* 52 C5
De Aar, *S. Africa* 84 E3
De Bilt, *Neths.* 16 D6
De Funiak Springs, *U.S.A.* 105 K2
De Grey, *Australia* 88 D2
De Grey →, *Australia* 88 D2
De Kalb, *U.S.A.* 108 E10
De Koog, *Neths.* 16 B5
De Land, *U.S.A.* 105 L5
De Leon, *U.S.A.* 109 J5
De Panne, *Belgium* 17 F1
De Pere, *U.S.A.* 104 C1
De Queen, *U.S.A.* 109 H7
De Quincy, *U.S.A.* 109 K8
De Ridder, *U.S.A.* 109 K8
De Rijp, *Neths.* 16 C5
De Smet, *U.S.A.* 108 C6
De Soto, *U.S.A.* 108 F9
De Tour, *U.S.A.* 104 C4
De Witt, *U.S.A.* 109 H9
Dead Sea, *Asia* 69 D4
Deadwood, *U.S.A.* 108 C3
Deadwood L., *Canada* 100 B3
Deakin, *Australia* 89 F4
Deal, *U.K.* 13 F9
Deal I., *Australia* 90 F4
Dealesville, *S. Africa* 84 D4
De'an, *China* 53 C10
Dean, Forest of, *U.K.* 13 F5
Deán Funes, *Argentina* 126 C3
Dearborn, *U.S.A.* 98 D3
Dease →, *Canada* 100 B3
Dease L., *Canada* 100 B2
Dease Lake, *Canada* 100 B2
Death Valley, *U.S.A.* 113 J10
Death Valley Junction, *U.S.A.* 113 J10
Death Valley Nat. Monument, *U.S.A.* 113 J10
Deauville, *France* 24 C7
Deba Habe, *Nigeria* 79 C7
Debaltsevo, *Ukraine* 42 B8
Debao, *China* 52 F6
Debar, *Macedonia, Yug.* 39 H3
Debden, *Canada* 101 C7
Debdou, *Morocco* 75 B4
Dębica, *Poland* 20 E11
Dęblin, *Poland* 20 D11
Débo, L., *Mali* 78 B4
Debolt, *Canada* 100 B5
Deborah East, L., *Australia* 89 F2
Deborah West, L., *Australia* 89 F2
Debre Birhan, *Ethiopia* 77 F4
Debre Markos, *Ethiopia* 77 E4
Debre May, *Ethiopia* 77 E4
Debre Sina, *Ethiopia* 77 F4
Debre Tabor, *Ethiopia* 77 E4
Debre Zebit, *Ethiopia* 77 E4
Debrecen, *Hungary* 21 H11
Dečani, *Serbia, Yug.* 21 N10
Decatur, *Ala., U.S.A.* 105 H2
Decatur, *Ga., U.S.A.* 105 J3
Decatur, *Ill., U.S.A.* 108 F10
Decatur, *Ind., U.S.A.* 104 E3
Decatur, *Tex., U.S.A.* 109 J6
Decazeville, *France* 26 D6
Deccan, *India* 60 M10
Deception L., *Canada* 101 B8
Dechang, *China* 52 D4
Děčín, *Czech.* 20 E4
Decize, *France* 25 F10
Deckerville, *U.S.A.* 106 C2
Decollatura, *Italy* 35 C9
Decorah, *U.S.A.* 108 D9
Dedéagach = Alexandroúpolis, *Greece* 39 J8
Dedegöl Dağları, *Turkey* 66 E4
Dedemsvaart, *Neths.* 16 C8
Dedham, *U.S.A.* 107 D13
Dedilovo, *Russia* 41 E10
Dédougou, *Burkina Faso* 78 C4
Dedza, *Malawi* 83 E3
Dee →, *Clwyd, U.K.* 12 D4
Dee →, *Gramp., U.K.* 14 D6
Deep B., *Canada* 100 A5
Deep Well, *Australia* 90 C1
Deepwater, *Australia* 91 D5
Deer →, *Canada* 101 B10
Deer Lake, *Nfld., Canada* 99 C8
Deer Lake, *Ont., Canada* 101 C10
Deer Lodge, *U.S.A.* 110 C7
Deer Park, *U.S.A.* 110 C5
Deer River, *U.S.A.* 108 B8
Deeral, *Australia* 90 B4
Deerdepoort, *S. Africa* 84 C4
Deerlijk, *Belgium* 17 G2
Deferiet, *U.S.A.* 107 B9
Defiance, *U.S.A.* 104 E3
Dêgê, *China* 52 B2
Degebe →, *Portugal* 31 G3
Degeh Bur, *Ethiopia* 68 F3
Degema, *Nigeria* 79 E6
Degersheim, *Switz.* 23 B8
Deggendorf, *Germany* 19 G8
Deh Bīd, *Iran* 65 D7
Deh-e Shīr, *Iran* 65 D7
Dehaj, *Iran* 65 D7
Dehdez, *Iran* 65 D6
Dehestān, *Iran* 65 D7
Dehgolān, *Iran* 64 C5
Dehi Titan, *Afghan.* 60 C3
Dehibat, *Tunisia* 75 B7
Dehlorān, *Iran* 64 C5
Dehnow-e Kūhestān, *Iran* 65 E8
Dehra Dun, *India* 62 D8
Dehri, *India* 63 G11
Dehua, *China* 53 E12
Dehui, *China* 51 B13
Deinze, *Belgium* 17 G3
Dej, *Romania* 38 B6
Dejiang, *China* 52 C7
Dekemhare, *Ethiopia* 77 D4
Dekese, *Zaïre* 80 E4
Del Mar, *U.S.A.* 113 N9
Del Norte, *U.S.A.* 111 H10
Del Rio, *U.S.A.* 109 L4
Delai, *Sudan* 76 D4
Delano, *U.S.A.* 113 K7
Delareyville, *S. Africa* 84 D4
Delavan, *U.S.A.* 108 D10
Delaware, *U.S.A.* 104 E4
Delaware □, *U.S.A.* 104 F8
Delaware →, *U.S.A.* 104 F8
Delaware B., *U.S.A.* 103 C12
Delegate, *Australia* 91 F4
Delémont, *Switz.* 22 B4
Delft, *Neths.* 16 D4
Delfzijl, *Neths.* 16 B9
Delgado, C., *Mozam.* 83 E5
Delgerhet, *Mongolia* 50 B6
Delgo, *Sudan* 76 C3
Delhi, *Canada* 106 D4
Delhi, *India* 62 E7
Delhi, *U.S.A.* 107 D10
Delia, *Canada* 100 C6
Delice, *Turkey* 66 D6
Delice →, *Turkey* 66 D6
Delicias, *Mexico* 114 B3
Delījān, *Iran* 65 C6
Delitzsch, *Germany* 18 D8
Dell City, *U.S.A.* 111 L11
Dell Rapids, *U.S.A.* 108 D6
Delle, *France* 25 E14
Dellys, *Algeria* 75 A5
Delmar, *U.S.A.* 107 D11
Delmenhorst, *Germany* 18 B4
Delmiro Gouveia, *Brazil* 122 C4
Delnice, *Croatia* 33 C11
Delong, Ostrova, *Russia* 45 B15
Deloraine, *Australia* 90 G4
Deloraine, *Canada* 101 D8
Delphi, *U.S.A.* 104 E2
Delphos, *U.S.A.* 104 E3
Delportshoop, *S. Africa* 84 D3
Delray Beach, *U.S.A.* 105 M5
Delsbo, *Sweden* 10 C10
Delta, *Colo., U.S.A.* 111 G9
Delta, *Utah, U.S.A.* 110 G7
Delta Amacuro □, *Venezuela* 121 B5
Delungra, *Australia* 91 D5
Delvina, *Albania* 39 K3
Delvinákion, *Greece* 39 K3
Demanda, Sierra de la, *Spain* 28 C1
Demba, *Zaïre* 80 F4
Dembecha, *Ethiopia* 77 E4
Dembi, *Ethiopia* 77 F4
Dembia, *Zaïre* 82 B2
Dembidolo, *Ethiopia* 77 F3
Demer →, *Belgium* 17 G5
Demerara □, *Guyana* 121 B6
Demidov, *Russia* 40 D7
Deming, *N. Mex., U.S.A.* 111 K10
Deming, *Wash., U.S.A.* 112 B4
Demini →, *Brazil* 121 D5
Demirci, *Turkey* 66 D3
Demirköy, *Turkey* 66 C2
Demmin, *Germany* 18 B9
Demnate, *Morocco* 74 B3
Demonte, *Italy* 32 D4
Demopolis, *U.S.A.* 105 J2
Dempo, *Indonesia* 56 E2
Demyansk, *Russia* 40 C8
Den Burg, *Neths.* 16 B5
Den Chai, *Thailand* 58 D3
Den Dungen, *Neths.* 17 E6
Den Haag = 's-Gravenhage, *Neths.* 16 D4
Den Ham, *Neths.* 16 D8
Den Helder, *Neths.* 16 C5
Den Hulst, *Neths.* 16 C8
Den Oever, *Neths.* 16 C6
Denain, *France* 25 B10
Denair, *U.S.A.* 112 H6
Denau, *Uzbekistan* 44 F7
Denbigh, *U.K.* 12 D4
Dendang, *Indonesia* 56 E3
Dender →, *Belgium* 17 F4
Denderhoutem, *Belgium* 17 G4
Denderleeuw, *Belgium* 17 G4
Dendermonde, *Belgium* 17 F4
Deneba, *Ethiopia* 77 F4
Denekamp, *Neths.* 16 D10
Deng Xian, *China* 53 A9
Dengchuan, *China* 52 E3
Denge, *Nigeria* 79 C6
Dengfeng, *China* 50 G7
Dengi, *Nigeria* 79 D6
Dengkou, *China* 50 D4
Denham, *Australia* 89 E1
Denham Ra., *Australia* 90 C4
Denham Sd., *Australia* 89 E1
Denia, *Spain* 29 G5
Denial B., *Australia* 91 E1
Deniliquin, *Australia* 91 F3
Denison, *Iowa, U.S.A.* 108 D7
Denison, *Tex., U.S.A.* 109 J6
Denison Plains, *Australia* 88 C4
Denizli, *Turkey* 66 E3
Denizli □, *Turkey* 66 E3
Denman Glacier, *Antarctica* 5 C7
Denmark, *Australia* 89 F2
Denmark ■, *Europe* 11 J3
Denmark Str., *Atl. Oc.* 4 C6
Dennison, *U.S.A.* 106 F3
Denpasar, *Indonesia* 56 F5
Denton, *Mont., U.S.A.* 110 C9
Denton, *Tex., U.S.A.* 109 J6
D'Entrecasteaux, Pt., *Australia* 89 F2
Dents du Midi, *Switz.* 22 D3
Denu, *Ghana* 79 D5
Denver, *U.S.A.* 108 F2
Denver City, *U.S.A.* 109 J3
Deoband, *India* 62 E7
Deoghar, *India* 63 G12
Deolali, *India* 60 K8
Deoli = Devli, *India* 62 G6
Deoria, *India* 63 F10
Deosai Mts., *Pakistan* 63 B6
Deping, *China* 51 F9
Deposit, *U.S.A.* 107 D9
Depot Springs, *Australia* 89 E3
Deputatskiy, *Russia* 45 C14
Dêqên, *China* 52 C2
Deqing, *China* 53 F8
Dera Ghazi Khan, *Pakistan* 62 D4
Dera Ismail Khan, *Pakistan* 62 D4
Derbent, *Russia* 43 E13
Derby, *Australia* 88 C3
Derby, *U.K.* 12 E6
Derby, *Conn., U.S.A.* 107 E11
Derby, *N.Y., U.S.A.* 106 D6
Derbyshire □, *U.K.* 12 E6
Dereli, *Turkey* 67 C8
Derg →, *U.K.* 15 B4
Derg, L., *Ireland* 15 D3
Dergachi, *Ukraine* 42 A7

Dergaon

Dergaon, *India* 61 F19
Derik, *Turkey* 67 E9
Derinkuyu, *Turkey* 66 D6
Dernieres Isles, *U.S.A.* 109 L9
Dêrong, *China* 52 C2
Derry = Londonderry, *U.K.* 15 B4
Derryveagh Mts., *Ireland* 15 B3
Derudub, *Sudan* 76 D4
Derval, *France* 24 E5
Dervéni, *Greece* 39 L5
Derwent, *Canada* 101 C6
Derwent →, *Derby, U.K.* 12 E6
Derwent →, *N. Yorks., U.K.* 12 D7
Derwent Water, *U.K.* 12 C4
Des Moines, *Iowa, U.S.A.* 108 E8
Des Moines, *N. Mex., U.S.A.* 109 G3
Des Moines →, *U.S.A.* 108 E9
Desaguadero →, *Argentina* 126 C2
Desaguadero →, *Bolivia* 124 D4
Descanso, Pta., *Mexico* 113 N9
Descartes, *France* 26 B4
Deschaillons, *Canada* 99 C5
Descharme →, *Canada* 101 B7
Deschutes →, *U.S.A.* 110 D3
Dese, *Ethiopia* 68 E2
Deseado, C., *Chile* 128 D2
Desenzano del Gardo, *Italy* 32 C7
Desert Center, *U.S.A.* 113 M11
Desert Hot Springs, *U.S.A.* 113 M10
Désirade, I., *Guadeloupe* 117 C7
Deskenatlata L., *Canada* 100 A6
Desna →, *Ukraine* 40 F7
Desnătui →, *Romania* 38 E6
Desolación, I., *Chile* 128 D2
Despeñaperros, Paso, *Spain* 29 G1
Despotovac, *Serbia, Yug.* 21 L11
Dessau, *Germany* 18 D8
Dessel, *Belgium* 17 F6
Dessye = Dese, *Ethiopia* 68 E2
D'Estrees B., *Australia* 91 F2
Desuri, *India* 62 G5
Desvres, *France* 25 B8
Det Udom, *Thailand* 58 E5
Dete, *Zimbabwe* 83 F2
Detinja →, *Serbia, Yug.* 21 M9
Detmold, *Germany* 18 D4
Detour Pt., *U.S.A.* 104 C2
Detroit, *Mich., U.S.A.* 98 D3
Detroit, *Tex., U.S.A.* 109 J7
Detroit Lakes, *U.S.A.* 108 B7
Deurne, *Belgium* 17 F4
Deurne, *Neths.* 17 F7
Deutsche Bucht, *Germany* 18 A4
Deutschlandsberg, *Austria* 21 J5
Deux-Sèvres □, *France* 24 F6
Deva, *Romania* 38 D5
Devakottai, *India* 60 Q11
Devaprayag, *India* 63 D8
Dévaványa, *Hungary* 21 H10
Deveci Dağı, *Turkey* 42 F7
Deveci Dağları, *Turkey* 66 C6
Develi, *Turkey* 66 D6
Deventer, *Neths.* 16 D8
Deveron →, *U.K.* 14 D6
Devgadh Bariya, *India* 62 H5
Devils Den, *U.S.A.* 112 K7
Devils Lake, *U.S.A.* 108 A5
Devils Paw, *Canada* 100 B2
Devizes, *U.K.* 13 F6
Devli, *India* 62 G6
Devnya, *Bulgaria* 38 F10
Devolii →, *Albania* 39 J3
Devon, *Canada* 100 C6
Devon □, *U.K.* 13 G4
Devon I., *Canada* 4 B3
Devonport, *Australia* 90 G4
Devonport, *N.Z.* 87 G5
Devonport, *U.K.* 13 G3
Devrek, *Turkey* 66 C4
Devrekâni, *Turkey* 66 C5
Devrez →, *Turkey* 66 C6
Dewas, *India* 62 H7
Dewetsdorp, *S. Africa* 84 D4
Dewsbury, *U.K.* 12 D6
Dexing, *China* 53 C11
Dexter, *Mo., U.S.A.* 109 G9
Dexter, *N. Mex., U.S.A.* 109 J2
Dey-Dey, L., *Australia* 89 E5
Deyang, *China* 52 B5
Deyhūk, *Iran* 65 C8
Deyyer, *Iran* 65 E6
Dezadeash L., *Canada* 100 A1
Dezfūl, *Iran* 65 C6
Dezhneva, Mys, *Russia* 45 C19
Dezhou, *China* 50 F9
Dháfni, *Greece* 37 D7
Dhahaban, *Si. Arabia* 76 C4
Dhahiriya = Aẓ Ẓāhirīyah, *Jordan* 69 D3
Dhahran = Aẓ Ẓahrān, *Si. Arabia* 65 E6
Dhaka, *Bangla.* 63 H14
Dhaka □, *Bangla.* 63 G14
Dhali, *Cyprus* 37 D12
Dhamar, *Yemen* 68 E3
Dhamási, *Greece* 39 K5
Dhampur, *India* 63 E8
Dhamtari, *India* 61 J12
Dhanbad, *India* 63 H12
Dhangarhi, *Nepal* 61 E12
Dhankuta, *Nepal* 63 F12
Dhar, *India* 62 H6
Dharampur, *India* 62 H6
Dharamsala = Dharmsala, *India* 62 C7
Dharmapuri, *India* 60 N11
Dharmsala, *India* 62 C7
Dharwad, *India* 60 M9
Dharwar, *India* 60 M9
Dhaulagiri, *Nepal* 63 E10
Dhebar, L., *India* 62 G6
Dheftera, *Cyprus* 37 D12
Dhenkanal, *India* 61 J14
Dhenoúsa, *Greece* 39 M8
Dherinia, *Cyprus* 37 D12
Dheskáti, *Greece* 39 K4
Dhespotikó, *Greece* 39 N7
Dhestina, *Greece* 39 L5
Dhiarrizos →, *Cyprus* 37 E11
Dhībān, *Jordan* 69 D4
Dhíkti Óros, *Greece* 37 D7
Dhimitsána, *Greece* 39 M5
Dhírfis, *Greece* 39 L6
Dhodhekánisos, *Greece* 39 N10
Dholiana, *Greece* 39 K3
Dholka, *India* 62 H5
Dhoraji, *India* 62 J4
Dhoxáton, *Greece* 39 H7
Dhráhstis, Ákra, *Greece* 37 A3
Dhrangadhra, *India* 62 H4
Dhrápanon, Ákra, *Greece* 37 D6
Dhrol, *India* 62 H4
Dhuburi, *India* 61 F16
Dhule, *India* 60 J9
Dhut →, *Somali Rep.* 68 E5
Di Linh, *Vietnam* 59 G7
Di Linh, Cao Nguyen, *Vietnam* 59 G7
Día, *Greece* 37 D7
Diablo, Mt., *U.S.A.* 112 H5
Diablo Range, *U.S.A.* 112 J5
Diafarabé, *Mali* 78 C4
Diala, *Mali* 78 C3
Dialakoro, *Mali* 78 C3
Diallassagou, *Mali* 78 C4
Diamante, *Argentina* 126 C3
Diamante →, *Argentina* 126 C2
Diamantina, *Brazil* 123 E3
Diamantina →, *Australia* 91 D2
Diamantino, *Brazil* 125 C6
Diamond Harbour, *India* 63 H13
Diamond Is., *Australia* 90 B5
Diamond Mts., *U.S.A.* 110 G6
Diamond Springs, *U.S.A.* 112 G6
Diamondville, *U.S.A.* 110 F8
Dianbai, *China* 53 G8
Diancheng, *China* 53 G8
Diano Marina, *Italy* 32 E5
Dianópolis, *Brazil* 123 D2
Dianra, *Ivory C.* 78 D3
Diapaga, *Burkina Faso* 79 C5
Diapangou, *Burkina Faso* 79 C5
Diariguila, *Guinea* 78 C2
Dībā, *Oman* 65 E8
Dibaya, *Zaïre* 80 F4
Dibaya-Lubue, *Zaïre* 80 E3
Dibbi, *Ethiopia* 68 G3
Dibete, *Botswana* 84 C4
Dibrugarh, *India* 61 F19
Dickinson, *U.S.A.* 108 B3
Dickson, *U.S.A.* 105 G2
Dickson City, *U.S.A.* 107 E9
Dicomano, *Italy* 33 E8
Didam, *Neths.* 16 E8
Didesa, W. →, *Ethiopia* 77 E4
Didiéni, *Mali* 78 C3
Didsbury, *Canada* 100 C6
Didwana, *India* 62 F6
Die, *France* 27 D9
Diébougou, *Burkina Faso* 78 C4
Diefenbaker L., *Canada* 101 C7
Diego Garcia, *Ind. Oc.* 3 E13
Diekirch, *Lux.* 17 J8
Diélette, *France* 24 C5
Diéma, *Mali* 78 C3
Diémbéring, *Senegal* 78 C1
Diemen, *Neths.* 16 D5
Dien Ban, *Vietnam* 58 E7
Dien Bien, *Vietnam* 58 B4
Dien Khanh, *Vietnam* 59 F7
Diepenbeek, *Belgium* 17 G6
Diepenheim, *Neths.* 16 D9
Diepenveen, *Neths.* 16 D8
Diepholz, *Germany* 18 C4
Diepoldsau, *Switz.* 23 B9
Dieppe, *France* 24 C8
Dieren, *Neths.* 16 D8
Dierks, *U.S.A.* 109 H7
Diessen, *Neths.* 17 F6
Diessenhofen, *Switz.* 23 A7
Diest, *Belgium* 17 G6
Dietikon, *Switz.* 23 B6
Dieulefit, *France* 27 D9
Dieuze, *France* 25 D13
Diever, *Neths.* 16 C8
Differdange, *Lux.* 17 J7
Dig, *India* 62 F7
Digba, *Zaïre* 82 B2
Digby, *Canada* 99 D6
Digges, *Canada* 101 B10
Digges Is., *Canada* 97 B12
Dighinala, *Bangla.* 61 H18
Dighton, *U.S.A.* 108 F4
Digne, *France* 27 D10
Digoin, *France* 26 B7
Digor, *Turkey* 67 C10
Digos, *Phil.* 55 H6
Digranes, *Iceland* 8 C6
Digul →, *Indonesia* 57 F9
Dihang →, *India* 61 F19
Dīhōk, *Iraq* 64 B3
Dijlah, Nahr →, *Asia* 64 D5
Dijle →, *Belgium* 17 G5
Dijon, *France* 25 E12
Dikala, *Sudan* 77 G3
Dikkil, *Djibouti* 77 E5
Dikomu di Kai, *Botswana* 84 C3
Diksmuide, *Belgium* 17 F1
Dikson, *Russia* 44 B9
Dikwa, *Nigeria* 79 C7
Dila, *Ethiopia* 77 F4
Dilbeek, *Belgium* 17 G4
Dili, *Indonesia* 57 F7
Dilizhan, *Armenia* 43 F11
Dillenburg, *Germany* 18 E4
Dilley, *U.S.A.* 109 L5
Dilling, *Sudan* 77 E2
Dillingen, *Germany* 19 G6
Dillingham, *U.S.A.* 96 C4
Dillon, *Canada* 101 B7
Dillon, *Mont., U.S.A.* 110 D7
Dillon, *S.C., U.S.A.* 105 H6
Dillon →, *Canada* 101 B7
Dilolo, *Zaïre* 80 G4
Dilsen, *Belgium* 17 F7
Dilston, *Australia* 90 G4
Dimas, *Mexico* 114 C3
Dimashq, *Syria* 69 B5
Dimashq □, *Syria* 69 B5
Dimbaza, *S. Africa* 85 E4
Dimbokro, *Ivory C.* 78 D4
Dimboola, *Australia* 91 F3
Dîmbovița →, *Romania* 38 E9
Dîmbovnic →, *Romania* 38 E8
Dimbulah, *Australia* 90 B4
Dimitrovgrad, *Bulgaria* 39 G8
Dimitrovgrad, *Russia* 41 D16
Dimitrovgrad, *Serbia, Yug.* 21 M12
Dimitrovo = Pernik, *Bulgaria* 38 G6
Dimmitt, *U.S.A.* 109 H3
Dimo, *Sudan* 77 F2
Dimona, *Israel* 69 D4
Dimovo, *Bulgaria* 38 F5
Dinagat, *Phil.* 55 F6
Dinajpur, *Bangla.* 61 G16
Dinan, *France* 24 D4
Dīnān Āb, *Iran* 65 C8
Dinant, *Belgium* 17 H5
Dinapur, *India* 63 G11
Dinar, *Turkey* 66 D4
Dinara Planina, *Croatia* 33 E13
Dinard, *France* 24 D4
Dinaric Alps = Dinara Planina, *Croatia* 33 E13
Dinder, Nahr ed →, *Sudan* 77 E3
Dindigul, *India* 60 P11
Ding Xian, *China* 50 E8
Dingalan, *Phil.* 55 D4
Dingbian, *China* 50 F4
Dingelstädt, *Germany* 18 D6
Dinghai, *China* 53 B14
Dingle, *Ireland* 15 D1
Dingle B., *Ireland* 15 D1
Dingmans Ferry, *U.S.A.* 107 E10
Dingnan, *China* 53 E10
Dingo, *Australia* 90 C4
Dingolfing, *Germany* 19 G8
Dingtao, *China* 50 G8
Dinguiraye, *Guinea* 78 C2
Dingwall, *U.K.* 14 D4
Dingxi, *China* 50 G3
Dingxiang, *China* 50 E7
Dingyuan, *China* 53 A11
Dinh, Mui, *Vietnam* 59 G7
Dinh Lap, *Vietnam* 58 B6
Dinkel →, *Neths.* 16 D9
Dinokwe, *Botswana* 84 C4
Dinosaur National Monument, *U.S.A.* 110 F9
Dinslaken, *Germany* 17 E9
Dintel →, *Neths.* 17 E4
Dinteloord, *Neths.* 17 E4
Dinuba, *U.S.A.* 111 H4
Dinxperlo, *Neths.* 16 E9
Diósgyör, *Hungary* 21 G10
Diourbel, *Senegal* 78 C1
Diplo, *Pakistan* 62 G3
Dipolog, *Phil.* 55 G5
Dipșa, *Romania* 38 C7
Dir, *Pakistan* 60 B7
Diré, *Mali* 78 B4
Dire Dawa, *Ethiopia* 68 F3
Diriamba, *Nic.* 116 D2
Dirico, *Angola* 81 H4
Dirk Hartog I., *Australia* 89 E1
Dirranbandi, *Australia* 91 D4
Disa, *India* 62 G5
Disa, *Sudan* 77 E3
Disappointment, C., *U.S.A.* 110 C1
Disappointment, L., *Australia* 88 D3
Disaster B., *Australia* 91 F4
Discovery B., *Australia* 91 F3
Disentis, *Switz.* 23 C7
Dishna, *Egypt* 76 B3
Disina, *Nigeria* 79 C6
Disko, *Greenland* 4 C5
Disko Bugt, *Greenland* 4 C5
Disna →, *Belorussia* 40 D6
Dison, *Belgium* 17 G7
Disteghil Sar, *Pakistan* 63 A6
Distrito Federal □, *Brazil* 123 E2
Distrito Federal □, *Venezuela* 120 A4
Disûq, *Egypt* 76 H7
Diu, *India* 62 J4
Dīvāndarreh, *Iran* 64 C5
Dives →, *France* 24 C6
Dives-sur-Mer, *France* 24 C6
Divichi, *Azerbaijan* 43 F13
Divide, *U.S.A.* 110 D7
Dividing Ra., *Australia* 89 E2
Divinópolis, *Brazil* 123 F3
Divisões, Serra dos, *Brazil* 123 E1
Divnoye, *Russia* 43 D10
Divo, *Ivory C.* 78 D3
Divriği, *Turkey* 67 D8
Dīwāl Kol, *Afghan.* 62 B2
Dixie Mt., *U.S.A.* 112 F6
Dixon, *Calif., U.S.A.* 112 G5
Dixon, *Ill., U.S.A.* 108 E10
Dixon, *Mont., U.S.A.* 110 C6
Dixon, *N. Mex., U.S.A.* 111 H11
Dixon Entrance, *U.S.A.* 100 C2
Dixonville, *Canada* 100 B5
Diyadin, *Turkey* 67 D10
Diyarbakır, *Turkey* 67 E9
Diyarbakir □, *Turkey* 67 E9
Djado, *Niger* 73 D7
Djakarta = Jakarta, *Indonesia* 57 G12
Djamâa, *Algeria* 75 B6
Djamba, *Angola* 84 B1
Djambala, *Congo* 80 E2
Djanet, *Algeria* 75 D6
Djawa = Jawa, *Indonesia* 57 G14
Djebiniana, *Tunisia* 75 A7
Djelfa, *Algeria* 75 B5
Djema, *C.A.R.* 82 A2
Djendel, *Algeria* 75 A5
Djeneïene, *Tunisia* 75 B7
Djenné, *Mali* 78 C4
Djenoun, Garet el, *Algeria* 75 C6
Djerba, *Tunisia* 75 B7
Djerba, I. de, *Tunisia* 73 B7
Djerid, Chott, *Tunisia* 75 B6
Djibo, *Burkina Faso* 79 C4
Djibouti, *Djibouti* 68 E3
Djibouti ■, *Africa* 68 E3
Djolu, *Zaïre* 80 D4
Djougou, *Benin* 79 D5
Djoum, *Cameroon* 80 D2
Djourab, *Chad* 73 E8
Djugu, *Zaïre* 82 B3
Djúpivogur, *Iceland* 8 D6
Djursholm, *Sweden* 10 E12
Djursland, *Denmark* 11 H4
Dmitriev-Lgovskiy, *Russia* 40 E9
Dmitriya Lapteva, Proliv, *Russia* 45 B15
Dmitrov, *Russia* 41 C10
Dmitrovsk-Orlovskiy, *Russia* 40 E9
Dnepr →, *Ukraine* 42 C5
Dneprodzerzhinsk, *Ukraine* 42 B6
Dneprodzerzhinskoye Vdkhr., *Ukraine* 42 B6
Dnepropetrovsk, *Ukraine* 42 B6
Dneprorudnoye, *Ukraine* 42 C6
Dnestr →, *Europe* 42 C4
Dnestrovski = Belgorod, *Russia* 41 F10
Dnieper = Dnepr →, *Ukraine* 42 C5
Dniester = Dnestr →, *Europe* 42 C4
Dno, *Russia* 40 C6
Doan Hung, *Vietnam* 58 B5
Doba, *Chad* 73 G8
Dobbiaco, *Italy* 33 B9
Dobbyn, *Australia* 90 B3
Döbeln, *Germany* 18 D9
Doberai, Jazirah, *Indonesia* 57 E8
Dobiegniew, *Poland* 20 C5
Doblas, *Argentina* 126 D3
Dobo, *Indonesia* 57 F8
Doboj, *Bos.-H., Yug.* 21 L8
Dobra, *Dîmbovita, Romania* 38 E8
Dobra, *Hunedoara, Romania* 38 D5
Dobreta-Turnu-Severin, *Romania* 38 E5
Dobrinishta, *Bulgaria* 39 H6
Dobrodzień, *Poland* 20 E8
Dobropole, *Ukraine* 42 B7
Dobruja, *Romania* 38 E11
Dobrush, *Belorussia* 40 E7
Dobtong, *Sudan* 77 F3
Doc, Mui, *Vietnam* 58 D6
Doce →, *Brazil* 123 E4
Doda, *India* 63 C6
Dodecanese = Dhodhekánisos, *Greece* 39 N10
Dodewaard, *Neths.* 16 E7
Dodge Center, *U.S.A.* 108 C8
Dodge City, *U.S.A.* 109 G5
Dodge L., *Canada* 101 B7
Dodgeville, *U.S.A.* 108 D9
Dodo, *Sudan* 77 F2
Dodola, *Ethiopia* 77 F4
Dodoma, *Tanzania* 82 D4
Dodoma □, *Tanzania* 82 D4
Dodsland, *Canada* 101 C7
Dodson, *U.S.A.* 110 B9
Doesburg, *Neths.* 16 D8
Doetinchem, *Neths.* 16 E8
Dog Creek, *Canada* 100 C4
Dog L., *Man., Canada* 101 C9
Dog L., *Ont., Canada* 98 C2
Doğanşehir, *Turkey* 67 D7
Dogger Bank, *N. Sea* 6 E6
Dogi, *Afghan.* 60 C3
Dogliani, *Italy* 32 D4
Dogondoutchi, *Niger* 79 C5
Dogran, *Pakistan* 62 D5
Doğubayazıt, *Turkey* 67 D11
Doguéraoua, *Niger* 79 C6
Dohazari, *Bangla.* 61 H18
Doi, *Indonesia* 57 D7
Doi Luang, *Thailand* 58 C3
Doi Saket, *Thailand* 58 C2
Doig →, *Canada* 100 B4
Dois Irmãos, Sa., *Brazil* 122 C3
Dokka, *Norway* 9 F11
Dokka →, *Norway* 10 D4
Dokkum, *Neths.* 16 B7
Dokkumer Ee →, *Neths.* 16 B7
Dokri, *Pakistan* 62 F3
Dol-de-Bretagne, *France* 24 D5
Doland, *U.S.A.* 108 C5
Dolbeau, *Canada* 99 C5
Dole, *France* 25 E12
Doleib, Wadi →, *Sudan* 77 E3
Dolgellau, *U.K.* 12 E4
Dolgelley = Dolgellau, *U.K.* 12 E4
Dolginovo, *Belorussia* 40 D5
Dolianova, *Italy* 34 C2
Dolinskaya, *Ukraine* 42 B5
Dollart, *Neths.* 16 B10
Dolna Banya, *Bulgaria* 38 G6
Dolni Dŭbnik, *Bulgaria* 38 F7
Dolo, *Ethiopia* 77 G5
Dolo, *Italy* 33 C9
Dolomites = Dolomiti, *Italy* 33 B8
Dolomiti, *Italy* 33 B8
Dolores, *Argentina* 126 D4
Dolores, *Uruguay* 126 C4
Dolores, *U.S.A.* 111 H9
Dolores →, *U.S.A.* 111 G9
Dolphin, C., *Falk. Is.* 128 D5
Dolphin and Union Str., *Canada* 96 B8
Dom, *Switz.* 22 D5
Dom Joaquim, *Brazil* 123 E3
Dom Pedrito, *Brazil* 127 C5
Dom Pedro, *Brazil* 122 B3
Doma, *Nigeria* 79 D6
Domaniç, *Turkey* 66 D3
Domasi, *Malawi* 83 F4
Domat Ems, *Switz.* 23 C8
Domazlice, *Czech.* 20 F2
Dombarovskiy, *Russia* 44 D6
Dombås, *Norway* 9 E10
Dombasle-sur-Meurthe, *France* 25 D13
Dombes, *France* 27 B8
Dombóvár, *Hungary* 21 J8
Domburg, *Neths.* 17 E3
Domérat, *France* 26 B6
Domeyko, *Chile* 126 B1
Domeyko, Cordillera, *Chile* 126 A2
Domfront, *France* 24 D6
Dominador, *Chile* 126 A2
Dominica ■, *W. Indies* 117 C7
Dominica Passage, *W. Indies* 117 C7
Dominican Rep. ■, *W. Indies* 117 C5
Dömitz, *Germany* 18 B7
Domme, *France* 26 D5
Dommel →, *Neths.* 17 E6
Domo, *Ethiopia* 68 F4
Domodóssola, *Italy* 32 B5
Dompaire, *France* 25 D13
Dompierre-sur-Besbre, *France* 26 B7
Dompim, *Ghana* 78 D4
Domrémy-la-Pucelle, *France* 25 D12
Domsjö, *Sweden* 10 A12
Domville, Mt., *Australia* 91 D5
Domvraína, *Greece* 39 L5
Domžale, *Slovenia* 33 B11
Don →, *Russia* 43 C8
Don →, *Gramp., U.K.* 14 D6
Don →, *S. Yorks., U.K.* 12 D7
Don, C., *Australia* 88 B5
Don Benito, *Spain* 31 G5
Don Duong, *Vietnam* 59 G7
Don Martín, Presa de, *Mexico* 114 B4
Dona Ana = Nhamaabué, *Mozam.* 83 F4
Donaghadee, *U.K.* 15 B6
Donald, *Australia* 91 F3
Donalda, *Canada* 100 C6
Donaldsonville, *U.S.A.* 109 K9
Donalsonville, *U.S.A.* 105 K3
Donau →, *Austria* 21 G7
Donaueschingen, *Germany* 19 H4
Donauwörth, *Germany* 19 G6
Doncaster, *U.K.* 12 D6

Dysart

Dondo, *Angola* 80 F2
Dondo, *Mozam.* 83 F3
Dondo, Teluk, *Indonesia* 57 D6
Dondra Head, *Sri Lanka* 60 S12
Donegal, *Ireland* 15 B3
Donegal □, *Ireland* 15 B4
Donegal B., *Ireland* 15 B3
Donets →, *Russia* 43 C9
Donetsk, *Ukraine* 42 C7
Dong Ba Thin, *Vietnam* 59 F7
Dong Dang, *Vietnam* 58 B6
Dong Giam, *Vietnam* 58 C5
Dong Ha, *Vietnam* 58 D6
Dong Hene, *Laos* 58 D5
Dong Hoi, *Vietnam* 58 D6
Dong Jiang →, *China* 53 F10
Dong Khe, *Vietnam* 58 A6
Dong Ujimqin Qi, *China* 50 B9
Dong Van, *Vietnam* 58 A5
Dong Xoai, *Vietnam* 59 G6
Donga, *Nigeria* 79 D7
Dong'an, *China* 53 D8
Dongara, *Australia* 89 E1
Dongbei, *China* 51 D13
Dongchuan, *China* 52 D4
Dongen, *Neths.* 17 E5
Donges, *France* 24 E4
Dongfang, *China* 58 C7
Dongfeng, *China* 51 C13
Donggala, *Indonesia* 57 E5
Donggan, *China* 52 F5
Donggou, *China* 51 E13
Dongguan, *China* 53 F9
Dongguang, *China* 50 F9
Donghai Dao, *China* 53 G8
Dongjingcheng, *China* 51 B15
Donglan, *China* 52 E6
Dongliu, *China* 53 B11
Dongmen, *China* 52 F6
Dongning, *China* 51 B16
Dongnyi, *China* 52 C3
Dongola, *Sudan* 76 D3
Dongou, *Congo* 80 D3
Dongping, *China* 50 G9
Dongshan, *China* 53 F11
Dongsheng, *China* 50 E6
Dongshi, *Taiwan* 53 E13
Dongtai, *China* 51 H11
Dongting Hu, *China* 53 C9
Dongxiang, *China* 53 C11
Dongxing, *China* 52 G7
Dongyang, *China* 53 C13
Dongzhi, *China* 53 B11
Donington, C., *Australia* 91 E2
Doniphan, *U.S.A.* 109 G9
Donja Stubica, *Croatia* 33 C13
Donji Dušnik, *Serbia, Yug.* 21 M12
Donji Miholjac, *Croatia* 21 K8
Donji Milanovac, *Serbia, Yug.* 21 L12
Donji Vakuf, *Bos.-H., Yug.* 21 L7
Dønna, *Norway* 8 C12
Donna, *U.S.A.* 109 M5
Donnaconna, *Canada* 99 C5
Donnelly's Crossing, *N.Z.* 87 F4
Donnybrook, *Australia* 89 F2
Donnybrook, *S. Africa* 85 D4
Donora, *U.S.A.* 106 F5
Donor's Hill, *Australia* 90 B3
Donostia = San Sebastián, *Spain* 28 B3
Donskoy, *Russia* 41 E11
Donsol, *Phil.* 55 E5
Donya Lendava, *Slovenia* 33 B13
Donzère, *France* 27 D8
Donzère-Mondragon, Barr. de, *France* 27 D8
Donzy, *France* 25 E10
Doon →, *U.K.* 14 F4
Doorn, *Neths.* 16 D6
Dora, L., *Australia* 88 D3
Dora Báltea →, *Italy* 32 C5
Dora Riparia →, *Italy* 32 C4
Doran L., *Canada* 101 A7
Dorchester, *U.K.* 13 G5
Dorchester, C., *Canada* 97 B12
Dordogne □, *France* 26 C4
Dordogne →, *France* 26 C3
Dordrecht, *Neths.* 16 E5
Dordrecht, *S. Africa* 84 E4
Dore →, *France* 26 C7
Dore, Mts., *France* 26 C6
Doré L., *Canada* 101 C7
Doré Lake, *Canada* 101 C7
Dores do Indaiá, *Brazil* 123 E2
Dorfen, *Germany* 19 G8
Dorgali, *Italy* 34 B2
Dori, *Burkina Faso* 79 C4
Doring →, *S. Africa* 84 E2
Doringbos, *S. Africa* 84 E2
Dorion, *Canada* 98 C5
Dormaa-Ahenkro, *Ghana* 78 D4
Dormo, Ras, *Ethiopia* 77 E5
Dornach, *Switz.* 22 B5
Dornberg, *Slovenia* 33 C10
Dornbirn, *Austria* 19 H5
Dornes, *France* 25 F10
Dornoch, *U.K.* 14 D4
Dornoch Firth, *U.K.* 14 D4
Dornogovĭ □, *Mongolia* 50 B6
Doro, *Mali* 79 B4
Dorogobuzh, *Russia* 40 D8
Dorohoi, *Romania* 38 B9
Döröö Nuur, *Mongolia* 54 B4
Dorr, *Iran* 65 C6
Dorre I., *Australia* 89 E1
Dorrigo, *Australia* 91 E5
Dorris, *U.S.A.* 110 F3
Dorset, *Canada* 106 A6
Dorset, *U.S.A.* 106 E4
Dorset □, *U.K.* 13 G5
Dorsten, *Germany* 18 D2
Dortmund, *Germany* 18 D3
Dörtyol, *Turkey* 66 E7
Dorum, *Germany* 18 B4
Doruma, *Zaïre* 82 B2
Dorūneh, *Iran* 65 C8
Dos Bahías, C., *Argentina* 128 B3
Dos Hermanas, *Spain* 31 H5
Dos Palos, *U.S.A.* 112 J6
Dosso, *Niger* 79 C5
Dothan, *U.S.A.* 105 K3
Dottignies, *Belgium* 17 G2
Doty, *U.S.A.* 112 D3
Douai, *France* 25 B10
Douala, *Cameroon* 79 E6
Douarnenez, *France* 24 D2
Double Island Pt., *Australia* 91 D5
Doubrava →, *Czech.* 20 F5
Doubs □, *France* 25 E13
Doubs →, *France* 25 F12
Doubtful Sd., *N.Z.* 87 L1
Doubtless B., *N.Z.* 87 F4
Doudeville, *France* 24 C7
Doué-la-Fontaine, *France* 24 E6
Douentza, *Mali* 78 C4
Douglas, *S. Africa* 84 D3
Douglas, *U.K.* 12 C3
Douglas, *Alaska, U.S.A.* 100 B2
Douglas, *Ariz., U.S.A.* 111 L9
Douglas, *Ga., U.S.A.* 105 K4
Douglas, *Wyo., U.S.A.* 108 D2
Douglastown, *Canada* 99 C7
Douglasville, *U.S.A.* 105 J3
Douirat, *Morocco* 74 B4
Doukáton, Ákra, *Greece* 39 L3
Doulevant-le-Château, *France* 25 D11
Doullens, *France* 25 B9
Doumé, *Cameroon* 80 D2
Douna, *Mali* 78 C3
Dounan, *Taiwan* 53 F13
Dounreay, *U.K.* 14 C5
Dour, *Belgium* 17 H3
Dourada, Serra, *Brazil* 123 D2
Dourados, *Brazil* 127 A5
Dourados →, *Brazil* 127 A5
Dourdan, *France* 25 D9
Douro →, *Europe* 30 D2
Douvaine, *France* 27 B10
Douz, *Tunisia* 75 B6
Douze →, *France* 26 E3
Dove →, *U.K.* 12 E6
Dove Creek, *U.S.A.* 111 H9
Dover, *Australia* 90 G4
Dover, *U.K.* 13 F9
Dover, *Del., U.S.A.* 104 F8
Dover, *N.H., U.S.A.* 107 C14
Dover, *N.J., U.S.A.* 107 F10
Dover, *Ohio, U.S.A.* 106 F3
Dover, Pt., *Australia* 89 F4
Dover, Str. of, *Europe* 24 B8
Dover-Foxcroft, *U.S.A.* 99 C6
Dover Plains, *U.S.A.* 107 E11
Dovey = Dyfi →, *U.K.* 13 E4
Dovrefjell, *Norway* 10 B3
Dow Rūd, *Iran* 65 C6
Dowa, *Malawi* 83 E3
Dowagiac, *U.S.A.* 104 E2
Dowgha'i, *Iran* 65 B8
Dowlatābād, *Iran* 65 D8
Down □, *U.K.* 15 B6
Downey, *Calif., U.S.A.* 113 M8
Downey, *Utah, U.S.A.* 110 E7
Downham Market, *U.K.* 13 E8
Downieville, *U.S.A.* 112 F6
Downpatrick, *U.K.* 15 B6
Downpatrick Hd., *Ireland* 15 B2
Dowsārī, *Iran* 65 D8
Doyle, *U.S.A.* 112 E6
Doylestown, *U.S.A.* 107 F9
Draa, C., *Morocco* 74 C2
Draa, Oued →, *Morocco* 74 C2
Drac →, *France* 27 C9
Drachten, *Neths.* 16 B8
Drăgăneşti, *Romania* 38 E7
Drăgăneşti-Viaşca, *Romania* 38 E8
Dragaš, *Serbia, Yug.* 21 N10
Drăgăşani, *Romania* 38 E7
Dragonera, I., *Spain* 36 B9
Draguignan, *France* 27 E10
Drain, *U.S.A.* 110 E2
Drake, *Australia* 91 D5
Drake, *U.S.A.* 108 B4
Drake Passage, *S. Ocean* 5 B17
Drakensberg, *S. Africa* 85 E4
Dráma, *Greece* 39 H7
Drammen, *Norway* 10 E4
Drangajökull, *Iceland* 8 C2
Drangedal, *Norway* 10 E3
Dranov, Ostrov, *Romania* 38 E12
Dras, *India* 63 B6
Drau = Drava →, *Croatia* 21 K8
Drava →, *Croatia* 21 K8
Draveil, *France* 25 D9
Dravograd, *Slovenia* 33 B12
Drawa →, *Poland* 20 C5
Drawno, *Poland* 20 B5
Drayton Valley, *Canada* 100 C6
Dreibergen, *Neths.* 16 D6
Drenthe □, *Neths.* 16 C9
Drentsche Hoofdvaart, *Neths.* 16 C8
Drepanum, C., *Cyprus* 37 E11
Dresden, *Canada* 106 D2
Dresden, *Germany* 18 D9
Dreux, *France* 24 D8
Driel, *Neths.* 16 E7
Driffield = Great Driffield, *U.K.* 12 C7
Driftwood, *U.S.A.* 106 E6
Driggs, *U.S.A.* 110 E8
Drin i zi →, *Albania* 39 H3
Drina →, *Bos.-H., Yug.* 21 L9
Drincea →, *Romania* 38 E5
Drini →, *Albania* 38 G3
Drinjača →, *Bos.-H., Yug.* 21 L9
Drivstua, *Norway* 10 B3
Drniš, *Croatia* 33 E13
Drøbak, *Norway* 10 E4
Drogheda, *Ireland* 15 C5
Drogichin, *Belorussia* 40 E4
Drogobych, *Ukraine* 40 G3
Droichead Nua, *Ireland* 15 C5
Droitwich, *U.K.* 13 E5
Drôme □, *France* 27 D9
Drôme →, *France* 27 D8
Dromedary, C., *Australia* 91 F5
Dronero, *Italy* 32 D4
Dronfield, *Australia* 90 C3
Dronne →, *France* 26 C3
Dronninglund, *Denmark* 11 G4
Dronrijp, *Neths.* 16 B7
Dropt →, *France* 26 D3
Drumbo, *Canada* 106 C4
Drumheller, *Canada* 100 C6
Drummond, *U.S.A.* 110 C7
Drummond I., *U.S.A.* 98 C3
Drummond Pt., *Australia* 91 E2
Drummond Ra., *Australia* 90 C4
Drummondville, *Canada* 98 C5
Drumright, *U.S.A.* 109 H6
Drunen, *Neths.* 17 E6
Druskininkai, *Lithuania* 40 D3
Drut →, *Belorussia* 40 E7
Druten, *Neths.* 16 E7
Druya, *Latvia* 40 D5
Druzhina, *Russia* 45 C15
Drvar, *Bos.-H., Yug.* 33 D13
Drvenik, *Croatia* 33 E13
Dry Tortugas, *U.S.A.* 116 B3
Dryanovo, *Bulgaria* 38 G8
Dryden, *Canada* 101 D10
Dryden, *U.S.A.* 109 K3
Drygalski I., *Antarctica* 5 C7
Drysdale →, *Australia* 88 B4
Drysdale I., *Australia* 90 A2
Dschang, *Cameroon* 79 D7
Du Bois, *U.S.A.* 106 E6
Du Quoin, *U.S.A.* 108 G10
Duanesburg, *U.S.A.* 107 D10
Duaringa, *Australia* 90 C4
Ḑubā, *Si. Arabia* 64 E2
Dubai = Dubayy, *U.A.E.* 65 E7
Dubawnt →, *Canada* 101 A8
Dubawnt, L., *Canada* 101 A8
Dubayy, *U.A.E.* 65 E7
Dubbeldam, *Neths.* 16 E5
Dubbo, *Australia* 91 E4
Dubele, *Zaïre* 82 B2
Dübendorf, *Switz.* 23 B7
Dubica, *Croatia* 33 C13
Dublin, *Ireland* 15 C5
Dublin, *Ga., U.S.A.* 105 J4
Dublin, *Tex., U.S.A.* 109 J5
Dublin □, *Ireland* 15 C5
Dublin B., *Ireland* 15 C5
Dubna, *Russia* 41 C10
Dubna, *Russia* 41 D10
Dubno, *Ukraine* 40 F4
Dubois, *U.S.A.* 110 D7
Dubossary, *Moldavia* 42 C3
Dubossary Vdkhr., *Moldavia* 42 C3
Dubovka, *Russia* 43 B11
Dubovskoye, *Russia* 43 C10
Dubrajpur, *India* 63 H12
Dubréka, *Guinea* 78 D2
Dubrovitsa, *Ukraine* 40 F5
Dubrovnik, *Croatia* 21 N8
Dubrovskoye, *Russia* 45 D12
Dubuque, *U.S.A.* 108 D9
Duchang, *China* 53 C11
Duchesne, *U.S.A.* 110 F8
Duchess, *Australia* 90 C2
Ducie I., *Pac. Oc.* 93 K15
Duck Cr. →, *Australia* 88 D2
Duck Lake, *Canada* 101 C7
Duck Mountain Prov. Park, *Canada* 101 C8
Duckwall, Mt., *U.S.A.* 112 H6
Düdelange, *Lux.* 17 K8
Duderstadt, *Germany* 18 D6
Dudhi, *India* 61 G13
Düdingen, *Switz.* 22 C4
Dudinka, *Russia* 45 C9
Dudley, *U.K.* 13 E5
Dueñas, *Spain* 30 D6
Dueré, *Brazil* 123 D2
Duero = Douro →, *Europe* 30 D2
Duffel, *Belgium* 17 F5
Dufftown, *U.K.* 14 D5
Dufourspitz, *Switz.* 22 E5
Dugi Otok, *Croatia* 33 E12
Dugo Selo, *Croatia* 33 C13
Duifken Pt., *Australia* 90 A3
Duisburg, *Germany* 18 D2
Duitama, *Colombia* 120 B3
Duiveland, *Neths.* 17 E4
Duiwelskloof, *S. Africa* 85 C5
Dūkdamīn, *Iran* 65 C8
Duke I., *U.S.A.* 100 C2
Dukhān, *Qatar* 65 E6
Dukhovshchina, *Russia* 40 D8
Duki, *Pakistan* 60 D6
Duku, *Bauchi, Nigeria* 79 C7
Duku, *Sokoto, Nigeria* 79 C5
Dulag, *Phil.* 55 F6
Dulce →, *Argentina* 126 C3
Dulce, G., *Costa Rica* 116 E3
Dulf, *Iraq* 64 C5
Dŭlgopol, *Bulgaria* 38 F10
Dulit, Banjaran, *Malaysia* 56 D4
Duliu, *China* 50 E9
Dullewala, *Pakistan* 62 D4
Dülmen, *Germany* 18 D3
Dulovo, *Bulgaria* 38 F10
Dulq Maghār, *Syria* 64 B3
Dululu, *Australia* 90 C5
Duluth, *U.S.A.* 108 B8
Dum Dum, *India* 63 H13
Dum Duma, *India* 61 F19
Dum Hadjer, *Chad* 73 F8
Dūmā, *Lebanon* 69 A4
Dūmā, *Syria* 69 B5
Dumaguete, *Phil.* 55 G5
Dumai, *Indonesia* 56 D2
Dumaran, *Phil.* 55 F3
Dumas, *Ark., U.S.A.* 109 J9
Dumas, *Tex., U.S.A.* 109 H4
Dumbarton, *U.K.* 14 F4
Dumbleyung, *Australia* 89 F2
Dumfries, *U.K.* 14 F5
Dumfries & Galloway □, *U.K.* 14 F5
Dumka, *India* 63 G12
Dümmersee, *Germany* 18 C4
Dumoine →, *Canada* 98 C4
Dumoine L., *Canada* 98 C4
Dumraon, *India* 63 G11
Dumyât, *Egypt* 76 H7
Dumyât, Masabb, *Egypt* 76 H7
Dun Laoghaire, *Ireland* 15 C5
Dun-le-Palestel, *France* 26 B5
Dun-sur-Auron, *France* 25 F9
Duna →, *Hungary* 21 K8
Dunaföldvár, *Hungary* 21 J8
Dunaj →, *Czech.* 21 H8
Dunajec →, *Poland* 20 E10
Dunajská Streda, *Czech.* 21 H7
Dunapatai, *Hungary* 21 J9
Dunărea →, *Romania* 38 D12
Dunaújváros, *Hungary* 21 J8
Dunav →, *Serbia, Yug.* 21 L11
Dunay, *Russia* 48 C6
Dunback, *N.Z.* 87 L3
Dunbar, *Australia* 90 B3
Dunbar, *U.K.* 14 E6
Dunblane, *U.K.* 14 E5
Duncan, *Canada* 100 D4
Duncan, *Ariz., U.S.A.* 111 K9
Duncan, *Okla., U.S.A.* 109 H6
Duncan, L., *Canada* 98 B4
Duncan L., *Canada* 100 A6
Duncan Town, *Bahamas* 116 B4
Duncannon, *U.S.A.* 106 F7
Dundalk, *Canada* 106 B4
Dundalk, *Ireland* 15 B5
Dundalk Bay, *Ireland* 15 C5
Dundas, *Canada* 98 D4
Dundas, L., *Australia* 89 F3
Dundas I., *Canada* 100 C2
Dundas Str., *Australia* 88 B5
Dundee, *S. Africa* 85 D5
Dundee, *U.K.* 14 E6
Dundgovĭ □, *Mongolia* 50 B4
Dundoo, *Australia* 91 D3
Dundrum, *U.K.* 15 B6
Dundrum B., *U.K.* 15 B6
Dundwara, *India* 63 F8
Dunedin, *N.Z.* 87 L3
Dunedin, *U.S.A.* 105 L4
Dunedin →, *Canada* 100 B4
Dunfermline, *U.K.* 14 E5
Dungannon, *Canada* 106 C3
Dungannon, *U.K.* 15 B5
Dungannon □, *U.K.* 15 B5
Dungarpur, *India* 62 H5
Dungarvan, *Ireland* 15 D4
Dungarvan Bay, *Ireland* 15 D4
Dungeness, *U.K.* 13 G8
Dungo, L. do, *Angola* 84 B2
Dungog, *Australia* 91 E5
Dungu, *Zaïre* 82 B2
Dungunâb, *Sudan* 76 C4
Dungunâb, Khalij, *Sudan* 76 C4
Dunhua, *China* 51 C15
Dunhuang, *China* 54 B4
Dunières, *France* 27 C8
Dunk I., *Australia* 90 B4
Dunkeld, *U.K.* 14 E5
Dunkerque, *France* 25 A9
Dunkery Beacon, *U.K.* 13 F4
Dunkirk = Dunkerque, *France* 25 A9
Dunkirk, *U.S.A.* 106 D5
Dunkuj, *Sudan* 77 E3
Dunkwa, *Central, Ghana* 78 D4
Dunkwa, *Central, Ghana* 79 D4
Dunlap, *U.S.A.* 108 E7
Dúnleary = Dun Laoghaire, *Ireland* 15 C5
Dunmanus B., *Ireland* 15 E2
Dunmara, *Australia* 90 B1
Dunmore, *U.S.A.* 107 E9
Dunmore Hd., *Ireland* 15 D1
Dunmore Town, *Bahamas* 116 A4
Dunn, *U.S.A.* 105 H6
Dunnellon, *U.S.A.* 105 L4
Dunnet Hd., *U.K.* 14 C5
Dunning, *U.S.A.* 108 E4
Dunnville, *Canada* 106 D5
Dunolly, *Australia* 91 F3
Dunoon, *U.K.* 14 F4
Dunqul, *Egypt* 76 C3
Duns, *U.K.* 14 F6
Dunseith, *U.S.A.* 108 A4
Dunsmuir, *U.S.A.* 110 F2
Dunstable, *U.K.* 13 F7
Dunstan Mts., *N.Z.* 87 L2
Dunster, *Canada* 100 C5
Dunvegan L., *Canada* 101 A7
Duolun, *China* 50 C9
Duong Dong, *Vietnam* 59 G4
Dupree, *U.S.A.* 108 C4
Dupuyer, *U.S.A.* 110 B7
Duque de Caxias, *Brazil* 123 F3
Duque de York, I., *Chile* 128 D1
Durack →, *Australia* 88 C4
Durack Ra., *Australia* 88 C4
Durağan, *Turkey* 66 C6
Durance →, *France* 27 E8
Durand, *U.S.A.* 104 D4
Durango = Victoria de Durango, *Mexico* 114 C4
Durango, *Spain* 28 B2
Durango, *U.S.A.* 111 H10
Durango □, *Mexico* 114 C4
Duranillin, *Australia* 89 F2
Durant, *U.S.A.* 109 J6
Duratón →, *Spain* 30 D6
Durazno, *Uruguay* 126 C4
Durazzo = Durrësi, *Albania* 39 H2
Durban, *France* 26 F6
Durban, *S. Africa* 85 D5
Dúrcal, *Spain* 31 J7
Düren, *Germany* 18 E2
Durg, *India* 61 J12
Durgapur, *India* 63 H12
Durham, *Canada* 98 D3
Durham, *U.K.* 12 C6
Durham, *Calif., U.S.A.* 112 F5
Durham, *N.C., U.S.A.* 105 G6
Durham □, *U.K.* 12 C6
Durham Downs, *Australia* 91 D4
Durmitor, *Montenegro, Yug.* 21 M9
Durness, *U.K.* 14 C4
Durrësi, *Albania* 39 H2
Durrie, *Australia* 90 D3
Dursunbey, *Turkey* 66 D3
Durtal, *France* 24 E6
Duru, *Zaïre* 82 B2
D'Urville, Tanjung, *Indonesia* 57 E9
D'Urville I., *N.Z.* 87 J4
Duryea, *U.S.A.* 107 E9
Dusa Mareb, *Somali Rep.* 68 F4
Dûsh, *Egypt* 76 C3
Dushak, *Turkmenistan* 44 F7
Dushan, *China* 52 E6
Dushanbe, *Tajikistan* 44 F7
Dusheti, *Georgia* 43 E11
Dusky Sd., *N.Z.* 87 L1
Dussejour, C., *Australia* 88 B4
Düsseldorf, *Germany* 18 D2
Dussen, *Neths.* 16 E5
Dutch Harbor, *U.S.A.* 96 C3
Dutlwe, *Botswana* 84 C3
Dutsan Wai, *Nigeria* 79 C6
Dutton, *Canada* 106 D3
Dutton →, *Australia* 90 C3
Duved, *Sweden* 10 A6
Duvno, *Bos.-H., Yug.* 21 M7
Duyun, *China* 52 D6
Düzce, *Turkey* 66 C4
Duzdab = Zāhedān, *Iran* 65 D9
Dvina, Sev. →, *Russia* 44 C5
Dvinsk = Daugavpils, *Latvia* 40 D5
Dvor, *Croatia* 33 C13
Dwarka, *India* 62 H3
Dwellingup, *Australia* 89 F2
Dwight, *Canada* 106 A5
Dwight, *U.S.A.* 104 E1
Dyakovskoya, *Russia* 41 A12
Dyatkovo, *Russia* 40 E9
Dyatlovo, *Belorussia* 40 E4
Dyer, C., *Canada* 97 B13
Dyer Plateau, *Antarctica* 5 D17
Dyersburg, *U.S.A.* 109 G10
Dyfed □, *U.K.* 13 E3
Dyfi →, *U.K.* 13 E4
Dyje →, *Czech.* 20 G6
Dyle →, *Belgium* 17 G5
Dynevor Downs, *Australia* 91 D3
Dynów, *Poland* 20 F12
Dysart, *Canada* 101 C8

Dzamin Üüd

Dzamin Üüd, *Mongolia* 50 C6
Dzerzhinsk, *Belorussia* 40 E5
Dzerzhinsk, *Russia* 41 C13
Dzhalinda, *Russia* 45 D13
Dzhambeyty, *Kazakhstan* 43 A15
Dzhambul, *Kazakhstan* 44 E8
Dzhankoi, *Ukraine* 42 D6
Dzhanybek, *Kazakhstan* 43 B12
Dzhardzhan, *Russia* 45 C13
Dzhelinde, *Russia* 45 C12
Dzhetygara, *Kazakhstan* 44 D7
Dzhezkazgan, *Kazakhstan* 44 E7
Dzhikimde, *Russia* 45 D13
Dzhizak, *Uzbekistan* 44 E7
Dzhugdzur, Khrebet, *Russia* 45 D14
Dzhvari, *Georgia* 43 E10
Działdowo, *Poland* 20 B10
Działoszyn, *Poland* 20 D8
Dzierzgoń, *Poland* 20 B9
Dzierzoniów, *Poland* 20 E6
Dzilam de Bravo, *Mexico* 115 C7
Dzioua, *Algeria* 75 B6
Dzungaria = Junggar Pendi, *China* 54 B3
Dzungarian Gate = Alataw Shankou, *China* 54 B3
Dzuumod, *Mongolia* 54 B5

E

Eabamet, L., *Canada* 98 B2
Eads, *U.S.A.* 108 F3
Eagle, *U.S.A.* 110 G10
Eagle →, *Canada* 99 B8
Eagle Butt, *U.S.A.* 108 C4
Eagle Grove, *U.S.A.* 108 D8
Eagle L., *Calif., U.S.A.* 110 F3
Eagle L., *Maine, U.S.A.* 99 C6
Eagle Lake, *U.S.A.* 109 L6
Eagle Mountain, *U.S.A.* 113 M11
Eagle Nest, *U.S.A.* 111 H11
Eagle Pass, *U.S.A.* 109 L4
Eagle Pk., *U.S.A.* 112 G7
Eagle Pt., *Australia* 88 C3
Eagle River, *U.S.A.* 108 C10
Ealing, *U.K.* 13 F7
Earaheedy, *Australia* 89 E3
Earl Grey, *Canada* 101 C8
Earle, *U.S.A.* 109 H9
Earlimart, *U.S.A.* 113 K7
Earn →, *U.K.* 14 E5
Earn, L., *U.K.* 14 E4
Earnslaw, Mt., *N.Z.* 87 L2
Earth, *U.S.A.* 109 H3
Easley, *U.S.A.* 105 H4
East Angus, *Canada* 99 C5
East Aurora, *U.S.A.* 106 D6
East B., *U.S.A.* 109 L10
East Bengal, *Bangla.* 61 G17
East Beskids = Vychodné Beskydy, *Europe* 20 F11
East Brady, *U.S.A.* 106 F5
East C., *N.Z.* 87 G7
East Chicago, *U.S.A.* 104 E2
East China Sea, *Asia* 54 C7
East Coulee, *Canada* 100 C6
East Falkland, *Falk. Is.* 128 D5
East Grand Forks, *U.S.A.* 108 B6
East Greenwich, *U.S.A.* 107 E13
East Hartford, *U.S.A.* 107 E12
East Helena, *U.S.A.* 110 C8
East Indies, *Asia* 57 E6
East Jordan, *U.S.A.* 104 C3
East Lansing, *U.S.A.* 104 D3
East Liverpool, *U.S.A.* 106 F4
East London, *S. Africa* 85 E4
East Main = Eastmain, *Canada* 98 B4
East Orange, *U.S.A.* 107 F10
East Pacific Ridge, *Pac. Oc.* 93 J17
East Pakistan = Bangladesh ■, *Asia* 61 H17
East Palestine, *U.S.A.* 106 F4
East Pine, *Canada* 100 B4
East Pt., *Canada* 99 C7
East Point, *U.S.A.* 105 J3
East Providence, *U.S.A.* 107 E13
East Retford, *U.K.* 12 D7
East St. Louis, *U.S.A.* 108 F9
East Schelde → = Oosterschelde, *Neths.* 17 E4
East Siberian Sea, *Russia* 45 B17
East Stroudsburg, *U.S.A.* 107 E9
East Sussex □, *U.K.* 13 G8
East Tawas, *U.S.A.* 104 C4
East Toorale, *Australia* 91 E4
East Walker →, *U.S.A.* 112 G7
Eastbourne, *N.Z.* 87 J5
Eastbourne, *U.K.* 13 G8
Eastend, *Canada* 101 D7
Easter Islands = Pascua, I. de, *Pac. Oc.* 93 K17
Eastern □, *Kenya* 82 B4
Eastern □, *Uganda* 82 B3
Eastern Cr. →, *Australia* 90 C3
Eastern Ghats, *India* 60 N11
Eastern Group = Lau Group, *Fiji* 87 C9
Eastern Group, *Australia* 89 F3
Eastern Province □, *S. Leone* 78 D2
Easterville, *Canada* 101 C9
Easthampton, *U.S.A.* 107 D12
Eastland, *U.S.A.* 109 J5
Eastleigh, *U.K.* 13 G6
Eastmain, *Canada* 98 B4
Eastmain →, *Canada* 98 B4
Eastman, *Canada* 107 A12
Eastman, *U.S.A.* 105 J4
Easton, *Md., U.S.A.* 104 F7
Easton, *Pa., U.S.A.* 107 F9
Easton, *Wash., U.S.A.* 112 C5
Eastport, *U.S.A.* 99 D6
Eastsound, *U.S.A.* 112 B4
Eaton, *U.S.A.* 108 E2
Eatonia, *Canada* 101 C7
Eatonton, *U.S.A.* 105 J4
Eatontown, *U.S.A.* 107 F10
Eatonville, *U.S.A.* 112 D4
Eau Claire, *Fr. Guiana* 121 C7
Eau Claire, *U.S.A.* 108 C9
Eauze, *France* 26 E4
Ebagoola, *Australia* 90 A3
Eban, *Nigeria* 79 D5
Ebbw Vale, *U.K.* 13 F4
Ebeggui, *Algeria* 75 C6
Ebeltoft, *Denmark* 9 H11
Ebensburg, *U.S.A.* 106 F6
Ebensee, *Austria* 21 H3
Eber Gölü, *Turkey* 66 D4
Eberbach, *Germany* 19 F4
Eberswalde, *Germany* 18 C9
Ebetsu, *Japan* 48 C10
Ebian, *China* 52 C4
Ebikon, *Switz.* 23 B6
Ebingen, *Germany* 19 G5
Ebnat-Kappel, *Switz.* 23 B8
Eboli, *Italy* 35 B8
Ebolowa, *Cameroon* 79 E7
Ebrach, *Germany* 19 F6
Ébrié, Lagune, *Ivory C.* 78 D4
Ebro →, *Spain* 28 E5
Ebro, Pantano del, *Spain* 30 B7
Ebstorf, *Germany* 18 B6
Ecaussines-d' Enghien, *Belgium* 17 G4
Eceabat, *Turkey* 66 C2
Ech Cheliff, *Algeria* 75 A5
Echallens, *Switz.* 22 C3
Echeng, *China* 53 B10
Echigo-Sammyaku, *Japan* 49 F9
Echizen-Misaki, *Japan* 49 G7
Echmiadzin, *Armenia* 43 F11
Echo Bay, *N.W.T., Canada* 96 B8
Echo Bay, *Ont., Canada* 98 C3
Echoing →, *Canada* 101 B10
Echt, *Neths.* 17 F7
Echternach, *Lux.* 17 J8
Echuca, *Australia* 91 F3
Ecija, *Spain* 31 H5
Eckernförde, *Germany* 18 A5
Eclipse Is., *Australia* 88 B4
Écommoy, *France* 24 E7
Ecoporanga, *Brazil* 123 E3
Écos, *France* 25 C8
Écouché, *France* 24 D6
Ecuador ■, *S. Amer.* 120 D2
Écueillé, *France* 24 E8
Ed, *Sweden* 11 F5
Ed Dabbura, *Sudan* 76 D3
Ed Dâmer, *Sudan* 76 D3
Ed Debba, *Sudan* 76 D3
Ed-Déffa, *Egypt* 76 A2
Ed Deim, *Sudan* 77 E2
Ed Dueim, *Sudan* 77 E3
Edah, *Australia* 89 E2
Edam, *Canada* 101 C7
Edam, *Neths.* 16 C6
Eday, *U.K.* 14 B6
Edd, *Ethiopia* 68 E3
Eddrachillis B., *U.K.* 14 C3
Eddystone, *U.K.* 13 G3
Eddystone Pt., *Australia* 90 G4
Ede, *Neths.* 16 D7
Ede, *Nigeria* 79 D5
Édea, *Cameroon* 79 E7
Edegem, *Belgium* 17 F4
Edehon L., *Canada* 101 A9
Edekel, Adrar, *Algeria* 75 D6
Eden, *Australia* 91 F4
Eden, *N.C., U.S.A.* 105 G6
Eden, *N.Y., U.S.A.* 106 D6
Eden, *Tex., U.S.A.* 109 K5
Eden, *Wyo., U.S.A.* 110 E9
Eden →, *U.K.* 12 C4
Eden L., *Canada* 101 B8
Edenburg, *S. Africa* 84 D4
Edendale, *S. Africa* 85 D5
Edenderry, *Ireland* 15 C4
Edenton, *U.S.A.* 105 G7
Edenville, *S. Africa* 85 D4
Eder →, *Germany* 18 D5
Ederstausee, *Germany* 18 D4
Edgar, *U.S.A.* 108 E5
Edgartown, *U.S.A.* 107 E14
Edge Hill, *U.K.* 13 E6
Edgefield, *U.S.A.* 105 J5
Edgeley, *U.S.A.* 108 B5
Edgemont, *U.S.A.* 108 D3
Edgeøya, *Svalbard* 4 B9
Edhessa, *Greece* 39 J5
Edievale, *N.Z.* 87 L2
Edina, *Liberia* 78 D2
Edina, *U.S.A.* 108 E8
Edinburg, *U.S.A.* 109 M5
Edinburgh, *U.K.* 14 F5
Edirne, *Turkey* 39 H9
Edirne □, *Turkey* 66 C2
Edison, *U.S.A.* 112 B4
Edithburgh, *Australia* 91 F2
Edjeleh, *Algeria* 75 C6
Edjudina, *Australia* 89 E3
Edmeston, *U.S.A.* 107 D9
Edmond, *U.S.A.* 109 H6
Edmonds, *U.S.A.* 112 C4
Edmonton, *Australia* 90 B4
Edmonton, *Canada* 100 C6
Edmund L., *Canada* 101 C10
Edmundston, *Canada* 99 C6
Edna, *U.S.A.* 109 L6
Edna Bay, *U.S.A.* 100 B2
Edolo, *Italy* 32 B7
Edremit, *Turkey* 66 D2
Edremit Körfezi, *Turkey* 66 D2
Edsbyn, *Sweden* 10 C9
Edsele, *Sweden* 10 A10
Edson, *Canada* 100 C5
Eduardo Castex, *Argentina* 126 D3
Edward →, *Australia* 91 F3
Edward, L., *Africa* 82 C2
Edward I., *Canada* 98 C2
Edward River, *Australia* 90 A3
Edward VII Land, *Antarctica* 5 E13
Edwards, *U.S.A.* 113 L9
Edwards Plateau, *U.S.A.* 109 K4
Edwardsville, *U.S.A.* 107 E9
Edzo, *Canada* 100 A5
Eefde, *Neths.* 16 D8
Eekloo, *Belgium* 17 F3
Eelde, *Neths.* 16 B9
Eem →, *Neths.* 16 D6
Eems →, *Neths.* 16 B9
Eems Kanaal, *Neths.* 16 B9
Eenrum, *Neths.* 16 B8
Eernegem, *Belgium* 17 F2
Eerste Valthermond, *Neths.* 16 C9
Eferi, *Algeria* 75 D6
Effingham, *U.S.A.* 104 F1
Effretikon, *Switz.* 23 B7
Eforie Sud, *Romania* 38 E11
Ega →, *Spain* 28 C3
Égadi, Ísole, *Italy* 34 E5
Eganville, *Canada* 98 C4
Egeland, *U.S.A.* 108 A5
Egenolf L., *Canada* 101 B9
Eger = Cheb, *Czech.* 20 E2
Eger, *Hungary* 21 H10
Eger →, *Hungary* 21 H10
Egersund, *Norway* 9 G9
Egg L., *Canada* 101 B7
Eggenburg, *Austria* 20 G5
Eggenfelden, *Germany* 19 G8
Eggiwil, *Switz.* 22 C5
Éghezée, *Belgium* 17 G5
Eginbah, *Australia* 88 D2
Égletons, *France* 26 C6
Eglisau, *Switz.* 23 A7
Egmond-aan-Zee, *Neths.* 16 C5
Egmont, C., *N.Z.* 87 H4
Egmont, Mt., *N.Z.* 87 H5
Eğridir, *Turkey* 66 E4
Eğridir Gölü, *Turkey* 66 E4
Egtved, *Denmark* 11 J3
Éguas →, *Brazil* 123 D3
Egume, *Nigeria* 79 D6
Éguzon, *France* 26 B5
Egvekinot, *Russia* 45 C19
Egypt ■, *Africa* 76 J7
Eha Amufu, *Nigeria* 79 D6
Ehime □, *Japan* 49 H6
Ehingen, *Germany* 19 G5
Ehrenberg, *U.S.A.* 113 M12
Ehrwald, *Austria* 19 H6
Eibar, *Spain* 28 B2
Eibergen, *Neths.* 16 D9
Eichstatt, *Germany* 19 G7
Eider →, *Germany* 18 A4
Eidsvold, *Australia* 91 D5
Eidsvoll, *Norway* 9 F11
Eifel, *Germany* 19 E2
Eiffel Flats, *Zimbabwe* 83 F3
Eigg, *U.K.* 14 E2
Eighty Mile Beach, *Australia* 88 C3
Eil, *Somali Rep.* 68 F4
Eil, L., *U.K.* 14 E3
Eildon, L., *Australia* 91 F4
Eileen L., *Canada* 101 A7
Eilenburg, *Germany* 18 D8
Ein el Luweiqa, *Sudan* 77 E3
Einasleigh, *Australia* 90 B3
Einasleigh →, *Australia* 90 B3
Einbeck, *Germany* 18 D5
Eindhoven, *Neths.* 17 F6
Einsiedeln, *Switz.* 23 B7
Eire ■, *Europe* 15 D4
Eiríksjökull, *Iceland* 8 D3
Eirlandsche Gat, *Neths.* 16 B5
Eirunepé, *Brazil* 124 B4
Eisden, *Belgium* 17 G7
Eisenach, *Germany* 18 E6
Eisenberg, *Germany* 18 E7
Eisenerz, *Austria* 21 H4
Eisenhüttenstadt, *Germany* 18 C10
Eisenstadt, *Austria* 21 H6
Eiserfeld, *Germany* 18 E3
Eisfeld, *Germany* 18 E6
Eisleben, *Germany* 18 D7
Ejby, *Denmark* 11 J3
Eje, Sierra del, *Spain* 30 C4
Ejea de los Caballeros, *Spain* 28 C3
Ejutla, *Mexico* 115 D5
Ekalaka, *U.S.A.* 108 C2
Ekeren, *Belgium* 17 F4
Eket, *Nigeria* 79 E6
Eketahuna, *N.Z.* 87 J5
Ekhínos, *Greece* 39 H8
Ekibastuz, *Kazakhstan* 44 D8
Ekimchan, *Russia* 45 D14
Ekoli, *Zaïre* 82 C1
Eksel, *Belgium* 17 F6
Ekwan →, *Canada* 98 B3
Ekwan Pt., *Canada* 98 B3
El Aaiún, *W. Sahara* 74 C2
El Aargub, *Mauritania* 74 D1
El Abiodh-Sidi-Cheikh, *Algeria* 75 B5
El 'Agrûd, *Egypt* 69 E3
El Aïoun, *Morocco* 75 B4
El 'Aiyat, *Egypt* 76 J7
El Alamein, *Egypt* 76 H6
El Alto, *Peru* 124 A1
El 'Aqaba, W. →, *Egypt* 69 E2
El 'Arag, *Egypt* 76 B2
El Arahal, *Spain* 31 H5
El Arenal, *Spain* 36 B9
El Aricha, *Algeria* 75 B4
El Arīhā, *Jordan* 69 D4
El Arish, *Australia* 90 B4
El 'Arîsh, *Egypt* 69 D2
El 'Arîsh, W. →, *Egypt* 69 D2
El Arrouch, *Algeria* 75 A6
El Asnam = Ech Cheliff, *Algeria* 75 A5
El Astillero, *Spain* 30 B7
El Badâri, *Egypt* 76 B3
El Bahrein, *Egypt* 76 B2
El Ballâs, *Egypt* 76 B3
El Balyana, *Egypt* 76 B3
El Banco, *Colombia* 120 B3
El Baqeir, *Sudan* 76 D3
El Barco de Ávila, *Spain* 30 E5
El Barco de Valdeorras, *Spain* 30 C4
El Bauga, *Sudan* 76 D3
El Baúl, *Venezuela* 120 B4
El Bawiti, *Egypt* 76 J6
El Bayadh, *Algeria* 75 B5
El Bierzo, *Spain* 30 C4
El Bluff, *Nic.* 116 D3
El Bolsón, *Argentina* 128 B2
El Bonillo, *Spain* 29 G2
El Brûk, W. →, *Egypt* 69 E2
El Buheirat □, *Sudan* 77 F2
El Caín, *Argentina* 128 B3
El Cajon, *U.S.A.* 113 N10
El Callao, *Venezuela* 121 B5
El Camp, *Spain* 28 D6
El Campo, *U.S.A.* 109 L6
El Carmen, *Bolivia* 125 C5
El Carmen, *Venezuela* 120 C4
El Castillo, *Spain* 31 H4
El Centro, *U.S.A.* 113 N11
El Cerro, *Bolivia* 125 D5
El Cerro, *Spain* 31 H4
El Cocuy, *Colombia* 120 B3
El Compadre, *Mexico* 113 N10
El Corcovado, *Argentina* 128 B2
El Coronil, *Spain* 31 H5
El Cuy, *Argentina* 128 A3
El Cuyo, *Mexico* 115 C7
El Dab'a, *Egypt* 76 H6
El Daheir, *Egypt* 69 D3
El Deir, *Egypt* 76 B3
El Dere, *Somali Rep.* 68 G4
El Descanso, *Mexico* 113 N10
El Desemboque, *Mexico* 114 A2
El Dilingat, *Egypt* 76 H7
El Diviso, *Colombia* 120 C2
El Djem, *Tunisia* 75 A7
El Djouf, *Mauritania* 70 D3
El Dorado, *Ark., U.S.A.* 109 J8
El Dorado, *Kans., U.S.A.* 109 G6
El Dorado, *Venezuela* 121 B5
El Eglab, *Algeria* 74 C4
El Escorial, *Spain* 30 E6
El Eulma, *Algeria* 75 A6
El Faiyûm, *Egypt* 76 J7
El Fâsher, *Sudan* 77 E2
El Fashn, *Egypt* 76 J7
El Ferrol, *Spain* 30 B2
El Fifi, *Sudan* 77 E1
El Fuerte, *Mexico* 114 B3
El Gal, *Somali Rep.* 68 E5
El Gebir, *Sudan* 77 E2
El Gedida, *Egypt* 76 B2
El Geteina, *Sudan* 77 E3
El Gezira □, *Sudan* 77 E3
El Gîza, *Egypt* 76 H7
El Goléa, *Algeria* 75 B5
El Guettar, *Algeria* 75 B5
El Hadeb, *W. Sahara* 74 C2
El Hadjira, *Algeria* 75 B6
El Hagiz, *Sudan* 77 D4
El Hajeb, *Morocco* 74 B3
El Hammam, *Egypt* 76 H6
El Hammâmi, *Mauritania* 74 D2
El Hank, *Mauritania* 74 D3
El Harrach, *Algeria* 75 A5
El Hasian, *W. Sahara* 74 C2
El Hawata, *Sudan* 77 E3
El Heiz, *Egypt* 76 B2
El 'Idisât, *Egypt* 76 B3
El Iskandarîya, *Egypt* 76 H6
El Jadida, *Morocco* 74 B3
El Jebelein, *Sudan* 77 E3
El Kab, *Sudan* 76 D3
El Kabrît, G., *Egypt* 69 F2
El Kala, *Algeria* 75 A6
El Kalâa, *Morocco* 74 B3
El Kamlin, *Sudan* 77 D3
El Kantara, *Algeria* 75 A6
El Kantara, *Tunisia* 75 B7
El Karaba, *Sudan* 76 D3
El Kef, *Tunisia* 75 A6
El Khandaq, *Sudan* 76 D3
El Khârga, *Egypt* 76 B3
El Khartûm, *Sudan* 77 D3
El Khartûm □, *Sudan* 77 D3
El Khartûm Bahrî, *Sudan* 77 D3
El Khroub, *Algeria* 75 A6
El Kseur, *Algeria* 75 A5
El Ksiba, *Morocco* 74 B3
El Kuntilla, *Egypt* 69 E3
El Laqâwa, *Sudan* 77 E2
El Laqeita, *Egypt* 76 B3
El Leiya, *Sudan* 77 D4
El Mafâza, *Sudan* 77 E3
El Mahalla el Kubra, *Egypt* 76 H7
El Mahârîq, *Egypt* 76 B3
El Mahmûdîya, *Egypt* 76 H7
El Maitén, *Argentina* 128 B2
El Maiz, *Algeria* 75 C4
El-Maks el-Bahari, *Egypt* 76 C3
El Manshâh, *Egypt* 76 B3
El Mansour, *Algeria* 75 C4
El Mansûra, *Egypt* 76 H7
El Mantico, *Venezuela* 121 B5
El Manzala, *Egypt* 76 H7
El Marâgha, *Egypt* 76 B3
El Masid, *Sudan* 77 D3
El Matariya, *Egypt* 76 H8
El Medano, *Canary Is.* 36 F3
El Meghaier, *Algeria* 75 B6
El Meraguen, *Algeria* 75 C4
El Metemma, *Sudan* 77 D3
El Miamo, *Venezuela* 121 B5
El Milagro, *Argentina* 126 C2
El Milia, *Algeria* 75 A6
El Minyâ, *Egypt* 76 J7
El Molar, *Spain* 28 E1
El Mreyye, *Mauritania* 78 B3
El Obeid, *Sudan* 77 E3
El Odaiya, *Sudan* 77 E2
El Oro, *Mexico* 115 D4
El Oro □, *Ecuador* 120 D2
El Oued, *Algeria* 75 B6
El Palmar, *Bolivia* 125 D5
El Palmar, *Venezuela* 121 B5
El Palmito, Presa, *Mexico* 114 B3
El Panadés, *Spain* 28 D6
El Pardo, *Spain* 30 E7
El Paso, *U.S.A.* 111 L10
El Paso Robles, *U.S.A.* 112 K6
El Pedernoso, *Spain* 29 F2
El Pedroso, *Spain* 31 H5
El Pobo de Dueñas, *Spain* 28 E3
El Portal, *U.S.A.* 111 H4
El Porvenir, *Mexico* 114 A3
El Prat de Llobregat, *Spain* 28 D7
El Progreso, *Honduras* 116 C2
El Provencío, *Spain* 29 F2
El Pueblito, *Mexico* 114 B3
El Pueblo, *Canary Is.* 36 F2
El Qâhira, *Egypt* 76 H7
El Qantara, *Egypt* 69 E1
El Qasr, *Egypt* 76 B2
El Quseima, *Egypt* 69 E3
El Qusîya, *Egypt* 76 B3
El Râshda, *Egypt* 76 B2
El Reno, *U.S.A.* 109 H6
El Ribero, *Spain* 30 C2
El Rîdisiya, *Egypt* 76 C3
El Rio, *U.S.A.* 113 L7
El Ronquillo, *Spain* 31 H4
El Roque, Pta., *Canary Is.* 36 F4
El Rosarito, *Mexico* 114 B2
El Rubio, *Spain* 31 H5
El Saff, *Egypt* 76 J7
El Saheira, W. →, *Egypt* 69 E2
El Salto, *Mexico* 114 C3
El Salvador ■, *Cent. Amer.* 116 D2
El Sancejo, *Spain* 31 H5
El Sauce, *Nic.* 116 D2
El Shallal, *Egypt* 76 C3
El Simbillawein, *Egypt* 76 H7
El Sombrero, *Venezuela* 120 B4
El Suweis, *Egypt* 76 J8
El Tamarâni, W. →, *Egypt* 69 E3
El Thamad, *Egypt* 69 F3
El Tigre, *Venezuela* 121 B5
El Tîh, G., *Egypt* 69 F2
El Tîna, Khalîg, *Egypt* 69 D1
El Tocuyo, *Venezuela* 120 B4
El Tofo, *Chile* 126 B1
El Tránsito, *Chile* 126 B1
El Tûr, *Egypt* 76 J8
El Turbio, *Argentina* 128 D2
El Uqsur, *Egypt* 76 B3
El Vado, *Spain* 28 D1
El Vallés, *Spain* 28 D7
El Venado, *Mexico* 114 C4
El Vigía, *Venezuela* 120 B3

Espinosa de los Monteros

El Wabeira, *Egypt* 69 F2
El Wak, *Kenya* 82 B5
El Waqf, *Egypt* 76 B3
El Wâsta, *Egypt* 76 J7
El Weguet, *Ethiopia* 77 F5
El Wuz, *Sudan* 77 D3
Elafónisos, *Greece* 39 N5
Elandsvlei, *S. Africa* 84 E2
Élassa, *Greece* 39 P9
Elassón, *Greece* 39 K5
Elat, *Israel* 69 F3
Elâzığ, *Turkey* 67 D8
Elâzığ □, *Turkey* 67 D8
Elba, *Italy* 32 F7
Elba, *U.S.A.* 105 K2
Elbasani, *Albania* 39 H3
Elbe, *U.S.A.* 112 D4
Elbe →, *Europe* 18 B4
Elbe-Seiten Kanal, *Germany* 18 C6
Elbert, Mt., *U.S.A.* 111 G10
Elberta, *U.S.A.* 104 C2
Elberton, *U.S.A.* 105 H4
Elbeuf, *France* 24 C8
Elbing = Elbląg, *Poland* 20 A9
Elbistan, *Turkey* 66 D7
Elbląg, *Poland* 20 A9
Elbow, *Canada* 101 C7
Elbrus, *Asia* 43 E10
Elburg, *Neths.* 16 D7
Elburz Mts. = Alborz, Reshteh-ye Kūhhā-ye, *Iran* 65 C7
Elche, *Spain* 29 G4
Elche de la Sierra, *Spain* 29 G2
Elcho I., *Australia* 90 A2
Elda, *Spain* 29 G4
Eldon, *Mo., U.S.A.* 108 F8
Eldon, *Wash., U.S.A.* 112 C3
Eldora, *U.S.A.* 108 D8
Eldorado, *Argentina* 127 B5
Eldorado, *Canada* 101 B7
Eldorado, *Mexico* 114 C3
Eldorado, *Ill., U.S.A.* 104 G1
Eldorado, *Tex., U.S.A.* 109 K4
Eldorado Springs, *U.S.A.* 109 G8
Eldoret, *Kenya* 82 B4
Eldred, *U.S.A.* 106 E6
Elea, C., *Cyprus* 37 D13
Electra, *U.S.A.* 109 H5
Elefantes →, *Mozam.* 85 C5
Elefantes, G., *Chile* 128 C2
Elektrogorsk, *Russia* 41 D11
Elektrostal, *Russia* 41 D11
Elele, *Nigeria* 79 D6
Elephant Butte Res., *U.S.A.* 111 K10
Elephant I., *Antarctica* 5 C18
Elesbão Veloso, *Brazil* 122 C3
Eleşkirt, *Turkey* 67 D10
Eleuthera, *Bahamas* 116 A4
Elgepiggen, *Norway* 10 B5
Elgeyo-Marakwet □, *Kenya* 82 B4
Elgg, *Switz.* 23 B7
Elgin, *N.B., Canada* 99 C6
Elgin, *Ont., Canada* 107 B8
Elgin, *U.K.* 14 D5
Elgin, *Ill., U.S.A.* 104 D1
Elgin, *N. Dak., U.S.A.* 108 B4
Elgin, *Nebr., U.S.A.* 108 E5
Elgin, *Nev., U.S.A.* 111 H6
Elgin, *Oreg., U.S.A.* 110 D5
Elgin, *Tex., U.S.A.* 109 K6
Elgon, Mt., *Africa* 82 B3
Eliase, *Indonesia* 57 F8
Elida, *U.S.A.* 109 J3
Elikón, *Greece* 39 L5
Elim, *S. Africa* 84 E2
Elisabethville = Lubumbashi, *Zaïre* 83 E2
Eliseu Martins, *Brazil* 122 C3
Elista, *Russia* 43 C11
Elizabeth, *Australia* 91 E2
Elizabeth, *U.S.A.* 107 F10
Elizabeth City, *U.S.A.* 105 G7
Elizabethton, *U.S.A.* 105 G4
Elizabethtown, *Ky., U.S.A.* 104 G3
Elizabethtown, *N.Y., U.S.A.* 107 B11
Elizabethtown, *Pa., U.S.A.* 107 F8
Elizondo, *Spain* 28 B3
Ełk, *Poland* 20 B12
Elk City, *U.S.A.* 109 H5
Elk Creek, *U.S.A.* 112 F4
Elk Grove, *U.S.A.* 112 G5
Elk Island Nat. Park, *Canada* 100 C6
Elk Lake, *Canada* 98 C3
Elk Point, *Canada* 101 C6
Elk River, *Idaho, U.S.A.* 110 C5
Elk River, *Minn., U.S.A.* 108 C8
Elkedra, *Australia* 90 C2
Elkedra →, *Australia* 90 C2
Elkhart, *Ind., U.S.A.* 104 E3
Elkhart, *Kans., U.S.A.* 109 G4
Elkhorn, *Canada* 101 D8
Elkhorn →, *U.S.A.* 108 E6
Elkhotovo, *Russia* 43 E11
Elkhovo, *Bulgaria* 38 G9
Elkin, *U.S.A.* 105 G5
Elkins, *U.S.A.* 104 F6
Elko, *Canada* 100 D5
Elko, *U.S.A.* 110 F6
Ell, L., *Australia* 89 E4
Ellecom, *Neths.* 16 D8
Ellef Ringnes I., *Canada* 4 B2
Ellendale, *Australia* 88 C3
Ellendale, *U.S.A.* 108 B5
Ellensburg, *U.S.A.* 110 C3
Ellenville, *U.S.A.* 107 E10
Ellery, Mt., *Australia* 91 F4
Ellesmere, L., *N.Z.* 87 M4
Ellesmere I., *Canada* 4 B4
Ellesmere Port, *U.K.* 12 D5
Ellezelles, *Belgium* 17 G3
Ellice Is. = Tuvalu ■, *Pac. Oc.* 92 H9
Ellinwood, *U.S.A.* 108 F5
Elliot, *Australia* 90 B1
Elliot, *S. Africa* 85 E4
Elliot Lake, *Canada* 98 C3
Elliotdale = Xhora, *S. Africa* 85 E4
Ellis, *U.S.A.* 108 F5
Elliston, *Australia* 91 E1
Ellisville, *U.S.A.* 109 K10
Ellon, *U.K.* 14 D6
Ellore = Eluru, *India* 61 L12
Ells →, *Canada* 100 B6
Ellsworth, *U.S.A.* 108 F5
Ellsworth Land, *Antarctica* 5 D16
Ellsworth Mts., *Antarctica* 5 D16
Ellwangen, *Germany* 19 G6
Ellwood City, *U.S.A.* 106 F4
Elm, *Switz.* 23 C8
Elma, *Canada* 101 D9
Elma, *U.S.A.* 112 D3
Elmadağ, *Turkey* 66 D5
Elmalı, *Turkey* 66 E3
Elmhurst, *U.S.A.* 104 E2
Elmina, *Ghana* 79 D4
Elmira, *Canada* 106 C4
Elmira, *U.S.A.* 106 D8
Elmore, *Australia* 91 F3
Elmore, *U.S.A.* 113 M11
Elmshorn, *Germany* 18 B5
Elmvale, *Canada* 106 B5
Elne, *France* 26 F6
Elora, *Canada* 106 C4
Elorza, *Venezuela* 120 B4
Eloúnda, *Greece* 37 D7
Eloy, *U.S.A.* 111 K8
Éloyes, *France* 25 D13
Elrose, *Canada* 101 C7
Elsas, *Canada* 98 C3
Elsie, *U.S.A.* 112 E3
Elsinore = Helsingør, *Denmark* 11 H6
Elsinore, *U.S.A.* 111 G7
Elspe, *Germany* 18 D4
Elspeet, *Neths.* 16 D7
Elst, *Neths.* 16 E7
Elster →, *Germany* 18 D7
Elsterwerda, *Germany* 18 D9
Elten, *Neths.* 16 E8
Eltham, *N.Z.* 87 H5
Elton, *Russia* 43 B12
Eluanbi, *Taiwan* 53 G13
Eluru, *India* 61 L12
Elvas, *Portugal* 31 G3
Elven, *France* 24 E4
Elverum, *Norway* 10 D5
Elvire →, *Australia* 88 C4
Elvo →, *Italy* 32 C5
Elvran, *Norway* 10 A5
Elwood, *Ind., U.S.A.* 104 E3
Elwood, *Nebr., U.S.A.* 108 E5
Ely, *U.K.* 13 E8
Ely, *Minn., U.S.A.* 108 B9
Ely, *Nev., U.S.A.* 110 G6
Elyria, *U.S.A.* 106 E2
Elz →, *Germany* 19 G3
Emāmrūd, *Iran* 65 B7
Emba, *Kazakhstan* 44 E6
Emba →, *Kazakhstan* 44 E6
Embarcación, *Argentina* 126 A3
Embarras Portage, *Canada* 101 B6
Embetsu, *Japan* 48 B10
Embira →, *Brazil* 124 B3
Embóna, *Greece* 37 C9
Embrach, *Switz.* 23 A7
Embrun, *France* 27 D10
Embu, *Kenya* 82 C4
Embu □, *Kenya* 82 C4
Emden, *Germany* 18 B3
Emerald, *Australia* 90 C4
Emerson, *Canada* 101 D9
Emery, *U.S.A.* 111 G8
Emet, *Turkey* 66 D3
Emi Koussi, *Chad* 73 E8
Emilia-Romagna □, *Italy* 32 D7
Emilius, Mte., *Italy* 32 C4
Eminabad, *Pakistan* 62 C6
Emirdağ, *Turkey* 66 D4
Emlenton, *U.S.A.* 106 E5
Emlichheim, *Germany* 18 C2
Emme →, *Switz.* 22 B5
Emmeloord, *Neths.* 16 C7
Emmen, *Neths.* 16 C9
Emmendingen, *Germany* 19 G3
Emmental, *Switz.* 22 C4
Emmer-Compascuum, *Neths.* 16 C10
Emmerich, *Germany* 18 D2
Emmet, *Australia* 90 C3
Emmetsburg, *U.S.A.* 108 D7
Emmett, *U.S.A.* 110 E5
Empalme, *Mexico* 114 B2
Empangeni, *S. Africa* 85 D5
Empedrado, *Argentina* 126 B4
Emperor Seamount Chain, *Pac. Oc.* 92 D9
Empoli, *Italy* 32 E7
Emporia, *Kans., U.S.A.* 108 F6
Emporia, *Va., U.S.A.* 105 G7
Emporium, *U.S.A.* 106 E6
Empress, *Canada* 101 C6
Emptinne, *Belgium* 17 H6
Empty Quarter = Rub' al Khali, *Si. Arabia* 68 D4
Ems →, *Germany* 18 B3
Emsdale, *Canada* 106 A5
Emsdetten, *Germany* 18 C3
Emu, *China* 51 C15
Emu Park, *Australia* 90 C5
'En 'Avrona, *Israel* 69 F3
En Nahud, *Sudan* 77 E2
Ena, *Japan* 49 G8
Enafors, *Sweden* 10 A6
Enambú, *Colombia* 120 C3
Enana, *Namibia* 84 B2
Enånger, *Sweden* 10 C11
Enaratoli, *Indonesia* 57 E9
Enard B., *U.K.* 14 C3
Enare = Inarijärvi, *Finland* 8 B19
Encantadas, Serra, *Brazil* 127 C5
Encanto, C., *Phil.* 57 A6
Encarnación, *Paraguay* 127 B4
Encarnación de Diaz, *Mexico* 114 C4
Enchi, *Ghana* 78 D4
Encinal, *U.S.A.* 109 L5
Encinitas, *U.S.A.* 113 M9
Encino, *U.S.A.* 111 J11
Encontrados, *Venezuela* 120 B3
Encounter B., *Australia* 91 F2
Encruzilhada, *Brazil* 123 E3
Ende, *Indonesia* 57 F6
Endeavour, *Canada* 101 C8
Endeavour Str., *Australia* 90 A3
Endelave, *Denmark* 11 J4
Enderbury I., *Kiribati* 92 H10
Enderby, *Canada* 100 C5
Enderby I., *Australia* 88 D2
Enderby Land, *Antarctica* 5 C5
Enderlin, *U.S.A.* 108 B6
Endicott, *N.Y., U.S.A.* 107 D8
Endicott, *Wash., U.S.A.* 110 C5
Endimari →, *Brazil* 124 B4
Endyalgout I., *Australia* 88 B5
Ene →, *Peru* 124 C3
Enewetak Atoll, *Pac. Oc.* 92 F8
Enez, *Turkey* 66 C2
Enfida, *Tunisia* 75 A7
Enfield, *U.K.* 13 F7
Engadin, *Switz.* 19 J6
Engaño, C., *Dom. Rep.* 117 C6
Engaño, C., *Phil.* 57 A6
Engcobo, *S. Africa* 85 E4
Engelberg, *Switz.* 23 C6
Engels = Pokrovsk, *Russia* 41 F15
Engemann L., *Canada* 101 B7
Enger, *Norway* 10 D4
Enggano, *Indonesia* 56 F2
Enghien, *Belgium* 17 G4
Engil, *Morocco* 74 B4
Engkilili, *Malaysia* 56 D4
England, *U.S.A.* 109 H9
England □, *U.K.* 7 E5
Englee, *Canada* 99 B8
Englehart, *Canada* 98 C4
Engler L., *Canada* 101 B7
Englewood, *Colo., U.S.A.* 108 F2
Englewood, *Kans., U.S.A.* 109 G5
English →, *Canada* 101 C10
English Bazar = Ingraj Bazar, *India* 63 G13
English Channel, *Europe* 13 G6
English River, *Canada* 98 C1
Enid, *U.S.A.* 109 G6
Enipévs →, *Greece* 39 K5
Enkhuizen, *Neths.* 16 C6
Enköping, *Sweden* 10 E11
Enle, *China* 52 E3
Enna, *Italy* 35 E7
Ennadai, *Canada* 101 A8
Ennadai L., *Canada* 101 A8
Ennedi, *Chad* 73 E9
Enngonia, *Australia* 91 D4
Ennis, *Ireland* 15 D3
Ennis, *Mont., U.S.A.* 110 D8
Ennis, *Tex., U.S.A.* 109 J6
Enniscorthy, *Ireland* 15 D5
Enniskillen, *U.K.* 15 B4
Ennistimon, *Ireland* 15 D2
Enns →, *Austria* 21 G4
Enontekiö, *Finland* 8 B17
Enping, *China* 53 F9
Enriquillo, L., *Dom. Rep.* 117 C5
Ens, *Neths.* 16 C7
Enschede, *Neths.* 16 D9
Ensenada, *Argentina* 126 C4
Ensenada, *Mexico* 114 A1
Enshi, *China* 52 B7
Ensiola, Pta., *Spain* 36 B9
Ensisheim, *France* 25 E14
Entebbe, *Uganda* 82 B3
Enter, *Neths.* 16 D9
Enterprise, *Canada* 100 A5
Enterprise, *Oreg., U.S.A.* 110 D5
Enterprise, *Utah, U.S.A.* 111 H7
Entlebuch, *Switz.* 22 C6
Entre Ríos, *Bolivia* 126 A3
Entre Rios, *Bahia, Brazil* 123 D4
Entre Rios, *Pará, Brazil* 125 B7
Entre Ríos □, *Argentina* 126 C4
Entrepeñas, Pantano de, *Spain* 28 E2
Enugu, *Nigeria* 79 D6
Enugu Ezike, *Nigeria* 79 D6
Enumclaw, *U.S.A.* 112 C5
Envermeu, *France* 24 C8
Envigado, *Colombia* 120 B2
Envira, *Brazil* 124 B3
Enz →, *Germany* 19 F5
Enza →, *Italy* 32 D7
Eólie, Is., *Italy* 35 D7
Epanomí, *Greece* 39 J5
Epe, *Neths.* 16 D7
Epe, *Nigeria* 79 D5
Épernay, *France* 25 C10
Épernon, *France* 25 D8
Ephesus, *Turkey* 66 E2
Ephraim, *U.S.A.* 110 G8
Ephrata, *U.S.A.* 110 C4
Epila, *Spain* 28 D3
Épinac-les-Mines, *France* 25 F11
Épinal, *France* 25 D13
Epira, *Guyana* 121 B6
Episkopi, *Cyprus* 37 E11
Episkopí, *Greece* 37 D6
Episkopi Bay, *Cyprus* 37 E11
Epping, *U.K.* 13 F8
Epukiro, *Namibia* 84 C2
Equatorial Guinea ■, *Africa* 80 D1
Equeipa, *Venezuela* 121 B5
Er Rahad, *Sudan* 77 E3
Er Rif, *Morocco* 75 A4
Er Roseires, *Sudan* 77 E3
Erāwadī Myit = Irrawaddy →, *Burma* 61 M19
Erba, *Italy* 32 C6
Erba, *Sudan* 76 D4
Erbaa, *Turkey* 66 C7
Erçek Gölü, *Turkey* 67 D10
Ercha, *Russia* 45 C15
Erçiş, *Turkey* 67 D10
Erciyaş Dağı, *Turkey* 66 D6
Erdao Jiang →, *China* 51 C14
Erdek, *Turkey* 66 C2
Erdemli, *Turkey* 66 E6
Erdene, *Mongolia* 50 B6
Erding, *Germany* 19 G7
Erdre →, *France* 24 E5
Erebato →, *Venezuela* 121 B5
Erebus, Mt., *Antarctica* 5 D11
Erechim, *Brazil* 127 B5
Ereğli, *Konya, Turkey* 66 E6
Ereğli, *Zonguldak, Turkey* 66 C4
Erei, Monti, *Italy* 35 E7
Erembodegem, *Belgium* 17 G4
Erenhot, *China* 50 C7
Eresma →, *Spain* 30 D6
Erewadi Myitwanya, *Burma* 61 M19
Erfenisdam, *S. Africa* 84 D4
Erfoud, *Morocco* 74 B4
Erft →, *Germany* 18 D2
Erfurt, *Germany* 18 E7
Ergani, *Turkey* 67 D8
Ergeni Vozvyshennost, *Russia* 43 C11
Ergli, *Latvia* 40 C4
Eria →, *Spain* 30 C5
Eriba, *Sudan* 77 D4
Eriboll, L., *U.K.* 14 C4
Erica, *Neths.* 16 C9
Érice, *Italy* 34 D5
Erie, *U.S.A.* 106 D4
Erie, L., *N. Amer.* 106 D3
Erie Canal, *U.S.A.* 106 C6
Erieau, *Canada* 106 D3
Erigavo, *Somali Rep.* 68 E4
Erikoúsa, *Greece* 37 A3
Eriksdale, *Canada* 101 C9
Erikslund, *Sweden* 10 B9
Erímanthos, *Greece* 39 M4
Erimo-misaki, *Japan* 48 D11
Eriswil, *Switz.* 22 B5
Erithraí, *Greece* 39 L6
Eritrea □, *Ethiopia* 77 E4
Erjas →, *Portugal* 31 F3
Erlangen, *Germany* 19 F7
Erldunda, *Australia* 90 D1
Erlin, *Taiwan* 53 F13
Ermelo, *Neths.* 16 D7
Ermelo, *S. Africa* 85 D4
Ermenak, *Turkey* 66 E5
Ermióni, *Greece* 39 M6
Ermones, *Greece* 37 A3
Ermoúpolis = Síros, *Greece* 39 M7
Ernakulam = Cochin, *India* 60 Q10
Erne →, *Ireland* 15 B3
Erne, Lower L., *U.K.* 15 B4
Erne, Upper L., *U.K.* 15 B4
Ernée, *France* 24 D6
Ernest Giles Ra., *Australia* 89 E3
Ernstberg, *Germany* 19 E2
Erode, *India* 60 P10
Eromanga, *Australia* 91 D3
Erongo, *Namibia* 84 C2
Erp, *Neths.* 17 E7
Erquelinnes, *Belgium* 17 H4
Erquy, *France* 24 D4
Erquy, C. d', *France* 24 D4
Err, Piz d', *Switz.* 23 C9
Errabiddy, *Australia* 89 E2
Erramala Hills, *India* 60 M11
Errer →, *Ethiopia* 77 F5
Errigal, *Ireland* 15 A3
Erris Hd., *Ireland* 15 B1
Erseka, *Albania* 39 J3
Erskine, *U.S.A.* 108 B7
Erstein, *France* 25 D14
Erstfeld, *Switz.* 23 C7
Ertil, *Russia* 41 F12
Ertvelde, *Belgium* 17 F3
Eruh, *Turkey* 67 E10
Eruwa, *Nigeria* 79 D5
Ervy-le-Châtel, *France* 25 D10
Erwin, *U.S.A.* 105 G4
Eryuan, *China* 52 D2
Erzgebirge, *Germany* 18 E9
Erzin, *Russia* 45 D10
Erzincan, *Turkey* 67 D8
Erzincan □, *Turkey* 67 D8
Erzurum, *Turkey* 67 D9
Erzurum □, *Turkey* 67 D9
Es Caló, *Spain* 36 C8
Es Caná, *Spain* 36 B8
Es Sahrâ' Esh Sharqîya, *Egypt* 76 B3
Es Sînâ', *Egypt* 76 J8
Es Sûkî, *Sudan* 77 E3
Esambo, *Zaïre* 82 C1
Esan-Misaki, *Japan* 48 D10
Esashi, *Hokkaidō, Japan* 48 B11
Esashi, *Hokkaidō, Japan* 48 D10
Esbjerg, *Denmark* 11 J2
Escada, *Brazil* 122 C4
Escalante, *U.S.A.* 111 H8
Escalante →, *U.S.A.* 111 H8
Escalón, *Mexico* 114 B4
Escalona, *Spain* 30 E6
Escambia →, *U.S.A.* 105 K2
Escanaba, *U.S.A.* 104 C2
Escaut →, *Belgium* 17 F3
Esch-sur-Alzette, *Lux.* 17 J7
Eschede, *Germany* 18 C6
Escholzmatt, *Switz.* 22 C5
Eschwege, *Germany* 18 D6
Eschweiler, *Germany* 18 E2
Escoma, *Bolivia* 124 D4
Escondido, *U.S.A.* 113 M9
Escuinapa, *Mexico* 114 C3
Escuintla, *Guatemala* 116 D1
Eséka, *Cameroon* 79 E7
Esens, *Germany* 18 B3
Esera →, *Spain* 28 C5
Eşfahān, *Iran* 65 C6
Esfīdeh, *Iran* 65 C8
Esgueva →, *Spain* 30 D6
Esh Sham = Dimashq, *Syria* 69 B5
Esh Shamâlîya □, *Sudan* 76 D2
Eshan, *China* 52 E4
Eshowe, *S. Africa* 85 D5
Esiama, *Ghana* 78 E4
Esino →, *Italy* 33 E10
Esk →, *Dumf. & Gall., U.K.* 14 G5
Esk →, *N. Yorks., U.K.* 12 C7
Eskifjörður, *Iceland* 8 D7
Eskilstuna, *Sweden* 10 E10
Eskimalatya, *Turkey* 67 D8
Eskimo Pt., *Canada* 101 A10
Eskişehir, *Turkey* 66 D4
Eskişehir □, *Turkey* 66 D4
Esla →, *Spain* 30 D4
Esla, Pantano del, *Spain* 30 D4
Eslāmābād-e Gharb, *Iran* 64 C5
Eslöv, *Sweden* 11 J7
Eşme, *Turkey* 66 D3
Esmeralda, I., *Chile* 128 C1
Esmeraldas, *Ecuador* 120 C2
Esmeraldas □, *Ecuador* 120 C2
Esmeraldas →, *Ecuador* 120 C2
Esneux, *Belgium* 17 G7
Espada, Pta., *Colombia* 120 A3
Espalion, *France* 26 D6
Espalmador, I., *Spain* 36 C7
Espanola, *Canada* 98 C3
Espardell, I. del, *Spain* 36 C7
Esparraguera, *Spain* 28 D6
Esparta, *Costa Rica* 116 E3
Espejo, *Spain* 31 H6
Esperança, *Brazil* 122 C4
Esperance, *Australia* 89 F3
Esperance B., *Australia* 89 F3
Esperantinópolis, *Brazil* 122 B3
Esperanza, *Santa Cruz, Argentina* 128 D2
Esperanza, *Santa Fe, Argentina* 126 C3
Esperanza, *Phil.* 55 G6
Espéraza, *France* 26 F6
Espichel, C., *Portugal* 31 G1
Espiel, *Spain* 31 G5
Espigão, Serra do, *Brazil* 127 B5
Espinal, *Colombia* 120 C3
Espinar, *Peru* 124 C3
Espinazo, Sierra del = Espinhaço, Serra do, *Brazil* 123 E3
Espinhaço, Serra do, *Brazil* 123 E3
Espinho, *Portugal* 30 D2
Espinilho, Serra do, *Brazil* 127 B5
Espino, *Venezuela* 120 B4
Espinosa de los Monteros, *Spain* 30 B7

Espírito Santo □, *Brazil* 123 F3
Espíritu Santo, B. del, *Mexico* 115 D7
Espíritu Santo, I., *Mexico* 114 C2
Espita, *Mexico* 115 C7
Espiye, *Turkey* 67 C8
Esplanada, *Brazil* 123 D4
Espluga de Francolí, *Spain* 28 D6
Espuña, Sierra, *Spain* 29 H3
Espungabera, *Mozam.* 85 C5
Esquel, *Argentina* 128 B2
Esquina, *Argentina* 126 B4
Essaouira, *Morocco* 74 B3
Essebie, *Zaïre* 82 B3
Essen, *Belgium* 17 F4
Essen, *Germany* 18 D2
Essendon, Mt., *Australia* 89 E3
Essequibo □, *Guyana* 121 B6
Essequibo →, *Guyana* 121 B6
Essex, *Canada* 106 D2
Essex, *Calif., U.S.A.* 113 L11
Essex, *N.Y., U.S.A.* 107 B11
Essex □, *U.K.* 13 F8
Esslingen, *Germany* 19 G5
Essonne □, *France* 25 D9
Essvik, *Sweden* 10 B11
Estaca, Pta. del, *Spain* 30 B3
Estadilla, *Spain* 28 C5
Estados, I. de Los, *Argentina* 128 D4
Estagel, *France* 26 F6
Eşţahbānāt, *Iran* 65 D7
Estallenchs, *Spain* 36 B9
Estância, *Brazil* 122 D4
Estancia, *U.S.A.* 111 J10
Estārm, *Iran* 65 D8
Estarreja, *Portugal* 30 E2
Estats, Pic d', *Spain* 28 C6
Estavayer-le-Lac, *Switz.* 22 C3
Estcourt, *S. Africa* 85 D4
Este, *Italy* 33 C8
Esteban, *Spain* 30 B4
Estelí, *Nic.* 116 D2
Estella, *Spain* 28 C2
Estelline, *S. Dak., U.S.A.* 108 C6
Estelline, *Tex., U.S.A.* 109 H4
Estena →, *Spain* 31 F6
Estepa, *Spain* 31 H6
Estepona, *Spain* 31 J5
Esterhazy, *Canada* 101 C8
Esternay, *France* 25 D10
Esterri de Aneu, *Spain* 28 C6
Estevan, *Canada* 101 D8
Estevan Group, *Canada* 100 C3
Estherville, *U.S.A.* 108 D7
Estissac, *France* 25 D10
Eston, *Canada* 101 C7
Estonia ■, *Europe* 40 B4
Estoril, *Portugal* 31 G1
Estouk, *Mali* 79 B5
Estrêla, Serra da, *Portugal* 30 E3
Estrella, *Spain* 29 G1
Estremoz, *Portugal* 31 G3
Estrondo, Serra do, *Brazil* 122 C2
Esztergom, *Hungary* 21 H8
Et Tîdra, *Mauritania* 78 B1
Étables-sur-Mer, *France* 24 D4
Etadunna, *Australia* 91 D2
Etah, *India* 63 F8
Étain, *France* 25 C12
Étalle, *Belgium* 17 J7
Etamamu, *Canada* 99 B8
Étampes, *France* 25 D9
Étang-sur-Arroux, *France* 27 B8
Etanga, *Namibia* 84 B1
Étaples, *France* 25 B8
Etawah, *India* 63 F8
Etawah →, *U.S.A.* 105 H3
Etawney L., *Canada* 101 B9
Ete, *Nigeria* 79 D6
Éthe, *Belgium* 17 J7
Ethel, *U.S.A.* 112 D4
Ethel, Oued el →, *Algeria* 74 C4
Ethel Creek, *Australia* 88 D3
Ethelbert, *Canada* 101 C8
Ethiopia ■, *Africa* 68 F3
Ethiopian Highlands, *Ethiopia* 70 E7
Etive, L., *U.K.* 14 E3
Etna, *Italy* 35 E8
Etoile, *Zaïre* 83 E2
Etolin I., *U.S.A.* 100 B2
Etosha Pan, *Namibia* 84 B2
Etowah, *U.S.A.* 105 H3
Étrépagny, *France* 25 C8
Étretat, *France* 24 C7
Ettelbruck, *Lux.* 17 J8
Etten, *Neths.* 17 E5
Ettlingen, *Germany* 19 G4
Ettrick Water →, *U.K.* 14 F6
Etuku, *Zaïre* 82 C2
Etzatlán, *Mexico* 114 C4
Eu, *France* 24 B8
Euboea = Évvoia, *Greece* 39 L7
Eucla Motel, *Australia* 89 F4
Euclid, *U.S.A.* 106 E3
Euclides da Cunha, *Brazil* 122 D4
Eucumbene, L., *Australia* 91 F4
Eudora, *U.S.A.* 109 J9
Eufaula, *Ala., U.S.A.* 105 K3
Eufaula, *Okla., U.S.A.* 109 H7
Eufaula, L., *U.S.A.* 109 H7
Eugene, *U.S.A.* 110 E2
Eugowra, *Australia* 91 E4
Eulo, *Australia* 91 D4
Eunice, *La., U.S.A.* 109 K8
Eunice, *N. Mex., U.S.A.* 109 J3
Eupen, *Belgium* 17 G8
Euphrates = Furāt, Nahr al →, *Asia* 64 D5
Eure □, *France* 24 C8
Eure →, *France* 24 C8
Eure-et-Loir □, *France* 24 D8
Eureka, *Canada* 4 B3
Eureka, *Calif., U.S.A.* 110 F1
Eureka, *Kans., U.S.A.* 109 G6
Eureka, *Mont., U.S.A.* 110 B6
Eureka, *Nev., U.S.A.* 110 G5
Eureka, *S. Dak., U.S.A.* 108 C5
Eureka, *Utah, U.S.A.* 110 G7
Eureka, Mt., *Australia* 89 E3
Euroa, *Australia* 91 F4
Europa, I., *Ind. Oc.* 81 J8
Europa, Picos de, *Spain* 30 B6
Europa, Pta. de, *Gib.* 31 J5
Europa Pt. = Europa, Pta. de, *Gib.* 31 J5
Europe 6 F10
Europoort, *Neths.* 16 E4
Euskirchen, *Germany* 18 E2
Eustis, *U.S.A.* 105 L5
Eutin, *Germany* 18 A6
Eutsuk L., *Canada* 100 C3
Eva, *Brazil* 121 D6
Eva Downs, *Australia* 90 B1
Evale, *Angola* 84 B2
Evans, *U.S.A.* 108 E2
Evans Head, *Australia* 91 D5
Evans L., *Canada* 98 B4
Evans Mills, *U.S.A.* 107 B9
Evanston, *Ill., U.S.A.* 104 D2
Evanston, *Wyo., U.S.A.* 110 F8
Evansville, *Ind., U.S.A.* 104 F2
Evansville, *Wis., U.S.A.* 108 D10
Évaux-les-Bains, *France* 26 B6
Evaz, *Iran* 65 E7
Eveleth, *U.S.A.* 108 B8
Evensk, *Russia* 45 C16
Evenstad, *Norway* 10 C5
Everard, L., *Australia* 91 E1
Everard Park, *Australia* 89 E5
Everard Ras., *Australia* 89 E5
Evere, *Belgium* 17 G4
Everest, Mt., *Nepal* 63 E12
Everett, *Pa., U.S.A.* 106 F6
Everett, *Wash., U.S.A.* 112 C4
Evergem, *Belgium* 17 F3
Everglades, *U.S.A.* 105 N5
Everglades City, *U.S.A.* 105 N5
Everglades Nat. Park., *U.S.A.* 105 N5
Evergreen, *U.S.A.* 105 K2
Everson, *U.S.A.* 110 B2
Evesham, *U.K.* 13 E6
Évian-les-Bains, *France* 27 B10
Evinayong, *Eq. Guin.* 80 D2
Évinos →, *Greece* 39 L4
Évisa, *France* 27 F12
Évora, *Portugal* 31 G3
Évora □, *Portugal* 31 G3
Evowghlī, *Iran* 64 B5
Évreux, *France* 24 C8
Évron, *France* 24 D6
Evrótas →, *Greece* 39 N5
Évvoia, *Greece* 39 L7
Évvoia □, *Greece* 39 L6
Ewe, L., *U.K.* 14 D3
Ewing, *U.S.A.* 108 D5
Ewo, *Congo* 80 E2
Exaltación, *Bolivia* 125 C4
Excelsior Springs, *U.S.A.* 108 F7
Excideuil, *France* 26 C5
Exe →, *U.K.* 13 G4
Exeter, *Canada* 106 C3
Exeter, *U.K.* 13 G4
Exeter, *Calif., U.S.A.* 111 H4
Exeter, *N.H., U.S.A.* 107 D14
Exeter, *Nebr., U.S.A.* 108 E6
Exloo, *Neths.* 16 C9
Exmes, *France* 24 D7
Exmoor, *U.K.* 13 F4
Exmouth, *Australia* 88 D1
Exmouth, *U.K.* 13 G4
Exmouth G., *Australia* 88 D1
Expedition Ra., *Australia* 90 C4
Extremadura □, *Spain* 31 F4
Exuma Sound, *Bahamas* 116 B4
Eyasi, L., *Tanzania* 82 C4
Eyeberry L., *Canada* 101 A8
Eyemouth, *U.K.* 14 F6
Eygurande, *France* 26 C6
Eyjafjörður, *Iceland* 8 C4
Eymet, *France* 26 D4
Eymoutiers, *France* 26 C5
Eynesil, *Turkey* 67 C8
Eyrarbakki, *Iceland* 8 E3
Eyre, *Australia* 89 F4
Eyre (North), L., *Australia* 91 D2
Eyre (South), L., *Australia* 91 D2
Eyre Cr. →, *Australia* 91 D2
Eyre Mts., *N.Z.* 87 L2
Eyre Pen., *Australia* 91 E2
Eyvānkī, *Iran* 65 C6
Ez Zeidab, *Sudan* 76 D3
Ezcaray, *Spain* 28 C2
Ezine, *Turkey* 66 D2
Ezmul, *Mauritania* 74 D1
Ezouza →, *Cyprus* 37 E11

F

Fabens, *U.S.A.* 111 L10
Fåborg, *Denmark* 11 J4
Fabriano, *Italy* 33 E9
Făcăeni, *Romania* 38 E10
Facatativá, *Colombia* 120 C3
Fachi, *Niger* 72 E7
Facture, *France* 26 D3
Fada, *Chad* 73 E9
Fada-n-Gourma, *Burkina Faso* 79 C5
Faddeyevskiy, Ostrov, *Russia* 45 B15
Fadghāmī, *Syria* 64 C4
Fadlab, *Sudan* 76 D3
Faenza, *Italy* 33 D8
Fafa, *Mali* 79 B5
Fafe, *Portugal* 30 D2
Fagam, *Nigeria* 79 C7
Făgăras, *Romania* 38 D7
Făgăras, Munţii, *Romania* 38 D7
Fågelsjö, *Sweden* 10 C8
Fagernes, *Norway* 9 F10
Fagersta, *Sweden* 9 F13
Făget, *Romania* 38 D5
Fagnano, L., *Argentina* 128 D3
Fagnano Castello, *Italy* 35 C9
Fagnières, *France* 25 D11
Fahlīān, *Iran* 65 D6
Fahraj, *Kermān, Iran* 65 D8
Fahraj, *Yazd, Iran* 65 D7
Faial, *Madeira* 36 D3
Faido, *Switz.* 23 D7
Fair Hd., *U.K.* 15 A5
Fair Oaks, *U.S.A.* 112 G5
Fairbank, *U.S.A.* 111 L8
Fairbanks, *U.S.A.* 96 B5
Fairbury, *U.S.A.* 108 E6
Fairfax, *U.S.A.* 109 G6
Fairfield, *Ala., U.S.A.* 105 J2
Fairfield, *Calif., U.S.A.* 112 G4
Fairfield, *Conn., U.S.A.* 107 E11
Fairfield, *Idaho, U.S.A.* 110 E6
Fairfield, *Ill., U.S.A.* 104 F1
Fairfield, *Iowa, U.S.A.* 108 E9
Fairfield, *Mont., U.S.A.* 110 C8
Fairfield, *Tex., U.S.A.* 109 K7
Fairford, *Canada* 101 C9
Fairhope, *U.S.A.* 105 K2
Fairlie, *N.Z.* 87 L3
Fairmead, *U.S.A.* 112 H6
Fairmont, *Minn., U.S.A.* 108 D7
Fairmont, *W. Va., U.S.A.* 104 F5
Fairmount, *U.S.A.* 113 L8
Fairplay, *U.S.A.* 111 G11
Fairport, *N.Y., U.S.A.* 106 C7
Fairport, *Ohio, U.S.A.* 106 E3
Fairview, *Australia* 90 B3
Fairview, *Canada* 100 B5
Fairview, *N. Dak., U.S.A.* 108 B2
Fairview, *Okla., U.S.A.* 109 G5
Fairview, *Utah, U.S.A.* 110 G8
Fairweather, Mt., *U.S.A.* 96 C6
Faisalabad, *Pakistan* 62 D5
Faith, *U.S.A.* 108 C3
Faizabad, *India* 63 F10
Fajardo, *Puerto Rico* 117 C6
Fakfak, *Indonesia* 57 E8
Fakobli, *Ivory C.* 78 D3
Fakse, *Denmark* 11 J6
Fakse B., *Denmark* 11 J6
Fakse Ladeplads, *Denmark* 11 J6
Faku, *China* 51 C12
Falaise, *France* 24 D6
Falaise, Mui, *Vietnam* 58 C5
Falam, *Burma* 61 H18
Falces, *Spain* 28 C3
Fălciu, *Romania* 38 C11
Falcón □, *Venezuela* 120 A4
Falcón, C., *Spain* 36 C7
Falcon, C., *Algeria* 75 A4
Falcon Dam, *U.S.A.* 109 M5
Falconara Marittima, *Italy* 33 E10
Falconer, *U.S.A.* 106 D5
Faléa, *Mali* 78 C2
Falenki, *Russia* 41 B17
Faleshty, *Moldavia* 42 C2
Falfurrias, *U.S.A.* 109 M5
Falher, *Canada* 100 B5
Falirakí, *Greece* 37 C10
Falkenberg, *Germany* 18 D9
Falkenberg, *Sweden* 11 H6
Falkensee, *Germany* 18 C9
Falkenstein, *Germany* 18 E8
Falkirk, *U.K.* 14 F5
Falkland, East, I., *Falk. Is.* 128 D5
Falkland, West, I., *Falk. Is.* 128 D4
Falkland Is., *Atl. Oc.* 128 D5
Falkland Is. Dependency □, *Atl. Oc.* 5 B1
Falkland Sd., *Falk. Is.* 128 D5
Falköping, *Sweden* 11 F7
Fall River, *U.S.A.* 107 E13
Fall River Mills, *U.S.A.* 110 F3
Fallbrook, *U.S.A.* 111 K5
Fallbrook, *U.S.A.* 113 M9
Fallon, *Mont., U.S.A.* 108 B2
Fallon, *Nev., U.S.A.* 110 G4
Falls City, *Nebr., U.S.A.* 108 E7
Falls City, *Oreg., U.S.A.* 110 D2
Falls Creek, *U.S.A.* 106 E6
Falmouth, *Jamaica* 116 C4
Falmouth, *U.K.* 13 G2
Falmouth, *U.S.A.* 104 F3
False B., *S. Africa* 84 E2
Falset, *Spain* 28 D5
Falso, C., *Honduras* 116 C3
Falster, *Denmark* 11 K5
Falsterbo, *Sweden* 11 J6
Fălticeni, *Romania* 38 B9
Falun, *Sweden* 9 F13
Famagusta, *Cyprus* 37 D12
Famagusta Bay, *Cyprus* 37 D13
Famatina, Sierra de, *Argentina* 126 B2
Family L., *Canada* 101 C9
Famoso, *U.S.A.* 113 K7
Fan Xian, *China* 50 G8
Fana, *Mali* 78 C3
Fandriana, *Madag.* 85 C8
Fang, *Thailand* 58 C2
Fang Xian, *China* 53 A8
Fangchang, *China* 53 B12
Fangcheng, *Guangxi Zhuangzu, China* 52 G7
Fangcheng, *Henan, China* 50 H7
Fangliao, *Taiwan* 53 F13
Fangshan, *China* 50 E6
Fangzi, *China* 51 F10
Fani i Madh →, *Albania* 39 H3
Fanjiatun, *China* 51 C13
Fannich, L., *U.K.* 14 D4
Fannūj, *Iran* 65 E8
Fanny Bay, *Canada* 100 D4
Fanø, *Denmark* 11 J2
Fano, *Italy* 33 E10
Fanshaw, *U.S.A.* 100 B2
Fanshi, *China* 50 E7
Fao = Al Fāw, *Iraq* 65 D6
Faqirwali, *Pakistan* 62 E5
Fara in Sabina, *Italy* 33 F9
Faradje, *Zaïre* 82 B2
Farafangana, *Madag.* 85 C8
Farâfra, El Wâhât el-, *Egypt* 76 B2
Farāh, *Afghan.* 60 C3
Farāh □, *Afghan.* 60 C3
Farahalana, *Madag.* 85 A9
Faraid, Gebel, *Egypt* 76 C4
Faramana, *Burkina Faso* 78 C4
Faranah, *Guinea* 78 C2
Farasān, Jazā'ir, *Si. Arabia* 68 D3
Farasan Is. = Farasān, Jazā'ir, *Si. Arabia* 68 D3
Faratsiho, *Madag.* 85 B8
Fardes →, *Spain* 29 H1
Fareham, *U.K.* 13 G6
Farewell, C., *N.Z.* 87 J4
Farewell C. = Farvel, Kap, *Greenland* 4 D5
Fargo, *U.S.A.* 108 B6
Fari'a →, *Jordan* 69 C4
Faribault, *U.S.A.* 108 C8
Faridkot, *India* 62 D6
Faridpur, *Bangla.* 63 H13
Färila, *Sweden* 10 C9
Farim, *Guinea-Biss.* 78 C1
Farīmān, *Iran* 65 C8
Farina, *Australia* 91 E2
Farinha →, *Brazil* 122 C2
Fariones, Pta., *Canary Is.* 36 E6
Fâriskûr, *Egypt* 76 H7
Farmerville, *U.S.A.* 109 J8
Farmington, *Calif., U.S.A.* 112 H6
Farmington, *N.H., U.S.A.* 107 C13
Farmington, *N. Mex., U.S.A.* 111 H9
Farmington, *Utah, U.S.A.* 110 F8
Farmington →, *U.S.A.* 107 E12
Farmville, *U.S.A.* 104 G6
Farnborough, *U.K.* 13 F7
Farne Is., *U.K.* 12 B6
Farnham, *Canada* 107 A12
Faro, *Brazil* 121 D6
Faro, *Portugal* 31 H3
Fårö, *Sweden* 9 H15
Faro □, *Portugal* 31 H2
Faroe Is. = Føroyar, *Atl. Oc.* 7 C4
Farquhar, C., *Australia* 89 D1
Farrars Cr. →, *Australia* 90 D3
Farrāshband, *Iran* 65 D7
Farrell, *U.S.A.* 106 E4
Farrell Flat, *Australia* 91 E2
Farrokhī, *Iran* 65 C8
Farruch, C., *Spain* 36 B10
Farrukhabad-cum-Fatehgarh, *India* 63 F8
Fārs □, *Iran* 65 D7
Fársala, *Greece* 39 K5
Farsø, *Denmark* 11 H3
Farsund, *Norway* 9 G9
Fartak, Râs, *Si. Arabia* 64 D2
Fartura, Serra da, *Brazil* 127 B5
Fārūj, *Iran* 65 B8
Farum, *Denmark* 11 J6
Farvel, Kap, *Greenland* 4 D5
Farwell, *U.S.A.* 109 H3
Fasā, *Iran* 65 D7
Fasano, *Italy* 35 B10
Fashoda, *Sudan* 77 F3
Fastnet Rock, *Ireland* 15 E2
Fastov, *Ukraine* 40 F6
Fatagar, Tanjung, *Indonesia* 57 E8
Fatehgarh, *India* 63 F8
Fatehpur, *Raj., India* 62 F6
Fatehpur, *Ut. P., India* 63 G9
Fatesh, *Russia* 41 E9
Fatick, *Senegal* 78 C1
Fatima, *Canada* 99 C7
Fátima, *Portugal* 31 F2
Fatoya, *Guinea* 78 C3
Faucille, Col de la, *France* 27 B10
Faulkton, *U.S.A.* 108 C5
Faulquemont, *France* 25 C13
Fauquembergues, *France* 25 B9
Faure I., *Australia* 89 E1
Făurei, *Romania* 38 D10
Fauresmith, *S. Africa* 84 D4
Fauske, *Norway* 8 C13
Fauvillers, *Belgium* 17 J7
Favara, *Italy* 34 E6
Favaritx, C., *Spain* 36 A11
Favignana, *Italy* 34 E5
Favignana, I., *Italy* 34 E5
Favourable Lake, *Canada* 98 B1
Fawn →, *Canada* 98 A2
Fawnskin, *U.S.A.* 113 L10
Faxaflói, *Iceland* 8 D2
Faya-Largeau, *Chad* 73 E8
Fayd, *Si. Arabia* 64 E4
Fayence, *France* 27 E10
Fayette, *Ala., U.S.A.* 105 J2
Fayette, *Mo., U.S.A.* 108 F8
Fayetteville, *Ark., U.S.A.* 109 G7
Fayetteville, *N.C., U.S.A.* 105 H6
Fayetteville, *Tenn., U.S.A.* 105 H2
Fayón, *Spain* 28 D5
Fazenda Nova, *Brazil* 123 E1
Fazilka, *India* 62 D6
Fazilpur, *Pakistan* 62 E4
Fdérik, *Mauritania* 74 D2
Feale →, *Ireland* 15 D2
Fear, C., *U.S.A.* 105 J7
Feather →, *U.S.A.* 110 G3
Feather Falls, *U.S.A.* 112 F5
Featherston, *N.Z.* 87 J5
Featherstone, *Zimbabwe* 83 F3
Fécamp, *France* 24 C7
Fedala = Mohammedia, *Morocco* 74 B3
Federación, *Argentina* 126 C4
Fedeshkūh, *Iran* 65 D7
Fedjadj, Chott el, *Tunisia* 75 B6
Fehmarn, *Germany* 18 A7
Fehmarn Bælt, *Denmark* 18 A7
Fei Xian, *China* 51 G9
Feijó, *Brazil* 124 B3
Feilding, *N.Z.* 87 J5
Feira de Santana, *Brazil* 123 D4
Feixiang, *China* 50 F8
Fejø, *Denmark* 11 K5
Feke, *Turkey* 66 E6
Felanitx, *Spain* 36 B10
Feldberg, *Baden-W., Germany* 19 H3
Feldberg, *Mecklenburg-Vorpommern, Germany* 18 B9
Feldkirch, *Austria* 19 H5
Felipe Carrillo Puerto, *Mexico* 115 D7
Felixlândia, *Brazil* 123 E3
Felixstowe, *U.K.* 13 F9
Felletin, *France* 26 C6
Felton, *U.K.* 12 B6
Felton, *U.S.A.* 112 H4
Feltre, *Italy* 33 B8
Femø, *Denmark* 11 K5
Femunden, *Norway* 10 B5
Fen He →, *China* 50 G6
Fenelon Falls, *Canada* 106 B6
Feneroa, *Ethiopia* 77 E4
Feng Xian, *Jiangsu, China* 50 G9
Feng Xian, *Shaanxi, China* 50 H4
Fengári, *Greece* 39 J8
Fengcheng, *Jiangxi, China* 53 C10
Fengcheng, *Liaoning, China* 51 D13
Fengdu, *China* 52 C6
Fengfeng, *China* 50 F8
Fenggang, *China* 52 D6
Fenghua, *China* 53 C13
Fenghuang, *China* 52 D7
Fenghuangzui, *China* 52 A7
Fengjie, *China* 52 B7
Fengkai, *China* 53 F8
Fengle, *China* 53 B9
Fengning, *China* 50 D9
Fengqing, *China* 52 E2
Fengqiu, *China* 50 G8
Fengrun, *China* 51 E10
Fengshan, *Guangxi Zhuangzu, China* 52 E7
Fengshan, *Guangxi Zhuangzu, China* 52 E6
Fengtai, *Anhui, China* 53 A11
Fengtai, *Beijing, China* 50 E9
Fengxian, *China* 53 B13
Fengxiang, *China* 50 G4
Fengxin, *China* 53 C10
Fengyang, *China* 51 H9
Fengyi, *China* 52 E3
Fengzhen, *China* 50 D7
Fenit, *Ireland* 15 D2
Fennimore, *U.S.A.* 108 D9
Feno, C. de, *France* 27 G12

Foum Assaka

Fenoarivo Afovoany, *Madag.* 85 B8
Fenoarivo Atsinanana, *Madag.* 85 B8
Fens, The, *U.K.* 12 E8
Fenton, *U.S.A.* 104 D4
Fenxi, *China* 50 F6
Fenyang, *China* 54 C6
Fenyang, *Shanxi, China* 50 F6
Fenyi, *China* 53 D10
Feodosiya, *Ukraine* 42 D6
Fer, C. de, *Algeria* 75 A6
Ferdows, *Iran* 65 C8
Fère-Champenoise, *France* 25 D10
Fère-en-Tardenois, *France* 25 C10
Ferentino, *Italy* 34 A6
Ferfer, *Somali Rep.* 68 F4
Fergana, *Uzbekistan* 44 E8
Fergus, *Canada* 98 D3
Fergus Falls, *U.S.A.* 108 B6
Fériana, *Tunisia* 75 B6
Feričanci, *Croatia* 21 K8
Ferkane, *Algeria* 75 B6
Ferkéssédougou, *Ivory C.* 78 D3
Ferlach, *Austria* 21 J4
Ferland, *Canada* 98 B2
Ferlo, Vallée du, *Senegal* 78 B2
Fermanagh □, *U.K.* 15 B4
Fermo, *Italy* 33 E10
Fermoselle, *Spain* 30 D4
Fermoy, *Ireland* 15 D3
Fernán Nuñéz, *Spain* 31 H6
Fernández, *Argentina* 126 B3
Fernandina Beach, *U.S.A.* 105 K5
Fernando de Noronha, *Brazil* 122 B5
Fernando Póo = Bioko, *Eq. Guin.* 79 E6
Fernandópolis, *Brazil* 123 F1
Ferndale, *Calif., U.S.A.* 110 F1
Ferndale, *Wash., U.S.A.* 112 B4
Fernie, *Canada* 100 D5
Fernlees, *Australia* 90 C4
Fernley, *U.S.A.* 110 G4
Ferozepore = Firozpur, *India* 62 D6
Férrai, *Greece* 39 J9
Ferrandina, *Italy* 35 B9
Ferrara, *Italy* 33 D8
Ferrato, C., *Italy* 34 C2
Ferreira do Alentejo, *Portugal* 31 G2
Ferreñafe, *Peru* 124 B2
Ferrerías, *Spain* 36 B11
Ferret, C., *France* 26 D2
Ferrette, *France* 25 E14
Ferriday, *U.S.A.* 109 K9
Ferrières, *France* 25 D9
Ferriete, *Italy* 32 D6
Ferrol, Pen. de, *Peru* 124 B2
Ferron, *U.S.A.* 111 G8
Ferros, *Brazil* 123 E3
Ferryland, *Canada* 99 C9
Fertile, *U.S.A.* 108 B6
Fertília, *Italy* 34 B1
Fès, *Morocco* 74 B4
Feschaux, *Belgium* 17 H5
Feshi, *Zaïre* 80 F3
Fessenden, *U.S.A.* 108 B5
Feteşti, *Romania* 38 E10
Fethiye, *Turkey* 66 E3
Fetlar, *U.K.* 14 A8
Feuerthalen, *Switz.* 23 A7
Feuilles →, *Canada* 97 C12
Feurs, *France* 27 C8
Fezzan, *Libya* 70 D5
Ffestiniog, *U.K.* 12 E4
Fiambalá, *Argentina* 126 B2
Fianarantsoa, *Madag.* 85 C8
Fianarantsoa □, *Madag.* 85 B8
Fianga, *Cameroon* 73 G8
Fichtelgebirge, *Germany* 19 E7
Ficksburg, *S. Africa* 85 D4
Fidenza, *Italy* 32 D7
Fiditi, *Nigeria* 79 D5
Field, *Canada* 98 C3
Field →, *Australia* 90 C2
Field I., *Australia* 88 B5
Fieri, *Albania* 39 J2
Fiesch, *Switz.* 22 D6
Fife □, *U.K.* 14 E5
Fife Ness, *U.K.* 14 E6
Fifth Cataract, *Sudan* 76 D3
Figeac, *France* 26 D6
Figline Valdarno, *Italy* 33 E8
Figtree, *Zimbabwe* 83 G2
Figueira Castelo Rodrigo, *Portugal* 30 E4
Figueira da Foz, *Portugal* 30 E2
Figueiró dos Vinhos, *Portugal* 30 F2
Figueras, *Spain* 28 C7
Figuig, *Morocco* 75 B4
Fihaonana, *Madag.* 85 B8
Fiherenana, *Madag.* 85 B8
Fiherenana →, *Madag.* 85 C7
Fiji ■, *Pac. Oc.* 87 C8
Fika, *Nigeria* 79 C7
Filabres, Sierra de los, *Spain* 29 H2
Filadelfia, *Bolivia* 124 C4
Filadélfia, *Brazil* 122 C2
Filadélfia, *Italy* 35 D9
Filer, *U.S.A.* 110 E6
Filey, *U.K.* 12 C7
Filfla, *Malta* 37 D1
Filiaşi, *Romania* 38 E6
Filiátes, *Greece* 39 K3
Filiatrá, *Greece* 39 M4
Filicudi, *Italy* 35 D7
Filiourí →, *Greece* 39 H8
Filipstad, *Sweden* 9 G13
Filisur, *Switz.* 23 C9
Fillmore, *Canada* 101 D8
Fillmore, *Calif., U.S.A.* 113 L8
Fillmore, *Utah, U.S.A.* 111 G7
Filottrano, *Italy* 33 E10
Filyos, *Turkey* 42 F5
Finale Lígure, *Italy* 32 D5
Finale nell' Emília, *Italy* 33 D8
Fiñana, *Spain* 29 H2
Finch, *Canada* 107 A9
Findhorn →, *U.K.* 14 D5
Findlay, *U.S.A.* 104 E4
Finger L., *Canada* 101 C10
Fíngõe, *Mozam.* 83 E3
Finike, *Turkey* 66 E4
Finistère □, *France* 24 D2
Finisterre, *Spain* 30 C1
Finisterre, C., *Spain* 30 C1
Finke, *Australia* 90 D1
Finke →, *Australia* 91 D2
Finland ■, *Europe* 9 E19
Finland, G. of, *Europe* 9 G19
Finlay →, *Canada* 100 B3
Finley, *Australia* 91 F4
Finley, *U.S.A.* 108 B6
Finn →, *Ireland* 15 B4
Finnigan, Mt., *Australia* 90 B4
Finniss, C., *Australia* 91 E1
Finnmark fylke □, *Norway* 8 B18
Finsteraarhorn, *Switz.* 22 C6
Finsterwalde, *Germany* 18 D9
Finsterwolde, *Neths.* 16 B10
Fiora →, *Italy* 33 F8
Fiorenzuola d'Arda, *Italy* 32 D6
Fīq, *Syria* 69 C4
Firat = Furāt, Nahr al →, *Asia* 64 D5
Fire River, *Canada* 98 C3
Firebag →, *Canada* 101 B6
Firebaugh, *U.S.A.* 112 J6
Firedrake L., *Canada* 101 A8
Firenze, *Italy* 33 E8
Firk →, *Iraq* 64 D5
Firmi, *France* 26 D6
Firminy, *France* 27 C8
Firozabad, *India* 63 F8
Firozpur, *India* 62 D6
Fīrūzābād, *Iran* 65 D7
Fīrūzkūh, *Iran* 65 C7
Firvale, *Canada* 100 C3
Fish →, *Namibia* 84 D2
Fish →, *S. Africa* 84 E3
Fisher, *Australia* 89 F5
Fisher B., *Canada* 101 C9
Fishguard, *U.K.* 13 F3
Fishing L., *Canada* 101 C9
Fismes, *France* 25 C10
Fitchburg, *U.S.A.* 107 D13
Fitero, *Spain* 28 C3
Fitri, L., *Chad* 73 F8
Fitz Roy, *Argentina* 128 C3
Fitzgerald, *Canada* 100 B6
Fitzgerald, *U.S.A.* 105 K4
Fitzmaurice →, *Australia* 88 B5
Fitzroy →, *Queens., Australia* 90 C5
Fitzroy →, *W. Austral., Australia* 88 C3
Fitzroy Crossing, *Australia* 88 C4
Fitzwilliam I., *Canada* 106 A3
Fiume = Rijeka, *Croatia* 33 C11
Fiumefreddo Brúzio, *Italy* 35 C9
Five Points, *U.S.A.* 112 J6
Fivizzano, *Italy* 32 D7
Fizi, *Zaïre* 82 C2
Fjellerup, *Denmark* 11 H4
Fjerritslev, *Denmark* 11 G3
Fkih ben Salah, *Morocco* 74 B3
Flå, *Norway* 10 A4
Flagler, *U.S.A.* 108 F3
Flagstaff, *U.S.A.* 111 J8
Flaherty I., *Canada* 98 A4
Flåm, *Norway* 9 F9
Flambeau →, *U.S.A.* 108 C9
Flamborough Hd., *U.K.* 12 C7
Flaming Gorge Dam, *U.S.A.* 110 F9
Flaming Gorge Res., *U.S.A.* 110 F9
Flamingo, Teluk, *Indonesia* 57 F9
Flanders = West-Vlaanderen □, *Belgium* 17 G2
Flandre Occidentale = West-Vlaanderen □, *Belgium* 17 G2
Flandre Orientale = Oost-Vlaanderen □, *Belgium* 17 F3
Flandreau, *U.S.A.* 108 C6
Flanigan, *U.S.A.* 112 E7
Flannan Is., *U.K.* 14 C1
Flåsjön, *Sweden* 8 D13
Flat →, *Canada* 100 A3
Flat River, *U.S.A.* 109 G9
Flatey, *Barðastrandarsýsla, Iceland* 8 C5
Flatey, *Suður-þingeyjarsýsla, Iceland* 8 D2
Flathead L., *U.S.A.* 110 C6
Flattery, C., *Australia* 90 A4
Flattery, C., *U.S.A.* 112 B2
Flavy-le-Martel, *France* 25 C10
Flawil, *Switz.* 23 B8
Flaxton, *U.S.A.* 108 A3
Fleetwood, *U.K.* 12 D4
Flekkefjord, *Norway* 9 G9
Flémalle, *Belgium* 17 G6
Flemington, *U.S.A.* 106 E7
Flensborg Fjord, *Germany* 11 K3
Flensburg, *Germany* 18 A5
Flers, *France* 24 D6
Flesherton, *Canada* 106 B4
Flesko, Tanjung, *Indonesia* 57 D6
Fleurance, *France* 26 E4
Fleurier, *Switz.* 22 C3
Fleurus, *Belgium* 17 H5
Flevoland □, *Neths.* 16 C7
Flims, *Switz.* 23 C8
Flin Flon, *Canada* 101 C8
Flinders, *Australia* 91 E2
Flinders →, *Australia* 90 B3
Flinders B., *Australia* 89 F2
Flinders Group, *Australia* 90 A3
Flinders I., *Australia* 90 F4
Flinders Reefs, *Australia* 90 B4
Flint, *U.K.* 12 D4
Flint, *U.S.A.* 104 D4
Flint →, *U.S.A.* 105 K3
Flint I., *Kiribati* 93 J12
Flinton, *Australia* 91 D4
Flix, *Spain* 28 D5
Flixecourt, *France* 25 B9
Flobecq, *Belgium* 17 G3
Flodden, *U.K.* 12 B5
Floodwood, *U.S.A.* 108 B8
Flora, *Norway* 10 A5
Flora, *U.S.A.* 104 F1
Florac, *France* 26 D7
Florala, *U.S.A.* 105 K2
Florânia, *Brazil* 122 C4
Floreffe, *Belgium* 17 H5
Florence = Firenze, *Italy* 33 E8
Florence, *Ala., U.S.A.* 105 H2
Florence, *Ariz., U.S.A.* 111 K8
Florence, *Colo., U.S.A.* 108 F2
Florence, *Oreg., U.S.A.* 110 E1
Florence, *S.C., U.S.A.* 105 H6
Florence, L., *Australia* 91 D2
Florennes, *Belgium* 17 H5
Florensac, *France* 26 E7
Florenville, *Belgium* 17 J6
Flores, *Brazil* 122 C4
Flores, *Guatemala* 116 C2
Flores, *Indonesia* 57 F6
Flores I., *Canada* 100 D3
Flores Sea, *Indonesia* 57 F6
Floresta, *Brazil* 122 C4
Floresville, *U.S.A.* 109 L5
Floriano, *Brazil* 122 C3
Florianópolis, *Brazil* 127 B6
Florida, *Cuba* 116 B4
Florida, *Uruguay* 127 C4
Florida □, *U.S.A.* 105 L5
Florida, Straits of, *U.S.A.* 116 B3
Florida B., *U.S.A.* 116 A3
Florida Keys, *U.S.A.* 116 B3
Florídia, *Italy* 35 E8
Floridsdorf, *Austria* 21 G6
Flórina, *Greece* 39 J4
Florø, *Norway* 9 F8
Flower Station, *Canada* 107 A8
Flower's Cove, *Canada* 99 B8
Floydada, *U.S.A.* 109 J4
Fluk, *Indonesia* 57 E7
Flumen →, *Spain* 28 D4
Flumendosa →, *Italy* 34 C2
Fluminimaggiore, *Italy* 34 C1
Flushing = Vlissingen, *Neths.* 17 F3
Fluviá →, *Spain* 28 C8
Flying Fish, C., *Antarctica* 5 D15
Foam Lake, *Canada* 101 C8
Foča, *Bos.-H., Yug.* 21 M8
Foça, *Turkey* 66 D2
Focşani, *Romania* 38 D10
Fogang, *China* 53 F9
Foggaret el Arab, *Algeria* 75 C5
Foggaret ez Zoua, *Algeria* 75 C5
Fóggia, *Italy* 35 A8
Foggo, *Nigeria* 79 C6
Foglia →, *Italy* 33 E9
Fogo, *Canada* 99 C9
Fogo I., *Canada* 99 C9
Fohnsdorf, *Austria* 21 H4
Föhr, *Germany* 18 A4
Foia, *Portugal* 31 H2
Foix, *France* 26 F5
Fokino, *Russia* 40 E9
Folda, *Nord-Trøndelag, Norway* 8 D11
Folda, *Nordland, Norway* 8 C13
Foleyet, *Canada* 98 C3
Folgefonn, *Norway* 9 F9
Foligno, *Italy* 33 F9
Folkestone, *U.K.* 13 F9
Folkston, *U.S.A.* 105 K5
Follett, *U.S.A.* 109 G4
Follónica, *Italy* 32 F7
Follónica, G. di, *Italy* 32 F7
Folsom Res., *U.S.A.* 112 G5
Fond-du-Lac, *Canada* 101 B7
Fond du Lac, *U.S.A.* 108 D10
Fond-du-Lac →, *Canada* 101 B7
Fonda, *U.S.A.* 107 D10
Fondi, *Italy* 34 A6
Fonfría, *Spain* 30 D4
Fongen, *Norway* 10 A5
Fonni, *Italy* 34 B2
Fonsagrada, *Spain* 30 B3
Fonseca, G. de, *Cent. Amer.* 116 D2
Fontaine-Française, *France* 25 E12
Fontainebleau, *France* 25 D9
Fontana, L., *Argentina* 128 B2
Fontas →, *Canada* 100 B4
Fonte Boa, *Brazil* 120 D4
Fontem, *Cameroon* 79 D6
Fontenay-le-Comte, *France* 26 B3
Fontur, *Iceland* 8 C6
Fonyód, *Hungary* 21 J7
Foochow = Fuzhou, *China* 53 D12
Foping, *China* 50 H4
Foppiano, *Italy* 32 B5
Forbach, *France* 25 C13
Forbes, *Australia* 91 E4
Forbesganj, *India* 63 F12
Forcados, *Nigeria* 79 D6
Forcados →, *Nigeria* 79 D6
Forcall →, *Spain* 28 E4
Forcalquier, *France* 27 E9
Forchheim, *Germany* 19 F7
Forclaz, Col de la, *Switz.* 22 D4
Ford City, *Calif., U.S.A.* 113 K7
Ford City, *Pa., U.S.A.* 106 F5
Ford's Bridge, *Australia* 91 D4
Fordyce, *U.S.A.* 109 J8
Forécariah, *Guinea* 78 D2
Forel, Mt., *Greenland* 4 C6
Foremost, *Canada* 100 D6
Forenza, *Italy* 35 B8
Forest, *Belgium* 17 G4
Forest, *Canada* 106 C3
Forest, *U.S.A.* 109 J10
Forest City, *Iowa, U.S.A.* 108 D8
Forest City, *N.C., U.S.A.* 105 H5
Forest City, *Pa., U.S.A.* 107 E9
Forest Grove, *U.S.A.* 112 E3
Forestburg, *Canada* 100 C6
Foresthill, *U.S.A.* 112 F6
Forestier Pen., *Australia* 90 G4
Forestville, *Canada* 99 C6
Forestville, *Calif., U.S.A.* 112 G4
Forestville, *Wis., U.S.A.* 104 C2
Forez, Mts. du, *France* 26 C7
Forfar, *U.K.* 14 E6
Forges-les-Eaux, *France* 25 C8
Forks, *U.S.A.* 112 C2
Forlì, *Italy* 33 D9
Forman, *U.S.A.* 108 B6
Formazza, *Italy* 32 B5
Formby Pt., *U.K.* 12 D4
Formentera, *Spain* 36 C7
Formentor, C. de, *Spain* 36 B10
Fórmia, *Italy* 34 A6
Formiga, *Brazil* 123 F2
Formigine, *Italy* 32 D7
Formiguères, *France* 26 F6
Formosa = Taiwan ■, *Asia* 53 F13
Formosa, *Argentina* 126 B4
Formosa, *Brazil* 123 E2
Formosa □, *Argentina* 126 B3
Formosa, Serra, *Brazil* 125 C6
Formosa Bay, *Kenya* 82 C5
Formoso →, *Brazil* 123 D2
Fornells, *Spain* 36 A11
Fornos de Algodres, *Portugal* 30 E3
Fornovo di Taro, *Italy* 32 D7
Føroyar, *Atl. Oc.* 7 C4
Forres, *U.K.* 14 D5
Forrest, *Vic., Australia* 91 F3
Forrest, *W. Austral., Australia* 89 F4
Forrest, Mt., *Australia* 89 D4
Forrest City, *U.S.A.* 109 H9
Forrières, *Belgium* 17 H6
Forsa, *Sweden* 10 C10
Forsayth, *Australia* 90 B3
Forsmo, *Sweden* 10 A11
Forst, *Germany* 18 D10
Forster, *Australia* 91 E5
Forsyth, *Ga., U.S.A.* 105 J4
Forsyth, *Mont., U.S.A.* 110 C10
Fort Albany, *Canada* 98 B3
Fort Apache, *U.S.A.* 111 K9
Fort Assiniboine, *Canada* 100 C6
Fort Augustus, *U.K.* 14 D4
Fort Beaufort, *S. Africa* 84 E4
Fort Benton, *U.S.A.* 110 C8
Fort Bragg, *U.S.A.* 110 G2
Fort Bridger, *U.S.A.* 110 F8
Fort Chipewyan, *Canada* 101 B6
Fort Collins, *U.S.A.* 108 E2
Fort-Coulonge, *Canada* 98 C4
Fort Davis, *U.S.A.* 109 K3
Fort-de-France, *Martinique* 117 D7
Fort de Possel = Possel, *C.A.R.* 80 C3
Fort Defiance, *U.S.A.* 111 J9
Fort Dodge, *U.S.A.* 108 D7
Fort Edward, *U.S.A.* 107 C11
Fort Frances, *Canada* 101 D10
Fort Franklin, *Canada* 96 B7
Fort Garland, *U.S.A.* 111 H11
Fort George, *Canada* 98 B4
Fort Good-Hope, *Canada* 96 B7
Fort Hancock, *U.S.A.* 111 L11
Fort Hertz = Putao, *Burma* 61 F20
Fort Hope, *Canada* 98 B2
Fort Irwin, *U.S.A.* 113 K10
Fort Jameson = Chipata, *Zambia* 83 E3
Fort Kent, *U.S.A.* 99 C6
Fort Klamath, *U.S.A.* 110 E3
Fort Lallemand, *Algeria* 75 B6
Fort-Lamy = Ndjamena, *Chad* 73 F7
Fort Laramie, *U.S.A.* 108 D2
Fort Lauderdale, *U.S.A.* 105 M5
Fort Liard, *Canada* 100 A4
Fort Liberté, *Haiti* 117 C5
Fort Lupton, *U.S.A.* 108 E2
Fort Mackay, *Canada* 100 B6
Fort McKenzie, *Canada* 99 A6
Fort Macleod, *Canada* 100 D6
Fort MacMahon, *Algeria* 75 C5
Fort McMurray, *Canada* 100 B6
Fort McPherson, *Canada* 96 B6
Fort Madison, *U.S.A.* 108 E9
Fort Meade, *U.S.A.* 105 M5
Fort Miribel, *Algeria* 75 C5
Fort Morgan, *U.S.A.* 108 E3
Fort Myers, *U.S.A.* 105 M5
Fort Nelson, *Canada* 100 B4
Fort Nelson →, *Canada* 100 B4
Fort Norman, *Canada* 96 B7
Fort Payne, *U.S.A.* 105 H3
Fort Peck, *U.S.A.* 110 B10
Fort Peck Dam, *U.S.A.* 110 C10
Fort Peck L., *U.S.A.* 110 C10
Fort Pierce, *U.S.A.* 105 M5
Fort Pierre, *U.S.A.* 108 C4
Fort Pierre Bordes = Ti-n-Zaouaténe, *Algeria* 75 E5
Fort Plain, *U.S.A.* 107 D10
Fort Portal, *Uganda* 82 B3
Fort Providence, *Canada* 100 A5
Fort Qu'Appelle, *Canada* 101 C8
Fort Resolution, *Canada* 100 A6
Fort Rixon, *Zimbabwe* 83 G2
Fort Rosebery = Mansa, *Zambia* 83 E2
Fort Ross, *U.S.A.* 112 G3
Fort Rupert, *Canada* 98 B4
Fort Saint, *Tunisia* 75 B6
Fort St. James, *Canada* 100 C4
Fort St. John, *Canada* 100 B4
Fort Sandeman, *Pakistan* 62 D3
Fort Saskatchewan, *Canada* 100 C6
Fort Scott, *U.S.A.* 109 G7
Fort Severn, *Canada* 98 A2
Fort Shevchenko, *Kazakhstan* 43 E14
Fort-Sibut, *C.A.R.* 73 G8
Fort Simpson, *Canada* 100 A4
Fort Smith, *Canada* 100 B6
Fort Smith, *U.S.A.* 109 H7
Fort Stanton, *U.S.A.* 111 K11
Fort Stockton, *U.S.A.* 109 K3
Fort Sumner, *U.S.A.* 109 H2
Fort Trinquet = Bir Mogrein, *Mauritania* 74 C2
Fort Valley, *U.S.A.* 105 J4
Fort Vermilion, *Canada* 100 B5
Fort Walton Beach, *U.S.A.* 105 K2
Fort Wayne, *U.S.A.* 104 E3
Fort William, *U.K.* 14 E3
Fort Worth, *U.S.A.* 109 J6
Fort Yates, *U.S.A.* 108 B4
Fort Yukon, *U.S.A.* 96 B5
Fortaleza, *Bolivia* 124 C4
Fortaleza, *Brazil* 122 B4
Forteau, *Canada* 99 B8
Forth →, *U.K.* 14 E5
Forth, Firth of, *U.K.* 14 E6
Forthassa Rharbia, *Algeria* 75 B4
Fortín Coronel Eugenio Garay, *Paraguay* 125 E5
Fortín Garrapatal, *Paraguay* 125 E5
Fortín General Pando, *Paraguay* 125 D6
Fortín Madrejón, *Paraguay* 125 E6
Fortín Uno, *Argentina* 128 A3
Fortore →, *Italy* 33 G12
Fortrose, *U.K.* 14 D4
Fortuna, *Spain* 29 G3
Fortuna, *Calif., U.S.A.* 110 F1
Fortuna, *N. Dak., U.S.A.* 108 A3
Fortune B., *Canada* 99 C8
Fos-sur-Mer, *France* 27 E8
Foshan, *China* 53 F9
Fossacesia, *Italy* 33 F11
Fossano, *Italy* 32 D4
Fosses-la-Ville, *Belgium* 17 H5
Fossil, *U.S.A.* 110 D3
Fossilbrook, *Australia* 90 B3
Fossombrone, *Italy* 33 E9
Fosston, *U.S.A.* 108 B7
Foster, *Canada* 107 A12
Foster →, *Canada* 101 B7
Fosters Ra., *Australia* 90 C1
Fostoria, *U.S.A.* 104 E4
Fougamou, *Gabon* 80 E2
Fougères, *France* 24 D5
Foul Pt., *Sri Lanka* 60 Q12
Foula, *U.K.* 14 A6
Foulness I., *U.K.* 13 F8
Foulpointe, *Madag.* 85 B8
Foum Assaka, *Morocco* 74 C2

Foum Zguid, *Morocco* ... 74 B3
Foumban, *Cameroon* ... 79 D7
Foundiougne, *Senegal* ... 78 C1
Fountain, *Colo., U.S.A.* ... 108 F2
Fountain, *Utah, U.S.A.* ... 110 G8
Fountain Springs, *U.S.A.* ... 113 K8
Fourchambault, *France* ... 25 E10
Fourchu, *Canada* ... 99 C7
Fouriesburg, *S. Africa* ... 84 D4
Fourmies, *France* ... 25 B11
Foúrnoi, *Greece* ... 39 M9
Fours, *France* ... 25 F10
Fouta Djalon, *Guinea* ... 78 C2
Foux, Cap-à-, *Haiti* ... 117 C5
Foveaux Str., *N.Z.* ... 87 M2
Fowey, *U.K.* ... 13 G3
Fowler, *Calif., U.S.A.* ... 111 H4
Fowler, *Colo., U.S.A.* ... 108 F2
Fowler, *Kans., U.S.A.* ... 109 G4
Fowlers B., *Australia* ... 89 F5
Fowlerton, *U.S.A.* ... 109 L5
Fox →, *Canada* ... 101 B10
Fox Valley, *Canada* ... 101 C7
Foxe Basin, *Canada* ... 97 B12
Foxe Chan., *Canada* ... 97 B11
Foxe Pen., *Canada* ... 97 B12
Foxhol, *Neths.* ... 16 B9
Foxpark, *U.S.A.* ... 110 F10
Foxton, *N.Z.* ... 87 J5
Foyle, Lough, *U.K.* ... 15 A4
Foynes, *Ireland* ... 15 D2
Foz, *Spain* ... 30 B3
Fóz do Cunene, *Angola* ... 84 B1
Foz do Gregório, *Brazil* ... 124 B3
Foz do Iguaçu, *Brazil* ... 127 B5
Foz do Riosinho, *Brazil* ... 124 B3
Frackville, *U.S.A.* ... 107 F8
Fraga, *Spain* ... 28 D5
Fraire, *Belgium* ... 17 H5
Frameries, *Belgium* ... 17 H3
Framingham, *U.S.A.* ... 107 D13
Franca, *Brazil* ... 123 F2
Francavilla al Mare, *Italy* ... 33 F11
Francavilla Fontana, *Italy* ... 35 B10
France ■, *Europe* ... 7 F6
Frances, *Australia* ... 91 F3
Frances →, *Canada* ... 100 A3
Frances L., *Canada* ... 100 A3
Francés Viejo, C., *Dom. Rep.* ... 117 C6
Franceville, *Gabon* ... 80 E2
Franche-Comté, *France* ... 25 F12
Franches Montagnes, *Switz.* ... 22 B4
Francisco de Orellana, *Ecuador* ... 120 D2
Francisco I. Madero, *Coahuila, Mexico* ... 114 B4
Francisco I. Madero, *Durango, Mexico* ... 114 C4
Francisco Sá, *Brazil* ... 123 E3
Francistown, *Botswana* ... 85 C4
Francofonte, *Italy* ... 35 E7
François, *Canada* ... 99 C8
François L., *Canada* ... 100 C3
Francorchamps, *Belgium* ... 17 H7
Franeker, *Neths.* ... 16 B7
Frankado, *Djibouti* ... 77 E5
Frankenberg, *Germany* ... 18 D4
Frankenthal, *Germany* ... 19 F4
Frankenwald, *Germany* ... 19 E7
Frankfort, *S. Africa* ... 85 D4
Frankfort, *Ind., U.S.A.* ... 104 E2
Frankfort, *Kans., U.S.A.* ... 108 F6
Frankfort, *Ky., U.S.A.* ... 104 F3
Frankfort, *Mich., U.S.A.* ... 104 C2
Frankfurt am Main, *Germany* ... 19 E4
Frankfurt an der Oder, *Germany* ... 18 C10
Fränkische Alb, *Germany* ... 19 F7
Fränkische Rezal →, *Germany* ... 19 F7
Fränkische Saale →, *Germany* ... 19 E5
Fränkische Schweiz, *Germany* ... 19 F7
Frankland →, *Australia* ... 89 G2
Franklin, *Ky., U.S.A.* ... 105 G2
Franklin, *La., U.S.A.* ... 109 L9
Franklin, *Mass., U.S.A.* ... 107 D13
Franklin, *N.H., U.S.A.* ... 107 C13
Franklin, *Nebr., U.S.A.* ... 108 E5
Franklin, *Pa., U.S.A.* ... 106 E5
Franklin, *Tenn., U.S.A.* ... 105 H2
Franklin, *Va., U.S.A.* ... 105 G7
Franklin, *W. Va., U.S.A.* ... 104 F6
Franklin, L., *U.S.A.* ... 110 F6
Franklin B., *Canada* ... 96 B7
Franklin D. Roosevelt L., *U.S.A.* ... 110 B4
Franklin I., *Antarctica* ... 5 D11
Franklin Mts., *Canada* ... 96 B7
Franklin Str., *Canada* ... 96 A10
Franklinton, *U.S.A.* ... 109 K9
Franklinville, *U.S.A.* ... 106 D6
Franks Peak, *U.S.A.* ... 110 E9
Frankston, *Australia* ... 91 F4
Fränsta, *Sweden* ... 10 B10
Frantsa Iosifa, Zemlya, *Russia* ... 44 A6
Franz, *Canada* ... 98 C3
Franz Josef Land = Frantsa Iosifa, Zemlya, *Russia* ... 44 A6
Franzburg, *Germany* ... 18 A8
Frascati, *Italy* ... 34 A5
Fraser →, *B.C., Canada* ... 100 D4
Fraser →, *Nfld., Canada* ... 99 A7
Fraser, Mt., *Australia* ... 89 E2
Fraser I., *Australia* ... 91 D5
Fraser Lake, *Canada* ... 100 C4
Fraserburg, *S. Africa* ... 84 E3
Fraserburgh, *U.K.* ... 14 D6
Fraserdale, *Canada* ... 98 C3
Frasne, *France* ... 25 F13
Frauenfeld, *Switz.* ... 23 A7
Fray Bentos, *Uruguay* ... 126 C4
Frazier Downs, *Australia* ... 88 C3
Frechilla, *Spain* ... 30 C6
Fredericia, *Denmark* ... 11 J3
Frederick, *Md., U.S.A.* ... 104 F7
Frederick, *Okla., U.S.A.* ... 109 H5
Frederick, *S. Dak., U.S.A.* ... 108 C5
Frederick Sd., *U.S.A.* ... 100 B2
Fredericksburg, *Tex., U.S.A.* ... 109 K5
Fredericksburg, *Va., U.S.A.* ... 104 F7
Frederickstown, *U.S.A.* ... 109 G9
Frederico I. Madero, Presa, *Mexico* ... 114 B3
Fredericton, *Canada* ... 99 C6
Fredericton Junc., *Canada* ... 99 C6
Frederikshåb, *Greenland* ... 4 C5
Frederikshavn, *Denmark* ... 11 G4
Frederikssund, *Denmark* ... 11 J6
Frederiksted, *Virgin Is.* ... 117 C7
Fredonia, *Ariz., U.S.A.* ... 111 H7
Fredonia, *Kans., U.S.A.* ... 109 G7
Fredonia, *N.Y., U.S.A.* ... 106 D5
Fredrikstad, *Norway* ... 10 E4
Freehold, *U.S.A.* ... 107 F10
Freel Pk., *U.S.A.* ... 112 G7
Freeland, *U.S.A.* ... 107 E9
Freels, C., *Canada* ... 99 C9
Freeman, *Calif., U.S.A.* ... 113 K9
Freeman, *S. Dak., U.S.A.* ... 108 D6
Freeport, *Bahamas* ... 116 A4
Freeport, *Canada* ... 99 D6
Freeport, *Ill., U.S.A.* ... 108 D10
Freeport, *N.Y., U.S.A.* ... 107 F11
Freeport, *Tex., U.S.A.* ... 109 L7
Freetown, *S. Leone* ... 78 D2
Frégate, L., *Canada* ... 98 B5
Fregenal de la Sierra, *Spain* ... 31 G4
Fregene, *Italy* ... 34 A5
Fréhel, C., *France* ... 24 D4
Freiberg, *Germany* ... 18 E9
Freibourg = Fribourg, *Switz.* ... 22 C4
Freiburg, *Baden-W., Germany* ... 19 H3
Freiburg, *Niedersachsen, Germany* ... 18 B5
Freiburger Alpen, *Switz.* ... 22 C4
Freire, *Chile* ... 128 A2
Freirina, *Chile* ... 126 B1
Freising, *Germany* ... 19 G7
Freistadt, *Austria* ... 20 G4
Freital, *Germany* ... 18 E9
Fréjus, *France* ... 27 E10
Fremantle, *Australia* ... 89 F2
Fremont, *Calif., U.S.A.* ... 111 H2
Fremont, *Mich., U.S.A.* ... 104 D3
Fremont, *Nebr., U.S.A.* ... 108 E6
Fremont, *Ohio, U.S.A.* ... 104 E4
Fremont →, *U.S.A.* ... 111 G8
Fremont, L., *U.S.A.* ... 110 E9
French Camp, *U.S.A.* ... 112 H5
French Cr. →, *U.S.A.* ... 106 E5
French Guiana ■, *S. Amer.* ... 121 C7
French Pass, *N.Z.* ... 87 J4
French Polynesia □, *Pac. Oc.* ... 93 J13
French Terr. of Afars & Issas = Djibouti ■, *Africa* ... 68 E3
Frenchglen, *U.S.A.* ... 110 E4
Frenchman →, *N. Amer.* ... 110 B10
Frenchman Butte, *Canada* ... 101 C7
Frenchman Creek →, *U.S.A.* ... 108 E4
Frenda, *Algeria* ... 75 A5
Fresco →, *Brazil* ... 125 B7
Freshfield, C., *Antarctica* ... 5 C10
Fresnay-sur-Sarthe, *France* ... 24 D7
Fresnillo, *Mexico* ... 114 C4
Fresno, *U.S.A.* ... 111 H4
Fresno Alhandiga, *Spain* ... 30 E5
Fresno Res., *U.S.A.* ... 110 B9
Freudenstadt, *Germany* ... 19 G4
Freux, *Belgium* ... 17 J6
Frévent, *France* ... 25 B9
Frew →, *Australia* ... 90 C2
Frewena, *Australia* ... 90 B2
Freycinet Pen., *Australia* ... 90 G4
Freyming-Merlebach, *France* ... 25 C13
Freyung, *Germany* ... 19 G9
Fria, *Guinea* ... 78 C2
Fria, C., *Namibia* ... 84 B1
Friant, *U.S.A.* ... 112 J7
Frías, *Argentina* ... 126 B2
Fribourg, *Switz.* ... 22 C4
Fribourg □, *Switz.* ... 22 C4
Frick, *Switz.* ... 22 A6
Friday Harbor, *U.S.A.* ... 112 B3
Friedberg, *Bayern, Germany* ... 19 G6
Friedberg, *Hessen, Germany* ... 19 E4
Friedland, *Germany* ... 18 B9
Friedrichshafen, *Germany* ... 19 H5
Friedrichskoog, *Germany* ... 18 A4
Friedrichstadt, *Germany* ... 18 A5
Friendly Is. = Tonga ■, *Pac. Oc.* ... 87 D11
Friesack, *Germany* ... 18 C8
Friesche Wad, *Neths.* ... 16 B7
Friesland □, *Neths.* ... 16 B7
Friesoythe, *Germany* ... 18 B3
Frillesås, *Sweden* ... 11 G6
Frio →, *U.S.A.* ... 109 L5
Friona, *U.S.A.* ... 109 H3
Frisian Is., *Europe* ... 18 B2
Fristad, *Sweden* ... 11 G7
Fritch, *U.S.A.* ... 109 H4
Fritsla, *Sweden* ... 11 G6
Fritzlar, *Germany* ... 18 D5
Friuli-Venezia Giulia □, *Italy* ... 33 B10
Frobisher B., *Canada* ... 97 B13
Frobisher Bay = Iqaluit, *Canada* ... 97 B13
Frobisher L., *Canada* ... 101 B7
Frohavet, *Norway* ... 8 E10
Froid, *U.S.A.* ... 108 A2
Froid-Chapelle, *Belgium* ... 17 H4
Frolovo, *Russia* ... 43 B10
Fromberg, *U.S.A.* ... 110 D9
Frome, *U.K.* ... 13 F5
Frome, L., *Australia* ... 91 E2
Frome Downs, *Australia* ... 91 E2
Frómista, *Spain* ... 30 C6
Front Range, *U.S.A.* ... 110 G11
Front Royal, *U.S.A.* ... 104 F6
Fronteira, *Portugal* ... 31 F3
Fronteiras, *Brazil* ... 122 C3
Frontera, *Canary Is.* ... 36 G2
Frontera, *Mexico* ... 115 D6
Frontignan, *France* ... 26 E7
Frosinone, *Italy* ... 34 A6
Frosolone, *Italy* ... 35 A7
Frostburg, *U.S.A.* ... 104 F6
Frostisen, *Norway* ... 8 B14
Frouard, *France* ... 25 D13
Frøya, *Norway* ... 8 E10
Fruges, *France* ... 25 B9
Frumoasa, *Romania* ... 38 C8
Frunze = Bishkek, *Kirghizia* ... 44 E8
Frutal, *Brazil* ... 123 F2
Frutigen, *Switz.* ... 22 C5
Frýdek-Místek, *Czech.* ... 20 F8
Frýdlant, *Czech.* ... 20 E5
Fu Jiang →, *China* ... 52 C6
Fu Xian, *Liaoning, China* ... 51 E11
Fu Xian, *Shaanxi, China* ... 50 F5
Fu'an, *China* ... 53 D12
Fubian, *China* ... 52 B4
Fucécchio, *Italy* ... 32 E7
Fucheng, *China* ... 50 F9
Fuchou = Fuzhou, *China* ... 53 D12
Fuchū, *Japan* ... 49 G6
Fuchuan, *China* ... 53 E8
Fuchun Jiang →, *China* ... 53 B13
Fúcino, Conca del, *Italy* ... 33 F10
Fuding, *China* ... 53 D13
Fuencaliente, *Canary Is.* ... 36 F2
Fuencaliente, *Spain* ... 31 G6
Fuencaliente, Pta., *Canary Is.* ... 36 F2
Fuengirola, *Spain* ... 31 J6
Fuente Alamo, *Albacete, Spain* ... 29 G3
Fuente Álamo, *Murcia, Spain* ... 29 H3
Fuente de Cantos, *Spain* ... 31 G4
Fuente del Maestre, *Spain* ... 31 G4
Fuente el Fresno, *Spain* ... 31 F7
Fuente Ovejuna, *Spain* ... 31 G5
Fuentes de Andalucía, *Spain* ... 31 H5
Fuentes de Ebro, *Spain* ... 28 D4
Fuentes de León, *Spain* ... 31 G4
Fuentes de Oñoro, *Spain* ... 30 E4
Fuentesaúco, *Spain* ... 30 D5
Fuerte →, *Mexico* ... 114 B3
Fuerte Olimpo, *Paraguay* ... 126 A4
Fuerteventura, *Canary Is.* ... 36 F6
Fufeng, *China* ... 50 G4
Fuga I., *Phil.* ... 55 B4
Fugløysund, *Norway* ... 8 A16
Fugong, *China* ... 52 D2
Fugou, *China* ... 50 G8
Fugu, *China* ... 50 E6
Fuhai, *China* ... 54 B3
Fuḩaymī, *Iraq* ... 64 C4
Fuji, *Japan* ... 49 G9
Fuji-San, *Japan* ... 49 G9
Fuji-yoshida, *Japan* ... 49 G9
Fujian □, *China* ... 53 E12
Fujinomiya, *Japan* ... 49 G9
Fujisawa, *Japan* ... 49 G9
Fukien = Fujian □, *China* ... 53 E12
Fukuchiyama, *Japan* ... 49 G7
Fukue-Shima, *Japan* ... 49 H4
Fukui, *Japan* ... 49 F8
Fukui □, *Japan* ... 49 G8
Fukuoka, *Japan* ... 49 H5
Fukuoka □, *Japan* ... 49 H5
Fukushima, *Japan* ... 48 F10
Fukushima □, *Japan* ... 48 F10
Fukuyama, *Japan* ... 49 G6
Fulda, *Germany* ... 18 E5
Fulda →, *Germany* ... 18 D5
Fuling, *China* ... 52 C6
Fullerton, *Calif., U.S.A.* ... 113 M9
Fullerton, *Nebr., U.S.A.* ... 108 E5
Fulongquan, *China* ... 51 B13
Fulton, *Mo., U.S.A.* ... 108 F9
Fulton, *N.Y., U.S.A.* ... 107 C8
Fulton, *Tenn., U.S.A.* ... 105 G1
Fuluälven →, *Sweden* ... 10 C7
Fulufjället, *Sweden* ... 10 C6
Fumay, *France* ... 25 C11
Fumel, *France* ... 26 D4
Fumin, *China* ... 52 E4
Funabashi, *Japan* ... 49 G10
Funchal, *Madeira* ... 36 D3
Fundación, *Colombia* ... 120 A3
Fundão, *Brazil* ... 123 E3
Fundão, *Portugal* ... 30 E3
Fundy, B. of, *Canada* ... 99 D6
Funing, *Hebei, China* ... 51 E10
Funing, *Jiangsu, China* ... 51 H10
Funing, *Yunnan, China* ... 52 F5
Funiu Shan, *China* ... 50 H7
Funsi, *Ghana* ... 78 C4
Funtua, *Nigeria* ... 79 C6
Fuping, *Hebei, China* ... 50 E8
Fuping, *Shaanxi, China* ... 50 G5
Fuqing, *China* ... 53 E12
Fuquan, *China* ... 52 D6
Fur, *Denmark* ... 11 H3
Furano, *Japan* ... 48 C11
Furāt, Nahr al →, *Asia* ... 64 D5
Fūrg, *Iran* ... 65 D7
Furkapass, *Switz.* ... 23 C7
Furmanov, *Russia* ... 41 C12
Furmanovo, *Kazakhstan* ... 43 B13
Furnás, *Spain* ... 36 B8
Furnas, Represa de, *Brazil* ... 123 F2
Furneaux Group, *Australia* ... 90 G4
Furness, *U.K.* ... 12 C4
Furqlus, *Syria* ... 69 A6
Fürstenau, *Germany* ... 18 C3
Fürstenberg, *Germany* ... 18 B9
Fürstenfeld, *Austria* ... 21 H6
Fürstenfeldbruck, *Germany* ... 19 G7
Fürstenwalde, *Germany* ... 18 C10
Fürth, *Germany* ... 19 F6
Furth im Wald, *Germany* ... 19 F8
Furtwangen, *Germany* ... 19 G4
Furukawa, *Japan* ... 48 E10
Furusund, *Sweden* ... 10 E12
Fury and Hecla Str., *Canada* ... 97 B11
Fusagasuga, *Colombia* ... 120 C3
Fuscaldo, *Italy* ... 35 C9
Fushan, *Shandong, China* ... 51 F11
Fushan, *Shanxi, China* ... 50 G6
Fushun, *Liaoning, China* ... 51 D12
Fushun, *Sichuan, China* ... 52 C5
Fusio, *Switz.* ... 23 D7
Fusong, *China* ... 51 C14
Füssen, *Germany* ... 19 H6
Fusui, *China* ... 52 F6
Futrono, *Chile* ... 128 B2
Futuna, *Wall. & F. Is.* ... 87 B8
Fuwa, *Egypt* ... 76 H7
Fuxin, *China* ... 51 C11
Fuyang, *Anhui, China* ... 50 H8
Fuyang, *Zhejiang, China* ... 53 B12
Fuyang He →, *China* ... 50 E9
Fuying Dao, *China* ... 53 D13
Fuyu, *China* ... 51 B13
Fuyuan, *Heilongjiang, China* ... 54 B8
Fuyuan, *Yunnan, China* ... 52 E5
Fuzhou, *China* ... 53 D12
Fylde, *U.K.* ... 12 D5
Fyn, *Denmark* ... 11 J4
Fyne, L., *U.K.* ... 14 F3
Fyns Amtskommune □, *Denmark* ... 11 J4
Fyresvatn, *Norway* ... 10 E2

G

Gaanda, *Nigeria* ... 79 C7
Gabarin, *Nigeria* ... 79 C7
Gabas →, *France* ... 26 E3
Gabela, *Angola* ... 80 G2
Gabès, *Tunisia* ... 75 B7
Gabès, G. de, *Tunisia* ... 75 B7
Gabgaba, W. →, *Egypt* ... 76 C3
Gabon ■, *Africa* ... 80 E2
Gaborone, *Botswana* ... 84 C4
Gabriels, *U.S.A.* ... 107 B10
Gābrīk, *Iran* ... 65 E8
Gabrovo, *Bulgaria* ... 38 G8
Gacé, *France* ... 24 D7
Gāch Sār, *Iran* ... 65 B6
Gachsārān, *Iran* ... 65 D6
Gacko, *Bos.-H., Yug.* ... 21 M8
Gadag, *India* ... 60 M9
Gadamai, *Sudan* ... 77 D4
Gadap, *Pakistan* ... 62 G2
Gadarwara, *India* ... 63 H8
Gadebusch, *Germany* ... 18 B7
Gadein, *Sudan* ... 77 F2
Gadhada, *India* ... 62 J4
Gadmen, *Switz.* ... 23 C6
Gádor, Sierra de, *Spain* ... 29 J2
Gadsden, *Ala., U.S.A.* ... 105 H2
Gadsden, *Ariz., U.S.A.* ... 111 K6
Gadwal, *India* ... 60 L10
Gadyach, *Ukraine* ... 40 F9
Găeşti, *Romania* ... 38 E8
Gaeta, *Italy* ... 34 A6
Gaeta, G. di, *Italy* ... 34 A6
Gaffney, *U.S.A.* ... 105 H5
Gafsa, *Tunisia* ... 75 B6
Gagarin = Gzhatsk, *Russia* ... 40 D9
Gagetown, *Canada* ... 99 C6
Gagino, *Russia* ... 41 D14
Gagliano del Capo, *Italy* ... 35 C11
Gagnoa, *Ivory C.* ... 78 D3
Gagnon, *Canada* ... 99 B6
Gagnon, L., *Canada* ... 101 A6
Gagra, *Georgia* ... 43 E9
Gahini, *Rwanda* ... 82 C3
Gahmar, *India* ... 63 G10
Gai Xian, *China* ... 51 D12
Gaïdhouronísi, *Greece* ... 37 E7
Gail, *U.S.A.* ... 109 J4
Gail →, *Austria* ... 21 J3
Gaillac, *France* ... 26 E5
Gaillon, *France* ... 24 C8
Gaimán, *Argentina* ... 128 B3
Gaines, *U.S.A.* ... 106 E7
Gainesville, *Fla., U.S.A.* ... 105 L4
Gainesville, *Ga., U.S.A.* ... 105 H4
Gainesville, *Mo., U.S.A.* ... 109 G8
Gainesville, *Tex., U.S.A.* ... 109 J6
Gainsborough, *U.K.* ... 12 D7
Gairdner, L., *Australia* ... 91 E2
Gairloch, L., *U.K.* ... 14 D3
Gais, *Switz.* ... 23 B8
Gakuch, *Pakistan* ... 63 A5
Galán, Cerro, *Argentina* ... 126 B2
Galana →, *Kenya* ... 82 C5
Galangue, *Angola* ... 81 G3
Galápagos, *Pac. Oc.* ... 93 H18
Galashiels, *U.K.* ... 14 F6
Galaţi, *Romania* ... 38 D11
Galatia, *Turkey* ... 66 D5
Galatina, *Italy* ... 35 B11
Galátone, *Italy* ... 35 B11
Galax, *U.S.A.* ... 105 G5
Galaxídhion, *Greece* ... 39 L5
Galbraith, *Australia* ... 90 B3
Galcaio, *Somali Rep.* ... 68 F4
Galdhøpiggen, *Norway* ... 10 C2
Galeana, *Mexico* ... 114 C4
Galela, *Indonesia* ... 57 D7
Galera, *Spain* ... 29 H2
Galera, Pta., *Chile* ... 128 A2
Galera Point, *Trin. & Tob.* ... 117 D7
Galesburg, *U.S.A.* ... 108 E9
Galeton, *U.S.A.* ... 106 E7
Galheirão →, *Brazil* ... 123 D2
Galheiros, *Brazil* ... 123 D2
Gali, *Georgia* ... 43 E9
Galich, *Russia* ... 41 B13
Galiche, *Bulgaria* ... 38 F6
Galicia □, *Spain* ... 30 C3
Galilee = Hagalil, *Israel* ... 69 C4
Galilee, L., *Australia* ... 90 C4
Galilee, Sea of = Yam Kinneret, *Israel* ... 69 C4
Galinoporni, *Cyprus* ... 37 D13
Galion, *U.S.A.* ... 106 F2
Galite, Is. de la, *Tunisia* ... 75 A6
Galiuro Mts., *U.S.A.* ... 111 K8
Gallabat, *Sudan* ... 77 E4
Gallardon, *France* ... 25 D8
Gallarte, *Italy* ... 32 C5
Gallatin, *U.S.A.* ... 105 G2
Galle, *Sri Lanka* ... 60 R12
Gállego →, *Spain* ... 28 D4
Gallegos →, *Argentina* ... 128 D3
Galley Hd., *Ireland* ... 15 E3
Galliate, *Italy* ... 32 C5
Gallinas, Pta., *Colombia* ... 120 A3
Gallipoli = Gelibolu, *Turkey* ... 39 J9
Gallípoli, *Italy* ... 35 B11
Gallipolis, *U.S.A.* ... 104 F4
Gällivare, *Sweden* ... 8 C16
Gallo, C., *Italy* ... 34 D6
Gallocanta, L. de, *Spain* ... 28 E3
Galloway, *U.K.* ... 14 G4
Galloway, Mull of, *U.K.* ... 14 G4
Gallup, *U.S.A.* ... 111 J9
Gallur, *Spain* ... 28 D3
Galong, *Australia* ... 91 E4
Galoya, *Sri Lanka* ... 60 Q12
Galt, *U.S.A.* ... 112 G5
Galtström, *Sweden* ... 10 B11
Galtür, *Austria* ... 19 J6
Galty Mts., *Ireland* ... 15 D3
Galtymore, *Ireland* ... 15 D3
Galva, *U.S.A.* ... 108 E9
Galvarino, *Chile* ... 128 A2
Galve de Sorbe, *Spain* ... 28 D1
Galveston, *U.S.A.* ... 109 L7
Galveston B., *U.S.A.* ... 109 L7
Gálvez, *Argentina* ... 126 C3
Gálvez, *Spain* ... 31 F6
Galway, *Ireland* ... 15 C2
Galway □, *Ireland* ... 15 C2
Galway B., *Ireland* ... 15 C2
Gam →, *Vietnam* ... 58 B5
Gamagori, *Japan* ... 49 G8
Gamari, L., *Ethiopia* ... 77 E5
Gamawa, *Nigeria* ... 79 C7

Gamay, *Phil.* 55 E6
Gambaga, *Ghana* 79 C4
Gambat, *Pakistan* 62 F3
Gambela, *Ethiopia* 77 F3
Gambia ■, *W. Afr.* 78 C1
Gambia →, *W. Afr.* 78 C1
Gambier, C., *Australia* 88 B5
Gambier Is., *Australia* 91 F2
Gamboli, *Pakistan* 62 E3
Gamboma, *Congo* 80 E3
Gamerco, *U.S.A.* 111 J9
Gamlakarleby = Kokkola, *Finland* 8 E17
Gammon →, *Canada* 101 C9
Gammouda, *Tunisia* 75 A6
Gamu-Gofa □, *Ethiopia* 77 F4
Gan, *France* 26 E3
Gan Gan, *Argentina* 128 B3
Gan Goriama, Mts., *Cameroon* 79 D7
Gan Jiang →, *China* 53 C10
Ganado, *Ariz., U.S.A.* 111 J9
Ganado, *Tex., U.S.A.* 109 L6
Gananoque, *Canada* 98 D4
Ganaveh, *Iran* 65 D6
Gand = Gent, *Belgium* 17 F3
Ganda, *Angola* 81 G2
Gandak →, *India* 63 G11
Gandava, *Pakistan* 62 E2
Gander, *Canada* 99 C9
Gander L., *Canada* 99 C9
Ganderowe Falls, *Zimbabwe* 83 F2
Gandesa, *Spain* 28 D5
Gandhi Sagar, *India* 62 G6
Gandi, *Nigeria* 79 C6
Gandía, *Spain* 29 G4
Gandino, *Italy* 32 C6
Gando, Pta., *Canary Is.* 36 G4
Gandole, *Nigeria* 79 D7
Gandu, *Brazil* 123 D4
Ganedidalem = Gani, *Indonesia* 57 E7
Ganetti, *Sudan* 76 D3
Ganga →, *India* 63 H14
Ganga, Mouths of the, *India* 63 J13
Ganganagar, *India* 62 E5
Gangapur, *India* 62 F7
Gangara, *Niger* 79 C6
Gangaw, *Burma* 61 H19
Gangdisê Shan, *China* 61 D12
Ganges = Ganga →, *India* 63 H14
Ganges, *France* 26 E7
Gangoh, *India* 62 E7
Gangtok, *India* 61 F16
Gangu, *China* 50 G3
Gangyao, *China* 51 B14
Gani, *Indonesia* 57 E7
Ganj, *India* 63 F8
Gannat, *France* 26 B7
Gannett Pk., *U.S.A.* 110 E9
Gannvalley, *U.S.A.* 108 C5
Ganquan, *China* 50 F5
Gänserdorf, *Austria* 21 G6
Ganshui, *China* 52 C6
Gansu □, *China* 50 G3
Ganta, *Liberia* 78 D3
Gantheaume, C., *Australia* 91 F2
Gantheaume B., *Australia* 89 E1
Gantsevichi, *Belorussia* 40 E5
Ganyem, *Indonesia* 57 E10
Ganyu, *China* 51 G10
Ganyushkino, *Kazakhstan* 43 C13
Ganzhou, *China* 53 E10
Gao, *Mali* 79 B5
Gao Xian, *China* 52 C5
Gao'an, *China* 53 C10
Gaohe, *China* 53 F9
Gaohebu, *China* 53 B11
Gaokeng, *China* 53 D9
Gaolan Dao, *China* 53 G9
Gaoligong Shan, *China* 52 E2
Gaomi, *China* 51 F10
Gaoping, *China* 50 G7
Gaotang, *China* 50 F9
Gaoua, *Burkina Faso* 78 C4
Gaoual, *Guinea* 78 C2
Gaoxiong, *Taiwan* 53 F13
Gaoyang, *China* 50 E8
Gaoyou, *China* 53 A12
Gaoyou Hu, *China* 51 H10
Gaoyuan, *China* 51 F9
Gaozhou, *China* 53 G8
Gap, *France* 27 D10
Gapan, *Phil.* 55 D4
Gar, *China* 54 C2
Garachico, *Canary Is.* 36 F3
Garachiné, *Panama* 116 E4
Garafia, *Canary Is.* 36 F2
Garajonay, *Canary Is.* 36 F2
Garanhuns, *Brazil* 122 C4
Garawe, *Liberia* 78 E3
Garba Tula, *Kenya* 82 B4
Garber, *U.S.A.* 109 G6
Garberville, *U.S.A.* 110 F2
Garça, *Brazil* 123 F2
Garças →, *Mato Grosso, Brazil* 125 D7
Garças →, *Pernambuco, Brazil* 122 C4
Garcias, *Brazil* 125 E7
Gard, *Somali Rep.* 68 F4
Gard □, *France* 27 D8
Gard →, *France* 27 E8
Garda, L. di, *Italy* 32 C7
Gardanne, *France* 27 E9
Garde L., *Canada* 101 A7
Gardelegen, *Germany* 18 C7
Garden City, *Kans., U.S.A.* 109 G4
Garden City, *Tex., U.S.A.* 109 K4
Garden Grove, *U.S.A.* 113 M9
Gardēz, *Afghan.* 62 C3
Gardiner, *U.S.A.* 110 D8
Gardiners I., *U.S.A.* 107 E12
Gardner, *U.S.A.* 107 D13
Gardner Canal, *Canada* 100 C3
Gardnerville, *U.S.A.* 112 G7
Gare Tigre, *Fr. Guiana* 121 C7
Garéssio, *Italy* 32 D5
Garey, *U.S.A.* 113 L6
Garfield, *U.S.A.* 110 C5
Gargan, Mt., *France* 26 C5
Gargano, Mte., *Italy* 35 A8
Gargouna, *Mali* 79 B5
Garhshankar, *India* 62 D7
Garibaldi Prov. Park, *Canada* 100 D4
Garies, *S. Africa* 84 E2
Garigliano →, *Italy* 34 A6
Garissa, *Kenya* 82 C4
Garissa □, *Kenya* 82 C5
Garkida, *Nigeria* 79 C7
Garko, *Nigeria* 79 C6
Garland, *U.S.A.* 110 F7
Garlasco, *Italy* 32 C5
Garm, *Tajikistan* 44 F8
Garmāb, *Iran* 65 C8
Garmisch-Partenkirchen, *Germany* 19 H7
Garmsār, *Iran* 65 C7
Garner, *U.S.A.* 108 D8
Garnett, *U.S.A.* 108 F7
Garo Hills, *India* 63 G14
Garoe, *Somali Rep.* 68 F4
Garonne →, *France* 26 C3
Garonne, Canal Latéral à la →, *France* 26 D4
Garoua, *Cameroon* 79 D7
Garrel, *Germany* 18 C3
Garrigue, *France* 26 E7
Garrison, *Mont., U.S.A.* 110 C7
Garrison, *N. Dak., U.S.A.* 108 B4
Garrison, *Tex., U.S.A.* 109 K7
Garrison Res. = Sakakawea, L., *U.S.A.* 108 B3
Garrovillas, *Spain* 31 F4
Garrucha, *Spain* 29 H3
Garry →, *U.K.* 14 E5
Garry, L., *Canada* 96 B9
Garsen, *Kenya* 82 C5
Garson L., *Canada* 101 B6
Gartempe →, *France* 26 B4
Gartz, *Germany* 18 B10
Garu, *Ghana* 79 C4
Garub, *Namibia* 84 D2
Garut, *Indonesia* 57 G12
Garvão, *Portugal* 31 H2
Garvie Mts., *N.Z.* 87 L2
Garwa = Garoua, *Cameroon* 79 D7
Garwa, *India* 63 G10
Garwolin, *Poland* 20 D11
Gary, *U.S.A.* 104 E2
Garz, *Germany* 18 A9
Garzê, *China* 52 B3
Garzón, *Colombia* 120 C2
Gas-San, *Japan* 48 E10
Gasan Kuli, *Turkmenistan* 44 F6
Gascogne, *France* 26 E4
Gascogne, G. de, *Europe* 28 B2
Gascony = Gascogne, *France* 26 E4
Gascoyne →, *Australia* 89 D1
Gascoyne Junc. T.O., *Australia* 89 E2
Gascueña, *Spain* 28 E2
Gash, Wadi →, *Ethiopia* 77 D4
Gashaka, *Nigeria* 79 D7
Gasherbrum, *Pakistan* 63 B7
Gashua, *Nigeria* 79 C7
Gaspé, *Canada* 99 C7
Gaspé, C. de, *Canada* 99 C7
Gaspé, Pén. de, *Canada* 99 C6
Gaspésie, Parc Prov. de la, *Canada* 99 C6
Gassaway, *U.S.A.* 104 F5
Gasselte, *Neths.* 16 C9
Gasselternijveen, *Neths.* 16 C9
Gássino Torinese, *Italy* 32 C4
Gassol, *Nigeria* 79 D7
Gastonia, *U.S.A.* 105 H5
Gastoúni, *Greece* 39 M4
Gastoúri, *Greece* 39 K2
Gastre, *Argentina* 128 B3
Gata, C., *Cyprus* 37 E12
Gata, C. de, *Spain* 29 J2
Gata, Sierra de, *Spain* 30 E4
Gataga →, *Canada* 100 B3
Gătaia, *Romania* 38 D4
Gatchina, *Russia* 40 B7
Gates, *U.S.A.* 106 C7
Gateshead, *U.K.* 12 C6
Gatesville, *U.S.A.* 109 K6
Gaths, *Zimbabwe* 83 G3
Gatico, *Chile* 126 A1
Gâtinais, *France* 25 D9
Gâtine, Hauteurs de, *France* 26 B3
Gatineau →, *Canada* 98 C4
Gatineau, Parc de la, *Canada* 98 C4
Gattaran, *Phil.* 55 B4
Gattinara, *Italy* 32 C5
Gatun, L., *Panama* 116 E4
Gatyana, *S. Africa* 85 E4
Gau, *Fiji* 87 D8
Gaucín, *Spain* 31 J5
Gauer L., *Canada* 101 B9
Gauhati, *India* 63 F14
Gauja →, *Latvia* 40 C4
Gaula →, *Norway* 8 E11
Gaurain-Ramecroix, *Belgium* 17 G3
Gausta, *Norway* 10 E2
Gāv Koshī, *Iran* 65 D8
Gavá, *Spain* 28 D6
Gāvakān, *Iran* 65 D7
Gavarnie, *France* 26 F3
Gavāter, *Iran* 65 E9
Gāvbandī, *Iran* 65 E7
Gavdhopoúla, *Greece* 37 E6
Gávdhos, *Greece* 37 E6
Gavere, *Belgium* 17 G3
Gavião, *Portugal* 31 F3
Gaviota, *U.S.A.* 113 L6
Gävleborgs län □, *Sweden* 10 C10
Gavorrano, *Italy* 32 F7
Gavray, *France* 24 D5
Gavrilov Yam, *Russia* 41 C11
Gawachab, *Namibia* 84 D2
Gawilgarh Hills, *India* 60 J10
Gawler, *Australia* 91 E2
Gaxun Nur, *China* 54 B5
Gaya, *India* 63 G11
Gaya, *Niger* 79 C5
Gaya, *Nigeria* 79 C6
Gaylord, *U.S.A.* 104 C3
Gayndah, *Australia* 91 D5
Gaysin, *Ukraine* 42 B3
Gayvoron, *Ukraine* 42 B3
Gaza, *Egypt* 69 D3
Gaza □, *Mozam.* 85 C5
Gaza Strip, *Egypt* 69 D3
Gazaoua, *Niger* 79 C6
Gāzbor, *Iran* 65 D8
Gazi, *Zaïre* 82 B1
Gaziantep, *Turkey* 66 E7
Gaziantep □, *Turkey* 66 E7
Gazipaşa, *Turkey* 66 E5
Gazli, *Uzbekistan* 44 E7
Gbarnga, *Liberia* 78 D3
Gbekebo, *Nigeria* 79 D5
Gboko, *Nigeria* 79 D6
Gbongan, *Nigeria* 79 D5
Gcuwa, *S. Africa* 85 E4
Gdańsk, *Poland* 20 A8
Gdańska, Zatoka, *Poland* 20 A9
Gdov, *Russia* 40 B5
Gdynia, *Poland* 20 A8
Gebe, *Indonesia* 57 D7
Gebeit Mine, *Sudan* 76 C4
Gebel Mûsa, *Egypt* 76 J8
Gebze, *Turkey* 66 C3
Gecha, *Ethiopia* 77 F4
Gedaref, *Sudan* 77 E4
Gede, Tanjung, *Indonesia* 56 F3
Gedinne, *Belgium* 17 J5
Gediz, *Turkey* 66 D3
Gediz →, *Turkey* 66 D2
Gedo, *Ethiopia* 77 F4
Gèdre, *France* 26 F4
Gedser, *Denmark* 11 K5
Gedser Odde, *Denmark* 11 K5
Geegully Cr. →, *Australia* 88 C3
Geel, *Belgium* 17 F5
Geelong, *Australia* 91 F3
Geelvink Chan., *Australia* 89 E1
Geer →, *Belgium* 17 G7
Geesthacht, *Germany* 18 B6
Geffen, *Neths.* 16 E6
Geidam, *Nigeria* 79 C7
Geikie →, *Canada* 101 B8
Geili, *Sudan* 77 D3
Geilo, *Norway* 10 D2
Geisingen, *Germany* 19 H4
Geislingen, *Germany* 19 G5
Geita, *Tanzania* 82 C3
Geita □, *Tanzania* 82 C3
Gejiu, *China* 52 F4
Gel →, *Sudan* 77 F2
Gel River, *Sudan* 77 F2
Gela, *Italy* 35 E7
Gela, G. di, *Italy* 35 F7
Geladi, *Ethiopia* 68 F4
Gelderland □, *Neths.* 16 D8
Geldermalsen, *Neths.* 16 E6
Geldern, *Germany* 18 D2
Geldrop, *Neths.* 17 F7
Geleen, *Neths.* 17 G7
Gelehun, *S. Leone* 78 D2
Gelendost, *Turkey* 66 D4
Gelendzhik, *Russia* 42 D8
Gelibolu, *Turkey* 39 J9
Gelidonya Burnu, *Turkey* 66 E4
Gelnhausen, *Germany* 19 E5
Gelsenkirchen, *Germany* 18 D3
Gelting, *Germany* 18 A5
Gemas, *Malaysia* 59 L4
Gembloux, *Belgium* 17 G5
Gemena, *Zaïre* 80 D3
Gemerek, *Turkey* 66 D7
Gemert, *Neths.* 17 E7
Gemlik, *Turkey* 66 C3
Gemona del Friuli, *Italy* 33 B10
Gemsa, *Egypt* 76 B3
Gemünden, *Germany* 19 E5
Genale, *Ethiopia* 77 F4
Genappe, *Belgium* 17 G4
Genç, *Turkey* 67 D9
Gençay, *France* 26 B4
Gendringen, *Neths.* 16 E8
Gendt, *Neths.* 16 E7
Geneina, Gebel, *Egypt* 76 J8
Genemuiden, *Neths.* 16 C8
General Acha, *Argentina* 126 D3
General Alvear, *Buenos Aires, Argentina* 126 D3
General Alvear, *Mendoza, Argentina* 126 D2
General Artigas, *Paraguay* 126 B4
General Belgrano, *Argentina* 126 D4
General Cabrera, *Argentina* 126 C3
General Carrera, L., *Chile* 128 C2
General Cepeda, *Mexico* 114 B4
General Conesa, *Argentina* 128 B4
General Guido, *Argentina* 126 D4
General Juan Madariaga, *Argentina* 126 D4
General La Madrid, *Argentina* 126 D3
General Lorenzo Vintter, *Argentina* 128 B4
General MacArthur, *Phil.* 55 F6
General Martin Miguel de Güemes, *Argentina* 126 A3
General Paz, *Argentina* 126 B4
General Pico, *Argentina* 126 D3
General Pinedo, *Argentina* 126 B3
General Pinto, *Argentina* 126 C3
General Sampaio, *Brazil* 122 B4
General Santos, *Phil.* 55 H6
General Toshevo, *Bulgaria* 38 F11
General Trevino, *Mexico* 115 B5
General Trías, *Mexico* 114 B3
General Viamonte, *Argentina* 126 D3
General Villegas, *Argentina* 126 D3
General Vintter, L., *Argentina* 128 B2
Generoso, Mte., *Switz.* 23 E8
Genesee, *Idaho, U.S.A.* 110 C5
Genesee, *Pa., U.S.A.* 106 E7
Genesee →, *U.S.A.* 106 C7
Geneseo, *Ill., U.S.A.* 108 E9
Geneseo, *Kans., U.S.A.* 108 F5
Geneseo, *N.Y., U.S.A.* 106 D7
Geneva = Genève, *Switz.* 22 D2
Geneva, *Ala., U.S.A.* 105 K3
Geneva, *N.Y., U.S.A.* 106 D7
Geneva, *Nebr., U.S.A.* 108 E6
Geneva, *Ohio, U.S.A.* 106 E4
Geneva, L. = Léman, Lac, *Switz.* 22 D3
Geneva, L., *U.S.A.* 104 D1
Genève, *Switz.* 22 D2
Genève □, *Switz.* 22 D2
Gengenbach, *Germany* 19 G4
Gengma, *China* 52 F2
Genichesk, *Ukraine* 42 C6
Genil →, *Spain* 31 H5
Génissiat, Barr. de, *France* 27 B9
Genk, *Belgium* 17 G7
Genlis, *France* 25 E12
Gennargentu, Mti. del, *Italy* 34 C2
Gennep, *Neths.* 17 E7
Gennes, *France* 24 E6
Genoa = Génova, *Italy* 32 D5
Genoa, *Australia* 91 F4
Genoa, *N.Y., U.S.A.* 107 D8
Genoa, *Nebr., U.S.A.* 108 E6
Genoa, *Nev., U.S.A.* 112 F7
Genoa →, *Argentina* 128 B2
Génova, *Italy* 32 D5
Génova, G. di, *Italy* 32 E6
Gent, *Belgium* 17 F3
Gentbrugge, *Belgium* 17 F3
Genthin, *Germany* 18 C8
Gentio do Ouro, *Brazil* 122 D3
Geographe B., *Australia* 89 F2
Geographe Chan., *Australia* 89 D1
Geokchay, *Azerbaijan* 43 F12
Georga, Zemlya, *Russia* 44 A5
George, *S. Africa* 84 E3
George →, *Canada* 99 A6
George, L., *N.S.W., Australia* 91 F4
George, L., *S. Austral., Australia* 91 F3
George, L., *W. Austral., Australia* 88 D3
George, L., *Uganda* 82 B3
George, L., *Fla., U.S.A.* 105 L5
George, L., *N.Y., U.S.A.* 107 C11
George Gill Ra., *Australia* 88 D5
George River = Port Nouveau-Québec, *Canada* 97 C13
George Sound, *N.Z.* 87 L1
George Town, *Bahamas* 116 B4
George Town, *Malaysia* 59 K3
George V Land, *Antarctica* 5 C10
George VI Sound, *Antarctica* 5 D17
George West, *U.S.A.* 109 L5
Georgetown, *Australia* 90 B3
Georgetown, *Ont., Canada* 98 D4
Georgetown, *P.E.I., Canada* 99 C7
Georgetown, *Cayman Is.* 116 C3
Georgetown, *Gambia* 78 C2
Georgetown, *Guyana* 121 B6
Georgetown, *Calif., U.S.A.* 112 G6
Georgetown, *Colo., U.S.A.* 110 G11
Georgetown, *Ky., U.S.A.* 104 F3
Georgetown, *S.C., U.S.A.* 105 J6
Georgetown, *Tex., U.S.A.* 109 K6
Georgia □, *U.S.A.* 105 J4
Georgia ■, *Asia* 43 E10
Georgia, Str. of, *Canada* 100 D4
Georgian B., *Canada* 98 C3
Georgievsk, *Russia* 43 D10
Georgina →, *Australia* 90 C2
Georgina Downs, *Australia* 90 C2
Georgiu-Dezh = Liski, *Russia* 41 F11
Gera, *Germany* 18 E8
Geraardsbergen, *Belgium* 17 G3
Geral, Serra, *Bahia, Brazil* 123 D3
Geral, Serra, *Goiás, Brazil* 122 D2
Geral, Serra, *Sta. Catarina, Brazil* 127 B6
Geral de Goiás, Serra, *Brazil* 123 D2
Geral do Paranã Serra, *Brazil* 123 E2
Geraldine, *U.S.A.* 110 C8
Geraldton, *Australia* 89 E1
Geraldton, *Canada* 98 C2
Gérardmer, *France* 25 D13
Gercüş, *Turkey* 67 E9
Gerede, *Turkey* 42 F5
Gereshk, *Afghan.* 60 D4
Gérgal, *Spain* 29 H2
Gerik, *Malaysia* 59 K3
Gering, *U.S.A.* 108 E3
Gerlach, *U.S.A.* 110 F4
Gerlachovka, *Czech.* 20 F10
Gerlogubi, *Ethiopia* 68 F4
Germansen Landing, *Canada* 100 B4
Germany ■, *Europe* 18 E6
Germersheim, *Germany* 19 F4
Germiston, *S. Africa* 85 D4
Gernsheim, *Germany* 19 F4
Gero, *Japan* 49 G8
Gerolstein, *Germany* 19 E2
Gerolzhofen, *Germany* 19 F6
Gerona, *Spain* 28 D7
Gerona □, *Spain* 28 C7
Gérouville, *Belgium* 17 J6
Gerrard, *Canada* 100 C5
Gers □, *France* 26 E4
Gers →, *France* 26 D4
Gersfeld, *Germany* 18 E5
Gerze, *Turkey* 66 C6
Geseke, *Germany* 18 D4
Geser, *Indonesia* 57 E8
Gesso →, *Italy* 32 D4
Gestro, Wabi →, *Ethiopia* 77 G5
Gesves, *Belgium* 17 H6
Getafe, *Spain* 30 E7
Gethsémani, *Canada* 99 B7
Gettysburg, *Pa., U.S.A.* 104 F7
Gettysburg, *S. Dak., U.S.A.* 108 C5
Getz Ice Shelf, *Antarctica* 5 D14
Geul →, *Neths.* 17 G7
Gevaş, *Turkey* 67 D10
Gévaudan, *France* 26 D7
Gevgelija, *Macedonia, Yug.* 39 H5
Gévora →, *Spain* 31 G4
Gex, *France* 27 B10
Geyser, *U.S.A.* 110 C8
Geyserville, *U.S.A.* 112 G4
Geysir, *Iceland* 8 D3
Geyve, *Turkey* 66 C4
Ghâbat el Arab = Wang Kai, *Sudan* 77 F2
Ghaghara →, *India* 63 G11
Ghalla, Wadi el →, *Sudan* 77 E2
Ghallamane, *Mauritania* 74 D3
Ghana ■, *W. Afr.* 79 D4
Ghansor, *India* 63 H9
Ghanzi, *Botswana* 84 C3
Ghanzi □, *Botswana* 84 C3
Gharb el Istiwa'iya □, *Sudan* 77 F2
Gharbîya, Es Sahrâ el, *Egypt* 76 B2
Ghard Abû Muharik, *Egypt* 76 B2
Ghardaïa, *Algeria* 75 B5
Ghârib, G., *Egypt* 76 J8
Ghârib, Râs, *Egypt* 76 J8
Gharyān, *Libya* 75 B7
Gharyān □, *Libya* 75 B7
Ghat, *Libya* 75 D7
Ghatal, *India* 63 H12
Ghatampur, *India* 63 F9
Ghaṭṭī, *Si. Arabia* 64 D3
Ghawdex = Gozo, *Malta* 37 C1
Ghazal, Bahr el →, *Chad* 73 F8
Ghazâl, Bahr el →, *Sudan* 77 F3
Ghazaouet, *Algeria* 75 A4
Ghaziabad, *India* 62 E7
Ghazipur, *India* 63 G10
Ghaznī, *Afghan.* 62 C3
Ghaznī □, *Afghan.* 60 C6
Ghedi, *Italy* 32 C7

Ghèlinsor, *Somali Rep.* 68 F4
Ghent = Gent, *Belgium* 17 F3
Gheorghe Gheorghiu-Dej, *Romania* 38 C9
Gheorgheni, *Romania* 38 C8
Ghergani, *Romania* 38 E8
Gherla, *Romania* 38 B6
Ghilarza, *Italy* 34 B1
Ghisonaccia, *France* 27 F13
Ghisoni, *France* 27 F13
Ghizao, *Afghan.* 62 C1
Ghizar →, *Pakistan* 63 A5
Ghogha, *India* 62 J5
Ghot Ogrein, *Egypt* 76 A2
Ghotaru, *India* 62 F4
Ghotki, *Pakistan* 62 E3
Ghowr □, *Afghan.* 60 C4
Ghudaf, W. al →, *Iraq* 64 C4
Ghudāmis, *Libya* 75 B6
Ghughri, *India* 63 H9
Ghugus, *India* 60 K11
Ghulam Mohammad Barrage, *Pakistan* 62 G3
Ghūrīān, *Afghan.* 60 B2
Gia Dinh, *Vietnam* 59 G6
Gia Lai = Pleiku, *Vietnam* 58 F7
Gia Nghia, *Vietnam* 59 G6
Gia Ngoc, *Vietnam* 58 E7
Gia Vuc, *Vietnam* 58 E7
Gian, *Phil.* 57 C7
Giannutri, *Italy* 32 F8
Giant Forest, *U.S.A.* 112 J8
Giant Mts. = Krkonoše, *Czech.* 20 E5
Giants Causeway, *U.K.* 15 A5
Giarabub = Al Jaghbūb, *Libya* 73 C9
Giarre, *Italy* 35 E8
Giaveno, *Italy* 32 C4
Gibara, *Cuba* 116 B4
Gibb River, *Australia* 88 C4
Gibbon, *U.S.A.* 108 E5
Gibe →, *Ethiopia* 77 F4
Gibellina, *Italy* 34 E6
Gibraléon, *Spain* 31 H4
Gibraltar, *Europe* 31 J5
Gibraltar, Str. of, *Medit. S.* 31 K5
Gibson Desert, *Australia* 88 D4
Gibsons, *Canada* 100 D4
Gibsonville, *U.S.A.* 112 F6
Giddings, *U.S.A.* 109 K6
Gidole, *Ethiopia* 77 F4
Gien, *France* 25 E9
Giessen, *Germany* 18 E4
Gieten, *Neths.* 16 B9
Gīfān, *Iran* 65 B8
Gifatin, Geziret, *Egypt* 76 B3
Gifford Creek, *Australia* 88 D2
Gifhorn, *Germany* 18 C6
Gifu, *Japan* 49 G8
Gifu □, *Japan* 49 G8
Gigant, *Russia* 43 C9
Giganta, Sa. de la, *Mexico* 114 B2
Gigen, *Bulgaria* 38 F7
Gigha, *U.K.* 14 F3
Giglio, *Italy* 32 F7
Gignac, *France* 26 E7
Gigüela →, *Spain* 29 F1
Gijón, *Spain* 30 B5
Gil I., *Canada* 100 C3
Gila →, *U.S.A.* 111 K6
Gila Bend, *U.S.A.* 111 K7
Gila Bend Mts., *U.S.A.* 111 K7
Gīlān □, *Iran* 65 B6
Gilbert →, *Australia* 90 B3
Gilbert Is., *Kiribati* 92 G9
Gilbert Plains, *Canada* 101 C8
Gilbert River, *Australia* 90 B3
Gilberton, *Australia* 90 B3
Gilbués, *Brazil* 122 C2
Gilf el Kebîr, Hadabat el, *Egypt* 76 C2
Gilford I., *Canada* 100 C3
Gilgandra, *Australia* 91 E4
Gilgil, *Kenya* 82 C4
Gilgit, *India* 63 B6
Gilgit →, *Pakistan* 63 B6
Giljeva Planina, *Serbia, Yug.* 21 M10
Gillam, *Canada* 101 B10
Gilleleje, *Denmark* 11 H6
Gillen, L., *Australia* 89 E3
Gilles, L., *Australia* 91 E2
Gillette, *U.S.A.* 108 C2
Gilliat, *Australia* 90 C3
Gillingham, *U.K.* 13 F8
Gilly, *Belgium* 17 H4
Gilmer, *U.S.A.* 109 J7
Gilmore, *Australia* 91 F4
Gilmore, L., *Australia* 89 F3
Gilmour, *Canada* 98 D4
Gilo →, *Ethiopia* 77 F3
Gilort →, *Romania* 38 E6
Gilroy, *U.S.A.* 111 H3
Gilze, *Neths.* 17 E5
Gimbi, *Ethiopia* 77 F4
Gimigliano, *Italy* 35 D9
Gimli, *Canada* 101 C9
Gimone →, *France* 26 E5
Gimont, *France* 26 E4
Gin Gin, *Australia* 91 D5
Ginâh, *Egypt* 76 B3
Gindie, *Australia* 90 C4
Gingin, *Australia* 89 F2
Gîngiova, *Romania* 38 F6
Ginir, *Ethiopia* 68 F3
Ginosa, *Italy* 35 B9
Ginzo de Limia, *Spain* 30 C3
Giohar, *Somali Rep.* 68 G4
Gióia, G. di, *Italy* 35 D8
Gióia del Colle, *Italy* 35 B9
Gióia Táuro, *Italy* 35 D8
Gioiosa Iónica, *Italy* 35 D9
Gióna, Óros, *Greece* 39 L5
Giovi, Passo dei, *Italy* 32 D5
Giovinazzo, *Italy* 35 A9
Gir Hills, *India* 62 J4
Girab, *India* 62 F4
Girâfi, W. →, *Egypt* 69 F3
Giraltovce, *Czech.* 20 F11
Girard, *Kans., U.S.A.* 109 G7
Girard, *Ohio, U.S.A.* 106 E4
Girard, *Pa., U.S.A.* 106 D4
Girardot, *Colombia* 120 C3
Girdle Ness, *U.K.* 14 D6
Giresun, *Turkey* 67 C8
Giresun □, *Turkey* 67 C8
Girga, *Egypt* 76 B3
Giridih, *India* 63 G12
Girifalco, *Italy* 35 D9
Girilambone, *Australia* 91 E4
Giro, *Nigeria* 79 C5
Giromagny, *France* 25 E13
Gironde □, *France* 26 D3
Gironde →, *France* 26 C2
Gironella, *Spain* 28 C6
Giru, *Australia* 90 B4
Girvan, *U.K.* 14 F4
Gisborne, *N.Z.* 87 H7
Gisenyi, *Rwanda* 82 C2
Gisors, *France* 25 C8
Gistel, *Belgium* 17 F1
Giswil, *Switz.* 22 C6
Gitega, *Burundi* 82 C2
Gits, *Belgium* 17 F2
Giuba →, *Somali Rep.* 68 G3
Giubiasco, *Switz.* 23 D8
Giugliano in Campania, *Italy* 35 B7
Giulianova, *Italy* 33 F10
Giurgeni, *Romania* 38 E10
Giurgiu, *Romania* 38 F8
Give, *Denmark* 11 J3
Givet, *France* 25 B11
Givors, *France* 27 C8
Givry, *Belgium* 17 H4
Givry, *France* 25 F11
Giyon, *Ethiopia* 77 F4
Giza = El Gîza, *Egypt* 76 H7
Gizhiga, *Russia* 45 C17
Gizhiginskaya Guba, *Russia* 45 C16
Giżycko, *Poland* 20 A11
Gizzeria, *Italy* 35 D9
Gjegjan, *Albania* 39 H3
Gjerstad, *Norway* 10 F3
Gjirokastra, *Albania* 39 J3
Gjoa Haven, *Canada* 96 B10
Gjøl, *Denmark* 11 G3
Gjøvik, *Norway* 10 D4
Glace Bay, *Canada* 99 C8
Glacier B., *U.S.A.* 100 B1
Glacier Nat. Park, *Canada* 100 C5
Glacier Park, *U.S.A.* 110 B7
Glacier Peak, *U.S.A.* 110 B3
Gladewater, *U.S.A.* 109 J7
Gladstone, *Queens., Australia* 90 C5
Gladstone, *S. Austral., Australia* 91 E2
Gladstone, *W. Austral., Australia* 89 E1
Gladstone, *Canada* 101 C9
Gladstone, *U.S.A.* 104 C2
Gladwin, *U.S.A.* 104 D3
Gladys L., *Canada* 100 B2
Gláma, *Iceland* 8 D2
Glåma →, *Norway* 10 E4
Glamis, *U.S.A.* 113 N11
Glamoč, *Bos.-H., Yug.* 33 D13
Glan, *Sweden* 11 F10
Glanerbrug, *Neths.* 16 D9
Glarner Alpen, *Switz.* 23 C8
Glärnisch, *Switz.* 23 C7
Glarus, *Switz.* 23 B8
Glarus □, *Switz.* 23 C8
Glasco, *Kans., U.S.A.* 108 F6
Glasco, *N.Y., U.S.A.* 107 D11
Glasgow, *U.K.* 14 F4
Glasgow, *Ky., U.S.A.* 104 G3
Glasgow, *Mont., U.S.A.* 110 B10
Glastonbury, *U.K.* 13 F5
Glastonbury, *U.S.A.* 107 E12
Glatt →, *Switz.* 23 B7
Glattfelden, *Switz.* 23 A7
Glauchau, *Germany* 18 E8
Glazov, *Russia* 41 B18
Gleiwitz = Gliwice, *Poland* 20 E8
Glen, *U.S.A.* 107 B13
Glen Affric, *U.K.* 14 D4
Glen Canyon Dam, *U.S.A.* 111 H8
Glen Canyon Nat. Recreation Area, *U.S.A.* 111 H8
Glen Coe, *U.K.* 14 E4
Glen Cove, *U.S.A.* 107 F11
Glen Garry, *U.K.* 14 D3
Glen Innes, *Australia* 91 D5
Glen Lyon, *U.S.A.* 107 E8
Glen Mor, *U.K.* 14 D4
Glen Moriston, *U.K.* 14 D4
Glen Orchy, *U.K.* 14 E4
Glen Spean, *U.K.* 14 E4
Glen Ullin, *U.S.A.* 108 B4
Glénan, Is. de, *France* 24 E2
Glenburgh, *Australia* 89 E2
Glencoe, *Canada* 106 D3
Glencoe, *S. Africa* 85 D5
Glencoe, *U.S.A.* 108 C7
Glendale, *Ariz., U.S.A.* 111 K7
Glendale, *Calif., U.S.A.* 113 L8
Glendale, *Oreg., U.S.A.* 110 E2
Glendale, *Zimbabwe* 83 F3
Glendive, *U.S.A.* 108 B2
Glendo, *U.S.A.* 108 D2
Glenelg, *Australia* 91 E2
Glenelg →, *Australia* 91 F3
Glenflorrie, *Australia* 88 D2
Glengarriff, *Ireland* 15 E2
Glengyle, *Australia* 90 C2
Glenmora, *U.S.A.* 109 K8
Glenmorgan, *Australia* 91 D4
Glenn, *U.S.A.* 112 F4
Glenns Ferry, *U.S.A.* 110 E6
Glenorchy, *Australia* 90 G4
Glenore, *Australia* 90 B3
Glenormiston, *Australia* 90 C2
Glenreagh, *Australia* 91 E5
Glenrock, *U.S.A.* 110 E11
Glenrothes, *U.K.* 14 E5
Glens Falls, *U.S.A.* 107 C11
Glenties, *Ireland* 15 B3
Glenville, *U.S.A.* 104 F5
Glenwood, *Alta., Canada* 100 D6
Glenwood, *Nfld., Canada* 99 C9
Glenwood, *Ark., U.S.A.* 109 H8
Glenwood, *Hawaii, U.S.A.* 102 J17
Glenwood, *Iowa, U.S.A.* 108 E7
Glenwood, *Minn., U.S.A.* 108 C7
Glenwood, *Wash., U.S.A.* 112 D5
Glenwood Springs, *U.S.A.* 110 G10
Gletsch, *Switz.* 23 C6
Glina, *Croatia* 33 C13
Glittertind, *Norway* 10 C2
Gliwice, *Poland* 20 E8
Globe, *U.S.A.* 111 K8
Glödnitz, *Austria* 21 J4
Głogów, *Poland* 20 D6
Glorieuses, Is., *Ind. Oc.* 85 A8
Glossop, *U.K.* 12 D6
Gloucester, *Australia* 91 E5
Gloucester, *U.K.* 13 F5
Gloucester, *U.S.A.* 107 D14
Gloucester I., *Australia* 90 B4
Gloucestershire □, *U.K.* 13 F5
Gloversville, *U.S.A.* 107 C10
Glovertown, *Canada* 99 C9
Główno, *Poland* 20 D9
Głubczyce, *Poland* 20 E7
Glubokiy, *Russia* 43 B9
Glubokoye, *Belorussia* 40 D5
Głuchołazy, *Poland* 20 E7
Glücksburg, *Germany* 18 A5
Glückstadt, *Germany* 18 B5
Glukhov, *Ukraine* 40 F8
Glussk, *Belorussia* 40 E6
Glyngøre, *Denmark* 11 H2
Gmünd, *Kärnten, Austria* 21 J3
Gmünd, *Niederösterreich, Austria* 20 G5
Gnarp, *Sweden* 10 B11
Gnesta, *Sweden* 10 E11
Gniew, *Poland* 20 B8
Gniezno, *Poland* 20 C7
Gnoien, *Germany* 18 B8
Gnowangerup, *Australia* 89 F2
Go Cong, *Vietnam* 59 G6
Gō-no-ura, *Japan* 49 H4
Go Quao, *Vietnam* 59 H5
Goa, *India* 60 M8
Goa □, *India* 60 M8
Goalen Hd., *Australia* 91 F5
Goalpara, *India* 61 F17
Goalundo Ghat, *Bangla.* 63 H13
Goaso, *Ghana* 78 D4
Goat Fell, *U.K.* 14 F3
Goba, *Ethiopia* 68 F2
Goba, *Mozam.* 85 D5
Gobabis, *Namibia* 84 C2
Gobernador Gregores, *Argentina* 128 C2
Gobi, *Asia* 50 C5
Gobō, *Japan* 49 H7
Gobo, *Sudan* 77 F3
Goch, *Germany* 18 D2
Gochas, *Namibia* 84 C2
Godavari →, *India* 61 L13
Godavari Point, *India* 61 L13
Godbout, *Canada* 99 C6
Godda, *India* 63 G12
Godegård, *Sweden* 11 F9
Goderich, *Canada* 98 D3
Goderville, *France* 24 C7
Godhavn, *Greenland* 4 C5
Godhra, *India* 62 H5
Gödöllö, *Hungary* 21 H9
Godoy Cruz, *Argentina* 126 C2
Gods →, *Canada* 101 B10
Gods L., *Canada* 101 C10
Godthåb, *Greenland* 97 B14
Godwin Austen = K2, Mt., *Pakistan* 63 B7
Goeie Hoop, Kaap die = Good Hope, C. of, *S. Africa* 84 E2
Goéland, L. au, *Canada* 98 C4
Goeree, *Neths.* 16 E4
Goes, *Neths.* 17 F3
Gogama, *Canada* 98 C3
Gogango, *Australia* 90 C5
Gogebic, L., *U.S.A.* 108 B10
Gogra = Ghaghara →, *India* 63 G11
Gogriâl, *Sudan* 77 F2
Goiana, *Brazil* 122 C5
Goianésia, *Brazil* 123 E2
Goiânia, *Brazil* 123 E2
Goiás, *Brazil* 123 E1
Goiás □, *Brazil* 122 D2
Goiatuba, *Brazil* 123 E2
Goio-Ere, *Brazil* 127 A5
Goirle, *Neths.* 17 E6
Góis, *Portugal* 30 E2
Gojam □, *Ethiopia* 77 E4
Gojeb, Wabi →, *Ethiopia* 77 F4
Gojō, *Japan* 49 G7
Gojra, *Pakistan* 62 D5
Gokarannath, *India* 63 F9
Gökçeada, *Turkey* 39 J8
Gökırmak →, *Turkey* 66 C6
Göksu →, *Turkey* 66 E6
Göksun, *Turkey* 66 D7
Gokteik, *Burma* 61 H20
Gokurt, *Pakistan* 62 E2
Gola, *India* 63 E9
Golakganj, *India* 63 F13
Golan Heights = Hagolan, *Syria* 69 B4
Golāshkerd, *Iran* 65 E8
Golaya Pristen, *Ukraine* 42 C5
Gölbaşı, *Adiyaman, Turkey* 67 E7
Gölbaşı, *Ankara, Turkey* 66 D5
Golchikha, *Russia* 4 B12
Golconda, *U.S.A.* 110 F5
Gölcük, *Kocaeli, Turkey* 66 C3
Gölcük, *Niğde, Turkey* 66 D6
Gold Beach, *U.S.A.* 110 E1
Gold Coast, *Australia* 91 D5
Gold Coast, *W. Afr.* 70 F3
Gold Hill, *U.S.A.* 110 E2
Goldach, *Switz.* 23 B8
Goldau, *Switz.* 23 B7
Goldberg, *Germany* 18 B8
Golden, *Canada* 100 C5
Golden, *U.S.A.* 108 F2
Golden B., *N.Z.* 87 J4
Golden Gate, *U.S.A.* 110 H2
Golden Hinde, *Canada* 100 D3
Golden Lake, *Canada* 106 A7
Golden Prairie, *Canada* 101 C7
Golden Vale, *Ireland* 15 D3
Goldendale, *U.S.A.* 110 D3
Goldfield, *U.S.A.* 111 H5
Goldfields, *Canada* 101 B7
Goldsand L., *Canada* 101 B8
Goldsboro, *U.S.A.* 105 H7
Goldsmith, *U.S.A.* 109 K3
Goldsworthy, *Australia* 88 D2
Goldthwaite, *U.S.A.* 109 K5
Golegã, *Portugal* 31 F2
Goleniów, *Poland* 20 B4
Golestānak, *Iran* 65 D7
Goleta, *U.S.A.* 113 L7
Golfito, *Costa Rica* 116 E3
Golfo Aranci, *Italy* 34 B2
Gölgeli Dağları, *Turkey* 66 E3
Goliad, *U.S.A.* 109 L6
Golija, *Serbia, Yug.* 21 M10
Gölköy, *Turkey* 67 C7
Golo →, *France* 27 F13
Golovanevsk, *Ukraine* 42 B4
Golpāyegān, *Iran* 65 C6
Gölpazarı, *Turkey* 66 C4
Golra, *Pakistan* 62 C5
Golspie, *U.K.* 14 D5
Golyama Kamchiya →, *Bulgaria* 38 F10
Goma, *Rwanda* 82 C2
Goma, *Zaïre* 82 C2
Gomati →, *India* 63 G10
Gombari, *Zaïre* 82 B2
Gombe, *Nigeria* 79 C7
Gombe →, *Tanzania* 82 C3
Gombi, *Nigeria* 79 C7
Gomel, *Belorussia* 40 E7
Gomera, *Canary Is.* 36 F2
Gómez Palacio, *Mexico* 114 B4
Gomīshān, *Iran* 65 B7
Gommern, *Germany* 18 C7
Gomogomo, *Indonesia* 57 F8
Gomoh, *India* 61 H15
Gompa = Ganta, *Liberia* 78 D3
Goms, *Switz.* 22 D6
Gonābād, *Iran* 65 C8
Gonaïves, *Haiti* 117 C5
Gonâve, G. de la, *Haiti* 117 C5
Gonâve, I. de la, *Haiti* 117 C5
Gonbab-e Kāvūs, *Iran* 65 B7
Gonda, *India* 63 F9
Gondal, *India* 62 J4
Gonder, *Ethiopia* 77 E4
Gonder □, *Ethiopia* 77 E4
Gondia, *India* 60 J12
Gondola, *Mozam.* 83 F3
Gondomar, *Portugal* 30 D2
Gondomar, *Spain* 30 C2
Gondrecourt-le-Château, *France* 25 D12
Gönen, *Turkey* 66 C2
Gong Xian, *China* 52 C5
Gong'an, *China* 53 B9
Gongcheng, *China* 53 E8
Gongga Shan, *China* 52 C3
Gongguan, *China* 52 G7
Gonghe, *China* 54 C5
Gongola □, *Nigeria* 79 D7
Gongola →, *Nigeria* 79 D7
Gongolgon, *Australia* 91 E4
Gongshan, *China* 52 D2
Gongtan, *China* 52 C7
Goniadz, *Poland* 20 B12
Goniri, *Nigeria* 79 C7
Gonjo, *China* 52 B2
Gonnesa, *Italy* 34 C1
Gónnos, *Greece* 39 K5
Gonnosfanadiga, *Italy* 34 C1
Gonzaga, *Phil.* 55 B5
Gonzales, *Calif., U.S.A.* 111 H3
Gonzales, *Tex., U.S.A.* 109 L6
González Chaves, *Argentina* 126 D3
Good Hope, C. of, *S. Africa* 84 E2
Gooderham, *Canada* 98 D4
Goodeve, *Canada* 101 C8
Gooding, *U.S.A.* 110 E6
Goodland, *U.S.A.* 108 F4
Goodnight, *U.S.A.* 109 H4
Goodooga, *Australia* 91 D4
Goodsoil, *Canada* 101 C7
Goodsprings, *U.S.A.* 111 J6
Goole, *U.K.* 12 D7
Goolgowi, *Australia* 91 E4
Goomalling, *Australia* 89 F2
Goombalie, *Australia* 91 D4
Goonda, *Mozam.* 83 F3
Goondiwindi, *Australia* 91 D5
Goongarrie, L., *Australia* 89 F3
Goonyella, *Australia* 90 C4
Goor, *Neths.* 16 D9
Gooray, *Australia* 91 D5
Goose →, *Canada* 99 B7
Goose L., *U.S.A.* 110 F3
Gop, *India* 60 H6
Gopalganj, *India* 63 F11
Goppenstein, *Switz.* 22 D5
Göppingen, *Germany* 19 G5
Gor, *Spain* 29 H2
Góra, *Poland* 20 D6
Gorakhpur, *India* 63 F10
Gorbatov, *Russia* 41 C13
Gorbea, Peña, *Spain* 28 B2
Gorda, *U.S.A.* 112 K5
Gorda, Pta., *Nic.* 116 D3
Gorda, Pta., *Canary Is.* 36 F2
Gordan B., *Australia* 88 B5
Gordon, *U.S.A.* 108 D3
Gordon →, *Australia* 90 G4
Gordon, I., *Chile* 128 D3
Gordon Downs, *Australia* 88 C4
Gordon L., *Alta., Canada* 101 B6
Gordon L., *N.W.T., Canada* 100 A6
Gordonia, *S. Africa* 84 D3
Gordonvale, *Australia* 90 B4
Gore, *Australia* 91 D5
Goré, *Chad* 73 G8
Gore, *Ethiopia* 77 F4
Gore, *N.Z.* 87 M2
Gore Bay, *Canada* 98 C3
Görele, *Turkey* 67 C8
Gorey, *Ireland* 15 D5
Gorg, *Iran* 65 D8
Gorgān, *Iran* 65 B7
Gorgona, *Italy* 32 E6
Gorgona, I., *Colombia* 124 A2
Gorgora, *Ethiopia* 77 E4
Gorham, *U.S.A.* 107 B13
Gori, *Georgia* 43 E11
Gorinchem, *Neths.* 16 E5
Gorinhatã, *Brazil* 123 E2
Goritsy, *Russia* 41 C10
Gorízia, *Italy* 33 C10
Gorki = Nizhniy Novgorod, *Russia* 41 C14
Gorki, *Belorussia* 40 D7
Gorkiy = Nizhniy Novgorod, *Russia* 41 C14
Gorkovskoye Vdkhr., *Russia* 41 C13
Gørlev, *Denmark* 11 J5
Gorlice, *Poland* 20 F11
Görlitz, *Germany* 18 D10
Gorlovka, *Ukraine* 42 B8
Gorman, *Calif., U.S.A.* 113 L8
Gorman, *Tex., U.S.A.* 109 J5
Gorna Dzhumayo = Blagoevgrad, *Bulgaria* 39 G6
Gorna Oryakhovitsa, *Bulgaria* 38 F8
Gornja Radgona, *Slovenia* 33 B13
Gornja Tuzla, *Bos.-H., Yug.* 21 L8
Gornji Grad, *Slovenia* 33 B11
Gornji Milanovac, *Serbia, Yug.* 21 M10
Gornji Vakuf, *Bos.-H., Yug.* 21 M7
Gorno-Altaysk, *Russia* 44 D9
Gorno Slinkino, *Russia* 44 C8
Gornyi, *Russia* 48 B6
Gornyy, *Russia* 41 F16
Gorodenka, *Ukraine* 42 B1

Grodzyanka

Gorodets, *Russia* 41 C13
Gorodishche, *Russia* 41 E14
Gorodishche, *Ukraine* 42 B4
Gorodnitsa, *Ukraine* 40 F5
Gorodnya, *Ukraine* 40 F7
Gorodok, *Belorussia* 40 D7
Gorodok, *Ukraine* 40 G3
Gorokhov, *Ukraine* 40 F4
Gorokhovets, *Russia* 41 C13
Gorom Gorom, *Burkina Faso* 79 C4
Goromonzi, *Zimbabwe* 83 F3
Gorongose →, *Mozam.* 85 C5
Gorongoza, *Mozam.* 83 F3
Gorongoza, Sa. da, *Mozam.* 83 F3
Gorontalo, *Indonesia* 57 D6
Goronyo, *Nigeria* 79 C6
Gorredijk, *Neths.* 16 C8
Gorron, *France* 24 D6
Gorssel, *Neths.* 16 D8
Gort, *Ireland* 15 C3
Gortis, *Greece* 37 D6
Gorzkowice, *Poland* 20 D9
Gorzów Śląski, *Poland* 20 D8
Gorzów Wielkopolski, *Poland* 20 C5
Göschenen, *Switz.* 23 C7
Gosford, *Australia* 91 E5
Goshen, *Calif., U.S.A.* 112 J7
Goshen, *Ind., U.S.A.* 104 E3
Goshen, *N.Y., U.S.A.* 107 E10
Goshogawara, *Japan* 48 D10
Goslar, *Germany* 18 D6
Gospič, *Croatia* 33 D12
Gosport, *U.K.* 13 G6
Gossau, *Switz.* 23 B8
Gosse →, *Australia* 90 B1
Gostivar, *Macedonia, Yug.* 39 H3
Gostyń, *Poland* 20 D7
Gostynin, *Poland* 20 C9
Göta älv →, *Sweden* 11 G5
Göta kanal, *Sweden* 9 G12
Göteborg, *Sweden* 11 G5
Göteborgs och Bohus län □, *Sweden* 9 G11
Götene, *Sweden* 11 F7
Gotha, *Germany* 18 E6
Gothenburg, *U.S.A.* 108 E4
Gotland, *Sweden* 9 H15
Gotse Delchev, *Bulgaria* 39 H6
Gotska Sandön, *Sweden* 9 G15
Gōtsu, *Japan* 49 G6
Göttingen, *Germany* 18 D5
Gottwald = Zmiyev, *Ukraine* 42 B7
Gottwaldov, *Czech.* 20 F7
Goubangzi, *China* 51 D11
Gouda, *Neths.* 16 D5
Goúdhoura, Ákra, *Greece* 37 E8
Goudiry, *Senegal* 78 C2
Gough I., *Atl. Oc.* 2 G9
Gouin, Rés., *Canada* 98 C5
Gouitafla, *Ivory C.* 78 D3
Goulburn, *Australia* 91 E4
Goulburn Is., *Australia* 90 A1
Goulia, *Ivory C.* 78 C3
Goulimine, *Morocco* 74 C3
Goulmina, *Morocco* 74 B4
Gounou-Gaya, *Chad* 73 G8
Goúra, *Greece* 39 M5
Gouraya, *Algeria* 75 A5
Gourdon, *France* 26 D5
Gouré, *Niger* 79 C7
Gouri, *Chad* 73 E8
Gourits →, *S. Africa* 84 E3
Gourma Rharous, *Mali* 79 B4
Goúrnais, *Greece* 37 D7
Gournay-en-Bray, *France* 25 C8
Gourock Ra., *Australia* 91 F4
Goursi, *Burkina Faso* 78 C4
Gouvêa, *Brazil* 123 E3
Gouverneur, *U.S.A.* 107 B9
Gouviá, *Greece* 37 A3
Gouzon, *France* 26 B6
Govan, *Canada* 101 C8
Governador Valadares, *Brazil* 123 E3
Governor's Harbour, *Bahamas* 116 A4
Gowan Ra., *Australia* 90 C4
Gowanda, *U.S.A.* 106 D6
Gowd-e Zirreh, *Afghan.* 60 E3
Gower, *U.K.* 13 F3
Gowna, L., *Ireland* 15 C4
Goya, *Argentina* 126 B4
Goyder Lagoon, *Australia* 91 D2
Goyllarisquisga, *Peru* 124 C2
Göynük, *Turkey* 66 C4
Goz Beïda, *Chad* 73 F9
Goz Regeb, *Sudan* 77 D4
Gozo, *Malta* 37 C1
Graaff-Reinet, *S. Africa* 84 E3
Grabow, *Germany* 18 B7
Grabs, *Switz.* 23 B8
Gračac, *Croatia* 33 D12
Gračanica, *Bos.-H., Yug.* 21 L8
Graçay, *France* 25 E8
Grace, *U.S.A.* 110 E8
Graceville, *U.S.A.* 108 C6
Gracias a Dios, C., *Honduras* 116 C3
Graciosa, I., *Canary Is.* 36 E6
Gradaús, *Brazil* 122 C1
Gradaús, Serra dos, *Brazil* 122 C1
Gradets, *Bulgaria* 38 G9
Grado, *Italy* 33 C10
Grado, *Spain* 30 B4
Gradule, *Australia* 91 D4
Grady, *U.S.A.* 109 H3
Graeca, Lacul, *Romania* 38 E9
Graénalon, L., *Iceland* 8 D5
Grafenau, *Germany* 19 G9
Gräfenberg, *Germany* 19 F7
Grafton, *Australia* 91 D5
Grafton, *U.S.A.* 108 A6
Gragnano, *Italy* 35 B7
Graham, *Canada* 98 C1
Graham, *N.C., U.S.A.* 105 G6
Graham, *Tex., U.S.A.* 109 J5
Graham →, *Canada* 100 B4
Graham Bell, Os., *Russia* 44 A7
Graham I., *Canada* 100 C2
Graham Land, *Antarctica* 5 C17
Graham Mt., *U.S.A.* 111 K9
Grahamdale, *Canada* 101 C9
Grahamstown, *S. Africa* 84 E4
Graïba, *Tunisia* 75 B7
Graide, *Belgium* 17 J6
Graie, Alpi, *Europe* 32 C4
Grain Coast, *W. Afr.* 70 F2
Grajaú, *Brazil* 122 C2
Grajaú →, *Brazil* 122 B3
Grajewo, *Poland* 20 B12
Gramada, *Bulgaria* 38 F5
Gramat, *France* 26 D5
Grammichele, *Italy* 35 E7
Grampian □, *U.K.* 14 D6
Grampian Highlands = Grampian Mts., *U.K.* 14 E5
Grampian Mts., *U.K.* 14 E5
Gran →, *Surinam* 121 C6
Gran Altiplanicie Central, *Argentina* 128 C3
Gran Canaria, *Canary Is.* 36 F4
Gran Chaco, *S. Amer.* 126 B3
Gran Paradiso, *Italy* 32 C4
Gran Sasso d'Italia, *Italy* 33 F10
Granada, *Nic.* 116 D2
Granada, *Spain* 29 H1
Granada, *U.S.A.* 109 F3
Granada □, *Spain* 31 H7
Granadilla de Abona, *Canary Is.* 36 F3
Granard, *Ireland* 15 C4
Granbury, *U.S.A.* 109 J6
Granby, *Canada* 98 C5
Grand →, *Mo., U.S.A.* 108 F8
Grand →, *S. Dak., U.S.A.* 108 C4
Grand Bahama, *Bahamas* 116 A4
Grand Bank, *Canada* 99 C8
Grand Bassam, *Ivory C.* 78 D4
Grand Béréby, *Ivory C.* 78 E3
Grand-Bourg, *Guadeloupe* 117 C7
Grand Canal = Yun Ho →, *China* 51 E9
Grand Canyon, *U.S.A.* 111 H7
Grand Canyon National Park, *U.S.A.* 111 H7
Grand Cayman, *Cayman Is.* 116 C3
Grand Cess, *Liberia* 78 E3
Grand Coulee, *U.S.A.* 110 C4
Grand Coulee Dam, *U.S.A.* 110 C4
Grand Erg Occidental, *Algeria* 75 B5
Grand Erg Oriental, *Algeria* 75 C6
Grand Falls, *Canada* 99 C8
Grand Forks, *Canada* 100 D5
Grand Forks, *U.S.A.* 108 B6
Grand-Fougeray, *France* 24 E5
Grand Haven, *U.S.A.* 104 D2
Grand I., *U.S.A.* 104 B2
Grand Island, *U.S.A.* 108 E5
Grand Isle, *U.S.A.* 109 L10
Grand Junction, *U.S.A.* 111 G9
Grand Lac Victoria, *Canada* 98 C4
Grand Lahou, *Ivory C.* 78 D3
Grand L., *N.B., Canada* 99 C6
Grand L., *Nfld., Canada* 99 C8
Grand L., *Nfld., Canada* 99 B7
Grand Lake, *U.S.A.* 110 F11
Grand L., *U.S.A.* 109 L8
Grand-Leez, *Belgium* 17 G5
Grand-Lieu, L. de, *France* 24 E5
Grand Manan I., *Canada* 99 D6
Grand Marais, *Canada* 108 B9
Grand Marais, *U.S.A.* 104 B3
Grand-Mère, *Canada* 98 C5
Grand Popo, *Benin* 79 D5
Grand Portage, *U.S.A.* 98 C2
Grand Rapids, *Canada* 101 C9
Grand Rapids, *Mich., U.S.A.* 104 D2
Grand Rapids, *Minn., U.S.A.* 108 B8
Grand St-Bernard, Col du, *Switz.* 22 E4
Grand Santi, *Fr. Guiana* 121 C7
Grand Teton, *U.S.A.* 110 E8
Grand Valley, *U.S.A.* 110 G9
Grand View, *Canada* 101 C8
Grandas de Salime, *Spain* 30 B4
Grande →, *Jujuy, Argentina* 126 A2
Grande →, *Mendoza, Argentina* 126 D2
Grande →, *Bolivia* 125 D5
Grande →, *Bahia, Brazil* 122 D3
Grande →, *Minas Gerais, Brazil* 123 F1
Grande →, *Spain* 29 F4
Grande →, *U.S.A.* 109 N6
Grande →, *Venezuela* 121 B5
Grande, B., *Argentina* 128 D3
Grande, I., *Brazil* 123 F3
Grande, Serra, *Goiás, Brazil* 122 D2
Grande, Serra, *Piauí, Brazil* 122 C2
Grande Baie, *Canada* 99 C5
Grande Baleine, R. de la →, *Canada* 98 A4
Grande Cache, *Canada* 100 C5
Grande de Santiago →, *Mexico* 114 C3
Grande Dixence, Barr. de la, *Switz.* 22 D4
Grande-Entrée, *Canada* 99 C7
Grande Prairie, *Canada* 100 B5
Grande-Rivière, *Canada* 99 C7
Grande Sauldre →, *France* 25 E9
Grande-Vallée, *Canada* 99 C6
Grandes-Bergeronnes, *Canada* 99 C6
Grandfalls, *U.S.A.* 109 K3
Grandoe Mines, *Canada* 100 B3
Grândola, *Portugal* 31 G2
Grandpré, *France* 25 C11
Grandson, *Switz.* 22 C3
Grandview, *U.S.A.* 110 C4
Grandvilliers, *France* 25 C8
Graneros, *Chile* 126 C1
Grangemouth, *U.K.* 14 E5
Granger, *Wash., U.S.A.* 110 C3
Granger, *Wyo., U.S.A.* 110 F9
Grangeville, *U.S.A.* 110 D5
Granite City, *U.S.A.* 108 F9
Granite Falls, *U.S.A.* 108 C7
Granite Mt., *U.S.A.* 113 M10
Granite Peak, *Australia* 89 E3
Granite Pk., *U.S.A.* 110 D9
Granity, *N.Z.* 87 J3
Granja, *Brazil* 122 B3
Granja de Moreruela, *Spain* 30 D5
Granja de Torrehermosa, *Spain* 31 G5
Granollers, *Spain* 28 D7
Gransee, *Germany* 18 B9
Grant, *U.S.A.* 108 E4
Grant, Mt., *U.S.A.* 110 G4
Grant City, *U.S.A.* 108 E7
Grant I., *Australia* 88 B5
Grant Range Mts., *U.S.A.* 111 G6
Grantham, *U.K.* 12 E7
Grantown-on-Spey, *U.K.* 14 D5
Grants, *U.S.A.* 111 J10
Grants Pass, *U.S.A.* 110 E2
Grantsburg, *U.S.A.* 108 C8
Grantsville, *U.S.A.* 110 F7
Granville, *France* 24 D5
Granville, *N. Dak., U.S.A.* 108 A4
Granville, *N.Y., U.S.A.* 104 D9
Granville L., *Canada* 101 B8
Grao de Gandía, *Spain* 29 F4
Grapeland, *U.S.A.* 109 K7
Gras, L. de, *Canada* 96 B8
Graskop, *S. Africa* 85 C5
Grass →, *Canada* 101 B9
Grass Range, *U.S.A.* 110 C9
Grass River Prov. Park, *Canada* 101 C8
Grass Valley, *Calif., U.S.A.* 112 F6
Grass Valley, *Oreg., U.S.A.* 110 D3
Grassano, *Italy* 35 B9
Grasse, *France* 27 E10
Grassmere, *Australia* 91 E3
Graubünden □, *Switz.* 23 C9
Graulhet, *France* 26 E5
Graus, *Spain* 28 C5
Gravatá, *Brazil* 122 C4
Grave, *Neths.* 16 E7
Grave, Pte. de, *France* 26 C2
's-Graveland, *Neths.* 16 D6
Gravelbourg, *Canada* 101 D7
Gravelines, *France* 25 B9
's-Gravendeel, *Neths.* 16 E5
's-Gravenhage, *Neths.* 16 D4
Gravenhurst, *Canada* 106 B5
's-Gravenpolder, *Neths.* 17 F3
's-Gravensande, *Neths.* 16 D4
Gravesend, *Australia* 91 D5
Gravesend, *U.K.* 13 F8
Gravina di Púglia, *Italy* 35 B9
Gravois, Pointe-à-, *Haiti* 117 C5
Gravone →, *France* 27 G12
Gray, *France* 25 E12
Grayling, *U.S.A.* 104 C3
Grayling →, *Canada* 100 B3
Grays Harbor, *U.S.A.* 110 C1
Grays L., *U.S.A.* 110 E8
Grays River, *U.S.A.* 112 D3
Grayson, *Canada* 101 C8
Graz, *Austria* 21 H5
Grazalema, *Spain* 31 J5
Greasy L., *Canada* 100 A4
Great Abaco I., *Bahamas* 116 A4
Great Artesian Basin, *Australia* 90 C3
Great Australian Bight, *Australia* 89 F5
Great Bahama Bank, *Bahamas* 116 B4
Great Barrier I., *N.Z.* 87 G5
Great Barrier Reef, *Australia* 90 B4
Great Barrington, *U.S.A.* 107 D11
Great Basin, *U.S.A.* 110 G5
Great Bear →, *Canada* 96 B7
Great Bear L., *Canada* 96 B8
Great Bena, *U.S.A.* 107 E9
Great Bend, *U.S.A.* 108 F5
Great Blasket I., *Ireland* 15 D1
Great Britain, *Europe* 6 E5
Great Central, *Canada* 100 D3
Great Dividing Ra., *Australia* 90 C4
Great Driffield, *U.K.* 12 C7
Great Exuma I., *Bahamas* 116 B4
Great Falls, *Canada* 101 C9
Great Falls, *U.S.A.* 110 C8
Great Fish = Groot Vis →, *S. Africa* 84 E4
Great Guana Cay, *Bahamas* 116 B4
Great Harbour Deep, *Canada* 99 B8
Great Inagua I., *Bahamas* 117 B5
Great Indian Desert = Thar Desert, *India* 62 F4
Great I., *Canada* 101 B9
Great Karoo, *S. Africa* 84 E3
Great Lake, *Australia* 90 G4
Great Ormes Head, *U.K.* 12 D4
Great Ouse →, *U.K.* 12 E8
Great Palm I., *Australia* 90 B4
Great Plains, *N. Amer.* 94 E9
Great Ruaha →, *Tanzania* 82 D4
Great Saint Bernard P. = Grand St-Bernard, Col du, *Switz.* 22 E4
Great Salt Lake, *U.S.A.* 110 F7
Great Salt Lake Desert, *U.S.A.* 110 F7
Great Salt Plains Res., *U.S.A.* 109 G5
Great Sandy Desert, *Australia* 88 D3
Great Scarcies →, *S. Leone* 78 D2
Great Slave L., *Canada* 100 A5
Great Smoky Mts. Nat. Park, *U.S.A.* 105 H4
Great Stour = Stour →, *U.K.* 13 F9
Great Victoria Desert, *Australia* 89 E4
Great Wall, *China* 50 E5
Great Whernside, *U.K.* 12 C6
Great Yarmouth, *U.K.* 12 E9
Greater Antilles, *W. Indies* 117 C5
Greater London □, *U.K.* 13 F7
Greater Manchester □, *U.K.* 12 D5
Greater Sunda Is., *Indonesia* 56 F4
Grebbestad, *Sweden* 11 F5
Grebenka, *Ukraine* 40 F8
Greco, C., *Cyprus* 37 E13
Greco, Mte., *Italy* 34 A6
Gredos, Sierra de, *Spain* 30 E5
Greece, *U.S.A.* 106 C7
Greece ■, *Europe* 39 K6
Greeley, *Colo., U.S.A.* 108 E2
Greeley, *Nebr., U.S.A.* 108 E5
Green →, *Ky., U.S.A.* 104 G2
Green →, *Utah, U.S.A.* 111 G9
Green B., *U.S.A.* 104 C2
Green Bay, *U.S.A.* 104 C2
Green C., *Australia* 91 F5
Green Cove Springs, *U.S.A.* 105 L5
Green River, *U.S.A.* 111 G8
Greenbank, *U.S.A.* 112 B4
Greenbush, *Mich., U.S.A.* 106 B1
Greenbush, *Minn., U.S.A.* 108 A6
Greencastle, *U.S.A.* 104 F2
Greene, *U.S.A.* 107 D9
Greenfield, *Calif., U.S.A.* 112 J5
Greenfield, *Calif., U.S.A.* 113 K8
Greenfield, *Ind., U.S.A.* 104 F3
Greenfield, *Iowa, U.S.A.* 108 E7
Greenfield, *Mass., U.S.A.* 107 D12
Greenfield, *Miss., U.S.A.* 109 G8
Greenfield Park, *Canada* 107 A11
Greenland ■, *N. Amer.* 4 C5
Greenland Sea, *Arctic* 4 B7
Greenock, *U.K.* 14 F4
Greenore, *Ireland* 15 B5
Greenore Pt., *Ireland* 15 D5
Greenough →, *Australia* 89 E1
Greenport, *U.S.A.* 107 E12
Greensboro, *Ga., U.S.A.* 105 J4
Greensboro, *N.C., U.S.A.* 105 G6
Greensburg, *Ind., U.S.A.* 104 F3
Greensburg, *Kans., U.S.A.* 109 G5
Greensburg, *Pa., U.S.A.* 106 F5
Greenville, *Liberia* 78 D3
Greenville, *Ala., U.S.A.* 105 K2
Greenville, *Calif., U.S.A.* 112 E6
Greenville, *Ill., U.S.A.* 108 F10
Greenville, *Maine, U.S.A.* 99 C6
Greenville, *Mich., U.S.A.* 104 D3
Greenville, *Miss., U.S.A.* 109 J9
Greenville, *N.C., U.S.A.* 105 H7
Greenville, *Ohio, U.S.A.* 104 E3
Greenville, *Pa., U.S.A.* 106 E4
Greenville, *S.C., U.S.A.* 105 H4
Greenville, *Tenn., U.S.A.* 105 G4
Greenville, *Tex., U.S.A.* 109 J6
Greenwater Lake Prov. Park, *Canada* 101 C8
Greenwich, *U.K.* 13 F8
Greenwich, *Conn., U.S.A.* 107 E11
Greenwich, *N.Y., U.S.A.* 107 C11
Greenwich, *Ohio, U.S.A.* 106 E2
Greenwood, *Canada* 100 D5
Greenwood, *Miss., U.S.A.* 109 J9
Greenwood, *S.C., U.S.A.* 105 H4
Greenwood, Mt., *Australia* 88 B5
Gregório →, *Brazil* 124 B3
Gregory, *U.S.A.* 108 D5
Gregory →, *Australia* 90 B2
Gregory, L., *S. Austral., Australia* 91 D2
Gregory, L., *W. Austral., Australia* 89 E2
Gregory Downs, *Australia* 90 B2
Gregory L., *Australia* 88 D4
Gregory Ra., *Queens., Australia* 90 B3
Gregory Ra., *W. Austral., Australia* 88 D3
Greiffenberg, *Germany* 18 B9
Greifswald, *Germany* 18 A9
Greifswalder Bodden, *Germany* 18 A9
Grein, *Austria* 21 G4
Greiz, *Germany* 18 E8
Gremikha, *Russia* 44 C4
Grenå, *Denmark* 11 H4
Grenada, *U.S.A.* 109 J10
Grenada ■, *W. Indies* 117 D7
Grenade, *France* 26 E5
Grenadines, *W. Indies* 117 D7
Grenchen, *Switz.* 22 B4
Grenen, *Denmark* 11 G4
Grenfell, *Australia* 91 E4
Grenfell, *Canada* 101 C8
Grenoble, *France* 27 C9
Grenora, *U.S.A.* 108 A3
Grenville, C., *Australia* 90 A3
Grenville Chan., *Canada* 100 C3
Gréoux-les-Bains, *France* 27 E9
Gresham, *U.S.A.* 112 E4
Gresik, *Indonesia* 57 G15
Grëssoney St. Jean, *Italy* 32 C4
Gretna Green, *U.K.* 14 F5
Grevelingen Krammer, *Neths.* 16 E4
Greven, *Germany* 18 C3
Grevená, *Greece* 39 J4
Grevenbroich, *Germany* 18 D2
Grevenmacher, *Lux.* 17 J8
Grevesmühlen, *Germany* 18 B7
Grevie, *Sweden* 11 H6
Grey →, *N.Z.* 87 K3
Grey, C., *Australia* 90 A2
Grey Ra., *Australia* 91 D3
Grey Res., *Canada* 99 C8
Greybull, *U.S.A.* 110 D9
Greymouth, *N.Z.* 87 K3
Greytown, *N.Z.* 87 J5
Greytown, *S. Africa* 85 D5
Gribanovskiy, *Russia* 41 F12
Gribbell I., *Canada* 100 C3
Gridley, *U.S.A.* 112 F5
Griekwastad, *S. Africa* 84 D3
Griffin, *U.S.A.* 105 J3
Griffith, *Australia* 91 E4
Grijpskerk, *Neths.* 16 B8
Grillby, *Sweden* 10 E11
Grimari, *C.A.R.* 73 G9
Grimaylov, *Ukraine* 40 G5
Grimbergen, *Belgium* 17 G4
Grimes, *U.S.A.* 112 F5
Grimma, *Germany* 18 D8
Grimmen, *Germany* 18 A9
Grimsby, *Canada* 106 C5
Grimsby, *U.K.* 12 D7
Grimselpass, *Switz.* 23 C6
Grímsey, *Iceland* 8 C5
Grimshaw, *Canada* 100 B5
Grimstad, *Norway* 11 F2
Grindelwald, *Switz.* 22 C6
Grindsted, *Denmark* 11 J2
Grindu, *Romania* 38 E9
Grinnell, *U.S.A.* 108 E8
Griñón, *Spain* 30 E7
Grintavec, *Slovenia* 33 B11
Grip, *Norway* 10 A1
Gris-Nez, C., *France* 25 B8
Grisolles, *France* 26 E5
Grisons = Graubünden □, *Switz.* 23 C9
Grivegnée, *Belgium* 17 G7
Grmeč Planina, *Bos.-H., Yug.* 33 D13
Groais I., *Canada* 99 B8
Groblersdal, *S. Africa* 85 D4
Grobming, *Austria* 21 H3
Grodno, *Belorussia* 40 E3
Grodzisk Mázowiecki, *Poland* 20 C10
Grodzisk Wielkopolski, *Poland* 20 C6
Grodzyanka, *Belorussia* 40 E6

Groenlo

Groenlo, *Neths.* 16 D9
Groesbeck, *U.S.A.* 109 K6
Groesbeek, *Neths.* 16 E7
Groix, *France* 24 E3
Groix, I. de, *France* 24 E3
Grójec, *Poland* 20 D10
Grolloo, *Neths.* 16 C9
Gronau, *Niedersachsen, Germany* 18 C5
Gronau, *Nordrhein-Westfalen, Germany* 18 C3
Grong, *Norway* 8 D12
Groningen, *Neths.* 16 B9
Groningen, *Surinam* 121 B6
Groningen □, *Neths.* 16 B9
Groninger Wad, *Neths.* 16 B9
Gronsveld, *Neths.* 17 G7
Groom, *U.S.A.* 109 H4
Groot →, *S. Africa* 84 E3
Groot Berg →, *S. Africa* 84 E2
Groot-Brakrivier, *S. Africa* 84 E3
Groot-Kei →, *S. Africa* 85 E4
Groot Vis →, *S. Africa* 84 E4
Groote Eylandt, *Australia* 90 A2
Grootebroek, *Neths.* 16 C6
Grootfontein, *Namibia* 84 B2
Grootlaagte →, *Africa* 84 C3
Grootvloer, *S. Africa* 84 E3
Gros C., *Canada* 100 A6
Grosa, Pta., *Spain* 36 B8
Grósio, *Italy* 32 B7
Grosne →, *France* 27 B8
Gross Glockner, *Austria* 21 H2
Grossenbrode, *Germany* 18 A7
Grossenhain, *Germany* 18 D9
Grosseto, *Italy* 32 F8
Groswater B., *Canada* 99 B8
Grote Gette →, *Neths.* 17 G6
Grote Nete →, *Belgium* 17 F5
Groton, *Conn., U.S.A.* 107 E12
Groton, *S. Dak., U.S.A.* 108 C5
Grottáglie, *Italy* 35 B10
Grottaminarda, *Italy* 35 A8
Grottammare, *Italy* 33 F10
Grouard Mission, *Canada* 100 B5
Grouin, Pte. du, *France* 24 D5
Groundhog →, *Canada* 98 C3
Grouse Creek, *U.S.A.* 110 F7
Grouw, *Neths.* 16 B7
Grove City, *U.S.A.* 106 E4
Groveland, *U.S.A.* 112 H6
Grover City, *U.S.A.* 113 K6
Groveton, *N.H., U.S.A.* 107 B13
Groveton, *Tex., U.S.A.* 109 K7
Grožnjan, *Croatia* 33 C10
Groznyy, *Russia* 43 E11
Grubbenvorst, *Neths.* 17 F8
Grudziądz, *Poland* 20 B8
Gruissan, *France* 26 E7
Grumo Áppula, *Italy* 35 A9
Grünberg, *Germany* 18 E4
Grundy Center, *U.S.A.* 108 D8
Gruver, *U.S.A.* 109 G4
Gruyères, *Switz.* 22 C4
Gryazi, *Russia* 41 E11
Gryazovets, *Russia* 41 B12
Gstaad, *Switz.* 22 D4
Gua, *India* 61 H14
Gua Musang, *Malaysia* 59 K3
Guacanayabo, G. de, *Cuba* 116 B4
Guacara, *Venezuela* 120 A4
Guachípas →, *Argentina* 126 B2
Guachiría →, *Colombia* 120 B3
Guadajoz →, *Spain* 31 H6
Guadalajara, *Mexico* 114 C4
Guadalajara, *Spain* 28 E1
Guadalajara □, *Spain* 28 E2
Guadalcanal, *Solomon Is.* 92 H8
Guadalcanal, *Spain* 31 G5
Guadalén →, *Spain* 31 G7
Guadales, *Argentina* 126 C2
Guadalete →, *Spain* 31 J4
Guadalhorce →, *Spain* 31 J6
Guadalimar →, *Spain* 29 G1
Guadalmena →, *Spain* 29 G2
Guadalmez →, *Spain* 31 G5
Guadalope →, *Spain* 28 D4
Guadalquivir →, *Spain* 31 J4
Guadalupe = Guadeloupe ■, *W. Indies* 117 C7
Guadalupe, *Brazil* 122 C3
Guadalupe, *Mexico* 113 N10
Guadalupe, *Spain* 31 F5
Guadalupe, *U.S.A.* 113 L6
Guadalupe →, *Mexico* 113 N10
Guadalupe →, *U.S.A.* 109 L6
Guadalupe, Sierra de, *Spain* 31 F5
Guadalupe Bravos, *Mexico* 114 A3
Guadalupe Pk., *U.S.A.* 111 L11
Guadalupe y Calvo, *Mexico* 114 B3
Guadarrama, Sierra de, *Spain* 30 E6
Guadeloupe ■, *W. Indies* 117 C7
Guadeloupe Passage, *W. Indies* 117 C7
Guadiamar →, *Spain* 31 J4
Guadiana →, *Portugal* 31 H3
Guadiana Menor →, *Spain* 29 H1
Guadiaro →, *Spain* 31 J5
Guadiato →, *Spain* 31 H5
Guadiela →, *Spain* 28 E2
Guadix, *Spain* 29 H1
Guafo, Boca del, *Chile* 128 B2
Guafo, I., *Chile* 128 B2
Guainía □, *Colombia* 120 C4
Guainía →, *Colombia* 120 C4
Guaíra, *Brazil* 127 A5
Guaitecas, Is., *Chile* 128 B2
Guajará-Mirim, *Brazil* 125 C4
Guajira □, *Colombia* 120 A3
Guajira, Pen. de la, *Colombia* 120 A3
Gualaceo, *Ecuador* 120 D2
Gualán, *Guatemala* 116 C2
Gualdo Tadino, *Italy* 33 E9
Gualeguay, *Argentina* 126 C4
Gualeguaychú, *Argentina* 126 C4
Gualicho, Salina, *Argentina* 128 B3
Gualjaina, *Argentina* 128 B2
Guam, *Pac. Oc.* 92 F6
Guamá, *Brazil* 122 B2
Guamá →, *Brazil* 122 B2
Guamblin, I., *Chile* 128 B1
Guaminí, *Argentina* 126 D3
Guamote, *Ecuador* 120 D2
Guampí, Sierra de, *Venezuela* 121 B4
Guamúchil, *Mexico* 114 B3
Guan Xian, *China* 52 B4
Guanabacoa, *Cuba* 116 B3
Guanacaste, Cordillera del, *Costa Rica* 116 D2
Guanacevi, *Mexico* 114 B3
Guanahani = San Salvador, *Bahamas* 117 B5
Guanajay, *Cuba* 116 B3
Guanajuato, *Mexico* 114 C4
Guanajuato □, *Mexico* 114 C4
Guanambi, *Brazil* 123 D3
Guanare, *Venezuela* 120 B4
Guanare →, *Venezuela* 120 B4
Guandacol, *Argentina* 126 B2
Guane, *Cuba* 116 B3
Guang'an, *China* 52 B6
Guangchang, *China* 53 D11
Guangde, *China* 53 B12
Guangdong □, *China* 53 F9
Guangfeng, *China* 53 C12
Guanghan, *China* 52 B5
Guanghua, *China* 53 A8
Guangji, *China* 53 C10
Guangling, *China* 50 E8
Guangning, *China* 53 F9
Guangrao, *China* 51 F10
Guangshun, *China* 52 D6
Guangwu, *China* 50 F3
Guangxi Zhuangzu Zizhiqu □, *China* 52 E7
Guangyuan, *China* 52 A5
Guangze, *China* 53 D11
Guangzhou, *China* 53 F9
Guanhães, *Brazil* 123 E3
Guanipa →, *Venezuela* 121 B5
Guanling, *China* 52 E5
Guannan, *China* 51 G10
Guanta, *Venezuela* 121 A5
Guantánamo, *Cuba* 117 B4
Guantao, *China* 50 F8
Guanyang, *China* 53 E8
Guanyun, *China* 51 G10
Guapí, *Colombia* 120 C2
Guápiles, *Costa Rica* 116 D3
Guaporé →, *Brazil* 125 C4
Guaqui, *Bolivia* 124 D4
Guara, Sierra de, *Spain* 28 C4
Guarabira, *Brazil* 122 C4
Guaranda, *Ecuador* 120 D2
Guarapari, *Brazil* 123 F3
Guarapuava, *Brazil* 123 G1
Guaratinguetá, *Brazil* 127 A6
Guaratuba, *Brazil* 127 B6
Guarda, *Portugal* 30 E3
Guarda □, *Portugal* 30 E3
Guardafui, C. = Asir, Ras, *Somali Rep.* 68 E5
Guardamar del Segura, *Spain* 29 G4
Guardavalle, *Italy* 35 D9
Guardiagrele, *Italy* 33 F11
Guardo, *Spain* 30 C6
Guareña, *Spain* 31 G4
Guareña →, *Spain* 30 D5
Guaria □, *Paraguay* 126 B4
Guárico □, *Venezuela* 120 B4
Guarrojo →, *Colombia* 120 C3
Guarujá, *Brazil* 127 A6
Guarus, *Brazil* 123 F3
Guasave, *Mexico* 114 B3
Guascama, Pta., *Colombia* 120 C2
Guasdualito, *Venezuela* 120 B3
Guasipati, *Venezuela* 121 B5
Guastalla, *Italy* 32 D7
Guatemala, *Guatemala* 116 D1
Guatemala ■, *Cent. Amer.* 116 C1
Guatire, *Venezuela* 120 A4
Guaviare □, *Colombia* 120 C3
Guaviare →, *Colombia* 120 C4
Guaxupé, *Brazil* 127 A6
Guayabero →, *Colombia* 120 C3
Guayama, *Puerto Rico* 117 C6
Guayaneco, Arch., *Chile* 128 C1
Guayaquil, *Ecuador* 120 D2
Guayaquil, G. de, *Ecuador* 120 D1
Guayaramerín, *Bolivia* 125 C4
Guayas →, *Ecuador* 120 D2
Guaymas, *Mexico* 114 B2
Guazhou, *China* 53 A12
Guba, *Zaïre* 83 E2
Gûbâl, Madîq, *Egypt* 76 B3
Gubat, *Phil.* 55 E6
Gúbbio, *Italy* 33 E9
Gubio, *Nigeria* 79 C7
Gubkin, *Russia* 41 F10
Gudata, *Georgia* 43 E9
Gudbrandsdalen, *Norway* 9 F10
Guddu Barrage, *Pakistan* 60 E6
Gudenå, *Denmark* 11 H3
Gudermes, *Russia* 43 E12
Gudivada, *India* 61 L12
Gudur, *India* 60 M11
Guebwiller, *France* 25 E14
Guecho, *Spain* 28 B2
Guékédou, *Guinea* 78 D2
Guelma, *Algeria* 75 A6
Guelph, *Canada* 98 D3
Guelt es Stel, *Algeria* 75 A5
Guelttara, *Algeria* 75 C4
Guemar, *Algeria* 75 B6
Guéméné-Penfao, *France* 24 E5
Guéméné-sur-Scorff, *France* 24 D3
Guéné, *Benin* 79 C5
Güepí, *Peru* 120 D2
Guer, *France* 24 E4
Güer Aike, *Argentina* 128 D3
Guérande, *France* 24 E4
Guercif, *Morocco* 75 B4
Guéréda, *Chad* 73 F9
Guéret, *France* 26 B5
Guérigny, *France* 25 E10
Guerneville, *U.S.A.* 112 G4
Guernica, *Spain* 28 B2
Guernsey, *U.K.* 13 H5
Guernsey, *U.S.A.* 108 D2
Guerrara, *Oasis, Algeria* 75 B5
Guerrara, *Saoura, Algeria* 75 C4
Guerrero □, *Mexico* 115 D5
Guerzim, *Algeria* 75 C4
Gueugnon, *France* 27 B8
Gueydan, *U.S.A.* 109 K8
Gügher, *Iran* 65 D8
Guglionesi, *Italy* 35 A7
Gui Jiang →, *China* 53 F8
Gui Xian, *China* 52 F7
Guia, *Canary Is.* 36 F4
Guia de Isora, *Canary Is.* 36 F3
Guia Lopes da Laguna, *Brazil* 127 A4
Guichi, *China* 53 B11
Guider, *Cameroon* 79 D7
Guidimouni, *Niger* 79 C6
Guiding, *China* 52 D6
Guidong, *China* 53 D9
Guiglo, *Ivory C.* 78 D3
Guijá, *Mozam.* 85 C5
Guijo de Coria, *Spain* 30 E4
Guildford, *U.K.* 13 F7
Guilford, *U.S.A.* 99 C6
Guilin, *China* 53 E8
Guillaumes, *France* 27 D10
Guillestre, *France* 27 D10
Guilvinec, *France* 24 E2
Güimar, *Canary Is.* 36 F3
Guimarães, *Brazil* 122 B3
Guimarães, *Portugal* 30 D2
Guimaras, *Phil.* 55 F5
Guinda, *U.S.A.* 112 G4
Guinea ■, *W. Afr.* 78 C2
Guinea, Gulf of, *Atl. Oc.* 70 F3
Guinea-Bissau ■, *Africa* 78 C2
Güines, *Cuba* 116 B3
Guingamp, *France* 24 D3
Guipavas, *France* 24 D2
Guiping, *China* 53 F8
Guipúzcoa □, *Spain* 28 B2
Guir, O. →, *Algeria* 75 B4
Guiratinga, *Brazil* 125 D7
Güiria, *Venezuela* 121 A5
Guiscard, *France* 25 C10
Guise, *France* 25 C10
Guitiriz, *Spain* 30 B3
Guiuan, *Phil.* 55 F6
Guixi, *China* 53 C11
Guiyang, *Guizhou, China* 52 D6
Guiyang, *Hunan, China* 53 E9
Guizhou □, *China* 52 D6
Gujan-Mestras, *France* 26 D2
Gujarat □, *India* 62 H4
Gujiang, *China* 53 D10
Gujranwala, *Pakistan* 62 C6
Gujrat, *Pakistan* 62 C6
Gukovo, *Russia* 43 B8
Gulbarga, *India* 60 L10
Gulbene, *Latvia* 40 C5
Gulf, The, *Asia* 65 E6
Gulfport, *U.S.A.* 109 K10
Gulgong, *Australia* 91 E4
Gulin, *China* 52 C5
Gulistan, *Pakistan* 62 D2
Gull Lake, *Canada* 101 C7
Gullegem, *Belgium* 17 G2
Güllük, *Turkey* 66 E2
Gulma, *Nigeria* 79 C5
Gulmarg, *India* 63 B6
Gülnar, *Turkey* 66 E5
Gulpen, *Neths.* 17 G7
Gülşehir, *Turkey* 66 D6
Gulshad, *Kazakhstan* 44 E8
Gulsvik, *Norway* 10 D3
Gulu, *Uganda* 82 B3
Gulwe, *Tanzania* 82 D4
Gulyaypole, *Ukraine* 42 C7
Gum Lake, *Australia* 91 E3
Gumal →, *Pakistan* 62 D4
Gumbaz, *Pakistan* 62 D3
Gumel, *Nigeria* 79 C6
Gumiel de Hizán, *Spain* 28 D1
Gumlu, *Australia* 90 B4
Gumma □, *Japan* 49 F9
Gummersbach, *Germany* 18 D3
Gummi, *Nigeria* 79 C6
Gümüşhaciköy, *Turkey* 42 F6
Gümüşhane, *Turkey* 67 C8
Gümüşhane □, *Turkey* 67 C8
Gumzai, *Indonesia* 57 F8
Guna, *Ethiopia* 77 E4
Guna, *India* 62 G7
Gundagai, *Australia* 91 F4
Gundelfingen, *Germany* 19 G6
Gundih, *Indonesia* 57 G14
Guneydogu Toroslar, *Turkey* 67 D9
Gungu, *Zaïre* 80 F3
Gunisao →, *Canada* 101 C9
Gunisao L., *Canada* 101 C9
Gunnbjørn Fjeld, *Greenland* 4 C6
Gunnedah, *Australia* 91 E5
Gunningbar Cr. →, *Australia* 91 E4
Gunnison, *Colo., U.S.A.* 111 G10
Gunnison, *Utah, U.S.A.* 110 G8
Gunnison →, *U.S.A.* 111 G9
Gunpowder, *Australia* 90 B2
Guntakal, *India* 60 M10
Guntersville, *U.S.A.* 105 H2
Guntong, *Malaysia* 59 K3
Guntur, *India* 61 L12
Gunungapi, *Indonesia* 57 F7
Gunungsitoli, *Indonesia* 56 D1
Günz →, *Germany* 19 G6
Gunza, *Angola* 80 G2
Günzburg, *Germany* 19 G6
Gunzenhausen, *Germany* 19 F6
Guo He →, *China* 51 H9
Guoyang, *China* 50 H9
Gupis, *Pakistan* 63 A5
Gura Humorului, *Romania* 38 B8
Gurag, *Ethiopia* 77 F4
Gurdaspur, *India* 62 C6
Gurdon, *U.S.A.* 109 J8
Gurdzhaani, *Georgia* 43 F11
Gurgaon, *India* 62 E7
Gürgentepe, *Turkey* 67 C8
Gurguéia →, *Brazil* 122 C3
Gurha, *India* 62 G4
Guri, Embalse de, *Venezuela* 121 B5
Gurk →, *Austria* 21 J4
Gurkha, *Nepal* 63 E11
Gurley, *Australia* 91 D4
Gurué, *Mozam.* 83 F4
Gurun, *Malaysia* 59 K3
Gürün, *Turkey* 66 D7
Gurupá, *Brazil* 121 D7
Gurupá, I. Grande de, *Brazil* 121 D7
Gurupi, *Brazil* 123 D2
Gurupi →, *Brazil* 122 B2
Gurupi, Serra do, *Brazil* 122 C2
Guryev, *Kazakhstan* 43 C14
Gus-Khrustalnyy, *Russia* 41 D12
Gusau, *Nigeria* 79 C6
Gusev, *Russia* 40 D3
Gushan, *China* 51 E12
Gushi, *China* 53 A10
Gushiago, *Ghana* 79 D4
Gusinje, *Montenegro, Yug.* 21 N9
Gusinoozersk, *Russia* 45 D11
Gúspini, *Italy* 34 C1
Gusťanj, *Slovenia* 33 B11
Gustine, *U.S.A.* 111 H3
Güstrow, *Germany* 18 B8
Gusum, *Sweden* 11 F10
Guta = Kalárovo, *Czech.* 21 H7
Gütersloh, *Germany* 18 D4
Gutha, *Australia* 89 E2
Guthalongra, *Australia* 90 B4
Guthrie, *U.S.A.* 109 H6
Gutian, *China* 53 D12
Gutiérrez, *Bolivia* 125 D5
Guttannen, *Switz.* 23 C6
Guttenberg, *U.S.A.* 108 D9
Guyana ■, *S. Amer.* 121 B6
Guyang, *China* 50 D6
Guyenne, *France* 26 D4
Guymon, *U.S.A.* 109 G4
Guyra, *Australia* 91 E5
Guyuan, *Hebei, China* 50 D8
Guyuan, *Ningxia Huizu, China* 50 F4
Guzhang, *China* 52 C7
Guzhen, *China* 51 H9
Guzmán, L. de, *Mexico* 114 A3
Gwa, *Burma* 61 L19
Gwaai, *Zimbabwe* 83 F2
Gwabegar, *Australia* 91 E4
Gwadabawa, *Nigeria* 79 C6
Gwādar, *Pakistan* 60 G3
Gwagwada, *Nigeria* 79 C6
Gwalia, *Australia* 89 E3
Gwalior, *India* 62 F8
Gwanda, *Zimbabwe* 83 G2
Gwandu, *Nigeria* 79 C5
Gwane, *Zaïre* 82 B2
Gwaram, *Nigeria* 79 C7
Gwarzo, *Nigeria* 79 C6
Gweebarra B., *Ireland* 15 B3
Gweedore, *Ireland* 15 A3
Gwent □, *U.K.* 13 F5
Gweru, *Zimbabwe* 83 F2
Gwi, *Nigeria* 79 D6
Gwinn, *U.S.A.* 104 B2
Gwio Kura, *Nigeria* 79 C7
Gwol, *Ghana* 78 C4
Gwoza, *Nigeria* 79 C7
Gwydir →, *Australia* 91 D4
Gwynedd □, *U.K.* 12 E4
Gyandzha, *Azerbaijan* 43 F12
Gyaring Hu, *China* 54 C4
Gydanskiy P-ov., *Russia* 44 C8
Gympie, *Australia* 91 D5
Gyoma, *Hungary* 21 J10
Gyöngyös, *Hungary* 21 H9
Györ, *Hungary* 21 H7
Gypsum Pt., *Canada* 100 A6
Gypsumville, *Canada* 101 C9
Gyula, *Hungary* 21 J11
Gzhatsk, *Russia* 40 D9

H

Ha 'Arava →, *Israel* 69 E4
Ha Coi, *Vietnam* 58 B6
Ha Dong, *Vietnam* 58 B5
Ha Giang, *Vietnam* 58 A5
Ha Tien, *Vietnam* 59 G5
Ha Tinh, *Vietnam* 58 C5
Ha Trung, *Vietnam* 58 C5
Haacht, *Belgium* 17 G5
Haag, *Germany* 19 G8
Haaksbergen, *Neths.* 16 D9
Haaltert, *Belgium* 17 G4
Haamstede, *Neths.* 17 E3
Haapamäki, *Finland* 8 E18
Haapsalu, *Estonia* 40 B3
Haarlem, *Neths.* 16 D5
Haast →, *N.Z.* 87 K2
Haast Bluff, *Australia* 88 D5
Haastrecht, *Neths.* 16 E5
Hab Nadi Chauki, *Pakistan* 62 G2
Habaswein, *Kenya* 82 B4
Habay, *Canada* 100 B5
Habay-la-Neuve, *Belgium* 17 J7
Habbānīyah, *Iraq* 64 C4
Haboro, *Japan* 48 B10
Haccourt, *Belgium* 17 G7
Hachenburg, *Germany* 18 E3
Hachijō-Jima, *Japan* 49 H9
Hachinohe, *Japan* 48 D10
Hachiōji, *Japan* 49 G9
Hachŏn, *N. Korea* 51 D15
Hachy, *Belgium* 17 J7
Hacıbektaş, *Turkey* 66 D6
Hacılar, *Turkey* 66 D6
Hackensack, *U.S.A.* 107 F10
Haçli Gölü, *Turkey* 67 D10
Hadali, *Pakistan* 62 C5
Hadarba, Ras, *Sudan* 76 C4
Hadarom □, *Israel* 69 E3
Haddington, *U.K.* 14 F6
Hadejia, *Nigeria* 79 C7
Hadejia →, *Nigeria* 79 C7
Haden, *Australia* 91 D5
Hadera, *Israel* 69 C3
Hadera, N. →, *Israel* 69 C3
Haderslev, *Denmark* 11 J3
Hadhramaut = Hadramawt, *Yemen* 68 D4
Hadım, *Turkey* 66 E5
Hadjeb El Aïoun, *Tunisia* 75 A6
Hadong, *S. Korea* 51 G14
Hadramawt, *Yemen* 68 D4
Hadrānīyah, *Iraq* 64 C4
Hadrian's Wall, *U.K.* 12 C5
Hadsten, *Denmark* 11 H4
Hadsund, *Denmark* 11 H4
Haeju, *N. Korea* 51 E13
Haenam, *S. Korea* 51 G14
Haerhpin = Harbin, *China* 51 B14
Hafar al Bāţin, *Si. Arabia* 64 D5
Hafik, *Turkey* 66 D7
Hafīrat al 'Aydā, *Si. Arabia* 64 E3
Hafizabad, *Pakistan* 62 C5
Haflong, *India* 61 G18
Hafnarfjörður, *Iceland* 8 D3
Hafun, Ras, *Somali Rep.* 68 E5
Hagalil, *Israel* 69 C4
Hagen, *Germany* 18 D3
Hagenow, *Germany* 18 B7
Hagerman, *U.S.A.* 109 J2
Hagerstown, *U.S.A.* 104 F7
Hagetmau, *France* 26 E3
Hagfors, *Sweden* 9 F12
Häggenås, *Sweden* 10 A8
Hagi, *Iceland* 8 D2
Hagi, *Japan* 49 G5
Hagolan, *Syria* 69 B4
Hagondange-Briey, *France* 25 C13
Hags Hd., *Ireland* 15 D2
Hague, C. de la, *France* 24 C5
Hague, The = 's-Gravenhage, *Neths.* 16 D4
Haguenau, *France* 25 D14
Hai □, *Tanzania* 82 C4
Hai Duong, *Vietnam* 58 B6

Hawzen

Hai'an, *Guangdong, China* 53 G8
Hai'an, *Jiangsu, China* 53 A13
Haicheng, *Fujian, China* 53 E11
Haicheng, *Liaoning, China* 51 D12
Haidar Khel, *Afghan.* 62 C3
Haifa = Ḩefa, *Israel* 69 C3
Haifeng, *China* 53 F10
Haig, *Australia* 89 F4
Haiger, *Germany* 18 E4
Haikang, *China* 53 G8
Haikou, *China* 54 D6
Ḩā'il, *Si. Arabia* 64 E4
Hailar, *China* 54 B6
Hailey, *U.S.A.* 110 E6
Haileybury, *Canada* 98 C4
Hailin, *China* 51 B15
Hailing Dao, *China* 53 G8
Hailong, *China* 51 C13
Hailun, *China* 54 B7
Hailuoto, *Finland* 8 D18
Haimen, *Guangdong, China* 53 F11
Haimen, *Jiangsu, China* 53 B13
Haimen, *Zhejiang, China* 53 C13
Hainan □, *China* 54 E5
Hainaut □, *Belgium* 17 H4
Haines, *U.S.A.* 110 D5
Haines City, *U.S.A.* 105 L5
Haines Junction, *Canada* 100 A1
Haining, *China* 53 B13
Haiphong, *Vietnam* 54 D5
Haiti ■, *W. Indies* 117 C5
Haiya Junction, *Sudan* 76 D4
Haiyan, *China* 53 B13
Haiyang, *China* 51 F11
Haiyuan, *Guangxi Zhuangzu, China* 52 F6
Haiyuan, *Ningxia Huizu, China* 50 F3
Haizhou, *China* 51 G10
Haizhou Wan, *China* 51 G10
Haja, *Indonesia* 57 E7
Hajar Bangar, *Sudan* 73 F9
Hajdúböszörmény, *Hungary* 21 H11
Hajdúszoboszló, *Hungary* 21 H11
Hajipur, *India* 63 G11
Hājjī Muḩsin, *Iraq* 64 C5
Ḩājjīābād, *Eşfahan, Iran* 65 C7
Ḩājjīābād, *Hormozgān, Iran* 65 D7
Hakansson, Mts., *Zaïre* 83 D2
Håkantorp, *Sweden* 11 F6
Hakkâri, *Turkey* 67 E10
Hakkâri □, *Turkey* 67 E10
Hakkâri Dağları, *Turkey* 67 E10
Hakken-Zan, *Japan* 49 G7
Hakodate, *Japan* 48 D10
Haku-San, *Japan* 49 F8
Hakui, *Japan* 49 F8
Hala, *Pakistan* 60 G6
Ḩalab, *Syria* 64 B3
Ḩalabjah, *Iraq* 64 C5
Halaib, *Sudan* 76 C4
Halanzy, *Belgium* 17 J7
Hālat' Ammār, *Si. Arabia* 64 D3
Halbā, *Lebanon* 69 A5
Halberstadt, *Germany* 18 D7
Halcombe, *N.Z.* 87 J5
Halcon, Mt., *Phil.* 57 B6
Halden, *Norway* 10 E5
Haldensleben, *Germany* 18 C7
Haldia, *India* 61 H16
Haldwani, *India* 63 E8
Hale →, *Australia* 90 C2
Haleakala Crater, *U.S.A.* 102 H16
Halen, *Belgium* 17 G6
Haleyville, *U.S.A.* 105 H2
Half Assini, *Ghana* 78 D4
Halfway →, *Canada* 100 B4
Haliburton, *Canada* 98 C4
Halifax, *Australia* 90 B4
Halifax, *Canada* 99 D7
Halifax, *U.K.* 12 D6
Halifax B., *Australia* 90 B4
Halifax I., *Namibia* 84 D2
Ḩalīl →, *Iran* 65 E8
Hall, *Austria* 19 H7
Hall Beach, *Canada* 97 B11
Hall Pt., *Australia* 88 C3
Hallands län □, *Sweden* 11 H6
Hallands Väderö, *Sweden* 11 H6
Hallandsås, *Sweden* 11 H7
Halle, *Belgium* 17 G4
Halle, *Nordrhein-Westfalen, Germany* 18 C4
Halle, *Sachsen-Anhalt, Germany* 18 D7
Hällefors, *Sweden* 9 G13
Hallein, *Austria* 21 H3
Hällekis, *Sweden* 11 F7
Hallett, *Australia* 91 E2
Hallettsville, *U.S.A.* 109 L6
Hällevadsholm, *Sweden* 11 F5
Halliday, *U.S.A.* 108 B3
Halliday L., *Canada* 101 A7
Hallim, *S. Korea* 51 H14
Hallingdal →, *Norway* 9 F10
Hällnäs, *Sweden* 8 D15
Hallock, *U.S.A.* 101 D9
Halls Creek, *Australia* 88 C4
Hallstahammar, *Sweden* 10 E10
Hallstead, *U.S.A.* 107 E9
Halmahera, *Indonesia* 57 D7
Halmeu, *Romania* 38 B6
Halmstad, *Sweden* 11 H6
Halq el Oued, *Tunisia* 75 A7
Hals, *Denmark* 11 H4
Halsafjorden, *Norway* 10 A2
Hälsingborg = Helsingborg, *Sweden* 11 H6
Halstad, *U.S.A.* 108 B6
Haltdalen, *Norway* 10 B5
Haltern, *Germany* 18 D3
Halul, *Qatar* 65 E7
Ḩalvān, *Iran* 65 C8
Ham, *France* 25 C10
Ham Tan, *Vietnam* 59 G6
Ham Yen, *Vietnam* 58 A5
Hamab, *Namibia* 84 D2
Hamad, *Sudan* 77 D3
Hamada, *Japan* 49 G6
Hamadān, *Iran* 65 C6
Hamadān □, *Iran* 65 C6
Hamadia, *Algeria* 75 A5
Hamāh, *Syria* 64 C3
Hamamatsu, *Japan* 49 G8
Hamar, *Norway* 10 D5
Hamarøy, *Norway* 8 B13
Hamâta, Gebel, *Egypt* 76 C3
Hambantota, *Sri Lanka* 60 R12
Hamber Prov. Park, *Canada* 100 C5
Hamburg, *Germany* 18 B5
Hamburg, *Ark., U.S.A.* 109 J9
Hamburg, *Iowa, U.S.A.* 108 E7
Hamburg, *N.Y., U.S.A.* 106 D6
Hamburg, *Pa., U.S.A.* 107 F9
Hamburg □, *Germany* 18 B6
Ḩamḑ, W. al →, *Si. Arabia* 64 E3
Hamden, *U.S.A.* 107 E12
Hame □ = Hämeen lääni □, *Finland* 9 F18
Hämeen lääni □, *Finland* 9 F18
Hämeenlinna, *Finland* 9 F18
Hamélé, *Ghana* 78 C4
Hamelin Pool, *Australia* 89 E1
Hameln, *Germany* 18 C5
Hamer Koke, *Ethiopia* 77 F4
Hamerkaz □, *Israel* 69 C3
Hamersley Ra., *Australia* 88 D2
Hamhung, *N. Korea* 51 E14
Hami, *China* 54 B4
Hamilton, *Australia* 91 F3
Hamilton, *Canada* 98 D4
Hamilton, *N.Z.* 87 G5
Hamilton, *U.K.* 14 F4
Hamilton, *Mo., U.S.A.* 108 F8
Hamilton, *Mont., U.S.A.* 110 C6
Hamilton, *N.Y., U.S.A.* 107 D9
Hamilton, *Ohio, U.S.A.* 104 F3
Hamilton, *Tex., U.S.A.* 109 K5
Hamilton →, *Australia* 90 C2
Hamilton City, *U.S.A.* 112 F4
Hamilton Hotel, *Australia* 90 C3
Hamilton Inlet, *Canada* 99 B8
Hamiota, *Canada* 101 C8
Hamlet, *U.S.A.* 105 H6
Hamley Bridge, *Australia* 91 E2
Hamlin = Hameln, *Germany* 18 C5
Hamlin, *N.Y., U.S.A.* 106 C7
Hamlin, *Tex., U.S.A.* 109 J4
Hamm, *Germany* 18 D3
Hammam Bouhadjar, *Algeria* 75 A4
Hammamet, *Tunisia* 75 A7
Hammamet, G. de, *Tunisia* 75 A7
Hammarstrand, *Sweden* 10 A10
Hamme, *Belgium* 17 F4
Hamme-Mille, *Belgium* 17 G5
Hammel, *Denmark* 11 H3
Hammelburg, *Germany* 19 E5
Hammerfest, *Norway* 8 A17
Hammond, *Ind., U.S.A.* 104 E2
Hammond, *La., U.S.A.* 109 K9
Hammonton, *U.S.A.* 104 F8
Hamoir, *Belgium* 17 H7
Hamont, *Belgium* 17 F7
Hamoyet, Jebel, *Sudan* 76 D4
Hampden, *N.Z.* 87 L3
Hampshire □, *U.K.* 13 F6
Hampshire Downs, *U.K.* 13 F6
Hampton, *Ark., U.S.A.* 109 J8
Hampton, *Iowa, U.S.A.* 108 D8
Hampton, *N.H., U.S.A.* 107 D14
Hampton, *S.C., U.S.A.* 105 J5
Hampton, *Va., U.S.A.* 104 G7
Hampton Tableland, *Australia* 89 F4
Hamrat esh Sheykh, *Sudan* 77 E2
Hamur, *Turkey* 67 D10
Hamyang, *S. Korea* 51 G14
Han Jiang →, *China* 53 F11
Han Shui →, *China* 53 B10
Hana, *U.S.A.* 102 H17
Hanak, *Si. Arabia* 64 E3
Hanamaki, *Japan* 48 E10
Hanang, *Tanzania* 82 C4
Hanau, *Germany* 19 E4
Hanbogd, *Mongolia* 50 C4
Hancheng, *China* 50 G6
Hanchuan, *China* 53 B9
Hancock, *Mich., U.S.A.* 108 B10
Hancock, *Minn., U.S.A.* 108 C7
Hancock, *Pa., U.S.A.* 107 E9
Handa, *Japan* 49 G8
Handa, *Somali Rep.* 68 E5
Handan, *China* 50 F8
Handen, *Sweden* 10 E12
Handeni, *Tanzania* 82 D4
Handeni □, *Tanzania* 82 D4
Handub, *Sudan* 76 D4
Handwara, *India* 63 B6
Handzame, *Belgium* 17 F2
Hanegev, *Israel* 69 E3
Haney, *Canada* 100 D4
Hanford, *U.S.A.* 111 H4
Hang Chat, *Thailand* 58 C2
Hang Dong, *Thailand* 58 C2
Hangang →, *S. Korea* 51 F14
Hangayn Nuruu, *Mongolia* 54 B4
Hangchou = Hangzhou, *China* 53 B13
Hanggin Houqi, *China* 50 D4
Hanggin Qi, *China* 50 E5
Hangö, *Finland* 9 G17
Hangu, *China* 51 E9
Hangzhou, *China* 53 B13
Hangzhou Wan, *China* 53 B13
Hanhongor, *Mongolia* 50 C3
Ḩanīdh, *Si. Arabia* 65 E6
Ḩanīsh, *Yemen* 68 E3
Hanjiang, *China* 53 E12
Hankinson, *U.S.A.* 108 B6
Hanko, *Finland* 9 G17
Hankou, *China* 53 B10
Hanksville, *U.S.A.* 111 G8
Hanle, *India* 63 C8
Hanmer Springs, *N.Z.* 87 K4
Hann →, *Australia* 88 C4
Hann, Mt., *Australia* 88 C4
Hanna, *Canada* 100 C6
Hannaford, *U.S.A.* 108 B5
Hannah, *U.S.A.* 108 A5
Hannah B., *Canada* 98 B4
Hannibal, *U.S.A.* 108 F9
Hannik, *Sudan* 76 D3
Hannover, *Germany* 18 C5
Hannut, *Belgium* 17 G6
Hanoi, *Vietnam* 54 D5
Hanover = Hannover, *Germany* 18 C5
Hanover, *Canada* 106 B3
Hanover, *S. Africa* 84 E3
Hanover, *N.H., U.S.A.* 107 C12
Hanover, *Ohio, U.S.A.* 106 F2
Hanover, *Pa., U.S.A.* 104 F7
Hanover, I., *Chile* 128 D2
Hanshou, *China* 53 C8
Hansi, *India* 62 E6
Hanson, L., *Australia* 91 E2
Hanyang, *China* 53 B10
Hanyin, *China* 52 A7
Hanyuan, *China* 52 C4
Hanzhong, *China* 50 H4
Hanzhuang, *China* 51 G9
Haora, *India* 63 H13
Haoxue, *China* 53 B9
Haparanda, *Sweden* 8 D18
Hapert, *Neths.* 17 F6
Happy, *U.S.A.* 109 H4
Happy Camp, *U.S.A.* 110 F2
Happy Valley-Goose Bay, *Canada* 99 B7
Hapsu, *N. Korea* 51 D15
Hapur, *India* 62 E7
Ḩaql, *Si. Arabia* 69 F3
Haquira, *Peru* 124 C3
Har, *Indonesia* 57 F8
Har-Ayrag, *Mongolia* 50 B5
Har Hu, *China* 54 C4
Har Us Nuur, *Mongolia* 54 B4
Har Yehuda, *Israel* 69 D3
Ḩaraḑ, *Si. Arabia* 68 C4
Haranomachi, *Japan* 48 F10
Harardera, *Somali Rep.* 68 G4
Harare, *Zimbabwe* 83 F3
Harat, *Ethiopia* 77 D4
Harazé, *Chad* 73 F8
Harbin, *China* 51 B14
Harbiye, *Turkey* 66 E7
Harboør, *Denmark* 11 H2
Harbor Beach, *U.S.A.* 104 D4
Harbor Springs, *U.S.A.* 104 C3
Harbour Breton, *Canada* 99 C8
Harbour Grace, *Canada* 99 C9
Harburg, *Germany* 18 B5
Hårby, *Denmark* 11 J4
Harda, *India* 62 H7
Hardangerfjorden, *Norway* 9 F8
Hardap Dam, *Namibia* 84 C2
Hardegarijp, *Neths.* 16 B7
Hardenberg, *Neths.* 16 C9
Harderwijk, *Neths.* 16 D7
Hardey →, *Australia* 88 D2
Hardin, *U.S.A.* 110 D10
Harding, *S. Africa* 85 E4
Harding Ra., *Australia* 88 C3
Hardisty, *Canada* 100 C6
Hardman, *U.S.A.* 110 D4
Hardoi, *India* 63 F9
Hardwar = Haridwar, *India* 62 E8
Hardwick, *U.S.A.* 107 B12
Hardy, *U.S.A.* 109 G9
Hardy, Pen., *Chile* 128 E3
Hare B., *Canada* 99 B8
Harelbeke, *Belgium* 17 G2
Haren, *Germany* 18 C3
Haren, *Neths.* 16 B9
Harer, *Ethiopia* 68 F3
Harerge □, *Ethiopia* 77 F5
Hareto, *Ethiopia* 77 F4
Harfleur, *France* 24 C7
Hargeisa, *Somali Rep.* 68 F3
Hargshamn, *Sweden* 9 F15
Hari →, *Indonesia* 56 E2
Haria, *Canary Is.* 36 E6
Haricha, Hamada el, *Mali* 74 D4
Haridwar, *India* 62 E8
Haringhata →, *Bangla.* 61 J16
Haringvliet, *Neths.* 16 E4
Harīrūd →, *Asia* 60 A2
Harlan, *Iowa, U.S.A.* 108 E7
Harlan, *Tenn., U.S.A.* 105 G4
Harlech, *U.K.* 12 E3
Harlem, *U.S.A.* 110 B9
Harlingen, *Neths.* 16 B6
Harlingen, *U.S.A.* 109 M6
Harlowton, *U.S.A.* 110 C9
Harmånger, *Sweden* 10 C11
Harmil, *Ethiopia* 77 D5
Harney Basin, *U.S.A.* 110 E4
Harney L., *U.S.A.* 110 E4
Harney Pk., *U.S.A.* 108 D3
Härnön, *Sweden* 10 B12
Härnösand, *Sweden* 10 B11
Haro, *Spain* 28 C2
Harp L., *Canada* 99 A7
Harper, *Liberia* 78 E3
Harplinge, *Sweden* 11 H6
Harrand, *Pakistan* 62 E4
Harriman, *U.S.A.* 105 H3
Harrington Harbour, *Canada* 99 B8
Harris, *U.K.* 14 D2
Harris, Sd. of, *U.K.* 14 D1
Harris L., *Australia* 91 E2
Harrisburg, *Ill., U.S.A.* 109 G10
Harrisburg, *Nebr., U.S.A.* 108 E3
Harrisburg, *Oreg., U.S.A.* 110 D2
Harrisburg, *Pa., U.S.A.* 106 F8
Harrismith, *S. Africa* 85 D4
Harrison, *Ark., U.S.A.* 109 G8
Harrison, *Idaho, U.S.A.* 110 C5
Harrison, *Nebr., U.S.A.* 108 D3
Harrison, C., *Canada* 99 B8
Harrison B., *U.S.A.* 96 A4
Harrison L., *Canada* 100 D4
Harrisonburg, *U.S.A.* 104 F6
Harrisonville, *U.S.A.* 108 F7
Harriston, *Canada* 98 D3
Harrisville, *U.S.A.* 106 B1
Harrogate, *U.K.* 12 D6
Harrow, *U.K.* 13 F7
Harsefeld, *Germany* 18 B5
Harsīn, *Iran* 64 C5
Harskamp, *Neths.* 16 D7
Harstad, *Norway* 8 B14
Hart, *U.S.A.* 104 D2
Hart, L., *Australia* 91 E2
Hartbees →, *S. Africa* 84 D3
Hartberg, *Austria* 21 H5
Hartford, *Conn., U.S.A.* 107 E12
Hartford, *Ky., U.S.A.* 104 G2
Hartford, *S. Dak., U.S.A.* 108 D6
Hartford, *Wis., U.S.A.* 108 D10
Hartford City, *U.S.A.* 104 E3
Hartland, *Canada* 99 C6
Hartland Pt., *U.K.* 13 F3
Hartlepool, *U.K.* 12 C6
Hartley Bay, *Canada* 100 C3
Hartmannberge, *Namibia* 84 B1
Hartney, *Canada* 101 D8
Harts →, *S. Africa* 84 D3
Hartselle, *U.S.A.* 105 H2
Hartshorne, *U.S.A.* 109 H7
Hartsville, *U.S.A.* 105 H5
Hartwell, *U.S.A.* 105 H4
Harunabad, *Pakistan* 62 E5
Harvand, *Iran* 65 D7
Harvey, *Australia* 89 F2
Harvey, *Ill., U.S.A.* 104 E2
Harvey, *N. Dak., U.S.A.* 108 B5
Harwich, *U.K.* 13 F9
Haryana □, *India* 62 E7
Harz, *Germany* 18 D6
Harzé, *Belgium* 17 H7
Harzgerode, *Germany* 18 D7
Hasaheisa, *Sudan* 77 E3
Hasan Kīādeh, *Iran* 65 B6
Ḩasanābād, *Iran* 65 C7
Hasanpur, *India* 62 E8
Haselünne, *Germany* 18 C3
Hashimoto, *Japan* 49 G7
Hashtjerd, *Iran* 65 C6
Håsjö, *Sweden* 10 A10
Haskell, *Okla., U.S.A.* 109 H7
Haskell, *Tex., U.S.A.* 109 J5
Haslach, *Germany* 19 G4
Haslev, *Denmark* 11 J5
Hasparren, *France* 26 E2
Hassa, *Turkey* 66 E7
Hasselt, *Belgium* 17 G6
Hasselt, *Neths.* 16 C8
Hassene, Adrar, *Algeria* 75 D5
Hassfurt, *Germany* 19 E6
Hassi Berrekrem, *Algeria* 75 B6
Hassi bou Khelala, *Algeria* 75 B4
Hassi Daoula, *Algeria* 75 B6
Hassi Djafou, *Algeria* 75 B5
Hassi el Abiod, *Algeria* 75 B5
Hassi el Biod, *Algeria* 75 C6
Hassi el Gassi, *Algeria* 75 B6
Hassi el Hadjar, *Algeria* 75 B5
Hassi er Rmel, *Algeria* 75 B5
Hassi Imoulaye, *Algeria* 75 C6
Hassi Inifel, *Algeria* 75 C5
Hassi Messaoud, *Algeria* 75 B6
Hassi Rhénami, *Algeria* 75 B6
Hassi Tartrat, *Algeria* 75 B6
Hassi Zerzour, *Morocco* 74 B4
Hastière-Lavaux, *Belgium* 17 H5
Hastings, *N.Z.* 87 H6
Hastings, *U.K.* 13 G8
Hastings, *Mich., U.S.A.* 104 D3
Hastings, *Minn., U.S.A.* 108 C8
Hastings, *Nebr., U.S.A.* 108 E5
Hastings Ra., *Australia* 91 E5
Hat Yai, *Thailand* 59 J3
Hatanbulag, *Mongolia* 50 C5
Hatay = Antalya, *Turkey* 66 E4
Hatay □, *Turkey* 66 E7
Hatch, *U.S.A.* 111 K10
Hatches Creek, *Australia* 90 C2
Hatchet L., *Canada* 101 B8
Haţeg, *Romania* 38 D5
Haţeg, Mţii., *Romania* 38 D6
Hatert, *Neths.* 16 E7
Hateruma-Shima, *Japan* 49 M1
Hatfield P.O., *Australia* 91 E3
Hatgal, *Mongolia* 54 A5
Hathras, *India* 62 F8
Hatia, *Bangla.* 61 H17
Hato de Corozal, *Colombia* 120 B3
Hato Mayor, *Dom. Rep.* 117 C6
Hattah, *Australia* 91 E3
Hattem, *Neths.* 16 D8
Hatteras, C., *U.S.A.* 105 H8
Hattiesburg, *U.S.A.* 109 K10
Hatvan, *Hungary* 21 H9
Hau Bon = Cheo Reo, *Vietnam* 58 F7
Hau Duc, *Vietnam* 58 E7
Haug, *Norway* 10 D4
Haugastøl, *Norway* 10 D1
Haugesund, *Norway* 9 G8
Haulerwijk, *Neths.* 16 B8
Haultain →, *Canada* 101 B7
Hauraki G., *N.Z.* 87 G5
Haut Atlas, *Morocco* 74 B3
Haut-Rhin □, *France* 25 E14
Haut Zaïre □, *Zaïre* 82 B2
Haute-Corse □, *France* 27 F13
Haute-Garonne □, *France* 26 E5
Haute-Loire □, *France* 26 C7
Haute-Marne □, *France* 25 D12
Haute-Saône □, *France* 25 E13
Haute-Savoie □, *France* 27 C10
Haute-Vienne □, *France* 26 C5
Hauterive, *Canada* 99 C6
Hautes-Alpes □, *France* 27 D10
Hautes Fagnes = Hohe Venn, *Belgium* 17 H8
Hautes Fagnes, *Belgium* 17 G8
Hautes-Pyrénées □, *France* 26 F4
Hauteville-Lompnès, *France* 27 C9
Hautmont, *France* 25 B10
Hautrage, *Belgium* 17 H3
Hauts-de-Seine □, *France* 25 D9
Hauts Plateaux, *Algeria* 75 B4
Hauzenberg, *Germany* 19 G9
Havana = La Habana, *Cuba* 116 B3
Havana, *U.S.A.* 108 E9
Havant, *U.K.* 13 G7
Havasu, L., *U.S.A.* 113 L12
Havel →, *Germany* 18 C8
Havelange, *Belgium* 17 H6
Havelian, *Pakistan* 62 B5
Havelock, *N.B., Canada* 99 C6
Havelock, *Ont., Canada* 98 D4
Havelock, *N.Z.* 87 J4
Havelte, *Neths.* 16 C8
Haverfordwest, *U.K.* 13 F3
Haverhill, *U.S.A.* 107 D13
Havering, *U.K.* 13 F8
Haverstraw, *U.S.A.* 107 E11
Håverud, *Sweden* 11 F6
Havlíčkův Brod, *Czech.* 20 F5
Havneby, *Denmark* 11 J2
Havre, *U.S.A.* 110 B9
Havre-Aubert, *Canada* 99 C7
Havre-St.-Pierre, *Canada* 99 B7
Havza, *Turkey* 66 C6
Haw →, *U.S.A.* 105 H6
Hawaii □, *U.S.A.* 102 H16
Hawaii I., *Pac. Oc.* 102 J17
Hawaiian Is., *Pac. Oc.* 102 H17
Hawaiian Ridge, *Pac. Oc.* 93 E11
Hawarden, *Canada* 101 C7
Hawarden, *U.S.A.* 108 D6
Hawea, L., *N.Z.* 87 L2
Hawera, *N.Z.* 87 H5
Hawick, *U.K.* 14 F6
Hawk Junction, *Canada* 98 C3
Hawke B., *N.Z.* 87 H6
Hawker, *Australia* 91 E2
Hawkesbury, *Canada* 98 C5
Hawkesbury I., *Canada* 100 C3
Hawkesbury Pt., *Australia* 90 A1
Hawkinsville, *U.S.A.* 105 J4
Hawkwood, *Australia* 91 D5
Hawley, *U.S.A.* 108 B6
Hawrān, *Syria* 69 C5
Hawsh Mūssá, *Lebanon* 69 B4
Hawthorne, *U.S.A.* 110 G4
Hawzen, *Ethiopia* 77 E4

Haxtun, *U.S.A.* 108 E3
Hay, *Australia* 91 E3
Hay →, *Australia* 90 C2
Hay →, *Canada* 100 A5
Hay, C., *Australia* 88 B4
Hay L., *Canada* 100 B5
Hay Lakes, *Canada* 100 C6
Hay-on-Wye, *U.K.* 13 E4
Hay River, *Canada* 100 A5
Hay Springs, *U.S.A.* 108 D3
Hayachine-San, *Japan* 48 E10
Hayange, *France* 25 C13
Hayden, *Ariz., U.S.A.* 111 K8
Hayden, *Colo., U.S.A.* 110 F10
Haydon, *Australia* 90 B3
Hayes, *U.S.A.* 108 C4
Hayes →, *Canada* 101 B10
Haymana, *Turkey* 66 D5
Haynesville, *U.S.A.* 109 J8
Hayrabolu, *Turkey* 66 C2
Hays, *Canada* 100 C6
Hays, *U.S.A.* 108 F5
Hayward, *Calif., U.S.A.* 112 H4
Hayward, *Wis., U.S.A.* 108 B9
Haywards Heath, *U.K.* 13 F7
Hazafon □, *Israel* 69 C4
Hazar Gölü, *Turkey* 67 D8
Hazarām, Kūh-e, *Iran* 65 D8
Hazard, *U.S.A.* 104 G4
Hazaribag, *India* 63 H11
Hazaribag Road, *India* 63 G11
Hazebrouck, *France* 25 B9
Hazelton, *Canada* 100 B3
Hazelton, *U.S.A.* 108 B4
Hazen, *N. Dak., U.S.A.* 108 B4
Hazen, *Nev., U.S.A.* 110 G4
Hazerswoude, *Neths.* 16 D5
Hazlehurst, *Ga., U.S.A.* 105 K4
Hazlehurst, *Miss., U.S.A.* 109 K9
Hazleton, *U.S.A.* 107 F9
Hazlett, L., *Australia* 88 D4
Hazor, *Israel* 69 B4
He Xian, *Anhui, China* 53 B12
He Xian, *Guangxi Zhuangzu, China* 53 E8
Head of Bight, *Australia* 89 F5
Headlands, *Zimbabwe* 83 F3
Healdsburg, *U.S.A.* 112 G4
Healdton, *U.S.A.* 109 H6
Healesville, *Australia* 91 F4
Heanor, *U.K.* 12 D6
Heard I., *Ind. Oc.* 3 G13
Hearne, *U.S.A.* 109 K6
Hearne B., *Canada* 101 A9
Hearne L., *Canada* 100 A6
Hearst, *Canada* 98 C3
Heart →, *U.S.A.* 108 B4
Heart's Content, *Canada* 99 C9
Heath →, *Bolivia* 124 C4
Heath Pt., *Canada* 99 C7
Heath Steele, *Canada* 99 C6
Heavener, *U.S.A.* 109 H7
Hebbronville, *U.S.A.* 109 M5
Hebei □, *China* 50 E9
Hebel, *Australia* 91 D4
Heber, *U.S.A.* 113 N11
Heber Springs, *U.S.A.* 109 H9
Hebert, *Canada* 101 C7
Hebgen, L., *U.S.A.* 110 D8
Hebi, *China* 50 G8
Hebrides, *U.K.* 14 D1
Hebron = Al Khalīl, *Jordan* 69 D4
Hebron, *Canada* 97 C13
Hebron, *N. Dak., U.S.A.* 108 B3
Hebron, *Nebr., U.S.A.* 108 E6
Hecate Str., *Canada* 100 C2
Hechi, *China* 52 E7
Hechingen, *Germany* 19 G4
Hechtel, *Belgium* 17 F6
Hechuan, *China* 52 B6
Hecla, *U.S.A.* 108 C5
Hecla I., *Canada* 101 C9
Heddal, *Norway* 10 E3
Hédé, *France* 24 D5
Hede, *Sweden* 10 B7
Hedemora, *Sweden* 9 F13
Hedley, *U.S.A.* 109 H4
Hedmark fylke □, *Norway* 10 C5
Hedrum, *Norway* 10 E4
Heeg, *Neths.* 16 C7
Heegermeer, *Neths.* 16 C7
Heemskerk, *Neths.* 16 C5
Heemstede, *Neths.* 16 D5
Heer, *Neths.* 17 G7
Heerde, *Neths.* 16 D8
's Heerenburg, *Neths.* 16 E8
Heerenveen, *Neths.* 16 C7
Heerhugowaard, *Neths.* 16 C5
Heerlen, *Neths.* 17 G7
Heers, *Belgium* 17 G6
Heesch, *Neths.* 16 E7
Heestert, *Belgium* 17 G2
Heeze, *Neths.* 17 F7
Hefa, *Israel* 69 C3
Hefa □, *Israel* 69 C4
Hefei, *China* 53 B11
Hegang, *China* 54 B8
Hegyalja, *Hungary* 21 G11
Heichengzhen, *China* 50 F4
Heide, *Germany* 18 A5
Heidelberg, *Germany* 19 F4
Heidelberg, *C. Prov., S. Africa* 84 E3
Heidelberg, *Trans., S. Africa* 85 D4
Heidenheim, *Germany* 19 G6
Heijing, *China* 52 E3
Heilbron, *S. Africa* 85 D4
Heilbronn, *Germany* 19 F5
Heiligenblut, *Austria* 21 H2
Heiligenhafen, *Germany* 18 A6
Heiligenstadt, *Germany* 18 D6
Heilongjiang □, *China* 51 B14
Heilunkiang = Heilongjiang □, *China* 51 B14
Heino, *Neths.* 16 D8
Heinola, *Finland* 9 F19
Heinsch, *Belgium* 17 J7
Heinze Is., *Burma* 61 M20
Heishan, *China* 51 D12
Heishui, *Liaoning, China* 51 C10
Heishui, *Sichuan, China* 52 A4
Heist, *Belgium* 17 F2
Heist-op-den-Berg, *Belgium* 17 F5
Hejaz = Al Ḩijāz, *Si. Arabia* 68 B2
Hejian, *China* 50 E9
Hejiang, *China* 52 C5
Hejin, *China* 50 G6
Hekelgem, *Belgium* 17 G4
Hekımhan, *Turkey* 67 D7
Hekla, *Iceland* 8 E4
Hekou, *Gansu, China* 50 F2
Hekou, *Guangdong, China* 53 F9
Hekou, *Yunnan, China* 54 D5
Helagsfjället, *Sweden* 10 B6
Helan Shan, *China* 50 E3
Helchteren, *Belgium* 17 F6
Helden, *Neths.* 17 F7
Helechosa, *Spain* 31 F6
Helena, *Ark., U.S.A.* 109 H9
Helena, *Mont., U.S.A.* 110 C7
Helendale, *U.S.A.* 113 L9
Helensburgh, *U.K.* 14 E4
Helensville, *N.Z.* 87 G5
Helgeroa, *Norway* 10 F3
Helgoland, *Germany* 18 A3
Heligoland = Helgoland, *Germany* 18 A3
Heliopolis, *Egypt* 76 H7
Hellebæk, *Denmark* 11 H6
Hellendoorn, *Neths.* 16 D8
Hellevoetsluis, *Neths.* 16 E4
Hellín, *Spain* 29 G3
Helmand □, *Afghan.* 60 D4
Helmand →, *Afghan.* 60 D2
Helme →, *Germany* 18 D7
Helmond, *Neths.* 17 F7
Helmsdale, *U.K.* 14 C5
Helmstedt, *Germany* 18 C7
Helnæs, *Denmark* 11 J4
Helong, *China* 51 C15
Helper, *U.S.A.* 110 G8
Helsingborg, *Sweden* 11 H6
Helsinge, *Denmark* 11 H6
Helsingfors, *Finland* 9 F18
Helsingør, *Denmark* 11 H6
Helsinki, *Finland* 9 F18
Helston, *U.K.* 13 G2
Helvellyn, *U.K.* 12 C4
Helvoirt, *Neths.* 17 E6
Helwân, *Egypt* 76 J7
Hemet, *U.S.A.* 113 M10
Hemingford, *U.S.A.* 108 D3
Hemphill, *U.S.A.* 109 K8
Hempstead, *U.S.A.* 109 K6
Hemse, *Sweden* 9 H15
Hemsö, *Sweden* 10 B12
Henan □, *China* 50 G8
Henares →, *Spain* 28 E1
Henashi-Misaki, *Japan* 48 D9
Hendaye, *France* 26 E2
Hendek, *Turkey* 66 C4
Henderson, *Argentina* 126 D3
Henderson, *Ky., U.S.A.* 104 G2
Henderson, *N.C., U.S.A.* 105 G6
Henderson, *Nev., U.S.A.* 113 J12
Henderson, *Pa., U.S.A.* 105 H1
Henderson, *Tex., U.S.A.* 109 J7
Hendersonville, *U.S.A.* 105 H4
Hendījān, *Iran* 65 D6
Hendon, *Australia* 91 D5
Heng Xian, *China* 52 F7
Hengcheng, *China* 50 E4
Hengdaohezi, *China* 51 B15
Hengelo, *Gelderland, Neths.* 16 D8
Hengelo, *Overijssel, Neths.* 16 D9
Hengfeng, *China* 53 C10
Hengshan, *Hunan, China* 53 D9
Hengshan, *Shaanxi, China* 50 F5
Hengshui, *China* 50 F8
Hengyang, *Hunan, China* 53 D9
Hengyang, *Hunan, China* 53 D9
Hénin-Beaumont, *France* 25 B9
Henlopen, C., *U.S.A.* 104 F8
Hennan, *Sweden* 10 B9
Hennebont, *France* 24 E3
Hennenman, *S. Africa* 84 D4
Hennessey, *U.S.A.* 109 G6
Hennigsdorf, *Germany* 18 C9
Henrichemont, *France* 25 E9
Henrietta, *U.S.A.* 109 J5
Henrietta, Ostrov, *Russia* 45 B16
Henrietta Maria C., *Canada* 98 A3
Henry, *U.S.A.* 108 E10
Henryetta, *U.S.A.* 109 H6
Hensall, *Canada* 106 C3
Hentiyn Nuruu, *Mongolia* 54 B5
Henty, *Australia* 91 F4
Henzada, *Burma* 61 L19
Heping, *China* 53 E10
Heppner, *U.S.A.* 110 D4
Hepu, *China* 52 G7
Hepworth, *Canada* 106 B3
Heqing, *China* 52 D3
Hequ, *China* 50 E6
Héraðsflói, *Iceland* 8 D6
Héraðsvötn →, *Iceland* 8 D4
Herald Cays, *Australia* 90 B4
Herāt, *Afghan.* 60 B3
Herāt □, *Afghan.* 60 B3
Hérault □, *France* 26 E7
Hérault →, *France* 26 E7
Herbault, *France* 24 E8
Herbert →, *Australia* 90 B4
Herbert Downs, *Australia* 90 C2
Herberton, *Australia* 90 B4
Herbignac, *France* 24 E4
Herborn, *Germany* 18 E4
Herby, *Poland* 20 E8
Hercegnovi, *Montenegro, Yug.* 21 N8
Herðubreið, *Iceland* 8 D5
Hereford, *U.K.* 13 E5
Hereford, *U.S.A.* 109 H3
Hereford and Worcester □, *U.K.* 13 E5
Herefoss, *Norway* 11 F2
Herent, *Belgium* 17 G5
Herentals, *Belgium* 17 F5
Herenthout, *Belgium* 17 F5
Herfølge, *Denmark* 11 J6
Herford, *Germany* 18 C4
Héricourt, *France* 25 E13
Herington, *U.S.A.* 108 F6
Herisau, *Switz.* 23 B8
Hérisson, *France* 26 B6
Herjehogna, *Norway* 9 F12
Herk →, *Belgium* 17 G6
Herkenbosch, *Neths.* 17 F8
Herkimer, *U.S.A.* 107 D10
Herlong, *U.S.A.* 112 E6
Herm, *Chan. Is.* 24 C4
Hermagor-Pressegger See, *Austria* 21 J3
Herman, *U.S.A.* 108 C6
Hermann, *U.S.A.* 108 F9
Hermannsburg, *Germany* 18 C6
Hermannsburg Mission, *Australia* 88 D5
Hermanus, *S. Africa* 84 E2
Herment, *France* 26 C6
Hermidale, *Australia* 91 E4
Hermiston, *U.S.A.* 110 D4
Hermitage, *N.Z.* 87 K3
Hermite, I., *Chile* 128 E3
Hermon, Mt. = Ash Shaykh, J., *Lebanon* 69 B4
Hermosillo, *Mexico* 114 B2
Hernád →, *Hungary* 21 H11
Hernandarias, *Paraguay* 127 B5
Hernandez, *U.S.A.* 112 J6
Hernando, *Argentina* 126 C3
Hernando, *U.S.A.* 109 H10
Herne, *Belgium* 17 G4
Herne, *Germany* 17 E10
Herne Bay, *U.K.* 13 F9
Herning, *Denmark* 11 H2
Heroica = Caborca, *Mexico* 114 A2
Heroica Nogales = Nogales, *Mexico* 114 A2
Heron Bay, *Canada* 98 C2
Herradura, Pta. de la, *Canary Is.* 36 F5
Herreid, *U.S.A.* 108 C4
Herrera, *Spain* 31 H6
Herrera de Alcántar, *Spain* 31 F3
Herrera de Pisuerga, *Spain* 30 C6
Herrera del Duque, *Spain* 31 F5
Herrick, *Australia* 90 G4
Herrin, *U.S.A.* 109 G10
Herrljunga, *Sweden* 11 F7
Hersbruck, *Germany* 19 F7
Herseaux, *Belgium* 17 G2
Herselt, *Belgium* 17 F5
Hersonissos, *Greece* 37 D7
Herstal, *Belgium* 17 G7
Hertford, *U.K.* 13 F7
Hertfordshire □, *U.K.* 13 F7
's-Hertogenbosch, *Neths.* 17 E6
Hertzogville, *S. Africa* 84 D4
Hervás, *Spain* 30 E5
Herve, *Belgium* 17 G7
Herwijnen, *Neths.* 16 E6
Herzberg, *Brandenburg, Germany* 18 D9
Herzberg, *Niedersachsen, Germany* 18 D6
Herzele, *Belgium* 17 G3
Herzliyya, *Israel* 69 C3
Herzogenbuchsee, *Switz.* 22 B5
Ḩeşār, *Fārs, Iran* 65 D6
Ḩeşār, *Markazī, Iran* 65 C6
Hesdin, *France* 25 B9
Hesel, *Germany* 18 B3
Heshui, *China* 50 G5
Heshun, *China* 50 F7
Hesperange, *Lux.* 17 J8
Hesperia, *U.S.A.* 113 L9
Hesse = Hessen □, *Germany* 18 E5
Hessen □, *Germany* 18 E5
Hetch Hetchy Aqueduct, *U.S.A.* 112 H5
Hettinger, *U.S.A.* 108 C3
Hettstedt, *Germany* 18 D7
Heugem, *Neths.* 17 G7
Heule, *Belgium* 17 G2
Heusden, *Belgium* 17 F6
Heusden, *Neths.* 16 E6
Hève, C. de la, *France* 24 C7
Heverlee, *Belgium* 17 G5
Hewett, C., *Canada* 97 A13
Hexham, *U.K.* 12 C5
Hexi, *Yunnan, China* 52 E4
Hexi, *Zhejiang, China* 53 D12
Hexigten Qi, *China* 51 C9
Hexrivier, *S. Africa* 84 E2
Ḩeydarābād, *Iran* 65 D7
Heyfield, *Australia* 91 F4
Heysham, *U.K.* 12 C5
Heythuysen, *Neths.* 17 F7
Heyuan, *China* 53 F10
Heywood, *Australia* 91 F3
Heze, *China* 50 G8
Hezhang, *China* 52 D5
Hi Vista, *U.S.A.* 113 L9
Hialeah, *U.S.A.* 105 N5
Hiawatha, *Kans., U.S.A.* 108 F7
Hiawatha, *Utah, U.S.A.* 110 G8
Hibbing, *U.S.A.* 108 B8
Hibbs B., *Australia* 90 G4
Hibernia Reef, *Australia* 88 B3
Hickory, *U.S.A.* 105 H5
Hicks, Pt., *Australia* 91 F4
Hicksville, *U.S.A.* 107 F11
Hida, *Romania* 38 B6
Hida-Gawa →, *Japan* 49 G8
Hida-Sammyaku, *Japan* 49 F8
Hidaka-Sammyaku, *Japan* 48 C11
Hidalgo, *Mexico* 115 C5
Hidalgo □, *Mexico* 115 C5
Hidalgo, Presa M., *Mexico* 114 B3
Hidalgo, Pta. del, *Canary Is.* 36 F3
Hidalgo del Parral, *Mexico* 114 B3
Hiddensee, *Germany* 18 A9
Hidrolândia, *Brazil* 123 E2
Hieflau, *Austria* 21 H4
Hiendelaencina, *Spain* 28 D1
Hierapolis, *Turkey* 66 E3
Hierro, *Canary Is.* 36 G1
Higashiajima-San, *Japan* 48 F10
Higashiōsaka, *Japan* 49 G7
Higgins, *U.S.A.* 109 G4
Higgins Corner, *U.S.A.* 112 F5
Higginsville, *Australia* 89 F3
High Atlas = Haut Atlas, *Morocco* 74 B3
High I., *Canada* 99 A7
High Island, *U.S.A.* 109 L7
High Level, *Canada* 100 B5
High Point, *U.S.A.* 105 H6
High Prairie, *Canada* 100 B5
High River, *Canada* 100 C6
High Springs, *U.S.A.* 105 L4
High Wycombe, *U.K.* 13 F7
Highbury, *Australia* 90 B3
Highland □, *U.K.* 14 D4
Highland Park, *U.S.A.* 104 D2
Highmore, *U.S.A.* 108 C5
Highrock L., *Canada* 101 B7
Higüay, *Dom. Rep.* 117 C6
Hihya, *Egypt* 76 H7
Hiiumaa, *Estonia* 40 B3
Híjar, *Spain* 28 D4
Ḩijāz □, *Si. Arabia* 68 C2
Hijken, *Neths.* 16 C8
Hijo = Tagum, *Phil.* 55 H6
Hikari, *Japan* 49 H5
Hiko, *U.S.A.* 111 H6
Hikone, *Japan* 49 G8
Hikurangi, *N.Z.* 87 F5
Hikurangi, Mt., *N.Z.* 87 H6
Hildburghhausen, *Germany* 19 E6
Hildesheim, *Germany* 18 C5
Hill →, *Australia* 89 F2
Hill City, *Idaho, U.S.A.* 110 E6
Hill City, *Kans., U.S.A.* 108 F5
Hill City, *Minn., U.S.A.* 108 B8
Hill City, *S. Dak., U.S.A.* 108 D3
Hill Island L., *Canada* 101 A7
Hillared, *Sweden* 11 G7
Hillcrest Center, *U.S.A.* 113 K8
Hillegom, *Neths.* 16 D5
Hillerød, *Denmark* 11 J6
Hillingdon, *U.K.* 13 F7
Hillman, *U.S.A.* 104 C4
Hillmond, *Canada* 101 C7
Hillsboro, *Kans., U.S.A.* 108 F6
Hillsboro, *N. Dak., U.S.A.* 108 B6
Hillsboro, *N.H., U.S.A.* 107 C13
Hillsboro, *N. Mex., U.S.A.* 111 K10
Hillsboro, *Oreg., U.S.A.* 112 E4
Hillsboro, *Tex., U.S.A.* 109 J6
Hillsborough, *Grenada* 117 D7
Hillsdale, *Mich., U.S.A.* 104 E3
Hillsdale, *N.Y., U.S.A.* 107 D11
Hillside, *Australia* 88 D2
Hillsport, *Canada* 98 C2
Hillston, *Australia* 91 E4
Hilo, *U.S.A.* 102 J17
Hilton, *U.S.A.* 106 C7
Hilvan, *Turkey* 67 E8
Hilvarenbeek, *Neths.* 17 F6
Hilversum, *Neths.* 16 D6
Himachal Pradesh □, *India* 62 D7
Himalaya, *Asia* 63 E11
Himamaylan, *Phil.* 55 F5
Himara, *Albania* 39 J2
Himatnagar, *India* 60 H8
Himeji, *Japan* 49 G7
Himi, *Japan* 49 F8
Himmerland, *Denmark* 11 H3
Ḩimş, *Syria* 69 A5
Ḩimş □, *Syria* 69 A5
Hinche, *Haiti* 117 C5
Hinchinbrook I., *Australia* 90 B4
Hinckley, *U.K.* 13 E6
Hinckley, *U.S.A.* 110 G7
Hindås, *Sweden* 11 G6
Hindaun, *India* 62 F7
Hindmarsh, L., *Australia* 91 F3
Hindsholm, *Denmark* 11 J4
Hindu Bagh, *Pakistan* 62 D2
Hindu Kush, *Asia* 60 B7
Hindubagh, *Pakistan* 60 D5
Hindupur, *India* 60 N10
Hines Creek, *Canada* 100 B5
Hinganghat, *India* 60 J11
Hingeon, *Belgium* 17 G5
Hingham, *U.S.A.* 110 B8
Hingoli, *India* 60 K10
Hinigaran, *Phil.* 55 F5
Hinis, *Turkey* 67 D9
Hinna = Imi, *Ethiopia* 68 F3
Hinna, *Nigeria* 79 C7
Hinojosa del Duque, *Spain* 31 G5
Hinsdale, *U.S.A.* 110 B10
Hinterrhein →, *Switz.* 23 C8
Hinton, *Canada* 100 C5
Hinton, *U.S.A.* 104 G5
Hinwil, *Switz.* 23 B7
Hınzır Burnu, *Turkey* 66 E6
Hippolytushoef, *Neths.* 16 C5
Hirado, *Japan* 49 H4
Hirakud Dam, *India* 61 J13
Hiratsuka, *Japan* 49 G9
Hirfanlı Baraji, *Turkey* 66 D5
Hirhafok, *Algeria* 75 D6
Hîrlău, *Romania* 38 B9
Hiroo, *Japan* 48 C11
Hirosaki, *Japan* 48 D10
Hiroshima, *Japan* 49 G6
Hiroshima □, *Japan* 49 G6
Hirsholmene, *Denmark* 11 G4
Hirson, *France* 25 C11
Hîrşova, *Romania* 38 E10
Hirtshals, *Denmark* 11 G3
Hisar, *India* 62 E6
Hisb →, *Iraq* 64 D5
Ḩismá, *Si. Arabia* 64 D3
Hispaniola, *W. Indies* 117 C5
Hīt, *Iraq* 64 C4
Hita, *Japan* 49 H5
Hitachi, *Japan* 49 F10
Hitchin, *U.K.* 13 F7
Hitoyoshi, *Japan* 49 H5
Hitra, *Norway* 8 E10
Hitzacker, *Germany* 18 B7
Ḩiyyon, N. →, *Israel* 69 E4
Hjalmar L., *Canada* 101 A7
Hjälmare kanal, *Sweden* 10 E9
Hjälmaren, *Sweden* 10 E9
Hjartdal, *Norway* 10 E2
Hjerkinn, *Norway* 10 B3
Hjørring, *Denmark* 11 G3
Hjortkvarn, *Sweden* 11 F9
Hlinsko, *Czech.* 20 F5
Hluhluwe, *S. Africa* 85 D5
Ho, *Ghana* 79 D5
Ho Chi Minh City = Phanh Bho Ho Chi Minh, *Vietnam* 59 G6
Ho Thuong, *Vietnam* 58 C5
Hoa Binh, *Vietnam* 58 B5
Hoa Da, *Vietnam* 59 G7
Hoa Hiep, *Vietnam* 59 G5
Hoai Nhon, *Vietnam* 58 E7
Hoare B., *Canada* 97 B13
Hobart, *Australia* 90 G4
Hobart, *U.S.A.* 109 H5
Hobbs, *U.S.A.* 109 J3
Hobbs Coast, *Antarctica* 5 D14
Hobo, *Colombia* 120 C2
Hoboken, *Belgium* 17 F4
Hoboken, *U.S.A.* 107 F10
Hobro, *Denmark* 11 H3
Hobscheid, *Lux.* 17 J7
Hoburgen, *Sweden* 9 H15
Hochdorf, *Switz.* 23 B6
Hochschwab, *Austria* 21 H5
Höchstadt, *Germany* 19 F6
Hockenheim, *Germany* 19 F4
Hodaka-Dake, *Japan* 49 F8
Hodgson, *Canada* 101 C9
Hódmezövásárhely, *Hungary* 21 J10
Hodna, Chott el, *Algeria* 75 A5
Hodna, Monts du, *Algeria* 75 A5
Hodonín, *Czech.* 20 G7
Hoeamdong, *N. Korea* 51 C16
Hœdic, I. de, *France* 24 E4
Hoegaarden, *Belgium* 17 G5
Hoek van Holland, *Neths.* 16 E4
Hoeksche Waard, *Neths.* 16 E4
Hoenderloo, *Neths.* 16 D7

Hoengsŏng, *S. Korea* 51 F14
Hoensbroek, *Neths.* 17 G7
Hoeryong, *N. Korea* 51 C15
Hoeselt, *Belgium* 17 G6
Hoeven, *Neths.* 17 E5
Hoeyang, *N. Korea* 51 E14
Hof, *Germany* 19 E7
Hof, *Iceland* 8 D6
Höfðakaupstaður, *Iceland* 8 D3
Hofgeismar, *Germany* 18 D5
Hofmeyr, *S. Africa* 84 E4
Hofsjökull, *Iceland* 8 D4
Hofsós, *Iceland* 8 D4
Hōfu, *Japan* 49 G5
Hogan Group, *Australia* 90 F4
Hogansville, *U.S.A.* 105 J3
Hogeland, *U.S.A.* 110 B9
Hoggar = Ahaggar, *Algeria* 75 D6
Högsäter, *Sweden* 11 F6
Hogsty Reef, *Bahamas* 117 B5
Hoh →, *U.S.A.* 112 C2
Hoh Xil Shan, *China* 54 C3
Hohe Rhön, *Germany* 19 E5
Hohe Tauern, *Austria* 21 H2
Hohe Venn, *Belgium* 17 H8
Hohenau, *Austria* 20 G6
Hohenems, *Austria* 19 H5
Hohenstein-Ernstthal, *Germany* 18 E8
Hohenwald, *U.S.A.* 105 H2
Hohenwestedt, *Germany* 18 A5
Hohhot, *China* 50 D6
Hóhlakas, *Greece* 37 D9
Hohoe, *Ghana* 79 D5
Hoi An, *Vietnam* 58 E7
Hoi Xuan, *Vietnam* 58 B5
Hoisington, *U.S.A.* 108 F5
Højer, *Denmark* 11 K2
Hōjō, *Japan* 49 H6
Hökerum, *Sweden* 11 G7
Hokianga Harbour, *N.Z.* 87 F4
Hokitika, *N.Z.* 87 K3
Hokkaidō □, *Japan* 48 C11
Hokksund, *Norway* 10 E3
Hol-Hol, *Djibouti* 77 E5
Holbæk, *Denmark* 11 J5
Holbrook, *Australia* 91 F4
Holbrook, *U.S.A.* 111 J8
Holden, *Canada* 100 C6
Holden, *U.S.A.* 110 G7
Holdenville, *U.S.A.* 109 H6
Holderness, *U.K.* 12 D7
Holdfast, *Canada* 101 C7
Holdich, *Argentina* 128 C3
Holdrege, *U.S.A.* 108 E5
Holguín, *Cuba* 116 B4
Hollabrunn, *Austria* 20 G6
Hollams Bird I., *Namibia* 84 C1
Holland, *U.S.A.* 104 D2
Hollandia = Jayapura, *Indonesia* 57 E10
Hollandsch Diep, *Neths.* 17 E5
Hollandsch IJssel →, *Neths.* 16 E5
Hollfeld, *Germany* 19 F7
Hollidaysburg, *U.S.A.* 106 F6
Hollis, *U.S.A.* 109 H5
Hollister, *Calif., U.S.A.* 111 H3
Hollister, *Idaho, U.S.A.* 110 E6
Hollum, *Neths.* 16 B7
Holly, *U.S.A.* 108 F3
Holly Hill, *U.S.A.* 105 L5
Holly Springs, *U.S.A.* 109 H10
Hollywood, *Calif., U.S.A.* 111 J4
Hollywood, *Fla., U.S.A.* 105 N5
Holm, *Sweden* 10 B10
Holman Island, *Canada* 96 A8
Hólmavík, *Iceland* 8 D3
Holmes Reefs, *Australia* 90 B4
Holmestrand, *Norway* 10 E4
Holmsbu, *Norway* 10 E4
Holmsjön, *Sweden* 10 B9
Holmsland Klit, *Denmark* 11 J2
Holmsund, *Sweden* 8 E16
Holroyd →, *Australia* 90 A3
Holstebro, *Denmark* 11 H2
Holsworthy, *U.K.* 13 G3
Holt, *Iceland* 8 E4
Holte, *Denmark* 11 J6
Holten, *Neths.* 16 D8
Holton, *Canada* 99 B8
Holton, *U.S.A.* 108 F7
Holtville, *U.S.A.* 113 N11
Holwerd, *Neths.* 16 B7
Holy Cross, *U.S.A.* 96 B4
Holy I., *Gwynedd, U.K.* 12 D3
Holy I., *Northumb., U.K.* 12 B6
Holyhead, *U.K.* 12 D3
Holyoke, *Colo., U.S.A.* 108 E3
Holyoke, *Mass., U.S.A.* 107 D12
Holyrood, *Canada* 99 C9
Holzkirchen, *Germany* 19 H7
Holzminden, *Germany* 18 D5
Homa Bay, *Kenya* 82 C3
Homa Bay □, *Kenya* 82 C3
Homalin, *Burma* 61 G19
Homand, *Iran* 65 C8
Homberg, *Germany* 18 D5
Hombori, *Mali* 79 B4
Homburg, *Germany* 19 F3
Home B., *Canada* 97 B13
Home Hill, *Australia* 90 B4
Homedale, *U.S.A.* 110 E5
Homer, *Alaska, U.S.A.* 96 C4
Homer, *La., U.S.A.* 109 J8
Homestead, *Australia* 90 C4
Homestead, *Fla., U.S.A.* 105 N5
Homestead, *Oreg., U.S.A.* 110 D5
Homewood, *U.S.A.* 112 F6
Hominy, *U.S.A.* 109 G6
Homoine, *Mozam.* 85 C6
Homoljske Planina, *Serbia, Yug.* 21 L11
Homorod, *Romania* 38 C8
Homs = Ḩimş, *Syria* 69 A5
Hon Chong, *Vietnam* 59 G5
Hon Me, *Vietnam* 58 C5
Hon Quan, *Vietnam* 59 G6
Honan = Henan □, *China* 50 G8
Honbetsu, *Japan* 48 C11
Honcut, *U.S.A.* 112 F5
Honda, *Colombia* 120 B3
Honda Bay, *Phil.* 55 G3
Hondeklipbaai, *S. Africa* 84 E2
Hondo, *Japan* 49 H5
Hondo, *U.S.A.* 109 L5
Hondo →, *Belize* 115 D7
Honduras ■, *Cent. Amer.* 116 D2
Honduras, G. de, *Caribbean* 116 C2
Hønefoss, *Norway* 9 F11
Honesdale, *U.S.A.* 107 E9
Honey L., *U.S.A.* 112 E6
Honfleur, *France* 24 C7
Hong Gai, *Vietnam* 58 B6
Hong He →, *China* 50 H8
Hong Kong ■, *Asia* 53 F10
Hong'an, *China* 53 B10
Hongchŏn, *S. Korea* 51 F14
Honghai Wan, *China* 53 F10
Honghu, *China* 53 C9
Hongjiang, *China* 52 D7
Hongliu He →, *China* 50 F5
Hongor, *Mongolia* 50 B7
Hongsa, *Laos* 58 C3
Hongshui He →, *China* 52 F7
Hongsŏng, *S. Korea* 51 F14
Hongtong, *China* 50 F6
Honguedo, Détroit d', *Canada* 99 C7
Hongwon, *N. Korea* 51 E14
Hongya, *China* 52 C4
Hongyuan, *China* 52 A4
Hongze Hu, *China* 51 H10
Honiara, *Solomon Is.* 92 H7
Honiton, *U.K.* 13 G4
Honjō, *Japan* 48 E10
Honkorâb, Ras, *Egypt* 76 C4
Honolulu, *U.S.A.* 102 H16
Honshū, *Japan* 49 G9
Hontoria del Pinar, *Spain* 28 D1
Hood, Pt., *Australia* 89 F2
Hood Mt., *U.S.A.* 110 D3
Hood River, *U.S.A.* 110 D3
Hoodsport, *U.S.A.* 112 C3
Hooge, *Germany* 18 A4
Hoogerheide, *Neths.* 17 F4
Hoogeveen, *Neths.* 16 C8
Hoogeveensche Vaart, *Neths.* 16 C8
Hoogezand, *Neths.* 16 B9
Hooghly = Hughli →, *India* 63 J13
Hooghly-Chinsura = Chunchura, *India* 63 H13
Hoogkerk, *Neths.* 16 B9
Hooglede, *Belgium* 17 G2
Hoogstraten, *Belgium* 17 F5
Hoogvliet, *Neths.* 16 E4
Hook Hd., *Ireland* 15 D5
Hook I., *Australia* 90 C4
Hook of Holland = Hoek van Holland, *Neths.* 16 E4
Hooker, *U.S.A.* 109 G4
Hooker Creek, *Australia* 88 C5
Hoopeston, *U.S.A.* 104 E2
Hoopstad, *S. Africa* 84 D4
Hoorn, *Neths.* 16 C6
Hoover Dam, *U.S.A.* 113 K12
Hooversville, *U.S.A.* 106 F6
Hop Bottom, *U.S.A.* 107 E9
Hopa, *Turkey* 43 F9
Hope, *Canada* 100 D4
Hope, *Ariz., U.S.A.* 113 M13
Hope, *Ark., U.S.A.* 109 J8
Hope, *N. Dak., U.S.A.* 108 B6
Hope, L., *Australia* 91 D2
Hope Pt., *U.S.A.* 96 B3
Hope Town, *Bahamas* 116 A4
Hopedale, *Canada* 99 A7
Hopefield, *S. Africa* 84 E2
Hopei = Hebei □, *China* 50 E9
Hopelchén, *Mexico* 115 D7
Hopetoun, *Vic., Australia* 91 F3
Hopetoun, *W. Austral., Australia* 89 F3
Hopetown, *S. Africa* 84 D3
Hopkins, *U.S.A.* 108 E7
Hopkins, L., *Australia* 88 D4
Hopkinsville, *U.S.A.* 105 G2
Hopland, *U.S.A.* 112 G3
Hoptrup, *Denmark* 11 J3
Hoquiam, *U.S.A.* 112 D3
Horasan, *Turkey* 67 C10
Horcajo de Santiago, *Spain* 28 F1
Hordaland fylke □, *Norway* 9 F9
Horden Hills, *Australia* 88 D5
Horezu, *Romania* 38 D6
Horgen, *Switz.* 23 B7
Horinger, *China* 50 D6
Horlick Mts., *Antarctica* 5 E15
Hormoz, *Iran* 65 E7
Hormoz, Jaz. ye, *Iran* 65 E8
Hormuz Str., *The Gulf* 65 E8
Horn, *Ísafjarðarsýsla, Iceland* 8 C2
Horn, *Suður-Múlasýsla, Iceland* 8 D7
Horn, *Neths.* 17 F7
Horn →, *Canada* 100 A5
Horn, Cape = Hornos, C. de, *Chile* 128 E3
Horn Head, *Ireland* 15 A3
Horn I., *Australia* 90 A3
Horn I., *U.S.A.* 105 K1
Horn Mts., *Canada* 100 A5
Hornachuelos, *Spain* 31 H5
Hornavan, *Sweden* 8 C14
Hornbæk, *Denmark* 11 H6
Hornbeck, *U.S.A.* 109 K8
Hornbrook, *U.S.A.* 110 F2
Hornburg, *Germany* 18 C6
Horncastle, *U.K.* 12 D7
Hornell, *U.S.A.* 106 D7
Hornell L., *Canada* 100 A5
Hornepayne, *Canada* 98 C3
Hornitos, *U.S.A.* 112 H6
Hornos, C. de, *Chile* 128 E3
Hornoy, *France* 25 C8
Hornsby, *Australia* 91 E5
Hornsea, *U.K.* 12 D7
Hornslandet, *Sweden* 10 C11
Hornslet, *Denmark* 11 H4
Hornu, *Belgium* 17 H3
Hörnum, *Germany* 18 A4
Horobetsu, *Japan* 48 C10
Horqin Youyi Qianqi, *China* 51 A12
Horqueta, *Paraguay* 126 A4
Horred, *Sweden* 11 G6
Horse Cr. →, *U.S.A.* 108 E3
Horse Is., *Canada* 99 B8
Horsefly L., *Canada* 100 C4
Horsens, *Denmark* 11 J3
Horsens Fjord, *Denmark* 11 J4
Horsham, *Australia* 91 F3
Horsham, *U.K.* 13 F7
Horst, *Neths.* 17 F8
Horten, *Norway* 10 E4
Hortobágy →, *Hungary* 21 H11
Horton, *U.S.A.* 108 F7
Horton →, *Canada* 96 B7
Horw, *Switz.* 23 B6
Horwood, L., *Canada* 98 C3
Hosaina, *Ethiopia* 77 F4
Hose, Gunung-Gunung, *Malaysia* 56 D4
Ḩoseynābād, *Khuzestān, Iran* 65 C6
Ḩoseynābād, *Kordestān, Iran* 64 C5
Hoshangabad, *India* 62 H7
Hoshiarpur, *India* 62 D6
Hosingen, *Lux.* 17 H8
Hosmer, *U.S.A.* 108 C5
Hospental, *Switz.* 23 C7
Hospet, *India* 60 M10
Hospitalet de Llobregat, *Spain* 28 D7
Hoste, I., *Chile* 128 E3
Hostens, *France* 26 D3
Hot, *Thailand* 58 C2
Hot Creek Ra., *U.S.A.* 110 G5
Hot Springs, *Ark., U.S.A.* 109 H8
Hot Springs, *S. Dak., U.S.A.* 108 D3
Hotagen, *Sweden* 8 E13
Hotan, *China* 54 C2
Hotazel, *S. Africa* 84 D3
Hotchkiss, *U.S.A.* 111 G10
Hotham, C., *Australia* 88 B5
Hoting, *Sweden* 8 D14
Hotte, Massif de la, *Haiti* 117 C5
Hottentotsbaai, *Namibia* 84 D1
Hotton, *Belgium* 17 H6
Houat, I. de, *France* 24 E4
Houck, *U.S.A.* 111 J9
Houdan, *France* 25 D8
Houdeng-Goegnies, *Belgium* 17 H4
Houei Sai, *Laos* 58 B3
Houffalize, *Belgium* 17 H7
Houghton, *U.S.A.* 108 B10
Houghton L., *U.S.A.* 104 C3
Houghton-le-Spring, *U.K.* 12 C6
Houhora Heads, *N.Z.* 87 F4
Houille →, *Belgium* 17 H5
Houlton, *U.S.A.* 99 C6
Houma, *U.S.A.* 109 L9
Houndé, *Burkina Faso* 78 C4
Hourtin, *France* 26 C2
Hourtin-Carcans, Étang d', *France* 26 C2
Houston, *Canada* 100 C3
Houston, *Mo., U.S.A.* 109 G9
Houston, *Tex., U.S.A.* 109 L7
Houten, *Neths.* 16 D6
Houthalen, *Belgium* 17 F6
Houthem, *Belgium* 17 G1
Houthulst, *Belgium* 17 G2
Houtman Abrolhos, *Australia* 89 E1
Houyet, *Belgium* 17 H6
Hov, *Denmark* 11 J4
Hova, *Sweden* 11 F8
Høvåg, *Norway* 11 F2
Hovd, *Mongolia* 54 B4
Hove, *U.K.* 13 G7
Hoveyzeh, *Iran* 65 D6
Hövsgöl, *Mongolia* 50 C5
Hövsgöl Nuur, *Mongolia* 54 A5
Howakil, *Ethiopia* 77 D5
Howar, Wadi →, *Sudan* 77 D2
Howard, *Australia* 91 D5
Howard, *Kans., U.S.A.* 109 G6
Howard, *Pa., U.S.A.* 106 E7
Howard, *S. Dak., U.S.A.* 108 C6
Howard I., *Australia* 90 A2
Howard L., *Canada* 101 A7
Howe, *U.S.A.* 110 E7
Howe, C., *Australia* 91 F5
Howell, *U.S.A.* 104 D4
Howick, *Canada* 107 A11
Howick, *S. Africa* 85 D5
Howick Group, *Australia* 90 A4
Howitt, L., *Australia* 91 D2
Howley, *Canada* 99 C8
Howrah = Haora, *India* 63 H13
Howth Hd., *Ireland* 15 C5
Höxter, *Germany* 18 D5
Hoy, *U.K.* 14 C5
Hoya, *Germany* 18 C5
Høyanger, *Norway* 9 F9
Hoyerswerda, *Germany* 18 D10
Hoyos, *Spain* 30 E4
Hpungan Pass, *Burma* 61 F20
Hradec Králové, *Czech.* 20 E5
Hranice, *Czech.* 20 F7
Hron →, *Czech.* 21 H8
Hrubieszów, *Poland* 20 E13
Hrvatska = Croatia ■, *Europe* 33 C13
Hsenwi, *Burma* 61 H20
Hsiamen = Xiamen, *China* 53 E12
Hsian = Xi'an, *China* 50 G5
Hsinhailien = Lianyungang, *China* 51 G10
Hsisha Chuntao, *Pac. Oc.* 56 A4
Hsüchou = Xuzhou, *China* 51 G9
Hu Xian, *China* 50 G5
Hua Hin, *Thailand* 58 F2
Hua Xian, *Henan, China* 50 G8
Hua Xian, *Shaanxi, China* 50 G5
Hua'an, *China* 53 E11
Huacaya, *Bolivia* 125 E5
Huacheng, *China* 53 E10
Huachinera, *Mexico* 114 A3
Huacho, *Peru* 124 C2
Huachón, *Peru* 124 C2
Huade, *China* 50 D7
Huadian, *China* 51 C14
Huai He →, *China* 53 A12
Huai Yot, *Thailand* 59 J2
Huai'an, *Hebei, China* 50 D8
Huai'an, *Jiangsu, China* 51 H10
Huaide, *China* 51 C13
Huaidezhen, *China* 51 C13
Huaihua, *China* 52 D7
Huaiji, *China* 53 F9
Huainan, *China* 53 A11
Huaining, *China* 53 B11
Huairen, *China* 50 E7
Huairou, *China* 50 D9
Huaiyang, *China* 50 H8
Huaiyuan, *Anhui, China* 51 H9
Huaiyuan, *Guangxi Zhuangzu, China* 52 E7
Huajianzi, *China* 51 D13
Huajuapan de Leon, *Mexico* 115 D5
Hualapai Pk., *U.S.A.* 111 J7
Hualian, *Taiwan* 53 F13
Huallaga →, *Peru* 124 B2
Huallanca, *Peru* 124 B2
Huamachuco, *Peru* 124 B2
Huambo, *Angola* 81 G3
Huan Jiang →, *China* 50 G5
Huan Xian, *China* 50 F4
Huancabamba, *Peru* 124 B2
Huancane, *Peru* 124 D4
Huancapi, *Peru* 124 C3
Huancavelica, *Peru* 124 C2
Huancavelica □, *Peru* 124 C3
Huancayo, *Peru* 124 C2
Huanchaca, *Bolivia* 124 E4
Huanchaca, Serranía de, *Bolivia* 125 C5
Huang Hai = Yellow Sea, *China* 51 G12
Huang He →, *China* 51 F10
Huang Xian, *China* 51 F11
Huangchuan, *China* 53 A10
Huanggang, *China* 53 B10
Huangling, *China* 50 G5
Huangliu, *China* 54 E5
Huanglong, *China* 50 G5
Huanglongtan, *China* 53 A8
Huangmei, *China* 53 B10
Huangpi, *China* 53 B10
Huangping, *China* 52 D6
Huangshi, *China* 53 B10
Huangsongdian, *China* 51 C14
Huangyan, *China* 53 C13
Huangyangsi, *China* 53 D8
Huaning, *China* 52 E4
Huanjiang, *China* 52 E7
Huanta, *Peru* 124 C3
Huantai, *China* 51 F9
Huánuco, *Peru* 124 B2
Huánuco □, *Peru* 124 B2
Huanuni, *Bolivia* 124 D4
Huanzo, Cordillera de, *Peru* 124 C3
Huaping, *China* 52 D3
Huaral, *Peru* 124 C2
Huaraz, *Peru* 124 B2
Huari, *Peru* 124 B2
Huarmey, *Peru* 124 C2
Huarochiri, *Peru* 124 C2
Huarocondo, *Peru* 124 C3
Huarong, *China* 53 C9
Huascarán, *Peru* 124 B2
Huascarán, Nevado, *Peru* 124 B2
Huasco, *Chile* 126 B1
Huasco →, *Chile* 126 B1
Huasna, *U.S.A.* 113 K6
Huatabampo, *Mexico* 114 B3
Huauchinango, *Mexico* 115 C5
Huautla de Jiménez, *Mexico* 115 D5
Huaxi, *China* 52 D6
Huay Namota, *Mexico* 114 C4
Huayin, *China* 50 G6
Huayllay, *Peru* 124 C2
Huayuan, *China* 52 C7
Huazhou, *China* 53 G8
Hubbard, *U.S.A.* 109 K6
Hubbart Pt., *Canada* 101 B10
Hubei □, *China* 53 B9
Hubli-Dharwad = Dharwad, *India* 60 M9
Huchang, *N. Korea* 51 D14
Hückelhoven, *Germany* 18 D2
Huddersfield, *U.K.* 12 D6
Hudi, *Sudan* 76 D3
Hudiksvall, *Sweden* 10 C11
Hudson, *Canada* 101 C10
Hudson, *Mass., U.S.A.* 107 D13
Hudson, *Mich., U.S.A.* 104 E3
Hudson, *N.Y., U.S.A.* 107 D11
Hudson, *Wis., U.S.A.* 108 C8
Hudson, *Wyo., U.S.A.* 110 E9
Hudson →, *U.S.A.* 107 F10
Hudson Bay, *N.W.T., Canada* 97 C11
Hudson Bay, *Sask., Canada* 101 C8
Hudson Falls, *U.S.A.* 107 C11
Hudson Mts., *Antarctica* 5 D16
Hudson Str., *Canada* 97 B13
Hudson's Hope, *Canada* 100 B4
Hue, *Vietnam* 58 D6
Huebra →, *Spain* 30 D4
Huechucuicui, Pta., *Chile* 128 B2
Huedin, *Romania* 38 C6
Huehuetenango, *Guatemala* 116 C1
Huejúcar, *Mexico* 114 C4
Huelgoat, *France* 24 D3
Huelma, *Spain* 29 H1
Huelva, *Spain* 31 H4
Huelva □, *Spain* 31 H4
Huelva →, *Spain* 31 H5
Huentelauquén, *Chile* 126 C1
Huércal Overa, *Spain* 29 H3
Huerta, Sa. de la, *Argentina* 126 C2
Huertas, C. de las, *Spain* 29 G4
Huerva →, *Spain* 28 D4
Huesca, *Spain* 28 C4
Huesca □, *Spain* 28 C5
Huéscar, *Spain* 29 H2
Huetamo, *Mexico* 114 D4
Huete, *Spain* 28 E2
Hugh →, *Australia* 90 D1
Hughenden, *Australia* 90 C3
Hughes, *Australia* 89 F4
Hughli →, *India* 63 J13
Hugo, *U.S.A.* 108 F3
Hugoton, *U.S.A.* 109 G4
Hui Xian, *Gansu, China* 50 H4
Hui Xian, *Henan, China* 50 G7
Hui'an, *China* 53 E12
Hui'anbu, *China* 50 F4
Huichang, *China* 53 E10
Huichapán, *Mexico* 115 C5
Huidong, *China* 52 D4
Huifa He →, *China* 51 C14
Huila □, *Colombia* 120 C2
Huila, Nevado del, *Colombia* 120 C2
Huilai, *China* 53 F11
Huili, *China* 52 D4
Huimin, *China* 51 F9
Huinan, *China* 51 C14
Huinca Renancó, *Argentina* 126 C3
Huining, *China* 50 G3
Huinong, *China* 50 E4
Huise, *Belgium* 17 G3
Huishui, *China* 52 D6
Huisne →, *France* 24 E7
Huissen, *Neths.* 16 E7
Huiting, *China* 50 G9
Huitong, *China* 52 D7
Huixtla, *Mexico* 115 D6
Huize, *China* 52 D4
Huizen, *Neths.* 16 D6
Huizhou, *China* 53 F10
Hukawng Valley, *Burma* 61 F20
Hukou, *China* 53 C11
Hukuntsi, *Botswana* 84 C3

Hula, *Ethiopia* 77 F4
Hulan, *China* 54 B7
Ḥulayfā', *Si. Arabia* 64 E4
Huld, *Mongolia* 50 B3
Hulin He →, *China* 51 B12
Hull = Kingston upon Hull, *U.K.* 12 D7
Hull, *Canada* 98 C4
Hull →, *U.K.* 12 D7
Hulst, *Neths.* 17 F4
Hulun Nur, *China* 54 B6
Humahuaca, *Argentina* 126 A2
Humaitá, *Brazil* 125 B5
Humaitá, *Paraguay* 126 B4
Humansdorp, *S. Africa* 84 E3
Humbe, *Angola* 84 B1
Humber →, *U.K.* 12 D7
Humberside □, *U.K.* 12 D7
Humbert River, *Australia* 88 C5
Humble, *U.S.A.* 109 L8
Humboldt, *Canada* 101 C7
Humboldt, *Iowa, U.S.A.* 108 D7
Humboldt, *Tenn., U.S.A.* 109 H10
Humboldt →, *U.S.A.* 110 F4
Humboldt Gletscher, *Greenland* 4 B4
Hume, *U.S.A.* 112 J8
Hume, L., *Australia* 91 F4
Humenné, *Czech.* 20 G11
Humphreys, Mt., *U.S.A.* 112 H8
Humphreys Pk., *U.S.A.* 111 J8
Humpolec, *Czech.* 20 F5
Humptulips, *U.S.A.* 112 C3
Hūn, *Libya* 73 C8
Hun Jiang →, *China* 51 D13
Húnaflói, *Iceland* 8 D3
Hunan □, *China* 53 D9
Hunchun, *China* 51 C16
Hundested, *Denmark* 11 J5
Hundred Mile House, *Canada* 100 C4
Hunedoara, *Romania* 38 D5
Hünfeld, *Germany* 18 E5
Hung Yen, *Vietnam* 58 B6
Hungary ■, *Europe* 21 H9
Hungary, Plain of, *Europe* 6 F9
Hungerford, *Australia* 91 D3
Hŭngnam, *N. Korea* 51 E14
Huni Valley, *Ghana* 78 D4
Hunsberge, *Namibia* 84 D2
Hunsrück, *Germany* 19 F3
Hunstanton, *U.K.* 12 E8
Hunte →, *Germany* 18 C4
Hunter, *N. Dak., U.S.A.* 108 B6
Hunter, *N.Y., U.S.A.* 107 D10
Hunter I., *Australia* 90 G3
Hunter I., *Canada* 100 C3
Hunter Ra., *Australia* 91 E5
Hunters Road, *Zimbabwe* 83 F2
Hunterville, *N.Z.* 87 H5
Huntingburg, *U.S.A.* 104 F2
Huntingdon, *Canada* 98 C5
Huntingdon, *U.K.* 13 E7
Huntingdon, *U.S.A.* 106 F6
Huntington, *Ind., U.S.A.* 104 E3
Huntington, *N.Y., U.S.A.* 107 F11
Huntington, *Oreg., U.S.A.* 110 D5
Huntington, *Utah, U.S.A.* 110 G8
Huntington, *W. Va., U.S.A.* 104 F4
Huntington Beach, *U.S.A.* 113 M8
Huntington Park, *U.S.A.* 111 K4
Huntly, *N.Z.* 87 G5
Huntly, *U.K.* 14 D6
Huntsville, *Canada* 98 C4
Huntsville, *Ala., U.S.A.* 105 H2
Huntsville, *Tex., U.S.A.* 109 K7
Hunyani →, *Zimbabwe* 83 F3
Hunyuan, *China* 50 E7
Hunza →, *India* 63 B6
Huo Xian, *China* 50 F6
Huong Hoa, *Vietnam* 58 D6
Huong Khe, *Vietnam* 58 C5
Huonville, *Australia* 90 G4
Huoqiu, *China* 53 A11
Huoshan, *Anhui, China* 53 A12
Huoshan, *Anhui, China* 53 B11
Huoshao Dao, *Taiwan* 53 F13
Hupeh = Hubei □, *China* 53 B9
Ḩūr, *Iran* 65 D8
Hure Qi, *China* 51 C11
Hurezani, *Romania* 38 E6
Hurghada, *Egypt* 76 B3
Hurley, *N. Mex., U.S.A.* 111 K9
Hurley, *Wis., U.S.A.* 108 B9
Huron, *Calif., U.S.A.* 112 J6
Huron, *Ohio, U.S.A.* 106 E2
Huron, *S. Dak., U.S.A.* 108 C5
Huron, L., *N. Amer.* 106 B2
Hurricane, *U.S.A.* 111 H7
Hurso, *Ethiopia* 77 F5
Hurum, *Norway* 10 C2
Hurunui →, *N.Z.* 87 K4
Hurup, *Denmark* 11 H2
Húsavík, *Iceland* 8 C5
Huşi, *Romania* 38 C11
Huskvarna, *Sweden* 9 H13
Hussar, *Canada* 100 C6
Husum, *Germany* 18 A5
Husum, *Sweden* 10 A13
Hutchinson, *Kans., U.S.A.* 109 F6
Hutchinson, *Minn., U.S.A.* 108 C7
Huttig, *U.S.A.* 109 J8
Hutton, Mt., *Australia* 91 D4
Huttwil, *Switz.* 22 B5
Huwun, *Ethiopia* 77 G5
Huy, *Belgium* 17 G6
Hvammur, *Iceland* 8 D3
Hvar, *Croatia* 33 E13
Hvarski Kanal, *Croatia* 33 E13
Hvítá, *Iceland* 8 D3
Hvítá →, *Iceland* 8 D3
Hvítárvatn, *Iceland* 8 D4
Hwachon-chosuji, *S. Korea* 51 E14
Hwang Ho = Huang He →, *China* 51 F10
Hwange, *Zimbabwe* 83 F2
Hwange Nat. Park, *Zimbabwe* 84 B4
Hyannis, *U.S.A.* 108 E4
Hyargas Nuur, *Mongolia* 54 B4
Hybo, *Sweden* 10 C10
Hyde Park, *Guyana* 121 B6
Hyden, *Australia* 89 F2
Hyderabad, *India* 60 L11
Hyderabad, *Pakistan* 62 G3
Hyères, *France* 27 E10
Hyères, Is. d', *France* 27 F10
Hyesan, *N. Korea* 51 D15
Hyland →, *Canada* 100 B3
Hyltebruk, *Sweden* 11 H7
Hymia, *India* 63 C8
Hyndman Pk., *U.S.A.* 110 E6
Hyōgo □, *Japan* 49 G7
Hyrum, *U.S.A.* 110 F8
Hysham, *U.S.A.* 110 C10
Hythe, *U.K.* 13 F9
Hyūga, *Japan* 49 H5
Hyvinge = Hyvinkää, *Finland* 9 F18
Hyvinkää, *Finland* 9 F18

I

I-n-Échaï, *Mali* 74 D4
I-n-Gall, *Niger* 79 B6
Iabès, Erg, *Algeria* 75 C4
Iaco →, *Brazil* 124 B4
Iaçu, *Brazil* 123 D3
Iakora, *Madag.* 85 C8
Iaşi, *Romania* 38 B10
Iauaretê, *Colombia* 120 C4
Iba, *Phil.* 55 D3
Ibadan, *Nigeria* 79 D5
Ibagué, *Colombia* 120 C2
Ibaiti, *Brazil* 123 F1
Iballja, *Albania* 38 G3
Ibăneşti, *Romania* 38 C7
Ibar →, *Serbia, Yug.* 21 M10
Ibaraki □, *Japan* 49 F10
Ibarra, *Ecuador* 120 C2
Ibba, *Sudan* 77 G2
Ibba, Bahr el →, *Sudan* 77 F2
Ibbenbüren, *Germany* 18 C3
Ibembo, *Zaïre* 82 B1
Ibera, L., *Argentina* 126 B4
Iberian Peninsula, *Europe* 6 H5
Iberico, Sistema, *Spain* 28 E2
Iberville, *Canada* 98 C5
Iberville, Lac d', *Canada* 98 A5
Ibi, *Nigeria* 79 D6
Ibiá, *Brazil* 123 E2
Ibicaraí, *Brazil* 123 D4
Ibicuí, *Brazil* 123 D4
Ibicuy, *Argentina* 126 C4
Ibioapaba, Sa. da, *Brazil* 122 B3
Ibipetuba, *Brazil* 122 D3
Ibitiara, *Brazil* 123 D3
Ibiza, *Spain* 36 C7
Íblei, Monti, *Italy* 35 E7
Ibo, *Mozam.* 83 E5
Ibonma, *Indonesia* 57 E8
Ibotirama, *Brazil* 123 D3
Ibrāhīm →, *Lebanon* 69 A4
Ibshawâi, *Egypt* 76 J7
Ibu, *Indonesia* 57 D7
Iburg, *Germany* 18 C4
Ibusuki, *Japan* 49 J5
Icá, *Peru* 124 C2
Ica □, *Peru* 124 C2
Iça →, *Brazil* 124 A4
Icabarú, *Venezuela* 121 C5
Icabarú →, *Venezuela* 121 C5
Içana, *Brazil* 120 C4
Içana →, *Brazil* 120 C4
Icatu, *Brazil* 122 B3
Içel = Mersin, *Turkey* 66 E6
Içel □, *Turkey* 66 E6
Iceland ■, *Atl. Oc.* 8 D4
Icha, *Russia* 45 D16
Ich'ang = Yichang, *China* 53 B8
Ichchapuram, *India* 61 K14
Ichihara, *Japan* 49 G10
Ichikawa, *Japan* 49 G9
Ichilo →, *Bolivia* 125 D5
Ichinohe, *Japan* 48 D10
Ichinomiya, *Japan* 49 G8
Ichinoseki, *Japan* 48 E10
Ichnya, *Ukraine* 40 F8
Ichŏn, *S. Korea* 51 F14
Icht, *Morocco* 74 C3
Ichtegem, *Belgium* 17 F2
Icó, *Brazil* 122 C4
Icod, *Canary Is.* 36 F3
Icoraci, *Brazil* 122 B2
Icy Str., *U.S.A.* 100 B1
Ida Grove, *U.S.A.* 108 D7
Ida Valley, *Australia* 89 E3
Idabel, *U.S.A.* 109 J7
Idaga Hamus, *Ethiopia* 77 E4
Idah, *Nigeria* 79 D6
Idaho □, *U.S.A.* 110 D6
Idaho City, *U.S.A.* 110 E6
Idaho Falls, *U.S.A.* 110 E7
Idaho Springs, *U.S.A.* 110 G11
Idanha-a-Nova, *Portugal* 30 F3
Idar-Oberstein, *Germany* 19 F3
Idd el Ghanam, *Sudan* 73 F9
Iddan, *Somali Rep.* 68 F4
Idehan, *Libya* 75 C7
Idehan Marzūq, *Libya* 73 D7
Idelès, *Algeria* 75 D6
Idfû, *Egypt* 76 C3
Ídhi Óros, *Greece* 37 D6
Ídhra, *Greece* 39 M6
Idi, *Indonesia* 56 C1
Idiofa, *Zaïre* 80 E3
Idku, Bahra el, *Egypt* 76 H7
Idlib, *Syria* 64 C3
Idria, *U.S.A.* 112 J6
Idrija, *Slovenia* 33 B11
Idritsa, *Russia* 40 C6
Idstein, *Germany* 19 E4
Idutywa, *S. Africa* 85 E4
Ieper, *Belgium* 17 G1
Ierápetra, *Greece* 37 E7
Ierissós, *Greece* 39 J6
Ierzu, *Italy* 34 C2
Iesi, *Italy* 33 E10
Ifach, Punta, *Spain* 29 G5
'Ifāl, W. al →, *Si. Arabia* 64 D2
Ifanadiana, *Madag.* 85 C8
Ife, *Nigeria* 79 D5
Iférouâne, *Niger* 79 B6
Iffley, *Australia* 90 B3
Ifni, *Morocco* 74 C2
Ifon, *Nigeria* 79 D6
Iforas, Adrar des, *Mali* 79 B5
Ifould, L., *Australia* 89 F5
Ifrane, *Morocco* 74 B3
Iganga, *Uganda* 82 B3
Igara Paraná →, *Colombia* 120 D3
Igarapava, *Brazil* 123 F2
Igarapé Açu, *Brazil* 122 B2
Igarapé-Mirim, *Brazil* 122 B2
Igarka, *Russia* 44 C9
Igatimi, *Paraguay* 127 A4
Igbetti, *Nigeria* 79 D5
Igbo-Ora, *Nigeria* 79 D5
Igboho, *Nigeria* 79 D5
Iğdır, *Turkey* 67 D11
Iggesund, *Sweden* 10 C11
Ighil Izane, *Algeria* 75 A5
Iglésias, *Italy* 34 C1
Igli, *Algeria* 75 B4
Igloolik, *Canada* 97 B11
Igma, Gebel el, *Egypt* 76 J8
Ignace, *Canada* 98 C1
İğneada Burnu, *Turkey* 66 C3
Igoshevo, *Russia* 41 B13
Iguaçu →, *Brazil* 127 B5
Iguaçu, Cat. del, *Brazil* 127 B5
Iguaçu Falls = Iguaçu, Cat. del, *Brazil* 127 B5
Iguala, *Mexico* 115 D5
Igualada, *Spain* 28 D6
Iguape, *Brazil* 123 F2
Iguassu = Iguaçu →, *Brazil* 127 B5
Iguatu, *Brazil* 122 C4
Iguéla, *Gabon* 80 E1
Igunga □, *Tanzania* 82 C3
Iheya-Shima, *Japan* 49 L3
Ihiala, *Nigeria* 79 D6
Ihosy, *Madag.* 85 C8
Ihotry, L., *Madag.* 85 C7
Ii, *Finland* 8 D18
Ii-Shima, *Japan* 49 L3
Iida, *Japan* 49 G8
Iijoki →, *Finland* 8 D18
Iisalmi, *Finland* 8 E19
Iiyama, *Japan* 49 F9
Iizuka, *Japan* 49 H5
Ijâfene, *Mauritania* 74 D3
Ijebu-Igbo, *Nigeria* 79 D5
Ijebu-Ode, *Nigeria* 79 D5
IJmuiden, *Neths.* 16 D5
IJssel →, *Neths.* 16 C7
IJsselmeer, *Neths.* 16 C6
IJsselmuiden, *Neths.* 16 C7
IJsselstein, *Neths.* 16 D6
Ijuí →, *Brazil* 127 B4
IJzendijke, *Neths.* 17 F3
IJzer →, *Belgium* 17 F1
Ikale, *Nigeria* 79 D6
Ikare, *Nigeria* 79 D6
Ikaría, *Greece* 39 M9
Ikast, *Denmark* 11 H3
Ikeda, *Japan* 49 G6
Ikeja, *Nigeria* 79 D5
Ikela, *Zaïre* 80 E4
Ikerre-Ekiti, *Nigeria* 79 D6
Ikhtiman, *Bulgaria* 38 G6
Iki, *Japan* 49 H4
Ikimba L., *Tanzania* 82 C3
Ikire, *Nigeria* 79 D5
İkizdere, *Turkey* 67 C9
Ikom, *Nigeria* 79 D6
Ikopa →, *Madag.* 85 B8
Ikot Ekpene, *Nigeria* 79 D6
Ikungu, *Tanzania* 82 C3
Ikurun, *Nigeria* 79 D5
Ila, *Nigeria* 79 D5
Ilagan, *Phil.* 55 C4
Īlām, *Iran* 64 C5
Ilam, *Nepal* 63 F12
Ilanskiy, *Russia* 45 D10
Ilanz, *Switz.* 23 C8
Ilaro, *Nigeria* 79 D5
Iława, *Poland* 20 B9
Ilbilbie, *Australia* 90 C4
Ile-à-la-Crosse, *Canada* 101 B7
Ile-à-la-Crosse, Lac, *Canada* 101 B7
Île-de-France, *France* 25 D9
Ilebo, *Zaïre* 80 E4
Ileje □, *Tanzania* 83 D3
Ilek, *Russia* 44 D6
Ilek →, *Russia* 44 D6
Ilero, *Nigeria* 79 D5
Ilesha, *Kwara, Nigeria* 79 D5
Ilesha, *Oyo, Nigeria* 79 D5
Ilford, *Canada* 101 B9
Ilfracombe, *Australia* 90 C3
Ilfracombe, *U.K.* 13 F3
Ilgaz, *Turkey* 66 C5
Ilgaz Dağları, *Turkey* 66 C5
Ilgın, *Turkey* 66 D4
Ilha Grande, *Brazil* 121 D4
Ilha Grande, B. da, *Brazil* 123 F3
Ílhavo, *Portugal* 30 E2
Ilhéus, *Brazil* 123 D4
Ili →, *Kazakhstan* 44 E8
Iliç, *Turkey* 67 D8
Ilich, *Kazakhstan* 44 E7
Iliff, *U.S.A.* 108 E3
Iligan, *Phil.* 55 G6
Iligan Bay, *Phil.* 55 G6
Ilíkí, L., *Greece* 39 L6
Ilin I., *Phil.* 55 E4
Iliodhrómia, *Greece* 39 K6
Ilion, *U.S.A.* 107 D9
Ilirska-Bistrica, *Slovenia* 33 C11
Ilkeston, *U.K.* 12 E6
Illampu = Ancohuma, Nevada, *Bolivia* 124 D4
Illana B., *Phil.* 55 H5
Illapel, *Chile* 126 C1
Ille-et-Vilaine □, *France* 24 D5
Ille-sur-Têt, *France* 26 F6
Iller →, *Germany* 19 G5
Illescas, *Spain* 30 E7
Illetas, *Spain* 36 B9
Illiers-Combray, *France* 24 D8
Illimani, *Bolivia* 124 D4
Illinois □, *U.S.A.* 103 C9
Illinois →, *U.S.A.* 103 C8
Illium = Troy, *Turkey* 66 D2
Illizi, *Algeria* 75 C6
Illora, *Spain* 31 H7
Ilm →, *Germany* 18 D7
Ilmen, Oz., *Russia* 40 B7
Ilmenau, *Germany* 18 E6
Ilo, *Peru* 124 D3
Ilobu, *Nigeria* 79 D5
Iloilo, *Phil.* 55 F5
Ilora, *Nigeria* 79 D5
Ilorin, *Nigeria* 79 D5
Iloulya, *Russia* 43 B11
Ilovatka, *Russia* 41 F14
Ilovlya →, *Russia* 43 B10
Ilubabor □, *Ethiopia* 77 F3
Ilukste, *Latvia* 40 D5
Ilva Mică, *Romania* 38 B7
Ilwaco, *U.S.A.* 112 D2
Ilwaki, *Indonesia* 57 F7
Ilyichevsk, *Ukraine* 42 C4
Imabari, *Japan* 49 G6
Imaloto →, *Madag.* 85 C8
İmamoğlu, *Turkey* 66 E6
Imandra, Oz., *Russia* 44 C4
Imari, *Japan* 49 H4
Imasa, *Sudan* 76 D4
Imbâbah, *Egypt* 76 H7
Imbabura □, *Ecuador* 120 C2
Imbaimadai, *Guyana* 121 B5
Imbler, *U.S.A.* 110 D5
Imdahane, *Morocco* 74 B3
imeni 26 Bakinskikh Komissarov, *Azerbaijan* 67 D13
Imeni Poliny Osipenko, *Russia* 45 D14
Imeri, Serra, *Brazil* 120 C4
Imerimandroso, *Madag.* 85 B8
Imesan, *Mauritania* 74 D1
Imi, *Ethiopia* 68 F3
Imishly, *Azerbaijan* 43 G13
Imitek, *Morocco* 74 C3
Imlay, *U.S.A.* 110 F4
Imlay City, *U.S.A.* 106 C1
Immenstadt, *Germany* 19 H6
Immingham, *U.K.* 12 D7
Immokalee, *U.S.A.* 105 M5
Imo □, *Nigeria* 79 D6
Imola, *Italy* 33 D8
Imotski, *Croatia* 21 M7
Imperatriz, *Amazonas, Brazil* 124 B4
Imperatriz, *Maranhão, Brazil* 122 C2
Impéria, *Italy* 32 E5
Imperial, *Canada* 101 C7
Imperial, *Peru* 124 C2
Imperial, *Calif., U.S.A.* 113 N11
Imperial, *Nebr., U.S.A.* 108 E4
Imperial Beach, *U.S.A.* 113 N9
Imperial Dam, *U.S.A.* 113 N12
Imperial Res., *U.S.A.* 113 N12
Imperial Valley, *U.S.A.* 113 N11
Imperieuse Reef, *Australia* 88 C2
Impfondo, *Congo* 80 D3
Imphal, *India* 61 G18
Imphy, *France* 26 B7
İmralı, *Turkey* 66 C3
Imranlı, *Turkey* 67 D8
İmroz = Gökçeada, *Turkey* 39 J8
Imst, *Austria* 19 H6
Imuruan B., *Phil.* 57 B5
In Belbel, *Algeria* 75 C5
In Delimane, *Mali* 79 B5
In Rhar, *Algeria* 75 C5
In Salah, *Algeria* 75 C5
In Tallak, *Mali* 79 B5
Ina, *Japan* 49 G8
Inajá, *Brazil* 122 C4
Inangahua Junction, *N.Z.* 87 J3
Inanwatan, *Indonesia* 57 E8
Iñapari, *Peru* 124 C4
Inari, *Finland* 8 B19
Inarijärvi, *Finland* 8 B19
Inawashiro-Ko, *Japan* 48 F10
Inca, *Spain* 36 B9
Incaguasi, *Chile* 126 B1
İnce-Burnu, *Turkey* 42 E6
İncekum Burnu, *Turkey* 66 E5
Inchon, *S. Korea* 51 F14
Incio, *Spain* 30 C3
İncirliova, *Turkey* 66 E2
Incomáti →, *Mozam.* 85 D5
Inda Silase, *Ethiopia* 77 E4
Indalsälven →, *Sweden* 10 B11
Indaw, *Burma* 61 G20
Indbir, *Ethiopia* 77 F4
Independence, *Calif., U.S.A.* 111 H4
Independence, *Iowa, U.S.A.* 108 D9
Independence, *Kans., U.S.A.* 109 G7
Independence, *Mo., U.S.A.* 108 F7
Independence, *Oreg., U.S.A.* 110 D2
Independence Fjord, *Greenland* 4 A6
Independence Mts., *U.S.A.* 110 F5
Independência, *Brazil* 122 C3
Independenţa, *Romania* 38 D10
Inderborskiy, *Kazakhstan* 43 B14
Index, *U.S.A.* 112 C5
India ■, *Asia* 60 K11
Indian →, *U.S.A.* 105 M5
Indian Cabins, *Canada* 100 B5
Indian Harbour, *Canada* 99 B8
Indian Head, *Canada* 101 C8
Indian Ocean 46 K11
Indian Springs, *U.S.A.* 113 J11
Indiana, *U.S.A.* 106 F5
Indiana □, *U.S.A.* 104 E3
Indianapolis, *U.S.A.* 104 F2
Indianola, *Iowa, U.S.A.* 108 E8
Indianola, *Miss., U.S.A.* 109 J9
Indiapora, *Brazil* 123 E1
Indiga, *Russia* 44 C5
Indigirka →, *Russia* 45 B15
Indija, *Serbia, Yug.* 21 K10
Indio, *U.S.A.* 113 M10
Indonesia ■, *Asia* 56 F5
Indore, *India* 62 H6
Indramayu, *Indonesia* 57 G13
Indravati →, *India* 61 K12
Indre □, *France* 25 F8
Indre →, *France* 24 E7
Indre-et-Loire □, *France* 24 E7
Indus →, *Pakistan* 62 G2
Indus, Mouth of the, *Pakistan* 62 H2
İnebolu, *Turkey* 66 C5
İnegöl, *Turkey* 66 C3
Inés, Mt., *Argentina* 128 C3
Ineu, *Romania* 38 C4
Inezgane, *Morocco* 74 B3
Infantes, *Spain* 29 G1
Infiernillo, Presa del, *Mexico* 114 D4
Infiesto, *Spain* 30 B5
Ingapirca, *Ecuador* 120 D2
Ingelmunster, *Belgium* 17 G2
Ingende, *Zaïre* 80 E3
Ingeniero Jacobacci, *Argentina* 128 B3
Ingenio, *Canary Is.* 36 G4
Ingenio Santa Ana, *Argentina* 126 B2
Ingersoll, *Canada* 106 C4
Ingham, *Australia* 90 B4
Ingleborough, *U.K.* 12 C5
Inglewood, *Queens., Australia* 91 D5
Inglewood, *Vic., Australia* 91 F3
Inglewood, *N.Z.* 87 H5
Inglewood, *U.S.A.* 113 M8
Ingólfshöfði, *Iceland* 8 E5
Ingolstadt, *Germany* 19 G7
Ingomar, *U.S.A.* 110 C10
Ingonish, *Canada* 99 C7
Ingore, *Guinea-Biss.* 78 C1
Ingraj Bazar, *India* 63 G13

Ingrid Christensen Coast, *Antarctica* 5 C6
Ingul →, *Ukraine* 42 C5
Ingulec, *Ukraine* 42 C5
Ingulets →, *Ukraine* 42 C5
Inguri →, *Georgia* 43 E9
Ingwavuma, *S. Africa* 85 D5
Inhaca, I., *Mozam.* 85 D5
Inhafenga, *Mozam.* 85 C5
Inhambane, *Mozam.* 85 C6
Inhambane □, *Mozam.* 85 C5
Inhambupe, *Brazil* 123 D4
Inhaminga, *Mozam.* 83 F4
Inharrime, *Mozam.* 85 C6
Inharrime →, *Mozam.* 85 C6
Inhuma, *Brazil* 122 C3
Inhumas, *Brazil* 123 E2
Iniesta, *Spain* 29 F3
Ining = Yining, *China* 54 B3
Inini □, *Fr. Guiana* 121 C7
Inírida →, *Colombia* 120 C4
Inishbofin, *Ireland* 15 C1
Inishmore, *Ireland* 15 C2
Inishowen, *Ireland* 15 A4
Injune, *Australia* 91 D4
Inklin, *Canada* 100 B2
Inklin →, *Canada* 100 B2
Inkom, *U.S.A.* 110 E7
Inle L., *Burma* 61 J20
Inn →, *Austria* 19 G9
Innamincka, *Australia* 91 D3
Inner Hebrides, *U.K.* 14 D2
Inner Mongolia = Nei Monggol Zizhiqu □, *China* 50 C6
Inner Sound, *U.K.* 14 D3
Innerkip, *Canada* 106 C4
Innerkirchen, *Switz.* 22 C6
Innerste →, *Germany* 18 C5
Innetalling I., *Canada* 98 A4
Innisfail, *Australia* 90 B4
Innisfail, *Canada* 100 C6
In'no-shima, *Japan* 49 G6
Innsbruck, *Austria* 19 H7
Inny →, *Ireland* 15 C4
Inocência, *Brazil* 123 E1
Inongo, *Zaïre* 80 E3
Inoucdjouac, *Canada* 97 C12
Inowrocław, *Poland* 20 C8
Inpundong, *N. Korea* 51 D14
Inquisivi, *Bolivia* 124 D4
Ins, *Switz.* 22 B4
Inscription, C., *Australia* 89 E1
Insein, *Burma* 61 L20
Însurăţei, *Romania* 38 E10
Intendente Alvear, *Argentina* 126 D3
Interior, *U.S.A.* 108 D4
Interlaken, *Switz.* 25 F14
International Falls, *U.S.A.* 108 A8
Intiyaco, *Argentina* 126 B3
Intragna, *Switz.* 23 D7
Intutu, *Peru* 120 D3
Inútil, B., *Chile* 128 D2
Inuvik, *Canada* 96 B6
Inveraray, *U.K.* 14 E3
Inverbervie, *U.K.* 14 E6
Invercargill, *N.Z.* 87 M2
Inverell, *Australia* 91 D5
Invergordon, *U.K.* 14 D4
Invermere, *Canada* 100 C5
Inverness, *Canada* 99 C7
Inverness, *U.K.* 14 D4
Inverness, *U.S.A.* 105 L4
Inverurie, *U.K.* 14 D6
Inverway, *Australia* 88 C4
Investigator Group, *Australia* 91 E1
Investigator Str., *Australia* 91 F2
Inya, *Russia* 44 D9
Inyanga, *Zimbabwe* 83 F3
Inyangani, *Zimbabwe* 83 F3
Inyantue, *Zimbabwe* 83 F2
Inyo Mts., *U.S.A.* 111 H5
Inyokern, *U.S.A.* 113 K9
Inza, *Russia* 41 E15
Inzhavino, *Russia* 41 E13
Iō-Jima, *Japan* 49 J5
Ioánnina, *Greece* 39 K3
Iola, *U.S.A.* 109 G7
Ion Corvin, *Romania* 38 E10
Iona, *U.K.* 14 E2
Ione, *Calif., U.S.A.* 112 G6
Ione, *Wash., U.S.A.* 110 B5
Ionia, *U.S.A.* 104 D3
Ionian Is. = Iónioi Nísoi, *Greece* 39 L3
Ionian Sea, *Europe* 6 H9
Iónioi Nísoi, *Greece* 39 L3
Iori →, *Azerbaijan* 43 F12
Íos, *Greece* 39 N8
Iowa □, *U.S.A.* 108 D8
Iowa City, *U.S.A.* 108 E9
Iowa Falls, *U.S.A.* 108 D8
Ipala, *Tanzania* 82 C3
Ipameri, *Brazil* 123 E2
Iparía, *Peru* 124 B3
Ipáti, *Greece* 39 L5
Ipatinga, *Brazil* 123 E3
Ipatovo, *Russia* 43 D10
Ipel →, *Europe* 21 G9
Ipiales, *Colombia* 120 C2
Ipiaú, *Brazil* 123 D4
Ipin = Yibin, *China* 52 C5
Ipirá, *Brazil* 123 D4
Ipiranga, *Brazil* 120 D4
Ipixuna, *Brazil* 124 B3
Ipixuna →, *Amazonas, Brazil* 124 B3
Ipixuna →, *Amazonas, Brazil* 125 B5
Ipoh, *Malaysia* 59 K3
Iporá, *Brazil* 123 D1
Ippy, *C.A.R.* 73 G9
Ipsala, *Turkey* 66 C2
Ipsárion Óros, *Greece* 39 J7
Ipswich, *Australia* 91 D5
Ipswich, *U.K.* 13 E9
Ipswich, *Mass., U.S.A.* 107 D14
Ipswich, *S. Dak., U.S.A.* 108 C5
Ipu, *Brazil* 122 B3
Ipueiras, *Brazil* 122 B3
Ipupiara, *Brazil* 123 D3
Iput →, *Belorussia* 40 E7
Iqaluit, *Canada* 97 B13
Iquique, *Chile* 124 E3
Iquitos, *Peru* 120 D3
Irabu-Jima, *Japan* 49 M2
Iracoubo, *Fr. Guiana* 121 B7
Īrafshān, *Iran* 65 E9
Irahuan, *Phil.* 55 G3
Iráklia, *Greece* 39 N8
Iráklion, *Greece* 37 D7
Iráklion □, *Greece* 37 D7
Irala, *Paraguay* 127 B5
Iramba □, *Tanzania* 82 C3
Iran ■, *Asia* 65 C7
Iran, Gunung-Gunung, *Malaysia* 56 D4
Iran Ra. = Iran, Gunung-Gunung, *Malaysia* 56 D4
Īrānshahr, *Iran* 65 E9
Irapa, *Venezuela* 121 A5
Irapuato, *Mexico* 114 C4
Iraq ■, *Asia* 64 C5
Irarrar, O. →, *Mali* 75 D5
Irati, *Brazil* 127 B5
Irbid, *Jordan* 69 C4
Irbid □, *Jordan* 69 C5
Irebu, *Zaïre* 80 E3
Irecê, *Brazil* 122 D3
Iregua →, *Spain* 28 C7
Ireland ■, *Europe* 15 D4
Ireland's Eye, *Ireland* 15 C5
Irele, *Nigeria* 79 D6
Ireng →, *Brazil* 121 C6
Iret, *Russia* 45 C16
Irgiz, Bolshaya →, *Russia* 41 E16
Irhârharene, *Algeria* 75 C6
Irharrhar, O. →, *Algeria* 75 C6
Irherm, *Morocco* 74 B3
Irhil Mgoun, *Morocco* 74 B3
Irhyangdong, *N. Korea* 51 D15
Iri, *S. Korea* 51 G14
Irian Jaya □, *Indonesia* 57 E9
Irié, *Guinea* 78 D3
Iriga, *Phil.* 55 E5
Iringa, *Tanzania* 82 D4
Iringa □, *Tanzania* 82 D4
Iriomote-Jima, *Japan* 49 M1
Iriona, *Honduras* 116 C2
Iriri →, *Brazil* 121 D7
Iriri Novo →, *Brazil* 125 B7
Irish Republic ■, *Europe* 15 D4
Irish Sea, *Europe* 12 D3
Irkineyeva, *Russia* 45 D10
Irkutsk, *Russia* 45 D11
Irma, *Canada* 101 C6
Irō-Zaki, *Japan* 49 G9
Iroise, Mer d', *France* 24 D2
Iron Baron, *Australia* 91 E2
Iron Gate = Portile de Fier, *Europe* 38 E5
Iron Knob, *Australia* 91 E2
Iron Mountain, *U.S.A.* 104 C1
Iron Ra., *Australia* 90 A3
Iron River, *U.S.A.* 108 B10
Ironbridge, *U.K.* 13 E5
Irondequoit, *U.S.A.* 106 C7
Ironstone Kopje, *Botswana* 84 D3
Ironton, *Mo., U.S.A.* 109 G9
Ironton, *Ohio, U.S.A.* 104 F4
Ironwood, *U.S.A.* 108 B9
Iroquois Falls, *Canada* 98 C3
Irosin, *Phil.* 55 E6
Irpen, *Ukraine* 40 F7
Irrara Cr. →, *Australia* 91 D4
Irrawaddy □, *Burma* 61 L19
Irrawaddy →, *Burma* 61 M19
Irsina, *Italy* 35 B9
Irtysh →, *Russia* 44 C7
Irumu, *Zaïre* 82 B2
Irún, *Spain* 28 B3
Irurzun, *Spain* 28 C3
Irvine, *Canada* 101 D6
Irvine, *U.K.* 14 F4
Irvine, *U.S.A.* 104 G4
Irvine, *Calif., U.S.A.* 113 M9
Irvinestown, *U.K.* 15 B4
Irvona, *U.S.A.* 106 F6
Irwin →, *Australia* 89 E1
Irymple, *Australia* 91 E3
Is-sur-Tille, *France* 25 E12
Isa, *Nigeria* 79 C6
Isaac →, *Australia* 90 C4
Isabel, *U.S.A.* 108 C4
Isabela, I., *Mexico* 114 C3
Isabella, *Phil.* 55 H5
Isabella, Cord., *Nic.* 116 D2
Isabella Ra., *Australia* 88 D3
Ísafjarðardjúp, *Iceland* 8 C2
Ísafjörður, *Iceland* 8 C2
Isagarh, *India* 62 G7
Isahaya, *Japan* 49 H5
Isaka, *Tanzania* 82 C3
Isana = Içana →, *Brazil* 120 C4
Isangi, *Zaïre* 80 D4
Isar →, *Germany* 19 G8
Isarco →, *Italy* 33 B8
Ísari, *Greece* 39 M5
Isbergues, *France* 25 B9
Iscayachi, *Bolivia* 125 E4
Íschia, *Italy* 34 B6
Iscuandé, *Colombia* 120 C2
Isdell →, *Australia* 88 C3
Ise, *Japan* 49 G8
Ise-Wan, *Japan* 49 G8
Isefjord, *Denmark* 11 J5
Iseltwald, *Switz.* 22 C5
Isenthal, *Switz.* 23 C7
Iseo, *Italy* 32 C7
Iseo, L. d', *Italy* 32 C7
Iseramagazi, *Tanzania* 82 C3
Isère □, *France* 27 C9
Isère →, *France* 27 D8
Iserlohn, *Germany* 18 D3
Isérnia, *Italy* 35 A7
Iseyin, *Nigeria* 79 D5
Isherton, *Guyana* 121 C6
Ishigaki-Shima, *Japan* 49 M2
Ishikari-Gawa →, *Japan* 48 C10
Ishikari-Sammyaku, *Japan* 48 C11
Ishikari-Wan, *Japan* 48 C10
Ishikawa □, *Japan* 49 F8
Ishim, *Russia* 44 D7
Ishim →, *Russia* 44 D8
Ishinomaki, *Japan* 48 E10
Ishioka, *Japan* 49 F10
Ishkuman, *Pakistan* 63 A5
Ishpeming, *U.S.A.* 104 B2
Isigny-sur-Mer, *France* 24 C5
Isil Kul, *Russia* 44 D8
Isiolo, *Kenya* 82 B4
Isiolo □, *Kenya* 82 B4
Isipingo Beach, *S. Africa* 85 E5
Isiro, *Zaïre* 82 B2
Isisford, *Australia* 90 C3
İskederun, *Turkey* 66 E7
İskenderun, *Turkey* 66 E7
İskenderun Körfezi, *Turkey* 66 E6
İskilip, *Turkey* 42 F6
Iskŭr →, *Bulgaria* 38 F7
Iskut →, *Canada* 100 B2
Isla →, *U.K.* 14 E5
Isla Cristina, *Spain* 31 H3
Isla Vista, *U.S.A.* 113 L7
İslâhiye, *Turkey* 66 E7
Islamabad, *Pakistan* 62 C5
Islamkot, *Pakistan* 62 G4
Island →, *Canada* 100 A4
Island Falls, *Canada* 98 C3
Island Falls, *U.S.A.* 99 C6
Island L., *Canada* 101 C10
Island Lagoon, *Australia* 91 E2
Island Pond, *U.S.A.* 107 B13
Islands, B. of, *Canada* 99 C8
Islay, *U.K.* 14 F2
Isle →, *France* 26 D3
Isle aux Morts, *Canada* 99 C8
Isle of Wight □, *U.K.* 13 G6
Isle Royale, *U.S.A.* 108 A10
Isleta, *U.S.A.* 111 J10
Isleton, *U.S.A.* 112 G5
Ismail, *Ukraine* 42 D3
Ismâ'ilîya, *Egypt* 76 H8
Ismaning, *Germany* 19 G7
Ismay, *U.S.A.* 108 B2
Isna, *Egypt* 76 B3
Isogstalo, *India* 63 B8
Isola del Gran Sasso d'Italia, *Italy* 33 F10
Ísola del Liri, *Italy* 34 A6
Ísola della Scala, *Italy* 32 C8
Ísola di Capo Rizzuto, *Italy* 35 D10
İsparta, *Turkey* 66 E4
İsparta □, *Turkey* 66 E4
Isperikh, *Bulgaria* 38 F9
Íspica, *Italy* 35 F7
İspir, *Turkey* 43 F9
Israel ■, *Asia* 69 D3
Issano, *Guyana* 121 B6
Issia, *Ivory C.* 78 D3
Issoire, *France* 26 C7
Issoudun, *France* 25 F8
Issyk-Kul, Ozero, *Kirghizia* 44 E8
Ist, *Croatia* 33 D11
Istaihah, *U.A.E.* 65 F7
İstanbul, *Turkey* 66 C3
İstanbul □, *Turkey* 66 C3
Istmina, *Colombia* 120 B2
Istok, *Serbia, Yug.* 21 N10
Istokpoga, L., *U.S.A.* 105 M5
Istra, *Croatia* 33 C11
Istra, *Russia* 41 D10
İstranca Dağları, *Turkey* 39 H10
Istres, *France* 27 E8
Istria = Istra, *Croatia* 33 C11
Itá, *Paraguay* 126 B4
Itabaiana, *Paraíba, Brazil* 122 C4
Itabaiana, *Sergipe, Brazil* 122 D4
Itabaianinha, *Brazil* 122 D4
Itaberaba, *Brazil* 123 D3
Itaberaí, *Brazil* 123 E2
Itabira, *Brazil* 123 E3
Itabirito, *Brazil* 123 F3
Itaboca, *Brazil* 121 D5
Itabuna, *Brazil* 123 D4
Itacajá, *Brazil* 122 C2
Itacaunas →, *Brazil* 122 C2
Itacoatiara, *Brazil* 121 D6
Itacuaí →, *Brazil* 124 A3
Itaguaçu, *Brazil* 123 E3
Itaguari →, *Brazil* 123 D3
Itaguatins, *Brazil* 122 C2
Itaim →, *Brazil* 122 C3
Itainópolis, *Brazil* 122 C3
Itaipu Dam, *Brazil* 127 B5
Itaituba, *Brazil* 121 D6
Itajaí, *Brazil* 127 B6
Itajubá, *Brazil* 123 F2
Itajuípe, *Brazil* 123 D4
Itaka, *Tanzania* 83 D3
Italy ■, *Europe* 7 G8
Itamataré, *Brazil* 122 B2
Itambacuri, *Brazil* 123 E3
Itambé, *Brazil* 123 E3
Itampolo, *Madag.* 85 C7
Itanhauã →, *Brazil* 121 D5
Itanhém, *Brazil* 123 E3
Itapaci, *Brazil* 123 D2
Itapagé, *Brazil* 122 B4
Itaparica, I. de, *Brazil* 123 D4
Itapebi, *Brazil* 123 E4
Itapecuru-Mirim, *Brazil* 122 B3
Itaperuna, *Brazil* 123 F3
Itapetinga, *Brazil* 123 E3
Itapetininga, *Brazil* 127 A6
Itapeva, *Brazil* 127 A6
Itapicuru →, *Bahia, Brazil* 122 D4
Itapicuru →, *Maranhão, Brazil* 122 B3
Itapinima, *Brazil* 125 B5
Itapipoca, *Brazil* 122 B4
Itapiranga, *Brazil* 121 D6
Itapiúna, *Brazil* 122 B4
Itaporanga, *Brazil* 122 C4
Itapuá □, *Paraguay* 127 B4
Itapuranga, *Brazil* 123 E2
Itaquari, *Brazil* 123 F3
Itaquatiara, *Brazil* 121 D6
Itaquí, *Brazil* 126 B4
Itararé, *Brazil* 127 A6
Itarsi, *India* 62 H7
Itarumã, *Brazil* 123 E1
Itatí, *Argentina* 126 B4
Itatira, *Brazil* 122 B4
Itatuba, *Brazil* 125 B5
Itatupa, *Brazil* 121 D7
Itaueira, *Brazil* 122 C3
Itaueira →, *Brazil* 122 C3
Itaúna, *Brazil* 123 F3
Itbayat, *Phil.* 55 A4
Itchen →, *U.K.* 13 G6
Ite, *Peru* 124 D3
Itezhi Tezhi, L., *Zambia* 83 F2
Ithaca = Itháki, *Greece* 39 L3
Ithaca, *U.S.A.* 107 D8
Itháki, *Greece* 39 L3
Itinga, *Brazil* 123 E3
Itiquira, *Brazil* 125 D7
Itiquira →, *Brazil* 125 D6
Itiruçu, *Brazil* 123 D3
Itiúba, *Brazil* 122 D4
Ito, *Japan* 49 G9
Itoigawa, *Japan* 49 F8
Iton →, *France* 24 C8
Itonamas →, *Bolivia* 125 C5
Itsa, *Egypt* 76 J7
Íttiri, *Italy* 34 B1
Ittoqqortoormiit = Scoresbysund, *Greenland* 4 B6
Itu, *Brazil* 127 A6
Itu, *Nigeria* 79 D6
Ituaçu, *Brazil* 123 D3
Ituango, *Colombia* 120 B2
Ituiutaba, *Brazil* 123 E2
Itumbiara, *Brazil* 123 E2
Ituna, *Canada* 101 C8
Itunge Port, *Tanzania* 83 D3
Ituni, *Guyana* 121 B6
Itupiranga, *Brazil* 122 C2
Iturama, *Brazil* 123 E1
Iturbe, *Argentina* 126 A2
Ituri →, *Zaïre* 82 B2
Iturup, Ostrov, *Russia* 45 E15
Ituverava, *Brazil* 123 F2
Ituxi →, *Brazil* 125 B5
Ituyuro →, *Argentina* 126 A3
Itzehoe, *Germany* 18 B5
Ivaí →, *Brazil* 127 A5
Ivalo, *Finland* 8 B19
Ivalojoki →, *Finland* 8 B19
Ivangorod, *Russia* 40 B6
Ivanhoe, *N.S.W., Australia* 91 E3
Ivanhoe, *W. Austral., Australia* 88 C4
Ivanhoe, *U.S.A.* 112 J7
Ivanhoe L., *Canada* 101 A7
Ivanić Grad, *Croatia* 33 C13
Ivanjica, *Serbia, Yug.* 21 M10
Ivanjšcice, *Croatia* 33 B13
Ivankoyskoye Vdkhr., *Russia* 41 C10
Ivano-Frankovsk, *Ukraine* 40 G4
Ivanovo, *Belorussia* 40 E4
Ivanovo, *Russia* 41 C12
Ivato, *Madag.* 85 C8
Ivaylovgrad, *Bulgaria* 39 H9
Ivinheima →, *Brazil* 127 A5
Iviza = Ibiza, *Spain* 36 C7
Ivohibe, *Madag.* 85 C8
Ivolândia, *Brazil* 123 E1
Ivory Coast ■, *Africa* 78 D3
Ivrea, *Italy* 32 C4
Ivugivik, *Canada* 97 B12
Iwahig, *Phil.* 56 C5
Iwaizumi, *Japan* 48 E10
Iwaki, *Japan* 49 F10
Iwakuni, *Japan* 49 G6
Iwamizawa, *Japan* 48 C10
Iwanai, *Japan* 48 C10
Iwata, *Japan* 49 G8
Iwate □, *Japan* 48 E10
Iwate-San, *Japan* 48 E10
Iwo, *Nigeria* 79 D5
Ixiamas, *Bolivia* 124 C4
Ixopo, *S. Africa* 85 E5
Ixtepec, *Mexico* 115 D5
Ixtlán del Río, *Mexico* 114 C4
Iyo, *Japan* 49 H6
Izabal, L. de, *Guatemala* 116 C2
Izamal, *Mexico* 115 C7
Izberbash, *Russia* 43 E12
Izegem, *Belgium* 17 G2
Izena-Shima, *Japan* 49 L3
Izhevsk, *Russia* 44 D6
İzmir, *Turkey* 66 D2
İzmir □, *Turkey* 66 D2
İzmit, *Turkey* 66 C3
Iznajar, *Spain* 31 H6
Iznalloz, *Spain* 29 H1
İznik Gölü, *Turkey* 66 C3
Izobil'nyy, *Russia* 43 D9
Izola, *Slovenia* 33 C10
Izozog, Bañados de, *Bolivia* 125 D5
Izra, *Syria* 69 C5
Iztochni Rodopi, *Bulgaria* 39 H8
Izu-Shotō, *Japan* 49 G10
Izumi-sano, *Japan* 49 G7
Izumo, *Japan* 49 G6
Izyaslav, *Ukraine* 40 F5
Izyum, *Ukraine* 42 B7

J

J.F. Rodrigues, *Brazil* 122 B1
Jaba, *Ethiopia* 77 F4
Jabal el Awlîya, *Sudan* 77 D3
Jabal Lubnān, *Lebanon* 69 B4
Jabalón →, *Spain* 31 G6
Jabalpur, *India* 63 H8
Jabbūl, *Syria* 64 B3
Jablah, *Syria* 64 C3
Jablanac, *Croatia* 33 D11
Jablonec, *Czech.* 20 E5
Jabłonowo, *Poland* 20 B9
Jaboatão, *Brazil* 122 C4
Jaboticabal, *Brazil* 127 A6
Jaburu, *Brazil* 125 B5
Jaca, *Spain* 28 C4
Jacaré →, *Brazil* 122 D3
Jacareí, *Brazil* 127 A6
Jacarèzinho, *Brazil* 127 A6
Jaciara, *Brazil* 125 D7
Jacinto, *Brazil* 123 E3
Jaciparaná, *Brazil* 125 B5
Jackman, *U.S.A.* 99 C5
Jacksboro, *U.S.A.* 109 J5
Jackson, *Australia* 91 D4
Jackson, *Ala., U.S.A.* 105 K2
Jackson, *Calif., U.S.A.* 112 G6
Jackson, *Ky., U.S.A.* 104 G4
Jackson, *Mich., U.S.A.* 104 D3
Jackson, *Minn., U.S.A.* 108 D7
Jackson, *Miss., U.S.A.* 109 J9
Jackson, *Mo., U.S.A.* 109 G10
Jackson, *Ohio, U.S.A.* 104 F4
Jackson, *Tenn., U.S.A.* 105 H1
Jackson, *Wyo., U.S.A.* 110 E8
Jackson, L., *U.S.A.* 110 E8
Jackson B., *N.Z.* 87 K2
Jacksons, *N.Z.* 87 K3
Jacksonville, *Ala., U.S.A.* 105 J3
Jacksonville, *Calif., U.S.A.* 112 H6
Jacksonville, *Fla., U.S.A.* 105 K5
Jacksonville, *Ill., U.S.A.* 108 F9
Jacksonville, *N.C., U.S.A.* 105 H7
Jacksonville, *Oreg., U.S.A.* 110 E2
Jacksonville, *Tex., U.S.A.* 109 K7
Jacksonville Beach, *U.S.A.* 105 K5
Jacmel, *Haiti* 117 C5
Jacob Lake, *U.S.A.* 111 H7
Jacobabad, *Pakistan* 62 E3
Jacobina, *Brazil* 122 D3
Jacques-Cartier, Mt., *Canada* 99 C6
Jacqueville, *Ivory C.* 78 D4
Jacuí →, *Brazil* 127 C5
Jacumba, *U.S.A.* 113 N10
Jacundá →, *Brazil* 122 B1
Jade, *Germany* 18 B4
Jadebusen, *Germany* 18 B4
Jadoigne, *Belgium* 17 G5
Jadotville = Likasi, *Zaïre* 83 E2
Jadraque, *Spain* 28 E2
Jādū, *Libya* 75 B7
Jaén, *Peru* 124 B2

Jaén, *Spain* 31 H7
Jaén □, *Spain* 31 H7
Jafène, *Africa* 74 D3
Jaffa = Tel Aviv-Yafo, *Israel* 69 C3
Jaffa, C., *Australia* 91 F2
Jaffna, *Sri Lanka* 60 Q12
Jagadhri, *India* 62 D7
Jagadishpur, *India* 63 G11
Jagdalpur, *India* 61 K12
Jagersfontein, *S. Africa* 84 D4
Jagraon, *India* 60 D9
Jagst →, *Germany* 19 F5
Jagtial, *India* 60 K11
Jaguaquara, *Brazil* 123 D4
Jaguariaíva, *Brazil* 127 A6
Jaguaribe, *Brazil* 122 C4
Jaguaribe →, *Brazil* 122 B4
Jaguaruana, *Brazil* 122 B4
Jagüey Grande, *Cuba* 116 B3
Jahangirabad, *India* 62 E8
Jahrom, *Iran* 65 D7
Jaicós, *Brazil* 122 C3
Jailolo, *Indonesia* 57 D7
Jailolo, Selat, *Indonesia* 57 D7
Jaipur, *India* 62 F6
Jājarm, *Iran* 65 B8
Jajce, *Bos.-H., Yug.* 21 L7
Jakarta, *Indonesia* 57 G12
Jakobstad, *Finland* 8 E17
Jakupica, *Macedonia, Yug.* 39 H4
Jal, *U.S.A.* 109 J3
Jalalabad, *Afghan.* 62 B4
Jalalabad, *India* 63 F8
Jalalpur Jattan, *Pakistan* 62 C6
Jalama, *U.S.A.* 113 L6
Jalapa, *Guatemala* 116 D2
Jalapa Enríquez, *Mexico* 115 D5
Jalaun, *India* 63 F8
Jales, *Brazil* 123 F1
Jaleswar, *Nepal* 63 F11
Jalgaon, *Maharashtra, India* 60 J10
Jalgaon, *Maharashtra, India* 60 J9
Jalhay, *Belgium* 17 G7
Jalībah, *Iraq* 64 D5
Jalingo, *Nigeria* 79 D7
Jalisco □, *Mexico* 114 C4
Jalkot, *Pakistan* 63 B5
Jallas →, *Spain* 30 C1
Jalna, *India* 60 K9
Jalón →, *Spain* 28 D3
Jalpa, *Mexico* 114 C4
Jalpaiguri, *India* 61 F16
Jaluit I., *Pac. Oc.* 92 G8
Jalūlā, *Iraq* 64 C5
Jamaari, *Nigeria* 79 C6
Jamaica ■, *W. Indies* 116 C4
Jamalpur, *Bangla.* 61 G16
Jamalpur, *India* 63 G12
Jamalpurganj, *India* 63 H13
Jamanxim →, *Brazil* 125 A6
Jamari, *Brazil* 125 B5
Jamari →, *Brazil* 125 B5
Jambe, *Indonesia* 57 E8
Jambes, *Belgium* 17 H5
Jambi, *Indonesia* 56 E2
Jambi □, *Indonesia* 56 E2
Jambusar, *India* 62 H5
James →, *U.S.A.* 108 D6
James B., *Canada* 97 C11
James Ras., *Australia* 88 D5
James Ross I., *Antarctica* 5 C18
Jamestown, *Australia* 91 E2
Jamestown, *S. Africa* 84 E4
Jamestown, *Ky., U.S.A.* 104 G3
Jamestown, *N. Dak., U.S.A.* 108 B5
Jamestown, *N.Y., U.S.A.* 106 D5
Jamestown, *Pa., U.S.A.* 106 E4
Jamestown, *Tenn., U.S.A.* 105 G3
Jamīlābād, *Iran* 65 C6
Jamiltepec, *Mexico* 115 D5
Jamkhandi, *India* 60 L9
Jammerbugt, *Denmark* 11 G3
Jammu, *India* 62 C6
Jammu & Kashmir □, *India* 63 B7
Jamnagar, *India* 62 H4
Jamoigne, *Belgium* 17 J6
Jampur, *Pakistan* 62 E4
Jamrud, *Pakistan* 62 C4
Jamshedpur, *India* 63 H12
Jamtara, *India* 63 H12
Jämtlands län □, *Sweden* 10 B7
Jan Kempdorp, *S. Africa* 84 D3
Jan L., *Canada* 101 C8
Jan Mayen, *Arctic* 4 B7
Janaúba, *Brazil* 123 E3
Janaucu, I., *Brazil* 122 A1
Jand, *Pakistan* 62 C5
Janda, L. de la, *Spain* 31 J5
Jandaia, *Brazil* 123 E1
Jandaq, *Iran* 65 C7
Jandia, *Canary Is.* 36 F5
Jandia, Pta. de, *Canary Is.* 36 F5
Jandiatuba →, *Brazil* 120 D4
Jandola, *Pakistan* 62 C4
Jandowae, *Australia* 91 D5
Jandrain-Jandrenouilles, *Belgium* 17 G5
Jándula →, *Spain* 31 G6
Janesville, *U.S.A.* 108 D10
Janga, *Ghana* 79 C4
Jango, *Brazil* 125 E6
Janīn, *Jordan* 69 C4
Janjina, *Croatia* 21 N7
Janos, *Mexico* 114 A3
Jánosháza, *Hungary* 21 H7
Janów Podlaski, *Poland* 20 C13
Januária, *Brazil* 123 E3
Janub Dârfûr □, *Sudan* 77 E2
Janub Kordofân □, *Sudan* 77 E3
Janubio, *Canary Is.* 36 F6
Janville, *France* 25 D8
Janzé, *France* 24 E5
Jaora, *India* 62 H6
Japan ■, *Asia* 49 G8
Japan, Sea of, *Asia* 48 E7
Japan Trench, *Pac. Oc.* 92 D6
Japen = Yapen, *Indonesia* 57 E9
Japurá →, *Brazil* 120 D4
Jaque, *Panama* 120 B2
Jarābulus, *Syria* 64 B3
Jaraguá, *Brazil* 123 E2
Jaraguari, *Brazil* 125 E7
Jaraicejo, *Spain* 31 F5
Jaraiz, *Spain* 30 E5
Jarama →, *Spain* 28 E1
Jaramillo, *Argentina* 128 C3
Jarandilla, *Spain* 30 E5
Jaranwala, *Pakistan* 62 D5
Jarash, *Jordan* 69 C4
Jarauçu →, *Brazil* 121 D7
Jardim, *Brazil* 126 A4
Jardín →, *Spain* 29 G2
Jardines de la Reina, Is., *Cuba* 116 B4
Jargalang, *China* 51 C12
Jargalant = Hovd, *Mongolia* 54 B4
Jargeau, *France* 25 E9
Jari →, *Brazil* 121 D7
Jarīr, W. al →, *Si. Arabia* 64 E4
Jarmen, *Germany* 18 B9
Jarnac, *France* 26 C3
Jarny, *France* 25 C12
Jarocin, *Poland* 20 D7
Jarosław, *Poland* 20 E12
Järpås, *Sweden* 11 F6
Järpen, *Sweden* 10 A7
Jarrahdale, *Australia* 89 F2
Jarres, Plaine des, *Laos* 58 C4
Jarso, *Ethiopia* 77 F4
Jartai, *China* 50 E3
Jaru, *Brazil* 125 C5
Jaru →, *Brazil* 125 C5
Jarud Qi, *China* 51 B11
Jarvis, *Canada* 106 D4
Jarvis I., *Pac. Oc.* 93 H12
Jarwa, *India* 63 F10
Jaša Tomić, *Serbia, Yug.* 21 K10
Jāsimīyah, *Iraq* 64 C5
Jasin, *Malaysia* 59 L4
Jāsk, *Iran* 65 E8
Jasło, *Poland* 20 F11
Jason, Is., *Falk. Is.* 128 D4
Jasper, *Alta., Canada* 100 C5
Jasper, *Ont., Canada* 107 B9
Jasper, *Ala., U.S.A.* 105 J2
Jasper, *Fla., U.S.A.* 105 K4
Jasper, *Minn., U.S.A.* 108 D6
Jasper, *Tex., U.S.A.* 109 K8
Jasper Nat. Park, *Canada* 100 C5
Jassy = Iaşi, *Romania* 38 B10
Jastrebarsko, *Croatia* 33 C12
Jastrzębie Zdrój, *Poland* 20 F8
Jászárokszállás, *Hungary* 21 H10
Jászberény, *Hungary* 21 H9
Jászladány, *Hungary* 21 H10
Jataí, *Brazil* 123 E1
Jatapu →, *Brazil* 121 D6
Jati, *Pakistan* 62 G3
Jatibarang, *Indonesia* 57 G13
Jatinegara, *Indonesia* 57 G12
Játiva, *Spain* 29 G4
Jatobal, *Brazil* 122 B2
Jaú, *Brazil* 127 A6
Jaú →, *Brazil* 121 D5
Jauaperí →, *Brazil* 121 D5
Jauche, *Belgium* 17 G5
Jauja, *Peru* 124 C2
Jaunjelgava, *Latvia* 40 C4
Jaunpur, *India* 63 G10
Jauru →, *Brazil* 125 D6
Java = Jawa, *Indonesia* 57 G14
Java Sea, *Indonesia* 56 E3
Java Trench, *Ind. Oc.* 92 H2
Jávea, *Spain* 29 G5
Javhlant = Ulyasutay, *Mongolia* 54 B4
Javier, I., *Chile* 128 C2
Javron, *France* 24 D6
Jawa, *Indonesia* 57 G14
Jawor, *Poland* 20 D6
Jaworzno, *Poland* 20 E9
Jay, *U.S.A.* 109 G7
Jaya, Puncak, *Indonesia* 57 E9
Jayanca, *Peru* 124 B2
Jayanti, *India* 61 F16
Jayapura, *Indonesia* 57 E10
Jayawijaya, Pegunungan, *Indonesia* 57 E9
Jaynagar, *India* 61 F15
Jayrūd, *Syria* 64 C3
Jayton, *U.S.A.* 109 J4
Jazīreh-ye Shīf, *Iran* 65 D6
Jazminal, *Mexico* 114 C4
Jazzīn, *Lebanon* 69 B4
Jean, *U.S.A.* 113 K11
Jean Marie River, *Canada* 100 A4
Jean Rabel, *Haiti* 117 C5
Jeanerette, *U.S.A.* 109 L9
Jeannette, Ostrov, *Russia* 45 B16
Jeannette, *U.S.A.* 106 F5
Jebba, *Morocco* 74 A4
Jebba, *Nigeria* 79 D5
Jebel, Bahr el →, *Sudan* 77 F3
Jebel Qerri, *Sudan* 77 D3
Jeberos, *Peru* 124 B2
Jedburgh, *U.K.* 14 F6
Jedda = Jiddah, *Si. Arabia* 68 C2
Jędrzejów, *Poland* 20 E10
Jedway, *Canada* 100 C2
Jeetzel →, *Germany* 18 B7
Jefferson, *Iowa, U.S.A.* 108 D7
Jefferson, *Ohio, U.S.A.* 106 E4
Jefferson, *Tex., U.S.A.* 109 J7
Jefferson, *Wis., U.S.A.* 108 D10
Jefferson, Mt., *Nev., U.S.A.* 110 G5
Jefferson, Mt., *Oreg., U.S.A.* 110 D3
Jefferson City, *Mo., U.S.A.* 108 F8
Jefferson City, *Tenn., U.S.A.* 105 G4
Jeffersonville, *U.S.A.* 104 F3
Jega, *Nigeria* 79 C5
Jekabpils, *Latvia* 40 C4
Jelenia Góra, *Poland* 20 E5
Jelgava, *Latvia* 9 H17
Jelli, *Sudan* 77 F3
Jellicoe, *Canada* 98 C2
Jemaja, *Indonesia* 56 D3
Jemaluang, *Malaysia* 59 L4
Jemappes, *Belgium* 17 H3
Jember, *Indonesia* 57 H15
Jembongan, *Malaysia* 56 C5
Jemeppe, *Belgium* 17 G7
Jemnice, *Czech.* 20 F5
Jena, *Germany* 18 E7
Jena, *U.S.A.* 109 K8
Jendouba, *Tunisia* 75 A6
Jenkins, *U.S.A.* 104 G4
Jenner, *U.S.A.* 112 G3
Jennings, *U.S.A.* 109 K8
Jennings →, *Canada* 100 B2
Jeparit, *Australia* 91 F3
Jequié, *Brazil* 123 D3
Jequitaí →, *Brazil* 123 E3
Jequitinhonha, *Brazil* 123 E3
Jequitinhonha →, *Brazil* 123 E4
Jerada, *Morocco* 75 B4
Jerantut, *Malaysia* 59 L4
Jérémie, *Haiti* 117 C5
Jeremoabo, *Brazil* 122 D4
Jerez, Punta, *Mexico* 115 C5
Jerez de García Salinas, *Mexico* 114 C4
Jerez de la Frontera, *Spain* 31 J4
Jerez de los Caballeros, *Spain* 31 G4
Jericho = Arīḩā, *Syria* 64 C3
Jericho = El Arīḩā, *Jordan* 69 D4
Jericho, *Australia* 90 C4
Jerichow, *Germany* 18 C8
Jerilderie, *Australia* 91 F4
Jermyn, *U.S.A.* 107 E9
Jerome, *U.S.A.* 111 J8
Jersey, *Chan. Is.* 13 H5
Jersey City, *U.S.A.* 107 F10
Jersey Shore, *U.S.A.* 106 E7
Jerseyville, *U.S.A.* 108 F9
Jerusalem, *Israel* 69 D4
Jervis B., *Australia* 91 F5
Jesenice, *Slovenia* 33 B11
Jesenké, *Czech.* 21 G10
Jesselton = Kota Kinabalu, *Malaysia* 56 C5
Jessnitz, *Germany* 18 D8
Jessore, *Bangla.* 61 H16
Jesup, *U.S.A.* 105 K5
Jesús, *Peru* 124 B2
Jesús Carranza, *Mexico* 115 D5
Jesús María, *Argentina* 126 C3
Jetmore, *U.S.A.* 109 F5
Jetpur, *India* 62 J4
Jette, *Belgium* 17 G4
Jevnaker, *Norway* 10 D4
Jewett, *Ohio, U.S.A.* 106 F3
Jewett, *Tex., U.S.A.* 109 K6
Jewett City, *U.S.A.* 107 E13
Jeyḩūnābād, *Iran* 65 C6
Jeypore, *India* 61 K13
Jeziorany, *Poland* 20 B10
Jhajjar, *India* 62 E7
Jhal Jhao, *Pakistan* 60 F4
Jhalawar, *India* 62 G7
Jhang Maghiana, *Pakistan* 62 D5
Jhansi, *India* 63 G8
Jharia, *India* 63 H12
Jharsaguda, *India* 61 J14
Jhelum, *Pakistan* 62 C5
Jhelum →, *Pakistan* 62 D5
Jhunjhunu, *India* 62 E6
Ji Xian, *Hebei, China* 50 F8
Ji Xian, *Henan, China* 50 G8
Ji Xian, *Shanxi, China* 50 F6
Jia Xian, *Henan, China* 50 H7
Jia Xian, *Shaanxi, China* 50 E6
Jiading, *China* 53 B13
Jiahe, *China* 53 E9
Jiali, *Taiwan* 53 F13
Jialing Jiang →, *China* 52 C6
Jiamusi, *China* 54 B8
Ji'an, *Jiangxi, China* 53 D10
Ji'an, *Jilin, China* 51 D14
Jianchang, *China* 51 D11
Jianchangying, *China* 51 D10
Jianchuan, *China* 52 D2
Jiande, *China* 53 C12
Jiangbei, *China* 52 C6
Jiangcheng, *China* 52 F3
Jiangdi, *China* 52 D4
Jiange, *China* 52 A5
Jiangjin, *China* 52 C6
Jiangkou, *China* 52 D7
Jiangle, *China* 53 D11
Jiangling, *China* 53 B9
Jiangmen, *China* 53 F9
Jiangshan, *China* 53 C12
Jiangsu □, *China* 51 H10
Jiangxi □, *China* 53 D10
Jiangyin, *China* 53 B13
Jiangyong, *China* 53 E8
Jiangyou, *China* 52 B5
Jianhe, *China* 52 D7
Jianli, *China* 53 C9
Jianning, *China* 53 D11
Jian'ou, *China* 53 D12
Jianshi, *China* 52 B7
Jianshui, *China* 52 F4
Jianyang, *Fujian, China* 53 D12
Jianyang, *Sichuan, China* 52 B5
Jiao Xian, *China* 51 F11
Jiaohe, *Hebei, China* 50 E9
Jiaohe, *Jilin, China* 51 C14
Jiaoling, *China* 53 E11
Jiaozhou Wan, *China* 51 F11
Jiaozuo, *China* 50 G7
Jiashan, *China* 53 A11
Jiawang, *China* 51 G9
Jiaxiang, *China* 50 G9
Jiaxing, *China* 53 B13
Jiayi, *Taiwan* 53 F13
Jiayu, *China* 53 C9
Jibão, Serra do, *Brazil* 123 D3
Jibiya, *Nigeria* 79 C6
Jibou, *Romania* 38 B6
Jibuti = Djibouti ■, *Africa* 68 E3
Jicarón, I., *Panama* 116 E3
Jičín, *Czech.* 20 E5
Jiddah, *Si. Arabia* 68 C2
Jido, *India* 61 E19
Jieshou, *China* 50 H8
Jiexiu, *China* 50 F6
Jieyang, *China* 53 F11
Jiggalong, *Australia* 88 D3
Jihlava, *Czech.* 20 F5
Jijel, *Algeria* 75 A6
Jijiga, *Ethiopia* 68 F3
Jijona, *Spain* 29 G4
Jikamshi, *Nigeria* 79 C6
Jilin, *China* 51 C14
Jilin □, *China* 51 C13
Jiloca →, *Spain* 28 D3
Jilong, *Taiwan* 53 E13
Jima, *Ethiopia* 77 F4
Jimbolia, *Romania* 38 D3
Jimena de la Frontera, *Spain* 31 J5
Jiménez, *Mexico* 114 B4
Jimo, *China* 51 F11
Jin Jiang →, *China* 53 C10
Jin Xian, *Hebei, China* 50 E8
Jin Xian, *Liaoning, China* 51 E11
Jinan, *China* 50 F9
Jincheng, *China* 50 G7
Jinchuan, *China* 52 B4
Jind, *India* 62 E7
Jindabyne, *Australia* 91 F4
Jindrichuv Hradeç, *Czech.* 20 F5
Jing He →, *China* 50 G5
Jing Shan, *China* 53 B8
Jing Xian, *Anhui, China* 53 B12
Jing Xian, *Hunan, China* 52 D7
Jing'an, *China* 53 C10
Jingbian, *China* 50 F5
Jingchuan, *China* 50 G4
Jingde, *China* 53 B12
Jingdezhen, *China* 53 C11
Jingdong, *China* 52 E3
Jinggu, *China* 52 F3
Jinghai, *China* 50 E9
Jinghong, *China* 52 F3
Jingjiang, *China* 53 A13
Jingle, *China* 50 E6
Jingmen, *China* 53 B9
Jingning, *China* 50 G3
Jingpo Hu, *China* 51 C15
Jingshan, *China* 53 B9
Jingtai, *China* 50 F3
Jingxi, *China* 52 F6
Jingxing, *China* 50 E8
Jingyang, *China* 50 G5
Jingyu, *China* 51 C14
Jingyuan, *China* 50 F3
Jingziguan, *China* 50 H6
Jinhua, *China* 53 C12
Jining, *Nei Mongol Zizhiqu, China* 50 D7
Jining, *Shandong, China* 50 G9
Jinja, *Uganda* 82 B3
Jinjang, *Malaysia* 59 L3
Jinji, *China* 50 F4
Jinjiang, *Fujian, China* 53 E12
Jinjiang, *Yunnan, China* 52 D3
Jinjie, *China* 52 F6
Jinjini, *Ghana* 78 D4
Jinkou, *China* 53 B10
Jinmen Dao, *China* 53 E12
Jinnah Barrage, *Pakistan* 60 C7
Jinning, *China* 52 E4
Jinotega, *Nic.* 116 D2
Jinotepe, *Nic.* 116 D2
Jinping, *Guizhou, China* 52 D7
Jinping, *Yunnan, China* 52 F4
Jinsha, *China* 52 D6
Jinsha Jiang →, *China* 52 C5
Jinshan, *China* 53 B13
Jinshi, *China* 53 C8
Jintan, *China* 53 B12
Jinxi, *Jiangxi, China* 53 D11
Jinxi, *Liaoning, China* 51 D11
Jinxian, *China* 53 C11
Jinxiang, *China* 50 G9
Jinyun, *China* 53 C13
Jinzhai, *China* 53 B10
Jinzhou, *China* 51 D11
Jiparaná →, *Brazil* 125 B5
Jipijapa, *Ecuador* 120 D1
Jiquilpan, *Mexico* 114 D4
Jishan, *China* 50 G6
Jishou, *China* 52 C7
Jishui, *China* 53 D10
Jisr ash Shughūr, *Syria* 64 C3
Jitarning, *Australia* 89 F2
Jitra, *Malaysia* 59 J3
Jiu →, *Romania* 38 F6
Jiudengkou, *China* 50 E4
Jiujiang, *Guangdong, China* 53 F9
Jiujiang, *Jiangxi, China* 53 C10
Jiuling Shan, *China* 53 C10
Jiulong, *China* 52 C3
Jiuquan, *China* 54 C4
Jiutai, *China* 51 B13
Jiuxiangcheng, *China* 50 H8
Jiuxincheng, *China* 50 E8
Jiuyuhang, *China* 53 B12
Jixi, *Anhui, China* 53 B12
Jixi, *Heilongjiang, China* 51 B16
Jiyang, *China* 51 F9
Jīzān, *Si. Arabia* 68 D3
Jize, *China* 50 F8
Jizera →, *Czech.* 20 E4
Jizō-Zaki, *Japan* 49 G6
Joaçaba, *Brazil* 127 B5
Joaíma, *Brazil* 123 E3
João, *Brazil* 122 B1
João Amaro, *Brazil* 123 D3
João Câmara, *Brazil* 122 C4
João Pessoa, *Brazil* 122 C5
João Pinheiro, *Brazil* 123 E2
Joaquim Távora, *Brazil* 123 F2
Joaquín V. González, *Argentina* 126 B3
Jobourg, Nez de, *France* 24 C5
Jódar, *Spain* 29 H1
Jodhpur, *India* 62 F5
Jœuf, *France* 25 C13
Jofane, *Mozam.* 85 C5
Joggins, *Canada* 99 C7
Jogjakarta = Yogyakarta, *Indonesia* 57 G14
Johannesburg, *S. Africa* 85 D4
Johannesburg, *U.S.A.* 113 K9
John Day, *U.S.A.* 110 D4
John Day →, *U.S.A.* 110 D3
John H. Kerr Res., *U.S.A.* 105 G6
John o' Groats, *U.K.* 14 C5
Johnnie, *U.S.A.* 113 J10
John's Ra., *Australia* 90 C1
Johnson, *U.S.A.* 109 G4
Johnson City, *N.Y., U.S.A.* 107 D9
Johnson City, *Tenn., U.S.A.* 105 G4
Johnson City, *Tex., U.S.A.* 109 K5
Johnsonburg, *U.S.A.* 106 E6
Johnsondale, *U.S.A.* 113 K8
Johnson's Crossing, *Canada* 100 A2
Johnston, L., *Australia* 89 F3
Johnston Falls = Mambilima Falls, *Zambia* 83 E2
Johnston I., *Pac. Oc.* 93 F11
Johnstone Str., *Canada* 100 C3
Johnstown, *N.Y., U.S.A.* 107 C10
Johnstown, *Pa., U.S.A.* 106 F6
Johor Baharu, *Malaysia* 59 M4
Joigny, *France* 25 E10
Joinvile, *Brazil* 127 B6
Joinville, *France* 25 D12
Joinville I., *Antarctica* 5 C18
Jojutla, *Mexico* 115 D5
Jokkmokk, *Sweden* 8 C15
Jökulsá á Bru →, *Iceland* 8 D6
Jökulsá á Fjöllum →, *Iceland* 8 C5
Jolfā, *Āzarbājān-e Sharqī, Iran* 64 B5
Jolfā, *Eşfahan, Iran* 65 C6
Joliet, *U.S.A.* 104 E1
Joliette, *Canada* 98 C5
Jolo, *Phil.* 55 J4
Jolon, *U.S.A.* 112 K5
Jomalig, *Phil.* 55 D5
Jombang, *Indonesia* 57 G15
Jomda, *China* 52 B2
Jome, *Indonesia* 57 E7
Jomfruland, *Norway* 11 F3
Jönåker, *Sweden* 11 F10
Jonava, *Lithuania* 40 D4

Jones Sound, *Canada* 4 B3
Jonesboro, *Ark., U.S.A.* 109 H9
Jonesboro, *Ill., U.S.A.* 109 G10
Jonesboro, *La., U.S.A.* 109 J8
Jonesport, *U.S.A.* 99 D6
Jonglei, *Sudan* 77 F3
Jonglei □, *Sudan* 77 F3
Joniskis, *Lithuania* 40 C3
Jönköping, *Sweden* 9 H13
Jönköpings län □, *Sweden* 9 H13
Jonquière, *Canada* 99 C5
Jonsberg, *Sweden* 11 F10
Jonsered, *Sweden* 11 G6
Jonzac, *France* 26 C3
Joplin, *U.S.A.* 109 G7
Jordan, *U.S.A.* 110 C10
Jordan ■, *Asia* 69 E5
Jordan →, *Asia* 69 D4
Jordan Valley, *U.S.A.* 110 E5
Jordânia, *Brazil* 123 E3
Jorge, C., *Chile* 128 D1
Jorhat, *India* 61 F19
Jörn, *Sweden* 8 D16
Jorong, *Indonesia* 56 E4
Jorquera →, *Chile* 126 B2
Jos, *Nigeria* 79 D6
José Batlle y Ordóñez, *Uruguay* 127 C4
José de San Martín, *Argentina* 128 B2
Joseph, *U.S.A.* 110 D5
Joseph, L., *Nfld., Canada* 99 B6
Joseph, L., *Ont., Canada* 106 A5
Joseph Bonaparte G., *Australia* 88 B4
Joseph City, *U.S.A.* 111 J8
Joshua Tree, *U.S.A.* 113 L10
Joshua Tree Nat. Mon., *U.S.A.* 113 M10
Josselin, *France* 24 E4
Jostedal, *Norway* 9 F9
Jotunheimen, *Norway* 10 C2
Jourdanton, *U.S.A.* 109 L5
Joure, *Neths.* 16 C7
Joussard, *Canada* 100 B5
Jovellanos, *Cuba* 116 B3
Joyeuse, *France* 27 D8
Józefów, *Poland* 20 C11
Ju Xian, *China* 51 F10
Juan Aldama, *Mexico* 114 C4
Juan Bautista Alberdi, *Argentina* 126 C3
Juan de Fuca Str., *Canada* 112 B2
Juan de Nova, *Ind. Oc.* 85 B7
Juan Fernández, Arch. de, *Pac. Oc.* 93 L20
Juan José Castelli, *Argentina* 126 B3
Juan L. Lacaze, *Uruguay* 126 C4
Juanjuí, *Peru* 124 B2
Juárez, *Argentina* 126 D4
Juárez, *Mexico* 113 N11
Juárez, Sierra de, *Mexico* 114 A1
Juatinga, Ponta de, *Brazil* 123 F3
Juàzeiro, *Brazil* 122 C3
Juàzeiro do Norte, *Brazil* 122 C4
Jubayl, *Lebanon* 69 A4
Jubbah, *Si. Arabia* 64 D4
Jubbulpore = Jabalpur, *India* 63 H8
Jübek, *Germany* 18 A5
Jubga, *Russia* 43 D8
Jubilee L., *Australia* 89 E4
Juby, C., *Morocco* 72 C2
Júcar →, *Spain* 29 F4
Júcaro, *Cuba* 116 B4
Juchitán, *Mexico* 115 D5
Judaea = Har Yehuda, *Israel* 69 D3
Judenburg, *Austria* 21 H4
Judith →, *U.S.A.* 110 C9
Judith Gap, *U.S.A.* 110 C9
Judith Pt., *U.S.A.* 107 E13
Jufari →, *Brazil* 121 D5
Jugoslavia = Yugoslavia ■, *Europe* 21 M10
Juigalpa, *Nic.* 116 D2
Juillac, *France* 26 C5
Juist, *Germany* 18 B2
Juiz de Fora, *Brazil* 123 F3
Jujuy □, *Argentina* 126 A2
Julesburg, *U.S.A.* 108 E3
Juli, *Peru* 124 D4
Julia Cr. →, *Australia* 90 C3
Julia Creek, *Australia* 90 C3
Juliaca, *Peru* 124 D3
Julian, *U.S.A.* 113 M10
Julian Alps = Julijske Alpe, *Slovenia* 33 B11
Julianakanaal, *Neths.* 17 F7
Julianatop, *Surinam* 121 C6
Julianehåb, *Greenland* 4 C5
Jülich, *Germany* 18 E2
Julierpass, *Switz.* 23 D9
Julijske Alpe, *Slovenia* 33 B11
Julimes, *Mexico* 114 B3
Jullundur, *India* 62 D6
Julu, *China* 50 F8
Jumbo, *Zimbabwe* 83 F3
Jumbo Pk., *U.S.A.* 113 J12
Jumentos Cays, *Bahamas* 117 B4
Jumet, *Belgium* 17 H4
Jumilla, *Spain* 29 G3
Jumla, *Nepal* 63 E10
Jumna = Yamuna →, *India* 63 G9
Junagadh, *India* 62 J4
Junction, *Tex., U.S.A.* 109 K5
Junction, *Utah, U.S.A.* 111 G7
Junction B., *Australia* 90 A1
Junction City, *Kans., U.S.A.* 108 F6
Junction City, *Oreg., U.S.A.* 110 D2
Junction Pt., *Australia* 90 A1
Jundah, *Australia* 90 C3
Jundiaí, *Brazil* 127 A6
Juneau, *U.S.A.* 96 C6
Junee, *Australia* 91 E4
Jungfrau, *Switz.* 22 C5
Junggar Pendi, *China* 54 B3
Junglinster, *Lux.* 17 J8
Jungshahi, *Pakistan* 62 G2
Juniata →, *U.S.A.* 106 F7
Junín, *Argentina* 126 C3
Junín, *Peru* 124 C2
Junín □, *Peru* 124 C3
Junín de los Andes, *Argentina* 128 A2
Jūniyah, *Lebanon* 69 B4
Juntura, *U.S.A.* 110 E4
Juparanã, L., *Brazil* 123 E3
Jupiter →, *Canada* 99 C7
Juquiá, *Brazil* 123 F2
Jur, Nahr el →, *Sudan* 77 F2
Jura, *Europe* 25 F13
Jura, *U.K.* 14 F3
Jura □, *France* 25 F12
Jura, Mts. du, *Europe* 27 B10
Jura, Sd. of, *U.K.* 14 F3
Jura Suisse, *Switz.* 22 B3
Jurado, *Colombia* 120 B2
Jurilovca, *Romania* 38 E11
Jurong, *China* 53 B12
Juruá →, *Brazil* 120 D4
Juruena, *Brazil* 125 C6
Juruena →, *Brazil* 125 B6
Juruti, *Brazil* 121 D6
Jussey, *France* 25 E12
Justo Daract, *Argentina* 126 C2
Jutaí, *Brazil* 124 B4
Jutaí →, *Brazil* 120 D4
Jüterbog, *Germany* 18 D9
Juticalpa, *Honduras* 116 D2
Jutland = Jylland, *Denmark* 11 H3
Jutphaas, *Neths.* 16 D6
Juventud, I. de la, *Cuba* 116 B3
Juvigny-sous-Andaine, *France* 24 D6
Juvisy-sur-Orge, *France* 25 D9
Juwain, *Afghan.* 60 D2
Jūy Zar, *Iran* 64 C5
Juye, *China* 50 G9
Juzennecourt, *France* 25 D11
Jylland, *Denmark* 11 H3
Jyväskylä, *Finland* 8 E18

K

K2, Mt., *Pakistan* 63 B7
Kaap die Goeie Hoop, *S. Africa* 84 E2
Kaap Plateau, *S. Africa* 84 D3
Kaapkruis, *Namibia* 84 C1
Kaapstad = Cape Town, *S. Africa* 84 E2
Kaatsheuvel, *Neths.* 17 E6
Kabaena, *Indonesia* 57 F6
Kabala, *S. Leone* 78 D2
Kabale, *Uganda* 82 C3
Kabalo, *Zaïre* 82 D2
Kabambare, *Zaïre* 82 C2
Kabango, *Zaïre* 83 D2
Kabanjahe, *Indonesia* 56 D1
Kabankalan, *Phil.* 55 G5
Kabara, *Mali* 78 B4
Kabardinka, *Russia* 42 D7
Kabardino-Balkar Republic □, *Russia* 43 E10
Kabare, *Indonesia* 57 E8
Kabarega Falls, *Uganda* 82 B3
Kabasalan, *Phil.* 55 H5
Kabba, *Nigeria* 79 D6
Kabin Buri, *Thailand* 58 F3
Kabinakagami L., *Canada* 98 C3
Kabīr, Zab al →, *Iraq* 64 C4
Kabkabīyah, *Sudan* 73 F9
Kabna, *Sudan* 76 D3
Kabompo, *Zambia* 83 E1
Kabompo →, *Zambia* 81 G4
Kabondo, *Zaïre* 83 D2
Kabongo, *Zaïre* 82 D2
Kabou, *Togo* 79 D5
Kaboudia, Rass, *Tunisia* 75 A7
Kabra, *Australia* 90 C5
Kabūd Gonbad, *Iran* 65 B8
Kabugao, *Phil.* 55 B4
Kābul, *Afghan.* 62 B3
Kābul □, *Afghan.* 60 B6
Kabul →, *Pakistan* 62 C5
Kabunga, *Zaïre* 82 C2
Kaburuang, *Indonesia* 57 D7
Kabushiya, *Sudan* 77 D3
Kabwe, *Zambia* 83 E2
Kačanik, *Serbia, Yug.* 21 N11
Kachanovo, *Russia* 40 C5
Kachchh, Gulf of, *India* 62 H3
Kachchh, Rann of, *India* 62 G4
Kachebera, *Zambia* 83 E3
Kachin □, *Burma* 61 F20
Kachira, L., *Uganda* 82 C3
Kachiry, *Kazakhstan* 44 D8
Kachisi, *Ethiopia* 77 F4
Kachot, *Cambodia* 59 G4
Kackar, *Turkey* 43 F9
Kadan Kyun, *Burma* 56 B1
Kadanai →, *Afghan.* 62 D1
Kadarkút, *Hungary* 21 J7
Kade, *Ghana* 79 D4
Kadi, *India* 62 H5
Kadina, *Australia* 91 E2
Kadınhanı, *Turkey* 66 D5
Kadirli, *Turkey* 66 E7
Kadiyevka, *Ukraine* 43 B8
Kadoka, *U.S.A.* 108 D4
Kadom, *Russia* 41 D13
Kadoma, *Zimbabwe* 83 F2
Kâdugli, *Sudan* 77 E2
Kaduna, *Nigeria* 79 C6
Kaduna □, *Nigeria* 79 C6
Kaédi, *Mauritania* 78 B2
Kaelé, *Cameroon* 79 C7
Kaeng Khoï, *Thailand* 58 E3
Kaesŏng, *N. Korea* 51 F14
Kāf, *Si. Arabia* 64 D3
Kafakumba, *Zaïre* 80 F4
Kafan, *Armenia* 67 D12
Kafanchan, *Nigeria* 79 D6
Kafareti, *Nigeria* 79 C7
Kaffrine, *Senegal* 78 C1
Kafia Kingi, *Sudan* 73 G9
Kafinda, *Zambia* 83 E3
Kafirévs, Ákra, *Greece* 39 L7
Kafr el Dauwâr, *Egypt* 76 H7
Kafr el Sheikh, *Egypt* 76 H7
Kafue, *Zambia* 83 F2
Kafue →, *Zambia* 81 H5
Kafue Flats, *Zambia* 83 F2
Kafue Nat. Park, *Zambia* 83 F2
Kafulwe, *Zambia* 83 D2
Kaga, *Afghan.* 62 B4
Kaga Bandoro, *C.A.R.* 73 G8
Kagan, *Uzbekistan* 44 F7
Kagawa □, *Japan* 49 G6
Kagera □, *Tanzania* 82 C3
Kagera →, *Uganda* 82 C3
Kağizman, *Turkey* 67 C10
Kagoshima, *Japan* 49 J5
Kagoshima □, *Japan* 49 J5
Kagul, *Moldavia* 42 D3
Kahak, *Iran* 65 B6
Kahama, *Tanzania* 82 C3
Kahama □, *Tanzania* 82 C3
Kahang, *Malaysia* 59 L4
Kahayan →, *Indonesia* 56 E4
Kahe, *Tanzania* 82 C4
Kahemba, *Zaïre* 80 F3
Kahil, Djebel bou, *Algeria* 75 B5
Kahniah →, *Canada* 100 B4
Kahnūj, *Iran* 65 E8
Kahoka, *U.S.A.* 108 E9
Kahoolawe, *U.S.A.* 102 H16
Kahramanmaraş, *Turkey* 66 E7
Kahramanmaraş □, *Turkey* 66 E7
Kâhta, *Turkey* 67 E8
Kahuta, *Pakistan* 62 C5
Kai, Kepulauan, *Indonesia* 57 F8
Kai Besar, *Indonesia* 57 F8
Kai Is. = Kai, Kepulauan, *Indonesia* 57 F8
Kai-Ketil, *Indonesia* 57 F8
Kai Xian, *China* 52 B7
Kaiama, *Nigeria* 79 D5
Kaiapoi, *N.Z.* 87 K4
Kaieteur Falls, *Guyana* 121 B6
Kaifeng, *China* 50 G8
Kaihua, *China* 53 C12
Kaikohe, *N.Z.* 87 F4
Kaikoura, *N.Z.* 87 K4
Kaikoura Ra., *N.Z.* 87 J4
Kailahun, *S. Leone* 78 D2
Kaili, *China* 52 D6
Kailu, *China* 51 C11
Kailua, *U.S.A.* 102 J17
Kaimana, *Indonesia* 57 E8
Kaimanawa Mts., *N.Z.* 87 H5
Kaimganj, *India* 63 F8
Kaimur Hills, *India* 63 G9
Kaingaroa Forest, *N.Z.* 87 H6
Kainji Res., *Nigeria* 79 C5
Kaipara Harbour, *N.Z.* 87 G5
Kaiping, *China* 53 F9
Kaipokok B., *Canada* 99 B8
Kairana, *India* 62 E7
Kaironi, *Indonesia* 57 E8
Kairouan, *Tunisia* 75 A7
Kaiserslautern, *Germany* 19 F3
Kaitaia, *N.Z.* 87 F4
Kaitangata, *N.Z.* 87 M2
Kaithal, *India* 62 E7
Kaitu →, *Pakistan* 62 C4
Kaiwi Channel, *U.S.A.* 102 H16
Kaiyang, *China* 52 D6
Kaiyuan, *Liaoning, China* 51 C13
Kaiyuan, *Yunnan, China* 52 F4
Kajaani, *Finland* 8 D19
Kajabbi, *Australia* 90 B3
Kajana = Kajaani, *Finland* 8 D19
Kajang, *Malaysia* 59 L3
Kajiado, *Kenya* 82 C4
Kajiado □, *Kenya* 82 C4
Kajo Kaji, *Sudan* 77 G3
Kaka, *Sudan* 77 E3
Kakabeka Falls, *Canada* 98 C2
Kakamas, *S. Africa* 84 D3
Kakamega, *Kenya* 82 B3
Kakamega □, *Kenya* 82 B3
Kakanj, *Bos.-H., Yug.* 21 L8
Kakanui Mts., *N.Z.* 87 L3
Kake, *Japan* 49 G6
Kakegawa, *Japan* 49 G9
Kakeroma-Jima, *Japan* 49 K4
Kakhib, *Russia* 43 E12
Kakhovka, *Ukraine* 42 C5
Kakhovskoye Vdkhr., *Ukraine* 42 C6
Kakinada, *India* 61 L13
Kakisa →, *Canada* 100 A5
Kakisa L., *Canada* 100 A5
Kakogawa, *Japan* 49 G7
Kakwa →, *Canada* 100 C5
Kāl Gūsheh, *Iran* 65 D8
Kal Safīd, *Iran* 64 C5
Kala, *Nigeria* 79 C7
Kalaa-Kebira, *Tunisia* 75 A7
Kalabagh, *Pakistan* 62 C4
Kalabahi, *Indonesia* 57 F6
Kalabáka, *Greece* 39 K4
Kalabo, *Zambia* 81 G4
Kalach, *Russia* 41 F12
Kalach na Donu, *Russia* 43 B10
Kaladan →, *Burma* 61 J18
Kaladar, *Canada* 106 B7
Kalahari, *Africa* 84 C3
Kalahari Gemsbok Nat. Park, *S. Africa* 84 D3
Kālak, *Iran* 65 E8
Kalakamati, *Botswana* 85 C4
Kalakan, *Russia* 45 D12
Kalakh, *Syria* 64 C3
K'alak'unlun Shank'ou, *Pakistan* 63 B7
Kalam, *Pakistan* 63 B5
Kalama, *U.S.A.* 112 E4
Kalama, *Zaïre* 82 C2
Kalamariá, *Greece* 39 J5
Kalamata, *Greece* 39 M5
Kalamazoo, *U.S.A.* 104 D3
Kalamazoo →, *U.S.A.* 104 D2
Kalambo Falls, *Tanzania* 83 D3
Kálamos, *Greece* 39 L3
Kalannie, *Australia* 89 F2
Kalāntarī, *Iran* 65 C7
Kalao, *Indonesia* 57 F6
Kalaotoa, *Indonesia* 57 F6
Kälarne, *Sweden* 10 B10
Kalárovo, *Czech.* 21 H7
Kalasin, *Thailand* 58 D4
Kalat, *Pakistan* 60 E5
Kalāteh, *Iran* 65 B7
Kalāteh-ye-Ganj, *Iran* 65 E8
Kálathos, *Greece* 39 N11
Kalaus →, *Russia* 43 D11
Kalávrita, *Greece* 39 L5
Kalbarri, *Australia* 89 E1
Kale, *Turkey* 66 E3
Kalecik, *Turkey* 42 F5
Kalegauk Kyun, *Burma* 61 M20
Kalehe, *Zaïre* 82 C2
Kalema, *Tanzania* 82 C3
Kalemie, *Zaïre* 82 D2
Kalety, *Poland* 20 E8
Kalewa, *Burma* 61 H19
Kálfafellsstaður, *Iceland* 8 D6
Kalgan = Zhangjiakou, *China* 50 D8
Kalgoorlie-Boulder, *Australia* 89 F3
Kaliakra, Nos, *Bulgaria* 38 F11
Kalianda, *Indonesia* 56 F3
Kalibo, *Phil.* 55 F5
Kaliganj, *Bangla.* 63 H13
Kalima, *Zaïre* 82 C2
Kalimantan, *Indonesia* 56 E4
Kalimantan Barat □, *Indonesia* 56 E4
Kalimantan Selatan □, *Indonesia* 56 E5
Kalimantan Tengah □, *Indonesia* 56 E4
Kalimantan Timur □, *Indonesia* 56 D5
Kálimnos, *Greece* 39 N10
Kalimpong, *India* 63 F13
Kalinin = Tver, *Russia* 41 C9
Kaliningrad, *Russia* 40 D2
Kaliningrad, *Russia* 41 D10
Kalinkovichi, *Belorussia* 40 E6
Kalinovik, *Bos.-H., Yug.* 21 M8
Kalipetrovo, *Bulgaria* 38 E10
Kaliro, *Uganda* 82 B3
Kalispell, *U.S.A.* 110 B6
Kalisz, *Poland* 20 D8
Kaliua, *Tanzania* 82 D3
Kalix →, *Sweden* 8 D17
Kalka, *India* 62 D7
Kalkan, *Turkey* 66 E3
Kalkaska, *U.S.A.* 104 C3
Kalkfeld, *Namibia* 84 C2
Kalkfontein, *Botswana* 84 C3
Kalkrand, *Namibia* 84 C2
Kållandsö, *Sweden* 11 F7
Kallithéa, *Greece* 39 M6
Kallonís, Kólpos, *Greece* 39 K9
Kallsjön, *Sweden* 8 E12
Kalmalo, *Nigeria* 79 C6
Kalmar, *Sweden* 9 H14
Kalmthout, *Belgium* 17 F4
Kalmyk Republic □, *Russia* 43 C12
Kalmykovo, *Kazakhstan* 43 B14
Kalna, *India* 63 H13
Kalocsa, *Hungary* 21 J9
Kalokhorio, *Cyprus* 37 E12
Kaloko, *Zaïre* 82 D2
Kalol, *Gujarat, India* 62 H5
Kalol, *Gujarat, India* 62 H5
Kalolímnos, *Greece* 39 M10
Kalomo, *Zambia* 83 F2
Kalpi, *India* 63 F8
Kaltbrunn, *Switz.* 23 B8
Kaltungo, *Nigeria* 79 D7
Kalu, *Pakistan* 62 G2
Kaluga, *Russia* 41 D10
Kalulushi, *Zambia* 83 E2
Kalundborg, *Denmark* 11 J5
Kalush, *Ukraine* 40 G4
Kałuszyn, *Poland* 20 C11
Kalutara, *Sri Lanka* 60 R11
Kalyazin, *Russia* 41 C10
Kama, *Zaïre* 82 C2
Kama →, *Russia* 44 D6
Kamachumu, *Tanzania* 82 C3
Kamaishi, *Japan* 48 E10
Kamalia, *Pakistan* 62 D5
Kamapanda, *Zambia* 83 E1
Kamaran, *Yemen* 68 D3
Kamativi, *Zimbabwe* 83 F2
Kamba, *Nigeria* 79 C5
Kambalda, *Australia* 89 F3
Kambar, *Pakistan* 62 F3
Kambia, *S. Leone* 78 D2
Kambolé, *Zambia* 83 D3
Kambos, *Cyprus* 37 D11
Kambove, *Zaïre* 83 E2
Kamchatka, P-ov., *Russia* 45 D16
Kamen, *Russia* 44 D9
Kamen Kashirskiy, *Ukraine* 40 F4
Kamen-Rybolov, *Russia* 48 B6
Kamenets-Podolskiy, *Ukraine* 42 B2
Kamenjak, Rt., *Croatia* 33 D10
Kamenka, *Russia* 41 E14
Kamenka, *Russia* 41 F11
Kamenka, *Ukraine* 42 B5
Kamenka Bugskaya, *Ukraine* 40 F4
Kamenka Dneprovskaya, *Ukraine* 42 C6
Kamenolomini, *Russia* 43 C9
Kamensk-Shakhtinskiy, *Russia* 43 B9
Kamensk Uralskiy, *Russia* 44 D7
Kamenskiy, *Russia* 41 F14
Kamenskiy, *Russia* 43 B9
Kamenskoye, *Russia* 45 C17
Kamenyak, *Bulgaria* 38 F9
Kamenz, *Germany* 18 D10
Kameoka, *Japan* 49 G7
Kamiah, *U.S.A.* 110 C5
Kamień Pomorski, *Poland* 20 B4
Kamieskroon, *S. Africa* 84 E2
Kamilukuak, L., *Canada* 101 A8
Kamina, *Zaïre* 83 D1
Kaminak L., *Canada* 101 A9
Kaminoyama, *Japan* 48 E10
Kamiros, *Greece* 37 C9
Kamituga, *Zaïre* 82 C2
Kamloops, *Canada* 100 C4
Kamnik, *Slovenia* 33 B11
Kamo, *Armenia* 43 F11
Kamo, *Japan* 48 F9
Kamoa Mts., *Guyana* 121 C6
Kamoke, *Pakistan* 62 C6
Kamp →, *Austria* 21 G5
Kampala, *Uganda* 82 B3
Kampar, *Malaysia* 59 K3
Kampar →, *Indonesia* 56 D2
Kampen, *Neths.* 16 C7
Kamperland, *Neths.* 17 E3
Kamphaeng Phet, *Thailand* 58 D2
Kampolombo, L., *Zambia* 83 E2
Kampong To, *Thailand* 59 J3
Kampot, *Cambodia* 59 G5
Kampti, *Burkina Faso* 78 C4
Kampuchea = Cambodia ■, *Asia* 58 F5
Kampung →, *Indonesia* 57 F9
Kampung Air Putih, *Malaysia* 59 K4
Kampung Jerangau, *Malaysia* 59 K4
Kampung Raja, *Malaysia* 59 K4
Kampungbaru = Tolitoli, *Indonesia* 57 D6
Kamrau, Teluk, *Indonesia* 57 E8
Kamsack, *Canada* 101 C8
Kamskoye Ustye, *Russia* 41 D16
Kamuchawie L., *Canada* 101 B8
Kamui-Misaki, *Japan* 48 C10
Kāmyārān, *Iran* 64 C5
Kamyshin, *Russia* 41 F14
Kamyzyak, *Russia* 43 C13
Kanaaupscow, *Canada* 98 B4
Kanab, *U.S.A.* 111 H7
Kanab Creek, *U.S.A.* 111 H7
Kanagi, *Japan* 48 D10

Kanairiktok

Kanairiktok →, *Canada* 99 A7
Kanália, *Greece* 39 K5
Kananga, *Zaïre* 80 F4
Kanarraville, *U.S.A.* 111 H7
Kanash, *Russia* 41 D15
Kanaskat, *U.S.A.* 112 C5
Kanawha →, *U.S.A.* 104 F4
Kanazawa, *Japan* 49 F8
Kanchanaburi, *Thailand* 58 E2
Kanchenjunga, *Nepal* 63 F13
Kanchipuram, *India* 60 N11
Kanda Kanda, *Zaïre* 80 F4
Kandahar = Qandahār, *Afghan.* 60 D4
Kandalaksha, *Russia* 44 C4
Kandalu, *Afghan.* 60 E3
Kandangan, *Indonesia* 56 E5
Kandanos, *Greece* 37 D5
Kander →, *Switz.* 22 C5
Kandersteg, *Switz.* 22 D5
Kandhíla, *Greece* 39 M5
Kandhkot, *Pakistan* 62 E3
Kandhla, *India* 62 E7
Kandi, *Benin* 79 C5
Kandi, *India* 63 H13
Kandıra, *Turkey* 66 C4
Kandla, *India* 62 H4
Kandos, *Australia* 91 E4
Kandy, *Sri Lanka* 60 R12
Kane, *U.S.A.* 106 E6
Kane Basin, *Greenland* 4 B4
Kanevskaya, *Russia* 43 C8
Kanfanar, *Croatia* 33 C10
Kangaba, *Mali* 78 C3
Kangal, *Turkey* 66 D7
Kangān, *Fārs, Iran* 65 E7
Kangān, *Hormozgān, Iran* 65 E8
Kangar, *Malaysia* 59 J3
Kangaroo I., *Australia* 91 F2
Kangavar, *Iran* 65 C6
Kangding, *China* 52 B3
Kăngdong, *N. Korea* 51 E14
Kangean, Kepulauan, *Indonesia* 56 F5
Kangean Is. = Kangean, Kepulauan, *Indonesia* 56 F5
Kanggye, *N. Korea* 51 D14
Kanggyŏng, *S. Korea* 51 F14
Kanghwa, *S. Korea* 51 F14
Kangnŭng, *S. Korea* 51 F15
Kango, *Gabon* 80 D2
Kangping, *China* 51 C12
Kangto, *India* 61 F18
Kani, *Ivory C.* 78 D3
Kaniama, *Zaïre* 82 D1
Kaniapiskau →, *Canada* 99 A6
Kaniapiskau L., *Canada* 99 B6
Kanin, P-ov., *Russia* 44 C5
Kanin Nos, Mys, *Russia* 44 C5
Kaniva, *Australia* 91 F3
Kanjiža, *Serbia, Yug.* 21 J10
Kanjut Sar, *Pakistan* 63 A6
Kankakee, *U.S.A.* 104 E2
Kankakee →, *U.S.A.* 104 E1
Kankan, *Guinea* 78 C3
Kanker, *India* 61 J12
Kankunskiy, *Russia* 45 D13
Kannapolis, *U.S.A.* 105 H5
Kannauj, *India* 63 F8
Kannod, *India* 60 H10
Kano, *Nigeria* 79 C6
Kano □, *Nigeria* 79 C6
Kan'onji, *Japan* 49 G6
Kanoroba, *Ivory C.* 78 D3
Kanowit, *Malaysia* 56 D4
Kanowna, *Australia* 89 F3
Kanoya, *Japan* 49 J5
Kanpetlet, *Burma* 61 J18
Kanpur, *India* 63 F9
Kansas □, *U.S.A.* 108 F6
Kansas →, *U.S.A.* 108 F7
Kansas City, *Kans., U.S.A.* 108 F7
Kansas City, *Mo., U.S.A.* 108 F7
Kansenia, *Zaïre* 83 E2
Kansk, *Russia* 45 D10
Kansŏng, *S. Korea* 51 E15
Kansu = Gansu □, *China* 50 G3
Kantang, *Thailand* 59 J2
Kantché, *Niger* 79 C6
Kanté, *Togo* 79 D5
Kantemirovka, *Russia* 43 B8
Kantharalak, *Thailand* 58 E5
Kantō □, *Japan* 49 F9
Kantō-Sanchi, *Japan* 49 G9
Kanturk, *Ireland* 15 D3
Kanuma, *Japan* 49 F9
Kanus, *Namibia* 84 D2
Kanye, *Botswana* 84 C4
Kanzenze, *Zaïre* 83 E2
Kanzi, Ras, *Tanzania* 82 D4
Kaohsiung = Gaoxiong, *Taiwan* 53 F13
Kaokoveld, *Namibia* 84 B1
Kaolack, *Senegal* 78 C1
Kaoshan, *China* 51 B13
Kapadvanj, *India* 62 H5
Kapanga, *Zaïre* 80 F4
Kapchagai, *Kazakhstan* 44 E8
Kapellen, *Belgium* 17 F4
Kapéllo, Ákra, *Greece* 39 N6
Kapema, *Zaïre* 83 E2
Kapfenberg, *Austria* 21 H5
Kapiri Mposhi, *Zambia* 83 E2
Kapiskau →, *Canada* 98 B3
Kapit, *Malaysia* 56 D4
Kapiti I., *N.Z.* 87 J5
Kaplice, *Czech.* 20 G4
Kapoe, *Thailand* 59 H2
Kapoeta, *Sudan* 77 G3
Kapos →, *Hungary* 21 J8
Kaposvár, *Hungary* 21 J7
Kapowsin, *U.S.A.* 112 D4
Kappeln, *Germany* 18 A5
Kapps, *Namibia* 84 C2
Kaprije, *Croatia* 33 E12
Kaprijke, *Belgium* 17 F3
Kapsan, *N. Korea* 51 D15
Kapsukas = Mariyampol, *Lithuania* 40 D3
Kapuas →, *Indonesia* 56 E3
Kapuas Hulu, Pegunungan, *Malaysia* 56 D4
Kapuas Hulu Ra. = Kapuas Hulu, Pegunungan, *Malaysia* 56 D4
Kapulo, *Zaïre* 83 D2
Kapunda, *Australia* 91 E2
Kapuni, *N.Z.* 87 H5
Kapurthala, *India* 62 D6
Kapuskasing, *Canada* 98 C3
Kapuskasing →, *Canada* 98 C3
Kapustin Yar, *Russia* 43 B11
Kaputar, *Australia* 91 E5
Kaputir, *Kenya* 82 B4
Kapuvár, *Hungary* 21 H7
Kara, *Russia* 44 C7
Kara Bogaz Gol, Zaliv, *Turkmenistan* 44 E6
Kara Kalpak Republic □, *Uzbekistan* 44 E6
Kara Kum = Karakum, Peski, *Turkmenistan* 44 F6
Kara Sea, *Russia* 44 B7
Karabük, *Turkey* 42 F5
Karaburun, *Turkey* 66 D2
Karaburuni, *Albania* 39 J2
Karabutak, *Kazakhstan* 44 E7
Karacabey, *Turkey* 66 C3
Karacasu, *Turkey* 66 E3
Karachala, *Azerbaijan* 43 G13
Karachayevsk, *Russia* 43 E9
Karachev, *Russia* 40 E9
Karachi, *Pakistan* 62 G2
Karad, *India* 60 L9
Karadeniz Boğazı, *Turkey* 66 C3
Karaga, *Ghana* 79 D4
Karaganda, *Kazakhstan* 44 E8
Karagayly, *Kazakhstan* 44 E8
Karaginskiy, Ostrov, *Russia* 45 D17
Karagüney Dağları, *Turkey* 66 C6
Karagwe □, *Tanzania* 82 C3
Karaikal, *India* 60 P11
Karaikkudi, *India* 60 P11
Karaisali, *Turkey* 66 E6
Karaj, *Iran* 65 C6
Karak, *Malaysia* 59 L4
Karakas, *Kazakhstan* 44 E9
Karakitang, *Indonesia* 57 D7
Karaklis, *Armenia* 43 F11
Karakoçan, *Turkey* 67 D9
Karakoram Pass, *Pakistan* 63 B7
Karakoram Ra., *Pakistan* 63 B7
Karakum, Peski, *Turkmenistan* 44 F6
Karakurt, *Turkey* 67 C10
Karalon, *Russia* 45 D12
Karaman, *Turkey* 66 E5
Karamay, *China* 54 B3
Karambu, *Indonesia* 56 E5
Karamea Bight, *N.Z.* 87 J3
Karamoja □, *Uganda* 82 B3
Karamsad, *India* 62 H5
Karand, *Iran* 64 C5
Karanganyar, *Indonesia* 57 G13
Karapınar, *Turkey* 66 E5
Karasburg, *Namibia* 84 D2
Karasino, *Russia* 44 C9
Karasjok, *Norway* 8 B18
Karasu, *Turkey* 66 C4
Karasu →, *Turkey* 67 D8
Karasuk, *Russia* 44 D8
Karasuyama, *Japan* 49 F10
Karataş Burnu, *Turkey* 66 E6
Karatau, *Kazakhstan* 44 E8
Karatau, Khrebet, *Kazakhstan* 44 E7
Karatepe, *Turkey* 66 E7
Karauli, *India* 62 F7
Karavostasi, *Cyprus* 37 D11
Karawang, *Indonesia* 57 G12
Karawanken, *Europe* 20 J4
Karayazı, *Turkey* 67 D10
Karazhal, *Kazakhstan* 44 E8
Karbalā, *Iraq* 64 C5
Kårböle, *Sweden* 10 C9
Karcag, *Hungary* 21 H10
Karcha →, *Pakistan* 63 B7
Karda, *Russia* 45 D11
Kardhámila, *Greece* 39 L9
Kardhítsa, *Greece* 39 K4
Kärdla, *Estonia* 40 B3
Kareeberge, *S. Africa* 84 E3
Kareima, *Sudan* 76 D3
Karelian Republic □, *Russia* 44 C4
Kārevāndar, *Iran* 65 E9
Kargasok, *Russia* 44 D9
Kargat, *Russia* 44 D9
Kargı, *Turkey* 42 F6
Kargil, *India* 63 B7
Karguéri, *Niger* 79 C7
Karia ba Mohammed, *Morocco* 74 B3
Karīān, *Iran* 65 E8
Kariba, *Zimbabwe* 83 F2
Kariba, L., *Zimbabwe* 83 F2
Kariba Dam, *Zimbabwe* 83 F2
Kariba Gorge, *Zambia* 83 F2
Karibib, *Namibia* 84 C2
Karimata, Kepulauan, *Indonesia* 56 E3
Karimata, Selat, *Indonesia* 56 E3
Karimata I. = Karimata, Kepulauan, *Indonesia* 56 E3
Karimnagar, *India* 60 K11
Karimunjawa, Kepulauan, *Indonesia* 56 F4
Karin, *Somali Rep.* 68 E4
Karīt, *Iran* 65 C8
Kariya, *Japan* 49 G8
Karkaralinsk, *Kazakhstan* 44 E8
Karkinitskiy Zaliv, *Ukraine* 42 D5
Karkur Tohl, *Egypt* 76 C2
Karl Libknekht, *Russia* 40 F9
Karl-Marx-Stadt = Chemnitz, *Germany* 18 E8
Karla, L. = Voiviïs Límni, *Greece* 39 K5
Karlobag, *Croatia* 33 D12
Karlovac, *Croatia* 33 C12
Karlovka, *Ukraine* 42 B6
Karlovy Vary, *Czech.* 20 E2
Karlsbad = Karlovy Vary, *Czech.* 20 E2
Karlsborg, *Sweden* 11 F8
Karlshamn, *Sweden* 9 H13
Karlskoga, *Sweden* 9 G13
Karlskrona, *Sweden* 9 H13
Karlsruhe, *Germany* 19 F4
Karlstad, *Sweden* 9 G12
Karlstad, *U.S.A.* 108 A6
Karlstadt, *Germany* 19 F5
Karnal, *India* 62 E7
Karnali →, *Nepal* 63 E9
Karnaphuli Res., *Bangla.* 61 H18
Karnataka □, *India* 60 N10
Karnes City, *U.S.A.* 109 L6
Karnische Alpen, *Europe* 21 J3
Karo, *Mali* 78 C4
Karoi, *Zimbabwe* 83 F2
Karonga, *Malawi* 83 D3
Karoonda, *Australia* 91 F2
Karora, *Sudan* 76 D4
Káros, *Greece* 39 N8
Karousádhes, *Greece* 39 K2
Karpasia □, *Cyprus* 37 D13
Kárpathos, *Greece* 39 P10
Kárpathos, Stenón, *Greece* 39 P10
Karrebæk, *Denmark* 11 J5
Kars, *Turkey* 43 F10
Kars □, *Turkey* 67 C10
Karsakpay, *Kazakhstan* 44 E7
Karsha, *Kazakhstan* 43 B14
Karshi, *Uzbekistan* 44 F7
Karsiyang, *India* 63 F13
Karst, *Croatia* 33 C11
Karsun, *Russia* 41 D15
Kartaly, *Russia* 44 D7
Kartapur, *India* 62 D6
Karthaus, *U.S.A.* 106 E6
Kartuzy, *Poland* 20 A8
Karufa, *Indonesia* 57 E8
Karumba, *Australia* 90 B3
Karumo, *Tanzania* 82 C3
Karumwa, *Tanzania* 82 C3
Karungu, *Kenya* 82 C3
Karup, *Denmark* 11 H3
Karviná, *Czech.* 20 F8
Karwar, *India* 60 M9
Karwi, *India* 63 G9
Kaş, *Turkey* 66 E3
Kasache, *Malawi* 83 E3
Kasai →, *Zaïre* 80 E3
Kasai Oriental □, *Zaïre* 82 C1
Kasaji, *Zaïre* 83 E1
Kasama, *Zambia* 83 E3
Kasan-dong, *N. Korea* 51 D14
Kasane, *Namibia* 84 B3
Kasanga, *Tanzania* 83 D3
Kasangulu, *Zaïre* 80 E3
Kasaragod, *India* 60 N9
Kasba L., *Canada* 101 A8
Kasba Tadla, *Morocco* 74 B3
Kāseh Garān, *Iran* 64 C5
Kasempa, *Zambia* 83 E2
Kasenga, *Zaïre* 83 E2
Kasese, *Uganda* 82 B3
Kasewa, *Zambia* 83 E2
Kasganj, *India* 63 F8
Kashabowie, *Canada* 98 C1
Kāshān, *Iran* 65 C6
Kashi, *China* 54 C2
Kashimbo, *Zaïre* 83 E2
Kashin, *Russia* 41 C10
Kashipur, *India* 63 E8
Kashira, *Russia* 41 D11
Kashiwazaki, *Japan* 49 F9
Kashk-e Kohneh, *Afghan.* 60 B3
Kāshmar, *Iran* 65 C8
Kashmir, *Asia* 63 C7
Kashmor, *Pakistan* 62 E3
Kashpirovka, *Russia* 41 E16
Kashun Noerh = Gaxun Nur, *China* 54 B5
Kasimov, *Russia* 41 D12
Kasinge, *Zaïre* 82 D2
Kasiruta, *Indonesia* 57 E7
Kaskaskia →, *U.S.A.* 108 G10
Kaskattama →, *Canada* 101 B10
Kaskinen, *Finland* 8 E16
Kaskö, *Finland* 8 E16
Kaslo, *Canada* 100 D5
Kasmere L., *Canada* 101 B8
Kasongo, *Zaïre* 82 C2
Kasongo Lunda, *Zaïre* 80 F3
Kásos, *Greece* 39 P9
Kásos, Stenón, *Greece* 39 P9
Kaspi, *Georgia* 43 F11
Kaspiysk, *Russia* 43 E12
Kaspiyskiy, *Russia* 43 D12
Kassab ed Doleib, *Sudan* 77 E3
Kassaba, *Egypt* 76 C2
Kassala, *Sudan* 77 D4
Kassalâ □, *Sudan* 77 D4
Kassel, *Germany* 18 D5
Kassinger, *Sudan* 76 D3
Kassiópi, *Greece* 37 A3
Kassue, *Indonesia* 57 F9
Kastamonu, *Turkey* 66 C5
Kastamonu □, *Turkey* 66 C5
Kastav, *Croatia* 33 C11
Kastélli, *Greece* 37 D5
Kastéllion, *Greece* 37 D7
Kastellou, Ákra, *Greece* 39 P10
Kasterlee, *Belgium* 17 F5
Kastóri, *Greece* 39 M5
Kastoría, *Greece* 39 J4
Kastornoye, *Russia* 41 F11
Kástron, *Greece* 39 K8
Kasulu, *Tanzania* 82 C3
Kasulu □, *Tanzania* 82 C3
Kasumi, *Japan* 49 G7
Kasumkent, *Azerbaijan* 43 F13
Kasungu, *Malawi* 83 E3
Kasur, *Pakistan* 62 D6
Kata, *Russia* 45 D11
Kataba, *Zambia* 83 F2
Katako Kombe, *Zaïre* 82 C1
Katákolon, *Greece* 39 M4
Katale, *Tanzania* 82 C3
Katamatite, *Australia* 91 F4
Katanda, *Kivu, Zaïre* 82 C2
Katanda, *Shaba, Zaïre* 82 D1
Katangi, *India* 60 J11
Katangli, *Russia* 45 D15
Katavi Swamp, *Tanzania* 82 D3
Kateríni, *Greece* 39 J5
Katha, *Burma* 61 G20
Katherîna, Gebel, *Egypt* 76 J8
Katherine, *Australia* 88 B5
Kathiawar, *India* 62 H4
Kathikas, *Cyprus* 37 E11
Kati, *Mali* 78 C3
Katihar, *India* 63 G12
Katima Mulilo, *Zambia* 84 B3
Katimbira, *Malawi* 83 E3
Katingan = Mendawai →, *Indonesia* 56 E4
Katiola, *Ivory C.* 78 D3
Katmandu, *Nepal* 63 F11
Kato Akhaïa, *Greece* 39 L4
Káto Arkhánai, *Greece* 37 D7
Káto Khorió, *Greece* 37 D7
Kato Pyrgos, *Cyprus* 37 D11
Káto Stavros, *Greece* 39 J6
Katompe, *Zaïre* 82 D2
Katonga →, *Uganda* 82 B3
Katoomba, *Australia* 91 E5
Katowice, *Poland* 20 E9
Katrine, L., *U.K.* 14 E4
Katrineholm, *Sweden* 10 E10
Katsepe, *Madag.* 85 B8
Katsina, *Nigeria* 79 C6
Katsina □, *Nigeria* 79 C6
Katsina Ala →, *Nigeria* 79 D6
Katsumoto, *Japan* 49 H4
Katsuura, *Japan* 49 G10
Katsuyama, *Japan* 49 F8
Kattaviá, *Greece* 37 D9
Kattegatt, *Denmark* 11 H5
Katumba, *Zaïre* 82 D2
Katungu, *Kenya* 82 C5
Katwa, *India* 63 H13
Katwijk-aan-Zee, *Neths.* 16 D4
Kauai, *U.S.A.* 102 H15
Kauai Chan., *U.S.A.* 102 H15
Kaub, *Germany* 19 E3
Kaufbeuren, *Germany* 19 H6
Kaufman, *U.S.A.* 109 J6
Kaukauna, *U.S.A.* 104 C1
Kaukauveld, *Namibia* 84 C3
Kaukonen, *Finland* 8 C18
Kauliranta, *Finland* 8 C17
Kaunas, *Lithuania* 40 D3
Kaura Namoda, *Nigeria* 79 C6
Kautokeino, *Norway* 8 B17
Kavacha, *Russia* 45 C17
Kavadarci, *Macedonia, Yug.* 39 H5
Kavaja, *Albania* 39 H2
Kavak, *Turkey* 66 C7
Kavalerovo, *Russia* 48 B7
Kavali, *India* 60 M12
Kavála, *Greece* 39 J7
Kavār, *Iran* 65 D7
Kavarna, *Bulgaria* 38 F11
Kavos, *Greece* 37 B4
Kaw, *Fr. Guiana* 121 C7
Kawa, *Sudan* 77 E3
Kawagama L., *Canada* 106 A6
Kawagoe, *Japan* 49 G9
Kawaguchi, *Japan* 49 G9
Kawaihae, *U.S.A.* 102 H17
Kawambwa, *Zambia* 83 D2
Kawanoe, *Japan* 49 G6
Kawardha, *India* 63 J9
Kawasaki, *Japan* 49 G9
Kawene, *Canada* 98 C1
Kawerau, *N.Z.* 87 H6
Kawhia Harbour, *N.Z.* 87 H5
Kawio, Kepulauan, *Indonesia* 57 D7
Kawnro, *Burma* 61 H21
Kawthoolei = Kawthule □, *Burma* 61 L20
Kawthule □, *Burma* 61 L20
Kaya, *Burkina Faso* 79 C4
Kayah □, *Burma* 61 K20
Kayan →, *Indonesia* 56 D5
Kaycee, *U.S.A.* 110 E10
Kayeli, *Indonesia* 57 E7
Kayenta, *U.S.A.* 111 H8
Kayes, *Mali* 78 C2
Kayima, *S. Leone* 78 D2
Kayl, *Lux.* 17 K8
Kayoa, *Indonesia* 57 D7
Kayomba, *Zambia* 83 E1
Kayoro, *Ghana* 79 C4
Kayrunnera, *Australia* 91 E3
Kaysatskoye, *Russia* 43 B12
Kayseri, *Turkey* 66 D6
Kayseri □, *Turkey* 66 D6
Kaysville, *U.S.A.* 110 F8
Kayuagung, *Indonesia* 56 E2
Kazachinskoye, *Russia* 45 D11
Kazachye, *Russia* 45 B14
Kazakhstan ■, *Asia* 44 E7
Kazan, *Russia* 41 D16
Kazan-Rettō, *Pac. Oc.* 92 E6
Kazanlúk, *Bulgaria* 38 G8
Kazanskaya, *Russia* 43 B9
Kazatin, *Ukraine* 42 B3
Kazbek, *Georgia* 43 E11
Kāzerūn, *Iran* 65 D6
Kazi Magomed, *Azerbaijan* 43 F13
Kazincbarcika, *Hungary* 21 G10
Kaztalovka, *Kazakhstan* 43 B13
Kazumba, *Zaïre* 80 F4
Kazuno, *Japan* 48 D10
Kazym →, *Russia* 44 C7
Kcynia, *Poland* 20 C7
Ké-Macina, *Mali* 78 C3
Kéa, *Greece* 39 M7
Keams Canyon, *U.S.A.* 111 J8
Kearney, *U.S.A.* 108 E5
Keban, *Turkey* 67 D8
Keban Baraji, *Turkey* 67 D8
Kébi, *Ivory C.* 78 D3
Kebili, *Tunisia* 75 B6
Kebnekaise, *Sweden* 8 C15
Kebri Dehar, *Ethiopia* 68 F3
Kebumen, *Indonesia* 57 G13
Kecel, *Hungary* 21 J9
Kechika →, *Canada* 100 B3
Kecskemét, *Hungary* 21 J9
Kedada, *Ethiopia* 77 F4
Kedainiai, *Lithuania* 40 D4
Kedgwick, *Canada* 99 C6
Kédhros Óros, *Greece* 37 D6
Kedia Hill, *Botswana* 84 C3
Kediri, *Indonesia* 57 G15
Kédougou, *Senegal* 78 C2
Kedzierzyn, *Poland* 20 E8
Keeler, *U.S.A.* 112 J9
Keeley L., *Canada* 101 C7
Keeling Is. = Cocos Is., *Ind. Oc.* 92 J1
Keene, *Calif., U.S.A.* 113 K8
Keene, *N.H., U.S.A.* 107 D12
Keeper Hill, *Ireland* 15 D3
Keer-Weer, C., *Australia* 90 A3
Keerbergen, *Belgium* 17 F5
Keeseville, *U.S.A.* 107 B11
Keeten Mastgat, *Neths.* 17 E4
Keetmanshoop, *Namibia* 84 D2
Keewatin, *U.S.A.* 108 B8
Keewatin □, *Canada* 101 A9
Keewatin →, *Canada* 101 B8
Kefa □, *Ethiopia* 77 F4
Kefallinía, *Greece* 39 L3
Kefamenanu, *Indonesia* 57 F6
Keffi, *Nigeria* 79 D6
Kefken, *Turkey* 66 C4
Keflavík, *Iceland* 8 D2
Keg River, *Canada* 100 B5
Kegaska, *Canada* 99 B7
Kehl, *Germany* 19 G3
Keighley, *U.K.* 12 D6
Keimoes, *S. Africa* 84 D3
Keita, *Niger* 79 C6
Keith, *Australia* 91 F3
Keith, *U.K.* 14 D6
Keith Arm, *Canada* 96 B7
Kejser Franz Joseph Fjord = Kong Franz Joseph Fd., *Greenland* 4 B6
Kekri, *India* 62 G6
Kël, *Russia* 45 C13
Kelamet, *Ethiopia* 77 D4
Kelan, *China* 50 E6

King I.

Kelang, *Malaysia* 59 L3
Kelantan →, *Malaysia* 59 J4
Kelheim, *Germany* 19 G7
Kelibia, *Tunisia* 75 A7
Kelkit, *Turkey* 67 C8
Kelkit →, *Turkey* 66 C7
Kellé, *Congo* 80 E2
Keller, *U.S.A.* 110 B4
Kellerberrin, *Australia* 89 F2
Kellett, C., *Canada* 4 B1
Kelleys I., *U.S.A.* 106 E2
Kellogg, *U.S.A.* 110 C5
Kelloselkä, *Finland* 8 C20
Kells = Ceanannus Mor, *Ireland* 15 C5
Kélo, *Chad* 73 G8
Kelokedhara, *Cyprus* 37 E11
Kelowna, *Canada* 100 D5
Kelsey Bay, *Canada* 100 C3
Kelseyville, *U.S.A.* 112 G4
Kelso, *N.Z.* 87 L2
Kelso, *U.K.* 14 F6
Kelso, *U.S.A.* 112 D4
Keluang, *Malaysia* 59 L4
Kelvington, *Canada* 101 C8
Kem, *Russia* 44 C4
Kem-Kem, *Morocco* 74 B4
Kema, *Indonesia* 57 D7
Kemah, *Turkey* 67 D8
Kemaliye, *Turkey* 67 D8
Kemano, *Canada* 100 C3
Kemasik, *Malaysia* 59 K4
Kembolcha, *Ethiopia* 77 E4
Kemer, *Turkey* 66 E4
Kemerovo, *Russia* 44 D9
Kemi, *Finland* 8 D18
Kemi älv = Kemijoki →, *Finland* 8 D18
Kemijärvi, *Finland* 8 C19
Kemijoki →, *Finland* 8 D18
Kemmel, *Belgium* 17 G1
Kemmerer, *U.S.A.* 110 F8
Kemmuna = Comino, *Malta* 37 C1
Kemp L., *U.S.A.* 109 J5
Kemp Land, *Antarctica* 5 C5
Kempsey, *Australia* 91 E5
Kempt, L., *Canada* 98 C5
Kempten, *Germany* 19 H6
Kemptville, *Canada* 98 C4
Kenadsa, *Algeria* 75 B4
Kendal, *Indonesia* 56 F4
Kendal, *U.K.* 12 C5
Kendall, *Australia* 91 E5
Kendall →, *Australia* 90 A3
Kendallville, *U.S.A.* 104 E3
Kendari, *Indonesia* 57 E6
Kendawangan, *Indonesia* 56 E4
Kende, *Nigeria* 79 C5
Kendenup, *Australia* 89 F2
Kendrapara, *India* 61 J15
Kendrew, *S. Africa* 84 E3
Kendrick, *U.S.A.* 110 C5
Kene Thao, *Laos* 58 D3
Kenedy, *U.S.A.* 109 L6
Kenema, *S. Leone* 78 D2
Keng Kok, *Laos* 58 D5
Keng Tawng, *Burma* 61 J21
Keng Tung, *Burma* 61 J21
Kenge, *Zaïre* 80 E3
Kengeja, *Tanzania* 82 D4
Kenhardt, *S. Africa* 84 D3
Kenitra, *Morocco* 74 B3
Kenli, *China* 51 F10
Kenmare, *Ireland* 15 E2
Kenmare, *U.S.A.* 108 A3
Kenmare →, *Ireland* 15 E2
Kennebec, *U.S.A.* 108 D5
Kennedy, *Zimbabwe* 83 F2
Kennedy Ra., *Australia* 89 D2
Kennedy Taungdeik, *Burma* 61 H18
Kennet →, *U.K.* 13 F7
Kenneth Ra., *Australia* 88 D2
Kennett, *U.S.A.* 109 G9
Kennewick, *U.S.A.* 110 C4
Kénogami, *Canada* 99 C5
Kenogami →, *Canada* 98 B3
Kenora, *Canada* 101 D10
Kenosha, *U.S.A.* 104 D2
Kensington, *Canada* 99 C7
Kensington, *U.S.A.* 108 F5
Kensington Downs, *Australia* 90 C3
Kent, *Ohio, U.S.A.* 106 E3
Kent, *Oreg., U.S.A.* 110 D3
Kent, *Tex., U.S.A.* 109 K2
Kent, *Wash., U.S.A.* 112 C4
Kent □, *U.K.* 13 F8
Kent Group, *Australia* 90 F4
Kent Pen., *Canada* 96 B9
Kentau, *Kazakhstan* 44 E7
Kentland, *U.S.A.* 104 E2
Kenton, *U.S.A.* 104 E4
Kentucky □, *U.S.A.* 104 G3
Kentucky →, *U.S.A.* 104 F3
Kentucky L., *U.S.A.* 105 G2
Kentville, *Canada* 99 C7
Kentwood, *U.S.A.* 109 K9
Kentwood, *La., U.S.A.* 109 K9
Kenya ■, *Africa* 82 B4
Kenya, Mt., *Kenya* 82 C4
Keo Neua, Deo, *Vietnam* 58 C5
Keokuk, *U.S.A.* 108 E9
Kep, *Cambodia* 59 G5
Kep, *Vietnam* 58 B6
Kepi, *Indonesia* 57 F9
Kępno, *Poland* 20 D7
Kepsut, *Turkey* 66 D3
Kerala □, *India* 60 P10
Kerama-Rettō, *Japan* 49 L3
Keran, *Pakistan* 63 B5
Kerang, *Australia* 91 F3
Keraudren, C., *Australia* 88 C2
Kerch, *Ukraine* 42 D7
Kerchenskiy Proliv, *Black Sea* 42 D7
Kerchoual, *Mali* 79 B5
Kerempe Burnu, *Turkey* 66 B5
Keren, *Ethiopia* 77 D4
Kerewan, *Gambia* 78 C1
Kerguelen, *Ind. Oc.* 3 G13
Keri Kera, *Sudan* 77 E3
Kericho, *Kenya* 82 C4
Kericho □, *Kenya* 82 C4
Kerinci, *Indonesia* 56 E2
Kerkdriel, *Neths.* 16 E6
Kerkenna, Is., *Tunisia* 75 B7
Kerki, *Turkmenistan* 44 F7
Kérkira, *Greece* 37 A3
Kerkrade, *Neths.* 17 G8
Kerma, *Sudan* 76 D3
Kermadec Is., *Pac. Oc.* 92 K10
Kermadec Trench, *Pac. Oc.* 92 L10
Kermān, *Iran* 65 D8
Kerman, *U.S.A.* 112 J6
Kermān □, *Iran* 65 D8
Kermānshāh = Bākhtarān, *Iran* 64 C5
Kerme Körfezi, *Turkey* 66 E2
Kermit, *U.S.A.* 109 K3
Kern →, *U.S.A.* 113 K7
Kerns, *Switz.* 23 C6
Kernville, *U.S.A.* 113 K8
Keroh, *Malaysia* 59 K3
Kerrobert, *Canada* 101 C7
Kerrville, *U.S.A.* 109 K5
Kerry □, *Ireland* 15 D2
Kerry Hd., *Ireland* 15 D2
Kersa, *Ethiopia* 77 F5
Kerteminde, *Denmark* 11 J4
Kertosono, *Indonesia* 57 G15
Kerulen →, *Asia* 54 B6
Kerzaz, *Algeria* 75 C4
Kerzers, *Switz.* 22 C4
Kesagami →, *Canada* 98 B4
Kesagami L., *Canada* 98 B3
Keşan, *Turkey* 66 C2
Kesch, Piz, *Switz.* 23 C9
Kesennuma, *Japan* 48 E10
Keshit, *Iran* 65 D8
Keşiş Dağ, *Turkey* 67 D8
Keski-Suomen lääni □, *Finland* 8 E18
Keskin, *Turkey* 66 D5
Kessel, *Belgium* 17 F5
Kessel, *Neths.* 17 F8
Kessel-Lo, *Belgium* 17 G5
Kestell, *S. Africa* 85 D4
Kestenga, *Russia* 44 C4
Kesteren, *Neths.* 16 E7
Keswick, *U.K.* 12 C4
Keszthely, *Hungary* 21 J7
Ket →, *Russia* 44 D9
Keta, *Ghana* 79 D5
Ketapang, *Indonesia* 56 E4
Ketchikan, *U.S.A.* 96 C6
Ketchum, *U.S.A.* 110 E6
Kete Krachi, *Ghana* 79 D4
Ketef, Khalîg Umm el, *Egypt* 76 C4
Ketelmeer, *Neths.* 16 C7
Keti Bandar, *Pakistan* 62 G2
Ketri, *India* 62 E6
Kętrzyn, *Poland* 20 A11
Kettering, *U.K.* 13 E7
Kettle →, *Canada* 101 B11
Kettle Falls, *U.S.A.* 110 B4
Kettleman City, *U.S.A.* 112 J7
Kevin, *U.S.A.* 110 B8
Kewanee, *U.S.A.* 108 E10
Kewaunee, *U.S.A.* 104 C2
Keweenaw B., *U.S.A.* 104 B1
Keweenaw Pen., *U.S.A.* 104 B2
Keweenaw Pt., *U.S.A.* 104 B2
Key Harbour, *Canada* 98 C3
Key West, *U.S.A.* 103 F10
Keyser, *U.S.A.* 104 F6
Keystone, *U.S.A.* 108 D3
Kezhma, *Russia* 45 D11
Kežmarok, *Czech.* 20 F10
Khabarovo, *Russia* 44 C7
Khabarovsk, *Russia* 45 E14
Khabr, *Iran* 65 D8
Khābūr →, *Syria* 64 C4
Khachmas, *Azerbaijan* 43 F13
Khachrod, *India* 62 H6
Khadari, W. el →, *Sudan* 77 E2
Khadro, *Pakistan* 62 F3
Khadyzhensk, *Russia* 43 D8
Khadzhilyangar, *India* 63 B8
Khagaria, *India* 63 G12
Khaipur, *Bahawalpur, Pakistan* 62 E5
Khaipur, *Hyderabad, Pakistan* 62 F3
Khair, *India* 62 F7
Khairabad, *India* 63 F9
Khairagarh, *India* 63 J9
Khairpur, *Pakistan* 60 F6
Khakhea, *Botswana* 84 C3
Khalafābād, *Iran* 65 D6
Khalfallah, *Algeria* 75 B5
Khalilabad, *India* 63 F10
Khalīlī, *Iran* 65 E7
Khalkhāl, *Iran* 65 B6
Khálki, *Greece* 39 K5
Khalkís, *Greece* 39 L6
Khalmer-Sede = Tazovskiy, *Russia* 44 C8
Khalmer Yu, *Russia* 44 C7
Khalturin, *Russia* 41 B16
Khalūf, *Oman* 68 C6
Kham Keut, *Laos* 58 C5
Khamas Country, *Botswana* 84 C4
Khambat, G. of, *India* 62 J5
Khambhaliya, *India* 62 H3
Khambhat, *India* 62 H5
Khamilonísion, *Greece* 39 P9
Khamīr, *Iran* 65 E7
Khamir, *Yemen* 68 D3
Khamsa, *Egypt* 69 E1
Khān Abū Shāmat, *Syria* 69 B5
Khān Azād, *Iraq* 64 C5
Khān Mujiddah, *Iraq* 64 C4
Khān Shaykhūn, *Syria* 64 C3
Khān Yūnis, *Egypt* 69 D3
Khānaqīn, *Iraq* 64 C5
Khānbāghī, *Iran* 65 B7
Khandrá, *Greece* 39 P9
Khandwa, *India* 60 J10
Khandyga, *Russia* 45 C14
Khāneh, *Iran* 64 B5
Khanewal, *Pakistan* 62 D4
Khanh Duong, *Vietnam* 58 F7
Khaniá, *Greece* 37 D6
Khaniá □, *Greece* 37 D6
Khaníon, Kólpos, *Greece* 37 D5
Khanka, Ozero, *Asia* 45 E14
Khankendy, *Azerbaijan* 67 D12
Khanna, *India* 62 D7
Khanpur, *Pakistan* 62 E4
Khanty-Mansiysk, *Russia* 44 C7
Khapalu, *Pakistan* 63 B7
Khapcheranga, *Russia* 45 E12
Kharagpur, *India* 63 H12
Khárakas, *Greece* 37 D7
Kharan Kalat, *Pakistan* 60 E4
Kharānaq, *Iran* 65 C7
Kharda, *India* 60 K9
Khardung La, *India* 63 B7
Khârga, El Wâhât el, *Egypt* 76 B3
Khargon, *India* 60 J9
Kharit, Wadi el →, *Egypt* 76 C3
Khārk, Jazireh, *Iran* 65 D6
Kharkov, *Ukraine* 42 B7
Kharmanli, *Bulgaria* 39 H8
Kharovsk, *Russia* 41 B12
Khartoum = El Khartûm, *Sudan* 77 D3
Khasan, *Russia* 48 C5
Khasavyurt, *Russia* 43 E12
Khāsh, *Iran* 60 E2
Khashm el Girba, *Sudan* 77 E4
Khashuri, *Georgia* 43 F10
Khaskovo, *Bulgaria* 39 H8
Khatanga, *Russia* 45 B11
Khatanga →, *Russia* 45 B11
Khatauli, *India* 62 E7
Khātūnābād, *Iran* 65 C6
Khatyrka, *Russia* 45 C18
Khaybar, Harrat, *Si. Arabia* 64 E4
Khāzimiyah, *Iraq* 64 C4
Khazzân Jabal el Awliyâ, *Sudan* 77 D3
Khe Bo, *Vietnam* 58 C5
Khe Long, *Vietnam* 58 B5
Khed Brahma, *India* 60 G8
Khekra, *India* 62 E7
Khemarak Phouminville, *Cambodia* 59 G4
Khemelnik, *Ukraine* 42 B2
Khemis Miliana, *Algeria* 75 A5
Khemissèt, *Morocco* 74 B3
Khemmarat, *Thailand* 58 D5
Khenāmān, *Iran* 65 D8
Khenchela, *Algeria* 75 A6
Khenifra, *Morocco* 74 B3
Kherrata, *Algeria* 75 A6
Kherson, *Ukraine* 42 C5
Khersónisos Akrotíri, *Greece* 37 D6
Kheta →, *Russia* 45 B11
Khilok, *Russia* 45 D12
Khimki, *Russia* 41 D10
Khíos, *Greece* 39 L9
Khirbat Qanāfār, *Lebanon* 69 B4
Khiuma = Hiiumaa, *Estonia* 40 B3
Khiva, *Uzbekistan* 44 E7
Khīyāv, *Iran* 64 B5
Khlong Khlung, *Thailand* 58 D2
Khmelnitskiy, *Ukraine* 40 G5
Khmer Rep. = Cambodia ■, *Asia* 58 F5
Khoai, Hon, *Vietnam* 59 H5
Khodzent, *Tajikistan* 44 E7
Khojak P., *Afghan.* 60 D5
Khok Kloi, *Thailand* 59 H2
Khok Pho, *Thailand* 59 J3
Khokholskiy, *Russia* 41 F11
Kholm, *Russia* 40 C7
Kholmsk, *Russia* 45 E15
Khomas Hochland, *Namibia* 84 C2
Khomayn, *Iran* 65 C6
Khon Kaen, *Thailand* 58 D4
Khong, *Laos* 58 E5
Khong Sedone, *Laos* 58 E5
Khonu, *Russia* 45 C15
Khoper →, *Russia* 41 G13
Khor el 'Atash, *Sudan* 77 E3
Khóra, *Greece* 39 M4
Khóra Sfakíon, *Greece* 37 D6
Khorāsān □, *Iran* 65 C8
Khorat = Nakhon Ratchasima, *Thailand* 58 E4
Khorat, Cao Nguyen, *Thailand* 58 E4
Khorb el Ethel, *Algeria* 74 C3
Khorixas, *Namibia* 84 C1
Khorog, *Tajikistan* 44 F8
Khorol, *Ukraine* 42 B5
Khorramābād, *Khorāsān, Iran* 65 C8
Khorramābād, *Lorestān, Iran* 65 C6
Khorrāmshahr, *Iran* 65 D6
Khosravī, *Iran* 65 D6
Khosrowābād, *Khuzestān, Iran* 65 D6
Khosrowābād, *Kordestān, Iran* 64 C5
Khosūyeh, *Iran* 65 D7
Khotin, *Ukraine* 42 B2
Khouribga, *Morocco* 74 B3
Khowai, *Bangla.* 61 G17
Khoyniki, *Belorussia* 40 F6
Khrami →, *Azerbaijan* 43 F11
Khrenovoye, *Russia* 41 F12
Khristianá, *Greece* 39 N8
Khrysokhou B., *Cyprus* 37 D11
Khu Khan, *Thailand* 58 E5
Khuff, *Si. Arabia* 64 E5
Khūgīānī, *Afghan.* 62 D1
Khulna, *Bangla.* 61 H16
Khulna □, *Bangla.* 61 H16
Khulo, *Georgia* 43 F10
Khumago, *Botswana* 84 C3
Khūnsorkh, *Iran* 65 E8
Khunzakh, *Russia* 43 E12
Khūr, *Iran* 65 C8
Khurai, *India* 62 G8
Khurayş, *Si. Arabia* 65 E6
Khūrīyā Mūrīyā, Jazā 'ir, *Oman* 68 D6
Khurja, *India* 62 E7
Khūsf, *Iran* 65 C8
Khush, *Afghan.* 60 C3
Khushab, *Pakistan* 62 C5
Khuzdar, *Pakistan* 62 F2
Khūzestān □, *Iran* 65 D6
Khvājeh, *Iran* 64 B5
Khvalynsk, *Russia* 41 E16
Khvānsār, *Iran* 65 D7
Khvatovka, *Russia* 41 E15
Khvor, *Iran* 65 C7
Khvorgū, *Iran* 65 E8
Khvormūj, *Iran* 65 D6
Khvoy, *Iran* 64 B5
Khvoynaya, *Russia* 40 B9
Khyber Pass, *Afghan.* 62 B4
Kiabukwa, *Zaïre* 83 D1
Kiama, *Australia* 91 E5
Kiamba, *Phil.* 55 H6
Kiambi, *Zaïre* 82 D2
Kiambu, *Kenya* 82 C4
Kiangsi = Jiangxi □, *China* 53 D10
Kiangsu = Jiangsu □, *China* 51 H10
Kibæk, *Denmark* 11 H2
Kibanga Port, *Uganda* 82 B3
Kibangou, *Congo* 80 E2
Kibara, *Tanzania* 82 C3
Kibare, Mts., *Zaïre* 82 D2
Kibombo, *Zaïre* 82 C2
Kibondo, *Tanzania* 82 C3
Kibondo □, *Tanzania* 82 C3
Kibumbu, *Burundi* 82 C2
Kibungu, *Rwanda* 82 C3
Kibuye, *Burundi* 82 C2
Kibuye, *Rwanda* 82 C2
Kibwesa, *Tanzania* 82 D2
Kibwezi, *Kenya* 82 C4
Kichiga, *Russia* 45 D17
Kicking Horse Pass, *Canada* 100 C5
Kidal, *Mali* 79 B5
Kidderminster, *U.K.* 13 E5
Kidete, *Tanzania* 82 D4
Kidira, *Senegal* 78 C2
Kidnappers, C., *N.Z.* 87 H6
Kidston, *Australia* 90 B3
Kidugallo, *Tanzania* 82 D4
Kiel, *Germany* 18 A6
Kiel Kanal = Nord-Ostsee Kanal, *Germany* 18 A5
Kielce, *Poland* 20 E10
Kieldrecht, *Belgium* 17 F4
Kieler Bucht, *Germany* 18 A6
Kien Binh, *Vietnam* 59 H5
Kien Tan, *Vietnam* 59 G5
Kienge, *Zaïre* 83 E2
Kiessé, *Niger* 79 C5
Kiev = Kiyev, *Ukraine* 40 F7
Kiffa, *Mauritania* 78 B2
Kifisiá, *Greece* 39 L6
Kifissós →, *Greece* 39 L6
Kifrī, *Iraq* 64 C5
Kigali, *Rwanda* 82 C3
Kigarama, *Tanzania* 82 C3
Kigoma □, *Tanzania* 82 D2
Kigoma-Ujiji, *Tanzania* 82 C2
Kigomasha, Ras, *Tanzania* 82 C4
Kihee, *Australia* 91 D3
Kii-Sanchi, *Japan* 49 G7
Kii-Suidō, *Japan* 49 H7
Kikaiga-Shima, *Japan* 49 K4
Kikinda, *Serbia, Yug.* 21 K10
Kikládhes, *Greece* 39 M7
Kikwit, *Zaïre* 80 E3
Kílalki, *Greece* 39 N10
Kilauea Crater, *U.S.A.* 102 J17
Kilchberg, *Switz.* 23 B7
Kilcoy, *Australia* 91 D5
Kildare, *Ireland* 15 C5
Kildare □, *Ireland* 15 C5
Kilgore, *U.S.A.* 109 J7
Kilifi, *Kenya* 82 C4
Kilifi □, *Kenya* 82 C4
Kilimanjaro, *Tanzania* 82 C4
Kilimanjaro □, *Tanzania* 82 C4
Kilindini, *Kenya* 82 C4
Kilis, *Turkey* 66 E7
Kiliya, *Ukraine* 42 D3
Kilju, *N. Korea* 51 D15
Kilkee, *Ireland* 15 D2
Kilkenny, *Ireland* 15 D4
Kilkenny □, *Ireland* 15 D4
Kilkieran B., *Ireland* 15 C2
Kilkís, *Greece* 39 J5
Killala, *Ireland* 15 B2
Killala B., *Ireland* 15 B2
Killaloe, *Ireland* 15 D3
Killaloe Sta., *Canada* 106 A7
Killam, *Canada* 100 C6
Killarney, *Australia* 91 D5
Killarney, *Canada* 98 C3
Killarney, *Ireland* 15 D2
Killarney, Lakes of, *Ireland* 15 E2
Killary Harbour, *Ireland* 15 C2
Killdeer, *Canada* 101 D7
Killdeer, *U.S.A.* 108 B3
Killeen, *U.S.A.* 109 K6
Killiecrankie, Pass of, *U.K.* 14 E5
Killin, *U.K.* 14 E4
Killíni, *Ilía, Greece* 39 M4
Killíni, *Korinthía, Greece* 39 M5
Killybegs, *Ireland* 15 B3
Kilmarnock, *U.K.* 14 F4
Kilmez, *Russia* 41 C17
Kilmez →, *Russia* 41 C17
Kilmore, *Australia* 91 F3
Kilondo, *Tanzania* 83 D3
Kilosa, *Tanzania* 82 D4
Kilosa □, *Tanzania* 82 D4
Kilrush, *Ireland* 15 D2
Kilwa □, *Tanzania* 83 D4
Kilwa Kisiwani, *Tanzania* 83 D4
Kilwa Kivinje, *Tanzania* 83 D4
Kilwa Masoko, *Tanzania* 83 D4
Kim, *U.S.A.* 109 G3
Kimaam, *Indonesia* 57 F9
Kimamba, *Tanzania* 82 D4
Kimba, *Australia* 91 E2
Kimball, *Nebr., U.S.A.* 108 E3
Kimball, *S. Dak., U.S.A.* 108 D5
Kimberley, *Canada* 100 D5
Kimberley, *S. Africa* 84 D3
Kimberley Downs, *Australia* 88 C3
Kimberly, *U.S.A.* 110 E6
Kimchaek, *N. Korea* 51 D15
Kimchŏn, *S. Korea* 51 F15
Kími, *Greece* 39 L7
Kimje, *S. Korea* 51 G14
Kímolos, *Greece* 39 N7
Kimovsk, *Russia* 41 D11
Kimparana, *Mali* 78 C4
Kimry, *Russia* 41 C10
Kimsquit, *Canada* 100 C3
Kimstad, *Sweden* 11 F9
Kinabalu, *Malaysia* 56 C5
Kínaros, *Greece* 39 N9
Kinaskan L., *Canada* 100 B2
Kinbasket L., *Canada* 100 C5
Kincaid, *Canada* 101 D7
Kincardine, *Canada* 98 D3
Kinda, *Zaïre* 83 D2
Kinder Scout, *U.K.* 12 D6
Kindersley, *Canada* 101 C7
Kindia, *Guinea* 78 C2
Kindu, *Zaïre* 82 C2
Kinel, *Russia* 41 E17
Kineshma, *Russia* 41 C13
Kinesi, *Tanzania* 82 C3
King, L., *Australia* 89 F2
King, Mt., *Australia* 90 D4
King City, *U.S.A.* 111 H3
King Cr. →, *Australia* 90 C2
King Edward →, *Australia* 88 B4
King Frederick VI Land = Kong Frederik VI.s Kyst, *Greenland* 4 C5
King George B., *Falk. Is.* 128 D4
King George I., *Antarctica* 5 C18
King George Is., *Canada* 97 C11
King I. = Kadan Kyun, *Burma* 56 B1

King I.

King I., *Australia* 90 F3
King I., *Canada* 100 C3
King Leopold Ras., *Australia* 88 C4
King Sd., *Australia* 88 C3
King William I., *Canada* 96 B10
King William's Town, *S. Africa* 84 E4
Kingaroy, *Australia* 91 D5
Kingfisher, *U.S.A.* 109 H6
Kingirbān, *Iraq* 64 C5
Kingisepp = Kuressaare, *Estonia* 40 B3
Kingisepp, *Russia* 40 B6
Kingman, *Ariz., U.S.A.* 113 K12
Kingman, *Kans., U.S.A.* 109 G5
Kingoonya, *Australia* 91 E2
Kings →, *U.S.A.* 111 H4
Kings Canyon National Park, *U.S.A.* 111 H4
King's Lynn, *U.K.* 12 E8
Kings Mountain, *U.S.A.* 105 H5
King's Peak, *U.S.A.* 110 F8
Kingsbridge, *U.K.* 13 G4
Kingsburg, *U.S.A.* 111 H4
Kingscote, *Australia* 91 F2
Kingscourt, *Ireland* 15 C5
Kingsley, *U.S.A.* 108 D7
Kingsport, *U.S.A.* 105 G4
Kingston, *Canada* 98 D4
Kingston, *Jamaica* 116 C4
Kingston, *N.Z.* 87 L2
Kingston, *N.Y., U.S.A.* 107 E10
Kingston, *Pa., U.S.A.* 107 E9
Kingston, *R.I., U.S.A.* 107 E13
Kingston Pk., *U.S.A.* 113 K11
Kingston South East, *Australia* 91 F2
Kingston upon Hull, *U.K.* 12 D7
Kingston-upon-Thames, *U.K.* 13 F7
Kingstown, *St. Vincent* 117 D7
Kingstree, *U.S.A.* 105 J6
Kingsville, *Canada* 98 D3
Kingsville, *U.S.A.* 109 M6
Kingussie, *U.K.* 14 D4
Kinistino, *Canada* 101 C7
Kinkala, *Congo* 80 E2
Kinki □, *Japan* 49 H8
Kinleith, *N.Z.* 87 H5
Kinmount, *Canada* 106 B6
Kinna, *Sweden* 11 G6
Kinnaird, *Canada* 100 D5
Kinnairds Hd., *U.K.* 14 D7
Kinnared, *Sweden* 11 G7
Kinnarodden, *Norway* 6 A11
Kino, *Mexico* 114 B2
Kinoje →, *Canada* 98 B3
Kinomoto, *Japan* 49 G8
Kinoni, *Uganda* 82 C3
Kinrooi, *Belgium* 17 F7
Kinross, *U.K.* 14 E5
Kinsale, *Ireland* 15 E3
Kinsale, Old Hd. of, *Ireland* 15 E3
Kinshasa, *Zaïre* 80 E3
Kinsley, *U.S.A.* 109 G5
Kinston, *U.S.A.* 105 H7
Kintampo, *Ghana* 79 D4
Kintap, *Indonesia* 56 E5
Kintore Ra., *Australia* 88 D4
Kintyre, *U.K.* 14 F3
Kintyre, Mull of, *U.K.* 14 F3
Kinushseo →, *Canada* 98 A3
Kinuso, *Canada* 100 B5
Kinyangiri, *Tanzania* 82 C3
Kinzig →, *Germany* 19 G3
Kinzua, *U.S.A.* 106 E6
Kinzua Dam, *U.S.A.* 106 E5
Kiosk, *Canada* 98 C4
Kiowa, *Kans., U.S.A.* 109 G5
Kiowa, *Okla., U.S.A.* 109 H7
Kipahigan L., *Canada* 101 B8
Kipanga, *Tanzania* 82 D4
Kiparissía, *Greece* 39 M4
Kiparissiakós Kólpos, *Greece* 39 M4
Kipembawe, *Tanzania* 82 D3
Kipengere Ra., *Tanzania* 83 D3
Kipili, *Tanzania* 82 D3
Kipini, *Kenya* 82 C5
Kipling, *Canada* 101 C8
Kippure, *Ireland* 15 C5
Kipushi, *Zaïre* 83 E2
Kiratpur, *India* 62 E8
Kirchberg, *Switz.* 22 B5
Kirchhain, *Germany* 18 E4
Kirchheim, *Germany* 19 G5
Kirchheim-Bolanden, *Germany* 19 F4
Kirensk, *Russia* 45 D11
Kirgella Rocks, *Australia* 89 F3
Kirghizia ■, *Asia* 44 E8
Kirgizia = Kirghizia ■, *Asia* 44 E8
Kiri, *Zaïre* 80 E3
Kiribati ■, *Pac. Oc.* 92 H9
Kırıkhan, *Turkey* 66 E7
Kırıkkale, *Turkey* 66 D5
Kirillov, *Russia* 41 B11
Kirin = Jilin, *China* 51 C14
Kirin = Jilin □, *China* 51 C13
Kirishi, *Russia* 40 B7
Kiritimati, *Kiribati* 93 G12
Kırka, *Turkey* 66 D4
Kirkcaldy, *U.K.* 14 E5
Kirkcudbright, *U.K.* 14 G4
Kirkee, *India* 60 K8
Kirkenær, *Norway* 10 D6
Kirkenes, *Norway* 8 B21
Kirkintilloch, *U.K.* 14 F4
Kirkjubæjarklaustur, *Iceland* 8 E4
Kirkland, *U.S.A.* 111 J7
Kirkland Lake, *Canada* 98 C3
Kırklareli, *Turkey* 39 H10
Kırklareli □, *Turkey* 66 C2
Kirksville, *U.S.A.* 108 E8
Kirkūk, *Iraq* 64 C5
Kirkwall, *U.K.* 14 C6
Kirkwood, *S. Africa* 84 E4
Kirn, *Germany* 19 F3
Kirov = Vyatka, *Russia* 41 B16
Kirov, *Russia* 40 D9
Kirovabad = Gyandzha, *Azerbaijan* 43 F12
Kirovakan = Karaklis, *Armenia* 43 F11
Kirovo-Chepetsk, *Russia* 41 B17
Kirovograd = Yelizavetgrad, *Ukraine* 42 B5
Kirovsk, *Russia* 44 C4
Kirovsk, *Turkmenistan* 44 F7
Kirovsk, *Ukraine* 43 B8
Kirovski, *Russia* 43 D13
Kirovskiy, *Russia* 45 D16
Kirovskiy, *Russia* 48 B6
Kirriemuir, *U.K.* 14 E6
Kirsanov, *Russia* 41 E13
Kırşehir, *Turkey* 66 D6
Kırşehir □, *Turkey* 66 D6
Kirstonia, *S. Africa* 84 D3
Kirtachi, *Niger* 79 C5
Kirthar Range, *Pakistan* 62 F2
Kiruna, *Sweden* 8 C16
Kirundu, *Zaïre* 82 C2
Kirup, *Australia* 89 F2
Kirya, *Russia* 41 D15
Kiryū, *Japan* 49 F9
Kisaga, *Tanzania* 82 C3
Kisalaya, *Nic.* 116 D3
Kisámou, Kólpos, *Greece* 37 D5
Kisanga, *Zaïre* 82 B2
Kisangani, *Zaïre* 82 B2
Kisar, *Indonesia* 57 F7
Kisaran, *Indonesia* 56 D1
Kisarawe, *Tanzania* 82 D4
Kisarawe □, *Tanzania* 82 D4
Kisarazu, *Japan* 49 G9
Kisbér, *Hungary* 21 H8
Kiselevsk, *Russia* 44 D9
Kishanganga →, *Pakistan* 63 B5
Kishanganj, *India* 63 F13
Kishangarh, *India* 62 F4
Kishi, *Nigeria* 79 D5
Kishinev, *Moldavia* 42 C3
Kishiwada, *Japan* 49 G7
Kishtwar, *India* 63 C6
Kisii, *Kenya* 82 C3
Kisii □, *Kenya* 82 C3
Kisiju, *Tanzania* 82 D4
Kısır Dağ, *Turkey* 43 F10
Kisizi, *Uganda* 82 C2
Kiska I., *U.S.A.* 96 C1
Kiskatinaw →, *Canada* 100 B4
Kiskittogisu L., *Canada* 101 C9
Kiskörös, *Hungary* 21 J9
Kiskundorozsma, *Hungary* 21 J10
Kiskunfélegyháza, *Hungary* 21 J9
Kiskunhalas, *Hungary* 21 J9
Kiskunmajsa, *Hungary* 21 J9
Kislovodsk, *Russia* 43 E10
Kiso-Gawa →, *Japan* 49 G8
Kiso-Sammyaku, *Japan* 49 G8
Kisofukushima, *Japan* 49 G8
Kisoro, *Uganda* 82 C2
Kispest, *Hungary* 21 H9
Kissidougou, *Guinea* 78 D2
Kissimmee, *U.S.A.* 105 L5
Kissimmee →, *U.S.A.* 105 M5
Kississing L., *Canada* 101 B8
Kissónerga, *Cyprus* 37 E11
Kistanje, *Croatia* 33 E12
Kisújszállás, *Hungary* 21 H10
Kisumu, *Kenya* 82 C3
Kisvárda, *Hungary* 21 G12
Kiswani, *Tanzania* 82 C4
Kiswere, *Tanzania* 83 D4
Kit Carson, *U.S.A.* 108 F3
Kita, *Mali* 78 C3
Kitab, *Uzbekistan* 44 F7
Kitaibaraki, *Japan* 49 F10
Kitakami, *Japan* 48 E10
Kitakami-Gawa →, *Japan* 48 E10
Kitakami-Sammyaku, *Japan* 48 E10
Kitakata, *Japan* 48 F9
Kitakyūshū, *Japan* 49 H5
Kitale, *Kenya* 82 B4
Kitami, *Japan* 48 C11
Kitami-Sammyaku, *Japan* 48 B11
Kitangiri, L., *Tanzania* 82 C3
Kitaya, *Tanzania* 83 E5
Kitchener, *Australia* 89 F3
Kitchener, *Canada* 98 D3
Kitega = Gitega, *Burundi* 82 C2
Kitengo, *Zaïre* 82 D1
Kiteto □, *Tanzania* 82 C4
Kitgum, *Uganda* 82 B3
Kíthira, *Greece* 39 N7
Kíthnos, *Greece* 39 M7
Kiti, *Cyprus* 37 E12
Kiti, C., *Cyprus* 37 E12
Kitikmeot □, *Canada* 96 B9
Kitimat, *Canada* 100 C3
Kitinen →, *Finland* 8 C19
Kitiyab, *Sudan* 77 D3
Kítros, *Greece* 39 J5
Kitsuki, *Japan* 49 H5
Kittakittaooloo, L., *Australia* 91 D2
Kittanning, *U.S.A.* 106 F5
Kittatinny Mts., *U.S.A.* 107 E10
Kittery, *U.S.A.* 105 D10
Kitui, *Kenya* 82 C4
Kitui □, *Kenya* 82 C4
Kitwe, *Zambia* 83 E2
Kitzbühel, *Austria* 19 H8
Kitzingen, *Germany* 19 F6
Kivalo, *Finland* 8 C19
Kivarli, *India* 62 G5
Kividhes, *Cyprus* 37 E11
Kivu □, *Zaïre* 82 C2
Kivu, L., *Zaïre* 82 C2
Kiyev, *Ukraine* 40 F7
Kiyevskoye Vdkhr., *Ukraine* 40 F7
Kiziguru, *Rwanda* 82 C3
Kızıl Irmak →, *Turkey* 42 F6
Kizil Jilga, *India* 63 B8
Kizil Yurt, *Russia* 43 E12
Kızılcahamam, *Turkey* 42 F5
Kızılhisar, *Turkey* 66 E3
Kızılırmak, *Turkey* 66 C5
Kızıltepe, *Turkey* 67 E9
Kizimkazi, *Tanzania* 82 D4
Kizlyar, *Russia* 43 E12
Kizyl-Arvat, *Turkmenistan* 44 F6
Kjellerup, *Denmark* 11 H3
Kladanj, *Bos.-H., Yug.* 21 L8
Kladno, *Czech.* 20 E4
Kladovo, *Serbia, Yug.* 21 L12
Klaeng, *Thailand* 58 F3
Klagenfurt, *Austria* 21 J4
Klagshamn, *Sweden* 11 J6
Klagstorp, *Sweden* 11 J7
Klaipeda, *Lithuania* 40 D2
Klamath →, *U.S.A.* 110 F1
Klamath Falls, *U.S.A.* 110 E3
Klamath Mts., *U.S.A.* 110 F2
Klanjec, *Croatia* 33 B12
Klappan →, *Canada* 100 B3
Klarälven →, *Sweden* 9 G12
Klaten, *Indonesia* 57 G14
Klatovy, *Czech.* 20 F3
Klawak, *U.S.A.* 100 B2
Klawer, *S. Africa* 84 E2
Klazienaveen, *Neths.* 16 C10
Kleczew, *Poland* 20 C8
Kleena Kleene, *Canada* 100 C4
Klein, *U.S.A.* 110 C9
Klein-Karas, *Namibia* 84 D2
Kleine Gette →, *Belgium* 17 G6
Kleine Nete →, *Belgium* 17 F5
Klekovača, *Bos.-H., Yug.* 33 D13
Klenovec, *Czech.* 20 G9
Klenovec, *Macedonia, Yug.* 39 H3
Klerksdorp, *S. Africa* 84 D4
Kletnya, *Russia* 40 E8
Kletsk, *Belorussia* 40 E5
Kletskiy, *Russia* 43 B10
Kleve, *Germany* 18 D2
Klickitat, *U.S.A.* 110 D3
Klickitat →, *U.S.A.* 112 E5
Klidhes, *Cyprus* 37 D13
Klimovichi, *Belorussia* 40 E8
Klin, *Russia* 41 C10
Klinaklini →, *Canada* 100 C3
Klintsey, *Russia* 40 E8
Klipdale, *S. Africa* 84 E2
Klipplaat, *S. Africa* 84 E3
Klitmøller, *Denmark* 11 G2
Kljajićevo, *Serbia, Yug.* 21 K9
Ključ, *Bos.-H., Yug.* 33 D13
Kłobuck, *Poland* 20 E8
Kłodzko, *Poland* 20 E6
Kloetinge, *Neths.* 17 F3
Klondike, *Canada* 96 B6
Klosterzande, *Neths.* 17 F4
Klosterneuburg, *Austria* 21 G6
Klosters, *Switz.* 23 C9
Kloten, *Switz.* 23 B7
Klötze, *Germany* 18 C7
Klouto, *Togo* 79 D5
Kluane L., *Canada* 96 B6
Kluczbork, *Poland* 20 E8
Klundert, *Neths.* 17 E5
Klyuchevskaya, Gora, *Russia* 45 D17
Knaresborough, *U.K.* 12 C6
Knee L., *Man., Canada* 101 B10
Knee L., *Sask., Canada* 101 B7
Kneïss, Is., *Tunisia* 75 B7
Knesselare, *Belgium* 17 F2
Knezha, *Bulgaria* 38 F7
Knić, *Serbia, Yug.* 21 M10
Knight Inlet, *Canada* 100 C3
Knighton, *U.K.* 13 E4
Knights Ferry, *U.S.A.* 112 H6
Knight's Landing, *U.S.A.* 112 G5
Knin, *Croatia* 33 D13
Knittelfeld, *Austria* 21 H4
Knjaževac, *Serbia, Yug.* 21 M12
Knob, C., *Australia* 89 F2
Knockmealdown Mts., *Ireland* 15 D4
Knokke, *Belgium* 17 F2
Knossós, *Greece* 37 D7
Knox, *U.S.A.* 104 E2
Knox, C., *Canada* 100 C2
Knox City, *U.S.A.* 109 J5
Knox Coast, *Antarctica* 5 C8
Knoxville, *Iowa, U.S.A.* 108 E8
Knoxville, *Tenn., U.S.A.* 105 H4
Knutshø, *Norway* 10 B3
Knysna, *S. Africa* 84 E3
Knyszyn, *Poland* 20 B12
Ko Kha, *Thailand* 58 C2
Ko Tao, *Thailand* 59 G2
Koartac, *Canada* 97 B13
Koba, *Aru, Indonesia* 57 F8
Koba, *Bangka, Indonesia* 56 E3
Kobarid, *Slovenia* 33 B10
Kobayashi, *Japan* 49 J5
Kobdo = Hovd, *Mongolia* 54 B4
Kōbe, *Japan* 49 G7
Kobelyaki, *Ukraine* 42 B6
København, *Denmark* 11 J6
Kōbi-Sho, *Japan* 49 M1
Koblenz, *Germany* 19 E3
Koblenz, *Switz.* 22 A6
Kobo, *Ethiopia* 77 E4
Kobrin, *Belorussia* 40 E4
Kobroor, Kepulauan, *Indonesia* 57 F8
Kobuleti, *Georgia* 43 F9
Kobyłka, *Poland* 20 C11
Kobylkino, *Russia* 41 D13
Kobylnik, *Belorussia* 40 D5
Kocaeli = İzmit, *Turkey* 66 C3
Kocaeli □, *Turkey* 66 C3
Kočani, *Macedonia, Yug.* 39 H5
Koceljevo, *Serbia, Yug.* 21 L9
Kočevje, *Slovenia* 33 C11
Koch Bihar, *India* 61 F16
Kochang, *S. Korea* 51 G14
Kochas, *India* 63 G10
Kocher →, *Germany* 19 F5
Kocheya, *Russia* 45 D13
Kōchi, *Japan* 49 H6
Kōchi □, *Japan* 49 H6
Kochiu = Gejiu, *China* 52 F4
Kodiak, *U.S.A.* 96 C4
Kodiak I., *U.S.A.* 96 C4
Kodinar, *India* 62 J4
Kodori →, *Georgia* 43 E9
Koekelare, *Belgium* 17 F1
Koersel, *Belgium* 17 F6
Koes, *Namibia* 84 D2
Koffiefontein, *S. Africa* 84 D4
Kofiau, *Indonesia* 57 E7
Koforidua, *Ghana* 79 D4
Kōfu, *Japan* 49 G9
Koga, *Japan* 49 F9
Kogaluk →, *Canada* 99 A7
Kogan, *Australia* 91 D5
Kogin Baba, *Nigeria* 79 D7
Koh-i-Bābā, *Afghan.* 60 B5
Koh-i-Khurd, *Afghan.* 62 C1
Kohat, *Pakistan* 62 C4
Kohima, *India* 61 G19
Kohkīlūyeh va Būyer Aḥmadi □, *Iran* 65 D6
Kohler Ra., *Antarctica* 5 D15
Kohtla Järve, *Estonia* 40 B5
Koin-dong, *N. Korea* 51 D14
Kojŏ, *N. Korea* 51 E14
Kojonup, *Australia* 89 F2
Kojūr, *Iran* 65 B6
Koka, *Sudan* 76 C3
Kokand, *Uzbekistan* 44 E8
Kokanee Glacier Prov. Park, *Canada* 100 D5
Kokas, *Indonesia* 57 E8
Kokchetav, *Kazakhstan* 44 D7
Kokemäenjoki, *Finland* 9 F16
Kokerite, *Guyana* 121 B6
Kokhma, *Russia* 41 C12
Kokkola, *Finland* 8 E17
Koko, *Nigeria* 79 C5
Koko Kyunzu, *Burma* 61 M18
Kokolopozo, *Ivory C.* 78 D3
Kokomo, *U.S.A.* 104 E2
Kokonau, *Indonesia* 57 E9
Kokoro, *Niger* 79 C5
Koksan, *N. Korea* 51 E14
Koksoak →, *Canada* 97 C13
Kokstad, *S. Africa* 85 E4
Kokubu, *Japan* 49 J5
Kokuora, *Russia* 45 B15
Kola, *Indonesia* 57 F8
Kola, *Russia* 44 C4
Kola Pen. = Kolskiy Poluostrov, *Russia* 44 C4
Kolahoi, *India* 63 B6
Kolahun, *Liberia* 78 D2
Kolaka, *Indonesia* 57 E6
Kolar, *India* 60 N11
Kolar Gold Fields, *India* 60 N11
Kolari, *Finland* 8 C17
Kolayat, *India* 60 F8
Kolby Kås, *Denmark* 11 J4
Kolchugino = Leninsk-Kuznetskiy, *Russia* 44 D9
Kolchugino, *Russia* 41 C11
Kolda, *Senegal* 78 C2
Kolding, *Denmark* 11 J3
Kole, *Zaïre* 80 E4
Koléa, *Algeria* 75 A5
Kolepom = Yos Sudarso, Pulau, *Indonesia* 57 F9
Kolguyev, Ostrov, *Russia* 44 C5
Kolham, *Neths.* 16 B9
Kolhapur, *India* 60 L9
Kolia, *Ivory C.* 78 D3
Kolín, *Czech.* 20 E5
Kolind, *Denmark* 11 H4
Kölleda, *Germany* 18 D7
Kollum, *Neths.* 16 B8
Kolmanskop, *Namibia* 84 D2
Köln, *Germany* 18 E2
Koło, *Poland* 20 C8
Kołobrzeg, *Poland* 20 A5
Kologriv, *Russia* 41 B14
Kolokani, *Mali* 78 C3
Kolomna, *Russia* 41 D11
Kolomyya, *Ukraine* 42 B1
Kolondiéba, *Mali* 78 C3
Kolonodale, *Indonesia* 57 E6
Kolosib, *India* 61 G18
Kolpashevo, *Russia* 44 D9
Kolpino, *Russia* 40 B7
Kolpny, *Russia* 41 E10
Kolskiy Poluostrov, *Russia* 44 C4
Kolubara →, *Serbia, Yug.* 21 L10
Koluszki, *Poland* 20 D9
Kolwezi, *Zaïre* 83 E2
Kolyberovo, *Russia* 41 D11
Kolyma →, *Russia* 45 C17
Kolymskoye, Okhotsko, *Russia* 45 C16
Kôm Ombo, *Egypt* 76 C3
Komandorskiye Ostrova, *Russia* 45 D17
Komárno, *Czech.* 21 H8
Komárom, *Hungary* 21 H8
Komarovo, *Russia* 40 B8
Komatipoort, *S. Africa* 85 D5
Komatou Yialou, *Cyprus* 37 D13
Komatsu, *Japan* 49 F8
Komatsujima, *Japan* 49 H7
Kombissiri, *Burkina Faso* 79 C4
Kombori, *Burkina Faso* 78 C4
Komen, *Slovenia* 33 C10
Komenda, *Ghana* 79 D4
Komi Republic □, *Russia* 44 C6
Komiža, *Croatia* 33 E13
Komló, *Hungary* 21 J8
Kommunarsk, *Ukraine* 43 B8
Kommunizma, Pik, *Tajikistan* 44 F8
Komodo, *Indonesia* 57 F5
Komoé, *Ivory C.* 78 D4
Komono, *Congo* 80 E2
Komoran, Pulau, *Indonesia* 57 F9
Komoro, *Japan* 49 F9
Komotini, *Greece* 39 H8
Kompasberg, *S. Africa* 84 E3
Kompong Bang, *Cambodia* 59 F5
Kompong Cham, *Cambodia* 59 F5
Kompong Chhnang, *Cambodia* 59 F5
Kompong Chikreng, *Cambodia* 58 F5
Kompong Kleang, *Cambodia* 58 F5
Kompong Luong, *Cambodia* 59 G5
Kompong Pranak, *Cambodia* 58 F5
Kompong Som, *Cambodia* 59 G4
Kompong Som, Chhung, *Cambodia* 59 G4
Kompong Speu, *Cambodia* 59 G5
Kompong Sralao, *Cambodia* 58 E5
Kompong Thom, *Cambodia* 58 F5
Kompong Trabeck, *Cambodia* 58 F5
Kompong Trabeck, *Cambodia* 59 G5
Kompong Trach, *Cambodia* 59 G5
Kompong Tralach, *Cambodia* 59 G5
Komrat, *Moldavia* 42 C3
Komsberg, *S. Africa* 84 E3
Komsomolets, Ostrov, *Russia* 45 A10
Komsomolsk, *Russia* 41 C12
Komsomolsk, *Russia* 45 D14
Komsomolskiy, *Russia* 41 E16
Konakovo, *Russia* 41 C10
Konarhá □, *Afghan.* 60 B7
Konārī, *Iran* 65 D6
Konawa, *U.S.A.* 109 H6
Konch, *India* 63 G8
Kondakovo, *Russia* 45 C16
Konde, *Tanzania* 82 C4
Kondinin, *Australia* 89 F2
Kondoa, *Tanzania* 82 C4
Kondoa □, *Tanzania* 82 D4
Kondókali, *Greece* 37 A3
Kondratyevo, *Russia* 45 D10
Konduga, *Nigeria* 79 C7
Kong, *Ivory C.* 78 D4
Kong →, *Cambodia* 58 F5
Kong, Koh, *Cambodia* 59 G4
Kong Christian IX.s Land, *Greenland* 4 C6
Kong Christian X.s Land, *Greenland* 4 B6

Kong Franz Joseph Fd., *Greenland* 4 B6
Kong Frederik IX.s Land, *Greenland* 4 C5
Kong Frederik VI.s Kyst, *Greenland* 4 C5
Kong Frederik VIII.s Land, *Greenland* 4 B6
Kong Oscar Fjord, *Greenland* 4 B6
Kongeå →, *Denmark* 11 J3
Kongju, *S. Korea* 51 F14
Konglu, *Burma* 61 F20
Kongolo, *Kasai Or., Zaïre* 82 D1
Kongolo, *Shaba, Zaïre* 82 D2
Kongor, *Sudan* 77 F3
Kongoussi, *Burkina Faso* 79 C4
Kongsberg, *Norway* 10 E3
Kongsvinger, *Norway* 10 D6
Kongwa, *Tanzania* 82 D4
Koni, *Zaïre* 83 E2
Koni, Mts., *Zaïre* 83 E2
Königsberg = Kaliningrad, *Russia* 40 D2
Königslutter, *Germany* 18 C6
Königswusterhausen, *Germany* 18 C9
Konin, *Poland* 20 C8
Kónitsa, *Greece* 39 J3
Köniz, *Switz.* 22 C4
Konjice, *Slovenia* 33 B12
Konkiep, *Namibia* 84 D2
Konkouré →, *Guinea* 78 D2
Könnern, *Germany* 18 D7
Kono, *S. Leone* 78 D2
Konolfingen, *Switz.* 22 C5
Konongo, *Ghana* 79 D4
Konosha, *Russia* 44 C5
Kōnosu, *Japan* 49 F9
Konotop, *Ukraine* 40 F8
Konqi He →, *China* 54 B4
Końskie, *Poland* 20 D10
Konstantinovka, *Ukraine* 42 B7
Konstantinovski, *Russia* 43 C9
Konstanz, *Germany* 19 H5
Kont, *Iran* 65 E9
Kontagora, *Nigeria* 79 C6
Kontich, *Belgium* 17 F4
Kontum, *Vietnam* 58 E7
Kontum, Plateau du, *Vietnam* 58 E7
Konya, *Turkey* 66 E5
Konya □, *Turkey* 66 E5
Konya Ovasi, *Turkey* 66 D5
Konz, *Germany* 19 F2
Konza, *Kenya* 82 C4
Kookynie, *Australia* 89 E3
Kooline, *Australia* 88 D2
Kooloonong, *Australia* 91 E3
Koolyanobbing, *Australia* 89 F2
Koondrook, *Australia* 91 F3
Koonibba, *Australia* 91 E1
Koorawatha, *Australia* 91 E4
Koorda, *Australia* 89 F2
Kooskia, *U.S.A.* 110 C6
Kootenai →, *Canada* 110 B5
Kootenay L., *Canada* 100 D5
Kootenay Nat. Park, *Canada* 100 C5
Kootjieskolk, *S. Africa* 84 E3
Kopanovka, *Russia* 43 C12
Kopaonik, *Serbia, Yug.* 21 M11
Kópavogur, *Iceland* 8 D3
Koper, *Slovenia* 33 C10
Kopervik, *Norway* 9 G8
Kopeysk, *Russia* 44 D7
Kopi, *Australia* 91 E2
Köping, *Sweden* 10 E10
Kopiste, *Croatia* 33 F13
Köpmanholmen, *Sweden* 10 A12
Koppang, *Norway* 10 C5
Kopparberg, *Sweden* 9 G13
Kopparbergs län □, *Sweden* 9 F13
Kopperå, *Norway* 10 A5
Koppies, *S. Africa* 85 D4
Koprivnica, *Croatia* 33 B13
Kopychintsy, *Ukraine* 40 G4
Kopys, *Belorussia* 40 D7
Korab, *Macedonia, Yug.* 39 H3
Korakiána, *Greece* 37 A3
Korba, *India* 63 H10
Korbach, *Germany* 18 D4
Korbu, G., *Malaysia* 59 K3
Korça, *Albania* 39 J3
Korce = Korça, *Albania* 39 J3
Korčula, *Croatia* 33 F14
Korčulanski Kanal, *Croatia* 33 E13
Kord Kūy, *Iran* 65 B7
Kord Sheykh, *Iran* 65 D7
Kordestān □, *Iran* 64 C5
Korea, North ■, *Asia* 51 E14
Korea, South ■, *Asia* 51 F15
Korea Bay, *Korea* 51 E13
Korea Strait, *Asia* 51 G15
Korenevo, *Russia* 40 F9
Korenovsk, *Russia* 43 D8
Korets, *Ukraine* 40 F5
Korgan, *Turkey* 67 C7
Korgus, *Sudan* 76 D3
Korhogo, *Ivory C.* 78 D3
Koribundu, *S. Leone* 78 D2
Korim, *Indonesia* 57 E9
Korinthiakós Kólpos, *Greece* 39 L5
Kórinthos, *Greece* 39 M5
Korioumé, *Mali* 78 B4
Koríssa, Límni, *Greece* 37 B3
Kōriyama, *Japan* 48 F10
Korkuteli, *Turkey* 66 E4
Kormakiti, C., *Cyprus* 37 D11
Körmend, *Hungary* 21 H6
Kornat, *Croatia* 33 E12
Korneshty, *Moldavia* 42 C3
Kornsjø, *Norway* 10 F5
Kornstad, *Norway* 10 B1
Koro, *Fiji* 87 C8
Koro, *Ivory C.* 78 D3
Koro, *Mali* 78 C4
Koro Sea, *Fiji* 87 C9
Korocha, *Russia* 41 F10
Köroğlu Dağları, *Turkey* 66 C4
Korogwe, *Tanzania* 82 D4
Korogwe □, *Tanzania* 82 D4
Koroit, *Australia* 91 F3
Koronadal, *Phil.* 55 H6
Koronowo, *Poland* 20 B7
Koror, *Pac. Oc.* 57 C8
Körös →, *Hungary* 21 J10
Korosten, *Ukraine* 40 F6
Korotoyak, *Russia* 41 F11
Korraraika, Helodranon' i, *Madag.* 85 B7
Korsakov, *Russia* 45 E15
Korshunovo, *Russia* 45 D12
Korsør, *Denmark* 9 J11
Korsun Shevchenkovskiy, *Ukraine* 42 B4
Korsze, *Poland* 20 A11
Kortemark, *Belgium* 17 F2
Kortessem, *Belgium* 17 G6
Korti, *Sudan* 76 D3
Kortrijk, *Belgium* 17 G2
Korwai, *India* 62 G8
Koryakskiy Khrebet, *Russia* 45 C18
Koryŏng, *S. Korea* 51 G15
Kos, *Greece* 39 N10
Kosa, *Ethiopia* 77 F4
Kosaya Gora, *Russia* 41 D10
Kościan, *Poland* 20 C6
Kościerzyna, *Poland* 20 A7
Kosciusko, *U.S.A.* 109 J10
Kosciusko, Mt., *Australia* 91 F4
Kosciusko I., *U.S.A.* 100 B2
Kösély →, *Hungary* 21 H11
Kosha, *Sudan* 76 C3
K'oshih = Kashi, *China* 54 C2
Koshiki-Rettō, *Japan* 49 J4
Kosi, *India* 62 F7
Kosi-meer, *S. Africa* 85 D5
Košice, *Czech.* 20 G11
Kosjerić, *Serbia, Yug.* 21 M9
Koskhinoú, *Greece* 37 C10
Kosŏng, *N. Korea* 51 E15
Kosovska-Mitrovica, *Serbia, Yug.* 21 N10
Kostajnica, *Croatia* 33 C13
Kostanjevica, *Slovenia* 33 C12
Kostelec, *Czech.* 20 E6
Koster, *S. Africa* 84 D4
Kôstî, *Sudan* 77 E3
Kostopol, *Ukraine* 40 F5
Kostroma, *Russia* 41 C12
Kostromskoye Vdkhr., *Russia* 41 C12
Kostyukovichi, *Belorussia* 40 E8
Koszalin, *Poland* 20 A6
Kőszeg, *Hungary* 21 H6
Kot Addu, *Pakistan* 62 D4
Kot Moman, *Pakistan* 62 C5
Kota, *India* 62 G6
Kota Baharu, *Malaysia* 59 J4
Kota Belud, *Malaysia* 56 C5
Kota Kinabalu, *Malaysia* 56 C5
Kota Tinggi, *Malaysia* 59 M4
Kotaagung, *Indonesia* 56 F2
Kotabaru, *Indonesia* 56 E5
Kotabumi, *Indonesia* 56 E2
Kotagede, *Indonesia* 57 G14
Kotamobagu, *Indonesia* 57 D6
Kotaneelee →, *Canada* 100 A4
Kotawaringin, *Indonesia* 56 E4
Kotcho L., *Canada* 100 B4
Kotelnich, *Russia* 41 B16
Kotelnikovo, *Russia* 43 C10
Kotelnyy, Ostrov, *Russia* 45 B14
Köthen, *Germany* 18 D7
Kothi, *India* 63 G9
Kotiro, *Pakistan* 62 F2
Kotka, *Finland* 9 F19
Kotlas, *Russia* 44 C5
Kotli, *Pakistan* 62 C5
Kotmul, *Pakistan* 63 B6
Kotonkoro, *Nigeria* 79 C6
Kotor, *Montenegro, Yug.* 21 N8
Kotoriba, *Croatia* 33 B13
Kotovo, *Russia* 41 F14
Kotovsk, *Ukraine* 42 C3
Kotputli, *India* 62 F7
Kotri, *Pakistan* 62 G3
Kótronas, *Greece* 39 N5
Kottayam, *India* 60 Q10
Kotturu, *India* 60 M10
Kotuy →, *Russia* 45 B11
Kotzebue, *U.S.A.* 96 B3
Kouango, *C.A.R.* 80 C4
Koudekerke, *Neths.* 17 F3
Koudougou, *Burkina Faso* 78 C4
Koufonísi, *Greece* 37 E8
Kougaberge, *S. Africa* 84 E3
Kouibli, *Ivory C.* 78 D3
Kouilou →, *Congo* 80 E2
Kouki, *C.A.R.* 80 C3
Koula Moutou, *Gabon* 80 E2
Koulen, *Cambodia* 58 F5
Koulikoro, *Mali* 78 C3
Kouloúra, *Greece* 37 A3
Koúm-bournoú, Ákra, *Greece* 37 C10
Koumala, *Australia* 90 C4
Koumankou, *Mali* 78 C3
Koumbia, *Burkina Faso* 78 C4
Koumbia, *Guinea* 78 C2
Koumboum, *Guinea* 78 C2
Koumpenntoum, *Senegal* 78 C2
Koumra, *Chad* 73 G8
Koundara, *Guinea* 78 C2
Kounradskiy, *Kazakhstan* 44 E8
Kountze, *U.S.A.* 109 K7
Koupéla, *Burkina Faso* 79 C4
Kouris →, *Cyprus* 37 E11
Kourou, *Fr. Guiana* 121 B7
Kouroussa, *Guinea* 78 C3
Koussané, *Mali* 78 C2
Kousseri, *Cameroon* 73 F7
Koutiala, *Mali* 78 C3
Kouto, *Ivory C.* 78 D3
Kouvé, *Togo* 79 D5
Kovačica, *Serbia, Yug.* 21 K10
Kovel, *Ukraine* 40 F4
Kovin, *Serbia, Yug.* 21 L10
Kovrov, *Russia* 41 C12
Kowanyama, *Australia* 90 B3
Kowkash, *Canada* 98 B2
Kowloon, *H.K.* 53 F10
Kowŏn, *N. Korea* 51 E14
Koyabuti, *Indonesia* 57 E10
Köyceğiz, *Turkey* 66 E3
Koyuk, *U.S.A.* 96 B3
Koyukuk →, *U.S.A.* 96 B4
Koyulhisar, *Turkey* 42 F7
Koza, *Japan* 49 L3
Kozan, *Turkey* 66 E6
Kozáni, *Greece* 39 J4
Kozara, *Bos.-H., Yug.* 33 D14
Kozarac, *Bos.-H., Yug.* 33 D13
Kozelsk, *Russia* 40 D9
Kozhikode = Calicut, *India* 60 P9
Kozje, *Slovenia* 33 B12
Kozlovets, *Bulgaria* 38 F8
Kozlu, *Turkey* 66 C4
Kozluk, *Turkey* 67 D9
Koźmin, *Poland* 20 D7
Kozmodemyansk, *Russia* 41 C15
Kpabia, *Ghana* 79 D4
Kpalimé, *Togo* 79 D5
Kpandae, *Ghana* 79 D4
Kpessi, *Togo* 79 D5
Kra, Isthmus of = Kra, Kho Khot, *Thailand* 59 G2
Kra, Kho Khot, *Thailand* 59 G2
Kra Buri, *Thailand* 59 G2
Krabbendijke, *Neths.* 17 F4
Krabi, *Thailand* 59 H2
Kragan, *Indonesia* 57 G14
Kragerø, *Norway* 10 F3
Kragujevac, *Serbia, Yug.* 21 L10
Krakatau = Rakata, Pulau, *Indonesia* 56 F3
Krakor, *Cambodia* 58 F5
Kraków, *Poland* 20 E9
Kraksaan, *Indonesia* 57 G15
Kråkstad, *Norway* 10 E4
Kralanh, *Cambodia* 58 F4
Králiky, *Czech.* 20 E6
Kraljevo, *Serbia, Yug.* 21 M10
Kralovice, *Czech.* 20 F3
Kralupy, *Czech.* 20 E4
Kramatorsk, *Ukraine* 42 B7
Kramfors, *Sweden* 10 B11
Kramis, C., *Algeria* 75 A5
Krångede, *Sweden* 10 A10
Kranj, *Slovenia* 33 B11
Kranjska Gora, *Slovenia* 33 B10
Krankskop, *S. Africa* 85 D5
Krapina, *Croatia* 33 B12
Krapina →, *Croatia* 33 C12
Krapivna, *Russia* 41 E10
Krapkowice, *Poland* 20 E7
Kraskino, *Russia* 45 E14
Kraslice, *Czech.* 20 E2
Krasnaya Gorbatka, *Russia* 41 D12
Krasnaya Polyana, *Russia* 43 E9
Kraśnik, *Poland* 20 E12
Kraśnik Fabryczny, *Poland* 20 E12
Krasnoarmeisk, *Ukraine* 42 B7
Krasnoarmeysk, *Russia* 41 F14
Krasnoarmeysk, *Russia* 43 B11
Krasnodar, *Russia* 43 D8
Krasnodon, *Ukraine* 43 B8
Krasnodonetskaya, *Russia* 43 B9
Krasnogorskiy, *Russia* 41 C16
Krasnograd, *Ukraine* 42 B6
Krasnogvardeyskoye, *Russia* 43 D9
Krasnogvardyesk, *Ukraine* 42 D6
Krasnokutsk, *Ukraine* 40 F9
Krasnoperekopsk, *Ukraine* 42 D5
Krasnorechenskiy, *Russia* 48 B7
Krasnoselkupsk, *Russia* 44 C9
Krasnoslobodsk, *Russia* 41 D13
Krasnoslobodsk, *Russia* 43 B11
Krasnoturinsk, *Russia* 44 D7
Krasnoufimsk, *Russia* 44 D6
Krasnouralsk, *Russia* 44 D7
Krasnovodsk, *Turkmenistan* 44 E6
Krasnoyarsk, *Russia* 45 D10
Krasnoye = Krasnyy, *Russia* 40 D7
Krasnoye, *Russia* 41 B15
Krasnoye, *Russia* 43 C11
Krasnozavodsk, *Russia* 41 C11
Krasny Liman, *Ukraine* 42 B7
Krasny Sulin, *Russia* 43 C9
Krasnystaw, *Poland* 20 E13
Krasnyy, *Russia* 40 D7
Krasnyy Kholm, *Russia* 41 B10
Krasnyy Kut, *Russia* 41 F15
Krasnyy Luch, *Ukraine* 43 B8
Krasnyy Profintern, *Russia* 41 C12
Krasnyy Yar, *Russia* 41 E17
Krasnyy Yar, *Russia* 41 F14
Krasnyy Yar, *Russia* 43 C13
Krasnyye Baki, *Russia* 41 C14
Krasnyyoskolskoye Vdkhr., *Ukraine* 42 B7
Kraszna →, *Hungary* 21 G12
Kratie, *Cambodia* 58 F6
Krau, *Indonesia* 57 E10
Kravanh, Chuor Phnum, *Cambodia* 59 G4
Krefeld, *Germany* 18 D2
Krémaston, Límni, *Greece* 39 L4
Kremenchug, *Ukraine* 42 B5
Kremenchugskoye Vdkhr., *Ukraine* 42 B5
Kremenets, *Ukraine* 42 A1
Kremennaya, *Ukraine* 42 B8
Kremges = Svetlovodsk, *Ukraine* 40 G8
Kremikovtsi, *Bulgaria* 38 G6
Kremmen, *Germany* 18 C9
Kremmling, *U.S.A.* 110 F10
Krems, *Austria* 21 G5
Kremsmünster, *Austria* 21 G4
Kretinga, *Lithuania* 40 D2
Krettamia, *Algeria* 74 C4
Krettsy, *Russia* 40 B8
Kreuzberg, *Germany* 19 E5
Kreuzlingen, *Switz.* 23 A8
Kribi, *Cameroon* 79 E6
Krichem, *Bulgaria* 38 G7
Krichev, *Belorussia* 40 E7
Krim, *Slovenia* 33 C11
Krimpen, *Neths.* 16 E5
Kriós, Ákra, *Greece* 37 D5
Krishna →, *India* 61 M12
Krishnanagar, *India* 63 H13
Kristiansand, *Norway* 9 G10
Kristianstad, *Sweden* 9 H13
Kristianstads län □, *Sweden* 9 H13
Kristiansund, *Norway* 10 A1
Kristiinankaupunki, *Finland* 8 E16
Kristinehamn, *Sweden* 9 G13
Kristinestad, *Finland* 8 E16
Kríti, *Greece* 37 D7
Kritsá, *Greece* 37 D7
Kriva →, *Macedonia, Yug.* 38 G4
Kriva Palanka, *Macedonia, Yug.* 38 G5
Krivaja →, *Bos.-H., Yug.* 21 L8
Krivoy Rog, *Ukraine* 42 C5
Križevci, *Croatia* 33 B13
Krk, *Croatia* 33 C11
Krka →, *Slovenia* 33 C12
Krkonoše, *Czech.* 20 E5
Krnov, *Czech.* 20 E7
Krobia, *Poland* 20 D6
Krokeaí, *Greece* 39 N5
Krokodil →, *Mozam.* 85 D5
Krokom, *Sweden* 10 A8
Krolevets, *Ukraine* 40 F8
Kroměříž, *Czech.* 20 F7
Krommenie, *Neths.* 16 D5
Kromy, *Russia* 40 E9
Kronach, *Germany* 19 E7
Kronobergs län □, *Sweden* 9 H13
Kronprins Olav Kyst, *Antarctica* 5 C5
Kronshtadt, *Russia* 40 A6
Kroonstad, *S. Africa* 84 D4
Kröpelin, *Germany* 18 A7
Kropotkin, *Russia* 43 D9
Kropotkin, *Russia* 45 D12
Kropp, *Germany* 18 A5
Krościenko, *Poland* 20 F10
Krosno, *Poland* 20 F11
Krosno Odrzańskie, *Poland* 20 C5
Krotoszyn, *Poland* 20 D7
Kroussón, *Greece* 37 D6
Krško, *Slovenia* 33 C12
Kruger Nat. Park, *S. Africa* 85 C5
Krugersdorp, *S. Africa* 85 D4
Kruiningen, *Neths.* 17 F4
Kruisfontein, *S. Africa* 84 E3
Kruishoutem, *Belgium* 17 G3
Kruisland, *Neths.* 17 E4
Kruja, *Albania* 39 H2
Krulevshchina, *Belorussia* 40 D5
Kruma, *Albania* 38 G3
Krumbach, *Germany* 19 G6
Krung Thep = Bangkok, *Thailand* 58 F3
Krupanj, *Serbia, Yug.* 21 L9
Krupinica →, *Czech.* 21 G8
Kruševac, *Serbia, Yug.* 21 M11
Kruzof I., *U.S.A.* 100 B1
Krymsk Abinsk, *Russia* 42 D8
Krymskiy Poluostrov, *Ukraine* 42 D5
Krynica Morska, *Poland* 20 A9
Krynki, *Poland* 20 B13
Krzywiń, *Poland* 20 D6
Krzyz, *Poland* 20 C6
Ksabi, *Morocco* 74 B4
Ksar Chellala, *Algeria* 75 A5
Ksar el Boukhari, *Algeria* 75 A5
Ksar el Kebir, *Morocco* 74 B3
Ksar es Souk = Ar Rachidiya, *Morocco* 74 B4
Ksar Rhilane, *Tunisia* 75 B6
Ksour, Mts. des, *Algeria* 75 B4
Kstovo, *Russia* 41 C14
Kuala, *Indonesia* 56 D3
Kuala Berang, *Malaysia* 59 K4
Kuala Dungun, *Malaysia* 59 K4
Kuala Kangsar, *Malaysia* 59 K3
Kuala Kelawang, *Malaysia* 59 L4
Kuala Kerai, *Malaysia* 59 K4
Kuala Kubu Baharu, *Malaysia* 59 L3
Kuala Lipis, *Malaysia* 59 K4
Kuala Lumpur, *Malaysia* 59 L3
Kuala Nerang, *Malaysia* 59 J3
Kuala Pilah, *Malaysia* 59 L4
Kuala Rompin, *Malaysia* 59 L4
Kuala Selangor, *Malaysia* 59 L3
Kuala Terengganu, *Malaysia* 59 K4
Kualajelai, *Indonesia* 56 E4
Kualakapuas, *Indonesia* 56 E4
Kualakurun, *Indonesia* 56 E4
Kualapembuang, *Indonesia* 56 E4
Kualasimpang, *Indonesia* 56 D1
Kuancheng, *China* 51 D10
Kuandang, *Indonesia* 57 D6
Kuandian, *China* 51 D13
Kuangchou = Guangzhou, *China* 53 F9
Kuantan, *Malaysia* 59 L4
Kuba, *Azerbaijan* 43 F13
Kuban →, *Russia* 42 D7
Kubenskoye, Oz., *Russia* 41 B11
Kuberle, *Russia* 43 C10
Kubokawa, *Japan* 49 H6
Kubrat, *Bulgaria* 38 F9
Kučevo, *Serbia, Yug.* 21 L11
Kucha Gompa, *India* 63 B7
Kuchaman, *India* 62 F6
Kuchino-eruba-Jima, *Japan* 49 J5
Kuchino-Shima, *Japan* 49 K4
Kuchinotsu, *Japan* 49 H5
Kucing, *Malaysia* 56 D4
Kuçove = Qytet Stalin, *Albania* 39 J2
Kud →, *Pakistan* 62 F2
Kuda, *India* 60 H7
Kudat, *Malaysia* 56 C5
Kudus, *Indonesia* 57 G14
Kudymkar, *Russia* 44 D6
Kueiyang = Guiyang, *China* 52 D6
Kufstein, *Austria* 19 H8
Kugong I., *Canada* 98 A4
Kūh-e Dīnār, *Iran* 65 D6
Kūh-e-Hazārām, *Iran* 65 D8
Kūhak, *Iran* 60 F3
Kūhbonān, *Iran* 65 D8
Kūhestak, *Iran* 65 E8
Kūhīn, *Iran* 65 C6
Kūhīrī, *Iran* 65 E9
Kuhnsdorf, *Austria* 21 J4
Kūhpāyeh, *Eşfahan, Iran* 65 C7
Kūhpāyeh, *Kermān, Iran* 65 D8
Kui Buri, *Thailand* 59 F2
Kuinre, *Neths.* 16 C7
Kuito, *Angola* 81 G3
Kujang, *N. Korea* 51 E14
Kuji, *Japan* 48 D10
Kujū-San, *Japan* 49 H5
Kukawa, *Nigeria* 79 C7
Kukerin, *Australia* 89 F2
Kukmor, *Russia* 41 C17
Kukup, *Malaysia* 59 M4
Kukvidze, *Russia* 41 F13
Kula, *Serbia, Yug.* 21 K9
Kulai, *Malaysia* 59 M4
Kulal, Mt., *Kenya* 82 B4
Kulaly, Os., *Kazakhstan* 43 D14
Kulasekarappattinam, *India* 60 Q11
Kuldiga, *Latvia* 40 C2
Kuldja = Yining, *China* 54 B3
Kuldu, *Sudan* 77 E2
Kulebaki, *Russia* 41 D13
Kulen Vakuf, *Bos.-H., Yug.* 33 D13
Kulgam, *India* 63 C6
Kuli, *Russia* 43 E12
Kulim, *Malaysia* 59 K3
Kulin, *Australia* 89 F2
Kulja, *Australia* 89 F2
Kulm, *U.S.A.* 108 B5
Kulmbach, *Germany* 19 E7
Kulp, *Turkey* 67 D9
Kulsary, *Kazakhstan* 44 E6
Kultay, *Kazakhstan* 43 D14
Kulti, *India* 63 H12
Kulu, *Turkey* 66 D5
Kulumbura, *Australia* 88 B4
Kulunda, *Russia* 44 D8
Kulungar, *Afghan.* 62 C3

Kūlvand

Kūlvand, *Iran* 65 D7
Kulwin, *Australia* 91 F3
Kulyab, *Tajikistan* 44 F7
Kum Tekei, *Kazakhstan* .. 44 E8
Kuma →, *Russia* 43 D12
Kumaganum, *Nigeria* 79 C7
Kumagaya, *Japan* 49 F9
Kumai, *Indonesia* 56 E4
Kumamba, Kepulauan,
  Indonesia 57 E9
Kumamoto, *Japan* 49 H5
Kumamoto □, *Japan* 49 H5
Kumanovo,
  Macedonia, Yug. 38 G4
Kumara, *N.Z.* 87 K3
Kumarl, *Australia* 89 F3
Kumasi, *Ghana* 78 D4
Kumayri, *Armenia* 43 F10
Kumba, *Cameroon* 79 E6
Kumbakonam, *India* 60 P11
Kumbarilla, *Australia* ... 91 D5
Kumbo, *Cameroon* 79 D7
Kŭmchŏn, *N. Korea* 51 E14
Kumdok, *India* 63 C8
Kume-Shima, *Japan* 49 L3
Kumeny, *Russia* 41 B16
Kŭmhwa, *S. Korea* 51 E14
Kumi, *Uganda* 82 B3
Kumla, *Sweden* 9 G13
Kumluca, *Turkey* 66 E4
Kummerower See,
  Germany 18 B8
Kumo, *Nigeria* 79 C7
Kumon Bum, *Burma* 61 F20
Kumtorkala, *Russia* 43 E12
Kumylzhenskaya, *Russia* . 43 B10
Kunama, *Australia* 91 F4
Kunashir, Ostrov, *Russia* . 45 E15
Kunda, *Estonia* 40 B5
Kundla, *India* 62 J4
Kungala, *Australia* 91 D5
Kungälv, *Sweden* 11 G5
Kunghit I., *Canada* 100 C2
Kungrad, *Uzbekistan* 44 E6
Kungsbacka, *Sweden* 11 G6
Kungur, *Russia* 44 D6
Kungurri, *Australia* 90 C4
Kunhar →, *Pakistan* 63 B5
Kunhegyes, *Hungary* 21 H10
Kuningan, *Indonesia* 57 G13
Kunlong, *Burma* 61 H21
Kunlun Shan, *Asia* 54 C3
Kunming, *China* 52 E4
Kunrade, *Neths.* 17 G7
Kunsan, *S. Korea* 51 G14
Kunshan, *China* 53 B13
Kununurra, *Australia* ... 88 C4
Kunwarara, *Australia* ... 90 C5
Kunya-Urgench,
  Turkmenistan 44 E6
Künzelsau, *Germany* 19 F5
Kuopio, *Finland* 8 E19
Kuopion lääni □, *Finland* . 8 E19
Kupa →, *Croatia* 33 C13
Kupang, *Indonesia* 57 F6
Kupres, *Bos.-H., Yug.* .. 21 L7
Kupyansk, *Ukraine* 42 B7
Kupyansk-Uzlovoi, *Ukraine* 42 B7
Kuqa, *China* 54 B3
Kuranda, *Australia* 90 B4
Kurashiki, *Japan* 49 G6
Kurayoshi, *Japan* 49 G6
Kurdistan, *Asia* 67 E10
Kŭrdzhali, *Bulgaria* 39 H8
Kure, *Japan* 49 G6
Küre, *Turkey* 66 C5
Küre Dağlari, *Turkey* ... 66 C6
Kuressaare, *Estonia* 40 B3
Kurgaldzhino, *Kazakhstan* 44 D8
Kurgan, *Russia* 44 D7
Kurganinsk, *Russia* 43 D9
Kurgannaya = Kurganinsk,
  Russia 43 D9
Kuria Maria Is. = Khūrīyā
  Mūrīyā, Jazā 'ir, *Oman* . 68 D6
Kuridala, *Australia* 90 C3
Kurigram, *Bangla.* 61 G16
Kuril Is. = Kurilskiye
  Ostrova, *Russia* 45 E15
Kuril Trench, *Pac. Oc.* . 92 C7
Kurilsk, *Russia* 45 E15
Kurilskiye Ostrova, *Russia* 45 E15
Kuringen, *Belgium* 17 G6
Kurino, *Japan* 49 J5
Kurkur, *Egypt* 76 C3
Kurlovskiy, *Russia* 41 D12
Kurmuk, *Sudan* 77 E3
Kurnool, *India* 60 M10
Kuro-Shima, *Kagoshima,*
  Japan 49 J4
Kuro-Shima, *Okinawa,*
  Japan 49 M2
Kurovskoye, *Russia* 41 D11
Kurow, *N.Z.* 87 L3
Kurrajong, *Australia* 91 E5
Kurram →, *Pakistan* 62 C4
Kurri Kurri, *Australia* ... 91 E5
Kursavka, *Russia* 43 D10
Kuršėnai, *Lithuania* 40 C3
Kursk, *Russia* 41 F10
Kuršumlija, *Serbia, Yug.* . 21 M11
Kurşunlu, *Turkey* 66 C5
Kurtalan, *Turkey* 67 E9
Kuru, Bahr el →, *Sudan* . 77 F2

Kurucaşile, *Turkey* 66 C5
Kuruktag, *China* 54 B3
Kuruman, *S. Africa* 84 D3
Kuruman →, *S. Africa* .. 84 D3
Kurume, *Japan* 49 H5
Kurunegala, *Sri Lanka* .. 60 R12
Kurupukari, *Guyana* ... 121 C6
Kurya, *Russia* 45 C11
Kus Gölü, *Turkey* 66 C2
Kuşadası, *Turkey* 66 E2
Kusatsu, *Japan* 49 F9
Kusawa L., *Canada* 100 A1
Kusel, *Germany* 19 F3
Kushchevskaya, *Russia* . 43 C8
Kushikino, *Japan* 49 J5
Kushima, *Japan* 49 J5
Kushimoto, *Japan* 49 H7
Kushiro, *Japan* 48 C12
Kushiro →, *Japan* 48 C12
Küshk, *Iran* 65 D8
Kushka, *Turkmenistan* .. 44 F7
Kūshkī, *Īlām, Iran* 64 C5
Kūshkī, *Khorāsān, Iran* . 65 B8
Kūshkū, *Iran* 65 E7
Kushol, *India* 63 C7
Kushtia, *Bangla.* 61 H16
Kushum →, *Kazakhstan* . 43 B14
Kuskokwim →, *U.S.A.* .. 96 B3
Kuskokwim Bay, *U.S.A.* . 96 C3
Küsnacht, *Switz.* 23 B7
Kussharo-Ko, *Japan* 48 C12
Küssnacht, *Switz.* 23 B6
Kustanay, *Kazakhstan* .. 44 D7
Kut, Ko, *Thailand* 59 G4
Kütahya, *Turkey* 66 D4
Kütahya □, *Turkey* 66 D3
Kutaisi, *Georgia* 43 E10
Kutaraja = Banda Aceh,
  Indonesia 56 C1
Kutch, Gulf of = Kachchh,
  Gulf of, *India* 62 H3
Kutch, Rann of =
  Kachchh, Rann of, *India* 62 G4
Kutina, *Croatia* 33 C13
Kutiyana, *India* 62 J4
Kutkashen, *Azerbaijan* . 43 F12
Kutná Hora, *Czech.* 20 F5
Kutno, *Poland* 20 C9
Kuttabul, *Australia* 90 C4
Kutu, *Zaïre* 80 E3
Kutum, *Sudan* 77 E1
Kuujjuaq, *Canada* 97 C13
Kuup-tong, *N. Korea* ... 51 D14
Kuurne, *Belgium* 17 G2
Kuvshinovo, *Russia* 40 C9
Kuwait = Al Kuwayt,
  Kuwait 64 D5
Kuwait ■, *Asia* 64 D5
Kuwana, *Japan* 49 G8
Kuybyshev = Samara,
  Russia 41 E17
Kuybyshev, *Russia* 44 D8
Kuybyshevo, *Russia* 42 C7
Kuybyshevskoye Vdkhr.,
  Russia 41 D16
Kuye He →, *China* 50 E6
Küyeh, *Iran* 64 B5
Küysanjaq, *Iraq* 64 B5
Kuyumba, *Russia* 45 C10
Kuzey Anadolu Dağlari,
  Turkey 66 C6
Kuznetsk, *Russia* 41 E15
Kvænangen, *Norway* ... 8 A16
Kvam, *Norway* 10 C3
Kvareli, *Georgia* 43 F11
Kvarner, *Croatia* 33 D11
Kvarnerič, *Croatia* 33 D11
Kviteseid, *Norway* 10 E2
Kwabhaca, *S. Africa* ... 85 E4
Kwadacha →, *Canada* . 100 B3
Kwakhanai, *Botswana* .. 84 C3
Kwakoegron, *Surinam* .. 121 B6
Kwale, *Kenya* 82 C4
Kwale, *Nigeria* 79 D6
Kwale □, *Kenya* 82 C4
KwaMashu, *S. Africa* ... 85 D5
Kwamouth, *Zaïre* 80 E3
Kwando →, *Africa* 84 B3
Kwangdaeri, *N. Korea* .. 51 D14
Kwangju, *S. Korea* 51 G14
Kwangsi-Chuang =
  Guangxi Zhuangzu
  Zizhiqu □, *China* 52 E7
Kwangtung =
  Guangdong □, *China* . 53 F9
Kwara □, *Nigeria* 79 D5
Kwataboahegan →,
  Canada 98 B3
Kwatisore, *Indonesia* ... 57 E8
Kweichow = Guizhou □,
  China 52 D6
Kwekwe, *Zimbabwe* ... 83 F2
Kwimba □, *Tanzania* ... 82 C3
Kwinana New Town,
  Australia 89 F2
Kwoka, *Indonesia* 57 E8
Kyabé, *Chad* 73 G8
Kyabra Cr. →, *Australia* . 91 D3
Kyabram, *Australia* 91 F4
Kyaikto, *Burma* 58 D1
Kyakhta, *Russia* 45 D11
Kyancutta, *Australia* ... 91 E2
Kyangin, *Burma* 61 K19
Kyaukpadaung, *Burma* . 61 J19

Kyaukpyu, *Burma* 61 K18
Kyaukse, *Burma* 61 J20
Kyburz, *U.S.A.* 112 G6
Kycen, *Russia* 45 D11
Kyenjojo, *Uganda* 82 B3
Kyle Dam, *Zimbabwe* .. 83 G3
Kyle of Lochalsh, *U.K.* . 14 D3
Kyll →, *Germany* 19 F2
Kyllburg, *Germany* 19 E2
Kyneton, *Australia* 91 F3
Kynuna, *Australia* 90 C3
Kyo-ga-Saki, *Japan* 49 G7
Kyoga, L., *Uganda* 82 B3
Kyogle, *Australia* 91 D5
Kyongju, *S. Korea* 51 G15
Kyongpyaw, *Burma* 61 L19
Kyōto, *Japan* 49 G7
Kyōto □, *Japan* 49 G7
Kyparissovouno, *Cyprus* 37 D11
Kyperounda, *Cyprus* ... 37 E11
Kyrenia, *Cyprus* 37 D12
Kyritz, *Germany* 18 C8
Kystatyam, *Russia* 45 C13
Kytal Ktakh, *Russia* 45 C13
Kythréa, *Cyprus* 37 D12
Kyulyunken, *Russia* 45 C14
Kyunhla, *Burma* 61 H19
Kyuquot, *Canada* 100 C3
Kyurdamir, *Azerbaijan* . 43 F13
Kyūshū, *Japan* 49 H5
Kyūshū □, *Japan* 49 H5
Kyūshū-Sanchi, *Japan* .. 49 H5
Kyustendil, *Bulgaria* 38 G5
Kyusyur, *Russia* 45 B13
Kywong, *Australia* 91 E4
Kyzyl, *Russia* 45 D10
Kyzyl-Kiya, *Kirghizia* ... 44 E8
Kyzylkum, Peski,
  Uzbekistan 44 E7
Kzyl-Orda, *Kazakhstan* . 44 E7

L

La Albuera, *Spain* 31 G4
La Alcarria, *Spain* 28 E2
La Algaba, *Spain* 31 H4
La Almarcha, *Spain* 28 F2
La Almunia de Doña
  Godina, *Spain* 28 D3
La Asunción, *Venezuela* 121 A5
La Banda, *Argentina* ... 126 B3
La Bañeza, *Spain* 30 C5
La Barca, *Mexico* 114 C4
La Barge, *U.S.A.* 110 E8
La Bassée, *France* 25 B9
La Bastide-Puylaurent,
  France 26 D7
La Baule, *France* 24 E4
La Belle, *U.S.A.* 105 M5
La Biche →, *Canada* .. 100 B4
La Bisbal, *Spain* 28 D8
La Blanquilla, *Venezuela* 121 A5
La Bomba, *Mexico* 114 A1
La Bresse, *France* 25 D13
La Bureba, *Spain* 28 C1
La Cal →, *Bolivia* 125 D6
La Calera, *Chile* 126 C1
La Campiña, *Spain* 31 H6
La Canal, *Spain* 36 C7
La Cañiza, *Spain* 30 C2
La Capelle, *France* 25 C10
La Carlota, *Argentina* .. 126 C3
La Carlota, *Phil.* 55 F5
La Carolina, *Spain* 31 G7
La Cavalerie, *France* ... 26 D7
La Ceiba, *Honduras* ... 116 C2
La Chaise-Dieu, *France* . 26 C7
La Chaize-le-Vicomte,
  France 24 F5
La Chapelle d'Angillon,
  France 25 E9
La Chapelle-Glain, *France* 24 E5
La Charité-sur-Loire,
  France 25 E10
La Chartre-sur-le-Loir,
  France 24 E7
La Châtaigneraie, *France* . 26 B3
La Châtre, *France* 26 B5
La Chaux de Fonds, *Switz.* 22 B3
La Chorrera, *Colombia* . 120 D3
La Ciotat, *France* 27 E9
La Clayette, *France* 27 B8
La Cocha, *Argentina* ... 126 B2
La Concepción = Ri-Aba,
  Eq. Guin. 79 E6
La Concepción, *Venezuela* 120 A3
La Concordia, *Mexico* .. 115 D6
La Conner, *U.S.A.* 110 B2
La Coruña, *Spain* 30 B2
La Coruña □, *Spain* 30 B2
La Côte, *Switz.* 22 D2
La Côte-St.-André, *France* 27 C9
La Courtine-le-Trucq,
  France 26 C6
La Crete, *Canada* 100 B5
La Crosse, *Kans., U.S.A.* 108 F5
La Crosse, *Wis., U.S.A.* . 108 D9
La Cruz, *Costa Rica* ... 116 D2
La Cruz, *Mexico* 114 C3

La Dorada, *Colombia* .. 120 B3
La Ensenada, *Chile* 128 B2
La Escondida, *Mexico* .. 114 C5
La Esmeralda, *Paraguay* 126 A3
La Esperanza, *Argentina* 128 B3
La Esperanza, *Cuba* ... 116 B3
La Esperanza, *Honduras* 116 D2
La Estrada, *Spain* 30 C2
La Fayette, *U.S.A.* 105 H3
La Fé, *Cuba* 116 B3
La Fère, *France* 25 C10
La Ferté-Bernard, *France* . 24 D7
La Ferté-Macé, *France* .. 24 D6
La Ferté-St.-Aubin, *France* 25 E8
La Ferté-sous-Jouarre,
  France 25 D10
La Ferté-Vidame, *France* . 24 D7
La Flèche, *France* 24 E6
La Follette, *U.S.A.* 105 G3
La Fregeneda, *Spain* ... 30 E4
La Fría, *Venezuela* 120 B3
La Fuente de San Esteban,
  Spain 30 E4
La Gineta, *Spain* 29 F2
La Gloria, *Colombia* ... 120 B3
La Gran Sabana, *Venezuela* 121 B5
La Grand-Combe, *France* . 27 D8
La Grande, *U.S.A.* 110 D4
La Grande-Motte, *France* . 27 E8
La Grange, *Australia* ... 88 C3
La Grange, *Ga., U.S.A.* . 105 J3
La Grange, *Ky., U.S.A.* . 104 F3
La Grange, *Tex., U.S.A.* 109 L6
La Grita, *Venezuela* 120 B3
La Guaira, *Venezuela* .. 120 A4
La Guardia, *Spain* 30 D2
La Gudiña, *Spain* 30 C3
La Güera, *Mauritania* .. 74 D1
La Guerche-de-Bretagne,
  France 24 E5
La Guerche-sur-l'Aubois,
  France 25 F9
La Habana, *Cuba* 116 B3
La Harpe, *U.S.A.* 108 E9
La Haye-du-Puits, *France* . 24 C5
La Horqueta, *Venezuela* 121 B5
La Horra, *Spain* 30 D7
La Independencia, *Mexico* 115 D6
La Isabela, *Dom. Rep.* . 117 C5
La Jara, *U.S.A.* 111 H11
La Joya, *Peru* 124 D3
La Junquera, *Spain* 28 C7
La Junta, *U.S.A.* 109 F3
La Laguna, *Canary Is.* . 36 F3
La Libertad, *Guatemala* 116 C1
La Libertad, *Mexico* ... 114 B2
La Libertad □, *Peru* 124 B2
La Ligua, *Chile* 126 C1
La Línea de la Concepción,
  Spain 31 J5
La Loche, *Canada* 101 B7
La Londe-les-Maures,
  France 27 E10
La Lora, *Spain* 30 C7
La Loupe, *France* 24 D8
La Louvière, *Belgium* ... 17 H4
La Machine, *France* 25 F10
La Maddalena, *Italy* 34 A2
La Malbaie, *Canada* 99 C5
La Mancha, *Spain* 29 F2
La Mariña, *Spain* 30 B3
La Mesa, *Calif., U.S.A.* 113 N9
La Mesa, *N. Mex., U.S.A.* 111 K10
La Misión, *Mexico* 114 A1
La Mothe-Achard, *France* 24 F5
La Motte, *France* 27 D10
La Motte-Chalançon,
  France 27 D9
La Moure, *U.S.A.* 108 B5
La Muela, *Spain* 28 D3
La Mure, *France* 27 D9
La Negra, *Chile* 126 A1
La Neuveville, *Switz.* ... 22 B4
La Oliva, *Canary Is.* ... 36 F6
La Oraya, *Peru* 124 C2
La Orotava, *Canary Is.* . 36 F3
La Pacaudière, *France* .. 26 B7
La Palma, *Canary Is.* .. 36 F2
La Palma, *Panama* 116 E4
La Palma, *Spain* 31 H4
La Paloma, *Chile* 126 C1
La Pampa □, *Argentina* 126 D2
La Paragua, *Venezuela* . 121 B5
La Paz, *Entre Ríos,*
  Argentina 126 C4
La Paz, *San Luis,*
  Argentina 126 C2
La Paz, *Bolivia* 124 D4
La Paz, *Honduras* 116 D2
La Paz, *Mexico* 114 C2
La Paz, *Phil.* 55 F5
La Paz □, *Bolivia* 124 D4
La Paz Centro, *Nic.* ... 116 D2
La Pedrera, *Colombia* .. 120 D4
La Perouse Str., *Asia* .. 48 B11
La Pesca, *Mexico* 115 C5
La Piedad, *Mexico* 114 C4
La Pine, *U.S.A.* 110 E3
La Plant, *U.S.A.* 108 C4
La Plata, *Argentina* 126 D4
La Plata, *Colombia* 120 C2
La Plata, L., *Argentina* . 128 B2
La Pobla de Lillet, *Spain* . 28 C6
La Pola de Gordón, *Spain* 30 C5

La Porte, *U.S.A.* 104 E2
La Puebla, *Spain* 28 F8
La Puebla de Cazalla,
  Spain 31 H5
La Puebla de los Infantes,
  Spain 31 H5
La Puebla de Montalbán,
  Spain 30 F6
La Puerta, *Spain* 29 G2
La Punt, *Switz.* 23 C9
La Purísima, *Mexico* ... 114 B2
La Push, *U.S.A.* 112 C2
La Quiaca, *Argentina* .. 126 A2
La Rambla, *Spain* 31 H6
La Reine, *Canada* 98 C4
La Réole, *France* 26 D3
La Restinga, *Canary Is.* . 36 G2
La Rioja, *Argentina* 126 B2
La Rioja □, *Argentina* .. 126 B2
La Rioja □, *Spain* 28 C2
La Robla, *Spain* 30 C5
La Roche, *Switz.* 22 C4
La Roche-Bernard, *France* 24 E4
La Roche-Canillac, *France* 26 C5
La Roche-en-Ardenne,
  Belgium 17 H7
La Roche-sur-Yon, *France* 24 F5
La Rochefoucauld, *France* 26 C4
La Rochelle, *France* 26 B2
La Roda, *Albacete, Spain* . 29 F2
La Roda, *Sevilla, Spain* . 31 H6
La Romana, *Dom. Rep.* 117 C6
La Ronge, *Canada* 101 B7
La Rumorosa, *Mexico* . 113 N10
La Sabina, *Spain* 36 C7
La Sagra, *Spain* 29 H2
La Salle, *U.S.A.* 108 E10
La Sanabria, *Spain* 30 C4
La Santa, *Canary Is.* ... 36 E6
La Sarraz, *Switz.* 22 C3
La Sarre, *Canada* 98 C4
La Scie, *Canada* 99 C8
La Selva, *Spain* 28 D7
La Selva Beach, *U.S.A.* 112 J5
La Serena, *Chile* 126 B1
La Serena, *Spain* 31 G5
La Seyne, *France* 27 E9
La Sila, *Italy* 35 C9
La Solana, *Spain* 29 G1
La Souterraine, *France* .. 26 B5
La Spézia, *Italy* 32 D6
La Suze-sur-Sarthe, *France* 24 E7
La Tagua, *Colombia* ... 120 C3
La Teste, *France* 26 D2
La Tortuga, *Venezuela* . 117 D6
La Tour-du-Pin, *France* . 27 C9
La Tranche-sur-Mer,
  France 24 F5
La Tremblade, *France* ... 26 C2
La Tuque, *Canada* 98 C5
La Unión, *Chile* 128 B2
La Unión, *Colombia* 120 C2
La Unión, *El Salv.* 116 D2
La Unión, *Mexico* 114 D4
La Unión, *Peru* 124 B2
La Unión, *Spain* 29 H4
La Urbana, *Venezuela* .. 120 B4
La Vecilla, *Spain* 30 C5
La Vega, *Dom. Rep.* ... 117 C5
La Vega, *Peru* 124 C2
La Vela, *Venezuela* 120 A4
La Veleta, *Spain* 31 H7
La Venta, *Mexico* 115 D6
La Ventura, *Mexico* 114 C4
La Venturosa, *Colombia* 120 B4
La Victoria, *Venezuela* . 120 A4
La Voulte-sur-Rhône,
  France 27 D8
La Zarza, *Spain* 31 H4
Laaber →, *Germany* ... 19 G8
Laage, *Germany* 18 B8
Laba →, *Russia* 43 D8
Labason, *Phil.* 55 G5
Labastide-Murat, *France* . 26 D5
Labastide-Rouairoux,
  France 26 E6
Labbézenga, *Mali* 79 B5
Labe = Elbe →, *Europe* . 18 B4
Labé, *Guinea* 78 C2
Laberec →, *Czech.* 20 G11
Laberge, L., *Canada* ... 100 A1
Labin, *Croatia* 33 C11
Labinsk, *Russia* 43 D9
Labis, *Malaysia* 59 L4
Labo, *Phil.* 55 D5
Laboe, *Germany* 18 A6
Labouheyre, *France* 26 D3
Laboulaye, *Argentina* .. 126 C3
Labra, Peña, *Spain* 30 B6
Labrador, Coast of □,
  Canada 99 B7
Labrador City, *Canada* . 99 B6
Lábrea, *Brazil* 125 B5
Labrède, *France* 26 D3
Labuan, Pulau, *Malaysia* 56 C5
Labuha, *Indonesia* 57 E7
Labuhan, *Indonesia* 57 G11
Labuhanbajo, *Indonesia* 57 F6
Labuissière, *Belgium* ... 17 H4
Labuk, Telok, *Malaysia* . 56 C5
Labyrinth, L., *Australia* . 91 E2
Labytnangi, *Russia* 44 C7
Lac Allard, *Canada* 99 B7
Lac Bouchette, *Canada* . 99 C5

Lac du Flambeau, *U.S.A.* 108 B10
Lac Édouard, *Canada* 98 C5
Lac La Biche, *Canada* 100 C6
Lac la Martre, *Canada* 96 B8
Lac-Mégantic, *Canada* 99 C5
Lac Seul, Res., *Canada* 98 B1
Lac Thien, *Vietnam* 58 F7
Lacanau, *France* 26 D2
Lacanau, Étang de, *France* 26 D2
Lacantúm →, *Mexico* 115 D6
Lacara →, *Spain* 31 G4
Lacaune, *France* 26 E6
Lacaune, Mts. de, *France* 26 E6
Laccadive Is. = Lakshadweep Is., *Ind. Oc.* 46 J11
Lacepede B., *Australia* 91 F2
Lacepede Is., *Australia* 88 C3
Lacerdónia, *Mozam.* 83 F4
Lacey, *U.S.A.* 112 C4
Lachay, Pta., *Peru* 124 C2
Lachen, *Switz.* 23 B7
Lachhmangarh, *India* 62 F6
Lachi, *Pakistan* 62 C4
Lachine, *Canada* 98 C5
Lachlan →, *Australia* 91 E3
Lachute, *Canada* 98 C5
Lackawanna, *U.S.A.* 106 D6
Lacolle, *Canada* 107 A11
Lacombe, *Canada* 100 C6
Lacona, *U.S.A.* 107 C8
Láconi, *Italy* 34 C2
Laconia, *U.S.A.* 107 C13
Lacq, *France* 26 E3
Lacrosse, *U.S.A.* 110 C5
Ladakh Ra., *India* 63 B8
Ladário, *Brazil* 125 D6
Ládhon →, *Greece* 39 M4
Lâdik, *Turkey* 42 F6
Ladismith, *S. Africa* 84 E3
Lādīz, *Iran* 65 D9
Ladnun, *India* 62 F6
Ladoga, L. = Ladozhskoye Ozero, *Russia* 44 C4
Ladon, *France* 25 D9
Ladozhskoye Ozero, *Russia* 44 C4
Ladrillero, G., *Chile* 128 C1
Lady Grey, *S. Africa* 84 E4
Ladybrand, *S. Africa* 84 D4
Ladysmith, *Canada* 100 D4
Ladysmith, *S. Africa* 85 D4
Ladysmith, *U.S.A.* 108 C9
Lae, *Papua N. G.* 92 H6
Laem Ngop, *Thailand* 59 F4
Laem Pho, *Thailand* 59 J3
Læsø, *Denmark* 11 G4
Læsø Rende, *Denmark* 11 G4
Lafayette, *Colo., U.S.A.* 108 F2
Lafayette, *Ind., U.S.A.* 104 E2
Lafayette, *La., U.S.A.* 109 K9
Lafayette, *Tenn., U.S.A.* 105 G3
Laferte →, *Canada* 100 A5
Lafia, *Nigeria* 79 D6
Lafiagi, *Nigeria* 79 D6
Lafleche, *Canada* 101 D7
Lafon, *Sudan* 77 F3
Laforsen, *Sweden* 10 C9
Lagan →, *Sweden* 11 H7
Lagan →, *U.K.* 15 B6
Lagarfljót →, *Iceland* 8 D6
Lagarto, *Brazil* 122 D4
Lage, *Germany* 18 D4
Lage, *Spain* 30 B2
Lage-Mierde, *Neths.* 17 F6
Lågen →, *Norway* 9 F11
Lägerdorf, *Germany* 18 B5
Laghouat, *Algeria* 75 B5
Lagnieu, *France* 27 C9
Lagny, *France* 25 D9
Lago, *Italy* 35 C9
Lago Posadas, *Argentina* 128 C2
Lago Ranco, *Chile* 128 B2
Lagôa, *Portugal* 31 H2
Lagoaça, *Portugal* 30 D4
Lagodekhi, *Georgia* 43 F12
Lagónegro, *Italy* 35 B8
Lagonoy Gulf, *Phil.* 55 E5
Lagos, *Nigeria* 79 D5
Lagos, *Portugal* 31 H2
Lagos de Moreno, *Mexico* 114 C4
Lagrange, *Australia* 88 C3
Lagrange B., *Australia* 88 C3
Laguardia, *Spain* 28 C2
Laguépie, *France* 26 D5
Laguna, *Brazil* 127 B6
Laguna, *U.S.A.* 111 J10
Laguna Beach, *U.S.A.* 113 M9
Laguna de la Janda, *Spain* 31 J5
Laguna Limpia, *Argentina* 126 B4
Laguna Madre, *U.S.A.* 115 B5
Lagunas, *Chile* 126 A2
Lagunas, *Peru* 124 B2
Lagunillas, *Bolivia* 125 D5
Lahad Datu, *Malaysia* 57 C5
Lahan Sai, *Thailand* 58 E4
Lahanam, *Laos* 58 D5
Laharpur, *India* 63 F9
Lahat, *Indonesia* 56 E2
Lahewa, *Indonesia* 56 D1
Lahiang Lahiang, *Phil.* 55 H4
Lahijan, *Iran* 65 B6
Lahn →, *Germany* 19 E3
Laholm, *Sweden* 11 H7
Laholmsbukten, *Sweden* 11 H6
Lahontan Res., *U.S.A.* 110 G4
Lahore, *Pakistan* 62 D6
Lahr, *Germany* 19 G3
Lahti, *Finland* 9 F18
Lahtis = Lahti, *Finland* 9 F18
Laï, *Chad* 73 G8
Lai Chau, *Vietnam* 58 A4
Lai'an, *China* 53 A12
Laibin, *China* 52 F7
Laidley, *Australia* 91 D5
Laifeng, *China* 52 C7
L'Aigle, *France* 24 D7
Laignes, *France* 25 E11
L'Aiguillon-sur-Mer, *France* 26 B2
Laikipia □, *Kenya* 82 B4
Laingsburg, *S. Africa* 84 E3
Lairg, *U.K.* 14 C4
Laishui, *China* 50 E8
Laiwu, *China* 51 F9
Laixi, *China* 51 F11
Laiyang, *China* 51 F11
Laiyuan, *China* 50 E8
Laizhou Wan, *China* 51 F10
Laja →, *Mexico* 114 C4
Lajere, *Nigeria* 79 C7
Lajes, *Rio Grande do N., Brazil* 122 C4
Lajes, *Sta. Catarina, Brazil* 127 B5
Lajinha, *Brazil* 123 F3
Lajkovac, *Serbia, Yug.* 21 L10
Lajosmizse, *Hungary* 21 H9
Lak Sao, *Laos* 58 C5
Lakaband, *Pakistan* 62 D3
Lakar, *Indonesia* 57 F7
Lake Alpine, *U.S.A.* 112 G7
Lake Andes, *U.S.A.* 108 D5
Lake Anse, *U.S.A.* 104 B1
Lake Arthur, *U.S.A.* 109 K8
Lake Cargelligo, *Australia* 91 E4
Lake Charles, *U.S.A.* 109 K8
Lake City, *Colo., U.S.A.* 111 G10
Lake City, *Fla., U.S.A.* 105 K4
Lake City, *Iowa, U.S.A.* 108 D7
Lake City, *Mich., U.S.A.* 104 C3
Lake City, *Minn., U.S.A.* 108 C8
Lake City, *Pa., U.S.A.* 106 D4
Lake City, *S.C., U.S.A.* 105 J6
Lake George, *U.S.A.* 107 C11
Lake Grace, *Australia* 89 F2
Lake Harbour, *Canada* 97 B13
Lake Havasu City, *U.S.A.* 113 L12
Lake Hughes, *U.S.A.* 113 L8
Lake Isabella, *U.S.A.* 113 K8
Lake King, *Australia* 89 F2
Lake Lenore, *Canada* 101 C8
Lake Louise, *Canada* 100 C5
Lake Mead Nat. Rec. Area, *U.S.A.* 113 K12
Lake Mills, *U.S.A.* 108 D8
Lake Nash, *Australia* 90 C2
Lake Providence, *U.S.A.* 109 J9
Lake River, *Canada* 98 B3
Lake Superior Prov. Park, *Canada* 98 C3
Lake Village, *U.S.A.* 109 J9
Lake Wales, *U.S.A.* 105 M5
Lake Worth, *U.S.A.* 105 M5
Lakefield, *Canada* 98 D4
Lakeland, *Australia* 90 B3
Lakeland, *U.S.A.* 105 L5
Lakemba, *Fiji* 87 D9
Lakeport, *U.S.A.* 112 F4
Lakes Entrance, *Australia* 91 F4
Lakeside, *Ariz., U.S.A.* 111 J9
Lakeside, *Calif., U.S.A.* 113 N10
Lakeside, *Nebr., U.S.A.* 108 D3
Lakeview, *U.S.A.* 110 E3
Lakewood, *Colo., U.S.A.* 108 F2
Lakewood, *N.J., U.S.A.* 107 F10
Lakewood, *Ohio, U.S.A.* 106 E3
Lakewood Center, *U.S.A.* 112 C4
Lakhaniá, *Greece* 37 D9
Lakhonpheng, *Laos* 58 E5
Lakhpat, *India* 62 H3
Laki, *Iceland* 8 D4
Lakin, *U.S.A.* 109 G4
Lakitusaki →, *Canada* 98 B3
Lákkoi, *Greece* 37 D5
Lakonikós Kólpos, *Greece* 39 N5
Lakota, *Ivory C.* 78 D3
Lakota, *U.S.A.* 108 A5
Laksefjorden, *Norway* 8 A19
Lakselv, *Norway* 8 A18
Lakshadweep Is., *Ind. Oc.* 46 J11
Lakshmikantapur, *India* 63 H13
Lala Ghat, *India* 61 G18
Lala Musa, *Pakistan* 62 C5
Lalago, *Tanzania* 82 C3
Lalapanzi, *Zimbabwe* 83 F3
Lalganj, *India* 63 G11
Lalibela, *Ethiopia* 77 E4
Lalin, *China* 51 B14
Lalín, *Spain* 30 C2
Lalin He →, *China* 51 B13
Lalinde, *France* 26 D4
Lalitapur = Patan, *Nepal* 61 F14
Lalitpur, *India* 63 G8
Lam, *Vietnam* 58 B6
Lam Pao Res., *Thailand* 58 D4
Lama Kara, *Togo* 79 D5
Lamaing, *Burma* 61 M20
Lamar, *Colo., U.S.A.* 108 F3
Lamar, *Mo., U.S.A.* 109 G7
Lamarque, *Argentina* 128 A3
Lamas, *Peru* 124 B2
Lamastre, *France* 27 D8
Lamballe, *France* 24 D4
Lambaréné, *Gabon* 80 E2
Lambasa, *Fiji* 87 C8
Lambay I., *Ireland* 15 C5
Lambayeque □, *Peru* 124 B2
Lambert, *U.S.A.* 108 B2
Lambert Glacier, *Antarctica* 5 D6
Lamberts Bay, *S. Africa* 84 E2
Lambesc, *France* 27 E9
Lámbia, *Greece* 39 M4
Lambro →, *Italy* 32 C6
Lame, *Nigeria* 79 C6
Lame Deer, *U.S.A.* 110 D10
Lamego, *Portugal* 30 D3
Lamèque, *Canada* 99 C7
Lameroo, *Australia* 91 F3
Lamesa, *U.S.A.* 109 J4
Lamía, *Greece* 39 L5
Lamitan, *Phil.* 55 H5
Lammermuir Hills, *U.K.* 14 F6
Lamon Bay, *Phil.* 55 D5
Lamont, *Canada* 100 C6
Lamont, *U.S.A.* 113 K8
Lampa, *Peru* 124 D3
Lampang, *Thailand* 58 C2
Lampasas, *U.S.A.* 109 K5
Lampaul, *France* 24 D1
Lampazos de Naranjo, *Mexico* 114 B4
Lampeter, *U.K.* 13 E3
Lampione, *Medit. S.* 75 A7
Lampman, *Canada* 101 D8
Lamprey, *Canada* 101 B10
Lampung □, *Indonesia* 56 F2
Lamu, *Kenya* 82 C5
Lamu □, *Kenya* 82 C5
Lamud, *Peru* 124 B2
Lamy, *U.S.A.* 111 J11
Lan Xian, *China* 50 E6
Lan Yu, *Taiwan* 53 F13
Lanai I., *U.S.A.* 102 H16
Lanak La, *India* 63 B8
Lanaken, *Belgium* 17 G7
Lanak'o Shank'ou = Lanak La, *India* 63 B8
Lanao, L., *Phil.* 55 H6
Lanark, *Canada* 107 A8
Lanark, *U.K.* 14 F5
Lancang, *China* 52 F2
Lancang Jiang →, *China* 52 G3
Lancashire □, *U.K.* 12 D5
Lancaster, *Canada* 107 A10
Lancaster, *U.K.* 12 C5
Lancaster, *Calif., U.S.A.* 113 L8
Lancaster, *Ky., U.S.A.* 104 G3
Lancaster, *N.H., U.S.A.* 107 B13
Lancaster, *N.Y., U.S.A.* 106 D6
Lancaster, *Pa., U.S.A.* 107 F8
Lancaster, *S.C., U.S.A.* 105 H5
Lancaster, *Wis., U.S.A.* 108 D9
Lancaster Sd., *Canada* 97 A11
Lancer, *Canada* 101 C7
Lanchow = Lanzhou, *China* 50 F2
Lanciano, *Italy* 33 F11
Lanco, *Chile* 128 A2
Lancones, *Peru* 124 A1
Lancun, *China* 51 F11
Łancut, *Poland* 20 E12
Lancy, *Switz.* 22 D2
Landau, *Bayern, Germany* 19 G8
Landau, *Rhld-Pfz., Germany* 19 F4
Landeck, *Austria* 19 H6
Landen, *Belgium* 17 G6
Lander, *U.S.A.* 110 E9
Lander →, *Australia* 88 D5
Landerneau, *France* 24 D2
Landeryd, *Sweden* 11 G7
Landes, *France* 26 D3
Landes □, *France* 26 E3
Landete, *Spain* 28 F3
Landi Kotal, *Pakistan* 62 B4
Landivisiau, *France* 24 D2
Landor, *Australia* 89 E2
Landquart, *Switz.* 23 C9
Landquart →, *Switz.* 23 C9
Landrecies, *France* 25 B10
Land's End, *U.K.* 13 G2
Landsberg, *Germany* 19 G6
Landsborough Cr. →, *Australia* 90 C3
Landshut, *Germany* 19 G8
Landskrona, *Sweden* 11 J6
Landstuhl, *Germany* 19 F3
Landvetter, *Sweden* 11 G6
Laneffe, *Belgium* 17 H5
Lanesboro, *U.S.A.* 107 E9
Lanett, *U.S.A.* 105 J3
Lang Bay, *Canada* 100 D4
Lang Qua, *Vietnam* 58 A5
Lang Shan, *China* 50 D4
Lang Son, *Vietnam* 58 B6
Lang Suan, *Thailand* 59 H2
La'nga Co, *China* 61 D12
Làngadhás, *Greece* 39 J6
Langádhia, *Greece* 39 M5
Långan →, *Sweden* 10 A8
Langar, *Iran* 65 C9
Langara I., *Canada* 100 C2
Langatabbetje, *Surinam* 121 C7
Langdai, *China* 52 D5
Langdon, *U.S.A.* 108 A5
Langdorp, *Belgium* 17 G5
Langeac, *France* 26 C7
Langeais, *France* 24 E7
Langeb Baraka →, *Sudan* 76 D4
Langeberg, *S. Africa* 84 E3
Langeberge, *S. Africa* 84 D3
Langeland, *Denmark* 11 K4
Langemark, *Belgium* 17 G1
Langen, *Germany* 19 F4
Langenburg, *Canada* 101 C8
Langeness, *Germany* 18 A4
Langenthal, *Switz.* 22 B5
Langeoog, *Germany* 18 B3
Langeskov, *Denmark* 11 J4
Langesund, *Norway* 10 F3
Länghem, *Sweden* 11 G7
Langhirano, *Italy* 32 D7
Langholm, *U.K.* 14 F6
Langhus, *Norway* 10 E4
Langjökull, *Iceland* 8 D3
Langkawi, P., *Malaysia* 59 J2
Langklip, *S. Africa* 84 D3
Langkon, *Malaysia* 56 C5
Langlade, *St- P. & M.* 99 C8
Langlois, *U.S.A.* 110 E1
Langnau, *Switz.* 22 C5
Langogne, *France* 26 D7
Langon, *France* 26 D3
Langøya, *Norway* 8 B13
Langres, *France* 25 E12
Langres, Plateau de, *France* 25 E12
Langsa, *Indonesia* 56 D1
Långsele, *Sweden* 10 A11
Langtry, *U.S.A.* 109 L4
Langu, *Thailand* 59 J2
Languedoc, *France* 26 E7
Langwies, *Switz.* 23 C9
Langxi, *China* 53 B12
Langxiangzhen, *China* 50 E9
Langzhong, *China* 52 B5
Lanigan, *Canada* 101 C7
Lankao, *China* 50 G8
Lannemezan, *France* 26 E4
Lannilis, *France* 24 D2
Lannion, *France* 24 D3
L'Annonciation, *Canada* 98 C5
Lanouaille, *France* 26 C5
Lanping, *China* 52 D2
Lansdale, *U.S.A.* 107 F9
Lansdowne, *Australia* 91 E5
Lansdowne, *Canada* 107 B8
Lansdowne House, *Canada* 98 B2
L'Anse, *U.S.A.* 98 C2
L'Anse au Loup, *Canada* 99 B8
Lansford, *U.S.A.* 107 F9
Lanshan, *China* 53 E9
Lansing, *U.S.A.* 104 D3
Lanslebourg-Mont-Cenis, *France* 27 C10
Lanta Yai, Ko, *Thailand* 59 J2
Lantian, *China* 50 G5
Lanus, *Argentina* 126 C4
Lanusei, *Italy* 34 C2
Lanuza, *Phil.* 55 G7
Lanxi, *China* 53 C12
Lanzarote, *Canary Is.* 36 E6
Lanzhou, *China* 50 F2
Lanzo Torinese, *Italy* 32 C4
Lao →, *Italy* 35 C8
Lao Bao, *Laos* 58 D6
Lao Cai, *Vietnam* 58 A4
Laoag, *Phil.* 55 B4
Laoang, *Phil.* 55 E6
Laoha He →, *China* 51 C11
Laois □, *Ireland* 15 D4
Laon, *France* 25 C10
Laona, *U.S.A.* 104 C1
Laos ■, *Asia* 58 D5
Lapa, *Brazil* 127 B6
Lapalisse, *France* 26 B7
Laparan, *Phil.* 57 C6
Lapeer, *U.S.A.* 104 D4
Lapi □ = Lapin lääni □, *Finland* 8 C19
Lapin lääni □, *Finland* 8 C19
Lapithos, *Cyprus* 37 D12
Lapland = Lappland, *Europe* 8 B18
Laporte, *U.S.A.* 107 E8
Lapovo, *Serbia, Yug.* 21 L11
Lappland, *Europe* 8 B18
Laprida, *Argentina* 126 D3
Laptev Sea, *Russia* 45 B13
Lăpuşul →, *Romania* 38 B6
L'Àquila, *Italy* 33 F10
Lār, *Āzarbājān-e Sharqī, Iran* 64 B5
Lār, *Fārs, Iran* 65 E7
Lara □, *Venezuela* 120 A4
Larabanga, *Ghana* 78 D4
Laracha, *Spain* 30 B2
Larache, *Morocco* 74 A3
Laragne-Montéglin, *France* 27 D9
Laramie, *U.S.A.* 108 E2
Laramie Mts., *U.S.A.* 108 E2
Laranjeiras, *Brazil* 122 D4
Laranjeiras do Sul, *Brazil* 127 B5
Larantuka, *Indonesia* 57 F6
Larap, *Phil.* 55 D5
Larat, *Indonesia* 57 F8
L'Arbresle, *France* 27 C8
Larde, *Mozam.* 83 F4
Larder Lake, *Canada* 98 C4
Lardhos, Ákra, *Greece* 37 C10
Lardhos, Órmos, *Greece* 37 C10
Laredo, *Spain* 28 B1
Laredo, *U.S.A.* 109 M5
Laredo Sd., *Canada* 100 C3
Laren, *Neths.* 16 D6
Largentière, *France* 27 D8
L'Argentière-la-Bessée, *France* 27 D10
Largs, *U.K.* 14 F4
Lari, *Italy* 32 E7
Lariang, *Indonesia* 57 E5
Larimore, *U.S.A.* 108 B6
Lārīn, *Iran* 65 C7
Larino, *Italy* 35 A7
Lárisa, *Greece* 39 K5
Larkana, *Pakistan* 62 F3
Larnaca, *Cyprus* 37 E12
Larnaca Bay, *Cyprus* 37 E12
Larne, *U.K.* 15 B6
Larned, *U.S.A.* 108 F5
Larochette, *Belgium* 17 J8
Laroquebrou, *France* 26 D6
Larrimah, *Australia* 88 C5
Larsen Ice Shelf, *Antarctica* 5 C17
Larvik, *Norway* 10 E4
Laryak, *Russia* 44 C8
Larzac, Causse du, *France* 26 E7
Las Alpujarras, *Spain* 29 J1
Las Animas, *U.S.A.* 108 F3
Las Anod, *Somali Rep.* 68 F4
Las Blancos, *Spain* 29 H4
Las Brenãs, *Argentina* 126 B3
Las Cabezas de San Juan, *Spain* 31 J5
Las Chimeneas, *Mexico* 113 N10
Las Coloradas, *Argentina* 128 A2
Las Cruces, *U.S.A.* 111 K10
Las Flores, *Argentina* 126 D4
Las Heras, *Argentina* 126 C2
Las Horquetas, *Argentina* 128 C2
Las Khoreh, *Somali Rep.* 68 E4
Las Lajas, *Argentina* 128 A2
Las Lomas, *Peru* 124 A1
Las Lomitas, *Argentina* 126 A3
Las Marismas, *Spain* 31 H4
Las Mercedes, *Venezuela* 120 B4
Las Navas de la Concepción, *Spain* 31 H5
Las Navas de Tolosa, *Spain* 31 G7
Las Navas del Marqués, *Spain* 30 E6
Las Palmas, *Argentina* 126 B4
Las Palmas, *Canary Is.* 36 F4
Las Palmas →, *Mexico* 113 N10
Las Piedras, *Uruguay* 127 C4
Las Pipinas, *Argentina* 126 D4
Las Plumas, *Argentina* 128 B3
Las Rosas, *Argentina* 126 C3
Las Tablas, *Panama* 116 E3
Las Termas, *Argentina* 126 B3
Las Truchas, *Mexico* 114 D4
Las Varillas, *Argentina* 126 C3
Las Vegas, *N. Mex., U.S.A.* 111 J11
Las Vegas, *Nev., U.S.A.* 113 J11
Lascano, *Uruguay* 127 C5
Lashburn, *Canada* 101 C7
Lashio, *Burma* 61 H20
Lashkar, *India* 62 F8
Łasin, *Poland* 20 B9
Lasíthi, *Greece* 37 D7
Lasíthi □, *Greece* 37 D7
Laško, *Slovenia* 33 B12
Lassance, *Brazil* 123 E3
Lassay, *France* 24 D6
Lassen Pk., *U.S.A.* 110 F3
Last Mountain L., *Canada* 101 C7
Lastchance Cr. →, *U.S.A.* 112 E5
Lastoursville, *Gabon* 80 E2
Lastovo, *Croatia* 33 F13
Lastovski Kanal, *Croatia* 33 F13
Lat Yao, *Thailand* 58 E2
Latacunga, *Ecuador* 120 D2
Latakia = Al Lādhiqīyah, *Syria* 64 C2
Latchford, *Canada* 98 C4
Laterza, *Italy* 35 B9
Latham, *Australia* 89 E2
Lathen, *Germany* 18 C3
Lathrop Wells, *U.S.A.* 113 J10
Latiano, *Italy* 35 B10
Latina, *Italy* 34 A5
Latisana, *Italy* 33 C10
Latium = Lazio □, *Italy* 33 F9
Laton, *U.S.A.* 112 J7
Latorica →, *Czech.* 21 G11
Latouche Treville, C., *Australia* 88 C3
Latrobe, *Australia* 90 G4
Latrobe, *U.S.A.* 106 F5
Latrónico, *Italy* 35 B9
Latvia ■, *Europe* 40 C3
Lau Group, *Fiji* 87 C9
Lauca →, *Bolivia* 124 D4
Lauchhammer, *Germany* 18 D9
Lauenburg, *Germany* 18 B6
Läufelfingen, *Switz.* 22 B5
Laufen, *Switz.* 22 B5
Lauffen, *Germany* 19 F5
Laugarbakki, *Iceland* 8 D3
Laujar, *Spain* 29 J2
Launceston, *Australia* 90 G4
Launceston, *U.K.* 13 G3

Laune →, *Ireland* 15 D2
Laupheim, *Germany* 19 G5
Laura, *Australia* 90 B3
Laureana di Borrello, *Italy* 35 D9
Laurel, *Miss., U.S.A.* 109 K10
Laurel, *Mont., U.S.A.* 110 D9
Laurencekirk, *U.K.* 14 E6
Laurens, *U.S.A.* 105 H4
Laurentian Plateau, *Canada* 99 B6
Laurentides, Parc Prov. des, *Canada* 99 C5
Lauria, *Italy* 35 B8
Laurie L., *Canada* 101 B8
Laurinburg, *U.S.A.* 105 H6
Laurium, *U.S.A.* 104 B1
Lausanne, *Switz.* 22 C3
Laut, *Indonesia* 56 D3
Laut Ketil, Kepulauan, *Indonesia* 56 E5
Lautaro, *Chile* 128 A2
Lauterbach, *Germany* 18 E5
Lauterbrunnen, *Switz.* 22 C5
Lauterecken, *Germany* 19 F3
Lautoka, *Fiji* 87 C7
Lauwe, *Belgium* 17 G2
Lauwers, *Neths.* 16 A8
Lauwers Zee, *Neths.* 16 B8
Lauzon, *Canada* 99 C5
Lava Hot Springs, *U.S.A.* 110 E7
Lavadores, *Spain* 30 C2
Lavagna, *Italy* 32 D6
Laval, *France* 24 D6
Lavalle, *Argentina* 126 B2
Lávara, *Greece* 39 H9
Lavardac, *France* 26 D4
Lavaur, *France* 26 E5
Lavaux, *Switz.* 22 D3
Lavelanet, *France* 26 F5
Lavello, *Italy* 35 A8
Laverne, *U.S.A.* 109 G5
Laverton, *Australia* 89 E3
Lavos, *Portugal* 30 E2
Lavras, *Brazil* 123 F3
Lavre, *Portugal* 31 G2
Lavrentiya, *Russia* 45 C19
Lávrion, *Greece* 39 M7
Lávris, *Greece* 37 D6
Lavumisa, *Swaziland* 85 D5
Lawas, *Malaysia* 56 D5
Lawele, *Indonesia* 57 F6
Lawn Hill, *Australia* 90 B2
Lawng Pit, *Burma* 61 G20
Lawqar, *Si. Arabia* 64 D4
Lawra, *Ghana* 78 C4
Lawrence, *N.Z.* 87 L2
Lawrence, *Kans., U.S.A.* 108 F7
Lawrence, *Mass., U.S.A.* 107 D13
Lawrenceburg, *Ind., U.S.A.* 104 F3
Lawrenceburg, *Tenn., U.S.A.* 105 H2
Lawrenceville, *U.S.A.* 105 J4
Laws, *U.S.A.* 112 H8
Lawton, *U.S.A.* 109 H5
Lawu, *Indonesia* 57 G14
Laxford, L., *U.K.* 14 C3
Laylān, *Iraq* 64 C5
Layon →, *France* 24 E6
Laysan I., *Pac. Oc.* 93 E11
Laytonville, *U.S.A.* 110 G2
Lazio □, *Italy* 33 F9
Lazo, *Russia* 48 C6
Le Barcarès, *France* 26 F7
Le Beausset, *France* 27 E9
Le Blanc, *France* 26 B5
Le Bleymard, *France* 26 D7
Le Bourgneuf-la-Fôret, *France* 24 D6
Le Bouscat, *France* 26 D3
Le Brassus, *Switz.* 22 C2
Le Bugue, *France* 26 D4
Le Canourgue, *France* 26 D7
Le Cateau, *France* 25 B10
Le Chambon-Feugerolles, *France* 27 C8
Le Château-d'Oléron, *France* 26 C2
Le Châtelard, *Switz.* 22 D3
Le Châtelet, *France* 26 B6
Le Châtelet-en-Brie, *France* 25 D9
Le Chesne, *France* 25 C11
Le Cheylard, *France* 27 D8
Le Conquet, *France* 24 D2
Le Creusot, *France* 25 F11
Le Croisic, *France* 24 E4
Le Donjon, *France* 26 B7
Le Dorat, *France* 26 B5
Le François, *Martinique* 117 D7
Le Grand-Lucé, *France* 24 E7
Le Grand-Pressigny, *France* 24 F7
Le Havre, *France* 24 C7
Le Lavandou, *France* 27 E10
Le Lion-d'Angers, *France* 24 E6
Le Locle, *Switz.* 22 B3
Le Louroux-Béconnais, *France* 24 E6
Le Luc, *France* 27 E10
Le Madonie, *Italy* 34 E6
Le Maire, Est. de, *Argentina* 128 D4
Le Mans, *France* 24 E7
Le Marinel, *Zaïre* 83 E2
Le Mars, *U.S.A.* 108 D6
Le Mêle-sur-Sarthe, *France* 24 D7
Le Merlerault, *France* 24 D7
Le Monastier-sur-Gazeille, *France* 26 D7
Le Monêtier-les-Bains, *France* 27 D10
Le Mont d'Or, *France* 25 F13
Le Mont-Dore, *France* 26 C6
Le Mont-St.-Michel, *France* 24 D5
Le Moule, *Guadeloupe* 117 C7
Le Muy, *France* 27 E10
Le Palais, *France* 24 E3
Le Perthus, *France* 26 F6
Le Pont, *Switz.* 22 C2
Le Pouldu, *France* 24 E3
Le Puy, *France* 26 C7
Le Quesnoy, *France* 25 B10
Le Roy, *U.S.A.* 109 F7
Le Sentier, *Switz.* 22 C2
Le Sueur, *U.S.A.* 108 C8
Le Teil, *France* 27 D8
Le Teilleul, *France* 24 D6
Le Theil, *France* 24 D7
Le Thillot, *France* 25 E13
Le Thuy, *Vietnam* 58 D6
Le Touquet-Paris-Plage, *France* 25 B8
Le Tréport, *France* 24 B8
Le Val-d'Ajol, *France* 25 E13
Le Verdon-sur-Mer, *France* 26 C2
Le Vigan, *France* 26 E7
Lea →, *U.K.* 13 F7
Leach, *Cambodia* 59 F4
Lead, *U.S.A.* 108 C3
Leader, *Canada* 101 C7
Leadhills, *U.K.* 14 F5
Leadville, *U.S.A.* 111 G10
Leaf →, *U.S.A.* 109 K10
Leakey, *U.S.A.* 109 L5
Leamington, *Canada* 98 D3
Leamington, *U.S.A.* 110 G7
Leamington Spa = Royal Leamington Spa, *U.K.* 13 E6
Le'an, *China* 53 D10
Leandro Norte Alem, *Argentina* 127 B4
Learmonth, *Australia* 88 D1
Leask, *Canada* 101 C7
Leavenworth, *Kans., U.S.A.* 108 F7
Leavenworth, *Wash., U.S.A.* 110 C3
Łeba, *Poland* 20 A7
Lebak, *Phil.* 55 H6
Lebam, *U.S.A.* 112 D3
Lebanon, *Ind., U.S.A.* 104 E2
Lebanon, *Kans., U.S.A.* 108 F5
Lebanon, *Ky., U.S.A.* 104 G3
Lebanon, *Mo., U.S.A.* 109 G8
Lebanon, *Oreg., U.S.A.* 110 D2
Lebanon, *Pa., U.S.A.* 107 F8
Lebanon, *Tenn., U.S.A.* 105 G2
Lebanon ■, *Asia* 69 B4
Lebbeke, *Belgium* 17 G4
Lebec, *U.S.A.* 113 L8
Lebedin, *Ukraine* 40 F9
Lebedyan, *Russia* 41 E11
Lebomboberge, *S. Africa* 85 C5
Lębork, *Poland* 20 A7
Lebrija, *Spain* 31 J4
Lebu, *Chile* 126 D1
Lecce, *Italy* 35 B11
Lecco, *Italy* 32 C6
Lecco, L. di, *Italy* 32 C6
Lécera, *Spain* 28 D4
Lech, *Austria* 19 H6
Lech →, *Germany* 19 G6
Lechang, *China* 53 E9
Lechtaler Alpen, *Austria* 19 H6
Lectoure, *France* 26 E4
Łęczyca, *Poland* 20 C9
Ledbury, *U.K.* 13 E5
Lede, *Belgium* 17 G3
Ledeberg, *Belgium* 17 F3
Ledesma, *Spain* 30 D5
Ledong, *China* 58 C7
Leduc, *Canada* 100 C6
Ledyczek, *Poland* 20 B6
Lee, *U.S.A.* 107 D11
Lee →, *Ireland* 15 E3
Lee Vining, *U.S.A.* 112 H7
Leech L., *U.S.A.* 108 B7
Leedey, *U.S.A.* 109 H5
Leeds, *U.K.* 12 D6
Leeds, *U.S.A.* 105 J2
Leek, *Neths.* 16 B8
Leek, *U.K.* 12 D5
Leende, *Neths.* 17 F7
Leer, *Germany* 18 B3
Leerdam, *Neths.* 16 E6
Leersum, *Neths.* 16 E6
Leesburg, *U.S.A.* 105 L5
Leesville, *U.S.A.* 109 K8
Leeton, *Australia* 91 E4
Leetonia, *U.S.A.* 106 F4
Leeu Gamka, *S. Africa* 84 E3
Leeuwarden, *Neths.* 16 B7
Leeuwin, C., *Australia* 89 F2
Leeward Is., *Atl. Oc.* 117 C7
Lefka, *Cyprus* 37 D11
Lefkoniko, *Cyprus* 37 D12
Lefors, *U.S.A.* 109 H4
Lefroy, L., *Australia* 89 F3
Legal, *Canada* 100 C6
Leganés, *Spain* 30 E7
Legazpi, *Phil.* 55 E5
Legendre I., *Australia* 88 D2
Leghorn = Livorno, *Italy* 32 E7
Legionowo, *Poland* 20 C10
Léglise, *Belgium* 17 J7
Legnago, *Italy* 33 C8
Legnano, *Italy* 32 C5
Legnica, *Poland* 20 D6
Legrad, *Croatia* 33 B13
Legume, *Australia* 91 D5
Leh, *India* 63 B7
Lehi, *U.S.A.* 110 F8
Lehighton, *U.S.A.* 107 F9
Lehrte, *Germany* 18 C5
Lehututu, *Botswana* 84 C3
Lei Shui →, *China* 53 D9
Leiah, *Pakistan* 62 D4
Leibnitz, *Austria* 21 J5
Leibo, *China* 52 C4
Leicester, *U.K.* 13 E6
Leicestershire □, *U.K.* 13 E6
Leichhardt →, *Australia* 90 B2
Leichhardt Ra., *Australia* 90 C4
Leiden, *Neths.* 16 D5
Leiderdorp, *Neths.* 16 D5
Leidschendam, *Neths.* 16 D4
Leie →, *Belgium* 25 A10
Leignon, *Belgium* 17 H6
Leine →, *Germany* 18 C5
Leinster, *Australia* 89 E3
Leinster □, *Ireland* 15 C4
Leinster, Mt., *Ireland* 15 D5
Leipzig, *Germany* 18 D8
Leiria, *Portugal* 31 F2
Leiria □, *Portugal* 31 F2
Leisler, Mt., *Australia* 88 D4
Leith, *U.K.* 14 F5
Leith Hill, *U.K.* 13 F7
Leitha →, *Europe* 21 H7
Leitrim, *Ireland* 15 B3
Leitrim □, *Ireland* 15 B3
Leiyang, *China* 53 D9
Leiza, *Spain* 28 B3
Leizhou Bandao, *China* 54 D6
Leizhou Wan, *China* 53 G8
Lek →, *Neths.* 16 E5
Leke, *Belgium* 17 F1
Lekkerkerk, *Neths.* 16 E5
Leksula, *Indonesia* 57 E7
Leland, *U.S.A.* 109 J9
Leland Lakes, *Canada* 101 A6
Leleque, *Argentina* 128 B2
Lelystad, *Neths.* 16 D6
Lema, *Nigeria* 79 C5
Léman, Lac, *Switz.* 22 D3
Lemelerveld, *Neths.* 16 D8
Lemera, *Zaïre* 82 C2
Lemery, *Phil.* 55 E4
Lemgo, *Germany* 18 C4
Lemhi Ra., *U.S.A.* 110 D7
Lemmer, *Neths.* 16 C7
Lemmon, *U.S.A.* 108 C3
Lemon Grove, *U.S.A.* 113 N9
Lemoore, *U.S.A.* 111 H4
Lempdes, *France* 26 C7
Lemsid, *W. Sahara* 74 C2
Lemvig, *Denmark* 11 H2
Lena →, *Russia* 45 B13
Lencloître, *France* 24 F7
Lençóis, *Brazil* 123 D3
Léndas, *Greece* 37 E6
Lendeh, *Iran* 65 D6
Lendelede, *Belgium* 17 G2
Lendinara, *Italy* 33 C8
Lengerich, *Germany* 18 C3
Lenggong, *Malaysia* 59 K3
Lenggries, *Germany* 19 H7
Lengua de Vaca, Pta., *Chile* 126 C1
Lenin, *Russia* 43 B9
Leninabad = Khodzent, *Tajikistan* 44 E7
Leninakan = Kumayri, *Armenia* 43 F10
Leningrad = Sankt-Peterburg, *Russia* 40 B7
Lenino, *Ukraine* 42 D6
Leninogorsk = Ridder, *Kazakhstan* 44 D9
Leninsk, *Russia* 43 B11
Leninsk, *Russia* 43 C10
Leninsk-Kuznetskiy, *Russia* 44 D9
Leninskaya Sloboda, *Russia* 41 C14
Leninskoye, *Russia* 41 B15
Leninskoye, *Russia* 45 E14
Lenk, *Switz.* 22 D4
Lenkoran, *Azerbaijan* 67 D13
Lenmalu, *Indonesia* 57 E8
Lenne →, *Germany* 18 D3
Lennox, I., *Chile* 128 E3
Lennoxville, *Canada* 107 A13
Leno, *Italy* 32 C7
Lenoir, *U.S.A.* 105 H5
Lenoir City, *U.S.A.* 105 H3
Lenora, *U.S.A.* 108 F4
Lenore L., *Canada* 101 C8
Lenox, *U.S.A.* 107 D11
Lens, *Belgium* 17 G3
Lens, *France* 25 B9
Lens St. Remy, *Belgium* 17 G6
Lensk, *Russia* 45 C12
Lenskoye, *Ukraine* 42 D6
Lent, *Neths.* 16 E7
Lentini, *Italy* 35 E8
Lentvaric, *Lithuania* 40 D4
Lenwood, *U.S.A.* 113 L9
Lenzburg, *Switz.* 22 B6
Lenzen, *Germany* 18 B7
Lenzerheide, *Switz.* 23 C9
Léo, *Burkina Faso* 78 C4
Leoben, *Austria* 21 H5
Leola, *U.S.A.* 108 C5
Leominster, *U.K.* 13 E5
Leominster, *U.S.A.* 107 D13
Léon, *France* 26 E2
León, *Mexico* 114 C4
León, *Nic.* 116 D2
León, *Spain* 30 C5
Leon, *U.S.A.* 108 E8
León □, *Spain* 30 C5
León, Montañas de, *Spain* 30 C4
Leonardtown, *U.S.A.* 104 F7
Leone, Mte., *Switz.* 22 D6
Leonforte, *Italy* 35 E7
Leongatha, *Australia* 91 F4
Leonídhion, *Greece* 39 M5
Leonora, *Australia* 89 E3
Léopold II, Lac = Mai-Ndombe, L., *Zaïre* 80 E3
Leopoldina, *Brazil* 123 F3
Leopoldo Bulhões, *Brazil* 123 E2
Leopoldsburg, *Belgium* 17 F6
Léopoldville = Kinshasa, *Zaïre* 80 E3
Leoti, *U.S.A.* 108 F4
Leoville, *Canada* 101 C7
Lépa, L. do, *Angola* 84 B2
Lepe, *Spain* 31 H3
Lepel, *Belorussia* 40 D6
Lepikha, *Russia* 45 C13
Leping, *China* 53 C11
Lepontine, Alpi, *Italy* 23 D6
Lequeitio, *Spain* 28 B2
Lercara Friddi, *Italy* 34 E6
Lerdo, *Mexico* 114 B4
Léré, *Chad* 73 G7
Lere, *Nigeria* 79 D6
Leribe, *Lesotho* 85 D4
Lérici, *Italy* 32 D6
Lérida, *Spain* 28 D5
Lérida □, *Spain* 28 C6
Lérins, Is. de, *France* 27 E11
Lerma, *Spain* 30 C7
Léros, *Greece* 39 M9
Lérouville, *France* 25 D12
Lerwick, *U.K.* 14 A7
Les Abrets, *France* 27 C9
Les Andelys, *France* 24 C8
Les Arcs, *France* 27 E10
Les Baux-de-Provence, *France* 27 E8
Les Bois, *Switz.* 22 B3
Les Cayes, *Haiti* 117 C5
Les Diablerets, *Switz.* 22 D4
Les Échelles, *France* 27 C9
Les Essarts, *France* 24 F5
Les Étroits, *Canada* 99 C6
Les Eyzies-de-Tayac-Sireuil, *France* 26 D5
Les Herbiers, *France* 24 F5
Les Minquiers, *Chan. Is.* 24 D4
Les Ponts-de-Cé, *France* 24 E6
Les Riceys, *France* 25 E11
Les Sables-d'Olonne, *France* 26 B2
Les Vans, *France* 27 D8
Les Verrières, *Switz.* 22 C2
Lesbos = Lésvos, *Greece* 39 K9
Leshan, *China* 52 C4
Lésina, L. di, *Italy* 33 G12
Lesja, *Norway* 10 B2
Lesjaverk, *Norway* 10 B2
Leskov I., *Antarctica* 5 B1
Leskovac, *Serbia, Yug.* 21 M11
Leslie, *U.S.A.* 109 H8
Lesneven, *France* 24 D2
Lešnica, *Serbia, Yug.* 21 L9
Lesnoye, *Russia* 40 B9
Lesopilnoye, *Russia* 48 A7
Lesotho ■, *Africa* 85 D4
Lesozavodsk, *Russia* 45 E14
Lesparre-Médoc, *France* 26 C3
Lessay, *France* 24 C5
Lesse →, *Belgium* 17 H5
Lesser Antilles, *W. Indies* 117 C7
Lesser Slave L., *Canada* 100 B5
Lesser Sunda Is., *Indonesia* 57 F6
Lessines, *Belgium* 17 G3
Lester, *U.S.A.* 112 C5
Lestock, *Canada* 101 C8
Lesuer I., *Australia* 88 B4
Lésvos, *Greece* 39 K9
Leszno, *Poland* 20 D6
Letchworth, *U.K.* 13 F7
Letea, Ostrov, *Romania* 38 D12
Lethbridge, *Canada* 100 D6
Lethem, *Guyana* 121 C6
Leti, Kepulauan, *Indonesia* 57 F7
Leti Is. = Leti, Kepulauan, *Indonesia* 57 F7
Letiahau →, *Botswana* 84 C3
Leticia, *Colombia* 120 D4
Leting, *China* 51 E10
Letjiesbos, *S. Africa* 84 E3
Letlhakeng, *Botswana* 84 C3
Letpadan, *Burma* 61 L19
Letpan, *Burma* 61 K19
Letterkenny, *Ireland* 15 B4
Leu, *Romania* 38 E7
Leucadia, *U.S.A.* 113 M9
Leucate, *France* 26 F7
Leucate, Étang de, *France* 26 F7
Leuk, *Switz.* 22 D5
Leukerbad, *Switz.* 22 D5
Leupegem, *Belgium* 17 G3
Leuser, G., *Indonesia* 56 D1
Leutkirch, *Germany* 19 H6
Leuven, *Belgium* 17 G5
Leuze, *Hainaut, Belgium* 17 G3
Leuze, *Namur, Belgium* 17 G5
Lev Tolstoy, *Russia* 41 E11
Levádhia, *Greece* 39 L5
Levan, *U.S.A.* 110 G8
Levanger, *Norway* 8 E11
Levant, I. du, *France* 27 E10
Lévanto, *Italy* 32 D6
Levanzo, *Italy* 34 E5
Levelland, *U.S.A.* 109 J3
Leven, *U.K.* 14 E6
Leven, L., *U.K.* 14 E5
Leven, Toraka, *Madag.* 85 A8
Levens, *France* 27 E11
Leveque C., *Australia* 88 C3
Leverano, *Italy* 35 B10
Leverkusen, *Germany* 18 D2
Levet, *France* 25 F9
Levice, *Czech.* 21 G8
Levico, *Italy* 33 C8
Levie, *France* 27 G13
Levier, *France* 25 F13
Levin, *N.Z.* 87 J5
Lévis, *Canada* 99 C5
Levis, L., *Canada* 100 A5
Levítha, *Greece* 39 M9
Levittown, *N.Y., U.S.A.* 107 F11
Levittown, *Pa., U.S.A.* 107 F10
Lévka Óri, *Greece* 37 D6
Levkás, *Greece* 39 L3
Levkímmi, *Greece* 37 B4
Levkímmi, Ákra, *Greece* 37 B4
Levkôsia = Nicosia, *Cyprus* 37 D12
Levoča, *Czech.* 20 F10
Levroux, *France* 25 F8
Levski, *Bulgaria* 38 F8
Levskigrad, *Bulgaria* 38 G7
Lewellen, *U.S.A.* 108 E3
Lewes, *U.K.* 13 G8
Lewes, *U.S.A.* 104 F8
Lewis, *U.K.* 14 C2
Lewis →, *U.S.A.* 112 E4
Lewis, Butt of, *U.K.* 14 C2
Lewis Ra., *Australia* 88 D4
Lewis Ra., *U.S.A.* 110 C7
Lewisburg, *Pa., U.S.A.* 106 F8
Lewisburg, *Tenn., U.S.A.* 105 H2
Lewisporte, *Canada* 99 C8
Lewiston, *Idaho, U.S.A.* 110 C5
Lewiston, *Maine, U.S.A.* 105 C11
Lewistown, *Mont., U.S.A.* 110 C9
Lewistown, *Pa., U.S.A.* 106 F7
Lexington, *Ill., U.S.A.* 108 E10
Lexington, *Ky., U.S.A.* 104 F3
Lexington, *Miss., U.S.A.* 109 J9
Lexington, *Mo., U.S.A.* 108 F8
Lexington, *N.C., U.S.A.* 105 H5
Lexington, *Nebr., U.S.A.* 108 E5
Lexington, *Ohio, U.S.A.* 106 F2
Lexington, *Oreg., U.S.A.* 110 D4
Lexington, *Tenn., U.S.A.* 105 H1
Lexington Park, *U.S.A.* 104 F7
Leye, *China* 52 E6
Leyre →, *France* 26 D2
Leysin, *Switz.* 22 D4
Leyte, *Phil.* 55 F6
Leyte Gulf, *Phil.* 55 F6
Lezay, *France* 26 B4
Lezha, *Albania* 39 H2
Lezhi, *China* 52 B5
Lézignan-Corbières, *France* 26 E6
Lezoux, *France* 26 C7
Lgov, *Russia* 40 F9
Lhasa, *China* 54 D4
Lhazê, *China* 54 D3
Lhokkruet, *Indonesia* 56 D1
Lhokseumawe, *Indonesia* 56 C1
Lhuntsi Dzong, *India* 61 F17
Li, *Thailand* 58 D2
Li Shui →, *China* 53 C9
Li Xian, *Gansu, China* 50 G3
Li Xian, *Hebei, China* 50 E8
Li Xian, *Hunan, China* 53 C8
Li Xian, *Sichuan, China* 52 B4
Liádhoi, *Greece* 39 N9
Lian Xian, *China* 53 E9
Liancheng, *China* 53 E11
Lianga, *Phil.* 55 G7
Liangcheng, *Nei Mongol Zizhiqu, China* 50 D7
Liangcheng, *Shandong, China* 51 G10
Liangdang, *China* 50 H4
Lianghekou, *China* 52 C7
Liangping, *China* 52 B6
Lianhua, *China* 53 D9
Lianjiang, *Fujian, China* 53 D12
Lianjiang, *Guangdong, China* 53 G8
Lianping, *China* 53 E10
Lianshan, *China* 53 E9
Lianshanguan, *China* 51 D12
Lianshui, *China* 51 H10

Lianyuan, *China* 53 D8
Lianyungang, *China* 51 G10
Liao He →, *China* 51 D11
Liaocheng, *China* 50 F8
Liaodong Bandao, *China* 51 E12
Liaodong Wan, *China* 51 D11
Liaoning □, *China* 54 B7
Liaoning □, *Liaoning, China* 51 D12
Liaoyang, *China* 51 D12
Liaoyuan, *China* 51 C13
Liaozhong, *China* 51 D12
Liapádhes, *Greece* 39 K2
Liard →, *Canada* 100 A4
Liari, *Pakistan* 62 G2
Líbano, *Colombia* 120 C2
Libau = Liepaja, *Latvia* 40 C2
Libby, *U.S.A.* 110 B6
Libenge, *Zaïre* 80 D3
Liberal, *Kans., U.S.A.* 109 G4
Liberal, *Mo., U.S.A.* 109 G7
Liberdade, *Brazil* 124 C3
Liberdade →, *Brazil* 125 B7
Liberec, *Czech.* 20 E5
Liberia, *Costa Rica* 116 D2
Liberia ■, *W. Afr.* 78 D3
Libertad, *Venezuela* 120 B4
Liberty, *Mo., U.S.A.* 108 F7
Liberty, *Tex., U.S.A.* 109 K7
Libin, *Belgium* 17 J6
Lîbîya, Sahrâ', *Africa* 73 C9
Libo, *China* 52 E6
Libobo, Tanjung, *Indonesia* 57 E7
Libode, *S. Africa* 85 E4
Libonda, *Zambia* 81 G4
Libourne, *France* 26 D3
Libramont, *Belgium* 17 J6
Libreville, *Gabon* 80 D1
Libya ■, *N. Afr.* 73 C8
Libyan Desert = Lîbîya, Sahrâ', *Africa* 73 C9
Libyan Plateau = Ed-Déffa, *Egypt* 76 A2
Licantén, *Chile* 126 D1
Licata, *Italy* 34 E6
Lice, *Turkey* 67 D9
Licheng, *China* 50 F7
Lichfield, *U.K.* 12 E6
Lichinga, *Mozam.* 83 E4
Lichtaart, *Belgium* 17 F5
Lichtenburg, *S. Africa* 84 D4
Lichtenfels, *Germany* 19 E7
Lichtenvoorde, *Neths.* 16 E9
Lichtervelde, *Belgium* 17 F2
Lichuan, *Hubei, China* 52 B7
Lichuan, *Jiangxi, China* 53 D11
Licosa, Punta, *Italy* 35 B7
Lida, *Belorussia* 40 E4
Lida, *U.S.A.* 111 H5
Lidingö, *Sweden* 10 E12
Lidköping, *Sweden* 11 F7
Lido, *Italy* 33 C9
Lido, *Niger* 79 C5
Lido di Roma = Óstia, Lido di, *Italy* 34 A5
Lidzbark Warminski, *Poland* 20 A10
Liebenwalde, *Germany* 18 C9
Lieberose, *Germany* 18 D10
Liebig, Mt., *Australia* 88 D5
Liechtenstein ■, *Europe* 23 B9
Liederkerke, *Belgium* 17 G4
Liège, *Belgium* 17 G7
Liège □, *Belgium* 17 G7
Liegnitz = Legnica, *Poland* 20 D6
Liempde, *Neths.* 17 E6
Lienart, *Zaïre* 82 B2
Lienyünchiangshih = Lianyungang, *China* 51 G10
Lienz, *Austria* 21 J2
Liepaja, *Latvia* 40 C2
Lier, *Belgium* 17 F5
Lierneux, *Belgium* 17 H7
Lieshout, *Neths.* 17 E7
Liestal, *Switz.* 22 B5
Liévin, *France* 25 B9
Lièvre →, *Canada* 98 C4
Liezen, *Austria* 21 H4
Liffey →, *Ireland* 15 C5
Lifford, *Ireland* 15 B4
Liffré, *France* 24 D5
Lifjell, *Norway* 10 E2
Lifudzin, *Russia* 48 B7
Ligao, *Phil.* 55 E5
Lightning Ridge, *Australia* 91 D4
Lignano, *Italy* 33 C10
Ligny-en-Barrois, *France* 25 D12
Ligny-le-Châtel, *France* 25 E10
Ligoúrion, *Greece* 39 M6
Ligueil, *France* 24 E7
Liguria □, *Italy* 32 D6
Ligurian Sea, *Italy* 32 E5
Lihou Reefs and Cays, *Australia* 90 B5
Lihue, *U.S.A.* 102 H15
Lijiang, *China* 52 D3
Likasi, *Zaïre* 83 E2
Likati, *Zaïre* 80 D4
Likhoslavl, *Russia* 40 C9
Likhovski, *Russia* 43 B9
Likoma I., *Malawi* 83 E3
Likumburu, *Tanzania* 83 D4
L'Île-Bouchard, *France* 24 E7
L'Ile-Rousse, *France* 27 F12
Liling, *China* 53 D9
Lille, *Belgium* 17 F5
Lille, *France* 25 B10
Lille Bælt, *Denmark* 11 J3
Lillebonne, *France* 24 C7
Lillehammer, *Norway* 10 C4
Lillers, *France* 25 B9
Lillesand, *Norway* 11 F2
Lilleshall, *U.K.* 13 E5
Lillestrøm, *Norway* 10 E5
Lillian Point, Mt., *Australia* 89 E4
Lillo, *Spain* 28 F1
Lillooet →, *Canada* 100 D4
Lilongwe, *Malawi* 83 E3
Liloy, *Phil.* 57 C6
Lim →, *Bos.-H., Yug.* 21 M9
Lima, *Indonesia* 57 E7
Lima, *Peru* 124 C2
Lima, *Mont., U.S.A.* 110 D7
Lima, *Ohio, U.S.A.* 104 E3
Lima □, *Peru* 124 C2
Lima →, *Portugal* 30 D2
Limages, *Canada* 107 A9
Liman, *Russia* 43 D12
Limassol, *Cyprus* 37 E12
Limavady, *U.K.* 15 A5
Limavady □, *U.K.* 15 B5
Limay →, *Argentina* 128 A3
Limay Mahuida, *Argentina* 126 D2
Limbang, *Brunei* 56 D5
Limbara, Monti, *Italy* 34 B2
Limbdi, *India* 62 H4
Limbe, *Cameroon* 79 E6
Limbourg, *Belgium* 17 G7
Limbri, *Australia* 91 E5
Limbunya, *Australia* 88 C4
Limburg, *Germany* 19 E4
Limburg □, *Belgium* 17 F6
Limburg □, *Neths.* 17 F7
Limeira, *Brazil* 127 A6
Limerick, *Ireland* 15 D3
Limerick □, *Ireland* 15 D3
Limestone, *U.S.A.* 106 D6
Limestone →, *Canada* 101 B10
Limfjorden, *Denmark* 11 H3
Limia = Lima →, *Portugal* 30 D2
Limmared, *Sweden* 11 G7
Limmat →, *Switz.* 23 B6
Limmen, *Neths.* 16 C5
Limmen Bight, *Australia* 90 A2
Limmen Bight →, *Australia* 90 B2
Límni, *Greece* 39 L6
Límnos, *Greece* 39 K8
Limoeiro, *Brazil* 122 C4
Limoeiro do Norte, *Brazil* 122 C4
Limoges, *France* 26 C5
Limón, *Costa Rica* 116 D3
Limon, *U.S.A.* 108 F3
Limone Piemonte, *Italy* 32 D4
Limousin, *France* 26 C5
Limousin, Plateaux du, *France* 26 C5
Limoux, *France* 26 E6
Limpopo →, *Africa* 85 D5
Limuru, *Kenya* 82 C4
Lin Xian, *China* 50 F6
Lin'an, *China* 53 B12
Linapacan I., *Phil.* 55 F3
Linapacan Str., *Phil.* 55 F3
Linares, *Chile* 126 D1
Linares, *Colombia* 120 C2
Linares, *Mexico* 115 C5
Linares, *Spain* 29 G1
Linares □, *Chile* 126 D1
Línas Mte., *Italy* 34 C1
Lincang, *China* 52 F3
Lincheng, *China* 50 F8
Linchuan, *China* 53 D11
Lincoln, *Argentina* 126 C3
Lincoln, *N.Z.* 87 K4
Lincoln, *U.K.* 12 D7
Lincoln, *Calif., U.S.A.* 112 G5
Lincoln, *Ill., U.S.A.* 108 E10
Lincoln, *Kans., U.S.A.* 108 F5
Lincoln, *Maine, U.S.A.* 99 C6
Lincoln, *N.H., U.S.A.* 107 B13
Lincoln, *N. Mex., U.S.A.* 111 K11
Lincoln, *Nebr., U.S.A.* 108 E6
Lincoln Hav = Lincoln Sea, *Arctic* 4 A5
Lincoln Sea, *Arctic* 4 A5
Lincoln Wolds, *U.K.* 12 D7
Lincolnshire □, *U.K.* 12 D7
Lincolnton, *U.S.A.* 105 H5
L'Incudine, *France* 27 G13
Lind, *U.S.A.* 110 C4
Linda, *U.S.A.* 112 F5
Lindau, *Germany* 19 H5
Linde →, *Neths.* 16 C7
Linden, *Guyana* 121 B6
Linden, *Calif., U.S.A.* 112 G5
Linden, *Tex., U.S.A.* 109 J7
Lindenheuvel, *Neths.* 17 G7
Lindenhurst, *U.S.A.* 107 F11
Linderöd, *Sweden* 11 J7
Linderödsåsen, *Sweden* 11 J7
Lindesnes, *Norway* 6 D7
Líndhos, *Greece* 37 C10
Lindi, *Tanzania* 83 D4
Lindi □, *Tanzania* 83 D4
Lindi →, *Zaïre* 82 B2
Lindoso, *Portugal* 30 D2
Lindow, *Germany* 18 C8
Lindsay, *Canada* 98 D4
Lindsay, *Calif., U.S.A.* 111 H4
Lindsay, *Okla., U.S.A.* 109 H6
Lindsborg, *U.S.A.* 108 F6
Linfen, *China* 50 F6
Ling Xian, *Hunan, China* 53 D9
Ling Xian, *Shandong, China* 50 F9
Lingao, *China* 58 C7
Lingayen, *Phil.* 57 A6
Lingayen G., *Phil.* 55 C4
Lingbi, *China* 51 H9
Lingchuan, *Guangxi Zhuangzu, China* 53 E8
Lingchuan, *Shanxi, China* 50 G7
Lingen, *Germany* 18 C3
Lingga, *Indonesia* 56 E2
Lingga, Kepulauan, *Indonesia* 56 E2
Lingga Arch. = Lingga, Kepulauan, *Indonesia* 56 E2
Lingle, *U.S.A.* 108 D2
Lingling, *China* 53 D8
Lingqiu, *China* 50 E8
Lingshan, *China* 52 F7
Lingshi, *China* 50 F6
Lingshou, *China* 50 E8
Lingshui, *China* 58 C8
Lingtai, *China* 50 G4
Linguéré, *Senegal* 78 B1
Lingwu, *China* 50 E4
Lingyuan, *China* 51 D10
Lingyun, *China* 52 E6
Linh Cam, *Vietnam* 58 C5
Linhai, *China* 53 C13
Linhares, *Brazil* 123 E3
Linhe, *China* 50 D4
Linjiang, *China* 51 D14
Linköping, *Sweden* 11 F9
Linkou, *China* 51 B16
Linli, *China* 53 C8
Linlithgow, *U.K.* 14 F5
Linnhe, L., *U.K.* 14 E3
Linosa, I., *Medit. S.* 75 A7
Linqi, *China* 50 G7
Linqing, *China* 50 F8
Linqu, *China* 51 F10
Linru, *China* 50 G7
Lins, *Brazil* 127 A6
Linshui, *China* 52 B6
Lintao, *China* 50 G2
Linth →, *Switz.* 19 H5
Linthal, *Switz.* 23 C8
Lintlaw, *Canada* 101 C8
Linton, *Canada* 99 C5
Linton, *Ind., U.S.A.* 104 F2
Linton, *N. Dak., U.S.A.* 108 B4
Lintong, *China* 50 G5
Linville, *Australia* 91 D5
Linwood, *Canada* 106 C4
Linwu, *China* 53 E9
Linxi, *China* 51 C10
Linxia, *China* 54 C5
Linxiang, *China* 53 C9
Linyanti →, *Africa* 84 B4
Linyi, *China* 51 G10
Linz, *Austria* 21 G4
Linz, *Germany* 18 E3
Linzhenzhen, *China* 50 F5
Linzi, *China* 51 F10
Lion, G. du, *France* 27 E8
Lionárisso, *Cyprus* 37 D13
Lioni, *Italy* 35 B8
Lion's Den, *Zimbabwe* 83 F3
Lion's Head, *Canada* 98 D3
Liozno, *Belorussia* 40 D7
Lipa, *Phil.* 55 E4
Lipali, *Mozam.* 83 F4
Lípari, *Italy* 35 D7
Lípari, Is., *Italy* 35 D7
Lipetsk, *Russia* 41 E11
Liping, *China* 52 D7
Lipkany, *Moldavia* 42 B2
Lipljan, *Serbia, Yug.* 21 N11
Lipno, *Poland* 20 C9
Lipova, *Romania* 38 C4
Lipovcy Manzovka, *Russia* 48 B6
Lipovets, *Ukraine* 42 B3
Lippe →, *Germany* 18 D2
Lippstadt, *Germany* 18 D4
Lipscomb, *U.S.A.* 109 G4
Lipsko, *Poland* 20 D11
Lipsói, *Greece* 39 M9
Liptovsky Svaty Milkulaš, *Czech.* 20 F9
Liptrap C., *Australia* 91 F4
Lipu, *China* 53 E8
Lira, *Uganda* 82 B3
Liri →, *Italy* 34 A6
Liria, *Spain* 28 F4
Lisala, *Zaïre* 80 D4
Lisboa, *Portugal* 31 G1
Lisboa □, *Portugal* 31 G1
Lisbon = Lisboa, *Portugal* 31 G1
Lisbon, *N. Dak., U.S.A.* 108 B6
Lisbon, *N.H., U.S.A.* 107 B13
Lisbon, *Ohio, U.S.A.* 106 F4
Lisburn, *U.K.* 15 B5
Lisburne, C., *U.S.A.* 96 B3
Liscannor B., *Ireland* 15 D2
Liscia →, *Italy* 34 A2
Lishe Jiang →, *China* 52 E3
Lishi, *China* 50 F6
Lishu, *China* 51 C13
Lishui, *Jiangsu, China* 53 B12
Lishui, *Zhejiang, China* 53 C12
Lisianski I., *Pac. Oc.* 92 E10
Lisichansk, *Ukraine* 42 B8
Lisieux, *France* 24 C7
Liski, *Russia* 41 F11
L'Isle-Adam, *France* 25 C9
L'Isle-Jourdain, *Gers, France* 26 E5
L'Isle-Jourdain, *Vienne, France* 26 B4
L'Isle-sur-le-Doubs, *France* 25 E13
Lisle-sur-Tarn, *France* 26 E5
Lismore, *Australia* 91 D5
Lismore, *Ireland* 15 D4
Lisse, *Neths.* 16 D5
List, *Germany* 18 A4
Lista, *Norway* 9 G9
Lista, *Sweden* 9 G14
Lister, Mt., *Antarctica* 5 D11
Liston, *Australia* 91 D5
Listowel, *Canada* 98 D3
Listowel, *Ireland* 15 D2
Lit-et-Mixe, *France* 26 D2
Litang, *Guangxi Zhuangzu, China* 52 F7
Litang, *Sichuan, China* 52 B3
Litang, *Malaysia* 57 C5
Litang Qu →, *China* 52 C3
Litani →, *Lebanon* 69 B4
Litchfield, *Calif., U.S.A.* 112 E6
Litchfield, *Conn., U.S.A.* 107 E11
Litchfield, *Ill., U.S.A.* 108 F10
Litchfield, *Minn., U.S.A.* 108 C7
Lithgow, *Australia* 91 E5
Líthinon, Ákra, *Greece* 37 E6
Lithuania ■, *Europe* 40 D3
Litija, *Slovenia* 33 B11
Litókhoron, *Greece* 39 J5
Litoměřice, *Czech.* 20 E4
Little Abaco I., *Bahamas* 116 A4
Little Barrier I., *N.Z.* 87 G5
Little Belt Mts., *U.S.A.* 110 C8
Little Blue →, *U.S.A.* 108 F6
Little Bushman Land, *S. Africa* 84 D2
Little Cadotte →, *Canada* 100 B5
Little Cayman, I., *Cayman Is.* 116 C3
Little Churchill →, *Canada* 101 B9
Little Colorado →, *U.S.A.* 111 H8
Little Current, *Canada* 98 C3
Little Current →, *Canada* 98 B3
Little Falls, *Minn., U.S.A.* 108 C7
Little Falls, *N.Y., U.S.A.* 107 C10
Little Fork →, *U.S.A.* 108 A8
Little Grand Rapids, *Canada* 101 C9
Little Humboldt →, *U.S.A.* 110 F5
Little Inagua I., *Bahamas* 117 B5
Little Karoo, *S. Africa* 84 E3
Little Lake, *U.S.A.* 113 K9
Little Laut Is. = Laut Ketil, Kepulauan, *Indonesia* 56 E5
Little Minch, *U.K.* 14 D2
Little Missouri →, *U.S.A.* 108 B3
Little Namaqualand, *S. Africa* 84 D2
Little Ouse →, *U.K.* 13 E8
Little Rann, *India* 62 H4
Little Red →, *U.S.A.* 109 H9
Little River, *N.Z.* 87 K4
Little Rock, *U.S.A.* 109 H8
Little Ruaha →, *Tanzania* 82 D4
Little Sable Pt., *U.S.A.* 104 D2
Little Sioux →, *U.S.A.* 108 E6
Little Smoky →, *Canada* 100 C5
Little Snake →, *U.S.A.* 110 F9
Little Valley, *U.S.A.* 106 D6
Little Wabash →, *U.S.A.* 104 G1
Littlefield, *U.S.A.* 109 J3
Littlefork, *U.S.A.* 108 A8
Littlehampton, *U.K.* 13 G7
Littleton, *U.S.A.* 107 B13
Liu He →, *China* 51 D11
Liu Jiang →, *China* 52 F7
Liuba, *China* 50 H4
Liucheng, *China* 52 E7
Liugou, *China* 51 D10
Liuhe, *China* 51 C13
Liuheng Dao, *China* 53 C14
Liukang Tenggaja, *Indonesia* 57 F5
Liuli, *Tanzania* 83 E3
Liuwa Plain, *Zambia* 81 G4
Liuyang, *China* 53 C9
Liuzhou, *China* 52 E7
Liuzhuang, *China* 51 H11
Livadherón, *Greece* 39 J4
Livadhia, *Cyprus* 37 E12
Livarot, *France* 24 D7
Live Oak, *Calif., U.S.A.* 112 F5
Live Oak, *Fla., U.S.A.* 105 K4
Liveras, *Cyprus* 37 D11
Liveringa, *Australia* 88 C3
Livermore, *U.S.A.* 112 H5
Livermore, Mt., *U.S.A.* 109 K2
Liverpool, *Australia* 91 E5
Liverpool, *Canada* 99 D7
Liverpool, *U.K.* 12 D5
Liverpool Plains, *Australia* 91 E5
Liverpool Ra., *Australia* 91 E5
Livingston, *Guatemala* 116 C2
Livingston, *Calif., U.S.A.* 112 H6
Livingston, *Mont., U.S.A.* 110 D8
Livingston, *Tex., U.S.A.* 109 K7
Livingstone, *Zambia* 83 F2
Livingstone Mts., *Tanzania* 83 D3
Livingstonia, *Malawi* 83 E3
Livny, *Russia* 41 E10
Livonia, *U.S.A.* 104 D4
Livorno, *Italy* 32 E7
Livramento, *Brazil* 127 C4
Livramento do Brumado, *Brazil* 123 D3
Livron-sur-Drôme, *France* 27 D8
Liwale, *Tanzania* 83 D4
Liwale □, *Tanzania* 83 D4
Lixi, *China* 52 D3
Liyang, *China* 53 B12
Lizard I., *Australia* 90 A4
Lizard Pt., *U.K.* 13 H2
Lizarda, *Brazil* 122 C2
Lizzano, *Italy* 35 B10
Ljubija, *Bos.-H., Yug.* 33 D13
Ljubljana, *Slovenia* 33 B11
Ljubno, *Slovenia* 33 B11
Ljubuški, *Bos.-H., Yug.* 21 M7
Ljung, *Sweden* 11 F7
Ljungan →, *Sweden* 10 B11
Ljungaverk, *Sweden* 10 B10
Ljungby, *Sweden* 9 H12
Ljusdal, *Sweden* 10 C10
Ljusnan →, *Sweden* 9 F14
Ljusne, *Sweden* 9 F14
Ljutomer, *Slovenia* 33 B13
Llagostera, *Spain* 28 D7
Llamellín, *Peru* 124 B2
Llancanelo, Salina, *Argentina* 126 D2
Llandeilo, *U.K.* 13 F3
Llandovery, *U.K.* 13 F4
Llandrindod Wells, *U.K.* 13 E4
Llandudno, *U.K.* 12 D4
Llanelli, *U.K.* 13 F3
Llanes, *Spain* 30 B6
Llangollen, *U.K.* 12 E4
Llanidloes, *U.K.* 13 E4
Llano, *U.S.A.* 109 K5
Llano →, *U.S.A.* 109 K5
Llano Estacado, *U.S.A.* 109 J3
Llanos, *S. Amer.* 118 B2
Llanquihue □, *Chile* 128 B2
Llanquihue, L., *Chile* 128 B1
Llebetx, C., *Spain* 36 B9
Llentrisca, C., *Spain* 36 C7
Llera, *Mexico* 115 C5
Llerena, *Spain* 31 G4
Llica, *Bolivia* 124 D4
Llico, *Chile* 126 C1
Llobregat →, *Spain* 28 D7
Lloret de Mar, *Spain* 28 D7
Lloyd B., *Australia* 90 A3
Lloyd L., *Canada* 101 B7
Lloydminster, *Canada* 101 C6
Lluchmayor, *Spain* 36 B9
Llullaillaco, Volcán, *S. Amer.* 126 A2
Lo, *Belgium* 17 G1
Lo →, *Vietnam* 58 B5
Loa, *U.S.A.* 111 G8
Loa →, *Chile* 126 A1
Loano, *Italy* 32 D5
Lobatse, *Botswana* 84 D4
Löbau, *Germany* 18 D10
Lobbes, *Belgium* 17 H4
Lobenstein, *Germany* 18 E7
Lobería, *Argentina* 126 D4
Lobito, *Angola* 81 G2
Lobón, Canal de, *Spain* 31 G4
Lobos, *Argentina* 126 D4
Lobos, I., *Mexico* 114 B2
Lobos, Is., *Peru* 118 C1
Lobos, I. de, *Canary Is.* 36 F6
Lobos de Tierra, I., *Peru* 124 B1
Loc Binh, *Vietnam* 58 B6
Loc Ninh, *Vietnam* 59 G6
Locarno, *Switz.* 23 D7
Lochaber, *U.K.* 14 E4
Lochcarron, *U.K.* 14 D3
Lochem, *Neths.* 16 D8
Loches, *France* 24 E8
Lochgelly, *U.K.* 14 E5
Lochgilphead, *U.K.* 14 E3
Lochinver, *U.K.* 14 C3
Lochnagar, *Australia* 90 C4
Lochnagar, *U.K.* 14 E5
Łochów, *Poland* 20 C11
Lochy →, *U.K.* 14 E3
Lock, *Australia* 91 E2
Lock Haven, *U.S.A.* 106 E7
Lockeford, *U.S.A.* 112 G5
Lockeport, *Canada* 99 D6
Lockerbie, *U.K.* 14 F5
Lockhart, *U.S.A.* 109 L6
Lockhart, L., *Australia* 89 F2
Lockney, *U.S.A.* 109 H4
Lockport, *U.S.A.* 106 C6
Locminé, *France* 24 E4
Locri, *Italy* 35 D9
Locronan, *France* 24 D2
Loctudy, *France* 24 E2
Lod, *Israel* 69 D3
Lodève, *France* 26 E7
Lodge Grass, *U.S.A.* 110 D10

Lodgepole

Lodgepole, *U.S.A.* 108 E3
Lodgepole Cr. →, *U.S.A.* 108 E2
Lodhran, *Pakistan* 62 E4
Lodi, *Italy* 32 C6
Lodi, *U.S.A.* 112 G5
Lodja, *Zaïre* 82 C1
Lodosa, *Spain* 28 C2
Lödöse, *Sweden* 11 F6
Lodwar, *Kenya* 82 B4
Łódź, *Poland* 20 D9
Loei, *Thailand* 58 D3
Loenen, *Neths.* 16 D8
Loengo, *Zaïre* 82 C2
Loeriesfontein, *S. Africa* 84 E2
Lofoten, *Norway* 8 B13
Lofsdalen, *Sweden* 10 B7
Lofsen →, *Sweden* 10 B7
Logan, *Kans., U.S.A.* ... 108 F5
Logan, *Ohio, U.S.A.* 104 F4
Logan, *Utah, U.S.A.* 110 F8
Logan, *W. Va., U.S.A.* .. 104 G5
Logan, Mt., *Canada* 96 B5
Logan Pass, *U.S.A.* 100 D6
Logandale, *U.S.A.* 113 J12
Logansport, *Ind., U.S.A.* 104 E2
Logansport, *La., U.S.A.* 109 K8
Logo, *Sudan* 77 F3
Logone →, *Chad* 73 F8
Logroño, *Spain* 28 C2
Logrosán, *Spain* 31 F5
Løgstør, *Denmark* 11 H3
Lohardaga, *India* 63 H11
Lohr, *Germany* 19 F5
Loi-kaw, *Burma* 61 K20
Loimaa, *Finland* 9 F17
Loir →, *France* 24 E6
Loir-et-Cher □, *France* . 24 E8
Loire □, *France* 27 C8
Loire →, *France* 24 E4
Loire-Atlantique □, *France* 24 E5
Loiret □, *France* 25 E9
Loitz, *Germany* 18 B9
Loja, *Ecuador* 124 A2
Loja, *Spain* 31 H6
Loja □, *Ecuador* 120 D2
Loji, *Indonesia* 57 E7
Loka, *Sudan* 77 G3
Lokandu, *Zaïre* 82 C2
Løken, *Norway* 10 E5
Lokeren, *Belgium* 17 F3
Lokhvitsa, *Ukraine* 40 F8
Lokichokio, *Kenya* 82 B3
Lokitaung, *Kenya* 82 B4
Lokka, *Finland* 8 C19
Løkken, *Denmark* 11 G3
Løkken Verk, *Norway* 10 A3
Loknya, *Russia* 40 C7
Lokoja, *Nigeria* 79 D6
Lokolama, *Zaïre* 80 E3
Lol →, *Sudan* 77 F2
Lola, *Guinea* 78 D3
Lola, Mt., *U.S.A.* 112 F6
Lolibai, Gebel, *Sudan* .. 77 G3
Lolimi, *Sudan* 77 G3
Loliondo, *Tanzania* 82 C4
Lolland, *Denmark* 11 K5
Lollar, *Germany* 18 E4
Lolo, *U.S.A.* 110 C6
Lolodorf, *Cameroon* 79 E7
Lom, *Bulgaria* 38 F6
Lom →, *Bulgaria* 38 F6
Lom Kao, *Thailand* 58 D3
Lom Sak, *Thailand* 58 D3
Loma, *U.S.A.* 110 C8
Loma Linda, *U.S.A.* 113 L9
Lomami →, *Zaïre* 82 B1
Lomas de Zamóra, *Argentina* 126 C4
Lombadina, *Australia* ... 88 C3
Lombardia □, *Italy* 32 C6
Lombardy = Lombardia □, *Italy* 32 C6
Lombez, *France* 26 E4
Lomblen, *Indonesia* 57 F6
Lombok, *Indonesia* 56 F5
Lomé, *Togo* 79 D5
Lomela, *Zaïre* 80 E4
Lomela →, *Zaïre* 80 E4
Lomello, *Italy* 32 C5
Lometa, *U.S.A.* 109 K5
Lomié, *Cameroon* 80 D2
Lomma, *Sweden* 11 J7
Lomme →, *Belgium* 17 H6
Lommel, *Belgium* 17 F6
Lomond, *Canada* 100 C6
Lomond, L., *U.K.* 14 E4
Lomonosov, *Russia* 40 B6
Lomphat, *Cambodia* 58 F6
Lompobatang, *Indonesia* . 57 F5
Lompoc, *U.S.A.* 113 L6
Lomsegga, *Norway* 10 C2
Łomża, *Poland* 20 B12
Loncoche, *Chile* 128 A2
Loncopuè, *Argentina* 128 A2
Londa, *India* 60 M9
Londerzeel, *Belgium* 17 G4
Londiani, *Kenya* 82 C4
Londinières, *France* 24 C8
London, *Canada* 98 D3
London, *U.K.* 13 F7
London, *Ky., U.S.A.* 104 G3
London, *Ohio, U.S.A.* ... 104 F4
London, Greater □, *U.K.* 13 F7
Londonderry, *U.K.* 15 B4

Londonderry □, *U.K.* 15 B4
Londonderry, C., *Australia* 88 B4
Londonderry, I., *Chile* . 128 E2
Londrina, *Brazil* 127 A5
Lone Pine, *U.S.A.* 111 H4
Long Beach, *Calif., U.S.A.* 113 M8
Long Beach, *N.Y., U.S.A.* 107 F11
Long Beach, *Wash., U.S.A.* 112 D2
Long Branch, *U.S.A.* 107 F11
Long Creek, *U.S.A.* 110 D4
Long Eaton, *U.K.* 12 E6
Long I., *Australia* 90 C4
Long I., *Bahamas* 117 B4
Long I., *U.S.A.* 107 F11
Long Island Sd., *U.S.A.* 107 E12
Long L., *Canada* 98 C2
Long Lake, *U.S.A.* 107 C10
Long Pine, *U.S.A.* 108 D5
Long Pt., *Nfld., Canada* 99 C8
Long Pt., *Ont., Canada* . 106 D4
Long Point B., *Canada* .. 106 D4
Long Range Mts., *Canada* 99 C8
Long Reef, *Australia* ... 88 B4
Long Str. = Longa, Proliv, *Russia* 4 C16
Long Thanh, *Vietnam* 59 G6
Long Xian, *China* 50 G4
Long Xuyen, *Vietnam* 59 G5
Longá, *Greece* 39 N4
Longa, Proliv, *Russia* .. 4 C16
Long'an, *China* 52 F6
Longarone, *Italy* 33 B9
Longchang, *China* 52 C5
Longchi, *China* 52 C4
Longchuan, *Guangdong, China* 53 E10
Longchuan, *Yunnan, China* 52 E1
Longde, *China* 50 G4
Longeau, *France* 25 E12
Longford, *Australia* 90 G4
Longford, *Ireland* 15 C4
Longford □, *Ireland* 15 C4
Longguan, *China* 50 D8
Longhua, *China* 51 D9
Longhui, *China* 53 D8
Longido, *Tanzania* 82 C4
Longiram, *Indonesia* 56 E5
Longkou, *Jiangxi, China* 53 D10
Longkou, *Shandong, China* 51 F11
Longlac, *Canada* 98 C2
Longli, *China* 52 D6
Longlier, *Belgium* 17 J6
Longlin, *China* 52 E5
Longling, *China* 52 E2
Longmen, *China* 53 F10
Longming, *China* 52 F6
Longmont, *U.S.A.* 108 E2
Longnan, *China* 53 E10
Longnawan, *Indonesia* ... 56 D4
Longobucco, *Italy* 35 C9
Longquan, *China* 53 C12
Longreach, *Australia* ... 90 C3
Longshan, *China* 52 C7
Longsheng, *China* 53 E8
Longton, *Australia* 90 C4
Longtown, *U.K.* 13 F5
Longué-Jumelles, *France* 24 E6
Longueau, *France* 25 C9
Longueuil, *Canada* 107 A11
Longuyon, *France* 25 C12
Longview, *Canada* 100 C6
Longview, *Tex., U.S.A.* . 109 J7
Longview, *Wash., U.S.A.* 112 D4
Longvilly, *Belgium* 17 H7
Longwy, *France* 25 C12
Longxi, *China* 50 G3
Longyou, *China* 53 C12
Longzhou, *China* 52 F6
Lonigo, *Italy* 33 C8
Löningen, *Germany* 18 C3
Lonja →, *Croatia* 33 C13
Lonoke, *U.S.A.* 109 H9
Lonquimay, *Chile* 128 A2
Lons-le-Saunier, *France* 25 F12
Lønstrup, *Denmark* 11 G3
Lookout, C., *Canada* 98 A3
Lookout, C., *U.S.A.* 105 H7
Loolmalasin, *Tanzania* .. 82 C4
Loon →, *Alta., Canada* . 100 B5
Loon →, *Man., Canada* .. 101 B8
Loon Lake, *Canada* 101 C7
Loon-op-Zand, *Neths.* ... 17 E6
Loongana, *Australia* 89 F4
Loop Hd., *Ireland* 15 D2
Loosduinen, *Neths.* 16 D4
Lop Buri, *Thailand* 58 E3
Lop Nor = Lop Nur, *China* 54 B4
Lop Nur, *China* 54 B4
Lopare, *Bos.-H., Yug.* .. 21 L8
Lopatin, *Russia* 43 E12
Lopatina, G., *Russia* ... 45 D15
Lopaye, *Sudan* 77 F3
Lopera, *Spain* 31 H6
Lopez, *Phil.* 55 E5
Lopez, C., *Gabon* 80 E1
Loppersum, *Neths.* 16 B9
Lopphavet, *Norway* 8 A16
Lora →, *Afghan.* 60 D4
Lora, Hamun-i-, *Pakistan* 60 E4
Lora Cr. →, *Australia* . 91 D2
Lora del Río, *Spain* 31 H5
Lorain, *U.S.A.* 106 E2
Loralai, *Pakistan* 62 D3
Lorca, *Spain* 29 H3

Lord Howe I., *Pac. Oc.* . 92 L7
Lord Howe Ridge, *Pac. Oc.* 92 L8
Lordsburg, *U.S.A.* 111 K9
Loreto, *Bolivia* 125 D5
Loreto, *Brazil* 122 C2
Loreto, *Italy* 33 E10
Loreto, *Mexico* 114 B2
Loreto □, *Peru* 120 D3
Loreto Aprutina, *Italy* . 33 F10
Lorgues, *France* 27 E10
Lorica, *Colombia* 120 B2
Lorient, *France* 24 E3
Lorn, *U.K.* 14 E3
Lorn, Firth of, *U.K.* ... 14 E3
Lorne, *Australia* 91 F3
Lorovouno, *Cyprus* 37 D11
Lörrach, *Germany* 19 H3
Lorraine, *France* 25 D12
Lorrainville, *Canada* ... 98 C4
Los, Îles de, *Guinea* ... 78 D2
Los Alamos, *Calif., U.S.A.* 113 L6
Los Alamos, *N. Mex., U.S.A.* 111 J10
Los Altos, *U.S.A.* 112 H4
Los Andes, *Chile* 126 C1
Los Angeles, *Chile* 126 D1
Los Angeles, *U.S.A.* 113 L8
Los Angeles Aqueduct, *U.S.A.* 113 K9
Los Antiguos, *Argentina* 128 C2
Los Banos, *U.S.A.* 111 H3
Los Barrios, *Spain* 31 J5
Los Blancos, *Argentina* . 126 A3
Los Cristianos, *Canary Is.* 36 F3
Los Gatos, *U.S.A.* 112 H5
Los Hermanos, *Venezuela* 117 D7
Los Islotes, *Canary Is.* 36 E6
Los Lagos, *Chile* 128 A2
Los Llanos de Aridane, *Canary Is.* 36 F2
Los Lomas, *Peru* 124 A1
Los Lunas, *U.S.A.* 111 J10
Los Menucos, *Argentina* . 128 B3
Los Mochis, *Mexico* 114 B3
Los Monegros, *Spain* 28 D4
Los Monos, *Argentina* ... 128 C3
Los Olivos, *U.S.A.* 113 L6
Los Palacios, *Cuba* 116 B3
Los Palacios y Villafranca, *Spain* 31 H5
Los Reyes, *Mexico* 114 D4
Los Ríos □, *Ecuador* 120 D2
Los Roques, *Venezuela* .. 120 A4
Los Santos de Maimona, *Spain* 31 G4
Los Teques, *Venezuela* .. 120 A4
Los Testigos, *Venezuela* 121 A5
Los Vilos, *Chile* 126 C1
Los Yébenes, *Spain* 31 F7
Losada →, *Colombia* 120 C3
Loshkalakh, *Russia* 45 C15
Lošinj, *Croatia* 33 D11
Losser, *Neths.* 16 D10
Lossiemouth, *U.K.* 14 D5
Lot □, *France* 26 D5
Lot →, *France* 26 D4
Lot-et-Garonne □, *France* 26 D4
Lota, *Chile* 126 D1
Løten, *Norway* 10 D5
Lotfābād, *Iran* 65 B8
Lothair, *S. Africa* 85 D5
Lothian □, *U.K.* 14 F5
Lothiers, *France* 25 F8
Lötschbergtunnel, *Switz.* 22 D5
Lotzwil, *Switz.* 22 B5
Loubomo, *Congo* 80 E2
Loudéac, *France* 24 D4
Loudi, *China* 53 D8
Loudon, *U.S.A.* 105 H3
Loudonville, *U.S.A.* 106 F2
Loudun, *France* 24 E7
Loué, *France* 24 E6
Loue →, *France* 25 E12
Louga, *Senegal* 78 B1
Loughborough, *U.K.* 12 E6
Loughrea, *Ireland* 15 C3
Loughros More B., *Ireland* 15 B3
Louhans, *France* 27 B9
Louis Trichardt, *S. Africa* 85 C4
Louis XIV, Pte., *Canada* 98 B4
Louisa, *U.S.A.* 104 F4
Louisbourg, *Canada* 99 C8
Louise I., *Canada* 100 C2
Louiseville, *Canada* 98 C5
Louisiade Arch., *Papua N. G.* 92 J7
Louisiana, *U.S.A.* 108 F9
Louisiana □, *U.S.A.* 109 K9
Louisville, *Ky., U.S.A.* 104 F3
Louisville, *Miss., U.S.A.* 109 J10
Loulay, *France* 26 B3
Loulé, *Portugal* 31 H2
Louny, *Czech.* 20 E3
Loup City, *U.S.A.* 108 E5
Lourdes, *France* 26 E3
Lourdes-du-Blanc-Sablon, *Canada* 99 B8
Lourenço, *Brazil* 121 C7
Lourenço-Marques = Maputo, *Mozam.* 85 D5
Loures, *Portugal* 31 G1
Lourinhã, *Portugal* 31 F1

Lousã, *Portugal* 30 E2
Louth, *Australia* 91 E4
Louth, *Ireland* 15 C5
Louth, *U.K.* 12 D7
Louth □, *Ireland* 15 C5
Louvain = Leuven, *Belgium* 17 G5
Louveigné, *Belgium* 17 G7
Louviers, *France* 24 C8
Louwsburg, *S. Africa* ... 85 D5
Lovat →, *Russia* 40 B7
Love, *Canada* 101 C8
Lovech, *Bulgaria* 38 F7
Loveland, *U.S.A.* 108 E2
Lovell, *U.S.A.* 110 D9
Lovelock, *U.S.A.* 110 F4
Lóvere, *Italy* 32 C7
Loviisa = Lovisa, *Finland* 9 F19
Loving, *U.S.A.* 109 J2
Lovington, *U.S.A.* 109 J3
Lovios, *Spain* 30 D2
Lovisa, *Finland* 9 F19
Lovran, *Croatia* 33 C11
Low Pt., *Australia* 89 F4
Lowa, *Zaïre* 82 C2
Lowa →, *Zaïre* 82 C2
Lowell, *U.S.A.* 107 D13
Lower Arrow L., *Canada* . 100 D5
Lower California = Baja California, *Mexico* 114 A1
Lower California = California, Baja, *Mexico* 114 A1
Lower Hutt, *N.Z.* 87 J5
Lower L., *U.S.A.* 110 F3
Lower Lake, *U.S.A.* 112 G4
Lower Post, *Canada* 100 B3
Lower Red L., *U.S.A.* ... 108 B7
Lower Saxony = Niedersachsen □, *Germany* 18 C5
Lower Tunguska = Tunguska, Nizhnyaya →, *Russia* 45 C9
Lowestoft, *U.K.* 13 E9
Łowicz, *Poland* 20 C9
Lowville, *U.S.A.* 107 C9
Loxton, *Australia* 91 E3
Loxton, *S. Africa* 84 E3
Loyalton, *U.S.A.* 112 F6
Loyalty Is. = Loyauté, Is., *N. Cal.* 92 K8
Loyang = Luoyang, *China* 50 G7
Loyauté, Is., *N. Cal.* .. 92 K8
Loyev, *Belorussia* 40 F7
Loyoro, *Uganda* 82 B3
Lož, *Slovenia* 33 C11
Lozère □, *France* 26 D7
Loznica, *Serbia, Yug.* .. 21 L9
Lozovaya, *Ukraine* 42 B7
Luachimo, *Angola* 80 F4
Luacono, *Angola* 80 G4
Lualaba →, *Zaïre* 82 B5
Luampa, *Zambia* 83 F1
Lu'an, *China* 53 B11
Luan Chau, *Vietnam* 58 B4
Luan He →, *China* 51 E10
Luan Xian, *China* 51 E10
Luancheng, *Guangxi Zhuangzu, China* 52 F7
Luancheng, *Hebei, China* 50 F8
Luanda, *Angola* 80 F2
Luang Prabang, *Laos* 58 C4
Luang Thale, *Thailand* .. 59 J3
Luangwa, *Zambia* 83 F3
Luangwa →, *Zambia* 83 E3
Luangwa Valley, *Zambia* . 83 E3
Luanne, *China* 51 D9
Luanping, *China* 51 D9
Luanshya, *Zambia* 83 E2
Luapula □, *Zambia* 83 E2
Luapula →, *Africa* 83 D2
Luarca, *Spain* 30 B4
Luashi, *Zaïre* 83 E1
Luau, *Angola* 80 G4
Lubalo, *Angola* 80 F3
Lubań, *Poland* 20 D5
Lubana, Ozero, *Latvia* .. 40 C5
Lubang, *Phil.* 55 E4
Lubang Is., *Phil.* 57 B6
Lubartów, *Poland* 20 D12
Lubawa, *Poland* 20 B9
Lubbeek, *Belgium* 17 G5
Lübben, *Germany* 18 D9
Lübbenau, *Germany* 18 D9
Lubbock, *U.S.A.* 109 J4
Lübeck, *Germany* 18 B6
Lübecker Bucht, *Germany* 18 A7
Lubefu, *Zaïre* 82 C1
Lubefu →, *Zaïre* 82 C1
Lubero = Luofu, *Zaïre* .. 82 C2
Lubicon L., *Canada* 100 B5
Lublin, *Poland* 20 D12
Lubliniec, *Poland* 20 E8
Lubnān, J., *Lebanon* 69 B4
Lubny, *Ukraine* 40 F8
Lubon, *Poland* 20 C6
Lubongola, *Zaïre* 82 C2
Lubsko, *Poland* 20 D4
Lübtheen, *Germany* 18 B7
Lubuagan, *Phil.* 55 C4
Lubudi, *Zaïre* 83 D2
Lubudi →, *Zaïre* 83 D2
Lubuk Antu, *Malaysia* ... 56 D4
Lubuklinggau, *Indonesia* 56 E2

Lubuksikaping, *Indonesia* 56 D2
Lubumbashi, *Zaïre* 83 E2
Lubunda, *Zaïre* 82 D2
Lubungu, *Zambia* 83 E2
Lubutu, *Zaïre* 82 C2
Luc An Chau, *Vietnam* ... 58 A5
Luc-en-Diois, *France* ... 27 D9
Lucan, *Canada* 106 C3
Lucban, *Phil.* 55 D4
Lucca, *Italy* 32 C8
Luce Bay, *U.K.* 14 G4
Lucea, *Jamaica* 116 C4
Lucedale, *U.S.A.* 105 K1
Lucena, *Phil.* 55 E4
Lucena, *Spain* 31 H6
Lucena del Cid, *Spain* .. 28 E4
Lučenec, *Czech.* 21 G9
Lucens, *Switz.* 22 C3
Lucera, *Italy* 35 A8
Lucerne = Luzern, *Switz.* 23 B6
Lucerne, *U.S.A.* 112 F4
Lucerne Valley, *U.S.A.* . 113 L10
Luchena →, *Spain* 29 H3
Lucheng, *China* 50 F7
Lucheringo →, *Mozam.* .. 83 E4
Lüchow, *Germany* 18 C7
Luchuan, *China* 53 F8
Lucie →, *Surinam* 121 C6
Lucira, *Angola* 81 G2
Luckau, *Germany* 18 D9
Luckenwalde, *Germany* ... 18 C9
Lucknow, *India* 63 F9
Luçon, *France* 26 B2
Lüda = Dalian, *China* ... 51 E11
Luda Kamchiya →, *Bulgaria* 38 F10
Ludbreg, *Croatia* 33 B13
Lüdenscheid, *Germany* ... 18 D3
Lüderitz, *Namibia* 84 D2
Ludewe →, *Tanzania* 83 D3
Ludhiana, *India* 62 D6
Ludian, *China* 52 D4
Luding Qiao, *China* 52 C3
Lüdinghausen, *Germany* .. 18 D3
Ludington, *U.S.A.* 104 D2
Ludlow, *U.K.* 13 E5
Ludlow, *Calif., U.S.A.* . 113 L10
Ludlow, *Vt., U.S.A.* 107 C12
Ludus, *Romania* 38 C7
Ludvika, *Sweden* 9 F13
Ludwigsburg, *Germany* ... 19 G5
Ludwigshafen, *Germany* .. 19 F4
Ludwigslust, *Germany* ... 18 B7
Ludza, *Latvia* 40 C5
Luebo, *Zaïre* 80 F4
Lueki, *Zaïre* 82 C2
Luena, *Zaïre* 83 D2
Luena, *Zambia* 83 E3
Luepa, *Venezuela* 121 B5
Lüeyang, *China* 50 H4
Lufeng, *Guangdong, China* 53 F10
Lufeng, *Yunnan, China* .. 52 E4
Lufira →, *Zaïre* 83 D2
Lufkin, *U.S.A.* 109 K7
Lufupa, *Zaïre* 83 E1
Luga, *Russia* 40 B6
Luga →, *Russia* 40 B6
Lugang, *Taiwan* 53 E13
Lugano, *Switz.* 23 D7
Lugano, L. di, *Switz.* .. 23 D7
Lugansk, *Ukraine* 43 B8
Lugard's Falls, *Kenya* .. 82 C4
Lugela, *Mozam.* 83 F4
Lugenda →, *Mozam.* 83 E4
Lugh Ganana, *Somali Rep.* 68 G3
Lugnaquilla, *Ireland* ... 15 D5
Lugnvik, *Sweden* 10 B11
Lugo, *Italy* 33 D8
Lugo, *Spain* 30 B3
Lugo □, *Spain* 30 C3
Lugoj, *Romania* 38 D4
Lugones, *Spain* 30 B5
Lugovoye, *Kazakhstan* ... 44 E8
Luhe, *China* 53 A12
Luhe →, *Germany* 18 B6
Luhuo, *China* 52 B3
Luiana, *Angola* 84 B3
Luino, *Italy* 32 C5
Luís Correia, *Brazil* ... 122 B3
Luís Gonçalves, *Brazil* . 122 C2
Luitpold Coast, *Antarctica* 5 D1
Luiza, *Zaïre* 80 F4
Luizi, *Zaïre* 82 D2
Luján, *Argentina* 126 C4
Lujiang, *China* 53 B11
Lukanga Swamp, *Zambia* .. 83 E2
Lukenie →, *Zaïre* 80 E3
Lukhisaral, *India* 63 G12
Lŭki, *Bulgaria* 39 H7
Lukolela, *Equateur, Zaïre* 80 E3
Lukolela, *Kasai Or., Zaïre* 82 D1
Lukosi, *Zimbabwe* 83 F2
Lukovit, *Bulgaria* 38 F7
Łuków, *Poland* 20 D12
Lukoyanov, *Russia* 41 D14
Lule älv →, *Sweden* 8 D17
Luleå, *Sweden* 8 D17
Lüleburgaz, *Turkey* 39 H10
Luliang, *China* 52 E4
Luling, *U.S.A.* 109 L6
Lulong, *China* 51 E10
Lulonga →, *Zaïre* 80 D3
Lulua →, *Zaïre* 80 E4

Luluabourg = Kananga, *Zaïre* 80 F4
Lumai, *Angola* 81 G4
Lumajang, *Indonesia* 57 H15
Lumbala N'guimbo, *Angola* 81 G4
Lumberton, *Miss., U.S.A.* 109 K10
Lumberton, *N.C., U.S.A.* 105 H6
Lumberton, *N. Mex., U.S.A.* 111 H10
Lumbres, *France* 25 B9
Lumbwa, *Kenya* 82 C4
Lummen, *Belgium* 17 G6
Lumsden, *N.Z.* 87 L2
Lumut, *Malaysia* 59 K3
Lumut, Tg., *Indonesia* 56 E3
Luna, *Phil.* 55 C4
Lunan, *China* 52 E4
Lunavada, *India* 62 H5
Lunca, *Romania* 38 B8
Lund, *Sweden* 11 J7
Lund, *U.S.A.* 110 G6
Lundazi, *Zambia* 83 E3
Lunde, *Norway* 10 E3
Lunderskov, *Denmark* 11 J3
Lundi →, *Zimbabwe* 83 G3
Lundu, *Malaysia* 56 D3
Lundy, *U.K.* 13 F3
Lune →, *U.K.* 12 C5
Lüneburg, *Germany* 18 B6
Lüneburg Heath = Lüneburger Heide, *Germany* 18 C6
Lüneburger Heide, *Germany* 18 C6
Lunel, *France* 27 E8
Lünen, *Germany* 18 D3
Lunenburg, *Canada* 99 D7
Lunéville, *France* 25 D13
Lunga →, *Zambia* 83 E2
Lungern, *Switz.* 22 C6
Lungi Airport, *S. Leone* 78 D2
Lunglei, *India* 61 H18
Luni, *India* 62 F5
Luni →, *India* 62 G4
Luninets, *Belorussia* 40 E5
Luning, *U.S.A.* 110 G4
Lunino, *Russia* 41 E14
Lunner, *Norway* 10 D4
Lunsemfwa →, *Zambia* 83 E3
Lunsemfwa Falls, *Zambia* 83 E2
Lunteren, *Neths.* 16 D7
Luo He →, *China* 50 G6
Luocheng, *China* 52 E7
Luochuan, *China* 50 G5
Luoci, *China* 52 E4
Luodian, *China* 52 E6
Luoding, *China* 53 F8
Luodong, *Taiwan* 53 E13
Luofu, *Zaïre* 82 C2
Luohe, *China* 50 H8
Luojiang, *China* 52 B5
Luonan, *China* 50 G6
Luoning, *China* 50 G6
Luoshan, *China* 53 A10
Luotian, *China* 53 B10
Luoyang, *China* 50 G7
Luoyuan, *China* 53 D12
Luozi, *Zaïre* 80 E2
Luozigou, *China* 51 C16
Lupeni, *Romania* 38 D6
Lupilichi, *Mozam.* 83 E4
Lupoing, *China* 52 E5
Luquan, *China* 52 E4
Luque, *Paraguay* 126 B4
Luque, *Spain* 31 H6
Luray, *U.S.A.* 104 F6
Lure, *France* 25 E13
Luremo, *Angola* 80 F3
Lurgan, *U.K.* 15 B5
Luribay, *Bolivia* 124 D4
Lurin, *Peru* 124 C2
Lusaka, *Zambia* 83 F2
Lusambo, *Zaïre* 82 C1
Lusangaye, *Zaïre* 82 C2
Luseland, *Canada* 101 C7
Lushan, *Henan, China* 50 H7
Lushan, *Sichuan, China* 52 B4
Lushi, *China* 50 G6
Lushnja, *Albania* 39 J2
Lushoto, *Tanzania* 82 C4
Lushoto □, *Tanzania* 82 C4
Lushui, *China* 52 E2
Lüshun, *China* 51 E11
Lusignan, *France* 26 B4
Lusigny-sur-Barse, *France* 25 D11
Lusk, *U.S.A.* 108 D2
Lussac-les-Châteaux, *France* 26 B4
Lussanvira, *Brazil* 123 F1
Luta = Dalian, *China* 51 E11
Luton, *U.K.* 13 F7
Lutong, *Malaysia* 56 D4
Lutry, *Switz.* 22 C3
Lutsk, *Ukraine* 40 F4
Lützow Holmbukta, *Antarctica* 5 C4
Lutzputs, *S. Africa* 84 D3
Luverne, *U.S.A.* 108 D6
Luvua, *Zaïre* 83 D2
Luvua →, *Zaïre* 82 D2
Luwegu →, *Tanzania* 83 D4
Luwuk, *Indonesia* 57 E6
Luxembourg, *Lux.* 17 J8
Luxembourg □, *Belgium* 17 J7
Luxembourg ■, *Europe* 17 J8
Luxeuil-les-Bains, *France* 25 E13
Luxi, *Hunan, China* 53 C8
Luxi, *Yunnan, China* 52 E4
Luxi, *Yunnan, China* 52 E2
Luxor = El Uqsur, *Egypt* 76 B3
Luy →, *France* 26 E2
Luy-de-Béarn →, *France* 26 E3
Luy-de-France →, *France* 26 E3
Luyi, *China* 50 H8
Luyksgestel, *Neths.* 17 F6
Luz-St.-Sauveur, *France* 26 F4
Luzern, *Switz.* 23 B6
Luzern □, *Switz.* 22 B5
Luzhai, *China* 52 E7
Luzhou, *China* 52 C5
Luziânia, *Brazil* 123 E2
Luzilândia, *Brazil* 122 B3
Luzon, *Phil.* 55 D4
Luzy, *France* 25 F10
Luzzi, *Italy* 35 C9
Lvov, *Ukraine* 40 G4
Lyakhovichi, *Belorussia* 40 E5
Lyakhovskiye, Ostrova, *Russia* 45 B15
Lyaki, *Azerbaijan* 43 F12
Lyallpur = Faisalabad, *Pakistan* 62 D5
Lycaonia, *Turkey* 66 D5
Lychen, *Germany* 18 B9
Lycia, *Turkey* 66 E3
Lycksele, *Sweden* 8 D15
Lydda = Lod, *Israel* 69 D3
Lydenburg, *S. Africa* 85 D5
Lydia, *Turkey* 66 D3
Lyell, *N.Z.* 87 J4
Lyell I., *Canada* 100 C2
Lygnern, *Sweden* 11 G6
Lyman, *U.S.A.* 110 F8
Lyme Regis, *U.K.* 13 G5
Lymington, *U.K.* 13 G6
Lynchburg, *U.S.A.* 104 G6
Lynd →, *Australia* 90 B3
Lynd Ra., *Australia* 91 D4
Lynden, *Canada* 106 C4
Lynden, *U.S.A.* 112 B4
Lyndhurst, *Queens., Australia* 90 B3
Lyndhurst, *S. Austral., Australia* 91 E2
Lyndon →, *Australia* 89 D1
Lyndonville, *N.Y., U.S.A.* 106 C6
Lyndonville, *Vt., U.S.A.* 107 B12
Lyngdal, *Norway* 10 E3
Lynher Reef, *Australia* 88 C3
Lynn, *U.S.A.* 107 D14
Lynn Canal, *U.S.A.* 100 B1
Lynn Lake, *Canada* 101 B8
Lynnwood, *U.S.A.* 112 C4
Lynton, *U.K.* 13 F4
Lyntupy, *Belorussia* 40 D5
Lynx L., *Canada* 101 A7
Lyø, *Denmark* 11 J4
Lyon, *France* 27 C8
Lyonnais, *France* 27 C8
Lyons = Lyon, *France* 27 C8
Lyons, *Colo., U.S.A.* 108 E2
Lyons, *Ga., U.S.A.* 105 J4
Lyons, *Kans., U.S.A.* 108 F5
Lyons, *N.Y., U.S.A.* 106 C8
Lyrestad, *Sweden* 11 F8
Lys = Leie →, *Belgium* 25 A10
Lysekil, *Sweden* 11 F5
Lyskovo, *Russia* 41 D14
Lyss, *Switz.* 22 B4
Lytle, *U.S.A.* 109 L5
Lyttelton, *N.Z.* 87 K4
Lytton, *Canada* 100 C4
Lyuban, *Russia* 40 B7
Lyubcha, *Belorussia* 40 E5
Lyubertsy, *Russia* 41 D10
Lyubim, *Russia* 41 B12
Lyuboml, *Ukraine* 40 F4
Lyubotin, *Ukraine* 42 B6
Lyubytino, *Russia* 40 B8
Lyudinovo, *Russia* 40 E9

M

Ma →, *Vietnam* 58 C5
Ma'adaba, *Jordan* 69 E4
Maamba, *Zambia* 84 B4
Ma'ān, *Jordan* 69 E4
Ma'ān □, *Jordan* 69 F5
Ma'anshan, *China* 53 B12
Maarheeze, *Neths.* 17 F7
Maarianhamina, *Finland* 9 F15
Maarn, *Neths.* 16 D6
Ma'arrat an Nu'mān, *Syria* 64 C3
Maarssen, *Neths.* 16 D6
Maartensdijk, *Neths.* 16 D6
Maas →, *Neths.* 16 E5
Maasbracht, *Belgium* 17 F7
Maasbree, *Neths.* 17 F8
Maasdam, *Neths.* 16 E5
Maasdijk, *Neths.* 16 E4
Maaseik, *Belgium* 17 F7
Maasland, *Neths.* 16 E4
Maasniel, *Neths.* 17 F8
Maassluis, *Neths.* 16 E4
Maastricht, *Neths.* 17 G7
Maave, *Mozam.* 85 C5
Mabaruma, *Guyana* 121 B6
Mabel L., *Canada* 100 C5
Mabenge, *Zaïre* 82 B1
Mabian, *China* 52 C4
Mablethorpe, *U.K.* 12 D8
Maboma, *Zaïre* 82 B2
Mabrouk, *Mali* 79 B4
Mabton, *U.S.A.* 110 C3
Mac Bac, *Vietnam* 59 H6
Macachín, *Argentina* 126 D3
Macaé, *Brazil* 123 F3
Macaíba, *Brazil* 122 C4
Macajuba, *Brazil* 123 D3
McAlester, *U.S.A.* 109 H7
McAllen, *U.S.A.* 109 M5
Macamic, *Canada* 98 C4
Macao = Macau ■, *China* 54 D6
Macão, *Portugal* 31 F3
Macapá, *Brazil* 121 C7
Macará, *Ecuador* 120 D2
Macarani, *Brazil* 123 E3
Macarena, Serranía de la, *Colombia* 120 C3
McArthur →, *Australia* 90 B2
McArthur, Port, *Australia* 90 B2
McArthur River, *Australia* 90 B2
Macas, *Ecuador* 120 D2
Macate, *Peru* 124 B2
Macau, *Brazil* 122 C4
Macau ■, *China* 54 D6
Macaúbas, *Brazil* 123 D3
Macaya →, *Colombia* 120 C3
McBride, *Canada* 100 C4
McCall, *U.S.A.* 110 D5
McCamey, *U.S.A.* 109 K3
McCammon, *U.S.A.* 110 E7
McCauley I., *Canada* 100 C2
McCleary, *U.S.A.* 112 C3
Macclesfield, *U.K.* 12 D5
McClintock, *Canada* 101 B10
McClintock Ra., *Australia* 88 C4
McCloud, *U.S.A.* 110 F2
McCluer I., *Australia* 88 B5
McClure, *U.S.A.* 106 F7
McClure, L., *U.S.A.* 112 H6
M'Clure Str., *Canada* 4 B2
McClusky, *U.S.A.* 108 B4
McComb, *U.S.A.* 109 K9
McConaughy, L., *U.S.A.* 108 E4
McCook, *U.S.A.* 108 E4
McCullough Mt., *U.S.A.* 113 K11
McCusker →, *Canada* 101 B7
McDame, *Canada* 100 B3
McDermitt, *U.S.A.* 110 F5
Macdonald, L., *Australia* 88 D4
McDonald Is., *Ind. Oc.* 3 G13
Macdonnell Ras., *Australia* 88 D5
McDouall Peak, *Australia* 91 D1
Macdougall L., *Canada* 96 B10
MacDowell L., *Canada* 98 B1
Macduff, *U.K.* 14 D6
Maceda, *Spain* 30 C3
Macedonia □, *Macedonia, Yug.* 39 H4
Maceió, *Brazil* 122 C4
Maceira, *Portugal* 31 F2
Macenta, *Guinea* 78 D3
Macerata, *Italy* 33 E10
McFarland, *U.S.A.* 113 K7
McFarlane →, *Canada* 101 B7
Macfarlane, L., *Australia* 91 E2
McGehee, *U.S.A.* 109 J9
McGill, *U.S.A.* 110 G6
Macgillycuddy's Reeks, *Ireland* 15 D2
MacGregor, *Canada* 101 D9
McGregor, *U.S.A.* 108 D9
McGregor →, *Canada* 100 B4
McGregor Ra., *Australia* 91 D3
Mach, *Pakistan* 60 E5
Māch Kowr, *Iran* 65 E9
Machacalis, *Brazil* 123 E3
Machado = Jiparaná →, *Brazil* 125 B5
Machagai, *Argentina* 126 B3
Machakos, *Kenya* 82 C4
Machakos □, *Kenya* 82 C4
Machala, *Ecuador* 120 D2
Machanga, *Mozam.* 85 C6
Machattie, L., *Australia* 90 C2
Machava, *Mozam.* 85 D5
Machece, *Mozam.* 83 F4
Machecoul, *France* 24 F5
Machelen, *Belgium* 17 G4
Macheng, *China* 53 B10
Machevna, *Russia* 45 C18
Machezo, *Spain* 31 F6
Machias, *U.S.A.* 99 D6
Machichaco, C., *Spain* 28 B2
Machichi →, *Canada* 101 B10
Machico, *Madeira* 36 D3
Machilipatnam, *India* 61 L12
Machiques, *Venezuela* 120 A3
Machupicchu, *Peru* 124 C3
Machynlleth, *U.K.* 13 E4
McIlwraith Ra., *Australia* 90 A3
Măcin, *Romania* 38 D11
Macina, *Mali* 78 C4
McIntosh, *U.S.A.* 108 C4
McIntosh L., *Canada* 101 B8
Macintosh Ra., *Australia* 89 E4
Macintyre →, *Australia* 91 D5
Macizo Galaico, *Spain* 30 C3
Mackay, *Australia* 90 C4
Mackay, *U.S.A.* 110 E7
MacKay →, *Canada* 100 B6
Mackay, L., *Australia* 88 D4
McKay Ra., *Australia* 88 D3
McKeesport, *U.S.A.* 106 F5
McKenna, *U.S.A.* 112 D4
Mackenzie, *Canada* 100 B4
Mackenzie, *Guyana* 121 B6
McKenzie, *U.S.A.* 105 G1
Mackenzie →, *Australia* 90 C4
Mackenzie →, *Canada* 96 B6
McKenzie →, *U.S.A.* 110 D2
Mackenzie City = Linden, *Guyana* 121 B6
Mackenzie Highway, *Canada* 100 B5
Mackenzie Mts., *Canada* 96 B7
Mackinaw City, *U.S.A.* 104 C3
McKinlay, *Australia* 90 C3
McKinlay →, *Australia* 90 C3
McKinley, Mt., *U.S.A.* 96 B4
McKinley Sea, *Arctic* 4 A7
McKinney, *U.S.A.* 109 J6
Mackinnon Road, *Kenya* 82 C4
Macksville, *Australia* 91 E5
McLaughlin, *U.S.A.* 108 C4
Maclean, *Australia* 91 D5
McLean, *U.S.A.* 109 H4
McLeansboro, *U.S.A.* 108 F10
Maclear, *S. Africa* 85 E4
Macleay →, *Australia* 91 E5
McLennan, *Canada* 100 B5
MacLeod, B., *Canada* 101 A7
McLeod, L., *Australia* 89 D1
MacLeod Lake, *Canada* 100 C4
M'Clintock Chan., *Canada* 96 A9
McLoughlin, Mt., *U.S.A.* 110 E2
McLure, *Canada* 100 C4
McMechen, *U.S.A.* 106 G4
McMillan L., *U.S.A.* 109 J2
McMinnville, *Oreg., U.S.A.* 110 D2
McMinnville, *Tenn., U.S.A.* 105 H3
McMorran, *Canada* 101 C7
McMurdo Sd., *Antarctica* 5 D11
McMurray = Fort McMurray, *Canada* 100 B6
McMurray, *U.S.A.* 112 B4
McNary, *U.S.A.* 111 J9
MacNutt, *Canada* 101 C8
Macodoene, *Mozam.* 85 C6
Macomb, *U.S.A.* 108 E9
Macomer, *Italy* 34 B1
Mâcon, *France* 27 B8
Macon, *Ga., U.S.A.* 105 J4
Macon, *Miss., U.S.A.* 105 J1
Macon, *Mo., U.S.A.* 108 F8
Macondo, *Angola* 81 G4
Macossa, *Mozam.* 83 F3
Macoun L., *Canada* 101 B8
Macovane, *Mozam.* 85 C6
McPherson, *U.S.A.* 108 F6
McPherson Pk., *U.S.A.* 113 L7
McPherson Ra., *Australia* 91 D5
Macquarie Harbour, *Australia* 90 G4
Macquarie Is., *Pac. Oc.* 92 N7
MacRobertson Land, *Antarctica* 5 D6
Macroom, *Ireland* 15 E3
Macroy, *Australia* 88 D2
MacTier, *Canada* 106 A5
Macubela, *Mozam.* 83 F4
Macugnaga, *Italy* 32 C4
Macuiza, *Mozam.* 83 F3
Macujer, *Colombia* 120 C3
Macusani, *Peru* 124 C3
Macuse, *Mozam.* 83 F4
Macuspana, *Mexico* 115 D6
Macusse, *Angola* 84 B3
McVille, *U.S.A.* 108 B5
Madadeni, *S. Africa* 85 D5
Madagali, *Nigeria* 79 C7
Madagascar ■, *Africa* 85 C8
Madā'in Sālih, *Si. Arabia* 64 E3
Madama, *Niger* 73 D7
Madame I., *Canada* 99 C7
Madaoua, *Niger* 79 C6
Madara, *Nigeria* 79 C7
Madaripur, *Bangla.* 61 H17
Madauk, *Burma* 61 L20
Madawaska, *Canada* 106 A7
Madawaska →, *Canada* 98 C4
Madaya, *Burma* 61 H20
Madbar, *Sudan* 77 F3
Maddaloni, *Italy* 35 A7
Made, *Neths.* 17 E5
Madeira, *Atl. Oc.* 36 D3
Madeira →, *Brazil* 121 D6
Madeleine, Is. de la, *Canada* 99 C7
Maden, *Turkey* 67 D8
Madera, *U.S.A.* 111 H3
Madha, *India* 60 L9
Madhubani, *India* 63 F12
Madhya Pradesh □, *India* 62 J7
Madian, *China* 53 A11
Madidi →, *Bolivia* 124 C4
Madikeri, *India* 60 N9
Madill, *U.S.A.* 109 H6
Madimba, *Zaïre* 80 E3
Ma'din, *Syria* 64 C3
Madīnat ash Sha'b, *Yemen* 68 E3
Madingou, *Congo* 80 E2
Madirovalo, *Madag.* 85 B8
Madison, *Calif., U.S.A.* 112 G5
Madison, *Fla., U.S.A.* 105 K4
Madison, *Ind., U.S.A.* 104 F3
Madison, *Nebr., U.S.A.* 108 E6
Madison, *Ohio, U.S.A.* 106 E3
Madison, *S. Dak., U.S.A.* 108 D6
Madison, *Wis., U.S.A.* 108 D10
Madison →, *U.S.A.* 110 D8
Madisonville, *Ky., U.S.A.* 104 G2
Madisonville, *Tex., U.S.A.* 109 K7
Madista, *Botswana* 84 C4
Madiun, *Indonesia* 57 G14
Madley, *U.K.* 13 E5
Madol, *Sudan* 77 F2
Madon →, *France* 25 D13
Madona, *Latvia* 40 C5
Madras = Tamil Nadu □, *India* 60 P10
Madras, *India* 60 N12
Madras, *U.S.A.* 110 D3
Madre, L., *Mexico* 115 B5
Madre, L., *U.S.A.* 109 M6
Madre, Sierra, *Phil.* 55 C5
Madre de Dios □, *Peru* 124 C3
Madre de Dios →, *Bolivia* 124 C4
Madre de Dios, I., *Chile* 128 D1
Madre del Sur, Sierra, *Mexico* 115 D5
Madre Occidental, Sierra, *Mexico* 114 B3
Madre Oriental, Sierra, *Mexico* 114 C4
Madri, *India* 62 G5
Madrid, *Spain* 30 E7
Madrid □, *Spain* 30 E7
Madridejos, *Spain* 31 F7
Madrigal de las Altas Torres, *Spain* 30 D6
Madrona, Sierra, *Spain* 31 G6
Madroñera, *Spain* 31 F5
Madu, *Sudan* 77 E2
Madura, Selat, *Indonesia* 57 G15
Madura Motel, *Australia* 89 F4
Madurai, *India* 60 Q11
Madurantakam, *India* 60 N11
Madzhalis, *Russia* 43 E12
Mae Chan, *Thailand* 58 B2
Mae Hong Son, *Thailand* 58 C2
Mae Khlong →, *Thailand* 58 F3
Mae Phrik, *Thailand* 58 D2
Mae Ramat, *Thailand* 58 D2
Mae Rim, *Thailand* 58 C2
Mae Sot, *Thailand* 58 D2
Mae Suai, *Thailand* 58 C2
Mae Tha, *Thailand* 58 C2
Maebashi, *Japan* 49 F9
Maella, *Spain* 28 D5
Măeruş, *Romania* 38 D8
Maesteg, *U.K.* 13 F4
Maestra, Sierra, *Cuba* 116 B4
Maestrazgo, Mts. del, *Spain* 28 E4
Maevatanana, *Madag.* 85 B8
Mafeking = Mafikeng, *S. Africa* 84 D4
Mafeking, *Canada* 101 C8
Maféré, *Ivory C.* 78 D4
Mafeteng, *Lesotho* 84 D4
Maffe, *Belgium* 17 H6
Maffra, *Australia* 91 F4
Mafia I., *Tanzania* 82 D4
Mafikeng, *S. Africa* 84 D4
Mafra, *Brazil* 127 B6
Mafra, *Portugal* 31 G1
Mafungabusi Plateau, *Zimbabwe* 83 F2
Magadan, *Russia* 45 D16
Magadi, *Kenya* 82 C4
Magadi, L., *Kenya* 82 C4
Magaliesburg, *S. Africa* 85 D4
Magallanes □, *Chile* 128 D2
Magallanes, Estrecho de, *Chile* 128 D2
Magangué, *Colombia* 120 B3
Magaria, *Niger* 79 C6
Magburaka, *S. Leone* 78 D2
Magdalena, *Argentina* 126 D4
Magdalena, *Bolivia* 125 C5
Magdalena, *Malaysia* 56 D5
Magdalena, *Mexico* 114 A2
Magdalena, *U.S.A.* 111 J10
Magdalena □, *Colombia* 120 A3
Magdalena →, *Colombia* 120 A3
Magdalena →, *Mexico* 114 A2
Magdalena, B., *Mexico* 114 C2
Magdalena, I., *Chile* 128 B2
Magdalena, Llano de la, *Mexico* 114 C2
Magdeburg, *Germany* 18 C7
Magdelaine Cays, *Australia* 90 B5
Magdub, *Sudan* 77 E2
Magee, *U.S.A.* 109 K10
Magee, I., *U.K.* 15 B6
Magelang, *Indonesia* 57 G14
Magellan's Str. = Magallanes, Estrecho de, *Chile* 128 D2
Magenta, *Italy* 32 C5
Magenta, L., *Australia* 89 F2
Maggia, *Switz.* 23 D7
Maggia →, *Switz.* 23 D7
Maggiorasca, Mte., *Italy* 32 D6
Maggiore, L., *Italy* 32 C5

Maghama, *Mauritania* 78 B2
Magherafelt, *U.K.* 15 B5
Maghnia, *Algeria* 75 B4
Magione, *Italy* 33 E9
Magliano in Toscana, *Italy* 33 F8
Máglie, *Italy* 35 B11
Magnac-Laval, *France* 26 B5
Magnetic Pole (North) = North Magnetic Pole, *Canada* 4 B2
Magnetic Pole (South) = South Magnetic Pole, *Antarctica* 5 C9
Magnitogorsk, *Russia* 44 D6
Magnolia, *Ark., U.S.A.* 109 J8
Magnolia, *Miss., U.S.A.* 109 K9
Magnor, *Norway* 10 E6
Magny-en-Vexin, *France* 25 C8
Magog, *Canada* 99 C5
Magoro, *Uganda* 82 B3
Magosa = Famagusta, *Cyprus* 37 D12
Magouládhes, *Greece* 37 A3
Magoye, *Zambia* 83 F2
Magpie L., *Canada* 99 B7
Magrath, *Canada* 100 D6
Magro →, *Spain* 29 F4
Magrur, Wadi →, *Sudan* 77 D2
Magu □, *Tanzania* 82 C3
Maguan, *China* 52 F5
Maguarinho, C., *Brazil* 122 B2
Maguse L., *Canada* 101 A9
Maguse Pt., *Canada* 101 A10
Magwe, *Burma* 61 J19
Maha Sarakham, *Thailand* 58 D4
Mahābād, *Iran* 64 B5
Mahabharat Lekh, *Nepal* 63 E9
Mahabo, *Madag.* 85 C7
Mahadeo Hills, *India* 62 H8
Mahagi, *Zaïre* 82 B3
Mahaicony, *Guyana* 121 B6
Mahajamba →, *Madag.* 85 B8
Mahajamba, Helodranon' i, *Madag.* 85 B8
Mahajan, *India* 62 E5
Mahajanga, *Madag.* 85 B8
Mahajanga □, *Madag.* 85 B8
Mahajilo →, *Madag.* 85 B8
Mahakam →, *Indonesia* 56 E5
Mahalapye, *Botswana* 84 C4
Maḩallāt, *Iran* 65 C6
Māhān, *Iran* 65 D8
Mahanadi →, *India* 61 J15
Mahanoro, *Madag.* 85 B8
Mahanoy City, *U.S.A.* 107 F8
Maharashtra □, *India* 60 J9
Maharès, *Tunisia* 75 B7
Mahari Mts., *Tanzania* 82 D2
Mahasham, W. →, *Egypt* 69 E3
Mahasolo, *Madag.* 85 B8
Mahattat ash Shīdīyah, *Jordan* 69 F4
Mahattat 'Unayzah, *Jordan* 69 E4
Mahaxay, *Laos* 58 D5
Mahbes, *W. Sahara* 74 C3
Mahbubnagar, *India* 60 L10
Maḩḑah, *Oman* 65 E7
Mahdia, *Guyana* 121 B6
Mahdia, *Tunisia* 75 A7
Mahe, *India* 63 C8
Mahenge, *Tanzania* 83 D4
Maheno, *N.Z.* 87 L3
Mahesana, *India* 62 H5
Mahia Pen., *N.Z.* 87 H6
Mahirija, *Morocco* 75 B4
Mahmiya, *Sudan* 77 D3
Mahmud Kot, *Pakistan* 62 D4
Mahmudia, *Romania* 38 D12
Mahnomen, *U.S.A.* 108 B7
Mahoba, *India* 63 G8
Mahón, *Spain* 36 B11
Mahone Bay, *Canada* 99 D7
Mahuta, *Nigeria* 79 C5
Mai-Ndombe, L., *Zaïre* 80 E3
Mai-Sai, *Thailand* 58 B2
Maicao, *Colombia* 120 A3
Maîche, *France* 25 E13
Maici →, *Brazil* 125 B5
Maicurú →, *Brazil* 121 D7
Máida, *Italy* 35 D9
Maidan Khula, *Afghan.* 62 C3
Maidenhead, *U.K.* 13 F7
Maidi, *Yemen* 77 D5
Maidstone, *Canada* 101 C7
Maidstone, *U.K.* 13 F8
Maiduguri, *Nigeria* 79 C7
Maignelay, *France* 25 C9
Maigo, *Phil.* 55 G5
Maigualida, Sierra, *Venezuela* 121 B4
Maigudo, *Ethiopia* 77 F4
Maijdi, *Bangla.* 61 H17
Maikala Ra., *India* 61 J12
Mailly-le-Camp, *France* 25 D11
Mailsi, *Pakistan* 62 E5
Main →, *Germany* 19 F4
Main →, *U.K.* 15 B5
Main Centre, *Canada* 101 C7
Mainburg, *Germany* 19 G7
Maine, *France* 24 E6
Maine □, *U.S.A.* 99 C6
Maine →, *Ireland* 15 D2
Maine-et-Loire □, *France* 24 E6
Maïne-Soroa, *Niger* 79 C7
Maingkwan, *Burma* 61 F20
Mainit, L., *Phil.* 55 G6
Mainland, *Orkney, U.K.* 14 C5
Mainland, *Shet., U.K.* 14 A7
Mainpuri, *India* 63 F8
Maintenon, *France* 25 D8
Maintirano, *Madag.* 85 B7
Mainvault, *Belgium* 17 G3
Mainz, *Germany* 19 F4
Maipú, *Argentina* 126 D4
Maiquetía, *Venezuela* 120 A4
Maira →, *Italy* 32 D4
Mairabari, *India* 61 F18
Mairipotaba, *Brazil* 123 E2
Maisí, *Cuba* 117 B5
Maisi, Pta. de, *Cuba* 117 B5
Maisse, *France* 25 D9
Maissin, *Belgium* 17 J6
Maitland, *N.S.W., Australia* 91 E5
Maitland, *S. Austral., Australia* 91 E2
Maitland →, *Canada* 106 C3
Maiyema, *Nigeria* 79 C5
Maiyuan, *China* 53 E11
Maiz, Is. del, *Nic.* 116 D3
Maizuru, *Japan* 49 G7
Majagual, *Colombia* 120 B3
Majalengka, *Indonesia* 57 G13
Majari →, *Brazil* 121 C5
Majene, *Indonesia* 57 E5
Majes →, *Peru* 124 D3
Maji, *Ethiopia* 77 F4
Majiang, *China* 52 D6
Major, *Canada* 101 C7
Majorca = Mallorca, *Spain* 36 B10
Majuriã, *Brazil* 125 B5
Maka, *Senegal* 78 C2
Makak, *Cameroon* 79 E7
Makale, *Indonesia* 57 E5
Makamba, *Burundi* 82 C2
Makari, *Cameroon* 80 B2
Makarikari = Makgadikgadi Salt Pans, *Botswana* 84 C4
Makarovo, *Russia* 45 D11
Makarska, *Croatia* 21 M7
Makaryev, *Russia* 41 C13
Makasar = Ujung Pandang, *Indonesia* 57 F5
Makasar, Selat, *Indonesia* 57 E5
Makasar, Str. of = Makasar, Selat, *Indonesia* 57 E5
Makat, *Kazakhstan* 44 E6
Makedonija = Macedonia □, *Macedonia, Yug.* 39 H4
Makena, *U.S.A.* 102 H16
Makeni, *S. Leone* 78 D2
Makeyevka, *Ukraine* 42 B7
Makgadikgadi Salt Pans, *Botswana* 84 C4
Makhachkala, *Russia* 43 E12
Makhambet, *Kazakhstan* 43 C14
Makharadze = Ozurgety, *Georgia* 43 F10
Makhmūr, *Iraq* 64 C4
Makian, *Indonesia* 57 D7
Makindu, *Kenya* 82 C4
Makinsk, *Kazakhstan* 44 D8
Makkah, *Si. Arabia* 68 C2
Makkovik, *Canada* 99 A8
Makkum, *Neths.* 16 B6
Makó, *Hungary* 21 J10
Makokou, *Gabon* 80 D2
Makongo, *Zaïre* 82 B2
Makoro, *Zaïre* 82 B2
Makoua, *Congo* 80 E3
Makrá, *Greece* 39 N8
Makrai, *India* 60 H10
Makran Coast Range, *Pakistan* 60 G4
Makrana, *India* 62 F6
Makriyialos, *Greece* 37 D7
Maksimkin Yar, *Russia* 44 D9
Maktar, *Tunisia* 75 A6
Mākū, *Iran* 64 B5
Makumbi, *Zaïre* 80 F4
Makunda, *Botswana* 84 C3
Makurazaki, *Japan* 49 J5
Makurdi, *Nigeria* 79 D6
Makūyeh, *Iran* 65 D7
Makwassie, *S. Africa* 84 D4
Mal B., *Ireland* 15 D2
Mal i Nemërçkës, *Albania* 39 J3
Mal i Tomorit, *Albania* 39 J3
Mala, *Peru* 124 C2
Mala, Pta., *Panama* 116 E3
Mala Kapela, *Croatia* 33 D12
Malabang, *Phil.* 55 H6
Malabar Coast, *India* 60 P9
Malabo = Rey Malabo, *Eq. Guin.* 79 E6
Malabon, *Phil.* 55 D4
Malacca, Str. of, *Indonesia* 59 L3
Malacky, *Czech.* 21 G7
Malad City, *U.S.A.* 110 E7
Málaga, *Colombia* 120 B3
Málaga, *Spain* 31 J6
Malaga, *U.S.A.* 109 J2
Málaga □, *Spain* 31 J6
Malagarasi, *Tanzania* 82 D3
Malagarasi →, *Tanzania* 82 D2
Malagón, *Spain* 31 F7
Malagón →, *Spain* 31 H3
Malaimbandy, *Madag.* 85 C8
Malakâl, *Sudan* 77 F3
Malakand, *Pakistan* 62 B4
Malakoff, *U.S.A.* 109 J7
Malamyzh, *Russia* 45 E14
Malang, *Indonesia* 57 G15
Malange, *Angola* 80 F3
Mälaren, *Sweden* 10 E11
Malargüe, *Argentina* 126 D2
Malartic, *Canada* 98 C4
Malatya, *Turkey* 67 D8
Malatya □, *Turkey* 67 D8
Malawi ■, *Africa* 83 E3
Malawi, L., *Africa* 83 E3
Malay Pen., *Asia* 59 J3
Malaya Belozërka, *Ukraine* 42 C6
Malaya Vishera, *Russia* 40 B8
Malaya Viska, *Ukraine* 42 B4
Malaybalay, *Phil.* 55 G6
Malāyer, *Iran* 65 C6
Malaysia ■, *Asia* 56 D4
Malazgirt, *Turkey* 67 D10
Malbon, *Australia* 90 C3
Malbooma, *Australia* 91 E1
Malbork, *Poland* 20 A9
Malcésine, *Italy* 32 C7
Malchin, *Germany* 18 B8
Malchow, *Germany* 18 B8
Malcolm, *Australia* 89 E3
Malcolm, Pt., *Australia* 89 F3
Maldegem, *Belgium* 17 F2
Malden, *Mass., U.S.A.* 107 D13
Malden, *Mo., U.S.A.* 109 G10
Malden I., *Kiribati* 93 H12
Maldives ■, *Ind. Oc.* 46 J11
Maldonado, *Uruguay* 127 C5
Maldonado, Punta, *Mexico* 115 D5
Malé, *Italy* 32 B7
Maléa, Ákra, *Greece* 39 N6
Malebo, Pool, *Africa* 70 G5
Malegaon, *India* 60 J9
Malei, *Mozam.* 83 F4
Malek Kandī, *Iran* 64 B5
Malela, *Zaïre* 82 C2
Malema, *Mozam.* 83 E4
Máleme, *Greece* 37 D5
Malerkotla, *India* 62 D6
Máles, *Greece* 37 D7
Malesherbes, *France* 25 D9
Malestroit, *France* 24 E4
Malfa, *Italy* 35 D7
Malgobek, *Russia* 43 E11
Malgomaj, *Sweden* 8 D14
Malgrat, *Spain* 28 D7
Malha, *Sudan* 77 D2
Malheur →, *U.S.A.* 110 D5
Malheur L., *U.S.A.* 110 E4
Mali, *Guinea* 78 C2
Mali ■, *Africa* 78 B4
Mali →, *Burma* 61 G20
Mali Kanal, *Serbia, Yug.* 21 K9
Malibu, *U.S.A.* 113 L8
Malik, *Indonesia* 57 E6
Malili, *Indonesia* 57 E6
Malimba, Mts., *Zaïre* 82 D2
Malin, *Ukraine* 40 F6
Malin Hd., *Ireland* 15 A4
Malindi, *Kenya* 82 C5
Malines = Mechelen, *Belgium* 17 F4
Maling, *Indonesia* 57 D6
Malinyi, *Tanzania* 83 D4
Malipo, *China* 52 F5
Maliqi, *Albania* 39 J3
Malita, *Phil.* 57 C7
Malkara, *Turkey* 66 C2
Małkinia Górna, *Poland* 20 C12
Malko Tŭrnovo, *Bulgaria* 39 H10
Mallacoota, *Australia* 91 F4
Mallacoota Inlet, *Australia* 91 F4
Mallaig, *U.K.* 14 E3
Mallawan, *India* 63 F9
Mallawi, *Egypt* 76 B3
Malleco □, *Chile* 128 A2
Mallemort, *France* 27 E9
Málles Venosta, *Italy* 32 B7
Mállia, *Greece* 37 D7
Mallión, Kólpos, *Greece* 37 D7
Mallorca, *Spain* 36 B10
Mallorytown, *Canada* 107 B9
Mallow, *Ireland* 15 D3
Malmberget, *Sweden* 8 C16
Malmédy, *Belgium* 17 H8
Malmesbury, *S. Africa* 84 E2
Malmö, *Sweden* 11 J6
Malmöhus län □, *Sweden* 11 J7
Malmslätt, *Sweden* 11 F9
Malmyzh, *Russia* 41 C17
Maloarkhangelsk, *Russia* 41 E10
Maloca, *Brazil* 121 C6
Maloja, *Switz.* 23 D9
Maloja, P., *Switz.* 23 D9
Malolos, *Phil.* 57 B6
Malombe L., *Malawi* 83 E4
Malone, *U.S.A.* 107 B10
Malong, *China* 52 E4
Malorita, *Belorussia* 40 F4
Maloyaroslovets, *Russia* 41 D10
Malpartida, *Spain* 31 F4
Malpaso, *Canary Is.* 36 G1
Malpelo, *Colombia* 124 A1
Malpica, *Spain* 30 B2
Malta, *Brazil* 122 C4
Malta, *Idaho, U.S.A.* 110 E7
Malta, *Mont., U.S.A.* 110 B10
Malta ■, *Europe* 37 D1
Malta Channel, *Medit. S.* 34 F6
Maltahöhe, *Namibia* 84 C2
Malters, *Switz.* 22 B6
Malton, *Canada* 106 C5
Malton, *U.K.* 12 C7
Maluku, *Indonesia* 57 E7
Maluku □, *Indonesia* 57 E7
Maluku Sea, *Indonesia* 57 E6
Malumfashi, *Nigeria* 79 C6
Malvan, *India* 60 L8
Malvern, *U.S.A.* 109 H8
Malvern Hills, *U.K.* 13 E5
Malvik, *Norway* 10 A4
Malvinas, Is. = Falkland Is., *Atl. Oc.* 128 D5
Malya, *Tanzania* 82 C3
Malyy Lyakhovskiy, Ostrov, *Russia* 45 B15
Mama, *Russia* 45 D12
Mamadysh, *Russia* 41 D17
Mamanguape, *Brazil* 122 C4
Mamasa, *Indonesia* 57 E5
Mambasa, *Zaïre* 82 B2
Mamberamo →, *Indonesia* 57 E9
Mambilima Falls, *Zambia* 83 E2
Mambirima, *Zaïre* 83 E2
Mambo, *Tanzania* 82 C4
Mambrui, *Kenya* 82 C5
Mamburao, *Phil.* 55 E4
Mameigwess L., *Canada* 98 B2
Mamer, *Lux.* 17 J8
Mamers, *France* 24 D7
Mamfe, *Cameroon* 79 D6
Mamiña, *Chile* 124 E4
Mámmola, *Italy* 35 D9
Mammoth, *U.S.A.* 111 K8
Mamoré →, *Bolivia* 125 C4
Mamou, *Guinea* 78 C2
Mampatá, *Guinea-Biss.* 78 C2
Mampong, *Ghana* 79 D4
Mamuil Malal, Paso, *S. Amer.* 128 A2
Mamuju, *Indonesia* 57 E5
Man, *Ivory C.* 78 D3
Man, I. of, *U.K.* 12 C3
Man Na, *Burma* 61 H20
Mana, *Fr. Guiana* 121 B7
Mana →, *Fr. Guiana* 121 B7
Måna →, *Norway* 10 E2
Manaar, G. of = Mannar, G. of, *Asia* 60 Q11
Manabí □, *Ecuador* 120 D1
Manacacías →, *Colombia* 120 C3
Manacapuru, *Brazil* 121 D5
Manacapuru →, *Brazil* 121 D5
Manacor, *Spain* 36 B10
Manado, *Indonesia* 57 D6
Manage, *Belgium* 17 G4
Managua, *Nic.* 116 D2
Managua, L., *Nic.* 116 D2
Manakara, *Madag.* 85 C8
Manambao →, *Madag.* 85 B7
Manambato, *Madag.* 85 A8
Manambolo →, *Madag.* 85 B7
Manambolosy, *Madag.* 85 B8
Mananara, *Madag.* 85 B8
Mananara →, *Madag.* 85 C8
Mananjary, *Madag.* 85 C8
Manantenina, *Madag.* 85 C8
Manaos = Manaus, *Brazil* 121 D6
Manapire →, *Venezuela* 120 B4
Manapouri, *N.Z.* 87 L1
Manapouri, L., *N.Z.* 87 L1
Manas, *China* 54 B3
Manas →, *India* 61 F17
Manaslu, *Nepal* 63 E11
Manasquan, *U.S.A.* 107 F10
Manassa, *U.S.A.* 111 H11
Manaung, *Burma* 61 K18
Manaus, *Brazil* 121 D6
Manavgat, *Turkey* 66 E4
Manawan L., *Canada* 101 B8
Manay, *Phil.* 55 H7
Manbij, *Syria* 64 B3
Mancelona, *U.S.A.* 104 C3
Mancha Real, *Spain* 31 H7
Manche □, *France* 24 C5
Manchester, *U.K.* 12 D5
Manchester, *Calif., U.S.A.* 112 G3
Manchester, *Conn., U.S.A.* 107 E12
Manchester, *Ga., U.S.A.* 105 J3
Manchester, *Iowa, U.S.A.* 108 D9
Manchester, *Ky., U.S.A.* 104 G4
Manchester, *N.H., U.S.A.* 107 D13
Manchester, *N.Y., U.S.A.* 106 D7
Manchester, *Vt., U.S.A.* 107 C11
Manchester L., *Canada* 101 A7
Manchuria = Dongbei, *China* 51 D13
Manciano, *Italy* 33 F8
Mancifa, *Ethiopia* 77 F5
Mancora, Pta., *Peru* 124 A1
Mand →, *Iran* 65 D7
Manda, *Chunya, Tanzania* 82 D3
Manda, *Ludewe, Tanzania* 83 E3
Mandabé, *Madag.* 85 C7
Mandaguari, *Brazil* 127 A5
Mandah, *Mongolia* 50 B5
Mandal, *Norway* 9 G9
Mandalay, *Burma* 61 J20
Mandale = Mandalay, *Burma* 61 J20
Mandalgovi, *Mongolia* 50 B4
Mandalī, *Iraq* 64 C5
Mandan, *U.S.A.* 108 B4
Mandaon, *Phil.* 55 E5
Mandar, Teluk, *Indonesia* 57 E5
Mandas, *Italy* 34 C2
Mandasor = Mandsaur, *India* 62 G6
Mandaue, *Phil.* 55 F5
Mandelieu-la-Napoule, *France* 27 E10
Mandera, *Kenya* 82 B5
Mandera □, *Kenya* 82 B5
Manderfeld, *Belgium* 17 H8
Mandi, *India* 62 D7
Mandimba, *Mozam.* 83 E4
Mandioli, *Indonesia* 57 E7
Mandioré, L., *S. Amer.* 125 D6
Mandla, *India* 63 H9
Mandø, *Denmark* 11 J2
Mandoto, *Madag.* 85 B8
Mandoúdhion, *Greece* 39 L6
Mandra, *Pakistan* 62 C5
Mandrare →, *Madag.* 85 D8
Mandritsara, *Madag.* 85 B8
Mandsaur, *India* 62 G6
Mandurah, *Australia* 89 F2
Mandúria, *Italy* 35 B10
Mandvi, *India* 62 H3
Mandya, *India* 60 N10
Mandzai, *Pakistan* 62 D2
Mané, *Burkina Faso* 79 C4
Maneh, *Iran* 65 B8
Manengouba, Mts., *Cameroon* 79 D6
Maneroo, *Australia* 90 C3
Maneroo Cr. →, *Australia* 90 C3
Manfalût, *Egypt* 76 B3
Manfred, *Australia* 91 E3
Manfredónia, *Italy* 35 A8
Manfredónia, G. di, *Italy* 35 A9
Manga, *Brazil* 123 D3
Manga, *Burkina Faso* 79 C4
Manga, *Niger* 79 C7
Mangabeiras, Chapada das, *Brazil* 122 D2
Mangalia, *Romania* 38 F11
Mangalore, *India* 60 N9
Manganeses, *Spain* 30 D5
Mangaweka, *N.Z.* 87 H5
Manggar, *Indonesia* 56 E3
Manggawitu, *Indonesia* 57 E8
Mangkalihat, Tanjung, *Indonesia* 57 D5
Mangla Dam, *Pakistan* 63 C5
Manglares, C., *Colombia* 120 C2
Manglaur, *India* 62 E7
Mangnai, *China* 54 C4
Mango, *Togo* 79 C5
Mangoche, *Malawi* 83 E4
Mangoky →, *Madag.* 85 C7
Mangole, *Indonesia* 57 E7
Mangombe, *Zaïre* 82 C2
Mangonui, *N.Z.* 87 F4
Mangualde, *Portugal* 30 E3
Mangueigne, *Chad* 73 F9
Mangueira, L. da, *Brazil* 127 C5
Manguéni, Hamada, *Niger* 75 D7
Mangum, *U.S.A.* 109 H5
Mangyshlak Poluostrov, *Kazakhstan* 43 D15
Mangyshlakskiy Zaliv, *Kazakhstan* 43 D14
Manhattan, *U.S.A.* 108 F6
Manhiça, *Mozam.* 85 D5
Manhuaçu, *Brazil* 123 F3
Manhumirim, *Brazil* 123 F3
Maní, *Colombia* 120 C3
Mania →, *Madag.* 85 B8
Maniago, *Italy* 33 B9
Manica, *Mozam.* 85 B5
Manica e Sofala □, *Mozam.* 85 B5
Manicaland □, *Zimbabwe* 83 F3
Manicoré, *Brazil* 125 B5
Manicoré →, *Brazil* 125 B5
Manicouagan →, *Canada* 99 C6
Manīfah, *Si. Arabia* 65 E6
Manifold, *Australia* 90 C5
Manifold, C., *Australia* 90 C5
Maniganggo, *China* 52 B2
Manigotagan, *Canada* 101 C9
Manihiki, *Cook Is.* 93 J11
Manika, Plateau de la, *Zaïre* 83 E2
Manila, *Phil.* 55 D4
Manila, *U.S.A.* 110 F9
Manila B., *Phil.* 55 D4
Manilla, *Australia* 91 E5
Manimpé, *Mali* 78 C3
Maningrida, *Australia* 90 A1
Manipur □, *India* 61 G18
Manipur →, *Burma* 61 H19
Manisa, *Turkey* 66 D2
Manisa □, *Turkey* 66 D2
Manistee, *U.S.A.* 104 C2
Manistee →, *U.S.A.* 104 C2
Manistique, *U.S.A.* 104 C2
Manito L., *Canada* 101 C7
Manitoba □, *Canada* 101 B9
Manitoba, L., *Canada* 101 C9
Manitou, *Canada* 101 D9
Manitou I., *U.S.A.* 98 C2
Manitou Is., *U.S.A.* 104 C2

Manitou L., *Canada*	99	B6
Manitou Springs, *U.S.A.* . .	108	F2
Manitoulin I., *Canada*	98	C3
Manitowaning, *Canada* . . .	98	C3
Manitowoc, *U.S.A.*	104	C2
Manitsauá-Missu →, *Brazil*	125	C7
Manizales, *Colombia*	120	B2
Manja, *Madag.*	85	C7
Manjacaze, *Mozam.*	85	C5
Manjakandriana, *Madag.* .	85	B8
Manjhand, *Pakistan*	62	G3
Manjil, *Iran*	65	B6
Manjimup, *Australia*	89	F2
Manjra →, *India*	60	K10
Mankato, *Kans., U.S.A.* . .	108	F5
Mankato, *Minn., U.S.A.* . .	108	C8
Mankayane, *Swaziland* . . .	85	D5
Mankono, *Ivory C.*	78	D3
Mankota, *Canada*	101	D7
Manlay, *Mongolia*	50	B4
Manlleu, *Spain*	28	C7
Manly, *Australia*	91	E5
Manmad, *India*	60	J9
Mann Ras., *Australia*	89	E5
Manna, *Indonesia*	56	E2
Mannahill, *Australia*	91	E3
Mannar, *Sri Lanka*	60	Q11
Mannar, G. of, *Asia*	60	Q11
Mannar I., *Sri Lanka* . . .	60	Q11
Männedorf, *Switz.*	23	B7
Mannheim, *Germany*	19	F4
Manning, *Canada*	100	B5
Manning, *Oreg., U.S.A.* . .	112	E3
Manning, *S.C., U.S.A.* . . .	105	J5
Manning Prov. Park,		
Canada	100	D4
Mannington, *U.S.A.*	104	F5
Mannu →, *Italy*	34	C2
Mannu, C., *Italy*	34	B1
Mannum, *Australia*	91	E2
Mano, *S. Leone*	78	D2
Manoa, *Bolivia*	125	B4
Manokwari, *Indonesia* . . .	57	E8
Manombo, *Madag.*	85	C7
Manono, *Zaïre*	82	D2
Manosque, *France*	27	E9
Manouane, L., *Canada* . . .	99	B5
Manpojin, *N. Korea*	51	D14
Manresa, *Spain*	28	D6
Mansa, *Gujarat, India* . . .	62	H5
Mansa, *Punjab, India* . . .	62	E6
Mansa, *Zambia*	83	E2
Mansehra, *Pakistan*	62	B5
Mansel I., *Canada*	97	B11
Mansfield, *Australia*	91	F4
Mansfield, *U.K.*	12	D6
Mansfield, *La., U.S.A.* . . .	109	J8
Mansfield, *Mass., U.S.A.* .	107	D13
Mansfield, *Ohio, U.S.A.* . .	104	F2
Mansfield, *Pa., U.S.A.* . . .	106	E7
Mansfield, *Wash., U.S.A.* .	110	C4
Mansidão, *Brazil*	122	D3
Mansilla de las Mulas,		
Spain	30	C5
Mansle, *France*	26	C4
Manso →, *Brazil*	123	D2
Mansoa, *Guinea-Biss.*	78	C1
Manson Creek, *Canada* . .	100	B4
Mansoura, *Algeria*	75	A5
Manta, *Ecuador*	120	D1
Manta, B. de, *Ecuador* . . .	120	D1
Mantalingajan, Mt., *Phil.* .	55	G2
Mantare, *Tanzania*	82	C3
Manteca, *U.S.A.*	111	H3
Mantecal, *Venezuela*	120	B4
Mantena, *Brazil*	123	E3
Manteo, *U.S.A.*	105	H8
Mantes-la-Jolie, *France* . .	25	D8
Manthani, *India*	60	K11
Manthelan, *France*	24	E7
Manti, *U.S.A.*	110	G8
Mantiqueira, Serra da,		
Brazil	123	F3
Manton, *U.S.A.*	104	C3
Mantorp, *Sweden*	11	F9
Mántova, *Italy*	32	C7
Mänttä, *Finland*	8	E18
Mantua = Mántova, *Italy* .	32	C7
Manturovo, *Russia*	41	B14
Manu, *Peru*	124	C3
Manu →, *Peru*	124	C3
Manua Is., *Amer. Samoa* .	87	B14
Manuae, *Cook Is.*	93	J12
Manuel Alves →, *Brazil* .	123	D2
Manuel Alves Grande →,		
Brazil	122	C2
Manuel Urbano, *Brazil* . .	124	B4
Manui, *Indonesia*	57	E6
Manuripi →, *Bolivia*	124	C4
Manville, *U.S.A.*	108	D2
Many, *U.S.A.*	109	K8
Manyara, L., *Tanzania* . . .	82	C4
Manych →, *Russia*	43	C8
Manych-Gudilo, Oz.,		
Russia	43	C10
Manyonga →, *Tanzania* . .	82	C3
Manyoni, *Tanzania*	82	D3
Manzai, *Pakistan*	62	C4
Manzala, Bahra el, *Egypt* .	76	H7
Manzanares, *Spain*	29	F1
Manzaneda, Cabeza de,		
Spain	30	C3
Manzanillo, *Cuba*	116	B4

Manzanillo, *Mexico*	114	D4
Manzanillo, Pta., *Panama*	116	E4
Manzano Mts., *U.S.A.* . . .	111	J10
Manẕarīyeh, *Iran*	65	C6
Manzhouli, *China*	54	B6
Manzini, *Swaziland*	85	D5
Mao, *Chad*	73	F8
Maoke, Pegunungan,		
Indonesia	57	E9
Maolin, *China*	51	C12
Maoming, *China*	53	G8
Maowen, *China*	52	B4
Maoxing, *China*	51	B13
Mapam Yumco, *China* . . .	54	C3
Mapastepec, *Mexico*	115	D6
Mapia, Kepulauan,		
Indonesia	57	D8
Mapimí, *Mexico*	114	B4
Mapimí, Bolsón de, *Mexico*	114	B4
Maping, *China*	53	B9
Mapinga, *Tanzania*	82	D4
Mapinhane, *Mozam.*	85	C6
Mapire, *Venezuela*	121	B5
Maple Creek, *Canada* . . .	101	D7
Maple Valley, *U.S.A.*	112	C4
Mapleton, *U.S.A.*	110	D2
Mapuera →, *Brazil*	121	D6
Maputo, *Mozam.*	85	D5
Maputo, B. de, *Mozam.* . .	85	D5
Maqiaohe, *China*	51	B16
Maqnā, *Si. Arabia*	64	D2
Maqteïr, *Mauritania*	74	D2
Maquela do Zombo,		
Angola	80	F3
Maquinchao, *Argentina* . .	128	B3
Maquoketa, *U.S.A.*	108	D9
Mar, Serra do, *Brazil*	127	B6
Mar Chiquita, L.,		
Argentina	126	C3
Mar del Plata, *Argentina* .	126	D4
Mar Menor, L., *Spain* . . .	29	H4
Mara, *Guyana*	121	B6
Mara, *Tanzania*	82	C3
Mara □, *Tanzania*	82	C3
Maraã, *Brazil*	120	D4
Marabá, *Brazil*	122	C2
Maracá, I. de, *Brazil*	121	C7
Maracaibo, *Venezuela* . . .	120	A3
Maracaibo, L. de,		
Venezuela	120	B3
Maracaju, *Brazil*	127	A4
Maracajú, Serra de, *Brazil*	125	E6
Maracanã, *Brazil*	122	B2
Maracás, *Brazil*	123	D3
Maracay, *Venezuela*	120	A4
Marādah, *Libya*	73	C8
Maradi, *Niger*	79	C6
Maradun, *Nigeria*	79	C6
Marāgheh, *Iran*	64	B5
Maragogipe, *Brazil*	123	D4
Marāh, *Si. Arabia*	64	E5
Marajó, B. de, *Brazil*	122	B2
Marajó, I. de, *Brazil*	122	B2
Marākand, *Iran*	64	B5
Maralal, *Kenya*	82	B4
Maralinga, *Australia*	89	F5
Marama, *Australia*	91	F3
Marampa, *S. Leone*	78	D2
Maran, *Malaysia*	59	L4
Marana, *U.S.A.*	111	K8
Maranboy, *Australia*	88	B5
Maranchón, *Spain*	28	D2
Marand, *Iran*	64	B5
Marang, *Malaysia*	59	K4
Maranguape, *Brazil*	122	B4
Maranhão = São Luís,		
Brazil	122	B3
Maranhão □, *Brazil*	122	B2
Marano, L. di, *Italy*	33	C10
Maranoa →, *Australia* . . .	91	D4
Marañón →, *Peru*	124	A3
Marão, *Mozam.*	85	C5
Marapi →, *Brazil*	121	C6
Marari, *Brazil*	124	B4
Maraş = Kahramanmaraş,		
Turkey	66	E7
Mărăşeşti, *Romania*	38	D10
Maratea, *Italy*	35	C8
Marateca, *Portugal*	31	G2
Marathasa □, *Cyprus*	37	E11
Marathókambos, *Greece* . .	39	M9
Marathon, *Australia*	90	C3
Marathon, *Canada*	98	C2
Marathón, *Greece*	39	L6
Marathon, *N.Y., U.S.A.* . .	107	D8
Marathon, *Tex., U.S.A.* . .	109	K3
Marathóvouno, *Cyprus* . .	37	D12
Maratua, *Indonesia*	57	D5
Maraú, *Brazil*	123	D4
Maravatío, *Mexico*	114	D4
Marawi City, *Phil.*	55	G6
Marāwih, *U.A.E.*	65	E7
Marbella, *Spain*	31	J6
Marble Bar, *Australia* . . .	88	D2
Marble Falls, *U.S.A.*	109	K5
Marblehead, *U.S.A.*	107	D14
Marburg, *Germany*	18	E4
Marby, *Sweden*	10	A8
Marcal →, *Hungary*	21	H7
Marcapata, *Peru*	124	C3
Marcaria, *Italy*	32	C7
March, *U.K.*	13	E8
Marchand = Rommani,		
Morocco	74	B3

Marche, *France*	26	B5
Marche □, *Italy*	33	E10
Marche-en-Famenne,		
Belgium	17	H6
Marchena, *Spain*	31	H5
Marches = Marche □, *Italy*	33	E10
Marciana Marina, *Italy* . .	32	F7
Marcianise, *Italy*	35	A7
Marcigny, *France*	27	B8
Marcillat-en-Combraille,		
France	26	B6
Marcinelle, *Belgium*	17	H4
Marck, *France*	25	B8
Marckolsheim, *France* . . .	25	D14
Marcona, *Peru*	124	D2
Marcos Juárez, *Argentina* .	126	C3
Marcus I. = Minami-Tori-		
Shima, *Pac. Oc.*	92	E7
Marcus Necker Ridge,		
Pac. Oc.	92	F9
Marcy Mt., *U.S.A.*	107	B11
Mardan, *Pakistan*	62	B5
Mardie, *Australia*	88	D2
Mardin, *Turkey*	67	E9
Marechal Deodoro, *Brazil*	122	C4
Maree L., *U.K.*	14	D3
Mareeba, *Australia*	90	B4
Marek = Stanke Dimitrov,		
Bulgaria	38	G6
Marek, *Indonesia*	57	E6
Maremma, *Italy*	32	F8
Marenberg, *Slovenia*	33	B12
Marengo, *U.S.A.*	108	E8
Marennes, *France*	26	C2
Marenyi, *Kenya*	82	C4
Marerano, *Madag.*	85	C7
Maréttimo, *Italy*	34	E5
Mareuil-sur-Lay, *France* . .	26	B2
Marfa, *U.S.A.*	109	K2
Marfa Pt., *Malta*	37	D1
Marganets, *Ukraine*	42	C6
Margaret →, *Australia* . . .	88	C4
Margaret Bay, *Canada* . . .	100	C3
Margaret L., *Canada*	100	B5
Margaret River, *Australia* .	88	C4
Margarita, I. de, *Venezuela*	121	A5
Margarítion, *Greece*	39	K3
Margaritovo, *Russia*	48	C7
Margate, *S. Africa*	85	E5
Margate, *U.K.*	13	F9
Margelan, *Uzbekistan* . . .	44	E8
Margeride, Mts. de la,		
France	26	D7
Margherita di Savola, *Italy*	35	A9
Margosatubig, *Phil.*	55	H5
Marguerite, *Canada*	100	C4
Marhoum, *Algeria*	75	B4
Mari Republic □, *Russia* .	41	C16
María Elena, *Chile*	126	A2
María Grande, *Argentina* .	126	C4
Maria I., *N. Terr.,*		
Australia	90	A2
Maria I., *Tas., Australia* . .	90	G4
Maria van Diemen, C.,		
N.Z.	87	F4
Mariager, *Denmark*	11	H4
Mariager Fjord, *Denmark* .	11	H4
Mariakani, *Kenya*	82	C4
Marian L., *Canada*	100	A5
Mariana Trench, *Pac. Oc.* .	92	F6
Marianao, *Cuba*	116	B3
Marianna, *Ark., U.S.A.* . .	109	H9
Marianna, *Fla., U.S.A.* . . .	105	K3
Mariánské Lázně, *Czech.* .	20	F2
Marias →, *U.S.A.*	110	C8
Mariato, Punta, *Panama* . .	116	E3
Mariazell, *Austria*	21	H5
Ma'rib, *Yemen*	68	D4
Maribo, *Denmark*	11	K5
Maribor, *Slovenia*	33	B12
Marico →, *Africa*	84	C4
Maricopa, *Ariz., U.S.A.* . .	111	K7
Maricopa, *Calif., U.S.A.* . .	113	K7
Marīdī, *Sudan*	77	G2
Maridi, Wadi →, *Sudan* . .	77	F2
Marié →, *Brazil*	120	D4
Marie Byrd Land,		
Antarctica	5	D14
Marie-Galante, *Guadeloupe*	117	C7
Mariecourt, *Canada*	97	B12
Mariefred, *Sweden*	10	E11
Mariehamn, *Finland*	9	F15
Marienbad = Mariánské		
Lázně, *Czech.*	20	F2
Marienberg, *Germany* . . .	18	E9
Marienberg, *Neths.*	16	D9
Marienbourg, *Belgium* . . .	17	H5
Mariental, *Namibia*	84	C2
Marienville, *U.S.A.*	106	E5
Mariestad, *Sweden*	11	F7
Marietta, *Ga., U.S.A.* . . .	105	J3
Marietta, *Ohio, U.S.A.* . . .	104	F5
Marieville, *Canada*	107	A11
Marignane, *France*	27	E9
Marquises, Is., *Pac. Oc.* . .	93	H14
Marra, Gebel, *Sudan*	77	F2
Marihatag, *Phil.*	55	G7
Mariinsk, *Russia*	44	D9
Mariinskiy Posad, *Russia* .	41	C15
Marília, *Brazil*	127	A5
Marillana, *Australia*	88	D2
Marín, *Spain*	30	C2
Marina, *U.S.A.*	112	J5
Marina di Cirò, *Italy*	35	C10
Marina Plains, *Australia* . .	90	A3

Marinduque, *Phil.*	55	E5
Marine City, *U.S.A.*	104	D4
Marineo, *Italy*	34	E6
Marinette, *U.S.A.*	104	C2
Maringá, *Brazil*	127	A5
Marinha Grande, *Portugal*	31	F2
Marion, *Ala., U.S.A.*	105	J2
Marion, *Ill., U.S.A.*	109	G10
Marion, *Ind., U.S.A.*	104	E3
Marion, *Iowa, U.S.A.* . . .	108	D9
Marion, *Kans., U.S.A.* . . .	108	F6
Marion, *Mich., U.S.A.* . . .	104	C3
Marion, *N.C., U.S.A.*	105	H4
Marion, *Ohio, U.S.A.*	104	E4
Marion, *S.C., U.S.A.*	105	H6
Marion, *Va., U.S.A.*	105	G5
Marion, L., *U.S.A.*	105	J5
Maripa, *Venezuela*	121	B4
Maripasoula, *Fr. Guiana* . .	121	C7
Mariposa, *U.S.A.*	111	H4
Mariscal Estigarribia,		
Paraguay	126	A3
Maritime Alps =		
Maritimes, Alpes,		
Europe	27	D11
Maritimes, Alpes, *Europe* .	27	D11
Maritsa, *Greece*	37	C10
Mariupol, *Ukraine*	42	C7
Marīvān, *Iran*	64	C5
Mariyampol, *Lithuania* . .	40	D3
Markam, *China*	52	C2
Markazī □, *Iran*	65	C6
Markdale, *Canada*	106	B4
Marke, *Belgium*	17	G2
Marked Tree, *U.S.A.*	109	H9
Markelsdorfer Huk,		
Germany	18	A6
Marken, *Neths.*	16	D6
Markermeer, *Neths.*	16	C6
Market Drayton, *U.K.* . . .	12	E5
Market Harborough, *U.K.* .	13	E7
Markham, *Canada*	106	C5
Markham, Mt., *Antarctica* .	5	E11
Markham L., *Canada*	101	A8
Marki, *Poland*	20	C11
Markleeville, *U.S.A.*	112	G7
Markoupoulon, *Greece* . . .	39	M6
Markovo, *Russia*	45	C17
Markoye, *Burkina Faso* . .	79	C5
Marks, *Russia*	41	F15
Marksville, *U.S.A.*	109	K8
Markt Schwaben, *Germany*	19	G7
Marktredwitz, *Germany* . .	19	E8
Marla, *Australia*	91	D1
Marlboro, *U.S.A.*	107	D13
Marlborough, *Australia* . .	90	C4
Marlborough Downs, *U.K.* .	13	F6
Marle, *France*	25	C10
Marlin, *U.S.A.*	109	K6
Marlow, *Germany*	18	A8
Marlow, *U.S.A.*	109	H6
Marly-le-Grand, *Switz.* . . .	22	C4
Marmagao, *India*	60	M8
Marmande, *France*	26	D4
Marmara, *France*	42	F2
Marmara, Sea of =		
Marmara Denizi, *Turkey*	66	C3
Marmara Denizi, *Turkey* .	66	C3
Marmara Gölü, *Turkey* . .	66	D3
Marmaris, *Turkey*	66	E3
Marmarth, *U.S.A.*	108	B3
Marmelos →, *Brazil*	125	B5
Marmion, Mt., *Australia* . .	89	E2
Marmion L., *Canada*	98	C1
Marmolada, Mte., *Italy* . . .	33	B8
Marmolejo, *Spain*	31	G6
Marmora, *Canada*	98	D4
Marnay, *France*	25	E12
Marne, *Germany*	18	B5
Marne □, *France*	25	D11
Marne →, *France*	25	D9
Marneuli, *Georgia*	43	F11
Maroa, *Venezuela*	120	C4
Maroala, *Madag.*	85	B8
Maroantsetra, *Madag.* . . .	85	B8
Maromandia, *Madag.*	85	A8
Marondera, *Zimbabwe* . . .	83	F3
Maroni →, *Fr. Guiana* . . .	121	B7
Maronne →, *France*	26	C5
Maroochydore, *Australia* . .	91	D5
Maroona, *Australia*	91	F3
Maros →, *Hungary*	21	J10
Marosakoa, *Madag.*	85	B8
Marostica, *Italy*	33	C8
Maroua, *Cameroon*	79	C7
Marovoay, *Madag.*	85	B8
Marowijne □, *Surinam* . . .	121	C7
Marowijne →, *Surinam* . .	121	B7
Marquard, *S. Africa*	84	D4
Marqueira, *Portugal*	31	G1
Marquesas Is. = Marquises,		
Is., *Pac. Oc.*	93	H14
Marquette, *U.S.A.*	104	B2
Marquise, *France*	25	B8
Marquises, Is., *Pac. Oc.* . .	93	H14
Marra, Gebel, *Sudan*	77	F2
Marracuene, *Mozam.*	85	D5
Marradi, *Italy*	33	D8
Marrakech, *Morocco*	74	B3
Marrawah, *Australia*	90	G3
Marrecas, Serra das, *Brazil*	122	C3
Marree, *Australia*	91	D2
Marrilla, *Australia*	88	D1
Marrimane, *Mozam.*	85	C5

Marromeu, *Mozam.*	85	B6
Marroquí, Punta, *Spain* . .	31	K5
Marrowie Cr. →, *Australia*	91	E4
Marrubane, *Mozam.*	83	F4
Marrum, *Neths.*	16	B7
Marrupa, *Mozam.*	83	E4
Marsá Matrûh, *Egypt* . . .	76	A2
Marsá Susah, *Libya*	73	B9
Marsabit, *Kenya*	82	B4
Marsabit □, *Kenya*	82	B4
Marsala, *Italy*	34	E5
Marsalforn, *Malta*	37	C1
Marsberg, *Germany*	18	D4
Marsciano, *Italy*	33	F9
Marsden, *Australia*	91	E4
Marsdiep, *Neths.*	16	C5
Marseillan, *France*	26	E7
Marseille, *France*	27	E9
Marseilles = Marseille,		
France	27	E9
Marsh I., *U.S.A.*	109	L9
Marsh L., *U.S.A.*	108	C6
Marshall, *Liberia*	78	D2
Marshall, *Ark., U.S.A.* . . .	109	H8
Marshall, *Mich., U.S.A.* . .	104	D3
Marshall, *Minn., U.S.A.* . .	108	C7
Marshall, *Mo., U.S.A.* . . .	108	F8
Marshall, *Tex., U.S.A.* . . .	109	J7
Marshall →, *Australia* . . .	90	C2
Marshall Is., *Pac. Oc.* . . .	92	G9
Marshalltown, *U.S.A.*	108	D8
Marshfield, *Mo., U.S.A.* . .	109	G8
Marshfield, *Wis., U.S.A.* . .	108	C9
Marshūn, *Iran*	65	B6
Mársico Nuovo, *Italy* . . .	35	B8
Märsta, *Sweden*	10	E11
Marstal, *Denmark*	11	K4
Marstrand, *Sweden*	11	G5
Mart, *U.S.A.*	109	K6
Marta →, *Italy*	33	F8
Martaban, *Burma*	61	L20
Martaban, G. of, *Burma* . .	61	L20
Martano, *Italy*	35	B11
Martapura, *Kalimantan,*		
Indonesia	56	E4
Martapura, *Sumatera,*		
Indonesia	56	E2
Marte, *Nigeria*	79	C7
Martel, *France*	26	D5
Martelange, *Belgium*	17	J7
Martés, Sierra, *Spain*	29	F4
Martha's Vineyard, *U.S.A.* .	107	E14
Martigné-Ferchaud, *France*	24	E5
Martigny, *Switz.*	22	D4
Martigues, *France*	27	E9
Martil, *Morocco*	74	A3
Martin, *Czech.*	20	F8
Martin, *S. Dak., U.S.A.* . .	108	D4
Martin, *Tenn., U.S.A.* . . .	109	G10
Martín →, *Spain*	28	D4
Martin, L., *U.S.A.*	105	J3
Martina, *Switz.*	23	C10
Martina Franca, *Italy* . . .	35	B10
Martinborough, *N.Z.*	87	J5
Martinez, *U.S.A.*	112	G4
Martinho Campos, *Brazil* .	123	E2
Martinique ■, *W. Indies* . .	117	D7
Martinique Passage,		
W. Indies	117	C7
Martínon, *Greece*	39	L6
Martinópolis, *Brazil*	127	A5
Martins Ferry, *U.S.A.*	106	F4
Martinsburg, *Pa., U.S.A.* . .	106	F6
Martinsburg, *W. Va.,*		
U.S.A.	104	F7
Martinsville, *Ind., U.S.A.* .	104	F2
Martinsville, *Va., U.S.A.* . .	105	G6
Marton, *N.Z.*	87	J5
Martorell, *Spain*	28	D6
Martos, *Spain*	31	H7
Martuni, *Armenia*	43	F11
Maru, *Nigeria*	79	C6
Marudi, *Malaysia*	56	D4
Ma'ruf, *Afghan.*	60	D5
Marugame, *Japan*	49	G6
Marúggio, *Italy*	35	B10
Maruim, *Brazil*	122	D4
Marulan, *Australia*	91	E5
Marum, *Neths.*	16	B8
Marunga, *Angola*	84	B3
Marungu, Mts., *Zaïre*	82	D2
Marvast, *Iran*	65	D7
Marvejols, *France*	26	D7
Marwar, *India*	62	G5
Mary, *Turkmenistan*	44	F7
Mary Frances L., *Canada* .	101	A7
Mary Kathleen, *Australia* .	90	C2
Maryborough = Port		
Laoise, *Ireland*	15	C4
Maryborough, *Queens.,*		
Australia	91	D5
Maryborough, *Vic.,*		
Australia	91	F3
Maryfield, *Canada*	101	D8
Maryland □, *U.S.A.*	104	F7
Maryland Junction,		
Zimbabwe	83	F3
Maryport, *U.K.*	12	C4
Mary's Harbour, *Canada* . .	99	B8
Marystown, *Canada*	99	C8
Marysvale, *U.S.A.*	111	G7
Marysville, *Canada*	100	D5
Marysville, *Calif., U.S.A.* .	112	F5
Marysville, *Kans., U.S.A.* .	108	F6

Marysville, *Mich., U.S.A.*	106	D2
Marysville, *Ohio, U.S.A.*	104	E4
Marysville, *Wash., U.S.A.*	112	B4
Maryvale, *Australia*	91	D5
Maryville, *U.S.A.*	105	H4
Marzo, Punta, *Colombia*	120	B2
Marzūq, *Libya*	73	C7
Masahunga, *Tanzania*	82	C3
Masai, *Malaysia*	59	M4
Masai Steppe, *Tanzania*	82	C4
Masaka, *Uganda*	82	C3
Masalembo, Kepulauan, *Indonesia*	56	F4
Masalima, Kepulauan, *Indonesia*	56	F5
Masamba, *Indonesia*	57	E6
Masan, *S. Korea*	51	G15
Masanasa, *Spain*	29	F4
Masasi, *Tanzania*	83	E4
Masasi □, *Tanzania*	83	E4
Masaya, *Nic.*	116	D2
Masba, *Nigeria*	79	C7
Masbate, *Phil.*	55	E5
Mascara, *Algeria*	75	A5
Mascota, *Mexico*	114	C4
Masela, *Indonesia*	57	F7
Maseru, *Lesotho*	84	D4
Mashaba, *Zimbabwe*	83	G3
Mashābih, *Si. Arabia*	64	E3
Mashan, *China*	52	F7
Masherbrum, *Pakistan*	63	B7
Mashhad, *Iran*	65	B8
Mashi, *Nigeria*	79	C6
Mashīz, *Iran*	65	D8
Mashkel, Hamun-i-, *Pakistan*	60	E3
Mashki Chāh, *Pakistan*	60	E3
Mashonaland Central □, *Zimbabwe*	85	B5
Mashonaland East □, *Zimbabwe*	85	B5
Mashonaland West □, *Zimbabwe*	85	B4
Mashtaga, *Azerbaijan*	43	F13
Masi, *Norway*	8	B17
Masi Manimba, *Zaïre*	80	E3
Masindi, *Uganda*	82	B3
Masindi Port, *Uganda*	82	B3
Masisea, *Peru*	124	B3
Masisi, *Zaïre*	82	C2
Masjed Soleyman, *Iran*	65	D6
Mask, L., *Ireland*	15	C2
Maslinica, *Croatia*	33	E13
Masnou, *Spain*	28	D7
Masoala, Tanjon' i, *Madag.*	85	B9
Masoarivo, *Madag.*	85	B7
Masohi, *Indonesia*	57	E7
Masomeloka, *Madag.*	85	C8
Mason, *Nev., U.S.A.*	112	G7
Mason, *Tex., U.S.A.*	109	K5
Mason City, *U.S.A.*	108	D8
Maspalomas, *Canary Is.*	36	G4
Maspalomas, Pta., *Canary Is.*	36	G4
Masqat, *Oman*	68	C6
Massa, *Italy*	32	D7
Massa, O. →, *Morocco*	74	B3
Massa Maríttima, *Italy*	32	E7
Massachusetts □, *U.S.A.*	107	D12
Massachusetts B., *U.S.A.*	107	D14
Massafra, *Italy*	35	B10
Massaguet, *Chad*	73	F8
Massakory, *Chad*	73	F8
Massanella, *Spain*	36	B9
Massangena, *Mozam.*	85	C5
Massapê, *Brazil*	122	B3
Massarosa, *Italy*	32	E7
Massat, *France*	26	F5
Massawa = Mitsiwa, *Ethiopia*	77	D4
Massena, *U.S.A.*	107	B10
Massénya, *Chad*	73	F8
Masset, *Canada*	100	C2
Massiac, *France*	26	C7
Massif Central, *France*	26	D7
Massillon, *U.S.A.*	106	F3
Massinga, *Mozam.*	85	C6
Masson, *Canada*	107	A9
Masson I., *Antarctica*	5	C7
Mastanli = Momchilgrad, *Bulgaria*	39	H8
Masterton, *N.Z.*	87	J5
Mástikho, Ákra, *Greece*	39	L9
Mastuj, *Pakistan*	63	A5
Mastung, *Pakistan*	60	E5
Mastūrah, *Si. Arabia*	76	C4
Masuda, *Japan*	49	G5
Masvingo, *Zimbabwe*	83	G3
Masvingo □, *Zimbabwe*	83	G3
Maswa □, *Tanzania*	82	C3
Maşyāf, *Syria*	64	C3
Mata de São João, *Brazil*	123	D4
Matabeleland North □, *Zimbabwe*	83	F2
Matabeleland South □, *Zimbabwe*	83	G2
Mataboor, *Indonesia*	57	E9
Matachel →, *Spain*	31	G4
Matachewan, *Canada*	98	C3
Matacuni →, *Venezuela*	121	C4
Matad, *Mongolia*	54	B6
Matadi, *Zaïre*	80	F2
Matagalpa, *Nic.*	116	D2
Matagami, *Canada*	98	C4

Matagami, L., *Canada*	98	C4
Matagorda, *U.S.A.*	109	L7
Matagorda B., *U.S.A.*	109	L6
Matagorda I., *U.S.A.*	109	L6
Matak, P., *Indonesia*	59	L6
Matakana, *Australia*	91	E4
Mátala, *Greece*	37	E6
Matalaque, *Peru*	124	D3
Matam, *Senegal*	78	B2
Matameye, *Niger*	79	C6
Matamoros, *Campeche, Mexico*	115	D6
Matamoros, *Coahuila, Mexico*	114	B4
Matamoros, *Puebla, Mexico*	115	D5
Matamoros, *Tamaulipas, Mexico*	115	B5
Ma'ṭan as Sarra, *Libya*	73	D9
Matandu →, *Tanzania*	83	D3
Matane, *Canada*	99	C6
Matang, *China*	52	F5
Matankari, *Niger*	79	C5
Matanzas, *Cuba*	116	B3
Matapan, C. = Taínaron, Ákra, *Greece*	39	N5
Matapédia, *Canada*	99	C6
Matara, *Sri Lanka*	60	S12
Mataram, *Indonesia*	56	F5
Matarani, *Peru*	124	D3
Mataranka, *Australia*	88	B5
Matarma, Râs, *Egypt*	69	E1
Mataró, *Spain*	28	D7
Matarraña →, *Spain*	28	D5
Matatiele, *S. Africa*	85	E4
Mataura, *N.Z.*	87	M2
Mategua, *Bolivia*	125	C5
Matehuala, *Mexico*	114	C4
Mateira, *Brazil*	123	E1
Mateke Hills, *Zimbabwe*	83	G3
Matélica, *Italy*	33	E10
Matera, *Italy*	35	B9
Mátészalka, *Hungary*	21	H12
Matetsi, *Zimbabwe*	83	F2
Mateur, *Tunisia*	75	A6
Matfors, *Sweden*	10	B11
Matha, *France*	26	C3
Matheson Island, *Canada*	101	C9
Mathis, *U.S.A.*	109	L6
Mathura, *India*	62	F7
Mati, *Phil.*	55	H7
Matías Romero, *Mexico*	115	D5
Matibane, *Mozam.*	83	E5
Matima, *Botswana*	84	C3
Matiri Ra., *N.Z.*	87	J4
Matlock, *U.K.*	12	D6
Matmata, *Tunisia*	75	B6
Matna, *Sudan*	77	E4
Mato →, *Venezuela*	121	B4
Mato, Serrania de, *Venezuela*	120	B4
Mato Grosso □, *Brazil*	125	C6
Mato Grosso, Planalto do, *Brazil*	125	C7
Mato Grosso do Sul □, *Brazil*	125	D7
Matochkin Shar, *Russia*	44	B6
Matopo Hills, *Zimbabwe*	83	G2
Matopos, *Zimbabwe*	83	G2
Matosinhos, *Portugal*	30	D2
Matour, *France*	27	B8
Matsena, *Nigeria*	79	C7
Matsesta, *Russia*	43	E8
Matsue, *Japan*	49	G6
Matsumae, *Japan*	48	D10
Matsumoto, *Japan*	49	F9
Matsusaka, *Japan*	49	G8
Matsuura, *Japan*	49	H4
Matsuyama, *Japan*	49	H6
Mattagami →, *Canada*	98	B3
Mattancheri, *India*	60	Q10
Mattawa, *Canada*	98	C4
Mattawamkeag, *U.S.A.*	99	C6
Matterhorn, *Switz.*	22	E5
Matthew Town, *Bahamas*	117	B5
Matthew's Ridge, *Guyana*	121	B5
Mattice, *Canada*	98	C3
Mattituck, *U.S.A.*	107	F12
Mattmar, *Sweden*	10	A7
Matuba, *Mozam.*	85	C5
Matucana, *Peru*	124	C2
Matun, *Afghan.*	62	C3
Maturín, *Venezuela*	121	B5
Matveyev Kurgan, *Russia*	43	C8
Mau, *India*	63	G10
Mau Escarpment, *Kenya*	82	C4
Mau Ranipur, *India*	63	G8
Maubeuge, *France*	25	B10
Maubourguet, *France*	26	E4
Maud, Pt., *Australia*	88	D1
Maude, *Australia*	91	E3
Maudin Sun, *Burma*	61	M19
Maués, *Brazil*	121	D6
Mauganj, *India*	61	G12
Maui, *U.S.A.*	102	H16
Maulamyaing = Moulmein, *Burma*	61	L20
Maule □, *Chile*	126	D1
Mauléon-Licharre, *France*	26	E3
Maullín, *Chile*	128	B2
Maumee, *U.S.A.*	104	E4
Maumee →, *U.S.A.*	104	E4
Maumere, *Indonesia*	57	F6
Maun, *Botswana*	84	B3

Mauna Kea, *U.S.A.*	102	J17
Mauna Loa, *U.S.A.*	102	H16
Maungmagan Kyunzu, *Burma*	61	M20
Maupin, *U.S.A.*	110	D3
Maure-de-Bretagne, *France*	24	E5
Maurepas L., *U.S.A.*	109	K9
Maures, *France*	27	E10
Mauriac, *France*	26	C6
Maurice, L., *Australia*	89	E5
Mauritania ■, *Africa*	74	D3
Mauritius ■, *Ind. Oc.*	3	F12
Mauron, *France*	24	E4
Maurs, *France*	26	D6
Mauston, *U.S.A.*	108	D9
Mauterndorf, *Austria*	21	H3
Mauvezin, *France*	26	E4
Mauzé-sur-le-Mignon, *France*	26	B3
Mavaca →, *Venezuela*	121	C4
Mavinga, *Angola*	81	H4
Mavli, *India*	62	G5
Mavrova, *Albania*	39	J2
Mavuradonha Mts., *Zimbabwe*	83	F3
Mawa, *Zaïre*	82	B2
Mawana, *India*	62	E7
Mawand, *Pakistan*	62	E3
Mawk Mai, *Burma*	61	J20
Mawlaik, *Burma*	61	H19
Mawquq, *Si. Arabia*	64	E4
Mawson Coast, *Antarctica*	5	C6
Max, *U.S.A.*	108	B4
Maxcanú, *Mexico*	115	C6
Maxesibeni, *S. Africa*	85	E4
Maxhamish L., *Canada*	100	B4
Maxixe, *Mozam.*	85	C6
Maxville, *Canada*	107	A10
Maxwell, *U.S.A.*	112	F4
Maxwelton, *Australia*	90	C3
May Downs, *Australia*	90	C4
May Pen, *Jamaica*	116	C4
Maya, *Spain*	28	B3
Maya →, *Russia*	45	D14
Maya Mts., *Belize*	115	D7
Mayaguana, *Bahamas*	117	B5
Mayagüez, *Puerto Rico*	117	C6
Mayahi, *Niger*	79	C6
Mayals, *Spain*	28	D5
Mayāmey, *Iran*	65	B7
Mayang, *China*	52	D7
Mayarí, *Cuba*	117	B4
Maybell, *U.S.A.*	110	F9
Maychew, *Ethiopia*	77	E4
Maydān, *Iraq*	64	C5
Maydena, *Australia*	90	G4
Mayen, *Germany*	19	E3
Mayenne, *France*	24	D6
Mayenne □, *France*	24	D6
Mayenne →, *France*	24	E6
Mayer, *U.S.A.*	111	J7
Mayerthorpe, *Canada*	100	C5
Mayfield, *U.S.A.*	105	G1
Mayhill, *U.S.A.*	111	K11
Maykop, *Russia*	43	D9
Maymyo, *Burma*	58	A1
Maynard, *U.S.A.*	112	C4
Maynard Hills, *Australia*	89	E2
Mayne →, *Australia*	90	C3
Maynooth, *Ireland*	15	C5
Mayo, *Canada*	96	B6
Mayo □, *Ireland*	15	C2
Mayo →, *Argentina*	128	C3
Mayo →, *Peru*	124	B2
Mayo L., *Canada*	96	B6
Mayon Volcano, *Phil.*	55	E5
Mayor I., *N.Z.*	87	G6
Mayorga, *Spain*	30	C5
Mayraira Pt., *Phil.*	55	B4
Mayskiy, *Russia*	43	E11
Mayson L., *Canada*	101	B7
Maysville, *U.S.A.*	104	F4
Mayu, *Indonesia*	57	D7
Mayville, *N. Dak., U.S.A.*	108	B6
Mayville, *N.Y., U.S.A.*	106	D5
Mayya, *Russia*	45	C14
Mazabuka, *Zambia*	83	F2
Mazagán = El Jadida, *Morocco*	74	B3
Mazagão, *Brazil*	121	D7
Mazamet, *France*	26	E6
Mazán, *Peru*	120	D3
Māzandarān □, *Iran*	65	B7
Mazapil, *Mexico*	114	C4
Mazar, O. →, *Algeria*	75	B5
Mazar del Vallo, *Italy*	34	E5
Mazarredo, *Argentina*	128	C3
Mazarrón, *Spain*	29	H3
Mazarrón, G. de, *Spain*	29	H3
Mazaruni →, *Guyana*	121	B6
Mazatán, *Mexico*	114	B2
Mazatenango, *Guatemala*	116	D1
Mazatlán, *Mexico*	114	C3
Mažeikiai, *Lithuania*	40	C3
Māzhān, *Iran*	65	C8
Mazīnān, *Iran*	65	B8
Mazoe, *Mozam.*	83	F3
Mazoe →, *Mozam.*	83	F3
Mazowe, *Zimbabwe*	83	F3
Mazrūb, *Sudan*	77	E2
Mazu Dao, *China*	53	D12
Mazurian Lakes = Mazurski, Pojezierze, *Poland*	20	B10

Mazurski, Pojezierze, *Poland*	20	B10
Mazzarino, *Italy*	35	E7
Mbaba, *Senegal*	78	C1
Mbabane, *Swaziland*	85	D5
Mbagne, *Mauritania*	78	B2
M'bahiakro, *Ivory C.*	78	D4
Mbaïki, *C.A.R.*	80	D3
Mbala, *Zambia*	83	D3
Mbale, *Uganda*	82	B3
Mbalmayo, *Cameroon*	79	E7
Mbamba Bay, *Tanzania*	83	E3
Mbandaka, *Zaïre*	80	D3
Mbanga, *Cameroon*	79	E6
Mbanza Congo, *Angola*	80	F2
Mbanza Ngungu, *Zaïre*	80	F2
Mbarara, *Uganda*	82	C3
Mbashe →, *S. Africa*	85	E4
Mbatto, *Ivory C.*	78	D4
Mbenkuru →, *Tanzania*	83	D4
Mberengwa, *Zimbabwe*	83	G2
Mberengwa, Mt., *Zimbabwe*	83	G2
Mberubu, *Nigeria*	79	D6
Mbesuma, *Zambia*	83	D3
Mbeya, *Tanzania*	83	D3
Mbeya □, *Tanzania*	82	D3
Mbinga, *Tanzania*	83	E4
Mbinga □, *Tanzania*	83	E3
Mbini □, *Eq. Guin.*	80	D2
Mboki, *C.A.R.*	77	F2
Mboro, *Senegal*	78	B1
Mboune, *Senegal*	78	C2
Mbour, *Senegal*	78	C1
Mbout, *Mauritania*	78	B2
Mbozi □, *Tanzania*	83	D3
Mbuji-Mayi, *Zaïre*	82	D1
Mbulu, *Tanzania*	82	C4
Mbulu □, *Tanzania*	82	C4
Mburucuyá, *Argentina*	126	B4
Mcherrah, *Algeria*	74	C4
Mchinja, *Tanzania*	83	D4
Mchinji, *Malawi*	83	E3
Mdennah, *Mauritania*	74	D3
Mead, L., *U.S.A.*	113	J12
Meade, *U.S.A.*	109	G4
Meadow, *Australia*	89	E1
Meadow Lake, *Canada*	101	C7
Meadow Lake Prov. Park, *Canada*	101	C7
Meadow Valley Wash →, *U.S.A.*	113	J12
Meadville, *U.S.A.*	106	E4
Meaford, *Canada*	98	D3
Mealhada, *Portugal*	30	E2
Mealy Mts., *Canada*	99	B8
Meander River, *Canada*	100	B5
Meares, C., *U.S.A.*	110	D2
Mearim →, *Brazil*	122	B3
Meath □, *Ireland*	15	C5
Meath Park, *Canada*	101	C7
Meaulne, *France*	26	B6
Meaux, *France*	25	D9
Mebechi-Gawa →, *Japan*	48	D10
Mecanhelas, *Mozam.*	83	F4
Mecaya →, *Colombia*	120	C2
Mecca = Makkah, *Si. Arabia*	68	C2
Mecca, *U.S.A.*	113	M10
Mechanicsburg, *U.S.A.*	106	F8
Mechanicville, *U.S.A.*	107	D11
Mechara, *Ethiopia*	77	F5
Mechelen, *Antwerpen, Belgium*	17	F4
Mechelen, *Limburg, Belgium*	17	G7
Mecheria, *Algeria*	75	B4
Mechernich, *Germany*	18	E2
Mechetinskaya, *Russia*	43	C9
Mechra Benâbbou, *Morocco*	74	B3
Mecitözü, *Turkey*	42	F6
Mecklenburg-Vorpommern □, *Germany*	18	B8
Mecklenburger Bucht, *Germany*	18	A7
Meconta, *Mozam.*	83	E4
Meda, *Australia*	88	C3
Meda, *Portugal*	30	E3
Medan, *Indonesia*	56	D1
Médanos, *Argentina*	128	A4
Medanosa, Pta., *Argentina*	128	C3
Medéa, *Algeria*	75	A5
Medeiros Neto, *Brazil*	123	E3
Medel, Pic, *Switz.*	23	C7
Medellín, *Colombia*	120	B2
Medemblik, *Neths.*	16	C6
Médenine, *Tunisia*	75	B7
Mederdra, *Mauritania*	78	B1
Medford, *Mass., U.S.A.*	107	D13
Medford, *Oreg., U.S.A.*	110	E2
Medford, *Wis., U.S.A.*	108	C9
Medgidia, *Romania*	38	E11
Medi, *Sudan*	77	F3
Media Agua, *Argentina*	126	C2
Media Luna, *Argentina*	126	C2
Mediaş, *Romania*	38	C7
Medical Lake, *U.S.A.*	110	C5
Medicina, *Italy*	33	D8
Medicine Bow, *U.S.A.*	110	F10
Medicine Bow Pk., *U.S.A.*	110	F10
Medicine Bow Ra., *U.S.A.*	110	F10
Medicine Hat, *Canada*	101	D6

Medicine Lake, *U.S.A.*	108	A2
Medicine Lodge, *U.S.A.*	109	G5
Medina = Al Madīnah, *Si. Arabia*	64	E3
Medina, *Brazil*	123	E3
Medina, *Colombia*	120	C3
Medina, *N. Dak., U.S.A.*	108	B5
Medina, *N.Y., U.S.A.*	106	C6
Medina, *Ohio, U.S.A.*	106	E3
Medina →, *U.S.A.*	109	L5
Medina de Ríoseco, *Spain*	30	D5
Medina del Campo, *Spain*	30	D6
Medina L., *U.S.A.*	109	L5
Medina-Sidonia, *Spain*	31	J5
Medinaceli, *Spain*	28	D2
Medinipur, *India*	63	H12
Mediterranean Sea, *Europe*	70	C5
Medjerda, O. →, *Tunisia*	75	A7
Medley, *Canada*	101	C6
Médoc, *France*	26	C3
Medstead, *Canada*	101	C7
Medulin, *Croatia*	33	D10
Medveda, *Serbia, Yug.*	21	N11
Medveditsa →, *Russia*	41	G13
Medveditsa →, *Russia*	41	C10
Medvedok, *Russia*	41	C17
Medvezhi, Ostrava, *Russia*	45	B17
Medvezhyegorsk, *Russia*	44	C4
Medway →, *U.K.*	13	F8
Medyn, *Russia*	41	D9
Medzilaborce, *Czech.*	20	F11
Meeberrie, *Australia*	89	E2
Meekatharra, *Australia*	89	E2
Meeker, *U.S.A.*	110	F10
Meer, *Belgium*	17	F5
Meerane, *Germany*	18	E8
Meerbeke, *Belgium*	17	G4
Meerhout, *Belgium*	17	F6
Meerle, *Belgium*	17	F5
Meersburg, *Germany*	19	H5
Meerssen, *Neths.*	17	G7
Meerut, *India*	62	E7
Meeteetse, *U.S.A.*	110	D9
Meeuwen, *Belgium*	17	F7
Mega, *Ethiopia*	77	G4
Megáli Petalí, *Greece*	39	M7
Megalópolis, *Greece*	39	M5
Meganísi, *Greece*	39	L3
Mégara, *Greece*	39	M6
Megarine, *Algeria*	75	B6
Megève, *France*	27	C10
Meghalaya □, *India*	61	G17
Meghezez, *Ethiopia*	77	F4
Mégiscane, L., *Canada*	98	C4
Mehadia, *Romania*	38	E5
Mehaigne →, *Belgium*	17	G5
Mehaïguene, O. →, *Algeria*	75	B5
Meheisa, *Sudan*	76	D3
Mehndawal, *India*	63	F10
Mehr Jān, *Iran*	65	C7
Mehrābād, *Iran*	64	B5
Mehrīz, *Iran*	65	D7
Mehun-sur-Yèvre, *France*	25	E9
Mei Jiang →, *China*	53	E11
Mei Xian, *Guangdong, China*	53	E11
Mei Xian, *Shaanxi, China*	50	G4
Meia Ponte →, *Brazil*	123	E2
Meicheng, *China*	53	C12
Meichengzhen, *China*	53	C8
Meichuan, *China*	53	B10
Meiganga, *Cameroon*	80	C2
Meijel, *Neths.*	17	F7
Meiktila, *Burma*	61	J19
Meilen, *Switz.*	23	B7
Meiningen, *Germany*	18	E6
Meio →, *Brazil*	123	D3
Meira, Sierra de, *Spain*	30	B3
Meiringen, *Switz.*	22	C6
Meishan, *China*	52	B4
Meissen, *Germany*	18	D9
Meissner, *Germany*	18	D5
Meitan, *China*	52	D6
Mejillones, *Chile*	126	A1
Meka, *Australia*	89	E2
Mékambo, *Gabon*	80	D2
Mekdela, *Ethiopia*	77	E4
Mekele, *Ethiopia*	77	E4
Mekhtar, *Pakistan*	60	D6
Meknès, *Morocco*	74	B3
Meko, *Nigeria*	79	D5
Mekong →, *Asia*	59	H6
Mekongga, *Indonesia*	57	E6
Melagiri Hills, *India*	60	N10
Melah, Sebkhet el, *Algeria*	75	C4
Melaka, *Malaysia*	59	L4
Melalap, *Malaysia*	56	C5
Mélambes, *Greece*	37	D6
Melanesia, *Pac. Oc.*	92	H7
Melbourne, *Australia*	91	F3
Melbourne, *U.S.A.*	105	L5
Melchor Múzquiz, *Mexico*	114	B4
Melchor Ocampo, *Mexico*	114	C4
Méldola, *Italy*	33	D9
Meldorf, *Germany*	18	A5
Melegnano, *Italy*	32	C6
Melenci, *Serbia, Yug.*	21	K10
Melenki, *Russia*	41	D12
Mélèzes →, *Canada*	97	C12
Melfi, *Chad*	73	F8
Melfi, *Italy*	35	B8
Melfort, *Canada*	101	C8

Melfort, *Zimbabwe*	83	F3
Melgaço, *Madeira*	30	C2
Melgar de Fernamental, *Spain*	30	C6
Melhus, *Norway*	10	A4
Melick, *Neths.*	17	F8
Melide, *Switz.*	23	E7
Meligalá, *Greece*	39	M4
Melilla, *Morocco*	75	A4
Melipilla, *Chile*	126	C1
Mélissa, Ákra, *Greece*	37	D6
Melita, *Canada*	101	D8
Mélito di Porto Salvo, *Italy*	35	E8
Melitopol, *Ukraine*	42	C6
Melk, *Austria*	21	G5
Mellansel, *Sweden*	8	E15
Melle, *Belgium*	17	G3
Melle, *France*	26	B3
Melle, *Germany*	18	C4
Mellégue, O. →, *Tunisia*	75	A6
Mellen, *U.S.A.*	108	B9
Mellerud, *Sweden*	11	F6
Mellette, *U.S.A.*	108	C5
Mellid, *Spain*	30	C2
Mellieha, *Malta*	37	D1
Mellit, *Sudan*	77	E2
Mellizo Sur, Cerro, *Chile*	128	C2
Mellrichstadt, *Germany*	19	E6
Mělník, *Czech.*	20	E4
Melo, *Uruguay*	127	C5
Melolo, *Indonesia*	57	F6
Melouprey, *Cambodia*	58	F5
Melovoye, *Ukraine*	43	B9
Melrhir, Chott, *Algeria*	75	B6
Melrose, N.S.W., *Australia*	91	E4
Melrose, W. Austral., *Australia*	89	E3
Melrose, *U.K.*	14	F6
Melrose, *U.S.A.*	109	H3
Mels, *Switz.*	23	B8
Melsele, *Belgium*	17	F4
Melstone, *U.S.A.*	110	C10
Melsungen, *Germany*	18	D5
Melton Mowbray, *U.K.*	12	E7
Melun, *France*	25	D9
Melut, *Sudan*	77	E3
Melville, *Canada*	101	C8
Melville, C., *Australia*	90	A3
Melville, L., *Canada*	99	B8
Melville B., *Australia*	90	A2
Melville I., *Australia*	88	B5
Melville I., *Canada*	4	B2
Melville Pen., *Canada*	97	B11
Melvin →, *Canada*	100	B5
Memaliaj, *Albania*	39	J2
Memba, *Mozam.*	83	E5
Memboro, *Indonesia*	57	F5
Membrilla, *Spain*	29	G1
Memel = Klaipeda, *Lithuania*	40	D2
Memel, S. *Africa*	85	D4
Memmingen, *Germany*	19	H6
Mempawah, *Indonesia*	56	D3
Memphis, Tenn., *U.S.A.*	109	H10
Memphis, Tex., *U.S.A.*	109	H4
Mena, *U.S.A.*	109	H7
Mena →, *Ethiopia*	77	F5
Menai Strait, *U.K.*	12	D3
Ménaka, *Mali*	79	B5
Menaldum, *Neths.*	16	B7
Menan = Chao Phraya →, *Thailand*	58	F3
Menarandra →, *Madag.*	85	D7
Menard, *U.S.A.*	109	K5
Menasha, *U.S.A.*	104	C1
Menate, *Indonesia*	56	E4
Mendawai →, *Indonesia*	56	E4
Mende, *France*	26	D7
Mendebo, *Ethiopia*	77	F4
Mendez, *Mexico*	115	B5
Mendhar, *India*	63	C6
Mendi, *Ethiopia*	77	F4
Mendip Hills, *U.K.*	13	F5
Mendocino, *U.S.A.*	110	G2
Mendocino, C., *U.S.A.*	110	F1
Mendota, Calif., *U.S.A.*	111	H3
Mendota, Ill., *U.S.A.*	108	E10
Mendoza, *Argentina*	126	C2
Mendoza □, *Argentina*	126	C2
Mendrisio, *Switz.*	23	E7
Mene Grande, *Venezuela*	120	B3
Menemen, *Turkey*	66	D2
Menen, *Belgium*	17	G2
Menéndez, L., *Argentina*	128	E2
Menfi, *Italy*	34	E5
Mengcheng, *China*	53	A11
Mengdingjie, *China*	52	F2
Mengeš, *Slovenia*	33	B11
Menggala, *Indonesia*	56	E3
Menghai, *China*	52	G3
Mengíbar, *Spain*	31	H7
Mengjin, *China*	50	G7
Mengla, *China*	52	G3
Menglian, *China*	52	F2
Mengoub, *Algeria*	74	C3
Mengshan, *China*	53	E8
Mengyin, *China*	51	G9
Mengzhe, *China*	52	F3
Mengzi, *China*	52	F4
Menihek L., *Canada*	99	B6
Menin = Menen, *Belgium*	17	G2
Menindee, *Australia*	91	E3
Menindee L., *Australia*	91	E3
Meningie, *Australia*	91	F2
Menlo Park, *U.S.A.*	112	H4
Menominee, *U.S.A.*	104	C2
Menominee →, *U.S.A.*	104	C2
Menomonie, *U.S.A.*	108	C9
Menongue, *Angola*	81	G3
Menorca, *Spain*	36	B11
Mentakab, *Malaysia*	59	L4
Mentawai, Kepulauan, *Indonesia*	56	E1
Menton, *France*	27	E11
Mentor, *U.S.A.*	106	E3
Mentz Dam, S. *Africa*	84	E4
Menzel-Bourguiba, *Tunisia*	75	A6
Menzel Chaker, *Tunisia*	75	B7
Menzel-Temime, *Tunisia*	75	A7
Menzies, *Australia*	89	E3
Me'ona, *Israel*	69	B4
Meoqui, *Mexico*	114	B3
Mepaco, *Mozam.*	83	F3
Meppel, *Neths.*	16	C8
Meppen, *Germany*	18	C3
Mequinenza, *Spain*	28	D5
Mer Rouge, *U.S.A.*	109	J9
Merabéllou, Kólpos, *Greece*	37	D7
Meramangye, L., *Australia*	89	E5
Meran = Merano, *Italy*	33	B8
Merano, *Italy*	33	B8
Merate, *Italy*	32	C6
Merauke, *Indonesia*	57	F10
Merbabu, *Indonesia*	57	G14
Merbein, *Australia*	91	E3
Merca, *Somali Rep.*	68	G3
Mercadal, *Spain*	36	B11
Mercato Saraceno, *Italy*	33	E9
Merced, *U.S.A.*	111	H3
Merced Pk., *U.S.A.*	112	H7
Mercedes, Buenos Aires, *Argentina*	126	C4
Mercedes, Corrientes, *Argentina*	126	B4
Mercedes, San Luis, *Argentina*	126	C2
Mercedes, *Uruguay*	126	C4
Merceditas, *Chile*	126	B1
Mercer, *N.Z.*	87	G5
Mercer, *U.S.A.*	106	E4
Merchtem, *Belgium*	17	G4
Mercier, *Bolivia*	124	C4
Mercury, *U.S.A.*	113	J11
Mercy C., *Canada*	97	B13
Merdrignac, *France*	24	D4
Mere, *Belgium*	17	G3
Meredith, C., *Falk. Is.*	128	D4
Meredith, L., *U.S.A.*	109	H4
Merelbeke, *Belgium*	17	G3
Méréville, *France*	25	D9
Merga = Nukheila, *Sudan*	76	D2
Mergenevsky, *Kazakhstan*	43	B14
Mergui Arch. = Myeik Kyunzu, *Burma*	59	G1
Mérida, *Mexico*	115	C7
Mérida, *Spain*	31	G4
Mérida, *Venezuela*	120	B3
Mérida □, *Venezuela*	120	B3
Mérida, Cord. de, *Venezuela*	118	B2
Meriden, *U.S.A.*	107	E12
Meridian, Calif., *U.S.A.*	112	F5
Meridian, Idaho, *U.S.A.*	110	E5
Meridian, Miss., *U.S.A.*	105	J1
Meridian, Tex., *U.S.A.*	109	K6
Mering, *Germany*	19	G7
Meriruma, *Brazil*	121	C7
Merkel, *U.S.A.*	109	J4
Merksem, *Belgium*	17	F4
Merksplas, *Belgium*	17	F5
Mermaid Reef, *Australia*	88	C2
Mern, *Denmark*	11	J6
Merowe, *Sudan*	76	D3
Merredin, *Australia*	89	F2
Merrick, *U.K.*	14	F4
Merrickville, *Canada*	107	B9
Merrill, Oreg., *U.S.A.*	110	E3
Merrill, Wis., *U.S.A.*	108	C10
Merriman, *U.S.A.*	108	D4
Merritt, *Canada*	100	C4
Merriwa, *Australia*	91	E5
Merriwagga, *Australia*	91	E4
Merry I., *Canada*	98	A4
Merrygoen, *Australia*	91	E4
Merryville, *U.S.A.*	109	K8
Mersa Fatma, *Ethiopia*	68	E3
Mersch, *Lux.*	17	J8
Merseburg, *Germany*	18	D7
Mersey →, *U.K.*	12	D5
Merseyside □, *U.K.*	12	D5
Mersin, *Turkey*	66	E6
Mersing, *Malaysia*	59	L4
Merta, *India*	62	F6
Mertert, *Lux.*	17	J8
Merthyr Tydfil, *U.K.*	13	F4
Mértola, *Portugal*	31	H3
Mertzig, *Lux.*	17	J8
Mertzon, *U.S.A.*	109	K4
Méru, *France*	25	C9
Meru, *Kenya*	82	B4
Meru, *Tanzania*	82	C4
Meru □, *Kenya*	82	B4
Merville, *France*	25	B9
Méry-sur-Seine, *France*	25	D10
Merzifon, *Turkey*	42	F6
Merzig, *Germany*	19	F2
Merzouga, Erg Tin, *Algeria*	75	D7
Mesa, *U.S.A.*	111	K8
Mesach Mellet, *Libya*	75	D7
Mesagne, *Italy*	35	B10
Mesanagrós, *Greece*	37	C9
Mesaoría □, *Cyprus*	37	D12
Mesarás, Kólpos, *Greece*	37	D6
Meschede, *Germany*	18	D4
Mesfinto, *Ethiopia*	77	E4
Mesgouez, L., *Canada*	98	B4
Meshchovsk, *Russia*	40	D9
Meshed = Mashhad, *Iran*	65	B8
Meshoppen, *U.S.A.*	107	E8
Meshra er Req, *Sudan*	77	F2
Mesick, *U.S.A.*	104	C3
Mesilinka →, *Canada*	100	B4
Mesilla, *U.S.A.*	111	K10
Meslay-du-Maine, *France*	24	E6
Mesocco, *Switz.*	23	D8
Mesolóngion, *Greece*	39	L4
Mesopotamia = Al Jazirah, *Iraq*	64	C5
Mesoraca, *Italy*	35	C9
Mesquite, *U.S.A.*	111	H6
Messac, *France*	24	E5
Messad, *Algeria*	75	B5
Messalo →, *Mozam.*	83	E4
Méssaména, *Cameroon*	79	E7
Messancy, *Belgium*	17	J7
Messier, Canal, *Chile*	128	C2
Messina, *Italy*	35	D8
Messina, S. *Africa*	85	C5
Messina, Str. di, *Italy*	35	D8
Messíni, *Greece*	39	M5
Messiniakós Kólpos, *Greece*	39	N5
Messkirch, *Germany*	19	H5
Messonghi, *Greece*	37	B3
Mesta →, *Bulgaria*	39	H7
Mestanza, *Spain*	31	G6
Mestre, *Italy*	33	C9
Mestre, Espigão, *Brazil*	123	D2
Městys Zelezná Ruda, *Czech.*	20	F3
Meta □, *Colombia*	120	C3
Meta →, S. *Amer.*	120	B4
Metairie, *U.S.A.*	109	L9
Metaline Falls, *U.S.A.*	110	B5
Metán, *Argentina*	126	B3
Metangula, *Mozam.*	83	E3
Metauro →, *Italy*	33	E10
Metema, *Ethiopia*	77	E4
Metengobalame, *Mozam.*	83	E3
Méthana, *Greece*	39	M6
Methven, *N.Z.*	87	K3
Methy L., *Canada*	101	B7
Metil, *Mozam.*	83	F4
Metlakatla, *U.S.A.*	100	B2
Metlaoui, *Tunisia*	75	B6
Metlika, *Slovenia*	33	C12
Metropolis, *U.S.A.*	109	G10
Mettet, *Belgium*	17	H5
Mettur Dam, *India*	60	P10
Metz, *France*	25	C13
Meulaboh, *Indonesia*	56	D1
Meulan, *France*	25	C8
Meung-sur-Loire, *France*	25	E8
Meureudu, *Indonesia*	56	C1
Meurthe →, *France*	25	D13
Meurthe-et-Moselle □, *France*	25	D12
Meuse □, *France*	25	C12
Meuse →, *Europe*	17	G7
Meuselwitz, *Germany*	18	D8
Mexborough, *U.K.*	12	D6
Mexia, *U.S.A.*	109	K6
Mexiana, I., *Brazil*	122	A2
Mexicali, *Mexico*	114	A1
México, *Mexico*	115	D5
Mexico, Maine, *U.S.A.*	107	B14
Mexico, Mo., *U.S.A.*	108	F9
México □, *Mexico*	114	D5
Mexico ■, Cent. Amer.	114	C4
Mexico, G. of, Cent. Amer.	115	C7
Meyenburg, *Germany*	18	B8
Meymac, *France*	26	C6
Meymaneh, *Afghan.*	60	B4
Meyrargues, *France*	27	E9
Meyrueis, *France*	26	D7
Meyssac, *France*	26	C5
Mezdra, *Bulgaria*	38	F6
Mèze, *France*	26	E7
Mezen, *Russia*	44	C5
Mezen →, *Russia*	44	C5
Mézenc, Mt., *France*	27	D8
Mezha →, *Russia*	40	D7
Mézidon, *France*	24	C6
Mézilhac, *France*	27	D8
Mézin, *France*	26	D4
Mezöberény, *Hungary*	21	J11
Mezökovácsháza, *Hungary*	21	J10
Mezökövesd, *Hungary*	21	H10
Mézos, *France*	26	D2
Mezötúr, *Hungary*	21	J10
Mezquital, *Mexico*	114	C4
Mezzolombardo, *Italy*	32	B8
Mglin, *Russia*	40	E8
Mhlaba Hills, *Zimbabwe*	83	F3
Mhow, *India*	62	H6
Miahuatlán, *Mexico*	115	D5
Miajadas, *Spain*	31	F5
Miallo, *Australia*	90	B4
Miami, Ariz., *U.S.A.*	111	K8
Miami, Fla., *U.S.A.*	105	N5
Miami, Tex., *U.S.A.*	109	H4
Miami →, *U.S.A.*	104	F3
Miami Beach, *U.S.A.*	105	N5
Miamisburg, *U.S.A.*	104	F3
Mian Xian, *China*	50	H4
Mianchi, *China*	50	G6
Mīāndowāb, *Iran*	64	B5
Miandrivazo, *Madag.*	85	B8
Mīāneh, *Iran*	64	B5
Mianning, *China*	52	C4
Mianwali, *Pakistan*	62	C4
Mianyang, Hubei, *China*	53	B9
Mianyang, Sichuan, *China*	52	B5
Mianzhu, *China*	52	B5
Miaoli, *Taiwan*	53	E13
Miarinarivo, *Madag.*	85	B8
Miass, *Russia*	44	D7
Miastko, *Poland*	20	A6
Michalovce, *Czech.*	20	G11
Michelstadt, *Germany*	19	F5
Michigan □, *U.S.A.*	103	B9
Michigan, L., *U.S.A.*	104	C2
Michigan City, *U.S.A.*	104	E2
Michikamau L., *Canada*	99	B7
Michipicoten, *Canada*	98	C3
Michipicoten I., *Canada*	98	C2
Michoacan □, *Mexico*	114	D4
Michurin, *Bulgaria*	38	G10
Michurinsk, *Russia*	41	E12
Miclere, *Australia*	90	C4
Mico, Pta. , *Nic.*	116	D3
Micronesia, Federated States of ■, Pac. Oc.	92	G7
Mid Glamorgan □, *U.K.*	13	F4
Midai, P., *Indonesia*	59	L6
Midale, *Canada*	101	D8
Middagsfjället, *Sweden*	10	A6
Middelbeers, *Neths.*	17	F6
Middelburg, *Neths.*	17	F3
Middelburg, C. Prov., S. *Africa*	84	E3
Middelburg, Trans., S. *Africa*	85	D4
Middelfart, *Denmark*	11	J3
Middelharnis, *Neths.*	16	E4
Middelkerke, *Belgium*	17	F1
Middelrode, *Neths.*	17	E6
Middelwit, S. *Africa*	84	C4
Middle Alkali L., *U.S.A.*	110	F3
Middle Fork Feather →, *U.S.A.*	112	F5
Middle I., *Australia*	89	F3
Middle Loup →, *U.S.A.*	108	E5
Middleboro, *U.S.A.*	107	E14
Middleburg, N.Y., *U.S.A.*	107	D10
Middleburg, Pa., *U.S.A.*	106	F7
Middlebury, *U.S.A.*	107	B11
Middleport, *U.S.A.*	104	F4
Middlesboro, *U.S.A.*	103	C10
Middlesboro, *U.S.A.*	105	G4
Middlesbrough, *U.K.*	12	C6
Middlesex, *Belize*	116	C2
Middlesex, *U.S.A.*	107	F10
Middleton, *Australia*	90	C3
Middleton, *Canada*	99	D6
Middletown, Calif., *U.S.A.*	112	G4
Middletown, Conn., *U.S.A.*	107	E12
Middletown, N.Y., *U.S.A.*	107	E10
Middletown, Ohio, *U.S.A.*	104	F3
Middletown, Pa., *U.S.A.*	107	F8
Midelt, *Morocco*	74	B4
Midi, Canal du →, *France*	26	E5
Midi d'Ossau, Pic du, *France*	26	F3
Midland, *Canada*	98	D4
Midland, Calif., *U.S.A.*	113	M12
Midland, Mich., *U.S.A.*	104	D3
Midland, Pa., *U.S.A.*	106	F4
Midland, Tex., *U.S.A.*	109	K3
Midlands □, *Zimbabwe*	83	F2
Midleton, *Ireland*	15	E3
Midlothian, *U.S.A.*	109	J6
Midongy, Tangorombohitr'i, *Madag.*	85	C8
Midongy Atsimo, *Madag.*	85	C8
Midou →, *France*	26	E3
Midouze →, *France*	26	E3
Midsayap, *Phil.*	55	H6
Midu, *China*	52	E3
Midway Wells, *U.S.A.*	113	N11
Midway Is., Pac. Oc.	92	E10
Midwest, *U.S.A.*	110	E10
Midwolda, *Neths.*	16	B9
Midyat, *Turkey*	67	E9
Mie □, *Japan*	49	G8
Miechów, *Poland*	20	E10
Międzychód, *Poland*	20	C5
Międzyrzec Podlaski, *Poland*	20	D12
Międzyrzecz, *Poland*	20	C5
Miélan, *France*	26	E4
Mielec, *Poland*	20	E11
Mienga, *Angola*	84	B2
Miercurea Ciuc, *Romania*	38	C8
Mieres, *Spain*	30	B5
Mierlo, *Neths.*	17	F7
Mieso, *Ethiopia*	77	F5
Mifflintown, *U.S.A.*	106	F7
Mifraz Ḥefa, *Israel*	69	C4
Migdāl, *Israel*	69	C4
Migennes, *France*	25	E10
Migliarino, *Italy*	33	D8
Miguel Alemán, Presa, *Mexico*	115	D5
Miguel Alves, *Brazil*	122	B3
Miguel Calmon, *Brazil*	122	D3
Mihaliçcik, *Turkey*	66	D4
Mihara, *Japan*	49	G6
Mijares →, *Spain*	28	F4
Mijas, *Spain*	31	J6
Mikese, *Tanzania*	82	D4
Mikha-Tskhakaya = Senaki, *Georgia*	43	E10
Mikhailovka, *Ukraine*	42	C6
Mikhaylovgrad, *Bulgaria*	38	F6
Mikhaylovka, *Azerbaijan*	43	F13
Mikhaylovka, *Russia*	41	D11
Mikhaylovka, *Russia*	41	F13
Mikhnevo, *Russia*	41	D10
Mikínai, *Greece*	39	M5
Mikkeli, *Finland*	9	F19
Mikkeli □ = Mikkelin lääni □, *Finland*	8	E19
Mikkelin lääni □, *Finland*	8	E19
Mikkwa →, *Canada*	100	B6
Mikniya, *Sudan*	77	D3
Mikołajki, *Poland*	20	B11
Míkonos, *Greece*	39	M8
Mikrón Dhérion, *Greece*	39	H9
Mikulov, *Czech.*	20	G6
Mikumi, *Tanzania*	82	D4
Milaca, *U.S.A.*	108	C8
Milagro, *Ecuador*	120	D2
Milagros, *Phil.*	55	E5
Milan = Milano, *Italy*	32	C6
Milan, Mo., *U.S.A.*	108	E8
Milan, Tenn., *U.S.A.*	105	H1
Milang, *Australia*	91	E2
Milange, *Mozam.*	83	F4
Milano, *Italy*	32	C6
Milâs, *Turkey*	66	E2
Milatos, *Greece*	37	D7
Milazzo, *Italy*	35	D8
Milbank, *U.S.A.*	108	C6
Milden, *Canada*	101	C7
Mildmay, *Canada*	106	B3
Mildura, *Australia*	91	E3
Mile, *China*	52	E4
Miléai, *Greece*	39	K6
Mileh Tharthār, *Iraq*	64	C4
Miles, *Australia*	91	D5
Miles, *U.S.A.*	109	K4
Miles City, *U.S.A.*	108	B2
Milestone, *Canada*	101	D8
Mileto, *Italy*	35	D9
Miletto, Mte., *Italy*	35	A7
Miletus, *Turkey*	66	E2
Mileura, *Australia*	89	E2
Milford, Calif., *U.S.A.*	112	E6
Milford, Conn., *U.S.A.*	107	E11
Milford, Del., *U.S.A.*	104	F8
Milford, Mass., *U.S.A.*	107	D13
Milford, Pa., *U.S.A.*	107	E10
Milford, Utah, *U.S.A.*	111	G7
Milford Haven, *U.K.*	13	F2
Milford Sd., *N.Z.*	87	L1
Milgun, *Australia*	89	D2
Milḥ, Baḥr al, *Iraq*	64	C4
Miliana, Aïn Salah, *Algeria*	75	C5
Miliana, Médéa, *Algeria*	75	A5
Miling, *Australia*	89	F2
Militello in Val di Catánia, *Italy*	35	E7
Milk →, N. *Amer.*	110	B10
Milk, Wadi el →, *Sudan*	76	D3
Milk River, *Canada*	100	D6
Mill, *Neths.*	17	E7
Mill City, *U.S.A.*	110	D2
Mill I., *Antarctica*	5	C8
Mill Valley, *U.S.A.*	112	H4
Millau, *France*	26	D7
Millbridge, *Canada*	106	B7
Millbrook, *Canada*	106	B6
Mille Lacs, L., *U.S.A.*	108	B8
Mille Lacs, L. des, *Canada*	98	C1
Milledgeville, *U.S.A.*	105	J4
Millen, *U.S.A.*	105	J5
Miller, *U.S.A.*	108	C5
Millerovo, *Russia*	43	B9
Millersburg, Ohio, *U.S.A.*	106	F3
Millersburg, Pa., *U.S.A.*	106	F8
Millerton, *U.S.A.*	107	E11
Millerton L., *U.S.A.*	112	J7
Millevaches, Plateau de, *France*	26	C6
Millicent, *Australia*	91	F3
Millingen, *Neths.*	16	E8
Millinocket, *U.S.A.*	99	C6
Millmerran, *Australia*	91	D5
Mills L., *Canada*	100	A5
Millsboro, *U.S.A.*	106	G4
Milltown Malbay, *Ireland*	15	D2
Millville, *U.S.A.*	104	F8
Millwood Res., *U.S.A.*	109	J8
Milly-la-Forêt, *France*	25	D9
Milna, *Croatia*	33	E13
Milne →, *Australia*	90	C2
Milne Inlet, *Canada*	97	A11
Milnor, *U.S.A.*	108	B6
Milo, *Canada*	100	C6
Mílos, *Greece*	39	N7
Milošévo, Serbia, Yug.	21	K10
Milparinka P.O., *Australia*	91	D3
Miltenberg, *Germany*	19	F5
Milton, *Canada*	106	C5
Milton, *N.Z.*	87	M2
Milton, *U.K.*	14	D4
Milton, Calif., *U.S.A.*	112	G6
Milton, Fla., *U.S.A.*	105	K2

Milton, *Pa., U.S.A.* 106 F8
Milton-Freewater, *U.S.A.* 110 D4
Milton Keynes, *U.K.* 13 E7
Miltou, *Chad* 73 F8
Milverton, *Canada* 106 C4
Milwaukee, *U.S.A.* 104 D2
Milwaukee Deep, *Atl. Oc.* 117 C6
Milwaukie, *U.S.A.* 112 E4
Mim, *Ghana* 78 D4
Mimizan, *France* 26 D2
Mimoso, *Brazil* 123 E2
Min Chiang →, *China* 53 E12
Min Jiang →, *China* 52 C5
Min Xian, *China* 50 G3
Mina, *U.S.A.* 111 G4
Mina Pirquitas, *Argentina* 126 A2
Mīnā Su'ud, *Si. Arabia* 65 D6
Mīnā'al Aḩmadī, *Kuwait* 65 D6
Mīnāb, *Iran* 65 E8
Minago →, *Canada* 101 C9
Minaki, *Canada* 101 D10
Minamata, *Japan* 49 H5
Minami-Tori-Shima, *Pac. Oc.* 92 E7
Minas, *Uruguay* 127 C4
Minas, Sierra de las, *Guatemala* 116 C2
Minas Basin, *Canada* 99 C7
Minas de Rio Tinto, *Spain* 31 H4
Minas de San Quintín, *Spain* 31 G6
Minas Gerais □, *Brazil* 123 E2
Minas Novas, *Brazil* 123 E3
Minatitlán, *Mexico* 115 D6
Minbu, *Burma* 61 J19
Mincio →, *Italy* 32 C7
Mindanao, *Phil.* 55 H6
Mindanao Sea = Bohol Sea, *Phil.* 57 C6
Mindanao Trench, *Pac. Oc.* 55 F7
Mindel →, *Germany* 19 G6
Mindelheim, *Germany* 19 G6
Minden, *Canada* 106 B6
Minden, *Germany* 18 C4
Minden, *La., U.S.A.* 109 J8
Minden, *Nev., U.S.A.* 112 G7
Mindiptana, *Indonesia* 57 F10
Mindoro, *Phil.* 55 E4
Mindoro Str., *Phil.* 55 E4
Mindouli, *Congo* 80 E2
Mine, *Japan* 49 G5
Minehead, *U.K.* 13 F4
Mineiros, *Brazil* 125 D7
Mineola, *U.S.A.* 109 J7
Mineral King, *U.S.A.* 112 J8
Mineral Wells, *U.S.A.* 109 J5
Mineralnyye Vody, *Russia* 43 D10
Minersville, *Pa., U.S.A.* 107 F8
Minersville, *Utah, U.S.A.* 111 G7
Minerva, *U.S.A.* 106 F3
Minervino Murge, *Italy* 35 A9
Minetto, *U.S.A.* 107 C8
Mingan, *Canada* 99 B7
Mingechaur, *Azerbaijan* 43 F12
Mingechaurskoye Vdkhr., *Azerbaijan* 43 F12
Mingela, *Australia* 90 B4
Mingenew, *Australia* 89 E2
Mingera Cr. →, *Australia* 90 C2
Minggang, *China* 53 A10
Mingin, *Burma* 61 H19
Minglanilla, *Spain* 28 F3
Minglun, *China* 52 E7
Mingorria, *Spain* 30 E6
Mingt'iehkaitafan = Mintaka Pass, *Pakistan* 63 A6
Mingxi, *China* 53 D11
Mingyuegue, *China* 51 C15
Minhou, *China* 53 E12
Minićevo, *Serbia, Yug.* 21 M12
Minidoka, *U.S.A.* 110 E7
Minigwal, L., *Australia* 89 E3
Minilya, *Australia* 89 D1
Minilya →, *Australia* 89 D1
Minipi, L., *Canada* 99 B7
Mink L., *Canada* 100 A5
Minna, *Nigeria* 79 D6
Minneapolis, *Kans., U.S.A.* 108 F6
Minneapolis, *Minn., U.S.A.* 108 C8
Minnedosa, *Canada* 101 C9
Minnesota □, *U.S.A.* 108 B7
Minnesund, *Norway* 10 D5
Minnie Creek, *Australia* 89 D2
Minnipa, *Australia* 91 E2
Minnitaki L., *Canada* 98 C1
Mino, *Japan* 49 G8
Miño →, *Spain* 30 D2
Minorca = Menorca, *Spain* 36 B11
Minore, *Australia* 91 E4
Minot, *U.S.A.* 108 A4
Minqin, *China* 50 E2
Minqing, *China* 53 D12
Minsen, *Germany* 18 B3
Minsk, *Belorussia* 40 E5
Mińsk Mazowiecki, *Poland* 20 C11
Mintaka Pass, *Pakistan* 63 A6
Minto, *U.S.A.* 96 B5
Minton, *Canada* 101 D8
Minturn, *U.S.A.* 110 G10
Minturno, *Italy* 34 A6
Minûf, *Egypt* 76 H7
Minusinsk, *Russia* 45 D10
Minutang, *India* 61 E20
Minvoul, *Gabon* 80 D2
Minya el Qamh, *Egypt* 76 H7
Mionica, *Serbia, Yug.* 21 L10
Mir, *Niger* 79 C7
Mir-Bashir, *Azerbaijan* 43 F12
Mīr Kūh, *Iran* 65 E8
Mīr Shahdād, *Iran* 65 E8
Mira, *Italy* 33 C9
Mira, *Portugal* 30 E2
Mira →, *Colombia* 120 C2
Mira →, *Portugal* 31 H2
Mira por vos Cay, *Bahamas* 117 B5
Mirabella Eclano, *Italy* 35 A7
Miracema do Norte, *Brazil* 122 C2
Mirador, *Brazil* 122 C3
Miraflores, *Colombia* 120 C3
Miraj, *India* 60 L9
Miram Shah, *Pakistan* 62 C4
Miramar, *Argentina* 126 D4
Miramar, *Mozam.* 85 C6
Miramas, *France* 27 E8
Mirambeau, *France* 26 C3
Miramichi B., *Canada* 99 C7
Miramont-de-Guyenne, *France* 26 D4
Miranda, *Brazil* 125 E6
Miranda □, *Venezuela* 120 A4
Miranda →, *Brazil* 125 D6
Miranda de Ebro, *Spain* 28 C2
Miranda do Corvo, *Spain* 30 E2
Miranda do Douro, *Portugal* 30 D4
Mirande, *France* 26 E4
Mirandela, *Portugal* 30 D3
Mirando City, *U.S.A.* 109 M5
Mirandola, *Italy* 32 D8
Mirandópolis, *Brazil* 127 A5
Mirango, *Malawi* 83 E3
Mirani, *Australia* 90 C4
Mirano, *Italy* 33 C9
Mirassol, *Brazil* 127 A6
Mirbāţ, *Oman* 68 D5
Mirear, *Egypt* 76 C4
Mirebeau, *Côte-d'Or, France* 25 E12
Mirebeau, *Vienne, France* 24 F7
Mirecourt, *France* 25 D13
Mirgorod, *Ukraine* 40 G8
Miri, *Malaysia* 56 D4
Miriam Vale, *Australia* 90 C5
Mirim, L., *S. Amer.* 127 C5
Mirimire, *Venezuela* 120 A4
Miriti, *Brazil* 125 B6
Mirnyy, *Russia* 45 C12
Mirond L., *Canada* 101 B8
Mirpur, *Pakistan* 63 C5
Mirpur Bibiwari, *Pakistan* 62 E2
Mirpur Khas, *Pakistan* 62 G3
Mirpur Sakro, *Pakistan* 62 G2
Mirria, *Niger* 79 C6
Mirror, *Canada* 100 C6
Mîrşani, *Romania* 38 E6
Miryang, *S. Korea* 51 G15
Mirzaani, *Georgia* 43 F12
Mirzapur, *India* 63 G10
Mirzapur-cum-Vindhyachal = Mirzapur, *India* 63 G10
Misantla, *Mexico* 115 D5
Misawa, *Japan* 48 D10
Miscou I., *Canada* 99 C7
Mish'āb, Ra'as al, *Si. Arabia* 65 D6
Mishagua →, *Peru* 124 C3
Mishan, *China* 54 B8
Mishawaka, *U.S.A.* 104 E2
Mishbih, Gebel, *Egypt* 76 C3
Mishima, *Japan* 49 G9
Misilmeri, *Italy* 34 D6
Misión, *Mexico* 113 N10
Misión Fagnano, *Argentina* 128 D3
Misiones □, *Argentina* 127 B5
Misiones □, *Paraguay* 126 B4
Miskah, *Si. Arabia* 64 E4
Miskitos, Cayos, *Nic.* 116 D3
Miskolc, *Hungary* 21 G10
Misoke, *Zaïre* 82 C2
Misool, *Indonesia* 57 E8
Misrātah, *Libya* 73 B8
Missanabie, *Canada* 98 C3
Missão Velha, *Brazil* 122 C4
Missinaibi →, *Canada* 98 B3
Missinaibi L., *Canada* 98 C3
Mission, *S. Dak., U.S.A.* 108 D4
Mission, *Tex., U.S.A.* 109 M5
Mission City, *Canada* 100 D4
Mission Viejo, *U.S.A.* 113 M9
Missisa L., *Canada* 98 B2
Mississagi →, *Canada* 98 C3
Mississippi □, *U.S.A.* 103 D9
Mississippi →, *U.S.A.* 109 L10
Mississippi, Delta of the, *U.S.A.* 109 L9
Mississippi L., *Canada* 107 A8
Mississippi Sd., *U.S.A.* 109 K10
Missoula, *U.S.A.* 110 C6
Missour, *Morocco* 74 B4
Missouri □, *U.S.A.* 108 F8
Missouri →, *U.S.A.* 108 F9
Missouri Valley, *U.S.A.* 108 E7
Mist, *U.S.A.* 112 E3
Mistake B., *Canada* 101 A10
Mistassini →, *Canada* 99 C5
Mistassini L., *Canada* 98 B5
Mistastin L., *Canada* 99 A7
Mistatim, *Canada* 101 C8
Mistelbach, *Austria* 20 G6
Misterbianco, *Italy* 35 E8
Mistretta, *Italy* 35 E7
Misty L., *Canada* 101 B8
Mît Ghamr, *Egypt* 76 H7
Mitatib, *Sudan* 77 D4
Mitchell, *Australia* 91 D4
Mitchell, *Canada* 106 C3
Mitchell, *Ind., U.S.A.* 104 F2
Mitchell, *Nebr., U.S.A.* 108 E3
Mitchell, *Oreg., U.S.A.* 110 D3
Mitchell, *S. Dak., U.S.A.* 108 D5
Mitchell →, *Australia* 90 B3
Mitchell, Mt., *U.S.A.* 105 H4
Mitchell Ras., *Australia* 90 A2
Mitchelstown, *Ireland* 15 D3
Mitha Tiwana, *Pakistan* 62 C5
Mitilíni, *Greece* 39 K9
Mito, *Japan* 49 F10
Mitsinjo, *Madag.* 85 B8
Mitsiwa, *Ethiopia* 77 D4
Mitsiwa Channel, *Ethiopia* 77 D5
Mitsukaidō, *Japan* 49 F9
Mittagong, *Australia* 91 E5
Mittelland, *Switz.* 22 C4
Mittelland Kanal, *Germany* 18 C3
Mittenwalde, *Germany* 18 C9
Mitterteich, *Germany* 19 F8
Mittweida, *Germany* 18 E8
Mitú, *Colombia* 120 C3
Mituas, *Colombia* 120 C4
Mitumba, *Tanzania* 82 D3
Mitumba, Chaîne des, *Zaïre* 82 D2
Mitwaba, *Zaïre* 83 D2
Mityana, *Uganda* 82 B3
Mitzic, *Gabon* 80 D2
Mixteco →, *Mexico* 115 D5
Miyagi □, *Japan* 48 E10
Miyâh, W. el →, *Egypt* 76 B3
Miyah, W. el →, *Syria* 64 C3
Miyake-Jima, *Japan* 49 G9
Miyako, *Japan* 48 E10
Miyako-Jima, *Japan* 49 M2
Miyako-Rettō, *Japan* 49 M2
Miyakonojō, *Japan* 49 J5
Miyanoura-Dake, *Japan* 49 J5
Miyazaki, *Japan* 49 J5
Miyazaki □, *Japan* 49 H5
Miyazu, *Japan* 49 G7
Miyet, Bahr el = Dead Sea, *Asia* 69 D4
Miyi, *China* 52 D4
Miyoshi, *Japan* 49 G6
Miyun, *China* 50 D9
Miyun Shuiku, *China* 51 D9
Mizamis = Ozamis, *Phil.* 55 G5
Mizdah, *Libya* 75 B7
Mizen Hd., *Cork, Ireland* 15 E2
Mizen Hd., *Wick., Ireland* 15 D5
Mizhi, *China* 50 F6
Mizil, *Romania* 38 E9
Mizoram □, *India* 61 H18
Mizpe Ramon, *Israel* 69 E3
Mizusawa, *Japan* 48 E10
Mjöbäck, *Sweden* 11 G6
Mjölby, *Sweden* 11 F9
Mjörn, *Sweden* 11 G6
Mjøsa, *Norway* 10 D5
Mkata, *Tanzania* 82 D4
Mkokotoni, *Tanzania* 82 D4
Mkomazi, *Tanzania* 82 C4
Mkomazi →, *S. Africa* 85 E5
Mkulwe, *Tanzania* 83 D3
Mkumbi, Ras, *Tanzania* 82 D4
Mkushi, *Zambia* 83 E2
Mkushi River, *Zambia* 83 E2
Mkuze, *S. Africa* 85 D5
Mkuze →, *S. Africa* 85 D5
Mladá Boleslav, *Czech.* 20 E4
Mladenovac, *Serbia, Yug.* 21 L10
Mlala Hills, *Tanzania* 82 D3
Mlange, *Malawi* 83 F4
Mlava →, *Serbia, Yug.* 21 L11
Mława, *Poland* 20 B10
Mlinište, *Bos.-H., Yug.* 33 D13
Mljet, *Croatia* 21 N7
Młynąry, *Poland* 20 A9
Mmabatho, *S. Africa* 84 D4
Mme, *Cameroon* 79 D7
Mo i Rana, *Norway* 8 C13
Moa, *Indonesia* 57 F7
Moa →, *S. Leone* 78 D2
Moab, *U.S.A.* 111 G9
Moabi, *Gabon* 80 E2
Moaco →, *Brazil* 124 B4
Moala, *Fiji* 87 D8
Moalie Park, *Australia* 91 D3
Moaña, *Spain* 30 C2
Moba, *Zaïre* 82 D2
Mobārakābād, *Iran* 65 D7
Mobārakīyeh, *Iran* 65 C6
Mobaye, *C.A.R.* 80 D4
Mobayi, *Zaïre* 80 D4
Moberly, *U.S.A.* 108 F8
Moberly →, *Canada* 100 B4
Mobile, *U.S.A.* 105 K1
Mobile B., *U.S.A.* 105 K2
Mobridge, *U.S.A.* 108 C4
Mobutu Sese Seko, L., *Africa* 82 B3
Moc Chau, *Vietnam* 58 B5
Moc Hoa, *Vietnam* 59 G5
Mocabe Kasari, *Zaïre* 83 D2
Mocajuba, *Brazil* 122 B2
Moçambique, *Mozam.* 83 F5
Moçâmedes = Namibe, *Angola* 81 H2
Mocapra →, *Venezuela* 120 B4
Mocha, I., *Chile* 128 A2
Mochudi, *Botswana* 84 C4
Mocimboa da Praia, *Mozam.* 83 E5
Moclips, *U.S.A.* 112 C2
Mocoa, *Colombia* 120 C2
Mococa, *Brazil* 127 A6
Mocorito, *Mexico* 114 B3
Moctezuma, *Mexico* 114 B3
Moctezuma →, *Mexico* 115 C5
Mocuba, *Mozam.* 83 F4
Mocúzari, Presa, *Mexico* 114 B3
Modane, *France* 27 C10
Modasa, *India* 62 H5
Modave, *Belgium* 17 H6
Modder →, *S. Africa* 84 D3
Modderrivier, *S. Africa* 84 D3
Módena, *Italy* 32 D7
Modena, *U.S.A.* 111 H7
Modesto, *U.S.A.* 111 H3
Módica, *Italy* 35 F7
Modigliana, *Italy* 33 D8
Modo, *Sudan* 77 F3
Modra, *Czech.* 21 G7
Moe, *Australia* 91 F4
Moebase, *Mozam.* 83 F4
Moëlan-sur-Mer, *France* 24 E3
Moengo, *Surinam* 121 B7
Moergestel, *Neths.* 17 E6
Moers, *Germany* 17 F9
Moësa →, *Switz.* 23 D8
Moffat, *U.K.* 14 F5
Moga, *India* 62 D6
Mogadishu = Muqdisho, *Somali Rep.* 68 G4
Mogador = Essaouira, *Morocco* 74 B3
Mogadouro, *Portugal* 30 D4
Mogalakwena →, *S. Africa* 85 C4
Mogami →, *Japan* 48 E10
Mogán, *Canary Is.* 36 G4
Mogaung, *Burma* 61 G20
Møgeltønder, *Denmark* 11 K2
Mogente, *Spain* 29 G4
Mogho, *Ethiopia* 77 G5
Mogi das Cruzes, *Brazil* 127 A6
Mogi-Guaçu →, *Brazil* 127 A6
Mogi-Mirim, *Brazil* 127 A6
Mogielnica, *Poland* 20 D10
Mogilev, *Belorussia* 40 E7
Mogilev-Podolskiy, *Moldavia* 42 B2
Mogilno, *Poland* 20 C7
Mogincual, *Mozam.* 83 F5
Mogliano Véneto, *Italy* 33 C9
Mogocha, *Russia* 45 D12
Mogoi, *Indonesia* 57 E8
Mogok, *Burma* 61 H20
Moguer, *Spain* 31 H4
Mogumber, *Australia* 89 F2
Mohács, *Hungary* 21 K8
Mohales Hoek, *Lesotho* 84 E4
Mohall, *U.S.A.* 108 A4
Moḩammadābād, *Iran* 65 B8
Mohammadia, *Algeria* 75 A5
Mohammedia, *Morocco* 74 B3
Mohave, L., *U.S.A.* 113 K12
Mohawk →, *U.S.A.* 107 D11
Möhne →, *Germany* 18 D3
Moholm, *Sweden* 11 F8
Mohoro, *Tanzania* 82 D4
Moia, *Sudan* 77 F2
Moidart, L., *U.K.* 14 E3
Moineşti, *Romania* 38 C9
Mointy, *Kazakhstan* 44 E8
Moirans, *France* 27 C9
Moirans-en-Montagne, *France* 27 B9
Moíres, *Greece* 37 D6
Moisakula, *Estonia* 40 B4
Moisie, *Canada* 99 B6
Moisie →, *Canada* 99 B6
Moissac, *France* 26 D5
Moïssala, *Chad* 73 G8
Moita, *Portugal* 31 G2
Mojácar, *Spain* 29 H3
Mojados, *Spain* 30 D6
Mojave, *U.S.A.* 113 K8
Mojave Desert, *U.S.A.* 113 L10
Mojiang, *China* 52 F3
Mojo, *Bolivia* 126 A2
Mojo, *Ethiopia* 77 F4
Mojokerto, *Indonesia* 57 G15
Mojos, Llanos de, *Bolivia* 125 D5
Moju →, *Brazil* 122 B2
Mokai, *N.Z.* 87 H5
Mokambo, *Zaïre* 83 E2
Mokameh, *India* 63 G11
Mokelumne →, *U.S.A.* 112 G5
Mokelumne Hill, *U.S.A.* 112 G6
Mokhós, *Greece* 37 D7
Mokhotlong, *Lesotho* 85 D4
Moknine, *Tunisia* 75 A7
Mokokchung, *India* 61 F19
Mokra Gora, *Serbia, Yug.* 21 N10
Mokronog, *Slovenia* 33 C12
Moksha →, *Russia* 41 D12
Mokshan, *Russia* 41 E14
Mol, *Belgium* 17 F6
Mola, C. de la, *Spain* 28 F9
Mola di Bari, *Italy* 35 A10
Moláoi, *Greece* 39 N5
Molat, *Croatia* 33 D11
Molchanovo, *Russia* 44 D9
Mold, *U.K.* 12 D4
Moldavia = Moldova, *Romania* 38 C10
Moldavia ■, *Europe* 42 C3
Molde, *Norway* 8 E9
Moldova, *Romania* 38 C10
Moldova Nouă, *Romania* 38 E4
Moldoveanu, *Romania* 38 D7
Molepolole, *Botswana* 84 C4
Moléson, *Switz.* 22 C4
Molfetta, *Italy* 35 A9
Molina de Aragón, *Spain* 28 E3
Moline, *U.S.A.* 108 E9
Molinella, *Italy* 33 D8
Molinos, *Argentina* 126 B2
Moliro, *Zaïre* 82 D3
Molise □, *Italy* 33 G11
Moliterno, *Italy* 35 B8
Mollahat, *Bangla.* 63 H13
Mölle, *Sweden* 11 H6
Molledo, *Spain* 30 B6
Mollendo, *Peru* 124 D3
Mollerin, L., *Australia* 89 F2
Mollerusa, *Spain* 28 D5
Mollina, *Spain* 31 H6
Mölln, *Germany* 18 B6
Mölltorp, *Sweden* 11 F8
Mölndal, *Sweden* 11 G6
Molochansk, *Ukraine* 42 C6
Molochnaya →, *Ukraine* 42 C6
Molodechno, *Belorussia* 40 D5
Molokai, *U.S.A.* 102 H16
Moloma →, *Russia* 41 B16
Molong, *Australia* 91 E4
Molopo →, *Africa* 84 D3
Mólos, *Greece* 39 L5
Molotov = Perm, *Russia* 44 D6
Moloundou, *Cameroon* 80 D3
Molsheim, *France* 25 D14
Molson L., *Canada* 101 C9
Molteno, *S. Africa* 84 E4
Molu, *Indonesia* 57 F8
Molucca Sea = Maluku Sea, *Indonesia* 57 E6
Moluccas = Maluku, *Indonesia* 57 E7
Moma, *Mozam.* 83 F4
Moma, *Zaïre* 82 C1
Mombaça, *Brazil* 122 C4
Mombasa, *Kenya* 82 C4
Mombetsu, *Japan* 48 B11
Mombuey, *Spain* 30 C4
Momchilgrad, *Bulgaria* 39 H8
Momi, *Zaïre* 82 C2
Momignies, *Belgium* 17 H4
Mompós, *Colombia* 120 B3
Møn, *Denmark* 11 K6
Mon →, *Burma* 61 J19
Mona, Canal de la, *W. Indies* 117 C6
Mona, I., *Puerto Rico* 117 C6
Mona, Pta., *Costa Rica* 116 E3
Mona, Pta., *Spain* 31 J7
Monach Is., *U.K.* 14 D1
Monaco ■, *Europe* 27 E11
Monadhliath Mts., *U.K.* 14 D4
Monagas □, *Venezuela* 121 B5
Monaghan, *Ireland* 15 B5
Monaghan □, *Ireland* 15 B5
Monahans, *U.S.A.* 109 K3
Monapo, *Mozam.* 83 E5
Monarch Mt., *Canada* 100 C3
Monastir = Bitola, *Macedonia, Yug.* 39 H4
Monastir, *Tunisia* 75 A7
Monastyriska, *Ukraine* 40 G4
Moncada, *Phil.* 55 D4
Moncada, *Spain* 28 F4
Moncalieri, *Italy* 32 D4
Moncalvo, *Italy* 32 C5
Moncão, *Portugal* 30 C2
Moncarapacho, *Portugal* 31 H3
Moncayo, Sierra del, *Spain* 28 D3
Mönchengladbach, *Germany* 18 D2
Monchique, *Portugal* 31 H2
Monclova, *Mexico* 114 B4
Moncontour, *France* 24 D4
Moncoutant, *France* 26 B3
Moncton, *Canada* 99 C7
Mondego →, *Portugal* 30 E2
Mondego, C., *Portugal* 30 E2
Mondeodo, *Indonesia* 57 E6
Mondolfo, *Italy* 33 E10
Mondoñedo, *Spain* 30 B3
Mondoví, *Italy* 32 D4
Mondovi, *U.S.A.* 108 C9
Mondragon, *France* 27 D8
Mondragon, *Phil.* 55 E6
Mondragone, *Italy* 34 A6
Mondrain I., *Australia* 89 F3
Monduli □, *Tanzania* 82 C4
Monemvasía, *Greece* 39 N6
Monessen, *U.S.A.* 106 F5
Monesterio, *Spain* 31 G4
Monestier-de-Clermont, *France* 27 D9
Monett, *U.S.A.* 109 G8

Monfalcone, *Italy* 33 C10
Monflanquin, *France* 26 D4
Monforte, *Portugal* 31 F3
Monforte de Lemos, *Spain* 30 C3
Mong Hsu, *Burma* 61 J21
Mong Kung, *Burma* 61 J20
Mong Nai, *Burma* 61 J20
Mong Pawk, *Burma* 61 H21
Mong Ton, *Burma* 61 J21
Mong Wa, *Burma* 61 J22
Mong Yai, *Burma* 61 H21
Mongalla, *Sudan* 77 F3
Mongers, L., *Australia* 89 E2
Monghyr = Munger, *India* 63 G12
Mongo, *Chad* 73 F8
Mongolia ■, *Asia* 54 B5
Mongonu, *Nigeria* 79 C7
Mongororo, *Chad* 73 F9
Mongu, *Zambia* 81 H4
Mônguá, *Angola* 84 B2
Monistrol-d'Allier, *France* 26 D7
Monistrol-sur-Loire, *France* 27 C8
Monkey Bay, *Malawi* 83 E4
Monkey River, *Belize* 115 D7
Monkira, *Australia* 90 C3
Monkoto, *Zaïre* 80 E4
Monmouth, *U.K.* 13 F5
Monmouth, *U.S.A.* 108 E9
Mono, L., *U.S.A.* 111 H4
Monolith, *U.S.A.* 113 K8
Monólithos, *Greece* 37 C9
Monongahela, *U.S.A.* 106 F5
Monópoli, *Italy* 35 B10
Monor, *Hungary* 21 H9
Monóvar, *Spain* 29 G4
Monqoumba, *C.A.R.* 80 D3
Monreal del Campo, *Spain* 28 E3
Monreale, *Italy* 34 D6
Monroe, *Ga., U.S.A.* 105 J4
Monroe, *La., U.S.A.* 109 J8
Monroe, *Mich., U.S.A.* 104 E4
Monroe, *N.C., U.S.A.* 105 H5
Monroe, *N.Y., U.S.A.* 107 E10
Monroe, *Utah, U.S.A.* 111 G7
Monroe, *Wash., U.S.A.* 112 C5
Monroe, *Wis., U.S.A.* 108 D10
Monroe City, *U.S.A.* 108 F9
Monroeville, *Ala., U.S.A.* 105 K2
Monroeville, *Pa., U.S.A.* 106 F5
Monrovia, *Liberia* 78 D2
Monrovia, *U.S.A.* 111 J4
Mons, *Belgium* 17 H3
Monsaraz, *Portugal* 31 G3
Monse, *Indonesia* 57 E6
Monsefú, *Peru* 124 B2
Monségur, *France* 26 D4
Monsélice, *Italy* 33 C8
Monster, *Neths.* 16 D4
Mont Cenis, Col du, *France* 27 C10
Mont-de-Marsan, *France* 26 E3
Mont-Joli, *Canada* 99 C6
Mont-Laurier, *Canada* 98 C4
Mont-St.-Michel, Le = Le Mont-St.-Michel, *France* 24 D5
Mont-sous-Vaudrey, *France* 25 F12
Mont-sur-Marchienne, *Belgium* 17 H4
Mont Tremblant Prov. Park, *Canada* 98 C5
Montabaur, *Germany* 18 E3
Montagnac, *France* 26 E7
Montagnana, *Italy* 33 C8
Montagu, *S. Africa* 84 E3
Montagu I., *Antarctica* 5 B1
Montague, *Canada* 99 C7
Montague, *U.S.A.* 110 F2
Montague, I., *Mexico* 114 A2
Montague Ra., *Australia* 89 E2
Montague Sd., *Australia* 88 B4
Montaigu, *France* 24 F5
Montalbán, *Spain* 28 E4
Montalbano di Elicona, *Italy* 35 D8
Montalbano Iónico, *Italy* 35 B9
Montalbo, *Spain* 28 F2
Montalcino, *Italy* 33 E8
Montalegre, *Portugal* 30 D3
Montalto di Castro, *Italy* 33 F8
Montalto Uffugo, *Italy* 35 C9
Montalvo, *U.S.A.* 113 L7
Montamarta, *Spain* 30 D5
Montaña, *Peru* 124 B3
Montana, *Switz.* 22 D4
Montana □, *U.S.A.* 102 A5
Montaña Clara, I., *Canary Is.* 36 E6
Montánchez, *Spain* 31 F4
Montañita, *Colombia* 120 C2
Montargis, *France* 25 E9
Montauban, *France* 26 D5
Montauk, *U.S.A.* 107 E13
Montauk Pt., *U.S.A.* 107 E13
Montbard, *France* 25 E11
Montbéliard, *France* 25 E13
Montblanch, *Spain* 28 D6
Montbrison, *France* 27 C8
Montcalm, Pic de, *France* 26 F5
Montceau-les-Mines, *France* 25 F11
Montchanin, *France* 27 B8
Montclair, *U.S.A.* 107 F10
Montcornet, *France* 25 C11
Montcuq, *France* 26 D5
Montdidier, *France* 25 C9
Monte Albán, *Mexico* 115 D5
Monte Alegre, *Brazil* 121 D7
Monte Alegre de Goiás, *Brazil* 123 D2
Monte Alegre de Minas, *Brazil* 123 E2
Monte Azul, *Brazil* 123 E3
Monte Bello Is., *Australia* 88 D2
Monte-Carlo, *Monaco* 27 E11
Monte Carmelo, *Brazil* 123 E2
Monte Caseros, *Argentina* 126 C4
Monte Comán, *Argentina* 126 C2
Monte Cristi, *Dom. Rep.* 117 C5
Monte Dinero, *Argentina* 128 D3
Monte Lindo →, *Paraguay* 126 A4
Monte Quemado, *Argentina* 126 B3
Monte Redondo, *Portugal* 30 F2
Monte Rio, *U.S.A.* 112 G4
Monte San Giovanni, *Italy* 34 A6
Monte San Savino, *Italy* 33 E8
Monte Sant' Ángelo, *Italy* 35 A8
Monte Santu, C. di, *Italy* 34 B2
Monte Vista, *U.S.A.* 111 H10
Monteagudo, *Argentina* 127 B5
Monteagudo, *Bolivia* 125 D5
Montealegre, *Spain* 29 G3
Montebello, *Canada* 98 C5
Montebelluna, *Italy* 33 C9
Montebourg, *France* 24 C5
Montecastrilli, *Italy* 33 F9
Montecatini Terme, *Italy* 32 E7
Montecito, *U.S.A.* 113 L7
Montecristi, *Ecuador* 120 D1
Montecristo, *Italy* 32 F7
Montefalco, *Italy* 33 F9
Montefiascone, *Italy* 33 F9
Montefrío, *Spain* 31 H6
Montegnée, *Belgium* 17 G7
Montego Bay, *Jamaica* 116 C4
Montegranaro, *Italy* 33 E10
Monteiro, *Brazil* 122 C4
Montejicar, *Spain* 29 H1
Montejinnie, *Australia* 88 C5
Montelíbano, *Colombia* 120 B2
Montélimar, *France* 27 D8
Montella, *Italy* 35 B8
Montellano, *Spain* 31 J5
Montello, *U.S.A.* 108 D10
Montelupo Fiorentino, *Italy* 32 E8
Montemor-o-Novo, *Portugal* 31 G2
Montemor-o-Velho, *Portugal* 30 E2
Montemorelos, *Mexico* 115 B5
Montendre, *France* 26 C3
Montenegro, *Brazil* 127 B5
Montenegro □, *Montenegro, Yug.* 21 N9
Montenero di Bisaccia, *Italy* 33 G11
Montepuez, *Mozam.* 83 E4
Montepuez →, *Mozam.* 83 E5
Montepulciano, *Italy* 33 E8
Montereale, *Italy* 33 F10
Montereau-Fault-Yonne, *France* 25 D9
Monterey, *U.S.A.* 111 H3
Monterey B., *U.S.A.* 112 J5
Montería, *Colombia* 120 B2
Monteros, *Bolivia* 125 D5
Monteros, *Argentina* 126 B2
Monterotondo, *Italy* 33 F9
Monterrey, *Mexico* 114 B4
Montes Altos, *Brazil* 122 C2
Montes Claros, *Brazil* 123 E3
Montesano, *U.S.A.* 112 D3
Montesárchio, *Italy* 35 A7
Montescaglioso, *Italy* 35 B9
Montesilvano, *Italy* 33 F11
Montevarchi, *Italy* 33 E8
Montevideo, *Uruguay* 127 C4
Montevideo, *U.S.A.* 108 C7
Montezuma, *U.S.A.* 108 E8
Montfaucon, *France* 25 C12
Montfaucon-en-Velay, *France* 27 C8
Montfort, *France* 24 D5
Montfort, *Neths.* 17 F7
Montfort-l'Amaury, *France* 25 D8
Montgenèvre, *France* 27 D10
Montgomery = Sahiwal, *Pakistan* 62 D5
Montgomery, *U.K.* 13 E4
Montgomery, *Ala., U.S.A.* 105 J2
Montgomery, *W. Va., U.S.A.* 104 F5
Montguyon, *France* 26 C3
Monthey, *Switz.* 22 D3
Monticelli d'Ongina, *Italy* 32 C6
Monticello, *Ark., U.S.A.* 109 J9
Monticello, *Fla., U.S.A.* 105 K4
Monticello, *Ind., U.S.A.* 104 E2
Monticello, *Iowa, U.S.A.* 108 D9
Monticello, *Ky., U.S.A.* 105 G3
Monticello, *Minn., U.S.A.* 108 C8
Monticello, *Miss., U.S.A.* 109 K9
Monticello, *N.Y., U.S.A.* 107 E10
Monticello, *Utah, U.S.A.* 111 H9
Montichiari, *Italy* 32 C7
Montier-en-Der, *France* 25 D11
Montignac, *France* 26 C5
Montignies-sur-Sambre, *Belgium* 17 H4
Montigny, *France* 25 C13
Montigny-sur-Aube, *France* 25 E11
Montijo, *Spain* 31 G4
Montijo, Presa de, *Spain* 31 G4
Montilla, *Spain* 31 H6
Montlhéry, *France* 25 D9
Montluçon, *France* 26 B6
Montmagny, *Canada* 99 C5
Montmarault, *France* 26 B6
Montmartre, *Canada* 101 C8
Montmédy, *France* 25 C12
Montmélian, *France* 27 C10
Montmirail, *France* 25 D10
Montmoreau-St.-Cybard, *France* 26 C4
Montmorency, *Canada* 99 C5
Montmorillon, *France* 26 B4
Montmort, *France* 25 D10
Monto, *Australia* 90 C5
Montoir-sur-le-Loir, *France* 24 E7
Montório al Vomano, *Italy* 33 F10
Montoro, *Spain* 31 G6
Montour Falls, *U.S.A.* 106 D8
Montpelier, *Idaho, U.S.A.* 110 E8
Montpelier, *Ohio, U.S.A.* 104 E3
Montpelier, *Vt., U.S.A.* 107 B12
Montpellier, *France* 26 E7
Montpezat-de-Quercy, *France* 26 D5
Montpon-Ménestérol, *France* 26 D4
Montréal, *Canada* 98 C5
Montréal, *France* 26 E6
Montreal L., *Canada* 101 C7
Montreal Lake, *Canada* 101 C7
Montredon-Labessonnié, *France* 26 E6
Montréjeau, *France* 26 E4
Montrésor, *France* 24 E8
Montreuil, *France* 25 B8
Montreuil-Bellay, *France* 24 E6
Montreux, *Switz.* 22 D3
Montrevault, *France* 24 E5
Montrevel-en-Bresse, *France* 27 B9
Montrichard, *France* 24 E8
Montrose, *U.K.* 14 E6
Montrose, *Colo., U.S.A.* 111 G10
Montrose, *Pa., U.S.A.* 107 E9
Monts, Pte. des, *Canada* 99 C6
Monts-sur-Guesnes, *France* 24 F7
Montsalvy, *France* 26 D6
Montsant, Sierra de, *Spain* 28 D5
Montsauche, *France* 25 E11
Montsech, Sierra del, *Spain* 28 C5
Montseny, *Spain* 28 D2
Montserrat, *Spain* 28 D6
Montserrat, *W. Indies* 117 C7
Montuenga, *Spain* 30 D6
Montuiri, *Spain* 36 B9
Monveda, *Zaïre* 80 D4
Monywa, *Burma* 61 H19
Monza, *Italy* 32 C6
Monze, *Zambia* 83 F2
Monze, C., *Pakistan* 62 G2
Monzón, *Spain* 28 D5
Mooi River, *S. Africa* 85 D4
Mook, *Neths.* 16 E7
Moolawatana, *Australia* 91 D2
Mooliabeenee, *Australia* 89 F2
Mooloogool, *Australia* 89 E2
Moomin Cr. →, *Australia* 91 D4
Moonah →, *Australia* 90 C2
Moonbeam, *Canada* 98 C3
Moonda, L., *Australia* 90 D3
Moonie, *Australia* 91 D5
Moonie →, *Australia* 91 D4
Moonta, *Australia* 91 E2
Moora, *Australia* 89 F2
Mooraberree, *Australia* 90 D3
Moorarie, *Australia* 89 E2
Moorcroft, *U.S.A.* 108 C2
Moore →, *Australia* 89 F2
Moore, L., *Australia* 89 E2
Moore Reefs, *Australia* 90 B4
Moorefield, *U.S.A.* 104 F6
Moores Res., *U.S.A.* 107 B13
Mooresville, *U.S.A.* 105 H5
Moorfoot Hills, *U.K.* 14 F5
Moorhead, *U.S.A.* 108 B6
Mooroopna, *Australia* 91 F4
Moorpark, *U.S.A.* 113 L8
Moorreesburg, *S. Africa* 84 E2
Moorslede, *Belgium* 17 G2
Moosburg, *Germany* 19 G7
Moose →, *Canada* 98 B3
Moose Factory, *Canada* 98 B3
Moose I., *Canada* 101 C9
Moose Jaw, *Canada* 101 C7
Moose Jaw →, *Canada* 101 C7
Moose Lake, *Canada* 101 C8
Moose Lake, *U.S.A.* 108 B8
Moose Mountain Cr. →, *Canada* 101 D8
Moose Mountain Prov. Park, *Canada* 101 D8
Moose River, *Canada* 98 B3
Moosehead L., *U.S.A.* 99 C6
Moosomin, *Canada* 101 C8
Moosonee, *Canada* 98 B3
Moosup, *U.S.A.* 107 E13
Mopeia Velha, *Mozam.* 83 F4
Mopipi, *Botswana* 84 C3
Mopoi, *C.A.R.* 82 A2
Mopti, *Mali* 78 C4
Moqatta, *Sudan* 77 E4
Moquegua, *Peru* 124 D3
Moquegua □, *Peru* 124 D3
Mór, *Hungary* 21 H8
Móra, *Portugal* 31 G2
Mora, *Sweden* 9 F13
Mora, *Minn., U.S.A.* 108 C8
Mora, *N. Mex., U.S.A.* 111 J11
Mora de Ebro, *Spain* 28 D5
Mora de Rubielos, *Spain* 28 E4
Mora la Nueva, *Spain* 28 D5
Morača →, *Montenegro, Yug.* 21 N9
Morada Nova, *Brazil* 122 C4
Morada Nova de Minas, *Brazil* 123 E2
Moradabad, *India* 63 E8
Morafenobe, *Madag.* 85 B7
Morąg, *Poland* 20 B9
Moral de Calatrava, *Spain* 29 G1
Moraleja, *Spain* 30 E4
Morales, *Colombia* 120 C2
Moramanga, *Madag.* 85 B8
Moran, *Kans., U.S.A.* 109 G7
Moran, *Wyo., U.S.A.* 110 E8
Moranbah, *Australia* 90 C4
Morano Cálabro, *Italy* 35 C9
Morant Cays, *Jamaica* 116 C4
Morant Pt., *Jamaica* 116 C4
Morar, L., *U.K.* 14 E3
Moratalla, *Spain* 29 G3
Moratuwa, *Sri Lanka* 60 R11
Morava →, *Czech.* 20 G6
Moravia, *U.S.A.* 108 E8
Moravian Hts. = Ceskomoravská Vrchovina, *Czech.* 20 F5
Moravica →, *Serbia, Yug.* 21 M10
Moravice →, *Czech.* 20 F7
Moraviţa, *Romania* 21 K11
Moravská Třebová, *Czech.* 20 F6
Morawa, *Australia* 89 E2
Morawhanna, *Guyana* 121 B6
Moray Firth, *U.K.* 14 D5
Morbach, *Germany* 19 F3
Morbegno, *Italy* 32 B6
Morbi, *India* 62 H4
Morbihan □, *France* 24 E4
Morcenx, *France* 26 D3
Mordelles, *France* 24 D5
Morden, *Canada* 101 D9
Mordovian Republic □, *Russia* 41 D14
Mordovo, *Russia* 41 E12
Møre og Romsdal fylke □, *Norway* 10 B2
Morea, *Australia* 91 F3
Morea, *Greece* 6 H10
Moreau →, *U.S.A.* 108 C4
Morecambe, *U.K.* 12 C5
Morecambe B., *U.K.* 12 C5
Moree, *Australia* 91 D4
Morehead, *U.S.A.* 104 F4
Morehead City, *U.S.A.* 105 H7
Morelia, *Mexico* 114 D4
Morella, *Australia* 90 C3
Morella, *Spain* 28 E4
Morelos, *Mexico* 114 B3
Morelos □, *Mexico* 115 D5
Morena, Sierra, *Spain* 31 G7
Morenci, *U.S.A.* 111 K9
Moreni, *Romania* 38 E8
Morero, *Bolivia* 125 C4
Moreru →, *Brazil* 125 C6
Moresby I., *Canada* 100 C2
Morestel, *France* 27 C9
Moret-sur-Loing, *France* 25 D9
Moreton, *Australia* 90 A3
Moreton I., *Australia* 91 D5
Moreuil, *France* 25 C9
Morey, *Spain* 36 B10
Morez, *France* 27 B10
Morgan, *Australia* 91 E2
Morgan, *U.S.A.* 110 F8
Morgan City, *U.S.A.* 109 L9
Morgan Hill, *U.S.A.* 112 H5
Morganfield, *U.S.A.* 104 G2
Morganton, *U.S.A.* 105 H5
Morgantown, *U.S.A.* 104 F6
Morgat, *France* 24 D2
Morgenzon, *S. Africa* 85 D4
Morges, *Switz.* 22 C3
Morghak, *Iran* 65 D8
Morhange, *France* 25 D13
Mori, *Italy* 32 C7
Morialmée, *Belgium* 17 H5
Morice L., *Canada* 100 C3
Morichal, *Colombia* 120 C3
Morichal Largo →, *Venezuela* 121 B5
Moriki, *Nigeria* 79 C6
Morinville, *Canada* 100 C6
Morioka, *Japan* 48 E10
Moris, *Mexico* 114 B3
Morlaàs, *France* 26 E3
Morlaix, *France* 24 D3
Morlanwelz, *Belgium* 17 H4
Mormanno, *Italy* 35 C8
Mormant, *France* 25 D9
Mornington, *Vic., Australia* 91 F4
Mornington, *W. Austral., Australia* 88 C4
Mornington, I., *Chile* 128 C1
Mornington I., *Australia* 90 B2
Mórnos →, *Greece* 39 L4
Moro, *Sudan* 77 E3
Moro G., *Phil.* 55 H5
Morocco ■, *N. Afr.* 74 B3
Morococha, *Peru* 124 C2
Morogoro, *Tanzania* 82 D4
Morogoro □, *Tanzania* 82 D4
Moroleón, *Mexico* 114 C4
Morombe, *Madag.* 85 C7
Moron, *Argentina* 126 C4
Morón, *Cuba* 116 B4
Mörön →, *Mongolia* 54 B6
Morón de Almazán, *Spain* 28 D2
Morón de la Frontera, *Spain* 31 H5
Morona →, *Peru* 120 D2
Morona-Santiago □, *Ecuador* 120 D2
Morondava, *Madag.* 85 C7
Morondo, *Ivory C.* 78 D3
Morongo Valley, *U.S.A.* 113 L10
Moronou, *Ivory C.* 78 D4
Morotai, *Indonesia* 57 D7
Moroto, *Uganda* 82 B3
Moroto Summit, *Kenya* 82 B3
Morozovsk, *Russia* 43 B9
Morpeth, *U.K.* 12 B6
Morphou, *Cyprus* 37 D11
Morphou Bay, *Cyprus* 37 D11
Morrilton, *U.S.A.* 109 H8
Morrinhos, *Ceara, Brazil* 122 B3
Morrinhos, *Minas Gerais, Brazil* 123 E2
Morrinsville, *N.Z.* 87 G5
Morris, *Canada* 101 D9
Morris, *Ill., U.S.A.* 104 E1
Morris, *Minn., U.S.A.* 108 C7
Morris, Mt., *Australia* 89 E5
Morrisburg, *Canada* 98 D4
Morrison, *U.S.A.* 108 E10
Morristown, *Ariz., U.S.A.* 111 K7
Morristown, *N.J., U.S.A.* 107 F10
Morristown, *S. Dak., U.S.A.* 108 C4
Morristown, *Tenn., U.S.A.* 105 G4
Morro, Pta., *Chile* 126 B1
Morro Bay, *U.S.A.* 111 J3
Morro del Jable, *Canary Is.* 36 F5
Morro do Chapéu, *Brazil* 123 D3
Morro Jable, Pta. de, *Canary Is.* 36 F5
Morros, *Brazil* 122 B3
Morrosquillo, G. de, *Colombia* 116 E4
Morrumbene, *Mozam.* 85 C6
Mors, *Denmark* 11 H2
Morshansk, *Russia* 41 E12
Mörsil, *Sweden* 10 A7
Mortagne →, *France* 25 D13
Mortagne-au-Perche, *France* 24 D7
Mortagne-sur-Gironde, *France* 26 C3
Mortagne-sur-Sèvre, *France* 24 F6
Mortain, *France* 24 D6
Mortara, *Italy* 32 C5
Morteau, *France* 25 E13
Morteros, *Argentina* 126 C3
Mortes, R. das →, *Brazil* 123 D1
Mortlake, *Australia* 91 F3
Morton, *Tex., U.S.A.* 109 J3
Morton, *Wash., U.S.A.* 112 D4
Mortsel, *Belgium* 17 F4
Morundah, *Australia* 91 E4
Moruya, *Australia* 91 F5
Morvan, *France* 25 E11
Morven, *Australia* 91 D4
Morvern, *U.K.* 14 E3
Morwell, *Australia* 91 F4
Mosalsk, *Russia* 40 D9
Mosbach, *Germany* 19 F5
Moščenice, *Croatia* 33 C11
Mosciano Sant' Ángelo, *Italy* 33 F10
Moscos Is., *Burma* 58 E1
Moscow = Moskva, *Russia* 41 D10
Moscow, *U.S.A.* 110 C5
Mosel →, *Europe* 19 E3
Moselle = Mosel →, *Europe* 19 E3
Moselle □, *France* 25 D13
Moses Lake, *U.S.A.* 110 C4
Mosgiel, *N.Z.* 87 L3
Moshi, *Tanzania* 82 C4
Moshi □, *Tanzania* 82 C4
Moshupa, *Botswana* 84 C4
Mosjøen, *Norway* 8 D12
Moskenesøya, *Norway* 8 C12
Moskenstraumen, *Norway* 8 C12
Moskva, *Russia* 41 D10
Moskva →, *Russia* 41 D11
Moslavačka Gora, *Croatia* 33 C13
Mosomane, *Botswana* 84 C4
Mosonmagyaróvár, *Hungary* 21 H7
Mospino, *Ukraine* 42 C7
Mosquera, *Colombia* 120 C2
Mosquero, *U.S.A.* 109 H3
Mosqueruela, *Spain* 28 E4
Mosquitia, *Honduras* 116 C3
Mosquitos, G. de los, *Panama* 116 E3
Moss, *Norway* 10 E4
Moss Vale, *Australia* 91 E5
Mossaka, *Congo* 80 E3

Mossâmedes, *Brazil* 123 E1
Mossbank, *Canada* 101 D7
Mossburn, *N.Z.* 87 L2
Mosselbaai, *S. Africa* 84 E3
Mossendjo, *Congo* 80 E2
Mosses, Col des, *Switz.* 22 D4
Mossgiel, *Australia* 91 E3
Mossman, *Australia* 90 B4
Mossoró, *Brazil* 122 C4
Mossuril, *Mozam.* 83 E5
Mossy →, *Canada* 101 C8
Most, *Czech.* 20 E3
Mosta, *Malta* 37 D1
Moştafáābād, *Iran* 65 C7
Mostaganem, *Algeria* 75 A5
Mostar, *Bos.-H., Yug.* 21 M7
Mostardas, *Brazil* 127 C5
Mostefa, Rass, *Tunisia* 75 A7
Mostiska, *Ukraine* 40 G3
Móstoles, *Spain* 30 E7
Mosty, *Belorussia* 40 E4
Mosul = Al Mawşil, *Iraq* 64 B4
Mosulpo, *S. Korea* 51 H14
Mota del Cuervo, *Spain* 28 F2
Mota del Marqués, *Spain* 30 D5
Motagua →, *Guatemala* 116 C2
Motala, *Sweden* 11 F9
Motherwell, *U.K.* 14 F5
Motihari, *India* 63 F11
Motilla del Palancar, *Spain* 28 F3
Motnik, *Slovenia* 33 B11
Motocurunya, *Venezuela* 121 C5
Motovun, *Croatia* 33 C10
Motozintla de Mendoza, *Mexico* 115 D6
Motril, *Spain* 29 J1
Motru →, *Romania* 38 E6
Mott, *U.S.A.* 108 B3
Móttola, *Italy* 35 B10
Motueka, *N.Z.* 87 J4
Motueka →, *N.Z.* 87 J4
Motul, *Mexico* 115 C7
Mouanda, *Gabon* 80 E2
Mouchalagane →, *Canada* 99 B6
Mouding, *China* 52 E3
Moudjeria, *Mauritania* 78 B2
Moudon, *Switz.* 22 C3
Mouila, *Gabon* 80 E2
Moulamein, *Australia* 91 F3
Moulianá, *Greece* 37 D7
Moulins, *France* 26 B7
Moulmein, *Burma* 61 L20
Moulouya, O. →, *Morocco* 75 A4
Moulton, *U.S.A.* 109 L6
Moultrie, *U.S.A.* 105 K4
Moultrie, L., *U.S.A.* 105 J5
Mound City, *Mo., U.S.A.* 108 E7
Mound City, *S. Dak., U.S.A.* 108 C4
Moúnda, Ákra, *Greece* 39 L3
Moundou, *Chad* 73 G8
Moundsville, *U.S.A.* 106 G4
Moung, *Cambodia* 58 F4
Mount Airy, *U.S.A.* 105 G5
Mount Albert, *Canada* 106 B5
Mount Amherst, *Australia* 88 C4
Mount Angel, *U.S.A.* 110 D2
Mount Augustus, *Australia* 88 D2
Mount Barker, *S. Austral., Australia* 91 F2
Mount Barker, *W. Austral., Australia* 89 F2
Mount Carmel, *U.S.A.* 104 F2
Mount Clemens, *U.S.A.* 98 D3
Mount Coolon, *Australia* 90 C4
Mount Darwin, *Zimbabwe* 83 F3
Mount Desert I., *U.S.A.* 99 D6
Mount Dora, *U.S.A.* 105 L5
Mount Douglas, *Australia* 90 C4
Mount Eba, *Australia* 91 E2
Mount Edgecumbe, *U.S.A.* 100 B1
Mount Elizabeth, *Australia* 88 C4
Mount Fletcher, *S. Africa* 85 E4
Mount Forest, *Canada* 98 D3
Mount Gambier, *Australia* 91 F3
Mount Garnet, *Australia* 90 B4
Mount Hope, *N.S.W., Australia* 91 E4
Mount Hope, *S. Austral., Australia* 91 E2
Mount Hope, *U.S.A.* 104 G5
Mount Horeb, *U.S.A.* 108 D10
Mount Howitt, *Australia* 91 D3
Mount Isa, *Australia* 90 C2
Mount Keith, *Australia* 89 E3
Mount Laguna, *U.S.A.* 113 N10
Mount Larcom, *Australia* 90 C5
Mount Lofty Ra., *Australia* 91 E2
Mount McKinley Nat. Park, *U.S.A.* 96 B5
Mount Magnet, *Australia* 89 E2
Mount Margaret, *Australia* 91 D3
Mount Maunganui, *N.Z.* 87 G6
Mount Molloy, *Australia* 90 B4
Mount Monger, *Australia* 89 F3
Mount Morgan, *Australia* 90 C5
Mount Morris, *U.S.A.* 106 D7
Mount Mulligan, *Australia* 90 B3
Mount Narryer, *Australia* 89 E2
Mount Olympus = Uludağ, *Turkey* 66 C3
Mount Oxide Mine, *Australia* 90 B2
Mount Pearl, *Canada* 99 C9
Mount Perry, *Australia* 91 D5
Mount Phillips, *Australia* 88 D2
Mount Pleasant, *Iowa, U.S.A.* 108 E9
Mount Pleasant, *Mich., U.S.A.* 104 D3
Mount Pleasant, *Pa., U.S.A.* 106 F5
Mount Pleasant, *S.C., U.S.A.* 105 J6
Mount Pleasant, *Tenn., U.S.A.* 105 H2
Mount Pleasant, *Tex., U.S.A.* 109 J7
Mount Pleasant, *Utah, U.S.A.* 110 G8
Mount Pocono, *U.S.A.* 107 E9
Mount Rainier Nat. Park., *U.S.A.* 112 D5
Mount Revelstoke Nat. Park, *Canada* 100 C5
Mount Robson Prov. Park, *Canada* 100 C5
Mount Sandiman, *Australia* 89 D2
Mount Shasta, *U.S.A.* 110 F2
Mount Signal, *U.S.A.* 113 N11
Mount Sterling, *Ill., U.S.A.* 108 F9
Mount Sterling, *Ky., U.S.A.* 104 F4
Mount Surprise, *Australia* 90 B3
Mount Union, *U.S.A.* 106 F7
Mount Vernon, *Australia* 88 D2
Mount Vernon, *Ind., U.S.A.* 108 F10
Mount Vernon, *N.Y., U.S.A.* 107 F11
Mount Vernon, *Ohio, U.S.A.* 106 F2
Mount Vernon, *Wash., U.S.A.* 112 B4
Mountain Center, *U.S.A.* 113 M10
Mountain City, *Nev., U.S.A.* 110 F6
Mountain City, *Tenn., U.S.A.* 105 G5
Mountain Grove, *U.S.A.* 109 G8
Mountain Home, *Ark., U.S.A.* 109 G8
Mountain Home, *Idaho, U.S.A.* 110 E6
Mountain Iron, *U.S.A.* 108 B8
Mountain Park, *Canada* 100 C5
Mountain Pass, *U.S.A.* 113 K11
Mountain View, *Ark., U.S.A.* 109 H8
Mountain View, *Calif., U.S.A.* 111 H2
Mountainair, *U.S.A.* 111 J10
Mountmellick, *Ireland* 15 C4
Moura, *Australia* 90 C4
Moura, *Brazil* 121 D5
Moura, *Portugal* 31 G3
Mourão, *Portugal* 31 G3
Mourdi, Dépression du, *Chad* 73 E9
Mourdiah, *Mali* 78 C3
Mourenx-Ville-Nouvelle, *France* 26 E3
Mouri, *Ghana* 79 D4
Mourilyan, *Australia* 90 B4
Mourmelon-le-Grand, *France* 25 C11
Mourne →, *U.K.* 15 B4
Mourne Mts., *U.K.* 15 B5
Mournies, *Greece* 37 D6
Mouscron, *Belgium* 17 G2
Moussoro, *Chad* 73 F8
Mouthe, *France* 25 F13
Moutier, *Switz.* 22 B4
Moûtiers, *France* 27 C10
Moutohara, *N.Z.* 87 H6
Moutong, *Indonesia* 57 D6
Mouy, *France* 25 C9
Mouzáki, *Greece* 39 K4
Movas, *Mexico* 114 B3
Moville, *Ireland* 15 A4
Moxhe, *Belgium* 17 G6
Moxotó →, *Brazil* 122 C4
Moy →, *Ireland* 15 B3
Moyale, *Kenya* 68 G2
Moyamba, *S. Leone* 78 D2
Moyen Atlas, *Morocco* 74 B3
Moyle □, *U.K.* 15 A5
Moyo, *Indonesia* 56 F5
Moyobamba, *Peru* 124 B2
Moyyero →, *Russia* 45 C11
Mozambique = Moçambique, *Mozam.* 83 F5
Mozambique ■, *Africa* 83 F4
Mozambique Chan., *Africa* 85 B7
Mozdok, *Russia* 43 E11
Mozdūrān, *Iran* 65 B9
Mozhaysk, *Russia* 41 D10
Mozhga, *Russia* 41 C18
Mozhnābād, *Iran* 65 C9
Mozirje, *Slovenia* 33 B11
Mozyr, *Belorussia* 40 E6
Mpanda, *Tanzania* 82 D3
Mpanda □, *Tanzania* 82 D3
Mpésoba, *Mali* 78 C3
Mpika, *Zambia* 83 E3
Mpulungu, *Zambia* 83 D3
Mpumalanga, *S. Africa* 85 D5
Mpwapwa, *Tanzania* 82 D4
Mpwapwa □, *Tanzania* 82 D4
Mrągowo, *Poland* 20 B11
Mramor, *Serbia, Yug.* 21 M11
Mrimina, *Morocco* 74 C3
Mrkonjić Grad, *Bos.-H., Yug.* 21 L7
Mrkopalj, *Croatia* 33 C11
Msab, Oued en →, *Algeria* 75 B6
Msaken, *Tunisia* 75 A7
Msambansovu, *Zimbabwe* 83 F3
M'sila, *Algeria* 75 A5
Msoro, *Zambia* 83 E3
Msta →, *Russia* 40 B7
Mstislavl, *Belorussia* 40 E7
Mtama, *Tanzania* 83 E4
Mtilikwe →, *Zimbabwe* 83 G3
Mtsensk, *Russia* 41 E10
Mtskheta, *Georgia* 43 F11
Mtubatuba, *S. Africa* 85 D5
Mtwara-Mikindani, *Tanzania* 83 E5
Mu Gia, Deo, *Vietnam* 58 D5
Mu Us Shamo, *China* 50 E5
Muaná, *Brazil* 122 B2
Muang Chiang Rai, *Thailand* 58 C2
Muang Lamphun, *Thailand* 58 C2
Muang Pak Beng, *Laos* 58 C3
Muar, *Malaysia* 59 L4
Muarabungo, *Indonesia* 56 E2
Muaraenim, *Indonesia* 56 E2
Muarajuloi, *Indonesia* 56 E4
Muarakaman, *Indonesia* 56 E5
Muaratebo, *Indonesia* 56 E2
Muaratembesi, *Indonesia* 56 E2
Muaratewe, *Indonesia* 56 E4
Mubarakpur, *India* 63 F10
Mubarraz = Al Mubarraz, *Si. Arabia* 65 E6
Mubende, *Uganda* 82 B3
Mubi, *Nigeria* 79 C7
Mubur, P., *Indonesia* 59 L6
Mucajaí →, *Brazil* 121 C5
Mucajaí, Serra do, *Brazil* 121 C5
Muchachos, Roque de los, *Canary Is.* 36 F2
Mücheln, *Germany* 18 D7
Muchinga Mts., *Zambia* 83 E3
Muchkapskiy, *Russia* 41 F13
Muck, *U.K.* 14 E2
Muckadilla, *Australia* 91 D4
Muco →, *Colombia* 120 C3
Muconda, *Angola* 80 G4
Mucuim →, *Brazil* 125 B5
Mucur, *Turkey* 66 D6
Mucura, *Brazil* 121 D5
Mucuri, *Brazil* 123 E4
Mucurici, *Brazil* 123 E3
Mucusso, *Angola* 84 B3
Muda, *Canary Is.* 36 F6
Mudan Jiang →, *China* 51 A15
Mudanjiang, *China* 51 B15
Mudanya, *Turkey* 42 F3
Muddy →, *U.S.A.* 111 H8
Mudgee, *Australia* 91 E4
Mudjatik →, *Canada* 101 B7
Mudurnu, *Turkey* 66 C4
Muecate, *Mozam.* 83 E4
Muêda, *Mozam.* 83 E4
Mueller Ra., *Australia* 88 C4
Muende, *Mozam.* 83 E3
Muerto, Mar, *Mexico* 115 D6
Muertos, Punta de los, *Spain* 29 J3
Mufindi □, *Tanzania* 83 D4
Mufu Shan, *China* 53 C10
Mufulira, *Zambia* 83 E2
Mufumbiro Range, *Africa* 82 C2
Mugardos, *Spain* 30 B2
Muge, *Portugal* 31 F2
Muge →, *Portugal* 31 F2
Múggia, *Italy* 33 C10
Mughayrā', *Si. Arabia* 64 D3
Mugi, *Japan* 49 H7
Mugia, *Spain* 30 B1
Mugila, Mts., *Zaïre* 82 D2
Muğla, *Turkey* 66 E3
Muğla □, *Turkey* 66 E3
Müglizh, *Bulgaria* 38 G8
Mugu, *Nepal* 63 E10
Muhammad, Râs, *Egypt* 76 B3
Muhammad Qol, *Sudan* 76 C4
Muhammadabad, *India* 63 F10
Muhesi →, *Tanzania* 82 D4
Muheza □, *Tanzania* 82 C4
Mühldorf, *Germany* 19 G8
Mühlhausen, *Germany* 18 D6
Mühlig Hofmann fjella, *Antarctica* 5 D3
Muhutwe, *Tanzania* 82 C3
Muiden, *Neths.* 16 D6
Muikamachi, *Japan* 49 F9
Muine Bheag, *Ireland* 15 D5
Muiños, *Spain* 30 D3
Muir, L., *Australia* 89 F2
Mukachevo, *Ukraine* 40 G3
Mukah, *Malaysia* 56 D4
Mukawwa, Geziret, *Egypt* 76 C4
Mukdahan, *Thailand* 58 D5
Mukden = Shenyang, *China* 51 D12
Mukhtolovo, *Russia* 41 D13
Mukhtuya = Lensk, *Russia* 45 C12
Mukinbudin, *Australia* 89 F2
Mukishi, *Zaïre* 83 D1
Mukomuko, *Indonesia* 56 E2
Mukomwenze, *Zaïre* 82 D2
Muktsar, *India* 62 D6
Mukur, *Afghan.* 62 C2
Mukutawa →, *Canada* 101 C9
Mukwela, *Zambia* 83 F2
Mula, *Spain* 29 G3
Mulange, *Zaïre* 82 C2
Mulchén, *Chile* 126 D1
Mulde →, *Germany* 18 D8
Mule Creek, *U.S.A.* 108 D2
Muleba, *Tanzania* 82 C3
Muleba □, *Tanzania* 82 C3
Mulegns, *Switz.* 23 C9
Muleshoe, *U.S.A.* 109 H3
Mulgathing, *Australia* 91 E1
Mulgrave, *Canada* 99 C7
Mulhacén, *Spain* 29 H1
Mülheim, *Germany* 18 D2
Mulhouse, *France* 25 E14
Muli, *China* 52 D3
Muling, *China* 51 B16
Mull, *U.K.* 14 E3
Mullaittvu, *Sri Lanka* 60 Q12
Mullen, *U.S.A.* 108 D4
Mullengudgery, *Australia* 91 E4
Mullens, *U.S.A.* 104 G5
Muller, Pegunungan, *Indonesia* 56 D4
Mullet Pen., *Ireland* 15 B1
Mullewa, *Australia* 89 E2
Müllheim, *Germany* 19 H3
Mulligan →, *Australia* 90 C2
Mullin, *U.S.A.* 109 K5
Mullingar, *Ireland* 15 C4
Mullins, *U.S.A.* 105 H6
Mullumbimby, *Australia* 91 D5
Mulobezi, *Zambia* 83 F2
Multan, *Pakistan* 62 D4
Multrå, *Sweden* 10 A11
Mulumbe, Mts., *Zaïre* 83 D2
Mulungushi Dam, *Zambia* 83 E2
Mulvane, *U.S.A.* 109 G6
Mulwad, *Sudan* 76 D3
Mulwala, *Australia* 91 F4
Mumbwa, *Zambia* 83 E2
Mumra, *Russia* 43 D12
Mun →, *Thailand* 58 E5
Muna, *Indonesia* 57 F6
Munamagi, *Estonia* 40 C5
Münchberg, *Germany* 19 E7
Müncheberg, *Germany* 18 C10
München, *Germany* 19 G7
Munchen-Gladbach = Mönchengladbach, *Germany* 18 D2
Muncho Lake, *Canada* 100 B3
Munchŏn, *N. Korea* 51 E14
Münchwilen, *Switz.* 23 B7
Muncie, *U.S.A.* 104 E3
Muncoonie, L., *Australia* 90 D2
Mundala, *Indonesia* 57 E10
Mundare, *Canada* 100 C6
Munday, *U.S.A.* 109 J5
Münden, *Germany* 18 D5
Mundiwindi, *Australia* 88 D3
Mundo →, *Spain* 29 G2
Mundo Novo, *Brazil* 123 D3
Mundra, *India* 62 H3
Mundrabilla, *Australia* 89 F4
Munducurus, *Brazil* 121 D6
Munera, *Spain* 29 F2
Mungallala, *Australia* 91 D4
Mungallala Cr. →, *Australia* 91 D4
Mungana, *Australia* 90 B3
Mungaoli, *India* 62 G8
Mungari, *Mozam.* 83 F3
Mungbere, *Zaïre* 82 B2
Munger, *India* 63 G12
Mungindi, *Australia* 91 D4
Munhango, *Angola* 81 G3
Munich = München, *Germany* 19 G7
Munising, *U.S.A.* 104 B2
Munka-Ljungby, *Sweden* 11 H6
Munkedal, *Sweden* 11 F5
Munku-Sardyk, *Russia* 45 D11
Münnerstadt, *Germany* 19 E6
Muñoz Gamero, Pen., *Chile* 128 D2
Munroe L., *Canada* 101 B9
Munsan, *S. Korea* 51 F14
Münsingen, *Switz.* 22 C5
Munster, *France* 25 D14
Munster, *Niedersachsen, Germany* 18 C6
Münster, *Nordrhein-Westfalen, Germany* 18 D3
Münster, *Switz.* 23 D6
Munster □, *Ireland* 15 D3
Muntadgin, *Australia* 89 F2
Muntele Mare, *Romania* 38 C6
Muntok, *Indonesia* 56 E3
Munyak, *Uzbekistan* 44 E6
Munyama, *Zambia* 83 F2
Muong Beng, *Laos* 58 B3
Muong Boum, *Vietnam* 58 A4
Muong Et, *Laos* 58 B5
Muong Hai, *Laos* 58 B3
Muong Hiem, *Laos* 58 B4
Muong Houn, *Laos* 58 B3
Muong Hung, *Vietnam* 58 B4
Muong Kau, *Laos* 58 E5
Muong Khao, *Laos* 58 C4
Muong Khoua, *Laos* 58 B4
Muong Liep, *Laos* 58 C3
Muong May, *Laos* 58 E6
Muong Ngeun, *Laos* 58 B3
Muong Ngoi, *Laos* 58 B4
Muong Nhie, *Vietnam* 58 A4
Muong Nong, *Laos* 58 D6
Muong Ou Tay, *Laos* 58 A3
Muong Oua, *Laos* 58 C3
Muong Peun, *Laos* 58 B4
Muong Phalane, *Laos* 58 D5
Muong Phieng, *Laos* 58 C3
Muong Phine, *Laos* 58 D6
Muong Sai, *Laos* 58 B3
Muong Saiapoun, *Laos* 58 C3
Muong Sen, *Vietnam* 58 C5
Muong Sing, *Laos* 58 B3
Muong Son, *Laos* 58 B4
Muong Soui, *Laos* 58 C4
Muong Va, *Laos* 58 B4
Muong Xia, *Vietnam* 58 B5
Muonio, *Finland* 8 C17
Muotathal, *Switz.* 23 C7
Mupa, *Angola* 81 H3
Muping, *China* 51 F11
Muqaddam, Wadi →, *Sudan* 76 D3
Muqdisho, *Somali Rep.* 68 G4
Mur-de-Bretagne, *France* 24 D4
Mura →, *Slovenia* 33 B13
Muradiye, *Turkey* 67 D10
Murakami, *Japan* 48 E9
Murallón, Cuerro, *Chile* 128 C2
Muralto, *Switz.* 23 D7
Muranda, *Rwanda* 82 C2
Murang'a, *Kenya* 82 C4
Murashi, *Russia* 41 B16
Murat, *France* 26 C6
Murat →, *Turkey* 67 D8
Muratlı, *Turkey* 66 C2
Muravera, *Italy* 34 C2
Murayama, *Japan* 48 E10
Murban, *U.A.E.* 65 F7
Murça, *Portugal* 30 D3
Murchison →, *Australia* 89 E1
Murchison, Mt., *Antarctica* 5 D11
Murchison Falls = Kabarega Falls, *Uganda* 82 B3
Murchison House, *Australia* 89 E1
Murchison Ra., *Australia* 90 C1
Murchison Rapids, *Malawi* 83 F3
Murcia, *Spain* 29 G3
Murcia □, *Spain* 29 H3
Murdo, *U.S.A.* 108 D4
Murdoch Pt., *Australia* 90 A3
Mureş →, *Romania* 38 C3
Mureşul = Mureş →, *Romania* 38 C3
Muret, *France* 26 E5
Murfatlar, *Romania* 38 E11
Murfreesboro, *U.S.A.* 105 H2
Murg, *Switz.* 23 B8
Murg →, *Germany* 19 G4
Murgab, *Tajikistan* 44 F8
Murgenthal, *Switz.* 22 B5
Murgon, *Australia* 91 D5
Murgoo, *Australia* 89 E2
Muri, *Switz.* 23 B6
Muria, *Indonesia* 57 G14
Muriaé, *Brazil* 123 F3
Murias de Paredes, *Spain* 30 C4
Murici, *Brazil* 122 C4
Muriel Mine, *Zimbabwe* 83 F3
Müritz See, *Germany* 18 B8
Murka, *Kenya* 82 C4
Murmansk, *Russia* 44 C4
Murmerwoude, *Neths.* 16 B8
Murnau, *Germany* 19 H7
Muro, *France* 27 F12
Muro, *Spain* 36 B10
Muro, C. de, *France* 27 G12
Muro Lucano, *Italy* 35 B8
Murom, *Russia* 41 D13
Muroran, *Japan* 48 C10
Muros, *Spain* 30 C1
Muros y de Noya, Ría de, *Spain* 30 C2
Muroto, *Japan* 49 H7
Muroto-Misaki, *Japan* 49 H7
Murphy, *U.S.A.* 110 E5
Murphys, *U.S.A.* 112 G6
Murphysboro, *U.S.A.* 109 G10
Murrat, *Sudan* 76 D2
Murray, *Ky., U.S.A.* 105 G1
Murray, *Utah, U.S.A.* 110 F8
Murray →, *Australia* 91 F2
Murray →, *Canada* 100 B4
Murray, L., *U.S.A.* 105 H5
Murray Bridge, *Australia* 91 F2
Murray Downs, *Australia* 90 C1
Murray Harbour, *Canada* 99 C7
Murraysburg, *S. Africa* 84 E3
Murree, *Pakistan* 62 C5
Murrieta, *U.S.A.* 113 M9
Murrin Murrin, *Australia* 89 E3
Murrumbidgee →, *Australia* 91 E3
Murrumburrah, *Australia* 91 E4
Murrurundi, *Australia* 91 E5
Mursala, *Indonesia* 56 D1
Murshid, *Sudan* 76 C3

Murshidabad, *India* 63 G13
Murska Sobota, *Slovenia* . 33 B13
Murten, *Switz.* 22 C4
Murtensee, *Switz.* 22 C4
Murtle L., *Canada* 100 C5
Murtoa, *Australia* 91 F3
Murtosa, *Portugal* 30 E2
Muru →, *Brazil* 124 B3
Murungu, *Tanzania* 82 C3
Murwara, *India* 63 H9
Murwillumbah, *Australia* . 91 D5
Mürz →, *Austria* 21 H5
Mürzzuschlag, *Austria* . . 21 H5
Muş, *Turkey* 67 D9
Muş □, *Turkey* 67 D9
Mûsa, G., *Egypt* 76 J8
Musa Khel, *Pakistan* 62 D3
Mūsá Qal'eh, *Afghan.* . . . 60 C4
Musaffargarh, *Pakistan* . . 60 D7
Musala, *Bulgaria* 38 G6
Musan, *N. Korea* 51 C15
Musangu, *Zaïre* 83 E1
Musasa, *Tanzania* 82 C3
Musay'īd, *Qatar* 65 E6
Muscat = Masqat, *Oman* . 68 C6
Muscat & Oman =
    Oman ■, *Asia* 68 C6
Muscatine, *U.S.A.* 108 E9
Musel, *Spain* 30 B5
Musgrave, *Australia* 90 A3
Musgrave Ras., *Australia* . 89 E5
Mushie, *Zaïre* 80 E3
Mushin, *Nigeria* 79 D5
Musi →, *Indonesia* 56 E2
Muskeg →, *Canada* 100 A4
Muskegon, *U.S.A.* 104 D2
Muskegon →, *U.S.A.* 104 D2
Muskegon Heights, *U.S.A.* 104 D2
Muskogee, *U.S.A.* 109 H7
Muskwa →, *Canada* 100 B4
Muslīmiyah, *Syria* 64 B3
Musmar, *Sudan* 76 D4
Musofu, *Zambia* 83 E2
Musoma, *Tanzania* 82 C3
Musoma □, *Tanzania* 82 C3
Musquaro, L., *Canada* . . . 99 B7
Musquodoboit Harbour,
    Canada 99 D7
Musselburgh, *U.K.* 14 F5
Musselkanaal, *Neths.* 16 C10
Musselshell →, *U.S.A.* . . 110 C10
Mussidan, *France* 26 C4
Mussomeli, *Italy* 34 E6
Musson, *Belgium* 17 J7
Mussoorie, *India* 62 D8
Mussuco, *Angola* 84 B2
Mustafakemalpaşa, *Turkey* 66 C3
Mustang, *Nepal* 63 E10
Musters, L., *Argentina* . . 128 C3
Musudan, *N. Korea* 51 D15
Muswellbrook, *Australia* . 91 E5
Mût, *Egypt* 76 B2
Mut, *Turkey* 66 E5
Mutanda, *Mozam.* 85 C5
Mutanda, *Zambia* 83 E2
Mutaray, *Russia* 45 C11
Mutare, *Zimbabwe* 83 F3
Muting, *Indonesia* 57 F10
Mutshatsha, *Zaïre* 83 E1
Mutsu, *Japan* 48 D10
Mutsu-Wan, *Japan* 48 D10
Muttaburra, *Australia* . . . 90 C3
Mutuáli, *Mozam.* 83 E4
Mutunópolis, *Brazil* 123 D2
Muweilih, *Egypt* 69 E3
Muxima, *Angola* 80 F2
Muy Muy, *Nic.* 116 D2
Muya, *Russia* 45 D12
Muyinga, *Burundi* 82 C3
Muzaffarabad, *Pakistan* . . 63 B5
Muzaffargarh, *Pakistan* . . 62 D4
Muzaffarnagar, *India* 62 E7
Muzaffarpur, *India* 63 F11
Muzhi, *Russia* 44 C7
Muzillac, *France* 24 E4
Muzon C., *U.S.A.* 100 C2
Muztag, *China* 54 C3
Mvôlô, *Sudan* 77 F2
Mvuma, *Zimbabwe* 83 F3
Mvurwi, *Zimbabwe* 83 F3
Mwadui, *Tanzania* 82 C3
Mwambo, *Tanzania* 83 E5
Mwandi, *Zambia* 83 F1
Mwanza, *Tanzania* 82 C3
Mwanza, *Zaïre* 82 D2
Mwanza, *Zambia* 83 F1
Mwanza □, *Tanzania* 82 C3
Mwaya, *Tanzania* 83 D3
Mweelrea, *Ireland* 15 C2
Mweka, *Zaïre* 80 E4
Mwenezi, *Zimbabwe* 83 G3
Mwenezi →, *Mozam.* 83 G3
Mwenga, *Zaïre* 82 C2
Mweru, L., *Zambia* 83 D2
Mweza Range, *Zimbabwe* 83 G3
Mwilambwe, *Zaïre* 82 D5
Mwimbi, *Tanzania* 83 D3
Mwinilunga, *Zambia* 83 E1
My Tho, *Vietnam* 59 G6
Mya, O. →, *Algeria* 75 B5
Myajlar, *India* 62 F4
Myanaung, *Burma* 61 K19
Myanmar = Burma ■, *Asia* 61 J20
Myaungmya, *Burma* 61 L19

Mycenae = Mikínai, *Greece* 39 M5
Myeik Kyunzu, *Burma* . . . 59 G1
Myerstown, *U.S.A.* 107 F8
Myingyan, *Burma* 61 J19
Myitkyina, *Burma* 61 G20
Myjava, *Czech.* 20 G7
Mymensingh, *Bangla.* . . . 61 G17
Mynydd Du, *U.K.* 13 F4
Mýrdalsjökull, *Iceland* . . . 8 E4
Myroodah, *Australia* 88 C3
Myrtle Beach, *U.S.A.* . . . 105 J6
Myrtle Creek, *U.S.A.* . . . 110 E2
Myrtle Point, *U.S.A.* . . . 110 E1
Myrtou, *Cyprus* 37 D12
Mysen, *Norway* 10 E5
Mysia, *Turkey* 66 D2
Myslenice, *Poland* 20 F9
Myślibórz, *Poland* 20 C4
Mysłowice, *Poland* 20 E9
Mysore = Karnataka □,
    India 60 N10
Mysore, *India* 60 N10
Mystic, *U.S.A.* 107 E13
Myszków, *Poland* 20 E9
Mythen, *Switz.* 23 B7
Mytishchi, *Russia* 41 D10
Myton, *U.S.A.* 110 F8
Mývatn, *Iceland* 8 D5
Mzimba, *Malawi* 83 E3
Mzimkulu →, *S. Africa* . . 85 E5
Mzimvubu →, *S. Africa* . . 85 E4
Mzuzu, *Malawi* 83 E3

N

N' Dioum, *Senegal* 78 B2
Na Noi, *Thailand* 58 C3
Na Phao, *Laos* 58 D5
Na Sam, *Vietnam* 58 A6
Na San, *Vietnam* 58 B5
Naab →, *Germany* 19 F8
Naaldwijk, *Neths.* 16 E4
Na'am, *Sudan* 77 F2
Naantali, *Finland* 9 F17
Naarden, *Neths.* 16 D6
Naas, *Ireland* 15 C5
Nababiep, *S. Africa* 84 D2
Nabadwip = Navadwip,
    India 63 H13
Nabari, *Japan* 49 G8
Nabawa, *Australia* 89 E1
Nabberu, L., *Australia* . . . 89 E3
Nabburg, *Germany* 19 F8
Naberezhnyye Chelny,
    Russia 44 D6
Nabeul, *Tunisia* 75 A7
Nabha, *India* 62 D7
Nabīd, *Iran* 65 D8
Nabire, *Indonesia* 57 E9
Nabisar, *Pakistan* 62 G3
Nabisipi →, *Canada* 99 B7
Nabiswera, *Uganda* 82 B3
Nablus = Nābulus, *Jordan* 69 C4
Naboomspruit, *S. Africa* . 85 C4
Nabua, *Phil.* 55 E5
Nābulus, *Jordan* 69 C4
Nābulus □, *Jordan* 69 C4
Nacala, *Mozam.* 83 E5
Nacala-Velha, *Mozam.* . . . 83 E5
Nacaome, *Honduras* 116 D2
Nacaroa, *Mozam.* 83 E4
Naches, *U.S.A.* 110 C3
Naches →, *U.S.A.* 112 D6
Nachingwea, *Tanzania* . . . 83 E4
Nachingwea □, *Tanzania* . 83 E4
Nachna, *India* 62 F4
Náchod, *Czech.* 20 E6
Nacimiento Res., *U.S.A.* . 112 K6
Nacka, *Sweden* 10 E12
Nackara, *Australia* 91 E2
Naco, *Mexico* 114 A3
Naco, *U.S.A.* 111 L9
Nacogdoches, *U.S.A.* . . . 109 K7
Nácori Chico, *Mexico* . . . 114 B3
Nacozari, *Mexico* 114 A3
Nadi, *Sudan* 76 D3
Nadiad, *India* 62 H5
Nădlac, *Romania* 38 C3
Nador, *Morocco* 75 A4
Nadur, *Malta* 37 C1
Nadūshan, *Iran* 65 C7
Nadvornaya, *Ukraine* 42 B1
Nadym, *Russia* 44 C8
Nadym →, *Russia* 44 C8
Næstved, *Denmark* 11 J5
Nafada, *Nigeria* 79 C7
Näfels, *Switz.* 23 B8
Naftshahr, *Iran* 64 C5
Nafūsah, Jabal, *Libya* 75 B7
Nag Hammâdi, *Egypt* 76 B3
Naga, *Phil.* 55 E5
Naga, Kreb en, *Africa* . . . 74 D3
Nagagami →, *Canada* 98 C3
Nagahama, *Japan* 49 G8
Nagai, *Japan* 48 E10
Nagaland □, *India* 61 F19
Nagano, *Japan* 49 F9
Nagano □, *Japan* 49 F9
Nagaoka, *Japan* 49 F9
Nagappattinam, *India* . . . 60 P11
Nagar Parkar, *Pakistan* . . 62 G4

Nagasaki, *Japan* 49 H4
Nagasaki □, *Japan* 49 H4
Nagato, *Japan* 49 G5
Nagaur, *India* 62 F5
Nagercoil, *India* 60 Q10
Nagina, *India* 63 E8
Nagīneh, *Iran* 65 C8
Nagir, *Pakistan* 63 A6
Nagold, *Germany* 19 G4
Nagold →, *Germany* 19 G4
Nagoorin, *Australia* 90 C5
Nagornyy, *Russia* 45 D13
Nagorsk, *Russia* 41 B17
Nagoya, *Japan* 49 G8
Nagpur, *India* 60 J11
Nagua, *Dom. Rep.* 117 C6
Nagykanizsa, *Hungary* . . . 21 J7
Nagykőrös, *Hungary* 21 H9
Nagyléta, *Hungary* 21 H11
Naha, *Japan* 49 L3
Nahanni Butte, *Canada* . 100 A4
Nahanni Nat. Park, *Canada* 100 A3
Nahariyya, *Israel* 64 C2
Nahāvand, *Iran* 65 C6
Nahe →, *Germany* 19 F3
Nahīya, Wadi →, *Egypt* . . 76 J7
Nahlin, *Canada* 100 B2
Nahuel Huapi, L.,
    Argentina 128 B2
Naicá, *Mexico* 114 B3
Naicam, *Canada* 101 C8
Nā'ifah, *Si. Arabia* 68 D5
Naila, *Germany* 19 E7
Nain, *Canada* 99 A7
Nā'īn, *Iran* 65 C7
Naini Tal, *India* 63 E8
Nainpur, *India* 60 H12
Naintré, *France* 24 F7
Naipu, *Romania* 38 E8
Naira, *Indonesia* 57 E7
Nairn, *U.K.* 14 D5
Nairobi, *Kenya* 82 C4
Naivasha, *Kenya* 82 C4
Naivasha, L., *Kenya* 82 C4
Najac, *France* 26 D5
Najafābād, *Iran* 65 C6
Nájera, *Spain* 28 C2
Najerilla →, *Spain* 28 C2
Najibabad, *India* 62 E8
Najin, *N. Korea* 51 C16
Najmah, *Si. Arabia* 65 E6
Naju, *S. Korea* 51 G14
Nakadōri-Shima, *Japan* . . 49 H4
Nakalagba, *Zaïre* 82 B2
Nakaminato, *Japan* 49 F10
Nakamura, *Japan* 49 H6
Nakano, *Japan* 49 F9
Nakano-Shima, *Japan* . . . 49 K4
Nakashibetsu, *Japan* 48 C12
Nakfa, *Ethiopia* 77 D4
Nakhichevan, *Azerbaijan* . 67 D11
Nakhichevan Republic □,
    Azerbaijan 44 F5
Nakhl, *Egypt* 69 F2
Nakhl-e Taqī, *Iran* 65 E7
Nakhodka, *Russia* 45 E14
Nakhon Nayok, *Thailand* . 58 E3
Nakhon Pathom, *Thailand* 58 F3
Nakhon Phanom, *Thailand* 58 D5
Nakhon Ratchasima,
    Thailand 58 E4
Nakhon Sawan, *Thailand* . 58 E3
Nakhon Si Thammarat,
    Thailand 59 H3
Nakhon Thai, *Thailand* . . 58 D3
Nakina, *B.C., Canada* . . 100 B2
Nakina, *Ont., Canada* . . . 98 B2
Nakło nad Notecią, *Poland* 20 B7
Nakodar, *India* 62 D6
Naksskov, *Denmark* 11 K5
Näkten, *Sweden* 10 B8
Naktong →, *S. Korea* 51 G15
Nakuru, *Kenya* 82 C4
Nakuru □, *Kenya* 82 C4
Nakuru, L., *Kenya* 82 C4
Nakusp, *Canada* 100 C5
Nal →, *Pakistan* 62 G1
Nalchik, *Russia* 43 E10
Nälden, *Sweden* 10 A8
Näldsjön, *Sweden* 10 A8
Nalerigu, *Ghana* 79 C4
Nalgonda, *India* 60 L11
Nalhati, *India* 63 G12
Nalinnes, *Belgium* 17 H4
Nallamalai Hills, *India* . . 60 M11
Nallıhan, *Turkey* 66 C4
Nalón →, *Spain* 30 B4
Nālūt, *Libya* 75 B7
Nam Can, *Vietnam* 59 H5
Nam Co, *China* 54 C4
Nam Dinh, *Vietnam* 58 B6
Nam Du, Hon, *Vietnam* . . 59 H5
Nam Ngum Dam, *Laos* . . 58 C4
Nam-Phan, *Vietnam* 59 G6
Nam Phong, *Thailand* . . . 58 D4
Nam Tha, *Laos* 58 B3
Nam Tok, *Thailand* 58 E2
Namacunde, *Angola* 84 B2
Namacurra, *Mozam.* 85 B6
Namak, Daryācheh-ye, *Iran* 65 C7
Namak, Kavir-e, *Iran* 65 C8
Namaland, *Namibia* 84 C2
Namangan, *Uzbekistan* . . 44 E8
Namapa, *Mozam.* 83 E4

Namaqualand, *S. Africa* . . 84 D2
Namasagali, *Uganda* 82 B3
Namber, *Indonesia* 57 E8
Nambour, *Australia* 91 D5
Nambucca Heads, *Australia* 91 E5
Namche Bazar, *Nepal* . . . 63 F12
Namchonjŏm, *N. Korea* . . 51 E14
Namêche, *Belgium* 17 H6
Namecunda, *Mozam.* 83 E4
Nameh, *Indonesia* 56 D5
Nameponda, *Mozam.* 83 F4
Nametil, *Mozam.* 83 F4
Namib Desert =
    Namibwoestyn, *Namibia* 84 C2
Namibe, *Angola* 81 H2
Namibe □, *Angola* 84 B1
Namibia ■, *Africa* 84 C2
Namibwoestyn, *Namibia* . 84 C2
Namlea, *Indonesia* 57 E7
Namoi →, *Australia* 91 E4
Namous, O. en →, *Algeria* 75 B4
Nampa, *U.S.A.* 110 E5
Nampō-Shotō, *Japan* 49 J10
Nampula, *Mozam.* 83 F4
Namrole, *Indonesia* 57 E7
Namse Shankou, *China* . . 61 E13
Namsen →, *Norway* 8 D11
Namsos, *Norway* 8 D11
Namtay, *Russia* 45 C13
Namtu, *Burma* 61 H20
Namtumbo, *Tanzania* 83 E4
Namu, *Canada* 100 C3
Namur, *Belgium* 17 H5
Namur □, *Belgium* 17 H6
Namutoni, *Namibia* 84 B2
Namwala, *Zambia* 83 F2
Namwŏn, *S. Korea* 51 G14
Namysłów, *Poland* 20 D7
Nan, *Thailand* 58 C3
Nan →, *Thailand* 58 E3
Nan Xian, *China* 53 C9
Nanaimo, *Canada* 100 D4
Nanam, *N. Korea* 51 D15
Nanan, *China* 53 E12
Nanango, *Australia* 91 D5
Nanao, *Japan* 49 F8
Nanbu, *China* 52 B6
Nanchang, *China* 53 C10
Nancheng, *China* 53 D11
Nanching = Nanjing, *China* 54 C6
Nanchong, *China* 52 B6
Nanchuan, *China* 52 C6
Nancy, *France* 25 D13
Nanda Devi, *India* 63 D8
Nandan, *China* 52 E6
Nandan, *Japan* 49 G7
Nanded, *India* 60 K10
Nandewar Ra., *Australia* . 91 E5
Nandi, *Fiji* 87 C7
Nandi □, *Kenya* 82 B4
Nandurbar, *India* 60 J9
Nandyal, *India* 60 M11
Nanfeng, *Guangdong,*
    China 53 F8
Nanfeng, *Jiangxi, China* . . 53 D11
Nanga, *Australia* 89 E1
Nanga-Eboko, *Cameroon* . 79 E7
Nanga Parbat, *Pakistan* . . 63 B6
Nangade, *Mozam.* 83 E4
Nangapinoh, *Indonesia* . . 56 E4
Nangarhár □, *Afghan.* . . . 60 B7
Nangatayap, *Indonesia* . . 56 E4
Nangeya Mts., *Uganda* . . 82 B3
Nangis, *France* 25 D10
Nangong, *China* 50 F8
Nanhua, *China* 52 E3
Nanhuang, *China* 51 F11
Nanhui, *China* 53 B13
Nanjeko, *Zambia* 83 F1
Nanji Shan, *China* 53 D13
Nanjian, *China* 52 E3
Nanjiang, *China* 52 A6
Nanjing, *Fujian, China* . . 53 E11
Nanjing, *Jiangsu, China* . . 54 C6
Nanjirinji, *Tanzania* 83 D4
Nankana Sahib, *Pakistan* . 62 D5
Nankang, *China* 53 E10
Nanking = Nanjing, *China* 54 C6
Nankoku, *Japan* 49 H6
Nanling, *China* 53 B12
Nanning, *China* 52 F7
Nannup, *Australia* 89 F2
Nanpan Jiang →, *China* . . 52 E6
Nanpara, *India* 63 F9
Nanpi, *China* 50 E9
Nanping, *Fujian, China* . . 53 D12
Nanping, *Henan, China* . . 53 C9
Nanri Dao, *China* 53 E12
Nanripe, *Mozam.* 83 E4
Nansei-Shotō = Ryūkyū-
    rettō, *Japan* 49 M2
Nansen Sd., *Canada* 4 A3
Nansio, *Tanzania* 82 C3
Nant, *France* 26 D7
Nantes, *France* 24 E5
Nanteuil-le-Haudouin,
    France 25 C9
Nantiat, *France* 26 B5
Nanticoke, *U.S.A.* 107 E8
Nanton, *Canada* 100 C6
Nantong, *China* 53 A13
Nantua, *France* 27 B9

Nantucket I., *U.S.A.* 94 E12
Nanuque, *Brazil* 123 E3
Nanutarra, *Australia* 88 D2
Nanxiong, *China* 53 E10
Nanyang, *China* 50 H7
Nanyi Hu, *China* 53 B12
Nanyuan, *China* 50 E9
Nanyuki, *Kenya* 82 B4
Nanzhang, *China* 53 B8
Náo, C. de la, *Spain* 29 G5
Naococane L., *Canada* . . . 99 B5
Naoetsu, *Japan* 49 F9
Náousa, *Greece* 39 J5
Naozhou Dao, *China* 53 G8
Napa, *U.S.A.* 112 G4
Napa →, *U.S.A.* 112 G4
Napanee, *Canada* 98 D4
Napanoch, *U.S.A.* 107 E10
Nape, *Laos* 58 C5
Nape Pass = Keo Neua,
    Deo, *Vietnam* 58 C5
Napf, *Switz.* 22 B5
Napier, *N.Z.* 87 H6
Napier Broome B.,
    Australia 88 B4
Napier Downs, *Australia* . 88 C3
Napier Pen., *Australia* . . . 90 A2
Naples = Nápoli, *Italy* . . . 35 B7
Naples, *U.S.A.* 105 M5
Napo, *China* 52 F5
Napo □, *Ecuador* 120 D2
Napo →, *Peru* 120 D3
Napoleon, *N. Dak., U.S.A.* 108 B5
Napoleon, *Ohio, U.S.A.* . 104 E3
Nápoli, *Italy* 35 B7
Nápoli, G. di, *Italy* 35 B7
Napopo, *Zaïre* 82 B2
Nappa Merrie, *Australia* . 91 D3
Naqâda, *Egypt* 76 B3
Naqqāsh, *Iran* 65 C6
Nara, *Japan* 49 G7
Nara, *Mali* 78 B3
Nara □, *Japan* 49 G8
Nara Canal, *Pakistan* 62 G3
Nara Visa, *U.S.A.* 109 H3
Naracoorte, *Australia* . . . 91 F3
Naradhan, *Australia* 91 E4
Narasapur, *India* 61 L12
Narathiwat, *Thailand* 59 J3
Narayanganj, *Bangla.* . . . 61 H17
Narayanpet, *India* 60 L10
Narbonne, *France* 26 E7
Narcea →, *Spain* 30 B4
Nardīn, *Iran* 65 B7
Nardò, *Italy* 35 B11
Narembeen, *Australia* . . . 89 F2
Nares Str., *Arctic* 94 B13
Naretha, *Australia* 89 F3
Narew →, *Poland* 20 C10
Nari →, *Pakistan* 62 E2
Narin, *Afghan.* 60 A6
Narindra, Helodranon' i,
    Madag. 85 A8
Narino □, *Colombia* 120 C2
Narita, *Japan* 49 G10
Narmada →, *India* 62 J5
Narman, *Turkey* 67 C9
Narnaul, *India* 62 E7
Narni, *Italy* 33 F9
Naro, *Ghana* 78 C4
Naro, *Italy* 34 E6
Naro Fominsk, *Russia* . . . 41 D10
Narodnaya, *Russia* 6 B17
Narok, *Kenya* 82 C4
Narok □, *Kenya* 82 C4
Narón, *Spain* 30 B2
Narooma, *Australia* 91 F5
Narowal, *Pakistan* 62 C6
Narrabri, *Australia* 91 E4
Narran →, *Australia* 91 D4
Narrandera, *Australia* . . . 91 E4
Narraway →, *Canada* . . . 100 B5
Narrogin, *Australia* 89 F2
Narromine, *Australia* 91 E4
Narsimhapur, *India* 63 H8
Nartkala, *Russia* 43 E10
Naruto, *Japan* 49 G7
Narva, *Estonia* 40 B6
Narva →, *Russia* 40 B6
Narvik, *Norway* 8 B14
Narvskoye Vdkhr., *Russia* 40 B6
Narwana, *India* 62 E7
Naryan-Mar, *Russia* 44 C6
Narylico, *Australia* 91 D3
Narym, *Russia* 44 D9
Narymskoye, *Kazakhstan* . 44 E9
Naryn, *Kirghizia* 44 E8
Nasa, *Norway* 8 C13
Nasarawa, *Nigeria* 79 D6
Năsăud, *Romania* 38 B7
Naseby, *N.Z.* 87 L3
Naselle, *U.S.A.* 112 D3
Naser, Buheirat en, *Egypt* 76 C3
Nashua, *Iowa, U.S.A.* . . . 108 D8
Nashua, *Mont., U.S.A.* . . 110 B10
Nashua, *N.H., U.S.A.* . . 107 D13
Nashville, *Ark., U.S.A.* . . 109 J8
Nashville, *Ga., U.S.A.* . . 105 K4
Nashville, *Tenn., U.S.A.* . 105 G2
Našice, *Croatia* 21 K8
Nasielsk, *Poland* 20 C10
Nasik, *India* 60 K8
Nasipit, *Phil.* 55 G6
Nasirabad, *India* 62 F6

Naskaupi →, Canada 99 B7
Naso, Italy 35 D7
Naṣrīān-e Pā'īn, Iran 64 C5
Nass →, Canada 100 B3
Nassau, Bahamas 116 A4
Nassau, U.S.A. 107 D11
Nassau, B., Chile 128 E3
Nasser, L. = Naser, Buheirat en, Egypt 76 C3
Nasser City = Kôm Ombo, Egypt 76 C3
Nassian, Ivory C. 78 D4
Nässjö, Sweden 9 H13
Nasugbu, Phil. 55 D4
Näsviken, Sweden 10 C10
Nat Kyizin, Burma 61 M20
Nata, Botswana 84 C4
Natagaima, Colombia 120 C2
Natal, Brazil 122 C4
Natal, Canada 100 D6
Natal, Indonesia 56 D1
Natal □, S. Africa 85 D5
Natalinci, Serbia, Yug. 21 L10
Naṭanz, Iran 65 C6
Natashquan, Canada 99 B7
Natashquan →, Canada 99 B7
Natchez, U.S.A. 109 K9
Natchitoches, U.S.A. 109 K8
Naters, Switz. 22 D5
Nathalia, Australia 91 F4
Nathdwara, India 62 G5
Nati, Pta., Spain 36 A10
Natimuk, Australia 91 F3
Nation →, Canada 100 B4
National City, U.S.A. 113 N9
Natitingou, Benin 79 C5
Natividad, I., Mexico 114 B1
Natoma, U.S.A. 108 F5
Natron, L., Tanzania 82 C4
Natrona Heights, U.S.A. 106 F5
Natrûn, W. el →, Egypt 76 H7
Natuna Besar, Kepulauan, Indonesia 59 L7
Natuna Is. = Natuna Besar, Kepulauan, Indonesia 59 L7
Natuna Selatan, Kepulauan, Indonesia 59 L7
Natural Bridge, U.S.A. 107 B9
Naturaliste, C., Australia 90 G4
Nau Qala, Afghan. 62 B3
Naubinway, U.S.A. 98 C2
Naucelle, France 26 D6
Nauders, Austria 19 J6
Nauen, Germany 18 C8
Naugatuck, U.S.A. 107 E11
Naujoji Vilnia, Lithuania 40 D4
Naumburg, Germany 18 D7
Nā'ūr at Tunayb, Jordan 69 D4
Nauru ■, Pac. Oc. 92 H8
Naushahra = Nowshera, Pakistan 60 B8
Nauta, Peru 120 D3
Nautanwa, India 61 F13
Nautla, Mexico 115 C5
Nava, Mexico 114 B4
Nava del Rey, Spain 30 D5
Navacerrada, Puerto de, Spain 30 E7
Navadwip, India 63 H13
Navahermosa, Spain 31 F6
Navajo Res., U.S.A. 111 H10
Navalcarnero, Spain 30 E6
Navalmoral de la Mata, Spain 30 F5
Navalvillar de Pela, Spain 31 F5
Navan = An Uaimh, Ireland 15 C5
Navarino, I., Chile 128 E3
Navarra □, Spain 28 C3
Navarre, U.S.A. 106 F3
Navarrenx, France 26 E3
Navarro, U.S.A. 112 F3
Navasota, U.S.A. 109 K6
Navassa, W. Indies 117 C4
Nave, Italy 32 C7
Naver →, U.K. 14 C4
Navia, Spain 30 B4
Navia →, Spain 30 B4
Navia de Suarna, Spain 30 C4
Navidad, Chile 126 C1
Navlya, Russia 40 E9
Navoi, Uzbekistan 44 E7
Navojoa, Mexico 114 B3
Navolato, Mexico 114 C3
Návpaktos, Greece 39 L4
Návplion, Greece 39 M5
Navrongo, Ghana 79 C4
Navsari, India 60 J8
Nawa Kot, Pakistan 62 E4
Nawabganj, Ut. P., India 63 F9
Nawabganj, Ut. P., India 63 E8
Nawabshah, Pakistan 62 F3
Nawada, India 63 G11
Nawakot, Nepal 63 F11
Nawalgarh, India 62 F6
Nawanshahr, India 63 C6
Nawi, Sudan 76 D3
Náxos, Greece 39 M8
Nay, France 26 E3
Nāy Band, Iran 65 E7
Naya →, Colombia 120 C2
Nayakhan, Russia 45 C16
Nayarit □, Mexico 114 C4
Nayé, Senegal 78 C2
Nayong, China 52 D5
Nayoro, Japan 48 B11
Nayyāl, W. →, Si. Arabia 64 D3
Nazaré, Bahia, Brazil 123 D4
Nazaré, Goiás, Brazil 122 C2
Nazaré, Pará, Brazil 125 B7
Nazaré, Portugal 31 F1
Nazareth = Nazerat, Israel 69 C4
Nazas, Mexico 114 B4
Nazas →, Mexico 114 B4
Naze, The, U.K. 13 F9
Nazerat, Israel 69 C4
Nāzīk, Iran 64 B5
Nazik Gölü, Turkey 67 D10
Nazilli, Turkey 66 E3
Nazir Hat, Bangla. 61 H17
Nazko, Canada 100 C4
Nazko →, Canada 100 C4
Nazret, Ethiopia 77 F4
Nchanga, Zambia 83 E2
Ncheu, Malawi 83 E3
Ndala, Tanzania 82 C3
Ndalatando, Angola 80 F2
Ndali, Benin 79 D5
Ndareda, Tanzania 82 C4
Ndélé, C.A.R. 73 G9
Ndendé, Gabon 80 E2
Ndjamena, Chad 73 F7
Ndjolé, Gabon 80 E2
Ndola, Zambia 83 E2
Ndoto Mts., Kenya 82 B4
Nduguti, Tanzania 82 C3
Nea →, Norway 10 A5
Néa Flippiás, Greece 39 K3
Neagh, Lough, U.K. 15 B5
Neah Bay, U.S.A. 112 B2
Neale, L., Australia 88 D5
Neápolis, Kozan, Greece 39 J4
Neápolis, Kríti, Greece 37 D7
Neápolis, Lakonia, Greece 39 N6
Near Is., U.S.A. 96 C1
Neath, U.K. 13 F4
Nebbou, Burkina Faso 79 C4
Nebine Cr. →, Australia 91 D4
Nebit Dag, Turkmenistan 44 F6
Nebolchy, Russia 40 B8
Nebraska □, U.S.A. 108 E5
Nebraska City, U.S.A. 108 E7
Nébrodi, Monti, Italy 35 E7
Necedah, U.S.A. 108 C9
Nechako →, Canada 100 C4
Neches →, U.S.A. 109 L8
Neckar →, Germany 19 F4
Necochea, Argentina 126 D4
Nedelišće, Croatia 33 B13
Neder Rijn →, Neths. 16 E8
Nederbrakel, Belgium 17 G3
Nederweert, Neths. 17 F7
Nédha →, Greece 39 M4
Nedroma, Algeria 75 A4
Neede, Neths. 16 D9
Needles, U.S.A. 113 L12
Needles, The, U.K. 13 G6
Ñeembucú □, Paraguay 126 B4
Neemuch = Nimach, India 62 G6
Neenah, U.S.A. 104 C1
Neepawa, Canada 101 C9
Neer, Neths. 17 F7
Neerpelt, Belgium 17 F6
Neft-chala = imeni 26 Bakinskikh Komissarov, Azerbaijan 67 D13
Nefta, Tunisia 75 B6
Neftah Sidi Boubekeur, Algeria 75 A5
Neftegorsk, Russia 43 D8
Neftekumsk, Russia 43 D11
Neftenbach, Switz. 23 A7
Negapatam = Nagappattinam, India 60 P11
Negaunee, U.S.A. 104 B2
Negele, Ethiopia 68 F2
Negev Desert = Hanegev, Israel 69 E3
Negombo, Sri Lanka 60 R11
Negotin, Serbia, Yug. 21 L12
Negra, Peña, Spain 30 C4
Negra, Pta., Mauritania 74 D1
Negra, Pta., Peru 124 B1
Negra Pt., Phil. 57 A6
Negreira, Spain 30 C2
Nègrine, Algeria 75 B6
Negro →, Argentina 128 B4
Negro →, Bolivia 125 C5
Negro →, Brazil 121 D6
Negro →, Uruguay 127 C4
Negros, Phil. 55 G5
Nehalem →, U.S.A. 112 E3
Nehāvand, Iran 65 C6
Nehbandān, Iran 65 D9
Neheim, Germany 18 D3
Nehoiaşu, Romania 38 D9
Nei Monggol Zizhiqu □, China 50 C6
Neidpath, Canada 101 C7
Neihart, U.S.A. 110 C8
Neijiang, China 52 C5
Neilton, U.S.A. 110 C2
Neiqiu, China 50 F8
Neira de Jusá, Spain 30 C3
Neisse →, Europe 18 C10
Neiva, Colombia 120 C2
Neixiang, China 50 H6
Nejanilini L., Canada 101 B9
Nejo, Ethiopia 77 F4
Nekā, Iran 65 B7
Nekemte, Ethiopia 77 F4
Nêkheb, Egypt 76 B3
Neksø, Denmark 9 J13
Nelas, Portugal 30 E3
Nelia, Australia 90 C3
Nelidovo, Russia 40 C8
Neligh, U.S.A. 108 D5
Nelkan, Russia 45 D14
Nellore, India 60 M11
Nelma, Russia 45 E14
Nelson, Canada 100 D5
Nelson, N.Z. 87 J4
Nelson, U.K. 12 D5
Nelson, U.S.A. 111 J7
Nelson →, Canada 101 C9
Nelson, C., Australia 91 F3
Nelson, Estrecho, Chile 128 D2
Nelson Forks, Canada 100 B4
Nelson House, Canada 101 B9
Nelson L., Canada 101 B8
Nelspoort, S. Africa 84 E3
Nelspruit, S. Africa 85 D5
Néma, Mauritania 78 B3
Neman →, Lithuania 40 D2
Nemeiben L., Canada 101 B7
Nemira, Romania 38 C9
Nemours, France 25 D9
Nemunas = Neman →, Lithuania 40 D2
Nemuro, Japan 48 C12
Nemuro-Kaikyō, Japan 48 C12
Nemuy, Russia 45 D14
Nen Jiang →, China 51 B13
Nenagh, Ireland 15 D3
Nenana, U.S.A. 96 B5
Nenasi, Malaysia 59 L4
Nene →, U.K. 12 E8
Nenjiang, China 54 B7
Neno, Malawi 83 F3
Nenusa, Kepulauan, Indonesia 57 D7
Neodesha, U.S.A. 109 G7
Neópolis, Brazil 122 D4
Neosho, U.S.A. 109 G7
Neosho →, U.S.A. 109 H7
Nepal ■, Asia 63 F11
Nepalganj, Nepal 63 E9
Nephi, U.S.A. 110 G8
Nephin, Ireland 15 B2
Neptune City, U.S.A. 107 F10
Néra →, Romania 38 E4
Nérac, France 26 D4
Nerchinsk, Russia 45 D12
Nerchinskiy Zavod, Russia 45 D12
Nereju, Romania 38 D9
Nerekhta, Russia 41 C12
Néret L., Canada 99 B5
Neringa, Lithuania 40 D2
Nerja, Spain 31 J7
Nerl →, Russia 41 C12
Nerpio, Spain 29 G2
Nerva, Spain 31 H4
Nes, Iceland 8 D5
Nes, Neths. 16 B7
Nesbyen, Norway 10 D3
Nesebŭr, Bulgaria 38 G10
Neskaupstaður, Iceland 8 D7
Nesland, Norway 10 E1
Neslandsvatn, Norway 10 F3
Nesle, France 25 C9
Nesodden, Norway 10 E4
Nesque →, France 27 E8
Ness, L., U.K. 14 D4
Nesslau, Switz. 23 B8
Néstos →, Greece 39 H7
Nesttun, Norway 9 F8
Nesvizh, Belorussia 40 E5
Netanya, Israel 69 C3
Nète →, Belgium 17 F4
Netherdale, Australia 90 C4
Netherlands ■, Europe 16 E6
Netherlands Antilles ■, S. Amer. 120 A4
Netherlands Guiana = Surinam ■, S. Amer. 121 C6
Neto →, Italy 35 C10
Nettancourt, France 25 D11
Nettilling L., Canada 97 B12
Nettuno, Italy 34 A5
Netzahualcoyotl, Presa, Mexico 115 D6
Neu-Isenburg, Germany 19 E4
Neu-Ulm, Germany 19 G6
Neubrandenburg, Germany 18 B9
Neubukow, Germany 18 A7
Neuburg, Germany 19 G7
Neuchâtel, Switz. 22 C3
Neuchâtel □, Switz. 22 C3
Neuchâtel, Lac de, Switz. 22 C3
Neudau, Austria 21 H6
Neuenegg, Switz. 22 C4
Neuenhaus, Germany 18 C2
Neuf-Brisach, France 25 D14
Neufahrn, Germany 19 G8
Neufchâteau, Belgium 17 J6
Neufchâteau, France 25 D12
Neufchâtel-en-Bray, France 24 C8
Neufchâtel-sur-Aisne, France 25 C11
Neuhaus, Germany 18 B6
Neuhausen, Switz. 23 A7
Neuillé-Pont-Pierre, France 24 E7
Neuilly-St.-Front, France 25 C10
Neukalen, Germany 18 B8
Neumarkt, Germany 19 F7
Neumarkt-Sankt Veit, Germany 19 G8
Neumünster, Germany 18 A5
Neung-sur-Beuvron, France 25 E8
Neunkirchen, Austria 21 H6
Neunkirchen, Germany 19 F3
Neuquén, Argentina 128 A3
Neuquén □, Argentina 126 D2
Neuquén →, Argentina 128 A3
Neuruppin, Germany 18 C8
Neuse →, U.S.A. 105 H7
Neusiedler See, Austria 21 H6
Neuss, Germany 17 F9
Neussargues-Moissac, France 26 C7
Neustadt, Baden-W., Germany 19 H4
Neustadt, Bayern, Germany 19 F8
Neustadt, Bayern, Germany 19 G7
Neustadt, Bayern, Germany 19 F6
Neustadt, Bayern, Germany 19 E7
Neustadt, Brandenburg, Germany 18 C8
Neustadt, Hessen, Germany 18 E5
Neustadt, Niedersachsen, Germany 18 C5
Neustadt, Rhld-Pfz., Germany 19 F4
Neustadt, Schleswig-Holstein, Germany 18 A6
Neustadt, Thüringen, Germany 18 E7
Neustrelitz, Germany 18 B9
Neuvic, France 26 C6
Neuville, Belgium 17 H5
Neuville-aux-Bois, France 25 D9
Neuville-de-Poitou, France 26 B4
Neuville-sur-Saône, France 27 C8
Neuvy-le-Roi, France 24 E7
Neuvy-St.-Sépulchre, France 26 B5
Neuvy-sur-Barangeon, France 25 E9
Neuwerk, Germany 18 B4
Neuwied, Germany 18 E3
Neva →, Russia 6 D12
Nevada, U.S.A. 109 G7
Nevada □, U.S.A. 110 G5
Nevada, Sierra, Spain 29 H1
Nevada, Sierra, U.S.A. 110 G3
Nevada City, U.S.A. 112 F6
Nevado, Cerro, Argentina 126 D2
Nevanka, Russia 45 D10
Nevel, Russia 40 D6
Nevele, Belgium 17 F3
Nevers, France 25 F10
Nevertire, Australia 91 E4
Neville, Canada 101 D7
Nevinnomyssk, Russia 43 D9
Nevis, W. Indies 117 C7
Nevrokop = Gotse Delchev, Bulgaria 39 H6
Nevşehir, Turkey 66 D6
Nevşehir □, Turkey 66 D6
New →, Guyana 121 C6
New Albany, Ind., U.S.A. 104 F3
New Albany, Miss., U.S.A. 109 H10
New Albany, Pa., U.S.A. 107 E8
New Amsterdam, Guyana 121 B6
New Angledool, Australia 91 D4
New Bedford, U.S.A. 107 E14
New Bern, U.S.A. 105 H7
New Bethlehem, U.S.A. 106 E5
New Bloomfield, U.S.A. 106 F7
New Boston, U.S.A. 109 J7
New Braunfels, U.S.A. 109 L5
New Brighton, N.Z. 87 K4
New Brighton, U.S.A. 106 F4
New Britain, Papua N. G. 92 H7
New Britain, U.S.A. 107 E12
New Brunswick, U.S.A. 107 F10
New Brunswick □, Canada 99 C6
New Bussa, Nigeria 79 D5
New Caledonia, Pac. Oc. 92 K8
New Castile = Castilla La Mancha □, Spain 31 F7
New Castle, Ind., U.S.A. 104 F3
New Castle, Pa., U.S.A. 106 E4
New City, U.S.A. 107 E11
New Cumberland, U.S.A. 106 F4
New Cuyama, U.S.A. 113 L7
New Delhi, India 62 E7
New Denver, Canada 100 D5
New Don Pedro Res., U.S.A. 112 H6
New England, U.S.A. 108 B3
New England Ra., Australia 91 E5
New Forest, U.K. 13 G6
New Glasgow, Canada 99 C7
New Guinea, Oceania 92 H5
New Hamburg, Canada 106 C4
New Hampshire □, U.S.A. 107 C13
New Hampton, U.S.A. 108 D8
New Hanover, S. Africa 85 D5
New Haven, Conn., U.S.A. 107 E12
New Haven, Mich., U.S.A. 106 D2
New Hazelton, Canada 100 B3
New Hebrides = Vanuatu ■, Pac. Oc. 92 J8
New Iberia, U.S.A. 109 K9
New Ireland, Papua N. G. 92 H7
New Jersey □, U.S.A. 107 F10
New Kensington, U.S.A. 106 F5
New Lexington, U.S.A. 104 F4
New Liskeard, Canada 98 C4
New London, Conn., U.S.A. 107 E12
New London, Minn., U.S.A. 108 C7
New London, Ohio, U.S.A. 106 E2
New London, Wis., U.S.A. 108 C10
New Madrid, U.S.A. 109 G10
New Meadows, U.S.A. 110 D5
New Melones L., U.S.A. 112 H6
New Mexico □, U.S.A. 102 D5
New Milford, Conn., U.S.A. 107 E11
New Milford, Pa., U.S.A. 107 E9
New Norcia, Australia 89 F2
New Norfolk, Australia 90 G4
New Orleans, U.S.A. 109 K9
New Philadelphia, U.S.A. 106 F3
New Plymouth, N.Z. 87 H5
New Plymouth, U.S.A. 110 E5
New Providence, Bahamas 116 A4
New Radnor, U.K. 13 E4
New Richmond, U.S.A. 108 C8
New Roads, U.S.A. 109 K9
New Rochelle, U.S.A. 107 F11
New Rockford, U.S.A. 108 B5
New Ross, Ireland 15 D5
New Salem, U.S.A. 108 B4
New Scone, U.K. 14 E5
New Siberian Is. = Novosibirskiye Ostrova, Russia 45 B15
New Smyrna Beach, U.S.A. 105 L5
New South Wales □, Australia 91 E4
New Springs, Australia 89 E3
New Town, U.S.A. 108 A3
New Ulm, U.S.A. 108 C7
New Waterford, Canada 99 C7
New Westminster, Canada 100 D4
New York □, U.S.A. 107 D9
New York City, U.S.A. 107 F11
New Zealand ■, Oceania 87 J5
Newala, Tanzania 83 E4
Newala □, Tanzania 83 E4
Newark, Del., U.S.A. 104 F8
Newark, N.J., U.S.A. 107 F10
Newark, N.Y., U.S.A. 106 C7
Newark, Ohio, U.S.A. 106 F2
Newark-on-Trent, U.K. 12 D7
Newaygo, U.S.A. 104 D3
Newberg, U.S.A. 110 D2
Newberry, Mich., U.S.A. 104 B3
Newberry, S.C., U.S.A. 105 H5
Newberry Springs, U.S.A. 113 L10
Newbrook, Canada 100 C6
Newburgh, U.S.A. 107 E10
Newbury, U.K. 13 F6
Newbury, U.S.A. 107 B12
Newburyport, U.S.A. 107 D14
Newcastle, Australia 91 E5
Newcastle, Canada 99 C6
Newcastle, S. Africa 85 D4
Newcastle, U.K. 15 B6
Newcastle, Calif., U.S.A. 112 G5
Newcastle, Wyo., U.S.A. 108 D2
Newcastle Emlyn, U.K. 13 E3
Newcastle Ra., Australia 88 C5
Newcastle-under-Lyme, U.K. 12 D5
Newcastle-upon-Tyne, U.K. 12 C6
Newcastle Waters, Australia 90 B1
Newdegate, Australia 89 F2
Newell, U.S.A. 108 C3
Newfoundland □, Canada 99 B8
Newhalem, U.S.A. 100 D4
Newhall, U.S.A. 113 L8
Newham, U.K. 13 F8
Newhaven, U.K. 13 G8
Newkirk, U.S.A. 109 G6
Newman, Australia 88 D2
Newman, U.S.A. 112 H5
Newmarket, Canada 106 B5
Newmarket, Ireland 15 D3
Newmarket, U.K. 13 E8
Newmarket, U.S.A. 107 C14
Newnan, U.S.A. 105 J3
Newport, Gwent, U.K. 13 F5
Newport, I. of W., U.K. 13 G6
Newport, Shrops., U.K. 13 E5
Newport, Ark., U.S.A. 109 H9
Newport, Ky., U.S.A. 104 F3
Newport, N.H., U.S.A. 107 C12
Newport, Oreg., U.S.A. 110 D1
Newport, Pa., U.S.A. 106 F7
Newport, R.I., U.S.A. 107 E13
Newport, Tenn., U.S.A. 105 H4
Newport, Vt., U.S.A. 107 B12
Newport, Wash., U.S.A. 110 B5
Newport Beach, U.S.A. 113 M9
Newport News, U.S.A. 104 G7
Newquay, U.K. 13 G2
Newry, U.K. 15 B5
Newry & Mourne □, U.K. 15 B5
Newton, Iowa, U.S.A. 108 E8
Newton, Mass., U.S.A. 107 D13
Newton, Miss., U.S.A. 109 J10
Newton, N.C., U.S.A. 105 H5
Newton, N.J., U.S.A. 107 E10
Newton, Tex., U.S.A. 109 K8

North Pole

Newton Abbot, *U.K.* 13 G4
Newton Boyd, *Australia* 91 D5
Newton Stewart, *U.K.* 14 G4
Newtonmore, *U.K.* 14 D4
Newtown, *U.K.* 13 E4
Newtownabbey □, *U.K.* 15 B6
Newtownards, *U.K.* 15 B6
Newville, *U.S.A.* 106 F7
Nexon, *France* 26 C5
Neya, *Russia* 41 B13
Neyrīz, *Iran* 65 D7
Neyshābūr, *Iran* 65 B8
Nezhin, *Ukraine* 40 F7
Nezperce, *U.S.A.* 110 C5
Ngabang, *Indonesia* 56 D3
Ngabordamlu, Tanjung, *Indonesia* 57 F8
Ngambé, *Cameroon* 79 D7
Ngami Depression, *Botswana* 84 C3
Ngamo, *Zimbabwe* 83 F2
Nganglong Kangri, *China* 61 C12
Nganjuk, *Indonesia* 57 G14
Ngao, *Thailand* 58 C2
Ngaoundéré, *Cameroon* 80 C2
Ngapara, *N.Z.* 87 L3
Ngara, *Tanzania* 82 C3
Ngara □, *Tanzania* 82 C3
Ngawi, *Indonesia* 57 G14
Nghia Lo, *Vietnam* 58 B5
Ngoma, *Malawi* 83 E3
Ngomahura, *Zimbabwe* 83 G3
Ngomba, *Tanzania* 83 D3
Ngop, *Sudan* 77 F3
Ngoring Hu, *China* 54 C4
Ngorkou, *Mali* 78 B4
Ngorongoro, *Tanzania* 82 C4
Ngozi, *Burundi* 82 C2
Ngudu, *Tanzania* 82 C3
Nguigmi, *Niger* 73 F7
Ngukurr, *Australia* 90 A1
Ngunga, *Tanzania* 82 C3
Nguru, *Nigeria* 79 C7
Nguru Mts., *Tanzania* 82 D4
Nguyen Binh, *Vietnam* 58 A5
Nha Trang, *Vietnam* 59 F7
Nhacoongo, *Mozam.* 85 C6
Nhamaabué, *Mozam.* 83 F4
Nhambiquara, *Brazil* 125 C6
Nhamundá, *Brazil* 121 D6
Nhamundá →, *Brazil* 121 D6
Nhangutazi, L., *Mozam.* 85 C5
Nhecolândia, *Brazil* 125 D6
Nhill, *Australia* 91 F3
Nho Quan, *Vietnam* 58 B5
Nhulunbuy, *Australia* 90 A2
Nia-nia, *Zaïre* 82 B2
Niafounké, *Mali* 78 B4
Niagara, *U.S.A.* 104 C1
Niagara Falls, *Canada* 98 D4
Niagara Falls, *U.S.A.* 106 C6
Niagara-on-the-Lake, *Canada* 106 C5
Niah, *Malaysia* 56 D4
Niamey, *Niger* 79 C5
Nianforando, *Guinea* 78 D2
Nianfors, *Sweden* 10 C10
Niangara, *Zaïre* 82 B2
Nias, *Indonesia* 56 D1
Niassa □, *Mozam.* 83 E4
Nibbiano, *Italy* 32 D6
Nibe, *Denmark* 11 H3
Nicaragua ■, *Cent. Amer.* 116 D2
Nicaragua, L. de, *Nic.* 116 D2
Nicastro, *Italy* 35 D9
Nice, *France* 27 E11
Niceville, *U.S.A.* 105 K2
Nichinan, *Japan* 49 J5
Nicholás, Canal, *W. Indies* 116 B3
Nicholasville, *U.S.A.* 104 G3
Nichols, *U.S.A.* 107 D8
Nicholson, *Australia* 88 C4
Nicholson, *U.S.A.* 107 E9
Nicholson →, *Australia* 90 B2
Nicholson Ra., *Australia* 89 E2
Nickerie □, *Surinam* 121 C6
Nickerie →, *Surinam* 121 B6
Nicobar Is., *Ind. Oc.* 46 J13
Nicoclí, *Colombia* 120 B2
Nicola, *Canada* 100 C4
Nicolet, *Canada* 98 C5
Nicolls Town, *Bahamas* 116 A4
Nicosia, *Cyprus* 37 D12
Nicosia, *Italy* 35 E7
Nicótera, *Italy* 35 D8
Nicoya, *Costa Rica* 116 D2
Nicoya, G. de, *Costa Rica* 116 E3
Nicoya, Pen. de, *Costa Rica* 116 E2
Nidau, *Switz.* 22 B4
Nidd →, *U.K.* 12 C6
Nidda, *Germany* 18 E5
Nidda →, *Germany* 19 E4
Nidwalden □, *Switz.* 23 C6
Nidzica, *Poland* 20 B10
Niebüll, *Germany* 18 A4
Nied →, *Germany* 25 C13
Niederaula, *Germany* 18 E5
Niederbipp, *Switz.* 22 B5
Niederbronn-les-Bains, *France* 25 D14
Niedere Tauern, *Austria* 21 H4
Niedersachsen □, *Germany* 18 C5
Niekerkshoop, *S. Africa* 84 D3
Niel, *Belgium* 17 F4
Niellé, *Ivory C.* 78 C3
Niemba, *Zaïre* 82 D2
Nienburg, *Germany* 18 C5
Niers →, *Germany* 18 D2
Niesen, *Switz.* 22 C5
Niesky, *Germany* 18 D10
Nieu Bethesda, *S. Africa* 84 E3
Nieuw-Amsterdam, *Neths.* 16 C9
Nieuw Amsterdam, *Surinam* 121 B6
Nieuw Beijerland, *Neths.* 16 E4
Nieuw-Dordrecht, *Neths.* 16 C9
Nieuw Loosdrecht, *Neths.* 16 D6
Nieuw Nickerie, *Surinam* 121 B6
Nieuw-Schoonebeek, *Neths.* 16 C10
Nieuw-Vennep, *Neths.* 16 D5
Nieuw-Vossemeer, *Neths.* 17 E4
Nieuwe-Niedorp, *Neths.* 16 C5
Nieuwe-Pekela, *Neths.* 16 B9
Nieuwe-Schans, *Neths.* 16 B10
Nieuwendijk, *Neths.* 16 E5
Nieuwerkerken, *Belgium* 17 G6
Nieuwkoop, *Neths.* 16 D5
Nieuwleusen, *Neths.* 16 C8
Nieuwnamen, *Neths.* 17 F4
Nieuwolda, *Neths.* 16 B9
Nieuwoudtville, *S. Africa* 84 E2
Nieuwpoort, *Belgium* 17 F1
Nieuwveen, *Neths.* 16 D5
Nieves, *Spain* 30 C2
Nieves, Pico de las, *Canary Is.* 36 G4
Nièvre □, *France* 25 E10
Niğde, *Turkey* 66 E6
Niğde □, *Turkey* 66 E6
Nigel, *S. Africa* 85 D4
Niger □, *Nigeria* 79 C6
Niger ■, *W. Afr.* 79 B6
Niger →, *W. Afr.* 79 D6
Nigeria ■, *W. Afr.* 79 D6
Nightcaps, *N.Z.* 87 L2
Nigríta, *Greece* 39 J6
Nihtaur, *India* 63 E8
Nii-Jima, *Japan* 49 G9
Niigata, *Japan* 48 F9
Niigata □, *Japan* 49 F9
Niihama, *Japan* 49 H6
Niihau, *U.S.A.* 102 H14
Niimi, *Japan* 49 G6
Niitsu, *Japan* 48 F9
Níjar, *Spain* 29 J2
Nijil, *Jordan* 69 E4
Nijkerk, *Neths.* 16 D7
Nijlen, *Belgium* 17 F5
Nijmegen, *Neths.* 16 E7
Nijverdal, *Neths.* 16 D8
Nīk Pey, *Iran* 65 B6
Nike, *Nigeria* 79 D6
Nikel, *Russia* 8 B21
Nikiniki, *Indonesia* 57 F6
Nikki, *Benin* 79 D5
Nikkō, *Japan* 49 F9
Nikolayev, *Ukraine* 42 C4
Nikolayevsk, *Russia* 41 G14
Nikolayevsk-na-Amur, *Russia* 45 D15
Nikolsk, *Russia* 41 B14
Nikolskoye, *Russia* 45 D17
Nikopol, *Bulgaria* 38 F7
Nikopol, *Ukraine* 42 C6
Niksar, *Turkey* 42 F7
Nīkshahr, *Iran* 65 E9
Nikšić, *Montenegro, Yug.* 21 N8
Nîl, Nahr en →, *Africa* 76 H7
Nîl el Abyad →, *Sudan* 77 D3
Nîl el Azraq →, *Sudan* 77 D3
Niland, *U.S.A.* 113 M11
Nile = Nîl, Nahr en →, *Africa* 76 H7
Nile □, *Uganda* 82 B3
Nile Delta, *Egypt* 76 H7
Niles, *U.S.A.* 106 E4
Nilo Peçanha, *Brazil* 123 D4
Nimach, *India* 62 G6
Nimbahera, *India* 62 G6
Nîmes, *France* 27 E8
Nimfaíon, Ákra-, *Greece* 39 J7
Nimmitabel, *Australia* 91 F4
Nimneryskiy, *Russia* 45 D13
Nimule, *Sudan* 77 G3
Nin, *Croatia* 33 D12
Nīnawá, *Iraq* 64 B4
Nindigully, *Australia* 91 D4
Ninemile, *U.S.A.* 100 B2
Nineveh = Nīnawá, *Iraq* 64 B4
Ning Xian, *China* 50 G4
Ningaloo, *Australia* 88 D1
Ning'an, *China* 51 B15
Ningbo, *China* 53 C13
Ningcheng, *China* 51 D10
Ningde, *China* 53 D12
Ningdu, *China* 53 D10
Ninggang, *China* 53 D9
Ningguo, *China* 53 B12
Ninghai, *China* 53 C13
Ninghua, *China* 53 D11
Ningjin, *China* 50 F8
Ningjing Shan, *China* 52 B2
Ninglang, *China* 52 D3
Ningling, *China* 50 G8
Ningming, *China* 52 F6
Ningnan, *China* 52 D4
Ningpo = Ningbo, *China* 53 C13
Ningqiang, *China* 50 H4
Ningshan, *China* 50 H5
Ningsia Hui A.R. = Ningxia Huizu Zizhiqu □, *China* 50 E3
Ningwu, *China* 50 E7
Ningxia Huizu Zizhiqu □, *China* 50 E3
Ningxiang, *China* 53 C9
Ningyang, *China* 50 G9
Ningyuan, *China* 53 E8
Ninh Binh, *Vietnam* 58 B5
Ninh Giang, *Vietnam* 58 B6
Ninh Hoa, *Vietnam* 58 F7
Ninh Ma, *Vietnam* 58 F7
Ninove, *Belgium* 17 G4
Nioaque, *Brazil* 127 A4
Niobrara, *U.S.A.* 108 D6
Niobrara →, *U.S.A.* 108 D6
Niono, *Mali* 78 C3
Nioro du Rip, *Senegal* 78 C1
Nioro du Sahel, *Mali* 78 B3
Niort, *France* 26 B3
Nipawin, *Canada* 101 C8
Nipawin Prov. Park, *Canada* 101 C8
Nipigon, *Canada* 98 C2
Nipigon, L., *Canada* 98 C2
Nipin →, *Canada* 101 B7
Nipishish L., *Canada* 99 B7
Nipissing L., *Canada* 98 C4
Nipomo, *U.S.A.* 113 K6
Nipton, *U.S.A.* 113 K11
Niquelândia, *Brazil* 123 D2
Nīr, *Iran* 64 B5
Nirasaki, *Japan* 49 G9
Nirmal, *India* 60 K11
Nirmali, *India* 63 F12
Niš, *Serbia, Yug.* 21 M11
Nisa, *Portugal* 31 F3
Nişāb, *Yemen* 68 E4
Nišava →, *Serbia, Yug.* 21 M11
Niscemi, *Italy* 35 E7
Nishinomiya, *Japan* 49 G7
Nishin'omote, *Japan* 49 J5
Nishiwaki, *Japan* 49 G7
Nísíros, *Greece* 39 N10
Niskibi →, *Canada* 98 A2
Nispen, *Neths.* 17 F4
Nisqually →, *U.S.A.* 112 C4
Nissáki, *Greece* 37 A3
Nissan →, *Sweden* 11 H6
Nissedal, *Norway* 10 E2
Nisser, *Norway* 10 E2
Nissum Fjord, *Denmark* 11 H2
Nistelrode, *Neths.* 17 E7
Nisutlin →, *Canada* 100 A2
Nitchequon, *Canada* 99 B5
Niterói, *Brazil* 123 F3
Nith →, *U.K.* 14 F5
Nitra, *Czech.* 21 G8
Nittedal, *Norway* 10 D4
Nittendau, *Germany* 19 F8
Niuafo'ou, *Tonga* 87 B11
Niue, *Cook Is.* 93 J11
Niulan Jiang →, *China* 52 D4
Niut, *Indonesia* 56 D4
Niutou Shan, *China* 53 C13
Niuzhuang, *China* 51 D12
Nivelles, *Belgium* 17 G4
Nivernais, *France* 25 E10
Nixon, *U.S.A.* 109 L6
Nizamabad, *India* 60 K11
Nizamghat, *India* 61 E19
Nizhne Kolymsk, *Russia* 45 C17
Nizhne-Vartovsk, *Russia* 44 C8
Nizhneangarsk, *Russia* 45 D11
Nizhnegorskiy, *Ukraine* 42 D6
Nizhnekamsk, *Russia* 41 D17
Nizhneudinsk, *Russia* 45 D10
Nizhneyansk, *Russia* 45 B14
Nizhniy Lomov, *Russia* 41 E13
Nizhniy Novgorod, *Russia* 41 C14
Nizhniy Tagil, *Russia* 44 D6
Nizip, *Turkey* 67 E7
Nizké Tatry, *Czech.* 20 G9
Nizza Monferrato, *Italy* 32 D5
Njakwa, *Malawi* 83 E3
Njanji, *Zambia* 83 E3
Njinjo, *Tanzania* 83 D4
Njombe, *Tanzania* 83 D3
Njombe □, *Tanzania* 83 D3
Njombe →, *Tanzania* 82 D4
Nkambe, *Cameroon* 79 D7
Nkana, *Zambia* 83 E2
Nkawkaw, *Ghana* 79 D4
Nkayi, *Zimbabwe* 83 F2
Nkhata Bay, *Malawi* 80 G6
Nkhota Kota, *Malawi* 83 E3
Nkongsamba, *Cameroon* 79 E6
Nkurenkuru, *Namibia* 84 B2
Nkwanta, *Ghana* 78 D4
Nmai →, *Burma* 61 G20
Noakhali = Maijdi, *Bangla.* 61 H17
Noatak, *U.S.A.* 96 B3
Nobel, *Canada* 106 A4
Nobeoka, *Japan* 49 H5
Noblejas, *Spain* 28 F1
Noblesville, *U.S.A.* 104 E3
Noce →, *Italy* 32 B8
Nocera Inferiore, *Italy* 35 B7
Nocera Terinese, *Italy* 35 C9
Nocera Umbra, *Italy* 33 E9
Noci, *Italy* 35 B10
Nockatunga, *Australia* 91 D3
Nocona, *U.S.A.* 109 J6
Noda, *Japan* 49 G9
Noel, *U.S.A.* 109 G7
Nogales, *Mexico* 114 A2
Nogales, *U.S.A.* 111 L8
Nōgata, *Japan* 49 H5
Nogent-en-Bassigny, *France* 25 D12
Nogent-le-Rotrou, *France* 24 D7
Nogent-sur-Seine, *France* 25 D10
Noggerup, *Australia* 89 F2
Noginsk, *Russia* 41 D11
Noginsk, *Sib., Russia* 45 C10
Nogoa →, *Australia* 90 C4
Nogoyá, *Argentina* 126 C4
Nogueira de Ramuin, *Spain* 30 C3
Noguera Pallaresa →, *Spain* 28 D5
Noguera Ribagorzana →, *Spain* 28 D5
Nohar, *India* 62 E6
Noire, Mt., *France* 24 D3
Noirétable, *France* 26 C7
Noirmoutier, I. de, *France* 24 F4
Noirmoutier-en-l'Ile, *France* 24 F4
Nojane, *Botswana* 84 C3
Nojima-Zaki, *Japan* 49 G9
Nok Kundi, *Pakistan* 60 E3
Nokaneng, *Botswana* 84 B3
Nokhtuysk, *Russia* 45 C12
Nokomis, *Canada* 101 C8
Nokomis L., *Canada* 101 B8
Nol, *Sweden* 11 G6
Nola, *C.A.R.* 80 D3
Nola, *Italy* 35 B7
Nolay, *France* 25 F11
Noli, C. di, *Italy* 32 D5
Nolinsk, *Russia* 41 C16
Noma Omuramba →, *Namibia* 84 B3
Noman L., *Canada* 101 A7
Nombre de Dios, *Panama* 116 E4
Nome, *U.S.A.* 96 B3
Nomo-Zaki, *Japan* 49 H4
Nonacho L., *Canada* 101 A7
Nonancourt, *France* 24 D8
Nonant-le-Pin, *France* 24 D7
Nonda, *Australia* 90 C3
Nong Chang, *Thailand* 58 E2
Nong Het, *Laos* 58 C4
Nong Khai, *Thailand* 58 D4
Nong'an, *China* 51 B13
Nongoma, *S. Africa* 85 D5
Nonoava, *Mexico* 114 B3
Nonthaburi, *Thailand* 58 F3
Nontron, *France* 26 C4
Nonza, *France* 27 F13
Noonamah, *Australia* 88 B5
Noonan, *U.S.A.* 108 A3
Noondoo, *Australia* 91 D4
Noonkanbah, *Australia* 88 C3
Noord-Bergum, *Neths.* 16 B8
Noord Brabant □, *Neths.* 17 E6
Noord Holland □, *Neths.* 16 D5
Noordbeveland, *Neths.* 17 E3
Noordeloos, *Neths.* 16 E5
Noordhollandsch Kanaal, *Neths.* 16 C5
Noordhorn, *Neths.* 16 B8
Noordoostpolder, *Neths.* 16 C7
Noordwijk aan Zee, *Neths.* 16 D4
Noordwijk-Binnen, *Neths.* 16 D4
Noordwijkerhout, *Neths.* 16 D5
Noordzee Kanaal, *Neths.* 16 D5
Noorwolde, *Neths.* 16 C8
Nootka, *Canada* 100 D3
Nootka I., *Canada* 100 D3
Nóqui, *Angola* 80 F2
Nora, *Ethiopia* 77 D5
Noranda, *Canada* 98 C4
Nórcia, *Italy* 33 F10
Norco, *U.S.A.* 113 M9
Nord □, *France* 25 B10
Nord-Ostsee Kanal, *Germany* 18 A5
Nord-Trøndelag fylke □, *Norway* 8 D12
Nordagutu, *Norway* 10 E3
Nordaustlandet, *Svalbard* 4 B9
Nordborg, *Denmark* 11 J3
Nordby, *Århus, Denmark* 11 J4
Nordby, *Ribe, Denmark* 11 J2
Norddeich, *Germany* 18 B3
Nordegg, *Canada* 100 C5
Norden, *Germany* 18 B3
Nordenham, *Germany* 18 B4
Norderhov, *Norway* 10 D4
Norderney, *Germany* 18 B3
Nordfriesische Inseln, *Germany* 18 A4
Nordhausen, *Germany* 18 D6
Nordhorn, *Germany* 18 C3
Nordjyllands Amtskommune □, *Denmark* 11 H4
Nordkapp, *Norway* 8 A18
Nordkapp, *Svalbard* 4 A9
Nordkinn = Kinnarodden, *Norway* 6 A11
Nordland fylke □, *Norway* 8 D12
Nördlingen, *Germany* 19 G6
Nordrhein-Westfalen □, *Germany* 18 D3
Nordstrand, *Germany* 18 A4
Nordvik, *Russia* 45 B12
Nore, *Norway* 10 D3
Norefjell, *Norway* 10 D3
Norembega, *Canada* 98 C3
Noresund, *Norway* 10 D3
Norfolk, *Nebr., U.S.A.* 108 D6
Norfolk, *Va., U.S.A.* 104 G7
Norfolk □, *U.K.* 12 E9
Norfolk Broads, *U.K.* 12 E9
Norfolk I., *Pac. Oc.* 92 K8
Norfork Res., *U.S.A.* 109 G8
Norg, *Neths.* 16 B8
Norilsk, *Russia* 45 C9
Norley, *Australia* 91 D3
Norma, Mt., *Australia* 90 C3
Normal, *U.S.A.* 108 E10
Norman, *U.S.A.* 109 H6
Norman →, *Australia* 90 B3
Norman Wells, *Canada* 96 B7
Normanby →, *Australia* 90 A3
Normandie, *France* 24 D7
Normandie, Collines de, *France* 24 D6
Normandin, *Canada* 98 C5
Normandy = Normandie, *France* 24 D7
Normanhurst, Mt., *Australia* 89 E3
Normanton, *Australia* 90 B3
Norquay, *Canada* 101 C8
Norquinco, *Argentina* 128 B2
Norrbotten □, *Sweden* 8 C17
Norrby, *Sweden* 8 D15
Nørre Åby, *Denmark* 11 J3
Nørre Nebel, *Denmark* 11 J2
Nørresundby, *Denmark* 11 G3
Norris, *U.S.A.* 110 D8
Norristown, *U.S.A.* 107 F9
Norrköping, *Sweden* 11 F10
Norrland, *Sweden* 8 E13
Norrtälje, *Sweden* 10 E12
Norseman, *Australia* 89 F3
Norsholm, *Sweden* 11 F9
Norsk, *Russia* 45 D14
Norte, Pta., *Argentina* 128 B4
Norte, Pta. del, *Canary Is.* 36 G2
Norte de Santander □, *Colombia* 120 B3
Nortelândia, *Brazil* 125 C6
North Adams, *U.S.A.* 107 D11
North America 94 F10
North Battleford, *Canada* 101 C7
North Bay, *Canada* 98 C4
North Belcher Is., *Canada* 98 A4
North Bend, *Canada* 100 D4
North Bend, *Oreg., U.S.A.* 110 E1
North Bend, *Pa., U.S.A.* 106 E7
North Bend, *Wash., U.S.A.* 112 C5
North Berwick, *U.K.* 14 E6
North Berwick, *U.S.A.* 107 C14
North Buganda □, *Uganda* 82 B3
North Canadian →, *U.S.A.* 109 H7
North C., *Canada* 99 C7
North C., *N.Z.* 87 F4
North Caribou L., *Canada* 98 B1
North Carolina □, *U.S.A.* 105 H5
North Channel, *Canada* 98 C3
North Channel, *U.K.* 14 G3
North Chicago, *U.S.A.* 104 D2
North Dakota □, *U.S.A.* 108 B5
North Dandalup, *Australia* 89 F2
North Down □, *U.K.* 15 B6
North Downs, *U.K.* 13 F8
North East, *U.S.A.* 106 D5
North East Frontier Agency = Arunachal Pradesh □, *India* 61 E19
North East Providence Chan., *W. Indies* 116 A4
North Eastern □, *Kenya* 82 B5
North Esk →, *U.K.* 14 E6
North European Plain, *Europe* 6 D11
North Foreland, *U.K.* 13 F9
North Fork, *U.S.A.* 112 H7
North Fork American →, *U.S.A.* 112 G5
North Fork Feather →, *U.S.A.* 112 F5
North Frisian Is. = Nordfriesische Inseln, *Germany* 18 A4
North Henik L., *Canada* 101 A9
North Highlands, *U.S.A.* 112 G5
North Horr, *Kenya* 82 B4
North I., *Kenya* 82 B4
North I., *N.Z.* 87 H5
North Kingsville, *U.S.A.* 106 E4
North Knife →, *Canada* 101 B10
North Koel →, *India* 63 G10
North Korea ■, *Asia* 51 E14
North Lakhimpur, *India* 61 F19
North Las Vegas, *U.S.A.* 113 J11
North Loup →, *U.S.A.* 108 E5
North Magnetic Pole, *Canada* 4 B2
North Minch, *U.K.* 14 C3
North Nahanni →, *Canada* 100 A4
North Olmsted, *U.S.A.* 106 E3
North Ossetian Republic □, *Russia* 43 E11
North Pagai, I. = Pagai Utara, *Indonesia* 56 E2
North Palisade, *U.S.A.* 111 H4
North Platte, *U.S.A.* 108 E4
North Platte →, *U.S.A.* 108 E4
North Pt., *Canada* 99 C7
North Pole, *Arctic* 4 A

North Portal

North Portal, *Canada* 101 D8
North Powder, *U.S.A.* ... 110 D5
North Ronaldsay, *U.K.* ... 14 B6
North Saskatchewan →, *Canada* 101 C7
North Sea, *Europe* 6 D6
North Sporades = Voríai Sporádhes, *Greece* 39 K6
North Sydney, *Canada* ... 99 C7
North Taranaki Bight, *N.Z.* 87 H5
North Thompson →, *Canada* 100 C4
North Tonawanda, *U.S.A.* 106 C6
North Troy, *U.S.A.* 107 B12
North Truchas Pk., *U.S.A.* 111 J11
North Twin I., *Canada* ... 98 B3
North Tyne →, *U.K.* 12 C5
North Uist, *U.K.* 14 D1
North Vancouver, *Canada* 100 D4
North Vernon, *U.S.A.* ... 104 F3
North Wabasca L., *Canada* 100 B6
North Walsham, *U.K.* 12 E9
North West C., *Australia* . 88 D1
North West Christmas I. Ridge, *Pac. Oc.* 93 G11
North West Frontier □, *Pakistan* 62 C4
North West Highlands, *U.K.* 14 D3
North West Providence Channel, *W. Indies* 116 A4
North West River, *Canada* 99 B7
North West Territories □, *Canada* 96 B9
North Western □, *Zambia* 83 E2
North York Moors, *U.K.* . 12 C7
North Yorkshire □, *U.K.* . 12 C6
Northallerton, *U.K.* 12 C6
Northam, *S. Africa* 84 C4
Northampton, *Australia* .. 89 E1
Northampton, *U.K.* 13 E7
Northampton, *Mass., U.S.A.* 107 D12
Northampton, *Pa., U.S.A.* 107 F9
Northampton Downs, *Australia* 90 C4
Northamptonshire □, *U.K.* 13 E7
Northbridge, *U.S.A.* 107 D13
Northcliffe, *Australia* 89 F2
Northeim, *Germany* 18 D6
Northern □, *Malawi* 83 E3
Northern □, *Uganda* 82 B3
Northern □, *Zambia* 83 E3
Northern Circars, *India* ... 61 L13
Northern Indian L., *Canada* 101 B9
Northern Ireland □, *U.K.* 15 B5
Northern Light, L., *Canada* 98 C1
Northern Marianas □, *Pac. Oc.* 92 F6
Northern Province □, *S. Leone* 78 D2
Northern Territory □, *Australia* 88 D5
Northfield, *U.S.A.* 108 C8
Northland □, *N.Z.* 87 F4
Northome, *U.S.A.* 108 B7
Northport, *Ala., U.S.A.* .. 105 J2
Northport, *Mich., U.S.A.* . 104 C3
Northport, *Wash., U.S.A.* 110 B5
Northumberland □, *U.K.* . 12 B5
Northumberland, C., *Australia* 91 F3
Northumberland Is., *Australia* 90 C4
Northumberland Str., *Canada* 99 C7
Northwich, *U.K.* 12 D5
Northwood, *Iowa, U.S.A.* 108 D8
Northwood, *N. Dak., U.S.A.* 108 B6
Norton, *U.S.A.* 108 F5
Norton, *Zimbabwe* 83 F3
Norton Sd., *U.S.A.* 96 B3
Nortorf, *Germany* 18 A5
Norwalk, *Calif., U.S.A.* .. 113 M8
Norwalk, *Conn., U.S.A.* .. 107 E11
Norwalk, *Ohio, U.S.A.* ... 106 E2
Norway, *U.S.A.* 104 C2
Norway ■, *Europe* 8 E11
Norway House, *Canada* .. 101 C9
Norwegian Sea, *Atl. Oc.* .. 4 C8
Norwich, *Canada* 106 D4
Norwich, *U.K.* 12 E9
Norwich, *Conn., U.S.A.* . 107 E12
Norwich, *N.Y., U.S.A.* ... 107 D9
Norwood, *Canada* 106 B7
Noshiro, *Japan* 48 D10
Nosok, *Russia* 44 B9
Nosovka, *Ukraine* 40 F7
Noss Hd., *U.K.* 14 C5
Nossa Senhora da Glória, *Brazil* 122 D4
Nossa Senhora das Dores, *Brazil* 122 D4
Nossa Senhora do Livramento, *Brazil* 125 D6
Nossebro, *Sweden* 11 F6
Nossob →, *S. Africa* 84 D3
Nosy Bé, *Madag.* 81 G9
Nosy Boraha, *Madag.* 85 B8
Nosy Mitsio, *Madag.* 81 G9
Nosy Varika, *Madag.* 85 C8
Noteć →, *Poland* 20 C5
Notigi Dam, *Canada* 101 B9
Notikewin →, *Canada* ... 100 B5
Notios Evvoïkos Kólpos, *Greece* 39 L7
Noto, *Italy* 35 F8
Noto, G. di, *Italy* 35 F8
Notodden, *Norway* 10 E3
Notre-Dame, *Canada* 99 C7
Notre Dame B., *Canada* .. 99 C8
Notre Dame de Koartac = Koartac, *Canada* 97 B13
Notre Dame d'Ivugivic = Ivugivik, *Canada* 97 B12
Notsé, *Togo* 79 D5
Nottaway →, *Canada* 98 B4
Nøtterøy, *Norway* 10 E4
Nottingham, *U.K.* 12 E6
Nottinghamshire □, *U.K.* . 12 D7
Nottoway →, *U.S.A.* 104 G7
Notwane →, *Botswana* ... 84 C4
Nouâdhibou, *Mauritania* .. 74 D1
Nouâdhibou, Ras, *Mauritania* 74 D1
Nouakchott, *Mauritania* .. 78 B1
Nouméa, *N. Cal.* 92 K8
Noupoort, *S. Africa* 84 E3
Nouveau Comptoir, *Canada* 98 B4
Nouvelle-Calédonie = New Caledonia, *Pac. Oc.* 92 K8
Nouzonville, *France* 25 C11
Nová Baňa, *Czech.* 21 G8
Nová Bystřice, *Czech.* 20 F5
Nova Casa Nova, *Brazil* .. 122 C3
Nova Cruz, *Brazil* 122 C4
Nova Era, *Brazil* 123 E3
Nova Esperança, *Brazil* .. 127 A5
Nova Friburgo, *Brazil* 123 F3
Nova Gaia = Cambundi-Catembo, *Angola* 80 G3
Nova Gradiška, *Croatia* .. 21 K7
Nova Granada, *Brazil* 123 F2
Nova Iguaçu, *Brazil* 123 F3
Nova Iorque, *Brazil* 122 C3
Nova Lamego, *Guinea-Biss.* 78 C2
Nova Lima, *Brazil* 127 A7
Nova Lisboa = Huambo, *Angola* 81 G3
Nova Lusitânia, *Mozam.* . 83 F3
Nova Mambone, *Mozam.* . 85 C6
Nova Mesto, *Slovenia* 33 C12
Nova Ponte, *Brazil* 123 E2
Nova Scotia □, *Canada* .. 99 C7
Nova Sofala, *Mozam.* 85 C5
Nova Venécia, *Brazil* 123 E3
Nova Vida, *Brazil* 125 C5
Nova Zagora, *Bulgaria* ... 38 G8
Novaleksandrovskaya, *Russia* 43 D9
Novannenskiy, *Russia* 41 F13
Novara, *Italy* 32 C5
Novata, *U.S.A.* 112 G4
Novaya Kakhovka, *Ukraine* 42 C5
Novaya Lyalya, *Russia* ... 44 D7
Novaya Sibir, Ostrov, *Russia* 45 B16
Novaya Zemlya, *Russia* ... 44 B6
Novelda, *Spain* 29 G4
Novellara, *Italy* 32 D7
Noventa Vicentina, *Italy* .. 33 C8
Novgorod, *Russia* 40 B7
Novgorod-Severskiy, *Ukraine* 40 E8
Novi Bečej, *Serbia, Yug.* . 21 K10
Novi Grad, *Croatia* 33 C10
Novi Krichim, *Bulgaria* ... 38 G7
Novi Lígure, *Italy* 32 D5
Novi Pazar, *Bulgaria* 38 F10
Novi Pazar, *Serbia, Yug.* . 21 M10
Novi Sad, *Serbia, Yug.* ... 21 K9
Novi Vinodolski, *Croatia* . 33 C11
Novigrad, *Croatia* 33 D12
Noville, *Belgium* 17 H7
Novo Acôrdo, *Brazil* 122 D2
Novo Aripuanã, *Brazil* ... 121 E5
Nôvo Cruzeiro, *Brazil* 123 E3
Nôvo Hamburgo, *Brazil* .. 127 B5
Novo Horizonte, *Brazil* ... 123 F2
Novo Remanso, *Brazil* 122 C3
Novo-Zavidovskiy, *Russia* 41 C10
Novoakrainka, *Ukraine* ... 42 B4
Novoataysk, *Russia* 44 D9
Novoazovsk, *Ukraine* 42 C8
Novobelitsa, *Belorussia* .. 40 E7
Novobogatinskoye, *Kazakhstan* 43 C14
Novocherkassk, *Russia* ... 43 C9
Novodevichye, *Russia* 41 E16
Novograd-Volynskiy, *Ukraine* 40 F5
Novogrudok, *Belorussia* .. 40 E4
Novokachalinsk, *Russia* .. 48 B6
Novokayakent, *Russia* 43 E12
Novokazalinsk, *Kazakhstan* 44 E7
Novokhopersk, *Russia* 41 F12
Novokuybyshevsk, *Russia* . 41 E16
Novokuznetsk, *Russia* 44 D9
Novomirgorod, *Ukraine* .. 42 B4
Novomoskovsk, *Russia* ... 41 D11
Novomoskovsk, *Ukraine* .. 42 B6
Novopolotsk, *Belorussia* .. 40 D6
Novorossiysk, *Russia* 42 D7
Novorybnoye, *Russia* 45 B11
Novorzhev, *Russia* 40 C6
Novoselitsa, *Ukraine* 42 B2
Novoshakhtinsk, *Russia* .. 43 C8
Novosibirsk, *Russia* 44 D9
Novosibirskiye Ostrova, *Russia* 45 B15
Novosil, *Russia* 41 E10
Novosokolniki, *Russia* 40 C7
Novotroitsk, *Russia* 44 D6
Novotulskiy, *Russia* 41 D10
Novouzensk, *Russia* 41 F16
Novovolynsk, *Ukraine* 40 F4
Novovyatsk, *Russia* 41 B16
Novozybkov, *Russia* 40 E8
Novska, *Croatia* 21 K6
Novvy Port, *Russia* 44 C8
Novy Bug, *Ukraine* 42 C5
Nový Bydzov, *Czech.* 20 E5
Novy Dwór Mazowiecki, *Poland* 20 C10
Novyy Afon, *Georgia* 43 E9
Novyy Oskol, *Russia* 41 F10
Now Shahr, *Iran* 65 B6
Nowa Deba, *Poland* 20 E11
Nowa Ruda, *Poland* 20 E6
Nowa Sól, *Poland* 20 D5
Nowbarān, *Iran* 65 C6
Nowe, *Poland* 20 B8
Nowghāb, *Iran* 65 C8
Nowgong, *India* 61 F18
Nowogard, *Poland* 20 B5
Nowogród, *Poland* 20 B11
Nowra, *Australia* 91 E5
Nowshera, *Pakistan* 60 B8
Nowy Korczyn, *Poland* ... 20 E10
Nowy Sącz, *Poland* 20 F10
Noxen, *U.S.A.* 107 E8
Noxon, *U.S.A.* 110 C6
Noya, *Spain* 30 C2
Noyant, *France* 24 E7
Noyers, *France* 25 E10
Noyes I., *U.S.A.* 100 B2
Noyon, *France* 25 C9
Noyon, *Mongolia* 50 C2
Nozay, *France* 24 E5
Nsa, O. en →, *Algeria* .. 75 B6
Nsanje, *Malawi* 83 F4
Nsawam, *Ghana* 79 D4
Nsomba, *Zambia* 83 E2
Nsukka, *Nigeria* 79 D6
Nu Jiang →, *China* 52 C1
Nu Shan, *China* 52 D2
Nuba Mts. = Nubah, Jibalan, *Sudan* 77 E3
Nubah, Jibalan, *Sudan* ... 77 E3
Nubian Desert = Nûbîya, Es Sahrâ En, *Sudan* 76 C3
Nûbîya, Es Sahrâ En, *Sudan* 76 C3
Ñuble □, *Chile* 126 D1
Nuboai, *Indonesia* 57 E9
Nubra →, *India* 63 B7
Nueces →, *U.S.A.* 109 M6
Nueltin L., *Canada* 101 A9
Nuenen, *Neths.* 17 F7
Nueva, I., *Chile* 128 E3
Nueva Antioquia, *Colombia* 120 B4
Nueva Asunción □, *Paraguay* 126 A3
Nueva Esparta □, *Venezuela* 121 A5
Nueva Gerona, *Cuba* 116 B3
Nueva Imperial, *Chile* ... 128 A2
Nueva Palmira, *Uruguay* .. 126 C4
Nueva Rosita, *Mexico* ... 114 B4
Nueva San Salvador, *El Salv.* 116 D2
Nuéve de Julio, *Argentina* 126 D3
Nuevitas, *Cuba* 116 B4
Nuevo, G., *Argentina* 128 B4
Nuevo Guerrero, *Mexico* . 115 B5
Nuevo Laredo, *Mexico* ... 115 B5
Nuevo León □, *Mexico* .. 114 C4
Nuevo Mundo, Cerro, *Bolivia* 124 E4
Nuevo Rocafuerte, *Ecuador* 120 D2
Nugget Pt., *N.Z.* 87 M2
Nugrus, Gebel, *Egypt* 76 C3
Nuhaka, *N.Z.* 87 H6
Nuits-St.-Georges, *France* . 25 E11
Nukey Bluff, *Australia* ... 91 E2
Nukheila, *Sudan* 76 D2
Nuku'alofa, *Tonga* 87 E11
Nukus, *Uzbekistan* 44 E6
Nuland, *Neths.* 16 E6
Nulato, *U.S.A.* 96 B4
Nules, *Spain* 28 F4
Nullagine →, *Australia* .. 88 D3
Nullarbor, *Australia* 89 F5
Nullarbor Plain, *Australia* . 89 F4
Numalla, L., *Australia* ... 91 D3
Numan, *Nigeria* 79 D7
Numansdorp, *Neths.* 16 E4
Numata, *Japan* 49 F9
Numatinna →, *Sudan* ... 77 F2
Numazu, *Japan* 49 G9
Numbulwar, *Australia* ... 90 A2
Numfoor, *Indonesia* 57 E8
Numurkah, *Australia* 91 F4
Nunaksaluk I., *Canada* ... 99 A7
Nuneaton, *U.K.* 13 E6
Nungo, *Mozam.* 83 E4
Nungwe, *Tanzania* 82 C3
Nunivak, *U.S.A.* 96 B3
Nunkun, *India* 63 C7
Nunspeet, *Neths.* 16 D7
Nuoro, *Italy* 34 B2
Nuquí, *Colombia* 120 B2
Nūrābād, *Iran* 65 E8
Nure →, *Italy* 32 C6
Nuremburg = Nürnberg, *Germany* 19 F7
Nuri, *Mexico* 114 B3
Nurina, *Australia* 89 F4
Nuriootpa, *Australia* 91 E2
Nurlat, *Russia* 41 D17
Nürnberg, *Germany* 19 F7
Nurran, L. = Terewah, L., *Australia* 91 D4
Nurrari Lakes, *Australia* .. 89 E5
Nurri, *Italy* 34 C2
Nusa Barung, *Indonesia* .. 57 H15
Nusa Kambangan, *Indonesia* 57 G13
Nusa Tenggara Barat □, *Indonesia* 56 F5
Nusa Tenggara Timur □, *Indonesia* 57 F6
Nushki, *Pakistan* 62 E2
Nutak, *Canada* 97 C13
Nuth, *Neths.* 17 G7
Nutwood Downs, *Australia* 90 B1
Nuuk = Godthåb, *Greenland* 97 B14
Nuwakot, *Nepal* 63 E10
Nuweiba', *Egypt* 76 B3
Nuweveldberge, *S. Africa* . 84 E3
Nuyts, C., *Australia* 89 F5
Nuyts Arch., *Australia* ... 91 E1
Nxau-Nxau, *Botswana* ... 84 B3
Nyaake, *Liberia* 78 E3
Nyack, *U.S.A.* 107 E11
Nyadal, *Sweden* 10 B11
Nyah West, *Australia* 91 F3
Nyahanga, *Tanzania* 82 C3
Nyahua, *Tanzania* 82 D3
Nyahururu, *Kenya* 82 B4
Nyainqentanglha Shan, *China* 54 C4
Nyakanazi, *Tanzania* 82 C3
Nyakrom, *Ghana* 79 D4
Nyâlâ, *Sudan* 77 E1
Nyamandhlovu, *Zimbabwe* 83 F2
Nyambiti, *Tanzania* 82 C3
Nyamwaga, *Tanzania* 82 C3
Nyandekwa, *Tanzania* 82 C3
Nyanding →, *Sudan* 77 F3
Nyangana, *Namibia* 84 B3
Nyanguge, *Tanzania* 82 C3
Nyankpala, *Ghana* 79 D4
Nyanza, *Burundi* 82 C2
Nyanza, *Rwanda* 82 C2
Nyanza □, *Kenya* 82 C3
Nyarling →, *Canada* 100 A6
Nyasa, L. = Malawi, L., *Africa* 83 E3
Nyazura, *Zimbabwe* 83 F3
Nyazwidzi →, *Zimbabwe* . 83 F3
Nyborg, *Denmark* 11 J4
Nybro, *Sweden* 9 H13
Nyda, *Russia* 44 C8
Nyeri, *Kenya* 82 C4
Nyerol, *Sudan* 77 F3
Nyhem, *Sweden* 10 B9
Nyiel, *Sudan* 77 F3
Nyinahin, *Ghana* 78 D4
Nyírbátor, *Hungary* 21 H12
Nyíregyháza, *Hungary* ... 21 H11
Nykarleby, *Finland* 8 E17
Nykøbing, *Sjælland, Denmark* 11 J5
Nykøbing, *Storstrøm, Denmark* 11 K5
Nykøbing, *Viborg, Denmark* 11 H2
Nyköping, *Sweden* 11 F11
Nykvarn, *Sweden* 10 E11
Nyland, *Sweden* 10 A11
Nylstroom, *S. Africa* 85 C4
Nymagee, *Australia* 91 E4
Nymburk, *Czech.* 20 E5
Nynäshamn, *Sweden* 10 F11
Nyngan, *Australia* 91 E4
Nyon, *Switz.* 22 D2
Nyong →, *Cameroon* 79 E6
Nyons, *France* 27 D9
Nyord, *Denmark* 11 J6
Nyou, *Burkina Faso* 79 C4
Nysa, *Poland* 20 E7
Nysa →, *Europe* 20 C4
Nyssa, *U.S.A.* 110 E5
Nysted, *Denmark* 11 K5
Nyunzu, *Zaïre* 82 D2
Nyurba, *Russia* 45 C12
Nzega, *Tanzania* 82 C3
Nzega □, *Tanzania* 82 C3
N'Zérékoré, *Guinea* 78 D3
Nzeto, *Angola* 80 F2
Nzilo, Chutes de, *Zaïre* ... 83 E2
Nzubuka, *Tanzania* 82 C3

O

Ō-Shima, *Nagasaki, Japan* 49 G4
Ō-Shima, *Shizuoka, Japan* 49 G9
Oacoma, *U.S.A.* 108 D5
Oahe Dam, *U.S.A.* 108 C4
Oahe L., *U.S.A.* 108 C4
Oahu, *U.S.A.* 102 H16
Oak Creek, *U.S.A.* 110 F10
Oak Harbour, *U.S.A.* 112 B4
Oak Hill, *U.S.A.* 104 G5
Oak Park, *U.S.A.* 104 E2
Oak Ridge, *U.S.A.* 105 G3
Oak View, *U.S.A.* 113 L7
Oakan-Dake, *Japan* 48 C12
Oakbank, *Australia* 91 E3
Oakdale, *Calif., U.S.A.* .. 111 H3
Oakdale, *La., U.S.A.* 109 K8
Oakengates, *U.K.* 12 E5
Oakes, *U.S.A.* 108 B5
Oakesdale, *U.S.A.* 110 C5
Oakey, *Australia* 91 D5
Oakham, *U.K.* 12 E7
Oakhurst, *U.S.A.* 112 H7
Oakland, *Calif., U.S.A.* .. 111 H2
Oakland, *Oreg., U.S.A.* .. 110 E2
Oakland City, *U.S.A.* 104 F2
Oakley, *Idaho, U.S.A.* ... 110 E7
Oakley, *Kans., U.S.A.* ... 108 F4
Oakover →, *Australia* ... 88 D3
Oakridge, *U.S.A.* 110 E2
Oakville, *U.S.A.* 112 D3
Oamaru, *N.Z.* 87 L3
Oasis, *Calif., U.S.A.* 113 M10
Oasis, *Nev., U.S.A.* 112 H9
Oates Land, *Antarctica* ... 5 C11
Oatman, *U.S.A.* 113 K12
Oaxaca, *Mexico* 115 D5
Oaxaca □, *Mexico* 115 D5
Ob →, *Russia* 44 C7
Oba, *Canada* 98 C3
Obala, *Cameroon* 79 E7
Obama, *Japan* 49 G7
Oban, *U.K.* 14 E3
Obbia, *Somali Rep.* 68 F4
Obdam, *Neths.* 16 C5
Obed, *Canada* 100 C5
Ober-Aagau, *Switz.* 22 B5
Obera, *Argentina* 127 B4
Oberalppass, *Switz.* 23 C7
Oberalpstock, *Switz.* 23 C7
Oberammergau, *Germany* . 19 H7
Oberdrauburg, *Austria* ... 21 J2
Oberengadin, *Switz.* 23 C9
Oberentfelden, *Switz.* 22 B6
Oberhausen, *Germany* ... 18 D2
Oberkirch, *Germany* 19 G4
Oberland, *Switz.* 22 C5
Oberlin, *Kans., U.S.A.* ... 108 F4
Oberlin, *La., U.S.A.* 109 K8
Oberlin, *Ohio, U.S.A.* 106 E2
Obernai, *France* 25 D14
Oberndorf, *Germany* 19 G4
Oberon, *Australia* 91 E4
Oberpfälzer Wald, *Germany* 19 F8
Obersiggenthal, *Switz.* 23 B6
Oberstdorf, *Germany* 19 H6
Oberwil, *Switz.* 22 A5
Obi, Kepulauan, *Indonesia* 57 E7
Obi Is. = Obi, Kepulauan, *Indonesia* 57 E7
Obiaruku, *Nigeria* 79 D6
Óbidos, *Brazil* 121 D6
Óbidos, *Portugal* 31 F1
Obihiro, *Japan* 48 C11
Obilatu, *Indonesia* 57 E7
Obilnoye, *Russia* 43 C11
Obing, *Germany* 19 H8
Öbisfelde, *Germany* 18 C6
Objat, *France* 26 C5
Obluchye, *Russia* 45 E14
Obninsk, *Russia* 41 D10
Obo, *C.A.R.* 82 A2
Obo, *Ethiopia* 77 G4
Oboa, Mt., *Uganda* 82 B3
Obock, *Djibouti* 77 E5
Oborniki, *Poland* 20 C6
Oboyan, *Russia* 41 F10
Obozerskaya, *Russia* 44 C5
Obrovac, *Croatia* 33 D12
Obruk, *Turkey* 66 D5
Observatory Inlet, *Canada* 100 B3
Obshchi Syrt, *Kazakhstan* . 6 E16
Obskaya Guba, *Russia* ... 44 C8
Obuasi, *Ghana* 79 D4
Obubra, *Nigeria* 79 D6
Obwalden □, *Switz.* 22 C6
Obzor, *Bulgaria* 38 G10
Ocala, *U.S.A.* 105 L4
Ocamo →, *Venezuela* ... 121 C4
Ocampo, *Mexico* 114 B3
Ocaña, *Colombia* 120 B3
Ocaña, *Spain* 28 F1
Oconomowoc, *U.S.A.* 108 D10
Ocate, *U.S.A.* 109 G2
Occidental, Cordillera, *Colombia* 120 C3
Occidental, Cordillera, *Peru* 124 C3
Ocean City, *N.J., U.S.A.* . 104 F8
Ocean City, *Wash., U.S.A.* 112 C2
Ocean I. = Banaba, *Kiribati* 92 H8
Ocean Park, *U.S.A.* 112 D2
Oceano, *U.S.A.* 113 K6
Oceanport, *U.S.A.* 107 F10
Oceanside, *U.S.A.* 113 M9
Ochagavia, *Spain* 28 C3
Ochamchire, *Georgia* 43 E9
Ochamps, *Belgium* 17 J6
Ochil Hills, *U.K.* 14 E5

Ochre River, *Canada* 101 C9
Ochsenfurt, *Germany* 19 F6
Ochsenhausen, *Germany* 19 G5
Ocilla, *U.S.A.* 105 K4
Ocmulgee →, *U.S.A.* 105 K4
Ocna Sibiului, *Romania* 38 D7
Ocoña, *Peru* 124 D3
Ocoña →, *Peru* 124 D3
Oconee →, *U.S.A.* 105 K4
Oconto, *U.S.A.* 104 C2
Oconto Falls, *U.S.A.* 104 C1
Ocosingo, *Mexico* 115 D6
Ocotal, *Nic.* 116 D2
Ocotlán, *Mexico* 114 C4
Ocquier, *Belgium* 17 H6
Ocreza →, *Portugal* 31 F3
Octave, *U.S.A.* 111 J7
Octeville, *France* 24 C5
Ocumare del Tuy, *Venezuela* 120 A4
Ocuri, *Bolivia* 125 D4
Oda, *Ghana* 79 D4
Ōda, *Japan* 49 G6
Oda, J., *Sudan* 76 C4
Ódáðahraun, *Iceland* 8 D5
Ödåkra, *Sweden* 11 H6
Odate, *Japan* 48 D10
Odawara, *Japan* 49 G9
Odda, *Norway* 9 F9
Odder, *Denmark* 11 J4
Oddur, *Somali Rep.* 68 G3
Ödeborg, *Sweden* 11 F5
Odei →, *Canada* 101 B9
Odemira, *Portugal* 31 H2
Ödemiş, *Turkey* 66 D3
Odendaalsrus, *S. Africa* 84 D4
Odense, *Denmark* 11 J4
Odenwald, *Germany* 19 F5
Oder →, *Germany* 18 B10
Oderzo, *Italy* 33 C9
Odessa, *Canada* 107 B8
Odessa, *Ukraine* 42 C4
Odessa, *Tex., U.S.A.* 109 K3
Odessa, *Wash., U.S.A.* 110 C4
Odiakwe, *Botswana* 84 C4
Odiel →, *Spain* 31 H4
Odienné, *Ivory C.* 78 D3
Odintsovo, *Russia* 41 D10
Odiongan, *Phil.* 55 E4
Odobeşti, *Romania* 38 D10
O'Donnell, *U.S.A.* 109 J4
Odoorn, *Neths.* 16 C9
Odorheiu Secuiesc, *Romania* 38 C8
Odoyevo, *Russia* 41 E10
Odra →, *Poland* 20 B4
Odra →, *Spain* 30 C6
Odžaci, *Serbia, Yug.* 21 K9
Odzi, *Zimbabwe* 85 B5
Oedelem, *Belgium* 17 F2
Oegstgeest, *Neths.* 16 D4
Oeiras, *Brazil* 122 C3
Oeiras, *Portugal* 31 G1
Oelrichs, *U.S.A.* 108 D3
Oelsnitz, *Germany* 18 E8
Oelwein, *U.S.A.* 108 D9
Oenpelli, *Australia* 88 B5
Of, *Turkey* 67 C9
Ofanto →, *Italy* 35 A9
Offa, *Nigeria* 79 D5
Offaly □, *Ireland* 15 C4
Offenbach, *Germany* 19 E4
Offenburg, *Germany* 19 G3
Offerdal, *Sweden* 10 A8
Offida, *Italy* 33 F10
Offranville, *France* 24 C8
Ofidhousa, *Greece* 39 N9
Ofotfjorden, *Norway* 8 B14
Ōfunato, *Japan* 48 E10
Oga, *Japan* 48 E9
Oga-Hantō, *Japan* 48 E9
Ogahalla, *Canada* 98 B2
Ōgaki, *Japan* 49 G8
Ogallala, *U.S.A.* 108 E4
Ogasawara Gunto, *Pac. Oc.* 92 E6
Ogbomosho, *Nigeria* 79 D5
Ogden, *Iowa, U.S.A.* 108 D8
Ogden, *Utah, U.S.A.* 110 F7
Ogdensburg, *U.S.A.* 107 B9
Ogeechee →, *U.S.A.* 105 K5
Ogilby, *U.S.A.* 113 N12
Oglio →, *Italy* 32 C7
Ogmore, *Australia* 90 C4
Ognon →, *France* 25 E12
Ogoja, *Nigeria* 79 D6
Ogoki →, *Canada* 98 B2
Ogoki L., *Canada* 98 B2
Ogoki Res., *Canada* 98 B2
Ogooué →, *Gabon* 80 E1
Ogosta →, *Bulgaria* 38 F6
Ogowe = Ogooué →, *Gabon* 80 E1
Ogr = Sharafa, *Sudan* 77 E2
Ogrein, *Sudan* 76 D3
Ogulin, *Croatia* 33 C12
Ogun □, *Nigeria* 79 D5
Oguta, *Nigeria* 79 D6
Ogwashi-Uku, *Nigeria* 79 D6
Ogwe, *Nigeria* 79 E6
Ohai, *N.Z.* 87 L2
Ohakune, *N.Z.* 87 H5
Ohanet, *Algeria* 75 C6
Ohata, *Japan* 48 D10
Ohau, L., *N.Z.* 87 L2
Ohey, *Belgium* 17 H6
Ohio □, *U.S.A.* 104 E3
Ohio →, *U.S.A.* 104 G1
Ohre →, *Czech.* 20 E4
Ohre →, *Germany* 18 C7
Ohrid, *Macedonia, Yug.* 39 H3
Ohridsko, Jezero, *Macedonia, Yug.* 39 H3
Ohrigstad, *S. Africa* 85 C5
Öhringen, *Germany* 19 F5
Oiapoque →, *Brazil* 121 C7
Oikou, *China* 51 E9
Oil City, *U.S.A.* 106 E5
Oildale, *U.S.A.* 113 K7
Oirschot, *Neths.* 17 E6
Oise □, *France* 25 C9
Oise →, *France* 25 D9
Oisterwijk, *Neths.* 17 E6
Ōita, *Japan* 49 H5
Ōita □, *Japan* 49 H5
Oiticica, *Brazil* 122 C3
Ojai, *U.S.A.* 113 L7
Ojinaga, *Mexico* 114 B4
Ojiya, *Japan* 49 F9
Ojos del Salado, Cerro, *Argentina* 126 B2
Oka →, *Russia* 41 C13
Okaba, *Indonesia* 57 F9
Okahandja, *Namibia* 84 C2
Okahukura, *N.Z.* 87 H5
Okanagan L., *Canada* 100 C5
Okandja, *Gabon* 80 E2
Okanogan, *U.S.A.* 110 B4
Okanogan →, *U.S.A.* 110 B4
Okaputa, *Namibia* 84 C2
Okara, *Pakistan* 62 D5
Okarito, *N.Z.* 87 K3
Okaukuejo, *Namibia* 84 B2
Okavango Swamps, *Botswana* 84 B3
Okaya, *Japan* 49 F9
Okayama, *Japan* 49 G6
Okayama □, *Japan* 49 G6
Okazaki, *Japan* 49 G8
Oke-Iho, *Nigeria* 79 D5
Okeechobee, *U.S.A.* 105 M5
Okeechobee, L., *U.S.A.* 105 M5
Okefenokee Swamp, *U.S.A.* 105 K4
Okehampton, *U.K.* 13 G3
Okene, *Nigeria* 79 D6
Oker →, *Germany* 18 C6
Okha, *Russia* 45 D15
Ókhi Óros, *Greece* 39 L7
Okhotsk, *Russia* 45 D15
Okhotsk, Sea of, *Asia* 45 D15
Okhotskiy Perevoz, *Russia* 45 C14
Okhotsko Kolymskoye, *Russia* 45 C16
Oki-Shotō, *Japan* 49 F6
Okiep, *S. Africa* 84 D2
Okigwi, *Nigeria* 79 D6
Okija, *Nigeria* 79 D6
Okinawa □, *Japan* 49 L3
Okinawa-Guntō, *Japan* 49 L3
Okinawa-Jima, *Japan* 49 L4
Okino-erabu-Shima, *Japan* 49 L4
Okitipupa, *Nigeria* 79 D5
Oklahoma □, *U.S.A.* 109 H6
Oklahoma City, *U.S.A.* 109 H6
Okmulgee, *U.S.A.* 109 H7
Oknitsa, *Ukraine* 42 B2
Okolo, *Uganda* 82 B3
Okolona, *U.S.A.* 109 H10
Okrika, *Nigeria* 79 E6
Oktabrsk, *Kazakhstan* 44 E6
Oktyabrsk, *Russia* 41 E16
Oktyabrskiy, *Belorussia* 40 E6
Oktyabrskoy Revolyutsii, Os., *Russia* 45 B10
Oktyabrskoye = Zhovtnevoye, *Ukraine* 42 C5
Oktyabrskoye, *Russia* 44 C7
Okulovka, *Russia* 40 B8
Okuru, *N.Z.* 87 K2
Okushiri-Tō, *Japan* 48 C9
Okuta, *Nigeria* 79 D5
Okwa →, *Botswana* 84 C3
Ola, *U.S.A.* 109 H8
Ólafsfjörður, *Iceland* 8 C4
Ólafsvík, *Iceland* 8 D2
Olancha, *U.S.A.* 113 J8
Olancha Pk., *U.S.A.* 113 J8
Olanchito, *Honduras* 116 C2
Öland, *Sweden* 9 H14
Olargues, *France* 26 E6
Olary, *Australia* 91 E3
Olascoaga, *Argentina* 126 D3
Olathe, *U.S.A.* 108 F7
Olavarría, *Argentina* 126 D3
Oława, *Poland* 20 E7
Ólbia, *Italy* 34 B2
Ólbia, G. di, *Italy* 34 B2
Old Bahama Chan. = Bahama, Canal Viejo de, *W. Indies* 116 B4
Old Baldy Pk. = San Antonio, Mt., *U.S.A.* 113 L9
Old Castile = Castilla y Leon □, *Spain* 30 D6
Old Castle, *Ireland* 15 C4
Old Cork, *Australia* 90 C3
Old Crow, *Canada* 96 B6
Old Dale, *U.S.A.* 113 L11
Old Dongola, *Sudan* 76 D3
Old Fletton, *U.K.* 13 E7
Old Forge, *N.Y., U.S.A.* 107 C10
Old Forge, *Pa., U.S.A.* 107 E9
Old Fort →, *Canada* 101 B6
Old Shinyanga, *Tanzania* 82 C3
Old Speck, Mt., *U.S.A.* 107 B14
Old Town, *U.S.A.* 99 D6
Old Wives L., *Canada* 101 C7
Oldbury, *U.K.* 13 F5
Oldeani, *Tanzania* 82 C4
Oldenburg, *Niedersachsen, Germany* 18 B4
Oldenburg, *Schleswig-Holstein, Germany* 18 A6
Oldenzaal, *Neths.* 16 D9
Oldham, *U.K.* 12 D5
Oldman →, *Canada* 100 D6
Olds, *Canada* 100 C6
Olean, *U.S.A.* 106 D6
Oléggio, *Italy* 32 C5
Oleiros, *Portugal* 30 F3
Olekma →, *Russia* 45 C13
Olekminsk, *Russia* 45 C13
Olema, *U.S.A.* 112 G4
Olen, *Belgium* 17 F5
Olenek, *Russia* 45 C12
Olenek →, *Russia* 45 B13
Olenino, *Russia* 40 C8
Oléron, I. d', *France* 26 C2
Oleśnica, *Poland* 20 D7
Olesno, *Poland* 20 E8
Olevsk, *Ukraine* 40 F5
Olga, *Russia* 45 E14
Olga, L., *Canada* 98 C4
Olga, Mt., *Australia* 89 E5
Ølgod, *Denmark* 11 J2
Olhão, *Portugal* 31 H3
Olib, *Croatia* 33 D11
Oliena, *Italy* 34 B2
Oliete, *Spain* 28 D4
Olifants →, *Africa* 85 C5
Olifantshoek, *S. Africa* 84 D3
Ólimbos, *Greece* 39 P10
Ólimbos, Óros, *Greece* 39 J5
Olímpia, *Brazil* 127 A6
Olinda, *Brazil* 122 C5
Olindiná, *Brazil* 122 D4
Olite, *Spain* 28 C3
Oliva, *Argentina* 126 C3
Oliva, *Spain* 29 G4
Oliva, Punta del, *Spain* 30 B5
Oliva de la Frontera, *Spain* 31 G4
Olivares, *Spain* 28 F2
Olivehurst, *U.S.A.* 112 F5
Oliveira, *Brazil* 123 F3
Oliveira de Azemeis, *Portugal* 30 E2
Oliveira dos Brejinhos, *Brazil* 123 D3
Olivenza, *Spain* 31 G3
Oliver, *Canada* 100 D5
Oliver L., *Canada* 101 B8
Olivone, *Switz.* 23 C7
Olkhovka, *Russia* 43 B11
Olkusz, *Poland* 20 E9
Ollagüe, *Chile* 126 A2
Olloy, *Belgium* 17 H5
Olmedo, *Spain* 30 D6
Olmos, *Peru* 124 B2
Olney, *Ill., U.S.A.* 104 F1
Olney, *Tex., U.S.A.* 109 J5
Oloma, *Cameroon* 79 E7
Olomane →, *Canada* 99 B7
Olomouc, *Czech.* 20 F7
Olongapo, *Phil.* 55 D4
Oloron, Gave d' →, *France* 26 E2
Oloron-Ste.-Marie, *France* 26 E3
Olot, *Spain* 28 C7
Olovo, *Bos.-H., Yug.* 21 L8
Olovyannaya, *Russia* 45 D12
Oloy →, *Russia* 45 C16
Olpe, *Germany* 18 D3
Olshanka, *Ukraine* 42 B4
Olshany, *Ukraine* 42 A6
Olst, *Neths.* 16 D8
Olsztyn, *Poland* 20 B10
Olt →, *Romania* 38 F7
Olten, *Switz.* 22 B5
Olteniţa, *Romania* 38 E9
Olton, *U.S.A.* 109 H3
Oltu, *Turkey* 67 C9
Olur, *Turkey* 67 C10
Olutanga, *Phil.* 55 H5
Olvega, *Spain* 28 D3
Olvera, *Spain* 31 J5
Olymbos, *Cyprus* 37 D12
Olympia, *Greece* 39 M4
Olympia, *U.S.A.* 112 D4
Olympic Mts., *U.S.A.* 112 C3
Olympic Nat. Park, *U.S.A.* 112 C3
Olympus, *Cyprus* 37 E11
Olympus, Mt. = Ólimbos, Óros, *Greece* 39 J5
Olympus, Mt., *U.S.A.* 112 C3
Olyphant, *U.S.A.* 107 E9
Om →, *Russia* 44 D8
Om Hajer, *Ethiopia* 77 E4
Om Koi, *Thailand* 58 D2
Ōma, *Japan* 48 D10
Ōmachi, *Japan* 49 F8
Omae-Zaki, *Japan* 49 G9
Ōmagari, *Japan* 48 E10
Omagh, *U.K.* 15 B4
Omagh □, *U.K.* 15 B4
Omaha, *U.S.A.* 108 E7
Omak, *U.S.A.* 110 B4
Omalos, *Greece* 37 D5
Oman ■, *Asia* 68 C6
Oman, G. of, *Asia* 65 E8
Omaruru, *Namibia* 84 C2
Omaruru →, *Namibia* 84 C1
Omate, *Peru* 124 D3
Ombai, Selat, *Indonesia* 57 F6
Omboué, *Gabon* 80 E1
Ombrone →, *Italy* 32 F8
Omdurmân, *Sudan* 77 D3
Omegna, *Italy* 32 C5
Omeonga, *Zaïre* 82 C1
Ometepe, I. de, *Nic.* 116 D2
Ometepec, *Mexico* 115 D5
Ominato, *Japan* 48 D10
Omineca →, *Canada* 100 B4
Omiš, *Croatia* 33 E13
Omišalj, *Croatia* 33 C11
Omitara, *Namibia* 84 C2
Ōmiya, *Japan* 49 G9
Omme Å →, *Denmark* 11 J2
Ommen, *Neths.* 16 C8
Ömnögovĭ □, *Mongolia* 50 C3
Omo →, *Ethiopia* 77 F4
Omodhos, *Cyprus* 37 E11
Omolon →, *Russia* 45 C16
Omono-Gawa →, *Japan* 48 E10
Omsk, *Russia* 44 D8
Omsukchan, *Russia* 45 C16
Ōmu, *Japan* 48 B11
Omul, Vf., *Romania* 38 D8
Ōmura, *Japan* 49 H4
Omuramba Omatako →, *Namibia* 81 H4
Omurtag, *Bulgaria* 38 F9
Ōmuta, *Japan* 49 H5
Omutninsk, *Russia* 41 B18
On, *Belgium* 17 H6
Oña, *Spain* 28 C1
Onaga, *U.S.A.* 108 F6
Onalaska, *U.S.A.* 108 D9
Onamia, *U.S.A.* 108 B8
Onancock, *U.S.A.* 104 G8
Onang, *Indonesia* 57 E5
Onaping L., *Canada* 98 C3
Oñate, *Spain* 28 B2
Onavas, *Mexico* 114 B3
Onawa, *U.S.A.* 108 D6
Onaway, *U.S.A.* 104 C3
Oncócua, *Angola* 84 B1
Onda, *Spain* 28 F4
Ondaejin, *N. Korea* 51 D15
Ondangua, *Namibia* 84 B2
Ondárroa, *Spain* 28 B2
Ondas →, *Brazil* 123 D3
Ondava →, *Czech.* 20 G11
Onderdijk, *Neths.* 16 C6
Ondjiva, *Angola* 84 B2
Ondo, *Nigeria* 79 D5
Ondo □, *Nigeria* 79 D6
Öndörhaan, *Mongolia* 54 B6
Öndörshil, *Mongolia* 50 B5
Öndverðarnes, *Iceland* 8 D1
Onega, *Russia* 44 C4
Onega →, *Russia* 6 C13
Onega, G. of = Onezhskaya Guba, *Russia* 44 C4
Onega, L. = Onezhskoye Ozero, *Russia* 44 C4
Onehunga, *N.Z.* 87 G5
Oneida, *U.S.A.* 107 C9
Oneida L., *U.S.A.* 107 C9
O'Neill, *U.S.A.* 108 D5
Onekotan, Ostrov, *Russia* 45 E16
Onema, *Zaïre* 82 C1
Oneonta, *Ala., U.S.A.* 105 J2
Oneonta, *N.Y., U.S.A.* 107 D9
Onezhskaya Guba, *Russia* 44 C4
Onezhskoye Ozero, *Russia* 44 C4
Ongarue, *N.Z.* 87 H5
Ongerup, *Australia* 89 F2
Ongjin, *N. Korea* 51 F13
Ongkharak, *Thailand* 58 E3
Ongniud Qi, *China* 51 C10
Ongoka, *Zaïre* 82 C2
Ongole, *India* 60 M12
Ongon, *Mongolia* 50 B7
Onguren, *Russia* 45 D11
Onhaye, *Belgium* 17 H5
Oni, *Georgia* 43 E10
Onida, *U.S.A.* 108 C4
Onilahy →, *Madag.* 85 C7
Onitsha, *Nigeria* 79 D6
Onoda, *Japan* 49 G5
Onpyŏng-ni, *S. Korea* 51 H14
Ons, Is. d', *Spain* 30 C2
Onsala, *Sweden* 11 G6
Onslow, *Australia* 88 D2
Onslow B., *U.S.A.* 105 H7
Onstwedde, *Neths.* 16 B10
Ontake-San, *Japan* 49 G8
Ontaneda, *Spain* 30 B7
Ontario, *Calif., U.S.A.* 113 L9
Ontario, *Oreg., U.S.A.* 110 D5
Ontario □, *Canada* 98 B2
Ontario, L., *N. Amer.* 98 D4
Onteniente, *Spain* 29 G4
Ontonagon, *U.S.A.* 108 B10
Ontur, *Spain* 29 G3
Onyx, *U.S.A.* 113 K8
Oodnadatta, *Australia* 91 D2
Ooldea, *Australia* 89 F5
Ooltgensplaat, *Neths.* 17 E4
Oombulgurri, *Australia* 88 C4
Oona River, *Canada* 100 C2
Oordegem, *Belgium* 17 G3
Oorindi, *Australia* 90 C3
Oost-Vlaanderen □, *Belgium* 17 F3
Oost-Vlieland, *Neths.* 16 B6
Oostakker, *Belgium* 17 F3
Oostburg, *Neths.* 17 F3
Oostduinkerke, *Belgium* 17 F1
Oostelijk-Flevoland, *Neths.* 16 C7
Oostende, *Belgium* 17 F1
Oosterbeek, *Neths.* 16 E7
Oosterdijk, *Neths.* 16 C6
Oosterend, *Friesland, Neths.* 16 B6
Oosterend, *Noord-Holland, Neths.* 16 B5
Oosterhout, *Noord-Brabant, Neths.* 17 E7
Oosterhout, *Noord-Brabant, Neths.* 17 E5
Oosterschelde, *Neths.* 17 E4
Oosterwolde, *Neths.* 16 B8
Oosterzele, *Belgium* 17 G3
Oostkamp, *Belgium* 17 F2
Oostmalle, *Belgium* 17 F5
Oostrozebekke, *Belgium* 17 G2
Oostvleteven, *Belgium* 17 G1
Oostvoorne, *Neths.* 16 E4
Oostzaan, *Neths.* 16 D5
Ootacamund, *India* 60 P10
Ootmarsum, *Neths.* 16 D9
Ootsa L., *Canada* 100 C3
Opala, *Russia* 45 D16
Opala, *Zaïre* 82 C1
Opanake, *Sri Lanka* 60 R12
Opasatika, *Canada* 98 C3
Opasquia, *Canada* 101 C10
Opatija, *Croatia* 33 C11
Opava, *Czech.* 20 F7
Opeinde, *Neths.* 16 B8
Opelousas, *U.S.A.* 109 K8
Opémisca, L., *Canada* 98 C5
Opglabbeek, *Belgium* 17 F7
Opheim, *U.S.A.* 110 B10
Ophthalmia Ra., *Australia* 88 D2
Opi, *Nigeria* 79 D6
Opinaca →, *Canada* 98 B4
Opinaca L., *Canada* 98 B4
Opiskotish, L., *Canada* 99 B6
Oploo, *Neths.* 17 E7
Opmeer, *Neths.* 16 C5
Opobo, *Nigeria* 79 E6
Opochka, *Russia* 40 C6
Opoczno, *Poland* 20 D10
Opol, *Phil.* 55 G6
Opole, *Poland* 20 E7
Oporto = Porto, *Portugal* 30 D2
Opotiki, *N.Z.* 87 H6
Opp, *U.S.A.* 105 K2
Oppenheim, *Germany* 19 F4
Opperdoes, *Neths.* 16 C6
Óppido Mamertina, *Italy* 35 D8
Oppland fylke □, *Norway* 10 C3
Oppstad, *Norway* 10 D5
Oprtalj, *Croatia* 33 C10
Opua, *N.Z.* 87 F5
Opunake, *N.Z.* 87 H4
Opuzen, *Croatia* 21 M7
Ora, *Cyprus* 37 E12
Ora, *Italy* 33 B8
Ora Banda, *Australia* 89 F3
Oracle, *U.S.A.* 111 K8
Oradea, *Romania* 38 B4
Öræfajökull, *Iceland* 8 D5
Orahovac, *Serbia, Yug.* 21 N10
Orai, *India* 63 G8
Oraison, *France* 27 E9
Oran, *Algeria* 75 A4
Oran, *Argentina* 126 A3
Orange = Oranje →, *S. Africa* 84 D2
Orange, *Australia* 91 E4
Orange, *France* 27 D8
Orange, *Calif., U.S.A.* 113 M9
Orange, *Mass., U.S.A.* 107 D12
Orange, *Tex., U.S.A.* 109 K8
Orange, *Va., U.S.A.* 104 F6
Orange, C., *Brazil* 121 C7
Orange Cove, *U.S.A.* 112 J7
Orange Free State □, *S. Africa* 84 D4
Orange Grove, *U.S.A.* 109 M6
Orange Walk, *Belize* 115 D7
Orangeburg, *U.S.A.* 105 J5
Orangeville, *Canada* 98 D3
Orani, *Phil.* 55 D4
Oranienburg, *Germany* 18 C9
Oranje →, *S. Africa* 84 D2
Oranje Vrystaat = Orange Free State □, *S. Africa* 84 D4
Oranjemund, *Namibia* 84 D2
Oranjerivier, *S. Africa* 84 D3
Oras, *Phil.* 55 E6
Orăştie, *Romania* 38 D6
Oraşul Stalin = Braşov, *Romania* 38 D8

Orava →, Czech. 20 F9
Oravita, Romania 38 D4
Orb →, France 26 E7
Orba →, Italy 32 D5
Ørbæk, Denmark 11 J4
Orbe, Switz. 22 C3
Orbec, France 24 C7
Orbetello, Italy 33 F8
Órbigo →, Spain 30 C5
Orbost, Australia 91 F4
Orce, Spain 29 H2
Orce →, Spain 29 H2
Orchies, France 25 B10
Orchila, I., Venezuela 120 A4
Orco →, Italy 32 C4
Orcopampa, Peru 124 D3
Orcutt, U.S.A. 113 L6
Ord →, Australia 88 C4
Ord, Mt., Australia 88 C4
Ordenes, Spain 30 B2
Orderville, U.S.A. 111 H7
Ording, Germany 18 A4
Ordos = Mu Us Shamo, China 50 E5
Ordu, Turkey 67 C7
Ordu □, Turkey 67 C7
Orduña, Álava, Spain 28 C7
Orduña, Granada, Spain 29 H1
Ordway, U.S.A. 108 F3
Ordzhonikidze = Vladikavkaz, Russia 43 E11
Ordzhonikidze, Ukraine 42 C6
Ore, Zaïre 82 B2
Ore Mts. = Erzgebirge, Germany 18 E9
Orealla, Guyana 121 B6
Orebić, Croatia 21 M7
Örebro, Sweden 9 G13
Örebro län □, Sweden 9 G13
Oregon, U.S.A. 108 D10
Oregon □, U.S.A. 110 E3
Oregon City, U.S.A. 112 E4
Orekhov, Ukraine 42 C6
Orekhovo-Zuyevo, Russia 41 D11
Orel, Russia 41 E10
Orel →, Ukraine 42 B6
Orellana, Canal de, Spain 31 F5
Orellana, Pantano de, Spain 31 F5
Orellana la Vieja, Spain 31 F5
Orem, U.S.A. 110 F8
Ören, Turkey 66 E2
Orenburg, Russia 44 D6
Orense, Spain 30 C3
Orense □, Spain 30 C3
Orepuki, N.Z. 87 M1
Orestiás, Greece 39 H9
Øresund, Europe 11 J6
Orford Ness, U.K. 13 E9
Orgañà, Spain 28 C6
Organos, Pta. de los, Canary Is. 36 F2
Orgaz, Spain 31 F7
Orgeyev, Moldavia 42 C3
Orgon, France 27 E9
Orhaneli, Turkey 66 D3
Orhangazi, Turkey 66 C3
Orhon Gol →, Mongolia 54 A5
Ória, Italy 35 B10
Orient, Australia 91 D3
Oriental, Cordillera, Bolivia 125 D4
Oriental, Cordillera, Colombia 120 B3
Oriente, Argentina 126 D3
Origny-Ste.-Benoîte, France 25 C10
Orihuela, Spain 29 G4
Orihuela del Tremedal, Spain 28 E3
Oriku, Albania 39 J2
Orinduik, Guyana 121 C5
Orinoco →, Venezuela 121 B5
Orissa □, India 61 K14
Oristano, Italy 34 C1
Oristano, G. di, Italy 34 C1
Orituco →, Venezuela 120 B4
Orizaba, Mexico 115 D5
Orizona, Brazil 123 E2
Orjen, Bos.-H., Yug. 21 N8
Orjiva, Spain 29 J1
Orkanger, Norway 10 A3
Örkelljunga, Sweden 11 H7
Örkény, Hungary 21 H9
Orkla →, Norway 10 A3
Orkney, S. Africa 84 D4
Orkney □, U.K. 14 C6
Orkney Is., U.K. 14 C6
Orland, U.S.A. 112 F4
Orlando, U.S.A. 105 L5
Orlando, C. d', Italy 35 D7
Orléanais, France 25 E9
Orléans, France 25 E8
Orleans, U.S.A. 107 B12
Orléans, I. d', Canada 99 C5
Orlice →, Czech. 20 E6
Orlov, Czech. 20 F10
Orlov Gay, Russia 41 F16
Ormara, Pakistan 60 G4
Ormea, Italy 32 D4
Ormília, Greece 39 J6
Ormoc, Phil. 55 F6
Ormond, N.Z. 87 H6
Ormond Beach, U.S.A. 105 L5
Ormož, Slovenia 33 B13
Ormstown, Canada 107 A11
Ornans, France 25 E13
Orne □, France 24 D7
Orne →, France 24 C6
Ørnhøj, Denmark 11 H2
Ornö, Sweden 10 E12
Örnsköldsvik, Sweden 10 A12
Oro, N. Korea 51 D14
Oro →, Mexico 114 B3
Oro Grande, U.S.A. 113 L9
Orobie, Alpi, Italy 32 B6
Orocué, Colombia 120 C3
Orodo, Nigeria 79 D6
Orogrande, U.S.A. 111 K10
Orol, Spain 30 B3
Oromocto, Canada 99 C6
Oron, Nigeria 79 E6
Oron, Switz. 22 C3
Orono, Canada 106 C6
Oropesa, Spain 30 F5
Oroquieta, Phil. 55 G5
Orós, Brazil 122 C4
Orosei, G. di, Italy 34 B2
Orosháza, Hungary 21 J10
Orotukan, Russia 45 C16
Oroville, Calif., U.S.A. 112 F5
Oroville, Wash., U.S.A. 110 B4
Oroville Res., U.S.A. 112 F5
Orroroo, Australia 91 E2
Orrville, U.S.A. 106 F3
Orsara di Púglia, Italy 35 A8
Orsha, Belorussia 40 D7
Orsières, Switz. 22 D4
Orsk, Russia 44 D6
Ørslev, Denmark 11 J5
Orsogna, Italy 33 F11
Orşova, Romania 38 E5
Ørsted, Denmark 11 H4
Orta, L. d', Italy 32 C5
Orta Nova, Italy 35 A8
Ortaca, Turkey 66 E3
Ortaköy, Çorum, Turkey 66 C6
Ortaköy, Niğde, Turkey 66 D6
Orte, Italy 33 F9
Ortegal, C., Spain 30 B3
Orteguaza →, Colombia 120 C2
Orthez, France 26 E3
Ortho, Belgium 17 H7
Ortigueira, Spain 30 B3
Orting, U.S.A. 112 C4
Ortles, Italy 32 B7
Ortón →, Bolivia 124 C4
Ortona, Italy 33 F11
Orūmīyeh, Iran 64 B5
Orūmīyeh, Daryācheh-ye, Iran 64 B5
Orune, Italy 34 B2
Oruro, Bolivia 124 D4
Oruro □, Bolivia 124 D4
Orust, Sweden 11 F5
Oruzgān □, Afghan. 60 C5
Orvault, France 24 E5
Orvieto, Italy 33 F9
Orwell, U.S.A. 106 E4
Orwell →, U.K. 13 E9
Oryakhovo, Bulgaria 38 F6
Orzinuovi, Italy 32 C6
Orzysz, Poland 20 B11
Osa, Pen. de, Costa Rica 116 E3
Osage, Iowa, U.S.A. 108 D8
Osage, Wyo., U.S.A. 108 D2
Osage →, U.S.A. 108 F9
Osage City, U.S.A. 108 F7
Ōsaka, Japan 49 G7
Osan, S. Korea 51 F14
Osawatomie, U.S.A. 108 F7
Osborne, U.S.A. 108 F5
Osceola, Ark., U.S.A. 109 H10
Osceola, Iowa, U.S.A. 108 E8
Oschatz, Germany 18 D9
Oschersleben, Germany 18 C7
Óschiri, Italy 34 B2
Oscoda, U.S.A. 106 B1
Ösel = Saaremaa, Estonia 40 B3
Osëry, Russia 41 D11
Osh, Kirghizia 44 E8
Oshawa, Canada 98 D4
Oshkosh, Nebr., U.S.A. 108 E3
Oshkosh, Wis., U.S.A. 108 C10
Oshmyany, Belorussia 40 D4
Oshnovīyeh, Iran 64 B5
Oshogbo, Nigeria 79 D5
Oshtorīnān, Iran 65 C6
Oshwe, Zaïre 80 E3
Osijek, Croatia 21 K8
Ósilo, Italy 34 B1
Osimo, Italy 33 E10
Osintorf, Belorussia 40 D7
Osipenko = Berdyansk, Ukraine 42 C7
Osipovichi, Belorussia 40 E6
Osizweni, S. Africa 85 D5
Oskaloosa, U.S.A. 108 E8
Oskarshamn, Sweden 9 H14
Oskélanéo, Canada 98 C4
Oskol →, Ukraine 41 G10
Oslo, Norway 10 E4
Oslob, Phil. 55 G5
Oslofjorden, Norway 10 E4
Osmanabad, India 60 K10
Osmancık, Turkey 42 F6
Osmaniye, Turkey 66 E7
Ösmo, Sweden 10 F11
Osnabrück, Germany 18 C4
Osor, Italy 33 D11
Osorio, Brazil 127 B5
Osorno, Chile 128 B2
Osorno, Spain 30 C6
Osorno □, Chile 128 B2
Osorno, Vol., Chile 128 B2
Osoyoos, Canada 100 D5
Ospika →, Canada 100 B4
Osprey Reef, Australia 90 A4
Oss, Neths. 16 E7
Ossa, Mt., Australia 90 G4
Óssa, Oros, Greece 39 K5
Ossa de Montiel, Spain 29 G2
Ossabaw I., U.S.A. 105 K5
Osse →, France 26 D4
Ossendrecht, Neths. 17 F4
Ossining, U.S.A. 107 E11
Ossipee, U.S.A. 107 C13
Ossokmanuan L., Canada 99 B7
Ossora, Russia 45 D17
Ostashkov, Russia 40 C8
Oste →, Germany 18 B5
Ostend = Oostende, Belgium 17 F1
Oster, Ukraine 40 F7
Osterburg, Germany 18 C7
Osterburken, Germany 19 F5
Österdalälven →, Sweden 9 F12
Östergötlands län □, Sweden 11 F9
Osterholz-Scharmbeck, Germany 18 B4
Østerild, Denmark 11 G2
Ostermundigen, Switz. 22 C4
Östersund, Sweden 10 A8
Østfold fylke □, Norway 10 E5
Ostfriesische Inseln, Germany 18 B3
Ostfriesland, Germany 18 B3
Óstia, Lido di, Italy 34 A5
Ostiglía, Italy 33 C8
Ostra, Italy 33 E10
Ostrava, Czech. 20 F8
Ostróda, Poland 20 B9
Ostrog, Ukraine 40 F5
Ostrogozhsk, Russia 41 F11
Ostrogróg Sźamotuły, Poland 20 C6
Ostrołęka, Poland 20 B11
Ostrov, Bulgaria 38 F7
Ostrov, Romania 38 E10
Ostrov, Russia 40 C6
Ostrów Mazowiecka, Poland 20 C11
Ostrów Wielkopolski, Poland 20 D7
Ostrowiec-Świętokrzyski, Poland 20 E11
Ostrzeszów, Poland 20 D7
Ostseebad-Külungsborn, Germany 18 A7
Osttirol □, Austria 19 J8
Ostuni, Italy 35 B10
Osum →, Bulgaria 38 F7
Osumi →, Albania 39 J3
Ōsumi-Kaikyō, Japan 49 J5
Ōsumi-Shotō, Japan 49 J5
Osuna, Spain 31 H5
Oswego, U.S.A. 107 C8
Oswestry, U.K. 12 E4
Oświecim, Poland 20 E9
Otago □, N.Z. 87 L2
Otago Harbour, N.Z. 87 L3
Ōtake, Japan 49 G6
Otaki, N.Z. 87 J5
Otaru, Japan 48 C10
Otaru-Wan = Ishikari-Wan, Japan 48 C10
Otava →, Czech. 20 F4
Otavalo, Ecuador 120 C2
Otavi, Namibia 84 B2
Otchinjau, Angola 84 B1
Otelec, Romania 38 D3
Otero de Rey, Spain 30 B3
Othello, U.S.A. 110 C4
Othonoí, Greece 39 K2
Óthris, Óros, Greece 39 K5
Otira Gorge, N.Z. 87 K3
Otis, U.S.A. 108 E3
Otjiwarongo, Namibia 84 C2
Otočac, Croatia 33 D12
Otoineppu, Japan 48 B11
Otorohanga, N.Z. 87 H5
Otoskwin →, Canada 98 B2
Otosquen, Canada 101 C8
Otranto, Italy 35 B11
Otranto, C. d', Italy 35 B11
Otranto, Str. of, Italy 35 B11
Otse, S. Africa 84 D4
Ōtsu, Japan 49 G7
Ōtsuki, Japan 49 G9
Otta, Norway 10 C3
Ottawa = Outaouais →, Canada 98 C5
Ottawa, Canada 98 C4
Ottawa, Ill., U.S.A. 108 E10
Ottawa, Kans., U.S.A. 108 F7
Ottawa Is., Canada 97 C11
Ottélé, Cameroon 79 E7
Otter L., Canada 101 B8
Otter Rapids, Ont., Canada 98 B3
Otter Rapids, Sask., Canada 101 B8
Otterndorf, Germany 18 B4
Otterup, Denmark 11 J4
Otterville, Canada 106 D4
Ottignies, Belgium 17 G5
Otto Beit Bridge, Zimbabwe 83 F2
Ottosdal, S. Africa 84 D4
Ottoshoop, S. Africa 84 D4
Ottsjön, Sweden 10 A7
Ottumwa, U.S.A. 108 E8
Otu, Nigeria 79 D5
Otukpa, Nigeria 79 D6
Oturkpo, Nigeria 79 D6
Otway, B., Chile 128 D2
Otway, C., Australia 91 F3
Otwock, Poland 20 C11
Ötz, Austria 19 H6
Ötz →, Austria 19 H6
Ötztaler Alpen, Austria 19 J7
Ou →, Laos 58 B4
Ou Neua, Laos 58 A3
Ou-Sammyaku, Japan 48 E10
Ouachita →, U.S.A. 109 K9
Ouachita, L., U.S.A. 109 H8
Ouachita Mts., U.S.A. 109 H7
Ouadâne, Mauritania 74 D2
Ouadda, C.A.R. 73 G9
Ouagadougou, Burkina Faso 79 C4
Ouahigouya, Burkina Faso 78 C4
Ouahila, Algeria 74 C3
Ouahran = Oran, Algeria 75 A4
Oualâta, Mauritania 78 B3
Ouallene, Algeria 75 D5
Ouanda Djallé, C.A.R. 73 G9
Ouango, C.A.R. 80 D4
Ouarâne, Mauritania 74 D2
Ouargla, Algeria 75 B6
Ouarkziz, Djebel, Algeria 74 C3
Ouarzazate, Morocco 74 B3
Ouatagouna, Mali 79 B5
Oubangi →, Zaïre 80 E3
Oubarakai, O. →, Algeria 75 C6
Ouche →, France 25 E12
Oud-Beijerland, Neths. 16 E4
Oud-Gastel, Neths. 17 E4
Oud Turnhout, Belgium 17 F6
Ouddorp, Neths. 16 E3
Oude-Pekela, Neths. 16 B10
Oude Rijn →, Neths. 16 D4
Oudega, Neths. 16 B8
Oudenaarde, Belgium 17 G3
Oudenbosch, Neths. 17 E5
Oudenburg, Belgium 17 F2
Ouderkerk, Utrecht, Neths. 16 D5
Ouderkerk, Zuid-Holland, Neths. 16 E5
Oudeschild, Neths. 16 B5
Oudewater, Neths. 16 D5
Oudkarspel, Neths. 16 C5
Oudon, France 24 E5
Oudtshoorn, S. Africa 84 E3
Oued Zem, Morocco 74 B3
Ouellé, Ivory C. 78 D4
Ouenza, Algeria 75 A6
Ouessa, Burkina Faso 78 C4
Ouessant, I. d', France 24 D1
Ouesso, Congo 80 D3
Ouest, Pte., Canada 99 C7
Ouezzane, Morocco 74 B3
Ouffet, Belgium 17 H6
Ouidah, Benin 79 D5
Ouistreham, France 24 C6
Oujda, Morocco 75 B4
Oujeft, Mauritania 74 D2
Ould Yenjé, Mauritania 78 B2
Ouled Djellal, Algeria 75 B6
Ouled Naïl, Mts. des, Algeria 75 B5
Oulmès, Morocco 74 B3
Oulu, Finland 8 D18
Oulu □ = Oulun lääni □, Finland 8 D19
Oulujärvi, Finland 8 D19
Oulujoki →, Finland 8 D18
Oulun lääni □, Finland 8 D19
Oulx, Italy 32 C3
Oum Chalouba, Chad 73 E9
Oum-el-Bouaghi, Algeria 75 A6
Oum el Ksi, Algeria 74 C3
Oum-er-Rbia, O. →, Morocco 74 B3
Oumè, Ivory C. 78 D3
Ounane, Dj., Algeria 75 C6
Ounguati, Namibia 84 C2
Ounianga-Kébir, Chad 73 E9
Ounianga Sérir, Chad 73 E9
Our →, Lux. 17 J8
Ouray, U.S.A. 111 G10
Ourcq →, France 25 C10
Oureg, Oued el →, Algeria 75 B5
Ourém, Brazil 122 B2
Ouricuri, Brazil 122 C3
Ourinhos, Brazil 127 A6
Ourique, Portugal 31 H2
Ouro Fino, Brazil 127 A6
Ouro Prêto, Brazil 123 F3
Ouro Sogui, Senegal 78 B2
Oursi, Burkina Faso 79 C4
Ourthe →, Belgium 17 H7
Ouse, Australia 90 G4
Ouse →, E. Susx., U.K. 13 G8
Ouse →, N. Yorks., U.K. 12 C8
Oust, France 26 F5
Oust →, France 24 E4
Outaouais →, Canada 98 C5
Outardes →, Canada 99 C6
Outat Oulad el Haj, Morocco 75 B4
Outer Hebrides, U.K. 14 D1
Outer I., Canada 99 B8
Outes, Spain 30 C2
Outjo, Namibia 84 C2
Outlook, Canada 101 C7
Outlook, U.S.A. 108 A2
Outreau, France 25 B8
Ouvèze →, France 27 E8
Ouyen, Australia 91 F3
Ouzouer-le-Marché, France 25 E8
Ovada, Italy 32 D5
Ovalau, Fiji 87 C8
Ovalle, Chile 126 C1
Ovar, Portugal 30 E2
Ovejas, Colombia 120 B2
Overdinkel, Neths. 16 D10
Overflakkee, Neths. 16 E4
Overijse, Belgium 17 G5
Overijssel □, Neths. 16 D9
Overijsselsch Kanaal →, Neths. 16 C8
Overpelt, Belgium 17 F6
Overton, U.S.A. 113 J12
Övertorneå, Sweden 8 C17
Ovid, U.S.A. 108 E3
Ovidiopol, Ukraine 42 C4
Oviedo, Spain 30 B5
Oviedo □, Spain 30 B5
Oviken, Sweden 10 A8
Oviksfjällen, Sweden 10 B7
Övör Hangay □, Mongolia 50 B2
Ovoro, Nigeria 79 D6
Ovruch, Ukraine 40 F6
Owaka, N.Z. 87 M2
Owase, Japan 49 G8
Owatonna, U.S.A. 108 C8
Owbeh, Afghan. 60 B3
Owego, U.S.A. 107 D8
Owen Falls, Uganda 82 B3
Owen Sound, Canada 98 D3
Owendo, Gabon 80 D1
Owens →, U.S.A. 112 J9
Owens L., U.S.A. 113 J9
Owensboro, U.S.A. 104 G2
Owensville, U.S.A. 108 F9
Owerri, Nigeria 79 D6
Owl →, Canada 101 B10
Owo, Nigeria 79 D6
Owosso, U.S.A. 104 D3
Owyhee, U.S.A. 110 F5
Owyhee →, U.S.A. 110 E5
Owyhee, L., U.S.A. 110 E5
Ox Mts., Ireland 15 B3
Oxapampa, Peru 124 C2
Oxelösund, Sweden 11 F11
Oxford, N.Z. 87 K4
Oxford, U.K. 13 F6
Oxford, Miss., U.S.A. 109 H10
Oxford, N.C., U.S.A. 105 G6
Oxford, Ohio, U.S.A. 104 F3
Oxford L., Canada 101 C9
Oxfordshire □, U.K. 13 F6
Oxley, Australia 91 E3
Oxnard, U.S.A. 113 L7
Oxus = Amudarya →, Uzbekistan 44 E6
Oya, Malaysia 56 D4
Oyama, Japan 49 F9
Oyapock →, Fr. Guiana 121 C7
Oyem, Gabon 80 D2
Oyen, Canada 101 C6
Øyeren, Norway 10 E5
Oykel →, U.K. 14 D4
Oymyakon, Russia 45 C15
Oyo, Nigeria 79 D5
Oyo □, Nigeria 79 D5
Oyón, Peru 124 C2
Oyonnax, France 27 B9
Oyster Bay, U.S.A. 107 F11
Ōyübari, Japan 48 C11
Özalp, Turkey 67 D10
Ozamis, Phil. 55 G5
Ozark, Ala., U.S.A. 105 K3
Ozark, Ark., U.S.A. 109 H8
Ozark, Mo., U.S.A. 109 G8
Ozark Plateau, U.S.A. 109 G9
Ozarks, L. of the, U.S.A. 108 F8
Ózd, Hungary 21 G10
Ozette, L., U.S.A. 112 B2
Ozieri, Italy 34 B2
Ozona, U.S.A. 109 K4
Ozorków, Poland 20 D9
Ozuluama, Mexico 115 C5
Ozurgety, Georgia 43 F10

P

P.K. le Roux Dam, S. Africa 84 E3
Pa, Burkina Faso 78 C4
Pa-an, Burma 61 L20
Pa Mong Dam, Thailand 58 D4
Paal, Belgium 17 F6
Paamiut = Frederikshåb, Greenland 4 C5
Paar →, Germany 19 G6
Paarl, S. Africa 84 E2

Paatsi →, *Russia* 8 B20
Paauilo, *U.S.A.* 102 H17
Pab Hills, *Pakistan* 62 F2
Pabianice, *Poland* 20 D9
Pabna, *Bangla.* 61 G16
Pabo, *Uganda* 82 B3
Pacaás Novos, Serra dos,
  Brazil 125 C5
Pacaipampa, *Peru* 124 B2
Pacaja →, *Brazil* 122 B1
Pacajus, *Brazil* 122 B4
Pacaraima, Sierra,
  Venezuela 121 C5
Pacarán, *Peru* 124 C2
Pacaraos, *Peru* 124 C2
Pacasmayo, *Peru* 124 B2
Paceco, *Italy* 34 E5
Pachacamac, *Peru* 124 C2
Pachhar, *India* 62 G7
Pachino, *Italy* 35 F8
Pachitea →, *Peru* 124 B3
Pachiza, *Peru* 124 B2
Pacho, *Colombia* 120 B3
Pachpadra, *India* 60 G8
Pachuca, *Mexico* 115 C5
Pacific, *Canada* 100 C3
Pacific-Antarctic Ridge,
  Pac. Oc. 93 M16
Pacific Grove, *U.S.A.* .. 111 H3
Pacific Ocean, *Pac. Oc.* . 93 G14
Pacifica, *U.S.A.* 112 H4
Pacitan, *Indonesia* 57 H14
Packwood, *U.S.A.* 112 D5
Pacuí →, *Brazil* 123 E2
Padaido, Kepulauan,
  Indonesia 57 E9
Padang, *Indonesia* 56 E2
Padangpanjang, *Indonesia* 56 E2
Padangsidempuan,
  Indonesia 56 D1
Padauari →, *Brazil* 121 D5
Padborg, *Denmark* 11 K3
Padcaya, *Bolivia* 125 E5
Paddockwood, *Canada* .. 101 C7
Paderborn, *Germany* 18 D4
Padilla, *Bolivia* 125 D5
Padloping Island, *Canada* . 97 B13
Pádova, *Italy* 33 C8
Padra, *India* 62 H5
Padrauna, *India* 63 F10
Padre I., *U.S.A.* 109 M6
Padro, Mte., *France* 27 F12
Padrón, *Spain* 30 C2
Padstow, *U.K.* 13 G3
Padua = Pádova, *Italy* .. 33 C8
Paducah, *Ky., U.S.A.* .. 104 G1
Paducah, *Tex., U.S.A.* . 109 H4
Padul, *Spain* 31 H7
Padula, *Italy* 35 B8
Paengnyong-do, *S. Korea* . 51 F13
Paeroa, *N.Z.* 87 G5
Paesana, *Italy* 32 D4
Pafúri, *Mozam.* 85 C5
Pag, *Croatia* 33 D11
Paga, *Ghana* 79 C4
Pagadian, *Phil.* 55 H5
Pagai Selatan, P., *Indonesia* 56 E2
Pagai Utara, *Indonesia* .. 56 E2
Pagalu = Annobón,
  Atl. Oc. 71 G4
Pagastikós Kólpos, *Greece* 39 K6
Pagatan, *Indonesia* 56 E5
Page, *Ariz., U.S.A.* 111 H8
Page, *N. Dak., U.S.A.* .. 108 B6
Paglieta, *Italy* 33 F11
Pagny-sur-Moselle, *France* 25 D13
Pago Pago, *Amer. Samoa* . 87 B13
Pagosa Springs, *U.S.A.* . 111 H10
Pagwa River, *Canada* ... 98 B2
Pahala, *U.S.A.* 102 J17
Pahang →, *Malaysia* 59 L4
Pahiatua, *N.Z.* 87 J5
Pahokee, *U.S.A.* 105 M5
Pahrump, *U.S.A.* 113 J11
Pahute Mesa, *U.S.A.* ... 112 H10
Pai, *Thailand* 58 C2
Paia, *U.S.A.* 102 H16
Paicines, *U.S.A.* 112 J5
Paide, *Estonia* 40 B4
Paignton, *U.K.* 13 G4
Paiján, *Peru* 124 B2
Päijänne, *Finland* 9 F18
Paimbœuf, *France* 24 E4
Paimpol, *France* 24 D3
Painan, *Indonesia* 56 E2
Painesville, *U.S.A.* 106 E3
Paint Hills = Nouveau
  Comptoir, *Canada* 98 B4
Paint L., *Canada* 101 B9
Paint Rock, *U.S.A.* 109 K5
Painted Desert, *U.S.A.* . 111 J8
Paintsville, *U.S.A.* 104 G4
País Vasco □, *Spain* 28 C2
Paisley, *Canada* 106 B3
Paisley, *U.K.* 14 F4
Paisley, *U.S.A.* 110 E3
Paita, *Peru* 124 B1
Paiva →, *Portugal* 30 D2
Paizhou, *China* 53 B9
Pajares, *Spain* 30 B5
Pajares, Puerto de, *Spain* . 30 C5
Pak Lay, *Laos* 58 C3
Pak Phanang, *Thailand* .. 59 H3
Pak Sane, *Laos* 58 C4

Pak Song, *Laos* 58 E6
Pak Suong, *Laos* 58 C4
Pakaraima Mts., *Guyana* . 121 B5
Pákhnes, *Greece* 37 D6
Pakistan ■, *Asia* 62 E3
Pakistan, East =
  Bangladesh ■, *Asia* .. 61 H17
Pakkading, *Laos* 58 C4
Pakokku, *Burma* 61 J19
Pakpattan, *Pakistan* ... 62 D5
Pakrac, *Croatia* 21 K7
Paks, *Hungary* 21 J8
Pakse, *Laos* 58 E5
Paktīā □, *Afghan.* 60 C6
Pakwach, *Uganda* 82 B3
Pala, *Chad* 73 G8
Pala, *U.S.A.* 113 M9
Pala, *Zaïre* 82 D2
Palabek, *Uganda* 82 B3
Palacios, *U.S.A.* 109 L6
Palafrugell, *Spain* ... 28 D8
Palagiano, *Italy* 35 B10
Palagonia, *Italy* 35 E7
Palagruža, *Croatia* ... 33 F13
Palaiokastron, *Greece* . 37 D8
Palaiokhóra, *Greece* .. 37 D5
Palam, *India* 60 K10
Palamás, *Greece* 39 K5
Palamós, *Spain* 28 D8
Palampur, *India* 62 C7
Palana, *Australia* 90 F4
Palana, *Russia* 45 D16
Palanan, *Phil.* 55 C5
Palanan Pt., *Phil.* 55 C5
Palanda, *Pakistan* 63 C5
Palangkaraya, *Indonesia* 56 E4
Palani Hills, *India* ... 60 P10
Palanpur, *India* 62 G5
Palapye, *Botswana* 84 C4
Palas, *Pakistan* 63 B5
Palatka, *Russia* 45 C16
Palatka, *U.S.A.* 105 L5
Palawan, *Phil.* 55 G3
Palayankottai, *India* .. 60 Q10
Palazzo, Pte., *France* .. 27 F12
Palazzo San Gervásio, *Italy* 35 B8
Palazzolo Acreide, *Italy* . 35 E7
Palca, *Chile* 124 D4
Paldiski, *Estonia* 40 B4
Paleleh, *Indonesia* 57 D6
Palembang, *Indonesia* . 56 E2
Palena →, *Chile* 128 B2
Palena, L., *Chile* 128 B2
Palencia, *Spain* 30 C6
Palencia □, *Spain* 30 C6
Paleokastrítsa, *Greece* . 37 A3
Paleometokho, *Cyprus* . 37 D12
Palermo, *Colombia* 120 C2
Palermo, *Italy* 34 D6
Palermo, *U.S.A.* 110 G3
Palestine, *Asia* 69 D4
Palestine, *U.S.A.* 109 K7
Palestrina, *Italy* 34 A5
Paletwa, *Burma* 61 J18
Palghat, *India* 60 P10
Palgrave, Mt., *Australia* 88 D2
Pali, *India* 62 G5
Palinuro, C., *Italy* ... 35 B8
Palisade, *U.S.A.* 108 E4
Paliseul, *Belgium* 17 J6
Palitana, *India* 62 J4
Palizada, *Mexico* 115 D6
Palizzi, *Italy* 35 E8
Palk Bay, *Asia* 60 Q11
Palk Strait, *Asia* 60 Q11
Palkānah, *Iraq* 64 C5
Palla Road = Dinokwe,
  Botswana 84 C4
Pallanza = Verbánia, *Italy* 32 C5
Pallasovka, *Russia* ... 41 F15
Pallisa, *Uganda* 82 B3
Pallu, *India* 62 E6
Palm Beach, *U.S.A.* ... 105 M6
Palm Desert, *U.S.A.* .. 113 M10
Palm Is., *Australia* ... 90 B4
Palm Springs, *U.S.A.* .. 113 M10
Palma, *Mozam.* 83 E5
Palma →, *Brazil* 123 D2
Palma, B. de, *Spain* ... 36 B9
Palma de Mallorca, *Spain* . 36 B9
Palma del Río, *Spain* .. 31 H5
Palma di Montechiaro, *Italy* 34 E6
Palma Soriano, *Cuba* .. 116 B4
Palmanova, *Italy* 33 C10
Palmares, *Brazil* 122 C4
Palmarito, *Venezuela* .. 120 B3
Palmarola, *Italy* 34 B5
Palmas, *Brazil* 127 B5
Palmas, C., *Liberia* ... 78 E3
Pálmas, G. di, *Italy* .. 34 C1
Palmas de Monte Alto,
  Brazil 123 D3
Palmdale, *U.S.A.* 113 L8
Palmeira, *Brazil* 123 G2
Palmeira dos Índios, *Brazil* 122 C4
Palmeirais, *Brazil* ... 122 C3
Palmeiras →, *Brazil* .. 123 D2
Palmeirinhas, Pta. das,
  Angola 80 F2
Palmela, *Portugal* 31 G2
Palmelo, *Brazil* 123 E2
Palmer, *U.S.A.* 96 B5
Palmer →, *Australia* .. 90 B3

Palmer Lake, *U.S.A.* ... 108 F2
Palmer Land, *Antarctica* . 5 D18
Palmerston, *Canada* ... 106 C4
Palmerston, *N.Z.* 87 L3
Palmerston North, *N.Z.* . 87 J5
Palmerton, *U.S.A.* 107 F9
Palmetto, *U.S.A.* 105 M4
Palmi, *Italy* 35 D8
Palmira, *Argentina* ... 126 C2
Palmira, *Colombia* 120 C2
Palmyra = Tudmur, *Syria* 64 C3
Palmyra, *Mo., U.S.A.* .. 108 F9
Palmyra, *N.Y., U.S.A.* . 106 C7
Palmyra Is., *Pac. Oc.* . 93 G11
Palo Alto, *U.S.A.* 111 H2
Palo del Colle, *Italy* .. 35 A9
Palo Verde, *U.S.A.* ... 113 M12
Palombara Sabina, *Italy* . 33 F9
Palompon, *Phil.* 55 F6
Palopo, *Indonesia* 57 E6
Palos, C. de, *Spain* ... 29 H4
Palos Verdes, *U.S.A.* .. 113 M8
Palos Verdes, Pt., *U.S.A.* 113 M8
Palouse, *U.S.A.* 110 C5
Palpa, *Peru* 124 C2
Palparara, *Australia* .. 90 C3
Pålsboda, *Sweden* 10 E9
Palu, *Indonesia* 57 E5
Paluan, *Phil.* 57 B6
Palwal, *India* 62 E7
Pama, *Burkina Faso* ... 79 C5
Pamanukan, *Indonesia* .. 57 G12
Pamekasan, *Indonesia* .. 57 G15
Pamiers, *France* 26 E5
Pamirs, *Tajikistan* ... 44 F8
Pamlico →, *U.S.A.* 105 H7
Pamlico Sd., *U.S.A.* .. 105 H8
Pampa, *U.S.A.* 109 H4
Pampa de Agma, *Argentina* 128 B3
Pampa de las Salinas,
  Argentina 126 C2
Pampa Grande, *Bolivia* .. 125 D5
Pampa Hermosa, *Peru* .. 124 B2
Pampanua, *Indonesia* .. 57 E6
Pamparato, *Italy* 32 D4
Pampas, *Argentina* ... 126 D3
Pampas, *Peru* 124 C3
Pampas →, *Peru* 124 C3
Pamphylia, *Turkey* ... 66 E4
Pamplona, *Colombia* ... 120 B3
Pamplona, *Spain* 28 C3
Pampoenpoort, *S. Africa* . 84 E3
Pamukkale, *Turkey* ... 66 E3
Pan Xian, *China* 52 E5
Pana, *U.S.A.* 108 F10
Panabo, *Phil.* 55 H6
Panaca, *U.S.A.* 111 H6
Panagyurishte, *Bulgaria* . 38 G7
Panaitan, *Indonesia* .. 57 G11
Panaji, *India* 60 M8
Panamá, *Panama* 116 E4
Panama ■, *Cent. Amer.* . 116 E4
Panamá, G. de, *Panama* . 116 E4
Panama Canal, *Panama* . 116 E4
Panama City, *U.S.A.* .. 105 K3
Panamint Ra., *U.S.A.* .. 113 J9
Panamint Springs, *U.S.A.* . 113 J9
Panão, *Peru* 124 B2
Panaon I., *Phil.* 55 F6
Panare, *Thailand* 59 J3
Panarea, *Italy* 35 D8
Panaro →, *Italy* 32 D8
Panarukan, *Indonesia* .. 57 G15
Panay, *Phil.* 55 F5
Panay, G., *Phil.* 57 B6
Pancake Ra., *U.S.A.* ... 111 G6
Pančevo, *Serbia, Yug.* . 21 L10
Pancorbo, Paso, *Spain* . 28 C1
Pandan, *Antique, Phil.* . 55 F5
Pandan, *Catanduanes, Phil.* 55 E6
Pandegelang, *Indonesia* . 57 G12
Pandharpur, *India* 60 L9
Pandilla, *Spain* 28 D1
Pando, *Uruguay* 127 C4
Pando, □, *Bolivia* 124 C4
Pando, L. = Hope, L.,
  Australia 91 D2
Pandokrátor, *Greece* .. 37 A3
Pandora, *Costa Rica* .. 116 E3
Panevezys, *Lithuania* .. 40 D4
Panfilov, *Kazakhstan* .. 44 E8
Panfilovo, *Russia* 41 F13
Pang-Long, *Burma* 61 H21
Pang-Yang, *Burma* 61 H21
Panga, *Zaïre* 82 B2
Pangalanes, Canal des,
  Madag. 85 C8
Pangani, *Tanzania* 82 D4
Pangani □, *Tanzania* ... 82 D4
Pangani →, *Tanzania* .. 82 D4
Pangfou = Bengbu, *China* 51 H9
Pangil, *Zaïre* 82 C2
Pangkah, Tanjung,
  Indonesia 57 G15
Pangkajene, *Indonesia* . 57 E5
Pangkalanbrandan,
  Indonesia 56 D1
Pangkalanbuun, *Indonesia* 56 E4
Pangkalansusu, *Indonesia* 56 D1
Pangkalpinang, *Indonesia* . 56 E3
Pangkoh, *Indonesia* ... 56 E4
Pangnirtung, *Canada* .. 97 B13
Pangrango, *Indonesia* .. 57 G12
Panguipulli, *Chile* 128 A2

Panguitch, *U.S.A.* 111 H7
Pangutaran Group, *Phil.* . 55 H4
Panhandle, *U.S.A.* 109 H4
Pani Mines, *India* 62 H5
Pania-Mutombo, *Zaïre* . 82 D1
Panipat, *India* 62 E7
Panjal Range, *India* ... 62 C7
Panjgur, *Pakistan* 60 F4
Panjim = Panaji, *India* . 60 M8
Panjinad Barrage, *Pakistan* 60 E7
Panjwai, *Afghan.* 62 D1
Pankshin, *Nigeria* 79 D6
Panmunjŏm, *N. Korea* . 51 F14
Panna, *India* 63 G9
Panna Hills, *India* 63 G9
Pano Lefkara, *Cyprus* . 37 E12
Pano Panayia, *Cyprus* . 37 E11
Panorama, *Brazil* 127 A5
Pánormon, *Greece* 37 D6
Panshan, *China* 51 D12
Panshi, *China* 51 C14
Pantar, *Indonesia* 57 F6
Pantelleria, *Italy* 34 F5
Pantón, *Spain* 30 C3
Pánuco, *Mexico* 115 C5
Panyam, *Nigeria* 79 D6
Panyu, *China* 53 F9
Pao →, *Anzoátegui,
  Venezuela* 121 B5
Pao →, *Apure, Venezuela* 120 B4
Páola, *Italy* 35 C9
Paola, *Malta* 37 D2
Paola, *U.S.A.* 108 F7
Paonia, *U.S.A.* 111 G10
Paoting = Baoding, *China* 50 E8
Paot'ou = Baotou, *China* . 50 D6
Paoua, *C.A.R.* 73 G8
Pápa, *Hungary* 21 H7
Papagayo →, *Mexico* .. 115 D5
Papagayo, G. de,
  Costa Rica 116 D2
Papakura, *N.Z.* 87 G5
Papantla, *Mexico* 115 C5
Papar, *Malaysia* 56 C5
Pápas, Ákra, *Greece* .. 39 L4
Papenburg, *Germany* .. 18 B3
Paphlagonia, *Turkey* .. 66 C5
Paphos, *Cyprus* 37 E11
Papien Chiang = Da →,
  Vietnam 58 B5
Papigochic →, *Mexico* . 114 B3
Papoose, *Chile* 126 B1
Papoutsa, *Cyprus* 37 E12
Papua New Guinea ■,
  Oceania 92 H6
Papuča, *Croatia* 33 D12
Papudo, *Chile* 126 C1
Papuk, *Croatia* 21 K7
Papun, *Burma* 61 K20
Papunya, *Australia* ... 88 D5
Pará = Belém, *Brazil* .. 122 B2
Pará □, *Brazil* 125 A7
Pará □, *Surinam* 121 B6
Parábita, *Italy* 35 B11
Paraburdoo, *Australia* . 88 D2
Paracale, *Phil.* 55 D5
Paracas, Pen., *Peru* ... 124 C2
Paracatu, *Brazil* 123 E2
Paracatu →, *Brazil* ... 123 E2
Paracel Is. = Hsisha
  Chuntao, *Pac. Oc.* .. 56 A4
Parachilna, *Australia* . 91 E2
Parachinar, *Pakistan* .. 62 C4
Paracín, *Serbia, Yug.* . 21 M11
Paracuru, *Brazil* 122 B4
Parada, Punta, *Peru* .. 124 D2
Paradas, *Spain* 31 H5
Paradela, *Spain* 30 C3
Paradhísi, *Greece* 37 C10
Paradip, *India* 61 J15
Paradise, *Calif., U.S.A.* . 112 F5
Paradise, *Mont., U.S.A.* . 110 C6
Paradise, *Nev., U.S.A.* . 113 J11
Paradise →, *Canada* .. 99 B8
Paradise Valley, *U.S.A.* . 110 F5
Parado, *Indonesia* 57 F5
Paragould, *U.S.A.* 109 G9
Paraguá →, *Bolivia* ... 125 C5
Paragua →, *Venezuela* . 121 B5
Paraguaçu →, *Brazil* .. 123 D4
Paraguaçu Paulista, *Brazil* 127 A5
Paraguaipoa, *Venezuela* . 120 A3
Paraguaná, Pen. de,
  Venezuela 120 A3
Paraguarí, *Paraguay* ... 126 B4
Paraguarí □, *Paraguay* . 126 B4
Paraguay ■, *S. Amer.* . 126 A4
Paraguay →, *Paraguay* . 126 B4
Paraíba = João Pessoa,
  Brazil 122 C5
Paraíba □, *Brazil* 122 C4
Paraíba do Sul →, *Brazil* . 123 F3
Parainen, *Finland* 9 F17
Paraiso, *Mexico* 115 D6
Parak, *Iran* 65 E7
Parakhino Paddubye,
  Russia 40 B8
Parakou, *Benin* 79 D5
Paralimni, *Cyprus* 37 D12
Paramaribo, *Surinam* .. 121 B6
Parambu, *Brazil* 122 C3
Paramillo, Nudo del,
  Colombia 120 B2
Paramirim, *Brazil* 123 D3

Paramirim →, *Brazil* ... 123 D3
Paramithiá, *Greece* 39 K3
Paramushir, Ostrov, *Russia* 45 D16
Paran →, *Israel* 69 E4
Paraná, *Argentina* 126 C3
Paraná, *Brazil* 123 D2
Paraná □, *Brazil* 127 A5
Paraná →, *Argentina* .. 126 C4
Paranaguá, *Brazil* 127 B6
Paranaíba, *Brazil* 123 E1
Paranaíba →, *Brazil* ... 127 A5
Paranapanema →, *Brazil* . 127 A5
Paranapiacaba, Serra do,
  Brazil 127 A6
Paranavaí, *Brazil* 127 A5
Parang, *Jolo, Phil.* ... 55 J4
Parang, *Mindanao, Phil.* . 57 C6
Parangaba, *Brazil* 122 B4
Parapóla, *Greece* 39 N6
Paraspóri, Ákra, *Greece* . 39 P10
Paratinga, *Brazil* 123 D3
Paratoo, *Australia* 91 E2
Parattah, *Australia* ... 90 G4
Paraúna, *Brazil* 123 E1
Paray-le-Monial, *France* . 27 B8
Parbati →, *India* 62 G7
Parbhani, *India* 60 K10
Parchim, *Germany* 18 B7
Parczew, *Poland* 20 D12
Pardes Hanna, *Israel* .. 69 C3
Pardilla, *Spain* 30 D7
Pardo →, *Bahia, Brazil* . 123 E4
Pardo →, *Mato Grosso,
  Brazil* 127 A5
Pardo →, *Minas Gerais,
  Brazil* 123 E3
Pardo →, *São Paulo,
  Brazil* 123 F2
Pardubice, *Czech.* 20 E5
Pare, *Indonesia* 57 G15
Pare □, *Tanzania* 82 C4
Pare Mts., *Tanzania* ... 82 C4
Parecis, Serra dos, *Brazil* 125 C6
Paredes de Nava, *Spain* . 30 C6
Pareh, *Iran* 64 B5
Parelhas, *Brazil* 122 C4
Paren, *Russia* 45 C17
Parent, *Canada* 98 C5
Parent, L., *Canada* ... 98 C4
Parentis-en-Born, *France* . 26 D2
Parepare, *Indonesia* .. 57 E5
Parfino, *Russia* 40 C7
Pargo, Pta. do, *Madeira* . 36 D2
Paria, G. of, *Venezuela* . 121 A5
Paria, Pen. de, *Venezuela* 121 A5
Pariaguán, *Venezuela* .. 121 B5
Pariaman, *Indonesia* .. 56 E2
Paricatuba, *Brazil* 121 D5
Paricutín, Cerro, *Mexico* . 114 D4
Parigi, *Java, Indonesia* . 57 G13
Parigi, *Sulawesi, Indonesia* 57 E6
Parika, *Guyana* 121 B6
Parima, Serra, *Brazil* .. 121 C5
Parinari, *Peru* 124 A3
Paring, *Romania* 38 D6
Parintins, *Brazil* 121 D6
Pariparit Kyun, *Burma* .. 61 M18
Paris, *Canada* 98 D3
Paris, *France* 25 D9
Paris, *Idaho, U.S.A.* .. 110 E8
Paris, *Ky., U.S.A.* 104 F3
Paris, *Tenn., U.S.A.* .. 105 G1
Paris, *Tex., U.S.A.* ... 109 J7
Paris, Ville de □, *France* . 25 D9
Parish, *U.S.A.* 107 C8
Pariti, *Indonesia* 57 F6
Park, *U.S.A.* 112 B4
Park City, *U.S.A.* 110 F8
Park Falls, *U.S.A.* 108 C9
Park Range, *U.S.A.* ... 110 G10
Park Rapids, *U.S.A.* ... 108 B7
Park River, *U.S.A.* ... 108 A6
Park Rynie, *S. Africa* .. 85 E5
Parkā Bandar, *Iran* ... 65 E8
Parker, *Ariz., U.S.A.* .. 113 L12
Parker, *S. Dak., U.S.A.* . 108 D6
Parker Dam, *U.S.A.* ... 113 L12
Parkersburg, *U.S.A.* ... 104 F5
Parkerview, *Canada* ... 101 C8
Parkes, *Australia* 91 E4
Parkfield, *U.S.A.* 112 K6
Parkland, *U.S.A.* 112 C4
Parkside, *Canada* 101 C7
Parkston, *U.S.A.* 108 D5
Parksville, *Canada* ... 100 D4
Parma, *Italy* 32 D7
Parma, *Idaho, U.S.A.* .. 110 E5
Parma, *Ohio, U.S.A.* .. 106 E3
Parma →, *Italy* 32 D7
Parnaguá, *Brazil* 122 D3
Parnaíba, *Piauí, Brazil* . 122 B3
Parnaíba, *São Paulo, Brazil* 125 D7
Parnaíba →, *Brazil* ... 122 B3
Parnamirim, *Brazil* ... 122 C4
Parnarama, *Brazil* 122 C3
Parnassós, *Greece* 39 L5
Párnis, *Greece* 39 L6
Párnon Óros, *Greece* .. 39 M5
Pärnu, *Estonia* 40 B4
Paroo →, *Australia* ... 91 E3
Páros, *Greece* 39 M8
Parowan, *U.S.A.* 111 H7
Parpaillon, *France* 27 D10
Parral, *Chile* 126 D1
Parramatta, *Australia* .. 91 E5

Parras, *Mexico* 114 B4
Parrett →, *U.K.* 13 F5
Parris I., *U.S.A.* 105 J5
Parrsboro, *Canada* 99 C7
Parry Is., *Canada* 4 B2
Parry Sound, *Canada* 98 C3
Parsberg, *Germany* 19 F7
Parshall, *U.S.A.* 108 B3
Parsnip →, *Canada* 100 B4
Parsons, *U.S.A.* 109 G7
Parsons Ra., *Australia* 90 A2
Partanna, *Italy* 34 E5
Parthenay, *France* 24 F6
Partinico, *Italy* 34 D6
Paru →, *Brazil* 121 D7
Parú →, *Venezuela* 120 C4
Paru de Oeste →, *Brazil* 121 C6
Parucito →, *Venezuela* 120 B4
Paruro, *Peru* 124 C3
Parvān □, *Afghan.* 60 B6
Parvatipuram, *India* 61 K13
Parys, *S. Africa* 84 D4
Pas-de-Calais □, *France* 25 B9
Pasádena, *Calif., U.S.A.* 113 L8
Pasadena, *Tex., U.S.A.* 109 L7
Pasaje, *Ecuador* 120 D2
Pasaje →, *Argentina* 126 B3
Pasay, *Phil.* 55 D4
Pascagoula, *U.S.A.* 109 K10
Pascagoula →, *U.S.A.* 109 K10
Paşcani, *Romania* 38 B9
Pasco, *U.S.A.* 110 C4
Pasco □, *Peru* 124 C2
Pasco, Cerro de, *Peru* 124 C2
Pascua, I. de, *Pac. Oc.* 93 K17
Pasewalk, *Germany* 18 B10
Pasfield L., *Canada* 101 B7
Pasha →, *Russia* 40 B8
Pashiwari, *Pakistan* 63 B6
Pashmakli = Smolyan, *Bulgaria* 39 H7
Pasinler, *Turkey* 67 D9
Pasirian, *Indonesia* 57 H15
Paskūh, *Iran* 65 E9
Pasley, C., *Australia* 89 F3
Pašman, *Croatia* 33 E12
Pasni, *Pakistan* 60 G3
Paso Cantinela, *Mexico* 113 N11
Paso de Indios, *Argentina* 128 B3
Paso de los Libres, *Argentina* 126 B4
Paso de los Toros, *Uruguay* 126 C4
Paso Flores, *Argentina* 128 B2
Paso Robles, *U.S.A.* 111 J3
Pasorapa, *Bolivia* 125 D5
Paspébiac, *Canada* 99 C6
Pasrur, *Pakistan* 62 C6
Passage West, *Ireland* 15 E3
Passaic, *U.S.A.* 107 F10
Passau, *Germany* 19 G9
Passendale, *Belgium* 17 G2
Passero, C., *Italy* 35 F8
Passo Fundo, *Brazil* 127 B5
Passos, *Brazil* 123 F2
Passow, *Germany* 18 B10
Passwang, *Switz.* 22 B5
Passy, *France* 27 C10
Pastaza □, *Ecuador* 120 D2
Pastaza →, *Peru* 120 D2
Pastęk, *Poland* 20 A9
Pasto, *Colombia* 120 C2
Pastos Bons, *Brazil* 122 C3
Pastrana, *Spain* 28 E2
Pasuruan, *Indonesia* 57 G15
Patagonia, *Argentina* 128 C2
Patagonia, *U.S.A.* 111 L8
Patambar, *Iran* 65 D9
Patan, *India* 60 H8
Patan, *Maharashtra, India* 60 H5
Patan, *Nepal* 61 F14
Patani, *Indonesia* 57 D7
Pataudi, *India* 62 E7
Patay, *France* 25 D8
Patchewollock, *Australia* 91 F3
Patchogue, *U.S.A.* 107 F11
Patea, *N.Z.* 87 H5
Pategi, *Nigeria* 79 D6
Patensie, *S. Africa* 84 E3
Paternò, *Italy* 35 E7
Pateros, *U.S.A.* 110 B4
Paterson, *U.S.A.* 107 F10
Paterson Ra., *Australia* 88 D3
Paterswolde, *Neths.* 16 B9
Pathankot, *India* 62 C6
Pathfinder Res., *U.S.A.* 110 E10
Pathiu, *Thailand* 59 G2
Pathum Thani, *Thailand* 58 E3
Pati, *Indonesia* 57 G14
Patía, *Colombia* 120 C2
Patía →, *Colombia* 120 C2
Patiala, *India* 62 D7
Patine Kouka, *Senegal* 78 C2
Pativilca, *Peru* 124 C2
Patkai Bum, *India* 61 F19
Pátmos, *Greece* 39 M9
Patna, *India* 63 G11
Patnos, *Turkey* 67 D10
Patonga, *Uganda* 82 B3
Patos, *Brazil* 122 C4
Patos, L. dos, *Brazil* 127 C5
Patos de Minas, *Brazil* 123 E2
Patquía, *Argentina* 126 C2
Pátrai, *Greece* 39 L4
Pátraikós Kólpos, *Greece* 39 L4
Patricio Lynch, I., *Chile* 128 C1
Patrocínio, *Brazil* 123 E2
Patta, *Kenya* 82 C5
Pattada, *Italy* 34 B2
Pattani, *Thailand* 59 J3
Patten, *U.S.A.* 99 C6
Patterson, *Calif., U.S.A.* 111 H3
Patterson, *La., U.S.A.* 109 L9
Patterson, Mt., *U.S.A.* 112 G7
Patti, *India* 62 D6
Patti, *Italy* 35 D7
Pattoki, *Pakistan* 62 D5
Patton, *U.S.A.* 106 F6
Patu, *Brazil* 122 C4
Patuakhali, *Bangla.* 61 H17
Patuca →, *Honduras* 116 C3
Patuca, Punta, *Honduras* 116 C3
Pâturages, *Belgium* 17 H3
Pátzcuaro, *Mexico* 114 D4
Pau, *France* 26 E3
Pau, Gave de →, *France* 26 E2
Pau d' Arco, *Brazil* 122 C2
Pau dos Ferros, *Brazil* 122 C4
Paucartambo, *Peru* 124 C3
Pauillac, *France* 26 C3
Pauini, *Brazil* 124 B4
Pauini →, *Brazil* 121 D5
Pauk, *Burma* 61 J19
Paul I., *Canada* 99 A7
Paul Isnard, *Fr. Guiana* 121 C7
Paulhan, *France* 26 E7
Paulis = Isiro, *Zaïre* 82 B2
Paulista, *Brazil* 122 C5
Paulistana, *Brazil* 122 C3
Paullina, *U.S.A.* 108 D7
Paulo Afonso, *Brazil* 122 C4
Paulo de Faria, *Brazil* 123 F2
Paulpietersburg, *S. Africa* 85 D5
Pauls Valley, *U.S.A.* 109 H6
Pauma Valley, *U.S.A.* 113 M10
Pausa, *Peru* 124 D3
Pauto →, *Colombia* 120 B3
Pāveh, *Iran* 64 C5
Pavelets, *Russia* 41 E11
Pavia, *Italy* 32 C6
Pavlikeni, *Bulgaria* 38 F8
Pavlodar, *Kazakhstan* 44 D8
Pavlograd, *Ukraine* 42 B6
Pavlovo, *Russia* 41 D13
Pavlovo, *Russia* 45 C12
Pavlovsk, *Russia* 41 F12
Pavlovskaya, *Russia* 43 C8
Pavlovskiy-Posad, *Russia* 41 D11
Pavullo nel Frignano, *Italy* 32 D7
Pawhuska, *U.S.A.* 109 G6
Pawling, *U.S.A.* 107 E11
Pawnee, *U.S.A.* 109 G6
Pawnee City, *U.S.A.* 108 E6
Pawtucket, *U.S.A.* 107 E13
Paximádhia, *Greece* 37 D6
Paxoí, *Greece* 39 K3
Paxton, *Ill., U.S.A.* 104 E1
Paxton, *Nebr., U.S.A.* 108 E4
Payakumbuh, *Indonesia* 56 E2
Payerne, *Switz.* 22 C3
Payette, *U.S.A.* 110 D5
Paymogo, *Spain* 31 H3
Payne Bay = Bellin, *Canada* 97 B13
Payne L., *Canada* 97 C12
Paynes Find, *Australia* 89 E2
Paynesville, *Liberia* 78 D2
Paynesville, *U.S.A.* 108 C7
Paysandú, *Uruguay* 126 C4
Payson, *Ariz., U.S.A.* 111 J8
Payson, *Utah, U.S.A.* 110 F8
Paz →, *Guatemala* 116 D1
Paz, B. la, *Mexico* 114 C2
Pāzanān, *Iran* 65 D6
Pazar, *Turkey* 67 C9
Pazarcık, *Turkey* 66 E7
Pazardzhik, *Bulgaria* 38 G7
Pazin, *Croatia* 33 C10
Pazña, *Bolivia* 124 D4
Pčinja →, *Macedonia, Yug.* 39 H4
Pe Ell, *U.S.A.* 112 D3
Peabody, *U.S.A.* 107 D14
Peace →, *Canada* 100 B6
Peace Point, *Canada* 100 B6
Peace River, *Canada* 100 B5
Peach Springs, *U.S.A.* 111 J7
Peak Downs, *Australia* 90 C4
Peak Downs Mine, *Australia* 90 C4
Peak Hill, *N.S.W., Australia* 91 E4
Peak Hill, *W. Austral., Australia* 89 E2
Peak Ra., *Australia* 90 C4
Peake, *Australia* 91 F2
Peake Cr. →, *Australia* 91 D2
Peale Mt., *U.S.A.* 111 G9
Pearblossom, *U.S.A.* 113 L9
Pearl →, *U.S.A.* 109 K10
Pearl City, *U.S.A.* 102 H16
Pearsall, *U.S.A.* 109 L5
Pearse I., *Canada* 100 C2
Peary Land, *Greenland* 4 A6
Pease →, *U.S.A.* 109 H5
Pebane, *Mozam.* 83 F4
Pebas, *Peru* 120 D3
Pebble, I., *Falk. Is.* 128 D5
Pebble Beach, *U.S.A.* 112 J5
Peč, *Serbia, Yug.* 21 N10
Peçanha, *Brazil* 123 E3
Péccioli, *Italy* 32 E7
Pechea, *Romania* 38 D10
Pechenezhin, *Ukraine* 42 B1
Pechenga, *Russia* 44 C4
Pechiguera, Pta., *Canary Is.* 36 F6
Pechnezhskoye Vdkhr., *Ukraine* 42 A7
Pechora →, *Russia* 44 C6
Pechorskaya Guba, *Russia* 44 C6
Pechory, *Russia* 40 C5
Pecica, *Romania* 38 C4
Pečka, *Serbia, Yug.* 21 L9
Pécora, C., *Italy* 34 C1
Pecos, *U.S.A.* 109 K3
Pecos →, *U.S.A.* 109 L3
Pécs, *Hungary* 21 J8
Pedder, L., *Australia* 90 G4
Peddie, *S. Africa* 85 E4
Pédernales, *Dom. Rep.* 117 C5
Pedieos →, *Cyprus* 37 D12
Pedirka, *Australia* 91 D2
Pedra Azul, *Brazil* 123 E3
Pedra Grande, Recifes de, *Brazil* 123 E4
Pedras Negras, *Brazil* 125 C5
Pedreiras, *Brazil* 122 B3
Pedro Afonso, *Brazil* 122 C2
Pedro Cays, *Jamaica* 116 C4
Pedro Chico, *Colombia* 120 C3
Pedro de Valdivia, *Chile* 126 A2
Pedro Juan Caballero, *Paraguay* 127 A4
Pedro Muñoz, *Spain* 29 F2
Pedrógão Grande, *Portugal* 30 F2
Peebinga, *Australia* 91 E3
Peebles, *U.K.* 14 F5
Peekskill, *U.S.A.* 107 E11
Peel, *U.K.* 12 C3
Peel →, *Australia* 91 E5
Peel →, *Canada* 96 B6
Peene →, *Germany* 18 A9
Peera Peera Poolanna L., *Australia* 91 D2
Peers, *Canada* 100 C5
Pegasus Bay, *N.Z.* 87 K4
Pegnitz, *Germany* 19 F7
Pegnitz →, *Germany* 19 F6
Pego, *Spain* 29 G4
Pegu, *Burma* 61 L20
Pegu Yoma, *Burma* 61 K19
Pehuajó, *Argentina* 126 D3
Pei Xian, *China* 50 G9
Peine, *Chile* 126 A2
Peine, *Germany* 18 C6
Peip'ing = Beijing, *China* 50 E9
Peissenberg, *Germany* 19 H7
Peitz, *Germany* 18 D10
Peixe, *Brazil* 123 D2
Peixe →, *Brazil* 123 F1
Peixoto de Azeredo →, *Brazil* 125 C6
Peize, *Neths.* 16 B8
Pek →, *Serbia, Yug.* 21 L11
Pekalongan, *Indonesia* 57 G13
Pekan, *Malaysia* 59 L4
Pekanbaru, *Indonesia* 56 D2
Pekin, *U.S.A.* 108 E10
Peking = Beijing, *China* 50 E9
Pelabuhan Kelang, *Malaysia* 59 L3
Pelabuhan Ratu, Teluk, *Indonesia* 57 G12
Pelabuhanratu, *Indonesia* 57 G12
Pélagos, *Greece* 39 K7
Pelaihari, *Indonesia* 56 E4
Pelat, Mt., *France* 27 D10
Peleaga, *Romania* 38 D5
Pelechuco, *Bolivia* 124 C4
Pelée, Mt., *Martinique* 117 D7
Pelee, Pt., *Canada* 98 D3
Pelee I., *Canada* 98 D3
Pelejo, *Peru* 124 B2
Pelekech, *Kenya* 82 B4
Peleng, *Indonesia* 57 E6
Pelham, *U.S.A.* 105 K3
Pelhřimov, *Czech.* 20 F5
Pelican L., *Canada* 101 C8
Pelican Narrows, *Canada* 101 B8
Pelican Rapids, *Canada* 101 C8
Pelkosenniemi, *Finland* 8 C19
Pella, *S. Africa* 84 D2
Pella, *U.S.A.* 108 E8
Péllaro, *Italy* 35 D8
Pellworm, *Germany* 18 A4
Pelly →, *Canada* 96 B6
Pelly Bay, *Canada* 97 B11
Pelly L., *Canada* 96 B9
Peloponnese = Pelopónnisos □, *Greece* 39 M5
Pelopónnisos □, *Greece* 39 M5
Peloritani, Monti, *Italy* 35 D8
Peloro, C., *Italy* 35 D8
Pelorus Sd., *N.Z.* 87 J4
Pelotas, *Brazil* 127 C5
Pelvoux, Massif de, *France* 27 D10
Pemalang, *Indonesia* 57 G13
Pematangsiantar, *Indonesia* 56 D1
Pemba, *Mozam.* 83 E5
Pemba, *Zambia* 83 F2
Pemba Channel, *Tanzania* 82 D4
Pemba I., *Tanzania* 82 D4
Pemberton, *Australia* 89 F2
Pemberton, *Canada* 100 C4
Pembina, *U.S.A.* 101 D9
Pembina →, *U.S.A.* 101 D9
Pembine, *U.S.A.* 104 C2
Pembino, *U.S.A.* 108 A6
Pembroke, *Canada* 98 C4
Pembroke, *U.K.* 13 F3
Pembroke, *U.S.A.* 105 J5
Pen-y-Ghent, *U.K.* 12 C5
Peña, Sierra de la, *Spain* 28 C4
Peña de Francia, Sierra de, *Spain* 30 E4
Penafiel, *Portugal* 30 D2
Peñafiel, *Spain* 30 D6
Peñaflor, *Spain* 31 H5
Peñalara, Pico, *Spain* 30 E7
Penalva, *Brazil* 122 B2
Penamacôr, *Portugal* 30 E3
Penang = Pinang, *Malaysia* 59 K3
Penápolis, *Brazil* 127 A6
Peñaranda de Bracamonte, *Spain* 30 E5
Peñarroya-Pueblonuevo, *Spain* 31 G5
Peñas, C. de, *Spain* 30 B5
Penas, G. de, *Chile* 128 C2
Peñas, Pta., *Venezuela* 121 A5
Peñas de San Pedro, *Spain* 29 G2
Peñas del Chache, *Canary Is.* 36 E6
Peñausende, *Spain* 30 D5
Pench'i = Benxi, *China* 51 D12
Pend Oreille →, *U.S.A.* 110 B5
Pend Oreille, L., *U.S.A.* 110 C5
Pendembu, *S. Leone* 78 D2
Pendências, *Brazil* 122 C4
Pender B., *Australia* 88 C3
Pendleton, *Calif., U.S.A.* 113 M9
Pendleton, *Oreg., U.S.A.* 110 D4
Penedo, *Brazil* 122 D4
Penetanguishene, *Canada* 98 D4
Peng Xian, *China* 52 B4
Pengalengan, *Indonesia* 57 G12
Penge, *Kasai Or., Zaïre* 82 D1
Penge, *Kivu, Zaïre* 82 C2
Penglai, *China* 51 F11
Pengshui, *China* 52 C7
Penguin, *Australia* 90 G4
Pengxi, *China* 52 B5
Pengze, *China* 53 C11
Penhalonga, *Zimbabwe* 83 F3
Peniche, *Portugal* 31 F1
Penicuik, *U.K.* 14 F5
Penida, *Indonesia* 56 F5
Peninsular Malaysia □, *Malaysia* 59 L4
Peñíscola, *Spain* 28 E5
Penitente, Serra dos, *Brazil* 122 C2
Penmarch, *France* 24 E2
Penmarch, Pte. de, *France* 24 E2
Penn Hills, *U.S.A.* 106 F5
Penn Yan, *U.S.A.* 106 D7
Pennabilli, *Italy* 33 E9
Pennant, *Canada* 101 C7
Penne, *Italy* 33 F10
Penner →, *India* 60 M12
Pennine, Alpi, *Alps* 32 B4
Pennines, *U.K.* 12 C5
Pennington, *U.S.A.* 112 F5
Pennino, Mte., *Italy* 33 E9
Pennsylvania □, *U.S.A.* 104 E6
Penny, *Canada* 100 C4
Peno, *Russia* 40 C8
Penola, *Australia* 91 F3
Penong, *Australia* 89 F5
Penonomé, *Panama* 116 E3
Penrith, *Australia* 91 E5
Penrith, *U.K.* 12 C5
Pensacola, *U.S.A.* 105 K2
Pensacola Mts., *Antarctica* 5 E1
Pense, *Canada* 101 C8
Penshurst, *Australia* 91 F3
Pentecoste, *Brazil* 122 B4
Penticton, *Canada* 100 D5
Pentland, *Australia* 90 C4
Pentland Firth, *U.K.* 14 C5
Pentland Hills, *U.K.* 14 F5
Penylan L., *Canada* 101 A7
Penza, *Russia* 41 E14
Penzance, *U.K.* 13 G2
Penzberg, *Germany* 19 H7
Penzhino, *Russia* 45 C17
Penzhinskaya Guba, *Russia* 45 C17
Penzlin, *Germany* 18 B9
Peoria, *Ariz., U.S.A.* 111 K7
Peoria, *Ill., U.S.A.* 108 E10
Pepingen, *Belgium* 17 G4
Pepinster, *Belgium* 17 G7
Pera Hd., *Australia* 90 A3
Perabumilih, *Indonesia* 56 E2
Perakhóra, *Greece* 39 L5
Perales de Alfambra, *Spain* 28 E3
Perales del Puerto, *Spain* 30 E4
Peralta, *Spain* 28 C3
Pérama, *Kérkira, Greece* 37 A3
Pérama, *Kríti, Greece* 37 D6
Percé, *Canada* 99 C7
Perche, *France* 24 D8
Perche, Collines du, *France* 24 D7
Percival Lakes, *Australia* 88 D4
Percy, *France* 24 D5
Percy Is., *Australia* 90 C5
Perdido →, *Argentina* 128 B3
Perdido, Mte., *Spain* 26 F4
Perdu, Mt. = Perdido, Mte., *Spain* 26 F4
Pereira, *Colombia* 120 C2
Pereira Barreto, *Brazil* 123 F1
Perekerten, *Australia* 91 E3
Perené →, *Peru* 124 C3
Perenjori, *Australia* 89 E2
Pereslavl-Zalesskiy, *Russia* 41 C11
Pereyaslav Khmelnitskiy, *Ukraine* 40 F7
Pérez, I., *Mexico* 115 C7
Pergamino, *Argentina* 126 C3
Pérgine Valsugano, *Italy* 33 B8
Pérgola, *Italy* 33 E9
Perham, *U.S.A.* 108 B7
Perhentian, Kepulauan, *Malaysia* 59 K4
Periam, *Romania* 38 C3
Péribonca →, *Canada* 99 C5
Péribonca, L., *Canada* 99 B5
Perico, *Argentina* 126 A2
Pericos, *Mexico* 114 B3
Périers, *France* 24 C5
Périgord, *France* 26 D4
Périgueux, *France* 26 C4
Perijá, Sierra de, *Colombia* 120 B3
Peristéra, *Greece* 39 K6
Peristerona →, *Cyprus* 37 D12
Perito Moreno, *Argentina* 128 C2
Peritoró, *Brazil* 122 B3
Perković, *Croatia* 33 E13
Perlas, Arch. de las, *Panama* 116 E4
Perlas, Punta de, *Nic.* 116 D3
Perleberg, *Germany* 18 B7
Perlevka, *Russia* 41 F11
Perm, *Russia* 44 D6
Pernambuco = Recife, *Brazil* 122 C5
Pernambuco □, *Brazil* 122 C4
Pernatty Lagoon, *Australia* 91 E2
Pernik, *Bulgaria* 38 G6
Peron, C., *Australia* 89 E1
Peron Is., *Australia* 88 B5
Peron Pen., *Australia* 89 E1
Péronne, *France* 25 C9
Péronnes, *Belgium* 17 H4
Perosa Argentina, *Italy* 32 D4
Perow, *Canada* 100 C3
Perpendicular Pt., *Australia* 91 E5
Perpignan, *France* 26 F6
Perris, *U.S.A.* 113 M9
Perros-Guirec, *France* 24 D3
Perry, *Fla., U.S.A.* 105 K4
Perry, *Ga., U.S.A.* 105 J4
Perry, *Iowa, U.S.A.* 108 E7
Perry, *Maine, U.S.A.* 105 C12
Perry, *Okla., U.S.A.* 109 G6
Perryton, *U.S.A.* 109 G4
Perryville, *U.S.A.* 109 G10
Perşembe, *Turkey* 67 C7
Perseverancia, *Bolivia* 125 C5
Persia = Iran ■, *Asia* 65 C7
Persian Gulf = Gulf, The, *Asia* 65 E6
Perstorp, *Sweden* 11 H7
Pertek, *Turkey* 67 D8
Perth, *Australia* 89 F2
Perth, *Canada* 98 D4
Perth, *U.K.* 14 E5
Perth Amboy, *U.S.A.* 107 F10
Pertuis, *France* 27 E9
Peru, *Ill., U.S.A.* 108 E10
Peru, *Ind., U.S.A.* 104 E2
Peru ■, *S. Amer.* 120 D2
Peru-Chile Trench, *Pac. Oc.* 93 K20
Perúgia, *Italy* 33 E9
Perušić, *Croatia* 33 D12
Péruwelz, *Belgium* 17 G3
Pervomaysk, *Russia* 41 D13
Pervomaysk, *Ukraine* 42 B4
Pervouralsk, *Russia* 44 D6
Perwez, *Belgium* 17 G5
Pes, Pta. del, *Spain* 36 C7
Pésaro, *Italy* 33 E9
Pescara, *Italy* 33 F11
Pescara →, *Italy* 33 F11
Peschanokopskoye, *Russia* 43 C9
Péscia, *Italy* 32 E7
Pescina, *Italy* 33 G10
Peseux, *Switz.* 22 C3
Peshawar, *Pakistan* 62 B4
Peshtigo, *U.S.A.* 104 C2
Peski, *Russia* 41 F13
Peskovka, *Russia* 41 B18
Pêso da Régua, *Portugal* 30 D3
Pesqueira, *Brazil* 122 C4
Pessac, *France* 26 D3
Pessoux, *Belgium* 17 H6
Pestovo, *Russia* 40 B9
Pestravka, *Russia* 41 E16
Petah Tiqwa, *Israel* 69 C3
Petaling Jaya, *Malaysia* 59 L3
Petaloudhes, *Greece* 37 C10
Petaluma, *U.S.A.* 112 G4
Petange, *Lux.* 17 J7
Petatlán, *Mexico* 114 D4
Petauke, *Zambia* 83 E3
Petawawa, *Canada* 98 C4
Petegem, *Belgium* 17 G3
Petén Itzá, L., *Guatemala* 116 C2
Peter I.s Øy, *Antarctica* 5 C16

Plattsburg

Peter Pond L., *Canada* 101 B7
Peterbell, *Canada* 98 C3
Peterborough, *Australia* 91 E2
Peterborough, *Canada* 106 B6
Peterborough, *U.K.* 13 E7
Peterborough, *U.S.A.* 107 D13
Peterhead, *U.K.* 14 D7
Petermann Bjerg, *Greenland* 94 B17
Peter's Mine, *Guyana* 121 B6
Petersburg, *Alaska, U.S.A.* 100 B2
Petersburg, *Ind., U.S.A.* 104 F2
Petersburg, *Va., U.S.A.* 104 G7
Petersburg, *W. Va., U.S.A.* 104 F6
Petford, *Australia* 90 B3
Petília Policastro, *Italy* 35 C9
Petit Bois I., *U.S.A.* 105 K1
Petit-Cap, *Canada* 99 C7
Petit Goâve, *Haiti* 117 C5
Petit Lac Manicouagan, *Canada* 99 B6
Petit Saint Bernard, Col du, *Italy* 32 C3
Petitcodiac, *Canada* 99 C6
Petite Baleine →, *Canada* 98 A4
Petite Saguenay, *Canada* 99 C5
Petitsikapau, L., *Canada* 99 B6
Petlad, *India* 62 H5
Peto, *Mexico* 115 C7
Petone, *N.Z.* 87 J5
Petoskey, *U.S.A.* 104 C3
Petra, *Jordan* 69 E4
Petra, *Spain* 36 B10
Petra, Ostrova, *Russia* 4 B13
Petra Velikogo, Zaliv, *Russia* 48 C5
Petralia, *Italy* 35 E7
Petrel, *Spain* 29 G4
Petreto-Bicchisano, *France* 27 G12
Petrich, *Bulgaria* 39 H6
Petrijanec, *Croatia* 33 B13
Petrikov, *Belorussia* 40 E6
Petrinja, *Croatia* 33 C13
Petrograd = Sankt-Peterburg, *Russia* 40 B7
Petrolândia, *Brazil* 122 C4
Petrolia, *Canada* 98 D3
Petrolina, *Brazil* 122 C3
Petropavlovsk, *Kazakhstan* 44 D7
Petropavlovsk-Kamchatskiy, *Russia* 45 D16
Petropavlovskiy = Akhtubinsk, *Russia* 43 B12
Petrópolis, *Brazil* 123 F3
Petroşeni, *Romania* 38 D6
Petrova Gora, *Croatia* 33 C12
Petrovac, *Montenegro, Yug.* 21 N8
Petrovsk, *Russia* 41 E14
Petrovsk-Zabaykalskiy, *Russia* 45 D11
Petrovskoye = Svetlograd, *Russia* 43 D10
Petrozavodsk, *Russia* 44 C4
Petrus Steyn, *S. Africa* 85 D4
Petrusburg, *S. Africa* 84 D4
Petukhovka, *Belorussia* 40 E7
Peumo, *Chile* 126 C1
Peureulak, *Indonesia* 56 D1
Pevek, *Russia* 45 C18
Peveragno, *Italy* 32 D4
Peyrehorade, *France* 26 E2
Peyruis, *France* 27 D9
Pézenas, *France* 26 E7
Pfaffenhofen, *Germany* 19 G7
Pfäffikon, *Switz.* 23 B7
Pfarrkirchen, *Germany* 19 G8
Pfeffenhausen, *Germany* 19 G7
Pforzheim, *Germany* 19 G4
Pfullendorf, *Germany* 19 H5
Pfungstadt, *Germany* 19 F4
Phagwara, *India* 60 D6
Phaistós, *Greece* 37 D6
Phala, *Botswana* 84 C4
Phalera = Phulera, *India* 62 F6
Phalodi, *India* 62 F5
Phalsbourg, *France* 25 D14
Phan, *Thailand* 58 C2
Phan Rang, *Vietnam* 59 G7
Phan Ri = Hoa Da, *Vietnam* 59 G7
Phan Thiet, *Vietnam* 59 G7
Phanat Nikhom, *Thailand* 58 F3
Phangan, Ko, *Thailand* 59 H3
Phangnga, *Thailand* 59 H2
Phanh Bho Ho Chi Minh, *Vietnam* 59 G6
Phanom Sarakham, *Thailand* 58 F3
Pharenda, *India* 63 F10
Phatthalung, *Thailand* 59 J3
Phayao, *Thailand* 58 C2
Phelps, *N.Y., U.S.A.* 106 D7
Phelps, *Wis., U.S.A.* 108 B10
Phelps L., *Canada* 101 B8
Phenix City, *U.S.A.* 105 J3
Phet Buri, *Thailand* 58 F2
Phetchabun, *Thailand* 58 D3
Phetchabun, Thiu Khao, *Thailand* 58 E3
Phetchaburi = Phet Buri, *Thailand* 58 F2
Phi Phi, Ko, *Thailand* 59 J2
Phiafay, *Laos* 58 E6
Phibun Mangsahan, *Thailand* 58 E5
Phichai, *Thailand* 58 D3
Phichit, *Thailand* 58 D3
Philadelphia, *Miss., U.S.A.* 109 J10
Philadelphia, *N.Y., U.S.A.* 107 B9
Philadelphia, *Pa., U.S.A.* 107 F9
Philip, *U.S.A.* 108 C4
Philippeville, *Belgium* 17 H5
Philippi L., *Australia* 90 C2
Philippines ■, *Asia* 55 F5
Philippolis, *S. Africa* 84 E4
Philippopolis = Plovdiv, *Bulgaria* 38 G7
Philipsburg, *Mont., U.S.A.* 110 C7
Philipsburg, *Pa., U.S.A.* 106 F6
Philipstown, *S. Africa* 84 E3
Phillip I., *Australia* 91 F4
Phillips, *Tex., U.S.A.* 109 H4
Phillips, *Wis., U.S.A.* 108 C9
Phillipsburg, *Kans., U.S.A.* 108 F5
Phillipsburg, *Pa., U.S.A.* 107 F9
Phillott, *Australia* 91 D4
Philmont, *U.S.A.* 107 D11
Philomath, *U.S.A.* 110 D2
Phimai, *Thailand* 58 E4
Phitsanulok, *Thailand* 58 D3
Phnom Dangrek, *Thailand* 58 E5
Phnom Penh, *Cambodia* 59 G5
Phoenix, *Ariz., U.S.A.* 111 K7
Phoenix, *N.Y., U.S.A.* 107 C8
Phoenix Is., *Kiribati* 92 H10
Phoenixville, *U.S.A.* 107 F9
Phon, *Thailand* 58 E4
Phon Tiou, *Laos* 58 D5
Phong →, *Thailand* 58 D4
Phong Saly, *Laos* 58 B4
Phong Tho, *Vietnam* 58 A4
Phonhong, *Laos* 58 C4
Phonum, *Thailand* 59 H2
Phosphate Hill, *Australia* 90 C2
Photharam, *Thailand* 58 F2
Phra Chedi Sam Ong, *Thailand* 58 E2
Phra Nakhon Si Ayutthaya, *Thailand* 58 E3
Phra Thong, Ko, *Thailand* 59 H2
Phrae, *Thailand* 58 C3
Phrom Phiram, *Thailand* 58 D3
Phrygia, *Turkey* 66 D3
Phu Dien, *Vietnam* 58 C5
Phu Loi, *Laos* 58 B4
Phu Ly, *Vietnam* 58 B5
Phu Tho, *Vietnam* 58 B5
Phuc Yen, *Vietnam* 58 B5
Phuket, *Thailand* 59 J2
Phuket, Ko, *Thailand* 59 J2
Phulera, *India* 62 F6
Phumiphon, Khuan, *Thailand* 58 D2
Phun Phin, *Thailand* 59 H2
Piacá, *Brazil* 122 C2
Piacenza, *Italy* 32 C6
Piaçubaçu, *Brazil* 122 D4
Piádena, *Italy* 32 C7
Pialba, *Australia* 91 D5
Pian Cr. →, *Australia* 91 E4
Piana, *France* 27 F12
Pianella, *Italy* 33 F11
Pianoro, *Italy* 33 D8
Pianosa, *Puglia, Italy* 33 F12
Pianosa, *Toscana, Italy* 32 F7
Piapot, *Canada* 101 D7
Piare →, *Italy* 33 C9
Pias, *Portugal* 31 G3
Piaseczno, *Poland* 20 C11
Piatã, *Brazil* 123 D3
Piatra, *Romania* 38 F8
Piatra Neamţ, *Romania* 38 C9
Piauí □, *Brazil* 122 C3
Piaui →, *Brazil* 122 C3
Piave →, *Italy* 33 C9
Piazza Ármerina, *Italy* 35 E7
Pibor →, *Sudan* 77 F3
Pibor Post, *Sudan* 77 F3
Pica, *Chile* 124 E4
Picardie, *France* 25 C9
Picardie, Plaine de, *France* 25 C9
Picardy = Picardie, *France* 25 C9
Picayune, *U.S.A.* 109 K10
Picerno, *Italy* 35 B8
Pichilemu, *Chile* 126 C1
Pichincha, □, *Ecuador* 120 D2
Pickerel L., *Canada* 98 C1
Pickle Lake, *Canada* 98 B1
Pico Truncado, *Argentina* 128 C3
Picos, *Brazil* 122 C3
Picos Ancares, Sierra de, *Spain* 30 C4
Picota, *Peru* 124 B2
Picquigny, *France* 25 C9
Picton, *Australia* 91 E5
Picton, *Canada* 98 D4
Picton, *N.Z.* 87 J5
Picton, I., *Chile* 128 E3
Pictou, *Canada* 99 C7
Picture Butte, *Canada* 100 D6
Picuí, *Brazil* 122 C4
Picún Leufú, *Argentina* 128 A3
Pidurutalagala, *Sri Lanka* 60 R12
Piedecuesta, *Colombia* 120 B3
Piedicavallo, *Italy* 32 C4
Piedmont = Piemonte □, *Italy* 32 D4
Piedmont, *U.S.A.* 105 J3
Piedmont Plateau, *U.S.A.* 105 J5
Piedmonte d'Alife, *Italy* 35 A7
Piedra →, *Spain* 28 D3
Piedra del Anguila, *Argentina* 128 B2
Piedra Lais, *Venezuela* 120 C4
Piedrabuena, *Spain* 31 F6
Piedrahita, *Spain* 30 E5
Piedras, R. de las →, *Peru* 124 C4
Piedras Negras, *Mexico* 114 B4
Piemonte □, *Italy* 32 D4
Pierce, *U.S.A.* 110 C6
Piercefield, *U.S.A.* 107 B10
Pierre, *U.S.A.* 108 C4
Pierre Bénite, Barrage de la, *France* 27 C8
Pierre-de-Bresse, *France* 27 B9
Pierrefeu-du-Var, *France* 27 E10
Pierrefonds, *France* 25 C9
Pierrefontaine-les-Varans, *France* 25 E13
Pierrefort, *France* 26 D6
Pierrelatte, *France* 27 D8
Pieštany, *Czech.* 20 G7
Piesting →, *Austria* 21 G6
Piet Retief, *S. Africa* 85 D5
Pietarsaari = Jakobstad, *Finland* 8 E17
Pietermaritzburg, *S. Africa* 85 D5
Pietersburg, *S. Africa* 85 C4
Pietraperzia, *Italy* 35 E7
Pietrasanta, *Italy* 32 E7
Pietrosu, *Romania* 38 B8
Pietrosul, *Romania* 38 B7
Pieve di Cadore, *Italy* 33 B9
Pieve di Teco, *Italy* 32 D4
Pievepélago, *Italy* 32 D7
Pigádhia, *Greece* 39 P10
Pigeon, *U.S.A.* 104 D4
Piggott, *U.S.A.* 109 G9
Pigna, *Italy* 32 E4
Pigüe, *Argentina* 126 D3
Pihani, *India* 63 F9
Pijnacker, *Neths.* 16 D4
Pikalevo, *Russia* 40 B9
Pikes Peak, *U.S.A.* 108 F2
Piketberg, *S. Africa* 84 E2
Pikeville, *U.S.A.* 104 G4
Pikou, *China* 51 E12
Pikwitonei, *Canada* 101 B9
Piła, *Poland* 20 B6
Pila, *Spain* 29 G3
Pilani, *India* 62 E6
Pilar, *Brazil* 122 C4
Pilar, *Paraguay* 126 B4
Pilas Group, *Phil.* 57 C6
Pilaya →, *Bolivia* 125 E5
Pilcomayo →, *Paraguay* 126 B4
Pilibhit, *India* 63 E8
Pilica →, *Poland* 20 D11
Pilkhawa, *India* 62 E7
Pillaro, *Ecuador* 120 D2
Pílos, *Greece* 39 N4
Pilot Mound, *Canada* 101 D9
Pilot Point, *U.S.A.* 109 J6
Pilot Rock, *U.S.A.* 110 D4
Pilsen = Plzeň, *Czech.* 20 F3
Pilštanj, *Slovenia* 33 B12
Pima, *U.S.A.* 111 K9
Pimba, *Australia* 91 E2
Pimenta Bueno, *Brazil* 125 C5
Pimentel, *Peru* 124 B2
Pina, *Spain* 28 D4
Pinamalayan, *Phil.* 55 E4
Pinang, *Malaysia* 59 K3
Pinar, C. del, *Spain* 36 B10
Pinar del Río, *Cuba* 116 B3
Pinarbaşi, *Turkey* 66 D7
Pinchang, *China* 52 B6
Pincher Creek, *Canada* 100 D6
Pinchi L., *Canada* 100 C4
Pinckneyville, *U.S.A.* 108 F10
Pîncota, *Romania* 38 C4
Pind Dadan Khan, *Pakistan* 62 C5
Pindar, *Australia* 89 E2
Pindaré →, *Brazil* 122 B3
Pindaré Mirim, *Brazil* 122 B2
Pindi Gheb, *Pakistan* 62 C5
Pindiga, *Nigeria* 79 D7
Pindobal, *Brazil* 122 B2
Pindos Óros, *Greece* 39 K4
Pindus Mts. = Pindos Óros, *Greece* 39 K4
Pine, *U.S.A.* 111 J8
Pine →, *Canada* 101 B7
Pine, C., *Canada* 99 C9
Pine Bluff, *U.S.A.* 109 H8
Pine City, *U.S.A.* 108 C8
Pine Falls, *Canada* 101 C9
Pine Flat Res., *U.S.A.* 112 J7
Pine Pass, *Canada* 100 B4
Pine Point, *Canada* 100 A6
Pine Ridge, *U.S.A.* 108 D3
Pine River, *Canada* 101 C8
Pine River, *U.S.A.* 108 B7
Pine Valley, *U.S.A.* 113 N10
Pinecrest, *U.S.A.* 112 G6
Pinedale, *U.S.A.* 112 J7
Pinega →, *Russia* 44 C5
Pinehill, *Australia* 90 C4
Pinerolo, *Italy* 32 D4
Pineto, *Italy* 33 F11
Pinetop, *U.S.A.* 111 J9
Pinetown, *S. Africa* 85 D5
Pinetree, *U.S.A.* 110 E11
Pineville, *Ky., U.S.A.* 105 G4
Pineville, *La., U.S.A.* 109 K8
Piney, *France* 25 D11
Ping →, *Thailand* 58 E3
Pingaring, *Australia* 89 F2
Pingba, *China* 52 D6
Pingchuan, *China* 52 D3
Pingding, *China* 50 F7
Pingdingshan, *China* 50 H7
Pingdong, *Taiwan* 53 F13
Pingdu, *China* 51 F10
Pingelly, *Australia* 89 F2
Pingguo, *China* 52 F6
Pinghe, *China* 53 E11
Pinghu, *China* 53 B13
Pingjiang, *China* 53 C9
Pingle, *China* 53 E8
Pingli, *China* 52 A7
Pingliang, *China* 50 G4
Pinglu, *China* 50 E7
Pingluo, *China* 50 E4
Pingnan, *Fujian, China* 53 D12
Pingnan, *Guangxi Zhuangzu, China* 53 F8
Pingquan, *China* 51 D10
Pingrup, *Australia* 89 F2
Pingtan, *China* 53 E12
Pingtang, *China* 52 E6
Pingwu, *China* 50 H3
Pingxiang, *Guangxi Zhuangzu, China* 52 F6
Pingxiang, *Jiangxi, China* 53 D9
Pingyao, *China* 50 F7
Pingyi, *China* 51 G9
Pingyin, *China* 50 F9
Pingyuan, *Guangdong, China* 53 E10
Pingyuan, *Shandong, China* 50 F9
Pingyuanjie, *China* 52 F4
Pinhal, *Brazil* 127 A6
Pinheiro, *Brazil* 122 B2
Pinhel, *Portugal* 30 E3
Pinhuá →, *Brazil* 125 B4
Pini, *Indonesia* 56 D1
Piniós →, *Ilía, Greece* 39 M4
Piniós →, *Trikkala, Greece* 39 K5
Pinjarra, *Australia* 89 F2
Pink →, *Canada* 101 B8
Pinnacles, *Australia* 89 E3
Pinnacles, *U.S.A.* 112 J5
Pinnaroo, *Australia* 91 F3
Pinneberg, *Germany* 18 B5
Pino Hachado, Paso, *S. Amer.* 128 A2
Pinon Hills, *U.S.A.* 113 L9
Pinos, *Mexico* 114 C4
Pinos, Mt., *U.S.A.* 113 L7
Pinos Pt., *U.S.A.* 111 H3
Pinos Puente, *Spain* 31 H7
Pinotepa Nacional, *Mexico* 115 D5
Pinrang, *Indonesia* 57 E5
Pinsk, *Belorussia* 40 E5
Pintados, *Chile* 124 E4
Pintumba, *Australia* 89 F5
Pinyang, *China* 53 D13
Pinyug, *Russia* 44 C5
Pinzolo, *Italy* 32 B7
Pio XII, *Brazil* 122 B2
Pioche, *U.S.A.* 111 H6
Piombino, *Italy* 32 F7
Piombino, Canale di, *Italy* 32 F7
Pioner, Os., *Russia* 45 B10
Pionki, *Poland* 20 D11
Piorini →, *Brazil* 121 D5
Piorini, L., *Brazil* 121 D5
Piotrków Trybunalski, *Poland* 20 D9
Piove di Sacco, *Italy* 33 C9
Pīp, *Iran* 65 E9
Pipar, *India* 62 F5
Piparia, *India* 62 H8
Pipestone, *U.S.A.* 108 D6
Pipestone →, *Canada* 98 B2
Pipestone Cr. →, *Canada* 101 D8
Pipmuacan, Rés., *Canada* 99 C5
Pippingarra, *Australia* 88 D2
Pipriac, *France* 24 E5
Piqua, *U.S.A.* 104 E3
Piquet Carneiro, *Brazil* 122 C4
Piquiri →, *Brazil* 127 A5
Pīr Sohrāb, *Iran* 65 E9
Piracanjuba, *Brazil* 123 E2
Piracicaba, *Brazil* 127 A6
Piracuruca, *Brazil* 122 B3
Piræus = Piraiévs, *Greece* 39 M6
Piraiévs, *Greece* 39 M6
Piráino, *Italy* 35 D7
Pirajuí, *Brazil* 127 A6
Piran, *Slovenia* 33 C10
Pirané, *Argentina* 126 B4
Piranhas, *Brazil* 122 C4
Pirano = Piran, *Slovenia* 33 C10
Pirapemas, *Brazil* 122 B3
Pirapora, *Brazil* 123 E3
Piray →, *Bolivia* 125 D5
Pires do Rio, *Brazil* 123 E2
Pírgos, *Ilía, Greece* 39 M4
Pírgos, *Messinia, Greece* 39 N5
Pirgovo, *Bulgaria* 38 F8
Piriac-sur-Mer, *France* 24 E4
Piribebuy, *Paraguay* 126 B4
Pirin Planina, *Bulgaria* 39 H6
Pirineos, *Spain* 28 C6
Piripiri, *Brazil* 122 B3
Piritu, *Venezuela* 120 B4
Pirmasens, *Germany* 19 F3
Pirna, *Germany* 18 E9
Pirot, *Serbia, Yug.* 21 M12
Piru, *Indonesia* 57 E7
Piru, *U.S.A.* 113 L8
Piryatin, *Ukraine* 40 F8
Pisa, *Italy* 32 E7
Pisac, *Peru* 124 C3
Pisagua, *Chile* 124 D3
Pisarovina, *Croatia* 33 C12
Pisciotta, *Italy* 35 B8
Pisco, *Peru* 124 C2
Písek, *Czech.* 20 F4
Pishan, *China* 54 C2
Pishin Lora →, *Pakistan* 62 E1
Pisidia, *Turkey* 66 E4
Pising, *Indonesia* 57 F6
Pismo Beach, *U.S.A.* 113 K6
Pissos, *France* 26 D3
Pissouri, *Cyprus* 37 E11
Pisticci, *Italy* 35 B9
Pistóia, *Italy* 32 E7
Pistol B., *Canada* 101 A10
Pisuerga →, *Spain* 30 D6
Pisz, *Poland* 20 B11
Pitalito, *Colombia* 120 C2
Pitanga, *Brazil* 123 F1
Pitangui, *Brazil* 123 E3
Pitarpunga, L., *Australia* 91 E3
Pitcairn I., *Pac. Oc.* 93 K14
Pite älv →, *Sweden* 8 D16
Piteå, *Sweden* 8 D16
Piterka, *Russia* 41 F15
Piteşti, *Romania* 38 E7
Pithapuram, *India* 61 L13
Pithara, *Australia* 89 F2
Píthion, *Greece* 39 H9
Pithiviers, *France* 25 D9
Pitigliano, *Italy* 33 F8
Pitlochry, *U.K.* 14 E5
Pitrufquén, *Chile* 128 A2
Pitsilia □, *Cyprus* 37 E12
Pitt I., *Canada* 100 C3
Pittem, *Belgium* 17 F2
Pittsburg, *Kans., U.S.A.* 109 G7
Pittsburg, *Tex., U.S.A.* 109 J7
Pittsburgh, *U.S.A.* 106 F5
Pittsfield, *Ill., U.S.A.* 108 F9
Pittsfield, *Mass., U.S.A.* 107 D11
Pittsfield, *N.H., U.S.A.* 107 C13
Pittston, *U.S.A.* 107 E9
Pittsworth, *Australia* 91 D5
Pituri →, *Australia* 90 C2
Piuí, *Brazil* 123 F2
Pium, *Brazil* 122 D2
Piura, *Peru* 124 B1
Piura □, *Peru* 124 A2
Pivijay, *Colombia* 120 A3
Pixley, *U.S.A.* 112 K7
Piyai, *Greece* 39 K4
Pizarro, *Colombia* 120 C2
Pizol, *Switz.* 23 C8
Pizzo, *Italy* 35 D9
Placentia, *Canada* 99 C9
Placentia B., *Canada* 99 C9
Placer, *Phil.* 55 F5
Placerville, *U.S.A.* 112 G6
Placetas, *Cuba* 116 B4
Plaffeien, *Switz.* 22 C4
Plain Dealing, *U.S.A.* 109 J8
Plainfield, *U.S.A.* 107 F10
Plains, *Kans., U.S.A.* 109 G4
Plains, *Mont., U.S.A.* 110 C6
Plains, *Tex., U.S.A.* 109 J3
Plainview, *Nebr., U.S.A.* 108 D6
Plainview, *Tex., U.S.A.* 109 H4
Plainville, *U.S.A.* 108 F5
Plainwell, *U.S.A.* 104 D3
Plaisance, *France* 26 E4
Pláka, *Greece* 39 J8
Pláka, Ákra, *Greece* 37 D8
Plakhino, *Russia* 44 C9
Plana Cays, *Bahamas* 117 B5
Planada, *U.S.A.* 112 H6
Plancoët, *France* 24 D4
Plandište, *Serbia, Yug.* 21 K11
Planeta Rica, *Colombia* 120 B2
Planina, *Slovenia* 33 B12
Planina, *Slovenia* 33 C11
Plankinton, *U.S.A.* 108 D5
Plano, *U.S.A.* 109 J6
Plant City, *U.S.A.* 105 L4
Plaquemine, *U.S.A.* 109 K9
Plasencia, *Spain* 30 E4
Plaški, *Croatia* 33 C12
Plaster City, *U.S.A.* 113 N11
Plaster Rock, *Canada* 99 C6
Plastun, *Russia* 48 B8
Plata, Río de la, *S. Amer.* 126 C4
Platani →, *Italy* 34 E6
Plátanos, *Greece* 37 D5
Plateau □, *Nigeria* 79 D6
Plateau du Coteau du Missouri, *U.S.A.* 108 B4
Plato, *Colombia* 120 B3
Platta, Piz, *Switz.* 23 D9
Platte, *U.S.A.* 108 D5
Platte →, *U.S.A.* 108 F7
Platteville, *U.S.A.* 108 E2
Plattling, *Germany* 19 G8
Plattsburg, *U.S.A.* 107 B11

Plattsmouth

Plattsmouth, *U.S.A.* 108 E7
Plau, *Germany* 18 B8
Plauen, *Germany* 18 E8
Plavinas, *Latvia* 40 C4
Plavnica, *Montenegro, Yug.* 21 N9
Plavsk, *Russia* 41 E10
Playa Blanca, *Canary Is.* 36 F6
Playa Blanca Sur, *Canary Is.* 36 F6
Playa de las Americas, *Canary Is.* 36 F3
Playa de Mogán, *Canary Is.* 36 G4
Playa del Inglés, *Canary Is.* 36 G4
Playa Esmerelda, *Canary Is.* 36 F5
Playgreen L., *Canada* 101 C9
Pleasant Bay, *Canada* 99 C7
Pleasant Hill, *Calif., U.S.A.* 112 H4
Pleasant Hill, *Mo., U.S.A.* 108 F7
Pleasanton, *U.S.A.* 109 L5
Pleasantville, *U.S.A.* 104 F8
Pléaux, *France* 26 C6
Pleiku, *Vietnam* 58 F7
Plélan-le-Grand, *France* 24 D4
Plémet-la-Pierre, *France* 24 D4
Pléneuf-Val-André, *France* 24 D4
Pleniţa, *Romania* 38 E6
Plenty →, *Australia* 90 C2
Plenty, B. of, *N.Z.* 87 G6
Plentywood, *U.S.A.* 108 A2
Plessisville, *Canada* 99 C5
Plestin-les-Grèves, *France* 24 D3
Pleszew, *Poland* 20 D7
Pleternica, *Croatia* 21 K7
Pletipi L., *Canada* 99 B5
Pleven, *Bulgaria* 38 F7
Plevlja, *Montenegro, Yug.* 21 M9
Płock, *Poland* 20 C9
Plöcken Passo, *Italy* 33 B9
Ploegsteert, *Belgium* 17 G1
Ploemeur, *France* 24 E3
Ploërmel, *France* 24 E4
Ploieşti, *Romania* 38 E9
Plombières-les-Bains, *France* 25 E13
Plomin, *Croatia* 33 C11
Plön, *Germany* 18 A6
Plöner See, *Germany* 18 A6
Plonge, Lac la, *Canada* 101 B7
Płońsk, *Poland* 20 C10
Płoty, *Poland* 20 B5
Plouaret, *France* 24 D3
Plouay, *France* 24 E3
Ploudalmézeau, *France* 24 D2
Plougasnou, *France* 24 D3
Plouha, *France* 24 D4
Plouhinec, *France* 24 E2
Plovdiv, *Bulgaria* 38 G7
Plum, *U.S.A.* 106 F5
Plum I., *U.S.A.* 107 E12
Plumas, *U.S.A.* 112 F7
Plummer, *U.S.A.* 110 C5
Plumtree, *Zimbabwe* 83 G2
Plunge, *Lithuania* 40 D2
Pluvigner, *France* 24 E3
Plymouth, *U.K.* 13 G3
Plymouth, *Calif., U.S.A.* 112 G6
Plymouth, *Ind., U.S.A.* 104 E2
Plymouth, *Mass., U.S.A.* 107 E14
Plymouth, *N.C., U.S.A.* 105 H7
Plymouth, *N.H., U.S.A.* 107 C13
Plymouth, *Pa., U.S.A.* 107 E9
Plymouth, *Wis., U.S.A.* 104 D2
Plynlimon = Pumlumon Fawr, *U.K.* 13 E4
Plyussa, *Russia* 40 B6
Plyussa →, *Russia* 40 B6
Plzeň, *Czech.* 20 F3
Pniewy, *Poland* 20 C6
Pô, *Burkina Faso* 79 C4
Po →, *Italy* 33 D9
Po, Foci del, *Italy* 33 D9
Po Hai = Bo Hai, *China* 51 E10
Pobé, *Benin* 79 D5
Pobeda, *Russia* 45 C15
Pobedino, *Russia* 45 E15
Pobedy Pik, *Kirghizia* 44 E8
Pobiedziska, *Poland* 20 C7
Pobla de Segur, *Spain* 28 C5
Pobladura de Valle, *Spain* 30 C5
Pocahontas, *Ark., U.S.A.* 109 G9
Pocahontas, *Iowa, U.S.A.* 108 D7
Pocatello, *U.S.A.* 110 E7
Pochep, *Russia* 40 E8
Pochinki, *Russia* 41 D14
Pochinok, *Russia* 40 D8
Pochutla, *Mexico* 115 D5
Poci, *Venezuela* 121 B5
Pocinhos, *Brazil* 122 C4
Pocito Casas, *Mexico* 114 B2
Poções, *Brazil* 123 D3
Pocomoke City, *U.S.A.* 104 F8
Poconé, *Brazil* 125 D6
Poços de Caldas, *Brazil* 127 A6
Poddebice, *Poland* 20 D8
Poděbrady, *Czech.* 20 E5
Podensac, *France* 26 D3
Podgorica = Titograd, *Montenegro, Yug.* 21 N9
Podkamennaya Tunguska →, *Russia* 45 C10
Podlapac, *Croatia* 33 D12
Podolsk, *Russia* 41 D10
Podor, *Senegal* 78 B1
Podravska Slatina, *Croatia* 21 K7
Podujevo, *Serbia, Yug.* 21 N11
Poel, *Germany* 18 B7
Pofadder, *S. Africa* 84 D2
Pogamasing, *Canada* 98 C3
Poggiardo, *Italy* 35 B11
Poggibonsi, *Italy* 33 E8
Pogoanele, *Romania* 38 E9
Pogradeci, *Albania* 39 J3
Pogranitšnyi, *Russia* 48 B5
Poh, *Indonesia* 57 E6
Pohang, *S. Korea* 51 F15
Pohnpei, *Pac. Oc.* 92 G7
Pohorelá, *Czech.* 20 G10
Pohorje, *Slovenia* 33 B12
Poiana Mare, *Romania* 38 F6
Poinsett, C., *Antarctica* 5 C8
Point Edward, *Canada* 98 D3
Point Pedro, *Sri Lanka* 60 Q12
Point Pleasant, *N.J., U.S.A.* 107 F10
Point Pleasant, *W. Va., U.S.A.* 104 F4
Pointe-à-la Hache, *U.S.A.* 109 L10
Pointe-à-Pitre, *Guadeloupe* 117 C7
Pointe Noire, *Congo* 80 E2
Poirino, *Italy* 32 D4
Poisonbush Ra., *Australia* 88 D3
Poissy, *France* 25 D9
Poitiers, *France* 24 F7
Poitou, *France* 26 B3
Poitou, Seuil du, *France* 26 B4
Poix de Picardie, *France* 25 C8
Poix-Terron, *France* 25 C11
Pojoaque Valley, *U.S.A.* 111 J11
Pokaran, *India* 60 F7
Pokataroo, *Australia* 91 D4
Poko, *Sudan* 77 F3
Poko, *Zaïre* 82 B2
Pokrov, *Russia* 41 D11
Pokrovsk, *Russia* 41 F15
Pokrovsk, *Russia* 45 C13
Pol, *Spain* 30 B3
Pola = Pula, *Croatia* 33 D10
Pola de Allande, *Spain* 30 B4
Pola de Lena, *Spain* 30 B5
Pola de Siero, *Spain* 30 B5
Pola de Somiedo, *Spain* 30 B4
Polacca, *U.S.A.* 111 J8
Polan, *Iran* 65 E9
Poland ■, *Europe* 20 C9
Polanów, *Poland* 20 A6
Polcura, *Chile* 126 D1
Polden Hills, *U.K.* 13 F5
Polessk, *Russia* 40 D2
Polesye, *Belorussia* 40 E6
Polewali, *Indonesia* 57 E5
Polgar, *Hungary* 21 H11
Pŏlgyo-ri, *S. Korea* 51 G14
Poli, *Cameroon* 80 C2
Políaigos, *Greece* 39 N7
Policastro, G. di, *Italy* 35 C8
Police, *Poland* 20 B4
Polignano a Mare, *Italy* 35 B10
Poligny, *France* 25 F12
Políkhnitas, *Greece* 39 K9
Polillo Is., *Phil.* 55 D4
Polillo Strait, *Phil.* 55 D4
Polis, *Cyprus* 37 D11
Polístena, *Italy* 35 D9
Políyiros, *Greece* 39 J6
Polk, *U.S.A.* 106 E5
Polla, *Italy* 35 B8
Pollachi, *India* 60 P10
Pollensa, *Spain* 36 B10
Pollensa, B. de, *Spain* 36 B10
Póllica, *Italy* 35 B8
Pollino, Mte., *Italy* 35 C9
Pollock, *U.S.A.* 108 C4
Polna, *Russia* 40 B6
Polnovat, *Russia* 44 C7
Polo, *U.S.A.* 108 E10
Pologi, *Ukraine* 42 C7
Polonnoye, *Ukraine* 40 F5
Polotsk, *Belorussia* 40 D6
Polson, *U.S.A.* 110 C6
Poltava, *Ukraine* 42 B6
Polunochnoye, *Russia* 44 C7
Polynesia, *Pac. Oc.* 93 H11
Pomarance, *Italy* 32 E7
Pomarico, *Italy* 35 B9
Pomaro, *Mexico* 114 D4
Pombal, *Brazil* 122 C4
Pombal, *Portugal* 30 F2
Pómbia, *Greece* 37 D6
Pomeroy, *Ohio, U.S.A.* 104 F4
Pomeroy, *Wash., U.S.A.* 110 C5
Pomona, *U.S.A.* 113 L9
Pomorie, *Bulgaria* 38 G10
Pomos, *Cyprus* 37 D11
Pomos, C., *Cyprus* 37 D11
Pomoshnaya, *Ukraine* 42 B4
Pompano Beach, *U.S.A.* 105 M5
Pompei, *Italy* 35 B7
Pompey, *France* 25 D13
Pompeys Pillar, *U.S.A.* 110 D10
Ponape = Pohnpei, *Pac. Oc.* 92 G7
Ponask, L., *Canada* 98 B1
Ponass L., *Canada* 101 C8
Ponca, *U.S.A.* 108 D6
Ponca City, *U.S.A.* 109 G6
Ponce, *Puerto Rico* 117 C6
Ponchatoula, *U.S.A.* 109 K9
Poncheville, L., *Canada* 98 B4
Poncin, *France* 27 B9
Pond, *U.S.A.* 113 K7
Pond Inlet, *Canada* 97 A12
Pondicherry, *India* 60 P11
Pondrôme, *Belgium* 17 H6
Ponds, I. of, *Canada* 99 B8
Ponferrada, *Spain* 30 C4
Pongo, Wadi →, *Sudan* 77 F2
Poniatowa, *Poland* 20 D12
Ponikva, *Slovenia* 33 B12
Ponnani, *India* 60 P9
Ponnyadaung, *Burma* 61 J19
Ponoi →, *Russia* 44 C5
Ponoka, *Canada* 100 C6
Ponorogo, *Indonesia* 57 G14
Pons, *France* 26 C3
Pons, *Spain* 28 D6
Ponsul →, *Portugal* 31 F3
Pont-à-Celles, *Belgium* 17 G4
Pont-à-Mousson, *France* 25 D13
Pont-Audemer, *France* 24 C7
Pont-Aven, *France* 24 E3
Pont Canavese, *Italy* 32 C4
Pont-de-Roide, *France* 25 E13
Pont-de-Salars, *France* 26 D6
Pont-de-Vaux, *France* 25 F11
Pont-de-Veyle, *France* 27 B8
Pont-l'Abbé, *France* 24 E2
Pont-l'Évêque, *France* 24 C7
Pont-St.-Esprit, *France* 27 D8
Pont-sur-Yonne, *France* 25 D10
Ponta de Pedras, *Brazil* 122 B2
Ponta do Sol, *Madeira* 36 D2
Ponta Grossa, *Brazil* 127 B5
Ponta Pora, *Brazil* 127 A4
Pontacq, *France* 26 E3
Pontailler-sur-Saône, *France* 25 E12
Pontal →, *Brazil* 122 C3
Pontalina, *Brazil* 123 E2
Pontarlier, *France* 25 F13
Pontassieve, *Italy* 33 E8
Pontaubault, *France* 24 D5
Pontaumur, *France* 26 C6
Pontcharra, *France* 27 C10
Pontchartrain, L., *U.S.A.* 109 K9
Pontchâteau, *France* 24 E4
Ponte Alta, Serra do, *Brazil* 123 E2
Ponte Alta do Norte, *Brazil* 122 D2
Ponte Branca, *Brazil* 125 D7
Ponte da Barca, *Portugal* 30 D2
Ponte de Sor, *Portugal* 31 F3
Ponte dell 'Olio, *Italy* 32 D6
Ponte di Legno, *Italy* 32 B7
Ponte do Lima, *Portugal* 30 D2
Ponte do Pungué, *Mozam.* 83 F3
Ponte-Leccia, *France* 27 F13
Ponte Macassar, *Indonesia* 57 F6
Ponte nell' Alpi, *Italy* 33 B9
Ponte Nova, *Brazil* 123 F3
Ponte San Martino, *Italy* 32 C4
Ponte San Pietro, *Italy* 32 C6
Pontebba, *Italy* 33 B10
Pontecorvo, *Italy* 34 A6
Pontedera, *Italy* 32 E7
Pontefract, *U.K.* 12 D6
Ponteix, *Canada* 101 D7
Pontelandolfo, *Italy* 35 A7
Pontevedra, *Spain* 30 C2
Pontevedra □, *Spain* 30 C2
Pontevedra, R. de →, *Spain* 30 C2
Pontevico, *Italy* 32 C7
Pontiac, *Ill., U.S.A.* 108 E10
Pontiac, *Mich., U.S.A.* 104 D4
Pontian Kecil, *Malaysia* 59 M4
Pontianak, *Indonesia* 56 E3
Pontic Mts. = Kuzey Anadolu Dağları, *Turkey* 66 C6
Pontine Is. = Ponziane, Isole, *Italy* 34 B5
Pontine Mts. = Kuzey Anadolu Dağları, *Turkey* 66 C6
Pontínia, *Italy* 34 A6
Pontivy, *France* 24 D4
Pontoise, *France* 25 C9
Ponton →, *Canada* 100 B5
Pontorson, *France* 24 D5
Pontrémoli, *Italy* 32 D6
Pontresina, *Switz.* 23 D9
Pontrieux, *France* 24 D3
Pontypool, *Canada* 106 B6
Pontypool, *U.K.* 13 F4
Pontypridd, *U.K.* 13 F4
Ponza, *Italy* 34 B5
Ponziane, Isole, *Italy* 34 B5
Poochera, *Australia* 91 E1
Poole, *U.K.* 13 G6
Pooley I., *Canada* 100 C3
Poona = Pune, *India* 60 K8
Pooncarie, *Australia* 91 E3
Poopelloe L., *Australia* 91 E3
Poopó, *Bolivia* 124 D4
Poopó, L. de, *Bolivia* 124 D4
Popanyinning, *Australia* 89 F2
Popayán, *Colombia* 120 C2
Poperinge, *Belgium* 17 G1
Popigay, *Russia* 45 B12
Popilta, L., *Australia* 91 E3
Popio L., *Australia* 91 E3
Poplar, *U.S.A.* 108 A2
Poplar →, *Man., Canada* 101 C9
Poplar →, *N.W.T., Canada* 100 A4
Poplar Bluff, *U.S.A.* 109 G9
Poplarville, *U.S.A.* 109 K10
Popocatepetl, *Mexico* 115 D5
Popokabaka, *Zaïre* 80 F3
Pópoli, *Italy* 33 F10
Popovača, *Croatia* 33 C13
Popovo, *Bulgaria* 38 F9
Poppel, *Belgium* 17 F6
Poprád, *Czech.* 20 F10
Poprád →, *Czech.* 20 F10
Porali →, *Pakistan* 62 G2
Porangaba, *Brazil* 124 B3
Porangatu, *Brazil* 123 D2
Porbandar, *India* 62 J3
Porce →, *Colombia* 120 B3
Porcher I., *Canada* 100 C2
Porco, *Bolivia* 125 D4
Porcos →, *Brazil* 123 D2
Porcuna, *Spain* 31 H6
Porcupine →, *Canada* 101 B8
Porcupine →, *U.S.A.* 96 B5
Pordenone, *Italy* 33 C9
Poreč, *Croatia* 33 C10
Porecatu, *Brazil* 123 F1
Poretskoye, *Russia* 41 D15
Pori, *Finland* 9 F16
Porjus, *Sweden* 8 C15
Porkhov, *Russia* 40 C6
Porkkala, *Finland* 9 G18
Porlamar, *Venezuela* 121 A5
Porlezza, *Italy* 32 B6
Porma →, *Spain* 30 C5
Pornic, *France* 24 E4
Poronaysk, *Russia* 45 E15
Póros, *Greece* 39 M6
Poroshiri-Dake, *Japan* 48 C11
Poroto Mts., *Tanzania* 83 D3
Porpoise B., *Antarctica* 5 C9
Porquerolles, I. de, *France* 27 F10
Porrentruy, *Switz.* 22 B4
Porreras, *Spain* 36 B10
Porretta, Passo di, *Italy* 32 D7
Porsangen, *Norway* 8 A18
Porsgrunn, *Norway* 10 E3
Port Adelaide, *Australia* 91 E2
Port Alberni, *Canada* 100 D4
Port Alfred, *Canada* 99 C5
Port Alfred, *S. Africa* 84 E4
Port Alice, *Canada* 100 C3
Port Allegany, *U.S.A.* 106 E6
Port Allen, *U.S.A.* 109 K9
Port Alma, *Australia* 90 C5
Port Angeles, *U.S.A.* 112 B3
Port Antonio, *Jamaica* 116 C4
Port Aransas, *U.S.A.* 109 M6
Port Arthur = Lüshun, *China* 51 E11
Port Arthur, *Australia* 90 G4
Port Arthur, *U.S.A.* 109 L8
Port au Port B., *Canada* 99 C8
Port-au-Prince, *Haiti* 117 C5
Port Augusta, *Australia* 91 E2
Port Augusta West, *Australia* 91 E2
Port Austin, *U.S.A.* 98 D3
Port Bell, *Uganda* 82 B3
Port Bergé Vaovao, *Madag.* 85 B8
Port Blandford, *Canada* 99 C9
Port Bou, *Spain* 28 C8
Port Bouët, *Ivory C.* 78 D4
Port Bradshaw, *Australia* 90 A2
Port Broughton, *Australia* 91 E2
Port Burwell, *Canada* 98 D3
Port Canning, *India* 63 H13
Port-Cartier, *Canada* 99 B6
Port Chalmers, *N.Z.* 87 L3
Port Chester, *U.S.A.* 107 F11
Port Clements, *Canada* 100 C2
Port Clinton, *U.S.A.* 104 E4
Port Colborne, *Canada* 98 D4
Port Coquitlam, *Canada* 100 D4
Port Credit, *Canada* 106 C5
Port Curtis, *Australia* 90 C5
Port Dalhousie, *Canada* 106 C5
Port Darwin, *Australia* 88 B5
Port Darwin, *Falk. Is.* 128 D5
Port Davey, *Australia* 90 G4
Port-de-Bouc, *France* 27 E8
Port-de-Paix, *Haiti* 117 C5
Port Dickson, *Malaysia* 59 L3
Port Douglas, *Australia* 90 B4
Port Dover, *Canada* 106 D4
Port Edward, *Canada* 100 C2
Port Elgin, *Canada* 98 D3
Port Elizabeth, *S. Africa* 84 E4
Port Ellen, *U.K.* 14 F2
Port-en-Bessin, *France* 24 C6
Port Erin, *I. of Man* 12 C3
Port Essington, *Australia* 88 B5
Port Etienne = Nouâdhibou, *Mauritania* 74 D1
Port Fairy, *Australia* 91 F3
Port Fouâd = Bûr Fuad, *Egypt* 76 H8
Port Gamble, *U.S.A.* 112 C4
Port-Gentil, *Gabon* 80 E1
Port Gibson, *U.S.A.* 109 K9
Port Glasgow, *U.K.* 14 F4
Port Harcourt, *Nigeria* 79 E6
Port Hardy, *Canada* 100 C3
Port Harrison = Inoucdjouac, *Canada* 97 C12
Port Hawkesbury, *Canada* 99 C7
Port Hedland, *Australia* 88 D2
Port Henry, *U.S.A.* 107 B11
Port Hood, *Canada* 99 C7
Port Hope, *Canada* 98 D4
Port Hueneme, *U.S.A.* 113 L7
Port Huron, *U.S.A.* 104 D4
Port Isabel, *U.S.A.* 109 M6
Port Jefferson, *U.S.A.* 107 F11
Port Jervis, *U.S.A.* 107 E10
Port-Joinville, *France* 24 F4
Port Katon, *Russia* 43 C8
Port Kembla, *Australia* 91 E5
Port Kenny, *Australia* 91 E1
Port-la-Nouvelle, *France* 26 E7
Port Laoise, *Ireland* 15 C4
Port Lavaca, *U.S.A.* 109 L6
Port-Leucate, *France* 26 F7
Port Lincoln, *Australia* 91 E2
Port Loko, *S. Leone* 78 D2
Port Louis, *France* 24 E3
Port Lyautey = Kenitra, *Morocco* 74 B3
Port MacDonnell, *Australia* 91 F3
Port Macquarie, *Australia* 91 E5
Port Maria, *Jamaica* 116 C4
Port Mellon, *Canada* 100 D4
Port-Menier, *Canada* 99 C7
Port Morant, *Jamaica* 116 C4
Port Moresby, *Papua N. G.* 92 H6
Port Mourant, *Guyana* 121 B6
Port Mouton, *Canada* 99 D7
Port Musgrave, *Australia* 90 A3
Port-Navalo, *France* 24 E4
Port Nelson, *Canada* 101 B10
Port Nolloth, *S. Africa* 84 D2
Port Nouveau-Québec, *Canada* 97 C13
Port O'Connor, *U.S.A.* 109 L6
Port of Spain, *Trin. & Tob.* 117 D7
Port Orchard, *U.S.A.* 112 C4
Port Orford, *U.S.A.* 110 E1
Port Pegasus, *N.Z.* 87 M1
Port Perry, *Canada* 98 D4
Port Phillip B., *Australia* 91 F3
Port Pirie, *Australia* 91 E2
Port Radium = Echo Bay, *Canada* 96 B8
Port Renfrew, *Canada* 100 D4
Port Roper, *Australia* 90 A2
Port Rowan, *Canada* 98 D3
Port Safaga = Bûr Safâga, *Egypt* 76 B3
Port Said = Bûr Sa'îd, *Egypt* 76 H8
Port St. Joe, *U.S.A.* 105 L3
Port St. Johns, *S. Africa* 85 E4
Port-St.-Louis-du-Rhône, *France* 27 E8
Port San Vicente, *Phil.* 55 B5
Port Sanilac, *U.S.A.* 98 D3
Port Saunders, *Canada* 99 B8
Port Severn, *Canada* 106 B5
Port Shepstone, *S. Africa* 85 E5
Port Simpson, *Canada* 100 C2
Port Stanley = Stanley, *Falk. Is.* 128 D5
Port Stanley, *Canada* 98 D3
Port Sudan = Bûr Sûdân, *Sudan* 76 D4
Port-sur-Saône, *France* 25 E13
Port Talbot, *U.K.* 13 F4
Port Taufîq = Bûr Taufiq, *Egypt* 76 J8
Port Townsend, *U.S.A.* 112 B4
Port-Vendres, *France* 26 F7
Port Wakefield, *Australia* 91 E2
Port Washington, *U.S.A.* 104 D2
Port Weld, *Malaysia* 59 K3
Portachuelo, *Bolivia* 125 D5
Portadown, *U.K.* 15 B5
Portage, *U.S.A.* 108 D10
Portage La Prairie, *Canada* 101 D9
Portageville, *U.S.A.* 109 G10
Portalegre, *Portugal* 31 F3
Portalegre □, *Portugal* 31 F3
Portales, *U.S.A.* 109 H3
Portarlington, *Ireland* 15 C4
Porteirinha, *Brazil* 123 E3
Portel, *Brazil* 122 B1
Portel, *Portugal* 31 G3
Porter L., *N.W.T., Canada* 101 A7
Porter L., *Sask., Canada* 101 B7
Porterville, *S. Africa* 84 E2
Porterville, *U.S.A.* 111 H4
Porthcawl, *U.K.* 13 F4
Porthill, *U.S.A.* 110 B5
Portile de Fier, *Europe* 38 E5
Portimão, *Portugal* 31 H2
Portland, *N.S.W., Australia* 91 E4
Portland, *Vic., Australia* 91 F3
Portland, *Canada* 107 B8
Portland, *Conn., U.S.A.* 107 E12
Portland, *Maine, U.S.A.* 99 D5
Portland, *Mich., U.S.A.* 104 D3
Portland, *Oreg., U.S.A.* 112 E4
Portland, I. of, *U.K.* 13 G5
Portland B., *Australia* 91 F3
Portland Bill, *U.K.* 13 G5
Portland Prom., *Canada* 97 C12
Portlands Roads, *Australia* 90 A3
Portneuf, *Canada* 99 C5

Pôrto, Brazil ... 122 B3
Porto, France ... 27 F12
Porto, Portugal ... 30 D2
Porto □, Portugal ... 30 D2
Porto, G. de, France ... 27 F12
Pôrto Acre, Brazil ... 124 B4
Pôrto Alegre, Pará, Brazil ... 121 D7
Pôrto Alegre, Rio Grande do S., Brazil ... 127 C5
Porto Amboim = Gunza, Angola ... 80 G2
Porto Argentera, Italy ... 32 D4
Porto Azzurro, Italy ... 32 F7
Porto Botte, Italy ... 34 C1
Pôrto Cajueiro, Brazil ... 125 C6
Porto Civitanova, Italy ... 33 E10
Porto Cristo, Spain ... 36 B10
Pôrto da Fôlha, Brazil ... 122 C4
Pôrto de Móz, Brazil ... 121 D7
Pôrto de Pedras, Brazil ... 122 C4
Pôrto des Meinacos, Brazil ... 125 C7
Porto Empédocle, Italy ... 34 E6
Pôrto Esperança, Brazil ... 125 D6
Pôrto Esperidão, Brazil ... 125 D6
Porto Franco, Brazil ... 122 C2
Porto Garibaldi, Italy ... 33 D9
Pôrto Grande, Brazil ... 121 C7
Pôrto Jofre, Brazil ... 125 D6
Pôrto Lágo, Greece ... 39 J8
Pôrto Mendes, Brazil ... 127 A5
Porto Moniz, Madeira ... 36 D2
Pôrto Murtinho, Brazil ... 125 E6
Pôrto Nacional, Brazil ... 122 D2
Porto Novo, Benin ... 79 D5
Porto Petro, Spain ... 36 B10
Porto Recanati, Italy ... 33 E10
Pôrto San Giórgio, Italy ... 33 E10
Pôrto Santana, Brazil ... 121 D7
Porto Santo, Madeira ... 72 B1
Porto Santo Stefano, Italy ... 32 F8
Pôrto São José, Brazil ... 127 A5
Pôrto Seguro, Brazil ... 123 E4
Porto Tolle, Italy ... 33 D9
Porto Tórres, Italy ... 34 B1
Pôrto União, Brazil ... 127 B5
Pôrto Válter, Brazil ... 124 B3
Porto-Vecchio, France ... 27 G13
Pôrto Velho, Brazil ... 125 B5
Portobelo, Panama ... 116 E4
Portoferráio, Italy ... 32 F7
Portogruaro, Italy ... 33 C9
Portola, U.S.A. ... 112 F6
Portomaggiore, Italy ... 33 D8
Portoscuso, Italy ... 34 C1
Portovénere, Italy ... 32 D6
Portovíejo, Ecuador ... 120 D1
Portpatrick, U.K. ... 14 G3
Portree, U.K. ... 14 D2
Portrush, U.K. ... 15 A5
Portsall, France ... 24 D2
Portsmouth, Domin. ... 117 C7
Portsmouth, U.K. ... 13 G6
Portsmouth, N.H., U.S.A. ... 107 C14
Portsmouth, Ohio, U.S.A. ... 104 F4
Portsmouth, R.I., U.S.A. ... 107 E13
Portsmouth, Va., U.S.A. ... 104 G7
Portsoy, U.K. ... 14 D6
Porttipahta, Finland ... 8 B19
Portugal ■, Europe ... 30 F3
Portugalete, Spain ... 28 B1
Portuguesa □, Venezuela ... 120 B4
Portuguese-Guinea = Guinea-Bissau ■, Africa ... 78 C2
Portuguese Timor ■ = Timor, Indonesia ... 57 F7
Portumna, Ireland ... 15 C3
Portville, U.S.A. ... 106 D6
Porvenir, Bolivia ... 124 C4
Porvenir, Chile ... 128 D2
Porvoo = Borgå, Finland ... 9 F18
Porzuna, Spain ... 31 F6
Posada →, Italy ... 34 B2
Posadas, Argentina ... 127 B4
Posadas, Spain ... 31 H5
Poschiavo, Switz. ... 23 D10
Posets, Spain ... 28 C5
Poshan = Boshan, China ... 51 F9
Posht-e-Badam, Iran ... 65 C7
Posídhion, Ákra, Greece ... 39 K6
Poso, Indonesia ... 57 E6
Posoegroenoe, Surinam ... 121 C6
Posong, S. Korea ... 51 G14
Posse, Brazil ... 123 D2
Possel, C.A.R. ... 80 C3
Possession I., Antarctica ... 5 D11
Pössneck, Germany ... 18 E7
Post, U.S.A. ... 109 J4
Post Falls, U.S.A. ... 110 C5
Postavy, Belorussia ... 40 D5
Poste Maurice Cortier, Algeria ... 75 D5
Postmasburg, S. Africa ... 84 D3
Postojna, Slovenia ... 33 C11
Poston, U.S.A. ... 113 M12
Potchefstroom, S. Africa ... 84 D4
Poté, Brazil ... 123 E3
Poteau, U.S.A. ... 109 H7
Poteet, U.S.A. ... 109 L5
Potelu, Lacul, Romania ... 38 F7
Potenza, Italy ... 35 B8
Potenza →, Italy ... 33 E10
Potenza Picena, Italy ... 33 E10
Poteriteri, L., N.Z. ... 87 M1
Potes, Spain ... 30 B6

Potgietersrus, S. Africa ... 85 C4
Poti, Georgia ... 43 E9
Potiraguá, Brazil ... 123 E4
Potiskum, Nigeria ... 79 C7
Potomac →, U.S.A. ... 104 F7
Potosí, Bolivia ... 125 D4
Potosí □, Bolivia ... 124 E4
Potosi Mt., U.S.A. ... 113 K11
Pototan, Phil. ... 55 F5
Potrerillos, Chile ... 126 B2
Potsdam, Germany ... 18 C9
Potsdam, U.S.A. ... 107 B10
Pottenstein, Germany ... 19 F7
Potter, U.S.A. ... 108 E3
Pottery Hill = Abû Ballas, Egypt ... 76 C2
Pottstown, U.S.A. ... 107 F9
Pottsville, U.S.A. ... 107 F8
Pottuvil, Sri Lanka ... 60 R12
Pouancé, France ... 24 E5
Pouce Coupé, Canada ... 100 B4
Poughkeepsie, U.S.A. ... 107 E11
Pouilly-sur-Loire, France ... 25 E9
Poulaphouca Res., Ireland ... 15 C5
Poulsbo, U.S.A. ... 112 C4
Pourri, Mt., France ... 27 C10
Pouso Alegre, Mato Grosso, Brazil ... 125 C6
Pouso Alegre, Minas Gerais, Brazil ... 127 A6
Pouzauges, France ... 24 F6
Povenets, Russia ... 44 C4
Poverty B., N.Z. ... 87 H7
Póvoa de Lanhosa, Portugal ... 30 D2
Póvoa de Varzim, Portugal ... 30 D2
Povorino, Russia ... 41 F13
Powassan, Canada ... 98 C4
Powder →, U.S.A. ... 108 B2
Powder River, U.S.A. ... 110 E10
Powell, U.S.A. ... 110 D9
Powell, L., U.S.A. ... 111 H8
Powell River, Canada ... 100 D4
Powers, Mich., U.S.A. ... 104 C2
Powers, Oreg., U.S.A. ... 110 E1
Powers Lake, U.S.A. ... 108 A3
Powys □, U.K. ... 13 E4
Poxoreu, Brazil ... 125 D7
Poyang Hu, China ... 53 C11
Poyarkovo, Russia ... 45 E13
Poza de la Sal, Spain ... 28 C1
Poza Rica, Mexico ... 115 C5
Pozanti, Turkey ... 66 E6
Požarevac, Serbia, Yug. ... 21 L11
Pozi, Taiwan ... 53 F13
Poznań, Poland ... 20 C6
Pozo, U.S.A. ... 113 K6
Pozo Alcón, Spain ... 29 H2
Pozo Almonte, Chile ... 124 E4
Pozo Colorado, Paraguay ... 126 A4
Pozo del Dátil, Mexico ... 114 B2
Pozoblanco, Spain ... 31 G6
Pozuzo, Peru ... 124 C2
Pozzallo, Italy ... 35 F7
Pozzuoli, Italy ... 35 B7
Pra →, Ghana ... 79 D4
Prachin Buri, Thailand ... 58 E3
Prachuap Khiri Khan, Thailand ... 59 G2
Pradelles, France ... 26 D7
Pradera, Colombia ... 120 C2
Prades, France ... 26 F6
Prado, Brazil ... 123 E4
Prado del Rey, Spain ... 31 J5
Præstø, Denmark ... 11 J6
Pragersko, Slovenia ... 33 B12
Prague = Praha, Czech. ... 20 E4
Praha, Czech. ... 20 E4
Prahecq, France ... 26 B3
Prahova →, Romania ... 38 E8
Prahovo, Serbia, Yug. ... 21 L12
Praid, Romania ... 38 C8
Prainha, Amazonas, Brazil ... 125 B5
Prainha, Pará, Brazil ... 121 D7
Prairie, Australia ... 90 C3
Prairie →, U.S.A. ... 109 H5
Prairie City, U.S.A. ... 110 D4
Prairie du Chien, U.S.A. ... 108 D9
Pramánda, Greece ... 39 K4
Pran Buri, Thailand ... 58 F2
Prang, Ghana ... 79 D4
Prapat, Indonesia ... 56 D1
Prasonísi, Ákra, Greece ... 37 D9
Prata, Brazil ... 123 E2
Pratapgarh, India ... 62 G6
Prática di Mare, Italy ... 34 A5
Prätigau, Switz. ... 23 C9
Prato, Italy ... 32 E8
Prátola Peligna, Italy ... 33 F10
Pratovécchio, Italy ... 33 E8
Prats-de-Mollo-la-Preste, France ... 26 F7
Pratt, U.S.A. ... 109 G5
Pratteln, Switz. ... 22 A5
Prattville, U.S.A. ... 105 J2
Pravdinsk, Russia ... 41 C13
Pravia, Spain ... 30 B4
Praya, Indonesia ... 56 F5
Pré-en-Pail, France ... 24 D6
Pré St. Didier, Italy ... 32 C4
Precordillera, Argentina ... 126 C2
Predáppio, Italy ... 33 D8
Predazzo, Italy ... 33 B8

Predejane, Serbia, Yug. ... 21 N12
Preeceville, Canada ... 101 C8
Préfailles, France ... 24 E4
Pregonero, Venezuela ... 120 B3
Pregrada, Croatia ... 33 B12
Preko, Croatia ... 33 D12
Prelate, Canada ... 101 C7
Prelog, Croatia ... 33 B13
Premier, Canada ... 100 B3
Premont, U.S.A. ... 109 M5
Premuda, Croatia ... 33 D11
Prenjasi, Albania ... 39 H3
Prentice, U.S.A. ... 108 C9
Prenzlau, Germany ... 18 B9
Preobrazheniye, Russia ... 48 C6
Prepansko Jezero, Macedonia, Yug. ... 39 J4
Preparis North Channel, Ind. Oc. ... 61 M18
Preparis South Channel, Ind. Oc. ... 61 M18
Přerov, Czech. ... 20 F7
Presanella, Italy ... 32 B7
Prescott, Canada ... 98 D4
Prescott, Ariz., U.S.A. ... 111 J7
Prescott, Ark., U.S.A. ... 109 J8
Preservation Inlet, N.Z. ... 87 M1
Preševo, Serbia, Yug. ... 21 N11
Presho, U.S.A. ... 108 D4
Presicce, Italy ... 35 C11
Presidencia de la Plaza, Argentina ... 126 B4
Presidencia Roque Saenz Peña, Argentina ... 126 B3
Presidente Epitácio, Brazil ... 123 F1
Presidente Hayes □, Paraguay ... 126 A4
Presidente Hermes, Brazil ... 125 C5
Presidente Prudente, Brazil ... 127 A5
Presidio, Mexico ... 114 B4
Presidio, U.S.A. ... 109 L2
Preslav, Bulgaria ... 38 F9
Prešov, Czech. ... 20 F11
Prespa, L. = Prepansko Jezero, Macedonia, Yug. ... 39 J4
Presque Isle, U.S.A. ... 99 C6
Prestbury, U.K. ... 13 F5
Prestea, Ghana ... 78 D4
Presteigne, U.K. ... 13 E5
Presto, Bolivia ... 125 D5
Preston, Canada ... 106 C4
Preston, U.K. ... 12 D5
Preston, Idaho, U.S.A. ... 110 E8
Preston, Minn., U.S.A. ... 108 D8
Preston, Nev., U.S.A. ... 110 G6
Preston, C., Australia ... 88 D2
Prestonpans, U.K. ... 14 F6
Prestwick, U.K. ... 14 F4
Prêto →, Amazonas, Brazil ... 121 D5
Prêto →, Bahia, Brazil ... 122 D3
Prêto do Igapó-Açu →, Brazil ... 121 D6
Pretoria, S. Africa ... 85 D4
Preuilly-sur-Claise, France ... 24 F7
Préveza, Greece ... 39 L3
Priazovskoye, Ukraine ... 42 C6
Pribilof Is., Bering S. ... 4 D17
Priboj, Serbia, Yug. ... 21 M9
Příbram, Czech. ... 20 F4
Price, U.S.A. ... 110 G8
Price I., Canada ... 100 C3
Prichalnaya, Russia ... 43 B11
Prichard, U.S.A. ... 105 K1
Priego, Spain ... 28 E2
Priego de Córdoba, Spain ... 31 H6
Priekule, Latvia ... 40 C2
Prien, Germany ... 19 H8
Prieska, S. Africa ... 84 D3
Priest →, U.S.A. ... 110 B5
Priest L., U.S.A. ... 110 B5
Priest River, U.S.A. ... 110 B5
Priest Valley, U.S.A. ... 112 J6
Priestly, Canada ... 100 C3
Prievidza, Czech. ... 20 G8
Prijedor, Bos.-H., Yug. ... 33 D13
Prikaspiyskaya Nizmennost, Asia ... 43 C13
Prilep, Macedonia, Yug. ... 39 H4
Priluki, Ukraine ... 40 F8
Prime Seal I., Australia ... 90 G4
Primeira Cruz, Brazil ... 122 B3
Primorsko-Akhtarsk, Russia ... 42 C8
Primorskoye, Ukraine ... 42 C7
Primrose L., Canada ... 101 C7
Prince Albert, Canada ... 101 C7
Prince Albert, S. Africa ... 84 E3
Prince Albert Mts., Antarctica ... 5 D11
Prince Albert Nat. Park, Canada ... 101 C7
Prince Albert Pen., Canada ... 96 A8
Prince Albert Sd., Canada ... 96 A8
Prince Alfred, C., Canada ... 4 B1
Prince Charles I., Canada ... 97 B12
Prince Charles Mts., Antarctica ... 5 D6
Prince Edward I. □, Canada ... 99 C7
Prince Edward Is., Ind. Oc. ... 3 G11
Prince George, Canada ... 100 C4
Prince of Wales, C., U.S.A. ... 94 C3
Prince of Wales I., Australia ... 90 A3
Prince of Wales I., Canada ... 96 A10

Prince of Wales I., U.S.A. ... 100 B2
Prince Patrick I., Canada ... 4 B2
Prince Regent Inlet, Canada ... 4 B3
Prince Rupert, Canada ... 100 C2
Princenhage, Neths. ... 17 F5
Princesa Isabel, Brazil ... 122 C4
Princess Charlotte B., Australia ... 90 A3
Princess May Ras., Australia ... 88 C4
Princess Royal I., Canada ... 100 C3
Princeton, Canada ... 100 D4
Princeton, Calif., U.S.A. ... 112 F4
Princeton, Ill., U.S.A. ... 108 E10
Princeton, Ind., U.S.A. ... 104 F2
Princeton, Ky., U.S.A. ... 104 G2
Princeton, Mo., U.S.A. ... 108 E8
Princeton, N.J., U.S.A. ... 107 F10
Princeton, W. Va., U.S.A. ... 104 G5
Principe, I. de, Atl. Oc. ... 70 F4
Principe Chan., Canada ... 100 C2
Principe da Beira, Brazil ... 125 C5
Prineville, U.S.A. ... 110 D3
Prins Harald Kyst, Antarctica ... 5 D4
Prinsesse Astrid Kyst, Antarctica ... 5 D3
Prinsesse Ragnhild Kyst, Antarctica ... 5 D4
Prinzapolca, Nic. ... 116 D3
Prior, C., Spain ... 30 B2
Pripet = Pripyat →, Europe ... 40 F7
Pripet Marshes = Polesye, Belorussia ... 40 E6
Pripyat →, Europe ... 40 F7
Pripyat Marshes = Polesye, Belorussia ... 40 E6
Prislop, Pasul, Romania ... 38 B8
Pristen, Russia ... 41 F10
Priština, Serbia, Yug. ... 21 N11
Pritzwalk, Germany ... 18 B8
Privas, France ... 27 D8
Priverno, Italy ... 34 A6
Privolzhsk, Russia ... 41 C12
Privolzhskaya Vozvyshennost, Russia ... 41 F15
Privolzhskiy, Russia ... 41 F15
Privolzhye, Russia ... 41 E16
Priyutnoye, Russia ... 43 C10
Prizren, Serbia, Yug. ... 21 N10
Prizzi, Italy ... 34 E6
Prnjavor, Bos.-H., Yug. ... 21 L7
Probolinggo, Indonesia ... 57 G15
Procida, Italy ... 35 B7
Proddatur, India ... 60 M11
Prodhromos, Cyprus ... 37 E11
Proença-a-Nova, Portugal ... 31 F3
Prof. Van Blommestein Meer, Surinam ... 121 C6
Profítis Ilías, Greece ... 37 C9
Profondeville, Belgium ... 17 H5
Progreso, Mexico ... 115 C7
Prokhladnyy, Russia ... 43 E11
Prokletije, Albania ... 38 G2
Prokopyevsk, Russia ... 44 D9
Prokuplje, Serbia, Yug. ... 21 M11
Proletarskaya, Russia ... 43 C9
Prome = Pyè, Burma ... 61 K19
Prophet →, Canada ... 100 B4
Propriá, Brazil ... 122 D4
Propriano, France ... 27 G12
Proserpine, Australia ... 90 C4
Prosser, U.S.A. ... 110 C4
Prostějov, Czech. ... 20 F7
Proston, Australia ... 91 D5
Próti, Greece ... 39 M4
Provadiya, Bulgaria ... 38 F10
Proven, Belgium ... 17 G1
Provence, France ... 27 E9
Providence, Ky., U.S.A. ... 104 G2
Providence, R.I., U.S.A. ... 107 E13
Providence B., Canada ... 98 C3
Providence Mts., U.S.A. ... 111 J6
Providencia, Ecuador ... 120 D2
Providencia, I. de, Colombia ... 116 D3
Provideniya, Russia ... 45 C19
Provins, France ... 25 D10
Provo, U.S.A. ... 110 F8
Provost, Canada ... 101 C6
Prozor, Bos.-H., Yug. ... 21 M7
Prudentópolis, Brazil ... 123 G1
Prud'homme, Canada ... 101 C7
Prudnik, Poland ... 20 E7
Prüm, Germany ... 19 E2
Pruszcz Gdański, Poland ... 20 A8
Pruszków, Poland ... 20 C10
Prut →, Romania ... 38 D11
Pruzhany, Belorussia ... 40 E4
Prvič, Croatia ... 33 D11
Prydz B., Antarctica ... 5 C6
Pryor, U.S.A. ... 109 G7
Przasnysz, Poland ... 20 B10
Przedbórz, Poland ... 20 D9
Przemyśl, Poland ... 20 E12
Przeworsk, Poland ... 20 E12
Przewóz, Poland ... 20 D4
Przhevalsk, Kirghizia ... 44 E8
Przysuchla, Poland ... 20 D10
Psakhná, Greece ... 39 L6
Psará, Greece ... 39 L8

Psel →, Ukraine ... 42 B5
Pserimos, Greece ... 39 N10
Psíra, Greece ... 37 D7
Pskov, Russia ... 40 C6
Psunj, Croatia ... 21 K7
Pszczyna, Poland ... 20 F8
Pteleón, Greece ... 39 K5
Ptich →, Belorussia ... 40 E6
Ptolemaís, Greece ... 39 J4
Ptuj, Slovenia ... 33 B12
Ptujska Gora, Slovenia ... 33 B12
Pu Xian, China ... 50 F6
Pua, Thailand ... 58 C3
Puán, Argentina ... 126 D3
Pu'an, China ... 52 E5
Puan, S. Korea ... 51 G14
Pubei, China ... 52 F7
Pucacuro →, Peru ... 120 D3
Pucallpa, Peru ... 124 B3
Pucará, Bolivia ... 125 D5
Pucará, Peru ... 124 D3
Pucarani, Bolivia ... 124 D4
Pucheng, China ... 53 D12
Pučišće, Croatia ... 33 E13
Pucka, Zatoka, Poland ... 20 A8
Puding, China ... 52 D5
Pudukkottai, India ... 60 P11
Puebla, Mexico ... 115 D5
Puebla □, Mexico ... 115 D5
Puebla de Alcocer, Spain ... 31 G5
Puebla de Don Fadrique, Spain ... 29 H2
Puebla de Don Rodrigo, Spain ... 31 F6
Puebla de Guzmán, Spain ... 31 H3
Puebla de Sanabria, Spain ... 30 C4
Puebla de Trives, Spain ... 30 C3
Puebla del Caramiñal, Spain ... 30 C2
Pueblo, U.S.A. ... 108 F2
Pueblo Hundido, Chile ... 126 B1
Pueblo Nuevo, Venezuela ... 120 B3
Puelches, Argentina ... 126 D2
Puelén, Argentina ... 126 D2
Puente Alto, Chile ... 126 C1
Puente del Arzobispo, Spain ... 30 F5
Puente-Genil, Spain ... 31 H6
Puente la Reina, Spain ... 28 C3
Puenteareas, Spain ... 30 C2
Puentedeume, Spain ... 30 B2
Puentes de Garcia Rodriguez, Spain ... 30 B3
Pu'er, China ... 52 F3
Puerco →, U.S.A. ... 111 J10
Puerto, Canary Is. ... 36 F2
Puerto Acosta, Bolivia ... 124 D4
Puerto Aisén, Chile ... 128 C2
Puerto Ángel, Mexico ... 115 D5
Puerto Arista, Mexico ... 115 D6
Puerto Armuelles, Panama ... 116 E3
Puerto Ayacucho, Venezuela ... 120 B4
Puerto Barrios, Guatemala ... 116 C2
Puerto Bermejo, Argentina ... 126 B4
Puerto Bermúdez, Peru ... 124 C3
Puerto Bolívar, Ecuador ... 120 D2
Puerto Cabello, Venezuela ... 120 A4
Puerto Cabezas, Nic. ... 116 D3
Puerto Cabo Gracias á Dios, Nic. ... 116 D3
Puerto Capaz = Jebba, Morocco ... 74 A4
Puerto Carreño, Colombia ... 120 B4
Puerto Castilla, Honduras ... 116 C2
Puerto Chicama, Peru ... 124 B2
Puerto Coig, Argentina ... 128 D3
Puerto Cortes, Costa Rica ... 116 E3
Puerto Cortés, Honduras ... 116 C2
Puerto Cumarebo, Venezuela ... 120 A4
Puerto de Alcudia, Spain ... 36 B10
Puerto de Andraitx, Spain ... 36 B9
Puerto de Cabrera, Spain ... 36 B9
Puerto de Gran Tarajal, Canary Is. ... 36 F5
Puerto de la Cruz, Canary Is. ... 36 F3
Puerto de Pozo Negro, Canary Is. ... 36 F6
Puerto de Santa María, Spain ... 31 J4
Puerto de Sóller, Spain ... 36 B9
Pto. del Carmen, Canary Is. ... 36 F6
Puerto del Rosario, Canary Is. ... 36 F6
Puerto Deseado, Argentina ... 128 C3
Puerto Guaraní, Paraguay ... 125 E6
Puerto Heath, Bolivia ... 124 C4
Puerto Huitoto, Colombia ... 120 C3
Puerto Inca, Peru ... 124 B3
Puerto Juárez, Mexico ... 115 C7
Puerto La Cruz, Venezuela ... 121 A5
Puerto Leguízamo, Colombia ... 120 D3
Puerto Limón, Colombia ... 120 C3
Puerto Lobos, Argentina ... 128 B3
Puerto López, Colombia ... 120 C3
Puerto Lumbreras, Spain ... 29 H3
Puerto Madryn, Argentina ... 128 B3
Puerto Maldonado, Peru ... 124 C4
Puerto Manotí, Cuba ... 116 B4
Puerto Mazarrón, Spain ... 29 H3

Puerto Mercedes, *Colombia* 120 C3
Puerto Miraña, *Colombia* 120 D3
Puerto Montt, *Chile* 128 B2
Puerto Morelos, *Mexico* 115 C7
Puerto Nariño, *Colombia* 120 C4
Puerto Natales, *Chile* 128 D2
Puerto Nuevo, *Colombia* 120 B4
Puerto Nutrias, *Venezuela* 120 B4
Puerto Ordaz, *Venezuela* 121 B5
Puerto Padre, *Cuba* 116 B4
Puerto Páez, *Venezuela* 120 B4
Puerto Peñasco, *Mexico* 114 A2
Puerto Pinasco, *Paraguay* 126 A4
Puerto Pirámides, *Argentina* 128 B4
Puerto Plata, *Dom. Rep.* 117 C5
Puerto Pollensa, *Spain* 36 B10
Puerto Portillo, *Peru* 124 B3
Puerto Princesa, *Phil.* 55 G3
Puerto Quellón, *Chile* 128 B2
Puerto Quepos, *Costa Rica* 116 E3
Puerto Real, *Spain* 31 J4
Puerto Rico, *Bolivia* 124 C4
Puerto Rico, *Canary Is.* 36 G4
Puerto Rico ■, *W. Indies* 117 C6
Puerto Rico Trench, *Atl. Oc.* 117 C6
Puerto Saavedra, *Chile* 128 A2
Puerto Sastre, *Paraguay* 126 A4
Puerto Siles, *Bolivia* 125 C4
Puerto Suárez, *Bolivia* 125 D6
Puerto Tejada, *Colombia* 120 C2
Puerto Umbría, *Colombia* 120 C2
Puerto Vallarta, *Mexico* 114 C3
Puerto Varas, *Chile* 128 B2
Puerto Villazón, *Bolivia* 125 C5
Puerto Wilches, *Colombia* 120 B3
Puertollano, *Spain* 31 G6
Puertomarin, *Spain* 30 C3
Puesto Cunambo, *Peru* 120 D2
Pueyrredón, L., *Argentina* 128 C2
Pugachev, *Kazakhstan* 41 F16
Puge, *China* 52 D4
Puge, *Tanzania* 82 C3
Puget Sd., *U.S.A.* 110 C2
Puget-Théniers, *France* 27 E10
Púglia □, *Italy* 35 B9
Pugŏdong, *N. Korea* 51 C16
Pugu, *Tanzania* 82 D4
Pūgūnzī, *Iran* 65 E8
Pui, *Romania* 38 D6
Puica, *Peru* 124 C3
Puig Mayor, *Spain* 36 B9
Puigcerdá, *Spain* 28 C6
Puigmal, *Spain* 28 C7
Puigpuñent, *Spain* 36 B9
Puisaye, Collines de la, *France* 25 E10
Puiseaux, *France* 25 D9
Pujilí, *Ecuador* 120 D2
Pujon-chosuji, *N. Korea* 51 D14
Puka, *Albania* 38 G2
Pukaki L., *N.Z.* 87 L3
Pukapuka, *Cook Is.* 93 J11
Pukatawagan, *Canada* 101 B8
Pukchin, *N. Korea* 51 D13
Pukchŏng, *N. Korea* 51 D15
Pukekohe, *N.Z.* 87 G5
Pukou, *China* 53 A12
Pula, *Croatia* 33 D10
Pula, *Italy* 34 D2
Pulacayo, *Bolivia* 124 E4
Pulaski, *N.Y., U.S.A.* 107 C8
Pulaski, *Tenn., U.S.A.* 105 H2
Pulaski, *Va., U.S.A.* 104 G5
Pulawy, *Poland* 20 D11
Pulga, *U.S.A.* 112 F5
Pulicat, L., *India* 60 N12
Pullman, *U.S.A.* 110 C5
Pulog, *Phil.* 55 C4
Pułtusk, *Poland* 20 C11
Pülümür, *Turkey* 67 D8
Pumlumon Fawr, *U.K.* 13 E4
Puna, *Bolivia* 125 D4
Puná, I., *Ecuador* 120 D1
Punakha, *Bhutan* 61 F16
Punasar, *India* 62 F5
Punata, *Bolivia* 125 D4
Punch, *India* 63 C6
Pune, *India* 60 K8
Pungsan, *N. Korea* 51 D15
Pungue, Ponte de, *Mozam.* 83 F3
Puning, *China* 53 F11
Punjab □, *India* 62 D6
Punjab □, *Pakistan* 62 E6
Puno, *Peru* 124 D3
Punta Alta, *Argentina* 128 A4
Punta Arenas, *Chile* 128 D2
Punta Cardón, *Venezuela* 120 A3
Punta Coles, *Peru* 124 D3
Punta de Bombón, *Peru* 124 D3
Punta de Díaz, *Chile* 126 B1
Punta Delgado, *Argentina* 128 B4
Punta Gorda, *Belize* 115 D7
Punta Gorda, *U.S.A.* 105 M5
Punta Prieta, *Mexico* 114 B2
Punta Prima, *Spain* 36 B11
Puntabie, *Australia* 91 E1
Puntarenas, *Costa Rica* 116 E3
Punto Fijo, *Venezuela* 120 A3
Punxsutawney, *U.S.A.* 106 F5
Puqi, *China* 53 C9
Puquio, *Peru* 124 C3
Pur →, *Russia* 44 C8
Purace, Vol., *Colombia* 120 C2
Purbeck, Isle of, *U.K.* 13 G5
Purcell, *U.S.A.* 109 H6
Purchena Tetica, *Spain* 29 H2
Puri, *India* 61 K14
Purificación, *Colombia* 120 C3
Purmerend, *Neths.* 16 C5
Purnia, *India* 63 G12
Purukcahu, *Indonesia* 56 E4
Puruliya, *India* 63 H12
Purus →, *Brazil* 121 D5
Pŭrvomay, *Bulgaria* 38 G8
Purwakarta, *Indonesia* 57 G12
Purwodadi, *Jawa, Indonesia* 57 G14
Purwodadi, *Jawa, Indonesia* 57 G13
Purwokerto, *Indonesia* 57 G13
Purworejo, *Indonesia* 57 G14
Puryŏng, *N. Korea* 51 C15
Pusan, *S. Korea* 51 G15
Pushchino, *Russia* 45 D16
Pushkin, *Russia* 40 B7
Pushkino, *Russia* 41 F15
Pushkino, *Russia* 41 C10
Püspökladány, *Hungary* 21 H11
Pustoshka, *Russia* 40 C6
Putahow L., *Canada* 101 B8
Putao, *Burma* 61 F20
Putaruru, *N.Z.* 87 H5
Putbus, *Germany* 18 A9
Puthein Myit →, *Burma* 61 M19
Putian, *China* 53 E12
Putignano, *Italy* 35 B10
Putina, *Peru* 124 C4
Puting, Tanjung, *Indonesia* 56 E4
Putlitz, *Germany* 18 B8
Putna →, *Romania* 38 D10
Putnam, *U.S.A.* 107 E13
Putorana, Gory, *Russia* 45 C10
Putre, *Chile* 124 D4
Puttalam, *Sri Lanka* 60 Q11
Putte, *Neths.* 17 F4
Putten, *Neths.* 16 D7
Puttgarden, *Germany* 18 A7
Putumayo →, *S. Amer.* 120 D4
Putuo, *China* 53 C14
Putussibau, *Indonesia* 56 D4
Puurs, *Belgium* 17 F4
Puy-de-Dôme, *France* 26 C6
Puy-de-Dôme □, *France* 26 C7
Puy-Guillaume, *France* 26 C7
Puy-l'Êvêque, *France* 26 D5
Puyallup, *U.S.A.* 112 C4
Puyang, *China* 50 G8
Puyehue, *Chile* 128 B2
Puylaurens, *France* 26 E6
Puyo, *Ecuador* 120 D2
Pūzeh Rīg, *Iran* 65 E8
Pwani □, *Tanzania* 82 D4
Pweto, *Zaïre* 83 D2
Pwllheli, *U.K.* 12 E3
Pyana →, *Russia* 41 D15
Pyapon, *Burma* 61 L19
Pyasina →, *Russia* 45 B9
Pyatigorsk, *Russia* 43 D10
Pyatikhatki, *Ukraine* 42 B5
Pyè, *Burma* 61 K19
Pyinmana, *Burma* 61 K20
Pyla, C., *Cyprus* 37 E12
Pyŏktong, *N. Korea* 51 D13
Pyŏnggang, *N. Korea* 51 E14
Pyŏngtaek, *S. Korea* 51 F14
P'yŏngyang, *N. Korea* 51 E13
Pyote, *U.S.A.* 109 K3
Pyramid L., *U.S.A.* 110 G4
Pyramid Pk., *U.S.A.* 113 J10
Pyramids, *Egypt* 76 J7
Pyrénées, *Europe* 26 F4
Pyrénées-Atlantiques □, *France* 26 E3
Pyrénées-Orientales □, *France* 26 F6
Pyrzyce, *Poland* 20 B4
Pyshchug, *Russia* 41 B14
Pytalovo, *Russia* 40 C5
Pyttegga, *Norway* 10 B1
Pyu, *Burma* 61 K20

Q

Qaanaaq = Thule, *Greenland* 4 B4
Qachasnek, *S. Africa* 85 E4
Qādib, *Yemen* 68 E5
Qa'el Jafr, *Jordan* 69 E5
Qa'emābād, *Iran* 65 D9
Qā'emshahr, *Iran* 65 B7
Qagan Nur, *China* 50 C8
Qahar Youyi Zhongqi, *China* 50 D7
Qahremānshahr = Bākhtarān, *Iran* 64 C5
Qaidam Pendi, *China* 54 C4
Qajarīyeh, *Iran* 65 D6
Qala, Ras il, *Malta* 37 C1
Qala-i-Jadid, *Afghan.* 62 D2
Qala Yangi, *Afghan.* 62 B2
Qal'at al Akhḍar, *Si. Arabia* 64 E3
Qal'at Sukkar, *Iraq* 64 D5
Qal'eh Darreh, *Iran* 64 B5
Qal'eh Shaharak, *Afghan.* 60 B4
Qalyûb, *Egypt* 76 H7
Qamar, Ghubbat al, *Yemen* 68 D5
Qamdo, *China* 52 B1
Qamruddin Karez, *Pakistan* 62 D3
Qandahār, *Afghan.* 60 D4
Qandahār □, *Afghan.* 60 D4
Qapān, *Iran* 65 B7
Qaqortoq = Julianehåb, *Greenland* 4 C5
Qâra, *Egypt* 76 B2
Qara Qash →, *India* 63 B8
Qārah, *Si. Arabia* 64 D4
Qardud, *Sudan* 77 E2
Qareh →, *Iran* 64 B5
Qareh Tekān, *Iran* 65 B6
Qarqan, *China* 54 C3
Qarqan He →, *China* 54 C3
Qarrasa, *Sudan* 77 E3
Qartabā, *Lebanon* 69 A4
Qaryat al Gharab, *Iraq* 64 D5
Qaryat al 'Ulyā, *Si. Arabia* 64 E5
Qasr 'Amra, *Jordan* 64 D3
Qaşr-e Qand, *Iran* 65 E9
Qasr Farâfra, *Egypt* 76 B2
Qatanā, *Syria* 69 B5
Qatar ■, *Asia* 65 E6
Qatlīsh, *Iran* 65 B8
Qattâra, *Egypt* 76 A2
Qattâra, Munkhafed el, *Egypt* 76 B2
Qattâra Depression = Qattâra, Munkhafed el, *Egypt* 76 B2
Qawām al Ḩamzah, *Iraq* 64 D5
Qāyen, *Iran* 65 C8
Qazvin, *Iran* 65 B6
Qena, *Egypt* 76 B3
Qena, Wadi →, *Egypt* 76 B3
Qeqertarsuag = Disko, *Greenland* 4 C5
Qeqertarsuaq = Godhavn, *Greenland* 4 C5
Qeshlāq, *Iran* 64 C5
Qeshm, *Iran* 65 E8
Qezi'ot, *Israel* 69 E3
Qi Xian, *China* 50 G8
Qian Gorlos, *China* 51 B13
Qian Xian, *China* 50 G5
Qiancheng, *China* 52 D7
Qianjiang, *Guangxi Zhuangzu, China* 52 F7
Qianjiang, *Hubei, China* 53 B9
Qianjiang, *Sichuan, China* 52 C7
Qianshan, *China* 53 B11
Qianwei, *China* 52 C4
Qianxi, *China* 52 D6
Qianyang, *Hunan, China* 53 D8
Qianyang, *Shaanxi, China* 50 G4
Qianyang, *Zhejiang, China* 53 B12
Qiaojia, *China* 52 D4
Qibā', *Si. Arabia* 64 E5
Qichun, *China* 53 B10
Qidong, *Hunan, China* 53 D9
Qidong, *Jiangsu, China* 53 B13
Qijiang, *China* 52 C6
Qila Safed, *Pakistan* 60 E2
Qila Saifullāh, *Pakistan* 62 D3
Qilian Shan, *China* 54 C4
Qimen, *China* 53 C11
Qin He →, *China* 50 G7
Qin Jiang →, *China* 53 D10
Qin Ling = Qinling Shandi, *China* 50 H5
Qin'an, *China* 50 G3
Qing Xian, *China* 50 E9
Qingcheng, *China* 51 F9
Qingdao, *China* 51 F11
Qingfeng, *China* 50 G8
Qinghai □, *China* 54 C4
Qinghai Hu, *China* 54 C5
Qinghecheng, *China* 51 D13
Qinghemen, *China* 51 D11
Qingjian, *China* 50 F6
Qingjiang, *Jiangsu, China* 51 H10
Qingjiang, *Jiangxi, China* 53 C10
Qingliu, *China* 53 D11
Qinglong, *China* 52 E5
Qingping, *China* 52 D6
Qingpu, *China* 53 B13
Qingshui, *China* 50 G4
Qingshuihe, *China* 50 E6
Qingtian, *China* 53 C13
Qingtongxia Shuiku, *China* 50 F3
Qingxi, *China* 52 D7
Qingxu, *China* 50 F7
Qingyang, *Anhui, China* 53 B11
Qingyang, *Gansu, China* 50 F4
Qingyi Jiang →, *China* 52 C4
Qingyuan, *Guangdong, China* 53 F9
Qingyuan, *Liaoning, China* 51 C13
Qingyuan, *Zhejiang, China* 53 D12
Qingyun, *China* 51 F9
Qingzhen, *China* 52 D6
Qinhuangdao, *China* 51 E10
Qinling Shandi, *China* 50 H5
Qinshui, *China* 50 G7
Qinyang, *China* 50 G7
Qinyuan, *China* 50 F7
Qinzhou, *China* 52 G7
Qionghai, *China* 58 C8
Qionglai, *China* 52 B4
Qionglai Shan, *China* 52 B4
Qiongshan, *China* 58 C8
Qiongzhou Haixia, *China* 58 B8
Qiqihar, *China* 54 B7
Qiraīya, W. →, *Egypt* 69 E3
Qiryat Ata, *Israel* 69 C4
Qiryat Gat, *Israel* 69 D3
Qiryat Mal'akhi, *Israel* 69 D3
Qiryat Shemona, *Israel* 69 B4
Qiryat Yam, *Israel* 69 C4
Qishan, *China* 50 G4
Qishan, *Taiwan* 53 F13
Qitai, *China* 54 B3
Qiubei, *China* 52 E5
Qixia, *China* 51 F11
Qiyang, *China* 53 D8
Qojūr, *Iran* 64 B5
Qom, *Iran* 65 C6
Qomsheh, *Iran* 65 D6
Qu Jiang →, *China* 52 B6
Qu Xian, *Sichuan, China* 52 B6
Qu Xian, *Zhejiang, China* 53 C12
Quackenbrück, *Germany* 18 C3
Quairading, *Australia* 89 F2
Quakertown, *U.S.A.* 107 F9
Qualeup, *Australia* 89 F2
Quambatook, *Australia* 91 F3
Quambone, *Australia* 91 E4
Quamby, *Australia* 90 C3
Quan Long, *Vietnam* 59 H5
Quanah, *U.S.A.* 109 H5
Quandialla, *Australia* 91 E4
Quang Ngai, *Vietnam* 58 E7
Quang Yen, *Vietnam* 58 B6
Quannan, *China* 53 E10
Quantock Hills, *U.K.* 13 F4
Quanzhou, *Fujian, China* 53 E12
Quanzhou, *Guangxi Zhuangzu, China* 53 E8
Quaraí, *Brazil* 126 C4
Quarré-les-Tombes, *France* 25 E10
Quartu Sant' Elena, *Italy* 34 C2
Quartzsite, *U.S.A.* 113 M12
Quatsino, *Canada* 100 C3
Quatsino Sd., *Canada* 100 C3
Qūchān, *Iran* 65 B8
Queanbeyan, *Australia* 91 F4
Québec, *Canada* 99 C5
Québec □, *Canada* 99 B6
Quedlinburg, *Germany* 18 D7
Queen Alexandra Ra., *Antarctica* 5 E11
Queen Charlotte, *Canada* 100 C2
Queen Charlotte Bay, *Falk. Is.* 128 D4
Queen Charlotte Is., *Canada* 100 C2
Queen Charlotte Str., *Canada* 100 C3
Queen Elizabeth Is., *Canada* 94 B10
Queen Elizabeth Nat. Park, *Uganda* 82 C3
Queen Mary Land, *Antarctica* 5 D7
Queen Maud G., *Canada* 96 B9
Queen Maud Land, *Antarctica* 5 D3
Queen Maud Mts., *Antarctica* 5 E13
Queens Chan., *Australia* 88 C4
Queenscliff, *Australia* 91 F3
Queensland □, *Australia* 90 C3
Queenstown, *Australia* 90 G4
Queenstown, *N.Z.* 87 L2
Queenstown, *S. Africa* 84 E4
Queets, *U.S.A.* 112 C2
Queguay Grande →, *Uruguay* 126 C4
Queimadas, *Brazil* 122 D4
Quela, *Angola* 80 F3
Quelimane, *Mozam.* 83 F4
Quelpart = Cheju Do, *S. Korea* 51 H14
Quemado, *N. Mex., U.S.A.* 111 J9
Quemado, *Tex., U.S.A.* 109 L4
Quemú-Quemú, *Argentina* 126 D3
Quequén, *Argentina* 126 D4
Querco, *Peru* 124 C3
Querétaro, *Mexico* 114 C4
Querétaro □, *Mexico* 114 C5
Querfurt, *Germany* 18 D7
Quesada, *Spain* 29 H1
Queshan, *China* 50 H8
Quesnel, *Canada* 100 C4
Quesnel →, *Canada* 100 C4
Quesnel L., *Canada* 100 C4
Questa, *U.S.A.* 111 H11
Questembert, *France* 24 E4
Quetena, *Bolivia* 124 E4
Quetico Prov. Park, *Canada* 98 C1
Quetrequile, *Argentina* 128 B3
Quetta, *Pakistan* 62 D2
Quevedo, *Ecuador* 120 D2
Quezaltenango, *Guatemala* 116 D1
Quezon City, *Phil.* 55 D4
Qufār, *Si. Arabia* 64 E4
Qui Nhon, *Vietnam* 58 F7
Quibaxe, *Angola* 80 F2
Quibdo, *Colombia* 120 B2
Quiberon, *France* 24 E3
Quíbor, *Venezuela* 120 B4
Quick, *Canada* 100 C3
Quickborn, *Germany* 18 B5
Quiet L., *Canada* 100 A2
Quiévrain, *Belgium* 17 H3
Quiindy, *Paraguay* 126 B4
Quila, *Mexico* 114 C3
Quilán, C., *Chile* 128 B2
Quilcene, *U.S.A.* 112 C4
Quilengues, *Angola* 81 G2
Quilimarí, *Chile* 126 C1
Quilino, *Argentina* 126 C3
Quillabamba, *Peru* 124 C3
Quillacollo, *Bolivia* 124 D4
Quillagua, *Chile* 126 A2
Quillaicillo, *Chile* 126 C1
Quillan, *France* 26 F6
Quillebeuf-sur-Seine, *France* 24 C7
Quillota, *Chile* 126 C1
Quilmes, *Argentina* 126 C4
Quilon, *India* 60 Q10
Quilpie, *Australia* 91 D3
Quilpué, *Chile* 126 C1
Quilua, *Mozam.* 83 F4
Quime, *Bolivia* 124 D4
Quimilí, *Argentina* 126 B3
Quimper, *France* 24 D2
Quimperlé, *France* 24 E3
Quinault →, *U.S.A.* 112 C2
Quincemil, *Peru* 124 C3
Quincy, *Calif., U.S.A.* 112 F6
Quincy, *Fla., U.S.A.* 105 K3
Quincy, *Ill., U.S.A.* 108 F9
Quincy, *Mass., U.S.A.* 107 D14
Quincy, *Wash., U.S.A.* 110 C4
Quines, *Argentina* 126 C2
Quinga, *Mozam.* 83 F5
Quingey, *France* 25 E12
Quintana de la Serena, *Spain* 31 G5
Quintana Roo □, *Mexico* 115 D7
Quintanar de la Orden, *Spain* 28 F1
Quintanar de la Sierra, *Spain* 28 D2
Quintanar del Rey, *Spain* 29 F3
Quintero, *Chile* 126 C1
Quintin, *France* 24 D4
Quinto, *Spain* 28 D4
Quinyambie, *Australia* 91 E3
Quípar →, *Spain* 29 G3
Quipungo, *Angola* 81 G2
Quirihue, *Chile* 126 D1
Quirindi, *Australia* 91 E5
Quiroga, *Spain* 30 C3
Quiruvilca, *Peru* 124 B2
Quissac, *France* 27 E8
Quissanga, *Mozam.* 83 E5
Quitilipi, *Argentina* 126 B3
Quitman, *Ga., U.S.A.* 105 K4
Quitman, *Miss., U.S.A.* 105 J1
Quitman, *Tex., U.S.A.* 109 J7
Quito, *Ecuador* 120 D2
Quixadá, *Brazil* 122 B4
Quixaxe, *Mozam.* 83 F5
Quixeramobim, *Brazil* 122 C4
Qujing, *China* 52 E4
Qul'ân, Jazâ'ir, *Egypt* 76 C4
Qumbu, *S. Africa* 85 E4
Quneitra, *Syria* 69 B4
Quoin I., *Australia* 88 B4
Quoin Pt., *S. Africa* 84 E2
Quondong, *Australia* 91 E3
Quorn, *Australia* 91 E2
Qurein, *Sudan* 77 E3
Qurnat as Sawdā', *Lebanon* 69 A5
Qûs, *Egypt* 76 B3
Qusaybah, *Iraq* 64 C4
Quseir, *Egypt* 76 B3
Qūshchī, *Iran* 64 B5
Quthing, *Lesotho* 85 E4
Qūţīābād, *Iran* 65 C6
Quwo, *China* 50 G6
Quyang, *China* 50 E8
Quynh Nhai, *Vietnam* 58 B4
Quzi, *China* 50 F4
Qytet Stalin, *Albania* 39 J2

R

Ra, Ko, *Thailand* 59 H2
Råå, *Sweden* 11 J6
Raahe, *Finland* 8 D18
Raalte, *Neths.* 16 D8
Raamsdonksveer, *Neths.* 17 E5
Raasay, *U.K.* 14 D2
Raasay, Sd. of, *U.K.* 14 D2
Rab, *Croatia* 33 D11
Raba, *Indonesia* 57 F5
Rába →, *Hungary* 21 H7
Rabaçal →, *Portugal* 30 D3
Rabah, *Nigeria* 79 C6
Rabai, *Kenya* 82 C4
Rabastens, *France* 26 E5
Rabastens-de-Bigorre, *France* 26 E4
Rabat, *Malta* 37 D1
Rabat, *Morocco* 74 B3
Rabaul, *Papua N. G.* 92 H7
Rabbit →, *Canada* 100 B3
Rabbit Lake, *Canada* 101 C7
Rabbitskin →, *Canada* 100 A4

Rabka, Poland	20	F9	
Rābor, Iran	65	D8	
Rácale, Italy	35	C11	
Racalmuto, Italy	34	E6	
Racconigi, Italy	32	D4	
Race, C., Canada	99	C9	
Rach Gia, Vietnam	59	G5	
Raciąż, Poland	20	C10	
Racibórz, Poland	20	E8	
Racine, U.S.A.	104	D2	
Rackerby, U.S.A.	112	F5	
Radama, Nosy, Madag.	85	A8	
Radama, Saikanosy, Madag.	85	A8	
Rădăuţi, Romania	38	B8	
Radbuza →, Czech.	20	F3	
Radeburg, Germany	18	D9	
Radeče, Slovenia	33	B12	
Radekhov, Ukraine	40	F4	
Radford, U.S.A.	104	G5	
Radhanpur, India	62	H4	
Radiska →, Macedonia, Yug.	39	H3	
Radisson, Canada	101	C7	
Radium Hot Springs, Canada	100	C5	
Radna, Romania	38	C4	
Radnor Forest, U.K.	13	E4	
Radolfzell, Germany	19	H4	
Radom, Poland	20	D11	
Radomir, Bulgaria	38	G6	
Radomsko, Poland	20	D9	
Radomyshl, Ukraine	40	F6	
Radoviš, Macedonia, Yug.	39	H5	
Radovljica, Slovenia	33	B11	
Radstock, U.K.	13	F5	
Radstock, C., Australia	91	E1	
Răducăneni, Romania	38	C10	
Radviliškis, Lithuania	40	D3	
Radville, Canada	101	D8	
Rae, Canada	100	A5	
Rae Bareli, India	63	F9	
Rae Isthmus, Canada	97	B11	
Raeren, Belgium	17	G8	
Raeside, L., Australia	89	E3	
Raetihi, N.Z.	87	H5	
Rafaela, Argentina	126	C3	
Rafah, Egypt	69	D3	
Rafai, C.A.R.	82	B1	
Raffadali, Italy	34	E6	
Rafḥā, Si. Arabia	64	D4	
Rafsanjān, Iran	65	D8	
Raft Pt., Australia	88	C3	
Ragag, Sudan	77	E1	
Ragama, Sri Lanka	60	R11	
Ragged, Mt., Australia	89	F3	
Raglan, Australia	90	C5	
Raglan, N.Z.	87	G5	
Ragunda, Sweden	10	A10	
Ragusa, Italy	35	F7	
Raha, Indonesia	57	E6	
Rahad, Nahr ed →, Sudan	77	E3	
Rahad al Bardī, Sudan	77	F9	
Rahaeng = Tak, Thailand	58	D2	
Rahden, Germany	18	C4	
Raheita, Ethiopia	77	E5	
Raḥīmah, Si. Arabia	65	E6	
Rahimyar Khan, Pakistan	62	E4	
Rāhjerd, Iran	65	C6	
Raichur, India	60	L10	
Raiganj, India	63	G13	
Raigarh, India	61	J13	
Raijua, Indonesia	57	F6	
Railton, Australia	90	G4	
Rainbow Lake, Canada	100	B5	
Rainier, U.S.A.	112	D4	
Rainier, Mt., U.S.A.	112	D5	
Rainy L., Canada	101	D10	
Rainy River, Canada	101	D10	
Raipur, India	61	J12	
Raj Nandgaon, India	61	J12	
Raja, Ujung, Indonesia	56	D1	
Raja Ampat, Kepulauan, Indonesia	57	E7	
Rajahmundry, India	61	L12	
Rajajooseppi, Finland	8	B20	
Rajang →, Malaysia	56	D4	
Rajapalaiyam, India	60	Q10	
Rajasthan □, India	62	F5	
Rajasthan Canal, India	62	E5	
Rajauri, India	63	C6	
Rajgarh, Mad. P., India	62	G7	
Rajgarh, Raj., India	62	F6	
Rajhenburg, Slovenia	33	B12	
Rajkot, India	62	H4	
Rajmahal Hills, India	63	G12	
Rajpipla, India	60	J8	
Rajpura, India	62	D7	
Rajshahi, Bangla.	61	G16	
Rajshahi □, Bangla.	63	G13	
Rakaia, N.Z.	87	K4	
Rakaia →, N.Z.	87	K4	
Rakan, Ra's, Qatar	65	E6	
Rakaposhi, Pakistan	63	A6	
Rakata, Pulau, Indonesia	56	F3	
Rakhni, Pakistan	62	D3	
Rakitnoye, Russia	48	B7	
Rakkestad, Norway	10	E5	
Rakops, Botswana	84	C3	
Rákospalota, Hungary	21	H9	
Rakov, Belorussia	40	E5	
Rakovica, Croatia	33	D12	
Rakovník, Czech.	20	E3	
Rakovski, Bulgaria	38	G7	
Rakvere, Estonia	40	B5	
Raleigh, U.S.A.	105	H6	
Raleigh B., U.S.A.	105	H7	
Ralja, Serbia, Yug.	21	L10	
Ralls, U.S.A.	109	J4	
Ram →, Canada	100	A4	
Rām Allāh, Jordan	69	D4	
Ram Hd., Australia	91	F4	
Rama, Nic.	116	D3	
Ramacca, Italy	35	E7	
Ramales de la Victoria, Spain	28	B1	
Ramalho, Serra do, Brazil	123	D3	
Raman, Thailand	59	J3	
Ramanathapuram, India	60	Q11	
Ramanetaka, B. de, Madag.	85	A8	
Ramat Gan, Israel	69	C3	
Ramatlhabama, S. Africa	84	D4	
Ramban, India	63	C6	
Rambervillers, France	25	D13	
Rambipuji, Indonesia	57	H15	
Rambouillet, France	25	D8	
Ramea, Canada	99	C8	
Ramechhap, Nepal	63	F12	
Ramelau, Indonesia	57	F7	
Ramenskoye, Russia	41	D11	
Ramgarh, Bihar, India	63	H11	
Ramgarh, Raj., India	62	F6	
Ramgarh, Raj., India	62	F4	
Rāmhormoz, Iran	65	D6	
Ramīān, Iran	65	B7	
Ramingining, Australia	90	A2	
Ramla, Israel	69	D3	
Ramlu, Ethiopia	77	E5	
Ramme, Denmark	11	H2	
Ramnad = Ramanathapuram, India	60	Q11	
Ramnagar, India	63	C6	
Ramnäs, Sweden	10	E10	
Ramon, Russia	41	F11	
Ramona, U.S.A.	113	M10	
Ramore, Canada	98	C3	
Ramotswa, Botswana	84	C4	
Rampur, H.P., India	62	D7	
Rampur, Mad. P., India	62	H5	
Rampur, Ut. P., India	63	E8	
Rampur Hat, India	63	G12	
Rampura, India	62	G6	
Ramree Kyun, Burma	61	K18	
Rāmsar, Iran	65	B6	
Ramsel, Belgium	17	F5	
Ramsey, Canada	98	C3	
Ramsey, U.K.	12	C3	
Ramsgate, U.K.	13	F9	
Ramsjö, Sweden	10	B9	
Ramtek, India	60	J11	
Ramvik, Sweden	10	B11	
Ranaghat, India	63	H13	
Ranahu, Pakistan	62	G3	
Ranau, Malaysia	56	C5	
Rancagua, Chile	126	C1	
Rance, Belgium	17	H4	
Rance →, France	24	D5	
Rance, Barrage de la, France	24	D4	
Rancharia, Brazil	123	F1	
Rancheria →, Canada	100	A3	
Ranchester, U.S.A.	110	D10	
Ranchi, India	63	H11	
Ranco, L., Chile	128	B2	
Randan, France	26	B7	
Randazzo, Italy	35	E7	
Randers, Denmark	11	H4	
Randers Fjord, Denmark	11	H4	
Randfontein, S. Africa	85	D4	
Randle, U.S.A.	112	D5	
Randolph, Mass., U.S.A.	107	D13	
Randolph, N.Y., U.S.A.	106	D6	
Randolph, Utah, U.S.A.	110	F8	
Randolph, Vt., U.S.A.	107	C12	
Randsfjord, Norway	10	D4	
Råne älv →, Sweden	8	D17	
Rangae, Thailand	59	J3	
Rangaunu B., N.Z.	87	F4	
Rångedala, Sweden	11	G7	
Rangeley, U.S.A.	107	B14	
Rangely, U.S.A.	110	F9	
Ranger, U.S.A.	109	J5	
Rangia, India	61	F17	
Rangiora, N.Z.	87	K4	
Rangitaiki →, N.Z.	87	G6	
Rangitata →, N.Z.	87	K3	
Rangkasbitung, Indonesia	57	G12	
Rangon →, Burma	61	L20	
Rangoon, Burma	61	L20	
Rangpur, Bangla.	61	G16	
Rangsit, Thailand	58	F3	
Ranibennur, India	60	M9	
Raniganj, India	63	H12	
Raniwara, India	60	G8	
Rāniyah, Iraq	64	B5	
Ranken →, Australia	90	C2	
Rankin, U.S.A.	109	K4	
Rankin Inlet, Canada	96	B10	
Rankins Springs, Australia	91	E4	
Rannoch, U.K.	14	E4	
Rannoch Moor, U.K.	14	E4	
Ranobe, Helodranon' i, Madag.	85	C7	
Ranohira, Madag.	85	C8	
Ranomafana, Toamasina, Madag.	85	B8	
Ranomafana, Toliara, Madag.	85	C8	
Ranong, Thailand	59	H2	
Rānsa, Iran	65	C6	
Ransiki, Indonesia	57	E8	
Rantau, Indonesia	56	E5	
Rantauprapat, Indonesia	56	D1	
Rantekombola, Indonesia	57	E5	
Rantoul, U.S.A.	104	E1	
Ranum, Denmark	11	H3	
Raon l'Étape, France	25	D13	
Raoui, Erg er, Algeria	75	C4	
Raoyang, China	50	E8	
Rapa, Pac. Oc.	93	K13	
Rapallo, Italy	32	D6	
Rāpch, Iran	65	E8	
Rapid →, Canada	100	B3	
Rapid City, U.S.A.	108	D3	
Rapid River, U.S.A.	104	C2	
Rapides des Joachims, Canada	98	C4	
Rapla, Estonia	40	B4	
Rapperswil, Switz.	23	B7	
Rapu Rapu I., Phil.	55	E6	
Rarotonga, Cook Is.	93	K12	
Ra's al' Ayn, Syria	64	B4	
Ra's al Khaymah, U.A.E.	65	E8	
Ra's al-Unuf, Libya	73	B8	
Ra's an Naqb, Jordan	69	F4	
Ras Bânâs, Egypt	76	C4	
Ras Dashen, Ethiopia	77	E4	
Ras el Ma, Algeria	75	B4	
Ras Mallap, Egypt	76	J8	
Rās Timirist, Mauritania	78	B1	
Rasa, Punta, Argentina	128	B4	
Rasca, Pta. de la, Canary Is.	36	G3	
Raseiniai, Lithuania	40	D3	
Rashad, Sudan	77	E3	
Rashīd, Egypt	76	H7	
Rashīd, Masabb, Egypt	76	H7	
Rasht, Iran	65	B6	
Rasi Salai, Thailand	58	E5	
Raška, Serbia, Yug.	21	M10	
Rason L., Australia	89	E3	
Rasova, Romania	38	E10	
Rasra, India	63	G10	
Rass el Oued, Algeria	75	A6	
Rasskazovo, Russia	41	E12	
Rastatt, Germany	19	G4	
Rat Buri, Thailand	58	F2	
Rat Is., U.S.A.	96	C1	
Rat River, Canada	100	A4	
Ratangarh, India	62	E6	
Raṭāwī, Iraq	64	D5	
Rath, India	63	G8	
Rath Luirc, Ireland	15	D3	
Rathdrum, Ireland	15	D5	
Rathenow, Germany	18	C8	
Rathkeale, Ireland	15	D3	
Rathlin, U.K.	15	A5	
Rathlin O'Birne I., Ireland	15	B3	
Ratibor = Racibórz, Poland	20	E8	
Ratlam, India	62	H6	
Ratnagiri, India	60	L8	
Raton, U.S.A.	109	G2	
Rattaphum, Thailand	59	J3	
Rattray Hd., U.K.	14	D7	
Ratz, Mt., Canada	100	B2	
Ratzeburg, Germany	18	B6	
Raub, Malaysia	59	L3	
Rauch, Argentina	126	D4	
Raufarhöfn, Iceland	8	C6	
Raufoss, Norway	10	D4	
Raukumara Ra., N.Z.	87	H6	
Raul Soares, Brazil	123	F3	
Rauland, Norway	10	E2	
Rauma, Finland	9	F16	
Rauma →, Norway	10	B1	
Raurkela, India	63	H11	
Rausu-Dake, Japan	48	B12	
Rava Russkaya, Ukraine	40	F3	
Ravānsar, Iran	64	C5	
Ravanusa, Italy	34	E6	
Rāvar, Iran	65	D8	
Ravels, Belgium	17	F6	
Ravena, U.S.A.	107	D11	
Ravenna, Italy	33	D9	
Ravenna, Nebr., U.S.A.	108	E5	
Ravenna, Ohio, U.S.A.	106	E3	
Ravensburg, Germany	19	H5	
Ravenshoe, Australia	90	B4	
Ravenstein, Neths.	16	E7	
Ravensthorpe, Australia	89	F3	
Ravenswood, Australia	90	C4	
Ravenswood, U.S.A.	104	F5	
Ravi →, Pakistan	62	D4	
Ravna Gora, Croatia	33	C11	
Rawa Mazowiecka, Poland	20	D10	
Rawalpindi, Pakistan	62	C5	
Rawāndūz, Iraq	64	B5	
Rawang, Malaysia	59	L3	
Rawdon, Canada	98	C5	
Rawene, N.Z.	87	F4	
Rawicz, Poland	20	D6	
Rawlinna, Australia	89	F4	
Rawlins, U.S.A.	110	F10	
Rawlinson Ra., Australia	89	D4	
Rawson, Argentina	128	B3	
Ray, U.S.A.	108	A3	
Ray, C., Canada	99	C8	
Rayadurg, India	60	M10	
Rayagada, India	61	K13	
Raychikhinsk, Russia	45	E13	
Rāyen, Iran	65	D8	
Raymond, Canada	100	D6	
Raymond, Calif., U.S.A.	112	H7	
Raymond, Wash., U.S.A.	112	D3	
Raymondville, U.S.A.	109	M6	
Raymore, Canada	101	C8	
Rayne, U.S.A.	109	K8	
Rayón, Mexico	114	B2	
Rayong, Thailand	58	F3	
Rayville, U.S.A.	109	J9	
Raz, Pte. du, France	24	D2	
Razan, Iran	65	C6	
Ražana, Serbia, Yug.	21	L9	
Ražanj, Serbia, Yug.	21	M11	
Razdel'naya, Ukraine	42	C4	
Razdolnoye, Russia	48	C5	
Razdolnoye, Ukraine	42	D5	
Razeh, Iran	65	C6	
Razelm, Lacul, Romania	38	E12	
Razgrad, Bulgaria	38	F9	
Razmak, Pakistan	62	C3	
Ré, I. de, France	26	B2	
Reading, U.K.	13	F7	
Reading, U.S.A.	107	F9	
Real, Cordillera, Bolivia	124	D4	
Realicó, Argentina	126	D3	
Réalmont, France	26	E6	
Reata, Mexico	114	B4	
Rebais, France	25	D10	
Rebecca, L., Australia	89	F3	
Rebi, Indonesia	57	F8	
Rebiana, Libya	73	D9	
Rebun-Tō, Japan	48	B10	
Recanati, Italy	33	E10	
Recaş, Romania	38	D4	
Recherche, Arch. of the, Australia	89	F3	
Rechitsa, Belorussia	40	E7	
Recht, Belgium	17	H8	
Recife, Brazil	122	C5	
Recklinghausen, Germany	17	E10	
Reconquista, Argentina	126	B4	
Recreio, Brazil	125	B6	
Recreo, Argentina	126	B2	
Recuay, Peru	124	B2	
Red →, N. Amer.	108	A6	
Red →, U.S.A.	109	K9	
Red Bank, U.S.A.	107	F10	
Red Bay, Canada	99	B8	
Red Bluff, U.S.A.	110	F2	
Red Bluff L., U.S.A.	109	K3	
Red Cliffs, Australia	91	E3	
Red Cloud, U.S.A.	108	E5	
Red Deer, Canada	100	C6	
Red Deer →, Alta., Canada	101	C6	
Red Deer →, Man., Canada	101	C8	
Red Deer L., Canada	101	C8	
Red Indian L., Canada	99	C8	
Red Lake, Canada	101	C10	
Red Lake Falls, U.S.A.	108	B6	
Red Lodge, U.S.A.	110	D9	
Red Mountain, U.S.A.	113	K9	
Red Oak, U.S.A.	108	E7	
Red Rock, Canada	98	C2	
Red Rock, L., U.S.A.	108	E8	
Red Rocks Pt., Australia	89	F4	
Red Sea, Asia	68	C2	
Red Slate Mt., U.S.A.	112	H8	
Red Sucker L., Canada	101	C10	
Red Tower Pass = Turnu Roşu Pasul, Romania	38	D7	
Red Wing, U.S.A.	108	C8	
Rédange, Lux.	17	J7	
Redbridge, U.K.	13	F8	
Redcar, U.K.	12	C6	
Redcliff, Canada	101	C6	
Redcliffe, Australia	91	D5	
Redcliffe, Mt., Australia	89	E3	
Reddersburg, S. Africa	84	D4	
Redding, U.S.A.	110	F2	
Redditch, U.K.	13	E6	
Redenção, Brazil	122	B4	
Redeye →, Canada	100	A5	
Redfield, U.S.A.	108	C5	
Redknife →, Canada	100	A5	
Redlands, U.S.A.	113	M9	
Redmond, Australia	89	F2	
Redmond, Oreg., U.S.A.	110	D3	
Redmond, Wash., U.S.A.	112	C4	
Redon, France	24	E4	
Redonda, Antigua	117	C7	
Redondela, Spain	30	C2	
Redondo, Portugal	31	G3	
Redondo Beach, U.S.A.	113	M8	
Redrock Pt., Canada	100	A5	
Redruth, U.K.	13	G2	
Redvers, Canada	101	D8	
Redwater, Canada	100	C6	
Redwood, U.S.A.	107	B9	
Redwood City, U.S.A.	111	H2	
Redwood Falls, U.S.A.	108	C7	
Ree, L., Ireland	15	C4	
Reed, L., Canada	101	C8	
Reed City, U.S.A.	104	D3	
Reeder, U.S.A.	108	B3	
Reedley, U.S.A.	111	H4	
Reedsburg, U.S.A.	108	D9	
Reedsport, U.S.A.	110	E1	
Reefton, N.Z.	87	K3	
Refahiye, Turkey	67	D8	
Refugio, U.S.A.	109	L6	
Rega →, Poland	20	A5	
Regalbuto, Italy	35	E7	
Regen, Germany	19	G9	
Regen →, Germany	19	F8	
Regeneração, Brazil	122	C3	
Regensburg, Germany	19	F8	
Regensdorf, Switz.	23	B6	
Réggio di Calábria, Italy	35	D8	
Réggio nell' Emilia, Italy	32	D7	
Regina, Canada	101	C8	
Régina, Fr. Guiana	121	C7	
Registro, Brazil	127	A6	
Reguengos de Monsaraz, Portugal	31	G3	
Rehar →, India	63	H10	
Rehoboth, Namibia	84	C2	
Rehovot, Israel	69	D3	
Rei-Bouba, Cameroon	73	G7	
Reichenbach, Germany	18	E8	
Reichenbach, Switz.	22	C5	
Reid, Australia	89	F4	
Reid River, Australia	90	B4	
Reiden, Switz.	22	B5	
Reidsville, U.S.A.	105	G6	
Reigate, U.K.	13	F7	
Reillo, Spain	28	F3	
Reims, France	25	C11	
Reina Adelaida, Arch., Chile	128	D2	
Reinach, Aargau, Switz.	22	B6	
Reinach, Basel, Switz.	22	B5	
Reinbeck, U.S.A.	108	D8	
Reindeer →, Canada	101	B8	
Reindeer I., Canada	101	C9	
Reindeer L., Canada	101	B8	
Reinga, C., N.Z.	87	F4	
Reinosa, Spain	30	B6	
Reinosa, Paso, Spain	30	C6	
Reitdiep, Neths.	16	B8	
Reitz, S. Africa	85	D4	
Reivilo, S. Africa	84	D3	
Rejmyre, Sweden	11	F9	
Reka →, Slovenia	33	C11	
Rekinniki, Russia	45	C17	
Reliance, Canada	101	A7	
Remad, Oued →, Algeria	75	B4	
Rémalard, France	24	D7	
Remarkable, Mt., Australia	91	E2	
Rembang, Indonesia	57	G14	
Remchi, Algeria	75	A4	
Remedios, Colombia	120	B3	
Remedios, Panama	116	E3	
Remeshk, Iran	65	E8	
Remich, Lux.	17	J8	
Rémire, Fr. Guiana	121	C7	
Remiremont, France	25	D13	
Remo, Ethiopia	77	F5	
Remontnoye, Russia	43	C10	
Remoulins, France	27	E8	
Remscheid, Germany	18	D3	
Ren Xian, China	50	F8	
Renascença, Brazil	120	D4	
Rende, Italy	35	C9	
Rendeux, Belgium	17	H7	
Rendína, Greece	39	K4	
Rendsburg, Germany	18	A5	
Rene, Russia	45	C19	
Renfrew, Canada	98	C4	
Renfrew, U.K.	14	F4	
Rengat, Indonesia	56	E2	
Rengo, Chile	126	C1	
Renhua, China	53	E9	
Renhuai, China	52	D6	
Reni, Moldavia	42	D3	
Renk, Sudan	77	E3	
Renkum, Neths.	16	E7	
Renmark, Australia	91	E3	
Rennell Sd., Canada	100	C2	
Renner Springs T.O., Australia	90	B1	
Rennes, France	24	D5	
Rennes, Bassin de, France	24	E5	
Reno, U.S.A.	112	F7	
Reno →, Italy	33	D9	
Renovo, U.S.A.	106	E7	
Renqiu, China	50	E9	
Rensselaer, Ind., U.S.A.	104	E2	
Rensselaer, N.Y., U.S.A.	107	D11	
Rentería, Spain	28	B3	
Renton, U.S.A.	112	C4	
Réo, Burkina Faso	78	C4	
Reotipur, India	63	G10	
Republic, Mich., U.S.A.	104	B2	
Republic, Wash., U.S.A.	110	B4	
Republican →, U.S.A.	108	F6	
Republican City, U.S.A.	108	E5	
Republiek, Surinam	121	B6	
Repulse Bay, Canada	97	B11	
Requena, Peru	124	B3	
Requena, Spain	29	F3	
Resadiye = Datça, Turkey	66	E2	
Reşadiye, Turkey	66	C7	
Resele, Sweden	10	A11	
Reserve, Canada	101	C8	
Reserve, U.S.A.	111	K9	
Resht = Rasht, Iran	65	B6	
Resistencia, Argentina	126	B4	
Reşiţa, Romania	38	D4	
Resolution I., Canada	97	B13	
Resolution I., N.Z.	87	L1	
Resplandes, Brazil	122	C2	
Resplendor, Brazil	123	E3	
Ressano Garcia, Mozam.	85	D5	
Reston, Canada	101	D8	
Retalhuleu, Guatemala	116	D1	
Reteag, Romania	38	B7	
Retenue, L. de, Zaïre	83	E2	

Rethel

Rethel, *France* 25 C11
Rethem, *Germany* 18 C5
Réthímnon, *Greece* 37 D6
Réthímnon □, *Greece* 37 D6
Retiche, Alpi, *Switz.* 23 D10
Retie, *Belgium* 17 F6
Retiers, *France* 24 E5
Retortillo, *Spain* 30 E4
Reuland, *Belgium* 17 H8
Réunion ■, *Ind. Oc.* 3 F12
Reus, *Spain* 28 D6
Reusel, *Neths.* 17 F6
Reuss →, *Switz.* 23 B6
Reutlingen, *Germany* 19 G5
Reutte, *Austria* 19 H6
Reuver, *Neths.* 17 F8
Reval = Tallinn, *Estonia* 40 B4
Revel, *France* 26 E6
Revelganj, *India* 63 G11
Revelstoke, *Canada* 100 C5
Reventazón, *Peru* 124 B1
Revigny-sur-Ornain, *France* 25 D11
Revilla Gigedo, Is., *Pac. Oc.* 93 F16
Revillagigedo I., *U.S.A.* 100 B2
Revin, *France* 25 C11
Revuè →, *Mozam.* 83 F3
Rewa, *India* 63 G9
Rewa →, *Guyana* 121 C6
Rewari, *India* 62 E7
Rexburg, *U.S.A.* 110 E8
Rey, *Iran* 65 C6
Rey, Rio del →, *Nigeria* 79 E6
Rey Malabo, *Eq. Guin.* 79 E6
Reyes, *Bolivia* 124 C4
Reyes, Pt., *U.S.A.* 112 H3
Reykjahlið, *Iceland* 8 D5
Reykjanes, *Iceland* 8 E2
Reykjavík, *Iceland* 8 D3
Reynolds, *Canada* 101 D9
Reynolds Ra., *Australia* 88 D5
Reynoldsville, *U.S.A.* 106 E6
Reynosa, *Mexico* 115 B5
Rezekne, *Latvia* 40 C5
Rezvān, *Iran* 65 E8
Rharis, O. →, *Algeria* 75 C6
Rhayader, *U.K.* 13 E4
Rheden, *Neths.* 16 D8
Rhein, *Canada* 101 C8
Rhein →, *Europe* 16 E8
Rhein-Main-Donau-Kanal, *Germany* 19 F7
Rheinbach, *Germany* 18 E2
Rheine, *Germany* 18 C3
Rheineck, *Switz.* 23 B9
Rheinfelden, *Switz.* 22 A5
Rheinland-Pfalz □, *Germany* 19 E2
Rheinsberg, *Germany* 18 B8
Rheinwaldhorn, *Switz.* 23 D8
Rhenen, *Neths.* 16 E7
Rheriss, Oued →, *Morocco* 74 B4
Rheydt, *Germany* 18 D2
Rhin = Rhein →, *Europe* 16 E8
Rhinau, *France* 25 D14
Rhine = Rhein →, *Europe* 16 E8
Rhineland-Palatinate □ = Rheinland-Pfalz □, *Germany* 19 E2
Rhinelander, *U.S.A.* 108 C10
Rhino Camp, *Uganda* 82 B3
Rhir, Cap, *Morocco* 74 B3
Rhisnes, *Belgium* 17 G5
Rho, *Italy* 32 C6
Rhode Island □, *U.S.A.* 107 E13
Rhodes = Ródhos, *Greece* 37 C10
Rhodesia = Zimbabwe ■, *Africa* 83 F2
Rhodope Mts. = Rhodopi Planina, *Bulgaria* 39 H7
Rhodopi Planina, *Bulgaria* 39 H7
Rhondda, *U.K.* 13 F4
Rhône □, *France* 27 C8
Rhône →, *France* 27 E8
Rhum, *U.K.* 14 E2
Rhyl, *U.K.* 12 D4
Rhymney, *U.K.* 13 F4
Ri-Aba, *Eq. Guin.* 79 E6
Riachão, *Brazil* 122 C2
Riacho de Santana, *Brazil* 123 D3
Rialma, *Brazil* 123 E2
Riaño, *Spain* 30 C5
Rians, *France* 27 E9
Riansares →, *Spain* 28 F1
Riasi, *India* 63 C6
Riau □, *Indonesia* 56 D2
Riau, Kepulauan, *Indonesia* 56 D2
Riau Arch. = Riau, Kepulauan, *Indonesia* 56 D2
Riaza, *Spain* 28 D1
Riaza →, *Spain* 28 D1
Riba de Saelices, *Spain* 28 E2
Ribadavia, *Spain* 30 C2
Ribadeo, *Spain* 30 B3
Ribadesella, *Spain* 30 B5
Ribamar, *Brazil* 122 B3
Ribas, *Spain* 28 C7
Ribas do Rio Pardo, *Brazil* 125 E7
Ribble →, *U.K.* 12 C5
Ribe, *Denmark* 11 J2
Ribeauvillé, *France* 25 D14
Ribécourt, *France* 25 C9
Ribeira, *Spain* 30 C2
Ribeira Brava, *Madeira* 36 D2
Ribeira do Pombal, *Brazil* 122 D4
Ribeirão Prêto, *Brazil* 127 A6
Ribeiro Gonçalves, *Brazil* 122 C2
Ribemont, *France* 25 C10
Ribera, *Italy* 34 E6
Ribérac, *France* 26 C4
Riberalta, *Bolivia* 125 C4
Ribnica, *Slovenia* 33 C11
Ribnitz-Damgarten, *Germany* 18 A8
Riccarton, *N.Z.* 87 K4
Riccia, *Italy* 35 A7
Riccione, *Italy* 33 D9
Rice, *U.S.A.* 113 L12
Rice L., *Canada* 106 B6
Rice Lake, *U.S.A.* 108 C9
Rich, *Morocco* 74 B4
Rich Hill, *U.S.A.* 109 F7
Richards Bay, *S. Africa* 85 D5
Richards L., *Canada* 101 B7
Richardson →, *Canada* 101 B6
Richardson Springs, *U.S.A.* 112 F5
Richardton, *U.S.A.* 108 B3
Riche, C., *Australia* 89 F2
Richelieu, *France* 24 E7
Richey, *U.S.A.* 108 B2
Richfield, *Idaho, U.S.A.* 110 E6
Richfield, *Utah, U.S.A.* 111 G8
Richford, *U.S.A.* 107 B12
Richibucto, *Canada* 99 C7
Richland, *Ga., U.S.A.* 105 J3
Richland, *Oreg., U.S.A.* 110 D5
Richland, *Wash., U.S.A.* 110 C4
Richland Center, *U.S.A.* 108 D9
Richlands, *U.S.A.* 104 G5
Richmond, *N.S.W., Australia* 91 E5
Richmond, *Queens., Australia* 90 C3
Richmond, *N.Z.* 87 J4
Richmond, *S. Africa* 85 D5
Richmond, *U.K.* 12 C6
Richmond, *Calif., U.S.A.* 112 H4
Richmond, *Ind., U.S.A.* 104 F3
Richmond, *Ky., U.S.A.* 104 G3
Richmond, *Mich., U.S.A.* 106 D2
Richmond, *Mo., U.S.A.* 108 F8
Richmond, *Tex., U.S.A.* 109 L7
Richmond, *Utah, U.S.A.* 110 F8
Richmond, *Va., U.S.A.* 104 G7
Richmond Ra., *Australia* 91 D5
Richmond-upon-Thames, *U.K.* 13 F7
Richterswil, *Switz.* 23 B7
Richton, *U.S.A.* 105 K1
Richwood, *U.S.A.* 104 F5
Ricla, *Spain* 28 D3
Ridder, *Kazakhstan* 44 D9
Ridderkerk, *Neths.* 16 E5
Riddes, *Switz.* 22 D4
Ridgecrest, *U.S.A.* 113 K9
Ridgedale, *Canada* 101 C8
Ridgefield, *U.S.A.* 112 E4
Ridgeland, *U.S.A.* 105 J5
Ridgelands, *Australia* 90 C5
Ridgetown, *Canada* 98 D3
Ridgewood, *U.S.A.* 107 F10
Ridgway, *U.S.A.* 106 E6
Riding Mountain Nat. Park, *Canada* 101 C8
Ridley, Mt., *Australia* 89 F3
Ried, *Austria* 21 G3
Riedlingen, *Germany* 19 G5
Riel, *Neths.* 17 E6
Rienza →, *Italy* 33 B8
Riesa, *Germany* 18 D9
Riesco, I., *Chile* 128 D2
Riesi, *Italy* 35 E7
Riet →, *S. Africa* 84 D3
Rieti, *Italy* 33 F9
Rieupeyroux, *France* 26 D6
Riez, *France* 27 E10
Riffe, L., *U.S.A.* 112 D4
Rifle, *U.S.A.* 110 G10
Rifstangi, *Iceland* 8 C5
Rift Valley □, *Kenya* 82 B4
Rig Rig, *Chad* 73 F7
Riga, *Latvia* 40 C4
Riga, G. of = Rīgas Jūras Līcis, *Latvia* 40 C3
Rīgān, *Iran* 65 D8
Rīgas Jūras Līcis, *Latvia* 40 C3
Rigaud, *Canada* 107 A10
Rigby, *U.S.A.* 110 E8
Rīgestān □, *Afghan.* 60 D4
Riggins, *U.S.A.* 110 D5
Rignac, *France* 26 D6
Rigolet, *Canada* 99 B8
Riihimäki, *Finland* 9 F18
Riiser-Larsen-halvøya, *Antarctica* 5 C4
Rijau, *Nigeria* 79 C6
Rijeka, *Croatia* 33 C11
Rijen, *Neths.* 17 E5
Rijkevorsel, *Belgium* 17 F5
Rijn →, *Neths.* 16 D4
Rijnsburg, *Neths.* 16 D4
Rijsbergen, *Neths.* 17 E5
Rijssen, *Neths.* 16 D9
Rijswijk, *Neths.* 16 D4
Rike, *Ethiopia* 77 E4
Rikuzentakada, *Japan* 48 E10
Rila Planina, *Bulgaria* 38 G6
Riley, *U.S.A.* 110 E4
Rima →, *Nigeria* 79 C6
Rimah, Wadi ar →, *Si. Arabia* 64 E4
Rimavská Sobota, *Czech.* 21 G10
Rimbey, *Canada* 100 C6
Rimbo, *Sweden* 10 E12
Rimi, *Nigeria* 79 C6
Rímini, *Italy* 33 D9
Rîmnicu Sărat, *Romania* 38 D10
Rîmnicu Vîlcea, *Romania* 38 D7
Rimouski, *Canada* 99 C6
Rimrock, *U.S.A.* 112 D5
Rinca, *Indonesia* 57 F5
Rincón de Romos, *Mexico* 114 C4
Rinconada, *Argentina* 126 A2
Ringarum, *Sweden* 11 F10
Ringe, *Denmark* 11 J4
Ringim, *Nigeria* 79 C6
Ringkøbing, *Denmark* 11 H2
Ringling, *U.S.A.* 110 C8
Ringsaker, *Norway* 10 D4
Ringsted, *Denmark* 11 J5
Ringvassøy, *Norway* 8 B15
Rinjani, *Indonesia* 56 F5
Rinteln, *Germany* 18 C5
Río, Punta del, *Spain* 29 J2
Rio Branco, *Brazil* 124 B4
Río Branco, *Uruguay* 127 C5
Rio Brilhante, *Brazil* 127 A5
Río Bueno, *Chile* 128 B2
Río Chico, *Venezuela* 120 A4
Rio Claro, *Brazil* 127 A6
Rio Claro, *Trin. & Tob.* 117 D7
Río Colorado, *Argentina* 128 A4
Río Cuarto, *Argentina* 126 C3
Rio das Pedras, *Mozam.* 85 C6
Rio de Contas, *Brazil* 123 D3
Rio de Janeiro, *Brazil* 123 F3
Rio de Janeiro □, *Brazil* 123 F3
Rio do Prado, *Brazil* 123 E3
Rio do Sul, *Brazil* 127 B6
Río Gallegos, *Argentina* 128 D3
Río Grande, *Argentina* 128 D3
Río Grande, *Bolivia* 124 E4
Rio Grande, *Brazil* 127 C5
Río Grande, *Mexico* 114 C4
Río Grande, *Nic.* 116 D3
Rio Grande →, *U.S.A.* 109 N6
Rio Grande City, *U.S.A.* 109 M5
Río Grande del Norte →, *N. Amer.* 103 E7
Rio Grande do Norte □, *Brazil* 122 C4
Rio Grande do Sul □, *Brazil* 127 C5
Río Hato, *Panama* 116 E3
Río Lagartos, *Mexico* 115 C7
Rio Largo, *Brazil* 122 C4
Rio Maior, *Portugal* 31 F2
Rio Marina, *Italy* 32 F7
Río Mayo, *Argentina* 128 C2
Río Mulatos, *Bolivia* 124 D4
Río Muni = Mbini □, *Eq. Guin.* 80 D2
Rio Negro, *Brazil* 127 B6
Río Negro, *Chile* 128 B2
Rio Negro, Pantanal do, *Brazil* 125 D6
Rio Pardo, *Brazil* 127 C5
Río Pico, *Argentina* 128 B2
Rio Real, *Brazil* 123 D4
Río Segundo, *Argentina* 126 C3
Río Tercero, *Argentina* 126 C3
Rio Tinto, *Brazil* 122 C4
Rio Tinto, *Portugal* 30 D2
Rio Verde, *Brazil* 123 E1
Río Verde, *Mexico* 115 C5
Rio Verde de Mato Grosso, *Brazil* 125 D7
Rio Vista, *U.S.A.* 112 G5
Ríobamba, *Ecuador* 120 D2
Ríohacha, *Colombia* 120 A3
Rioja, *Peru* 124 B2
Riom, *France* 26 C7
Riom-ès-Montagnes, *France* 26 C6
Rion-des-Landes, *France* 26 E3
Rionegro, *Colombia* 120 B2
Rionero in Vúlture, *Italy* 35 B8
Rioni →, *Georgia* 43 E9
Rios, *Spain* 30 D3
Riosucio, *Caldas, Colombia* 120 B2
Ríosucio, *Choco, Colombia* 120 B2
Riou L., *Canada* 101 B7
Rioz, *France* 25 E13
Riozinho →, *Brazil* 120 D4
Riparia, Dora →, *Italy* 32 C4
Ripatransone, *Italy* 33 F10
Ripley, *Canada* 106 B3
Ripley, *Calif., U.S.A.* 113 M12
Ripley, *N.Y., U.S.A.* 106 D5
Ripley, *Tenn., U.S.A.* 109 H10
Ripoll, *Spain* 28 C7
Ripon, *U.K.* 12 C6
Ripon, *Calif., U.S.A.* 112 H5
Ripon, *Wis., U.S.A.* 104 D1
Riposto, *Italy* 35 E8
Risalpur, *Pakistan* 62 B4
Risan, *Montenegro, Yug.* 21 N8
Risaralda □, *Colombia* 120 B2
Riscle, *France* 26 E3
Rishā', W. ar →, *Si. Arabia* 64 E5
Rishiri-Tō, *Japan* 48 B10
Rishon le Ẕiyyon, *Israel* 69 D3
Risle →, *France* 24 C7
Rison, *U.S.A.* 109 J8
Risør, *Norway* 11 F3
Rissani, *Morocco* 74 B4
Riti, *Nigeria* 79 D6
Rittman, *U.S.A.* 106 F3
Ritzville, *U.S.A.* 110 C4
Riva Bella, *France* 24 C6
Riva del Garda, *Italy* 32 C7
Rivadavia, *Buenos Aires, Argentina* 126 D3
Rivadavia, *Mendoza, Argentina* 126 C2
Rivadavia, *Salta, Argentina* 126 A3
Rivadavia, *Chile* 126 B1
Rivarolo Canavese, *Italy* 32 C4
Rivas, *Nic.* 116 D2
Rive-de-Gier, *France* 27 C8
River Cess, *Liberia* 78 D3
Rivera, *Uruguay* 127 C4
Riverdale, *U.S.A.* 112 J7
Riverdsale, *S. Africa* 84 E3
Riverhead, *U.S.A.* 107 F12
Riverhurst, *Canada* 101 C7
Riverina, *Australia* 89 E3
Rivers, *Canada* 101 C8
Rivers □, *Nigeria* 79 E6
Rivers, L. of the, *Canada* 101 D7
Rivers Inlet, *Canada* 100 C3
Riverside, *Calif., U.S.A.* 113 M9
Riverside, *Wyo., U.S.A.* 110 F10
Riversleigh, *Australia* 90 B2
Riverton, *Australia* 91 E2
Riverton, *Canada* 101 C9
Riverton, *N.Z.* 87 M1
Riverton, *U.S.A.* 110 E9
Riverton Heights, *U.S.A.* 112 C4
Rives, *France* 27 C9
Rivesaltes, *France* 26 F6
Riviera, *Europe* 32 E5
Rivière-à-Pierre, *Canada* 99 C5
Rivière-au-Renard, *Canada* 99 C7
Rivière-du-Loup, *Canada* 99 C6
Rivière-Pentecôte, *Canada* 99 C6
Rivière-Pilot, *Martinique* 117 D7
Rívoli, *Italy* 32 C4
Rivoli B., *Australia* 91 F3
Rixensart, *Belgium* 17 G5
Riyadh = Ar Riyāḍ, *Si. Arabia* 64 E5
Rize, *Turkey* 67 C9
Rize □, *Turkey* 67 C9
Rizhao, *China* 51 G10
Rizokarpaso, *Cyprus* 37 D13
Rizzuto, C., *Italy* 35 D10
Rjukan, *Norway* 10 E2
Roa, *Norway* 10 D4
Roa, *Spain* 30 D7
Road Town, *Virgin Is.* 117 C7
Roag, L., *U.K.* 14 C2
Roanne, *France* 27 B8
Roanoke, *Ala., U.S.A.* 105 J3
Roanoke, *Va., U.S.A.* 104 G6
Roanoke →, *U.S.A.* 105 H7
Roanoke I., *U.S.A.* 105 H8
Roanoke Rapids, *U.S.A.* 105 G7
Roatán, *Honduras* 116 C2
Robbins I., *Australia* 90 G4
Robe →, *Australia* 88 D2
Robe →, *Ireland* 15 C2
Röbel, *Germany* 18 B8
Robert Lee, *U.S.A.* 109 K4
Roberts, *U.S.A.* 110 E7
Robertsganj, *India* 63 G10
Robertson, *S. Africa* 84 E2
Robertson I., *Antarctica* 5 C18
Robertson Ra., *Australia* 88 D3
Robertsport, *Liberia* 78 D2
Robertstown, *Australia* 91 E2
Roberval, *Canada* 99 C5
Robeson Chan., *Greenland* 4 A4
Robinson →, *Australia* 90 B2
Robinson Ra., *Australia* 89 E2
Robinson River, *Australia* 90 B2
Robinvale, *Australia* 91 E3
Roblin, *Canada* 101 C8
Roboré, *Bolivia* 125 D6
Robson, Mt., *Canada* 100 C5
Robstown, *U.S.A.* 109 M6
Roca, C. da, *Portugal* 6 H4
Roca Partida, I., *Mexico* 114 D2
Rocas, I., *Brazil* 122 B5
Rocca d'Aspidé, *Italy* 35 B8
Rocca San Casciano, *Italy* 33 D8
Roccalbegna, *Italy* 33 F8
Roccastrada, *Italy* 33 F8
Roccella Iónica, *Italy* 35 D9
Rocha, *Uruguay* 127 C5
Rochdale, *U.K.* 12 D5
Rochechouart, *France* 26 C4
Rochedo, *Brazil* 125 D7
Rochefort, *Belgium* 17 H6
Rochefort, *France* 26 C3
Rochefort-en-Terre, *France* 24 E4
Rochelle, *U.S.A.* 108 E10
Rocher River, *Canada* 100 A6
Rocherath, *Belgium* 17 H8
Rocheservière, *France* 24 F5
Rochester, *Canada* 100 C6
Rochester, *U.K.* 13 F8
Rochester, *Ind., U.S.A.* 104 E2
Rochester, *Minn., U.S.A.* 108 C8
Rochester, *N.H., U.S.A.* 107 C14
Rochester, *N.Y., U.S.A.* 106 C7
Rociana, *Spain* 31 H4
Rociu, *Romania* 38 E8
Rock →, *Canada* 100 A3
Rock Hill, *U.S.A.* 105 H5
Rock Island, *U.S.A.* 108 E9
Rock Rapids, *U.S.A.* 108 D6
Rock River, *U.S.A.* 110 F11
Rock Sound, *Bahamas* 116 B4
Rock Springs, *Mont., U.S.A.* 110 C10
Rock Springs, *Wyo., U.S.A.* 110 F9
Rock Valley, *U.S.A.* 108 D6
Rockall, *Atl. Oc.* 6 D3
Rockanje, *Neths.* 16 E4
Rockdale, *Tex., U.S.A.* 109 K6
Rockdale, *Wash., U.S.A.* 112 C5
Rockefeller Plateau, *Antarctica* 5 E14
Rockford, *U.S.A.* 108 D10
Rockglen, *Canada* 101 D7
Rockhampton, *Australia* 90 C5
Rockhampton Downs, *Australia* 90 B2
Rockingham, *Australia* 89 F2
Rockingham B., *Australia* 90 B4
Rockingham Forest, *U.K.* 13 E7
Rocklake, *U.S.A.* 108 A5
Rockland, *Canada* 107 A9
Rockland, *Idaho, U.S.A.* 110 E7
Rockland, *Maine, U.S.A.* 99 D6
Rockland, *Mich., U.S.A.* 108 B10
Rocklin, *U.S.A.* 112 G5
Rockmart, *U.S.A.* 105 H3
Rockport, *Mo., U.S.A.* 108 E7
Rockport, *Tex., U.S.A.* 109 L6
Rocksprings, *U.S.A.* 109 K4
Rockville, *Conn., U.S.A.* 107 E12
Rockville, *Md., U.S.A.* 104 F7
Rockwall, *U.S.A.* 109 J6
Rockwell City, *U.S.A.* 108 D7
Rockwood, *U.S.A.* 105 H3
Rocky Ford, *U.S.A.* 108 F3
Rocky Gully, *Australia* 89 F2
Rocky Lane, *Canada* 100 B5
Rocky Mount, *U.S.A.* 105 H7
Rocky Mountain House, *Canada* 100 C6
Rocky Mts., *N. Amer.* 100 C4
Rockyford, *Canada* 100 C6
Rocroi, *France* 25 C11
Rod, *Pakistan* 60 E3
Rødberg, *Norway* 10 D2
Rødby, *Denmark* 11 K5
Rødbyhavn, *Denmark* 11 K5
Roddickton, *Canada* 99 B8
Rødding, *Denmark* 11 J3
Rødekro, *Denmark* 11 J3
Roden, *Neths.* 16 B8
Rødenes, *Norway* 10 E5
Rodenkirchen, *Germany* 18 B4
Roderick I., *Canada* 100 C3
Rodez, *France* 26 D6
Rodholívas, *Greece* 39 J6
Rodhopoú, *Greece* 37 D5
Ródhos, *Greece* 37 C10
Rodi Garganico, *Italy* 35 A8
Rodna, *Romania* 38 B7
Rodney, *Canada* 106 D3
Rodney, C., *N.Z.* 87 G5
Rodniki, *Russia* 41 C12
Rodriguez, *Ind. Oc.* 3 E13
Roe →, *U.K.* 15 A5
Roebling, *U.S.A.* 107 F10
Roebourne, *Australia* 88 D2
Roebuck B., *Australia* 88 C3
Roebuck Plains, *Australia* 88 C3
Roer →, *Neths.* 17 F7
Roermond, *Neths.* 17 F7
Roes Welcome Sd., *Canada* 97 B11
Roeselare, *Belgium* 17 G2
Rœulx, *Belgium* 17 G4
Rogachev, *Belorussia* 40 E7
Rogagua, L., *Bolivia* 124 C4
Rogaland fylke □, *Norway* 9 G9
Rogaška Slatina, *Slovenia* 33 B12
Rogatec, *Slovenia* 33 B12
Rogatin, *Ukraine* 40 G4
Rogdhia, *Greece* 37 D7
Rogers, *U.S.A.* 109 G7
Rogers City, *U.S.A.* 104 C4
Rogerson, *U.S.A.* 110 E6
Rogersville, *U.S.A.* 105 G4
Roggan River, *Canada* 98 B4
Roggel, *Neths.* 17 F7
Roggeveldberge, *S. Africa* 84 E3
Roggiano Gravina, *Italy* 35 C9
Rogliano, *France* 27 F13
Rogliano, *Italy* 35 C9
Rogoaguado, L., *Bolivia* 125 C4
Rogue →, *U.S.A.* 110 E1
Rohan, *France* 24 D4
Róhda, *Greece* 37 A3
Rohnert Park, *U.S.A.* 112 G4
Rohrbach-lès-Bitche, *France* 25 C14
Rohri, *Pakistan* 62 F3
Rohri Canal, *Pakistan* 62 F3
Rohtak, *India* 62 E7
Roi Et, *Thailand* 58 D4
Roisel, *France* 25 C10
Rojas, *Argentina* 126 C3
Rojo, C., *Mexico* 115 C5

Rokan →, Indonesia 56 D2
Rokeby, Australia 90 A3
Rokiskis, Lithuania 40 D4
Rokitno, Russia 40 F9
Rolândia, Brazil 127 A5
Rolde, Neths. 16 C9
Rolette, U.S.A. 108 A5
Rolla, Kans., U.S.A. 109 G4
Rolla, Mo., U.S.A. 109 G9
Rolla, N. Dak., U.S.A. 108 A5
Rollag, Norway 10 D3
Rolle, Switz. 22 D2
Rolleston, Australia 90 C4
Rollingstone, Australia 90 B4
Rom, Sudan 77 F3
Roma, Australia 91 D4
Roma, Italy 34 A5
Roma, Sweden 9 H15
Roman, Romania 38 C9
Roman, Russia 45 C12
Roman-Kosh, Gora, Ukraine 42 D6
Romanche →, France 27 C9
Romang, Indonesia 57 F7
Români, Egypt 69 E1
Romania ■, Europe 38 D8
Romano, Cayo, Cuba 116 B4
Romano di Lombardía, Italy 32 C6
Romanovka = Bessarabka, Moldavia 42 C3
Romans-sur-Isère, France 27 C9
Romanshorn, Switz. 23 A8
Romblon, Phil. 55 E5
Rombo □, Tanzania 82 C4
Rome = Roma, Italy 34 A5
Rome, Ga., U.S.A. 105 H3
Rome, N.Y., U.S.A. 107 C9
Romeleåsen, Sweden 11 J7
Romenay, France 27 B9
Romerike, Norway 10 D5
Romilly-sur-Seine, France 25 D10
Romîni, Romania 38 E7
Rommani, Morocco 74 B3
Romney, U.S.A. 104 F6
Romney Marsh, U.K. 13 F8
Romny, Ukraine 40 F8
Rømø, Denmark 11 J2
Romodan, Ukraine 40 G8
Romodanovo, Russia 41 D14
Romont, Switz. 22 C3
Romorantin-Lanthenay, France 25 E8
Romsdalen, Norway 10 B2
Ron, Vietnam 58 D6
Rona, U.K. 14 D3
Ronan, U.S.A. 110 C6
Roncador, Cayos, Caribbean 116 D3
Roncador, Serra do, Brazil 123 D1
Roncesvalles, Paso, Spain 28 B3
Ronceverte, U.S.A. 104 G5
Ronciglione, Italy 33 F9
Ronco →, Italy 33 D9
Ronda, Spain 31 J5
Ronda, Serranía de, Spain 31 J5
Rondane, Norway 10 C3
Rondón, Colombia 120 B3
Rondônia, Brazil 125 C5
Rondônia □, Brazil 125 C5
Rondonópolis, Brazil 125 D7
Rong Jiang →, China 52 E7
Rong Xian, Guangxi Zhuangzu, China 53 F8
Rong Xian, Sichuan, China 52 C5
Rong'an, China 52 E7
Rongchang, China 52 C5
Ronge, L. la, Canada 101 B7
Rongjiang, China 52 E7
Rongshui, China 52 E7
Ronne Ice Shelf, Antarctica 5 D18
Ronsard, C., Australia 89 D1
Ronse, Belgium 17 G3
Ronuro →, Brazil 125 C7
Roodepoort, S. Africa 85 D4
Roodeschool, Neths. 16 B9
Roof Butte, U.S.A. 111 H9
Roompot, Neths. 17 E3
Roorkee, India 62 E7
Roosendaal, Neths. 17 E4
Roosevelt, Minn., U.S.A. 108 A7
Roosevelt, Utah, U.S.A. 110 F8
Roosevelt →, Brazil 125 B5
Roosevelt, Mt., Canada 100 B3
Roosevelt I., Antarctica 5 D12
Roosevelt Res., U.S.A. 111 K8
Roper →, Australia 90 A2
Ropesville, U.S.A. 109 J3
Roque Pérez, Argentina 126 D4
Roquefort, France 26 D3
Roquemaure, France 27 D8
Roquetas, Spain 28 E5
Roquevaire, France 27 E9
Roraima □, Brazil 121 C5
Roraima, Mt., Venezuela 121 B5
Rorketon, Canada 101 C9
Røros, Norway 10 B5
Rorschach, Switz. 23 B8
Rosa, Zambia 83 D3
Rosa, C., Algeria 75 A6
Rosa, Monte, Europe 22 E5
Rosal, Spain 30 D2
Rosal de la Frontera, Spain 31 H3
Rosalia, U.S.A. 110 C5
Rosamond, U.S.A. 113 L8
Rosans, France 27 D9
Rosario, Argentina 126 C3
Rosário, Brazil 122 B3
Rosario, Baja Calif. N., Mexico 114 A1
Rosario, Sinaloa, Mexico 114 C3
Rosario, Paraguay 126 A4
Rosario, Villa del, Venezuela 120 A3
Rosario de la Frontera, Argentina 126 B3
Rosario de Lerma, Argentina 126 A2
Rosario del Tala, Argentina 126 C4
Rosário do Sul, Brazil 127 C5
Rosário Oeste, Brazil 125 C6
Rosarito, U.S.A. 113 N9
Rosarno, Italy 35 D8
Rosas, Spain 28 C8
Roscoe, U.S.A. 108 C5
Roscoff, France 24 D3
Roscommon, Ireland 15 C3
Roscommon, U.S.A. 104 C3
Roscommon □, Ireland 15 C3
Roscrea, Ireland 15 D4
Rose →, Australia 90 A2
Rose Blanche, Canada 99 C8
Rose Harbour, Canada 100 C2
Rose Pt., Canada 100 C2
Rose Valley, Canada 101 C8
Roseau, Domin. 117 C7
Roseau, U.S.A. 108 A7
Rosebery, Australia 90 G4
Rosebud, U.S.A. 109 K6
Roseburg, U.S.A. 110 E2
Rosedale, Australia 90 C5
Rosedale, U.S.A. 109 J9
Rosée, Belgium 17 H5
Roseland, U.S.A. 112 G4
Rosemary, Canada 100 C6
Rosenberg, U.S.A. 109 L7
Rosendaël, France 25 A9
Rosenheim, Germany 19 H8
Roseto degli Abruzzi, Italy 33 F11
Rosetown, Canada 101 C7
Rosetta = Rashîd, Egypt 76 H7
Roseville, U.S.A. 112 G5
Rosewood, N. Terr., Australia 88 C4
Rosewood, Queens., Australia 91 D5
Roshkhvār, Iran 65 C8
Rosières-en-Santerre, France 25 C9
Rosignano Marittimo, Italy 32 E7
Rosignol, Guyana 121 B6
Roşiori de Vede, Romania 38 E8
Rositsa, Bulgaria 38 F10
Rositsa →, Bulgaria 38 F8
Roskilde, Denmark 11 J6
Roskilde Amtskommune □, Denmark 11 J6
Roskilde Fjord, Denmark 11 J6
Roslavl, Russia 40 E8
Roslyn, Australia 91 E4
Rosmaninhal, Portugal 31 F3
Rosmead, S. Africa 84 E4
Røsnæs, Denmark 11 J4
Rosolini, Italy 35 F7
Rosporden, France 24 E3
Ross, Australia 90 G4
Ross, N.Z. 87 K3
Ross I., Antarctica 5 D11
Ross Ice Shelf, Antarctica 5 E12
Ross L., U.S.A. 110 B3
Ross-on-Wye, U.K. 13 F5
Ross Sea, Antarctica 5 D11
Rossa, Switz. 23 D8
Rossan Pt., Ireland 15 B3
Rossano Cálabro, Italy 35 C9
Rossburn, Canada 101 C8
Rosseau, Canada 106 A5
Rossignol, L., Canada 98 B5
Rossignol Res., Canada 99 D6
Rossland, Canada 100 D5
Rosslare, Ireland 15 D5
Rosslau, Germany 18 D8
Rosso, Mauritania 78 B1
Rossosh, Russia 43 A8
Rossport, Canada 98 C2
Rossum, Neths. 16 E6
Røssvatnet, Norway 8 D13
Rossville, Australia 90 B4
Rosthern, Canada 101 C7
Rostock, Germany 18 A8
Rostov, Russia 41 C11
Rostov, Russia 43 C8
Rostrenen, France 24 D3
Roswell, U.S.A. 109 J2
Rosyth, U.K. 14 E5
Rota, Spain 31 J4
Rotälven →, Sweden 10 C8
Rotan, U.S.A. 109 J4
Rotem, Belgium 17 F7
Rotenburg, Germany 18 B5
Roth, Germany 19 F7
Rothaargebirge, Germany 18 E4
Rothenburg, Switz. 23 B6
Rothenburg ob der Tauber, Germany 19 F6
Rother →, U.K. 13 G8
Rotherham, U.K. 12 D6
Rothes, U.K. 14 D5
Rothesay, Canada 99 C6
Rothesay, U.K. 14 F3
Rothrist, Switz. 22 B5
Roti, Indonesia 57 F6
Roto, Australia 91 E4
Rotondella, Italy 35 B9
Rotoroa, L., N.Z. 87 J4
Rotorua, N.Z. 87 H6
Rotorua, L., N.Z. 87 H6
Rotselaar, Belgium 17 G5
Rott →, Germany 19 G9
Rotten →, Switz. 22 D5
Rottenburg, Germany 19 G4
Rotterdam, Neths. 16 E5
Rottnest I., Australia 89 F2
Rottumeroog, Neths. 16 A9
Rottweil, Germany 19 G4
Rotuma, Fiji 92 J9
Roubaix, France 25 B10
Rouen, France 24 C8
Rouillac, France 26 C3
Rouleau, Canada 101 C8
Round Mt., Australia 91 E5
Round Mountain, U.S.A. 110 G5
Roundup, U.S.A. 110 C9
Roura, Fr. Guiana 121 C7
Rousay, U.K. 14 B5
Rouses Point, U.S.A. 107 B11
Roussillon, Isère, France 27 C8
Roussillon, Pyrénées-Or., France 26 F6
Rouveen, Neths. 16 C8
Rouxville, S. Africa 84 E4
Rouyn, Canada 98 C4
Rovaniemi, Finland 8 C18
Rovato, Italy 32 C7
Rovenki, Ukraine 43 B8
Rovereto, Italy 32 C8
Rovigo, Italy 33 C8
Rovinari, Romania 38 E6
Rovinj, Croatia 33 C10
Rovira, Colombia 120 C2
Rovno, Ukraine 40 F5
Rovnoye, Russia 41 F15
Rovuma →, Tanzania 83 E5
Row'ān, Iran 65 C6
Rowena, Australia 91 D4
Rowley Shoals, Australia 88 C2
Roxa, Guinea-Biss. 78 C1
Roxas, Capiz, Phil. 55 F5
Roxas, Isabela, Phil. 55 C4
Roxas, Mindoro, Phil. 55 E4
Roxboro, U.S.A. 105 G6
Roxborough Downs, Australia 90 C2
Roxburgh, N.Z. 87 L2
Roxen, Sweden 11 F9
Roy, Mont., U.S.A. 110 C9
Roy, N. Mex., U.S.A. 109 H2
Roy Hill, Australia 88 D2
Roya, Peña, Spain 28 E4
Royal Leamington Spa, U.K. 13 E6
Royan, France 26 C2
Roye, France 25 C9
Røyken, Norway 10 E4
Rožaj, Montenegro, Yug. 21 N10
Rozay-en-Brie, France 25 D9
Rozhishche, Ukraine 40 F4
Rožňava, Czech. 20 G10
Rozoy-sur-Serre, France 25 C11
Rtishchevo, Russia 41 D13
Rúa, Spain 30 C3
Ruacaná, Angola 84 B1
Ruahine Ra., N.Z. 87 H6
Ruapehu, N.Z. 87 H5
Ruapuke I., N.Z. 87 M2
Ruâq, W. →, Egypt 69 F2
Rub' al Khali, Si. Arabia 68 D4
Rubeho Mts., Tanzania 82 D4
Rubezhnoye, Ukraine 42 B8
Rubh a' Mhail, U.K. 14 F2
Rubha Hunish, U.K. 14 D2
Rubiataba, Brazil 123 E2
Rubicon →, U.S.A. 112 G5
Rubicone →, Italy 33 D9
Rubinéia, Brazil 123 F1
Rubino, Ivory C. 78 D4
Rubio, Venezuela 120 B3
Rubtsovsk, Russia 44 D9
Ruby L., U.S.A. 110 F6
Ruby Mts., U.S.A. 110 F6
Rucava, Latvia 40 C2
Rucheng, China 53 E9
Rud, Norway 10 D4
Rūd Sar, Iran 65 B6
Ruda Śląska, Poland 20 E8
Rudall, Australia 91 E2
Rudall →, Australia 88 D3
Ruden, Germany 18 A9
Rüdersdorf, Germany 18 C9
Rudewa, Tanzania 83 E3
Rudkøbing, Denmark 11 K4
Rudnik, Serbia, Yug. 21 L10
Rudnogorsk, Russia 45 D11
Rudnya, Russia 40 D7
Rudnyy, Kazakhstan 44 D7
Rudolf, Ostrov, Russia 44 A6
Rudolstadt, Germany 18 E7
Rudong, China 53 A13
Rudozem, Bulgaria 39 H7
Rudyard, U.S.A. 104 B3
Rue, France 25 B8
Ruelle, France 26 C4
Rufa'a, Sudan 77 E3
Ruffec, France 26 B4
Rufiji □, Tanzania 82 D4
Rufiji →, Tanzania 82 D4
Rufino, Argentina 126 C3
Rufisque, Senegal 78 C1
Rufunsa, Zambia 83 F2
Rugao, China 53 A13
Rugby, U.K. 13 E6
Rugby, U.S.A. 108 A5
Rügen, Germany 18 A9
Rugles, France 24 D7
Ruhengeri, Rwanda 82 C2
Ruhla, Germany 18 E6
Ruhland, Germany 18 D9
Ruhr →, Germany 18 D2
Ruhuhu →, Tanzania 83 E3
Rui Barbosa, Brazil 123 D3
Rui'an, China 53 D13
Ruichang, China 53 C10
Ruidosa, U.S.A. 109 L2
Ruidoso, U.S.A. 111 K11
Ruili, China 52 E1
Ruinen, Neths. 16 C8
Ruinerwold, Neths. 16 C8
Ruiten A Kanaal →, Neths. 16 C10
Ruivo, Pico, Madeira 36 D3
Rujm Tal'at al Jamā'ah, Jordan 69 E4
Ruk, Pakistan 62 F3
Rukwa □, Tanzania 82 D3
Rukwa L., Tanzania 82 D3
Rulhieres, C., Australia 88 B4
Rulles, Belgium 17 J7
Rum Cay, Bahamas 117 B5
Rum Jungle, Australia 88 B5
Ruma, Serbia, Yug. 21 K9
Rumāḩ, Si. Arabia 64 E5
Rumania = Romania ■, Europe 38 D8
Rumaylah, Iraq 64 D5
Rumbalara, Australia 90 D1
Rumbêk, Sudan 77 F2
Rumbeke, Belgium 17 G2
Rumelange, Lux. 17 K8
Rumford, U.S.A. 107 B14
Rumilly, France 27 C9
Rumoi, Japan 48 C10
Rumonge, Burundi 82 C2
Rumsey, Canada 100 C6
Rumula, Australia 90 B4
Rumuruti, Kenya 82 B4
Runan, China 50 H8
Runanga, N.Z. 87 K3
Runaway, C., N.Z. 87 G6
Runcorn, U.K. 12 D5
Rungwa, Tanzania 82 D3
Rungwa →, Tanzania 82 D3
Rungwe, Tanzania 83 D3
Rungwe □, Tanzania 83 D3
Runka, Nigeria 79 C6
Runton Ra., Australia 88 D3
Ruoqiang, China 54 C3
Rupa, India 61 F18
Rupar, India 62 D7
Rupat, Indonesia 56 D2
Rupert →, Canada 98 B4
Rupert House = Fort Rupert, Canada 98 B4
Rupununi →, Guyana 121 C6
Rur →, Germany 18 E2
Rurrenabaque, Bolivia 124 C4
Rus →, Spain 29 F2
Rusambo, Zimbabwe 83 F3
Rusape, Zimbabwe 83 F3
Ruschuk = Ruse, Bulgaria 38 F8
Ruse, Bulgaria 38 F8
Ruşeţu, Romania 38 E10
Rushan, China 51 F11
Rushden, U.K. 13 E7
Rushford, U.S.A. 108 D9
Rushville, Ill., U.S.A. 108 E9
Rushville, Ind., U.S.A. 104 F3
Rushville, Nebr., U.S.A. 108 D3
Rushworth, Australia 91 F4
Russas, Brazil 122 B4
Russell, Canada 101 C8
Russell, U.S.A. 108 F5
Russell L., Man., Canada 101 B8
Russell L., N.W.T., Canada 100 A5
Russellkonda, India 61 K14
Russellville, Ala., U.S.A. 105 H2
Russellville, Ark., U.S.A. 109 H8
Russellville, Ky., U.S.A. 105 G2
Russi, Italy 33 D9
Russian →, U.S.A. 112 G3
Russian Federation ■, Eurasia 45 C11
Russkaya Polyana, Kazakhstan 44 D8
Russkoye Ustie, Russia 4 B15
Rustam, Pakistan 62 B5
Rustam Shahr, Pakistan 62 F2
Rustavi, Georgia 43 F11
Rustenburg, S. Africa 84 D4
Ruston, U.S.A. 109 J8
Ruswil, Switz. 22 B6
Rutana, Burundi 82 C2
Rute, Spain 31 H6
Ruteng, Indonesia 57 F6
Ruth, Mich., U.S.A. 106 C2
Ruth, Nev., U.S.A. 110 G6
Rutherford, U.S.A. 112 G4
Rutherglen, U.K. 14 F4
Rüti, Switz. 23 B7
Rutigliano, Italy 35 A10
Rutland Plains, Australia 90 B3
Rutledge →, Canada 101 A6
Rutledge L., Canada 101 A6
Rutshuru, Zaïre 82 C2
Ruurlo, Neths. 16 D8
Ruvo di Púglia, Italy 35 A9
Ruvu, Tanzania 82 D4
Ruvu →, Tanzania 82 D4
Ruvuma □, Tanzania 83 E4
Ruwais, U.A.E. 65 E7
Ruwenzori, Africa 82 B2
Ruyigi, Burundi 82 C3
Ruyuan, China 53 E9
Ruzayevka, Russia 41 D14
Ružomberok, Czech. 20 F9
Rwanda ■, Africa 82 C3
Ry, Denmark 11 H3
Ryakhovo, Bulgaria 38 F9
Ryan, L., U.K. 14 G3
Ryazan, Russia 41 D11
Ryazhsk, Russia 41 E12
Rybache, Kazakhstan 44 E9
Rybinsk, Russia 41 B11
Rybinskoye Vdkhr., Russia 41 B11
Rybnik, Poland 20 E8
Rybnitsa, Moldavia 42 C3
Rybnoye, Russia 41 D11
Rychwał, Poland 20 C8
Ryde, U.K. 13 G6
Ryderwood, U.S.A. 112 D3
Rydöbruk, Sweden 11 H7
Rydułtowy, Poland 20 E8
Rye, U.K. 13 G8
Rye →, U.K. 12 C7
Rye Patch Res., U.S.A. 110 F4
Ryegate, U.S.A. 110 C9
Rylsk, Russia 40 F9
Rylstone, Australia 91 E4
Ryōthu, Japan 48 E9
Rypin, Poland 20 B9
Ryūgasaki, Japan 49 G10
Ryūkyū Is. = Ryūkyū-rettō, Japan 49 M2
Ryūkyū-rettō, Japan 49 M2
Rzeszów, Poland 20 E11
Rzhev, Russia 40 C9

S

Sa, Thailand 58 C3
Sa Dec, Vietnam 59 G5
Sa'ādatābād, Fārs, Iran 65 D7
Sa'ādatābād, Kermān, Iran 65 D7
Saale →, Germany 18 D7
Saaler Bodden, Germany 18 A8
Saalfeld, Germany 18 E7
Saane →, Switz. 22 B4
Saar →, Europe 25 C13
Saarbrücken, Germany 19 F2
Saarburg, Germany 19 F2
Saaremaa, Estonia 40 B3
Saariselkä, Finland 8 B20
Saarland □, Germany 25 C13
Saarlouis, Germany 19 F2
Saas Fee, Switz. 22 D5
Sab 'Bi'ār, Syria 64 C3
Saba, W. Indies 117 C7
Šabac, Serbia, Yug. 21 L9
Sabadell, Spain 28 D7
Sabah □, Malaysia 56 C5
Sabak Bernam, Malaysia 59 L3
Sábana de la Mar, Dom. Rep. 117 C6
Sábanalarga, Colombia 120 A3
Sabang, Indonesia 56 C1
Sabará, Brazil 123 E3
Sabarania, Indonesia 57 E9
Sabattis, U.S.A. 107 B10
Sabáudia, Italy 34 A6
Sabaya, Bolivia 124 D4
Sabhah, Libya 73 C7
Sabie, S. Africa 85 D5
Sabinal, Mexico 114 A3
Sabinal, U.S.A. 109 L5
Sabinal, Punta del, Spain 29 J2
Sabinas, Mexico 114 B4
Sabinas →, Mexico 114 B4
Sabinas Hidalgo, Mexico 114 B4
Sabine →, U.S.A. 109 L8
Sabine L., U.S.A. 109 L8
Sabine Pass, U.S.A. 109 L8
Sabinópolis, Brazil 123 E3
Sabinov, Czech. 20 F11
Sabirabad, Azerbaijan 43 F13
Sabkhet el Bardawîl, Egypt 69 D2
Sablayan, Phil. 55 E4
Sable, C., Canada 99 D6
Sable, C., U.S.A. 103 E10
Sable I., Canada 99 D8
Sablé-sur-Sarthe, France 24 E6
Saboeiro, Brazil 122 C4
Sabolev, Russia 45 D16
Sabor →, Portugal 30 D3
Sabou, Burkina Faso 78 C4
Sabrātah, Libya 75 B7
Sabria, Tunisia 75 B6

Sabrina Coast, *Antarctica* 5 C9
Sabugal, *Portugal* 30 E3
Sabulubek, *Indonesia* 56 E1
Sabzevār, *Iran* 65 B8
Sabzvārān, *Iran* 65 D8
Sac City, *U.S.A.* 108 D7
Sacedón, *Spain* 28 E2
Sachigo →, *Canada* 98 A2
Sachigo, L., *Canada* 98 B1
Sachkhere, *Georgia* 43 E10
Sachseln, *Switz.* 23 C6
Sachsen □, *Germany* 18 E9
Sachsen-Anhalt □, *Germany* 18 D8
Sacile, *Italy* 33 C9
Sackets Harbor, *U.S.A.* 107 C8
Saco, *Maine, U.S.A.* 105 D10
Saco, *Mont., U.S.A.* 110 B10
Sacramento, *Brazil* 123 E2
Sacramento, *U.S.A.* 112 G5
Sacramento →, *U.S.A.* 112 G5
Sacramento Mts., *U.S.A.* 111 K11
Sacramento Valley, *U.S.A.* 112 G5
Sacratif, C., *Spain* 29 J1
Săcueni, *Romania* 38 B5
Sada, *Spain* 30 B2
Sádaba, *Spain* 28 C3
Sadani, *Tanzania* 82 D4
Sadao, *Thailand* 59 J3
Sadd el Aali, *Egypt* 76 C3
Saddle Mt., *U.S.A.* 112 E3
Sade, *Nigeria* 79 C7
Sadimi, *Zaïre* 83 D1
Sado, *Japan* 48 E9
Sado →, *Portugal* 31 G2
Sadon, *Burma* 61 G20
Sadon, *Russia* 43 E10
Sæby, *Denmark* 11 G4
Saegerstown, *U.S.A.* 106 E4
Saelices, *Spain* 28 F2
Safaga, *Egypt* 76 B3
Şafājah, *Si. Arabia* 64 E3
Säffle, *Sweden* 9 G12
Safford, *U.S.A.* 111 K9
Saffron Walden, *U.K.* 13 E8
Safi, *Morocco* 74 B3
Şafīābād, *Iran* 65 B8
Safīd Dasht, *Iran* 65 C6
Safīd Kūh, *Afghan.* 60 B3
Safonovo, *Russia* 40 D8
Safranbolu, *Turkey* 42 F5
Safwān, *Iraq* 64 D5
Sag Harbor, *U.S.A.* 107 F12
Saga, *Indonesia* 57 E8
Saga, *Japan* 49 H5
Saga □, *Japan* 49 H5
Sagae, *Japan* 48 E10
Sagala, *Mali* 78 C3
Sagar, *India* 60 M9
Sagara, L., *Tanzania* 82 D3
Sagay, *Phil.* 55 F5
Sagil, *Mongolia* 54 A4
Saginaw, *U.S.A.* 104 D4
Saginaw B., *U.S.A.* 104 D4
Sagīr, Zab as →, *Iraq* 64 C4
Sagleipie, *Liberia* 78 D3
Saglouc, *Canada* 97 B12
Sagŏ-ri, *S. Korea* 51 G14
Sagone, *France* 27 F12
Sagone, G. de, *France* 27 F12
Sagres, *Portugal* 31 J2
Sagua la Grande, *Cuba* 116 B3
Saguache, *U.S.A.* 111 G10
Saguenay →, *Canada* 99 C5
Sagunto, *Spain* 28 F4
Sahaba, *Sudan* 76 D3
Sahagún, *Colombia* 120 B2
Sahagún, *Spain* 30 C5
Saḥam al Jawlān, *Syria* 69 C4
Sahand, Kūh-e, *Iran* 64 B5
Sahara, *Africa* 70 D4
Saharan Atlas = Saharien, Atlas, *Algeria* 75 B5
Saharanpur, *India* 62 E7
Saharien, Atlas, *Algeria* 75 B5
Sahasinaka, *Madag.* 85 C8
Sahaswan, *India* 63 E8
Sahel, Canal du, *Mali* 78 C3
Sahibganj, *India* 63 G12
Sahiwal, *Pakistan* 62 D5
Şahneh, *Iran* 64 C5
Sahtaneh →, *Canada* 100 B4
Sahuaripa, *Mexico* 114 B3
Sahuarita, *U.S.A.* 111 L8
Sahuayo, *Mexico* 114 C4
Sahy, *Czech.* 21 G8
Sai Buri, *Thailand* 59 J3
Sai-Cinza, *Brazil* 125 B6
Sa'id Bundas, *Sudan* 73 G9
Saïda, *Algeria* 75 B5
Saʻīdābād, *Kermān, Iran* 65 D7
Saʻīdābād, *Semnān, Iran* 65 B7
Saïdia, *Morocco* 75 A4
Saʻīdiyeh, *Iran* 65 B6
Saidpur, *Bangla.* 61 G16
Saidu, *Pakistan* 63 B5
Saignelégier, *Switz.* 22 B3
Saignes, *France* 26 C6
Saigon = Phanh Bho Ho Chi Minh, *Vietnam* 59 G6
Saijō, *Japan* 49 H6
Saikhoa Ghat, *India* 61 F19
Saiki, *Japan* 49 H5
Saillans, *France* 27 D9
Sailolof, *Indonesia* 57 E8
Saimbeyli, *Turkey* 66 E7
Şa'in Dezh, *Iran* 64 B5
St. Abb's Head, *U.K.* 14 F6
St. Aegyd, *Austria* 21 H5
St.-Affrique, *France* 26 E6
St.-Agrève, *France* 27 C8
St.-Aignan, *France* 24 E8
St. Alban's, *Canada* 99 C8
St. Albans, *U.K.* 13 F7
St. Albans, *Vt., U.S.A.* 107 B11
St. Albans, *W. Va., U.S.A.* 104 F5
St. Alban's Head, *U.K.* 13 G5
St. Albert, *Canada* 100 C6
St.-Amand-en-Puisaye, *France* 25 E10
St.-Amand-les-Eaux, *France* 25 B10
St.-Amand-Mont-Rond, *France* 26 B6
St.-Amarin, *France* 25 E14
St.-Amour, *France* 27 B9
St.-André-de-Cubzac, *France* 26 D3
St.-André-de-l'Eure, *France* 24 D8
St.-André-les-Alpes, *France* 27 E10
St. Andrew's, *Canada* 99 C8
St. Andrews, *U.K.* 14 E6
St-Anicet, *Canada* 107 A10
St. Ann B., *Canada* 99 C7
St. Anne, *U.K.* 24 C4
St. Ann's Bay, *Jamaica* 116 C4
St. Anthony, *Canada* 99 B8
St. Anthony, *U.S.A.* 110 E8
St.-Antonin-Noble-Val, *France* 26 D5
St. Arnaud, *Australia* 91 F3
St. Arthur, *Canada* 99 C6
St. Asaph, *U.K.* 12 D4
St.-Astier, *France* 26 C4
St.-Aubin, *Switz.* 22 C3
St.-Aubin-du-Cormier, *France* 24 D5
St-Augustin-Saguenay, *Canada* 99 B8
St. Augustine, *U.S.A.* 105 L5
St. Austell, *U.K.* 13 G3
St.-Avold, *France* 25 C13
St.-Barthélemy, I., *W. Indies* 117 C7
St. Bee's Hd., *U.K.* 12 C4
St.-Benoît-du-Sault, *France* 26 B5
St.-Bernard, Col du Grand, *Europe* 22 E4
St.-Bernard, Col du Petit, *France* 27 C10
St.-Blaise, *Switz.* 22 B3
St. Boniface, *Canada* 101 D9
St.-Bonnet, *France* 27 D10
St.-Brévin-les-Pins, *France* 24 E4
St.-Brice-en-Coglès, *France* 24 D5
St. Bride's, *Canada* 99 C9
St. Brides B., *U.K.* 13 F2
St.-Brieuc, *France* 24 D4
St.-Calais, *France* 24 E7
St.-Cast-le-Guildo, *France* 24 D4
St. Catharines, *Canada* 98 D4
St. Catherines I., *U.S.A.* 105 K5
St. Catherine's Pt., *U.K.* 13 G6
St.-Céré, *France* 26 D5
St.-Cergue, *Switz.* 22 D2
St.-Cernin, *France* 26 C6
St.-Chamond, *France* 27 C8
St. Charles, *Ill., U.S.A.* 104 E1
St. Charles, *Mo., U.S.A.* 108 F9
St.-Chély-d'Apcher, *France* 26 D7
St.-Chinian, *France* 26 E6
St. Christopher, *W. Indies* 117 C7
St. Christopher-Nevis ■, *W. Indies* 117 C7
St.-Ciers-sur-Gironde, *France* 26 C3
St. Clair, *Mich., U.S.A.* 106 D2
St. Clair, *Pa., U.S.A.* 107 F8
St. Clair, L., *Canada* 98 D3
St. Clairsville, *U.S.A.* 106 F4
St.-Claud, *France* 26 C4
St. Claude, *Canada* 101 D9
St.-Claude, *France* 27 B9
St. Cloud, *Fla., U.S.A.* 105 L5
St. Cloud, *Minn., U.S.A.* 108 C7
St-Coeur de Marie, *Canada* 99 C5
St. Cricq, C., *Australia* 89 E1
St. Croix, *Virgin Is.* 117 C7
St. Croix →, *U.S.A.* 108 C8
St. Croix Falls, *U.S.A.* 108 C8
St.-Cyr-sur-Mer, *France* 27 E9
St. David's, *Canada* 99 C8
St. David's, *U.K.* 13 F2
St. David's Head, *U.K.* 13 F2
St.-Denis, *France* 25 D9
St.-Denis-d'Orques, *France* 24 D6
St.-Dié, *France* 25 D13
St.-Dizier, *France* 25 D11
St.-Égrève, *France* 27 C9
St. Elias, Mt., *U.S.A.* 96 B5
St. Elias Mts., *Canada* 100 A1
St.-Élie, *Fr. Guiana* 121 C7
St.-Eloy-les-Mines, *France* 26 B6
St.-Émilion, *France* 26 D3
St.-Étienne, *France* 27 C8
St.-Étienne-de-Tinée, *France* 27 D10
St. Eugène, *Canada* 107 A10
St. Eustatius, *W. Indies* 117 C7
St-Félicien, *Canada* 98 C5
St.-Florent, *France* 27 F13
St.-Florent-sur-Cher, *France* 25 F9
St.-Florentin, *France* 25 D10
St.-Flour, *France* 26 C7
St.-Fons, *France* 27 C8
St. Francis, *U.S.A.* 108 F4
St. Francis →, *U.S.A.* 109 H9
St. Francis, C., *S. Africa* 84 E3
St. Francisville, *U.S.A.* 109 K9
St-François, L., *Canada* 107 A10
St.-Fulgent, *France* 24 F5
St-Gabriel-de-Brandon, *Canada* 98 C5
St.-Gaudens, *France* 26 E4
St.-Gengoux-le-National, *France* 27 B8
St.-Geniez-d'Olt, *France* 26 D6
St. George, *Australia* 91 D4
St. George, *Canada* 99 C6
St. George, *S.C., U.S.A.* 105 J5
St. George, *Utah, U.S.A.* 111 H7
St. George, C., *Canada* 99 C8
St. George, C., *U.S.A.* 105 L3
St. George Ra., *Australia* 88 C4
St-Georges, *Belgium* 17 G6
St. George's, *Canada* 99 C8
St-Georges, *Canada* 99 C5
St.-Georges, *Fr. Guiana* 121 C7
St. George's, *Grenada* 117 D7
St. George's B., *Canada* 99 C8
St. Georges Basin, *Australia* 88 C4
St. George's Channel, *U.K.* 15 E6
St.-Georges-de-Didonne, *France* 26 C3
St. Georges Hd., *Australia* 91 F5
St.-Gérard, *Belgium* 17 H5
St.-Germain-de-Calberte, *France* 26 D7
St.-Germain-des-Fossés, *France* 26 B7
St.-Germain-du-Plain, *France* 25 F11
St.-Germain-en-Laye, *France* 25 D9
St.-Germain-Laval, *France* 27 C8
St.-Germain-Lembron, *France* 26 C7
St.-Gervais-d'Auvergne, *France* 26 B6
St.-Gervais-les-Bains, *France* 27 C10
St.-Gildas, Pte. de, *France* 24 E4
St.-Gilles, *France* 27 E8
St.-Gilles-Croix-de-Vie, *France* 26 B2
St.-Gingolph, *Switz.* 22 D3
St.-Girons, *France* 26 F5
St. Gotthard P. = San Gottardo, Paso del, *Switz.* 23 C7
St.-Gualtier, *France* 24 F8
St.-Guénolé, *France* 24 E2
St. Helena, *Atl. Oc.* 2 E9
St. Helena, *U.S.A.* 110 G2
St. Helena, Mt., *U.S.A.* 112 G4
St. Helena B., *S. Africa* 84 E2
St. Helens, *Australia* 90 G4
St. Helens, *U.K.* 12 D5
St. Helens, *U.S.A.* 112 E4
St. Helens, Mt., *U.S.A.* 112 D4
St. Helier, *U.K.* 13 H5
St.-Hilaire-du-Harcouët, *France* 24 D5
St.-Hippolyte, *France* 25 E13
St.-Hippolyte-du-Fort, *France* 26 E7
St.-Honoré-les-Bains, *France* 25 F10
St.-Hubert, *Belgium* 17 H6
St-Hyacinthe, *Canada* 98 C5
St. Ignace, *U.S.A.* 104 C3
St. Ignace I., *Canada* 98 C2
St. Ignatius, *U.S.A.* 110 C6
St.-Imier, *Switz.* 22 B3
St. Ives, *Cambs., U.K.* 13 E7
St. Ives, *Corn., U.K.* 13 G2
St.-James, *France* 24 D5
St. James, *U.S.A.* 108 D7
St-Jean, *Canada* 98 C5
St-Jean →, *Canada* 99 B7
St-Jean, L., *Canada* 99 C5
St. Jean Baptiste, *Canada* 101 D9
St.-Jean-d'Angély, *France* 26 C3
St.-Jean-de-Bournay, *France* 27 C9
St.-Jean-de-Luz, *France* 26 E2
St.-Jean-de-Maurienne, *France* 27 C10
St.-Jean-de-Monts, *France* 24 F4
St.-Jean-du-Gard, *France* 26 D7
St.-Jean-en-Royans, *France* 27 C9
St-Jean-Port-Joli, *Canada* 99 C5
St-Jérôme, *Qué., Canada* 98 C5
St-Jérôme, *Qué., Canada* 99 C5
St. John, *Canada* 99 C6
St. John, *Kans., U.S.A.* 109 G5
St. John, *N. Dak., U.S.A.* 108 A5
St. John →, *N. Amer.* 99 C6
St. John, C., *Canada* 99 B8
St. John's, *Antigua* 117 C7
St. John's, *Canada* 99 C9
St. Johns, *Ariz., U.S.A.* 111 J9
St. Johns, *Mich., U.S.A.* 104 D3
St. John's →, *U.S.A.* 105 K5
St. Johnsbury, *U.S.A.* 107 B12
St. Johnsville, *U.S.A.* 107 C10
St. Joseph, *La., U.S.A.* 109 K9
St. Joseph, *Mich., U.S.A.* 104 D2
St. Joseph, *Mo., U.S.A.* 108 F7
St. Joseph →, *U.S.A.* 104 D2
St. Joseph, I., *Canada* 98 C3
St. Joseph, L., *Canada* 98 B1
St-Jovite, *Canada* 98 C5
St.-Juéry, *France* 26 E6
St.-Julien-Chapteuil, *France* 27 C8
St.-Julien-du-Sault, *France* 25 D10
St.-Julien-en-Genevois, *France* 27 B10
St.-Junien, *France* 26 C4
St.-Just-en-Chaussée, *France* 25 C9
St.-Just-en-Chevalet, *France* 26 C7
St.-Justin, *France* 26 E3
St. Kilda, *N.Z.* 87 L3
St. Kitts = St. Christopher, *W. Indies* 117 C7
St. Laurent, *Canada* 101 C9
St.-Laurent, *Fr. Guiana* 121 B7
St.-Laurent-du-Pont, *France* 27 C9
St.-Laurent-en-Grandvaux, *France* 27 B9
St. Lawrence, *Australia* 90 C4
St. Lawrence, *Canada* 99 C8
St. Lawrence →, *Canada* 99 C6
St. Lawrence, Gulf of, *Canada* 99 C7
St. Lawrence I., *U.S.A.* 96 B3
St.-Léger, *Belgium* 17 J7
St. Leonard, *Canada* 99 C6
St.-Léonard-de-Noblat, *France* 26 C5
St. Lewis →, *Canada* 99 B8
St.-Lô, *France* 24 C5
St-Louis, *Senegal* 78 B1
St. Louis, *Mich., U.S.A.* 104 D3
St. Louis, *Mo., U.S.A.* 108 F9
St. Louis →, *U.S.A.* 108 B8
St.-Loup-sur-Semouse, *France* 25 E13
St. Lucia ■, *W. Indies* 117 D7
St. Lucia, L., *S. Africa* 85 D5
St. Lucia Channel, *W. Indies* 117 D7
St. Lunaire-Griquet, *Canada* 99 B8
St. Maarten, *W. Indies* 117 C7
St.-Maixent-l'École, *France* 26 B3
St.-Malo, *France* 24 D4
St.-Malo, G. de, *France* 24 D4
St.-Mandrier-sur-Mer, *France* 27 E9
St-Marc, *Haiti* 117 C5
St.-Marcellin, *France* 27 C9
St.-Marcouf, Is., *France* 24 C5
St. Maries, *U.S.A.* 110 C5
St-Martin, *W. Indies* 117 C7
St. Martin, L., *Canada* 101 C9
St.-Martin-de-Ré, *France* 26 B2
St.-Martin-Vésubie, *France* 27 D11
St. Martins, *Canada* 99 C6
St. Martinsville, *U.S.A.* 109 K9
St.-Martory, *France* 26 E4
St. Mary Pk., *Australia* 91 E2
St. Marys, *Australia* 90 G4
St. Marys, *Canada* 106 C3
St. Mary's, *U.K.* 13 H1
St. Marys, *U.S.A.* 106 E6
St. Mary's, C., *Canada* 99 C9
St. Mary's B., *Canada* 99 C9
St. Marys Bay, *Canada* 99 D6
St.-Mathieu, Pte., *France* 24 D2
St. Matthews, I. = Zadetkyi Kyun, *Burma* 59 H2
St.-Maur-des-Fossés, *France* 25 D9
St. Maurice, *Switz.* 22 D4
St-Maurice →, *Canada* 98 C5
St.-Médard-de-Guizières, *France* 26 C3
St.-Méen-le-Grand, *France* 24 D4
St. Michael's Mount, *U.K.* 13 G2
St.-Michel-de-Maurienne, *France* 27 C10
St.-Mihiel, *France* 25 D12
St.-Nazaire, *France* 24 E4
St. Neots, *U.K.* 13 E7
St.-Nicolas-de-Port, *France* 25 D13
St. Niklaus, *Switz.* 22 D5
St.-Omer, *France* 25 B9
St-Pacome, *Canada* 99 C6
St.-Palais-sur-Mer, *France* 26 C2
St-Pamphile, *Canada* 99 C6
St.-Pardoux-la-Rivière, *France* 26 C4
St. Pascal, *Canada* 99 C6
St. Paul, *Canada* 100 C6
St. Paul, *Minn., U.S.A.* 108 C8
St. Paul, *Nebr., U.S.A.* 108 E5
St. Paul, I., *Ind. Oc.* 3 F13
St.-Paul-de-Fenouillet, *France* 26 F6
St. Paul I., *Canada* 99 C7
St.-Paul-lès-Dax, *France* 26 E2
St.-Péray, *France* 27 D8
St.-Père-en-Retz, *France* 24 E4
St. Peter, *U.S.A.* 108 C8
St. Peter Port, *Chan. Is.* 13 H5
St. Peters, *N.S., Canada* 99 C7
St. Peters, *P.E.I., Canada* 99 C7
St. Petersburg = Sankt-Peterburg, *Russia* 40 B7
St. Petersburg, *U.S.A.* 105 M4
St.-Philbert-de-Grand-Lieu, *France* 24 E5
St.-Pierre, *St- P. & M.* 99 C8
St-Pierre, L., *Canada* 98 C5
St.-Pierre-d'Oléron, *France* 26 C2
St.-Pierre-Église, *France* 24 C5
St.-Pierre-en-Port, *France* 24 C7
St.-Pierre et Miquelon □, *St- P. & M.* 99 C8
St.-Pierre-le-Moûtier, *France* 25 F10
St.-Pierre-sur-Dives, *France* 24 C6
St.-Pieters Leew, *Belgium* 17 G4
St.-Pol-de-Léon, *France* 24 D2
St.-Pol-sur-Mer, *France* 25 A9
St.-Pol-sur-Ternoise, *France* 25 B9
St.-Pons, *France* 26 E6
St.-Pourçain-sur-Sioule, *France* 26 B7
St.-Quay-Portrieux, *France* 24 D4
St.-Quentin, *France* 25 C10
St.-Rambert-d'Albon, *France* 27 C8
St.-Raphaël, *France* 27 E10
St. Regis, *U.S.A.* 110 C6
St.-Rémy-de-Provence, *France* 27 E8
St.-Renan, *France* 24 D2
St.-Saëns, *France* 24 C8
St.-Sauveur-en-Puisaye, *France* 25 E10
St.-Sauveur-le-Vicomte, *France* 24 C5
St.-Savin, *France* 26 B4
St.-Savinien, *France* 26 C3
St. Sebastien, Tanjon' i, *Madag.* 85 A8
St.-Seine-l'Abbaye, *France* 25 E11
St.-Sernin-sur-Rance, *France* 26 E6
St.-Servan-sur-Mer, *France* 24 D4
St.-Sever, *France* 26 E3
St.-Sever-Calvados, *France* 24 D5
St-Siméon, *Canada* 99 C6
St. Stephen, *Canada* 99 C6
St.-Sulpice, *France* 26 E5
St.-Sulpice-Laurière, *France* 26 B5
St.-Syprien, *France* 26 F7
St.-Thégonnec, *France* 24 D3
St. Thomas, *Canada* 98 D3
St. Thomas, *Virgin Is.* 117 C7
St-Tite, *Canada* 98 C5
St.-Tropez, *France* 27 E10
St. Troud = Sint Truiden, *Belgium* 17 G6
St.-Vaast-la-Hougue, *France* 24 C5
St.-Valéry-en-Caux, *France* 24 C7
St.-Valéry-sur-Somme, *France* 25 B8
St.-Vallier, *France* 27 C8
St.-Vallier-de-Thiey, *France* 27 E10
St.-Varent, *France* 24 F6
St. Vincent, *W. Indies* 117 D7
St. Vincent, G., *Australia* 91 F2
St. Vincent and the Grenadines ■, *W. Indies* 117 D7
St.-Vincent-de-Tyrosse, *France* 26 E2
St. Vincent Passage, *W. Indies* 117 D7
St-Vith, *Belgium* 17 H8
St.-Yrieix-la-Perche, *France* 26 C5
Ste.-Adresse, *France* 24 C7
Ste-Agathe-des-Monts, *Canada* 98 C5
Ste-Anne de Beaupré, *Canada* 99 C5
Ste-Anne-des-Monts, *Canada* 99 C6
Ste-Croix, *Switz.* 22 C3
Ste.-Enimie, *France* 26 D7
Ste.-Foy-la-Grande, *France* 26 D4
Ste. Genevieve, *U.S.A.* 108 G9
Ste.-Hermine, *France* 26 B2
Ste.-Livrade-sur-Lot, *France* 26 D4
Ste-Marguerite →, *Canada* 99 B6
Ste-Marie, *Martinique* 117 D7
Ste.-Marie-aux-Mines, *France* 25 D14
Ste-Marie de la Madeleine, *Canada* 99 C5
Ste.-Maure-de-Touraine, *France* 24 E7
Ste.-Maxime, *France* 27 E10
Ste.-Menehould, *France* 25 C11
Ste.-Mère-Église, *France* 24 C5
Ste-Rose, *Guadeloupe* 117 C7
Ste. Rose du Lac, *Canada* 101 C9
Saintes, *France* 26 C3
Saintes, I. des, *Guadeloupe* 117 C7
Stes.-Maries-de-la-Mer, *France* 27 E8
Saintonge, *France* 26 C3
Saipan, *Pac. Oc.* 92 F6
Sairang, *India* 61 H18

Sairecábur, Cerro, *Bolivia* 126 A2
Saitama □, *Japan* 49 F9
Sajama, *Bolivia* 124 D4
Sajum, *India* 63 C8
Sak →, *S. Africa* 84 E3
Sakai, *Japan* 49 G7
Sakaide, *Japan* 49 G6
Sakaiminato, *Japan* 49 G6
Sakākah, *Si. Arabia* 64 D4
Sakakawea, L., *U.S.A.* 108 B3
Sakami, L., *Canada* 98 B4
Sâkâne, 'Erg i-n, *Mali* 74 D4
Sakania, *Zaïre* 83 E2
Sakarya = Adapazarı, *Turkey* 66 C4
Sakarya □, *Turkey* 66 C4
Sakarya →, *Turkey* 42 F4
Sakashima-Guntō, *Japan* 49 M2
Sakata, *Japan* 48 E9
Sakchu, *N. Korea* 51 D13
Sakeny →, *Madag.* 85 C8
Sakété, *Benin* 79 D5
Sakhalin, *Russia* 45 D15
Sakhalinskiy Zaliv, *Russia* 45 D15
Saki, *Ukraine* 42 D5
Sakiai, *Lithuania* 40 D3
Sakon Nakhon, *Thailand* 58 D5
Sakrand, *Pakistan* 62 F3
Sakrivier, *S. Africa* 84 E3
Sakskøbing, *Denmark* 11 K5
Sakuma, *Japan* 49 G8
Sakurai, *Japan* 49 G7
Sal →, *Russia* 43 C9
Sala, *Sweden* 9 G14
Sala Consilina, *Italy* 35 B8
Sala-y-Gómez, *Pac. Oc.* 93 K17
Salaberry-de-Valleyfield, *Canada* 98 C5
Saladas, *Argentina* 126 B4
Saladillo, *Argentina* 126 D4
Salado →, *Buenos Aires, Argentina* 126 D4
Salado →, *La Pampa, Argentina* 128 A3
Salado →, *Río Negro, Argentina* 128 B3
Salado →, *Santa Fe, Argentina* 126 C3
Salado →, *Mexico* 114 B5
Salaga, *Ghana* 79 D4
Sālah, *Syria* 69 C5
Sálakhos, *Greece* 37 C9
Salala, *Liberia* 78 D2
Salala, *Sudan* 76 C4
Salālah, *Oman* 68 D5
Salamanca, *Chile* 126 C1
Salamanca, *Spain* 30 E5
Salamanca, *U.S.A.* 106 D6
Salamanca □, *Spain* 30 E5
Salāmatābād, *Iran* 64 C5
Salamina, *Colombia* 120 B2
Salamis, *Cyprus* 37 D12
Salamis, *Greece* 39 M6
Salar de Atacama, *Chile* 126 A2
Salar de Uyuni, *Bolivia* 124 E4
Sălard, *Romania* 38 B5
Salas, *Spain* 30 B4
Salas de los Infantes, *Spain* 28 C1
Salatiga, *Indonesia* 57 G14
Salaverry, *Peru* 124 B2
Salawati, *Indonesia* 57 E8
Salayar, *Indonesia* 57 F6
Salazar →, *Spain* 28 C3
Salbris, *France* 25 E9
Salcombe, *U.K.* 13 G4
Salda Gölü, *Turkey* 66 E3
Saldaña, *Spain* 30 C6
Saldanha, *S. Africa* 84 E2
Saldanha B., *S. Africa* 84 E2
Saldus, *Latvia* 40 C3
Sale, *Australia* 91 F4
Salé, *Morocco* 74 B3
Sale, *U.K.* 12 D5
Salekhard, *Russia* 44 C7
Salem, *India* 60 P11
Salem, *Ind., U.S.A.* 104 F2
Salem, *Mass., U.S.A.* 107 D14
Salem, *Mo., U.S.A.* 109 G9
Salem, *N.J., U.S.A.* 104 F8
Salem, *Ohio, U.S.A.* 106 F4
Salem, *Oreg., U.S.A.* 110 D2
Salem, *S. Dak., U.S.A.* 108 D6
Salem, *Va., U.S.A.* 104 G5
Salemi, *Italy* 34 E5
Salernes, *France* 27 E10
Salerno, *Italy* 35 B7
Salerno, G. di, *Italy* 35 B7
Salford, *U.K.* 12 D5
Salgir →, *Ukraine* 42 D6
Salgótarján, *Hungary* 21 G9
Salgueiro, *Brazil* 122 C4
Salida, *U.S.A.* 102 C5
Salies-de-Béarn, *France* 26 E3
Salihli, *Turkey* 66 D3
Salima, *Malawi* 81 G6
Salina, *Italy* 35 D7
Salina, *U.S.A.* 108 F6
Salina Cruz, *Mexico* 115 D5
Salinas, *Brazil* 123 E3
Salinas, *Chile* 126 A2
Salinas, *Ecuador* 120 D1
Salinas, *U.S.A.* 111 H3
Salinas →, *Guatemala* 115 D6
Salinas →, *U.S.A.* 111 H3
Salinas, B. de, *Nic.* 116 D2
Salinas, C. de, *Spain* 36 B10
Salinas, Pampa de las, *Argentina* 126 C2
Salinas Ambargasta, *Argentina* 126 B3
Salinas de Hidalgo, *Mexico* 114 C4
Salinas Grandes, *Argentina* 126 B2
Saline →, *Ark., U.S.A.* 109 J8
Saline →, *Kans., U.S.A.* 108 F6
Salines, *Spain* 36 B10
Salinópolis, *Brazil* 122 B2
Salins-les-Bains, *France* 25 F12
Salir, *Portugal* 31 H2
Salisbury = Harare, *Zimbabwe* 83 F3
Salisbury, *Australia* 91 E2
Salisbury, *U.K.* 13 F6
Salisbury, *Md., U.S.A.* 104 F8
Salisbury, *N.C., U.S.A.* 105 H5
Salisbury Plain, *U.K.* 13 F6
Săliște, *Romania* 38 D6
Salitre →, *Brazil* 122 C3
Salka, *Nigeria* 79 C5
Salkhad, *Jordan* 69 C5
Sallent, *Spain* 28 D6
Salles-Curan, *France* 26 D6
Salling, *Denmark* 11 H2
Sallisaw, *U.S.A.* 109 H7
Sallom Junction, *Sudan* 76 D4
Salmās, *Iran* 64 B5
Salmerón, *Spain* 28 E2
Salmo, *Canada* 100 D5
Salmon, *U.S.A.* 110 D7
Salmon →, *Canada* 100 C4
Salmon →, *U.S.A.* 110 D5
Salmon Arm, *Canada* 100 C5
Salmon Falls, *U.S.A.* 110 E6
Salmon Gums, *Australia* 89 F3
Salmon Res., *Canada* 99 C8
Salmon River Mts., *U.S.A.* 110 D6
Salo, *Finland* 9 F17
Salò, *Italy* 32 C7
Salobreña, *Spain* 31 J7
Salome, *U.S.A.* 113 M13
Salon-de-Provence, *France* 27 E9
Salonica = Thessaloníki, *Greece* 39 J5
Salonta, *Romania* 38 C4
Salor →, *Spain* 31 F3
Salou, C., *Spain* 28 D6
Salsacate, *Argentina* 126 C2
Salses, *France* 26 F6
Salsk, *Russia* 43 C9
Salso →, *Italy* 34 E6
Salsomaggiore, *Italy* 32 D6
Salt →, *Canada* 100 B6
Salt →, *U.S.A.* 111 K7
Salt Creek, *Australia* 91 F2
Salt Fork →, *U.S.A.* 109 G6
Salt Lake City, *U.S.A.* 110 F8
Salt Range, *Pakistan* 62 C5
Salta, *Argentina* 126 A2
Salta □, *Argentina* 126 A2
Saltcoats, *U.K.* 14 F4
Saltee Is., *Ireland* 15 D5
Saltfjorden, *Norway* 8 C13
Saltholm, *Denmark* 11 J6
Salthólmavík, *Iceland* 8 D3
Saltillo, *Mexico* 114 B4
Salto, *Argentina* 126 C3
Salto, *Uruguay* 126 C4
Salto da Divisa, *Brazil* 123 E4
Salton City, *U.S.A.* 113 M11
Salton Sea, *U.S.A.* 113 M11
Saltpond, *Ghana* 79 D4
Saltsjöbaden, *Sweden* 10 E12
Saltville, *U.S.A.* 104 G5
Saluda →, *U.S.A.* 105 H5
Salûm, *Egypt* 76 A2
Salûm, Khâlig el, *Egypt* 76 A2
Salur, *India* 61 K13
Salut, Is. du, *Fr. Guiana* 121 B7
Saluzzo, *Italy* 32 D4
Salvación, B., *Chile* 128 D1
Salvador, *Brazil* 123 D4
Salvador, *Canada* 101 C7
Salvador, L., *U.S.A.* 109 L9
Salvaterra, *Brazil* 122 B2
Salvaterra de Magos, *Portugal* 31 F2
Sálvora, I., *Spain* 30 C2
Salween →, *Burma* 61 L20
Salyany, *Azerbaijan* 67 D13
Salyersville, *U.S.A.* 104 G4
Salza →, *Austria* 21 H4
Salzach →, *Austria* 21 G2
Salzburg, *Austria* 21 H3
Salzgitter, *Germany* 18 C6
Salzwedel, *Germany* 18 C7
Sam Neua, *Laos* 58 B5
Sam Ngao, *Thailand* 58 D2
Sam Rayburn Res., *U.S.A.* 109 K7
Sam Son, *Vietnam* 58 C5
Sam Teu, *Laos* 58 C5
Sama, *Russia* 44 C7
Sama de Langreo, *Spain* 30 B5
Samagaltai, *Russia* 45 D10
Samaipata, *Bolivia* 125 D5
Samales Group, *Phil.* 55 J4
Samâlût, *Egypt* 76 J7
Samana, *India* 62 D7
Samana Cay, *Bahamas* 117 B5
Samandağı, *Turkey* 66 E6
Samanga, *Tanzania* 83 D4
Samangwa, *Zaïre* 82 C1
Samani, *Japan* 48 C11
Samar, *Phil.* 55 F6
Samara, *Russia* 41 E17
Samaria = Shōmrōn, *Jordan* 69 C4
Samariá, *Greece* 37 D5
Samarinda, *Indonesia* 56 E5
Samarkand, *Uzbekistan* 44 F7
Sāmarrā, *Iraq* 64 C4
Samastipur, *India* 63 G11
Samatan, *France* 26 E4
Samaúma, *Brazil* 125 B5
Samba, *India* 63 C6
Samba, *Zaïre* 82 C2
Sambaíba, *Brazil* 122 C2
Sambalpur, *India* 61 J14
Sambar, Tanjung, *Indonesia* 56 E4
Sambas, *Indonesia* 56 D3
Sambava, *Madag.* 85 A9
Sambawizi, *Zimbabwe* 83 F2
Sambhal, *India* 63 E8
Sambhar, *India* 62 F6
Sambiase, *Italy* 35 D9
Sambonifacio, *Italy* 32 C8
Sambor, *Cambodia* 58 F6
Sambor, *Ukraine* 40 G3
Sambre →, *Europe* 17 H5
Sambuca di Sicilia, *Italy* 34 E6
Samburu □, *Kenya* 82 B4
Samchŏk, *S. Korea* 51 F15
Samchonpo, *S. Korea* 51 G15
Same, *Tanzania* 82 C4
Samedan, *Switz.* 23 C9
Samer, *France* 25 B8
Samfya, *Zambia* 83 E2
Sámi, *Greece* 39 L3
Samnah, *Si. Arabia* 64 E3
Samnaun, *Switz.* 23 C10
Samo Alto, *Chile* 126 C1
Samobor, *Croatia* 33 C12
Samoëns, *France* 27 B10
Samokov, *Bulgaria* 38 G6
Samoorombón, B., *Argentina* 126 D4
Samorogouan, *Burkina Faso* 78 C4
Sámos, *Greece* 39 M9
Samoš, *Serbia, Yug.* 21 K10
Samos, *Spain* 30 C3
Samothráki, *Évros, Greece* 39 J8
Samothráki, *Kérkira, Greece* 37 A3
Samoylovka, *Russia* 41 F13
Sampa, *Ghana* 78 D4
Sampacho, *Argentina* 126 C3
Sampang, *Indonesia* 57 G15
Samper de Calanda, *Spain* 28 D4
Sampit, *Indonesia* 56 E4
Sampit, Teluk, *Indonesia* 56 E4
Samrée, *Belgium* 17 H7
Samrong, *Cambodia* 58 E4
Samrong, *Thailand* 58 E3
Samsø, *Denmark* 11 J4
Samsø Bælt, *Denmark* 11 J4
Samsun, *Turkey* 66 C7
Samtredia, *Georgia* 43 E10
Samui, Ko, *Thailand* 59 H3
Samun □, *Turkey* 66 C7
Samur →, *Azerbaijan* 43 F13
Samusole, *Zaïre* 83 E1
Samut Prakan, *Thailand* 58 F3
Samut Sakhon, *Thailand* 58 F3
Samut Songkhram →, *Thailand* 58 F3
Samwari, *Pakistan* 62 E2
San, *Mali* 78 C4
San →, *Cambodia* 58 F5
San →, *Poland* 20 E11
San Adrián, C. de, *Spain* 30 B2
San Agustín, *Colombia* 120 C2
San Agustin, C., *Phil.* 55 H7
San Agustín de Valle Fértil, *Argentina* 126 C2
San Ambrosio, *Pac. Oc.* 93 K20
San Andreas, *U.S.A.* 112 G6
San Andrés, I. de, *Caribbean* 116 D3
San Andres Mts., *U.S.A.* 111 K10
San Andrés Tuxtla, *Mexico* 115 D5
San Angelo, *U.S.A.* 109 K4
San Anselmo, *U.S.A.* 112 H4
San Antonio, *Belize* 115 D7
San Antonio, *Chile* 126 C1
San Antonio, *Phil.* 55 D4
San Antonio, *N. Mex., U.S.A.* 111 K10
San Antonio, *Tex., U.S.A.* 109 L5
San Antonio, *Venezuela* 120 C4
San Antonio →, *U.S.A.* 109 L6
San Antonio, C., *Argentina* 126 D4
San Antonio, C., *Cuba* 116 B3
San Antonio, C. de, *Spain* 29 G5
San Antonio, Mt., *U.S.A.* 113 L9
San Antonio Abad, *Spain* 36 C7
San Antonio de los Baños, *Cuba* 116 B3
San Antonio de los Cobres, *Argentina* 126 A2
San Antonio Oeste, *Argentina* 128 B4
San Arcángelo, *Italy* 35 B9
San Ardo, *U.S.A.* 112 J6
San Augustín, *Canary Is.* 36 G4
San Augustine, *U.S.A.* 109 K7
San Bartolomé, *Canary Is.* 36 F6
San Bartolomé de Tirajana, *Canary Is.* 36 G4
San Bartolomeo in Galdo, *Italy* 35 A8
San Benedetto, *Italy* 32 C7
San Benedetto del Tronto, *Italy* 33 F10
San Benedicto, I., *Mexico* 114 D2
San Benito, *U.S.A.* 109 M6
San Benito →, *U.S.A.* 112 J5
San Benito Mt., *U.S.A.* 112 J6
San Bernardino, *U.S.A.* 113 L9
San Bernardino, Paso del, *Switz.* 23 D8
San Bernardino Mts., *U.S.A.* 113 L10
San Bernardino Str., *Phil.* 55 E6
San Bernardo, *Chile* 126 C1
San Bernardo, I. de, *Colombia* 120 B2
San Blas, *Mexico* 114 B3
San Blas, Arch. de, *Panama* 116 E4
San Blas, C., *U.S.A.* 105 L3
San Borja, *Bolivia* 124 C4
San Buenaventura, *Bolivia* 124 C4
San Buenaventura, *Mexico* 114 B4
San Carlos = Butuku-Luba, *Eq. Guin.* 79 E6
San Carlos, *Argentina* 126 C2
San Carlos, *Bolivia* 125 D5
San Carlos, *Chile* 126 D1
San Carlos, *Mexico* 114 B4
San Carlos, *Nic.* 116 D3
San Carlos, *Negros, Phil.* 55 F5
San Carlos, *Pangasinan, Phil.* 55 D4
San Carlos, *Spain* 36 B8
San Carlos, *Uruguay* 127 C5
San Carlos, *U.S.A.* 111 K8
San Carlos, *Amazonas, Venezuela* 120 C4
San Carlos, *Cojedes, Venezuela* 120 B4
San Carlos de Bariloche, *Argentina* 128 B2
San Carlos de la Rápita, *Spain* 28 E5
San Carlos del Zulia, *Venezuela* 120 B3
San Carlos L., *U.S.A.* 111 K8
San Cataldo, *Italy* 34 E6
San Celoni, *Spain* 28 D7
San Clemente, *Chile* 126 D1
San Clemente, *Spain* 29 F2
San Clemente, *U.S.A.* 113 M9
San Clemente I., *U.S.A.* 113 N8
San Constanzo, *Italy* 33 E10
San Cristóbal, *Argentina* 126 C3
San Cristóbal, *Colombia* 120 D3
San Cristóbal, *Dom. Rep.* 117 C5
San Cristóbal, *Mexico* 115 D6
San Cristóbal, *Spain* 36 B11
San Cristóbal, *Venezuela* 120 B3
San Damiano d'Asti, *Italy* 32 D5
San Daniele del Friuli, *Italy* 33 B10
San Demétrio Corone, *Italy* 35 C9
San Diego, *Calif., U.S.A.* 113 N9
San Diego, *Tex., U.S.A.* 109 M5
San Diego, C., *Argentina* 128 D3
San Diego de la Unión, *Mexico* 114 C4
San Dimitri, Ras, *Malta* 37 C1
San Donà di Piave, *Italy* 33 C9
San Elpídio a Mare, *Italy* 33 E10
San Estanislao, *Paraguay* 126 A4
San Esteban de Gormaz, *Spain* 28 D1
San Felice sul Panaro, *Italy* 32 D8
San Felipe, *Chile* 126 C1
San Felipe, *Colombia* 120 C4
San Felipe, *Mexico* 114 A2
San Felipe, *Venezuela* 120 A4
San Felipe →, *U.S.A.* 113 M11
San Felíu de Guíxols, *Spain* 28 D8
San Felíu de Llobregat, *Spain* 28 D7
San Félix, *Pac. Oc.* 93 K20
San Fernando, *Chile* 126 C1
San Fernando, *Mexico* 114 B1
San Fernando, *La Union, Phil.* 55 C4
San Fernando, *Pampanga, Phil.* 55 D4
San Fernando, *Baleares, Spain* 36 C7
San Fernando, *Cádiz, Spain* 31 J4
San Fernando, *Trin. & Tob.* 117 D7
San Fernando, *U.S.A.* 113 L8
San Fernando →, *Mexico* 114 C5
San Fernando de Apure, *Venezuela* 120 B4
San Fernando de Atabapo, *Venezuela* 120 C4
San Fernando di Púglia, *Italy* 35 A9
San Francisco, *Argentina* 126 C3
San Francisco, *Bolivia* 125 D4
San Francisco, *U.S.A.* 111 H2
San Francisco →, *U.S.A.* 111 K9
San Francisco, Paso de, *S. Amer.* 126 B2
San Francisco de Macorîs, *Dom. Rep.* 117 C5
San Francisco del Monte de Oro, *Argentina* 126 C2
San Francisco del Oro, *Mexico* 114 B3
San Francisco Javier, *Spain* 36 C7
San Francisco Solano, Pta., *Colombia* 120 B2
San Fratello, *Italy* 35 D7
San Gabriel, *Ecuador* 120 C2
San Gavino Monreale, *Italy* 34 C1
San Gil, *Colombia* 120 B3
San Gimignano, *Italy* 32 E8
San Giórgio di Nogaro, *Italy* 33 C10
San Giórgio Iónico, *Italy* 35 B10
San Giovanni Bianco, *Italy* 32 C6
San Giovanni in Fiore, *Italy* 35 C9
San Giovanni in Persiceto, *Italy* 33 D8
San Giovanni Rotondo, *Italy* 35 A8
San Giovanni Valdarno, *Italy* 33 E8
San Giuliano Terme, *Italy* 32 E7
San Gorgonio Mt., *U.S.A.* 113 L10
San Gottardo, Paso del, *Switz.* 23 C7
San Gregorio, *Uruguay* 127 C4
San Gregorio, *U.S.A.* 112 H4
San Guiseppe Iato, *Italy* 34 E6
San Ignacio, *Belize* 115 D7
San Ignacio, *Bolivia* 125 D5
San Ignacio, *Mexico* 114 B2
San Ignacio, *Paraguay* 126 B4
San Ignacio, L., *Mexico* 114 B2
San Ildefonso, C., *Phil.* 55 C5
San Isidro, *Argentina* 126 C4
San Jacinto, *Colombia* 120 B2
San Jacinto, *U.S.A.* 113 M10
San Jaime, *Spain* 36 B11
San Javier, *Misiones, Argentina* 127 B4
San Javier, *Santa Fe, Argentina* 126 C4
San Javier, *Beni, Bolivia* 125 C5
San Javier, *Santa Cruz, Bolivia* 125 D5
San Javier, *Chile* 126 D1
San Javier, *Spain* 29 H4
San Jerónimo, Sa. de, *Colombia* 120 B2
San Jeronimo Taviche, *Mexico* 115 D5
San Joaquín, *Bolivia* 125 C5
San Joaquin, *U.S.A.* 112 J6
San Joaquín, *Venezuela* 120 A4
San Joaquín →, *Bolivia* 125 C5
San Joaquin →, *U.S.A.* 111 G3
San Joaquin Valley, *U.S.A.* 112 J6
San Jordi, *Spain* 36 B9
San Jorge, *Argentina* 126 C3
San Jorge, *Spain* 36 C7
San Jorge, B. de, *Mexico* 114 A2
San Jorge, G., *Argentina* 128 C3
San Jorge, G. de, *Spain* 28 E4
San José, *Bolivia* 125 D5
San José, *Costa Rica* 116 E3
San José, *Guatemala* 116 D1
San José, *Mexico* 114 C2
San Jose, *Phil.* 55 D4
San José, *Spain* 36 C7
San Jose, *U.S.A.* 111 H3
San Jose →, *U.S.A.* 111 J10
San Jose de Buenovista, *Phil.* 55 E4
San José de Feliciano, *Argentina* 126 C4
San José de Jáchal, *Argentina* 126 C2
San José de Mayo, *Uruguay* 126 C4
San José de Ocune, *Colombia* 120 C3
San José de Uchapiamonas, *Bolivia* 124 C4
San José del Cabo, *Mexico* 114 C3
San José del Guaviare, *Colombia* 120 C3
San José do Anauá, *Brazil* 121 C5
San Juan, *Argentina* 126 C2
San Juan, *Colombia* 120 B2
San Juan, *Mexico* 114 C4
San Juan, *Ica, Peru* 124 D2
San Juan, *Puno, Peru* 124 C4
San Juan, *Phil.* 55 G7
San Juan, *Puerto Rico* 117 C6
San Juan □, *Argentina* 126 C2
San Juan →, *Argentina* 126 C2
San Juan →, *Bolivia* 125 E4
San Juan →, *Colombia* 120 C2
San Juan →, *Nic.* 116 D3
San Juan →, *Calif., U.S.A.* 112 J5
San Juan →, *Utah, U.S.A.* 111 H8
San Juan →, *Venezuela* 121 A5
San Juan, C., *Eq. Guin.* 80 D1
San Juan Bautista, *Paraguay* 126 B4
San Juan Bautista, *Spain* 36 B8
San Juan Bautista, *U.S.A.* 111 H3
San Juan Bautista Valle Nacional, *Mexico* 115 D5

San Juan Capistrano, *U.S.A.* 113 M9
San Juan de Guadalupe, *Mexico* 114 C4
San Juan de los Morros, *Venezuela* 120 B4
San Juan del César, *Colombia* 120 A3
San Juan del Norte, *Nic.* 116 D3
San Juan del Norte, B. de, *Nic.* 116 D3
San Juan del Puerto, *Spain* 31 H4
San Juan del Río, *Mexico* 115 C5
San Juan del Sur, *Nic.* 116 D2
San Juan I., *U.S.A.* 112 B3
San Juan Mts., *U.S.A.* 111 H10
San Julián, *Argentina* 128 C3
San Just, Sierra de, *Spain* 28 E4
San Justo, *Argentina* 126 C3
San Kamphaeng, *Thailand* 58 C2
San Lázaro, C., *Mexico* 114 C2
San Lázaro, Sa., *Mexico* 114 C3
San Leandro, *U.S.A.* 111 H2
San Leonardo, *Spain* 28 D1
San Lorenzo, *Argentina* 126 C3
San Lorenzo, *Beni, Bolivia* 125 D4
San Lorenzo, *Tarija, Bolivia* 125 E5
San Lorenzo, *Ecuador* 120 C2
San Lorenzo, *Paraguay* 126 B4
San Lorenzo, *Spain* 36 B10
San Lorenzo, *Venezuela* 120 B3
San Lorenzo →, *Mexico* 114 C3
San Lorenzo, I., *Mexico* 114 B2
San Lorenzo, I., *Peru* 124 C2
San Lorenzo, Mt., *Argentina* 128 C2
San Lorenzo de la Parrilla, *Spain* 28 F2
San Lorenzo de Morunys, *Spain* 28 C6
San Lucas, *Bolivia* 125 E4
San Lucas, *Baja Calif. S., Mexico* 114 C3
San Lucas, *Baja Calif. S., Mexico* 114 B2
San Lucas, *U.S.A.* 112 J5
San Lucas, C., *Mexico* 114 C3
San Lúcido, *Italy* 35 C9
San Luis, *Argentina* 126 C2
San Luis, *Cuba* 116 B3
San Luis, *Guatemala* 116 C2
San Luis, *U.S.A.* 111 H11
San Luis □, *Argentina* 126 C2
San Luis, I., *Mexico* 114 B2
San Luis, L. de, *Bolivia* 125 C5
San Luis, Sierra de, *Argentina* 126 C2
San Luis de la Paz, *Mexico* 114 C4
San Luis Obispo, *U.S.A.* 113 K6
San Luis Potosí, *Mexico* 114 C4
San Luis Potosí □, *Mexico* 114 C4
San Luis Res., *U.S.A.* 112 H5
San Luis Río Colorado, *Mexico* 114 A2
San Marco Argentano, *Italy* 35 C9
San Marco dei Cavoti, *Italy* 35 A7
San Marco in Lámis, *Italy* 35 A8
San Marcos, *Colombia* 120 B2
San Marcos, *Guatemala* 116 D1
San Marcos, *Mexico* 114 B2
San Marcos, *U.S.A.* 109 L6
San Marino ■, *Europe* 33 E9
San Martín, *Argentina* 126 C2
San Martín, *Colombia* 120 C3
San Martín →, *Bolivia* 125 C5
San Martín, L., *Argentina* 128 C2
San Martín de los Andes, *Argentina* 128 B2
San Martín de Valdeiglesias, *Spain* 30 E6
San Martino de Calvi, *Italy* 32 C6
San Mateo, *Phil.* 55 C4
San Mateo, *Baleares, Spain* 36 B7
San Mateo, *Valencia, Spain* 28 E5
San Mateo, *U.S.A.* 111 H2
San Matías, *Bolivia* 125 D6
San Matías, G., *Argentina* 128 B4
San Miguel, *El Salv.* 116 D2
San Miguel, *Panama* 116 E4
San Miguel, *Spain* 36 B7
San Miguel, *U.S.A.* 111 J3
San Miguel, *Venezuela* 120 B4
San Miguel →, *Bolivia* 125 C5
San Miguel →, *S. Amer.* 120 C2
San Miguel de Huachi, *Bolivia* 124 D4
San Miguel de Salinas, *Spain* 29 H4
San Miguel de Tucumán, *Argentina* 126 B2
San Miguel del Monte, *Argentina* 126 D4
San Miguel I., *U.S.A.* 113 L6
San Miniato, *Italy* 32 E7
San Narciso, *Phil.* 55 D4
San Nicolás, *Canary Is.* 36 G4
San Nicolas, *Phil.* 55 B4
San Nicolás de los Arroyas, *Argentina* 126 C3
San Nicolas I., *U.S.A.* 113 M7
San Onofre, *Colombia* 120 B2
San Onofre, *U.S.A.* 113 M9
San Pablo, *Bolivia* 126 A2
San Pablo, *Phil.* 55 D4
San Paolo di Civitate, *Italy* 35 A8
San Pedro, *Buenos Aires, Argentina* 127 B5
San Pedro, *Jujuy, Argentina* 126 A3
San Pedro, *Colombia* 120 C3
San-Pédro, *Ivory C.* 78 E3
San Pedro, *Mexico* 114 C2
San Pedro, *Peru* 124 C3
San Pedro □, *Paraguay* 126 A4
San Pedro →, *Chihuahua, Mexico* 114 B3
San Pedro →, *Michoacan, Mexico* 114 D4
San Pedro →, *Nayarit, Mexico* 114 C3
San Pedro →, *U.S.A.* 111 K8
San Pedro, Pta., *Chile* 126 B1
San Pedro, Sierra de, *Spain* 31 F4
San Pedro Channel, *U.S.A.* 113 M8
San Pedro de Arimena, *Colombia* 120 C3
San Pedro de Atacama, *Chile* 126 A2
San Pedro de Jujuy, *Argentina* 126 A3
San Pedro de las Colonias, *Mexico* 114 B4
San Pedro de Lloc, *Peru* 124 B2
San Pedro de Macorís, *Dom. Rep.* 117 C6
San Pedro del Norte, *Nic.* 116 D3
San Pedro del Paraná, *Paraguay* 126 B4
San Pedro del Pinatar, *Spain* 29 H4
San Pedro Mártir, Sierra, *Mexico* 114 A1
San Pedro Mixtepec, *Mexico* 115 D5
San Pedro Ocampo = Melchor Ocampo, *Mexico* 114 C4
San Pedro Sula, *Honduras* 116 C2
San Pietro, I., *Italy* 34 C1
San Pietro Vernótico, *Italy* 35 B11
San Quintín, *Mexico* 114 A1
San Rafael, *Argentina* 126 C2
San Rafael, *Calif., U.S.A.* 112 H4
San Rafael, *N. Mex., U.S.A.* 111 J10
San Rafael, *Venezuela* 120 A3
San Rafael Mt., *U.S.A.* 113 L7
San Rafael Mts., *U.S.A.* 113 L7
San Ramón, *Bolivia* 125 C5
San Ramón, *Peru* 124 C2
San Ramón de la Nueva Orán, *Argentina* 126 A3
San Remo, *Italy* 32 E4
San Román, C., *Venezuela* 120 A3
San Roque, *Argentina* 126 B4
San Roque, *Spain* 31 J5
San Rosendo, *Chile* 126 D1
San Saba, *U.S.A.* 109 K5
San Salvador, *Bahamas* 117 B5
San Salvador, *El Salv.* 116 D2
San Salvador, *Spain* 36 B10
San Salvador de Jujuy, *Argentina* 126 A3
San Salvador I., *Bahamas* 117 B5
San Sebastián, *Argentina* 128 D3
San Sebastián, *Spain* 28 B3
San Sebastián, *Venezuela* 120 B4
San Sebastian de la Gomera, *Canary Is.* 36 F2
San Serra, *Spain* 36 B10
San Serverino Marche, *Italy* 33 E10
San Simeon, *U.S.A.* 112 K5
San Simon, *U.S.A.* 111 K9
San Stéfano di Cadore, *Italy* 33 B9
San Telmo, *Mexico* 114 A1
San Telmo, *Spain* 36 B9
San Tiburcio, *Mexico* 114 C4
San Valentin, Mte., *Chile* 128 C2
San Vicente de Alcántara, *Spain* 31 F3
San Vicente de la Barquera, *Spain* 30 B6
San Vicente del Caguán, *Colombia* 120 C3
San Vincenzo, *Italy* 32 E7
San Vito, *Italy* 34 C2
San Vito, C., *Italy* 34 D5
San Vito al Tagliamento, *Italy* 33 C9
San Vito Chietino, *Italy* 33 F11
San Vito dei Normanni, *Italy* 35 B10
San Yanaro, *Colombia* 120 C4
San Ygnacio, *U.S.A.* 109 M5
Saña, *Peru* 124 B2
Sana', *Yemen* 68 D3
Sana →, *Bos.-H., Yug.* 33 C13
Sanaba, *Burkina Faso* 78 C4
Şanāfīr, *Si. Arabia* 76 B3
Sanaga →, *Cameroon* 79 E6
Sanaloa, Presa, *Mexico* 114 C3
Sanana, *Indonesia* 57 E7
Sanand, *India* 62 H5
Sanandaj, *Iran* 64 C5
Sanandita, *Bolivia* 126 A3
Sanary-sur-Mer, *France* 27 E9
Sanawad, *India* 62 H7
Sancellas, *Spain* 36 B9
Sancergues, *France* 25 E9
Sancerre, *France* 25 E9
Sancerrois, Collines du, *France* 25 E9
Sancha He →, *China* 52 D6
Sanchahe, *China* 51 B14
Sánchez, *Dom. Rep.* 117 C6
Sanchor, *India* 62 G4
Sanco Pt., *Phil.* 57 C7
Sancoins, *France* 25 F9
Sancti-Spíritus, *Cuba* 116 B4
Sancy, Puy de, *France* 26 C6
Sand →, *S. Africa* 85 C5
Sand Springs, *U.S.A.* 109 G6
Sanda, *Japan* 49 G7
Sandakan, *Malaysia* 56 C5
Sandan = Sambor, *Cambodia* 58 F6
Sandanski, *Bulgaria* 39 H6
Sandaré, *Mali* 78 C2
Sanday, *U.K.* 14 B6
Sandefjord, *Norway* 10 E4
Sanders, *U.S.A.* 111 J9
Sanderson, *U.S.A.* 109 K3
Sandfly L., *Canada* 101 B7
Sandgate, *Australia* 91 D5
Sandía, *Peru* 124 C4
Sandıklı, *Turkey* 66 D4
Sandnes, *Norway* 9 G8
Sandness, *U.K.* 14 A7
Sandoa, *Zaïre* 80 F4
Sandona, *Colombia* 120 C2
Sandover →, *Australia* 90 C2
Sandoway, *Burma* 61 K19
Sandpoint, *U.S.A.* 110 B5
Sandringham, *U.K.* 12 E8
Sandslån, *Sweden* 10 A11
Sandspit, *Canada* 100 C2
Sandstone, *Australia* 89 E2
Sandu, *China* 52 E6
Sandusky, *Mich., U.S.A.* 98 D3
Sandusky, *Ohio, U.S.A.* 106 E2
Sandvig, *Sweden* 11 J8
Sandviken, *Sweden* 9 F14
Sandwich, C., *Australia* 90 B4
Sandwich B., *Canada* 99 B8
Sandwich B., *Namibia* 84 C1
Sandwip Chan., *Bangla.* 61 H17
Sandy, *Nev., U.S.A.* 113 K11
Sandy, *Oreg., U.S.A.* 112 E4
Sandy Bight, *Australia* 89 F3
Sandy C., *Queens., Australia* 90 C5
Sandy C., *Tas., Australia* 90 G3
Sandy Cay, *Bahamas* 117 B4
Sandy Cr. →, *U.S.A.* 110 F9
Sandy L., *Canada* 98 B1
Sandy Lake, *Canada* 98 B1
Sandy Narrows, *Canada* 101 B8
Sanford, *Fla., U.S.A.* 105 L5
Sanford, *Maine, U.S.A.* 107 C14
Sanford, *N.C., U.S.A.* 105 H6
Sanford →, *Australia* 89 E2
Sanford Mt., *U.S.A.* 96 B5
Sang-i-Masha, *Afghan.* 62 C2
Sanga, *Mozam.* 83 E4
Sanga →, *Congo* 80 E3
Sanga-Tolon, *Russia* 45 C15
Sangamner, *India* 60 K9
Sangar, *Afghan.* 62 C1
Sangar, *Russia* 45 C13
Sangar Sarai, *Afghan.* 62 B4
Sangasangadalam, *Indonesia* 56 E5
Sangay, *Ecuador* 120 D2
Sange, *Zaïre* 82 D2
Sangeang, *Indonesia* 57 F5
Sanger, *U.S.A.* 111 H4
Sangerhausen, *Germany* 18 D7
Sanggan He →, *China* 50 E9
Sanggau, *Indonesia* 56 D4
Sangihe, Kepulauan, *Indonesia* 57 D7
Sangihe, P., *Indonesia* 57 D7
Sangju, *S. Korea* 51 F15
Sangkapura, *Indonesia* 56 F4
Sangkhla, *Thailand* 58 E2
Sangli, *India* 60 L9
Sangmélina, *Cameroon* 79 E7
Sangonera →, *Spain* 29 H3
Sangre de Cristo Mts., *U.S.A.* 109 G2
Sangro →, *Italy* 33 F11
Sangudo, *Canada* 100 C6
Sangue →, *Brazil* 125 C6
Sangüesa, *Spain* 28 C3
Sanguinaires, Is., *France* 27 G12
Sangzhi, *China* 53 C8
Sanhala, *Ivory C.* 78 C3
Sāniyah, *Iraq* 64 C4
Sanje, *Uganda* 82 C3
Sanjiang, *China* 52 E7
Sanjo, *Japan* 48 F9
Sankt Antönien, *Switz.* 23 C9
Sankt Blasien, *Germany* 19 H4
Sankt Gallen, *Switz.* 23 B8
Sankt Gallen □, *Switz.* 23 B8
Sankt Goar, *Germany* 19 E3
Sankt Ingbert, *Germany* 19 F3
Sankt Margrethen, *Switz.* 23 B9
Sankt Moritz, *Switz.* 23 D9
Sankt-Peterburg, *Russia* 40 B7
Sankt Pölten, *Austria* 21 G5
Sankt Valentin, *Austria* 21 G4
Sankt Veit, *Austria* 21 J4
Sankt Wendel, *Germany* 19 F3
Sankuru →, *Zaïre* 80 E4
Sanlúcar de Barrameda, *Spain* 31 J4
Sanlúcar la Mayor, *Spain* 31 H4
Sanluri, *Italy* 34 C1
Sanmenxia, *China* 50 G6
Sanming, *China* 53 D11
Sannaspos, *S. Africa* 84 D4
Sannicandro Gargánico, *Italy* 35 A8
Sannidal, *Norway* 10 F3
Sannieshof, *S. Africa* 84 D4
Sannīn, J., *Lebanon* 69 B4
Sanok, *Poland* 20 F12
Sanquhar, *U.K.* 14 F5
Sansanding Dam, *Mali* 78 C3
Sansepolcro, *Italy* 33 E9
Sansha, *China* 53 D13
Sanshui, *China* 53 F9
Sanski Most, *Bos.-H., Yug.* 33 D13
Sansui, *China* 52 D7
Santa, *Peru* 124 B2
Sant' Ágata de Goti, *Italy* 35 A7
Sant' Ágata di Militello, *Italy* 35 D7
Santa Ana, *Beni, Bolivia* 125 C4
Santa Ana, *Santa Cruz, Bolivia* 125 D6
Santa Ana, *Santa Cruz, Bolivia* 125 D5
Santa Ana, *Ecuador* 120 D1
Santa Ana, *El Salv.* 116 D2
Santa Ana, *Mexico* 114 A2
Santa Ana, *U.S.A.* 113 M9
Santa Ana →, *Venezuela* 120 B3
Sant' Ángelo Lodigiano, *Italy* 32 C6
Sant' Antíoco, *Italy* 34 C1
Sant' Arcángelo di Romagna, *Italy* 33 D9
Santa Bárbara, *Colombia* 120 B2
Santa Bárbara, *Honduras* 116 D2
Santa Bárbara, *Mexico* 114 B3
Santa Bárbara, *Spain* 28 E5
Santa Barbara, *U.S.A.* 113 L7
Santa Bárbara, *Venezuela* 120 B3
Santa Bárbara, Mt., *Spain* 29 H2
Santa Barbara Channel, *U.S.A.* 113 L7
Santa Barbara I., *U.S.A.* 113 M7
Santa Catalina, *Colombia* 120 A2
Santa Catalina, *Mexico* 114 B2
Santa Catalina, G. of, *U.S.A.* 113 N9
Santa Catalina I., *U.S.A.* 113 M8
Santa Catarina □, *Brazil* 127 B6
Santa Catarina, I. de, *Brazil* 127 B6
Santa Caterina Villarmosa, *Italy* 35 E7
Santa Cecília, *Brazil* 127 B5
Santa Clara, *Cuba* 116 B4
Santa Clara, *Calif., U.S.A.* 111 H3
Santa Clara, *Utah, U.S.A.* 111 H7
Santa Clara de Olimar, *Uruguay* 127 C5
Santa Clotilde, *Peru* 120 D3
Santa Coloma de Farners, *Spain* 28 D7
Santa Coloma de Gramanet, *Spain* 28 D7
Santa Comba, *Spain* 30 B2
Santa Croce Camerina, *Italy* 35 F7
Santa Croce di Magliano, *Italy* 35 A7
Santa Cruz, *Argentina* 128 D3
Santa Cruz, *Bolivia* 125 D5
Santa Cruz, *Brazil* 122 C4
Santa Cruz, *Chile* 126 C1
Santa Cruz, *Costa Rica* 116 D2
Santa Cruz, *Madeira* 36 D3
Santa Cruz, *Peru* 124 B2
Santa Cruz, *Phil.* 55 D4
Santa Cruz, *U.S.A.* 111 H2
Santa Cruz, *Venezuela* 121 B5
Santa Cruz □, *Argentina* 128 C3
Santa Cruz □, *Bolivia* 125 D5
Santa Cruz →, *Argentina* 128 D3
Santa Cruz Cabrália, *Brazil* 123 E4
Santa Cruz de la Palma, *Canary Is.* 36 F2
Santa Cruz de Mudela, *Spain* 29 G1
Santa Cruz de Tenerife, *Canary Is.* 36 F3
Santa Cruz del Norte, *Cuba* 116 B3
Santa Cruz del Retamar, *Spain* 30 E6
Santa Cruz del Sur, *Cuba* 116 B4
Santa Cruz do Rio Pardo, *Brazil* 127 A6
Santa Cruz do Sul, *Brazil* 127 B5
Santa Cruz I., *Solomon Is.* 92 J8
Santa Cruz I., *U.S.A.* 113 M7
Santa Domingo, Cay, *Bahamas* 116 B4
Santa Elena, *Argentina* 126 C4
Santa Elena, *Ecuador* 120 D1
Santa Elena, C., *Costa Rica* 116 D2
Sant' Eufémia, G. di, *Italy* 35 D9
Santa Eugenia, Pta., *Mexico* 114 B1
Santa Eulalia, *Spain* 36 C8
Santa Fe, *Argentina* 126 C3
Santa Fe, *Spain* 31 H7
Santa Fe, *U.S.A.* 111 J11
Santa Fé □, *Argentina* 126 C3
Santa Filomena, *Brazil* 122 C2
Santa Galdana, *Spain* 36 B10
Santa Gertrudis, *Spain* 36 B7
Santa Helena, *Brazil* 122 B2
Santa Helena de Goiás, *Brazil* 123 E1
Santa Inês, *Brazil* 123 D4
Santa Inés, *Baleares, Spain* 36 B7
Santa Inés, *Extremadura, Spain* 31 G5
Santa Inés, I., *Chile* 128 D2
Santa Isabel = Rey Malabo, *Eq. Guin.* 79 E6
Santa Isabel, *Argentina* 126 D2
Santa Isabel, *Brazil* 123 D1
Santa Isabel, Pico, *Eq. Guin.* 79 E6
Santa Isabel do Araguaia, *Brazil* 122 C2
Santa Isabel do Morro, *Brazil* 123 D1
Santa Lucía, *Corrientes, Argentina* 126 B4
Santa Lucía, *San Juan, Argentina* 126 C2
Santa Lucía, *Spain* 29 H4
Santa Lucía, *Uruguay* 126 C4
Santa Lucia Range, *U.S.A.* 111 J3
Santa Magdalena, I., *Mexico* 114 C2
Santa Margarita, *Argentina* 126 D3
Santa Margarita, *Mexico* 114 C2
Santa Margarita, *Spain* 36 B10
Santa Margarita, *U.S.A.* 112 K6
Santa Margarita →, *U.S.A.* 113 M9
Santa Margherita, *Italy* 32 D6
Santa María, *Argentina* 126 B2
Santa Maria, *Brazil* 127 B5
Santa Maria, *Phil.* 55 C4
Santa Maria, *Spain* 36 B9
Santa Maria, *Switz.* 23 C10
Santa Maria, *U.S.A.* 113 L6
Santa María →, *Mexico* 114 A3
Santa María, B. de, *Mexico* 114 B3
Santa Maria, C. de, *Portugal* 31 J3
Santa Maria Capua Vetere, *Italy* 35 A7
Santa Maria da Vitória, *Brazil* 123 D3
Santa María de Ipire, *Venezuela* 121 B4
Santa Maria di Leuca, C., *Italy* 35 C11
Santa Maria do Suaçuí, *Brazil* 123 E3
Santa Maria dos Marmelos, *Brazil* 125 B5
Santa María la Real de Nieva, *Spain* 30 D6
Santa Marta, *Colombia* 120 A3
Santa Marta, *Spain* 31 G4
Santa Marta, Ría de, *Spain* 30 B3
Santa Marta, Sierra Nevada de, *Colombia* 120 A3
Santa Marta Grande, C., *Brazil* 127 B6
Santa Maura = Levkás, *Greece* 39 L3
Santa Monica, *U.S.A.* 113 M8
Santa Olalla, *Huelva, Spain* 31 H4
Santa Olalla, *Toledo, Spain* 30 E6
Sant' Onofrio, *Italy* 35 D9
Santa Pola, *Spain* 29 G4
Santa Ponsa, *Spain* 36 B9
Santa Quitéria, *Brazil* 122 B3
Santa Rita, *U.S.A.* 111 K10
Santa Rita, *Guarico, Venezuela* 120 B4
Santa Rita, *Zulia, Venezuela* 120 A3
Santa Rita do Araquaia, *Brazil* 125 D7
Santa Rosa, *La Pampa, Argentina* 126 D3
Santa Rosa, *San Luis, Argentina* 126 C2
Santa Rosa, *Bolivia* 124 C4
Santa Rosa, *Brazil* 127 B5
Santa Rosa, *Colombia* 120 C4
Santa Rosa, *Ecuador* 120 D2
Santa Rosa, *Peru* 124 C3
Santa Rosa, *Calif., U.S.A.* 112 G4
Santa Rosa, *N. Mex., U.S.A.* 109 H2
Santa Rosa, *Venezuela* 120 C4
Santa Rosa de Cabal, *Colombia* 120 C2
Santa Rosa de Copán, *Honduras* 116 D2
Santa Rosa de Osos, *Colombia* 120 B2
Santa Rosa de Río Primero, *Argentina* 126 C3
Santa Rosa de Viterbo, *Colombia* 120 B3
Santa Rosa del Palmar, *Bolivia* 125 D5
Santa Rosa I., *Calif., U.S.A.* 113 M6
Santa Rosa I., *Fla., U.S.A.* 105 K2

Santa Rosa Ra., U.S.A. 110 F5
Santa Rosalía, Mexico 114 B2
Santa Sofia, Italy 33 E8
Santa Sylvina, Argentina 126 B3
Santa Tecla = Nueva San Salvador, El Salv. 116 D2
Santa Teresa, Argentina 126 C3
Santa Teresa, Brazil 123 E3
Santa Teresa, Mexico 115 B5
Santa Teresa, Venezuela 121 C5
Santa Teresa di Riva, Italy 35 E8
Santa Teresa Gallura, Italy 34 A2
Santa Vitória, Brazil 123 E1
Santa Vitória do Palmar, Brazil 127 C5
Santa Ynez, U.S.A. 113 L6
Santa Ynez →, U.S.A. 113 L6
Santa Ysabel, U.S.A. 113 M10
Santadi, Italy 34 C1
Santai, China 52 B5
Santaluz, Brazil 122 D4
Santana, Brazil 123 D3
Santana, Madeira 36 D3
Santana, Coxilha de, Brazil 127 C4
Santana do Ipanema, Brazil 122 C4
Santana do Livramento, Brazil 127 C4
Santanayi, Spain 36 B10
Santander, Colombia 120 C2
Santander, Spain 30 B7
Santander Jiménez, Mexico 115 C5
Santaquin, U.S.A. 110 G8
Santarém, Brazil 121 D7
Santarém, Portugal 31 F2
Santarém □, Portugal 31 F2
Santaren Channel, W. Indies 116 B4
Santee, U.S.A. 113 N10
Santéramo in Colle, Italy 35 B9
Santerno →, Italy 33 D8
Santhia, Italy 32 C5
Santiago, Bolivia 125 D6
Santiago, Brazil 127 B5
Santiago, Chile 126 C1
Santiago, Panama 116 E3
Santiago, Peru 124 C2
Santiago, Phil. 55 C4
Santiago □, Chile 126 C1
Santiago →, Peru 120 D2
Santiago, C., Chile 128 D1
Santiago, Punta de, Eq. Guin. 79 E6
Santiago, Serranía de, Bolivia 125 D6
Santiago de Chuco, Peru 124 B2
Santiago de Compostela, Spain 30 C2
Santiago de Cuba, Cuba 116 C4
Santiago de los Cabelleros, Dom. Rep. 117 C5
Santiago del Estero, Argentina 126 B3
Santiago del Estero □, Argentina 126 B3
Santiago del Teide, Canary Is. 36 F3
Santiago do Cacém, Portugal 31 G2
Santiago Ixcuintla, Mexico 114 C3
Santiago Papasquiaro, Mexico 114 B3
Santiaguillo, L. de, Mexico 114 C4
Santillana del Mar, Spain 30 B6
Säntis, Switz. 23 B8
Santisteban del Puerto, Spain 29 G1
Santo →, Peru 124 B2
Santo Amaro, Brazil 123 D4
Santo Anastácio, Brazil 127 A5
Santo André, Brazil 127 A6
Santo Ângelo, Brazil 127 B5
Santo Antonio, Brazil 125 D6
Santo Antônio de Jesus, Brazil 123 D4
Santo Antônio do Içá, Brazil 120 D4
Santo Antônio do Leverger, Brazil 125 D6
Santo Corazón, Bolivia 125 D6
Santo Domingo, Dom. Rep. 117 C6
Santo Domingo, Baja Calif. N., Mexico 114 A1
Santo Domingo, Baja Calif. S., Mexico 114 B2
Santo Domingo, Nic. 116 D3
Santo Domingo de la Calzada, Spain 28 C2
Santo Domingo de los Colorados, Ecuador 120 D2
Santo Stéfano di Camastro, Italy 35 D7
Santo Stino di Livenza, Italy 33 C9
Santo Tirso, Portugal 30 D2
Santo Tomás, Mexico 114 A1
Santo Tomás, Peru 124 C3
Santo Tomé, Argentina 127 B4
Santo Tomé de Guayana = Ciudad Guayana, Venezuela 121 B5
Santoña, Spain 30 B7
Santos, Brazil 127 A6
Santos, Sierra de los, Spain 31 G5
Santos Dumont, Brazil 123 F3
Santpoort, Neths. 16 D5
Sanvignes-les-Mines, France 25 F11
Sanyuan, China 50 G5
Sanza Pombo, Angola 80 F3
São Anastácio, Brazil 127 A5
São Bartolomeu de Messines, Portugal 31 H2
São Benedito, Brazil 122 B3
São Bento, Brazil 122 B3
São Bento do Norte, Brazil 122 C4
São Bernado de Campo, Brazil 123 F2
São Borja, Brazil 127 B4
São Bras d'Alportel, Portugal 31 H3
São Caitano, Brazil 122 C4
São Carlos, Brazil 127 A6
São Cristóvão, Brazil 122 D4
São Domingos, Brazil 123 D2
São Domingos do Maranhão, Brazil 122 C3
São Félix, Brazil 123 D1
São Francisco, Brazil 123 E3
São Francisco →, Brazil 122 D4
São Francisco do Maranhão, Brazil 122 C3
São Francisco do Sul, Brazil 127 B6
São Gabriel, Brazil 127 C5
São Gabriel da Palha, Brazil 123 E3
São Gonçalo, Brazil 123 F3
São Gotardo, Brazil 123 E2
Sao Hill, Tanzania 83 D4
São João da Boa Vista, Brazil 127 A6
São João da Pesqueira, Portugal 30 D3
São João da Ponte, Brazil 123 E3
São João del Rei, Brazil 123 F3
São João do Araguaia, Brazil 122 C2
São João do Paraíso, Brazil 123 E3
São João do Piauí, Brazil 122 C3
São João dos Patos, Brazil 122 C3
São Joaquim da Barra, Brazil 123 F2
São Jorge, Pta. de, Madeira 36 D3
São José, B. de, Brazil 122 B3
São José da Laje, Brazil 122 C4
São José de Mipibu, Brazil 122 C4
São José do Peixe, Brazil 122 C3
São José do Rio Prêto, Brazil 127 A6
São José dos Campos, Brazil 127 A6
São Leopoldo, Brazil 127 B5
São Lourenço, Brazil 123 F2
São Lourenço →, Brazil 125 D6
São Lourenço, Pantanal do, Brazil 125 D6
São Lourenço, Pta. de, Madeira 36 D3
São Luís, Brazil 122 B3
São Luís do Curu, Brazil 122 B4
São Luís Gonzaga, Brazil 127 B5
São Marcos →, Brazil 123 E2
São Marcos, B. de, Brazil 122 B3
São Martinho, Portugal 30 E2
São Mateus, Brazil 123 E4
São Mateus →, Brazil 123 E4
São Miguel do Araguaia, Brazil 123 D1
São Miguel dos Campos, Brazil 122 C4
São Nicolau →, Brazil 122 C3
São Paulo, Brazil 127 A6
São Paulo □, Brazil 127 A6
São Paulo, I., Atl. Oc. 2 D8
São Paulo de Olivença, Brazil 120 D4
São Pedro do Sul, Portugal 30 E2
São Rafael, Brazil 122 C4
São Raimundo das Mangabeiras, Brazil 122 C2
São Raimundo Nonato, Brazil 122 C3
São Romão, Brazil 123 E2
São Roque, Madeira 36 D3
São Roque, C. de, Brazil 122 C4
São Sebastião, I. de, Brazil 127 A6
São Sebastião do Paraíso, Brazil 127 A6
São Simão, Brazil 123 E1
São Teotónio, Portugal 31 H2
São Tomé, Atl. Oc. 70 F4
São Tomé, Brazil 122 C4
São Tomé, C. de, Brazil 123 F3
São Tomé & Principe ■, Africa 71 F4
São Vicente, Brazil 127 A6
São Vicente, Madeira 36 D2
São Vicente, C. de, Portugal 31 H2
Saona, I., Dom. Rep. 117 C6
Saône →, France 27 C8
Saône-et-Loire □, France 25 F11
Saonek, Indonesia 57 E8
Saoura, O. →, Algeria 75 C4
Sapanca, Turkey 66 C4
Sapão →, Brazil 122 D2
Saparua, Indonesia 57 E7
Sapé, Brazil 122 C4
Sapele, Nigeria 79 D6
Sapelo I., U.S.A. 105 K5
Sapiéntza, Greece 39 N4
Sapone, Burkina Faso 79 C4
Saposoa, Peru 124 B2
Sapozhok, Russia 41 E12
Sappemeer, Neths. 16 B9
Sappho, U.S.A. 112 B2
Sapporo, Japan 48 C10
Sapri, Italy 35 B8
Sapudi, Indonesia 57 G16
Sapulpa, U.S.A. 109 G7
Saqqez, Iran 64 B5
Sar Dasht, Iran 65 C6
Sar Gachīneh, Iran 65 D6
Sar Planina, Macedonia, Yug. 38 G4
Sara, Burkina Faso 78 C4
Sara, Phil. 55 F5
Sara Buri, Thailand 58 E3
Sarāb, Iran 64 B5
Sarabadi, Iraq 64 C5
Sarada →, India 61 F12
Saragossa = Zaragoza, Spain 28 D4
Saraguro, Ecuador 120 D2
Sarajevo, Bos.-H., Yug. 21 M8
Saramacca □, Surinam 121 C6
Saramacca →, Surinam 121 B6
Saran, G., Indonesia 56 E4
Saranac Lake, U.S.A. 107 B10
Saranda, Tanzania 82 D3
Sarandí del Yi, Uruguay 127 C4
Sarandí Grande, Uruguay 126 C4
Sarangani B., Phil. 55 J6
Sarangani Is., Phil. 55 J6
Sarangarh, India 61 J13
Saransk, Russia 41 D14
Sarapul, Russia 44 D6
Sarasota, U.S.A. 105 M4
Saratoga, Calif., U.S.A. 112 H4
Saratoga, Wyo., U.S.A. 110 F10
Saratoga Springs, U.S.A. 107 C11
Saratov, Russia 41 F15
Saravane, Laos 58 E6
Sarawak □, Malaysia 56 D4
Saray, Turkey 67 D11
Saraya, Senegal 78 C2
Sarayköy, Turkey 66 E3
Sarayönü, Turkey 66 D5
Sarbāz, Iran 65 E9
Sarbīsheh, Iran 65 C8
Sarca →, Italy 32 C7
Sardalas, Libya 75 C7
Sardarshahr, India 62 E6
Sardegna, Italy 34 B2
Sardhana, India 62 E7
Sardina, Pta., Canary Is. 36 F4
Sardinata, Colombia 120 B3
Sardinia = Sardegna, Italy 34 B2
Sardis, Turkey 66 D3
Sārdūīyeh = Dar Mazār, Iran 65 D8
Saréyamou, Mali 78 B4
Sargent, U.S.A. 108 E5
Sargodha, Pakistan 62 C5
Sarh, Chad 73 G8
Sarhro, Djebel, Morocco 74 B3
Sārī, Iran 65 B7
Sária, Greece 39 P10
Sarıgöl, Turkey 66 D3
Sarikamiş, Turkey 67 C10
Sarıkaya, Turkey 66 D6
Sarikei, Malaysia 56 D4
Sarina, Australia 90 C4
Sariñena, Spain 28 D4
Sarita, U.S.A. 109 M6
Sariwŏn, N. Korea 51 E13
Sark, Chan. Is. 13 H5
Sarkad, Hungary 21 J11
Şarkışla, Turkey 66 D7
Şarköy, Turkey 66 C2
Sarlat-la-Canéda, France 26 D5
Sarles, U.S.A. 108 A5
Sărmaşu, Romania 38 C7
Sarmi, Indonesia 57 E9
Sarmiento, Argentina 128 C3
Särna, Sweden 10 C7
Sarnano, Italy 33 E10
Sarnen, Switz. 22 C6
Sarnia, Canada 98 D3
Sarno, Italy 35 B7
Sarny, Ukraine 40 F5
Särö, Sweden 11 G5
Sarolangun, Indonesia 56 E2
Saronikós Kólpos, Greece 39 M6
Saronno, Italy 32 C6
Saros Körfezi, Turkey 66 C2
Sárospatak, Hungary 21 G11
Sarova, Russia 41 D13
Sarpsborg, Norway 10 E5
Sarracín, Spain 28 C1
Sarralbe, France 25 D14
Sarre = Saar →, Europe 25 C13
Sarre-Union, France 25 D14
Sarrebourg, France 25 D14
Sarreguemines, France 25 C14
Sarriá, Spain 30 C3
Sarrión, Spain 28 E4
Sarro, Mali 78 C3
Sarstedt, Germany 18 C5
Sartène, France 27 G12
Sarthe □, France 24 E7
Sarthe →, France 24 E6
Sartilly, France 24 D5
Sartynya, Russia 44 C7
Sárvár, Hungary 21 H6
Sarvestān, Iran 65 D7
Särvfjället, Sweden 10 B7
Sárviz →, Hungary 21 J8
Sary-Tash, Kirghizia 44 F8
Sarych, Mys, Ukraine 42 D5
Saryshagan, Kazakhstan 44 E8
Sarzana, Italy 32 D6
Sarzeau, France 24 E4
Sas van Gent, Neths. 17 F3
Sasabeneh, Ethiopia 68 F3
Sasaram, India 63 G11
Sasebo, Japan 49 H4
Saser, India 63 B7
Saskatchewan □, Canada 101 C7
Saskatchewan →, Canada 101 C8
Saskatoon, Canada 101 C7
Saskylakh, Russia 45 B12
Sasnovka, Russia 41 C17
Sasolburg, S. Africa 85 D4
Sasovo, Russia 41 D12
Sassandra, Ivory C. 78 E3
Sassandra →, Ivory C. 78 E3
Sássari, Italy 34 B1
Sassenheim, Neths. 16 D5
Sassnitz, Germany 18 A9
Sasso Marconi, Italy 33 D8
Sassocorvaro, Italy 33 E9
Sassoferrato, Italy 33 E9
Sassuolo, Italy 32 D7
Sástago, Spain 28 D4
Sastown, Liberia 78 E3
Sasumua Dam, Kenya 82 C4
Sata-Misaki, Japan 49 J5
Satadougou, Mali 78 C2
Satanta, U.S.A. 109 G4
Satara, India 60 L8
Satilla →, U.S.A. 105 K5
Satipo, Peru 124 C3
Satmala Hills, India 60 J9
Satna, India 63 G9
Šator, Bos.-H., Yug. 33 D13
Sátoraljaújhely, Hungary 21 G11
Satpura Ra., India 62 J7
Satrup, Germany 18 A5
Satsuna-Shotō, Japan 49 K5
Sattahip, Thailand 58 F3
Satu Mare, Romania 38 B5
Satui, Indonesia 56 E5
Satun, Thailand 59 J3
Saturnina →, Brazil 125 C6
Sauce, Argentina 126 C4
Sauceda, Mexico 114 B4
Saucillo, Mexico 114 B3
Sauda, Norway 9 G9
Saúde, Brazil 122 D3
Sauðarkrókur, Iceland 8 D4
Saudi Arabia ■, Asia 68 B3
Sauer →, Germany 17 J9
Saugeen →, Canada 106 B3
Saugerties, U.S.A. 107 D11
Saugues, France 26 D7
Sauherad, Norway 10 E3
Saujon, France 26 C3
Sauk Centre, U.S.A. 108 C7
Sauk Rapids, U.S.A. 108 C7
Saül, Fr. Guiana 121 C7
Saulgau, Germany 19 G5
Saulieu, France 25 E11
Sault, France 27 D9
Sault Ste. Marie, Canada 98 C3
Sault Ste. Marie, U.S.A. 104 B3
Saumlaki, Indonesia 57 F8
Saumur, France 24 E6
Saunders C., N.Z. 87 L3
Saunders I., Antarctica 5 B1
Saunders Point, Australia 89 E4
Saurbær, Borgarfjarðarsýsla, Iceland 8 D3
Saurbær, Eyjafjarðarsýsla, Iceland 8 D4
Sauri, Nigeria 79 C6
Saurimo, Angola 80 F4
Sausalito, U.S.A. 112 H4
Sautatá, Colombia 120 B2
Sauveterre-de-Béarn, France 26 E3
Sauzé-Vaussais, France 26 B4
Savá, Honduras 116 C2
Sava →, Serbia, Yug. 21 L10
Savage, U.S.A. 108 B2
Savage I. = Niue, Cook Is. 93 J11
Savai'i, W. Samoa 87 A12
Savalou, Benin 79 D5
Savane, Mozam. 83 F4
Savanna, U.S.A. 108 D9
Savanna la Mar, Jamaica 116 C4
Savannah, Ga., U.S.A. 105 J5
Savannah, Mo., U.S.A. 108 F7
Savannah, Tenn., U.S.A. 105 H1
Savannah →, U.S.A. 105 J5
Savannakhet, Laos 58 D5
Savant L., Canada 98 B1
Savant Lake, Canada 98 B1
Savanur, India 60 M9
Savé, Benin 79 D5
Save →, France 26 E5
Save →, Mozam. 85 C5
Sāveh, Iran 65 C6
Savelugu, Ghana 79 D4
Savenay, France 24 E5
Saverdun, France 26 E5
Saverne, France 25 D14
Savièse, Switz. 22 D4
Savigliano, Italy 32 D4
Savigny-sur-Braye, France 24 E7
Saviñao, Spain 30 C3
Savio →, Italy 33 D9
Savognin, Switz. 23 C9
Savoie □, France 27 C10
Savona, Italy 32 D5
Sawahlunto, Indonesia 56 E2
Sawai, Indonesia 57 E7
Sawai Madhopur, India 62 F7
Sawang Daen Din, Thailand 58 D4
Sawankhalok, Thailand 58 D2
Sawara, Japan 49 G10
Sawatch Mts., U.S.A. 111 G10
Sawel, U.K. 15 B4
Sawi, Thailand 59 G2
Sawmills, Zimbabwe 83 F2
Sawu, Indonesia 57 F6
Sawu Sea, Indonesia 57 F6
Saxby →, Australia 90 B3
Saxon, Switz. 22 D4
Saxony, Lower = Niedersachsen □, Germany 18 C5
Saxton, U.S.A. 106 F6
Say, Niger 79 C5
Saya, Nigeria 79 D5
Sayabec, Canada 99 C6
Sayaboury, Laos 58 C3
Sayán, Peru 124 C2
Sayan, Vostochnyy, Russia 45 D10
Sayan, Zapadnyy, Russia 45 D10
Sayasan, Russia 43 E12
Saydā, Lebanon 69 B4
Sayhan-Ovoo, Mongolia 50 B2
Sayhandulaan, Mongolia 50 B5
Sayḩut, Yemen 68 D5
Saynshand, Mongolia 50 B6
Sayre, Okla., U.S.A. 109 H5
Sayre, Pa., U.S.A. 107 E8
Sayula, Mexico 114 D4
Sazin, Pakistan 63 B5
Sazlika →, Bulgaria 39 H8
Sbeïtla, Tunisia 75 A6
Scaër, France 24 D3
Scafell Pikes, U.K. 12 C4
Scalea, Italy 35 C8
Scalpay, U.K. 14 D2
Scandia, Canada 100 C6
Scandiano, Italy 32 D7
Scandinavia, Europe 8 E12
Scansano, Italy 33 F8
Scapa Flow, U.K. 14 C5
Scappoose, U.S.A. 112 E4
Scarborough, Trin. & Tob. 117 D7
Scarborough, U.K. 12 C7
Scebeli, Wabi →, Somali Rep. 68 G3
Šćedro, Croatia 33 E13
Scenic, U.S.A. 108 D3
Schaal See, Germany 18 B6
Schaan, Liech. 23 B9
Schaesberg, Neths. 17 G8
Schaffen, Belgium 17 G6
Schaffhausen, Switz. 23 A7
Schaffhausen □, Switz. 23 A7
Schagen, Neths. 16 C5
Schaijk, Neths. 16 E7
Schalkhaar, Neths. 16 D8
Schalkwijk, Neths. 16 E6
Schangnau, Switz. 22 C5
Schänis, Switz. 23 B8
Schärding, Austria 20 G3
Scharhörn, Germany 18 B4
Scharnitz, Austria 19 H7
Scheessel, Germany 18 B5
Schefferville, Canada 99 B6
Schelde →, Belgium 17 F4
Schell Creek Ra., U.S.A. 110 G6
Schenectady, U.S.A. 107 D11
Scherfede, Germany 18 D5
Scherpenheuvel, Belgium 17 G5
Scherpenisse, Neths. 17 E4
Scherpenzeel, Neths. 16 D7
Schesaplana, Switz. 23 B9
Schesslitz, Germany 19 F7
Scheveningen, Neths. 16 D4
Schiedam, Neths. 16 E4
Schiermonnikoog, Neths. 16 B8
Schiers, Switz. 23 C9
Schifferstadt, Germany 19 F4
Schifflange, Lux. 17 K8
Schijndel, Neths. 17 E6
Schiltigheim, France 25 D14
Schio, Italy 33 C8
Schipbeek, Neths. 16 D8
Schipluiden, Neths. 16 E4
Schirmeck, France 25 D14
Schlei →, Germany 18 A5
Schleiden, Germany 18 E2
Schleiz, Germany 18 E7
Schleswig, Germany 18 A5
Schleswig-Holstein □, Germany 18 A5
Schlieren, Switz. 23 B6
Schlüchtern, Germany 19 E5
Schmalkalden, Germany 18 E6
Schmölln, Brandenburg, Germany 18 B10
Schmölln, Thüringen, Germany 18 E8
Schneeberg, Austria 21 H5
Schneeberg, Germany 18 E8
Schoenberg, Belgium 17 H8
Schofield, U.S.A. 108 C10

Scholls, *U.S.A.* 112 E4
Schönberg, *Mecklenburg-Vorpommern, Germany* 18 B6
Schönberg, *Schleswig-Holstein, Germany* 18 A6
Schönebeck, *Germany* 18 C7
Schönenwerd, *Switz.* 22 B5
Schongau, *Germany* 19 H6
Schöningen, *Germany* 18 C6
Schoondijke, *Neths.* 17 F3
Schoonebeek, *Neths.* 16 C9
Schoonhoven, *Neths.* 16 E5
Schoorl, *Neths.* 16 C5
Schortens, *Germany* 18 B3
Schoten, *Belgium* 17 F5
Schouten I., *Australia* 90 G4
Schouten Is. = Supriori, Kepulauan, *Indonesia* 57 E9
Schouwen, *Neths.* 17 E3
Schramberg, *Germany* 19 G4
Schrankogl, *Austria* 19 H7
Schreckhorn, *Switz.* 22 C6
Schreiber, *Canada* 98 C2
Schrobenhausen, *Germany* 19 G7
Schruns, *Austria* 19 H5
Schuler, *Canada* 101 C6
Schuls, *Switz.* 23 C10
Schumacher, *Canada* 98 C3
Schüpfen, *Switz.* 22 B4
Schüpfheim, *Switz.* 22 C6
Schurz, *U.S.A.* 110 G4
Schuyler, *U.S.A.* 108 E6
Schuylkill Haven, *U.S.A.* 107 F8
Schwabach, *Germany* 19 F7
Schwäbisch Gmünd, *Germany* 19 G5
Schwäbisch Hall, *Germany* 19 F5
Schwäbische Alb, *Germany* 19 G5
Schwabmünchen, *Germany* 19 G6
Schwanden, *Switz.* 23 C8
Schwandorf, *Germany* 19 F8
Schwaner, Pegunungan, *Indonesia* 56 E4
Schwarmstedt, *Germany* 18 C5
Schwärze, *Germany* 18 C9
Schwarze Elster →, *Germany* 18 D8
Schwarzenberg, *Germany* 18 E8
Schwarzenburg, *Switz.* 22 C4
Schwarzwald, *Germany* 19 H4
Schwaz, *Austria* 19 H7
Schwedt, *Germany* 18 B10
Schweinfurt, *Germany* 19 E6
Schweizer Mittelland, *Switz.* 22 C4
Schweizer-Reneke, *S. Africa* 84 D4
Schwenningen, *Germany* 19 G4
Schwerin, *Germany* 18 B7
Schweriner See, *Germany* 18 B7
Schwetzingen, *Germany* 19 F4
Schwyz, *Switz.* 23 B7
Schwyz □, *Switz.* 23 B7
Sciacca, *Italy* 34 E6
Scicli, *Italy* 35 F7
Scilla, *Italy* 35 D8
Scilly, Isles of, *U.K.* 13 H1
Ścinawa, *Poland* 20 D6
Scioto →, *U.S.A.* 104 F4
Scobey, *U.S.A.* 108 A2
Scone, *Australia* 91 E5
Scordia, *Italy* 35 E7
Scoresbysund, *Greenland* 4 B6
Scorno, Punta dello, *Italy* 34 A1
Scotia, *Calif., U.S.A.* 110 F1
Scotia, *N.Y., U.S.A.* 107 D11
Scotia Sea, *Antarctica* 5 B18
Scotland, *U.S.A.* 108 D6
Scotland □, *U.K.* 14 E5
Scotland Neck, *U.S.A.* 105 G7
Scott, C., *Australia* 88 B4
Scott City, *U.S.A.* 108 F4
Scott Glacier, *Antarctica* 5 C8
Scott I., *Antarctica* 5 C11
Scott Inlet, *Canada* 97 A12
Scott Is., *Canada* 100 C3
Scott L., *Canada* 101 B7
Scott Reef, *Australia* 88 B3
Scottburgh, *S. Africa* 85 E5
Scottdale, *U.S.A.* 106 F5
Scottsbluff, *U.S.A.* 108 E3
Scottsboro, *U.S.A.* 105 H2
Scottsburg, *U.S.A.* 104 F3
Scottsdale, *Australia* 90 G4
Scottsville, *Ky., U.S.A.* 105 G2
Scottsville, *N.Y., U.S.A.* 106 C7
Scottville, *U.S.A.* 104 D2
Scranton, *U.S.A.* 107 E9
Scugog, L., *Canada* 106 B6
Scunthorpe, *U.K.* 12 D7
Scuol, *Switz.* 23 C10
Scusciuban, *Somali Rep.* 68 E5
Scutari = Üsküdar, *Turkey* 39 H12
Seabra, *Brazil* 123 D3
Seabrook, L., *Australia* 89 F2
Seaford, *U.S.A.* 104 F8
Seaforth, *Canada* 98 D3
Seagraves, *U.S.A.* 109 J3
Seal →, *Canada* 101 B10
Seal Cove, *Canada* 99 C8
Seal L., *Canada* 99 B7
Sealy, *U.S.A.* 109 L6
Searchlight, *U.S.A.* 113 K12
Searcy, *U.S.A.* 109 H9
Searles L., *U.S.A.* 113 K9
Seaside, *Calif., U.S.A.* 112 J5
Seaside, *Oreg., U.S.A.* 112 E3
Seaspray, *Australia* 91 F4
Seattle, *U.S.A.* 112 C4
Seaview Ra., *Australia* 90 B4
Sebastián Vizcaíno, B., *Mexico* 114 B2
Sebastopol = Sevastopol, *Ukraine* 42 D5
Sebastopol, *U.S.A.* 112 G4
Sebderat, *Ethiopia* 77 D4
Sebdou, *Algeria* 75 B4
Seben, *Turkey* 66 C4
Sebewaing, *U.S.A.* 104 D4
Sebezh, *Russia* 40 C6
Sébi, *Mali* 78 B4
Şebinkarahisar, *Turkey* 42 F8
Sebiş, *Romania* 38 C5
Sebkhet Te-n-Dghâmcha, *Mauritania* 78 B1
Sebkra Azzel Mati, *Algeria* 75 C5
Sebkra Mekerghene, *Algeria* 75 C5
Sebnitz, *Germany* 18 E10
Sebou, Oued →, *Morocco* 74 B3
Sebring, *Fla., U.S.A.* 105 M5
Sebring, *Ohio, U.S.A.* 106 F3
Sebringville, *Canada* 106 C3
Sebta = Ceuta, *Morocco* 74 A3
Sebuku, *Indonesia* 56 E5
Sebuku, Teluk, *Malaysia* 56 D5
Secchia →, *Italy* 32 C8
Sechelt, *Canada* 100 D4
Sechura, *Peru* 124 B1
Sechura, Desierto de, *Peru* 124 B1
Seclin, *France* 25 B10
Secondigny, *France* 24 F6
Secretary I., *N.Z.* 87 L1
Secunderabad, *India* 60 L11
Sécure →, *Bolivia* 125 D5
Sedalia, *U.S.A.* 108 F8
Sedan, *Australia* 91 E2
Sedan, *France* 25 C11
Sedan, *U.S.A.* 109 G6
Sedano, *Spain* 28 C1
Seddon, *N.Z.* 87 J5
Seddonville, *N.Z.* 87 J4
Sedeh, *Fārs, Iran* 65 D7
Sedeh, *Khorāsān, Iran* 65 C8
Sederot, *Israel* 69 D3
Sedgewick, *Canada* 100 C6
Sedhiou, *Senegal* 78 C1
Sedičany, *Czech.* 20 F4
Sedico, *Italy* 33 B9
Sedley, *Canada* 101 C8
Sedova, Pik, *Russia* 44 B6
Sedrata, *Algeria* 75 A6
Sedro Woolley, *U.S.A.* 112 B4
Sedrun, *Switz.* 23 C7
Seduva, *Lithuania* 40 D3
Seebad Ahlbeck, *Germany* 18 B10
Seehausen, *Germany* 18 C7
Seeheim, *Namibia* 84 D2
Seekoei →, *S. Africa* 84 E4
Seelaw, *Germany* 18 C10
Sées, *France* 24 D7
Seesen, *Germany* 18 D6
Sefadu, *S. Leone* 78 D2
Seferihisar, *Turkey* 66 D2
Séfeto, *Mali* 78 C3
Sefrou, *Morocco* 74 B4
Sefwi Bekwai, *Ghana* 78 D4
Seg-ozero, *Russia* 40 A8
Segamat, *Malaysia* 59 L4
Segarcea, *Romania* 38 E6
Segbwema, *S. Leone* 78 D2
Seget, *Indonesia* 57 E8
Seggueur, O. →, *Algeria* 75 B5
Segonzac, *France* 26 C3
Segorbe, *Spain* 28 F4
Ségou, *Mali* 78 C3
Segovia = Coco →, *Cent. Amer.* 116 D3
Segovia, *Colombia* 120 B3
Segovia, *Spain* 30 E6
Segovia □, *Spain* 30 E6
Segré, *France* 24 E6
Segre →, *Spain* 28 D5
Séguéla, *Ivory C.* 78 D3
Seguin, *U.S.A.* 109 L6
Segundo →, *Argentina* 126 C3
Segura →, *Spain* 29 G4
Segura, Sierra de, *Spain* 29 G2
Seh Qal'eh, *Iran* 65 C8
Sehitwa, *Botswana* 84 C3
Sehore, *India* 62 H7
Sehwan, *Pakistan* 62 F2
Şeica Mare, *Romania* 38 C7
Seiland, *Norway* 8 A17
Seiling, *U.S.A.* 109 G5
Seille →, *France* 27 B8
Seilles, *Belgium* 17 G6
Sein, I. de, *France* 24 D2
Seinäjoki →, *Finland* 8 E17
Seine →, *France* 24 C7
Seine, B. de la, *France* 24 C6
Seine-et-Marne □, *France* 25 D9
Seine-Maritime □, *France* 24 C7
Seine-St.-Denis □, *France* 25 D9
Seistan, *Iran* 65 D9
Sejerø, *Denmark* 11 J5
Sejerø Bugt, *Denmark* 11 J5
Seka, *Ethiopia* 77 F4
Sekayu, *Indonesia* 56 E2
Seke, *Tanzania* 82 C3
Sekenke, *Tanzania* 82 C3
Sekken Veøy, *Norway* 10 B1
Sekondi-Takoradi, *Ghana* 78 E4
Sekuma, *Botswana* 84 C3
Selah, *U.S.A.* 110 C3
Selama, *Malaysia* 59 K3
Selárgius, *Italy* 34 C2
Selaru, *Indonesia* 57 F8
Selb, *Germany* 19 E8
Selby, *U.K.* 12 D6
Selby, *U.S.A.* 108 C4
Selca, *Croatia* 33 E13
Selçuk, *Turkey* 66 E2
Selden, *U.S.A.* 108 F4
Sele →, *Italy* 35 B7
Selemdzha →, *Russia* 45 D13
Selenga = Selenge Mörön →, *Asia* 54 A5
Selenge Mörön →, *Asia* 54 A5
Selenica, *Albania* 39 J2
Selenter See, *Germany* 18 A6
Sélestat, *France* 25 D14
Seletan, Tg., *Indonesia* 56 E4
Seletin, *Romania* 38 B8
Selfridge, *U.S.A.* 108 B4
Sélibabi, *Mauritania* 78 B2
Seliger, Oz., *Russia* 40 C8
Seligman, *U.S.A.* 111 J7
Şelim, *Turkey* 43 F10
Selîma, El Wâhât el, *Sudan* 76 C2
Selinda Spillway, *Botswana* 84 B3
Selinoús, *Greece* 39 M4
Selizharovo, *Russia* 40 C8
Seljord, *Norway* 10 E2
Selkirk, *Canada* 101 C9
Selkirk, *U.K.* 14 F6
Selkirk I., *Canada* 101 C9
Selkirk Mts., *Canada* 100 C5
Selles-sur-Cher, *France* 25 E8
Selliá, *Greece* 37 D6
Sellières, *France* 25 F12
Sells, *U.S.A.* 111 L8
Sellye, *Hungary* 21 K7
Selma, *Ala., U.S.A.* 105 J2
Selma, *Calif., U.S.A.* 111 H4
Selma, *N.C., U.S.A.* 105 H6
Selmer, *U.S.A.* 105 H1
Selongey, *France* 25 E12
Selowandoma Falls, *Zimbabwe* 83 G3
Selpele, *Indonesia* 57 E8
Selsey Bill, *U.K.* 13 G7
Seltz, *France* 25 D15
Selu, *Indonesia* 57 F8
Sélune →, *France* 24 D5
Selva, *Argentina* 126 B3
Selva, *Italy* 33 B8
Selva, *Spain* 28 D6
Selvas, *Brazil* 124 B4
Selwyn, *Australia* 90 C3
Selwyn L., *Canada* 101 A8
Selwyn Ra., *Australia* 90 C3
Seman →, *Albania* 39 J2
Semara, *W. Sahara* 74 C2
Semarang, *Indonesia* 57 G14
Semau, *Indonesia* 57 F6
Sembabule, *Uganda* 82 C3
Sémé, *Senegal* 78 B2
Semeih, *Sudan* 77 E3
Semenov, *Russia* 41 C14
Semenovka, *Ukraine* 40 E8
Semenovka, *Ukraine* 42 B5
Semeru, *Indonesia* 57 H15
Semiluki, *Russia* 41 F11
Seminoe Res., *U.S.A.* 110 E10
Seminole, *Okla., U.S.A.* 109 H6
Seminole, *Tex., U.S.A.* 109 J3
Semiozernoye, *Kazakhstan* 44 D7
Semipalatinsk, *Kazakhstan* 44 D9
Semirara Is., *Phil.* 55 F4
Semisopochnoi, *U.S.A.* 96 C2
Semitau, *Indonesia* 56 D4
Semiyarskoye, *Kazakhstan* 44 D8
Semmering Pass, *Austria* 21 H5
Semnān, *Iran* 65 C7
Semnān □, *Iran* 65 C7
Semois →, *Europe* 17 J5
Semporna, *Malaysia* 57 D5
Semuda, *Indonesia* 56 E4
Semur-en-Auxois, *France* 25 E11
Sena, *Bolivia* 124 C4
Senā, *Iran* 65 D6
Sena, *Mozam.* 83 F3
Sena →, *Bolivia* 124 C4
Sena Madureira, *Brazil* 124 B4
Senador Pompeu, *Brazil* 122 C4
Senaja, *Malaysia* 56 C5
Senaki, *Georgia* 43 E10
Senanga, *Zambia* 84 B3
Senatobia, *U.S.A.* 109 H10
Sendafa, *Ethiopia* 77 F4
Sendai, *Kagoshima, Japan* 49 J5
Sendai, *Miyagi, Japan* 48 E10
Sendai-Wan, *Japan* 48 E10
Sendenhorst, *Germany* 18 D3
Seneca, *Oreg., U.S.A.* 110 D4
Seneca, *S.C., U.S.A.* 105 H4
Seneca Falls, *U.S.A.* 107 D8
Seneca L., *U.S.A.* 106 D8
Seneffe, *Belgium* 17 G4
Senegal ■, *W. Afr.* 78 C2
Senegal →, *W. Afr.* 78 B1
Senegambia, *Africa* 70 E2
Senekal, *S. Africa* 85 D4
Senftenberg, *Germany* 18 D10
Senga Hill, *Zambia* 83 D3
Senge Khambab = Indus →, *Pakistan* 62 G2
Sengerema □, *Tanzania* 82 C3
Sengiley, *Russia* 41 E16
Sengkang, *Indonesia* 57 E6
Sengua →, *Zimbabwe* 83 F2
Senguerr →, *Argentina* 128 C3
Senhor-do-Bonfim, *Brazil* 122 D3
Senica, *Czech.* 20 G7
Senigállia, *Italy* 33 E10
Senio →, *Italy* 33 D9
Senirkent, *Turkey* 66 D4
Senise, *Italy* 35 B9
Senj, *Croatia* 33 D11
Senja, *Norway* 8 B14
Senlis, *France* 25 C9
Senmonorom, *Cambodia* 58 F6
Sennâr, *Sudan* 77 E3
Senne →, *Belgium* 17 G4
Senneterre, *Canada* 98 C4
Senniquelle, *Liberia* 78 D3
Senno, *Belorussia* 40 D6
Sennori, *Italy* 34 B1
Seno, *Laos* 58 D5
Senonches, *France* 24 D8
Senorbì, *Italy* 34 C2
Senožeče, *Slovenia* 33 C11
Sens, *France* 25 D10
Senta, *Serbia, Yug.* 21 K10
Sentery, *Zaïre* 82 D2
Sentinel, *U.S.A.* 111 K7
Sentolo, *Indonesia* 57 G14
Senya Beraku, *Ghana* 79 D4
Seo de Urgel, *Spain* 28 C6
Seohara, *India* 63 E8
Seoni, *India* 63 H8
Seoul = Sŏul, *S. Korea* 51 F14
Separation Point, *Canada* 99 B8
Sepīdān, *Iran* 65 D7
Sepo-ri, *N. Korea* 51 E14
Sepone, *Laos* 58 D6
Sept-Îles, *Canada* 99 B6
Septemvri, *Bulgaria* 38 G7
Sepúlveda, *Spain* 30 D7
Sequeros, *Spain* 30 E4
Sequim, *U.S.A.* 112 B3
Sequoia Nat. Park, *U.S.A.* 111 H4
Serafimovich, *Russia* 43 B10
Seraing, *Belgium* 17 G7
Seraja, *Indonesia* 59 L7
Serakhis →, *Cyprus* 37 D11
Seram, *Indonesia* 57 E7
Seram Laut, Kepulauan, *Indonesia* 57 E8
Seram Sea, *Indonesia* 57 E7
Serang, *Indonesia* 57 G12
Serasan, *Indonesia* 59 L7
Seravezza, *Italy* 32 E7
Serbia □, *Serbia, Yug.* 21 M11
Serdo, *Ethiopia* 77 E5
Serdobsk, *Russia* 41 E14
Seredka, *Russia* 40 B6
Şereflikoçhisar, *Turkey* 66 D5
Seregno, *Italy* 32 C6
Seremban, *Malaysia* 59 L3
Serengeti □, *Tanzania* 82 C3
Serengeti Plain, *Tanzania* 82 C3
Serenje, *Zambia* 83 E3
Sereth = Siret →, *Romania* 38 D11
Sergach, *Russia* 41 D14
Serge →, *Spain* 28 D5
Sergino, *Russia* 44 C7
Sergipe □, *Brazil* 122 D4
Sergiyev Posad, *Russia* 41 C11
Seria, *Brunei* 56 D4
Serian, *Malaysia* 56 D4
Seriate, *Italy* 32 C6
Seribu, Kepulauan, *Indonesia* 56 F3
Sérifontaine, *France* 25 C8
Sérifos, *Greece* 39 M7
Sérignan, *France* 26 E7
Serik, *Turkey* 66 E4
Seringapatam Reef, *Australia* 88 B3
Sermaize-les-Bains, *France* 25 D11
Sermata, *Indonesia* 57 F7
Sérmide, *Italy* 33 C8
Sernovodsk, *Russia* 41 E17
Serny Zavod, *Turkmenistan* 44 F6
Serón, *Spain* 29 H2
Serós, *Spain* 28 D5
Serov, *Russia* 44 D7
Serowe, *Botswana* 84 C4
Serpa, *Portugal* 31 H3
Serpeddi, Punta, *Italy* 34 C2
Serpentara, *Italy* 34 C2
Serpentine, *Australia* 89 F2
Serpentine Lakes, *Australia* 89 E4
Serpis →, *Spain* 29 G4
Serpukhov, *Russia* 41 D10
Serra do Navio, *Brazil* 121 C7
Serra San Bruno, *Italy* 35 D9
Serra Talhada, *Brazil* 122 C4
Serracapriola, *Italy* 35 A8
Serradilla, *Spain* 30 F4
Sérrai, *Greece* 39 H6
Serramanna, *Italy* 34 C1
Serrat, C., *Tunisia* 75 A6
Serre-Ponçon, L. de, *France* 27 D10
Serres, *France* 27 D9
Serrezuela, *Argentina* 126 C2
Serrinha, *Brazil* 123 D4
Serrita, *Brazil* 122 C4
Sersale, *Italy* 35 C9
Sertã, *Portugal* 30 F2
Sertânia, *Brazil* 122 C4
Sertanópolis, *Brazil* 127 A5
Sêrtar, *China* 52 A3
Sertig, *Switz.* 23 C9
Serua, *Indonesia* 57 F8
Serui, *Indonesia* 57 E9
Serule, *Botswana* 84 C4
Sérvia, *Greece* 39 J4
Sese Is., *Uganda* 82 C3
Sesepe, *Indonesia* 57 E7
Sesfontein, *Namibia* 84 B1
Sesheke, *Zambia* 84 B3
Sesia →, *Italy* 32 C5
Sesimbra, *Portugal* 31 G1
Sessa Aurunca, *Italy* 34 A6
S'estañol, *Spain* 36 B9
Sesto San Giovanni, *Italy* 32 C6
Sestri Levante, *Italy* 32 D6
Sestrières, *Italy* 32 D3
Sestrunj, *Croatia* 33 D12
Sestu, *Italy* 34 C2
Sesvenna, *Switz.* 23 C10
Setana, *Japan* 48 C9
Sète, *France* 26 E7
Sete Lagôas, *Brazil* 123 E3
Sétif, *Algeria* 75 A6
Seto, *Japan* 49 G8
Setonaikai, *Japan* 49 G6
Settat, *Morocco* 74 B3
Setté-Cama, *Gabon* 80 E1
Séttimo Tor, *Italy* 32 C4
Setting L., *Canada* 101 B9
Settle, *U.K.* 12 C5
Settlement Pt., *Bahamas* 105 M6
Setto Calende, *Italy* 32 C5
Setúbal, *Portugal* 31 G2
Setúbal □, *Portugal* 31 G2
Setúbal, B. de, *Portugal* 31 G2
Seugne →, *France* 26 C3
Seulimeum, *Indonesia* 56 C1
Seuzach, *Switz.* 23 A7
Sevan, *Armenia* 43 F11
Sevan, Ozero, *Armenia* 43 F11
Sevastopol, *Ukraine* 42 D5
Sevelen, *Switz.* 23 B8
Seven Emu, *Australia* 90 B2
Seven Sisters, *Canada* 100 C3
Sevenum, *Neths.* 17 F8
Sever →, *Spain* 31 F3
Sévérac-le-Château, *France* 26 D7
Severn →, *Canada* 98 A2
Severn →, *U.K.* 13 F5
Severn L., *Canada* 98 B1
Severnaya Zemlya, *Russia* 45 B10
Severo-Kurilsk, *Russia* 45 D16
Severo-Yeniseyskiy, *Russia* 45 C10
Severodonetsk, *Ukraine* 43 B8
Severodvinsk, *Russia* 44 C4
Sevier, *U.S.A.* 111 G7
Sevier →, *U.S.A.* 111 G7
Sevier L., *U.S.A.* 110 G7
Sevilla, *Colombia* 120 C2
Sevilla, *Spain* 31 H5
Sevilla □, *Spain* 31 H5
Seville = Sevilla, *Spain* 31 H5
Sevnica, *Slovenia* 33 B12
Sèvre-Nantaise →, *France* 24 E5
Sèvre-Niortaise →, *France* 26 B3
Sevsk, *Russia* 40 E9
Seward, *Alaska, U.S.A.* 96 B5
Seward, *Nebr., U.S.A.* 108 E6
Seward Pen., *U.S.A.* 96 B3
Sewell, *Chile* 126 C1
Sewer, *Indonesia* 57 F8
Sewickley, *U.S.A.* 106 F4
Sexbierum, *Neths.* 16 B6
Sexsmith, *Canada* 100 B5
Seychelles ■, *Ind. Oc.* 47 K9
Seyðisfjörður, *Iceland* 8 D7
Seydvān, *Iran* 64 B5
Seyfe Gölü, *Turkey* 66 D6
Seyhan Baraji, *Turkey* 66 E6
Seyitgazi, *Turkey* 66 D4
Seym →, *Ukraine* 40 F8
Seymchan, *Russia* 45 C16
Seymour, *Australia* 91 F4
Seymour, *S. Africa* 85 E4
Seymour, *Conn., U.S.A.* 107 E11
Seymour, *Ind., U.S.A.* 104 F3
Seymour, *Tex., U.S.A.* 109 J5
Seymour, *Wis., U.S.A.* 104 C1
Seyne, *France* 27 D10
Seyssel, *France* 27 C9
Sežana, *Slovenia* 33 C10
Sézanne, *France* 25 D10
Sezze, *Italy* 34 A6
Sfax, *Tunisia* 75 B7
Sfîntu Gheorghe, *Romania* 38 D8
Sfîntu Gheorghe, Braţul →, *Romania* 38 E12
Sha Xi →, *China* 53 D12
Sha Xian, *China* 53 D11
Shaanxi □, *China* 50 G5
Shaba □, *Zaïre* 82 D2
Shabunda, *Zaïre* 82 C2
Shache, *China* 54 C2
Shackleton Ice Shelf, *Antarctica* 5 C8
Shackleton Inlet, *Antarctica* 5 E11

Shādegān, *Iran* 65 **D6**
Shadi, *China* 53 **D10**
Shadi, *India* 63 **C7**
Shadrinsk, *Russia* 44 **D7**
Shaffa, *Nigeria* 79 **C7**
Shafter, *Calif., U.S.A.* 113 **K7**
Shafter, *Tex., U.S.A.* 109 **L2**
Shaftesbury, *U.K.* 13 **F5**
Shagamu, *Nigeria* 79 **D5**
Shagram, *Pakistan* 63 **A5**
Shah Bunder, *Pakistan* 62 **G2**
Shahabad, *Punjab, India* 62 **D7**
Shahabad, *Raj., India* 62 **G7**
Shahabad, *Ut. P., India* 63 **F8**
Shahadpur, *Pakistan* 62 **G3**
Shahba, *Syria* 69 **C5**
Shahdād, *Iran* 65 **D8**
Shahdadkot, *Pakistan* 62 **F2**
Shahe, *China* 50 **F8**
Shahganj, *India* 63 **F10**
Shahgarh, *India* 60 **F6**
Shaḥḥāt, *Libya* 73 **B9**
Shahjahanpur, *India* 63 **F8**
Shahpur, *India* 62 **H7**
Shahpur, *Pakistan* 62 **E3**
Shahpura, *India* 63 **H9**
Shahr Kord, *Iran* 65 **C6**
Shāhrakht, *Iran* 65 **C9**
Shahrig, *Pakistan* 62 **D2**
Shahukou, *China* 50 **D7**
Shaikhabad, *Afghan.* 62 **B3**
Shajapur, *India* 62 **H7**
Shakargarh, *Pakistan* 62 **C6**
Shakawe, *Botswana* 84 **B3**
Shaker Heights, *U.S.A.* 106 **E3**
Shakhty, *Russia* 43 **C9**
Shakhunya, *Russia* 41 **C15**
Shaki, *Nigeria* 79 **D5**
Shakopee, *U.S.A.* 108 **C8**
Shala, L., *Ethiopia* 77 **F4**
Shallow Lake, *Canada* 106 **B3**
Shaluli Shan, *China* 52 **B2**
Shām, *Iran* 65 **E8**
Shamâl Dârfûr □, *Sudan* 77 **D2**
Shamâl Kordofân □, *Sudan* 77 **D2**
Shamattawa, *Canada* 101 **B10**
Shamattawa →, *Canada* 98 **A2**
Shambe, *Sudan* 77 **F3**
Shambu, *Ethiopia* 77 **F4**
Shamīl, *Iran* 65 **E8**
Shamkhor, *Azerbaijan* 43 **F12**
Shāmkūh, *Iran* 65 **C8**
Shamli, *India* 62 **E7**
Shamo = Gobi, *Asia* 50 **C5**
Shamo, L., *Ethiopia* 77 **F4**
Shamokin, *U.S.A.* 107 **F8**
Shamrock, *U.S.A.* 109 **H4**
Shamva, *Zimbabwe* 83 **F3**
Shan □, *Burma* 61 **J21**
Shan Xian, *China* 50 **G9**
Shanan →, *Ethiopia* 77 **F5**
Shanchengzhen, *China* 51 **C13**
Shāndak, *Iran* 65 **D9**
Shandon, *U.S.A.* 112 **K6**
Shandong □, *China* 51 **F10**
Shandong Bandao, *China* 51 **F11**
Shang Xian, *China* 50 **H5**
Shangalowe, *Zaïre* 83 **E2**
Shangani →, *Zimbabwe* 83 **F2**
Shangbancheng, *China* 51 **D10**
Shangcai, *China* 53 **A10**
Shangcheng, *China* 53 **B10**
Shangchuan Dao, *China* 53 **G9**
Shangdu, *China* 50 **D7**
Shanggao, *China* 53 **C10**
Shanghai, *China* 53 **B13**
Shanghang, *China* 53 **E11**
Shanghe, *China* 51 **F9**
Shangjin, *China* 53 **A8**
Shanglin, *China* 52 **F7**
Shangnan, *China* 50 **H6**
Shangqiu, *China* 50 **G8**
Shangrao, *China* 53 **C11**
Shangshui, *China* 50 **H8**
Shangsi, *China* 52 **F6**
Shangyou, *China* 53 **E10**
Shangzhi, *China* 51 **B14**
Shanhetun, *China* 51 **B14**
Shani, *Nigeria* 79 **C7**
Shaniko, *U.S.A.* 110 **D3**
Shannon, *Greenland* 4 **B7**
Shannon, *N.Z.* 87 **J5**
Shannon →, *Ireland* 15 **D2**
Shansi = Shanxi □, *China* 50 **F7**
Shantar, Ostrov Bolshoy, *Russia* 45 **D14**
Shantipur, *India* 63 **H13**
Shantou, *China* 53 **F11**
Shantung = Shandong □, *China* 51 **F10**
Shanxi □, *China* 50 **F7**
Shanyang, *China* 50 **H5**
Shanyin, *China* 50 **E7**
Shaoguan, *China* 53 **E9**
Shaowu, *China* 53 **D11**
Shaoxing, *China* 53 **C13**
Shaoyang, *Hunan, China* 53 **D8**
Shaoyang, *Hunan, China* 53 **D8**
Shapinsay, *U.K.* 14 **B6**
Shaqra', *Si. Arabia* 64 **E5**
Shaqrā', *Yemen* 68 **E4**
Sharafa, *Sudan* 77 **E2**
Sharbot Lake, *Canada* 107 **B8**
Shari, *Japan* 48 **C12**
Sharjah = Ash Shāriqah, *U.A.E.* 65 **E7**
Shark B., *Australia* 89 **E1**
Sharm el Sheikh, *Egypt* 76 **B3**
Sharon, *Mass., U.S.A.* 107 **D13**
Sharon, *Pa., U.S.A.* 106 **E4**
Sharon Springs, *U.S.A.* 108 **F4**
Sharp Pt., *Australia* 90 **A3**
Sharpe L., *Canada* 101 **C10**
Sharpsville, *U.S.A.* 106 **E4**
Sharq el Istiwa'iya □, *Sudan* 77 **F3**
Sharya, *Russia* 41 **B14**
Shasha, *Ethiopia* 77 **F4**
Shashemene, *Ethiopia* 77 **F4**
Shashi, *Botswana* 85 **C4**
Shashi, *China* 53 **B9**
Shashi →, *Africa* 83 **G2**
Shasta, Mt., *U.S.A.* 110 **F2**
Shasta L., *U.S.A.* 110 **F2**
Shatsk, *Russia* 41 **D12**
Shatt al'Arab →, *Iraq* 65 **D6**
Shattuck, *U.S.A.* 109 **G5**
Shatura, *Russia* 41 **D11**
Shaumyani, *Georgia* 43 **F11**
Shaunavon, *Canada* 101 **D7**
Shaver Lake, *U.S.A.* 112 **H7**
Shaw →, *Australia* 88 **D2**
Shaw I., *Australia* 90 **C4**
Shawan, *China* 54 **B3**
Shawanaga, *Canada* 106 **A4**
Shawano, *U.S.A.* 104 **C1**
Shawinigan, *Canada* 98 **C5**
Shawnee, *U.S.A.* 109 **H6**
Shaybārā, *Si. Arabia* 64 **E3**
Shayib el Banat, Gebel, *Egypt* 76 **B3**
Shaykh Sa'īd, *Iraq* 64 **C5**
Shchekino, *Russia* 41 **D10**
Shcherbakov = Rybinsk, *Russia* 41 **B11**
Shchigri, *Russia* 41 **F10**
Shchors, *Ukraine* 40 **F7**
Shchuchiosk, *Kazakhstan* 44 **D8**
She Xian, *Anhui, China* 53 **C12**
She Xian, *Hebei, China* 50 **F7**
Shea, *Guyana* 121 **C6**
Shebekino, *Russia* 41 **F10**
Shebele = Scebeli, Wabi →, *Somali Rep.* 68 **G3**
Sheboygan, *U.S.A.* 104 **D2**
Shediac, *Canada* 99 **C7**
Sheelin, L., *Ireland* 15 **C4**
Sheep Haven, *Ireland* 15 **A4**
Sheerness, *U.K.* 13 **F8**
Sheet Harbour, *Canada* 99 **D7**
Sheffield, *U.K.* 12 **D6**
Sheffield, *Ala., U.S.A.* 105 **H2**
Sheffield, *Mass., U.S.A.* 107 **D11**
Sheffield, *Pa., U.S.A.* 106 **E5**
Sheffield, *Tex., U.S.A.* 109 **K4**
Sheho, *Canada* 101 **C8**
Shehojele, *Ethiopia* 77 **E4**
Shehong, *China* 52 **B5**
Shehuen →, *Argentina* 128 **C3**
Sheikhpura, *India* 63 **G11**
Shek Hasan, *Ethiopia* 77 **E4**
Shekhupura, *Pakistan* 62 **D5**
Sheki, *Azerbaijan* 43 **F12**
Sheksna →, *Russia* 41 **B11**
Shelburne, *N.S., Canada* 99 **D6**
Shelburne, *Ont., Canada* 98 **D3**
Shelburne, *U.S.A.* 107 **B11**
Shelburne B., *Australia* 90 **A3**
Shelburne Falls, *U.S.A.* 107 **D12**
Shelby, *Mich., U.S.A.* 104 **D2**
Shelby, *Mont., U.S.A.* 110 **B8**
Shelby, *N.C., U.S.A.* 105 **H5**
Shelby, *Ohio, U.S.A.* 106 **F2**
Shelbyville, *Ill., U.S.A.* 108 **F10**
Shelbyville, *Ind., U.S.A.* 104 **F3**
Shelbyville, *Tenn., U.S.A.* 105 **H2**
Sheldon, *U.S.A.* 108 **D7**
Sheldrake, *Canada* 99 **B7**
Shelikhova, Zaliv, *Russia* 45 **D16**
Shell Lake, *Canada* 101 **C7**
Shell Lakes, *Australia* 89 **E4**
Shellbrook, *Canada* 101 **C7**
Shellharbour, *Australia* 91 **E5**
Shelling Rocks, *Ireland* 15 **E1**
Shelon →, *Russia* 40 **B7**
Shelton, *Conn., U.S.A.* 107 **E11**
Shelton, *Wash., U.S.A.* 112 **C3**
Shemakha, *Azerbaijan* 43 **F13**
Shen Xian, *China* 50 **F8**
Shenandoah, *Iowa, U.S.A.* 108 **E7**
Shenandoah, *Pa., U.S.A.* 107 **F8**
Shenandoah, *Va., U.S.A.* 104 **F6**
Shenandoah →, *U.S.A.* 104 **F7**
Shenchi, *China* 50 **E7**
Shendam, *Nigeria* 79 **D6**
Shendî, *Sudan* 77 **D3**
Sheng Xian, *China* 53 **C13**
Shengfang, *China* 50 **E9**
Shëngjergji, *Albania* 39 **H3**
Shëngjini, *Albania* 39 **H2**
Shenjingzi, *China* 51 **B13**
Shenmu, *China* 50 **E6**
Shennongjia, *China* 53 **B8**
Shenqiu, *China* 50 **H8**
Shenqiucheng, *China* 50 **H8**
Shensi = Shaanxi □, *China* 50 **G5**
Shenyang, *China* 51 **D12**
Sheopur Kalan, *India* 60 **G10**
Shepetovka, *Ukraine* 40 **F5**
Shepparton, *Australia* 91 **F4**
Sheqi, *China* 50 **H7**
Sher Qila, *Pakistan* 63 **A6**
Sherborne, *U.K.* 13 **G5**
Sherbro I., *S. Leone* 78 **D2**
Sherbrooke, *Canada* 99 **C5**
Shereik, *Sudan* 76 **D3**
Sheridan, *Ark., U.S.A.* 109 **H8**
Sheridan, *Wyo., U.S.A.* 110 **D10**
Sherkot, *India* 63 **E8**
Sherman, *U.S.A.* 109 **J6**
Sherridon, *Canada* 101 **B8**
Sherwood, *N. Dak., U.S.A.* 108 **A4**
Sherwood, *Tex., U.S.A.* 109 **K4**
Sherwood Forest, *U.K.* 12 **D6**
Sheslay, *Canada* 100 **B2**
Sheslay →, *Canada* 100 **B2**
Shethanei L., *Canada* 101 **B9**
Shetland □, *U.K.* 14 **A7**
Shetland Is., *U.K.* 14 **A7**
Shewa □, *Ethiopia* 77 **F4**
Shewa Gimira, *Ethiopia* 77 **F4**
Sheyenne, *U.S.A.* 108 **B5**
Sheyenne →, *U.S.A.* 108 **B6**
Shibām, *Yemen* 68 **D4**
Shibata, *Japan* 48 **F9**
Shibecha, *Japan* 48 **C12**
Shibetsu, *Japan* 48 **B11**
Shibîn el Kôm, *Egypt* 76 **H7**
Shibîn el Qanâtir, *Egypt* 76 **H7**
Shibing, *China* 52 **D7**
Shibogama L., *Canada* 98 **B2**
Shibushi, *Japan* 49 **J5**
Shicheng, *China* 53 **D11**
Shidao, *China* 51 **F12**
Shidian, *China* 52 **E2**
Shido, *Japan* 49 **G7**
Shiel, L., *U.K.* 14 **E3**
Shield, C., *Australia* 90 **A2**
Shiga □, *Japan* 49 **G8**
Shigaib, *Sudan* 73 **E9**
Shigu, *China* 52 **D2**
Shiguaigou, *China* 50 **D6**
Shihchiachuangi = Shijiazhuang, *China* 50 **E8**
Shijiazhuang, *China* 50 **E8**
Shijiu Hu, *China* 53 **B12**
Shikarpur, *India* 62 **E8**
Shikarpur, *Pakistan* 62 **F3**
Shikoku □, *Japan* 49 **H6**
Shikoku-Sanchi, *Japan* 49 **H6**
Shilabo, *Ethiopia* 68 **F3**
Shiliguri, *India* 61 **F16**
Shilka, *Russia* 45 **D12**
Shilka →, *Russia* 45 **D13**
Shillelagh, *Ireland* 15 **D5**
Shillong, *India* 61 **G17**
Shilo, *Jordan* 69 **C4**
Shilong, *China* 53 **F9**
Shilou, *China* 50 **F6**
Shilovo, *Russia* 41 **D12**
Shimabara, *Japan* 49 **H5**
Shimada, *Japan* 49 **G9**
Shimane □, *Japan* 49 **G6**
Shimanovsk, *Russia* 45 **D13**
Shimen, *China* 53 **C8**
Shimenjie, *China* 53 **C11**
Shimian, *China* 52 **C4**
Shimizu, *Japan* 49 **G9**
Shimodate, *Japan* 49 **F9**
Shimoga, *India* 60 **N9**
Shimoni, *Kenya* 82 **C4**
Shimonoseki, *Japan* 49 **H5**
Shimpuru Rapids, *Angola* 84 **B2**
Shimsk, *Russia* 40 **B7**
Shin, L., *U.K.* 14 **C4**
Shin-Tone →, *Japan* 49 **G10**
Shinan, *China* 52 **F7**
Shinano →, *Japan* 49 **F9**
Shīndand, *Afghan.* 60 **C3**
Shingleton, *U.S.A.* 98 **C2**
Shingū, *Japan* 49 **H7**
Shinjō, *Japan* 48 **E10**
Shinkafe, *Nigeria* 79 **C6**
Shinshār, *Syria* 69 **A5**
Shinyanga, *Tanzania* 82 **C3**
Shinyanga □, *Tanzania* 82 **C3**
Shiogama, *Japan* 48 **E10**
Shiojiri, *Japan* 49 **F8**
Ship I., *U.S.A.* 109 **K10**
Shipehenski Prokhod, *Bulgaria* 38 **G8**
Shiping, *China* 52 **F4**
Shipki La, *India* 60 **D11**
Shippegan, *Canada* 99 **C7**
Shippensburg, *U.S.A.* 106 **F7**
Shiprock, *U.S.A.* 111 **H9**
Shiqian, *China* 52 **D7**
Shiqma, N. →, *Israel* 69 **D3**
Shiquan, *China* 50 **H5**
Shīr Kūh, *Iran* 65 **D7**
Shiragami-Misaki, *Japan* 48 **D10**
Shirakawa, *Fukushima, Japan* 49 **F10**
Shirakawa, *Gifu, Japan* 49 **F8**
Shirane-San, *Gumma, Japan* 49 **F9**
Shirane-San, *Yamanashi, Japan* 49 **G9**
Shiraoi, *Japan* 48 **C10**
Shīrāz, *Iran* 65 **D7**
Shirbin, *Egypt* 76 **H7**
Shire →, *Africa* 83 **F4**
Shiretoko-Misaki, *Japan* 48 **B12**
Shirinab →, *Pakistan* 62 **D2**
Shiringushi, *Russia* 41 **E13**
Shiriya-Zaki, *Japan* 48 **D10**
Shiroishi, *Japan* 48 **E10**
Shīrvān, *Iran* 65 **B8**
Shirwa, L. = Chilwa, L., *Malawi* 83 **F4**
Shishou, *China* 53 **C9**
Shitai, *China* 53 **B11**
Shivpuri, *India* 62 **G7**
Shixian, *China* 51 **C15**
Shixing, *China* 53 **E10**
Shiyan, *China* 53 **A8**
Shiyata, *Egypt* 76 **B2**
Shizhu, *China* 52 **C7**
Shizong, *China* 52 **E5**
Shizuishan, *China* 50 **E4**
Shizuoka, *Japan* 49 **G9**
Shizuoka □, *Japan* 49 **G9**
Shklov, *Belorussia* 40 **D7**
Shkoder = Shkodra, *Albania* 38 **G2**
Shkodra, *Albania* 38 **G2**
Shkumbini →, *Albania* 39 **H2**
Shmidta, O., *Russia* 45 **A10**
Shō-Gawa →, *Japan* 49 **F8**
Shoal Lake, *Canada* 101 **C8**
Shōdo-Shima, *Japan* 49 **G7**
Shoeburyness, *U.K.* 13 **F8**
Sholapur = Solapur, *India* 60 **L9**
Shologontsy, *Russia* 45 **C12**
Shōmrōn, *Jordan* 69 **C4**
Shoshone, *Calif., U.S.A.* 113 **K10**
Shoshone, *Idaho, U.S.A.* 110 **E6**
Shoshone L., *U.S.A.* 110 **D8**
Shoshone Mts., *U.S.A.* 110 **G5**
Shoshong, *Botswana* 84 **C4**
Shoshoni, *U.S.A.* 110 **E9**
Shostka, *Ukraine* 40 **F8**
Shou Xian, *China* 53 **A11**
Shouchang, *China* 53 **C12**
Shouguang, *China* 51 **F10**
Shouning, *China* 53 **D12**
Shouyang, *China* 50 **F7**
Show Low, *U.S.A.* 111 **J9**
Shpola, *Ukraine* 42 **B4**
Shreveport, *U.S.A.* 109 **J8**
Shrewsbury, *U.K.* 12 **E5**
Shrirampur, *India* 63 **H13**
Shropshire □, *U.K.* 13 **E5**
Shuangbai, *China* 52 **E3**
Shuangcheng, *China* 51 **B14**
Shuangfeng, *China* 53 **D9**
Shuanggou, *China* 51 **G9**
Shuangjiang, *China* 52 **F2**
Shuangliao, *China* 51 **C12**
Shuangshanzi, *China* 51 **D10**
Shuangyang, *China* 51 **C13**
Shuangyashan, *China* 54 **B8**
Shucheng, *China* 53 **B11**
Shuguri Falls, *Tanzania* 83 **D4**
Shuicheng, *China* 52 **D5**
Shuiji, *China* 53 **D12**
Shuiye, *China* 50 **F8**
Shujalpur, *India* 62 **H7**
Shukpa Kunzang, *India* 63 **B8**
Shulan, *China* 51 **B14**
Shule, *China* 54 **C2**
Shumagin Is., *U.S.A.* 96 **C4**
Shumerlya, *Russia* 41 **D15**
Shumikha, *Russia* 44 **D7**
Shunchang, *China* 53 **D11**
Shunde, *China* 53 **F9**
Shungay, *Kazakhstan* 43 **B12**
Shungnak, *U.S.A.* 96 **B4**
Shuo Xian, *China* 50 **E7**
Shūr →, *Iran* 65 **D7**
Shūr Āb, *Iran* 65 **C6**
Shūr Gaz, *Iran* 65 **D8**
Shūrāb, *Iran* 65 **C8**
Shūrjestān, *Iran* 65 **D7**
Shurma, *Russia* 41 **C17**
Shurugwi, *Zimbabwe* 83 **F3**
Shūsf, *Iran* 65 **D9**
Shūshtar, *Iran* 65 **D6**
Shuswap L., *Canada* 100 **C5**
Shuya, *Russia* 41 **C12**
Shuyang, *China* 51 **G10**
Shūzū, *Iran* 65 **D7**
Shwebo, *Burma* 61 **H19**
Shwegu, *Burma* 61 **G20**
Shweli →, *Burma* 61 **H20**
Shyok, *India* 63 **B8**
Shyok →, *Pakistan* 63 **B6**
Si Chon, *Thailand* 59 **H2**
Si Kiang = Xi Jiang →, *China* 53 **F9**
Si Prachan, *Thailand* 58 **E3**
Si Racha, *Thailand* 58 **F3**
Si Xian, *China* 51 **H9**
Siahan Range, *Pakistan* 60 **F4**
Siaksrindrapura, *Indonesia* 56 **D2**
Sialkot, *Pakistan* 62 **C6**
Siam = Thailand ■, *Asia* 58 **E4**
Sian = Xi'an, *China* 50 **G5**
Siantan, P., *Indonesia* 59 **L6**
Siàpo →, *Venezuela* 120 **C4**
Sīāreh, *Iran* 65 **D9**
Siargao, *Phil.* 55 **G7**
Siari, *Pakistan* 63 **B7**
Siasi, *Phil.* 57 **C6**
Siasi I., *Phil.* 55 **J4**
Siátista, *Greece* 39 **J4**
Siau, *Indonesia* 57 **D7**
Siauliai, *Lithuania* 40 **D3**
Siaya □, *Kenya* 82 **B3**
Siazan, *Azerbaijan* 43 **F13**
Sibâi, Gebel el, *Egypt* 76 **B3**
Sibari, *Italy* 35 **C9**
Sibasa, *S. Africa* 85 **C5**
Sibayi, L., *S. Africa* 85 **D5**
Šibenik, *Croatia* 33 **E12**
Siberia, *Russia* 4 **D13**
Siberut, *Indonesia* 56 **E1**
Sibi, *Pakistan* 62 **E2**
Sibil, *Indonesia* 57 **E10**
Sibiti, *Congo* 80 **E2**
Sibiu, *Romania* 38 **D7**
Sibley, *Iowa, U.S.A.* 108 **D7**
Sibley, *La., U.S.A.* 109 **J8**
Sibolga, *Indonesia* 56 **D1**
Sibret, *Belgium* 17 **J7**
Sibsagar, *India* 61 **F19**
Sibu, *Malaysia* 56 **D4**
Sibuco, *Phil.* 55 **H5**
Sibuguey B., *Phil.* 55 **H5**
Sibutu, *Phil.* 57 **D5**
Sibutu Group, *Phil.* 55 **J3**
Sibutu Passage, *E. Indies* 57 **D5**
Sibuyan, *Phil.* 55 **E5**
Sibuyan Sea, *Phil.* 55 **E5**
Sicamous, *Canada* 100 **C5**
Sichuan □, *China* 52 **B5**
Sicilia, *Italy* 35 **E7**
Sicilia □, *Italy* 35 **E7**
Sicilia, Canale di, *Italy* 34 **E5**
Sicilian Channel = Sicilia, Canale di, *Italy* 34 **E5**
Sicily = Sicilia, *Italy* 35 **E7**
Sicuani, *Peru* 124 **C3**
Siculiana, *Italy* 34 **E6**
Sidamo □, *Ethiopia* 77 **G4**
Sidaouet, *Niger* 79 **B6**
Sidári, *Greece* 37 **A3**
Siddeburen, *Neths.* 16 **B9**
Siddhapur, *India* 62 **H5**
Siddipet, *India* 60 **K11**
Side, *Turkey* 66 **E4**
Sidéradougou, *Burkina Faso* 78 **C4**
Siderno Marina, *Italy* 35 **D9**
Sídheros, Ákra, *Greece* 37 **D8**
Sidhirókastron, *Greece* 39 **H6**
Sîdi Abd el Rahmân, *Egypt* 76 **H6**
Sîdi Barrâni, *Egypt* 76 **A2**
Sidi-bel-Abbès, *Algeria* 75 **A4**
Sidi Bennour, *Morocco* 74 **B3**
Sidi Haneish, *Egypt* 76 **A2**
Sidi Kacem, *Morocco* 74 **B3**
Sidi Omar, *Egypt* 76 **A1**
Sidi Slimane, *Morocco* 74 **B3**
Sidi Smaïl, *Morocco* 74 **B3**
Sidlaw Hills, *U.K.* 14 **E5**
Sidley, Mt., *Antarctica* 5 **D14**
Sidmouth, *U.K.* 13 **G4**
Sidmouth, C., *Australia* 90 **A3**
Sidney, *Canada* 100 **D4**
Sidney, *Mont., U.S.A.* 108 **B2**
Sidney, *N.Y., U.S.A.* 107 **D9**
Sidney, *Nebr., U.S.A.* 108 **E3**
Sidney, *Ohio, U.S.A.* 104 **E3**
Sidoarjo, *Indonesia* 57 **G15**
Sidon = Saydā, *Lebanon* 69 **B4**
Sidra, G. of = Surt, Khalīj, *Libya* 73 **B8**
Siedlce, *Poland* 20 **C12**
Sieg →, *Germany* 18 **E3**
Siegburg, *Germany* 18 **E3**
Siegen, *Germany* 18 **E4**
Siem Pang, *Cambodia* 58 **E6**
Siem Reap, *Cambodia* 58 **F4**
Siena, *Italy* 33 **E8**
Sieradź, *Poland* 20 **D8**
Sierck-les-Bains, *France* 25 **C13**
Sierpc, *Poland* 20 **C9**
Sierpe, Bocas de la, *Venezuela* 121 **B5**
Sierra Blanca, *U.S.A.* 111 **L11**
Sierra Blanca Pk., *U.S.A.* 111 **K11**
Sierra City, *U.S.A.* 112 **F6**
Sierra Colorada, *Argentina* 128 **B3**
Sierra de Yeguas, *Spain* 31 **H6**
Sierra Gorda, *Chile* 126 **A2**
Sierra Grande, *Argentina* 128 **B3**
Sierra Leone ■, *W. Afr.* 78 **D2**
Sierra Madre, *Mexico* 115 **D6**
Sierra Mojada, *Mexico* 114 **B4**
Sierraville, *U.S.A.* 112 **F6**
Sierre, *Switz.* 22 **D5**
Sif Fatima, *Algeria* 75 **B6**
Sífnos, *Greece* 39 **N7**
Sifton, *Canada* 101 **C8**
Sifton Pass, *Canada* 100 **B3**
Sig, *Algeria* 75 **A4**
Sigdal, *Norway* 10 **D3**
Sigean, *France* 26 **E6**
Sighetu-Marmatiei, *Romania* 38 **B6**
Sighişoara, *Romania* 38 **C7**
Sigli, *Indonesia* 56 **C1**
Siglufjörður, *Iceland* 8 **C4**
Sigmaringen, *Germany* 19 **G5**
Signakhi, *Georgia* 43 **F11**
Signal, *U.S.A.* 113 **L13**
Signal Pk., *U.S.A.* 113 **M12**
Signau, *Switz.* 22 **C5**
Signy-l'Abbaye, *France* 25 **C11**
Sigsig, *Ecuador* 120 **D2**
Sigtuna, *Sweden* 10 **E11**
Sigüenza, *Spain* 28 **D2**
Siguiri, *Guinea* 78 **C3**

Sigulda, *Latvia* 40 C4
Sigurd, *U.S.A.* 111 G8
Sihanoukville = Kompong Som, *Cambodia* 59 G4
Sihaus, *Peru* 124 B2
Sihui, *China* 53 F9
Siirt, *Turkey* 67 E9
Siirt □, *Turkey* 67 E9
Sijarira Ra., *Zimbabwe* 83 F2
Sikao, *Thailand* 59 J2
Sikar, *India* 62 F6
Sikasso, *Mali* 78 C3
Sikeston, *U.S.A.* 109 G10
Sikhote Alin, Khrebet, *Russia* 45 E14
Sikiá, *Greece* 39 J6
Síkinos, *Greece* 39 N8
Sikkani Chief →, *Canada* 100 B4
Sikkim □, *India* 61 F16
Sikotu-Ko, *Japan* 48 C10
Sil →, *Spain* 30 C3
Silacayoapan, *Mexico* 115 D5
Silandro, *Italy* 32 B7
Silay, *Phil.* 55 F5
Silba, *Croatia* 33 D11
Silchar, *India* 61 G18
Silcox, *Canada* 101 B10
Şile, *Turkey* 66 C3
Silenrieux, *Belgium* 17 H4
Siler City, *U.S.A.* 105 H6
Silesia = Śląsk, *Poland* 20 E6
Silet, *Algeria* 75 D5
Silgarhi Doti, *Nepal* 63 E9
Silghat, *India* 61 F18
Silifke, *Turkey* 66 E5
Siling Co, *China* 54 C3
Silíqua, *Italy* 34 C1
Silistra, *Bulgaria* 38 E10
Silivri, *Turkey* 66 C3
Siljan, *Sweden* 9 F13
Silkeborg, *Denmark* 11 H3
Sillajhuay, Cordillera, *Chile* 124 D4
Sillé-le-Guillaume, *France* 24 D6
Sillustani, *Peru* 124 D3
Siloam Springs, *U.S.A.* 109 G7
Silopi, *Turkey* 67 E10
Silsbee, *U.S.A.* 109 K7
Silute, *Lithuania* 40 D2
Silva Porto = Kuito, *Angola* 81 G3
Silvan, *Turkey* 67 D9
Silvaplana, *Switz.* 23 D9
Silver City, *N. Mex., U.S.A.* 111 K9
Silver City, *Nev., U.S.A.* 110 G4
Silver Cr. →, *U.S.A.* 110 E4
Silver Creek, *U.S.A.* 106 D5
Silver L., *U.S.A.* 112 G6
Silver Lake, *Calif., U.S.A.* 113 K10
Silver Lake, *Oreg., U.S.A.* 110 E3
Silver Streams, *S. Africa* 84 D3
Silverton, *Colo., U.S.A.* 111 H10
Silverton, *Tex., U.S.A.* 109 H4
Silves, *Portugal* 31 H2
Silvi, *Italy* 33 F11
Silvia, *Colombia* 120 C2
Silvies →, *U.S.A.* 110 E4
Silvolde, *Neths.* 16 E8
Silvretta-Gruppe, *Switz.* 23 C10
Silwa Bahari, *Egypt* 76 C3
Silz, *Austria* 19 H6
Sim, C., *Morocco* 74 B3
Simanggang, *Malaysia* 56 D4
Simao, *China* 52 F3
Simão Dias, *Brazil* 122 D4
Simard, L., *Canada* 98 C4
Simav, *Turkey* 66 D3
Simba, *Tanzania* 82 C4
Simbach, *Germany* 19 G9
Simbirsk, *Russia* 41 D16
Simbo, *Tanzania* 82 C2
Simcoe, *Canada* 98 D3
Simcoe, L., *Canada* 98 D4
Simenga, *Russia* 45 C11
Simeto →, *Italy* 35 E8
Simeulue, *Indonesia* 56 D1
Simferopol, *Ukraine* 42 D6
Sími, *Greece* 39 N10
Simi Valley, *U.S.A.* 113 L8
Simikot, *Nepal* 63 E9
Simití, *Colombia* 120 B3
Simla, *India* 62 D7
Şimleu-Silvaniei, *Romania* 38 B5
Simme →, *Switz.* 22 C4
Simmern, *Germany* 19 F3
Simmie, *Canada* 101 D7
Simmler, *U.S.A.* 113 K7
Simões, *Brazil* 122 C3
Simojärvi, *Finland* 8 C19
Simojoki →, *Finland* 8 D18
Simojovel, *Mexico* 115 D6
Simonette →, *Canada* 100 B5
Simonstown, *S. Africa* 84 E2
Simplício Mendes, *Brazil* 122 C3
Simplon, *Switz.* 22 D6
Simplon Pass = Simplonpass, *Switz.* 22 D6
Simplon Tunnel, *Switz.* 22 D6
Simplonpass, *Switz.* 22 D6
Simpson Desert, *Australia* 90 D2
Simpungdong, *N. Korea* 51 D15
Simunjan, *Malaysia* 56 D4
Simushir, Ostrov, *Russia* 45 E16
Sinabang, *Indonesia* 56 D1
Sinadogo, *Somali Rep.* 68 F4
Sinai = Es Sînâ', *Egypt* 76 J8
Sinai, Mt. = Mûsa, G., *Egypt* 76 J8
Sinai Peninsula, *Egypt* 69 F2
Sinaia, *Romania* 38 D8
Sinaloa □, *Mexico* 114 C3
Sinaloa de Levya, *Mexico* 114 B3
Sinalunga, *Italy* 33 E8
Sinan, *China* 52 D7
Sinarádhes, *Greece* 37 A3
Sīnāwan, *Libya* 75 B7
Sincé, *Colombia* 120 B2
Sincelejo, *Colombia* 120 B2
Sinchang, *N. Korea* 51 D15
Sinchang-ni, *N. Korea* 51 E14
Sinclair, *U.S.A.* 110 F10
Sinclair Mills, *Canada* 100 C4
Sincorá, Serra do, *Brazil* 123 D3
Sind, *Pakistan* 62 G3
Sind □, *Pakistan* 62 F3
Sind →, *India* 63 B6
Sind Sagar Doab, *Pakistan* 62 D4
Sindal, *Denmark* 11 G4
Sindangan, *Phil.* 55 G5
Sindangbarang, *Indonesia* 57 G12
Sinde, *Zambia* 83 F2
Sinegorski, *Russia* 43 C9
Sinelnikovo, *Ukraine* 42 B6
Sines, *Portugal* 31 H2
Sines, C. de, *Portugal* 31 H2
Sineu, *Spain* 36 B10
Sinfra, *Ivory C.* 78 D3
Sing Buri, *Thailand* 58 E3
Singa, *Sudan* 77 E3
Singapore ■, *Asia* 59 M4
Singapore, Straits of, *Asia* 59 M5
Singaraja, *Indonesia* 56 F5
Singen, *Germany* 19 H4
Singida, *Tanzania* 82 C3
Singida □, *Tanzania* 82 D3
Singitikós Kólpos, *Greece* 39 J6
Singkaling Hkamti, *Burma* 61 G19
Singkawang, *Indonesia* 56 D3
Singleton, *Australia* 91 E5
Singleton, Mt., *N. Terr., Australia* 88 D5
Singleton, Mt., *W. Austral., Australia* 89 E2
Singoli, *India* 62 G6
Singora = Songkhla, *Thailand* 59 J3
Singosan, *N. Korea* 51 E14
Sinhung, *N. Korea* 51 D14
Sînî □, *Egypt* 69 F2
Siniscóla, *Italy* 34 B2
Sinj, *Croatia* 33 E13
Sinjai, *Indonesia* 57 F6
Sinjār, *Iraq* 64 B4
Sinkat, *Sudan* 76 D4
Sinkiang Uighur = Xinjiang Uygur Zizhiqu □, *China* 54 B3
Sinmak, *N. Korea* 51 E14
Sinnai, *Italy* 34 C2
Sinni →, *Italy* 35 B9
Sinnuris, *Egypt* 76 J7
Sinoe, L., *Romania* 38 E11
Sinop, *Turkey* 42 E6
Sinop □, *Turkey* 66 C6
Sinpo, *N. Korea* 51 E15
Sins, *Switz.* 23 B6
Sinskoye, *Russia* 45 C13
Sint-Amandsberg, *Belgium* 17 F3
Sint Annaland, *Neths.* 17 E4
Sint Annaparoch, *Neths.* 16 B7
Sint-Denijs, *Belgium* 17 G2
Sint Eustatius, I., *Neth. Ant.* 117 C7
Sint-Genesius-Rode, *Belgium* 17 G4
Sint-Gillis-Waas, *Belgium* 17 F4
Sint-Huibrechts-Lille, *Belgium* 17 F6
Sint-Katelinje-Waver, *Belgium* 17 F5
Sint-Kruis, *Belgium* 17 F2
Sint-Laureins, *Belgium* 17 F3
Sint Maarten, I., *W. Indies* 117 C7
Sint-Michiels, *Belgium* 17 F2
Sint Nicolaasga, *Neths.* 16 C7
Sint Niklaas, *Belgium* 17 F4
Sint Oedenrode, *Neths.* 17 E6
Sint Pancras, *Neths.* 16 C5
Sint Philipsland, *Neths.* 17 E4
Sint Truiden, *Belgium* 17 G6
Sint Willebrord, *Neths.* 17 E5
Sîntana, *Romania* 38 C4
Sintang, *Indonesia* 56 D4
Sintjohannesga, *Neths.* 16 C7
Sinton, *U.S.A.* 109 L6
Sintra, *Portugal* 31 G1
Sinŭiju, *N. Korea* 51 D13
Sinyukha →, *Ukraine* 42 B4
Siocon, *Phil.* 55 H5
Siófok, *Hungary* 21 J8
Sioma, *Zambia* 84 B3
Sion, *Switz.* 22 D4
Sioux City, *U.S.A.* 108 D6
Sioux Falls, *U.S.A.* 108 D6
Sioux Lookout, *Canada* 98 B1
Sip Song Chau Thai, *Vietnam* 58 B4
Sipalay, *Phil.* 55 G5
Siping, *China* 51 C13
Sipiwesk L., *Canada* 101 B9
Sipora, *Indonesia* 56 E1
Siquia →, *Nic.* 116 D3
Siquijor, *Phil.* 55 G5
Siquirres, *Costa Rica* 116 D3
Siquisique, *Venezuela* 120 A4
Sir Edward Pellew Group, *Australia* 90 B2
Sir Graham Moore Is., *Australia* 88 B4
Siracusa, *Italy* 35 E8
Sirajganj, *Bangla.* 63 G13
Sirakoro, *Mali* 78 C3
Şiran, *Turkey* 67 C8
Sirasso, *Ivory C.* 78 D3
Sīrdān, *Iran* 65 B6
Sirer, *Spain* 36 C7
Siret, *Romania* 38 B9
Siret →, *Romania* 38 D11
Şiria, *Romania* 38 C4
Sirino, Monte, *Italy* 35 B8
Sírna, *Greece* 39 N9
Sirnach, *Switz.* 23 B7
Şirnak, *Turkey* 67 E10
Sirohi, *India* 62 G5
Sironj, *India* 62 G7
Síros, *Greece* 39 M7
Sirretta Pk., *U.S.A.* 113 K8
Sirsa, *India* 62 E6
Siruela, *Spain* 31 G5
Sisak, *Croatia* 33 C13
Sisaket, *Thailand* 58 E5
Sisante, *Spain* 29 F2
Sisargas, Is., *Spain* 30 B2
Sishen, *S. Africa* 84 D3
Sishui, *Henan, China* 50 G7
Sishui, *Shandong, China* 51 G9
Sisipuk L., *Canada* 101 B8
Sisophon, *Cambodia* 58 F4
Sissach, *Switz.* 22 B5
Sisseton, *U.S.A.* 108 C6
Sissonne, *France* 25 C10
Sīstān va Balūchestān □, *Iran* 65 E9
Sisteron, *France* 27 D9
Sisters, *U.S.A.* 110 D3
Sitamarhi, *India* 63 F11
Sitapur, *India* 63 F9
Siteki, *Swaziland* 85 D5
Sitges, *Spain* 28 D6
Sitía, *Greece* 37 D8
Sítio da Abadia, *Brazil* 123 D2
Sitka, *U.S.A.* 96 C6
Sitoti, *Botswana* 84 C3
Sitra, *Egypt* 76 B2
Sittang Myit →, *Burma* 61 L20
Sittard, *Neths.* 17 G7
Sittensen, *Germany* 18 B5
Sittona, *Ethiopia* 77 E4
Sittwe, *Burma* 61 J18
Siuna, *Nic.* 116 D3
Siuri, *India* 63 H12
Sivana, *India* 62 E8
Sīvand, *Iran* 65 D7
Sivas, *Turkey* 66 D7
Sivas □, *Turkey* 66 D7
Siverek, *Turkey* 67 E8
Sivrihisar, *Turkey* 66 D4
Sivry, *Belgium* 17 H4
Sîwa, *Egypt* 76 B2
Sîwa, El Wâhât es, *Egypt* 76 B2
Siwalik Range, *Nepal* 63 F10
Siwan, *India* 63 F11
Siyâl, Jazâ'ir, *Egypt* 76 C4
Sizewell, *U.K.* 13 E9
Siziwang Qi, *China* 50 D6
Sjælland, *Denmark* 11 J5
Sjællands Odde, *Denmark* 11 J5
Själevad, *Sweden* 10 A12
Sjenica, *Serbia, Yug.* 21 M10
Sjoa, *Norway* 10 C3
Sjöbo, *Sweden* 11 J7
Sjösa, *Sweden* 11 F11
Sjumen = Šumen, *Bulgaria* 38 F9
Skadovsk, *Ukraine* 42 C5
Skagafjörður, *Iceland* 8 D4
Skagastølstindane, *Norway* 9 F9
Skagen, *Denmark* 11 G4
Skagerrak, *Denmark* 11 G3
Skagit →, *U.S.A.* 112 B4
Skagway, *U.S.A.* 100 B1
Skaidi, *Norway* 8 A18
Skala Podolskaya, *Ukraine* 42 B2
Skalat, *Ukraine* 40 G4
Skalni Dol = Kamenyak, *Bulgaria* 38 F9
Skals, *Denmark* 11 H3
Skanderborg, *Denmark* 11 H3
Skanör, *Sweden* 11 J6
Skara, *Sweden* 9 G12
Skaraborgs län □, *Sweden* 9 G12
Skardu, *Pakistan* 63 B6
Skarrild, *Denmark* 11 J2
Skarzysko Kamienna, *Poland* 20 D10
Skebokvarn, *Sweden* 10 E10
Skeena →, *Canada* 100 C2
Skeena Mts., *Canada* 100 B3
Skegness, *U.K.* 12 D8
Skeldon, *Guyana* 121 B6
Skellefte älv →, *Sweden* 8 D16
Skellefteå, *Sweden* 8 D16
Skelleftehamn, *Sweden* 8 D16
Skender Vakuf, *Bos.-H., Yug.* 21 L7
Skene, *Sweden* 11 G6
Skerries, The, *U.K.* 12 D3
Skhoinoúsa, *Greece* 39 N8
Ski, *Norway* 10 E4
Skíathos, *Greece* 39 K6
Skibbereen, *Ireland* 15 E2
Skiddaw, *U.K.* 12 C4
Skien, *Norway* 10 E3
Skierniewice, *Poland* 20 D10
Skikda, *Algeria* 75 A6
Skilloura, *Cyprus* 37 D12
Skinári, Ákra, *Greece* 39 M3
Skipton, *Australia* 91 F3
Skipton, *U.K.* 12 D5
Skirmish Pt., *Australia* 90 A1
Skíros, *Greece* 39 L7
Skivarp, *Sweden* 11 J7
Skive, *Denmark* 11 H3
Skjálfandafljót →, *Iceland* 8 D5
Skjálfandi, *Iceland* 8 C5
Skjeberg, *Norway* 10 E5
Skjern, *Denmark* 11 J2
Škofja Loka, *Slovenia* 33 B11
Skoghall, *Sweden* 9 G12
Skole, *Ukraine* 40 G3
Skópelos, *Greece* 39 K6
Skopí, *Greece* 37 D8
Skopin, *Russia* 41 E11
Skopje, *Macedonia, Yug.* 39 G4
Skórcz, *Poland* 20 B8
Skövde, *Sweden* 9 G12
Skovorodino, *Russia* 45 D13
Skowhegan, *U.S.A.* 99 D6
Skownan, *Canada* 101 C9
Skradin, *Croatia* 33 E12
Skreanäs, *Sweden* 11 H6
Skudeneshavn, *Norway* 9 G8
Skull, *Ireland* 15 E2
Skultorp, *Sweden* 11 F7
Skunk →, *U.S.A.* 108 E9
Skuodas, *Lithuania* 40 C2
Skurup, *Sweden* 11 J7
Skutskär, *Sweden* 10 D11
Skvira, *Ukraine* 42 B3
Skwierzyna, *Poland* 20 C5
Skye, *U.K.* 14 D2
Skykomish, *U.S.A.* 110 C3
Skyros = Skíros, *Greece* 39 L7
Slagelse, *Denmark* 11 J5
Slagharen, *Neths.* 16 C9
Slamet, *Indonesia* 56 F3
Slaney →, *Ireland* 15 D5
Slangerup, *Denmark* 11 J6
Slano, *Croatia* 21 N7
Slantsy, *Russia* 40 B6
Śląsk, *Poland* 20 E6
Slate Is., *Canada* 98 C2
Slatina, *Romania* 38 E7
Slaton, *U.S.A.* 109 J4
Slave →, *Canada* 100 A6
Slave Coast, *W. Afr.* 70 F4
Slave Lake, *Canada* 100 B6
Slave Pt., *Canada* 100 A5
Slavgorod, *Russia* 44 D8
Slavnoye, *Belorussia* 40 D6
Slavonska Požega, *Croatia* 21 K7
Slavonski Brod, *Croatia* 21 K8
Slavuta, *Ukraine* 40 F5
Slavyanka, *Russia* 48 C5
Slavyansk, *Ukraine* 42 B7
Slavyansk-na-Kubani, *Russia* 42 D8
Sławno, *Poland* 20 A6
Sławoborze, *Poland* 20 B5
Sleaford, *U.K.* 12 E7
Sleaford B., *Australia* 91 E2
Sleat, Sd. of, *U.K.* 14 D3
Sleeper Is., *Canada* 97 C11
Sleepy Eye, *U.S.A.* 108 C7
Sleidinge, *Belgium* 17 F3
Sleman, *Indonesia* 57 G14
Slemon L., *Canada* 100 A5
Slidell, *U.S.A.* 109 K10
Sliedrecht, *Neths.* 16 E5
Sliema, *Malta* 37 D2
Slieve Aughty, *Ireland* 15 C3
Slieve Bloom, *Ireland* 15 C4
Slieve Donard, *U.K.* 15 B6
Slieve Gullion, *U.K.* 15 B5
Slieve Mish, *Ireland* 15 D2
Slievenamon, *Ireland* 15 D4
Sligo, *Ireland* 15 B3
Sligo □, *Ireland* 15 B3
Sligo B., *Ireland* 15 B3
Slijpe, *Belgium* 17 F1
Slikkerveer, *Neths.* 16 E5
Slite, *Sweden* 9 H15
Sliven, *Bulgaria* 38 G9
Slivnitsa, *Bulgaria* 38 G6
Sljeme, *Croatia* 33 C12
Sloan, *U.S.A.* 113 K11
Sloansville, *U.S.A.* 107 D10
Slobodskoy, *Russia* 41 B17
Slobozia, *Romania* 38 E10
Slocan, *Canada* 100 D5
Slochteren, *Neths.* 16 B9
Slöinge, *Sweden* 11 H6
Slonim, *Belorussia* 40 E4
Slotermeer, *Neths.* 16 C7
Slough, *U.K.* 13 F7
Sloughhouse, *U.S.A.* 112 G5
Slovakian Ore Mts. = Slovenské Rudohorie, *Czech.* 20 G9
Slovenia ■, *Europe* 33 C11
Slovenija = Slovenia ■, *Europe* 33 C11
Slovenj Gradec, *Slovenia* 33 B12
Slovenska Bistrica, *Slovenia* 33 B12
Slovenské Rudohorie, *Czech.* 20 G9
Słubice, *Poland* 20 C4
Sluch →, *Ukraine* 40 F5
Sluis, *Neths.* 17 F2
Slunj, *Croatia* 33 C12
Słupca, *Poland* 20 C7
Słupsk, *Poland* 20 A7
Slurry, *S. Africa* 84 D4
Slutsk, *Belorussia* 40 E5
Slyne Hd., *Ireland* 15 C1
Slyudyanka, *Russia* 45 D11
Smålandsfarvandet, *Denmark* 11 J5
Smålandsstenar, *Sweden* 11 G7
Smalltree L., *Canada* 101 A7
Smara, *Morocco* 72 B3
Smarje, *Slovenia* 33 B12
Smartt Syndicate Dam, *S. Africa* 84 E3
Smartville, *U.S.A.* 112 F5
Smeaton, *Canada* 101 C8
Smederevo, *Serbia, Yug.* 21 L10
Smederevska Palanka, *Serbia, Yug.* 21 L10
Smela, *Ukraine* 42 B4
Smethport, *U.S.A.* 106 E6
Smidovich, *Russia* 45 E14
Smilde, *Neths.* 16 C8
Smiley, *Canada* 101 C7
Smith, *Canada* 100 B6
Smith →, *Canada* 100 B3
Smith Arm, *Canada* 96 B7
Smith Center, *U.S.A.* 108 F5
Smith Sund, *Greenland* 4 B4
Smithburne →, *Australia* 90 B3
Smithers, *Canada* 100 C3
Smithfield, *S. Africa* 85 E4
Smithfield, *N.C., U.S.A.* 105 H6
Smithfield, *Utah, U.S.A.* 110 F8
Smiths Falls, *Canada* 98 D4
Smithton, *Australia* 90 G4
Smithtown, *Australia* 91 E5
Smithville, *Canada* 106 C5
Smithville, *U.S.A.* 109 K6
Smoky →, *Canada* 100 B5
Smoky Bay, *Australia* 91 E1
Smoky Falls, *Canada* 98 B3
Smoky Hill →, *U.S.A.* 108 F6
Smoky Lake, *Canada* 100 C6
Smøla, *Norway* 10 A2
Smolensk, *Russia* 40 D8
Smolikas, Óros, *Greece* 39 J3
Smolník, *Czech.* 20 G10
Smolyan, *Bulgaria* 39 H7
Smooth Rock Falls, *Canada* 98 C3
Smoothstone L., *Canada* 101 C7
Smorgon, *Belorussia* 40 D5
Smyadovo, *Bulgaria* 38 F10
Smyrna = İzmir, *Turkey* 66 D2
Snaefell, *U.K.* 12 C3
Snæfellsjökull, *Iceland* 8 D2
Snake →, *U.S.A.* 110 C4
Snake I., *Australia* 91 F4
Snake L., *Canada* 101 B7
Snake Ra., *U.S.A.* 110 G6
Snake River Plain, *U.S.A.* 110 E7
Snarum, *Norway* 10 D3
Snedsted, *Denmark* 11 H2
Sneek, *Neths.* 16 B7
Sneeker-meer, *Neths.* 16 B7
Sneeuberge, *S. Africa* 84 E3
Snejbjerg, *Denmark* 11 H2
Snelling, *U.S.A.* 112 H6
Snezhnoye, *Ukraine* 43 C8
Snežnik, *Slovenia* 33 C11
Snigirevka, *Ukraine* 42 C5
Snizort, L., *U.K.* 14 D2
Snøhetta, *Norway* 10 B3
Snohomish, *U.S.A.* 112 C4
Snoul, *Cambodia* 59 F6
Snow Hill, *U.S.A.* 104 F8
Snow Lake, *Canada* 101 C8
Snow Mt., *U.S.A.* 112 F4
Snowbird L., *Canada* 101 A8
Snowdon, *U.K.* 12 D3
Snowdrift, *Canada* 101 A6
Snowdrift →, *Canada* 101 A6
Snowflake, *U.S.A.* 111 J8
Snowshoe Pk., *U.S.A.* 110 B6
Snowtown, *Australia* 91 E2
Snowville, *U.S.A.* 110 F7
Snowy →, *Australia* 91 F4
Snowy Mts., *Australia* 91 F4
Snug Corner, *Bahamas* 117 B5
Snyatyn, *Ukraine* 42 B1
Snyder, *Okla., U.S.A.* 109 H5
Snyder, *Tex., U.S.A.* 109 J4
Soacha, *Colombia* 120 C3
Soahanina, *Madag.* 85 B7
Soalala, *Madag.* 85 B8
Soan →, *Pakistan* 62 C4
Soanierana-Ivongo, *Madag.* 85 B8
Soap Lake, *U.S.A.* 110 C4
Sobat, Nahr →, *Sudan* 77 F3
Sobhapur, *India* 62 H8
Sobinka, *Russia* 41 D12
Sobótka, *Poland* 20 E6
Sobrado, *Spain* 30 B2
Sobral, *Brazil* 122 B3
Sobreira Formosa, *Portugal* 31 F3
Soc Giang, *Vietnam* 58 A6
Soc Trang, *Vietnam* 59 H5

Soča →, *Europe* 33 B10
Sochaczew, *Poland* 20 C10
Soch'e = Shache, *China* 54 C2
Sochi, *Russia* 43 E8
Société, Is. de la, *Pac. Oc.* 93 J12
Society Is. = Société, Is. de la, *Pac. Oc.* 93 J12
Socompa, Portezuelo de, *Chile* 126 A2
Socorro, *Colombia* 120 B3
Socorro, *U.S.A.* 111 J10
Socorro, I., *Mexico* 114 D2
Socotra, *Ind. Oc.* 68 E5
Socúellmos, *Spain* 29 F2
Soda L., *U.S.A.* 111 J5
Soda Plains, *India* 63 B8
Soda Springs, *U.S.A.* 110 E8
Söderhamn, *Sweden* 9 F14
Söderköping, *Sweden* 9 G14
Södermanlands län □, *Sweden* 10 E10
Södertälje, *Sweden* 10 E11
Sodiri, *Sudan* 77 E2
Sodo, *Ethiopia* 77 F4
Sodražica, *Slovenia* 33 C11
Sodus, *U.S.A.* 106 C7
Soekmekaar, *S. Africa* 85 C4
Soest, *Germany* 18 D4
Soest, *Neths.* 16 D6
Soestdijk, *Neths.* 16 D6
Sofádhes, *Greece* 39 K5
Sofara, *Mali* 78 C4
Sofia = Sofiya, *Bulgaria* 38 G6
Sofia →, *Madag.* 85 B8
Sofievka, *Ukraine* 42 B5
Sofiiski, *Russia* 45 D14
Sofikón, *Greece* 39 M6
Sofiya, *Bulgaria* 38 G6
Sōfu-Gan, *Japan* 49 K10
Sogakofe, *Ghana* 79 D5
Sogamoso, *Colombia* 120 B3
Sogār, *Iran* 65 E8
Sögel, *Germany* 18 C3
Sogn og Fjordane fylke □, *Norway* 9 F9
Sogndalsfjøra, *Norway* 9 F9
Sognefjorden, *Norway* 9 F8
Söğüt, *Turkey* 66 C4
Söğüt Gölü, *Turkey* 66 E3
Sŏgwi-po, *S. Korea* 51 H14
Soh, *Iran* 65 C6
Sohâg, *Egypt* 76 B3
Sŏhori, *N. Korea* 51 D15
Soignies, *Belgium* 17 G4
Soira, *Ethiopia* 77 E4
Soissons, *France* 25 C10
Sōja, *Japan* 49 G6
Sojat, *India* 62 G5
Sok →, *Russia* 41 E17
Sokal, *Ukraine* 40 F4
Söke, *Turkey* 66 E2
Sokelo, *Zaïre* 83 D1
Sokki, Oued In →, *Algeria* 75 C5
Sokna, *Norway* 10 D3
Soknedal, *Norway* 10 B4
Soko Banja, *Serbia, Yug.* 21 M11
Sokodé, *Togo* 79 D5
Sokol, *Russia* 41 B12
Sokółka, *Poland* 20 B13
Sokolo, *Mali* 78 C3
Sokołów Małpolski, *Poland* 20 E12
Sokołów Podlaski, *Poland* 20 C12
Sokoto, *Nigeria* 79 C6
Sokoto □, *Nigeria* 79 C6
Sokoto →, *Nigeria* 79 C5
Sol Iletsk, *Russia* 44 D6
Solai, *Kenya* 82 B4
Solano, *Phil.* 55 C4
Solapur, *India* 60 L9
Solares, *Spain* 30 B7
Soléa □, *Cyprus* 37 D12
Solec Kujawski, *Poland* 20 B8
Soledad, *Colombia* 120 A3
Soledad, *U.S.A.* 111 H3
Soledad, *Venezuela* 121 B5
Solent, The, *U.K.* 13 G6
Solenzara, *France* 27 G13
Solesmes, *France* 25 B10
Solfonn, *Norway* 9 F9
Solhan, *Turkey* 67 D9
Soligalich, *Russia* 41 B13
Soligorsk, *Belorussia* 40 E5
Solikamsk, *Russia* 44 D6
Solila, *Madag.* 85 C8
Solimões = Amazonas →, *S. Amer.* 121 D7
Solingen, *Germany* 17 F10
Sollebrunn, *Sweden* 11 F6
Sollefteå, *Sweden* 10 A11
Sollentuna, *Sweden* 10 E11
Sóller, *Spain* 36 B9
Solling, *Germany* 18 D5
Solna, *Sweden* 10 E12
Solnechnogorsk, *Russia* 41 C10
Sologne, *France* 25 E8
Solok, *Indonesia* 56 E2
Sololá, *Guatemala* 116 D1
Solomon, N. Fork →, *U.S.A.* 108 F5
Solomon, S. Fork →, *U.S.A.* 108 F5
Solomon Is. ■, *Pac. Oc.* 92 H7
Solon, *China* 54 B7
Solon Springs, *U.S.A.* 108 B9
Solonópole, *Brazil* 122 C4
Solor, *Indonesia* 57 F6
Solotcha, *Russia* 41 D11
Solothurn, *Switz.* 22 B5
Solothurn □, *Switz.* 22 B5
Solsona, *Spain* 28 D6
Solta, *Croatia* 33 E13
Solṭānābād, *Khorāsān, Iran* 65 C8
Solṭānābād, *Khorāsān, Iran* 65 B8
Solṭānābād, *Markazī, Iran* 65 C6
Soltau, *Germany* 18 C5
Soltsy, *Russia* 40 B7
Solunska Glava, *Macedonia, Yug.* 39 H4
Solvang, *U.S.A.* 113 L6
Solvay, *U.S.A.* 107 C8
Solway Firth, *U.K.* 12 C4
Solwezi, *Zambia* 83 E2
Sōma, *Japan* 48 F10
Soma, *Turkey* 66 D2
Somali Rep. ■, *Africa* 68 F4
Sombernon, *France* 25 E11
Sombor, *Serbia, Yug.* 21 K9
Sombra, *Canada* 106 D2
Sombrerete, *Mexico* 114 C4
Sombrero, *Anguilla* 117 C7
Someren, *Neths.* 17 F7
Somers, *U.S.A.* 110 B6
Somerset, *Canada* 101 D9
Somerset, *Colo., U.S.A.* 111 G10
Somerset, *Ky., U.S.A.* 104 G3
Somerset, *Mass., U.S.A.* 107 E13
Somerset, *Pa., U.S.A.* 106 F5
Somerset □, *U.K.* 13 F5
Somerset East, *S. Africa* 84 E4
Somerset I., *Canada* 96 A10
Somerset West, *S. Africa* 84 E2
Somerton, *U.S.A.* 111 K6
Somerville, *U.S.A.* 107 F10
Someş →, *Romania* 38 B5
Someşul Mare →, *Romania* 38 B7
Somma Lombardo, *Italy* 32 C5
Somma Vesuviana, *Italy* 35 B7
Sommariva, *Australia* 91 D4
Sommatino, *Italy* 34 E6
Somme □, *France* 25 C9
Somme →, *France* 25 B8
Somme, B. de la, *France* 24 B8
Sommelsdijk, *Neths.* 16 E4
Sommepy-Tahure, *France* 25 C11
Sömmerda, *Germany* 18 D7
Sommesous, *France* 25 D11
Sommières, *France* 27 E8
Somoto, *Nic.* 116 D2
Sompolno, *Poland* 20 C8
Somport, Paso, *Spain* 28 C4
Somport, Puerto de, *Spain* 28 C4
Somuncurá, Meseta de, *Argentina* 128 B3
Son, *Neths.* 17 E6
Son, *Norway* 10 E4
Son, *Spain* 30 C2
Son Ha, *Vietnam* 58 E7
Son Hoa, *Vietnam* 58 F7
Son La, *Vietnam* 58 B4
Son Tay, *Vietnam* 58 B5
Soná, *Panama* 116 E3
Sonamarg, *India* 63 B6
Sonamukhi, *India* 63 H12
Sŏnchŏn, *N. Korea* 51 E13
Soncino, *Italy* 32 C6
Sondags →, *S. Africa* 84 E4
Sondalo, *Italy* 32 B7
Sondar, *India* 63 C6
Sønder Omme, *Denmark* 11 J2
Sønder Tornby, *Denmark* 11 G3
Sønderborg, *Denmark* 11 K3
Sønderjyllands Amtskommune □, *Denmark* 11 J3
Sondershausen, *Germany* 18 D6
Sóndrio, *Italy* 32 B6
Sone, *Mozam.* 83 F3
Sonepur, *India* 61 J13
Song, *Thailand* 58 C3
Song Cau, *Vietnam* 58 F7
Song Xian, *China* 50 G7
Songchŏn, *N. Korea* 51 E14
Songea, *Tanzania* 83 E4
Songea □, *Tanzania* 83 E4
Songeons, *France* 25 C8
Songhua Hu, *China* 51 C14
Songhua Jiang →, *China* 54 B8
Songjiang, *China* 53 B13
Songjin, *N. Korea* 51 D15
Songjŏng-ni, *S. Korea* 51 G14
Songkan, *China* 52 C6
Songkhla, *Thailand* 59 J3
Songming, *China* 52 E4
Songnim, *N. Korea* 51 E13
Songpan, *China* 52 A4
Songtao, *China* 52 C7
Songwe, *Zaïre* 82 C2
Songwe →, *Africa* 83 D3
Songxi, *China* 53 D12
Songzi, *China* 53 B8
Sonid Youqi, *China* 50 C7
Sonipat, *India* 62 E7
Sonkovo, *Russia* 41 C10
Sonmiani, *Pakistan* 62 G2
Sonnino, *Italy* 34 A6
Sono →, *Goiás, Brazil* 122 C2
Sono →, *Minas Gerais, Brazil* 123 E2
Sonogno, *Switz.* 23 D7
Sonora, *Calif., U.S.A.* 111 H3
Sonora, *Tex., U.S.A.* 109 K4
Sonora □, *Mexico* 114 B2
Sonora →, *Mexico* 114 B2
Sonora Desert, *U.S.A.* 113 M12
Sonoyta, *Mexico* 114 A2
Sŏnsan, *S. Korea* 51 F15
Sonsonate, *El Salv.* 116 D2
Sonthofen, *Germany* 19 H6
Soochow = Suzhou, *China* 53 B13
Sop Hao, *Laos* 58 B5
Sop Prap, *Thailand* 58 D2
Sopachuy, *Bolivia* 125 D5
Sopi, *Indonesia* 57 D7
Sopo, Nahr →, *Sudan* 77 F2
Sopot, *Poland* 20 A8
Sopotnica, *Macedonia, Yug.* 39 H4
Sopron, *Hungary* 21 H6
Sop's Arm, *Canada* 99 C8
Sopur, *India* 63 B6
Sør-Rondane, *Antarctica* 5 D4
Sør-Trøndelag fylke □, *Norway* 10 B3
Sora, *Italy* 34 A6
Sorah, *Pakistan* 62 F3
Söråker, *Sweden* 10 B11
Sorano, *Italy* 33 F8
Sorata, *Bolivia* 124 D4
Sorbas, *Spain* 29 H2
Sorel, *Canada* 98 C5
Sörenberg, *Switz.* 22 C6
Soreq, N. →, *Israel* 69 D3
Soresina, *Italy* 32 C6
Sorgono, *Italy* 34 B2
Sorgues, *France* 27 D8
Sorgun, *Turkey* 66 D6
Soria, *Spain* 28 D2
Soria □, *Spain* 28 D2
Soriano, *Uruguay* 126 C4
Soriano nel Cimino, *Italy* 33 F9
Sorkh, Kuh-e, *Iran* 65 C8
Sorø, *Denmark* 11 J5
Soro, *Guinea* 78 C3
Sorocaba, *Brazil* 127 A6
Soroki, *Moldavia* 42 B3
Soron, *India* 63 F8
Sorong, *Indonesia* 57 E8
Soroní, *Greece* 37 C10
Soroti, *Uganda* 82 B3
Sørøya, *Norway* 8 A17
Sørøysundet, *Norway* 8 A17
Sorraia →, *Portugal* 31 G2
Sorrento, *Australia* 91 F3
Sorrento, *Italy* 35 B7
Sorsele, *Sweden* 8 D14
Sorso, *Italy* 34 B1
Sorsogon, *Phil.* 55 E6
Sortino, *Italy* 35 E8
Sorvizhi, *Russia* 41 C16
Sos, *Spain* 28 C3
Sŏsan, *S. Korea* 51 F14
Soscumica, L., *Canada* 98 B4
Sosna →, *Russia* 41 E11
Sosnovka, *Russia* 41 E12
Sosnovka, *Russia* 45 D11
Sosnowiec, *Poland* 20 E9
Sospel, *France* 27 E11
Sostanj, *Slovenia* 33 B12
Sŏsura, *N. Korea* 51 C16
Soto la Marina →, *Mexico* 115 C5
Soto y Amío, *Spain* 30 C5
Sotteville-lès-Rouen, *France* 24 C8
Sotuta, *Mexico* 115 C7
Souanké, *Congo* 80 D2
Soúdha, *Greece* 37 D6
Soúdhas, Kólpos, *Greece* 37 D6
Sougne-Remouchamps, *Belgium* 17 H7
Souillac, *France* 26 D5
Souk-Ahras, *Algeria* 75 A6
Souk el Arba du Rharb, *Morocco* 74 B3
Soukhouma, *Laos* 58 E5
Sŏul, *S. Korea* 51 F14
Soulac-sur-Mer, *France* 26 C2
Soultz-sous-Forêts, *France* 25 D14
Soumagne, *Belgium* 17 G7
Sound, The = Øresund, *Europe* 11 J6
Sound, The, *U.K.* 13 G3
Soúnion, Ákra, *Greece* 39 M7
Sour el Ghozlane, *Algeria* 75 A5
Sources, Mt. aux, *Lesotho* 85 D4
Sourdeval, *France* 24 D6
Soure, *Brazil* 122 B2
Soure, *Portugal* 30 E2
Souris, *Man., Canada* 101 D8
Souris, *P.E.I., Canada* 99 C7
Souris →, *Canada* 108 A5
Sousa, *Brazil* 122 C4
Sousel, *Brazil* 122 B1
Sousel, *Portugal* 31 G3
Souss, O. →, *Morocco* 74 B3
Sousse, *Tunisia* 75 A7
Soustons, *France* 26 E2
South Africa ■, *Africa* 84 E3
South Aulatsivik I., *Canada* 99 A7
South Australia □, *Australia* 91 E2
South Baldy, *U.S.A.* 111 J10
South Bend, *Ind., U.S.A.* 104 E2
South Bend, *Wash., U.S.A.* 112 D3
South Boston, *U.S.A.* 105 G6
South Branch, *Canada* 99 C8
South Brook, *Canada* 99 C8
South Buganda □, *Uganda* 82 C3
South Carolina □, *U.S.A.* 105 J5
South Charleston, *U.S.A.* 104 F5
South China Sea, *Asia* 56 C4
South Dakota □, *U.S.A.* 108 C5
South Downs, *U.K.* 13 G7
South East C., *Australia* 90 G4
South East Is., *Australia* 89 F3
South Esk →, *U.K.* 14 E5
South Foreland, *U.K.* 13 F9
South Fork →, *U.S.A.* 110 C7
South Fork, American →, *U.S.A.* 112 G5
South Fork, Feather →, *U.S.A.* 112 F5
South Georgia, *Antarctica* 5 B1
South Glamorgan □, *U.K.* 13 F4
South Haven, *U.S.A.* 104 D2
South Henik, L., *Canada* 101 A9
South Honshu Ridge, *Pac. Oc.* 92 E6
South Horr, *Kenya* 82 B4
South I., *Kenya* 82 B4
South I., *N.Z.* 87 L3
South Invercargill, *N.Z.* 87 M2
South Knife →, *Canada* 101 B10
South Korea ■, *Asia* 51 F15
South Lake Tahoe, *U.S.A.* 112 G6
South Loup →, *U.S.A.* 108 E5
South Magnetic Pole, *Antarctica* 5 C9
South Milwaukee, *U.S.A.* 104 D2
South Molton, *U.K.* 13 F4
South Nahanni →, *Canada* 100 A4
South Negril Pt., *Jamaica* 116 C4
South Orkney Is., *Antarctica* 5 C18
South Pagai, I. = Pagai Selatan, P., *Indonesia* 56 E2
South Pass, *U.S.A.* 110 E9
South Pittsburg, *U.S.A.* 105 H3
South Platte →, *U.S.A.* 108 E4
South Pole, *Antarctica* 5 E
South Porcupine, *Canada* 98 C3
South River, *Canada* 98 C4
South River, *U.S.A.* 107 F10
South Ronaldsay, *U.K.* 14 C6
South Sandwich Is., *Antarctica* 5 B1
South Saskatchewan →, *Canada* 101 C7
South Seal →, *Canada* 101 B9
South Shetland Is., *Antarctica* 5 C18
South Shields, *U.K.* 12 C6
South Sioux City, *U.S.A.* 108 D6
South Taranaki Bight, *N.Z.* 87 H5
South Thompson →, *Canada* 100 C4
South Twin I., *Canada* 98 B4
South Tyne →, *U.K.* 12 C5
South Uist, *U.K.* 14 D1
South West Africa = Namibia ■, *Africa* 84 C2
South West C., *Australia* 90 G4
South Yorkshire □, *U.K.* 12 D6
Southampton, *Canada* 98 D3
Southampton, *U.K.* 13 G6
Southampton, *U.S.A.* 107 F12
Southampton I., *Canada* 97 B11
Southbridge, *N.Z.* 87 K4
Southbridge, *U.S.A.* 107 D12
Southend, *Canada* 101 B8
Southend-on-Sea, *U.K.* 13 F8
Southern □, *Malawi* 83 F4
Southern □, *S. Leone* 78 D2
Southern □, *Zambia* 83 F2
Southern Alps, *N.Z.* 87 K3
Southern Cross, *Australia* 89 F2
Southern Hills, *Australia* 89 F3
Southern Indian L., *Canada* 101 B9
Southern Ocean, *Antarctica* 5 C6
Southern Pines, *U.S.A.* 105 H6
Southern Uplands, *U.K.* 14 F5
Southington, *U.S.A.* 107 E12
Southold, *U.S.A.* 107 E12
Southport, *Australia* 91 D5
Southport, *U.K.* 12 D4
Southport, *U.S.A.* 105 J6
Southwest C., *N.Z.* 87 M1
Southwold, *U.K.* 13 E9
Soutpansberg, *S. Africa* 85 C4
Souvigny, *France* 26 B7
Sovetsk, *Lithuania* 40 D2
Sovetsk, *Russia* 41 C16
Sovetskaya Gavan, *Russia* 45 E15
Sovicille, *Italy* 33 E8
Soviet Union = Commonwealth of Independent States ■, *Eurasia* 45 D11
Sovra, *Croatia* 21 N7
Soweto, *S. Africa* 85 D4
Sōya-Kaikyō = La Perouse Str., *Asia* 48 B11
Sōya-Misaki, *Japan* 48 B10
Soyo, *Angola* 80 F2
Sozh →, *Belorussia* 40 F7
Sozopol, *Bulgaria* 38 G10
Spa, *Belgium* 17 H7
Spain ■, *Europe* 7 H5
Spakenburg, *Neths.* 16 D6
Spalding, *Australia* 91 E2
Spalding, *U.K.* 12 E7
Spalding, *U.S.A.* 108 E5
Spangler, *U.S.A.* 106 F6
Spaniard's Bay, *Canada* 99 C9
Spanish, *Canada* 98 C3
Spanish Fork, *U.S.A.* 110 F8
Spanish Town, *Jamaica* 116 C4
Sparks, *U.S.A.* 112 F7
Sparta = Spárti, *Greece* 39 M5
Sparta, *Ga., U.S.A.* 105 J4
Sparta, *Wis., U.S.A.* 108 D9
Spartanburg, *U.S.A.* 105 H4
Spartansburg, *U.S.A.* 106 E5
Spartel, C., *Morocco* 74 A3
Spárti, *Greece* 39 M5
Spartivento, C., *Calabria, Italy* 35 E9
Spartivento, C., *Sard., Italy* 34 D1
Spas-Demensk, *Russia* 40 D8
Spas-Klepiki, *Russia* 41 D12
Spassk-Dalniy, *Russia* 45 E14
Spassk-Ryazanskiy, *Russia* 41 D12
Spátha, Ákra, *Greece* 37 D5
Spatsizi →, *Canada* 100 B3
Spearfish, *U.S.A.* 108 C3
Spearman, *U.S.A.* 109 G4
Speer, *Switz.* 23 B8
Speers, *Canada* 101 C7
Speightstown, *Barbados* 117 D8
Speke Gulf, *Tanzania* 82 C3
Spekholzerheide, *Neths.* 17 G8
Spence Bay, *Canada* 96 B10
Spencer, *Idaho, U.S.A.* 110 D7
Spencer, *Iowa, U.S.A.* 108 D7
Spencer, *N.Y., U.S.A.* 107 D8
Spencer, *Nebr., U.S.A.* 108 D5
Spencer, *W. Va., U.S.A.* 104 F5
Spencer, C., *Australia* 91 F2
Spencer B., *Namibia* 84 D1
Spencer G., *Australia* 91 E2
Spencerville, *Canada* 107 B9
Spences Bridge, *Canada* 100 C4
Spenser Mts., *N.Z.* 87 K4
Sperkhiós →, *Greece* 39 L5
Sperrin Mts., *U.K.* 15 B5
Spessart, *Germany* 19 E5
Spétsai, *Greece* 39 M6
Spey →, *U.K.* 14 D5
Speyer, *Germany* 19 F4
Speyer →, *Germany* 19 F4
Spezzano Albanese, *Italy* 35 C9
Spiekeroog, *Germany* 18 B3
Spielfeld, *Austria* 33 B12
Spiez, *Switz.* 22 C5
Spijk, *Neths.* 16 B9
Spijkenisse, *Neths.* 16 E4
Spíli, *Greece* 37 D6
Spilimbergo, *Italy* 33 B9
Spin Baldak = Qala-i-Jadid, *Afghan.* 62 D2
Spinalónga, *Greece* 37 D7
Spinazzola, *Italy* 35 B9
Spirit Lake, *Idaho, U.S.A.* 110 C5
Spirit Lake, *Wash., U.S.A.* 112 D4
Spirit River, *Canada* 100 B5
Spiritwood, *Canada* 101 C7
Spišská Nová Ves, *Czech.* 20 G10
Spithead, *U.K.* 13 G6
Spittal, *Austria* 21 J3
Spitzbergen = Svalbard, *Arctic* 4 B8
Split, *Croatia* 33 E13
Split L., *Canada* 101 B9
Splitski Kanal, *Croatia* 33 E13
Splügen, *Switz.* 23 C8
Splügenpass, *Switz.* 23 C8
Spoffard, *U.S.A.* 109 L4
Spokane, *U.S.A.* 110 C5
Spoleto, *Italy* 33 F9
Spooner, *U.S.A.* 108 C9
Sporyy Navolok, Mys, *Russia* 44 B7
Spragge, *Canada* 98 C3
Sprague, *U.S.A.* 110 C5
Sprague River, *U.S.A.* 110 E3
Spratly I., *S. China Sea* 56 C4
Spray, *U.S.A.* 110 D4
Spree →, *Germany* 18 C9
Spremberg, *Germany* 18 D10
Sprimont, *Belgium* 17 G7
Spring City, *U.S.A.* 110 G8
Spring Garden, *U.S.A.* 112 F6
Spring Mts., *U.S.A.* 111 H6
Spring Valley, *Calif., U.S.A.* 113 N10
Spring Valley, *Minn., U.S.A.* 108 D8
Springbok, *S. Africa* 84 D2
Springdale, *Canada* 99 C8
Springdale, *Ark., U.S.A.* 109 G7
Springdale, *Wash., U.S.A.* 110 B5
Springe, *Germany* 18 C5
Springer, *U.S.A.* 109 G2
Springerville, *U.S.A.* 111 J9
Springfield, *Canada* 106 D4
Springfield, *N.Z.* 87 K3
Springfield, *Colo., U.S.A.* 109 G3
Springfield, *Ill., U.S.A.* 108 F10
Springfield, *Mass., U.S.A.* 107 D12
Springfield, *Mo., U.S.A.* 109 G8
Springfield, *Ohio, U.S.A.* 104 F4
Springfield, *Oreg., U.S.A.* 110 D2
Springfield, *Tenn., U.S.A.* 105 G2
Springfield, *Vt., U.S.A.* 107 C12
Springfontein, *S. Africa* 84 E4
Springhill, *Canada* 99 C7

Springhouse, *Canada* 100 C4
Springhurst, *Australia* 91 F4
Springs, *S. Africa* 85 D4
Springsure, *Australia* 90 C4
Springvale, *Queens., Australia* 90 C3
Springvale, *W. Austral., Australia* 88 C4
Springvale, *U.S.A.* 107 C14
Springville, *Calif., U.S.A.* 112 J8
Springville, *N.Y., U.S.A.* 106 D6
Springville, *Utah, U.S.A.* 110 F8
Springwater, *Canada* 101 C7
Spruce-Creek, *U.S.A.* 106 F6
Spur, *U.S.A.* 109 J4
Spurn Hd., *U.K.* 12 D8
Spuž, *Montenegro, Yug.* 21 N9
Spuzzum, *Canada* 100 D4
Squam L., *U.S.A.* 107 C13
Squamish, *Canada* 100 D4
Square Islands, *Canada* 99 B8
Squillace, G. di, *Italy* 35 D9
Squinzano, *Italy* 35 B11
Squires, Mt., *Australia* 89 E4
Sragen, *Indonesia* 57 G14
Srbac, *Bos.-H., Yug.* 21 K7
Srbija = Serbia □, *Serbia, Yug.* 21 M11
Srbobran, *Serbia, Yug.* 21 K9
Sre Khtum, *Cambodia* 59 F6
Sre Umbell, *Cambodia* 59 G4
Srebrnica, *Bos.-H., Yug.* 21 L9
Sredinnyy Khrebet, *Russia* 45 D16
Sredinnyy Ra. = Sredinnyy Khrebet, *Russia* 45 D16
Središče, *Slovenia* 33 B13
Sredna Gora, *Bulgaria* 38 G7
Sredne Tambovskoye, *Russia* 45 D14
Srednekolymsk, *Russia* 45 C16
Srednevilyuysk, *Russia* 45 C13
Śrem, *Poland* 20 C7
Sremska Mitrovica, *Serbia, Yug.* 21 L9
Srepok →, *Cambodia* 58 F6
Sretensk, *Russia* 45 D12
Sri Lanka ■, *Asia* 60 R12
Srikakulam, *India* 61 K13
Srinagar, *India* 63 B6
Środa Wielkopolski, *Poland* 20 C7
Srpska Itabej, *Serbia, Yug.* 21 K10
Staaten →, *Australia* 90 B3
Staberhuk, *Germany* 18 A7
Stabroek, *Belgium* 17 F4
Stad Delden, *Neths.* 16 D9
Stade, *Germany* 18 B5
Staden, *Belgium* 17 G2
Staðarhólskirkja, *Iceland* 8 D3
Städjan, *Sweden* 10 C6
Stadlandet, *Norway* 8 E8
Stadskanaal, *Neths.* 16 B9
Stadthagen, *Germany* 18 C5
Stadtlohn, *Germany* 18 D2
Stadtroda, *Germany* 18 E7
Stäfa, *Switz.* 23 B7
Stafafell, *Iceland* 8 D6
Staffa, *U.K.* 14 E2
Stafford, *U.K.* 12 E5
Stafford, *U.S.A.* 109 G5
Stafford Springs, *U.S.A.* 107 E12
Staffordshire □, *U.K.* 12 E5
Stagnone, *Italy* 34 E5
Staines, *U.K.* 13 F7
Stakhanov = Kadiyevka, *Ukraine* 43 B8
Stalden, *Switz.* 22 D5
Stalingrad = Volgograd, *Russia* 43 B11
Staliniri = Tskhinvali, *Georgia* 43 E11
Stalino = Donetsk, *Ukraine* 42 C7
Stalinogorsk = Novomoskovsk, *Russia* 41 D11
Stalis, *Greece* 37 D7
Stalowa Wola, *Poland* 20 E12
Stalybridge, *U.K.* 12 D5
Stamford, *Australia* 90 C3
Stamford, *U.K.* 13 E7
Stamford, *Conn., U.S.A.* 107 E11
Stamford, *Tex., U.S.A.* 109 J5
Stamps, *U.S.A.* 109 J8
Stanberry, *U.S.A.* 108 E7
Stančevo = Kalipetrovo, *Bulgaria* 38 E10
Standerton, *S. Africa* 85 D4
Standish, *U.S.A.* 104 D4
Stanford, *U.S.A.* 110 C8
Stange, *Norway* 10 D5
Stanger, *S. Africa* 85 D5
Stanislaus →, *U.S.A.* 112 H5
Stanislav = Ivano-Frankovsk, *Ukraine* 40 G4
Stanke Dimitrov, *Bulgaria* 38 G6
Stanley, *Australia* 90 G4
Stanley, *N.B., Canada* 99 C6
Stanley, *Sask., Canada* 101 B8
Stanley, *Falk. Is.* 128 D5
Stanley, *Idaho, U.S.A.* 110 D6
Stanley, *N. Dak., U.S.A.* 108 A3
Stanley, *N.Y., U.S.A.* 106 D7
Stanley, *Wis., U.S.A.* 108 C9
Stanovoy Khrebet, *Russia* 45 D13
Stanovoy Ra. = Stanovoy Khrebet, *Russia* 45 D13
Stans, *Switz.* 23 C6
Stansmore Ra., *Australia* 88 D4
Stanthorpe, *Australia* 91 D5
Stanton, *U.S.A.* 109 J4
Stanwood, *U.S.A.* 112 B4
Staphorst, *Neths.* 16 C8
Staples, *U.S.A.* 108 B7
Stapleton, *U.S.A.* 108 E4
Star City, *Canada* 101 C8
Stara-minskaya, *Russia* 43 C8
Stara Moravica, *Serbia, Yug.* 21 K9
Stara Planina, *Bulgaria* 38 F6
Stara Zagora, *Bulgaria* 38 G8
Starachowice, *Poland* 20 D11
Starashcherbinovskaya, *Russia* 43 C8
Staraya Russa, *Russia* 40 C7
Starbuck I., *Kiribati* 93 H12
Stargard Szczeciński, *Poland* 20 B5
Stari Trg, *Slovenia* 33 C12
Staritsa, *Russia* 40 C9
Starke, *U.S.A.* 105 K4
Starkville, *Colo., U.S.A.* 109 G2
Starkville, *Miss., U.S.A.* 105 J1
Starnberg, *Germany* 19 G7
Starnberger See, *Germany* 19 H7
Starobelsk, *Ukraine* 43 B8
Starodub, *Russia* 40 E8
Starogard, *Poland* 20 B8
Starokonstantinov, *Ukraine* 42 B2
Start Pt., *U.K.* 13 G4
Staryy Biryuzyak, *Russia* 43 D12
Staryy Chartoriysk, *Ukraine* 40 F4
Staryy Kheydzhan, *Russia* 45 C15
Staryy Krym, *Ukraine* 42 D6
Staryy Oskol, *Russia* 41 F10
Stassfurt, *Germany* 18 D7
State College, *U.S.A.* 106 F7
Stateline, *U.S.A.* 112 G7
Staten, I. = Estados, I. de Los, *Argentina* 128 D4
Staten I., *U.S.A.* 107 F10
Statesboro, *U.S.A.* 105 J5
Statesville, *U.S.A.* 105 H5
Stauffer, *U.S.A.* 113 L7
Staunton, *Ill., U.S.A.* 108 F10
Staunton, *Va., U.S.A.* 104 F6
Stavanger, *Norway* 9 G8
Staveley, *N.Z.* 87 K3
Stavelot, *Belgium* 17 H7
Stavenhagen, *Germany* 18 B8
Stavenisse, *Neths.* 17 E4
Staveren, *Neths.* 16 C6
Stavern, *Norway* 10 F4
Stavre, *Sweden* 10 B9
Stavropol, *Russia* 43 D10
Stavros, *Cyprus* 37 D11
Stavrós, *Greece* 37 D6
Stavros, Ákra, *Greece* 37 D6
Stavroúpolis, *Greece* 39 H7
Stawell, *Australia* 91 F3
Stawell →, *Australia* 90 C3
Stawiszyn, *Poland* 20 D8
Stayner, *Canada* 106 B4
Steamboat Springs, *U.S.A.* 110 F10
Steckborn, *Switz.* 23 A7
Steele, *U.S.A.* 108 B5
Steelton, *U.S.A.* 106 F8
Steelville, *U.S.A.* 109 G9
Steen River, *Canada* 100 B5
Steenbergen, *Neths.* 17 E4
Steenkool = Bintuni, *Indonesia* 57 E8
Steenvoorde, *France* 25 B9
Steenwijk, *Neths.* 16 C8
Steep Pt., *Australia* 89 E1
Steep Rock, *Canada* 101 C9
Ştefăneşti, *Romania* 38 B10
Stefanie L. = Chew Bahir, *Ethiopia* 77 G4
Stefansson Bay, *Antarctica* 5 C5
Steffisburg, *Switz.* 22 C5
Stege, *Denmark* 11 K6
Steiermark □, *Austria* 21 H5
Steigerwald, *Germany* 19 F6
Steilacoom, *U.S.A.* 112 C4
Stein, *Neths.* 17 G7
Steinbach, *Canada* 101 D9
Steinfort, *Lux.* 17 J7
Steinfurt, *Germany* 18 C3
Steinheim, *Germany* 18 D5
Steinhuder Meer, *Germany* 18 C5
Steinkjer, *Norway* 8 E11
Steinkopf, *S. Africa* 84 D2
Stekene, *Belgium* 17 F4
Stellarton, *Canada* 99 C7
Stellenbosch, *S. Africa* 84 E2
Stellendam, *Neths.* 16 E4
Stelvio, Paso dello, *Italy* 23 C10
Stemshaug, *Norway* 10 A2
Stendal, *Germany* 18 C7
Stene, *Belgium* 17 F1
Stensele, *Sweden* 8 D14
Stenstorp, *Sweden* 11 F7
Stepanakert = Khankendy, *Azerbaijan* 67 D12
Stephan, *U.S.A.* 108 A6
Stephens Creek, *Australia* 91 E3
Stephens I., *Canada* 100 C2
Stephenville, *Canada* 99 C8
Stephenville, *U.S.A.* 109 J5
Stepnica, *Poland* 20 B4
Stepnoi = Elista, *Russia* 43 C11
Stepnyak, *Kazakhstan* 44 D8
Steppe, *Asia* 46 E9
Sterkstroom, *S. Africa* 84 E4
Sterling, *Colo., U.S.A.* 108 E3
Sterling, *Ill., U.S.A.* 108 E10
Sterling, *Kans., U.S.A.* 108 F5
Sterling City, *U.S.A.* 109 K4
Sterling Run, *U.S.A.* 106 E6
Sterlitamak, *Russia* 44 D6
Šternberg, *Germany* 18 B7
Šternberk, *Czech.* 20 F7
Stérnes, *Greece* 37 D6
Stettin = Szczecin, *Poland* 20 B4
Stettiner Haff, *Germany* 18 B10
Stettler, *Canada* 100 C6
Steubenville, *U.S.A.* 106 F4
Stevens Point, *U.S.A.* 108 C10
Stevenson, *U.S.A.* 112 E5
Stevenson L., *Canada* 101 C9
Stevns Klint, *Denmark* 11 J6
Stewart, *B.C., Canada* 100 B3
Stewart, *N.W.T., Canada* 96 B6
Stewart, *U.S.A.* 112 F7
Stewart, C., *Australia* 90 A1
Stewart, I., *Chile* 128 D2
Stewart I., *N.Z.* 87 M1
Stewarts Point, *U.S.A.* 112 G3
Stewiacke, *Canada* 99 C7
Steynsburg, *S. Africa* 84 E4
Steyr, *Austria* 21 G4
Steytlerville, *S. Africa* 84 E3
Stia, *Italy* 33 E8
Stiens, *Neths.* 16 B7
Stigler, *U.S.A.* 109 H7
Stigliano, *Italy* 35 B9
Stigsnæs, *Denmark* 11 J5
Stigtomta, *Sweden* 11 F10
Stikine →, *Canada* 100 B2
Stilfontein, *S. Africa* 84 D4
Stilís, *Greece* 39 L5
Stillwater, *N.Z.* 87 K3
Stillwater, *Minn., U.S.A.* 108 C8
Stillwater, *N.Y., U.S.A.* 107 D11
Stillwater, *Okla., U.S.A.* 109 G6
Stillwater Ra., *U.S.A.* 110 G4
Stilwell, *U.S.A.* 109 H7
Štip, *Macedonia, Yug.* 39 H5
Stíra, *Greece* 39 L7
Stirling, *Australia* 90 B3
Stirling, *Canada* 100 D6
Stirling, *U.K.* 14 E5
Stirling Ra., *Australia* 89 F2
Stittsville, *Canada* 107 A9
Stockach, *Germany* 19 H5
Stockerau, *Austria* 21 G6
Stockett, *U.S.A.* 110 C8
Stockholm, *Sweden* 10 E12
Stockholms län □, *Sweden* 10 E12
Stockhorn, *Switz.* 22 C5
Stockport, *U.K.* 12 D5
Stockton, *Calif., U.S.A.* 111 H3
Stockton, *Kans., U.S.A.* 108 F5
Stockton, *Mo., U.S.A.* 109 G8
Stockton-on-Tees, *U.K.* 12 C6
Stockvik, *Sweden* 10 B11
Stöde, *Sweden* 10 B10
Stogovo, *Macedonia, Yug.* 39 H3
Stoke on Trent, *U.K.* 12 D5
Stokes Bay, *Canada* 98 C3
Stokes Pt., *Australia* 90 G3
Stokes Ra., *Australia* 88 C5
Stokkseyri, *Iceland* 8 E3
Stokksnes, *Iceland* 8 D6
Stolac, *Bos.-H., Yug.* 21 M7
Stolberg, *Germany* 18 E2
Stolbovaya, *Russia* 41 D10
Stolbovaya, *Russia* 45 C16
Stolbovoy, Ostrov, *Russia* 45 D17
Stolbtsy, *Belorussia* 40 E5
Stolin, *Belorussia* 40 F5
Stolwijk, *Neths.* 16 E5
Stomíon, *Greece* 37 D5
Ston, *Croatia* 21 N7
Stonehaven, *U.K.* 14 E6
Stonehenge, *Australia* 90 C3
Stonewall, *Canada* 101 C9
Stony L., *Man., Canada* 101 B9
Stony L., *Ont., Canada* 106 B6
Stony Rapids, *Canada* 101 B7
Stony Tunguska = Podkamennaya Tunguska →, *Russia* 45 C10
Stonyford, *U.S.A.* 112 F4
Stopnica, *Poland* 20 E10
Stora Lulevatten, *Sweden* 8 C15
Stora Sjöfallet, *Sweden* 8 C15
Storavan, *Sweden* 8 D15
Store Bælt, *Denmark* 11 J5
Store Creek, *Australia* 91 E4
Store Heddinge, *Denmark* 11 J6
Støren, *Norway* 10 A4
Storm B., *Australia* 90 G4
Storm Lake, *U.S.A.* 108 D7
Stormberge, *S. Africa* 84 E4
Stormsrivier, *S. Africa* 84 E3
Stornoway, *U.K.* 14 C2
Storozhinets, *Ukraine* 42 B1
Storsjö, *Sweden* 10 B7
Storsjøen, *Hedmark, Norway* 10 D5
Storsjøen, *Hedmark, Norway* 10 C5
Storsjön, *Sweden* 10 B7
Storstrøms Amt. □, *Denmark* 11 K5
Storuman, *Sweden* 8 D14
Stoughton, *Canada* 101 D8
Stour →, *Dorset, U.K.* 13 G5
Stour →, *Here. & Worcs., U.K.* 13 E5
Stour →, *Kent, U.K.* 13 F9
Stour →, *Suffolk, U.K.* 13 F9
Stourbridge, *U.K.* 13 E5
Stout, L., *Canada* 101 C10
Stove Pipe Wells Village, *U.S.A.* 113 J9
Stowmarket, *U.K.* 13 E9
Strabane, *U.K.* 15 B4
Strabane □, *U.K.* 15 B4
Stracin, *Macedonia, Yug.* 38 G5
Stradella, *Italy* 32 C6
Strahan, *Australia* 90 G4
Strakonice, *Czech.* 20 F3
Straldzha, *Bulgaria* 38 G9
Stralsund, *Germany* 18 A9
Strand, *S. Africa* 84 E2
Strangford L., *U.K.* 15 B6
Strängnäs, *Sweden* 10 E11
Strangsville, *U.S.A.* 106 E3
Stranraer, *U.K.* 14 G3
Strasbourg, *Canada* 101 C8
Strasbourg, *France* 25 D14
Strasburg, *Germany* 18 B9
Strasburg, *U.S.A.* 108 B4
Strassen, *Lux.* 17 J8
Stratford, *Canada* 98 D3
Stratford, *N.Z.* 87 H5
Stratford, *Calif., U.S.A.* 111 H4
Stratford, *Conn., U.S.A.* 107 E11
Stratford, *Tex., U.S.A.* 109 G3
Stratford-upon-Avon, *U.K.* 13 E6
Strath Spey, *U.K.* 14 D5
Strathalbyn, *Australia* 91 F2
Strathclyde □, *U.K.* 14 F4
Strathcona Prov. Park, *Canada* 100 D3
Strathmore, *Australia* 90 B3
Strathmore, *Canada* 100 C6
Strathmore, *U.K.* 14 E5
Strathmore, *U.S.A.* 112 J7
Strathnaver, *Canada* 100 C4
Strathpeffer, *U.K.* 14 D4
Strathroy, *Canada* 98 D3
Strathy Pt., *U.K.* 14 C4
Stratton, *U.S.A.* 108 F3
Straubing, *Germany* 19 G8
Straumnes, *Iceland* 8 C2
Strausberg, *Germany* 18 C9
Strawberry Res., *U.S.A.* 110 F8
Strawn, *U.S.A.* 109 J5
Strážnice, *Czech.* 20 G7
Streaky B., *Australia* 91 E1
Streaky Bay, *Australia* 91 E1
Streator, *U.S.A.* 108 E10
Streé, *Belgium* 17 H4
Streeter, *U.S.A.* 108 B5
Streetsville, *Canada* 106 C5
Strehaia, *Romania* 38 E6
Strelcha, *Bulgaria* 38 G7
Strelka, *Russia* 45 D10
Streng →, *Cambodia* 58 F4
Strésa, *Italy* 32 C5
Strezhevoy, *Russia* 44 C8
Stříbro, *Czech.* 20 F3
Strijen, *Neths.* 16 E5
Strimón →, *Greece* 39 J6
Strimonikós Kólpos, *Greece* 39 J6
Stroeder, *Argentina* 128 B4
Strofádhes, *Greece* 39 M4
Strömbacka, *Sweden* 10 C10
Strómboli, *Italy* 35 D8
Stromeferry, *U.K.* 14 D3
Stromness, *U.K.* 14 C5
Ströms vattudal, *Sweden* 8 D13
Strömstad, *Sweden* 9 G11
Strömsund, *Sweden* 8 E13
Stróngoli, *Italy* 35 C10
Stronsay, *U.K.* 14 B6
Stronsburg, *U.S.A.* 108 E6
Stroud, *U.K.* 13 F5
Stroud Road, *Australia* 91 E5
Stroudsberg, *U.S.A.* 107 F9
Stroumbi, *Cyprus* 37 E11
Struer, *Denmark* 11 H2
Struga, *Macedonia, Yug.* 39 H3
Strugi Krasnyye, *Russia* 40 B6
Strumica, *Macedonia, Yug.* 39 H5
Strumica →, *Europe* 39 H6
Struthers, *Canada* 98 C2
Struthers, *U.S.A.* 106 E4
Stryi, *Ukraine* 40 G3
Stryker, *U.S.A.* 110 B6
Strzegom, *Poland* 20 E6
Strzelce Krajeńskie, *Poland* 20 C5
Strzelecki Cr. →, *Australia* 91 D2
Strzelin, *Poland* 20 E7
Strzelno, *Poland* 20 C8
Strzyżów, *Poland* 20 F11
Stuart, *Fla., U.S.A.* 105 M5
Stuart, *Nebr., U.S.A.* 108 D5
Stuart →, *Canada* 100 C4
Stuart Bluff Ra., *Australia* 88 D5
Stuart L., *Canada* 100 C4
Stuart Ra., *Australia* 91 D1
Stubbekøbing, *Denmark* 11 K6
Stugun, *Sweden* 10 A9
Stull, L., *Canada* 98 B1
Stung Treng, *Cambodia* 58 F5
Stupart →, *Canada* 101 B10
Stupino, *Russia* 41 D11
Sturgeon B., *Canada* 101 C9
Sturgeon Bay, *U.S.A.* 104 C2
Sturgeon Falls, *Canada* 98 C4
Sturgeon L., *Alta., Canada* 100 B5
Sturgeon L., *Ont., Canada* 106 B6
Sturgeon L., *Ont., Canada* 98 B1
Sturgis, *Mich., U.S.A.* 104 E3
Sturgis, *S. Dak., U.S.A.* 108 C3
Sturt Cr. →, *Australia* 88 C4
Sturt Creek, *Australia* 88 C4
Stutterheim, *S. Africa* 84 E4
Stuttgart, *Germany* 19 G5
Stuttgart, *U.S.A.* 109 H9
Stuyvesant, *U.S.A.* 107 D11
Stykkishólmur, *Iceland* 8 D2
Styr →, *Belorussia* 40 E5
Styria = Steiermark □, *Austria* 21 H5
Su Xian, *China* 50 H9
Suakin, *Sudan* 76 D4
Suan, *N. Korea* 51 E14
Suapure →, *Venezuela* 120 B4
Suaqui, *Mexico* 114 B3
Suatá →, *Venezuela* 121 B4
Subang, *Indonesia* 57 G12
Subansiri →, *India* 61 F18
Subayhah, *Si. Arabia* 64 D3
Subi, *Indonesia* 59 L7
Subiaco, *Italy* 33 G10
Subotica, *Serbia, Yug.* 21 J9
Success, *Canada* 101 C7
Suceava, *Romania* 38 B9
Suceava →, *Romania* 38 B9
Sucha-Beskidzka, *Poland* 20 F9
Suchan, *Poland* 20 B5
Suchan, *Russia* 48 C6
Suchitoto, *El Salv.* 116 D2
Suchou = Suzhou, *China* 53 B13
Süchow = Xuzhou, *China* 51 G9
Suchowola, *Poland* 20 B13
Sucio →, *Colombia* 120 B2
Suck →, *Ireland* 15 C3
Sucre, *Bolivia* 125 D4
Sucre, *Colombia* 120 B3
Sucre □, *Colombia* 120 B2
Sucre □, *Venezuela* 121 A5
Sucuaro, *Colombia* 120 C4
Sućuraj, *Croatia* 33 E14
Sucuriju, *Brazil* 122 A2
Sucuriú →, *Brazil* 125 E7
Sud, Pte., *Canada* 99 C7
Sud-Ouest, Pte. du, *Canada* 99 C7
Suda →, *Russia* 41 B10
Sudak, *Ukraine* 42 D6
Sudan, *U.S.A.* 109 H3
Sudan ■, *Africa* 77 E3
Suday, *Russia* 41 B13
Sudbury, *Canada* 98 C3
Sudbury, *U.K.* 13 E8
Sûdd, *Sudan* 77 F2
Suddie, *Guyana* 121 B6
Süderbrarup, *Germany* 18 A5
Süderlügum, *Germany* 18 A4
Süderoog-Sand, *Germany* 18 A4
Sudeten Mts. = Sudety, *Europe* 20 E6
Sudety, *Europe* 20 E6
Sudi, *Tanzania* 83 E4
Sudirman, Pegunungan, *Indonesia* 57 E9
Sudogda, *Russia* 41 D12
Sudr, *Egypt* 76 J8
Sudzha, *Russia* 40 F9
Sueca, *Spain* 29 F4
Suedala, *Sweden* 11 J7
Suez = El Suweis, *Egypt* 76 J8
Suez, G. of = Suweis, Khalîg el, *Egypt* 76 J8
Suez Canal = Suweis, Qanâl es, *Egypt* 76 H8
Suffield, *Canada* 101 C6
Suffolk, *U.S.A.* 104 G7
Suffolk □, *U.K.* 13 E9
Sugar City, *U.S.A.* 108 F3
Suğla Gölü, *Turkey* 66 E5
Sugluk = Saglouc, *Canada* 97 B12
Sugny, *Belgium* 17 J5
Suhaia, L., *Romania* 38 F8
Suḥār, *Oman* 65 E8
Suhbaatar, *Mongolia* 54 A5
Sühbaatar □, *Mongolia* 50 B8
Suhl, *Germany* 18 E6
Suhr, *Switz.* 22 B6
Şuhut, *Turkey* 66 D4
Sui Xian, *Henan, China* 50 G8
Sui Xian, *Henan, China* 53 B9
Suiá Missu →, *Brazil* 125 C7
Suichang, *China* 53 C12
Suichuan, *China* 53 D10
Suide, *China* 50 F6
Suifenhe, *China* 51 B16
Suihua, *China* 54 B7
Suijiang, *China* 52 C4
Suining, *Hunan, China* 53 D8
Suining, *Jiangsu, China* 51 H9
Suining, *Sichuan, China* 52 B5
Suiping, *China* 50 H7
Suippes, *France* 25 C11
Suir →, *Ireland* 15 D4
Suixi, *China* 53 G8
Suiyang, *Guizhou, China* 52 D6
Suiyang, *Heilongjiang, China* 51 B16
Suizhong, *China* 51 D11
Sujangarh, *India* 62 F6
Sukabumi, *Indonesia* 57 G12

Sukadana, *Kalimantan, Indonesia* 56 E3
Sukadana, *Sumatera, Indonesia* 56 F3
Sukagawa, *Japan* 49 F10
Sukaraja, *Indonesia* 56 E4
Sukarnapura = Jayapura, *Indonesia* 57 E10
Sukchŏn, *N. Korea* 51 E13
Sukhinichi, *Russia* 40 D9
Sukhona →, *Russia* 44 D4
Sukhothai, *Thailand* 58 D2
Sukhumi, *Georgia* 43 E9
Sukkur, *Pakistan* 62 F3
Sukkur Barrage, *Pakistan* 62 F3
Sukumo, *Japan* 49 H6
Sukunka →, *Canada* 100 B4
Sul, Canal do, *Brazil* 122 B2
Sula →, *Ukraine* 40 G8
Sula, Kepulauan, *Indonesia* 57 E7
Sulaco →, *Honduras* 116 C2
Sulaiman Range, *Pakistan* 62 D3
Sulak →, *Russia* 43 E12
Sūlār, *Iran* 65 D6
Sulawesi □, *Indonesia* 57 E6
Sulechów, *Poland* 20 C5
Sulejów, *Poland* 20 D9
Sulgen, *Switz.* 23 A8
Sulima, *S. Leone* 78 D2
Sulina, *Romania* 38 D12
Sulina, Braţul →, *Romania* 38 D12
Sulingen, *Germany* 18 C4
Sulitälma, *Sweden* 8 C14
Sulitjelma, *Norway* 8 C14
Sullana, *Peru* 124 A1
Sullivan, *Ill., U.S.A.* 108 F10
Sullivan, *Ind., U.S.A.* 104 F2
Sullivan, *Mo., U.S.A.* 108 F9
Sullivan Bay, *Canada* 100 C3
Sully-sur-Loire, *France* 25 E9
Sulmona, *Italy* 33 F10
Sulphur, *La., U.S.A.* 109 K8
Sulphur, *Okla., U.S.A.* 109 H6
Sulphur Pt., *Canada* 100 A6
Sulphur Springs, *U.S.A.* 109 J7
Sulphur Springs Draw →, *U.S.A.* 109 J4
Sultan, *Canada* 98 C3
Sultan, *U.S.A.* 112 C5
Sultanpur, *India* 63 F10
Sulu Arch., *Phil.* 55 J4
Sulu Sea, *E. Indies* 55 G4
Sülüklü, *Turkey* 66 D5
Sululta, *Ethiopia* 77 F4
Suluova, *Turkey* 66 C6
Suluq, *Libya* 73 B9
Sulzbach, *Germany* 19 F3
Sulzbach-Rosenberg, *Germany* 19 F7
Sulzberger Ice Shelf, *Antarctica* 5 D10
Sumalata, *Indonesia* 57 D6
Sumampa, *Argentina* 126 B3
Sumatera □, *Indonesia* 56 D2
Sumatra = Sumatera □, *Indonesia* 56 D2
Sumatra, *U.S.A.* 110 C10
Sumba, *Indonesia* 57 F5
Sumba, Selat, *Indonesia* 57 F5
Sumbawa, *Indonesia* 56 F5
Sumbawa Besar, *Indonesia* 56 F5
Sumbawanga □, *Tanzania* 82 D3
Sumbe, *Angola* 80 G2
Sumburgh Hd., *U.K.* 14 B7
Sumdo, *India* 63 B8
Sumé, *Brazil* 122 C4
Sumedang, *Indonesia* 57 G12
Šumen, *Bulgaria* 38 F9
Sumenep, *Indonesia* 57 G15
Sumgait, *Azerbaijan* 43 F13
Sumiswald, *Switz.* 22 B5
Summer L., *U.S.A.* 110 E3
Summerland, *Canada* 100 D5
Summerside, *Canada* 99 C7
Summerville, *Ga., U.S.A.* 105 H3
Summerville, *S.C., U.S.A.* 105 J5
Summit Lake, *Canada* 100 C4
Summit Pk., *U.S.A.* 111 H10
Sumner, *Iowa, U.S.A.* 108 D8
Sumner, *Wash., U.S.A.* 112 C4
Sumoto, *Japan* 49 G7
Sumter, *U.S.A.* 105 J5
Sumy, *Ukraine* 40 F9
Sun City, *Ariz., U.S.A.* 111 K7
Sun City, *Calif., U.S.A.* 113 M9
Sunagawa, *Japan* 48 C10
Sunan, *N. Korea* 51 E13
Sunart, L., *U.K.* 14 E3
Sunburst, *U.S.A.* 110 B8
Sunbury, *Australia* 91 F3
Sunbury, *U.S.A.* 107 F8
Sunchales, *Argentina* 126 C3
Suncho Corral, *Argentina* 126 B3
Sunchon, *S. Korea* 51 G14
Suncook, *U.S.A.* 107 C13
Sunda, Selat, *Indonesia* 56 F3
Sunda Is., *Indonesia* 92 H2
Sunda Str. = Sunda, Selat, *Indonesia* 56 F3
Sundance, *U.S.A.* 108 C2
Sundarbans, The, *Asia* 61 J16
Sundargarh, *India* 61 H14
Sundays = Sondags →, *S. Africa* 84 E4
Sundbyberg, *Sweden* 10 E11
Sunderland, *Canada* 106 B5
Sunderland, *U.K.* 12 C6
Sundre, *Canada* 100 C6
Sundridge, *Canada* 98 C4
Sunds, *Denmark* 11 H3
Sundsjö, *Sweden* 10 B9
Sundsvall, *Sweden* 10 B11
Sung Hei, *Vietnam* 59 G6
Sungai Kolok, *Thailand* 59 J3
Sungai Lembing, *Malaysia* 59 L4
Sungai Patani, *Malaysia* 59 K3
Sungaigerong, *Indonesia* 56 E2
Sungailiat, *Indonesia* 56 E3
Sungaipakning, *Indonesia* 56 D2
Sungaipenuh, *Indonesia* 56 E2
Sungaitiram, *Indonesia* 56 E5
Sungari = Songhua Jiang →, *China* 54 B8
Sungguminasa, *Indonesia* 57 F5
Sunghua Chiang = Songhua Jiang →, *China* 54 B8
Sungikai, *Sudan* 77 E2
Sungurlu, *Turkey* 42 F6
Sunja, *Croatia* 33 C13
Sunnyside, *Utah, U.S.A.* 110 G8
Sunnyside, *Wash., U.S.A.* 110 C3
Sunnyvale, *U.S.A.* 111 H2
Sunray, *U.S.A.* 109 G4
Suntar, *Russia* 45 C12
Sunyani, *Ghana* 78 D4
Supai, *U.S.A.* 111 H7
Supamo →, *Venezuela* 121 B5
Supaul, *India* 63 F12
Supe, *Peru* 124 C2
Superior, *Ariz., U.S.A.* 111 K8
Superior, *Mont., U.S.A.* 110 C6
Superior, *Nebr., U.S.A.* 108 E5
Superior, *Wis., U.S.A.* 108 B8
Superior, L., *N. Amer.* 98 C2
Supetar, *Croatia* 33 E13
Suphan Buri, *Thailand* 58 E3
Suphan Daği, *Turkey* 67 D10
Supriori, Kepulauan, *Indonesia* 57 E9
Supung Sk., *China* 51 D13
Sūq Suwayq, *Si. Arabia* 64 E3
Suqian, *China* 51 H10
Sūr, *Lebanon* 69 B4
Sur, Pt., *U.S.A.* 111 H3
Sura →, *Russia* 41 C15
Surab, *Pakistan* 62 E2
Surabaja = Surabaya, *Indonesia* 57 G15
Surabaya, *Indonesia* 57 G15
Suraia, *Romania* 38 D10
Surakarta, *Indonesia* 57 G14
Surakhany, *Azerbaijan* 43 F14
Surat, *Australia* 91 D4
Surat, *India* 60 J8
Surat Thani, *Thailand* 59 H2
Suratgarh, *India* 62 E5
Surazh, *Belorussia* 40 D7
Surazh, *Russia* 40 E8
Surduc Pasul, *Romania* 38 D6
Surdulica, *Serbia, Yug.* 21 N12
Sûre = Sauer →, *Germany* 17 J9
Surendranagar, *India* 62 H4
Surf, *U.S.A.* 113 L6
Surgères, *France* 26 B3
Surgut, *Russia* 44 C8
Surhuisterveen, *Neths.* 16 B8
Suriapet, *India* 60 L11
Surigao, *Phil.* 55 G6
Surigao Strait, *Phil.* 55 F6
Surin, *Thailand* 58 E4
Surin Nua, Ko, *Thailand* 59 H1
Surinam ■, *S. Amer.* 121 C6
Suriname □, *Surinam* 121 B6
Suriname →, *Surinam* 121 B6
Sürmaq, *Iran* 65 D7
Sürmene, *Turkey* 43 F9
Surovikino, *Russia* 43 B10
Surprise L., *Canada* 100 B2
Surrey □, *U.K.* 13 F7
Sursee, *Switz.* 22 B6
Sursk, *Russia* 41 E14
Surt, *Libya* 73 B8
Surt, Khalīj, *Libya* 73 B8
Surtsey, *Iceland* 8 E3
Surubim, *Brazil* 122 C4
Sürüç, *Turkey* 67 E8
Suruga-Wan, *Japan* 49 G9
Surumu →, *Brazil* 121 C5
Susa, *Italy* 32 C4
Susă →, *Denmark* 11 J5
Sušac, *Croatia* 33 F13
Susak, *Croatia* 33 D11
Susaki, *Japan* 49 H6
Süsangerd, *Iran* 65 D6
Susanino, *Russia* 45 D15
Susanville, *U.S.A.* 110 F3
Susch, *Switz.* 23 C10
Suşehri, *Turkey* 67 C8
Susong, *China* 53 B11
Susquehanna →, *U.S.A.* 107 G8
Susquehanna Depot, *U.S.A.* 107 E9
Susques, *Argentina* 126 A2
Sussex, *Canada* 99 C6
Sussex, *U.S.A.* 107 E10
Sussex, E. □, *U.K.* 13 G8
Sussex, W. □, *U.K.* 13 G7
Susteren, *Neths.* 17 F7
Sustut →, *Canada* 100 B3
Susuman, *Russia* 45 C15
Susunu, *Indonesia* 57 E8
Susurluk, *Turkey* 66 D3
Susuz, *Turkey* 67 C10
Sütçüler, *Turkey* 66 E4
Sutherland, *S. Africa* 84 E3
Sutherland, *U.S.A.* 108 E4
Sutherland Falls, *N.Z.* 87 L1
Sutherlin, *U.S.A.* 110 E2
Sutivan, *Croatia* 33 E13
Sutlej →, *Pakistan* 62 E4
Sutter, *U.S.A.* 112 F5
Sutter Creek, *U.S.A.* 112 G6
Sutton, *Canada* 107 A12
Sutton, *U.S.A.* 108 E6
Sutton →, *Canada* 98 A3
Sutton in Ashfield, *U.K.* 12 D6
Suttor →, *Australia* 90 C4
Suttsu, *Japan* 48 C10
Suva, *Fiji* 87 D8
Suva Reka, *Serbia, Yug.* 21 N10
Suvo Rudište, *Serbia, Yug.* 21 M10
Suvorov, *Russia* 41 D10
Suvorov Is. = Suwarrow Is., *Cook Is.* 93 J11
Suwałki, *Poland* 20 A12
Suwannaphum, *Thailand* 58 E4
Suwannee →, *U.S.A.* 105 L4
Suwanose-Jima, *Japan* 49 K4
Suwarrow Is., *Cook Is.* 93 J11
Suwayq aş Şuqban, *Iraq* 64 D5
Suweis, Khalîg el, *Egypt* 76 J8
Suweis, Qanâl es, *Egypt* 76 H8
Suwŏn, *S. Korea* 51 F14
Suzdal, *Russia* 41 C12
Suzhou, *China* 53 B13
Suzu, *Japan* 49 F8
Suzu-Misaki, *Japan* 49 F8
Suzuka, *Japan* 49 G8
Suzzara, *Italy* 32 C7
Svalbard, *Arctic* 4 B8
Svalbarð, *Iceland* 8 C6
Svalöv, *Sweden* 11 J7
Svanvik, *Norway* 8 B21
Svappavaara, *Sweden* 8 C16
Svarstad, *Norway* 10 E3
Svartisen, *Norway* 8 C12
Svartvik, *Sweden* 10 B11
Svatovo, *Ukraine* 42 B8
Svay Chek, *Cambodia* 58 F4
Svay Rieng, *Cambodia* 59 G5
Svealand □, *Sweden* 9 G13
Sveg, *Sweden* 9 E13
Svendborg, *Denmark* 11 J4
Svene, *Norway* 10 E3
Svenljunga, *Sweden* 11 G7
Svenstrup, *Denmark* 11 H3
Sverdlovsk = Yekaterinburg, *Russia* 44 D7
Sverdlovsk, *Ukraine* 43 B8
Sverdrup Is., *Canada* 4 B3
Svetac, *Croatia* 33 E12
Sveti Ivan Zelina, *Croatia* 33 C13
Sveti Jurij, *Slovenia* 33 B12
Sveti Lenart, *Slovenia* 33 B12
Sveti Nikole, *Macedonia, Yug.* 39 H4
Sveti Trojica, *Slovenia* 33 B12
Svetlaya, *Russia* 48 A9
Svetlogorsk, *Belorussia* 40 E6
Svetlograd, *Russia* 43 D10
Svetlovodsk, *Ukraine* 40 G8
Svetozarevo, *Serbia, Yug.* 21 L11
Svidník, *Czech.* 20 F11
Svilaja Planina, *Croatia* 33 E13
Svilengrad, *Bulgaria* 39 H9
Svir →, *Russia* 6 C12
Svishtov, *Bulgaria* 38 F8
Svisloch, *Belorussia* 40 E4
Svitava →, *Czech.* 20 F6
Svitavy, *Czech.* 20 F6
Svobodnyy, *Russia* 45 D13
Svolvær, *Norway* 8 B13
Svratka →, *Czech.* 20 F6
Svrljig, *Serbia, Yug.* 21 M12
Swabian Alps = Schwäbische Alb, *Germany* 19 G5
Swainsboro, *U.S.A.* 105 J4
Swakopmund, *Namibia* 84 C1
Swale →, *U.K.* 12 C6
Swalmen, *Neths.* 17 F8
Swan Hill, *Australia* 91 F3
Swan Hills, *Canada* 100 C5
Swan Is., *W. Indies* 116 C3
Swan L., *Canada* 101 C8
Swan River, *Canada* 101 C8
Swanage, *U.K.* 13 G6
Swansea, *Australia* 91 E5
Swansea, *U.K.* 13 F4
Swar →, *Pakistan* 63 B5
Swartberge, *S. Africa* 84 E3
Swartmodder, *S. Africa* 84 D3
Swartruggens, *S. Africa* 84 D4
Swarzędz, *Poland* 20 C7
Swastika, *Canada* 98 C3
Swatow = Shantou, *China* 53 F11
Swaziland ■, *Africa* 85 D5
Sweden ■, *Europe* 9 H13
Swedru, *Ghana* 79 D4
Sweet Home, *U.S.A.* 110 D2
Sweetwater, *Nev., U.S.A.* 112 G7
Sweetwater, *Tex., U.S.A.* 109 J4
Sweetwater →, *U.S.A.* 110 E10
Swellendam, *S. Africa* 84 E3
Świdnica, *Poland* 20 E6
Świdnik, *Poland* 20 D12
Świdwin, *Poland* 20 B5
Świebodzin, *Poland* 20 C5
Świecie, *Poland* 20 B8
Świętokrzyskie, Góry, *Poland* 20 E10
Swift Current, *Canada* 101 C7
Swiftcurrent →, *Canada* 101 C7
Swilly, L., *Ireland* 15 A4
Swindle, I., *Canada* 100 C3
Swindon, *U.K.* 13 F6
Swinemünde = Świnoujście, *Poland* 20 B4
Świnoujście, *Poland* 20 B4
Switzerland ■, *Europe* 22 D6
Swords, *Ireland* 15 C5
Syasstroy, *Russia* 40 A8
Sychevka, *Russia* 40 D9
Sydney, *Australia* 91 E5
Sydney, *Canada* 99 C7
Sydney Mines, *Canada* 99 C7
Sydprøven, *Greenland* 4 C5
Sydra G. of = Surt, Khalīj, *Libya* 73 B8
Syke, *Germany* 18 C4
Syktyvkar, *Russia* 44 C6
Sylacauga, *U.S.A.* 105 J2
Sylarna, *Sweden* 8 E12
Sylhet, *Bangla.* 61 G17
Sylt, *Germany* 18 A4
Sylvan Lake, *Canada* 100 C6
Sylvania, *U.S.A.* 105 J5
Sylvester, *U.S.A.* 105 K4
Sym, *Russia* 44 C9
Symón, *Mexico* 114 C4
Synnott Ra., *Australia* 88 C4
Syracuse, *Kans., U.S.A.* 109 F4
Syracuse, *N.Y., U.S.A.* 107 C8
Syrdarya →, *Kazakhstan* 44 E7
Syria ■, *Asia* 64 C3
Syul'dzhyukyor, *Russia* 45 C12
Syzran, *Russia* 41 E16
Szaraz →, *Hungary* 21 J10
Szarvas, *Hungary* 21 J10
Szczebrzeszyn, *Poland* 20 E12
Szczecin, *Poland* 20 B4
Szczecinek, *Poland* 20 B6
Szczekocimy, *Poland* 20 E9
Szczytno, *Poland* 20 B11
Szechwan = Sichuan □, *China* 52 B5
Szeged, *Hungary* 21 J10
Szeghalom, *Hungary* 21 H11
Székesfehérvár, *Hungary* 21 H8
Szekszárd, *Hungary* 21 J8
Szendrö, *Hungary* 21 G10
Szentendre, *Hungary* 21 H9
Szentes, *Hungary* 21 J10
Szentgotthárd, *Hungary* 21 J6
Szentlörinc, *Hungary* 21 J8
Szigetvár, *Hungary* 21 J7
Szolnok, *Hungary* 21 H10
Szombathely, *Hungary* 21 H6
Szprotawa, *Poland* 20 D5
Szydłowiec, *Poland* 20 D10
Szypliszki, *Poland* 20 A13

T

't Harde, *Neths.* 16 D7
't Zandt, *Neths.* 16 B9
Ta Khli Khok, *Thailand* 58 E3
Ta Lai, *Vietnam* 59 G6
Tabacal, *Argentina* 126 A3
Tabaco, *Phil.* 55 E5
Tabagné, *Ivory C.* 78 D4
Ţābah, *Si. Arabia* 64 E4
Tabajara, *Brazil* 125 B5
Tabalos, *Peru* 124 B2
Tabarca, I. de, *Spain* 29 G4
Tabarka, *Tunisia* 75 A6
Ţabas, *Khorāsān, Iran* 65 C9
Ţabas, *Khorāsān, Iran* 65 C8
Tabasará, Serranía de, *Panama* 116 E3
Tabasco □, *Mexico* 115 D6
Tabatinga, Serra da, *Brazil* 122 D3
Tabāzīn, *Iran* 65 D8
Tabelbala, Kahal de, *Algeria* 75 C4
Taber, *Canada* 100 D6
Tabernas, *Spain* 29 H2
Tabernes de Valldigna, *Spain* 29 F4
Tabira, *Brazil* 122 C4
Tablas, *Phil.* 55 E5
Tablas Strait, *Phil.* 55 E4
Table B. = Tafelbaai, *S. Africa* 84 E2
Table B., *Canada* 99 B8
Table Mt., *S. Africa* 84 E2
Tableland, *Australia* 88 C4
Tabletop, Mt., *Australia* 90 C4
Tábor, *Czech.* 20 F4
Tabora, *Tanzania* 82 D3
Tabora □, *Tanzania* 82 D3
Tabou, *Ivory C.* 78 E3
Tabrīz, *Iran* 64 B5
Tabuaeran, *Pac. Oc.* 93 G12
Tabuelan, *Phil.* 55 F5
Tabuenca, *Spain* 28 D3
Tabūk, *Si. Arabia* 64 D3
Tacámbaro de Codallos, *Mexico* 114 D4
Tacheng, *China* 54 B3
Tach'ing Shan = Daqing Shan, *China* 50 D6
Táchira □, *Venezuela* 120 B3
Tácina →, *Italy* 35 D9
Tacloban, *Phil.* 55 F6
Tacna, *Peru* 124 D3
Tacna □, *Peru* 124 D3
Tacoma, *U.S.A.* 112 C4
Tacuarembó, *Uruguay* 127 C4
Tacutu →, *Brazil* 121 C5
Tademaït, Plateau du, *Algeria* 75 C5
Tadent, O. →, *Algeria* 75 D6
Tadjerdjeri, O. →, *Algeria* 75 C6
Tadjerouna, *Algeria* 75 B5
Tadjettaret, O. →, *Algeria* 75 D6
Tadjmout, *Oasis, Algeria* 75 B5
Tadjmout, *Saoura, Algeria* 75 C5
Tadjoura, *Djibouti* 68 E3
Tadjoura, Golfe de, *Djibouti* 77 E5
Tadmor, *N.Z.* 87 J4
Tadoule, L., *Canada* 101 B9
Tadoussac, *Canada* 99 C6
Tadzhikistan = Tajikistan ■, *Asia* 44 F8
Taechŏn-ni, *S. Korea* 51 F14
Taegu, *S. Korea* 51 G15
Taegwan, *N. Korea* 51 D13
Taejŏn, *S. Korea* 51 F14
Tafalla, *Spain* 28 C3
Tafar, *Sudan* 77 F2
Tafassasset, O. →, *Algeria* 75 D6
Tafelbaai, *S. Africa* 84 E2
Tafelney, C., *Morocco* 74 B3
Tafermaar, *Indonesia* 57 F8
Taffermit, *Morocco* 74 C3
Tafí Viejo, *Argentina* 126 B2
Tafīhān, *Iran* 65 D7
Tafiré, *Ivory C.* 78 D3
Tafnidilt, *Morocco* 74 C2
Tafraoute, *Morocco* 74 C3
Taft, *Iran* 65 D7
Taft, *Phil.* 55 F6
Taft, *Calif., U.S.A.* 113 K7
Taft, *Tex., U.S.A.* 109 M6
Taga Dzong, *Bhutan* 61 F16
Taganrog, *Russia* 43 C8
Taganrogskiy Zaliv, *Russia* 42 C8
Tagânt, *Mauritania* 78 B2
Tagatay, *Phil.* 55 D4
Tagbilaran, *Phil.* 55 G5
Tággia, *Italy* 32 E4
Taghzout, *Morocco* 74 B4
Tagish, *Canada* 100 A2
Tagish L., *Canada* 100 A2
Tagliacozzo, *Italy* 33 F10
Tagliamento →, *Italy* 33 C10
Táglio di Po, *Italy* 33 D9
Tagna, *Colombia* 120 D3
Tago, *Phil.* 55 G7
Tagomago, I. de, *Spain* 36 B8
Taguatinga, *Brazil* 123 D3
Tagudin, *Phil.* 55 C4
Tagum, *Phil.* 55 H6
Tagus = Tejo →, *Europe* 31 G1
Tahakopa, *N.Z.* 87 M2
Tahala, *Morocco* 74 B4
Tahan, Gunong, *Malaysia* 59 K4
Tahat, *Algeria* 75 D6
Tāherī, *Iran* 65 E7
Tahiti, *Pac. Oc.* 93 J13
Tahoe, L., *U.S.A.* 112 G6
Tahoe City, *U.S.A.* 112 F6
Taholah, *U.S.A.* 112 C2
Tahoua, *Niger* 79 C6
Tahta, *Egypt* 76 B3
Tahtali Dağlari, *Turkey* 66 D6
Tahuamanu →, *Bolivia* 124 C4
Tahulandang, *Indonesia* 57 D7
Tahuna, *Indonesia* 57 D7
Taï, *Ivory C.* 78 D3
Tai Hu, *China* 54 C7
Tai Shan, *China* 51 F9
Tai Xian, *China* 53 A13
Tai'an, *China* 51 F9
Taibei, *Taiwan* 53 E13
Taibique, *Canary Is.* 36 G2
Taibus Qi, *China* 50 D8
T'aichung = Taizhong, *Taiwan* 53 E13
Taidong, *Taiwan* 53 F13
Taieri →, *N.Z.* 87 M3
Taigu, *China* 50 F7
Taihang Shan, *China* 50 G7
Taihape, *N.Z.* 87 H5
Taihe, *Anhui, China* 50 H8
Taihe, *Jiangxi, China* 53 D10
Taihu, *China* 53 B11
Taijiang, *China* 52 D7
Taikang, *China* 50 G8
Tailem Bend, *Australia* 91 F2
Tailfingen, *Germany* 19 G5
Taimyr Peninsula = Taymyr, Poluostrov, *Russia* 45 B11
Tain, *U.K.* 14 D4
Tainan, *Taiwan* 53 F13
Taínaron, Ákra, *Greece* 39 N5
Taining, *China* 53 D11
Taintignies, *Belgium* 17 G2
Taiobeiras, *Brazil* 123 E3

T'aipei

T'aipei = Taibei, *Taiwan* 53 E13
Taiping, *China* 53 B12
Taiping, *Malaysia* 59 K3
Taipingzhen, *China* 50 H6
Taipu, *Brazil* 122 C4
Taishan, *China* 53 F9
Taishun, *China* 53 D12
Taita □, *Kenya* 82 C4
Taita Hills, *Kenya* 82 C4
Taitao, C., *Chile* 128 C1
Taitao, Pen. de, *Chile* 128 C2
Taivalkoski, *Finland* 8 D20
Taiwan ■, *Asia* 53 F13
Taiwan Shan, *Taiwan* 53 F13
Taixing, *China* 53 A13
Taïyetos Óros, *Greece* 39 N5
Taiyiba, *Israel* 69 C4
Taiyuan, *China* 50 F7
Taizhong, *Taiwan* 53 E13
Taizhou, *China* 53 A12
Taizhou Liedao, *China* 53 C13
Ta'izz, *Yemen* 68 E3
Tājābād, *Iran* 65 D7
Tajapuru, Furo do, *Brazil* 122 B1
Tajikistan ■, *Asia* 44 F8
Tajima, *Japan* 49 F9
Tajo = Tejo →, *Europe* 31 G1
Tajrīsh, *Iran* 65 C6
Tājūrā, *Libya* 73 B7
Tak, *Thailand* 58 D2
Takāb, *Iran* 64 B5
Takachiho, *Japan* 49 H5
Takada, *Japan* 49 F9
Takahagi, *Japan* 49 F10
Takaka, *N.Z.* 87 J4
Takamatsu, *Japan* 49 G7
Takaoka, *Japan* 49 F8
Takapuna, *N.Z.* 87 G5
Takasaki, *Japan* 49 F9
Takatsuki, *Japan* 49 G7
Takaungu, *Kenya* 82 C4
Takayama, *Japan* 49 F8
Take-Shima, *Japan* 49 J5
Takefu, *Japan* 49 G8
Takengon, *Indonesia* 56 D1
Takeo, *Cambodia* 59 G5
Takeo, *Japan* 49 H5
Tåkern, *Sweden* 11 F8
Tākestān, *Iran* 65 C6
Taketa, *Japan* 49 H5
Takh, *India* 63 C7
Takhman, *Cambodia* 59 G5
Takikawa, *Japan* 48 C10
Takla L., *Canada* 100 B3
Takla Landing, *Canada* 100 B3
Takla Makan = Taklamakan Shamo, *China* 54 C3
Taklamakan Shamo, *China* 54 C3
Taku →, *Canada* 100 B2
Takum, *Nigeria* 79 D6
Takutu →, *Guyana* 121 C5
Tal Halāl, *Iran* 65 D7
Tala, *Uruguay* 127 C4
Talacogan, *Phil.* 55 G6
Talagante, *Chile* 126 C1
Talaïnt, *Morocco* 74 C3
Talak, *Niger* 79 B6
Talamanca, Cordillera de, *Cent. Amer.* 116 E3
Talara, *Peru* 124 A1
Talas, *Kirghizia* 44 E8
Talas, *Turkey* 66 D6
Talâta, *Egypt* 69 E1
Talata Mafara, *Nigeria* 79 C6
Talaud, Kepulauan, *Indonesia* 57 D7
Talaud Is. = Talaud, Kepulauan, *Indonesia* 57 D7
Talavera de la Reina, *Spain* 30 F6
Talawana, *Australia* 88 D3
Talayan, *Phil.* 55 H6
Talbert, Sillon de, *France* 24 D3
Talbot, C., *Australia* 88 B4
Talbragar →, *Australia* 91 E4
Talca, *Chile* 126 D1
Talca □, *Chile* 126 D1
Talcahuano, *Chile* 126 D1
Talcher, *India* 61 J14
Talcho, *Niger* 79 C5
Taldy Kurgan, *Kazakhstan* 44 E8
Talesh, *Iran* 65 B6
Ţalesh, Kūhhā-ye, *Iran* 65 B6
Talguharai, *Sudan* 76 D4
Tali Post, *Sudan* 77 F3
Taliabu, *Indonesia* 57 E6
Talibon, *Phil.* 57 B6
Talibong, Ko, *Thailand* 59 J2
Talihina, *U.S.A.* 109 H7
Talisayan, *Phil.* 55 G6
Taliwang, *Indonesia* 56 F5
Tall 'Asūr, *Jordan* 69 D4
Tall Kalakh, *Syria* 69 A5
Talla, *Egypt* 76 J7
Talladega, *U.S.A.* 105 J2
Tallahassee, *U.S.A.* 105 K3
Tallangatta, *Australia* 91 F4
Tallarook, *Australia* 91 F4
Tallering Pk., *Australia* 89 E2
Tallinn, *Estonia* 40 B4
Tallulah, *U.S.A.* 109 J9
Talmest, *Morocco* 74 B3
Talmont, *France* 26 B2
Talnoye, *Ukraine* 42 B4
Talodi, *Sudan* 77 E3
Talovaya, *Russia* 41 F12
Talpa de Allende, *Mexico* 114 C4
Talsi, *Latvia* 40 C3
Talsinnt, *Morocco* 75 B4
Taltal, *Chile* 126 B1
Taltson →, *Canada* 100 A6
Talwood, *Australia* 91 D4
Talyawalka Cr. →, *Australia* 91 E3
Tam Chau, *Vietnam* 59 G5
Tam Ky, *Vietnam* 58 E7
Tam Quan, *Vietnam* 58 E7
Tama, *U.S.A.* 108 E8
Tamala, *Australia* 89 E1
Tamalameque, *Colombia* 120 B3
Tamale, *Ghana* 79 D4
Taman, *Russia* 42 D7
Tamanar, *Morocco* 74 B3
Tamano, *Japan* 49 G6
Tamanrasset, *Algeria* 75 D6
Tamanrasset, O. →, *Algeria* 75 D5
Tamaqua, *U.S.A.* 107 F9
Tamar →, *U.K.* 13 G3
Támara, *Colombia* 120 B3
Tamarang, *Australia* 91 E5
Tamarinda, *Spain* 36 B10
Tamarite de Litera, *Spain* 28 D5
Tamashima, *Japan* 49 G6
Tamaské, *Niger* 79 C6
Tamaulipas □, *Mexico* 115 C5
Tamaulipas, Sierra de, *Mexico* 115 C5
Tamazula, *Mexico* 114 C3
Tamazunchale, *Mexico* 115 C5
Tamba-Dabatou, *Guinea* 78 C2
Tambacounda, *Senegal* 78 C2
Tambelan, Kepulauan, *Indonesia* 56 D3
Tambellup, *Australia* 89 F2
Tambo, *Australia* 90 C4
Tambo, *Peru* 124 C3
Tambo →, *Peru* 124 C3
Tambo de Mora, *Peru* 124 C2
Tambobamba, *Peru* 124 C3
Tambohorano, *Madag.* 85 B7
Tambopata →, *Peru* 124 C4
Tambora, *Indonesia* 56 F5
Tambov, *Russia* 41 E12
Tambre →, *Spain* 30 C2
Tambuku, *Indonesia* 57 G15
Tamburâ, *Sudan* 77 F2
Tâmchekket, *Mauritania* 78 B2
Tame, *Colombia* 120 B3
Tamega →, *Portugal* 30 D2
Tamelelt, *Morocco* 74 B3
Tamenglong, *India* 61 G18
Tamerza, *Tunisia* 75 B6
Tamgak, Mts., *Niger* 72 E6
Tamiahua, L. de, *Mexico* 115 C5
Tamil Nadu □, *India* 60 P10
Tamines, *Belgium* 17 H5
Tamis →, *Serbia, Yug.* 38 E3
Tamluk, *India* 63 H12
Tammerfors = Tampere, *Finland* 9 F17
Tammisaari, *Finland* 9 F17
Tamo Abu, Pegunungan, *Malaysia* 56 D5
Tampa, *U.S.A.* 105 M4
Tampa B., *U.S.A.* 105 M4
Tampere, *Finland* 9 F17
Tampico, *Mexico* 115 C5
Tampin, *Malaysia* 59 L4
Tamri, *Morocco* 74 B3
Tamrida = Qādib, *Yemen* 68 E5
Tamsagbulag, *Mongolia* 54 B6
Tamsalu, *Estonia* 40 B5
Tamu, *Burma* 61 G19
Tamuja →, *Spain* 31 F4
Tamworth, *Australia* 91 E5
Tamworth, *U.K.* 13 E6
Tamyang, *S. Korea* 51 G14
Tan An, *Vietnam* 59 G6
Tan-tan, *Morocco* 74 C2
Tana, *Norway* 8 A20
Tana →, *Kenya* 82 C5
Tana →, *Norway* 8 A20
Tana, L., *Ethiopia* 77 E4
Tana River, *Kenya* 82 C4
Tanabe, *Japan* 49 H7
Tanabi, *Brazil* 123 F2
Tanafjorden, *Norway* 8 A20
Tanaga, Pta., *Canary Is.* 36 G1
Tanagro →, *Italy* 35 B8
Tanahbala, *Indonesia* 56 E1
Tanahgrogot, *Indonesia* 56 E5
Tanahjampea, *Indonesia* 57 F6
Tanahmasa, *Indonesia* 56 E1
Tanahmerah, *Indonesia* 57 F10
Tanakura, *Japan* 49 F10
Tanami, *Australia* 88 C4
Tanami Desert, *Australia* 88 C5
Tanana, *U.S.A.* 96 B4
Tanana →, *U.S.A.* 96 B4
Tananarive = Antananarivo, *Madag.* 85 B8
Tanannt, *Morocco* 74 B3
Tånaro →, *Italy* 32 C5
Tanaunella, *Italy* 34 B2
Tanbar, *Australia* 90 D3
Tancarville, *France* 24 C7
Tancheng, *China* 51 G10
Tanchŏn, *N. Korea* 51 D15
Tanda, *Ut. P., India* 63 F10
Tanda, *Ut. P., India* 63 E8
Tanda, *Ivory C.* 78 D4
Tandag, *Phil.* 55 G7
Tandaia, *Tanzania* 83 D3
Tăndărei, *Romania* 38 E10
Tandaué, *Angola* 84 B2
Tandil, *Argentina* 126 D4
Tandil, Sa. del, *Argentina* 126 D4
Tandlianwala, *Pakistan* 62 D5
Tando Adam, *Pakistan* 62 G3
Tandou L., *Australia* 91 E3
Tandsbyn, *Sweden* 10 A8
Tane-ga-Shima, *Japan* 49 J5
Taneatua, *N.Z.* 87 H6
Tanen Tong Dan, *Burma* 58 D2
Tanezrouft, *Algeria* 75 D5
Tang, Koh, *Cambodia* 59 G4
Tang Krasang, *Cambodia* 58 F5
Tanga, *Tanzania* 82 D4
Tanga □, *Tanzania* 82 D4
Tanganyika, L., *Africa* 82 D2
Tanger, *Morocco* 74 A3
Tangerang, *Indonesia* 57 G12
Tangerhütte, *Germany* 18 C7
Tangermünde, *Germany* 18 C7
Tanggu, *China* 51 E9
Tanggula Shan, *China* 54 C4
Tanghe, *China* 50 H7
Tangier = Tanger, *Morocco* 74 A3
Tangorin P.O., *Australia* 90 C3
Tangshan, *China* 51 E10
Tangtou, *China* 51 G10
Tanguiéta, *Benin* 79 C5
Tangxi, *China* 53 C12
Tangyan He →, *China* 52 C7
Tanimbar, Kepulauan, *Indonesia* 57 F8
Tanimbar Is. = Tanimbar, Kepulauan, *Indonesia* 57 F8
Taninges, *France* 27 B10
Tanjay, *Phil.* 55 G5
Tanjong Malim, *Malaysia* 59 L3
Tanjore = Thanjavur, *India* 60 P11
Tanjung, *Indonesia* 56 E5
Tanjungbalai, *Indonesia* 56 D1
Tanjungbatu, *Indonesia* 56 D5
Tanjungkarang Telukbetung, *Indonesia* 56 F3
Tanjungpandan, *Indonesia* 56 E3
Tanjungpinang, *Indonesia* 56 D2
Tanjungpriok, *Indonesia* 57 G12
Tanjungredeb, *Indonesia* 56 D5
Tanjungselor, *Indonesia* 56 D5
Tank, *Pakistan* 62 C4
Tänndalen, *Sweden* 10 B6
Tannis Bugt, *Denmark* 11 G4
Tannu-Ola, *Russia* 45 D10
Tano →, *Ghana* 78 D4
Tanon Str., *Phil.* 55 F5
Tanout, *Niger* 79 C6
Tanquinho, *Brazil* 123 D4
Tanta, *Egypt* 76 H7
Tantoyuca, *Mexico* 115 C5
Tantung = Dandong, *China* 51 D13
Tanumshede, *Sweden* 11 F5
Tanunda, *Australia* 91 E2
Tanus, *France* 26 D6
Tanyeri, *Turkey* 67 D8
Tanzania ■, *Africa* 82 D3
Tanzilla →, *Canada* 100 B2
Tao Ko, *Thailand* 59 G2
Tao'an, *China* 51 B12
Tao'er He →, *China* 51 B13
Taohua Dao, *China* 53 C14
Taolanaro, *Madag.* 85 D8
Taole, *China* 50 E4
Taormina, *Italy* 35 E8
Taos, *U.S.A.* 111 H11
Taoudenni, *Mali* 74 D4
Taoudrart, Adrar, *Algeria* 75 D5
Taounate, *Morocco* 74 B4
Taourirt, *Algeria* 75 C5
Taourirt, *Morocco* 75 B4
Taouz, *Morocco* 74 B4
Taoyuan, *China* 53 C8
Taoyuan, *Taiwan* 53 E13
Tapa, *Estonia* 40 B4
Tapa Shan = Daba Shan, *China* 52 B7
Tapachula, *Mexico* 115 E6
Tapah, *Malaysia* 59 K3
Tapajós →, *Brazil* 121 D7
Tapaktuan, *Indonesia* 56 D1
Tapanahoni →, *Surinam* 121 C7
Tapanui, *N.Z.* 87 L2
Tapauá, *Brazil* 125 B5
Tapauá →, *Brazil* 125 B5
Tapeta, *Liberia* 78 D3
Taphan Hin, *Thailand* 58 D3
Tapi →, *India* 60 J8
Tapia, *Spain* 30 B4
Tápiószele, *Hungary* 21 H9
Tapiraí, *Brazil* 123 E2
Tapirapé →, *Brazil* 122 D1
Tapirapecó, Serra, *Venezuela* 121 C5
Tapirapuã, *Brazil* 125 C6
Tapoeripa, *Surinam* 121 B6
Tapolca, *Hungary* 21 J7
Tappahannock, *U.S.A.* 104 G7
Tapuaenuku, Mt., *N.Z.* 87 J4
Tapul Group, *Phil.* 55 J4
Tapurucuará, *Brazil* 121 D4
Taqīābād, *Iran* 65 C8
Ţaqţaq, *Iraq* 64 C5
Taquara, *Brazil* 127 B5
Taquari →, *Brazil* 125 D6
Taquaritinga, *Brazil* 123 F2
Tara, *Australia* 91 D5
Tara, *Canada* 106 B3
Tara, *Russia* 44 D8
Tara, *Zambia* 83 F2
Tara →, *Russia* 44 D8
Tarabagatay, Khrebet, *Kazakhstan* 44 E9
Tarabuco, *Bolivia* 125 D5
Tarābulus, *Lebanon* 69 A4
Tarābulus, *Libya* 75 B7
Tarahouahout, *Algeria* 75 D6
Tarajalejo, *Canary Is.* 36 F5
Tarakan, *Indonesia* 56 D5
Tarakit, Mt., *Kenya* 82 B4
Taralga, *Australia* 91 E4
Tarama-Jima, *Japan* 49 M2
Taranagar, *India* 62 E6
Taranaki □, *N.Z.* 87 H5
Tarancón, *Spain* 28 E1
Taranga, *India* 62 H5
Taranga Hill, *India* 62 H5
Táranto, *Italy* 35 B10
Táranto, G. di, *Italy* 35 B10
Tarapacá, *Colombia* 120 D4
Tarapacá □, *Chile* 126 A2
Tarapoto, *Peru* 124 B2
Taraquá, *Brazil* 120 C4
Tarare, *France* 27 C8
Tararua Ra., *N.Z.* 87 J5
Tarascon, *France* 27 E8
Tarascon-sur-Ariège, *France* 26 F5
Tarashcha, *Ukraine* 42 B4
Tarata, *Peru* 124 D3
Tarauacá, *Brazil* 124 B3
Tarauacá →, *Brazil* 124 B4
Taravo →, *France* 27 G12
Tarawera, *N.Z.* 87 H6
Tarawera L., *N.Z.* 87 H6
Tarazona, *Spain* 28 D3
Tarazona de la Mancha, *Spain* 29 F3
Tarbat Ness, *U.K.* 14 D5
Tarbela Dam, *Pakistan* 62 B5
Tarbert, *Strath., U.K.* 14 F3
Tarbert, *W. Isles, U.K.* 14 D2
Tarbes, *France* 26 E4
Tarboro, *U.S.A.* 105 H7
Tarbrax, *Australia* 90 C3
Tarcento, *Italy* 33 B10
Tarcoola, *Australia* 91 E1
Tarcoon, *Australia* 91 E4
Tardets-Sorholus, *France* 26 E3
Tardoire →, *France* 26 C4
Taree, *Australia* 91 E5
Tarentaise, *France* 27 C10
Tarf, Ras, *Morocco* 74 A3
Tarfa, Wadi el →, *Egypt* 76 J7
Tarfaya, *Morocco* 74 C2
Targon, *France* 26 D3
Targuist, *Morocco* 74 B3
Tarhbalt, *Morocco* 74 B3
Tarhit, *Algeria* 75 B4
Táriba, *Venezuela* 120 B3
Tarifa, *Spain* 31 J5
Tarija, *Bolivia* 126 A3
Tarija □, *Bolivia* 126 A3
Tariku →, *Indonesia* 57 E9
Tarim Basin = Tarim Pendi, *China* 54 C3
Tarim He →, *China* 54 C3
Tarim Pendi, *China* 54 C3
Tarime □, *Tanzania* 82 C3
Taritatu →, *Indonesia* 57 E9
Tarka →, *S. Africa* 84 E4
Tarkastad, *S. Africa* 84 E4
Tarkhankut, Mys, *Ukraine* 42 D5
Tarko Sale, *Russia* 44 C8
Tarkwa, *Ghana* 78 D4
Tarlac, *Phil.* 55 D4
Tarlton Downs, *Australia* 90 C2
Tarm, *Denmark* 11 J2
Tarma, *Peru* 124 C2
Tarn □, *France* 26 E6
Tarn →, *France* 26 D5
Tarn-et-Garonne □, *France* 26 D5
Tarna →, *Hungary* 21 H9
Tårnby, *Denmark* 11 J6
Tarnobrzeg, *Poland* 20 E11
Tarnów, *Poland* 20 F11
Táro →, *Italy* 32 D7
Taroom, *Australia* 91 D4
Taroudannt, *Morocco* 74 B3
Tarp, *Germany* 18 A5
Tarpon Springs, *U.S.A.* 105 L4
Tarquínia, *Italy* 33 F8
Tarragona, *Spain* 28 D6
Tarragona □, *Spain* 28 D6
Tarrasa, *Spain* 28 D7
Tárrega, *Spain* 28 D6
Tarrytown, *U.S.A.* 107 E11
Tarshiha = Me'ona, *Israel* 69 B4
Tarso Emissi, *Chad* 73 D8
Tarsus, *Turkey* 66 E6
Tartagal, *Argentina* 126 A3
Tartas, *France* 26 E3
Tartu, *Estonia* 40 B5
Ţarţūs, *Syria* 64 C2
Tarumirim, *Brazil* 123 E3
Tarumizu, *Japan* 49 J5
Tarussa, *Russia* 41 D10
Tarutao, Ko, *Thailand* 59 J2
Tarutung, *Indonesia* 56 D1
Tarvisio, *Italy* 33 B10
Tarz Ulli, *Libya* 75 C7
Tasāwah, *Libya* 73 C7
Taschereau, *Canada* 98 C4
Taseko →, *Canada* 100 C4
Tash-Kumyr, *Kirghizia* 44 E8
Tashauz, *Turkmenistan* 44 E6
Tashi Chho Dzong = Thimphu, *Bhutan* 61 F16
Tashkent, *Uzbekistan* 44 E7
Tashtagol, *Russia* 44 D9
Tasikmalaya, *Indonesia* 57 G13
Tåsjön, *Sweden* 8 D13
Taskan, *Russia* 45 C16
Taşköprü, *Turkey* 42 F6
Tasman B., *N.Z.* 87 J4
Tasman Mts., *N.Z.* 87 J4
Tasman Pen., *Australia* 90 G4
Tasman Sea, *Pac. Oc.* 92 L8
Tasmania □, *Australia* 90 G4
Tăşnad, *Romania* 38 B5
Tassil Tin-Rerhoh, *Algeria* 75 D5
Tassili n-Ajjer, *Algeria* 75 C6
Tassili-Oua-n-Ahaggar, *Algeria* 75 D6
Tasu Sd., *Canada* 100 C2
Tata, *Morocco* 74 C3
Tatabánya, *Hungary* 21 H8
Tatahouine, *Tunisia* 75 B7
Tatar Republic □, *Russia* 44 D6
Tatarbunary, *Ukraine* 42 D3
Tatarsk, *Russia* 44 D8
Tateyama, *Japan* 49 G9
Tathlina L., *Canada* 100 A5
Tathra, *Australia* 91 F4
Tatinnai L., *Canada* 101 A9
Tatnam, C., *Canada* 101 B10
Tatra = Tatry, *Czech.* 20 F9
Tatry, *Czech.* 20 F9
Tatsuno, *Japan* 49 G7
Tatta, *Pakistan* 62 G2
Tatuī, *Brazil* 127 A6
Tatum, *U.S.A.* 109 J3
Tat'ung = Datong, *China* 50 D7
Tatvan, *Turkey* 67 D10
Tauá, *Brazil* 122 C3
Taubaté, *Brazil* 127 A6
Tauberbischofsheim, *Germany* 19 F5
Taucha, *Germany* 18 D8
Taufikia, *Sudan* 77 F3
Taumarunui, *N.Z.* 87 H5
Taumaturgo, *Brazil* 124 B3
Taung, *S. Africa* 84 D3
Taungdwingyi, *Burma* 61 J19
Taunggyi, *Burma* 61 J20
Taungup, *Burma* 61 K19
Taungup Pass, *Burma* 61 K19
Taungup Taunggya, *Burma* 61 K18
Taunsa Barrage, *Pakistan* 62 D4
Taunton, *U.K.* 13 F4
Taunton, *U.S.A.* 107 E13
Taunus, *Germany* 19 E4
Taupo, *N.Z.* 87 H6
Taupo, L., *N.Z.* 87 H5
Taurage, *Lithuania* 40 D3
Tauranga, *N.Z.* 87 G6
Tauranga Harb., *N.Z.* 87 G6
Taurianova, *Italy* 35 D9
Taurus Mts. = Toros Dağları, *Turkey* 66 E5
Tauste, *Spain* 28 D3
Tauz, *Azerbaijan* 43 F11
Tavannes, *Switz.* 22 B4
Tavda, *Russia* 44 D7
Tavda →, *Russia* 44 D7
Taverny, *France* 25 C9
Taveta, *Tanzania* 82 C4
Taveuni, *Fiji* 87 C9
Tavignano →, *France* 27 F13
Tavira, *Portugal* 31 H3
Tavistock, *Canada* 106 C4
Tavistock, *U.K.* 13 G3
Tavolara, *Italy* 34 B2
Távora →, *Portugal* 30 D3
Tavoy, *Burma* 58 E2
Tavşanlı, *Turkey* 66 D3
Taw →, *U.K.* 13 F3
Tawas City, *U.S.A.* 104 C4
Tawau, *Malaysia* 56 D5
Tawitawi, *Phil.* 55 J4
Taxila, *Pakistan* 62 C5
Tay →, *U.K.* 14 E5
Tay, Firth of, *U.K.* 14 E5
Tay, L., *Australia* 89 F3
Tay, L., *U.K.* 14 E4
Tay Ninh, *Vietnam* 59 G6
Tayabamba, *Peru* 124 B2
Tayabas Bay, *Phil.* 55 E4
Taylakovy, *Russia* 44 D8
Taylor, *Canada* 100 B4
Taylor, *Nebr., U.S.A.* 108 E5
Taylor, *Pa., U.S.A.* 107 E9
Taylor, *Tex., U.S.A.* 109 K6
Taylor Mt., *U.S.A.* 111 J10
Taylorville, *U.S.A.* 108 F10
Taymā, *Si. Arabia* 64 E3
Taymyr, Oz., *Russia* 45 B11
Taymyr, Poluostrov, *Russia* 45 B11
Tayport, *U.K.* 14 E6
Tayshet, *Russia* 45 D10
Tayside □, *U.K.* 14 E5
Taytay, *Phil.* 55 F3

Taz →, *Russia* 44 C8
Taza, *Morocco* 74 B4
Tāzah Khurmātū, *Iraq* 64 C5
Tazawa-Ko, *Japan* 48 E10
Tazenakht, *Morocco* 74 B3
Tazin L., *Canada* 101 B7
Tazoult, *Algeria* 75 A6
Tazovskiy, *Russia* 44 C8
Tbilisi, *Georgia* 43 F11
Tchad = Chad ■, *Africa* 73 E8
Tchad, L., *Chad* 73 F7
Tchaourou, *Benin* 79 D5
Tch'eng-tou = Chengdu, *China* 52 B5
Tchentlo L., *Canada* 100 B4
Tchibanga, *Gabon* 80 E2
Tchien, *Liberia* 78 D3
Tchin Tabaraden, *Niger* 79 B6
Tch'ong-k'ing = Chongqing, *China* 52 C6
Tczew, *Poland* 20 A8
Te Anau, L., *N.Z.* 87 L1
Te Aroha, *N.Z.* 87 G5
Te Awamutu, *N.Z.* 87 H5
Te Kuiti, *N.Z.* 87 H5
Te Puke, *N.Z.* 87 G6
Te Waewae B., *N.Z.* 87 M1
Tea →, *Brazil* 120 D4
Tea Tree, *Australia* 90 C1
Teague, *U.S.A.* 109 K6
Teano, *Italy* 35 A7
Teapa, *Mexico* 115 D6
Teba, *Spain* 31 J6
Tebakang, *Malaysia* 56 D4
Teberda, *Russia* 43 E9
Tébessa, *Algeria* 75 A6
Tebicuary →, *Paraguay* 126 B4
Tebingtinggi, *Indonesia* 56 D1
Tébourba, *Tunisia* 75 A6
Téboursouk, *Tunisia* 75 A6
Tebulos, *Russia* 43 E11
Tecate, *Mexico* 113 N10
Tecer Dağı, *Turkey* 66 D7
Tech →, *France* 26 F7
Techiman, *Ghana* 78 D4
Tecka, *Argentina* 128 B2
Tecomán, *Mexico* 114 D4
Tecopa, *U.S.A.* 113 K10
Tecoripa, *Mexico* 114 B3
Tecuala, *Mexico* 114 C3
Tecuci, *Romania* 38 D10
Tecumseh, *U.S.A.* 104 D4
Tedzhen, *Turkmenistan* 44 F7
Tees →, *U.K.* 12 C6
Teesside, *U.K.* 12 C6
Teeswater, *Canada* 106 C3
Tefé, *Brazil* 121 D5
Tefé →, *Brazil* 121 D5
Tefenni, *Turkey* 66 E3
Tegal, *Indonesia* 57 G13
Tegelen, *Neths.* 17 F8
Tegernsee, *Germany* 19 H7
Teggiano, *Italy* 35 B8
Teghra, *India* 63 G11
Tegid, L. = Bala, L., *U.K.* 12 E4
Tegina, *Nigeria* 79 C6
Tegucigalpa, *Honduras* 116 D2
Tehachapi, *U.S.A.* 113 K8
Tehachapi Mts., *U.S.A.* 113 L8
Tehamiyam, *Sudan* 76 D4
Tehilla, *Sudan* 76 D4
Téhini, *Ivory C.* 78 D4
Tehrān, *Iran* 65 C6
Tehuacán, *Mexico* 115 D5
Tehuantepec, *Mexico* 115 D5
Tehuantepec, G. de, *Mexico* 115 D5
Tehuantepec, Istmo de, *Mexico* 115 D6
Teide, *Canary Is.* 36 F3
Teifi →, *U.K.* 13 E3
Teign →, *U.K.* 13 G4
Teignmouth, *U.K.* 13 G4
Teixeira, *Brazil* 122 C4
Teixeira Pinto, *Guinea-Biss.* 78 C1
Tejo →, *Europe* 31 G1
Tejon Pass, *U.S.A.* 113 L8
Tekamah, *U.S.A.* 108 E6
Tekapo, L., *N.Z.* 87 K3
Tekax, *Mexico* 115 C7
Tekeli, *Kazakhstan* 44 E8
Tekeze →, *Ethiopia* 77 E4
Tekija, *Serbia, Yug.* 21 L12
Tekirdağ, *Turkey* 66 C2
Tekirdağ □, *Turkey* 66 C2
Tekkali, *India* 61 K14
Tekke, *Turkey* 66 C7
Tekman, *Turkey* 67 D9
Tekoa, *U.S.A.* 110 C5
Tekouiât, O. →, *Algeria* 75 D5
Tel Aviv-Yafo, *Israel* 69 C3
Tel Lakhish, *Israel* 69 D3
Tel Megiddo, *Israel* 69 C4
Tela, *Honduras* 116 C2
Télagh, *Algeria* 75 B4
Telanaipura = Jambi, *Indonesia* 56 E2
Telavi, *Georgia* 43 F11
Telde, *Canary Is.* 36 G4
Telegraph Creek, *Canada* 100 B2
Telekhany, *Belorussia* 40 E4
Telemark fylke □, *Norway* 10 E2
Telén, *Argentina* 126 D2
Teleng, *Iran* 65 E9
Teleño, *Spain* 30 C4
Teleorman →, *Romania* 38 E8
Teles Pires →, *Brazil* 125 B6
Telescope Peak, *U.S.A.* 113 J9
Teletaye, *Mali* 79 B5
Telford, *U.K.* 12 E5
Telfs, *Austria* 19 H7
Télimélé, *Guinea* 78 C2
Telkwa, *Canada* 100 C3
Tell City, *U.S.A.* 104 G2
Tellicherry, *India* 60 P9
Tellin, *Belgium* 17 H6
Telluride, *U.S.A.* 111 H10
Teloloapán, *Mexico* 115 D5
Telpos Iz, *Russia* 6 C17
Telsen, *Argentina* 128 B3
Telšiai, *Lithuania* 40 D3
Teltow, *Germany* 18 C9
Teluk Anson, *Malaysia* 59 K3
Teluk Betung = Tanjungkarang Telukbetung, *Indonesia* 56 F3
Teluk Intan = Teluk Anson, *Malaysia* 59 K3
Telukbutun, *Indonesia* 59 K7
Telukdalem, *Indonesia* 56 D1
Tema, *Ghana* 79 D5
Temanggung, *Indonesia* 57 G14
Temapache, *Mexico* 115 C5
Temax, *Mexico* 115 C7
Temba, *S. Africa* 85 D4
Tembe, *Zaïre* 82 C2
Temblador, *Venezuela* 121 B5
Tembleque, *Spain* 28 F1
Temblor Ra., *U.S.A.* 113 K7
Teme →, *U.K.* 13 E5
Temecula, *U.S.A.* 113 M9
Temerloh, *Malaysia* 59 L4
Temir, *Kazakhstan* 44 E6
Temirtau, *Kazakhstan* 44 D8
Temirtau, *Russia* 44 D9
Témiscaming, *Canada* 98 C4
Temma, *Australia* 90 G3
Temnikov, *Russia* 41 D13
Temo →, *Italy* 34 B1
Temora, *Australia* 91 E4
Temosachic, *Mexico* 114 B3
Tempe, *U.S.A.* 111 K8
Tempe Downs, *Australia* 88 D5
Témpio Pausania, *Italy* 34 B2
Tempiute, *U.S.A.* 112 H11
Temple, *U.S.A.* 109 K6
Temple B., *Australia* 90 A3
Templemore, *Ireland* 15 D4
Templeton, *U.S.A.* 112 K6
Templeton →, *Australia* 90 C2
Templeuve, *Belgium* 17 G2
Templin, *Germany* 18 B9
Tempoal, *Mexico* 115 C5
Temryuk, *Russia* 42 D7
Temse, *Belgium* 17 F4
Temska →, *Serbia, Yug.* 21 M12
Temuco, *Chile* 128 A2
Temuka, *N.Z.* 87 L3
Ten Boer, *Neths.* 16 B9
Tena, *Ecuador* 120 D2
Tenabo, *Mexico* 115 C6
Tenaha, *U.S.A.* 109 K7
Tenali, *India* 60 L12
Tenancingo, *Mexico* 115 D5
Tenango, *Mexico* 115 D5
Tenasserim, *Burma* 59 F2
Tenasserim □, *Burma* 58 F2
Tenay, *France* 27 C9
Tenby, *U.K.* 13 F3
Tenda, Col di, *France* 27 D11
Tendaho, *Ethiopia* 68 E3
Tende, *France* 27 D11
Tendelti, *Sudan* 77 E3
Tendjedi, Adrar, *Algeria* 75 D6
Tendrara, *Morocco* 75 B4
Tendre, Mt., *Switz.* 22 C2
Teneida, *Egypt* 76 B2
Tenente Marques →, *Brazil* 125 C6
Ténéré, *Niger* 79 B7
Tenerife, *Canary Is.* 36 F3
Tenerife, Pico, *Canary Is.* 36 G1
Ténès, *Algeria* 75 A5
Teng Xian, *Guangxi Zhuangzu, China* 53 F8
Teng Xian, *Shandong, China* 51 G9
Tengah □, *Indonesia* 57 E6
Tengah Kepulauan, *Indonesia* 56 F5
Tengchong, *China* 52 E2
Tengchowfu = Penglai, *China* 51 F11
Tenggara □, *Indonesia* 57 E6
Tenggarong, *Indonesia* 56 E5
Tenggol, P., *Malaysia* 59 K4
Tengiz, Ozero, *Kazakhstan* 44 D7
Tenigerbad, *Switz.* 23 C7
Tenino, *U.S.A.* 112 D4
Tenkasi, *India* 60 Q10
Tenke, *Shaba, Zaïre* 83 E2
Tenke, *Shaba, Zaïre* 83 E2
Tenkodogo, *Burkina Faso* 79 C4
Tenna →, *Italy* 33 E10
Tennant Creek, *Australia* 90 B1
Tennessee □, *U.S.A.* 103 C9
Tennessee →, *U.S.A.* 104 G1
Tenneville, *Belgium* 17 H7
Tennille, *U.S.A.* 105 J4
Tennsift, Oued →, *Morocco* 74 B3
Teno, Pta. de, *Canary Is.* 36 F3
Tenom, *Malaysia* 56 C5
Tenosique, *Mexico* 115 D6
Tenryū-Gawa →, *Japan* 49 G8
Tent L., *Canada* 101 A7
Tenterfield, *Australia* 91 D5
Teófilo Otoni, *Brazil* 123 E3
Teotihuacán, *Mexico* 115 D5
Tepa, *Indonesia* 57 F7
Tepalcatepec →, *Mexico* 114 D4
Tepehuanes, *Mexico* 114 B3
Tepequem, Serra, *Brazil* 121 C5
Tepetongo, *Mexico* 114 C4
Tepic, *Mexico* 114 C4
Tepoca, C., *Mexico* 114 A2
Tequila, *Mexico* 114 C4
Ter →, *Spain* 28 C8
Ter Apel, *Neths.* 16 C10
Téra, *Niger* 79 C5
Tera →, *Spain* 30 D5
Teraina, *Kiribati* 93 G11
Téramo, *Italy* 33 F10
Terang, *Australia* 91 F3
Terborg, *Neths.* 16 E8
Tercan, *Turkey* 67 D9
Tercero →, *Argentina* 126 C3
Terebovlya, *Ukraine* 40 G4
Terek →, *Russia* 43 E12
Terenos, *Brazil* 125 E7
Tereshka →, *Russia* 41 F15
Teresina, *Brazil* 122 C3
Teresinha, *Brazil* 121 C7
Terewah, L., *Australia* 91 D4
Terges →, *Portugal* 31 H3
Tergnier, *France* 25 C10
Terhazza, *Mali* 74 D3
Terheijden, *Neths.* 17 E5
Teridgerie Cr. →, *Australia* 91 E4
Terlizzi, *Italy* 35 A9
Terme, *Turkey* 42 F7
Termez, *Uzbekistan* 44 F7
Términi Imerese, *Italy* 34 E6
Términos, L. de, *Mexico* 115 D6
Térmoli, *Italy* 33 F12
Ternate, *Indonesia* 57 D7
Terneuzen, *Neths.* 17 F3
Terney, *Russia* 45 E14
Terni, *Italy* 33 F9
Ternitz, *Austria* 21 H6
Ternopol, *Ukraine* 42 B1
Terowie, *N.S.W., Australia* 91 E4
Terowie, *S. Austral., Australia* 91 E2
Terra Bella, *U.S.A.* 113 K7
Terrace, *Canada* 100 C3
Terrace Bay, *Canada* 98 C2
Terracina, *Italy* 34 A6
Terralba, *Italy* 34 C1
Terranova = Ólbia, *Italy* 34 B2
Terranuova Bracciolini, *Italy* 33 E8
Terrasini Favarotta, *Italy* 34 D6
Terrasson-la-Villedieu, *France* 26 C5
Terre Haute, *U.S.A.* 104 F2
Terrebonne B., *U.S.A.* 109 L9
Terrecht, *Mali* 75 D4
Terrell, *U.S.A.* 109 J6
Terrenceville, *Canada* 99 C9
Terrick Terrick, *Australia* 90 C4
Terry, *U.S.A.* 108 B2
Terschelling, *Neths.* 16 B6
Terter →, *Azerbaijan* 43 F12
Teruel, *Spain* 28 E3
Teruel □, *Spain* 28 E4
Tervel, *Bulgaria* 38 F10
Tervola, *Finland* 8 C18
Teryaweyna L., *Australia* 91 E3
Tešanj, *Bos.-H., Yug.* 21 L7
Teseney, *Ethiopia* 77 D4
Tesha →, *Russia* 41 D13
Teshio, *Japan* 48 B10
Teshio-Gawa →, *Japan* 48 B10
Tesiyn Gol →, *Mongolia* 54 A4
Teslin, *Canada* 100 A2
Teslin →, *Canada* 100 A2
Teslin L., *Canada* 100 A2
Tesouro, *Brazil* 125 D7
Tessalit, *Mali* 79 A5
Tessaoua, *Niger* 79 C6
Tessenderlo, *Belgium* 17 F6
Tessin, *Germany* 18 A8
Tessit, *Mali* 79 B5
Test →, *U.K.* 13 F6
Testa del Gargano, *Italy* 35 A9
Têt →, *France* 26 F7
Tetachuck L., *Canada* 100 C3
Tetas, Pta., *Chile* 126 A1
Tete, *Mozam.* 83 F3
Tete □, *Mozam.* 83 F3
Teterev →, *Ukraine* 40 F7
Teteringen, *Neths.* 17 E5
Teterow, *Germany* 18 B8
Teteven, *Bulgaria* 38 G7
Tethul →, *Canada* 100 A6
Tetiyev, *Ukraine* 42 B3
Teton →, *U.S.A.* 110 C8
Tétouan, *Morocco* 74 A3
Tetovo, *Macedonia, Yug.* 38 G4
Tetuán = Tétouan, *Morocco* 74 A3
Tetyukhe Pristan, *Russia* 48 B7
Tetyushi, *Russia* 41 D16
Teuco →, *Argentina* 126 B3
Teufen, *Switz.* 23 B8
Teulada, *Italy* 34 D1
Teulon, *Canada* 101 C9
Teun, *Indonesia* 57 F7
Teutoburger Wald, *Germany* 18 C4
Tevere →, *Italy* 33 G9
Teverya, *Israel* 69 C4
Teviot →, *U.K.* 14 F6
Tewantin, *Australia* 91 D5
Tewkesbury, *U.K.* 13 F5
Texada I., *Canada* 100 D4
Texarkana, *Ark., U.S.A.* 109 J8
Texarkana, *Tex., U.S.A.* 109 J7
Texas, *Australia* 91 D5
Texas □, *U.S.A.* 109 K5
Texas City, *U.S.A.* 109 L7
Texel, *Neths.* 16 B5
Texhoma, *U.S.A.* 109 G4
Texline, *U.S.A.* 109 G3
Texoma L., *U.S.A.* 109 J6
Teykovo, *Russia* 41 C12
Teza →, *Russia* 41 C12
Tezin, *Afghan.* 62 B3
Teziutlán, *Mexico* 115 D5
Tezpur, *India* 61 F18
Tezzeron L., *Canada* 100 C4
Tha-anne →, *Canada* 101 A10
Tha Deua, *Laos* 58 D4
Tha Deua, *Laos* 58 C3
Tha Pla, *Thailand* 58 D3
Tha Rua, *Thailand* 58 E3
Tha Sala, *Thailand* 59 H2
Tha Song Yang, *Thailand* 58 D1
Thaba Nchu, *S. Africa* 84 D4
Thaba Putsoa, *Lesotho* 85 D4
Thabana Ntlenyana, *Lesotho* 85 D4
Thabazimbi, *S. Africa* 85 C4
Thai Binh, *Vietnam* 58 B6
Thai Hoa, *Vietnam* 58 C5
Thai Muang, *Thailand* 59 H2
Thai Nguyen, *Vietnam* 58 B5
Thailand ■, *Asia* 58 E4
Thailand, G. of, *Asia* 59 G3
Thakhek, *Laos* 58 D5
Thal, *Pakistan* 62 C4
Thal Desert, *Pakistan* 62 D4
Thala, *Tunisia* 75 A6
Thala La, *Burma* 61 E20
Thalabarivat, *Cambodia* 58 F5
Thalkirch, *Switz.* 23 C8
Thallon, *Australia* 91 D4
Thalwil, *Switz.* 23 B7
Thame →, *U.K.* 13 F6
Thames, *N.Z.* 87 G5
Thames →, *Canada* 98 D3
Thames →, *U.K.* 13 F8
Thames →, *U.S.A.* 107 E12
Thamesford, *Canada* 106 C3
Thamesville, *Canada* 106 D3
Than Uyen, *Vietnam* 58 B4
Thane, *India* 60 K8
Thanesar, *India* 62 D7
Thanet, I. of, *U.K.* 13 F9
Thangoo, *Australia* 88 C3
Thangool, *Australia* 90 C5
Thanh Hoa, *Vietnam* 58 C5
Thanh Hung, *Vietnam* 59 H5
Thanh Pho Ho Chi Minh = Phanh Bho Ho Chi Minh, *Vietnam* 59 G6
Thanh Thuy, *Vietnam* 58 A5
Thanjavur, *India* 60 P11
Thann, *France* 25 E14
Thaon-les-Vosges, *France* 25 D13
Thap Sakae, *Thailand* 59 G2
Thap Than, *Thailand* 58 E2
Thar Desert, *India* 62 F4
Tharad, *India* 62 G4
Thargomindah, *Australia* 91 D3
Tharrawaddy, *Burma* 61 L19
Tharthar, W. →, *Iraq* 64 C4
Thásos, *Greece* 39 J7
That Khe, *Vietnam* 58 A6
Thatcher, *Ariz., U.S.A.* 111 K9
Thatcher, *Colo., U.S.A.* 109 G2
Thaton, *Burma* 61 L20
Thau, Bassin de, *France* 26 E7
Thaungdut, *Burma* 61 G19
Thayer, *U.S.A.* 109 G9
Thayetmyo, *Burma* 61 K19
Thayngen, *Switz.* 23 A7
Thazi, *Burma* 61 J20
The Alberga →, *Australia* 91 D2
The Bight, *Bahamas* 117 B4
The Coorong, *Australia* 91 F2
The Dalles, *U.S.A.* 110 D3
The English Company's Is., *Australia* 90 A2
The Frome →, *Australia* 91 D2
The Grampians, *Australia* 91 F3
The Great Divide = Great Dividing Ra., *Australia* 90 C4
The Hague = 's-Gravenhage, *Neths.* 16 D4
The Hamilton →, *Australia* 91 D2
The Macumba →, *Australia* 91 D2
The Neales →, *Australia* 91 D2
The Officer →, *Australia* 89 E5
The Pas, *Canada* 101 C8
The Range, *Zimbabwe* 83 F3
The Rock, *Australia* 91 F4
The Salt L., *Australia* 91 E3
The Stevenson →, *Australia* 91 D2
The Warburton →, *Australia* 91 D2
Thebes = Thívai, *Greece* 39 L6
Thebes, *Egypt* 76 B3
Thedford, *Canada* 106 C3
Thedford, *U.S.A.* 108 E4
Theebine, *Australia* 91 D5
Thekulthili L., *Canada* 101 A7
Thelon →, *Canada* 101 A8
Thénezay, *France* 24 F6
Thenia, *Algeria* 75 A5
Thenon, *France* 26 C5
Theodore, *Australia* 90 C5
Thepha, *Thailand* 59 J3
Thérain →, *France* 25 C9
Theresa, *U.S.A.* 107 B9
Thermaïkos Kólpos, *Greece* 39 J5
Thermopolis, *U.S.A.* 110 E9
Thermopylae P., *Greece* 39 L5
Thessalía □, *Greece* 39 L4
Thessalon, *Canada* 98 C3
Thessaloníki, *Greece* 39 J5
Thessaloniki, Gulf of = Thermaïkos Kólpos, *Greece* 39 J5
Thessaly = Thessalía □, *Greece* 39 L4
Thetford, *U.K.* 13 E8
Thetford Mines, *Canada* 99 C5
Theun →, *Laos* 58 C5
Theunissen, *S. Africa* 84 D4
Theux, *Belgium* 17 G7
Thevenard, *Australia* 91 E1
Thiámis →, *Greece* 39 K3
Thiberville, *France* 24 C7
Thibodaux, *U.S.A.* 109 L9
Thicket Portage, *Canada* 101 B9
Thief River Falls, *U.S.A.* 108 A6
Thiel Mts., *Antarctica* 5 E16
Thiene, *Italy* 33 C8
Thiérache, *France* 25 C10
Thiers, *France* 26 C7
Thies, *Senegal* 78 C1
Thiet, *Sudan* 77 F2
Thika, *Kenya* 82 C4
Thikombia, *Fiji* 87 B9
Thille-Boubacar, *Senegal* 78 B1
Thimphu, *Bhutan* 61 F16
þingvallavatn, *Iceland* 8 D3
Thionville, *France* 25 C13
Thíra, *Greece* 39 N8
Thirasía, *Greece* 39 N8
Thirsk, *U.K.* 12 C6
Thisted, *Denmark* 9 H10
Thistle I., *Australia* 91 F2
Thívai, *Greece* 39 L6
Thiviers, *France* 26 C4
Thizy, *France* 27 B8
þjórsá →, *Iceland* 8 E3
Thlewiaza →, *Man., Canada* 101 B8
Thlewiaza →, *N.W.T., Canada* 101 A10
Thmar Puok, *Cambodia* 58 F4
Tho Vinh, *Vietnam* 58 C5
Thoa →, *Canada* 101 A7
Thoen, *Thailand* 58 D2
Thoeng, *Thailand* 58 C3
Thoissey, *France* 27 B8
Tholdi, *Pakistan* 63 B7
Tholen, *Neths.* 17 E4
Thomas, *Okla., U.S.A.* 109 H5
Thomas, *W. Va., U.S.A.* 104 F6
Thomas, L., *Australia* 91 D2
Thomaston, *U.S.A.* 105 J3
Thomasville, *Ala., U.S.A.* 105 K2
Thomasville, *Ga., U.S.A.* 105 K3
Thomasville, *N.C., U.S.A.* 105 H5
Thommen, *Belgium* 17 H8
Thompson, *Canada* 101 B9
Thompson, *U.S.A.* 111 G9
Thompson →, *Canada* 100 C4
Thompson →, *U.S.A.* 108 F8
Thompson Falls, *U.S.A.* 110 C6
Thompson Landing, *Canada* 101 A6
Thompson Pk., *U.S.A.* 110 F2
Thomson's Falls = Nyahururu, *Kenya* 82 B4
Thon Buri, *Thailand* 59 F3
Thônes, *France* 27 C10
Thonon-les-Bains, *France* 27 B10
Thorez, *Ukraine* 43 B8
þórisvatn, *Iceland* 8 D4
þorlákshöfn, *Iceland* 8 E3
Thornaby on Tees, *U.K.* 12 C6
Thornbury, *Canada* 106 B4
Thorold, *Canada* 106 C5
þórshöfn, *Iceland* 8 C6
Thouarcé, *France* 24 E6
Thouars, *France* 24 F6
Thouin, C., *Australia* 88 D2
Thousand Oaks, *U.S.A.* 113 L8
Thrace, *Turkey* 66 C2
Thrakikón Pélagos, *Greece* 39 J8
Three Forks, *U.S.A.* 110 D8
Three Hills, *Canada* 100 C6
Three Hummock I., *Australia* 90 G3
Three Lakes, *U.S.A.* 108 C10

Three Points, C., *Ghana* 78 E4
Three Rivers, *Australia* 89 E2
Three Rivers, *Calif., U.S.A.* 112 J8
Three Rivers, *Tex., U.S.A.* 109 L5
Three Sisters, *U.S.A.* 110 D3
Throssell, L., *Australia* 89 E3
Throssell Ra., *Australia* 88 D3
Thuan Hoa, *Vietnam* 59 H5
Thubun Lakes, *Canada* 101 A6
Thueyts, *France* 27 D8
Thuillies, *Belgium* 17 H4
Thuin, *Belgium* 17 H4
Thuir, *France* 26 F6
Thule, *Greenland* 4 B4
Thun, *Switz.* 22 C5
Thundelarra, *Australia* 89 E2
Thunder B., *U.S.A.* 106 B1
Thunder Bay, *Canada* 98 C2
Thunersee, *Switz.* 22 C5
Thung Song, *Thailand* 59 H2
Thunkar, *Bhutan* 61 F17
Thuong Tra, *Vietnam* 58 D6
Thur →, *Switz.* 23 A8
Thurgau □, *Switz.* 23 A8
Thüringen □, *Germany* 18 E7
Thüringer Wald, *Germany* 18 E7
Thurles, *Ireland* 15 D4
Thurloo Downs, *Australia* 91 D3
Thurn P., *Austria* 19 H8
Thursday I., *Australia* 90 A3
Thurso, *Canada* 98 C4
Thurso, *U.K.* 14 C5
Thurston I., *Antarctica* 5 D16
Thury-Harcourt, *France* 24 D6
Thusis, *Switz.* 23 C8
Thutade L., *Canada* 100 B3
Thyborøn, *Denmark* 11 H2
Thylungra, *Australia* 91 D3
Thyolo, *Malawi* 83 F4
Thysville = Mbanza Ngungu, *Zaïre* 80 F2
Ti-n-Barraouene, O. →, *Africa* 79 B5
Ti-n-Medjerdam, O. →, *Algeria* 75 C5
Ti-n-Tarabine, O. →, *Algeria* 75 D6
Ti-n-Zaouaténe, *Algeria* 75 E5
Tia, *Australia* 91 E5
Tiahuanacu, *Bolivia* 124 D4
Tian Shan, *China* 54 B3
Tianchang, *China* 53 A12
Tiandong, *China* 52 F6
Tian'e, *China* 52 E6
Tianguá, *Brazil* 122 B3
Tianhe, *China* 52 E7
Tianjin, *China* 51 E9
Tiankoura, *Burkina Faso* 78 C4
Tianlin, *China* 52 E6
Tianmen, *China* 53 B9
Tianquan, *China* 52 B4
Tianshui, *China* 50 G3
Tiantai, *China* 53 C13
Tianyang, *China* 52 F6
Tianzhen, *China* 50 D8
Tianzhu, *China* 52 D7
Tianzhuangtai, *China* 51 D12
Tiaret, *Algeria* 75 A5
Tiassalé, *Ivory C.* 78 D4
Tibagi, *Brazil* 127 A5
Tibagi →, *Brazil* 127 A5
Tibati, *Cameroon* 79 D7
Tiber = Tevere →, *Italy* 33 G9
Tiber Res., *U.S.A.* 110 B8
Tiberias = Teverya, *Israel* 69 C4
Tiberias, L. = Yam Kinneret, *Israel* 69 C4
Tibesti, *Chad* 73 D8
Tibet = Xizang □, *China* 54 C3
Tibiao, *Phil.* 55 F5
Tibiri, *Niger* 79 C6
Ţibleş, *Romania* 38 B7
Tibnī, *Syria* 64 C3
Tibooburra, *Australia* 91 D3
Tibro, *Sweden* 11 F8
Tibugá, G. de, *Colombia* 120 B2
Tiburón, *Mexico* 114 B2
Ticao I., *Phil.* 55 E5
Tîchît, *Mauritania* 78 B3
Tichla, *Mauritania* 74 D2
Ticho, *Ethiopia* 77 F4
Ticino □, *Switz.* 23 D7
Ticino →, *Italy* 32 C6
Ticonderoga, *U.S.A.* 107 C11
Ticul, *Mexico* 115 C7
Tidaholm, *Sweden* 11 F7
Tiddim, *Burma* 61 H18
Tideridjaouine, Adrar, *Algeria* 75 D5
Tidikelt, *Algeria* 75 C5
Tidjikja, *Mauritania* 78 B2
Tidore, *Indonesia* 57 D7
Tiébissou, *Ivory C.* 78 D3
Tiefencastel, *Switz.* 23 C9
Tiel, *Neths.* 16 E6
Tiel, *Senegal* 78 C1
Tieling, *China* 51 C12
Tielt, *Belgium* 17 F2
Tien Shan, *Asia* 46 E11
Tien-tsin = Tianjin, *China* 51 E9
Tien Yen, *Vietnam* 58 B6
T'ienching = Tianjin, *China* 51 E9
Tienen, *Belgium* 17 G5
Tiénigbé, *Ivory C.* 78 D3
Tientsin = Tianjin, *China* 51 E9
Tierra Amarilla, *Chile* 126 B1
Tierra Amarilla, *U.S.A.* 111 H10
Tierra Colorada, *Mexico* 115 D5
Tierra de Barros, *Spain* 31 G4
Tierra de Campos, *Spain* 30 C6
Tierra del Fuego □, *Argentina* 128 D3
Tierra del Fuego, I. Gr. de, *Argentina* 128 D3
Tierralta, *Colombia* 120 B2
Tiétar →, *Spain* 30 F4
Tieté →, *Brazil* 127 A5
Tieyon, *Australia* 91 D1
Tifarati, *W. Sahara* 74 C2
Tiffin, *U.S.A.* 104 E4
Tiflèt, *Morocco* 74 B3
Tiflis = Tbilisi, *Georgia* 43 F11
Tifton, *U.S.A.* 105 K4
Tifu, *Indonesia* 57 E7
Tigil, *Russia* 45 D16
Tignish, *Canada* 99 C7
Tigray □, *Ethiopia* 77 E4
Tigre →, *Peru* 120 D3
Tigre →, *Venezuela* 121 B5
Tigris = Dijlah, Nahr →, *Asia* 64 D5
Tiguentourine, *Algeria* 75 C6
Tigyaing, *Burma* 61 H20
Tigzerte, O. →, *Morocco* 74 C3
Tîh, Gebel el, *Egypt* 76 J8
Tihodaine, Dunes de, *Algeria* 75 C6
Tijesno, *Croatia* 33 E12
Tījī, *Libya* 75 B7
Tijuana, *Mexico* 113 N9
Tikal, *Guatemala* 116 C2
Tikamgarh, *India* 63 G8
Tikhoretsk, *Russia* 43 D9
Tikhvin, *Russia* 40 B8
Tikkadouine, Adrar, *Algeria* 75 D5
Tiko, *Cameroon* 79 E6
Tikrīt, *Iraq* 64 C4
Tiksi, *Russia* 45 B13
Tilamuta, *Indonesia* 57 D6
Tilburg, *Neths.* 17 E6
Tilbury, *Canada* 98 D3
Tilbury, *U.K.* 13 F8
Tilcara, *Argentina* 126 A2
Tilden, *Nebr., U.S.A.* 108 D6
Tilden, *Tex., U.S.A.* 109 L5
Tilemses, *Niger* 79 B5
Tilemsi, Vallée du, *Mali* 79 B5
Tilhar, *India* 63 F8
Tilia, O. →, *Algeria* 75 C5
Tilichiki, *Russia* 45 C17
Tiligul →, *Ukraine* 42 C4
Tililane, *Algeria* 75 C4
Tílissos, *Greece* 37 D7
Till →, *U.K.* 12 B5
Tillabéri, *Niger* 79 C5
Tillamook, *U.S.A.* 110 D2
Tillberga, *Sweden* 10 E10
Tillia, *Niger* 79 B5
Tillsonburg, *Canada* 98 D3
Tillyeria □, *Cyprus* 37 D11
Tílos, *Greece* 39 N10
Tilpa, *Australia* 91 E3
Tilrhemt, *Algeria* 75 B5
Tilsit = Sovetsk, *Lithuania* 40 D2
Tilt →, *U.K.* 14 E5
Tilton, *U.S.A.* 107 C13
Timagami L., *Canada* 98 C3
Timaru, *N.Z.* 87 L3
Timashevsk, *Russia* 43 D8
Timau, *Italy* 33 B10
Timau, *Kenya* 82 B4
Timbákion, *Greece* 37 D6
Timbaúba, *Brazil* 122 C4
Timbedgha, *Mauritania* 78 B3
Timber Lake, *U.S.A.* 108 C4
Timber Mt., *U.S.A.* 112 H10
Timbío, *Colombia* 120 C2
Timbiqui, *Colombia* 120 C2
Timboon, *Australia* 91 F3
Timbuktu = Tombouctou, *Mali* 78 B4
Timellouline, *Algeria* 75 C6
Timétrine Montagnes, *Mali* 79 B4
Timfristós, Óros, *Greece* 39 L4
Timhadit, *Morocco* 74 B3
Timi, *Cyprus* 37 E11
Tîmia, *Niger* 79 B6
Timimoun, *Algeria* 75 C5
Timiş = Tamis →, *Serbia, Yug.* 38 E3
Timişoara, *Romania* 38 D4
Timmins, *Canada* 98 C3
Timok →, *Serbia, Yug.* 21 L12
Timon, *Brazil* 122 C3
Timor, *Indonesia* 57 F7
Timor □, *Indonesia* 57 F7
Timor Sea, *Ind. Oc.* 88 B4
Tin Alkoum, *Algeria* 75 D7
Tin Gornai, *Mali* 79 B4
Tin Mt., *U.S.A.* 112 J9
Tîna, Khalîg el, *Egypt* 76 H8
Tinaca Pt., *Phil.* 55 J6
Tinaco, *Venezuela* 120 B4
Tinafak, O. →, *Algeria* 75 C6
Tinajo, *Canary Is.* 36 E6
Tinaquillo, *Venezuela* 120 B4
Tinca, *Romania* 38 C4
Tinchebray, *France* 24 D6
Tindouf, *Algeria* 74 C3
Tinée →, *France* 27 E11
Tineo, *Spain* 30 B4
Tinerhir, *Morocco* 74 B3
Tinfouchi, *Algeria* 74 C3
Ting Jiang →, *China* 53 E11
Tinggi, Pulau, *Malaysia* 59 L5
Tinglev, *Denmark* 11 K3
Tingo Maria, *Peru* 124 B2
Tinh Bien, *Vietnam* 59 G5
Tinharé, I. de, *Brazil* 123 D4
Tinjoub, *Algeria* 72 C3
Tinkurrin, *Australia* 89 F2
Tinnevelly = Tirunelveli, *India* 60 Q10
Tinnoset, *Norway* 10 E3
Tinnsjø, *Norway* 10 E2
Tinogasta, *Argentina* 126 B2
Tínos, *Greece* 39 M8
Tiñoso, C., *Spain* 29 H3
Tinta, *Peru* 124 C3
Tintigny, *Belgium* 17 J7
Tintina, *Argentina* 126 B3
Tintinara, *Australia* 91 F3
Tinto →, *Spain* 31 H4
Tioga, *U.S.A.* 106 E7
Tioman, Pulau, *Malaysia* 59 L5
Tione di Trento, *Italy* 32 B7
Tionesta, *U.S.A.* 106 E5
Tior, *Sudan* 77 F3
Tioulilin, *Algeria* 75 C4
Tipongpani, *India* 61 F19
Tipperary, *Ireland* 15 D3
Tipperary □, *Ireland* 15 D4
Tipton, *U.K.* 13 E5
Tipton, *Calif., U.S.A.* 111 H4
Tipton, *Ind., U.S.A.* 104 E2
Tipton, *Iowa, U.S.A.* 108 E9
Tipton, Mt., *U.S.A.* 113 K12
Tiptonville, *U.S.A.* 109 G10
Tiquié →, *Brazil* 120 C4
Tiracambu, Serra do, *Brazil* 122 B2
Tīrān, *Iran* 65 C6
Tīrān, *Si. Arabia* 76 B3
Tirana, *Albania* 39 H2
Tiranë = Tirana, *Albania* 39 H2
Tirano, *Italy* 32 B7
Tiraspol, *Moldavia* 42 C3
Tirat Karmel, *Israel* 69 C3
Tiratimine, *Algeria* 75 C5
Tirdout, *Mali* 79 B4
Tire, *Turkey* 66 D2
Tirebolu, *Turkey* 67 C8
Tiree, *U.K.* 14 E2
Tîrgovişte, *Romania* 38 E8
Tîrgu Frumos, *Romania* 38 B10
Tîrgu-Jiu, *Romania* 38 D6
Tîrgu Mureş, *Romania* 38 C7
Tîrgu Neamţ, *Romania* 38 B9
Tîrgu Ocna, *Romania* 38 C9
Tîrgu Secuiesc, *Romania* 38 D9
Tirich Mir, *Pakistan* 60 A7
Tiriola, *Italy* 35 D9
Tiririca, Serra da, *Brazil* 123 E2
Tiris, *W. Sahara* 74 D2
Tîrnava Mare →, *Romania* 38 C7
Tîrnava Mică →, *Romania* 38 C7
Tîrnăveni, *Romania* 38 C7
Tírnavos, *Greece* 39 K5
Tirodi, *India* 60 J11
Tiros, *Brazil* 123 E2
Tirschenreuth, *Germany* 19 F8
Tirso →, *Italy* 34 C1
Tirso, L. del, *Italy* 34 B1
Tiruchchirappalli, *India* 60 P11
Tirunelveli, *India* 60 Q10
Tirupati, *India* 60 N11
Tiruppur, *India* 60 P10
Tiruvannamalai, *India* 60 N11
Tisa →, *Hungary* 21 J10
Tisa →, *Serbia, Yug.* 21 K10
Tisdale, *Canada* 101 C8
Tishomingo, *U.S.A.* 109 H6
Tisnaren, *Sweden* 10 F9
Tisovec, *Czech.* 20 G9
Tissemsilt, *Algeria* 75 A5
Tissint, *Morocco* 74 C3
Tissø, *Denmark* 11 J5
Tisza = Tisa →, *Hungary* 21 J10
Tiszafüred, *Hungary* 21 H10
Tiszavasvári, *Hungary* 21 H11
Tit, *Ahaggar, Algeria* 75 D6
Tit, *Tademait, Algeria* 75 C5
Tit-Ary, *Russia* 45 B13
Titaguas, *Spain* 28 F3
Titel, *Serbia, Yug.* 21 K10
Tithwal, *Pakistan* 63 B5
Titicaca, L., *S. Amer.* 124 D4
Titiwa, *Nigeria* 79 C7
Titlis, *Switz.* 23 C6
Titograd, *Montenegro, Yug.* 21 N9
Titov Veles, *Macedonia, Yug.* 39 H4
Titova Korenica, *Croatia* 33 D12
Titovo Užice, *Serbia, Yug.* 21 M9
Titule, *Zaïre* 82 B2
Titumate, *Colombia* 120 B2
Titusville, *Fla., U.S.A.* 105 L5
Titusville, *Pa., U.S.A.* 106 E5
Tivaouane, *Senegal* 78 C1
Tiveden, *Sweden* 11 F8
Tiverton, *U.K.* 13 G4
Tívoli, *Italy* 33 G9
Tiyo, *Ethiopia* 77 E5
Tizga, *Morocco* 74 B3
Ti'zi N'Isli, *Morocco* 74 B3
Tizi-Ouzou, *Algeria* 75 A5
Tizimín, *Mexico* 115 C7
Tiznados →, *Venezuela* 120 B4
Tiznit, *Morocco* 74 C3
Tjeggelvas, *Sweden* 8 C14
Tjeukemeer, *Neths.* 16 C7
Tjirebon = Cirebon, *Indonesia* 57 G13
Tjøme, *Norway* 10 E4
Tjonger Kanaal, *Neths.* 16 C7
Tjörn, *Sweden* 11 G5
Tkibuli, *Georgia* 43 E10
Tkvarcheli, *Georgia* 43 E9
Tlacotalpan, *Mexico* 115 D5
Tlahualilo, *Mexico* 114 B4
Tlaquepaque, *Mexico* 114 C4
Tlaxcala, *Mexico* 115 D5
Tlaxcala □, *Mexico* 115 D5
Tlaxiaco, *Mexico* 115 D5
Tlell, *Canada* 100 C2
Tlemcen, *Algeria* 75 B4
Tleta Sidi Bouguedra, *Morocco* 74 B3
Tlumach, *Ukraine* 42 B1
Tlyarata, *Russia* 43 E12
Tmassah, *Libya* 73 C8
Tnine d'Anglou, *Morocco* 74 C3
To Bong, *Vietnam* 58 F7
Toad →, *Canada* 100 B4
Toamasina, *Madag.* 85 B8
Toamasina □, *Madag.* 85 B8
Toay, *Argentina* 126 D3
Toba, *Japan* 49 G8
Toba Kakar, *Pakistan* 62 D3
Toba Tek Singh, *Pakistan* 62 D5
Tobago, *W. Indies* 117 D7
Tobarra, *Spain* 29 G3
Tobelo, *Indonesia* 57 D7
Tobermorey, *Australia* 90 C2
Tobermory, *Canada* 98 C3
Tobermory, *U.K.* 14 E2
Tobin, *U.S.A.* 112 F5
Tobin, L., *Australia* 88 D4
Tobin L., *Canada* 101 C8
Toboali, *Indonesia* 56 E3
Tobol, *Kazakhstan* 44 D7
Tobol →, *Russia* 44 D7
Toboli, *Indonesia* 57 E6
Tobolsk, *Russia* 44 D7
Tobruk = Tubruq, *Libya* 73 B9
Tobyhanna, *U.S.A.* 107 E9
Tocache Nuevo, *Peru* 124 B2
Tocantínia, *Brazil* 122 C2
Tocantinópolis, *Brazil* 122 C2
Tocantins →, *Brazil* 122 B2
Toccoa, *U.S.A.* 105 H4
Toce →, *Italy* 32 C5
Tochigi, *Japan* 49 F9
Tochigi □, *Japan* 49 F9
Tocina, *Spain* 31 H5
Tocopilla, *Chile* 126 A1
Tocumwal, *Australia* 91 F4
Tocuyo →, *Venezuela* 120 A4
Tocuyo de la Costa, *Venezuela* 120 A4
Todd →, *Australia* 90 C2
Todeli, *Indonesia* 57 E6
Todenyang, *Kenya* 82 B4
Todi, *Italy* 33 F9
Tödi, *Switz.* 23 C7
Todos os Santos, B. de, *Brazil* 123 D4
Todos Santos, *Mexico* 114 C2
Todtnau, *Germany* 19 H3
Toecé, *Burkina Faso* 79 C4
Tofield, *Canada* 100 C6
Tofino, *Canada* 100 D3
Töfsingdalens nationalpark, *Sweden* 10 B6
Toftlund, *Denmark* 11 J3
Tofua, *Tonga* 87 D11
Tōgane, *Japan* 49 G10
Togba, *Mauritania* 78 B2
Toggenburg, *Switz.* 23 B8
Togian, Kepulauan, *Indonesia* 57 E6
Togliatti, *Russia* 41 E16
Togo ■, *W. Afr.* 79 D5
Togtoh, *China* 50 D6
Tohma →, *Turkey* 67 D8
Tōhoku □, *Japan* 48 E10
Toinya, *Sudan* 77 F2
Tojo, *Indonesia* 57 E6
Tōjō, *Japan* 49 G6
Toka, *Guyana* 121 C6
Tokachi-Dake, *Japan* 48 C11
Tokachi-Gawa →, *Japan* 48 C11
Tokaj, *Hungary* 21 G11
Tokala, *Indonesia* 57 E6
Tōkamachi, *Japan* 49 F9
Tokanui, *N.Z.* 87 M2
Tokar, *Sudan* 76 D4
Tokara-Rettō, *Japan* 49 K4
Tokarahi, *N.Z.* 87 L3
Tokashiki-Shima, *Japan* 49 L3
Tokat, *Turkey* 66 C7
Tokat □, *Turkey* 66 C7
Tŏkchŏn, *N. Korea* 51 E14
Tokeland, *U.S.A.* 112 D3
Tokelau Is., *Pac. Oc.* 92 H10
Tokmak, *Kirghizia* 44 E8
Toko Ra., *Australia* 90 C2
Tokoro-Gawa →, *Japan* 48 B12
Tokuno-Shima, *Japan* 49 L4
Tokushima, *Japan* 49 G7
Tokushima □, *Japan* 49 H7
Tokuyama, *Japan* 49 G5
Tōkyō, *Japan* 49 G9
Tolaga Bay, *N.Z.* 87 H7
Tolbukhin, *Bulgaria* 38 F10
Toledo, *Spain* 30 F6
Toledo, *Ohio, U.S.A.* 104 E4
Toledo, *Oreg., U.S.A.* 110 D2
Toledo, *Wash., U.S.A.* 110 C2
Toledo, Montes de, *Spain* 31 F6
Tolentino, *Italy* 33 E10
Tolga, *Algeria* 75 B6
Tolga, *Norway* 10 B5
Toliara, *Madag.* 85 C7
Toliara □, *Madag.* 85 C8
Tolima, *Colombia* 120 C2
Tolima □, *Colombia* 120 C2
Tolitoli, *Indonesia* 57 D6
Tolkamer, *Neths.* 16 E8
Tolleson, *U.S.A.* 111 K7
Tollhouse, *U.S.A.* 112 H7
Tolmachevo, *Russia* 40 B6
Tolmezzo, *Italy* 33 B10
Tolmin, *Slovenia* 33 B10
Tolo, *Zaïre* 80 E3
Tolo, Teluk, *Indonesia* 57 E6
Tolochin, *Belorussia* 40 D6
Tolosa, *Spain* 28 B2
Tolox, *Spain* 31 J6
Toltén, *Chile* 128 A2
Toluca, *Mexico* 115 D5
Tom Burke, *S. Africa* 85 C4
Tom Price, *Australia* 88 D2
Tomah, *U.S.A.* 108 D9
Tomahawk, *U.S.A.* 108 C10
Tomakomai, *Japan* 48 C10
Tomales, *U.S.A.* 112 G4
Tomales B., *U.S.A.* 112 G3
Tomar, *Portugal* 31 F2
Tomarza, *Turkey* 66 D6
Tomás Barrón, *Bolivia* 124 D4
Tomaszów Mazowiecki, *Poland* 20 D9
Tomatlán, *Mexico* 114 D3
Tombador, Serra do, *Brazil* 125 C6
Tombé, *Sudan* 77 F3
Tombigbee →, *U.S.A.* 105 K2
Tombouctou, *Mali* 78 B4
Tombstone, *U.S.A.* 111 L8
Tombua, *Angola* 84 B1
Tomé, *Chile* 126 D1
Tomé-Açu, *Brazil* 122 B2
Tomelilla, *Sweden* 11 J7
Tomelloso, *Spain* 29 F1
Tomingley, *Australia* 91 E4
Tomini, *Indonesia* 57 D6
Tomini, Teluk, *Indonesia* 57 E6
Tominian, *Mali* 78 C4
Tomiño, *Spain* 30 D2
Tomkinson Ras., *Australia* 89 E4
Tommot, *Russia* 45 D13
Tomnavoulin, *U.K.* 14 D5
Tomnop Ta Suos, *Cambodia* 59 G5
Tomo, *Colombia* 120 C4
Tomo →, *Colombia* 120 B4
Toms Place, *U.S.A.* 112 H8
Toms River, *U.S.A.* 107 G10
Tomsk, *Russia* 44 D9
Tonalá, *Mexico* 115 D6
Tonale, Passo del, *Italy* 32 B7
Tonalea, *U.S.A.* 111 H8
Tonantins, *Brazil* 120 D4
Tonasket, *U.S.A.* 110 B4
Tonate, *Fr. Guiana* 121 C7
Tonawanda, *U.S.A.* 106 D6
Tonbridge, *U.K.* 13 F8
Tondano, *Indonesia* 57 D6
Tondela, *Portugal* 30 E2
Tønder, *Denmark* 11 K2
Tondi Kiwindi, *Niger* 79 C5
Tondibi, *Mali* 79 B4
Tonekābon, *Iran* 65 B6
Tong Xian, *China* 50 E9
Tonga ■, *Pac. Oc.* 87 D11
Tonga Trench, *Pac. Oc.* 92 J10
Tongaat, *S. Africa* 85 D5
Tong'an, *China* 53 E12
Tongareva, *Cook Is.* 93 H12
Tongatapu, *Tonga* 87 E11
Tongbai, *China* 53 A9
Tongcheng, *Anhui, China* 53 B11
Tongcheng, *Hubei, China* 53 C9
Tongchŏn-ni, *N. Korea* 51 E14
Tongchuan, *China* 50 G5
Tongdao, *China* 52 D7
Tongeren, *Belgium* 17 G6
Tonggu, *China* 53 C10
Tongguan, *China* 50 G6
Tonghai, *China* 52 E4
Tonghua, *China* 51 D13
Tongjiang, *Heilongjiang, China* 54 B8
Tongjiang, *Sichuan, China* 52 B6
Tongjosŏn Man, *N. Korea* 51 E14
Tongking, G. of = Tonkin, G. of, *Asia* 58 B7
Tongliang, *China* 52 C6
Tongliao, *China* 51 C12
Tongling, *China* 53 B11
Tonglu, *China* 53 C12
Tongnae, *S. Korea* 51 G15
Tongnan, *China* 52 B5
Tongobory, *Madag.* 85 C7

Tongoy, *Chile* 126 C1
Tongren, *China* 52 D7
Tongres = Tongeren, *Belgium* 17 G6
Tongsa Dzong, *Bhutan* 61 F17
Tongue, *U.K.* 14 C4
Tongue →, *U.S.A.* 108 B2
Tongwei, *China* 50 G3
Tongxin, *China* 50 F3
Tongyang, *N. Korea* 51 E14
Tongyu, *China* 51 B12
Tongzi, *China* 52 C6
Tonj, *Sudan* 77 F2
Tonk, *India* 62 F6
Tonkawa, *U.S.A.* 109 G6
Tonkin = Bac Phan, *Vietnam* 58 B5
Tonkin, G. of, *Asia* 58 B7
Tonlé Sap, *Cambodia* 58 F4
Tonnay-Charente, *France* 26 C3
Tonneins, *France* 26 D4
Tonnerre, *France* 25 E10
Tönning, *Germany* 18 A4
Tono, *Japan* 48 E10
Tonopah, *U.S.A.* 111 G5
Tonosí, *Panama* 116 E3
Tønsberg, *Norway* 10 E4
Tooele, *U.S.A.* 110 F7
Toompine, *Australia* 91 D3
Toonpan, *Australia* 90 B4
Toora, *Australia* 91 F4
Toora-Khem, *Russia* 45 D10
Toowoomba, *Australia* 91 D5
Topalu, *Romania* 38 E11
Topaz, *U.S.A.* 112 G7
Topeka, *U.S.A.* 108 F7
Topki, *Russia* 44 D9
Topl'a →, *Czech.* 20 G11
Topley, *Canada* 100 C3
Toplica →, *Serbia, Yug.* 21 M11
Toplița, *Romania* 38 C8
Topocalma, Pta., *Chile* 126 C1
Topock, *U.S.A.* 113 L12
Topola, *Serbia, Yug.* 21 L10
Topoľčany, *Czech.* 20 G8
Topoli, *Kazakhstan* 43 C14
Topolnitsa →, *Bulgaria* 38 G7
Topolobampo, *Mexico* 114 B3
Topolovgrad, *Bulgaria* 38 G9
Toppenish, *U.S.A.* 110 C3
Topusko, *Croatia* 33 C12
Toquepala, *Peru* 124 D3
Torá, *Spain* 28 D6
Tora Kit, *Sudan* 77 E3
Toraka Vestale, *Madag.* 85 B7
Torata, *Peru* 124 D3
Torbalı, *Turkey* 66 D2
Torbay, *Canada* 99 C9
Torbay, *U.K.* 13 G4
Tørdal, *Norway* 10 E2
Tordesillas, *Spain* 30 D6
Tordoya, *Spain* 30 B2
Töreboda, *Sweden* 11 F8
Torfajökull, *Iceland* 8 E4
Torgau, *Germany* 18 D8
Torgelow, *Germany* 18 B9
Torhout, *Belgium* 17 F2
Tori, *Ethiopia* 77 F3
Tori-Shima, *Japan* 49 J10
Torigni-sur-Vire, *France* 24 C6
Torija, *Spain* 28 E1
Torin, *Mexico* 114 B2
Toriñana, C., *Spain* 30 B1
Torino, *Italy* 32 C4
Torit, *Sudan* 77 G3
Torkovichi, *Russia* 40 B7
Tormes →, *Spain* 30 D4
Tornado Mt., *Canada* 100 D6
Torne älv →, *Sweden* 8 D18
Torneå = Tornio, *Finland* 8 D18
Torneträsk, *Sweden* 8 B15
Tornio, *Finland* 8 D18
Tornionjoki →, *Finland* 8 D18
Tornquist, *Argentina* 126 D3
Toro, *Baleares, Spain* 36 B11
Toro, *Zamora, Spain* 30 D5
Torö, *Sweden* 11 F11
Toro, Cerro del, *Chile* 126 B2
Toro Pk., *U.S.A.* 113 M10
Törökszentmiklós, *Hungary* 21 H10
Toroníios Kólpos, *Greece* 39 J6
Toronto, *Australia* 91 E5
Toronto, *Canada* 98 D4
Toronto, *U.S.A.* 106 F4
Toropets, *Russia* 40 C7
Tororo, *Uganda* 82 B3
Toros Dağları, *Turkey* 66 E5
Torotoro, *Bolivia* 125 D4
Torpshammar, *Sweden* 10 B10
Torquay, *Canada* 101 D8
Torquay, *U.K.* 13 G4
Torquemada, *Spain* 30 C6
Torralba de Calatrava, *Spain* 31 F7
Torrance, *U.S.A.* 113 M8
Torrão, *Portugal* 31 G2
Torre Annunziata, *Italy* 35 B7
Tôrre de Moncorvo, *Portugal* 30 D3
Torre del Greco, *Italy* 35 B7
Torre del Mar, *Spain* 31 J6
Torre-Pacheco, *Spain* 29 H4
Torre Pellice, *Italy* 32 D4
Torreblanca, *Spain* 28 E5
Torrecampo, *Spain* 31 G6
Torrecilla en Cameros, *Spain* 28 C2
Torredembarra, *Spain* 28 D6
Torredonjimeno, *Spain* 31 H7
Torrejoncillo, *Spain* 30 F4
Torrelaguna, *Spain* 28 E1
Torrelavega, *Spain* 30 B6
Torremaggiore, *Italy* 35 A8
Torremolinos, *Spain* 31 J6
Torrens, L., *Australia* 91 E2
Torrens Cr. →, *Australia* 90 C4
Torrens Creek, *Australia* 90 C4
Torrente, *Spain* 29 F4
Torrenueva, *Spain* 29 G1
Torreón, *Mexico* 114 B4
Torreperogil, *Spain* 29 G1
Torres, *Mexico* 114 B2
Torres Novas, *Portugal* 31 F2
Torres Strait, *Australia* 92 H6
Torres Vedras, *Portugal* 31 F1
Torrevieja, *Spain* 29 H4
Torrey, *U.S.A.* 111 G8
Torridge →, *U.K.* 13 G3
Torridon, L., *U.K.* 14 D3
Torrijos, *Spain* 30 F6
Torrington, *Conn., U.S.A.* 107 E11
Torrington, *Wyo., U.S.A.* 108 D2
Torroella de Montgri, *Spain* 28 C8
Torrox, *Spain* 31 J7
Torsö, *Sweden* 11 F7
Tortola, *Virgin Is.* 117 C7
Tórtoles de Esgueva, *Spain* 30 D6
Tortona, *Italy* 32 D5
Tortoreto, *Italy* 33 F10
Tortorici, *Italy* 35 D7
Tortosa, *Spain* 28 E5
Tortosa, C., *Spain* 28 E5
Tortosendo, *Portugal* 30 E3
Tortue, I. de la, *Haiti* 117 B5
Tortum, *Turkey* 67 C9
Torūd, *Iran* 65 C7
Torul, *Turkey* 67 C8
Toruń, *Poland* 20 B8
Torup, *Denmark* 11 G3
Torup, *Sweden* 11 H7
Tory I., *Ireland* 15 A3
Torysa →, *Czech.* 20 G11
Torzhok, *Russia* 40 C9
Tosa, *Japan* 49 H6
Tosa-Shimizu, *Japan* 49 H6
Tosa-Wan, *Japan* 49 H6
Toscana, *Italy* 32 E8
Toscano, Arcipelago, *Italy* 32 F7
Tosno, *Russia* 40 B7
Tossa, *Spain* 28 D7
Tostado, *Argentina* 126 B3
Tostedt, *Germany* 18 B5
Tostón, Pta. de, *Canary Is.* 36 F5
Tosu, *Japan* 49 H5
Tosya, *Turkey* 66 C6
Totana, *Spain* 29 H3
Toten, *Norway* 10 D4
Toteng, *Botswana* 84 C3
Tôtes, *France* 24 C8
Tótkomlós, *Hungary* 21 J10
Totma, *Russia* 41 B13
Totnes, *U.K.* 13 G4
Totness, *Surinam* 121 B6
Totonicapán, *Guatemala* 116 D1
Totora, *Bolivia* 125 D4
Totten Glacier, *Antarctica* 5 C8
Tottenham, *Australia* 91 E4
Tottenham, *Canada* 106 B5
Tottori, *Japan* 49 G7
Tottori □, *Japan* 49 G7
Touat, *Algeria* 75 C5
Touba, *Ivory C.* 78 D3
Toubkal, Djebel, *Morocco* 74 B3
Toucy, *France* 25 E10
Tougan, *Burkina Faso* 78 C4
Touggourt, *Algeria* 75 B6
Tougué, *Guinea* 78 C2
Toukmatine, *Algeria* 75 D6
Toul, *France* 25 D12
Toulepleu, *Ivory C.* 78 D3
Toulon, *France* 27 E9
Toulouse, *France* 26 E5
Toummo, *Niger* 73 D7
Toumodi, *Ivory C.* 78 D3
Tounassine, Hamada, *Algeria* 74 C3
Toungoo, *Burma* 61 K20
Touques →, *France* 24 C7
Touraine, *France* 24 E7
Tourane = Da Nang, *Vietnam* 58 D7
Tourcoing, *France* 25 B10
Tourine, *Mauritania* 74 D2
Tournai, *Belgium* 17 G2
Tournan-en-Brie, *France* 25 D9
Tournay, *France* 26 E4
Tournon, *France* 27 C8
Tournon-St.-Martin, *France* 24 F7
Tournus, *France* 27 B8
Touros, *Brazil* 122 C4
Tours, *France* 24 E7
Touwsrivier, *S. Africa* 84 E3
Tovar, *Venezuela* 120 B3
Tovarkovskiy, *Russia* 41 E11
Tovdal, *Norway* 11 F2
Tovdalselva →, *Norway* 11 F2
Towada, *Japan* 48 D10
Towada-Ko, *Japan* 48 D10
Towamba, *Australia* 91 F4
Towanda, *U.S.A.* 107 E8
Towang, *India* 61 F17
Tower, *U.S.A.* 108 B8
Towerhill Cr. →, *Australia* 90 C3
Towner, *U.S.A.* 108 A4
Townsend, *U.S.A.* 110 C8
Townshend I., *Australia* 90 C5
Townsville, *Australia* 90 B4
Towson, *U.S.A.* 104 F7
Toya-Ko, *Japan* 48 C10
Toyah, *U.S.A.* 109 K3
Toyahvale, *U.S.A.* 109 K3
Toyama, *Japan* 49 F8
Toyama □, *Japan* 49 F8
Toyama-Wan, *Japan* 49 F8
Toyohashi, *Japan* 49 G8
Toyokawa, *Japan* 49 G8
Toyonaka, *Japan* 49 G7
Toyooka, *Japan* 49 G7
Toyota, *Japan* 49 G8
Tozeur, *Tunisia* 75 B6
Tra On, *Vietnam* 59 H5
Trabancos →, *Spain* 30 D5
Traben Trarbach, *Germany* 19 F3
Trabzon, *Turkey* 42 F8
Trabzon □, *Turkey* 67 C8
Tracadie, *Canada* 99 C7
Tracy, *Calif., U.S.A.* 111 H3
Tracy, *Minn., U.S.A.* 108 C7
Tradate, *Italy* 32 C5
Tradovoye, *Russia* 48 C6
Trafalgar, C., *Spain* 31 J4
Traiguén, *Chile* 128 A2
Trail, *Canada* 100 D5
Trainor L., *Canada* 100 A4
Traíra →, *Brazil* 120 D4
Trákhonas, *Cyprus* 37 D12
Tralee, *Ireland* 15 D2
Tralee B., *Ireland* 15 D2
Tramelan, *Switz.* 22 B4
Tramore, *Ireland* 15 D4
Tran Ninh, Cao Nguyen, *Laos* 58 C4
Tranås, *Sweden* 9 G13
Trancas, *Argentina* 126 B2
Trancoso, *Portugal* 30 E3
Tranebjerg, *Denmark* 11 J4
Tranemo, *Sweden* 11 G7
Trang, *Thailand* 59 J2
Trangahy, *Madag.* 85 B7
Trangan, *Indonesia* 57 F8
Trangie, *Australia* 91 E4
Trångsviken, *Sweden* 10 A8
Trani, *Italy* 35 A9
Tranoroa, *Madag.* 85 C8
Tranqueras, *Uruguay* 127 C4
Trans Nzoia □, *Kenya* 82 B3
Transantarctic Mts., *Antarctica* 5 E12
Transcaucasia = Zakavkazye, *Asia* 43 F11
Transcona, *Canada* 101 D9
Transilvania, *Romania* 38 D8
Transkei □, *S. Africa* 85 E4
Transvaal □, *S. Africa* 84 D4
Transylvania = Transilvania, *Romania* 38 D8
Transylvanian Alps, *Romania* 6 F10
Trápani, *Italy* 34 D5
Trapper Peak, *U.S.A.* 110 D6
Traralgon, *Australia* 91 F4
Trarza, *Mauritania* 78 B2
Trasacco, *Italy* 33 G10
Trăscău, Munții, *Romania* 38 C6
Trasimeno, L., *Italy* 33 E9
Trat, *Thailand* 59 F4
Traun, *Austria* 21 G4
Traunstein, *Germany* 19 H8
Tråvad, *Sweden* 11 F7
Traveller's L., *Australia* 91 E3
Travemünde, *Germany* 18 B6
Travers, Mt., *N.Z.* 87 K4
Traverse City, *U.S.A.* 104 C3
Travnik, *Bos.-H., Yug.* 21 L7
Trayning, *Australia* 89 F2
Trazo, *Spain* 30 B2
Trbovlje, *Slovenia* 33 B12
Trébbia →, *Italy* 32 C6
Trebel →, *Germany* 18 B9
Trebinje, *Bos.-H., Yug.* 21 N8
Trebisacce, *Italy* 35 C9
Trebišnica →, *Bos.-H., Yug.* 21 N8
Trebišov, *Czech.* 20 G11
Trebižat →, *Bos.-H., Yug.* 21 M7
Trebnje, *Slovenia* 33 C12
Třeboň, *Czech.* 20 G4
Trebujena, *Spain* 31 J4
Trecate, *Italy* 32 C5
Trece Martires, *Phil.* 55 D4
Tredegar, *U.K.* 13 F4
Tregaron, *U.K.* 13 E4
Trégastel-Plage, *France* 24 D3
Tregnago, *Italy* 33 C8
Tregrosse Is., *Australia* 90 B5
Tréguier, *France* 24 D3
Trégunc, *France* 24 E3
Treherne, *Canada* 101 D9
Tréia, *Italy* 33 E10
Treignac, *France* 26 C5
Treinta y Tres, *Uruguay* 127 C5
Treis, *Germany* 19 E3
Trekveld, *S. Africa* 84 E2
Trelde Næs, *Denmark* 11 J3
Trelew, *Argentina* 128 B3
Trélissac, *France* 26 C4
Trelleborg, *Sweden* 11 J7
Trélon, *France* 25 B11
Tremiti, *Italy* 33 F12
Tremonton, *U.S.A.* 110 F7
Tremp, *Spain* 28 C5
Trenche →, *Canada* 98 C5
Trenčín, *Czech.* 20 G8
Trenggalek, *Indonesia* 57 H14
Trenque Lauquen, *Argentina* 126 D3
Trent →, *U.K.* 12 D7
Trentino-Alto Adige □, *Italy* 32 B8
Trento, *Italy* 32 B8
Trenton, *Canada* 98 D4
Trenton, *Mo., U.S.A.* 108 E8
Trenton, *N.J., U.S.A.* 107 F10
Trenton, *Nebr., U.S.A.* 108 E4
Trenton, *Tenn., U.S.A.* 109 H10
Trepassey, *Canada* 99 C9
Trepuzzi, *Italy* 35 B11
Tres Arroyos, *Argentina* 126 D3
Três Corações, *Brazil* 123 F2
Três Lagoas, *Brazil* 123 F1
Tres Lagos →, *Argentina* 128 C2
Tres Marías, *Mexico* 114 C3
Três Marias, Represa, *Brazil* 123 E2
Tres Montes, C., *Chile* 128 C1
Tres Pinos, *U.S.A.* 112 J5
Três Pontas, *Brazil* 123 F2
Tres Puentes, *Chile* 126 B1
Tres Puntas, C., *Argentina* 128 C3
Três Rios, *Brazil* 123 F3
Tres Valles, *Mexico* 115 D5
Treska →, *Macedonia, Yug.* 39 H4
Trespaderne, *Spain* 28 C1
Trets, *France* 27 E9
Treuchtlingen, *Germany* 19 G6
Treuenbrietzen, *Germany* 18 C8
Treungen, *Norway* 9 G10
Trevíglio, *Italy* 32 C6
Trevínca, Peña, *Spain* 30 C4
Treviso, *Italy* 33 C9
Trévoux, *France* 27 C8
Treysa, *Germany* 18 E5
Trgovište, *Serbia, Yug.* 21 N12
Triabunna, *Australia* 90 G4
Triánda, *Greece* 37 C10
Triang, *Malaysia* 59 L4
Triaucourt-en-Argonne, *France* 25 D12
Tribsees, *Germany* 18 A8
Tribulation, C., *Australia* 90 B4
Tribune, *U.S.A.* 108 F4
Tricárico, *Italy* 35 B9
Tricase, *Italy* 35 C11
Trichinopoly = Tiruchchirappalli, *India* 60 P11
Trichur, *India* 60 P10
Trida, *Australia* 91 E4
Trier, *Germany* 19 F2
Trieste, *Italy* 33 C10
Trieste, G. di, *Italy* 33 C10
Trieux →, *France* 24 D3
Triggiano, *Italy* 35 A9
Triglav, *Slovenia* 33 B10
Trigno →, *Italy* 33 F11
Trigueros, *Spain* 31 H4
Trikhonis, Límni, *Greece* 39 L4
Tríkkala, *Greece* 39 K4
Trikomo, *Cyprus* 37 D12
Trikora, Puncak, *Indonesia* 57 E9
Trilj, *Croatia* 33 E13
Trillo, *Spain* 28 E2
Trim, *Ireland* 15 C5
Trincomalee, *Sri Lanka* 60 Q12
Trindade, *Brazil* 123 E2
Trindade, I., *Atl. Oc.* 2 F8
Trinidad, *Bolivia* 125 C5
Trinidad, *Colombia* 120 B3
Trinidad, *Cuba* 116 B3
Trinidad, *Uruguay* 126 C4
Trinidad, *U.S.A.* 109 G2
Trinidad, *W. Indies* 117 D7
Trinidad →, *Mexico* 115 D5
Trinidad, G., *Chile* 128 C1
Trinidad, I., *Argentina* 128 A4
Trinidad & Tobago ■, *W. Indies* 117 D7
Trinitápoli, *Italy* 35 A9
Trinity, *Canada* 99 C9
Trinity, *U.S.A.* 109 K7
Trinity →, *Calif., U.S.A.* 110 F2
Trinity →, *Tex., U.S.A.* 109 L7
Trinity B., *Canada* 99 C9
Trinity Mts., *U.S.A.* 110 F4
Trinkitat, *Sudan* 76 D4
Trino, *Italy* 32 C5
Trion, *U.S.A.* 105 H3
Trionto, C., *Italy* 35 C9
Triora, *Italy* 32 E4
Tripoli = Tarābulus, *Lebanon* 69 A4
Tripoli = Tarābulus, *Libya* 75 B7
Tripp, *U.S.A.* 108 D6
Tripura □, *India* 61 H17
Tripylos, *Cyprus* 37 E11
Trischen, *Germany* 18 A4
Tristan da Cunha, *Atl. Oc.* 2 F9
Trivandrum, *India* 60 Q10
Trivento, *Italy* 35 A7
Trnava, *Czech.* 21 G7
Trochu, *Canada* 100 C6
Trodely I., *Canada* 98 B4
Trogir, *Croatia* 33 E13
Troglav, *Croatia* 33 E13
Trøgstad, *Norway* 10 E5
Tróia, *Italy* 35 A8
Troilus, L., *Canada* 98 B5
Troina, *Italy* 35 E7
Trois Fourches, Cap des, *Morocco* 75 A4
Trois-Pistoles, *Canada* 99 C6
Trois-Rivières, *Canada* 98 C5
Troisvierges, *Belgium* 17 H8
Troitsk, *Russia* 44 D7
Troitsko Pechorsk, *Russia* 44 C6
Trölladyngja, *Iceland* 8 D5
Trollhättan, *Sweden* 11 F6
Trollheimen, *Norway* 10 B3
Trombetas →, *Brazil* 121 D6
Troms fylke □, *Norway* 8 B15
Tromsø, *Norway* 8 B15
Trona, *U.S.A.* 113 K9
Tronador, *Argentina* 128 B2
Trondheim, *Norway* 10 A4
Trondheimsfjorden, *Norway* 8 E11
Trönninge, *Sweden* 11 H6
Trönö, *Sweden* 10 C10
Tronto →, *Italy* 33 F10
Troodos, *Cyprus* 37 E11
Troon, *U.K.* 14 F4
Tropea, *Italy* 35 D8
Tropic, *U.S.A.* 111 H7
Tropoja, *Albania* 38 G3
Trossachs, The, *U.K.* 14 E4
Trostan, *U.K.* 15 A5
Trostberg, *Germany* 19 G8
Trostyanets, *Ukraine* 40 F9
Trotternish, *U.K.* 14 D2
Troup, *U.S.A.* 109 J7
Trout →, *Canada* 100 A5
Trout L., *N.W.T., Canada* 100 A4
Trout L., *Ont., Canada* 101 C10
Trout Lake, *Mich., U.S.A.* 98 C2
Trout Lake, *Wash., U.S.A.* 112 E5
Trout River, *Canada* 99 C8
Trouville-sur-Mer, *France* 24 C7
Trowbridge, *U.K.* 13 F5
Troy, *Turkey* 66 D2
Troy, *Ala., U.S.A.* 105 K3
Troy, *Idaho, U.S.A.* 110 C5
Troy, *Kans., U.S.A.* 108 F7
Troy, *Mo., U.S.A.* 108 F9
Troy, *Mont., U.S.A.* 110 B6
Troy, *N.Y., U.S.A.* 107 D11
Troy, *Ohio, U.S.A.* 104 E3
Troyan, *Bulgaria* 38 G7
Troyes, *France* 25 D11
Trpanj, *Croatia* 21 M7
Trstena, *Czech.* 20 F9
Trstenik, *Serbia, Yug.* 21 M10
Trubchevsk, *Russia* 40 E8
Trucial States = United Arab Emirates ■, *Asia* 65 F7
Truckee, *U.S.A.* 112 F6
Trujillo, *Colombia* 120 C2
Trujillo, *Honduras* 116 C2
Trujillo, *Peru* 124 B2
Trujillo, *Spain* 31 F5
Trujillo, *U.S.A.* 109 H2
Trujillo, *Venezuela* 120 B3
Trujillo □, *Venezuela* 120 B3
Truk, *Pac. Oc.* 92 G7
Trumann, *U.S.A.* 109 H9
Trumbull, Mt., *U.S.A.* 111 H7
Trun, *France* 24 D7
Trun, *Switz.* 23 C7
Trundle, *Australia* 91 E4
Trung-Phan, *Vietnam* 58 E7
Truro, *Canada* 99 C7
Truro, *U.K.* 13 G2
Truslove, *Australia* 89 F3
Trustrup, *Denmark* 11 H4
Truth or Consequences, *U.S.A.* 111 K10
Trutnov, *Czech.* 20 E5
Truyère →, *France* 26 D6
Tryavna, *Bulgaria* 38 G8
Tryon, *U.S.A.* 105 H4
Tryonville, *U.S.A.* 106 E5
Trzcianka, *Poland* 20 B6
Trzebiatów, *Poland* 20 A5
Trzebiez, *Poland* 20 B4
Trzebinia-Siersza, *Poland* 20 E9
Trzebnica, *Poland* 20 D7
Tržič, *Slovenia* 33 B11
Tsageri, *Georgia* 43 E10
Tsaratanana, *Madag.* 85 B8
Tsaratanana, Mt. de, *Madag.* 85 A8
Tsarevo = Michurin, *Bulgaria* 38 G10
Tsarichanka, *Ukraine* 42 B6
Tsau, *Botswana* 84 C3
Tsebrikovo, *Ukraine* 42 C4
Tselinograd, *Kazakhstan* 44 D8
Tsetserleg, *Mongolia* 54 B5
Tshabong, *Botswana* 84 D3
Tshane, *Botswana* 84 C3
Tshela, *Zaïre* 80 E2
Tshesebe, *Botswana* 85 C4
Tshibeke, *Zaïre* 82 C2
Tshibinda, *Zaïre* 82 C2
Tshikapa, *Zaïre* 80 F4
Tshilenge, *Zaïre* 82 D1

Tshinsenda, *Zaïre* 83 E2
Tshofa, *Zaïre* 82 D2
Tshwane, *Botswana* 84 C3
Tsigara, *Botswana* 84 C4
Tsihombe, *Madag.* 85 D8
Tsimlyansk, *Russia* 43 C10
Tsimlyanskoye Vdkhr., *Russia* 43 B10
Tsinan = Jinan, *China* 50 F9
Tsineng, *S. Africa* 84 D3
Tsinghai = Qinghai □, *China* 54 C4
Tsingtao = Qingdao, *China* 51 F11
Tsinjomitondraka, *Madag.* 85 B8
Tsiroanomandidy, *Madag.* 85 B8
Tsivilsk, *Russia* 41 D15
Tsivory, *Madag.* 85 C8
Tskhinvali, *Georgia* 43 E11
Tsna →, *Russia* 41 D12
Tso Moriri, L., *India* 63 C8
Tsodilo Hill, *Botswana* 84 B3
Tsogttsetsiy, *Mongolia* 50 C3
Tsolo, *S. Africa* 85 E4
Tsomo, *S. Africa* 85 E4
Tsu, *Japan* 49 G8
Tsu L., *Canada* 100 A6
Tsuchiura, *Japan* 49 F10
Tsugaru-Kaikyō, *Japan* 48 D10
Tsumeb, *Namibia* 84 B2
Tsumis, *Namibia* 84 C2
Tsuruga, *Japan* 49 G8
Tsurugi-San, *Japan* 49 H7
Tsuruoka, *Japan* 48 E9
Tsushima, *Gifu, Japan* 49 G8
Tsushima, *Nagasaki, Japan* 49 G4
Tsvetkovo, *Ukraine* 42 B4
Tua →, *Portugal* 30 D3
Tual, *Indonesia* 57 F8
Tuam, *Ireland* 15 C3
Tuamotu Is., *Pac. Oc.* 93 J13
Tuamotu Ridge, *Pac. Oc.* 93 K14
Tuanfeng, *China* 53 B10
Tuanxi, *China* 52 D6
Tuao, *Phil.* 55 C4
Tuapse, *Russia* 43 D8
Tuatapere, *N.Z.* 87 M1
Tuba City, *U.S.A.* 111 H8
Tuban, *Indonesia* 57 G15
Tubarão, *Brazil* 127 B6
Tūbās, *Jordan* 69 C4
Tubau, *Malaysia* 56 D4
Tubbergen, *Neths.* 16 D9
Tübingen, *Germany* 19 G5
Tubize, *Belgium* 17 G4
Tubruq, *Libya* 73 B9
Tubuai Is., *Pac. Oc.* 93 K12
Tuc Trung, *Vietnam* 59 G6
Tucacas, *Venezuela* 120 A4
Tucano, *Brazil* 122 D4
Tuchang, *Taiwan* 53 E13
Tuchodi →, *Canada* 100 B4
Tuchola, *Poland* 20 B7
Tucson, *U.S.A.* 111 K8
Tucumán □, *Argentina* 126 B2
Tucumcari, *U.S.A.* 109 H3
Tucunaré, *Brazil* 125 B6
Tucupido, *Venezuela* 120 B4
Tucupita, *Venezuela* 121 B5
Tucuruí, *Brazil* 122 B2
Tudela, *Spain* 28 C3
Tudela de Duero, *Spain* 30 D6
Tudmur, *Syria* 64 C3
Tudor, L., *Canada* 99 A6
Tudora, *Romania* 38 B9
Tuella →, *Portugal* 30 D3
Tuen, *Australia* 91 D4
Tueré →, *Brazil* 122 B1
Tugela →, *S. Africa* 85 D5
Tuguegarao, *Phil.* 55 C4
Tugur, *Russia* 45 D14
Tuineje, *Canary Is.* 36 F5
Tukangbesi, Kepulauan, *Indonesia* 57 F6
Tukarak I., *Canada* 98 A4
Tukayyid, *Iraq* 64 D5
Tûkh, *Egypt* 76 H7
Tukobo, *Ghana* 78 D4
Tūkrah, *Libya* 73 B9
Tuktoyaktuk, *Canada* 96 B6
Tukums, *Latvia* 40 C3
Tukuyu, *Tanzania* 83 D3
Tula, *Hidalgo, Mexico* 115 C5
Tula, *Tamaulipas, Mexico* 115 C5
Tula, *Nigeria* 79 D7
Tula, *Russia* 41 D10
Tulancingo, *Mexico* 115 C5
Tulare, *U.S.A.* 111 H4
Tulare Lake Bed, *U.S.A.* 111 J4
Tularosa, *U.S.A.* 111 K10
Tulbagh, *S. Africa* 84 E2
Tulcán, *Ecuador* 120 C2
Tulcea, *Romania* 38 D11
Tulchin, *Ukraine* 42 B3
Tūleh, *Iran* 65 C7
Tulemalu L., *Canada* 101 A9
Tuli, *Indonesia* 57 E6
Tuli, *Zimbabwe* 83 G2
Tulia, *U.S.A.* 109 H4
Ţulkarm, *Jordan* 69 C4
Tullahoma, *U.S.A.* 105 H2
Tullamore, *Australia* 91 E4
Tullamore, *Ireland* 15 C4
Tulle, *France* 26 C5
Tullibigeal, *Australia* 91 E4
Tullins, *France* 27 C9
Tulln, *Austria* 21 G6
Tullow, *Ireland* 15 D4
Tullus, *Sudan* 77 E1
Tully, *Australia* 90 B4
Ţulmaythah, *Libya* 73 B9
Tulmur, *Australia* 90 C3
Tulnici, *Romania* 38 D9
Tulovo, *Bulgaria* 38 G8
Tulsa, *U.S.A.* 109 G7
Tulsequah, *Canada* 100 B2
Tulu Milki, *Ethiopia* 77 F4
Tulu Welel, *Ethiopia* 77 F3
Tulua, *Colombia* 120 C2
Tulun, *Russia* 45 D11
Tulungagung, *Indonesia* 56 F4
Tum, *Indonesia* 57 E8
Tuma, *Russia* 41 D12
Tuma →, *Nic.* 116 D3
Tumaco, *Colombia* 120 C2
Tumaco, Ensenada, *Colombia* 120 C2
Tumatumari, *Guyana* 121 B6
Tumba, *Sweden* 10 E11
Tumba, L., *Zaïre* 80 E3
Tumbarumba, *Australia* 91 F4
Tumbaya, *Argentina* 126 A2
Túmbes, *Peru* 124 A1
Tumbes □, *Peru* 124 A1
Tumbwe, *Zaïre* 83 E2
Tumby Bay, *Australia* 91 E2
Tumd Youqi, *China* 50 D6
Tumen, *China* 51 C15
Tumen Jiang →, *China* 51 C16
Tumeremo, *Venezuela* 121 B5
Tumiritinga, *Brazil* 123 E3
Tumkur, *India* 60 N10
Tummel, L., *U.K.* 14 E5
Tump, *Pakistan* 60 F3
Tumpat, *Malaysia* 59 J4
Tumu, *Ghana* 78 C4
Tumucumaque, Serra, *Brazil* 121 C7
Tumupasa, *Bolivia* 124 C4
Tumut, *Australia* 91 F4
Tumwater, *U.S.A.* 110 C2
Tunas de Zaza, *Cuba* 116 B4
Tunbridge Wells, *U.K.* 13 F8
Tunceli, *Turkey* 67 D8
Tunceli □, *Turkey* 67 D8
Tuncurry, *Australia* 91 E5
Tunduru, *Tanzania* 83 E4
Tunduru □, *Tanzania* 83 E4
Tundzha →, *Bulgaria* 39 H9
Tunga Pass, *India* 61 E19
Tungabhadra →, *India* 60 M11
Tungaru, *Sudan* 77 E3
Tungla, *Nic.* 116 D3
Tungnafellsjökull, *Iceland* 8 D5
Tungsten, *Canada* 100 A3
Tungurahua □, *Ecuador* 120 D2
Tunguska, Nizhnyaya →, *Russia* 45 C9
Tunia, *Colombia* 120 C2
Tunica, *U.S.A.* 109 H9
Tunis, *Tunisia* 75 A7
Tunis, Golfe de, *Tunisia* 75 A7
Tunisia ■, *Africa* 75 B6
Tunja, *Colombia* 120 B3
Tunkhannock, *U.S.A.* 107 E9
Tunliu, *China* 50 F7
Tunnsjøen, *Norway* 8 D12
Tunungayualok I., *Canada* 99 A7
Tunuyán, *Argentina* 126 C2
Tunuyán →, *Argentina* 126 C2
Tunxi, *China* 53 C12
Tuo Jiang →, *China* 52 C5
Tuolumne, *U.S.A.* 111 H3
Tuolumne →, *U.S.A.* 112 H5
Tuoy-Khaya, *Russia* 45 C12
Tūp Āghāj, *Iran* 64 B5
Tupã, *Brazil* 127 A5
Tupaciguara, *Brazil* 123 E2
Tupelo, *U.S.A.* 105 H1
Tupik, *Russia* 40 D8
Tupik, *Russia* 45 D12
Tupinambaranas, *Brazil* 121 D6
Tupirama, *Brazil* 122 C2
Tupiratins, *Brazil* 122 C2
Tupiza, *Bolivia* 126 A2
Tupman, *U.S.A.* 113 K7
Tupper, *Canada* 100 B4
Tupper Lake, *U.S.A.* 107 B10
Tupungato, Cerro, *S. Amer.* 126 C2
Tuquan, *China* 51 B11
Túquerres, *Colombia* 120 C2
Tura, *Russia* 45 C11
Turabah, *Si. Arabia* 64 D4
Turagua, Serranía, *Venezuela* 121 B5
Tūrān, *Iran* 65 C8
Turan, *Russia* 45 D10
Turayf, *Si. Arabia* 64 D3
Turbenthal, *Switz.* 23 B7
Turégano, *Spain* 30 D6
Turek, *Poland* 20 C8
Turen, *Venezuela* 120 B4
Turfan = Turpan, *China* 54 B3
Turfan Depression = Turpan Hami, *China* 54 B3
Tŭrgovishte, *Bulgaria* 38 F9
Turgutlu, *Turkey* 66 D2
Turhal, *Turkey* 42 F7
Turia →, *Spain* 29 F4
Turiaçu, *Brazil* 122 B2
Turiaçu →, *Brazil* 122 B2
Turin = Torino, *Italy* 32 C4
Turin, *Canada* 100 D6
Turka, *Ukraine* 40 G3
Turkana □, *Kenya* 82 B4
Turkana, L., *Africa* 82 B4
Turkestan, *Kazakhstan* 44 E7
Túrkeve, *Hungary* 21 H10
Turkey ■, *Eurasia* 66 D7
Turkey Creek, *Australia* 88 C4
Turki, *Russia* 41 F13
Turkmenistan ■, *Asia* 44 F6
Türkoğlu, *Turkey* 66 E7
Turks Is., *W. Indies* 117 B5
Turks Island Passage, *W. Indies* 117 B5
Turku, *Finland* 9 F17
Turkwe →, *Kenya* 82 B4
Turlock, *U.S.A.* 111 H3
Turnagain →, *Canada* 100 B3
Turnagain, C., *N.Z.* 87 J6
Turneffe Is., *Belize* 115 D7
Turner, *Australia* 88 C4
Turner, *U.S.A.* 110 B9
Turner Pt., *Australia* 90 A1
Turner Valley, *Canada* 100 C6
Turners Falls, *U.S.A.* 107 D12
Turnhout, *Belgium* 17 F5
Turnor L., *Canada* 101 B7
Tŭrnovo, *Bulgaria* 38 F8
Turnu Măgurele, *Romania* 38 F7
Turnu Rosu Pasul, *Romania* 38 D7
Turon, *U.S.A.* 109 G5
Turpan, *China* 54 B3
Turpan Hami, *China* 54 B3
Turriff, *U.K.* 14 D6
Tursāq, *Iraq* 64 C5
Tursha, *Russia* 41 C15
Tursi, *Italy* 35 B9
Turtle Head I., *Australia* 90 A3
Turtle L., *Canada* 101 C7
Turtle Lake, *N. Dak., U.S.A.* 108 B4
Turtle Lake, *Wis., U.S.A.* 108 C8
Turtleford, *Canada* 101 C7
Turukhansk, *Russia* 45 C9
Turun ja Porin lääni □, *Finland* 9 F17
Turzovka, *Czech.* 20 F8
Tuscaloosa, *U.S.A.* 105 J2
Tuscánia, *Italy* 33 F8
Tuscany = Toscana, *Italy* 32 E8
Tuscola, *Ill., U.S.A.* 104 F1
Tuscola, *Tex., U.S.A.* 109 J5
Tuscumbia, *U.S.A.* 105 H2
Tuskar Rock, *Ireland* 15 D5
Tuskegee, *U.S.A.* 105 J3
Tustna, *Norway* 10 A2
Tutak, *Turkey* 67 D10
Tutayev, *Russia* 41 C11
Tuticorin, *India* 60 Q11
Tutin, *Serbia, Yug.* 21 N10
Tutóia, *Brazil* 122 B3
Tutong, *Brunei* 56 D4
Tutova →, *Romania* 38 C10
Tutrakan, *Bulgaria* 38 E9
Tutshi L., *Canada* 100 B2
Tuttle, *U.S.A.* 108 B5
Tuttlingen, *Germany* 19 H4
Tutuala, *Indonesia* 57 F7
Tutuila, *Amer. Samoa* 87 B13
Tututepec, *Mexico* 115 D5
Tuva Republic □, *Russia* 45 D10
Tuvalu ■, *Pac. Oc.* 92 H9
Tuxpan, *Mexico* 115 C5
Tuxtla Gutiérrez, *Mexico* 115 D6
Tuy, *Spain* 30 C2
Tuy An, *Vietnam* 58 F7
Tuy Duc, *Vietnam* 59 F6
Tuy Hoa, *Vietnam* 58 F7
Tuy Phong, *Vietnam* 59 G7
Tuya L., *Canada* 100 B2
Tuyen Hoa, *Vietnam* 58 D6
Tuyen Quang, *Vietnam* 58 B5
Tūysarkān, *Iran* 65 C6
Tuz Gölü, *Turkey* 66 D5
Ţūz Khurmātū, *Iraq* 64 C5
Tuzla, *Bos.-H., Yug.* 21 L8
Tuzla Gölü, *Turkey* 66 D6
Tuzlov →, *Russia* 43 C8
Tvååker, *Sweden* 11 G6
Tvedestrand, *Norway* 11 F2
Tver, *Russia* 41 C9
Tvŭrditsa, *Bulgaria* 38 G8
Twain, *U.S.A.* 112 E5
Twain Harte, *U.S.A.* 112 G6
Tweed, *Canada* 106 B7
Tweed →, *U.K.* 14 F7
Tweed Heads, *Australia* 91 D5
Tweedsmuir Prov. Park, *Canada* 100 C3
Twello, *Neths.* 16 D8
Twentynine Palms, *U.S.A.* 113 L10
Twillingate, *Canada* 99 C9
Twin Bridges, *U.S.A.* 110 D7
Twin Falls, *U.S.A.* 110 E6
Twin Valley, *U.S.A.* 108 B6
Twisp, *U.S.A.* 110 B3
Twistringen, *Germany* 18 C4
Two Harbors, *U.S.A.* 108 B9
Two Hills, *Canada* 100 C6
Two Rivers, *U.S.A.* 104 C2
Twofold B., *Australia* 91 F4
Tychy, *Poland* 20 E8
Tykocin, *Poland* 20 B12
Tyldal, *Norway* 10 B4
Tyler, *U.S.A.* 103 D7
Tyler, *Minn., U.S.A.* 108 C6
Tyler, *Tex., U.S.A.* 109 J7
Týn nad Vltavou, *Czech.* 20 F4
Tynda, *Russia* 45 D13
Tyne →, *U.K.* 12 C6
Tyne & Wear □, *U.K.* 12 C6
Tynemouth, *U.K.* 12 B6
Tynset, *Norway* 10 B4
Tyre = Sūr, *Lebanon* 69 B4
Tyrifjorden, *Norway* 10 D4
Tyringe, *Sweden* 11 H7
Tyristrand, *Norway* 10 D4
Tyrnyauz, *Russia* 43 E10
Tyrone, *U.S.A.* 106 F6
Tyrrell →, *Australia* 91 F3
Tyrrell, L., *Australia* 91 F3
Tyrrell Arm, *Canada* 101 A9
Tyrrell L., *Canada* 101 A7
Tyrrhenian Sea, *Europe* 34 B5
Tysfjorden, *Norway* 8 B14
Tystberga, *Sweden* 11 F11
Tyub Karagan, Mys, *Kazakhstan* 43 D14
Tyuleniy, *Russia* 43 D12
Tyumen, *Russia* 44 D7
Tywi →, *U.K.* 13 F3
Tywyn, *U.K.* 13 E3
Tzaneen, *S. Africa* 85 C5
Tzermiádhes, *Greece* 37 D7
Tzermiádhes Neápolis, *Greece* 39 P8
Tzoumérka, Óros, *Greece* 39 K4
Tzukong = Zigong, *China* 52 C5
Tzummarum, *Neths.* 16 B7

U

U Taphao, *Thailand* 58 F3
Uachadi, Sierra, *Venezuela* 121 C4
Uainambi, *Colombia* 120 C4
Uanda, *Australia* 90 C3
Uarsciek, *Somali Rep.* 68 G4
Uasin □, *Kenya* 82 B4
Uato-Udo, *Indonesia* 57 F7
Uatumã →, *Brazil* 121 D6
Uauá, *Brazil* 122 C4
Uaupés, *Brazil* 120 D4
Uaupés →, *Brazil* 120 C4
Uaxactún, *Guatemala* 116 C2
Ubá, *Brazil* 123 F3
Ubaitaba, *Brazil* 123 D4
Ubangi = Oubangi →, *Zaïre* 80 E3
Ubaté, *Colombia* 120 B3
Ubauro, *Pakistan* 62 E3
Ubaye →, *France* 27 D10
Ube, *Japan* 49 H5
Ubeda, *Spain* 29 G1
Uberaba, *Brazil* 123 E2
Uberaba, L., *Brazil* 125 D6
Uberlândia, *Brazil* 123 E2
Überlingen, *Germany* 19 H5
Ubiaja, *Nigeria* 79 D6
Ubolratna Res., *Thailand* 58 D4
Ubombo, *S. Africa* 85 D5
Ubon Ratchathani, *Thailand* 58 E5
Ubondo, *Zaïre* 82 C2
Ubort →, *Belorussia* 40 E6
Ubrique, *Spain* 31 J5
Ubundu, *Zaïre* 82 C2
Ucayali →, *Peru* 124 A3
Uccle, *Belgium* 17 G4
Uchi Lake, *Canada* 101 C10
Uchiura-Wan, *Japan* 48 C10
Uchiza, *Peru* 124 B2
Uchte, *Germany* 18 C4
Uchur →, *Russia* 45 D14
Ucluelet, *Canada* 100 D3
Ucuriş, *Romania* 38 C4
Uda →, *Russia* 45 D14
Udaipur, *India* 62 G5
Udaipur Garhi, *Nepal* 63 F12
Udbina, *Croatia* 33 D12
Uddel, *Neths.* 16 D7
Uddevalla, *Sweden* 11 F5
Uddjaur, *Sweden* 8 D16
Uden, *Neths.* 17 E7
Udgir, *India* 60 K10
Udhampur, *India* 63 C6
Udi, *Nigeria* 79 D6
Údine, *Italy* 33 B10
Udmurt Republic □, *Russia* 44 D6
Udon Thani, *Thailand* 58 D4
Udupi, *India* 60 N9
Udvoy Balkan, *Bulgaria* 38 G9
Udzungwa Range, *Tanzania* 83 D4
Ueckermünde, *Germany* 18 B10
Ueda, *Japan* 49 F9
Uedineniya, Os., *Russia* 4 B12
Uele →, *Zaïre* 80 D4
Uelen, *Russia* 45 C19
Uelzen, *Germany* 18 C6
Uetendorf, *Switz.* 22 C5
Ufa, *Russia* 44 D6
Uffenheim, *Germany* 19 F6
Ugab →, *Namibia* 84 C1
Ugalla →, *Tanzania* 82 D3
Uganda ■, *Africa* 82 B3
Ugchelen, *Neths.* 16 D7
Ugento, *Italy* 35 C11
Ugep, *Nigeria* 79 D6
Ugie, *S. Africa* 85 E4
Ugijar, *Spain* 29 J1
Ugine, *France* 27 C10
Uglegorsk, *Russia* 45 E15
Uglich, *Russia* 41 C11
Ugljane, *Croatia* 33 E13
Ugolyak, *Russia* 45 C13
Ugra →, *Russia* 41 D10
Ugûn Mûsa, *Egypt* 69 F1
Ugŭrchin, *Bulgaria* 38 F7
Uh →, *Czech.* 21 G11
Uherske Hradiště, *Czech.* 20 F7
Uhrichsville, *U.S.A.* 106 F3
Uíge, *Angola* 80 F2
Uijŏngbu, *S. Korea* 51 F14
Ŭiju, *N. Korea* 51 D13
Uinta Mts., *U.S.A.* 110 F8
Uitenhage, *S. Africa* 84 E4
Uitgeest, *Neths.* 16 C5
Uithoorn, *Neths.* 16 D5
Uithuizen, *Neths.* 16 B9
Uitkerke, *Belgium* 17 F2
Újfehértó, *Hungary* 21 H11
Ujhani, *India* 63 F8
Uji-guntō, *Japan* 49 J4
Ujjain, *India* 62 H6
Újpest, *Hungary* 21 H9
Újszász, *Hungary* 21 H10
Ujung Pandang, *Indonesia* 57 F5
Uka, *Russia* 45 D17
Ukara I., *Tanzania* 82 C3
Uke-Shima, *Japan* 49 K4
Ukerewe □, *Tanzania* 82 C3
Ukerewe I., *Tanzania* 82 C3
Ukholovo, *Russia* 41 E12
Ukhrul, *India* 61 G19
Ukhta, *Russia* 44 C6
Ukiah, *U.S.A.* 112 F3
Ukki Fort, *India* 63 C7
Ukmerge, *Lithuania* 40 D4
Ukraine ■, *Europe* 42 B4
Ukwi, *Botswana* 84 C3
Ulaanbaatar, *Mongolia* 54 B5
Ulaangom, *Mongolia* 54 A4
Ulamba, *Zaïre* 83 D1
Ulan Bator = Ulaanbaatar, *Mongolia* 54 B5
Ulan Ude, *Russia* 45 D11
Ulanga □, *Tanzania* 83 D4
Ulanów, *Poland* 20 E12
Ulaş, *Turkey* 66 D7
Ulaya, *Morogoro, Tanzania* 82 D4
Ulaya, *Tabora, Tanzania* 82 C3
Ulcinj, *Montenegro, Yug.* 39 H2
Ulco, *S. Africa* 84 D3
Ulfborg, *Denmark* 11 H2
Ulft, *Neths.* 16 E8
Ulhasnagar, *India* 60 K8
Uljma, *Serbia, Yug.* 21 K11
Ulla →, *Spain* 30 C2
Ulladulla, *Australia* 91 F5
Ullånger, *Sweden* 10 B12
Ullapool, *U.K.* 14 D3
Ullared, *Sweden* 11 G6
Ulldecona, *Spain* 28 E5
Ullswater, *U.K.* 12 C5
Ullung-do, *S. Korea* 51 F16
Ulm, *Germany* 19 G5
Ulmarra, *Australia* 91 D5
Ulmeni, *Romania* 38 D9
Ulonguè, *Mozam.* 83 E3
Ulricehamn, *Sweden* 9 H12
Ulrum, *Neths.* 16 B8
Ulsan, *S. Korea* 51 G15
Ulsberg, *Norway* 10 B3
Ulster □, *U.K.* 15 B5
Ulubaria, *India* 63 H13
Ulubat Gölü, *Turkey* 66 C3
Ulubey, *Turkey* 66 D3
Uluborlu, *Turkey* 66 D4
Uludağ, *Turkey* 66 C3
Uludere, *Turkey* 67 E10
Uluguru Mts., *Tanzania* 82 D4
Ulukışla, *Turkey* 66 E6
Ulungur He →, *China* 54 B3
Ulutau, *Kazakhstan* 44 E7
Ulvenhout, *Neths.* 17 E5
Ulverston, *U.K.* 12 C4
Ulverstone, *Australia* 90 G4
Ulya, *Russia* 45 D15
Ulyanovsk = Simbirsk, *Russia* 41 D16
Ulyasutay, *Mongolia* 54 B4
Ulysses, *U.S.A.* 109 G4
Umag, *Croatia* 33 C10
Umala, *Bolivia* 124 D4
Uman, *Ukraine* 42 B4
Umaria, *India* 61 H12
Umarkot, *Pakistan* 60 G6
Umatilla, *U.S.A.* 110 D4
Umba, *Russia* 44 C4
Umbertide, *Italy* 33 E9
Umbrella Mts., *N.Z.* 87 L2
Umbria □, *Italy* 33 F9
Ume älv →, *Sweden* 8 E16
Umeå, *Sweden* 8 E16
Umera, *Indonesia* 57 E7
Umfuli →, *Zimbabwe* 83 F2
Umgusa, *Zimbabwe* 83 F2
Umka, *Serbia, Yug.* 21 L10

Umkomaas, *S. Africa* 85 E5
Umm ad Daraj, J., *Jordan* 69 C4
Umm al Qaywayn, *U.A.E.* 65 E7
Umm al Qittayn, *Jordan* 69 C5
Umm Arda, *Sudan* 77 D3
Umm Bāb, *Qatar* 65 E6
Umm Bel, *Sudan* 77 E2
Umm Dubban, *Sudan* 77 D3
Umm el Fahm, *Israel* 69 C4
Umm Koweika, *Sudan* ... 77 E3
Umm Lajj, *Si. Arabia* ... 64 E3
Umm Merwa, *Sudan* 76 D3
Umm Ruwaba, *Sudan* ... 77 E3
Umm Sidr, *Sudan* 77 E2
Ummanz, *Germany* 18 A9
Umnak, *U.S.A.* 96 C3
Umniati →, *Zimbabwe* .. 83 F2
Umpqua →, *U.S.A.* 110 E1
Umreth, *India* 62 H5
Umtata, *S. Africa* 85 E4
Umuahia, *Nigeria* 79 D6
Umuarama, *Brazil* 127 A5
Umvukwe Ra., *Zimbabwe* 83 F3
Umzimvubu = Port St.
 Johns, *S. Africa* 85 E4
Umzingwane →,
 Zimbabwe 83 G2
Umzinto, *S. Africa* 85 E5
Una, *India* 62 J4
Una →, *Bos.-H., Yug.* .. 33 C13
Una →, *Bos.-H., Yug.* .. 33 D13
Unac →, *Bos.-H., Yug.* . 33 D13
Unadilla, *U.S.A.* 107 D9
Unalaska, *U.S.A.* 96 C3
Uncastillo, *Spain* 28 C3
Uncía, *Bolivia* 124 D4
Uncompahgre Pk., *U.S.A.* 111 G10
Unden, *Sweden* 11 F8
Underberg, *S. Africa* ... 85 D4
Underbool, *Australia* ... 91 F3
Undersaker, *Sweden* 10 A7
Undersvik, *Sweden* 10 C10
Unecha, *Russia* 40 E8
Uneiuxi →, *Brazil* 120 D4
Ungarie, *Australia* 91 E4
Ungarra, *Australia* 91 E2
Ungava B., *Canada* 97 C13
Ungava Pen., *Canada* ... 97 C12
Ungeny, *Moldavia* 42 C2
Unggi, *N. Korea* 51 C16
Ungwatiri, *Sudan* 77 D4
Uni, *Russia* 41 C17
União da Vitória, *Brazil* 127 B5
União dos Palmares, *Brazil* 122 C4
Unije, *Croatia* 33 D11
Unimak, *U.S.A.* 96 C3
Unini →, *Brazil* 121 D5
Union, *Miss., U.S.A.* ... 109 J10
Union, *Mo., U.S.A.* 108 F9
Union, *S.C., U.S.A.* 105 H5
Union, *Mt., U.S.A.* 111 J7
Union City, *Calif., U.S.A.* 112 H4
Union City, *N.J., U.S.A.* 107 F10
Union City, *Pa., U.S.A.* 106 E5
Union City, *Tenn., U.S.A.* 109 G10
Union Gap, *U.S.A.* 110 C3
Union of Soviet Socialist
 Republics =
 Commonwealth of
 Independent States ■,
 Eurasia 45 D11
Union Springs, *U.S.A.* . 105 J3
Uniondale, *S. Africa* ... 84 E3
Uniontown, *U.S.A.* 104 F6
Unionville, *U.S.A.* 108 E8
United Arab Emirates ■,
 Asia 65 F7
United Kingdom ■, *Europe* 7 E5
United States of
 America ■, *N. Amer.* . 102 C7
Unity, *Canada* 101 C7
Universales, Mtes., *Spain* 28 E3
Unjha, *India* 62 H5
Unnao, *India* 63 F9
Uno, Ilha, *Guinea-Biss.* 78 C1
Unst, *U.K.* 14 A8
Unstrut →, *Germany* ... 18 D7
Unter-engadin, *Switz.* .. 23 C10
Unterägeri, *Switz.* 23 B7
Unterkulm, *Switz.* 23 B6
Unterseen, *Switz.* 22 C5
Unterwaldner Alpen, *Switz.* 23 C6
Unuk →, *Canada* 100 B2
Ünye, *Turkey* 42 F7
Unzha, *Russia* 41 B14
Unzha →, *Russia* 41 C13
Uors, *Switz.* 23 C8
Upa →, *Czech.* 20 E6
Upata, *Venezuela* 121 B5
Upemba, L., *Zaïre* 83 D2
Upernavik, *Greenland* .. 4 B5
Upington, *S. Africa* 84 D3
Upleta, *India* 62 J4
Upolu, *W. Samoa* 87 A13
Upper Alkali Lake, *U.S.A.* 110 F3
Upper Arrow L., *Canada* 100 C5
Upper Foster L., *Canada* 101 B7
Upper Hutt, *N.Z.* 87 J5
Upper Klamath L., *U.S.A.* 110 E3
Upper Lake, *U.S.A.* 112 F4
Upper Musquodoboit,
 Canada 99 C7
Upper Red L., *U.S.A.* .. 108 A7
Upper Sandusky, *U.S.A.* . 104 E4

Upper Volta = Burkina
 Faso ■, *Africa* 78 C4
Upphärad, *Sweden* 11 F6
Uppsala, *Sweden* 10 E11
Uppsala län □, *Sweden* . 9 G14
Upshi, *India* 63 C7
Upstart, C., *Australia* .. 90 B4
Upton, *U.S.A.* 108 C2
Ur, *Iraq* 64 D5
Urabá, G. de, *Colombia* 120 B2
Uracara, *Brazil* 121 D6
Urad Qianqi, *China* 50 D5
Urakawa, *Japan* 48 C11
Ural, *Australia* 91 E4
Ural →, *Kazakhstan* ... 43 C14
Ural Mts. = Uralskie Gory,
 Russia 44 D6
Uralla, *Australia* 91 E5
Uralsk, *Kazakhstan* 44 D6
Uralskie Gory, *Russia* .. 44 D6
Urambo, *Tanzania* 82 D3
Urambo □, *Tanzania* ... 82 D3
Urandangi, *Australia* ... 90 C2
Uranium City, *Canada* .. 101 B7
Uranquinty, *Australia* .. 91 F4
Uraricaá →, *Brazil* 121 C5
Uraricuera →, *Brazil* .. 121 C5
Urawa, *Japan* 49 G9
Uray, *Russia* 44 C7
'Uray'irah, *Si. Arabia* .. 65 E6
Urbana, *Ill., U.S.A.* 104 E1
Urbana, *Ohio, U.S.A.* .. 104 E4
Urbánia, *Italy* 33 E9
Urbano Santos, *Brazil* . 122 B3
Urbel →, *Spain* 28 C1
Urbino, *Italy* 33 E9
Urbión, Picos de, *Spain* 28 C2
Urcos, *Peru* 124 C3
Urda, *Kazakhstan* 43 B12
Urda, *Spain* 31 F7
Urdinarrain, *Argentina* . 126 C4
Urdos, *France* 26 F3
Urdzhar, *Kazakhstan* ... 44 E9
Ure →, *U.K.* 12 C6
Uren, *Russia* 41 C14
Ures, *Mexico* 114 B2
Urfa, *Turkey* 67 E8
Urfa □, *Turkey* 67 E8
Urfahr, *Austria* 21 G4
Urgench, *Uzbekistan* ... 44 E7
Uri, *India* 63 B6
Uri □, *Switz.* 23 C7
Uribante →, *Venezuela* 120 B3
Uribe, *Colombia* 120 C3
Uribia, *Colombia* 120 A3
Uriondo, *Bolivia* 126 A3
Urique, *Mexico* 114 B3
Urique →, *Mexico* 114 B3
Urirotstock, *Switz.* 23 C7
Urk, *Neths.* 16 C7
Urla, *Turkey* 66 D2
Urlati, *Romania* 38 E9
Urmia = Orūmīyeh, *Iran* 64 B5
Urmia, L. = Orūmīyeh,
 Daryācheh-ye, *Iran* .. 64 B5
Urner Alpen, *Switz.* 23 C7
Uroševac, *Serbia, Yug.* 21 N11
Urrao, *Colombia* 120 B2
Ursus, *Poland* 20 C10
Uruaçu, *Brazil* 123 D2
Uruana, *Brazil* 123 E2
Uruapan, *Mexico* 114 D4
Uruará →, *Brazil* 121 D7
Urubamba, *Peru* 124 C3
Urubamba →, *Peru* 124 C3
Urubaxi →, *Brazil* 121 D5
Urubu →, *Brazil* 121 D6
Uruçara, *Brazil* 121 D6
Uruçuí, *Brazil* 122 C3
Uruçuí, Serra do, *Brazil* 122 C3
Uruçuí Prêto, →, *Brazil* 122 C3
Urucuia →, *Brazil* 123 E2
Urucurituba, *Brazil* 121 D6
Uruguai →, *Brazil* 127 B5
Uruguaiana, *Brazil* 126 B4
Uruguay ■, *S. Amer.* .. 126 C4
Uruguay →, *S. Amer.* . 126 C4
Urumchi = Ürümqi, *China* 54 B3
Ürümqi, *China* 54 B3
Urup, →, *Russia* 43 D9
Urup, Os., *Russia* 45 E16
Urutaí, *Brazil* 123 E2
Uryung-Khaya, *Russia* . 45 B12
Uryupinsk, *Russia* 41 F12
Urzhum, *Russia* 41 C16
Urziceni, *Romania* 38 E9
Uşak, *Turkey* 66 D3
Uşak □, *Turkey* 66 D3
Usakos, *Namibia* 84 C2
Usborne, Mt., *Falk. Is.* . 128 D5
Ušče, *Serbia, Yug.* 21 M10
Usedom, *Germany* 18 B9
'Usfān, *Si. Arabia* 76 C4
Ush-Tobe, *Kazakhstan* . 44 E8
Ushakova, Os., *Russia* . 4 A12
Ushant = Ouessant, I. d',
 France 24 D1
Ushashi, *Tanzania* 82 C3
Ushat, *Sudan* 77 F2
Ushibuka, *Japan* 49 H5
Ushuaia, *Argentina* 128 D3
Ushumun, *Russia* 45 D13
Usk →, *U.K.* 13 F5
Üsküdar, *Turkey* 39 H12

Uslar, *Germany* 18 D5
Usman, *Russia* 41 E11
Usoke, *Tanzania* 82 D3
Usolye Sibirskoye, *Russia* 45 D11
Usoro, *Nigeria* 79 D6
Uspallata, P. de, *Argentina* 126 C2
Uspenskiy, *Kazakhstan* . 44 E8
Usquert, *Neths.* 16 B9
Ussel, *France* 26 C6
Ussuri →, *Asia* 48 A7
Ussuriysk, *Russia* 45 E14
Ussurka, *Russia* 48 B6
Ust-Aldan = Batamay,
 Russia 45 C13
Ust Amginskoye =
 Khandyga, *Russia* ... 45 C14
Ust-Bolsheretsk, *Russia* . 45 D16
Ust Buzulukskaya, *Russia* 41 F13
Ust Chaun, *Russia* 45 C18
Ust-Donetskiy, *Russia* .. 43 C9
Ust'-Ilga, *Russia* 45 D11
Ust Ilimpeya = Yukti,
 Russia 45 C11
Ust-Ilimsk, *Russia* 45 D11
Ust Ishim, *Russia* 44 D8
Ust-Kamchatsk, *Russia* . 45 D17
Ust-Kamenogorsk,
 Kazakhstan 44 E9
Ust-Karenga, *Russia* ... 45 D12
Ust Khayryuzova, *Russia* 45 D16
Ust-Kut, *Russia* 45 D11
Ust Kuyga, *Russia* 45 B14
Ust-Labinsk, *Russia* 43 D8
Ust Luga, *Russia* 40 B6
Ust Maya, *Russia* 45 C14
Ust-Mil, *Russia* 45 D14
Ust-Nera, *Russia* 45 C15
Ust-Nyukzha, *Russia* ... 45 D13
Ust Olenek, *Russia* 45 B12
Ust-Omchug, *Russia* ... 45 C15
Ust Port, *Russia* 44 C9
Ust Tsilma, *Russia* 44 C6
Ust-Tungir, *Russia* 45 D13
Ust Urt = Ustyurt, Plato,
 Kazakhstan 44 E6
Ust Vorkuta, *Russia* 44 C7
Ustaoset, *Norway* 10 D2
Ustaritz, *France* 26 E2
Uste, *Russia* 41 B11
Uster, *Switz.* 23 B7
Ústí nad Labem, *Czech.* 20 E4
Ústí nad Orlicí, *Czech.* . 20 F6
Ustica, *Italy* 34 D6
Ustinov = Izhevsk, *Russia* 44 D6
Ustka, *Poland* 20 A6
Ustrzyki Dolne, *Poland* . 20 F12
Ustye, *Russia* 45 D10
Ustyurt, Plato, *Kazakhstan* 44 E6
Ustyuzhna, *Russia* 41 B10
Usu, *China* 54 B3
Usuki, *Japan* 49 H5
Usulután, *El Salv.* 116 D2
Usumacinta →, *Mexico* 115 D6
Usumbura = Bujumbura,
 Burundi 82 C2
Usure, *Tanzania* 82 C3
Uta, *Indonesia* 57 E9
Utah □, *U.S.A.* 110 G8
Utah, L., *U.S.A.* 110 F8
Ute Cr. →, *U.S.A.* 109 H3
Utena, *Lithuania* 40 D4
Ütersen, *Germany* 18 B5
Utete, *Tanzania* 82 D4
Uthai Thani, *Thailand* .. 58 E3
Uthal, *Pakistan* 62 G2
Utiariti, *Brazil* 125 C6
Utica, *N.Y., U.S.A.* 107 C9
Utica, *Ohio, U.S.A.* 106 F2
Utiel, *Spain* 28 F3
Utik L., *Canada* 101 B9
Utikuma L., *Canada* 100 B5
Utinga, *Brazil* 123 D3
Utrecht, *Neths.* 16 D6
Utrecht, *S. Africa* 85 D5
Utrecht □, *Neths.* 16 D6
Utrera, *Spain* 31 H5
Utsjoki, *Finland* 8 B19
Utsunomiya, *Japan* 49 F9
Uttar Pradesh □, *India* . 63 F9
Uttaradit, *Thailand* 58 D3
Uttoxeter, *U.K.* 12 E6
Ütze, *Germany* 18 C6
Uudenmaan lääni □,
 Finland 9 F18
Uusikaarlepyy, *Finland* . 8 E17
Uusikaupunki, *Finland* .. 9 F16
Uva →, *Russia* 41 C18
Uva →, *Colombia* 120 C3
Uvalde, *U.S.A.* 109 L5
Uvarovo, *Russia* 41 F13
Uvat, *Russia* 44 D7
Uvinza, *Tanzania* 82 D3
Uvira, *Zaïre* 82 C2
Uvs Nuur, *Mongolia* ... 54 A4
Uwajima, *Japan* 49 H6
Uweinat, Jebel, *Sudan* . 76 C1
Uxbridge, *Canada* 106 B5
Uxin Qi, *China* 50 E5
Uxmal, *Mexico* 115 C7
Uyandi, *Russia* 45 C15
Uyo, *Nigeria* 79 D6
Uyuni, *Bolivia* 124 E4
Uzbekistan ■, *Asia* 44 E7
Uzen, Bol. →, *Kazakhstan* 41 G16
Uzen, Mal. →, *Kazakhstan* 41 G16

Uzerche, *France* 26 C5
Uzès, *France* 27 D8
Uzh →, *Ukraine* 40 F7
Uzhgorod, *Ukraine* 40 G3
Uzlovaya, *Russia* 41 E11
Uzunköprü, *Turkey* 39 H9
Uzwil, *Switz.* 23 B8

V

Vaal →, *S. Africa* 84 D3
Vaal Dam, *S. Africa* ... 85 D4
Vaals, *Neths.* 17 G8
Vaalwater, *S. Africa* ... 85 C4
Vaasa, *Finland* 8 E16
Vaasan lääni □, *Finland* 8 E17
Vaassen, *Neths.* 16 D7
Vabre, *France* 26 E6
Vác, *Hungary* 21 H9
Vacaria, *Brazil* 127 B5
Vacaville, *U.S.A.* 112 G5
Vaccarès, Étang de, *France* 27 E8
Vach →, *Russia* 44 C8
Vache, I.-à-, *Haiti* 117 C5
Vadnagar, *India* 62 H5
Vado Lígure, *Italy* 32 D5
Vadodara, *India* 62 H5
Vadsø, *Norway* 8 A20
Vadstena, *Sweden* 11 F8
Vaduz, *Liech.* 23 B9
Værøy, *Norway* 8 C12
Vagnhärad, *Sweden* 10 F11
Vagos, *Portugal* 30 E2
Váh →, *Czech.* 21 H8
Vahsel B., *Antarctica* .. 5 D1
Vaï, *Greece* 37 D8
Vaigach, *Russia* 44 B6
Vaiges, *France* 24 D6
Vaihingen, *Germany* ... 19 G4
Vailly-sur-Aisne, *France* 25 C10
Vaison-la-Romaine, *France* 27 D9
Vakfikebir, *Turkey* 67 C8
Val-de-Marne □, *France* 25 D9
Val-d'Oise □, *France* ... 25 C9
Val d'Or, *Canada* 98 C4
Val Marie, *Canada* 101 D7
Valadares, *Portugal* 30 D2
Valahia, *Romania* 38 E8
Valais □, *Switz.* 22 D5
Valais, Alpes du, *Switz.* 22 D5
Valandovo,
 Macedonia, Yug. 39 H5
Valcheta, *Argentina* 128 B3
Valdagno, *Italy* 33 C8
Valday, *Russia* 40 C8
Valdayskaya
 Vozvyshennost, *Russia* . 40 C8
Valdeazogues →, *Spain* 31 G6
Valdemarsvik, *Sweden* .. 11 F10
Valdepeñas, *Ciudad Real,*
 Spain 31 G7
Valdepeñas, *Jaén, Spain* 31 H7
Valderaduey →, *Spain* . 30 D5
Valderrobres, *Spain* 28 E5
Valdés, Pen., *Argentina* 128 B4
Valdez, *Ecuador* 120 C2
Valdez, *U.S.A.* 96 B5
Valdivia, *Chile* 128 A2
Valdivia, *Colombia* 120 B2
Valdivia, *Chile* 128 B2
Valdobbiádene, *Italy* ... 33 C9
Valdosta, *U.S.A.* 105 K4
Valdoviño, *Spain* 30 B2
Valdres, *Norway* 10 D3
Vale, *Georgia* 43 F10
Vale, *U.S.A.* 110 E5
Valea lui Mihai, *Romania* 38 B5
Valença, *Brazil* 123 D4
Valença, *Portugal* 30 C2
Valença do Piauí, *Brazil* 122 C3
Valençay, *France* 25 E8
Valence, *Drôme, France* 27 D8
Valence, *Tarn-et-Garonne,*
 France 26 D4
Valencia, *Spain* 29 F4
Valencia, *Venezuela* 120 A4
Valencia □, *Spain* 29 F4
Valencia, Albufera de,
 Spain 29 F4
Valencia, G. de, *Spain* .. 29 F5
Valencia de Alcántara,
 Spain 31 F3
Valencia de Don Juan,
 Spain 30 C5
Valencia del Ventoso,
 Spain 31 G4
Valenciennes, *France* ... 25 B10
Valensole, *France* 27 E9
Valentia Harbour, *Ireland* 15 E1
Valentia I., *Ireland* 15 E1
Valentim, Sa. do, *Brazil* 122 C3
Valentin, *Russia* 48 C7
Valentine, *Nebr., U.S.A.* 108 D4
Valentine, *Tex., U.S.A.* . 109 K2
Valenza, *Italy* 32 C5
Valera, *Venezuela* 120 B3
Valga, *Estonia* 40 C5
Valguarnera Caropepe,
 Italy 35 E7
Valier, *U.S.A.* 110 B7
Valinco, G. de, *France* .. 27 G12
Valjevo, *Serbia, Yug.* ... 21 L9

Valkeakoski, *Finland* 9 F18
Valkenburg, *Neths.* 17 G7
Valkenswaard, *Neths.* ... 17 F6
Vall de Uxó, *Spain* 28 F4
Valla, *Sweden* 10 E10
Valladolid, *Mexico* 115 C7
Valladolid, *Spain* 30 D6
Valladolid □, *Spain* 30 D6
Vallata, *Italy* 35 A8
Valldemosa, *Spain* 36 B9
Valle d'Aosta □, *Italy* .. 32 C4
Valle de Arán, *Spain* ... 28 C5
Valle de Cabuérnga, *Spain* 30 B6
Valle de la Pascua,
 Venezuela 120 B4
Valle de las Palmas, *Mexico* 113 N10
Valle de Santiago, *Mexico* 114 C4
Valle de Suchil, *Mexico* 114 C4
Valle de Zaragoza, *Mexico* 114 B3
Valle del Cauca □,
 Colombia 120 C2
Valle Fértil, Sierra del,
 Argentina 126 C2
Valle Hermoso, *Mexico* 115 B5
Vallecas, *Spain* 30 E7
Valledupar, *Colombia* ... 120 A3
Vallehermoso, *Canary Is.* 36 F2
Vallejo, *U.S.A.* 112 G4
Vallenar, *Chile* 126 B1
Valleraugue, *France* 26 D7
Vallet, *France* 24 E5
Valletta, *Malta* 37 D2
Valley Center, *U.S.A.* .. 113 M9
Valley City, *U.S.A.* 108 B6
Valley Falls, *U.S.A.* 110 E3
Valley Springs, *U.S.A.* . 112 G6
Valley Wells, *U.S.A.* ... 113 K11
Valleyview, *Canada* 100 B5
Valli di Comácchio, *Italy* 33 D9
Vallimanca, Arroyo,
 Argentina 126 D4
Vallo della Lucánia, *Italy* 35 B8
Vallon-Pont-d'Arc, *France* 27 D8
Vallorbe, *Switz.* 22 C2
Valls, *Spain* 28 D6
Vallsta, *Sweden* 10 C10
Valmaseda, *Spain* 28 B1
Valmiera, *Latvia* 40 C4
Valmont, *France* 24 C7
Valmontone, *Italy* 34 A5
Valmy, *France* 25 C11
Valnera, Mte., *Spain* ... 28 B1
Valognes, *France* 24 C5
Valona = Vlóra, *Albania* 39 J2
Valongo, *Portugal* 30 D2
Valpaços, *Portugal* 30 D3
Valparaíso, *Chile* 126 C1
Valparaiso, *Mexico* 114 C4
Valparaiso, *U.S.A.* 104 E2
Valparaíso □, *Chile* 126 C1
Valpovo, *Croatia* 21 K8
Valréas, *France* 27 D8
Vals, *Switz.* 23 C8
Vals →, *S. Africa* 84 D4
Vals, *Tanjung, Indonesia* 57 F9
Vals-les-Bains, *France* .. 27 D8
Valsad, *India* 60 J8
Valskog, *Sweden* 10 E9
Válta, *Greece* 39 J6
Valtellina, *Italy* 32 B6
Valuyki, *Russia* 41 F11
Valverde, *Canary Is.* ... 36 G2
Valverde del Camino,
 Spain 31 H4
Valverde del Fresno, *Spain* 30 E4
Vama, *Romania* 38 B8
Vámos, *Greece* 37 D6
Van, *Turkey* 67 D10
Van □, *Turkey* 67 D10
Van, L. = Van Gölü,
 Turkey 67 D10
Van Alstyne, *U.S.A.* ... 109 J6
Van Bruyssel, *Canada* .. 99 C5
Van Buren, *Canada* 99 C6
Van Buren, *Ark., U.S.A.* 109 H7
Van Buren, *Maine, U.S.A.* 105 B11
Van Buren, *Mo., U.S.A.* 109 G9
Van Canh, *Vietnam* 58 F7
Van Diemen, C., *N. Terr.,*
 Australia 88 B5
Van Diemen, C., *Queens.,*
 Australia 90 B2
Van Diemen G., *Australia* 88 B5
Van Gölü, *Turkey* 67 D10
Van Horn, *U.S.A.* 109 K2
Van Ninh, *Vietnam* 58 F7
Van Reenen P., *S. Africa* 85 D4
Van Rees, Pegunungan,
 Indonesia 57 E9
Van Tassell, *U.S.A.* 108 D2
Van Wert, *U.S.A.* 104 E3
Van Yen, *Vietnam* 58 B5
Vanavara, *Russia* 45 C11
Vancouver, *Canada* 100 D4
Vancouver, *U.S.A.* 112 E4
Vancouver, C., *Australia* 89 G2
Vancouver I., *Canada* ... 100 D3
Vandalia, *Ill., U.S.A.* ... 108 F10
Vandalia, *Mo., U.S.A.* .. 108 F9
Vandenburg, *U.S.A.* 113 L6
Vanderbijlpark, *S. Africa* 85 D4
Vandergrift, *U.S.A.* 106 F5
Vanderhoof, *Canada* 100 C4
Vanderlin I., *Australia* .. 90 B2
Vandyke, *Australia* 90 C4

Vänern

Vänern, *Sweden* 11 F7
Vänersborg, *Sweden* 11 F6
Vang Vieng, *Laos* 58 C4
Vanga, *Kenya* 82 C4
Vangaindrano, *Madag.* 85 C8
Vanguard, *Canada* 101 D7
Vanier, *Canada* 98 C4
Vankarem, *Russia* 45 C18
Vankleek Hill, *Canada* 98 C5
Vanna, *Norway* 8 A15
Vännäs, *Sweden* 8 E15
Vannes, *France* 24 E4
Vanoise, Massif de la, *France* 27 C10
Vanrhynsdorp, *S. Africa* 84 E2
Vanrook, *Australia* 90 B3
Vansbro, *Sweden* 9 F13
Vansittart B., *Australia* 88 B4
Vanthli, *India* 62 J4
Vanua Levu, *Fiji* 87 C8
Vanua Mbalavu, *Fiji* 87 C9
Vanuatu ■, *Pac. Oc.* 92 J8
Vanwyksvlei, *S. Africa* 84 E3
Vanzylsrus, *S. Africa* 84 D3
Vapnyarka, *Ukraine* 42 B3
Var □, *France* 27 E10
Var →, *France* 27 E11
Vara, *Sweden* 11 F6
Varades, *France* 24 E5
Varaita →, *Italy* 32 D4
Varallo, *Italy* 32 C5
Varanasi, *India* 63 G10
Varangerfjorden, *Norway* 8 A20
Varaždin, *Croatia* 33 B13
Varazze, *Italy* 32 D5
Varberg, *Sweden* 11 G6
Vardar = Axiós →, *Greece* 39 J5
Varde, *Denmark* 11 J2
Varde Å →, *Denmark* 11 J2
Varel, *Germany* 18 B4
Varella, Mui, *Vietnam* 58 F7
Varena, *Lithuania* 40 D4
Varennes-sur-Allier, *France* 26 B7
Vareš, *Bos.-H., Yug.* 21 L8
Varese, *Italy* 32 C5
Varese Lígure, *Italy* 32 D6
Vårgårda, *Sweden* 11 F6
Vargem Bonita, *Brazil* 123 F2
Vargem Grande, *Brazil* 122 B3
Varginha, *Brazil* 127 A6
Vargön, *Sweden* 11 F6
Variadero, *U.S.A.* 109 H2
Varillas, *Chile* 126 A1
Väring, *Sweden* 11 F8
Värmlands län □, *Sweden* 9 G12
Varna, *Bulgaria* 38 F10
Värnamo, *Sweden* 9 H13
Värö, *Sweden* 11 G6
Vars, *Canada* 107 A9
Varsseveld, *Neths.* 16 E8
Varto, *Turkey* 67 D9
Varvarin, *Serbia, Yug.* 21 M11
Varzaneh, *Iran* 65 C7
Várzea Alegre, *Brazil* 122 C4
Várzea da Palma, *Brazil* 123 E3
Várzea Grande, *Brazil* 125 D6
Varzi, *Italy* 32 D6
Varzo, *Italy* 32 B5
Varzy, *France* 25 E10
Vasa, *Finland* 8 E16
Vasa Barris →, *Brazil* 122 D4
Vascâo →, *Portugal* 31 H3
Vaşcău, *Romania* 38 C5
Vascongadas = País Vasco □, *Spain* 28 C2
Vasht = Khāsh, *Iran* 60 E2
Vasilevichi, *Belorussia* 40 E6
Vasilikón, *Greece* 39 L6
Vasilkov, *Ukraine* 40 F7
Vaslui, *Romania* 38 C10
Vassar, *Canada* 101 D9
Vassar, *U.S.A.* 104 D4
Västerås, *Sweden* 10 E10
Västerbottens län □, *Sweden* 8 D14
Västernorrlands län □, *Sweden* 10 A11
Västervik, *Sweden* 9 H14
Västmanlands län □, *Sweden* 9 G14
Vasto, *Italy* 33 F11
Vasvár, *Hungary* 21 H6
Vatan, *France* 25 E8
Vathí, *Greece* 39 M10
Váthia, *Greece* 39 N5
Vatican City ■, *Italy* 33 G9
Vaticano, C., *Italy* 35 D8
Vatili, *Cyprus* 37 D12
Vatnajökull, *Iceland* 8 D5
Vatnås, *Norway* 10 E3
Vatneyri, *Iceland* 8 D2
Vatoa, *Fiji* 87 D9
Vatólakkos, *Greece* 37 D5
Vatoloha, *Madag.* 85 B8
Vatomandry, *Madag.* 85 B8
Vatra-Dornei, *Romania* 38 B8
Vättern, *Sweden* 11 F8
Vättis, *Switz.* 23 C8
Vaucluse □, *France* 27 E9
Vaucouleurs, *France* 25 D12
Vaud □, *Switz.* 22 C2
Vaughn, *Mont., U.S.A.* 110 C8
Vaughn, *N. Mex., U.S.A.* 111 J11
Vaulruz, *Switz.* 22 C3
Vaupés = Uaupés →, *Brazil* 120 C4
Vaupes □, *Colombia* 120 C3
Vauvert, *France* 27 E8
Vauxhall, *Canada* 100 C6
Vava'u, *Tonga* 87 D11
Vavoua, *Ivory C.* 78 D3
Vaxholm, *Sweden* 10 E12
Växjö, *Sweden* 9 H13
Vaygach, Ostrov, *Russia* 44 C6
Váyia, Ákra, *Greece* 37 C10
Veadeiros, *Brazil* 123 D2
Vechta, *Germany* 18 C4
Vechte →, *Neths.* 16 C8
Vecsés, *Hungary* 21 H9
Veddige, *Sweden* 11 G6
Vedea →, *Romania* 38 F8
Vedia, *Argentina* 126 C3
Vedra, I. del, *Spain* 36 C7
Vedrin, *Belgium* 17 G5
Veendam, *Neths.* 16 B9
Veenendaal, *Neths.* 16 D7
Veerle, *Belgium* 17 F5
Vefsna →, *Norway* 8 D12
Vega, *Norway* 8 D11
Vega, *U.S.A.* 109 H3
Vegadeo, *Spain* 30 B3
Vegafjorden, *Norway* 8 D12
Veghel, *Neths.* 17 E7
Vegorritis, Límni, *Greece* 39 J4
Vegreville, *Canada* 100 C6
Vegusdal, *Norway* 11 F2
Veii, *Italy* 33 F9
Vejen, *Denmark* 11 J3
Vejer de la Frontera, *Spain* 31 J5
Vejle, *Denmark* 11 J3
Vejle Fjord, *Denmark* 11 J3
Vela Luka, *Croatia* 33 F13
Velas, C., *Costa Rica* 116 D2
Velasco, Sierra de, *Argentina* 126 B2
Velay, Mts. du, *France* 26 D7
Velddrif, *S. Africa* 84 E2
Veldegem, *Belgium* 17 F2
Velden, *Neths.* 17 F8
Veldhoven, *Neths.* 17 F6
Velebit Planina, *Croatia* 33 D12
Velebitski Kanal, *Croatia* 33 D11
Veleka →, *Bulgaria* 38 G10
Velenje, *Slovenia* 33 B12
Velestínon, *Greece* 39 K5
Vélez, *Colombia* 120 B3
Vélez Blanco, *Spain* 29 H2
Vélez Málaga, *Spain* 31 J6
Vélez Rubio, *Spain* 29 H2
Velhas →, *Brazil* 123 E3
Velika, *Croatia* 21 K7
Velika Gorica, *Croatia* 33 C13
Velika Kapela, *Croatia* 33 C12
Velika Kladuša, *Bos.-H., Yug.* 33 C12
Velika Morava →, *Serbia, Yug.* 21 L11
Velikaya →, *Russia* 40 C6
Velikaya Kema, *Russia* 48 B8
Velikaya Lepetikha, *Ukraine* 42 C5
Velike Lašče, *Slovenia* 33 C11
Velikiye Luki, *Russia* 40 C7
Velikonda Range, *India* 60 M11
Velikoye, Oz., *Russia* 41 D12
Velingrad, *Bulgaria* 39 G6
Velino, Mte., *Italy* 33 F10
Velizh, *Russia* 40 D7
Velke Meziřici, *Czech.* 20 F6
Velletri, *Italy* 34 A5
Vellinge, *Sweden* 11 J7
Vellore, *India* 60 N11
Velp, *Neths.* 16 D7
Velsen-Noord, *Neths.* 16 D5
Velten, *Germany* 18 C9
Veluwe Meer, *Neths.* 16 D7
Velva, *U.S.A.* 108 A4
Veme, *Norway* 10 D4
Ven, *Sweden* 11 J6
Venaco, *France* 27 F13
Venado Tuerto, *Argentina* 126 C3
Venafro, *Italy* 35 A7
Venarey-les-Laumes, *France* 25 E11
Venaria, *Italy* 32 C4
Venčane, *Serbia, Yug.* 21 L10
Vence, *France* 27 E11
Venda □, *S. Africa* 85 C5
Vendas Novas, *Portugal* 31 G2
Vendée □, *France* 24 F5
Vendée →, *France* 24 F5
Vendéen, Bocage, *France* 26 B2
Vendeuvre-sur-Barse, *France* 25 D11
Vendôme, *France* 24 E8
Vendrell, *Spain* 28 D6
Vendsyssel, *Denmark* 11 G4
Véneta, L., *Italy* 33 C9
Véneto □, *Italy* 33 C8
Venev, *Russia* 41 D11
Venézia, *Italy* 33 C9
Venézia, G. di, *Italy* 33 C10
Venezuela ■, *S. Amer.* 120 B4
Venezuela, G. de, *Venezuela* 120 A3
Vengurla, *India* 60 M8
Venice = Venézia, *Italy* 33 C9
Venkatapuram, *India* 61 K12
Venlo, *Neths.* 17 F8
Venraij, *Neths.* 17 E7
Venta de Cardeña, *Spain* 31 G6
Venta de San Rafael, *Spain* 30 E6
Ventana, Punta de la, *Mexico* 114 C3
Ventana, Sa. de la, *Argentina* 126 D3
Ventersburg, *S. Africa* 84 D4
Venterstad, *S. Africa* 84 E4
Ventimíglia, *Italy* 32 E4
Ventnor, *U.K.* 13 G6
Ventotene, *Italy* 34 B6
Ventoux, Mt., *France* 27 D9
Ventspils, *Latvia* 9 H16
Ventuarí →, *Venezuela* 120 C4
Ventucopa, *U.S.A.* 113 L7
Ventura, *U.S.A.* 113 L7
Venus B., *Australia* 91 F4
Vera, *Argentina* 126 B3
Vera, *Spain* 29 H3
Veracruz, *Mexico* 115 D5
Veracruz □, *Mexico* 115 D5
Veraval, *India* 62 J4
Verbánia, *Italy* 32 C5
Verbicaro, *Italy* 35 C8
Verbier, *Switz.* 22 D4
Vercelli, *Italy* 32 C5
Verchovchevo, *Ukraine* 42 B6
Verdalsøra, *Norway* 8 E11
Verde →, *Argentina* 128 B3
Verde →, *Goiás, Brazil* 123 E1
Verde →, *Goiás, Brazil* 123 E1
Verde →, *Mato Grosso, Brazil* 125 E7
Verde →, *Mato Grosso, Brazil* 125 C6
Verde →, *Chihuahua, Mexico* 114 B3
Verde →, *Oaxaca, Mexico* 115 D5
Verde →, *Veracruz, Mexico* 114 C4
Verde →, *Paraguay* 126 A4
Verde, Cay, *Bahamas* 116 B4
Verde Grande →, *Brazil* 123 E3
Verde Island Pass, *Phil.* 55 E4
Verde Pequeno →, *Brazil* 123 D3
Verden, *Germany* 18 C5
Verdi, *U.S.A.* 112 F7
Verdigre, *U.S.A.* 108 D5
Verdon →, *France* 27 E9
Verdun, *France* 25 C12
Verdun-sur-le-Doubs, *France* 25 F12
Vereeniging, *S. Africa* 85 D4
Vérendrye, Parc Prov. de la, *Canada* 98 C4
Verga, C., *Guinea* 78 C2
Vergato, *Italy* 32 D8
Vergemont, *Australia* 90 C3
Vergemont Cr. →, *Australia* 90 C3
Vergennes, *U.S.A.* 107 B11
Vergt, *France* 26 C4
Verín, *Spain* 30 D3
Veriña, *Spain* 30 B5
Verkhnedvinsk, *Belorussia* 40 D5
Verkhnevilyuysk, *Russia* 45 C13
Verkhneye Kalinino, *Russia* 45 D11
Verkhniy Baskunchak, *Russia* 43 B12
Verkhovye, *Russia* 41 E10
Verkhoyansk, *Russia* 45 C14
Verkhoyansk Ra. = Verkhoyanskiy Khrebet, *Russia* 45 C13
Verkhoyanskiy Khrebet, *Russia* 45 C13
Verlo, *Canada* 101 C7
Verma, *Norway* 10 B2
Vermenton, *France* 25 E10
Vermilion, *Canada* 101 C6
Vermilion →, *Alta., Canada* 101 C6
Vermilion →, *Qué., Canada* 98 C5
Vermilion, B., *U.S.A.* 109 L9
Vermilion Bay, *Canada* 101 D10
Vermilion Chutes, *Canada* 100 B6
Vermilion L., *U.S.A.* 108 B8
Vermillion, *U.S.A.* 108 D6
Vermont □, *U.S.A.* 107 C12
Vernal, *U.S.A.* 110 F9
Vernalis, *U.S.A.* 112 H5
Vernayaz, *Switz.* 22 D4
Verner, *Canada* 98 C3
Verneuil-sur-Avre, *France* 24 D7
Verneukpan, *S. Africa* 84 D3
Vernier, *Switz.* 22 D2
Vernon, *Canada* 100 C5
Vernon, *France* 24 C8
Vernon, *U.S.A.* 109 H5
Vernonia, *U.S.A.* 112 E3
Vero Beach, *U.S.A.* 105 M5
Véroia, *Greece* 39 J5
Verolanuova, *Italy* 32 C7
Véroli, *Italy* 34 A6
Verona, *Italy* 32 C8
Veropol, *Russia* 45 C17
Versailles, *France* 25 D9
Versalles, *Bolivia* 125 C5
Versoix, *Switz.* 22 D2
Vert, C., *Senegal* 78 C1
Vertou, *France* 24 E5
Vertus, *France* 25 D11
Verulam, *S. Africa* 85 D5
Verviers, *Belgium* 17 G7
Vervins, *France* 25 C10
Verzej, *Slovenia* 33 B13
Vescavoto, *France* 27 F13
Vesdre →, *Belgium* 17 G7
Veselí nad Lužnicí, *Czech.* 20 F4
Veselovskoye Vdkhr., *Russia* 43 C9
Veshenskaya, *Russia* 43 B9
Vesle →, *France* 25 C10
Vesoul, *France* 25 E13
Vessigebro, *Sweden* 11 H6
Vest-Agder fylke □, *Norway* 9 G9
Vesterålen, *Norway* 8 B13
Vestersche Veld, *Neths.* 16 C8
Vestfjorden, *Norway* 8 C13
Vestfold fylke □, *Norway* 9 G11
Vestmannaeyjar, *Iceland* 8 E3
Vestmarka, *Norway* 10 E5
Vestone, *Italy* 32 C7
Vestsjællands Amtskommune □, *Denmark* 11 J5
Vestspitsbergen, *Svalbard* 4 B8
Vestvågøy, *Norway* 8 B12
Vesuvio, *Italy* 35 B7
Vesuvius, Mt. = Vesuvio, *Italy* 35 B7
Vesyegonsk, *Russia* 41 B10
Veszprém, *Hungary* 21 H7
Vésztö, *Hungary* 21 J11
Vetlanda, *Sweden* 9 H13
Vetluga, *Russia* 41 C14
Vetlugu →, *Russia* 41 C15
Vetluzhskiy, *Russia* 41 C14
Vetovo, *Bulgaria* 38 F9
Vetralia, *Italy* 33 F9
Vettore, Monte, *Italy* 33 F10
Veurne, *Belgium* 17 F1
Vevey, *Switz.* 22 D3
Veynes, *France* 27 D9
Veys, *Iran* 65 D6
Vézelise, *France* 25 D13
Vézère →, *France* 26 D4
Vezirköprü, *Turkey* 66 C6
Vi Thanh, *Vietnam* 59 H5
Viacha, *Bolivia* 124 D4
Viadana, *Italy* 32 D7
Viamão, *Brazil* 127 C5
Viana, *Brazil* 122 B3
Viana, *Spain* 28 C2
Viana del Bollo, *Spain* 30 C3
Viana do Alentejo, *Portugal* 31 G3
Viana do Castelo, *Portugal* 30 D2
Vianden, *Belgium* 17 J8
Vianen, *Neths.* 16 E6
Vianna do Castelo □, *Portugal* 30 D2
Vianópolis, *Brazil* 123 E2
Viar →, *Spain* 31 H5
Viaréggio, *Italy* 32 E7
Viaur →, *France* 26 D5
Vibank, *Canada* 101 C8
Vibo Valéntia, *Italy* 35 D9
Viborg, *Denmark* 11 H3
Vibraye, *France* 24 D7
Vic-en-Bigorre, *France* 26 E4
Vic-Fézensac, *France* 26 E4
Vic-sur-Cère, *France* 26 D6
Vicenza, *Italy* 33 C8
Vich, *Spain* 28 D7
Vichada □, *Colombia* 120 C4
Vichada →, *Colombia* 120 C4
Vichuga, *Russia* 41 C12
Vichy, *France* 26 B7
Vicksburg, *Ariz., U.S.A.* 113 M13
Vicksburg, *Mich., U.S.A.* 104 D3
Vicksburg, *Miss., U.S.A.* 109 J9
Vico, L. di, *Italy* 33 F9
Vico del Gargaro, *Italy* 35 A8
Viçosa, *Brazil* 122 C4
Viçosa do Ceará, *Brazil* 122 B3
Vicosoprano, *Switz.* 23 D9
Victor, *India* 62 J4
Victor, *Colo., U.S.A.* 108 F2
Victor, *N.Y., U.S.A.* 106 D7
Victor Harbor, *Australia* 91 F2
Victoria, *Argentina* 126 C3
Victoria, *Canada* 100 D4
Victoria, *Chile* 128 A2
Victoria, *Guinea* 78 C2
Victoria, *Malaysia* 56 C5
Victoria, *Malta* 37 C1
Victoria, *Phil.* 55 D4
Victoria, *Kans., U.S.A.* 108 F5
Victoria, *Tex., U.S.A.* 109 L6
Victoria □, *Australia* 91 F3
Victoria →, *Australia* 88 C4
Victoria, Grand L., *Canada* 98 C4
Victoria, L., *Africa* 82 C3
Victoria, L., *Australia* 91 E3
Victoria Beach, *Canada* 101 C9
Victoria de Durango, *Mexico* 114 C4
Victoria de las Tunas, *Cuba* 116 B4
Victoria Falls, *Zimbabwe* 83 F2
Victoria Harbour, *Canada* 98 D4
Victoria I., *Canada* 96 A8
Victoria Ld., *Antarctica* 5 D11
Victoria Nile →, *Uganda* 82 B3
Victoria Res., *Canada* 99 C8
Victoria River Downs, *Australia* 88 C5
Victoria Taungdeik, *Burma* 61 J18
Victoria West, *S. Africa* 84 E3
Victorias, *Phil.* 55 F5
Victoriaville, *Canada* 99 C5
Victorica, *Argentina* 126 D2
Victorville, *U.S.A.* 113 L9
Vicuña, *Chile* 126 C1
Vicuña Mackenna, *Argentina* 126 C3
Vidal, *U.S.A.* 113 L12
Vidal Junction, *U.S.A.* 113 L12
Vidalia, *U.S.A.* 105 J4
Vidauban, *France* 27 E10
Vídho, *Greece* 37 A3
Vidigueira, *Portugal* 31 G3
Vidin, *Bulgaria* 38 F5
Vidio, C., *Spain* 30 B4
Vidisha, *India* 62 H7
Vidzy, *Belorussia* 40 D5
Viechtach, *Germany* 19 F8
Viedma, *Argentina* 128 B4
Viedma, L., *Argentina* 128 C2
Vieira, *Portugal* 30 D2
Viella, *Spain* 28 C5
Vielsalm, *Belgium* 17 H7
Vienenburg, *Germany* 18 D6
Vieng Pou Kha, *Laos* 58 B3
Vienna = Wien, *Austria* 21 G6
Vienna, *U.S.A.* 109 G10
Vienne, *France* 27 C8
Vienne □, *France* 26 B4
Vienne →, *France* 24 E7
Vientiane, *Laos* 58 D4
Vientos, Paso de los, *Caribbean* 117 C5
Vierlingsbeek, *Neths.* 17 E8
Viersen, *Germany* 18 D2
Vierwaldstättersee, *Switz.* 23 C7
Vierzon, *France* 25 E9
Vieste, *Italy* 35 A9
Vietnam ■, *Asia* 58 C5
Vieux-Boucau-les-Bains, *France* 26 E2
Vif, *France* 27 C9
Vigan, *Phil.* 55 C4
Vigévano, *Italy* 32 C5
Vigia, *Brazil* 122 B2
Vigía Chico, *Mexico* 115 D7
Víglas, Ákra, *Greece* 37 D9
Vignemale, Pic du, *France* 26 F3
Vigneulles-lès-Hattonchâtel, *France* 25 D12
Vignola, *Italy* 32 D8
Vigo, *Spain* 30 C2
Vigo, Ría de, *Spain* 30 C2
Vihiers, *France* 24 E6
Vijayawada, *India* 61 L12
Vijfhuizen, *Neths.* 16 D5
Viken, *Sweden* 11 F8
Viking, *Canada* 100 C6
Vikna, *Norway* 8 D11
Viksjö, *Sweden* 10 B11
Vikulovo, *Russia* 44 D8
Vila da Maganja, *Mozam.* 83 F4
Vila de João Belo = Xai-Xai, *Mozam.* 85 D5
Vila de Rei, *Portugal* 31 F2
Vila do Bispo, *Portugal* 31 H2
Vila do Chibuto, *Mozam.* 85 C5
Vila do Conde, *Portugal* 30 D2
Vila Franca de Xira, *Portugal* 31 G2
Vila Gamito, *Mozam.* 83 E3
Vila Gomes da Costa, *Mozam.* 85 C5
Vila Machado, *Mozam.* 83 F3
Vila Mouzinho, *Mozam.* 83 E3
Vila Nova de Foscôa, *Portugal* 30 D3
Vila Nova de Ourém, *Portugal* 31 F2
Vila Novo de Gaia, *Portugal* 30 D2
Vila Pouca de Aguiar, *Portugal* 30 D3
Vila Real, *Portugal* 30 D3
Vila Real de Santo António, *Portugal* 31 H3
Vila Vasco da Gama, *Mozam.* 83 E3
Vila Velha, *Amapá, Brazil* 121 C7
Vila Velha, *Espírito Santo, Brazil* 123 F3
Vila Viçosa, *Portugal* 31 G3
Vilaboa, *Spain* 30 C2
Vilaine →, *France* 24 E4
Vilanandro, Tanjona, *Madag.* 85 B7
Vilanculos, *Mozam.* 85 C6
Vilar Formosa, *Portugal* 30 E4
Vilareal □, *Portugal* 30 D3
Vilaseca-Salou, *Spain* 28 D6
Vilcabamba, Cordillera, *Peru* 124 C3
Vilcanchos, *Peru* 124 C3
Vileyka, *Belorussia* 40 D5
Vilhelmina, *Sweden* 8 D14
Vilhena, *Brazil* 125 C5
Viliga, *Russia* 45 C16
Viliya →, *Lithuania* 40 D3
Viljandi, *Estonia* 40 B4
Vilkovo, *Ukraine* 42 D3
Villa Abecia, *Bolivia* 126 A2
Villa Ahumada, *Mexico* 114 A3
Villa Ana, *Argentina* 126 B4

Villa Ángela, *Argentina* .. 126 B3
Villa Bella, *Bolivia* 125 C4
Villa Bens = Tarfaya, *Morocco* 74 C2
Villa Cañás, *Argentina* ... 126 C3
Villa Carlos, *Spain* 36 B11
Villa Cisneros = Dakhla, *Mauritania* 74 D1
Villa Colón, *Argentina* ... 126 C2
Villa Constitución, *Argentina* 126 C3
Villa de Cura, *Venezuela* . 120 A4
Villa de María, *Argentina* . 126 B3
Villa del Rosario, *Venezuela* 120 A3
Villa Dolores, *Argentina* .. 126 C2
Villa Frontera, *Mexico* ... 114 B4
Villa Guillermina, *Argentina* 126 B4
Villa Hayes, *Paraguay* 126 B4
Villa Iris, *Argentina* 126 D3
Villa Juárez, *Mexico* 114 B4
Villa María, *Argentina* 126 C3
Villa Mazán, *Argentina* ... 126 B2
Villa Minozzo, *Italy* 32 D7
Villa Montes, *Bolivia* 126 A3
Villa Ocampo, *Argentina* . 126 B4
Villa Ocampo, *Mexico* 114 B3
Villa Ojo de Agua, *Argentina* 126 B3
Villa San Giovanni, *Italy* . 35 D8
Villa San José, *Argentina* . 126 C4
Villa San Martín, *Argentina* 126 B3
Villa Santina, *Italy* 33 B9
Villa Unión, *Mexico* 114 C3
Villablino, *Spain* 30 C4
Villacañas, *Spain* 28 F1
Villacarriedo, *Spain* 28 B1
Villacarrillo, *Spain* 29 G1
Villacastín, *Spain* 30 E6
Villach, *Austria* 21 J3
Villaciado, *Italy* 34 C1
Villada, *Spain* 30 C6
Villadiego, *Spain* 30 C6
Villadóssola, *Italy* 32 B5
Villafeliche, *Spain* 28 D3
Villafranca, *Spain* 28 C3
Villafranca de los Barros, *Spain* 31 G4
Villafranca de los Caballeros, *Spain* 29 F1
Villafranca de los Caballeros, *Spain* 36 B10
Villafranca del Bierzo, *Spain* 30 C4
Villafranca del Cid, *Spain* . 28 E4
Villafranca del Panadés, *Spain* 28 D6
Villafranca di Verona, *Italy* 32 C7
Villagarcía de Arosa, *Spain* 30 C2
Villagrán, *Mexico* 115 C5
Villaguay, *Argentina* 126 C4
Villaharta, *Spain* 31 G6
Villahermosa, *Mexico* 115 D6
Villahermosa, *Spain* 29 G2
Villaines-la-Juhel, *France* . 24 D6
Villajoyosa, *Spain* 29 G4
Villalba, *Spain* 30 B3
Villalba de Guardo, *Spain* 30 C6
Villalcampo, Pantano de, *Spain* 30 D4
Villalón de Campos, *Spain* 30 C5
Villalpando, *Spain* 30 D5
Villaluenga, *Spain* 30 E7
Villamanán, *Spain* 30 C5
Villamartín, *Spain* 31 J5
Villamayor, *Spain* 28 F2
Villamblard, *France* 26 C4
Villanova Monteleone, *Italy* 34 B1
Villanueva, *Colombia* 120 A3
Villanueva, *U.S.A.* 111 J11
Villanueva de Castellón, *Spain* 29 F4
Villanueva de Córdoba, *Spain* 31 G6
Villanueva de la Fuente, *Spain* 29 G2
Villanueva de la Serena, *Spain* 31 G5
Villanueva de la Sierra, *Spain* 30 E4
Villanueva de los Castillejos, *Spain* 31 H3
Villanueva del Arzobispo, *Spain* 29 G1
Villanueva del Duque, *Spain* 31 G5
Villanueva del Fresno, *Spain* 31 G3
Villanueva y Geltrú, *Spain* 28 D6
Villaodrid, *Spain* 30 B3
Villaputzu, *Italy* 34 C2
Villar del Arzobispo, *Spain* 28 F4
Villar del Rey, *Spain* 31 F4
Villarcayo, *Spain* 28 C1
Villard-Bonnot, *France* ... 27 C9
Villard-de-Lans, *France* .. 27 C9
Villarino de los Aires, *Spain* 30 D4
Villarosa, *Italy* 35 E7
Villarramiel, *Spain* 30 C6
Villarreal, *Spain* 28 F4
Villarrica, *Chile* 128 A2
Villarrica, *Paraguay* 126 B4
Villarrobledo, *Spain* 29 F2
Villarroya de la Sierra, *Spain* 28 D3
Villarrubia de los Ojos, *Spain* 29 F1
Villars-les-Dombes, *France* 27 B9
Villarta de San Juan, *Spain* 29 F1
Villasayas, *Spain* 28 D2
Villaseca de los Gamitos, *Spain* 30 D4
Villastar, *Spain* 28 E3
Villatobas, *Spain* 28 F1
Villavicencio, *Argentina* .. 126 C2
Villavicencio, *Colombia* .. 120 C3
Villaviciosa, *Spain* 30 B5
Villazón, *Bolivia* 126 A2
Ville-Marie, *Canada* 98 C4
Ville Platte, *U.S.A.* 109 K8
Villedieu-les-Poêlles, *France* 24 D5
Villefort, *France* 26 D7
Villefranche-de-Lauragais, *France* 26 E5
Villefranche-de-Rouergue, *France* 26 D6
Villefranche-du-Périgord, *France* 26 D5
Villefranche-sur-Cher, *France* 25 E8
Villefranche-sur-Saône, *France* 27 C8
Villegrande, *Bolivia* 125 D5
Villel, *Spain* 28 E3
Villemaur-sur-Vanne, *France* 25 D10
Villemur-sur-Tarn, *France* 26 E5
Villena, *Spain* 29 G4
Villenauxe-la-Grande, *France* 25 D10
Villenave-d'Ornon, *France* 26 D3
Villeneuve, *Italy* 32 C4
Villeneuve, *Switz.* 22 D3
Villeneuve-l'Archevêque, *France* 25 D10
Villeneuve-lès-Avignon, *France* 27 E8
Villeneuve-St.-Georges, *France* 25 D9
Villeneuve-sur-Allier, *France* 26 B7
Villeneuve-sur-Lot, *France* 26 D4
Villeréal, *France* 26 D4
Villers-Bocage, *France* ... 24 C6
Villers-Bretonneux, *France* 25 C9
Villers-Cotterêts, *France* .. 25 C10
Villers-le-Bouillet, *Belgium* 17 G6
Villers-le-Gambon, *Belgium* 17 H5
Villers-sur-Mer, *France* ... 24 C6
Villersexel, *France* 25 E13
Villerupt, *France* 25 C12
Villerville, *France* 24 C7
Villiers, *S. Africa* 85 D4
Villingen, *Germany* 19 G4
Villisca, *U.S.A.* 108 E7
Vilna, *Canada* 100 C6
Vilnius, *Lithuania* 40 D4
Vils →, *Germany* 19 G9
Vilsbiburg, *Germany* 19 G8
Vilshofen, *Germany* 19 G9
Vilskutskogo, Proliv, *Russia* 45 B11
Vilusi, *Montenegro, Yug.* . 21 N8
Vilvoorde, *Belgium* 17 G4
Vilyuy →, *Russia* 45 C13
Vilyuysk, *Russia* 45 C13
Vimercate, *Italy* 32 C6
Vimiosa, *Portugal* 30 D4
Vimoutiers, *France* 24 D7
Vimperk, *Czech.* 20 F3
Viña del Mar, *Chile* 126 C1
Vinaroz, *Spain* 28 E5
Vincennes, *U.S.A.* 104 F2
Vincent, *U.S.A.* 113 L8
Vinces, *Ecuador* 120 D2
Vinchina, *Argentina* 126 B2
Vindel älven →, *Sweden* . 8 E15
Vindeln, *Sweden* 8 D15
Vinderup, *Denmark* 11 H2
Vindhya Ra., *India* 62 H7
Vineland, *U.S.A.* 104 F8
Vinga, *Romania* 38 D4
Vingnes, *Norway* 10 C4
Vinh, *Vietnam* 58 C5
Vinh Linh, *Vietnam* 58 D6
Vinh Long, *Vietnam* 59 G5
Vinh Yen, *Vietnam* 58 B5
Vinhais, *Portugal* 30 D3
Vinica, *Croatia* 33 B13
Vinica, *Slovenia* 33 C12
Vinita, *U.S.A.* 109 G7
Vinkeveen, *Neths.* 16 D5
Vinkovci, *Croatia* 21 K8
Vinnitsa, *Ukraine* 42 B3
Vinstra, *Norway* 10 C3
Vinton, *Calif., U.S.A.* ... 112 F6
Vinton, *Iowa, U.S.A.* 108 D8
Vinton, *La., U.S.A.* 109 K8
Vinţu de Jos, *Romania* ... 38 D6
Viöl, *Germany* 18 A5
Vipava, *Slovenia* 33 C10
Vipiteno, *Italy* 33 B8
Viqueque, *Indonesia* 57 F7
Vir, *Croatia* 33 D12
Virac, *Phil.* 55 E6
Virachei, *Cambodia* 58 F6
Virago Sd., *Canada* 100 C2
Viramgam, *India* 62 H5
Viranşehir, *Turkey* 67 E8
Virden, *Canada* 101 D8
Vire, *France* 24 D6
Vire →, *France* 24 C5
Virgem da Lapa, *Brazil* .. 123 E3
Vírgenes, C., *Argentina* .. 128 D3
Virgin →, *Canada* 101 B7
Virgin →, *U.S.A.* 111 H6
Virgin Gorda, *Virgin Is.* .. 117 C7
Virgin Is., *W. Indies* 117 C7
Virginia, *S. Africa* 84 D4
Virginia, *U.S.A.* 108 B8
Virginia □, *U.S.A.* 104 G7
Virginia Beach, *U.S.A.* ... 104 G8
Virginia City, *Mont., U.S.A.* 110 D8
Virginia City, *Nev., U.S.A.* 112 F7
Virginia Falls, *Canada* 100 A3
Virginiatown, *Canada* 98 C4
Virieu-le-Grand, *France* .. 27 C9
Viroqua, *U.S.A.* 108 D9
Virovitica, *Croatia* 21 K7
Virton, *Belgium* 17 J7
Virtsu, *Estonia* 40 B3
Virú, *Peru* 124 B2
Virudunagar, *India* 60 Q10
Vis, *Croatia* 33 E13
Vis Kanal, *Croatia* 33 E13
Visalia, *U.S.A.* 111 H4
Visayan Sea, *Phil.* 55 F5
Visby, *Sweden* 9 H15
Viscount Melville Sd., *Canada* 4 B2
Visé, *Belgium* 17 G7
Višegrad, *Bos.-H., Yug.* .. 21 M9
Viseu, *Brazil* 122 B2
Viseu, *Portugal* 30 E3
Viseu □, *Portugal* 30 E3
Vişeu de Sus, *Romania* ... 38 B7
Vishakhapatnam, *India* ... 61 L13
Viskafors, *Sweden* 11 G6
Visnagar, *India* 62 H5
Višnja Gora, *Slovenia* 33 C11
Viso, Mte., *Italy* 32 D4
Viso del Marqués, *Spain* .. 29 G1
Visoko, *Bos.-H., Yug.* 21 M8
Visokoi I., *Antarctica* 5 B1
Visp, *Switz.* 22 D5
Vispa →, *Switz.* 22 D5
Visselhövede, *Germany* ... 18 C5
Vissoie, *Switz.* 22 D5
Vista, *U.S.A.* 113 M9
Vistula = Wisła →, *Poland* 20 A8
Vit →, *Bulgaria* 38 F7
Vitanje, *Slovenia* 33 B12
Vitebsk, *Belorussia* 40 D7
Viterbo, *Italy* 33 F9
Viti Levu, *Fiji* 87 C7
Vitigudino, *Spain* 30 D4
Vitim, *Russia* 45 D12
Vitim →, *Russia* 45 D12
Vitória, *Brazil* 123 F3
Vitoria, *Spain* 28 C2
Vitória da Conquista, *Brazil* 123 D3
Vitória de São Antão, *Brazil* 122 C4
Vitorino Friere, *Brazil* ... 122 B2
Vitré, *France* 24 D5
Vitry-le-François, *France* . 25 D11
Vitsi, Óros, *Greece* 39 J4
Vitteaux, *France* 25 E11
Vittel, *France* 25 D12
Vittória, *Italy* 35 F7
Vittório Véneto, *Italy* 33 C9
Vivario, *France* 27 F13
Vivegnis, *Belgium* 17 G7
Viver, *Spain* 28 F4
Vivero, *Spain* 30 B3
Viviers, *France* 27 D8
Vivonne, *France* 26 B4
Vizcaíno, Desierto de, *Mexico* 114 B2
Vizcaíno, Sierra, *Mexico* .. 114 B2
Vizcaya □, *Spain* 28 B2
Vize, *Turkey* 66 C2
Vizianagaram, *India* 61 K13
Vizille, *France* 27 C9
Viziñada, *Croatia* 33 C10
Viziru, *Romania* 38 E10
Vizovice, *Czech.* 20 F7
Vizzini, *Italy* 35 E7
Vlaardingen, *Neths.* 16 E4
Vlădeasa, *Romania* 38 C5
Vladikavkaz, *Russia* 43 E11
Vladimir, *Russia* 41 C12
Vladimir Volynskiy, *Ukraine* 40 F4
Vladimirovac, *Serbia, Yug.* 21 K10
Vladimirovka, *Russia* 43 B12
Vladimirovka, *Russia* 43 D11
Vladislavovka, *Ukraine* ... 42 D6
Vladivostok, *Russia* 45 E14
Vlamertinge, *Belgium* 17 G1
Vlasenica, *Bos.-H., Yug.* . 21 L8
Vlasinsko Jezero, *Serbia, Yug.* 21 N12
Vleuten, *Neths.* 16 D6
Vlieland, *Neths.* 16 B5
Vliestroom, *Neths.* 16 B6
Vlijmen, *Neths.* 17 E6
Vlissingen, *Neths.* 17 F3
Vlóra, *Albania* 39 J2
Vlorës, Gjiri i, *Albania* ... 39 J2
Vltava →, *Czech.* 20 E4
Vo Dat, *Vietnam* 59 G6
Vobarno, *Italy* 32 C7
Voćin, *Croatia* 21 K7
Vodice, *Croatia* 33 E12
Vodnjan, *Croatia* 33 D10
Vogelkop = Doberai, Jazirah, *Indonesia* 57 E8
Vogelsberg, *Germany* 18 E5
Voghera, *Italy* 32 D6
Vohibinany, *Madag.* 85 B8
Vohimarina, *Madag.* 85 A9
Vohimena, Tanjon' i, *Madag.* 85 D8
Vohipeno, *Madag.* 85 C8
Voi, *Kenya* 82 C4
Void, *France* 25 D12
Voiron, *France* 27 C9
Voisey B., *Canada* 99 A7
Voitsberg, *Austria* 21 H5
Voiviïs Límni, *Greece* 39 K5
Vojens, *Denmark* 11 J3
Vojmsjön, *Sweden* 8 D14
Vojnić, *Croatia* 33 C12
Vojnik, *Italy* 33 B12
Vokhma, *Russia* 41 B15
Vokhma →, *Russia* 41 C15
Vokhtoga, *Russia* 41 B12
Volborg, *U.S.A.* 108 C2
Volcano Is. = Kazan-Rettō, *Pac. Oc.* 92 E6
Volchansk, *Ukraine* 42 A7
Volchayevka, *Russia* 45 E14
Volchya →, *Ukraine* 42 C7
Volda, *Norway* 8 E9
Volendam, *Neths.* 16 D6
Volga, *Russia* 41 C11
Volga →, *Russia* 43 C13
Volga Hts. = Privolzhskaya Vozvyshennost, *Russia* . 41 F15
Volgodonsk, *Russia* 43 C10
Volgograd, *Russia* 43 B11
Volgogradskoye Vdkhr., *Russia* 41 F14
Volgorechensk, *Russia* ... 41 C12
Volkach, *Germany* 19 F6
Volkerak, *Neths.* 17 E4
Volkhov, *Russia* 40 B8
Volkhov →, *Russia* 40 A8
Völklingen, *Germany* 19 F2
Volkovysk, *Belorussia* 40 E4
Volksrust, *S. Africa* 85 D4
Vollenhove, *Neths.* 16 C7
Vol'n'ansk, *Ukraine* 42 C6
Volnovakha, *Ukraine* 42 C7
Volochanka, *Russia* 45 B10
Volodarsk, *Russia* 41 C13
Vologda, *Russia* 41 B11
Volokolamsk, *Russia* 41 C9
Volokonovka, *Russia* 41 F10
Vólos, *Greece* 39 K5
Volosovo, *Russia* 40 B6
Volozhin, *Belorussia* 40 D5
Volsk, *Russia* 41 E15
Volta →, *Ghana* 70 F4
Volta, L., *Ghana* 79 D5
Volta Blanche = White Volta →, *Ghana* 79 D4
Volta Redonda, *Brazil* ... 123 F3
Voltaire, C., *Australia* ... 88 B4
Volterra, *Italy* 32 E7
Voltri, *Italy* 32 D5
Volturara Áppula, *Italy* ... 35 A8
Volturno →, *Italy* 34 A6
Volubilis, *Morocco* 74 B3
Volvo, *Australia* 91 E3
Volzhsk, *Russia* 41 D16
Volzhskiy, *Russia* 43 B11
Vondrozo, *Madag.* 85 C8
Voorburg, *Neths.* 16 D4
Voorne Putten, *Neths.* 16 E4
Voorst, *Neths.* 16 D8
Voorthuizen, *Neths.* 16 D7
Vopnafjörður, *Iceland* 8 D6
Vóras Óros, *Greece* 39 J4
Vorbasse, *Denmark* 11 J3
Vorden, *Neths.* 16 D8
Vorderrhein →, *Switz.* ... 23 C8
Vordingborg, *Denmark* ... 11 K5
Voreppe, *France* 27 C9
Voríai Sporádhes, *Greece* . 39 K6
Vórios Evvoïkos Kólpos, *Greece* 39 L6
Vorkuta, *Russia* 44 C7
Vorma →, *Norway* 10 D5
Vorona →, *Russia* 41 F13
Voronezh, *Russia* 41 F11
Voronezh, *Ukraine* 40 F8
Voronezh →, *Russia* 41 F10
Vorontsovo-Aleksandrovskoye = Zelenokumsk, *Russia* ... 43 D10
Voroshilovgrad = Lugansk, *Ukraine* 43 B8
Voroshilovsk = Kommunarsk, *Ukraine* . 43 B8
Vorovskoye, *Russia* 45 D16
Vorselaar, *Belgium* 17 F5
Vorskla →, *Ukraine* 42 B6
Vōru, *Estonia* 40 C5
Vorupør, *Denmark* 11 H2
Vosges, *France* 25 D14
Vosges □, *France* 25 D13
Voskopoja, *Albania* 39 J3
Voskresensk, *Russia* 41 D11
Voskresenskoye, *Russia* .. 41 C14
Voss, *Norway* 9 F9
Vosselaar, *Belgium* 17 F5
Vostok I., *Kiribati* 93 J12
Vouga →, *Portugal* 30 E2
Vouillé, *France* 24 F7
Vouvray, *France* 24 E7
Vouvry, *Switz.* 22 D3
Voúxa, Ákra, *Greece* 37 D5
Vouzela, *Portugal* 30 E2
Vouziers, *France* 25 C11
Voves, *France* 25 D8
Voxna, *Sweden* 10 C9
Vozhgaly, *Russia* 41 B17
Voznesenka, *Russia* 45 D10
Voznesensk, *Ukraine* 42 C4
Voznesenye, *Russia* 44 C4
Vrådal, *Norway* 10 E2
Vrakhnéïka, *Greece* 39 L4
Vrancei, Munţii, *Romania* 38 D9
Vrangelya, Ostrov, *Russia* 45 B19
Vranica, *Bos.-H., Yug.* ... 21 M7
Vranje, *Serbia, Yug.* 21 N11
Vransko, *Slovenia* 33 B11
Vratsa, *Bulgaria* 38 F6
Vrbas, *Serbia, Yug.* 21 K9
Vrbas →, *Bos.-H., Yug.* . 21 K7
Vrbnik, *Croatia* 33 C11
Vrbovec, *Croatia* 33 C13
Vrbovsko, *Croatia* 33 C12
Vrchlabí, *Czech.* 20 E5
Vrede, *S. Africa* 85 D4
Vredefort, *S. Africa* 84 D4
Vredenburg, *S. Africa* 84 E2
Vredendal, *S. Africa* 84 E2
Vreeswijk, *Neths.* 16 D6
Vrena, *Sweden* 11 F10
Vrgorac, *Croatia* 21 M7
Vrhnika, *Slovenia* 33 C11
Vrïdi, *Ivory C.* 78 D4
Vries, *Neths.* 16 B9
Vriezenveen, *Neths.* 16 D9
Vrindavan, *India* 62 F7
Vríses, *Greece* 37 D6
Vrnograč, *Bos.-H., Yug.* . 33 C12
Vroomshoop, *Neths.* 16 D9
Vršac, *Serbia, Yug.* 21 K11
Vrsacki Kanal, *Serbia, Yug.* 21 K11
Vryburg, *S. Africa* 84 D3
Vryheid, *S. Africa* 85 D5
Vsetín, *Czech.* 20 F8
Vu Liet, *Vietnam* 58 C5
Vucha →, *Bulgaria* 39 G7
Vught, *Neths.* 17 E6
Vukovar, *Croatia* 21 K8
Vulcan, *Canada* 100 C6
Vulcan, *U.S.A.* 104 C2
Vulcano, *Italy* 35 D7
Vŭlchedruma, *Bulgaria* ... 38 F6
Vulci, *Italy* 33 F8
Vulkaneshty, *Moldavia* ... 42 D3
Vunduzi →, *Mozam.* 83 F3
Vung Tau, *Vietnam* 59 G6
Vŭrbitsa, *Bulgaria* 38 G9
Vyasniki, *Russia* 41 C13
Vyatka, *Russia* 41 B16
Vyatka →, *Russia* 41 C17
Vyatskiye Polyany, *Russia* 41 C17
Vyazemskiy, *Russia* 45 E14
Vyazma, *Russia* 40 D9
Vyborg, *Russia* 44 C3
Vychegda →, *Russia* 44 C5
Vychodné Beskydy, *Europe* 20 F11
Vyksa, *Russia* 41 D13
Vyrnwy, L., *U.K.* 12 E4
Vyshniy Volochek, *Russia* 40 C9
Vyškov, *Czech.* 20 F6
Vysoké Mýto, *Czech.* 20 F6
Vysokovsk, *Russia* 41 C10
Vysotsk, *Ukraine* 40 F5

W

W.A.C. Bennett Dam, *Canada* 100 B4
Wa, *Ghana* 78 C4
Waal →, *Neths.* 16 E6
Waalwijk, *Neths.* 17 E6
Waarschoot, *Belgium* 17 F3
Waasmunster, *Belgium* 17 F4
Wabakimi L., *Canada* 98 B2
Wabana, *Canada* 99 C9
Wabasca, *Canada* 100 B6
Wabash, *U.S.A.* 104 E3
Wabash →, *U.S.A.* 104 G1
Wabeno, *U.S.A.* 104 C1
Wabi →, *Ethiopia* 77 F5
Wabigoon L., *Canada* 101 D10
Wabowden, *Canada* 101 C9
Wąbrzeźno, *Poland* 20 B8
Wabu Hu, *China* 53 A11
Wabuk Pt., *Canada* 98 A2
Wabush, *Canada* 99 B6
Wabuska, *U.S.A.* 110 G4
Wachtebeke, *Belgium* 17 F3
Wächtersbach, *Germany* ... 19 E5
Waco, *U.S.A.* 109 K6
Waconichi, L., *Canada* ... 98 B5
Wad Ban Naqa, *Sudan* ... 77 D3
Wad Banda, *Sudan* 77 E2
Wad el Haddad, *Sudan* ... 77 E3
Wad en Nau, *Sudan* 77 E3
Wad Hamid, *Sudan* 77 D3

Wâd Medanî

Wâd Medanî, *Sudan* 77 E3
Wad Thana, *Pakistan* 62 F2
Wadayama, *Japan* 49 G7
Waddeneilanden, *Neths.* 16 B6
Waddenzee, *Neths.* 16 B6
Wadderin Hill, *Australia* 89 F2
Waddington, *U.S.A.* 107 B9
Waddington, Mt., *Canada* 100 C3
Waddinxveen, *Neths.* 16 D5
Waddy Pt., *Australia* 91 C5
Wadena, *Canada* 101 C8
Wadena, *U.S.A.* 108 B7
Wädenswil, *Switz.* 23 B7
Wadesboro, *U.S.A.* 105 H5
Wadhams, *Canada* 100 C3
Wādī as Sīr, *Jordan* 69 D4
Wadi Gemâl, *Egypt* 76 C4
Wadi Halfa, *Sudan* 76 C3
Wadian, *China* 53 A9
Wadowice, *Poland* 20 F9
Wadsworth, *U.S.A.* 110 G4
Waegwan, *S. Korea* 51 G15
Wafrah, *Si. Arabia* 64 D5
Wagenberg, *Neths.* 17 E5
Wageningen, *Neths.* 16 E7
Wageningen, *Surinam* 121 B6
Wager B., *Canada* 97 B11
Wager Bay, *Canada* 97 B10
Wagga Wagga, *Australia* 91 F4
Waghete, *Indonesia* 57 E9
Wagin, *Australia* 89 F2
Wagon Mound, *U.S.A.* 109 G2
Wagoner, *U.S.A.* 109 G7
Wagrowiec, *Poland* 20 C7
Wah, *Pakistan* 62 C5
Wahai, *Indonesia* 57 E7
Wahiawa, *U.S.A.* 102 H15
Wâḥid, *Egypt* 69 E1
Wahnai, *Afghan.* 62 C1
Wahoo, *U.S.A.* 108 E6
Wahpeton, *U.S.A.* 108 B6
Wai, Koh, *Cambodia* 59 H4
Waiau →, *N.Z.* 87 K4
Waibeem, *Indonesia* 57 E8
Waiblingen, *Germany* 19 G5
Waidhofen, *Niederösterreich, Austria* 20 G5
Waidhofen, *Niederösterreich, Austria* 21 H4
Waigeo, *Indonesia* 57 E8
Waihi, *N.Z.* 87 G5
Waihou →, *N.Z.* 87 G5
Waika, *Zaïre* 82 C2
Waikabubak, *Indonesia* 57 F5
Waikari, *N.Z.* 87 K4
Waikato →, *N.Z.* 87 G5
Waikerie, *Australia* 91 E2
Waikokopu, *N.Z.* 87 H6
Waikouaiti, *N.Z.* 87 L3
Waimakariri →, *N.Z.* 87 K4
Waimate, *N.Z.* 87 L3
Waimes, *Belgium* 17 H8
Wainganga →, *India* 60 K11
Waingapu, *Indonesia* 57 F6
Waini →, *Guyana* 121 B6
Wainwright, *Canada* 101 C6
Wainwright, *U.S.A.* 96 A3
Waiouru, *N.Z.* 87 H5
Waipara, *N.Z.* 87 K4
Waipawa, *N.Z.* 87 H6
Waipiro, *N.Z.* 87 H7
Waipu, *N.Z.* 87 F5
Waipukurau, *N.Z.* 87 J6
Wairakei, *N.Z.* 87 H6
Wairarapa, L., *N.Z.* 87 J5
Wairoa, *N.Z.* 87 H6
Waitaki →, *N.Z.* 87 L3
Waitara, *N.Z.* 87 H5
Waitsburg, *U.S.A.* 110 C5
Waiuku, *N.Z.* 87 G5
Wajima, *Japan* 49 F8
Wajir, *Kenya* 82 B5
Wajir □, *Kenya* 82 B5
Wakasa, *Japan* 49 G7
Wakasa-Wan, *Japan* 49 G7
Wakatipu, L., *N.Z.* 87 L2
Wakaw, *Canada* 101 C7
Wakayama, *Japan* 49 G7
Wakayama-ken □, *Japan* 49 H7
Wake Forest, *U.S.A.* 105 H6
Wake I., *Pac. Oc.* 92 F8
Wakefield, *N.Z.* 87 J4
Wakefield, *U.K.* 12 D6
Wakefield, *Mass., U.S.A.* 107 D13
Wakefield, *Mich., U.S.A.* 108 B10
Wakema, *Burma* 61 L19
Wakkanai, *Japan* 48 B10
Wakkerstroom, *S. Africa* 85 D5
Wakool, *Australia* 91 F3
Wakool →, *Australia* 91 F3
Wakre, *Indonesia* 57 E8
Wakuach L., *Canada* 99 A6
Walamba, *Zambia* 83 E2
Wałbrzych, *Poland* 20 E6
Walbury Hill, *U.K.* 13 F6
Walcha, *Australia* 91 E5
Walcheren, *Neths.* 17 E3
Walcott, *U.S.A.* 110 F10
Wałcz, *Poland* 20 B6
Wald, *Switz.* 23 B7
Waldbröl, *Germany* 18 E3
Waldburg Ra., *Australia* 88 D2
Waldeck, *Germany* 18 D5
Walden, *Colo., U.S.A.* 110 F10
Walden, *N.Y., U.S.A.* 107 E10
Waldenburg, *Switz.* 22 B5
Waldport, *U.S.A.* 110 D1
Waldron, *U.S.A.* 109 H7
Waldshut, *Germany* 19 H4
Walembele, *Ghana* 78 C4
Walensee, *Switz.* 23 B8
Walenstadt, *Switz.* 23 B8
Wales □, *U.K.* 13 E4
Walewale, *Ghana* 79 C4
Walgett, *Australia* 91 E4
Walgreen Coast, *Antarctica* 5 D15
Walhalla, *Australia* 91 F4
Walhalla, *U.S.A.* 101 D9
Walker, *U.S.A.* 108 B7
Walker L., *Man., Canada* 101 C9
Walker L., *Qué., Canada* 99 B6
Walker L., *U.S.A.* 110 G4
Walkerston, *Australia* 90 C4
Walkerton, *Canada* 106 B3
Wall, *U.S.A.* 108 C3
Walla Walla, *U.S.A.* 110 C4
Wallabadah, *Australia* 90 B3
Wallace, *Idaho, U.S.A.* 110 C6
Wallace, *N.C., U.S.A.* 105 H7
Wallace, *Nebr., U.S.A.* 108 E4
Wallaceburg, *Canada* 98 D3
Wallachia = Valahia, *Romania* 38 E8
Wallal, *Australia* 91 D4
Wallal Downs, *Australia* 88 C3
Wallambin, L., *Australia* 89 F2
Wallaroo, *Australia* 91 E2
Wallasey, *U.K.* 12 D4
Walldürn, *Germany* 19 F5
Wallerawang, *Australia* 91 E5
Wallhallow, *Australia* 90 B2
Wallingford, *U.S.A.* 107 E12
Wallis & Futuna, Is., *Pac. Oc.* 92 J10
Wallisellen, *Switz.* 23 B7
Wallowa, *U.S.A.* 110 D5
Wallowa Mts., *U.S.A.* 110 D5
Wallsend, *Australia* 91 E5
Wallsend, *U.K.* 12 C6
Wallula, *U.S.A.* 110 C4
Wallumbilla, *Australia* 91 D4
Walmsley, L., *Canada* 101 A7
Walney, I. of, *U.K.* 12 C4
Walnut Creek, *U.S.A.* 112 H4
Walnut Ridge, *U.S.A.* 109 G9
Walsall, *U.K.* 13 E6
Walsenburg, *U.S.A.* 109 G2
Walsh, *U.S.A.* 109 G3
Walsh →, *Australia* 90 B3
Walsh P.O., *Australia* 90 B3
Walshoutem, *Belgium* 17 G6
Walsrode, *Germany* 18 C5
Walterboro, *U.S.A.* 105 J5
Walters, *U.S.A.* 109 H5
Waltershausen, *Germany* 18 E6
Waltham, *U.S.A.* 107 D13
Waltham Station, *Canada* 98 C4
Waltman, *U.S.A.* 110 E10
Walton, *U.S.A.* 107 D9
Walvisbaai, *S. Africa* 84 C1
Wamba, *Kenya* 82 B4
Wamba, *Zaïre* 82 B2
Wamego, *U.S.A.* 108 F6
Wamena, *Indonesia* 57 E9
Wamsasi, *Indonesia* 57 E7
Wan Xian, *China* 50 E8
Wana, *Pakistan* 62 C3
Wanaaring, *Australia* 91 D3
Wanaka, *N.Z.* 87 L2
Wanaka L., *N.Z.* 87 L2
Wan'an, *China* 53 D10
Wanapiri, *Indonesia* 57 E9
Wanapitei L., *Canada* 98 C3
Wanbi, *Australia* 91 E3
Wandaik, *Guyana* 121 C6
Wandarrie, *Australia* 89 E2
Wanderer, *Zimbabwe* 83 F3
Wandoan, *Australia* 91 D4
Wandre, *Belgium* 17 G7
Wanfercée-Baulet, *Belgium* 17 H5
Wanfu, *China* 51 D12
Wang →, *Thailand* 58 D2
Wang Kai, *Sudan* 77 F2
Wang Noi, *Thailand* 58 E3
Wang Saphung, *Thailand* 58 D3
Wang Thong, *Thailand* 58 D3
Wanga, *Zaïre* 82 B2
Wangal, *Indonesia* 57 F8
Wanganella, *Australia* 91 F3
Wanganui, *N.Z.* 87 H5
Wangaratta, *Australia* 91 F4
Wangary, *Australia* 91 E2
Wangcang, *China* 52 A6
Wangdu, *China* 50 E8
Wangerooge, *Germany* 18 B3
Wangi, *Kenya* 82 C5
Wangiwangi, *Indonesia* 57 F6
Wangjiang, *China* 53 B11
Wangmo, *China* 52 E6
Wangqing, *China* 51 C15
Wankaner, *India* 62 H4
Wanless, *Canada* 101 C8
Wannian, *China* 53 C11
Wanon Niwat, *Thailand* 58 D4
Wanquan, *China* 50 D8
Wanrong, *China* 50 G6
Wanshan, *China* 52 D7
Wanshengchang, *China* 52 C6
Wanssum, *Neths.* 17 E8
Wanxian, *China* 52 B7
Wanyuan, *China* 52 A7
Wanzai, *China* 53 C10
Wanze, *Belgium* 17 G6
Wapakoneta, *U.S.A.* 104 E3
Wapato, *U.S.A.* 110 C3
Wapawekka L., *Canada* 101 C8
Wapikopa L., *Canada* 98 B2
Wappingers Falls, *U.S.A.* 107 E11
Wapsipinicon →, *U.S.A.* 108 E9
Warangal, *India* 60 L11
Waratah, *Australia* 90 G4
Waratah B., *Australia* 91 F4
Warburg, *Germany* 18 D5
Warburton, *Vic., Australia* 91 F4
Warburton, *W. Austral., Australia* 89 E4
Warburton Ra., *Australia* 89 E4
Ward, *N.Z.* 87 J5
Ward →, *Australia* 91 D4
Ward Cove, *U.S.A.* 100 B2
Ward Mt., *U.S.A.* 112 H8
Warden, *S. Africa* 85 D4
Wardha, *India* 60 J11
Wardha →, *India* 60 K11
Wardlow, *Canada* 100 C6
Ware, *Canada* 100 B3
Ware, *U.S.A.* 107 D12
Waregem, *Belgium* 17 G2
Wareham, *U.S.A.* 107 E14
Waremme, *Belgium* 17 G6
Waren, *Germany* 18 B8
Warendorf, *Germany* 18 D3
Warialda, *Australia* 91 D5
Wariap, *Indonesia* 57 E8
Warin Chamrap, *Thailand* 58 E5
Warkopi, *Indonesia* 57 E8
Warley, *U.K.* 13 E6
Warm Springs, *U.S.A.* 111 G5
Warman, *Canada* 101 C7
Warmbad, *Namibia* 84 D2
Warmbad, *S. Africa* 85 C4
Warmenhuizen, *Neths.* 16 C5
Warmeriville, *France* 25 C11
Warmond, *Neths.* 16 D5
Warnambool Downs, *Australia* 90 C3
Warnemünde, *Germany* 18 A8
Warner, *Canada* 100 D6
Warner Mts., *U.S.A.* 110 F3
Warner Robins, *U.S.A.* 105 J4
Warnes, *Bolivia* 125 D5
Warneton, *Belgium* 17 G1
Warnow →, *Germany* 18 A8
Warnsveld, *Neths.* 16 D8
Waroona, *Australia* 89 F2
Warracknabeal, *Australia* 91 F3
Warragul, *Australia* 91 F4
Warrawagine, *Australia* 88 D3
Warrego →, *Australia* 91 E4
Warrego Ra., *Australia* 90 C4
Warren, *Australia* 91 E4
Warren, *Ark., U.S.A.* 109 J8
Warren, *Mich., U.S.A.* 104 D4
Warren, *Minn., U.S.A.* 108 A6
Warren, *Ohio, U.S.A.* 106 E4
Warren, *Pa., U.S.A.* 106 E5
Warrenpoint, *U.K.* 15 B5
Warrensburg, *U.S.A.* 108 F8
Warrenton, *S. Africa* 84 D3
Warrenton, *U.S.A.* 112 D3
Warrenville, *Australia* 91 D4
Warri, *Nigeria* 79 D6
Warrina, *Australia* 91 D2
Warrington, *U.K.* 12 D5
Warrington, *U.S.A.* 105 K2
Warrnambool, *Australia* 91 F3
Warroad, *U.S.A.* 108 A7
Warsa, *Indonesia* 57 E9
Warsaw = Warszawa, *Poland* 20 C11
Warsaw, *Ind., U.S.A.* 104 E3
Warsaw, *N.Y., U.S.A.* 106 D6
Warsaw, *Ohio, U.S.A.* 106 F2
Warstein, *Germany* 18 D4
Warszawa, *Poland* 20 C11
Warta →, *Poland* 20 C4
Warthe = Warta →, *Poland* 20 C4
Waru, *Indonesia* 57 E8
Warwick, *Australia* 91 D5
Warwick, *U.K.* 13 E6
Warwick, *U.S.A.* 107 E13
Warwickshire □, *U.K.* 13 E6
Wasaga Beach, *Canada* 106 B4
Wasatch Ra., *U.S.A.* 110 F8
Wasbank, *S. Africa* 85 D5
Wasco, *Calif., U.S.A.* 113 K7
Wasco, *Oreg., U.S.A.* 110 D3
Waseca, *U.S.A.* 108 C8
Wasekamio L., *Canada* 101 B7
Wash, The, *U.K.* 12 E8
Washago, *Canada* 106 B5
Washburn, *N. Dak., U.S.A.* 108 B4
Washburn, *Wis., U.S.A.* 108 B9
Washim, *India* 60 J10
Washington, *D.C., U.S.A.* 104 F7
Washington, *Ga., U.S.A.* 105 J4
Washington, *Ind., U.S.A.* 104 F2
Washington, *Iowa, U.S.A.* 108 E9
Washington, *Mo., U.S.A.* 108 F9
Washington, *N.C., U.S.A.* 105 H7
Washington, *N.J., U.S.A.* 107 F10
Washington, *Pa., U.S.A.* 106 F4
Washington, *Utah, U.S.A.* 111 H7
Washington □, *U.S.A.* 110 C3
Washington, Mt., *U.S.A.* 107 B13
Washington I., *U.S.A.* 104 C2
Washougal, *U.S.A.* 112 E4
Wasian, *Indonesia* 57 E8
Wasior, *Indonesia* 57 E8
Waskaiowaka, L., *Canada* 101 B9
Waskesiu Lake, *Canada* 101 C7
Wasmes, *Belgium* 17 H3
Waspik, *Neths.* 17 E5
Wassen, *Switz.* 23 C7
Wassenaar, *Neths.* 16 D4
Wasserburg, *Germany* 19 G8
Wasserkuppe, *Germany* 18 E5
Wassy, *France* 25 D11
Waswanipi, *Canada* 98 C4
Waswanipi, L., *Canada* 98 C4
Watangpone, *Indonesia* 57 E6
Water Park Pt., *Australia* 90 C5
Water Valley, *U.S.A.* 109 H10
Waterberge, *S. Africa* 85 C4
Waterbury, *Conn., U.S.A.* 107 E11
Waterbury, *Vt., U.S.A.* 107 B12
Waterbury L., *Canada* 101 B8
Waterdown, *Canada* 106 C5
Waterford, *Canada* 106 D4
Waterford, *Ireland* 15 D4
Waterford, *U.S.A.* 112 H6
Waterford □, *Ireland* 15 D4
Waterford Harbour, *Ireland* 15 D5
Waterhen L., *Man., Canada* 101 C9
Waterhen L., *Sask., Canada* 101 C7
Wateringen, *Neths.* 16 D4
Waterloo, *Belgium* 17 G4
Waterloo, *Ont., Canada* 98 D3
Waterloo, *Qué., Canada* 107 A12
Waterloo, *S. Leone* 78 D2
Waterloo, *Ill., U.S.A.* 108 F9
Waterloo, *Iowa, U.S.A.* 108 D8
Waterloo, *N.Y., U.S.A.* 106 D8
Watermeal-Boitsford, *Belgium* 17 G4
Watersmeet, *U.S.A.* 108 B10
Waterton-Glacier Int. Peace Park, *U.S.A.* 110 B7
Watertown, *Conn., U.S.A.* 107 E11
Watertown, *N.Y., U.S.A.* 107 C9
Watertown, *S. Dak., U.S.A.* 108 C6
Watertown, *Wis., U.S.A.* 108 D10
Waterval-Boven, *S. Africa* 85 D5
Waterville, *Canada* 107 A13
Waterville, *Maine, U.S.A.* 99 D6
Waterville, *N.Y., U.S.A.* 107 D9
Waterville, *Pa., U.S.A.* 106 E7
Waterville, *Wash., U.S.A.* 110 C3
Watervliet, *Belgium* 17 F3
Watervliet, *U.S.A.* 107 D11
Wates, *Indonesia* 57 G14
Watford, *Canada* 106 D3
Watford, *U.K.* 13 F7
Watford City, *U.S.A.* 108 B3
Wathaman →, *Canada* 101 B8
Watheroo, *Australia* 89 F2
Wating, *China* 50 G4
Watkins Glen, *U.S.A.* 106 D8
Watling I. = San Salvador, *Bahamas* 117 B5
Watonga, *U.S.A.* 109 H5
Watou, *Belgium* 17 G1
Watrous, *Canada* 101 C7
Watrous, *U.S.A.* 109 H2
Watsa, *Zaïre* 82 B2
Watseka, *U.S.A.* 104 E2
Watson, *Australia* 89 F5
Watson, *Canada* 101 C8
Watson Lake, *Canada* 100 A3
Watsonville, *U.S.A.* 111 H3
Wattenwil, *Switz.* 22 C5
Wattiwarriganna Cr. →, *Australia* 91 D2
Wattwil, *Switz.* 23 B8
Watuata = Batuata, *Indonesia* 57 F6
Watubela, Kepulauan, *Indonesia* 57 E8
Watubela Is. = Watubela, Kepulauan, *Indonesia* 57 E8
Waubach, *Neths.* 17 G8
Waubamik, *Canada* 106 A4
Waubay, *U.S.A.* 108 C6
Waubra, *Australia* 91 F3
Wauchope, *Australia* 91 E5
Wauchula, *U.S.A.* 105 M5
Waugh, *Canada* 101 D9
Waukarlycarly, L., *Australia* 88 D3
Waukegan, *U.S.A.* 104 D2
Waukesha, *U.S.A.* 104 D1
Waukon, *U.S.A.* 108 D9
Wauneta, *U.S.A.* 108 E4
Waupaca, *U.S.A.* 108 C10
Waupun, *U.S.A.* 108 D10
Waurika, *U.S.A.* 109 H6
Wausau, *U.S.A.* 108 C10
Wautoma, *U.S.A.* 108 C10
Wauwatosa, *U.S.A.* 104 D2
Wave Hill, *Australia* 88 C5
Waveney →, *U.K.* 13 E9
Waverley, *N.Z.* 87 H5
Waverly, *Iowa, U.S.A.* 108 D8
Waverly, *N.Y., U.S.A.* 107 D8
Wavre, *Belgium* 17 G5
Wavreille, *Belgium* 17 H6
Wâw, *Sudan* 77 F2
Wāw al Kabīr, *Libya* 73 C8
Wawa, *Canada* 98 C3
Wawa, *Nigeria* 79 D5
Wawa, *Sudan* 76 C3
Wawanesa, *Canada* 101 D9
Wawona, *U.S.A.* 112 H7
Waxahachie, *U.S.A.* 109 J6
Way, L., *Australia* 89 E3
Wayabula Rau, *Indonesia* 57 D7
Wayatinah, *Australia* 90 G4
Waycross, *U.S.A.* 105 K4
Wayi, *Sudan* 77 F3
Wayne, *Nebr., U.S.A.* 108 D6
Wayne, *W. Va., U.S.A.* 104 F4
Waynesboro, *Ga., U.S.A.* 105 J4
Waynesboro, *Miss., U.S.A.* 105 K1
Waynesboro, *Pa., U.S.A.* 104 F7
Waynesboro, *Va., U.S.A.* 104 F6
Waynesburg, *U.S.A.* 104 F5
Waynesville, *U.S.A.* 105 H4
Waynoka, *U.S.A.* 109 G5
Wāzin, *Libya* 75 B7
Wazirabad, *Pakistan* 62 C6
We, *Indonesia* 56 C1
Weald, The, *U.K.* 13 F8
Wear →, *U.K.* 12 C6
Weatherford, *Okla., U.S.A.* 109 H5
Weatherford, *Tex., U.S.A.* 109 J6
Weaverville, *U.S.A.* 110 F2
Webb City, *U.S.A.* 109 G7
Webo = Nyaake, *Liberia* 78 E3
Webster, *Mass., U.S.A.* 107 D13
Webster, *N.Y., U.S.A.* 106 C7
Webster, *S. Dak., U.S.A.* 108 C6
Webster, *Wis., U.S.A.* 108 C8
Webster City, *U.S.A.* 108 D8
Webster Green, *U.S.A.* 108 F9
Webster Springs, *U.S.A.* 104 F5
Weda, *Indonesia* 57 D7
Weda, Teluk, *Indonesia* 57 D7
Weddell I., *Falk. Is.* 128 D4
Weddell Sea, *Antarctica* 5 D1
Wedderburn, *Australia* 91 F3
Wedgeport, *Canada* 99 D6
Wedza, *Zimbabwe* 83 F3
Wee Waa, *Australia* 91 E4
Weed, *U.S.A.* 110 F2
Weed Heights, *U.S.A.* 112 G7
Weedsport, *U.S.A.* 107 C8
Weedville, *U.S.A.* 106 E6
Weemelah, *Australia* 91 D4
Weenen, *S. Africa* 85 D5
Weener, *Germany* 18 B3
Weert, *Neths.* 17 F7
Weesp, *Neths.* 16 D6
Weggis, *Switz.* 23 B6
Wegliniec, *Poland* 20 D5
Węgorzewo, *Poland* 20 A11
Węgrów, *Poland* 20 C12
Wehl, *Neths.* 16 E8
Wei He →, *Hebei, China* 50 F8
Wei He →, *Shaanxi, China* 50 G6
Weichang, *China* 51 D9
Weichuan, *China* 50 G7
Weida, *Germany* 18 E8
Weiden, *Germany* 19 F8
Weifang, *China* 51 F10
Weihai, *China* 51 F12
Weilburg, *Germany* 18 E4
Weilheim, *Germany* 19 H7
Weimar, *Germany* 18 E7
Weinan, *China* 50 G5
Weinfelden, *Switz.* 23 A8
Weingarten, *Germany* 19 H5
Weinheim, *Germany* 19 F4
Weining, *China* 52 D5
Weipa, *Australia* 90 A3
Weir →, *Australia* 91 D4
Weir →, *Canada* 101 B10
Weir River, *Canada* 101 B10
Weirton, *U.S.A.* 106 F4
Weisen, *Switz.* 23 C9
Weiser, *U.S.A.* 110 D5
Weishan, *Shandong, China* 51 G9
Weishan, *Yunnan, China* 52 E3
Weissenburg, *Germany* 19 F6
Weissenfels, *Germany* 18 D8
Weisshorn, *Switz.* 22 D5
Weissmies, *Switz.* 22 D6
Weisstannen, *Switz.* 23 C8
Weisswasser, *Germany* 18 D10
Weiswampach, *Belgium* 17 H8
Weixi, *China* 52 D2
Weixin, *China* 52 D5
Weiyuan, *China* 50 G3
Weiz, *Austria* 21 H5
Weizhou Dao, *China* 52 G7
Wejherowo, *Poland* 20 A8
Wekusko L., *Canada* 101 C9
Welbourn Hill, *Australia* 91 D1
Welch, *U.S.A.* 104 G5
Weldya, *Ethiopia* 77 E4
Welega □, *Ethiopia* 77 F3
Welkenraedt, *Belgium* 17 G7
Welkite, *Ethiopia* 77 F4
Welkom, *S. Africa* 84 D4
Welland, *Canada* 98 D4
Welland →, *U.K.* 12 E7
Wellen, *Belgium* 17 G6
Wellesley Is., *Australia* 90 B2
Wellin, *Belgium* 17 H6
Wellingborough, *U.K.* 13 E7

Wellington, *Australia* 91 E4
Wellington, *Canada* 98 D4
Wellington, *N.Z.* 87 J5
Wellington, *S. Africa* 84 E2
Wellington, *Shrops., U.K.* 12 E5
Wellington, *Somst., U.K.* 13 G4
Wellington, *Colo., U.S.A.* 108 E2
Wellington, *Kans., U.S.A.* 109 G6
Wellington, *Nev., U.S.A.* 112 G7
Wellington, *Ohio, U.S.A.* 106 E2
Wellington, *Tex., U.S.A.* 109 H4
Wellington, I., *Chile* 128 C2
Wellington, L., *Australia* 91 F4
Wells, *Norfolk, U.K.* 12 E8
Wells, *Somst., U.K.* 13 F5
Wells, *Maine, U.S.A.* 107 C14
Wells, *Minn., U.S.A.* 108 D8
Wells, *Nev., U.S.A.* 110 F6
Wells, L., *Australia* 89 E3
Wells Gray Prov. Park, *Canada* 100 C4
Wells River, *U.S.A.* 107 B12
Wellsboro, *U.S.A.* 106 E7
Wellsburg, *U.S.A.* 106 F4
Wellsville, *Mo., U.S.A.* 108 F9
Wellsville, *N.Y., U.S.A.* 106 D7
Wellsville, *Ohio, U.S.A.* 106 F4
Wellsville, *Utah, U.S.A.* 110 F8
Wellton, *U.S.A.* 111 K6
Welmel, Wabi →, *Ethiopia* 77 F5
Welo □, *Ethiopia* 77 E4
Wels, *Austria* 21 G4
Welshpool, *U.K.* 13 E4
Wem, *U.K.* 12 E5
Wembere →, *Tanzania* 82 C3
Wemmel, *Belgium* 17 G4
Wen Xian, *Gansu, China* 50 H3
Wen Xian, *Henan, China* 50 G7
Wenatchee, *U.S.A.* 110 C3
Wenchang, *China* 58 C8
Wencheng, *China* 53 D13
Wenchi, *Ghana* 78 D4
Wenchow = Wenzhou, *China* 53 C13
Wenchuan, *China* 52 B4
Wendell, *U.S.A.* 110 E6
Wendeng, *China* 51 F12
Wendesi, *Indonesia* 57 E8
Wendo, *Ethiopia* 77 F4
Wendon, *U.S.A.* 113 M13
Wendover, *U.S.A.* 110 F6
Wenduine, *Belgium* 17 F2
Weng'an, *China* 52 D6
Wengcheng, *China* 53 E9
Wengen, *Switz.* 22 C5
Wengyuan, *China* 53 E10
Wenjiang, *China* 52 B4
Wenling, *China* 53 C13
Wenlock →, *Australia* 90 A3
Wenshan, *China* 52 F5
Wenshang, *China* 50 G9
Wenshui, *Guizhou, China* 52 C6
Wenshui, *Shanxi, China* 50 F7
Wensu, *China* 54 B3
Wentworth, *Australia* 91 E3
Wenut, *Indonesia* 57 E8
Wenxi, *China* 50 G6
Wenzhou, *China* 53 C13
Weott, *U.S.A.* 110 F2
Wepener, *S. Africa* 84 D4
Werbomont, *Belgium* 17 H7
Werda, *Botswana* 84 D3
Werdau, *Germany* 18 E8
Werder, *Ethiopia* 68 F4
Werder, *Germany* 18 C8
Werdohl, *Germany* 18 D3
Wereilu, *Ethiopia* 77 E4
Weri, *Indonesia* 57 E8
Werkendam, *Neths.* 16 E5
Werne, *Germany* 18 D3
Werneck, *Germany* 19 F6
Wernigerode, *Germany* 18 D6
Werra →, *Germany* 18 D5
Werribee, *Australia* 91 F3
Werrimull, *Australia* 91 E3
Werris Creek, *Australia* 91 E5
Wersar, *Indonesia* 57 E8
Wertach →, *Germany* 19 G6
Wertheim, *Germany* 19 F5
Wertingen, *Germany* 19 G6
Wervershoof, *Neths.* 16 C6
Wervik, *Belgium* 17 G2
Wesel, *Germany* 18 D2
Weser →, *Germany* 18 B4
Wesiri, *Indonesia* 57 F7
Wesley Vale, *U.S.A.* 111 J10
Wesleyville, *Canada* 99 C9
Wesleyville, *U.S.A.* 106 D4
Wessel, C., *Australia* 90 A2
Wessel Is., *Australia* 90 A2
Wesselburen, *Germany* 18 A4
Wessem, *Neths.* 17 F7
Wessington, *U.S.A.* 108 C5
Wessington Springs, *U.S.A.* 108 C5
West, *U.S.A.* 109 K6
West B., *U.S.A.* 109 L10
West Baines →, *Australia* 88 C4
West Bend, *U.S.A.* 104 D1
West Bengal □, *India* 63 H12
West Branch, *U.S.A.* 104 C3
West Bromwich, *U.K.* 13 E5
West Cape Howe, *Australia* 89 G2
West Chazy, *U.S.A.* 107 B11
West Chester, *U.S.A.* 104 F8
West Columbia, *U.S.A.* 109 L7
West Covina, *U.S.A.* 113 L9
West Des Moines, *U.S.A.* 108 E8
West End, *Bahamas* 116 A4
West Falkland, *Falk. Is.* 128 D4
West Frankfort, *U.S.A.* 108 G10
West Glamorgan □, *U.K.* 13 F4
West Hartford, *U.S.A.* 107 E12
West Haven, *U.S.A.* 107 E12
West Helena, *U.S.A.* 109 H9
West Ice Shelf, *Antarctica* 5 C7
West Indies, *Cent. Amer.* 117 C7
West Lorne, *Canada* 106 D3
West Lunga →, *Zambia* 83 E1
West Memphis, *U.S.A.* 109 H9
West Midlands □, *U.K.* 13 E6
West Mifflin, *U.S.A.* 106 F5
West Monroe, *U.S.A.* 109 J8
West Newton, *U.S.A.* 106 F5
West Nicholson, *Zimbabwe* 83 G2
West Palm Beach, *U.S.A.* 105 M5
West Plains, *U.S.A.* 109 G9
West Pt., *Australia* 91 F2
West Point, *Ga., U.S.A.* 105 J3
West Point, *Miss., U.S.A.* 105 J1
West Point, *Nebr., U.S.A.* 108 E6
West Point, *Va., U.S.A.* 104 G7
West Pokot □, *Kenya* 82 B4
West Road →, *Canada* 100 C4
West Rutland, *U.S.A.* 107 C11
West Schelde = Westerschelde →, *Neths.* 17 F2
West Seneca, *U.S.A.* 106 D6
West Siberian Plain, *Russia* 46 C11
West Sussex □, *U.K.* 13 G7
West-Terschelling, *Neths.* 16 B6
West Virginia □, *U.S.A.* 104 F5
West-Vlaanderen □, *Belgium* 17 G2
West Walker →, *U.S.A.* 112 G7
West Wyalong, *Australia* 91 E4
West Yellowstone, *U.S.A.* 110 D8
West Yorkshire □, *U.K.* 12 D6
Westall Pt., *Australia* 91 E1
Westbrook, *Maine, U.S.A.* 105 D10
Westbrook, *Tex., U.S.A.* 109 J4
Westbury, *Australia* 90 G4
Westby, *U.S.A.* 108 A2
Westend, *U.S.A.* 113 K9
Westerbork, *Neths.* 16 C9
Westerland, *Germany* 18 A4
Western □, *Kenya* 82 B3
Western □, *Uganda* 82 B3
Western □, *Zambia* 83 F1
Western Australia □, *Australia* 89 E2
Western Ghats, *India* 60 N9
Western Isles □, *U.K.* 14 D1
Western Sahara ■, *Africa* 74 D2
Western Samoa ■, *Pac. Oc.* 87 A13
Westernport, *U.S.A.* 104 F6
Westerschelde →, *Neths.* 17 F2
Westerstede, *Germany* 18 B3
Westervoort, *Neths.* 16 E7
Westerwald, *Germany* 18 E4
Westfield, *Mass., U.S.A.* 107 D12
Westfield, *N.Y., U.S.A.* 106 D5
Westfield, *Pa., U.S.A.* 106 E7
Westgat, *Neths.* 17 E3
Westhope, *U.S.A.* 108 A4
Westkapelle, *Belgium* 17 F2
Westkapelle, *Neths.* 17 E2
Westland Bight, *N.Z.* 87 K3
Westlock, *Canada* 100 C6
Westmalle, *Belgium* 17 F5
Westmeath □, *Ireland* 15 C4
Westminster, *U.S.A.* 104 F7
Westmorland, *U.S.A.* 111 K6
Weston, *Malaysia* 56 C5
Weston, *Oreg., U.S.A.* 110 D4
Weston, *W. Va., U.S.A.* 104 F5
Weston I., *Canada* 98 B4
Weston-super-Mare, *U.K.* 13 F5
Westport, *Canada* 107 B8
Westport, *Ireland* 15 C2
Westport, *N.Z.* 87 J3
Westport, *Oreg., U.S.A.* 112 D3
Westport, *Wash., U.S.A.* 110 C1
Westray, *Canada* 101 C8
Westray, *U.K.* 14 B6
Westree, *Canada* 98 C3
Westville, *Calif., U.S.A.* 112 F6
Westville, *Ill., U.S.A.* 104 E2
Westville, *Okla., U.S.A.* 109 G7
Westwood, *U.S.A.* 110 F3
Wetar, *Indonesia* 57 F7
Wetaskiwin, *Canada* 100 C6
Wethersfield, *U.S.A.* 107 E12
Wetteren, *Belgium* 17 G3
Wettingen, *Switz.* 23 B6
Wetzikon, *Switz.* 23 B7
Wetzlar, *Germany* 18 E4
Wevelgem, *Belgium* 17 G2
Wewaka, *U.S.A.* 109 H6
Wexford, *Ireland* 15 D5
Wexford □, *Ireland* 15 D5
Wexford Harbour, *Ireland* 15 D5
Weyburn, *Canada* 101 D8
Weyburn L., *Canada* 100 A5
Weyer, *Austria* 21 H4
Weyib →, *Ethiopia* 77 F5
Weymouth, *Canada* 99 D6
Weymouth, *U.K.* 13 G5
Weymouth, *U.S.A.* 107 D14
Weymouth, C., *Australia* 90 A3
Wezemaal, *Belgium* 17 G5
Wezep, *Neths.* 16 D7
Whakatane, *N.Z.* 87 G6
Whale →, *Canada* 99 A6
Whale Cove, *Canada* 101 A10
Whales, B. of, *Antarctica* 5 D12
Whalsay, *U.K.* 14 A7
Whangamomona, *N.Z.* 87 H5
Whangarei, *N.Z.* 87 F5
Whangarei Harb., *N.Z.* 87 F5
Wharfe →, *U.K.* 12 D6
Wharfedale, *U.K.* 12 C5
Wharton, *N.J., U.S.A.* 107 F10
Wharton, *Pa., U.S.A.* 106 E6
Wharton, *Tex., U.S.A.* 109 L6
Wheatland, *Calif., U.S.A.* 112 F5
Wheatland, *Wyo., U.S.A.* 108 D2
Wheatley, *Canada* 106 D2
Wheaton, *U.S.A.* 108 C6
Wheelbarrow Pk., *U.S.A.* 112 H10
Wheeler, *Oreg., U.S.A.* 110 D2
Wheeler, *Tex., U.S.A.* 109 H4
Wheeler →, *Canada* 101 B7
Wheeler Pk., *N. Mex., U.S.A.* 111 H11
Wheeler Pk., *Nev., U.S.A.* 111 G6
Wheeler Ridge, *U.S.A.* 113 L8
Wheeling, *U.S.A.* 106 F4
Whernside, *U.K.* 12 C5
Whidbey I., *U.S.A.* 100 D4
Whiskey Gap, *Canada* 100 D6
Whiskey Jack L., *Canada* 101 B8
Whistleduck Cr. →, *Australia* 90 C2
Whitby, *Canada* 106 C6
Whitby, *U.K.* 12 C7
White →, *Ark., U.S.A.* 109 J9
White →, *Colo., U.S.A.* 110 F9
White →, *Ind., U.S.A.* 104 F2
White →, *S. Dak., U.S.A.* 108 D5
White →, *Wash., U.S.A.* 112 C4
White, L., *Australia* 88 D4
White B., *Canada* 99 B8
White Bear Res., *Canada* 99 C8
White Bird, *U.S.A.* 110 D5
White Butte, *U.S.A.* 108 B3
White City, *U.S.A.* 108 F6
White Cliffs, *Australia* 91 E3
White Deer, *U.S.A.* 109 H4
White Hall, *U.S.A.* 108 F9
White Haven, *U.S.A.* 107 E9
White I., *N.Z.* 87 G6
White L., *Canada* 107 A8
White L., *U.S.A.* 109 L8
White Mts., *Calif., U.S.A.* 111 H4
White Mts., *N.H., U.S.A.* 107 B13
White Nile = Nîl el Abyad →, *Sudan* 77 D3
White Nile Dam = Khazzân Jabal el Awliyâ, *Sudan* 77 D3
White Otter L., *Canada* 98 C1
White Pass, *Canada* 100 B1
White Pass, *U.S.A.* 112 D5
White Plains, *U.S.A.* 107 E11
White River, *Canada* 98 C2
White River, *S. Africa* 85 D5
White River, *U.S.A.* 108 D4
White Russia = Belorussia ■, *Europe* 40 E5
White Sea = Beloye More, *Russia* 44 C4
White Sulphur Springs, *Mont., U.S.A.* 110 C8
White Sulphur Springs, *W. Va., U.S.A.* 104 G5
White Swan, *U.S.A.* 112 D6
White Volta →, *Ghana* 79 D4
Whitecliffs, *N.Z.* 87 K3
Whitecourt, *Canada* 100 C5
Whiteface, *U.S.A.* 109 J3
Whitefield, *U.S.A.* 107 B13
Whitefish, *U.S.A.* 110 B6
Whitefish L., *Canada* 101 A7
Whitefish Pt., *U.S.A.* 104 B3
Whitegull, L., *Canada* 99 A7
Whitehall, *Mich., U.S.A.* 104 D2
Whitehall, *Mont., U.S.A.* 110 D7
Whitehall, *N.Y., U.S.A.* 107 C11
Whitehall, *Wis., U.S.A.* 108 C9
Whitehaven, *U.K.* 12 C4
Whitehorse, *Canada* 100 A1
Whitehorse, Vale of, *U.K.* 13 F6
Whitemark, *Australia* 90 G4
Whitemouth, *Canada* 101 D9
Whiteplains, *Liberia* 78 D2
Whitesboro, *N.Y., U.S.A.* 107 C9
Whitesboro, *Tex., U.S.A.* 109 J6
Whiteshell Prov. Park, *Canada* 101 C9
Whiteside, Canal, *Chile* 128 D2
Whitetail, *U.S.A.* 108 A2
Whiteville, *U.S.A.* 105 H6
Whitewater, *U.S.A.* 104 D1
Whitewater Baldy, *U.S.A.* 111 K9
Whitewater L., *Canada* 98 B2
Whitewood, *Australia* 90 C3
Whitewood, *Canada* 101 C8
Whitfield, *Australia* 91 F4
Whithorn, *U.K.* 14 G4
Whitianga, *N.Z.* 87 G5
Whitman, *U.S.A.* 107 D14
Whitmire, *U.S.A.* 105 H5
Whitney, *Canada* 98 C4
Whitney, Mt., *U.S.A.* 111 H4
Whitney Point, *U.S.A.* 107 D9
Whitstable, *U.K.* 13 F9
Whitsunday I., *Australia* 90 C4
Whittier, *U.S.A.* 113 M8
Whittlesea, *Australia* 91 F4
Whitwell, *U.S.A.* 105 H3
Wholdaia L., *Canada* 101 A8
Whyalla, *Australia* 91 E2
Whyjonta, *Australia* 91 D3
Wiarton, *Canada* 98 D3
Wiawso, *Ghana* 78 D4
Wibaux, *U.S.A.* 108 B2
Wichabai, *Guyana* 121 C6
Wichian Buri, *Thailand* 58 E3
Wichita, *U.S.A.* 109 G6
Wichita Falls, *U.S.A.* 109 J5
Wick, *U.K.* 14 C5
Wickenburg, *U.S.A.* 111 K7
Wickepin, *Australia* 89 F2
Wickham, C., *Australia* 90 F3
Wickliffe, *U.S.A.* 106 E3
Wicklow, *Ireland* 15 D5
Wicklow □, *Ireland* 15 D5
Wicklow Hd., *Ireland* 15 D5
Widgiemooltha, *Australia* 89 F3
Widnes, *U.K.* 12 D5
Wiedenbrück, *Germany* 18 D4
Wiek, *Germany* 18 A9
Wielbark, *Poland* 20 B10
Wieliczka, *Poland* 20 F10
Wieluń, *Poland* 20 D8
Wien, *Austria* 21 G6
Wiener Neustadt, *Austria* 21 H6
Wieprz →, *Koszalin, Poland* 20 A6
Wieprz →, *Lublin, Poland* 20 D11
Wierden, *Neths.* 16 D9
Wiers, *Belgium* 17 H3
Wiesbaden, *Germany* 19 E4
Wiesental, *Germany* 19 F4
Wigan, *U.K.* 12 D5
Wiggins, *Colo., U.S.A.* 108 E2
Wiggins, *Miss., U.S.A.* 109 K10
Wight, I. of □, *U.K.* 13 G6
Wigtown, *U.K.* 14 G4
Wigtown B., *U.K.* 14 G4
Wijchen, *Neths.* 16 E7
Wijhe, *Neths.* 16 D8
Wijk bij Duurstede, *Neths.* 16 E6
Wil, *Switz.* 23 B8
Wilber, *U.S.A.* 108 E6
Wilberforce, *Canada* 106 A6
Wilberforce, C., *Australia* 90 A2
Wilburton, *U.S.A.* 109 H7
Wilcannia, *Australia* 91 E3
Wilcox, *U.S.A.* 106 E6
Wildbad, *Germany* 19 G4
Wildervank, *Neths.* 16 B9
Wildeshausen, *Germany* 18 C4
Wildhorn, *Switz.* 22 D4
Wildrose, *Calif., U.S.A.* 113 J9
Wildrose, *N. Dak., U.S.A.* 108 A3
Wildspitze, *Austria* 19 J6
Wildstrubel, *Switz.* 22 D5
Wildwood, *U.S.A.* 104 F8
Wilge →, *S. Africa* 85 D4
Wilhelm II Coast, *Antarctica* 5 C7
Wilhelm-Pieck-Stadt Guben, *Germany* 18 D10
Wilhelmina, Geb., *Surinam* 121 C6
Wilhelmina Kanaal, *Neths.* 17 E6
Wilhelmsburg, *Austria* 21 G5
Wilhelmshaven, *Germany* 18 B4
Wilhelmstal, *Namibia* 84 C2
Wilkes Barre, *U.S.A.* 107 E9
Wilkesboro, *U.S.A.* 105 G5
Wilkie, *Canada* 101 C7
Wilkinsburg, *U.S.A.* 106 F5
Wilkinson Lakes, *Australia* 89 E5
Willamina, *U.S.A.* 110 D2
Willandra Billabong Creek →, *Australia* 91 E4
Willapa, B., *U.S.A.* 110 C2
Willapa Hills, *U.S.A.* 112 D3
Willard, *N. Mex., U.S.A.* 111 J10
Willard, *Utah, U.S.A.* 110 F7
Willcox, *U.S.A.* 111 K9
Willebroek, *Belgium* 17 F4
Willemstad, *Neth. Ant.* 117 D6
Willeroo, *Australia* 88 C5
William →, *Canada* 101 B7
William Creek, *Australia* 91 D2
Williambury, *Australia* 89 D2
Williams, *Australia* 89 F2
Williams, *Ariz., U.S.A.* 111 J7
Williams, *Calif., U.S.A.* 112 F4
Williams Lake, *Canada* 100 C4
Williamsburg, *Ky., U.S.A.* 105 G3
Williamsburg, *Pa., U.S.A.* 106 F6
Williamsburg, *Va., U.S.A.* 104 G7
Williamson, *N.Y., U.S.A.* 106 C7
Williamson, *W. Va., U.S.A.* 104 G4
Williamsport, *U.S.A.* 106 E7
Williamston, *U.S.A.* 105 H7
Williamstown, *Australia* 91 F3
Williamstown, *Mass., U.S.A.* 107 D11
Williamstown, *N.Y., U.S.A.* 107 C9
Williamsville, *U.S.A.* 109 G9
Willimantic, *U.S.A.* 107 E12
Willis Group, *Australia* 90 B5
Willisau, *Switz.* 22 B6
Williston, *S. Africa* 84 E3
Williston, *Fla., U.S.A.* 105 L4
Williston, *N. Dak., U.S.A.* 108 A3
Williston L., *Canada* 100 B4
Willits, *U.S.A.* 110 G2
Willmar, *U.S.A.* 108 C7
Willoughby, *U.S.A.* 106 E3
Willow Bunch, *Canada* 101 D7
Willow L., *Canada* 100 A5
Willow Lake, *U.S.A.* 108 C6
Willow Springs, *U.S.A.* 109 G8
Willow Wall, The, *China* 51 C12
Willowlake →, *Canada* 100 A4
Willowmore, *S. Africa* 84 E3
Willows, *Australia* 90 C4
Willows, *U.S.A.* 112 F4
Willowvale = Gatyana, *S. Africa* 85 E4
Wills, L., *Australia* 88 D4
Wills Cr. →, *Australia* 90 C3
Wills Point, *U.S.A.* 109 J7
Willunga, *Australia* 91 F2
Wilmette, *U.S.A.* 104 D2
Wilmington, *Australia* 91 E2
Wilmington, *Del., U.S.A.* 104 F8
Wilmington, *Ill., U.S.A.* 104 E1
Wilmington, *N.C., U.S.A.* 105 H7
Wilmington, *Ohio, U.S.A.* 104 F4
Wilpena Cr. →, *Australia* 91 E2
Wilrijk, *Belgium* 17 F4
Wilsall, *U.S.A.* 110 D8
Wilson, *U.S.A.* 105 H7
Wilson →, *Queens., Australia* 91 D3
Wilson →, *W. Austral., Australia* 88 C4
Wilson Bluff, *Australia* 89 F4
Wilsons Promontory, *Australia* 91 F4
Wilster, *Germany* 18 B5
Wilton, *U.K.* 13 F6
Wilton, *U.S.A.* 108 B4
Wilton →, *Australia* 90 A1
Wiltshire □, *U.K.* 13 F6
Wiltz, *Lux.* 17 J7
Wiluna, *Australia* 89 E3
Wimereux, *France* 25 B8
Wimmera →, *Australia* 91 F3
Winam G., *Kenya* 82 C3
Winburg, *S. Africa* 84 D4
Winchendon, *U.S.A.* 107 D12
Winchester, *U.K.* 13 F6
Winchester, *Conn., U.S.A.* 107 E11
Winchester, *Idaho, U.S.A.* 110 C5
Winchester, *Ind., U.S.A.* 104 E3
Winchester, *Ky., U.S.A.* 104 G3
Winchester, *N.H., U.S.A.* 107 D12
Winchester, *Nev., U.S.A.* 113 J11
Winchester, *Tenn., U.S.A.* 105 H2
Winchester, *Va., U.S.A.* 104 F6
Wind →, *U.S.A.* 110 E9
Wind River Range, *U.S.A.* 110 E9
Windber, *U.S.A.* 106 F6
Windermere, L., *U.K.* 12 C5
Windfall, *Canada* 100 C5
Windflower L., *Canada* 100 A5
Windhoek, *Namibia* 84 C2
Windom, *U.S.A.* 108 D7
Windorah, *Australia* 90 D3
Window Rock, *U.S.A.* 111 J9
Windrush →, *U.K.* 13 F6
Windsor, *Australia* 91 E5
Windsor, *N.S., Canada* 99 D7
Windsor, *Nfld., Canada* 99 C8
Windsor, *Ont., Canada* 98 D3
Windsor, *U.K.* 13 F7
Windsor, *Colo., U.S.A.* 108 E2
Windsor, *Conn., U.S.A.* 107 E12
Windsor, *Mo., U.S.A.* 108 F8
Windsor, *N.Y., U.S.A.* 107 D9
Windsor, *Vt., U.S.A.* 107 C12
Windsorton, *S. Africa* 84 D3
Windward Is., *W. Indies* 117 D7
Windward Passage = Vientos, Paso de los, *Caribbean* 117 C5
Windy L., *Canada* 101 A8
Winefred L., *Canada* 101 B6
Winejok, *Sudan* 77 F2
Winfield, *U.S.A.* 109 G6
Wingate Mts., *Australia* 88 B5
Wingen, *Australia* 91 E5
Wingene, *Belgium* 17 F2
Wingham, *Australia* 91 E5
Wingham, *Canada* 98 D3
Winifred, *U.S.A.* 110 C9
Winisk, *Canada* 98 A2
Winisk →, *Canada* 98 A2
Winisk L., *Canada* 98 B2
Wink, *U.S.A.* 109 K3
Winkler, *Canada* 101 D9
Winlock, *U.S.A.* 112 D4
Winneba, *Ghana* 79 D4
Winnebago, *U.S.A.* 108 D7
Winnebago L., *U.S.A.* 104 D1
Winnecke Cr. →, *Australia* 88 C5
Winnemucca, *U.S.A.* 110 F5
Winnemucca, L., *U.S.A.* 110 F4
Winner, *U.S.A.* 108 D5
Winnett, *U.S.A.* 110 C9
Winnfield, *U.S.A.* 109 K8
Winnibigoshish L., *U.S.A.* 108 B7
Winning, *Australia* 88 D1
Winnipeg, *Canada* 101 D9
Winnipeg →, *Canada* 101 C9

Winnipeg, L., Canada 101 C9
Winnipeg Beach, Canada 101 C9
Winnipegosis, Canada 101 C9
Winnipegosis L., Canada 101 C9
Winnipesaukee, L., U.S.A. 107 C13
Winnsboro, La., U.S.A. 109 J9
Winnsboro, S.C., U.S.A. 105 H5
Winnsboro, Tex., U.S.A. 109 J7
Winokapau, L., Canada 99 B7
Winona, Miss., U.S.A. 109 J10
Winona, Wis., U.S.A. 108 C9
Winooski, U.S.A. 107 B11
Winschoten, Neths. 16 B10
Winsen, Germany 18 B6
Winslow, Ariz., U.S.A. 111 J8
Winslow, Wash., U.S.A. 112 C4
Winsted, U.S.A. 107 E11
Winston-Salem, U.S.A. 105 G5
Winsum, Neths. 16 B9
Winter Garden, U.S.A. 105 L5
Winter Haven, U.S.A. 105 M5
Winter Park, U.S.A. 105 L5
Winterberg, Germany 18 D4
Winterhaven, U.S.A. 113 N12
Winters, Calif., U.S.A. 112 G5
Winters, Tex., U.S.A. 109 K5
Winterset, U.S.A. 108 E7
Wintersville, U.S.A. 106 F4
Winterswijk, Neths. 16 E9
Winterthur, Switz. 23 B7
Winthrop, Minn., U.S.A. 108 C7
Winthrop, Wash., U.S.A. 110 B3
Winton, Australia 90 C3
Winton, N.Z. 87 M2
Winton, U.S.A. 105 G7
Wintzenheim, France 25 D14
Wipper →, Germany 18 D7
Wirral, U.K. 12 D4
Wirrulla, Australia 91 E1
Wisbech, U.K. 12 E8
Wisconsin □, U.S.A. 108 C10
Wisconsin →, U.S.A. 108 D9
Wisconsin Dells, U.S.A. 108 D10
Wisconsin Rapids, U.S.A. 108 C10
Wisdom, U.S.A. 110 D7
Wishaw, U.K. 14 F5
Wishek, U.S.A. 108 B5
Wisła, Poland 20 F8
Wisła →, Poland 20 A8
Wisłok →, Poland 20 E12
Wisłoka →, Poland 20 E11
Wismar, Germany 18 B7
Wismar, Guyana 121 B6
Wisner, U.S.A. 108 E6
Wissant, France 25 B8
Wissembourg, France 25 C14
Wissenkerke, Neths. 17 E3
Witbank, S. Africa 85 D4
Witdraai, S. Africa 84 D3
Witham →, U.K. 12 D7
Withernsea, U.K. 12 D8
Witmarsum, Neths. 16 B6
Witney, U.K. 13 F6
Witnossob →, Namibia 84 D3
Wittdün, Germany 18 A4
Witten, Germany 17 F10
Wittenberg, Germany 18 D8
Wittenberge, Germany 18 B7
Wittenburg, Germany 18 B7
Wittenoom, Australia 88 D2
Wittingen, Germany 18 C6
Wittlich, Germany 19 F2
Wittmund, Germany 18 B3
Wittow, Germany 18 A9
Wittstock, Germany 18 B8
Witzenhausen, Germany 18 D5
Wlingi, Indonesia 57 H15
Włocławek, Poland 20 C9
Włodawa, Poland 20 D13
Włoszczowa, Poland 20 E9
Woburn, U.S.A. 107 D13
Wodian, China 50 H7
Wodonga, Australia 91 F4
Woerden, Neths. 16 D5
Woerth, France 25 D14
Woëvre, France 25 C12
Wognum, Neths. 16 C6
Wohlen, Switz. 23 B6
Woinbogoin, China 52 A2
Wokam, Indonesia 57 F8
Wolbrom, Poland 20 E9
Woldegk, Germany 18 B9
Wolf →, Canada 100 A2
Wolf Creek, U.S.A. 110 C7
Wolf L., Canada 100 A2
Wolf Point, U.S.A. 108 A2
Wolfe I., Canada 98 D4
Wolfenbüttel, Germany 18 C6
Wolfheze, Neths. 16 D7
Wolfsberg, Austria 21 J4
Wolfsburg, Germany 18 C6
Wolgast, Germany 18 A9
Wolhusen, Switz. 22 B6
Wolin, Poland 20 B4
Wollaston, Is., Chile 128 E3
Wollaston L., Canada 101 B8
Wollaston Pen., Canada 96 B8
Wollogorang, Australia 90 B2
Wollongong, Australia 91 E5
Wolmaransstad, S. Africa 84 D4
Wolmirstedt, Germany 18 C7
Wolseley, Australia 91 F3
Wolseley, Canada 101 C8
Wolseley, S. Africa 84 E2
Wolstenholme, C., Canada 94 C12
Wolsztyn, Poland 20 C6
Wolvega, Neths. 16 C7
Wolverhampton, U.K. 13 E5
Wommels, Neths. 16 B7
Wonarah, Australia 90 B2
Wonck, Belgium 17 G7
Wondai, Australia 91 D5
Wondelgem, Belgium 17 F3
Wongalarroo L., Australia 91 E3
Wongan Hills, Australia 89 F2
Wongawol, Australia 89 E3
Wŏnju, S. Korea 51 F14
Wonosari, Indonesia 57 G14
Wŏnsan, N. Korea 51 E14
Wonthaggi, Australia 91 F4
Woocalla, Australia 91 E2
Wood Buffalo Nat. Park, Canada 100 B6
Wood Is., Australia 88 C3
Wood L., Canada 101 B8
Wood Lake, U.S.A. 108 D4
Woodah I., Australia 90 A2
Woodanilling, Australia 89 F2
Woodbridge, Canada 106 C5
Woodburn, Australia 91 D5
Woodenbong, Australia 91 D5
Woodend, Australia 91 F3
Woodfords, U.S.A. 112 G7
Woodgreen, Australia 90 C1
Woodlake, U.S.A. 112 J7
Woodland, U.S.A. 112 G5
Woodlands, Australia 88 D2
Woodpecker, Canada 100 C4
Woodridge, Canada 101 D9
Woodroffe, Mt., Australia 89 E5
Woodruff, Ariz., U.S.A. 111 J8
Woodruff, Utah, U.S.A. 110 F8
Woods, L., Australia 90 B1
Woods, L., Canada 99 B6
Woods, L. of the, Canada 101 D10
Woodstock, Queens., Australia 90 B4
Woodstock, W. Austral., Australia 88 D2
Woodstock, N.B., Canada 99 C6
Woodstock, Ont., Canada 98 D3
Woodstock, U.K. 13 F6
Woodstock, Ill., U.S.A. 108 D10
Woodstock, Vt., U.S.A. 107 C12
Woodsville, U.S.A. 107 B13
Woodville, N.Z. 87 J5
Woodville, U.S.A. 109 K7
Woodward, U.S.A. 109 G5
Woody, U.S.A. 113 K8
Woolamai, C., Australia 91 F4
Woolgoolga, Australia 91 E5
Woombye, Australia 91 D5
Woomera, Australia 91 E2
Woonsocket, R.I., U.S.A. 107 D13
Woonsocket, S. Dak., U.S.A. 108 C5
Wooramel, Australia 89 E1
Wooramel →, Australia 89 E1
Wooroloo, Australia 89 F2
Wooster, U.S.A. 106 F3
Worb, Switz. 22 C5
Worcester, S. Africa 84 E2
Worcester, U.K. 13 E5
Worcester, Mass., U.S.A. 107 D13
Worcester, N.Y., U.S.A. 107 D10
Wörgl, Austria 19 H8
Workington, U.K. 12 C4
Worksop, U.K. 12 D6
Workum, Neths. 16 C6
Worland, U.S.A. 110 D10
Wormerveer, Neths. 16 D5
Wormhoudt, France 25 B9
Worms, Germany 19 F4
Wörth, Germany 19 F8
Wortham, U.S.A. 109 K6
Wörther See, Austria 21 J4
Worthing, U.K. 13 G7
Worthington, U.S.A. 108 D7
Wosi, Indonesia 57 E7
Wou-han = Wuhan, China 53 B10
Woubrugge, Neths. 16 D5
Woudenberg, Neths. 16 D6
Woudsend, Neths. 16 C7
Wour, Chad 73 D8
Wouw, Neths. 17 E4
Wowoni, Indonesia 57 E6
Woy Woy, Australia 91 E5
Wrangel I. = Vrangelya, Ostrov, Russia 45 B19
Wrangell, U.S.A. 96 C6
Wrangell I., U.S.A. 100 B2
Wrangell Mts., U.S.A. 96 B5
Wrath, C., U.K. 14 C3
Wray, U.S.A. 108 E3
Wrekin, The, U.K. 12 E5
Wrens, U.S.A. 105 J4
Wrexham, U.K. 12 D4
Wriezen, Germany 18 C10
Wright, Canada 100 C4
Wright, Phil. 55 F6
Wrightson, Mt., U.S.A. 111 L8
Wrightwood, U.S.A. 113 L9
Wrigley, Canada 96 B7
Wrocław, Poland 20 D7
Września, Poland 20 C7
Wschowa, Poland 20 D6
Wu Jiang →, China 52 C6
Wu'an, China 50 F8
Wubin, Australia 89 F2
Wubu, China 50 F6
Wuchang, China 51 B14
Wucheng, China 50 F9
Wuchuan, Guangdong, China 53 G8
Wuchuan, Guizhou, China 52 C7
Wuchuan, Nei Mongol Zizhiqu, China 50 D6
Wudi, China 51 F9
Wuding, China 52 E4
Wuding He →, China 50 F6
Wudu, China 50 H3
Wufeng, China 53 B8
Wugang, China 53 D8
Wugong Shan, China 53 D9
Wuhan, China 53 B10
Wuhe, China 51 H9
Wuhsi = Wuxi, China 53 B13
Wuhu, China 53 B12
Wujiang, China 53 B13
Wukari, Nigeria 79 D6
Wulajie, China 51 B14
Wulanbulang, China 50 D6
Wulehe, Ghana 79 D5
Wulian, China 51 G10
Wuliang Shan, China 52 E3
Wuliaru, Indonesia 57 F8
Wulumuchi = Ürümqi, China 54 B3
Wum, Cameroon 79 D7
Wuming, China 52 F7
Wuning, China 53 C10
Wunnummin L., Canada 98 B2
Wunsiedel, Germany 19 E8
Wunstorf, Germany 18 C5
Wuntho, Burma 61 H19
Wuping, China 53 E11
Wuppertal, Germany 18 D3
Wuppertal, S. Africa 84 E2
Wuqing, China 51 E9
Würenlingen, Switz. 23 A6
Wurung, Australia 90 B3
Würzburg, Germany 19 F5
Wurzen, Germany 18 D8
Wushan, Gansu, China 50 G3
Wushan, Sichuan, China 52 B7
Wusuli Jiang = Ussuri →, Asia 48 A7
Wutach →, Germany 19 H4
Wutai, China 50 E7
Wuting = Huimin, China 51 F9
Wutong, China 53 E8
Wutonghaolai, China 51 C11
Wutongqiao, China 52 C4
Wuustwezel, Belgium 17 F5
Wuwei, Anhui, China 53 B11
Wuwei, Gansu, China 54 C5
Wuxi, Jiangsu, China 53 B13
Wuxi, Sichuan, China 52 B7
Wuxiang, China 50 F7
Wuxing, China 53 B13
Wuxuan, China 52 F7
Wuyang, China 50 H7
Wuyi, Hebei, China 50 F8
Wuyi, Zhejiang, China 53 C12
Wuyi Shan, China 53 D11
Wuyo, Nigeria 79 C7
Wuyuan, Jiangxi, China 53 C11
Wuyuan, Nei Mongol Zizhiqu, China 50 D5
Wuzhai, China 50 E6
Wuzhi Shan, China 54 E5
Wuzhong, China 50 E4
Wuzhou, China 53 F8
Wyaaba Cr. →, Australia 90 B3
Wyalkatchem, Australia 89 F2
Wyalusing, U.S.A. 107 E8
Wyandotte, U.S.A. 104 D4
Wyandra, Australia 91 D4
Wyangala Res., Australia 91 E4
Wyara, L., Australia 91 D3
Wycheproof, Australia 91 F3
Wye →, U.K. 13 F5
Wyemandoo, Australia 89 E2
Wyk, Germany 18 A4
Wymondham, U.K. 13 E7
Wymore, U.S.A. 108 E6
Wynbring, Australia 91 E1
Wyndham, Australia 88 C4
Wyndham, N.Z. 87 M2
Wyndmere, U.S.A. 108 B6
Wynne, U.S.A. 109 H9
Wynnum, Australia 91 D5
Wynyard, Australia 90 G4
Wynyard, Canada 101 C8
Wyola, L., Australia 89 E5
Wyoming □, U.S.A. 102 B5
Wyong, Australia 91 E5
Wyszków, Poland 20 C11
Wyszogród, Poland 20 C10
Wytheville, U.S.A. 104 G5

X

Xai-Xai, Mozam. 85 D5
Xainza, China 54 C3
Xambioá, Brazil 122 C2
Xangongo, Angola 84 B2
Xanten, Germany 18 D2
Xánthi, Greece 39 H7
Xanthos, Turkey 66 E3
Xapuri, Brazil 124 C4
Xar Moron He →, China 51 C11
Xau, L., Botswana 84 C3
Xavantina, Brazil 127 A5
Xenia, U.S.A. 104 F4
Xeropotamos →, Cyprus 37 E11
Xhora, S. Africa 85 E4
Xhumo, Botswana 84 C3
Xi Jiang →, China 53 F9
Xi Xian, Henan, China 53 A10
Xi Xian, Shanxi, China 50 F6
Xia Xian, China 50 G6
Xiachengzi, China 51 B16
Xiachuan Dao, China 53 G9
Xiaguan, China 52 E3
Xiajiang, China 53 D10
Xiajin, China 50 F8
Xiamen, China 53 E12
Xi'an, China 50 G5
Xian Xian, China 50 E9
Xianfeng, China 52 C7
Xiang Jiang →, China 53 C9
Xiangcheng, Henan, China 50 H8
Xiangcheng, Henan, China 50 H7
Xiangcheng, Sichuan, China 52 C2
Xiangdu, China 52 F6
Xiangfan, China 53 A9
Xianghuang Qi, China 50 C7
Xiangning, China 50 G6
Xiangquan, China 50 F7
Xiangshan, China 53 C13
Xiangshui, China 51 G10
Xiangtan, China 53 D9
Xiangxiang, China 53 D9
Xiangyin, China 53 C9
Xiangyun, China 52 E3
Xiangzhou, China 52 F7
Xianju, China 53 C13
Xianning, China 53 C10
Xianshui He →, China 52 B3
Xianyang, China 50 G5
Xianyou, China 53 E12
Xiao Hinggan Ling, China 54 B7
Xiao Xian, China 50 G9
Xiaofeng, China 53 B12
Xiaogan, China 53 B9
Xiaojin, China 52 B4
Xiaolan, China 53 F9
Xiaoshan, China 53 B13
Xiaoyi, China 50 F6
Xiapu, China 53 D12
Xiawa, China 51 C11
Xiayi, China 50 G9
Xichang, China 52 D4
Xichong, China 52 B5
Xichuan, China 50 H6
Xiemahe, China 53 B8
Xieng Khouang, Laos 58 C4
Xifei He →, China 50 H9
Xifeng, Guizhou, China 52 D6
Xifeng, Liaoning, China 51 C13
Xifengzhen, China 50 G4
Xigazê, China 54 D3
Xihe, China 50 G3
Xihua, China 50 H8
Xiliao He →, China 51 C12
Xilin, China 52 E5
Xilókastron, Greece 39 L5
Xin Jiang →, China 53 C11
Xin Xian, China 50 E7
Xinavane, Mozam. 85 D5
Xinbin, China 51 D13
Xincai, China 53 A10
Xinchang, China 53 C13
Xincheng, Guangxi Zhuangzu, China 52 E7
Xincheng, Jiangxi, China 53 D10
Xinfeng, Guangdong, China 53 E10
Xinfeng, Jiangxi, China 53 D11
Xinfeng, Jiangxi, China 53 E10
Xing Xian, China 50 E6
Xing'an, Guangxi Zhuangzu, China 53 E8
Xingan, Jiangxi, China 53 D10
Xingcheng, China 51 D11
Xingguo, China 53 D10
Xinghe, China 50 D7
Xinghua, China 51 H10
Xinghua Wan, China 53 E12
Xinglong, China 51 D9
Xingning, China 53 E10
Xingping, China 50 G5
Xingren, China 52 E5
Xingshan, China 53 B8
Xingtai, China 50 F8
Xingu →, Brazil 121 D7
Xingyang, China 50 G7
Xinhe, China 50 F8
Xinhua, China 53 D8
Xinhuang, China 52 D7
Xinhui, China 53 F9
Xining, China 54 C5
Xinjiang, China 50 G6
Xinjiang Uygur Zizhiqu □, China 54 B3
Xinjie, China 52 D3
Xinjin, Liaoning, China 51 E11
Xinjin, Sichuan, China 52 B4
Xinkai He →, China 51 C12
Xinle, China 50 E8
Xinlitun, China 51 D12
Xinlong, China 52 B3
Xinmin, China 51 D12
Xinning, China 53 D8
Xinping, China 52 E3
Xinshao, China 53 D8
Xintai, China 51 G9
Xintian, China 53 E9
Xinxiang, China 50 G7
Xinxing, China 53 F9
Xinyang, China 53 A10
Xinye, China 53 A9
Xinyi, China 53 F8
Xinyu, China 53 D10
Xinzhan, China 51 C14
Xinzheng, China 50 G7
Xinzhou, China 53 B10
Xinzhu, Taiwan 53 E13
Xiong Xian, China 50 E9
Xiongyuecheng, China 51 D12
Xiping, Henan, China 50 H8
Xiping, Henan, China 50 H6
Xiping, Zhejiang, China 53 C12
Xique-Xique, Brazil 122 D3
Xiruá →, Brazil 124 B4
Xisha Qundao = Hsisha Chuntao, Pac. Oc. 56 A4
Xishui, China 53 B10
Xituozhen, China 52 B7
Xiuning, China 53 C12
Xiuren, China 53 E8
Xiushan, China 52 C7
Xiushui, China 53 C10
Xiuwen, China 52 D6
Xiuyan, China 51 D12
Xixabangma Feng, China 61 E14
Xixia, China 50 H6
Xixiang, China 50 H4
Xiyang, China 50 F7
Xizang □, China 54 C3
Xlendi, Malta 37 C1
Xu Jiang →, China 53 D11
Xuan Loc, Vietnam 59 G6
Xuancheng, China 53 B12
Xuan'en, China 52 C7
Xuanhan, China 52 B6
Xuanhua, China 50 D8
Xuchang, China 50 G7
Xuefeng Shan, China 53 D8
Xuejiaping, China 53 B8
Xun Jiang →, China 53 F8
Xun Xian, China 50 G8
Xundian, China 52 E4
Xunwu, China 53 E10
Xunyang, China 50 H5
Xunyi, China 50 G5
Xupu, China 53 D8
Xushui, China 50 E8
Xuwen, China 53 G8
Xuyen Moc, Vietnam 59 G6
Xuyong, China 52 C5
Xuzhou, China 51 G9
Xylophagou, Cyprus 37 E12

Y

Ya Xian, China 58 C7
Yaamba, Australia 90 C5
Ya'an, China 52 C4
Yaapeet, Australia 91 F3
Yabassi, Cameroon 79 E6
Yabelo, Ethiopia 77 G4
Yablonovy Khrebet, Russia 45 D12
Yablonovy Ra. = Yablonovy Khrebet, Russia 45 D12
Yabrai Shan, China 50 E2
Yabrūd, Syria 69 B5
Yacuiba, Bolivia 126 A3
Yacuma →, Bolivia 125 C4
Yadgir, India 60 L10
Yadkin →, U.S.A. 105 H5
Yadrin, Russia 41 D15
Yagaba, Ghana 79 C4
Yagodnoye, Russia 45 C15
Yagoua, Cameroon 80 B3
Yaguas →, Peru 120 D3
Yaha, Thailand 59 J3
Yahila, Zaïre 82 B1
Yahk, Canada 100 D5
Yahuma, Zaïre 80 D4
Yahyalı, Turkey 66 D6
Yaita, Japan 49 F9
Yaiza, Canary Is. 36 F6
Yajiang, China 52 B3
Yajua, Nigeria 79 C7
Yakima, U.S.A. 110 C3
Yakima →, U.S.A. 110 C3
Yako, Burkina Faso 78 C4
Yakoruda, Bulgaria 39 G6
Yakovlevka, Russia 48 B6
Yaku-Shima, Japan 49 J5
Yakut Republic □, Russia 45 C13
Yakutat, U.S.A. 96 C6
Yakutsk, Russia 45 C13
Yala, Thailand 59 J3
Yalbalgo, Australia 89 E1
Yalboroo, Australia 90 C4
Yale, U.S.A. 106 C2
Yalgoo, Australia 89 E2
Yalinga, C.A.R. 73 G9
Yalkubul, Punta, Mexico 115 C7
Yalleroi, Australia 90 C4

Yuscarán

Yalobusha →, *U.S.A.* 109 J9
Yalong Jiang →, *China* 52 D3
Yalova, *Turkey* 66 C3
Yalpukh, Oz., *Ukraine* 38 D11
Yalta, *Ukraine* 42 D6
Yalu Jiang →, *China* 51 E13
Yalutorovsk, *Russia* 44 D7
Yalvaç, *Turkey* 66 D4
Yam Ha Melah = Dead Sea, *Asia* 69 D4
Yam Kinneret, *Israel* 69 C4
Yamada, *Japan* 49 H5
Yamagata, *Japan* 48 E10
Yamagata □, *Japan* 48 E10
Yamaguchi, *Japan* 49 G5
Yamaguchi □, *Japan* 49 G5
Yamal, Poluostrov, *Russia* 44 B8
Yamanashi □, *Japan* 49 G9
Yamantau, Gora, *Russia* 44 D6
Yamba, *N.S.W., Australia* 91 D5
Yamba, *S. Austral., Australia* 91 E3
Yambah, *Australia* 90 C1
Yambarran Ra., *Australia* 88 C5
Yâmbiô, *Sudan* 77 G2
Yambol, *Bulgaria* 38 G9
Yamdena, *Indonesia* 57 F8
Yame, *Japan* 49 H5
Yamethin, *Burma* 61 J20
Yamil, *Nigeria* 79 C6
Yamma-Yamma, L., *Australia* 91 D3
Yamoussoukro, *Ivory C.* 78 D3
Yampa →, *U.S.A.* 110 F9
Yampi Sd., *Australia* 88 C3
Yampol, *Ukraine* 42 B3
Yamrat, *Nigeria* 79 C6
Yamrukchal, *Bulgaria* 38 G7
Yamuna →, *India* 63 G9
Yamzho Yumco, *China* 54 D4
Yan, *Nigeria* 79 C7
Yana →, *Russia* 45 B14
Yanac, *Australia* 91 F3
Yanagawa, *Japan* 49 H5
Yanai, *Japan* 49 H6
Yan'an, *China* 50 F5
Yanbian, *China* 52 D3
Yanbu 'al Baḩr, *Si. Arabia* 64 F3
Yancannia, *Australia* 91 E3
Yanchang, *China* 50 F6
Yancheng, *Henan, China* 50 H7
Yancheng, *Jiangsu, China* 51 H11
Yanchi, *China* 50 F4
Yanchuan, *China* 50 F6
Yanco Cr. →, *Australia* 91 F4
Yandal, *Australia* 89 E3
Yandanooka, *Australia* 89 E2
Yandaran, *Australia* 90 C5
Yandoon, *Burma* 61 L19
Yanfeng, *China* 52 E3
Yanfolila, *Mali* 78 C3
Yang Xian, *China* 50 H4
Yangambi, *Zaïre* 82 B1
Yangbi, *China* 52 E2
Yangcheng, *China* 50 G7
Yangch'ü = Taiyuan, *China* 50 F7
Yangchun, *China* 53 F8
Yanggao, *China* 50 D7
Yanggu, *China* 50 F8
Yangi-Yer, *Kazakhstan* 44 E7
Yangjiang, *China* 53 G8
Yangliuqing, *China* 51 E9
Yangping, *China* 53 B8
Yangpingguan, *China* 50 H4
Yangquan, *China* 50 F7
Yangshan, *China* 53 E9
Yangshuo, *China* 53 E8
Yangtze Kiang = Chang Jiang →, *China* 53 B13
Yangxin, *China* 53 C10
Yangyang, *S. Korea* 51 E15
Yangyuan, *China* 50 D8
Yangzhou, *China* 53 A12
Yanhe, *China* 52 C7
Yanji, *China* 51 C15
Yanjin, *China* 52 C5
Yanjing, *China* 52 C2
Yankton, *U.S.A.* 108 D6
Yanna, *Australia* 91 D4
Yanonge, *Zaïre* 82 B1
Yanqi, *China* 54 B3
Yanqing, *China* 50 D8
Yanshan, *Hebei, China* 51 E9
Yanshan, *Jiangxi, China* 53 C11
Yanshan, *Yunnan, China* 52 F5
Yanshou, *China* 51 B15
Yantabulla, *Australia* 91 D4
Yantai, *China* 51 F11
Yanting, *China* 52 B5
Yantra →, *Bulgaria* 38 F8
Yanwa, *China* 52 D2
Yanyuan, *China* 52 D3
Yanzhou, *China* 50 G9
Yao, *Chad* 73 F8
Yao Xian, *China* 50 G5
Yao Yai, Ko, *Thailand* 59 J2
Yao'an, *China* 52 E3
Yaodu, *China* 52 A5
Yaoundé, *Cameroon* 79 E7
Yaowan, *China* 51 G10
Yap I., *Pac. Oc.* 92 G5
Yapen, *Indonesia* 57 E9
Yapen, Selat, *Indonesia* 57 E9
Yappar →, *Australia* 90 B3
Yaqui →, *Mexico* 114 B2
Yar, *Russia* 41 B18
Yar-Sale, *Russia* 44 C8
Yaracuy □, *Venezuela* 120 A4
Yaracuy →, *Venezuela* 120 A4
Yaraka, *Australia* 90 C3
Yarangüme, *Turkey* 66 E3
Yaransk, *Russia* 41 C15
Yaratishky, *Belorussia* 40 D4
Yardea P.O., *Australia* 91 E2
Yare →, *U.K.* 13 E9
Yarensk, *Russia* 44 C5
Yarí →, *Colombia* 120 D3
Yaritagua, *Venezuela* 120 A4
Yarkand = Shache, *China* 54 C2
Yarker, *Canada* 107 B8
Yarkhun →, *Pakistan* 63 A5
Yarmouth, *Canada* 99 D6
Yarmūk →, *Syria* 69 C4
Yaroslavl, *Russia* 41 C11
Yarqa, W. →, *Egypt* 69 F2
Yarra Yarra Lakes, *Australia* 89 E2
Yarraden, *Australia* 90 A3
Yarraloola, *Australia* 88 D2
Yarram, *Australia* 91 F4
Yarraman, *Australia* 91 D5
Yarranvale, *Australia* 91 D4
Yarras, *Australia* 91 E5
Yarrowmere, *Australia* 90 C4
Yartsevo, *Russia* 40 D8
Yartsevo, *Russia* 45 C10
Yarumal, *Colombia* 120 B2
Yasawa Group, *Fiji* 87 C7
Yaselda →, *Belorussia* 40 E5
Yashi, *Nigeria* 79 C6
Yasin, *Pakistan* 63 A5
Yasinovataya, *Ukraine* 42 B7
Yasinski, L., *Canada* 98 B4
Yasothon, *Thailand* 58 E5
Yass, *Australia* 91 E4
Yata →, *Bolivia* 125 C4
Yatağan, *Turkey* 66 E3
Yates Center, *U.S.A.* 109 G7
Yathkyed L., *Canada* 101 A9
Yatsushiro, *Japan* 49 H5
Yatta Plateau, *Kenya* 82 C4
Yauca, *Peru* 124 D3
Yauya, *Peru* 124 B2
Yauyos, *Peru* 124 C2
Yavari →, *Peru* 124 A3
Yavatmal, *India* 60 J11
Yavne, *Israel* 69 D3
Yavorov, *Ukraine* 40 G3
Yavuzeli, *Turkey* 67 E7
Yawatahama, *Japan* 49 H6
Yawri B., *S. Leone* 78 D2
Yaxi, *China* 52 D6
Yayama-Rettō, *Japan* 49 M1
Yazd, *Iran* 65 D7
Yazd □, *Iran* 65 D7
Yazoo →, *U.S.A.* 109 J9
Yazoo City, *U.S.A.* 109 J9
Yding Skovhøj, *Denmark* 9 J10
Ye Xian, *Henan, China* 50 H7
Ye Xian, *Shandong, China* 51 F10
Yealering, *Australia* 89 F2
Yebyu, *Burma* 61 M21
Yechŏn, *S. Korea* 51 F15
Yecla, *Spain* 29 G3
Yécora, *Mexico* 114 B3
Yedintsy, *Moldavia* 42 B2
Yeeda, *Australia* 88 C3
Yeelanna, *Australia* 91 E2
Yefremov, *Russia* 41 E11
Yegorlyk →, *Russia* 43 C9
Yegorlykskaya, *Russia* 43 C9
Yegoryevsk, *Russia* 41 D11
Yegros, *Paraguay* 126 B4
Yehuda, Midbar, *Israel* 69 D4
Yei, *Sudan* 77 G3
Yei, Nahr →, *Sudan* 77 F3
Yekaterinburg, *Russia* 44 D7
Yekaterinodar = Krasnodar, *Russia* 43 D8
Yelan, *Russia* 41 F13
Yelan-Kolenovskiy, *Russia* 41 F12
Yelanskoye, *Russia* 45 C13
Yelarbon, *Australia* 91 D5
Yelatma, *Russia* 41 D12
Yelcho, L., *Chile* 128 B2
Yelets, *Russia* 41 E11
Yélimané, *Mali* 78 B2
Yelizavetgrad, *Ukraine* 42 B5
Yell, *U.K.* 14 A7
Yell Sd., *U.K.* 14 A7
Yellow Sea, *China* 51 G12
Yellowhead Pass, *Canada* 100 C5
Yellowknife, *Canada* 100 A6
Yellowknife →, *Canada* 100 A6
Yellowstone →, *U.S.A.* 108 B3
Yellowstone L., *U.S.A.* 110 D8
Yellowstone National Park, *U.S.A.* 110 D8
Yellowtail Res., *U.S.A.* 110 D9
Yelnya, *Russia* 40 D8
Yelsk, *Belorussia* 40 F6
Yelvertoft, *Australia* 90 C2
Yelwa, *Nigeria* 79 C5
Yemen ■, *Asia* 68 E3
Yen Bai, *Vietnam* 58 B5
Yenakiyevo, *Ukraine* 42 B8
Yenangyaung, *Burma* 61 J19
Yenda, *Australia* 91 E4
Yendéré, *Ivory C.* 78 C4
Yendi, *Ghana* 79 D4
Yenice, *Turkey* 66 D2
Yenice →, *Turkey* 66 E6
Yenisaía, *Greece* 39 H7
Yenişehir, *Turkey* 66 C3
Yenisey →, *Russia* 44 B9
Yeniseysk, *Russia* 45 D10
Yeniseyskiy Zaliv, *Russia* 44 B9
Yennádhi, *Greece* 37 C9
Yenne, *France* 27 C9
Yenotayevka, *Russia* 43 C12
Yenyuka, *Russia* 45 D13
Yeo, L., *Australia* 89 E3
Yeola, *India* 60 J9
Yeoryioúpolis, *Greece* 37 D6
Yeovil, *U.K.* 13 G5
Yepes, *Spain* 28 F1
Yeppoon, *Australia* 90 C5
Yeráki, *Greece* 39 N4
Yerbent, *Turkmenistan* 44 F6
Yerbogachen, *Russia* 45 C11
Yerevan, *Armenia* 43 F11
Yerilla, *Australia* 89 E3
Yerköy, *Turkey* 66 D6
Yermak, *Kazakhstan* 44 D8
Yermakovo, *Russia* 45 D13
Yermo, *U.S.A.* 113 L10
Yerofey Pavlovich, *Russia* 45 D13
Yerólakkos, *Cyprus* 37 D12
Yeropótamos →, *Greece* 37 D6
Yeroskipos, *Cyprus* 37 E11
Yerseke, *Neths.* 17 F4
Yershov, *Russia* 41 F16
Yerunaja, Cerro, *Peru* 124 C2
Yerushalayim = Jerusalem, *Israel* 69 D4
Yerville, *France* 24 C7
Yes Tor, *U.K.* 13 G4
Yesan, *S. Korea* 51 F14
Yeşilhisar, *Turkey* 66 D6
Yeşilırmak →, *Turkey* 66 C7
Yesilkent, *Turkey* 66 E7
Yesnogorsk, *Russia* 41 D10
Yeso, *U.S.A.* 109 H2
Yessentuki, *Russia* 43 D10
Yessey, *Russia* 45 C11
Yeste, *Spain* 29 G2
Yeu, I. d', *France* 24 F4
Yevlakh, *Azerbaijan* 43 F12
Yevpatoriya, *Ukraine* 42 D5
Yevstratovskiy, *Russia* 41 F11
Yeya →, *Russia* 43 C8
Yeysk, *Russia* 42 C8
Yezd = Yazd, *Iran* 65 D7
Yhati, *Paraguay* 126 B4
Yhú, *Paraguay* 127 B4
Yi →, *Uruguay* 126 C4
Yi 'Allaq, G., *Egypt* 69 E2
Yi He →, *China* 51 G10
Yi Xian, *Anhui, China* 53 C11
Yi Xian, *Hebei, China* 50 E8
Yi Xian, *Liaoning, China* 51 D11
Yiali, *Greece* 39 N10
Yialiás →, *Cyprus* 37 D12
Yi'allaq, G., *Egypt* 76 H8
Yialousa, *Cyprus* 37 D13
Yiáltra, *Greece* 39 L5
Yianisádhes, *Greece* 37 D8
Yiannitsa, *Greece* 39 J5
Yibin, *China* 52 C5
Yichang, *China* 53 B8
Yicheng, *Henan, China* 53 B9
Yicheng, *Shanxi, China* 50 G6
Yichuan, *China* 50 F6
Yichun, *Heilongjiang, China* 54 B7
Yichun, *Jiangxi, China* 53 D10
Yidu, *Hubei, China* 53 B8
Yidu, *Shandong, China* 51 F10
Yidun, *China* 52 B2
Yihuang, *China* 53 D11
Yijun, *China* 50 G5
Yilan, *Taiwan* 53 E13
Yıldızeli, *Turkey* 66 D7
Yiliang, *Yunnan, China* 52 D5
Yiliang, *Yunnan, China* 52 E4
Yilong, *China* 52 B6
Yimen, *China* 52 E4
Yimianpo, *China* 51 B15
Yinchuan, *China* 50 E4
Yindarlgooda, L., *Australia* 89 F3
Ying He →, *China* 50 H9
Ying Xian, *China* 50 E7
Yingcheng, *China* 53 B9
Yingde, *China* 53 E9
Yingjiang, *China* 52 E1
Yingjing, *China* 52 C4
Yingkou, *China* 51 D12
Yingshan, *Henan, China* 53 B9
Yingshan, *Hubei, China* 53 B10
Yingshan, *Sichuan, China* 52 B6
Yingshang, *China* 53 A11
Yingtan, *China* 54 D6
Yining, *China* 54 B3
Yinjiang, *China* 52 C7
Yinmabin, *Burma* 61 H19
Yinnietharra, *Australia* 88 D2
Yiofiros →, *Greece* 37 D7
Yioúra, *Greece* 39 K7
Yipinglang, *China* 52 E3
Yirga Alem, *Ethiopia* 77 F4
Yishan, *China* 52 E7
Yishui, *China* 51 G10
Yíthion, *Greece* 39 N5
Yitiaoshan, *China* 50 F3
Yitong, *China* 51 C13
Yiwu, *China* 53 C13
Yixing, *China* 53 B12
Yiyang, *Henan, China* 50 G7
Yiyang, *Hunan, China* 53 C9
Yiyang, *Jiangxi, China* 53 C11
Yizhang, *China* 53 E9
Yizheng, *China* 53 A12
Ylitornio, *Finland* 8 C17
Ylivieska, *Finland* 8 D18
Yngaren, *Sweden* 11 F10
Ynykchanskiy, *Russia* 45 C14
Yoakum, *U.S.A.* 109 L6
Yog Pt., *Phil.* 57 B6
Yogan, *Togo* 79 D5
Yogyakarta, *Indonesia* 57 G14
Yoho Nat. Park, *Canada* 100 C5
Yojoa, L. de, *Honduras* 116 D2
Yŏju, *S. Korea* 51 F14
Yokadouma, *Cameroon* 80 D2
Yokkaichi, *Japan* 49 G8
Yoko, *Cameroon* 79 D7
Yokohama, *Japan* 49 G9
Yokosuka, *Japan* 49 G9
Yokote, *Japan* 48 E10
Yola, *Nigeria* 79 D7
Yolaina, Cordillera de, *Nic.* 116 D3
Yonago, *Japan* 49 G6
Yonaguni-Jima, *Japan* 49 M1
Yŏnan, *N. Korea* 51 F14
Yonezawa, *Japan* 48 F10
Yong Peng, *Malaysia* 59 L4
Yong Sata, *Thailand* 59 J2
Yongampo, *N. Korea* 51 E13
Yong'an, *China* 53 E11
Yongcheng, *China* 50 H9
Yŏngchŏn, *S. Korea* 51 G15
Yongchuan, *China* 52 C5
Yongchun, *China* 53 E12
Yongdeng, *China* 50 F2
Yongding, *China* 53 E11
Yŏngdŏk, *S. Korea* 51 F15
Yŏngdŭngpo, *S. Korea* 51 F14
Yongfeng, *China* 53 D10
Yongfu, *China* 52 E7
Yonghe, *China* 50 F6
Yŏnghŭng, *N. Korea* 51 E14
Yongji, *China* 50 G6
Yŏngju, *S. Korea* 51 F15
Yongkang, *Yunnan, China* 52 E2
Yongkang, *Zhejiang, China* 53 C13
Yongnian, *China* 50 F8
Yongning, *Guangxi Zhuangzu, China* 52 F7
Yongning, *Ningxia Huizu, China* 50 E4
Yongping, *China* 52 E2
Yongqing, *China* 50 E9
Yongren, *China* 52 D3
Yongshan, *China* 52 C4
Yongsheng, *China* 52 D3
Yongshun, *China* 52 C7
Yongtai, *China* 53 E12
Yŏngwŏl, *S. Korea* 51 F15
Yongxin, *China* 53 D10
Yongxing, *China* 53 D9
Yongxiu, *China* 53 C10
Yonibana, *S. Leone* 78 D2
Yonkers, *U.S.A.* 107 F11
Yonne □, *France* 25 E10
Yonne →, *France* 25 D9
York, *Australia* 89 F2
York, *U.K.* 12 D6
York, *Ala., U.S.A.* 105 J1
York, *Nebr., U.S.A.* 108 E6
York, *Pa., U.S.A.* 104 F7
York, C., *Australia* 90 A3
York, Kap, *Greenland* 4 B4
York Sd., *Australia* 88 B4
Yorke Pen., *Australia* 91 E2
Yorkshire Wolds, *U.K.* 12 D7
Yorkton, *Canada* 101 C8
Yorktown, *U.S.A.* 109 L6
Yorkville, *U.S.A.* 112 G3
Yornup, *Australia* 89 F2
Yoro, *Honduras* 116 C2
Yoron-Jima, *Japan* 49 L4
Yos Sudarso, Pulau, *Indonesia* 57 F9
Yosemite National Park, *U.S.A.* 111 H4
Yosemite Village, *U.S.A.* 112 H7
Yoshkar Ola, *Russia* 41 C15
Yŏsu, *S. Korea* 51 G14
Yotala, *Bolivia* 125 D4
Yotvata, *Israel* 69 F4
You Xian, *China* 53 D9
Youbou, *Canada* 100 D4
Youghal, *Ireland* 15 E4
Youghal B., *Ireland* 15 E4
Youkounkoun, *Guinea* 78 C2
Young, *Australia* 91 E4
Young, *Canada* 101 C7
Young, *Uruguay* 126 C4
Younghusband, L., *Australia* 91 E2
Younghusband Pen., *Australia* 91 F2
Youngstown, *Canada* 101 C6
Youngstown, *N.Y., U.S.A.* 106 C5
Youngstown, *Ohio, U.S.A.* 106 E4
Youngsville, *U.S.A.* 106 E5
Youssoufia, *Morocco* 74 B3
Youxi, *China* 53 D12
Youyang, *China* 52 C7
Youyu, *China* 50 D7
Yoweragabbie, *Australia* 89 E2
Yozgat, *Turkey* 66 D6
Yozgat □, *Turkey* 66 D6
Ypané →, *Paraguay* 126 A4
Yport, *France* 24 C7
Ypres = Ieper, *Belgium* 17 G1
Ypsilanti, *U.S.A.* 104 D4
Yreka, *U.S.A.* 110 F2
Ysleta, *U.S.A.* 111 L10
Yssingeaux, *France* 27 C8
Ystad, *Sweden* 11 J7
Ythan →, *U.K.* 14 D7
Ytterhogdal, *Sweden* 10 B8
Ytyk-Kel, *Russia* 45 C14
Yu Jiang →, *China* 54 D6
Yu Shan, *Taiwan* 53 F13
Yu Xian, *Hebei, China* 50 E8
Yu Xian, *Henan, China* 50 G7
Yu Xian, *Shanxi, China* 50 E7
Yuan Jiang →, *Hunan, China* 53 C8
Yuan Jiang →, *Yunnan, China* 52 F4
Yuan'an, *China* 53 B8
Yuanjiang, *Hunan, China* 53 C9
Yuanjiang, *Yunnan, China* 52 F4
Yuanli, *Taiwan* 53 E13
Yuanlin, *Taiwan* 53 F13
Yuanling, *China* 53 C8
Yuanmou, *China* 52 E3
Yuanqu, *China* 50 G6
Yuanyang, *Henan, China* 50 G7
Yuanyang, *Yunnan, China* 52 F4
Yuba →, *U.S.A.* 112 F5
Yuba City, *U.S.A.* 112 F5
Yūbari, *Japan* 48 C10
Yūbetsu, *Japan* 48 B11
Yucatán □, *Mexico* 115 C7
Yucatán, Canal de, *Caribbean* 116 B2
Yucatan Str. = Yucatán, Canal de, *Caribbean* 116 B2
Yucca, *U.S.A.* 113 L12
Yucca Valley, *U.S.A.* 113 L10
Yucheng, *China* 50 F9
Yuci, *China* 50 F7
Yudino, *Russia* 41 D16
Yudino, *Russia* 44 D7
Yudu, *China* 53 E10
Yuendumu, *Australia* 88 D5
Yueqing, *China* 53 C13
Yueqing Wan, *China* 53 C13
Yuexi, *Anhui, China* 53 B11
Yuexi, *Sichuan, China* 52 C4
Yueyang, *China* 53 C9
Yugan, *China* 53 C11
Yugoslavia ■, *Europe* 21 M10
Yuhuan, *China* 53 C13
Yujiang, *China* 53 C11
Yukhnov, *Russia* 40 D9
Yukon →, *N. Amer.* 96 B3
Yukon Territory □, *Canada* 96 B6
Yüksekova, *Turkey* 67 E11
Yukti, *Russia* 45 C11
Yukuhashi, *Japan* 49 H5
Yule →, *Australia* 88 D2
Yuli, *Nigeria* 79 D7
Yulin, *Guangxi Zhuangzu, China* 53 F8
Yulin, *Shaanxi, China* 50 E5
Yuma, *Ariz., U.S.A.* 113 N12
Yuma, *Colo., U.S.A.* 108 E3
Yuma, B. de, *Dom. Rep.* 117 C6
Yumbe, *Uganda* 82 B3
Yumbi, *Zaïre* 82 C2
Yumbo, *Colombia* 120 C2
Yumen, *China* 54 C4
Yumurtalık, *Turkey* 66 E6
Yun Ho →, *China* 51 E9
Yun Xian, *Hubei, China* 53 A8
Yun Xian, *Yunnan, China* 52 E3
Yunak, *Turkey* 66 D4
Yunan, *China* 53 F8
Yuncheng, *Henan, China* 50 G8
Yuncheng, *Shanxi, China* 50 G6
Yundamindra, *Australia* 89 E3
Yunfu, *China* 53 F9
Yungas, *Bolivia* 125 D4
Yungay, *Chile* 126 D1
Yungay, *Peru* 124 B2
Yunhe, *China* 53 C12
Yunlin, *Taiwan* 53 F13
Yunling, *China* 52 D2
Yunlong, *China* 52 E2
Yunmeng, *China* 53 B9
Yunnan □, *China* 52 E4
Yunquera de Henares, *Spain* 28 E1
Yunta, *Australia* 91 E2
Yunxi, *China* 50 H6
Yunxiao, *China* 53 F11
Yunyang, *China* 52 B7
Yuping, *China* 52 D7
Yupukarri, *Guyana* 121 C6
Yupyongdong, *N. Korea* 51 D15
Yuqing, *China* 52 D6
Yur, *Russia* 45 D14
Yurgao, *Russia* 44 D9
Yuribei, *Russia* 44 B8
Yurimaguas, *Peru* 124 B2
Yurya, *Russia* 41 B16
Yuryev-Polskiy, *Russia* 41 C11
Yuryevets, *Russia* 41 C13
Yuscarán, *Honduras* 116 D2

Yushanzhen, *China* 52 C7
Yushe, *China* 50 F7
Yushu, *Jilin, China* 51 B14
Yushu, *Qinghai, China* 54 C4
Yutai, *China* 50 G9
Yutian, *China* 51 E9
Yuxi, *China* 52 E4
Yuyao, *China* 53 B13
Yuzawa, *Japan* 48 E10
Yuzha, *Russia* 41 C13
Yuzhno-Sakhalinsk, *Russia* 45 E15
Yvelines □, *France* 25 D8
Yverdon, *Switz.* 22 C3
Yvetot, *France* 24 C7
Yvonand, *Switz.* 22 C3

Z

Zaamslag, *Neths.* 17 F3
Zaan →, *Neths.* 16 D5
Zaandam, *Neths.* 16 D5
Zab, Monts du, *Algeria* 75 B6
Žabalj, *Serbia, Yug.* 21 K10
Žabari, *Serbia, Yug.* 21 L11
Zabarjad, *Egypt* 76 C4
Zabaykalskiy, *Russia* 45 E12
Zabid, *Yemen* 68 E3
Ząbkowice Śląskie, *Poland* 20 E6
Zabłudów, *Poland* 20 B13
Zābol, *Iran* 65 D9
Zābolī, *Iran* 65 E9
Zabré, *Burkina Faso* 79 C4
Zabrze, *Poland* 20 E8
Zacapa, *Guatemala* 116 D2
Zacapu, *Mexico* 114 D4
Zacatecas, *Mexico* 114 C4
Zacatecas □, *Mexico* 114 C4
Zacatecoluca, *El Salv.* 116 D2
Zacoalco, *Mexico* 114 C4
Zacualtipán, *Mexico* 115 C5
Zadar, *Croatia* 33 D12
Zadawa, *Nigeria* 79 C7
Zadetkyi Kyun, *Burma* 59 H2
Zadonsk, *Russia* 41 E11
Zafarqand, *Iran* 65 C7
Zafra, *Spain* 31 G4
Żagań, *Poland* 20 D5
Zagazig, *Egypt* 76 H7
Zāgheh, *Iran* 65 C6
Zaghouan, *Tunisia* 75 A7
Zaglivérion, *Greece* 39 J6
Zaglou, *Algeria* 75 C4
Zagnanado, *Benin* 79 D5
Zagorá, *Greece* 39 K6
Zagora, *Morocco* 74 B3
Zagorsk = Sergiyev Posad, *Russia* 41 C11
Zagreb, *Croatia* 33 C12
Zāgros, Kuhhā-ye, *Iran* 65 C6
Zagros Mts. = Zāgros, Kuhhā-ye, *Iran* 65 C6
Zaguinaso, *Ivory C.* 78 C3
Zāhedān, *Fārs, Iran* 65 D7
Zāhedān, *Sīstān va Balūchestān, Iran* 65 D9
Zahlah, *Lebanon* 69 B4
Zahna, *Germany* 18 D8
Zahrez Chergui, *Algeria* 75 A5
Zahrez Rharbi, *Algeria* 75 B5
Zaïre ■, *Africa* 80 E4
Zaïre →, *Africa* 80 F2
Zaječar, *Serbia, Yug.* 21 M12
Zakamensk, *Russia* 45 D11
Zakataly, *Azerbaijan* 43 F12
Zakavkazye, *Asia* 43 F11
Zākhū, *Iraq* 64 B4
Zákinthos, *Greece* 39 M3
Zakopane, *Poland* 20 F9
Zákros, *Greece* 37 D8
Zala →, *Hungary* 21 J7
Zalaegerszeg, *Hungary* 21 J6
Zalalövö, *Hungary* 21 J6
Zalamea de la Serena, *Spain* 31 G5
Zalamea la Real, *Spain* 31 H4
Zalazna, *Russia* 41 B18
Žalec, *Slovenia* 33 B12
Zaleshchiki, *Ukraine* 42 B1
Zalingei, *Sudan* 73 F9
Zaltbommel, *Neths.* 16 E6
Zambeke, *Zaïre* 82 B2
Zambeze →, *Africa* 83 F4
Zambezi = Zambeze →, *Africa* 83 F4
Zambezi, *Zambia* 81 G4
Zambezia □, *Mozam.* 83 F4
Zambia ■, *Africa* 83 E2
Zamboanga, *Phil.* 55 H5
Zamboanguita, *Phil.* 55 G5
Zambrano, *Colombia* 120 B3
Zambrów, *Poland* 20 C12
Zametchino, *Russia* 41 E13
Zamora, *Ecuador* 120 D2
Zamora, *Mexico* 114 C4
Zamora, *Spain* 30 D5
Zamora □, *Spain* 30 D5
Zamora-Chinchipe □, *Ecuador* 120 D2
Zamość, *Poland* 20 E13
Zamuro, Sierra del, *Venezuela* 121 C5
Zan, *Ghana* 79 D4
Zanaga, *Congo* 80 E2
Záncara →, *Spain* 29 F1
Zandijk, *Neths.* 16 D5
Zandvoort, *Neths.* 16 D5
Zanesville, *U.S.A.* 106 G2
Zangābād, *Iran* 64 B5
Zangue →, *Mozam.* 83 F4
Zanjan, *Iran* 65 B6
Zanjān □, *Iran* 65 B6
Zannone, *Italy* 34 B6
Zante = Zákinthos, *Greece* 39 M3
Zanthus, *Australia* 89 F3
Zanzibar, *Tanzania* 82 D4
Zanzūr, *Libya* 75 B7
Zaouiet El-Kala = Bordj Omar Driss, *Algeria* 75 C6
Zaouiet Reggane, *Algeria* 75 C5
Zaoyang, *China* 53 A9
Zaozhuang, *China* 51 G9
Zapadna Morava →, *Serbia, Yug.* 21 M11
Zapadnaya Dvina, *Russia* 40 C8
Zapadnaya Dvina →, *Belorussia* 40 C4
Západné Beskydy, *Europe* 20 F9
Zapala, *Argentina* 128 A2
Zapaleri, Cerro, *Bolivia* 126 A2
Zapata, *U.S.A.* 109 M5
Zapatón →, *Spain* 31 G4
Zapiga, *Chile* 124 D4
Zaporozhye, *Ukraine* 42 C6
Zapponeta, *Italy* 35 A8
Zara, *Turkey* 67 D7
Zaragoza, *Colombia* 120 B3
Zaragoza, *Coahuila, Mexico* 114 B4
Zaragoza, *Nuevo León, Mexico* 115 C5
Zaragoza, *Spain* 28 D4
Zaragoza □, *Spain* 28 D4
Zarand, *Kermān, Iran* 65 D8
Zarand, *Markazī, Iran* 65 C6
Zărandului, Munţii, *Romania* 38 C5
Zaranj, *Afghan.* 60 D2
Zarasai, *Lithuania* 40 D5
Zarate, *Argentina* 126 C4
Zaraysk, *Russia* 41 D11
Zaraza, *Venezuela* 121 B4
Zāreh, *Iran* 65 C6
Zarembo I., *U.S.A.* 100 B2
Zaria, *Nigeria* 79 C6
Zarneh, *Iran* 64 C5
Zarós, *Greece* 37 D6
Zarqā' →, *Jordan* 69 C4
Zarrīn, *Iran* 65 C7
Zaruma, *Ecuador* 120 D2
Żary, *Poland* 20 D5
Zarza de Alange, *Spain* 31 G4
Zarza de Granadilla, *Spain* 30 E4
Zarzaïtine, *Algeria* 75 C6
Zarzal, *Colombia* 120 C2
Zarzis, *Tunisia* 75 B7
Zas, *Spain* 30 B2
Zashiversk, *Russia* 45 C15
Zaskar →, *India* 63 B7
Zaskar Mts., *India* 63 C7
Zastron, *S. Africa* 84 E4
Zavāreh, *Iran* 65 C7
Zaventem, *Belgium* 17 G4
Zavetnoye, *Russia* 43 C10
Zavidovići, *Bos.-H., Yug.* 21 L8
Zavitinsk, *Russia* 45 D13
Zavodovski, I., *Antarctica* 5 B1
Zavolzhsk, *Russia* 41 C13
Zavolzhye, *Russia* 41 C13
Zawiercie, *Poland* 20 E9
Zāwiyat al Bayḑā, *Libya* 73 B9
Zâwyet Shammâs, *Egypt* 76 A2
Zâwyet Um el Rakham, *Egypt* 76 A2
Zâwyet Ungeîla, *Egypt* 76 A2
Zāyā, *Iraq* 64 C5
Zayarsk, *Russia* 45 D11
Zaysan, *Kazakhstan* 44 E9
Zaysan, Oz., *Kazakhstan* 44 E9
Zayü, *China* 52 C1
Zazir, O. →, *Algeria* 75 D6
Zbarazh, *Ukraine* 40 G4
Zbąszyń, *Poland* 20 C5
Zblewo, *Poland* 20 B8
Zdolbunov, *Ukraine* 40 F5
Ždrelo, *Serbia, Yug.* 21 L11
Zduńska Wola, *Poland* 20 D8
Zeballos, *Canada* 100 D3
Zebediela, *S. Africa* 85 C4
Zedelgem, *Belgium* 17 F2
Zeebrugge, *Belgium* 17 F2
Zeehan, *Australia* 90 G4
Zeeland, *Neths.* 17 E7
Zeeland □, *Neths.* 17 F3
Zeelst, *Neths.* 17 F6
Zeerust, *S. Africa* 84 D4
Zefat, *Israel* 69 C4
Zegdou, *Algeria* 74 C4
Zege, *Ethiopia* 77 E4
Zegelsem, *Belgium* 17 G3
Zégoua, *Mali* 78 C3
Zehdenick, *Germany* 18 C9
Zeil, Mt., *Australia* 88 D5
Zeila, *Somali Rep.* 68 E3
Zeist, *Neths.* 16 D6
Zeitz, *Germany* 18 D8
Zele, *Belgium* 17 F4
Zelenodolsk, *Russia* 41 D16
Zelenograd, *Russia* 41 C10
Zelenogradsk, *Russia* 40 D2
Zelenokumsk, *Russia* 43 D10
Zelënyy, *Kazakhstan* 43 B14
Zelhem, *Neths.* 16 D8
Zell, *Baden-W., Germany* 19 H3
Zell, *Rhld-Pfz., Germany* 19 E3
Zell am See, *Austria* 21 H2
Zella Mehlis, *Germany* 18 E6
Zelzate, *Belgium* 17 F3
Zembra, I., *Tunisia* 75 A7
Zémio, *C.A.R.* 82 A2
Zemmora, *Algeria* 75 A5
Zemmur, *W. Sahara* 74 C2
Zemoul, O. →, *Algeria* 74 C3
Zemst, *Belgium* 17 G4
Zemun, *Serbia, Yug.* 21 L10
Zengbe, *Cameroon* 79 D7
Zengcheng, *China* 53 F9
Zenica, *Bos.-H., Yug.* 21 L7
Zenina, *Algeria* 75 B5
Žepče, *Bos.-H., Yug.* 21 L8
Zeraf, Bahr ez →, *Sudan* 77 F3
Zerbst, *Germany* 18 D8
Zermatt, *Switz.* 22 D5
Zernez, *Switz.* 23 C10
Zernograd, *Russia* 43 C9
Zerqani, *Albania* 39 H3
Zestafoni, *Georgia* 43 E10
Zetel, *Germany* 18 B3
Zetten, *Neths.* 16 E7
Zeulenroda, *Germany* 18 E7
Zeven, *Germany* 18 B5
Zevenaar, *Neths.* 16 E8
Zevenbergen, *Neths.* 17 E5
Zévio, *Italy* 32 C8
Zeya, *Russia* 45 D13
Zeya →, *Russia* 45 D13
Zêzere →, *Portugal* 31 F2
Zghartā, *Lebanon* 69 A4
Zgierz, *Poland* 20 D9
Zgorzelec, *Poland* 20 D5
Zhabinka, *Belorussia* 40 E4
Zhailma, *Kazakhstan* 44 D7
Zhangbei, *China* 50 D8
Zhangguangcai Ling, *China* 51 B15
Zhanghua, *Taiwan* 53 E13
Zhangjiakou, *China* 50 D8
Zhangping, *China* 53 E11
Zhangpu, *China* 53 E11
Zhangwu, *China* 51 C12
Zhangye, *China* 54 C5
Zhangzhou, *China* 53 E11
Zhanhua, *China* 51 F10
Zhanjiang, *China* 53 G8
Zhanyi, *China* 52 E4
Zhanyu, *China* 51 B12
Zhao Xian, *China* 50 F8
Zhao'an, *China* 53 F11
Zhaocheng, *China* 50 F6
Zhaojue, *China* 52 C4
Zhaoping, *China* 53 E8
Zhaoqing, *China* 53 F9
Zhaotong, *China* 52 D4
Zhaoyuan, *Heilongjiang, China* 51 B13
Zhaoyuan, *Shandong, China* 51 F11
Zharkovskiy, *Russia* 40 D8
Zhashkov, *Ukraine* 42 B4
Zhashui, *China* 50 H5
Zhdanov = Mariupol, *Ukraine* 42 C7
Zhecheng, *China* 50 G8
Zhegao, *China* 53 B11
Zhejiang □, *China* 53 C13
Zheleznogorsk, *Russia* 40 E9
Zheleznogorsk-Ilimskiy, *Russia* 45 D11
Zheltyye Vody, *Ukraine* 42 B5
Zhen'an, *China* 50 H5
Zhenfeng, *China* 52 E5
Zheng'an, *China* 52 C6
Zhengding, *China* 50 E8
Zhenghe, *China* 53 D12
Zhengyang, *China* 53 A10
Zhengyangguan, *China* 53 A11
Zhengzhou, *China* 50 G7
Zhenhai, *China* 53 C13
Zhenjiang, *China* 53 A12
Zhenlai, *China* 51 B12
Zhenning, *China* 52 D5
Zhenping, *Henan, China* 50 H7
Zhenping, *Shaanxi, China* 52 B7
Zhenxiong, *China* 52 D5
Zhenyuan, *Gansu, China* 50 G4
Zhenyuan, *Guizhou, China* 52 D7
Zherdevka, *Russia* 41 F12
Zherong, *China* 53 D12
Zhidan, *China* 50 F5
Zhigansk, *Russia* 45 C13
Zhigulevsk, *Russia* 41 E16
Zhijiang, *Hubei, China* 53 B8
Zhijiang, *Hunan, China* 52 D7
Zhijin, *China* 52 D5
Zhirnovsk, *Russia* 41 F14
Zhitomir, *Ukraine* 40 F6
Zhizdra, *Russia* 40 E9
Zhlobin, *Belorussia* 40 E6
Zhmerinka, *Ukraine* 42 B3
Zhodino, *Belorussia* 40 D6
Zhokhova, Ostrov, *Russia* 45 B16
Zhong Xian, *China* 52 B7
Zhongdian, *China* 52 D2
Zhongdong, *China* 52 F6
Zhongdu, *China* 52 E7
Zhongning, *China* 50 F3
Zhongshan, *Guangdong, China* 53 F9
Zhongshan, *Guangxi Zhuangzu, China* 53 E8
Zhongtiao Shan, *China* 50 G6
Zhongwei, *China* 50 F3
Zhongxiang, *China* 53 B9
Zhongyang, *China* 50 F6
Zhoucun, *China* 51 F9
Zhouning, *China* 53 D12
Zhoushan Dao, *China* 53 C14
Zhouzhi, *China* 50 G5
Zhovtnevoye, *Ukraine* 42 C5
Zhuanghe, *China* 51 E12
Zhucheng, *China* 51 G10
Zhugqu, *China* 50 H3
Zhuhai, *China* 53 F9
Zhuji, *China* 53 C13
Zhukovka, *Russia* 40 E8
Zhumadian, *China* 50 H8
Zhuo Xian, *China* 50 E8
Zhuolu, *China* 50 D8
Zhuozi, *China* 50 D7
Zhupanovo, *Russia* 45 D16
Zhushan, *China* 53 A8
Zhuxi, *China* 52 A7
Zhuzhou, *China* 53 D9
Zi Shui →, *China* 53 C9
Zīārān, *Iran* 65 B6
Ziarat, *Pakistan* 62 D2
Zibo, *China* 51 F10
Zichang, *China* 50 F5
Zichem, *Belgium* 17 F5
Zielona Góra, *Poland* 20 D5
Zierikzee, *Neths.* 17 E3
Ziesar, *Germany* 18 C8
Zifta, *Egypt* 76 H7
Zigey, *Chad* 73 F8
Zigong, *China* 52 C5
Zigui, *China* 53 B8
Ziguinchor, *Senegal* 78 C1
Zihuatanejo, *Mexico* 114 D4
Zijin, *China* 53 F10
Zile, *Turkey* 66 C6
Žilina, *Czech.* 20 F8
Zillah, *Libya* 73 C8
Zillertaler Alpen, *Austria* 19 H7
Zima, *Russia* 45 D11
Zimane, Adrar in, *Algeria* 75 D5
Zimapán, *Mexico* 115 C5
Zimba, *Zambia* 83 F2
Zimbabwe, *Zimbabwe* 83 G3
Zimbabwe ■, *Africa* 83 F2
Zimovniki, *Russia* 43 C10
Zinal, *Switz.* 22 D5
Zinder, *Niger* 79 C6
Zinga, *Tanzania* 83 D4
Zingem, *Belgium* 17 G3
Zingst, *Germany* 18 A8
Ziniaré, *Burkina Faso* 79 C4
Zinkgruvan, *Sweden* 11 F9
Zinnowitz, *Germany* 18 A9
Zion Nat. Park, *U.S.A.* 111 H7
Zipaquirá, *Colombia* 120 C3
Zirc, *Hungary* 21 H7
Žiri, *Slovenia* 33 B11
Žirje, *Croatia* 33 E12
Zirl, *Austria* 19 H7
Ziros, *Greece* 37 D8
Zitácuaro, *Mexico* 114 D4
Zitava →, *Czech.* 21 G8
Zittau, *Germany* 18 E10
Zitundo, *Mozam.* 85 D5
Živinice, *Bos.-H., Yug.* 21 L8
Ziway, L., *Ethiopia* 77 F4
Zixi, *China* 53 D11
Zixing, *China* 53 E9
Ziyang, *Shaanxi, China* 50 H5
Ziyang, *Sichuan, China* 52 B5
Ziyun, *China* 52 E6
Ziz, Oued →, *Morocco* 74 B4
Zizhixian, *China* 53 E8
Zizhong, *China* 52 C5
Zlarin, *Croatia* 33 E12
Zlatar, *Croatia* 33 B13
Zlataritsa, *Bulgaria* 38 F8
Zlatitsa, *Bulgaria* 38 G7
Zlatograd, *Bulgaria* 39 H8
Zlatoust, *Russia* 44 D6
Zletovo, *Macedonia, Yug.* 39 H5
Zlin = Gottwaldov, *Czech.* 20 F7
Zlītan, *Libya* 73 B7
Złocieniec, *Poland* 20 B6
Złoczew, *Poland* 20 D8
Zlotoryja, *Poland* 20 D5
Złotów, *Poland* 20 B7
Zmeinogorsk, *Kazakhstan* 44 D9
Żmigród, *Poland* 20 D6
Zmiyev, *Ukraine* 42 B7
Znamenka, *Ukraine* 42 B5
Znamensk, *Russia* 40 D2
Żnin, *Poland* 20 C7
Znojmo, *Czech.* 20 G6
Zoar, *S. Africa* 84 E3
Zobeyrī, *Iran* 64 C5
Zobia, *Zaïre* 82 B2
Zoetermeer, *Neths.* 16 D5
Zofingen, *Switz.* 22 B5
Zogang, *China* 52 C1
Zogno, *Italy* 32 C6
Zogqên, *China* 52 A2
Zolder, *Belgium* 17 F6
Zollikofen, *Switz.* 22 C4
Zollikon, *Switz.* 23 B7
Zolochev, *Ukraine* 40 G4
Zolotonosha, *Ukraine* 42 B5
Zomba, *Malawi* 83 F4
Zomergem, *Belgium* 17 F3
Zongo, *Zaïre* 80 D3
Zonguldak, *Turkey* 42 F4
Zonguldak □, *Turkey* 66 C4
Zonhoven, *Belgium* 17 G6
Zonqor Pt., *Malta* 37 D2
Zonza, *France* 27 G13
Zorgo, *Burkina Faso* 79 C4
Zorita, *Spain* 31 F5
Zorritos, *Peru* 124 A1
Zorzor, *Liberia* 78 D3
Zossen, *Germany* 18 C9
Zottegem, *Belgium* 17 G3
Zou Xiang, *China* 50 G9
Zouar, *Chad* 73 D8
Zouérate, *Mauritania* 74 D2
Zousfana, O. →, *Algeria* 75 B4
Zoushan Dao, *China* 53 B14
Zoutkamp, *Neths.* 16 B8
Zrenjanin, *Serbia, Yug.* 21 K10
Zuarungu, *Ghana* 79 C4
Zuba, *Nigeria* 79 D6
Zubayr, *Yemen* 77 D5
Zubia, *Spain* 31 H7
Zubtsov, *Russia* 40 C9
Zudáñez, *Bolivia* 125 D5
Zuénoula, *Ivory C.* 78 D3
Zuera, *Spain* 28 D4
Zuetina, *Libya* 73 B9
Zufar, *Oman* 68 D5
Zug, *Switz.* 23 B7
Zug □, *Switz.* 23 B7
Zugdidi, *Georgia* 43 E9
Zugersee, *Switz.* 23 B7
Zugspitze, *Germany* 19 H6
Zuid-Holland □, *Neths.* 16 E5
Zuidbeveland, *Neths.* 17 F3
Zuidbroek, *Neths.* 16 B9
Zuidelijk-Flevoland, *Neths.* 16 D6
Zuidhorn, *Neths.* 16 B8
Zuidlaarder meer, *Neths.* 16 B9
Zuidlaren, *Neths.* 16 B9
Zuidwolde, *Neths.* 16 C8
Zújar, *Spain* 29 H2
Zújar →, *Spain* 31 F5
Zújar, Pantano del, *Spain* 31 G5
Zula, *Ethiopia* 77 D4
Zulia □, *Venezuela* 120 B3
Zulpich, *Germany* 18 E2
Zumaya, *Spain* 28 B2
Zumbo, *Mozam.* 83 F3
Zummo, *Nigeria* 79 D7
Zumpango, *Mexico* 115 D5
Zundert, *Neths.* 17 F5
Zungeru, *Nigeria* 79 D6
Zunhua, *China* 51 D9
Zuni, *U.S.A.* 111 J9
Zunyi, *China* 52 D6
Zuoquan, *China* 50 F7
Zuozhou, *China* 52 F6
Županja, *Croatia* 21 K8
Zurbātīyah, *Iraq* 64 C5
Zürich, *Switz.* 23 B7
Zürich □, *Switz.* 23 B7
Zürichsee, *Switz.* 23 B7
Zuromin, *Poland* 20 B9
Zuru, *Nigeria* 79 C6
Zurzach, *Switz.* 23 A6
Žut, *Croatia* 33 E12
Zutendaal, *Belgium* 17 G7
Zutphen, *Neths.* 16 D8
Zuwārah, *Libya* 75 B7
Zuyevka, *Russia* 41 B17
Zūzan, *Iran* 65 C8
Žužemberk, *Slovenia* 33 C11
Zvenigorodka, *Ukraine* 42 B4
Zverinogolovskoye, *Russia* 44 D7
Zvezdets, *Bulgaria* 38 G10
Zvishavane, *Zimbabwe* 83 G3
Zvolen, *Czech.* 20 G9
Zvonce, *Serbia, Yug.* 21 N12
Zvornik, *Bos.-H., Yug.* 21 L9
Zwaag, *Neths.* 16 C6
Zwanenburg, *Neths.* 16 D5
Zwarte Meer, *Neths.* 16 C7
Zwarte Waler, *Neths.* 16 C8
Zwartemeer, *Neths.* 16 C10
Zwartsluis, *Neths.* 16 C8
Zwedru = Tchien, *Liberia* 78 D3
Zweibrücken, *Germany* 19 F3
Zwenkau, *Germany* 18 D8
Zwevegem, *Belgium* 17 G2
Zwickau, *Germany* 18 E8
Zwiesel, *Germany* 19 F9
Zwijnaarde, *Belgium* 17 F3
Zwijndrecht, *Belgium* 17 F4
Zwijndrecht, *Neths.* 16 E5
Zwischenahn, *Germany* 18 B4
Zwolle, *Neths.* 16 C8
Zwolle, *U.S.A.* 109 K8
Zymoetz →, *Canada* 100 C3
Żyrardów, *Poland* 20 C10
Zyrya, *Azerbaijan* 43 F14
Zyryanka, *Russia* 45 C16
Zyryanovsk, *Kazakhstan* 44 E9
Zyyi, *Cyprus* 37 E12

NORTH
AMERICA

ARCTIC
OCEAN
4

96-97

8-9

Arctic Circle

8

14

15

12-13

16

24-25

30-31

26-27

32-3

100-101

98-99

104-105

106-107

74-75

36

36

36

28-29

A T L A N T I C

O C E A N

112-
113

110-111

108-109

116-117

Tropic of Cancer

102

PACIFIC
OCEAN
92-93

114-115

120-121

122-123

Equator

AFRICA

72-73

78

SOUTH
AMERICA

124-125

Tropic of Capricorn

P A C I F I C   O C E A N

126-127

128

KEY TO WORLD MAP PAGES